RAND McNALLY
GOODE'S WORLD ATLAS
17th EDITION

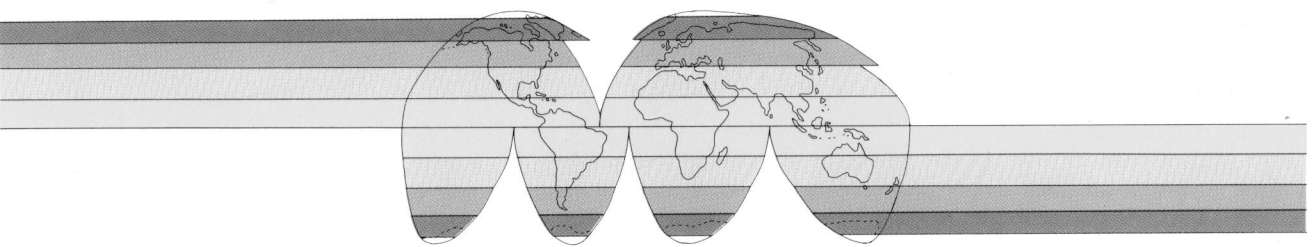

EDWARD B. ESPENSHADE, JR., *Editor*
Professor Emeritus of Geography
Northwestern University

JOEL L. MORRISON, *Senior Consultant*
United States Geological Survey

RAND McNALLY & COMPANY / *Chicago • New York • San Francisco*

Photo credits:
Figures 22, 23 - United States Geological Survey;
Figures 1, 2, 18, 19, 20 - National Aeronautics & Space Administration

contents

acknowledgments

This is the seventeenth edition of the Rand McNally *Goode's World Atlas* which was first published over sixty years ago. The name of Dr. J. Paul Goode, the original editor and distinguished cartographer who designed the early editions, has been retained to affirm the high standards which all those who have participated in the preparation of the book during these years have sought to attain.

Through the years, general-reference maps coverage has been expanded; the number of thematic maps has been increased and their kinds extended; and systematic improvements in symbolism, cartographic presentation, and map production and printing have been incorporated.

This seventeenth edition has been expanded to include United States thematic maps on water resources, minorities, income, education, life expectancy, population change, labor structure, and westward expansion. We have thus added to the sixteenth edition's seven world maps on nutrition and health, and eighteen continent maps covering energy resources, water resources, natural hazards, landform regions, ethnic groups, and political change. In line with our policy of periodic revision, most of the thematic maps and graphs have been revised. A new reference map of the Middle East (scale of 1:12,000,000) supplements the map coverage of that strategic region. To the ocean-floor section, we have added material on the theory of plate tectonics and continental drift. The World Political Information Table, added in the sixteenth edition, has been revised, as have the World Comparisons and Principal Cities of the World tables. For this edition, the Major Cities Map Index has been combined with the main Pronouncing Index. Thus one universal index serves the user as a reference for places on all the maps. These additions and the other revisions to the atlas reflect the editors' and publisher's commitment to maintaining the Rand McNally *Goode's World Atlas* as a standard of world atlases.

Sources

Every effort was made to assemble the latest and most authentic source materials to use in this edition. In the general physical-political maps, data from national and state surveys, recent military maps, and hydrographic charts were utilized. Source materials for the specialized maps were even more varied. They included both published and unpublished items in the form of maps, descriptions in articles and books, statistics, and correspondence with geographers and others. To the various agencies and organizations, official and unofficial, that cooperated, appreciation and thanks are expressed. Noteworthy among these organizations and agencies were: The United Nations (for demographic and trade statistics); the Food and Agriculture Organization of The United Nations (for production statistics on livestock, crops, and forest products and for statistics on world trade); the Population Reference Bureau (for population data); the Office of the Geographer, Department of State (for the map "Surface Transport Facilities" and other items); the office of Foreign Agricultural Relations, Department of Agriculture (for information on crop and livestock production and distribution); the Bureau of Mines, Department of the Interior (for information on mineral production); various branches of the national military establishment and the Weather Bureau, Department of Commerce (for information on temperature, wind, pressure, and ocean currents); the Maritime Commission and the Department of Commerce (for statistics on ocean trade); the American Geographical Society (for use of its library and permission to use the Miller cylindrical projection); the University of Chicago Press, owners of the copyright (for permission to use Goode's Homolosine equal-area projection); the McGraw-Hill Book Company (for cooperation in permitting the use of Glenn Trewartha's map of climatic regions and Petterssen's diagram of zones of precipitation); the Association of American Geographers (for permission to use Richard Murphy's map of landforms); and publications of the World Bank (for nutrition, health, and economic information).

Some additional sources of specific data and information are as follows: *World Oil* (for oil and gas data); International Labour Organisation (for labor statistics); International Road Federation (for transportation data); Miller Freeman Publications, Inc. (for data on coal, copper, tin, and iron ore); Organisation for Economic Co-operation and Development (for data on ocean transportation and uranium); and Textile Economics Bureau, Inc. (for data on fibers).

Other Acknowledgments

The variety and complexity of the problems involved in the preparation of a world atlas make highly desirable the participation of specialists in the fields concerned. In the preparation of the new edition of the Rand McNally *Goode's World Atlas*, the editors have been ably assisted by several such experts. They express their deep appreciation and thanks to all of them.

They are particularly indebted to the following experts who have cooperated over the years: A. W. Kuchler, Department of Geography, University of Kansas; Richard E. Murphy, late professor of geography, University of New Mexico; Erwin Raisz, late cartographer, Cambridge, Massachusetts; Glenn T. Trewartha, late professor of geography, University of Wisconsin; Derwent Whittlesey, late professor of geography, Harvard University; and Bogdan Zaborski, professor emeritus of geography, University of Ottawa.

The editors thank the entire Cartographic and Design staff of Rand McNally & Company for their continued outstanding contributions.

EDWARD B. ESPENSHADE, JR.
JOEL L. MORRISON

introduction: maps and imagery

The map is a unique means of recording and communicating geographic information. By reducing the world to a smaller scale, it enables us to see regions of the earth well beyond our ordinary range of vision. Thus, a map represents one of the most convenient, accurate, and effective ways to learn about size, distance, direction, and the geographic features of our planet.

An atlas is a collection of general reference maps and thematic maps (maps that depict specialized information) along with related graphic and statistical data. Whether readers are interested in the political boundaries of the Middle East or in the distribution of oil reserves, an atlas is an indispensable aid to understanding the many facets of our complex earth and the general course of world events.

The maps in *Goode's World Atlas* are grouped into four sections, beginning with World Thematic Maps, portraying the distribution of climatic regions, raw materials, landforms, and other major worldwide features. The second section, Major Cities Maps, focuses on individual cities and their environs. The main body of the atlas is the Regional Section, providing detailed physical-political reference maps for all inhabited land areas. Finally, the section Plate Tectonics / Ocean Floor Maps discusses the theory of plate tectonics and continental drift while maps vividly depict the terrain beneath the world's seas.

Geographical tables and indexes complete the atlas, providing comparative data, a glossary of foreign geographical terms, and a universal pronouncing index for place-names on the general reference maps. Each of the four map sections contains a separate introduction and appropriate legends to help readers understand and interpret the material.

CARTOGRAPHIC COMMUNICATION:
Mapmakers, Maps, and the Reader

To communicate information through a map, cartographers must assemble the geographic data, use their personal perception of the world to select the relevant information, and apply graphic techniques to produce the map. Readers must then be able to interpret the mapped data and relate it to their own experience and need for information. Thus, the success of any map depends on both the cartographer's and the map reader's knowledge and perception of the world and on their common understanding of a map's purpose and limitations.

Maps can present an almost infinite variety of information about our world. However, when reduced to fundamentals, the map shows only existence, associative existence, and spatially associated existence. *Existence* refers simply to the notation on a map that a point or area exists. *Associative existence* implies adding an absolute or relative quantity to the identified point or area (e.g., its elevation or annual rainfall). *Spatially associated existence* indicates spatial relationships between points or areas (e.g., distances and directions between cities)

Technological advances in gathering geographic information through satellites and high-altitude photography have greatly expanded the cartographer's ability to collect data and create accurate maps. These pictures and images enable us to see the world through infrared, radar, and other spectral wavelengths. The images created can be used as background for maps or manipulated to show us totally new ways of viewing natural and human patterns and landforms on the earth's surface.

The ability to understand maps and related imagery depends first on the reader's skill at recognizing how a curved, three-dimensional world is symbolized on a flat, two-dimensional map. Normally, we view the world horizontally (that is, our line of vision parallels the horizon), at an eye level about five and one-half to six feet above the ground. Images appear directly in front and to either side of us, with our eyes encompassing all details as nonselectively as a camera. Less frequently, when we are atop a high platform or in an airplane, we view the world obliquely, as shown in Figure 1, in which both vertical and horizontal facets of objects can be seen. And only those persons at very high altitudes will view the world at a vertical angle (Figure 2). Yet maps are based on our ability to visualize the world from an overhead, or vertical, perspective.

A map differs from a purely vertical photograph in two important respects. First, in contrast to the single focal point of a photograph, a map is created as if the viewer were directly overhead at all points (see Figure 3). Second, just as our brains select from the myriad items in our field of vision those objects of interest or importance to us, so each map presents only those details necessary for a particular purpose—a map is not an inventory of all that is visible. Selectivity is one of a map's most important and useful characteristics.

Imagery gained from high altitudes and satellites can have properties of both photographs and maps, for it can show complex detail or selected features; but its focal point may be that of neither a photograph nor a map. Because these remotely sensed images often look odd or unfamiliar, map readers need more-detailed explanations to help them interpret the information.

Skill in reading maps is basically a matter of practice, but a fundamental grasp of cartographic principles and the symbols, scales, and projections commonly employed in creating maps is essential to comprehensive map use.

Map Data

When creating a map, the cartographer must select the objects and information to be shown, evaluate their relative importance, and find some way to simplify their form. The combined process is called *cartographic generalization*. In attempting to generalize data, the cartographer is limited by the purpose of the map, its scale, the technical methods used to produce it, and the accuracy and reliability of the data. Because a well-drawn map creates an aura of truth and exactness, the cartographer should caution the reader against interpreting the generalized data too literally.

Figure 1. Oblique aerial photograph of New York City.

Figure 2. High-altitude vertical photograph of New York City area.

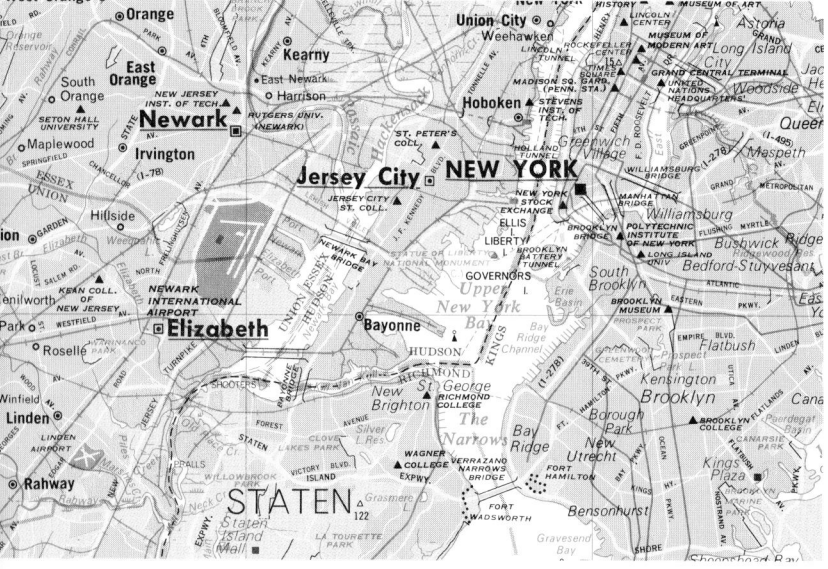

Figure 3. Map of New York City and environs.

Cartographic generalization consists of simplification, classification, symbolization, and induction.

Simplification involves omitting details that will clutter the map and confuse the reader. The degree of simplification depends on the purpose and scale of the map. If the cartographer is creating a detailed map of Canada and merely wants to show the location of the United States, he or she can draw a simplified outline of the country. However, if the map requires a precise identification of the states in New England and the Great Lakes region, the mapmaker will have to draw a more detailed outline, still being careful not to distract the reader from the main features of the Canadian map.

Classification of data is a way of reducing the information to a form that can be easily presented on a map. For example, portraying precise urban populations in the United States would require using as many different symbols as there are cities. Instead, the cartographer groups cities into population categories and assigns a distinct symbol to each one. With the help of a legend, the reader can easily decode the classifications (for an example, see page 51).

Symbolization of information depends largely on the nature of the original data. Information can be *nominal* (showing differences in kind, such as land versus water, grassland versus forest); or *ordinal* (showing relative differences in quantities as well as kind, such as *major* versus *minor* ore deposits); or *interval* (degrees of temperature, inches of rainfall) or *ratio* (population densities), both expressing quantitative details about the data being mapped.

Cartographers use various shapes, colors, or patterns to symbolize these categories of data, and the particular nature of the information being communicated often determines how it is symbolized. Population density, for example, can be shown by the use of small dots or different intensities of color. However, if nominal data is being portrayed—for instance, the desert and fertile areas of Egypt—the mapmaker may want to use a different method of symbolizing the data, perhaps pattern symbols. The color, size, and style of type used for the different elements on a map are also important to symbolization.

Induction is the term cartographers use to describe the process whereby more information is represented on a map than is actually supplied by the original data. For instance, in creating a rainfall map, a cartographer may start with precise rainfall records for relatively few points on the map. After deciding the interval categories into which the data will be divided (e.g., thirty inches or more, fifteen to thirty inches, under fifteen inches), the mapmaker infers from the particular data points that nearby places receive the same or nearly the same amount of rainfall and draws the lines that distinguish the various rainfall regions accordingly. Obviously, generalizations arrived at through induction can never be as precise as the real-world patterns they represent. The map will only tell the reader that all the cities in a given area received about the same amount of rainfall; it will not tell exactly how much rain fell in any particular city in any particular time period.

Cartographers must also be aware of the map reader's perceptual limitations and preferences. During the past two decades, numerous experiments have helped determine how much information readers actually glean from a map and how symbols, colors, and shapes are recognized and interpreted. As a result, cartographers now have a better idea of what kind of rectangle to use; what type of layout or lettering suggests qualities such as power, stability, movement; and what colors are most appropriate.

Map Scale

Since part or all of the earth's surface may be portrayed on a single page of an atlas, the reader's first question should be: What is the relation of map size to the area represented? This proportional relationship is known as the *scale* of a map.

Scale is expressed as a ratio between the distance or area on the map and the same distance or area on the earth. The map scale is commonly represented in three ways: (1) as a simple fraction or ratio called the representative fraction, or RF; (2) as a written statement of map distance in relation to earth distance; and (3) as a graphic representation or a bar scale. All three forms of scale for distances are expressed on Maps A–D.

The RF is usually written as 1:62,500 (as in Map A), where 1 always refers to a unit of distance on the map. The ratio means that 1 centimeter or 1 millimeter or 1 foot on the map represents 62,500 centimeters or millimeters or feet on the earth's surface. The units of measure on both sides of the ratio must always be the same.

Maps may also include a *written statement* expressing distances in terms more familiar to the reader. In Map A the scale 1:62,500 is expressed as being (approximately) 1 inch to 1 mile; that is, 1 inch on the map represents roughly 1 mile on the earth's surface.

The *graphic scale* for distances is usually a bar scale, as shown in Maps A–D. A bar scale is normally subdivided, enabling the reader to measure distance directly on the map.

An *area scale* can also be used, in which one unit of area (square inches, square centimeters) is proportional to the same square units on the earth. The scale may be expressed as either $1:62,500^2$ or 1 to the square of 62,500. Area scales are used when the transformation of the globe to the flat map has been made so areas are represented in true relation to their respective area on the earth.

When comparing map scales, it is helpful to remember that the *larger* the scale (see Map A) the smaller the area represented and the greater the amount of detail that a map can include. The *smaller* the scale (see Maps B, C, D) the larger the area covered and the less detail that can be presented.

Large-scale maps are useful when readers need such detailed information as the location of roadways, major buildings, city plans, and the like. On a smaller scale, the reader is able to place cities in relation to one another and recognize other prominent features of the region. At the smallest scale, the reader can get a broad view of several states and an idea of the total area. Finer details cannot be shown.

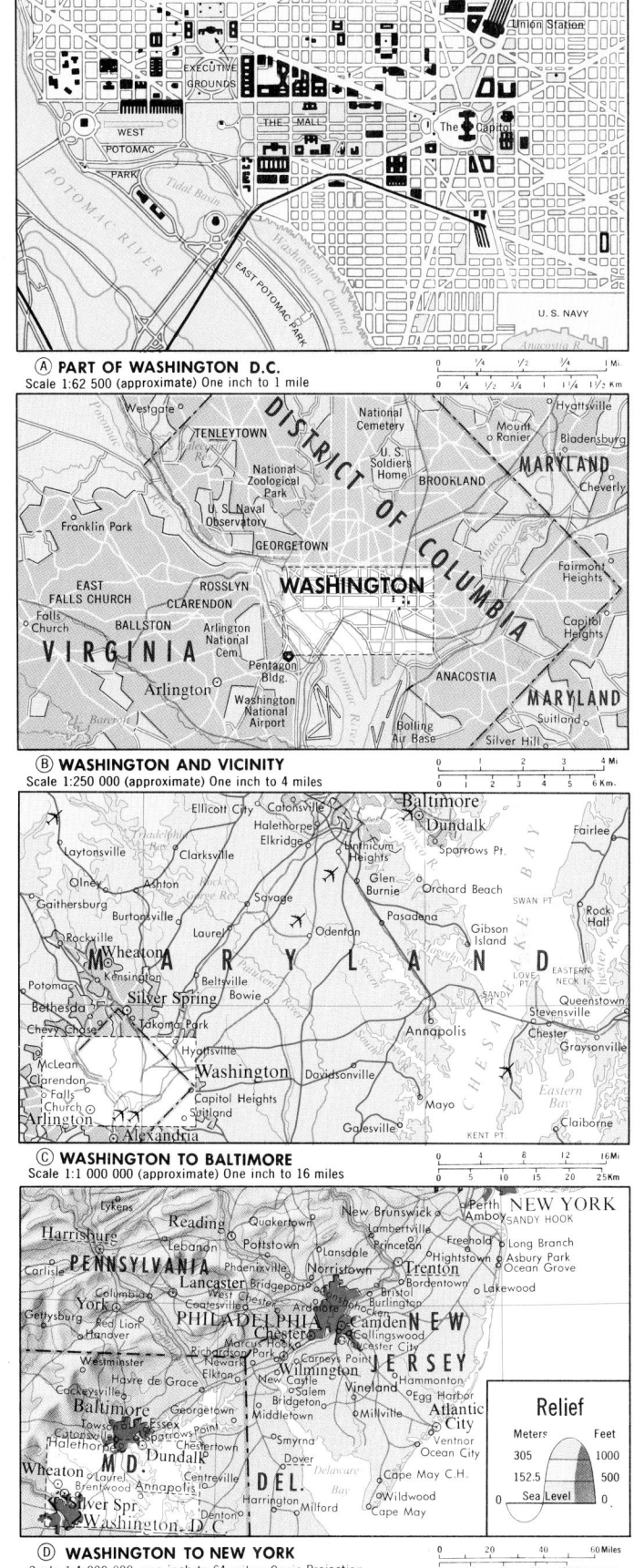

Ⓐ **PART OF WASHINGTON D.C.**
Scale 1:62 500 (approximate) One inch to 1 mile

Ⓑ **WASHINGTON AND VICINITY**
Scale 1:250 000 (approximate) One inch to 4 miles

Ⓒ **WASHINGTON TO BALTIMORE**
Scale 1:1 000 000 (approximate) One inch to 16 miles

Ⓓ **WASHINGTON TO NEW YORK**
Scale 1:4 000 000 one inch to 64 miles. Conic Projection

Map Projections

Every cartographer is faced with the problem of transforming the curved surface of the earth onto a flat plane with a minimum of distortion. The systematic transformation of locations on the earth (spherical surface) to locations on a map (flat surface) is called projection.

It is not possible to represent on a flat map the spatial relationships of angle, distance, direction, and area that only a globe can show faithfully. As a result, projection systems inevitably involve some distortion. On large-scale maps representing a few square miles, the distortion is generally negligible. But on maps depicting large countries, continents, or the entire world, the amount of distortion can be significant. Some maps of the Western Hemisphere, because of their projection, incorrectly portray Canada and Alaska as larger than the United States and Mexico, while South America looks considerably smaller than its northern neighbors.

One of the more practical ways map readers can become aware of projection distortions and learn how to make allowances for them is to compare the projection grid of a flat map with the grid of a globe. Some important characteristics of the globe grid are found listed on page xii.

There are an infinite number of possible map projections, all of which distort one or more of the characteristics of the globe in varying degrees. The projection system that a cartographer chooses depends on the size and location of the area being projected and the purpose of the map. In this atlas, most of the maps are drawn on projections that give a consistent area scale; good land and ocean shape; parallels that are parallel; and as consistent a linear scale as possible throughout the projection.

The transformation process is actually a mathematical one, but to aid in visualizing this process, it is helpful to consider the earth reduced to the scale of the intended map and then projected onto a simple geometric shape—a cylinder, cone, or plane. These geometric forms are then flattened to two dimensions to produce cylindrical, conic, and plane projections (see Figures 4, 5, and 6). Some of the projection systems used in this atlas are described on the following pages. By comparing these systems with the characteristics of a globe grid, readers can gain a clearer understanding of map distortion.

Mercator: This transformation—bearing the name of a famous sixteenth century cartographer—is conformal; that is, land masses are represented in their true shapes. Thus, for every point on the map, the angles shown are correct in every direction within a limited area. To achieve this, the projection increases latitudinal and longitudinal distances away from the equator. As a result, land *shapes* are correct, but their *areas* are distorted. The farther away from the equator, the greater the area distortion. For example, on a Mercator map, Alaska appears far larger than Mexico, whereas in fact Mexico's land area is greater. The Mercator projection is used in nautical navigation, because a line connecting any two points gives the compass direction between them. (See Figure 4.)

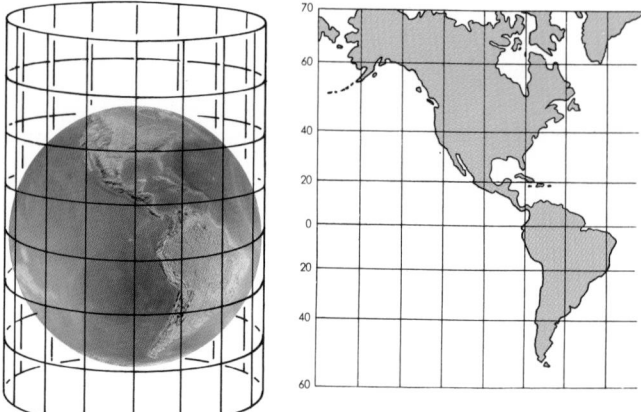

Figure 4. Mercator Projection (right), based upon the projection of the globe onto a cylinder.

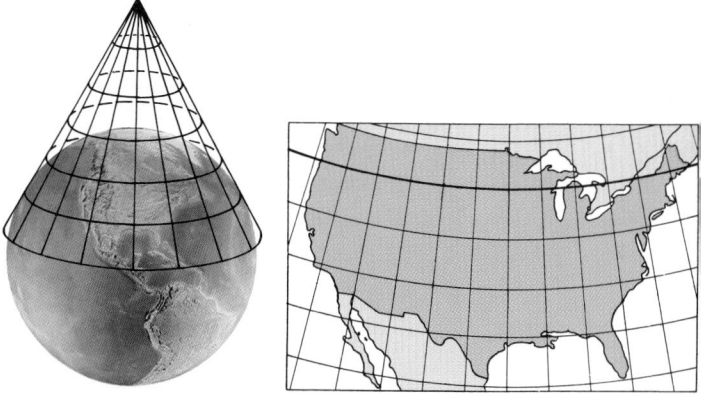

Figure 5. Projection of the globe onto a cone and a resultant Conic Projection.

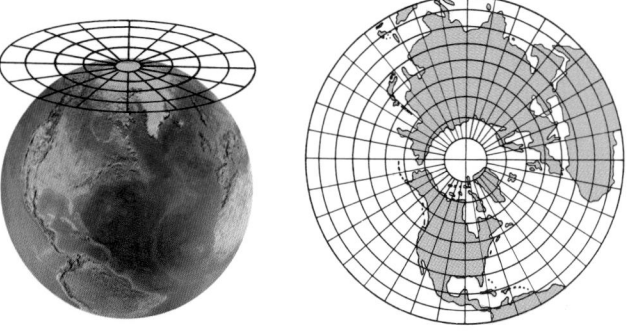

Figure 6. Lambert Equal-Area Projection (right), which assumes the projection of the globe onto a plane surface.

Conic: In this transformation—a globe projected onto a tangent cone—meridians of longitude appear as straight lines, and lines of latitude appear as parallel arcs. The parallel of tangency (that is, where the cone is presumed to touch the globe) is called a standard parallel. In this projection, distortion increases in bands away from the standard parallel. Conic projections are helpful in depicting middle-latitude areas of east-west extension. (See Figure 5.)

Lambert Equal Area *(polar case):* This projection assumes a plane touching the globe at a single point. It shows true distances close to the center (the tangent point) but increasingly distorted ones away from it. The equal-area quality (showing land areas in their correct proportion) is maintained throughout; but in regions away from the center, distortion of shape increases. (See Figure 6.)

Miller Cylindrical: O. M. Miller suggested a modification to the Mercator projection to lessen the severe area distortion in the higher latitudes. The Miller projection is neither conformal nor equal-area. Thus, while shapes are less accurate than on the Mercator, the exaggeration of *size* of areas has been somewhat decreased. The Miller cylindrical is useful for showing the entire world in a rectangular format. (See Figure 7.)

Mollweide Homolographic: The Mollweide is an equal-area projection; the least distorted areas are ovals centered just above and below the center of the projection. Distance distortions increase toward the edges of the map. The Mollweide is used for world-distribution maps where a pleasing oval look is desired along with the equal-area quality. It is one of the bases used in the Goode's Interrupted Homolosine projection. (See Figure 8.)

Sinusoidal, or Sanson-Flamsteed: In this equal-area projection the scale is the same along all parallels and the central meridian. Distortion of shapes is less along the two main axes of the projection but increases markedly toward the edges. Maps depicting areas such as South America or Africa can make good use of the Sinusoidal's favorable characteristics by situating the land masses along the central meridian, where the shapes will be virtually undistorted. The Sinusoidal is also one of the bases used in the Goode's Interrupted Homolosine. (See Figure 9.)

Goode's Interrupted Homolosine: An equal-area projection, Goode's is composed of the Sinusoidal grid from the equator to about 40° N and 40° S latitudes; beyond these latitudes, the Mollweide is used. This grid is interrupted so that land masses can be projected with a minimum of shape distortion by positioning each section on a separate central meridian. Thus, the shapes as well as the sizes of land masses are represented with a high degree of fidelity. Oceans can also be positioned in this manner. (See Figure 10.)

Robinson: This recently devised transformation is a projection that serves as a compromise of all the distortions that can occur on a world map. Though no single attribute is maintained, the projection minimizes visually disturbing distortions. As a result, the continental outlines "look" appropriate.

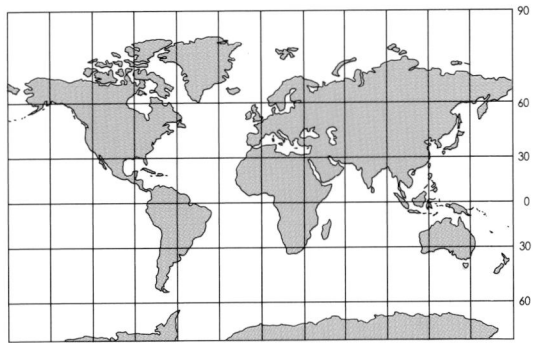

Figure 7. Miller Cylindrical Projection.

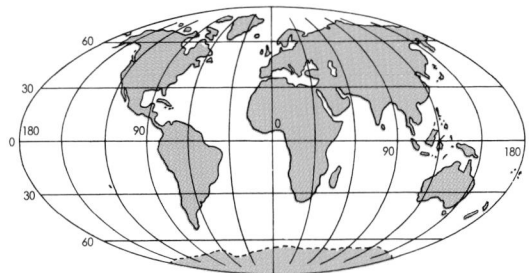

Figure 8. Mollweide Homolographic Projection.

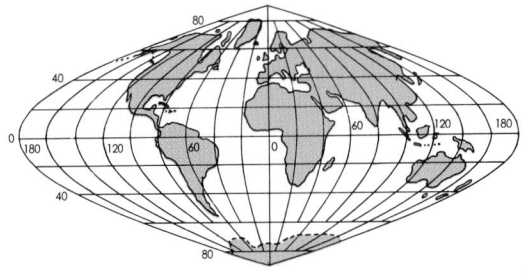

Figure 9. Sinusoidal Projection.

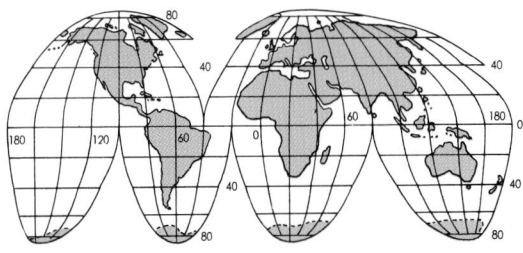

Figure 10. Goode's Interrupted Homolosine Projection.

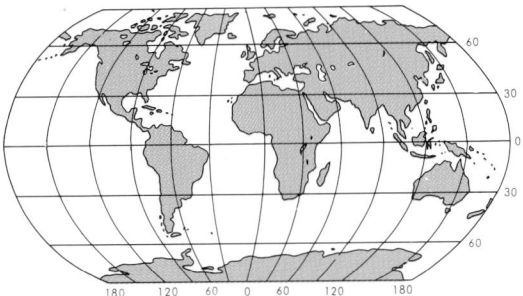

Figure 11. Robinson Projection.

Bonne: This equal-area transformation is mathematically related to the Sinusoidal. Distances are true along all parallels and the central meridian. Farther out from the central meridian, however, the increasing obliqueness of the grid's angles distorts shape and distance. This limits the area that can be usefully projected. Bonne projections, like conics, are best employed for relatively small areas in middle latitudes. (See Figure 12.)

Conic with Two Standard Parallels: The linear scale of this projection is consistent along two standard parallels instead of only one as in the simple conic. Since the spacing of the other parallels is reduced somewhat between the standard parallels and progressively enlarged beyond them, the projection does not exhibit the equal-area property. Careful selection of the standard parallels, however, provides good representation of limited areas. Like the Bonne projection, this system is widely used for areas in middle latitudes. (See Figure 13.)

Polyconic: In this system, the globe is projected onto a series of strips taken from tangent cones. Parallels are nonconcentric circles, and each is divided equally by the meridians, as on the globe. While distances along the straight central meridian are true, they are increasingly exaggerated along the curving meridians. Likewise, general representation of areas and shapes is good near the central meridian but progressively distorted away from it. Polyconic projections are used for middle-latitude areas to minimize all distortions and were employed for large-scale topographic maps. (See Figure 14.)

Lambert Conformal Conic: This conformal transformation system usually employs two standard parallels. Distortion increases away from the standard parallels, being greatest at the edges of the map. It is useful for projecting elongated east-west areas in the middle latitudes and is ideal for depicting the forty-eight contiguous states. It is also widely used for aeronautical and meteorological charts. (See Figure 15.)

Lambert Equal Area *(oblique and polar cases):* This equal-area projection can be centered at any point on the earth's surface, perpendicular to a line drawn through the globe. It maintains correct angles to all points on the map from its center (point of tangency), but distances become progressively distorted toward the edges. It is most useful for roughly circular areas or areas whose dimensions are nearly equal in two perpendicular directions.

The two most common forms of the Lambert projection are the oblique and the polar, shown in Figures 6 and 16. Although the meridians and parallels for the forms are different, the distortion characteristics are the same.

Important characteristics of the globe grid

1. All meridians of longitude are equal in length and meet at the Poles.
2. All lines of latitude are parallel and equally spaced on meridians.
3. The length, or circumference, of the parallels of latitude decreases as one moves from the equator to the Poles. For instance, the circumference of the parallel at 60° latitude is one-half the circumference of the equator.
4. Meridians of longitude are equally spaced on each parallel, but the distance between them decreases toward the Poles.
5. All parallels and meridians meet at right angles.

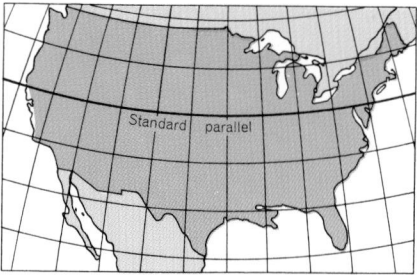

Figure 12.
Bonne Projection.

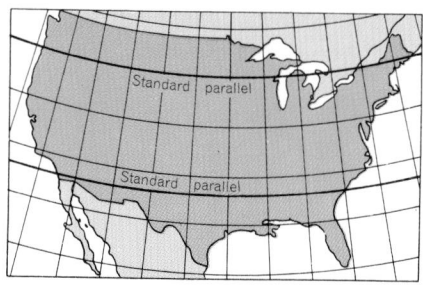

Figure 13.
Conic Projection with Two Standard Parallels.

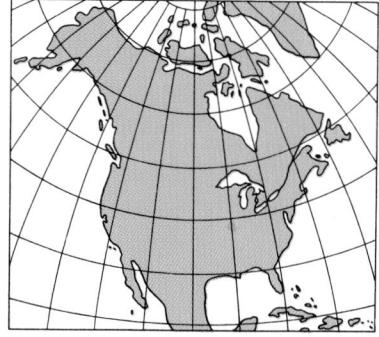

Figure 14.
Polyconic Projection.

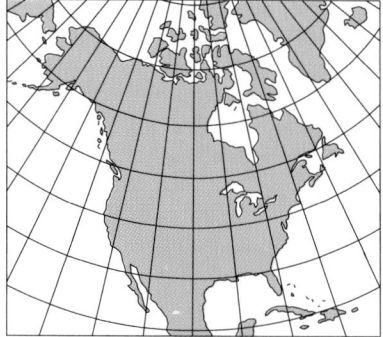

Figure 15.
Lambert Conformal Conic Projection.

Figure 16.
Lambert Equal-Area Projection (oblique case).

REMOTELY SENSED IMAGERY

Recent technological advances have greatly expanded our ability to "see" surface features on the earth. *Remote sensing* can be defined as gathering and recording from a distance information about many types of geographic features. Human beings have been using a form of remote sensing for thousands of years. To gather information about terrain, people have climbed trees or hilltops and used their eyes, ears, and even their sense of smell to detect what lay in the distance. Now, with highly sophisticated cameras and electronic sensing equipment as our remote sensors, we can learn a great deal more about our world than we have been able to gather with our physical senses.

Remote sensing is based on two fundamental principles. First, each type of surface material (rock, soil, vegetation) absorbs and reflects solar energy in a characteristic manner. In addition, a certain amount of internal energy is emitted by each surface. Remote-sensing instruments can detect this absorbed, reflected, and emitted energy and produce photographs or images.

Second, while the human eye is sensitive to only a small portion of the electromagnetic spectrum (shown as A in the top illustration of Figure 17), remote-sensing instruments can work in longer and shorter wavelengths, generally in the infrared and radar, or microwave, regions. These areas of the spectrum are often referred to as bands.

In remote-sensing photography, the most commonly used bands, in addition to those in the visible spectrum, are the near-infrared bands of 0.7 to 0.8μ (micrometers) and 0.8 to 1.1μ. Infrared photography has proved invaluable in studying agricultural areas. Since healthy plants reflect a considerable amount of near-infrared light, high-altitude photographs using this band of the spectrum can detect diseased vegetation before the problem is visible to the naked eye.

Multispectral photographic techniques are also being used. In this type of remote sensing, reflected energy from a surface is isolated into a number of given wavelength bands (shown in the bottom illustration of Figure 17). Each band can be separately recorded on film, or bands can be recorded simultaneously. These restricted wavelengths include a blue band of 0.4 to 0.5μ, a green band of 0.5 to 0.6μ, and a red band of 0.6 to 0.7μ. Scientists can select various band widths in order to highlight certain features within an area. The photographs in Figure 18 demonstrate the different effects that multispectral photography can produce and the types of information that can be revealed.

Thermal infrared (shown as B in the top illustration in Figure 17) and radar, or microwave, (shown as C) have also been important for gathering geographical data. Thermal imagery records the temperatures of surface features and is collected through electronic sensing instruments, not by cameras. These images show "hot spots" in lakes, rivers, and coastal areas where waste discharges are affecting the water temperature. Thermal-infrared sensing can also pick up animal populations that may be camouflaged to the naked eye. Heat loss from buildings can also be measured.

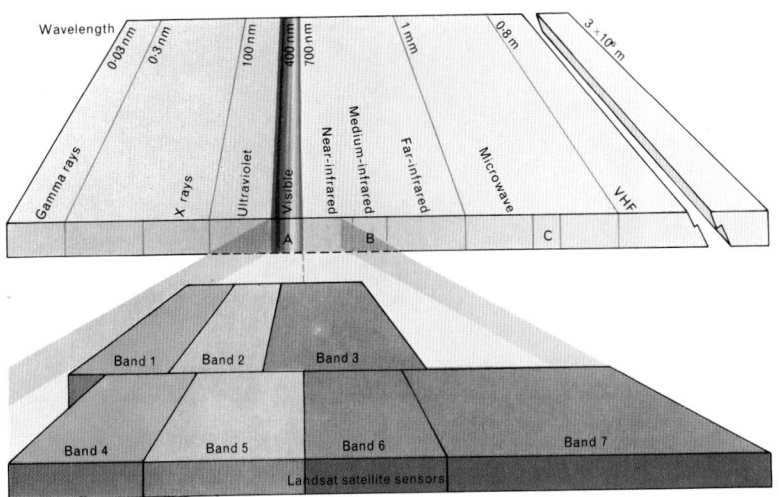

Figure 17. Top: The electromagnetic spectrum.
Bottom: Visible portion of the spectrum.

0.7 to 0.8μ band: Black-and-white, infrared.

0.8 to 0.9μ band: Black-and-white, infrared.

0.5 to $0.8\ \mu$ band: Color infrared.

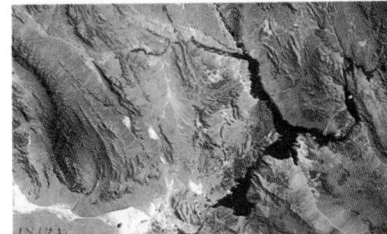

0.4 to 0.7μ band: Color.

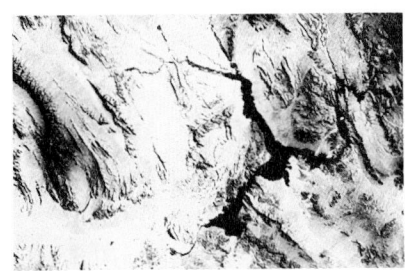

0.6 to 0.7μ band: Black-and-white, visible.

0.5 to 0.6μ band: Black-and-white, visible.

Figure 18. Images taken over Lake Mead, Nevada, by a multispectral camera. Each of the images has been derived from a different wavelength band of the spectrum.

Figure 19. Landsat (satellite) image of southeastern Colorado.

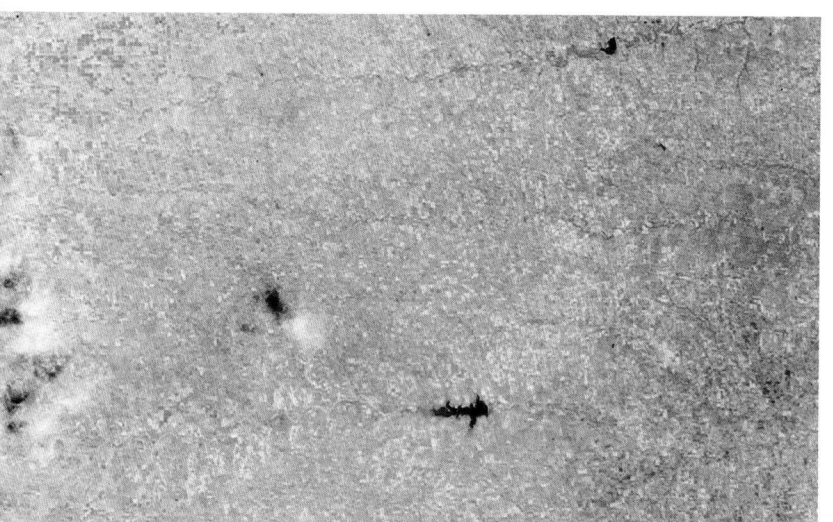

Figure 20. Landsat (satellite) image of western Kansas.

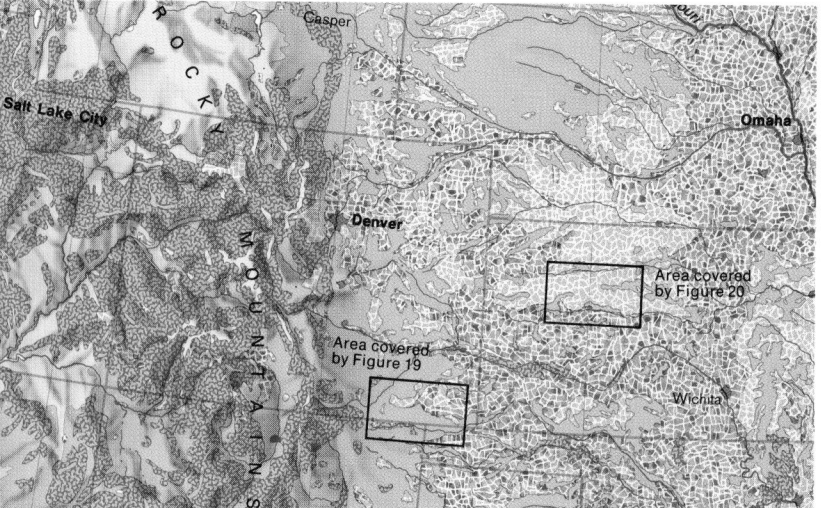

Figure 21. Land use (environment) map derived by using information from the satellite images in Figures 19 and 20.

Radar differs from other sensing methods in that a signal is sent out by the sensor, and the intensity of the reflected "echo" is recorded electronically. (The images may then be printed as a photograph.) Radar has the advantage of being unaffected by weather conditions, and in areas with persistent cloud cover it has proved to be the most reliable instrument available. This type of remote sensing can record surface relief features with remarkable accuracy. It is also useful in searching for mineral deposits and in detecting the types and extent of land ice, sea ice, and groundwater.

Landsat

Perhaps the most well-known examples of remotely sensed imagery are the pictures gathered by the Landsat satellites. Originally known as ERTS (Earth Resource Technology Satellite), Landsat 1 was launched in 1972 and functioned until 1979. Landsat 2 and Landsat 3—launched in 1975 and 1978, respectively—are still collecting data.

These satellites carry a system that views the earth in two visible and two near-infrared bands. The images are gathered electronically by sensors that scan the terrain directly beneath the satellite and record energy from individual areas on the ground. The size of these areas is determined by the spot size, or resolution capacity, of the optical scanner on board the satellite.

The smallest individual area distinguished by the scanner is called a picture element, or *pixel.* Each Landsat pixel covers about an acre of the earth's surface, with approximately 7,800,000 pixels composing each image (an image covers 115 x 115 mi or 185 x 185 km). The pixels are recorded as digits and transmitted to a ground receiving station. The digits represent brightness values and are stored in a computer as four separate arrays, one for each band of the visible and near-infrared light used. The digits can be electronically manipulated to produce false-color pictures like those shown in Figure 19 and Figure 20. A single Landsat satellite can gather some thirty million bits of data for each frame in about twenty-five seconds.

This form of data gathering has a number of advantages over conventional photography. Chiefly, the digits can be computer enhanced to bring out specific features more clearly and reveal subtle changes that may not appear on a conventional photograph of the same area.

Scientists are still discovering new uses for Landsat images. The uniform orbits of the Landsat satellites allow for coverage of the same terrain every eighteen days. As a result, the scanners can detect changes in crops, vegetation, and farming patterns; damage resulting from earthquakes, hurricanes, floods, and fires; and movements of desert sands, erosion patterns, and levels of some pollutants discharged into waterways.

Landsat images are particularly helpful to cartographers in correcting existing maps or creating new ones, as the striking resemblance between the environmental map (Figure 21) and the two pictures above it shows.

High-Altitude Imagery

Cartographers also benefit from the increased use of high-altitude photography. Figure 22 is a good example of an infrared photograph taken with a high-altitude camera mounted in an aircraft. The imagery gathered is limited by the sensitivity of the film, which can record only in the 0.3 to 1.1μ range of the spectrum. Even within this range, and using only black-and-white film, the data collected can be used to generate highly accurate 1:24,000 topographic maps, such as the one shown in Figure 23. Side benefits of this form of photography can be the production of orthophotomaps and digital elevation models (DEM). A DEM is composed of a set of equally spaced surface elevations for an area of the earth.

High-altitude photographs, like satellite pictures, can be used to monitor changes. Often these pictures will record shifts in land use, transportation lines, erosion, drainage patterns, soil characteristics, and surface structures.

Although *Goode's World Atlas* does not employ topographic maps, they are used as a reference source for the volume. High-altitude photography makes it possible to update such features as highway networks, metropolitan areas, the shape and flow of rivers and lakes, ocean currents, and ice formations.

Recent and future technological advances in collecting geographic information promise to make the cartographer's job somewhat easier. More important, these advances will allow us to give the atlas user more-detailed and up-to-date knowledge about our world and the impact of human activity around the globe.

Joel L. Morrison

Edward B. Espenshade, Jr.

Figure 22. High-altitude infrared image of the Goodland, Kansas, area.

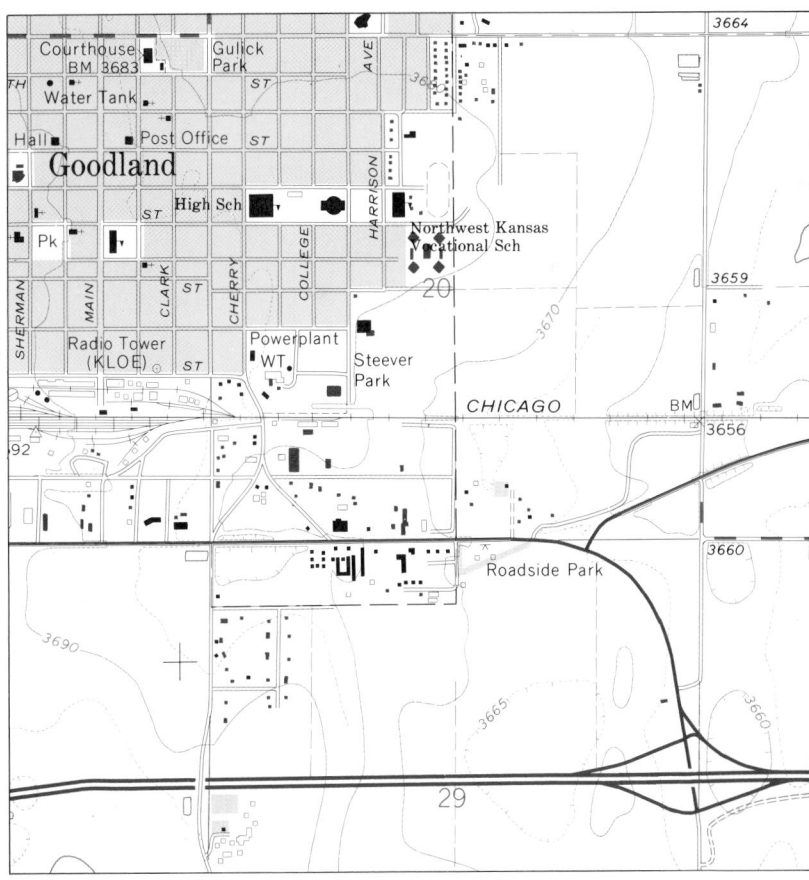

Figure 23. 1:24,000 United States Geological Survey map of the Goodland, Kansas, area.

THE SEASONS (NORTHERN HEMISPHERE)

SUMMER SOLSTICE
Noon sun is directly overhead at 23½° N. Longest day of year.

VERNAL EQUINOX
Noon sun is directly overhead at the equator, on its apparent migration North. Day and night are equal.

SPRING

NIGHT — JUNE 21 — DAY

NIGHT — MAR. 21 — DAY

TANGENT SUN RAY
ARCTIC CIRCLE
OBLIQUE SUN RAYS
TROPIC OF CANCER
EQUATOR
VERTICAL SUN RAY
TROPIC OF CAPRICORN
OBLIQUE SUN RAYS
ANTARCTIC CIRCLE
SOUTH POLE
TANGENT SUN RAY

Aphelion July 1
AXIS OF
Aphelion 94.5 million miles
EARTH'S ORBIT

SUMMER

SUN

WINTER

EARTH'S ORBIT
EARTH'S ORBIT
EARTH'S ORBIT
Perihelion 91.5 million miles
Perihelion Jan. 1

TANGENT SUN RAY
NORTH POLE
ARCTIC CIRCLE
OBLIQUE SUN RAYS
TROPIC OF CANCER
EQUATOR
VERTICAL SUN RAY
TROPIC OF CAPRICORN
OBLIQUE SUN RAYS
ANTARCTIC CIRCLE
TANGENT SUN RAY

DAY — SEPT. 23 — NIGHT

DAY — DEC. 22 — NIGHT

AUTUMN

AUTUMNAL EQUINOX
Noon sun is directly overhead at the equator, on its apparent migration South. Day and night are equal.

WINTER SOLSTICE
Noon sun is directly overhead at 23½° S. Shortest day of year.

NEW MOON — WANING CRESCENT — LAST QUARTER — GIBBOUS MOON — FULL MOON — GIBBOUS MOON — FIRST QUARTER — WAXING CRESCENT — NEW MOON

PATH OF MOON
EARTH
PATH OF EARTH
SUN RAYS
SUN RAYS
EARTH
EARTH
NEW MOON
SUN RAYS
SUN RAYS
NEW MOON

PATHS OF EARTH AND MOON DURING ONE LUNAR MONTH

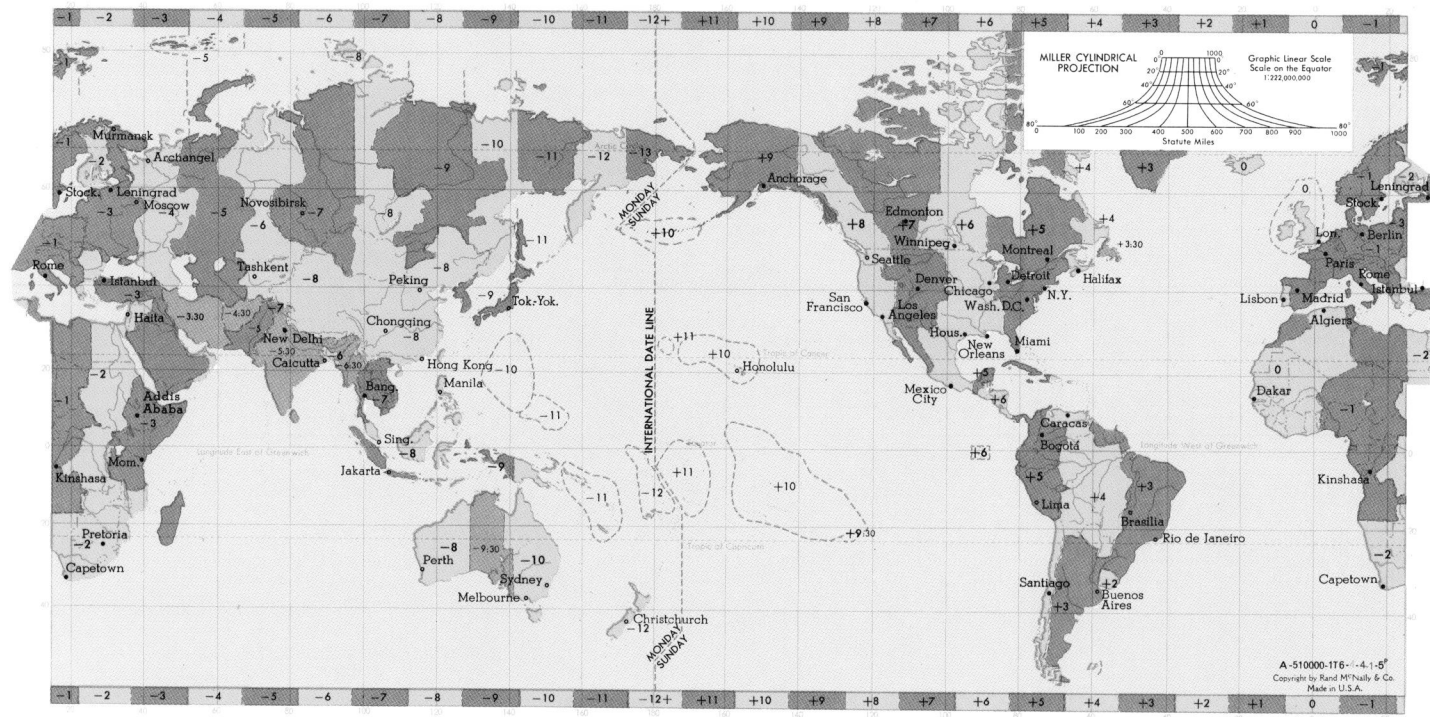

MILLER CYLINDRICAL PROJECTION
Graphic Linear Scale
Scale on the Equator
1:222,000,000

Time Zones

The surface of the earth is divided into 24 time zones. Each zone represents 15° of longitude or one hour of time. The time of the initial, or zero, zone is based on the central meridian of Greenwich and is adopted eastward and westward for a distance of 7½° of longitude. Each of the zones in turn is designated by a number representing the hours (+ or −) by which its standard time differs from Greenwich mean time. These standard time zones are indicated by bands of orange and yellow. Areas which have a fractional deviation from standard time are shown in an intermediate color. The irregularities in the zones and the fractional deviations are due to political and economic factors.
(Revised to 1980. After U.S. Defense Mapping Agency)

A-510000-1T6-·-4·1-5°
Copyright by Rand McNally & Co.
Made in U.S.A.

world thematic maps

This section of the atlas consists of more than sixty thematic maps presenting world patterns and distributions. Together with accompanying graphs, these maps communicate basic information on mineral resources, agricultural products, trade, transportation, and other selected aspects of the natural and cultural geographical environment.

A thematic map uses symbols to show certain characteristics of, generally, one class of geographical information. This "theme" of a thematic map is presented upon a background of basic locational information—coastline, country boundaries, major drainage, etc. The map's primary concern is to communicate visually basic impressions of the distribution of the theme. For instance, on page 39 the distribution of cattle shown by point symbols impresses the reader with relative densities—the distribution of cattle is much more uniform throughout the United States than it is in China, and cattle are more numerous in the United States than in China.

Although it is possible to use a thematic map to obtain exact values of a quantity or commodity, it is not the purpose intended, any more than a thematic map is intended to be used to give precise distances from New York to Moscow. If one seeks precise statistics for each country, he may consult the bar graph on the map or a statistical table.

The map on this page is an example of a special class of thematic maps called cartograms. The cartogram assigns to a named earth region an area based on some value other than land surface area. In the cartogram below the areas assigned are proportional to their countries' populations and tinted according to their rate of natural increase. The result of mapping on this base is a meaningful way of portraying this distribution since natural increase is causally related to existing size of population. On the other hand, natural increase is not causally related to earth area. In the other thematic maps in this atlas, relative earth sizes have been considered when presenting the distributions.

Real and hypothetical geographical distributions of interest to man are practically limitless but can be classed into point, line, area, or volume information relative to a specific location or area in the world. The thematic map, in communicating these fundamental classes of information, utilizes point, line, and area symbols. The symbols may be employed to show *qualitative* differences (differences in *kind*) of a certain category of information and may also show *quantitative* differences in the information (differences in *amount*). For example, the natural-vegetation map (page 16) was based upon information gathered by many observations over a period of time. It utilizes area symbols (color and pattern) to show the difference in the *kind* of vegetation as well as the extent. Quantitative factual information was shown on the annual-precipitation map, page 14, by means of isohyets (lines connecting points of equal rainfall). Also, area symbols were employed to show the intervals between the lines. In each of these thematic maps, there is one primary theme, or subject; the map communicates the information far better than volumes of words and tables could.

One of the most important aspects of the thematic-map section is use of the different maps to show comparisons and relationships among the distributions of various types of geographical information. For example, the relationship of dense population (page 20) to areas of intensive subsistence agriculture (page 30) and to manufacturing and commerce (page 28) is an important geographic concept.

The statistics communicated by the maps and graphs in this section are intended to give an idea of the relative importance of countries in the distributions mapped. The maps are not intended to take the place of statistical reference works. No single year affords a realistic base for production, trade, and certain economic and demographic statistics. Therefore, averages of data for three or four years have been used. Together with the maps, the averages and percentages provide the student with a realistic idea of the importance of specific areas.

POPULATION

Size of each country is proportional to population.
Tints indicate rate of natural increase.

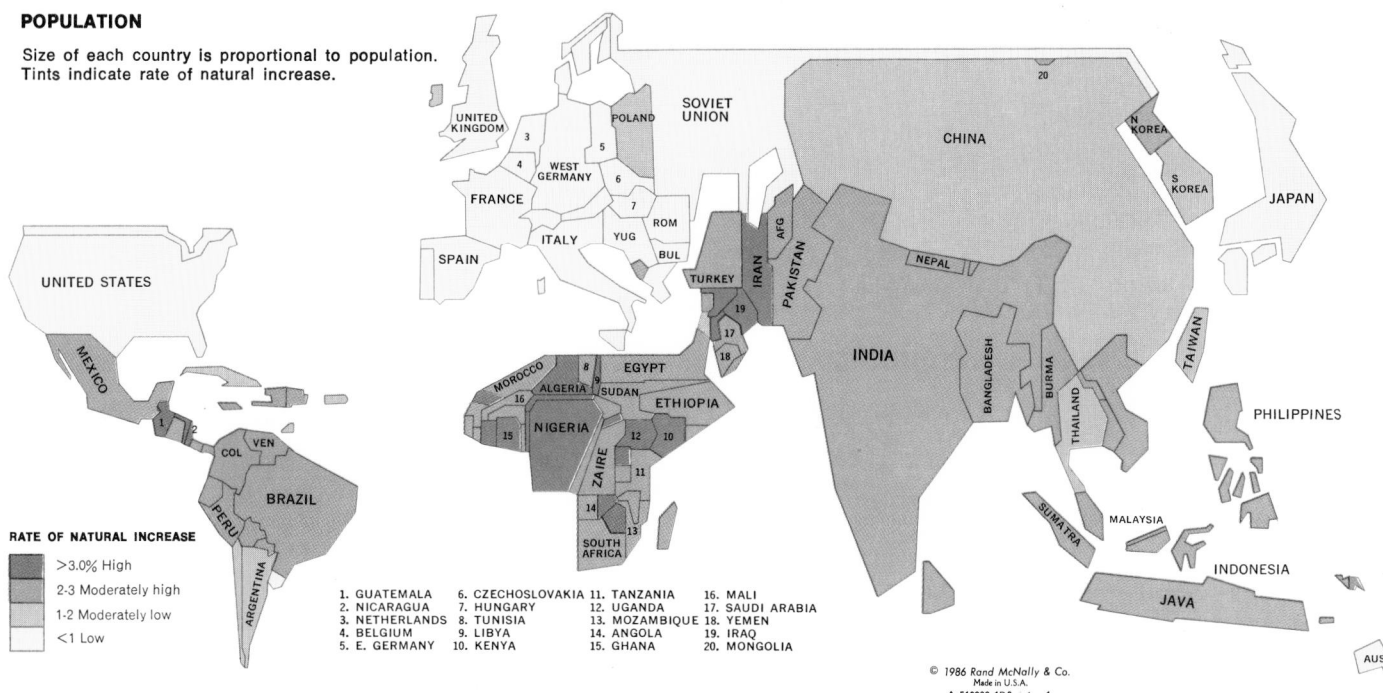

RATE OF NATURAL INCREASE

- >3.0% High
- 2-3 Moderately high
- 1-2 Moderately low
- <1 Low

1. GUATEMALA	6. CZECHOSLOVAKIA	11. TANZANIA	16. MALI
2. NICARAGUA	7. HUNGARY	12. UGANDA	17. SAUDI ARABIA
3. NETHERLANDS	8. TUNISIA	13. MOZAMBIQUE	18. YEMEN
4. BELGIUM	9. LIBYA	14. ANGOLA	19. IRAQ
5. E. GERMANY	10. KENYA	15. GHANA	20. MONGOLIA

© 1986 Rand McNally & Co.
Made in U.S.A.
A-510000-1P6 -1 -1

POLITICAL

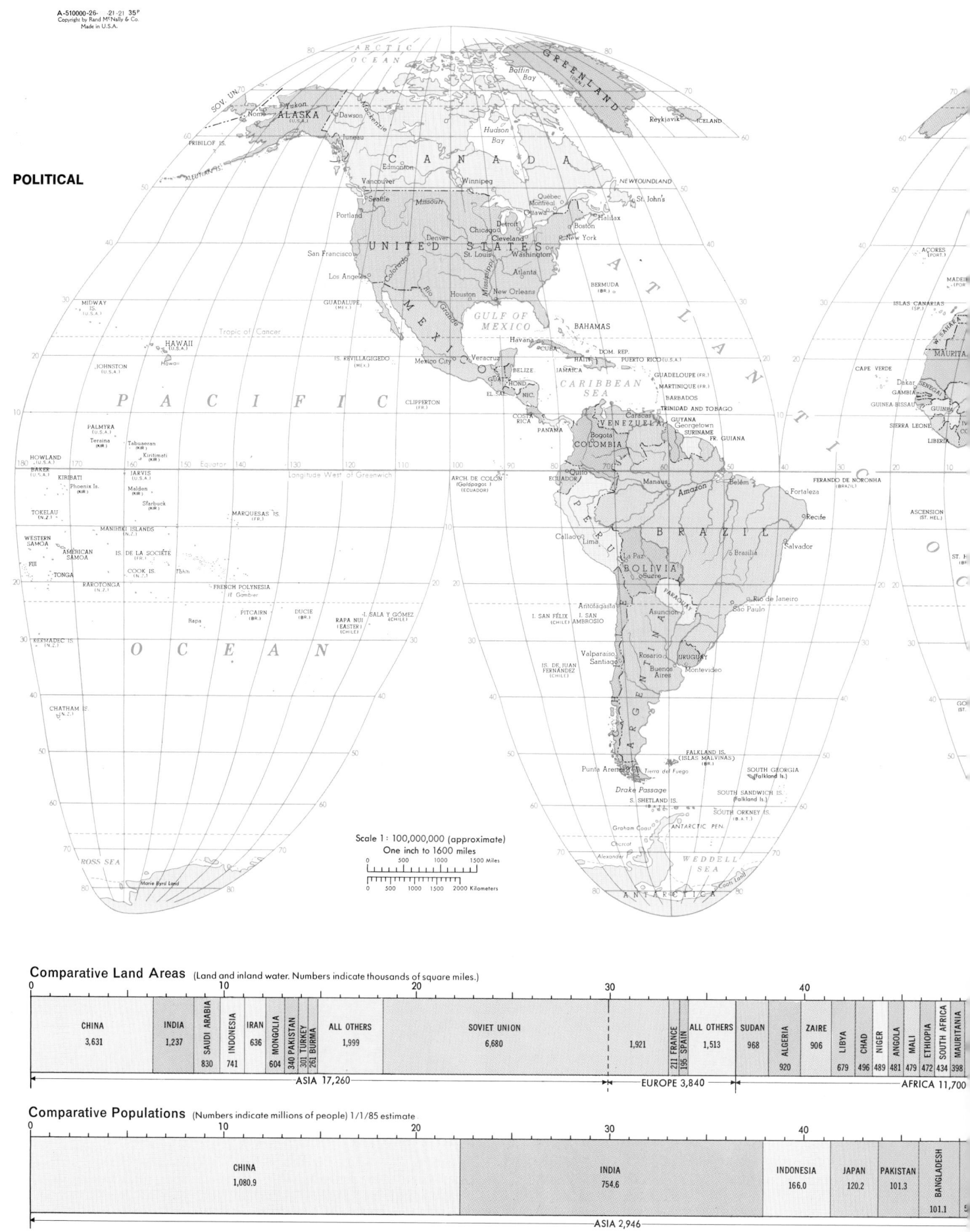

Scale 1 : 100,000,000 (approximate)
One inch to 1600 miles

0   500   1000   1500 Miles

0   500   1000   1500   2000 Kilometers

Comparative Land Areas (Land and inland water. Numbers indicate thousands of square miles.)

0	10	20	30	40

| CHINA 3,631 | INDIA 1,237 | SAUDI ARABIA | INDONESIA | IRAN 636 | MONGOLIA | PAKISTAN | TURKEY | BURMA | ALL OTHERS 1,999 | SOVIET UNION 6,680 | | 1,921 | FRANCE | SPAIN | ALL OTHERS 1,513 | SUDAN 968 | ALGERIA 920 | ZAIRE 906 | LIBYA 679 | CHAD 496 | NIGER 489 | ANGOLA 481 | MALI 479 | ETHIOPIA 472 | SOUTH AFRICA 434 | MAURITANIA 398 |

830 | 741 | 604 | 340 | 301 | 261 | 211 | 195

ASIA 17,260 ◄─────► EUROPE 3,840 ◄────► AFRICA 11,700

Comparative Populations (Numbers indicate millions of people) 1/1/85 estimate

0	10	20	30	40

| CHINA 1,080.9 | INDIA 754.6 | INDONESIA 166.0 | JAPAN 120.2 | PAKISTAN 101.3 | BANGLADESH 101.1 |

ASIA 2,946

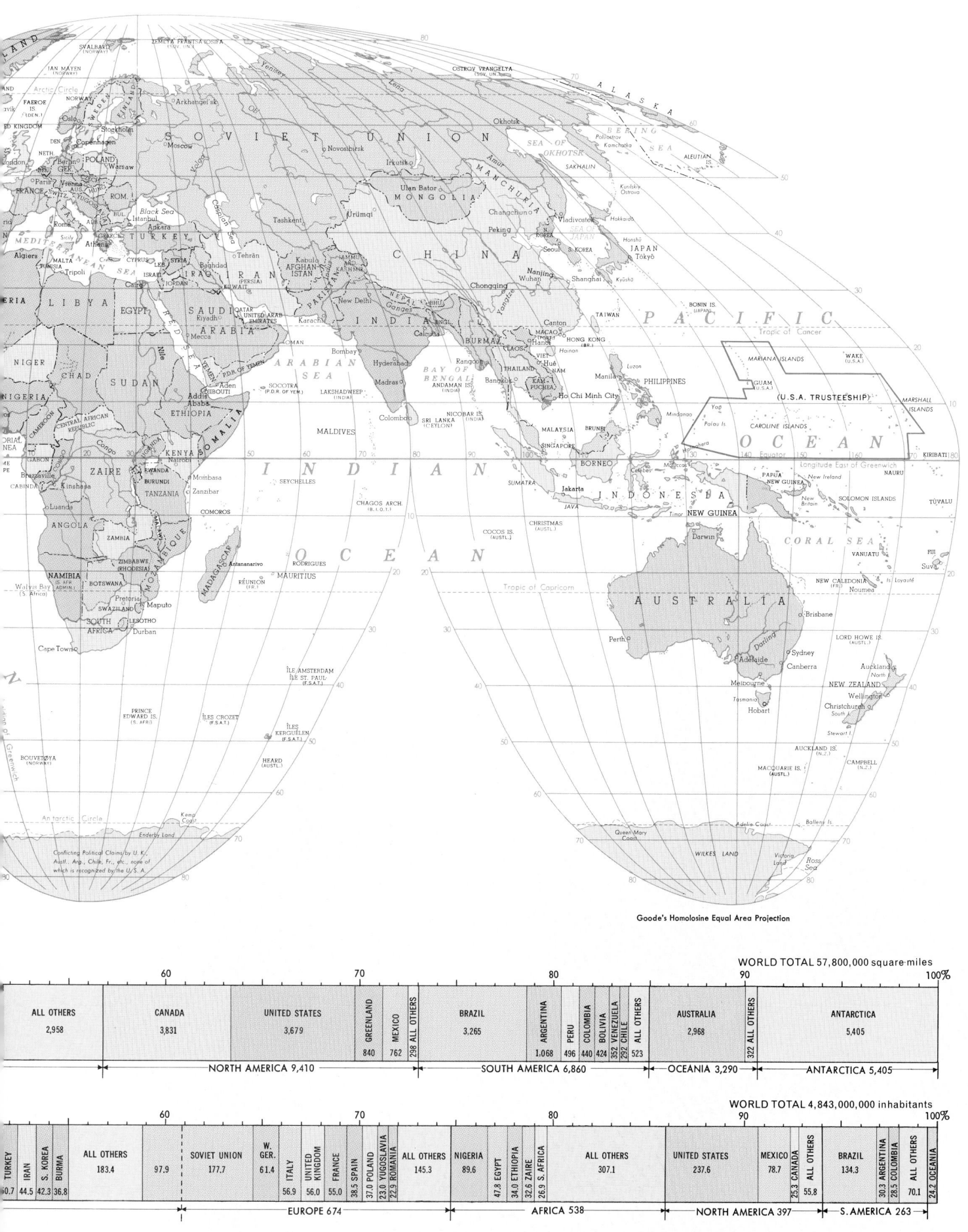

Goode's Homolosine Equal Area Projection

WORLD TOTAL 57,800,000 square miles

60	70	80	90	100%

| ALL OTHERS 2,958 | CANADA 3,831 | UNITED STATES 3,679 | GREENLAND 840 | MEXICO 762 | ALL OTHERS 298 | BRAZIL 3,265 | ARGENTINA 1,068 | PERU 496 | COLOMBIA 440 | BOLIVIA 424 | VENEZUELA 352 | CHILE 292 | ALL OTHERS 523 | AUSTRALIA 2,968 | ALL OTHERS 322 | ANTARCTICA 5,405 |

|← NORTH AMERICA 9,410 →|← SOUTH AMERICA 6,860 →|← OCEANIA 3,290 →|← ANTARCTICA 5,405 →|

WORLD TOTAL 4,843,000,000 inhabitants

60	70	80	90	100%

| TURKEY 50.7 | IRAN 44.5 | S. KOREA 42.3 | BURMA 36.8 | ALL OTHERS 183.4 | SOVIET UNION 97.9 | W. GER. 61.4 | ITALY 56.9 | UNITED KINGDOM 56.0 | FRANCE 55.0 | SPAIN 38.5 | POLAND 37.0 | YUGOSLAVIA 23.0 | ROMANIA 22.9 | ALL OTHERS 145.3 | NIGERIA 89.6 | EGYPT 47.8 | ETHIOPIA 34.0 | ZAIRE 32.6 | S. AFRICA 26.9 | ALL OTHERS 307.1 | UNITED STATES 237.6 | MEXICO 78.7 | CANADA 25.3 | ALL OTHERS 55.8 | BRAZIL 134.3 | ARGENTINA 30.3 | COLOMBIA 28.5 | ALL OTHERS 70.1 | OCEANIA 24.2 |

|← EUROPE 674 →|← AFRICA 538 →|← NORTH AMERICA 397 →|← S. AMERICA 263 →|

PHYSICAL

North Pole

ARCTIC OCEAN

ASIA

PT. BARROW
Beaufort Sea
Magnetic Pole
BANKS I.
Victoria Island
Bear I.
GREENLAND
Baffin Bay
BAFFIN ISLAND
Hekla (Vol.) 4 747
ICELAND
KAP FARVEL
GRE

Nunivak
Mt. McKinley 20 320
Mt. Logan 19 520
Gulf of Alaska
PRIBILOF IS.
Alaska Pen.
BERING SEA
ALEUTIAN ISLANDS
ALEUTIAN TRENCH

Great Slave L.
GREAT CENTRAL LOWLAND
L. Winnipeg
HUDSON BAY
Belcher
NORTHERN LOWLAND
LABRADOR PENINSULA AND PLATEAU
Str. of Belle Isle
NEWFOUNDLAND
KAP FARVEL

NORTH AMERICA

VANCOUVER I.
Mt. Rainier 14 410
C. Mendocino
San Francisco Bay
Mt. Whitney 14 494
GREAT BASIN
ROCKY MTS.
Pikes Peak
Mt. Mitchell
APPALACHIAN
C. COD
C. SABLE
C. HATTERAS
BERMUDA

MIDWAY IS.

Guadalupe
PENINSULA DE BAJA CALIFORNIA
C. SAN LUCAS
IS. REVILLAGIGEDO
GULF OF MEXICO
FLORIDA PEN.
C. Sable
BAHAMA ISLANDS
Cuba
GREATER ANTILLES
NORTH AMERICAN BASIN

HAWAIIAN ISLANDS
Hawaii
Mauna Kea (Vol.) 13 796
Johnston

Citlaltépetl 18 701
ISTMO DE TEHUANTEPEC
Bahia de Campeche
Pen. de Yucatán
G. de Honduras
Jamaica
WEST INDIES
Puerto Rico
LESSER ANTILLES
Guadeloupe
Martinique
Barbados
WINDWARD ISLANDS
CARIBBEAN SEA
Trinidad

Palmyra
Teraina
Tabuaeran
Kiritimati
Clipperton
Irazú (Vol.) 11 260
ISTMO DE PANAMÁ
G. de Panamá
Pta. de Gallinas

Howland
Baker
Jarvis
Malden
Starbuck
MANIHIKI IS.
PHOENIX ISLANDS
MARQUESAS IS.
ARCH. DE COLÓN (GALÁPAGOS IS.)
PTA. PARIÑAS
G. de Guayaquil
Chimborazo 20 561
ORINOCO
LLANOS
GUIANA HIGHLANDS
MARAJÓ I.
Fernando de Noronha

TOKELAU IS.
WESTERN SAMOA
Tutuila
ÍLES
SOCIETY IS.
Tahiti
Amazonas
SELVAS
CABO DE SÃO ROQUE

SOUTH AMERICA

FIJI IS.
TONGA
COOK IS.
ÍLES AUSTRALES
TUAMOTU
Is. Gambier
Pitcairn
Ducie
Rapa Nui (Easter)
Rapa
L. Titicaca
ATACAMA TRENCH
CAMPOS
PLATEAU OF MATO GROSSO
Pico da Bandeira 9 482
C. FRIO

PACIFIC OCEAN

KERMADEC IS.
KERMADEC TRENCH
I. San Félix
I. San Ambrosio
Aconcagua (Vol.) 22 831
IS. DE JUAN FERNÁNDEZ
PAMPA
Río de la Plata
TRISTAN DA CUNHA
GOU

CHATHAM IS.
ARCH. DE LOS CHONOS
G. de Peñas
G. San Matías
G. San Jorge
PATAGONIA

Tierra del Fuego
FALKLAND IS.
SHAG ROCKS
SOUTH GEORGIA
SOUTH SANDWICH IS.
CABO DE HORNOS
Drake Passage
SOUTH SHETLAND IS.
SOUTH ORKNEY IS.

ROSS SEA
Graham Coast
ANTARCTIC PENINSULA
Alexander I.
WEDDELL SEA
Scott Land

Marie Byrd Land
South Pole

ATLANTIC OCEAN

AÇORES (AZORES)
MADEIRA
Jebel Toubkal 13 665
IS. CANARIAS
ARQUIPELAGO DE CABO VERDE
C. VERT
ASCENSION
ST.

Scale 1:100,000,000 (approximate)
One inch to 1600 miles

0 500 1000 1500 Miles
0 500 1000 1500 2000 Kilometers

Meters		Feet
3 050		10 000
1 525		5 000
610		2 000
305		1 000
0	SEA L.	0
		BELOW SEA LEVEL
152.5		500
3 050		10 000
6 100		20 000

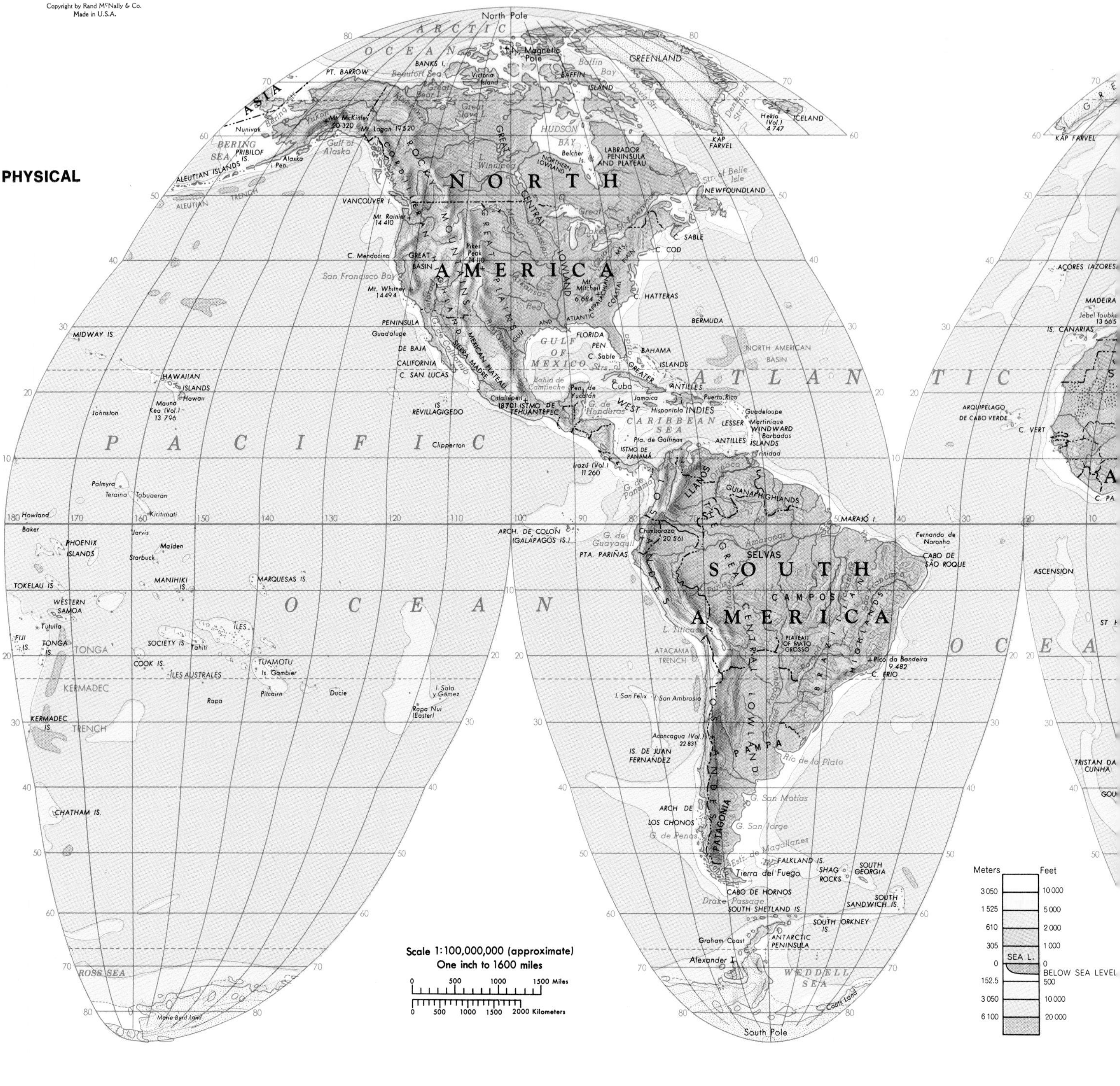

Land Elevations in Profile

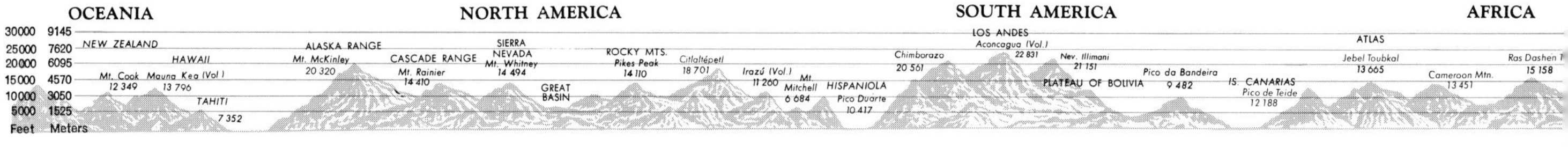

OCEANIA   NORTH AMERICA   SOUTH AMERICA   AFRICA

Feet	Meters
30000	9145
25000	7620
20000	6095
15000	4570
10000	3050
5000	1525

NEW ZEALAND
HAWAII
Mt. Cook 12 349
Mauna Kea (Vol.) 13 796
TAHITI 7 352
ALASKA RANGE
Mt. McKinley 20 320
CASCADE RANGE
Mt. Rainier 14 410
SIERRA NEVADA
Mt. Whitney 14 494
GREAT BASIN
ROCKY MTS.
Pikes Peak 14 110
Citlaltépetl 18 701
Irazú (Vol.) 11 260
Mt. Mitchell 6 684
HISPANIOLA
Pico Duarte 10 417
LOS ANDES
Aconcagua 22 831
Chimborazo 20 561
Nev. Illimani 21 151
PLATEAU OF BOLIVIA
Pico da Bandeira 9 482
IS. CANARIAS
Pico de Teide 12 188
ATLAS
Jebel Toubkal 13 665
Cameroon Mtn. 13 451
Ras Dashen 15 158

Ocean Depths in Profile

PACIFIC OCEAN   ATLANTIC

INDOCHINA HAINAN
MARIANA IS.
Sea Level
HAWAII
MEXICO
NOVA SCOTIA
GRAND BANK
ATLANTIC

Feet	Meters
5000	1525
10000	3050
15000	4570
20000	6095
25000	7620
30000	9145
35000	10670

PHILIPPINES BASIN 20 364
PHILIPPINES TRENCH 34 436
JAPAN TRENCH 34 036
MARIANA TRENCH 36 201
ALEUTIAN TRENCH 26 574
A Section along 20°N. Lat.
PUERTO RICO TRENCH 28 374
BRAZIL 20 0
A Section along 45

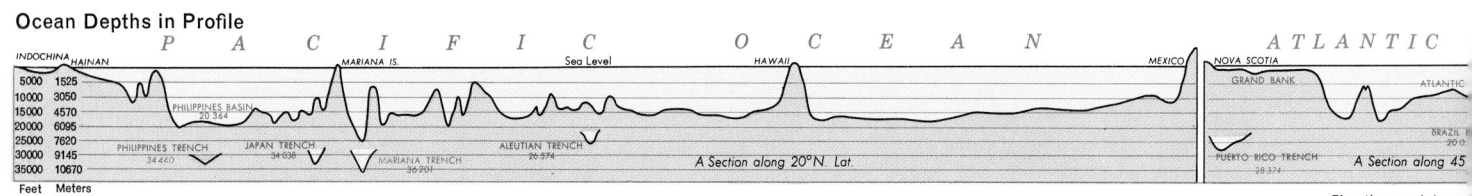

Elevations and depres

North Pole
ARCTIC OCEAN
ZEMLYA
SVALBARD
FRANTSA IOSIFA
NOVAYA
ZEMLYA
Jan Mayen
NORDKAPP
Karskoye More
POLUOSTROV TAYMYR
NOVOSIBIRSKIYE OSTROVA
Ostrov Vrangelya
N. AMERICA
ICELAND
FAEROE IS.
NORTH BRITISH SEA ISLES
SCANDINAVIAN PEN.
Gulf of Bothnia
Beloye More (White Sea)
Onezhskoye Oz.
WEST SIBERIAN PLAIN
C E N T R A L S I B E R I A N
St. Lawrence
BERING SEA
SEA OF OKHOTSK
Klyuchevskaya (Vol.) 15 584
KAMCHATKA
SAKHALIN
Mys Lopatka
KURIL'SKIY OSTROVA
ALEUTIAN

EUROPE
Mt. Blanc 15 771
Corse
MEDITERRANEAN SEA
Sardegna
Sicilia
Etna (Vol.) 11 122
Balkhash
Plateau of ASIA MINOR
CYPRUS
SYRIAN PLATEAU
Black Sea
CAUCASUS
Gora El'brus
CASPIAN DEPRESSION
Ararat 16 804
Aralskoye More
ALTAI MTS.
KHREBET KHANGAY
PLATEAU OF MONGOLIA
GOBI DESERT
STANOVOY KHREBET
MANCHURIAN PLAIN
HOKKAIDO
JAPAN TRENCH
SEA OF JAPAN
KOREAN PEN.
HONSHU
Fuji-San (Vol.) 12 388
KYUSHU

A S I A
HIGHLAND
TARIM BASIN
PAMIRS
KUNLUN SHAN
PLATEAU OF TIBET
Everest 29 028
HIMALAYAS
NORTH CHINA PLAIN
Yellow Sea
Hsinkao Shan 13 113
TAIWAN
EAST CHINA SEA
RYUKYU RETTO
BONIN IS.

SAHARA
LIBYAN DESERT
OASES OF FEZZAN
TASSILI
NUBIAN DESERT
RED SEA
IRAN
GREAT SALT DESERT
PLATEAU OF IRAN
AN NAFUD
ARABIAN PEN.
Ras al Hadd
GREAT INDIAN DESERT
PENINSULA OF INDIA
DECCAN PLATEAU
HAINAN
LUZON
MARIANA ISLANDS
Guam
WAKE
MARIANA TRENCH

AFRICA
ADAMAWA HIGHLANDS
Cameroon Mtn. 13 451
Gulf of Aden
Socotra
ETHIOPIAN
CASEYR
Ras Dashan 15 158
C. COMORIN
SRI LANKA
NICOBAR IS.
ANDAMAN ISLANDS
ISTHMUS OF KRA
Gulf of Thailand
MALAY PENINSULA
Strait of Malacca
SOUTH CHINA SEA
MINDANAO
PHILIPPINES
Kinabalu 13 455
PALAU IS.
CAROLINE ISLANDS
YAP
PHILIPPINE TRENCH
MARSHALL ISLANDS

BAY OF BENGAL
LAKSHADWEEP
MALDIVE ISLANDS
C E N T R A L
Kilimanjaro 19 340
Zanzibar
Lake Victoria
Lake Tanganyika
Lake Nyasa
CHAGOS ARCH.
DIEGO GARCIA
AMIRANTE IS.
ALDABRA IS.
COMORO IS.
C. d'Ambre
BORNEO
CELEBES
Moluccas
Celebes Sea
Banda Sea
Puncak Jaya 16 503
NEW GUINEA
New Ireland
New Britain
SOLOMON ISLANDS
Nauru
GILBERT ISLANDS
TUVALU

PLATEAU
KALAHARI DESERT
Mozambique Channel
MADAGASCAR
Maromokotro
C. FRIO
Mont aux Sources 10 822
Baía Delagoa
C. Ste. Marie
MASCARENE IS.
Rodrigues
Réunion
Mauritius
I N D I A N O C E A N
COCOS IS.
CHRISTMAS
JAVA TRENCH
JAVA
SUMATRA
SUNDA ISLANDS
Java Sea
Timor
Timor Sea
Arafura Sea
Torres Str.
C. YORK
Gulf of Carpentaria
GREAT BARRIER REEF
C O R A L S E A
NEW HEBRIDES
FIJI IS.
Viti Levu
NEW CALEDONIA

C. OF GOOD HOPE
C. AGULHAS
GREAT KARROO
ÎLE AMSTERDAM
ÎLE ST. PAUL
NORTH WEST CAPE
GT. SANDY DESERT
WESTERN PLATEAU
A U S T R A L I A
GT. VICTORIA DESERT
C. LEEUWIN
Shark Bay
Great Australian Bight
THE GREAT DIVIDING RANGE
NORTH CAPE
Mt. Kosciusko 7 310
C. HOWE
NORTH ISLAND
NEW ZEALAND
Mt. Cook 12 349
SOUTH ISLAND
Stewart
BOUNTY IS.
ANTIPODES
AUCKLAND IS.
Campbell
MACQUARIE IS.

BOUVETØYA
Heard
PRINCE EDWARD IS.
ÎLES CROZET
ÎLES KERGUÉLEN
Enderby Land
A N T A R C T I C A
DAVIS SEA
WILKES LAND
VICTORIA LAND
BALLENY IS.
Ross Sea
South Pole

For Glossary of Foreign Geographical Terms see page 248

Goode's Homolosine Equal Area Projection

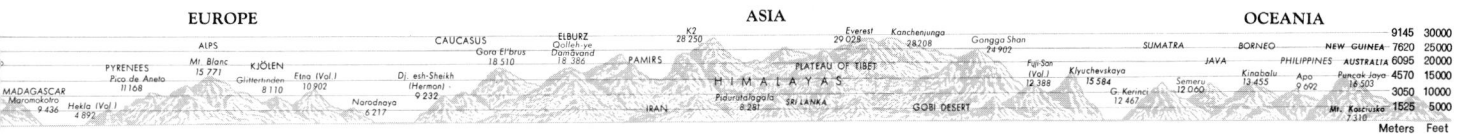

EUROPE					ASIA						OCEANIA				

EUROPE
ALPS
PYRENEES
Pico de Aneto 11 168
Mt. Blanc 15 771
KJÖLEN
Glittertinden 8 110
MADAGASCAR
Maromokotro 9 436
Hekla (Vol.) 4 892
Etna (Vol.) 10 902
Norodnaya 6 217

ASIA
CAUCASUS
Gora El'brus 18 510
ELBURZ
Qolleh-ye Damavand 18 386
PAMIRS
K2 28 250
Everest 29 028
Kanchenjunga 28 208
Gangga Shan 24 902
PLATEAU OF TIBET
HIMALAYAS
Dj. esh-Sheikh (Hermon) 9 232
Pidurutalagala 8 297
SRI LANKA
IRAN
GOBI DESERT

OCEANIA
9145 30000
SUMATRA
BORNEO
NEW GUINEA 7620 25000
JAVA
PHILIPPINES
AUSTRALIA 6095 20000
Fuji-San (Vol.) 12 388
Klyuchevskaya 15 584
Kinabalu 13 455
Apo 9 692
Puncak Jaya 16 503 4570 15000
Semeru 12 060
G. Kerinci 12 467
3050 10000
Mt. Kosciusko 7 310 1525 5000
Meters Feet

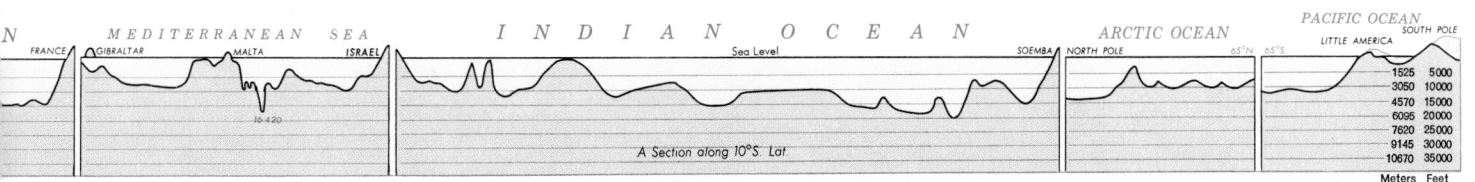

N
FRANCE
MEDITERRANEAN SEA
GIBRALTAR
MALTA 10 420
ISRAEL
I N D I A N O C E A N
Sea Level
SOEMBA
ARCTIC OCEAN
NORTH POLE
65°N
65°S
PACIFIC OCEAN
SOUTH POLE
LITTLE AMERICA
1525 5000
3050 10000
4570 15000
6095 20000
7620 25000
9145 30000
10670 35000
Meters Feet

A Section along 10°S. Lat.

en in feet

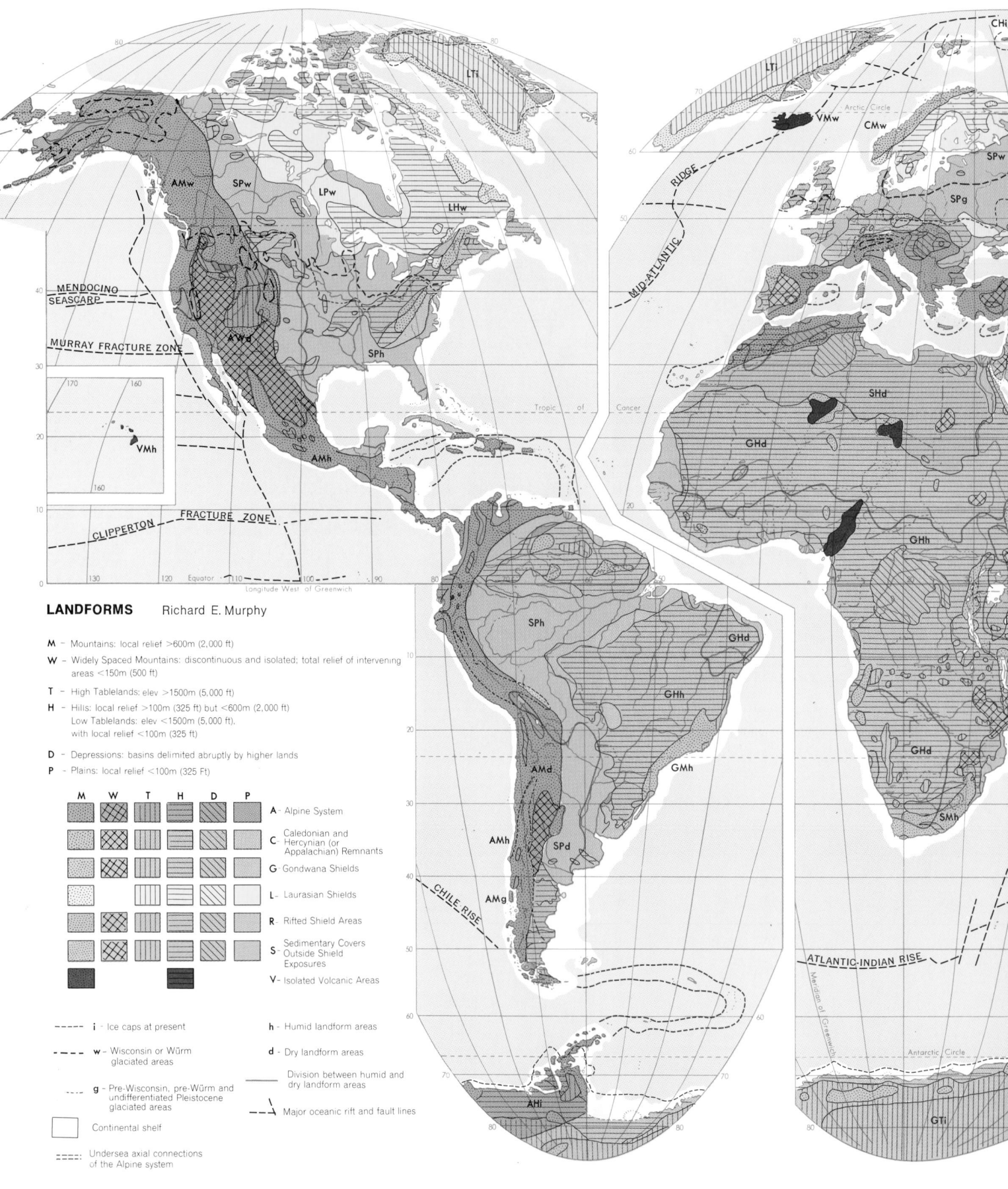

6

LANDFORMS Richard E. Murphy

M – Mountains: local relief >600m (2,000 ft)

W – Widely Spaced Mountains: discontinuous and isolated; total relief of intervening areas <150m (500 ft)

T – High Tablelands: elev >1500m (5,000 ft)

H – Hills: local relief >100m (325 ft) but <600m (2,000 ft)
Low Tablelands: elev <1500m (5,000 ft), with local relief <100m (325 ft)

D – Depressions: basins delimited abruptly by higher lands

P – Plains: local relief <100m (325 Ft)

M	W	T	H	D	P	
						A – Alpine System
						C – Caledonian and Hercynian (or Appalachian) Remnants
						G – Gondwana Shields
						L – Laurasian Shields
						R – Rifted Shield Areas
						S – Sedimentary Covers Outside Shield Exposures
						V – Isolated Volcanic Areas

- - - - - i – Ice caps at present

- - - - - w – Wisconsin or Würm glaciated areas

- - - - - g – Pre-Wisconsin, pre-Würm and undifferentiated Pleistocene glaciated areas

☐ Continental shelf

- - - - - Undersea axial connections of the Alpine system

h – Humid landform areas

d – Dry landform areas

──── Division between humid and dry landform areas

- - - - - Major oceanic rift and fault lines

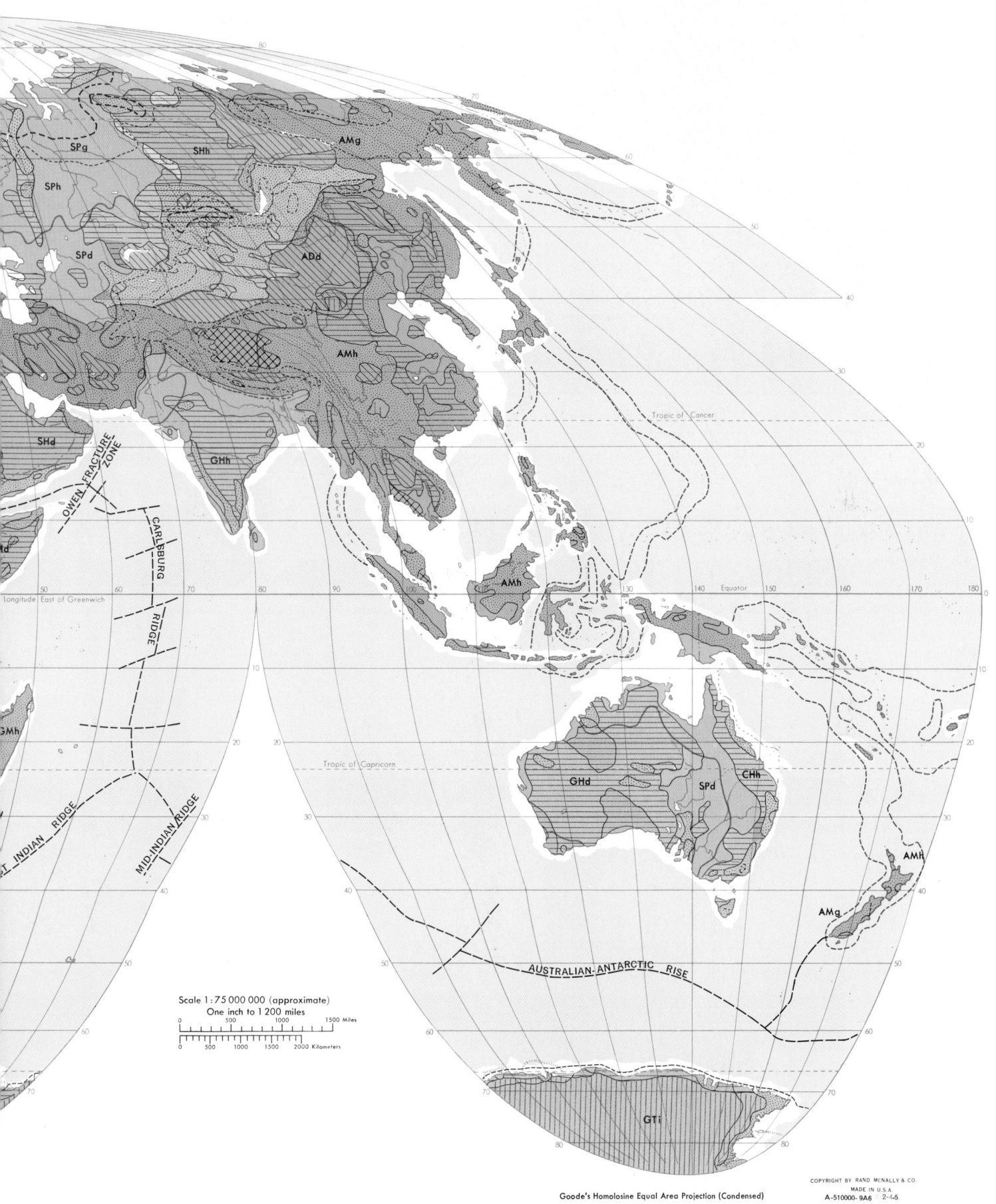

SPg

SHh

AMg

SPh

SPd

ADd

AMh

SHd

GHh

OWEN FRACTURE ZONE

CARLSBURG RIDGE

Longitude East of Greenwich

Tropic of Cancer

AMh

GMh

I INDIAN RIDGE

MID-INDIAN RIDGE

Tropic of Capricorn

GHd

SPd

CHh

AMh

AUSTRALIAN-ANTARCTIC RISE

AMg

Equator

GTi

Scale 1:75 000 000 (approximate)
One inch to 1 200 miles

0   500   1000   1500 Miles

0   500   1000   1500   2000 Kilometers

Goode's Homolosine Equal Area Projection (Condensed)

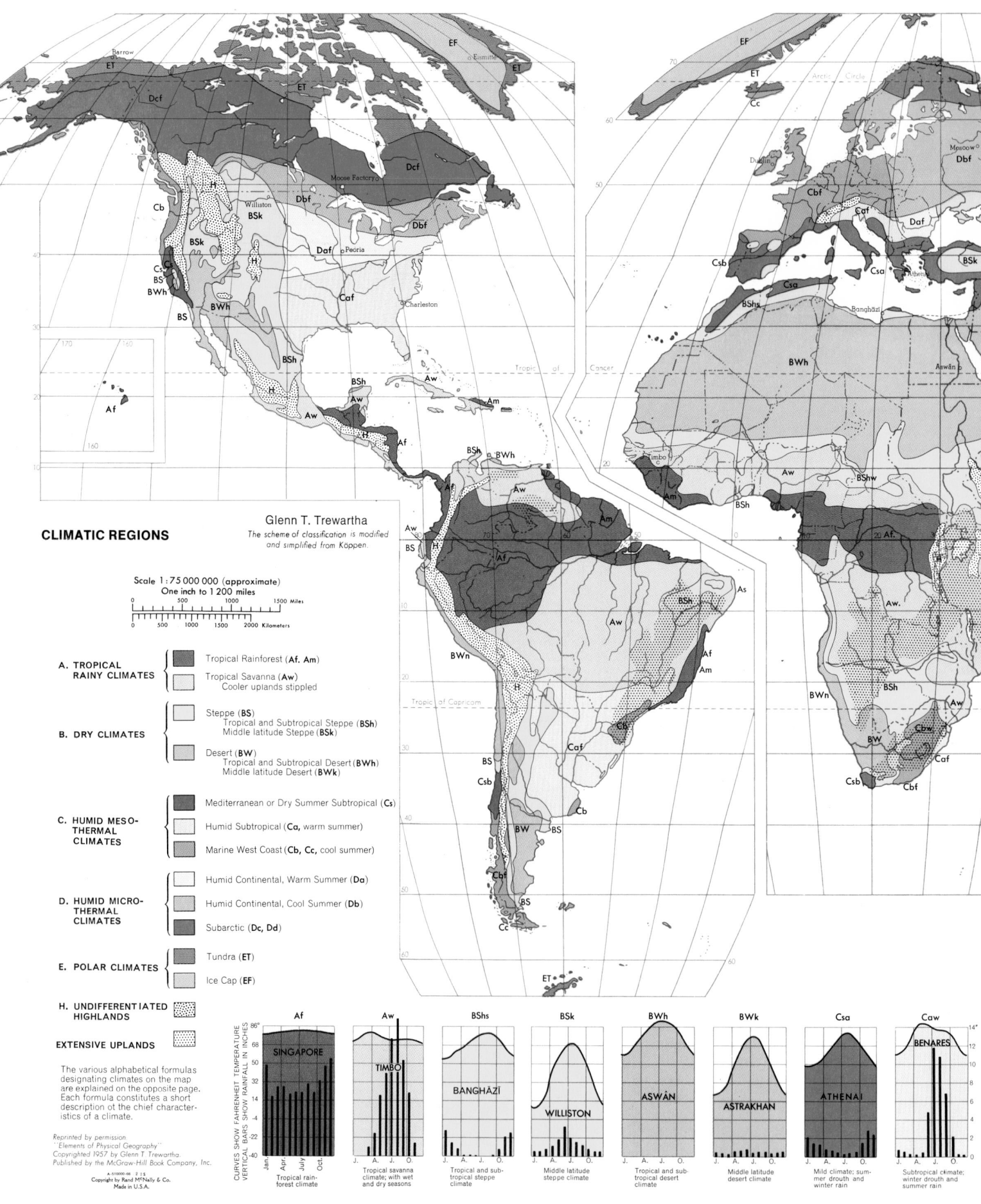

8

CLIMATIC REGIONS

Glenn T. Trewartha
The scheme of classification is modified and simplified from Köppen.

Scale 1 : 75 000 000 (approximate)
One inch to 1 200 miles

A. TROPICAL RAINY CLIMATES
- Tropical Rainforest (**Af, Am**)
- Tropical Savanna (**Aw**)
  Cooler uplands stippled

B. DRY CLIMATES
- Steppe (**BS**)
  Tropical and Subtropical Steppe (**BSh**)
  Middle latitude Steppe (**BSk**)
- Desert (**BW**)
  Tropical and Subtropical Desert (**BWh**)
  Middle latitude Desert (**BWk**)

C. HUMID MESO-THERMAL CLIMATES
- Mediterranean or Dry Summer Subtropical (**Cs**)
- Humid Subtropical (**Ca**, warm summer)
- Marine West Coast (**Cb, Cc**, cool summer)

D. HUMID MICRO-THERMAL CLIMATES
- Humid Continental, Warm Summer (**Da**)
- Humid Continental, Cool Summer (**Db**)
- Subarctic (**Dc, Dd**)

E. POLAR CLIMATES
- Tundra (**ET**)
- Ice Cap (**EF**)

H. UNDIFFERENTIATED HIGHLANDS

EXTENSIVE UPLANDS

The various alphabetical formulas designating climates on the map are explained on the opposite page. Each formula constitutes a short description of the chief characteristics of a climate.

CURVES SHOW FAHRENHEIT TEMPERATURE
VERTICAL BARS SHOW RAINFALL IN INCHES

Af	Aw	BShs	BSk	BWh	BWk	Csa	Caw
SINGAPORE	TIMBO	BANGHÂZÎ	WILLISTON	ASWÂN	ASTRAKHAN	ATHENAI	BENARES
Tropical rainforest climate	Tropical savanna climate; with wet and dry seasons	Tropical and subtropical steppe climate	Middle latitude steppe climate	Tropical and subtropical desert climate	Middle latitude desert climate	Mild climate; summer drouth and winter rain	Subtropical climate; winter drouth and summer rain

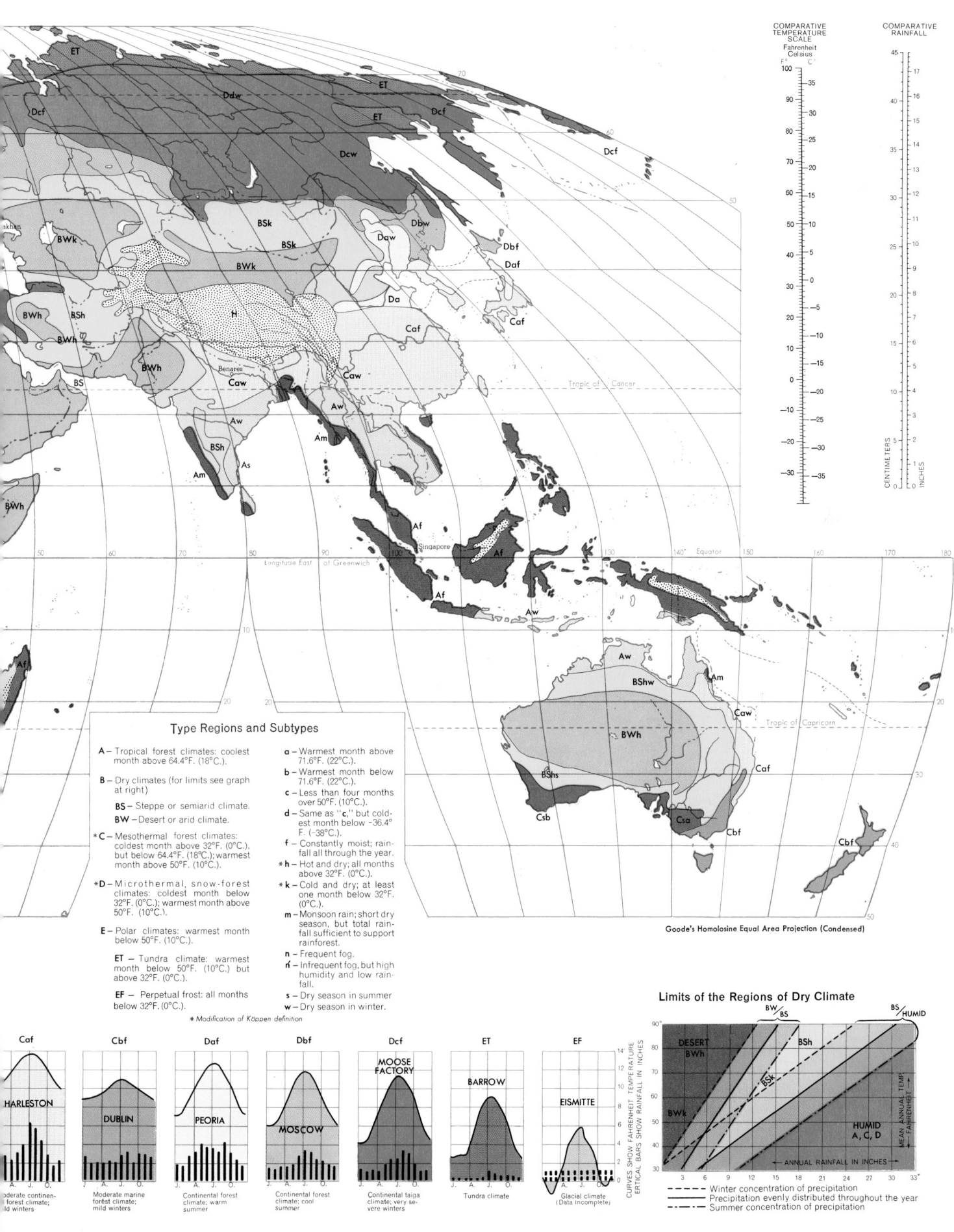

COMPARATIVE
TEMPERATURE
SCALE
Fahrenheit
Celsius

COMPARATIVE
RAINFALL

Goode's Homolosine Equal Area Projection (Condensed)

Type Regions and Subtypes

A – Tropical forest climates: coolest month above 64.4°F. (18°C.).

B – Dry climates (for limits see graph at right)

  BS – Steppe or semiarid climate.

  BW – Desert or arid climate.

*****C** – Mesothermal forest climates: coldest month above 32°F. (0°C.), but below 64.4°F. (18°C.); warmest month above 50°F. (10°C.).

*****D** – Microthermal, snow-forest climates: coldest month below 32°F. (0°C.); warmest month above 50°F. (10°C.).

E – Polar climates: warmest month below 50°F. (10°C.).

  ET – Tundra climate: warmest month below 50°F. (10°C.) but above 32°F. (0°C.).

  EF – Perpetual frost: all months below 32°F. (0°C.).

a – Warmest month above 71.6°F. (22°C.).

b – Warmest month below 71.6°F. (22°C.).

c – Less than four months over 50°F. (10°C.).

d – Same as "c," but coldest month below −36.4° F. (−38°C.).

f – Constantly moist; rainfall all through the year.

*****h** – Hot and dry; all months above 32°F. (0°C.).

*****k** – Cold and dry; at least one month below 32°F. (0°C.).

m – Monsoon rain; short dry season, but total rainfall sufficient to support rainforest.

n – Frequent fog.

ń – Infrequent fog, but high humidity and low rainfall.

s – Dry season in summer

w – Dry season in winter.

Modification of Köppen definition

Limits of the Regions of Dry Climate

DESERT
BWh
BWk

BSh
BSk

HUMID
A, C, D

CURVES SHOW FAHRENHEIT TEMPERATURE
VERTICAL BARS SHOW RAINFALL IN INCHES

ANNUAL RAINFALL IN INCHES

MEAN ANNUAL TEMP.—FAHRENHEIT

- - - - Winter concentration of precipitation
——— Precipitation evenly distributed throughout the year
-·-·- Summer concentration of precipitation

Caf
HARLESTON

Moderate continental-forest climate; mild winters

Cbf
DUBLIN

Moderate marine forest climate; mild winters

Daf
PEORIA

Continental forest climate; warm summer

Dbf
MOSCOW

Continental forest climate; cool summer

Dcf
MOOSE FACTORY

Continental taiga climate; very severe winters

ET
BARROW

Tundra climate

EF
EISMITTE

Glacial climate (Data incomplete)

CURVES SHOW FAHRENHEIT TEMPERATURE
VERTICAL BARS SHOW RAINFALL IN INCHES

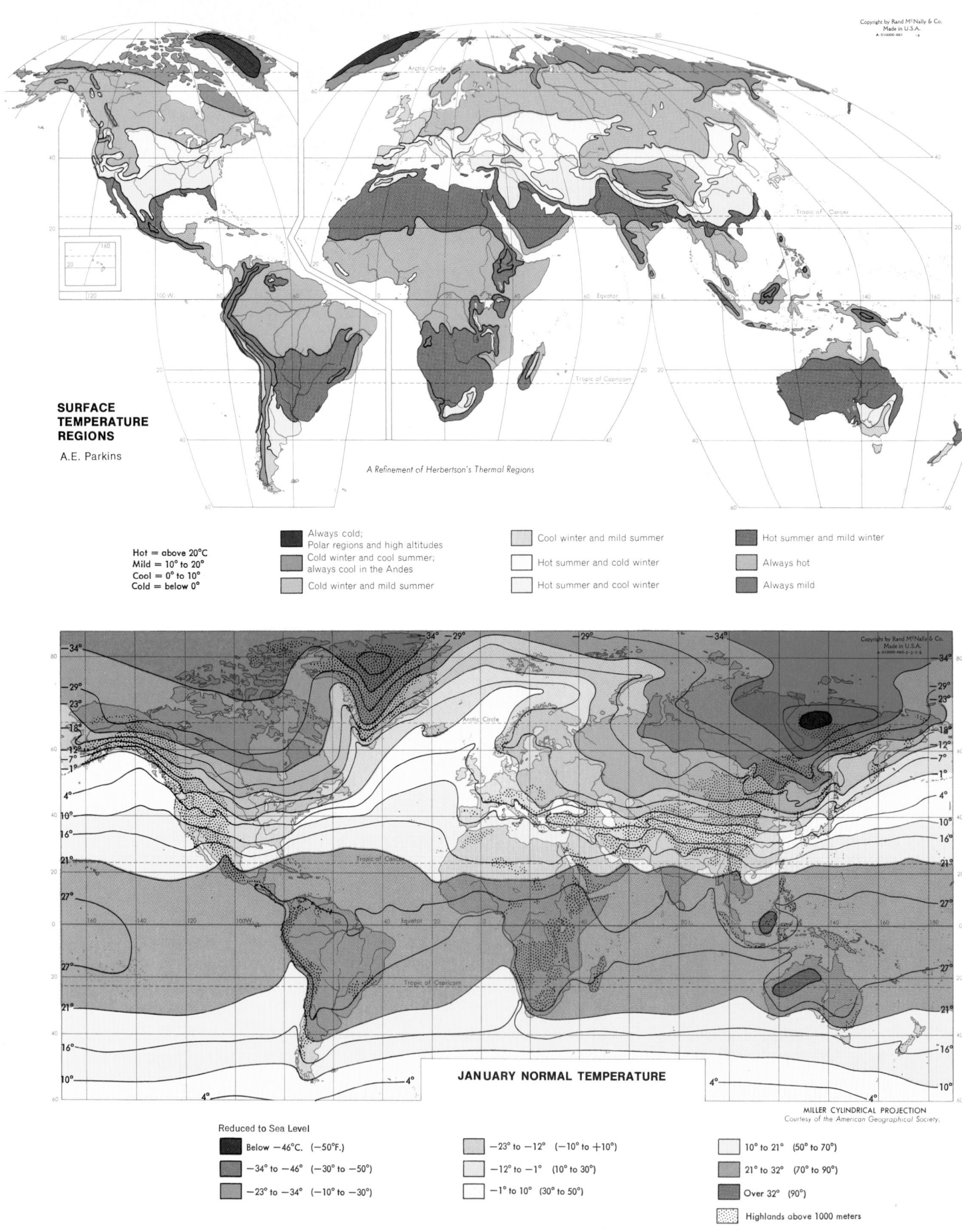

**SURFACE
TEMPERATURE
REGIONS**

A.E. Parkins

A Refinement of Herbertson's Thermal Regions

Hot = above 20°C
Mild = 10° to 20°
Cool = 0° to 10°
Cold = below 0°

	Always cold; Polar regions and high altitudes
	Cold winter and cool summer; always cool in the Andes
	Cold winter and mild summer
	Cool winter and mild summer
	Hot summer and cold winter
	Hot summer and cool winter
	Hot summer and mild winter
	Always hot
	Always mild

JANUARY NORMAL TEMPERATURE

MILLER CYLINDRICAL PROJECTION
Courtesy of the American Geographical Society.

Reduced to Sea Level

	Below −46°C. (−50°F.)
	−34° to 46° (−30° to −50°)
	−23° to −34° (−10° to −30°)
	−23° to −12° (−10° to +10°)
	−12° to −1° (10° to 30°)
	−1° to 10° (30° to 50°)
	10° to 21° (50° to 70°)
	21° to 32° (70° to 90°)
	Over 32° (90°)
	Highlands above 1000 meters

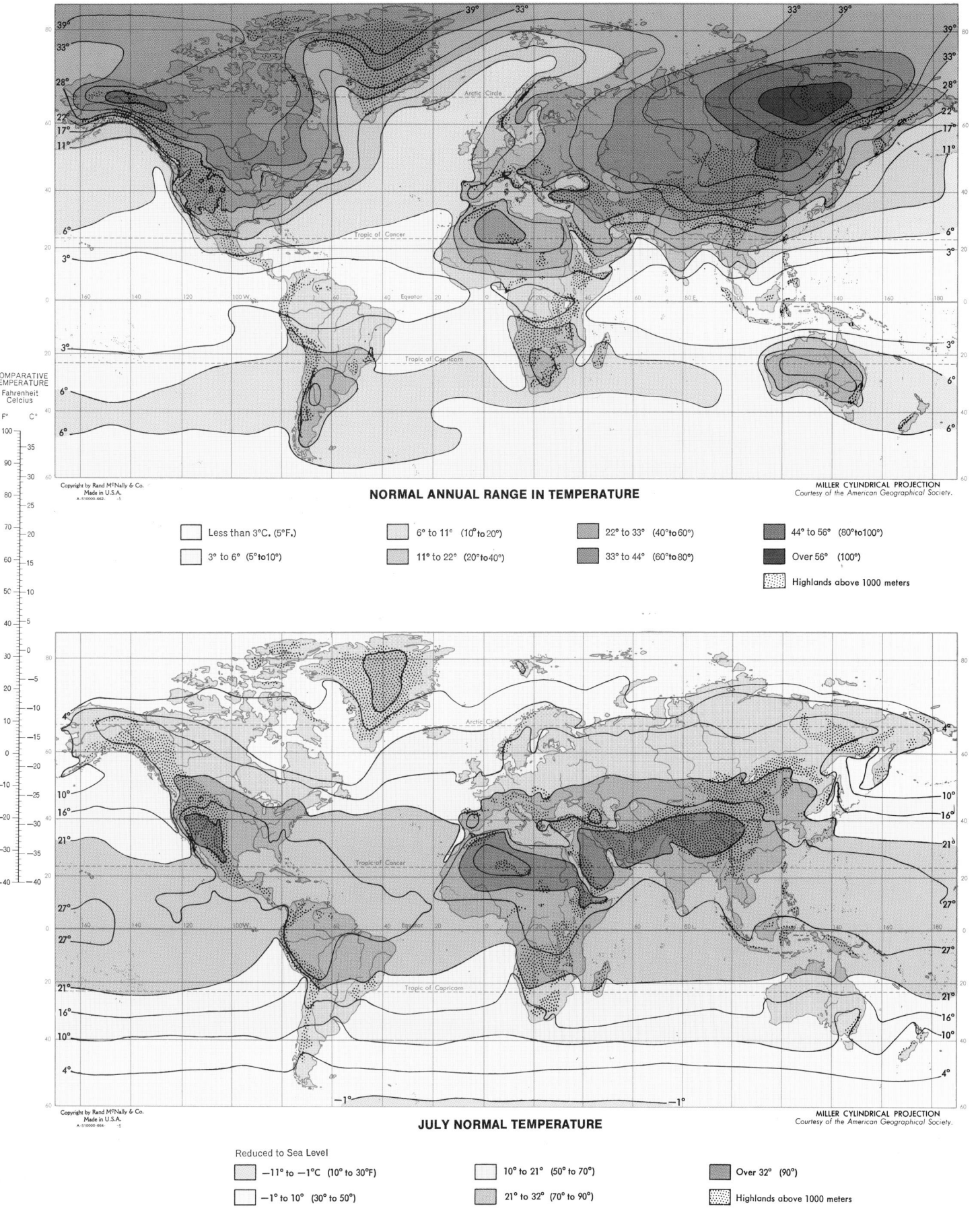

COMPARATIVE
TEMPERATURE
Fahrenheit
Celcius

F°   C°
100 ─ 35
90 ─ 30
80 ─ 25
70 ─ 20
60 ─ 15
50 ─ 10
40 ─ 5
─ 0
─ -5
─ -10
─ -15
-40 ─ -40

Copyright by Rand McNally & Co.
Made in U.S.A.
A-510000-062-   -5

NORMAL ANNUAL RANGE IN TEMPERATURE

MILLER CYLINDRICAL PROJECTION
Courtesy of the American Geographical Society.

Less than 3°C. (5°F.)	6° to 11° (10° to 20°)	22° to 33° (40° to 60°)	44° to 56° (80° to 100°)
3° to 6° (5° to 10°)	11° to 22° (20° to 40°)	33° to 44° (60° to 80°)	Over 56° (100°)

Highlands above 1000 meters

Copyright by Rand McNally & Co.
Made in U.S.A.
A-510000-064-   -5

JULY NORMAL TEMPERATURE

MILLER CYLINDRICAL PROJECTION
Courtesy of the American Geographical Society.

Reduced to Sea Level

−11° to −1°C (10° to 30°F)	10° to 21° (50° to 70°)	Over 32° (90°)
−1° to 10° (30° to 50°)	21° to 32° (70° to 90°)	Highlands above 1000 meters

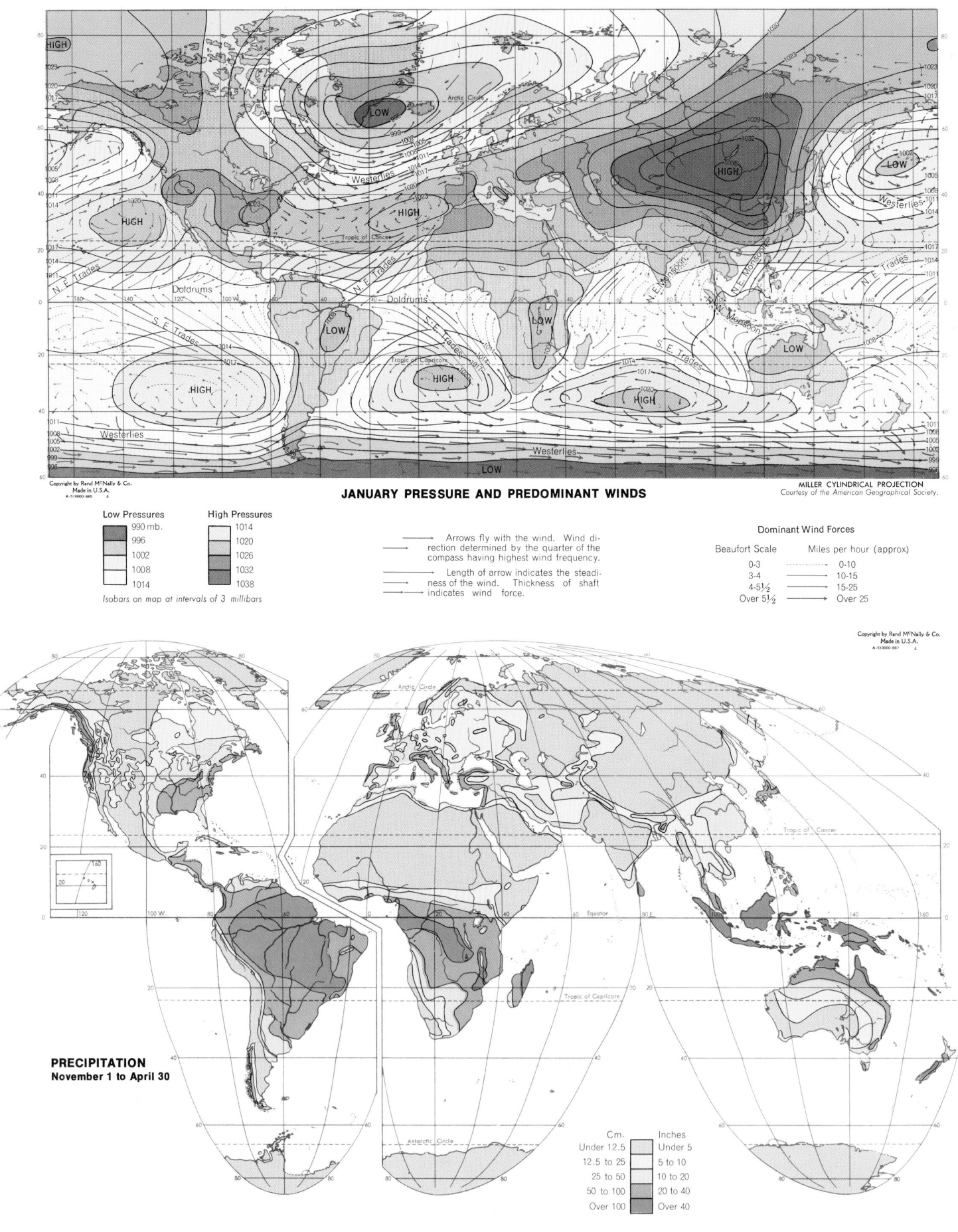

JANUARY PRESSURE AND PREDOMINANT WINDS

MILLER CYLINDRICAL PROJECTION
Courtesy of the American Geographical Society.

Copyright by Rand McNally & Co.
Made in U.S.A.
A-510000-665 4

Low Pressures	High Pressures
990 mb.	1014
996	1020
1002	1026
1008	1032
1014	1038

Isobars on map at intervals of 3 millibars

Arrows fly with the wind. Wind direction determined by the quarter of the compass having highest wind frequency.

Length of arrow indicates the steadiness of the wind. Thickness of shaft indicates wind force.

Dominant Wind Forces

Beaufort Scale	Miles per hour (approx)
0-3	0-10
3-4	10-15
4-5½	15-25
Over 5½	Over 25

Copyright by Rand McNally & Co.
Made in U.S.A.
A-510000-667 4

PRECIPITATION
November 1 to April 30

Cm.	Inches
Under 12.5	Under 5
12.5 to 25	5 to 10
25 to 50	10 to 20
50 to 100	20 to 40
Over 100	Over 40

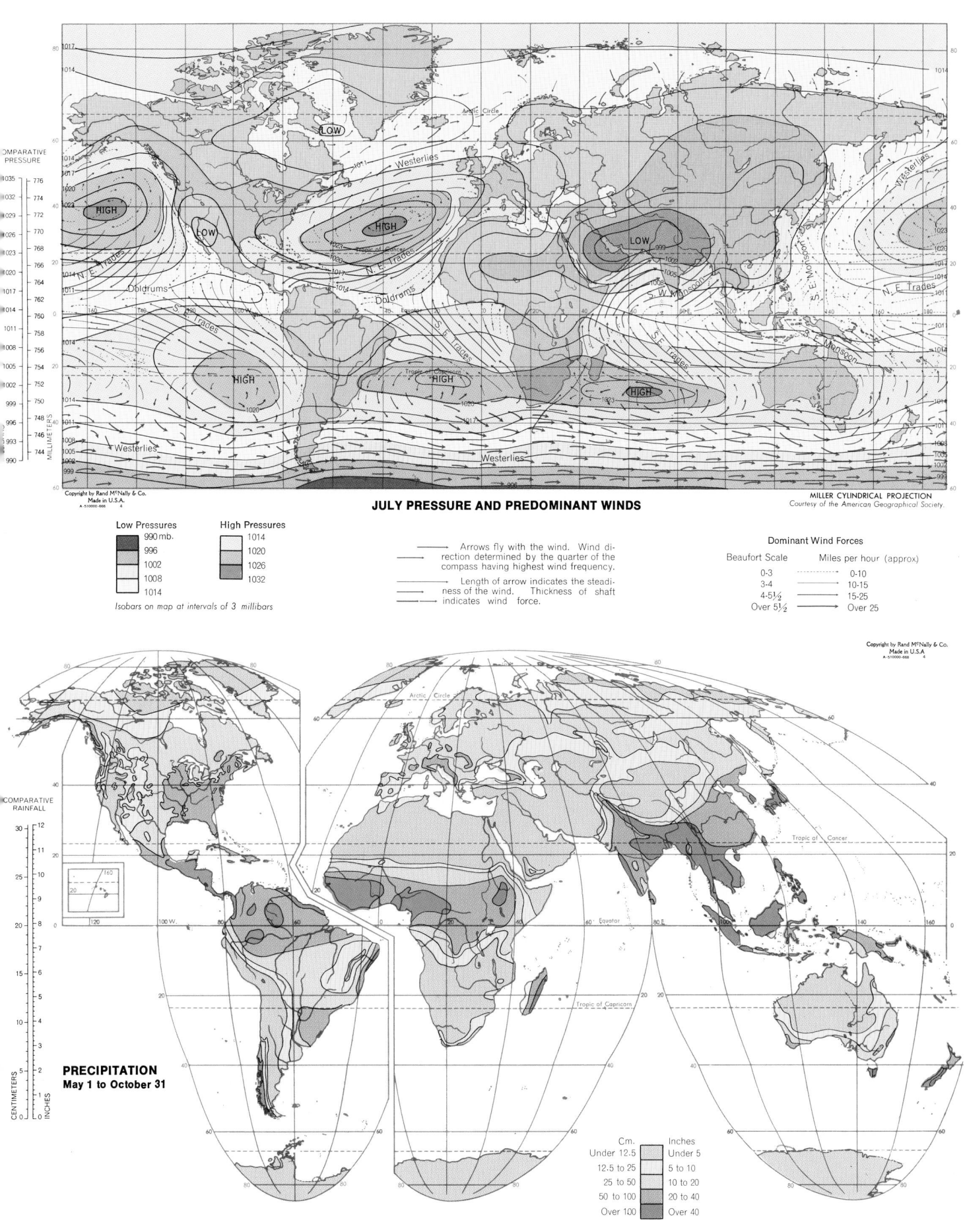

COMPARATIVE
PRESSURE

JULY PRESSURE AND PREDOMINANT WINDS

MILLER CYLINDRICAL PROJECTION
Courtesy of the American Geographical Society.

Low Pressures	High Pressures
990 mb.	1014
996	1020
1002	1026
1008	1032
1014	

Isobars on map at intervals of 3 millibars

Arrows fly with the wind. Wind direction determined by the quarter of the compass having highest wind frequency.

Length of arrow indicates the steadiness of the wind. Thickness of shaft indicates wind force.

Dominant Wind Forces

Beaufort Scale	Miles per hour (approx)
0-3	0-10
3-4	10-15
4-5½	15-25
Over 5½	Over 25

COMPARATIVE
RAINFALL

PRECIPITATION
May 1 to October 31

Cm.	Inches
Under 12.5	Under 5
12.5 to 25	5 to 10
25 to 50	10 to 20
50 to 100	20 to 40
Over 100	Over 40

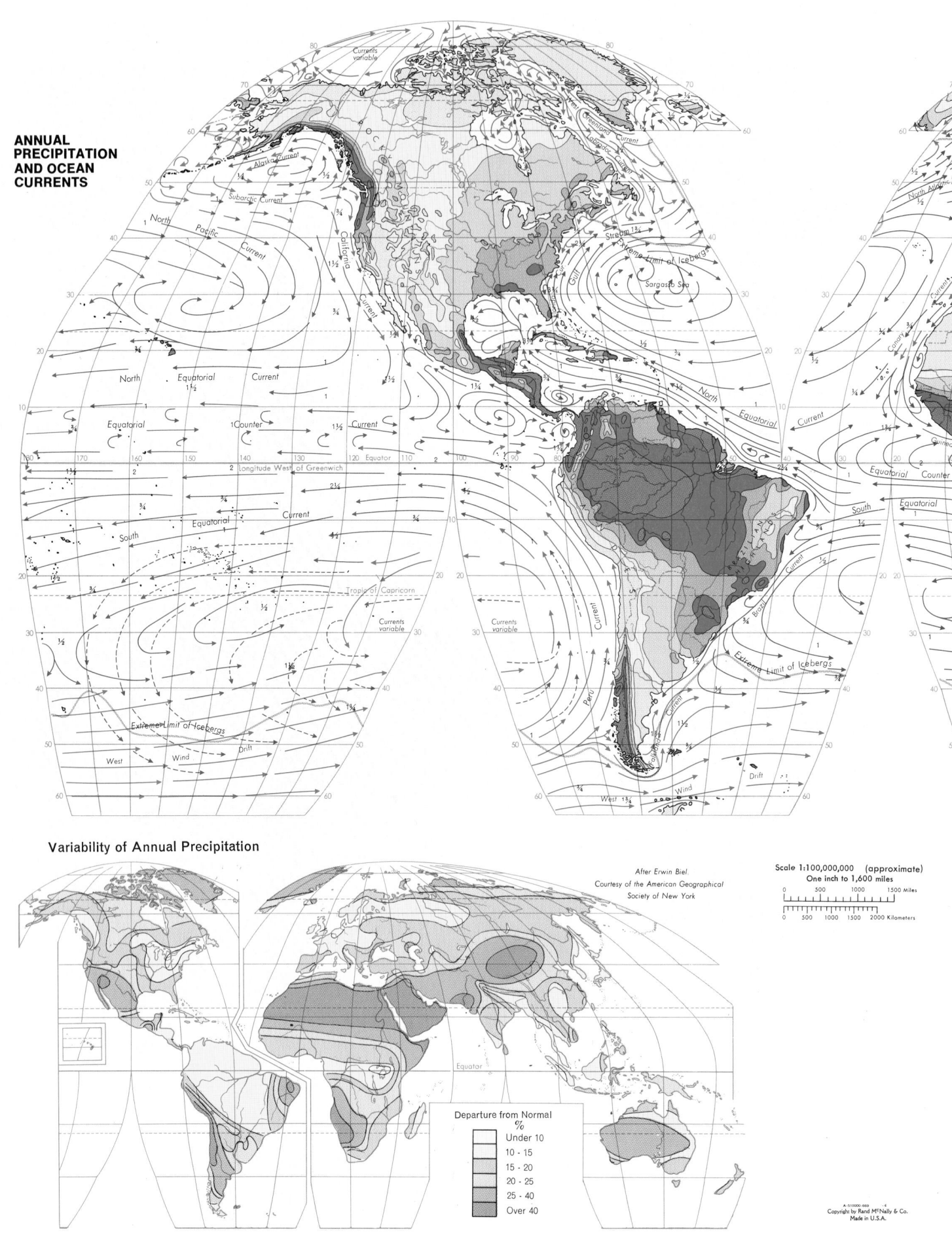

ANNUAL
PRECIPITATION
AND OCEAN
CURRENTS

Variability of Annual Precipitation

After Erwin Biel.
Courtesy of the American Geographical
Society of New York

Scale 1:100,000,000   (approximate)
One inch to 1,600 miles

0   500   1000   1500 Miles

0   500   1000   1500   2000 Kilometers

Departure from Normal
%
Under 10
10 - 15
15 - 20
20 - 25
25 - 40
Over 40

A-510000-669
Copyright by Rand McNally & Co.
Made in U.S.A.

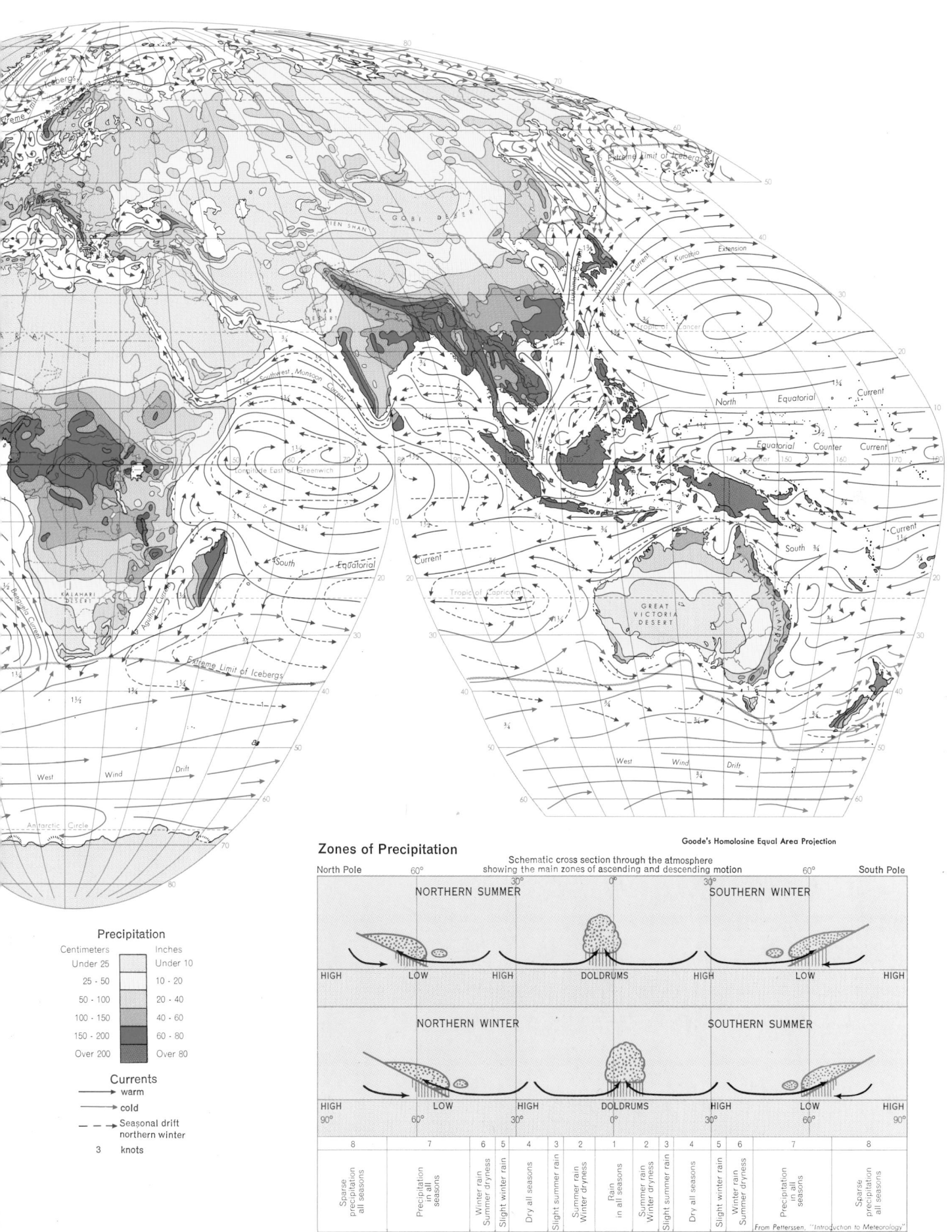

Goode's Homolosine Equal Area Projection

Zones of Precipitation

Schematic cross section through the atmosphere
showing the main zones of ascending and descending motion

North Pole	60°		30°	0°		30°		60°	South Pole

NORTHERN SUMMER   **SOUTHERN WINTER**

HIGH	LOW	HIGH	DOLDRUMS	HIGH	LOW	HIGH

NORTHERN WINTER   **SOUTHERN SUMMER**

HIGH	LOW	HIGH	DOLDRUMS	HIGH	LOW	HIGH
90°	60°	30°	0°	30°	60°	90°

8	7	6	5	4	3	2	1	2	3	4	5	6	7	8
Sparse precipitation all seasons	Precipitation in all seasons	Winter rain Summer dryness	Slight winter rain	Dry all seasons	Slight summer rain	Summer rain Winter dryness	Rain in all seasons	Summer rain Winter dryness	Slight summer rain	Dry all seasons	Slight winter rain	Winter rain Summer dryness	Precipitation in all seasons	Sparse precipitation all seasons

From Petterssen, "Introduction to Meteorology"

Precipitation

Centimeters	Inches
Under 25	Under 10
25 - 50	10 - 20
50 - 100	20 - 40
100 - 150	40 - 60
150 - 200	60 - 80
Over 200	Over 80

Currents

→ warm
→ cold
--- Seasonal drift northern winter

3   knots

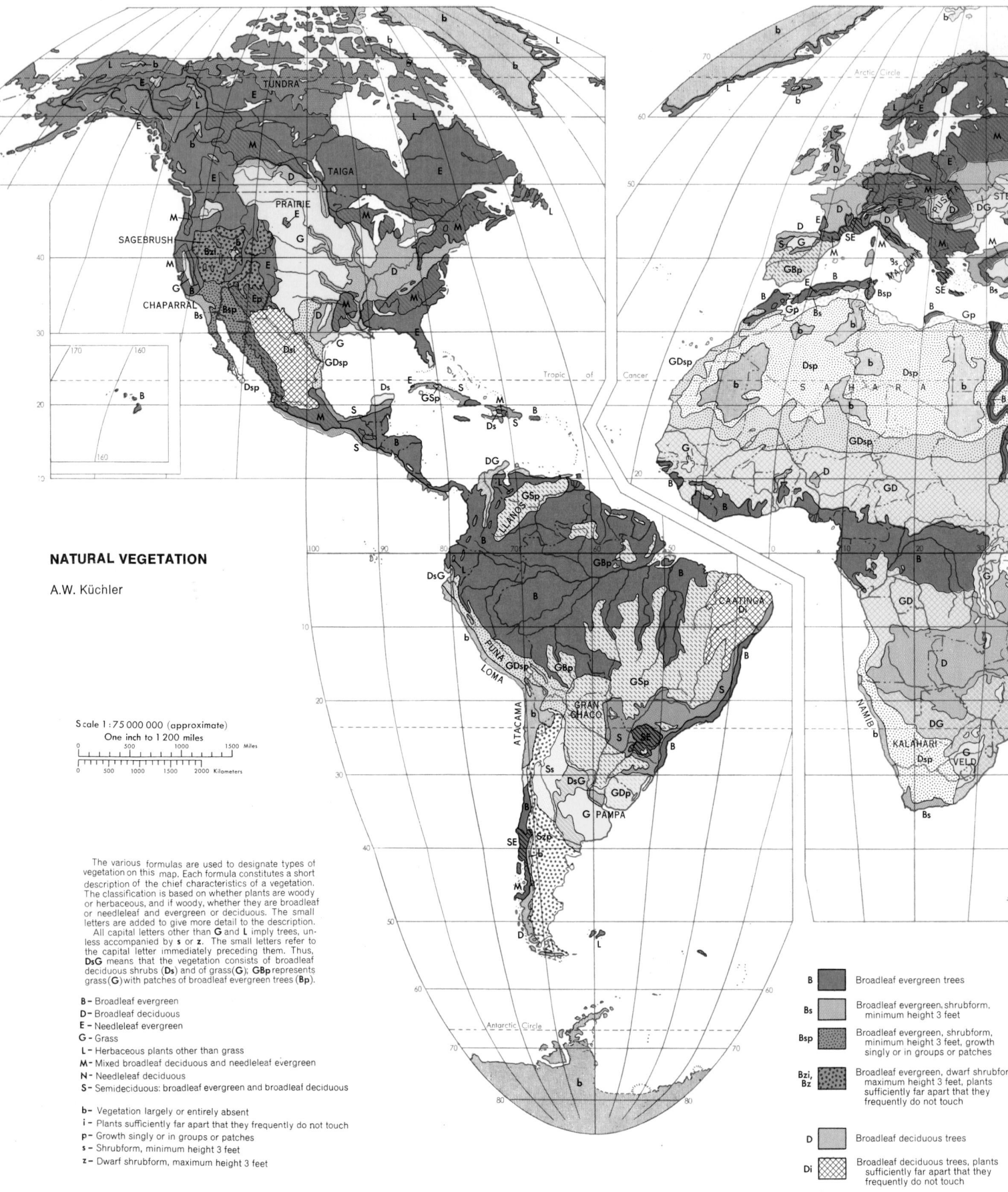

NATURAL VEGETATION

A.W. Küchler

The various formulas are used to designate types of
vegetation on this map. Each formula constitutes a short
description of the chief characteristics of a vegetation.
The classification is based on whether plants are woody
or herbaceous, and if woody, whether they are broadleaf
or needleleaf and evergreen or deciduous. The small
letters are added to give more detail to the description.

All capital letters other than **G** and **L** imply trees, un-
less accompanied by **s** or **z**. The small letters refer to
the capital letter immediately preceding them. Thus,
DsG means that the vegetation consists of broadleaf
deciduous shrubs (**Ds**) and of grass (**G**); **GBp** represents
grass (**G**) with patches of broadleaf evergreen trees (**Bp**).

B – Broadleaf evergreen
D – Broadleaf deciduous
E – Needleleaf evergreen
G – Grass
L – Herbaceous plants other than grass
M – Mixed broadleaf deciduous and needleleaf evergreen
N – Needleleaf deciduous
S – Semideciduous: broadleaf evergreen and broadleaf deciduous

b – Vegetation largely or entirely absent
i – Plants sufficiently far apart that they frequently do not touch
p – Growth singly or in groups or patches
s – Shrubform, minimum height 3 feet
z – Dwarf shrubform, maximum height 3 feet

Scale 1 : 75 000 000 (approximate)
One inch to 1 200 miles

B	Broadleaf evergreen trees
Bs	Broadleaf evergreen, shrubform, minimum height 3 feet
Bsp	Broadleaf evergreen, shrubform, minimum height 3 feet, growth singly or in groups or patches
Bzi, Bz	Broadleaf evergreen, dwarf shrubform, maximum height 3 feet, plants sufficiently far apart that they frequently do not touch
D	Broadleaf deciduous trees
Di	Broadleaf deciduous trees, plants sufficiently far apart that they frequently do not touch

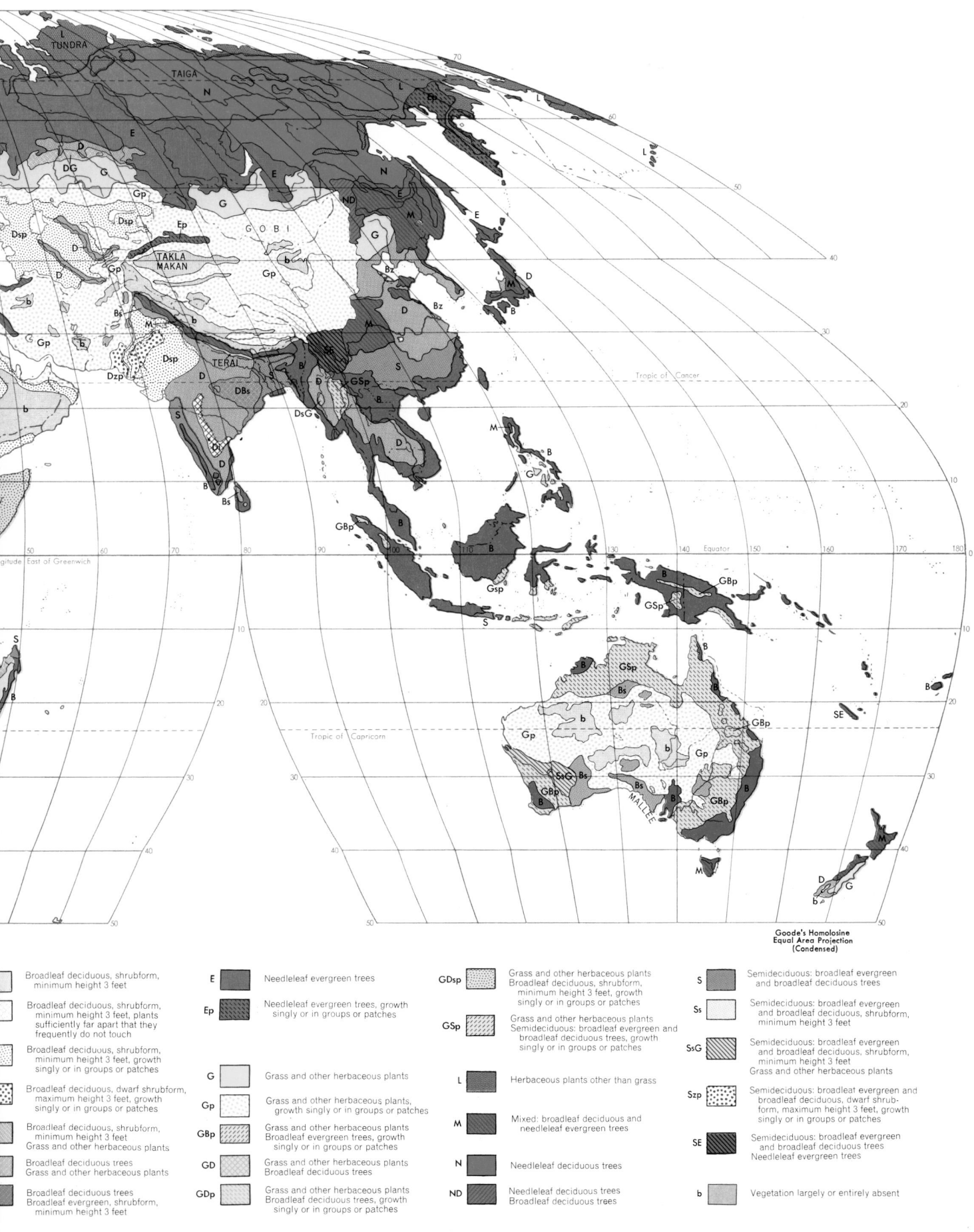

TUNDRA

TAIGA

GOBI

TAKLA MAKAN

TERAI

Tropic of Cancer

Longitude East of Greenwich

Equator

Tropic of Capricorn

MALLEE

Goode's Homolosine
Equal Area Projection
(Condensed)

	Broadleaf deciduous, shrubform, minimum height 3 feet	**E**	Needleleaf evergreen trees	**GDsp**	Grass and other herbaceous plants Broadleaf deciduous, shrubform, minimum height 3 feet, plants singly or in groups or patches	**S**	Semideciduous: broadleaf evergreen and broadleaf deciduous trees
	Broadleaf deciduous, shrubform, minimum height 3 feet, plants sufficiently far apart that they frequently do not touch	**Ep**	Needleleaf evergreen trees, growth singly or in groups or patches	**GSp**	Grass and other herbaceous plants Semideciduous: broadleaf evergreen and broadleaf deciduous trees, growth singly or in groups or patches	**Ss**	Semideciduous: broadleaf evergreen and broadleaf deciduous, shrubform, minimum height 3 feet
	Broadleaf deciduous, shrubform, minimum height 3 feet, growth singly or in groups or patches	**G**	Grass and other herbaceous plants	**L**	Herbaceous plants other than grass	**SsG**	Semideciduous: broadleaf evergreen and broadleaf deciduous, shrubform, minimum height 3 feet Grass and other herbaceous plants
	Broadleaf deciduous, dwarf shrubform, maximum height 3 feet, growth singly or in groups or patches	**Gp**	Grass and other herbaceous plants, growth singly or in groups or patches	**M**	Mixed: broadleaf deciduous and needleleaf evergreen trees	**Szp**	Semideciduous: broadleaf evergreen and broadleaf deciduous, dwarf shrub-form, maximum height 3 feet, growth singly or in groups or patches
	Broadleaf deciduous, shrubform, minimum height 3 feet Grass and other herbaceous plants	**GBp**	Grass and other herbaceous plants Broadleaf evergreen, shrubform, growth singly or in groups or patches	**N**	Needleleaf deciduous trees	**SE**	Semideciduous: broadleaf evergreen and broadleaf deciduous trees Needleleaf evergreen trees
	Broadleaf deciduous trees Grass and other herbaceous plants	**GD**	Grass and other herbaceous plants Broadleaf deciduous trees	**ND**	Needleleaf deciduous trees Broadleaf deciduous trees	**b**	Vegetation largely or entirely absent
	Broadleaf deciduous trees Broadleaf evergreen, shrubform, minimum height 3 feet	**GDp**	Grass and other herbaceous plants Broadleaf deciduous trees, growth singly or in groups or patches				

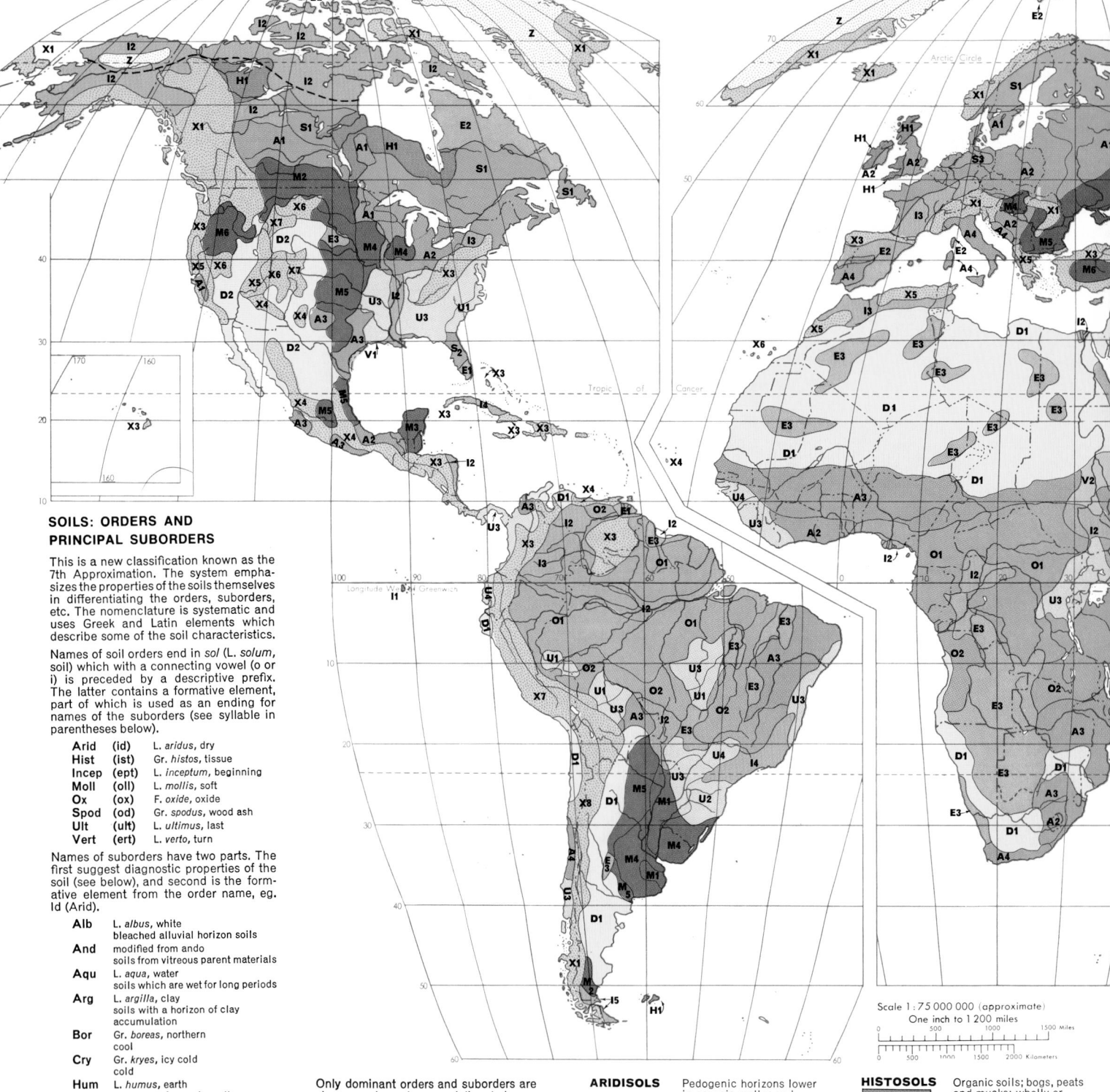

SOILS: ORDERS AND PRINCIPAL SUBORDERS

This is a new classification known as the 7th Approximation. The system emphasizes the properties of the soils themselves in differentiating the orders, suborders, etc. The nomenclature is systematic and uses Greek and Latin elements which describe some of the soil characteristics.

Names of soil orders end in *sol* (L. *solum*, soil) which with a connecting vowel (o or i) is preceded by a descriptive prefix. The latter contains a formative element, part of which is used as an ending for names of the suborders (see syllable in parentheses below).

Arid	(id)	L. *aridus*, dry
Hist	(ist)	Gr. *histos*, tissue
Incep	(ept)	L. *inceptum*, beginning
Moll	(oll)	L. *mollis*, soft
Ox	(ox)	F. *oxide*, oxide
Spod	(od)	Gr. *spodus*, wood ash
Ult	(ult)	L. *ultimus*, last
Vert	(ert)	L. *verto*, turn

Names of suborders have two parts. The first suggest diagnostic properties of the soil (see below), and second is the formative element from the order name, eg. Id (Arid).

Alb	L. *albus*, white bleached alluvial horizon soils
And	modified from ando soils from vitreous parent materials
Aqu	L. *aqua*, water soils which are wet for long periods
Arg	L. *argilla*, clay soils with a horizon of clay accumulation
Bor	Gr. *boreas*, northern cool
Cry	Gr. *kryes*, icy cold cold
Hum	L. *humus*, earth presence of organic matter
Ochr	Gr. *orchras*, pale soils with little organic matter
Psamm	Gr. *psammas*, sand sandy soils
Rend	from Rendzina high carbonate content
Torr	L. *torridus*, hot and dry soils of very dry climate
Ud	L. *udus*, humid soils of humid climate
Umbr	L. *umbra*, shade dark color reflecting relatively high organic matter
Ust	L. *ustus*, burnt soils of dry climates with summer rains
Xer	Gr. *xeros*, dry soils of dry climates with winter rains

Only dominant orders and suborders are shown and each area delineated may include other kinds of soil.

ALFISOLS
Podzolic soils of middle latitudes: soils with gray to brown surface horizons; subsurface horizons of clay accumulation; medium to high base supply.

Boralfs A1	Cool to cold, freely drained.
Udalfs A2	Temperate to hot; usually moist (Gray-brown Podzolic*)
Ustalfs A3	Warm subhumid to semi-arid; dry > 90 days (some Reddish Chestnut and Red & Yellow Podzolic soils*)
Xeralfs A4	Warm, dry in summer; moist in winter.

ARIDISOLS
Pedogenic horizons lower in organic matter and dry for > 6 mo. of the year. (Desert and Reddish Desert*) Salts may accumulate on or near surface.

Aridisols D1	Undifferentiated.
Argids D2	With horizon of clay accumulation.

ENTISOLS
Soils without pedogenic horizons on recent alluvium, dune sands, etc.; varied in appearance.

Aquents E1	Seasonally or perennially wet; bluish or gray and mottled.
Orthents E2	Shallow; or recent erosional surfaces (Lithosols*). A few on recent loams.
Psamments E3	Sandy soils on shifting and stabilized sands.

HISTOSOLS
Organic soils; bogs, peats and mucks; wholly or partly saturated with water.

INCEPTISOLS
Immature, weakly developed soils; pedogenic horizons show alteration but little illuviation; usually moist.

Andepts I1	Soil formed on amorphous clay or vitric volcanic ash.
Aquepts I2	Seasonally saturated with water (includes some Humic Gley, alluvial tundra soils*).
Ochrepts I3	Thin, light-colored surface horizons; little organic matter.
Tropepts I4	Continuously warm to hot; brownish to reddish.
Umbrepts I5	Dark colored surface horizons; rich in organic matter; medium to low base supply.

Scale 1:75 000 000 (approximate)
One inch to 1 200 miles

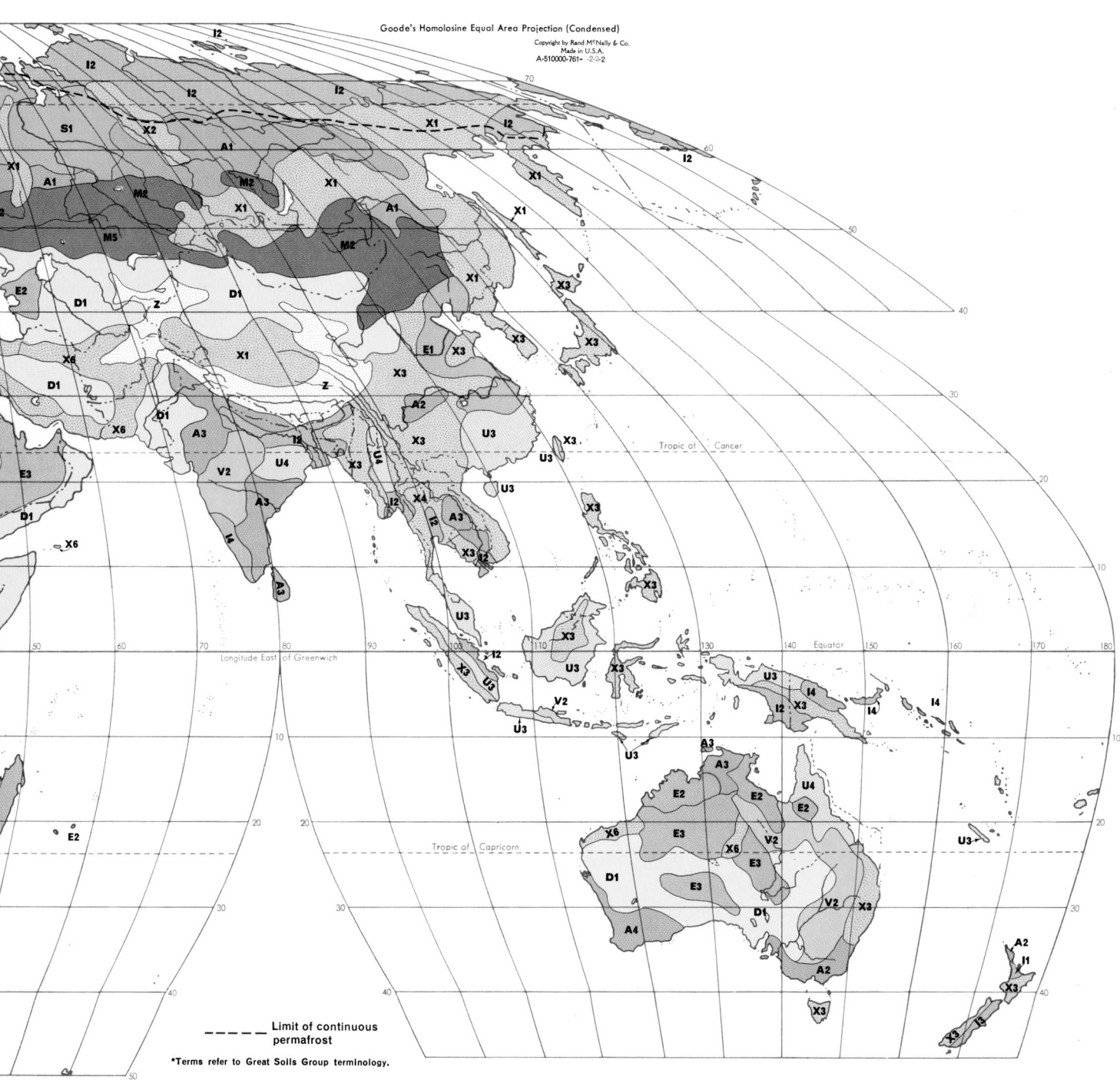

Goode's Homolosine Equal Area Projection (Condensed)

Copyright by Rand McNally & Co.
Made in U.S.A.
A-510000-761- -2-2-2

------ Limit of continuous
permafrost

*Terms refer to Great Soils Group terminology.

MOLLISOLS		Soils of the steppe (incl. Chernozem and Chestnut soils*). Thick, black organic rich surface horizons and high base supply.
Albolls M1		Seasonally saturated with water; light gray subsurface horizon.
Borolls M2		Cool or cold (incl. some Chernozem, Chestnut and Brown soils*).
Rendolls M3		Formed on highly calcareous parent materials (Rendzina*).
Udolls M4		Temperate to warm; usually moist (Prairie soils*).
Ustolls M5		Temperate to hot; dry for > 90 days (incl. some Chestnut and Brown soils*).
Xerolls M6		Cool to warm; dry in summer; moist in winter.

OXISOLS		Deeply weathered tropical and subtropical soils (Laterites*); rich in sesquioxides of iron and aluminum; low in nutrients; limited productivity without fertilizer.
Orthox O1		Hot and nearly always moist.
Ustox O2		Warm or hot; dry for long periods but moist > 90 consecutive days.
SPODOSOLS		Soils with a subsurface accumulation of amorphous materials overlaid by a light colored, leached sandy horizon.
Spodosols S1		Undifferentiated (mostly high latitudes).
Aquods S2		Seasonally saturated with water; sandy parent materials.
Humods S3		Considerable accumulations of organic matter in subsurface horizon.
Orthods S4		With subsurface accumulations of iron, aluminum and organic matter (Podzols*).

ULTISOLS		Soils with some subsurface clay accumulation; low base supply; usually moist and low inorganic matter; usually moist and low in organic matter; can be productive with fertilization.
Aquults U1		Seasonally saturated with water; subsurface gray or mottled horizon.
Humults U2		High in organic matter; dark colored; moist, warm to temperate all year.
Udults U3		Low in organic matter; moist, temperate to hot (Red-Yellow Podzolic; some Reddish-Brown Lateritic soils*).
Ustults U4		Warm to hot; dry > 90 days.
VERTISOLS		Soils with high content of swelling clays; deep, wide cracks in dry periods dark colored.
Uderts V1		Usually moist; cracks open < 90 days.
Usterts V2		Cracks open > 90 days; difficult to till (Black tropical soils*).

MOUNTAIN SOILS		Soils with various moisture and temperature regimes; steep slopes and variable relief and elevation; soils vary greatly within short distance.
X1		Cryic great groups of Entisols, Inceptisols and Spodosols.
X2		Boralfs and Cryic groups of Entisols and Inceptisols.
X3		Udic great groups of Alfisols, Entisols and Ultisols; Inceptisols.
X4		Ustic great groups of Alfisols, Entisols, Inceptisols, Mollisols and Ultisols.
X5		Xeric great groups of Alfisols, Entisols, Inceptisols, Mollisols and Ultisols.
X6		Torric great groups of Entisols; Aridisols.
X7		Ustic and cryic great groups of Alfisols, Entisols; Inceptisols and Mollisols; ustic great groups of Ultisols; cryic great groups of Spodosols.
X8		Aridisols; torric and cryic great groups of Entisols, and cryic great groups of Spodosols and Inceptisols.
z		Areas with little or no soil; icefields, and rugged mountain.

20

POPULATION DENSITY

Scale 1 : 75 000 000 (approximate)
One inch to 1 200 miles

0   500   1000   1500 Miles

0   500   1000   1500   2000 Kilometers

Population Density
per square kilometer (per square mile)

	of Total Area		of Cultivated Land	
ARGENTINA	11(28)		86(223)	
AUSTRALIA	2(5)		36(93)	
BRAZIL	16(41)		183(475)	
CHINA	115(298)		1071(2775)	
EGYPT	48(124)		1170(4324)	
FRANCE	101(261)		295(764)	
GERMANY	219(566)		624(1616)	
INDIA & PAKISTAN	214(555)		461(1194)	
JAPAN	318(824)		2477(6415)	
SOVIET UNION	12(32)		119(307)	
UNITED KINGDOM	230(596)		803(2079)	
UNITED STATES	25(65)		125(323)	

Goode's Homolosine Equal Area Projection (Condensed)

Population

Per Sq. Km.	Per Sq. Mile
Uninhabited	Uninhabited
Under 1	Under 2
1-10	2-25
10-25	25-60
25-50	60-125
50-100	125-250
Over 100	Over 250

▫ Metropolitan areas over 2,000,000 population
○ Metropolitan areas 1,000,000 to 2,000,000 population

Some cities are identified by initial letter only.

Rural/Urban Population Ratios

Rural		Urban
18%	ARGENTINA	82%
14	AUSTRALIA	86
32	BRAZIL	68
24	CANADA	76
79	CHINA	21
27	FRANCE	73
77	INDIA	23
24	JAPAN	76
36	SOVIET UNION	64
55	TURKEY	45
24	UNITED KINGDOM	76
26	UNITED STATES	74

A-510000-16 -7-3-9°
Copyright by Rand M°Nally & Co.
Made in U.S.A.

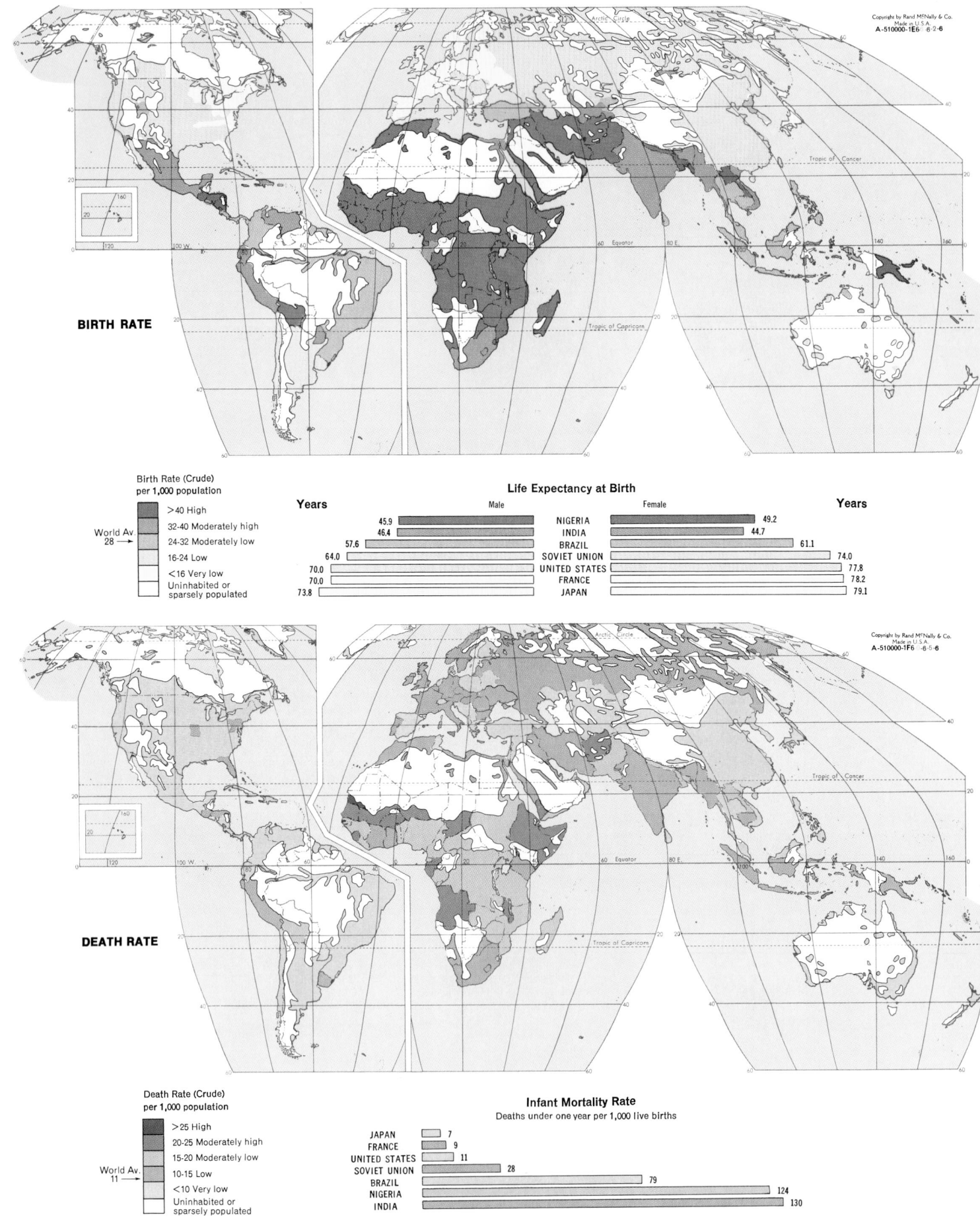

BIRTH RATE

Birth Rate (Crude)
per 1,000 population

- >40 High
- 32-40 Moderately high
- 24-32 Moderately low
- 16-24 Low
- <16 Very low
- Uninhabited or sparsely populated

World Av.
28 →

Life Expectancy at Birth

Years	Male		Female	Years
45.9	NIGERIA		49.2	
46.4	INDIA		44.7	
57.6	BRAZIL		61.1	
64.0	SOVIET UNION		74.0	
70.0	UNITED STATES		77.8	
70.0	FRANCE		78.2	
73.8	JAPAN		79.1	

DEATH RATE

Death Rate (Crude)
per 1,000 population

- >25 High
- 20-25 Moderately high
- 15-20 Moderately low
- 10-15 Low
- <10 Very low
- Uninhabited or sparsely populated

World Av.
11 →

Infant Mortality Rate

Deaths under one year per 1,000 live births

JAPAN	7
FRANCE	9
UNITED STATES	11
SOVIET UNION	28
BRAZIL	79
NIGERIA	124
INDIA	130

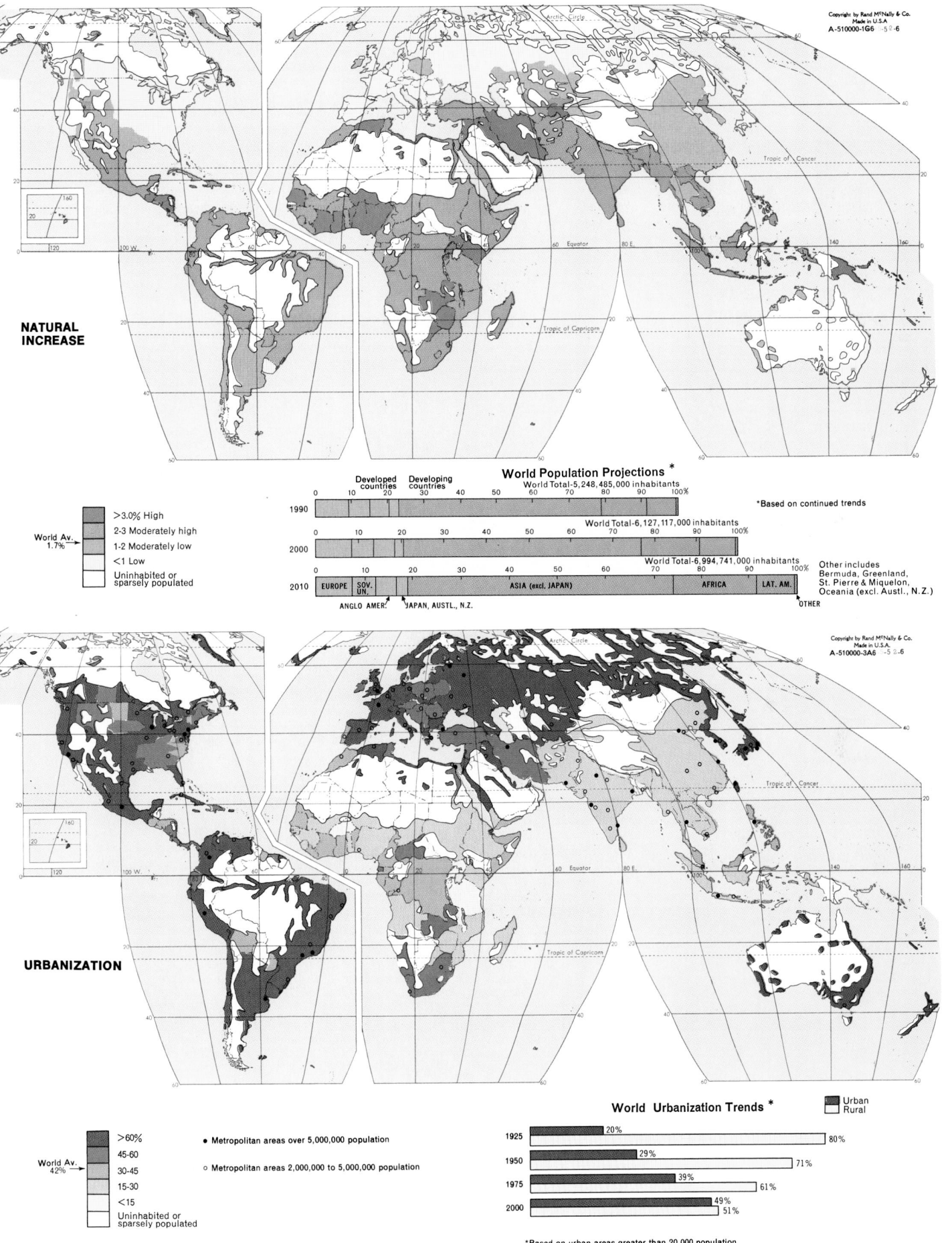

NATURAL INCREASE

World Av. 1.7% →
- >3.0% High
- 2-3 Moderately high
- 1-2 Moderately low
- <1 Low
- Uninhabited or sparsely populated

World Population Projections *

*Based on continued trends

Other includes Bermuda, Greenland, St. Pierre & Miquelon, Oceania (excl. Austl., N.Z.)

1990 — World Total-5,248,485,000 inhabitants
2000 — World Total-6,127,117,000 inhabitants
2010 — World Total-6,994,741,000 inhabitants

Developed countries
Developing countries

EUROPE   SOV. UN.   ASIA (excl. JAPAN)   AFRICA   LAT. AM.
ANGLO AMER.   JAPAN, AUSTL., N.Z.   OTHER

URBANIZATION

World Av. 42% →
- >60%
- 45-60
- 30-45
- 15-30
- <15
- Uninhabited or sparsely populated

● Metropolitan areas over 5,000,000 population

○ Metropolitan areas 2,000,000 to 5,000,000 population

World Urbanization Trends *

■ Urban
□ Rural

	Urban	Rural
1925	20%	80%
1950	29%	71%
1975	39%	61%
2000	49%	51%

*Based on urban areas greater than 20,000 population

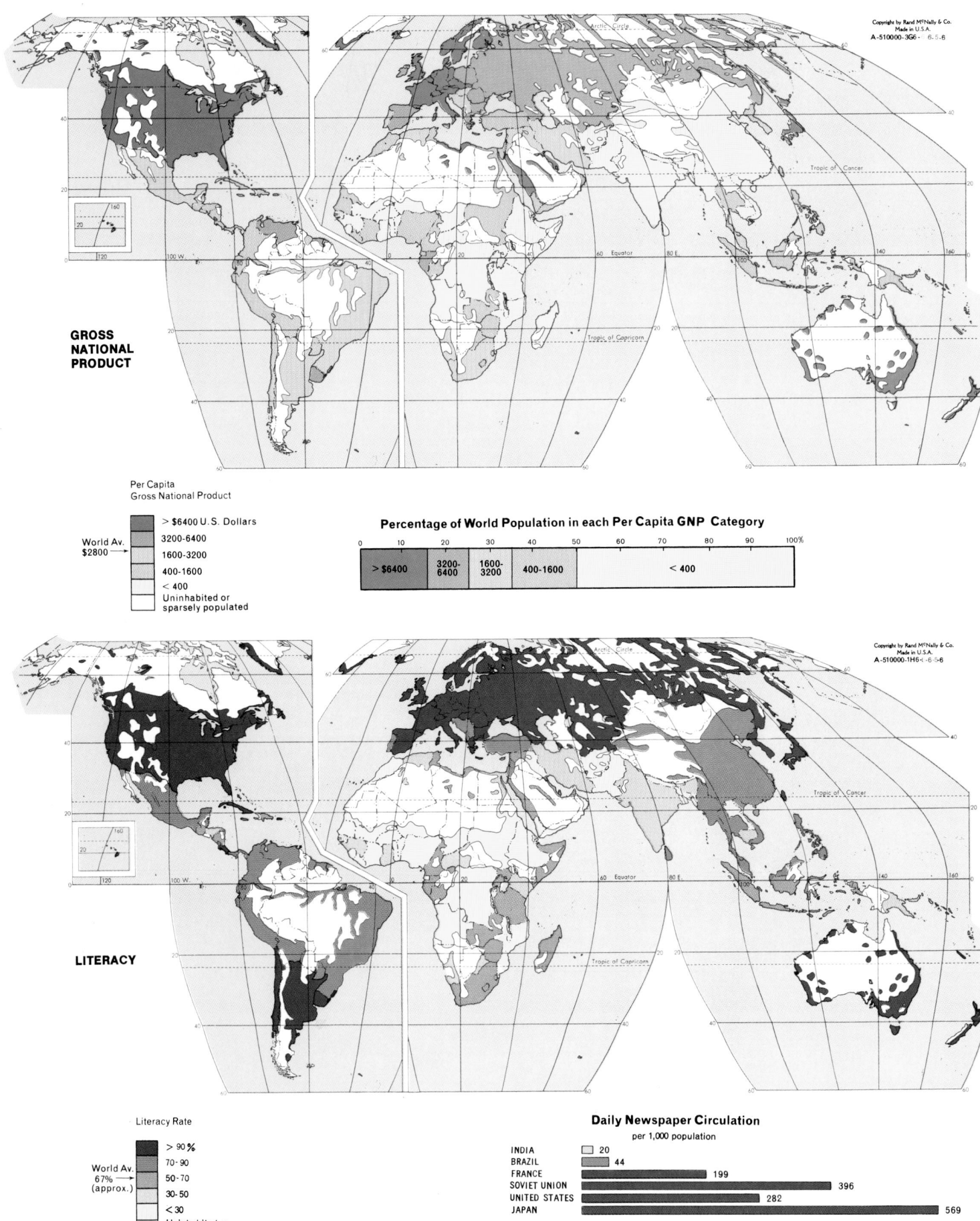

GROSS NATIONAL PRODUCT

Per Capita
Gross National Product

> $6400 U.S. Dollars
3200-6400
World Av.
$2800 → 1600-3200
400-1600
< 400
Uninhabited or
sparsely populated

Percentage of World Population in each Per Capita GNP Category

| 0 | 10 | 20 | 30 | 40 | 50 | 60 | 70 | 80 | 90 | 100% |

| > $6400 | 3200-6400 | 1600-3200 | 400-1600 | < 400 |

LITERACY

Literacy Rate

> 90 %
70-90
World Av.
67% → 50-70
(approx.) 30-50
< 30
Uninhabited or
sparsely populated

Based on Population 15 years
and over who can read and write

Daily Newspaper Circulation
per 1,000 population

INDIA	20
BRAZIL	44
FRANCE	199
SOVIET UNION	396
UNITED STATES	282
JAPAN	569

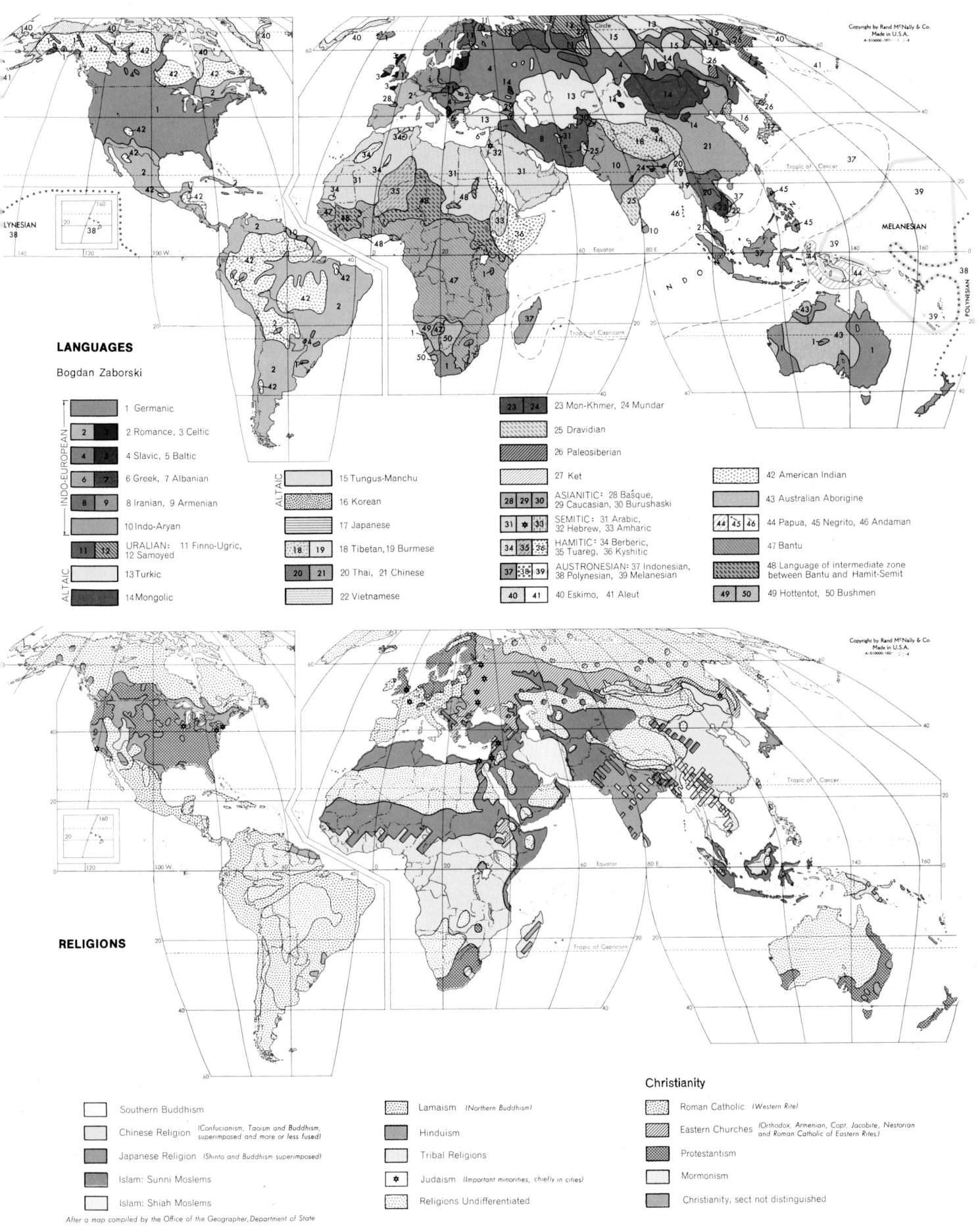

LANGUAGES

Bogdan Zaborski

INDO-EUROPEAN
- 1 Germanic
- 2 Romance, 3 Celtic
- 4 Slavic, 5 Baltic
- 6 Greek, 7 Albanian
- 8 Iranian, 9 Armenian
- 10 Indo-Aryan
- URALIAN: 11 Finno-Ugric, 12 Samoyed
- 13 Turkic
- 14 Mongolic

ALTAIC
- 15 Tungus-Manchu
- 16 Korean
- 17 Japanese
- 18 Tibetan, 19 Burmese
- 20 Thai, 21 Chinese
- 22 Vietnamese

- 23 Mon-Khmer, 24 Mundar
- 25 Dravidian
- 26 Paleosiberian
- 27 Ket
- ASIANITIC: 28 Basque, 29 Caucasian, 30 Burushaski
- SEMITIC: 31 Arabic, 32 Hebrew, 33 Amharic
- HAMITIC: 34 Berberic, 35 Tuareg, 36 Kyshitic
- AUSTRONESIAN: 37 Indonesian, 38 Polynesian, 39 Melanesian
- 40 Eskimo, 41 Aleut

- 42 American Indian
- 43 Australian Aborigine
- 44 Papua, 45 Negrito, 46 Andaman
- 47 Bantu
- 48 Language of intermediate zone between Bantu and Hamit-Semit
- 49 Hottentot, 50 Bushmen

Copyright by Rand McNally & Co.
Made in U.S.A.
A-510000-161-

RELIGIONS

- Southern Buddhism
- Chinese Religion *(Confucianism, Taoism and Buddhism, superimposed and more or less fused)*
- Japanese Religion *(Shinto and Buddhism superimposed)*
- Islam: Sunni Moslems
- Islam: Shiah Moslems

- Lamaism *(Northern Buddhism)*
- Hinduism
- Tribal Religions
- ✷ Judaism *(Important minorities, chiefly in cities)*
- Religions Undifferentiated

Christianity

- Roman Catholic *(Western Rite)*
- Eastern Churches *(Orthodox, Armenian, Copt, Jacobite, Nestorian and Roman Catholic of Eastern Rites.)*
- Protestantism
- Mormonism
- Christianity, sect not distinguished

After a map compiled by the Office of the Geographer, Department of State

Copyright by Rand McNally & Co.
Made in U.S.A.
A-510000-182-

CALORIE SUPPLY

Note: Size of each country is proportional to population

Calorie supply per capita
(percentage of requirements*)

≥120%	Well above requirements
110 to 120	Above requirements
100 to 110	Adequate nutrition
90 to 100	Some malnutrition
<90	Serious malnutrition and/or hunger
n.a.	Data not available

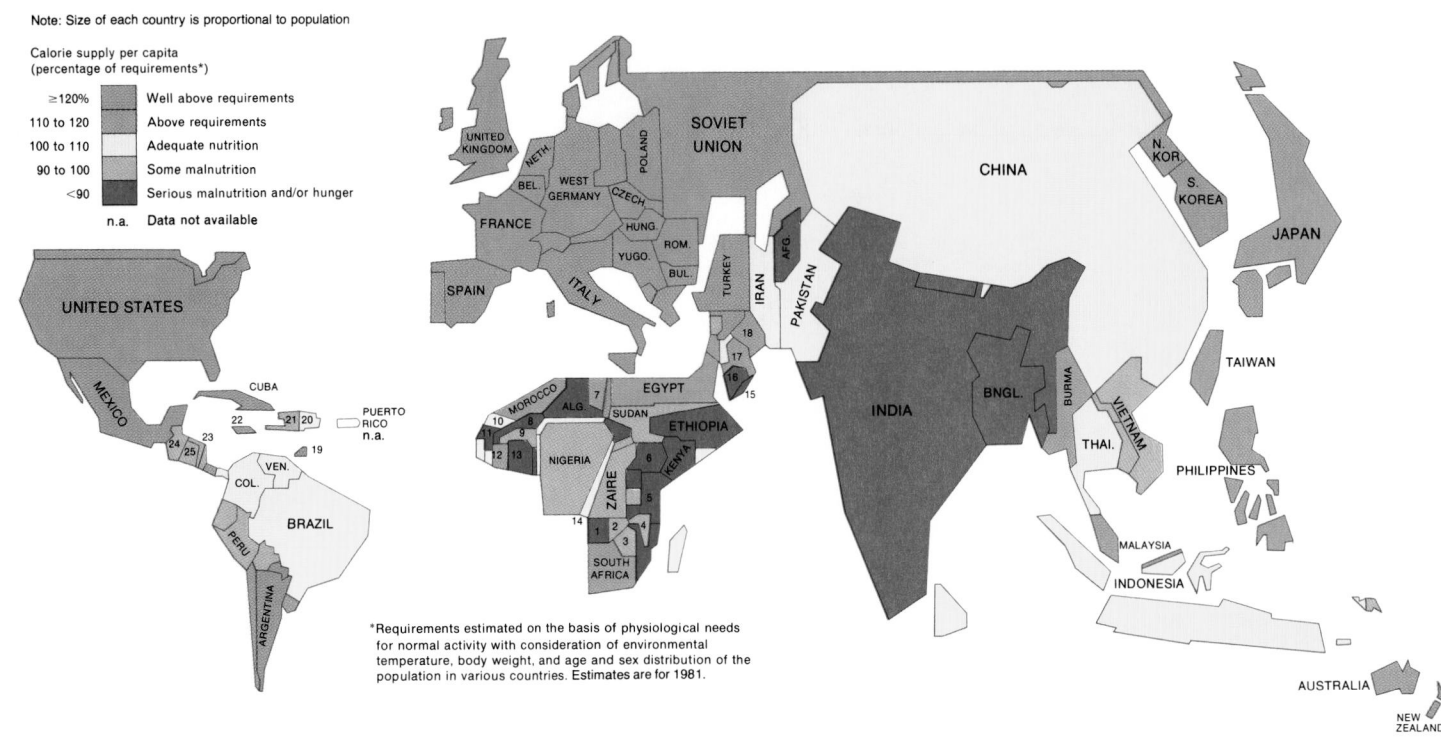

*Requirements estimated on the basis of physiological needs for normal activity with consideration of environmental temperature, body weight, and age and sex distribution of the population in various countries. Estimates are for 1981.

1. ANGOLA	6. UGANDA	11. GUINEA	16. YEMEN	21. HAITI
2. ZAMBIA	7. TUNISIA	12. IVORY COAST	17. SAUDI ARABIA	22. JAMAICA
3. ZIMBABWE	8. MALI	13. GHANA	18. IRAQ	23. HONDURAS
4. MALAWI	9. BURKINA FASO	14. CAMEROON	19. TRIN. & TOBAGO	24. GUATEMALA
5. TANZANIA	10. SENEGAL	15. P.D.R. YEMEN	20. DOM. REPUBLIC	25. EL SALVADOR

© 1986 Rand McNally & Co.
Made in U.S.A.
A-510000-1V6 -2 -2-2

PROTEIN CONSUMPTION

Note: size of each country is proportional to population

n.a. Data not available

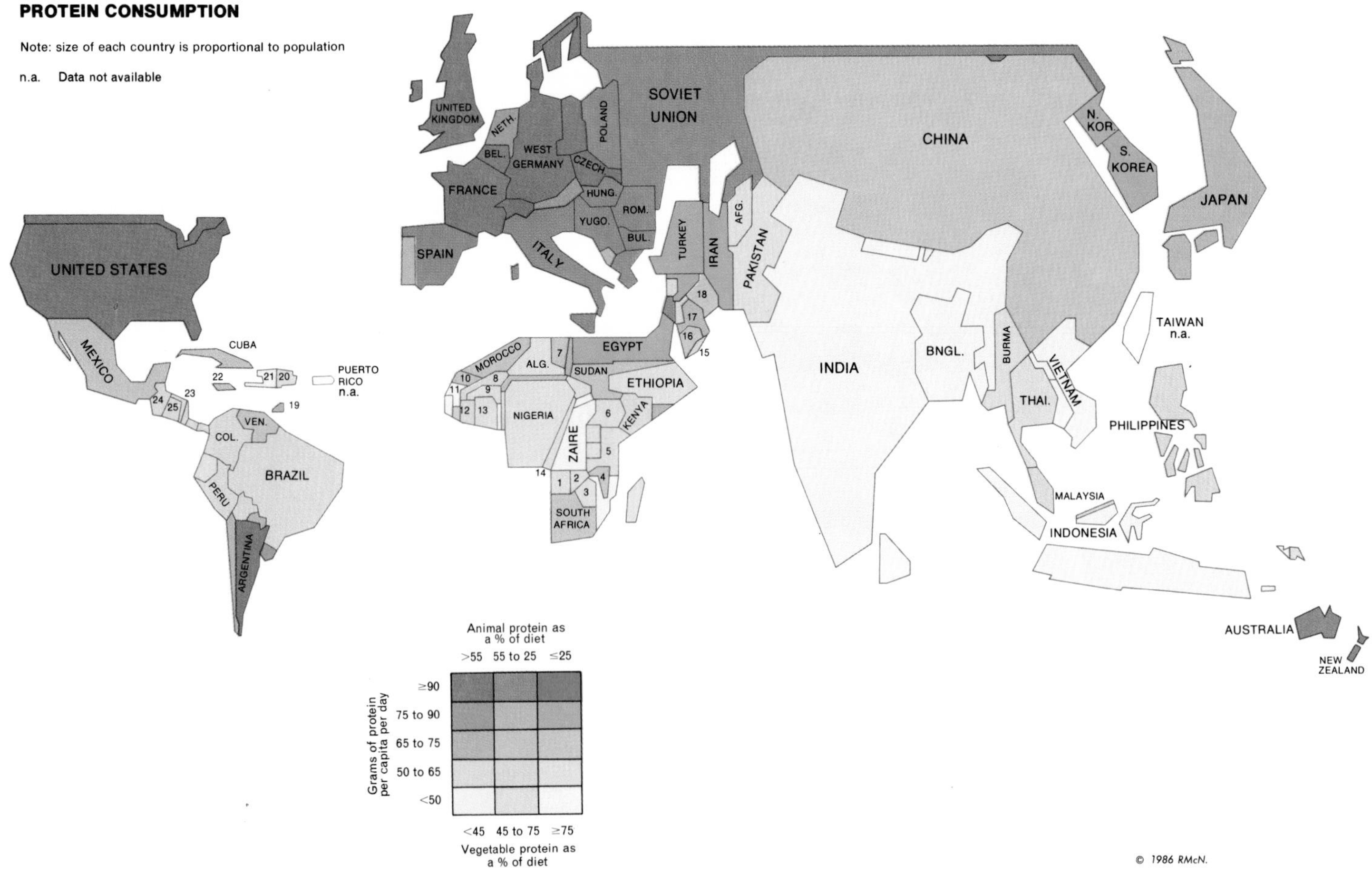

Animal protein as
a % of diet
>55   55 to 25   ≤25

Grams of protein per capita per day			
≥90			
75 to 90			
65 to 75			
50 to 65			
<50			

<45   45 to 75   ≥75
Vegetable protein as
a % of diet

© 1986 RMcN.

PHYSICIANS

Note: Size of each country is proportional to population

Population per physician

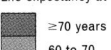

- <1000
- 1000 to 6000
- 6000 to 18000
- ≥18000

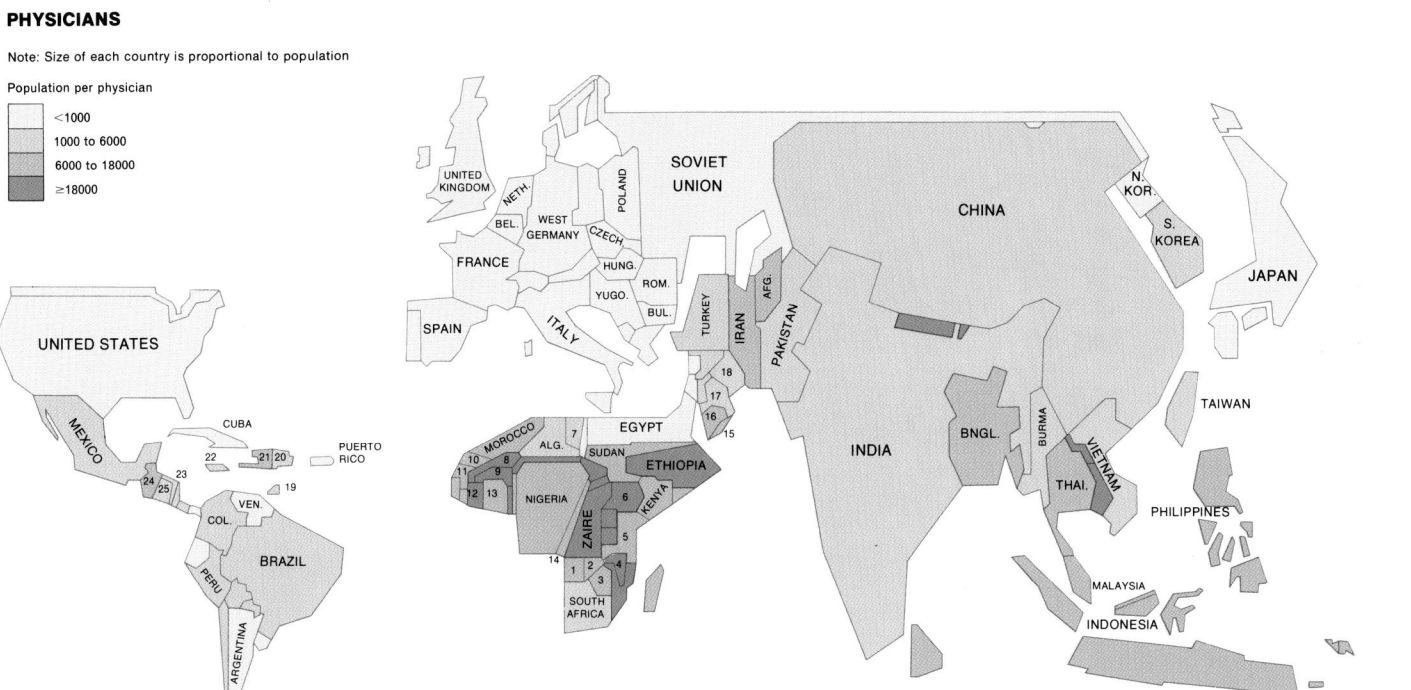

1. ANGOLA	6. UGANDA	11. GUINEA	16. YEMEN	21. HAITI
2. ZAMBIA	7. TUNISIA	12. IVORY COAST	17. SAUDI ARABIA	22. JAMAICA
3. ZIMBABWE	8. MALI	13. GHANA	18. IRAQ	23. HONDURAS
4. MALAWI	9. BURKINA FASO	14. CAMEROON	19. TRIN. & TOBAGO	24. GUATEMALA
5. TANZANIA	10. SENEGAL	15. P.D.R. YEMEN	20. DOM. REPUBLIC	25. EL SALVADOR

© 1986 Rand McNally & Co.
Made in U.S.A.
A-510000-1L6 -2-2-2

LIFE EXPECTANCY

Note: Size of each country is proportional to population

Life expectancy at birth

- ≥70 years
- 60 to 70
- 50 to 60
- <50

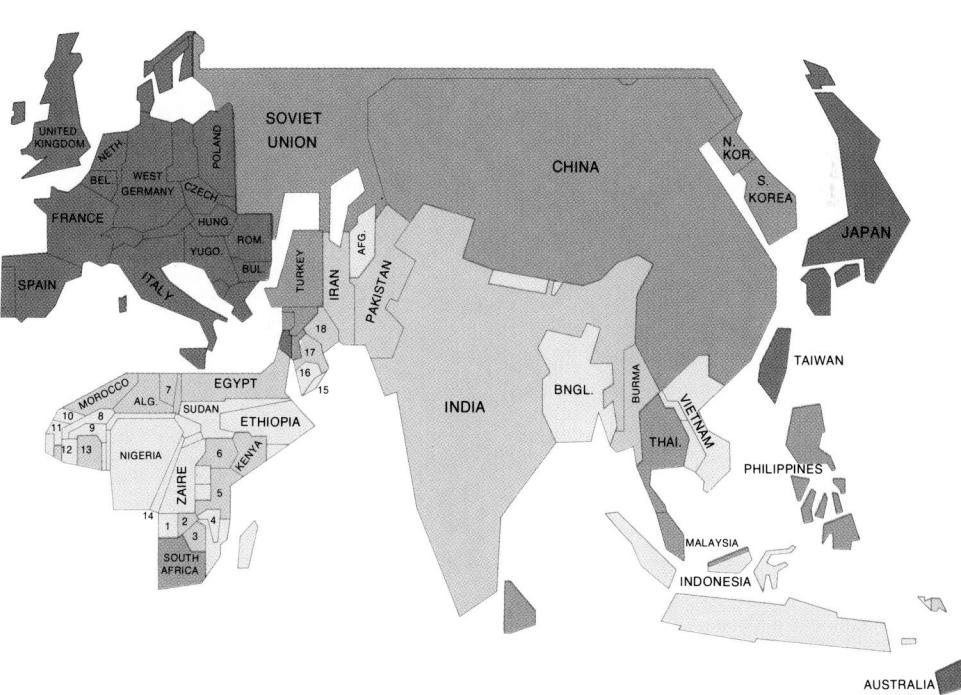

Deaths by Age Group as a % of Total Deaths

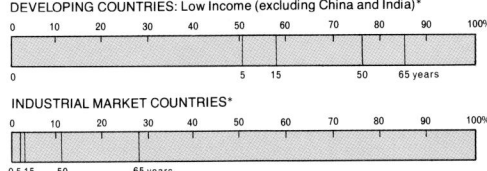

DEVELOPING COUNTRIES: Low Income (excluding China and India)*

INDUSTRIAL MARKET COUNTRIES*

Life Expectancy at Birth

DEVELOPING: Low Income*	56.1 years
DEVELOPING: Middle Income*	59.0
OIL EXPORTING*	57.3
EAST EUROPEAN NONMARKET*	69.6
INDUSTRIAL MARKET*	74.1

*as defined by the World Bank

© 1986 RMcN.

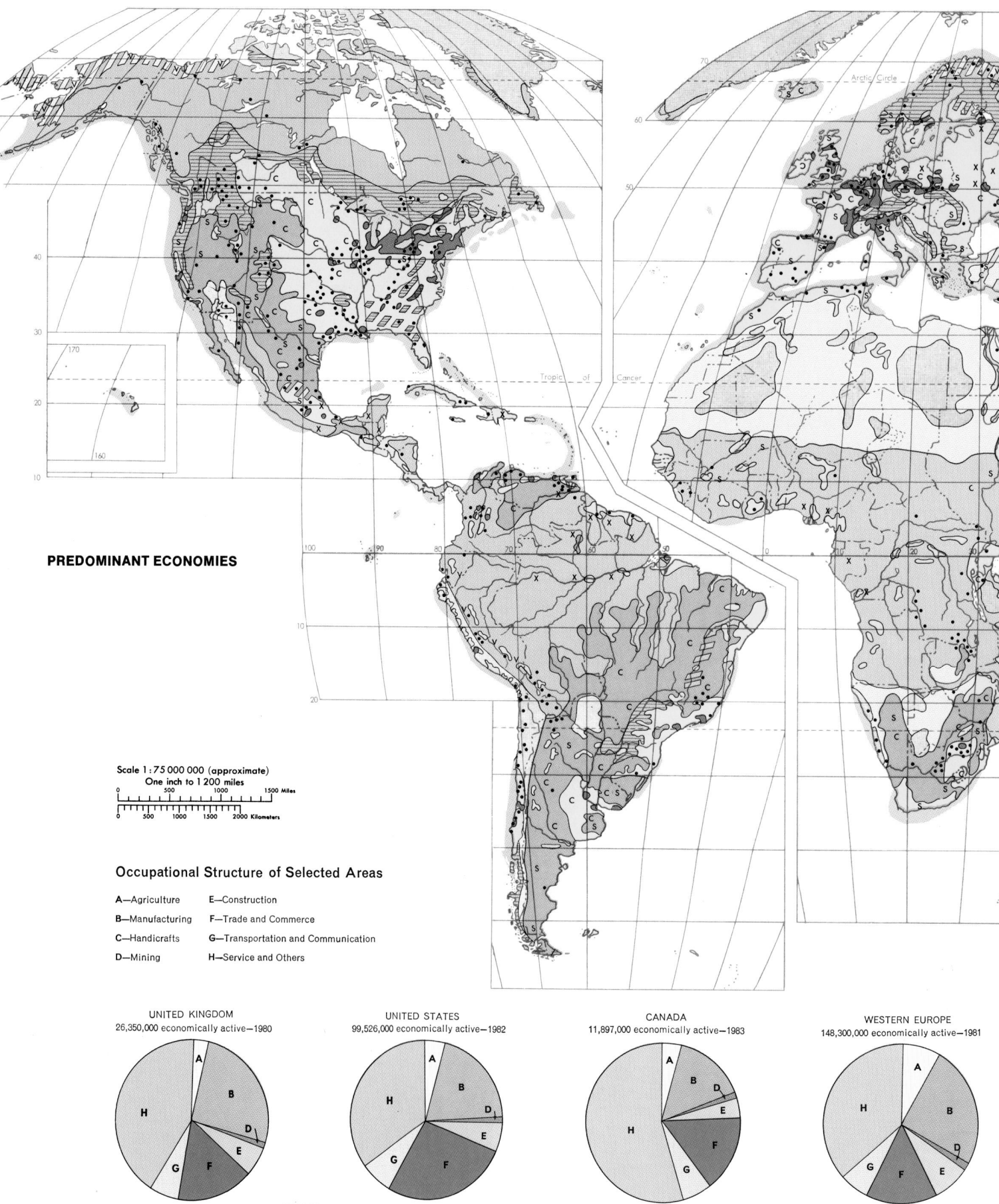

PREDOMINANT ECONOMIES

Scale 1 : 75 000 000 (approximate)
One inch to 1 200 miles

| 0 | 500 | 1000 | 1500 Miles |

| 0 | 500 | 1000 | 1500 | 2000 Kilometers |

Occupational Structure of Selected Areas

A—Agriculture   **E**—Construction

B—Manufacturing   **F**—Trade and Commerce

C—Handicrafts   **G**—Transportation and Communication

D—Mining   **H**—Service and Others

UNITED KINGDOM
26,350,000 economically active—1980

UNITED STATES
99,526,000 economically active—1982

CANADA
11,897,000 economically active—1983

WESTERN EUROPE
148,300,000 economically active—1981

A-810000-36 -5-5-4 5
Copyright by Rand McNally & Co.
Made in U.S.A.

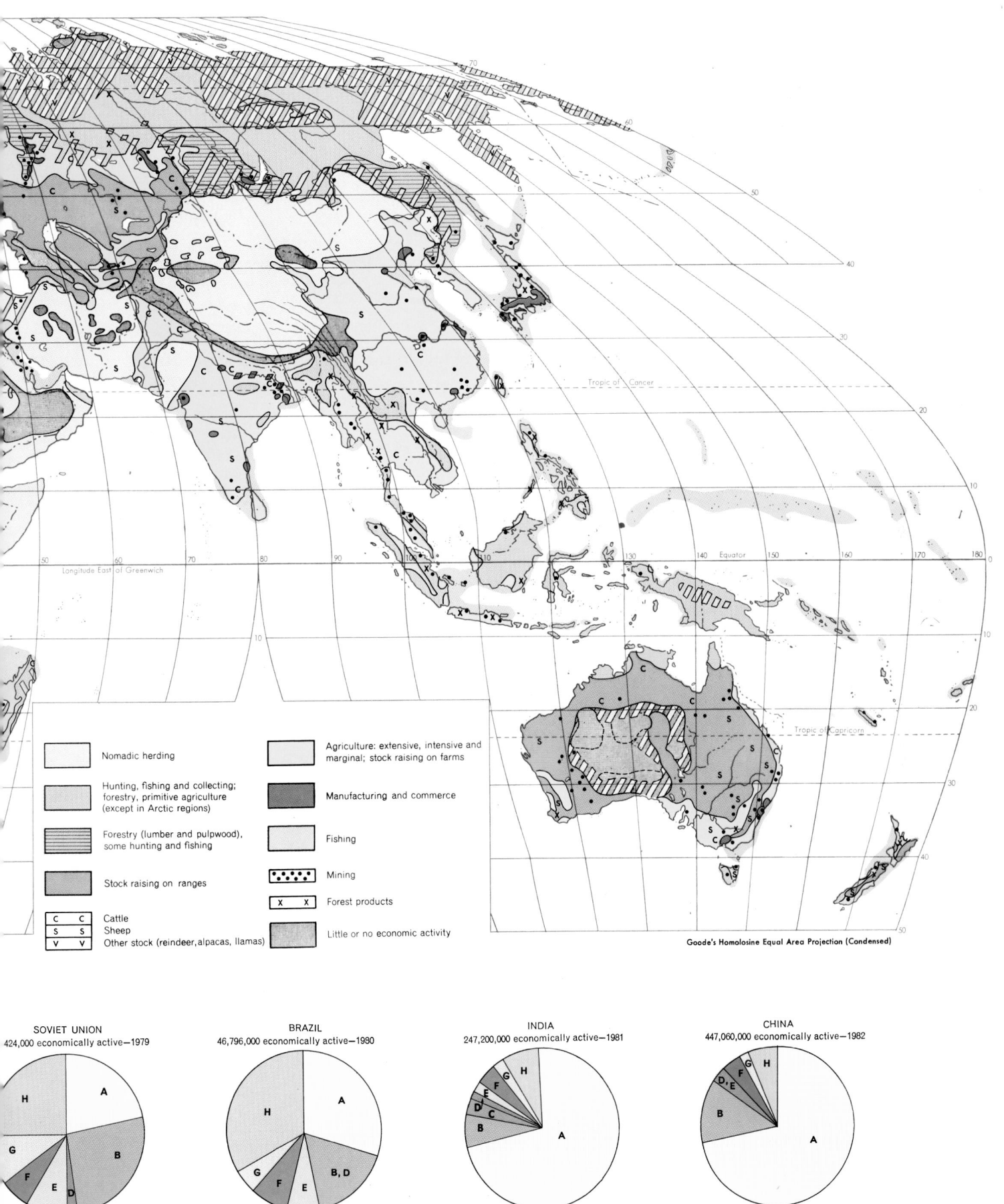

Nomadic herding

Hunting, fishing and collecting; forestry, primitive agriculture (except in Arctic regions)

Forestry (lumber and pulpwood), some hunting and fishing

Stock raising on ranges

C   C   Cattle
S   S   Sheep
V   V   Other stock (reindeer, alpacas, llamas)

Agriculture: extensive, intensive and marginal; stock raising on farms

Manufacturing and commerce

Fishing

Mining

X   X   Forest products

Little or no economic activity

Goode's Homolosine Equal Area Projection (Condensed)

SOVIET UNION
424,000 economically active—1979

BRAZIL
46,796,000 economically active—1980

INDIA
247,200,000 economically active—1981

CHINA
447,060,000 economically active—1982

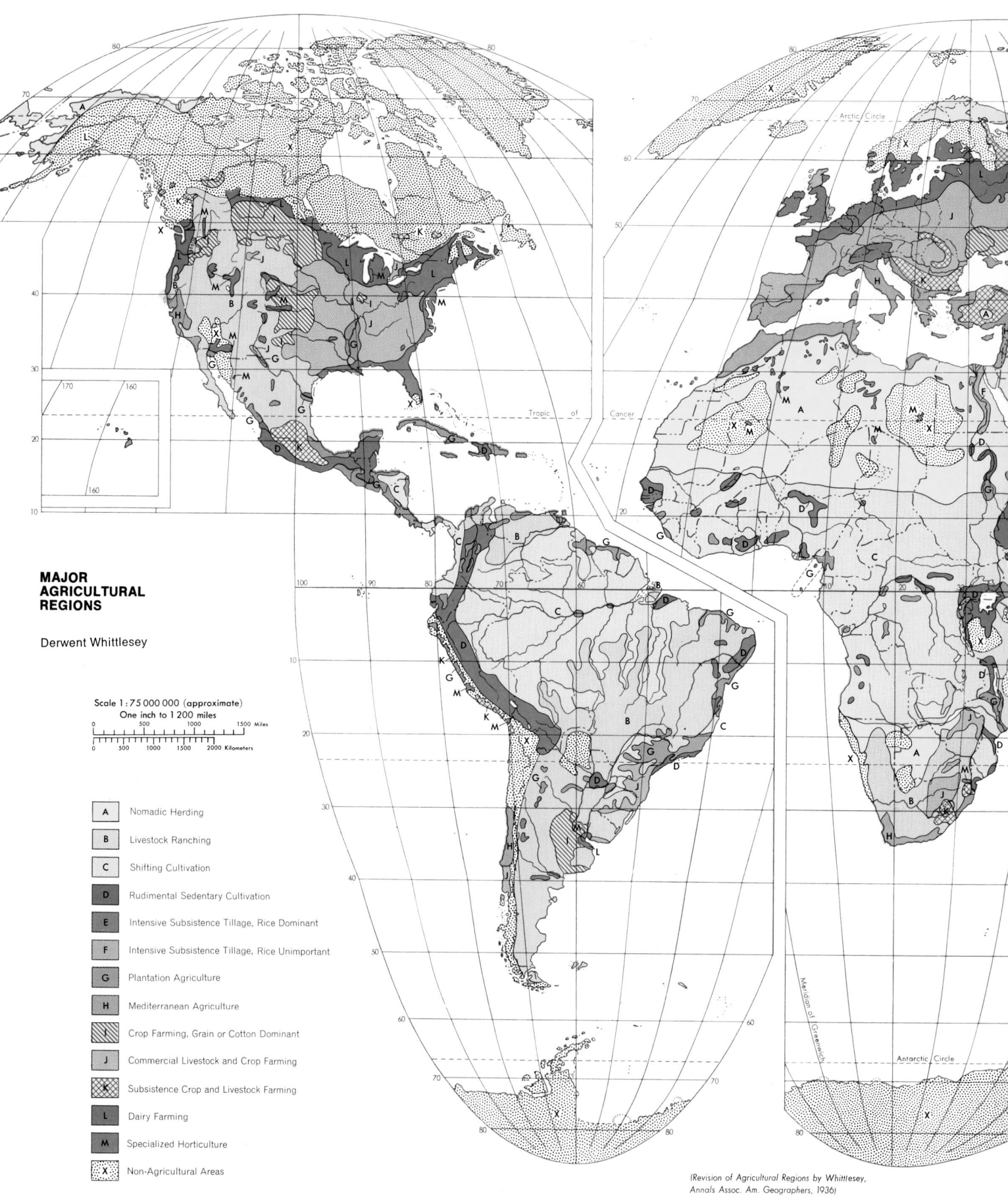

**MAJOR
AGRICULTURAL
REGIONS**

Derwent Whittlesey

Scale 1 : 75 000 000 (approximate)
One inch to 1 200 miles

0   500   1000   1500 Miles

0   500   1000   1500   2000 Kilometers

A	Nomadic Herding
B	Livestock Ranching
C	Shifting Cultivation
D	Rudimental Sedentary Cultivation
E	Intensive Subsistence Tillage, Rice Dominant
F	Intensive Subsistence Tillage, Rice Unimportant
G	Plantation Agriculture
H	Mediterranean Agriculture
I	Crop Farming, Grain or Cotton Dominant
J	Commercial Livestock and Crop Farming
K	Subsistence Crop and Livestock Farming
L	Dairy Farming
M	Specialized Horticulture
X	Non-Agricultural Areas

*(Revision of Agricultural Regions by Whittlesey,
Annals Assoc. Am. Geographers, 1936)*

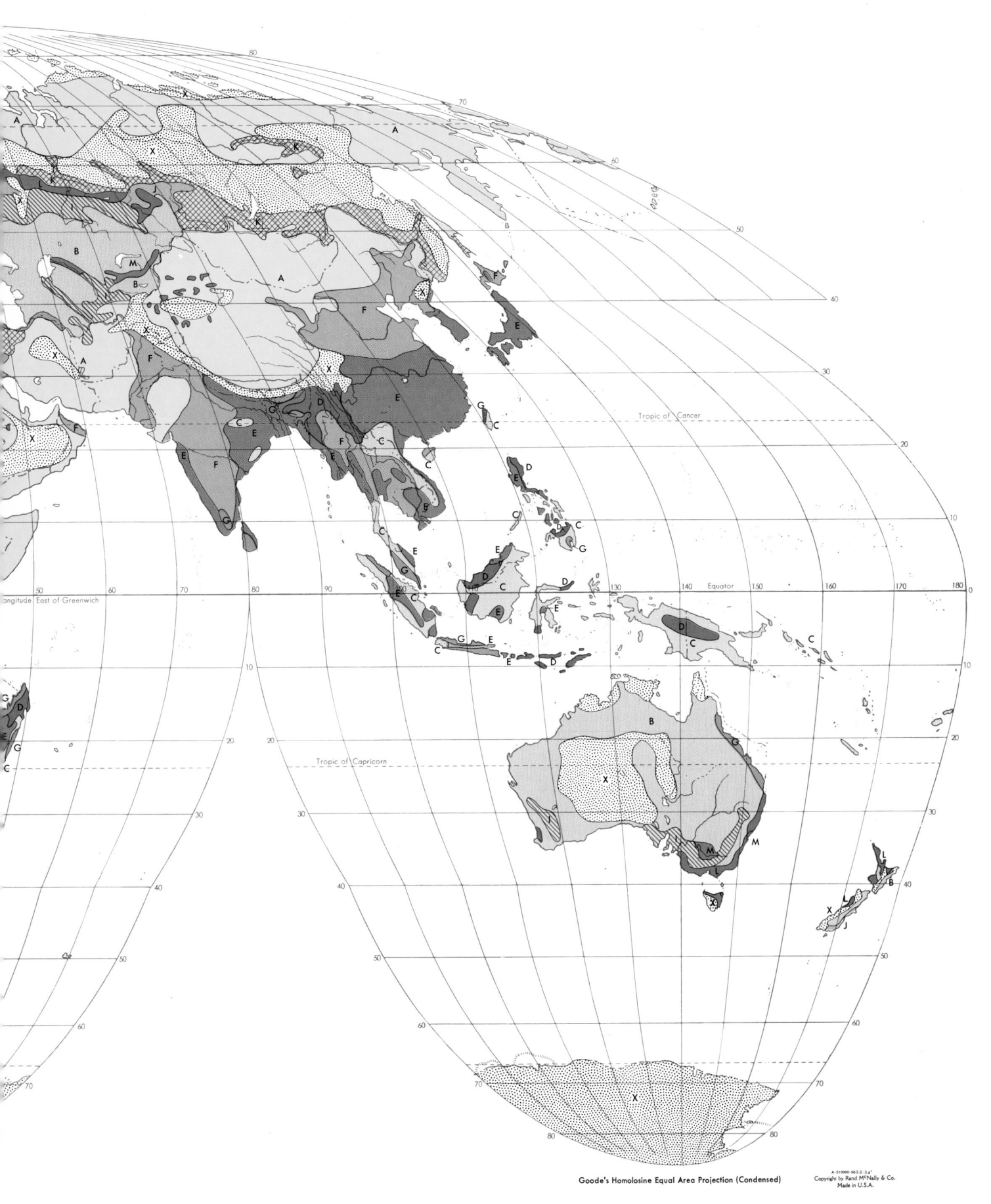

Goode's Homolosine Equal Area Projection (Condensed)

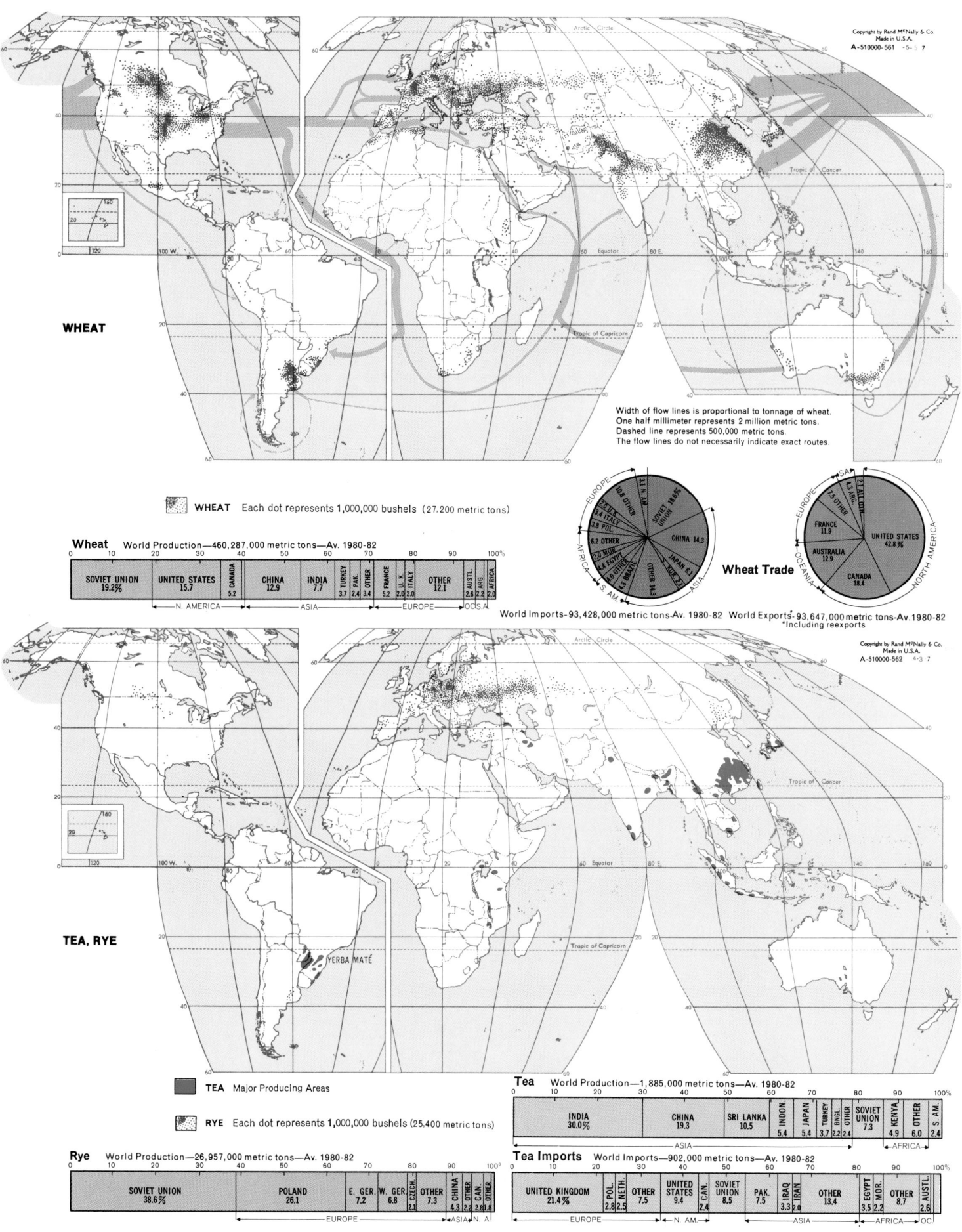

Copyright by Rand McNally & Co.
Made in U.S.A.
A-510000-561

WHEAT

Width of flow lines is proportional to tonnage of wheat.
One half millimeter represents 2 million metric tons.
Dashed line represents 500,000 metric tons.
The flow lines do not necessarily indicate exact routes.

WHEAT Each dot represents 1,000,000 bushels (27,200 metric tons)

Wheat World Production—460,287,000 metric tons—Av. 1980-82

0	10	20	30	40	50	60	70	80	90	100%

| SOVIET UNION 19.2% | UNITED STATES 15.7 | CANADA 5.2 | CHINA 12.9 | INDIA 7.7 | TURKEY 3.7 | PAK. 2.4 | OTHER 3.4 | FRANCE 5.2 | U.K. 2.0 | ITALY 2.0 | OTHER 12.1 | AUSTL. 2.6 | ARG. 2.2 | AFRICA 2.0 |

N. AMERICA — ASIA — EUROPE — OCS.A

Wheat Trade

World Imports-93,428,000 metric tons-Av. 1980-82   World Exports*-93,647,000 metric tons-Av. 1980-82
*Including reexports

Copyright by Rand McNally & Co.
Made in U.S.A.
A-510000-562

TEA, RYE

YERBA MATÉ

TEA Major Producing Areas

RYE Each dot represents 1,000,000 bushels (25,400 metric tons)

Rye World Production—26,957,000 metric tons—Av. 1980-82

0	10	20	30	40	50	60	70	80	90	100%

| SOVIET UNION 38.6% | POLAND 26.1 | E. GER. 7.2 | W. GER. 6.8 | CZECH. 2.1 | OTHER 7.3 | CHINA 4.3 | OTHER 2.2 | CAN. 2.8 | OTHER 1.8 |

EUROPE — ASIA | N. A

Tea World Production—1,885,000 metric tons—Av. 1980-82

0	10	20	30	40	50	60	70	80	90	100%

| INDIA 30.0% | CHINA 19.3 | SRI LANKA 10.5 | INDON. 5.4 | JAPAN 5.4 | TURKEY 3.7 | BNGL. 2.2 | OTHER 2.4 | SOVIET UNION 7.3 | KENYA 4.9 | OTHER 6.0 | S. AM. 2.4 |

ASIA — AFRICA

Tea Imports World Imports—902,000 metric tons—Av. 1980-82

0	10	20	30	40	50	60	70	80	90	100%

| UNITED KINGDOM 21.4% | POL. 2.8 | NETH. 2.5 | OTHER 7.5 | UNITED STATES 9.4 | CAN. 2.4 | SOVIET UNION 8.5 | PAK. 7.5 | IRAQ 3.3 | IRAN 2.0 | OTHER 13.4 | EGYPT 3.5 | MOR. 2.2 | OTHER 8.7 | AUSTL. 2.6 |

EUROPE — N. AM. — ASIA — AFRICA | OC

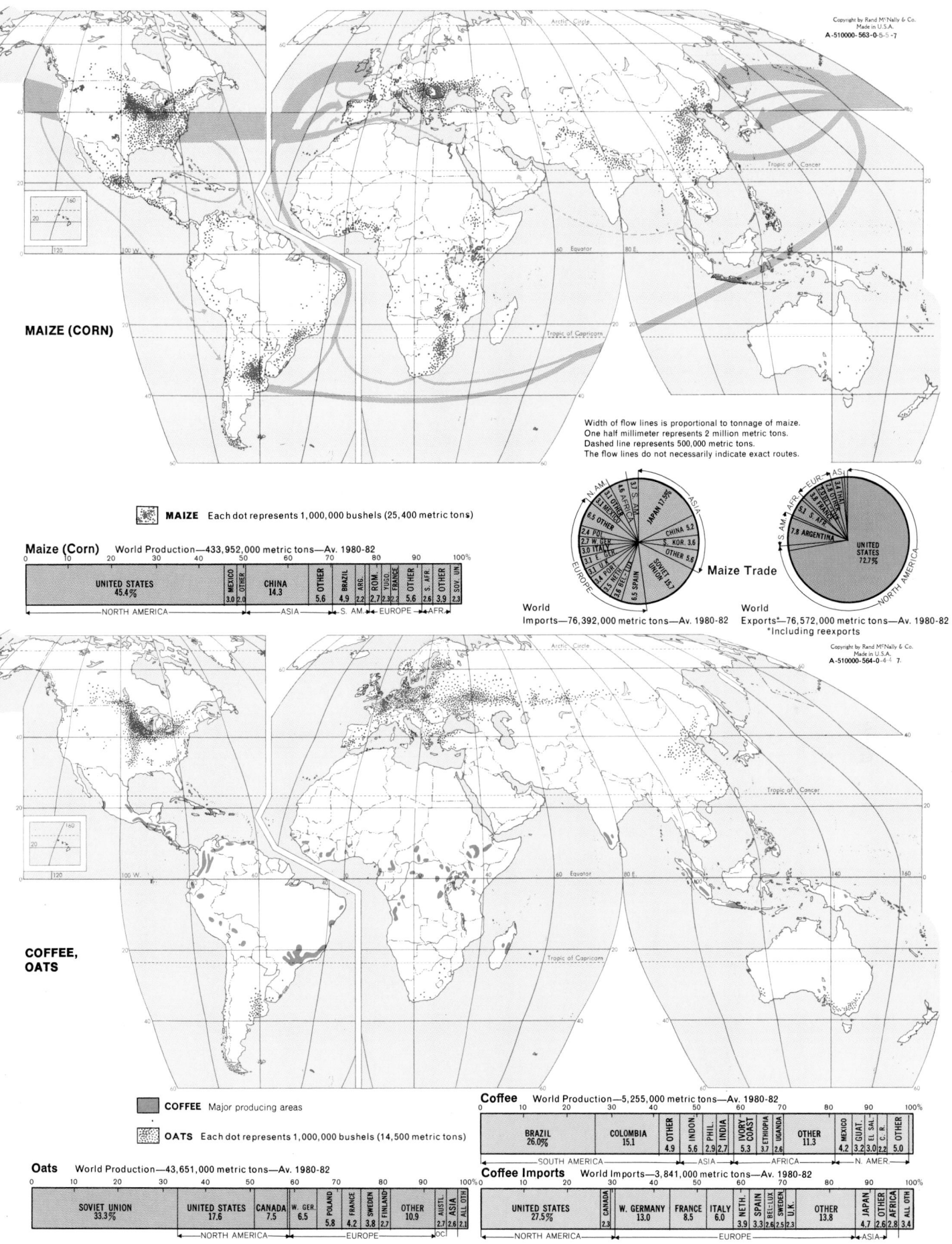

MAIZE (CORN)

Width of flow lines is proportional to tonnage of maize.
One half millimeter represents 2 million metric tons.
Dashed line represents 500,000 metric tons.
The flow lines do not necessarily indicate exact routes.

MAIZE Each dot represents 1,000,000 bushels (25,400 metric tons)

Maize (Corn) World Production—433,952,000 metric tons—Av. 1980-82

UNITED STATES 45.4%	MEXICO 3.0	OTHER 2.0	CHINA 14.3	OTHER 5.6	BRAZIL 4.9	ARG. 2.2	ROM. 2.7	YUGO 2.3	FRANCE 2.7	OTHER 5.6	S. AFR. 2.6	OTHER 3.9	SOV. UN. 2.3

NORTH AMERICA — ASIA — S. AM. — EUROPE — AFR.

Maize Trade

World Imports—76,392,000 metric tons—Av. 1980-82

World Exports—76,572,000 metric tons—Av. 1980-82
*Including reexports

COFFEE, OATS

COFFEE Major producing areas

OATS Each dot represents 1,000,000 bushels (14,500 metric tons)

Oats World Production—43,651,000 metric tons—Av. 1980-82

SOVIET UNION 33.3%	UNITED STATES 17.6	CANADA 7.5	W. GER. 6.5	POLAND 5.8	FRANCE 4.2	SWEDEN 3.8	FINLAND 2.7	OTHER 10.9	AUSTL. 2.7	ASIA 2.6	ALL OTH. 2.1

NORTH AMERICA — EUROPE — OC.

Coffee World Production—5,255,000 metric tons—Av. 1980-82

BRAZIL 26.0%	COLOMBIA 15.1	OTHER 4.9	INDON. 5.6	PHIL. 2.9	INDIA 2.7	IVORY COAST 5.3	ETHIOPIA 3.7	UGANDA 2.6	OTHER 11.3	MEXICO 4.2	GUAT. 3.2	EL SAL. 3.0	C.R. 2.2	OTHER 5.0

SOUTH AMERICA — ASIA — AFRICA — N. AMER.

Coffee Imports World Imports—3,841,000 metric tons—Av. 1980-82

UNITED STATES 27.5%	CANADA 2.3	W. GERMANY 13.0	FRANCE 8.5	ITALY 6.0	NETH. 3.9	SPAIN 3.3	BEL-LUX 2.6	SWEDEN 2.5	U.K. 2.3	OTHER 13.8	JAPAN 4.7	AFRICA 2.8	ALL OTH 3.4

NORTH AMERICA — EUROPE — ASIA

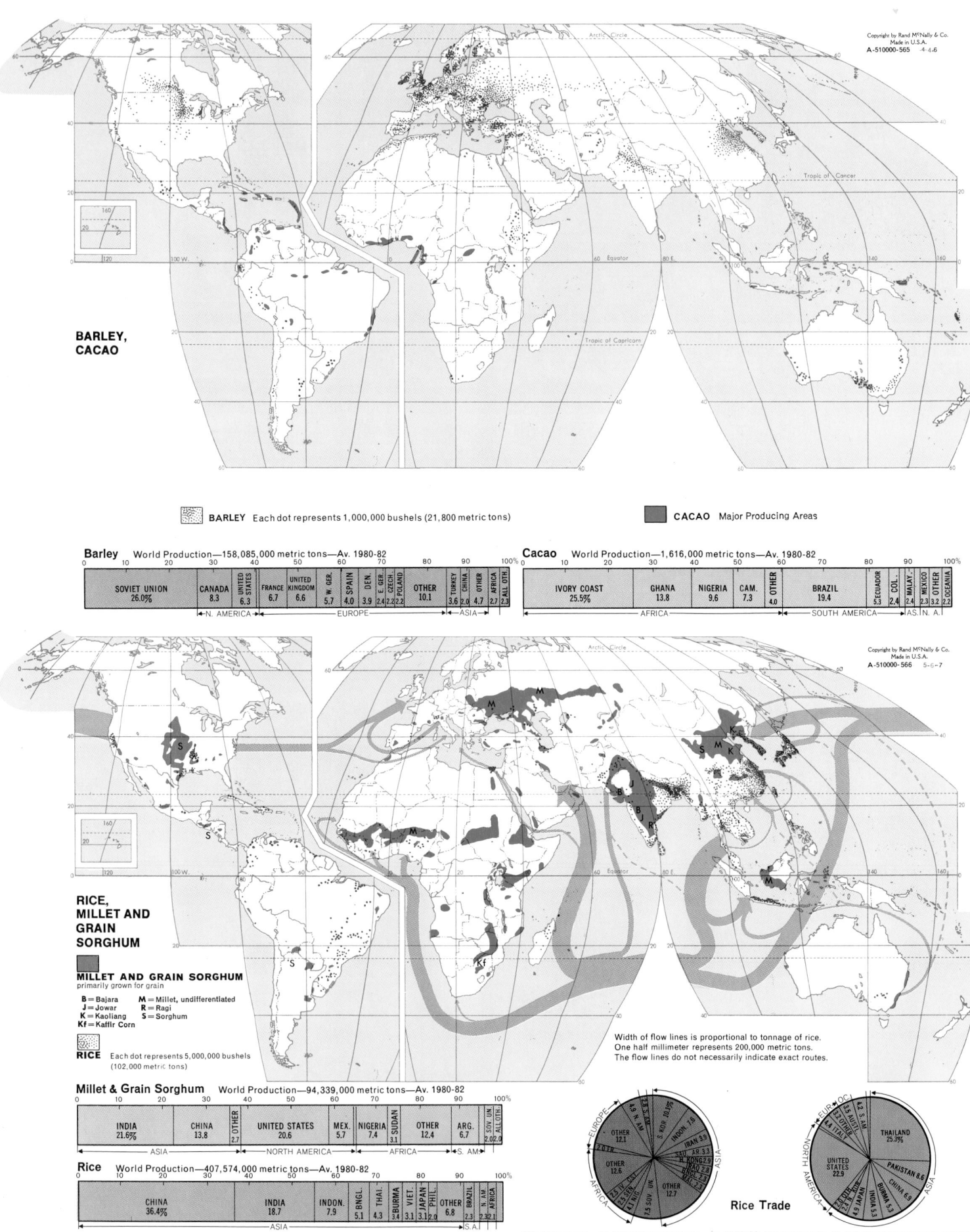

**BARLEY,
CACAO**

BARLEY Each dot represents 1,000,000 bushels (21,800 metric tons)

CACAO Major Producing Areas

Barley World Production—158,085,000 metric tons—Av. 1980-82

0	10	20	30	40	50	60	70	80	90	100%
SOVIET UNION 26.0%		CANADA 8.3	UNITED STATES 6.3	FRANCE 6.7	UNITED KINGDOM 6.6	W. GER. 5.7	SPAIN 4.0	DEN. 3.9	E. GER. 2.4	CZECH. 2.2	POLAND 2.2	OTHER 10.1	TURKEY 3.6	CHINA 2.0	OTHER 4.7	AFRICA 2.7	ALL OTH. 2.3

← N. AMERICA →   EUROPE   ← ASIA →

Cacao World Production—1,616,000 metric tons—Av. 1980-82

0	10	20	30	40	50	60	70	80	90	100%
IVORY COAST 25.5%		GHANA 13.8	NIGERIA 9.6	CAM. 7.3	OTHER 4.0	BRAZIL 19.4	ECUADOR 5.3	COL. 2.4	MALAY. 2.4	MEXICO 3.2	OTHER 3.2	OCEANIA 2.2

← AFRICA →   ← SOUTH AMERICA →   AS. N. A.

**RICE,
MILLET AND
GRAIN
SORGHUM**

MILLET AND GRAIN SORGHUM
primarily grown for grain

B = Bajara   M = Millet, undifferentiated
J = Jowar   R = Ragi
K = Kaoliang   S = Sorghum
Kf = Kaffir Corn

RICE Each dot represents 5,000,000 bushels
(102,000 metric tons)

Width of flow lines is proportional to tonnage of rice.
One half millimeter represents 200,000 metric tons.
The flow lines do not necessarily indicate exact routes.

Millet & Grain Sorghum World Production—94,339,000 metric tons—Av. 1980-82

0	10	20	30	40	50	60	70	80	90	100%
INDIA 21.6%		CHINA 13.8	OTHER 2.7	UNITED STATES 20.6	MEX. 5.7	NIGERIA 7.4	SUDAN 3.1	OTHER 12.4	ARG. 6.7	SOV. UN. 2.0	ALL OTH. 2.9

← ASIA →   ← NORTH AMERICA →   ← AFRICA →   ← S. AM. →

Rice World Production—407,574,000 metric tons—Av. 1980-82

0	10	20	30	40	50	60	70	80	90	100%
CHINA 36.4%		INDIA 18.7	INDON. 7.9	BNGL. 5.1	THAI. 4.3	BURMA 3.4	VIET. 3.1	JAPAN 3.1	PHIL. 2.0	OTHER 6.8	BRAZIL 2.3	N. AM. OTHER	AFRICA 2.1

← ASIA →   S.A.

Rice Trade

World Imports—12,569,000 metric tons—Av. 1980-82   World Exports*-12,703,000 metric tons-Av. 1980-82
*Including reexports

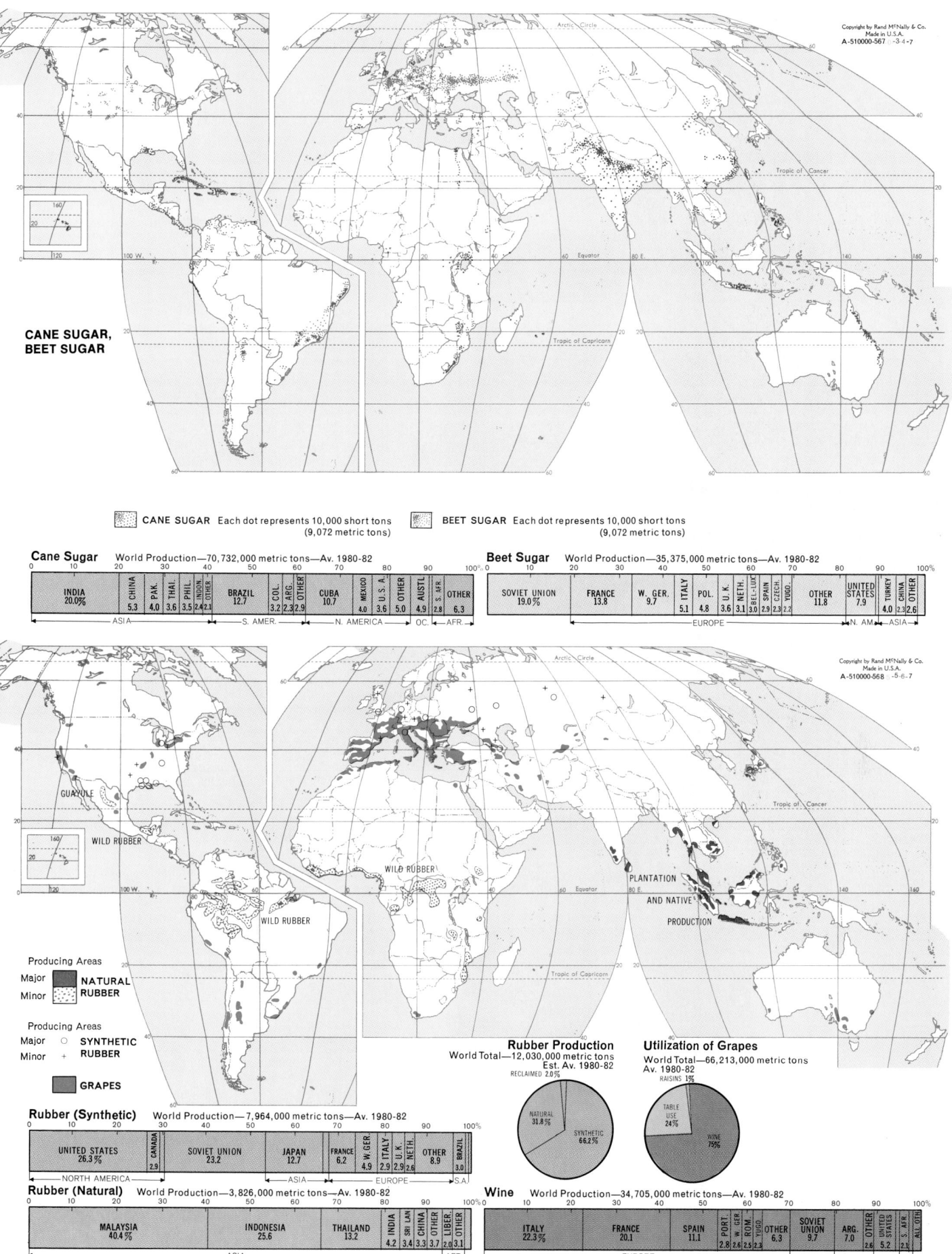

CANE SUGAR, BEET SUGAR

CANE SUGAR Each dot represents 10,000 short tons (9,072 metric tons)

BEET SUGAR Each dot represents 10,000 short tons (9,072 metric tons)

Cane Sugar World Production—70,732,000 metric tons—Av. 1980-82

INDIA 20.0%	CHINA 5.3	PAK. 4.0	THAI. 3.6	PHIL. 3.5	INDON. 2.4	OTHER 2.1	BRAZIL 12.7	COL. 3.2	ARG. 2.3	OTHER 2.9	CUBA 10.7	MEXICO 4.0	U.S.A. 3.6	OTHER 5.0	AUSTL. 4.9	S. AFR. 2.8	OTHER 6.3
◄———— ASIA ————►							◄——— S. AMER. ———►				◄———— N. AMERICA ————►				◄ OC. ►	◄— AFR. —►	

Beet Sugar World Production—35,375,000 metric tons—Av. 1980-82

SOVIET UNION 19.0%	FRANCE 13.8	W. GER. 9.7	ITALY 5.1	POL. 4.8	U.K. 3.6	NETH. 3.1	BEL-LUX. 3.0	SPAIN 2.9	CZECH. 2.3	YUGO. 2.2	OTHER 11.8	UNITED STATES 7.9	TURKEY 4.0	CHINA 2.3	OTHER 2.6
			◄———————————————————— EUROPE ————————————————————►									◄—— N. AM. ——►	◄—— ASIA ——►		

GUAYULE
WILD RUBBER
WILD RUBBER
WILD RUBBER
WILD RUBBER
PLANTATION
AND NATIVE
PRODUCTION

Producing Areas
Major / Minor NATURAL RUBBER

Producing Areas
Major ○ / Minor + SYNTHETIC RUBBER

GRAPES

Rubber Production
World Total—12,030,000 metric tons
Est. Av. 1980-82
RECLAIMED 2.0%
NATURAL 31.8%
SYNTHETIC 66.2%

Utilization of Grapes
World Total—66,213,000 metric tons
Av. 1980-82
RAISINS 1%
TABLE USE 24%
WINE 75%

Rubber (Synthetic) World Production— 7,964,000 metric tons—Av. 1980-82

UNITED STATES 26.3%	CANADA 2.9	SOVIET UNION 23.2	JAPAN 12.7	FRANCE 6.2	W. GER. 4.9	ITALY 2.9	U.K. 2.9	NETH. 2.6	OTHER 8.9	BRAZIL 3.0
◄——— NORTH AMERICA ———►			◄——— ASIA ———►		◄——— EUROPE ———►					◄ S.A. ►

Rubber (Natural) World Production—3,826,000 metric tons—Av. 1980-82

MALAYSIA 40.4%	INDONESIA 25.6	THAILAND 13.2	INDIA 4.2	SRI LAN 3.4	CHINA 3.3	OTHER 3.7	LIBER. 2.0	OTHER 3.1
	◄———————————————— ASIA ————————————————►						◄—— AFR. ——►	

Wine World Production—34,705,000 metric tons—Av. 1980-82

ITALY 22.3%	FRANCE 20.1	SPAIN 11.1	PORT. 2.8	W. GER. 2.6	ROM. 2.5	YUGO. 2.2	OTHER 6.3	SOVIET UNION 9.7	ARG. 7.0	OTHER 2.6	UNITED STATES 5.2	S. AFR. 2.1	ALL OTH.
		◄————————————————————— EUROPE —————————————————————►							◄— S. AM. —►		◄— N. AM. —►		

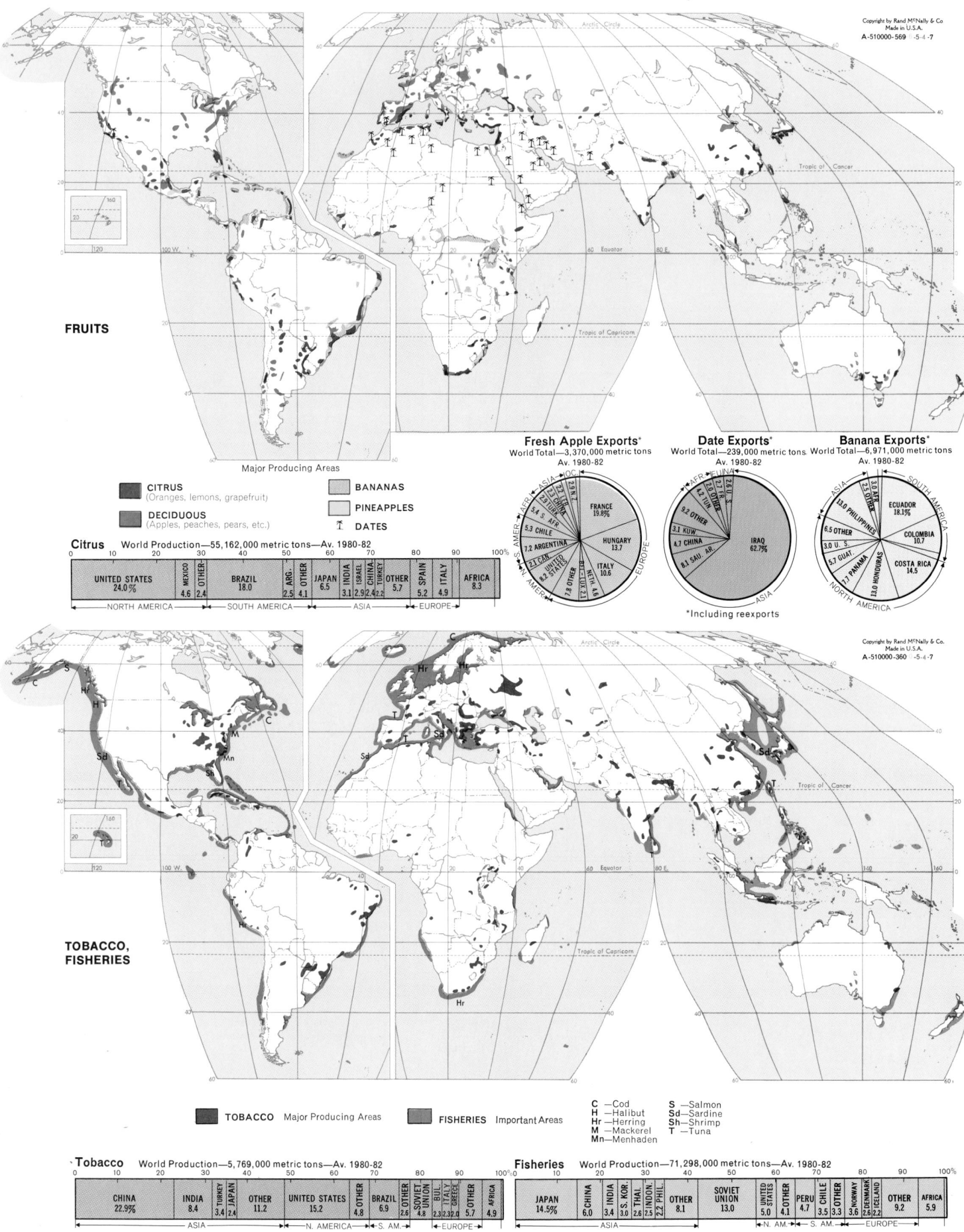

FRUITS

Major Producing Areas

■ **CITRUS**
(Oranges, lemons, grapefruit)

■ **DECIDUOUS**
(Apples, peaches, pears, etc.)

■ **BANANAS**

■ **PINEAPPLES**

🌴 **DATES**

Copyright by Rand McNally & Co
Made in U.S.A.
A-510000-569 -5-4-7

Citrus World Production—55,162,000 metric tons—Av. 1980-82

UNITED STATES 24.0%	MEXICO 4.6	OTHER 2.4	BRAZIL 18.0	ARG. 2.5	OTHER 4.1	JAPAN 6.5	INDIA 3.1	ISRAEL 2.9	CHINA 2.4	TURKEY 2.2	OTHER 5.7	SPAIN 5.2	ITALY 4.9	AFRICA 8.3

←NORTH AMERICA→ ←SOUTH AMERICA→ ←ASIA→ ←EUROPE→

Fresh Apple Exports*
World Total—3,370,000 metric tons
Av. 1980-82

FRANCE 19.8%
HUNGARY 13.7
ITALY 10.6
NETH. 4.6
U.S. 2.1
UNITED STATES 8.2
CAN. 2.1
ARGENTINA 7.2
CHILE 5.3
S. AFR. 5.4
CHINA 2.5
N. ZEAL. 2.7
AUS. 2.9
OC.
S. AMER.
N. AMER.
AFR.
ASIA
EUROPE

Date Exports*
World Total—239,000 metric tons
Av. 1980-82

IRAQ 62.7%
SAU. AR. 8.1
KUW. 3.1
CHINA 4.7
OTHER 9.2
TUN. 4.2
EUN. 2.7
AFR.
U.S.
ASIA

Banana Exports*
World Total—6,971,000 metric tons.
Av. 1980-82

ECUADOR 18.1%
COLOMBIA 10.7
COSTA RICA 14.5
HONDURAS 13.0
PANAMA 7.7
GUAT. 5.7
U.S. 3.0
OTHER 6.5
PHILIPPINES 13.0
ASIA 2.5
OC. 3.0
SOUTH AMERICA
NORTH AMERICA

*Including reexports

Copyright by Rand McNally & Co.
Made in U.S.A.
A-510000-360 -5-4-7

TOBACCO, FISHERIES

■ **TOBACCO** Major Producing Areas

■ **FISHERIES** Important Areas

C —Cod
H —Halibut
Hr —Herring
M —Mackerel
Mn—Menhaden

S —Salmon
Sd—Sardine
Sh—Shrimp
T —Tuna

Tobacco World Production—5,769,000 metric tons—Av. 1980-82

CHINA 22.9%	INDIA 8.4	TURKEY 3.4	JAPAN 2.4	OTHER 11.2	UNITED STATES 15.2	OTHER 4.8	BRAZIL 6.9	OTHER 4.8	SOVIET UNION 7.4	BUL. 2.3	ITALY 2.3	GREECE 2.0	OTHER 5.7	AFRICA 4.9

←ASIA→ ←N. AMERICA→ ←S. AM.→ ←EUROPE→

Fisheries World Production—71,298,000 metric tons—Av. 1980-82

JAPAN 14.5%	CHINA 6.0	INDIA 3.4	S. KOR. 3.0	THAI. 2.6	INDON. 2.5	PHIL. 2.2	OTHER 8.1	SOVIET UNION 13.0	UNITED STATES 5.0	OTHER 4.1	PERU 4.7	CHILE 3.5	NORWAY 3.3	DENMARK 3.6	ICELAND 2.2	OTHER 9.2	AFRICA 5.9

←ASIA→ ←N. AM.→ ←S. AM.→ ←EUROPE→

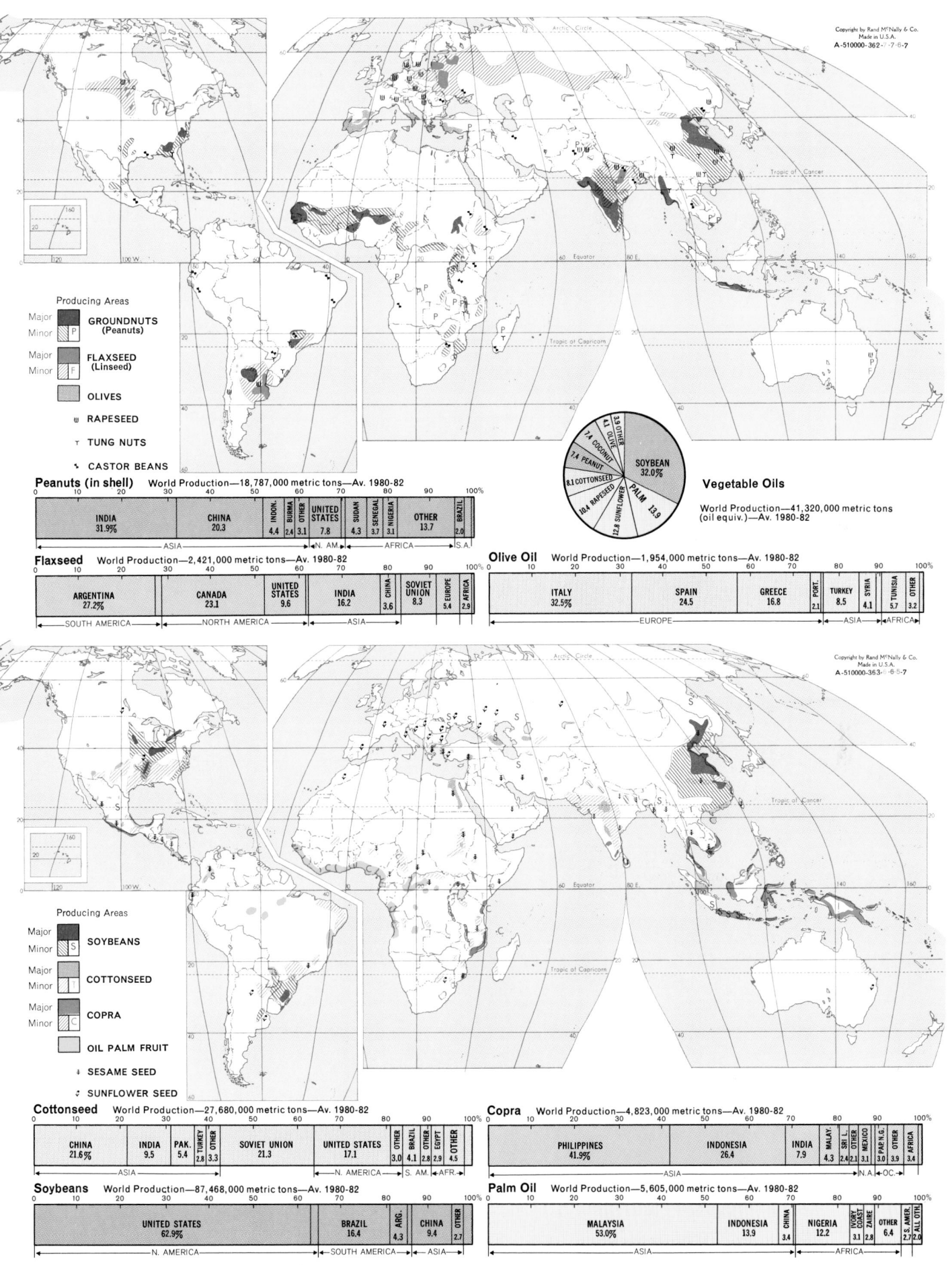

Producing Areas

Major / Minor		
Major ▓ Minor ▒	**GROUNDNUTS** (Peanuts)	
Major ▓ Minor ⫽	**FLAXSEED** (Linseed)	
░	**OLIVES**	
ψ	**RAPESEED**	
τ	**TUNG NUTS**	
⟡	**CASTOR BEANS**	

Vegetable Oils

Pie chart: SOYBEAN 32.0%, PALM 13.9, SUNFLOWER 12.8, RAPESEED 10.4, COTTONSEED 8.1, PEANUT 7.4, COCONUT 7.4, OLIVE 4.1, OTHER 3.9

World Production—41,320,000 metric tons (oil equiv.)—Av. 1980-82

Peanuts (in shell)   World Production—18,787,000 metric tons—Av. 1980-82

INDIA 31.9%	CHINA 20.3	INDON. 4.4	BURMA 2.4	OTHER 3.1	UNITED STATES 7.8	SUDAN 4.3	SENEGAL 3.7	NIGERIA 3.1	OTHER 13.7	BRAZIL 2.0
←————————ASIA————————→					←N. AM.→	←————AFRICA————→				←S.A.→

Flaxseed   World Production—2,421,000 metric tons—Av. 1980-82

ARGENTINA 27.2%	CANADA 23.1	UNITED STATES 9.6	INDIA 16.2	CHINA 3.6	SOVIET UNION 8.3	EUROPE 5.4	AFRICA 2.9
←SOUTH AMERICA→	←———NORTH AMERICA———→		←————ASIA————→				

Olive Oil   World Production—1,954,000 metric tons—Av. 1980-82

ITALY 32.5%	SPAIN 24.5	GREECE 16.8	PORT. 2.1	TURKEY 8.5	SYRIA 4.1	TUNISIA 5.7	OTHER 3.2
←————————————EUROPE————————————→				←————ASIA————→		←AFRICA→	

Producing Areas

Major / Minor	
Major ▓ Minor ⧅ S	**SOYBEANS**
Major ░ Minor ▫	**COTTONSEED**
Major ▓ Minor ⧄ C	**COPRA**
░	**OIL PALM FRUIT**
⚹	**SESAME SEED**
⚘	**SUNFLOWER SEED**

Cottonseed   World Production—27,680,000 metric tons—Av. 1980-82

CHINA 21.6%	INDIA 9.5	PAK. 5.4	TURKEY 2.8	OTHER 3.3	SOVIET UNION 21.3	UNITED STATES 17.1	OTHER 3.0	BRAZIL 4.1	OTHER 2.8	EGYPT 2.9	OTHER 4.5
←————————ASIA————————→						←N. AMERICA→		←S. AM.→		←AFR.→	

Copra   World Production—4,823,000 metric tons—Av. 1980-82

PHILIPPINES 41.9%	INDONESIA 26.4	INDIA 7.9	MALAY. 4.3	SRI L. 2.4	OTHER 2.1	MEXICO 3.1	PAP. N.G. 3.0	OTHER 3.9	AFRICA 3.4
←————————————ASIA————————————→						←N.A.→	←OC.→		

Soybeans   World Production—87,468,000 metric tons—Av. 1980-82

UNITED STATES 62.9%	BRAZIL 16.4	ARG. 4.3	CHINA 9.4	OTHER 2.7
←———N. AMERICA———→	←———SOUTH AMERICA———→		←ASIA→	

Palm Oil   World Production—5,605,000 metric tons—Av. 1980-82

MALAYSIA 53.0%	INDONESIA 13.9	CHINA 3.4	NIGERIA 12.2	IVORY COAST 3.1	ZAIRE 2.4	OTHER 6.4	S. AMER. 2.7	ALL OTH. 2.0
←————————————ASIA————————————→			←————————AFRICA————————→					

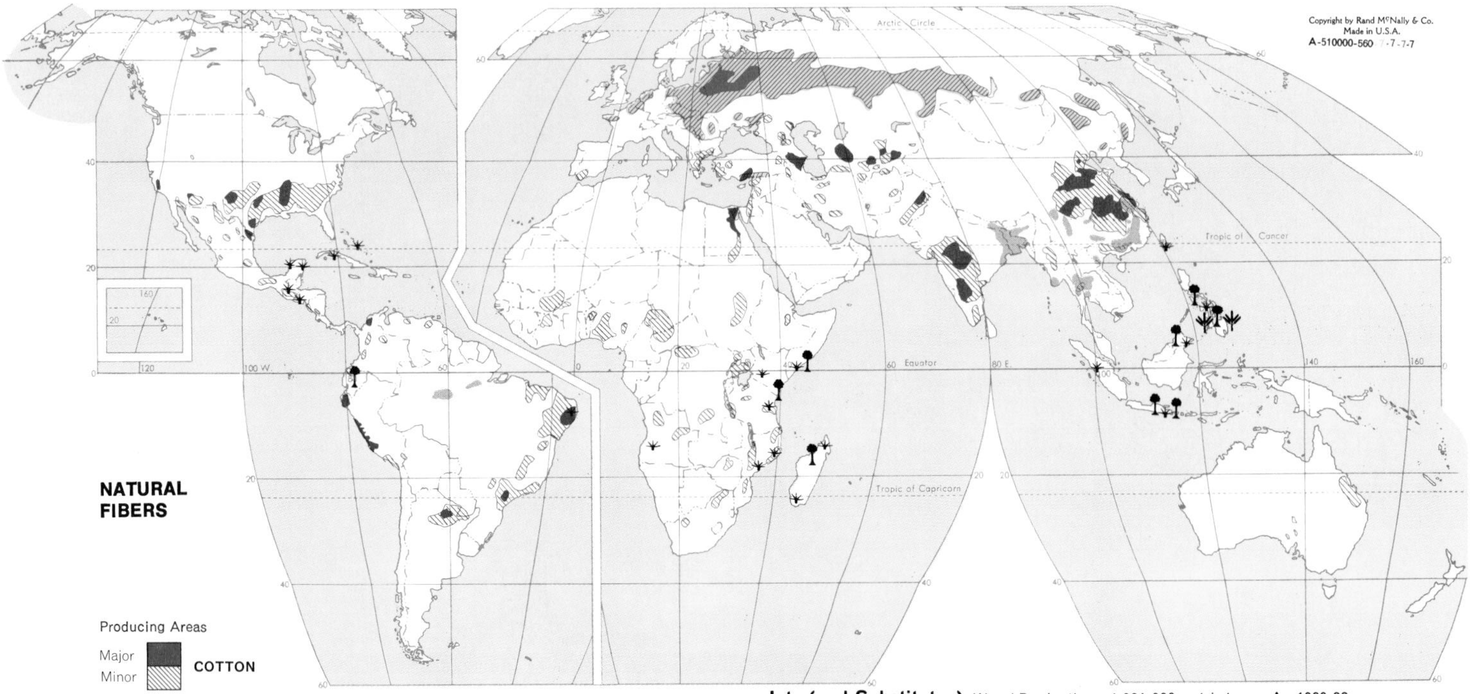

Copyright by Rand McNally & Co.
Made in U.S.A.
A-510000-560 · -7·-7-7

NATURAL FIBERS

Producing Areas

Major	COTTON
Minor	
Major	FLAX (Fiber)
Minor	
	JUTE

✷ SISAL

♠ KAPOK

✷ ABACA (Manila Hemp)

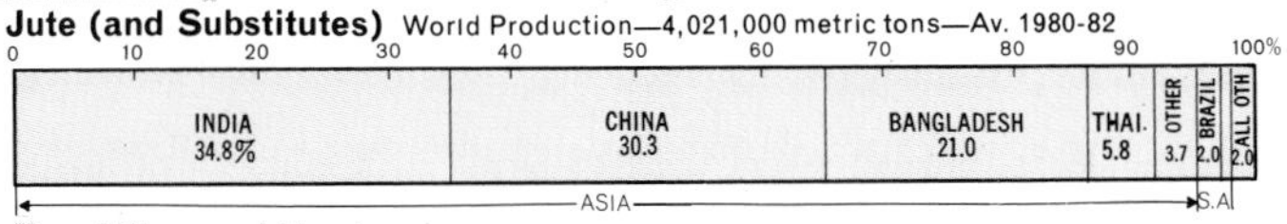

Cotton (Lint) World Production—14,647,000 metric tons—Av. 1980-82

0	10	20	30	40	50	60	70	80	90	100%

CHINA 20.4%	INDIA 9.0	PAK. 5.1	TURKEY 3.3	OTHER 3.0	SOVIET UNION 19.6	UNITED STATES 19.2	MEXICO 2.0	BRAZIL 4.0	EGYPT 2.9	OTHER 3.4	OTHER 4.6

←————— ASIA —————→ ←— N. AMERICA —→ ←S. AM.→ ←AFR.→

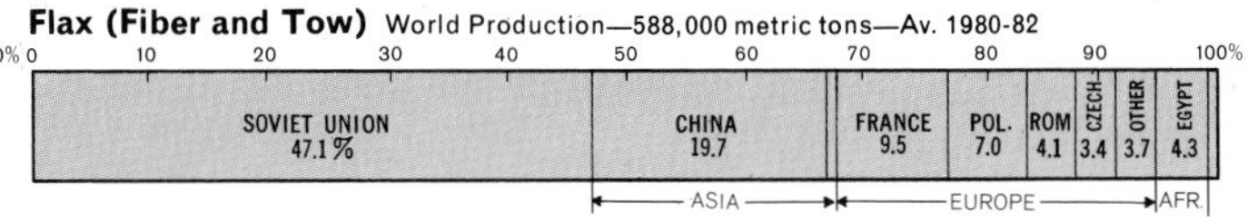

Jute (and Substitutes) World Production—4,021,000 metric tons—Av. 1980-82

0	10	20	30	40	50	60	70	80	90	100%

INDIA 34.8%	CHINA 30.3	BANGLADESH 21.0	THAI. 5.8	OTHER 3.7	BRAZIL 2.0	ALL OTH 2.0

←———————————————————— ASIA ————————————————————→ ←S.A.→

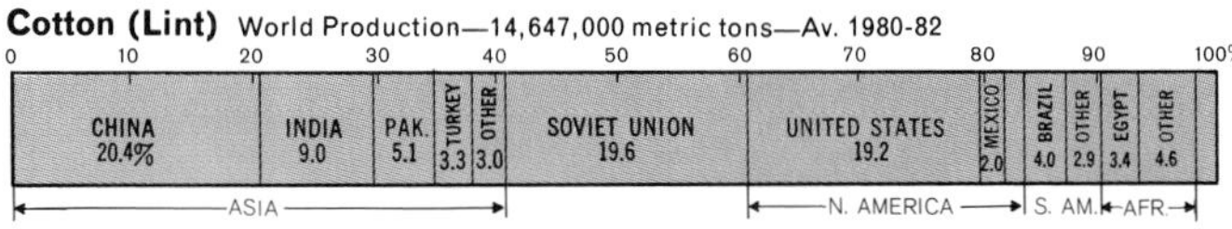

Flax (Fiber and Tow) World Production—588,000 metric tons—Av. 1980-82

0	10	20	30	40	50	60	70	80	90	100%

SOVIET UNION 47.1%	CHINA 19.7	FRANCE 9.5	POL. 7.0	ROM 4.1	CZECH. 3.4	OTHER 3.7	EGYPT 4.3

←————————— ASIA —————————→ ←———— EUROPE ————→ ←AFR.→

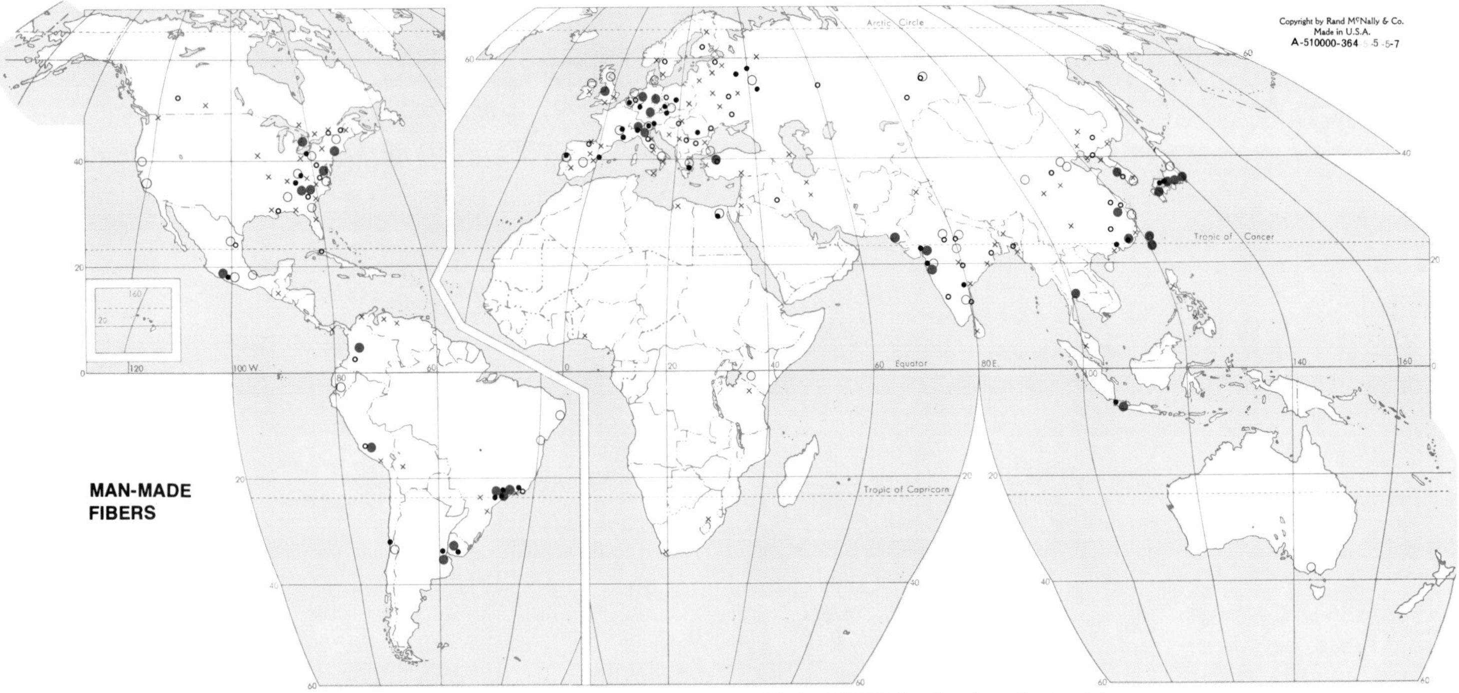

Copyright by Rand McNally & Co.
Made in U.S.A.
A-510000-364 · -5·-5-7

MAN-MADE FIBERS

CELLULOSIC (rayon, acetate)

• 2–3 plants

○ 1 plant

NONCELLULOSIC (acrylic, nylon, polyester, etc.)

● 6–10 plants

○ 3–5 plants

× 1–2 plants

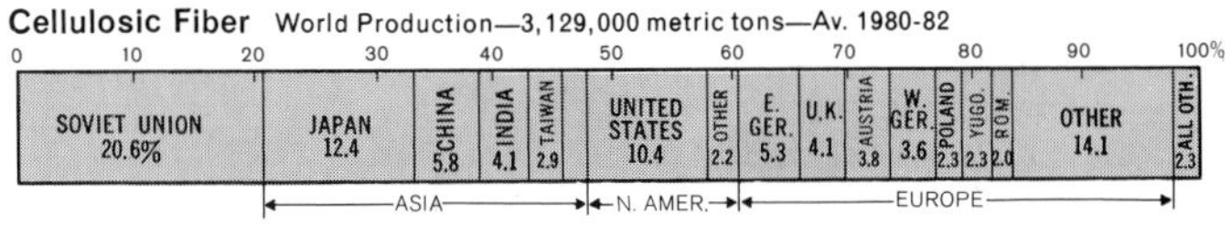

Cellulosic Fiber World Production—3,129,000 metric tons—Av. 1980-82

0	10	20	30	40	50	60	70	80	90	100%

SOVIET UNION 20.6%	JAPAN 12.4	CHINA 5.8	INDIA 4.1	TAIWAN 2.9	UNITED STATES 10.4	OTHER 2.2	E. GER. 5.3	U.K. 4.1	AUSTRIA 3.8	W. GER. 3.6	POLAND 2.3	YUGO. 2.3	ROM 2.0	OTHER 14.1	ALL OTH 2.3

←——————— ASIA ———————→ ←N. AMER.→ ←———————— EUROPE ————————→

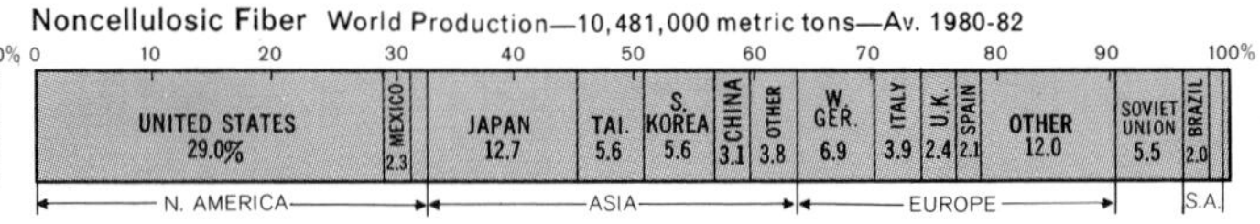

Noncellulosic Fiber World Production—10,481,000 metric tons—Av. 1980-82

0	10	20	30	40	50	60	70	80	90	100%

UNITED STATES 29.0%	MEXICO 2.3	JAPAN 12.7	TAI. 5.6	S. KOREA 5.6	CHINA 3.1	OTHER 3.8	W. GER. 6.9	ITALY 3.9	U.K. 2.4	SPAIN 2.1	OTHER 12.0	SOVIET UNION 5.5	BRAZIL 2.0

←———— N. AMERICA ————→ ←————— ASIA —————→ ←————— EUROPE —————→ ←S.A.→

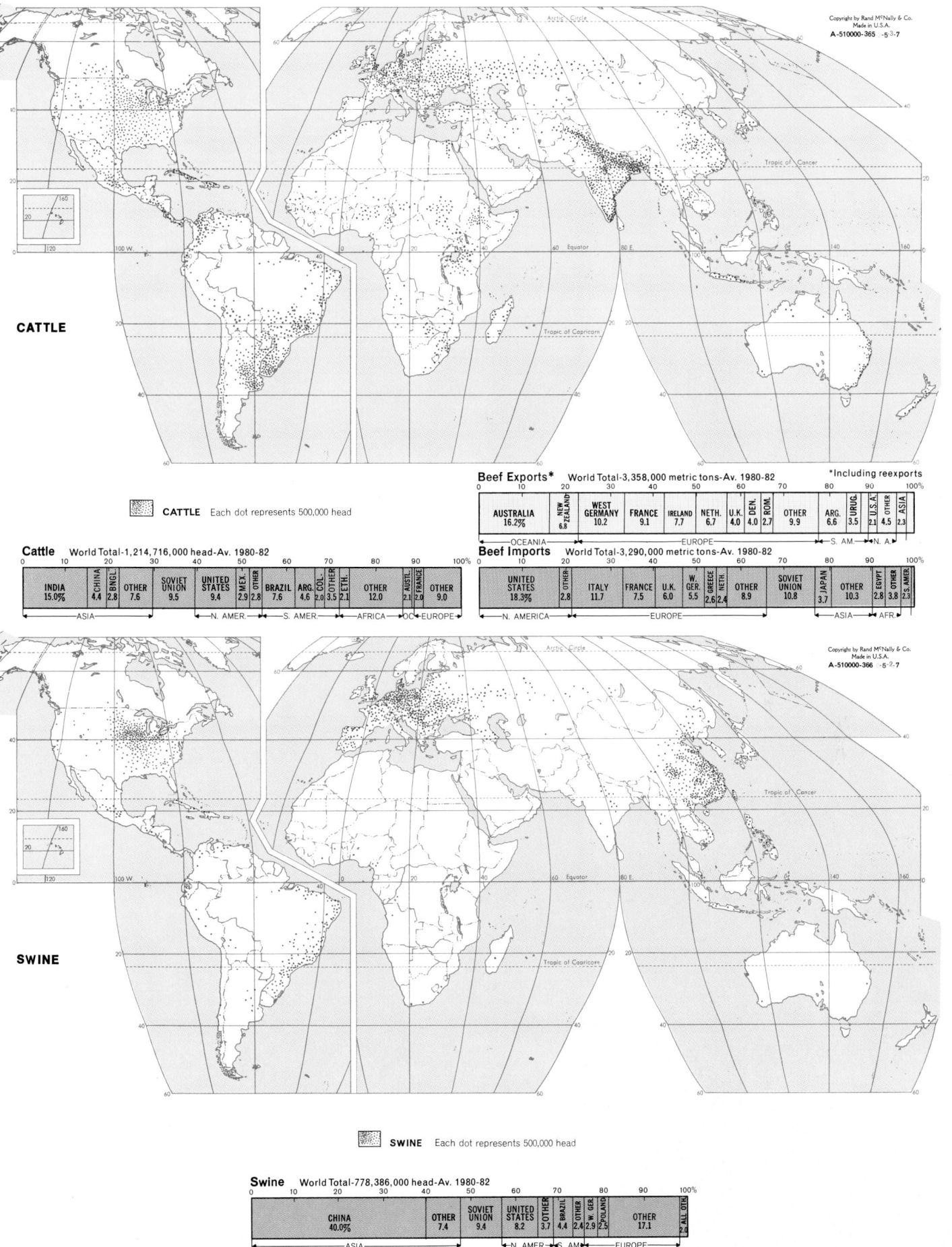

CATTLE

CATTLE   Each dot represents 500,000 head

Cattle   World Total-1,214,716,000 head-Av. 1980-82

| | 0 | 10 | 20 | 30 | 40 | 50 | 60 | 70 | 80 | 90 | 100% |

| INDIA 15.0% | CHINA 4.4 | BNGL. 2.8 | OTHER 7.6 | SOVIET UNION 9.5 | UNITED STATES 9.4 | MEX. 2.9 | OTHER 2.8 | BRAZIL 7.6 | ARG. 4.6 | COL. 2.0 | OTHER 3.5 | ETH. 2.1 | OTHER 12.0 | AUSTL. 2.1 | FRANCE 2.0 | OTHER 9.0 |

←—ASIA—→   ←—N. AMER.—→   ←—S. AMER.—→   ←—AFRICA—→ ←OC ←—EUROPE—→

Beef Exports*   World Total-3,358,000 metric tons-Av. 1980-82   *Including reexports

| 0 | 10 | 20 | 30 | 40 | 50 | 60 | 70 | 80 | 90 | 100% |

| AUSTRALIA 16.2% | NEW ZEALAND 6.8 | WEST GERMANY 10.2 | FRANCE 9.1 | IRELAND 7.7 | NETH. 6.7 | U.K. 4.0 | DEN. 4.0 | ROM. 2.7 | OTHER 9.9 | ARG. 6.6 | URUG. 3.5 | U.S.A. 2.1 | OTHER 4.5 | ASIA 2.3 |

←——OCEANIA——→   ←————————EUROPE————————→   ←S. AM.→ ←N. A.→

Beef Imports   World Total-3,290,000 metric tons-Av. 1980-82

| UNITED STATES 18.3% | OTHER 2.8 | ITALY 11.7 | FRANCE 7.5 | U.K. 6.0 | W. GER. 5.5 | GREECE 2.6 | NETH. 2.4 | OTHER 8.9 | SOVIET UNION 10.8 | JAPAN 3.7 | OTHER 10.3 | EGYPT 2.8 | OTHER 3.8 | S. AMER. 2.3 |

←——N. AMERICA——→   ←————————EUROPE————————→   ←——ASIA——→ ←AFR.→

SWINE

SWINE   Each dot represents 500,000 head

Swine   World Total-778,386,000 head-Av. 1980-82

| 0 | 10 | 20 | 30 | 40 | 50 | 60 | 70 | 80 | 90 | 100% |

| CHINA 40.0% | OTHER 7.4 | SOVIET UNION 9.4 | UNITED STATES 8.2 | OTHER 3.7 | BRAZIL 4.4 | W. GER. 2.4 | POLAND 2.5 | OTHER 17.1 | ALL OTH. 2.0 |

←————————ASIA————————→   ←N. AMER.→ ←S. AM→ ←——EUROPE——→

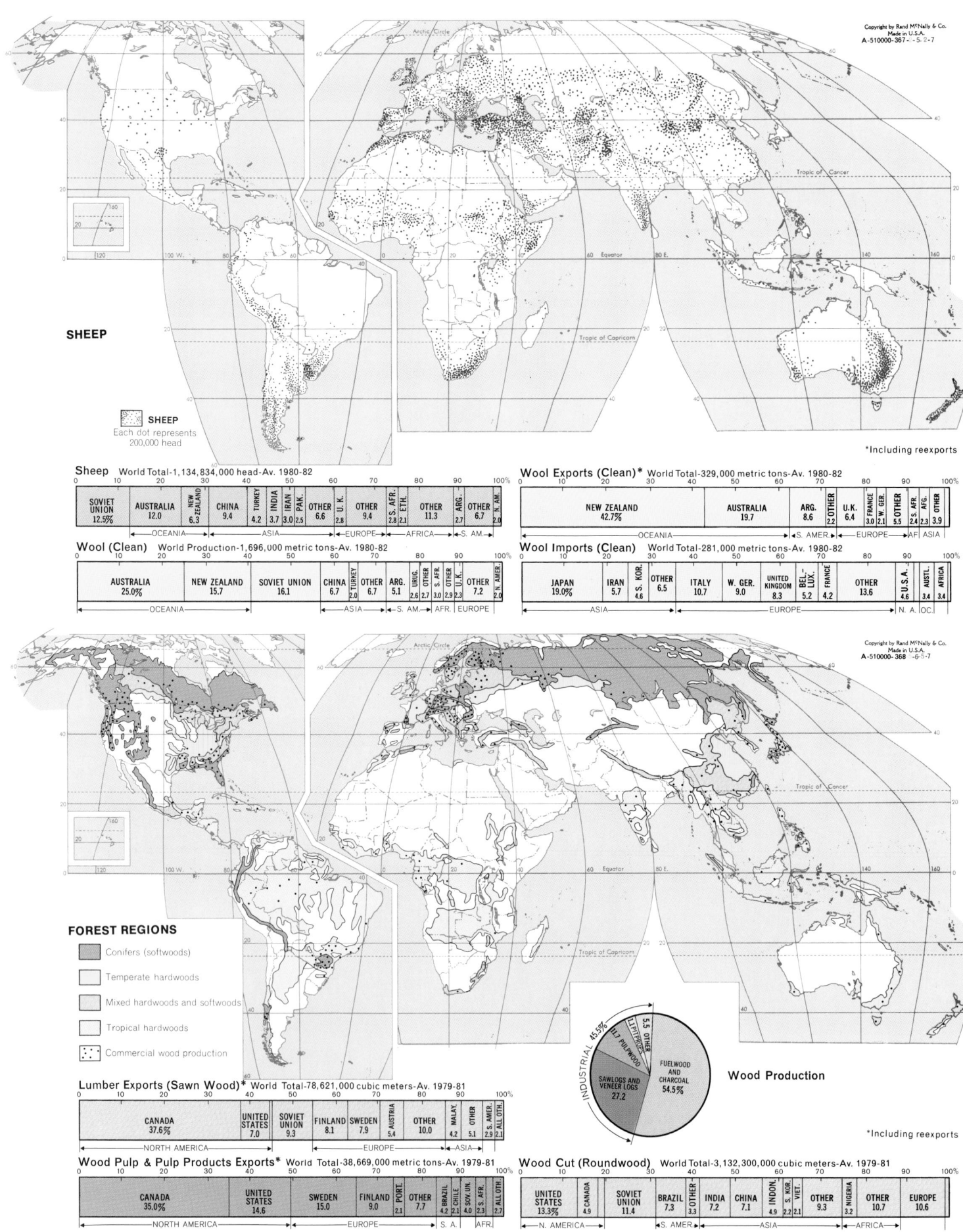

SHEEP

SHEEP
Each dot represents
200,000 head

*Including reexports

Sheep World Total-1,134,834,000 head-Av. 1980-82

SOVIET UNION 12.5%	AUSTRALIA 12.0	NEW ZEALAND 6.3	CHINA 9.4	TURKEY 4.2	INDIA 3.7	IRAN 3.0	PAK. 2.5	OTHER 6.6	U.K. 2.8	OTHER 9.4	S. AFR. 2.8	ETH. 2.1	OTHER 11.3	ARG. 2.7	OTHER 6.7	N. AM. 2.0

OCEANIA — ASIA — EUROPE — AFRICA — S. AM.

Wool (Clean) World Production-1,696,000 metric tons-Av. 1980-82

| AUSTRALIA 25.0% | NEW ZEALAND 15.7 | SOVIET UNION 16.1 | CHINA 6.7 | TURKEY 2.0 | OTHER 6.7 | ARG. 5.1 | URUG. 2.6 | OTHER 2.7 | S. AFR. 3.0 | OTHER 2.3 | U.K. 7.2 | OTHER 7.2 | N. AMER 2.0 |

OCEANIA — ASIA — S. AM. — AFR. — EUROPE

Wool Exports (Clean)* World Total-329,000 metric tons-Av. 1980-82

| NEW ZEALAND 42.7% | AUSTRALIA 19.7 | ARG. 8.6 | OTHER 2.2 | U.K. 6.4 | FRANCE 3.0 | W. GER. 2.1 | OTHER 5.5 | S. AFR. 2.4 | AFG. 2.3 | Other 3.9 |

OCEANIA — S. AMER. — EUROPE — AF — ASIA

Wool Imports (Clean) World Total-281,000 metric tons-Av. 1980-82

| JAPAN 19.0% | IRAN 5.7 | S. KOR. 4.6 | OTHER 6.5 | ITALY 10.7 | W. GER. 9.0 | UNITED KINGDOM 8.3 | BEL.- LUX. 5.2 | FRANCE 4.2 | OTHER 13.6 | U.S.A. 3.4 | AUSTL. | AFRICA 3.4 |

ASIA — EUROPE — N. A. OC.

FOREST REGIONS

- Conifers (softwoods)
- Temperate hardwoods
- Mixed hardwoods and softwoods
- Tropical hardwoods
- Commercial wood production

Wood Production

INDUSTRIAL 45.5%
5.5 OTHER
1.1 PLYWOOD
11.7 PULPWOOD
SAWLOGS AND VENEER LOGS 27.2
FUELWOOD AND CHARCOAL 54.5%

*Including reexports

Lumber Exports (Sawn Wood)* World Total-78,621,000 cubic meters-Av. 1979-81

| CANADA 37.6% | UNITED STATES 7.0 | SOVIET UNION 9.3 | FINLAND 8.1 | SWEDEN 7.9 | AUSTRIA 5.4 | OTHER 10.0 | MALAY. 4.2 | OTHER 2.9 | S. AMER. 2.1 | ALL OTH. |

NORTH AMERICA — EUROPE — ASIA

Wood Pulp & Pulp Products Exports* World Total-38,669,000 metric tons-Av. 1979-81

| CANADA 35.0% | UNITED STATES 14.6 | SWEDEN 15.0 | FINLAND 9.0 | PORT. 2.1 | OTHER 7.7 | BRAZIL 4.2 | CHILE 2.1 | SOV. UN. 4.0 | S. AFR. 2.3 | ALL OTH. 2.7 |

NORTH AMERICA — EUROPE — S. A. AFR.

Wood Cut (Roundwood) World Total-3,132,300,000 cubic meters-Av. 1979-81

| UNITED STATES 13.3% | CANADA 4.9 | SOVIET UNION 11.4 | BRAZIL 7.3 | OTHER 3.3 | INDIA 7.2 | CHINA 7.1 | INDON. 4.9 | S. KOR. 2.2 | VIET. 2.1 | OTHER 9.3 | NIGERIA 3.2 | OTHER 10.7 | EUROPE 10.6 |

N. AMERICA — S. AMER — ASIA — AFRICA

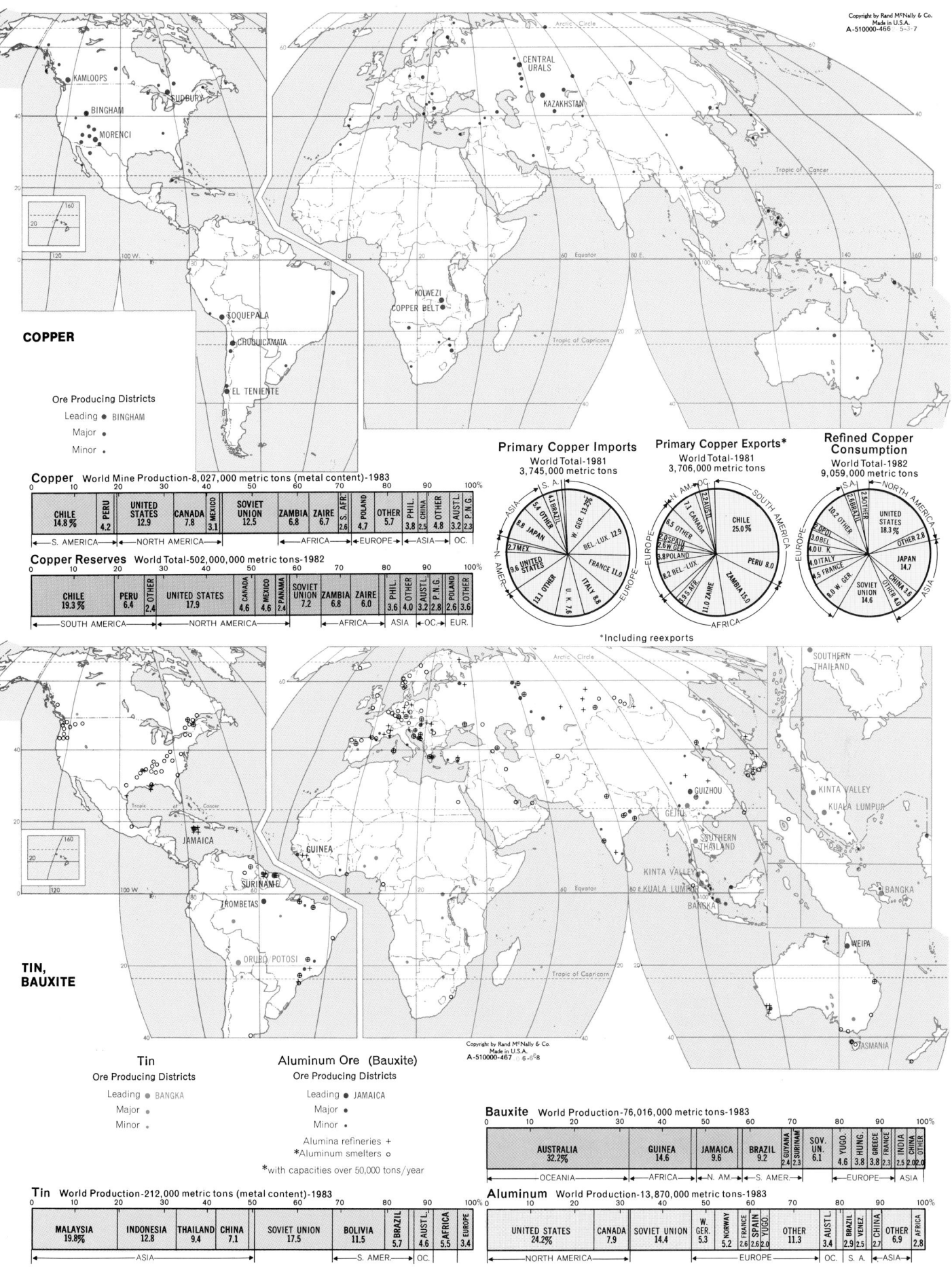

Copyright by Rand McNally & Co.
Made in U.S.A.
A-510000-466 5-3-7

COPPER

KAMLOOPS
SUDBURY
BINGHAM
MORENCI
CENTRAL URALS
KAZAKHSTAN
TOQUEPALA
CHUQUICAMATA
EL TENIENTE
KOLWEZI
COPPER BELT

Ore Producing Districts

Leading ● BINGHAM

Major ●

Minor ●

Copper World Mine Production-8,027,000 metric tons (metal content)-1983

0	10	20	30	40	50	60	70	80	90	100%

| CHILE 14.8% | PERU 4.2 | UNITED STATES 12.9 | CANADA 7.8 | MEXICO 3.1 | SOVIET UNION 12.5 | ZAMBIA 6.8 | ZAIRE 6.7 | S. AFR. 2.6 | POLAND 4.7 | OTHER 5.7 | PHIL. 3.8 | CHINA 2.5 | OTHER 4.8 | AUSTL. 3.2 | P.N.G. 2.3 |

◄— S. AMERICA —► ◄— NORTH AMERICA —► ◄————— AFRICA —————► ◄—EUROPE—► ◄—ASIA—► OC.

Copper Reserves World Total-502,000,000 metric tons-1982

0	10	20	30	40	50	60	70	80	90	100%

| CHILE 19.3% | PERU 6.4 | OTHER 2.4 | UNITED STATES 17.9 | CANADA 4.6 | MEXICO 4.6 | PANAMA 2.4 | SOVIET UNION 7.2 | ZAMBIA 6.8 | ZAIRE 6.0 | PHIL. 3.6 | AUSTL. 4.0 | P.N.G. 3.2 | POLAND 2.6 | OTHER 3.6 |

◄—SOUTH AMERICA—► ◄— NORTH AMERICA —► ◄— AFRICA —► ◄ ASIA ► ◄OC.► EUR.

Primary Copper Imports
World Total-1981
3,745,000 metric tons

S.A. · 4.1 BRAZIL · 5.4 OTHER · 8.8 JAPAN · 2.7 MEX. · 9.6 UNITED STATES · 13.1 OTHER · U.K. 7.6 · ITALY 8.8 · FRANCE 11.0 · BEL.-LUX. 12.9 · W. GER. 13.2%

Primary Copper Exports*
World Total-1981
3,706,000 metric tons

2.8 AUST. · 7.1 CANADA · 6.5 OTHER · 2.0 SPAIN · 2.6 W. GER. · 3.8 BEL.-LUX. · 8.2 S. AFR. · 11.0 ZAIRE · ZAMBIA 15.0 · PERU 8.0 · CHILE 25.0%

Refined Copper Consumption
World Total-1982
9,059,000 metric tons

S.A. · 2.5 OTHER · 2.6 BRAZIL · 10.2 OTHER · 2.0 BEL. · 3.0 BEL. · 4.0 U.K. · 4.0 ITALY · 4.5 FRANCE · 8.0 W. GER. · SOVIET UNION 14.6 · CHINA 3.8 · OTHER 4.0 · JAPAN 14.7 · OTHER 2.8 · UNITED STATES 18.3%

*Including reexports

TIN, BAUXITE

SOUTHERN THAILAND
KINTA VALLEY
KUALA LUMPUR
BANGKA
GUIZHOU
GEJIU
SOUTHERN THAILAND
KINTA VALLEY
KUALA LUMPUR
BANGKA
WEIPA
JAMAICA
GUINEA
SURINAME
TROMBETAS
ORURO/POTOSI
TASMANIA

Copyright by Rand McNally & Co.
Made in U.S.A.
A-510000-467 6-6-8

Tin
Ore Producing Districts

Leading ● BANGKA

Major ●

Minor ●

Aluminum Ore (Bauxite)
Ore Producing Districts

Leading ● JAMAICA

Major ●

Minor ●

Alumina refineries +

*Aluminum smelters ○

*with capacities over 50,000 tons/year

Bauxite World Production-76,016,000 metric tons-1983

0	10	20	30	40	50	60	70	80	90	100%

| AUSTRALIA 32.2% | GUINEA 14.6 | JAMAICA 9.6 | BRAZIL 9.2 | GUYANA 2.4 | SURINAM 2.3 | SOV. UN. 6.1 | YUGO. 4.6 | HUNG. 3.8 | GREECE 3.8 | FRANCE 2.3 | INDIA 2.5 | CHINA 2.0 | OTHER 2.0 |

◄————— OCEANIA —————► ◄— AFRICA —► ◄N. AM.► ◄ S. AMER. ► ◄————— EUROPE —————► ◄ ASIA ►

Tin World Production-212,000 metric tons (metal content)-1983

0	10	20	30	40	50	60	70	80	90	100%

| MALAYSIA 19.8% | INDONESIA 12.8 | THAILAND 9.4 | CHINA 7.1 | SOVIET UNION 17.5 | BOLIVIA 11.5 | BRAZIL 5.7 | AUSTL. 4.6 | AFRICA 5.5 | EUROPE 3.4 |

◄————————— ASIA —————————► ◄— S. AMER. —► ◄OC.►

Aluminum World Production-13,870,000 metric tons-1983

0	10	20	30	40	50	60	70	80	90	100%

| UNITED STATES 24.2% | CANADA 7.9 | SOVIET UNION 14.4 | W. GER. 5.3 | NORWAY 5.2 | FRANCE 2.6 | SPAIN 2.6 | YUGO. 2.0 | OTHER 11.3 | AUSTL. 3.4 | BRAZIL 2.9 | VENEZ. 2.5 | CHINA 2.7 | OTHER 6.9 | AFRICA 2.8 |

◄————— NORTH AMERICA —————► ◄————————— EUROPE —————————► ◄OC.► ◄ S. A. ► ◄—ASIA—►

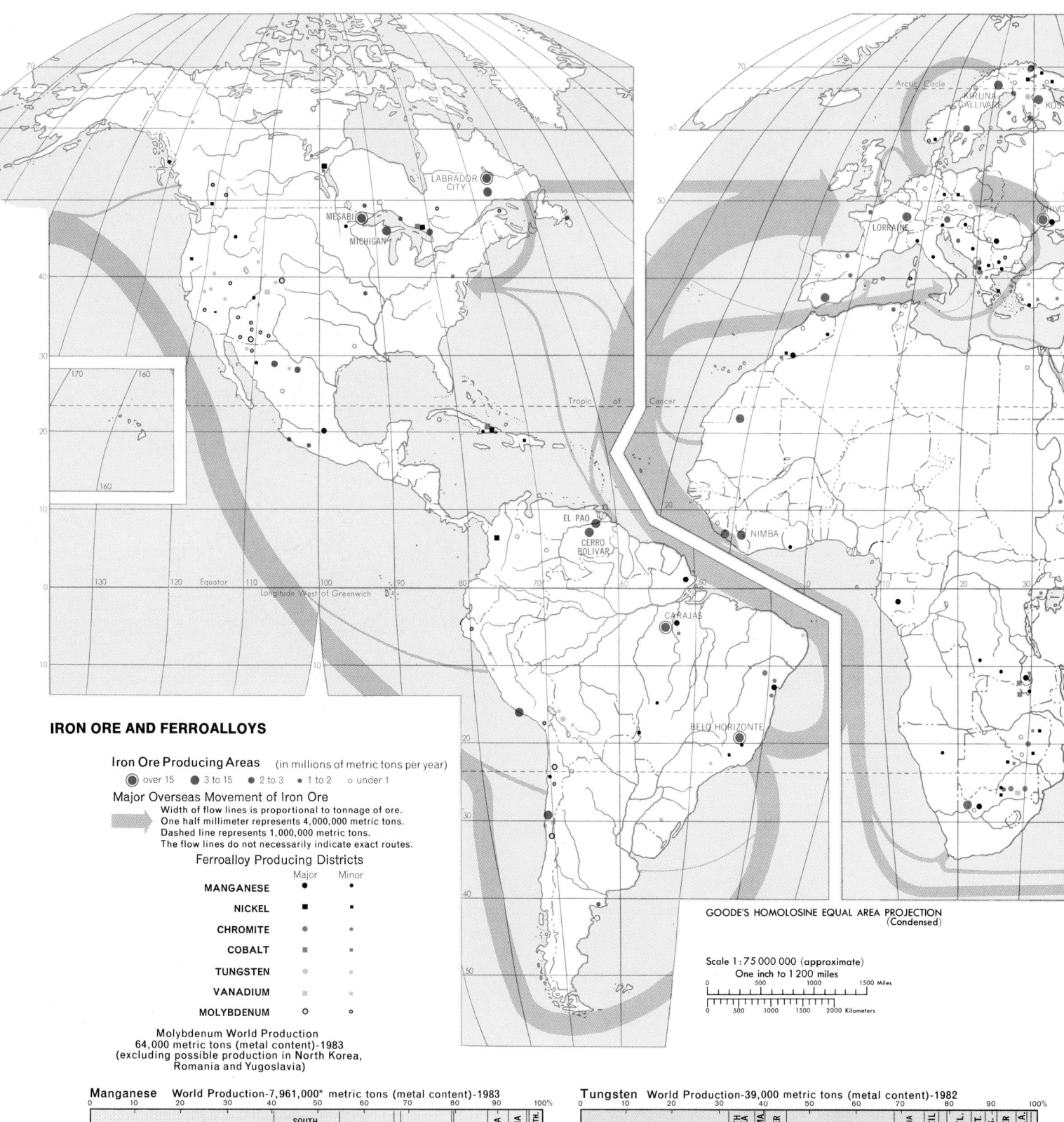

IRON ORE AND FERROALLOYS

Iron Ore Producing Areas (in millions of metric tons per year)

◉ over 15 ● 3 to 15 ■ 2 to 3 • 1 to 2 ○ under 1

Major Overseas Movement of Iron Ore

Width of flow lines is proportional to tonnage of ore.
One half millimeter represents 4,000,000 metric tons.
Dashed line represents 1,000,000 metric tons.
The flow lines do not necessarily indicate exact routes.

Ferroalloy Producing Districts

	Major	Minor
MANGANESE	●	•
NICKEL	■	■
CHROMITE	●	•
COBALT	■	■
TUNGSTEN	●	•
VANADIUM	■	■
MOLYBDENUM	○	○

Molybdenum World Production
64,000 metric tons (metal content)-1983
(excluding possible production in North Korea,
Romania and Yugoslavia)

GOODE'S HOMOLOSINE EQUAL AREA PROJECTION
(Condensed)

Scale 1 : 75 000 000 (approximate)
One inch to 1 200 miles

0 500 1000 1500 Miles

0 500 1000 1500 2000 Kilometers

Manganese World Production-7,961,000* metric tons (metal content)-1983

0	10	20	30	40	50	60	70	80	90	100%
SOVIET UNION 40.6%					SOUTH AFRICA 14.1	GABON 11.9	BRAZIL 11.5	AUSTL. 7.6	INDIA 5.3	CHINA 4.0	ALL OTH. 2.9

←————AFRICA————→ ←S. AMER.→ ←OC.→ ←ASIA→

*Excluding possible production in Cuba and Namibia

Tungsten World Production-39,000 metric tons (metal content)-1982

0	10	20	30	40	50	60	70	80	90	100%
CHINA 32.1%				SOUTH KOREA 5.9	BURMA 2.4	OTHER 4.6	SOVIET UNION 23.4		BOLIVIA 6.2	BRAZIL 3.1	AUSTL. 5.3	PORT. 3.5	AUS. 2.9	OTHER 4.1	U.S.A. 2.5

←————ASIA————→ ←S. AMER.→ ←OC.→ ←EUR.→ ←N.A.→

Nickel World Production-689,000 metric tons (metal content)-1983

0	10	20	30	40	50	60	70	80	90	100%
SOVIET UNION 24.6%			CANADA 17.7	CUBA 5.4	DOM. REP. 2.9	AUSTRALIA 13.1	NEW CALEDONIA 9.1	INDON. 6.8	PHIL. 2.8	S. AFR. 3.0	BOTS. 2.5	GREECE 2.2	OTHER 4.1	COL. 2.0

←——NORTH AMERICA——→ ←———OCEANIA———→ ←—ASIA—→ ←AFR.→ ←EUR.→ ←S.A→

Vanadium World Mine Production-29,000 metric tons (metal content)-1983

0	10	20	30	40	50	60	70	80	90	100%
SOVIET UNION 33.1%				SOUTH AFRICA 28.0		CHINA 15.8	JAPAN 2.4	FINLAND 11.1	UNITED STATES 9.7

←————AFRICA————→ ←——ASIA——→ ←EUROPE→ ←N. AMER.→

NIZHNIY TAGIL
GORSK
KUSTANAY
KUZNETSK
MAANSHAN
SINGHBHUM
GOA
MT. NEWMAN
HAMERSLEY

Tropic of Cancer
Tropic of Capricorn
Equator
Longitude East of Greenwich

Iron Ore Imports
World Total-323,900,000 metric tons
1982

N. AM.
4.5 U.S.A.
7.8 OTHER
3.3 U.K.
3.6 CZECH.
4.2 POL.
4.4 ROM.
4.8 FRANCE
5.0 ITALY
5.1 BEL.-LUX.
W. GERMANY 12.0
JAPAN 37.6%
KOR. 3.8
OTHER 2.0
ASIA
EUROPE

mite World Production-8,093,000** metric tons-1983

	10	20	30	40	50	60	70	80	90	100%
SOVIET UNION 30.3%			SOUTH AFRICA 27.6			ZIMB. 5.3	ALBANIA 11.1	FINLAND 4.2	TURKEY 4.9	INDIA 4.5	PHIL. 4.1	BRAZIL 3.5

AFRICA — EUROPE — ASIA — S.A

**Excluding possible production in Bulgaria, China and North Korea

lt World Mine Production-24,000† metric tons (metal content)-1983

10	20	30	40	50	60	70	80	90	100%
ZAIRE 46.2%			ZAMBIA 13.1	SOVIET UNION 9.6	AUSTL. 7.4	CUBA 6.7	CANADA 6.5	FINLAND 3.7	PHIL. 2.4

AFRICA — OC. — N. AMER. — EUR. AS

†Excluding possible production in Bulgaria, Cyprus, East Germany,
Greece, Indonesia, Poland, South Africa, Spain and Uganda

Iron Ore World Production-422,954,000†† metric tons (metal content)-1983

10	20	30	40	50	60	70	80	90	100%
SOVIET UNION 31.3%			AUSTRALIA 11.1	CHINA 8.4	INDIA 5.7	BRAZIL 6.5	OTHER 10.3	UNITED STATES 5.8	CANADA 5.0	S. AFR. 2.5	LIBERIA 2.1	OTHER 2.0	SWEDEN 2.0	OTHER 4.1

OCEANIA — ASIA — S. AMERICA — N. AMER. — AFR. — EUR.

††Excluding possible production in Cuba and Vietnam

Iron Ore Reserves World Total-65,500,000,000 metric tons (metal content)-1984

10	20	30	40	50	60	70	80	90	100%
SOVIET UNION 34.6%			BRAZIL 15.0	OTHER 2.3	AUSTRALIA 14.0	INDIA 6.6	CHINA 4.8	CANADA 6.2	U.S.A. 5.1	S. AFR. 4.0	SWEDEN 2.2	OTHER 2.4

S. AMERICA — OCEANIA — ASIA — N. AMER. — AFR. — EUR.

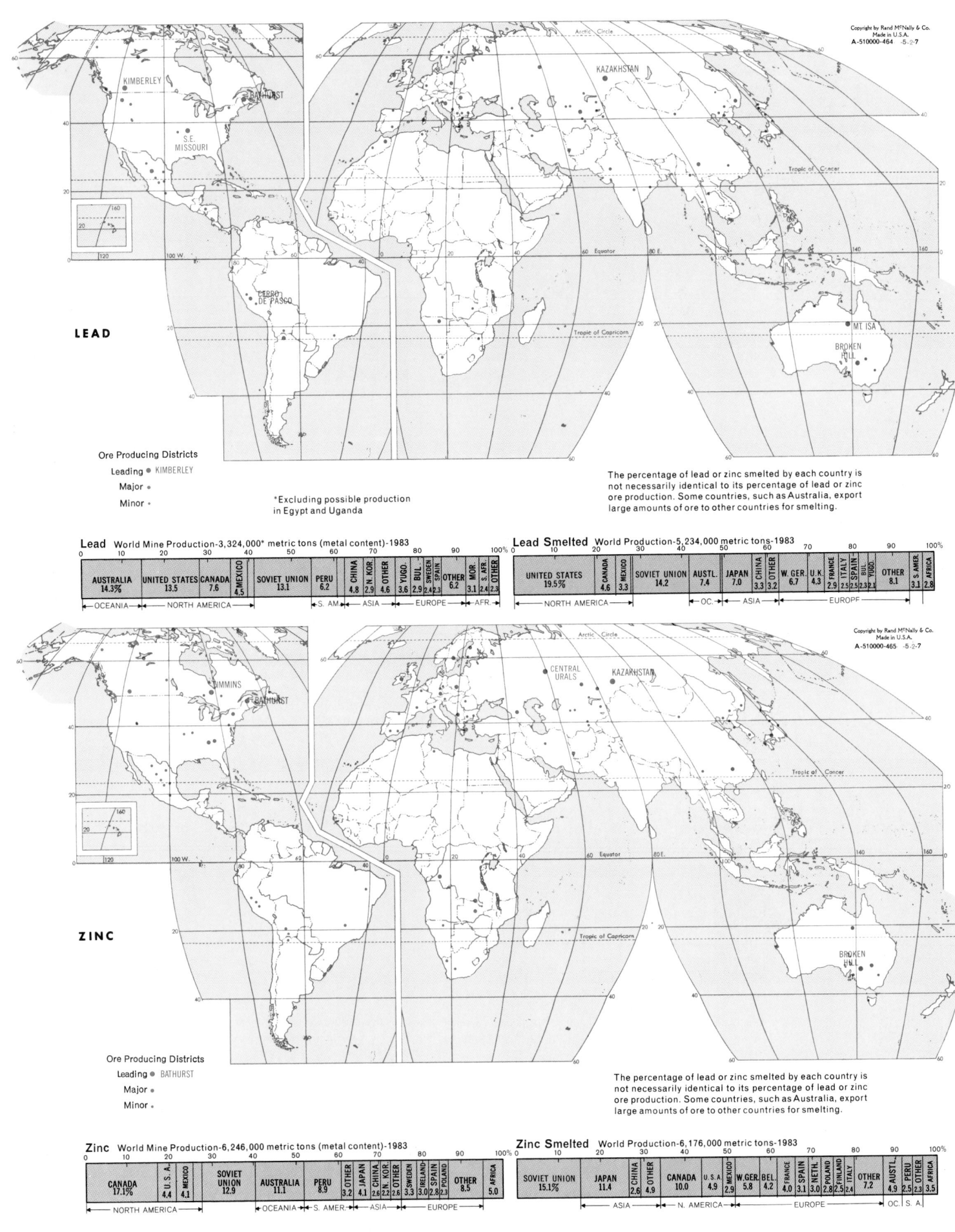

Copyright by Rand McNally & Co.
Made in U.S.A.
A-510000-464 -5-2-7

KIMBERLEY

BATHURST

S.E.
MISSOURI

KAZAKHSTAN

CERRO
DE PASCO

LEAD

MT. ISA

BROKEN
HILL

Ore Producing Districts

Leading ● KIMBERLEY

Major ●

Minor ·

*Excluding possible production
in Egypt and Uganda

The percentage of lead or zinc smelted by each country is
not necessarily identical to its percentage of lead or zinc
ore production. Some countries, such as Australia, export
large amounts of ore to other countries for smelting.

Lead World Mine Production-3,324,000* metric tons (metal content)-1983

0	10	20	30	40	50	60	70	80	90	100%
AUSTRALIA 14.3%	UNITED STATES 13.5	CANADA 7.6	MEXICO 4.5	SOVIET UNION 13.1	PERU 6.2	CHINA 4.8	N. KOR. 2.9	OTHER 4.6	YUGO. 3.6	BUL. 2.9	SWEDEN 2.4	SPAIN 2.3	OTHER 6.2	MOR. 3.1	S. AFR. 2.4	OTHER 2.3

← OCEANIA → ← NORTH AMERICA → ← S. AM. → ← ASIA → ← EUROPE → ← AFR. →

Lead Smelted World Production-5,234,000 metric tons-1983

0	10	20	30	40	50	60	70	80	90	100%
UNITED STATES 19.5%	CANADA 4.6	MEXICO 3.3	SOVIET UNION 14.2	AUSTL. 7.4	JAPAN 7.0	CHINA 3.3	OTHER 3.2	W. GER. 6.7	U.K. 4.3	FRANCE 2.9	ITALY 2.5	SPAIN 2.5	BUL. 2.3	YUGO. 2.1	OTHER 8.1	S. AMER. 3.1	AFRICA 2.8

← NORTH AMERICA → ← OC. → ← ASIA → ← EUROPE →

Copyright by Rand McNally & Co.
Made in U.S.A.
A-510000-465 -5-2-7

TIMMINS

BATHURST

CENTRAL
URALS

KAZAKHSTAN

ZINC

BROKEN
HILL

Ore Producing Districts

Leading ● BATHURST

Major ●

Minor ·

The percentage of lead or zinc smelted by each country is
not necessarily identical to its percentage of lead or zinc
ore production. Some countries, such as Australia, export
large amounts of ore to other countries for smelting.

Zinc World Mine Production-6,246,000 metric tons (metal content)-1983

0	10	20	30	40	50	60	70	80	90	100%
CANADA 17.1%	U.S.A. 4.4	MEXICO 4.1	SOVIET UNION 12.9	AUSTRALIA 11.1	PERU 8.9	OTHER 3.2	JAPAN 4.1	CHINA 2.6	N. KOR. 2.2	OTHER 2.6	SWEDEN 3.3	IRELAND 3.0	SPAIN 2.8	POLAND 2.3	OTHER 8.5	AFRICA 5.0

← NORTH AMERICA → ← OCEANIA → ← S. AMER. → ← ASIA → ← EUROPE →

Zinc Smelted World Production-6,176,000 metric tons-1983

0	10	20	30	40	50	60	70	80	90	100%
SOVIET UNION 15.1%	JAPAN 11.4	CHINA 2.6	OTHER 4.9	CANADA 10.0	U.S.A. 4.9	MEXICO 2.9	W. GER. 5.8	BEL. 4.2	FRANCE 4.0	SPAIN 3.1	NETH. 3.0	POLAND 2.8	FINLAND 2.5	ITALY 2.4	OTHER 7.2	AUSTL. 4.9	PERU 2.5	OTHER 3.0	AFRICA 3.5

← ASIA → ← N. AMERICA → ← EUROPE → ← OC. → ← S. A. →

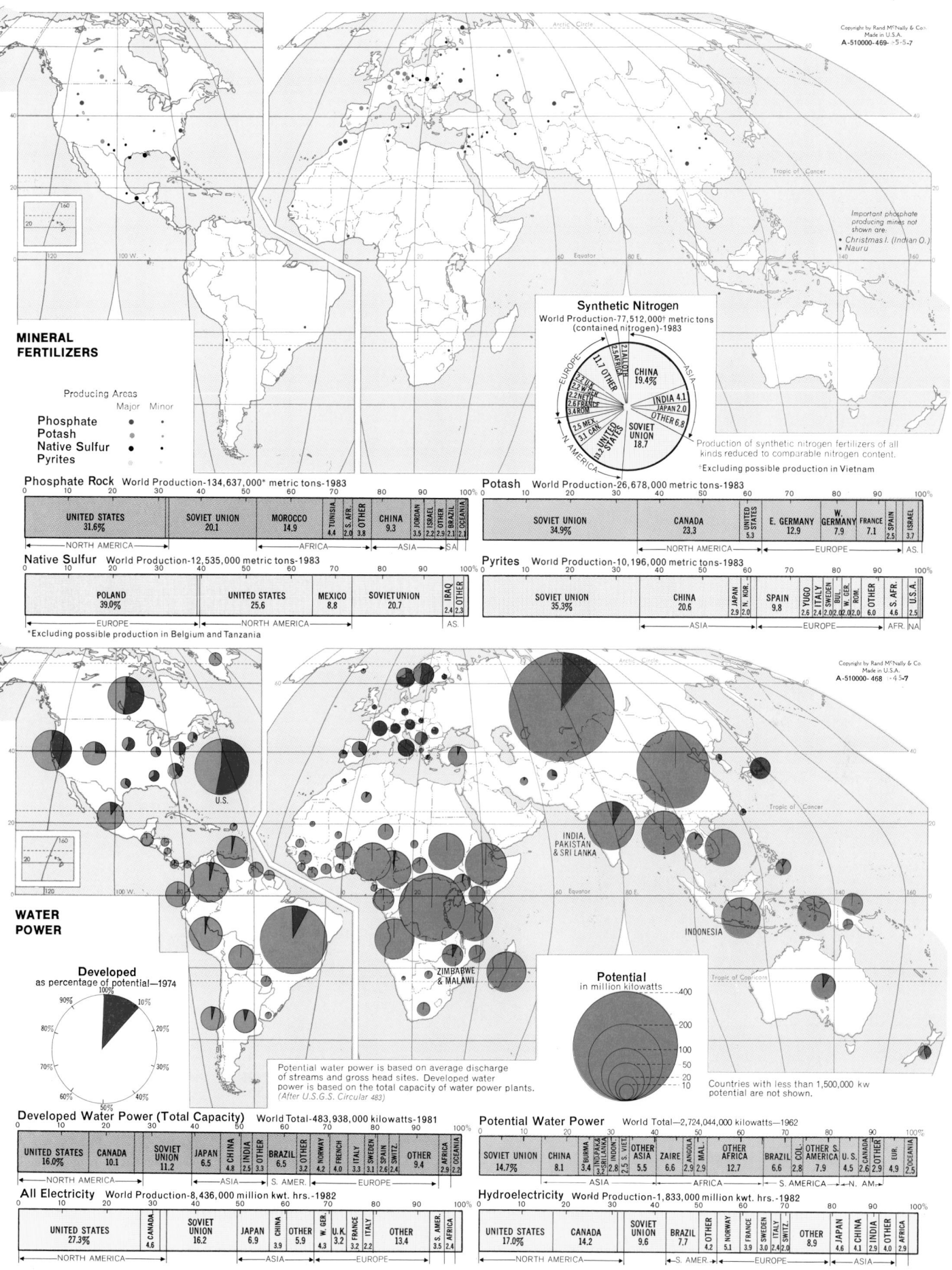

Copyright by Rand McNally & Co.
Made in U.S.A.
A-510000-469- -5-5-7

Important phosphate producing mines not shown are:
• *Christmas I. (Indian O.)*
• *Nauru*

MINERAL FERTILIZERS

Producing Areas

	Major	Minor
Phosphate		
Potash		
Native Sulfur		
Pyrites		

Synthetic Nitrogen
World Production-77,512,000† metric tons
(contained nitrogen)-1983

CHINA 19.4%
INDIA 4.1
JAPAN 2.0
OTHER 6.8
SOVIET UNION 18.7
UNITED STATES 13.2
3.1 CAN.
2.5 MEX.
3.4 ROM.
2.6 FRANCE
2.2 NETH.
2.2 W.GER.
2.3 U.K.
11.7 OTHER
2.6 AFRICA
2.1 AUST.

Production of synthetic nitrogen fertilizers of all kinds reduced to comparable nitrogen content.
†Excluding possible production in Vietnam

Phosphate Rock World Production-134,637,000* metric tons-1983

UNITED STATES 31.6%	SOVIET UNION 20.1	MOROCCO 14.9	TUNISIA 4.4	S. AFR. 2.0	OTHER 3.8	CHINA 9.3	JORDAN	ISRAEL	OTHER	BRAZIL 2.1	OCEANIA 2.1

NORTH AMERICA — AFRICA — ASIA — SA

Native Sulfur World Production-12,535,000 metric tons-1983

POLAND 39.0%	UNITED STATES 25.6	MEXICO 8.8	SOVIET UNION 20.7	IRAQ 2.4	OTHER 2.3

EUROPE — NORTH AMERICA — AS.

*Excluding possible production in Belgium and Tanzania

Potash World Production-26,678,000 metric tons-1983

SOVIET UNION 34.9%	CANADA 23.3	UNITED STATES 5.3	E. GERMANY 12.9	W. GERMANY 7.9	FRANCE 7.1	SPAIN 2.5	ISRAEL 3.7

NORTH AMERICA — EUROPE — AS.

Pyrites World Production-10,196,000 metric tons-1983

SOVIET UNION 35.3%	CHINA 20.6	JAPAN 2.9	N. KOR. 2.0	SPAIN 9.8	YUGO. 2.6	ITALY 2.4	SWEDEN 2.0	BUL. 2.0	W. GER. 2.0	ROM. 2.0	OTHER 6.0	S. AFR. 2.9	U.S.A. 2.5

ASIA — EUROPE — AFR. NA

Copyright by Rand McNally & Co.
Made in U.S.A.
A-510000- 468 - -4-5-7

WATER POWER

U.S.
INDIA, PAKISTAN & SRI LANKA
INDONESIA
ZIMBABWE & MALAWI

Developed
as percentage of potential—1974

100% 90% 80% 70% 60% 50% 40% 30% 20% 10%

Potential water power is based on average discharge of streams and gross head sites. Developed water power is based on the total capacity of water power plants.
(After U.S.G.S. Circular 483)

Potential
in million kilowatts

400
200
100
50
20
10

Countries with less than 1,500,000 kw potential are not shown.

Developed Water Power (Total Capacity) World Total-483,938,000 kilowatts-1981

UNITED STATES 16.0%	CANADA 10.1	SOVIET UNION 11.2	JAPAN 6.5	CHINA 4.8	INDIA 2.5	OTHER 3.3	BRAZIL 6.5	NORWAY 3.2	FRENCH 4.2	ITALY 4.0	SWEDEN 3.3	SPAIN 2.2	SWITZ. 2.6	OTHER 9.4	AFRICA 2.9	OCEANIA 2.4

NORTH AMERICA — ASIA — S. AMER. — EUROPE

Potential Water Power World Total-2,724,044,000 kilowatts-1962

SOVIET UNION 14.7%	CHINA 8.1	BURMA 3.4	INDIA-PAK. & SRI LANKA 2.8	INDON. 2.5	VIET 2.5	OTHER ASIA 5.5	ZAIRE 6.6	ANGOLA 2.9	MAL. 2.9	OTHER AFRICA 12.7	BRAZIL 6.6	COL. 2.8	OTHER S. AMERICA 7.9	U.S. 4.5	CANADA 4.5	EUR. 2.9	OCEANIA 4.9

ASIA — AFRICA — S. AMERICA — N. AM.

All Electricity World Production-8,436,000 million kwt. hrs.-1982

UNITED STATES 27.3%	CANADA 4.6	SOVIET UNION 16.2	JAPAN 6.9	CHINA 3.9	OTHER 5.9	W. GER. 4.3	U.K. 3.2	FRANCE 3.2	ITALY 2.2	OTHER 13.4	S. AMER. 3.5	AFRICA 2.4

NORTH AMERICA — ASIA — EUROPE

Hydroelectricity World Production-1,833,000 million kwt. hrs.-1982

UNITED STATES 17.0%	CANADA 14.2	SOVIET UNION 9.6	BRAZIL 7.7	OTHER 4.2	NORWAY 5.1	FRANCE 3.9	SWEDEN 3.0	ITALY 2.4	SWITZ. 2.0	OTHER 8.9	JAPAN 4.6	CHINA 4.1	OTHER 4.0	AFRICA 2.9

NORTH AMERICA — S. AMER. — EUROPE — ASIA

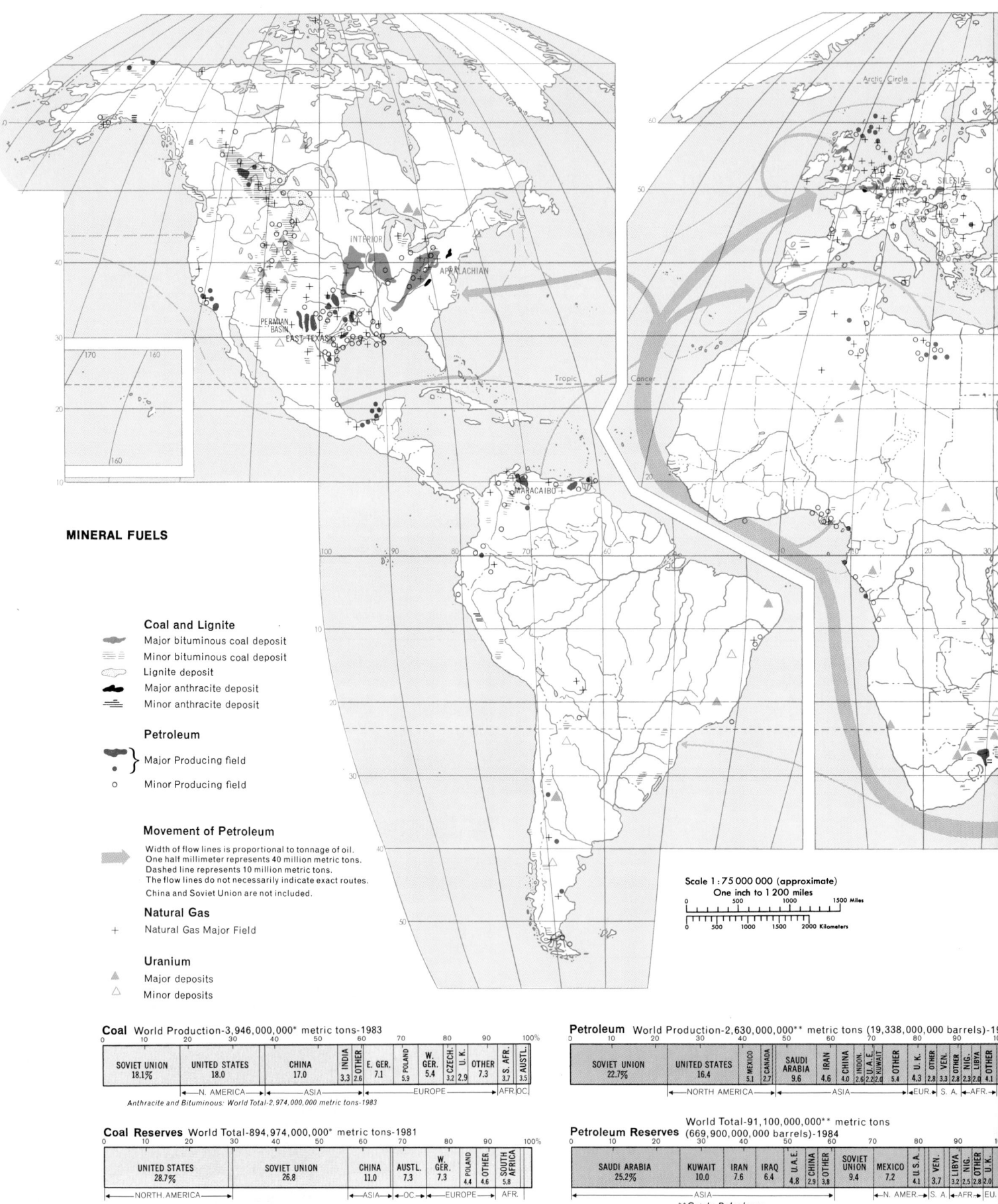

MINERAL FUELS

Coal and Lignite
▬ Major bituminous coal deposit
☰ Minor bituminous coal deposit
⬭ Lignite deposit
◆ Major anthracite deposit
☰ Minor anthracite deposit

Petroleum
⬛
⦁ } Major Producing field

○ Minor Producing field

Movement of Petroleum
➡ Width of flow lines is proportional to tonnage of oil.
One half millimeter represents 40 million metric tons.
Dashed line represents 10 million metric tons.
The flow lines do not necessarily indicate exact routes.
China and Soviet Union are not included.

Natural Gas
+ Natural Gas Major Field

Uranium
▲ Major deposits
△ Minor deposits

Scale 1:75 000 000 (approximate)
One inch to 1 200 miles
0   500   1000   1500 Miles
0   500   1000   1500   2000 Kilometers

Coal World Production-3,946,000,000* metric tons-1983

SOVIET UNION 18.1%	UNITED STATES 18.0	CHINA 17.0	INDIA 3.3	OTHER 2.6	E. GER. 7.1	POLAND 5.9	W. GER. 5.4	CZECH. 3.2	U.K. 2.9	OTHER 7.3	S. AFR. 3.7 / AUSTL. 3.5

◄─ N. AMERICA ─► ◄──── ASIA ────► ◄──── EUROPE ────► ◄AFR.│OC.►
Anthracite and Bituminous: World Total-2,974,000,000 metric tons-1983

Coal Reserves World Total-894,974,000,000* metric tons-1981

UNITED STATES 28.7%	SOVIET UNION 26.8	CHINA 11.0	AUSTL. 7.3	W. GER. 7.3	POLAND 4.4 / OTHER 4.6	SOUTH AFRICA 5.8

◄── NORTH AMERICA ──► ◄ASIA► ◄OC.► ◄─── EUROPE ───► ◄AFR.►
Anthracite and Bituminous: World Total-657,180,000,000 metric tons-1981
**Includes anthracite, subanthracite, bituminous, subbituminous, lignite and brown coal*

Petroleum World Production-2,630,000,000** metric tons (19,338,000,000 barrels)-19

SOVIET UNION 22.7%	UNITED STATES 16.4	MEXICO 5.1	CANADA 2.7	SAUDI ARABIA 9.6	IRAN 4.6	CHINA 4.0	INDON. 2.6	U.A.E. 2.2	KUWAIT 2.0	OTHER 5.4	U.K. 4.3	VEN. 3.3	NIG. 2.8 / LIBYA 2.0	OTHER 4.1

◄────NORTH AMERICA────► ◄──────── ASIA ────────► ◄EUR.► S. A. ◄─AFR.─►

World Total-91,100,000,000** metric tons
Petroleum Reserves (669,900,000,000 barrels)-1984

SAUDI ARABIA 25.2%	KUWAIT 10.0	IRAN 7.6	IRAQ 6.4	U.A.E. 4.8	CHINA 2.9	OTHER 3.8	SOVIET UNION 9.4	MEXICO 7.2	U.S.A. 4.1	VEN. 3.7	NIG. 2.5 / LIBYA 2.8	OTHER 2.0	

◄──────────────── ASIA ────────────────► ◄─N. AMER.─► S. A. ◄AFR.► EU.
**Crude Petroleum*

KANSK-ACHINSK
KUZNETS
EKIBASTUZ
KARAGANDA
URAL-VOLGA
BAKU
KIRKUK
PERSIAN GULF FIELDS
KUWAIT
GHAWAR
SHANXI
SHAANXI

Tropic of Cancer
Equator
Longituae East of Greenwich
Tropic of Capricorn

Goode's Homolosine Equal Area Projection (Condensed)

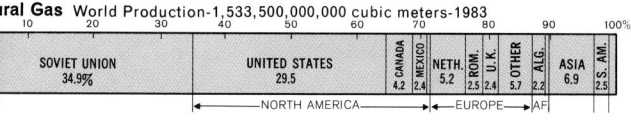

ıral Gas World Production-1,533,500,000,000 cubic meters-1983

10	20	30	40	50	60	70	80	90	100%

SOVIET UNION 34.9%	UNITED STATES 29.5	CANADA 4.2	MEXICO 2.4	NETH. 5.2	ROM. 2.5	U.K. 2.4	OTHER 2.8	ALG. 2.2	ASIA 6.9	S. AM. 2.5

NORTH AMERICA — EUROPE — AF

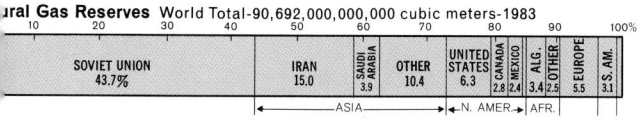

ıral Gas Reserves World Total-90,692,000,000,000 cubic meters-1983

10	20	30	40	50	60	70	80	90	100%

SOVIET UNION 43.7%	IRAN 15.0	SAUDI ARABIA 3.9	OTHER 10.4	UNITED STATES 6.3	CANADA 2.8	MEXICO 2.4	ALG. 3.4	OTHER 2.5	EUROPE 5.5	S. AM. 3.1

ASIA — N. AMER. — AFR.

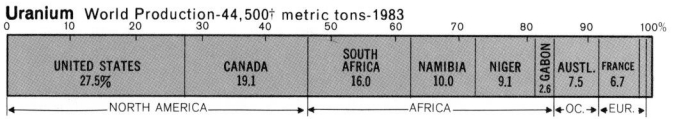

Uranium World Production-44,500† metric tons-1983

0	10	20	30	40	50	60	70	80	90	100%

UNITED STATES 27.5%	CANADA 19.1	SOUTH AFRICA 16.0	NAMIBIA 10.0	NIGER 9.1	GABON 2.6	AUSTL. 7.5	FRANCE 6.7

NORTH AMERICA — AFRICA — OC. — EUR.

†Excluding possible production in China, India, Israel, Mexico, Soviet Union and Eastern Europe

Uranium Reserves World Total-2,000,000†† metric tons-1983

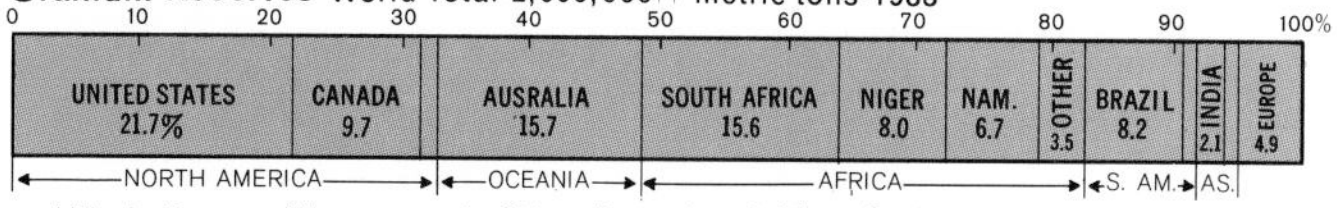

0	10	20	30	40	50	60	70	80	90	100%

UNITED STATES 21.7%	CANADA 9.7	AUSRALIA 15.7	SOUTH AFRICA 15.6	NIGER 8.0	NAM. 6.7	OTHER 3.5	BRAZIL 8.2	INDIA 2.1	EUROPE 4.9

NORTH AMERICA — OCEANIA — AFRICA — S. AM. — AS.

††Excluding possible reserves in China, Egypt, Israel, Libya, Soviet Union and Eastern Europe

BE-NE-LUX

ENERGY PRODUCTION

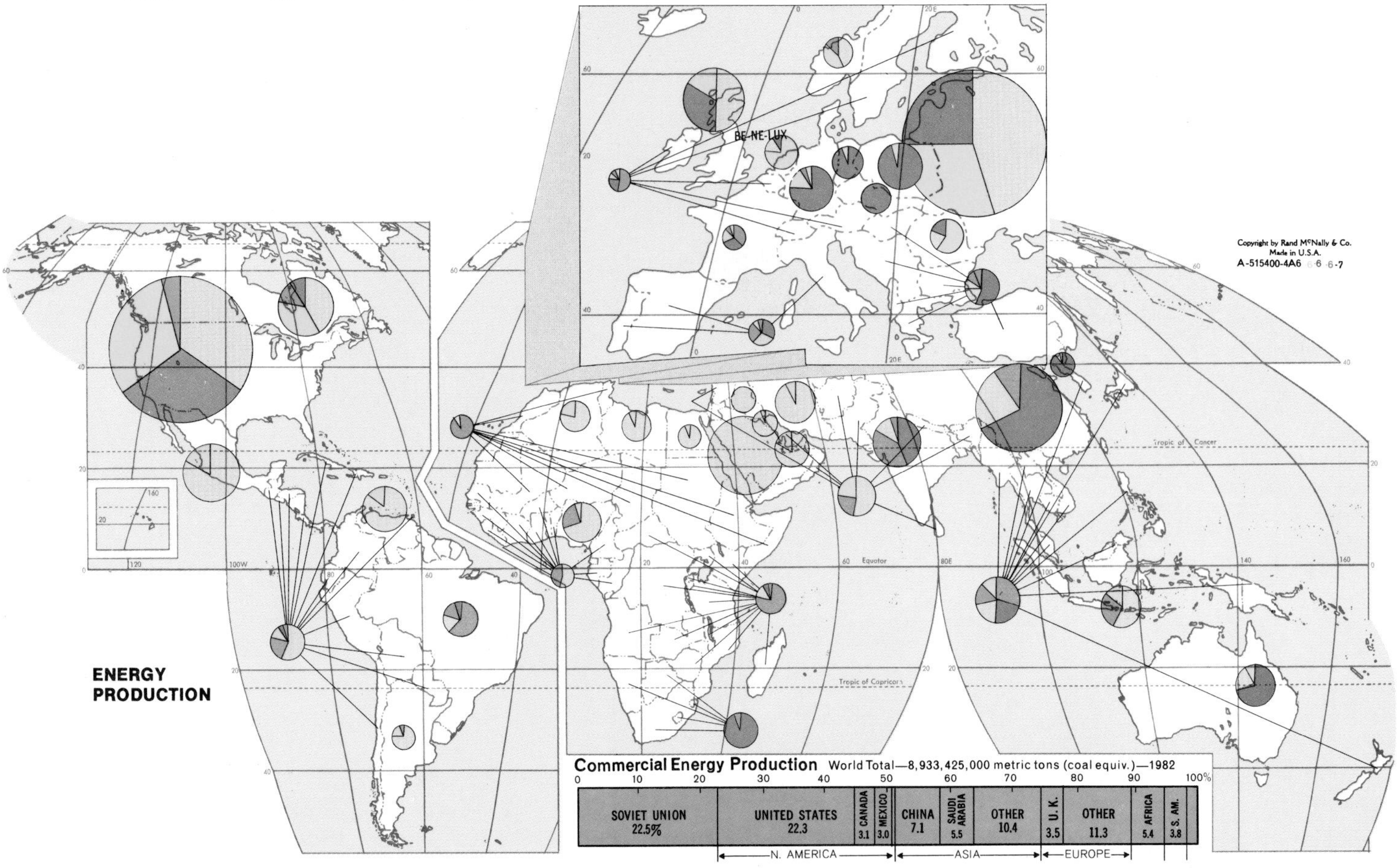

Commercial Energy Production World Total—8,933,425,000 metric tons (coal equiv.)—1982

0	10	20	30	40	50	60	70	80	90	100%

| SOVIET UNION 22.5% | UNITED STATES 22.3 | CANADA 3.1 | MEXICO 3.0 | CHINA 7.1 | SAUDI ARABIA 5.5 | OTHER 10.4 | U.K. 3.5 | OTHER 11.3 | AFRICA 5.4 | S. AM. 3.8 |

← N. AMERICA → ← ASIA → ← EUROPE →

Volume of Energy
in millions of metric tons
(Coal equivalent)—1982

2,500

1,000
500
250
100
40

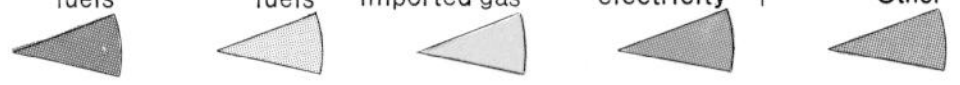

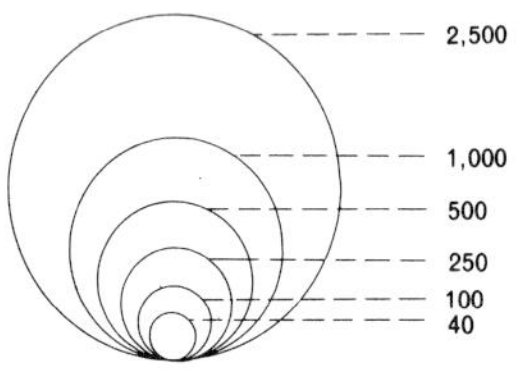

Volume data is not shown for countries with less than
1 million metric tons (coal equivalent)

Composition of Energy
Commercial Energy

| Solid fuels | Liquid fuels | Natural and imported gas | Hydro, nuclear & imported electricity | Other |

Per Capita Consumption of
Commercial Energy (coal
equivalent in kg. per capita—1982)

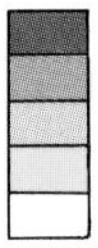

- 4,500–13,500 kg*
- 1,500–4,500
- 500–1,500
- <500
- Uninhabited or sparsely populated

*The Netherlands Antilles, Qatar, United Arab Emirates,
and U.S. Virgin Islands exceed this level.

BE-NE-LUX

ENERGY CONSUMPTION

Commercial Energy Consumption World Total—8,405,445,000 metric tons (coal equiv.)—1982

0	10	20	30	40	50	60	70	80	90	100%

| UNITED STATES 26.0% | CANADA 2.8 | OTHER 2.2 | SOVIET UNION 18.6 | CHINA 7.0 | JAPAN 4.9 | OTHER 7.3 | W. GER. 4.0 | U.K. 3.0 | FRANCE 2.6 | OTHER 14.7 | S. AM. 3.0 | AFRICA 2.4 |

← NORTH AMERICA → ← ASIA → ← EUROPE →

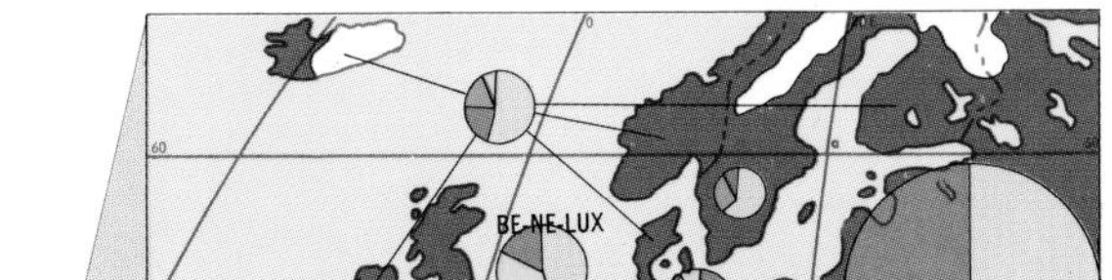

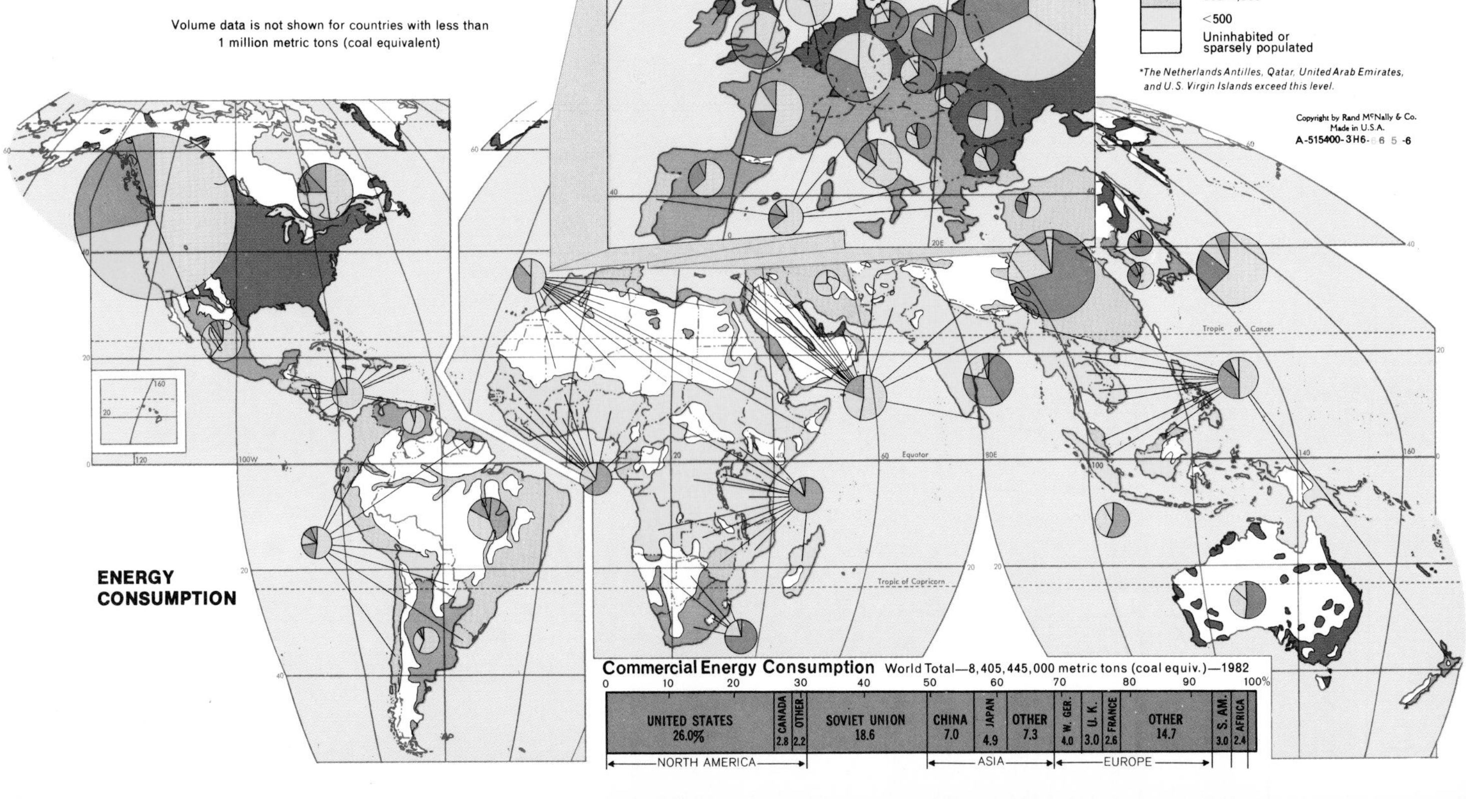

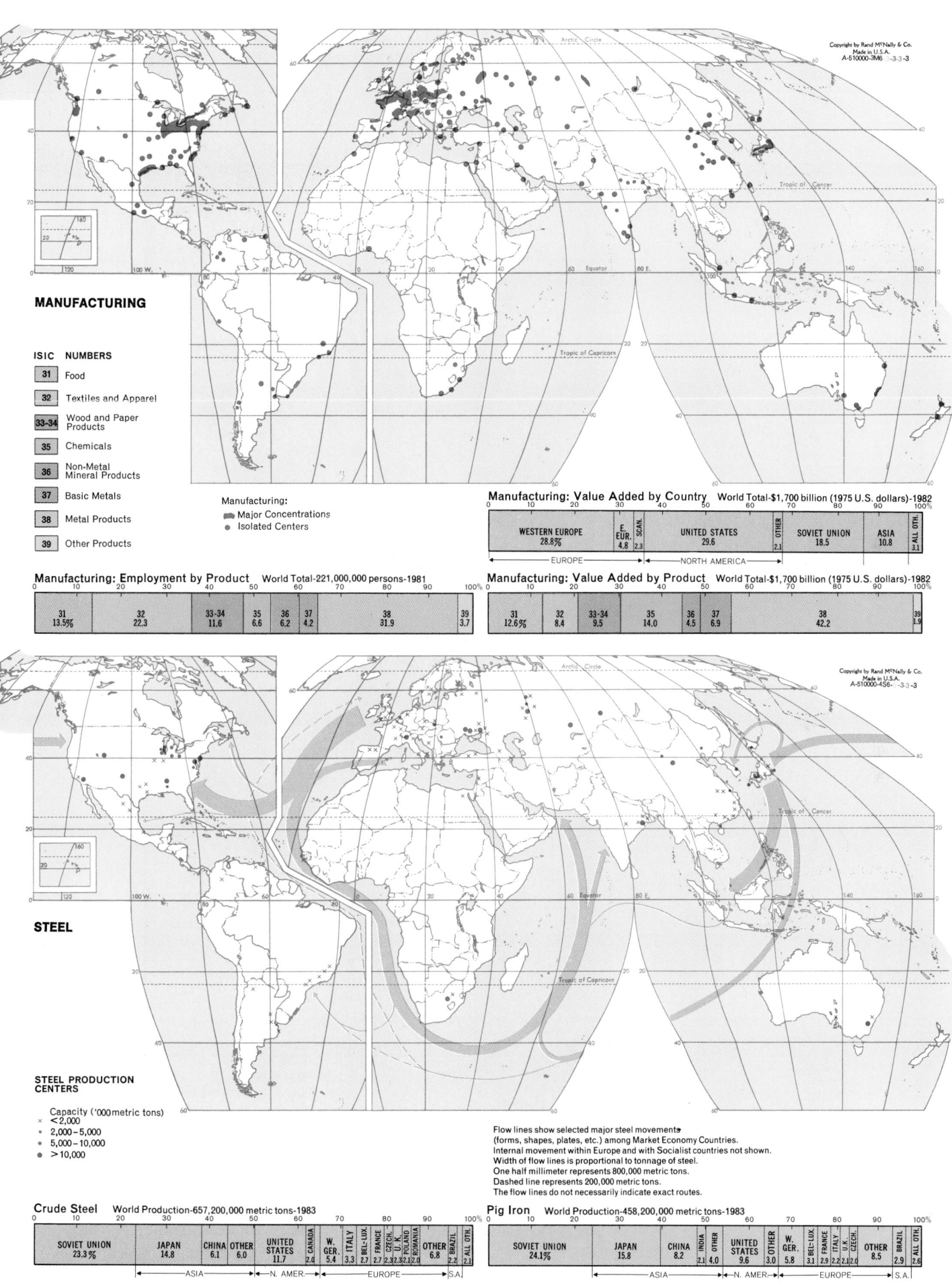

Copyright by Rand McNally & Co.
Made in U.S.A.
A-510000-3M6- -3-3-3

MANUFACTURING

ISIC NUMBERS

31	Food
32	Textiles and Apparel
33-34	Wood and Paper Products
35	Chemicals
36	Non-Metal Mineral Products
37	Basic Metals
38	Metal Products
39	Other Products

Manufacturing:
🢒 Major Concentrations
● Isolated Centers

Manufacturing: Value Added by Country   World Total-$1,700 billion (1975 U.S. dollars)-1982

0	10	20	30	40	50	60	70	80	90	100%

WESTERN EUROPE 28.8%	E. EUR. 4.8	SCAN. 2.3	UNITED STATES 29.6	OTHER 2.1	SOVIET UNION 18.5	ASIA 10.8	ALL OTH. 3.1

←——— EUROPE ———→ ←——— NORTH AMERICA ———→

Manufacturing: Employment by Product   World Total-221,000,000 persons-1981

0	10	20	30	40	50	60	70	80	90	100%

31 13.5%	32 22.3	33-34 11.6	35 6.6	36 6.2	37 4.2	38 31.9	39 3.7

Manufacturing: Value Added by Product   World Total-$1,700 billion (1975 U.S. dollars)-1982

0	10	20	30	40	50	60	70	80	90	100%

31 12.6%	32 8.4	33-34 9.5	35 14.0	36 4.5	37 6.9	38 42.2	39 1.9

Copyright by Rand McNally & Co.
Made in U.S.A.
A-510000-4S6- -3-3-3

STEEL

STEEL PRODUCTION CENTERS

Capacity ('000 metric tons)
× <2,000
● 2,000-5,000
● 5,000-10,000
● >10,000

Flow lines show selected major steel movements (forms, shapes, plates, etc.) among Market Economy Countries.
Internal movement within Europe and with Socialist countries not shown.
Width of flow lines is proportional to tonnage of steel.
One half millimeter represents 800,000 metric tons.
Dashed line represents 200,000 metric tons.
The flow lines do not necessarily indicate exact routes.

Crude Steel   World Production-657,200,000 metric tons-1983

0	10	20	30	40	50	60	70	80	90	100%

SOVIET UNION 23.3%	JAPAN 14.8	CHINA 6.1	OTHER 6.0	UNITED STATES 11.7	CANADA 2.0	W. GER. 5.4	ITALY 3.3	BEL.-LUX. 2.7	FRANCE 2.3	CZECH. 2.3	U.K. 2.1	ROMANIA 2.0	OTHER 6.8	BRAZIL 2.2	ALL OTH. 2.1

←———ASIA———→ ←N. AMER.→ ←———————EUROPE———————→ →S.A.

Pig Iron   World Production-458,200,000 metric tons-1983

0	10	20	30	40	50	60	70	80	90	100%

SOVIET UNION 24.1%	JAPAN 15.8	CHINA 8.2	INDIA 2.1	OTHER 4.0	UNITED STATES 9.6	OTHER 3.0	W. GER. 5.8	BEL.-LUX. 2.9	FRANCE 2.2	ITALY 2.2	U.K. 2.0	CZECH. 2.0	OTHER 8.5	BRAZIL 2.9	ALL OTH. 2.6

←———ASIA———→ ←N. AMER.→ ←———————EUROPE———————→ →S.A.

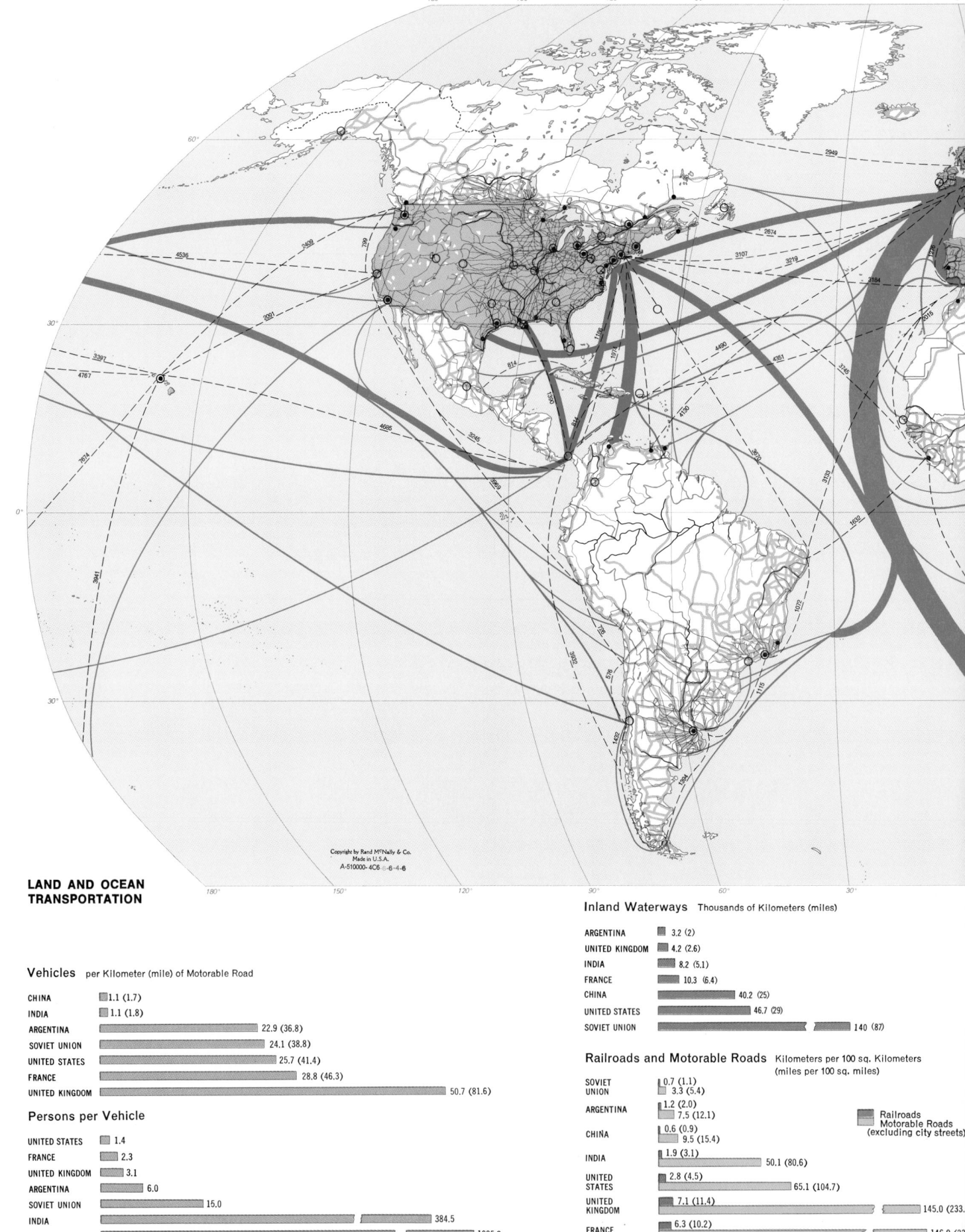

LAND AND OCEAN TRANSPORTATION

Vehicles per Kilometer (mile) of Motorable Road

CHINA	1.1 (1.7)
INDIA	1.1 (1.8)
ARGENTINA	22.9 (36.8)
SOVIET UNION	24.1 (38.8)
UNITED STATES	25.7 (41.4)
FRANCE	28.8 (46.3)
UNITED KINGDOM	50.7 (81.6)

Persons per Vehicle

UNITED STATES	1.4
FRANCE	2.3
UNITED KINGDOM	3.1
ARGENTINA	6.0
SOVIET UNION	15.0
INDIA	384.5
CHINA	1025.8

Inland Waterways Thousands of Kilometers (miles)

ARGENTINA	3.2 (2)
UNITED KINGDOM	4.2 (2.6)
INDIA	8.2 (5.1)
FRANCE	10.3 (6.4)
CHINA	40.2 (25)
UNITED STATES	46.7 (29)
SOVIET UNION	140 (87)

Railroads and Motorable Roads Kilometers per 100 sq. Kilometers (miles per 100 sq. miles)

Railroads
Motorable Roads (excluding city streets)

	Railroads	Motorable Roads
SOVIET UNION	0.7 (1.1)	3.3 (5.4)
ARGENTINA	1.2 (2.0)	7.5 (12.1)
CHINA	0.6 (0.9)	9.5 (15.4)
INDIA	1.9 (3.1)	50.1 (80.6)
UNITED STATES	2.8 (4.5)	65.1 (104.7)
UNITED KINGDOM	7.1 (11.4)	145.0 (233.6)
FRANCE	6.3 (10.2)	146.9 (236)

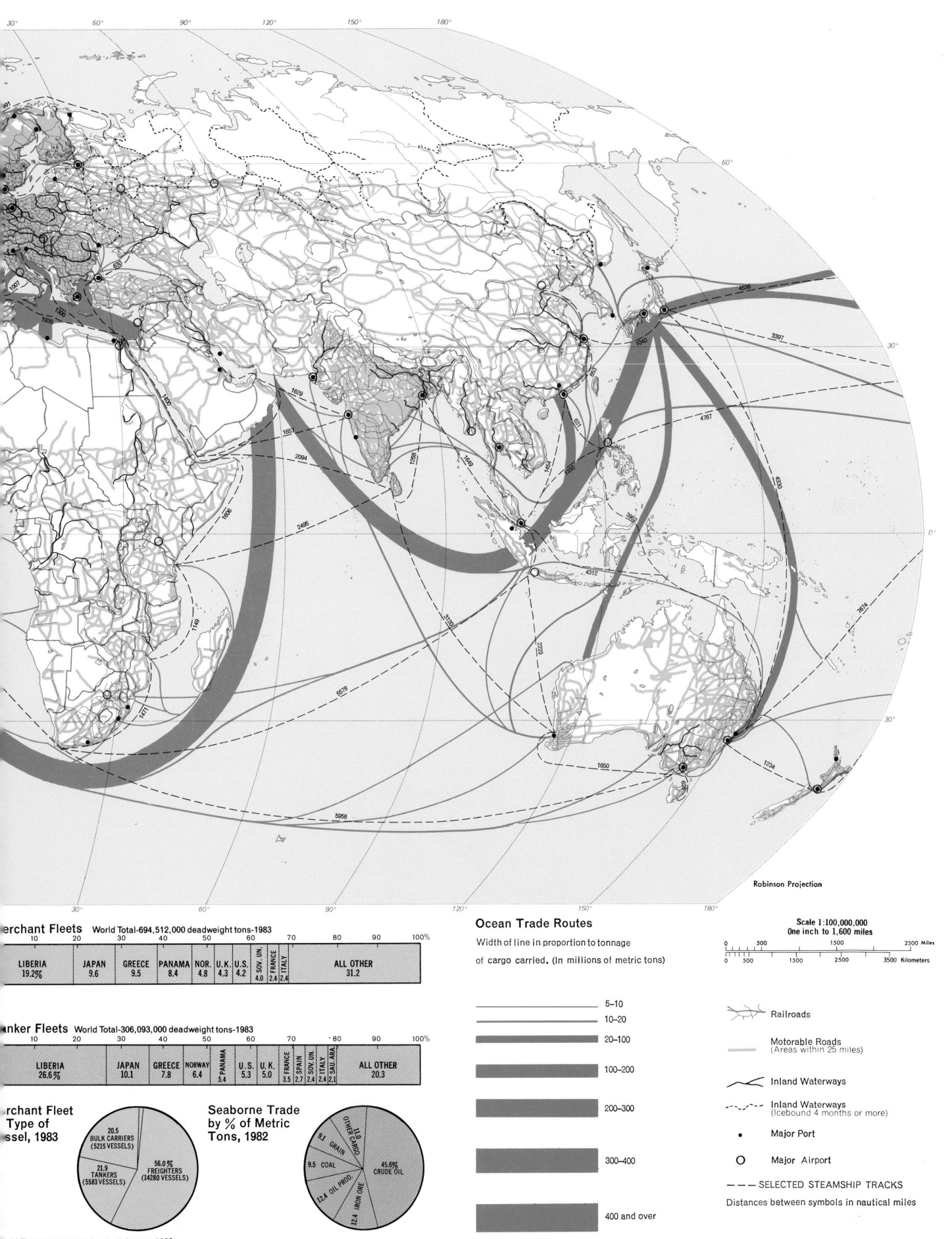

Robinson Projection

Ocean Trade Routes

Width of line in proportion to tonnage
of cargo carried. (In millions of metric tons)

	5–10
	10–20
	20–100
	100–200
	200–300
	300–400
	400 and over

Scale 1:100,000,000
One inch to 1,600 miles

0   500   1500   2500 Miles
0   500   1500   2500   3500 Kilometers

- Railroads
- Motorable Roads (Areas within 25 miles)
- Inland Waterways
- Inland Waterways (Icebound 4 months or more)
- • Major Port
- O Major Airport
- – – – SELECTED STEAMSHIP TRACKS

Distances between symbols in nautical miles

erchant Fleets   World Total–694,512,000 deadweight tons-1983

	10	20	30	40	50	60	70	80	90	100%

| LIBERIA 19.2% | JAPAN 9.6 | GREECE 9.5 | PANAMA 8.4 | NOR. 4.8 | U.K. 4.3 | U.S. 4.2 | SOV. UN. 4.0 | FRANCE 2.4 | ITALY 2.4 | ALL OTHER 31.2 |

anker Fleets   World Total-306,093,000 deadweight tons-1983

	10	20	30	40	50	60	70	80	90	100%

| LIBERIA 26.5% | JAPAN 10.1 | GREECE 7.8 | NORWAY 6.4 | PANAMA 5.4 | U.S. 5.3 | U.K. 5.0 | FRANCE 3.5 | SPAIN 2.7 | SOV. UN. 2.4 | ITALY 2.4 | SAU. ARA. 2.1 | ALL OTHER 20.3 |

erchant Fleet Type of essel, 1983

20.5 BULK CARRIERS (5215 VESSELS)
21.9 TANKERS (5583 VESSELS)
56.0% FREIGHTERS (14280 VESSELS)

orld Total-694,512,000 deadweight tons-1983

Seaborne Trade by % of Metric Tons, 1982

11.0 OTHER CARGO
9.1 GRAIN
9.5 COAL
12.4 OIL PROD.
12.4 IRON ORE
45.6% CRUDE OIL

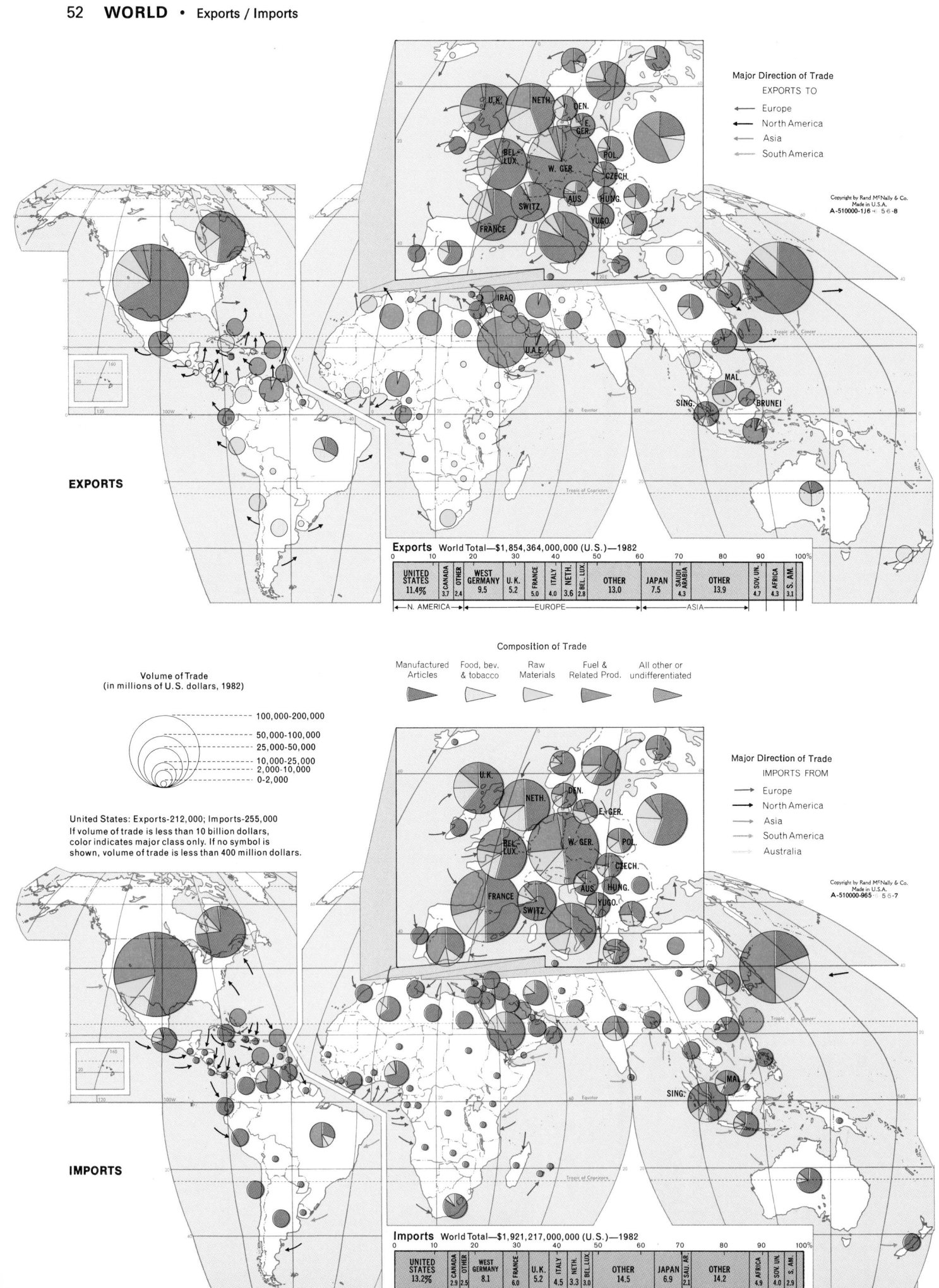

Major Direction of Trade

EXPORTS TO
→ Europe
→ North America
→ Asia
→ South America

Copyright by Rand McNally & Co.
Made in U.S.A.
A-510000-1J6-| 5-6-8

EXPORTS

Exports World Total—$1,854,364,000,000 (U.S.)—1982

	0	10			20		30	40	50		60	70	80	90	100%

| UNITED STATES 11.4% | CANADA 3.7 | OTHER 2.4 | WEST GERMANY 9.5 | U.K. 5.2 | FRANCE 5.0 | ITALY 4.0 | NETH. 3.6 | BEL. LUX. 2.8 | OTHER 13.0 | JAPAN 7.5 | SAUDI ARABIA 4.3 | OTHER 13.9 | SOV. UN. 4.7 | AFRICA 4.3 | S. AM. 3.1 |

←— N. AMERICA —→ ←———— EUROPE ————→ ←———— ASIA ————→

Composition of Trade

Manufactured Articles	Food, bev. & tobacco	Raw Materials	Fuel & Related Prod.	All other or undifferentiated

Volume of Trade
(in millions of U.S. dollars, 1982)

100,000-200,000
50,000-100,000
25,000-50,000
10,000-25,000
2,000-10,000
0-2,000

United States: Exports-212,000; Imports-255,000
If volume of trade is less than 10 billion dollars,
color indicates major class only. If no symbol is
shown, volume of trade is less than 400 million dollars.

Major Direction of Trade

IMPORTS FROM
→ Europe
→ North America
→ Asia
→ South America
→ Australia

Copyright by Rand McNally & Co.
Made in U.S.A.
A-510000-965-| 5-6-7

IMPORTS

Imports World Total—$1,921,217,000,000 (U.S.)—1982

	0	10		20	30		40		50	60	70	80	90	100%

| UNITED STATES 13.2% | CANADA 2.9 | OTHER | WEST GERMANY 8.1 | FRANCE 6.0 | U.K. 5.2 | ITALY | NETH. 3.3 | BEL. LUX. 3.0 | OTHER 14.5 | JAPAN 6.9 | SAU. AR. 2.1 | OTHER 14.2 | AFRICA 4.9 | SOV. UN 4.0 | S. AM. 2.9 |

←— N. AMERICA —→ ←———— EUROPE ————→ ←———— ASIA ————→

major cities maps

This section consists of 62 maps of the world's most populous metropolitan areas. In order to make comparison easier, all the metropolitan areas are shown at the same scale, 1:300,000.

Detailed urban maps are an important reference requirement for a world atlas. The names of many large settlements, towns, suburbs, and neighborhoods can be located on these large-scale maps. From a thematic standpoint the maps show generalized land-use patterns. Included were the total urban extent, major industrial areas, parks, public land, wooded areas, airports, shopping centers, streets, and railroads. A special effort was made to portray the various metropolitan areas in a manner as standard and comparable as possible. (For the symbols used, see the legend below.)

Notable differences occur in the forms of cities. In most of North America these forms were conditioned by a rectangular pattern of streets; land-use zones (residential, commercial, industrial) are well defined. The basic structure of most European cities is noticeably different and more complex; street patterns are irregular and zones are less well defined. In Asia, Africa, and South America the form tends to be even more irregular and complex. Widespread dispersion of craft and trade activities has lessened zonation, there may be cities with no identifiable city centers, and sometimes there may be dual centers (old and modern). Higher population densities result in more limited, compact urban places in these areas of the world.

Inhabited Localities

The symbol represents the number of inhabitants within the locality

- · 0—10,000
- ° 10,000—25,000
- ◉ 25,000—100,000
- ▣ 100,000—250,000
- ▤ 250,000—1,000,000
- ■ >1,000,000

The size of type indicates the relative economic and political importance of the locality

Écommoy
Trouville
Lisieux

St.-Denis

PARIS

Hollywood   Section of a City,
Westminster Neighborhood
Northland ■
Center   Major Shopping Center

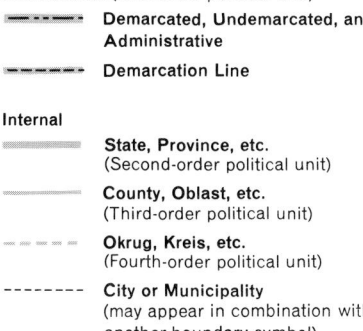
Urban Area (area of continuous industrial, commercial, and residential development)

Major Industrial Area

Wooded Area

Political Boundaries

International (First-order political unit)
━ ▪ ━ ▪ ━ Demarcated, Undemarcated, and Administrative
━ ━ ━ ━ Demarcation Line

Internal
━━━━━ State, Province, etc. (Second-order political unit)
─────── County, Oblast, etc. (Third-order political unit)
─ ─ ─ ─ Okrug, Kreis, etc. (Fourth-order political unit)
- - - - - City or Municipality (may appear in combination with another boundary symbol)

Capitals of Political Units

BUDAPEST Independent Nation

Recife State, Province, etc.

White Plains County, Oblast, etc.

Iserlohn Okrug, Kreis, etc.

Transportation

Road

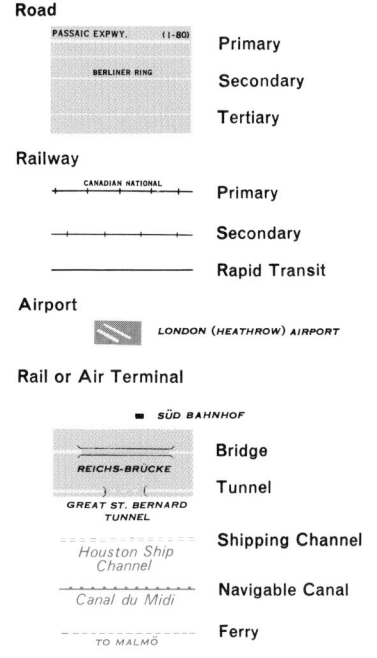

PASSAIC EXPWY.   (1-80)   Primary

BERLINER RING   Secondary

Tertiary

Railway

CANADIAN NATIONAL   Primary

Secondary

Rapid Transit

Airport

LONDON (HEATHROW) AIRPORT

Rail or Air Terminal

■ SÜD BAHNHOF

REICHS-BRÜCKE   Bridge

GREAT ST. BERNARD TUNNEL   Tunnel

Houston Ship Channel   Shipping Channel

Canal du Midi   Navigable Canal

TO MALMÖ   Ferry

Hydrographic Features

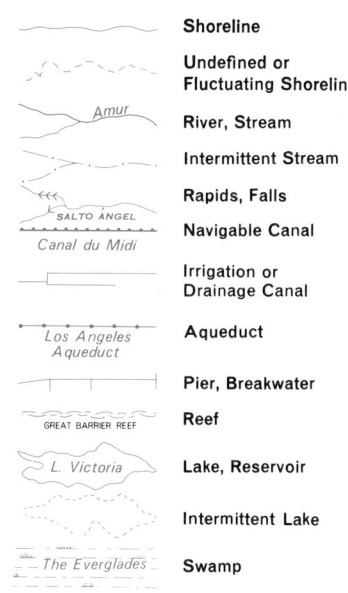

Shoreline

Undefined or Fluctuating Shoreline

River, Stream

Amur

Intermittent Stream

Rapids, Falls

SALTO ÁNGEL

Navigable Canal

Canal du Midi

Irrigation or Drainage Canal

Los Angeles Aqueduct   Aqueduct

Pier, Breakwater

GREAT BARRIER REEF   Reef

L. Victoria   Lake, Reservoir

Intermittent Lake

The Everglades   Swamp

Miscellaneous Cultural Features

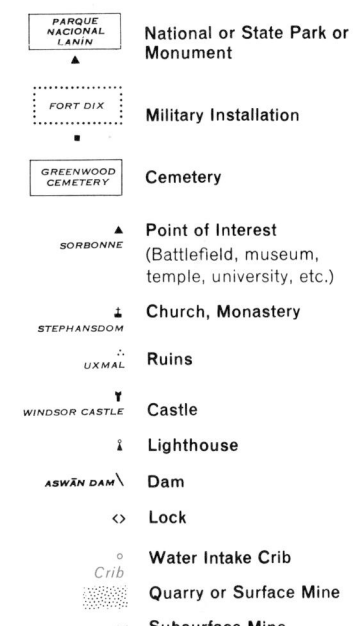

PARQUE NACIONAL LANÍN   National or State Park or Monument

FORT DIX   Military Installation

GREENWOOD CEMETERY   Cemetery

SORBONNE   ▲ Point of Interest (Battlefield, museum, temple, university, etc.)

STEPHANSDOM   Church, Monastery

UXMAL   Ruins

WINDSOR CASTLE   Castle

Lighthouse

ASWĀN DAM   Dam

<> Lock

°   Water Intake Crib
Crib

Quarry or Surface Mine

Subsurface Mine

Topographic Features

Mt. Kenya 5199 △ Elevation Above Sea Level

Elevations are given in meters

⋆ Rock

A N D E S Mountain Range, Plateau,
KUNLUNSHANMAI Valley, etc.

BAFFIN ISLAND Island

POLUOSTROV KAMČATKA Peninsula, Cape, Point, etc.
CABO DE HORNOS

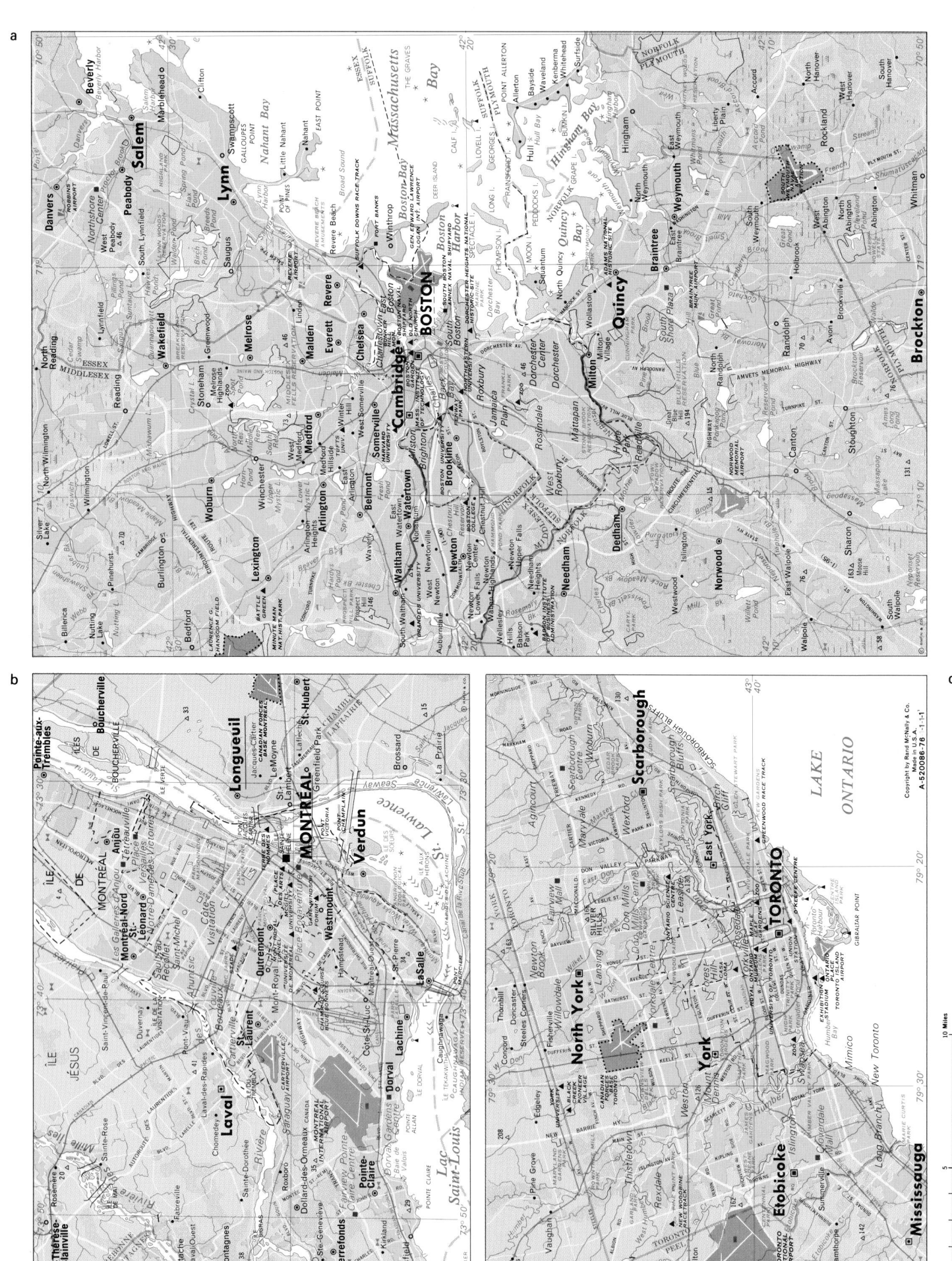

Scale 1:300,000; one inch to 4.7 miles.

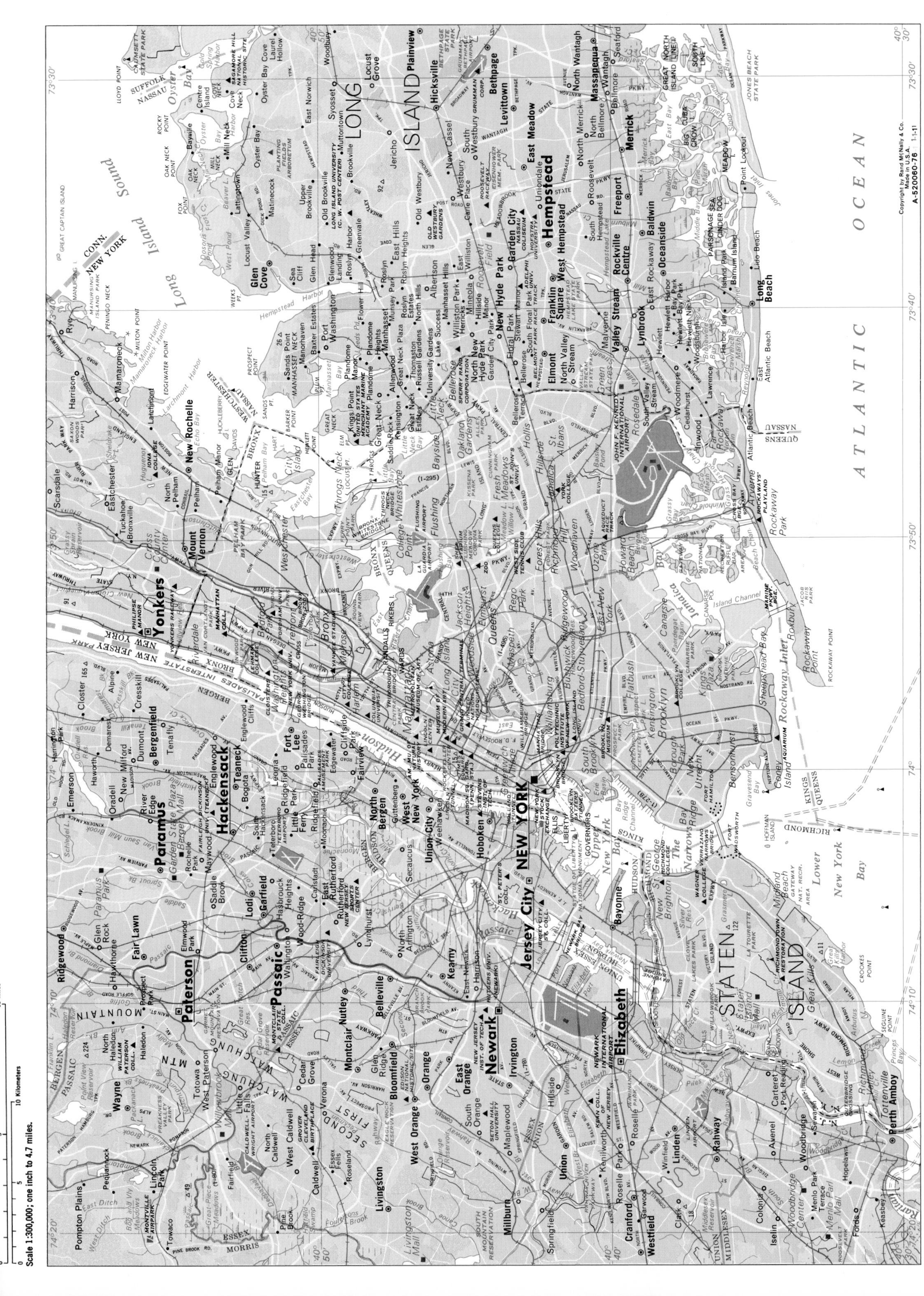

Scale 1:300,000; one inch to 4.7 miles.

0 5 10 Kilometers

CONN.
NEW YORK

Long Island Sound

ATLANTIC OCEAN

LONG ISLAND

STATEN ISLAND

NEW YORK

Jersey City

Newark

Elizabeth

Yonkers

Paterson

Passaic

Paramus

Hackensack

Hempstead

Garden City

New Hyde Park

Franklin Square

Valley Stream

Long Beach

Glen Cove

Hicksville

Bethpage

Plainview

Levittown

East Meadow

Merrick

Lynbrook

New Rochelle

Mount Vernon

Wayne

Ridgewood

Fair Lawn

Clifton

Lodi

Garfield

Bloomfield

Montclair

Nutley

Belleville

East Orange

Orange

West Orange

Union

Rahway

Linden

Perth Amboy

Copyright by Rand McNally & Co.
Made in U.S.A.
A-520060-76   1-11

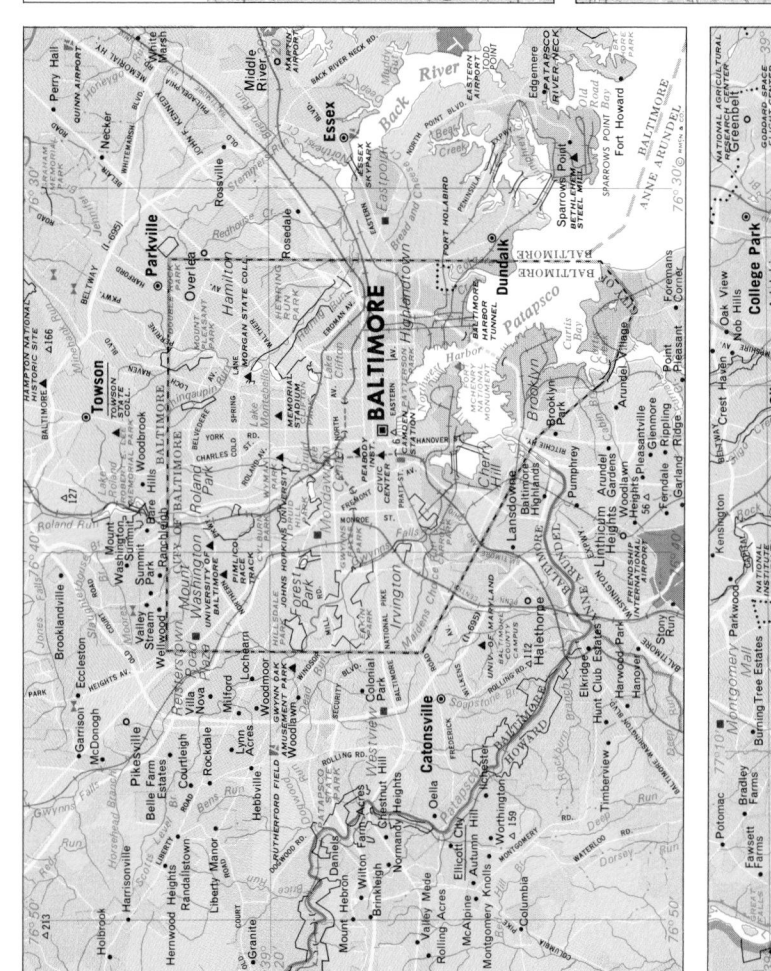
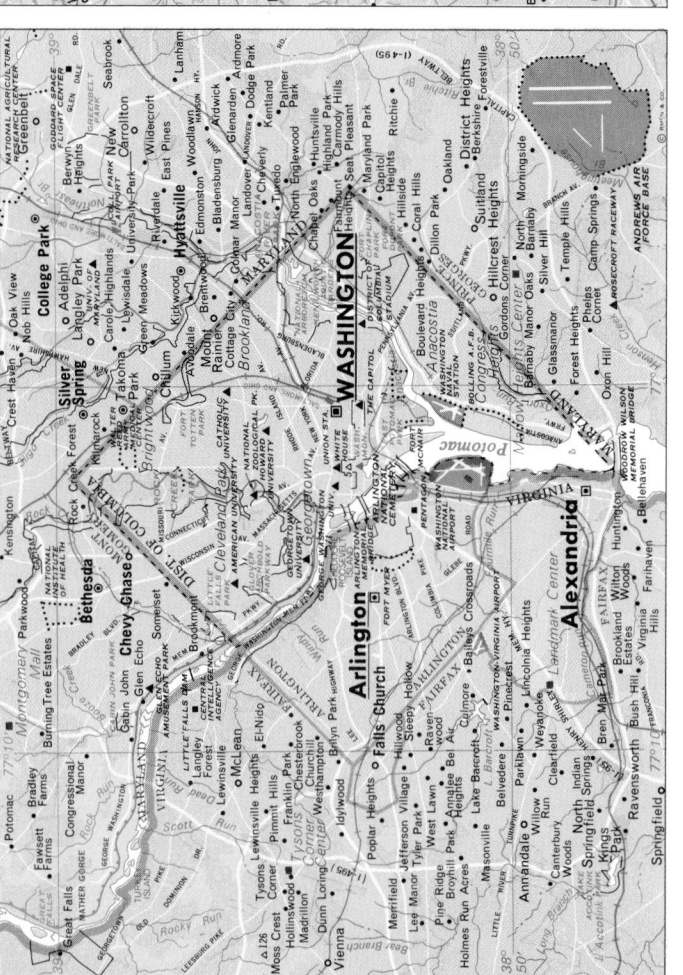

Scale 1:300,000: one inch to 4.7 miles

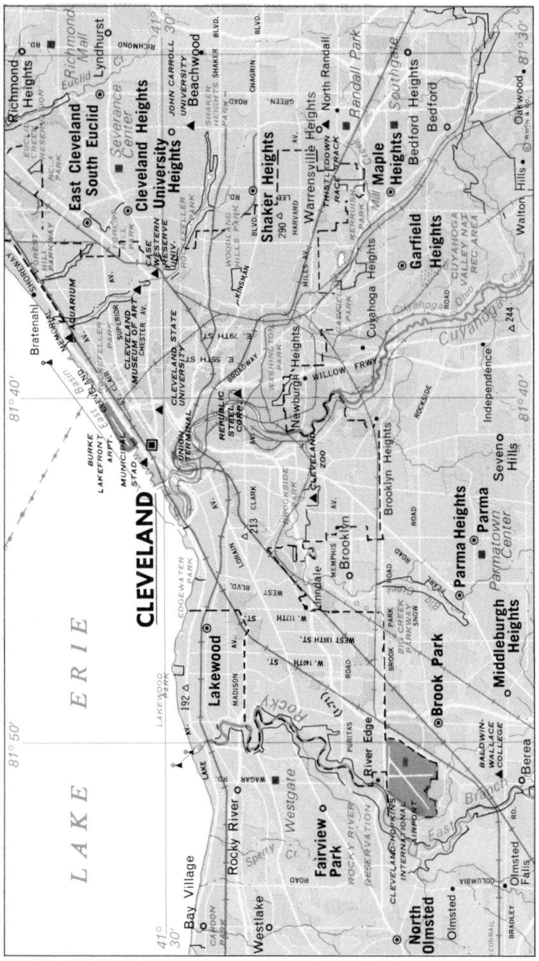

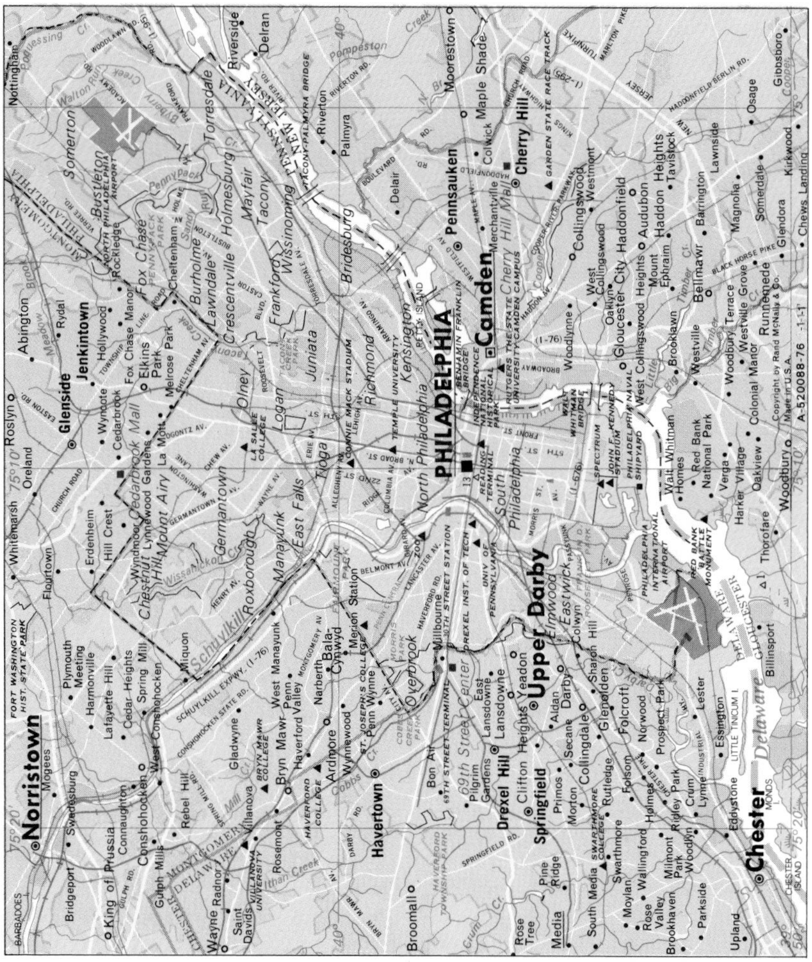

a

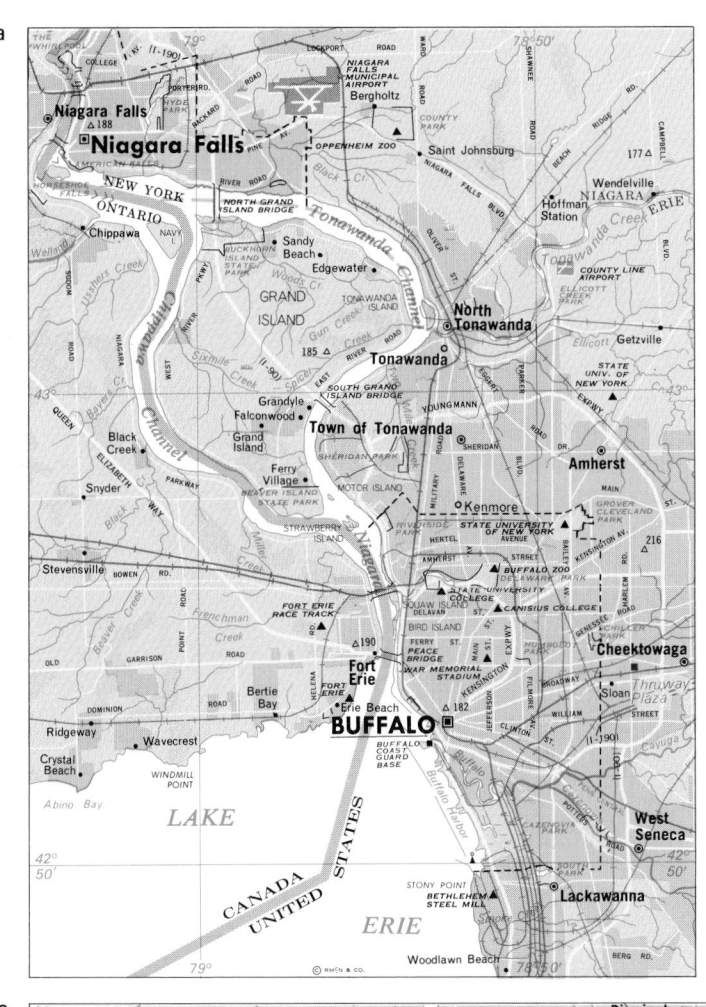

b

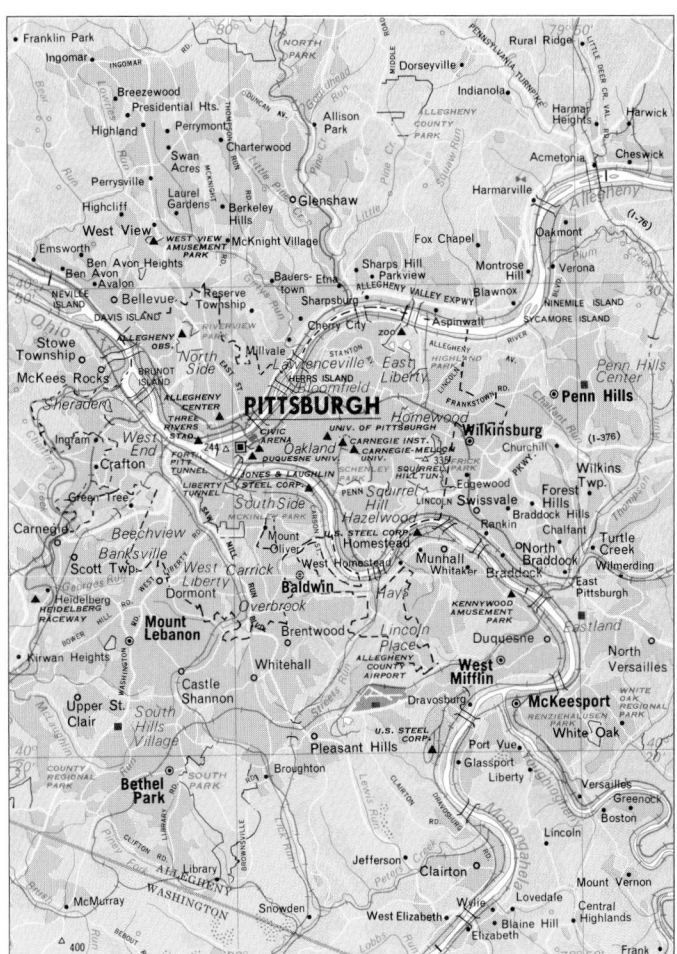

c

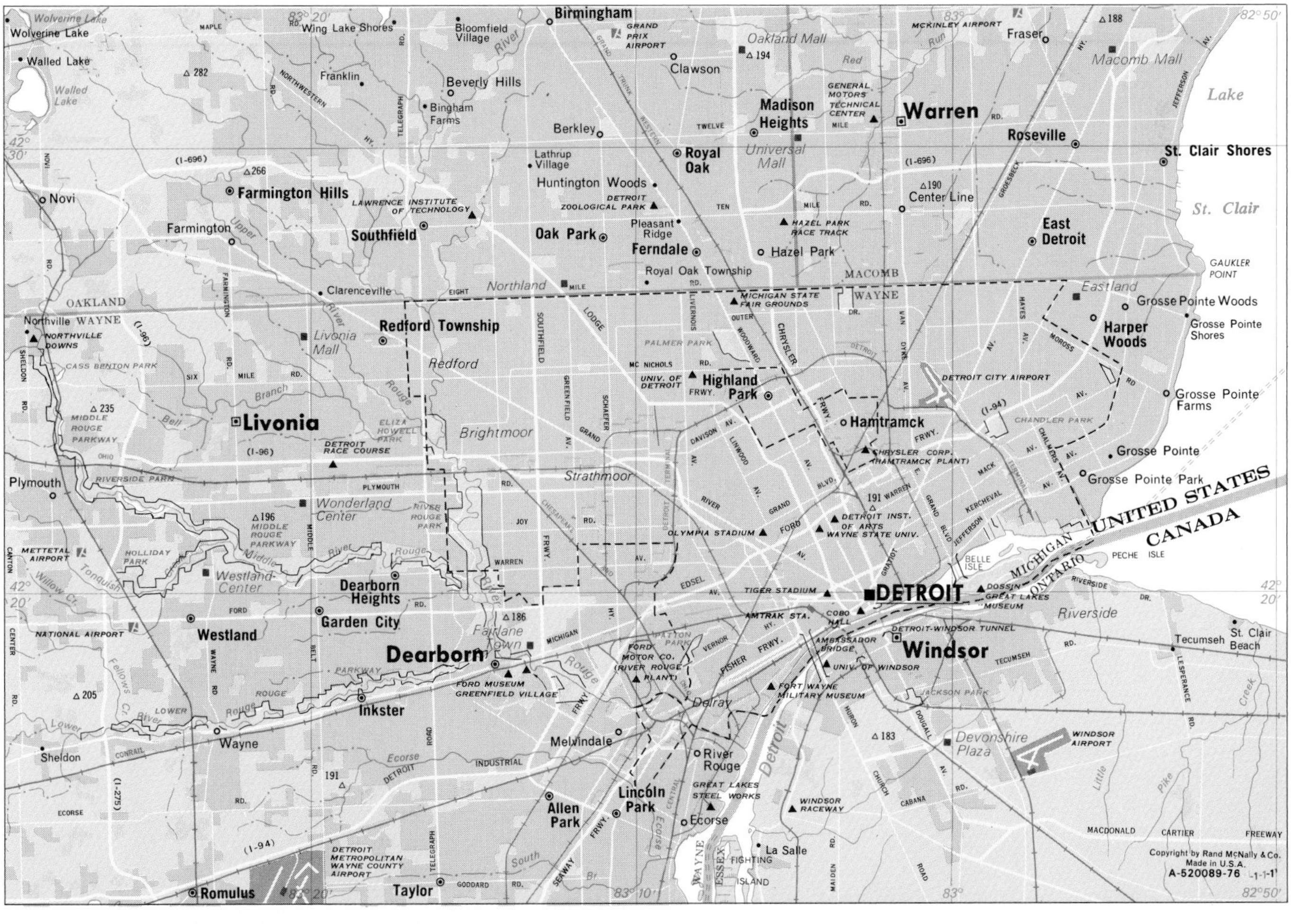

Scale 1:300,000; one inch to 4.7 miles.

10 Kilometers

5

Copyright by Rand McNally & Co.
Made in U.S.A.
A-520089-76 -1-1-1'

a

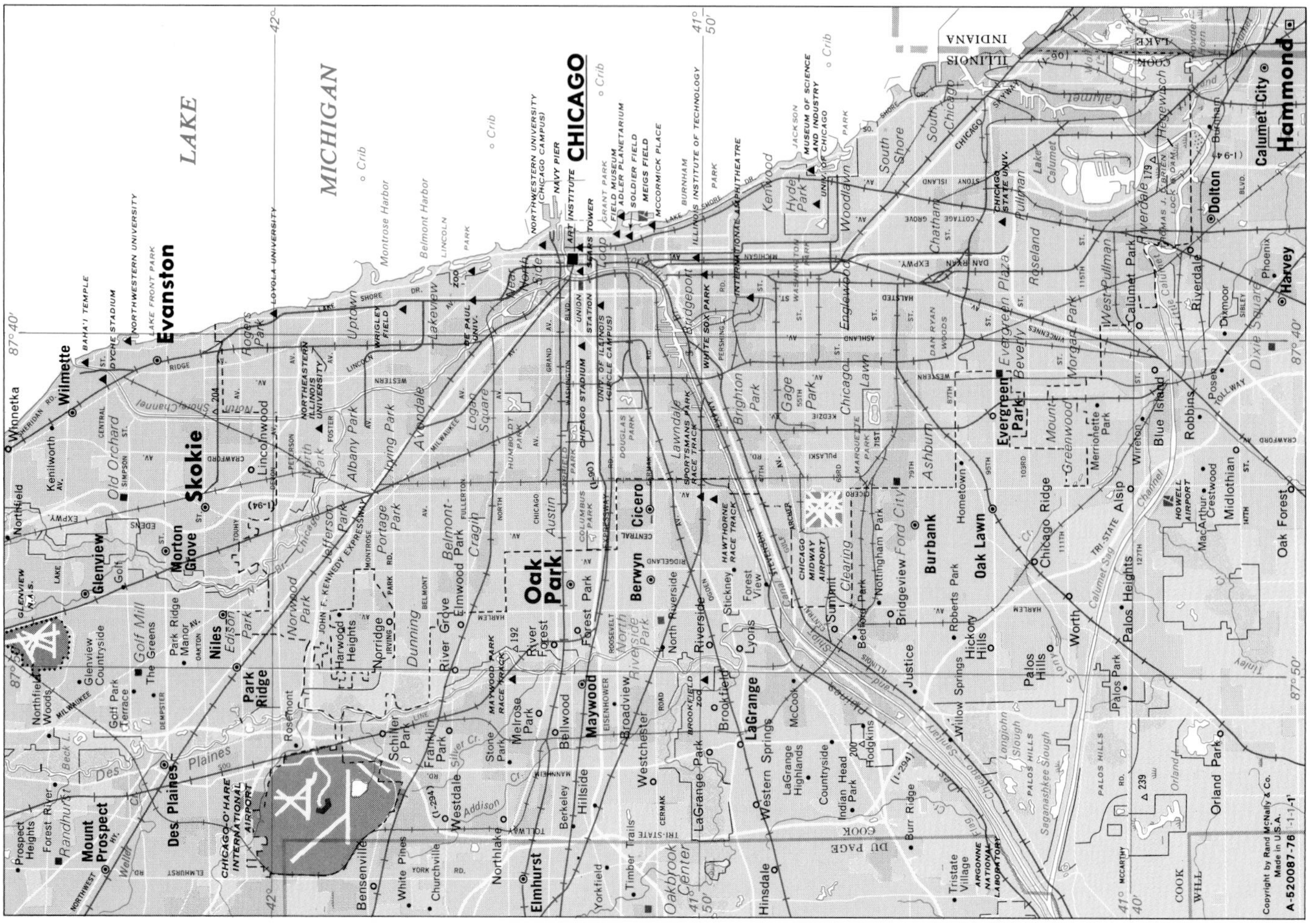

LAKE MICHIGAN

ILLINOIS
INDIANA

CHICAGO

Evanston

Wilmette

Winnetka

Skokie

Glenview

Morton Grove

Niles

Park Ridge

Des Plaines

Mount Prospect

Prospect Heights

Oak Park

Cicero

Berwyn

Maywood

Melrose Park

LaGrange

Elmhurst

Evergreen Park

Burbank

Oak Lawn

Chicago Ridge

Palos Hills

Calumet City

Hammond

Dolton

Harvey

CHICAGO-O'HARE INTERNATIONAL AIRPORT

CHICAGO MIDWAY AIRPORT

Copyright by Rand McNally & Co.
Made in U.S.A.
A-520087-76

b

PACIFIC OCEAN

San Francisco Bay

San Pablo Bay

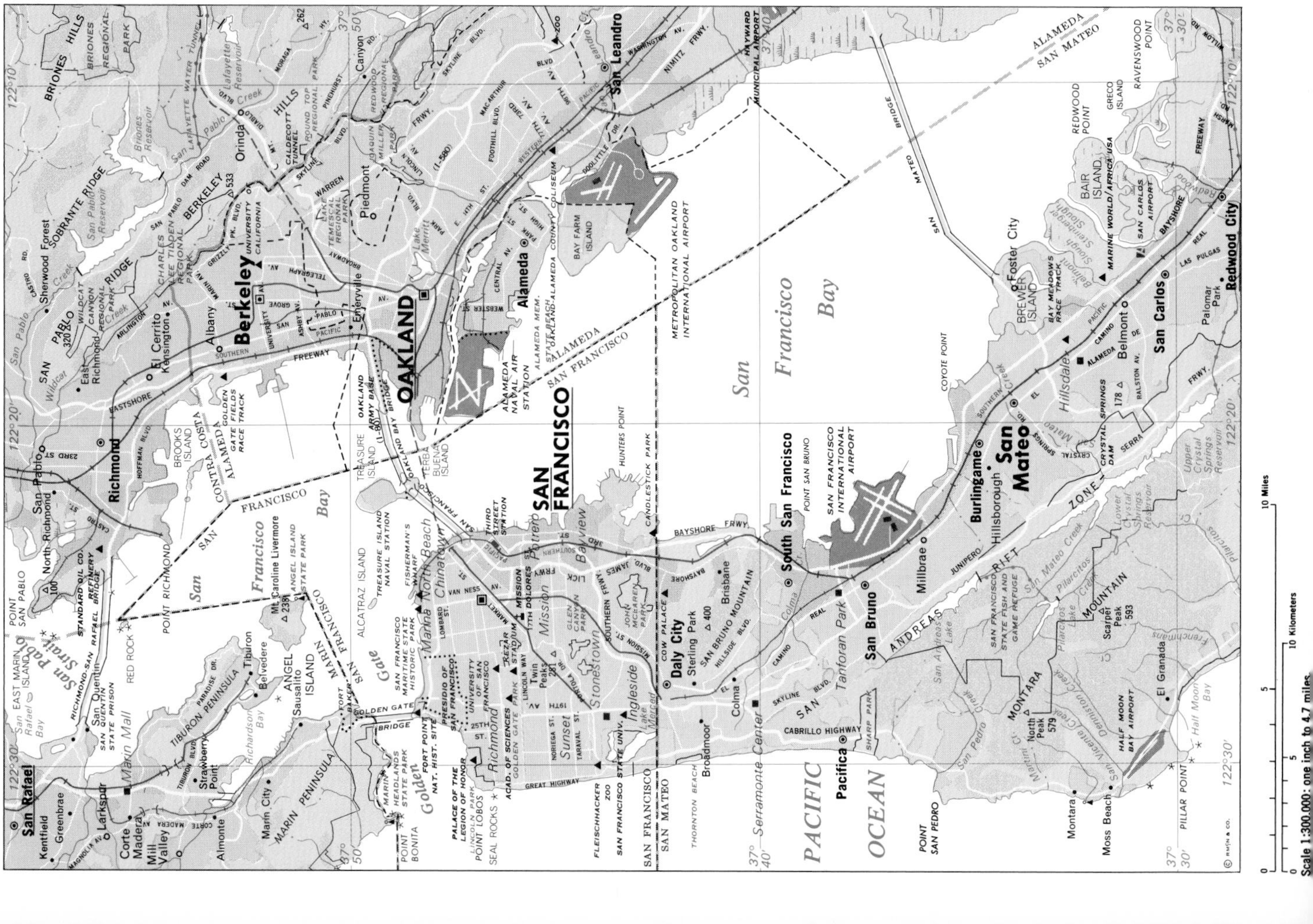

SAN FRANCISCO

OAKLAND

Berkeley

Richmond

Alameda

San Leandro

San Rafael

San Mateo

San Carlos

Redwood City

Burlingame

Hillsborough

San Bruno

South San Francisco

Daly City

Pacifica

Foster City

Belmont

SAN FRANCISCO INTERNATIONAL AIRPORT

METROPOLITAN OAKLAND INTERNATIONAL AIRPORT

Golden Gate

Alcatraz Island

Angel Island

Treasure Island

Scale 1:300,000: one inch to 4.7 miles.

10 Miles

10 Kilometers

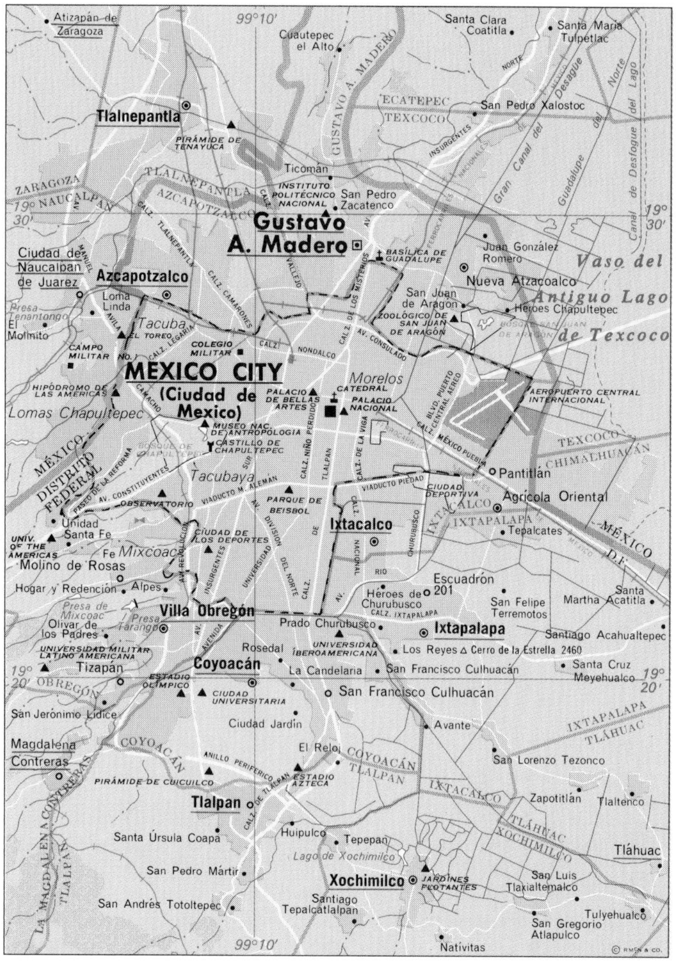

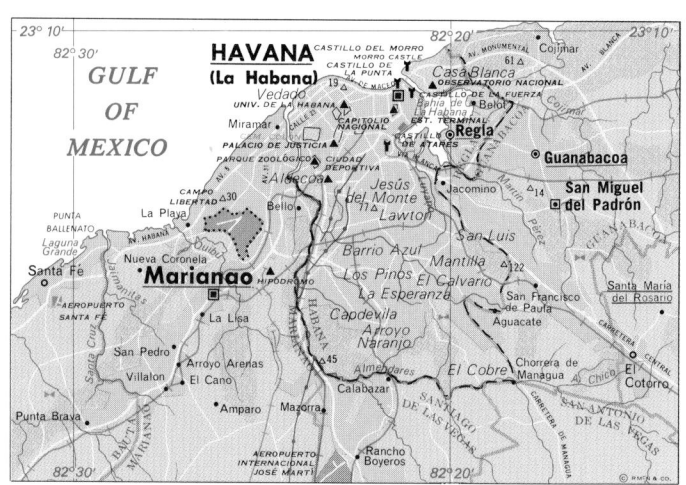

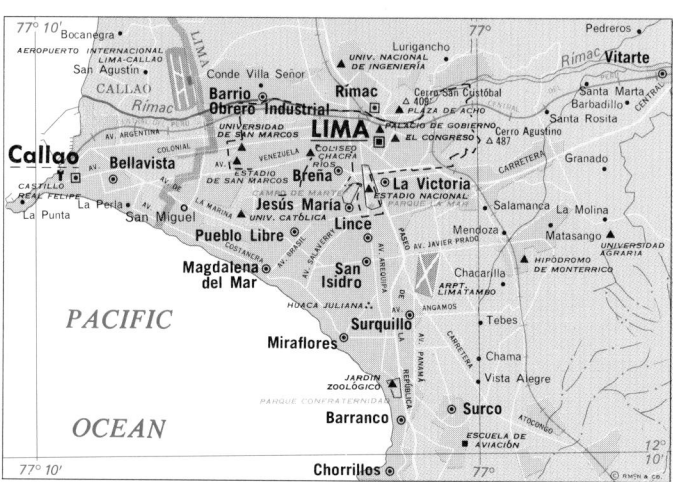

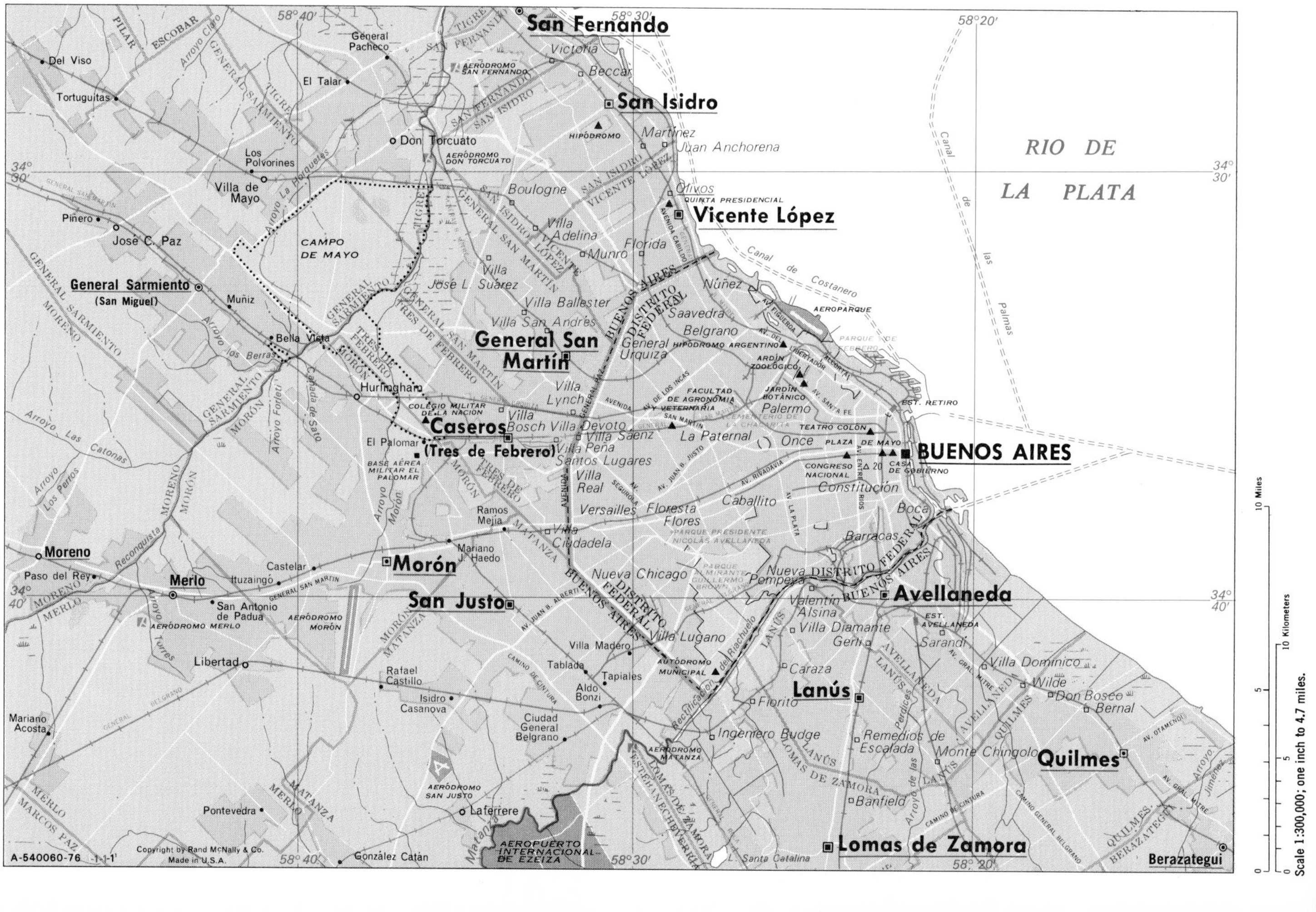

a
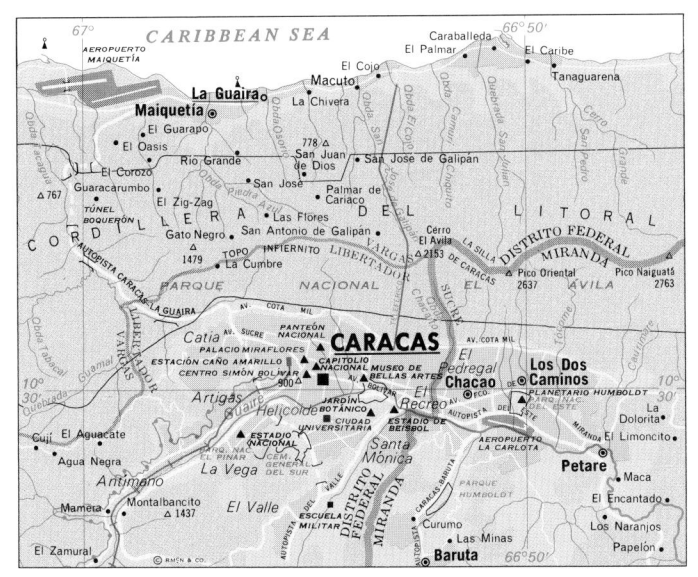

b

c
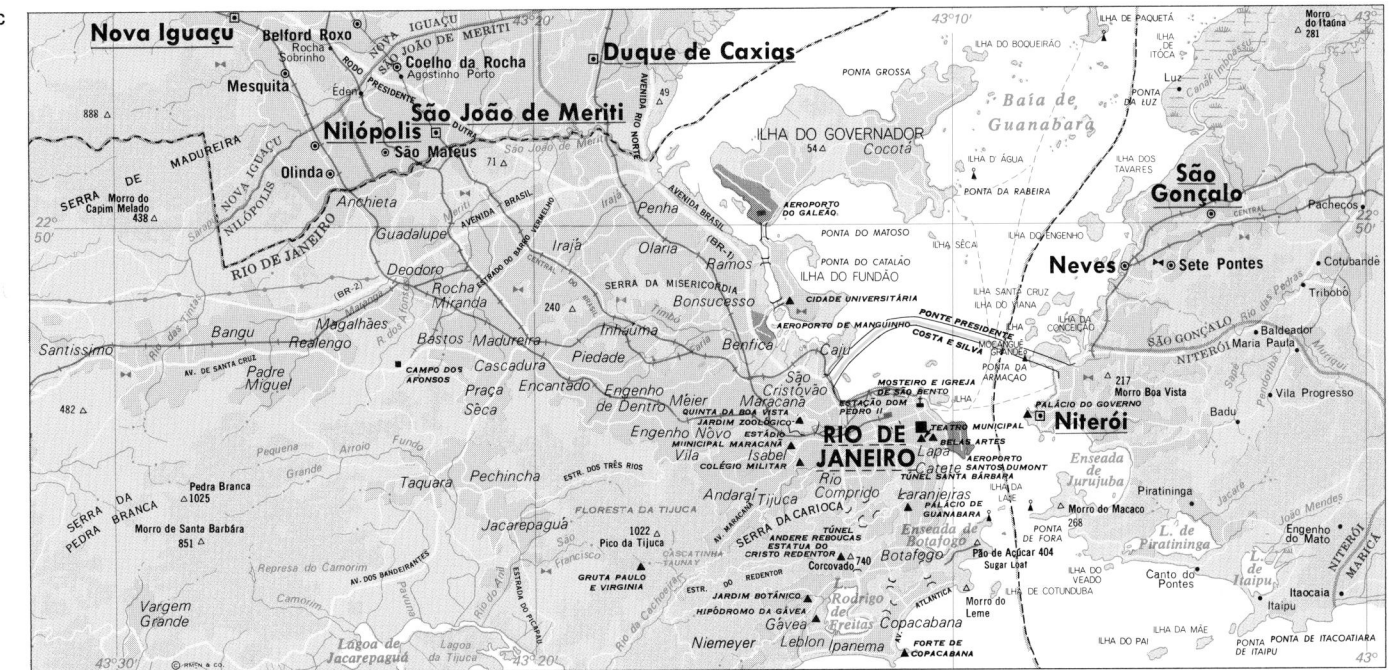

d
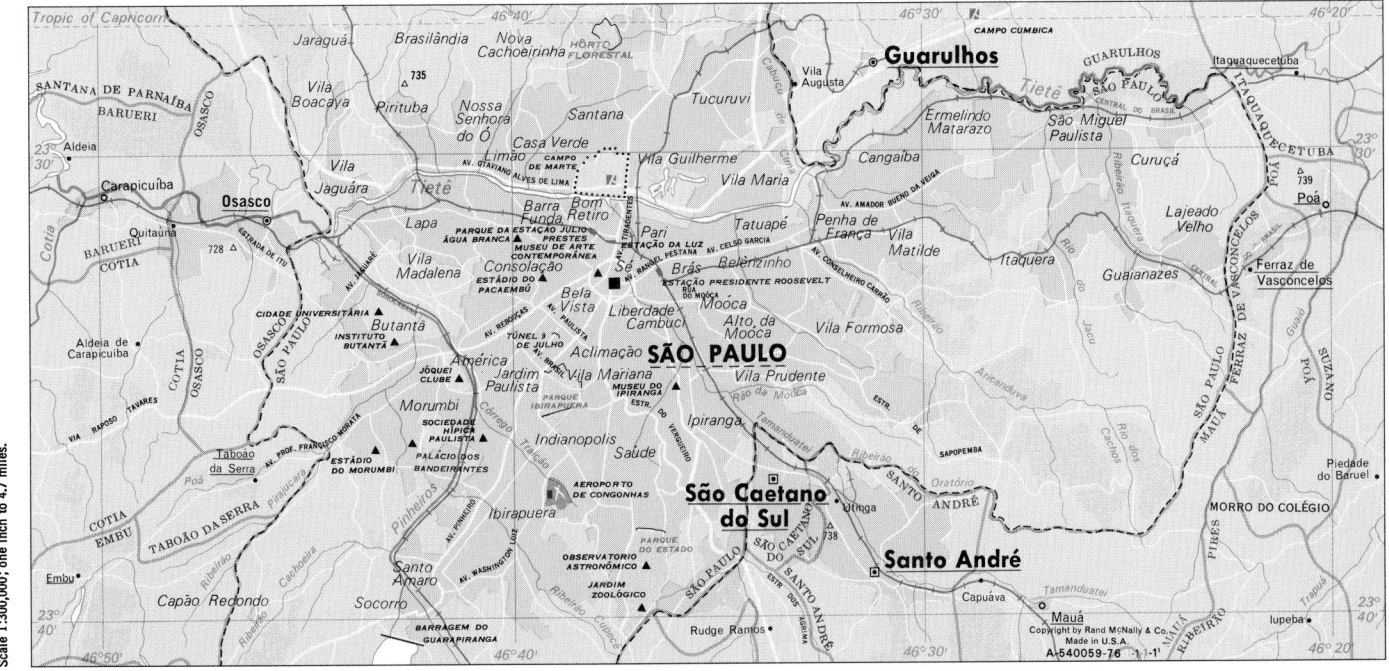

Scale 1:300,000; one inch to 4.7 miles.

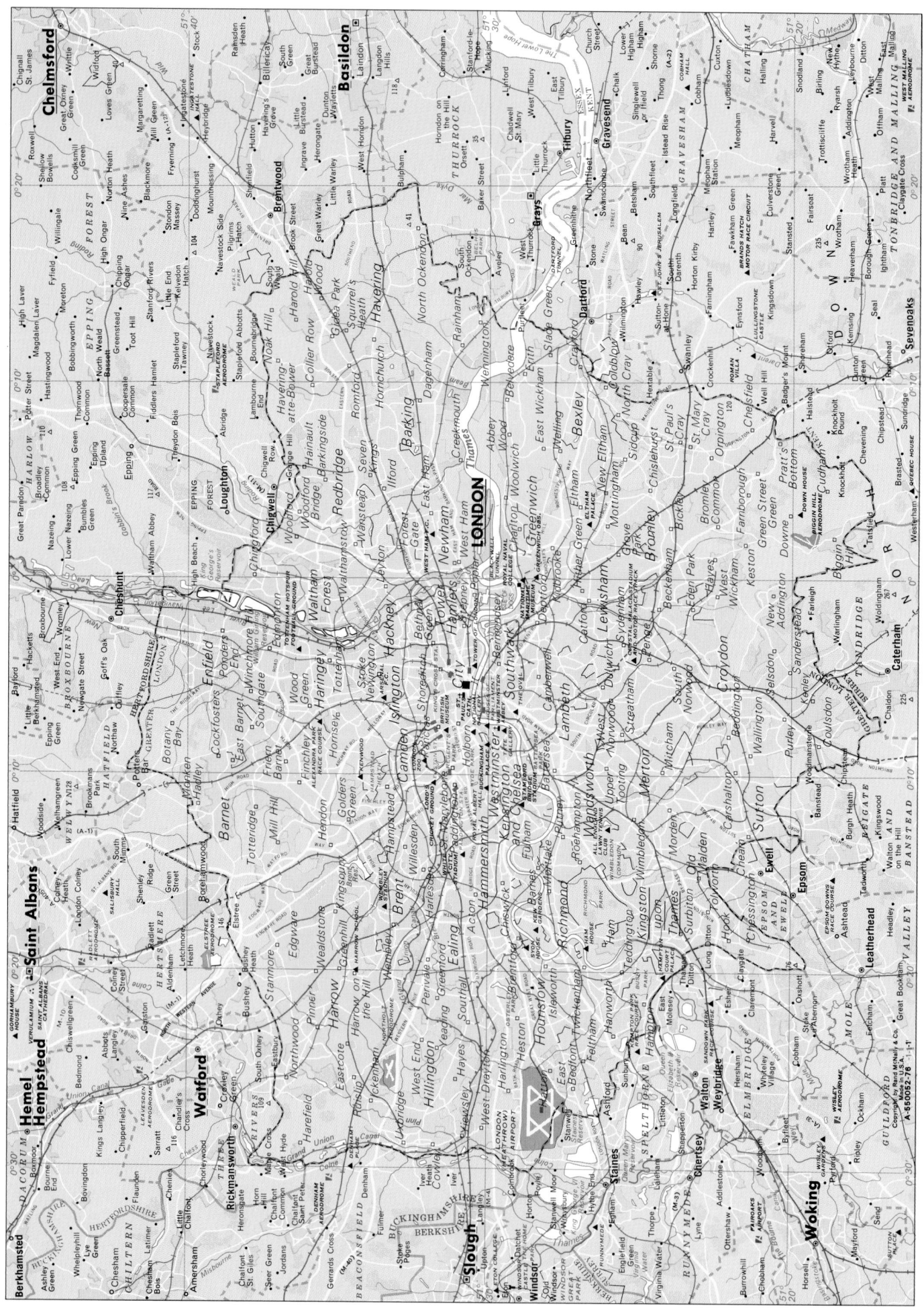

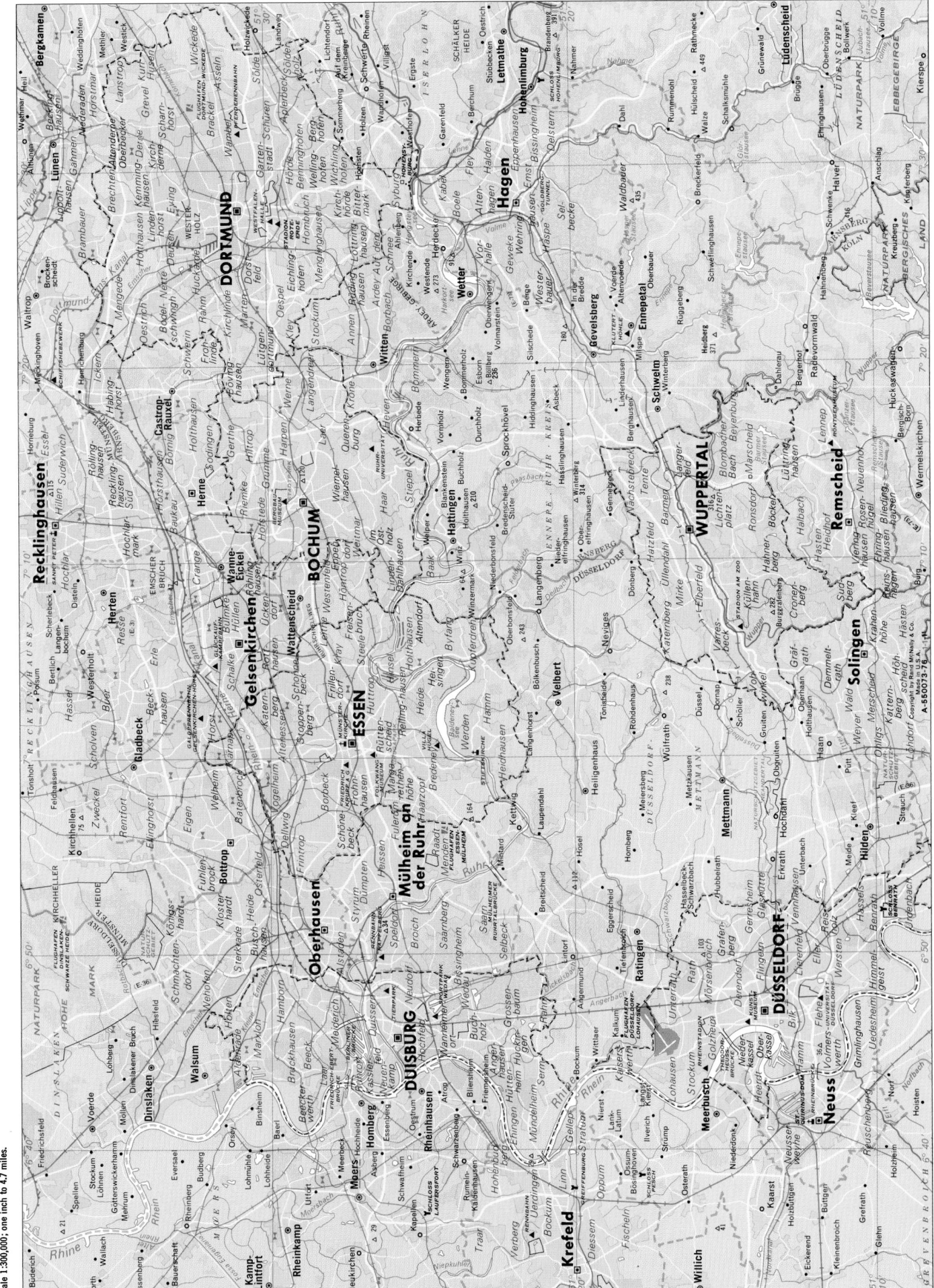

Scale 1:300,000; one inch to 4.7 miles.

Scale 1:300,000; one inch to 4.7 miles.

Copyright by Rand McNally & Co.
Made in U.S.A.
A-550078-76   -1-1-1

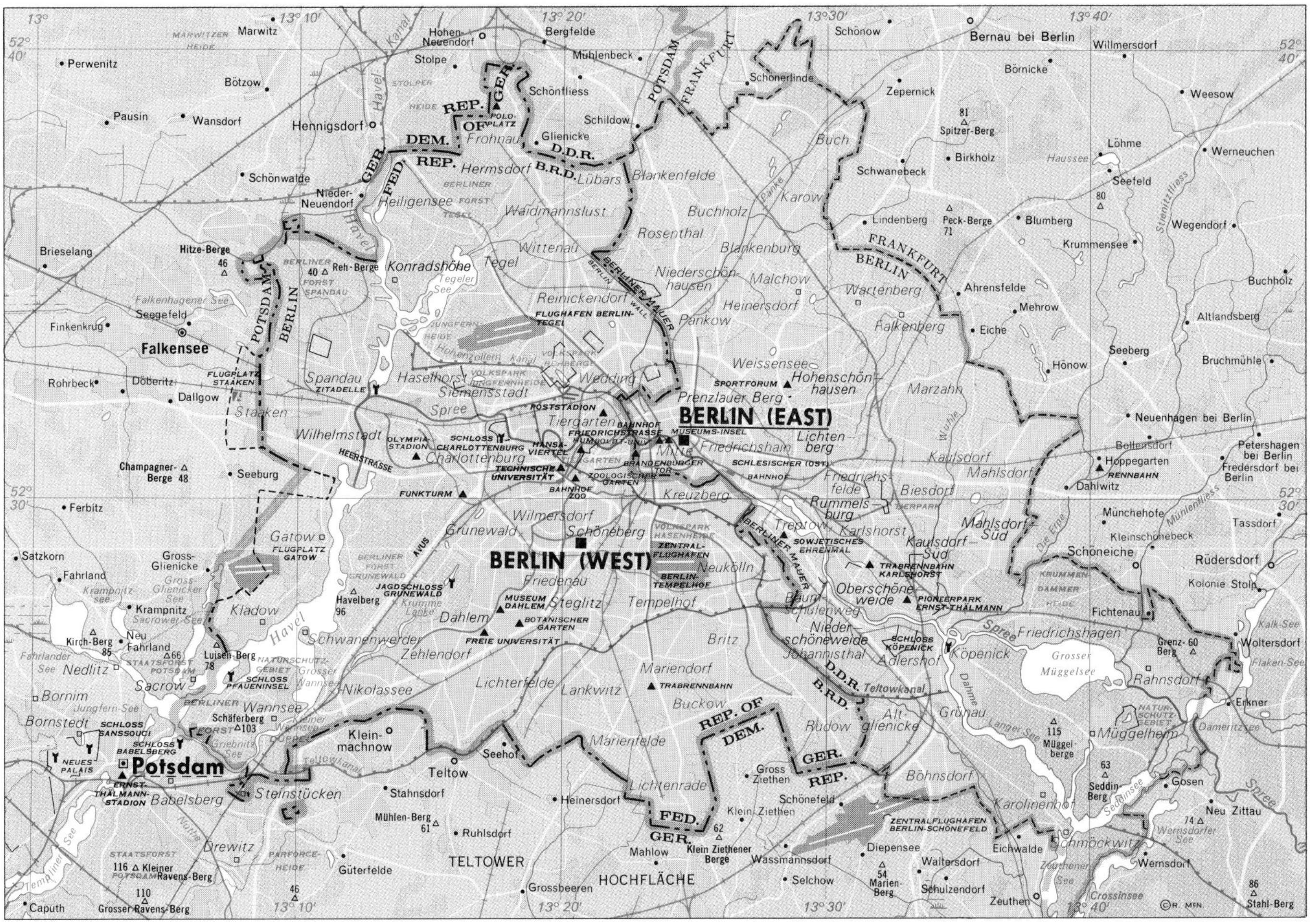

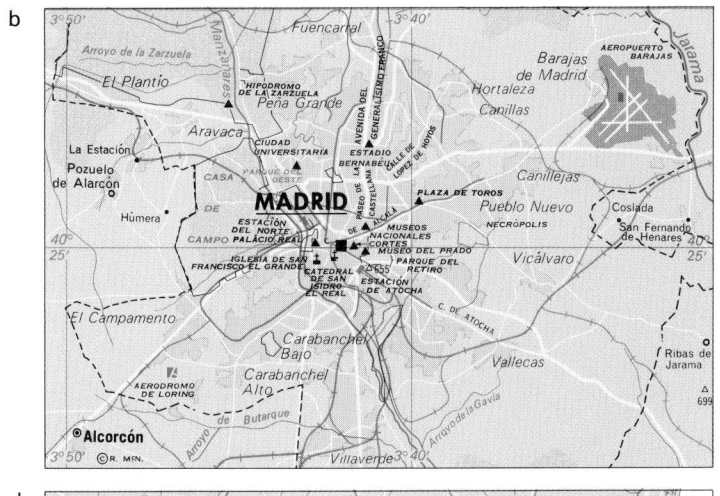

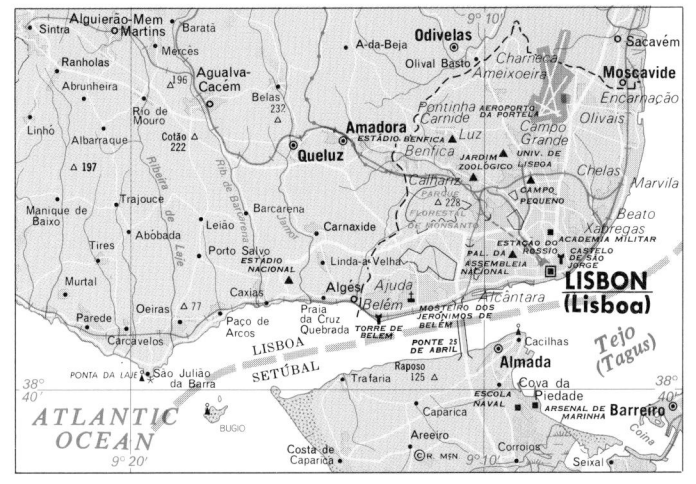
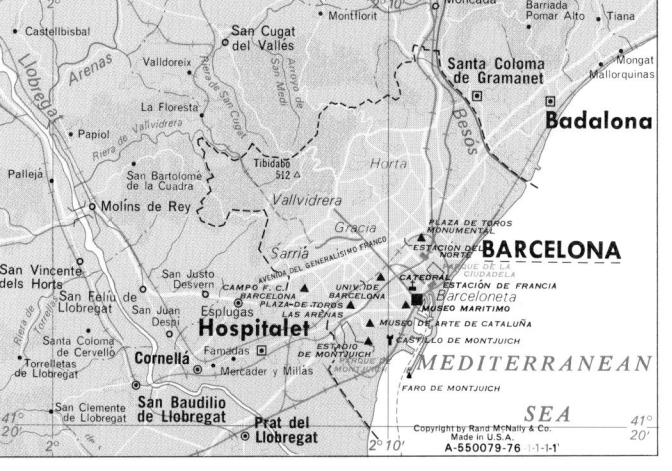

a

Gulf of Finland

STADION IMENI S.M. KIROVA
OSTROV VASIL'EVSKIJ
PETROPAVLOVSKAJA KREPOST'
AVRORA
AKADEMIJA NAUK
UNIVERSITET
ERMITAŽ
SMOL'NYJ
Bol'šaja Ochta
Malaja Ochta
PÁM'ATNIK PETRU I
DRAMATIČESKIJ TEATR
OPERA
LENINGRAD
MOSKOVSKIJ VOKZAL
TAVRIČESKIJ DVOREC
VITEBSKIJ VOKZAL
VARŠAVSKIJ VOKZAL
BALTIJSKIJ VOKZAL
ALEKSANDRO-NEVSKAJA LAVRA
Neva
Kudrovo
Ves'oly Pos'olok
Avtovo

AEROPORT KOLOM'AGI
CEL'USKINCEV PARK
Udel naja
Ručji
Rybackaja
Ozero Lachtinskij Razliv
Lachta
Staraja Derevn'a
Lesnoj
Graždanka
Rževka
Novoje Koval'ovo
Pol'ustrovo
LESNOJ PARK
Malaja Neva
BOTANIČESKIJ SAD
KIROVSKIE OSTROVA
MORSKOJ UNIVERSITET
OSTROV VOLNYJ
MORSKOJ PASSAŽIRSKIJ PORT
OSTROV KANONERSKIJ
OSTROV GUTUJEVSKIJ
KLADBIŠČE VOLKOVO

b

Chimki (Khimki)
Novoarchangel'skoje
MOSKVA GOROD MOSKVA
Jauza
Mytishchi
Tajninka
Kurkino
Lianozovo
DMITROVSKOE ŠOSSE
Beskudnikovo
Medvedkovo
157
Putilkovo
Novochovrino
Degunino
Vladykino
Babuškin (Babuškin)
Chimkinskoje Vodochranilišče
Chimki-Chovrino
VYSTAVKA DOSTIŽENIJ NARODNOGO CHOZ'AJSTVA S.S.S.R.
Abramcevo
Tušino (Tushino)
SAVELOVSKOE ŠOSSE
Petrovsko-Razumovskoe
MONUMENT KOSMOSA
Bogorodskoje
Goljanovo
Strogino
Makino
Pokrovskoe-Strešnevo
SAVELOVSKIJ VOKZAL
Ostankino
PARK SOKOL'NIKI
Sokol'niki
POSTOJANNYJ VYSTAVOČNYJ PAVIL'ON
ŠČOLKOVSKOE ŠOSSE
Izmajlovo
Serebr'anyj Bor
MOSKOVSKIJ AEROVOKZAL
Mnevniki
LENINGRADSKIJ VOKZAL
RIŽSKIJ VOKZAL
STADION DINAMO
IPPODROM
BELORUSSKIJ VOKZAL
LENINGRADSKIJ VOKZAL
JAROSLAVSKIJ VOKZAL
150
IZMAJLOVSKIJ PARK
Tatarovo
MUZEJ REVOL'UCII
ISTORIČESKIJ MUZEJ
CIRK
KAZANSKIJ VOKZAL
KURSKIJ VOKZAL
Reutov
Krylatskoje
120
Fili
BOL'ŠOJ TEATR
KREML'
KIEVSKIJ VOKZAL
TRET'AKOVSKAJA GALEREJA
ENTUZIASTOV
Novogirejevo
Perovo
Kuskovo
Mazilovo
MOSCOW (Moskva)
Kunc ovo (Kuncevo)
CENTRAL'NYJ PARK IMENI GOR'KOGO
PAVELECKIJ VOKZAL
Vešn'aki
Nemčinovka
Luzniki
CENTRALNYJ STADION IMENI V.I. LENINA
UNIVERSITET IMENI M.V. LOMONOSOVA
AKADEMIJA NAUK S.S.S.R.
Kosino
Očakovo
Gora Lenina
191
Čeromuski
Kuz'minki
Zareče
Ramenka
Nagatino
L'ublino (Ljublino)
Meščerskij
Nikulino
Jugo-Zapad
Kolomenskoje
Solncevo
Tropar'ovo
Volchonka-Zil
Z'uzino
Djakovo
Orlovo
250
Čertanovka
Saburovo
Kapotn'a
Bratejevo
Dzeržinskij
Rum'ancevo
Uzkoje
Čertanovo
Lenino
Borisovo
(Moscow)
Salarjovo
T'oplyj Stan
Jasenevo
Pokrovskoje
Besedy
Nikolo-Chovanskoje
Krasnyj Stroitel'
Bir'ul'ovo (Birjulevo)
Mamonovo
Ascerino
Letovo
Baturino
Michajlovskoje
Ostrov
Sosenki
Kommunarka
Bitca
Misailovo

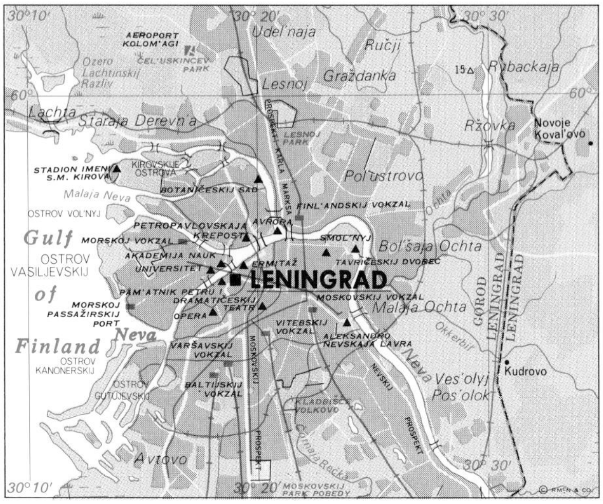

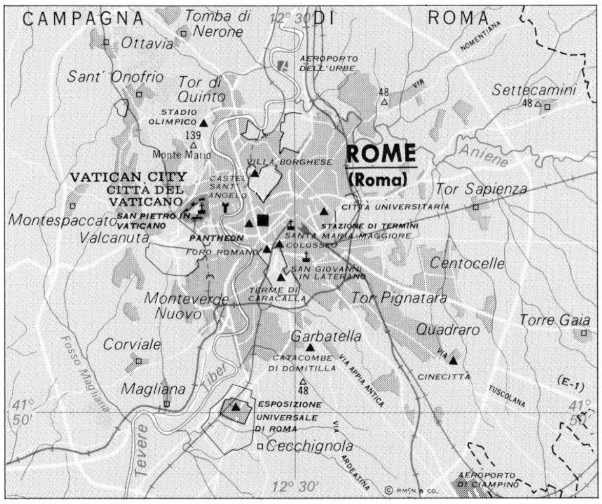

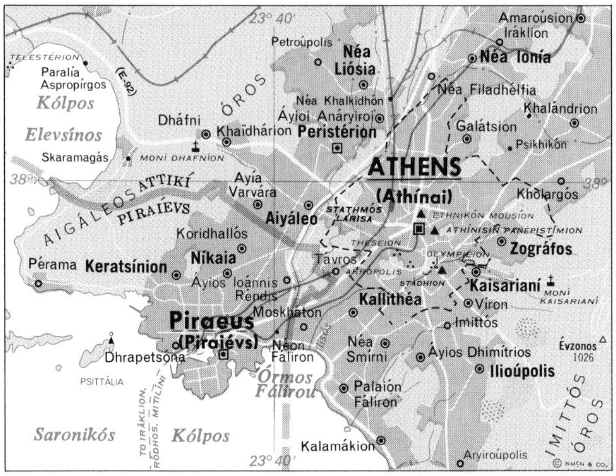

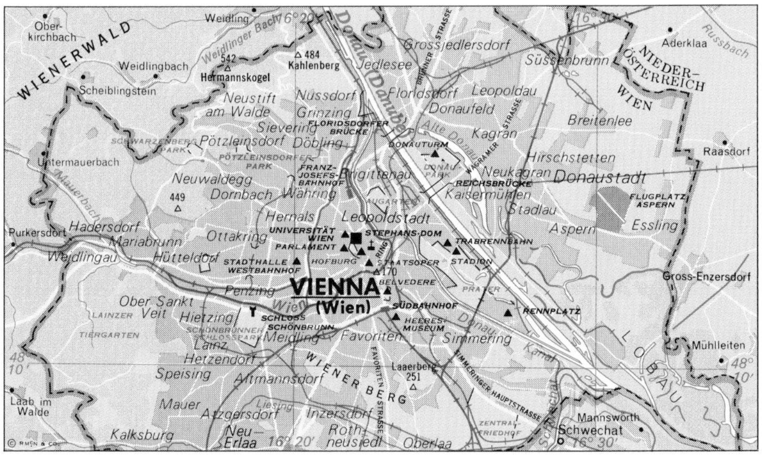

c

CAMPAGNA DI ROMA
Tomba di Nerone
Ottavia
Sant' Onofrio
Tor di Quinto
AEROPORTO DELL'URBE
NOMENTANA
Settecamini
Settebagni
48
STADIO OLIMPICO
139
Monte Mario
VILLA BORGHESE
Sant' Sapienza
Aniene
VATICAN CITY CITTA DEL VATICANO
CASTEL SANT'ANGELO
CITTÀ UNIVERSITARIA
STAZIONE DI TERMINI
SAN PIETRO IN VATICANO
PANTHEON
ROME (Roma)
SANTA MARIA MAGGIORE
Montespaccato
FORO ROMANO
COLOSSEO
SAN GIOVANNI IN LATERANO
Centocelle
Valcanuta
Tor Pignatara
Monteverde Nuovo
TERME DI CARACALLA
Torre Gaia
Corviale
Garbatella
Quadraro
VIA
Magliana
CATACOMBE DI DOMITILLA
48
CINECITTA
VIA APPIA ANTICA
TUSCOLANA
(E-1)
Tevere
ESPOSIZIONE UNIVERSALE DI ROMA
Cecchignola
AEROPORTO DI CIAMPINO

d

TELESTERION
(E-92)
Amaroúsion
Iráklion
Petroúpolis
Néa Liósia
Néa Ioínia
Paralía Aspropírgos
ÓROS
Néa Khalkidhón
Néa Filadhélfia
Kólpos Elevsínos
Dháfni
MONÍ DHAFNÍ
Áyioi Anáryiroi
Peristérion
Khalándrion
Skaramagás
Khaidhárion
Psikhikón
Áyia Varvára
AIGÁLEOS ATTIKÍ PIRAIEVS
Aiyáleo
ATHENS (Athínai)
Kholargós
Koridhallós
STATHMÓS LARISA
ETHNIKÓN MOUSÍON
ATHINÍSIN PANEPISTÍMION
Párama
Keratsínion
Níkaia
Áyios Ioánnis Renpis
THESEION
OLYMPEION
ACROPOLIS
Zográfos
Tavros
Péráma
Moskháton
Kallithéa
STADION
Kaisarianí
MONÍ KAISARIANÍ
Piraeus (Piraiévs)
Néon Fáliron
Víron
Néa Smírni
Ímittos
Néa Fáliron
Áyios Dhimítrios
Évzonos 1026
Dhrapetsóna
PSITTÁLIA
Órmos Fálirou
Palaión Fáliron
Ilioúpolis
Saronikós Kólpos
IMITTÓS ÓROS
Kalamákion
Aryiroúpolis
TO IRÁKLION, RÓDHOS, MÍTILINI

e

Ober-kirchbach
WIENERWALD
Weidling
Weidlingbach
Weidlinger Bach
542
484 Kahlenberg
Gross/edlersdorf
NIEDER-ÖSTERREICH
Aderklaa
Scheiblingstein
Hermannskogel
Jedlesee
Floridsdorf
Leopoldau
Russbach
Süssenbrunn
WIEN
Neustift am Walde
Nüssdorf
Grinzing
Donaufeld
Breitenlee
Untermauerbach
Pötzleinsdorf
Sievering
FLORIDSDORFER BRÜCKE
DONAUTURM
Kagran
Döbling
449
POTZLEINSDORFER PARK
FRANZ-JOSEFS-BAHNHOF
Brigittenau
Neukagran
Donaustadt
Neuwaldegg
Dornbach
Währing
REICHSBRÜCKE
Hirschstetten
Purkersdorf
Hernals
UNIVERSITÄT WIEN
Kaisermühlen
Stadlau
FLUGPLATZ ASPERN
Hadersdorf
Mariabrunn
Ottakring
PARLAMENT
STEPHANS-DOM
TRABRENNBAHN
Aspern
Hütteldorf
STADTHALLE WESTBAHNHOF
HOFBURG
PRATER
Essling
Weidlingau
Penzing
STADION
Ober Sankt Veit
Wien
BELVEDERE
Gross-Enzersdorf
VIENNA (Wien)
SÜDBAHNHOF
SCHÖNBRUNN
HEERES-MUSEUM
Simmering
Lainzer Tiergarten
Hietzing
Meidling
Favoriten
LOBAU
Lanz
RENNPLATZ
Mühlleiten
Hetzendorf
251
Speising
WIENER BERG
Laaerberg
Kalksburg
Mauer
Atzgersdorf
Inzersdorf
Mannsworth
Laab im Walde
Neu-Erlaa
Roth-neusiedl
ZENTRAL-FRIEDHOF
Oberlaa
Schwechat
Kaltenleutgeben

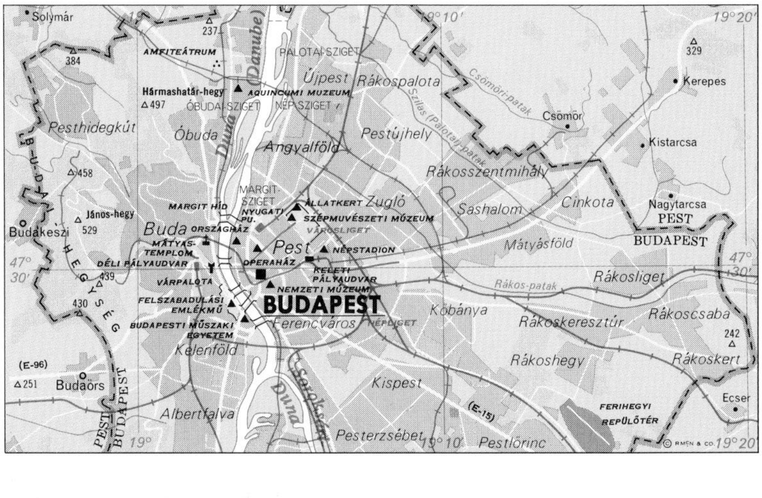

f

Alibey
Boyacıköy
Kanlıca
128
Kâğıthane
Rumelihisarı
RUMELIHISARI
Anadoluhisarı
ROBERT COLLEGE
EMALI BEND
Küçükköy
Alibeyköy
Bebek
Kandilli
İstanbul Boğazı
Atışalan
Şişli
Kuruçeşme
Vaniköy
İstanbul Bogazı
Eyüp
Hasköy
Ortaköy
Çengelköy
Eseler
Beyoğlu
Beşiktaş
Beylerbeyi
Güngören
Topkapı
Kasımpaşa
DOLMABAHÇE SARAY
GALATA KULESİ
GALATA
GALATA KÖPRÜSÜ
Kısıklı
Üsküdar
İSTANBUL
YENİ CAMİİ
BEYAZIT
SÜLEYMANİYE CAMİİ
ATATÜRK
İSTANBUL ÜNİVERSİTESİ
TOPKAPI MÜZESİ
AYASOFYA CAMİİ
FATİH
HEYKELİ
Yenikapı
Samatya
AHMET CAMİİ
Kadıköy
Fenerbahçe
FENERBAHÇE STADYUMU
YEDIKULE SURLARI
Yedikule
Zeytinburnu
Kızıltoprak
Yeniköy
Bakırköy
İSTANBUL (YEŞİLKÖY) HAVA ALANI
Marmara Denizi (Sea of Marmara)
Erenköy
Bostancı

g

Solymár
237
AMFITEÁTRUM
PALOTA-SZIGET
384
Újpest
Rákospalota
329
Kerepes
Hármashatár-hegy
497
AQUINCUMI MUZEUM
ÓBUDAI-SZIGET
NÉP-SZIGET
Csömör
Pesthidegkút
ÓBUDA
Pestújhely
Kistarcsa
Duna
Angyalföld
Rákosszentmihály
458
Buda-keszi
Zugló
Sashalom
Cinkota
Nagytarcsa
János-hegy
529
MARGIT-SZIGET
ÁLLATKERT
SZÉPMŰVÉSZETI MÚZEUM
MÁTYÁSFÖLD
PEST
BUDAPEST
MARGIT HÍD
NYUGAT
VÁROSLIGET
Rákosliget
Buda
ORSZÁGHÁZ
MÁTYÁS-TEMPLOM
Pest
OPERAHÁZ
NÉPSTADION
Kőbánya
Rákoscsaba
439
VÁRPALOTA
KELETI
PÁLYAUDVAR
NEMZETI MÚZEUM
Rákoskeresztúr
430
FELSZABADULÁSI EMLÉKMŰ
DÉLI PÁLYAUDVAR
FELSZABADULÁSI EMLÉKMŰ
BUDAPESTI MŰSZAKI EGYETEM
Ferencváros
Kelenföld
251
Budaörs
Albertfalva
(E-96)
Kispest
(E-15)
Pesterzsébet
FERIHEGYI REPÜLŐTÉR
Pestlőrinc
Ecser
242

Scale 1:1,300,000; one inch to 4.7 miles
10 Miles
10 Kilometers

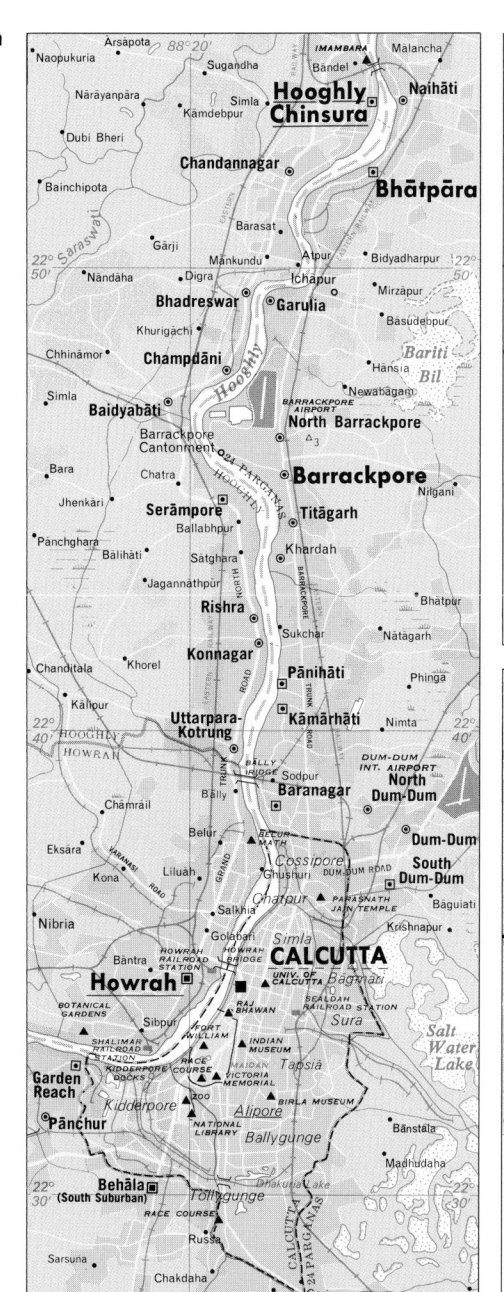

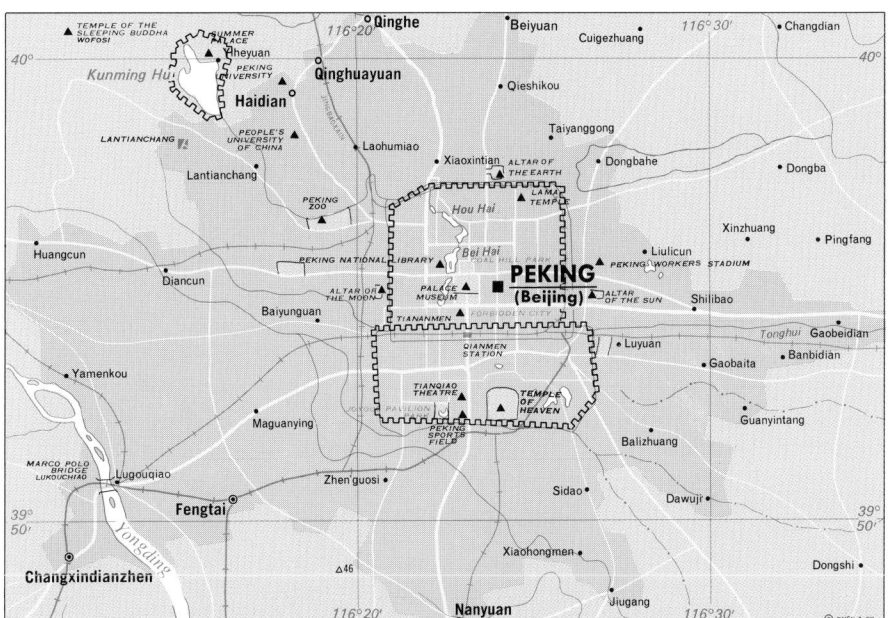

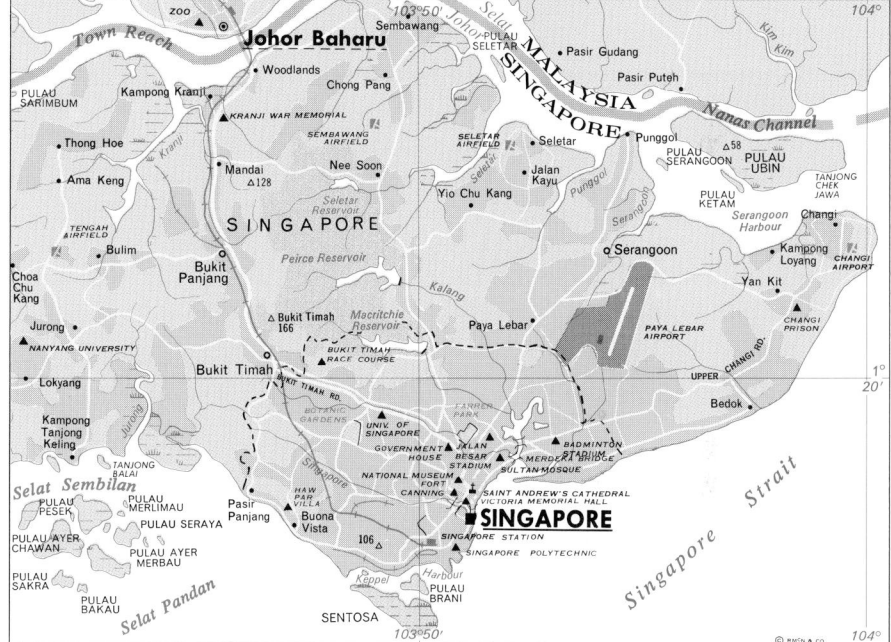

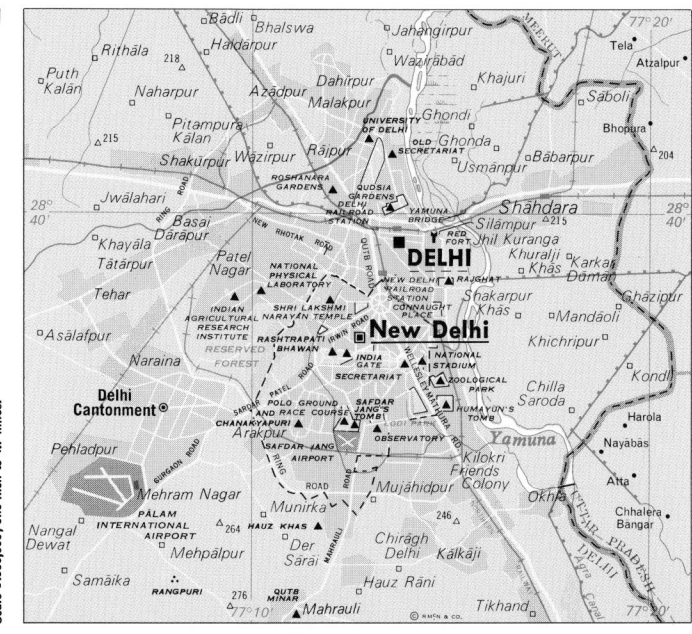

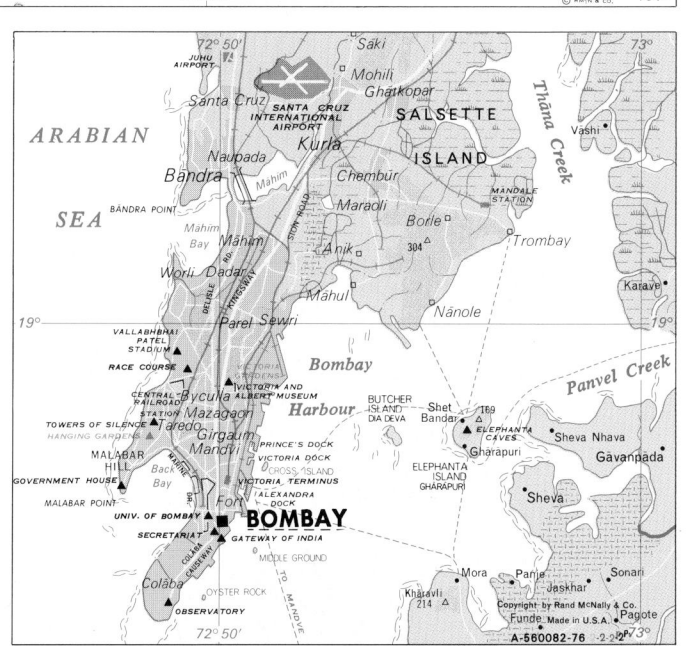

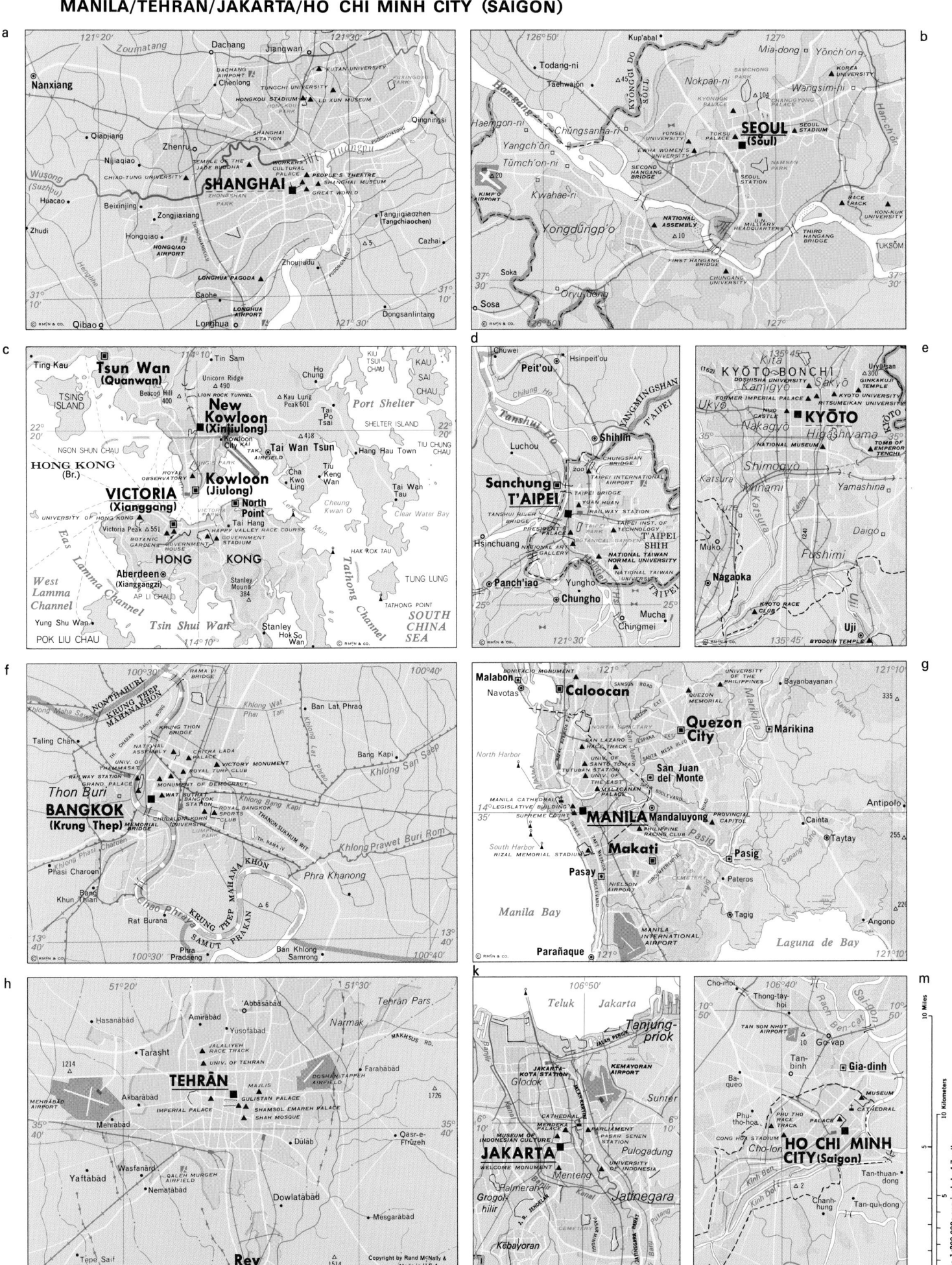

Scale 1:300,000; one inch to 4.7 miles.

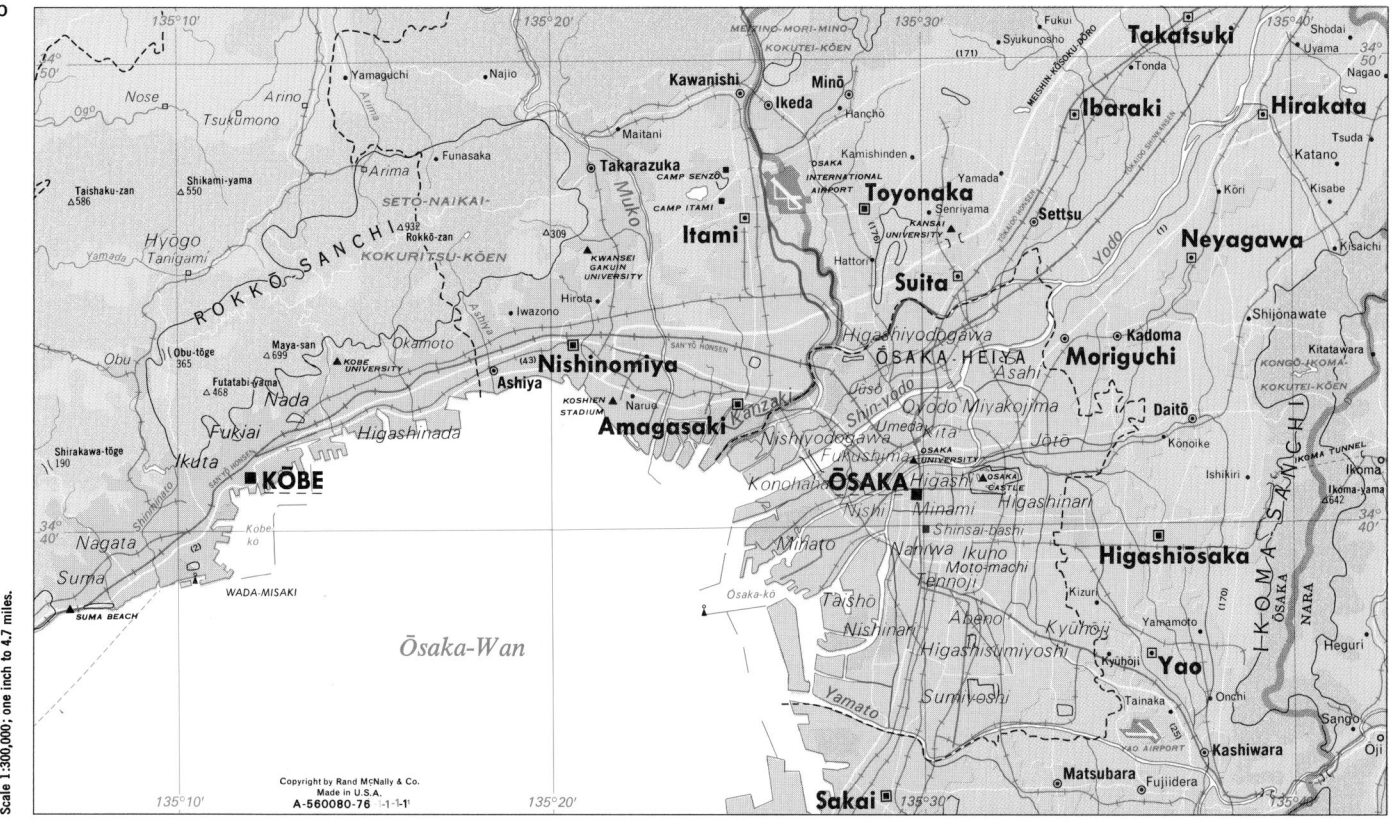

a

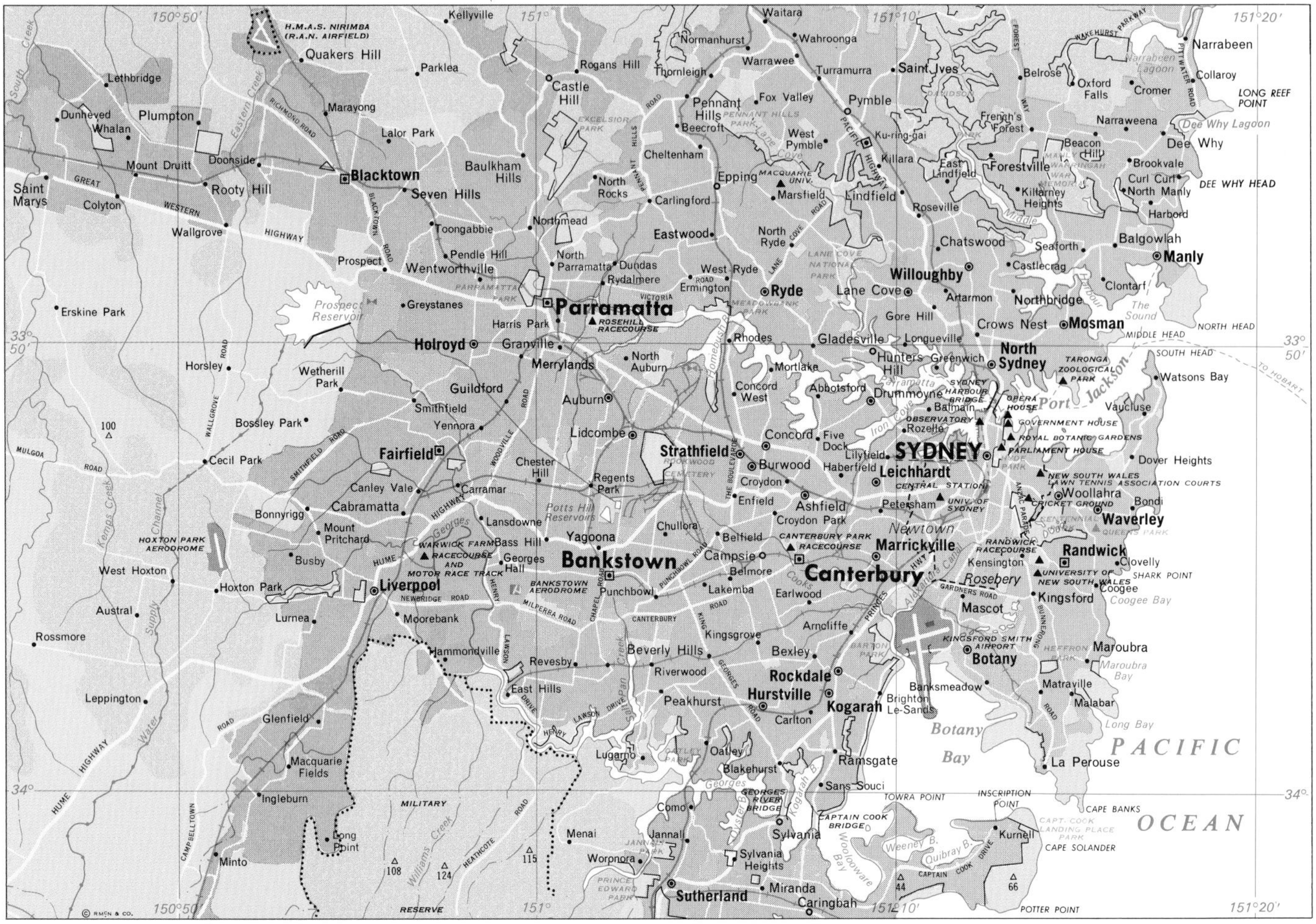

150°50'   150°50'   151°   151°10'   151°20'

H.M.A.S. NIRIMBA (R.A.N. AIRFIELD)
Quakers Hill
Kellyville
Rogans Hill
Waitara
Normanhurst
Wahroonga
Narrabeen
Collaroy
LONG REEF POINT
Lethbridge
Parklea
Castle Hill
Thornleigh
Warrawee
Turramurra
Saint Ives
Belrose
Oxford Falls
Cromer
Dunheved
Whalan
Plumpton
Marayong
Lalor Park
Beecroft
Pennant Hills
Fox Valley
Pymble
Ku-ring-gai
French's Forest
Narraweena
Dee Why
Dee Why Lagoon
Mount Druitt
Doonside
Baulkham Hills
Cheltenham
West Pymble
Epping
Killara
East Lindfield
Forestville
Brookvale
Curl Curl
North Manly
DEE WHY HEAD
Blacktown
Seven Hills
North Rocks
Carlingford
Marsfield
Lindfield
Roseville
Chatswood
Seaforth
Balgowlah
Saint Marys
Colyton
Rooty Hill
Toongabbie
Northmead
North Parramatta
Eastwood
North Ryde
Willoughby
Castlecrag
Manly
Wallgrove
Prospect
Wentworthville
Pendle Hill
Dundas
West Ryde
Ryde
Lane Cove
Artarmon
Northbridge
Clontarf
The Sound
NORTH HEAD
Erskine Park
Greystanes
Harris Park
Rydalmere
Ermington
Rhodes
Gladesville
Longueville
Crows Nest
Mosman
Prospect Reservoir
Parramatta
Holroyd
Granville
Merrylands
North Auburn
Concord West
Hunters Hill
Greenwich
North Sydney
TARONGA ZOOLOGICAL PARK
MIDDLE HEAD
Horsley
Wetherill Park
Guildford
Smithfield
Yennora
Auburn
Lidcombe
Concord
Five Dock
Abbotsford
Drummoyne
Balmain
SYDNEY HARBOUR BRIDGE
OPERA HOUSE
Watsons Bay
SOUTH HEAD
TO HOBART
Fairfield
Chester Hill
Regents Park
Rozelle
OBSERVATORY
GOVERNMENT HOUSE
ROYAL BOTANIC GARDENS
PARLIAMENT HOUSE
SYDNEY
Dover Heights
Bossley Park
Cecil Park
Canley Vale
Carramar
Lansdowne
Yagoona
Belmore
Croydon
Enfield
Ashfield
Haberfield
Leichhardt
UNIV. OF SYDNEY
Petersham
Newtown
NEW SOUTH WALES LAWN TENNIS ASSOCIATION COURTS
SYDNEY CRICKET GROUND
Woollahra
Bondi
Bonnyrigg
Busby
Mount Pritchard
Bass Hill
WARWICK FARM RACECOURSE AND MOTOR RACE TRACK
Georges Hall
BANKSTOWN AERODROME
Punchbowl
Belfield
Campsie
CANTERBURY PARK RACECOURSE
Marrickville
Waverley
West Hoxton
Liverpool
Moorebank
Lurnea
Bankstown
Lakemba
Earlwood
Arncliffe
RANDWICK RACECOURSE
UNIVERSITY OF NEW SOUTH WALES
Randwick
Coogee
Clovelly
SHARK POINT
Coogee Bay
Austral
Rossmore
Hammondville
Revesby
Beverly Hills
Kingsgrove
Bexley
Kingsford
Mascot
Rosebery
KINGSFORD SMITH AIRPORT
Maroubra
Maroubra Bay
Leppington
Glenfield
East Hills
Peakhurst
Riverwood
Carlton
Rockdale
Hurstville
Kogarah
Brighton Le-Sands
Botany
Banksmeadow
Matraville
Malabar
Long Bay
Macquarie Fields
Ingleburn
MILITARY
Como
Lugarno
Blakehurst
Oatley
Ramsgate
Sans Souci
Botany Bay
La Perouse
PACIFIC
Minto
108   124   115
Menai
Jannali
Sylvania
GEORGES RIVER BRIDGE
CAPTAIN COOK BRIDGE
Kurnell
CAPE BANKS
CAPT. COOK LANDING PLACE PARK
CAPE SOLANDER
OCEAN
PRINCE EDWARD PARK
Sutherland
Sylvania Heights
Worpnora
Miranda
Caringbah
TOWRA POINT
INSCRIPTION POINT
44   66
POTTER POINT
RESERVE
© RMcN & Co.
A-590056-76 -2-2-2'

33°50'   33°50'
34°   34°

b

144°50'   145°   145°10'   145°20'

Broadmeadows
Thomastown
Diamond Creek
Little Sugarloaf
271
Sydenham
CALDER HIGHWAY
TULLAMARINE INTERNATIONAL AIRPORT
Tullamarine
Campbellfield
143
Kangaroo Ground
237
Mount Lofty
Keilor
Jacana
Glenroy
Keon Park
Bundoora
Greensborough
Research
Airport West
Oak Park
Hadfield
Reservoir
Watsonia
Mont Park
Montmorency
Saint Albans
Merlynston
Pascoe Vale
Fawkner
Macleod
Eltham
Lower Plenty
CLIFFORD PARK
Wonga Park
North Essendon
ESSENDON AIRPORT
Coburg
Regent
Preston
West Heidelberg
Rosanna
FELTHAM LOWER PARK
Warrandyte
VICTORIA STATE CAR CLUB RACE CIRCUIT
Avondale Heights
Essendon
Brunswick
Thornbury
Heidelberg
Ivanhoe
Templestowe
Warrandyte South
Black Springs
205
Lilydale
Albion
Maribyrnong
Braybrook
MOONEE VALLEY RACECOURSE
North Fitzroy
Northcote
Park Orchards
Black Springs Hill
Deer Park
Maidstone
FLEMINGTON RACECOURSE
UNIV. OF MELBOURNE
ZOO
Fitzroy
Collingwood
North Balwyn
Doncaster
Ringwood North
Mooroolbark
Sunshine
Footscray
MELBOURNE
STATE PARLIAMENT HOUSE
CARLTON GARDENS
Richmond
Kew
Hawthorn
Balwyn
North Box Hill
Doncaster East
Croydon
Kilsyth
Yarraville
Spotswood
MELBOURNE CRICKET GROUND
GOVERNMENT HOUSE
Camberwell
Canterbury
Box Hill
Mitcham
Ringwood
Montrose
Kingsville
Newport
Paisley
Port Melbourne
ROYAL BOTANIC GARDENS
VICTORIAN LAWN TENNIS ASSOCIATION COURTS
Kooyong
Toorak
Burwood
Nunawading
Forest Hill
Heathmont
Bayswater North
Mount Dandenong
633
Altona North
Galvin
Seaholme
South Melbourne
Prahran
Malvern
Ashburton
East Burwood
Vermont
Wantirna
Bayswater
The Basin
Olinda
Laverton
Altona
POINT GELLIBRAND
Williamstown
Hobsons Bay
Saint Kilda
Caulfield
Mount Waverley
Holmesglen
Syndal
Wantirna South
Boronia
One Tree Hill
Sassafras
502
Elwood
CAULFIELD RACE COURSE
Glenhuntly
Chadstone
Glen Waverley
Wheelers Hill
Scoresby
Knox
Upper Ferntree Gully
Perny Creek
11
POINT COOK
Point Cook
Brighton
Ormond
Bentleigh
Notting Hill
MONASH UNIVERSITY
Mulgrave
Rowville
Upwey
Belgrave
POINT COOK ROYAL AUSTRALIAN AIR FORCE STATION
Moorabbin
Hampton
Oakleigh
Oakleigh South
Clayton
Lysterfield
Mount Morton
276
Sandringham
MOORABBIN AIRPORT
Heatherton
SANDOWN PARK RACECOURSE
Springvale
Noble Park
Harrisfield
Lysterfield Hills
225
Sugarloaf Hill
184
Black Rock
Half Moon Bay
Cheltenham
Dingley
Springvale South
Dandenong
Narre Warren North
Beaumaris
Beaumaris Bay
RICKETTS POINT
Braeside
Keysborough
Hallam
Harkaway
Doveton
Mordialloc
Port Phillip Bay

37°50'   37°50'
38°   38°

Copyright by Rand McNally & Co.
Made in U.S.A.

Scale 1-300,000: one inch to 4.7 miles.
10 Miles
10 Kilometers

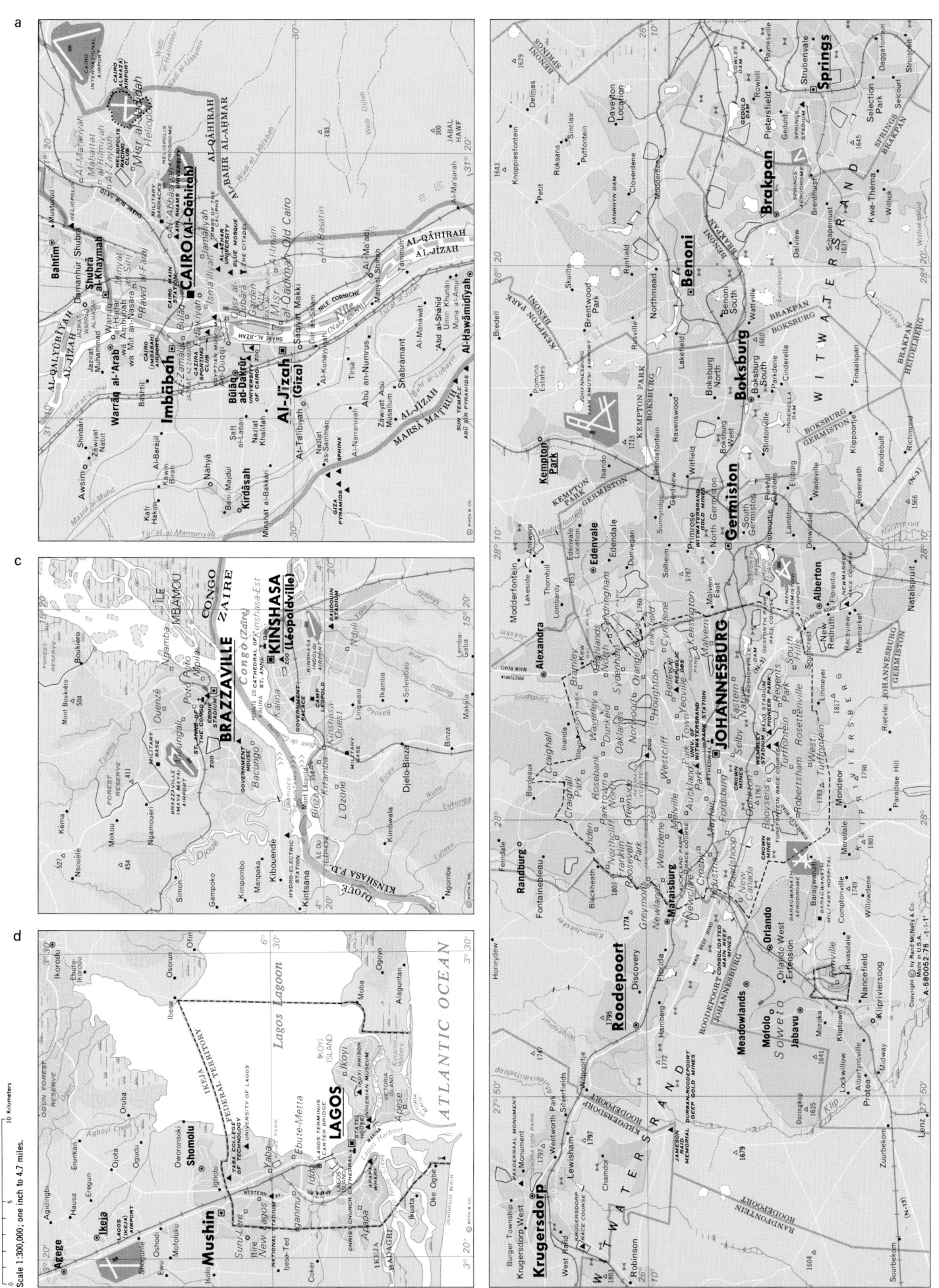

regional section

physical-political reference maps

Basic continental and regional coverage of the world's land areas is provided by the following section of physical-political reference maps. The section falls into a continental arrangement: North America, South America, Europe, Asia, Australia, and Africa. (Introducing each regional reference-map section are basic thematic maps and the environment maps.)

To aid the student in acquiring concepts of the relative sizes of continents and of some of the countries and regions, uniform scales for comparable areas were used so far as possible. Continental maps are at a uniform scale of 1:40,000,000. In addition, most of the world is covered by a series of regional maps at scales of 1:16,000,000 and 1:12,000,000.

Maps at 1:10,000,000 provide even greater detail for parts of Europe, Africa, and Southeast Asia. The United States, parts of Canada, and much of Europe and the Soviet Union are mapped at 1:4,000,000. Seventy-six urbanized areas are shown at 1:1,000,000. The new, separate metropolitan-area section contains larger-scale maps of selected urban areas.

Many of the symbols used are self-explanatory. A complete legend below provides a key to the symbols on the reference maps in this atlas.

General elevation above sea level is shown by layer tints for altitudinal zones, each of which has a different hue and is defined by a generalized contour line. A legend is given on each map, reflecting this color gradation.

The surface configuration is represented by hill-shading, which gives the three-dimensional impression of landforms. This terrain representation is superimposed on the layer tints to convey a realistic and readily visualized impression of the surface. The combination of altitudinal tints and hill-shading best shows elevation, relief, steepness of slope, and ruggedness of terrain.

If the world used one alphabet and one language, no particular difficulty would arise in understanding place-names. However, some of the people of the world, the Chinese and the Japanese, for example, use nonalphabetic languages. Their symbols are transliterated into the Roman alphabet. In this atlas a "local-name" policy generally was used for naming cities and towns and all local topographic and water features. However, for a few major cities the Anglicized name was preferred and the local name given in parentheses, for instance, Moscow (*Moskva*), Vienna (*Wien*), Cologne (*Köln*). In countries where more than one official language is used, a name is in the dominant local language. The generic parts of local names for topographic and water features are self-explanatory in many cases because of the associated map symbols or type styles. A complete list of foreign generic names is given in the Glossary, on page 248.

Place-names on the reference maps are listed in the Pronouncing Index, which is a distinctive feature of *Goode's World Atlas*.

Physical-Political Reference Map Legend

Cultural Features

Political Boundaries

— International (over water) (Demarcated, Undemarcated, and Administrative)

— Disputed de facto

— Claim Boundary

— Indefinite or Undefined

— Secondary, State, Provincial, etc. (over water)

Parks, Indian Reservations

City Limits — Urbanized Areas

□ Neighborhoods, Sections of City

Populated Places

⊙ 1,000,000 and over

◎ 250,000 to 1,000,000

⊙ 100,000 to 250,000

• 25,000 to 100,000

○ 0 to 25,000

TŌKYŌ National Capitals

Boise Secondary Capitals

Note: On maps at 1:20,000,000 and smaller the town symbols do not follow the specific population classification shown above. On all maps, type size indicates the relative importance of the city.

Transportation

— Railroads

— Railroads On 1:1,000,000 scale maps

---------- Railroad Ferries

Roads

— Major On 1:1,000,000 scale maps
— Other

— Major On 1:4,000,000 scale maps
— Other

— On other scale maps

.... Caravan Routes

✈ Airports

Other Cultural Features

— Dams

+++++++ Pipelines

▲ Points of Interest

∴ Ruins

Land Features

△ Peaks, Spot Heights

= Passes

Sand

Contours

Water Features

Lakes and Reservoirs

Fresh Water

Fresh Water: Intermittent

Salt Water

Salt Water: Intermittent

Other Water Features

Salt Basins, Flats

Swamps

Ice Caps and Glaciers

Rivers

Intermittent Rivers

Aqueducts and Canals

Ship Channels

Falls

Rapids

Springs

△ Water Depths

Fishing Banks

Sand Bars

Reefs

environment maps

The environment-map series shows the general nature of the environment, whether natural or modified by man. The appearance and/or general activity which characterize an area were the conditions for its being classified in one of the map categories. Inclusion in a category was determined largely by the percent of the area covered by urban development, crops (including pasture), trees, or grass. On these small-scale maps, no attempt was made to depict specific crops or the productivity of the area.

Ten major environments were depicted and the categories identified and described in the legend below. The colors and patterns for each category were chosen to illustrate the results of man's activity. Hill shading was used to show land configuration. Together, these design elements create a visual impression of the surface environment.

Naturally, when mapping any distribution it is necessary to limit the number of categories. Therefore, some gradations of meaning exist within the limits of the chosen categories. For example, the grassland, grazing-land category identifies the lush pampas of Argentina and the savanna of Africa as well as the steppes of the Soviet Union. Furthermore, in areas of cropland certain enclaves which might not be defined as cropland are included within the boundary. Tracts such as these, through the process of generalization were included within the boundary of

the dominant environment surrounding them. Finally, it should be pointed out that boundaries on these maps, as on all maps, are never absolute but mark the center of transitional zones between categories.

Actual urban shapes were shown where metropolitan areas are of a large areal extent. A red dot indicates concentrated urbanized development where actual shapes would be indistinguishable at the map scale. Black dots were used to locate selected places important as locational reference points.

From these maps one may make comprehensive observations about the extent and distribution of the major world environments. For example, the urban areas of the world are limited in extent, although over 40 percent of the world's population lives in these areas. Together, the categories of cropland and cropland associated with woodland or grazing land apply to relatively small portions of the earth's surface. Conversely, vast areas of each continent show man's limited influence on the natural environment. The barren lands, wasteland, and tundra, the sparse grass and steppe land, and the tropical rain forests are notable in this respect.

Use of the environment-series maps with the world and continental thematic maps of population, landforms, transportation, and gross national product, for instance, allows further insights into the nature of the world's major environments.

Environment Map Legend

URBAN
Major areas of contiguous residential, commercial, and industrial development.

FOREST, WOODLAND
Extensive wooded areas with little or no cropland.

CROPLAND
Cultivated land predominates (includes pasture, irrigated land, and land in crop rotation).

SWAMP, MARSHLAND
Extensive wetland areas (includes mangroves).

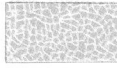
CROPLAND AND WOODLAND
Cultivated land interrupted by small wooded areas.

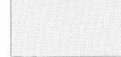
TUNDRA
Areas of lichen, shrubs, small trees, and wetland.

CROPLAND AND GRAZING LAND
Cultivated land with grassland and rangeland.

SHRUB, SPARSE GRASS;
WASTELAND
Desert shrub and short grass, growing singly or in patches. Wasteland includes sand, salt flats, etc. (Extensive wastelands shown by pattern).

GRASSLAND, GRAZING LAND
Extensive grassland and rangeland with little or no cropland.

BARREN LAND
Icefields, glaciers, permanent snow, with exposed rock.

· OASIS
Important small areas of cultivation within grassland or wasteland.

· Selected cities as points of reference.

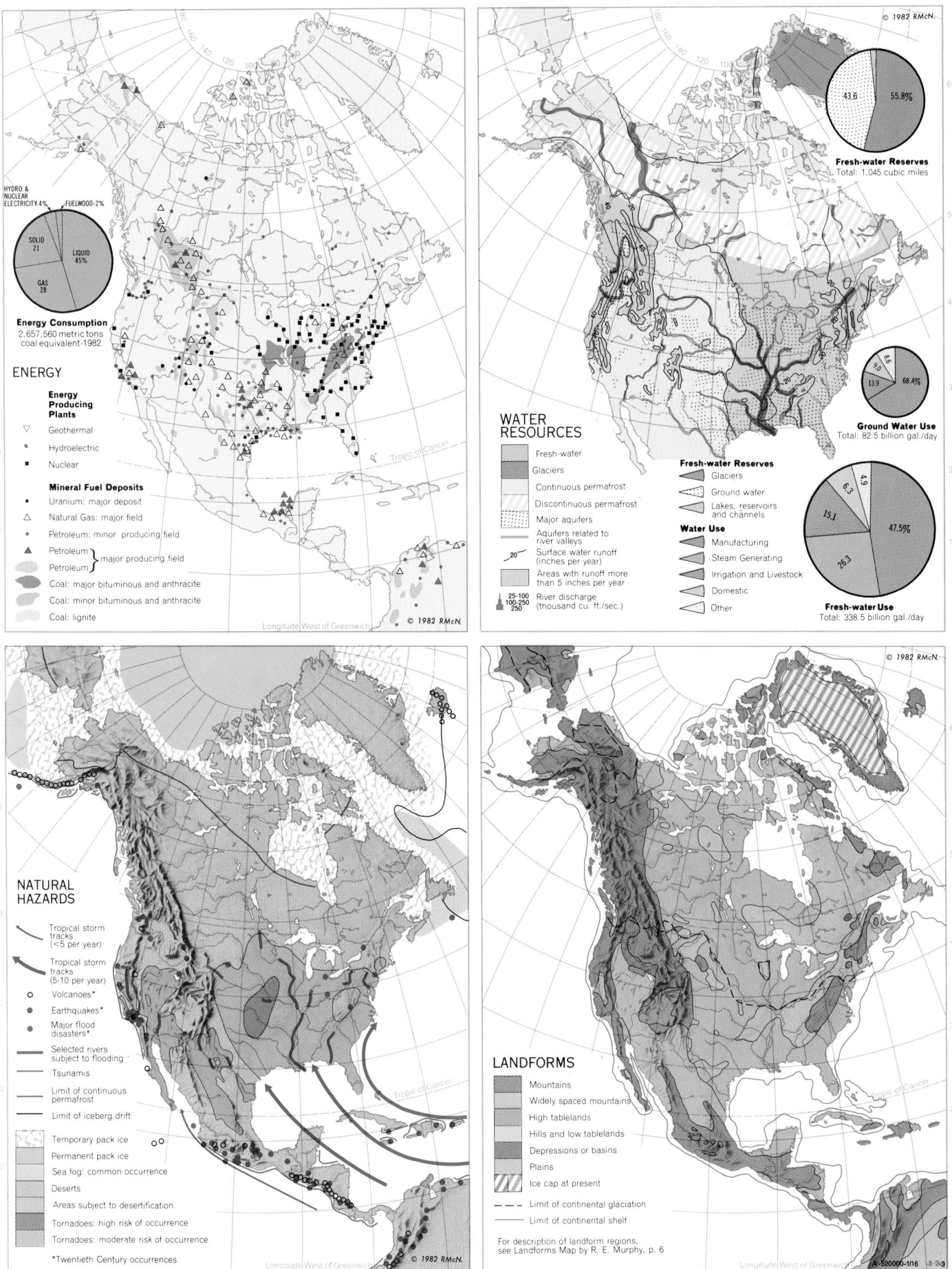

ENERGY

Energy Consumption
2,657,560 metric tons
coal equivalent-1982

HYDRO. & NUCLEAR ELECTRICITY–4%
FUELWOOD–2%
SOLID 21
LIQUID 45%
GAS 28

Energy Producing Plants
▽ Geothermal
• Hydroelectric
■ Nuclear

Mineral Fuel Deposits
• Uranium: major deposit
△ Natural Gas: major field
• Petroleum: minor producing field
▲ Petroleum: major producing field
Coal: major bituminous and anthracite
Coal: minor bituminous and anthracite
Coal: lignite

WATER RESOURCES

Fresh-water
Glaciers
Continuous permafrost
Discontinuous permafrost
Major aquifers
Aquifers related to river valleys
Surface water runoff (inches per year)
Areas with runoff more than 5 inches per year
25-100 / 100-250 / 250 River discharge (thousand cu. ft./sec.)

Fresh-water Reserves
Glaciers
Ground water
Lakes, reservoirs and channels

Water Use
Manufacturing
Steam Generating
Irrigation and Livestock
Domestic
Other

Fresh-water Reserves
Total: 1,045 cubic miles
43.6 55.8%

Ground Water Use
Total: 82.5 billion gal./day
8.6 9.0 13.9 68.4%

Fresh-water Use
Total: 338.5 billion gal./day
4.9 6.3 15.1 26.3 47.5%

NATURAL HAZARDS

Tropical storm tracks (<5 per year)
Tropical storm tracks (5-10 per year)
○ Volcanoes*
• Earthquakes*
• Major flood disasters*
Selected rivers subject to flooding
Tsunamis
Limit of continuous permafrost
Limit of iceberg drift
Temporary pack ice
Permanent pack ice
Sea fog: common occurrence
Deserts
Areas subject to desertification
Tornadoes: high risk of occurrence
Tornadoes: moderate risk of occurrence

*Twentieth Century occurrences

LANDFORMS

Mountains
Widely spaced mountains
High tablelands
Hills and low tablelands
Depressions or basins
Plains
Ice cap at present
Limit of continental glaciation
Limit of continental shelf

For description of landform regions,
see Landforms Map by R. E. Murphy, p. 6

© 1982 RMcN.

A-520000-1n6   3-2-3

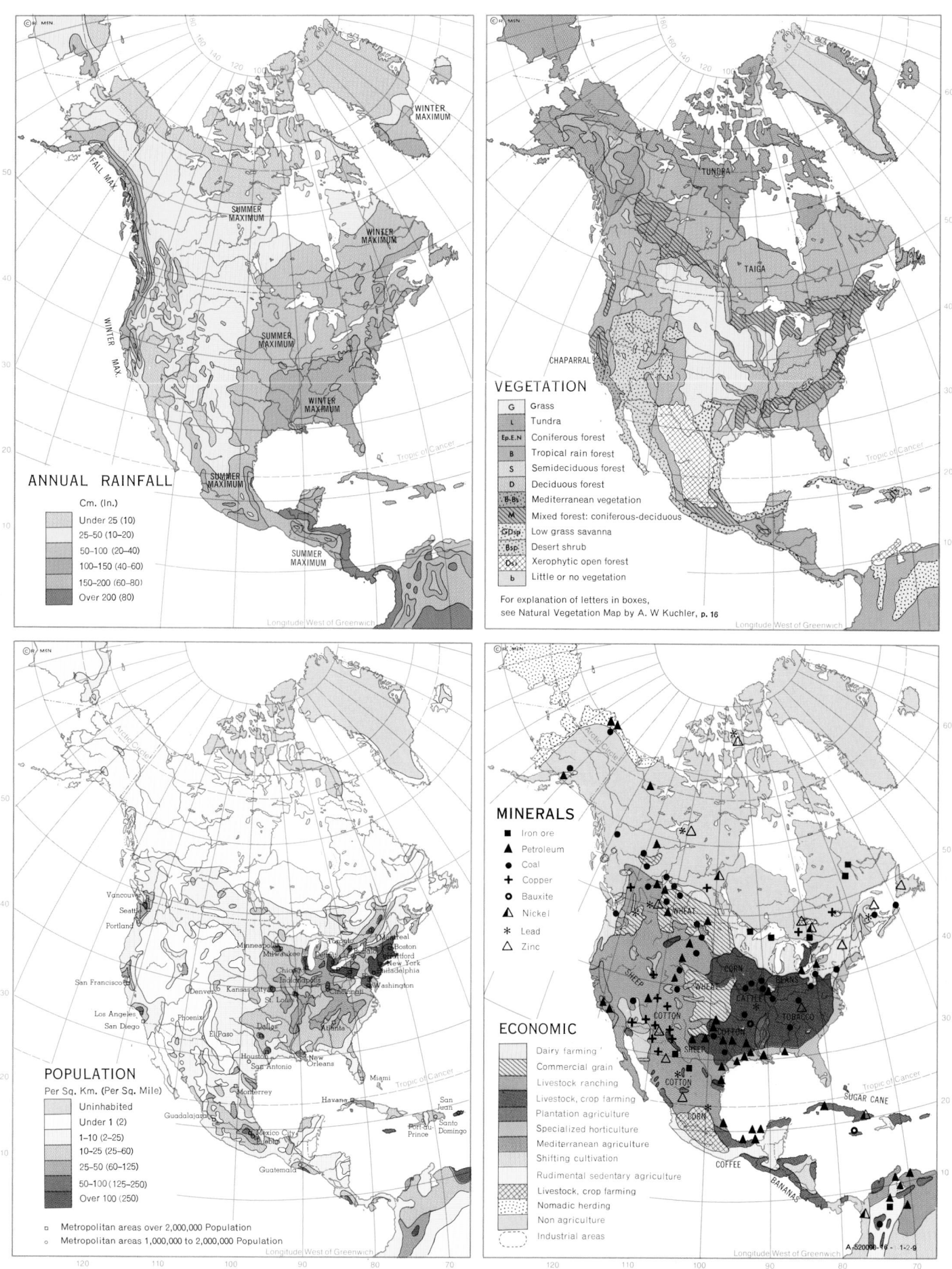

ANNUAL RAINFALL

WINTER MAXIMUM
FALL MAX.
SUMMER MAXIMUM
WINTER MAXIMUM
WINTER MAX.
SUMMER MAXIMUM
SUMMER MAXIMUM
WINTER MAXIMUM
SUMMER MAXIMUM
SUMMER MAXIMUM

Cm. (In.)
Under 25 (10)
25–50 (10–20)
50–100 (20–40)
100–150 (40–60)
150–200 (60–80)
Over 200 (80)

Longitude West of Greenwich

VEGETATION

TUNDRA
TAIGA
CHAPARRAL

G	Grass
L	Tundra
Ep.E.N	Coniferous forest
B	Tropical rain forest
S	Semideciduous forest
D	Deciduous forest
B-Bs	Mediterranean vegetation
M	Mixed forest: coniferous-deciduous
GDsp	Low grass savanna
Bsp	Desert shrub
Oxi	Xerophytic open forest
b	Little or no vegetation

For explanation of letters in boxes,
see Natural Vegetation Map by A. W Kuchler, **p. 16**

Longitude West of Greenwich

POPULATION

Vancouver
Seattle
Portland
Minneapolis
Milwaukee
Toronto
Montreal
Boston
Hartford
New York
Philadelphia
Washington
San Francisco
Denver
Kansas City
St. Louis
Chicago
Indianapolis
Cincinnati
Los Angeles
San Diego
Phoenix
El Paso
Dallas
Atlanta
Houston
San Antonio
New Orleans
Miami
Monterrey
Havana
San Juan
Guadalajara
Mexico City
Puebla
Port-au-Prince
Santo Domingo
Guatemala

Per Sq. Km. (Per Sq. Mile)
Uninhabited
Under 1 (2)
1–10 (2–25)
10–25 (25–60)
25–50 (60–125)
50–100 (125–250)
Over 100 (250)

▫ Metropolitan areas over 2,000,000 Population
○ Metropolitan areas 1,000,000 to 2,000,000 Population

Longitude West of Greenwich

MINERALS
■ Iron ore
▲ Petroleum
● Coal
✛ Copper
○ Bauxite
△ Nickel
✳ Lead
△ Zinc

WHEAT
SHEEP
WHEAT
CORN
BEANS
COTTON
CATTLE
TOBACCO
COTTON
SHEEP
COTTON
CORN
SUGAR CANE
COFFEE
BANANAS

ECONOMIC
Dairy farming
Commercial grain
Livestock ranching
Livestock, crop farming
Plantation agriculture
Specialized horticulture
Mediterranean agriculture
Shifting cultivation
Rudimentary sedentary agriculture
Livestock, crop farming
Nomadic herding
Non agriculture
Industrial areas

Tropic of Cancer

Longitude West of Greenwich
A 520000-16 - 1-2-9

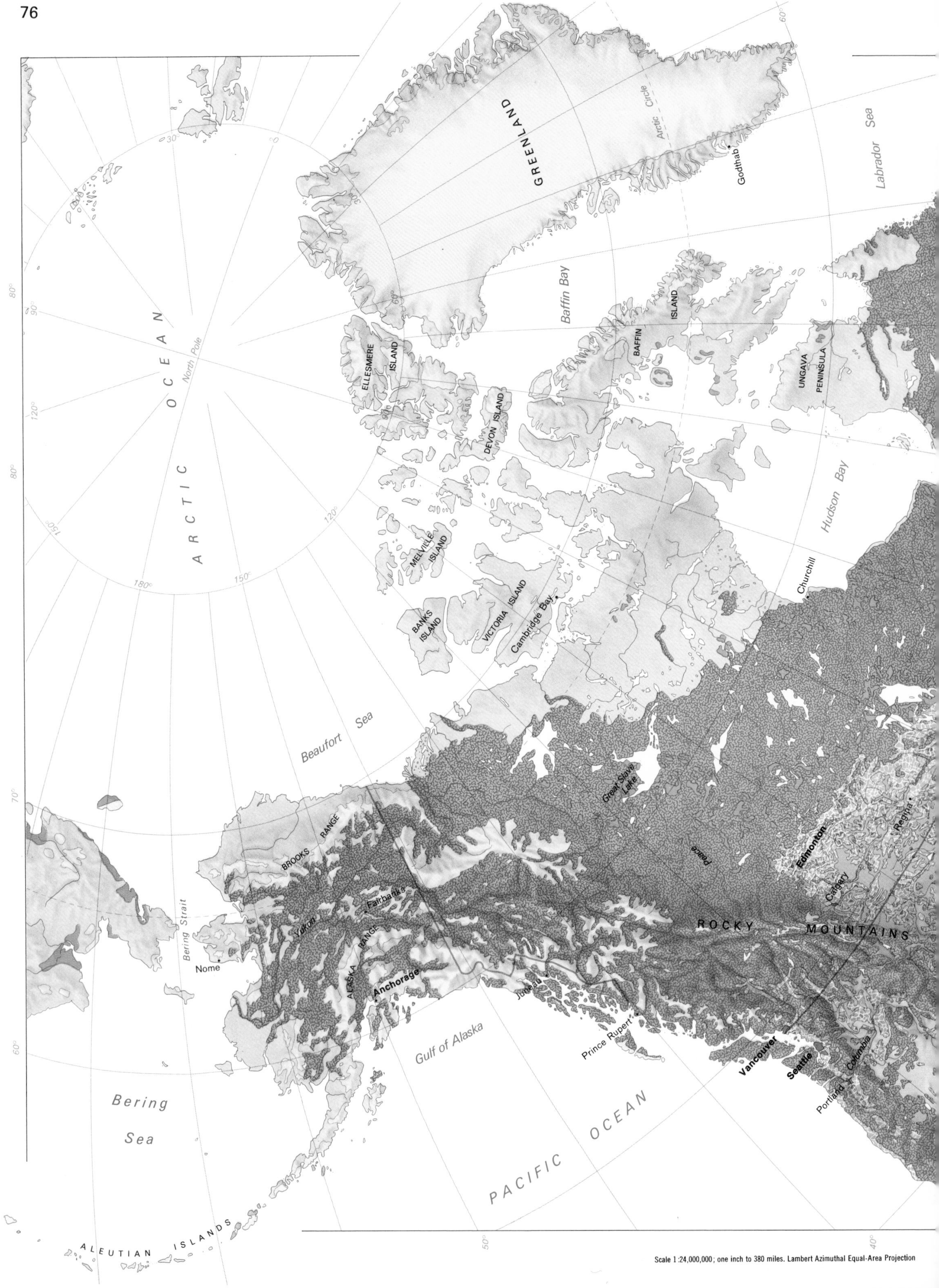
GREENLAND
Arctic Circle
Godthab
Labrador Sea
ARCTIC OCEAN
North Pole
Baffin Bay
BAFFIN ISLAND
ELLESMERE ISLAND
DEVON ISLAND
UNGAVA PENINSULA
Hudson Bay
MELVILLE ISLAND
BANKS ISLAND
VICTORIA ISLAND
Cambridge Bay
Churchill
Beaufort Sea
Great Slave Lake
BROOKS RANGE
Peace
Edmonton
Regina
Calgary
Fairbanks
Yukon
ALASKA RANGE
ROCKY MOUNTAINS
Bering Strait
Nome
Anchorage
Juneau
Prince Rupert
Gulf of Alaska
Vancouver
Seattle
Columbia
Portland
Bering Sea
PACIFIC OCEAN
ALEUTIAN ISLANDS
30°
0°
60°
90°
120°
150°
180°
80°
70°
50°
40°

Scale 1:24,000,000; one inch to 380 miles. Lambert Azimuthal Equal-Area Projection

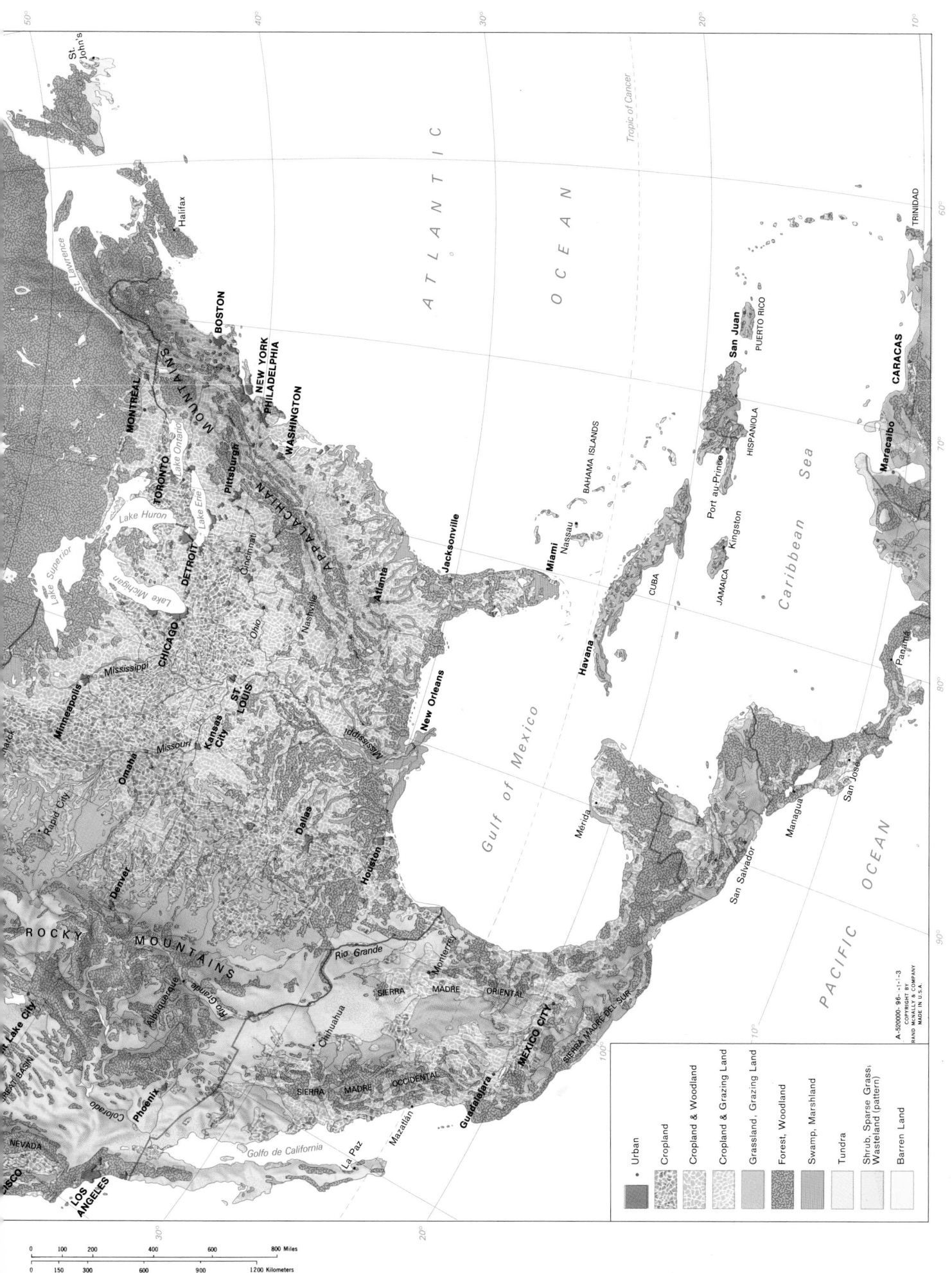

St. John's

Halifax

St. Lawrence

MONTREAL

MOUNTAINS

Lake Ontario

TORONTO

Lake Erie

Pittsburgh

BOSTON

NEW YORK
PHILADELPHIA

WASHINGTON

APPALACHIAN

DETROIT

Lake Huron

Cincinnati

Lake Michigan

Lake Superior

CHICAGO

Nashville

Ohio

Atlanta

Jacksonville

Miami

Nassau

BAHAMA ISLANDS

Havana

CUBA

JAMAICA

Kingston

Port au-Prince

HISPANIOLA

San Juan

PUERTO RICO

TRINIDAD

CARACAS

Maracaibo

Caribbean Sea

Panama

Minneapolis

Mississippi

ST.
LOUIS

Kansas
City

Missouri

Omaha

Rapid City

New Orleans

Dallas

Houston

Gulf of Mexico

Mérida

Managua

San Jose

San Salvador

PACIFIC OCEAN

Denver

ROCKY MOUNTAINS

Rio Grande

Monterrey

SIERRA MADRE ORIENTAL

Chihuahua

Albuquerque

Rio Grande

SIERRA MADRE OCCIDENTAL

MEXICO CITY

SIERRA MADRE DEL SUR

Guadalajara

Mazatlán

La Paz

Golfo de California

Phoenix

Colorado

NEVADA

GREAT BASIN

Salt Lake City

LOS
ANGELES

ATLANTIC

OCEAN

Tropic of Cancer

A-509000-96-1-1-3
COPYRIGHT BY
RAND MCNALLY & COMPANY
MADE IN U.S.A.

Urban
Cropland
Cropland & Woodland
Cropland & Grazing Land
Grassland, Grazing Land
Forest, Woodland
Swamp, Marshland
Tundra
Shrub, Sparse Grass,
Wasteland (pattern)
Barren Land

0   100   200   400   600   800 Miles

0   150   300   600   900   1200 Kilometers

78

PACIFIC
OCEAN

Vancouver

Seattle

Spokane

Portland

R A N G E

C A S C A D E

Columbia

Medford

Boise

SAN
FRANCISCO

Reno

GREAT BASIN

Great Salt
Lake

Salt Lake City

Fresno

S I E R R A

N E V A D A

Las Vegas

LOS ANGELES

San Diego

Colorado

Phoenix

PACIFIC

OCEAN

Hermosillo

Gulf
of
California

S I E R R A

M A D R E

O C C I D E N T A L

Chihuahua

Torreon

R O C K Y

M O U N T A I N S

Calgary

Regina

Billings

Rapid City

Casper

R O C K Y   M O U N T A I N S

Denver

Albuquerque

Amarillo

El Paso

Odessa

Rio Grande

San Antonio

S I E R R A

M A D R E

O R I E N T A L

Rio Grande

Monterrey

Lake Winnipeg

Win

Bismarck

Missouri

Omah

Wichita

Oklahc
City

Red

50°

45°

125°

40°

35°

30°

120°

25°

115°

110°

Scale 1:12,000,000; one inch to 190 miles. Polyconic Projection

	Urban
	Cropland
	Cropland & Woodland
	Cropland & Grazing Land
	Grassland, Grazing Land
	Forest, Woodland
	Swamp, Marshland
	Shrub, Sparse Grass, Wasteland (pattern)
	Barren Land

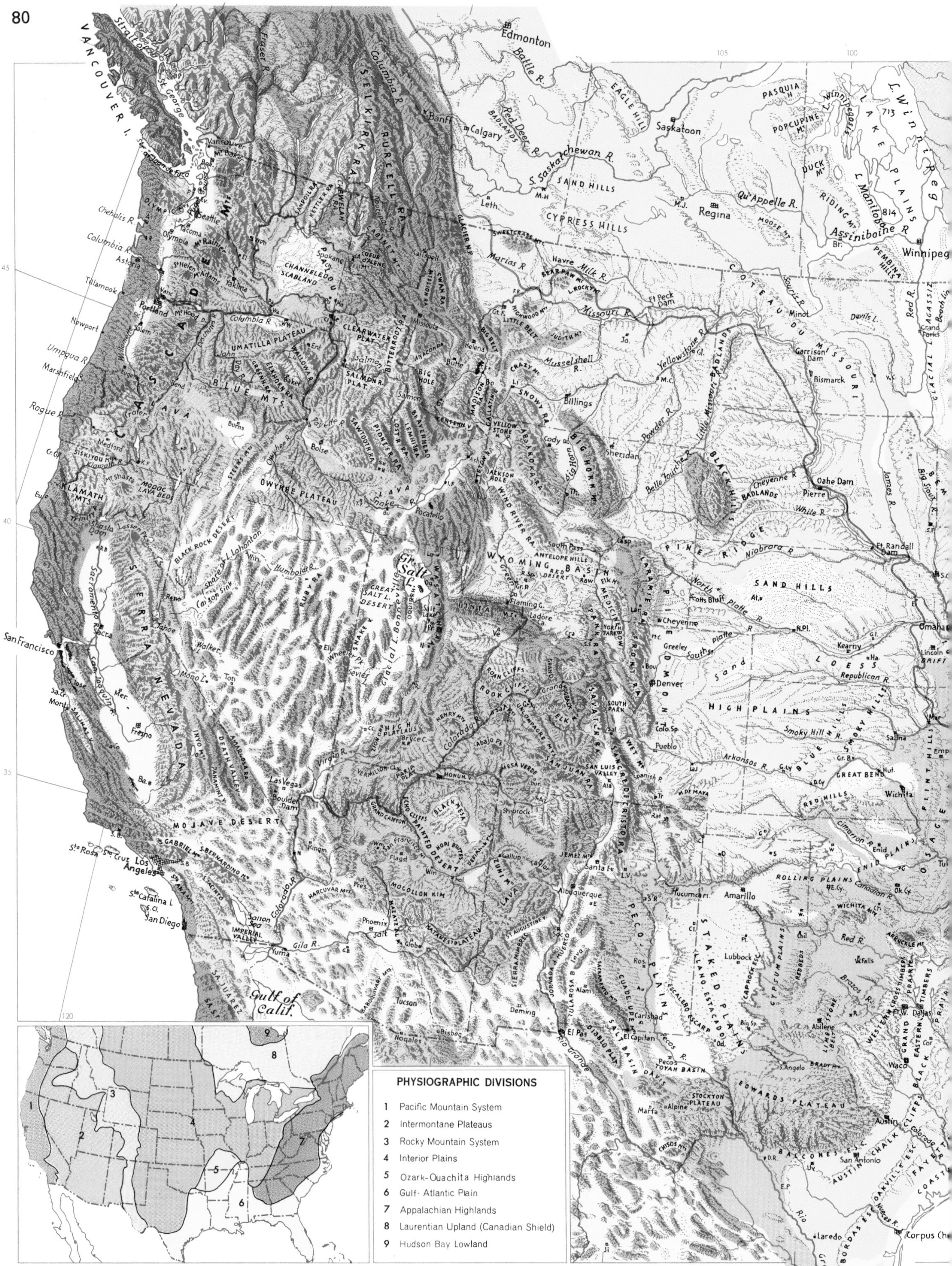

PHYSIOGRAPHIC DIVISIONS

1 Pacific Mountain System
2 Intermontane Plateaus
3 Rocky Mountain System
4 Interior Plains
5 Ozark-Ouachita Highlands
6 Gulf-Atlantic Plain
7 Appalachian Highlands
8 Laurentian Upland (Canadian Shield)
9 Hudson Bay Lowland

Scale 1: 12 000 000; One inch to 190 miles.   POLYCONIC PROJECTION

0 25 50 75 100   200   300   400   500 Miles
0 50 100   200   400   600   800 Kilometers

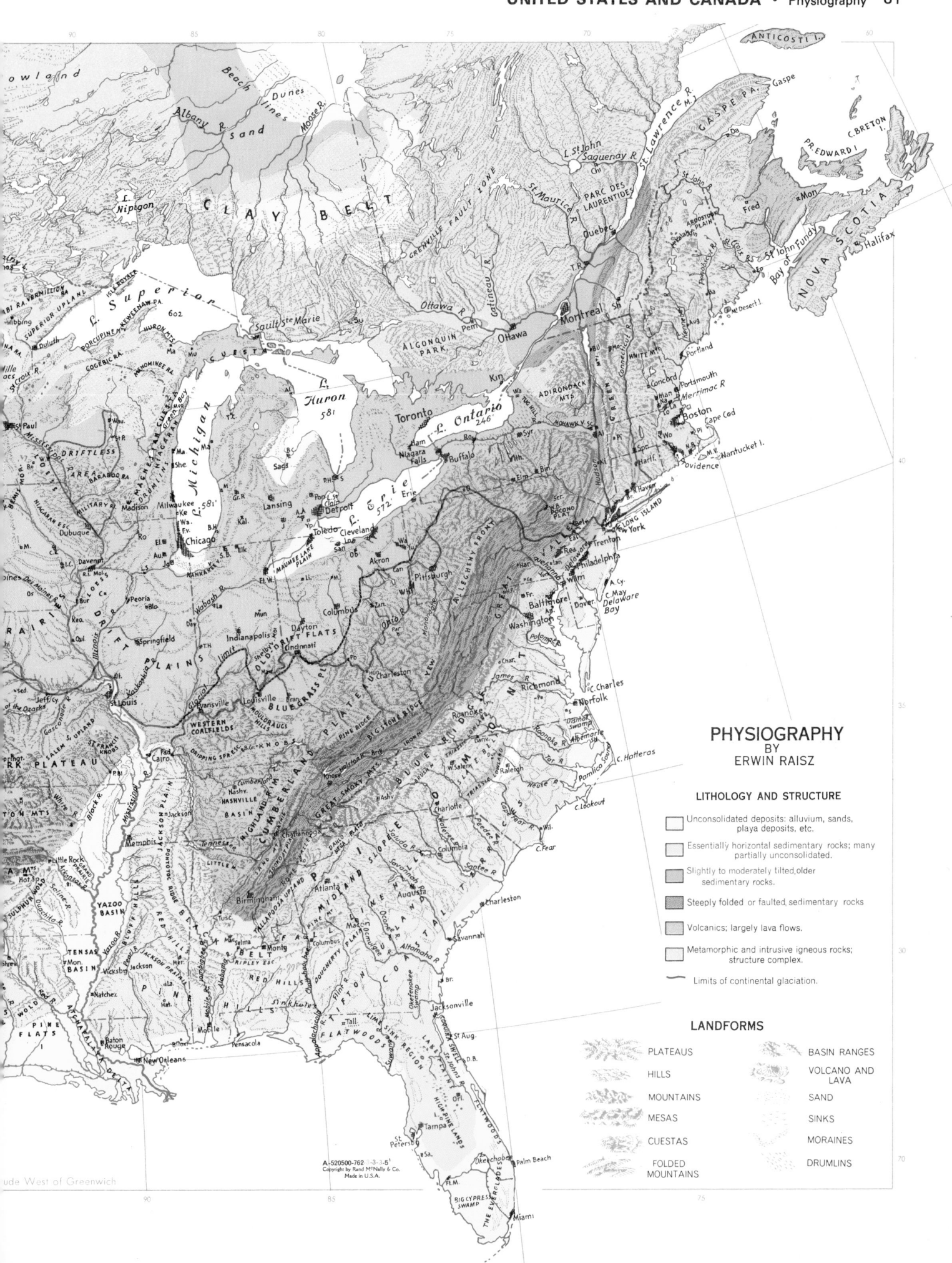

PHYSIOGRAPHY
BY
ERWIN RAISZ

LITHOLOGY AND STRUCTURE

Unconsolidated deposits: alluvium, sands, playa deposits, etc.

Essentially horizontal sedimentary rocks; many partially unconsolidated.

Slightly to moderately tilted, older sedimentary rocks.

Steeply folded or faulted, sedimentary rocks

Volcanics; largely lava flows.

Metamorphic and intrusive igneous rocks; structure complex.

Limits of continental glaciation.

LANDFORMS

PLATEAUS

HILLS

MOUNTAINS

MESAS

CUESTAS

FOLDED MOUNTAINS

BASIN RANGES

VOLCANO AND LAVA

SAND

SINKS

MORAINES

DRUMLINS

A-520500-762
Copyright by Rand McNally & Co.
Made in U.S.A.

Longitude West of Greenwich

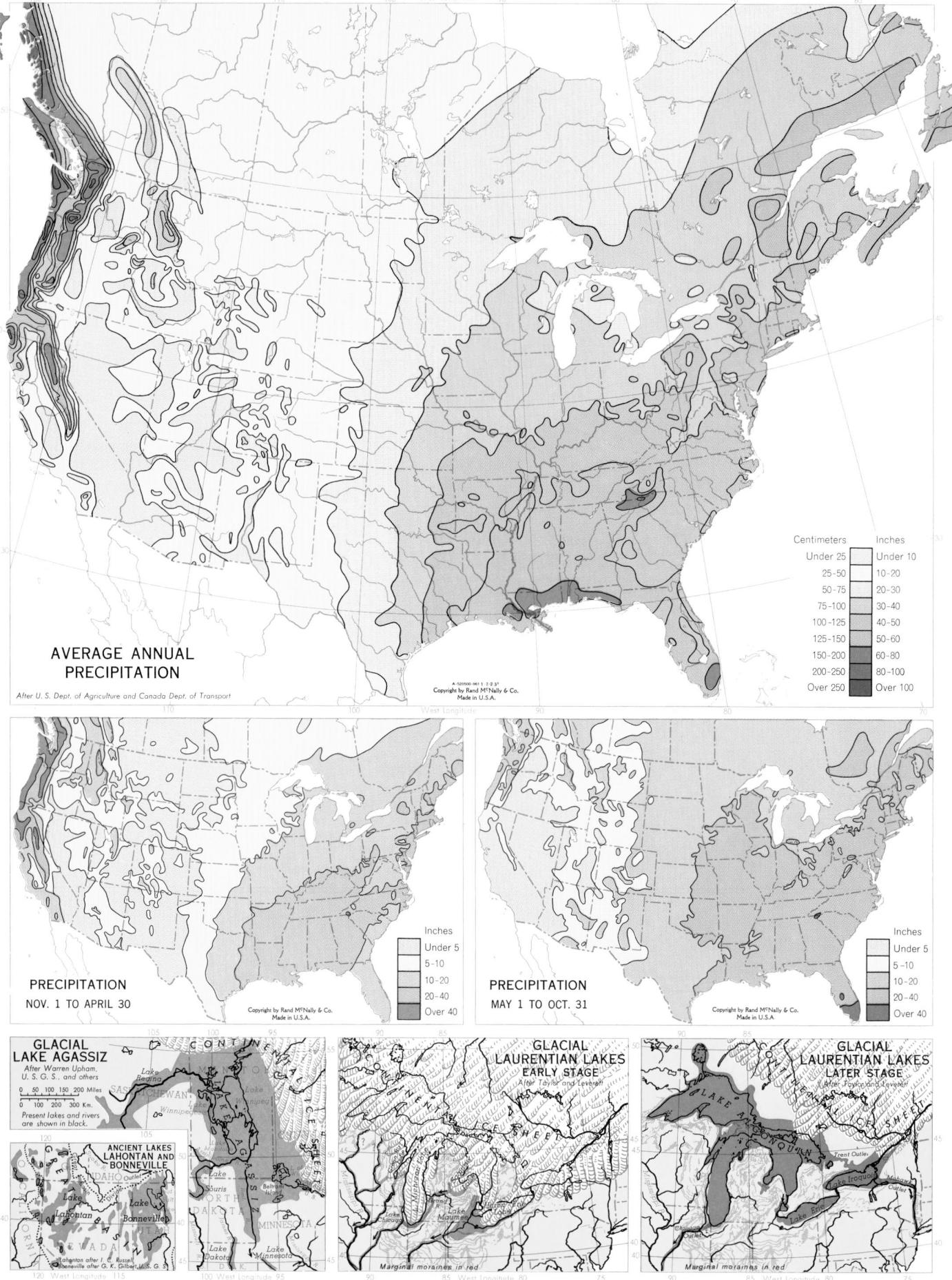

AVERAGE ANNUAL
PRECIPITATION

After U. S. Dept. of Agriculture and Canada Dept. of Transport

A-520500-961 1-2-2'31'
Copyright by Rand McNally & Co.
Made in U.S.A.

Centimeters	Inches
Under 25	Under 10
25-50	10-20
50-75	20-30
75-100	30-40
100-125	40-50
125-150	50-60
150-200	60-80
200-250	80-100
Over 250	Over 100

PRECIPITATION
NOV. 1 TO APRIL 30

Copyright by Rand McNally & Co.
Made in U.S.A.

Inches
Under 5
5-10
10-20
20-40
Over 40

PRECIPITATION
MAY 1 TO OCT. 31

Copyright by Rand McNally & Co.
Made in U.S.A.

Inches
Under 5
5-10
10-20
20-40
Over 40

GLACIAL
LAKE AGASSIZ
After Warren Upham,
U. S. G. S., and others

0 50 100 150 200 Miles
0 100 200 300 Km.
Present lakes and rivers
are shown in black.

ANCIENT LAKES
LAHONTAN AND
BONNEVILLE

Lahontan after I. C. Russell
Bonneville after G. K. Gilbert, U. S. G. S.

GLACIAL
LAURENTIAN LAKES
EARLY STAGE
After Taylor and Leverett

Marginal moraines in red

GLACIAL
LAURENTIAN LAKES
LATER STAGE
After Taylor and Leverett

Marginal moraines in red

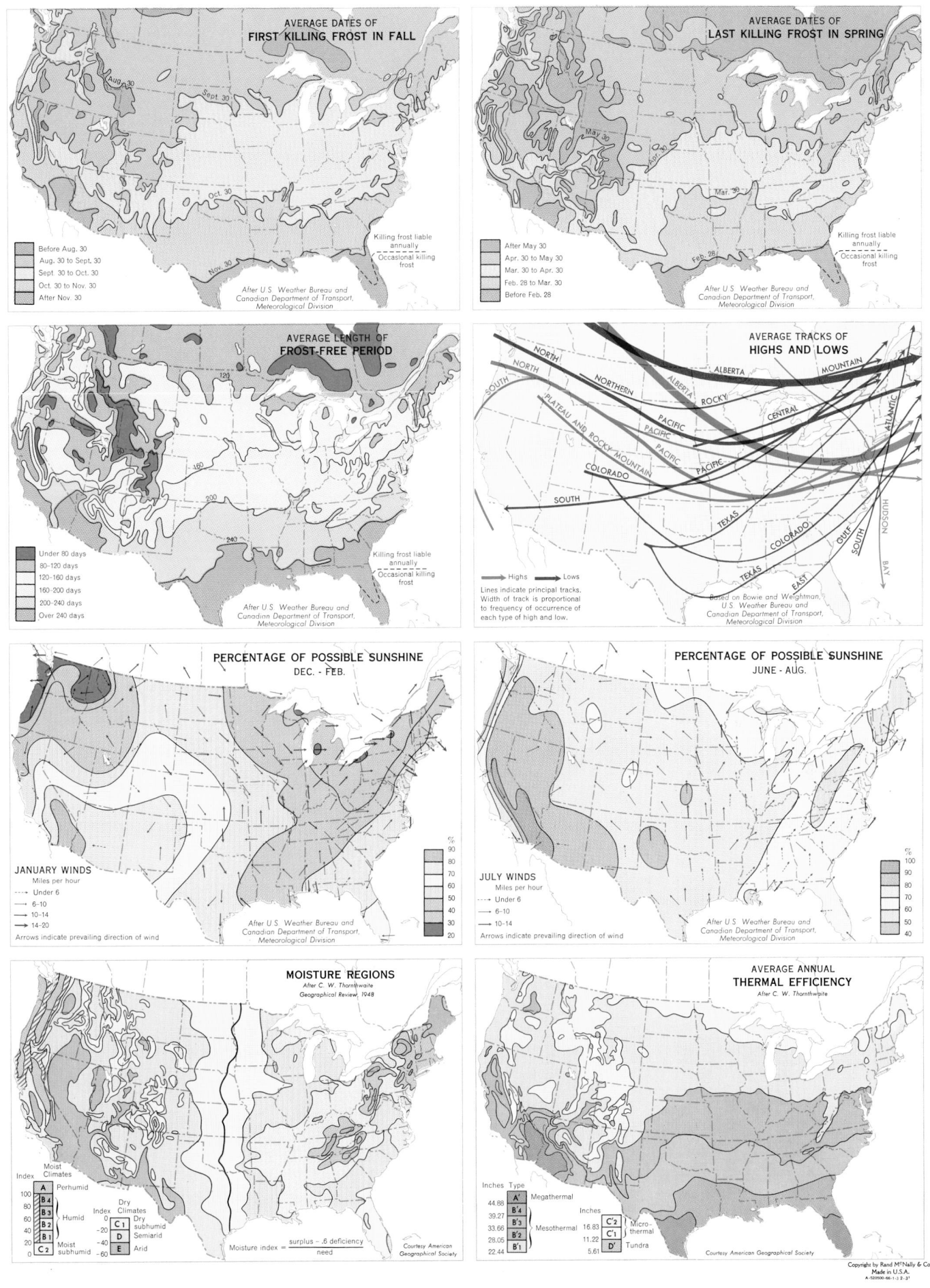

AVERAGE DATES OF FIRST KILLING FROST IN FALL

Aug. 30
Sept. 30
Oct. 30
Nov. 30

Before Aug. 30
Aug. 30 to Sept. 30
Sept. 30 to Oct. 30
Oct. 30 to Nov. 30
After Nov. 30

Killing frost liable annually
Occasional killing frost

After U.S. Weather Bureau and Canadian Department of Transport, Meteorological Division

AVERAGE DATES OF LAST KILLING FROST IN SPRING

May 30
Apr. 30
Mar. 30
Feb. 28

After May 30
Apr. 30 to May 30
Mar. 30 to Apr. 30
Feb. 28 to Mar. 30
Before Feb. 28

Killing frost liable annually
Occasional killing frost

After U.S. Weather Bureau and Canadian Department of Transport, Meteorological Division

AVERAGE LENGTH OF FROST-FREE PERIOD

120
80
160
200
240

Under 80 days
80-120 days
120-160 days
160-200 days
200-240 days
Over 240 days

Killing frost liable annually
Occasional killing frost

After U.S. Weather Bureau and Canadian Department of Transport, Meteorological Division

AVERAGE TRACKS OF HIGHS AND LOWS

NORTH
NORTH
SOUTH
NORTHERN
PLATEAU AND ROCKY MOUNTAIN
PACIFIC
PACIFIC
PACIFIC
PACIFIC
ALBERTA
ROCKY
ALBERTA
MOUNTAIN
CENTRAL
ATLANTIC
COLORADO
SOUTH
TEXAS
COLORADO
GULF
SOUTH
HUDSON
BAY
TEXAS
EAST

Highs   Lows
Lines indicate principal tracks. Width of track is proportional to frequency of occurrence of each type of high and low.

Based on Bowie and Weightman, U.S. Weather Bureau and Canadian Department of Transport, Meteorological Division

PERCENTAGE OF POSSIBLE SUNSHINE DEC. - FEB.

JANUARY WINDS
Miles per hour
Under 6
6-10
10-14
14-20
Arrows indicate prevailing direction of wind

%
90
80
70
60
50
40
30
20

After U.S. Weather Bureau and Canadian Department of Transport, Meteorological Division

PERCENTAGE OF POSSIBLE SUNSHINE JUNE - AUG.

JULY WINDS
Miles per hour
Under 6
6-10
10-14
Arrows indicate prevailing direction of wind

%
100
90
80
70
60
50
40

After U.S. Weather Bureau and Canadian Department of Transport, Meteorological Division

MOISTURE REGIONS
After C. W. Thornthwaite
Geographical Review, 1948

Moist
Climates
Index
100 A Perhumid
80 B4
60 B3 Humid
40 B2
20 B1 Moist
0 C2 subhumid

Dry Climates
Index
0 C1 Dry
-20 D subhumid
-40 D Semiarid
-60 E Arid

Moisture index = surplus − .6 deficiency / need

Courtesy American Geographical Society

AVERAGE ANNUAL THERMAL EFFICIENCY
After C. W. Thornthwaite

Inches Type
44.88 A' Megathermal
39.27 B'4
33.66 B'3 Mesothermal
28.05 B'2
22.44 B'1

Inches
16.83 C'2 Micro-
11.22 C'1 thermal
5.61 D' Tundra

Courtesy American Geographical Society

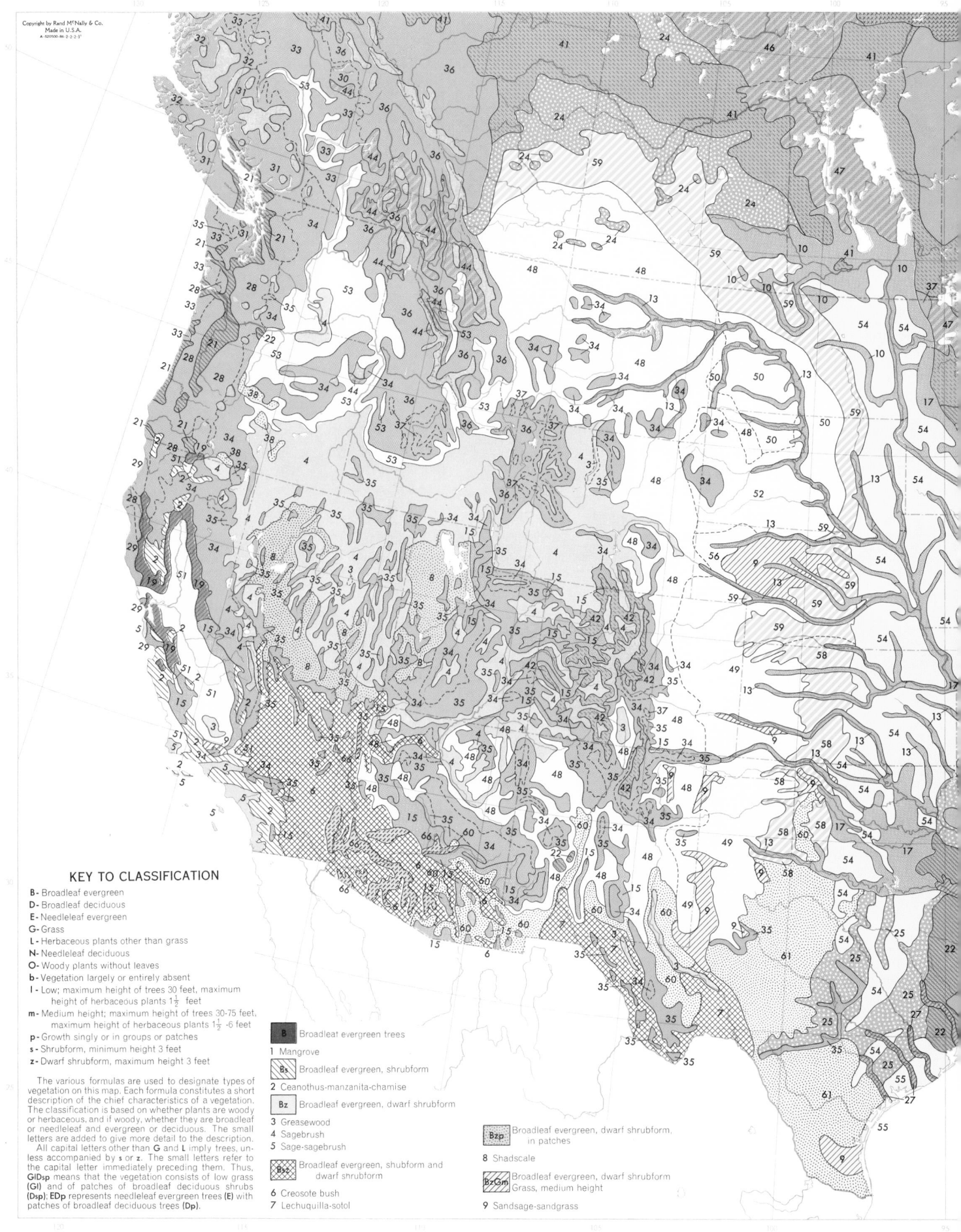

Copyright by Rand McNally & Co.
Made in U.S.A.
A-520500-86-2-2-2-1⁴

KEY TO CLASSIFICATION

B - Broadleaf evergreen
D - Broadleaf deciduous
E - Needleleaf evergreen
G - Grass
L - Herbaceous plants other than grass
N - Needleleaf deciduous
O - Woody plants without leaves
b - Vegetation largely or entirely absent
l - Low; maximum height of trees 30 feet, maximum
 height of herbaceous plants 1½ feet
m - Medium height; maximum height of trees 30-75 feet,
 maximum height of herbaceous plants 1½ -6 feet
p - Growth singly or in groups or patches
s - Shrubform, minimum height 3 feet
z - Dwarf shrubform, maximum height 3 feet

The various formulas are used to designate types of
vegetation on this map. Each formula constitutes a short
description of the chief characteristics of a vegetation.
The classification is based on whether plants are woody
or herbaceous, and if woody, whether they are broadleaf
or needleleaf and evergreen or deciduous. The small
letters are added to give more detail to the description.
 All capital letters other than **G** and **L** imply trees, un-
less accompanied by **s** or **z**. The small letters refer to
the capital letter immediately preceding them. Thus,
GlDsp means that the vegetation consists of low grass
(**Gl**) and of patches of broadleaf deciduous shrubs
(**Dsp**); **EDp** represents needleleaf evergreen trees (**E**) with
patches of broadleaf deciduous trees (**Dp**).

B   Broadleaf evergreen trees

1   Mangrove

Bs   Broadleaf evergreen, shrubform

2   Ceanothus-manzanita-chamise

Bz   Broadleaf evergreen, dwarf shrubform

3   Greasewood

4   Sagebrush

5   Sage-sagebrush

Bsz   Broadleaf evergreen, shubform and
   dwarf shrubform

6   Creosote bush

7   Lechuquilla-sotol

Bzp   Broadleaf evergreen, dwarf shrubform,
   in patches

8   Shadscale

BzGm   Broadleaf evergreen, dwarf shrubform
   Grass, medium height

9   Sandsage-sandgrass

0 25 50 .75 100   200   300   400   500 Miles

0 50 100   200   400   600   800 Kilometers

Scale 1:14 000 000;   One inch to 220

NATURAL VEGETATION

BY A. W. KÜCHLER

Based on "A Physiognomic Classification of Vegetation"
Annals of the Assoc. of American Geographers, Vol 39, September, 1949

EDp Needleleaf evergreen trees
Broadleaf deciduous trees, in patches

39 Douglas fir-pine-aspen
40 Pine-spruce-birch
41 Spruce-aspen
42 Spruce-fir-aspen
43 Spruce-poplar-birch

EN Needleleaf evergreen trees
Needleleaf deciduous trees

44 Hemlock-arbor vitae-Douglas fir-larch
45 Pine-bald cypress
46 Pine-spruce-larch
47 Spruce-larch

Gl Grass, low

48 Grama grass
49 Grama grass-buffalo grass
50 Grama grass-needle grass
51 Needle grass-blue grass
52 Wheat grass
53 Wheat grass-blue grass

Gm Grass, medium height

54 Bluestem
55 Broom grass-water grass
56 Marsh grass
57 Saw grass

Gml Grass, medium and low height

58 Bluestem-bunch grass
59 Needle grass-wheat grass

Gl/Dsp Grass, low
Broadleaf deciduous, shrubform, in patches

60 Bunch grass-oak

Gm/Dsp Grass, medium height
Broadleaf deciduous, shrubform, in patches

61 Mesquite grass-mesquite

L Herbaceous plants other than grass

62 Lichens, etc.

LEp Herbaceous plants other than grass
Needleleaf evergreen trees, in patches

63 Lichens-spruce

LEp/Np Herbaceous plants other than grass
Needleleaf evergreen trees, in patches
Needleleaf deciduous trees, in patches

64 Lichens-spruce-larch

N Needleleaf deciduous trees

65 Bald cypress

Op Woody plants without leaves, in patches

66 Palo verde-cacti-ocotillo

b Vegetation largely or entirely absent

D Broadleaf deciduous trees

10 Aspen-oak
11 Beech-maple
12 Beech-tulip tree-maple-basswood
13 Cottonwood-willow
14 Maple-basswood
15 Oak
16 Oak-ash-maple
17 Oak-hickory
18 Oak-tulip tree

DB Broadleaf deciduous trees
Broadleaf evergreen trees

19 Oak-madrone

DE Broadleaf deciduous trees
Needleleaf evergreen trees

20 Maple-yellow birch-hemlock-pine
21 Oak-Douglas fir
22 Oak-pine
23 Maple-beech-hemlock

D/Gmp Broadleaf deciduous trees
Grass, medium height, in patches

24 Aspen-needle grass-wheat grass
25 Oak-hickory-bluestem

DN Broadleaf deciduous trees
Needleleaf deciduous trees

26 Bay trees-bald cypress
27 Tupelo-gum-bald cypress

E Needleleaf evergreen trees

28 Douglas fir
29 Douglas fir-redwood
30 Hemlock-arbor vitae
31 Hemlock-arbor vitae-Douglas fir
32 Hemlock-arbor vitae-fir
33 Hemlock-spruce
34 Pine
35 Pine-juniper
36 Pine-spruce
37 Spruce-fir

Esp Needleleaf evergreen, shrubform,
in patches

38 Juniper

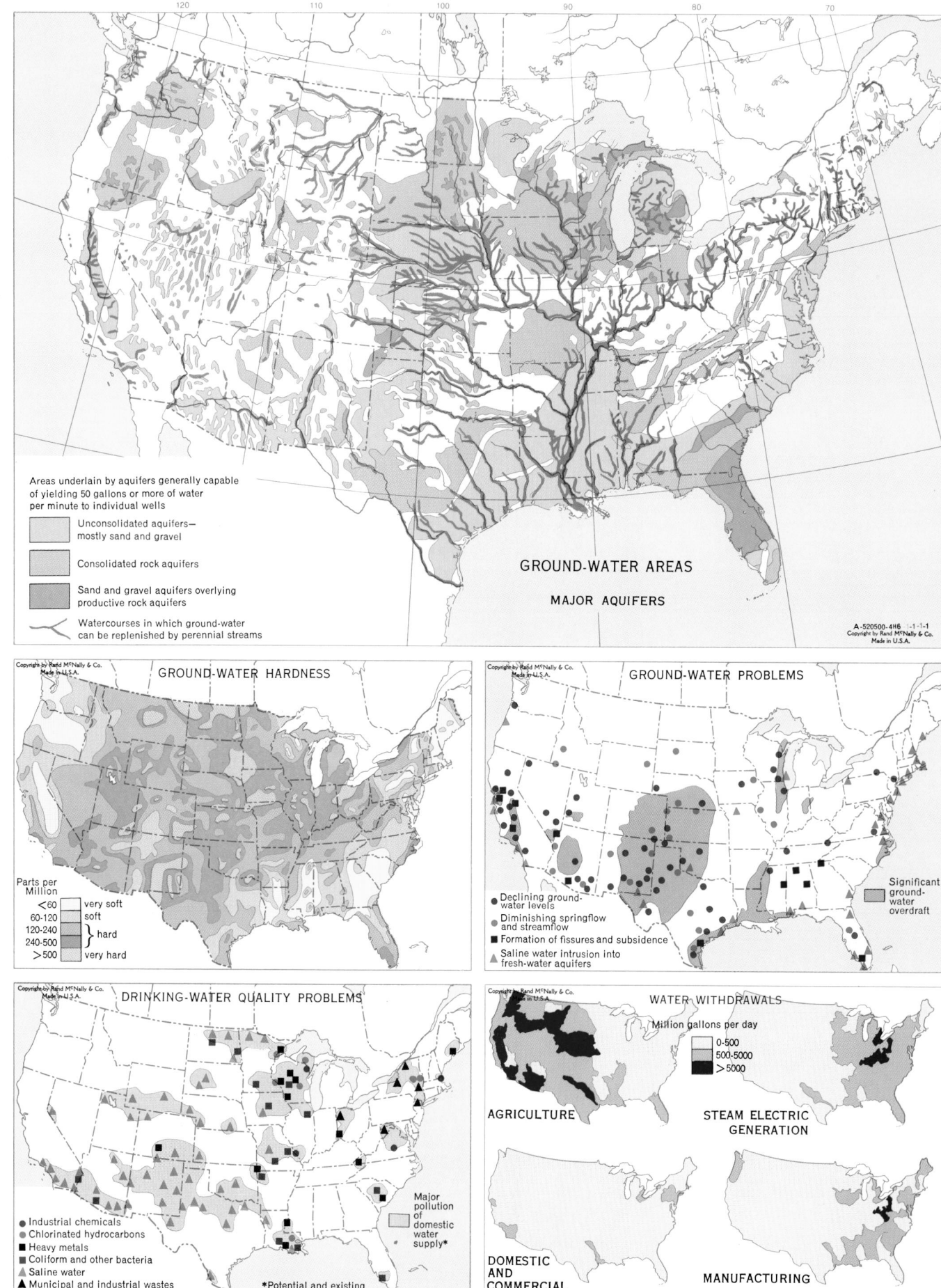

GROUND-WATER AREAS

MAJOR AQUIFERS

Areas underlain by aquifers generally capable
of yielding 50 gallons or more of water
per minute to individual wells

Unconsolidated aquifers—
mostly sand and gravel

Consolidated rock aquifers

Sand and gravel aquifers overlying
productive rock aquifers

Watercourses in which ground-water
can be replenished by perennial streams

A-520500-4H6
Copyright by Rand McNally & Co.
Made in U.S.A.

GROUND-WATER HARDNESS

Parts per
Million
<60   very soft
60-120   soft
120-240   } hard
240-500
>500   very hard

GROUND-WATER PROBLEMS

Significant
ground-
water
overdraft

● Declining ground-
   water levels
● Diminishing springflow
   and streamflow
■ Formation of fissures and subsidence
▲ Saline water intrusion into
   fresh-water aquifers

DRINKING-WATER QUALITY PROBLEMS

Major
pollution
of
domestic
water
supply*

● Industrial chemicals
● Chlorinated hydrocarbons
■ Heavy metals
■ Coliform and other bacteria
▲ Saline water
▲ Municipal and industrial wastes

*Potential and existing

WATER WITHDRAWALS

Million gallons per day
0-500
500-5000
>5000

AGRICULTURE

**STEAM ELECTRIC
GENERATION**

**DOMESTIC
AND
COMMERCIAL**

MANUFACTURING

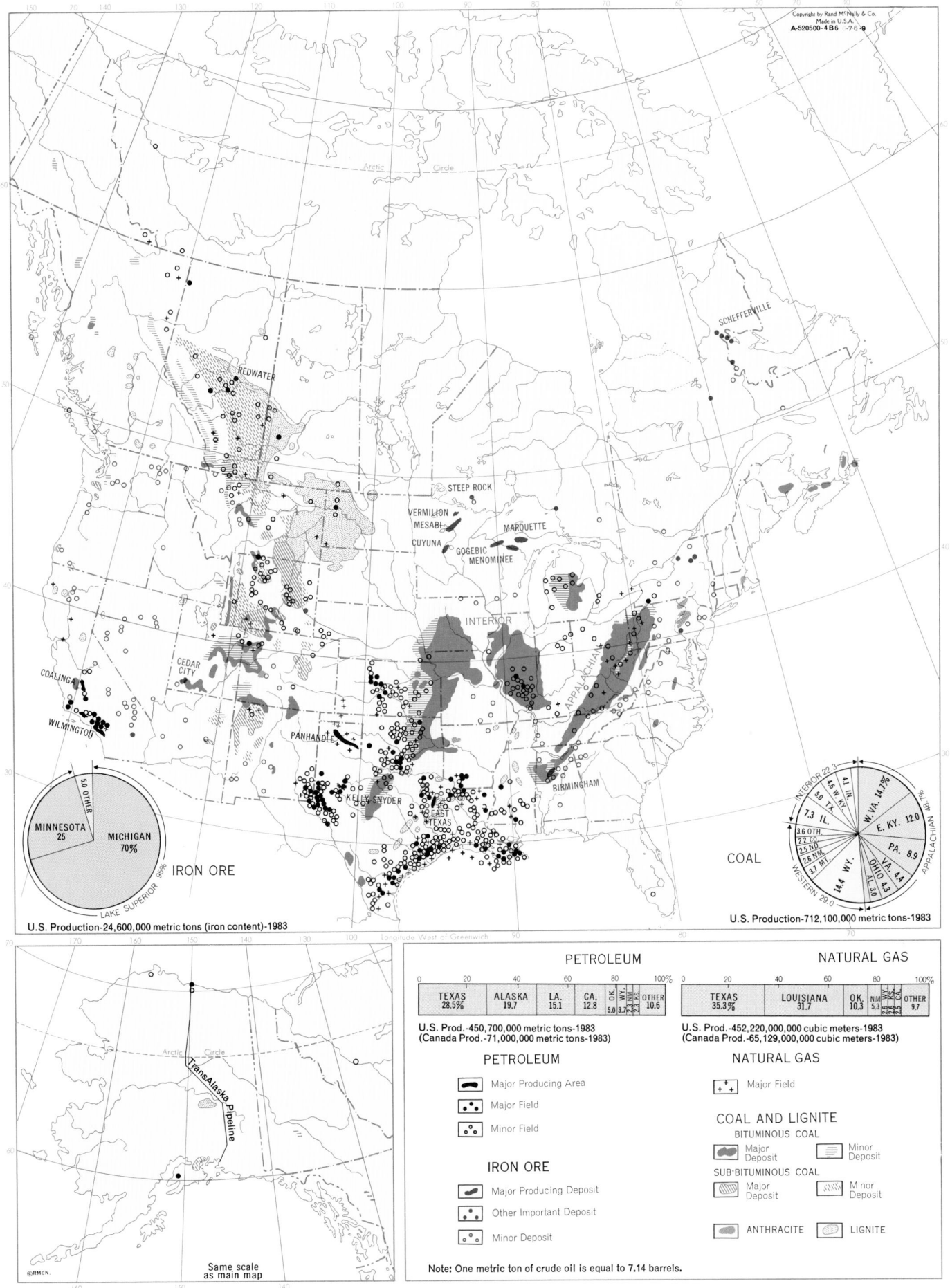

SCHEFFERVILLE

REDWATER

STEEP ROCK

VERMILION
MESABI
CUYUNA
GOGEBIC
MENOMINEE

MARQUETTE

INTERIOR

APPALACHIAN

COALINGA

CEDAR
CITY

WILMINGTON

PANHANDLE

KELLY-SNYDER

EAST
TEXAS

BIRMINGHAM

IRON ORE

5.0 OTHER
MINNESOTA
25
MICHIGAN
70%
LAKE SUPERIOR 95%

U.S. Production-24,600,000 metric tons (iron content)-1983

COAL

INTERIOR 22.3
44.6 W. KY.
5.0 OTH.
7.3 IL.
3.6 OTH.
2.2 CO.
2.5 ND.
2.6 NM.
3.7 MT.
14.4 WY.
WESTERN 29.0
41 IN.
W.VA. 14.7%
E. KY. 12.0
PA. 8.9
OHIO 4.3
VA. 4.4
AL. 3.0
APPALACHIAN 48.7%

U.S. Production-712,100,000 metric tons-1983

Longitude West of Greenwich

TransAlaska Pipeline

Arctic Circle

Same scale
as main map

©RMcN.

PETROLEUM

	TEXAS 28.5%	ALASKA 19.7	LA. 15.1	CA. 12.8	OK. 5.0	WY. 3.7	KS. 2.3	OTHER 10.6

U.S. Prod.-450,700,000 metric tons-1983
(Canada Prod.-71,000,000 metric tons-1983)

NATURAL GAS

	TEXAS 35.3%	LOUISIANA 31.7	OK. 10.3	NM 5.3	WY 2.3	CA. 2.2	OTHER 9.7

U.S. Prod.-452,220,000,000 cubic meters-1983
(Canada Prod.-65,129,000,000 cubic meters-1983)

PETROLEUM

- Major Producing Area
- Major Field
- Minor Field

IRON ORE

- Major Producing Deposit
- Other Important Deposit
- Minor Deposit

NATURAL GAS

- Major Field

COAL AND LIGNITE

BITUMINOUS COAL
- Major Deposit
- Minor Deposit

SUB-BITUMINOUS COAL
- Major Deposit
- Minor Deposit

- ANTHRACITE
- LIGNITE

Note: One metric ton of crude oil is equal to 7.14 barrels.

Scale 1:32 000 000; One inch to 500 miles.   LAMBERT CONFORMAL CONIC PROJECTION

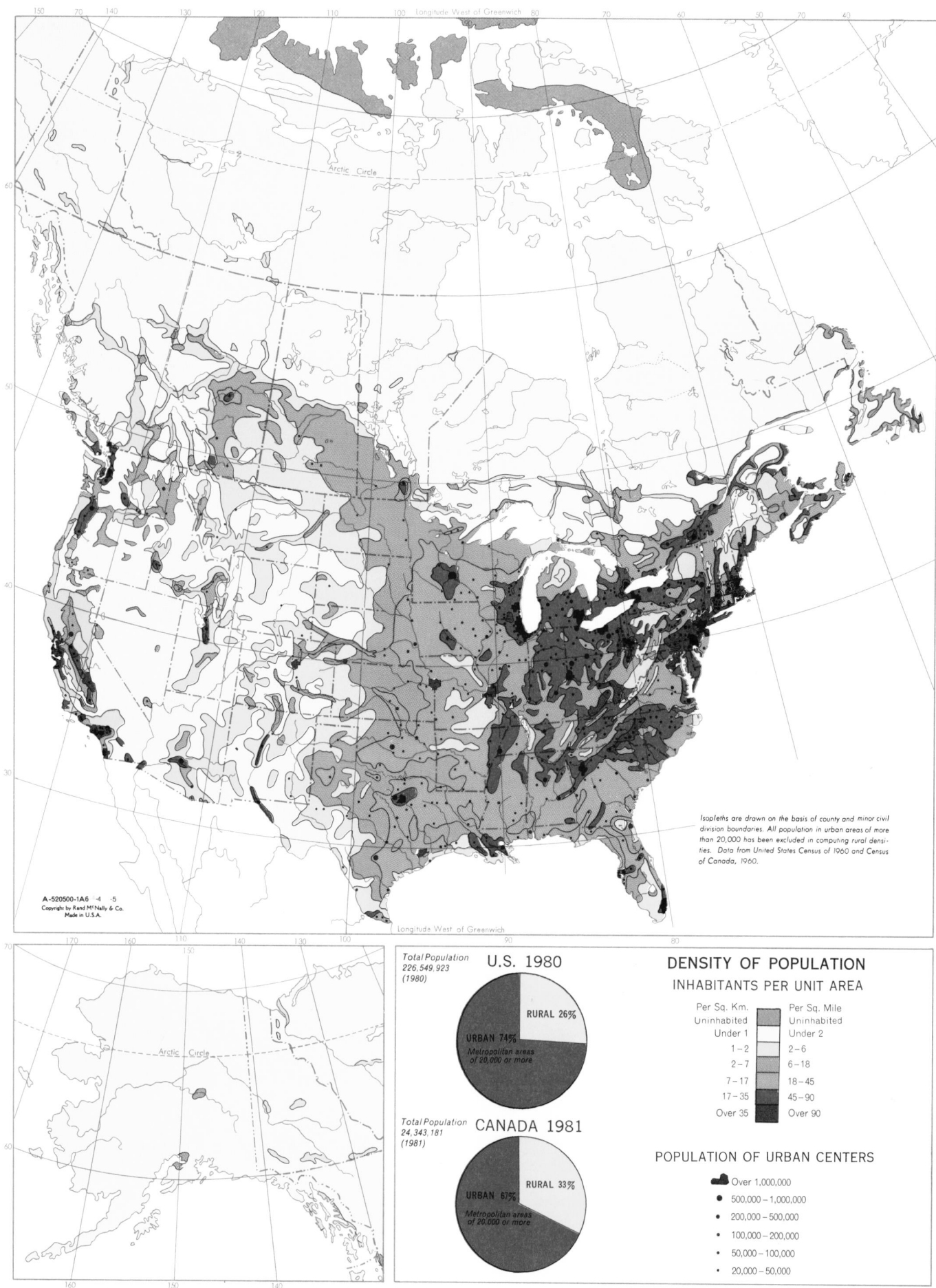

Isopleths are drawn on the basis of county and minor civil division boundaries. All population in urban areas of more than 20,000 has been excluded in computing rural densities. Data from United States Census of 1960 and Census of Canada, 1960.

A-520500-1A6   -4   -5
Copyright by Rand McNally & Co.
Made in U.S.A.

Total Population
226,549,923
(1980)

U.S. 1980

RURAL 26%

URBAN 74%

Metropolitan areas of 20,000 or more

Total Population
24,343,181
(1981)

CANADA 1981

RURAL 33%

URBAN 67%

Metropolitan areas of 20,000 or more

DENSITY OF POPULATION

INHABITANTS PER UNIT AREA

Per Sq. Km.	Per Sq. Mile
Uninhabited	Uninhabited
Under 1	Under 2
1 – 2	2 – 6
2 – 7	6 – 18
7 – 17	18 – 45
17 – 35	45 – 90
Over 35	Over 90

POPULATION OF URBAN CENTERS

Over 1,000,000
500,000 – 1,000,000
200,000 – 500,000
100,000 – 200,000
50,000 – 100,000
20,000 – 50,000

Scale 1: 32 000 000; One inch to 500 miles.   LAMBERT CONFORMAL CONIC PROJECTION

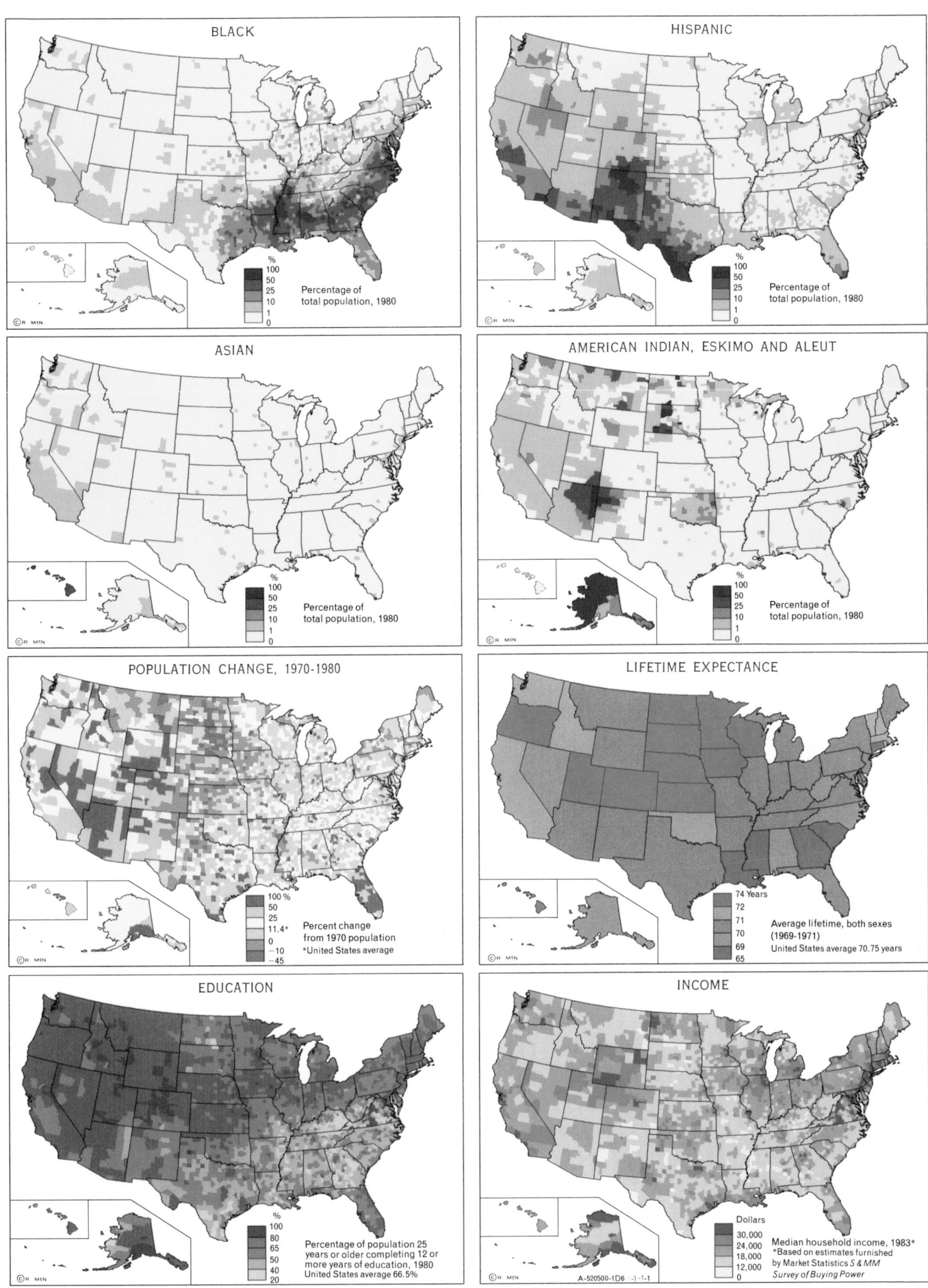

BLACK

%
100
50
25
10
1
0

Percentage of
total population, 1980

HISPANIC

%
100
50
25
10
1
0

Percentage of
total population, 1980

ASIAN

%
100
50
25
10
1
0

Percentage of
total population, 1980

AMERICAN INDIAN, ESKIMO AND ALEUT

%
100
50
25
10
1
0

Percentage of
total population, 1980

POPULATION CHANGE, 1970-1980

100 %
50
25
11.4*
0
-10
-45

Percent change
from 1970 population
*United States average

LIFETIME EXPECTANCE

74 Years
72
71
70
69
65

Average lifetime, both sexes
(1969-1971)
United States average 70.75 years

EDUCATION

%
100
80
65
50
40
20

Percentage of population 25
years or older completing 12 or
more years of education, 1980
United States average 66.5%

INCOME

Dollars
30,000
24,000
18,000
12,000
0

Median household income, 1983*
*Based on estimates furnished
by Market Statistics S & MM
Survey of Buying Power

A-520500-1D6 -1 -1-1

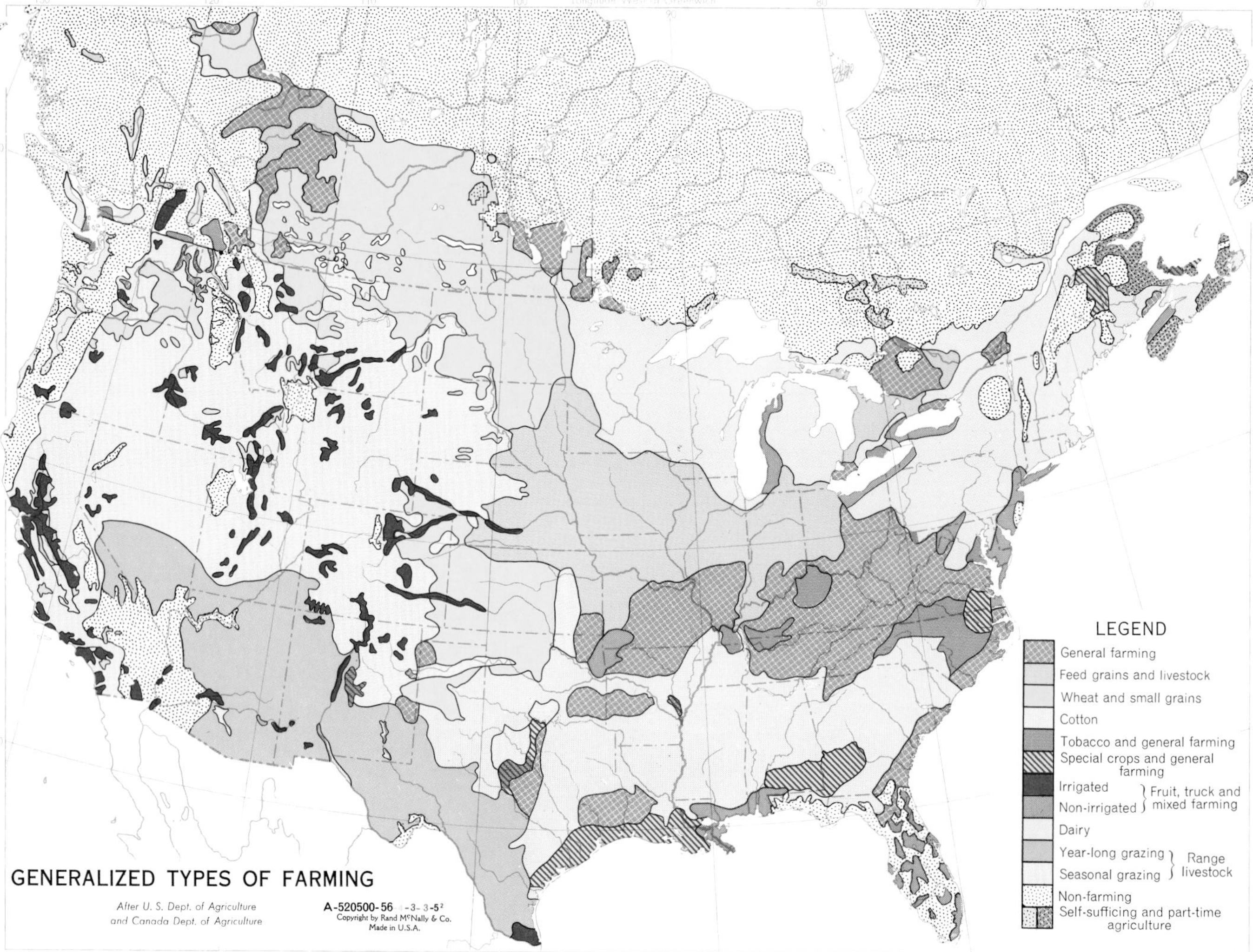

GENERALIZED TYPES OF FARMING

*After U. S. Dept. of Agriculture
and Canada Dept. of Agriculture*

A-520500-56 -3-3-5²
Copyright by Rand M°Nally & Co.
Made in U.S.A.

LEGEND

- General farming
- Feed grains and livestock
- Wheat and small grains
- Cotton
- Tobacco and general farming
- Special crops and general farming
- Irrigated ⎫ Fruit, truck and
- Non-irrigated ⎭ mixed farming
- Dairy
- Year-long grazing ⎫ Range
- Seasonal grazing ⎭ livestock
- Non-farming
- Self-sufficing and part-time agriculture

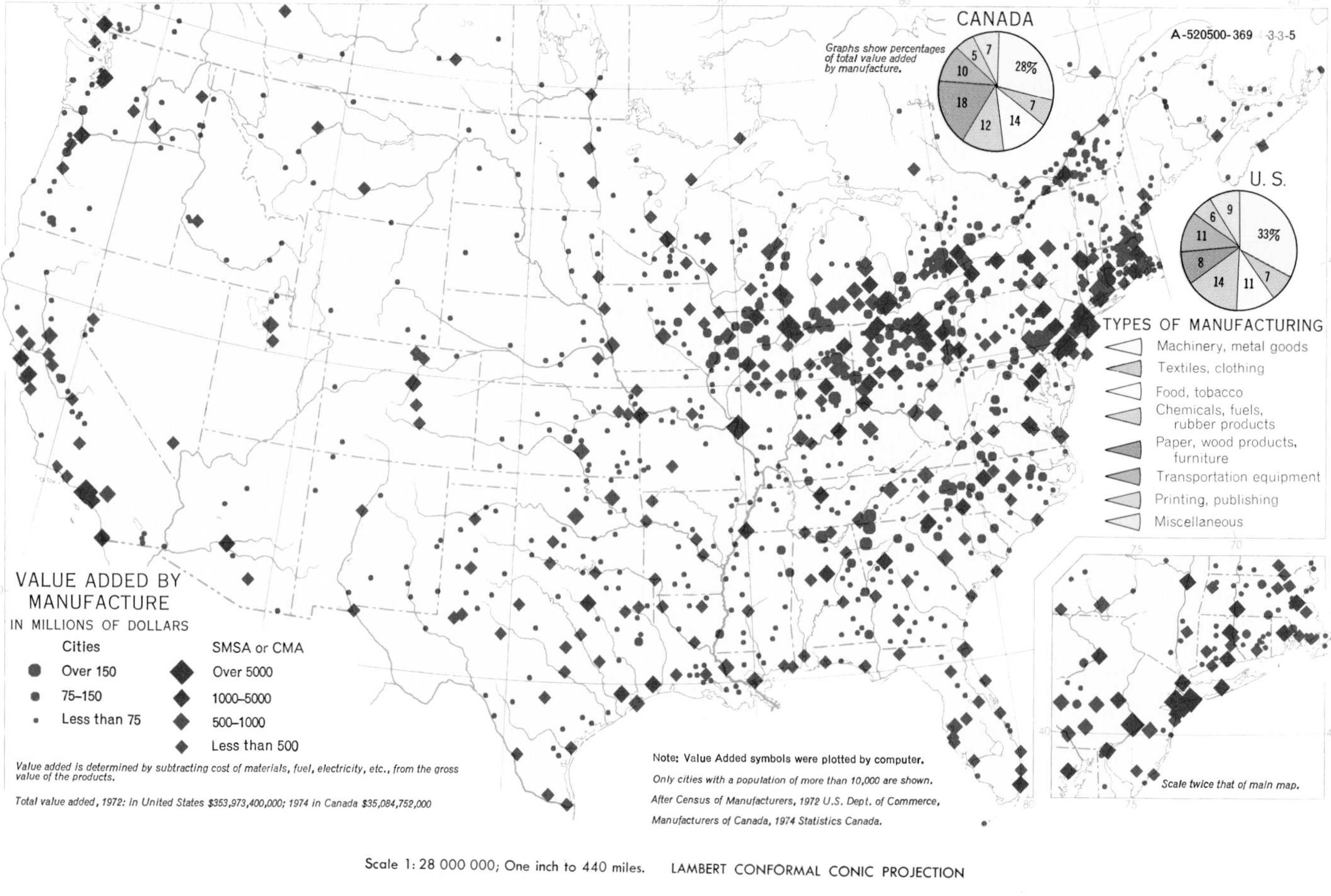

CANADA

A-520500-369 -3-3-5

*Graphs show percentages
of total value added
by manufacture.*

7
5
28%
10
18
7
12 14

U.S.

6 9
33%
11
8 7
14 11

TYPES OF MANUFACTURING

- Machinery, metal goods
- Textiles, clothing
- Food, tobacco
- Chemicals, fuels, rubber products
- Paper, wood products, furniture
- Transportation equipment
- Printing, publishing
- Miscellaneous

VALUE ADDED BY MANUFACTURE

IN MILLIONS OF DOLLARS

Cities	SMSA or CMA
Over 150	Over 5000
75–150	1000–5000
Less than 75	500–1000
	Less than 500

*Value added is determined by subtracting cost of materials, fuel, electricity, etc., from the gross
value of the products.*

Total value added, 1972: In United States $353,973,400,000; 1974 in Canada $35,084,752,000

Note: Value Added symbols were plotted by computer.

Only cities with a population of more than 10,000 are shown.

*After Census of Manufacturers, 1972 U.S. Dept. of Commerce,
Manufacturers of Canada, 1974 Statistics Canada.*

Scale twice that of main map.

Scale 1: 28 000 000; One inch to 440 miles.   LAMBERT CONFORMAL CONIC PROJECTION

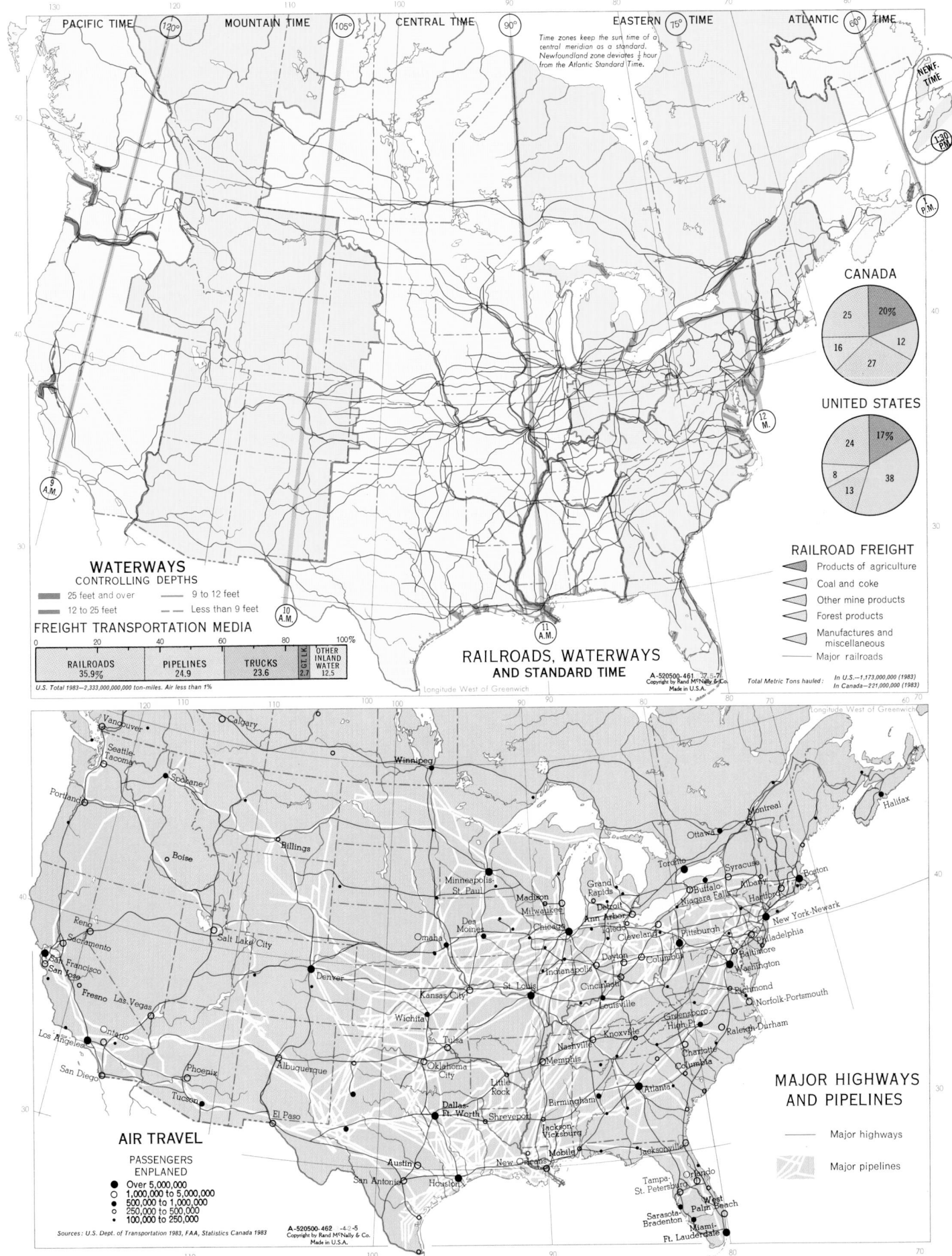

PACIFIC TIME   MOUNTAIN TIME   CENTRAL TIME   EASTERN TIME   ATLANTIC TIME

Time zones keep the sun time of a
central meridian as a standard.
Newfoundland zone deviates ½ hour
from the Atlantic Standard Time.

CANADA

20%
25
12
16
27

UNITED STATES

17%
24
38
8
13

RAILROAD FREIGHT

◁ Products of agriculture
◁ Coal and coke
◁ Other mine products
◁ Forest products
◁ Manufactures and
  miscellaneous
— Major railroads

WATERWAYS
CONTROLLING DEPTHS

▬ 25 feet and over   — 9 to 12 feet
▬ 12 to 25 feet   --- Less than 9 feet

FREIGHT TRANSPORTATION MEDIA

0	20	40	60	80	100%
RAILROADS 35.9%	PIPELINES 24.9	TRUCKS 23.6	GT LK 2.7	OTHER INLAND WATER 12.5	

U.S. Total 1983—2,333,000,000 ton-miles. Air less than 1%

RAILROADS, WATERWAYS
AND STANDARD TIME

A-520500-461   27.5-7
Copyright by Rand McNally & Co.
Made in U.S.A.

Longitude West of Greenwich

Total Metric Tons hauled: In U.S.—1,173,000,000 (1983)
                             In Canada—221,000,000 (1983)

MAJOR HIGHWAYS
AND PIPELINES

— Major highways

◁ Major pipelines

AIR TRAVEL

PASSENGERS
ENPLANED

● Over 5,000,000
● 1,000,000 to 5,000,000
◉ 500,000 to 1,000,000
○ 250,000 to 500,000
○ 100,000 to 250,000

Sources: U.S. Dept. of Transportation 1983, FAA, Statistics Canada 1983

A-520500-462   4.2-5
Copyright by Rand McNally & Co.
Made in U.S.A.

Scale 1: 28 000 000; One inch to 440 miles.   LAMBERT CONFORMAL CONIC PROJECTION

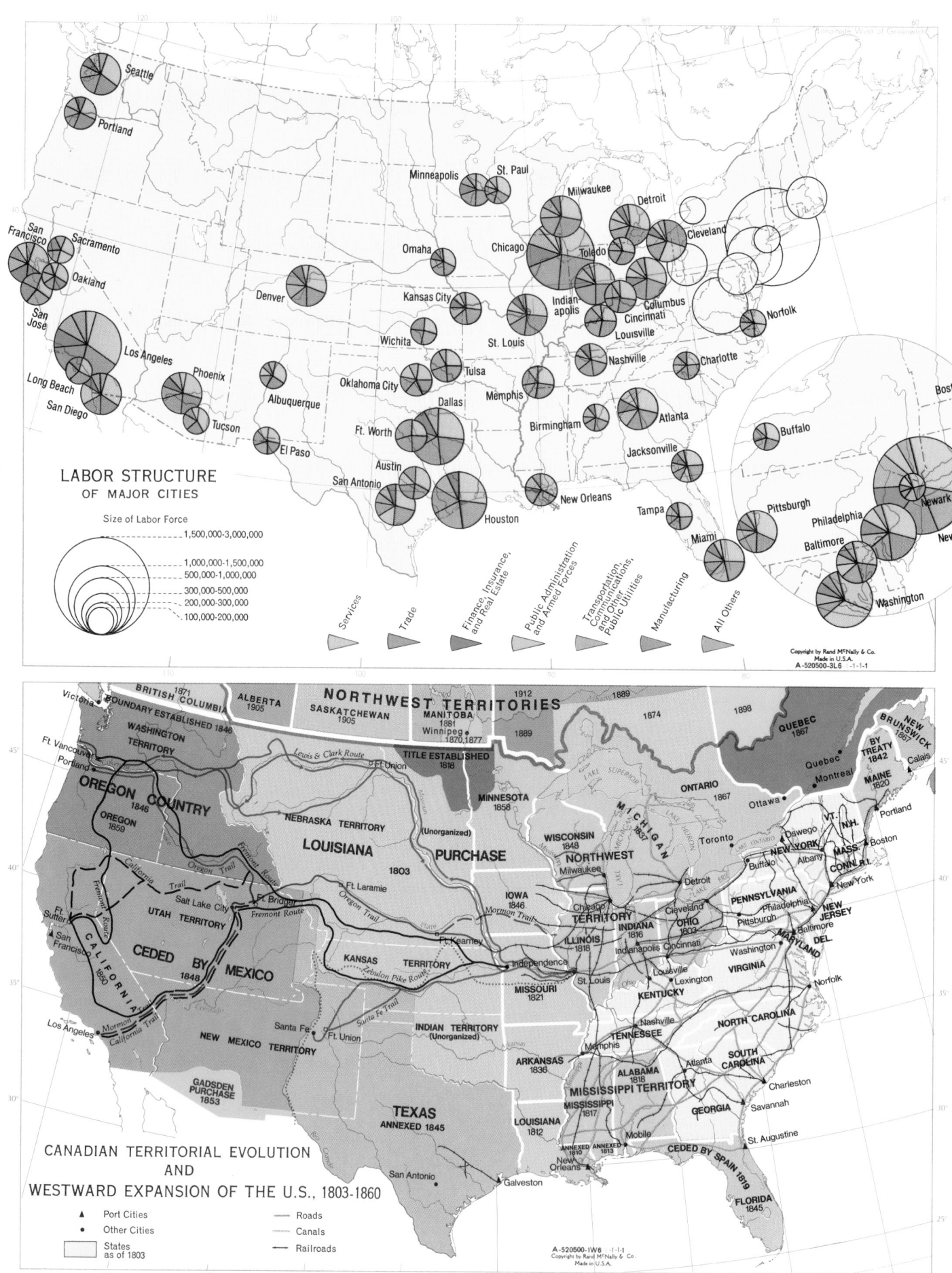

LABOR STRUCTURE
OF MAJOR CITIES

Size of Labor Force

1,500,000–3,000,000
1,000,000–1,500,000
500,000–1,000,000
300,000–500,000
200,000–300,000
100,000–200,000

Services

Trade

Finance, Insurance, and Real Estate

Public Administration and Armed Forces

Transportation, Communications, and Other Public Utilities

Manufacturing

All Others

Copyright by Rand McNally & Co.
Made in U.S.A.
A-520500-3L6 -1-1-1

CANADIAN TERRITORIAL EVOLUTION
AND
WESTWARD EXPANSION OF THE U.S., 1803-1860

▲ Port Cities
• Other Cities
States as of 1803

Roads
Canals
Railroads

A-520500-1W6 -1-1-1
Copyright by Rand McNally & Co.
Made in U.S.A.

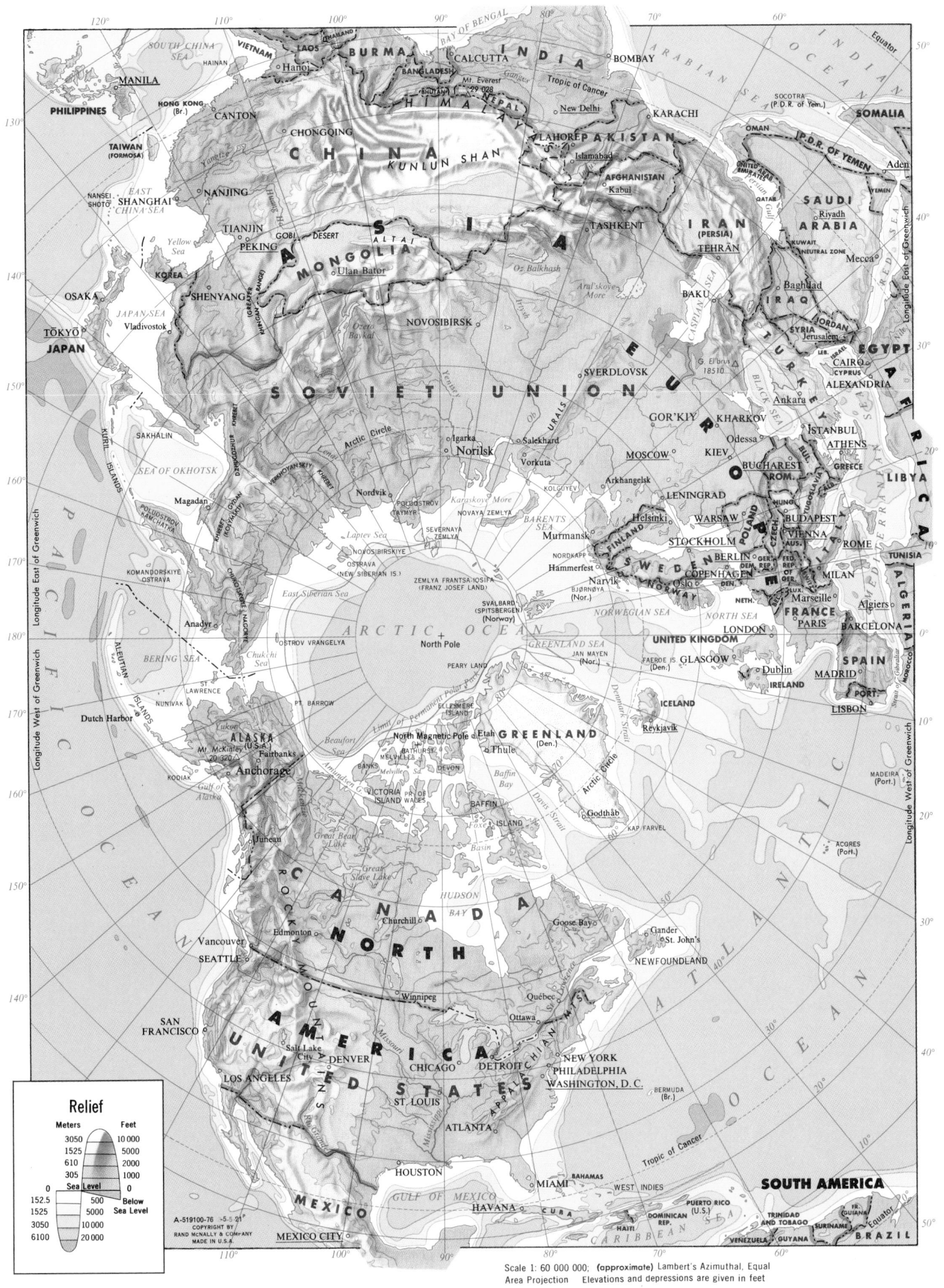

Relief

Meters		Feet
3050		10 000
1525		5000
610		2000
305		1000
0	Sea Level	
152.5		500 Below
1525		5000 Sea Level
3050		10 000
6100		20 000

A-519100-76 -5-5-21
COPYRIGHT BY
RAND M^cNALLY & COMPANY
MADE IN U.S.A.

Scale 1: 60 000 000; (approximate) Lambert's Azimuthal, Equal
Area Projection   Elevations and depressions are given in feet

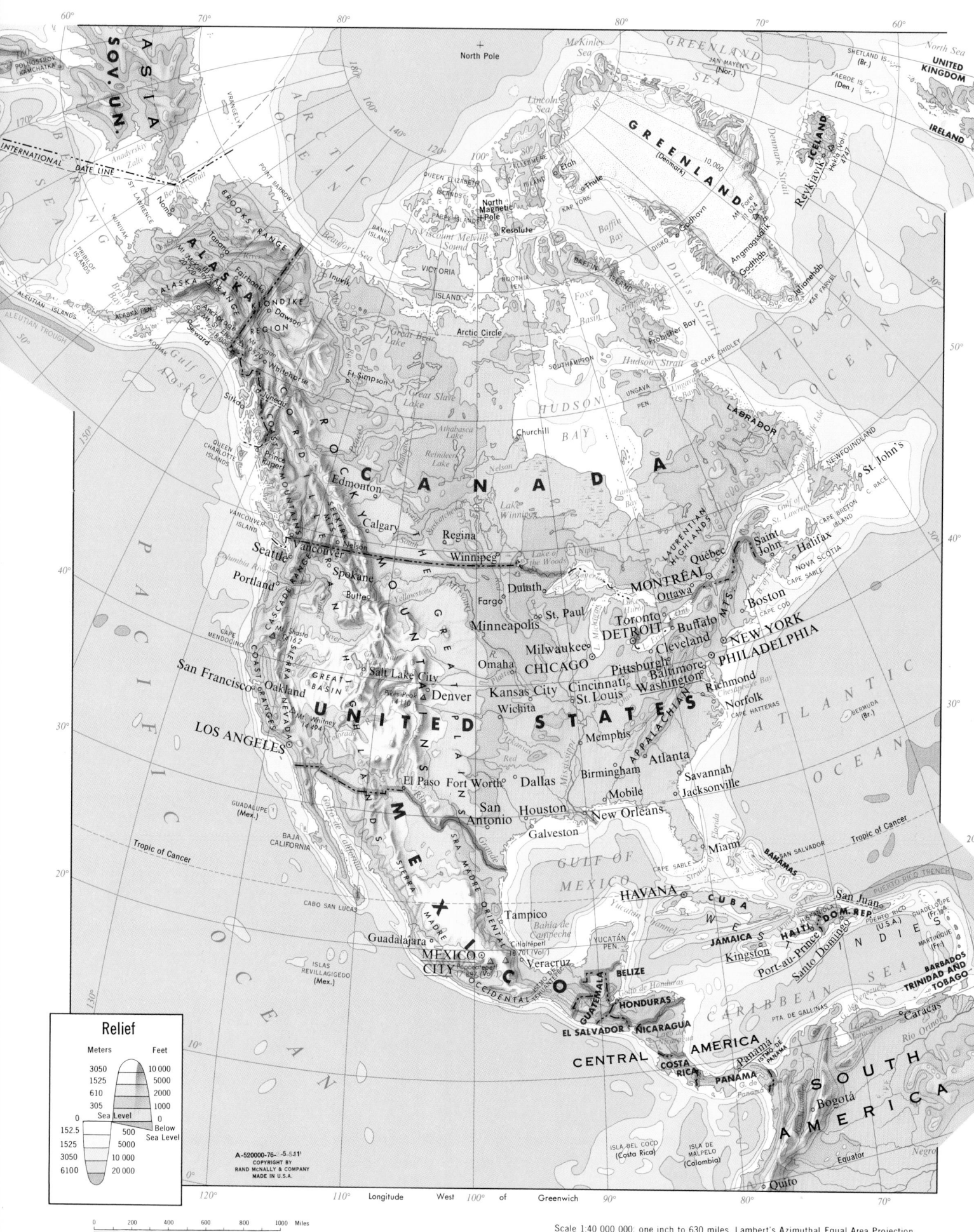

ASIA
SOV. UN.

UNITED
KINGDOM

IRELAND

North Pole

GREENLAND
(Denmark)

ICELAND
Reykjavík

INTERNATIONAL DATE LINE

ARCTIC OCEAN

Lincoln Sea

Baffin Bay

Denmark Strait

Davis Strait

BROOKS RANGE

ALASKA

ALASKA RANGE

Fairbanks

Nome

Seward

Sitka

Juneau

Whitehorse

KLONDIKE REGION

Dawson

Arctic Circle

Great Bear Lake

Great Slave Lake

Ft. Simpson

VICTORIA ISLAND

BANKS ISLAND

QUEEN ELIZABETH ISLANDS

Resolute

North Magnetic Pole

BAFFIN ISLAND

Foxe Basin

BOOTHIA PEN.

Frobisher Bay

HUDSON BAY

SOUTHAMPTON

UNGAVA PEN.

LABRADOR

NEWFOUNDLAND

St. John's

C. RACE

Churchill

Reindeer Lake

Athabasca Lake

Lake Winnipeg

CANADA

Edmonton

Calgary

Regina

Winnipeg

Lake of the Woods

ROCKY MOUNTAINS

SELKIRK MTS.

THE GREAT PLAINS

Nelson

Saskatchewan

VANCOUVER ISLAND

Vancouver

Prince Rupert

QUEEN CHARLOTTE ISLANDS

Nelson

Seattle

Portland

Spokane

Butte

COAST RANGE

CASCADE RANGE

COLUMBIA R.

Yellowstone

GREAT BASIN

Salt Lake City

Great Salt Lake

Fargo

Duluth

St. Paul

Minneapolis

Milwaukee

Omaha

CHICAGO

L. Superior

L. Michigan

L. Huron

DETROIT

Toronto

Buffalo

Cleveland

MONTRÉAL

Ottawa

Québec

LAURENTIAN HIGHLANDS

Saint John

Halifax

NOVA SCOTIA

CAPE BRETON ISLAND

CAPE SABLE

Boston

CAPE COD

NEW YORK

PHILADELPHIA

Pittsburgh

Baltimore

Washington

Richmond

Norfolk

Chesapeake Bay

APPALACHIAN MTS.

CAPE HATTERAS

BERMUDA (Br.)

San Francisco

Oakland

COAST RANGES

SIERRA NEVADA

Mt. Whitney 14 494

LOS ANGELES

Mt. Shasta 14 162

Cape Mendocino

UNITED STATES

Denver

Pikes Peak 14 110

Kansas City

Wichita

Cincinnati

St. Louis

Memphis

Colorado R.

Red R.

GREAT PLAINS

HIGH PLAINS

El Paso

Fort Worth

Dallas

San Antonio

Houston

Galveston

New Orleans

Birmingham

Atlanta

Mobile

Savannah

Jacksonville

Miami

ATLANTIC OCEAN

PACIFIC OCEAN

GUADALUPE (Mex.)

BAJA CALIFORNIA

CABO SAN LUCAS

Golfo de California

SIERRA MADRE OCCIDENTAL

SIERRA MADRE ORIENTAL

MEXICO

Guadalajara

MEXICO CITY

Popocatépetl 17 887 (Vol.)

Orizaba 18 701 (Vol.)

Veracruz

Tampico

Bahía de Campeche

YUCATÁN PEN.

Tropic of Cancer

GULF OF MEXICO

CAPE SABLE

Yucatan Channel

HAVANA

CUBA

BAHAMAS

SAN SALVADOR

San Juan

PUERTO RICO (U.S.)

GUADELOUPE (Fr.)

MARTINIQUE (Fr.)

HAITI

DOM. REP.

JAMAICA

Kingston

Port-au-Prince

Santo Domingo

HISPANIOLA

PUERTO RICO TRENCH

WEST INDIES

BARBADOS

TRINIDAD AND TOBAGO

CARIBBEAN SEA

BELIZE

GUATEMALA

HONDURAS

EL SALVADOR

NICARAGUA

COSTA RICA

PANAMA

CENTRAL AMERICA

PTA. DE GALLINAS

Caracas

L. de Maracaibo

Rio Orinoco

Bogotá

SOUTH AMERICA

Quito

Equator

ISLAS REVILLAGIGEDO (Mex.)

ISLA DEL COCO (Costa Rica)

ISLA DE MALPELO (Colombia)

Golfo de Panamá

ISTMO DE PANAMÁ

Tropic of Cancer

Relief

Meters		Feet
3050		10 000
1525		5000
610		2000
305		1000
0	Sea Level	0
152.5		500 Below Sea Level
1525		5000
3050		10 000
6100		20 000

A-520000-76- -5-S41'
COPYRIGHT BY
RAND McNALLY & COMPANY
MADE IN U.S.A.

Longitude West of Greenwich

| 0 | 200 | 400 | 600 | 800 | 1000 Miles |

| 0 | 400 | 800 | 1200 | 1600 Kilometers |

Scale 1:40 000 000; one inch to 630 miles. Lambert's Azimuthal Equal Area Projection
Elevations and depressions are given in feet

a

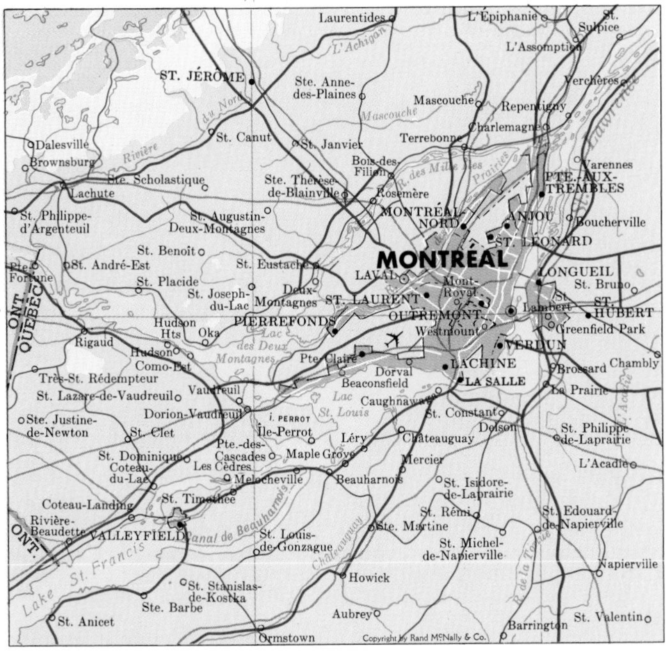

MONTRÉAL

b

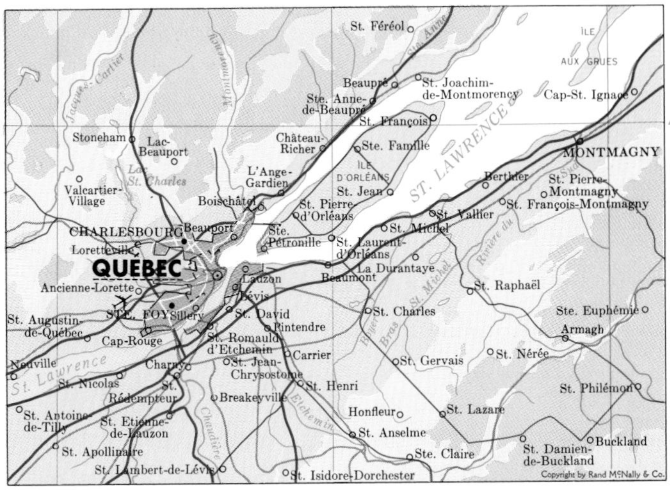

QUEBEC

c

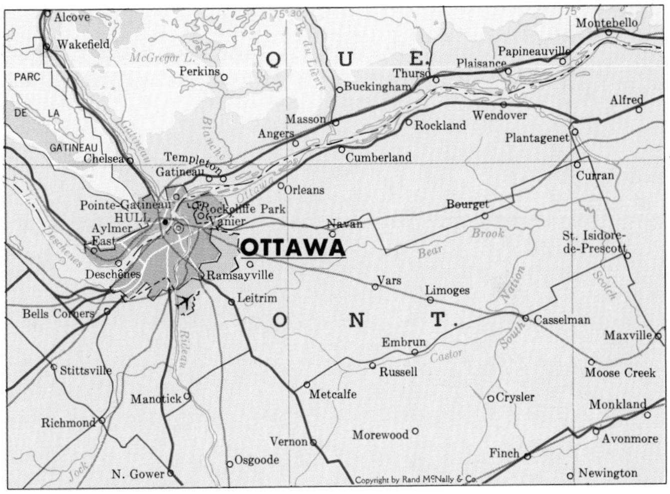

OTTAWA

d

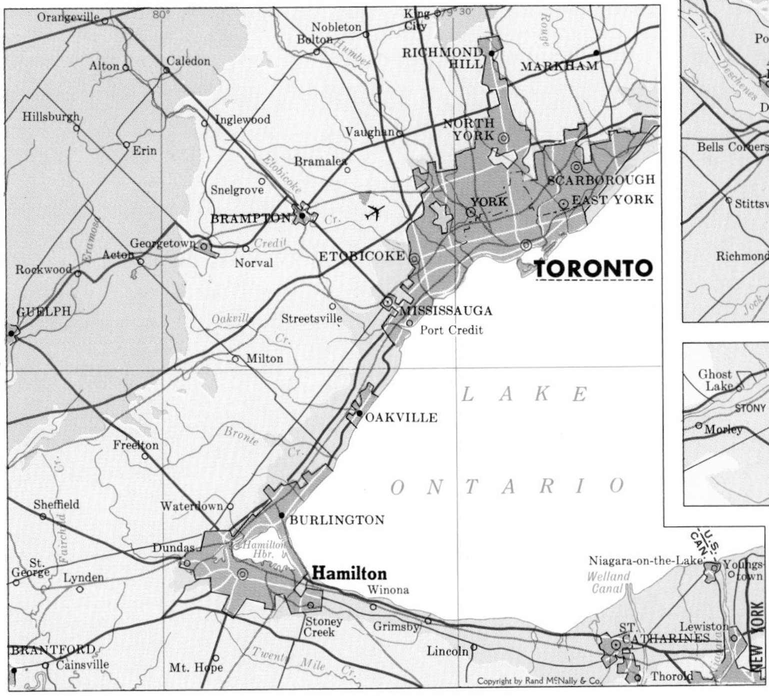

TORONTO

LAKE ONTARIO

Hamilton

e

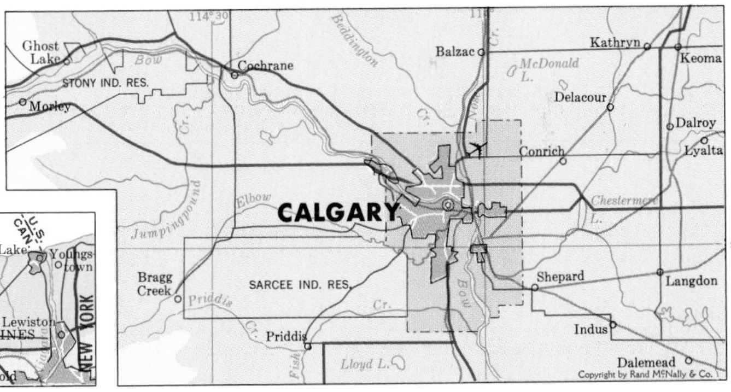

CALGARY

f

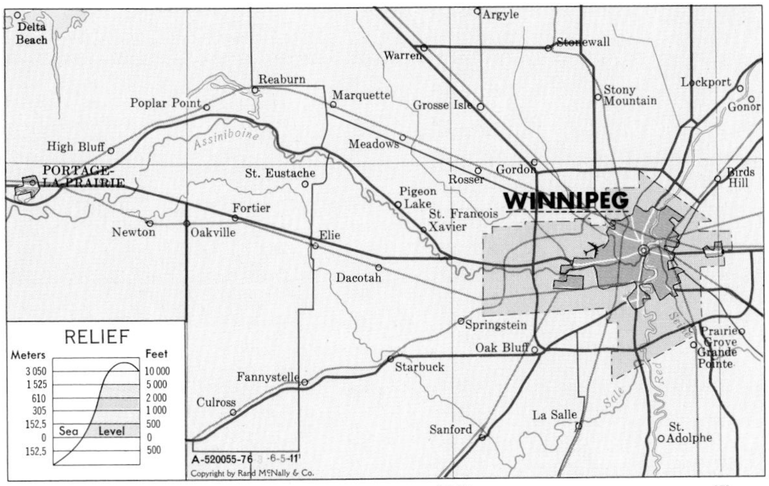

WINNIPEG

g

EDMONTON

RELIEF

Meters	Feet
3 050	10 000
1 525	5 000
610	2 000
305	1 000
152.5	500
Sea Level	0
152.5	500

A-520055-76   -6-5-11'
Copyright by Rand McNally & Co.

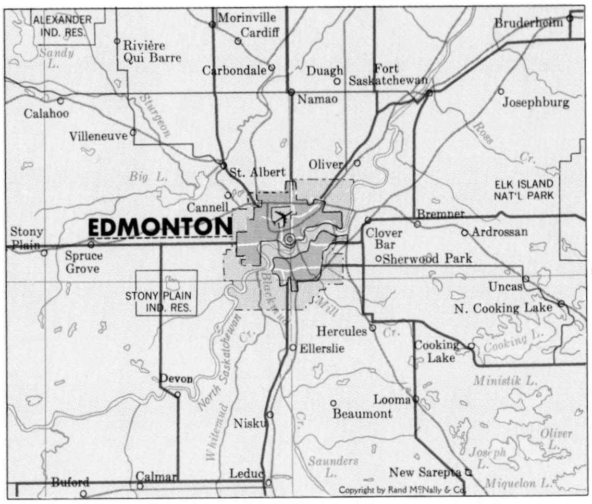

Scale 1:1 000 000; One inch to 16 miles.
Elevations and depressions are given in feet.

0 2 4 6 8 10 12 14 16 18 20 22 24   Miles
0 4 8 12 16 20 24 28 32 36 40   Kilometers

For larger scale coverage of Montréal and Toronto see page 54.

Longitude West of Greenwich

Scale 1: 12 000 000; one inch to 190 miles. Conic Projection

Elevations and depressions are given in feet

60° Longitude West of Greenwich 55°

Same scale as main map

QUEBEC

CAPE BAULD

Gulf of
St. Lawrence

GROS MORNE
NAT'L PARK
Deer Lake
Corner Brook
Stephenville
St. George's
St. George's Bay

Botwood
Grand Falls
TERRA NOVA
NAT'L PARK

Windsor
Gander
Bonavista
Bonavista Bay

NEWFOUNDLAND
Trinity

CAPE RAY
Channel-Port-aux-Basques
Grand Bank
Burin
CAPE NORTH
CAPE BRETON
ISLAND
ST. PIERRE AND MIQUELON (Fr.)

Fortune Bay
Placentia Bay

St. John's

ATLANTIC OCEAN

©RMcN a

FRANKLIN

MELVILLE
PENINSULA

BAFFIN ISLAND

BAFFIN ISLAND NAT'L PARK

Foxe
Basin

Arctic Circle

Igloolik

PRINCE CHARLES ISLAND

Pangnirtung

Nettilling

Cumberland Sound

CUMBERLAND PEN.

MERCY

Foxe Channel

SOUTHAMPTON ISLAND

COATS

MANSEL

NOTTINGHAM ISLAND

SALISBURY

Frobisher Bay
HALL PEN.
Lake Harbour
Frobisher Bay
EVERETT MTS.
RESOLUTION

C. DE NOUVELLE FRANCE

Hudson Strait

C. HOPES ADVANCE
AKPATOK
CAPE CHIDLEY

KEEWATIN

HUDSON BAY

All islands within bays and straits lie within Northwest Territories.

OTTAWA ISLANDS

Povungnituk

PENINSULE D'UNGAVA

Payne

Ungava Bay

Ft. Chimo

TORNGAT MTS.

Hebron

Nain

NEWFOUNDLAND

Hopedale
Makkovik
Cartwright

Hamilton Inlet
Rigolet

BELCHER ISLANDS

Minto

aux Feuilles

Lac Bienville

Grande de la Baleine

MEALY MTS.

Battle Harbour
Anthony

LONG RANGE MTS.

GROS MORNE NAT'L PARK

Corner Brook
Stephenville
St. George's

Churchill Falls
Goose Bay

LABRADOR

Ft. Severn

C. HENRIETTA MARIA

PTE. LOUIS-XIV

James Bay

Ft. George

AKIMISKI

Ft. Albany

Moosonee

Nichicun

MTS. OTISH

Schefferville

Mistassini

Sept-Îles

ILE D'ANTICOSTI

Gulf of St. Lawrence

Channel-Port-aux-Basques

ONTARIO

Winisk

Severn

Trout Lake

Sioux Lookout

Lac Seul

Dryden

Lake of the Woods
Rainy

St. Joseph

Armstrong Sta.

Nakina

Geraldton
Longlac

Nipigon

Lake Nipigon

Marathon

PUKASKWA NAT'L PARK

Thunder Bay

MICHIPICOTEN I.

Lake Superior

Marquette

Escanaba

Duluth
Superior

MINNESOTA

WISCONSIN

St. Paul

Green Bay

MINNEAPOLIS

Madison

MILWAUKEE

CHICAGO

Grand Rapids

Lansing

Flint

Saginaw

DETROIT

Windsor

Toledo

Leamington

Hearst

Kapuskasing
Cochrane
Iroquois Falls
Timmins
Kirkland Lake

Chapleau

Sudbury

Sault Ste. Marie
Thessalon
Blind River
Espanola

MANITOULIN

Georgian Bay

Wiarton
Owen Sound

Kincardine

Port Huron

Sarnia

Chatham

Lake Huron

London

St. Thomas

Lake Erie

Coral Rapids
Fraserdale

La Sarre

Rouyn

Malartic

Ville-Marie
Témiscaming

Cobalt

North Bay

Sturgeon Falls

Huntsville
Parry Sound

Midland
Barrie

Orillia

Lindsay

Peterborough

Oshawa
Whitby

TORONTO

Hamilton
Niagara
St. Catharines

Buffalo

Rochester

ONTARIO

Amos
Senneterre

Val-d'Or

QUEBEC

MTS. OTISH

Chibougamau

Dolbeau
Mistassini
Roberval
Chambord
St. Félicien
Lac St-Jean

Chicoutimi
Jonquière

Baie Comeau

Malbaie
St. Paul

Clarke City

Baie St. Paul

La Tuque

Grand'Mère
Shawinigan
Trois-Rivières
Sorel
Drummondville
Victoriaville
Nicolet

Parent

Réservoir Gouin

St. Maurice

Quebec
Lévis

MONTREAL
Laval
Longueuil
St. Hyacinthe
Granby
Sherbrooke

Valleyfield

MAINE

NEW BRUNSWICK

Edmundston

Fredericton
Saint John

St. Stephen

FUNDY NAT'L PARK

Moncton

Bathurst

Chatham

Newcastle

CHIC-CHOCS MTS.

Gaspé

New Carlisle

Matane
Rimouski
Rivière-du-Loup

GASPÉ PEN.

ILES DE LA MADELEINE

P.E.I.

PRINCE EDWARD ISLAND NAT'L PARK

Summerside
Charlottetown

Amherst

NOVA SCOTIA

Truro

Sydney
Glace Bay

Glasgow

New Waterford

CAPE BRETON HIGHLANDS NAT'L PARK

Kentville
Bridgewater
Lunenburg
Liverpool
Shelburne

Yarmouth

CAPE SABLE

Halifax

Digby

NEW HAMPSHIRE

VERMONT

Augusta

Portland

Concord

Hartford

Providence

Boston

ATLANTIC OCEAN

CAPE COD

NEW YORK

Ottawa
Hull
Pembroke
Renfrew
Bancroft
Smiths Falls
Kingston
Brockville
Ogdensburg
Alexandria Bay

Albany

Newark

NEW YORK

N.J.

PENNSYLVANIA

Scranton

OHIO

CONN.

MASS.

R.I.

80°

75°

70°

65°

60°

55°

Relief

Meters		Feet
3050		10 000
1525		5000
610		2000
305		1000
152.5		500
0	Sea Level	0
152.5		500
1525		5000
3050		10 000

A-520200-76
COPYRIGHT BY
RAND McNALLY & COMPANY
MADE IN U.S.A.

0 25 50 75 100   200   300   400   500 Miles

0   100   200   300   400   500   600   700   800 Kilometers

134° 132° 130° 128° 126° 124°

BRINCE
Klawock
WALES
Hydaburg
Copper Mtn
3916
OF
DALL
ISLAND
ISLAND
Metlakatla
Ketchikan
ANNETTE
ISLAND
Mt. Reid
4592
REVILLAGIGEDO
ISLAND

UNITED STATES
CANADA

Dixon Entrance

CAPE KNOX
DUNDAS
ISLAND

Alice Arm
Hazelton
SKEENA
MOUNTAINS
Shedin Pk
8750
OMINECA
MOUNTAINS
Williston
Lake

HAZELTON

Mt. Thomlinson
8050

Smithers
Takla
Lake
Thentlo
Lake
McLeod

Prince Rupert
Terrace
Skeena
BULKLEY
MOUNTAINS
BULKLEY RANGES
Howson Pk
9050

Babine
Lake
Stuart
Lake
Fort
St. James
Salmon

Masset
PORCHER
ISLAND

Kitimat
Morice Lake
Burns Lake
NECHAKO
Endako
Vanderhoof

QUEEN
Masset
Inlet
GRAHAM ISLAND
PITT
ISLAND
KITIMAT
COAST

Ootsa
Lake
Tahtsa
Lake
Michel Pk
7396
Nechako
Reservoir
KENNEY DAM
PLATEAU

CHARLOTTE
Skidegate Inlet
BANKS
ISLAND
Hartley Bay
Whitesail
Lake
Eutsuk Lake
Tetachuck
Lake
West
NECHAKO
RANGE

MORESBY ISLAND
Mount Kermode
3550
Hecate
ESTEVAN
GROUP
PRINCESS
ROYAL
ISLAND
RANGES
Eutsuk Lake
West Road
Dean

ISLANDS
Strait
ARISTAZABAL
ISLAND
Mt Born
3450
RODERICK
ISLAND
Dean
BRITISH
Chilcotin

CAPE ST. JAMES
Ocean Falls
Bella Coola
Charlotte
Lake
FRASE
Redstone

Queen
Bella Bella
COLUM
PLAT

Charlotte
Namu
Monarch Mtn
11506
Chilko
Lake

Sound
Rivers Inlet
PACIFIC
Razorback Mtn
10432
Silverthrone Mtn
Mt Tatlow
10058

CALVERT ISLAND
Mt Waddington
Mt. Queen Bess
10791
Good Hope Mtn
10613
Monmouth Mtn
10040

PACIFIC
CAPE
CAUTION
Queen Charlotte Strait
Knight
Mt Gilbert
3109
Bra

Bull Harbour
CAPE SCOTT
Port Hardy
Simood
Sound
RANGES
Wedg

OCEAN
Quatsino Sound
Port Alice
Kelsey Bay
VANCOUVER
Powell
Mt Gorde
8787
Squamish

CAPE COOK
Victoria Pk
7095
Bloedel
Campbell
River
Powell River

VANCOUVER
NOOTKA
ISLAND
Golden Hinde
7291
Courtenay
Comox
Vanando
ISLAND
RANGES
North Vancouver
Vancouver
Burnaby
New Westmin

ISLAND
Nootka
Sound
Tofino
Port Alberni
Nanaimo
Mt Whymper
5056
Lake Cowichan
Ladysmith

PACIFIC RIM
NATIONAL PARK
Barkley
Sound
CAPE BEALE

CAPE FLATTERY
Strait of Juan de Fuca
Esquimalt
Victo

OLYMPIC
NATIONAL
PARK
OLYMPIC
NATIONAL
PARK
Port
Angeles

PACIFIC

54°
52°
50°
48°

132°

A-520220-76 6-5-7
COPYRIGHT BY
RAND MCNALLY & COMPANY
MADE IN U.S.A.

Relief		
Meters		Feet
3050		10 000
1525		5000
610		2000
305		1000
152.5		500
0	Sea Level	0
152.5		500
1525		5000

130° Continued on pages 116-117 128° Longitude West of Greenwich 126° 124°

Scale 1:4 000 000; one inch to 64 miles. Conic Projection
Elevations and depressions are given in feet.

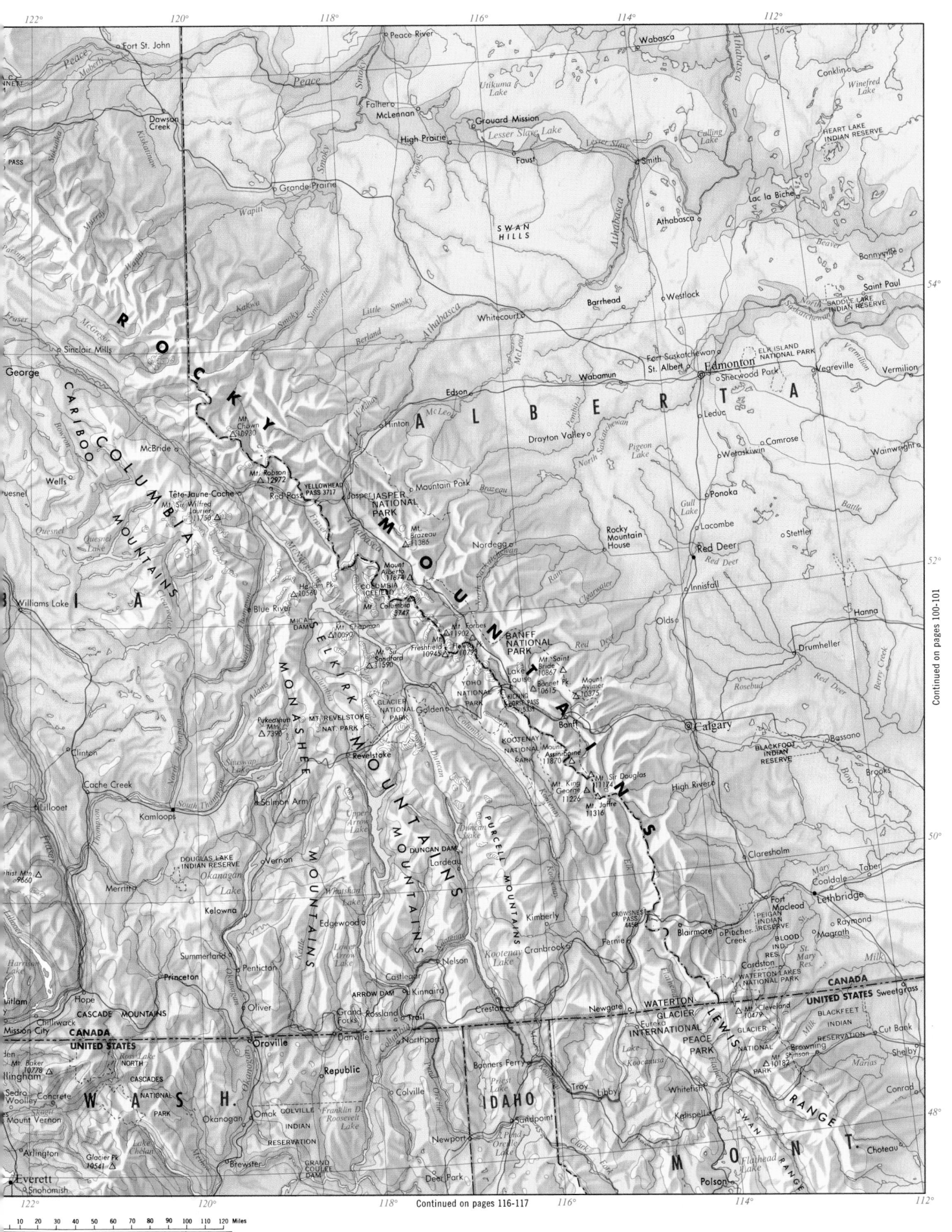

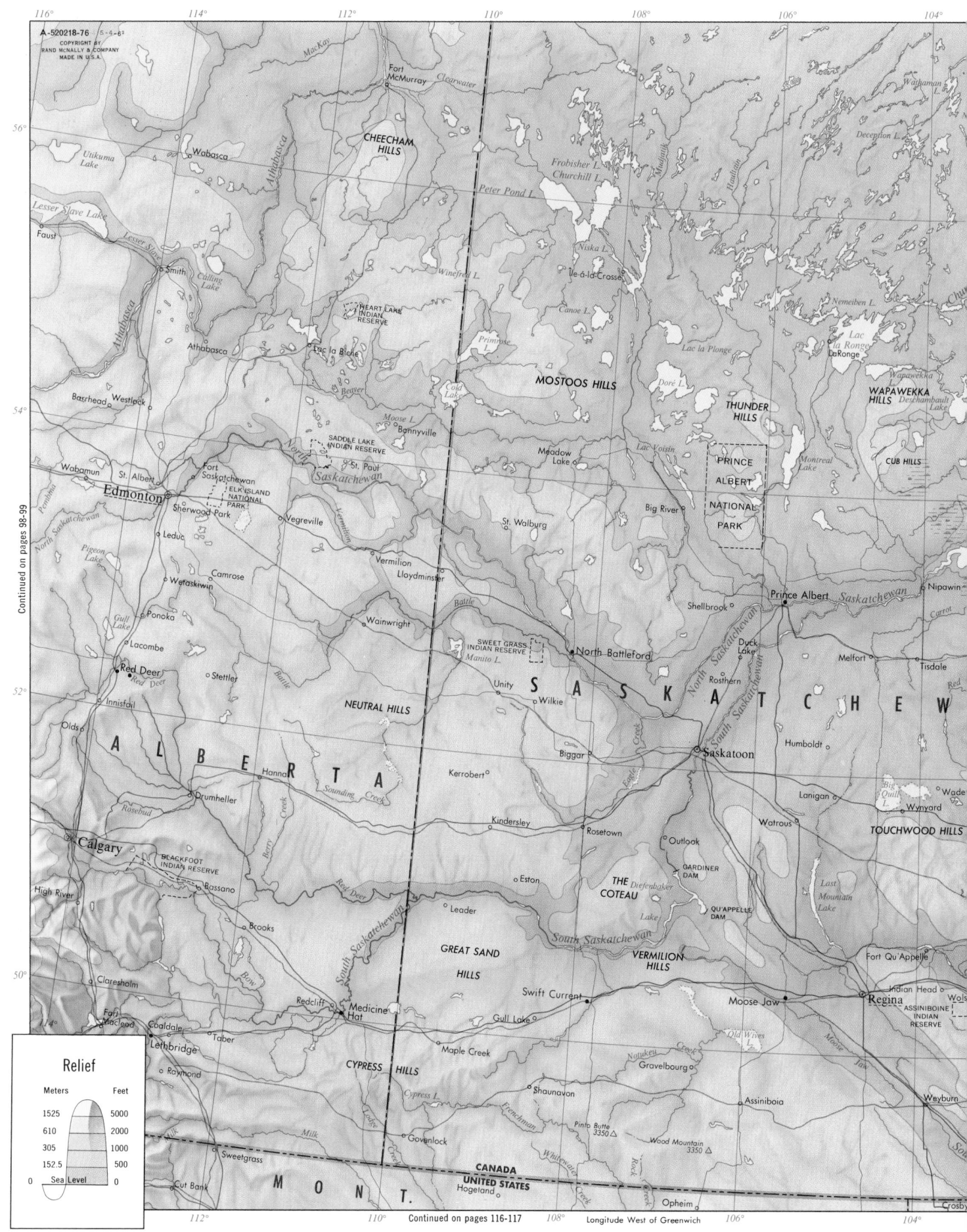

A-520218-76 5-4-63
COPYRIGHT BY
RAND McNALLY & COMPANY
MADE IN U.S.A.

116°   114°   112°   110°   108°   106°   104°

56°

Utikuma
Lake
Faust

Lesser Slave Lake

CHEECHAM
HILLS

Fort
McMurray   Clearwater

MacKay

Frobisher L.
Churchill L.

Peter Pond L.

Wabasca

Deception L.

Wathaman L.

Smith
Calling
Lake

Lesser Slave

Athabasca

Barrhead   Westlock

Athabasca

HEART LAKE
INDIAN
RESERVE

Lac la Biche

Beaver

Winefred L.

Niska L.

Île-à-la-Crosse

Canoe L.

Primrose

Cold
L.

MOSTOOS HILLS

Lac la Plonge

Doré L.

Nemeiben L.

Lac
la Ronge
LaRonge   Wapawekka L.

WAPAWEKKA
HILLS   Deschambault
Lake

54°

Wabamun   St. Albert

North

Saddle Lake
Indian Reserve

Moose L.

Bonnyville

St. Paul

Meadow
Lake

Lac Voisin

THUNDER
HILLS

Montreal
Lake

CUB HILLS

Edmonton

Fort
Saskatchewan

Elk Island
National
Park

Sherwood Park

Leduc

Saskatchewan

Vegreville

Vermilion

Big River

PRINCE
ALBERT
NATIONAL
PARK

Nipawin

Camrose

Wetaskiwin

Vermilion

Lloydminster

St. Walburg

Shellbrook

Prince Albert   Saskatchewan

Carrot

Ponoka

Pigeon
Lake

Gull
Lake

Battle

Wainwright

Sweet Grass
Indian Reserve

Rosthern

Melfort

Tisdale

Red

Lacombe

North Saskatchewan

Red Deer

Stettler

Battle

Manito L.

North Battleford

Duck
Lake

Humboldt

52°

Innisfail

Olds

NEUTRAL HILLS

Unity   Wilkie

SASKATCHEW

Saskatoon

Lanigan

Big
Quill
L.   Wade

Wynyard

Drumheller

A   L   B   E   R   T   A

Hanna

Kerrobert

Biggar

Sounding   Creek

Watrous

TOUCHWOOD HILLS

Rosebud

Berry   Creek

Kindersley

Rosetown

Outlook

GARDINER
DAM

Last
Mountain
Lake

Calgary

BLACKFOOT
INDIAN RESERVE

Bassano

Red   Deer

Eston

THE
COTEAU   Diefenbaker
Lake

QU'APPELLE
DAM

High River

Brooks

South Saskatchewan

Leader

Bow

Saskatchewan

GREAT SAND
HILLS

VERMILION
HILLS

Fort Qu'Appelle

Claresholm

50°

Fort
Macleod

Redcliff   Medicine
Hat

Swift Current

Gull Lake

Moose Jaw

Regina

Wols

Coaldale

Taber

Maple Creek

Old Wives
L.

Gravelbourg

Indian Head

ASSINIBOINE
INDIAN
RESERVE

Lethbridge

Raymond

CYPRESS   HILLS

Cypress L.

Notukeu   Creek

Assiniboia

Weyburn

Milk

Ledge

Shaunavon

Frenchman

Pinto Butte
△3350

Wood Mountain
△3350

Whitewater

Rock   Creek

Moose Jaw

Sweetgrass

Milk

Govenlock

CANADA
UNITED STATES

Cut Bank

M   O   N   T.

Hogeland

Opheim

Crosby

Continued on pages 98-99

Continued on pages 116-117

Longitude West of Greenwich

112°   110°   108°   106°   104°

Relief

Meters	Feet
1525	5000
610	2000
305	1000
152.5	500
0 Sea Level	0

Scale 1:4 000 000; one inch to 64 miles. Conic Projection

Elevations and depressions are given in feet.

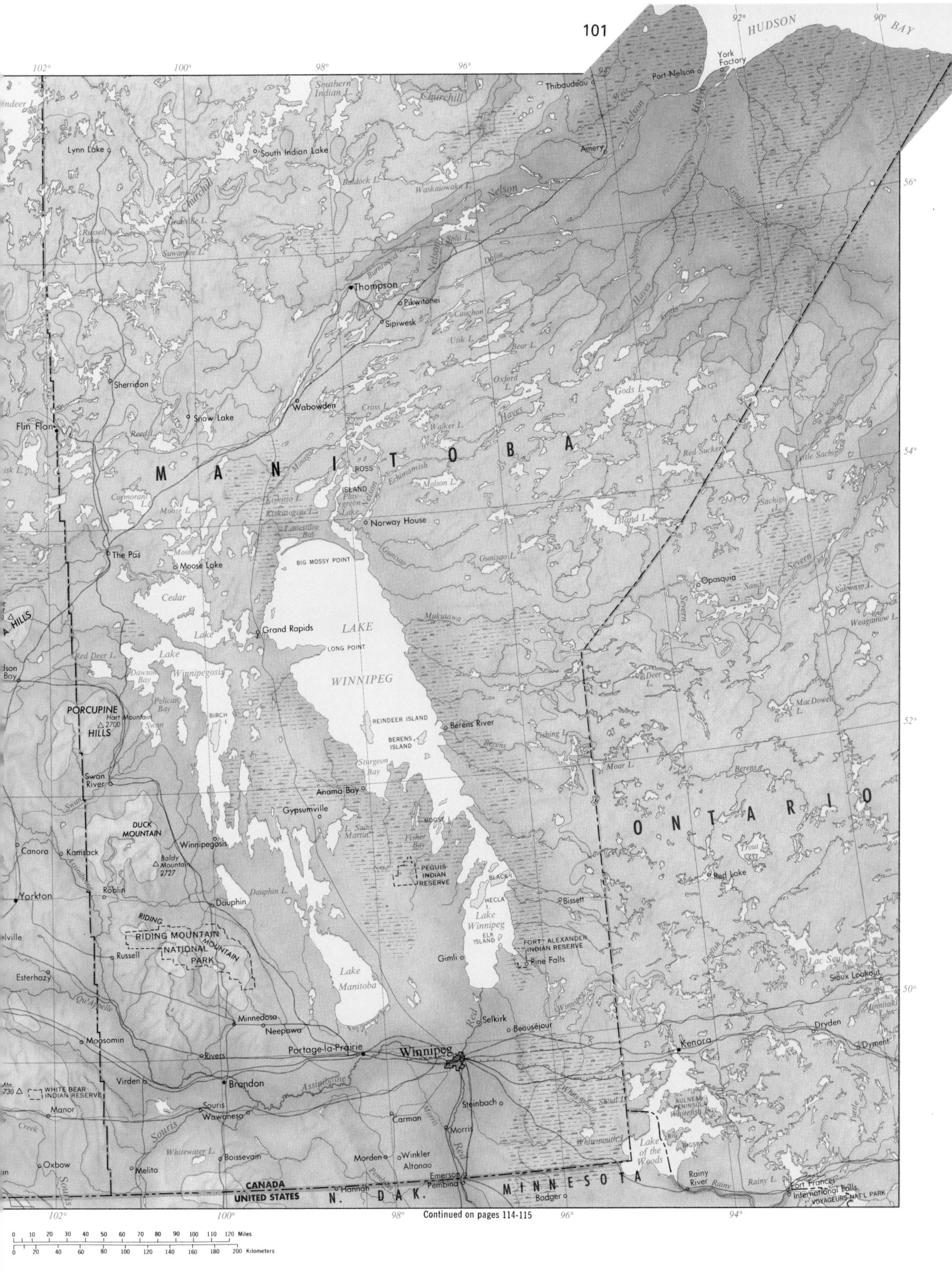

HUDSON BAY

92°   90°

York Factory
Port Nelson
Thibaudeau
Amery

M A N I T O B A

Lynn Lake
South Indian Lake
Baldock L.
Southern Indian L.
Churchill

Sherridon
Snow Lake
Wabowden
Thompson
Pikwitonei
Sipiwesk
Cross L.
Utik L.
Bear L.
Oxford L.
Gods L.
Red Sucker L.
Little Sachigo

Flin Flon
Reed L.
Cormorant L.
Minago L.
ROSS ISLAND
Playgreen Lake
Norway House
Walker L.
Molson L.
Echimamish
Island L.
Opasquia
Sandy L.
Salowagow L.

The Pas
Moose Lake
Moose L.
Cedar Lake
Limestone Bay
BIG MOSSY POINT
Gunisao L.
Mukutawa
Red Lake
Weagamow L.

PORCUPINE HILLS
Hart Mountain △2700
Pelican Bay
BIRCH I.
Dawson Bay
Winnipegosis
Grand Rapids
LONG POINT
LAKE WINNIPEG
REINDEER ISLAND
BERENS ISLAND
Berens River
Fishing L.
Deer L.
MacDowell L.

Swan River
Swan L.
Sturgeon Bay
Berens
Moar L.
Berens R.
Trout L.

DUCK MOUNTAIN
Baldy Mountain △ 2727
Anama Bay
Gypsumville
L. Saint Martin
MOOSE I.
Fisher Bay
O N T A R I O

Canora
Kamsack
Winnipegosis
PEGUIS INDIAN RESERVE

Yorkton
Roblin
Dauphin L.
Dauphin
BLACK I.
HECLA I.
Lake Winnipeg
Bissett

elville
RIDING MOUNTAIN
RIDING MOUNTAIN NATIONAL PARK
Russell
ELK ISLAND
FORT ALEXANDER INDIAN RESERVE
Lac Seul
Sioux Lookout

Esterhazy
Minnedosa
Neepawa
Lake Manitoba
Gimli
Pine Falls
Dryden
Dyment

Moosomin
Rivers
Portage-la-Prairie
Winnipeg
Selkirk
Beauséjour
Kenora

Mtn. 730 △
WHITE BEAR INDIAN RESERVE
Virden
Brandon
Assiniboine
AULNEAU PENINSULA Whitefish Bay

Manor
Souris
Wawanesa
Carman
Steinbach
Morris
BIGSBY

Oxbow
Melita
Boissevain
Whitewater L.
Morden
Winkler
Altonao
Emerson
Pembina
Lake of the Woods
Rainy River
Fort Frances
International Falls VOYAGEURS NAT'L PARK

CANADA
UNITED STATES
N.   D A K.   MINNESOTA
Hannah
Badger

Continued on pages 114-115

102°   100°   98°   96°   94°

0 10 20 30 40 50 60 70 80 90 100 110 120 Miles
0 20 40 60 80 100 120 140 160 180 200 Kilometers

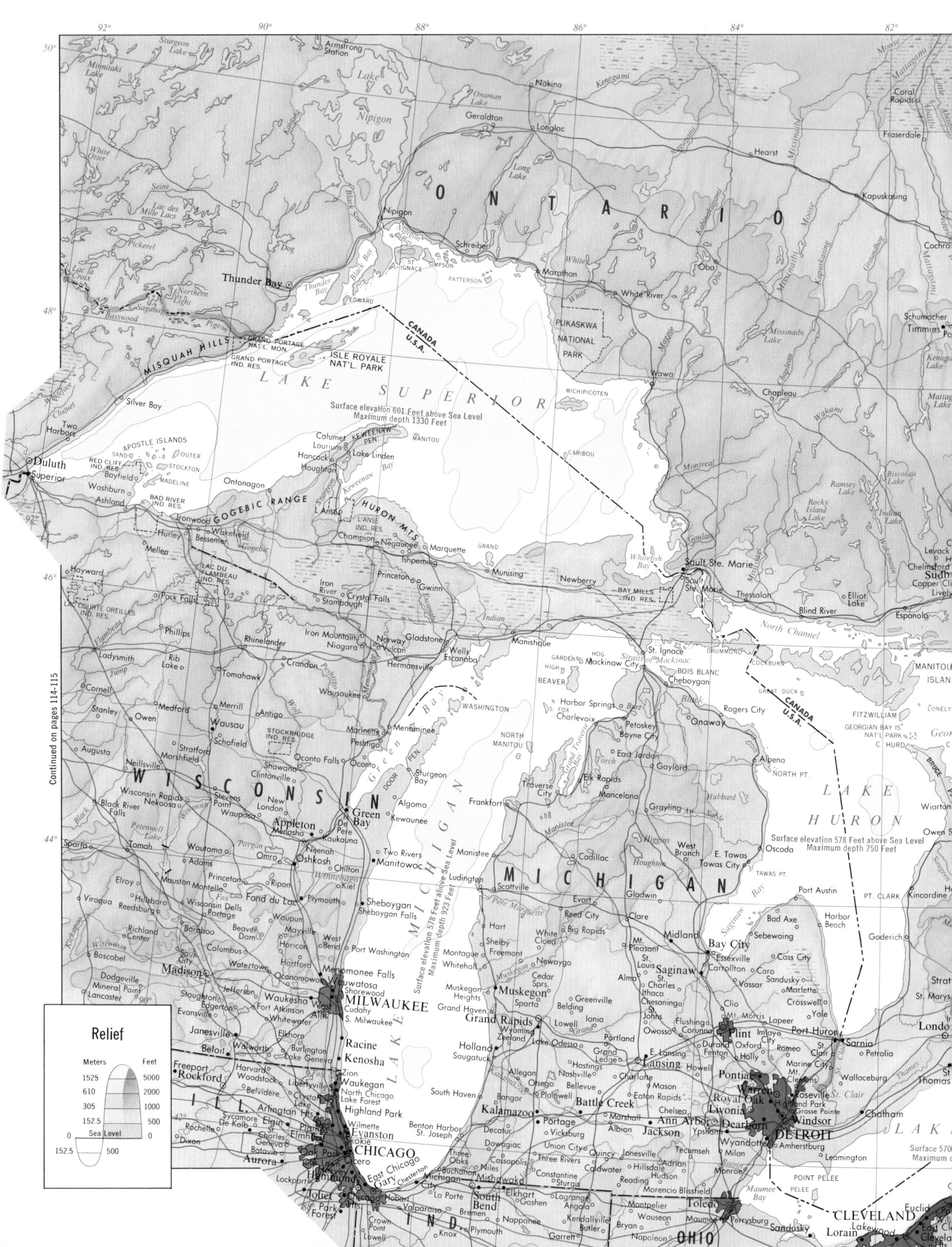

Continued on pages 114-115

Relief

Meters	Feet
1525	5000
610	2000
305	1000
152.5	500
Sea Level	0
152.5	500

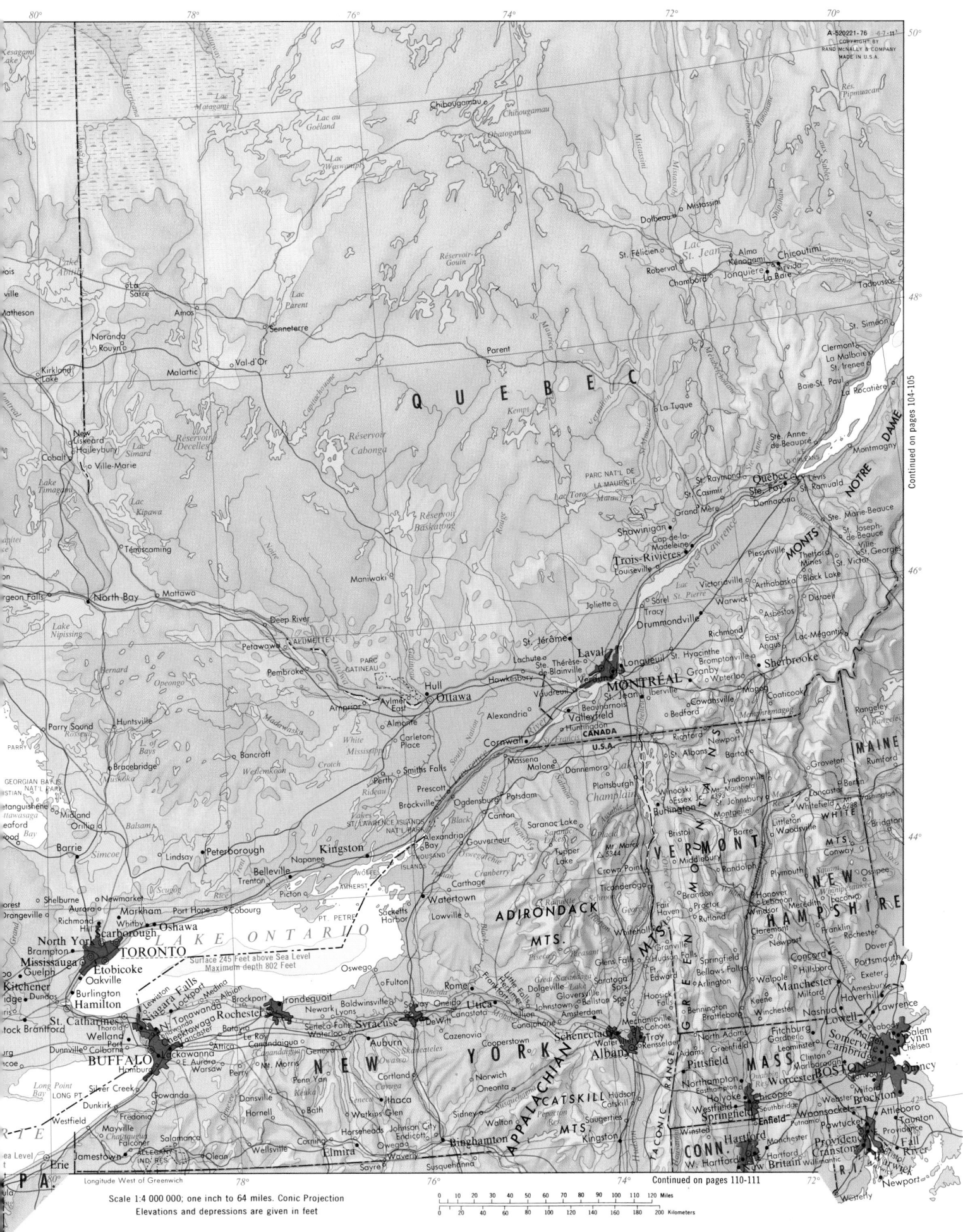

Continued on pages 104-105

A-520021-76   6-7-11'
COPYRIGHT BY
RAND McNALLY & COMPANY
MADE IN U.S.A.

80°   78°   76°   74°   72°   70°   50°

Kesagami Lake
Lac Matagami
Lac au Goéland
Chibougamau
Chibougamau
Obatogamau
Rés. Pipmuacan
48°

Lac Waswanipi
Mistassini
Dolbeau   Mistassini

ois
ville
Matheson
Lac Simard
Lac Parent
Réservoir-Gouin
St. Félicien   Lac St. Jean   Alma   Chicoutimi
Roberval   Kénogami   Arvida   La Baie
Chambord   Jonquière
Saguenay
St. Siméon

Noranda   Amos   Senneterre
Rouyn
Kirkland Lake
Val-d'Or   Parent
St. Irenee
La Malbaie
St. Irenee
Baie-St. Paul
La Rocatière

New Liskeard (Haileybury)   Malartic
Réservoir Decelles
Q U E B E C
Montmagny
46°

Cobalt   Ville-Marie
Lac Simard
Lac Kipawa
Réservoir Cabonga
Kempt
La Tuque
PARC NAT'L DE LA MAURICIE
St. Raymond   Québec   Lévis
Ste. Foy   St. Romuald

Témiscaming
Réservoir Baskatong
Lac Toro
St. Casimir
Donnacona
Ste. Marie-Beauce
St. Joseph-de-Beauce
Ville
St. Victor   St. Georges

rgeon Falls   North Bay   Mattawa
Maniwaki
Grand Mère
Shawinigan
Cap-de-la-Madeleine
Plessisville   Thetford Mines
Black Lake
MONTS

Lake Nipissing
Deep River
Trois-Rivières
Louiseville
Victoriaville   Arthabaska
Disraeli
Lac-Mégantic

PARRY
Parry Sound   Huntsville
Petawawa   ALUMETTE
PARC GATINEAU
St. Jérôme
Joliette
Sorel   Warwick   Asbestos
Richmond   East Angus
NOTRE DAME

Bernard   Opeongo
Pembroke   Amprior   Aylmer East   Hull   Ottawa
Lachute   Ste. Thérèse-de-Blainville   Laval   Longueuil   St. Hyacinthe
Drummondville   Sherbrooke
Rangeley

Bracebridge   Bancroft
Madawaska
Almonte   Carleton Place
Vaudreuil   MONTRÉAL   St. Jean   Iberville
Granby   Waterloo   Magog
Coaticook
Rangeley

GEORGIAN BAY IS.
NAT'L PARK
Muskoka   White Mississippi   Crotch
Smiths Falls   Perth
CANADA
U.S.A.
Hawkesbury   Beauharnois   St. Jean
Bedford   Cowansville
Memphremagog
MAINE

tanguishene
eaford
ood
Midland   Orillia   Balsam   Lindsay
Rideau
Brockville   Ogdensburg   Potsdam
Alexandria   Cornwall   Valleyfield   Huntingdon
Massena   Malone   Dannemora   St. Albans   Newport   Barton
Groveton   Rumford

Bay   Barrie   Simcoe   Peterborough
Napanee   Kingston
Prescott
Perth
Yokes   ST. LAWRENCE ISLANDS NAT'L PARK
Canton
Gouverneur
Plattsburgh   Lake Champlain
Lyndonville
St. Johnsbury   Lancaster
Berlin   WHITE MTS.
Whitefield
Mt. Washington 6288

Shelburne   Newmarket
Aurora   Markham   Port Hope   Cobourg
Belleville   WOLFE   AMHERST   THOUSAND ISLANDS
Black
Saranac Lake   Saranac Lakes   Lake Placid   Mt. Marcy 5344   Crown Point
Montpelier   Barre   Littleton   Woodsville
Middlebury   Randolph

orest
Orangeville
Richmond Hill   Whitby   Oshawa
Trenton   Picton
PT. PETRE
Watertown   Lowville   Carthage
Cranberry Lake
Tupper Lake   Ticonderoga
VERMONT   Hanover   Lebanon   Meredith   Laconia   Ossipee
Brandon   Proctor   Rutland   Windsor   Plymouth
Conway
NEW HAMPSHIRE

North York   Scarborough   TORONTO
LAKE ONTARIO
Surface 245 Feet above Sea Level
Maximum depth 802 Feet
Oswego
ADIRONDACK
MTS.
Whitehall   Granville
Glens Falls   Hudson Falls   Fair Haven   Springfield
Claremont   Newport   Franklin   Rochester   Dover
Keene   Winchester   Manchester   Milford   Nashua   Haverhill   Lawrence

Brampton
Mississauga   Etobicoke   Oakville
Burlington
Guelph
Kitchener   Hamilton
St. Catharines
Niagara Falls   Lewiston   Lockport   Medina   Albion   Brockport
Irondequoit   Newark   Lyons   Baldwinsville   Oneida   Utica
Fulton   Rome   Ilion   Herkimer   Little Falls   Gloversville   Johnstown   Amsterdam
Saratoga Sprs.   Ballston Spa   Mechanicville   Cohoes
Hoosick Falls   Bennington   Brattleboro
GREEN   North Adams   Greenfield   Gardner   Fitchburg   Leominster
TACONIC RANGE   Pittsfield   Adams
Walpole   Hillsboro   Exeter
MASS.

N. Tonawanda   Tonawanda   Cheektowaga   Lancaster   Attica
Batavia   Le Roy   Canandaigua   Geneva   Seneca Falls   Waterloo   Syracuse   DeWitt
Auburn   Skaneateles   Cazenovia
Schenectady   Troy   Rensselaer   Albany   Watervliet
Northampton   Easthampton   Worcester   BOSTON
Marlborough   Framingham

BUFFALO   Lackawanna   Hamburg   E. Aurora   Warsaw   Perry
Penn Yan   Mt. Morris   Cortland   Cayuga   Owasco
Norwich   Oneonta   Cooperstown
N E W   Y O R K
Hudson   Catskill
CATSKILL   Saugerties
APPALACHIAN MTS.   Kingston
Holyoke   Chicopee   Springfield   Webster
Westfield   Enfield   Hartford   Manchester
Southbridge   Woonsocket   Pawtucket   Attleboro   Taunton
Providence   Cranston   Fall River
CONN.   New Britain   Willimantic   R.I.
Newport

St. Catharines
Thorold   Welland   Port Colborne
Dunnville
coe
Silver Creek   Gowanda
Dunkirk
Westfield
Fredonia
Mayville
Jamestown   Falconer   Salamanca
Chautauqua   ALLEGANY IND. RES.
Olean
Hornell
Dansville   Wayland
Bath
Watkins Glen   Horseheads   Elmira
Corning   Johnson City   Endicott   Owego   Waverly
Binghamton   Susquehanna
Sidney   Walton   Hancock
Deposit
Sayre

LAKE ERIE
LONG PT.
Long Point Bay
Silver Creek
a Level
ea Level
P A
Erie
P A
Longitude West of Greenwich
80°   78°   76°   74°

Continued on pages 110-111

42°

Scale 1:4 000 000; one inch to 64 miles. Conic Projection
Elevations and depressions are given in feet

0   10   20   30   40   50   60   70   80   90   100   110   120 Miles
0   20   40   60   80   100   120   140   160   180   200 Kilometers

104

50°

74° 72° 70° 68° 66°

Chibougamau
Chibougamau
Chibougamau

Mistassini

Manouane

Rés. Pipmuacan

Rivière

B
E

Clarke City
Sept-Îles
Port-Cartier

Mingar

Détroit de

48°

Dolbeau
Mistassini

St. Félicien

Roberval
Lac
St-Jean
Chambord
Kenogami
Janquière
Arvida
La Baie

Chicoutimi

Forestville

Portneuf-Sur-Mer

Sault-au-Mouton

Hauterive
Baie-Comeau
Betsiamites

Baie-Trinité
POINTE DES MONTS

St.
Lawrence
River

Cap-Chat
Mt. Jacques-Cartier
4160

Matane

Ste. Felicité

Mont-Joli
Rimouski
Amqui
Causapscal

MTS.
CHIC-CHOCS

GASPÉ

Gaspé
PARC
FORIL
Percé
Grand-Rivière

Q
U
E
E

Q

St. Siméon
La Tuque

St. Maurice

Vermilion

Kemp

Clermont
La Malbaie
St. Irénée
Baie-St. Paul

ILE
AUX
COUDRES

Bic

Rivière-Trois-Pistoles

Cacouna
Rivière-du-Loup
Témiscouata

Matapédia

Nouvelle
Dalhousie
Campbellton
Jacquet River

Maria

Kedgwick

Chandler
New
Carlisle

Chaleur
Bay

MISCOU PT.
MISCOU
SHIPPEGAN

Caraquet
Burnsville
Shippegan

Tigni

Miramichi
Bay

La Tuque

Grand'Mère
Shawinigan
Cap-de-la-Madeleine
Trois-Rivières
Louiseville

Joliette

Tracy
Sorel

St. Raymond
St. Casimir

Québec
Ste. Foy
St. Romuald
Donnacana

Montmagny

Ste. Anne
de Beaupré
ILE D'ORLEANS

St. Pascal
La Pocatière

Notre-Dame
du-Lac

Cabano

Edmundston

Fort
Kent
Eagle
Lake

Van Buren
St. Leonard
Grand Falls

Plaster Rock

NEW

Newcastle
Chatham
Millerton
Blackville
Richibucto

Alberton
O'Leary

Buctouche
Harcourt

46°

MONTRÉAL
Laval
Longueuil
Verdun
Beauharnois

St. Jean

Hyacinthe
Granby

Iberville
Bedford

Richford

Hemmingford

St. Albans
Newport

CANADA
U.S.A.

St.
Pierre
Lac

DAME
CANADA
U.S.A.

NOTRE

MONTS

Plessisville

Victoriaville
Arthabaska
Warwick
Black Lake

Thetford
Mines
St. Victor
Ville-St. Georges

Ste. Marie-Beauce
St.
Joseph-
Beauce

Lac-Frontière

Fish
River

Ashland

Stockholm
Caribou
Washburn

Presque
Isle

Mars Hill
Monticello

Oakfield
Patten

Fort Fairfield

Bath

Woodstock

Houlton

Benton

CANADA
U.S.A.

Grand Falls

Hartland
Stanley

Marysville
Fredericton

Minto

Chipman

Salmon

BRUNSWICK

Moncton
Salisbury
Havelock
Petitcodiac
Sussex

Dieppe
Port Elgin
Sackville

Shediac

Summ

NOVA

Drummondville

Waterloo

Magog
Coaticook

Asbestos
Disraeli

Lac-Mégantic

Rockwood

Moosehead
Lake

Mt. Katahdin
5267

Millinocket

Danforth
McAdam

Oromocto

Grand

Minas Basin
COBEQUID

Amherst
Joggins
COBEQUID
Londonderry

Springhi

Richmond
Bromptonville
East
Angus

Sherbrooke

Memphremagog
Lake

CANADA
U.S.A.

Brandon

Burlington
Essex Jc.

GREEN

Barton

St. Johnsbury
Lyndonville

Lancaster

Whitefield

Berlin

Greenville
Brownville
Junction
Monson
Milo

Lincoln

MAINE

Parsboro

Minas Channel
Bridgetown

St. Stephen
St. George
St. Andrews
Calais
Eastport
Lubec

St. John

St. Martins

FUNDY
NAT'L
PARK
Hampton
Rothesay

Alma

Chignecto Bay

Joggins
Springhi

Bay
of
Fundy

Minas
Basin
Canning
Wolfville
Hantsport

VT.

Platts-
burg
Winooski

Mt. Mansfield
4393

Middlebury

Montpelier
Barre

Bristol

Proctor
Rutland

VERMONT

MONTS

Randolph

Woodsville

Littleton
Woodstock

WHITE

MTS.
Mt. Washington
6288

Rangeley

Madison
Farmington
Mexico
Rumford
Norway
S. Paris

Bingham

Dover-
Foxcroft
Dexter
Newport

Skowhegan

Old Town

Bangor
Brewer

Cherryfield

Machias

Ellsworth

Bar Harbor
ACADIA NAT'L PARK
MT. DESERT

GRAND
MANAN

Campobello
LONG I.
BRIER I.

St. Mary's Bay

Middleton
Windsor

Bridgewater
Lunenburg

Dartmout

Halifax

NEW

Lebanon

Hanover

Windsor
Claremont
Newport

Franklin

HAMPSHIRE

Winthrop
Waterville

Fairfield

Pittsfield

Augusta

Gardiner

Winchendon
Meredith
Laconia
Winnipesaukee
Lake

Plymouth

Ossipee

Conway

Mechanic Falls
Lewiston
Auburn
Lisbon Falls

Camden
Rockland

Belfast
Searsport

Penobscot
Bay

DEER
ISLE AU HAUT

KEJIMKUJIK
NAT'L PARK

Mahone Bay

Liverpool

Lake
Champlain

NEW
YORK

Bellows
Falls

Springfield

Arlington

Bennington
Brattleboro
N. Adams
Adams

Claremont
Newport

Keene
Winchester
Nashua

Manchester
Milford

Hillsboro
Concord

Franklin
Exeter
Amesbury

Dover
Somersworth
Berwick
Rochester
Sanford
Biddeford
Kennebunk

Saco

Portland
S. Portland

Brunswick
Bath

Boothbay Harbor

Wedgeport

Yarmouth

Shelburne

Lockeport

Clark's Harbour
CAPE SABLE

A
T
L
A
N
T
I
C

44°

Greenfield
MASS.
Northampton
Easthampton

Fitchburg
Gardner
Leominster
Clinton
Marlborough

Lowell
Lawrence
Haverhill
Peabody
Salem
Malden

CAPE ANN
Gloucester

Lynn

Continued on pages 110-111

42°

Holyoke
Chicopee
Springfield

Southbridge
Webster
Putnam

Worcester

Dedham
Norwood
Milford
Woonsocket
Pawtucket
Prov.

Chelsea
Cambridge
Somerville
BOSTON
Quincy
Weymouth
Brockton

Massachusetts
Bay

Provincetown
Plymouth

CAPE COD

CONN.
Hartford

R.I.

Taunton
Attleboro

68° 66° 64°

Longitude West of Greenwich

Scale 1:4 000 000; one inch to 64 miles. Conic Project

Elevations and depressions are given in feet.

Relief

Meters	Feet
1525	5000
610	2000
305	1000
152.5	500
0 Sea Level	0
152.5	500
1525	5000

LABRADOR (Newf.)

LABRADOR SEA

GULF OF ST. LAWRENCE

NEWFOUNDLAND

LONG RANGE MTS.

ANNIEOPSQUOTCH MTS.

ÎLE D'ANTICOST (Que.)

Natashquan
Wolf Bay
Mutton Bay

St. Pierre

GROS-MÉCATINA
PETIT-MÉCATINA

Robertson

Blue Mtn. 2085 △
△ Gros Pate 2115

St. Anthony
Hare Bay
GROAIS
BELL

Canada Bay
Englee

Strait of Belle Isle

HORSE IS.

CAPE ST. JOHN

NORTH TWILLINGATE
Twillingate
FOGO
Foga

Notre Dame Bay

Springdale
Lewisporte
Botwood
Glenwood
Gander
Glovertown

Wesleyville
C. FREELS

Bonavista Bay
Bonavista

Gros Morne 2644
NAT'L PARK
Mt. St. Gregory △ 2251

GROS MORNE
Bonne Bay

Deer Lake
Corner Brook
Humbermouth
Lewis Hills 2672
Red Indian Lake
GLOVER I.
Buchans
Millertown
Hodges Hill 1870 △
Windsor
Grand Falls

TERRA NOVA NAT'L PARK
Trinity

RANDOM I.
Bay de Verde
Heart's Content
Carbonear
Harbour Grace
Bay Roberts
Brigus
St. John's
SPEAR

GRATES PT.

Trinity Bay
Conception Bay
Torbay

Long Pt.
Port au Port
C. ST. GEORGE
Stephenville
St. George's
Robinson

St. George's Bay
Victoria Lake
Meelpaeg Lake

Crooked Lake

Kepenkeck Lake

AVALON PEN.
Placentia
Ferryland

C. ANGUILLE

Granite Lake
Jeddore Lake
Round Pond

LONG RANGE MTS.

GRINDSTONE Island
ÎLES DE LA (Que.)
BRION

Cabot Strait

C. RAY
Channel-Port-aux-Basques

Burgeo

La Poile Bay

Hermitage Bay

Belleoram
Belle Bay
Harbour Breton

Marystown
Placentia Bay

MERASHEEN

St. Mary's Bay

C. FREELS
C. RACE
Trepassey Bay
Trepassey

ST. PAUL I.
CAPE NORTH
Aspy Bay

BRUNETTE

Grand Bank
Fortune
BURIN
Burin
St. Lawrence

ST. PIERRE & MIQUELON (Fr.)
St. Pierre

CAPE BRETON HIGHLANDS NAT'L PARK

St. Ann's Bay

CE EDWARD ISLAND

ISLAND PARK
Mount Stewart
Souris
arlottetown
ontague
Georgetown
Murray Harbour

Inverness
Sydney Mines
N. Sydney
New Waterford
Dominion
Glace Bay
Sydney
SCATARI

ctou
New Glasgow
arton
Trenton
Antigonish
St. Georges Bay
Havre Boucher
Port Hawkesbury
St. Peters

CAPE BRETON ISLAND

Louisburg
CAPE BRETON

L. Ainslie
Port Hood

S C O T I A

N O V A

Bras d'Or Lake
Mulgrave
ARICHAT
MADAME

Guysborough
Canso
CAPE CANSO

Chedabucto Bay

O C E A N

SABLE (N.S.)

a

Scale 1:1 000 000

0 4 8 12 16 Kilometers
0 5 10 Miles

Derry
Hubbard
Amesbury
Merrimack
Merrimac
Newburyport
W. Newbury
Newbury
Merrimack R.

South Merrimack
Nashua
Salem
Haverhill
Groveland

Brookline
Hollis
Pelham
Methuen
Georgetown
Rowley
Ipswich
Rockport

Townsend
N.H.
MASS.
Dracut
Lawrence
N. Andover
Andover
Hamilton
Essex
Gloucester

Pepperell

Fitchburg
Lunenburg
Groton
Chelmsford
Lowell
Tewksbury
Wilmington
Middleton
N. Reading
Danvers
Wenham
Manchester

Leominster
Shirley
Ayer
Littleton
Billerica
Reading
Peabody
Salem
Beverly

Harvard
Acton
Bedford
Burlington
Wakefield
Marblehead

Sterling
Lancaster
Stow
Maynard
Lincoln
Lexington
Woburn
Melrose
Saug
Lynn
Swampscott
Nahant

Holden
Clinton
Hudson
Sudbury
Arlington
Medford
Malden
Everett
Chelsea
Revere

W. Boylston
Marlborough
Weston
Somerville
Cambridge
BOSTON

MASSACHUSETTS BAY

Worcester
Northborough
Southborough
Shrewsbury
Framingham
Ashland
Natick
Wellesley
Newton
Brookline
Needham
Hull

Westborough
Grafton
Hopkinton
Holliston
Dedham
Westwood
Norwood
Quincy
Hingham
Cohasset
Scituate

Millbury
Upton
Medfield
Canton
Randolph
Holbrook
Weymouth
Braintree
Rockland
Hanover
Marshfield

Auburn
Sutton
Northbridge
Hopedale
Millis
Medway
Walpole
Sharon
Stoughton
Avon
Abington
Whitman
Hanson
Pembroke

Oxford
Whitinsville
Uxbridge
Bellingham
Franklin
Wrentham
Foxboro
Brockton

Webster
Holden

10 20 30 40 50 60 70 80 90 100 110 120 Miles
20 40 60 80 100 120 140 160 180 200 Kilometers

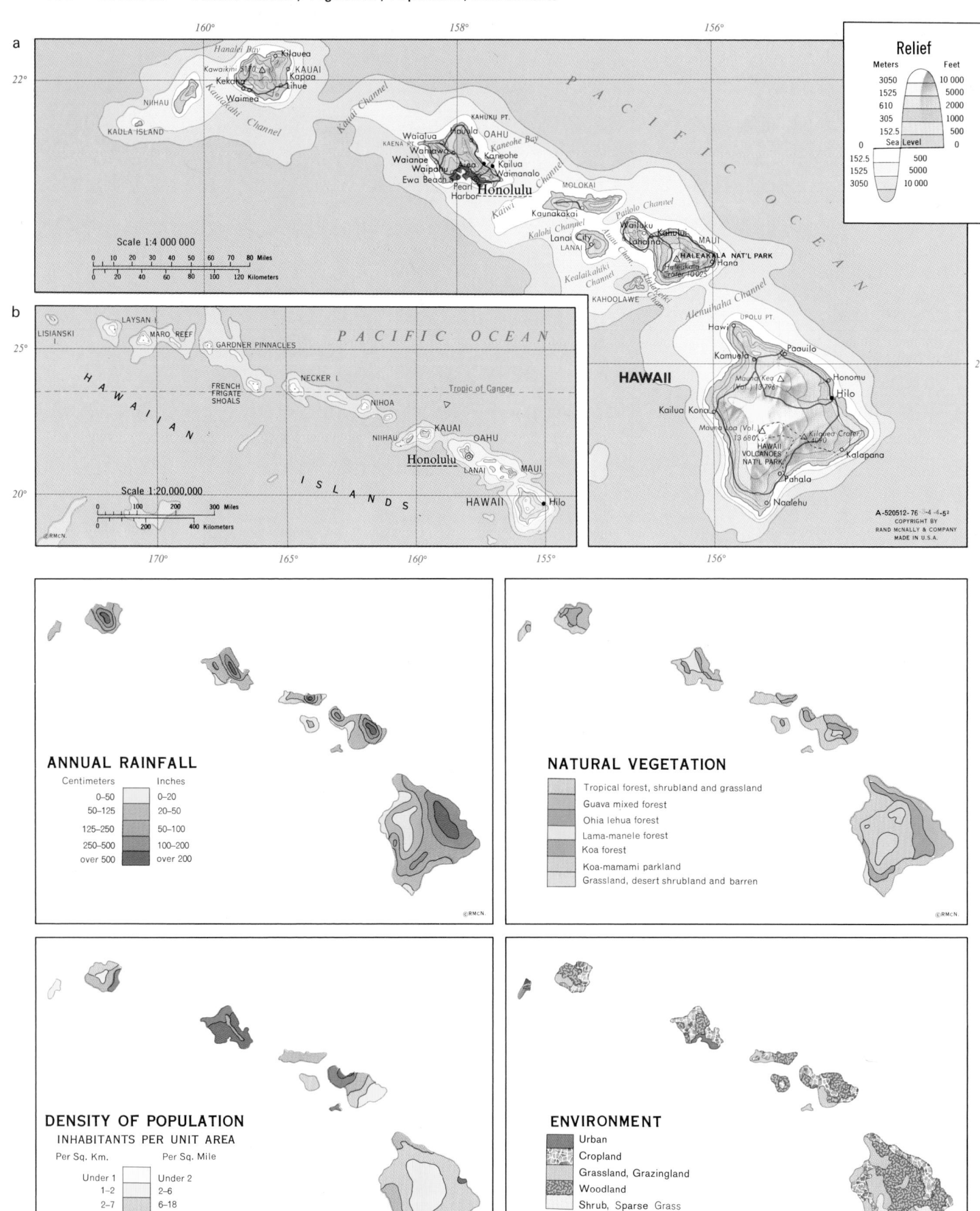

a

Relief

Meters	Feet
3050	10 000
1525	5000
610	2000
305	1000
152.5	500
0	Sea Level	0
152.5	500
1525	5000
3050	10 000

Scale 1:4 000 000

b

Scale 1:20,000,000

A-520512-76
COPYRIGHT BY
RAND MCNALLY & COMPANY
MADE IN U.S.A.

ANNUAL RAINFALL

Centimeters	Inches
0–50	0–20
50–125	20–50
125–250	50–100
250–500	100–200
over 500	over 200

NATURAL VEGETATION

Tropical forest, shrubland and grassland
Guava mixed forest
Ohia lehua forest
Lama-manele forest
Koa forest
Koa-mamami parkland
Grassland, desert shrubland and barren

DENSITY OF POPULATION

INHABITANTS PER UNIT AREA

Per Sq. Km.	Per Sq. Mile
Under 1	Under 2
1–2	2–6
2–7	6–18
7–17	18–45
17–35	45–90
over 35	over 90

ENVIRONMENT

Urban
Cropland
Grassland, Grazingland
Woodland
Shrub, Sparse Grass

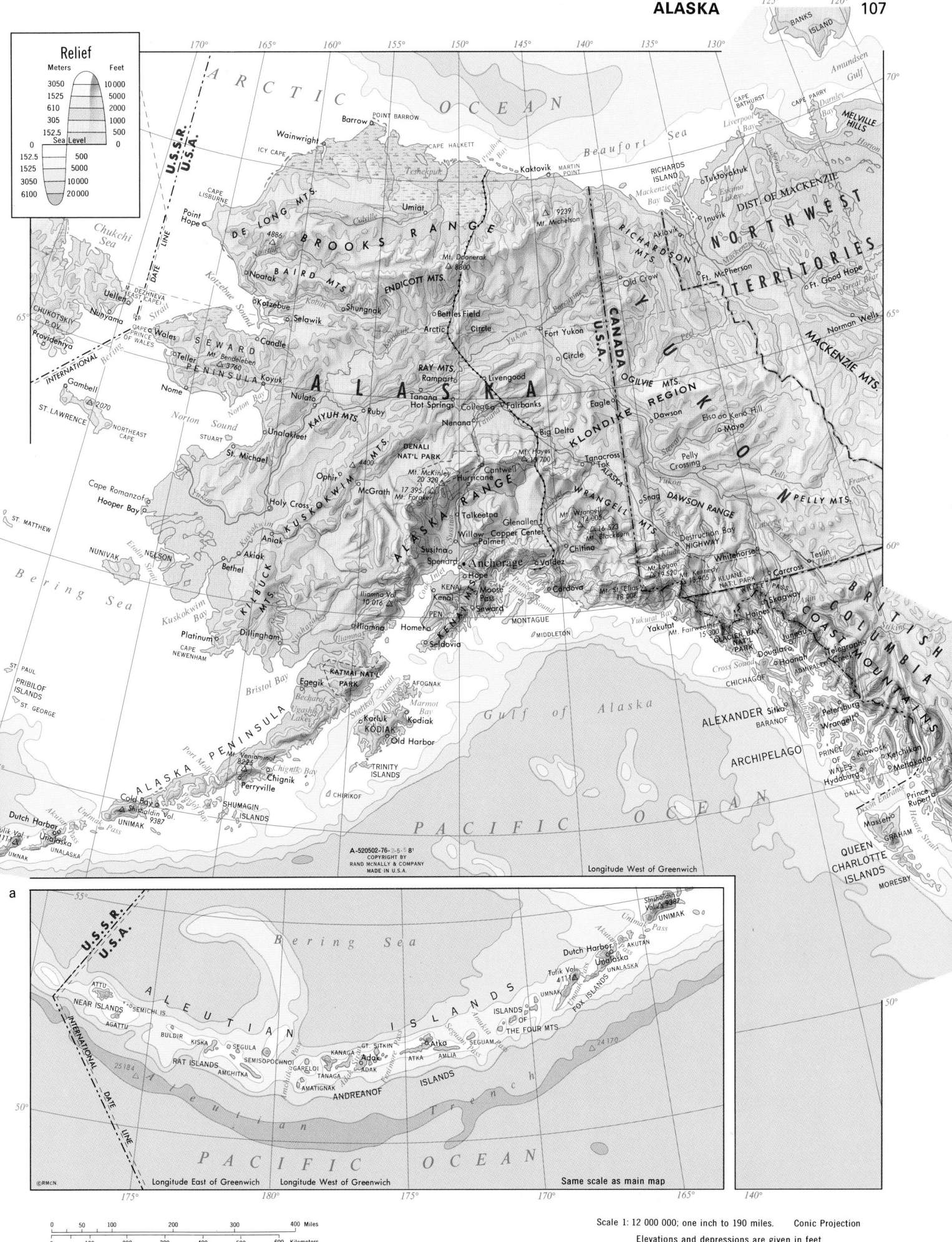

Relief

Meters	Feet
3050	10 000
1525	5000
610	2000
305	1000
152.5	500
Sea Level	Sea Level
0	0
152.5	500
1525	5000
3050	10 000
6100	20 000

ARCTIC OCEAN

U.S.S.R.
U.S.A.
DATE LINE

Chukchi Sea

Beaufort Sea

Barrow
Point Barrow
Wainwright
ICY CAPE
CAPE HALKETT
Teshekpuk
Kaktovik
MARTIN POINT

CAPE LISBURNE

Point Hope

DE LONG MTS.
BROOKS RANGE
△ 9239
Mt. Michelson

BAIRD MTS.
ENDICOTT MTS.
Mt. Doonerak △ 8800

RICHARDS ISLAND
Mackenzie Bay
Tuktoyaktuk

Eskimo Lakes
Inuvik

DIST. OF MACKENZIE

NORTHWEST TERRITORIES

Noatak
Kotzebue
Kobuk
Shungnak
Selawik
Bettles Field

Aklavik
Old Crow
Ft. McPherson
Ft. Good Hope

Great Bear Lake

Kotzebue Sound

Uelen
DEZHNEVA EAST CAPE
CAPE PRINCE OF WALES

Wales
Teller
SEWARD
Candle
Arctic
Circle
Yukon
Fort Yukon
CANADA U.S.A.

RICHARDSON MTS.

Norman Wells

MACKENZIE MTS.

CHUKOTSKIY P.OV.
Providenya
INTERNATIONAL
Gambell △ 2070
ST. LAWRENCE

Nunyama
BERING
Strait
Mt. Bendeleben △ 3760
PENINSULA
Koyuk
Nome
Norton Bay

Teller
RAY MTS.
Rampart
Livengood
Circle
Eagle
Dawson
Elsa o do Keno Hill
Mayo

OGILVIE MTS.

KLONDIKE REGION

Y U K O N

NORTHEAST CAPE
STUART

Nulato
Tanana
Hot Springs
College
Fairbanks
Big Delta

Nenana
Pelly Crossing

Pelly

Frances

NELSON
Norton Sound

St. Michael
Ophir
KAIYUH MTS.
Ruby
Tanana
△ 4400
DENALI NAT'L PARK
Mt. Hayes △ 13 700

Tanacross
Tok
ALASKA

DAWSON RANGE

Snag
PELLY MTS.

Cape Romanzof
Hooper Bay

Holy Cross
McGrath
Mt. McKinley 20 320
Mt. Foraker 17 395
Hurricane

ST. MATTHEW

Aniak
KUSKOKWIM MTS.
KILBUCK MTS.
ALASKA RANGE
Talkeetna
Cantwell

Mt. Wrangell △ 12 005
Mt. Blackburn △ 16 523
WRANGELL MTS.

Destruction Bay
HIGHWAY

NUNIVAK
Akiak
Bethel

Susitna
Willow
Glennallen
Copper Center
Palmer
Chitina

Mt. Logan 19 520
Mt. Kennedy △ 13 905
KLUANE NAT'L PARK

Whitehorse
Carcross

Teslin

Iliamna Vol. 10 016
Spenard
Anchorage
Hope
Moose Pass
Cordova
Mt. St. Elias 18 000

Skagway
Haines
Teslin

BRITISH COLUMBIA

Bering Sea

Platinum
Dillingham

Homer
Seldovia
KENAI
Kenai
PEN.
Seward
Valdez
MONTAGUE
MIDDLETON

Yakutat Bay
Yakutat
Mt. Fairweather 15 300
GLACIER BAY NAT'L PARK

Juneau
Douglas
Haonah
Telegraph Creek

COAST MOUNTAINS

ST. MATTHEW

ST. PAUL
PRIBILOF ISLANDS
ST. GEORGE

Bristol Bay

KATMAI NAT'L PARK
Egegik
Becharof Lakes

Ugashik Lakes
AFOGNAK
Marmot Bay
Shelikof Strait

Gulf of Alaska

CHICHAGOF
ADMIRALTY
Sitka
BARANOF

ALEXANDER
ARCHIPELAGO

Cross Sound

Petersburg
Wrangell
PRINCE OF WALES

Sakine

ALASKA PENINSULA
Port Moller
Mt. Veniaminof 8225
Chignik
Perryville
Chignik Bay
SHUMAGIN ISLANDS

Korluk
Kodiak
KODIAK
Old Harbor
TRINITY ISLANDS

CHIROF

Klawock
Ketchikan
Metlakatla
Hydaburg
DALL

Prince Rupert

Cold Bay
UNIMAK
Shishaldin Vol. △ 9387

Dutch Harbor
Unalaska
UNALASKA

Tulik Vol. △ 4111
UNIMAK
Unimak Pass

PACIFIC OCEAN

QUEEN CHARLOTTE ISLANDS
GRAHAM
Masseh
MORESBY

A-520502-76-2-5-5 81
COPYRIGHT BY
RAND McNALLY & COMPANY
MADE IN U.S.A.

Longitude West of Greenwich

a

U.S.S.R.
U.S.A.
DATE LINE

Bering Sea

ATTU
NEAR ISLANDS
SEMICHI IS.
AGATTU

A L E U T I A N   I S L A N D S

Shishaldin Vol. △ 9387
UNIMAK

Unimak Pass
AKUTAN
Dutch Harbor
Unalaska
UNALASKA

Tulik Vol. 4111 △
UMNAK

ISLANDS OF THE FOUR MTS.

FOX ISLANDS
UNALASKA

INTERNATIONAL
25 184 △

BULDIR
KISKA
SEGULA
SEMISOPOCHNOI
RAT ISLANDS
AMCHITKA

KANAGA
GT. SITKIN
GARELOI
TANAGA
ADAK
AMATIGNAK
AMATIGNAK
ANDREANOF ISLANDS
ADAK
ATKA
AMLIA

SEGUAM
Seguam Pass
AMUKTA

△ 24 170

Aleutian Trench

PACIFIC OCEAN

©RMCN
Longitude East of Greenwich
Longitude West of Greenwich
Same scale as main map

0	50	100	200	300	400 Miles
0	100	200	300	400	500	600 Kilometers

Scale 1: 12 000 000; one inch to 190 miles.   Conic Projection

Elevations and depressions are given in feet

108

Continued on pages 96-97

130°   125°   120°   115°   110°   105°   100°

BRITISH COLUMBIA

Vancouver
Victoria

ALBERTA
Lethbridge
Cardston
Medicine Hat
Moose Jaw

SASKATCHEWAN
Regina
Brandon

MANI C A
Win

WASHINGTON
SEATTLE
Everett
Tacoma
Olympia
Aberdeen
OLYMPIC NAT'L PARK
MT. RAINIER NAT'L PARK
Spokane
Coeur d'Alene
Kalispell
Havre
Great Falls
Lewistown
Williston
Minot
Devils Lake

NORTH DAKOTA
Bismarck
Dickinson
Mandan
Jamestown
Valley City

Astoria
Portland
Vancouver
Salem
Corvallis
Albany
Eugene

OREGON
Bend
The Dalles
Pendleton
La Grande
Baker

Walla Walla
Lewiston
Moscow

MONTANA
Missoula
Helena
Anaconda
Butte
Bozeman
Livingston
Billings
Miles City
Glendive

Great Falls
Glasgow
Wolf Point

SOUTH DAKOTA
Rapid City
Lead
Deadwood
Pierre
Aberdeen
Mitchell
Yankton
Huron
Watert

Medford
Klamath Falls
Roseburg

CRATER LAKE NAT'L PARK

Eureka
Santa Rosa

NEVADA
Winnemucca
Elko
Reno
Carson City
Tonopah
Ely

IDAHO
Boise
Nampa
Twin Falls
Idaho Falls
Pocatello

WYOMING
YELLOWSTONE NAT'L PARK
GRAND TETON NAT'L PARK
Cody
Sheridan
Casper
Rawlins
Laramie
Cheyenne
Rock Springs

NEBRASKA
Chadron
Valentine
Alliance
North Platte
Grand Island
Norfolk
Hastin

CALIFORNIA
SAN FRANCISCO
Berkeley
Oakland
Alameda
San Jose
Santa Cruz
Monterey
Sacramento
Stockton
Vallejo
Napa
Fresno

SEQUOIA NAT'L PARK
KINGS CANYON NAT'L PARK
YOSEMITE
Mt. Whitney 14,494

UTAH
Salt Lake City
Ogden
Provo
Logan

GREAT SALT LAKE
GREAT SALT LAKE DESERT

COLORADO
Grand Junction
Fort Collins
Boulder
DENVER
Colorado Springs
Pueblo
Trinidad
Raton

ROCKY MT. NAT'L PARK
Longs Peak 14,255
Mt. Massive 14,418
Mt. Elbert 14,433
Pikes Peak 14,110

MESA VERDE NAT'L PARK

KANSAS
Dodge City
Hutchinson
Wichita
Man

San Luis Obispo
Bakersfield
Santa Barbara
Santa Monica
LOS ANGELES
Glendale
Pasadena
Pomona
Long Beach
Santa Ana
Riverside
San Bernardino
SAN DIEGO
Tijuana

DEATH VALLEY
Telescope Peak 11,045
MOJAVE DESERT
Las Vegas
Boulder City
HOOVER DAM
PARKER DAM

ARIZONA
GRAND CANYON NAT'L PARK
Humphreys Peak 12,633
Flagstaff
Prescott
Phoenix
Miami
Globe
Tucson
Yuma

GLEN CANYON DAM
Lake Powell
ZION NAT'L PARK
BRYCE CANYON NAT'L PARK

SAN JUAN MTS.
Blanca Peak 14,317

NEW MEXICO
Gallup
Mt. Taylor 11,301
Santa Fe
Las Vegas
Albuquerque
Clovis
Las Cruces
Roswell
Deming
El Paso

Truchas Pk. 13,110
SANGRE DE CRISTO RANGE
Sierra Blanca 12,003
BLACK RANGE
SAN ANDRES MTS.
MOGOLLON PLATEAU
Baldy Peak

OKLAHOMA
Oklahoma City
Chickasha
Lawton
Pampa
Amarillo
Wichita Falls
Ardmore
Enid

LLANO ESTACADO
Lubbock
Sweetwater
Abilene
Cleburne
Ranger

TEXAS
San Angelo
Brownwood
Waco
Fort Worth
Dallas
Austin
Del Rio
Eagle Pass
San Antonio

EDWARDS PLATEAU
BIG BEND NAT'L PARK
STOCKTON PLATEAU

BAJA CALIFORNIA NORTE
Mexicali
Ensenada
Brawley
Calexico

SONORA
Nogales
Nogales
Bisbee
Douglas
Cananea
Magdalena
Ciudad Juárez

CHIHUAHUA M E X I C O
Ojinaga

COAHUILA
Piedras Negras
Nueva Rosita
Laredo
Nuevo Laredo

NUEVO LEÓN
Monterrey
Saltillo

DUR.
Torreón
Gómez Palacio

TAMAUL
Reynosa
Matamoros
Brownsville
Harlingen

45°
40°
35°
30°

PACIFIC OCEAN

A-520500-76- -7-9 -14²
COPYRIGHT BY
RAND McNALLY & COMPANY
MADE IN U.S.A.

Continued on pages 96-97

a
170°   160°   150°   140°   130°   120°
ARCTIC OCEAN
C. LISBURNE
Barrow
SOVIET UNION
Kotzebue
Nome
BROOKS RANGE
Umiat
Inuvik
Great Bear Lake
Arctic Circle
ALASKA
Yukon
CANADA
NORTHWEST TERR.
Ruby
Circle
Dawson
Fairbanks
McGrath
DENALI NAT'L PARK
Mt. McKinley 20,320
Anchorage
YUKON
Whitehorse
Burwash Landing
Watson Lake
Bethel
ST. LAWRENCE
NUNIVAK
Dillingham
KATMAI NAT'L PARK
Seward
Cordova
Skagway
Juneau
GLACIER BAY NAT'L PARK
BRITISH COLUMBIA
Kodiak
Sitka
Wrangell
Ketchikan
QUEEN CHARLOTTE IS.
Dutch Harbor
PACIFIC OCEAN

b
Scale 1: 36 000 000
Dutch Harbor
ATTU
KISKA
ANDREANOF
ALEUTIAN IS.
UMNAK
UNALASKA
ATKA
©RMCN
Scale 1: 36 000 000
One inch to 570 miles
©RMCN

c
160°   155°
Longitude West of Greenwich
HAWAIIAN IS.
NIIHAU
KAUAI
Lihue
OAHU
Honolulu
Kaitua
MOLOKAI
LANAI
Wailuku
Kahului
KAHOOLAWE
MAUI
HAWAII
Hilo
Mauna Kea 13,796
Mauna Loa 13,680
HAWAII VOLCANOES NAT'L PARK
Kaneohe Bay
©RMCN
PEARL HARBOR
Honolulu
Same scale as main map

d
Scale 1: 3 400 000
KAHUKU PT.
OAHU
Kahuku
Wahiawa
Waipahu
Kailua
KAENA PT.
©RMCN
PEARL HARBOR
Honolulu

100° Longitude West of Greer

Scale 1:12 000 000; one inch to 190 miles. Polyconic Projec
Elevations and depressions are given in feet

Relief

Meters		Feet
3050		10 000
1525		5000
610		2000
305		1000
152.5		500
0	Sea Level	0
152.5		500 Below
1525		5 000 Sea Level
3050		10 000
6100		20 000

Cities and Towns

0 to 50,000 ○   500,000 to 1,000,000 ◎

50,000 to 500,000 ⊙   1,000,000 and over

50 75 100   200   300   400   500 Miles

100   200   400   600   800 Kilometers

Continued on pages 114-115

Continued on pages 126-127

Cities
and
Towns

0 to 50,000   500,000 to 1,000,000

50,000 to 500,000   1,000,000 and over

Longitude West of Greenwich

Scale 1:4 000 000; one inch to 64 miles.   Conic Projection
Elevations and depressions are given in feet

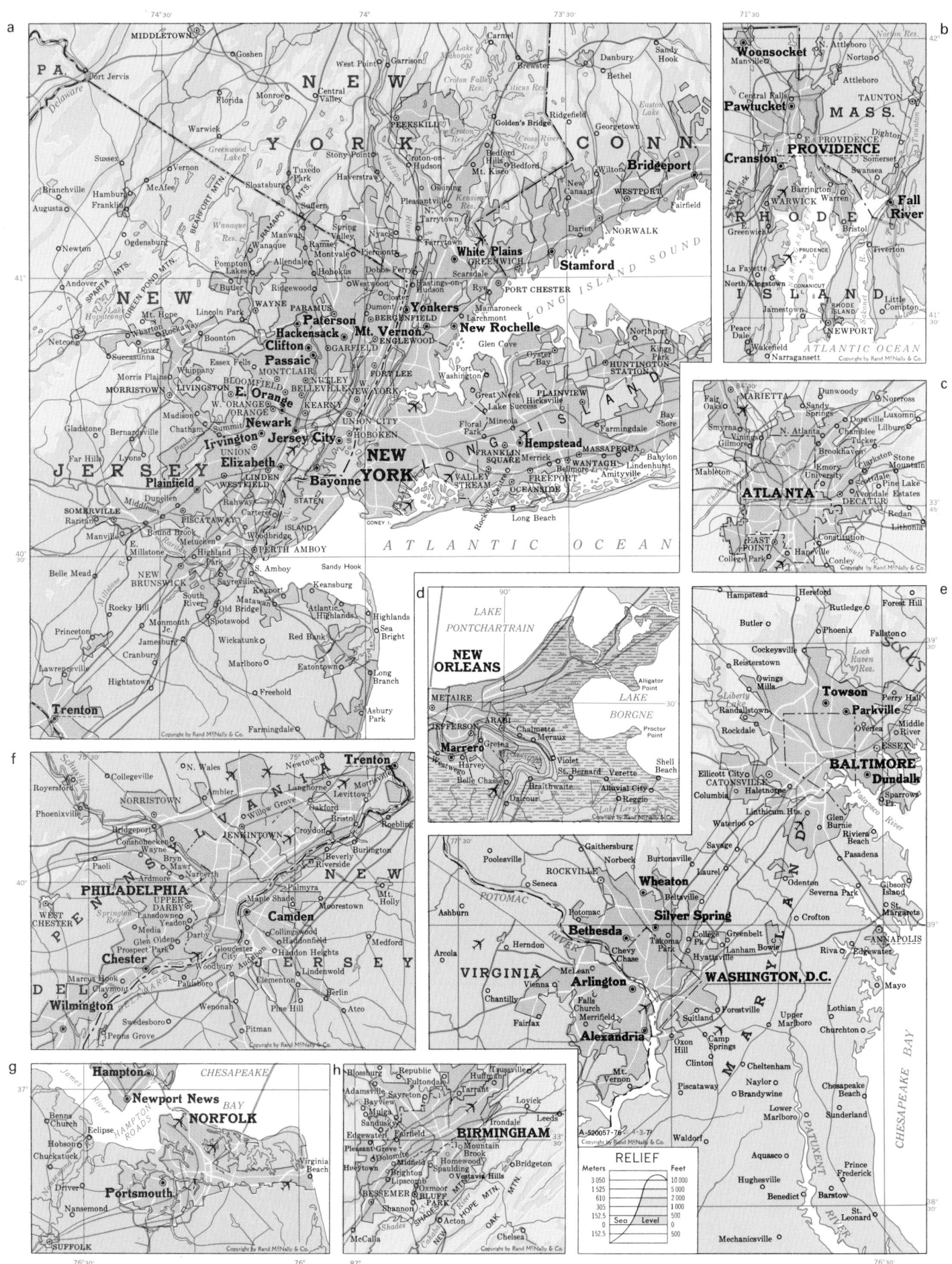

Scale 1:1 000 000; One inch to 16 miles.
Elevations and depressions are given in feet.

For larger scale coverage of New York, Baltimore, Washington, D. C. and Philadelphia see pages 55 and 56.

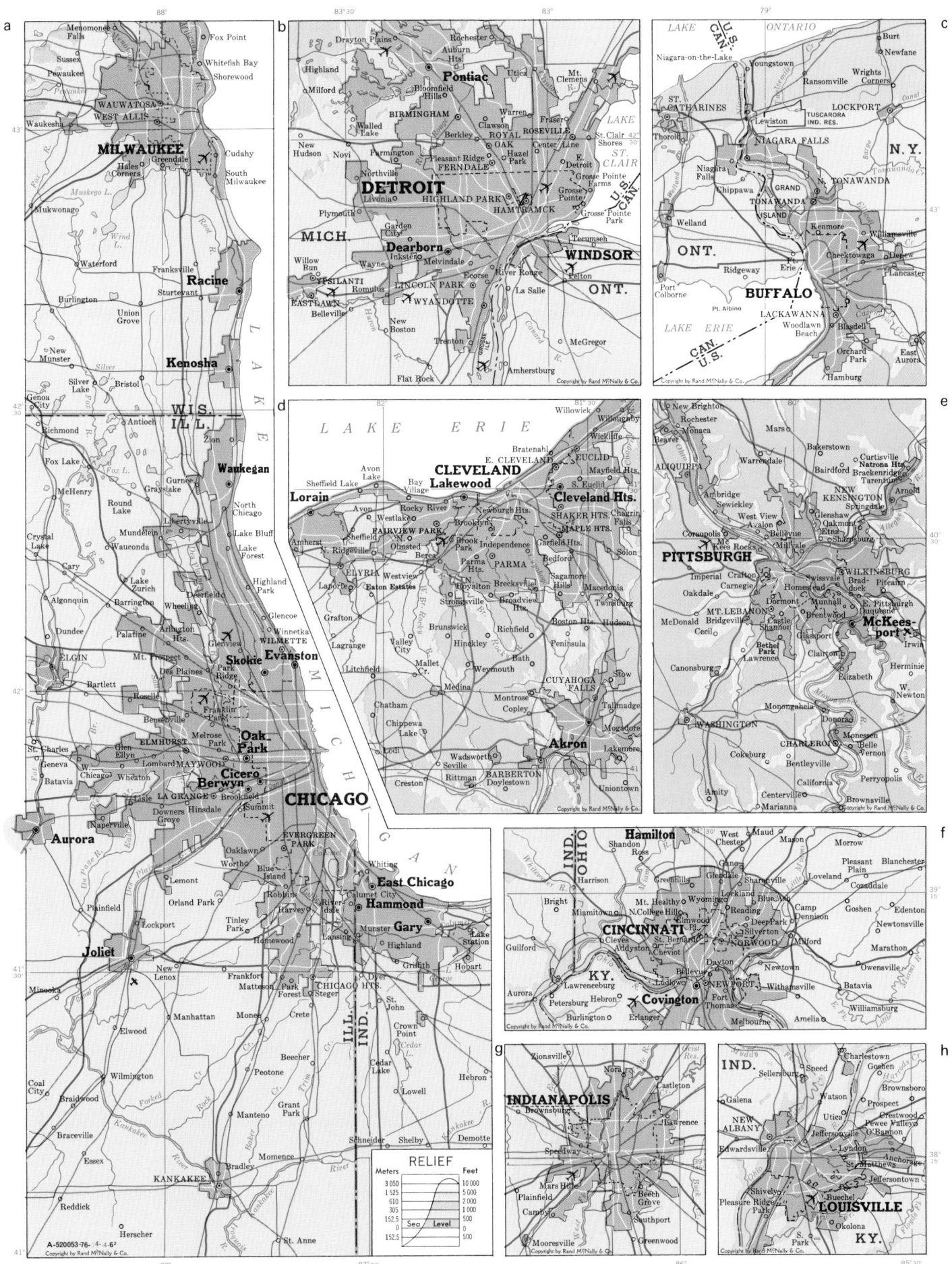

RELIEF

Meters		Feet
3 050		10 000
1 525		5 000
610		2 000
305		1 000
152.5		500
	Sea Level	
152.5		500

Scale 1:1 000 000; One inch to 16 miles.
Elevations and depressions are given in feet.

0 2 4 6 8 10 12 14 16 18 20 22 24 Miles
0 4 8 12 16 20 24 28 32 36 40 Kilometers

For larger scale coverage of Chicago see page 58.

A-520053-76- 4-4-6²
Copyright by Rand McNally & Co.

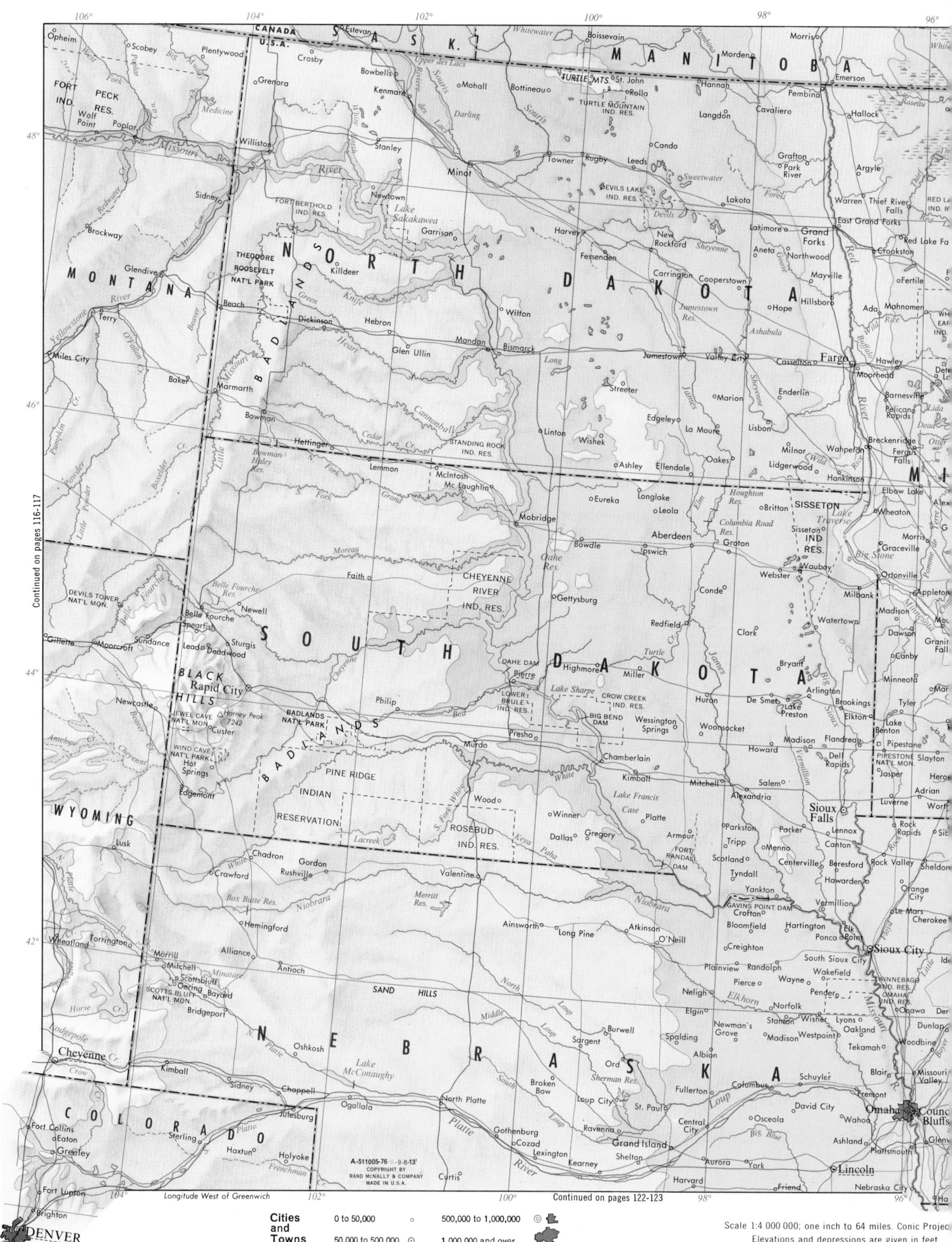

Continued on pages 116-117

Continued on pages 122-123

Longitude West of Greenwich

A-511005-76 9-8-13
COPYRIGHT BY
RAND McNALLY & COMPANY
MADE IN U.S.A.

Cities and Towns	0 to 50,000	500,000 to 1,000,000
	50,000 to 500,000	1,000,000 and over

Scale 1:4 000 000; one inch to 64 miles. Conic Projection
Elevations and depressions are given in feet

Continued on pages 110-111

Continued on pages 122-123

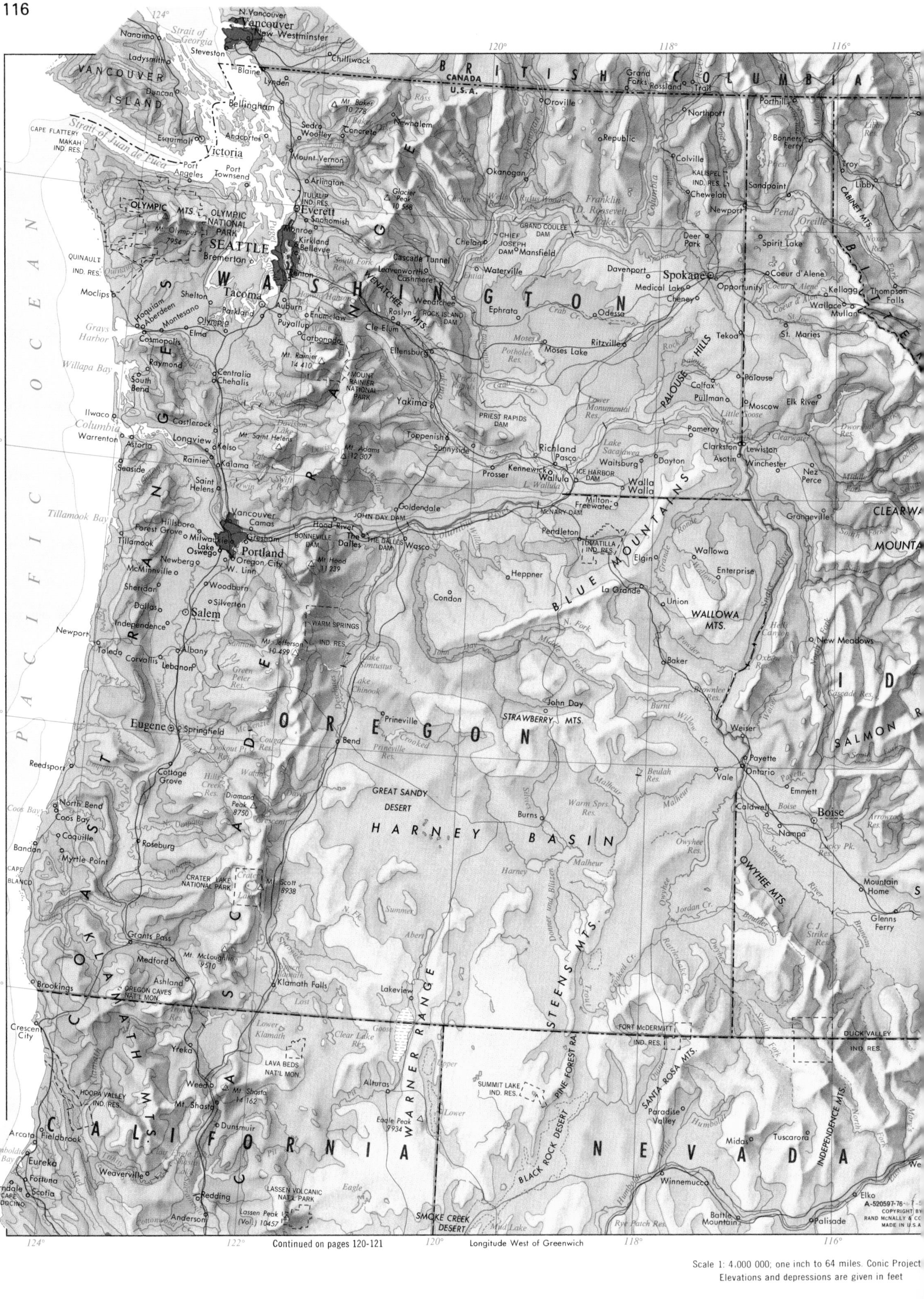

Longitude West of Greenwich

A-520597-76
COPYRIGHT BY
RAND M9NALLY & CO
MADE IN U.S.A.

Scale 1: 4,000 000; one inch to 64 miles. Conic Project
Elevations and depressions are given in feet

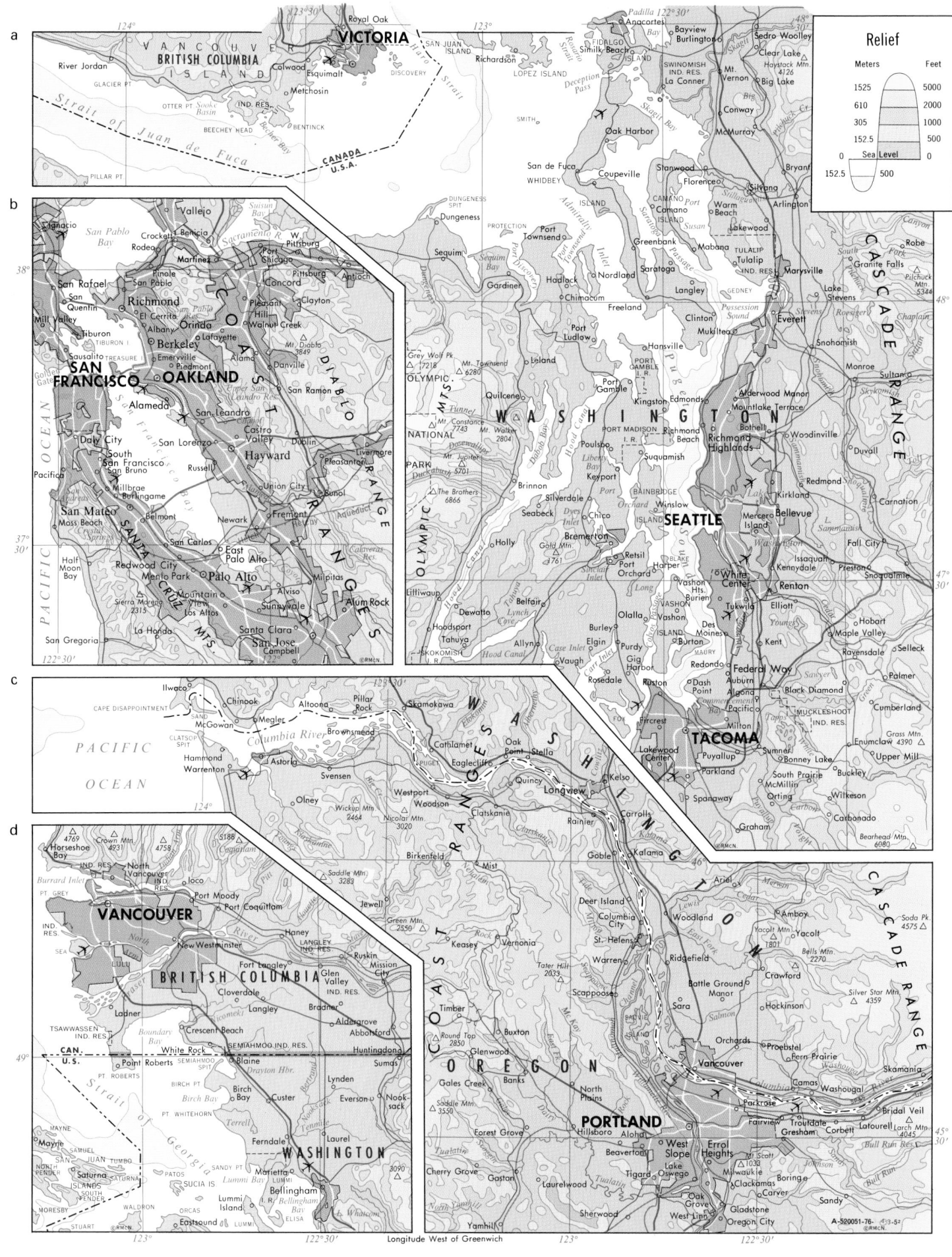

Relief

Meters		Feet
1525		5000
610		2000
305		1000
152.5		500
0	Sea Level	0
152.5		500

Longitude West of Greenwich

Scale 1:1 000 000; one inch to 16 miles.
Elevations and depressions are given in feet.

A-520051-76—

0   5   10   15   20 Miles
0   4   8   12   16   20   24   28   32 Kilometers

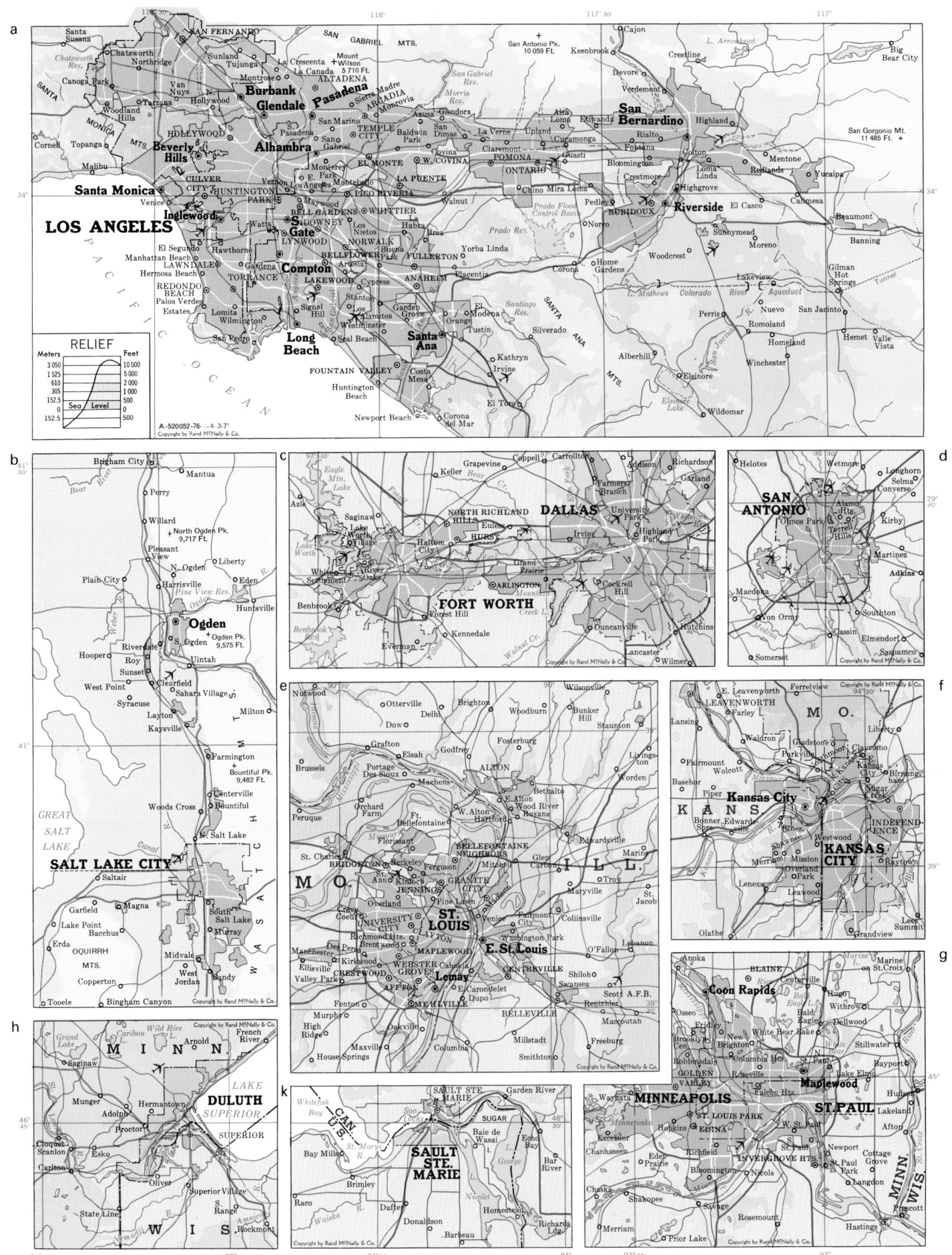

a

Santa Susana Santa Susana SAN FERNANDO SAN GABRIEL MTS. Cajon L. Arrowhead Crestline Big Bear City
Chatsworth Chatsworth Northridge Sunland Tujunga La Crescenta Mount Wilson 5,710 Ft. San Antonio Pk. 10,059 Ft. Keenbrook Devore Verdemont
Chatsworth Res. La Canada ALTADENA Sierra Madre Res. Morris Res. Highland
Canoga Park Van Nuys N. Hollywood **Burbank** **Glendale** **Pasadena** ARCADIA Monrovia Azusa Glendora Alta Loma Etiwanda **San Bernardino** San Gorgonio Mt. 11,485 Ft.
Cornell Topanga Tarzana Woodland Hills HOLLYWOOD San Marino TEMPLE CITY Baldwin Park San Dimas La Verne Upland Cucamonga Rialto Fontana Highland
Beverly Hills **Alhambra** Pasadena E. Pasadena Sano San Gabriel El Monte W. COVINA Claremont POMONA Guasti Bloomington Colton Loma Linda Redlands Mentone
Malibu CULVER CITY Vernon Los Angeles Montebello PICO RIVERA La Puente ONTARIO Chino Mira Loma Crestmore Highgrove Yucaipa
Santa Monica HUNTINGTON PARK Maywood WHITTIER Walnut Prado Flood Control Basin Pedley **RUBIDOUX** **Riverside** El Casco Beaumont
Venice **Inglewood** S. Gate BELL GARDENS DOWNEY Los Nietos Brea Habra Prado Res. Norco Wooderest Sunnymead Moreno Banning
LOS ANGELES Watts LYNWOOD NORWALK BELLFLOWER Buena Park FULLERTON Yorba Linda Home Gardens Lakeview Gilman Hot Springs
El Segundo Hawthorne Gardena Artesia Cypress ANAHEIM Placentia Corona L. Mathews Colorado River Aqueduct Tunnel
Manhattan Beach LAWNDALE **Compton** LAKEWOOD Stanton Garden Grove El Modena Santiago Res. Perris Nuevo San Jacinto
Hermosa Beach TORRANCE Signal Hill Los Alamitos **Santa Ana** Orange Tustin Silverado Alberhill Romoland Hemet Valle Vista
REDONDO BEACH Palos Verdes Estates Lomita Wilmington **Long Beach** Seal Beach Westminster Kathryn SANTA ANA MTS. Elsinore Homeland Winchester
San Pedro FOUNTAIN VALLEY Irvine Elsinore Lake Wildomar
Huntington Beach Costa Mesa El Toro
Newport Beach Corona del Mar

RELIEF
Meters Feet
3,050 10,000
1,525 5,000
610 2,000
305 1,000
152.5 500
0 0
152.5 500
Sea Level
A-520052-76- -4-3-7'
Copyright by Rand McNally & Co.

PACIFIC OCEAN

SANTA MONICA MTS.

b

Brigham City Mantua
Bear River Perry
Willard North Ogden Pk. 9,717 Ft.
Plain City Pleasant View N. Ogden Liberty
Harrisville Eden
Ogden + Ogden Pk. 9,575 Ft.
Hooper Riverdale Pine View Res. Huntsville
Roy S. Ogden Uintah
Sunset Clearfield Sahara Village
West Point Layton Milton
Syracuse Kaysville
Farmington + Bountiful Pk. 9,482 Ft.
GREAT SALT LAKE Centerville Bountiful
Woods Cross
N. Salt Lake
SALT LAKE CITY
Saltair
Garfield Magna South Salt Lake Murray
Lake Point Bacchus
OQUIRRH MTS. Midvale
Erda Copperton West Jordan Sandy
Tooele Bingham Canyon
WASATCH

c

Eagle Mtn. Lake Grapevine Coppell Carrollton Addison Richardson Helotes Wetmore Longhorn
Keller Bear Creek Farmers Branch Garland
Azle Saginaw Keller University Park **DALLAS**
Lake Worth NORTH RICHLAND HILLS Euless HURST Irving Highland Park
White Settlement Haltom City Grand Prairie Cockrell Hill
FORT WORTH Arlington Mountain Creek L.
Benbrook Forest Hill Duncanville Hutchins
Benbrook Res. Kennedale Lancaster
Everman Walnut Cr. Wilmer
Copyright by Rand McNally & Co.

d

Helotes Wetmore Longhorn Selma Converse
SAN ANTONIO Olmos Park Alamo Hts. Kirby
Terrell Hills Martinez
Macdona Von Ormy Adkins
Cassin Elmendorf Southton
Somerset Saspamco
Copyright by Rand McNally & Co.

e

Nutwood Otterville Brighton Woodburn Wilsonville
Delhi Bunker Hill Staunton
Dow Fosterburg Livingston
Grafton Elsah Godfrey ALTON Worden
Brussels Portage Des Sioux Machens E. Alton Wood River Roxana Bethalto Edwardsville
Orchard Farm W. Alton Hartford
Peruque Ft. Bellefontaine Florissant BELLEFONTAINE NEIGHBORS Marine Glen Carbon
St. Charles Berkeley Ferguson Mitchell Troy Maryville
MO. BRIDGETON St. Ann Jennings GRANITE CITY St. Jacob
Creve Coeur Overland Pine Lawn Venice Fairmont Collinsville
UNIVERSITY CITY Richmond Hts. Clayton **ST. LOUIS** Washington Park O'Fallon Lebanon
Manchester Des Peres Brentwood MAPLEWOOD **E. St. Louis** Scott A.F.B.
Ellisville Kirkwood WEBSTER GROVES Cahokia CENTREVILLE Shiloh Rentchler
Valley Park CRESTWOOD **Lemay** Dupo Swansea Mascoutah
Fenton AFFTON Carondelet Belleville Freeburg
High Ridge Oakville MEHLVILLE
Maxville Columbia Millstadt Smithton
House Springs Copyright by Rand McNally & Co.

f

E. Leavenworth Ferrelview Copyright by Rand McNally & Co.
LEAVENWORTH Farley **MO.** Liberty
Lansing Gladstone Claycomo
Fairmount Wolcott Parkville **Kansas City** Birmingham
Basehor Piper Sugar Cr.
KANS. Bonner Springs Edwardsville INDEPENDENCE
Merriam Shawnee Westwood **KANSAS CITY** Raytown
Lenexa Overland Park Mission Leawood
Olathe Grandview Lee's Summit

g

Anoka BLAINE Centerville Marine on St. Croix
Coon Rapids Hugo Withrow
Osseo Fridley Eagle Dellwood
New Brighton White Bear Lake
Brooklyn Center Columbia Hts. Lake Elmo
Robbinsdale Roseville Stillwater
GOLDEN VALLEY New Brighton Bayport
MINNEAPOLIS ST. LOUIS PARK **ST. PAUL** Lakeland
Wayzata Hopkins EDINA W. St. Paul Afton
Excelsior Richfield Newport Cottage Grove
Eden Prairie Bloomington INVERGROVE HTS. St. Paul Park Langdon
Chaska Nicols **MINN.** **WIS.**
Shakopee Savage Rosemount
Prior Lake Hastings
Merriam Copyright by Rand McNally & Co.
Maplewood
Chanhassen Minnetonka

h

Grand Lake Caribou L. Wild Rice L. Arnold French River Copyright by Rand McNally & Co.
Saginaw Munger Hermantown LAKE SUPERIOR
Adolph Proctor **DULUTH**
Cloquet Esko SUPERIOR
Scanlon Superior
Carlton Oliver
State Line Superior Village
MINN. **WIS.** Range Rockmont

k

Whitefish Bay SAULT STE. MARIE Garden River
CAN. Soo Locks SUGAR I.
U.S. Bay Mills Baie de Wasai
Raco St. Marys R. Echo Bay
Brimley GEORGE Bar River
Dafter Nicolet Homestead
Waiska R. Donaldson Richards Ldg.
Barbeau
Copyright by Rand McNally & Co.

0 2 4 6 8 10 12 14 16 18 20 22 24 Miles
0 4 8 12 16 20 24 28 32 36 40 Kilometers

Scale 1:1 000 000; One inch to 16 miles.
Elevations and depressions are given in feet.

For larger scale coverage of Los Angeles see page 59.

Cities
and
Towns

0 to 50,000   500,000 to 1,000,000

50,000 to 500,000   1,000,000 and over

Relief

Meters		Feet
3050		10000
1525		5000
610		2000
305		1000
152.5		500
0	Sea Level	Sea Level
152.5		500 Below
1525		5000 Sea Level
3050		10000

Continued on pages 116-117

NEVADA

CALIFORNIA

PACIFIC OCEAN

SIERRA NEVADA

COAST RANGES

SAN JOAQUIN VALLEY

MOJAVE DESERT

DEATH VALLEY

DEATH VALLEY NATL. MON.

YOSEMITE NATIONAL PARK

KINGS CANYON NATL. PARK

SEQUOIA NATL. PARK

JOSHUA TREE NATL. MON.

PINNACLES NATL. MON.

Sacramento
San Francisco
Oakland
Berkeley
Richmond
Alameda
San Rafael
Sausalito
Daly City
San Mateo
Redwood City
Palo Alto
Santa Clara
San Jose
Los Gatos
Santa Cruz
Watsonville
Pacific Grove
Monterey
Salinas
Hollister
King City
Coalinga
Fresno
Selma
Reedley
Dinuba
Visalia
Exeter
Tulare
Hanford
Madera
Sanger
Porterville
Delano
Bakersfield
Taft
Santa Maria
Lompoc
Santa Barbara
Ventura
Oxnard
Santa Paula
LOS ANGELES
Burbank
Glendale
Pasadena
Monrovia
Santa Monica
Inglewood
Alhambra
Pomona
San Bernardino
Redlands
Riverside
Palm Springs
Compton
Redondo Beach
Orange
Santa Ana
Newport Beach
Long Beach
Huntington Beach
Elsinore
Avalon
Oceanside
Escondido
SAN DIEGO
Coronado
National City
Chula Vista
Tijuana
El Centro
Calexico
Mexicali
Brawley
Calipatria
Holtville

Reno
Sparks
Carson City
Virginia City
Yerington
Hawthorne
Fallon
Lovelock
Winnemucca
Battle Mountain
Austin
Eureka
Ruth
Tonopah
Goldfield
Coaldale
Beatty
Henderson
Boulder
Las Vegas

Anderson
Red Bluff
Redding
Willows
Chico
Oroville
Gridley
Colusa
Marysville
Yuba City
Woodland
Lincoln
Roseville
Auburn
Placerville
Folsom City
Lodi
Stockton
Tracy
Livermore
Oakdale
Modesto
Turlock
Merced
Mariposa
Los Banos
Gilroy

Ukiah
Cloverdale
Healdsburg
Sebastopol
Santa Rosa
Petaluma
Napa
Vallejo
Benicia
Pittsburg
Lakeport

Susanville
Westwood
Portola
Downieville
Nevada City
Grass Valley
Truckee

PYRAMID LAKE
INDIAN RESERVATION
SMOKE CREEK DESERT
PYRAMID LAKE
Walker Lake
WALKER RIVER IND. RES.
WASSUK RANGE
TOIYABE RANGE
PANAMINT RA.
INYO MTS.
WHITE MTS.
PANAMINT MTS.
SPRING MTS.
RUBY MTS.
FRANKLIN MTS.
STILLWATER RA.
HUMBOLT RA.
Humboldt Salt Marsh
Carson Sink
Humboldt Sink
FRENCHMAN FLAT

Lassen Peak (Vol.) 10,457
LASSEN VOLCANIC NATL. PARK
Sonora Pk. 11,429
Mt. Lyell 13,095
Dana Mtn. 13,053
DEVILS POSTPILE N.M.
Boundary Peak 13,145
Mt. Whitney 14,494
White Mt. Peak 14,246
Telescope Peak 11,045
Arc Dome 11,775
Duckwater Pk. 11,493
282 ft. below sea level

Mono Lake
Owens Lake
Searles Lake
Tulare Basin
Buena Vista Lake Reservoir

TEHACHAPI MTS.
SAN BERNARDINO MTS.
SANTA ROSA IND. RES.
MORONGO IND. RES.
AGUA CALIENTE IND. RES.
TORRES MARTINEZ IND. RES.
CABAZON IND. RES.
TULE RIVER IND. RES.
CUYAPAIPE IND. RES.
INAJA IND. RES.
SANTA YSABEL IND. RES.
CAMP IND. RES.
Salton Sea
Bottom 235 ft. below sea level
IMPERIAL VALLEY
Laguna Salada

POINT ARENA
POINT REYES
MUIR WOODS NATL. MON.
San Pablo Bay
Burlingame
Monterey Bay
Estero Bay
San Luis Obispo
San Luis Bay
POINT ARGUELLO
POINT CONCEPTION
Santa Barbara Channel
SAN MIGUEL
SANTA ROSA
SANTA CRUZ
SANTA BARBARA ISLANDS
SANTA BARBARA CHANNEL ISLANDS NAT'L PARK
San Pedro
Santa Catalina
SAN NICOLAS
SAN CLEMENTE
Gulf of Santa Catalina
SAN PEDRO
CABRILLO NATL. MON.

Jackson
Angels Camp
San Andreas
Sonora
Bodie
Bishop
Benton
Lone Pine
Keeler
Trona
Inyokern
Mojave
Barstow
Daggett
Cadiz
Goffs
FORT
Palisade
Alamo
MOAPA IND. RES.
HOOVER
SPRING MTS.

BAJA CALIFORNIA NORTE

San Diego inset (a)

PACIFIC OCEAN
CALIFORNIA
SAN DIEGO
Del Mar
La Jolla
Lakeside
Santee
El Cajon
La Mesa
Spring Valley
Lemon Grove
National City
Chula Vista
Coronado
Imperial Beach
Tijuana
Otay
Sweetwater Reservoir
Lower Otay Reservoir
CABRILLO NATL. MON.
USA
MEXICO
BAJA CALIFORNIA NORTE

Scale 1:1 000 000
0   5   10 Miles
0   4   8   12   16 Kilometers

A-520599-76
COPYRIGHT BY
RAND McNALLY & COMPANY
MADE IN U.S.A.
©RMcN.

Longitude West of Greenwich

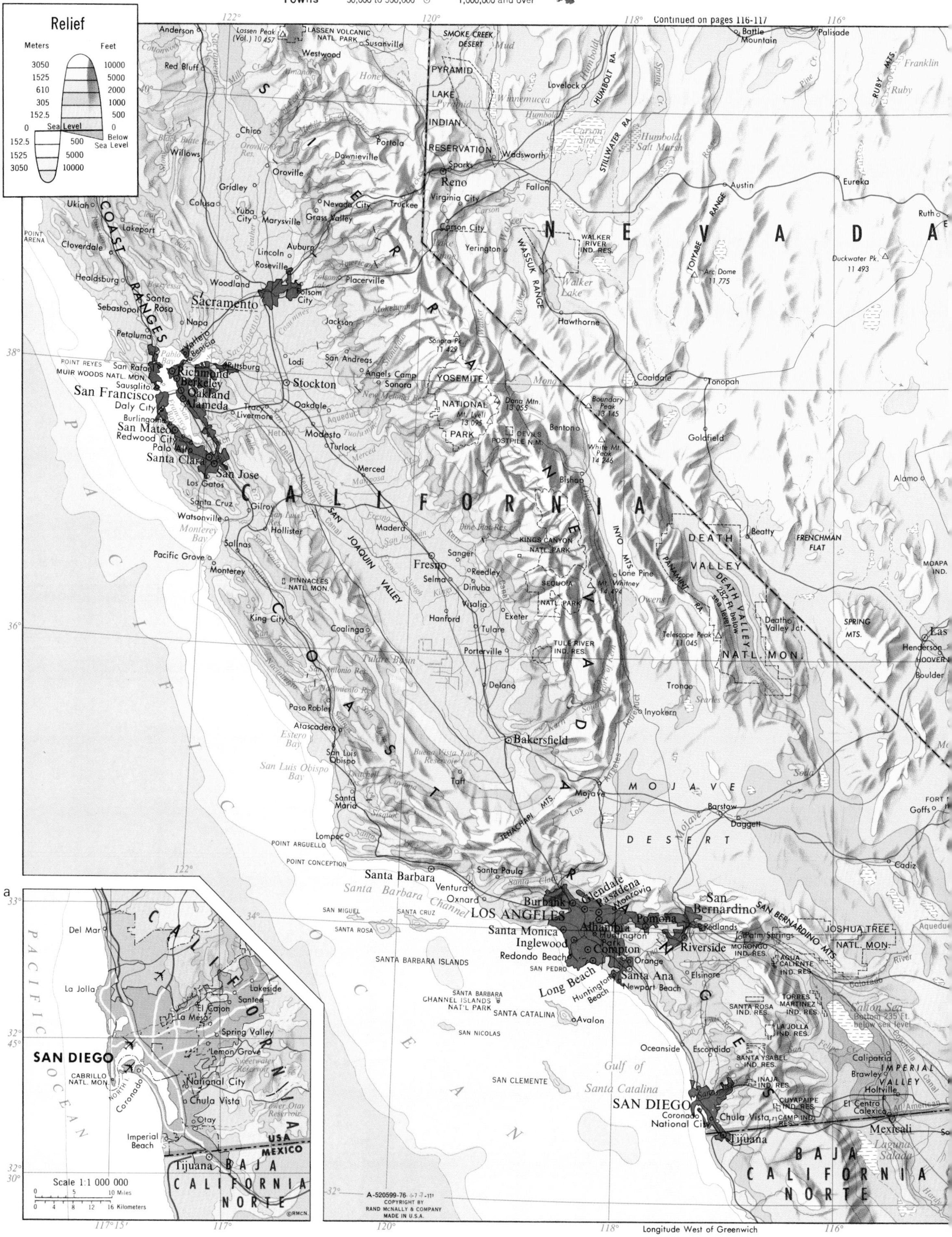

Scale 1:4 000 000; one inch to 64 miles. Conic Projection
Elevations and depressions are given in feet

0   20   40   60   80   100   120 MILES
0   20   40   60   80   100   120   140   160   180   200 KILOMETERS

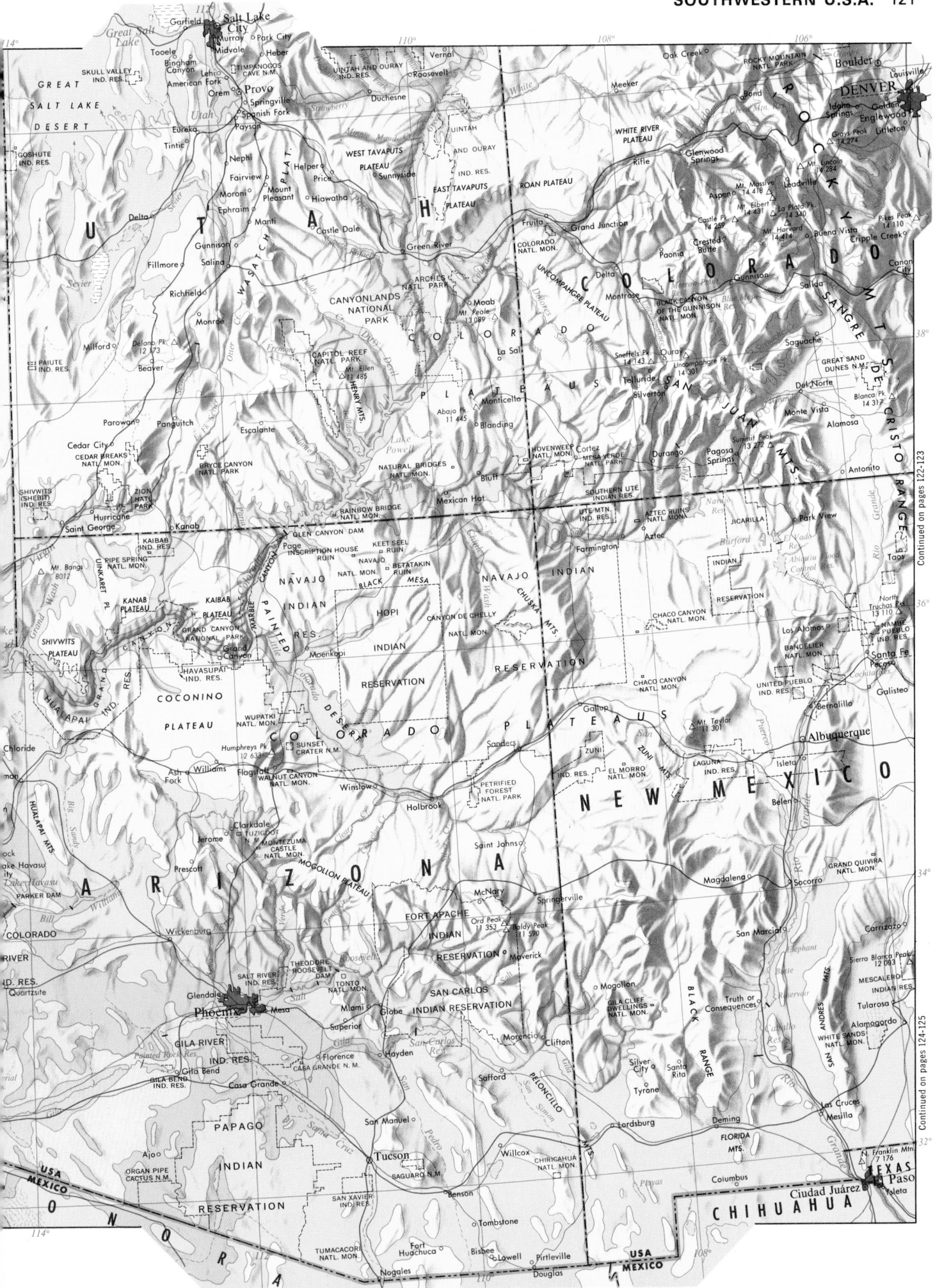

Continued on pages 114-115 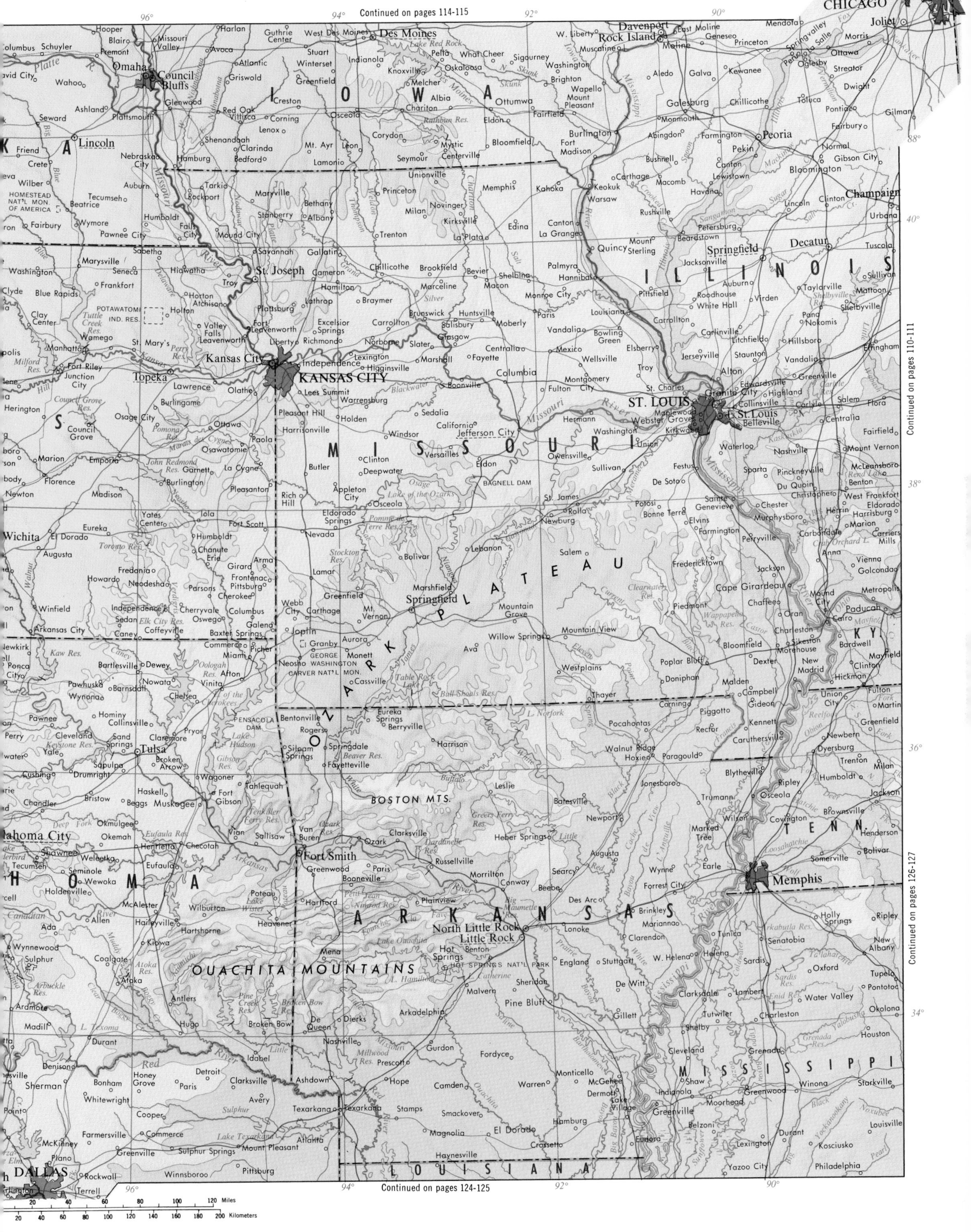
Continued on pages 110-111
Continued on pages 126-127
Continued on pages 124-125

CHICAGO

IOWA

ILLINOIS

MISSOURI

KANSAS

OKLAHOMA

ARKANSAS

TENN.

MISSISSIPPI

KY.

LOUISIANA

OZARK PLATEAU

BOSTON MTS.

OUACHITA MOUNTAINS

Omaha
Council Bluffs
Lincoln
Kansas City
KANSAS CITY
Topeka
St. Joseph
Des Moines
St. Louis
ST. LOUIS
Springfield
Peoria
Decatur
Champaign
Tulsa
Oklahoma City
Wichita
Fort Smith
Little Rock
North Little Rock
Hot Springs
Memphis
Dallas
Paducah
Cairo

HOMESTEAD NAT'L MON. OF AMERICA

GEORGE WASHINGTON CARVER NAT'L MON.

HOT SPRINGS NAT'L PARK

BAGNELL DAM

PENSACOLA DAM

Lake of the Ozarks

Table Rock Lake

Bull Shoals Res.

L. Norfork

Lake Texoma

20 40 60 80 100 120 Miles
20 40 60 80 100 120 140 160 180 200 Kilometers

Continued on pages 122-123

Continued on pages 130-131

Longitude West of Greenwich

Scale 1:4 000 000; one inch to 64 miles. Conic Projection
Elevations and depressions are given in feet

Continued on pages 122-123

Continued on pages 126-127

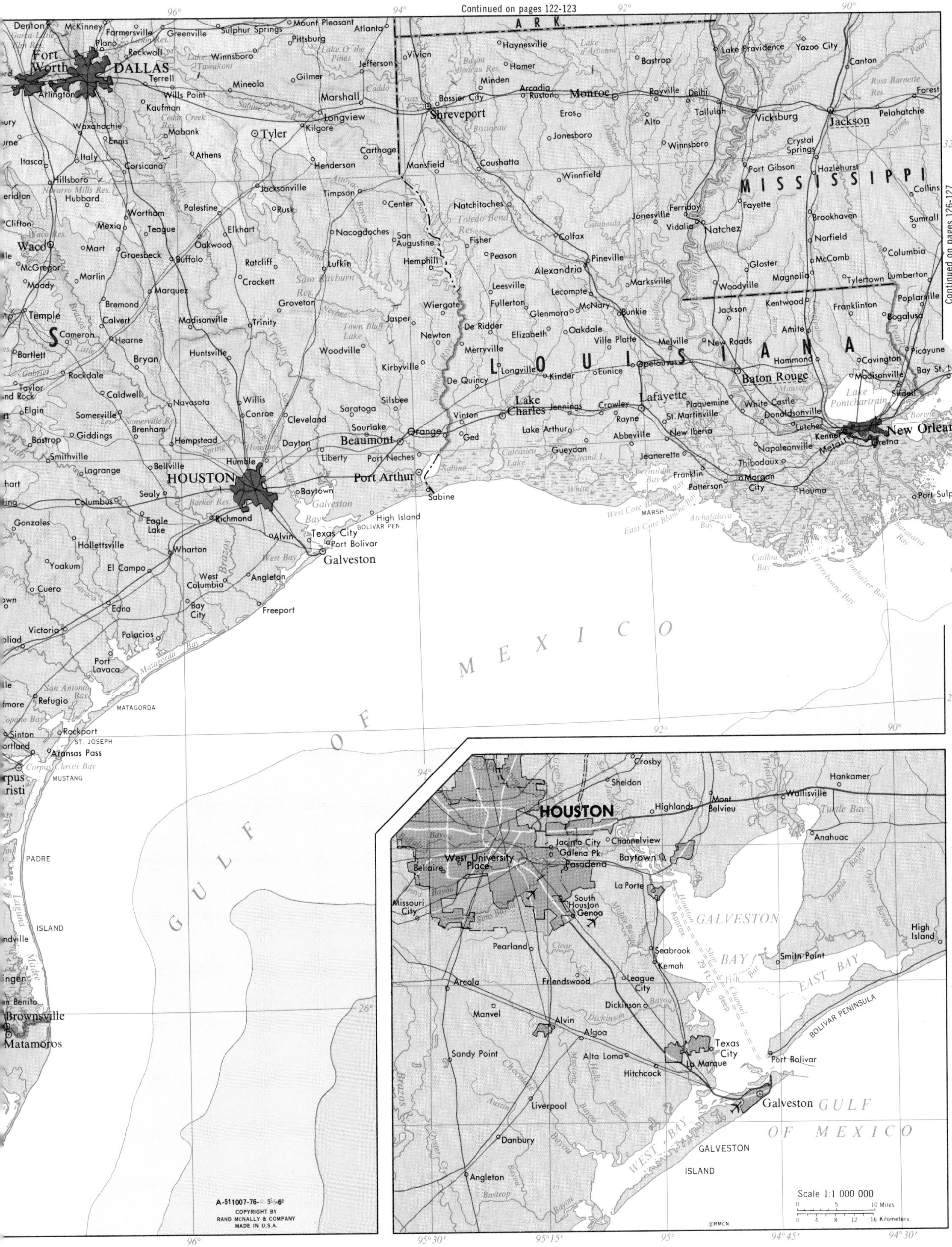

ARK.

MISSISSIPPI

LOUISIANA

Denton McKinney Farmersville Greenville Sulphur Springs Mount Pleasant Atlanta
Fort Worth DALLAS Plano Rockwall Lake Winnsboro Pittsburg Jefferson Vivian Haynesville Homer Bastrop Lake Providence Yazoo City Canton
Arlington Terrell Wills Point Gilmer Marshall Bossier City Arcadia Rustono Monroe Rayville Delhi Vicksburg Jackson Pelahatchie
Kaufman Mineola Longview Shreveport Eros Tallulah Forest
Waxahachie Mabank Tyler Kilgore Carthage Mansfield Coushatta Winnsboro Jonesboro Alto Winnfield Crystal Springs Port Gibson Hazlehurst Collins
Itasca Italy Corsicana Athens Henderson Catahoula Natchitoches Fisher Colfax Pineville Jonesville Vidalia Natchez Fayette Brookhaven Sumrall
Hillsboro Hubbard Jacksonville Timpson Center San Augustine Peason Alexandria Marksville Woodville Magnolia McComb Tylertown Lumberton Columbia
Waco Mexia Palestine Nacogdoches Hemphill Leesville Lecompte McNary Bunkie Jackson Kentwood Franklinton Poplarville Bogalusa
McGregor Moody Teague Elkhart Lufkin Wiergate De Ridder Glenmora Oakdale Ville Platte Melville New Roads Amite Picayune
Temple Groesbeck Buffalo Ratcliff Crockett Jasper Newton Elizabeth Longville Eunice Opelousas Hammond Covington Bay St. Louis
Cameron Hearne Madisonville Trinity Woodville Kirbyville Kinder Crowley Baton Rouge Madisonville Slidell
Bartlett Bryan Groveton Merryville De Quincy Jennings Rayne Lafayette Plaquemine White Castle Donaldsonville Lutcher Lake Pontchartrain NEW ORLEANS
Rockdale Huntsville Saratoga Silsbee Lake Charles Lake Arthur Abbeville New Iberia Napoleonville Kenner Metairie Gretna
Taylor Caldwell Navasota Willis Conroe Cleveland Dayton Vinton Orange Beaumont Ged Gueydan Jeanerette Franklin Thibodaux Morgan City Houma Port Sulphur
Elgin Somerville Brenham Hempstead Liberty Port Neches Port Arthur Patterson
Bastrop Giddings Smithville Bellville HOUSTON Humble Baytown Sabine Galveston Bay
Columbus Sealy Richmond Texas City High Island
Gonzales Eagle Lake Wharton Alvin Port Bolivar
Cuero Yoakum Hollettsville El Campo West Columbia Angleton Galveston
Victoria Edna Bay City Freeport
Goliad Palacios
Refugio Port Lavaca
Sinton Rockport St. Joseph
Portland Aransas Pass
Corpus Christi Bay Mustang
Corpus Christi
Padre Island
Harlingen San Benito
Brownsville
Matamoros

GULF OF MEXICO

Inset map (a)

Crosby Hankamer
Sheldon Highlands Mont Belvieu Wallisville
HOUSTON Jacinto City Channelview Anahuac
West University Place Galena Pk. Baytown
Bellaire Pasadena La Porte
Missouri City South Houston Genoa
Pearland Seabrook
Kemah GALVESTON BAY
Areola Friendswood League City Smith Point High Island
Manvel Dickinson EAST BAY
Alvin Algoa
Sandy Point Alta Loma Texas City BOLIVAR PENINSULA
Hitchcock La Marque Port Bolivar
Liverpool Galveston GULF OF MEXICO
Danbury WEST BAY
Angleton GALVESTON ISLAND
Bastrop

Scale 1:1 000 000

Cities and Towns

Symbol	Population
o	0 to 50,000
⊙	50,000 to 500,000
◉	500,000 to 1,000,000
(shape)	1,000,000 and over

Continued on pages 110-111

Continued on pages 122-123

Continued on pages 124-125

MISSOURI

ILL.

KENTUCKY

TENNESSEE

ARKANSAS

APPALACHIAN

CUMBERLAND PLATEAU

BLUE

MISSISSIPPI

ALABAMA

GEOR

LOUISIANA

FLOR

GULF OF MEXICO

Scale 1:4 000 000; one inch to 64 miles. Conic Projectio
Elevations and depressions are given in feet

Longitude West of Greenwich

A-520598-76- -6-6 -9-
COPYRIGHT BY
RAND McNALLY & COMPANY
MADE IN U.S.A.

Relief

Meters	Feet
1525	5000
610	2000
305	1000
152.5	500
Sea Level	0
152.5	500
1525	5000

Same scale as main map

a

WEST VIRGINIA

Welch
Filbert
Princeton
Bluefield
Radford
Pulaski
Christiansburg
Wytheville

VIRGINIA

Salem
Roanoke
Altavista
Lynchburg
Farmville
Crewe
Chester
Petersburg
Blackstone
Victoria
Lawrenceville
Franklin
Emporia
Suffolk
Chase City
South Hill
Hopewell
Williamsburg
Yorktown
Dendron
Newport News
Hampton
Norfolk
Portsmouth
Virginia Beach

Richmond
Appomattox River
James River
Chesapeake Bay
Cape Charles
CAPE CHARLES
CAPE HENRY

NORTH CAROLINA

Elizabeth City
Hertford
Edenton
Kitty Hawk
Manteo
Windsor
Plymouth
Bethaven
New Holland
Washington
Ayden
Greenville
Farmville
Wilson
Tarboro
Williamston
Scotland Neck
Enfield
Weldon
Roanoke Rapids
Henderson
Louisburg
Oxford
Roxboro
Reidsville
Madison
Spray
Mayodan
Mount Airy
Elkin
North Wilkesboro
Winston-Salem
Greensboro
Burlington
Graham
Durham
Raleigh
Chapel Hill
High Point
Siler City
Thomasville
Lexington
Spencer
Salisbury
Randleman
Asheboro
Sanford
Smithfield
Selma
Clayton
Wake Forest
Goldsboro
Kinston
New Bern
Mount Olive
Warsaw
Clinton
Dunn
Erwin
Fayetteville
Southern Pines
Carthage
Troy
Norwood
Albemarle
Badin
Concord
Kannapolis
Mooresville
Statesville
Cooleemee
Granite Falls
Lenoir
Hickory
Newton
Lincolnton
Cherryville
Bessemer City
Gastonia
Kings Mt.
Charlotte
Fort Mill
Monroe
Wadesboro
Rockingham
Hamlet
Raeford
Laurinburg
St. Pauls
Lumberton
Burgaw
Morehead City
Beaufort
Atlantic
CAPE HATTERAS
CAPE LOOKOUT
Pamlico Sound
Raleigh Bay
OCEAN
Neuse
Cape Fear
Onslow Bay

SOUTH CAROLINA

Columbia
W. Columbia
Sumter
Camden
Bishopville
Hartsville
Darlington
Florence
Timmonsville
Lake City
Manning
Kingstree
Andrews
Georgetown
Myrtle Beach
Conway
Waccamaw
Long Bay
Chester
Cheraw
McColl
Bennettsville
Dillon
Marion
Mullins
Whiteville
Chadbourn
Wilmington
Southport
CAPE FEAR
Lancaster
Rock Hill
York
Winnsboro
Great Falls
Blackville
Denmark
Bamberg
Branchville
Orangeburg
St. George
Summerville
North Charleston
Charleston
Mount Pleasant
FORT SUMTER NAT'L MON.
Edisto Island
Beaufort
SEA ISLANDS

GEORGIA

Augusta
Waynesboro
Louisville
Wadley
Millen
Sylvania
Swainsboro
Statesboro
Metter
Lyons
Claxton
Glennville
Savannah
FORT PULASKI NAT'L MON.
Hazlehurst
Baxley
Jesup
Brunswick
FORT FREDERICA NAT'L MON.
Waycross
Folkston
St. Marys
Fernandina Beach
Okefenokee Swamp
Altamaha River
Satilla River
Ocmulgee River

ATLANTIC

OCEAN

FLORIDA

Jacksonville
Jacksonville Beach
Green Cove Springs
Starke
CASTILLO DE SAN MARCOS NAT'L MON.
St. Augustine
Palatka
FORT MATANZAS NAT'L MON.
Crescent City
Ormond Beach
Daytona Beach
New Smyrna Beach
De Land
Gainesville
Ocala
Dunnellon
Eustis
Mount Dora
Sanford
Winter Park
Titusville
Apopka
Orlando
Winter Garden
Cocoa
Cocoa Beach
CAPE CANAVERAL
Kissimmee
St. Cloud
Melbourne
Haines City
Lakeland
Winter Haven
Lake Wales
Vero Beach
Fort Pierce
Avon Park
Sebring
Okeechobee
Stuart
Brooksville
Inverness
Leesburg
Dade City
Tarpon Springs
Dunedin
Clearwater
Tampa
St. Petersburg
Port Tampa
Bartow
Fort Meade
Wauchula
Arcadia
Palmetto
Bradenton
Sarasota
Punta Gorda
SEMINOLE INDIAN RES.
Lake Okeechobee
Pahokee
Clewiston
Belle Glade
Chosen
W. Palm Beach
Lake Worth
Delray Beach
Pompano Beach
Riviera Beach
Fort Lauderdale
Hollywood
Dania
Hialeah
MIAMI
Miami Beach
Coral Gables
Fort Myers
Naples
SANIBEL I.
Pine I. Sound
Charlotte Harbor
Caloosahatchee
Big Cypress
SEMINOLE INDIAN RES.
THE EVERGLADES
Everglades
Tamiami
CAPE ROMANO
TEN THOUSAND IS.
EVERGLADES NATIONAL PARK
Homestead
CAPE SABLE
Whitewater Bay
Flamingo
Florida Bay
KEY LARGO

GULF

OF

MEXICO

FORT JEFFERSON N.M.
DRY TORTUGAS
MARQUESAS KEYS
Key West
Marathon
FLORIDA KEYS
PINE IS

Jacksonville
Jacksonville Beach
Green Cove Springs
Starke
CASTILLO DE SAN MARCOS NAT'L MON.
St. Augustine
Palatka
FORT MATANZAS NAT'L MON.
Crescent City
Ormond Beach
Daytona Beach
New Smyrna Beach
De Land
Eustis
Leesburg
Dunnellon
Ocala
Inverness

©RMcN.

0 10 20 30 40 50 60 70 80 90 100 110 120 Miles
0 20 40 60 80 100 120 140 160 180 200 Kilometers

120°   115°   110°   105°   100°   95°   90°

KANSAS   MISSOURI
Santa Fe   Evansville
Springfield   ILL. Cairo   KEN
CALIFORNIA   ARIZONA   NEW MEXICO   Joplin   Bowling Gre
Prescott   Albuquerque   Oklahoma City   Tulsa   Nashville   Hopkinsv
SAN DIEGO   Phoenix   Amarillo   OKLAHOMA   Fort Smith   Memphis   TENNESS
Tijuana   Mexicali   Socorro   Muskogee   ARKANSAS   Chattano
Ensenada   Yuma   Gila   Las Cruces   Wichita Falls   Lawton   Hot Springs   Little Rock
30°   BAJA   Cerro Pinacate   Deming   Lubbock   Pine Bluff   Birmingha
CALIFORNIA   Tucson   El Paso   Fort Worth   Texarkana   Vicksburg   ALABAM
NORTE   Nogales   Bisbee   Ciudad Juárez   San Angelo   DALLAS   Shreveport   Jackson   Montgo
GUADALUPE   Nogales   Douglas   Del Rio   Pecos   Corsicana   LOUISIANA   Natchez   Gree
(Mex.)   Cananea   Waco   Austin   Beaumont   Baton Rouge   Mobile
SONORA   CHIHUAHUA   Chihuahua   Piedras Negras   Columbus   HOUSTON   New Orleans   Pensaco
Hermosillo   TEXAS   San Antonio   CAPE SAN
Guaymas   Ciudad Camargo   Eagle Pass   Galveston
Ciudad Obregón   Hidalgo del Parral   BOLSON   Laredo   Corpus Christi
25°   Navojoa   Jiménez   COAHUILA   Nuevo Laredo   GULF   OF   MEX
BAJA   Topolobampo   San Francisco del Oro   DE   Monclova   Brownsville
CALIFORNIA   Gómez Palacio   MAPIMI   Matamoros
SUR   Culiacán   DURANGO   Lerdo   Torreón   NUEVO   Monterrey
Durango   Saltillo   LEÓN   Montemorelos
Mazatlán   Concepción del Oro   Linares
MEXICO   ZACATECAS   Ciudad Victoria   Tropic of Cancer
La Paz   Fresnillo   Matehuala   Ciudad Mante
20°   Escuinapa   Zacatecas   SAN LUIS   Tampico
NAYARIT   Aguascalientes   Salinas   POTOSÍ
Tepic   León   Guanajuato   Tuxpan
Guadalajara   Querétaro   HIDALGO   Papantla de Olarte
JALISCO   Celaya   Pachuca   Nautla
Ciudad Guzmán   Morelia   MEXICO CITY   Jalapa Enríquez   Mérida   YUCATÁN
Colima   Toluca   Puebla   Veracruz   Campeche   QUINTANA ROO
Manzanillo   MICHOACAN   Orizaba   TABASCO   CAMPECHE   Ciudad Chetumal
15°   GUERRERO   OAXACA   Minatitlán   Villahermosa   BELIZE
Acapulco   Oaxaca   CHIAPAS   Belize City
SIERRA MADRE   Tuxtla Gutiérrez   BELIZE   GUATEMALA
Golfo de   GUATEMALA   HONDURAS
Tehuantepec   Quezaltenango   Guatemala   EL SALVADOR
Santa Ana   San Salvador   NICA
León   Managua

a   Caribbean Sea
Colón   2200
Coco Solito   Isaacs Mt.
Rainbow City   1847
Margarita
GATUN   Gatun   Salud Mt.   Nuevo San Juan
LOCKS   1162
West Mt.   East Mt.   Chilibre
537   608
North Gamboa
Balboa Mt.   GAILLARD CUT   Gold Hill   Paraiso
1149   662   Pedro Miguel   Río Abajo
PEDRO MIGUEL LOCKS   Miguel
MIRAFLORES LOCKS   Cocoli
PANAMA   Diablo Hts.   Ancon   Panamá
Cerro Galera   Balboa Heights
1205
La Chorrera
Scale 1:1 000 000
0   10 Miles   Bahía de Panamá
0 4 8 12 15 Kilometers   TABOGA   TABOGUILLA

80°   79°30'

CENTRAL

A-530000 76-   9-6-21'
COPYRIGHT BY
RAND McNALLY & COMPANY

Scale 1:16 000 000; one inch to 250 miles. Polyconic Projection
Elevations and depressions are given in feet

b

ATLANTIC OCEAN

Arecibo ○San Juan
Aguadilla Bayamón CABEZAS DE ST. THOMAS
Utuado SAN JUAN (U.S.A.) TORTOLA
PUERTO RICO Fajardo Charlotte (Br.)
Mayagüez (U.S.A.) Caguas CULEBRA Amalie ST. JOHN
Coamo ○Cayey Humacao Vieques (U.S.A.)
CABO ROJO Ponce Salinas Guayama VIEQUES
Christiansted
CARIBBEAN SEA SAINT CROIX
(U.S.A.)

Scale 1:4 000 000
0 10 20 30 40 Miles
0 10 20 30 40 50 60 Kilometers

©RMcN

c

LITTLE 64°50′
OUTER BRASS HANS LOLLICK 65°
INNER BRASS HANS LOLLICK
PICARA PT GRASS
STORMY PT THATCH CAY CAY
ST THOMAS (U.S.A.)
Crown Mt. PICARA PT
1558 Charlotte Amalie 18°
WATER (St. Thomas) 20′
FLAMINGO PT St. Thomas Nadir
Harbor
©RMcN Scale 1:500 000

Continued on pages 124-125

106°   104°   102°   100°

24°

22°

20°

18°

16°

DURANGO

SINALOA

NAYARIT

S I E R R A   M A D R E   D E   N A Y A R I T

SIERRA DE VALLEJO

S I E R R A   M A D R E   O C C I D E N T A L

JALISCO

COLIMA

SIERRA DE COALCOMAN

SA. DEL CUALE

Z A C A T E C A S

A L T I P L A N I C I E

M E X I C A N A

AGUASCALIENTES

S A N   L U I S A

P O T O S I

S   NUEVO   LEON

TAMAULIP

GUANAJUATO

QUERÉTARO

HIDALGO

MICHOACÁN

MORELOS

G U E R R E R O

S I E R R A   M A D R E

DISTRITO FEDERAL

San Dimas
El Salto
Durango
Nombre de Dios
Miguel Auza
Juan Aldama
Nieves
Gruñidora
Ascensión
Aramberri
Hidalgo
Jiménez
Pánuco
Siqueros
Concordia
Pueblo Nuevo
Villa Unión
Mezquital
Muleros
Río Grande
Sombrerete
Chalchihuites
11 700
Sain Alto
Cañitas
Vanegas
Cedral
Catorce
La Paz
Doctor Arroyo
Zaragoza
Ciudad Victoria
Peña Nevada
13 300
Miquihuana
Padilla
Soto la Marina
Rosario
Escuinapa
San Felipe
Santa María de Ocotán
C. Pimal
Valparaíso
Huejuquilla el Alto
Ciudad García
Zacatecas
Calera
Víctor Rosales
Morelos
Troncoso
Ramos
Moctezuma
Charcas
Venado
Matehuala
Jaumave
Llera
Xicotencatl
Ocampo
Magiscatzin
Ciudad Mante
Huajícori
Acaponeta
Tecuala
San Felipe
Rosamorada
Mezquitic
Monte Escobedo
Sta. María de los Angeles
Colotlán
Villanueva
Luis Moya
Rincón de Romos
Asientos
Tepezalá
Villa García
Ojocaliente
Salinas
11 000
Bocas
Peotillos
San Luis Potosí
Zaragoza
Pozos
Soledad Diez Gutiérrez
Cerritos
Guadalcázar
Ciudad del Maíz
El Ebano
Tamuín
Cárdenas
Ciudad de Valles
Laguna de Agua Brava
Ruiz
Tuxpan
San Blas
Jalisco
Tepic
Pochotitlán
Sta. María del Oro
Compostela
San Pedro Lagunillas
Jala
Ixtlán del Río
Ahuacatlán
Amatlán de Cañas
Tabasco
Calvillo
Aguascalientes
Gogorrón
Ciudad Fernández
Ojo Caliente
Sta. María del Río
Villa de Reyes
San Felipe
Ríoverde
Pastora
Rayón
Alaquines
Xilitla
San Martín Chalchi
Tamazunchale
Jalpa
Villa Hidalgo
Encarnación de Díaz
San Diego de la Unión
Dolores Hidalgo
San Luis de la Paz
Arroyo Seco
Jalpan
General Pedro Antonio Santos
Huehuetlán
Jaltocan
Huejutla
Jiménez del Téul
Teocaltiche
Nochistlán
Lagos de Moreno
León
La Luz
Guanajuato
San José Iturbide
Tierra Blanca
Toliman
Jalpan
Calnali
Huichapan
Metztitlán
García de la Cadena
Moyahua
Juchipila
San Juan de los Lagos
Unión de San Antonio
San Francisco del Rincón
Silao
San Miguel de Allende
Comonfort
Colón
Cadereyta
Zimapán
Tasquillo
Ixmiquilpan
Atotonilco
Mineral del Chico
Puerta Vallarta
Mascota
Talpa de Allende
Tenamaxtlán
Ahualulco
Etzatlán
Ameca
Tala
Zapopan
Guadalajara
Tlaquepaque
Tonalá
Zapotlanejo
Arandas
Atotonilco el Alto
Tepatitlán de Morelos
San Miguel el Alto
Yahualica
Jalostotitlán
Cuquío
Ciudad Manuel Doblado
Irapuato
Juventino Rosas
Salamanca
Cortazar
Celaya
Querétaro
Cayetano Rubio
Tequisquiapan
San Juan del Río
Amealco
Tecozautla
Huichapan
Mixquiahuala
Actopan
Tula
Pachuca
Tulancingo
Minatitlán
Cocula
Ameca
Tala
Jocotepec
Chapala
Ocotlán
Tizapán
Jamay
La Barca
Yurécuaro
La Piedad
Cabadas
Penjamillo
Pénjamo
Abasolo
Valle de Santiago
Jaral del Progreso
Salvatierra
Yuriria
Moroleón
Acámbaro
Contepec
Maravatío
Tlalpujahua
El Oro
Ixtlahuaca
Temascalcingo
Jilotepec
Tepeji del Río
Teoloyucan
Tula
Otumba
Zumpango
Apizaco
Autlán
Unión de Tula
El Grullo
Purificación
Ayutla
Juchitlán
Tecolotlán
Zacoalco de Torres
Tomatlán
Venustiano Carranza
Sayula
Tamazula de Gordiano
Tuxpan
Ciudad Guzmán
Zapotiltic
Tecalitlán
Tuxcueca
Sahuayo de Díaz
Jiquilpan de Juárez
Chavinda
Zamora
Tangancícuaro
Purépero
Chilchota
Zacapu
Coeneo de la Libertad
Zinapécuaro
Ciudad Hidalgo
Zitácuaro
Angangueo
Tlacotepec
Toluca
Metepec
Tenango
Amecameca
Chalco
Tlalpan
Coyoacán
MEXICO CITY
Azcapotzalco
G.A. Madero
Texcoco
Teotihuacán
Nevado de Colima
13 993
Colima de Colima
12 620
Comala
Villa de Álvarez
Colima
Tecomán
Cuyutlán
Minatitlán
Cihuatlán
Manzanillo
Bahía de Manzanillo
Tepalcatepec
Tancítaro
Apatzingán de la Constitución
Parácuaro
Los Reyes
Cerro de Tancítaro
12 660
Uruapan
Paracho
Cherán
Pátzcuaro
Erongarícuaro
Tacámbaro de Cadallos
Turicato
Morelia
Quiroga
Puruándiro
Villa Morelos
Cuitzeo
Tlalpujahua
El Oro
Valle de Bravo
Temascaltepec
Tejupilco de Hidalgo
Tenancingo
Sultepec
Malinalco
Texcaltitlán
 Tonatico
Ixtapan de la Sal
Cuernavaca
Cuautla
Yautepec
Jojutla
Tepoztlán
Zacualpan
Tlatlaya
Coalcomán de Matamoros
Aguililla
Churumuco
Huetamo de Núñez
Tumbiscatío
Coahuayutla
Zirándaro
Ciudad Altamirano
Coyuca de Catalán
Ajuchitlán del Progreso
Tlapehuala
Arcelia
Teloloapan
Iguala
Huitzuco
Taxco
Ixcateopan
Pilcaya
Apipilulco
Tepecoacuilco de Trujano
Tlapehuala
Acapetlahuaya
Cutzamala de Pinzón
Tlalchapa
Atoyac de Álvarez
Coyuca de Benítez
Acapulco
San Marcos
Cuautepec
Cruz Grande
San Jerónimo de Juárez
Tecpan de Galeana
Petatlán
La Unión
Coahuayutla
Río Balsas
Xochihuet
Chilpancingo
Chilapa
Tixtla de Guerrero
Mochitlán
Huexcafenango
Atliaca
Apango
Zitlala
Olinalá
Zapotitlán
Huamuxtitlán
Tlaxcala
Cuetzalá del Progreso
Coatepec Costales
Chiapa
Pta. Farallón
Cabo Corrientes
Punta de Mita
Bahía de Banderas
Pta. Tejupan
Pta. Maldonado
Bahía de Pétacalco
Laguna Papagayo
Puerto

P A C I F I C   O C E A N

Longitude West of Greenwich

Relief

Meters		Feet
3050		10000
1525		5000
610		2000
305		1000
152.5		500
0	Sea Level	0
152.5		500
1525		5000
3050		10000

Cities and Towns

0 to 50,000 ○	500,000 to 1,000,000 ◎	
50,000 to 500,000 ⊙	1,000,000 and over	

Scale 1:4 000 000; one inch to 64 miles. Conic Project
Elevations and depressions are given in feet

For larger scale coverage of Mexico City see page 60.

Continued on pages 132-133

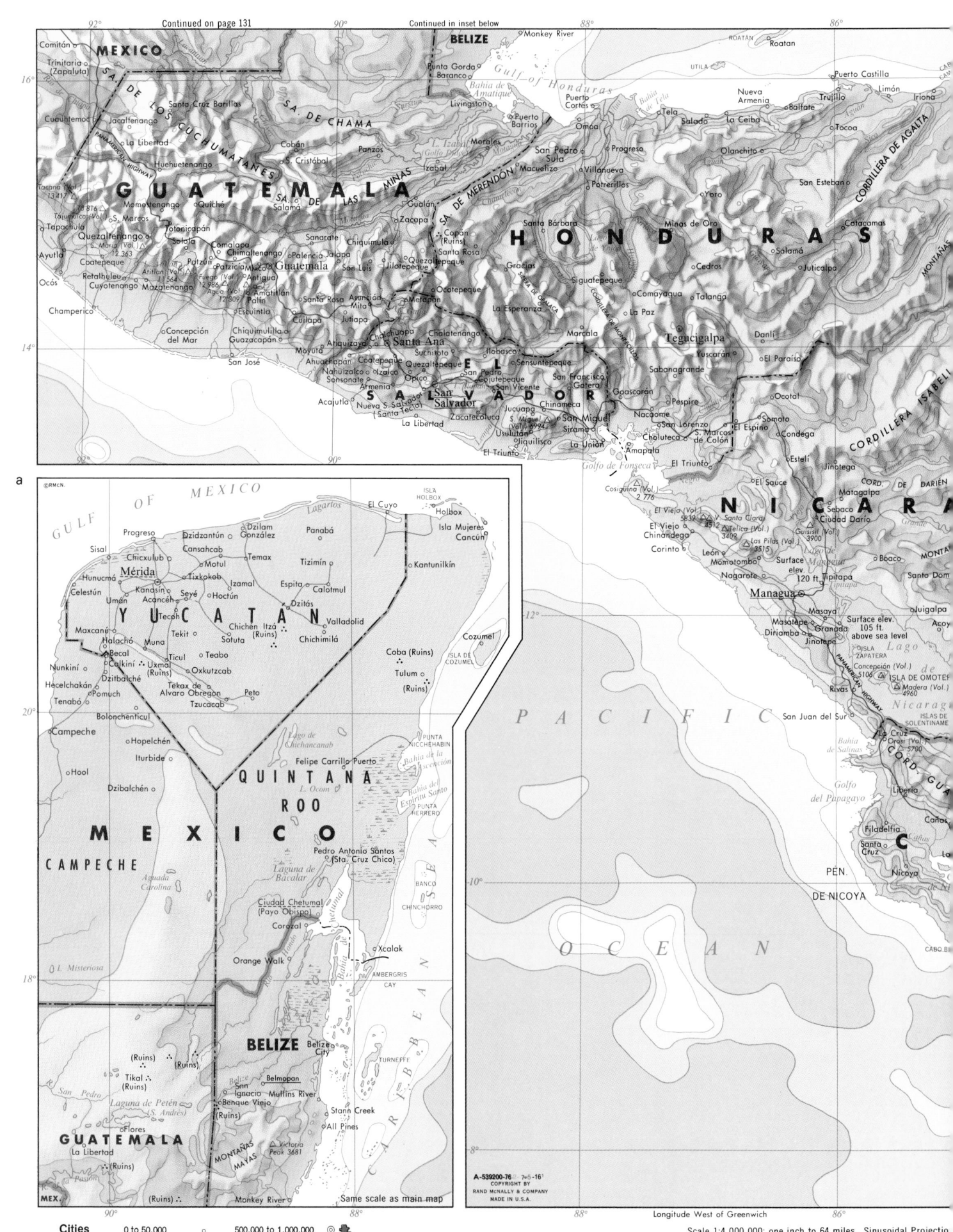

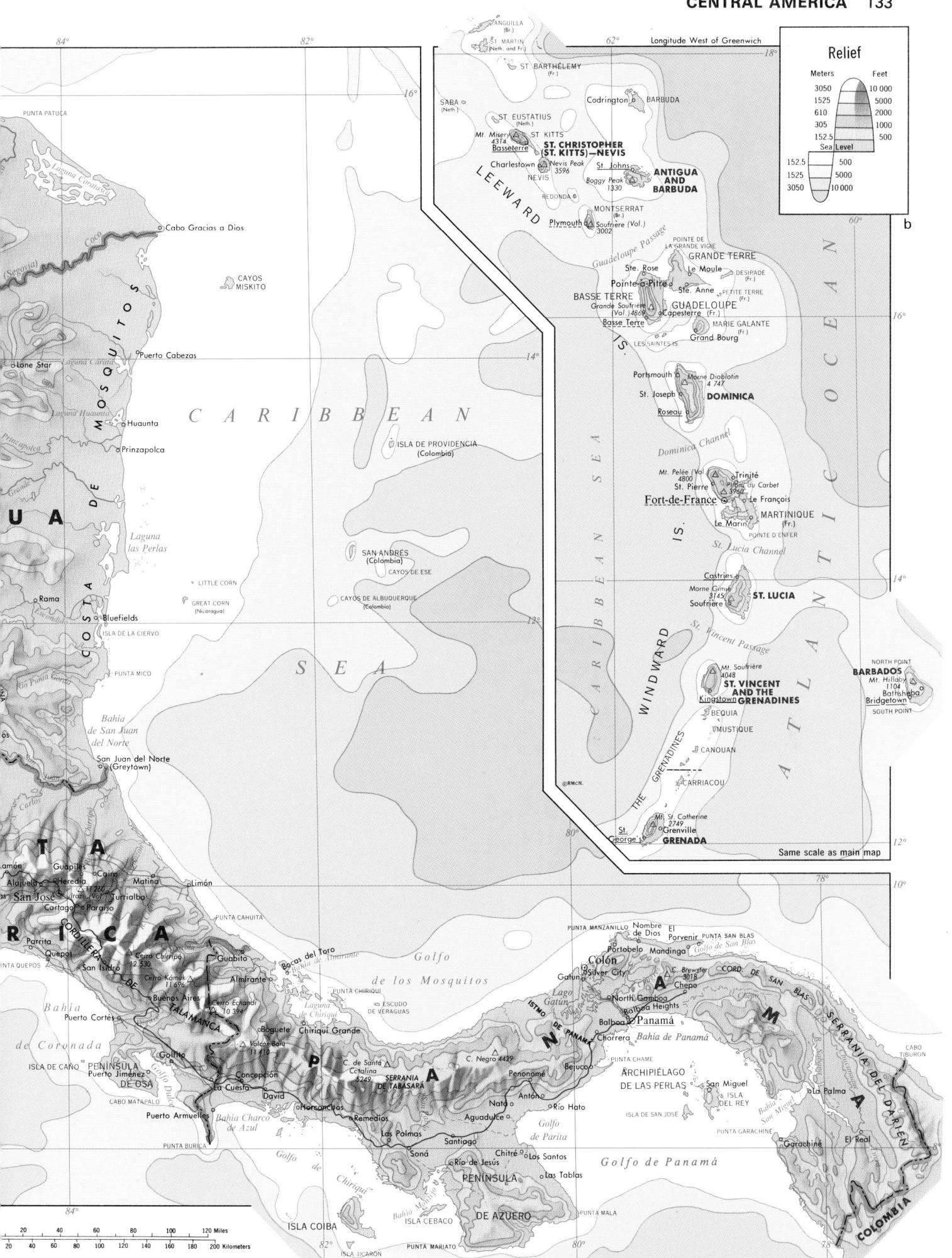

Relief

Meters		Feet
3050		10 000
1525		5000
610		2000
305		1000
152.5		500
Sea Level		0
152.5		500
1525		5000
3050		10 000
6100		20 000

A-533200-76- 6-4-9²
COPYRIGHT BY
RAND McNALLY & COMPANY
MADE IN U.S.A.

Cities	0 to 50,000	○	500,000 to 1,000,000	◎
and				
Towns	50,000 to 500,000	⊙	1,000,000 and over	

Longitude West of Greenwich

Scale 1:4 000 000; one inch to 64 miles. Conic Proje

Elevations and depressions are given in feet.

Scale 1:1 000 000

HAVANA
(La Habana)

GULF OF MEXICO

Cojímar
Playa de Guanabo

Guanabacoa
Playa de Santa Fé
Regla
Campo Florido
Baracoa
Marianao
San Francisco de Paula
Cotorro
Arroya Arena
Calabazar
Cuatro Caminos
Bauta
Rancho Boyeros
Managua
San José de las Lajas
Caimito del Guayabal
Santiago de las Vegas
La Sabina
Bejucal
L. de Ariguanabo
Buenaventura
△ 950
Ceiba del Agua
San Antonio de los Baños
San Antonio de las Vegas
©rmcn.

76° 74° 72° 26° 82°30' 82°15' 70°

MES PT.
Governor's Harbour
PALMETTO PT.
ELEUTHERA
Rock Sound

ERA PT.
Arthur's Town
NORTHEAST PT.
LITTLE
SAN SALVADOR
CAT

Old Bight
HAWKS NEST PT.
COLUMBUS PT.
SAN SALVADOR
(WATLING)
(Columbus, Oct. 12, 1492)
SOUTHWEST PT.

REAT
ANA CAY

CONCEPTIÓN

ATLANTIC

OCEAN

LEE STOCKING
Rolleville
CAPE STA. MARIA
RUM CAY

GREAT
EXUMA
George Town

Tropic of Cancer

24°

LITTLE EXUMA
HOG CAY
LONG

JUMENTO CAYS
WATER CAY
FLAMINGO CAY
Clarence Town
SAMANA OR ATWOOD CAY

B A H A M A S

JAMAICA CAY
CAP VERDE
BIRD ROCK
CROOKED
NORTHEAST PT.

SEAL CAYS
FORTUNE
PLANA OR FLAT CAYS
Man of War Channel
DIANA BANK
FISH CAY
ACKLINS

NURSE CAY
RACCOON CAY
SALINA PT.
Abraham's Bay
MAYAGUANA
CASTLE

INOS
GREAT RAGGED
COLUMBUS BANK
MIRA POR VOS ISLETS
CAY VERDE
Mira Por Vos Pass

KS
CAY STA. DOMINGO
HOGSTY REEF

BROWN BANK
Caicos Passage

NORTH CAICOS
GRAND CAICOS
PROVIDENCIALES
CAPE COMETE
EAST CAICOS
CAICOS IS.
(Br.)
GRAND TURK
WEST CAICOS
Grand Turk
LITTLE INAGUA
CAICOS BANK
SOUTH CAICOS
TURKS IS. (Br.)
SALT CAY
NORTHEAST PT.
WEST SAND SPIT
AMBERGRIS CAYS
Turks I. Passage
PALMETTO PT.
SEAL CAYS
MOUCHOIR PASSAGE
Ocean Bight
The Lake
GREAT INAGUA
MOUCHOIR BANK
Man of War Bay
Matthew Town
South Bay

22°

SILVER BANK

CABO LUCRECIA
Banes
Holguín
Antilla
Bahía de Nipe
GUÍN
Mayari
Sagua de Tánamo
NAVIDAD BANK
Silver Bank Passage
20°
SA. DE NIPE
CUCHILLAS DE TOAR
Baracoa
SANTIAGO DE CUBA
1100
SA. DE PURIAL
Alto Songo
PUNTA MAISÍ
oriano
San Luis
Caney
Gran Piedra
401
Yateras
Bahía de Ovando
GUANTÁNAMO
Santiago de Cuba
Caimanero
Guantánamo
Yateras
Naval Station
(U.S.A.)
Bahía de Guantánamo
ÍLE DE LA TORTUE
CABO ISABELA
CAP ST. NICOLAS
Canal de la Tortue
Monte Cristi
Puerto Plata
CORDILLERA SEPTENTRIONAL
CABO FRANCÉS VIEJO
Le Môle
Port de Paix
Cap-Haïtien
Baie de l'Acul
Guayubin
Diego
Gaspar Hernández
Le Borgne
Limbé
Fort Liberté
Dajabón
Santiago Rodríguez
Bahía Escocesa
PTE. PLATEFORME
Ouanaminthe
Santiago de los Caballeros
Salcedo
Nagua
Windward Passage
Gonaïves
Vallière
VEGA
San Francisco
CABO SAMANÁ
A
St. Michel-de-l'Atalaye
La Vega
Riva
Bahía de Samaná
Sánchez
Samaná
GOLFE DES GONAÏVES
Pic Bonhomme
D O M I N I C A N
CABO SAN RAFAEL
St. Marc
5883
Mte. Mira Pico Duarte
Jarabacoa
7431
10417
CORDILLERA ORIENTAL
POINT OUEST
Mirebalais
Mte. Tina
Cotuí
Hato Mayor
H A I T I
ÍLE DE LA GONÂVE
Lascahobas
7295
Bayaguana
Los Llanos
Seibo
Jérémie
ÍLE GRANDE CAYEMITE
2500
Báníca
San Juan
Cayos
Yamasá
Higüey
CAP DAME MARIE
Petit-Goâve
Port-au-Prince
SIERRA DE NEIBA
Azua
San Cristóbal
La Romana
Anse d'Hainault
Miragoâne
Léogâne
Pétionville
CORDILLERA CENTRAL
Catalina
CAP DES IROIS
Anse à Veau
R E P U B L I C
Tiburon
Aquin
Neiba
Bani
S. Pedro de Macoris
FORMIGAS BANK
Pico de Macaya
7920
CUL DE SAC
Barahona
Santo Domingo
SAONA
NAVASSA
(U.S.A.)
MASSIF DE LA HOTTE
Duverge
Bahía de Neiba
Coteaux
MASSIF DE LA SELLE
7792
SAONA
Les Cayes
Jacmel Belle-Anse
Enriquillo
PTA. PALENQUE
Roche à Bateau
SIERRA DE BAHORUCO
H I S P A N I O L A
CABO FALSO
POINTE À GRAVOIS
ÍLE À VACHE
Oviedo
Trujin
MORANT PT.
CABO BEATA
BEATA
CABO BEATA
ALTO VELO

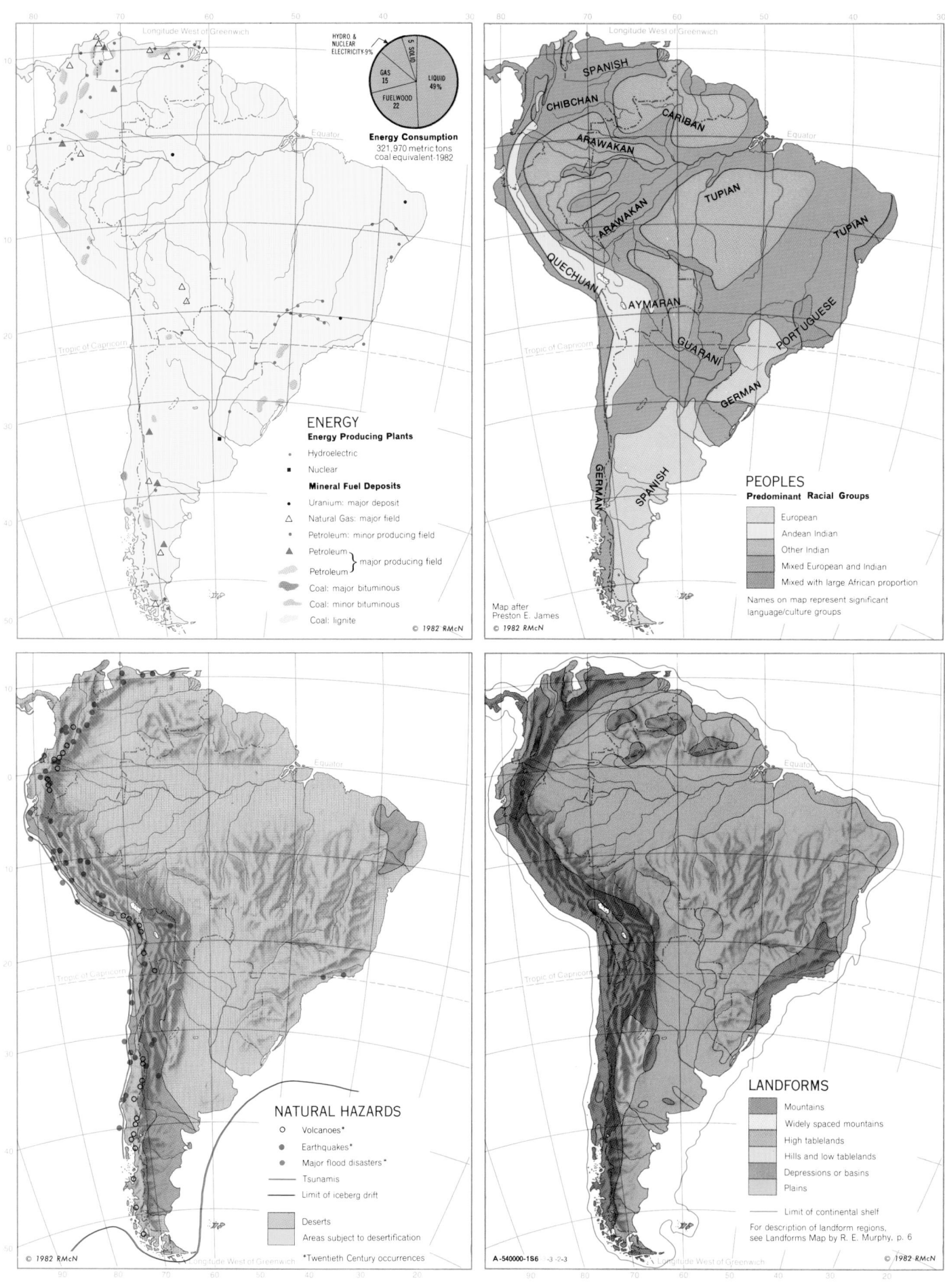

ENERGY

Energy Producing Plants

- • Hydroelectric
- ■ Nuclear

Mineral Fuel Deposits

- ▲ Uranium: major deposit
- △ Natural Gas: major field
- • Petroleum: minor producing field
- ▲ Petroleum } major producing field
-   Petroleum
-   Coal: major bituminous
-   Coal: minor bituminous
-   Coal: lignite

© 1982 RMcN

HYDRO & NUCLEAR ELECTRICITY-9%
GAS 15
FUELWOOD 22
LIQUID 49%
S SOLID

Energy Consumption
321,970 metric tons
coal equivalent-1982

PEOPLES

Predominant Racial Groups

- European
- Andean Indian
- Other Indian
- Mixed European and Indian
- Mixed with large African proportion

Names on map represent significant
language/culture groups

Map after
Preston E. James
© 1982 RMcN

NATURAL HAZARDS

- ○ Volcanoes*
- ● Earthquakes*
- ● Major flood disasters*
- ⎯ Tsunamis
- ⎯ Limit of iceberg drift
-   Deserts
-   Areas subject to desertification

*Twentieth Century occurrences

© 1982 RMcN

LANDFORMS

- Mountains
- Widely spaced mountains
- High tablelands
- Hills and low tablelands
- Depressions or basins
- Plains
- ⎯ Limit of continental shelf

For description of landform regions,
see Landforms Map by R. E. Murphy, p. 6

A-540000-1S6   -3-2-3   © 1982 RMcN

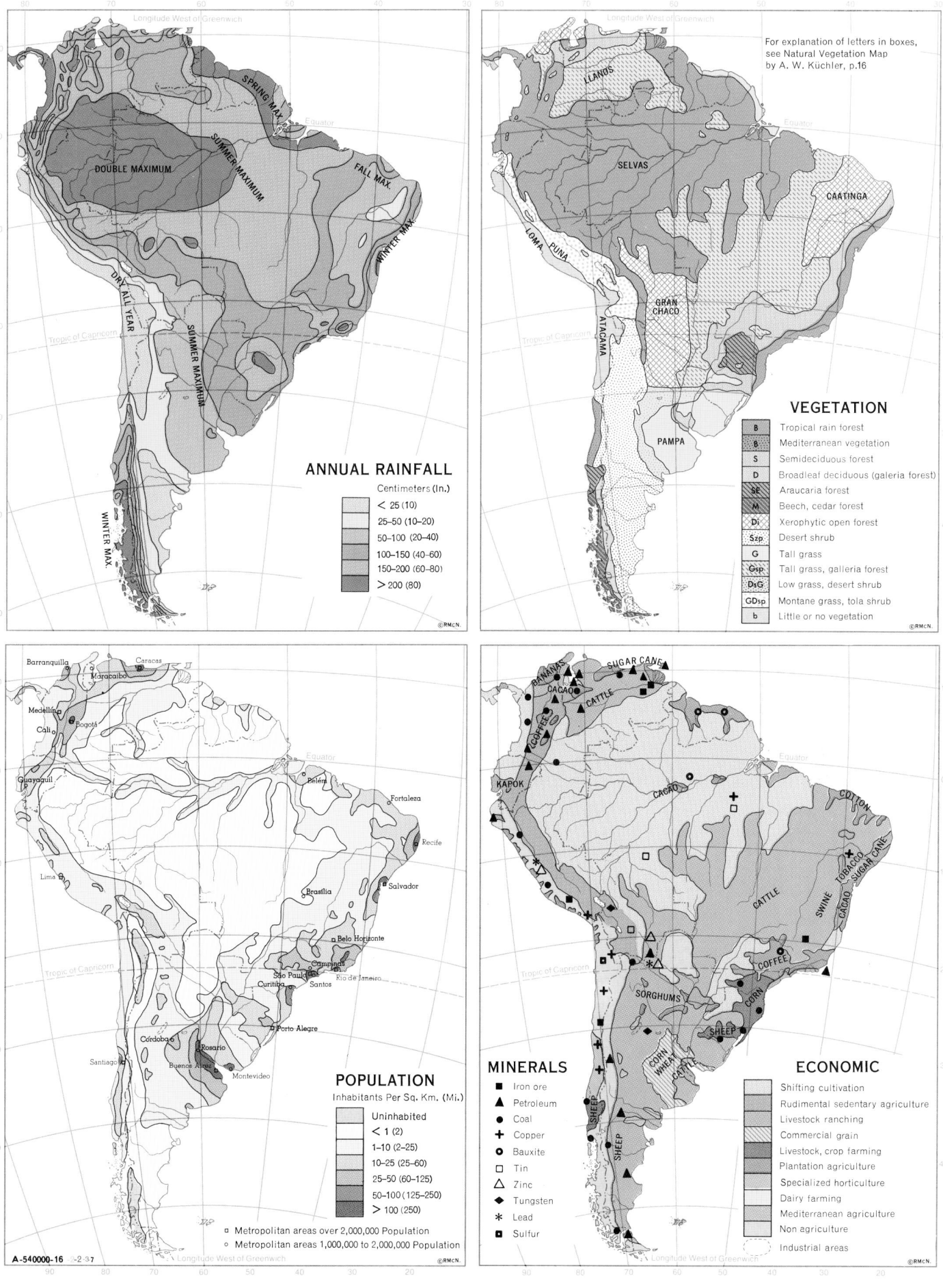

ANNUAL RAINFALL

SPRING MAX.
SUMMER MAXIMUM
DOUBLE MAXIMUM
FALL MAX.
WINTER MAX.
DRY ALL YEAR
SUMMER MAXIMUM
WINTER MAX.

Centimeters (In.)

- < 25 (10)
- 25–50 (10–20)
- 50–100 (20–40)
- 100–150 (40–60)
- 150–200 (60–80)
- > 200 (80)

©RMCN.

VEGETATION

For explanation of letters in boxes, see Natural Vegetation Map by A. W. Küchler, p.16

LLANOS
SELVAS
CAATINGA
LOMA
PUNA
ATACAMA
GRAN CHACO
PAMPA

B	Tropical rain forest
B	Mediterranean vegetation
S	Semideciduous forest
D	Broadleaf deciduous (galeria forest)
SE	Araucaria forest
M	Beech, cedar forest
Di	Xerophytic open forest
Szp.	Desert shrub
G	Tall grass
Gsp	Tall grass, galleria forest
DsG	Low grass, desert shrub
GDsp	Montane grass, tola shrub
b	Little or no vegetation

©RMCN.

POPULATION

Barranquilla
Caracas
Maracaibo
Medellín
Cali
Bogotá
Guayaquil
Lima
Belém
Fortaleza
Recife
Brasília
Salvador
Belo Horizonte
Campinas
São Paulo
Santos
Curitiba
Rio de Janeiro
Porto Alegre
Córdoba
Rosario
Santiago
Buenos Aires
Montevideo

Inhabitants Per Sq. Km. (Mi.)

- Uninhabited
- < 1 (2)
- 1–10 (2–25)
- 10–25 (25–60)
- 25–50 (60–125)
- 50–100 (125–250)
- > 100 (250)

□ Metropolitan areas over 2,000,000 Population
○ Metropolitan areas 1,000,000 to 2,000,000 Population

A-540000-16   -2-37

©RMCN.

MINERALS

- ■ Iron ore
- ▲ Petroleum
- ● Coal
- + Copper
- ◉ Bauxite
- □ Tin
- △ Zinc
- ◆ Tungsten
- ✳ Lead
- ▣ Sulfur

ECONOMIC

BANANAS
CACAO
COFFEE
CATTLE
SUGAR CANE
KAPOK
CACAO
CACAO
COTTON
CATTLE
TOBACCO
SWINE
CACAO-SUGAR CANE
COFFEE
SORGHUMS
CORN
CORN WHEAT
CATTLE
SHEEP
SHEEP
SHEEP
SHEEP

- Shifting cultivation
- Rudimental sedentary agriculture
- Livestock ranching
- Commercial grain
- Livestock, crop farming
- Plantation agriculture
- Specialized horticulture
- Dairy farming
- Mediterranean agriculture
- Non agriculture
- Industrial areas

©RMCN.

138

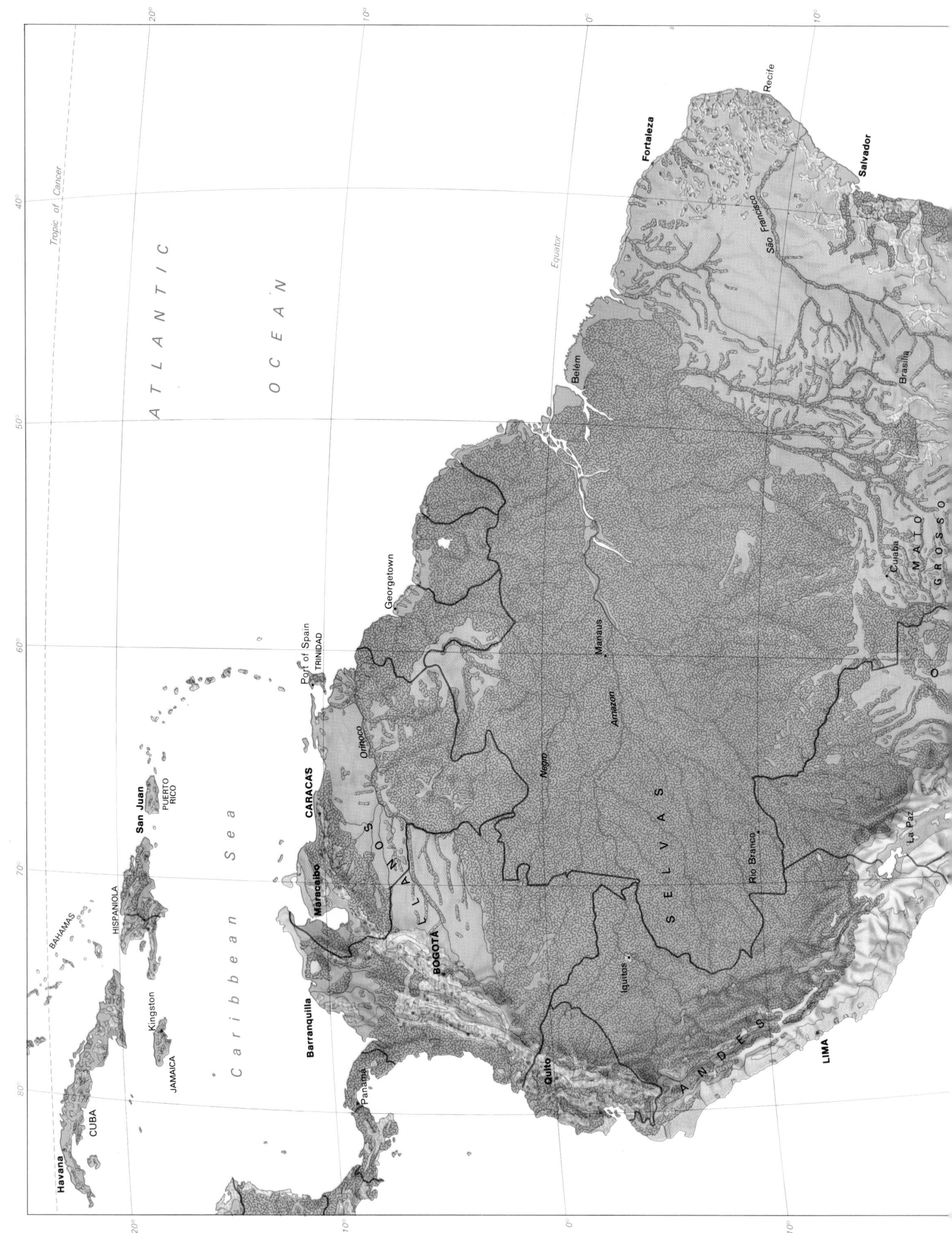

ATLANTIC

OCEAN

Tropic of Cancer

40°

50°

60°

70°

80°

20°

10°

0°

10°

20°

20°

10°

0°

10°

Equator

Havana

CUBA

BAHAMAS

Kingston

JAMAICA

HISPANIOLA

San Juan

PUERTO RICO

Caribbean Sea

Barranquilla

Panamá

Maracaibo

CARACAS

Port of Spain

TRINIDAD

Georgetown

BOGOTA

Quito

Iquitos

Orinoco

L L A N O S

A M A Z O N

Negro

Amazon

Manaus

Belém

Fortaleza

Recife

São Francisco

Salvador

Brasília

Cuiabá

MATO GROSSO

S E L V A S

Rio Branco

La Paz

A N D E S

LIMA

B

Scale 1:24,000,000; one inch to 380 miles. Lambert Azimuthal Equal-Area Projection

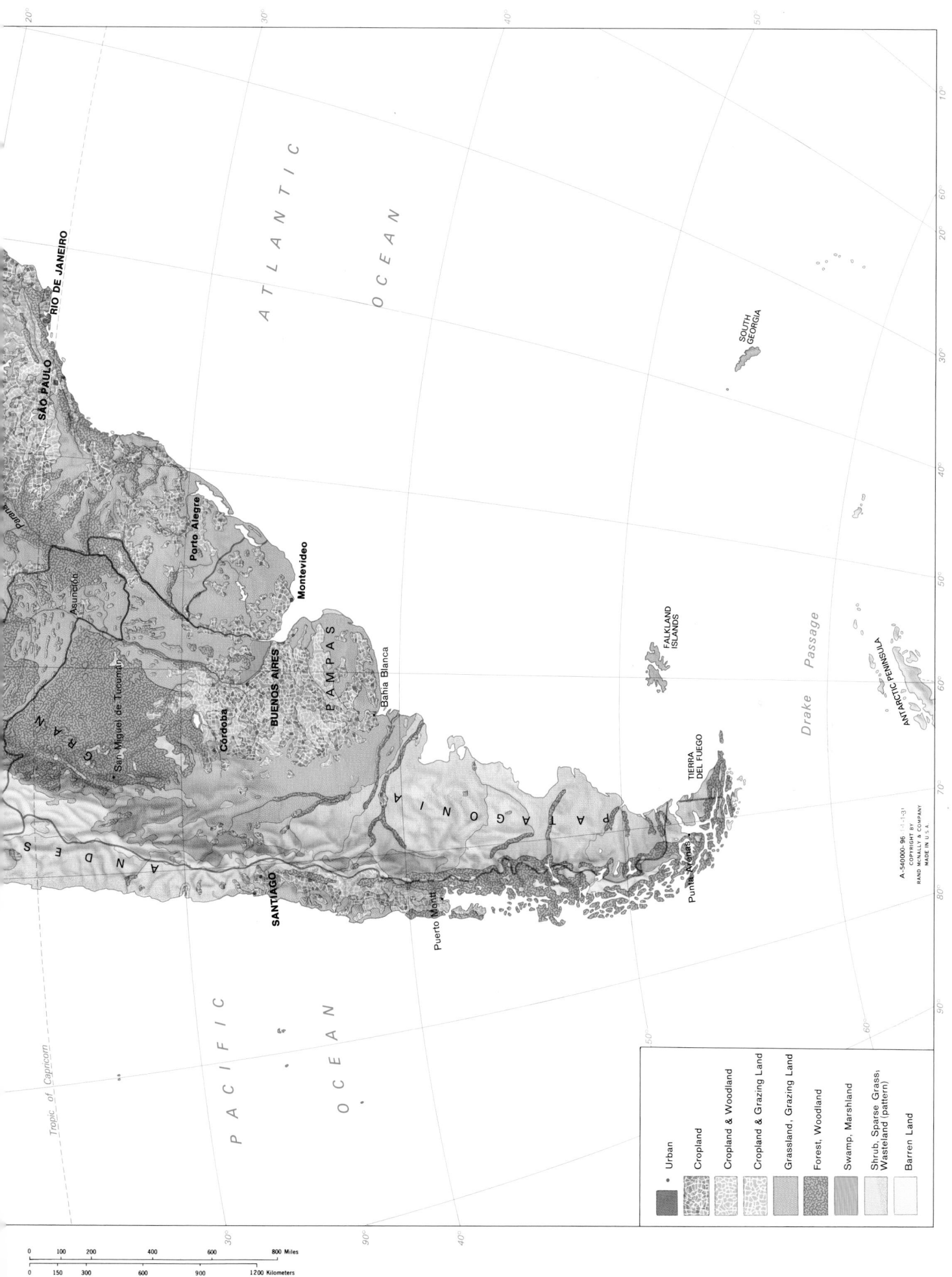

ATLANTIC

OCEAN

RIO DE JANEIRO

SÃO PAULO

SOUTH
GEORGIA

Porto Alegre

Montevideo

Asunción

FALKLAND
ISLANDS

Drake   Passage

BUENOS AIRES

P A M P A S

Bahía Blanca

San Miguel de Tucumán

Córdoba

ANTARCTIC PENINSULA

G R A N

TIERRA
DEL FUEGO

P A T A G O N I A

SANTIAGO

Punta Arenas

A N D E S

Puerto Montt

PACIFIC

OCEAN

Tropic of Capricorn

A-540000-96
COPYRIGHT BY
RAND McNALLY & COMPANY
MADE IN U.S.A.

Paraná

•	Urban
	Cropland
	Cropland & Woodland
	Cropland & Grazing Land
	Grassland, Grazing Land
	Forest, Woodland
	Swamp, Marshland
	Shrub, Sparse Grass, Wasteland (pattern)
	Barren Land

0   100   200   400   600   800 Miles

0   150   300   600   900   1200 Kilometers

HAVANA
CUBA
Bahía de Campeche
PEN DE YUCATÁN
Gulf of Honduras
JAMAICA
HISPANIOLA
San Juan
PUERTO RICO (U.S.)
PUERTO RICO TRENCH
NORTH AMERICAN BASIN
GUADELOUPE (Fr.)
MARTINIQUE (Fr.)
Tropic of Cancer
CARIBBEAN SEA
WEST INDIES
BARBADOS

ATLANTIC OCEAN

CENTRAL AMERICA
Lago de Nicaragua
ISLA DEL COCO (Costa Rica)
PUNTA DE GALLINAS
Golfo de Venezuela
Barranquilla
Cartagena
Panamá
Golfo de Panamá
ST. OF PAN.
Gulf of Darien
Medellín
BOGOTÁ
COLOMBIA
ISLA DE MALPELO (Colombia)
Nevado del Tolima 17,110
Maracaibo
Mérida
Valencia
VENEZUELA
Ciudad Bolívar
Cerro Icutú 7800
Orinoco
La Guaira
CARACAS
Port of Spain
TRINIDAD AND TOBAGO
Georgetown
GUYANA
Paramaribo
SURINAME
FR. GUIANA
Cayenne
GUIANA HIGHLANDS
Boa Vista do Rio Branco

Quito
ECUADOR
Cotopaxi 19,347
Chimborazo 20,561
Guayaquil
Golfo de Guayaquil
ARCHIPIÉLAGO DE COLÓN (GALÁPAGOS ISLANDS) (Ec.)
Iquitos
Leticia
Putumayo
Japurá
Rio Negro
Rio Solimões (Amazonas)
Manaus (Manáos)
Rio Amazonas
Equator
ILHA DE MARAJÓ
Belém (Pará)
São Luís (Maranhão)
ROCEDOS SÃO PEDRO E SÃO PAULO (Brazil)
ARQUIPÉLAGO FERNANDO DE NORONHA (Brazil)

Chiclayo
Trujillo
PERU
Nevs. Huascarán 22,205
LIMA
Callao
Cuzco
ANDES MTS.
Volcán Misti 19,098
Arequipa
Mollendo
Lago Titicaca
La Paz
Nev. Illimani 21,151
BOLIVIA
Sucre
Potosí
Rio Branco
Pôrto Velho
Juruá
Purús
Rio Madeira
Beni
Mamoré
Tapajós
Xingu
Tocantins
Teresina
Fortaleza (Ceará)
CABO DE SÃO ROQUE
Natal
João Pessoa (Paraíba)
RECIFE (Pernambuco)
Maceió
BRAZIL
CHAPADA DE MATO GROSSO
Cuiabá
Brasília
Diamantina
BRAZILIAN HIGHLANDS
SERRA DO ESPINHAÇO
SERRA DO PIAUÍ
Salvador (Bahia)

Antofagasta
Tropic of Capricorn
ISLA DE SAN FÉLIX (Chile)
ISLA DE SAN AMBROSIO (Chile)
Cerro Azufre (Copiapó) Vol.
Salta
GRAN CHACO
Tucumán
Asunción
PARAGUAY
Corrientes
Belo Horizonte
Pico da Bandeira 9492
Vitória
SÃO PAULO
Santos
CABO FRIO
RIO DE JANEIRO
Florianópolis
Iguaçú Falls
DESIERTO DE ATACAMA
Iquique
Copiapó
Coquimbo
Valparaíso
SANTIAGO
Córdoba
Aconcagua 22,835
Mendoza
Rosario
Santa Fe
Salto
URUGUAY
Rio Grande
Pôrto Alegre
Concepción
BUENOS AIRES
La Plata
Rio de la Plata
MONTEVIDEO
PAMPAS
Colorado
Bahía Blanca
Valdivia
ARGENTINA
Viedma
Golfo San Matías
Chubut
Puerto Montt
ISLA DE CHILOE
ARCHIPIÉLAGO DE LOS CHONOS
ANDES MTS.
Monte Valentín 13,314
Comodoro Rivadavia
Golfo San Jorge

ATLANTIC OCEAN
ISLAS DE JUAN FERNÁNDEZ (Chile)
PACIFIC OCEAN

WELLINGTON
HANOVER
Punta Arenas
DESOLACIÓN
Mt. Sarmiento 8100
Río Gallegos
Stanley
FALKLAND IS. (ISLAS MALVINAS) (Br.)
Estrecho de Magallanes
TIERRA DEL FUEGO
ISLA DE LOS ESTADOS
CABO DE HORNOS (CAPE HORN)
Drake Passage
SOUTH GEORGIA (Falkland Is.)
SOUTH SHETLAND ISLANDS (B.A.T.)
SOUTH ORKNEY IS. (B.A.T.)
Joinville
JAMES/ROSS
Antarctic Circle
SOUTH SANDWICH ISLANDS
PALMER PENINSULA

Longitude West of Greenwich

A-540000-76 3-5-12
COPYRIGHT BY
RAND MCNALLY & COMPANY
MADE IN U.S.A.

Relief		
Meters		Feet
3050		10 000
1525		5000
610		2000
305		1000
0	Sea Level	0
152.5		500
1525		5000
3050		10 000
6100		20 000

0 200 400 600 800 1000 Miles
0 400 800 1200 1600 Kilometers

Scale 1:40 000 000; one inch to 630 miles. Lambert's Azimuthal, Equal Area Projection
Elevations and depressions are given in feet

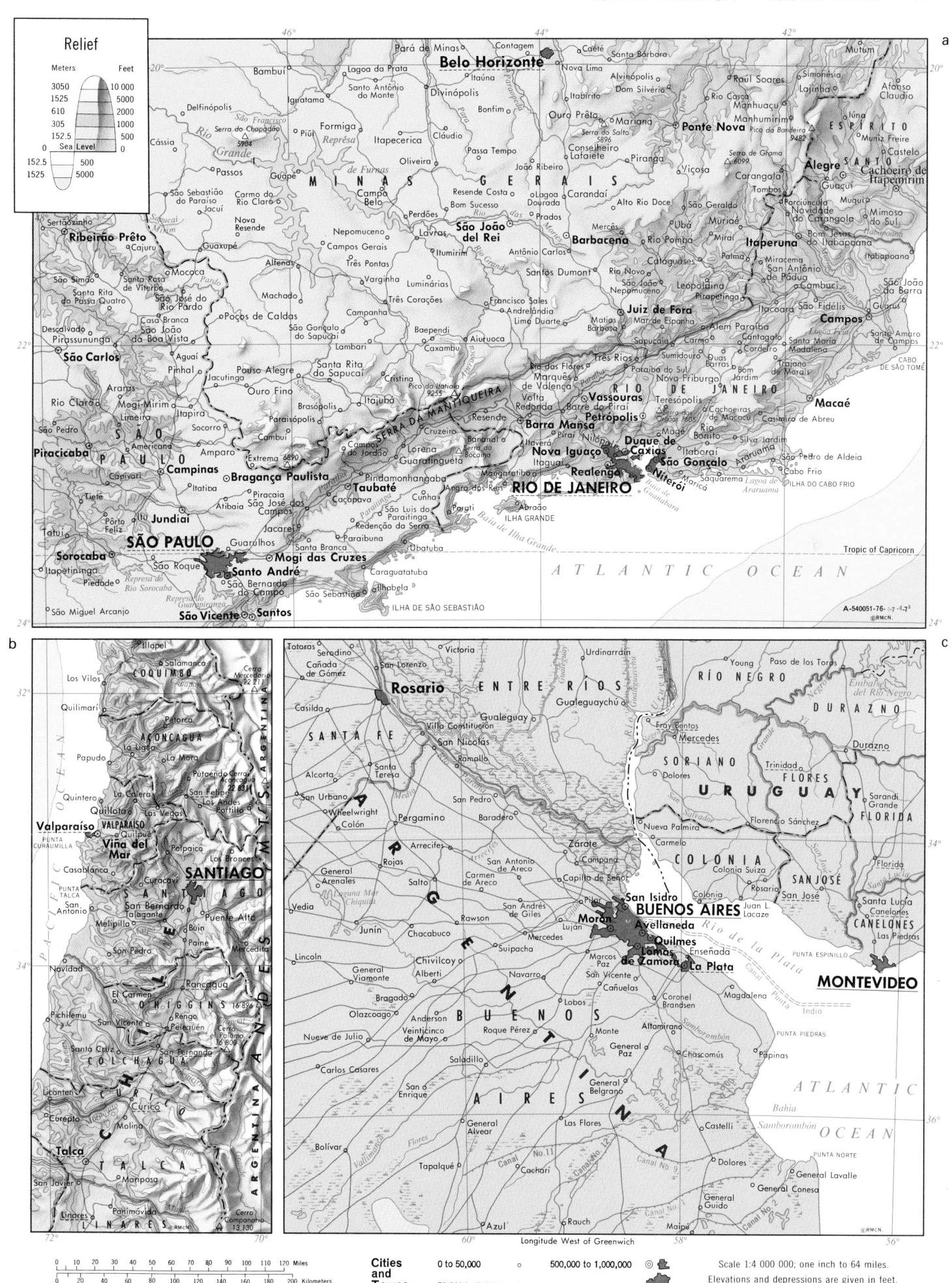

Cities
and
Towns

0 to 50,000 · 500,000 to 1,000,000
50,000 to 500,000 ⊙ 1,000,000 and over

Scale 1:16 000 000; one inch to 250 miles. Sinusoidal Projec
Elevations and depressions are given in feet

Continued on page 144

Continued on pages 142-143

a

BUENOS AIRES

Scale 1:1 000 000

b

RIO DE JANEIRO

Scale 1:1 000 000

Relief

Meters	Feet
3050	10 000
1525	5000
610	2000
305	1000
152.5	500
0 Sea Level	0 Sea Level
152.5	500 Below Sea Level
1525	5000
3050	10 000
6100	20 000

A-549200-76 -10-7-11
COPYRIGHT BY
RAND McNALLY & COMPANY
MADE IN U.S.A.

Longitude West of Greenwich

Scale 1:16 000 000; one inch to 250 miles. Sinusoidal Projection
Elevations and depressions are given in feet

For larger scale coverage of Buenos Aires,
Rio de Janeiro, and São Paulo see pages 60 and 61

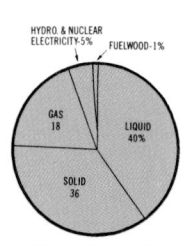

HYDRO. & NUCLEAR
ELECTRICITY-5%   FUELWOOD-1%

GAS
18

LIQUID
40%

SOLID
36

Energy Consumption
2,061,530 metric tons
coal equivalent-1982

ENERGY

Energy Producing Plants

▽ Geothermal

• Hydroelectric

■ Nuclear

Mineral Fuel Deposits

• Uranium: major deposit

△ Natural Gas: major field

• Petroleum: minor producing field

▲ Petroleum }
   Petroleum } major producing field

   Coal: major bituminous and anthracite

   Coal: minor bituminous and anthracite

   Coal: lignite

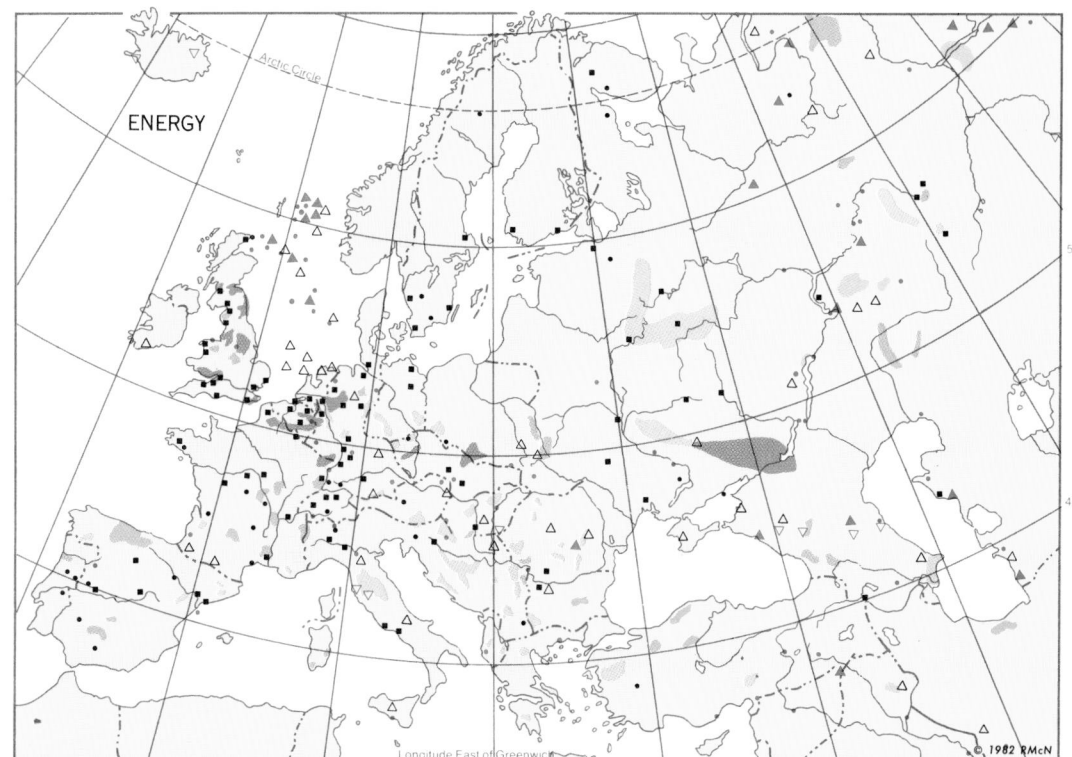

NATURAL HAZARDS

○ Volcanoes*

● Earthquakes*

● Major flood disasters*

——— Tsunamis

——— Limit of iceberg drift

   Temporary pack ice

   Areas subject to desertification

*Twentieth Century occurrences

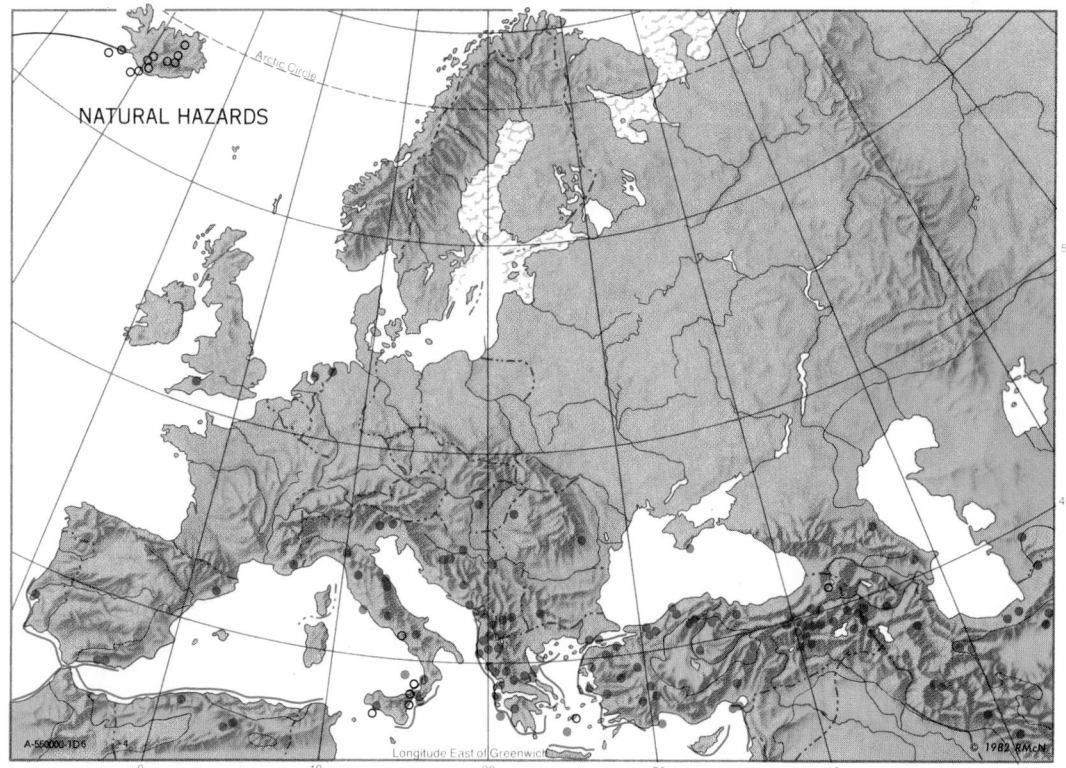

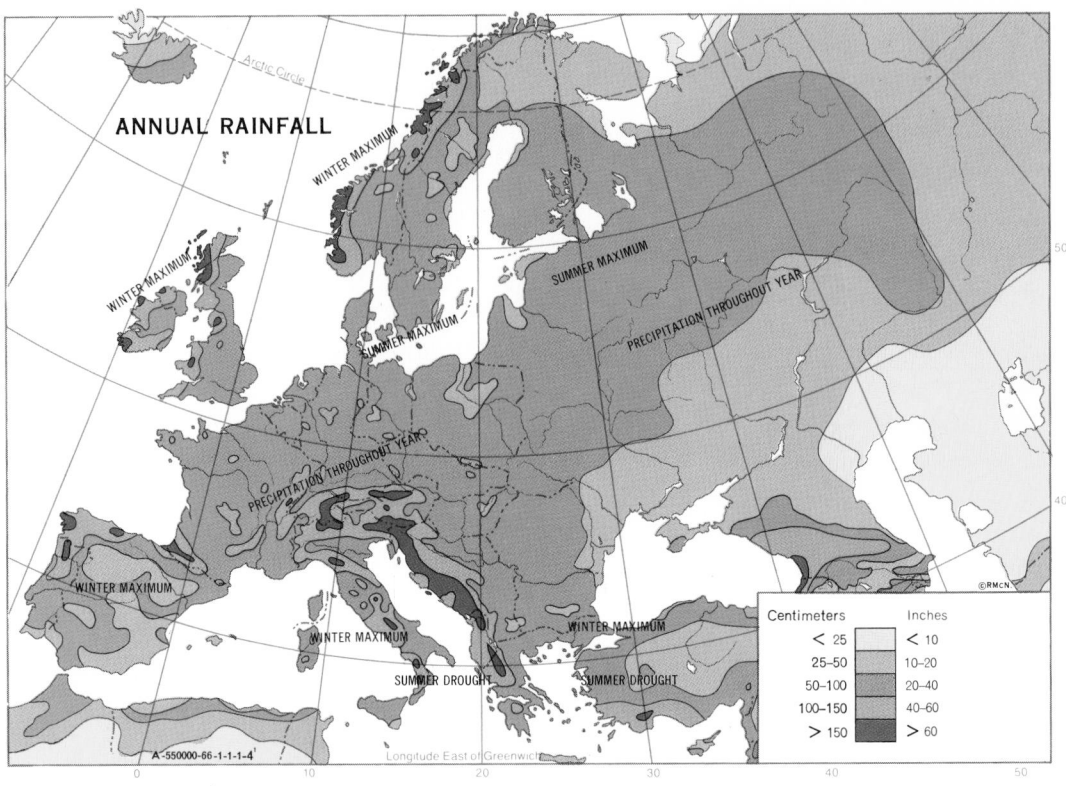

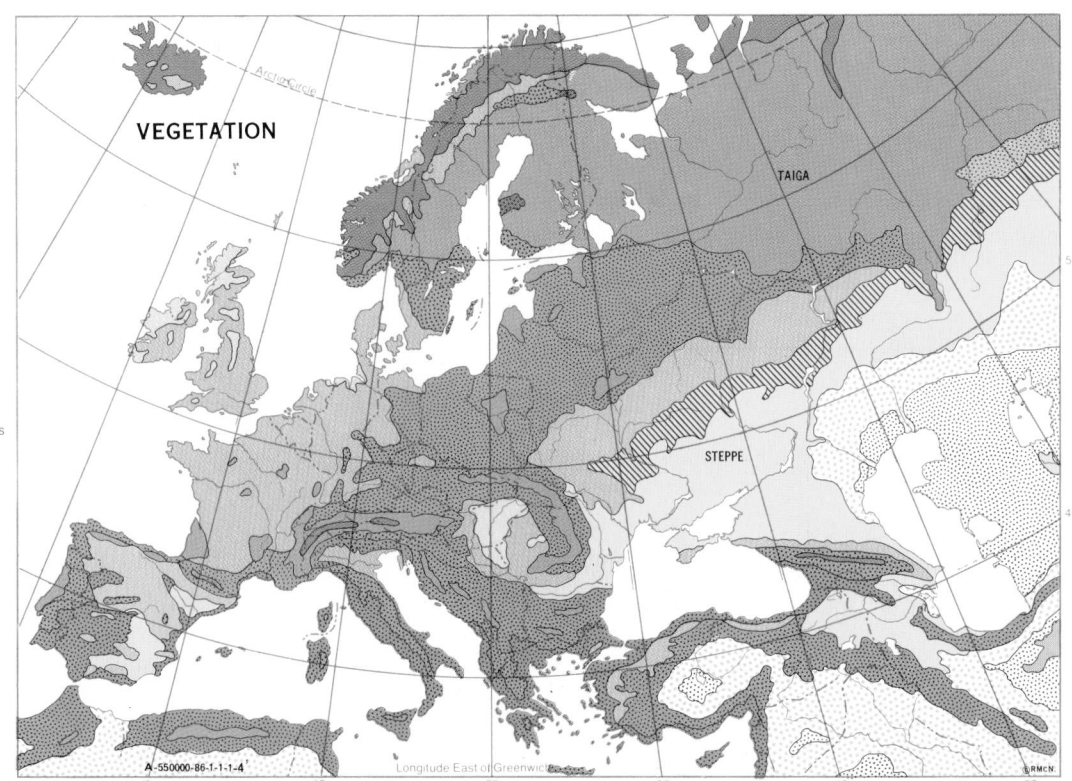

VEGETATION

E	Coniferous forest
B,Bs	Mediterranean vegetation
M	Mixed forest: coniferous-deciduous
S	Semi-deciduous forest
D	Deciduous forest
DG	Wooded steppe
G	Grass (steppe)
Gp	Short grass
Dsh	Desert shrub
L	Heath and moor
L	Alpine vegetation, tundra
b	Little or no vegetation

For explanation of letters in boxes,
see Natural Vegetation Map
by A. W. Kuchler, **p. 16**

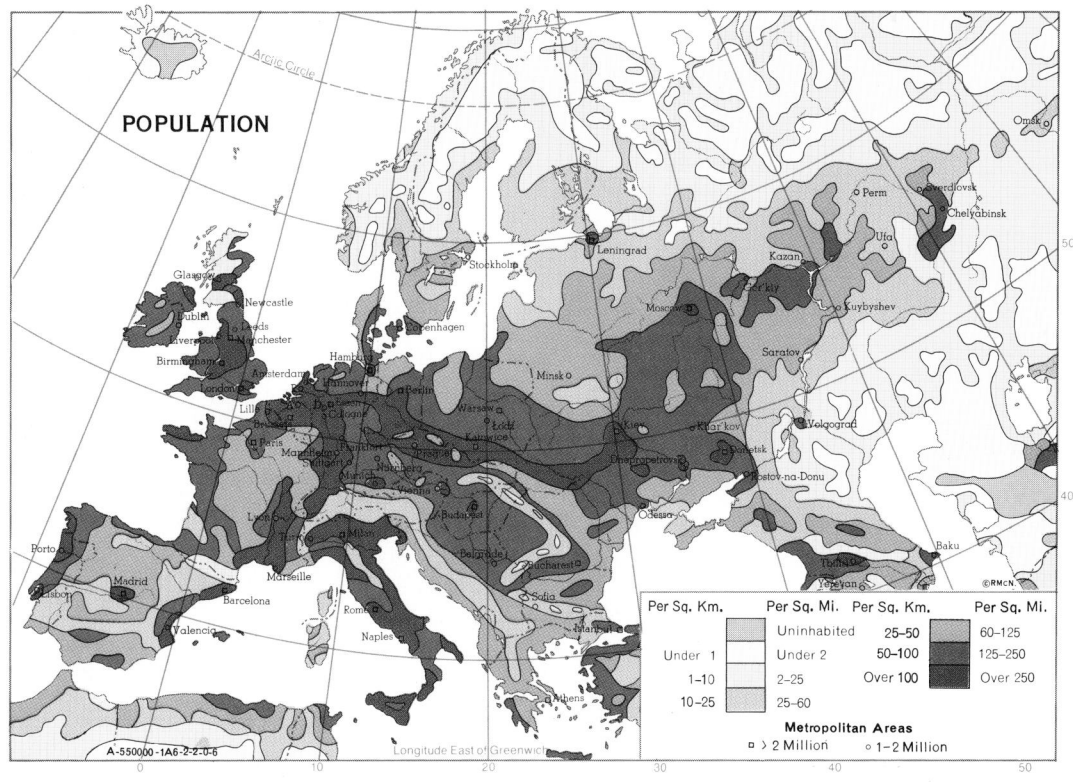

POPULATION

Per Sq. Km.	Per Sq. Mi.	Per Sq. Km.	Per Sq. Mi.
	Uninhabited	25–50	60–125
Under 1	Under 2	50–100	125–250
1–10	2–25	Over 100	Over 250
10–25	25–60		

Metropolitan Areas
□ > 2 Million   ○ 1–2 Million

A-550000-1A6-2-2-0-5

Longitude East of Greenwich

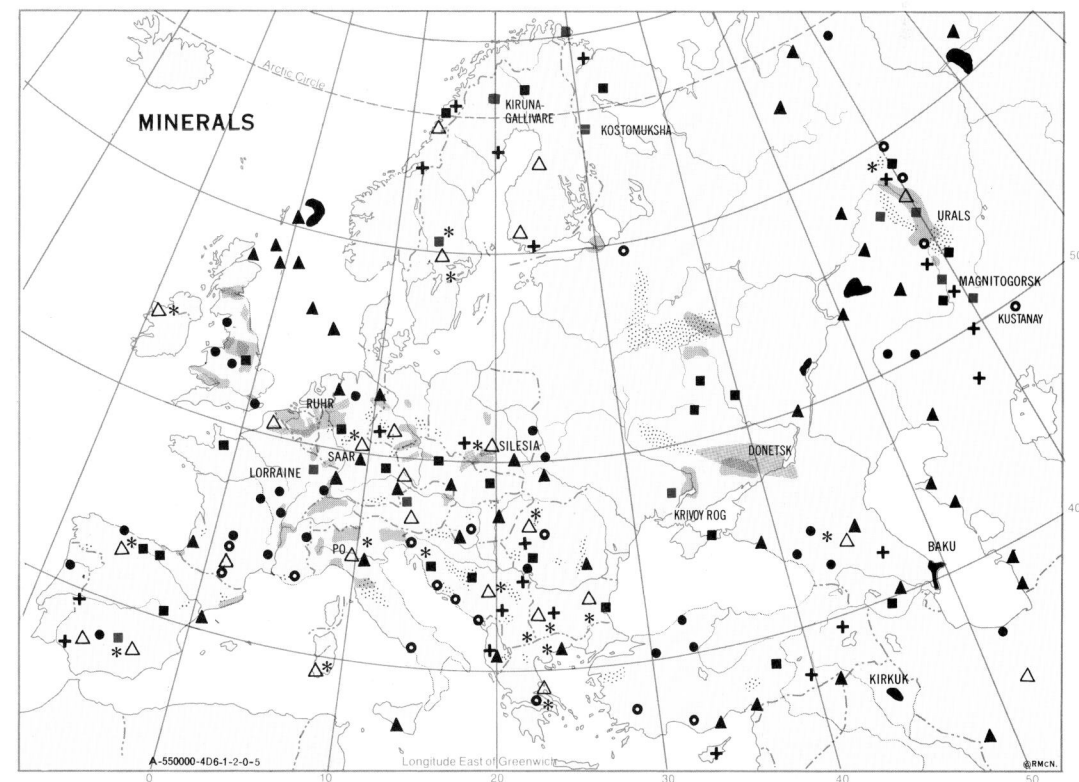

MINERALS

- Industrial areas
- Major coal deposits
- Major petroleum deposits
- Lignite deposits
- ▲ Minor petroleum deposits
- ● Minor coal deposits
- ■ Major iron ore
- ■ Minor iron ore
- * Lead
- ○ Bauxite
- △ Zinc
- + Copper

A-550000-4D6-1-2-0-5

Longitude East of Greenwich

Urban

Cropland

Cropland & Woodland

Cropland & Grazing Land

Grassland, Grazing Land

Forest, Woodland

Swamp, Marshland

Tundra

Shrub, Sparse Grass,
Wasteland (pattern)

Barren Land

Oasis

ATLANTIC OCEAN

North Sea

Reykjavík

Narvik

Ume

Gulf of Bothnia

Trondheim

Bergen

Oslo

Stockholm

Göteborg

Helsinki

LENINGRAD

Tallinn

Rīga

Minsk

Copenhagen

Baltic Sea

Kaliningrad

Glasgow

Belfast

MANCHESTER

Dublin

LONDON

Amsterdam

Hamburg

Elbe

BERLIN

Oder

Warsaw

Prip

Antwerp

Essen

Leipzig

Frankfurt

Kraków

L'vov

Brest

PARIS

Seine

Loire

Strasbourg

Rhine

Prague

Danube

VIENNA

CARPATHIANS

Munich

Bay of Biscay

Bordeaux

Garonne

Zürich

ALPS

Lyon

Rhône

MILAN

Venice

Zagreb

Save

Tisza

BUDAPEST

La Coruña

Bilbao

PYRENEES

Douro

Ebro

MADRID

Marseille

Genoa

Belgrade

Bucharest

Danube

Lisbon

BARCELONA

CORSICA

ROME

Sofia

Adriatic Sea

Sevilla

SARDINIA

Naples

Tirane

ISLAS BALEARES

Tyrrhenian Sea

Tanger

Athens

Aegean Sea

Algiers

Oran

Palermo

SICILY

Casablanca

ATLAS MOUNTAINS

Tunis

Mediterranean Sea

MALTA

CRETE

Longitude West of Greenwich   0°   Longitude East of Greenwich

Scale 1: 16,000,000; one inch to 250 miles. Conic Projection

0   50   100   200   300   400   500 Miles

0   100   200   400   600   800 Kilometers

Sea

Nar'yan-Mar

Pechora

Archangelsk

Ob'

Irtysh

Novosibirsk

Ob'

Omsk

U R A L S

SVERDLOVSK

Perm'

Kirov

Vologda

Kama

Volga

Ufa

Karaganda

Kazan'

Magnitogorsk

GORKIY

Balkhash

Kuybyshev

Orsk

MOSCOW

Volga

Tula

Kzyl-Orda

Syr-Dar'ya

Saratov

Ural

Aral'skoye
More
(Aral Sea)

PESKI
KYZYLKUM

Khar'kov

VOLGOGRAD

DEPRESSION

CASPIAN

Amu Dar'ya

Don

Volga

Astrakhan'

PESKI KARAKUMY

Dnepropetrovsk

Donetsk

MANYCH

DEPRESSION

Dnepr

Krasnodar

Ashkhabad

Odessa

C A U C A S U S   M T S.

TBILISI

BAKU

C
a
s
p
i
a
n

Black   Sea

Yerevan

S
e
a

NBUL

ELBURZ   MTS.

Ankara

TEHRAN

DASHT-E KAVIR

POROS

Kerman

Tigris

ZAGROS

Euphrates

MOUNTAINS

Nicosia

Baghdad

CYPRUS

Beirut

Ābādān

150

I C E L A N D

Ice

Lava

Re

A T L A N T I C   O C E A N

Arctic Circle

Nord Cape

LAPPLAND

Narvik

Kiruna

Knobs

LOWLAND

Muskeg Region

Rock and Drift

Inari Basin

Elongat

Lakes

Gulf of Bothnia

Granite Upland

Moraine

Faeröerne

Trondh.

Dovre

Sylarna

Östersund

Clay Basin

Northern Driftland

Viborg Massif

Shetland Is.

Sogne Fiord

Bergene

Hardanger Fiord

Hallingdal

Numdal

Oslo

Staw

Nor.

Vänern Basin

Glacial channel

Malar Basin

Lowland

Helsinki

Gulf of Finland

Orkney Is.

NW. HIGH'DS

Stockholm

Cuestas

Pei

GRAMPIAN MTS

Ed.

SO. HIGHLANDS

N O R T H   S E A

Skagerrak

Kattegat

Southern Driftland

Gotland

Öland

Riga

Lowland

Dau.

Bo.

Gl.

PENNINE CHAIN

Cleveland Hills

Skåne Plain

Copenhagen

Kiel

B

Niemen R.

Lowland

Kau.

Vilnyus

Shannon Is.

Wicklow Mts

Snowdon

LAKE DIST.

Elbe R.

Weser R.

Hamb.

Hann.

BALTIC LAKE PLAINS

Kal.

Po.

Danzig

Mazurian lakes

P O L

WELSH HIGHLDS

Cotswold

Chiltern Hills

E. Anglian H.

Amsterdam

Rhine

dunes

Lakes

Berlin

Mazurian Plain

Warsaw

Brest

Sw

Limit of Glaciation Exmoor

London

N. Downs

Hague

NETHERLANDS

Br.

A.

Col.

Dusses.

Har.

L.

Dr.

SILESIAN PLAIN

Wr.

Cz.

Łódz

Lyso Gory

Lublin

Moro

English Channel

Dartmoor

S. Downs

Flandrian Plain

Ant.

Br.

Sauerland

Westerwald

ORE M.

SUDETES

Galician Basin

Podoli

Cotentin Penins.

Seine R.

L.H.

Ardenne

Eifel

Taunus

Vogelsbg

Rhon.

Fr.

Prague

Pl.

Cracow

Pr.

Lvov

ARMORICAN MASSIVE

PARIS BASIN

CHAMPAGNE LOWLD

Lorrain Basin

Str.

Hunsruck

Black forest

Schwabian Jura

Frank.

BOHEMIAN FOR.

Bohemian Basin

Moravian Hills

Tatry

Podoli

Paris

Orl.

Nur.

Cher.

Loire R.

Nan.

LOIRE BASIN

Langres Plat.

Vosges

Stu.

M.

Chor.

Bordeaux

F AQUITANIAN LOWLD

CENTRAL MASSIVE

MORVAN PLAT.

JURA

SWISS

BAVARIAN BASIN

Austrian Plain

Vienna

Little Alföld

Mor.

Tol

Garonne R.

Lyons

Geneva

Munich

Inns.

BIHARM

CANTABRIAN MTS

Bu.

dunes Landes

Tou.

CAUSSES PLAT.

CEVENNES

Carc.

Per.

Po.

Milan

PO VALLEY

Turin

Genoa

Venice

Triest.

Savo

Zagreb

Papuk

Bakony

Balaton

Mecsek

HUNGARIAN (Alföld) BASIN

Tran-sylvanian Basin

Cluj

Bay of Biscay

656 feet

Douro

LEON-OLD CASTILIAN BASIN

IBERIAN MTS

EBRO BASIN

CATALAN MTS

Pa.

Sal.

S. de Guadarrama

Madrid

S. de Gredos

Riviera

Monaco

Marseilles

Barcelona

ADRIATIC SEA

Sava R.

Belgrade

Nis

Iron Gate

WALLACHIAN P.

Danube R.

Lisbon

Tagus R.

NEW CAST. BASIN

Cuen.

LA MANCHA BASIN

Ebro R.

Far.

CORSICA

M. Gargano

KAPELA

KARST

DINARIC ALPS

Kasovo Polje

Skoplje

Rila M.

BALKAN

ANTIBALKANS

Sof.

RODOPE M.

Danubian Pl.

S. de Estrela

S. de Gata

Guadiana R.

ANDALUSIAN LOWLD

SA. MORENA

Cor.

Sevilla

R. Segura

S. de Flobres

S. de Pila

Valencia

BALEARIC ISLANDS

Rome

VOLCANIC BELT

Naples

Vesuvius

APULIAN V.

MURGE PLAT.

ABRUZZI

PINDUS

Dur.

Olympus R.

Tess.

Str.

Maritsa

Skopie R.

Pass

Dardanelles

AEGEA

Strait of Gibraltar

Tangiers

S. Nevada

Mal.

Cart.

SARDINIA

TYRRHENIAN SEA

Lipari Volcanoes

Palermo

Etna

CALABRIAN M.

IONIAN SEA

Athens

M E D I T E R R A N E A N

Rabat

Cas.

COASTAL PLAIN

S. RIF

M. Fes

Fes

Oran

Algiers

TELL ATLAS

Bône

Biz.

Tunis

SICILY

Sousse

Malta

S E A

C R E T

HIGH ATLAS

MOROCCO MESETA

MIDDLE ATLAS

MOULOUYA BASIN

H I G H   P L A T E A U S

SAHARAN ATLAS

Biskra

JEB. AURES

Const.

B.S.

TUNISIAN ATLAS

EUROPE LANGUAGES
BY
BOGDAN ZABORSKI

Longitude West of Greenwich Longitude East of Greenwich

COPYRIGHT BY
RAND McNALLY & COMPANY
MADE IN U.S.A.

Scale 1:16,500,000; one inch to 260 miles Conic Projection

| 0 | 100 | 200 | 300 | 400 | 500 | 600 Miles |

| 0 | 200 | 400 | 600 | 800 | 1000 Kilometers |

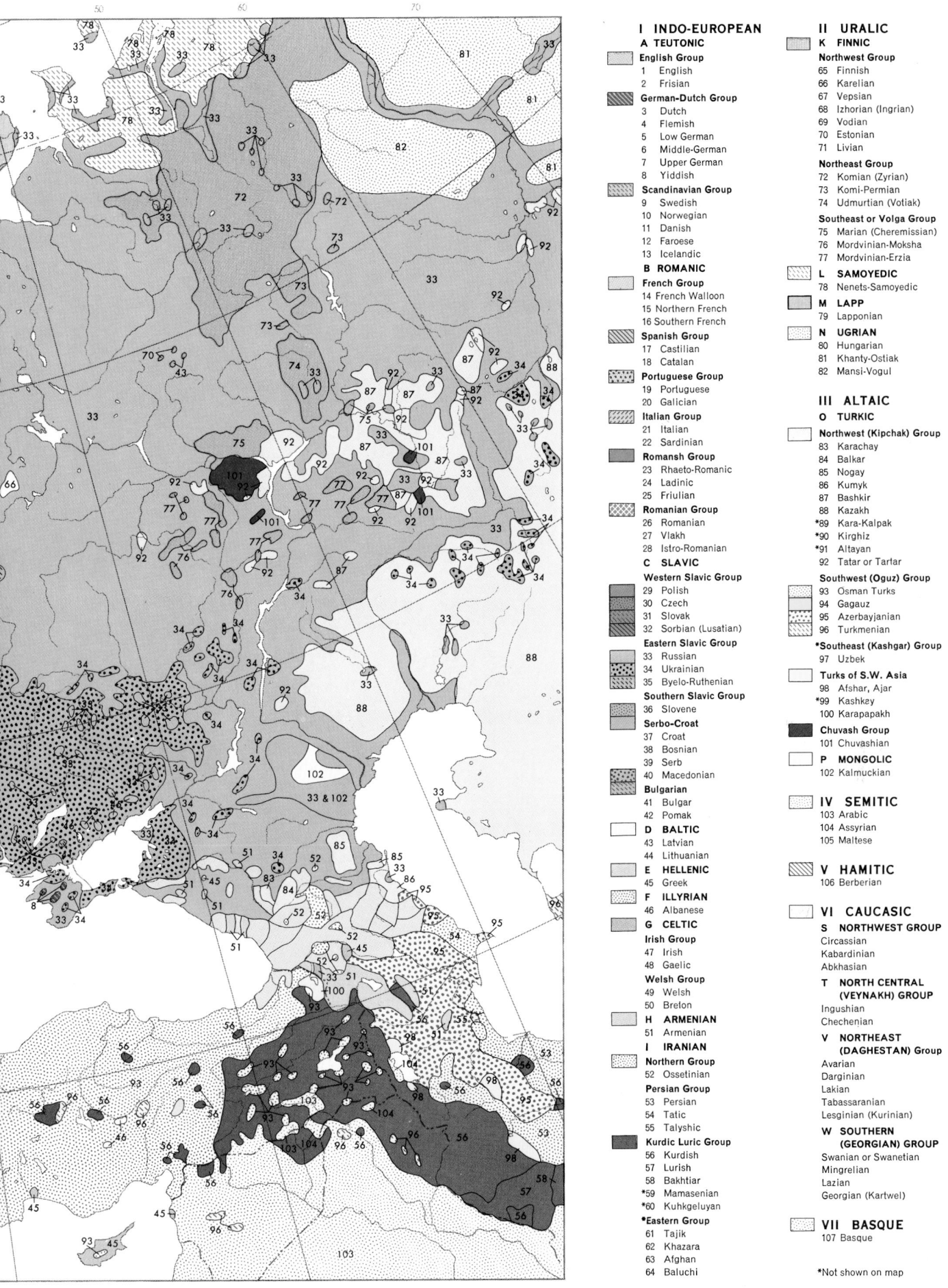

I INDO-EUROPEAN

A TEUTONIC

English Group
1 English
2 Frisian

German-Dutch Group
3 Dutch
4 Flemish
5 Low German
6 Middle-German
7 Upper German
8 Yiddish

Scandinavian Group
9 Swedish
10 Norwegian
11 Danish
12 Faroese
13 Icelandic

B ROMANIC

French Group
14 French Walloon
15 Northern French
16 Southern French

Spanish Group
17 Castilian
18 Catalan

Portuguese Group
19 Portuguese
20 Galician

Italian Group
21 Italian
22 Sardinian

Romansh Group
23 Rhaeto-Romanic
24 Ladinic
25 Friulian

Romanian Group
26 Romanian
27 Vlakh
28 Istro-Romanian

C SLAVIC

Western Slavic Group
29 Polish
30 Czech
31 Slovak
32 Sorbian (Lusatian)

Eastern Slavic Group
33 Russian
34 Ukrainian
35 Byelo-Ruthenian

Southern Slavic Group
36 Slovene

Serbo-Croat
37 Croat
38 Bosnian
39 Serb
40 Macedonian

Bulgarian
41 Bulgar
42 Pomak

D BALTIC
43 Latvian
44 Lithuanian

E HELLENIC
45 Greek

F ILLYRIAN
46 Albanese

G CELTIC

Irish Group
47 Irish
48 Gaelic

Welsh Group
49 Welsh
50 Breton

H ARMENIAN
51 Armenian

I IRANIAN

Northern Group
52 Ossetinian

Persian Group
53 Persian
54 Tatic
55 Talyshic

Kurdic Luric Group
56 Kurdish
57 Lurish
58 Bakhtiar
*59 Mamasenian
*60 Kuhkgeluyan

*Eastern Group
61 Tajik
62 Khazara
63 Afghan
64 Baluchi

II URALIC

K FINNIC

Northwest Group
65 Finnish
66 Karelian
67 Vepsian
68 Izhorian (Ingrian)
69 Vodian
70 Estonian
71 Livian

Northeast Group
72 Komian (Zyrian)
73 Komi-Permian
74 Udmurtian (Votiak)

Southeast or Volga Group
75 Marian (Cheremissian)
76 Mordvinian-Moksha
77 Mordvinian-Erzia

L SAMOYEDIC
78 Nenets-Samoyedic

M LAPP
79 Lapponian

N UGRIAN
80 Hungarian
81 Khanty-Ostiak
82 Mansi-Vogul

III ALTAIC

O TURKIC

Northwest (Kipchak) Group
83 Karachay
84 Balkar
85 Nogay
86 Kumyk
87 Bashkir
88 Kazakh
*89 Kara-Kalpak
*90 Kirghiz
*91 Altayan
92 Tatar or Tartar

Southwest (Oguz) Group
93 Osman Turks
94 Gagauz
95 Azerbayjanian
96 Turkmenian

*Southeast (Kashgar) Group
97 Uzbek

Turks of S.W. Asia
98 Afshar, Ajar
*99 Kashkey
100 Karapapakh

Chuvash Group
101 Chuvashian

P MONGOLIC
102 Kalmuckian

IV SEMITIC
103 Arabic
104 Assyrian
105 Maltese

V HAMITIC
106 Berberian

VI CAUCASIC

S NORTHWEST GROUP
Circassian
Kabardinian
Abkhasian

**T NORTH CENTRAL
(VEYNAKH) GROUP**
Ingushian
Chechenian

**V NORTHEAST
(DAGHESTAN) Group**
Avarian
Darginian
Lakian
Tabassaranian
Lesginian (Kurinian)

**W SOUTHERN
(GEORGIAN) GROUP**
Swanian or Swanetian
Mingrelian
Lazian
Georgian (Kartwel)

VII BASQUE
107 Basque

*Not shown on map

Scale 1: 16 000 000; one inch to 250 miles. Conic Projection

Elevations and depressions are given in feet

Continued on pages 224-225

Continued on pages 180-181

Continued on pages 192-193

A-519697-76 · 6 1·16
COPYRIGHT BY
RAND McNALLY & COMPANY
MADE IN U.S.A.

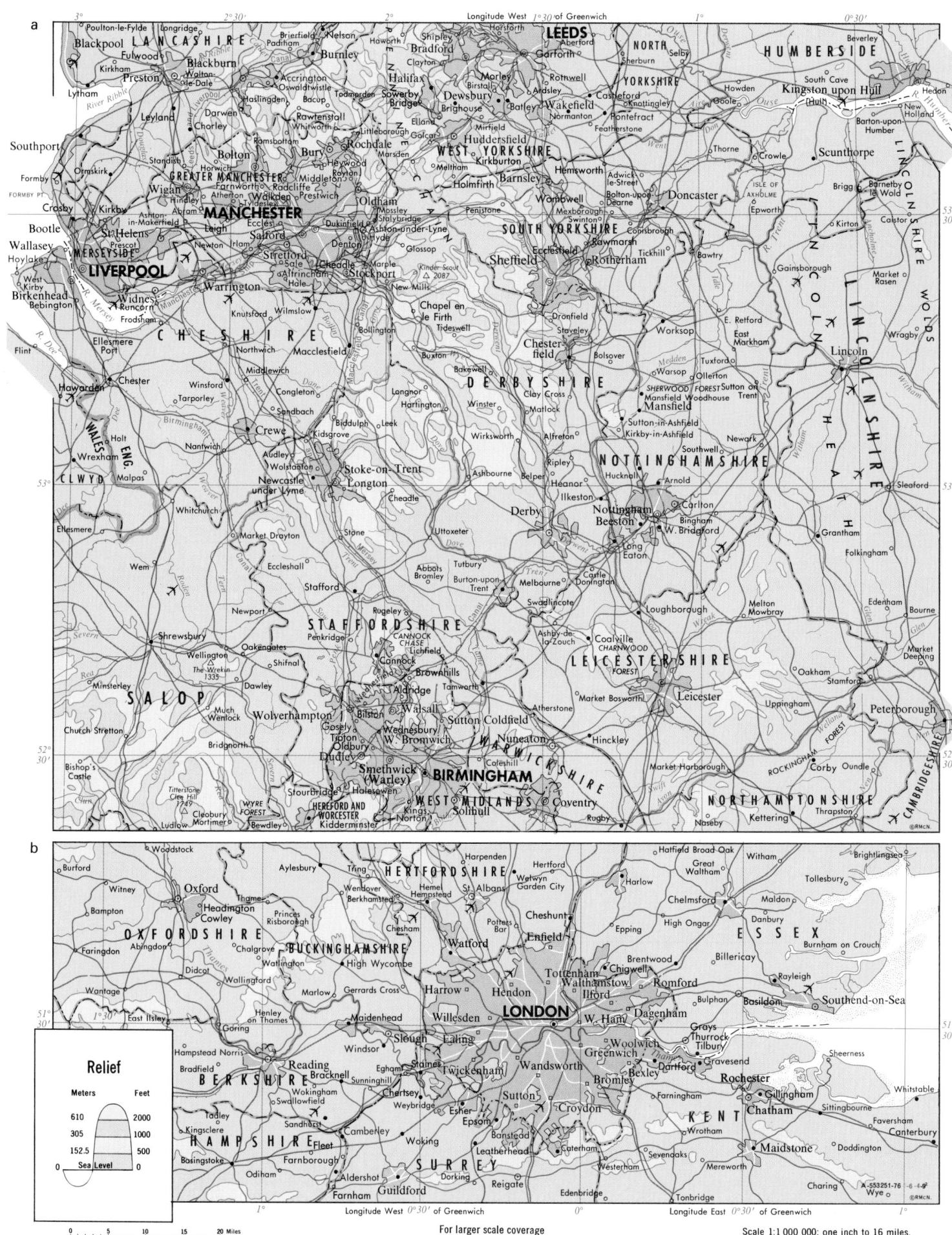

a

Poulton-le-Fylde Longridge
Blackpool LANCASHIRE Brierfield Nelson NORTH
Fulwood Padiham Haworth Shipley LEEDS Aberford
Kirkham Blackburn Accrington Burnley Bradford Horsforth YORKSHIRE Sherburn Selby HUMBERSIDE
Lytham Preston Walton-le-Dale Oswaldtwistle Halifax Morley Clayton Garforth Beverley
Haslingden Todmorden Sowerby Dewsbury Rothwell Castleford South Cave Kingston upon Hull
Southport Leyland Chorley Darwen Rawtenstall Whitworth Bridge Brighouse Batley Wakefield Knottingley Pontefract Howden (Hull)
Formby Ormskirk Standish Ramsbottom WEST YORKSHIRE Elland Mirfield Normanton Featherstone Goole New Holland
Formby PT Kirkham GREATER MANCHESTER Bury Rochdale Marsden Huddersfield Kirkburton Barton-upon-Humber Scunthorpe
Crosby Kirkby Wigan Radcliffe Heywood Royton Oldham Meltham Holmfirth Hemsworth Adwick le-Street Doncaster Thorne Crowle Epworth Brigg Barnetby le Wold
Bootle MANCHESTER Salford Ashton-under-Lyne Penistone Barnsley Wombwell Bolton-upon-Dearne Mexborough ISLE OF AXHOLME Kirton
Wallasey Bebington St Helens Prescot Eccles Denton Hyde Glossop SOUTH YORKSHIRE Swinton Conisbrough Bawtry Gainsborough Market Rasen
LIVERPOOL Warrington Stretford Sale Stockport New Mills Sheffield Ecclesfield Rotherham Tickhill E. Retford Kirton
Birkenhead Widnes Runcorn Altrincham Hale Marple Kinder Scout Chapel en le Firth Dronfield East Markham Lincoln
Hoylake MERSEYSIDE Frodsham Knutsford Wilmslow Bollington Tideswell Staveley Worksop Lincoln
West Kirby Flint Ellesmere Port CHESHIRE Macclesfield Buxton Chesterfield Bolsover Warsop Tuxford Wragby WOLDS
Hawarden Chester Northwich Middlewich Bakewell Clay Cross Mansfield Woodhouse Sutton on Trent
WALES ENG. Tarporley Winsford Congleton Dane Langnor DERBYSHIRE Matlock SHERWOOD FOREST Mansfield Ollerton Newark Sleaford
CLWYD Holt Sandbach Biddulph Leek Wirksworth Alfreton Sutton-in-Ashfield Kirkby-in-Ashfield Southwell Grantham
Wrexham Crewe Kidsgrove Ashbourne Belper Ripley Heanor Hucknall Arnold NOTTINGHAMSHIRE
Malpas Nantwich Audley Wolstanton Newcastle Stoke-on-Trent Ilkeston Nottingham Carlton Folkingham
Whitchurch under Lyme Longton Cheadle Uttoxeter Derby Beeston W. Bridgford Grantham
Ellesmere Market Drayton Stone Dove Tutbury Burton-upon-Trent Melbourne Long Eaton Castle Donington LEICESTERSHIRE Sleaford
Wem Eccleshall Abbots Bromley Swadlincote Loughborough Melton Mowbray Edenham
Shrewsbury Stafford Rugeley Ashby-de-la-Zouch Coalville CHARNWOOD FOREST Oakham Stamford Bourne
Wellington Oakengates Shifnal STAFFORDSHIRE CANNOCK CHASE Lichfield Tamworth Market Bosworth Uppingham Market Deeping
The Wrekin 1335 Dawley Penkridge Cannock Brownhills Atherstone Leicester Peterborough
Minsterley SALOP Much Wenlock Wellington Aldridge Walsall Sutton Coldfield WARWICKSHIRE ROCKINGHAM FOREST Corby Oundle
Church Stretton Bridgnorth Wolverhampton Bilston Wednesbury Nuneaton Hinckley Market Harborough Thrapston NORTHAMPTONSHIRE
Bishop's Castle Gosely Tipton Oldbury W. Bromwich Coleshill Naseby Kettering
Titterstone Clee Hill 1749 Smethwick (Warley) Dudley BIRMINGHAM WEST MIDLANDS Solihull Coventry Rugby
Cleobury Mortimer Stourbridge Halesowen WYRE FOREST Kings Norton Kings Coventry
Ludlow Bewdley HEREFORD AND WORCESTER Kidderminster

b

Woodstock Harpenden Hatfield Broad Oak Brightlingsea
Burford Witney Oxford Thame Tring HERTFORDSHIRE Hertford Great Witham Tollesbury
Bampton Headington Cowley Aylesbury Wendover Hemel Welwyn Garden City Waltham
Faringdon OXFORDSHIRE Abingdon Princes Risborough Berkhamsted St Albans Harlow Chelmsford Maldon ESSEX
Chalgrove BUCKINGHAMSHIRE Chesham Potters Watford Cheshunt Epping High Ongar Danbury Burnham on Crouch
Wantage Didcot Watlington High Wycombe Bar Enfield Brentwood Billericay
Wallingford Marlow Gerrards Cross Harrow Hendon Tottenham Chigwell Romford Basildon Rayleigh
East Ilsley Goring Henley on Thames Maidenhead Slough Ealing LONDON Walthamstow Ilford Bulphan Southend-on-Sea
Hampstead Norris Bradfield Windsor Staines Willesden W. Ham Dagenham Grays Thurrock Tilbury Sheerness
Reading Egham Twickenham Wandsworth Woolwich Greenwich Bexley Dartford Gravesend Rochester Whitstable
BERKSHIRE Bracknell Sunninghill Chertsey Weybridge Esher Sutton Bromley Farningham Gillingham KENT Chatham
Tadley Wokingham Swallowfield Camberley Woking Croydon Banstead Epsom Leatherhead Caterham Wrotham Faversham Canterbury
Kingsclere Sandhurst Basingstoke Farnborough Fleet HAMPSHIRE Odiham Aldershot Farnham Guildford SURREY Dorking Reigate Westerham Sevenoaks Mereworth Maidstone Doddington
Woking Leatherhead Edenbridge Tonbridge Wye

Relief

Meters		Feet
610		2000
305		1000
152.5		500
0	Sea Level	0

20 Miles
0 5 10 15 20 Miles
0 4 8 12 16 20 24 28 32 Kilometers

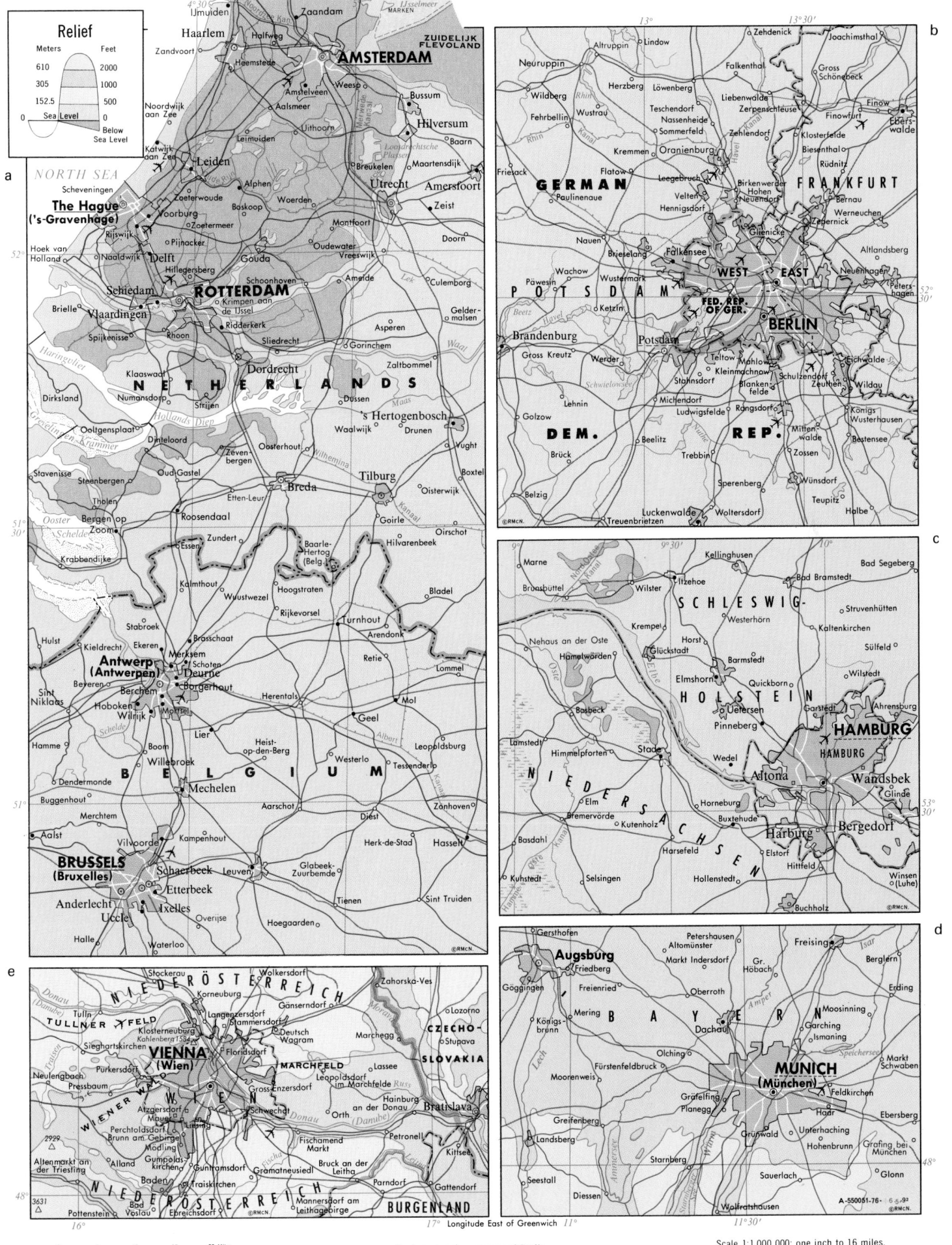

EUROPE • Cities and Environs 157

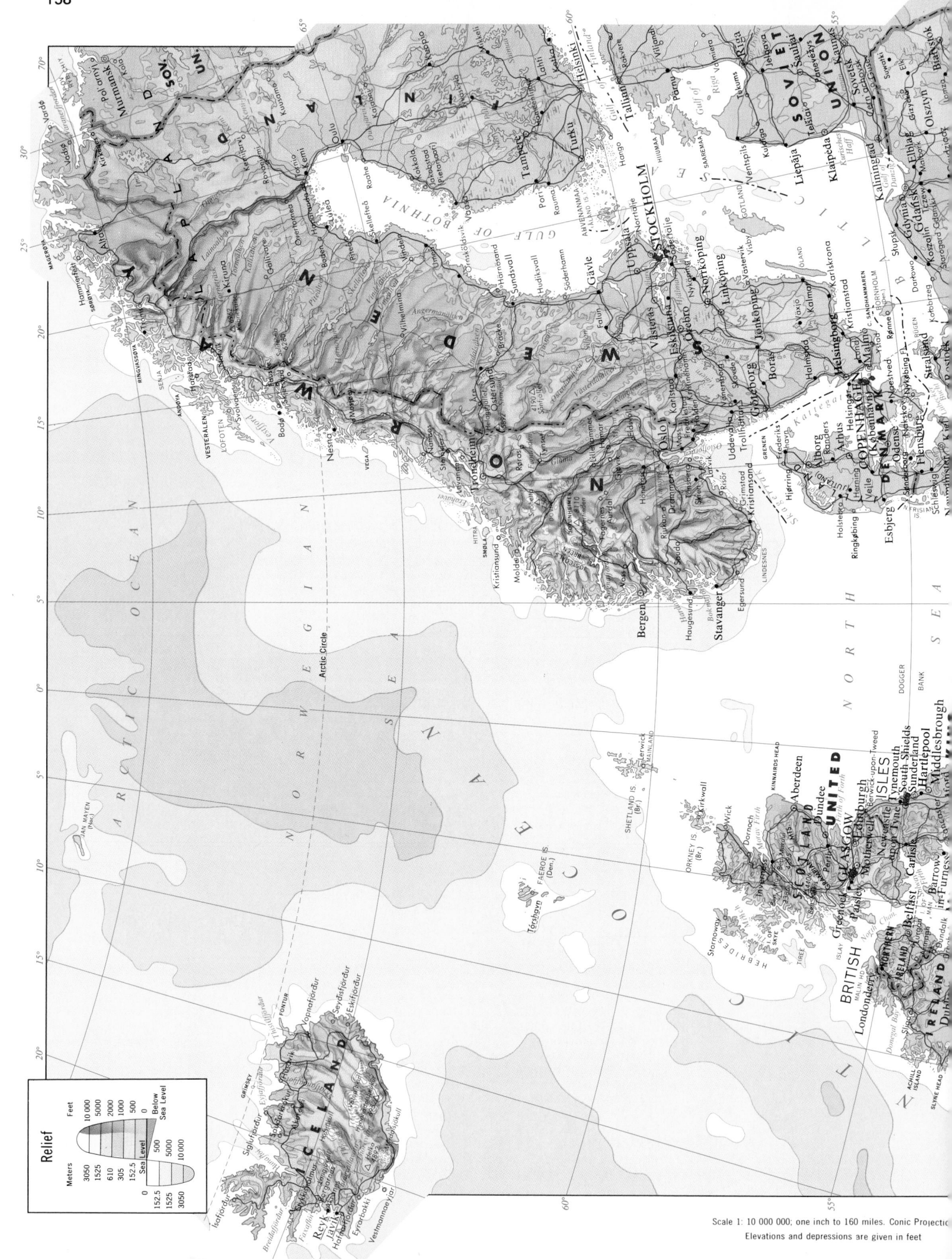

Relief

Meters	Feet
3050	10 000
1525	5000
610	2000
305	1000
152.5	500
0	Sea Level / Below Sea Level
152.5	500
1525	5000
3050	10000

Scale 1: 10 000 000; one inch to 160 miles. Conic Projection
Elevations and depressions are given in feet

ROMANIA

YUGOSLAVIA

ALBANIA

HUNGARY

CZECHOSLOVAKIA

POLAND

GERMAN FEDERAL REPUBLIC

GERMANY

NETHERLANDS

BELGIUM

SWITZERLAND

AUSTRIA

ITALY

FRANCE

SPAIN

PORTUGAL

ENGLAND

WALES

MOROCCO

ALGERIA

TUNISIA

ANDORRA

MONACO

MALTA

ATLAS MOUNTAINS

SIERRA MORENA

CORDILLERA CANTÁBRICA

CORSICA (Fr.)

SARDINIA (It.)

SICILY

BALEARES (Sp.)

ADRIATIC SEA

TYRRHENIAN SEA

IONIAN SEA

LIGURIAN SEA

MEDITERRANEAN SEA

BAY OF BISCAY

ENGLISH CHANNEL

ATLANTIC

ISLES OF SCILLY

LAND'S END

CHANNEL IS. (Br.)

GUERNSEY

JERSEY

Major cities: LONDON, BIRMINGHAM, PARIS, BRUSSELS, AMSTERDAM, The Hague, Rotterdam, COLOGNE, DÜSSELDORF, FRANKFURT, STUTTGART, MUNICH, PRAGUE, VIENNA, BUDAPEST, BELGRADE, ROME, Vatican City, NAPLES, Venice, Milan, Genoa, MADRID, Barcelona, Valencia, LISBON, Porto, Sevilla, Córdoba, Málaga, Granada, Palermo, Catania, Messina, Siracusa, Cagliari, Algiers, Oran, Tunis, Bizerte, Constantine

A-559400.76—7-6-14
COPYRIGHT BY
RAND McNALLY & COMPANY
MADE IN U.S.A.

Longitude East of Greenwich

Longitude West of Greenwich

50   100   150   200   250   300 Miles

100   200   300   400   500 Kilometers

Continued on pages 158-159

ATLANTIC OCEAN

BAY OF BISCAY

FRANCE

PARIS

SPAIN

MADRID

LISBON

PORTUGAL

SIERRA MORENA

ANDORRA

BARCELONA

BALEARES (Sp.)

ISLAS BALEARES

MALLORCA

MENORCA

IBIZA

FORMENTERA

MEDITERRANEAN

CORSICA (Fr.)

SARDINIA (It.)

LIGURIAN SEA

TYRRHENIAN SEA

ROME (Roma)

NAPLES (Napoli)

VATICAN CITY

SAN MARINO

MONACO

SWITZERLAND

FED. REP. OF GER.

FRANKFURT

MANNHEIM

MUNICH

STUTTGART

MILAN

TURIN

Genoa

Venice

PRAGUE (Praha)

MOROCCO

ALGERIA

TUNISIA

SAHARAN ATLAS MOUNTAINS

GRAND ERG OCCIDENTAL

GRAND ERG ORIENTAL

ATLAS

HAUT ATLAS

MOYEN ATLAS

Algiers (El Djazaïr)

Oran (Wahran)

Rabat

TARABULU (TRIPOLITANIA)

Tripoli (Tarābul)

SICILY

Palermo

MALTA

A-558300-76   12-8-21
COPYRIGHT BY
RAND McNALLY & COMPANY
MADE IN U.S.A.

Relief

Meters	Feet
3050	10000
1525	5000
610	2000
305	1000
152.5	500
0 Sea Level	0 Below Sea Level
152.5	500
1525	5000
3050	10000

Longitude West of Greenwich 0° Longitude East of Greenwich

Scale 1: 10 000 000; one inch to 160 miles Bonne's Project
Elevations and depressions are given in feet

NORWAY

Egersund
Flekkefjord
Farsund
Kristiansand
Mandal
LINDESNES
Arendal
Grimstad
Lillesand

Kungälv
Göteborg
Mölndal
Borås
SWEDEN
Varberg
Falkenberg
Oskarström
Halmstad
Laholm
Ängelholm
Helsingborg
Landskrona
Lund
Malmö
Trelleborg

Skagerrak
Kattegat

Skagen
GRENEN
Hjørring
Frederikshavn
LÆSØ
Brønderslev
 Ålborg
Thisted
Nykøbing
Hobro
Mariager
Skive
Viborg
Randers
Struer
Silkeborg
Grenå
Holstebro
Skanderborg
Århus
Ringkøbing
Herning
ANHOLT
Skälderviken
Helsingør
København
COPENHAGEN
SJAELLAND
Roskilde
Hillerød
Nykøbing S.

JYLLAND
DENMARK

Horsens
Varde
Vejle
Fredericia
Kolding
Esbjerg
Ribe
Haderslev
Åbenrå
Tønder
Sønderborg
Flensburg
FØHR
SYLT
RØMØ
FANØ
NORTH FRISIAN IS.

Kalundborg
Holbæk
Ringsted
Slagelse
Korsør
Næstved
Køge
SAMSØ
Odense
FYN
Assens
Nyborg
Faborg
Svendborg
Vordingborg
Rudkøbing
MØN
Maribo
Nykøbing
FALSTER
LOLLAND
LANGELAND
AERØ
Store Bælt
Lille Bælt

Middelfart
Bogense

BALTIC SEA

DOGGER
BANK
60–120 Ft.

NORTH

SEA

Nissum
Fjord
Ringkøbing
Fjord

Kiel Bay
Kiel
Eckernförde
Rendsburg
SCHLESWIG
Schleswig
Husum
Tønning
Heide
HOLSTEIN
Neumünster
Itzehoe
Bad Oldesloe
Elmshorn
Lübeck
LÜBECKER BUCHT
Neustadt i. Holstein
FEHMARN
Rostock
Wismar
Güstrow
Teterow
Schwerin
GERMAN
DEMOCRATIC
REPUBLIC
MECKLENBURG
Parchim
Ludwigslust
Pritzwalk
Perleberg
Wittenberge
Salzwedel
Gardelegen
Tangermünde
Stendal
HELGOLAND

Cuxhaven
Bremerhaven
Stade
HAMBURG
Lüneburg
LÜNEBURGER HEIDE
Soltau
Uelzen
Harburg

FRISIAN ISLANDS
NORDERNEY LANGEOOG
JUIST
BORKUM
Norden
Wilhelmshaven
Emden
Delfzijl
Groningen
Oldenburg
Papenburg
Delmenhorst
Bremen
Verden
HEIDE

TERSCHELLING
AMELAND
VLIELAND
Leeuwarden
Harlingen
TEXEL
Waddenzee
Assen
Emmen
Meppen
Lingen
Nordhorn
NIEDERSACHSEN
Nienburg
Celle
Gifhorn
Hadersleben
Haldensleben
Magdeburg
Tangerhütte

Den Helder
Alkmaar
IJsselmeer
Meppel
Zwolle
Almelo
Hengelo
Rheine
Osnabrück
Minden
Hannover
Braunschweig
Helmstedt
Schöneck

NETHERLANDS
Haarlem
Zaandam
AMSTERDAM
Apeldoorn
Deventer
Enschede
Gronau
Münster
Herford
Bielefeld
Detmold
Hameln
Hildesheim
Wolfenbüttel
Goslar
Halberstadt
Blankenburg
Quedlinburg
Stassfurt
Bernburg
Aschersleben
HARZ
THÜRINGEN

The Hague
('s-Gravenhage)
Leiden
Utrecht
Arnhem
Ahlen
Gütersloh
Paderborn
Einbeck
Northeim
Göttingen
Nordhausen
Heiligenstadt
Mühlhausen
Sondershausen
Sangerhausen
Halle
Merseburg

Vlaardingen
Delft
ROTTERDAM
Dordrecht
Nijmegen
Kleve
Wesel
Gelsenkirchen
Bochum
Dortmund
Arnsberg
Iserlohn
Hamm
Lippstadt
Soest
Kassel
Eschwege
Eisenach
Erfurt
Weimar
Jena
Gotha
Arnstadt
Rudolstadt

Southend-
on-Sea
Thames
Harwich
Bergen
op Zoom
Breda
'sHertogenbosch
Helmond
Tilburg
Eindhoven
Weert
Mönchengladbach
Duisburg
Oberhausen
ESSEN
Wuppertal
Solingen
Hagen
Lüdenscheid
Siegen
Marburg an
der Lahn
Bad Hersfeld
Fulda
Bad Kissingen
Meiningen
Suhl
Schmalkalden
Zella-Mehlis
Hildburghausen
Sonneberg
Coburg
Neustadt b.C.
HESSEN

Vlissingen
Turnhout
ANTWERP
Mechelen
Heerlen
DÜSSELDORF
Neuss
COLOGNE
(Köln)
Siegen
Siegburg
Bonn
Aachen
Düren
Gummersbach
Giessen
Schweinfurt

Oostende
Brugge
Gent
Aalst
BELGIUM
BRUSSELS
Leuven
Maastricht
Herstal
Liège
Eupen
Verviers
Spa
Malmédy
Euskirchen
Ahrweiler
Neuwied
Andernach
Koblenz
Bad Homburg
Hanau
Offenbach
FRANKFURT
AM MAIN
Wiesbaden
Bad Kreuznach
Mainz
Darmstadt
Würzburg
Aschaffenburg
Kitzingen
Bayreuth
Bamberg
Erlangen

Dunkerque
Calais
Boulogne-
sur-Mer
St. Omer
Armentières
FLANDERS
Lille
Roubaix
Tourcoing
Roeselare
Kortrijk
Ieper
Béthune
Douai
Arras
Denain
Valenciennes
Cambrai
Maubeuge
Charleroi
Namur
Dinant
Givet
Fourmies
Hautmont
Abbeville
Somme
St. Valéry-
sur-Somme
Le Tréport
Étaples
FRANCE
ARDENNES
Bastogne
LUX
EIFEL
RHEINLAND
PFALZ
HUNSRÜCK
Kirn
Bingen
Wittlich
Bad Herrenalb
Coburg

Lynn
Norwich
Great
Yarmouth
Lowestoft
Thetford
Ipswich
Margate
Ramsgate
Canterbury
Dover
Folkestone
Maidstone
NORTH FORELAND
Strait of Dover

Longitude East of Greenwich

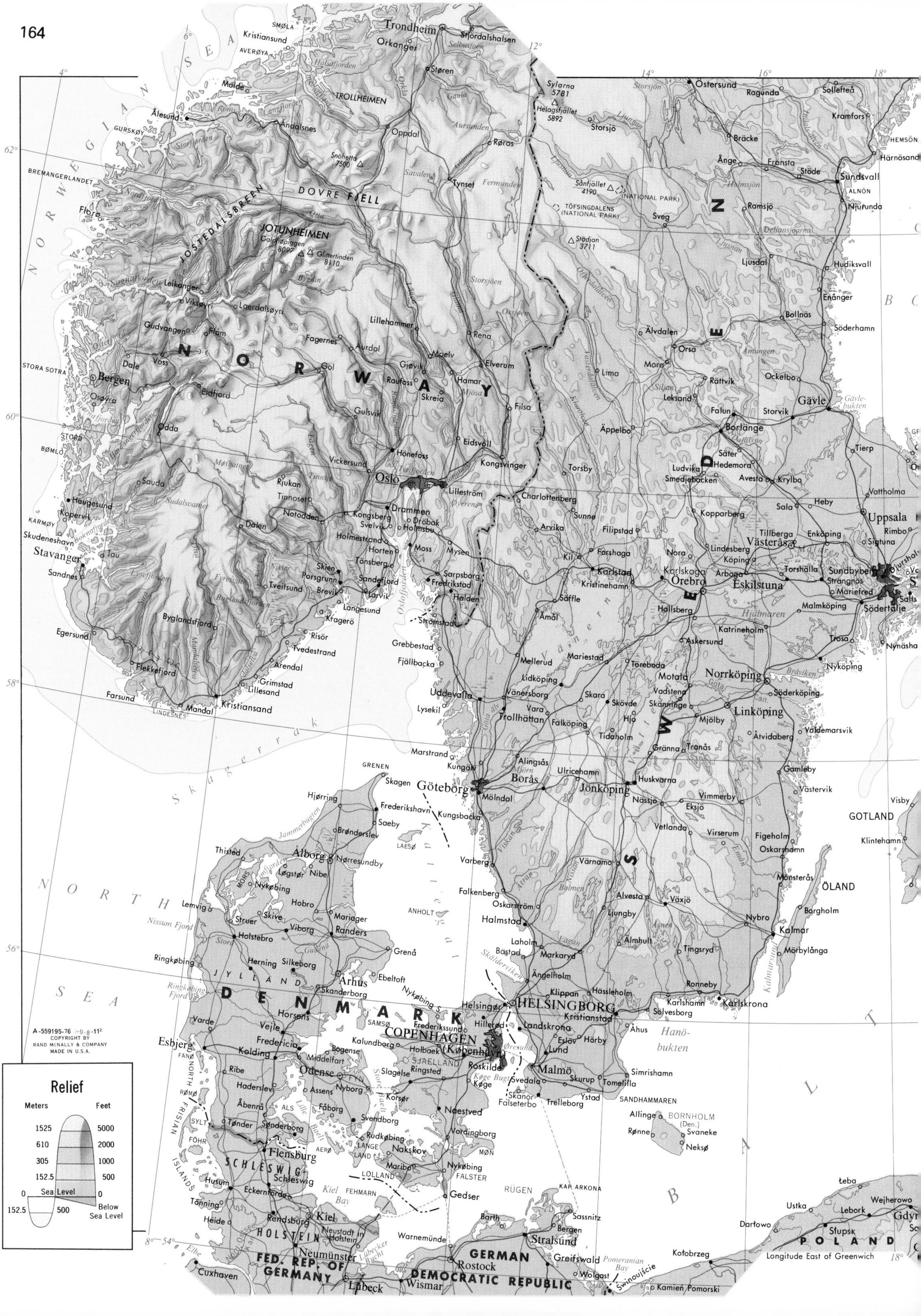

NORWEGIAN SEA

N O R W A Y

S W E D E N

DENMARK

FED. REP. OF GERMANY

GERMAN DEMOCRATIC REPUBLIC

POLAND

NORTH SEA

BALTIC

Skagerrak

Kattegat

GOTLAND

ÖLAND

BORNHOLM (Den.)

Trondheim · Orkanger · Støren · Stjørdalshalsen · Sylarna 5781 · Helagsfjället 5892 · Storsjön · Östersund · Ragunda · Sollefteå · Kramfors · HÄRNÖSAND · HEMSÖN

Kristiansund · Averøya · SMØLA · Molde · Åndalsnes · TROLLHEIMEN · Oppdal · Røros · Tynset · Sånfjället 4190 (NATIONAL PARK) · Töfsingdalens (NATIONAL PARK) · Sveg · Storsjö · Ånge · Fränsta · Stöde · Sundsvall · ALNÖN · Njurunda

Ålesund · GURSKØY · DOVRE FJELL · Snøhetta 7500 · Strädian 3711 · Ramsjö · Ljusdal · Hudiksvall

Florø · BREMANGERLANDET · Nord Fjord · JOSTEDALSBREEN · JOTUNHEIMEN · Galdhøpiggen 8097 · Glittertinden 8110 · Lillehammer · Rena · Älvdalen · Orsa · Mora · Lima · Enånger · Bollnäs · Söderhamn

Leikanger · Viksøyri · Lærdalsøyri · Fagernes · Aurdal · Gjøvik · Moelv · Elverum · Åppelbo · Rättvik · Ockelbo · Gävle · Gävle-bukten

Gudvangen · Flåm · Dale · Voss · Gol · Raufoss · Hamar · Mjøsa · Filsa · Siljan · Leksand · Falun · Storvik · Borlänge · Säter · Hedemora · Avesta · Krylbo · Tierp

Bergen · Eidfjord · Gulsvik · Eidsvoll · Kongsvinger · Torsby · Sunne · Ludvika · Smedjebacken · Kopparberg · Sala · Heby · Vattholma · Uppsala · Rimbo · Sigtuna

Odda · Rjukan · Vickersund · Hønefoss · Oslo · Lillestrøm · Charlottenberg · Arvika · Filipstad · Nora · Lindesberg · Köping · Arboga · Tillberga · Enköping

Stavanger · Sandnes · Egersund · Dalen · Natodden · Kongsberg · Svelvik · Drammen · Drøbak · Holmsbu · Mysen · Sarpsborg · Fredrikstad · Halden · Kil · Karlstad · Kristinehamn · Karlskoga · Örebro · Eskilstuna · Strängnäs · Mariefred · Södertälje · Salts

Skudeneshavn · KARMØY · Haugesund · Kopervik · Tau · Skien · Porsgrunn · Brevik · Larvik · Sandefjord · Tønsberg · Horten · Moss · Säffle · Åmål · Hällsta · Malmköping · Katrineholm · Trosa · Nynäshamn

Flekkefjord · Arendal · Grimstad · Lillesand · Risør · Tvedestrand · Grebbestad · Strømstad · Mellerud · Mariestad · Töreboda · Askersund · Motala · Norrköping · Söderköping · Nyköping

Farsund · Mandal · Kristiansand · LINDESNES · Fjällbacka · Uddevalla · Vänersborg · Skara · Skövde · Vadstena · Linköping · Valdemarsvik · Gamleby · Västervik

Lysekil · Trollhättan · Vara · Falköping · Hjo · Skänninge · Mjölby · Åtvidaberg

Marstrand · Kungälv · Alingsås · Tidaholm · Gränna · Tranås · Nässjö · Eksjö · Vimmerby · Figeholm · Oskarshamn

GRENEN · Skagen · Hjørring · Frederikshavn · Sæby · Brønderslev · Göteborg · Mölndal · Kungsbacka · Borås · Ulricehamn · Huskvarna · Jönköping · Vetlanda · Virserum · Visby · Klintehamn

Thisted · Ålborg · Nibe · Nørresundby · LÆSØ · Varberg · Värnamo · Mönsterås · Bergholm

Lemvig · MORS · Løgstør · Nykøbing · Hobro · ANHOLT · Falkenberg · Oskarström · Alvesta · Växjö · Nybro · Kalmar

Struer · Skive · Viborg · Mariager · Halmstad · Ljungby · Åsnen · Almhult · Tingsryd · Mörbylånga

Ringkøbing · Holstebro · Herning · Silkeborg · Randers · Grenå · Laholm · Båstad · Markaryd · Ronneby · Karlshamn · Karlskrona

JYLLAND · Århus · Skanderborg · Ebeltoft · Nykøbing S. · Ängelholm · Klippan · Hässleholm · Sölvesborg · Åhus · Hanö-bukten · Mörbylånga

Varde · Horsens · Vejle · Helsingør · HELSINGBORG · Kristianstad · Simrishamn

Esbjerg · FANØ · Fredericia · Kolding · Middelfart · SAMSØ · Frederikssund · Hillerød · Landskrona · Eslöv · Hörby · SANDHAMMAREN · Allinge · Svaneke

COPENHAGEN · København · Malmö · Skurup · Tomelilla · Rønne · Neksø

Ribe · Odense · FYN · Bogense · Holbæk · Roskilde · Lund · Svedala · Køge · Køge Bugt

Haderslev · Åbenrå · Assens · Nyborg · Slagelse · Ringsted · SJÆLLAND · Skanør · Falsterbo · Trelleborg · Ystad

ALS · Fåborg · Korsør · Svendborg · Næstved

RØMØ · SYLT · Tønder · Sønderborg · AERØ · Rudkøbing · Vordingborg · MØN

FØHR · NORTH FRISIAN ISLANDS · Flensburg · LANGE-LAND · Nakskov · Maribo · Nykøbing FALSTER · KAP ARKONA

Husum · Schleswig · Svendborg · LOLLAND · RÜGEN · Sassnitz · Barth · Bergen

SCHLESWIG · Tønning · Eckernförde · Kiel · Kiel Bay · FEHMARN · Gedser · Greifswald · Pomeranian Bay · Wolgast · Świnoujście · Kamień Pomorski

Heide · Rendsburg · HOLSTEIN · Neustadt in Holstein · Warnemünde · Stralsund · Kołobrzeg · Darłowo · Słupsk · Ustka · Lębork · Wejherowo · Gdynia

Cuxhaven · Neumünster · Lübeck · Lübecker Bucht · Rostock · Wismar · German Democratic Republic · POLAND · Longitude East of Greenwich

Relief

Meters		Feet
1525		5000
610		2000
305		1000
152.5		500
0	Sea Level	0
152.5		500 Below Sea Level

A-559195-76 |-9-8-11²
COPYRIGHT BY
RAND McNALLY & COMPANY
MADE IN U.S.A.

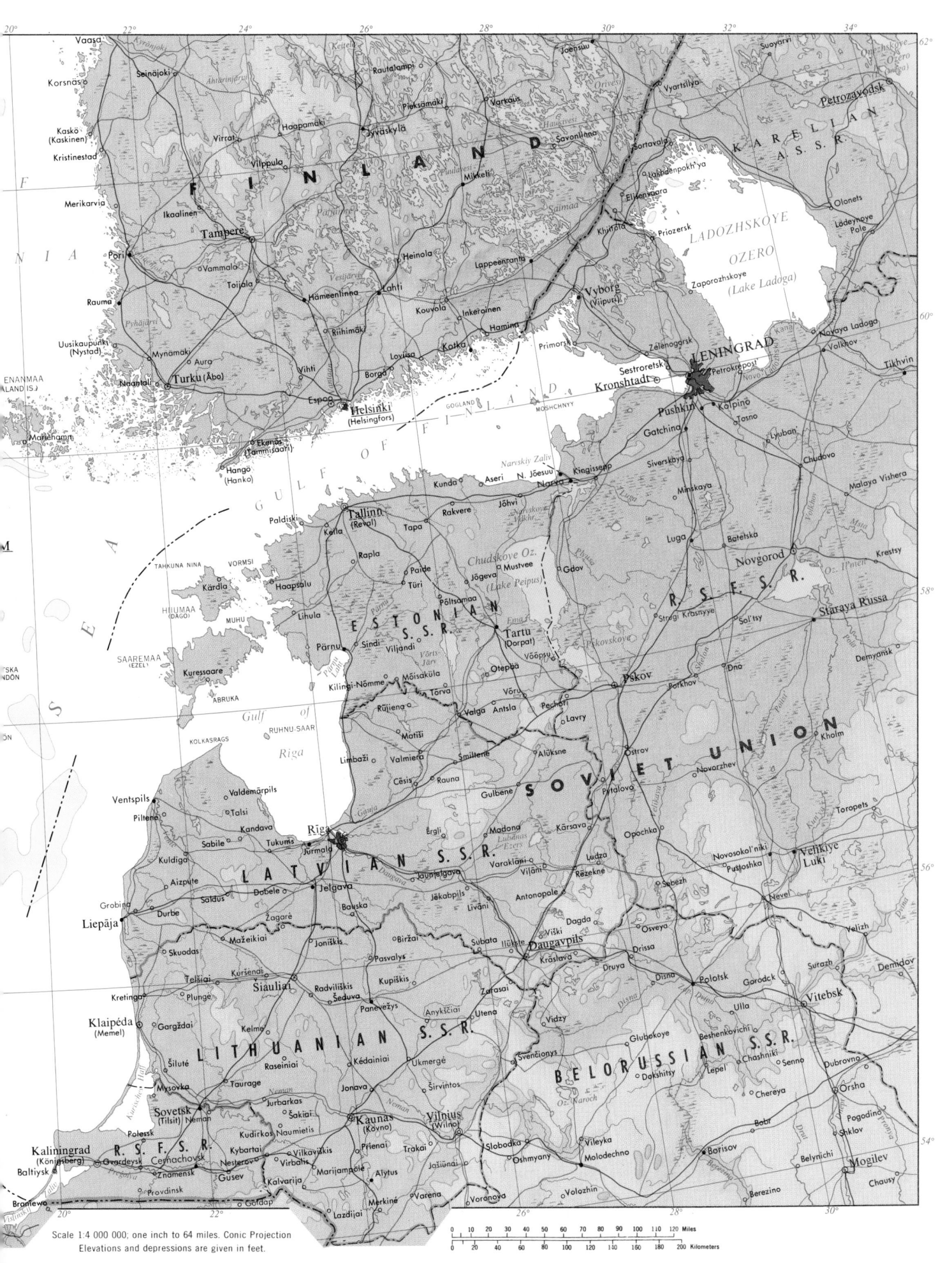

Scale 1:4 000 000; one inch to 64 miles. Conic Projection
Elevations and depressions are given in feet.

0 10 20 30 40 50 60 70 80 90 100 110 120 Miles

0 20 40 60 80 100 120 140 160 180 200 Kilometers

NORTH SEA

DENMARK

Svendborg
Tønder
Flensburg
Sønderborg
Rødbybing
Nakskov
MØN
Nykøbing
FALSTER
Gedser

SCHLESWIG
Schleswig
Husum
Eckernförde
Kiel
Kiel Bay
Rendsburg
Neustadt in Holstein
Lübecker Bucht
HOLSTEIN
Heide
Itzehoe
Neumünster
Bad Oldesloe
Elmshorn
Stade
HAMBURG
Lübeck

FRISIAN ISLANDS
Norderney
Wangerooge
Cuxhaven

Rostock
Stralsund
Sassnitz
RÜGEN
Bergen
Barth
Greifswald
Wolgast
Wismar
Schwerin
Güstrow
Teterow
Neubrandenburg
Pasewalk
Anklam
Demmin
MECKLENBURG

GERMAN DEMOCRATIC REPUBLIC
(EAST GERMANY)

Den Helder
Alkmaar
NETHERLANDS
AMSTERDAM
Utrecht
Apeldoorn
Leeuwarden
Groningen
Emden
Wilhelmshaven
Bremerhaven
Oldenburg
Delmenhorst
Bremen
LÜNEBURGER HEIDE
Lüneburg
Soltau
Uelzen
Ludwigslust
Parchim
Waren
Neustrelitz
Neu Ruppin
Templin
Prenzlau
Angermünde

Szczecin
(Stettin)
POMERANIA

FEDERAL REPUBLIC

Nijmegen
Arnhem
Enschede
Osnabrück
Minden
Hannover
Celle
Wolfsburg
Braunschweig
Magdeburg
Brandenburg
Potsdam
BERLIN
East Berlin
Frankfurt an der Oder

BRANDENBURG

Münster
Bielefeld
Herford
Hameln
Hildesheim
Wolfenbüttel
Helmstedt
Halberstadt
Quedlinburg
Dessau
Wittenberg
Cottbus
Zielona Góra

DÜSSELDORF
ESSEN
Dortmund
Hagen
Wuppertal
Solingen
Kassel
Göttingen
Nordhausen
HARZ
Eisleben
Halle
Leipzig
Dresden
Görlitz

COLOGNE (Köln)
Aachen
Bonn
Siegen
Marburg an der Lahn
Giessen
Fulda
Eisenach
Gotha
Erfurt
Weimar
Jena
Gera
THÜRINGEN
Karl-Marx-Stadt
Zwickau
Reichenbach
Plauen
Hof

ERZGEBIRGE
Prague (Praha)
CZECHOSLOVAKIA
BOHEMIA
Plzeň
Brno

Koblenz
GERMANY
FRANKFURT AM MAIN
Wiesbaden
Mainz
Offenbach
Hanau
Aschaffenburg
Darmstadt
Worms
Würzburg
Bamberg
Bayreuth
Schweinfurt

Luxembourg
Trier
Kaiserslautern
SAARLAND
Saarbrücken
MANNHEIM
Ludwigshafen
Heidelberg
(WEST GERMANY)
Heilbronn
Nürnberg
Fürth
Erlangen
Regensburg
BOHEMIAN FOREST

Metz
Nancy
Strasbourg
Karlsruhe
Pforzheim
STUTTGART
Esslingen
Tübingen
Reutlingen
Ulm
Neu Ulm
Augsburg
Ingolstadt
Landshut
Passau

FRANCE
Colmar
Freiburg
SCHWARZWALD
WÜRTTEMBERG
(BAVARIA)
Munich (München)
Freising
Rosenheim
Salzburg
Linz
VIENNA (Wien)

Mulhouse
Belfort
Basel
Schaffhausen
Konstanz
Winterthur
Zürich
Friedrichshafen
Bregenz
Kempten
Garmisch-Partenkirchen
Innsbruck
AUSTRIA
Graz

SWITZERLAND
Lausanne
Geneva (Genève)
Bern
Luzern
LIECHTENSTEIN
VORARLBERG
ALPS
HOHE TAUERN
Klagenfurt
Maribor

ALPI ORIE
Bolzano
Trento
YUGOSLAVIA

Continued on pages 172-173

Longitude East of Greenwich

Scale 1:4 000 000; one inch to 64 miles. Conic Projection
Elevations and depressions are given in feet.

COPYRIGHT BY RAND M9NALLY & COMPANY
MADE IN U.S.A.

Continued on pages 174-175

Relief

Meters	Feet
3050	10 000
1525	5000
610	2000
305	1000
152.5	500
0 Sea Level	0
	Below Sea Level

0 10 20 30 40 50 60 70 80 90 100 110 120 Miles

0 20 40 60 80 100 120 140 160 180 200 Kilometers

Relief

Meters		Feet
3050		10 000
1525		5000
610		2000
305		1000
152.5		500
0	Sea Level	0
152.5		500
1525		5000

A-550900-76-37-5-10²
COPYRIGHT BY
RAND McNALLY & COMPANY
MADE IN U.S.A.

a

Scale 1:1 000 000

0   10 Miles
0 4   8   12 16 Kilometers

©RMcN.

Scale 1:4 000 000; one inch to 64 miles. Conic Projection
Elevations and depressions are given in feet

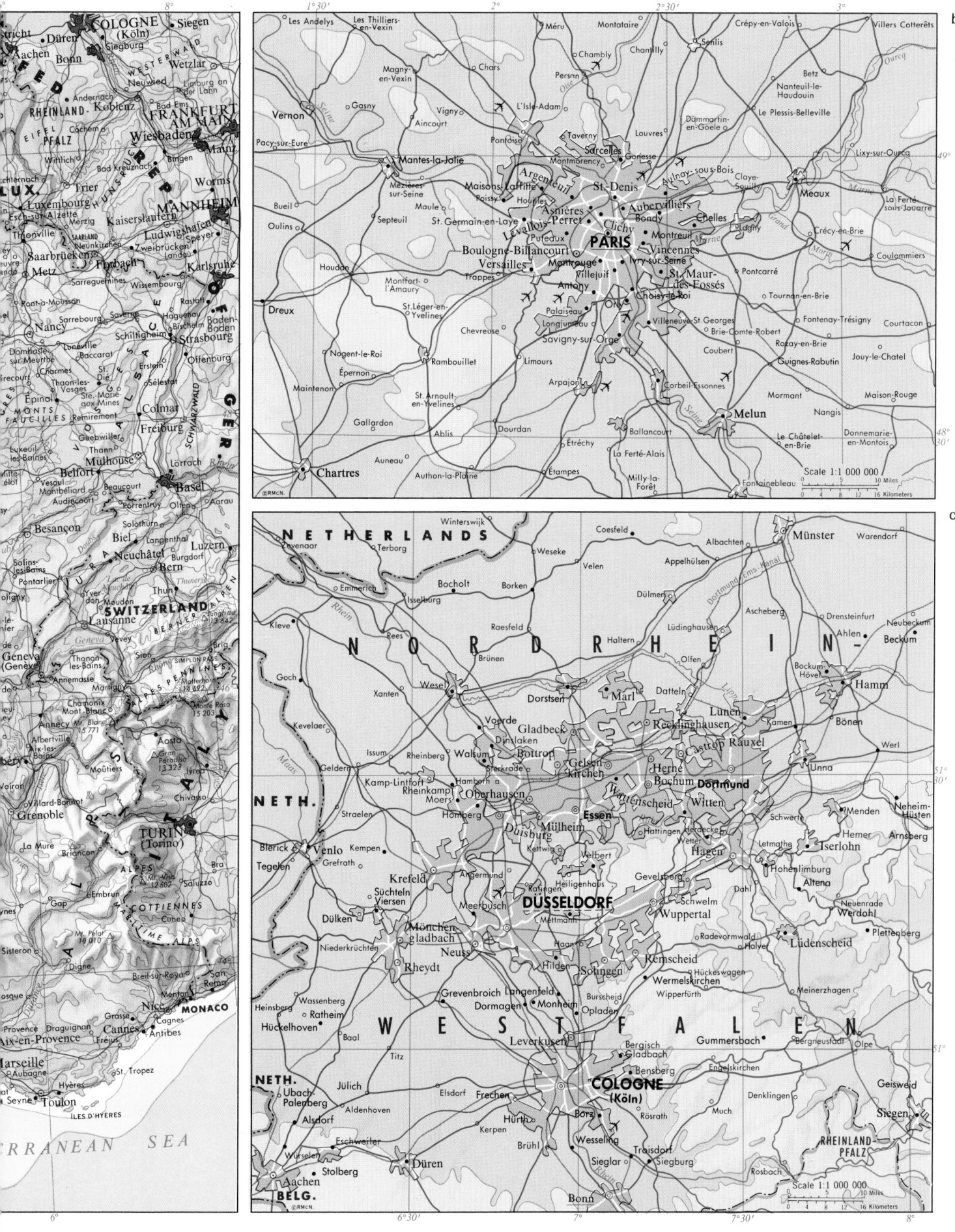

b

Les Andelys Les Thilliers-en-Vexin Méru Montataire Crépy-en-Valois Villers Cotterêts
Magny-en-Vexin Chars Chambly Chantilly Senlis Betz Ourcq
Vernon Gasny Vigny Persan Nanteuil-le-Haudouin Le Plessis-Belleville
Pacy-sur-Eure L'Isle-Adam Dammartin-en-Goele Lixy-sur-Ourcq 49°
Pontoise Taverny Louvres
Mantes-la-Jolie Sarcelles Goussainville Meaux La Ferté-sous-Jouarre
Mézières-sur-Seine Montmorency Aulnay-sous-Bois Claye-Souilly Marne
Maisons-Laffitte Argenteuil St-Denis Chelles Lagny Crécy-en-Brie
Bueil Poissy Houilles Asnières-Perret Bondy Coulommiers
Maule St-Germain-en-Laye Levallois-Perret Clichy Montreuil Morin
Septeuil Puteaux PARIS Vincennes Pontcarré Crécy-en-Brie
Oulins Boulogne-Billancourt Montrouge St-Maur-des-Fossés Tournan-en-Brie
Houdan Versailles Villejuif Choisy-le-Roi Fontenay-Trésigny
Montfort-l'Amaury Antony ORLY Villeneuve-St Georges Brie-Comte-Robert Courtacon
Dreux Trappes Palaiseau Rozay-en-Brie Jouy-le-Chatel
St-Léger-en-Yvelines Longjumeau Corbeil-Essonnes Guignes-Rabutin
Chevreuse Savigny-sur-Orge Coubert
Nogent-le-Roi Limours Maison-Rouge
Maintenon Rambouillet Arpajon Mormant
St-Arnoult-en-Yvelines Ballancourt Melun Nangis
Gallardon Dourdan Le Châtelet-en-Brie Donnemarie-en-Montois 48° 30'
Ablis Étrechy La Ferté-Alais
Auneau Authon-la-Plaine Étampes Milly-la-Forêt
Chartres Fontainebleau

Scale 1:1 000 000
©RMcN

c

N E T H E R L A N D S Winterswijk Coesfeld Warendorf
Zevenaar Terborg Weseke Albachten Münster
Emmerich Velen Appelhülsen
Bocholt Borken Dülmen Ascheberg Drensteinfurt Neubeckum
N O R D R H E I N - Lüdinghausen Ahlen Beckum
Kleve Rees Raesfeld Haltern Olfen Bockum-Hövel Hamm
Brünen Lippe Werl
Goch Xanten Wesel Marl Datteln Lünen Kamen Bönen
Kevelaer Dorstsen Recklinghausen Unna
Voerde Gladbeck Castrop Rauxel
Issum Dinslaken Bottrop Gelsenkirchen Herne Werl
Rheinberg Walsum Wattenscheid Bochum Dortmund
Geldern Steckrade Essen Witten Schwerte Menden
Kamp-Lintfort Hamborn a Oberhausen Herdecke Neheim-Hüsten
N E T H. Moers Rheinkamp Mülheim Hattingen Wetter Hemer Arnsberg
Straelen Homberg Duisburg Velbert Hagen Letmathe Iserlohn
Blerick Kempen Kettwig Gevelsberg Hohenlimburg
Venlo Grefrath Angermund Heiligenhaus Schwelm Altena
Tegelen Krefeld Ratingen Dahl Neuenrade Werdohl
Dülken Süchteln Meerbusch **DÜSSELDORF** Wuppertal Lüdenscheid
Viersen Mettmann Radevormwald Plettenberg
Niederkrüchten Haan Halver
M ö n c h e n - Neuss Hilden Solingen Remscheid Meinerzhagen
gladbach Hückeswagen
Rheydt Grevenbroich Langenfeld Monheim Wermelskirchen Wipperfürth
Heinsberg Wassenberg Dormagen Burscheid Opladen
Hückelhoven Ratheim **W E S T F A L E N** 51°
Baal Leverkusen Bergisch-Gladbach Gummersbach Bergneustadt
Titz Bensberg Engelskirchen Olpe
N E T H. Jülich Elsdorf Frechen **COLOGNE (Köln)** Denklingen
Ubach-Palenberg Aldenhoven Hürth Rösrath Much Geisweid
Alsdorf Kerpen Borr Siegen
Würselen Eschweiler Brühl Wesseling Troisdorf **RHEINLAND-PFALZ** 51°
Aachen Stolberg Düren Sieglar Siegburg Rosbach
BELG. Bonn

Scale 1:1 000 000
©RMcN

For larger scale coverage of Düsseldorf and Paris see pages 63 and 64.

COLOGNE (Köln) Siegen
Düren Siegburg
Aachen Bonn Westerwald Wetzlar
Andernach Neuwied Limburg an der Lahn
RHEINLAND Koblenz Bad Ems
EIFEL Cochem FRANKFURT AM MAIN
PFALZ Wiesbaden Mainz
Wittlich Bingen
Trier Bad Kreuznach Worms
LUX. Luxembourg MANNHEIM
Esch-sur-Alzette Merzig Kaiserslautern Ludwigshafen Speyer
Thionville SAARLAND Neunkirchen Zweibrücken Landau Karlsruhe
Saarbrücken Forbach Wissembourg Rastatt
Metz Sarreguemines Haguenau Baden-Baden
Pont-à-Mousson Sarrebourg Saverne Bischheim Offenburg
Nancy Lunéville Strasbourg
Dombasle-sur-Meurthe Baccarat Schiltigheim GER.
Charmes St-Dié Erstein Sélestat
Thaon-les-Vosges Ste-Marie-aux-Mines Freiburg
Épinal Remiremont Colmar SCHWARZWALD
Luxeuil-les-Bains Guebwiller Thann Rhein
Vesoul Belfort Mulhouse Lörrach
Montbéliard Beaucourt Basel
Audincourt Porrentruy Olten Aarau
Besançon Solothurn
Biel Langenthal Luzern
Salins-les-Bains Neuchâtel Burgdorf
Pontarlier Moudon Bern Thun Thunersee
SWITZERLAND Brig SIMPLON PASS
Lausanne Vevey Sion PENNINES
Geneva (Genève) Thonon-les-Bains Martigny Matterhorn Monte Rosa
Annemasse Chamonix Mont-Blanc
Albertville Aosta Gran Paradiso Ivrea
Aix-les-Bains Moûtiers Chivasso
Grenoble Villard-Bonnot **TURIN (Torino)**
La Mure Briançon ALPES Bra Saluzzo
Embrun COTTIENNES Cuneo
Gap MARITIME ALPS
Sisteron Digne Breil-sur-Roya San Remo
Draguignan Grasse Menton Nice **MONACO**
Aix-en-Provence Cannes Cagnes Antibes
Marseille Fréjus
Aubagne St-Tropez
Seyne Hyères Toulon ÎLES D'HYÈRES
MEDITERRANEAN SEA

10 20 30 40 50 60 70 80 90 100 110 120 Miles
20 40 60 80 100 120 140 160 180 200 Kilometers

Relief

Meters		Feet
3050		10000
1525		5000
610		2000
305		1000
152.5		500
0	Sea Level	0
152.5		500
1525		5000
3050		10000

A-552900-76- -6-5-8²
COPYRIGHT BY
RAND McNALLY & COMPANY
MADE IN U.S.A.

Scale 1:4 000 000, one inch to 64 miles. Conic Projection
Elevations and depressions are given in feet

Longitude West of Greenwich

FRANCE

Toulouse
Montpellier
Béziers
Narbonne
Carcassonne
Perpignan
Pau
Tarbes
Lourdes
St. Gaudens
Foix
ANDORRA
Andorra

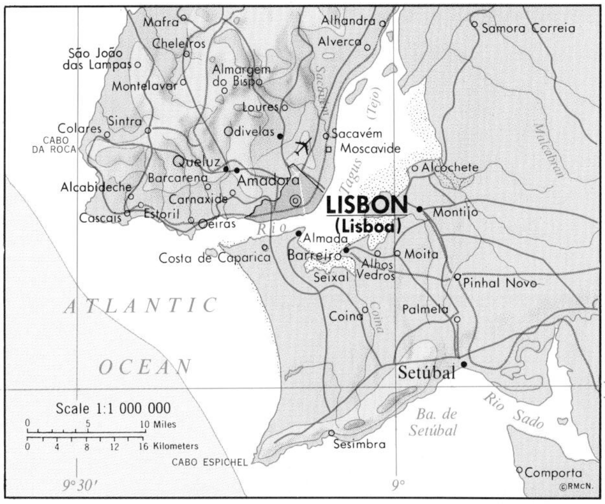

PYRENEES

Golfe du Lion

CABO DE CREUS
Golfo de Rosas

Gerona
Manresa
Sabadell
Tarrasa
BARCELONA
Badalona
Mataró
Villanueva y Geltrú
Tarragona

Lérida
Reus
Tortosa
CABO DE TORTOSA

CATALUÑA

BALEARIC SEA

BALEARES
(SP.)
ISLANDS
ISLAS BALEARIC

MENORCA
(MINORCA)
Ciudadela
Mahón

Pollensa
La Puebla
Inca
Sóller
Palma
Manacor
Lluchmayor
Felanitx
Santañy
MALLORCA
(MAJORCA)
Ba. de Palma
CABE SALINAS
CABRERA

IBIZA
(IVIZA)
San Antonio Abad
Ibiza
Sta. Eulalia del Río
FORMENTERA

Castellón de la Plana
Villarreal
Burriana
Sagunto
Valencia
Catarroja
Sueca
Cullera
Gandía
Oliva
Denia
Jávea
CABO DE LA NAO
Alcoy
Villajoyosa
Alicante
Elche
Torrevieja
Mar Menor
CABO DE PALOS

MEDITERRANEAN SEA

Algiers
(Alger)
Blida
Médéa
ATLAS MOUNTAINS
ALGERIA
Mostaganem
Mascara

Longitude East of Greenwich

20 40 60 80 100 120 Miles
20 40 60 80 100 120 140 160 180 200 Kilometers

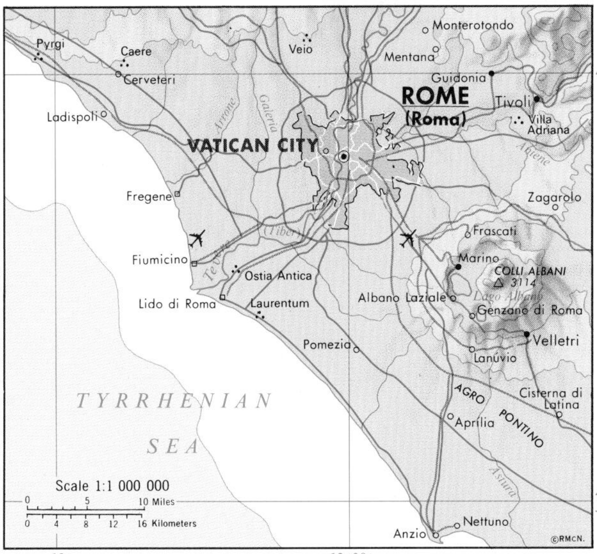

For larger scale coverage of Lisbon, Madrid, and Rome see pages 65 and 66.

a

SA. DEL HOYO
El Escorial
Galapagar
El Pardo
Las Rozas de Madrid
Fuencarral
Barajas
Torrejón de Ardoz
Alcalá de Henares
Pozuelo de Alarcón
Valdemorillo
Brunete
MADRID
Vicálvaro
Alcorcón
Leganés
Móstoles
Getafe
Vallecas
Arganda
Campo Real
Parla
Pinto
S. Martín de la Vega
Marata de Tajuña

Scale 1:1 000 000
0   5   10 Miles
0 4 8 12 16 Kilometers

b

Mafra
Cheleiros
Alhandra
Alverca
Samora Correia
São João das Lampas
Montelavar
Sintra
Colares
CABO DA ROCA
Odivelas
Sacavém
Moscavide
Alcochete
Queluz
Barcarena
Amadora
Carnaxide
Cascais
Estoril
Oeiras
LISBON
(Lisboa)
Montijo
Almada
Costa de Caparica
Barreiro
Alhos Vedros
Moita
Seixal
Pinhal Novo
Coina
Palmela

ATLANTIC OCEAN

Setúbal
Ba. de Setúbal
Sesimbra
CABO ESPICHEL
Comporta

Scale 1:1 000 000
0   5   10 Miles
0 4 8 12 16 Kilometers

c

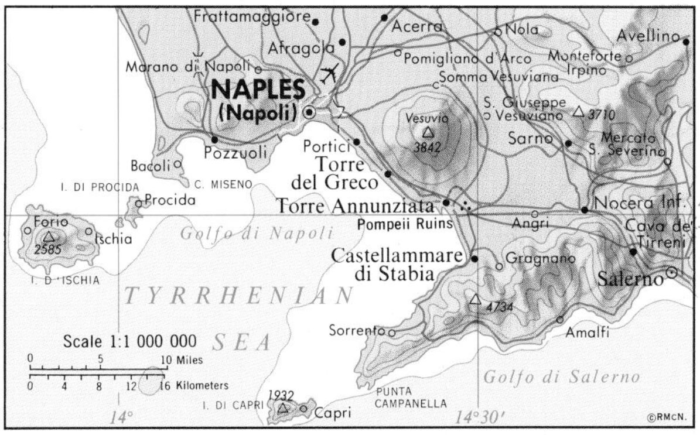

Frattamaggiore
Acerra
Nola
Afragola
Pomigliano d'Arco
Monteforte Irpino
Avellino
Marano di Napoli
Somma Vesuviana
NAPLES
(Napoli)
S. Giuseppe Vesuviano
Sarno
Mercato Severino
Pozzuoli
Bacoli
Portici
Vesuvio
Torre del Greco
C. MISENO
Torre Annunziata
Nocera Inf.
I. DI PROCIDA
Procida
Pompeii Ruins
Angri
Cava de Tirreni
Forio
Ischia
Castellammare di Stabia
Gragnano
Salerno
I. D'ISCHIA
Golfo di Napoli
TYRRHENIAN SEA
Sorrento
Amalfi
Golfo di Salerno
PUNTA CAMPANELLA
I. DI CAPRI
Capri

Scale 1:1 000 000
0   5   10 Miles
0 4 8 12 16 Kilometers

d

Pyrgi
Caere
Cerveteri
Veio
Monterotondo
Mentana
Guidonia
ROME
(Roma)
Tivoli
Villa Adriana
Ladispoli
VATICAN CITY
Fregene
Zagarolo
Frascati
Fiumicino
Marino
COLLI ALBANI
Ostia Antica
Lido di Roma
Laurentum
Albano Laziale
Genzano di Roma
Pomezia
Lanuvio
Velletri
Aprilia
Cisterna di Latina
TYRRHENIAN SEA
AGRO PONTINO
Anzio
Nettuno

Scale 1:1 000 000
0   5   10 Miles
0 4 8 12 16 Kilometers

Continued on pages 166-167

Continued on pages 168-169

Scale 1:4 000 000; one inch to 64 miles. Conic Projection
Elevations and depressions are given in feet

Relief

Meters	Feet
3050	10 000
1525	5000
610	2000
305	1000
152.5	500
0 Sea Level	0
152.5	500
1525	5000
3050	10 000

A-558396-76- 5-7-11*
COPYRIGHT BY
RAND McNALLY & COMPANY
MADE IN U.S.A.

18°   Longitude East of Greenwich   20°

0 10 20 30 40 50 60 70 80 90 100 110 120 Miles
0   20   40   60   80   100   120   140   160   180   200 Kilometers

Relief

Feet	Meters
5000	1525
2000	610
1000	305
500	152.5
Sea Level	0
500	152.5

Cities and Towns

0 to 50,000   500,000 to 1,000,000

50,000 to 500,000   1,000,000 and over

Scale 1:4 000 000; one inch to 64 miles. Conic Proje

Elevations and depressions are given in feet

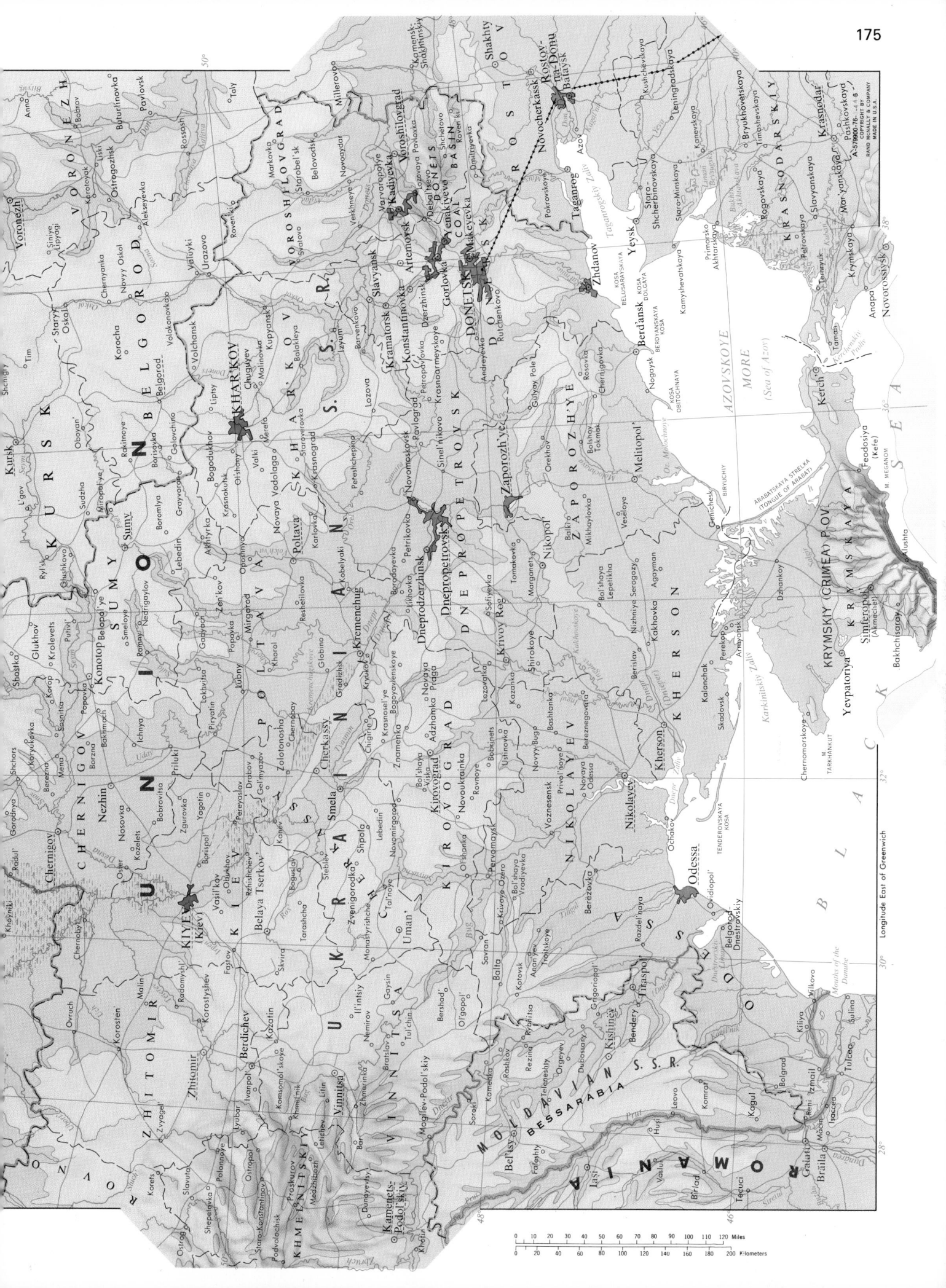

Scale 1:20 000 000; one inch to 315 m
Lambert's Azimuthal, Equal Area Proj
Elevations and depressions are given

Relief

Meters		Feet
3050		10 000
1525		5000
610		2000
305		1000
152.5		500
0	Sea Level	
152.5		500
1525		5000
3050		10 000
		Below Sea Level

SEVERNAYA ZEMLYA (NORTHERN LAND)

P-OV GORY

TAYMYR GORY BYRRANGA

M. CHELYUSKIN

NORDENSHEL'DA

LAPTEV SEA

DE-LONGA

FADDEYA

NOVAYA SIBIR

NOVOSIBIRSKIYE O-VA (NEW SIBERIAN ISLANDS)

MALYY LYAKHOVSKIYE

KOTEL'NYY

BOL'SHOY BEGICHEV

M. BUOR-KHAYA

SVYATOY NOS

M. SHELAGSKIY

VRANGELYA (WRANGEL)

CHUKOTSKOYE NAGOR'YE

M. CHELAGSKIY

AYON

Ambarchik

ARCTIC OCEAN

EAST SIBERIAN SEA

MEDVEZH'I

Anadyrskiy Zaliv

ril'sk

GORY PUTORANA

G. Polkan 3543

'anhsk

Nizhnyaya Tunguska

Podkamennaya Tunguska

artsevo

DERATIVE

Baykit

Tura

Khatanga

Nordvik

Ust'-Olenek

Taymyr Khatangskiy Zaliv

Tiksi

Bulun

Kozach'ye

Olenek

Zhigansk

VERKHOYANSKIY KHREBET

YAKUT

Suntar

Vilyuysk

Vilyuy

Aldan

Yakutsk

Olekminsk

Lena

Amga

CIALIST REPUBLIC

A.S.S.R.

KHREBET CHERSKOGO

Verkhoyansk

Gora Chen 10171

Oymyakon

Ust'-Moya

Aldanskoye

Tommot

Aldan

DZHUGDZHUR KHREBET

Nel'kan

Ayan

Chumikan

Uchur

Udskaya Guba

SHANTAR

KHREBET GYDAN (KOLYMSKIY)

Zyryanka

Srednekolymsk

Kolyma

Nizhne-Kolymsk

Magadan

Okhotsk

M. ALEVINA

Gizhiga

KORYAKSKIY KHREBET

Markovo

Penzhino

Palana

M. OL'KHOVSKIY

P-OV KAMCHATKA

M. Kamchatka

KAMCHATKA

Verkhne-Kamchatsk

Petropavlovsk-Kamchatskiy

Ust' Bol'sheretsk

SEA OF OKHOTSK

M. YELIZAVETY

Okha

Aleksandrovsk

SAKHALIN (Sov. Union)

Poronaysk

Uglegorsk

M. TERPENIYA

Kholmsk

Yuzhno-Sakhalinsk

Korsakov

P-OV MUNKU SARDYK 3543

GORY PUTORANA

Baykit

Nizhnyaya Tunguska

K Krasnoyarsk

Kansk

Balakhta

Nizhneudinsk

Minusinsk

Abakan

Kyzyl

TANNU-OLA

Uyu Nuur

Har Us Nuur

Hovd

Uliastay

Tsast Bogd 13 419

A MISA

AIMTS

MONGOLIA

Ulan Bator (Ulaanbaatar)

Ondorhaan

Sayr Usa

GOBI OR SHAMO (DESERT)

HANGAYN NURUU

NHANGAI

Selenge

Kerulen

Wenquan

Tao an

Jarud Qi

Chifeng

Chengde

Weichang

Zhangjiakou

Fengzhen

PEKING (Beijing)

Baoding

TIANJIN

Lushun

Lüda

Bo Hai

SHANDONG BANDAO

YELLOW SEA

Tayshet

Bratsk

Tulun

Nizhneudinsk

Zhigalovo

Kachuga

Cheremhovo

Angarsk

Irkutsk

Kyren

Kutulik

Goradek

Kyakhta

Petrovsk-Zabaykal'skiy

Ulan-Ude

Aginskoye

Akska

Borzya

BAYKAL'SKIY KHREBET

Bargusin

Ozero Baykal (Baykal) Surface elev. 1535 ft. above sea level

BURYAT A.S.S.R.

Golets Purpula 6377

Peleduy

Vitim

Bodaybo

Golets Skalistyy 9186

PATOM PLATEAU

Mukhtuya

Kirensk

Ilimsk

YABLONOVYY KHREBET

Vitim

Chita

Nerchinsk

Nerchinskiy Zavod

Sretensk

NERCHINSKIY KHREBET

STANOVOY KHREBET

Tyndinskiy

Zeya

Skovorodino

YABLONOVYY KHREBET

Amur

Shilka

Onon

GREATER KHINGAN

LESSER KHINGAN

KHINGAN

Nenjiang

Goukou

Hailun

Suihua

Fuyu

Qiqihar

Tao an

Shuangliao

CHANGCHUN

Jilin

HARBIN

Mudanjiang

Dunhua

Boli

Spassk-Dal'niy

Artem

Huchun

Nojin

Chongjin

MANCHURIA

SHENYANG

FUSHUN

Svobodnyy

Belogorsk

Ust' Tyrma

Bureya

Blagoveshchensk

Birobidzhan

Khabarovsk

Nikolayevsk-na-Amure

Komsomol'sk-na-Amure

KHREBET BUREINSKIY

Soyetskaya

Gavan'

Dal'nerechensk

USSURIYSKIY KHREBET

SIKHOTE ALIN'

Iman

Ussuri

Pozharskoye

Nakhodka

Ol'ga

Vladivostok

Pyongyang

NORTH KOREA

SOUTH KOREA

SEOUL

Kaesong

Andong

Taegu

PUSAN

Korea Bay

J A P A N

HOKKAIDO

Wakkanai

Otaru

Sapporo

Esashi

HONSHU

Kanazawa

Tottori

Matsue

KYOTO

KOBE

Okayama

OSAKA

Hiroshima

Kōchi

SEA OF JAPAN

Tatarskiy Proliv

KHREBET SIKHOTE ALIN'

100 200 300 400 500 600 Miles

200 400 600 800 1000 Kilometers

A-570000-76

COPYRIGHT BY RAND McNALLY & COMPANY MADE IN U.S.A.

Continued on pages 158-159

Scale 1:10 000 000; one inch to 160 miles. Conic Projection
Elevations and depressions are given in feet.

Continued on pages 160-161

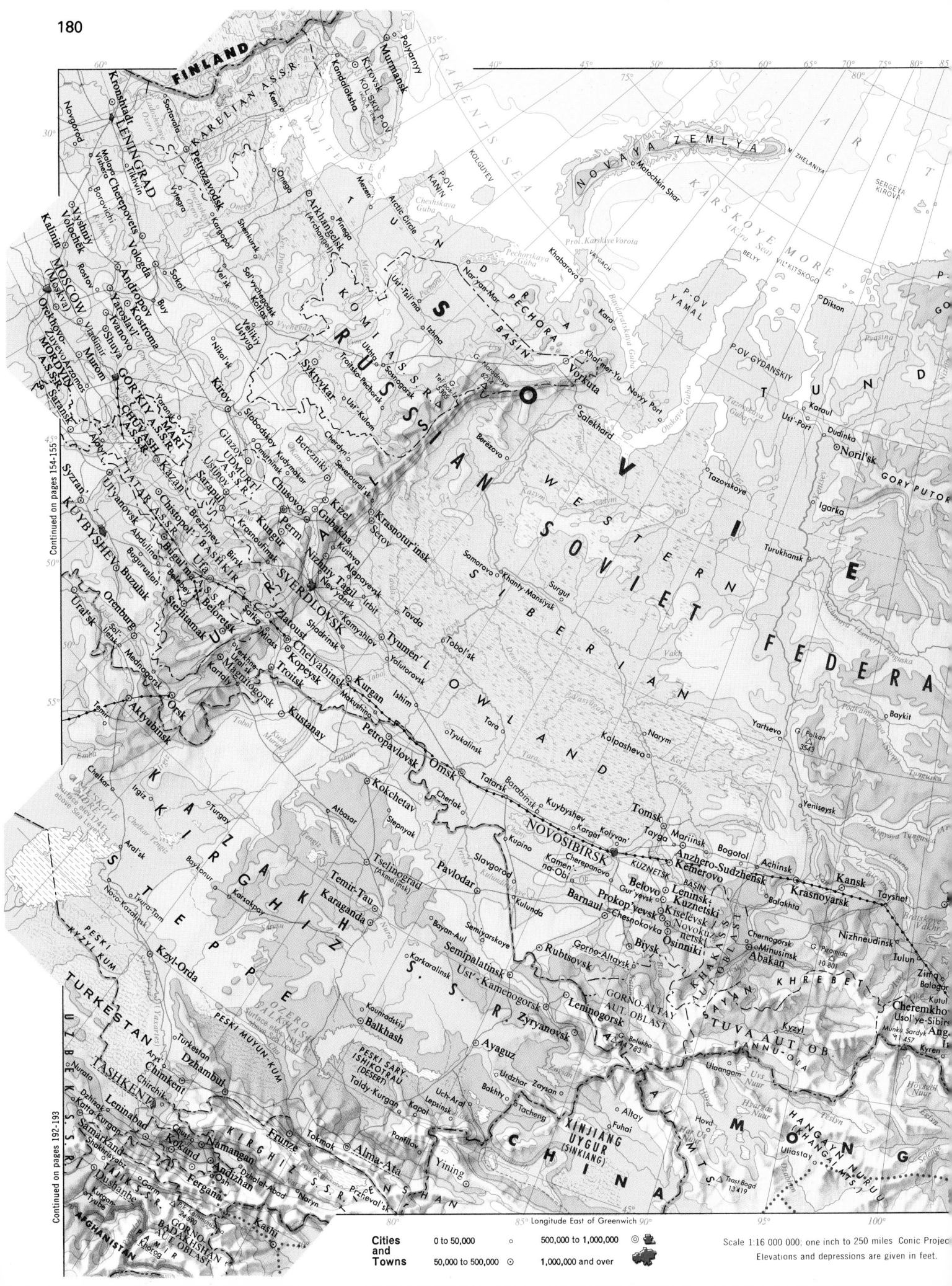

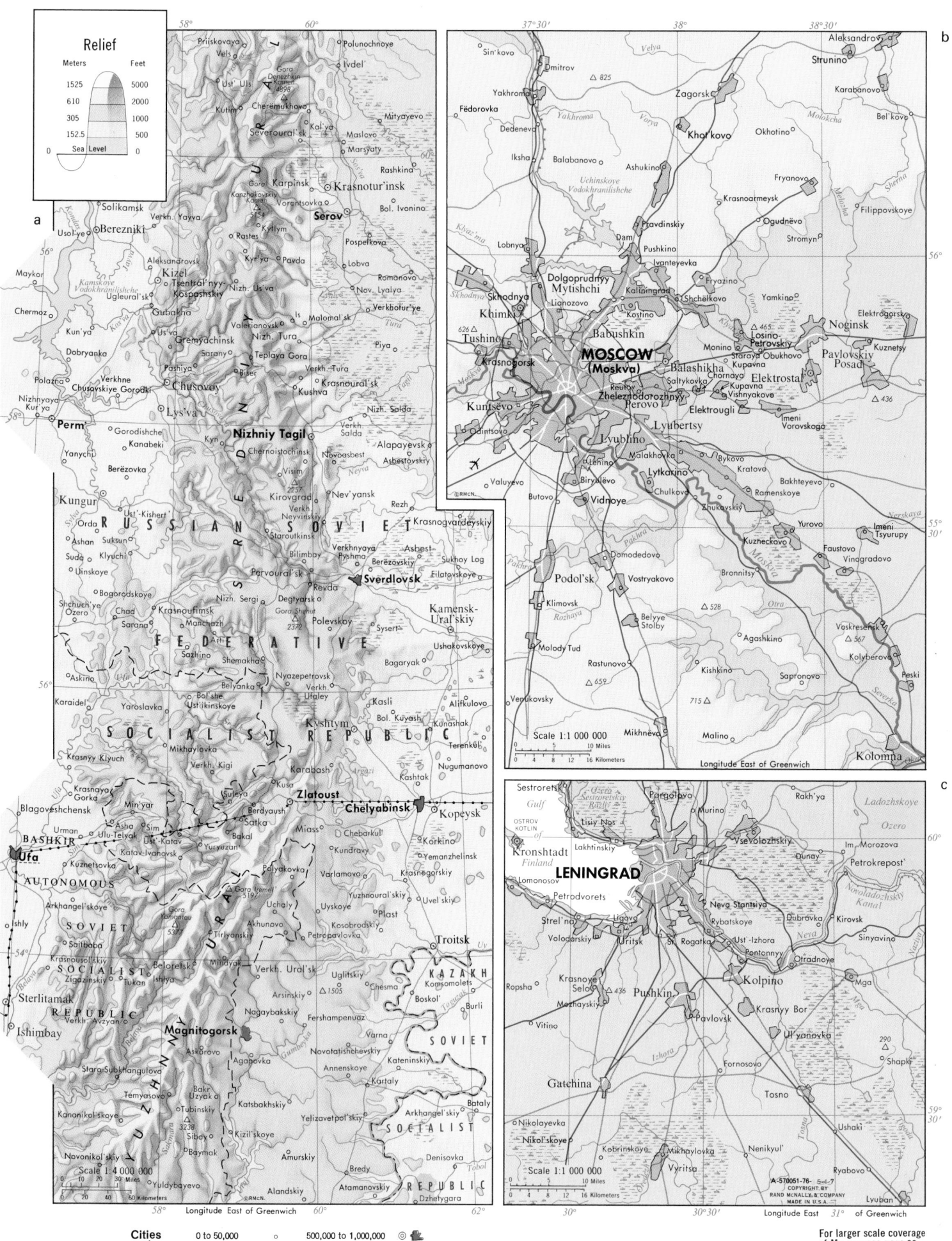

Relief

Meters		Feet
1525		5000
610		2000
305		1000
152.5		500
0	Sea Level	

a

b

c

MOSCOW (Moskva)

Scale 1:1 000 000

0 — 5 — 10 Miles
0 — 4 — 8 — 12 — 16 Kilometers

Longitude East of Greenwich

LENINGRAD

Scale 1:1 000 000

0 — 5 — 10 Miles
0 — 4 — 8 — 12 — 16 Kilometers

Longitude East 31° of Greenwich

A-570051-76 5-4-7
COPYRIGHT BY
RAND MCNALLY & COMPANY
MADE IN U.S.A.

For larger scale coverage of Moscow see page 66.

Magnitogorsk

Chelyabinsk

Zlatoust

Sverdlovsk

Nizhniy Tagil

Serov

Perm'

Ufa

Scale 1:4 000 000

0 — 10 — 20 — 30 Miles
0 — 20 — 40 — 60 Kilometers

Longitude East of Greenwich

Cities and Towns

0 to 50,000 — o
50,000 to 500,000 — ⊙
500,000 to 1,000,000 — ◎
1,000,000 and over

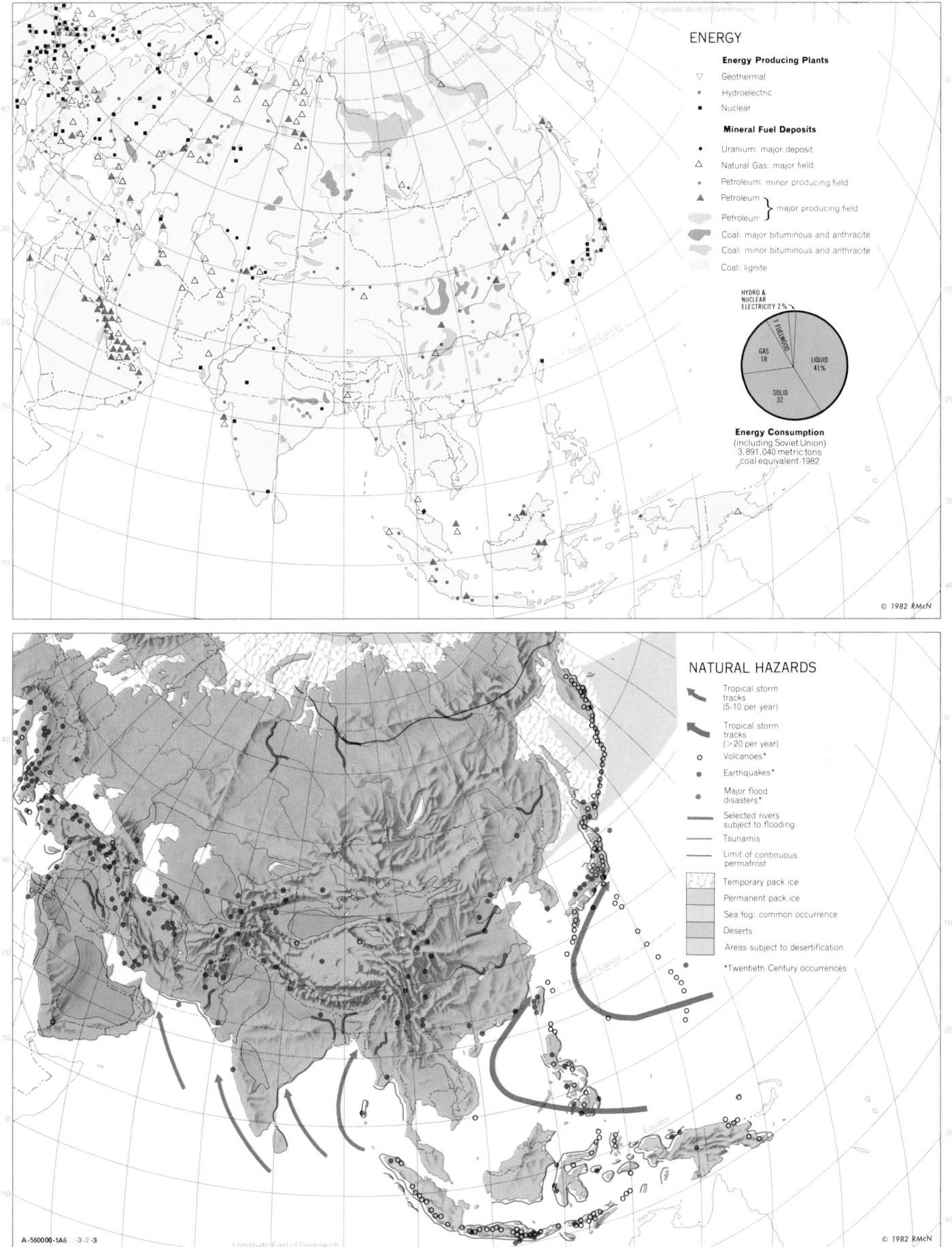

ENERGY

Energy Producing Plants

▽ Geothermal

• Hydroelectric

■ Nuclear

Mineral Fuel Deposits

• Uranium: major deposit

△ Natural Gas: major field

• Petroleum: minor producing field

▲ Petroleum

Petroleum } major producing field

Coal: major bituminous and anthracite

Coal: minor bituminous and anthracite

Coal: lignite

HYDRO & NUCLEAR ELECTRICITY 2%

FUELWOOD 7

GAS 18

LIQUID 41%

SOLID 32

Energy Consumption
(including Soviet Union)
3,891,040 metric tons
coal equivalent·1982

© 1982 RMcN

NATURAL HAZARDS

Tropical storm tracks (5·10 per year)

Tropical storm tracks (>20 per year)

○ Volcanoes*

• Earthquakes*

• Major flood disasters*

Selected rivers subject to flooding

Tsunamis

Limit of continuous permafrost

Temporary pack ice

Permanent pack ice

Sea fog: common occurrence

Deserts

Areas subject to desertification

*Twentieth Century occurrences

A-560000-1A6 3-2-3

© 1982 RMcN

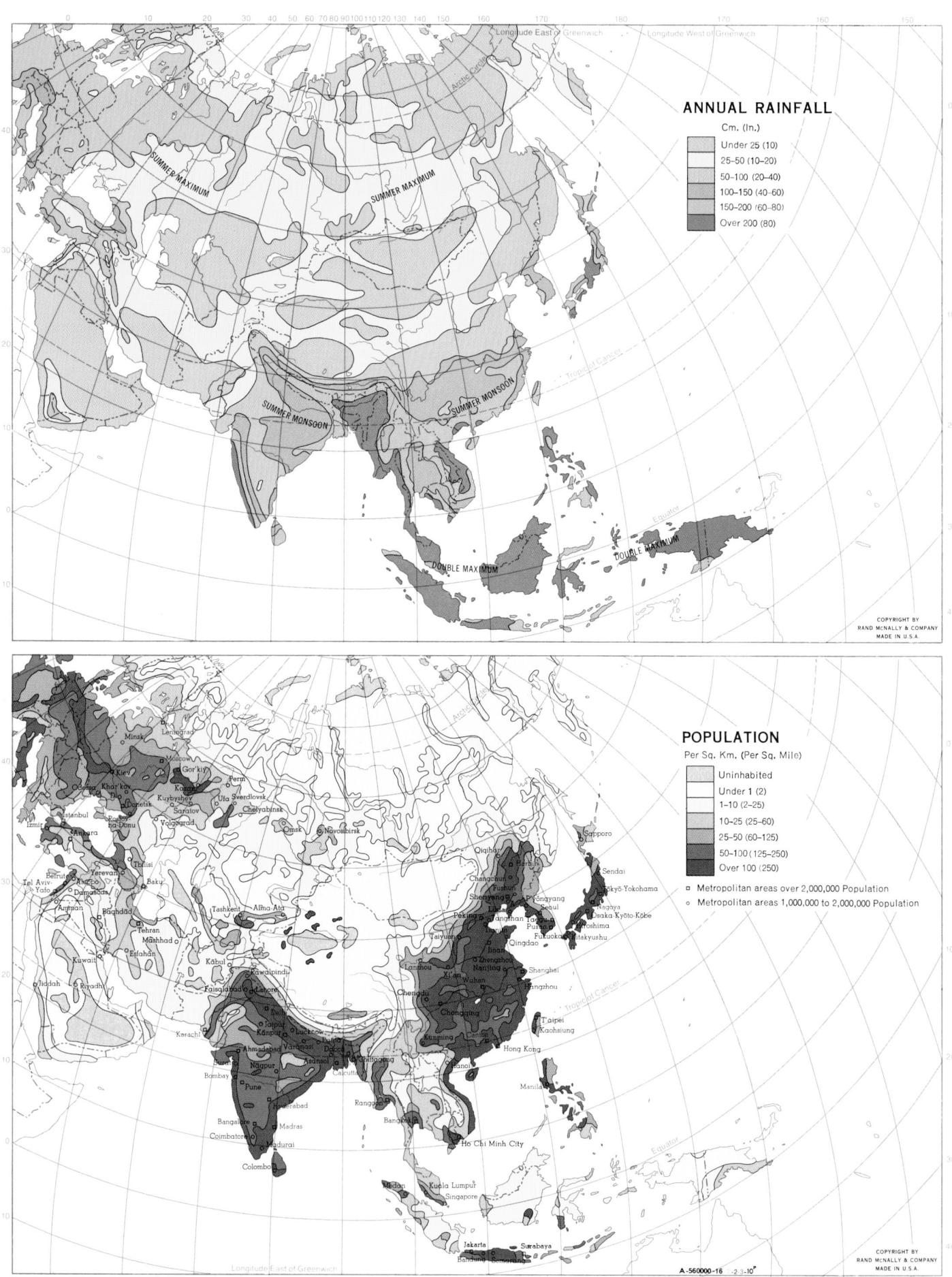

ANNUAL RAINFALL

Cm. (In.)

Under 25 (10)
25–50 (10–20)
50–100 (20–40)
100–150 (40–60)
150–200 (60–80)
Over 200 (80)

SUMMER MAXIMUM
SUMMER MAXIMUM
SUMMER MONSOON
SUMMER MONSOON
DOUBLE MAXIMUM
DOUBLE MAXIMUM

POPULATION

Per Sq. Km. (Per Sq. Mile)

Uninhabited
Under 1 (2)
1–10 (2–25)
10–25 (25–60)
25–50 (60–125)
50–100 (125–250)
Over 100 (250)

□ Metropolitan areas over 2,000,000 Population
○ Metropolitan areas 1,000,000 to 2,000,000 Population

A-560000-16 -2 3-10°

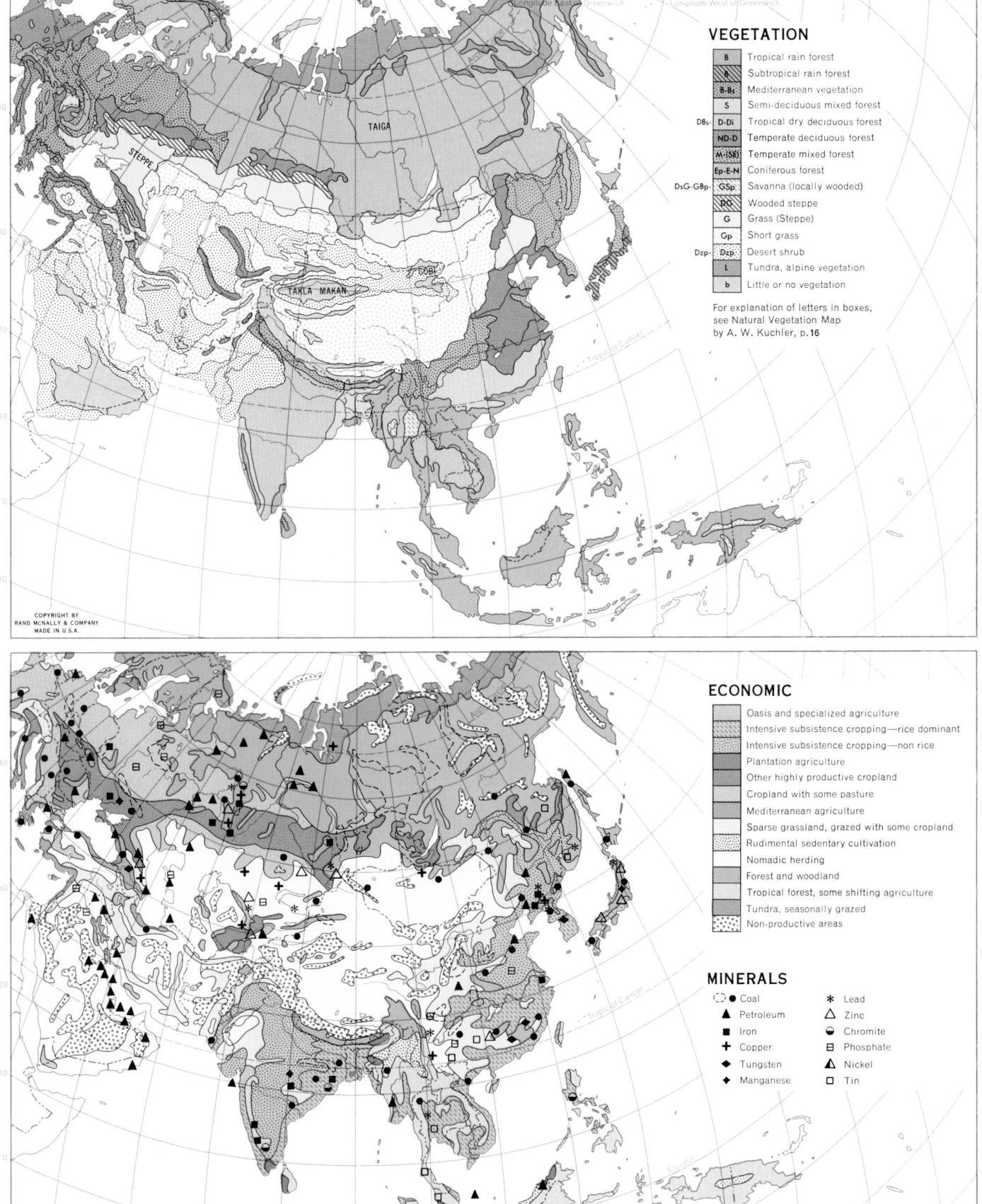

VEGETATION

B	Tropical rain forest
B	Subtropical rain forest
B-Bs	Mediterranean vegetation
S	Semi-deciduous mixed forest
DBs- / D-Di	Tropical dry deciduous forest
ND-D	Temperate deciduous forest
M-(SE)	Temperate mixed forest
Ep-E-N	Coniferous forest
DsG-GBp- / GSp	Savanna (locally wooded)
DG	Wooded steppe
G	Grass (Steppe)
Gp	Short grass
Dzp- / Dzp	Desert shrub
L	Tundra, alpine vegetation
b	Little or no vegetation

For explanation of letters in boxes,
see Natural Vegetation Map
by A. W. Kuchler, p.16

TAIGA
STEPPE
GOBI
TAKLA MAKAN

ECONOMIC

	Oasis and specialized agriculture
	Intensive subsistence cropping—rice dominant
	Intensive subsistence cropping—non rice
	Plantation agriculture
	Other highly productive cropland
	Cropland with some pasture
	Mediterranean agriculture
	Sparse grassland, grazed with some cropland
	Rudimental sedentary cultivation
	Nomadic herding
	Forest and woodland
	Tropical forest, some shifting agriculture
	Tundra, seasonally grazed
	Non-productive areas

MINERALS

●	Coal	✳	Lead
▲	Petroleum	△	Zinc
■	Iron	⬯	Chromite
✚	Copper	⊟	Phosphate
◆	Tungsten	◭	Nickel
◆	Manganese	☐	Tin

A-560000-1B6 -2-3-10

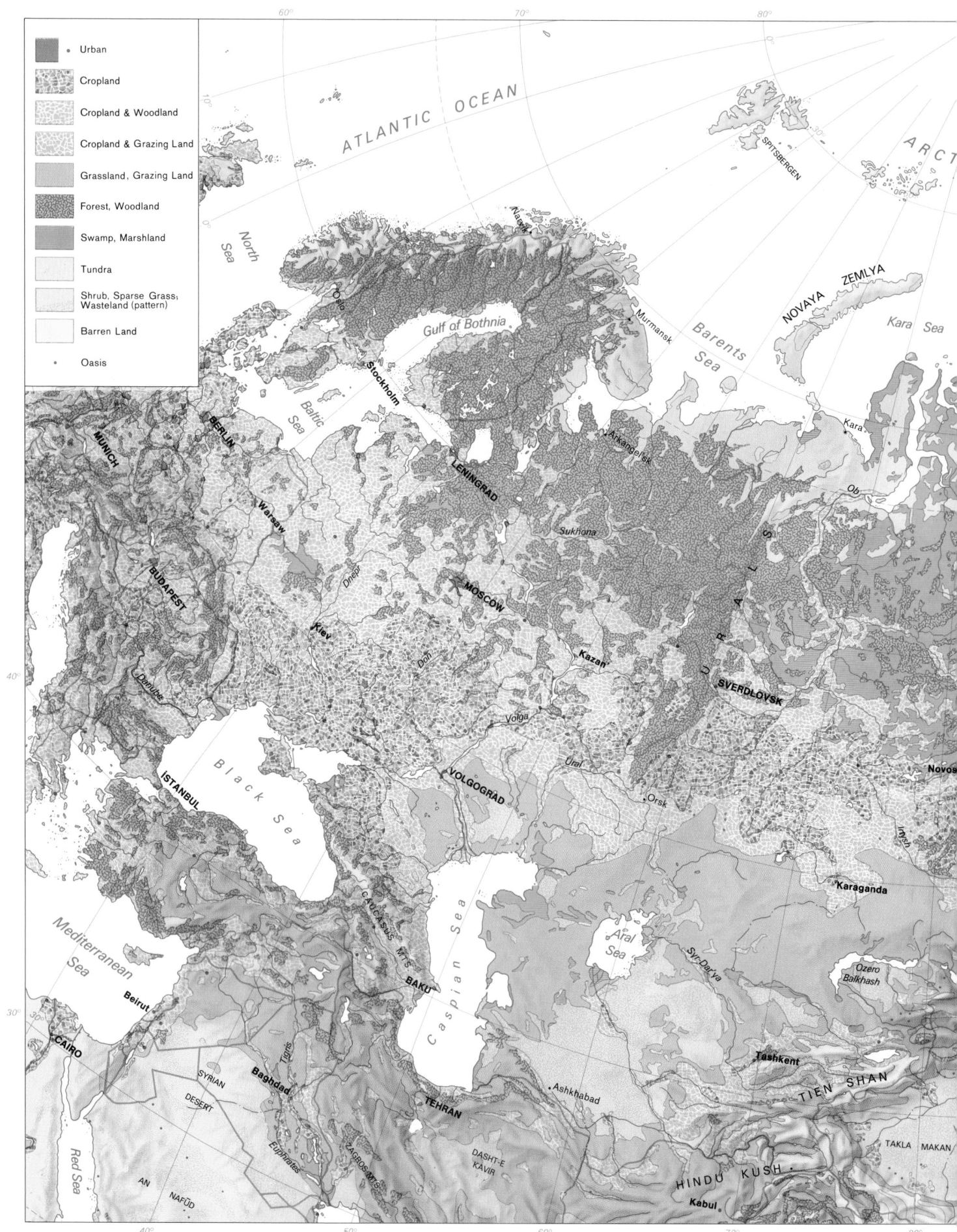

Urban

Cropland

Cropland & Woodland

Cropland & Grazing Land

Grassland, Grazing Land

Forest, Woodland

Swamp, Marshland

Tundra

Shrub, Sparse Grass;
Wasteland (pattern)

Barren Land

Oasis

ATLANTIC OCEAN

SPITSBERGEN

ARCT

NOVAYA ZEMLYA

Kara Sea

North Sea

Barents Sea

Murmansk

Oslo

Gulf of Bothnia

Narvik

Stockholm

Baltic Sea

Arkangelsk

Kara

Ob

BERLIN

MUNICH

Warsaw

LENINGRAD

Sukhona

U
R
A
L
S

MOSCOW

BUDAPEST

Dnepr

Kiev

Don

Kazan

SVERDLOVSK

Danube

Volga

Ural

Orsk

Novos

ISTANBUL

Black Sea

VOLGOGRAD

Karaganda

Irtish

CAUCASUS Mts.

Caspian Sea

Aral Sea

Syr-Dar'ya

Ozero
Balkhash

Mediterranean Sea

Beirut

BAKU

TEHRAN

Tashkent

TIEN SHAN

CAIRO

SYRIAN DESERT

Baghdad

Tigris

Ashkhabad

DASHT-E KAVIR

Red Sea

Euphrates

AN NAFŪD

ZAGROS MTS.

TAKLA MAKAN

HINDU KUSH

Kabul

Scale 1:24,000,000; one inch to 380 miles. Lambert Azimuthal Equal-Area Projection

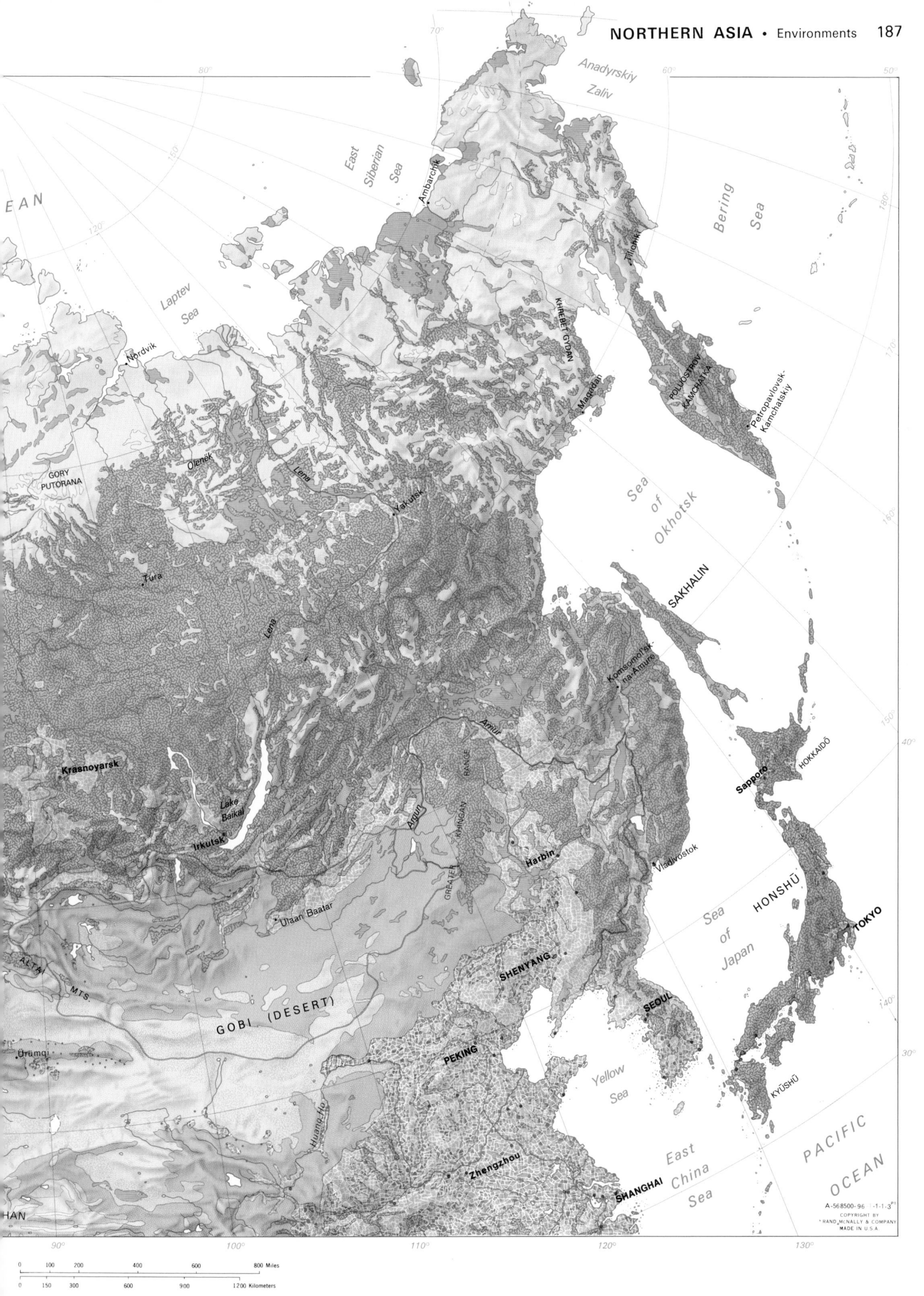

70°
80°
60°
50°

Anadyrskiy
Zaliv

East
Siberian
Sea

Ambarchik

150°

Bering
Sea

120°

Laptev
Sea

180°

EAN

170°

Pilginki

Nordvik

KHREBET GYDAN

POLUOSTROV
KAMCHATKA

Magadan

Petropavlovsk-
Kamchatskiy

160°

GORY
PUTORANA

Olenek

Lena

Yakutsk

Sea
of
Okhotsk

Tura

SAKHALIN

Lena

150°

Komsomol'sk
na-Amure

HOKKAIDŌ

40°

Krasnoyarsk

Amur

Sapporo

Lake
Baikal

RANGE

Irkutsk

Argun

KHINGAN

Harbin

Vladivostok

HONSHŪ

Uaan Baatar

GREATER

Sea
of
Japan

TOKYO

ALTAI
MTS.

SHENYANG

40°

GOBI (DESERT)

SEOUL

Ürümqi

30°

PEKING

Yellow
Sea

KYŪSHŪ

130°

Huang Ho

Zhengzhou

East
China
Sea

PACIFIC

HAN

SHANGHAI

OCEAN

A-568500-96 1-1-3
COPYRIGHT BY
RAND McNALLY & COMPANY
MADE IN U.S.A.

90°
100°
110°
120°

0 100 200   400   600   800 Miles
0 150 300   600   900   1200 Kilometers

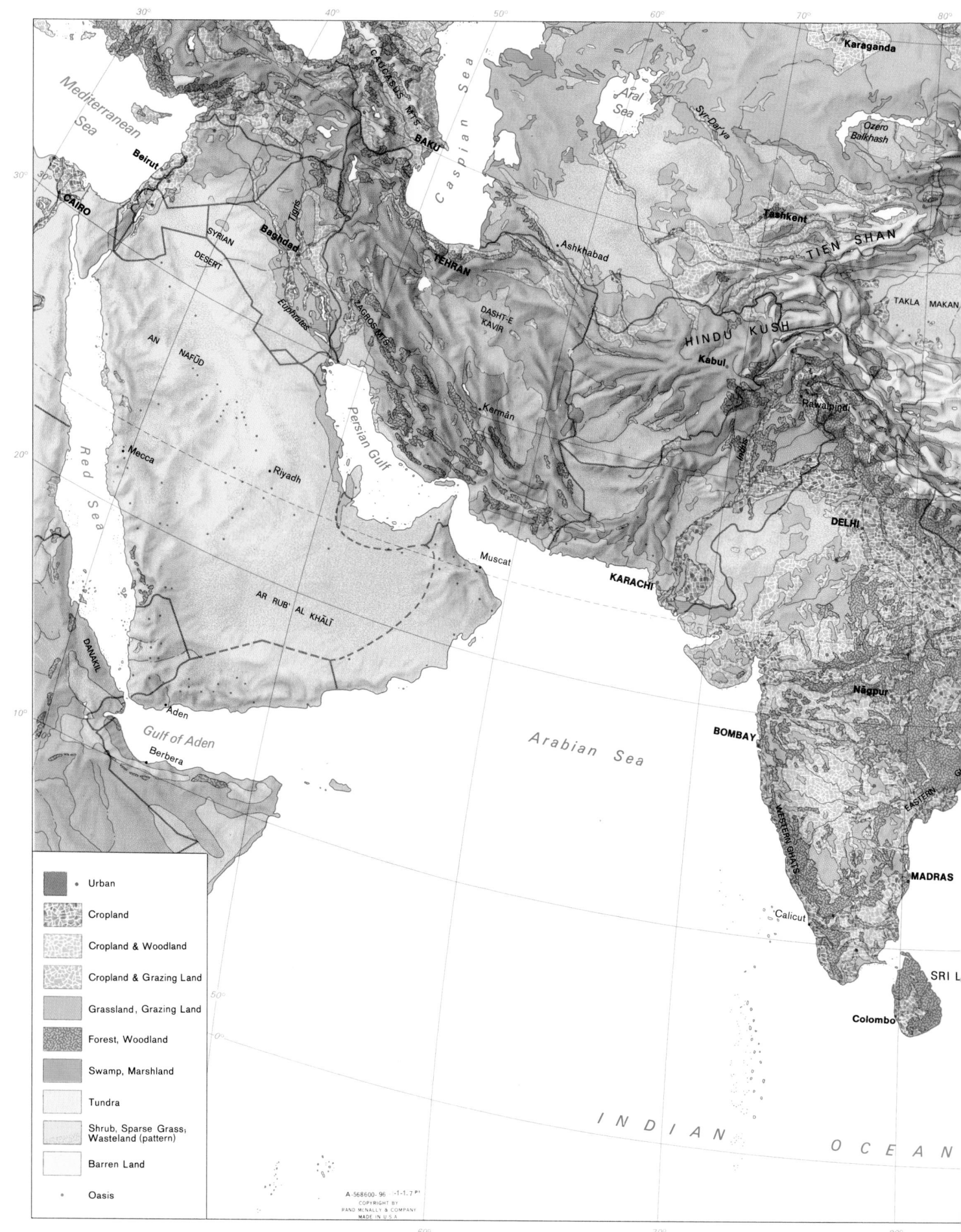

Mediterranean Sea

Beirut

CAIRO

30°

SYRIAN DESERT

Baghdad

Tigris

Euphrates

ZAGROS MTS

AN NAFŪD

Red Sea

Mecca

Riyadh

Persian Gulf

20°

DANAKIL

AR RUB' AL KHĀLĪ

Aden

Gulf of Aden

Berbera

10°

CAUCASUS MTS

BAKU

Caspian Sea

Aral Sea

Syr-Darya

Karaganda

Ozero Balkhash

Tashkent

TIEN SHAN

TAKLA MAKAN

Ashkhabad

TEHRAN

DASHT-E KAVIR

HINDU KUSH

Kabul

Kermān

Rawalpindi

Indus

DELHI

Muscat

KARACHI

Nāgpur

BOMBAY

Arabian Sea

WESTERN GHATS

EASTERN G

MADRAS

Calicut

SRI L

Colombo

INDIAN OCEAN

	Urban
	Cropland
	Cropland & Woodland
	Cropland & Grazing Land
	Grassland, Grazing Land
	Forest, Woodland
	Swamp, Marshland
	Tundra
	Shrub, Sparse Grass, Wasteland (pattern)
	Barren Land
•	Oasis

Scale 1:24,000,000, one inch to 380 miles. Lambert Azimuthal Equal-Area Projection

ALTAI MTS.

Ulaan Baatar

GOBI (DESERT)

Ürümqi

HAN

Huang He

TIBET

MALAYAS

Brahmaputra

Mekong

ges

LCUTTA

Mandalay

Salween

Bay of Bengal

Rangoon

Andaman Sea

BANGKOK

Medan

SUMATRA

SINGAPORE

Equator

GREATER KHINGAN RA.

Harbin

SHENYANG

PEKING

Zhengzhou

WUHAN

CHONGQING

Kunming

Hanoi

CANTON

HAINAN DAO

Mekong

HO CHI MINH CITY

Kuching

Vladivostok

Sea of Japan

HONSHŪ

TOKYO

SEOUL

Yellow Sea

East China Sea

KYŪSHŪ

PACIFIC OCEAN

SHANGHAI

T'aipei

Tropic of Cancer

TAIWAN

Philippine Sea

MANILA

Cebu

MINDANAO

South China Sea

Celebes Sea

Kota Kinabalu

Manado

BORNEO

CELEBES

Ujung Pandang

JAKARTA

JAVA

Java Sea

40°

30°

20°

10°

0°

10°

140°

140°

130°

120°

90°

100°

0   100   200   400   600   800 Miles

0   150   300   600   900   1200 Kilometers

ATLANTIC OCEAN

ARCTIC OCEAN

North Pole

GREENLAND (Den.)

Meridian of Greenwich

Arctic Circle

ICELAND

BARENTS SEA

SVALBARD (Spitsbergen) (Nor.)

ZEMLYA FRANTSA IOSIFA (FRANZ JOSEF LAND)

NOVAYA ZEMLYA

SEVERNAYA ZEMLYA (NORTHERN LAND)

KARA SEA

LAPTEV SEA

LISBON

MADRID

C. DE SÃO VICENTE

C. DE FINISTERRE

BIRMINGHAM

LONDON

Edinburgh

Liverpool

COPENHAGEN

HAMBURG

STOCKHOLM

Oslo

Bergen

SCANDINAVIAN PENINSULA

Helsinki

Gulf of Bothnia

Arkhangel'sk (Archangel)

SOVIET

PARIS

BERLIN

WARSAW

PRAGUE

VIENNA

BUDAPEST

ROME

NAPLES

MOSCOW

LENINGRAD

GOR'KIY

Perm

Kazan

KUYBYSHEV

SVERDLOVSK

Tobol'sk

SIBERIA

UNION

BELGRADE

BUCHAREST

ISTANBUL

ATHENS

DONETSK

Odessa

Rostov-na-Donu

KIEV

Astrakhan

CASPIAN DEPRESSION

KARGHIZ STEPPE

Orenburg

Omsk

Tomsk

Krasnoyarsk

NOVOSIBIRSK

Tselinograd

Semipalatinsk

SAYAN

Irkutsk

ALGIERS

Tunis

ATLAS MTS

MEDITERRANEAN SEA

TURKEY

Ankara

Izmir

CYPRUS

SYRIA

Tbilisi

BAKU

TURKESTAN

Ozero Balkhash

Alma-Ata

TIEN SHAN

ALTAI MTS

MONGOLIA

Ulan Bator

ALEXANDRIA

CAIRO

Jerusalem

ISRAEL

LEB.

Beirut

Damascus

IRAQ

Baghdad

TEHRAN

Tabriz

Ashkhabad

Mashhad

Bukhara

Samarkand

TASHKENT

Kokand

Dushanbe

PAMIRS

Kashi

Shache

TARIM BASIN

TAKLA MAKAN (DESERT)

ALTUN SHAN

KUNLUN SHAN

PLATEAU OF TIBET

CHINA

Lanzhou

LIBYAN DESERT

Suez

Amman

JORDAN

Al Başrah

IRAN

Eşfahān

Kuwait

Shiraz

Kerman

Herat

Kābul

Peshāwar

AFGHANISTAN

Quetta

HINDU KUSH

Srinagar

Rawalpindi

Islāmābād

KARAKORAM

LAHORE

Khartoum

Mitsiwa

Jiddah

Mecca

Al Madinah

NAJD

Riyadh

AL HASA

QATAR

UNITED ARAB EMIRATES

OMAN

Muscat

KARĀCHI

PAKISTAN

DELHI

New Delhi

GREAT INDIAN DESERT

Āgra

KANPUR

Kathmandu

NEPAL

Everest

BHUTAN

Lhasa

CHENGDU

CHONGQING

KUNMING

San'a

YEMEN

P.D.R. OF YEMEN

Aden

Gulf of Aden

Berbera

ETHIOPIAN PLATEAU

Addis Ababa

SOCOTRA (P.D.R. of Yemen)

ARABIAN SEA

BOMBAY

HYDERĀBĀD

DECCAN

Nāgpur

Ahmadābād

INDIA

Allahābād

Vāranāsi

Patna

Dacca

BNGL

CALCUTTA

Mandalay

BURMA

Rangoon

THAI

BANGKOK (Krung Thep)

Moulmein

BANGALORE

MADRAS

Coimbatore

Calicut

Madurai

CAPE COMORIN

SRI LANKA (CEYLON)

Colombo

LAKSHADWEEP (India)

MALDIVES

ANDAMAN ISLANDS (India)

NICOBAR ISLANDS (India)

George Town

Banda Aceh

SUMATRA

INDIAN OCEAN

BAY OF BENGAL

Equator

Tropic of Cancer

Continued on page 222

Relief

Meters		Feet
3050		10 000
1525		5000
610		2000
305		1000
0	Sea Level	0
		Below Sea Level
152.5		500
1525		5000
3050		10 000
6100		20 000

A-519695-76- -13-11 24

COPYRIGHT BY
RAND McNALLY & COMPANY
MADE IN U.S.A.

Longitude East of Greenwich

Scale 1:40 000 000; one inch to 630 miles. Lambert's Azimuthal, Equal Area Projection
Elevations and depressions are given in feet

NORTH AMERICA

Bering Str.

M. DEZHNEVA
(EAST CAPE)

PRIBILOF IS.
(USA)

ST. LAWRENCE

Arctic Circle

ALEUTIAN ISLANDS
(USA)

ALEUTIAN TRENCH

BERING SEA

KORYAKSKIY KHREBET

KOMANDORSKIYE OSTROVA
(Sov. Union)

West Longitude

East Longitude

Petropavlovsk-
Kamchatskiy

SEA OF OKHOTSK

M. LOPATKA

KURIL ISLANDS
(Sov. Union)

SAKHALIN

HOKKAIDO TRENCH

Okhotsk

Komsomolsk

Sovétskaya Gavan'

Khabarovsk

Blagoveshchensk

Vladivostok

Komsomolsk

Tatar Strait

SIKHOTE-ALIN'

Hakodate

Sendai

HONSHU

TOKYO
YOKOHAMA

KYOTO
OSAKA
KOBE

SHIKOKU

JAPAN

Nagasaki

KYUSHU

NANSEI SHOTO

PACIFIC OCEAN

Tropic of Cancer

MANCHURIA

HARBIN

CHANGCHUN

SHENYANG

Zhangjiakou

TIANJIN

Jinan

QINGDAO

TAIYUAN

NANJING

SHANGHAI

WUHAN

KITAKYUSHU

CHINA

EAST CHINA SEA

P'YONGYANG

NORTH KOREA

SEOUL

SOUTH KOREA

Bo Hai

Lüda

Jilin

STANOVOY KHREBET

NAN LING

Fuzhou

Xiamen

Shantou

CANTON

HONG KONG (Br.)

Macao (Port.)

HAINAN DAO

TAIPEI

TAIWAN
(FORMOSA)

Taiwan Strait

PHILIPPINE SEA

LUZON

Quezon City

MANILA

MINDORO

SAMAR

LEYTE

PANAY

NEGROS

PALAWAN

MINDANAO

PHILIPPINES

SULU SEA

PHILIPPINE TRENCH

CELEBES SEA

Kota Kinabalu

Sandakan

BRUNEI

MALAYSIA

Kuching

BORNEO

CELEBES

NEW GUINEA

HALMAHERA

Equator

SOUTH CHINA SEA

HO CHI MINH CITY
(Saigon)

Penh

CYPRUS

Néa Páfos

Episkopi

Lemesós

Lárnax

Kólpos
Lárnakos

AKR. PIDÁLION

AKR. GÁTAS

Ólimbos
6401

Longitude 35° East of Greenwich 36°

Halba

Tarābulus
(Tripoli)

Al Qusayr

Al Hirmil

Zgharta

Al Batrūn

Amyūn

LEBANON

Jubayl (Byblos)

Ba'labakk

Beirut
(Bayrūt)

Zahlah

Ad Dāmūr

Az Zabdānī

Şaydā
(Sidon)

Jazzīn

Rāshayyā

Damascus
(Dimashq)

Dūmā

Şūr
(Tyre)

Marj 'Uyūn

Al Kiswah

Qiryat Shemona

SYRIA

Tibnin

Al Qunaytirah

Nahariyya

'Akko

Zefat

As Sanamayn

MEDITERRANEAN SEA

Haifa
(Hefa)

Teverya

Dar'ā

Nazerat

Irbid

'Afula

Bet She'an

Al Mafraq

Hadera

Tulkarm

Jenin

Jarash

Netanya

Shechem
(Ruins)

Nābulus

As Salt

Herzliyya

Petah Tiqwa

Az Zarqā'

Tel Aviv-Yafo

Rishon leZiyyon

Lod

Amman

Rehovot

Jerusalem

Jericho

Madabā

Ashdod

Bayt Lahm
(Bethlehem)

Zuwayza

Ashqelon

Qiryat Gat

Dhibān

Gaza
(Ghazzah)

Al Khalīl
(Hebron)

Al Mazra'ah

Maḩaṭṭat al Qaṭrānah

Khān Yūnus

Be'er Sheva

Arad

Al Karak

Rafah

Dimona

Al Mazār

Sedom

At Ṭafīlah

The Gaza Strip and West Bank areas are occupied by Israel. Status undetermined.

Port Said (Būr Sa'īd)

Khalīj aţ
Tinah

Sabkhat al
Bardawil

Mahaṭṭat Jurf
ad Darāwīsh

Al 'Arish

Ḩorʼot Shiva
(Ruins)

Ma'ān

Qezi'ot

Petra
(Ruins)

Rummānah

Ash Shawbak

Wādī Mūsā

Al Qanṭarah

Al Qusaymah

QA' AL JAFR

Daphnae
(Ruins)

Ismailia
(Al Ismā'īlīyah)

NEGEV

Fā'id

Ra's Abū Qurūn

JABAL
YU 'ALLIQ

JORDAN

Great Bitter
Lake

Suez
(As Suways)

MITLA PASS

EGYPT

Al Kuntillah

Ra's an Naqb

An Nakhl

Ath Thamad

Mahaṭṭat
'Aqabat al Ḩijāzīyah

JABAL
JALĀLAH
AL BAHRĪYAH

Elat

Al 'Aqaba

Mahaṭṭat
ar Ramlah

Bi'r Za farānah

Abū Zanīmah

Ra's al Junaynah

SAUDI ARABIA

JABAL AT TĪH

JABAL AL 'AJMAH

Nuwaybi' al
Muzayyinah

JABAL MAZHAFAH

Scale 1:4 000 000

JABAL AL JALĀLAT
AL QIBLĪYAH

SINAI PEN
(SHIBH JAZĪRAT SĪNĀ)

Haql

Scale 1:4 000 000

Kuala Lumpur

Kelang

Kajang

PAHANG

Kuala Klawang

Gunung Telapa

SELANGOR

Bahau

Telok Datok

Rembau

NEGERI SEMBILAN

Seremban

Rompin

Gemas

Padang Endau

TIOMAN

Gunong Kajang
3444

PEMANGGIL

Sepang

Rantau

Tampin

Segamat

Gunong Besar

Mersing

AUR

Port Dickson

CAPE RACHADO

Alor Gajah

Jasin

Labis

SOUTH

Mt Ophir
4187

MALAYSIA

Paloh

TINGGI

Melaka
(Malacca)

Panchor

MALAY

Bandar
Maharani

JOHOR

Keluang

Gunong Blumut

PENINSULA

STRAIT OF MALACCA

TANJONG
TOHOR

Rengam

Batu
Pahat

Ayer
Hitam

Layang Layang

Kota Tinggi

SOUTH CHINA SEA

Jumrah

RUPAT

Teluklecak

Batupanjang

Pontian Kechil

Johor
Baharu

TANJONG
RAMUNIA

Dumai

SINGAPORE

SINGAPORE

Bengkalis

BENGKALIS

TANJONG PIAI

KARIMUN
BESAR

Philip Channel

Singapore Strait

TANJUNG
BERAKIT

Kudap

Ketamputih

BATAM

SUMATRA

Telesung

KEPULAUAN RIAU

Pinggir

Tanjungbalai

Tanjungpinang

BINTAN

RIAU

PADANG

REMPANG

INDONESIA

Minas

Buatan

Siaksriindrapura

KUNDUR

Baranpauh

Serangung

Selat Riau

MARMARA DENIZI
Marmara Denizi
Troy (Ruins)
İstanbul Boğazı (Bosporus)
Üsküdar
ISTANBUL
Mithilini
İzmir
Bergama
Balıkesir
Bursa
Kütahya
Eskişehir
Afyon
Aydın
Muğla
İsparta
Eğridir Gölü
Konya
RHODOS
MEDITERRANEAN SEA
CYPRUS
Nicosia

BLACK SEA

Zonguldak
Kastamonu
Sinop
Samsun
Giresun
Trabzon
Çankırı
Merzifon
Çorum
Yozgat
Tokat
Sivas
Ankara
Kayseri
TOROS DAĞLAR
Mersin
Adana
Tarsus
İskenderun
Antakya
Maraş
Malatya
Elâzığ
Diyarbakır
Siverek
Mardin
Cizre
Urfa
Gaziantep
Al Lādhiqīyah (Latakia)
Ḥamāh
Ḥimş
TURKEY
KURDISTAN

CAUCASUS MTS.
Ordzhonikidze
Grozny
Makhachkala
Kutaisi
Poti
Batumi
GEORGIAN S.S.R.
Tbilisi
Leninakan
Kars
Kirovabad
ARMENIAN S.S.R.
Yerevan
AZERBAIJAN S.S.R.
Baku
Erzurum
Erzincan
Van Gölü
Van
Bitlis
Rawanduz
Tabriz
Ardabīl
Khvoy
Orūmīyeh
Miāneh
Lenkoran

SOVIET
Fort Shevchenko
KAZAK
CASPIAN SEA
Surface 92 feet below Sea Level
Krasnovodsk
Nebit-Dag
Bandar-e Anzali
Rasht
Bandar-e Torkeman
Gorgān

KAZAK
MANGYSHLAK
PLATO UST-URT
Aral
Kungrad
Chimbay
Nukus
Turtkul
Khiva
TURKESTAN
PESKI KYZYL KUM (DESERT)
PESKI KARAKUMY (DESERT)
TURKMEN S.S.R.
Chardzhou
Ashkhabad
KOPPEH DAĞH
Bojnūrd
Mary
Kushka

Aleppo
Dayr az Zawr
As Sulaymānīyah
Irbil
Kirkūk
Mosul
As
Nineveh
Tikrīt
Abū Kamāl
Palmyra (Ruins)
SYRIA
Damascus (Dimashq)
As Suwaydā
Al Mawşil
Zanjān
Sanandaj
Hamadān
Bakhtarān
Qom
TEHRAN
ELBURZ MTS.
Qolleh-ye Damāvand
Dāmghān
Neyshābūr
Mashhad
Bābol

Şaydā (Sidon)
LEBANON
Beirut
Haifa
Tel Aviv-Yafo
ISRAEL
Jerusalem
Gaza
Al Turayf
Amman
JORDAN
Ar Ramādī
BAGHDAD
Karbalā
An Najaf
Babylon (Ruins)
Borūjerd
Arāk
Kāshān
DASHT-E KAVĪR DESERT
Bejestan
Ferdows

Tarābulus (Tripoli)
Rashid
Damietta
Port Said
ALEXANDRIA (Al Iskandarīyah)
CAIRO (Al Qāhirah)
Suez (As Suwayş)
SINAI PEN.
Jabal Katrīnā 8651
IRAQ
Dezfūl
Shūshtar
Masjed Soleymān
Ahvāz
Khorramshahr
Abādān
Esfahān
Shahreżā
Yazd
Bāfq
PLATEAU OF IRAN
(DASHT-E LŪT DESERT)
Qāyen
Bīrjand
Farāh
AFGH

Bür Safājah
Al Quşayr
An Nafūd
Taymā
JABAL SHAMMAR
Ḥā'il
Khaybar
Al Jawf
Sakākah
Rafḥā
Al Qayşūmah
AD DAHNĀ
An Nāşirīyah
Al Başrah
Neutral Zone
KUWAIT
Kuwait (Al Kuwayt)
Būshehr
PERSIAN GULF
Kāzerūn
Shīrāz
Borāzjān
Daryācheh-ye Bakhtegān
Jahrom
Lār
Kermān
Rafsanjān
Zāhedān
Rīgān
Bampūr
Khāsh
CHĀG
GULF OF OMAN

EGYPT
Al Madīnah (Medina)
Yanbu
SAUDI NAJD
Burayadah
Unayzah
Sudayr
Ash Shagrā
Riyadh (Ar Riyāḑ)
AL HASA
Dammām
Al Qaţīf
Az Zahrān (Dhahran)
BAHRAIN
Al Manāmah
Al Hufūf
QATAR
Ad Dawhah
Abū Zaby
UNITED ARAB EMIRATES
Al Buraymī
Bandar-e Lengeh
Qeshm
Bandar 'Abbās
Jāsk
OMAN
Ajman
Dubayy
Al Khābūrah
Matrah
Muscat
JABAL AL AKHDAR
Jabal ash Sham
CHĀH BAHĀR
Gwādar

Jiddah
Mecca (Makkah)
Aţ Ţā'if
AL HIJAZ
AL AFLAJ
Ad Dilam
Nafūd Al Mubarraz
NAFŪD AD DAHY
JABAL TUWAYQ
Al Khurmah
Al Lidām
Wādī ad Dawāsir
ARABIA
AR RUB' AL KHĀLĪ
RAS AL HADD
Şūr
OMAN
RAS AL MADRAKAH

SUDAN
Bür Sūdān
Sawākin
Tawkar
Al Qunfudhah
Abhā
Qal'at Bīshah
ASĪR
NAJRAN
RAMLAT AS SAB'ATAYN
Najran
Shibām
Tarīm
Say'ūn
HADRAMAWT
KHŪRYĀN MŪRYĀN (Oman)
Mirbāt
RAS FARTAK

Tropic of Cancer

Kassalā
Keren
Mitsiwa (Massawa)
Akordat
Barentu
Asmera
Adi Ugri
ETHIOPIA
Qizān
Abū 'Arīsh
JAZĀ'IR FARASĀN
Sa'dah
Şan'ā
DAHLAK ARCH.
KAMARAN (P.D.R. of Yem.)
Al Luḥayyah
YEMEN
Al Hudaydah
Al Mukhā (Mocha)
Madīnat ash Sha'b
Aden ('Adan)
P.D.R. OF YEMEN
Al Hawtah
Shuqrah
Ash Shiḥr
Al Mukallā
Sayḥūt
Ghaydah
SUQUTRA (SOCOTRA) (P.D.R. of Yemen)
Hadībū

Sebderat
DENAKIL
Ed
Beylul
DJIBOUTI
Tadjoura
Djibouti
Aysha
Dese
Seylac
GULF OF ADEN
Caluula
CASEYR
Berbera
Lass Qoray
SOMALIA

A-569400-76 13·10·25 P
COPYRIGHT BY
RAND McNALLY & COMPANY
MADE IN U.S.A.

Continued on pages 224–225

ADMINISTR. BDY.

The Gaza Strip and West Bank areas are occupied by Israel. Status undetermined.

Relief

Meters	Feet
3050	10 000
1525	5000
610	2000
305	1000
152.5	500
0 Sea Level	0 Sea Level
152.5	500
1525	5000
3050	10 000

Below Sea Level

Ⓐ Area occupied by Pakistan and claimed by India.
Ⓑ Area occupied by India and claimed by Pakistan.
Ⓒ Area occupied by China and claimed by India and Pakistan.
Ⓓ Area occupied by China and claimed by India.
Ⓔ Area occupied by India and claimed by China.

Longitude East of Greenwich

Scale 1:16 000 000; one inch to 250 miles. Polyconic Projection
Elevations and depressions are given in feet

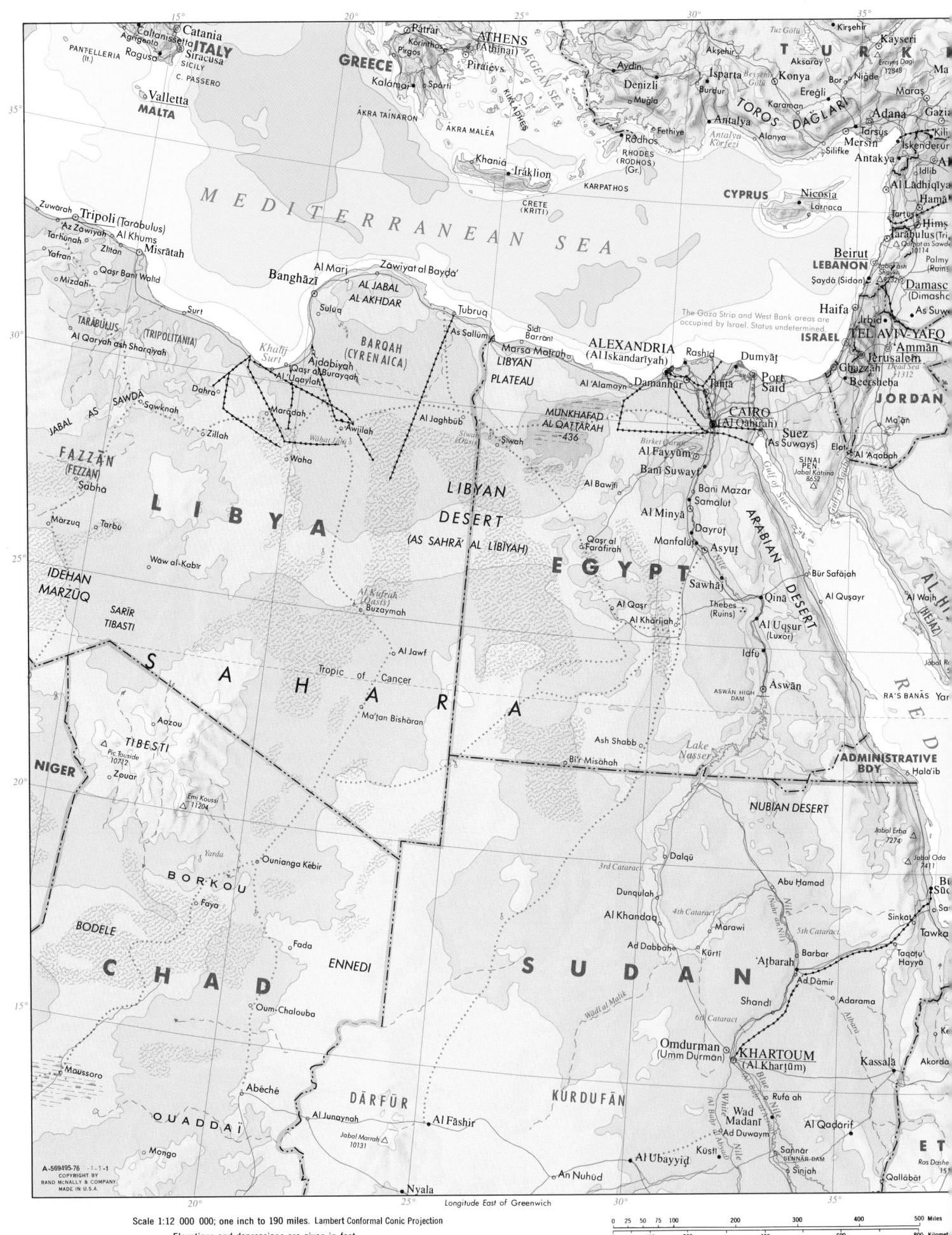

Scale 1:12 000 000; one inch to 190 miles. Lambert Conformal Conic Projection

Elevations and depressions are given in feet

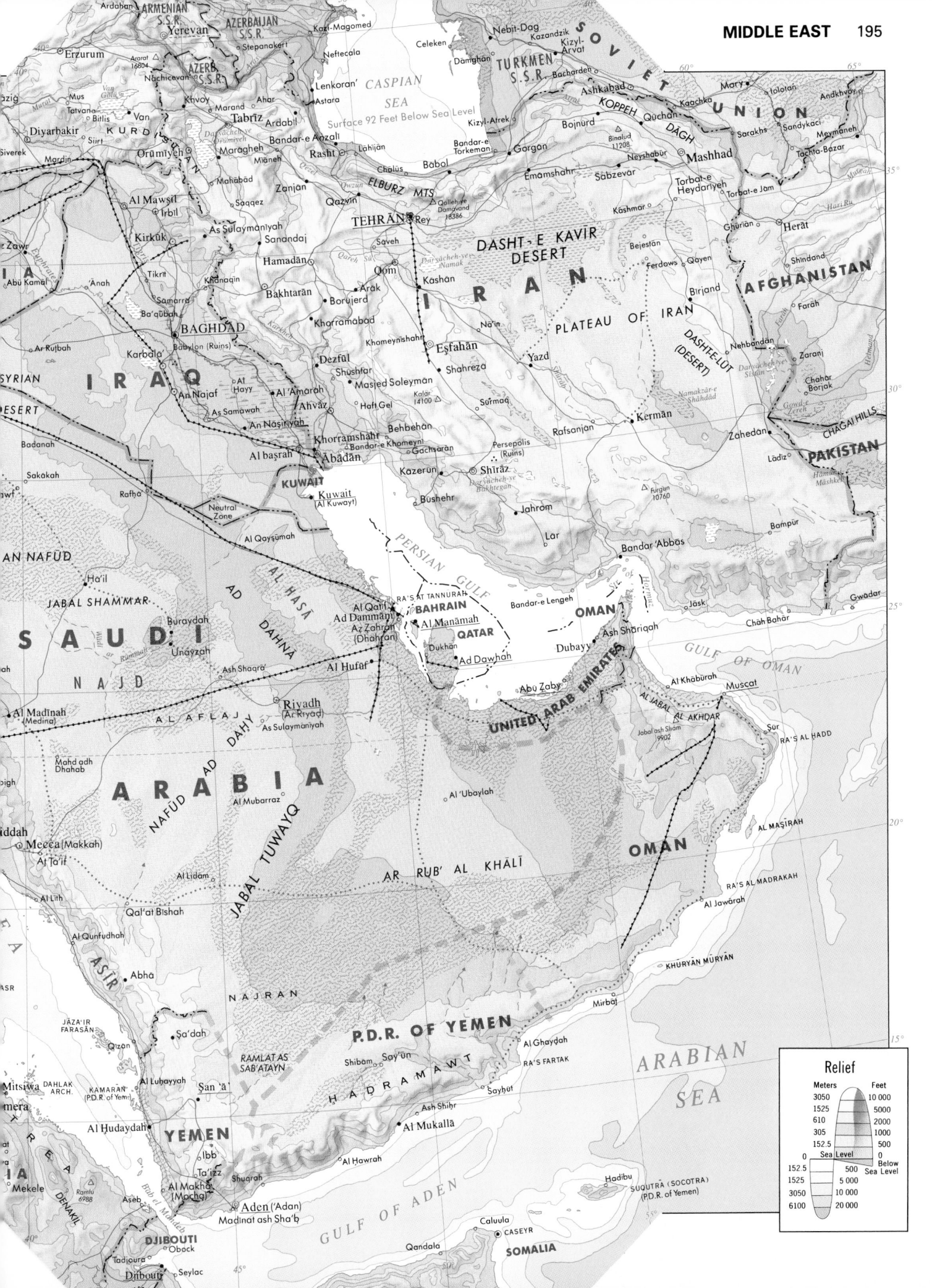

Relief

Meters	Feet
3050	10 000
1525	5000
610	2000
305	1000
152.5	500
0 Sea Level	0 Below Sea Level
152.5	500
1525	5 000
3050	10 000
6100	20 000

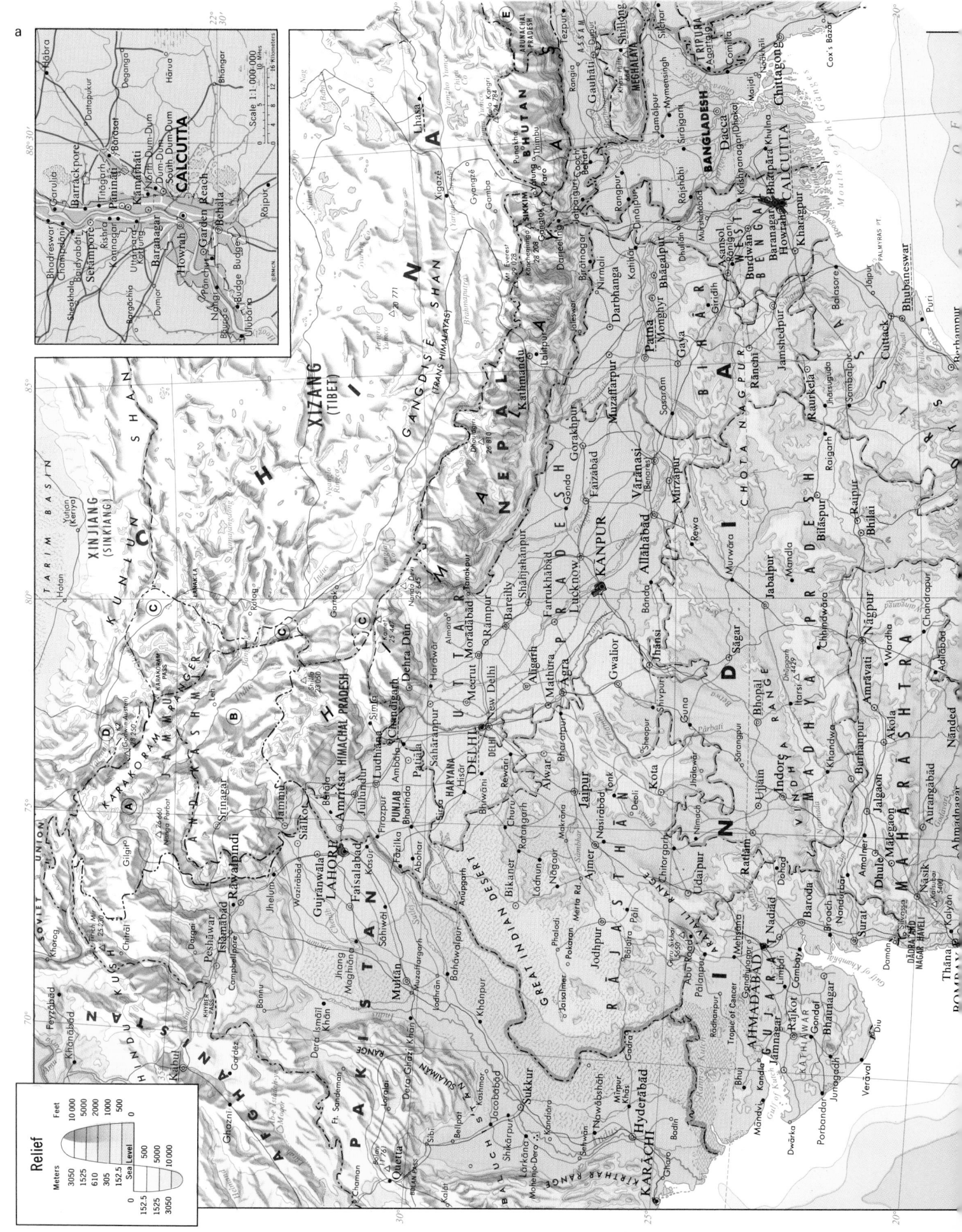

a

CALCUTTA

Scale 1:1 000 000

Relief

Meters	Feet
3050	10 000
1525	5000
610	2000
305	1000
152.5	500
Sea Level	0
	Sea Level
152.5	500
1525	5000
3050	10 000

Scale 1:10 000 000; one inch to 160 miles. Lambert Conformal Conic Projection
Elevations and depressions are given in feet

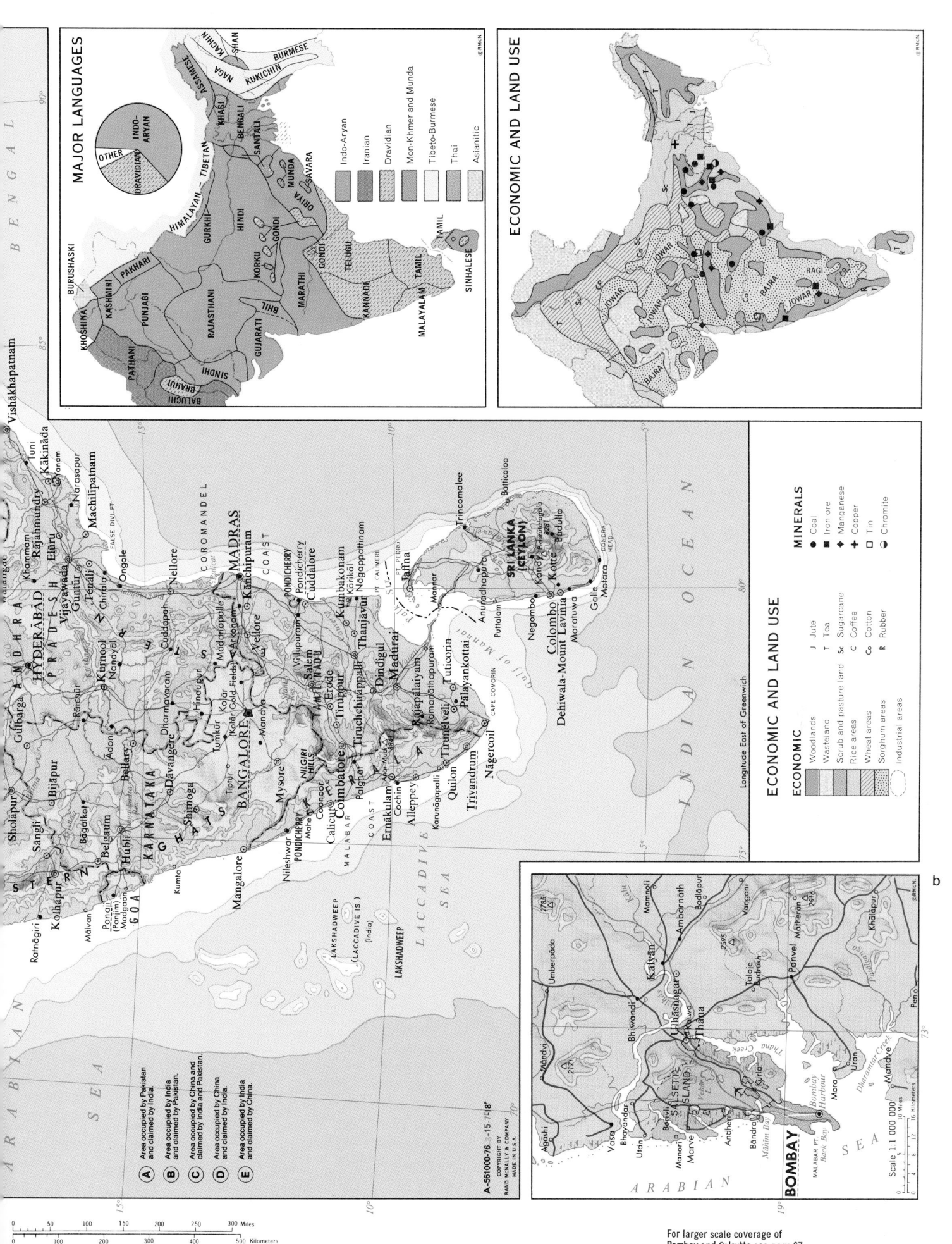

For larger scale coverage of
Bombay and Calcutta see page 67.

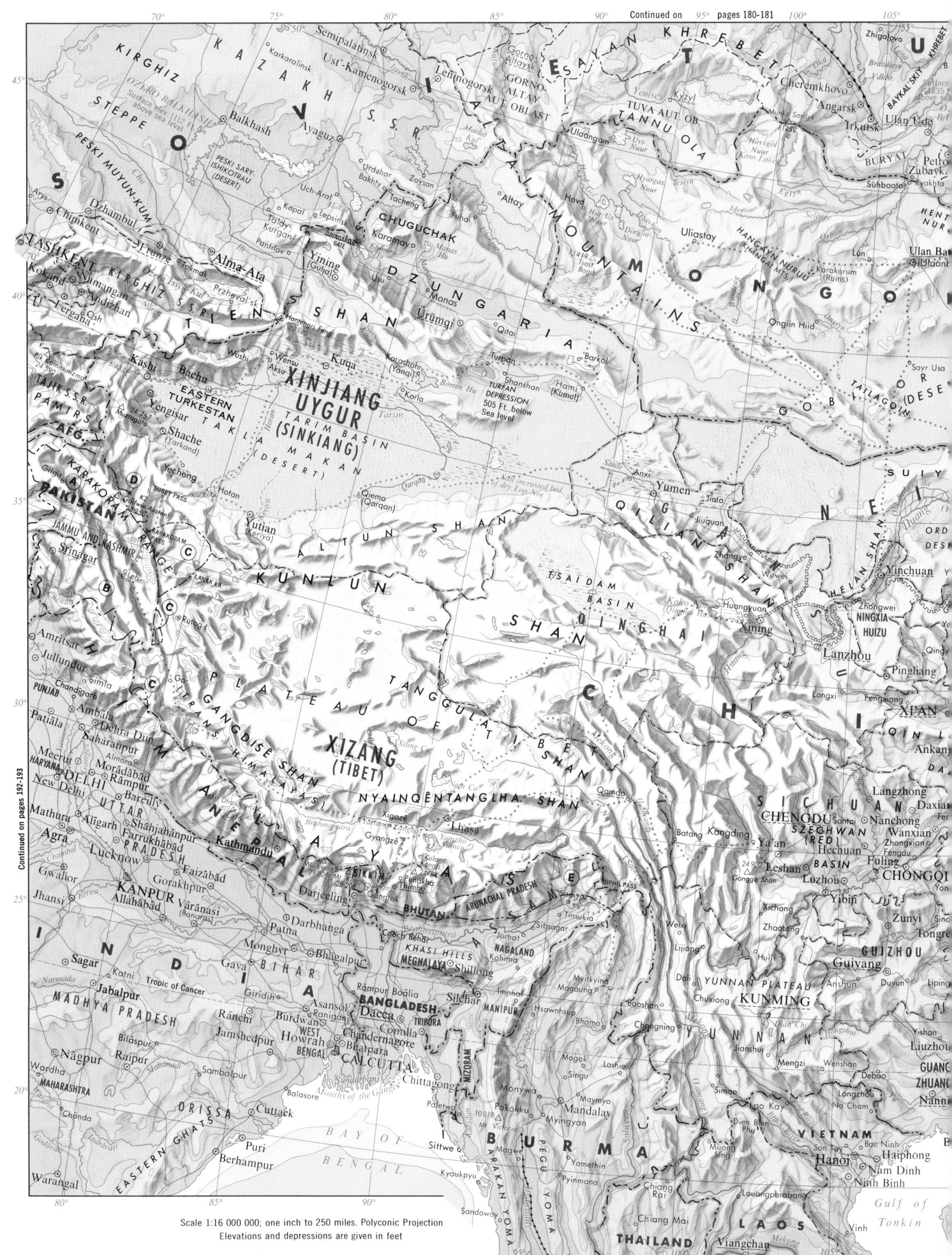

Continued on 95° pages 180-181

Scale 1:16 000 000; one inch to 250 miles. Polyconic Projection
Elevations and depressions are given in feet

Chinese Provinces,
Autonomous Regions (AR)
and Municipalities (M)

Conventional Form — Pinyin Form

Conventional Form	Pinyin Form
Anhwei	Anhui
Chekiang	Zhejiang
Fukien	Fujian
Heilungkiang	Heilongjiang
Honan	Henan
Hopeh	Hebei
Hunan	Hunan
Hupeh	Hubei
Inner Mongolia (AR)	Nei Monggol
Kansu	Gansu
Kiangsi	Jiangxi
Kiangsu	Jiangsu
Kirin	Jilin
Kwangsi (AR)	Guangxi Zhuangzu
Kwangtung	Guangdong
Kweichow	Guizhou
Liaoning	Liaoning
Ningsia Hui (AR)	Ningxia Huizu
Peking (M)	Beijing
Shanghai (M)	Shanghai
Shansi	Shanxi
Shantung	Shandong
Shensi	Shaanxi
Sinkiang (AR)	Xinjiang Uygur
Szechwan	Sichuan
Tibet (AR)	Xizang
Tientsin (M)	Tianjin
Tsinghai	Qinghai
Yunnan	Yunnan

Ⓐ Area occupied by Pakistan and claimed by India.

Ⓑ Area occupied by India and claimed by Pakistan.

Ⓒ Area occupied by India and claimed by India and Pakistan.

Ⓓ Area occupied by China and claimed by India.

Ⓔ Area occupied by India and claimed by China.

Habomai, Shikotan, Kunashiri and Etorofu, occupied by the U.S.S.R. since 1945, are claimed by Japan pending a final peace treaty.

Relief

Meters	Feet
3050	10 000
1525	5000
610	2000
305	1000
152.5	500
Sea Level	0
152.5	Below Sea Level
1525	500
3050	5000
6100	10 000
	20 000

A-569700-76 -12-9-20P
COPYRIGHT BY
RAND MCNALLY & COMPANY
MADE IN U.S.A.

Cities and Towns

0 to 50,000 ○   500,000 to 1,000,000 ◎
50,000 to 500,000 ⊙   1,000,000 and over

Continued on pages 206-207

Longitude East of Greenwich

0 50 100 200 300 400 500 Miles
0 100 200 300 400 600 800 Kilometers

Relief

Meters	Feet
1525	5000
610	2000
305	1000
152.5	500
0 Sea Level	0

LIAONING

Xincheng
JUHUA DAO
Gaixian
Xiongyuecheng
LIAODONG
WAN
Suizhong
Qianwei
3714
LIAODONG
Qianwei
LIAONING
Xiheying
BEIJING
SHI
Shunyi Zhanggezhuang
Haidian PEKING
(Beijing)
Tongxian
Xianghe
Baodi
Zhuoxian
Caiyu
Anci
Huanghuadian Wangqingtuo
TIANJIN
TIANJIN
SHI
Gegu
Dagu
Tanggu

Sanhe
Jixian
Yutian
Zunhua
Jianchangying
Lulong
Fuzhoucheng
Fuxian
Shanhaiguan
Qinhuangdao
Changli
TANGSHAN
Leting
HEBEI
Luanxian
Fening
Guye
Fengrun
Yahongqiao
Ninghe

CHANGXING DAO
XIZHONG DAO
FENGMING DAO

Fuxian
Xinjin
DACHANGSHAN
DAO
GUANGLU
DAO
ZHANGZI DAO
Jinzhou Wan
Lüshun
Lüda
Dalian Wan
Jinxian
CHANGSHAN
QUNDAO

Xiheying
Dingxing
Gucheng
Wanxian
Tangxian
Baoding
Renqiu
Baiyang
Dian
Wen'an
Shengfang
Baigou
Qingxian
Qikou
Huanghua

Hejian
Lixian
Anguo
Dingxian
Lingshou
Zhengding
Wuji
Shenze
Raoyang
Shanglin
Cangzhou
Yang'erzhuang
Yanshan
BOHAI
Bohai Haixia
BEIHUANGCHENG DAO
DAQIN DAO   NANHUANGCHENG DAO
TUOJI DAO
MIAODAO QUNDAO
DAHEISHAN DAO   NANCHANGSHAN DAO

Yangquan
Yuanshi
Huolu
Shijiazhuang
Zhaoxian
Gaoyi
Ningjin
Neiqiu
Xingjiawan
Nangong
Jixian
Dezhou
Wuqiao
Qingyun
Shanghe
Pingyuan
Wucheng
Xiajin
Qingping
Gaotang
Linqing
Xiping
Quzhou
Weixian
Jiuyongnian
Guantao
Dong'e
Liaocheng
Jinan
Changqing
Bucun
Zhoucun
Zibo
Huang
Zhangqiu
Xinhai
Zhangdian
Qingcheng
Boxing
Guangrao
Houzhen
Shouguang
Changyi
Pingdu
Gaomi
Jiaoxian
Jimo
HEBEI
Lianxian
Zhaoyang
Shenxian
Hengshui
Jingxian
Deping
Huimin
Binxian
Lijia
Luozhen
Zhanhua
Yangxin
Qingyun
Wangsi
Dongguang
Bozhen

Shanxi
Xiyang
SHAN
TAIHANG
SHAN
Yongnian
Shexian
Pengcheng
Handan
Cixian
Guangping
Linzhang
Daming
Shuiye
Liyuan
Anyang
Chuwang
Nanle
Qingfeng
Jiushouzhang
Yanggu
Shenxian
Dong'erzen
Dongping
Hu
Feicheng
TAI SHAN
5000
Tai'an
Kouzhen
Boshan
3284
Linqu
Anqiu
Weifang
Yidu
Yuezhuang
Jingzhi
AI
SHAN
2743
Zhaoyuan
Huangxian
Longkou
Chaoshui
Penglai
2285
Laiyang
2707
SHANDONG BANDAO
Xiyou
Yexian
2861
Muping
Yantai
Weihai
Jiurongcheng
Wendeng
Rushan
1968
Laishan
Wan
3877

SHANDONG
Xintai
Mengshan
4100
Pingyi
Sishui
Yishui
Juxian
2427
Rizhao
Andongwei
Ganyu
Haizhou
Wan
Lianyungang
(Xinpu)
Guanyun
YELLOW
SEA

Jiaozuo
Jixian
Xinxiang
Changyuan
Yanjin
HENAN
Zhengzhou
Xinzheng
Weishi
Kaifeng
Qixian
Heze
Dongming
Juye
Juncheng
Shan Xian
Longgu
Fengxian
Jing'anji
Yucheng
Tongshan
Xiayi
Zhecheng
Shangqiu
Guyang
Caoxian
Zaozhuang
Tai'erzhuang
Guanhu
Tancheng
Xuzhou
Suining
Suqian
Shuyang
Guannan
Linyi
Feixian
Tengxian
Zouxian
Qufu
Jining
Wenshang
Ningyang
Yanzhou
Nanyang
Hu
Jinxiang
Pingyi

Xuchang
Yanling
Linying
Yancheng
Luohe
Xiping
Shangcai
Suiping
Runan
Xiangcheng
Shengli
Jieshou
Taihe
Luyi
Zhoukouzhen
Huaiyang
Guoyang
Mengcheng
Hugou
Guzhen
Haocheng
Suxian
Lingbi
Sixian
Sihong
Xuyi
Boxian
Linhuanji
Shicun
Liji
Buzi
Yanghe
Siyang
Lianshui
Qingjiang
Huai'an
Baoying
Funing
Lianshui

JIANGSU
Yancheng
Wuyou
Baiju
Xinghua
Dongtai
Hai'an
Rugao
Baipu
Qi'anzhen
Tangzha
Nantong
Haifuzhen
Lingdianzhen

HENAN
Zhengyang
Xixian
Wulidian
Mangzhangdian
Huangchuan
Gushi
Longtansi
Fuyang
Huaiyuan
Huainan
Shouxian
Huoqiu
ANHUI
Dingyuan
Chengdong
Hu
Chengxi
Hu
Weibu
Hu
Lai'an
1135
Chihe
Bengbu
Fengyang
Jiashan
Shaobo
Hu
Gaoyou
Hu
Gaoyou
Hu
Shaobo
Luhe
Yangzhou
Taixian
Qutang
Taizhou
Banjin
Jijiashi
Zhenjiang

DABIE
SHAN
Xinyang
Guangshan
Dawu
Xyanhuadian
Yuwangcheng
Xinxian
Shangcheng
Jinzhai
6200
Changzhuyuanlihua
Qiliping
HUBEI
Yeji
Lu'an
Dushan
Shuanghe
Jinqiao
Hefei
Feidong
Zhegao
Hexian
Hanshan
Chuxian
Chaoxian
Zhenjiang
Danyang
Jintan
Liyang
Yixing
Huangli
Changzhou
Dayiqiao
Wuxi
Changshu
Jiangyin
Miaozhen
Taicang
Baoshan
HENG
SHA
SHANGHAI
SHI
CHONGMING
DAO
Jiading
Dachang
Zhouqu
Nanhui

Longtansi
Yejian
Huaibin
Wuhan
Shijikou
Huaili
Shuhedon
Wuwei
Dongba
Daibu
Shiju
Hu
Caishiji
Wuhu
Dangtu
Meizhou
Wanzhi
Qingpu
Nanxiang
Wujiang
Wusong
Zhoupu
Taicang

NANJING
Jurong
Lishui
Jintan
Jiangning
Taixing
Nantong

Scale 1:4 000 000 one inch to 64 miles. Conic Projection
Elevations and depressions are given in feet

Longitude East of Greenwich

0   10   20   30   40 Miles
0   10   20   30   40   50   60 Kilometers

A-560796-76-   -6- 4P-   -7P
COPYRIGHT BY
RAND McNALLY & COMPANY
MADE IN U.S.A.

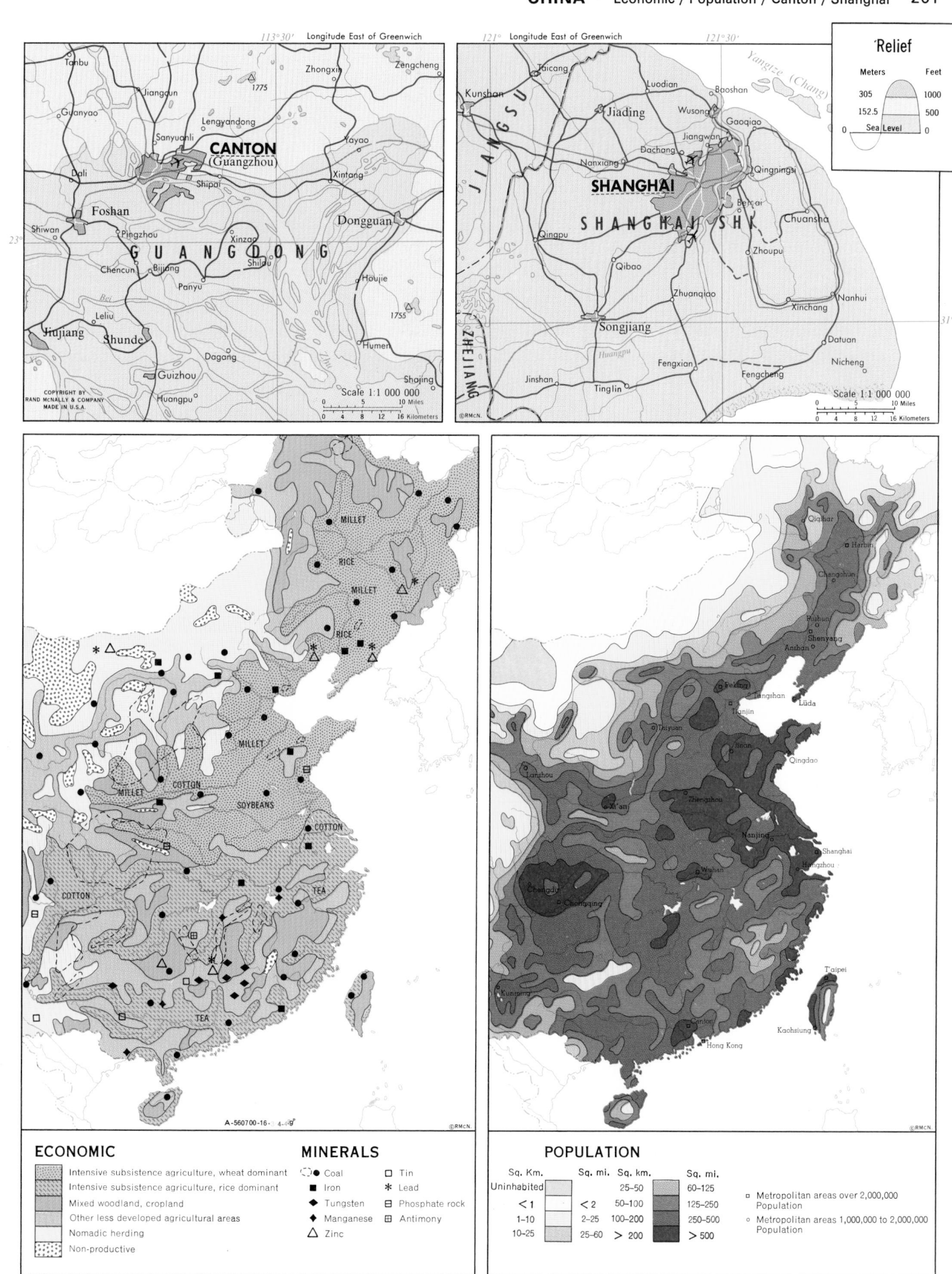

Relief

Meters	Feet
305	1000
152.5	500
0	Sea Level	0

Longitude East of Greenwich 113°30'

Tonbu Zhongxin Zengcheng
Jiangjun 1775
Guanyao Lengyandong
Sanyuanli **CANTON**
(Guangzhou) Yayao
Dali Shipai Xintang
Foshan Dongguan
Shiwan Pingzhou Xinzao
GUANGDONG Shilou
Chencun Bijiang Houjie
Panyu
Leliu Dagang
Hujiang Shunde 1755
Guizhou Humen
Huangpu Shojing

COPYRIGHT BY
RAND McNALLY & COMPANY
MADE IN U.S.A.

Scale 1:1 000 000
0 5 10 Miles
0 4 8 12 16 Kilometers

Longitude East of Greenwich 121° 121°30'

Yangtze (Chang)
Taicang Luodian Baoshan
Kunshan Wusong
Jiading Gaoqiao
JIANGSU Nanxiang Dachang Jiangwan
SHANGHAI Qingningsi
SHANGHAI SHI Beicai
Qingpu Chuansha
Qibao Zhoupu
Zhuanqiao Nanhui
Xinchang
ZHEJIANG Songjiang Datuan
Huangpu Fengxian Nicheng
Jinshan Tinglin Fengcheng

Scale 1:1 000 000
0 5 10 Miles
0 4 8 12 16 Kilometers

A-560700-16 4-69

ECONOMIC

- Intensive subsistence agriculture, wheat dominant
- Intensive subsistence agriculture, rice dominant
- Mixed woodland, cropland
- Other less developed agricultural areas
- Nomadic herding
- Non-productive

MINERALS

- ● Coal
- ■ Iron
- ◆ Manganese
- △ Zinc
- □ Tin
- ✳ Lead
- ⊟ Phosphate rock
- ⊞ Antimony
- Tungsten

POPULATION

Sq. Km.	Sq. mi.	Sq. km.	Sq. mi.
Uninhabited		25–50	60–125
< 1	< 2	50–100	125–250
1–10	2–25	100–200	250–500
10–25	25–60	> 200	> 500

- □ Metropolitan areas over 2,000,000 Population
- ○ Metropolitan areas 1,000,000 to 2,000,000 Population

For larger scale coverage of Shanghai see page 68.

Continued on page 204

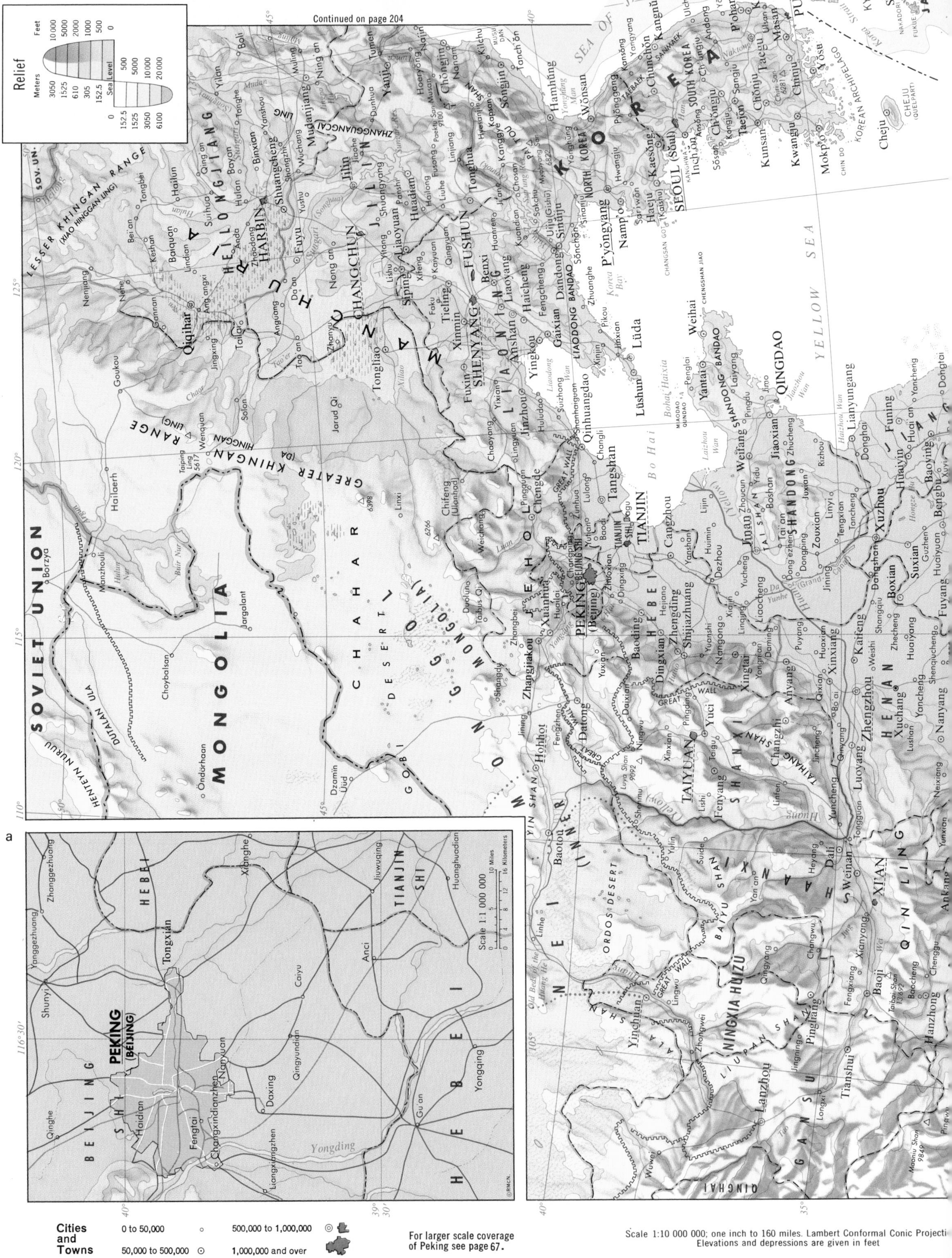

Relief

Feet	
10,000	
5000	
2000	
1000	
0	

Meters	
3050	
1525	
610	
305	
152.5	
Sea Level	500

| 500 | 5000 |
| 10,000 | 20,000 |

0 152.5 3050 6100
152.5 1525 3050

SEA OF JAPAN

JAPAN
KYŪSHŪ
TSU SHIMA
IKI SHIMA
NAGOOSO
FUKUE
PUSAN
Korea Strait
KOREAN ARCHIPELAGO
CHEJU (QUELPART)
CHEJU
CHIN DO

SOUTH KOREA
SEOUL (Soul)
Inch'ŏn
Suwŏn
Ch'ŏngju
Taejŏn
Chŏnju
Kunsan
Kwangju
Mokp'o
Taegu
Masan
Sangju
Andong
Yŏngju
Kyŏngju
Pohang
Ulsan

NORTH KOREA
PYŎNGYANG
Namp'o
Haeju
Kaesŏng
Wŏnsan
Hamhŭng
Hŭngnam
Ch'ŏngjin
Najin
Sinŭiju
Sinanju
Anju
Sariwŏn
Kanggye

SOVIET UNION
SOV. UN.

HEILONGJIANG
HARBIN
Qiqihar
Boli
Yichun
Jiamusi
Tonghe
Yilan
Hailun
Bayan
Binxian
Shuangcheng
Shangzhi
Wangqing
Tongbei
Keshan
Beian
Nehe
Nenjiang
Suihua
Hulan
Anda
Fuyu

LESSER KHINGAN RANGE (XIAO HINGGAN LING)

JILIN
CHANGCHUN
Jilin
Siping
Liaoyuan
Dunhua
Tonghua
Meihekou
Panshi
Yanji
Tumen
Hunchun
Huadian
Jiaohe
Dehui
Nong'an

GREATER KHINGAN (DA HINGGAN LING)

LIAONING
SHENYANG
FUSHUN
Benxi
Anshan
Liaoyang
Yingkou
Jinzhou
Fuxin
Tieling
Xinmin
Haicheng
Dandong
Fengcheng
Gaixian
Chaoyang
Lingyuan
Suizhong

LIAODONG BANDAO
Lüda
Lüshun
Jinxian

MONGOLIA
Choybalsan
Öndörhaan
Jargalant

GOBI
GOBI DESERT

CHAHAR

INNER MONGOLIA

JEHO

HEBEI
PEKING (BEIJING)
TIANJIN
Tangshan
Baoding
Zhangjiakou
Shijiazhuang
Chengde
Qinhuangdao

BOHAI
Bo Hai
Bohai Haixia
Laizhou Wan
Liaodong Wan

YELLOW SEA

SHANDONG
QINGDAO
Jinan
Zibo
Weifang
Yantai
Weihai
Zaozhuang
Dezhou
Linyi
Yanzhou
Jining

SHANXI
TAIYUAN
Datong
Yangquan
Linfen
Yuci

SHAANXI
XIAN
Baoji
Xianyang
Weinan

HENAN
Zhengzhou
Kaifeng
Luoyang
Xuchang
Anyang
Xinxiang
Nanyang

NINGXIA HUIZU
Yinchuan

GANSU
Lanzhou
Tianshui
Pingliang

QINGHAI

ORDOS DESERT
Baotou
Hohhot

QIN LING
QINLING

GREAT WALL

TAIHANG SHAN

YIN SHAN

---

a

| HEBEI |
| TIANJIN SHI |
| BEIJING SHI |

PEKING (BEIJING)
Shunyi
Qinghe
Haidian
Fengtai
Changxindianzhen
Liangxiangzhen
Nanyuan
Daxing
Tongxian
Xianghe
Anci
Caiyu
Qingyundian
Gu'an
Yongqing
Huangchuang
Jiuwuqing
Zhanggezhuang
Yonglezhuang
Zhangezhuang

Scale 1:1 000 000

0 ... 10 Miles
0 ... 16 Kilometers

Yongding

RMcN.

Cities and Towns

0 to 50,000	o
50,000 to 500,000	⊙
500,000 to 1,000,000	◎
1,000,000 and over	

For larger scale coverage of Peking see page 67.

Scale 1:10 000 000; one inch to 160 miles. Lambert Conformal Conic Projection
Elevations and depressions are given in feet

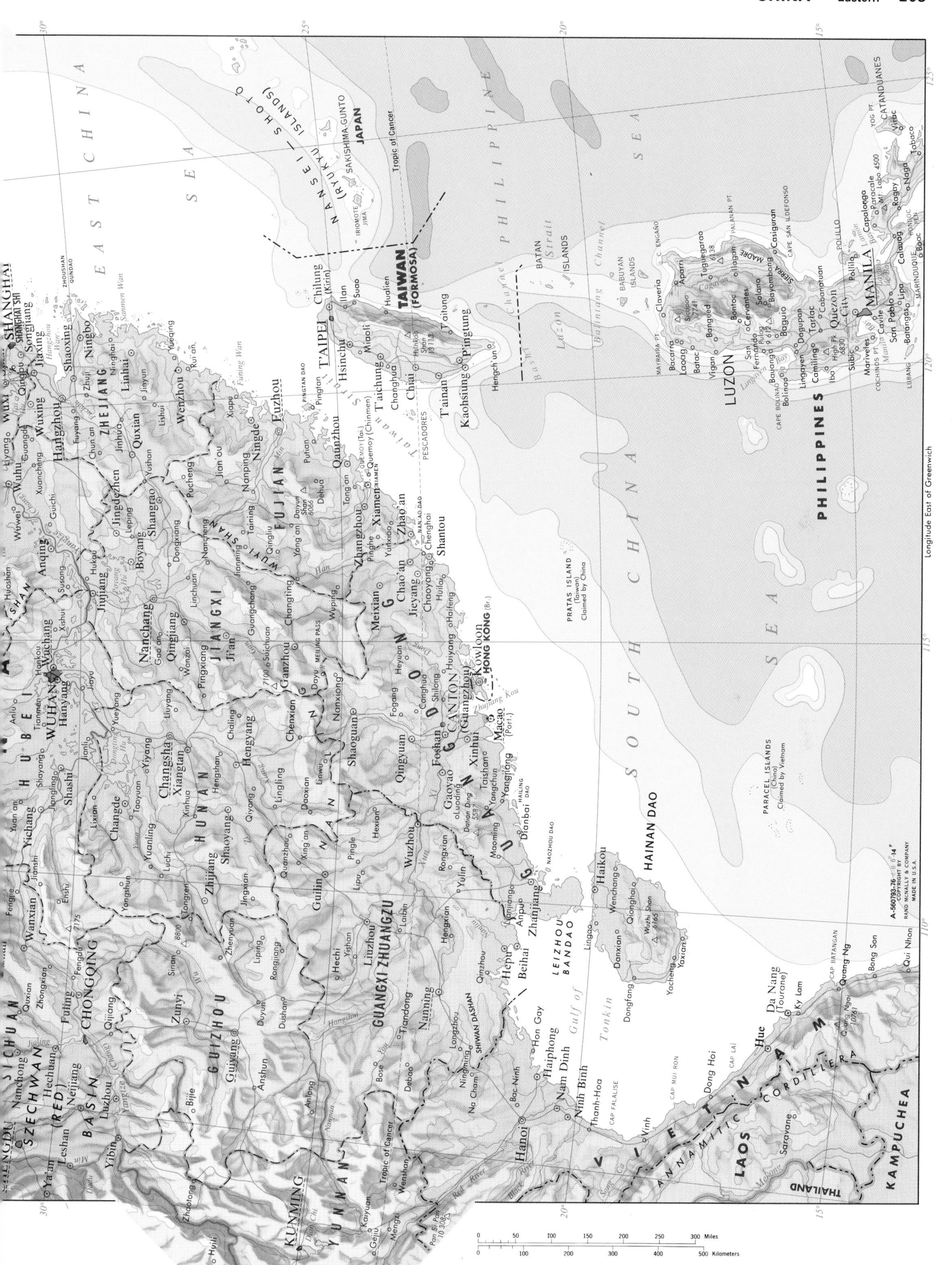

EAST CHINA SEA

PHILIPPINE SEA

SOUTH CHINA SEA

JAPAN

TAIWAN (FORMOSA)

T'AIPEI

NANSEI-SHOTO (RYUKYU ISLANDS)

SAKISHIMA-GUNTO

IRIOMOTE JIMA

Tropic of Cancer

CATANDUANES

PHILIPPINES

LUZON

SIERRA MADRE

MANILA

Manila Bay

BABUYAN ISLANDS

BATAN ISLANDS

Balintang Channel

Babuyan Channel

Luzon Strait

Bashi Channel

Chilung (Kirin)

Ilan

Suao

Hualien

T'aichung

Changhua

Chiai

Tainan

Kaohsiung

Pingtung

Hsinchu

Miaoli

Heng ch'un

SHANGHAI

Songjiang

Jiaxing

Shaoxing

Ningbo

Zhoushan

ZHEJIANG

Hangzhou

Wuxing

Huzhou

Huangd

Qingdu

Fuyang

Chun an

Jinhua

Quxian

Lishui

Wenzhou

Yueqing

Linhai

Rui an

Jinyun

Fuding

Xiapu

Ningde

FUJIAN

Fuzhou

Nanping

WUYI SHAN

Jian ou

Qingliu

Taining

Shaowu

Yong an

Dehua

Zhangzhou

Xiamen (Amoy)

Quanzhou

Putian

Pingtan DAO

MACAO DAO

Zhao'an

Chenghai

Shantou

Chao'an

Huilai

Meixian

Wiping

Changting

Ganzhou

Dayu

Nanxiong

JIANGXI

Nanchang

Qingjiang

Ji'an

Xingguo

Jian

Suichuan

Guangchang

Guixi

Boyang

Jingdezhen

Shangrao

Dongxiang

Nancheng

Linchuan

HUNAN

Changsha

Xiangtan

Shaoyang

Hengyang

Lingling

Daoxian

Qiyang

Changde

Yuanling

Luchi

GUIZHOU

Guiyang

Zunyi

Anshun

Duyun

Kaili

Bijie

SICHUAN

CHONGQING

Chongqing

Hechuan

Neijiang

Fuling

Wanxian

Fengjie

Yichang

Yueyang

WUHAN

Wuchang

Hanyang

Hankou

HUBEI

GUANGXI ZHUANGZU

Nanning

Liuzhou

Guilin

Wuzhou

Yulin

Beihai

Hepu

Qinzhou

Fangchenggang

Zhanjiang

LEIZHOU BANDAO

HAINAN DAO

Haikou

Qionghai

Wenchang

Danxian

Yaxian

Wuzhi Shan

GUANGDONG

CANTON (Guangzhou)

Kowloon

HONG KONG (Br.)

Macao (Port.)

Foshan

Xinhui

Taishan

Yangjiang

Maoming

HAILING DAO

NAOZHOU DAO

PRATAS ISLAND (Taiwan) Claimed by China

PARACEL ISLANDS Claimed by Vietnam

VIETNAM

Hanoi

Haiphong

Nam Dinh

Ninh Binh

Thanh-Hoa

Vinh

Dong Hoi

Hue

Da Nang (Tourane)

Quang Ngai

Qui Nhon

Bong Son

ANNAMITIC CORDILLERA

LAOS

THAILAND

KAMPUCHEA

Gulf of Tonkin

YUNNAN

KUNMING

Longitude East of Greenwich

A-560793-76

COPYRIGHT BY

RAND McNALLY & COMPANY

MADE IN U.S.A.

0   50 100 150 200 250 300 Miles

0 100 200 300 400 500 Kilometers

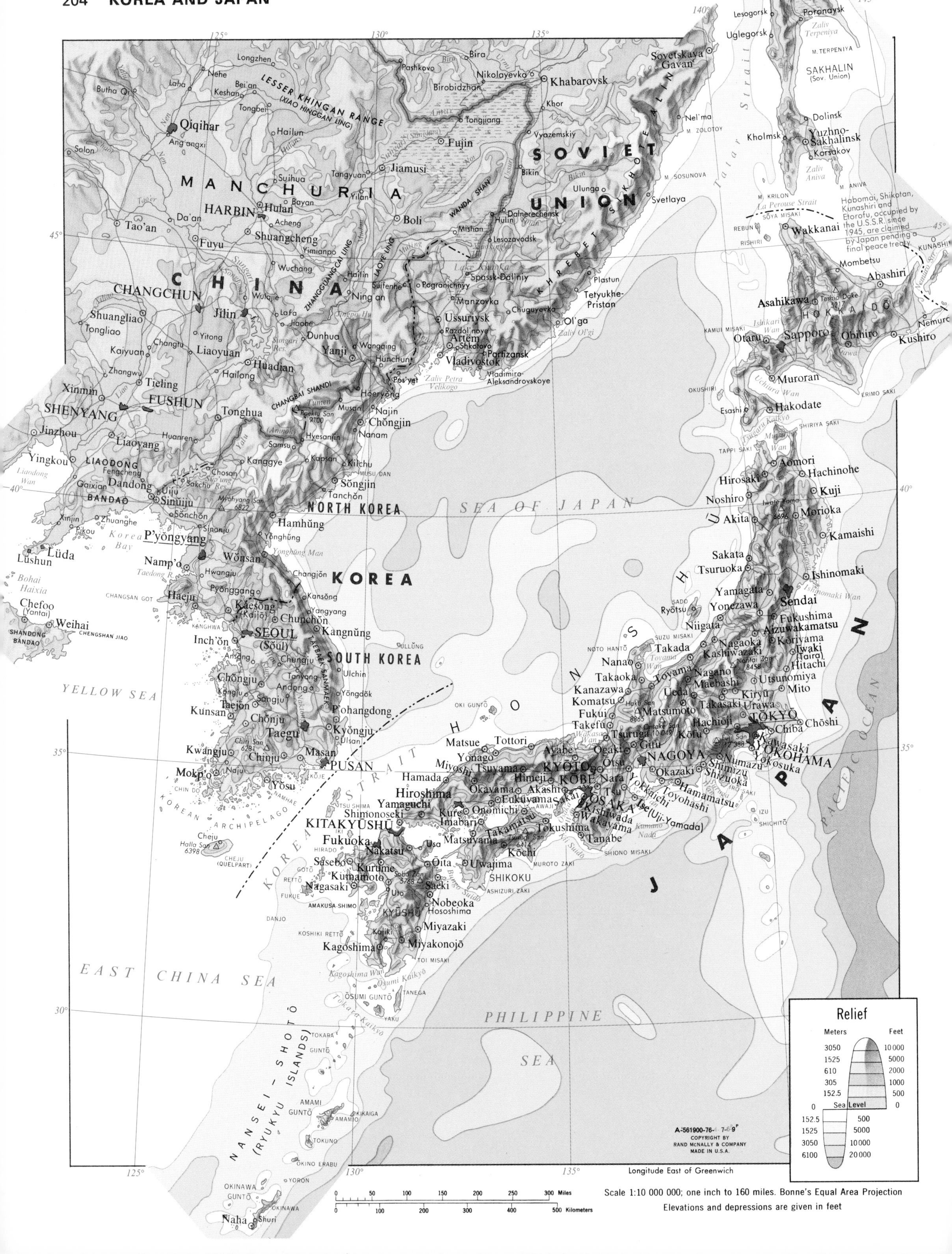

MANCHURIA

CHINA

SOVIET UNION

SAKHALIN (Sov. Union)

Qiqihar
Ang'angxi
Nehe
Longzhen
Butha Qi
Laha
Keshan
Bei'an
Tongbei
Hailun
Suihua
Tangyuan
Jiamusi
Fujin
Pashkovo
Bira
Bira
Nikolayevka
Birobidzhan
Khabarovsk
Sovetskaya Gavan'
Uglegorsk
Lesogorsk
Poronaysk
Zaliv Terpeniya
M. TERPENIYA

HARBIN
Hulan
Acheng
Bayan
Yilan
Boli
Wanda Shan
Bikin
Khor
Vyazemskiy
Dolinsk
Yuzhno-Sakhalinsk
Korsakov
Zaliv Aniva

Tao'an
Da'an
Fuyu
Shuangcheng
Yimianpo
Wuchang
Hulin
Dalnerechensk
Lesozavodsk
Mishan
Svetlaya
Kholmsk

CHANGCHUN
Jilin
Lafa
Jiaohe
Dunhua
Suifenhe
Pogranichnyy
Manzovka
Spassk-Dal'niy
Chuguyevka
Plastun
M. ZOLOTOY

Shuangliao
Tongliao
Changtu
Yitong
Wangqing
Yanji
Hunchun
Razdol'noye
Artëm
Ussuriysk
Ol'ga
Zaliv Ol'ga

Kaiyuan
Zhangwu
Hailong
Huadian
Tonghua
Vladivostok
Shkotovo
Partizansk
Vladimiro-Aleksandrovskoye

Xinmin
Tieling
Liaoyuan
Huanren
Pos'yet
Zaliv Petra Velikogo

SHENYANG
FUSHUN
Liaoyang
Changbai Shandi
Hoeryŏng
Musan
Najin

Jinzhou
LIAODONG
Fengcheng
Dandong
Tonghua
Hyesanjin
Kapsan
Kilchu
Chŏngjin
Nanam

Yingkou
Gaixian
Xinyi
Zhuanghe
Uiju
Sinŭiju
Sŏnchŏn
Kanggye
Myohyang San 6822
MUSU DAN
Tanchŏn
Sŏngjin

Liaodong Wan
Pikou
Sinanju
Hamhŭng

Lüshun
Lüda
Namp'o
P'yŏngyang
Hwangju
Wŏnsan
Yŏnghŭng Man

Bohai Haixia
Chefoo (Yantai)
Changsan got
Haeju
Yŏnan
Changjŏn
Kansŏng

NORTH KOREA

KOREA

SOUTH KOREA

SEA OF JAPAN

Weihai
SHANDONG BANDAO
CHENGSHAN JIAO
KANGHWA
Kaesŏng (Kaijo)
Chunchŏn
Yangyang

Inch'ŏn
SEOUL (Sŏul)
Ansŏng
Kangnŭng

Ullŭng

YELLOW SEA
Chŏngju
Chungju
Tanyang
Ulchin

Kunsan
T'aebaek Sanmaek
Yŏngdŏk
Taejŏn
Sangju
Andong

Kwangju
Chŏnju
Chŏngju
Pohangdong

Mokp'o
Naju
Taegu
Kyŏngju
Ulsan

Chinju
Masan
PUSAN
KOJE

Cheju
Halla San 6398
CHEJU (QUELPART)

Oki Guntō

Matsue
Tottori
Yonago
Tsuyama

Miyoshi
Tsuyama
Himeji
Akashi

KOREA STRAIT

KOREAN ARCHIPELAGO
CHIN DO
NAMHAE

Hamada
Yamaguchi
Hiroshima
Okayama
Fukuyama
Onomichi

KITAKYŪSHŪ
IKI
Shimonoseki
Kure
Imabari
Matsuyama

Fukuoka
Nakatsu
Usa
Takamatsu
Tokushima

Sasebo
Kurume
Ōita
Kōchi

Nagasaki
Uto
Saeki
SHIKOKU
MURO TO ZAKI

AMAKUSA-SHIMO
Hososhima
Nobeoka
ASHIZURI ZAKI
SHIONO MISAKI

KYŪSHŪ
Miyazaki
Miyakonojō

KOSHIKI RETTŌ
Kagoshima
Kagoshima Wan
TOI MISAKI

DANJO
ŌSUMI GUNTŌ
TANEGA
Tokara Kaikyō

EAST CHINA SEA

NANSEI-SHOTŌ (RYUKYU ISLANDS)

TOKARA
GUNTŌ
YAKU

AMAMI
GUNTŌ
KIKAIGA
AMAMIO

TOKUNO

OKINAWA
GUNTŌ
OKINO ERABU
YORON

Naha
Shuri
OKINAWA

PHILIPPINE SEA

HOKKAIDO
Wakkanai
REBUN
RISHIRI
SOYA MISAKI
La Perouse Strait
M. KRILON

Asahikawa
Otaru
Sapporo
Obihiro
Kushiro
Mombetsu
Abashiri
Nemuro

Muroran
Hakodate
Uchiura Wan
ERIMO SAKI
OKUSHIRI
Esashi

Habomai, Shikotan, Kunashiri and Etorofu, occupied by the U.S.S.R. since 1945, are claimed by Japan pending final peace treaty.

KUNASHIRI

Aomori
Hachinohe
Hirosaki
Kuji
Noshiro
IWATE YAMA 6696
Morioka
Akita
Kamaishi

Sakata
Ishinomaki
Tsuruoka
Yamagata
Sendai
Yonezawa
Fukushima

SADO
Ryōtsu
Niigata
Nagaoka
Aizuwakamatsu
Kōriyama
Iwaki (Taira)
Hitachi

NOTO HANTŌ
Nanao
Takada
Kashiwazaki
Nagano
Maebashi
Utsunomiya
Mito

Takaoka
Toyama Wan
Toyama
Ueda
Takasaki
Kiryū

Kanazawa
Komatsu
Matsumoto
Urawa
TOKYO
Chiba
Chōshi

Fukui
Takefu
Gifu
Kōfu
Kawasaki
YOKOHAMA
Yokosuka

Tsuruga
Ōtsu
KYŌTO
Nara
NAGOYA
Hamamatsu
IZU

Wakasa Wan
Ayabe
Tsu
Okazaki
Shimizu
Shizuoka

OSAKA
KŌBE
Yokkaichi
Toyohashi

Kishiwada
Ise (Uji-Yamada)
Kumano Nada

Wakayama
Tanabe

HONSHU

JAPAN

PACIFIC OCEAN

SHICHITŌ

Scale 1:10 000 000; one inch to 160 miles. Bonne's Equal Area Projection
Elevations and depressions are given in feet

Longitude East of Greenwich

A-561900-76- 7-6-9
COPYRIGHT BY
RAND McNALLY & COMPANY
MADE IN U.S.A.

Relief

Meters		Feet
3050		10 000
1525		5000
610		2000
305		1000
152.5		500
0	Sea Level	0
152.5		500
1525		5000
3050		10 000
6100		20 000

0 50 100 150 200 250 300 Miles
0 100 200 300 400 500 Kilometers

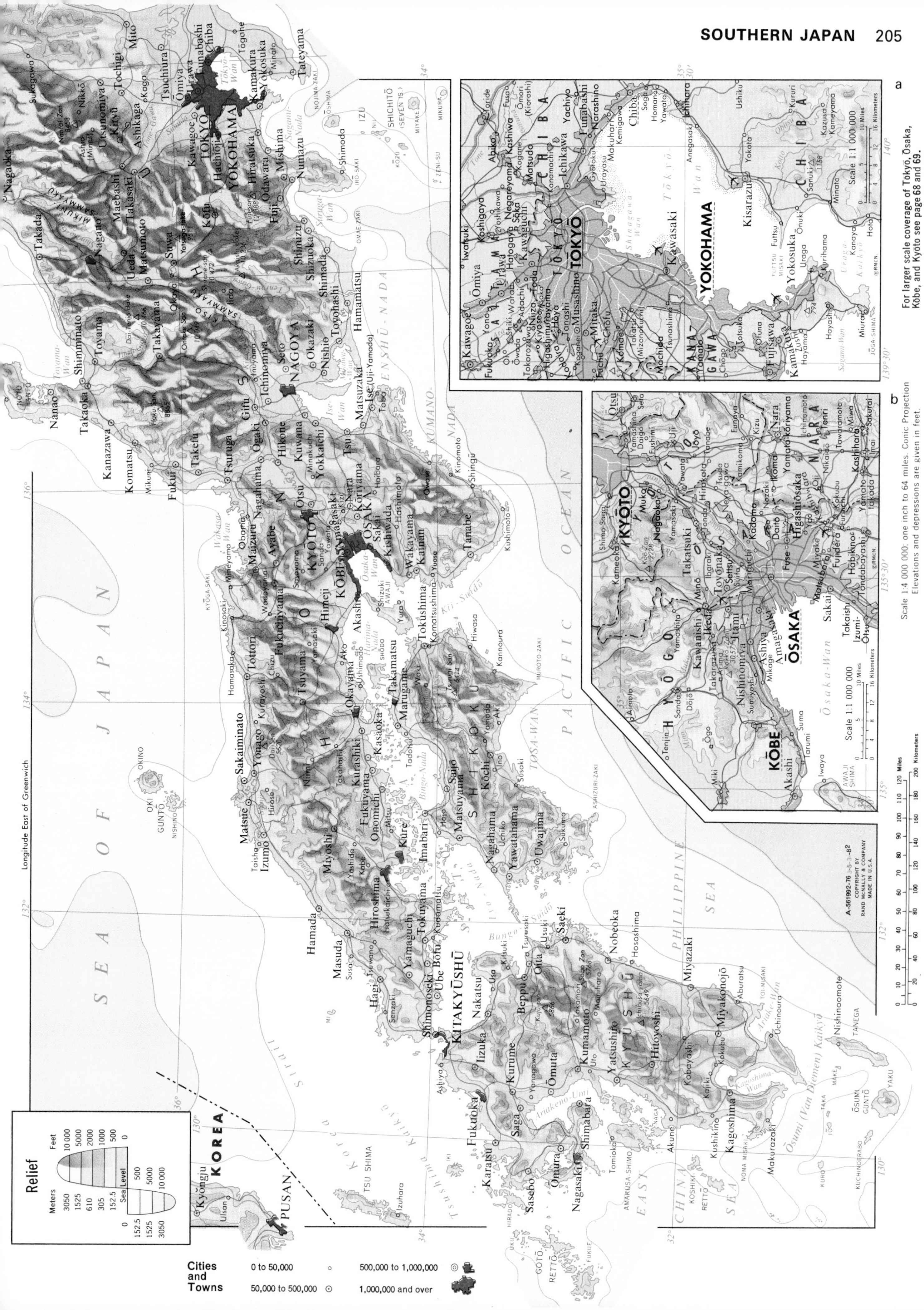

For larger scale coverage of Tōkyō, Ōsaka,
Kōbe, and Kyōto see page 68 and 69.

Scale 1:1 000 000

a

b

Scale 1:4 000 000; one inch to 64 miles. Conic Projection
Elevations and depressions are given in feet.

Scale 1:1 000 000

A-561992-76 —5-3—82
COPYRIGHT BY
RAND McNALLY COMPANY
MADE IN U.S.A.

Relief

Meters	Feet
3050	10 000
1525	5000
610	2000
305	1000
152.5	500
0	Sea Level
152.5	500
1525	5000
3050	10 000

Cities and Towns

0 to 50,000 ○
50,000 to 500,000 ⊙
500,000 to 1,000,000 ◎
1,000,000 and over

SEA OF JAPAN

PACIFIC OCEAN

PHILIPPINE SEA

EAST CHINA SEA

KOREA

PUSAN

TOKYO

YOKOHAMA

NAGOYA

KYOTO

OSAKA

KOBE

KITAKYUSHU

Longitude East of Greenwich

Scale 1:16 000 000; one inch to 250 miles. Polyconic Projection
Elevations and depressions are given in feet

Relief

Meters	Feet
3050	10 000
1525	5000
610	2000
305	1000
152.5	500
Sea Level	
152.5	500
1525	5000
3050	10 000
6100	20 000

A-569800-76 9-8-10-23
COPYRIGHT BY
RAND MCNALLY & COMPANY
MADE IN U.S.A.

Continued on pages 198-199

130°

135°

20°

120°

Cabugao

Iguig

Tuguegarao

224°

15°

Vigan

Banguéd

Lubuagan

Cabagan

Divilacan Bay

Narvacan

Bontoc

Ilagan

Palanan Bay

PALANAN PT.

Condon

Mt. Amuyao
8799

Cauayán

Cervantes

Santiago

DIJOHAN PT.

Luna

Jones

Echague

Pulog
9626

Casiguran

PHILIPPINE

San Fernando

Bagabag

S. Juan

Solano

CABARRUYAN

Baguio

Bayombong

Bauang

Bambang

Bolinao

Aringay

Dupax

16°

SANTIAGO

Lingayen

CAPE SAN ILDEFONSO

Bani

Alaminos

Gulf

San
Fabian

S. Nicolas

Agno

Dagupan

Binmaloy

S. Tayug

Burgos

Urdaneta

S. Quintin

CAIMAN PT.

San Carlos

Rosales

Baler Bay

Lingayen

Dasol Bay

Santa Cruz

Mangatarem

Bayambang

San Jose

Baler

CAPE ENCANTO

Infanta

Camiling

Muñoz

Candelaria

High Pk.
6683

Gerona

Victoria

Dingalan Bay

LUZON

Tarlac

Cabanatuan

PHILIPPINES

Palauig

Concepcion

Gapan

Iba

S. Miguel

Pinatubo
5771

Angeles

Arayat

S. Fernando

SEA

S. Narciso

Guagua

Malolos

Polillo Str.

POLILLO IS.

S. Antonio

Subic

Sto.
Maria

POLILLO

Olongapo

Orani

Malabon

Infanta

Polillo

Patnanongan

JOMALIG

Balanga

Malabon

Quezon
City

SAMPALOC PT.

Orion

Manila

Pasig

Lamon Bay

CALAGUAS ISLAND

Mariveles

MANILA

Cavite

BALESIN

Capalonga

Paracale

Talisay

Naic

Laguna

Sta. Cruz

Mauban

CABALETE

Labo

Daet

CORREGIDOR ISLAND

de Bay

Calamba

Nagcarlan

ALABAT

Silang

Mt. Banahao

Atimonan

Mt. Labo
5066

Ragay

Nasugbu

S. Pablo

Lucena

Gumaca

Macalelon

San Miguel
Bay

Lipa

Unisan

Catanauan

Naga

Mt. Isarog
6450

Balayan
Bay

Lemery

Batangas

Tayabas Bay

Pili

Bato

Buhi

LUBANG

AMBIL
ISLAND

Rosario

Lobo

S. Narciso

Tabaco

Polangui

Mayon
8077

IS.

GOLD
ISLAND

MARICABAN

VERDE

Boac

S. Cruz

Torrijos

BURIAS PASS

Ligao

CAPE CALAVITE

Verde I. Passage

Calapan

Gasan

Legazpi

Paluan

Mt. Halcon
8471

Naujan

MARINDUQUE
ISLAND

DUMALI PT.

San Pascual

BURIAS

Mamburao

MINDORO

Pinamalayan

Jones

BANTON

SIBUYAN

TICAO
ISLAND

Scale 1:4 000 000

Sablayan

Mt. Baco
8163

Knob Pk.
3031

ROMBLON ISLAND

S. Jacinto

Aroroy

0 10 20 30 40 Miles

DONGON PT.

Romblon

0 10 20 30 40 50 60 Kilometers

TABLAS

MASBATE

BUSUANGA

S. Jose

Bulalacao

Odiongan

Looc

SIBUYAN

TARA

ILIN ISLAND

SEA

®RMCN.

Continued on pages 198-199 (left panel)

PHILIPPINE

15°

PHILIPPINES

SAMAR

Catbalogan

CATANDUANES
ISLAND

rsogon

LEYTE

PHILIPPINE

Tacloban

DINAGAT ISLAND

bu

OHOL

34 578

SEA

10°

Butuan

TRENCH

Cagayan

MINDANAO

Apo
9692

Davao

PALAU IS.

Danao Gulf

(T.T.P.I.)

5°

PULAU MIANGAS

SONSOROL
ISLANDS

KEPULAUAN
TALAUD

do

PULAU SANGIHE

Tondano

Equator

0°

Ternate

PULAU SIAU

HALMAHERA

MOROTAI

Laut

PULAU
WAIGEO

KEPULAUAN
MAPIA

Maluku

Halmahera

Selat Dampier

JAN

(Molucca Sea)

(Halmahera Sea)

Sorong

Manokwari

BIAK

NINIGO GROUP

MUSSAU
ISLAND

AI

PULAU BACAN

Labuha

JAZIRAH
DOBERAI

SALAWATI

PULAU YAPEN

HERMIT IS.

ADMIRALTY ISLANDS

EMIRA
ISLAND

PULAU
TALIBU

PULAU
MANGOLE

KEPULAUAN OBI

PULAU
MISOOL

PULAU NUMFOOR

TG. PERKAM

Jayapura
(Sukarnapura)

MANUS
ISLAND

NEW HANOVER

KEPULAUAN
SULA

PULAU OBI

Teluk Berau

Teluk
Cenderawasih

Aitape

Kavieng

Piru

SERAM

Fakfak

Kaimana

Wewak

BISMARCK

BURU

(MOLUCCAS)

PEGUNUNGAN VAN REES

Sepik

NEW
IRELAND

Ambon

PULAU AMBON

Bula

PEGUNUNGAN MAOKE

Namatanai

I A

PULAU ADI

Puncak Jaya
16 503

Puncak Trikora
15 584

Rabaul

ARCH.

KEPULAUAN
BANDA

NEW GUINEA

BISMARCK

WITU
ISLANDS

KARKAR ISLAND

Kokopo

KEPULAUAN
LUCIPARA

LAUT BANDA

KEPULAUAN KAI

Mt. Wilhelm 14 793

Madang

LONG ISLAND

Talasea

The Father
7546

(BANDA SEA)

KAI KECIL

Dobo

Mt. Giluwe 14 330

Mt. Bangeta
13 529

PULAU WETAR

KEPULAUAN
ARU

PAPUA

NEW BRITAIN

PULAU
DAMAR

PULAU
TRANGAN

Lae

NEW BRITAIN TRENCH

PULAUU
KANGBESI

YAMDENA

NEW GUINEA

Huon Gulf

Alor

PULAU BABAR

KEPULAUAN
TANIMBAR

PULAU
YOS
SUDARSA

Morobe

WOODLARK
ISLAND

DE ATAURO

PULAU MOA

PULAU SELARU

Mt. Albert Edward
13 090

Buna

TROBRIAND IS.

Dili

TIMOR

TANJUNG VALS

Merauke

Gulf
of Papua

OWEN STANLEY RA.

D'ENTRECASTEAUX IS.

ARAFURA

Daru

Mt. Victoria
13 240

SEA

SEA

MELVILLE
ISLAND

COBOURG
PEN.

CROKER ISLAND

Port Moresby

Torres

CAPE
YORK

GREAT

CORAL SEA

10°

BATHURST
ISLAND

WESSEL IS.

Van
Diemen Gulf

Darwin

C. ARNHEM

Gulf of Carpentaria

STRAIT

CAPE
YORK
PEN.

BARRIER

Samarai

AUSTRALIA

Continued on pages 214-215

125°

130°

135°

140°

145°

150°

50 100 200 300 400 500 Miles

100 200 400 600 800 Kilometers

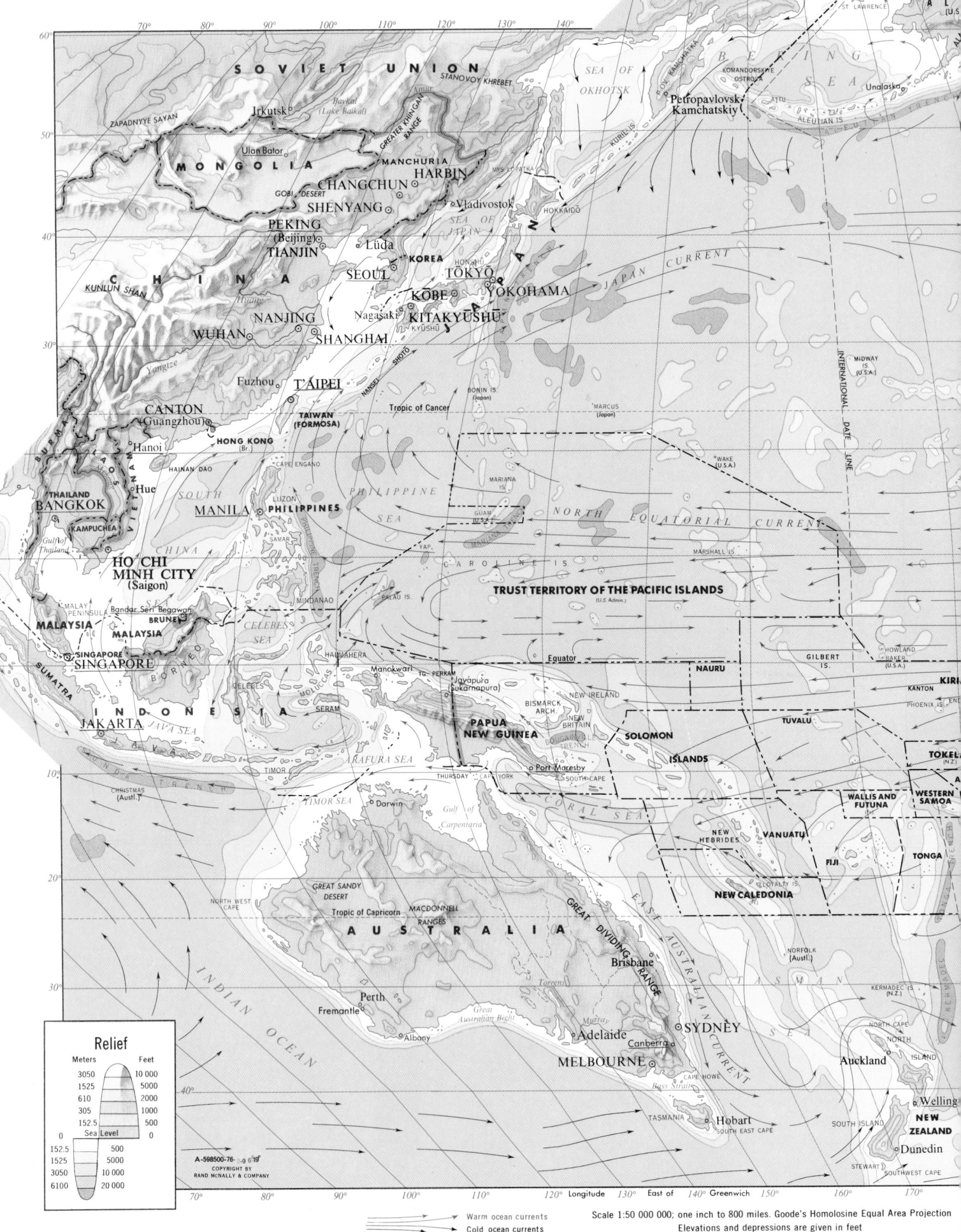

Relief

Meters		Feet
3050		10 000
1525		5000
610		2000
305		1000
152.5		500
0	Sea Level	0
152.5		500
1525		5000
3050		10 000
6100		20 000

A-598500-76
COPYRIGHT BY
RAND McNALLY & COMPANY

→ Warm ocean currents
→ Cold ocean currents

Scale 1:50 000 000; one inch to 800 miles. Goode's Homolosine Equal Area Projection
Elevations and depressions are given in feet

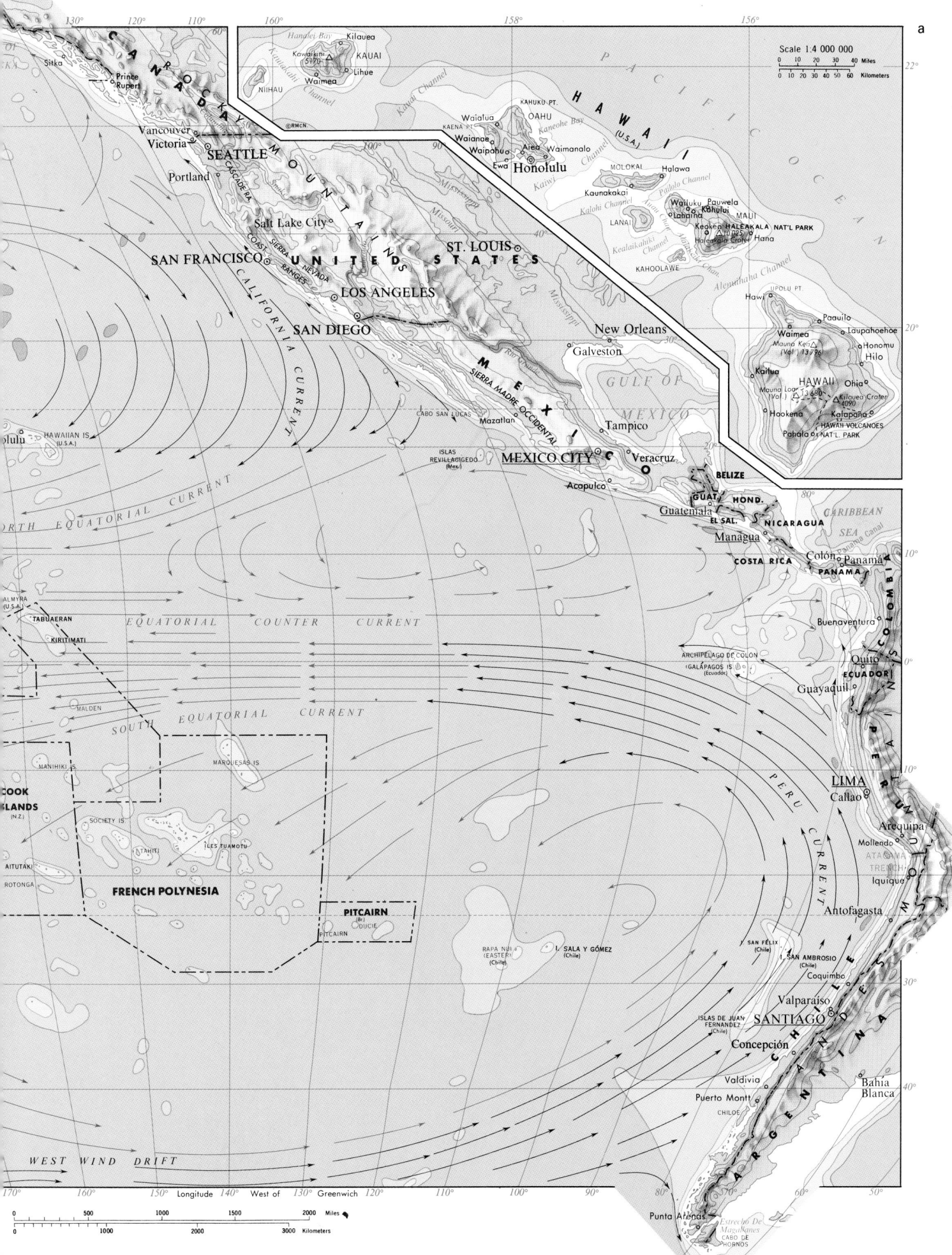

a

Scale 1:4 000 000

0 10 20 30 40 Miles
0 10 20 30 40 50 60 Kilometers

Handei Bay • Kilauea
Kawaikini △ • KAUAI
5170 •
Kaumahina Channel   Lihue
Waimea
NIIHAU

KAHUKU PT.
Waialua   OAHU
Waianae   Aiea • Waimanalo
Waipahu   Ewa **Honolulu**
Kaena Pt

HAWAII
(U.S.A.)

MOLOKAI Halawa
Kaunakakai
Wailuku • Pauwela
Kalohi Channel Kahului MAUI
LANAI Lahaina Keokea • HALEAKALA NAT'L PARK
△ 10 025
Haleakala Crater • Hana
KAHOOLAWE
Kealaikahiki Chan.
Alenuihaha Channel

UPOLU PT.
Hawi • Paauilo
Waimea • Laupahoehoe
Mauna Kea △ • Honomu
(Vol.) 13 796 • Hilo
Kailua
HAWAII • Ohia
Mauna Loa • Kilauea Crater
(Vol.) △ 13 680 4090
Hoopena HAWAII VOLCANOES
Pahala NAT'L PARK
Kalapana

CANADA
ROCKY
Sitka
Prince Rupert

Vancouver
Victoria
SEATTLE MOUNTAINS
Portland CASCADE
SIERRA
COAST NEVADA
Salt Lake City
RANGES
SAN FRANCISCO **UNITED STATES** St. LOUIS
LOS ANGELES
CALIFORNIA
SAN DIEGO
CURRENT
SIERRA MADRE OCCIDENTAL
MEXICO
CABO SAN LUCAS
Mazatlan
ISLAS
REVILLAGIGEDO
(Mex.)
MEXICO CITY • Veracruz
Acapulco

New Orleans
Galveston
GULF OF
MEXICO
Tampico

BELIZE
GUAT. HOND.
Guatemala
EL SAL. NICARAGUA CARIBBEAN
Managua SEA
COSTA RICA Colón • Panamá
PANAMA Panama Canal

olulu • HAWAIIAN IS.
(U.S.A.)

ORTH EQUATORIAL CURRENT

ALMYRA
(U.S.A.)
TABUAERAN
KIRITIMATI

EQUATORIAL COUNTER CURRENT

Buenaventura

ARCHIPÉLAGO DE COLÓN
(GALÁPAGOS IS.)
(Ecuador)

Quito
COLOMBIA
ECUADOR
Guayaquil

MALDEN

SOUTH EQUATORIAL CURRENT

MANIHIKI IS.
MARQUESAS IS.

COOK
ISLANDS
(N.Z.)
SOCIETY IS.
AITUTAKI TAHITI
ROTONGA ÎLES TUAMOTU

FRENCH POLYNESIA

PERU
LIMA
Callao
Arequipa
Mollendo
ATACAMA
TRENCH
Iquique
Antofagasta

CURRENT

PITCAIRN
(Br.)
DUCIE
PITCAIRN

RAPA NUI
(EASTER)
(Chile)
I. SALA Y GÓMEZ
(Chile)

SAN FÉLIX
(Chile)
I. SAN AMBROSIO
(Chile)
Coquimbo

Valparaíso
ISLAS DE JUAN **SANTIAGO**
FERNÁNDEZ
(Chile)
Concepción
ANDES
ARGENTINA
CHILE
Valdivia
Puerto Montt
CHILOE
Bahía
Blanca

WEST WIND DRIFT

Punta Arenas
Estrecho De
Magallanes
CABO DE
HORNOS

0   500   1000   1500   2000 Miles
0   1000   2000   3000 Kilometers

170° 160° 150° Longitude 140° West of 130° Greenwich 120° 110° 100° 90° 80° 70° 60° 50°

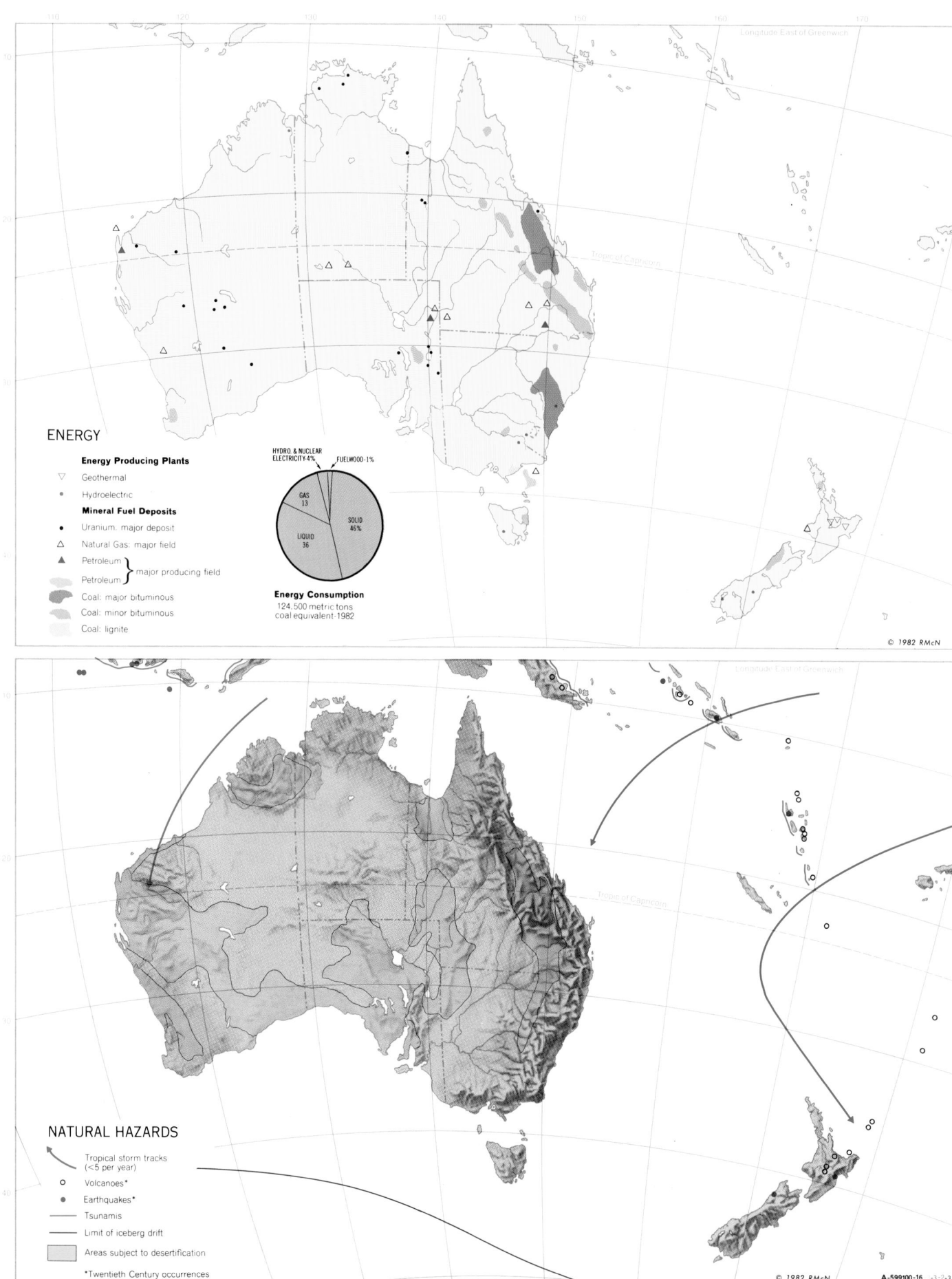

ENERGY

Energy Producing Plants

▽ Geothermal

• Hydroelectric

Mineral Fuel Deposits

• Uranium: major deposit

△ Natural Gas: major field

▲ Petroleum

Petroleum } major producing field

Coal: major bituminous

Coal: minor bituminous

Coal: lignite

HYDRO. & NUCLEAR ELECTRICITY-4%   FUELWOOD-1%

GAS 13

SOLID 46%

LIQUID 36

Energy Consumption
124,500 metric tons
coal equivalent-1982

© 1982 RMcN

NATURAL HAZARDS

Tropical storm tracks (<5 per year)

○ Volcanoes*

• Earthquakes*

Tsunamis

Limit of iceberg drift

Areas subject to desertification

*Twentieth Century occurrences

© 1982 RMcN   A-599100-16   -3-2-3

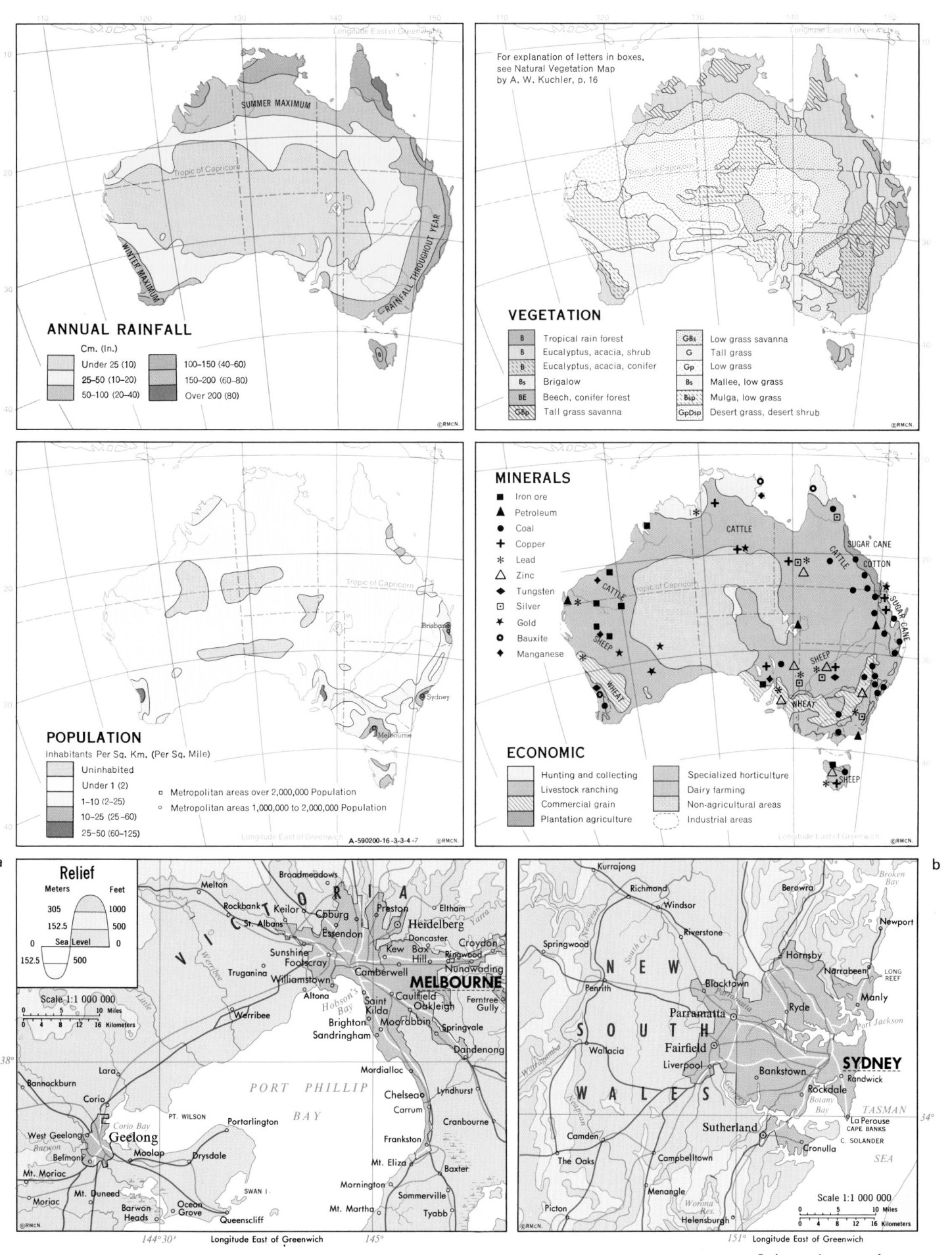

ANNUAL RAINFALL

Cm. (In.)

- Under 25 (10)
- 25–50 (10–20)
- 50–100 (20–40)
- 100–150 (40–60)
- 150–200 (60–80)
- Over 200 (80)

©RMCN.

VEGETATION

For explanation of letters in boxes,
see Natural Vegetation Map
by A. W. Kuchler, p. 16

B	Tropical rain forest	GBs	Low grass savanna
B	Eucalyptus, acacia, shrub	G	Tall grass
B	Eucalyptus, acacia, conifer	Gp	Low grass
Bs	Brigalow	Bs	Mallee, low grass
BE	Beech, conifer forest	Bsp	Mulga, low grass
GBp	Tall grass savanna	GpDsp	Desert grass, desert shrub

©RMCN.

POPULATION

Inhabitants Per Sq. Km. (Per Sq. Mile)

- Uninhabited
- Under 1 (2)
- 1–10 (2–25)
- 10–25 (25–60)
- 25–50 (60–125)

□ Metropolitan areas over 2,000,000 Population
○ Metropolitan areas 1,000,000 to 2,000,000 Population

A-590200-16-3-3-4-7   ©RMCN.

MINERALS

- ■ Iron ore
- ▲ Petroleum
- ● Coal
- + Copper
- ✳ Lead
- △ Zinc
- ◆ Tungsten
- ⊡ Silver
- ✲ Gold
- ○ Bauxite
- ◆ Manganese

ECONOMIC

- Hunting and collecting
- Livestock ranching
- Commercial grain
- Plantation agriculture
- Specialized horticulture
- Dairy farming
- Non-agricultural areas
- Industrial areas

©RMCN.

a

Relief

Meters	Feet
305	1000
152.5	500
0	Sea Level 0
152.5	500

Scale 1:1 000 000

0   5   10 Miles
0   4   8   12   16 Kilometers

©RMCN.   144°30'   Longitude East of Greenwich   145°

b

Scale 1:1 000 000

0   5   10 Miles
0   4   8   12   16 Kilometers

©RMCN.   151° Longitude East of Greenwich

For larger scale coverage of
Melbourne and Sydney see page 70

SINGAPORE

BORNEO

Palembang

SUMATRA

Banjarmasin

JAKARTA

Surabaya

JAVA

CELEBES

SERAM

Java Sea

Ujung Pandang

SUMBA

TIMOR

Arafura Sea

Timor Sea

Darwin

Daly

INDIAN OCEAN

Gulf of Carpentaria

PEN

KIMBERLEY PLATEAU

Victoria

Broome

Fitzroy

Mount Isa

GREAT SANDY DESERT

Alice Springs

GIBSON DESERT

SIMPSON DESERT

GREA ARTES BASI

Carnarvon

Tropic of Capricorn

GREAT VICTORIA DESERT

Lake Eyre

Kalgoorlie

NULLARBOR PLAIN

Lake Gairdner

FLINDERS RANGES

Broken Hill

Murray

DARLING RA.

Great Australian Bight

Adelaide

Perth

INDIAN OCEAN

▪	Urban
▦	Cropland
▨	Cropland & Woodland
▨	Cropland & Grazing Land
▒	Grassland, Grazing Land
▓	Forest, Woodland
▤	Swamp, Marshland
░	Shrub, Sparse Grass, Wasteland (pattern)
□	Barren Land

Scale 1:24,000,000; one inch to 380 miles. Lambert Azimuthal Equal-Area Projection

150°   160°   170°   180°

0°

Equator

KIRIBATI

NEW GUINEA

NEW BRITAIN

resby •

SOLOMON ISLANDS

P A C I F I C   O C E A N

Coral   Sea

airns

Townsville

VANUATU

SAMOA ISLANDS

Pago Pago

FIJI ISLANDS

Suva

NEW CALEDONIA

ÎLES LOYAUTÉ

Rockhampton

Nouméa

10°

G RANGE

TONGA ISLANDS

20°

Brisbane

DIVIDING RANGE

SYDNEY

Canberra •

EAT

Tasman   Sea

ELBOURNE

30°

P A C I F I C   O C E A N

Auckland

NORTH ISLAND

TASMANIA

Hobart

SOUTHERN ALPS

Wellington

Christchurch

SOUTH ISLAND

STEWART ISLAND

Dunedin

A-590200-96 -1-1-7'

40°

150°   160°   170°   180°   170°   160°

0   100   200   400   600   800 Miles
0   150   300   600   900   1200 Kilometers

Continued on pages 206-207

Relief

Meters	Feet
3050	10 000
1525	5000
610	2000
305	1000
152.5	500
0 Sea Level	0
152.5	500
1525	5000 Below Sea Level
3050	10 000
6100	20 000

A-590200-76- -5-5-14
COPYRIGHT BY
RAND McNALLY & COMPANY
MADE IN U.S.A.

Longitude 115° East of Greenwich

Scale 1:16 000 000; one inch to 250 miles. Lambert's Azimuthal, Equal Area Projec
Elevations and depressions are given in feet

W. GUINEA
PAPUA NEW GUINEA
Mt. Albert Edward 13 100
Mt. Victoria 13 363
Port Moresby
Buna
OWEN STANLEY RA.
TROBRIAND IS.
WOODLARK
D'ENTRECASTEAUX ISLANDS
Samarai
SOUTH CAPE
LOUISIADE ARCHIPELAGO
TAGULA
ROSSEL

Torres Strait
BANKS
DARU
HORN I.
CAPE YORK

VELLA LAVELLA
CHOISEUL
NEW GEORGIA
SANTA ISABEL
RENDOVA
RUSSELL IS.
FLORIDA
MALAITA
S O L O M O N   I S L A N D S
Honiara
TULAGI
GUADALCANAL
SAN CRISTÓBAL
RENNELL

CAPE YORK
PENINSULA

Princess Charlotte Bay
CAPE MELVILLE
OSPREY REEF

C O R A L   S E A

SANTA CRUZ ISLANDS

Laura
Cooktown
Palmerville
ATHERTON
Munganna
PLATEAU
Croydon
Mt. Bartle Frere 5287
Cairns
HINCHINBROOK I.
HOLMES REEFS
WILLIS IS.
FLINDERS REEFS
TREGROSSE IS.
LIHOU REEFS

Forsayth
Ingham
Halifax Bay
Townsville

MARION REEF

P A C I F I C

ESPÍRITU SANTO
MAEWO
NEW
PENTECOST
HEBRIDES
MALEKULA
AMBRIM
ERI
AMBRYM
VANUATU
EFATE
Port Vila

Richmond
Hughenden
Charters Towers
Bowen
WHITSUNDAY
CUMBERLAND IS.
Repulse Bay
Mackay

Kynuna
Winton
Mt. Dalrymple 4190
NORTHUMBERLAND IS.
SWAIN REEFS

ÎLES CHESTERFIELD (Fr.)
ÎLES BÉLEP
OUVÉA
LIFOU
ÎLES LOYAUTÉ (French)
MARE
TANA
ANEITYUM

QUEENSLAND
Longreach
Barcaldine
Jericho
Clermont
Emerald
Dingo
Rockhampton
Mount Morgan
CURTIS
Gladstone

Yaraka
Blackall
Tambo
BUCKLAND TABLELAND
Bundaberg
Hervey Bay
SANDY CAPE
FRASER

WRECK REEFS

NEW CALEDONIA (Fr.)
Nouméa
ÎLE DES PINS

Tropic of Capricorn

ARTESIAN RANGE
Quilpie
Charleville
Roma
Maryborough
Gympie

O C E A N

Thargomindah
Cunnamulla
St. George
Dalby
Toowoomba
Warwick
Ipswich
Brisbane
N. STRADBROKE I.
Southport

Brewarrina
Walgett
Moree
Tenterfield
Glen Innes
Inverell
NEW ENGLAND RANGE
Lismore
Grafton

Bourke
Coonamble
Narrabri
Armidale
Tamworth
The Round Mountain
Kempsey
Port Macquarie

Cobar
Nyngan
Dubbo
WARRUMBUNGLE RA.
LIVERPOOL RA.

NEW SOUTH WALES
Forbes
Bathurst
Orange
Lithgow
BLUE MTS.
Maitland
Cessnock
Newcastle
SYDNEY
Botany Bay
Wollongong

MURRAY
RIVERINA
REGION
West Wyalong
Narrandera
Wagga Wagga
Canberra
AUSTL. CAP. TER.
Goulburn
Jervis Bay

Hay
Albury
Tumbarumba
Kosciusko 7310
SNOWY MTS.
Cooma
Bombala

VICTORIA
Bendigo
Benalla
GREAT
Bega
Bairnsdale
CAPE HOWE

Ballarat
Maryborough
MELBOURNE
Geelong
WONTHAGGI
NINETY MILE BEACH
WILSON'S PROMONTORY

T A S M A N   S E A

LORD HOWE I. (NEW S. WALES)

PORT PHILLIP
CAPE OTWAY
KING I.
BASS STRAIT
FLINDERS I.
FURNEAUX GROUP
CAPE BARREN

TASMANIA
Burnie
Ulverstone
Devonport
Mt. OSSA 5305
Launceston
Strahan
BRUNY
SOUTH EAST CAPE
Hobart
New Norfolk
Risdon

50 0 50 100 200 300 400 500 Miles
0 100 200 400 600 800 Kilometers

a

P A C I F I C
NORTH CAPE
Kaitaia
Russell
GREAT BARRIER
O C E A N
Devonport
Auckland
NORTH ISLAND
Hamilton
Bay of Plenty
EAST CAPE

NEW ZEALAND

North Taranaki Bight
New Plymouth
C. EGMONT
Egmont Vol. 8 125
South Taranaki Bight
Wanganui
Gisborne
Napier
Hastings
Palmerston North

T A S M A N
S E A
CAPE FAREWELL
Tasman Bay
Nelson
Cook Strait
Lower Hutt
Wellington

CAPE FOULWIND
Karamea Bight
Greymouth
Hokitika
SOUTHERN ALPS
Mt. Cook 12 349
Pegasus Bay
Christchurch
SOUTH ISLAND
CASCADE PT.
Canterbury Bight
Timaru

P A C I F I C

RESOLUTION ISLAND
Dunedin
CAPE SAUNDERS
Foveaux Strait
Invercargill
STEWART ISLAND
SOUTHWEST CAPE

O C E A N

Same scale as main map

Cities and Towns

0 to 50,000	○	500,000 to 1,000,000	◎
50,000 to 500,000	⊙	1,000,000 and over	

SIMPSON DESERT

QUEENSLAND

GREAT ARTESIAN BASIN

GREY RANGE

WARREGO RA.

CHESTERTON RA.

EXPEDITION RA.

DARLING DOWNS

GREAT DIVIDING RANGE

NEW ENGLAND RANGE

SOUTH AUSTRALIA

FLINDERS RANGES

NORTH FLINDERS RANGES

GAWLER RANGES

NORTH-MOUNT LOFTY RANGES

EYRE PEN.

NEW SOUTH WALES

MAIN BARRIER RANGE

WARRUMBUNGLE RANGE

BLUE MTS.

MURRAY REGION

RIVERINA

VICTORIA

AUSTRALIAN ALPS

SNOWY MTS.

AUSTL. CAP. TER.

GIPPSLAND

INDIAN OCEAN

BASS STRAIT

FURNEAUX GROUP

KING

FLINDERS

TASMANIA

TASMAN SEA

KANGAROO

EYRE PEN.

Cities and towns:

Gladstone, Biloela, Mt. Fort William 2420, Bundaberg, Hervey Bay, Theodore, Pialba, FRASER, Maryborough, Gayndah, Gympie, Kingaroy, Yarraman, MORETON, Redcliffe, Brisbane, Ipswich, Southport, Mt. Roberts 3495, Murwillumbah, Warwick, Lismore, Casino, Ballina, Tenterfield, Capompeta 5000, Glen Innes, Grafton, Guyra, The Round Mountain 5300, Coff's Harbour, Mt. Banda Banda 4144, Kempsey, Port Macquarie

Welford, Windorah, Yaraka, Tambo, Augathella, Charleville, Quilpie, Injune, Wandoan, Miles, Barakula, Chinchilla, Roma, Mt. Mowbullan 3611, Dalby, Durham Downs, Surat, Meandarra, Millmerran, Inglewood, Thargomindah, Cunnamulla, St. George, Dirranbandi, Goondiwindi, Texas, Innamincka, Naryilco, Hungerford, Mungindi, Moree, Lightning Ridge, Pokataroo, Wariolda, Inverell, Barraba, Gwabegar, Coonamble, Gunnedah, Tamworth, Mt. Kaputar 4999, Narrabri, Armidale 5300, Brewarrina, Bourke, Walgett, Wee Waa, Narran Lake, Nyngan, Coonabarabran, Dubbo, Coolah, Merriwa, Muswellbrook, Barrington Tops 5200, Taree, Sugarloaf Pt., Liverpool, Maitland, Cessnock, Port Stephens, Wellington, Mudgee, Newcastle, Gosford, Broken Bay, Sydney, Botany Bay, Lithgow, Mt. Reeves 4470, Cowra, Bathurst, Orange, Parkes, Forbes, Eugowra, Young, Cootamundra, Crookwell, Goulburn, Mossvale, Nowra, Wollongong, Beecroft Head, Canberra, Batlow, Tumbarumba, Albury, Bimberi Pk. 6274, Wagga Wagga, Cooma, Bega, Bombala, Eden, Cape Howe, Mallacoota Inlet, Bateman's Bay

Marree, Andamooka, Woomera, Pimba, Lake Torrens, Leigh Creek, Hawker, Quorn, Iron Knob, Whyalla, Kimba, Wilmington, Peterborough, Port Augusta, Port Pirie, Gladstone, Wallaroo, Moonta, YORKE PENINSULA, Riverton, Morgan, Wakefield, Gawler, Adelaide, Waikerie, Loxton, Renmark, Mildura, Wentworth, Red Cliffs, Morkalla, Robinvale, Murray Bridge, Tailem Bend, Pinnaroo, Peebinga, Ouyen, Kulwin, Swan Hill, Balranald, Hay, Deniliquin, Griffith, Narrandera, Coolamon, Temora, Hillston, West Wyalong, Lake Cowal, L. Cargelligo, Roto, Ivanhoe, Menindee, L. Tandou, Wilcannia, Cobar, Nymagee, White Cliffs, Broken Hill, Mt. Sturt 1400, Tottenham, Narromine, Binnaway

Thistle, Kingscote, KANGAROO, Victor Harbour, Encounter Bay, Lake Alexandrina, The Coorong, Keith, Kingston, CAPE JAFFA, Naracoorte, Millicent, Mount Gambier, Casterton, Hamilton, Portland, CAPE NELSON, Warrnambool, Colac, Geelong, CAPE OTWAY, Wonthaggi, PHILLIP I., Phillip Bay, Dandenong, MELBOURNE, Ballarat, Ararat, Horsham, Gotoke, Rockland Res., Maryborough, Castlemaine, Bendigo, Seymour, Fildon Res., Mansfield, Mt. Torbreck 4495, Mt. Cobberas 6025, Mt. Baw Baw 5127, Bairnsdale, Orbost, Lakes Entrance, NINETY MILE BEACH, Sale, Moe, Traralgon, Yarram, Corner Inlet, WILSON'S PROMONTORY, KENT GROUP, Warracknabeal, Charlton, Echuca, Shepparton, Wangaratta, Benalla, Bright, Mt. Bogong 6508, Mt. Kosciusko 7316, Corowa, Cohuna, Kerang, Hopetoun, Yanac, Kaniva, Dimboola, Nhill, Stawell

Grassy, Smithton, Burnie, Ulverstone, Devonport, WEST PT., CAPE GRIM, HUNTER IS., Deloraine, Launceston, Legges Pk. 5160, Scottsdale, St. Marys, Mt. Ossa 5305, Queenstown, Campbell Town, CAPE SORELL, Strahan, FREYCINET PENINSULA, Bridgewater, New Norfolk, Hobart, TASMAN PENINSULA, FLINDERS, FURNEAUX GROUP, CAPE BARREN, CAPE BARREN, Banks Strait, EDDYSTONE PT.

Rivers and lakes:

L. Machattie, L. Moonda, Lake Yamma Yamma, L. Goyder, Coopers Creek, Diamantina R., Whitula Cr., Bulloo R., Carapundy Swamp, Barwon (Macintyre), Narran R., Namoi R., Macquarie R., Bogan R., Lachlan R., Murrumbidgee R., Billabong Cr., Lake Eyre 39 Ft., L. Gregory, L. Blanche, Lake Callabonna, Lake Frome, Strzelecki Cr., The Warburton, Peera Peera Poolanna L., L. Howitt, Cooper Cr., Lake Torrens, Lake Gairdner, Lake Macfarlane, Spencer Gulf, Gulf St. Vincent, Investigator Strait, Lake Alexandrina, Murray R., Darling R., Lake Hindmarsh, Glenelg R., Goulburn R., Snowy R., Tambo R., Grampians, Lake Victoria

A-590298-76- 5-4 82
COPYRIGHT BY
RAND McNALLY & COMPANY
MADE IN U.S.A.

Relief

Meters	Feet
1525	5000
610	2000
305	1000
152.5	500
Sea Level	Sea Level
152.5	500
1525	5000
3050	10 000
	Below Sea Level

140° Longitude East of Greenwich

0   50   100   150   200 Miles
0   50   100   150   200   250   300 Kilometers

Scale 1:8 000 000; one inch to 126 miles.
Lambert's Azimuthal, Equal Area Projection.
Elevations and depressions are given in feet.

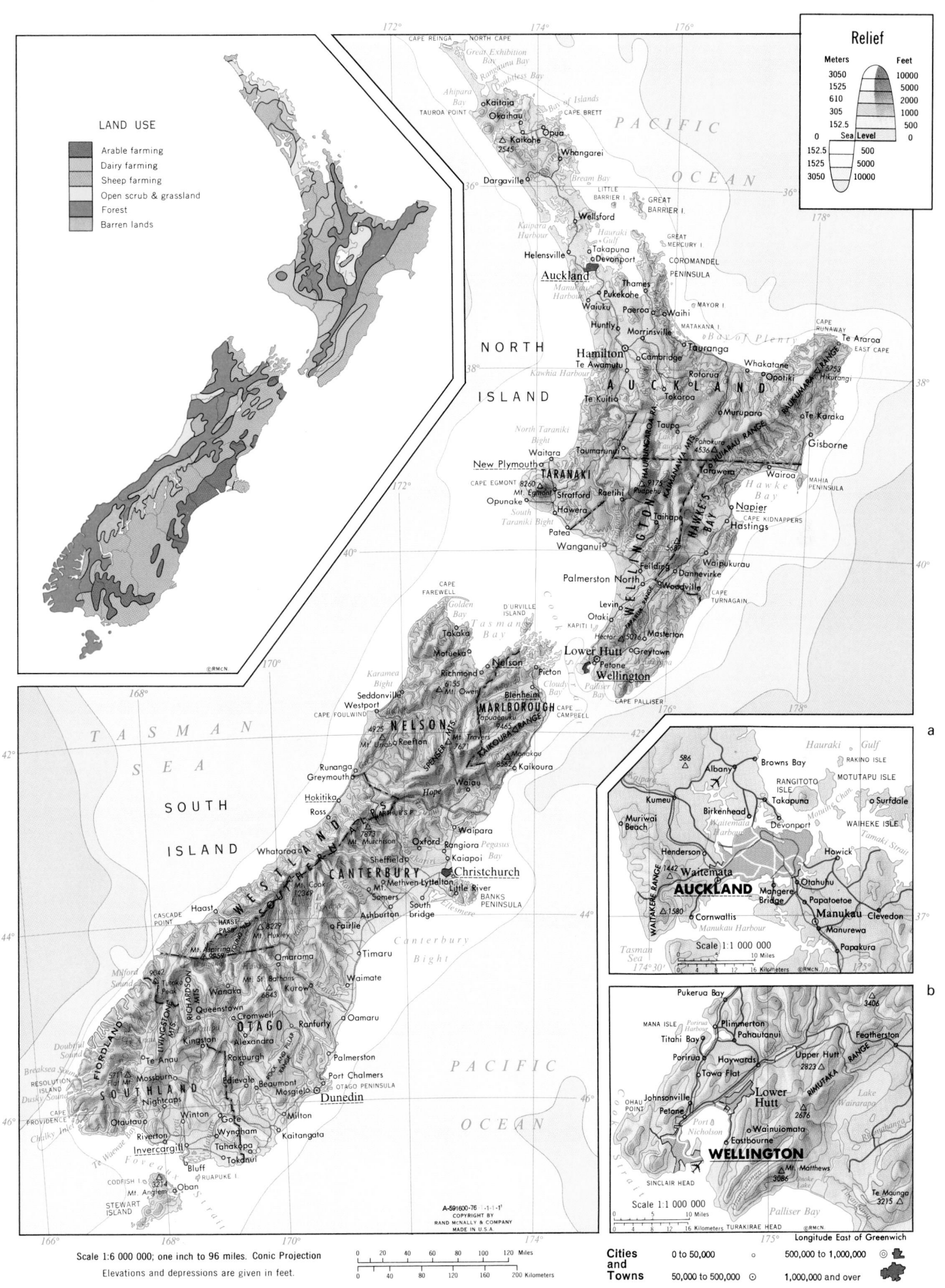

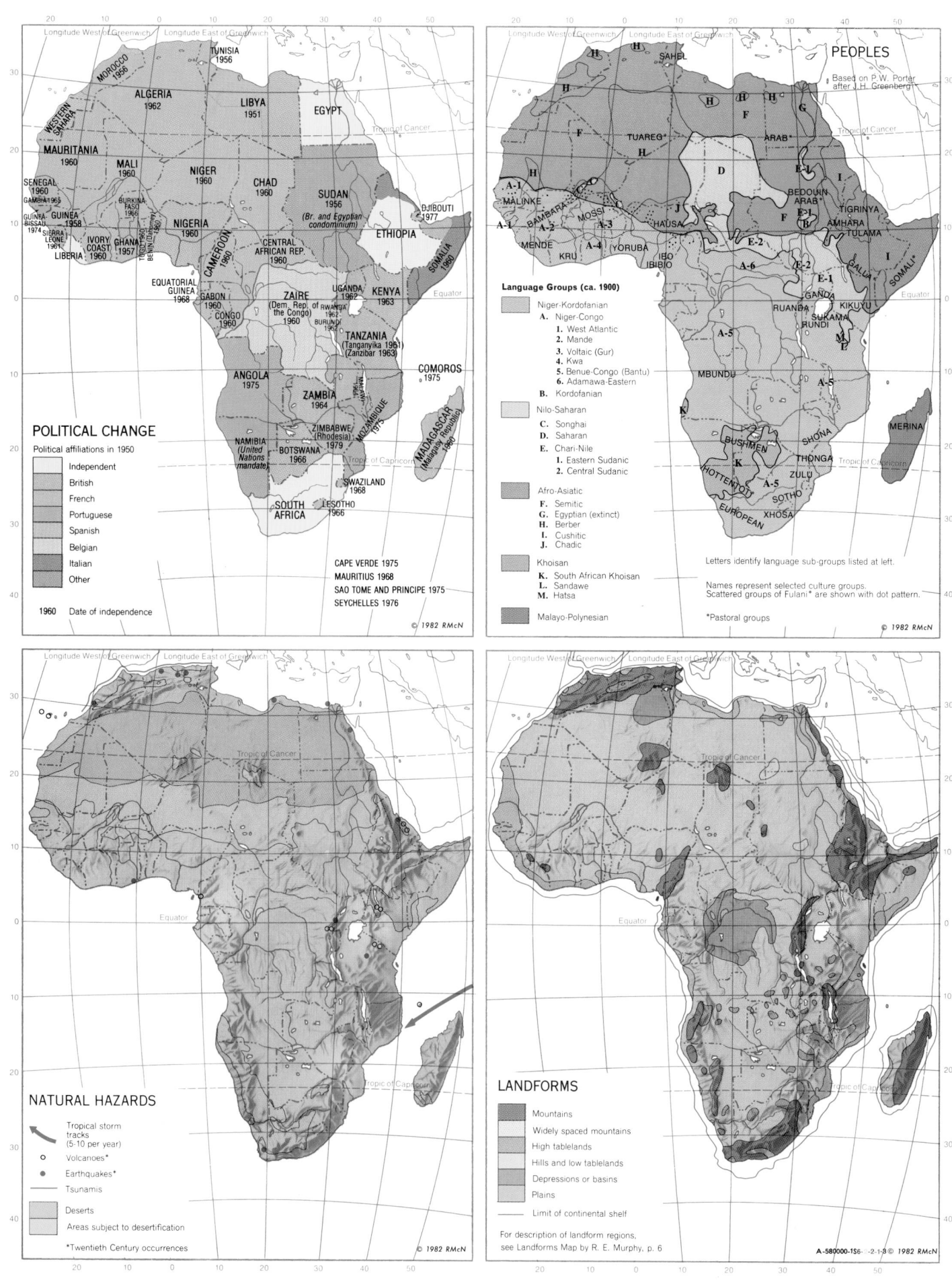

POLITICAL CHANGE

Political affiliations in 1950

Independent
British
French
Portuguese
Spanish
Belgian
Italian
Other

1960   Date of independence

CAPE VERDE 1975
MAURITIUS 1968
SAO TOME AND PRINCIPE 1975
SEYCHELLES 1976

© 1982 RMcN

TUNISIA 1956
MOROCCO 1956
ALGERIA 1962
LIBYA 1951
EGYPT
WESTERN SAHARA
MAURITANIA 1960
MALI 1960
NIGER 1960
CHAD 1960
SUDAN 1956 (Br. and Egyptian condominium)
DJIBOUTI 1977
SENEGAL 1960
GAMBIA 1965
GUINEA BISSAU 1974
GUINEA 1958
SIERRA LEONE 1961
BURKINA FASO 1960
NIGERIA 1960
CENTRAL AFRICAN REP. 1960
ETHIOPIA
SOMALIA 1960
LIBERIA 1960
IVORY COAST 1957
GHANA 1957
TOGO 1960
BENIN (Dahomey) 1960
CAMEROON 1960
EQUATORIAL GUINEA 1968
GABON 1960
CONGO 1960
ZAIRE (Dem. Rep.) of the Congo 1960
UGANDA 1962
RWANDA 1962
BURUNDI 1962
KENYA 1963
TANZANIA (Tanganyika 1961) (Zanzibar 1963)
COMOROS 1975
ANGOLA 1975
ZAMBIA 1964
MALAWI
MOZAMBIQUE 1975
MADAGASCAR (Malagasy Republic) 1960
MERINA
NAMIBIA (United Nations mandate)
BOTSWANA 1966
ZIMBABWE (Rhodesia) 1979
SWAZILAND 1968
SOUTH AFRICA
LESOTHO 1966

PEOPLES

Based on P. W. Porter
after J. H. Greenberg

Language Groups (ca. 1900)

Niger-Kordofanian
   A. Niger-Congo
     1. West Atlantic
     2. Mande
     3. Voltaic (Gur)
     4. Kwa
     5. Benue-Congo (Bantu)
     6. Adamawa-Eastern
   B. Kordofanian

Nilo-Saharan
   C. Songhai
   D. Saharan
   E. Chari-Nile
     1. Eastern Sudanic
     2. Central Sudanic

Afro-Asiatic
   F. Semitic
   G. Egyptian (extinct)
   H. Berber
   I. Cushitic
   J. Chadic

Khoisan
   K. South African Khoisan
   L. Sandawe
   M. Hatsa

Malayo-Polynesian

Letters identify language sub-groups listed at left.

Names represent selected culture groups.
Scattered groups of Fulani* are shown with dot pattern.

*Pastoral groups

© 1982 RMcN

SAHEL
TUAREG
ARAB
BEDOUIN ARAB
MALINKE
BAMBARA
MOSSI
HAUSA
MENDE
KRU
YORUBA
IBO
IBIBIO
TIGRINYA
AMHARA
TULAMA
GALLA
SOMALI*
GANDA
KIKUYU
RUANDA
RUNDI
SUKAMA
MBUNDU
SHONA
THONGA
ZULU
SOTHO
XHOSA
BUSHMEN
HOTTENTOT
EUROPEAN
MERINA

NATURAL HAZARDS

Tropical storm tracks (5-10 per year)
○ Volcanoes*
● Earthquakes*
Tsunamis
Deserts
Areas subject to desertification

*Twentieth Century occurrences

© 1982 RMcN

LANDFORMS

Mountains
Widely spaced mountains
High tablelands
Hills and low tablelands
Depressions or basins
Plains
Limit of continental shelf

For description of landform regions,
see Landforms Map by R. E. Murphy, p. 6

A-580000-1S6--2-1-3 © 1982 RMcN

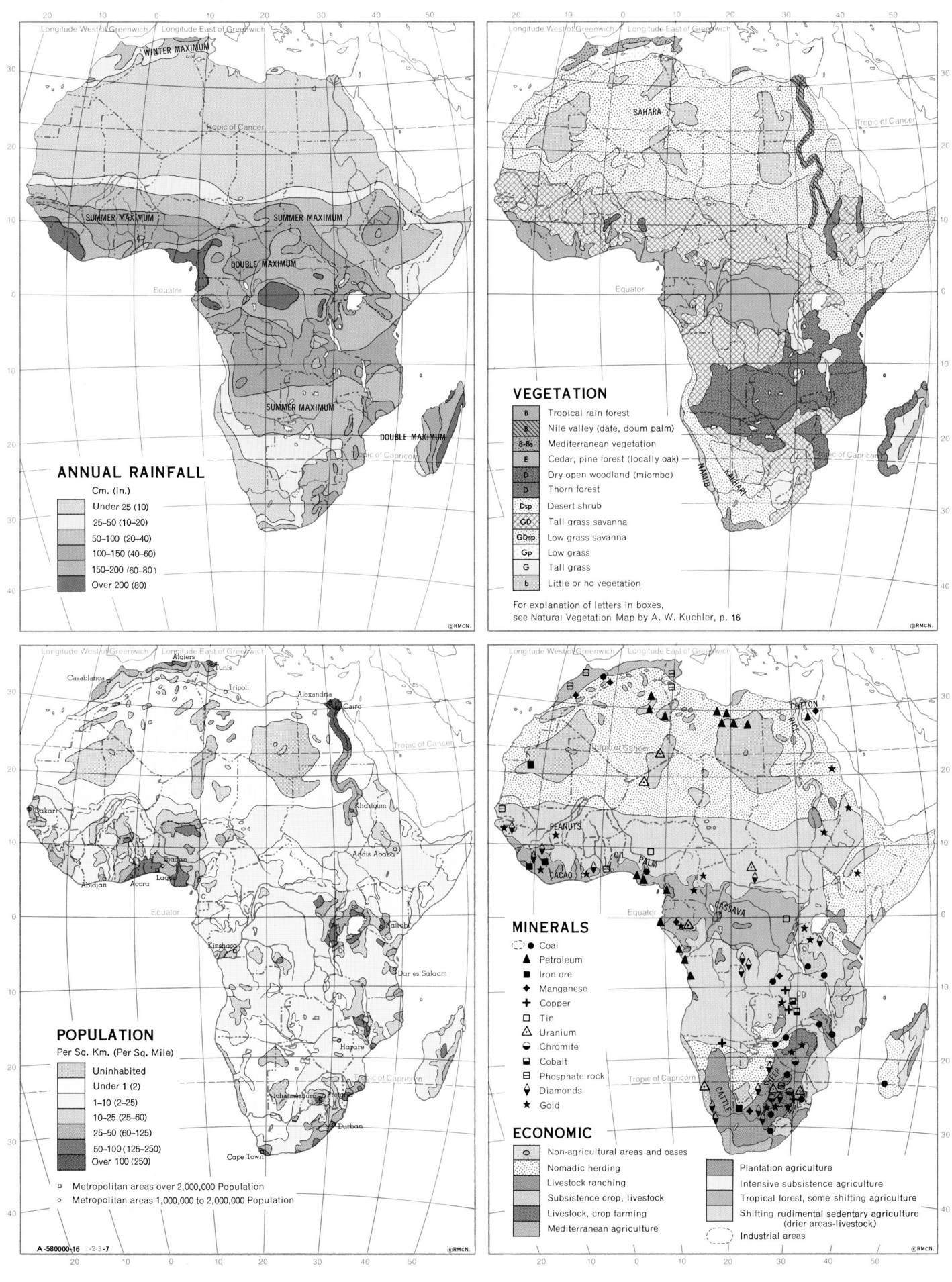

ANNUAL RAINFALL

Cm. (In.)

	Under 25 (10)
	25–50 (10–20)
	50–100 (20–40)
	100–150 (40–60)
	150–200 (60–80)
	Over 200 (80)

WINTER MAXIMUM
SUMMER MAXIMUM
SUMMER MAXIMUM
DOUBLE MAXIMUM
SUMMER MAXIMUM
DOUBLE MAXIMUM

©RMCN.

VEGETATION

B	Tropical rain forest
B	Nile valley (date, doum palm)
B–Bs	Mediterranean vegetation
E	Cedar, pine forest (locally oak)
D	Dry open woodland (miombo)
D	Thorn forest
Dsp	Desert shrub
GD	Tall grass savanna
GDsp	Low grass savanna
Gp	Low grass
G	Tall grass
b	Little or no vegetation

For explanation of letters in boxes,
see Natural Vegetation Map by A. W. Kuchler, p. **16**

SAHARA
NAMIB
KALAHARI

©RMCN.

POPULATION

Per Sq. Km. (Per Sq. Mile)

	Uninhabited
	Under 1 (2)
	1–10 (2–25)
	10–25 (25–60)
	25–50 (60–125)
	50–100 (125–250)
	Over 100 (250)

◦ Metropolitan areas over 2,000,000 Population
◦ Metropolitan areas 1,000,000 to 2,000,000 Population

Algiers
Tunis
Casablanca
Tripoli
Alexandria
Cairo
Dakar
Khartoum
Ibadan
Addis Ababa
Lagos
Abidjan
Accra
Nairobi
Kinshasa
Dar es Salaam
Harare
Johannesburg Pretoria
Durban
Cape Town

A-580000-16   -2-3-7

©RMCN.

MINERALS

●	Coal
▲	Petroleum
■	Iron ore
◆	Manganese
+	Copper
□	Tin
△	Uranium
◔	Chromite
▱	Cobalt
⊟	Phosphate rock
◇	Diamonds
★	Gold

COTTON
RICE
PEANUTS
CACAO
OIL PALM
CASSAVA
SHEEP
CATTLE

ECONOMIC

	Non-agricultural areas and oases
	Nomadic herding
	Livestock ranching
	Subsistence crop, livestock
	Livestock, crop farming
	Mediterranean agriculture
	Plantation agriculture
	Intensive subsistence agriculture
	Tropical forest, some shifting agriculture
	Shifting rudimental sedentary agriculture (drier areas-livestock)
	Industrial areas

©RMCN.

220

BERLIN

LONDON

PARIS

MADRID

ALPS

ROME

CORSICA

SARDINIA

SICILY

MALTA

PYRENEES

ATLAS MOUNTAINS

Casablanca

Algiers

Tunis

Tripoli

Banghāzī

Athens

CRETE

Alexandria

CAIRO

Nile

Lake Nasser

ARABIAN DESERT

NUBIAN DESERT

Nile

LIBYAN DESERT

A

R

N

ENNEDI

TIBESTI

A

A

H

A

G

G

A

R

D

U

S

S

A

Lake Chad

Ndjamena

Kano

Yaoundé

Niger

Lagos

Gulf of Guinea

GRAND ERG OCCIDENTAL

GRAND ERG ORIENTAL

AHAGGAR

Tamanrasset

ATLAS

ADRAR DES IFORAS

EL DJOUF

Tombouctou

Niger

Bamako

Lake Volta

Abidjan

CANARY ISLANDS

El Aaiun

Dakar

CAPE VERDE ISLANDS

Freetown

Mediterranean Sea

Red Sea

ATLANTIC OCEAN

Tropic of Cancer

ATLANTIC OCEAN

Scale 1:24,000,000; one inch to 380 miles. Lambert Azimuthal Equal-Area Projection

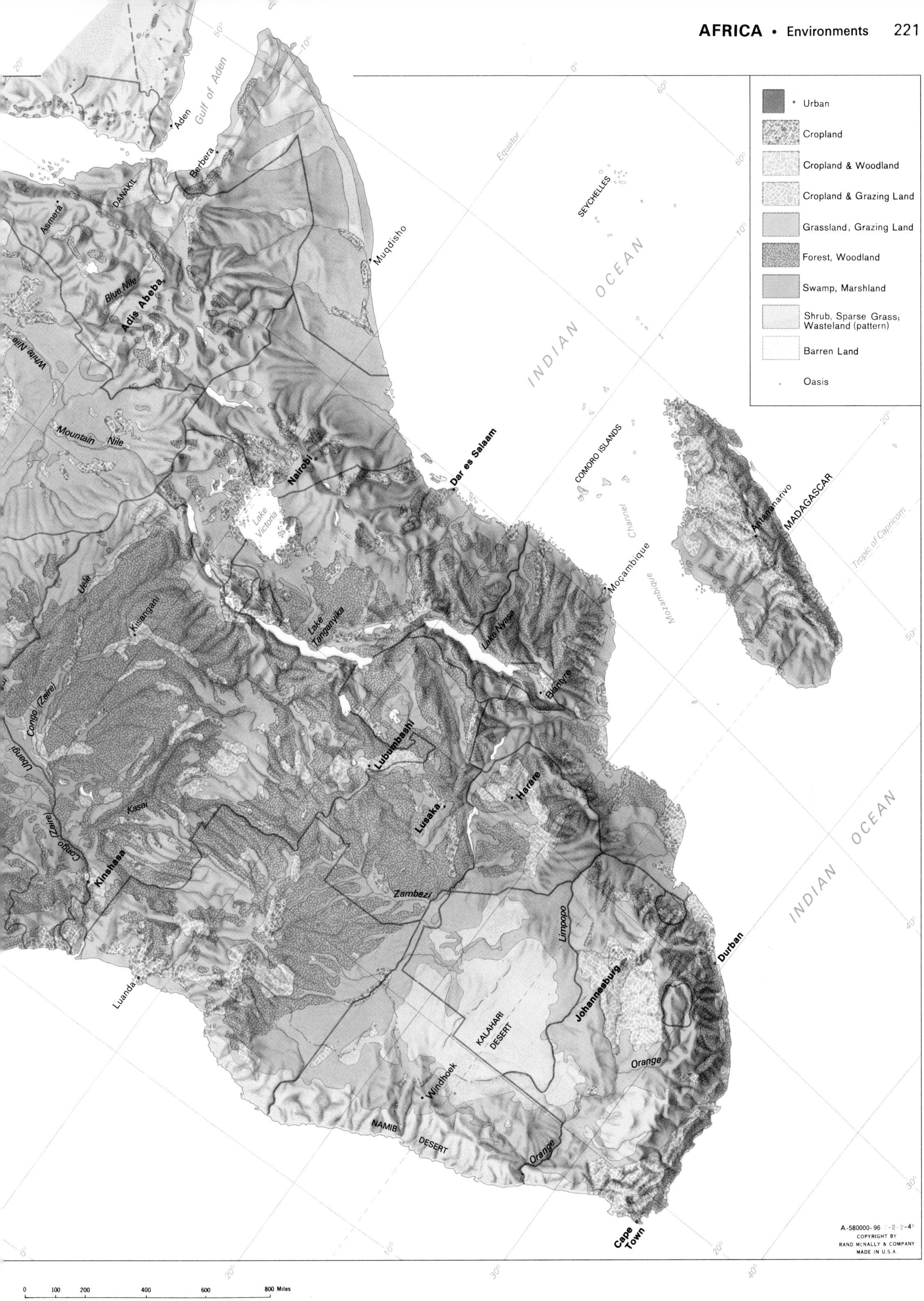

Legend

- Urban
- Cropland
- Cropland & Woodland
- Cropland & Grazing Land
- Grassland, Grazing Land
- Forest, Woodland
- Swamp, Marshland
- Shrub, Sparse Grass; Wasteland (pattern)
- Barren Land
- Oasis

Gulf of Aden
Aden
Berbera
DANAKIL
Asmera
Blue Nile
Adis Abeba
White Nile
Mountain Nile
Muqdisho
SEYCHELLES
INDIAN OCEAN
Nairobi
Dar es Salaam
COMORO ISLANDS
Lake Victoria
Uele
Kisangani
Lake Tanganyika
Lake Nyasa
MADAGASCAR
Antananarivo
Congo (Zaïre)
Ubangi
Kasai
Lubumbashi
Blantyre
Kinshasa
Lusaka
Harare
Zambezi
Mozambique Channel
Luanda
Limpopo
Johannesburg
Durban
KALAHARI DESERT
Orange
Windhoek
NAMIB DESERT
Orange
INDIAN OCEAN
Cape Town

0 100 200 400 600 800 Miles
0 150 300 600 900 1200 Kilometers

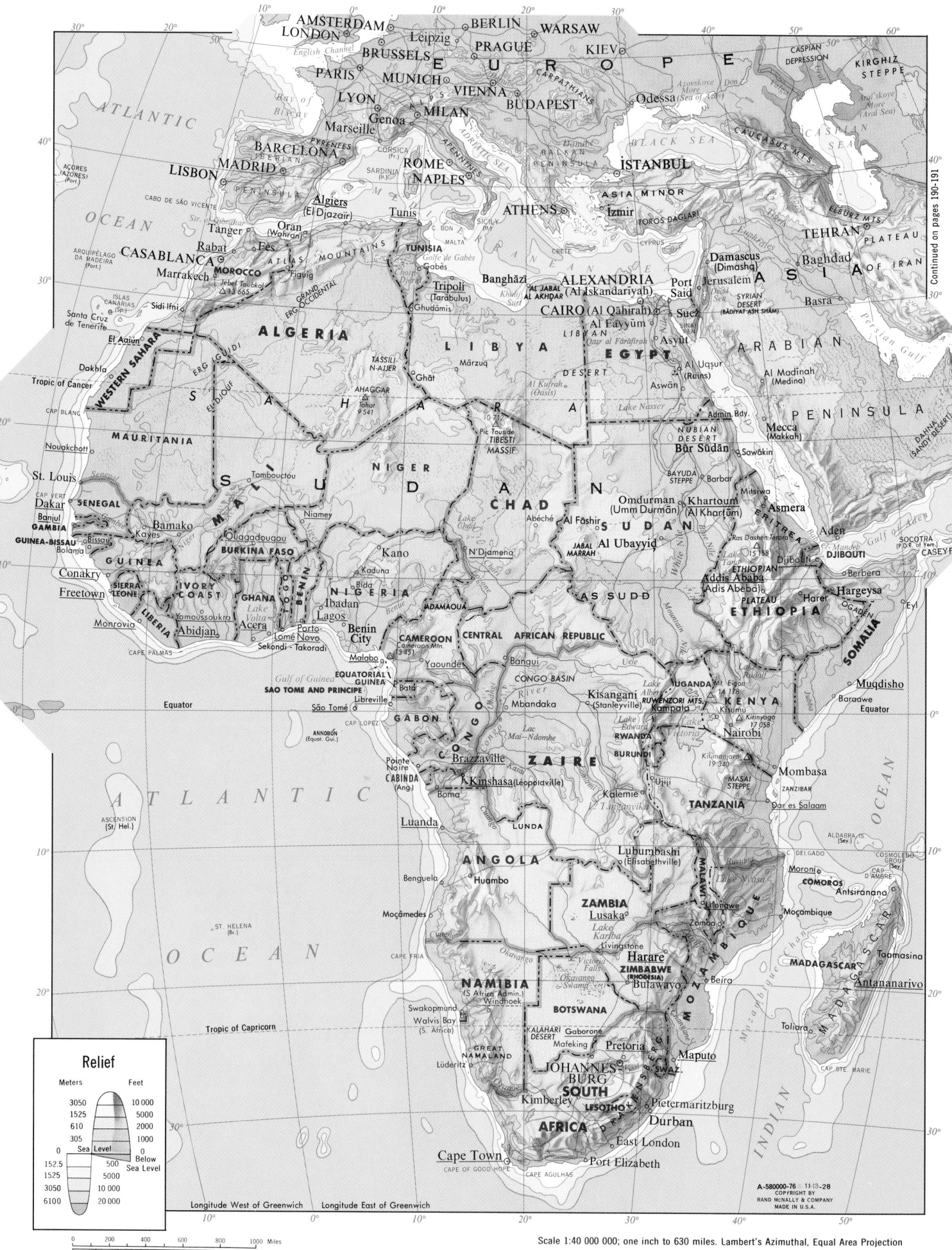

Relief

Meters	Feet
3050	10 000
1525	5000
610	2000
305	1000
0 Sea Level	0 Sea Level
152.5	500 Below Sea Level
1525	5000
3050	10 000
6100	20 000

0 200 400 600 800 1000 Miles
0 400 800 1200 1600 Kilometers

Longitude West of Greenwich   Longitude East of Greenwich

A-580000-76 11-13-28
COPYRIGHT BY
RAND McNALLY & COMPANY
MADE IN U.S.A.

Scale 1:40 000 000; one inch to 630 miles. Lambert's Azimuthal, Equal Area Projection
Elevations and depressions are given in feet.

Continued on pages 190-191

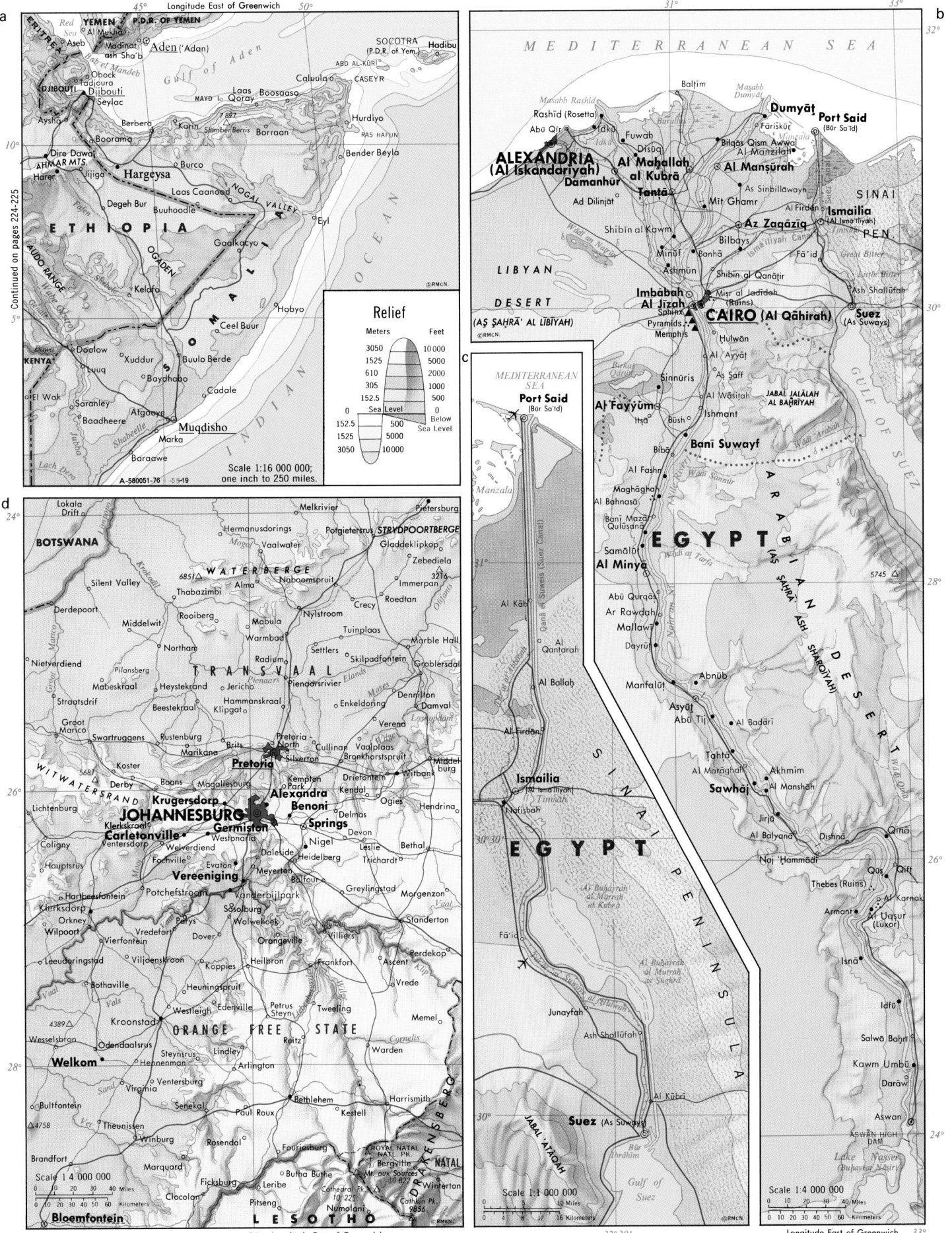

Continued on pages 154-155

a AÇORES (AZORES) (Port.)
GRACIOSA · TERCEIRA · SÃO JORGE · FAIAL · PICO · SÃO MIGUEL · STA. MARIA · Ponta Delgada
Same scale as main map

b CAPE VERDE
SANTO ANTÃO · SÃO VICENTE · SAL · SÃO NICOLAU · BOA VISTA · SÃO TIAGO · MAIO · FOGO · Praia
Same scale as main map

ATLANTIC OCEAN

SPAIN

Cádiz · Gibraltar (U.K.) · Tanger (Tangier) · Tetouan · Larache · Ceuta (Sp.) · Melilla (Sp.)

CASABLANCA · Rabat · Salé · Meknès · Fès · Taza

Algiers (El Djazair) · Oran · Constantine · Annaba

MOROCCO · ATLAS MOUNTAINS · ALGERIA

Marrakech · Agadir · Tindouf

WESTERN SAHARA · El Aaiún · Dakhla · Tropic of Cancer

The Western Sahara is occupied by Morocco

ISLAS CANARIAS (Sp.) · La Palma · Tenerife · Gran Canaria · Las Palmas de Gran Canaria

S A H A R A · GRAND ERG OCCIDENTAL · GRAND ERG ORIENTAL · ERG IGUIDI · ERG CHECH · EL DJOUF · TANEZROUFT · AHAGGAR · TUAREG

MAURITANIA · Nouakchott · Nouadhibou · Atar · EL MREYYÉ · OUARANE

Taoudenni · Araouane · Tombouctou (Timbuktu) · Gao · Kidal · ADRAR DES IFÔGHAS

M A L I · Bamako · Ségou · Mopti · AÏR · Agadez

SENEGAL · Dakar · Saint-Louis · Kaolack · Thiès
GAMBIA · Banjul (Bathurst)
GUINEA-BISSAU · Bissau
GUINEA · Conakry · FOUTA DJALLON · Kankan
SIERRA LEONE · Freetown
LIBERIA · Monrovia
IVORY COAST · Yamoussoukro · Abidjan · Bouaké
GHANA · Accra · Kumasi
BURKINA FASO · Ouagadougou · Bobo-Dioulasso
TOGO · Lomé · BENIN · Porto-Novo
N I G E R · Niamey
NIGERIA · Lagos · Ibadan · Kano · Kaduna · Zaria · Enugu · Port Harcourt · Benin City · Onitsha
EQUATORIAL GUINEA · Malabo · SÃO TOME AND PRINCIPE
CAMEROON · Douala
GULF OF GUINEA · Bight of Benin · ATLANTIC OCEAN

Longitude West of Greenwich · Longitude East of Greenwich

Scale 1:16 000 000; one inch to 250 miles. Sinusoidal Projection
Elevations and depressions are given in feet

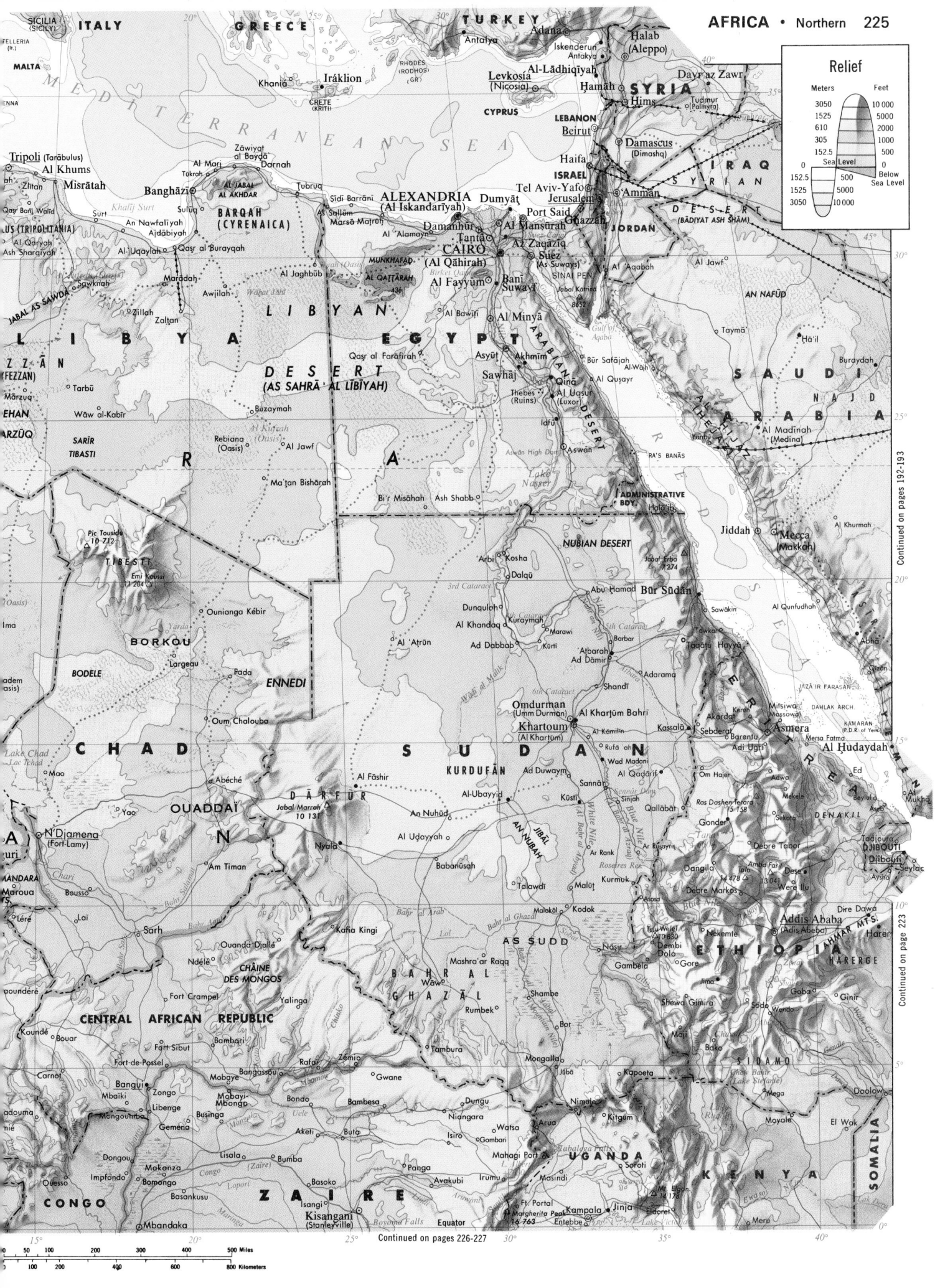

Continued on pages 192-193
Continued on page 223
Continued on pages 226-227

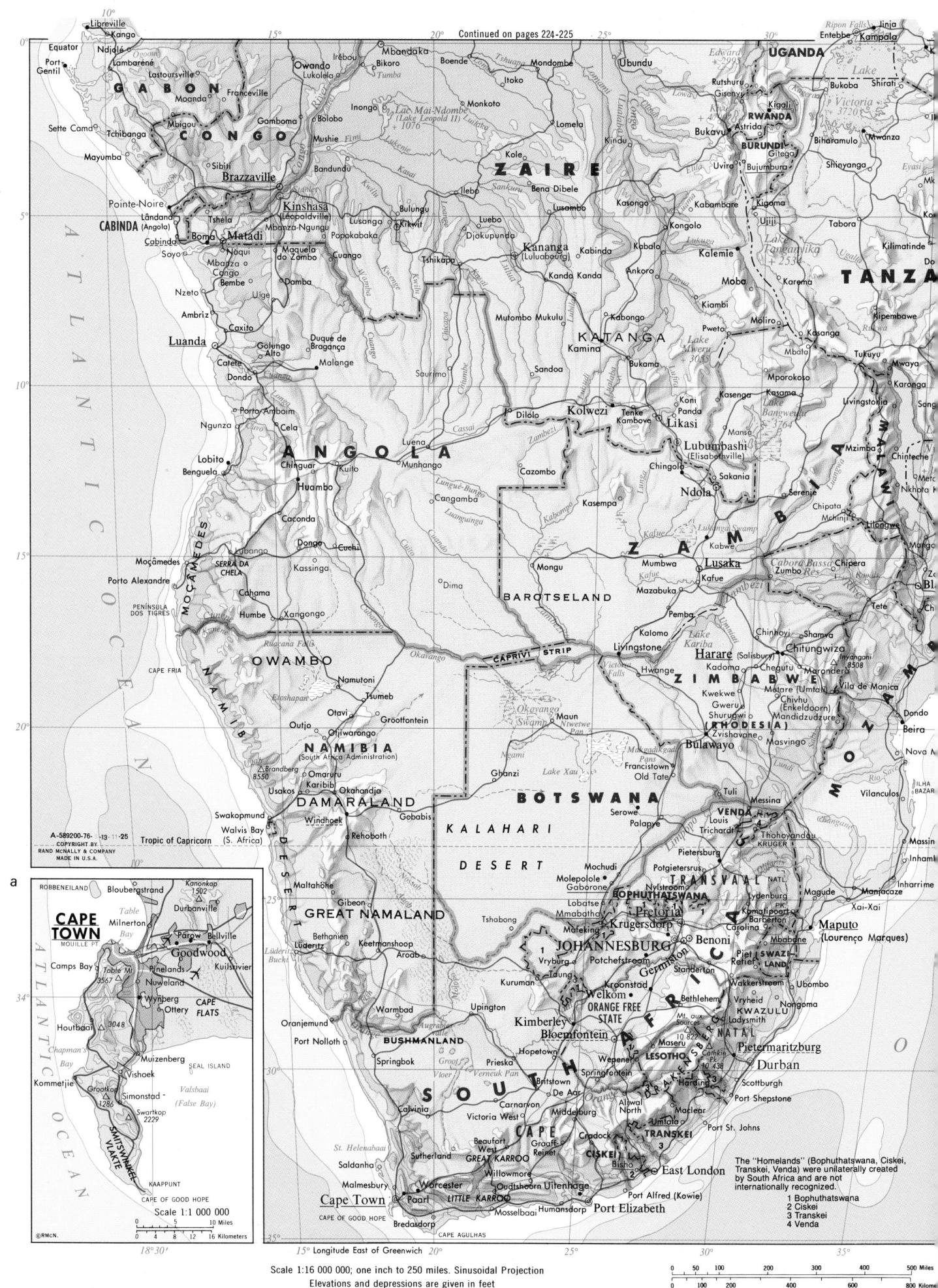

Continued on pages 224-225

ATLANTIC OCEAN

GABON

CONGO

ZAIRE

UGANDA

RWANDA

BURUNDI

TANZA

Libreville
Kango
Equator
Ndjolé
Lambaréné
Port Gentil
Sette Cama
Tchibanga
Mbigou
Moanda
Franceville
Lastoursville
Mayumba
Sibiti

Brazzaville
Pointe-Noire
Lândana
CABINDA
Cabinda (Angola)
Boma Matadi
Nóqui
Soyo
Mbanza Congo
Bembe

Ogooué
Owando
Lukolela
Irébou
Bikoro
Boende
Bandundu
Inongo
Lac Mai-Ndombe
(Lake Leopold II)
1076
Monkoto
Lomela
Ubundu

Mbandaka
Mondombe
Lomela

Kinshasa
(Leopoldville)
Mbanza-Ngungu
Popokabaka
Ilebo
Bena Dibele
Lusambo

Kole

Mbata
Bolobo
Mushie

Kikwit
Bulungu
Lusanga
Tshikapa

Kindu
Kongolo
Kabambare
Kigoma
Tabora

Kananga
(Luluabourg)
Kabinda
Ankoro
Kabalo
Ujiji

Kalemie

Kilimatinde

Maquela do Zombo
Cuango
Damba

KATANGA
Kamina
Sandoa
Bukama
Kabongo
Pweto
Moliro
Karema
Kipembawe

Luena
Munhango
Cazombo

Dilolo
Kolwezi
Tenke
Kambove
Likasi
Chingola
Sakania
Mansa

Mwaya
Karonga

Uige
Ambriz
Nzeto

Luanda
Catete
Dondo
Golungo Alto
Duque de Bragança
Malange

Porto Amboim
Ngunza
Cela

ANGOLA

Lubumbashi
(Elisabethville)
Ndola

Serenje
Chipata
Mchinji
Mzimba

Chinteche
Nkhata

Lobito
Benguela
Metc

Chinguar
Kuito
Huambo
Caconda

ZAMBIA

Cabora Bassa
Zumbo Res.

Cangamba
Luanguinga

Mumbwa
Mazabuka
Lusaka
Kafue
Pemba

Chinhoyi
Shamva
Kadoma
Chegutu
Marondera

Harare (Salisbury)
Chitungwiza

Lake Kariba

Livingstone
Victoria Falls

ZIMBABWE
(RHODESIA)

Motare (Umtali)
Vila de Manica

Kwekwe
Gweru
Shurugwi

Dondo
Beira
Nova Sofala

Moçâmedes
Porto Alexandre
PENÍNSULA DOS TIGRES

SERRA DA CHELA
Lubango
Kassinga
Cahama
Humbe
Xangongo

Ruacana Falls

CAPE FRIA

OWAMBO
Etoshapan
Namutoni

Donge
Cuchi

Dima

BAROTSELAND

Mongu

CAPRIVI STRIP

Okavango Swamp
Nxwetwe Pan

Bulawayo
Zvishavane
Masvingo

Mandidzudzure

VENDA
Messina

NAMIBIA
(South Africa Administration)

Tsumeb
Otavi
Grootfontein
Outjo
Otjiwarongo

Ngami
Lake Xau
Ghanzi

BOTSWANA

Maun

Makgadikgadi Pans
Francistown
Old Tate

Tuli

DAMARALAND
Brandberg 8550
Omaruru
Karibib
Okahandja
Usakos
Windhoek
Rehoboth
Gobabis

KALAHARI

DESERT

Serowe
Palapye

Thohoyandou
KRUGER

Louis Trichardt

Pietersburg

Swakopmund
Walvis Bay (S. Africa)

Tropic of Capricorn

Mochudi
Molepolole
Gaborone

Potgietersrus

TRANSVAAL

Lydenburg
Carolina
Barberton
Komatipoort

Magude
Manjacaze
Xai-Xai

Maputo
(Lourenço Marques)

A-589200-76-
COPYRIGHT BY
RAND McNALLY & COMPANY
MADE IN U.S.A.
13-11-25

GREAT NAMALAND

Gibeon
Maltahöhe

Lüderitz
Lüderitz Bucht

Bethanien
Keetmanshoop
Aroab

Tshabong
Mmabatho
Lobatse
Mafeking
Vryburg

BOPHUTHATSWANA

Pretoria
Krugersdorp
JOHANNESBURG
Benoni

Germiston
Nylstroom

SWAZI LAND
Mbabane

Piet Retief
Ubombo

Nongoma

Mbane

Oranjemund
Port Nolloth

Warmbad

BUSHMANLAND

Upington
Kuruman
Taung
Potchefstroom
Kroonstad

Welkom
ORANGE FREE STATE
Bethlehem
Vryheid

Wakkerstroom

KWAZULU
Ladysmith

NATAL

Springbok

Kimberley
Hopetown
Bloemfontein

Maseru
LESOTHO

Pietermaritzburg
Durban

Calvinia

Prieska
Britstown
Springfontein
Wepener
Mt. aux Sources
10,822

Cathkin Pk
10,438
BRAKENSBERG

Harding
Scottburgh
Port Shepstone

Victoria West
Carnarvon
De Aar
Middelburg
Aliwal North
Maclear

Umtata
TRANSKEI

Port St. Johns

Sutherland

CAPE

Beaufort West
Graaff Reinet
Cradock

CISKEI
Bisho

East London

Saldanha
St. Helenabaai

GREAT KARROO
Willowmore
Oudtshoorn
Uitenhage

Port Alfred (Kowie)

Malmesbury
Worcester
Paarl

LITTLE KARROO
Mosselbaai
Humansdorp

Port Elizabeth

Cape Town
CAPE OF GOOD HOPE
Bredasdorp
Cape Agulhas

SOUTH AFRICA

The "Homelands" (Bophuthatswana, Ciskei, Transkei, Venda) were unilaterally created by South Africa and are not internationally recognized.
1 Bophuthatswana
2 Ciskei
3 Transkei
4 Venda

15° Longitude East of Greenwich

Scale 1:16 000 000; one inch to 250 miles. Sinusoidal Projection
Elevations and depressions are given in feet

0   50   100   200   300   400   500 Miles
0   100   200   400   600   800 Kilom

a

CAPE TOWN
MOUILLE PT.

ROBBENEILAND
Bloubergstrand
Kanonkop 1502
Milnerton
Durbanville
Parow Bellville
Table Bay
Goodwood
Kuilsrivier
Camps Bay
Table Mt. 3567
Pinelands
Nuweland
Wynberg
Ottery
CAPE FLATS
Houtbaai
Chapman's Bay
Muizenberg
SEAL ISLAND
Kommetjie
Vishoek
Simonstad
Grootkop 1286
Swartkop 2229
Valsbaai
(False Bay)
SMITSWINKEL VLAKTE
KAAPPUNT
CAPE OF GOOD HOPE

Scale 1:1 000 000

0   10 Miles
0   4   8   12   16 Kilometers

18°30'

b

c

SOMALIA

Kismaayo
Buur Gaabo
Equator

Witu
Lamu
Malindi
Takaungu
Mombasa
Vanga
PEMBA ISLAND
Tanga
Pangani
Zanzibar
Bagamoyo
Dar es Salaam
Morogoro
Kisaki
Utete
MAFIA
Kilwa Kivinje
Lindi
Mikindani
Masasi

INDIAN

Moçímboa
da Praia
CABO DELGADO
Ibo
Pemba
Lúrio
Memba
Nacala
Moçambique
ILHA ANGOCHE
António Enes

ZAMBIQUE CHANNEL

ALDABRA IS.
(Sey.)
COSMOLEDO GROUP
(Sey.)

Moroni
GRANDE
COMORE
Mohéli
ANJOUAN
COMOROS
ÎLES GLORIEUSES
(Fr.)
CAP D'AMBRE
Antsiranana
Dzaoudzi
MAYOTTE
(Fr.)
Iharana
NOSY BE
Maromokotra
2436

Mahajanga
Mandritsara
Maroantsetra
NOSY BORAHA
Fenoarivo
Afsinanana
CAP SAINT-
ANDRÉ
Helodrano
Antongila
Besalampy
ÎLE JUAN DE NOVA
(Fr.)
Ambatondra-
zaka
Toamasina
Maintirano
NOSY BARREN
Moramanga
MADAGASCAR
Antananarivo
Tsiafajavona
8671
Vatomandry
Mahanoro
Antsirabe
Ambositra
Mananjary
Morondava
Fianarantsoa
Manakara
BASSAS DA INDIA
(Fr.)
Ivohibé
Manakara
Morombe
EUROPA
(Fr.)
Farafangana
Betroka
Toliara
Mahaly
Trafanomby
4417
Faradofay
CAP STE. MARIE

ORANGE FREE STATE
Arlington
Paul Roux
Bethlehem
Senekal
Fouriesburg
Clarens
ROYAL NATAL
NAT'L. PK.
Harrismith
Kestell
Dannhauser
Glencoe
Dundee
Nqutu
Mahlabatini
Wasbank
Ladysmith
Pomeroy
Nkandla
Melmoth
Ficksburg
Butha Buthe
Leribe
MALOTI MTS.
10 822
Mt. aux
Sources
Bergville
Winterton
Cathedral Pk.
9856
Colenso
Weenen
Estcourt
Tugela Ferry
Greytown
Eshowe
Clocolan
Pitseng
Cathkin Pk.
10438
Mooirivier
New
Hanover
Dalton
Stanger
Wartburg
Teyateyaneng
Mokhotlong
Mt.
Gilboa
5803
Howick
LESOTHO
Machache
9464
Thabana
Ntlenyana
11425
Impendle
Ntshoni
5851
Pietermaritzburg
Roma
Underberg
Bulwer
Richmond
Camper-
down
Pinetown
Verulam
10159
Mohale's
Hoek
The Twins
8820
Sacha's Nek
Donnybrook
Mid Illovo
Durban
Isipingo
Zastron
Quthing
The Twins
Swartberg
7619
Creighton
Ixopo
Umkomaas
Matatiele
Franklin
TRANSKEI
Umzinto
Scottburgh
Park Rynie
Cedarville
Mt. Currie
7297
Kokstad
Harding
Sezela
TRANSKEI
Wilberg
7853
Ben Macdhui
9846
Mount
Fletcher
9684
7426
Bizana
Umtentweni
Port Shepstone
Uvongo Beach
Margate
Herschel
Lady Grey
Rhodes
Mount Frere
Maclear
Mount Ayliff
Tabankulu
Flagstaff
Port Edward
Barkly East
Jamestown
Rossouw
8430
Elliot
Ugie
Qumbu
Lusikisiki
Molteno
Dordrecht
Indwe
Cala
Tsolo
Libode
STORMBERG
Sterkstroom
Lady Frere
Engcobo
Umtata
Ngqeleni
Port St. Johns
RAME HEAD
Waverly
Queenstown
Tarkastad
Tylden
Cofimvaba
Tsomo
Mqanduli
Elliotdale
SOUTH AFRICA
CAPE
BANKBERG
6606
WINTERBERG
7778
Cradock
Whittlesea
Carthcart
Idutywa
Willowvale
Seymour
Stutterheim
Kamga
Butterworth
Pearston
Adelaide
CISKEI
Keiskammahoek
Frankfort
Kentani
Kei Mouth
Morgan's Bay
Somerset East
Bedford
Fort
Beaufort
Fort Alice
Bisho
King William's
Town
Berlin
Breidbach
Gonubie
Macleantown
East London
SUURBERGE
Riebeek-Oos
Peddie
Kidd's Beach
Alicedale
Grahamstown
Hamburg
Kirkwood
Addo
Salem
Bathurst
Alexandria
Port Alfred (Kowie)
Uitenhage
SAINT CROIX
ISLAND
BIRD ISLAND
Port Elizabeth
KAAP RECIFE

INDIAN

OCEAN

@RMCN.
Wolhuterskop
Pretoria
North
Cullinan
Jacksonstuin
Magaliesberg
Hartbeespoort
Pretoria
Swartspruit
Silverton
Rayton
Skeerpoort
4549
Kosmos
Hartbeespoortdam
Voortrekkerhoogte
Vathalla
4426
Foothills
Hennopsrivier
Irene
Tierpoort
WITWATERSBERG
Olievenhoutpoort
4602
Lyttelton
Tarlton
Halfway
House
Bapsfontein
Krugersdorp
Modderfontein
Kaalfontein
Kempton Park
Randfontein
Roodepoort
JOHANNESBURG
Alexandra
Putfontein
5725
Discovery
Edenvale
5557
Florida
Maraisburg
Primrose
Benoni
Orlando
Turffontein
Rosettenville
Germiston
Brakpan
Pimville
Albertan
Boksburg
Springs
WITWATERSRAND

Scale 1:1 000 000
0   5   10 Miles
0 4 8 12 16 Kilometers

Scale 1:4 000 000
0   10   20   30   40 Miles
0 10 20 30 40 50 60 Kilometers

Longitude East of Greenwich

Relief

Meters		Feet
3050		10 000
1525		5000
610		2000
305		1000
152.5		500
0	Sea Level	0
152.5		500
1525		5000
3050		10 000

@RMCN.

Relief

Meters	Feet
3050	10 000
1525	5000
610	2000
305	1000
152.5	500
0	Sea Level
152.5	500
1525	5000
3050	10 000

Copyright by Rand McNally & Co.
Made in U.S.A.
A-589400-76 2-1-8

Scale 1:10,000,000; one inch to 160 miles. Lambert Azimuthal Equal Area Projection
Elevations and depressions are given in feet.

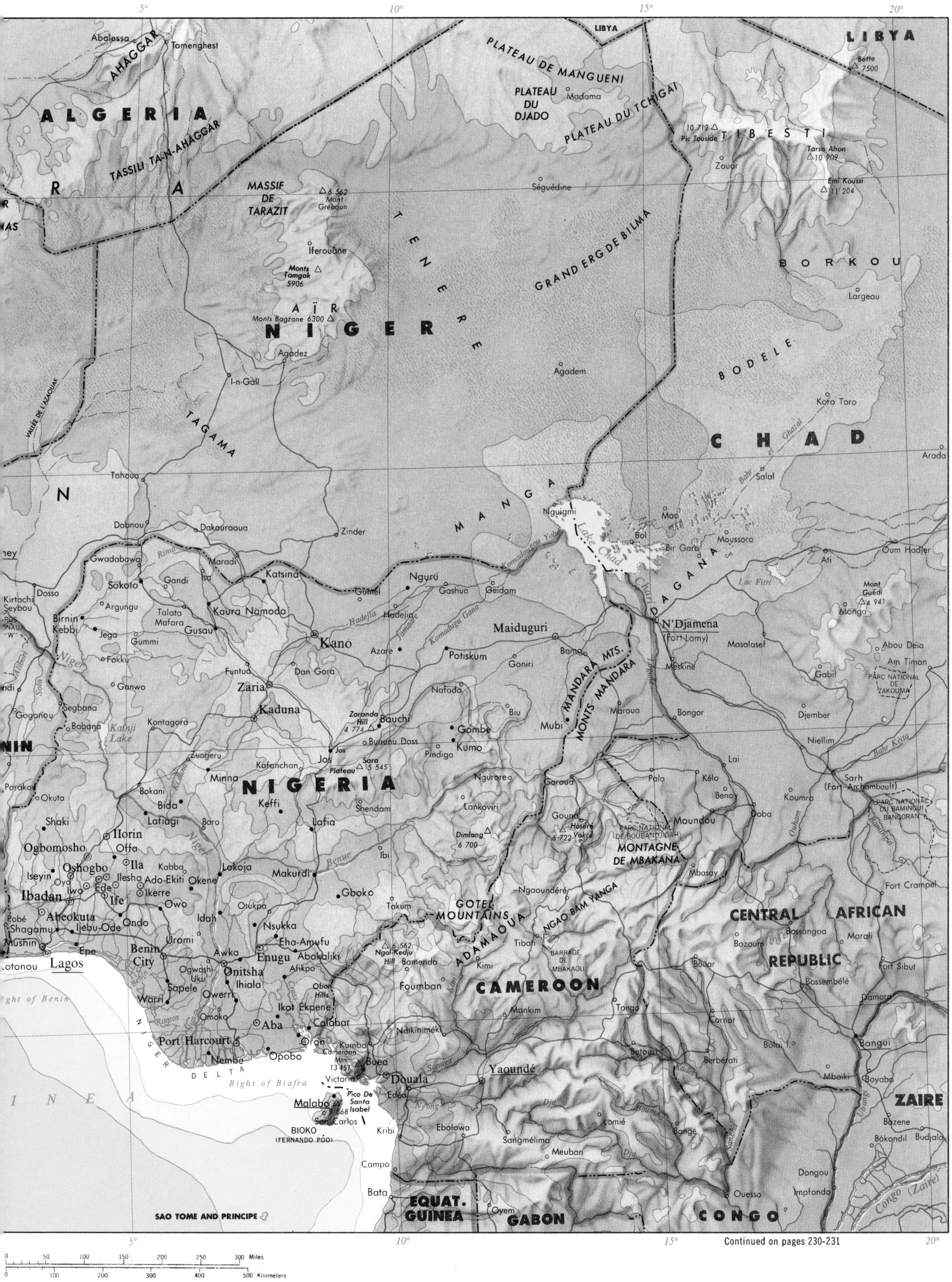

LIBYA

ALGERIA

AHAGGAR

Abalessa   Tamenghest

TASSILI TA-N-AHAGGAR

PLATEAU DE MANGUENI

PLATEAU DU DJADO

Madama

PLATEAU DU TCHIGAI

LIBYA

Bette △ 7500

TIBESTI

10 712 △ Pic Tousside

Tarso Ahon △ 10 909

Zouar

Emi Koussi △ 11 204

20°

MASSIF DE TARAZIT   △ 6 562 Mont Grébaun

BORKOU

Iferouâne

AÏR

Monts Tamgak 5906 △

TENERE

GRAND ERG DE BILMA

Largeau

NIGER

Monts Bagzane 6300 △

Agadez

BODELE

Agadem

Koro Toro

I-n-Gall

TAGAMA

CHAD

Arada

15°

Tahoua

MANGA

Salal

Ghazal

Nguigmi

Mao

Moussoro

Oum Hadjer

Dabnou

Dakouraoua

Zinder

Komadougou Yobé

Lake Chad

Bol

Bir Gara

DAGANA

Lac Firi

Ati

N

Gwadabawa

Maradi

Isa

Katsina

Gumel

Ngyru

Gashua

Geidam

N'Djamena (Fort-Lamy)

Masalasef

Mont Guédi △ 4 941

Mongo

Abou Deïa

Am Timan

Dosso

Sokoto

Gandi

Argungu

Talata Mafara

Kaura Namoda

Gusau

Hadejia

Hadejia

Maiduguri

Bama

Meskine

Gabil

PARC NATIONAL DE ZAKOUMA

Kirtachi Seybou

Birnin Kebbi

Jega

Gummi

Fokku

Kano

Azare

Potiskum

Goniri

Mubi

Maroua

Bongor

Djember

Niellim

10°

Dosso

Ganwo

Funtua

Dan Gora

Nafada

Biu

MANDARA MTS.

MONTS MANDARA

Lai

Bahr Keita

Gogoro

Segbana

Babana

Kainji Lake

Kontagora

Zaria

Kaduna

Zaranda Hill 4 774 △

Bauchi

Bununu Dass

Gombe

Kumo

Pindiga

Nguroreo

Garoua

Gouna

Pala

Kélo

Benoy

Koumra

Doba

Sarh (Fort-Archambault)

Zungeru

Jos

Jos Plateau

Sara 5 545 △

PARC NATIONAL DU BAMINGUI BANGORAN

Parakou

Okuta

Minna

Bokani

Bido

Kafanchan

NIGERIA

Keffi

Lafia

Shendam

Lankoviri

Dimlang 6 700 △

Hosséré 6 722 △ Yoko

PARC NATIONAL DE BOUBANDJIDAH

Moundou

Mbasay

Fort Crampel

Shaki

Lafiagi

Baro

Ogbomosho

Ilorin

Offa

Ila

Kabba

Lokoja

Lafia

Ibi

MONTAGNE DE MBAKANA

Gounda

Ngaoundéré

Tibati

BARRAGE DE MBAKAOU

Bouar

Bossangoa

Bozoum

Marali

Iseyin

Oyo

Oshogbo

Ilesha

Ado-Ekiti

Okene

Makurdi

Gboko

Takum

GOTEL MOUNTAINS

ADAMAOUA

NGAO BAM YANGA

CENTRAL

AFRICAN

Fort Sibut

Ibadan

Iwo

Ede

Ife

Ikerre

Owo

Otukpa

Nsukka

Eha-Amufu

Ngol Kedju Hill 6 562 △

Bamenda

Kimi

Foumban

Mankim

Tonga

REPUBLIC

Bossembélé

Carnot

Damara

Pobé

Abeokuta

Ijebu-Ode

Ondo

Idah

Awka

Enugu

Abakaliki

Afikpo

CAMEROON

Betou

Bossa

Bangui

Mushin

Epe

Benin City

Ogwashi-Uku

Onitsha

Ihiala

Oban Hills

Ndikiniméki

Yaoundé

Mbaiki

Boyabo

Lagos

Otonou

Bight of Benin

Sapele

Owerri

Ikot Ekpene

Calabar

Edéa

Dja

ZAIRE

Warri

Omoko

Aba

Oron

Kumba

Buea

Douala

Lomié

Bazene

Bokondil

Budjala

Port Harcourt

Nembe

Opobo

DELTA

Kumba Cameroon Mtn. 13 451 △

Victoria

Nyong

Kribi

Sangmélima

Meuban

Sanaga

Sangha

Dongou

Impfondo

Bight of Biafra

Malabo

Pico De Santa Isabel △ 9 868

San Carlos

BIOKO (FERNANDO PÓO)

Campo

Bata

Ebolowa

SAO TOME AND PRINCIPE

EQUAT. GUINEA

Oyem

GABON

Ouesso

CONGO

Congo (Zaïre)

GUINEA

NIGER

N

5°   10°   15°   20°

Continued on pages 230-231

0 50 100 150 200 250 300 Miles
0 100 200 300 400 500 Kilometers

Continued on pages 228-229

CENTRAL AFRICAN REPUBLIC

NIGERIA

Bight of Biafra

Opobo
Cameroon Mtn.
13 451 △
Douala
Buéa
Malabo
San Carlos
BIOKO
(FERNANDO PÓO)

EQUATORIAL GUINEA

Bata
Kribi
Campo
Acalayong

CAMEROON

Yaoundé
Edéa
Ebolowa
Sangmelima
Doumé
Batou
Lomié
Yokadouma
Meuban
Nyong
Djoum
Oyem
Souanké
Moloundou
Bangui
Kongbo
Bossou
Bossembélé
Boali
Fort de Possel
Bangassou
Mobaye
Yakoma
Bondo
Bata
Berberati
Bolai I.
Mbaiki
Boyabo
Gemena
Businga
Bodalang
Yandongi
Aket
Buta
Gi

PRÍNCIPE

SAO TOME AND PRINCIPE

CABO SAN JUAN
ISLA DE CORISCO

São Tomé
SÃO TOMÉ

MONTS DE CRISTAL

Libreville
Kango
Booué
Bifoum
Makokou
Mékambo
Lebango
Djokoumatombi
Equator

GABON

Port-Gentil
CAP LOPEZ
Lambaréné
Mount Iboundji 5 184 △
Koula-Moutou
Mouila
Franceville
St. François de Boundji
Gamboma
Djambala
Monts De La Lékéti
3 412

Ombooué
Petit Loango

Owando

CONGO

Mbandaka
(Coquilhatville)
Bikoro
Lac Tumba

ZAIRE

Kisanga
(Stanleyville)
Simba
Lifanga
Isangi
Bengc
Basoko
Yangambi
Boende
Bokungu
Yahuma
Lokolama
Ekanga
Ekoli
Monkoto
Kiri

Tchibanga
Mossendjo
Sibiti
Kindamba
Mayumba
Madingo
Madingou
Brazzaville
Loubomo
Pointe-Noire
Chutes De Livingstone
(Livingstone Falls)
Tshela

Kinshasa
(Léopoldville)
Kisantu
Mbanza-Ngungu
Popokabaka
Kimvula

Bandundu
Makaw
Dekese
Esambo
Lac Mai-Ndombe
Fimi
Lukenie
Kwilu
Idiofa
Tebo (Port-Francqui)
Domiongo
Lusambo
Mbuji-Mayi (Bakwanga)

CABINDA (Ang.)
Cabinda
Boma
Matadi
Nóqui
Mbanza Congo
SERRA DO CONGO
PONTA DO PADRÃO
Soyo

Kikwit
Kilembe
Djokupunda
Bulunga
Kananga
(Luluabourg)
Tshikapa
Kanda-Kanda
Demba

Nzeto
Damba
Quimbele
Mabaia
Uíge
Ambriz

Kitenda
Kahemba
Kibenga
Luachimo

Kapanga
KATANGA
Kangowa

Luanda
PONTA DAS PALMEIRINHAS
Caxito
Catete
Duque de Bragança
Ndalatando
Dondo
Malange
Marimba
Quimbonge
Caluango
Sambungo
Saurimo

Quela
Nova Gaia
Cacolo

Luao
Lucano
Malanga
Nasc

CABO DAS TRÊS PONTAS
Porto Amboim
Ngunza
Gabela
Cela
Calucinga
Cuvo
Mussende
Saútar

ANGOLA

PARQUE NACIONAL DA CAMEIA
Luena
Calunda
Curunga
Lur

KASHIJI PLAIN
Chitokoloki

Covelo
Lobito
Benguela
SERRA CAMBONDA
SERRA MOCO
8 596 △
Huambo
(Nova Lisboa)
Catumbela
Alto-Uama
Kuito
Coemba
Chitembo
Chá Pungana
Cangamba
Lungue-Bungo

LIUWA PLAIN
Mussuma
Ninda

SERRE DO CHILENGUE
Caconda
Caluquembe
Cacula

SERRA DA NEVE
São Nicolau
CABO DE SANTA MARTA

Folgares
Menongue
Lunga

Mongu
BAROTSE PLAIN

Moçâmedes
Lubango
PONTA ALBINA
PARQUE NACIONAL DO BIKUAR
Chiange

Kassinga
Caiundo
Mavinga

SILOANA PLAINS

PONTA DA MARCA
Baía dos Tigres
Porto Alexandre
PARQUE NACIONAL DO IONA
Foz do Cunene
Oncocua
Cuamato
Cahama
Catuala
Melunga
Cuando
Cuangar
Sambungo

CAPRIVI STRIP
Kasinka

NAMIBIA
BOTS.
CHOBE NAT'L

ATLANTIC OCEAN

Scale 1:10,000,000; one inch to 160 miles. Lambert Azimuthal Equal Area Projection
Elevations and depressions are given in feet.

Relief

Meters	Feet
3050	10 000
1525	5000
610	2000
305	1000
152.5	500
0 Sea Level	0
152.5	500
1525	5000
3050	10 000

SUDAN

ETHIOPIA

UGANDA

KENYA

SOMALIA

RWANDA

BURUNDI

TANZANIA

INDIAN

OCEAN

ZAMBIA

MALAWI

MOZAMBIQUE

COMOROS

ZIMBABWE

(RHODESIA)

Maridi   Juba
Yambio   Kapoeta   Didinga Hills
Gobur   Keyala
Bagbele   Aba   Nimule   LOTIKIPI PLAIN   Lokitaung
Niangara   Arua   Padibe   CHALBI   Royale   Baidoa
Watsa   Gulu   Lodwar   DESERT
Isiro (Paulis)   Moroto   Marsabit   SOMALIA
Mungbere   Lira   Kitale   NDOTO MOUNTAINS   Baardheere
Wamba   Nabiswera   CHERANGANY HILLS   Marsabit   BUR PLAINS
Bunia   Mbale   Mount Elgon 14,178   Eldoret   Laisamis   Wajir   Solola   Jamaame
Panga   Mubende   Thomson's Falls   Nakuru   Nanyuki   Kismaayo
Kampala   Jinja   Kisumu   Kirinyaga (Mt. Kenya) 17,058   Alanga Arba   Baardheere
Entebbe   Kericho   Nyeri   Embu   Garissa   Kolbio   Kiunga
Masaka   Thika   Mwingi   Kaningo   Bura   LAMU ISLAND
Mbarara   Nairobi   Machakos   Garsen   Lamu
Lake Victoria   Magadi   Makindu   TSAVO NATIONAL PARK   Malindi
Bukoba   SERENGETI NATIONAL PARK   Loliondo   Longido   Kilifi
Mwanza   SERENGETI PLAIN   Kilimanjaro 19,340   Moshi   Mombasa
Geita   Arusha   Mackinnon Road   Chake Chake   PEMBA ISLAND
Nyakanazi   Mount Meru 14,978
Biharamulo   Shinyanga   Mwanga   Tanga
Nzega   Bereku   MASAI STEPPE   ZANZIBAR
Tabora   Hanang 11,215   Zanzibar
Dodoma   Bagamoyo
Igalula   Mpwapwa   Dar es Salaam
Mbogo   RUAHA NATIONAL PARK   Morogoro   MAFIA ISLAND
Iringa   Mahenge   Kibiti   Kilindoni
Mbeya   Sao Hill   Mahenge   Somanga
Njombe   Kilwa Kisiwani
KIPENGERE RANGE   Litoo   Lindi
NYIKA PLATEAU   Livingstonia   Songea   Tunduru   Mtwara
Liuli   Mbamba Bay   Masasi   Mikindani   Quionga   CABO DELGADO
Mzuzu   Newala   Mocimboa da Praia
COMOROS   GRANDE COMORE
Moroni   Karthala 7,746   ANJOUAN   MOHÉLI
Mzimba   Côbué   Diaca   Ibo   Pemba
Lichinga   Marrupa   Montepuez
Chipata   MALAWI   Chamama
Mchinji   Salima   Lilongwe   Mucojo
Katete   Monkey Bay   Mandimba   Maúa   Nampuecha
Mtakataka   Cuamba   Mucata   Nampula
LUSAKA   Furancungo   Malema   Ribauè   Murrupula   Nametil
SERRA NAMULI 7,936   Blantyre   Zomba   Alto Molócuè   Errego   Mogincual
Cabora Bassa Res.   Fingoè   Casula   Mlanje   Sapitwa 9,843   Nampula   Moçambique
Tete   Vila Caldas Xavier   Macubela   Mucubela   ILHA ANGOCHE
Changara   Chemba   Nsanje   Moma
HARARE (Salisbury)   Chitungwiza   Pebane

Copyright by Rand McNally & Co.
Made in U.S.A.
A-589500-76

0   50   100   150   200   250   300 Miles
0   100   200   300   400   500 Kilometers

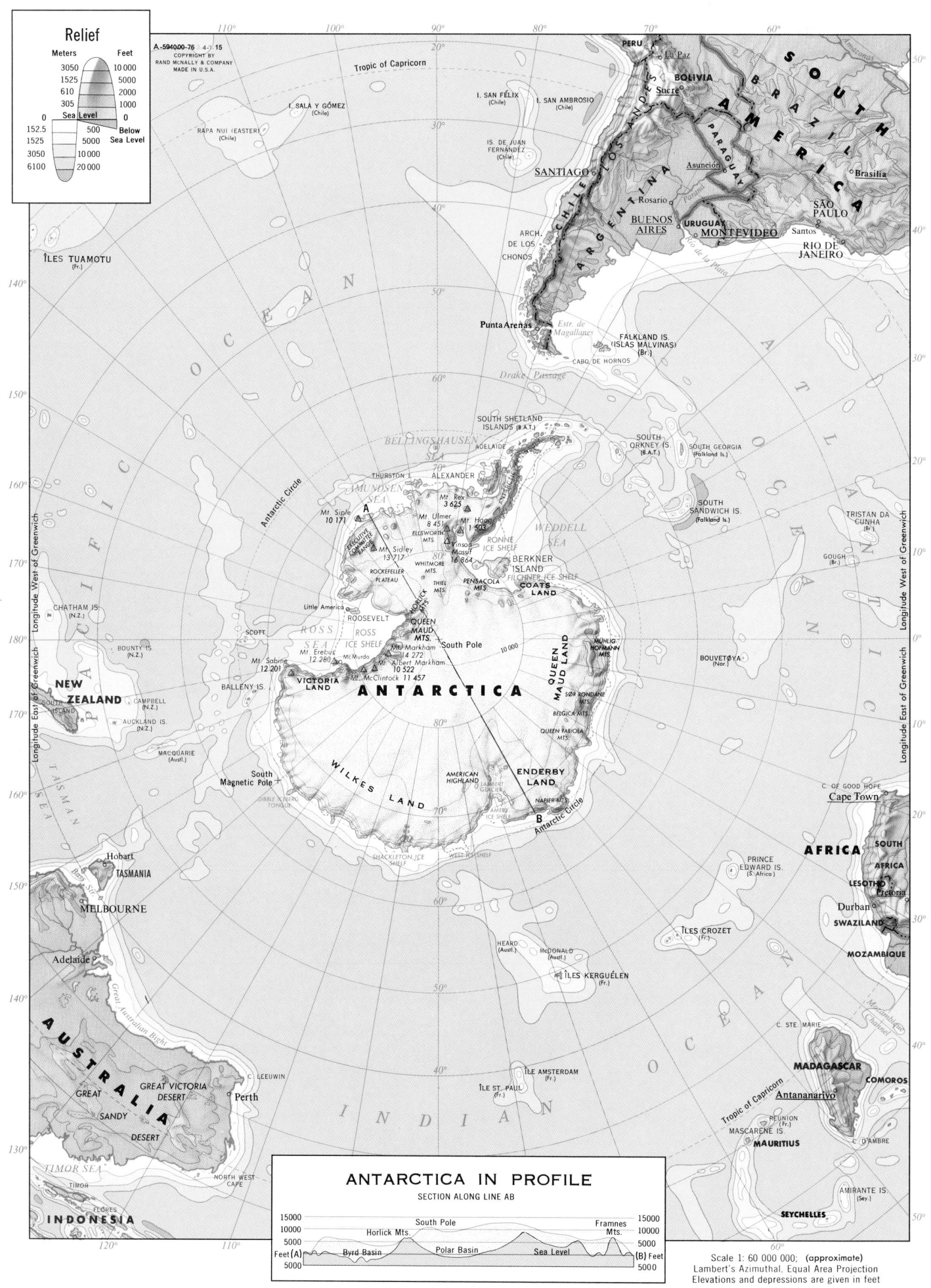

Relief

Meters		Feet
3050		10 000
1525		5000
610		2000
305		1000
0	Sea Level	0
152.5		500
		Below
1525		Sea Level
3050		5000
6100		10 000
		20 000

A-594000-76 4-1 15
COPYRIGHT BY
RAND McNALLY & COMPANY
MADE IN U.S.A.

SOUTH AMERICA

BRAZIL

PERU
BOLIVIA
La Paz
Sucre
PARAGUAY
Asunción
Brasilia

CHILE
ARGENTINA
SANTIAGO
Rosario
BUENOS AIRES
URUGUAY
MONTEVIDEO
Santos
SÃO PAULO
RIO DE JANEIRO

Tropic of Capricorn

I. SALA Y GÓMEZ (Chile)
RAPA NUI (EASTER) (Chile)
I. SAN FÉLIX (Chile)
I. SAN AMBROSIO (Chile)
IS. DE JUAN FERNÁNDEZ (Chile)

ÎLES TUAMOTU (Fr.)

ARCH. DE LOS CHONOS

Punta Arenas
Estr. de Magallanes
FALKLAND IS. (ISLAS MALVINAS) (Br.)
CABO DE HORNOS

Drake Passage

SOUTH SHETLAND ISLANDS (B.A.T.)
Adelaide
SOUTH ORKNEY IS. (B.A.T.)
SOUTH GEORGIA (Falkland Is.)

BELLINGSHAUSEN SEA

THURSTON I.
ALEXANDER
Mt. Rex 3 625

SOUTH SANDWICH IS. (Falkland Is.)

TRISTAN DA CUNHA (Br.)

AMUNDSEN SEA

Mt. Siple 10 171
Mt. Ulmer 8 451
ELLSWORTH MTS.
Vinson Massif 16 864
Mt. Hope 1 503
Mt. Sidley 13 717
EXECUTIVE COMMITTEE RANGE
WHITMORE MTS.
ROCKEFELLER PLATEAU
THIEL MTS.
HORLICK MTS.
Little America
ROOSEVELT
Scott
RONNE ICE SHELF
BERKNER ISLAND
PENSACOLA MTS.
COATS LAND
FILCHNER ICE SHELF
WEDDELL SEA

GOUGH (Br.)

QUEEN MAUD MTS.
South Pole
10 000
QUEEN MAUD LAND
MÜHLIG HOFMANN MTS.
SØR RONDANE MTS.
BELGICA MTS.
QUEEN FABIOLA MTS.

BOUVETØYA (Nor.)

ROSS ICE SHELF
ROSS SEA
Mt. Erebus 12 280
McMurdo
Mt. Markham 14 272
Mt. Albert Markham 10 522
Mt. McClintock 11 457
Mt. Sabine 12 201
VICTORIA LAND

ANTARCTICA

NEW ZEALAND
SOUTH ISLAND
CHATHAM IS. (N.Z.)
BOUNTY IS. (N.Z.)
CAMPBELL (N.Z.)
AUCKLAND IS. (N.Z.)
MACQUARIE (Austl.)
BALLENY IS.

South Magnetic Pole
DIBBLE ICEBERG TONGUE
WILKES LAND

AMERICAN HIGHLAND
LAMBERT GLACIER
AMERY ICE SHELF
ENDERBY LAND
NAPIER MTS.

C. OF GOOD HOPE
Cape Town

AFRICA
SOUTH AFRICA
LESOTHO
Pretoria
Durban
SWAZILAND
MOZAMBIQUE

PRINCE EDWARD IS. (S. Africa)

ÎLES CROZET (Fr.)

SHACKLETON ICE SHELF
WEST ICE SHELF

HEARD (Austl.)
McDONALD (Austl.)
ÎLES KERGUÉLEN (Fr.)

Hobart
TASMANIA

MELBOURNE
Adelaide

AUSTRALIA
GREAT VICTORIA DESERT
GREAT SANDY DESERT
Perth
C. LEEUWIN

C. STE MARIE

MADAGASCAR
COMOROS
Antananarivo
RÉUNION (Fr.)
MASCARENE IS.
MAURITIUS
C. D'AMBRE

AMIRANTE IS. (Sey.)
SEYCHELLES

TIMOR SEA
TIMOR
NORTH WEST CAPE
FLORES
INDONESIA

Tropic of Capricorn

ÎLE AMSTERDAM (Fr.)
ÎLE ST. PAUL (Fr.)

INDIAN OCEAN

PACIFIC OCEAN

ATLANTIC OCEAN

TASMAN SEA

Antarctic Circle

Longitude West of Greenwich
Longitude East of Greenwich

ANTARCTICA IN PROFILE

SECTION ALONG LINE AB

15000	South Pole		15000
10000	Horlick Mts.		Framnes Mts.	10000
5000				5000
Feet (A)	Byrd Basin	Polar Basin	Sea Level	(B) Feet
5000				5000

Scale 1: 60 000 000; (approximate)
Lambert's Azimuthal, Equal Area Projection
Elevations and depressions are given in feet

plate tectonics and ocean floor maps

Plate Tectonics

Maps and atlases portray the position of the land and water masses and the surface features of the earth. In general they answer the question *where?* The plate tectonic theory of the earth's actions relates the physics of the earth's subsurface and its surface to explain *how* and *why* the surface features are where they are.

Stated concisely, the theory presumes the lithosphere—the outside crust and uppermost mantle of the earth—is divided into six major rigid plates and several smaller platelets that move relative to one another. The position and names of the plates are shown on the map below.

The motor that drives the plates is found deep in the mantle. The theory states that because of temperature differences in the mantle, slow convection currents circulate. Where two molten currents converge and move upward, they separate, causing the crustal plates to bulge and move apart in midoceanic regions. Lava wells up at these points to cause ridges and volcanic activity. The plates grow larger by accretion along these midocean regions, cause vast regions of the crust to move apart, and force different plates to move into one another. As the plates do so, they are destroyed at subduction zones, where the plates are consumed downward to form deep ocean trenches. Movement along these zones prompts earthquakes as well as changes in the coastline. Further movement results as plates slide past one another along transcurrent faults. The diagrams to the right illustrate the processes.

The overall result of tectonic movements is that the crustal plates move slowly and inexorably as relatively rigid entities, carrying the continents along with them. It is now accepted that the continents have moved and changed their positions during the past millions of years. The sequence of this continental drifting is illustrated on the following page. It begins with a single landmass, called the supercontinent of Pangaea, and the ancestral ocean, the Panthalassa Ocean. Pangaea first split into a northern landmass called Laurasia and a southern block called Gondwanaland and subsequently into the continents we map today.

Subduction Zone

Ocean Ridge Zone

World-Wide Distribution of Tectonic Plates

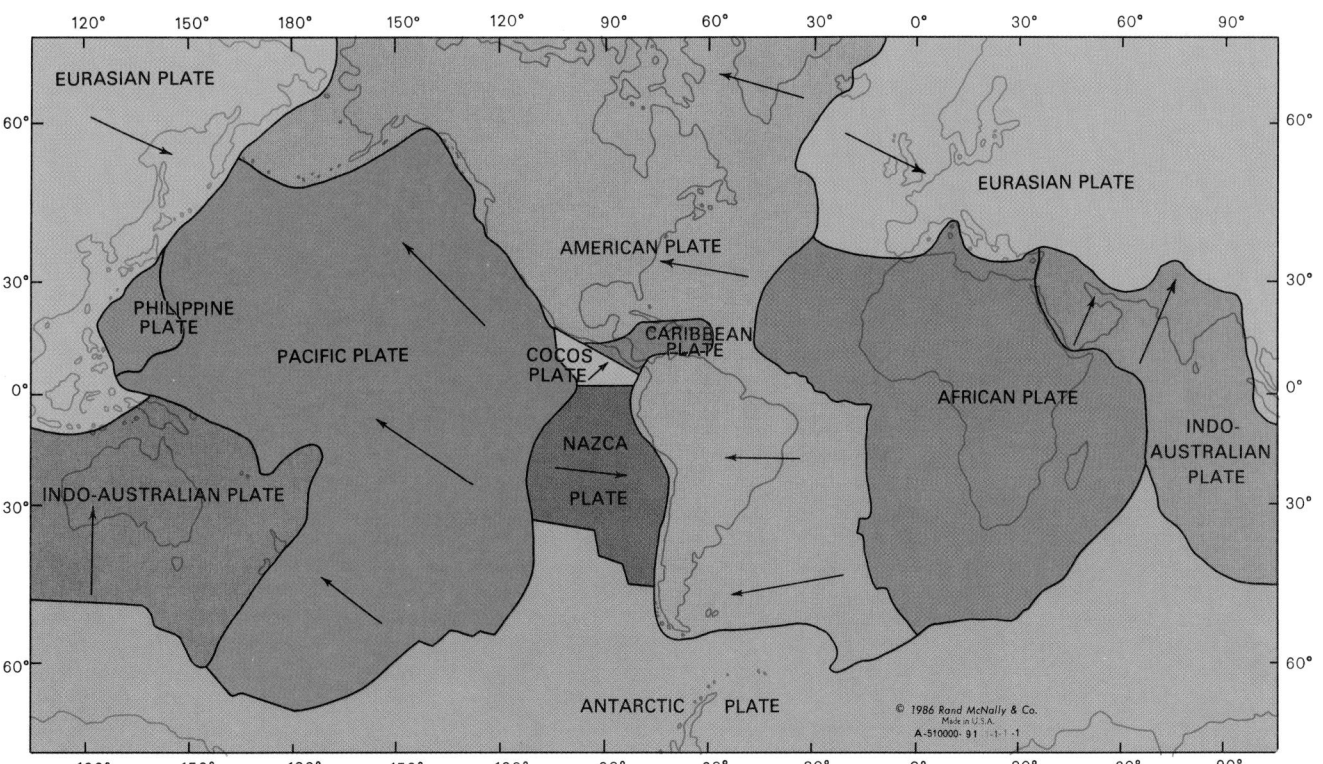

Credit: adapted from a drawing by Scripps Institution of Oceanography

Continental Drift

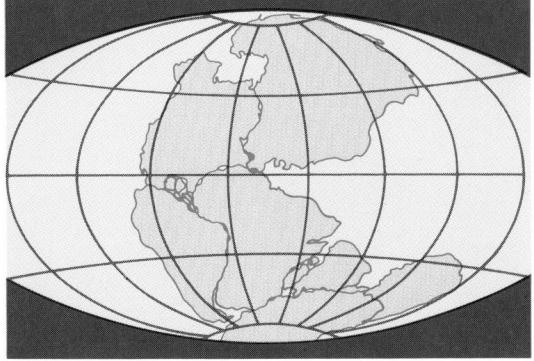

225 million years ago the supercontinent of Pangaea exists and Panthalassa forms the ancestral ocean. Tethys Sea separates Eurasia and Africa.

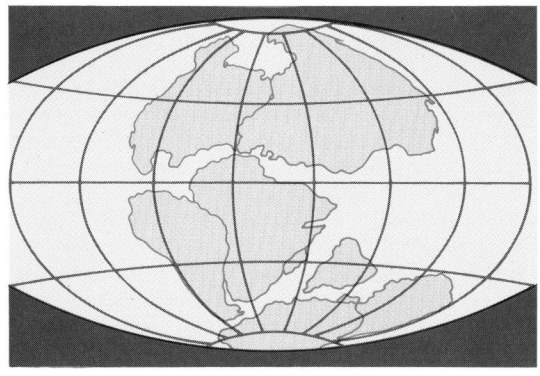

180 million years ago Pangaea splits, Laurasia drifts north. Gondwanaland breaks into South America/Africa, India, and Australia/Antarctica.

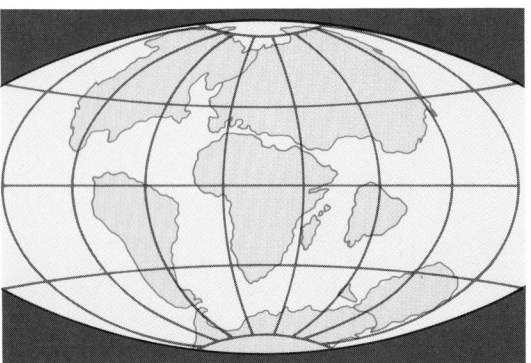

65 million years ago ocean basins take shape as South America and India move from Africa and the Tethys Sea closes to form the Mediterranean Sea.

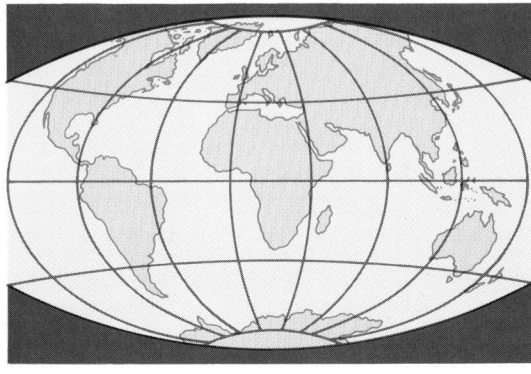

The present day: India has merged with Asia, Australia is free of Antarctica, and North America is free of Eurasia.

Ocean Floor Maps

The maps in this section convey an impression of the physical nature of the world's ocean floors. In general, the colors are those thought to exist on the ocean floors. For continental shelves or shallow inland seas, gray-green is used to correspond to terrigenous oozes, sediments washed from the continental areas. In deeper parts of the oceans, calcareous oozes derived from the skeletons of marine life appear in white, and the fine mud from land is red. In the Atlantic, materials accumulate relatively rapidly, have a high iron content, and thus are brighter red than elsewhere. Slower sedimentation in the Pacific and Indian oceans results in more manganese and hence darker colors. Undersea ridges are shown in black to suggest recent upswelling of molten rock. Small salt-and-pepper patches portray areas where manganese nodules are found. Around certain islands, white is used to show coral reefs. Differences in subsurface form are shown by relief-shading.

Many different features on the ocean floor are recognizable. Towering mountain ranges, vast canyons, broad plains, and a variety of other physiographic forms exceed in magnitude those found on the continents. One of the more pronounced is the Mid-Atlantic Ridge, a chain of mountains bisecting the Atlantic Ocean. One distinct characteristic of this ridge is a trough that runs along the entire center, in effect producing twin ridge lines. Away from the center there are parallel and lower crests, while at right angles to the crests are numerous fracture zones.

Measurements of temperature and magnetism indicate that the troughs in the Mid-Atlantic Ridge are younger than the paralleling crests, whose ages increase with distance from the center. It is believed that the central troughs mark a line where molten materials from the earth's interior rise to the ocean floor, where they form gigantic plates that move slowly apart. Where the plates meet certain continental areas or island chains, they plunge downward to replenish inner-earth materials and form trenches of profound depths. Along the northern and western edges of the Pacific Ocean, several lines of such gutters include some of the deepest known spots—Mariana Trench, Tonga Trench, Kuril Trench. Deep trenches also parallel the western coasts of Central and South America, the northern coasts of Puerto Rico and the Virgin Islands, and other coastal areas. Other identifiable features include the great sub-marine canyons that lead from the edges of the continents; seamounts that rise above the ocean floors; and the continental shelves, which appear to be underwater extensions of landmasses and which vary in shape from narrow fringes to broad plains.

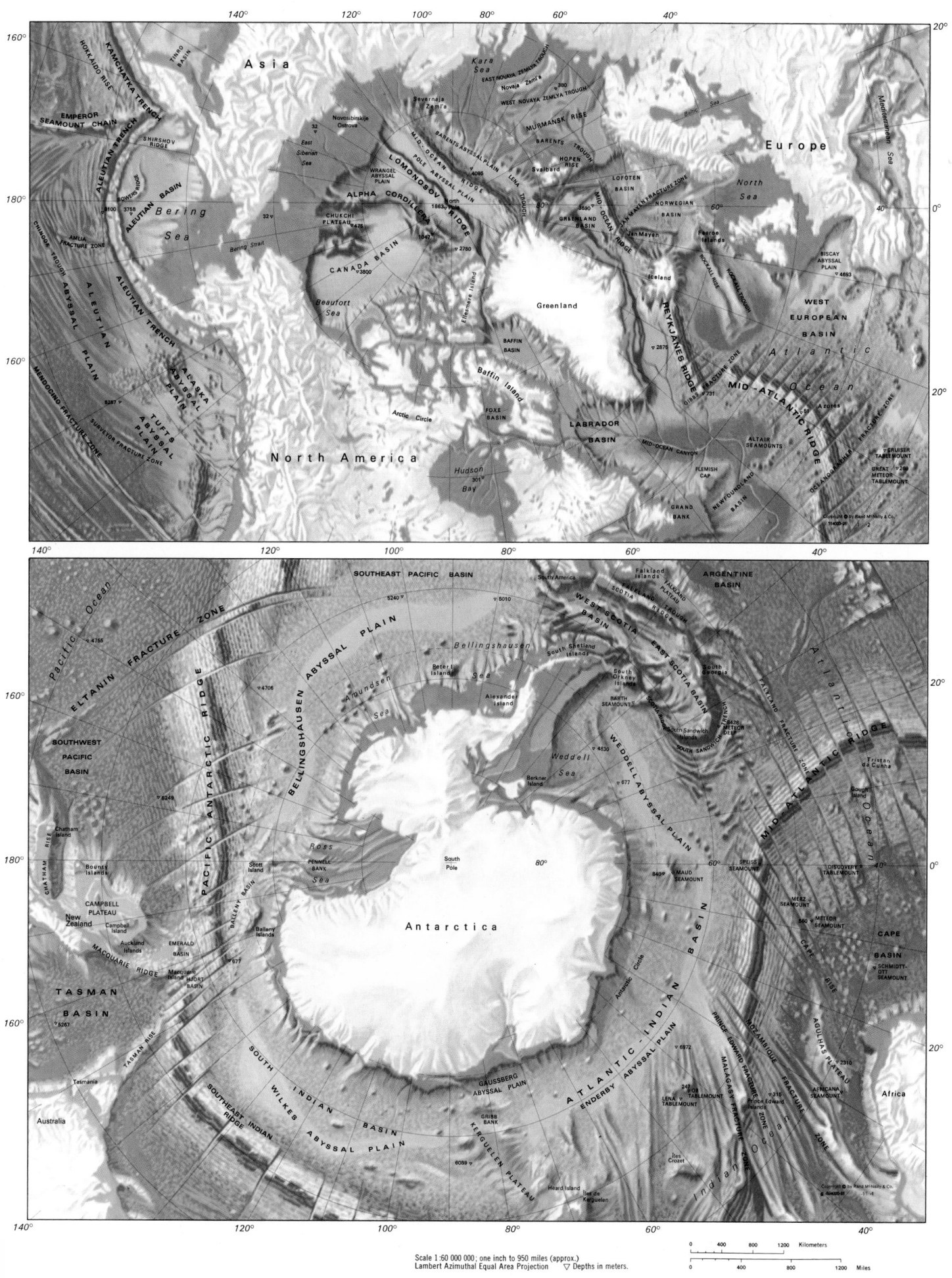

Scale 1:60 000 000; one inch to 950 miles (approx.)
Lambert Azimuthal Equal Area Projection   ▽ Depths in meters.

Scale 1:44,000,000; one inch to 700 miles (approx.)
Modified Cylindrical Projection   ▽ Depths in meters.

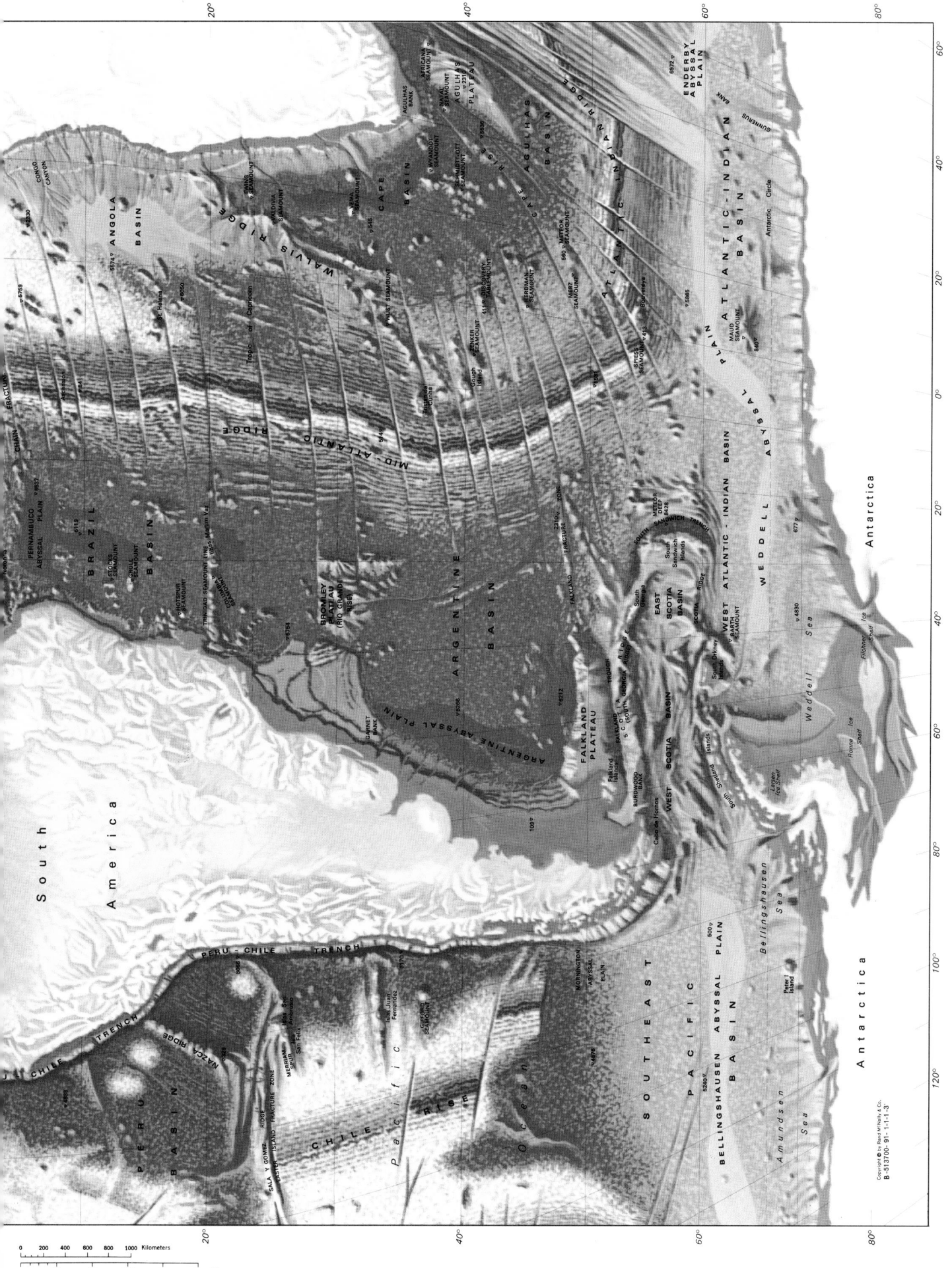

South America

Antarctica

Antarctica

CONGO CANYON

ANGOLA BASIN

WALVIS RIDGE

BRAZIL BASIN

CHAIN FRACTURE

MID-ATLANTIC RIDGE

PERNAMBUCO ABYSSAL PLAIN

St. Helena

Tropic of Capricorn

Ascension

SLOMAN SEAMOUNT

COLUMBIA SEAMOUNT

HOTSPUR SEAMOUNT

BROMLEY PLATEAU TRIO GRANDE RISE

ARGENTINE BASIN

ARGENTINE ABYSSAL PLAIN

GARNET BANK

FALKLAND PLATEAU

Falkland Islands

BURDWOOD BANK

Cabo de Hornos

WEST SCOTIA BASIN

AGULHAS BANK

AGULHAS PLATEAU

AFRICANA SEAMOUNT

NATAL SEAMOUNT

EWING SEAMOUNT

MALLORY SEAMOUNT

WUST SEAMOUNT

CAPE BASIN

CAPE RISE

SCHMIDT-OTT SEAMOUNT

VEMA SEAMOUNT

AGULHAS BASIN

CAPE AGULHAS BASIN

METEOR SEAMOUNT

DISCOVERY SEAMOUNT

SCHWABENLAND

BERGMAN SEAMOUNT

MEYER SEAMOUNT

SPIESS SEAMOUNT

Gough Island

Bristol Gough

Tristan da Cunha

FRACTURE ZONE

FALKLAND FRACTURE

SOUTH GEORGIA RIDGE

S. (SOUTH GEORGIA) RIDGE

South Georgia

SCOTIA RIDGE

South Orkney Islands

SCOTIA SEA

South Shetland Islands

South Sandwich Islands

SOUTH SANDWICH TRENCH

METEOR DEEP

EAST SCOTIA BASIN

ATLANTIC - INDIAN RIDGE

ENDERBY ABYSSAL PLAIN

GUNNERUS BANK

Antarctic Circle

ATLANTIC - INDIAN BASIN

MAUD SEAMOUNT

WEST ATLANTIC - INDIAN BASIN

ASTRID SEAMOUNT

WEDDELL ABYSSAL PLAIN

Weddell Sea

Filchner Ice Shelf

Ronne Ice Shelf

Larsen Ice Shelf

PERU - CHILE TRENCH

CHILE TRENCH

NAZCA RIDGE

PERU BASIN

SALA Y GOMEZ RIDGE

EASTER ISLAND FRACTURE ZONE

MENDANA SPUR

Isla Juan Fernández

San Felix

Islas Juan Fernández

San Ambrosio

GIFFORD SEAMOUNT

CHILE RISE

Pacific Ocean

EAST PACIFIC RISE

MORNINGTON ABYSSAL PLAIN

SOUTHEAST PACIFIC BASIN

BELLINGSHAUSEN ABYSSAL PLAIN

Bellingshausen Sea

Peter I Island

Amundsen Sea

Antarctica

0   200   400   600   800   1000 Kilometers

0   200   400   600   800   1000 Miles

Scale 1:58 000 000; one inch to 900 miles (approx.)
Modified Cylindrical Projection   ▽ Depths in meters.

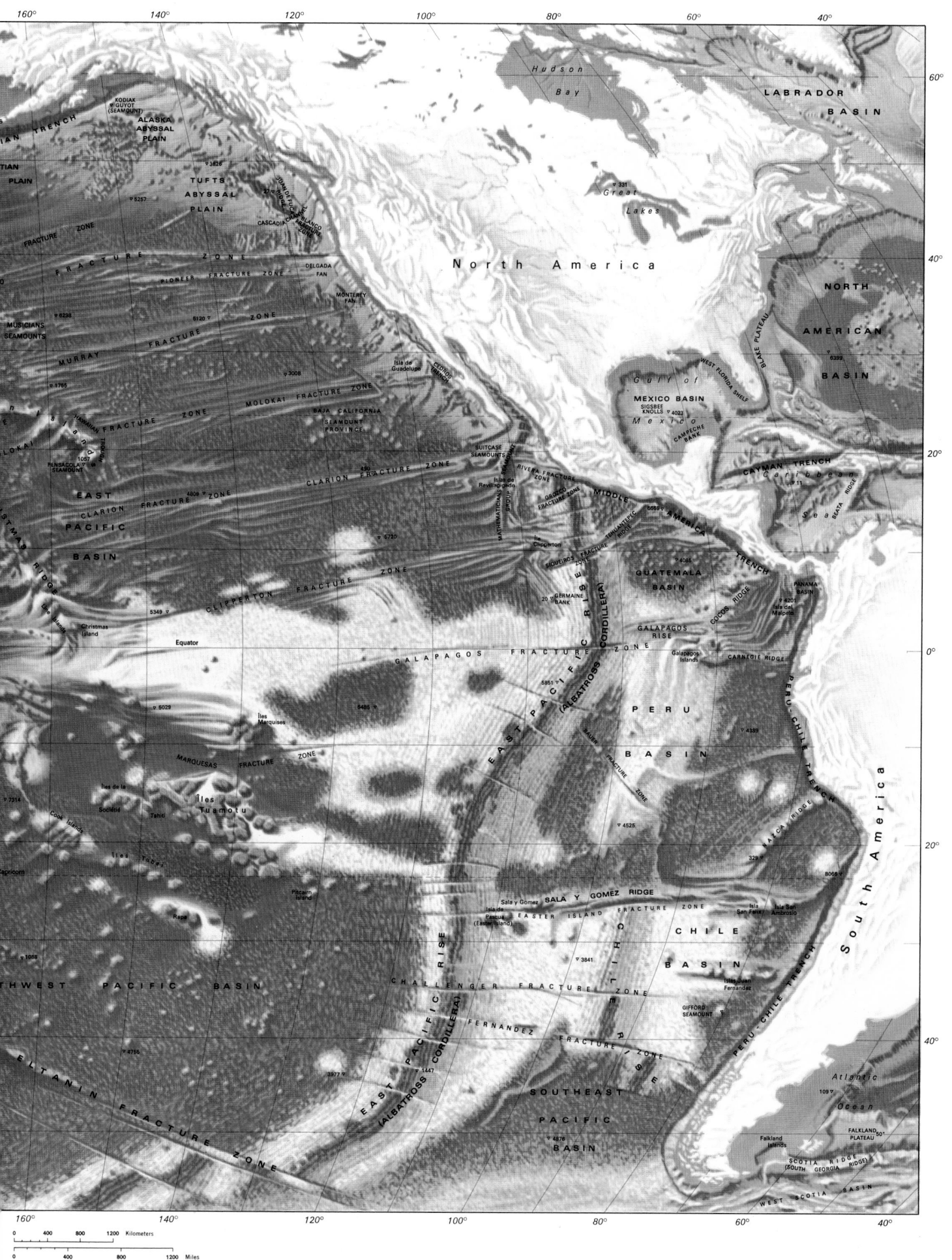

60°

LABRADOR
BASIN

*Hudson
Bay*

NORTH

AMERICAN

BASIN

40°

North America

♢331
*Great
Lakes*

Gulf of
MEXICO BASIN
SIGSBEE
KNOLLS ♢4023
Mexico

WEST FLORIDA SHELF
BLAKE PLATEAU

♢6399

CAMPECHE
BANK

CAYMAN TRENCH
Caribbean

BEATA RIDGE

♢11
Sea

MIDDLE
AMERICA
TRENCH

GUATEMALA
BASIN

♢4066

PANAMA
BASIN

♢4201
Isla del
Malpelo

COCOS RIDGE

GALAPAGOS
RISE

0°

South America

CARNEGIE RIDGE

Galapagos
Islands

PERU

BASIN

♢4389

NAZCA RIDGE

20°

♢329

♢8066

Isla
San Felix
Isla San
Ambrosio

CHILE

BASIN

Isla Juan
Fernandez

GIFFORD
SEAMOUNT

♢109

Atlantic

Ocean

40°

FALKLAND
PLATEAU

Falkland
Islands

SCOTIA RIDGE
(SOUTH GEORGIA RIDGE)

WEST SCOTIA BASIN

IAN TRENCH

KODIAK
♢GUYOT
(SEAMOUNT)

ALASKA
ABYSSAL
PLAIN

TIAN

PLAIN

♢3826

TUFTS

♢5257

ABYSSAL

PLAIN

JUAN DE FUCA RIDGE
CAPE BLANCO
FRACTURE ZONE
CASCADIA

PIONEER FRACTURE ZONE

DELGADA
FAN

MONTEREY FAN

MUSICIANS
SEAMOUNTS

♢6238

MURRAY

FRACTURE

♢1766

MOLOKAI FRACTURE ZONE

ZONE

Isla de
Guadalupe

CEDROS
TRENCH

♢3008

BAJA CALIFORNIA
SEAMOUNT
PROVINCE

HAWAIIAN FRACTURE ZONE

PENSACOLA
SEAMOUNT

♢1057

SUITCASE
SEAMOUNTS

RIVERA FRACTURE
ZONE

EAST

CLARION FRACTURE ZONE

CLARION FRACTURE ZONE

♢490

Isla de
Revillagigedo

OROZCO
FRACTURE ZONE
MATHEMATICIANS SEAMOUNTS
TEHUANTEPEC
RIDGE

♢8689

PACIFIC

♢4808

Ile
Clipperton

BASIN

♢6720

SIQUEIROS FRACTURE
ZONE

MAS RIDGE

GALAPAGOS FRACTURE

20°
GERMAINE
BANK

ZONE

♢5349

♢5851

Equator

GALAPAGOS FRACTURE ZONE

Christmas
Island

Leen Islands

Christmas
Island

♢5029

Îles
Marquises

♢5486

PERU

♢4525

MARQUESAS FRACTURE ZONE

JUAREZ
FRACTURE ZONE

♢7314

Îles de la
Société

Tahiti

Îles
Tuamotu

Cook Islands

20°

Îles Tubuaï

Capricorn

Pitcairn
Island

Sala y Gomez
Isla de
Pascua
(Easter Island)

SALA Y GOMEZ RIDGE

EASTER ISLAND FRACTURE ZONE

Rapa

♢1066

♢3841

CHILE

THWEST

PACIFIC

BASIN

CHALLENGER FRACTURE ZONE

FERNANDEZ

♢4755

FRACTURE

ZONE

ELTANIN FRACTURE ZONE

♢3977

♢1447

SOUTHEAST

PACIFIC

BASIN

♢4876

EAST PACIFIC RISE
(ALBATROSS CORDILLERA)

EAST PACIFIC RISE (ALBATROSS CORDILLERA)

PERU-CHILE TRENCH

PERU-CHILE TRENCH

160°   140°   120°   100°   80°   60°   40°

0   400   800   1200   Kilometers

0   400   800   1200   Miles

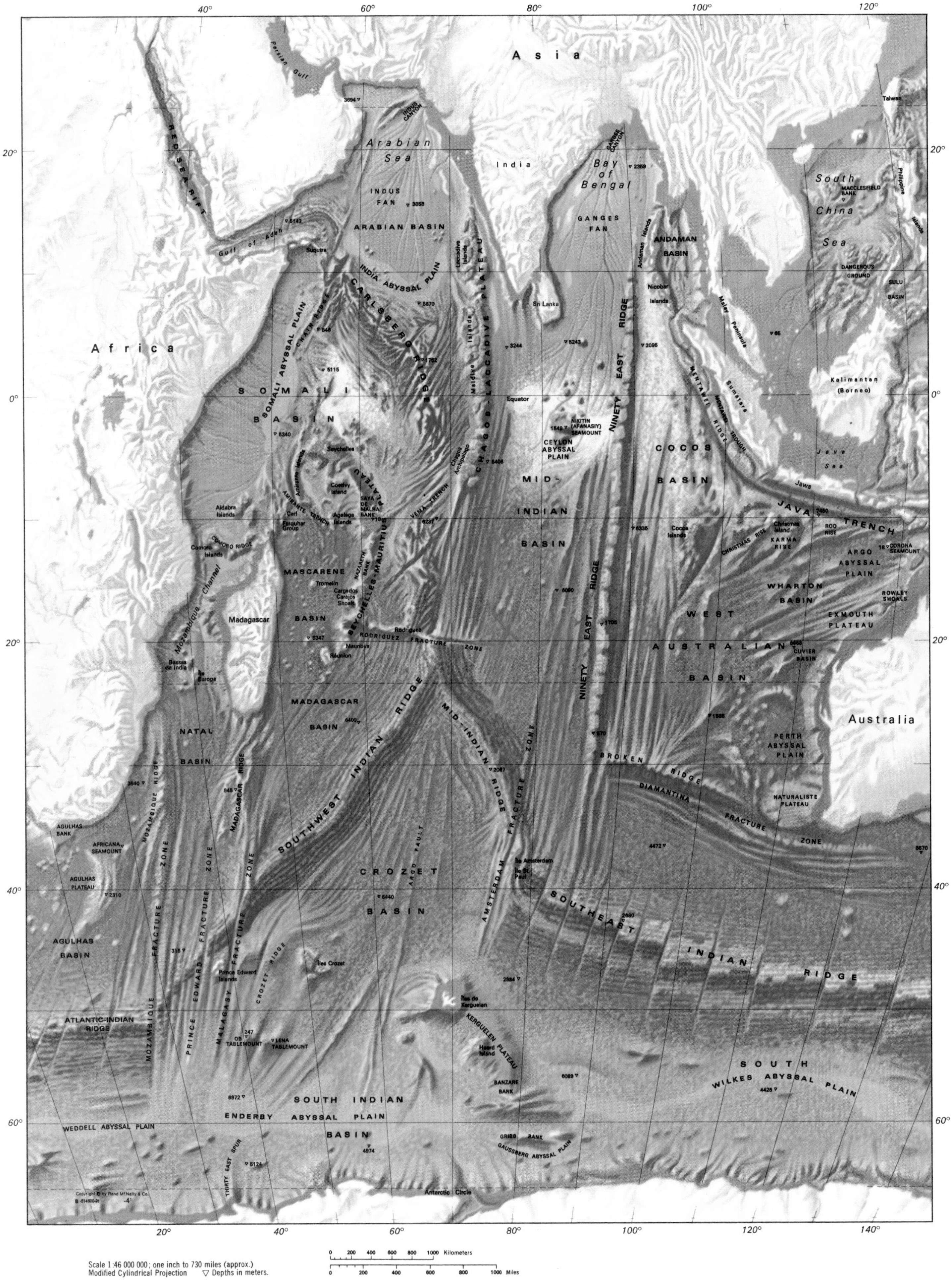

Asia

RED SEA RIFT

Persian Gulf

Arabian Sea

India

Bay of Bengal

South China Sea

Taiwan

Philippine Islands

MACCLESFIELD BANK

INDUS FAN

ARABIAN BASIN

Gulf of Aden

Suqutra

Africa

INDIA ABYSSAL PLAIN

CARLSBERG RIDGE

SOMALI BASIN

Seychelles

Coetivy Island

Laccadive Islands

Maldive Islands

CHAGOS-LACCADIVE PLATEAU

Sri Lanka

Equator

NIKITIN (AFANASIY) SEAMOUNT

CEYLON ABYSSAL PLAIN

GANGES FAN

ANDAMAN BASIN

Andaman Islands

Nicobar Islands

NINETY EAST RIDGE

MENTAWAI RIDGE

Sumatra

DANGEROUS GROUND

SULU BASIN

Kalimantan (Borneo)

Java Sea

COCOS BASIN

Christmas Island

Cocos Islands

CHRISTMAS RISE

KARMA RISE

ROO RISE

CORONA SEAMOUNT

ARGO ABYSSAL PLAIN

ROWLEY SHOALS

Jawa

JAVA TRENCH

MID-INDIAN BASIN

WHARTON BASIN

EXMOUTH PLATEAU

WEST AUSTRALIAN BASIN

CUVIER BASIN

Aldabra Islands

Cerf

Farquhar Group

Agalega Islands

AMIRANTE TRENCH

VEMA TRENCH

SAYA DE MALHA BANK

Cargados Carajos Shoals

MASCARENE BASIN

Tromelin

SEYCHELLES-MAURITIUS RIDGE

Rodrigues

Mauritius

Réunion

RODRIGUES FRACTURE ZONE

Comoro Islands

COMORO RIDGE

MOZAMBIQUE Channel

Madagascar

MADAGASCAR BASIN

MADAGASCAR RIDGE

MID-INDIAN RIDGE

Basses da India

Ile Europe

NATAL BASIN

Australia

PERTH ABYSSAL PLAIN

NATURALISTE PLATEAU

AGULHAS BANK

AFRICANA SEAMOUNT

AGULHAS PLATEAU

AGULHAS BASIN

MOZAMBIQUE FRACTURE ZONE

PRINCE EDWARD FRACTURE ZONE

MALAGASY FRACTURE ZONE

SOUTHWEST INDIAN RIDGE

CROZET BASIN

CROZET RIDGE

Iles Crozet

Prince Edward Islands

Ile Amsterdam
Ile St. Paul

AMSTERDAM FRACTURE ZONE

ARGO FAULT

BROKEN RIDGE

DIAMANTINA FRACTURE ZONE

SOUTHEAST INDIAN RIDGE

ATLANTIC-INDIAN RIDGE

DB TABLEMOUNT

LENA TABLEMOUNT

Iles de Kerguelen

KERGUELEN PLATEAU

Heard Island

BANZARE BANK

GAUSSBERG ABYSSAL PLAIN

GRIEG BANK

SOUTH WILKES ABYSSAL PLAIN

THIRTY EAST SPUR

WEDDELL ABYSSAL PLAIN

SOUTH INDIAN BASIN

ENDERBY ABYSSAL PLAIN

Antarctic Circle

Scale 1:46 000 000; one inch to 730 miles (approx.)
Modified Cylindrical Projection   ▽ Depths in meters.

Copyright © by Rand McNally & Co.

0 200 400 600 800 1000 Kilometers

0 200 400 600 800 1000 Miles

This table lists all countries and dependencies in the world, U.S. States, Canadian provinces, and other important regions and political subdivisions. Besides specifying the form of government for all political areas, the table classifies them into five groups according to their political status. Units labeled A are independent sovereign nations. (Several of these are designated as members of the British Commonwealth of Nations.) Units labeled B are independent as regards internal affairs, but for purposes of foreign affairs they are under the protection of another country. Units labeled C are colonies, overseas territories, dependencies, etc., of other countries. Together the A, B, and C areas comprise practically the entire inhabited area of the world. Units labeled D are states, provinces, soviet republics, or similar major administrative subdivisions of important countries. Units in the table with no letter designation are regions or other areas that do not constitute separate political units by themselves.

REGION OR POLITICAL DIVISION	Area* Sq. Mi.	Est. Pop. 1/1/85	Pop. Per. Sq. Mi.	Form of Government and Ruling Power		Capital; Largest City (if other)	Predominant Languages
Afars & Issas, see Djibouti							
Afghanistan†	250,000	14,650,000	59	Socialist Republic	A	Kâbul	Dari, Pushtu
Africa	11,700,000	538,000,000	46			...; Cairo	
Alabama	51,704	4,015,000	78	State (U.S.)	D	Montgomery; Birmingham	English
Alaska	591,004	515,000	0.9	State (U.S.)	D	Juneau; Anchorage	English, Amerindian languages, Eskimo
Albania†	11,100	2,935,000	264	Socialist Republic	A	Tiranë	Albanian
Alberta	255,285	2,370,000	9.3	Province (Canada)	D	Edmonton	English
Algeria†	919,595	21,695,000	24	Socialist Republic	A	Algiers (El Djazaïr)	Arabic, Berber, French
American Samoa	77	35,000	455	Unincorporated Territory (U.S.)	C	Pago Pago	Samoan, English
Andaman & Nicobar Is.	3,202	195,000	61	Territory (India)	D	Port Blair	Andaman, Nicobar Malay
Andorra	175	39,000	223	Coprincipality (French and Spanish protection)	B	Andorra	French, Spanish
Angola†	481,353	7,875,000	16	Socialist Republic	A	Luanda	Portuguese, indigenous languages
Anguilla	35	7,000	200	Associated State (U.K.)	B	The Valley; South Hill	English
Anhui	54,054	53,400,000	988	Province (China)	D	Hefei; Huainan	Chinese
Antarctica	5,400,000						
Antigua and Barbuda†	170	78,000	459	Parliamentary State (Comm. of Nations)	A	St. John's	English
Arabian Peninsula	1,160,000	24,270,000	21			...; Riyadh	Arabic
Argentina†	1,068,301	30,340,000	28	Republic	A	Buenos Aires	Spanish
Arizona	114,002	3,040,000	27	State (U.S.)	D	Phoenix	English
Arkansas	53,191	2,375,000	45	State (U.S.)	D	Little Rock	English
Armenian S.S.R.	11,506	3,280,000	285	Soviet Socialist Republic (Sov. Un.)	D	Yerevan	Armenian, Russian
Aruba	75	65,000	867	Division of Netherlands Antilles (Neth.)	D	Oranjestad	Dutch, Spanish, English, Papiamento
Ascension	34	1,400	41	Dependency of St. Helena (U.K.)	C	Georgetown	English
Asia	17,250,000	2,946,200,000	171			...; Tōkyō	
Australia†	2,967,909	15,565,000	5.2	Parliamentary State (Federal) (Commonwealth of Nations)	A	Canberra; Sydney	English
Australian Capital Territory	939	245,000	261	Territory (Australia)	D	Canberra	English
Austria†	32,377	7,580,000	234	Federal Republic	A	Vienna (Wien)	German
Azerbaijan S.S.R.	33,436	6,505,000	195	Soviet Socialist Republic (Sov. Un.)	D	Baku	Turkish, Russian, Armenian
Azores (Açores)	868	255,000	294	Autonomous Region (Portugal)	D	Ponta Delgada	Portuguese
Bahamas†	5,382	230,000	43	Parliamentary State (Commonwealth of Nations)	A	Nassau	English
Bahrain†	256	415,000	1,621	Constitutional Monarchy	A	Al Manāmah	Arabic, English
Balearic Is. (Islas Baleares)	1,936	695,000	359	Province (Spain)	D	Palma [de Mallorca]	Spanish
Baltic Republics	67,182	7,720,000	115	Part of Sov. Un. (3 Republics)		Rīga	Lithuanian, Latvian, Estonian, Russian
Bangladesh†	55,598	101,130,000	1,819	Republic (Commonwealth of Nations)	A	Dacca (Dhaka)	Bangla, English
Barbados†	166	250,000	1,506	Parliamentary State (Commonwealth of Nations)	A	Bridgetown	English
Beijing Shi	6,487	10,055,000	1,550	Autonomous City (China)	D	Peking (Beijing)	Chinese
Belgium†	11,783	9,875,000	838	Constitutional Monarchy	A	Brussels (Bruxelles)	Dutch (Flemish), French
Belize (British Honduras)†	8,866	160,000	18	Parliamentary State (Commonwealth of Nations)	A	Belmopan; Belize City	English, Spanish, indigenous languages
Belorussian S.S.R.†	80,155	9,975,000	124	Soviet Socialist Republic (Sov. Un.)	D	Minsk	Byelorussian, Polish, Russian
Benelux	28,823	24,705,000	857	Economic Union		...; Brussels	Dutch, French, Luxembourgish
Benin†	43,484	3,970,000	91	Socialist Republic	A	Porto- Novo; Cotonou	French, Fon, Adja, indigenous languages
Bermuda	21	70,000	3,333	Colony (U.K.)	C	Hamilton	English
Bhutan†	18,147	1,435,000	79	Monarchy (Indian protection)	B	Thimbu	Dzongkha, English, Nepalese dialects
Bolivia†	424,164	6,115,000	14	Republic	A	La Paz and Sucre;	Spanish, Quechua, Aymara
Bophuthatswana	15,610	1,440,000	92	Bantu Homeland (South Africa)††	B	Mmabatho	Sesotho, Afrikaans
Borneo, Indonesian (Kalimantan)	208,287	7,575,000	36	Part of Indonesia (4 Provinces)		...; Banjarmasin	Indonesian
Botswana†	231,805	1,055,000	4.6	Republic (Commonwealth of Nations)	A	Gaborone	English, Setswana
Brazil†	3,286,487	134,340,000	41	Federal Republic	A	Brasília; São Paulo	Portuguese
British Columbia	366,255	2,885,000	7.9	Province (Canada)	D	Victoria; Vancouver	English
British Honduras, see Belize							
British Indian Ocean Territory	23			Colony (U.K.)	C	Administered from London	
British Solomon Is., see Solomon Is.							
Brunei†	2,226	220,000	99	Constitutional Monarchy (Commonwealth of Nations)	A	Bandar Seri Begawan (Brunei)	Malay, English, Chinese
Bulgaria†	42,823	8,980,000	210	Socialist Republic	A	Sofia (Sofiya)	Bulgarian
Burkina Faso†	105,869	6,820,000	64	Provisional Military Government	A	Ouagadougou	French, indigenous languages
Burma†	261,228	36,795,000	141	Socialist Republic	A	Rangoon	Burmese, indigenous languages
Burundi†	10,747	4,760,000	443	Republic	A	Bujumbura	Kirundi, French, Swahili
California	158,704	25,620,000	161	State (U.S.)	D	Sacramento; Los Angeles	English
Cambodia, see Kampuchea							
Cameroon†	183,569	9,640,000	53	Republic	A	Yaoundé; Douala	English, French, indigenous languages
Canada†	3,831,033	25,270,000	6.6	Parliamentary State (Federal) (Commonwealth of Nations)	A	Ottawa; Toronto	English, French
Canary Is. (Islas Canarias)	2,808	1,475,000	525	Part of Spain (2 Provinces)		...; Las Palmas de Gran Canaria	Spanish
Cape Verde†	1,557	300,000	193	Republic	A	Praia	Portuguese, Crioulo
Cayman Is.	100	220,000	220	Colony (U.K.)	C	Georgetown	English
Celebes (Sulawesi)	73,057	11,725,000	160	Part of Indonesia (4 Provinces)		...; Ujung Pandang	Indonesian, Malay-Polynesian languages
Central African Republic†	240,535	2,620,000	11	Republic	A	Bangui	French, Sangho
Central America	202,000	25,495,000	126			...; Guatemala	Spanish, Amerindian languages
Central Asia, Soviet	493,090	28,545,000	58	Part of Sov. Un (4 Republics)		...; Tashkent	Uzbek, Russian, Kirghiz, Turkish, Tajik
Ceylon, see Sri Lanka							
Chad†	495,755	5,180,000	10	Republic	A	N'Djamena	French, Arabic, indigenous languages
Channel Is. (Guernsey, Jersey, etc.)	75	132,000	1,760	Dependency (U.K.)	C	...; St. Helier	English, French
Chile†	292,135	11,740,000	40	Republic	A	Santiago	Spanish
China (excl. Taiwan)†	3,718,783	1,080,980,000	291	Socialist Republic	A	Peking (Beijing); Shanghai	Chinese dialects

† Member of the United Nations (1984).
* Areas include inland water.
†† Bophuthatswana, Ciskei, Transkei and Venda are not recognized by the United Nations.

REGION OR POLITICAL DIVISION	Area* Sq. Mi.	Est. Pop. 1/1/85	Pop. Per. Sq. Mi.	Form of Government and Ruling Power		Capital; Largest City (if other)	Predominant Languages
China (Nationalist), see Taiwan ..							
Christmas I. (Indian Ocean)	52	3,300	63	External Territory (Australia)	C	.........; Flying Fish Cove	English, Tahitian
Ciskei	3,205	740,000	231	Bantu Homeland (South Africa)††	B	Bisho; Mdantsane	Xhosa, Afrikaans
Cocos (Keeling) Is.	5.4	600	111	Part of Australia	C		Malay, English
Colombia†	439,737	28,545,000	65	Republic	A	Bogotá	Spanish
Colorado	104,094	3,210,000	31	State (U.S.)	D	Denver	English
Commonwealth of Nations	10,650,000	1,196,620,000	112			.........; London	
Comoros†	838	460,000	549	Republic	A	Moroni	Arabic, French, Swahili
Congo†	132,047	1,770,000	13	Republic	A	Brazzaville	French, indigenous languages
Connecticut	5,019	3,160,000	630	State (U.S.)	D	Hartford	English
Cook Is.	91	16,000	176	Self-governing Territory (New Zealand)	B	Avarua	Malay-Polynesian languages, English
Corsica	3,352	220,000	66	Part of France (2 Departments)		.........; Ajaccio	French, Italian
Costa Rica†	19,730	2,725,000	138	Republic	A	San José	Spanish
Cuba†	44,218	9,770,000	221	Socialist Republic	A	Havana (La Habana)	Spanish
Curaçao	171	165,000	965	Division of Netherlands Antilles (Neth.)	D	Willemstad	Dutch, Spanish, English, Papiamento
Cyprus†	3,572	675,000	189	Republic (Commonwealth of Nations)	A	Nicosia	Greek, Turkish
Czechoslovakia†	49,381	15,490,000	314	Socialist Republic	A	Prague (Praha)	Czech, Slovak, Hungarian
Dahomey, see Benin							
Delaware	2,045	620,000	303	State (U.S.)	D	Dover; Wilmington	English
Denmark†	16,633	5,010,000	301	Constitutional Monarchy	A	Copenhagen (København)	Danish
Denmark and Possessions	857,177	5,110,000	6.0			Copenhagen	Danish, Faeroese, Eskimo
District of Columbia	69	610,000	8,841	District (U.S.)	D	Washington	English
Djibouti†	8,880	360,000	41	Republic	A	Djibouti	French, Somali, Afar, Arabic
Dominica†	290	74,000	255	Republic (Commonwealth of Nations)	A	Roseau	English, French
Dominican Republic†	18,704	6,205,000	332	Republic	A	Santo Domingo	Spanish
Ecuador†	109,483	9,235,000	84	Republic	A	Quito; Guayaquil	Spanish, Quechua
Egypt††	386,643	47,755,000	124	Socialist Republic	A	Cairo (Al Qāhirah)	Arabic
Ellice Is., see Tuvalu							
El Salvador†	8,124	4,905,000	604	Republic	A	San Salvador	Spanish
England	50,207	46,540,000	927	Administrative division of U.K.	D	London	English
Equatorial Guinea†	10,831	280,000	26	Republic	A	Malabo	Spanish, indigenous languages, English
Estonian S.S.R.	17,413	1,545,000	89	Soviet Socialist Republic (Sov. Un.)	D	Tallinn	Estonian, Russian
Ethiopia†	472,434	34,050,000	72	Provisional Military Government	A	Addis Ababa	Amharic, Arabic, indigenous languages
Eurasia	21,150,000	3,644,370,000	172			.........; Tōkyō	
Europe	3,800,000	673,900,000	177			.........; London	
Faeroe Is.	540	45,000	83	Part of Danish Realm	B	Tórshavn	Danish, Faeroese
Falkland Is. (excl. Deps.)	4,700	2,000	0.4	Colony (U.K.)△	C	Stanley	English
Fiji†	7,055	695,000	99	Parliamentary State (Commonwealth of Nations)	A	Suva	English, Fijian, Hindustani
Finland†	130,558	4,885,000	37	Republic	A	Helsinki	Finnish, Swedish
Florida	58,668	10,925,000	186	State (U.S.)	D	Tallahassee; Miami	English
France (excl. Overseas Depts)† ..	211,208	55,020,000	261	Republic	A	Paris	French
France and Possessions	260,661	56,680,000	217			Paris	French
French Guiana	35,135	81,000	2.3	Overseas Department (France)	D	Cayenne	French
French Polynesia	1,544	160,000	104	Overseas Territory (France)	C	Papeete	French, Tahitian,
French West Indies	1,112	640,000	576			.........; Fort-de-France	French
Fujian	47,491	27,890,000	587	Province (China)	D	Fuzhou	Chinese
Gabon†	103,347	975,000	9.4	Republic	A	Libreville	French, indigenous languages
Galapagos Is.	3,075	6,600	2.1	Province (Ecuador)	D	Puerto Baquerizo Moreno	Spanish
Gambia†	4,361	715,000	164	Republic (Commonwealth of Nations)	A	Banjul (Bathurst)	English, indigenous languages
Gansu	150,580	21,080,000	140	Province (China)	D	Lanzhou	Chinese, Mongolian, Tibetan dialects
Georgia	58,914	5,820,000	99	State (U.S.)	D	Atlanta	English
Georgian S.S.R.	26,911	5,210,000	194	Soviet Socialist Republic (Sov. Union)	D	Tbilisi	Georgic, Armenian, Russian
Germany (Entire)	137,794	77,990,000	566			.........; Essen	German
German Democratic Republic (East Germany)†	41,768	16,600,000	397	Socialist Republic	A	Berlin (East)	German
Germany, Federal Republic of (West Germany)†	96,019	61,390,000	639	Federal Republic	A	Bonn; Essen	German
Ghana†	92,100	14,030,000	152	Republic (Commonwealth of Nations)	A	Accra	English, Akan, indigenous languages
Gibraltar	2.3	30,000	13,043	Colony (U.K.)	C	Gibraltar	English, Spanish
Gilbert Is., see Kiribati							
Great Britain & Northern Ireland, see United Kingdom							
Greece†	50,944	10,030,000	197	Republic	A	Athens (Athínai)	Greek
Greenland	840,004	53,000	0.06	Part of Danish Realm	B	Godthåb	Danish, indigenous languages
Grenada†	133	114,000	857	Parliamentary State (Commonwealth of Nations)	A	St. George's	English
Guadeloupe (incl. Dependencies)	687	320,000	466	Overseas Department (France)	C	Basse-Terre; Pointe-à-Pitre	French, Creole
Guam	209	116,000	555	Unincorporated Territory (U.S.)	C	Agana	English, Chamorro
Guangdong	89,190	63,775,000	715	Province (China)	D	Canton (Guangzhou)	Chinese, Miao-Yao
Guangxi Zhuangzu	91,506	39,240,000	429	Autonomous Region (China)	D	Nanning	Chinese, Thai, Miao-Yao
Guatemala†	42,042	8,080,000	192	Republic	A	Guatemala	Spanish, indigenous languages
Guernsey (incl. Dependencies) ..	30	78,000	2,600	Bailiwick of Channel Islands (U.K.)	C	St. Peter Port	English, French
Guinea†	94,926	5,655,000	60	Republic	A	Conakry	French, indigenous languages
Guinea-Bissau†	13,948	850,000	61	Republic	A	Bissau	Portuguese, indigenous languages
Guizhou	67,182	30,810,000	459	Province (China)	D	Guiyang	Chinese, Thai, Miao-Yao
Guyana†	83,000	840,000	10	Republic (Commonwealth of Nations)	A	Georgetown	English
Haiti†	10,714	5,305,000	495	Republic	A	Port-au-Prince	French
Hawaii	6,473	1,045,000	161	State (U.S.)	D	Honolulu	English, Japanese, Hawaiian
Hebei	78,379	56,970,000	727	Province (China)	D	Shijiazhuang; Tangshan	Chinese
Heilongjiang	177,607	35,130,000	198	Province (China)	D	Harbin	Chinese, Mongolian, Tungus
Henan	64,479	79,990,000	1,241	Province (China)	D	Zhengzhou	Chinese
Hispaniola	29,418	11,510,000	391			.........; Santo Domingo	French, Spanish, Creole
Holland, see Netherlands							
Honduras†	43,277	4,500,000	104	Republic	A	Tegucigalpa	Spanish
Hong Kong	410	5,435,000	13,256	Colony (U.K.)	C	Hong Kong	Cantonese, English
Hubei	72,587	51,455,000	709	Province (China)	D	Wuhan	Chinese
Hunan	81,468	58,050,000	713	Province (China)	D	Changsha	Chinese, Miao-Yao
Hungary†	35,921	10,675,000	297	Socialist Republic	A	Budapest	Hungarian
Iceland†	39,769	240,000	6.0	Republic	A	Reykjavik	Icelandic
Idaho	83,566	1,020,000	12	State (U.S.)	D	Boise	English
Illinois	57,872	11,620,000	201	State (U.S.)	D	Springfield; Chicago	English
India (incl. part of Jammu and Kashmir)†	1,237,061	754,600,000	610	Federal Republic (Commonwealth of Nations)	A	New Delhi; Calcutta	Hindi, English, indigenous languages
Indiana	36,417	5,585,000	153	State (U.S.)	D	Indianapolis	English
Indonesia†	741,101	166,070,000	224	Republic	A	Jakarta	Indonesian, Malay-Polynesian languages
Inner Mongolia, see Nei Monggol							
Iowa	56,275	2,970,000	53	State (U.S.)	D	Des Moines	English

† Member of the United Nations (1984).
△ Claimed by Argentina.
* Areas include inland water.
†† Bophuthatswana, Ciskei, Transkei and Venda are not recognized by the United Nations.

REGION OR POLITICAL DIVISION	Area* Sq. Mi.	Est. Pop. 1/1/85	Pop. Per Sq. Mi.	Form of Government and Ruling Power		Capital; Largest City (if other)	Predominant Languages
ran†	636,296	44,500,000	70	Republic	A	Tehrān	Farsi, Turkish, Kurdish, Arabic
raq†	167,925	15,255,000	91	Republic	A	Baghdād	Arabic, Kurdish
reland†	27,136	3,595,000	132	Republic	A	Dublin	Irish Gaelic, English
sle of Man	227	67,000	295	Self-governing Territory (U.K.)	B	Douglas	English
srael†	8,302	4,189,000	505	Republic	A	Jerusalem; Tel Aviv-Yafo	Hebrew, Arabic, English
sraeli Occupied Territories	2,239	1,281,000	572			........; Gaza	Hebrew, Arabic
taly†	116,319	56,940,000	490	Republic	A	Rome (Roma); Milan (Milano)	Italian
vory Coast†	123,847	9,325,000	75	Republic	A	Abidjan and Yamoussoukro; Abidjan	French, indigenous languages
amaica†	4,244	2,170,000	511	Parliamentary State (Commonwealth of Nations)	A	Kingston	English
apan†	145,834	120,200,000	824	Constitutional Monarchy	A	Tōkyō	Japanese
ava (Jawa) (incl. Madura)	51,038	102,760,000	2,013	Part of Indonesia (5 Provinces)		........; Jakarta	Indonesian, Chinese, English
ersey	45	54,000	1,200	Bailiwick of Channel Islands (U.K.)	C	St. Helier	English, French
iangsu	39,382	65,075,000	1,652	Province (China)	D	Nanjing	Chinese
iangxi	63,707	35,780,000	562	Province (China)	D	Nanchang	Chinese
ilin	72,201	24,320,000	337	Province (China)	D	Changchun	Chinese, Mongolian, Korean
ordan†	35,135	2,475,000	70	Constitutional Monarchy	A	'Ammān	Arabic, English
ampuchea†	69,898	6,180,000	88	Socialist Republic	A	Phnom Penh	Khmer
ansas	82,282	2,450,000	30	State (U.S.)	D	Topeka; Wichita	English
ashmir, Jammu and	86,024	9,210,000	107	In dispute (India & Pakistan)		Srīnagar and Jammu; Srīnagar	Urdu, Kashmiri, Punjabi
azakh S.S.R.	1,049,155	15,710,000	15	Soviet Socialist Republic (Sov. Un.)	D	Alma-Ata	Turkish, Russian
entucky	40,414	3,780,000	94	State (U.S.)	D	Frankfort; Louisville	English
enya†	224,961	18,970,000	84	Republic (Commonwealth of Nations)	A	Nairobi	English, Swahili, indigenous languages
irghiz S.S.R.	76,641	3,855,000	50	Soviet Socialist Republic (Sov. Un.)	D	Frunze	Turkish, Farsi, Russian
iribati (Gilbert Is.)	275	62,000	225	Republic (Commonwealth of Nations)	A	Bairiki; Bikenibeu	English, Gilbertese
orea (Entire)	85,052‡	62,170,000	731			........; Seoul (Sŏul)	Korean
orea, North	46,540	19,855,000	427	Socialist Republic	A	P'yŏngyang	Korean
orea, South	38,025	42,315,000	1,113	Republic	A	Seoul (Sŏul)	Korean
uwait†	6,880	1,815,000	264	Constitutional Monarchy	A	Kuwait (Al Kuwayt)	Arabic, English
abrador	112,826	32,000	0.3	Part of Newfoundland Province (Canada)		........; Labrador City	English, Eskimo dialects
aos†	91,429	3,775,000	41	Socialist Republic	A	Viangchan	Lao, French
atin America	8,000,000	397,610,000	50			........; Mexico City	Spanish, Portuguese
atvian S.S.R.	24,595	2,620,000	107	Soviet Socialist Republic (Sov. Un.)	D	Rīga	Latvian, Russian
ebanon†	4,015	2,610,000	650	Republic	A	Beirut (Bayrūt)	Arabic, French, English
esotho†	11,720	1,495,000	128	Monarchy (Commonwealth of Nations)	A	Maseru	English, Sesotho
iaoning	58,301	38,485,000	660	Province (China)	D	Shenyang (Mukden)	Chinese, Mongolian
iberia†	43,000	2,195,000	51	Provisional Military Government	A	Monrovia	English, indigenous languages
ibya†	679,362	3,785,000	5.6	Socialist Republic	A	Tripoli	Arabic
iechtenstein	62	27,000	435	Constitutional Monarchy	A	Vaduz	German
ithuanian S.S.R.	25,174	3,555,000	141	Soviet Socialist Republic (Sov. Un.)	D	Vilnius	Lithuanian, Polish, Russian
ouisiana	47,750	4,515,000	95	State (U.S.)	D	Baton Rouge; New Orleans	English
uxembourg†	998	365,000	366	Constitutional Monarchy	A	Luxembourg	Luxembourgish, French, German
Macao	6.0	310,000	51,667	Overseas Province (Portugal)	D	Macao	Portuguese, Chinese dialects
Madagascar (Malagasy Republic)†	226,658	9,775,000	43	Socialist Republic	A	Antananarivo	French, Malagasy
Madeira Is. (Arquipélago da Madeira)	307	260,000	847	Autonomous Region (Portugal)	D	Funchal	Portuguese
Maine	33,265	1,165,000	35	State (U.S.)	D	Augusta; Portland	English
Malagasy Republic see Madagascar							
Malawi†	45,747	6,940,000	152	Republic (Commonwealth of Nations)	A	Lilongwe; Blantyre	Chichewa, English
Malaya	50,700	12,850,000	253	Part of Malaysia (11 States)		........; Kuala Lumpur	Malay, Chinese, English, Tamil
Malaysia†	128,430	15,500,000	121	Constitutional Monarchy (Comm. of Nations)	A	Kuala Lumpur	Malay, Chinese, English, Tamil
Maldives†	115	175,000	1,522	Republic (Commonwealth of Nations)	A	Male	Divehi
Mali†	478,766	7,650,000	16	Republic	A	Bamako	French, Bambara, indigenous languages
Malta†	122	360,000	2,951	Republic (Commonwealth of Nations)	A	Valletta	Maltese, English
Manitoba	251,000	1,060,000	4.2	Province (Canada)	D	Winnipeg	English
Maritime Provinces (excl. Newfoundland)	51,963	1,715,000	33	Part of Canada (3 Provinces)		........; Halifax	English
Marshall Is.	70	34,000	486	Part of Trust Terr. of the Pacific Is.	B	Majuro (island); Jarej-Uliga-Delap	Malay-Polynesian languages, English
Martinique	425	320,000	753	Overseas Department (France)	D	Fort-de-France	French, Creole
Maryland	10,461	4,375,000	418	State (U.S.)	D	Annapolis; Baltimore	English
Massachusetts	8,286	5,820,000	702	State (U.S.)	D	Boston	English
Mauritania†	397,955	1,640,000	4.1	Provisional Military Government	A	Nouakchott	Arabic, French
Mauritius (incl. Dependencies)†	790	1,025,000	1,297	Parliamentary State (Commonwealth of Nations)	A	Port Louis	French, English
Mayotte	144	63,000	438	Overseas Department (France)	D	Dzaoudzi	Swahili, French
Mexico†	761,604	78,670,000	103	Federal Republic	A	Mexico City	Spanish
Michigan	97,107	9,090,000	94	State (U.S.)	D	Lansing; Detroit	English
Micronesia, Federated States of	271	80,000	295	Part of Trust Terr. of the Pacific Is.	B	Kolonia	Malay-Polynesian languages, English
Middle America	1,056,000	134,310,000	127			........; Mexico City	Spanish, English
Midway Is.	2.0	500	250	Unincorporated Territory (U.S.)	C	Administered from Washington, D.C.	English
Minnesota	86,614	4,205,000	49	State (U.S.)	D	St. Paul; Minneapolis	English
Mississippi	47,691	2,640,000	55	State (U.S.)	D	Jackson	English
Missouri	69,697	5,040,000	72	State (U.S.)	D	Jefferson City; St. Louis	English
Moldavian S.S.R.	13,012	4,105,000	315	Soviet Socialist Republic (Sov. Un.)	D	Kishinĕv	Moldavian, Russian, Ukrainian
Monaco	0.6	28,000	46,667	Constitutional Monarchy	A	Monaco	French, Italian, English, Monegasque
Mongolia†	604,250	1,885,000	3.1	Socialist Republic	A	Ulan Bator	Khalka Mongol
Montana	147,045	830,000	5.6	State (U.S.)	D	Helena; Billings	English
Montserrat	40	12,000	300	Colony (U.K.)	C	Plymouth	English
Morocco (excl. Western Sahara)†	172,414	21,750,000	126	Constitutional Monarchy	A	Rabat; Casablanca	Arabic, Berber dialects, French
Mozambique†	308,642	13,700,000	44	Socialist Republic	A	Maputo	Portuguese, indigenous languages
Namibia (excl. Walvis Bay)	318,261	1,095,000	3.4	Under South African Administration**	C	Windhoek	Afrikaans, indigenous languages
Nauru	8.2	7,800	951	Republic (Commonwealth of Nations)	A	Yaren District; ...	Nauruan, English
Nebraska	77,350	1,615,000	21	State (U.S.)	D	Lincoln; Omaha	English
Nei Monggol (Inner Mongolia)	463,323	20,865,000	45	Autonomous Region (China)	D	Hohhot; Baotou	Mongolian
Nepal†	56,135	16,785,000	299	Constitutional Monarchy	A	Kathmandu	Nepali
Netherlands†	16,042	14,465,000	902	Constitutional Monarchy	A	Amsterdam and The Hague ('s-Gravenhage); Amsterdam	Dutch
Netherlands Antilles	383	250,000	653	Self-governing Territory (Netherlands)	B	Willemstad	Dutch, Spanish, English, Papiamento
Netherlands Guiana, see Surinam							
Nevada	110,562	945,000	8.5	State (U.S.)	D	Carson City; Las Vegas	English
New Brunswick	28,354	715,000	25	Province (Canada)	D	Fredericton; Saint John	English, French
New Caledonia (incl. Deps.)	7,358	149,000	20	Overseas Territory (France)	C	Nouméa	French, Malay-Polynesian languages
New England	66,674	12,630,000	189	Part of U.S. (6 States)		........; Boston	English
Newfoundland	156,185	585,000	3.7	Province (Canada)	D	St. John's	English

* Member of the United Nations (1984). ‡ Includes 487 sq. miles of demilitarized zone, not included in North or South Korea figures.
** The United Nations declared an end to the mandate of South Africa over Namibia in October 1966. Administration of the territory by South Africa is not recognized by the United Nations.
* Areas include inland water.

REGION OR POLITICAL DIVISION	Area* Sq. Mi.	Est. Pop. 1/1/85	Pop. Per. Sq. Mi.	Form of Government and Ruling Power		Capital; Largest City (if other)	Predominant Languages
Newfoundland (excl. Labrador) ..	43,359	553,000	13	Part of Newfoundland Province, Canada		......; St. John's	English
New Hampshire	9,278	975,000	105	State (U.S.)	D	Concord; Manchester	English
New Hebrides, see Vanuatu							
New Jersey	7,787	7,555,000	970	State (U.S.)	D	Trenton; Newark	English
New Mexico	121,594	1,425,000	12	State (U.S.)	D	Santa Fe; Albuquerque	English, Spanish
New South Wales	309,433	5,415,000	17	State (Australia)	D	Sydney	English
New York	52,737	17,895,000	339	State (U.S.)	D	Albany; New York	English
New Zealand†	103,515	3,155,000	30	Parliamentary State (Commonwealth of Nations)	A	Wellington; Auckland	English, Maori
Nicaragua†	50,193	2,970,000	59	Republic	A	Managua	Spanish, English
Niger†	489,191	6,390,000	13	Provisional Military Government	A	Niamey	French, Hausa, indigenous languages
Nigeria†	356,669	89,650,000	251	Federal Republic (Commonwealth of Nations)	A	Lagos	English, Hausa, Yoruba, Ibo, indigenous languages
Ningxia Huizu	25,483	4,325,000	170	Autonomous Region (China)	D	Yinchuan	Chinese
Niue	102	2,900	28	Self-governing Territory (New Zealand)	B	Alofi	Malay-Polynesian languages, English
Norfolk Island	14	1,700	121	Part of Australia	C	Kingston	English
North America	9,400,000	397,400,000	42			......; New York	
North Borneo, see Sabah							
North Carolina	52,669	6,180,000	117	State (U.S.)	D	Raleigh; Charlotte	English
North Dakota	70,702	690,000	9.8	State (U.S.)	D	Bismarck; Fargo	English
Northern Ireland	5,452	1,555,000	285	Administrative division of United Kingdom	D	Belfast	English
Northern Mariana Is.	184	19,000	103	Part of Trust Terr. of the Pacific Is.	B	Saipan (island); Chalan Kanoa	Malay-Polynesian languages, English
Northern Territory	520,280	140,000	0.3	Territory (Australia)	D	Darwin	English, Aboriginal languages
Northwest Territories	1,304,903	51,000	0.04	Territory (Canada)	D	Yellowknife	English, Eskimo, indigenous languages
Norway (incl. Svalbard and Jan Mayen)†	149,158	4,150,000	28	Constitutional Monarchy	A	Oslo	Norwegian (Riksmål and Landsmål), Lappish
Nova Scotia	21,425	875,000	41	Province (Canada)	D	Halifax	English
Oceania (incl. Australia)	3,300,000	24,200,000	7.3			......; Sydney	
Ohio	44,786	10,760,000	240	State (U.S.)	D	Columbus; Cleveland	English
Oklahoma	69,957	3,375,000	48	State (U.S.)	D	Oklahoma City	English
Oman†	82,030	1,025,000	12	Monarchy	A	Muscat; Maṭraḥ	Arabic, Farsi
Ontario	412,582	8,985,500	22	Province (Canada)	D	Toronto	English
Oregon	97,076	2,710,000	28	State (U.S.)	D	Salem; Portland	English
Orkney Is.	376	19,000	51	Part of Scotland, U.K.		Kirkwall	English
Pacific Islands, Trust Territory of the	717	146,000	203	U.N. Trusteeship (U.S. Administration)	B	Saipan (island); Jarej-Uliga-Delap	Malay-Polynesian languages, English
Pakistan (incl. part of Jammu and Kashmir)†	339,732	101,300,000	298	Federal Republic	A	Islāmābād; Karāchi	Urdu, English, Punjabi, Sindhi
Palau (Belau)	192	13,000	68	Part of Trust Terr. of the Pacific Is.	B	Koror	Malay-Polynesian languages, English
Panama†	29,762	2,155,000	72	Republic	A	Panamá	Spanish, English
Papua New Guinea†	178,703	3,400,000	19	Parliamentary State (Commonwealth of Nations)	A	Port Moresby	English, Papuan and Negrito languages
Paraguay†	157,048	3,230,000	21	Republic	A	Asunción	Spanish, Guarani
Peking, see Beijing							
Pennsylvania	46,047	12,025,000	261	State (U.S.)	D	Harrisburg; Philadelphia	English
Peru†	496,224	19,520,000	39	Republic	A	Lima	Spanish, Quechua, Aymara
Philippines†	115,831	55,140,000	476	Republic	A	Manila	Pilipino, Spanish, English, Malay-Polynesian languages
Pitcairn (incl. Dependencies)	19	50	0.3	Colony (U.K.)	C	Adamstown	English, Tahitian
Poland†	120,728	37,055,000	307	Socialist Republic	A	Warsaw (Warszawa); Katowice	Polish
Portugal†	35,516	10,065,000	283	Republic	A	Lisbon (Lisboa)	Portuguese
Portuguese Guinea, see Guinea-Bissau							
Prairie Provinces	757,985	4,440,000	5.9	Part of Canada (3 Provinces)		......; Winnipeg	English
Prince Edward Island	2,184	126,000	58	Province (Canada)	D	Charlottetown	English
Puerto Rico	3,515	3,350,000	953	Commonwealth (U.S.)	B	San Juan	Spanish, English
Qatar†	4,247	280,000	65	Monarchy	A	Ad Dawhah (Doha)	Arabic, English
Qinghai	278,380	4,325,000	16	Province (China)	D	Xining	Tibetan dialects, Mongolian, Turkish, Chinese
Quebec	594,860	6,585,000	11	Province (Canada)	D	Québec; Montréal	French, English
Queensland	667,000	2,500,000	3.7	State (Australia)	D	Brisbane	English
Reunion	969	545,000	562	Overseas Department (France)	D	St. Denis	French
Rhode Island	1,212	975,000	804	State (U.S.)	D	Providence	English
Rhodesia, see Zimbabwe							
Rodrigues	40	35,000	875	Part of Mauritius		......; Port Mathurin	English, French
Romania†	91,699	22,860,000	249	Socialist Republic	A	Bucharest (Bucureşti)	Romanian
Russian S.F.S.R.	6,592,846	143,280,000	22	Soviet Federated Socialist Republic (Sov. Un.)	D	Moscow (Moskva)	Russian, Finno-Ugric languages, Farsi, Turkish, Mongolian
Rwanda†	10,169	5,935,000	584	Republic	A	Kigali	Kinyarwanda, French
Sabah (North Borneo)	29,388	1,155,000	39	State (Malaysia)	D	Kota Kinabalu; Sandakan	Malay, Chinese, English, indigenous languages
St. Christopher-Nevis†	104	45,000	433	Parliamentary State (Commonwealth of Nations)	A	Basseterre	English
St. Helena (incl. Dependencies) ...	162	6,900	43	Colony (U.K.)	C	Jamestown	English
St. Lucia†	238	120,000	504	Parliamentary State (Commonwealth of Nations)	A	Castries	English, French
St. Pierre and Miquelon	93	6,200	67	Overseas Department (France)	D	St.-Pierre	French
St. Vincent and the Grenadines† .	150	140,000	933	Parliamentary State (Commonwealth of Nations)	A	Kingstown	English
San Marino	24	23,000	958	Republic	A	San Marino	Italian
Sao Tome and Principe†	372	89,000	239	Republic	A	São Tomé	Portuguese, indigenous languages
Sarawak	48,342	1,495,000	31	State (Malaysia)	D	Kuching	Malay, Chinese, English, indigenous languages
Sardinia	9,301	1,600,000	172	Part of Italy (Sardegna Autonomous Region)	D	Cagliari	Italian
Saskatchewan	251,700	1,010,000	4.0	Province (Canada)	D	Regina	English
Saudi Arabia†	830,000	10,970,000	13	Monarchy	A	Riyadh; Jiddah	Arabic
Scandinavia (incl. Finland and Iceland)	510,000	22,665,000	44			......; Copenhagen (København)	Swedish, Danish, Norwegian, Finnish, Icelandic
Scotland	30,416	5,130,000	169	Administrative division of United Kingdom	D	Edinburgh; Glasgow	English, Scots Gaelic
Senegal†	75,955	6,650,000	88	Republic	A	Dakar	French, Wolof, indigenous languages
Seychelles†	171	66,000	386	Republic (Commonwealth of Nations)	A	Victoria	French, English
Shaanxi (Shensi)	75,676	31,130,000	411	Province (China)	D	Xi'an	Chinese
Shandong	59,074	79,990,000	1,354	Province (China)	D	Jinan; Qingdao	Chinese
Shanghai Shi	2,239	12,865,000	5,745	Autonomous City (China)	D	Shanghai	Chinese
Shanxi (Shansi)	60,618	27,240,000	449	Province (China)	D	Taiyuan	Chinese
Shetland Is.	551	29,000	53	Part of Scotland, U.K.		Lerwick	English
Sichuan (Szechwan)	219,692	107,125,000	488	Province (China)	D	Chengdu; Chongqing	Chinese, Tiberan dialects, Miao-Yao
Sicily	9,926	4,925,000	496	Part of Italy (Sicilia Autonomous Region)	D	Palermo	Italian
Sierra Leone†	27,925	3,855,000	138	Republic (Commonwealth of Nations)	A	Freetown	English, Krio, indigenous languages
Singapore†	224	2,545,000	11,361	Republic (Commonwealth of Nations)	A	Singapore	English, Chinese, Malay, Tamil
Soloman Is.†	11,506	270,000	23	Parliamentary State (Commonwealth of Nations)	A	Honiara	English, Malay-Polynesian languages
Somalia†	246,200	6,465,000	26	Socialist Republic	A	Muqdisho (Mogadishu)	Somali, Arabic, English, Italian
South Africa (incl. Walvis Bay)† .	433,680	26,855,000	62	Republic		Pretoria, Cape Town, and Bloemfontein; Johannesburg	Afrikaans, English, indigenous languages
South America	6,900,000	263,300,000	38			......; São Paulo	
South Australia	380,070	1,355,000	3.6	State (Australia)	D	Adelaide	English

† Member of the United Nations (1984).
*Areas include inland water.

REGION OR POLITICAL DIVISION	Area* Sq. Mi.	Est. Pop. 1/1/85	Pop. Per. Sq. Mi.	Form of Government and Ruling Power	Capital; Largest City (if other)	Predominant Languages
South Carolina	31,116	3,325,000	107	State (U.S.) .... D	Columbia; Charleston	English
South Dakota	77,120	715,000	9.3	State (U.S.) .... D	Pierre; Sioux Falls	English
Southern Yemen, see Yemen, People's Democratic Republic of				....		
South Georgia (incl. Dependencies)	1,580	22	0.01	Dependency of Falkland Is. (U.K.) C		English, Norwegian
South West Africa, see Namibia						
Soviet Union (Union of Soviet Socialist Republics)†	8,600,383	275,590,000	32	Federal Socialist Republic .... A	Moscow (Moskva)	Russian and other Slavic languages, various Altaic and Indo-European languages
Soviet Union in Europe	1,920,789	177,710,000	93	Part of Soviet Union	...; Moscow	Russian and other Slavic languages
Spain†	194,882	38,515,000	198	Constitutional Monarchy .... A	Madrid	Spanish
Spanish North Africa	12	137,000	11,417	Five Possessions (no central government) (Spain) C	...; Ceuta	Spanish, Arabic, Berber
Spanish Sahara, see Western Sahara						
Sri Lanka (Ceylon)†	24,962	16,070,000	644	Socialist Republic (Commonwealth of Nations) .... A	Colombo	Sinhala, Tamil, English
Sudan†	967,500	21,390,000	22	Republic .... A	Al Kharṭum (Khartoum)	Arabic, indigenous languages, English
Sumatra (Sumatera)	182,860	31,555,000	173	Part of Indonesia (7 Provinces)	...; Medan	Indonesian, English, Chinese
Suriname†	63,037	375,000	5.9	Republic .... A	Paramaribo	Dutch, English, Hindi, Sranang Tongo, Javanese
Svalbard	23,958	4,200	0.2	Part of Norway	...; Longyearbyen	Norwegian, Russian
Swaziland†	6,704	660,000	98	Monarchy (Commonwealth of Nations) .... A	Mbabane	English, siSwati
Sweden†	173,780	8,335,000	48	Constitutional Monarchy .... A	Stockholm	Swedish
Switzerland	15,943	6,485,000	408	Federal Republic .... A	Bern; Zürich	German, French, Italian
Syria†	71,498	10,485,000	147	Socialist Republic .... A	Damascus (Dimashq)	Arabic
Taiwan†	13,900	19,090,000	1,373	Republic .... A	T'aipei	Chinese dialects
Tajik S.S.R.	55,251	4,300,000	78	Soviet Socialist Republic (Sov. Un.) .... D	Dushanbe	Tajik, Turkish, Russian
Tanzania†	364,900	21,525,000	59	Republic (Commonwealth of Nations) .... A	Dar es Salaam	Swahili, English, indigenous languages
Tasmania	26,383	440,000	17	State (Australia) .... D	Hobart	English
Tennessee	42,143	4,755,000	113	State (U.S.) .... D	Nashville; Memphis	English
Texas	266,805	16,090,000	60	State (U.S.) .... D	Austin; Dallas	English, Spanish
Thailand†	198,115	52,220,000	264	Constitutional Monarchy .... A	Bangkok (Krung Thep)	Thai
Tianjin Shi	4,247	8,430,000	1,985	Autonomous City (China) .... D	Tianjin (Tientsin)	Chinese
Tibet, see Xizang				....		
Togo†	21,925	2,965,000	135	Republic .... A	Lomé	French, indigenous languages
Tokelau (Union Is.)	3.9	1,500	384	Island Territory (New Zealand) C	...; Fakaofo	Malay-Polynesian languages, English
Tonga	270	107,000	396	Constitutional Monarchy (Comm. of Nations) .... A	Nuku'alofa	Tongan, English
Transcaucasia	71,853	14,995,000	209	Part of Soviet Union (3 Republics)	...; Baku	Russian, Armenian, Georgic, Turkish
Transkei	15,831	2,560,000	162	Bantu Homeland (South Africa)†† .... B	Umtata	Xhosa; Afrikaans
Trinidad and Tobago†	1,980	1,240,000	626	Republic (Commonwealth of Nations) .... A	Port of Spain	English
Tristan da Cunha	40	300	7.5	Dependency of St. Helena (U.K.) C	Edinburgh	English
Tunisia†	63,170	7,295,000	115	Republic .... A	Tunis	Arabic, French
Turkey†	300,948	50,730,000	169	Republic .... A	Ankara; İstanbul	Turkish, Kurdish
Turkey in Europe	9,175	4,780,000	521	Part of Turkey	İstanbul	Turkish
Turkmen S.S.R.	188,456	3,085,000	16	Soviet Socialist Republic (Sov. Un.) .... D	Ashkhabad	Turkish, Russian
Turks and Caicos Is.	166	8,100	49	Colony (U.K.) C	Grand Turk	English
Tuvalu (Ellice Is.)	10	8,200	820	Parliamentary State (Commonwealth of Nations) .... A	Funafuti	Tuvaluan, English
Uganda†	91,134	14,505,000	159	Republic (Commonwealth of Nations) .... A	Kampala	English, Swahili, Luganda, indigenous languages
Ukrainian S.S.R.†	233,090	51,260,000	220	Federal Socialist Republic (Sov. Un.) .... D	Kiev	Ukrainian, Russian
Union of Soviet Socialist Republics, see Soviet Union				....		
United Arab Emirates†	32,278	1,600,000	50	Federation of Monarchs .... A	Abū Ẓaby (Abu Dhabi)	Arabic, Farsi, English
United Arab Republic, see Egypt				....		
United Kingdom†	94,092	56,040,000	596	Constitutional Monarchy (Commonwealth of Nations) .. A	London	English
United Kingdom & Possessions	102,111	61,820,000	605		London	English
United States†	3,679,245	237,640,000	65	Federal Republic .... A	Washington; New York	English
United States & Possessions	3,683,901	241,390,000	66		Washington; New York	English, Spanish
Upper Volta, see Burkina Faso						
Uruguay†	68,037	2,930,000	43	Republic .... A	Montevideo	Spanish
Utah	84,902	1,690,000	20	State (U.S.) .... D	Salt Lake City	English
Uzbek S.S.R.	172,742	17,305,000	100	Soviet Socialist Republic (Sov. Un.) .... D	Tashkent	Turkish, Sart, Russian
Vanuatu (New Hebrides)†	5,714	130,000	23	Republic (Commonwealth of Nations) .... A	Port-Vila	Bislama, English, French
Vatican City (Holy See)	0.2	700	3,500	Ecclesiastical State .... A	Vatican City	Italian, Latin
Venda	2,774	400,000	144	Bantu Homeland (South Africa)†† .... B	Thohoyandou; Makearela	Venda, Afrikaans
Venezuela†	352,144	16,040,000	46	Federal Republic .... A	Caracas	Spanish
Vermont	9,614	535,000	56	State (U.S.) .... D	Montpelier; Burlington	English
Victoria	87,884	4,080,000	46	State (Australia) .... D	Melbourne	English
Vietnam†	127,242	58,930,000	463	Socialist Republic .... A	Ha-noi; Ho Chi Minh City (Saigon)	Vietnamese
Virginia	40,763	5,630,000	138	State (U.S.) .... D	Richmond; Norfolk	English
Virgin Is., British	59	13,000	220	Colony (U.K.) C	Road Town	English
Virgin Is. (U.S.)	133	105,000	789	Unincorporated Territory (U.S.) C	Charlotte Amalie	English, Spanish
Wake I.	3.0	300	100	Unincorporated Territory (U.S.) C	Administered from Washington, D.C.	English
Wales	8,017	2,815,000	351	Administrative division of U.K. .... D	Cardiff	English, Welsh
Wallis and Futuna	98	12,000	122	Overseas Territory (France) C	Mata-Utu	Uvean, Futunan, French
Washington	68,139	4,395,000	65	State (U.S.) .... D	Olympia; Seattle	English
Western Australia	975,920	1,390,000	1.4	State (Australia) .... D	Perth	English
Western Sahara	102,703	170,000	1.7	Occupied by Morocco	El Aaiún	Arabic
Western Samoa†	1,097	160,000	146	Constitutional Monarchy (Comm. of Nations) .... A	Apia	Samoan, English
West Indies	92,000	30,150,000	328		...; Havana	Spanish, English, French, Creole
West Virginia	24,236	1,995,000	82	State (U.S.) .... D	Charleston; Huntington	English
White Russia, see Belorussian S.S.R.				....		
Wisconsin	66,213	4,800,000	72	State (U.S.) .... D	Madison; Milwaukee	English
World	57,850,000	4,843,000,000	84	....	...; Tōkyō	
Wyoming	97,808	525,000	5.4	State (U.S.) .... D	Cheyenne	English
Xinjiang Uygur	635,910	14,160,000	22	Autonomous Region (China) .... D	Ürümqi	Turkish, Mongolian, Tungus
Xizang (Tibet)	471,817	2,160,000	4.6	Autonomous Region (China) .... D	Lhasa	Tibetan dialects
Yemen†	75,290	5,985,000	79	Republic .... A	Șan'ā'	Arabic
Yemen, People's Democratic Republic of,†	128,560	2,180,000	17	Socialist Republic .... A	Aden	Arabic
Yugoslavia†	98,766	23,075,000	234	Socialist Federal Republic .... A	Belgrade (Beograd)	Serbo-Croatian, Slovene, Macedonian
Yukon Territory	186,300	23,000	0.1	Territory (Canada) .... D	Whitehorse	English, Eskimo, Indian
Yunnan	168,341	35,025,000	208	Province (China) .... D	Kunming	Chinese, Tibetan dialects, Khmer, Miao-Yao
Zaire†	905,567	32,625,000	36	Republic .... A	Kinshasa	French, Lingala, Swahili, Kikongo, Tshiluba
Zambia†	290,586	6,660,000	23	Republic (Commonwealth of Nations) .... A	Lusaka	English, indigenous languages
Zanzibar	641	555,000	866	Part of Tanzania	...; Zanzibar	Swahili, English, indigenous languages
Zhejiang	39,382	41,835,000	1,062	Province (China) .... D	Hangzhou	Chinese
Zimbabwe (Rhodesia)†	150,804	8,190,000	54	Republic (Commonwealth of Nations) .... A	Harare	English, ChiShona, SiNdebele

† Member of the United Nations (1984).
* Areas include inland water.
†† Bophuthatswana, Ciskei, Transkei and Venda are not recognized by the United Nations.

world comparisons

General Information

Equatorial diameter of the earth, 7,926.68 miles
Polar diameter of the earth, 7,899.99 miles
Diameter of the mean sphere of the earth, 7,918.78 miles
Equatorial circumference of the earth, 24,901.46 miles
Polar circumference of the earth, 24,859.73 miles
Mean distance from the earth to the sun, 93,020,000 miles
Mean distance from the earth to the moon, 238,857 miles
Total area of the earth, 196,940,400 square miles

Highest elevation on the earth's surface, Mt. Everest, Asia, 29,028 feet
Lowest elevation on the earth's land surface, shores of the Dead Sea, Asia—1,312 feet below sea level
Greatest known depth of the ocean, south of the Mariana Islands, Pacific Ocean, 35,810 feet
Total land area of the earth, including inland water and Antarctica, 57,850,000 square miles.

Area of Africa, 11,700,000 square miles
Area of Antarctica, 5,400,000 square miles
Area of Asia, 17,250,000 square miles
Area of Europe, 3,800,000 square miles
Area of North America, 9,400,000 square miles
Area of Oceania, incl. Australia, 3,300,000 square miles
Area of South America, 6,900,000 square miles
Population of the earth (est. 1/1/85), 4,843,000,000

Principal Islands and Their Areas

ISLAND	Area (Sq. Mi.)
Baffin, Canada	183,810
Banks, Canada	27,038
Borneo, Asia	258,855
Bougainville, Papua New Guinea	3,880
Cape Breton, Canada	3,981
Celebes, Indonesia	73,057
Corsica, France	3,352
Crete, Greece	3,217
Cuba, North America	44,218
Cyprus, Asia	3,572
Devon, Canada	21,331
Ellesmere, Canada	83,896
Flores, Indonesia	5,513
Great Britain, U.K.	88,787
Greenland, North America	840,004
Guadalcanal, Solomon Is.	2,500
Hainan, China	13,127
Hawaii, U.S.	4,021
Hispaniola, North America	29,418
Hokkaidō, Japan	30,144
Honshū, Japan	87,805
Iceland, Europe	39,769
Ireland, Europe	32,588
Jamaica, North America	4,244
Jawa (Java), Indonesia	50,745
Kodiak, U.S.	3,670
Kyūshū, Japan	16,215
Leyte, Philippines	2,785
Luzon, Philippines	40,420
Madagascar, Africa	226,658
Melville, Canada	16,274
Mindanao, Philippines	36,537
Mindoro, Philippines	3,759
Negros, Philippines	4,907
New Britain, Papua New Guinea	14,592
New Caledonia, Oceania	5,671
Newfoundland, Canada	43,359
New Guinea, Oceania	303,090
New Ireland, Papua New Guinea	3,205
North East Land, Norway	6,350
North Island, New Zealand	44,279
Novaya Zemlya, Soviet Union	18,882
Palawan, Philippines	4,550
Panay, Philippines	4,446
Prince of Wales, Canada	12,872
Puerto Rico, North America	3,515
Sakhalin, Soviet Union	29,498
Samar, Philippines	5,050
Sardinia, Italy	9,301
Seram, Indonesia	6,046
Sicily, Italy	9,926
Shikoku, Japan	7,245
Somerset, Canada	9,570
Southampton, Canada	15,913
South Island, New Zealand	57,862
Spitsbergen, Norway	15,260
Sri Lanka, Asia	24,962
Sumatra, Indonesia	182,860
Taiwan, Asia	13,900
Tasmania, Australia	26,383
Tierra del Fuego, S. America	18,600
Timor, Indonesia	13,094
Vancouver, Canada	12,079
Victoria, Canada	81,930
Vrangelya, Soviet Union	2,819

Principal Lakes, Oceans, Seas, and Their Areas

LAKE Country	Area (Sq. Mi.)
Aral'skoye More (Aral Sea), Sov. Un	24,909
Arctic Ocean	5,400,000
Athabasca, L., Can	3,064
Atlantic Ocean	31,800,000
Balkhash, Ozero (L.), Sov. Un	7,115
Baltic Sea, Eur.	163,000
Baykal, Ozero (L. Baikal), Sov. Un	12,160
Bering Sea, Asia-N.A.	876,000
Black Sea, Eur.-Asia	178,000
Caribbean Sea, N.A.-S.A.	1,063,000
Caspian Sea, Asia	143,240
Chad, L., Chad-Cam.-Nig.	6,300
East China Sea, Asia	482,000
Erie, L., U.S.-Can.	9,910
Eyre, L., Austl.	2,970
Gairdner, L., Austl.	1,840
Great Bear L., Can.	12,028
Great Salt L., U.S.	1,680
Great Slave L., Can.	11,030
Hudson Bay, Can.	475,000
Huron, L., U.S.-Can.	23,000
Indian Ocean	28,900,000
Japan, Sea of, Asia	389,000
Koko Nor (Qinghai Hu) (L.), China	1,650
Ladozhskoye Ozero (Lake Ladoga), Sov. Un.	6,835
Mai-Ndombe, Lac, (L.), Zaire	3,100
Manitoba, L., Can.	1,800
Mediterranean Sea., Eur.-Afr.-Asia	967,000
Mexico, Gulf of, N.A.	596,000
Michigan, L., U.S.	22,300
Nicaragua, Lago de (L.), Nic.	3,150
North Sea, Eur.	222,000
Nyasa, L., Mwi,-Moz.-Tan	11,150
Okhotsk, Sea of, Asia	610,000
Onezhskoye Ozero (Lake Onega), Sov. Un.	3,720
Ontario, L., U.S.-Can.	7,540
Pacific Ocean	63,800,000
Red Sea, Afr.-Asia	169,000
Rudolf, L., Ken.-Eth.	2,473
Superior, L., U.S.-Can.	31,700
Tanganyika, L., Tan.-Zaire-Bdi.-Zam.	12,350
Titicaca, Lago (L.), Bol.-Peru	3,200
Torrens, L., Austl.	2,230
Vänern (L.), Swe.	2,156
Van Gölü (L.), Tur.	1,434
Victoria, L., Tan.-Ken.-Ug.	26,820
Winnipeg, L., Can.	9,417
Winnipegosis, L., Can.	2,075
Yellow Sea, China	480,000

Principal Mountains and Their Heights

MOUNTAIN Country	Elev. (Ft.)
Aconcagua, Argentina	22,831
Albert Edward, Papua New Guinea	13,091
Annapurna, Nepal	26,504
Antofalla, Argentina	20,013
Apo, Philippines	9,692
Ararat, Turkey	16,804
Bandeira, Brazil	9,482
Barú, Panama	11,410
Belukha, Soviet Union	14,783
Blanc, France-Italy	15,771
Blanca, Colorado, U.S.	14,317
Bolívar (La Columna), Venezuela	16,411
Borah, Idaho, U.S.	12,662
Cameroon, Cam	13,451
Chimborazo, Ecuador	20,561
Citlaltépetl, Mexico	18,701
Colima, Mexico	13,993
Cook, New Zealand	12,349
Cotopaxi, Ecuador	19,347
Cristóbal Colón, Colombia	19,029
Damāvand, Iran	18,386
Dhaulagiri, Nepal	26,810
Duarte, Dom. Rep.	10,417
Dykh-Tau, Soviet Union	17,070
Elbert, Colorado, U.S.	14,431
El'brus, Soviet Union	18,510
Elgon, Kenya	14,178
eNjesuthi, S. Africa	11,306
Erciyeş, Turkey	12,848
Erebus, Antarctia	12,280
Etna, Italy	10,902
Everest, Nepal-China	29,028
Finsteraarhorn, Switzerland	14,022
Foraker, Alaska, U.S.	17,395
Fuji, Japan	12,388
Gannett, Wyo., U.S.	13,785
Gasherbrum, Pak	26,470
Gerlachovský, Czech.	8,710
Glittertinden, Norway	8,110
Gongga Shan, China	24,902
Gosainthan, China	26,289
Grand Teton, Wyo., U.S.	13,766
Gran Paradiso, Italy	13,323
Grossglockner, Austria	12,461
Gunnbjørns, Greenland	12,139
Gurla Mandhata, China	25,354
Hekla, Iceland	4,892
Hood, Oregon, U.S.	11,239
Huascarán, Peru	22,205
Huila, Colombia	18,865
Hvannadalshnukur, Iceland	6,952
Illimani, Bolivia	21,151
Incahuasi, Argentina-Chile	21,719
Iztaccihuatl, Mexico	17,343
Jaya, Indonesia	16,503
Jungfrau, Switzerland	13,668
K2 (Godwin Austen), Pak	28,250
Kailas, China (Tibet)	22,028
Kāmet, India	25,447
Kanchenjunga, Nepal-India	28,208
Kātrīnā, Egypt	8,652
Kazbek, Soviet Union	16,558
Kebnekaise, Sweden	6,926
Kerinci, Indonesia	12,467
Kilimanjaro, Tanzania	19,340
Kinabalu, Malaysia	13,455
Kirinyaga, Kenya	17,058
Klyuchevskaya, Soviet Union	15,584
Kommunizma, Soviet Union	24,590
Korab, Albania	9,026
Kosciusko, Australia	7,310
Koussi, Chad	11,204
Kula Kangri, Bhutan	24,784
Kwanmo, Korea	8,337
Lassen, California, U.S.	10,457
Lenina, Soviet Union	23,406
Llullaillaco, Argentina-Chile	22,057
Logan, Canada	19,524
McKinley, Alaska, U.S.	20,320
Makālu, China-Nepal	27,824
Margherita, Zaire-Uganda	16,763
Markham, Antarctica	14,272
Maromokotro, Madagascar	9,436
Matterhorn, Switz.-Italy	14,685
Mauna Kea, Hawaii, U.S.	13,796
Mauna Loa, Hawaii, U.S.	13,680
Mercedario, Argentina	22,211
Meru, Tanzania	14,978
Midi d'Ossau, France	10,322
Misti, Peru	19,098
Mitchell, North Carolina, U.S.	6,684
Moldaveneau, Romania	8,343
Munku-Sardyk, Mong. Soviet Union	11,457
Musala, Bulgaria	9,592
Muztag, China	25,338
Muztagata, China	24,388
Namcha Barwa, China	25,443
Nanda Devi, India	25,645
Nanga Parbat, Pak.	26,660
Narodnaya, Sov. Un.	6,217
Neblina, Brazil	9,888
Neiges, Reunion	10,069
Nevis, U.K.	4,406
Ntlenyana, Lesotho	11,424
Ojos del Salado, Argentina-Chile	22,615
Ólimbos, Greece	9,550
Orohena, Tahiti	7,352
Paektu, N. Korea-Sov. Un.	9,100
Paricutín, Mexico	9,213
Pelée, Martinique	4,800
Pico, Cape Verde	9,281
Pidurutalagala, Sri Lanka	8,281
Pikes Peak, Colorado, U.S.	14,110
Pissis, Argentina	22,241
Pobedy, China-Soviet Union	24,406
Popocatépetl, Mexico	17,887
Pulog, Philippines	9,626
Rainier, Washington, U.S.	14,410
Rakaposhi, Pak	25,550
Ras Dashen, Ethiopia	15,158
Rinjani, Indonesia	12,224
Rosa, Italy-Switzerland	15,200
Ruapehu, New Zealand	9,175
St. Elias, U.S.-Canada	18,008
Sajama, Bolivia	21,391
Sawdā, Lebanon	10,115
Semeru, Indonesia	12,060
Shām, Oman	9,902
Shasta, California, U.S.	14,162
Shkhara, Soviet Union	16,594
Sources, Lesotho-S. Afr.	10,822
Tahat, Algeria	9,541
Tajumulco, Guat.	13,816
Tirich Mīr, Pak.	25,230
Tocorpuri, Bolivia-Chile	19,137
Toubkal, Morocco	13,665
Trikora, Indonesia	15,584
Tsast Bogd, Mongolia	13,419
Tupungato, Argentina-Chile	22,310
Vesuvio (Vesuvius), Italy	3,842
Victoria, Papau New Guinea	13,242
Vinson Massif, Ant	16,864
Waddington, Canada	13,260
Washington, N.H., U.S.	6,288
Weisshorn, Switzerland	14,783
Whitney, California, U.S.	14,494
Wilhelm, Papua New Guinea	14,794
Wrangell, Alaska, U.S.	14,005
Yerupaja, Peru	21,765
Zugspitze, Austria	9,721

Principal Rivers and Their Lengths

RIVER Continent	Length (Mi.)
Albany, North America	610
Aldan, Asia	1,392
Amazonas-Ucayali, South America	3,902
Amu Dar'ya (Oxus), Asia	1,616
Amur, Asia	2,744
Araguaia, South America	1,367
Arkansas, North America	1,459
Athabasca, North America	765
Brahmaputra, Asia	1,802
Branco, South America	580
Brazos, North America	870
Canadian, North America	906
Churchill, North America	1,000
Colorado, North America	1,450
Columbia, North America	1,243
Congo (Zaïre), Africa	2,610
Cumberland, North America	720
Danube, Europe	1,777
Darling, Australia	1,690
Dnepr (Dnieper), Europe	1,368
Dnestr (Dniester), Europe	876
Don, Europe	1,162
Donets, Europe	735
Elbe, Europe	720
Euphrates, Asia	1,715
Fraser, North America	850
Gambia, Africa	470
Ganges, Asia	1,678
Gila, North America	630
Godāvari, Asia	930
Huang (Yellow), Asia	3,395
Indus, Asia	1,976
Irrawaddy, Asia	1,425
Japurá, South America	1,400
Juruá, South America	1,250
Kama, Europe	1,263
Kasai, Africa	1,338
Kolyma, Asia	1,600
Lena, Asia	2,734
Limpopo, Africa	1,100
Loire, Europe	625
Mackenzie, North America	2,635
Madeira-Mamore, South America	1,988
Magdalena, South America	950
Marañón, South America	1,000
Mekong, Asia	2,796
Meuse, Europe	575
Mississippi, North America	2,348
Mississippi-Missouri, North America	3,740
Missouri, North America	2,314
Murray, Australia	1,609
Negro, South America	1,305
Nelson-Saskatchewan, North America	1,600
Neman, Europe	582
Niger, Africa	2,585
Nile-Kagera, Africa	4,145
Ob'-Irtysh, Asia	3,362
Oder, Europe	565
Ohio, North America	981
Oka, Europe	920
Orange, Africa	1,300
Orinoco, South America	1,700
Ottawa, North America	696
Paraguay, South America	1,584
Paraná, South America	2,796
Paranaíba, South America	850
Peace, North America	1,195
Pechora, Europe	1,124
Pecos, North America	735
Pilcomayo, South America	1,550
Plata-Paraná, South America	2,920
Purús, South America	1,988
Red, North America	1,270
Rhine, Europe	820
Rhône, Europe	500
Rio Grande, North America	1,885
Roosevelt, South America	950
St. Lawrence, North America	800
Salado, South America	870
Salween, Asia	1,770
São Francisco, South America	1,802
Saskatchewan, North America	1,660
Sava, Europe	585
Snake, North America	1,038
Sungari (Songhua), Asia	1,140
Syr-Dar'ya, Asia	1,859
Tagus (Tajo, Tejo), Europe	625
Tarim, Asia	1,328
Tennessee, North America	652
Tigris, Asia	1,181
Tisza, Europe	607
Tobol, Asia	1,093
Tocantins, South America	1,640
Ucayali, South America	1,220
Ural, Asia	1,509
Uruguay, South America	1,025
Verkhnyaya Tunguska (Angara), Asia	1,549
Vilyuy, Asia	1,513
Volga, Europe	2,194
White, North America	720
Wisla (Vistula), Europe	630
Xingú, South America	1,230
Yangtze, Asia	3,915
Yellowstone, North America	671
Yenisey, Asia	2,543
Yukon, North America	1,979
Zambezi, Africa	1,653

principal cities of the world

bidjan, Ivory Coast ... 1,500,000
ccra, Ghana (1,142,690) ... 1,045,381
ddis Ababa, Ethiopia ... 1,408,068
delaide, Australia (931,886) ... 12,656
hmadābād, India (2,400,000) ... 2,024,917
leppo (Halab), Syria ... 962,954
lexandria (Al Iskandarīyah), Egypt (2,850,000) ... 2,409,000
lgiers (El Djazaïr), Algeria (1,724,705) ... 1,523,000
l Kharṭūm (Khartoum), Sudan, (790,000) ... 333,921
lma-Ata, Soviet Union (1,075,000) ... 1,046,000
mmān, Jordan ... 648,587
msterdam, Netherlands (1,810,000) ... 687,397
nkara (Angora), Turkey (1,975,000) ... 1,877,755
nshan, China (1,210,000†) ... 1,030,000
ntwerp (Antwerpen), Belgium (1,100,000) ... 490,524
sunción, Paraguay (700,000) ... 455,517
thens (Athínai), Greece (3,027,331) ... 885,737
tlanta, Georgia (2,112,400) ... 425,022
uckland, New Zealand (778,200) ... 144,400
aghdād, Iraq (2,183,800) ... 1,300,000
aku, Soviet Union (1,880,000) ... 1,084,000
altimore, Maryland (1,901,100) ... 786,741
andung, Indonesia (1,525,000) ... 1,462,637
angalore, India (2,950,000) ... 2,482,507
angkok (Krung Thep), Thailand (5,700,000) ... 5,153,902
arcelona, Spain (3,975,000) ... 1,754,900
eirut, Lebanon (1,675,000) ... 474,870
elfast, No. Ireland (710,000) ... 295,223
elgrade (Beograd), Yugoslavia (1,400,000) ... 936,200
elo Horizonte, Brazil (2,500,000) ... 1,781,924
erlin, East, Ger. Dem. Rep. (*Berlin, West) ... 1,152,529
erlin, West, Fed. Rep. of Ger. (3,790,000) ... 1,869,584
ilbao, Spain (965,000) ... 433,030
irmingham, England (2,675,000) ... 1,022,300
ogotá, Colombia (4,150,000) ... 4,067,000
ombay, India (9,950,000) ... 8,227,332
onn, Fed. Rep. of Ger. (570,000) ... 293,852
oston, Massachusetts (3,732,300) ... 562,994
rasilia, Brazil ... 1,177,393
remen, Fed. Rep. of Ger. (800,000) ... 547,619
risbane, Australia (1,028,527) ... 689,378
russels (Bruxelles), Belgium (2,395,000) ... 137,738
ucharest (Bucureşti), Romania (2,175,000) ... 1,929,360
udapest, Hungary (2,540,000) ... 2,064,000
uenos Aires, Argentina (10,700,000) ... 2,908,001
uffalo, New York (1,133,800) ... 357,870
airo (Al Qāhirah), Egypt (8,500,000) ... 5,278,000
alcutta, India (11,100,000) ... 3,291,655
ali, Colombia (1,340,000) ... 1,293,000
anberra, Australia (239,798) ... 219,323
anton (Guangzhou), China (3,120,000†) ... 2,380,000
ape Town, South Africa (1,790,000) ... 859,940
aracas, Venezuela (3,600,000) ... 3,041,000
ardiff, Wales (625,000) ... 281,300
asablanca, Morocco (1,575,000) ... 1,506,373
hangchun, China (1,740,000†) ... 1,340,000
helyabinsk, Soviet Union (1,245,000) ... 1,086,000
hengdu, China (2,470,000) ... 1,410,000
hicago, Illinois (7,823,000) ... 3,005,072
hongqing (Chungking), China (2,650,800†) ... 1,940,000
incinnati, Ohio (1,472,200) ... 385,409
leveland, Ohio (2,160,800) ... 573,822
ologne (Köln), Fed. Rep. of Ger. (1,810,000) ... 961,777
olombo, Sri Lanka (1,600,000) ... 585,776
olumbus, Ohio (949,200) ... 565,032
openhagen (København), Denmark (1,470,000) ... 498,850
acca (Dhaka), Bangladesh (3,458,602) ... 1,850,000
akar, Senegal ... 979,000
allas, Texas (3,126,500) ... 904,570
amascus (Dimashq), Syria (1,575,000) ... 1,201,000
ar es Salaam, Tanzania ... 757,346
elhi, India (7,200,000) ... 4,865,077
enver, Colorado (1,559,200) ... 492,686
etroit, Michigan (4,254,800) ... 1,203,368
nepropetrovsk, Soviet Union (1,525,000) ... 1,140,000

Donetsk (Stalino), Soviet Union (2,140,000) ... 1,064,000
Dresden, Ger. Dem. Rep. (640,000) ... 516,225
Dublin (Baile Atha Cliath), Ireland (1,110,000) ... 525,882
Durban, South Africa (1,550,000) ... 677,760
Düsseldorf, Fed. Rep. of Ger. (1,215,000) ... 583,445
Edinburgh, Scotland (630,000) ... 446,361
Essen, Fed. Rep. of Ger. (5,050,000) ... 638,812
Florence (Firenze), Italy (650,000) ... 453,293
Fortaleza, Brazil (1,550,000) ... 1,308,919
Frankfurt am Main, Fed. Rep. of Ger. (1,880,000) ... 620,186
Fukuoka, Japan (1,575,000) ... 1,088,588
Fushun, China (1,190,000†) ... 1,040,000
Gdańsk (Danzig), Poland (875,000) ... 464,600
Geneva (Génève), Switzerland (435,000) ... 158,900
Genoa (Genova), Italy (830,000) ... 760,300
Glasgow, Scotland (1,800,000) ... 767,456
Gor'kiy, Soviet Union (1,940,000) ... 1,392,000
Guadalajara, Mexico (2,300,000) ... 1,626,152
Guatemala, Guatemala (1,100,000) ... 749,784
Guayaquil, Ecuador ... 1,278,908
Hamburg, Fed. Rep. of Ger. (2,250,000) ... 1,623,848
Hannover, Fed. Rep. of Ger. (1,005,000) ... 526,253
Hanoi, Vietnam (1,500,000) ... 819,913
Harare, Zimbabwe (870,000) ... 656,011
Harbin, China (2,550,000†) ... 2,150,000
Hartford, Connecticut (1,058,800) ... 136,392
Havana (La Habana), Cuba (1,975,000) ... 1,924,886
Helsinki, Finland (900,000) ... 483,051
Hiroshima, Japan (1,525,000) ... 899,399
Ho Chi Minh City (Saigon), Vietnam (3,100,000) ... 2,441,185
Hong Kong, Hong Kong (4,515,000) ... 1,183,621
Honolulu, Hawaii (806,100) ... 365,048
Houston, Texas (3,085,700) ... 1,595,138
Hyderābād, India (2,750,000) ... 2,142,087
Ibadan, Nigeria ... 1,009,000
Indianapolis, Indiana (1,115,100) ... 700,807
Irkutsk, Soviet Union ... 589,000
İstanbul, Turkey (4,650,000) ... 2,772,708
İzmir, Turkey (1,200,000) ... 757,854
Jakarta (Batavia), Indonesia (7,000,000) ... 6,503,449
Jerusalem, Israel (440,000) ... 415,000
Jinan, China (1,320,000†) ... 1,040,000
Johannesburg, South Africa (3,650,000) ... 703,980
Kābul, Afghanistan ... 913,164
Kānpur, India (1,875,000) ... 1,531,345
Kansas City, Missouri (1,264,600) ... 448,028
Kaohsiung, Taiwan (1,640,000) ... 1,227,454
Karāchi, Pakistan (5,150,000) ... 4,776,000
Kathmandu, Nepal (320,000) ... 235,160
Katowice, Poland (2,720,000) ... 361,300
Kawasaki, Japan (*Tōkyō) ... 1,040,802
Kazan', Soviet Union (1,080,000) ... 1,039,000
Khar'kov, Soviet Union (1,825,000) ... 1,536,000
Kiev, Soviet Union (2,635,000) ... 2,409,000
Kingston, Jamaica ... 671,000
Kinshasa, Zaire ... 2,700,000
Kitakyūshū, Japan (1,515,000) ... 1,065,078
Kōbe, Japan (*Ōsaka) ... 1,367,390
Kowloon, Hong Kong (*Hong Kong) ... 799,123
Kuala Lumpur, Malaysia (1,250,000) ... 937,817
Kunming, China (1,430,000†) ... 1,020,000
Kuwait (Al Kuwayt), Kuwait (1,085,000) ... 60,365
Kuybyshev, Soviet Union (1,460,000) ... 1,250,000
Kyōto, Japan (*Ōsaka) ... 1,473,065
Lagos, Nigeria (2,000,000) ... 1,404,000
Lahore, Pakistan (2,975,000) ... 2,685,000
Lanzhou, China (1,430,000†) ... 1,080,000
La Paz, Bolivia ... 719,780
Leeds, England (1,540,000) ... 718,100
Leipzig, Ger. Dem. Rep. (710,000) ... 562,480
Leningrad, Soviet Union (5,550,000) ... 4,295,000
Liège, Belgium (755,000) ... 207,496
Lille, France (1,020,000) ... 168,424
Lima, Peru (4,608,010) ... 371,122
Lisbon (Lisboa), Portugal (2,250,000) ... 807,200

Liverpool, England (1,525,000) ... 518,900
Łódź, Poland (1,045,000) ... 848,500
London, England (11,100,000) ... 6,851,400
Los Angeles, California (10,339,800) ... 2,968,579
Louisville, Kentucky (882,700) ... 298,694
Luanda, Angola ... 475,328
Lucknow, India (1,060,000) ... 895,947
Lüda (Dairen), China (1,480,000†) ... 1,240,000
Lyon, France (1,180,000) ... 413,095
Madras, India (4,475,000) ... 3,266,034
Madrid, Spain (4,515,000) ... 3,188,297
Managua, Nicaragua ... 644,588
Manchester, England (2,775,000) ... 464,200
Manila, Philippines (6,800,000) ... 1,626,249
Mannheim, Fed. Rep. of Ger. (1,410,000) ... 302,621
Maracaibo, Venezuela ... 929,000
Marseille, France (1,090,000) ... 874,436
Mecca (Makkah), Saudi Arabia ... 550,000
Medan, Indonesia (1,450,000) ... 1,378,955
Medellín, Colombia (2,025,000) ... 1,477,000
Melbourne, Australia (2,722,817) ... 63,388
Memphis, Tennessee (847,300) ... 646,174
Mexico City, Mexico (14,600,000) ... 9,373,400
Miami, Florida (3,097,300) ... 346,865
Milan (Milano), Italy (3,775,000) ... 1,634,638
Milwaukee, Wisconsin (1,347,000) ... 636,297
Minneapolis, Minnesota (2,025,600) ... 370,951
Minsk, Soviet Union (1,450,000) ... 1,442,000
Monterrey, Mexico (2,015,000) ... 1,090,009
Montevideo, Uruguay (1,350,000) ... 1,229,748
Montréal, Canada (2,828,349) ... 980,354
Moscow (Moskva), Soviet Union (12,400,000) ... 8,202,000
Munich (München), Fed. Rep. of Ger. (1,955,000) ... 1,287,080
Nagoya, Japan (4,625,000) ... 2,087,902
Nāgpur, India (1,325,000) ... 1,215,425
Nairobi, Kenya ... 827,775
Nanjing, China (2,130,000) ... 1,740,000
Naples (Napoli), Italy (2,765,000) ... 1,210,503
Newcastle upon Tyne, England (1,300,000) ... 285,300
New Delhi, India (*Delhi) ... 271,990
New Orleans, Louisiana (1,236,500) ... 557,927
New York, New York (16,635,500) ... 7,071,639
Norfolk, Virginia (830,900) ... 266,979
Novosibirsk, Soviet Union (1,515,000) ... 1,384,000
Nürnberg, Fed. Rep. of Ger. (1,040,000) ... 479,035
Odessa, Soviet Union (1,165,000) ... 1,113,000
Oklahoma City, Oklahoma (813,300) ... 404,014
Omsk, Soviet Union (1,100,000) ... 1,094,000
Osaka, Japan (15,900,000) ... 2,648,180
Oslo, Norway (725,000) ... 448,747
Ottawa, Canada (717,978) ... 295,163
Palermo, Italy ... 699,691
Panamá, Panama (625,000) ... 388,638
Paris, France (9,450,000) ... 2,176,243
Peking (Beijing), China (6,100,000) ... 5,597,972
Perm', Soviet Union (1,105,000) ... 1,048,000
Perth, Australia (898,918) ... 79,398
Philadelphia, Pennsylvania (5,157,900) ... 1,688,210
Phnom Penh, Kampuchea ... 400,000
Phoenix, Arizona (1,652,700) ... 790,160
Pittsburgh, Pennsylvania (2,119,100) ... 423,959
Port-au-Prince, Haiti (800,000) ... 745,700
Portland, Oregon (1,249,600) ... 368,139
Porto (Oporto), Portugal (1,225,000) ... 327,400
Porto Alegre, Brazil (2,200,000) ... 1,125,901
Prague (Praha), Czechoslovakia (1,270,000) ... 1,185,693
Pretoria, South Africa (960,000) ... 435,100
Providence, Rhode Island (903,700) ... 156,804
Pune, India (1,775,000) ... 1,202,848
Pusan, Korea (South) ... 3,395,000
P'yŏngyang, Korea (North) ... 1,700,000
Qingdao, China (1,180,000†) ... 1,080,000
Qiqihar, China (1,222,000†) ... 920,000
Québec, Canada (576,075) ... 166,474
Quezon City, Philippines (*Manila) ... 1,165,865
Quito, Equador ... 918,884
Rabat, Morocco (540,000) ... 367,620

Rangoon, Burma (3,000,000) ... 2,276,000
Rawalpindi, Pakistan (1,040,000) ... 452,000
Recife (Pemambuco), Brazil (2,300,000) ... 1,204,738
Rīga, Soviet Union (950,000) ... 875,000
Rio de Janerio, Brazil (9,200,000) ... 5,093,232
Riyadh, Saudi Arabia ... 1,000,000
Rochester, New York (826,000) ... 241,741
Rome (Roma), Italy (3,115,000) ... 2,830,569
Rosario, Argentina (1,045,000) ... 935,471
Rostov-na-Donu, Soviet Union (1,110,000) ... 983,000
Rotterdam, Netherlands (1,090,000) ... 558,832
Sacramento, California (926,600) ... 275,741
St. Louis, Missouri (2,225,500) ... 452,801
St. Paul, Minnesota (*Minneapolis) ... 270,230
Salt Lake City, Utah (756,600) ... 163,034
Salvador, Brazil (1,700,000) ... 1,506,602
San Antonio, Texas, (1,104,500) ... 785,940
San Diego, California (1,746,500) ... 875,538
San Francisco, California (4,884,300) ... 678,974
San José, Costa Rica (560,000) ... 259,126
San Juan, Puerto Rico (1,535,000) ... 422,701
San Salvador, El Salvador (720,000) ... 397,100
Santiago, Chile (3,992,509) ... 425,924
Santo Domingo, Dominican Rep. ... 1,313,172
São Paulo, Brazil (12,700,000) ... 8,493,598
Sapporo, Japan (1,450,000) ... 1,401,757
Saratov, Soviet Union (1,125,000) ... 893,000
Seattle, Washington (2,173,800) ... 493,846
Seoul (Sŏul), Korea (South) (11,200,000) ... 8,366,756
Shanghai, China (9,000,000) ... 6,292,960
Sheffield, England (710,000) ... 547,600
Shenyang (Mukden), China (4,020,000†) ... 3,030,000
Singapore, Singapore (2,760,000) ... 2,502,000
Sofia (Sofiya), Bulgaria (1,142,582) ... 1,056,945
Stockholm, Sweden (1,402,426) ... 649,686
Stuttgart, Fed. Rep. of Ger. (1,935,000) ... 573,577
Surabaya, Indonesia (2,150,000) ... 2,027,913
Sverdlovsk, Soviet Union (1,505,000) ... 1,286,000
Sydney, Australia (3,204,696) ... 51,836
Taegu, Korea (South) ... 1,959,000
T'aipei, Taiwan (5,050,000) ... 2,270,983
Taiyuan, China (1,750,000†) ... 1,280,000
Tashkent, Soviet Union (2,165,000) ... 1,986,000
Tbilisi, Soviet Union (1,295,000) ... 1,140,000
Tegucigalpa, Honduras ... 444,749
Tehrān, Iran (4,700,000) ... 4,496,159
Tel Aviv-Yafo, Israel (1,380,000) ... 329,500
The Hague ('s-Gravenhage), Netherlands (775,000) ... 449,338
Tianjin (Tientsin), China (7,764,141†) ... 4,300,000
Tiranë, Albania ... 198,000
Tōkyō, Japan (26,200,000) ... 8,351,893
Toronto, Canada (2,998,947) ... 599,217
Tripoli (Tarābulus), Libya ... 858,500
Tunis, Tunisia (915,000) ... 550,404
Turin (Torino), Italy (1,600,000) ... 1,103,520
Ufa, Soviet Union (1,050,000) ... 1,048,000
Ulan Bator, Mongolia ... 435,400
Valencia, Spain (1,270,000) ... 751,734
Valparaíso, Chile (530,000) ... 266,502
Vancouver, Canada (1,268,183) ... 414,281
Venice (Venezia), Italy (415,000) ... 332,775
Vienna (Wien), Austria (1,875,000) ... 1,515,666
Vladivostok, Soviet Union ... 590,000
Volgograd (Stalingrad), Soviet Union (1,275,000) ... 969,000
Warsaw (Warszawa), Poland (2,145,000) ... 1,628,900
Washington, D.C. (3,329,800) ... 618,400
Wellington, New Zealand (343,200) ... 134,900
Winnipeg, Canada (584,842) ... 564,473
Wuhan, China (3,230,000†) ... 2,730,000
Wuppertal, Fed. Rep. of Ger. (855,000) ... 387,951
Xi'an, China (2,180,000†) ... 1,610,000
Xuzhou, China (773,000†) ... 668,000
Yerevan, Soviet Union (1,220,000) ... 1,114,000
Yokohama, Japan (*Tōkyō) ... 2,773,674
Zagreb, Yugoslavia ... 768,700
Zhengzhou, China (1,424,000†) ... 895,000
Zürich, Switzerland (780,000) ... 356,800

Metropolitan area populations are shown in parentheses.
City is located within the metropolitan area of another city; for example, Kyōto, Japan (*Ōsaka).
Population of entire municipality or district, including rural area.

glossary of foreign geographical terms

Annam . . . Annamese
Arab . . . Arabic
Bantu . . . Bantu
Bur . . . Burmese
Camb . . . Cambodian
Celt . . . Celtic
Chn . . . Chinese
Czech . . . Czech
Dan . . . Danish
Du . . . Dutch
Fin . . . Finnish
Fr . . . French
Ger . . . German
Gr . . . Greek
Hung . . . Hungarian
Ice . . . Icelandic
India . . . India
Indian . . . American Indian
Indon . . . Indonesian
It . . . Italian
Jap . . . Japanese
Kor . . . Korean
Mal . . . Malayan
Mong . . . Mongolian
Nor . . . Norwegian
Per . . . Persian
Pol . . . Polish
Port . . . Portuguese
Rom . . . Romanian
Rus . . . Russian
Siam . . . Siamese
So. Slav . . . Southern Slavonic
Sp . . . Spanish
Swe . . . Swedish
Tib . . . Tibetan
Tur . . . Turkish
Yugo . . . Yugoslav

å, Nor., Swe . . . **brook, river**
aa, Dan., Nor . . . **brook**
aas, Dan., Nor . . . **ridge**
āb, Per . . . **water, river**
abad, India, Per . . . **town, city**
ada, Tur . . . **island**
adrar, Berber . . . **mountain**
air, Indon . . . **stream**
akrotírion, Gr . . . **cape**
älf, Swe . . . **river**
alp, Ger . . . **mountain**
altipiano, It . . . **plateau**
alto, Sp . . . **height**
archipel, Fr . . . **archipelago**
archipiélago, Sp . . . **archipelago**
arquipélago, Port . . . **archipelago**
arroyo, Sp . . . **brook, stream**
ås, Nor., Swe . . . **ridge**
austral, Sp . . . **southern**
baai, Du . . . **bay**
bab, Arab . . . **gate, port**
bach, Ger . . . **brook, stream**
backe, Swe . . . **hill**
bad, Ger . . . **bath, spa**
bahía, Sp . . . **bay, gulf**
bahr, Arab . . . **river, sea, lake**
baia, It . . . **bay, gulf**
baía, Port . . . **bay**
baie, Fr . . . **bay, gulf**
bajo, Sp . . . **depression**
bak, Indon . . . **stream**
bakke, Dan., Nor . . . **hill**
balkan, Tur . . . **mountain range**
bana, Jap . . . **point, cape**
banco, Sp . . . **bank**
bandar, Mal., Per. . . . **town, port, harbor**
bang, Siam . . . **village**
bassin, Fr . . . **basin**
batang, Indon., Mal . . . **river**
ben, Celt . . . **mountain, summit**
bender, Arab . . . **harbor, port**
bereg, Rus . . . **coast, shore**
berg, Du., Ger., Nor., Swe. . . . **mountain, hill**
bir, Arab . . . **well**
birkat, Arab . . . **lake, pond, pool**
bit, Arab . . . **house**
bjaerg, Dan., Nor . . . **mountain**
bocche, It . . . **mouth**
boğazı, Tur . . . **strait**
bois, Fr . . . **forest, wood**
boloto, Rus . . . **marsh**
bolsón, Sp. . . . **flat-floored desert valley**
boreal, Sp . . . **northern**
borg, Dan., Nor., Swe . . . **castle, town**
borgo, It . . . **town, suburb**
bosch, Du . . . **forest, wood**
bouche, Fr . . . **river mouth**
bourg, Fr . . . **town, borough**
bro, Dan., Nor., Swe . . . **bridge**
brücke, Ger . . . **bridge**
bucht, Ger . . . **bay, bight**
bugt, Dan., Nor., Swe . . . **bay, gulf**
bulu, Indon . . . **mountain**
burg, Du., Ger . . . **castle, town**
buri, Siam . . . **town**
burun, burnu, Tur . . . **cape**
by, Dan., Nor., Swe . . . **village**
caatinga, Port. (Brazil) . . . **open brushland**
cabezo, Sp . . . **summit**
cabo, Port., Sp . . . **cape**
campo, It., Port., Sp . . . **plain, field**
campos, Port. (Brazil) . . . **plains**
cañón, Sp . . . **canyon**
cap, Fr . . . **cape**
capo, It . . . **cape**
casa, It., Port., Sp . . . **house**
castello, It., Port . . . **castle, fort**
castillo, Sp . . . **castle**
càte, Fr . . . **hill**
çay, Tur . . . **stream, river**
cayo, Sp . . . **rock, shoal, islet**
cerro, Sp . . . **mountain, hill**
champ, Fr . . . **field**
chang, Chn . . . **village, middle**
château, Fr . . . **castle**
chen, Chn . . . **market town**
chiang, Chn . . . **river**
chott, Arab . . . **salt lake**
chou, Chn. **capital of district; island**
chu, Tib . . . **water, stream**
cidade, Port . . . **town, city**
cima, Sp . . . **summit, peak**
città, It . . . **town, city**
ciudad, Sp . . . **town, city**
cochilha, Port . . . **ridge**
col, Fr . . . **pass**
colina, Sp . . . **hill**
cordillera, Sp . . . **mountain chain**
costa, It., Port., Sp . . . **coast**
côte, Fr . . . **coast**
cuchilla, Sp . . . **mountain ridge**
dağ, Tur . . . **mountain(s)**
dake, Jap . . . **peak, summit**
dal, Dan., Du., Nor., Swe . . . **valley**
dan, Kor . . . **point, cape**
danau, Indon . . . **lake**
dar, Arab . . . **house, abode, country**
darya, Per . . . **river, sea**
dasht, Per . . . **plain, desert**
deniz, Tur . . . **sea**
désert, Fr . . . **desert**
deserto, It . . . **desert**
desierto, Sp . . . **desert**
détroit, Fr . . . **strait**
dijk, Du . . . **dam, dike**
djebel, Arab . . . **mountain**
do, Kor . . . **island**
dorf, Ger . . . **village**
dorp, Du . . . **village**
duin, Du . . . **dune**
dzong, Tib. . . . **fort, administrative capital**
eau, Fr . . . **water**
ecuador, Sp . . . **equator**
eiland, Du . . . **island**
elv, Dan., Nor . . . **river, stream**
embalse, Sp . . . **reservoir**
erg, Arab . . . **dune, sandy desert**
est, Fr., It . . . **east**
estado, Sp . . . **state**
este, Port., Sp . . . **east**
estrecho, Sp . . . **strait**
étang, Fr . . . **pond, lake**
état, Fr . . . **state**
eyjar, Ice . . . **islands**
feld, Ger . . . **field, plain**
festung, Ger . . . **fortress**
fiume, It . . . **river**
fjäll, Swe . . . **mountain**
fjärd, Swe . . . **bay, inlet**
fjeld, Nor . . . **mountain, hill**
fjord, Dan., Nor . . . **fiord, inlet**
fjördur, Ice . . . **fiord, inlet**
fleuve, Fr . . . **river**
flod, Dan., Swe . . . **river**
flói, Ice . . . **bay, marshland**
fluss, Ger . . . **river**
foce, It . . . **river mouth**
fontein, Du . . . **a spring**
forêt, Fr . . . **forest**
fors, Swe . . . **waterfall**
forst, Ger . . . **forest**
fos, Dan., Nor . . . **waterfall**
fu, Chn . . . **town, residence**
fuente, Sp . . . **spring, fountain**
fuerte, Sp . . . **fort**
furt, Ger . . . **ford**
gang, Kor . . . **stream, river**
gangri, Tib . . . **mountain**
gat, Dan., Nor . . . **channel**
gàve, Fr . . . **stream**
gawa, Jap . . . **river**
gebergte, Du . . . **mountain range**
gebiet, Ger . . . **district, territory**
gebirge, Ger . . . **mountains**
ghat, India . . . **pass, mountain range**
gobi, Mong . . . **desert**
gol, Mong . . . **river**
göl, gölü, Tur . . . **lake**
golf, Du., Ger . . . **gulf, bay**
golfe, Fr . . . **gulf, bay**
golfo, It., Port., Sp . . . **gulf, bay**
gomba, gompa, Tib . . . **monastery**
gora, Rus., So. Slav . . . **mountain**
góra, Pol . . . **mountain**
gorod, Rus . . . **town**
grad, Rus., So. Slav . . . **town**
guba, Rus . . . **bay, gulf**
gundung, Indon . . . **mountain**
guntō, Jap . . . **archipelago**
gunung, Mal . . . **mountain**
haf, Swe . . . **sea, ocean**
hafen, Ger . . . **port, harbor**
haff, Ger . . . **gulf, inland sea**
hai, Chn . . . **sea, lake**
hama, Jap . . . **beach, shore**
hamada, Arab . . . **rocky plateau**
hamn, Swe . . . **harbor**
hāmūn, Per . . . **swampy lake, plain**
hantō, Jap . . . **peninsula**
hassi, Arab . . . **well, spring**
haus, Ger . . . **house**
haut, Fr . . . **summit, top**
hav, Dan., Nor . . . **sea, ocean**
havn, Dan., Nor . . . **harbor, port**
havre, Fr . . . **harbor, port**
háza, Hung . . . **house, dwelling of**
heim, Ger . . . **hamlet, home**
hem, Swe . . . **hamlet, home**
higashi, Jap . . . **east**
hisar, Tur . . . **fortress**
hissar, Arab . . . **fort**
ho, Chn . . . **river**
hoek, Du . . . **cape**
hof, Ger . . . **court, farmhouse**
höfn, Ice . . . **harbor**
hoku, Jap . . . **north**
holm, Dan., Nor., Swe . . . **island**
hora, Czech . . . **mountain**
horn, Ger . . . **peak**
hoved, Dan., Nor . . . **cape**
hsien, Chn . . . **district, district capital**
hu, Chn . . . **lake**
hügel, Ger . . . **hill**
huk, Dan., Swe . . . **point**
hus, Dan., Nor., Swe . . . **house**
île, Fr . . . **island**
ilha, Port . . . **island**
indsö, Dan., Nor . . . **lake**
insel, Ger . . . **island**
insjö, Swe . . . **lake**
irmak, irmagi, Tur . . . **river**
isla, Sp . . . **island**
isola, It . . . **island**
istmo, It., Sp . . . **isthmus**
järvi, jaur, Fin . . . **lake**
jebel, Arab . . . **mountain**
jima, Jap . . . **island**
jökel, Nor . . . **glacier**
joki, Fin . . . **river**
jökull, Ice . . . **glacier**
kaap, Du . . . **cape**
kai, Jap . . . **bay, gulf, sea**
kaikyō, Jap . . . **channel, strait**
kalat, Per . . . **castle, fortress**
kale, Tur . . . **fort**
kali, Mal . . . **creek, river**
kand, Per . . . **village**
kang, Chn . . . **mountain ridge; village**
kap, Dan., Ger . . . **cape**
kapp, Nor., Swe . . . **cape**
kasr, Arab . . . **fort, castle**
kawa, Jap . . . **river**
kefr, Arab . . . **village**
kei, Jap . . . **creek, river**
ken, Jap . . . **prefecture**
khor, Arab . . . **bay, inlet**
khrebet, Rus . . . **mountain range**
kiang, Chn . . . **large river**
king, Chn . . . **capital city, town**
kita, Jap . . . **north**
ko, Jap . . . **lake**
köbstad, Dan . . . **market-town**
kol, Mong . . . **lake**
kólpos, Gr . . . **gulf**
kong, Chn . . . **river**
kopf, Ger . . . **head, summit, peak**
köpstad, Swe . . . **market-town**
körfezi, Tur . . . **gulf**
kosa, Rus . . . **spit**
kou, Chn . . . **river mouth**
köy, Tur . . . **village**
kraal, Du. (Africa) . . . **native village**
ksar, Arab . . . **fortified village**
kuala, Mal . . . **bay, river mouth**
kuh, Per . . . **mountain**
kum, Tur . . . **sand**
kuppe, Ger . . . **summit**
küste, Ger . . . **coast**
kyo, Jap . . . **town, capital**
la, Tib . . . **mountain pass**
labuan, Mal . . . **anchorage, port**
lac, Fr . . . **lake**
lago, It., Port., Sp . . . **lake**
lagoa, Port . . . **lake, marsh**
laguna, It., Port., Sp . . . **lagoon, lake**
lahti, Fin . . . **bay, gulf**
län, Swe . . . **county**
landsby, Dan., Nor . . . **village**
liehtao, Chn . . . **archipelago**
liman, Tur . . . **bay, port**
ling, Chn . . . **pass, ridge, mountain**
llanos, Sp . . . **plains**
loch, Celt. (Scotland) . . . **lake, bay**
loma, Sp . . . **long, low hill**
lough, Celt. (Ireland) . . . **lake, bay**
machi, Jap . . . **town**
man, Kor . . . **bay**
mar, Port., Sp . . . **sea**
mare, It., Rom . . . **sea**
marisma, Sp . . . **marsh, swamp**
mark, Ger . . . **boundary, limit**
massif, Fr . . . **block of mountains**
mato, Port . . . **forest, thicket**
me, Siam . . . **river**
meer, Du., Ger . . . **lake, sea**
mer, Fr . . . **sea**
mesa, Sp . . . **flat-topped mountain**
meseta, Sp . . . **plateau**
mina, Port., Sp . . . **mine**
minami, Jap . . . **south**
minato, Jap . . . **harbor, haven**
misaki, Jap . . . **cape, headland**
mont, Fr . . . **mount, mountain**
montagna, It . . . **mountain**
montagne, Fr . . . **mountain**
montaña, Sp . . . **mountain**
monte, It., Port., Sp. . . . **mount, mountain**
more, Rus., So. Slav . . . **sea**
morro, Port., Sp . . . **hill, bluff**
mühle, Ger . . . **mill**
mund, Ger . . . **mouth, opening**
mündung, Ger . . . **river mouth**
mura, Jap . . . **township**
myit, Bur . . . **river**
mys, Rus . . . **cape**
nada, Jap . . . **sea**
nadi, India . . . **river, creek**
naes, Dan., Nor . . . **cape**
nafud, Arab . . . **desert of sand dunes**
nagar, India . . . **town, city**
nahr, Arab . . . **river**
nam, Siam . . . **river, water**
nan, Chn., Jap . . . **south**
näs, Nor., Swe . . . **cape**
nez, Fr . . . **point, cape**
nishi, nisi, Jap . . . **west**
njarga, Fin . . . **peninsula**
nong, Siam . . . **marsh**
noord, Du . . . **north**
nor, Mong . . . **lake**
nord, Dan., Fr., Ger., It., Nor., Swe . . . **north**
norte, Port., Sp . . . **north**
nos, Rus . . . **cape**
nyasa, Bantu . . . **lake**
ö, Dan., Nor., Swe . . . **island**
occidental, Sp . . . **western**
ocna, Rom . . . **salt mine**
odde, Dan., Nor . . . **point, cape**
oeste, Port., Sp . . . **west**
oka, Jap . . . **hill**
oost, Du . . . **east**
oriental, Sp . . . **eastern**
óros, Gr . . . **mountain**
ost, Ger., Swe . . . **east**
öster, Dan., Nor., Swe . . . **eastern**
ostrov, Rus . . . **island**
oued, Arab . . . **river, stream**
ouest, Fr . . . **west**
ozero, Rus . . . **lake**
pää, Fin . . . **mountain**
padang, Mal . . . **plain, field**
pampas, Sp. (Argentina) . . . **grassy plains**
pará, Indian (Brazil) . . . **river**
pas, Fr . . . **channel, passage**
paso, Sp . . . **mountain pass, passage**
passo, It., Port. **mountain pass, passage, strait**
patam, India . . . **city, town**
pei, Chn . . . **north**
pélagos, Gr . . . **open sea**
pegunungan, Indon . . . **mountains**
peña, Sp . . . **rock**
peresheyek, Rus . . . **isthmus**
pertuis, Fr . . . **strait**
peski, Rus . . . **desert**
pic, Fr . . . **mountain peak**
pico, Port., Sp . . . **mountain peak**
piedra, Sp . . . **stone, rock**
ping, Chn . . . **plain, flat**
planalto, Port . . . **plateau**
planina, Yugo . . . **mountains**
playa, Sp . . . **shore, beach**
pnom, Camb . . . **mountain**
pointe, Fr . . . **point**
polder, Du., Ger . . . **reclaimed marsh**
polje, So. Slav . . . **plain, field**
poluostrov, Rus . . . **peninsula**
pont, Fr . . . **bridge**
ponta, Port . . . **point, headland**
ponte, It., Port . . . **bridge**
pore, India . . . **city, town**
porthmós, Gr . . . **strait**
porto, It., Port . . . **port, harbor**
potamós, Gr . . . **river**
p'ov, Rus . . . **peninsula**
prado, Sp . . . **field, meadow**
presqu'île, Fr . . . **peninsula**
proliv, Rus . . . **strait**
pu, Chn . . . **commercial village**
pueblo, Sp . . . **town, village**
puerto, Sp . . . **port, harbor**
pulau, Indon . . . **island**
punkt, Ger . . . **point**
punt, Du . . . **point**
punta, It., Sp . . . **point**
pur, India . . . **city, town**
puy, Fr . . . **peak**
qal'a, qal'at, Arab . . . **fort, village**
qasr, Arab . . . **fort, castle**
rann, India . . . **wasteland**
ra's, Arab . . . **cape, head**
reka, Rus., So. Slav . . . **river**
reprêsa, Port . . . **reservoir**
rettō, Jap . . . **island chain**
ría, Sp . . . **estuary**
ribeira, Port . . . **stream**
riberão, Port . . . **river**
rio, It., Port . . . **stream, river**
río, Sp . . . **river**
rivière, Fr . . . **river**
roca, Sp . . . **rock**
rt, Yugo . . . **cape**
rūd, Per . . . **river**
saari, Fin . . . **island**
sable, Fr . . . **sand**
sahara, Arab . . . **desert, plain**
saki, Jap . . . **cape**
sal, Sp . . . **salt**
salar, Sp . . . **salt flat, salt lak**
salto, Sp . . . **waterfa**
san, Jap., Kor . . . **mountain, h**
sat, satul, Rom . . . **villag**
schloss, Ger . . . **cast**
sebkha, Arab . . . **salt mars**
see, Ger . . . **lake, se**
şehir, Tur . . . **town, cit**
selat, Indon . . . **strea**
selvas, Port. (Brazil) . . . **tropical rain fores**
seno, Sp . . . **ba**
serra, Port . . . **mountain chai**
serranía, Sp . . . **mountain ridg**
seto, Jap . . . **stra**
severnaya, Rus . . . **norther**
shahr, Per . . . **town, cit**
shan, Chn . . . **mountain, hill, islan**
shatt, Arab . . . **rive**
shi, Jap . . . **cit**
shima, Jap . . . **islan**
shōtō, Jap . . . **archipelag**
si, Chn . . . **west, wester**
sierra, Sp . . . **mountain rang**
sjö, Nor., Swe . . . **lake, se**
sö, Dan., Nor . . . **lake, se**
söder, södra, Swe . . . **sout**
song, Annam . . . **rive**
sopka, Rus . . . **peak, volcar**
source, Fr . . . **a sprin**
spitze, Ger . . . **summit, poir**
staat, Ger . . . **stat**
stad, Dan., Du., Nor., Swe. . . . **city, tow**
stadt, Ger . . . **city, tow**
stato, It . . . **sta**
step', Rus . . . **treeless plain, stepp**
straat, Du . . . **stra**
strand, Dan., Du., Ger., Nor., Swe . . . **shore, beac**
stretto, It . . . **stra**
strom, Ger . . . **river, strea**
ström, Dan., Nor., Swe. . . . **stream, riv**
stroom, Du . . . **stream, riv**
su, suyu, Tur . . . **water, rive**
sud, Fr., Sp . . . **sout**
süd, Ger . . . **sout**
suidō, Jap . . . **chann**
sul, Port . . . **sout**
sund, Dan., Nor., Swe . . . **soun**
sungai, sungei, Indon., Mal . . . **riv**
sur, Sp . . . **sout**
syd, Dan., Nor., Swe . . . **sout**
tafelland, Ger . . . **platea**
take, Jap . . . **peak, summ**
tal, Ger . . . **valle**
tanjung, tanjong, Mal . . . **cap**
tao, Chn . . . **islan**
târg, târgul, Rom . . . **market, tow**
tell, Arab . . . **hi**
teluk, Indon . . . **bay, gu**
terra, It . . . **lar**
terre, Fr . . . **earth, lar**
thal, Ger . . . **valle**
tierra, Sp . . . **earth, lar**
tō, Jap . . . **east; islar**
tonle, Camb . . . **river, lak**
top, Du . . . **pea**
torp, Swe . . . **hamlet, cottag**
tsangpo, Tib . . . **riv**
tsi, Chn . . . **village, boroug**
tso, Tib . . . **lak**
tsu, Jap . . . **harbor, po**
tundra, Rus . . . **treeless arctic plair**
tung, Chn . . . **ea**
tuz, Tur . . . **sa**
udde, Swe . . . **cap**
ufer, Ger . . . **shore, riverbar**
ujung, Indon . . . **point, cap**
umi, Jap . . . **sea, gu**
ura, Jap . . . **bay, coast, cree**
ust'ye, Rus . . . **river mout**
valle, It., Port., Sp . . . **valle**
vallée, Fr . . . **valle**
valli, It . . . **lak**
vár, Hung . . . **fortres**
város, Hung . . . **tow**
varoš, So. Slav . . . **tow**
veld, Du . . . **open plain, fie**
verkh, Rus . . . **top, summ**
ves, Czech . . . **villag**
vest, Dan., Nor., Swe . . . **we**
vik, Swe . . . **cove, ba**
vila, Port . . . **tow**
villa, Sp . . . **tow**
villar, Sp . . . **village, haml**
ville, Fr . . . **town, cit**
vostok, Rus . . . **ea**
wad, wādī, Arab. . . . **intermittent strea**
wald, Ger . . . **forest, woodlar**
wan, Chn., Jap . . . **bay, gu**
weiler, Ger . . . **hamlet, villag**
westersch, Du . . . **wester**
wüste, Ger . . . **dese**
yama, Jap . . . **mountai**
yarimada, Tur . . . **peninsu**
yug, Rus . . . **sou**
zaki, Jap . . . **cap**
zaliv, Rus . . . **bay, gu**
zapad, Rus . . . **we**
zee, Du . . . **se**
zemlya, Rus . . . **lan**
zuid, Du . . . **sou**

abbreviations of geographical names and terms

.fg.	.Afghanistan
.fr.	.Africa
.k.	.Alaska
.l.	.Alabama
.lb.	.Albania
.lg.	.Algeria
.nd.	.Andorra
.ng.	.Angola
.nt.	.Antarctica
.r.	.Arkansas
.rch.	.Archipelago
rc. O.	.Arctic Ocean
.rg.	.Argentina
. S. S. R.	.Autonomous Soviet Socialist Republic
tl. O.	.Atlantic Ocean
.us.	.Austria
.ustl.	.Australia
.ug.	.Autonomous
.z.	.Arizona
..	.Bay, Bahia
.a.	.Bahamas
.A.T.	.British Antarctic Territory
ngl.	.Bangladesh
arb.	.Barbados
dy.	.Boundary
el.	.Belgium
g.	.Berg
hu.	.Bhutan
k.	.Bank
ol.	.Bolivia
oph.	.Bophuthatswana
ots.	.Botswana
r.	.British
raz.	.Brazil
ru.	.Brunei
ul.	.Bulgaria
urkina	.Burkina Faso
ur.	.Burma
.	.Cerro, Cape
a.	.California
am.	.Cameroon
an.	.Canal, Canada
an. Is.	.Canary Is.
en. Afr. Rep.	.Central African Republic
han.	.Channel
o.	.County, Colorado
ol.	.Colombia
on.	.Congo
omm.	.Commonwealth
. R.	.Costa Rica
r.	.Creek
t.	.Connecticut
. V.	.Cape Verde
zech.	.Czechoslovakia
C	.District of Columbia
e.	.Delaware
en.	.Denmark
ept.	.Department
es.	.Desert
. F.	.Distrito Federal
ist.	.District
iv.	.Division
om. Rep.	.Dominican Republic
.	.East
.	.Ecuador
ng.	.England
quat. Gui.	.Equatorial Guinea
th.	.Ethiopia
ur.	.Europe
aer.	.Faeroe Is.
alk. Is.	.Falkland Is.
ed. Rep. of Ger., F.R.G.	.Federal Republic of Germany
in.	.Finland
k.	.Fork
l.	.Florida
or.	.Forest
r.	.France
r. Gu.	.French Guiana
t.	.Fort
.	.Golfo, Gulf
a.	.Georgia
am.	.Gambia
er. Dem. Rep., G.D.R.	.German Democratic Republic
ib.	.Gibraltar
rc.	.Greece
rnld.	.Greenland
t.	.Great
t. Brit.	.Great Britain
uad.	.Guadeloupe
uat.	.Guatemala
ui.	.Guinea
uy.	.Guyana
ai.	.Haiti
ar., Hbr.	.Harbor, Harbour

Abbreviation	Full form
Hd.	.Head
Hi.	.Hawaii
Hond.	.Honduras
Hts.	.Heights
Hung.	.Hungary
I.	.Island
Ia.	.Iowa
Ice.	.Iceland
Id.	.Idaho
Ill.	.Illinois
In.	.Inset, Indiana
Ind. O.	.Indian Ocean
Indon.	.Indonesia
Ind. Res.	.Indian Reservation
Int., Intl.	.International
Ire.	.Ireland
Is.	.Islands
Isr.	.Israel
Isth.	.Isthmus
It.	.Italy
Jam.	.Jamaica
Jap.	.Japan
Jc.	.Junction
Kamp.	.Kampuchea
Ken.	.Kenya
Km.	.Kilometer, Kilometers
Kor.	.Korea
Ks.	.Kansas
Kuw.	.Kuwait
Ky.	.Kentucky
L.	.Lago, Lake, Loch, Lough
La.	.Louisiana
Lat.	.Latitude
Leb.	.Lebanon
Leso.	.Lesotho
Lib.	.Liberia
Liech.	.Liechtenstein
Long.	.Longitude
Lux.	.Luxembourg
M.	.Mile, Miles
Ma.	.Massachusetts
Md.	.Madagascar
Md. Is.	.Madeira Islands
Mala.	.Malaysia
Mand.	.Mandate
Mart.	.Martinique
Max.	.Maximum
Max. surf. elev.	.Maximum surface elevation
Md.	.Maryland
Me.	.Maine
Medit.	.Mediterranean
Mex.	.Mexico
Mi.	.Mile, Miles, Michigan
Mn.	.Minnesota
Mo.	.Missouri
Mong.	.Mongolia
Mor.	.Morocco
Moz.	.Mozambique
Ms.	.Mississippi
Mt.	.Mount, Montana
Mtn.	.Mountain
Mts.	.Mountains
N. A.	.North America
Natl.	.National
Ntal. Mon.	.National Monument
Ne.	.Nebraska
NC	.North Carolina
N. Cal.	.New Caledonia
ND	.North Dakota
Neigh.	.Neighborhood
Nep.	.Nepal
Neth.	.Netherlands
NH	.New Hampshire
Nic.	.Nicaragua
Nig.	.Nigeria
N. Ire.	.Northern Ireland
NJ	.New Jersey
NM	.New Mexico
Nor.	.Norway
Nv.	.Nevada
NY	.New York
N. Z.	.New Zealand
O.	.Ocean
Obs.	.Observatory
Oh.	.Ohio
Ok.	.Oklahoma
Om.	.Oman
Or.	.Oregon
O-va.	.Ostrova
P.	.Pass
Pa.	.Pennsylvania
Pac. O.	.Pacific Ocean
Pak.	.Pakistan
Pan.	.Panama

Abbreviation	Full form
Pap. N. Gui.	.Papua New Guinea
Par.	.Paraguay
Pass.	.Passage
P.D.R. of Yem.	.Yemen, People's Democratic Republic of
Pen.	.Peninsula
Phil.	.Philippines
P. Int.	.Point of Interest
Pk.	.Peak, Park
Plat.	.Plateau
Pln.	.Plain
Pol.	.Poland
Port.	.Portugal
P-Ov.	.Poluostrov
P. R.	.Puerto Rico
Prov.	.Province
Pt.	.Point
Pta.	.Punta
Pte.	.Pointe
R.	.River, Rio, Rivière
Ra.	.Range, Ranges
Reg.	.Region
Rep.	.Republic
Res.	.Reservation, Reservoir
Rf.	.Reef
RI	.Rhode Island
Rom.	.Romania
R. R.	.Railroad
R. S. F. S. R.	.Russian Soviet Federated Socialist Republic
Rw.	.Rwanda
Ry.	.Railway
Rys.	.Railways
S.	.San, Santo, South
Sa.	.Serra, Sierra
S. A.	.South America
S. Afr.	.South Africa
Sal.	.El Salvador
SC	.South Carolina
Scot.	.Scotland
SD	.South Dakota
Sd.	.Sound
S. L.	.Sierra Leone
Sol. Is.	.Solomon Is.
Som.	.Somalia
Sov. Un.	.Soviet Union
Sp.	.Spain
Spr., Sprs.	.Spring, Springs
S. S. R.	.Soviet Socialist Republic
St.	.Saint
Sta.	.Santa
Ste.	.Sainte
Str.	.Strait
Strm.	.Stream
Sud.	.Sudan
Sur.	.Surinam
Swaz.	.Swaziland
Swe.	.Sweden
Switz.	.Switzerland
Swp.	.Swamp
Syr.	.Syria
Tan.	.Tanzania
Tas.	.Tasmania
Ter.	.Territory
Thai.	.Thailand
Tn.	.Tennessee
Trans.	.Transkei
Trin.	.Trinidad and Tobago
Tun.	.Tunisia
Tur.	.Turkey
Tx.	.Texas
U.A.E.	.United Arab Emirates
Ug.	.Uganda
U. K.	.United Kingdom of Gt. Brit. and N. Ire.
Ur.	.Uruguay
U. S., U. S. A.	.United States of America
Ut.	.Utah
Va.	.Virginia
Val.	.Valley
Vdkhr.	.Vodokhranilishche
Ven.	.Venezuela
Viet.	.Vietnam
Vir. Is.	.Virgin Is.
Vol.	.Volcano
Vt.	.Vermont
Wa.	.Washington
Wi.	.Wisconsin
W. Sah.	.Western Sahara
W. Sam.	.Western Samoa
WV	.West Virginia
Wy.	.Wyoming
Yugo.	.Yugoslavia
Zimb.	.Zimbabwe

pronunciation of geographical names

key to the sound values of letters and symbols used in the index to indicate pronunciation

ă – ăt, căt, băttle
ă – ăppeal, finăl
ā – rāte, elāte
å – inanimåte, senåte
ä – cälm, ärm
à – àsk, bàth
a – màrine, sofà (short neutral or indeterminate sound)
â – fâre, prepâre
ch – church, choose
dh – as th in other, either
ē – bē, ēve
ė – crėate, ėvent
ĕ – bĕt, ĕnd
ĕ – recĕnt (short neutral or indeterminate sound)
ē – cratēr, cindēr
g – gŏ, găme
gh – gutteral g
ĭ – wĭll, bĭt
i – short neutral or indeterminate sound
ī – rīde, bīte
κ – gutteral k as ch in German ich
ng – sing
ŋ – baŋk, liŋger
N – indicates nasalized preceding vowel
ŏ – nŏd, ŏdd
ŏ – cŏmmit, cŏnnect
ō – ōld, bōld
ô – ôbey, hôtel
ô – ôrder, nôrth
oi – boil
oo – food, root
oo – foot, wood
ou – thou, out
s – as in soft, so, sane
sh – dish, finish
th – thin, thick
ū – pūre, cūre
û – ûnite, ûsûrp
û – ûrn, fûr
ŭ – stŭd, ŭp
ü – as in French tu
u – circŭs, sŭbmit
zh – as z in azure
' – indeterminate vowel sound

In many cases the spelling of foreign geographic names does not even remotely indicate the pronunciation to an American, i. e., Słupsk in Poland is pronounced swoopsk; Jujuy in Argentina is pronounced hoohwē'; La Spezia in Italy is lä-spē'zyä.

This condition is hardly surprising, however, when we consider that in our own language Worcester, Massachusetts, is pronounced woos'tēr; Sioux City, Iowa, soo si'tĭ; Schuylkill Haven, Pennsylvania, skool'kĭl hä-vĕn; Poughkeepsie, New York, pŏ-kĭp'se.

The indication of pronunciation of geographic names presents several peculiar problems:

1. Many foreign tongues use sounds that are not present in the English language and which an American cannot normally articulate. Thus, though the nearest English equivalent sound has been indicated, only approximate results are possible.

2. There are several dialects in each foreign tongue which cause variation in the local pronunciation of names. This also occurs in identical names in the various divisions of a great language group, as the Slavic or the Latin.

3. Within the United States there are marked differences in pronunciation, not only of local geographic names, but also of common words, indicating that the sound and tone values for letters as well as the placing of the emphasis vary considerably from one part of the country to another.

4. A number of different letter and diacritical combinations could be used to indicate essentially the same or approximate pronunciations.

Some variation in pronunciation other than that indicated in this index may be encountered, but such a difference does not necessarily indicate that either is in error, and in many cases it is a matter of individual choice as to which is preferred. In fact, an exact indication of pronunciation of many foreign names using English letters and diacritical marks is extremely difficult and sometimes impossible.

a pronouncing index

of over 30,000 geographical names

This universal index includes in a single alphabetical list the important names that appear on the reference maps. Each place name is followed by the country or continent in which it is located, the pronunciation of the name, the page number of the map on which it appears, and the approximate geographic coordinates.

Local official names are used on the maps for nearly all cities and towns, with the exception of about 50 major world cities for which Anglicized conventional names have been preferred. For these exceptions, the index gives a cross-reference to the official local name.

The system of alphabetizing used in the index is standard. When more than one name (including political and physical names) with the same spelling is shown, the order of precedence is as follows: first, place names; second, political divisions; and third, physical features.

An explanation of the pronunciation system for names appears on page 249.

If a place is indexed to an inset map, the page number is followed by a lower-case letter which refers to the appropriate inset on that page.

Country names are followed by the continent in which they are located. Places in the U.S. are followed by their state. All other places are identified by the country in which they are located.

All minor political divisions are followed by a descriptive term (Dist., Reg., Prov., State, etc.) and the country in which they are located. The names of physical features and points of interest shown on the maps are listed in the index. Each of these entries is followed by a descriptive term (Bay, Hill, Island, etc.) to indicate its nature. A key to the abbreviations used for these descriptive terms appears on page 249.

PLACE (Pronounciation)	PAGE	Lat. °′	Long. °′
Aachen, F.R.G. (ä′kĕn)	169c	50.46 N	6.07 E
Aalen, F.R.G. (ä′lĕn)	166	48.49 N	10.08 E
Aalsmeer, Neth.	157a	52.16 N	4.44 E
Aalst, Bel.	157a	50.58 N	4.00 E
Aarau, Switz. (är′ou)	166	47.22 N	8.03 E
Aarschot, Bel.	157a	50.59 N	4.51 E
Aba, Nig.	229	5.06 N	7.21 E
Aba, Zaïre	231	3.52 N	30.14 E
Ābādān, Iran (ä-bŭ-dän′)	192	30.15 N	48.30 E
Abaetetuba, Braz. (ä′bȧĕ-tĕ-tōō′bȧ)	143	1.44 S	48.45 W
Abajo Pk., Ut. (ä-bȧ′hŏ)	121	37.51 N	109.28 W
Abakaliki, Nig.	229	6.21 N	8.06 E
Abakan (R.), Sov. Un.	180	53.00 N	91.06 E
Abakan, Sov. Un. (ŭ-bȧ-kän′)	180	53.43 N	91.28 E
Abancay, Peru (ä-bän-kä′ē)	142	13.44 S	72.46 W
Abashiri, Jap. (ä-bä-shē′rē)	204	44.00 N	144.13 E
Abasolo, Mex. (ä-bä-sō′lô)	130	24.05 N	98.24 W
Abasolo, Mex.	124	27.13 N	101.25 W
Abay (R.), **see Blue Nile**			
Abaya L., Eth. (ȧ-bä′yȧ)	225	6.24 N	38.22 E
'Abbāsābād, Iran	68h	35.44 N	51.25 E
'Abbāsah, Tur'at al (Can.), Egypt	223c	30.45 N	32.15 E
Abbeville, Al. (ăb′ē-vĭl)	126	31.35 N	85.15 W
Abbeville, Fr. (ȧb-vēl′)	168	50.08 N	1.49 E
Abbeville, Ga. (ăb′ē-vĭl)	126	31.53 N	83.23 W
Abbeville, La.	125	29.59 N	92.07 W
Abbeville, SC	127	34.09 N	82.25 W
Abbey Wood (Neigh.), Eng.	62	51.29 N	0.08 E
Abbiategrasso, It. (äb-byä′tȧ-gräs′sō)	172	45.23 N	8.52 E
Abbots Bromley, Eng. (ăb′ŭts brŭm′lē)	156	52.49 N	1.52 W
Abbotsford, Can. (ăb′ŭts-fērd)	118d	49.03 N	122.17 W
Abbots Langley, Eng.	62	51.43 N	0.25 W
Abd Al Kuri (I.), P.D.R. of Yem. (ăbd-ĕl-kōō′rē)	223a	12.12 N	51.00 E
'Abd al-Shāhīd, Egypt	71a	29.55 N	31.13 E
Abdulino, Sov. Un. (äb-dōō-lē′nō)	178	53.40 N	53.45 E
Abéché, Chad (ȧ-bĕ-shā′)	225	13.48 N	20.39 E
Abengourou, Ivory Coast	228	6.44 N	3.29 W
Åbenrå, Den. (ô′bĕn-rô)	164	55.03 N	9.20 E
Abeokuta, Nig. (ä-bȧ-ô-kōō′tä)	229	7.10 N	3.26 E
Abercorn, see Mbala			
Aberdare, Wales (ăb-ēr-dâr′)	162	51.45 N	3.35 W
Aberdeen (Xianggangzi), Hong Kong	68c	22.15 N	114.09 E
Aberdeen, Ms. (ăb-ēr-dēn′)	126	33.49 N	88.33 W
Aberdeen, Scot.	162	57.10 N	2.05 W
Aberdeen, SD	114	45.28 N	98.29 W
Aberdeen, Wa.	116	47.00 N	123.48 W
Aberford, Eng. (ăb′ēr-fērd)	156	53.49 N	1.21 W
Abergavenny, Wales (ăb′ēr-gȧ-vĕn′ĭ)	162	51.45 N	3.05 W
Abert L., Or. (ā′bērt)	116	42.39 N	120.24 W
Aberystwyth, Wales (ă-bēr-ĭst′wĭth)	162	52.25 N	4.04 W
Abhā, Sau. Ar.	192	18.13 N	42.29 E
Abidjan, Ivory Coast (ä-bēd-zhäɴ′)	228	5.19 N	4.02 W
Abiko, Jap. (ä-bē-kō)	205a	35.53 N	140.01 E
Abilene, Ks. (ăb′ĭ-lēn)	123	38.54 N	97.12 W
Abilene, Tx.	124	32.25 N	99.45 W
Abingdon, Eng.	156b	51.38 N	1.17 W
Abingdon, Il. (ăb′ĭng-dŭn)	115	40.48 N	90.21 W
Abingdon, Va.	127	36.42 N	81.57 W
Abington, Ma. (ăb′ĭng-tŭn)	105a	42.07 N	70.57 W
Abington, Pa.	56b	40.07 N	75.08 W
Abiquiu Res., NM	121	36.26 N	106.42 W
Abitibi (L.), Can. (ăb-ĭ-tĭb′ĭ)	97	48.27 N	80.20 W
Abitibi (R.), Can.	97	49.30 N	81.10 W
Abkhaz A.S.S.R., Sov. Un.	179	43.10 N	40.45 E
Ablis, Fr. (ȧ-blē′)	169b	48.31 N	1.50 E
Ablon-sur-Seine, Fr.	64c	48.43 N	2.25 E
Abnūb, Egypt (ȧb-nōōb′)	223b	27.18 N	31.11 E
Abóbada, Port.	65d	38.43 N	9.20 W
Abohar, India	196	30.12 N	74.13 E
Aboisso, Ivory Coast	228	5.28 N	3.12 W
Abomey, Benin (ȧb-ô-mā′)	229	7.11 N	1.59 E
Abony, Hung. (ŏ′bô-ny′)	167	47.12 N	20.00 E
Åbo, see Turku			
Abou Deïa, Chad	229	11.27 N	19.17 E
Abra (R.), Phil (ä′brä)	207a	17.16 N	120.38 E
Abraão, Braz. (äbrȧ-ouɴ′)	141a	23.10 S	44.10 W
Abraham's B., Ba.	135	22.20 N	73.50 W
Abram, Eng. (ā′brăm)	156	53.31 N	2.36 W
Abramcevo, Sov. Un.	66b	55.50 N	37.50 E
Abrantes, Port. (ȧ-brän′tĕs)	170	39.28 N	8.13 W
Abridge, Eng.	62	51.39 N	0.07 E
Abrolhos, Arquipélago dos (Arch.), Braz. (ä-rōōē-pĕ′lä-gô dôs ä-brô′l-yōs)	143	17.58 S	38.40 W
Abruka (I.), Sov. Un. (ȧ-brōō′kȧ)	165	58.09 N	22.30 E
Abrunheira, Port.	65d	38.46 N	9.21 W
Abruzzi E Molise (Reg.), It. (ä-brōōt′sē, mô′lē-zā)	172	42.10 N	13.55 E
Absaroka Ra. (Mts.), Wy. (ȧb-să-rō-kă)	117	44.50 N	109.47 W
Abū an-Numrus, Egypt	71a	29.57 N	31.12 E
Abū Arīsh, Sau. Ar. (ä-bōō ȧ-rēsh′)	192	16.48 N	43.00 E
Abu Ḩamad, Sud. (ä′bōō hä′-mĕd)	225	19.37 N	33.21 E
Abū Kamāl, Syr.	192	34.45 N	40.46 E
Abunã (R.), Bol-Braz. (ȧ-bōō-nä′)	142	10.25 S	67.00 W
Abū Qīr, Egypt (ä′bōō kēr′)	223b	31.18 N	30.06 E
Abū Qurqāş, Egypt (ā′bōō kōōr-käs′)	223b	27.57 N	30.51 E
Abū Qurūn, Ra's (Mtn.), Egypt	191a	30.22 N	33.32 E
Aburatsu, Jap. (ä′bōō-rät′sōō)	205	31.33 N	131.20 E
Abu Road, India (ȧ′bōō)	196	24.38 N	72.45 E
Abū Şīr Pyramids (P. Int.), Egypt	71a	29.54 N	31.12 E
Abū Tīj, Egypt	223b	27.03 N	31.19 E
Abū Ẓaby, U.A.E.	192	24.15 N	54.28 E
Abū Zanīmah, Egypt	191a	29.03 N	33.08 E
Abyad, Al-Bahr al- (R.), **see White Nile**			
Abyy, Sov. Un.	181	68.24 N	134.00 E
Acacias, Col. (ȧ-kȧ′sēäs)	142a	3.59 N	73.44 W
Acadia Natl. Park, Me. (ă-kā′dĭ-ȧ)	104	44.19 N	68.01 W
Acajutla, Sal. (ä-kä-hōōt′lä)	132	13.37 N	89.50 W
Acala, Mex. (ä-kä′lä)	131	16.38 N	92.49 W
Acalayong, Equat. Gui.	230	1.05 N	9.40 E
Acȧmbaro, Mex. (ä-käm′bä-rō)	130	20.03 N	100.42 W
Acancéh, Mex. (ä-kän-sĕ′)	132a	20.50 N	89.27 W
Acapetlahuaya, Mex. (ä-kä-pĕt′lä-hwä′yä)	130	18.24 N	100.04 W
Acaponeta, Mex. (ä-kä-pô-nā′tă)	130	22.31 N	105.25 W
Acaponeta (R.), Mex.	130	22.47 N	105.23 W
Acapulco, Mex. (ä-kä-pōōl′kō)	130	16.49 N	99.57 W
Acaraí Mts., Braz.	143	1.30 N	57.40 W
Acaraú, Braz. (ä-kȧrhȧ-ōō′)	143	2.55 S	40.04 W
Acarigua, Ven. (äkä-rē′gwä)	142	9.29 N	69.11 W
Acatlán de Osorio, Mex. (ä-kät-län′dā ô-sō′rē-ō)	130	18.11 N	98.04 W
Acatzingo de Hidalgo, Mex. (ä-kät-zĭŋ′gō dā ē-dhäl′gō)	131	18.58 N	97.47 W
Acayucan, Mex. (ä-kä-yōō′kän)	131	17.56 N	94.55 W
Accord, Ma.	54a	42.10 N	70.53 W
Accoville, WV (äk′kô-vĭl)	110	37.45 N	81.50 W
Accra, Ghana (ă′krȧ)	228	5.33 N	0.13 W
Accrington, Eng. (ăk′rĭng-tŭn)	156	53.45 N	2.22 W
Acerra, It. (ä-chĕ′r-rä)	171c	40.42 N	14.22 E
Achacachi, Bol. (ä-chä-kä′chē)	142	16.11 S	68.32 W
Acheng, China (ä′chĕng′)	204	45.32 N	126.59 E
Achill I., Ire. (ă-chĭl′)	162	53.55 N	10.05 W
Achinsk, Sov. Un. (ȧ-chēnsk′)	180	56.13 N	90.32 E
Acireale, It. (ä-chē-rā-ä′lā)	172	37.37 N	15.12 E
Ackia Battle Ground Natl. Mon., Ms. (ă-ĸyū′)	126	34.22 N	89.05 W
Acklins (I.), Ba. (ăk′lĭns)	135	22.30 N	73.55 W
Acklins, The Bight of (B.), Ba.	135	22.35 N	74.20 W
Acolman, Mex. (ä-kôl-mȧ′n)	131a	19.38 N	98.56 W
Aconcagua (Prov.), Chile (ä-kôn-kä′gwä)	141b	32.20 S	71.00 W
Aconcagua (R.), Chile	141b	32.43 S	70.53 W
Aconcagua, Cerro (Mtn.), Arg.	141b	32.38 S	70.00 W
Açores (Azores) (Is.), Atl. O. (ä-zô′rēs) (ȧ-zōrz′)	224a	37.44 N	29.25 W
Acoyapa, Nic. (ä-kô-yä′pä)	132	11.54 N	85.11 W
Acqui, It. (äk′kwē)	172	44.41 N	8.22 W
Acre (R.), Braz.	142	10.33 S	68.34 W
Acre (State), Braz. (ä′krā)	142	8.40 S	70.45 W
Acton, Al. (ăk′tŭn)	112h	33.21 N	86.49 W
Acton, Can.	95d	43.38 N	80.02 W
Acton, Ma.	105a	42.29 N	71.26 W
Acton (Neigh.), Eng.	62	51.30 N	0.16 W
Actopan, Mex. (äk-tô-pän′)	130	20.16 N	98.57 W
Actópan (R.), Mex. (äk-tŏ′pän)	131	19.25 N	96.31 W
Acuitzio del Canje, Mex. (ä-kwēt′zē-ō dĕl kän′hȧ)	130	19.28 N	101.21 W
Acul, Baie de l' (B.), Hai. (ä-kōōl′)	135	19.55 N	72.20 W
Ada, Mn. (ā′dŭ)	114	47.17 N	96.32 W
Ada, Oh.	110	40.45 N	83.45 W
Ada, Ok.	123	34.45 N	96.43 W
Ada, Yugo. (ä′dä)	173	45.48 N	20.06 E
Adachi, Jap.	205a	35.50 N	39.36 E
Adachi (Neigh.), Jap.	69a	35.45 N	139.48 E
Adak, Ak. (ă-dăk′)	107a	56.50 N	176.48 W
Adak (I.), Ak.	107a	51.40 N	176.28 W
Adak Str., Ak.	107a	51.42 N	177.16 W
Adalia, see Antalya			
Adamaoua (Mts.), Cam.-Nig.	229	6.30 N	11.50 E
Adams, Ma. (ăd′ămz)	111	42.35 N	73.10 W
Adams (R.), Can.	99	51.30 N	119.20 W
Adams, Wi.	115	43.55 N	89.48 W
Adams, Mt., Wa.	116	46.15 N	121.19 W
Adamsville, Al. (ăd′ămz-vĭl)	112h	33.36 N	86.57 W
Adana, Tur. (ä′dä-nä)	179	37.05 N	35.20 E
Adapazari, Tur. (ä-dä-pä-zä′rē)	179	40.45 N	30.20 E
Adarama, Sud. (ä-dä-rä′mä)	225	17.11 N	34.56 E
Adda (R.), It. (äd′dä)	172	45.43 N	9.31 E
Ad Dabbah, Sud.	225	18.04 N	30.58 E
Ad Dahnā (Des.), Sau. Ar.	192	26.05 N	47.15 E
Ad-Dāmir, Sud. (ad-dä′mĕr)	225	17.38 N	33.57 E
Ad Dammān, Sau. Ar.	192	26.27 N	49.59 E
Ad Dāmūr, Leb.	191a	33.44 N	35.27 E
Ad Dawhah, Qatar	192	25.02 N	51.28 E
Ad Dilam, Sau. Ar.	192	23.47 N	47.03 E
Ad Dilinjāt, Egypt	223b	30.48 N	30.32 E
Addington, Eng.	62	51.18 N	0.23 E
Addis Ababa (Ādis Abeda), Eth.	225	9.00 N	38.44 E
Addison, Tx. (ă′dĭ-sŭn)	119c	32.58 N	96.50 W
Addlestone, Eng.	62	51.22 N	0.30 W
Addo, S. Afr. (ădō)	227c	33.33 S	25.43 E
Ad-Duqqī, Egypt	71a	30.04 N	31.15 E
Ad Duwaym, Sud. (dōō-ām′)	225	13.56 N	32.22 E
Addyston, Oh. (ăd′ē-stŭn)	113f	39.09 N	84.42 W
Adel, Ga. (ā-dĕl′)	126	31.08 N	83.55 W
Adelaide, Austl. (ăd′ē-lād)	216	34.46 S	139.08 E
Adelaide, S. Afr. (ăd-ĕl′ād)	227c	32.41 S	26.07 E

ăt; finăl; rāte; senȧte; ärm; ȧsk; sofȧ; fâre; ch-choose; dh-as th in other; bē; ēvent; bĕt; recĕnt; cratēr; g-gō; gh-guttural g; bĭt; ĭ-short neutral; rīde; ĸ-guttural k as ch in German ich;

PRONOUNCING INDEX

Adelaide I. – Albertville 251

PLACE (Pronounciation)	PAGE	Lat. °′	Long. °′
Adelaide I., Ant.	232	67.15 S	68.40 W
Adelphi, Md.	56d	39.00 N	76.58 W
Aden ('Adan), P.D.R. of Yem. (ä'dĕn)	192	12.48 N	45.00 E
Aden, G. of, Asia	192	11.45 N	45.45 E
Aderklaa, Aus.	66e	48.17 N	16.32 E
Adige (R.), It. (ä'dē-jā)	172	46.38 N	10.43 E
Adige R., Aus.-Switz.	160	46.34 N	10.51 E
Adigrat, Eth.	195	14.17 N	39.28 E
Adilābād, India (ŭ-dĭl-ä-bäd')	196	19.47 N	78.30 E
Adi, Pulau (I.), Indon. (ä'dē)	207	4.25 S	133.52 E
Adirondack, Mts., NY (ăd-ĭ-rŏn'dăk)	111	43.45 N	74.40 W
Adis Abeba, see Addis Ababa			
Adi Ugri, Eth. (ä-dē o͞o'grē)	225	14.54 N	38.52 E
Adjud, Rom. (äd'zho͞od)	167	46.05 N	27.12 E
Adkins, Tx.	119d	29.22 N	98.18 W
Adlershof (Neigh.), G.D.R.	65a	52.26 N	13.33 E
Admiralty (I.), Ak.	107	57.50 N	133.50 W
Admiralty Inlet, Wa. (ăd'mĭrăl-tē)	118a	48.10 N	122.45 W
Admiralty Is., Pap. N. Gui.	207	1.40 S	146.45 E
Ado-Ekiti, Nig.	229	7.38 N	5.12 E
Adolph, Mn. (ā'dolf)	119h	46.47 N	92.17 W
Adoni, India	197	15.42 N	77.18 E
Adour (R.), Fr. (á-do͞or')	168	43.43 N	0.38 W
Adra, Sp. (ä'drä)	170	36.45 N	3.02 W
Adrano, It. (ä-drä'nō)	172	37.42 N	14.52 E
Adria, It. (ä'drē-ä)	172	45.03 N	12.01 E
Adrian, Mi. (ā'drĭ-ăn)	110	41.55 N	84.00 W
Adrian, Mn.	114	43.39 N	95.56 W
Adrianople, see Edirne			
Adriatic Sea, Eur.	172	43.30 N	14.27 E
Adrir, Alg.	224	27.53 N	0.15 W
Adwa, Eth.	225	14.02 N	38.58 E
Adwick-le-Street, Eng. (ăd'wĭk-lē-strēt')	156	53.35 N	1.11 W
Adycha (R.), Sov. Un. (ä'dĭ-chà)	181	66.11 N	136.45 E
Adzhamka, Sov. Un. (ád-zhäm'ká)	175	48.33 N	32.28 E
Adzopé, Ivory Coast	228	6.06 N	3.52 W
Adz'va (R.), Sov. Un. (ädz'vá)	178	67.00 N	59.20 E
Aegean Sea, Asia-Eur. (ē-jē'ăn)	161	39.04 N	24.56 E
Aerø (I.), Den. (âr'ö)	163	54.52 N	10.22 E
Affton, Mo.	119e	38.33 N	90.20 W
Afghanistan, Asia (ăf-găn-ĭ-stăn')	190	33.00 N	63.00 E
Afgoi, Som. (äf-gô'ĭ)	223a	2.08 N	45.08 E
Afikpo, Nig.	229	5.53 N	7.56 E
Aflou, Alg. (ä-flo͞o')	224	33.59 N	2.04 E
Afognak (I.), Ak. (ä-fŏg-nák')	107	58.28 N	151.35 W
Afragola, It. (ä-frä'gō-lä)	171c	40.40 N	14.19 E
Africa (ăf'rĭ-ká)	218		
Afton, Mn. (ăf'tŭn)	119g	44.54 N	92.47 W
Afton, Ok.	123	36.42 N	94.56 W
Afton, Wy.	117	42.42 N	110.52 W
'Afula, Isr. (ä-fo͞o'lá)	191a	32.36 N	35.17 E
Afyon, Tur. (ä-fē-ōn)	179	38.45 N	30.20 E
Agadem, Niger (ä'gá-dĕm)	229	16.50 N	13.17 E
Agadez, Niger (ä'gá-dĕs)	229	16.58 N	7.59 E
Agadir, Mor. (ä-gá-dēr)	224	30.30 N	9.37 W
Agalta, Cord. de (Mts.), Hond. (kôr-dēl-yĕ'rä-dĕ-ä-gä'l-tä)	132	15.15 N	85.42 W
Agapovka, Sov. Un. (ä-gä-pôv'kä)	182a	53.18 N	59.10 E
Agartala, India	196	23.53 N	91.22 E
Agāshi, India	197b	19.28 N	72.46 E
Agashkino, Sov. Un. (á-gäsh'kĭ-nô)	182b	55.18 N	38.13 E
Agattu (I.), Ak. (á'gä-to͞o)	107a	52.14 N	173.40 E
Agayman, Sov. Un. (á-gä-ē-män')	175	46.39 N	34.20 E
Agboville, Ivory Coast	228	5.56 N	4.13 W
Agdam, Sov. Un. (āg'dăm)	179	40.00 N	47.00 E
Agde, Fr. (ägd)	168	43.19 N	3.30 E
Agege, Nig.	71d	6.37 N	3.20 E
Agen, Fr. (á-zhäN')	168	44.13 N	0.31 E
Agincourt (Neigh.), Can.	54c	43.48 N	79.17 W
Aginskoye, Sov. Un. (ä-hĭn'skô-yĕ)	181	51.15 N	113.15 E
Agno, Phil. (äg'nō)	207a	16.07 N	119.49 E
Agno (R.), Phil.	207a	15.42 N	120.28 E
Agnone, It. (än-yō'nā)	172	41.49 N	14.23 E
Agogo, Ghana	228	6.47 N	1.04 W
Agostinho Pôrto, Braz.	61c	22.47 S	43.23 W
Agra, India (ä'grä)	196	27.18 N	78.00 E
Ağri, Tur	179	39.50 N	43.10 E
Agri (R.), It. (ä'grē)	172	40.15 N	16.21 E
Agrícola Oriental, Mex.	60a	19.24 N	99.05 W
Agrínion, Grc. (á-grē'nyôn)	173	38.38 N	21.06 E
Agua (Vol.), Guat. (ä'gwä)	132	14.28 N	90.43 W
Agua Blanca, Río (R.), Mex. (rē'ō-ä-gwä-blä'n-kä)	130	21.46 N	102.54 W
Agua Brava, Laguna de (L.), Mex. (lä-go͞o'nä-dĕ-ä'gwä-brä'vä)	130	22.04 N	105.40 W
Agua Caliente Ind. Res., Ca. (ä'gwä kal-yĕn'tä)	120	33.50 N	116.24 W
Aguacate, Cuba	60b	22.59 N	81.49 W
Aguada, Cuba (ä-gwä'dá)	134	22.25 N	80.50 W
Aguada L., Mex.	132a	18.46 N	89.40 W
Aguadas, Col. (ä-gwä'dás)	142a	5.37 N	75.27 W
Aguadilla, P.R. (ä-gwä-dēl'yä)	129b	18.27 N	67.10 W
Aguadulce, Pan. (ä-gwä-do͞ol'sä)	133	8.15 N	80.33 W
Agua Escondida, Meseta de (Plat.), Mex. (mĕ-sĕ'tä-dĕ-ä'gwä-ĕs-kôn-dē'dä)	131	16.54 N	91.35 W
Agua Fria (R.), Az. (ä'gwä frē-ä)	121	33.43 N	112.22 W
Aguai, Braz. (ägwä-ē')	141a	22.04 S	46.57 W
Agualeguas, Mex. (ä-gwä-lä'gwäs)	124	26.19 N	99.33 W
Agualva-Cacém, Port.	65d	38.46 N	9.18 W
Aguanaval, R., Mex. (ä-guä-nä-väl')	124	25.12 N	103.28 W
Aguán R., Hond. (ä-gwä'n)	132	15.22 N	87.00 W
Aguanus (R.), Can. (á-gwä'nŭs)	105	50.45 N	62.03 W
Aguascalientes, Mex. (ä'gwäs-käl-yĕn'tās)	130	21.52 N	102.17 W
Aguascalientes (State), Mex.	130	22.00 N	102.18 W
Águeda, Port. (ä-gwā'dá)	170	40.36 N	8.26 W
Agueda (R.), Sp. (ä-gĕ-dä)	170	40.50 N	6.44 W
Aguelhok, Mali	228	19.28 N	0.52 E
Aguilar, Co. (ä-gē-lär')	122	37.24 N	104.38 W
Aguilar, Sp.	170	37.32 N	4.39 W
Aguilas, Sp. (ä-gē-läs)	170	37.26 N	1.35 W

PLACE (Pronounciation)	PAGE	Lat. °′	Long. °′
Aguililla, Mex. (ä-gē-lēl-yä)	130	18.44 N	102.44 W
Aguililla (R.), Mex.	130	18.30 N	102.48 W
Aguja, Pta. (Pt.), Peru (pŭn'tá á-go͞o' hä)	142	6.00 S	81.15 W
Agulhas, C., S. Afr. (ä-go͞ol'yäs)	226	34.47 S	20.00 E
Agusan (R.), Phil. (ä-go͞o'sän)	207	8.12 N	126.07 E
Ahaggar (Mts.), Alg. (á-há-gär')	224	23.14 N	6.00 E
Ahar, Iran	195	38.28 N	47.04 E
Ahlen, F.R.G. (ä'lĕn)	169c	51.45 N	7.52 E
Ahlenberg, F.R.G.	63	51.25 N	7.28 E
Ahmadābād, India (ŭ-mĕd-ā-bäd')	196	23.04 N	72.38 E
Ahmadnagar, India (ä'mûd-nû-gûr)	196	19.09 N	74.45 E
Ahmar Mts., Eth.	223a	9.22 N	42.00 E
Ahoskie, NC (ā-hŏs'kē)	127	36.15 N	77.00 W
Ahrensburg, F.R.G. (ä'rĕns-bo͝org)	157c	53.40 N	10.14 E
Ahrensfelde, G.D.R.	65a	52.35 N	13.35 E
Ahrweiler, F.R.G. (är'vī-lĕr)	166	50.34 N	7.05 E
Ähtärinjärvi (L.), Fin.	165	62.46 N	24.25 E
Ahuacatlán, Mex. (ä-wä-kät-län')	130	21.05 N	104.28 W
Ahuachapan, Sal. (ä-wä-chä-pän')	132	13.57 N	89.53 W
Ahualulco, Mex. (ä-wä-lo͞ol'kō)	130	20.43 N	103.57 W
Ahuatempan, Mex. (ä-wä-tĕm-pän)	130	18.11 N	98.02 W
Ahuntsic (Neigh.), Can.	54b	45.33 N	73.39 W
Åhus, Swe. (ô'ho͞os)	164	55.56 N	14.19 E
Ahvāz, Iran	192	31.15 N	48.54 E
Ahvenanmaa (Åland Is.), Fin. (ä'vĕ-nán-mô) (ô'länd)	165	60.36 N	19.55 E
Aiea, Hi.	106a	21.18 N	157.52 W
Aigburth (Neigh.), Eng.	64a	53.22 N	2.55 W
Aiken, SC (ā'kĕn)	127	33.32 N	81.43 W
Aimorès, Serra dos (Mts.), Braz. (sĕ'r-rä-dôs-ī-mō-rĕ's)	143	17.40 S	42.38 W
Aimoto, Jap. (ī-mô-tō)	205b	34.59 N	135.09 E
Aincourt, Fr. (âN-ko͞o'r)	169b	49.04 N	1.47 E
Ainsworth, Eng.	64b	53.35 N	2.22 W
Ainsworth, Ne. (ānz'wûrth)	114	42.32 N	99.51 W
Aintree, Eng.	64a	53.29 N	2.56 W
Aipe, Col. (ī'pĕ)	142a	3.13 N	75.15 W
Aire (R.), Eng.	156	53.42 N	1.00 W
Aire-sur-l'Adour, Fr. (âr)	168	43.42 N	0.17 W
Airhitam, Selat (Str.), Indon.	191b	0.58 N	102.38 E
Airport West, Austl.	70b	37.44 S	144.53 E
Aisne (R.), Fr. (ĕn)	168	49.28 N	3.32 E
Aitape, Pap. N. Gui. (ä-ē-tä'pā)	207	3.00 S	142.10 E
Aitkin, Mn. (āt'kĭn)	115	46.32 N	93.43 W
Aïn Beïtda, Alg. (ä'ēn bä-dä')	224	35.57 N	7.25 E
Aïn Oussera, Alg. (ĕn o͞o-sâ-rá)	171	35.25 N	2.50 E
Aïn Salah, Alg.	224	27.13 N	2.22 E
Aïn Témouchent, Alg. (ä'ĕntĕ-mo͞o-shäN')	159	35.20 N	1.23 W
Aitolikón, Grc. (å-tō'lĭ-kôn)	173	38.27 N	21.21 E
Aitos, Bul. (ä-ē'tōs)	173	42.42 N	27.17 E
Aïr (Mts.), Niger	229	18.00 N	8.30 E
Aitutaki (I.), Cook Is. (ī-to͞o-tä'kē)	209	19.00 S	162.00 W
Aiud, Rom. (ä'ē-o͞od)	167	46.19 N	23.40 E
Aiuruoca, Braz. (aē'o͞o-ro͞oō'-kà)	141a	21.57 S	44.36 W
Aiuruoca (R.), Braz.	141a	22.11 S	44.35 W
Aíyina, Grc.	173	37.37 N	22.12 E
Aíyina (I.), Grc.	173	37.43 N	23.35 E
Aíyion, Grc.	173	38.13 N	22.04 E
Aix-en-Provence, Fr. (ĕks-prô-väNs)	168a	43.32 N	5.27 E
Aix-les-Bains, Fr. (ĕks'-lā-băN')	169	45.42 N	5.56 E
Aiyáleo, Grc.	66d	37.59 N	23.41 E
Aizpute, Sov. Un. (ä'ēz-po͞o-tĕ)	165	56.44 N	21.37 E
Aizuwakamatsu, Jap.	205	37.27 N	139.51 E
Ajaccio, Fr. (ä-yät'chō)	172	41.55 N	8.42 E
Ajalpan, Mex. (ä-häl'pän)	131	18.21 N	97.14 W
Ajana, Austl. (āj-än'ēr)	214	28.00 S	114.45 E
Ajax Mt., Mt. (ā'jăks)	117	45.19 N	113.43 W
Ajdābiyah, Libya	225	30.56 N	20.16 E
Ajmah, Jabal al (Mts.), Egypt	191a	29.12 N	34.03 E
Ajman, U.A.E.	192	25.15 N	54.30 E
Ajmer, India (ŭj-mēr')	196	26.26 N	74.42 E
Ajo, Az. (ä'hō)	121	32.20 N	112.55 W
Ajuchitlán del Progreso, Mex. (ä-ho͞o-chet-lān)	130	18.11 N	100.32 W
Ajuda (Neigh.), Port.	65d	38.43 N	9.12 W
Ajusco, Mex. (ä-ho͞o's-kō)	131a	19.13 N	99.12 W
Ajusco, Cerro (Mtn.), Mex. (sĕ'r-rô-ä-ho͞o's-kō)	131a	19.12 N	99.16 W
Akaishi-dake (Mtn.), Jap. (ä-kī-shē dä'kā)	205	35.30 N	138.00 E
Akashi, Jap. (ä'kä-shē)	205b	34.38 N	134.59 E
Akbarābād, Iran	68h	35.41 N	51.21 E
Aketi, Zaire (ä-kă-tē)	230	2.44 N	23.46 E
Akhaltsikhe, Sov. Un. (äkà'l-tsĭ-kĕ)	179	41.40 N	42.50 E
Akhdar, Al Jabal al (Mts.), Libya	225	32.00 N	22.00 E
Akhelóös (R.), Grc. (ä-hĕ'lō-ōs)	173	38.45 N	21.26 E
Akhisar, Tur. (äk-hĭs-sär')	179	38.58 N	27.58 E
Akhtarskaya, Bukhta (B.), Sov. Un. (bo͝ok'tä äK-tär'skä-yá)	175	45.53 N	38.22 E
Akhtopol, Bul. (äK'tô-pōl)	173	42.08 N	27.54 E
Akhtyrka, Sov. Un. (äK-tür'ká)	175	50.18 N	34.53 E
Akhunovo, Sov. Un. (ä-kû'nô-vô)	182a	54.13 N	59.36 E
Aki, Jap. (ä'kē)	205	33.31 N	133.51 E
Akiak, Ak. (äk'yák)	107	61.00 N	161.02 W
Akimiski (I.), Can. (ä-kĭ-mĭ'skĭ)	97	52.54 N	80.22 W
Akishima, Jap.	69a	35.41 N	139.22 E
Akita, Jap. (ä'kē-tä)	204	39.40 N	140.12 E
Akjoujt, Mauritania	228	19.45 N	14.23 W
'Akko, Isr.	191a	32.56 N	35.05 E
Aklavik, Can. (äk'lä-vĭk)	96	68.28 N	135.26 W
'Aklé'Âouâna (Dunes), Mali-Mauritania	228	18.07 N	6.00 W
Ako, Jap. (ä'kô)	205	34.44 N	134.22 E
Akola, India (á-kō'lä)	196	20.47 N	77.00 E
Akordat, Eth.	225	15.34 N	37.54 E
Akpatok (I.), Can. (ák'pá-tŏk)	97	60.30 N	67.10 W
Akranes, Ice.	158	64.18 N	21.40 W
Akron, Co. (ăk'rŭn)	122	40.09 N	103.14 W
Akron, Oh.	113d	41.05 N	81.30 W
Akrópolis (P. Int.), Grc.	66d	37.58 N	23.43 E
Aksaray, Tur. (äk-sá-rī')	179	38.30 N	34.05 E

PLACE (Pronounciation)	PAGE	Lat. °′	Long. °′
Aksehir (L.), Tur.	179	38.40 N	31.30 E
Aksehir, Tur. (äk'shå-hēr)	179	38.20 N	31.20 E
Aksha, Sov.Un. (äk'shá)	181	50.28 N	113.00 E
Aksu, China (ä-kŭ-so͞o)	198	41.29 N	80.15 E
Aktyubinsk, Sov. Un. (äk'tyo͞o-bĕnsk)	179	50.20 N	57.00 E
Akune, Jap. (ä'ko͞o-nå)	205	32.03 N	130.16 E
Akureyri, Ice. (ä-ko͞o-rå'rē)	158	65.39 N	18.01 W
Akutan (I.), Ak. (ä-ko͞o-tän')	107a	53.58 N	169.54 W
Akwatia, Ghana	228	6.04 N	0.49 W
Alabama (State), U.S. (ăl-á-băm'á)	109	32.50 N	87.30 W
Alabama (R.), Al.	126	31.20 N	87.39 W
Alabat (I.), Phil. (ä-lä-bät')	207a	14.14 N	122.05 E
Alacam, Tur. (ä-lä-chäm')	179	41.30 N	35.40 E
Alacranes, Cuba (ä-lä-krä'nås)	134	22.45 N	81.35 W
Al Aflaj (Des.), Sau. Ar.	192	24.00 N	44.47 E
Alagôas (State), Braz. (ä-lä-gō'äzh)	143	9.50 S	36.33 W
Alagoinhas, Braz. (ä-lä-gō-ēn'yäzh)	143	12.13 S	38.12 W
Alagón (R.), Sp.	170	39.53 N	6.42 W
Alagón, Sp. (ä-lä-gōn')	170	41.46 N	1.07 W
Alaguntan, Nig.	71d	6.26 N	3.30 E
Alahuatán (R.), Mex. (ä-lä-wä-tà'n)	130	18.30 N	100.00 W
Alajuela, C.R. (ä-lä-hwa'lä)	133	10.01 N	84.14 W
Alajuela, L., Pan.	128a	9.15 N	79.34 W
Alakol (L.), Sov. Un.	180	45.45 N	81.13 E
Alalakeiki Chan., Hi. (ä-lä-lä-kā'kē)	106a	20.40 N	156.30 W
Al 'Alamayn, Egypt	225	30.53 N	28.52 E
Al 'Amārah, Iraq	195	31.50 N	47.09 E
Alameda, Ca. (ăl-á-mā'dá)	118b	37.46 N	122.15 W
Alameda (R.), Ca.	118b	37.36 N	122.02 W
Alaminos, Phil. (ä-lä-mē'nôs)	207a	16.09 N	119.58 E
Al 'Amirīyah, Egypt	161	31.01 N	29.52 E
Alamo, Ca. (ă'lá-mō)	118b	37.51 N	122.02 W
Alamo, Mex. (ä'lä-mô)	131	20.55 N	97.41 W
Alamo, Nv. (ă'lá-mō)	120	37.22 N	115.10 W
Alamogordo, NM (ăl-á-mō-gôr'dō)	121	32.55 N	106.00 W
Alamo Heights, Tx. (ă'lá-mō)	119d	29.28 N	98.27 W
Alamo Pk., NM (ă'lá-mō pēk)	124	32.50 N	105.55 W
Alamo, R., Mex. (ä'lä-mô)	124	26.33 N	99.35 W
Alamosa, Co. (ăl-á-mō'sá)	121	37.25 N	105.50 W
Alandskiy, Sov. Un. (ä-länt'skĭ)	182a	52.14 N	59.48 E
Alanga Arba, Ken.	231	0.07 N	40.25 E
Alanya, Tur.	179	36.40 N	32.10 E
Alaotra (L.), Mad. (ä-lä-ō'trá)	227	17.15 S	48.17 E
Alapayevsk, Sov. Un. (ä-lä-pä'yĕfsk)	182a	57.50 N	61.35 E
Al 'Aqabah, Jordan	191a	29.32 N	35.00 E
Alaquines, Mex. (ä-lä-kē'nås)	130	22.07 N	99.35 W
Al 'Arīsh, Egypt (a-rēsh')	191a	31.08 N	33.48 E
Alaska (State), U.S. (á-lăs'ká)	108a	64.00 N	150.00 W
Alaska, G. of, Ak.	107	57.42 N	147.40 W
Alaska Hy., Ak.	107	63.00 N	142.00 W
Alaska Pen., Ak.	107	55.50 N	162.10 W
Alaska Ra., Ak.	107	62.00 N	152.18 W
Al-'Aṭrūn, Sud.	225	18.13 N	26.44 E
Alatyr', Sov.Un. (ä'lä-tür)	178	54.55 N	46.30 E
Alausí, Ec. (á-lou-sē')	142	2.15 S	78.45 W
Al 'Ayyāṭ, Egypt (ä-ē-yät')	223b	29.38 N	31.18 E
Alba, It. (äl'bä)	172	44.41 N	8.02 E
Albacete, Sp. (äl-bä-thā'tā)	170	39.00 N	1.49 W
Albachten, F.R.G. (äl-bä'K-tĕn)	169c	51.55 N	7.31 E
Al Badārī, Egypt	223b	26.59 N	31.29 E
Alba de Tormes, Sp. (äl-bà dā tôr'mās)	170	40.48 N	5.28 W
Al Bahnasā, Egypt	223b	28.35 N	30.30 E
Alba Iulia, Rom. (äl-bä yo͞o'lyá)	167	46.05 N	23.32 E
Al Ballaḩ, Egypt (bä'lä)	223c	30.46 N	32.20 E
Al Balyanā, Egypt	223b	26.12 N	32.00 E
Albania, Eur. (ăl-bā'nĭ-á)	154	41.45 N	20.00 E
Albani, Colli (Mtn.), It.	171d	41.46 N	12.45 E
Albano, Lago (L.), It. (lä'-gō äl-bä'nō)	171d	41.45 N	12.44 E
Albano Laziale, It. (äl-bä'nō lät-zē-ä'lā)	171d	41.44 N	12.43 E
Albany, Austl. (ôl'bá-nĭ)	214	35.00 S	118.00 E
Albany, Ca.	118b	37.54 N	122.18 W
Albany, Ga.	126	31.35 N	84.10 W
Albany, Mo.	123	40.14 N	94.18 W
Albany, NY	111	42.40 N	73.50 W
Albany, Or.	116	44.38 N	123.06 W
Albany (R.), Can.	97	51.45 N	83.30 W
Albany Park (Neigh.), Il.	58a	41.58 N	87.43 W
Al-Barājīl, Egypt	71a	30.04 N	31.09 E
Al Başrah, Iraq	192	30.35 N	47.59 E
Al Batrūn, Leb. (bä-tro͞on')	191a	34.16 N	35.39 E
Al Bawīṭī, Egypt	225	28.19 N	29.00 E
Al Bayḑā, Libya	194	32.46 N	21.43 E
Albemarle, NC (ăl'bē-märl)	127	35.24 N	80.36 W
Albemarle Sd., NC	127	36.00 N	76.17 W
Albenga, It. (äl-bĕŋ'gä)	172	44.04 N	8.13 E
Alberche (R.), Sp. (äl-bĕr'chå)	170	40.08 N	4.19 W
Albergaria a-Velha, Port. (äl-bĕr-gá-rē' á-ä-väl'yá)	170	40.47 N	8.31 W
Alberga, The (R.), Austl. (ăl-bûr'gá)	214	27.15 S	135.00 E
Alberhill, Ca. (ăl'bēr-hĭl)	119a	33.43 N	117.23 W
Albert, Fr. (ál-bâr')	168	50.00 N	2.49 E
Albert (L.), Afr. (ăl'bērt) (ál-bâr')	231	1.50 N	30.40 E
Alberta (Prov.), Can. (ăl-bûr'tá)	96	54.33 N	117.10 W
Alberta, Mt., Can.	99	52.18 N	117.28 W
Albert Edward, Mt., Pap. N. Gui. (ăl'bērt ĕd'wērd)	207	8.25 S	147.25 E
Albertfalva (Neigh.), Hung.	66g	47.27 N	19.02 E
Alberti, Arg. (àl-bĕ'r-tē)	141c	35.01 S	60.16 W
Albert Kanaal (Can.), Bel.	157a	51.07 N	5.07 E
Albert Lea, Mn. (ăl'bērt lē')	115	43.38 N	93.24 W
Albert Nile (R.), Ug.	231	3.25 N	31.35 E
Alberton, Can. (ăl'bēr-tŭn)	104	46.49 N	64.04 W
Alberton, S. Afr.	227b	26.16 S	28.08 E
Albert, Parc Natl. (Natl. Pk.), Zaire	231	0.05 N	29.30 E
Albertson, NY	55	40.46 N	73.39 W
Albertville, Al. (ăl'bērt-vĭl)	126	34.15 N	86.10 W
Albertville, Fr. (ál-bĕr-vēl')	169	45.42 N	6.25 E
Albertville (Neigh.), S. Afr.	71b	26.10 S	27.59 E

ng-sing; nŋ-banŋk; N-nasalized n; nŏd; cŏmmit; ōld; ôbey; ôrder; oi-boil; fo͞od; fo͝ot; ou-out; s-soft; sh-dish; th-thin; pūre; ůnite; ûrn; stŭd; circŭs; ü-as in French tu; '-indeterminate vowel.

252 Albertville – Alpine

PLACE (Pronounciation)	PAGE	Lat. °′	Long. °′
Albertville, see Kalemie			
Albi, Fr. (äl-bē')	168	43.54 N	2.07 E
Albia, Ia. (ăl-bĭ-à)	115	41.01 N	92.44 W
Albina, Sur. (äl-bē'nä)	143	5.30 N	54.33 W
Albina, Ponta (Pt.), Ang.	230	15.51 S	11.44 E
Albino, Pt., Can. (ăl-bī'nō)	113c	42.50 N	79.05 W
Albion, Austl.	70b	37.47 S	144.49 E
Albion, Mi. (ăl'bĭ-ŭn)	110	42.15 N	84.50 W
Albion, Ne.	114	41.42 N	98.00 W
Albion, NY	111	43.15 N	78.10 W
Alboran, Isla del (I.), Sp. (ē's-lä-děl-äl-bō-rä'n)	170	35.58 N	3.02 W
Ålborg, Den. (ôl'bŏr)	164	57.02 N	9.55 E
Al Buḩayrah al Murrah al Kubrā (Great Bitter) (Salt L.), Egypt	223c	30.24 N	32.27 E
Al Buḩayrah al Murrah aş Şughrā (Little Bitter) (Salt L.), Egypt	223c	30.10 N	32.36 E
Albuquerque, NM (ăl-bŭ-kûr'kē)	121	35.05 N	106.40 W
Albuquerque, Cayus de (I.), Col. (ăl-bŭ-kûr'kē)	133	12.12 N	81.24 W
Al Buraymī, Om.	192	23.45 N	55.39 E
Alburquerque, Sp. (äl-bōōr-kĕr'kä)	170	39.13 N	6.58 W
Albury, Austl. (ôl'bēr-ē)	216	36.00 S	147.00 E
Alcabideche, Port. (äl-kȧ-bē-dā'chå)	171b	38.43 N	9.24 W
Alcácer do Sal, Port. (äl-kä'sĕr dōō säl')	170	38.24 N	8.33 W
Alcalá de Henares, Sp. (äl-kä-lä' dā ā-na'rās)	171a	40.29 N	3.22 W
Alcalá la Real, Sp. (äl-kä-lä'lä rā-äl')	170	37.27 N	3.57 W
Alcamo, It. (äl'kȧ-mō)	172	37.58 N	13.03 E
Alcanadre (R.), Sp. (äl-kä-nä'drå)	171	41.41 N	0.18 W
Alcanar, Sp. (äl-kä-när')	171	40.35 N	0.27 E
Alcañiz, Sp. (äl-kän-yēth')	171	41.03 N	0.08 W
Alcântara, Braz. (äl-kän'tȧ-rȧ)	143	2.17 S	44.29 W
Alcântara (Neigh.), Port.	65d	38.42 N	9.10 W
Alcaraz, Sp. (äl-kä-räth')	170	38.39 N	2.28 W
Alcaudete, Sp. (äl-kou-dhā'tā)	170	37.38 N	4.05 W
Alcázar de San Juan, Sp. (äl-kä'thär dā sän hwän')	170	39.22 N	3.12 W
Alcira, Sp. (ä-thē'rä)	171	39.09 N	0.26 W
Alcoa, Tn. (ăl-kō'ȧ)	126	35.45 N	84.00 W
Alcobendas, Sp. (äl-kō-bĕn'dȧs)	171a	40.32 N	3.39 W
Alcochete, Port. (äl-kō-chā'tȧ)	171b	38.45 N	8.58 W
Alcorón, Sp. (äl-kô-rō'n)	171a	40.22 N	3.50 W
Alcorta, Arg. (äl-kôr'tä)	141c	33.32 S	61.08 W
Alcova Res., Wy. (ăl-kō'vȧ)	117	42.31 N	106.33 W
Alcove, Can. (ăl-kōv')	95c	45.41 N	75.55 W
Alcoy, Sp. (äl-koi')	171	38.42 N	0.30 W
Alcudia, Bahia de (B.), Sp. (bä-ē'ä-dē-äl-kōō-dhē'ȧ)	171	39.48 N	3.20 E
Aldabra Is., Afr. (äl-dä'brä)	227	9.16 S	46.17 E
Aldama, Mex. (äl-dä'mä)	130	22.54 N	98.04 W
Aldama, Mex.	124	28.50 N	105.54 W
Aldan (R.), Sov. Un.	181	63.30 N	132.14 E
Aldan, Sov.Un.	181	58.46 N	125.19 E
Aldan Plat., Sov. Un.	181	57.42 N	130.28 E
Aldanskaya, Sov. Un.	181	61.52 N	135.29 E
Aldeia, Braz.	61d	23.30 S	46.51 E
Aldeia de Carapicuiba, Braz.	61d	23.35 S	46.48 W
Aldenham, Eng.	62	51.40 N	0.21 W
Aldenhoven, F.R.G. (äl'dĕn-hō'vĕn)	169c	50.54 N	6.18 E
Aldenrade (Neigh.), F.R.G.	63	51.31 N	6.44 E
Aldergrove, Can. (ôl'dēr-grōv)	118d	49.03 N	122.28 W
Alderney (I.), Guernsey (ôl'dēr-nĭ)	168	49.43 N	2.11 W
Aldershot, Eng. (ôl'dēr-shŏt)	156b	51.14 N	0.46 W
Alderson, WV (ôl-dēr-sŭn)	110	37.40 N	80.40 W
Alderwood Manor, Wa. (ôl'dēr-wo͝od măn'ŏr)	118a	47.49 N	122.18 W
Aldridge-Brownhills, Eng.	156	52.38 N	1.55 W
Aledo, Il. (ȧ-le'dō)	123	41.12 N	90.47 W
Aleg, Mauritania	228	17.03 N	13.55 W
Alegre, Braz. (ȧlĕ'grĕ)	141a	20.41 S	41.32 W
Alegre (R.), Braz.	144b	22.22 S	43.34 W
Alegrete, Braz. (ä-lā-grā'tā)	144	29.46 S	55.44 W
Aleksandrov, Sov. Un. (ä-lyĕk-sän' drôf)	182b	56.24 N	38.45 E
Aleksandrovsk, Sov. Un. (ä-lyĕk-sän'drôfsk)	182a	59.11 N	57.36 E
Aleksandrovsk, Sov. Un.	181	51.02 N	142.21 E
Aleksandrów Kujawski, Pol. (ä-lĕk-säh'drōōv kōō-yav'skē)	167	52.54 N	18.45 E
Alekseyevka, Sov. Un. (ä-lyĕk-sâ-yĕf'kȧ)	175	50.39 N	38.40 E
Aleksin, Sov. Un. (ä-lyĕk-sĭn)	174	54.31 N	37.07 E
Aleksinac, Yugo. (ȧ-lyĕk-sē-nȧk')	173	43.33 N	21.42 E
Alem Paraíba, Braz. (ä-lĕ'm-pȧ-rȧē'bȧ)	141a	21.54 S	42.40 W
Alençon, Fr. (ȧ-läɴ-sôɴ')	168	48.26 N	0.08 E
Alenquer, Braz. (ä-lĕŋ-kĕr')	143	1.58 S	54.44 W
Alenquer, Port.	170	39.04 N	9.01 W
Alentjo (Reg.), Port. (ä-lĕŋ-tä'zhōō)	170	38.05 N	7.45 W
Alenuihaha Chan., Hi. (ä'lå-nōō-ē-hä'hä)	106a	20.20 N	156.05 W
Aleppo, Syr. (ȧ-lĕp-ō)	161	36.10 N	37.18 E
Alès, Fr. (ä-lĕs')	168	44.07 N	4.06 E
Alessandria, It. (ä-lĕs-sän'drē-ä)	172	44.53 N	8.35 E
Alessio, see Lesh			
Ålesund, Nor. (ô'lē-sōōn')	164	62.28 N	6.14 E
Aleutian Is., Ak. (ȧ-lu'shăn)	107a	52.40 N	177.30 W
Aleutian Trench, Ak.	107a	50.40 N	177.10 E
Alevina, Mys (C.), Sov. Un.	181	58.49 N	151.44 E
Alexander Arch., Ak. (ăl-ĕg-zăn'dēr)	107	57.05 N	138.10 W
Alexander City, Al.	126	32.55 N	85.55 W
Alexander I., Ant.	232	71.00 S	71.00 W
Alexander Ind. Res., Can.	95g	53.47 N	114.00 W
Alexandra, S. Afr. (ăl-ex-än'drȧ)	227b	26.07 S	28.07 E
Alexandria, Austl. (ăl-ĕg-zăn'drĭ-ȧ)	214	19.00 S	136.56 E
Alexandria, Can.	111	45.50 N	74.35 W
Alexandria, In.	110	40.20 N	85.20 W
Alexandria, La.	125	31.18 N	92.28 W
Alexandria, Mn.	114	45.53 N	95.23 W
Alexandria, Rom.	173	43.55 N	25.21 E

PLACE (Pronounciation)	PAGE	Lat. °′	Long. °′
Alexandria, S. Afr. (ăl-ĕx-än-drĭ-ȧ)	227c	33.40 S	26.26 E
Alexandria, SD	114	43.39 N	97.45 W
Alexandria, Va. (ăl-ĕg-zăn'drĭ-ȧ)	112e	38.50 N	77.05 W
Alexandria Bay, NY	111	44.20 N	75.55 W
Alexandria, see Al Iskandarīyah			
Alexandroúpolis (Dedeagats), Grc. (ä-lĕk-sän-drōō'pō-lĭs) (de'dĕ-ä-gäts)	173	40.41 N	25.51 E
Alfaro, Sp. (äl-färō)	170	42.08 N	1.43 W
Al-Fāshir, Sud. (fä'shēr)	225	13.38 N	25.21 E
Al Fashn, Egypt	223b	28.47 N	30.53 E
Al Fayyūm, Egypt	225	29.14 N	30.48 E
Alfenas, Braz. (äl-fĕ'nȧs)	141a	21.26 S	45.55 W
Alfiós (R.), Grc.	173	37.33 N	21.50 E
Al Firdān, Egypt (fer-dän')	223b	30.43 N	32.20 E
Alfonso Claudio, Braz. (äl-fōn'sō-klou'dēō)	141a	20.05 S	41.05 W
Alfortville, Fr.	64c	48.49 N	2.25 E
Alfred, Can. (ăl'frĕd)	95c	45.34 N	74.52 W
Alfreton, Eng. (ăl'fēr-tŭn)	156	53.06 N	1.23 W
Algarve (Reg.), Port. (äl-gär'vĕ)	170	37.15 N	8.12 W
Algeciras, Sp. (äl-hā-thē'räs)	170	36.08 N	5.25 W
Algeria, Afr. (ăl-gē'rĭ-ȧ)	222	28.45 N	1.00 E
Algés, Port.	65d	38.42 N	9.13 W
Algete, Sp. (äl-hā'tā)	171a	40.36 N	3.30 W
Al Ghayḑah, P.D.R. of Yem.	195	16.12 N	52.15 E
Alghero, It. (äl-gâ'rō)	172	40.32 N	8.22 E
Algiers, (El Djazaïr), Alg. (ăl-jērs)	224	36.51 N	2.56 E
Algoa, Tx. (ăl-gō'ȧ)	125a	29.24 N	95.11 W
Algoabaai (B.), S. Afr. (ăl'gôȧ)	227c	33.51 S	24.50 E
Algoma, Wa.	118a	47.17 N	122.15 W
Algoma, Wi.	115	44.38 N	87.29 W
Algona, Ia.	115	43.04 N	94.11 W
Algonac, Mi. (ăl'gō-năk)	110	42.35 N	82.30 W
Algonquin, Il. (ăl-gŏŋ'kwĭn)	113a	42.10 N	88.17 W
Algonquin Provincial Park, Can.	111	45.50 N	78.20 W
Alguierão-Mem Martins, Port.	65d	38.48 N	9.20 W
Alhama de Granada, Sp. (äl-hä'mä)	170	37.00 N	3.59 W
Alhama de Murcia, Sp.	170	37.50 N	1.24 W
Alhambra, Ca. (ăl-hăm'brȧ)	119a	34.05 N	118.08 W
Al Ḩammām, Egypt	161	30.46 N	29.42 E
Alhandra, Port. (äl-yän'drȧ)	171b	38.55 N	9.01 W
Al Hasā (Plain), Sau. Ar.	192	27.00 N	47.48 E
Alhaurín, Sp. (ä-lou-rēn')	170	36.40 N	4.40 W
Al-Hawāmidīyah, Egypt	71a	29.54 N	31.15 E
Al Hawrah, P.D.R. of Yem.	195	13.49 N	47.37 E
Al Hayy, Iraq	195	32.10 N	46.03 E
Al Ḩijāz (Reg.), Sau. Ar.	192	23.45 N	39.08 E
Al Hirmil, Leb.	191a	34.23 N	36.22 E
Al-Hoceima, Sp.	170	35.15 N	3.55 W
Alhos Vedros, Port. (äl'yōs'vā'drōs)	171b	38.39 N	9.02 W
Alhucemas, Baie d' (B.), Mor.	170	35.18 N	3.50 W
Al Hudaydah, Yemen	192	14.43 N	43.03 E
Al Hufūf, Sau. Ar.	192	25.15 N	49.43 E
Aliákmon (R.), Grc. (ăl-ē-ák'mōn)	173	40.26 N	22.17 E
Alibori (R.), Benin	229	11.40 N	2.55 E
Alicante, Sp. (ä-lē-kän'tä)	171	38.20 N	0.30 W
Alice, S. Afr. (ăl-ĭs)	227c	32.47 S	26.51 E
Alice, Tx. (ăl'ĭs)	124	27.45 N	98.04 W
Alice Arm, Can.	98	55.29 N	129.29 W
Alicedale, S. Afr. (ăl'ĭs-dāl)	227c	33.18 S	26.04 E
Alice, Punta (Pt.), It. (ä-lē'chĕ)	173	39.23 N	17.10 E
Alice Springs, Austl. (ăl'ĭs)	214	23.38 S	133.56 E
Alicudi (I.), It. (ä-lē-kōō'dē)	172	38.34 N	14.21 E
Alifkulovo, Sov. Un. (ä-lĭf-kû'lô-vô)	182a	55.57 N	62.06 E
Al-Imām (Neigh.), Egypt	71a	30.01 N	31.10 E
Alingsås, Swe. (á'lĭŋ-sôs)	164	57.57 N	12.30 E
Alīgarh, India (ä-lē-gŭr')	196	27.58 N	78.08 E
Alipore (Neigh.), India	67a	22.31 N	88.18 E
Aliquippa, Pa. (ăl-ĭ-kwĭp'ȧ)	113e	40.37 N	80.15 W
Al Iskandarīyah (Alexandria), Egypt	223b	31.12 N	29.58 E
Al Ismā'īlīyah, see Ismailia			
Aliwal North, S. Afr. (ä-lē-wäl')	226	31.09 S	28.26 E
Al-Jabal Al-Akhdar (Mts.), Om.	192	23.30 N	56.43 W
Al Jafr, Qa'al (L.), Jordan	191a	30.15 N	36.24 E
Al Jaghbūb, Libya	225	29.46 N	24.32 E
Al Jawārah, Om.	195	18.55 N	57.17 E
Al Jawf, Libya	225	24.14 N	23.15 E
Al Jawf, Sau. Ar.	192	29.45 N	39.30 E
Aljezur, Port. (äl-zhä-zōōr')	170	37.18 N	8.52 W
Al Jīzah, Egypt	223b	30.01 N	31.12 E
Al Jufrah (Oasis), Libya	224	29.30 N	15.16 E
Al Junaynah, Sud.	194	13.27 N	22.27 E
Aljustrel, Port. (äl-zhōō-strĕl')	170	37.44 N	8.23 W
Al Kāb, Egypt	223c	30.56 N	32.19 E
Al Kāmilīn, Sud. (käm-lēn')	225	15.09 N	33.06 E
Al Karak, Jordan (kĕ-räk')	191a	31.11 N	35.42 E
Al Karnak, Egypt (kär'nak)	223b	25.42 N	32.43 E
Al Khābūrah, Om.	192	23.45 N	57.30 E
Al Khalīl (Hebron), Jordan	191a	31.31 N	35.07 E
Al Khandaq, Sud. (kän-däk')	225	18.38 N	30.29 E
Al Khārijah, Egypt	194	25.26 N	30.33 E
Al Kharṭūm, see Khartoum			
Al Kharṭūm Baḩrī, Sud.	225	15.43 N	32.41 E
Al Khums, Libya	225	32.35 N	14.10 E
Al Khurmah, Sau. Ar.	192	21.37 N	41.44 E
Al Kiswah, Syr.	191a	33.31 N	36.13 E
Alkmaar, Neth. (älk-mär')	163	52.39 N	4.42 E
Al Kubrī, Egypt (kōō'brē)	223c	30.01 N	32.35 E
Al Kufrah (Oasis), Libya	225	24.45 N	22.45 E
Al-Kunayyisah, Egypt	71a	29.59 N	31.11 E
Al Kuntillah, Egypt	191a	29.59 N	34.42 E
Al Kuwayt (Kuwait), Kuw. (kōō-wit)	192	29.04 N	47.59 E
Al Lādhiqīyah (Latakia), Syr.	161	35.32 N	35.51 E
Allagash (R.), Me. (ăl'ȧ-găsh)	104	46.50 N	69.24 W
Allāhābād, India (ŭl-ŭ-hä-bäd')	196	25.32 N	81.53 E
All American Can., Ca. (âl ȧ-mĕr'ĭ-kăn)	120	32.43 N	115.12 W
Alland, Aus.	157e	48.04 N	16.05 E
Allariz, Sp. (äl-yä-rēth')	170	42.10 N	7.48 W
Allatoona (R.), Ga. (ăl'ȧ-tōōn'ȧ)	126	34.05 N	84.57 W
Allauch, Fr. (ä-lĕ'ōō)	168a	43.21 N	5.30 E

PLACE (Pronounciation)	PAGE	Lat. °′	Long. °′
Allaykha, Sov.Un. (ä-lī'ĸȧ)	181	70.32 N	148.53 E
Allegan, Mi. (ăl'ē-găn)	102	42.30 N	85.55 W
Allegany Ind. Res., NY (ăl-ē-gā'nĭ)	111	42.05 N	78.55 W
Allegheny (R.), Pa.	111	41.10 N	79.20 W
Allegheny Front (Mts.), U.S.	111	38.12 N	80.03 W
Allegheny Mts., U.S.	109	37.35 N	81.55 W
Allegheny Plat, U.S.	110	39.00 N	81.15 W
Allegheny Res., Pa.	111	41.50 N	78.55 W
Allen, Ok. (ăl'ĕn)	123	34.51 N	96.26 W
Allendale, NJ (ăl'ĕn-dāl)	112a	41.02 N	74.08 W
Allendale, SC	127	33.00 N	81.19 W
Allende, Mex. (äl-yĕn'då)	131	18.23 N	92.49 W
Allende, Mex.	124	28.20 N	100.50 W
Allen, Lough (B.), Ire. (lŏk ăl'ĕn)	162	54.07 N	8.09 W
Allen Park, Mi.	57c	42.15 N	83.13 W
Allentown, Pa. (ăl'en-toun)	111	40.35 N	75.30 W
Alleppey, India (ȧ-lĕp'ē)	197	9.33 N	76.22 E
Aller R., F.R.G. (äl'ēr)	166	52.43 N	9.50 E
Allerton, Ma.	54a	42.18 N	70.53 W
Allerton (Neigh.), Eng.	64a	53.22 N	2.53 W
Alliance, Ne. (ȧ-lī'ăns)	114	42.06 N	102.53 W
Alliance, Oh.	110	40.55 N	81.10 W
Al Lidām, Sau.Ar.	192	20.45 N	44.12 E
Allier (R.), Fr. (ȧ-lyā')	168	46.43 N	3.03 E
Alligator Pt., La. (ăl'ĭ-gā-tēr)	112d	30.57 N	89.41 W
Allinge, Den. (äl'ĭŋ-ĕ)	164	55.16 N	14.48 E
Allison Park, Pa.	57b	40.34 N	79.57 W
Al Līth, Sau. Ar.	195	20.09 N	40.16 E
All Pines, Belize (ôl pĭnz)	132a	16.55 N	88.15 W
Allston (Neigh.), Ma.	54a	42.22 N	71.08 W
Al Luḩayyah, Yemen	192	15.58 N	42.48 E
Alluvial City, La.	112d	29.51 N	89.42 W
Allyn, Wa. (ăl'ĭn)	118a	47.23 N	122.51 W
Alma, Can. (ăl'mȧ)	104	45.36 N	64.59 W
Alma, Can.	104	48.29 N	71.42 W
Alma, Ga.	127	31.33 N	82.31 W
Alma, Mi.	110	43.25 N	84.40 W
Alma, Ne.	122	40.08 N	99.21 W
Alma, S. Afr.	223d	24.30 S	28.05 E
Alma, Wi.	115	44.21 N	91.57 W
Alma-Ata, Sov. Un. (äl'mȧ ȧ'tȧ)	180	43.19 N	77.08 E
Al Mabrak (R.), Sau. Ar.	191a	29.16 N	35.12 E
Almacuzac (R.), Mex. (ä-mä-kōō-zȧk)	130	18.00 N	99.03 W
Almada, Port. (äl-mä'dä)	171b	38.40 N	9.09 W
Almadén, Sp. (äl-mȧ-dhān)	170	38.47 N	4.50 W
Al Madīnah (Medina), Sau. Ar.	192	24.26 N	39.42 E
Al Mafraq, Jordan	191a	32.21 N	36.13 E
Almagre, Laguna (L.), Mex. (lä-gōō'nä-äl-mä'grĕ)	131	23.48 N	97.45 W
Almagro, Sp. (äl-mä'grō)	170	38.52 N	3.41 W
Al Maḩallah al Kubrā, Egypt	223b	31.00 N	31.10 E
Al Manāmah, Bahrain	192	26.01 N	50.33 E
Al-Manāwāt, Egypt	71a	29.55 N	31.14 E
Almanor (R.), Ca. (ăl-măn'ôr)	120	40.11 N	121.20 W
Almansa, Sp. (äl-män'sä)	170	38.52 N	1.09 W
Al Manshāh, Egypt	223b	26.31 N	31.46 E
Almansor (R.), Port. (äl-män-sôr)	170	38.41 N	8.27 W
Al Manşūrah, Egypt	223b	31.02 N	31.25 E
Al Manzilah, Egypt (män'za-la)	223b	31.09 N	32.05 E
Almanzora (R.), Sp. (äl-män-thō'rä)	170	37.20 N	2.25 W
Al Marāghah, Egypt	223b	26.41 N	31.35 E
Almargem do Bispo, Port. (äl-mär-zhĕɴ)	171b	38.51 N	9.16 W
Al-Marj, Libya	225	32.44 N	21.08 E
Al-Marj (Neigh.), Egypt	71a	30.09 N	31.20 E
Al Maşīrah (I.), Om.	192	20.43 N	58.58 E
Al Mawsil, Iraq	192	36.00 N	42.53 E
Almazán, Sp. (äl-mä-thän')	170	41.30 N	2.33 W
Al Mazār, Jordan	191a	31.04 N	35.41 E
Al Mazra'ah, Jordan	191a	31.17 N	35.33 E
Almeirim, Port. (äl-māĭ-rēɴ')	170	39.13 N	8.31 W
Almelo, Neth. (äl'mē-lō)	163	52.20 N	6.42 E
Almendra, Embalse de (Res.), Sp.	170	41.15 N	6.10 W
Almendralejo, Sp. (äl-män-drä-lā'hō)	170	38.43 N	6.24 W
Almería, Sp. (äl-mȧ-rē'ä)	170	36.52 N	2.28 W
Almería, Golfo de (G.), Sp. (gôl-fô-dĕ-äl-māĭ-reɴ')	170	36.45 N	2.26 W
Älmhult, Swe. (älm'hōōlt)	164	56.35 N	14.08 E
Almina, Pta., Mor. (äl-mē'nä)	170	35.58 N	5.17 W
Al Minyā, Egypt	223b	28.04 N	30.45 E
Almirante, Pan. (äl-mē-rän'tä)	133	9.18 N	82.24 W
Almirante, Bahia de (B.), Pan. (bä-ē'ä-dĕ-äl-mē-rän'tä)	133	9.22 N	82.07 W
Almirós, Grc.	173	39.13 N	22.47 E
Almodóvar del Campo, Sp. (äl-mō-dhō'vär)	170	38.43 N	4.10 W
Almoi, India	196	29.41 N	79.42 E
Almoloya, Mex. (äl-mō-lō'yä)	130	19.32 N	99.44 W
Almoloya, Mex.	131a	19.11 N	99.28 W
Almonte, Can. (ăl-mŏn'tē)	111	45.15 N	76.15 W
Almonte (R.), Sp.	170	39.35 N	5.50 W
Almonte, Sp. (äl-mōn'tā)	170	37.16 N	6.32 W
Almora, India	196	29.20 N	79.40 E
Al Mubarraz, Sau.Ar.	192	22.31 N	46.27 E
Al Mudawwarah, Jordan	191a	29.20 N	36.01 E
Al Mukallā, P.D.R. of Yem.	192	14.27 N	49.05 E
Al Mukhā, Yemen	192	13.19 N	43.15 E
Almuñécar, Sp. (äl-mōōn-yā'kär)	170	36.44 N	3.43 W
Alnön (I.), Swe.	164	62.20 N	17.39 E
Aloha, Or. (ä'lô-hä)	118c	45.29 N	122.52 W
Alondra, Ca.	59	33.54 N	118.19 W
Alora, Sp. (ä'lô-rä)	170	36.49 N	4.42 W
Alor Gajah, Mala	191b	2.23 N	102.13 E
Alor, Pulau (I.), Indon. (ä'lôr)	207	8.07 S	125.00 E
Alor Setar, Mala. (ä'lôr stär)	206	6.10 N	100.16 E
Alouette (R.), Can. (ä-lōō-ĕt')	118d	49.16 N	122.32 W
Alpena, Mi. (ăl-pē'nȧ)	110	45.05 N	83.30 W
Alphen, Neth.	157a	52.07 N	4.38 E
Alpiarça, Port. (äl-pyär'sȧ)	170	39.38 N	8.37 W
Alpine, NJ	55	40.56 N	73.56 W

PRONOUNCING INDEX

Alpine – Ang'angxi 253

PLACE (Pronounciation)	PAGE	Lat. °'	Long. °'
Alpine, Tx. (ăl'pīn)	124	30.21 N	103.41 W
Alps (Mts.), Eur. (ălps)	160	46.18 N	8.42 E
Alpujarra, Col. (ál-pōō-ká'rà)	142a	3.23 N	74.56 W
Alpujarras (Mts.), Sp. (äl-pōō-här'räs)	170	36.55 N	3.25 W
Al Qaḍārif, Sud.	225	14.03 N	35.11 E
Al Qāhirah (Cairo), Egypt	223b	30.00 N	31.17 E
Al Qanṭarah, Egypt	223c	30.51 N	32.20 E
Al Qaryah ash Sharqiyah, Libya	225	30.36 N	13.13 E
Al Qaṣr, Egypt	194	25.42 N	28.53 E
Al Qaṭīf, Sau. Ar.	192	26.30 N	50.00 E
Al Qayṣūmah, Sau. Ar.	192	28.15 N	46.20 E
Al Qunaytirah, Syr.	191a	33.09 N	35.49 E
Al Qunfudhah, Sau. Ar.	195	19.08 N	41.05 E
Al Quṣaymah, Egypt	191a	30.40 N	34.23 E
Al Qusayr, Egypt	191a	34.32 N	36.33 E
Al Quṣayr, Egypt	225	26.14 N	34.11 E
Als (I.), Den. (äls)	164	55.06 N	9.40 E
Alsace (Reg.), Fr. (äl-sá's)	169	48.25 N	7.24 E
Al Shan (Mts.), China (äī'shän)	200	37.27 N	120.35 E
Alsip, Il.	58a	41.40 N	87.44 W
Altadena, Ca. (äl-tä-dē'nä)	119a	34.12 N	118.08 W
Alta Gracia, Arg. (äl'tä grä'sē-ä)	144	31.41 S	64.19 W
Altagracia, Ven.	142	10.42 N	71.34 W
Altagracia de Orituco, Ven. (ä'l-tá-grá'sēä-dĕ-ôrē-tōō'kô)	143b	9.53 N	66.22 W
Altai Mts., Asia (äl'tī')	198	49.11 N	87.15 E
Alta Loma, Ca. (äl'tă lō'mä)	119a	34.07 N	117.35 W
Alta Loma, Tx. (ăl'tá lō-má)	125a	29.22 N	95.05 W
Altamaha (R.), Ga. (ôl-tá-má-hô')	127	31.50 N	82.00 W
Altamira, Braz. (äl-tä-mē'rä)	143	3.13 S	52.14 W
Altamira, Mex.	131	22.25 N	97.55 W
Altamirano, Arg. (äl-tá-mē-rä'nō)	144	35.26 S	58.12 W
Altamura, It. (äl-tä-mōō'rä)	172	40.40 N	16.35 E
Altar of Heaven (P. Int.), China	67b	39.53 N	116.25 E
Altar of the Earth (P. Int.), China	67b	39.57 N	116.24 E
Altar of the Moon (P. Int.), China	67b	39.55 N	116.20 E
Altar of the Sun (P. Int.), China	67b	39.54 N	116.27 E
Altavista, Va. (äl-tä-vĭs'tá)	127	37.08 N	79.14 W
Altay, China (äl-tä)	198	47.52 N	86.50 E
Altenburg, G.D.R. (äl-tĕn-bōōrgh)	166	50.59 N	12.27 E
Altenderne Oberbecker (Neigh.), F.R.G.	63	51.35 N	7.33 E
Altenessen (Neigh.), F.R.G.	63	51.29 N	7.00 E
Altenhagen (Neigh.), F.R.G.	63	51.22 N	7.28 E
Altenmarkt an der Triesting, Aus.	157e	48.02 N	16.00 E
Altenvoerde, F.R.G.	63	51.18 N	7.22 E
Alter do Chão, Port. (äl-tĕr'dōō shäN'ōN)	170	39.13 N	7.38 W
Altiplanicie Mexicana (Plat.), Mex. (äl-tē-plä-nē'syē-mĕ-kē-ká-nä)	130	22.38 N	102.33 W
Altiplano (Plat.), Bol. (äl-tē-plá'nō)	142	18.38 S	68.20 W
Altlandsberg, G.D.R. (ält länts'bĕrgh)	157b	52.34 N	13.44 E
Altlünun, F.R.G.	63	51.38 N	7.31 E
Altmannsdorf, (Neigh.), Aus.	66e	48.10 N	16.20 E
Alto, La. (äl'tō)	125	32.21 N	91.52 W
Alto da Moóca, (Neigh.), Braz.	61d	23.34 S	46.35 W
Alto Marañón, Rio (R.), Peru (rē'ō-ál'tô-mä-rän-yŏ'n)	142	8.18 S	77.13 W
Alto Molócuè, Moz.	231	15.38 S	37.42 E
Altomünster, F.R.G. (äl'tō-mün'stĕr)	157d	48.24 N	11.16 E
Alton, Can. (ôl'tŭn)	95d	43.52 N	80.05 W
Alton, Il.	119e	38.53 N	90.11 W
Altona, Austl.	206a	37.52 S	144.50 E
Altona, Can.	101	49.06 N	97.33 W
Altona, F.R.G. (äl'tō-ná)	157c	53.33 N	9.54 E
Altona North, Austl.	70b	37.50 S	144.51 E
Altoona, Al. (ăl-tōō'ná)	126	34.01 N	86.15 W
Altoona, Pa.	111	40.25 N	78.25 W
Altoona, Wa.	118c	46.16 N	123.39 W
Alto Rio Doce, Braz. (äl'tô-rē'ô-dō'sĕ)	141a	21.02 S	43.23 W
Alto Songo, Cuba (äl-fō-sôŋ'gō)	135	20.10 N	75.45 W
Altotonga, Mex. (äl-tō-tôŋ'gä)	131	19.44 N	97.13 W
Alto-Uama, Ang.	230	12.14 S	15.33 E
Alto Velo (I.), Dom. Rep. (äl-tô-vĕ'lō)	135	17.30 N	71.35 W
Altrincham, Eng. (ôl'trĭng-ăm)	156	53.18 N	2.21 W
Altruppin, G.D.R. (ält rōō'ppēn)	157b	52.56 N	12.50 E
Altun Shan (Mts.), China (äl-tōōn shän)	198	36.58 N	85.09 E
Alturas, Ca. (äl-tōō'rás)	116	41.29 N	120.33 W
Alturas, Serra das (Mts.), Port. (sĕ'r-rä-däs-äl-tōō'räs)	170	40.43 N	7.48 W
Altus, Ok. (ăl'tŭs)	122	34.38 N	99.20 W
Al 'Ubaylah, Sau. Ar.	195	21.59 N	50.57 E
Al-Ubayyiḍ, Sud.	225	13.15 N	30.15 E
Al-Uḍayyah, Sud.	225	12.06 N	28.16 E
Al-'Ugaylah, Libya	225	30.15 N	19.07 E
Alūksne, Sov. Un. (ä'lŏŏks-nĕ)	174	57.24 N	27.04 E
Alumette I., Can. (á-lü-mĕt')	111	45.50 N	77.00 W
Alum Rock, Ca.	118b	37.23 N	121.50 W
Al Uqṣur (Luxor), Egypt	223b	25.38 N	32.59 E
Alushta, Sov. Un. (ä'lshōō-tá)	175	44.39 N	34.23 E
Alva, Ok. (ăl'vá)	122	36.46 N	98.41 W
Alvanley, Eng.	64a	53.16 N	2.45 W
Alvarado, Mex. (äl-vä-rä'dhō)	131	18.48 N	95.45 W
Alvarado, Luguna de (L.), Mex. (lä-gōō'nä-dĕ-äl-vä-rá'dô)	131	18.44 N	96.45 W
Älvdalen, Swe. (ĕlv'dä-lĕn)	164	61.14 N	14.04 E
Alverca, Port. (al-vĕr'ká)	171b	38.53 N	9.02 W
Alvesta, Swe. (äl-vĕs'tä)	164	56.55 N	14.29 E
Alvin, Tx. (ăl'vĭn)	125a	29.25 N	95.14 W
Alvinópolis, Braz. (äl-vēnō'pō-lēs)	141a	20.07 S	43.03 W
Alviso, Ca. (äl-vī'sō)	118b	37.26 N	121.59 W
Al Wajh, Sau. Ar.	192	26.15 N	36.32 E
Alwar, India (ŭl'wŭr)	196	27.39 N	76.39 E
Al Wāsiṭah, Egypt	223b	29.21 N	31.15 E
Alytus, Sov. Un. (ä'lē-tōōs)	165	54.25 N	24.05 E
Amadeus, (L.), Austl. (ăm-á-dē'ŭs)	214	24.30 S	131.25 E
Amadjuak (L.), Can. (ä-mädj'wăk)	97	64.50 N	69.20 W
Amadora, Port.	65d	38.45 N	9.14 W
Amagasaki, Jap. (ä'mä-gä-sä'kē)	205b	34.43 N	135.25 E
Ama Keng, Singapore	67c	1.24 N	103.42 E
Amakusa-Shimo (I.), Jap. (ämä-kōō'sä shē-mō)	205	32.24 N	129.35 E
Åmål, Swe. (ô'môl)	164	59.05 N	12.40 E
Amalfi, Col. (ä'mä'l-fē)	142a	6.55 N	75.04 W
Amalfi, It. (ä-mä'l-fē)	171c	40.23 N	14.36 E
Amaliás, Grc. (á-măl'yás)	173	37.48 N	21.23 E
Amalner, India	196	21.07 N	75.06 E
Amambai, Serra de (Mts.), Braz.	143	20.06 S	57.08 W
Amami Guntō (Is.), Jap. (ä'mä'mē gōōn'tō')	204	28.25 N	129.00 E
Amamio (I.), Jap. (ä-mä'mē-ō)	204	28.10 N	129.55 E
Amapá, Braz. (ä-mä-pá')	143	2.14 N	50.48 W
Amapá (State), Braz.	143	1.15 N	52.15 W
Amapala, Hond. (ä-mä-pä'lä)	132	13.16 N	87.39 W
Amarante, Braz. (ä-mä-rän'tā)	143	6.17 S	42.43 W
Amargosa (R.), Ca. (á'mär-gō'sá)	120	35.55 N	116.45 W
Amarillo, Tx. (ăm-á-rĭl'ō)	122	35.14 N	101.49 W
Amaro, Mt., It. (ä-mä'rō)	172	42.07 N	14.07 E
Amaroúsion, Grc.	66d	38.03 N	23.49 E
Amasya, Tur. (ä-mä'sē-à)	179	40.40 N	35.50 E
Amatenango, Mex. (ä-mä-tā-näŋ'gō)	131	16.30 N	92.29 W
Amatignak (I.), Ak. (ä-mä'tē-năk)	107a	51.12 N	178.30 W
Amatique, Bahía de (B.), Belize-Guat. (bä-ē'ä-dĕ-ä-mä-tē'kā)	132	15.58 N	88.50 W
Amatitlán, Guat. (ä-mä-tē-tlän')	132	14.27 N	90.39 W
Amatlán de Cañas, Mex. (ä-mät-län'dā kän-yäs)	130	20.50 N	104.22 W
Amazonas (State), Braz. (ä-mä-thō'näs)	142	4.15 S	64.30 W
Amazonas, Rio (R.), Braz. (rē'ō-ä-mä-thō'näs)	143	2.03 S	53.18 W
Ambāla, India (ŭm-bä'lŭ)	196	30.31 N	76.48 E
Ambalema, Col. (äm-bä-lā'mä)	142a	4.47 N	74.45 W
Ambarchik, Sov. Un. (ŭm-bär'chĭk)	181	69.39 N	162.18 E
Ambarnāth, India	197b	19.12 N	73.10 E
Ambato, Ec. (äm-bä'tō)	142	1.15 S	78.30 W
Ambatondrazaka, Mad.	227	17.58 S	48.43 E
Amberg, F.R.G. (äm'bĕrgh)	166	49.26 N	11.51 E
Ambergris Cay (I.), Belize (ăm'bēr-grēs kāz)	132	18.04 N	87.43 W
Ambergris Cays (Is.), Turks & Caicos Is.	135	21.20 N	71.40 W
Ambérieu-en-Bugey, Fr. (äN-bā-rē-u')	169	45.57 N	5.21 E
Ambert, Fr. (äN-bĕr')	168	45.32 N	3.41 E
Ambil I., Phil. (äm'bēl)	207a	13.51 N	120.25 E
Ambler, Pa. (ăm'blēr)	112f	40.09 N	75.13 W
Amboise, Fr. (äN-bwăz')	168	47.25 N	0.56 E
Ambon, Indon.	207	3.45 S	128.17 E
Ambon, Pulau (I.), Indon.	207	4.50 S	128.45 E
Ambositra, Mad. (äN-bô-sē'trä)	227	20.31 S	47.28 E
Amboy, Il. (ăm'boi)	110	41.41 N	89.15 W
Amboy, Wa.	118c	45.55 N	122.27 W
Ambre, Cap d' (C.), Mad.	227	12.06 S	49.15 E
Ambridge, Pa. (ăm'brĭdj)	113e	40.36 N	80.13 W
Ambrim (I.), Vanuatu	215	16.25 S	168.15 E
Ambriz, Ang.	230	7.50 S	13.06 E
Amchitka (I.), Ak. (ăm-chĭt'ká)	107a	51.25 N	178.10 E
Amchitka Pass., Ak.	107a	51.30 N	179.36 W
Amealco, Mex. (ä-mā-äl'kō)	130	20.12 N	100.08 W
Ameca, Mex. (ä-mĕ'kä)	130	20.34 N	104.02 W
Amecameca, Mex. (ä-mā-kä-mä'kä)	131a	19.06 N	98.46 W
Ameide, Neth.	157a	51.57 N	4.57 E
Ameixoera (Neigh.), Port.	65d	38.47 N	9.10 W
Ameland (I.), Neth.	163	53.29 N	5.54 E
Amelia, Oh. (á-mēl'yá)	113f	39.01 N	84.12 W
American (R.), Ca. (á-mĕr'ĭ-kăn)	120	38.43 N	120.45 W
Americana, Braz. (ä-mĕ-rē-ká'ná)	141a	22.46 S	47.19 W
American Falls, Id. (á-mĕ-ĭ-kăn)	117	42.45 N	112.53 W
American Falls Res., Id.	117	42.56 N	113.18 W
American Fork, Ut.	121	40.20 N	111.50 W
American Highland, Ant.	232	72.00 S	79.00 E
American Samoa, (I.) Oceania	208	14.20 S	170.00 W
Americus, Ga. (á-mĕr'ĭ-kŭs)	126	32.04 N	84.15 W
Amersfoort, Neth. (ä'mĕrz-fōrt)	157a	52.08 N	5.23 E
Amersham, Eng.	62	51.40 N	0.38 W
Amery, Can. (ā'mĕr-ē)	101	56.34 N	94.03 W
Amery, Wi.	115	45.19 N	92.24 W
Ames, Ia. (āmz)	115	42.00 N	93.36 W
Amesbury, Ma. (āmz'bĕr-ē)	105a	42.51 N	70.56 W
Amfissa, Grc. (àm-fĭ'sá)	173	38.32 N	22.26 E
Amga (R.), Sov. Un.	181	61.41 N	133.11 E
Amga, Sov. Un. (ŭm-gä')	181	61.08 N	132.09 E
Amgun (R.), Sov. Un.	181	53.33 N	137.57 E
Amherst, Can. (ăm'hērst)	104	45.49 N	64.14 W
Amherst (I.), Can.	103	44.08 N	76.45 W
Amherst, NY	57a	42.58 N	78.48 W
Amherst, Oh.	113d	41.24 N	82.13 W
Amiens, Fr. (ä-myăN')	168	49.54 N	2.18 E
Amirante Is., Sey.	232	6.02 S	52.30 E
Amisk L., Can.	101	54.35 N	102.13 W
Amistad Res., Tx.	124	29.20 N	101.00 W
Amite, La. (á-mēt')	125	30.43 N	90.32 W
Amite R., La.	125	30.45 N	90.48 W
Amity, Pa. (ăm'ĭ-tĭ)	113e	40.02 N	80.11 W
Amityville, NY (ăm'ĭ-tĭ-vĭl)	112a	40.41 N	73.24 W
Amlia (I.), Ak. (á'mlēä)	107a	52.00 N	173.28 W
'Ammān, Jordan (äm'mán)	191a	31.57 N	35.57 E
Ammersee (I.), F.R.G. (äm'mĕr)	157d	48.00 N	11.08 E
Amnicon R., Wi. (ăm'nē-kŏn)	119h	46.35 N	91.56 W
Amnok (R.), see Yalu			
Amorgós (I.), Grc. (ä-môr'gōs)	173	36.47 N	25.47 E
Amory, Ms. (ām'o-rē)	126	33.58 N	88.27 W
Amos, Can. (ā'mŭs)	103	48.31 N	78.04 W
Amoy, see Xiamen			
Amparo, Braz. (äm-pá'-rô)	141a	22.43 S	46.44 W
Amper R., F.R.G. (äm'pĕr)	157d	48.18 N	11.32 E
Amposta, Sp. (äm-pōs'tä)	171	40.42 N	0.34 E
Amqui, Can.	104	48.28 N	67.28 W
Amrāvati, India	196	20.58 N	77.47 E
Amritsar, India (ŭm-rĭt'sŭr)	196	31.43 N	74.52 E
Amstelveen, Neth.	157a	52.18 N	4.51 E
Amsterdam, Neth. (äm-stĕr-däm')	157a	52.21 N	4.52 E
Amsterdam, NY (ăm'stĕr-dăm)	111	42.55 N	74.10 W
Amsterdam, Île (I.), Ind. O.	232	37.52 S	77.32 E
Amstetten, Aus. (äm'stĕt-ĕn)	166	48.09 N	14.53 E
Am Timan, Chad (äm'tē-män')	225	11.18 N	20.30 E
Amu Darya (R.), Asia (ä-mōō-dä'rēä)	192	40.40 N	62.00 E
Amukta Pass., Ak. (ä-mōōk'tá)	107a	52.30 N	172.00 W
Amundsen G., Can. (ä'mŭn-sĕn)	96	70.17 N	123.28 W
Amundsen Sea, Ant.	232	72.00 S	110.00 W
Amungen (L.), Swe.	164	61.07 N	16.00 E
Amurskiy, Sov. Un. (ä-mûr'skĭ)	182a	52.35 N	59.36 E
Amurskiy, Zaliv (B.), Sov. Un. (zä'lĭf ä-mōōr'skĭ)	204	43.20 N	131.40 E
Amusgos (San Pedro), Mex. (ä-mōō's-gôs) (săn-pē'drō)	130	16.39 N	98.09 W
Amuyao, Mt., Phil. (ä-mōō-yä'ō)	207a	17.04 N	121.09 E
Amvrakikos Kólpos (G.), Grc.	173	39.00 N	21.00 E
Amyun, Leb.	191a	34.18 N	35.48 E
Anabar (R.), Sov. Un. (ăn-á-băr')	181	71.15 N	113.00 E
Anaco, Ven. (ä-ná'kô)	143b	9.29 N	64.27 W
Anaconda, Mt. (ăn-á-kŏn'dá)	117	46.07 N	112.55 W
Anacortes, Wa. (ăn-á-kôr'tĕz)	118a	48.30 N	122.37 W
Anacostia (Neigh.), DC.	56d	38.52 N	76.59 W
Anadarko, Ok. (ăn-á-där'kō)	122	35.05 N	98.14 W
Anadoluhisarı (P. Int.), Tur.	66f	41.04 N	29.03 E
Anadyr', Sov.Un. (ŭ-ná-dĭr')	181	64.47 N	177.01 E
Anadyr (R.), Sov. Un.	181	65.30 N	172.45 E
Anadyrskiy Zaliv (B.), Sov. Un.	191	64.10 N	178.00 W
'Ānah, Iraq	195	34.28 N	41.56 E
Anaheim, Ca. (ăn'á-hīm)	119a	33.50 N	117.55 W
Anahuac, Tx. (ä-nä'wăk)	125a	29.46 N	94.41 W
Anai Mudi (Mtn.), India	197	10.10 N	77.00 E
Anama Bay, Can.	101	51.56 N	98.05 W
Ana María, Cayos (Is.), Cuba (kä'yōs-ä'ná má-rē'á)	134	21.55 N	78.50 W
Anambas, Kepulauan (Is.), Indon. (ä-näm-bäs)	206	2.41 N	106.38 E
Anamosa, Ia. (ăn-á-mō'sá)	115	42.06 N	91.18 W
Anan'yev, Sov. Un. (á-nä'nyĕf)	175	47.43 N	29.59 E
Anapa, Sov. Un. (á-nä'pä)	175	44.54 N	37.19 E
Anápolis, Braz. (ä-ná'pō-lēs)	143	16.17 S	48.47 W
Añatuya, Arg. (ä-nyä-tōō'yá)	144	28.22 S	62.45 W
Anchieta, Braz. (än-chyĕ'tä)	144b	22.49 S	43.24 W
Ancholme (R.), Eng. (ăn'chŭm)	156	53.28 N	0.27 W
Anchorage, Ak. (ăŋ'kēr-āj)	107	61.12 N	149.48 W
Anchorage, Ky.	113b	38.16 N	85.32 W
Anci, China (än-tsŭ)	202a	39.31 N	116.41 E
Ancienne-Lorette, Can. (äN-syĕn' lō-rĕt')	95b	46.48 N	71.21 W
Ancon, Pan. (ăŋ-kōn')	128a	8.55 N	79.32 W
Ancona, It. (än-kō'nä)	172	43.37 N	13.32 E
Ancud, Chile (äŋ-kōōdh')	144	41.52 S	73.45 W
Ancud, G. de, Chile (gôl-fô-dĕ-äŋ-kōōdh')	144	41.15 S	73.00 W
Anda, China	202	46.20 N	125.20 E
Andalgalá, Arg. (á'n-däl-gä-lá')	144	27.35 S	66.14 W
Åndalsnes, Nor.	164	62.33 N	7.46 E
Andalucia (Reg.), Sp. (än-dä-lōō-sē'ä)	170	37.35 N	5.40 W
Andalusia, Al. (ăn-dá-lōō'zhá)	126	31.19 N	86.19 W
Andaman Is., Andaman & Nicobar Is. (ăn-dá-măn')	206	11.38 N	92.17 E
Andaman Sea, Asia	206	12.44 N	95.45 E
Andarax (R.), Sp.	170	37.00 N	2.40 W
Anderlecht, Bel. (än'dĕr-lĕkt)	157a	50.49 N	4.16 E
Andernach, F.R.G. (än'dĕr-näk)	166	50.25 N	7.23 E
Anderson, Arg. (á'n-dĕr-sōn)	141c	35.15 S	60.15 W
Anderson, Ca. (ăn'dēr-sŭn)	116	40.28 N	122.19 W
Anderson, In.	110	40.05 N	85.50 W
Anderson, SC	127	34.30 N	82.40 W
Anderson (R.), Can.	96	68.32 N	125.12 W
Andes Mts., S. A. (ăn'dēz) (än'dās)	140	13.00 S	75.00 W
Andheri (Neigh.), India	197b	19.08 N	72.50 E
Andhra Pradesh (State), India	197	16.00 N	79.00 E
Andikíthira (I.), Grc.	161	35.50 N	23.20 E
Andizhan, Sov. Un. (än-dē-zhän')	180	40.51 N	72.39 E
Andong, Kor. (än'dŭng')	204	36.31 N	128.42 E
Andongwei, China (än-dôŋ-wā)	200	35.08 N	119.19 E
Andorra, And. (än-dôr'rä)	171	42.38 N	1.30 E
Andorra, Eur.	159	42.30 N	2.00 E
Andover, Ma. (ăn'dō-vēr)	105a	42.39 N	71.08 W
Andover, NJ	112a	40.59 N	74.45 W
Andøya (I.), Nor. (änd-ûĕ)	158	69.12 N	14.58 E
Andreanof Is., Ak. (än-drā-ä'nôf)	107a	51.10 N	177.00 W
Andrelândia, Braz. (än-drĕ-lá'n-dyá)	141a	21.45 S	44.18 W
Andrésy, Fr.	64c	48.59 N	2.04 E
Andrew Johnson Natl. Mon., Tn. (ăn'drōō jŏn'sŭn)	126	36.15 N	82.55 W
Andrews, NC (ăn'drōōz)	126	35.12 N	83.48 W
Andrews, SC	127	33.25 N	79.32 W
Andrews Air Force Base (P. Int.), Md.	56d	38.48 N	76.52 W
Andreyevka, Sov. Un. (än-drā-yĕf'ká)	175	48.03 N	37.03 E
Andria, It. (än'drē-ä)	172	41.17 N	15.55 E
Andropov (Rybinsk), Sov. Un.	174	58.02 N	38.52 E
Andros, Grc. (án'dhrôs)	173	37.50 N	24.54 E
Ándros (I.), Grc. (án'drôs)	173	37.59 N	24.55 E
Androscoggin (R.), Me. (ăn-drŭs-kŏg'ĭn)	104	44.25 N	70.45 W
Andros I., Ba. (ăn'drŏs)	134	24.30 N	78.00 W
Anefis i-n-Darane, Mali	228	18.03 N	0.36 E
Anegasaki, Jap. (ä'nā-gä-sä'kē)	205a	35.29 N	140.02 E
Aneityum (I.), Vanuatu (ä-nā-ē'tē-ŭm)	215	20.15 S	169.49 E
Aneta, ND (ă-nē'tá)	114	47.41 N	97.57 W
Angamacutiro, Mex. (än'gä-mä-kōō-tē'rô)	130	20.08 N	101.44 W
Angangueo, Mex. (än-gäŋ'gwā-ō)	130	19.36 N	100.18 W
Ang'angxi, China (äŋ-äŋ-shyē)	202	47.05 N	123.58 E

PLACE (Pronounciation)	PAGE	Lat. °′	Long. °′
Angara (R.), **see Verkhnyaya Tunguska**			
Angarsk, Sov. Un.	180	52.48 N	104.15 E
Ange, Swe. (ông'ā)	164	62.31 N	15.39 E
Angel De La Guarda (I.), Mex. (ȧ'n-hĕl-dĕ-lä-gwä'r-dä)	128	29.30 N	113.00 W
Angeles, Phil. (än'hā-lās)	207a	15.09 N	120.35 E
Ängelholm, Swe. (ĕng'ĕl-hôlm)	164	56.14 N	12.50 E
Angelina R., Tx. (ăn-jē lē'nȧ)	125	31.30 N	94.53 W
Angel, Salto (Falls), Ven. (säl'tō-ȧ'n-hĕl)	142	5.44 N	62.27 W
Angels Camp, Ca. (ān'jĕls kămp')	120	38.03 N	120.33 W
Angerhausen, (Neigh.), F.R.G.	63	51.23 N	6.44 E
Ångermanälven (R.), Swe.	158	64.10 N	18.35 E
Angermund, F.R.G. (ȧn'ngĕr-mŭnd)	169c	51.20 N	6.47 E
Angermünde, G.D.R. (äng'ēr-mûn-dĕ)	166	53.02 N	14.00 E
Angers, Can. (äN-zhā')	95c	41.31 N	75.29 W
Angers, Fr.	168	47.29 N	0.36 W
Angkor (Ruins), Kamp. (äng'kôr)	206	13.52 N	103.50 E
Anglesey, (I.), Wales (ăŋ'g'l-sē)	162	53.35 N	4.28 W
Angleton, Tx. (aŋ'g'l-tŭn)	125a	29.10 N	95.25 W
Angmagssalik, Grnld. (ȧŋ-mȧ'sȧ-lĭk)	94	65.40 N	37.40 W
Angoche, Ilha (I.), Moz. (ē'lä-ăn-gō'chā)	231	16.20 S	40.00 E
Angol, Chile (aŋ-gōl')	144	37.47 S	72.43 W
Angola, Afr.	222	14.15 S	16.00 E
Angola, In. (ăŋ-gō'lȧ)	110	41.35 S	85.00 W
Angono, Phil.	68g	14.31 N	121.08 E
Angora, see Ankara			
Angoulême, Fr. (äŋ'gōō-lâm')	168	45.40 N	0.09 E
Angra dos Reis, Braz. (aŋ'grä dōs rā'ēs)	141a	23.01 S	44.17 W
Angri, It. (ä'n-grē)	171c	40.30 N	14.35 E
Anguang, China (än-gŭäŋ)	202	45.28 N	123.42 E
Anguilla, N.A.	129	18.15 N	62.54 W
Anguilla, Cays (Is.), Ba. (ăŋ-gwĭl'ȧ)	134	23.30 N	79.35 W
Anguille, C., Can. (äŋ-gē'yĕ)	105	47.55 N	59.25 W
Anguo, China (än-gwō)	200	38.27 N	115.19 E
Angyalföld (Neigh.), Hung.	66g	47.33 N	19.05 E
Anholt (I.), Den. (än'hŏlt)	164	56.43 N	11.34 E
Anhui (Prov.), China (än-hwā)	199	31.30 N	117.15 E
Aniak, Ak. (ä-nyȧ'k)	107	61.32 N	159.35 W
Anik (Neigh.), India	67e	19.02 N	72.53 E
Animas (R.), Co. (ä'nē-mȧs)	121	37.03 N	107.50 W
Anina, Rom. (ä-nē'nä)	173	45.03 N	21.50 E
Anita, Pa. (ȧ-nē'ȧ)	111	41.05 N	79.00 W
Aniva, Mys (Pt.), Sov.Un. (mĭs ȧ-nē'vȧ)	204	46.08 N	143.13 E
Aniva, Zaliv (B.), Sov. Un. (zä'lĭf ȧ-nē'vȧ)	204	46.28 N	143.30 E
Anjou, Can.	95a	45.37 N	73.33 W
Anjouan (I.), Comoros (äN-zhwäN)	227	12.14 S	44.47 E
Ankang, China (än-Käŋ)	202	32.38 N	109.10 E
Ankara (Angora), Tur. (än'kȧ-rȧ) (ăn-gō'rȧ)	179	39.55 N	32.50 E
Anklam, G.D.R. (än'kläm)	166	53.52 N	13.43 E
Ankoro, Zaire (ăŋ-kō'rō)	231	6.45 S	26.57 E
Anloga, Ghana	228	5.47 N	0.50 E
Anlong, China (än-loŋ)	203	25.01 N	105.32 E
Anlu, China (än'lōō')	203	31.18 N	113.40 E
Anna, Il. (ăn'ȧ)	123	37.28 N	89.15 W
Anna, Sov. Un. (än'ä)	175	51.31 N	40.27 E
Annaba (Bône), Alg.	224	36.57 N	7.39 E
Annaberg-Bucholz, G.D.R. (än'ä-bĕrgh)	166	50.35 N	13.02 E
An Nafūd (Des.), Sau. Ar.	192	28.30 N	40.30 E
An Najaf, Iraq (än nä-jäf')	192	32.00 N	44.25 E
An Nakhl, Egypt	191a	29.55 N	33.45 E
Annamese Cordillera (Mts.), Laos-Viet.	206	17.34 N	105.38 E
Annandale, Va.	56d	38.50 N	77.12 W
Annapolis, Md. (ă-năp'ō-lĭs)	112e	39.00 N	76.25 W
Annapolis Royal, Can.	104	44.45 N	65.31 W
Ann Arbor, Mi. (ăn är'bēr)	110	42.15 N	83.45 W
An-Narrānīyah, Egypt	71a	29.58 N	31.10 E
An Nāşirīyah, Iraq	192	31.08 N	46.15 E
An Nawfalīyah, Libya	225	30.57 N	17.38 E
Ann, C., Ma. (ăn)	111	42.40 N	70.40 W
Annecy, Fr. (ȧn sē')	169	45.54 N	6.07 E
Annemasse, Fr. (än'mäs')	169	46.09 N	6.13 E
Annen (Neigh.), F.R.G.	63	51.27 N	7.22 E
Annenskoye, Sov. Un. (ä-nĕn'skô-yĕ)	182a	53.09 N	60.25 E
Annet-sur-Marne, Fr.	64c	48.56 N	2.43 E
Annette I., Ak.	98	55.13 N	131.30 W
An-nhon, Viet.	206	13.55 N	109.00 E
Annieopsquotch Mts., Can.	105	48.37 N	57.17 W
Anniston, Al. (ăn'ĭs-tŭn)	126	33.39 N	85.47 W
Annobón (I.), Equat. Gui.	222	2.00 S	3.30 E
Annonay, Fr. ȧ-nō-nĕ')	168	45.16 N	4.36 E
Annotto Bay, Jam. (än-nō'tō)	134	18.15 N	76.45 W
An Nuhūd, Sud.	225	12.39 N	28.18 E
Anoka, Mn. (ȧ-nō'kȧ)	119g	45.12 N	93.24 W
Anori, Col. (ȧ-nō'rē)	142a	7.01 N	75.09 W
Áno Viánnos, Grc.	172a	35.02 N	25.26 E
Anpu, China (än-pōō)	203	21.28 N	110.00 E
Anqing, China (än-chĭŋ)	203	30.32 N	117.00 E
Anqiu, China (än-chyō)	200	36.26 N	119.12 E
Ansbach, F.R.G. (äns'bäk)	166	49.18 N	10.35 E
Anschlag, F.R.G.	63	51.10 N	7.29 E
Anse à Veau, Hai. (äNs' ä-vō')	135	18.30 N	73.25 W
Anse d' Hainault, Hai. (äNs'dĕnō)	135	18.45 N	74.25 W
Anserma, Col. (ȧ'n-sĕ'r-mȧ)	142a	5.13 N	75.47 W
Ansermanuevo, Col. (ȧ'n-sĕ'r-mȧ-nwĕ'vō)	142a	4.47 N	75.59 W
Anshan, China	202	41.00 N	123.00 E
Anshun, China (än-shōōn')	203	26.12 N	105.50 E
Anson, Tx. (ăn'sŭn)	124	32.45 N	99.52 W
Anson B., Austl.	214	13.10 S	130.00 E
Ansŏng, Kor. (än'sŭng')	204	37.00 N	127.12 E
Ansongo, Mali	228	15.40 N	0.30 E
Ansonia, Ct. (ăn-sōnĭ-ȧ)	111	41.20 N	73.05 W
Antakya, Tur. (än-täk'yä)	179	36.20 N	36.10 E
Antalya (Adalia), Tur. (än-tä'lē-ä) (ä-dä'lē-ä)	179	37.00 N	30.50 E
Antalya Körfezi (G.), Tur.	179	36.40 N	31.20 E
Antananarivo, Mad.	227	18.51 S	47.40 E
Antarctica,	232	80.15 S	127.00 E
Antartic Pen., Ant.	232	70.00 S	65.00 W
Antelope Cr., Wy. (ăn'tē-lōp)	117	43.29 N	105.42 W
Antequera, Sp. (än-tĕ-kĕ'rä)	170	37.01 N	4.34 W
Anthony, Ks. (ăn'thō-nē)	122	37.08 N	98.01 W
Anti Atlas (Mts.), Mor.	224	28.45 N	9.30 W
Antibes, Fr. (äN-tēb')	169	43.36 N	7.12 E
Anticosti, Île d' (I.), Can. (ăn-tĭ-kŏs'tē)	105	49.30 N	62.00 W
Antigo, Wi. (ăn'tĭ-gō)	115	45.09 N	89.11 W
Antigonish, Can. (ăn-tĭ-gō-nēsh')	105	45.35 N	61.55 W
Antigua, Guat. (än-tē'gwä)	132	14.32 N	90.43 W
Antigua, N.A.	129	17.15 N	61.15 W
Antigua (R.), Mex.	131	19.16 N	96.36 W
Antigua and Barbuda, N.A.	129	17.15 N	61.15 W
Antigua Veracruz, Mex. (än-tē'gwä vā-rä-krōōz')	131	19.18 N	96.17 W
Antiguo Lago de Texcoco, Vaso del (L.), Mex.	60a	19.30 N	99.00 W
Antilla, Cuba (än-tē'lyä)	135	20.50 N	75.50 W
Antilles, Greater (Is.), N.A.	129	20.30 N	79.15 W
Antilles, Lesser (Is.), N.A.	129	12.15 N	65.00 W
Antioch, Ca. (ăn'tĭ-ŏk)	118b	38.00 N	121.48 W
Antioch, Il.	113a	42.29 N	88.06 W
Antioch, Ne.	114	42.05 N	102.36 W
Antioquia, Col. (än-tē-ō'kēä)	142a	6.34 N	75.49 W
Antioquia (Dept.), Col.	142a	6.48 N	75.42 W
Antímano (Neigh.), Ven.	61a	10.28 N	66.59 W
Antlers, Ok. (ănt'lērz)	123	34.14 N	95.38 W
Antofagasta, Chile (än-tō-fä-gäs'tä)	144	23.32 N	70.21 W
Antofalla, Salar de (Des.), Arg. (sȧ-lȧr'de ȧn'tō-fä'lä)	144	26.00 S	67.52 W
Antón, Pan. (än-tōn')	133	8.24 N	80.15 W
Antongila, Helodrano (B.), Mad.	227	16.15 S	50.15 E
Antônio Carlos, Braz. (än-tō'nēōō-kȧ'r-lōs)	141a	21.19 S	43.45 W
António Enes, Moz. (ăn-to'nyŏ ĕn'ēs)	231	16.14 S	39.58 E
Antonito, Co. (ăn-tō-nē'tō)	122	37.04 N	106.01 W
Antonopole, Sov. Un. (än'tō-nō-pō lyĕ)	174	56.19 N	27.11 E
Antony, Fr.	64c	48.45 N	2.18 E
Antsirabe, Mad. (änt-sē-rä'bā)	227	19.49 S	47.16 E
Antsiranana, Mad.	227	12.18 S	49.16 E
Antsla, Sov. Un. (änt'slȧ)	174	57.49 N	26.29 E
Antuco (Vol.), Chile (än-tōō'kō)	144	37.30 S	72.30 W
Antwerp, S. Afr.	71b	26.06 S	28.10 E
Antwerpen (Antwerp), Bel. (ănt'wērpĕn)	157a	51.13 N	4.24 E
Antwerp, see Antwerpen			
Anūpgarh, India (ŭ-nōōp'gŭr)	196	29.22 N	73.20 E
Anuradhapura, Sri Lanka (ŭ-nōō'rä-dŭ-pōō'rŭ)	197	8.24 N	80.25 E
Anxi, China (än-shyē)	198	40.36 N	95.49 E
Anyang, China (än'yäng)	200	36.05 N	114.22 E
Anykščiai, Sov. Un. (anĭksh-chȧ'ē)	165	55.34 N	25.04 E
Anzá, Col. (ȧn-zȧ')	142a	6.19 N	75.51 W
Anzhero-Sudzhensk, Sov. Un. (än'zhâ-rō-sōōd'zhĕnsk)	180	56.08 N	86.08 E
Anzio, It. (änt'zē-ō)	171d	41.28 N	12.39 E
Anzoátegui (State), Ven. (ȧn-zōȧ'tĕ-gē)	143b	9.38 N	64.45 W
Aomori, Jap. (äō-mō'rē)	204	40.45 N	140.52 E
Aosta, It. (ä-ôs'tä)	172	45.45 N	7.20 E
Aoukâr (Pln.), Mauritania	228	18.00 N	9.40 W
Aouk, Bahr (R.), Chad-Cen. Afr. Rep. (ä-ōōk')	225	9.30 N	20.45 E
Aozou, Chad	194	21.49 N	17.25 E
Apalachicola, Fl. (ăp-ȧ-lăch-ĭ-kō'lȧ)	126	29.43 N	84.59 W
Apan, Mex. (ä-pȧ'n)	131a	19.43 N	98.27 W
Apango, Mex. (ä-päŋ'gō)	130	17.41 N	99.22 W
Apaporis (R.), Col. (ä-pä-pō'rĭs)	142	0.48 N	72.32 W
Aparri, Phil. (ä-pär'rē)	206	18.15 N	121.40 E
Apasco, Mex. (ä-pȧ's-kō)	130	20.33 N	100.43 W
Apatin, Yugo. (ŏ'pō-tĭn)	173	45.40 N	19.00 E
Apatzingán de la Constitución, Mex. (ä-pät-zĭŋ-gän'dā lä cōn-stĭ-tōō-sē-ōn')	130	19.07 N	102.21 W
Apeldoorn, Neth. (ä'pĕl-dōōrn)	163	52.14 N	5.55 E
Apese (Neigh.), Nig.	71d	6.25 N	3.25 E
Apía, Col. (ȧ-pē'ä)	142a	5.07 N	75.58 W
Apipilulco, Mex. (ä-pĭ-pĭ-lōōl'kō)	130	18.09 N	99.40 W
Apishapa (R.), Co. (ăp-ĭ-shä'pȧ)	122	37.40 N	104.08 W
Apizaco, Mex. (ä-pē-zä'kō)	130	19.18 N	98.11 W
Aplerbeck (Neigh.), F.R.G.	63	51.29 N	7.33 E
Apo (Mtn.), Phil. (ä'pō)	207	6.56 N	125.05 E
Apopka, Fl. (ä-pŏp'kȧ)	127a	28.37 N	81.30 W
Apopka (L.), Fl.	127a	28.38 N	81.50 W
Apoquindo, Chile	61b	33.24 S	70.32 W
Apostle Is., Wi. (ă-pŏs'l)	115	47.05 N	90.55 W
Appalachia, Va. (ăpȧ-lăch'ĭ-ȧ)	126	36.54 N	82.49 W
Appalachian Mts., U.S. (ăp-ȧ-lăch'ĭ-ȧn)	109	37.20 N	82.00 W
Appalachicola R., Fl. (ăpȧ-lăch'ĭ-cōlă)	126	30.11 N	85.00 W
Äppelbo, Swe. (ĕp-ĕl-bōō)	164	60.30 N	14.02 E
Appelhülsen, F.R.G. (ä'pĕl-hül'sĕn)	169c	51.55 N	7.26 E
Appennino (Mts.), It. (äp-pĕn-nē'nō)	172	43.48 N	11.06 E
Appleton, Mn. (ăp'l-tŭn)	114	45.10 N	96.01 W
Appleton, Wi.	115	44.14 N	88.27 W
Appleton City, Mo.	123	38.10 N	94.02 W
Appomattox (R.), Va. (ăp-ō-măt'ŭks)	127	37.22 N	78.09 W
Aprília, It. (ȧ-prē'lyȧ)	171d	41.36 N	12.40 E
Apsheronskiy, P-Ov. (Pen.), Sov. Un.	179	40.20 N	50.30 E
Apt, Fr. (äpt)	169	43.54 N	5.19 E
Apulia (Reg.), **see Puglia**			
Apure (R.), Ven. (ä-pōō'rā)	142	8.08 N	68.46 W
Apurimac (R.), Peru (ä-pōō-rē-mäk')	142	11.39 S	73.48 W
Aqaba, G. of, Asia (ä'kȧ-bȧ)	161	28.30 N	34.40 E
Aqabah, Wādī al (R.), Egypt	191a	29.48 N	34.05 E
Aquasco, Md. (ȧ'gwȧ'scō)	112e	38.35 N	76.44 W
Aquidauana, Braz. (ä-kē-däwä'nä)	143	20.24 S	55.46 W
Aquin, Hai. (ä-kăn')	135	18.20 N	73.25 W
Ara (R.), Jap. (ä-rä)	205a	35.40 N	139.52 E
'Arabah, Wādī, Egypt	223b	29.02 N	32.10 E
Arabatskaya Strelka (Tongue of Arabat) (Spit), Sov. Un. (ä-rä-băt' skȧ-yȧ strĕl'kȧ) (ă-rȧ-băt')	175	45.50 N	35.05 E
Arab, Baḩr al- (R.), Sud.	225	9.46 N	26.52 E
Arabi, La.	112d	29.58 N	90.01 W
Arabian Des. (Aş Şaḩrā' ash Sharqīyah), Egypt (ȧ-rā'bĭ-ăn)	223b	27.06 N	32.49 E
Arabian Pen., Asia	222	28.00 N	40.00 E
Arabian Sea, Asia (ȧ-rā'bĭ-ăn)	190	16.00 N	65.15 E
Aracaju, Braz. (ä-rä'kä-zhōō')	143	11.00 S	37.01 W
Aracati, Braz. (ä-rä'kä-tē')	143	4.31 S	37.41 W
Araçatuba, Braz. (ä-rä-sȧ-tōō'bä)	143	21.14 S	50.19 W
Aracena, Sp.	170	37.53 N	6.34 W
Aracruz, Braz. (ä-rä-krōō's)	143	19.58 S	40.11 W
Araçuaí, Braz. (ä-rä-sōō-ä-ē')	143	16.57 S	41.56 W
'Arad, Isr.	191a	31.20 N	35.15 E
Arad, Rom. (ŏ'rŏd)	167	46.10 N	21.18 E
Aradabīl, Iran	192	38.15 N	48.00 E
Arafura Sea, Oceania (ä-rä-fōō'rä)	208	8.40 S	130.00 E
Aragon (Reg.), Sp. (ä-rä-gōn')	171	40.55 N	0.45 W
Aragón (R.), Sp.	170	42.35 N	1.10 W
Aragua (State), Ven. (ä-rä'gwä)	143b	10.00 N	67.05 W
Aragua de Barcelona, Ven. (ä-rä'gwä dā bär-thā-lō'nä)	143b	9.29 N	64.48 W
Araguaía (R.), Braz. (ä-rä-gwä'yä)	143	8.37 S	49.43 W
Araguari, Braz. (ä-rä-gwä'rē)	143	18.43 S	48.03 W
Araguatins, Braz. (ä-rä-gwä-tēns)	143	5.41 S	48.04 W
Aragüita, Ven. (ärȧ-gwē'tȧ)	143b	10.13 N	66.28 W
Araj (Oasis), Egypt (ä-räj')	161	29.05 N	26.51 E
Arāk, Iran	192	34.08 N	49.57 E
Arakan Yoma (Mts.), Bur. (ŭ-rŭ-kŭn'yō'mȧ)	198	19.51 N	94.13 E
Arakawa (Neigh.), Jap.	69a	35.47 N	139.44 E
Arakhthos (R.), Grc. (är'äK-thōs)	173	39.10 N	21.05 E
Arakpur (Neigh.), India	67d	28.35 N	77.10 E
Aral Sea, see Aral'skoye More			
Aral'sk, Sov. Un. (ȧ-rälsk')	180	46.47 N	62.00 E
Aral'skoye More (Aral Sea), Sov. Un.	155	45.17 N	60.02 E
Aralsor (L.), Sov. Un. (ȧ-räl'sôr')	179	49.00 N	48.20 E
Aramberri, Mex. (ä-rȧm-bĕr-rē')	130	24.05 N	99.47 W
Arana, Sierra (Mts.), Sp.	170	37.17 N	3.28 W
Aranda de Duero, Sp. (ä-rän'dä dā dwā'rō)	170	41.43 N	3.45 W
Arandas, Mex. (ä-rän'däs)	130	20.43 N	102.18 W
Aran I., Ire. (ăr'ăn)	162	54.58 N	8.33 W
Aran Is., Ire.	162	53.04 N	9.59 W
Aranjuez, Sp. (ä-rän-hwāth')	170	40.02 N	3.24 W
Aransas Pass, Tx. (ȧ-răn'sȧs pȧs)	125	27.55 N	97.09 W
Araouane, Mali	228	18.54 N	3.33 W
Arapkir, Tur. (ä-räp-kēr')	179	39.00 N	38.10 E
Araraquara, Braz. (ä-rä-rä-kwȧ'rä)	143	21.47 S	48.08 W
Araras, Braz. (ä-rȧ'răs)	141a	22.21 S	47.22 W
Araras, Serra das (Mts.), Braz. (sĕ'r-rä-däs-ä-rä'räs)	143	18.03 S	53.23 W
Araras, Serra das (Mts.), Braz.	144b	22.24 S	43.15 W
Araras, Serra das (Mts.), Braz.	144	23.30 S	53.00 W
Ararat, Austl. (ăr'ȧrăt)	216	37.17 S	142.56 E
Ararat (Mtn.), Tur.	179	39.50 N	44.20 E
Arari (L.), Braz. (ä-rȧ'rē)	143	0.30 S	48.50 W
Araripe, Chapada do (Plain), Braz. (shä-pä'dä-dō-ä-rä-rē'pĕ)	143	5.55 S	40.42 W
Araruama, Braz. (ä-rä-rōō-ä'mä)	141a	22.53 S	42.19 W
Araruama, Lagoa de (L.), Braz. (lȧ-gôä-dĕ-ä-rä-rōō-ä'mä)	141a	23.00 S	42.15 W
Aras (R.), Iran-Sov. Un. (ȧ-räs)	179	39.15 N	47.10 E
Aratuípe, Braz. (ä-rä-tōō-ē'pĕ)	143	13.12 S	38.58 W
Arauca, Col. (ä-rou'kä)	142	6.56 N	70.45 W
Arauca (R.), Ven.	142	7.13 N	68.43 W
Aravaca (Neigh.), Sp.	65b	40.28 N	3.46 W
Aravalli Ra., India (ä-rä'vŭ-lē)	196	24.15 N	72.40 E
Araxá, Braz. (ä-rä-shȧ')	143	19.41 S	46.46 W
Araya, Punta de (Pt.), Ven. (pŭn'tȧ-dĕ-ä-rä'yȧ)	143b	10.40 N	64.15 W
Arayat, Phil. (ä-rä'yät)	207a	15.10 N	120.44 E
'Arbi, Sud.	225	20.36 N	29.57 E
Arboga, Swe. (är-bō'gä)	164	59.26 N	15.50 E
Arborea, It. (är-bō-rĕ'ä)	172	39.50 N	8.36 E
Arbroath, Scot. (är-brōth')	162	56.36 N	2.25 W
Arcachon, Fr. (är-Kä-shôN')	168	44.39 N	1.12 W
Arcachon, Bassin d' (Basin), Fr. (bä-sĕn' där-kä-shôn')	168	44.42 N	1.50 W
Arcadia, Ca. (är-kā'dĭ-ȧ)	119a	34.08 N	118.02 W
Arcadia, Fl.	127a	27.12 N	81.51 W
Arcadia, La.	125	32.33 N	92.56 W
Arcadia, Wi.	115	44.15 N	91.30 W
Arcata, Ca. (är-kȧ'tȧ)	116	40.54 N	124.05 W
Arc de Triomphe (P. Int.), Fr.	64c	48.53 N	2.17 E
Arc Dome Mtn., Nv. (ärk dōm)	120	38.51 N	117.21 W
Arcelia, Mex. (är-sā'lē-ä)	130	18.19 N	100.14 W
Archbald, Pa. (ärch'bôld)	111	41.30 N	75.35 W
Arches Natl. Park, Ut. (är'ches)	121	38.45 N	109.35 W
Archidona, Ec. (är-chē-do'nä)	142	1.01 S	77.49 W
Archidona, Sp. (är-chē-dō'nä)	170	37.08 N	4.24 W
Arcis-sur-Aube, Fr. (är-sēs'sûr-ōb')	168	48.31 N	4.04 E
Arco, Id. (är'kō)	117	43.39 N	113.15 W
Arcola, Tx.	125a	29.30 N	95.28 W
Arcola, Va. (ăr'cōlă)	112e	38.57 N	77.32 W
Arcos de la Frontera, Sp. (är'kōs-dĕ-lä-frōn-tĕ'rä)	170	36.44 N	5.48 W
Arctic Ocean (ärk'tĭk)	91		
Arcueil, Fr.	64c	48.48 N	2.20 E
Arda (R.), Bul. (är'dä)	173	41.36 N	25.18 E
Ardabīl, Iran	195	38.15 N	48.18 E
Ardahan, Tur. (är-dȧ-hän')	179	41.10 N	42.40 E
Ardatov, Sov. Un. (är-dȧ-tôf')	178	54.58 N	46.10 E

ăt; finăl; rāte; senāte; ärm; ȧsk; sofȧ; fâre; ch-choose; dh-as th in other; bē; ēvent; bĕt; recĕnt; cratēr; g-gō; gh-guttural g; bĭt; ĭ-short neutral; rīde; K-guttural k as ch in German ich;

PLACE (Pronounciation)	PAGE	Lat. °'	Long. °'
Ardennes (Mts.), Bel. (ȧr-dĕn')	163	50.01 N	5.12 E
Ardey (Neigh.), F.R.G.	63	51.26 N	7.23 E
Ardila (R.), Port. (är-dē'lä)	170	38.10 N	7.15 W
Ardmore, Md.	56d	38.56 N	76.52 W
Ardmore, Ok. (ärd'mōr)	123	34.10 N	97.08 W
Ardmore, Pa.	112f	40.01 N	75.18 W
Ardrossan, Can. (är-dros'ȧn)	95g	53.33 N	113.08 W
Ardsley, Eng. (ärdz'lē)	156	53.43 N	1.33 W
Åre, Swe.	158	63.12 N	13.12 E
Arecibo, P.R. (ä-rā-sē'bō)	129b	18.28 N	66.45 W
Areeiro, Port.	65d	38.39 N	9.12 W
Areia Branca, Braz. (ä-rĕ'yä-brä'n-kä)	143	4.58 S	37.02 W
Arena, Pt., Ca. (ä-rā'nȧ)	120	38.57 N	123.40 W
Arenas de San Pedro, Sp. (ä-rā'nȧs dā sän pā'drō)	170	40.12 N	5.04 W
Arenas, Punta (Pt.), Ven. (pōō'n-tä-rĕ'näs)	143b	10.57 N	64.24 W
Arendal, Nor. (ä'rĕn-däl)	164	58.29 N	8.44 E
Arendonk, Bel.	157a	51.19 N	5.07 E
Arequipa, Peru (ä-rā-kē'pä)	142	16.27 S	71.30 W
Arezzo, It. (ä-rĕt'sō)	172	43.28 N	11.54 E
Arga (R.), Sp. (är'gä)	170	42.35 N	1.55 W
Arganda, Sp. (är-gän'dä)	171a	40.18 N	3.27 W
Argazi (L.), Sov. Un. (är'gä-zĭ)	182a	55.24 N	60.37 E
Argazi R., Sov. Un.	182a	55.33 N	57.30 E
Argentan, Fr. (ȧr-zhäN-täN')	168	48.45 N	0.01 W
Argentat, Fr. (ȧr-zhäN-tȧ')	168	45.07 N	1.57 E
Argenteuil, Fr. (är-zhäN-tû'y')	169b	48.56 N	2.15 E
Argentina, S.A. (är-jĕn-tē'nȧ)	140	35.30 S	67.00 W
Argentino (L.), Arg. (är-Kĕn-tē'nō)	144	50.15 S	72.45 W
Argenton-sur-Creuse, Fr. (är-zhäN'tôN-sür-krôs)	168	46.34 N	1.28 E
Argeş (R.), Rom. (ȧr'zhĕsh)	173	44.27 N	25.22 E
Argolikos Kólpos (G.), Grc.	173	37.20 N	23.00 E
Argonne (Mts.), Fr. (ä'r-gôn)	168	49.21 N	5.54 E
Argos, Grc. (är'gŏs)	173	37.38 N	22.45 E
Argostólion, Grc. (är-gŏs-tŏ'lē-ōn)	173	38.10 N	20.30 E
Arguello, Pt., Ca. (är-gwāl'yō)	120	34.35 N	120.40 W
Argungu, Nig.	229	12.45 N	4.31 E
Argun R., China-Sov. Un. (ár-gōōn')	181	50.15 N	118.45 E
Argyle, Can. (är'gīl)	95f	50.11 N	97.27 W
Argyle, Mn.	114	48.21 N	96.48 W
Århus, Den. (ôr'hōōs)	164	56.09 N	10.10 E
Ariakeno-Umi (Sea), Jap. (ä-rē'ä-Kä'nō ōō'nē)	205	33.03 N	130.18 E
Ariake-Wan (B.), Jap. (ä'rē-ä'kȧ wän)	205	31.19 N	131.15 E
Ariano, It. (ä-rē-ä'nō)	172	41.09 N	15.11 E
Ariari (R.), Col. (ä-ryȧ'rē)	142a	3.34 N	73.42 W
Aribinda, Upper Volta	228	14.14 N	0.52 W
Arica, Chile (ä-rē'kä)	142	18.34 S	70.14 W
Arichat, Can. (ä-rĭ-shät')	105	45.31 N	61.01 W
Ariège (R.), Fr. (ȧ-rē-ĕzh')	168	43.26 N	1.29 E
Ariel, Wa. (â'rĭ-ĕl)	118c	45.57 N	122.34 W
Arieşul (R.), Rom. (ä-rē-ā'shōōl)	167	46.25 N	23.15 E
Ariguanabo, L. de, Cuba (lä'gô-dĕ-ä-rē-gwä-nä'bō)	135a	22.17 N	82.33 W
Arikaree (R.), Co. (ä-rĭ-kȧ-rē')	122	39.51 N	102.18 W
Arima, Jap. (ä'rē-mä')	205b	34.48 N	135.16 E
Aringay, Phil. (ä-rĭŋ-gä'ē)	207a	16.25 N	120.20 E
Arino (Neigh.), Jap.	69b	34.50 N	135.14 E
Arinos (R.), Braz. (ä-rē'nôzsh)	143	12.09 S	56.49 W
Arīḥā (Jericho), Jordan	191a	31.51 N	35.28 E
'Arīsh, Wādī al (R.), Egypt (ȧ-rēsh')	191a	30.36 N	34.07 E
Aripuanã (R.), Braz. (ȧ-rē-pwän'yȧ)	143	7.06 S	60.29 W
Aristazabal I., Can.	98	52.30 N	129.20 W
Arizona (State), U.S. (ăr-ĭ-zō'nȧ)	108	34.00 N	113.00 W
Arjona, Sp. (är-hō'nä)	170	37.58 N	4.03 W
Arka (R.), Sov. Un.	181	60.12 N	142.30 E
Arkabutla Res., Ms. (är-kȧ-bŭt'lȧ)	126	34.48 N	90.00 W
Arkadelphia, Ar. (är-kȧ-dĕl'fĭ-ȧ)	123	34.06 N	93.05 W
Arkansas (State), U.S. (är'kăn-sô) (är-kăn'sȧs)	109	34.50 N	93.40 W
Arkansas City, Ks.	123	37.04 N	97.02 W
Arkansas R., Ok.	123	35.20 N	94.56 W
Arkhangelsk (Archangel), Sov. Un. (ȧr-Kän'gĕlsk)	178	64.30 N	40.25 E
Arkhangel'skiy, Sov. Un. (är-kän-gĕl'skĭ)	182a	52.52 N	61.53 E
Arkhangel'skoye, Sov. Un. (är-kän-gĕl'skô-yĕ)	182a	54.25 N	56.48 E
Arklow, Ire. (ärk'lō)	162	52.47 N	6.10 W
Arkona, Kap (C.), G.D.R. (är'kō-nä)	164	54.43 N	13.43 E
Arkonam, India (är-kō-näm')	197	13.05 N	79.43 E
Arlanza (R.), Sp. (är-län-thä')	170	42.08 N	3.45 W
Arlanzón (R.), Sp. (är-län-thōn')	170	42.12 N	3.58 W
Arlberg Tun., Aus. (ärl'bĕrgh)	166	47.05 N	10.15 E
Arles, Fr. (ärl)	168	43.42 N	4.38 E
Arlington, Ga. (är'lĭng-tun')	126	31.25 N	84.42 W
Arlington, Ma.	105a	42.26 N	71.13 W
Arlington, S. Afr.	223d	28.02 S	27.52 E
Arlington, SD (är'lĕng-tŭn)	114	44.23 N	97.09 W
Arlington, Tx. (ȧr'lĭng-tŭn)	119c	32.44 N	97.07 W
Arlington, Va.	112e	38.55 N	77.10 W
Arlington, Vt.	111	43.05 N	73.05 W
Arlington, Wa.	118a	48.11 N	122.08 W
Arlington Heights, Il. (ar'lĕng-tŭn-hī'ts)	113a	42.05 N	87.59 W
Arlington National Cemetery (P. Int.), Va.	56d	38.53 N	77.04 W
Arltunga, Austl. (ärl-tōōŋ'gȧ)	214	23.19 S	134.45 E
Arma, Ks. (är'mȧ)	123	37.34 N	94.43 W
Armagh, Can. (är-mä') (är-mäK')	95b	46.45 N	70.36 W
Armagh, N. Ire.	162	54.21 N	6.25 W
Armant, Egypt (är-mänt')	223b	25.37 N	32.32 E
Armaro, Col. (är-mȧ'rō)	142a	4.58 N	74.54 W
Armavir, Sov. Un. (ȧr-mȧ-vĭr')	179	45.00 N	41.00 E
Armenia, Col. (är-mĕ'nēȧ)	142a	4.33 N	75.40 W
Armenia, Sal. (är-mā'nē-ä)	132	13.44 N	89.31 W
Armenian, S. S. R., Sov. Un.	176	41.00 N	44.39 E
Armentières, Fr. (ȧr-män-tyâr')	168	50.43 N	2.53 E
Armeria, Rio de (R.), Mex. (rē'ō-dĕ-är-mȧ-rē'ä)	130	19.36 N	104.10 W
Armherstburg, Can. (ärm'hĕrst-bōōrgh)	113b	42.06 N	83.06 W
Armidale, Austl. (är'mĭ-dāl)	216	30.27 S	151.50 E
Armour, SD (är'mẽr)	114	43.18 N	98.21 W
Armstrong Station, Can. (ärm'strŏng)	102	50.21 N	89.00 W
Armyansk, Sov. Un. (ärm'yȧnsk)	175	46.06 N	33.42 E
Arnedo, Sp. (är-nā'dō)	170	42.12 N	2.03 W
Arnhem, Neth. (ärn'hĕm)	163	51.58 N	5.56 E
Arnhem, C., Austl.	214	12.15 S	137.00 E
Arnhem Land, (Reg.), Austl. (ärn'hĕm-lănd)	214	13.15 S	133.00 E
Arno (R.), It. (ä'r-nō)	172	43.45 N	10.42 E
Arnold, Eng. (är'nŭld)	156	53.00 N	1.08 W
Arnold, Mn. (ȧr'nŭld)	119h	46.53 N	92.06 W
Arnold, Pa.	113e	40.35 N	79.45 W
Arnouville-lès-Gonesse, Fr.	64c	49.00 N	2.25 E
Arnprior, Can. (ärn-prī'ēr)	111	45.25 N	76.20 W
Arnsberg, F.R.G. (ärns'bĕrgh)	163	51.25 N	8.02 E
Arnstadt, G.D.R. (ärn'shtät)	166	50.51 N	10.57 E
Aroab, Namibia (är'ō-ȧb)	226	25.40 S	19.45 E
Aroostook (R.), Me. (ȧ-rōōs'tŏŏk)	104	46.44 N	68.15 W
Aroroy, Phil. (ä-rō-rō'ē)	207a	12.30 N	123.24 E
Arpajon, Fr. (ăr-pä-jō'n)	169b	48.35 N	2.15 E
Arpoador, Ponta do (Pt.), Braz. (pô'n-tä-dō-är'pōä-dō'r)	144b	22.59 S	43.11 W
Arraiolos, Port. (är-rī-ō'lōzh)	170	38.47 N	7.59 W
Ar Ramādī, Iraq	192	33.30 N	43.12 E
Arran, Island of, Scot. (ă'răn)	162	55.25 N	5.25 W
Ar Rank, Sud.	225	11.45 N	32.53 E
Arras, Fr. (ȧ-räs')	168	50.21 N	2.40 E
Ar Rawḍah, Egypt	223b	27.47 N	30.52 E
Arrecifes, Arg. (är-rā-sē'fās)	141c	34.03 S	60.05 W
Arrecifes (R.), Arg.	141c	34.07 S	59.50 W
Arrée, Mts. d', Fr. (är-rā')	168	48.27 N	4.00 W
Arriaga, Mex. (är-rēä'gä)	131	16.15 N	93.54 W
Ar Riyāḍ, see Riyadh			
Arrone (R.), It.	171d	41.57 N	12.17 E
Arrowhead, L., Ca. (lăk ăr'ōhĕd)	119a	34.17 N	117.13 W
Arrow R., Mt. (ăr'ō)	117	47.29 N	109.53 W
Arrowrock Res., Id. (ăr'ō-rŏk)	116	43.40 N	115.30 W
Arroya Arena, Cuba (är-rô'yä-rē'nä)	135a	23.01 N	82.30 W
Arroyo de la Luz, Sp. (är-rō'yō-dĕ-lä-lōō'z)	170	39.39 N	6.46 W
Arroyo Grande (R.), Mex. (är-rô'yō-grä'n-dĕ)	130	23.30 N	98.45 W
Arroyo Seco, Mex. (är-rō'yō sä'kō)	130	21.31 N	99.44 W
Ar Rub' Al Khālī (Des.), Sau. Ar.	192	20.30 N	49.15 E
Ar-Ruşayriş, Sud.	225	11.38 N	34.42 E
Ar-Ruṭbah, Iraq	195	33.02 N	40.17 E
Arsen'yev, Sov. Un.	181	44.13 N	133.32 E
Arsinskiy, Sov. Un. (är-sĭn'skĭ)	182a	53.46 N	59.54 E
Árta, Grc. (är'tä)	173	39.08 N	21.02 E
Artarmon, Austl.	70a	33.49 S	151.11 E
Arteaga, Mex. (är-tä-ä'gä)	124	25.28 N	100.50 W
Artëm, Sov. Un. (ȧr-tyôm')	181	43.28 N	132.29 E
Artemisa, Cuba (är-tȧ-mē'sä)	134	22.50 N	82.45 W
Artëmovsk, Sov. Un. (ȧr-tyŏm'ŏfsk)	175	48.37 N	38.00 E
Arteria, Ca.	59	33.52 N	118.05 W
Artesia, NM (är-tē'sĭ-ȧ)	122	32.44 N	104.23 W
Artesian Basin, The, Austl. (är-tē'zhăn)	216	26.45 S	141.40 E
Arthabaska, Can.	104	46.03 N	71.54 W
Arthur's Town, Ba.	135	24.40 N	75.40 W
Arti, Sov. Un. (är'tĭ)	182a	56.20 N	58.38 E
Artibonite (R.), Hai. (är-tē-bō-nē'tä)	135	19.00 N	72.25 W
Artigas (Neigh.), Ven.	61a	10.30 N	66.56 W
Arua, Ug. (ä'rōō-ä)	231	3.01 N	30.55 E
Aruba, (I.), Neth. Antilles (ä-rōō'bȧ)	142	12.29 N	70.00 W
Aru, Kepulauan (Is.), Indon.	207	6.20 S	133.00 E
Arunachal Pradesh (Union Ter.), India	198	27.35 N	92.56 E
Arundel Gardens, Md.	56c	39.13 N	76.37 W
Arundel Village, Md.	56c	39.13 N	76.36 W
Arusha, Tan. (ȧ-rōō'shä)	231	3.22 S	36.41 E
Arvida, Can.	103	48.26 N	71.11 W
Arvika, Swe. (är-vē'kȧ)	164	59.41 N	12.35 E
Arzamas, Sov. Un. (är-zä-mäs')	178	55.20 N	43.52 E
Arziw, Alg.	160	35.50 N	0.20 W
Arzua, Sp. (är-thōō'ä)	170	42.54 N	8.19 W
As, Czech. (äsh')	166	50.12 N	12.13 E
Asahi-Gawa (Strm.), Jap. (ä-sä'hē-gä'wä)	205	35.01 N	133.40 E
Asahikawa, Jap.	204	43.50 N	142.09 E
Asaka, Jap. (ä-sä'kä)	205a	35.47 N	139.36 E
Asālafpur (Neigh.), India	67d	28.38 N	77.05 E
Asansol, India	196	23.45 N	86.58 E
Asbest, Sov. Un. (äs-bĕst')	182a	57.02 N	61.28 E
Asbestos, Can. (ăs-bĕs'tŏs)	104	45.49 N	71.52 W
Asbestovskiy, Sov. Un.	182a	57.46 N	61.23 E
Asbury Park, NJ (ăz'bĕr-ĭ)	112a	40.13 N	74.01 W
Ascención, Bahía de la (B.), Mex. (bä-ē'ä-dĕ-lä-äs-sĕn-sē-ōn')	132a	19.39 N	87.30 W
Ascensión, Mex. (äs-sĕn-sē-ōn')	130	24.21 N	99.54 W
Ascension (I.), Atl. O. (ȧ-sĕn'shŭn)	222	8.00 S	13.00 W
Ascent, S. Afr. (ȧs-ĕnt')	223d	27.14 S	29.06 E
Aschaffenburg, F.R.G. (ä-shäf'ĕn-bōōrgh)	166	49.58 N	9.12 E
Ascheberg, F.R.G. (ä'shĕ-bĕrg)	169c	51.47 N	7.38 E
Aschersleben, G.D.R. (äsh'ērs-lā-bĕn)	166	51.46 N	11.28 E
Ascoli Piceno, It. (äs'kô-lēpē-chā'nō)	172	42.50 N	13.55 E
Aseb, Eth.	223a	12.52 N	43.39 E
Asenovgrad, Bul.	173	42.00 N	24.49 E
Aseri, Sov. Un. (ȧ'sĕ-rĭ)	174	59.26 N	26.58 E
Asfi, see Safi			
Asha, Sov. Un. (ä'shä)	182a	55.01 N	57.17 E
Ashabula (L.), ND (ăsh'ȧ-bū-lä)	114	47.07 N	97.51 W
Ashan, Sov. Un. (ä'shän)	182a	57.08 N	56.25 E
Ashbourne, Eng. (ăsh'bŭrn)	156	53.01 N	1.44 W
Ashburn, Ga. (ăsh'bŭrn)	126	31.42 N	83.42 W
Ashburn, Va.	112e	39.02 N	77.30 W
Ashburton (R.), Austl. (ăsh'bûr-tŭn)	214	22.30 S	115.30 E
Ashby-de-la-Zouch, Eng. (ăsh'bĭ-dĕ-lȧ zōōsh')	156	52.44 N	1.23 W
Ashdod, Isr.	191a	31.46 N	34.39 E
Ashdown, Ar. (ăsh'doun)	123	33.41 N	94.07 W
Asheboro, NC (ăsh'bŭr-ô)	127	35.41 N	79.50 W
Asherton, Tx. (ăsh'ēr-tŭn)	124	28.26 N	99.45 W
Asheville, NC (ăsh'vĭl)	127	35.35 N	82.35 W
Ashfield, Austl.	70a	33.53 S	151.08 E
Ashford, Eng.	62	51.26 N	0.27 W
Ash Fork, Az.	121	35.13 N	112.29 W
Ashikaga, Jap. (ä'shē-kä'gȧ)	205	36.22 N	139.26 E
Ashiya, Jap. (ä'shē-yä')	205	33.54 N	130.40 E
Ashiya, Jap.	205b	34.44 N	135.18 E
Ashizuri-Zaki (Pt.), Jap. (ä-shē-zōō-rē zä-kē)	205	32.43 N	133.04 E
Ashkhabad, Sov. Un. (ŭsh-kä-bät')	155	39.45 N	58.13 E
Ashland, Al. (ăsh'lănd)	126	33.15 N	85.50 W
Ashland, Ks.	122	37.11 N	99.46 W
Ashland, Ky.	110	38.25 N	82.40 W
Ashland, Ma.	105a	42.16 N	71.28 W
Ashland, Me.	104	46.37 N	68.26 W
Ashland, Ne.	114	41.02 N	96.23 W
Ashland, Oh.	110	40.50 N	82.15 W
Ashland, Or.	116	42.12 N	122.42 W
Ashland, Pa.	111	40.45 N	76.20 W
Ashland, Wi.	115	46.34 N	90.55 W
Ashley, Eng.	64b	53.21 N	2.20 W
Ashley, ND (ăsh'lē)	114	46.03 N	99.23 W
Ashley, Pa.	111	41.15 N	75.55 W
Ashley Green, Eng.	62	51.44 N	0.35 W
Ashmore Rf., Indon. (ăsh'mōr)	206	12.08 S	122.45 E
Ashmūn, Egypt (ȧsh-mōōn')	223b	30.19 N	30.57 E
Ashqelon, Isr. (äsh'kĕ-lōn)	191a	31.40 N	34.36 E
Ash Shabb, Egypt (shĕb)	225	22.34 N	29.52 E
Ash Shallūfah, Egypt (shäl'lōō-fȧ)	223c	30.09 N	32.33 E
Ash Shaqrā', Sau. Ar.	192	25.10 N	45.08 E
Ash Shāriqah, U.A.E.	195	25.22 N	55.23 E
Ash Shawbak, Jordan	191a	30.31 N	35.35 E
Ash Shiḥr, P.D.R. of Yem.	192	14.45 N	49.32 E
Ashtabula, Oh. (ăsh-tȧ-bū'lȧ)	110	41.55 N	80.50 W
Ashtead, Eng.	62	51.19 N	0.18 W
Ashton, Id. (ăsh'tŭn)	117	44.04 N	111.28 W
Ashton-in-Makerfield, Eng. (ăsh'tŭn-ĭn-māk'ēr-fēld)	156	53.29 N	2.39 W
Ashton-under-Lyne, Eng. (ăsh'tŭn-ŭn-dēr-līn')	156	53.29 N	2.04 W
Ashton upon Mersey, Eng.	64b	53.26 N	2.19 W
Ashuanipi (L.), Can. (ăsh-wȧ-nĭp'ĭ)	97	52.40 N	67.42 W
Ashukino, Sov. Un. (ȧ-shōō'kĭnô)	182b	56.10 N	37.57 E
Asia Minor, Asia (ā'zhȧ)	155	38.18 N	31.18 E
Asia (ā'zhȧ)	190		
Asientos, Mex. (ä-sē-ĕn'tōs)	130	22.13 N	102.05 W
Asilah, Mor.	170	35.30 N	6.05 W
Asinara (I.), It.	172	41.02 N	8.22 E
Asinara, Golfo dell' (G.), It. (gôl'fō-dĕl-ä-sē-nä'rä)	172	40.58 N	8.28 E
Asīr (Reg.), Sau. Ar. (ä-sēr')	192	19.30 N	42.00 E
Asir, Ras (C.), Som.	223a	11.55 N	51.30 E
Askarovo, Sov. Un. (äs-kä-rô'vô)	182a	53.21 N	58.32 E
Askersund, Swe. (äs'kĕr-sōōnd)	164	58.43 N	14.53 E
Askino, Sov. Un. (äs'kĭ-nô)	182a	56.06 N	56.29 E
Asmera, Eth. (äs-mä'rä)	225	15.17 N	38.56 E
Asnieres, Fr. (ä-nyâr')	169b	48.55 N	2.18 E
Asosa, Eth.	225	10.13 N	34.28 E
Asotin, Wa. (ȧ-sō'tĭn)	116	46.19 N	117.01 W
Aspen, Co. (ăs'pĕn)	121	39.15 N	106.55 W
Asperen, Neth.	157a	51.52 N	5.07 E
Aspern (Neigh.), Aus.	66e	48.13 N	16.29 E
Aspinwall, Pa.	57b	40.30 N	79.55 W
Aspy B., Can. (ăs'pē)	105	46.55 N	60.25 W
Aş Şaff, Egypt	223b	29.33 N	31.23 E
Aş Şahrā' al Lībīyah, see Libyan Des.			
Aş Şaḥrā' ash Sharqīyah, see Arabian Des.			
As Sallūm, Egypt	225	31.34 N	25.09 E
As Salt, Jordan	191a	32.02 N	35.44 E
Assam (State), India (ăs-săm')	196	26.00 N	91.00 E
As Samāwah, Iraq	195	31.18 N	45.17 E
Asseln (Neigh.), F.R.G.	63	51.32 N	7.35 E
Assens, Den. (äs'sĕns)	164	55.16 N	9.54 E
As Sinbillāwayn, Egypt	223b	30.53 N	31.37 E
Assini, Ivory Coast. (ä-sē-nē')	224	4.52 N	3.16 W
Assiniboia, Can.	100	49.38 N	105.59 W
Assiniboine (R.), Can. (ă-sĭn'ĭ-boin)	100	50.03 N	97.57 W
Assiniboine, Mt., Can.	99	50.52 N	115.39 W
Assis, Braz. (ä-sē's)	143	22.39 S	50.21 W
Assisi, It.	172	43.04 N	12.37 E
As-Sudd (Reg.), Sud.	225	8.45 N	30.45 E
As Sulaymānīyah, Iraq	192	35.47 N	45.23 E
As Sulaymānīyah, Sau. Ar.	195	24.09 N	46.19 E
As Suwaydā', Syr.	192	32.41 N	36.41 E
As Suways (Suez), Egypt	223c	29.58 N	32.34 E
Astakós, Grc. (äs'tä-kôs)	173	38.42 N	21.00 E
Astara, Sov. Un.	179	38.30 N	48.50 E
Asti, It. (äs'tē)	172	44.54 N	8.12 E
Astipálaia (I.), Grc.	161	36.31 N	26.19 E
Astley Bridge, Eng.	64b	53.36 N	2.26 W
Astorga, Sp. (äs-tôr'gä)	170	42.28 N	6.03 W
Astoria (Neigh.), NY	55	40.46 N	73.55 W
Astoria, Or. (ăs-tō'rĭ-ȧ)	118c	46.11 N	123.51 W
Astrakhan' Sov. Un. (äs-trȧ-kän')	179	46.15 N	48.00 E
Astrida, Rw. (äs-trē'dȧ)	226	2.37 S	29.48 E
Asturias (Reg.), Sp. (äs-tōō'ryäs)	170	43.21 N	6.00 W
Asunción, Par. (ä-sōōn-syōn')	144	25.25 S	57.30 W
Asunción Mita, Guat. (ä-sōōn-syō'n-mē'tä)	132	14.19 N	89.43 W
Asunción, see Ixtaltepec			
Asunción, see Nochixtlán			
Åsunden (L.), Swe. (ô'sōōn-dĕn)	163	57.46 N	13.16 E
Aswān, Egypt (ä-swän')	223b	24.05 N	32.57 E

ng-sing; ŋ-baŋk; N-nasalized n; nŏd; cŏmmit; ōld; ôbey; ôrder; oi-boil; fōōd; fŏŏt; ou-out; s-soft; sh-dish; th-thin; pūre; ûnite; ûrn; stŭd; circŭs; ü-as in French tu; '-indeterminate vowel.

PLACE (Pronunciation)	PAGE	Lat. °'	Long. °'
Aswān High Dam, Egypt	223b	23.58 N	32.53 E
Asyūṭ, Egypt (ä-syo͞ot')	223b	27.10 N	31.10 E
Atacama, Desierto de (Des.), Chile-Peru (dĕ-syĕ'r-tô-dĕ-ä-tä-kà'mä)	140	23.50 S	69.00 W
Atacama, Puna de (Plat.), Bol. (po͞o'nä-dĕ-ä-tä-kà'mä)	142	21.35 S	66.58 W
Atacama, Puna de (Reg.), Chile (po͞o'nä-dĕ-àtä-kà'mä)	144	23.15 S	68.45 W
Atacama, Salar de (L.), Chile (sà-lär'dĕ-àtä-kà'mä)	144	23.38 S	68.15 W
Atacama Trench, S.A.	144	25.00 S	71.30 W
Ataco, Col. (ä-tà'kō)	142a	3.36 N	75.22 W
Atacora, Chaîne de l' (Mts.), Benin	228	10.15 N	1.15 E
Atā 'itah, Jabal al (Mts.), Jordan	191a	30.48 N	35.19 E
Atakpamé, Togo (ä'tàk-pà-mā')	228	7.32 N	1.08 E
Atamanovskiy, Sov. Un. (ä-tä-mä'nôv-skĭ)	182a	52.15 N	60.47 E
'Atāqah, Jabal (Mts.), Egypt	223c	29.59 N	32.20 E
Atar, Mauritania (ä-tär')	224	20.45 N	13.16 W
Atascadero, Ca. (ăt-ăs-kà-dâ'rō)	120	35.29 N	120.40 W
Atascosa R., Tx. (ăt-ăs-kō'sà)	124	28.50 N	98.17 W
Atauro, Ilha de (I.), Indon. (dĕ-ä-tä'o͞o-rô)	207	8.20 S	126.15 E
'Aṭbarah, Sud. (ät'bà-rä)	225	17.45 N	33.15 E
Atbara R., Sud.	225	17.14 N	34.27 E
Atbasar, Sov. Un. (ät'bä-sär')	180	51.42 N	68.28 E
Atchafalaya B., La. (ăch-à-fà-lī'à)	125	29.25 N	91.30 W
Atchafalaya R., La.	125	30.53 N	91.51 W
Atchison, Ks. (ăch'ĭ-sŭn)	123	39.33 N	95.08 W
Atco, NJ (ăt'kō)	112f	39.46 N	74.53 W
Atempan, Mex. (ä-tĕm-pà'n)	131	19.49 N	97.25 W
Atenguillo (R.), Mex. (ä-tĕn-gē'l-yô)	130	20.18 N	104.35 W
Athabasca, Can. (ăth-à-băs'kà)	96	54.43 N	113.17 W
Athabasca (L.), Can.	96	59.04 N	109.10 W
Athabasca (R.), Can.	99	56.00 N	112.35 W
Athens, Al. (ăth'ĕnz)	126	34.47 N	86.58 W
Athens, Ga.	126	33.55 N	83.24 W
Athens, Oh.	110	39.20 N	82.10 W
Athens, Pa.	111	42.00 N	76.30 W
Athens, Tn.	126	35.26 N	84.36 W
Athens, Tx.	125	32.13 N	95.51 W
Athens, see Athínai			
Atherstone, Eng. (ăth'ēr-stŭn)	156	52.34 N	1.33 W
Atherton, Eng. (ăth'ēr-tŭn)	156	53.32 N	2.29 W
Atherton Plat., Austl. (ădh-ēr-tŏn)	215	17.00 S	144.30 E
Athi (R.), Ken. (ä'tē)	231	2.43 S	38.30 E
Athis-Mons, Fr.	64c	48.43 N	2.24 E
Athínai (Athens), Grc. (ä-thē'nĕ)	173	38.00 N	23.38 E
Athlone, Ire. (ăth-lōn')	162	53.24 N	7.30 W
Athos (Mtn.), Grc. (ăth'ŏs)	173	40.10 N	24.15 E
Ath Thamad, Egypt	191a	29.41 N	34.17 E
Athy, Ire. (à-thī)	162	52.59 N	7.08 W
Ati, Chad	229	13.13 N	18.20 E
Atibaia, Braz. (ä-tē-bà'yà)	141a	23.08 S	46.32 W
Atikonak (L.), Can.	97	52.34 N	63.49 W
Atimonan, Phil. (ä-tē-mō'nän)	207a	13.59 N	121.56 E
Atiquizaya, Sal. (ä'tē-kē-zä'yä)	132	14.00 N	89.42 W
Atitlan (Vol.), Guat. (ä-tē-tlän')	132	14.35 N	91.11 W
Atitlan L., Guat. (ä-tē-tlän')	132	14.35 N	91.23 W
Atizapán, Mex. (ä'tē-zà-pän')	131a	19.33 N	99.16 W
Atka, Ak. (ăt'kà)	107a	52.18 N	174.18 W
Atka (I.), Ak.	107a	51.58 N	174.30 W
Atkarsk, Sov. Un. (åt-kärsk')	179	51.50 N	45.00 E
Atkinson, Ne. (ăt'kĭn-sŭn)	114	42.32 N	98.58 W
Atlanta, Ga. (ăt-lăn'tà)	112c	33.45 N	84.23 W
Atlanta, Tx.	123	33.09 N	94.09 W
Atlantic, Ia. (ăt-lăn'tĭk)	115	41.23 N	94.58 W
Atlantic, NC	127	34.54 N	76.20 W
Atlantic Beach, NY	55	40.35 N	73.44 W
Atlantic City, NJ	111	39.20 N	74.30 W
Atlantic Highlands, NJ	112a	40.25 N	74.04 W
Atlantic O.	93	23.30 N	40.00 W
Atlas Mts., Alg.-Mor. (ăt'lăs)	224	31.22 N	4.57 W
Atliaca, Mex. (ät-lē-ä'kä)	130	17.38 N	99.24 W
Atlin (L.), Can. (ăt'lĭn)	96	59.34 N	133.20 W
Atlixco, Mex. (ät-lēz'kō)	130	18.52 N	98.27 W
Atmore, Al. (ăt'mōr)	126	31.01 N	87.31 W
Atoka, Ok. (à-tō'kà)	123	34.23 N	96.07 W
Atoka Res., Ok.	123	34.30 N	96.05 W
Atotonilco el Alto, Mex. (ä'tô-tô-nēl'kō ĕl äl'tō)	130	20.35 N	102.32 W
Atotonilco el Grande, Mex. (ä'tô-tô-nēl-kō ĕl grän'dä)	130	20.17 N	98.41 W
Atoui R., Mauritania-W. Sah. (à-to͞o-ē')	224	21.00 N	15.32 W
Atoyac, Mex. (ä-tô-yäk')	130	20.01 N	103.28 W
Atoyac (R.), Mex.	130	18.35 N	98.16 W
Atoyac (R.), Mex.	131	16.27 N	97.28 W
Atoyac de Alvarez, Mex. (ä-tô-yäk'dā äl'vä-räz)	130	17.13 N	100.29 W
Atoyatempan, Mex. (ä-tō'yà-tĕm-pän')	131	18.47 N	97.54 W
Atrak (R.), Iran	192	37.45 N	56.30 E
Atran (R.), Swe.	164	57.02 N	12.43 E
Atrato (R.), Col. (ä-trä'tō)	142a	5.48 N	76.19 W
Atrato, Rio (R.), Col. (rē'ō-ä-trä'tō)	142	7.15 N	77.18 W
Atsugi, Jap.	69a	35.27 N	139.22 E
Atta, India	67d	28.34 N	77.20 E
Aṭ Ṭafīlah, Jordan (tä-fē'la)	191a	30.50 N	35.36 E
Aṭ Ṭā'if, Sau. Ar.	192	21.03 N	41.00 E
At-Ṭalibīyah, Egypt	71a	30.00 N	31.11 E
Attalla, Al. (à-tăl'yà)	126	34.01 N	86.05 W
Attawapiskat (R.), Can. (ăt'à-wà-pĭs'kăt)	97	52.31 N	86.22 W
Attersee (L.) (Kammer), Aus.	166	47.57 N	13.25 E
Attica, NY (ăt'ĭ-kà)	111	42.55 N	78.15 W
Attleboro, Ma. (ăt''l-bŭr-ô)	112b	41.56 N	71.15 W
Attow, Ben (Mtn.), Scot. (bĕn ăt'tō)	162	57.15 N	5.25 W
Attoyac Bay, Tx. (ă-toi'yăk)	125	31.45 N	94.23 W
Attu (I.), Ak. (ät-to͞o')	107a	53.08 N	173.18 E
Aṭ Ṭūr, Egypt	161	28.09 N	33.47 E
Aṭ Ṭurayf, Sau. Ar.	192	31.32 N	38.30 E
Åtvidaberg, Swe. (ôt-vē'dá-bĕrgh)	164	58.12 N	15.55 E
Atwood, Ks. (ăt'wo͝od)	122	39.48 N	101.06 W
Atzalpur, India	67d	28.43 N	77.21 E
Atzcapotzalco, Mex. (ät'zkä-pô-tzäl'kō)	131a	19.29 N	99.11 W
Atzgersdorf, Aus.	157e	48.10 N	16.17 E
Auau Chan., Hi. (ä'o͞o-ä'o͞o)	106a	20.55 N	156.50 W
Aubagne, Fr. (ō-bän'y')	169	43.18 N	5.34 E
Aube (R.), Fr. (ōb)	168	48.42 N	3.49 E
Aubenas, Fr. (ōb-nä')	168	44.37 N	4.22 E
Aubervilliers, Fr. (ō-bĕr-vē-yā')	169b	48.54 N	2.23 E
Aubin, Fr. (ō-băN')	168	44.29 N	2.12 E
Aubrey, Can. (ô-brē')	95a	45.08 N	73.47 W
Auburn, Al. (ô'bŭrn)	126	32.35 N	85.26 W
Auburn, Austl.	70a	33.51 S	151.02 E
Auburn, Ca.	120	38.52 N	121.05 W
Auburn, Il.	123	39.36 N	89.46 W
Auburn, In.	110	41.20 N	85.05 W
Auburn, Ma.	105a	42.11 N	71.51 W
Auburn, Me.	104	44.04 N	70.24 W
Auburn, Ne.	123	40.23 N	95.50 W
Auburn, NY	111	42.55 N	76.35 W
Auburn, Wa.	118a	47.18 N	122.14 W
Auburndale, Ma.	54a	42.21 N	71.22 W
Auburn Hts., Mi.	113b	42.37 N	83.13 W
Aubusson, Fr. (ō-bü-sôN')	168	45.57 N	2.10 E
Auch, Fr. (ōsh)	168	43.38 N	0.35 E
Aucilla (R.), Fl.-Ga. (ô-sĭl'à)	126	30.15 N	83.55 W
Auckland, N.Z. (ôk'lănd)	215a	36.53 S	174.45 E
Auckland Is., N.Z.	232	50.30 S	166.30 E
Auckland Park (Neigh.), S. Afr.	71b	26.11 S	28.00 E
Aude (R.), Fr. (ōd)	168	42.55 N	2.08 E
Audenshaw, Eng.	64b	53.28 N	2.08 W
Audierne, Fr. (ō-dyĕrn')	168	48.02 N	4.31 W
Audincourt, Fr. (ō-dăN-ko͞or')	169	47.30 N	6.49 E
Audley, Eng. (ôd'lĭ)	156	53.03 N	2.18 W
Audo Ra., Eth.	223a	6.58 N	41.18 E
Audubon, Ia. (ô'do͞o-bŏn)	115	41.43 N	94.57 W
Audubon, NJ	112f	39.54 N	75.04 W
Aue, G.D.R. (ou'ē)	166	50.35 N	12.44 E
Auf dem Kreinberge, F.R.G.	63	51.27 N	7.36 E
Auf dem Schnee (Neigh.), F.R.G.	63	51.26 N	7.25 E
Augathella, Austl. (ôr'gà'thē-là)	216	25.49 S	146.40 E
Aughton, Eng.	64a	53.32 N	2.56 W
Aughton Park, Eng.	64a	53.33 N	2.53 W
Augrabiesvalle (Falls), S. Afr.	226	28.30 S	20.00 E
Augsburg, F.R.G. (ouks'bo͝orgh)	157d	48.23 N	10.55 E
Augusta, Ar. (ô-gŭs'tà)	123	35.16 N	91.21 W
Augusta, Ga.	127	33.26 N	82.00 W
Augusta, Ks.	123	37.41 N	96.58 W
Augusta, Ky.	110	38.45 N	84.00 W
Augusta, Me.	104	44.19 N	69.42 W
Augusta, NJ	112a	41.07 N	74.44 W
Augusta, Wi.	115	44.40 N	91.09 W
Augustow, Pol. (ou-go͞os'to͞of)	167	53.52 N	23.00 E
Aulnay-sous-Bois, Fr. (ō-nĕ'so͞o-bwä')	169b	48.56 N	2.30 E
Aulne (R.), Fr. (ōn)	168	48.08 N	3.53 W
Auneau, Fr. (ō-nëü)	169b	48.28 N	1.45 E
Auob (R.), Namibia (ä'wŏb)	226	25.00 S	19.00 E
Aur (I.), Mala.	191b	2.27 N	104.51 E
Aura, Fin.	165	60.38 N	22.32 E
Aurangābād, India (ou-rŭŋ-gä-bäd')	196	19.56 N	75.19 E
Aurdal, Nor. (äür-däl)	164	60.54 N	9.24 E
Aurès, Massif de l' (Mts.), Alg.	160	35.16 N	5.53 E
Aurillac, Fr. (ō-rē-yàk')	168	44.57 N	2.27 E
Aurora, Can.	103	43.59 N	79.25 W
Aurora, Il. (ô-rō'rà)	113a	41.45 N	88.18 W
Aurora, In.	113f	39.04 N	84.55 W
Aurora, Mn.	115	47.31 N	92.17 W
Aurora, Mo.	123	36.58 N	93.42 W
Aurora, Ne.	122	40.54 N	98.01 W
Aursunden (L.), Nor. (äûr-sûndĕn)	164	62.42 N	11.10 E
Au Sable (R.), Mi. (ô-sä'b'l)	110	44.40 N	84.25 W
Ausable (R.), NY	111	44.25 N	73.50 W
Austerlitz (P. Int.), Fr.	64c	48.50 N	2.22 E
Austin (L.), Austl.	214	27.45 S	117.30 E
Austin, Mn. (ôs'tĭn)	115	43.40 N	92.58 W
Austin (Neigh.), Il.	58a	41.54 N	87.45 W
Austin, Nv.	120	39.30 N	117.05 W
Austin, Tx.	125	30.15 N	97.42 W
Austin Bayou, Tx. (ôs'tĭn bī-o͞o')	125a	29.17 N	95.21 W
Austral, Austl.	70a	33.56 S	150.48 E
Australian Alps (Mts.), Austl.	216	37.10 S	147.55 E
Australian Capital Ter., Austl. (ôs-trā'lĭ-ăn)	216	35.30 S	148.40 E
Australia, Eur. (ôs-trā'lĭ-à)	214	25.00 S	135.00 E
Austria, Eur. (ôs'trĭ-à)	154	47.15 N	11.53 E
Authon-la-Plaine, Fr. (ō-tôN-lă-plĕ'n)	169b	48.27 N	1.58 E
Autlán, Mex. (ä-o͞ot-län')	130	19.47 N	104.24 W
Autun, Fr. (ō-tŭN')	168	46.58 N	4.14 E
Auvergne (Mts.), Fr. (ō-vĕrn'y')	168	45.12 N	2.31 E
Auxerre, Fr. (ō-sâr')	168	47.48 N	3.32 E
Ava, Mo. (ā'và)	123	36.56 N	92.40 W
Avakubi, Zaire (ä-vá-ko͞o'bē)	231	1.20 N	27.34 E
Avallon, Fr. (à-và-lôN')	168	47.30 N	3.58 E
Avalon, Ca.	120	33.21 N	118.22 W
Avalon, Pa. (ăv'à-lŏn)	113e	40.31 N	80.05 W
Avanley, Eng.	64b	53.16 N	2.45 W
Aveiro, Port. (ä-vā'ro͞o)	170	40.38 N	8.38 W
Avelar, Braz. (ä'vē-là'r)	144b	22.20 S	43.25 W
Aveley, Eng.	62	51.30 N	0.16 E
Avellaneda, Arg. (ä-vĕl-yä-nä'dhä)	144a	34.25 S	58.23 W
Avellino, It. (ä-vĕl-lē'nō)	171c	40.40 N	14.46 E
Avenel, NJ	55	40.35 N	74.17 W
Averøya (I.), Nor. (ävĕr-ûê)	164	63.40 N	7.16 E
Aversa, It. (ä-vĕr'sä)	172	40.58 N	14.13 E
Avery, Tx. (ā'vēr-ĭ)	123	33.34 N	94.46 W
Avesta, Swe. (ä-vĕs'tä)	164	60.16 N	16.09 E
Aveyron (R.), Fr. (ä-vâ-rôN)	168	44.07 N	1.45 E
Avezzano, It. (ä-vät-sä'nō)	172	42.03 N	13.27 E
Avigliano, It. (ä-vēl-yä'nō)	172	40.45 N	15.44 E
Avignon, Fr. (à-vē-nyôN')	168	43.55 N	4.50 E
Ávila, Sp. (ä-vē-lä)	170	40.39 N	4.42 W
Avilés, Sp. (ä-vē-lās')	170	43.33 N	5.55 W
Avoca, Ia. (à-vō'kà)	123	41.29 N	95.16 W
Avocado Heights, Ca.	59	34.03 N	118.00 W
Avon, Ct. (ā'vŏn)	111	41.40 N	72.50 W
Avon, Ma. (ā'vŏn)	105a	42.08 N	71.03 W
Avon, Oh.	113d	41.27 N	82.02 W
Avon (R.), Eng. (ā'vŭn)	162	52.05 N	1.55 W
Avondale, Ga.	112c	33.47 N	84.16 W
Avondale Heights, Austl.	70b	37.46 S	144.51 E
Avon Lake, Oh.	113d	41.31 N	82.01 W
Avonmore, Can. (ä'vŏN-mōr)	95c	45.11 N	74.58 W
Avon Park, Fl. (ā'vŏn pärk')	127a	27.35 N	81.29 W
Avranches, Fr. (à-vräNsh')	168	48.43 N	1.34 W
Awaji-Shima (I.), Jap. (ä'wä-jē shē-mä)	205b	34.32 N	135.02 E
Awe, Loch (L.), Scot. (lŏK ôr)	162	56.22 N	5.04 W
Awīn, Iran	68h	35.48 N	51.24 E
Awjilah, Libya	225	29.07 N	21.21 E
Awsīm, Egypt	71a	30.07 N	31.08 E
Ax-les-Thermes, Fr. (äks'lā tĕrm')	168	42.43 N	1.50 E
Axochiapan, Mex. (äks-ō-chyä'pän)	130	18.29 N	98.49 W
Ay (R.), Sov. Un.	178	55.55 N	57.55 E
Ayabe, Jap. (ä'yä-bē)	205	35.16 N	135.17 E
Ayachi, Arin' (Mtn.), Mor.	160	32.29 N	4.57 W
Ayacucho, Arg. (ä-yä-ko͞o'chō)	144	37.05 S	58.30 W
Ayacucho, Peru	142	12.12 S	74.03 W
Ayaguz, Sov. Un. (ä-yà-go͞oz')	180	48.00 N	80.12 E
Ayamonte, Sp. (ä-yä-mō'n-tĕ)	170	37.14 N	7.28 W
Ayan, Sov. Un. (à-yän')	181	56.26 N	138.18 E
Ayase, Jap.	69a	35.26 N	139.26 E
Ayata, Bol. (ä-yä'tä)	142	15.17 S	68.43 W
Ayaviri, Peru (ä-yä-vē'rē)	142	14.46 S	70.38 W
Aydar (R.), Sov. Un. (ī-där')	175	49.15 N	38.48 E
Ayden, NC (ā'dĕn)	127	35.27 N	77.25 W
Aydın, Tur. (āīy-dĕn)	179	37.40 N	27.40 E
Ayer, Ma. (âr)	105a	42.33 N	71.36 W
Ayer Hitam, Mala.	191b	1.55 N	103.11 E
Ayiassos, Grc.	173	39.06 N	26.25 E
Áyion Óros (Mount Athos) (Reg.), Grc.	173	40.20 N	24.15 E
Áyios Evstrátios (I.), Grc.	173	39.30 N	24.58 E
Ayía Varvára, Grc.	66d	37.59 N	23.39 E
Ayíou Orous, Kólpos (G.), Grc.	173	40.15 N	24.00 E
Aylesbury, Eng. (ālz'bēr-ĭ)	156b	51.47 N	0.49 W
Aylmer (L.), Can. (āl'mēr)	96	64.27 N	108.22 W
Aylmer East, Can. (āl'mēr)	95c	45.24 N	75.50 W
Aylmer, Mt., Can.	99	51.19 N	115.26 W
Ayo el Chico, Mex. (ä'yō el chē'kō)	130	20.31 N	102.21 W
Ayon (I.), Sov. Un. (ī-ôn')	181	69.50 N	168.40 E
Ayorou, Niger	228	14.44 N	0.55 E
Ayotla, Mex. (ä-yōt'lä)	131a	19.18 N	98.55 W
Ayoun el Atrous, Mauritania	228	16.40 N	9.37 W
Ayr, Scot. (âr)	162	55.27 N	4.40 W
Aysha, Eth.	223a	10.48 N	42.32 E
Ayutla, Guat. (ä-yo͞ot'lä)	132	14.44 N	92.11 W
Ayutla, Mex.	130	16.50 N	99.16 W
Ayutla, Mex.	130	20.09 N	104.20 W
Ayvalik, Tur. (āīy-wă-lĭk)	173	39.19 N	26.40 E
Azādpur (Neigh.), India	67d	28.43 N	77.11 E
Azaouad (Dunes), Mali	228	18.00 N	3.20 W
Azaouak, Vallée de l' (Val.), Mali	229	15.50 N	3.10 E
Azare, Nig.	229	11.40 N	10.11 E
Azcapotzalco, Mex.	60a	19.28 N	99.12 W
Azemmour, Mor. (à-zē-mo͞or')	224	33.20 N	8.21 W
Azerbaijan (S.S.R.), Sov. Un. (ä'zēr-bä-ē-jän')	176	40.38 N	47.25 E
Azle, Tx. (āz'lē)	119c	35.54 N	97.33 W
Azogues, Ec. (ä-sō'gās)	142	2.47 S	78.45 W
Azores (Is.), see Açores			
Azov, Sov. Un. (à-zôf') (ä-zôf)	175	47.07 N	39.19 E
Azov, Sea of, see Azovskoye More			
Azovskoye More (Sea of Azov), Sov. Un. (à-zôf'skô-yĕ mô'rĕ)	175	46.00 N	36.20 E
Azoyú, Mex. (ä-zô-yo͞o')	130	16.42 N	98.46 W
Azraq, Al-Bahr al- (R.), see Blue Nile			
Aztec, NM (ăz'tĕk)	121	36.40 N	108.00 W
Aztec Ruins Natl. Mon., NM	121	36.50 N	108.00 W
Azua, Dom. Rep. (ä'swä)	135	18.30 N	70.45 W
Azuaga, Sp. (ä-thwä'gä)	170	38.15 N	5.42 W
Azucar, Presa de (Res.), Mex. (prĕ'sä-dĕ-ä-zo͞o'kär)	124	26.06 N	98.44 W
Azuero, Peninsula de (Pen.), Pan. (ä-swä'rō)	133	7.30 N	80.34 W
Azufre, Cerro (Copiapó) (Vol.), Chile (sĕr'rō ä-so͞o'frā) (kō-pē-äpō')	144	26.10 S	69.00 W
Azul, Arg. (ä-so͞ol')	141c	36.46 S	59.51 W
Azul, Cordillera (Mts.), Peru (kô'r-dē-lyĕ'rä-zo͞o'l)	142	7.15 S	75.30 W
Azul, Sierra (Mts.), Mex. (sē-ĕ'r-rä-zo͞o'l)	130	23.20 N	98.28 W
Azusa, Ca. (à-zo͞o'sà)	119a	34.08 N	117.55 W
Az Zabdānī, Syr.	191a	33.45 N	36.06 E
Aẓ Ẓahrān (Dhahran, Sau. Ar. (dä-rän')	192	26.13 N	50.00 E
Az-Zamālik (Neigh.), Egypt	71a	30.04 N	31.13 E
Az Zaqāzīq, Egypt	223b	30.36 N	31.36 E
Az Zarqā', Jordan	191a	32.03 N	36.07 E
Az Zawiyah, Libya	225	32.28 N	11.55 E

ăt; finăl; rāte; senåte; ärm; àsk; sofà; fâre; ch-choose; dh-as th in other; bē; ēvent; bĕt; recĕnt; cratēr; g-gō; gh-guttural g; bĭt; ĭ-short neutral; rīde; K-guttural k as ch in German ich;

PLACE (Pronunciation)	PAGE	Lat. °′	Long. °′
B			
Baak, F.R.G.	63	51.25 N	7.10 E
Baal, F.R.G. (bäl)	169c	51.02 N	6.17 E
Baao, Phil. (bä'ō)	207a	13.27 N	123.22 E
Baardheere, Som.	223a	2.13 N	42.24 E
Baarle-Hertog, Bel.	157a	51.26 N	4.57 E
Baarn, Neth.	157a	52.12 N	5.18 E
Babaeski, Tur. (bä'bä-ĕs'kĭ)	173	41.25 N	27.05 E
Babahoyo, Ec. (bä-bä-ō'yō)	142	1.56 S	79.24 W
Babana, Nig.	229	10.36 N	3.50 E
Babanango, S. Afr.	227c	28.24 S	31.11 E
Babanūsah, Sud.	225	11.30 N	27.55 E
Babar, Pulau (I.), Indon. (bä'bär)	207	7.50 S	129.15 E
Bābarpur (Neigh.), India	67d	28.41 N	77.17 E
Bab-el-Mandeb, Str. of, Afr.-Asia (bäb'ĕl män-dĕb')	223a	13.17 N	42.49 E
Babelsberg (Neigh.), G.D.R.	65a	52.24 N	13.05 E
Babia, Arroyo de la, Mex. (är-rō'yō dā lä bä'bē-ä)	124	28.26 N	101.50 W
Babine (R.), Can.	98	55.10 N	127.00 W
Babine L., Can. (băb'ēn)	98	54.45 N	126.00 W
Bābol, Iran	192	36.30 N	52.48 E
Babson Park, Ma.	54a	42.18 N	71.23 W
Babushkin, Sov. Un. (bä'bo͝osh-kĭn)	181	51.47 N	106.08 W
Babushkin, Sov. Un.	182b	55.52 N	37.42 E
Babuyan Is., Phil. (bä-bo͞o-yän')	206	19.30 N	122.38 E
Babyak, Bul. (bäb'zhȧk)	173	41.59 N	23.42 E
Babylon, NY (băb'ĭ-lŏn)	112a	40.42 N	73.19 W
Babylon (Ruins), Iraq	192	32.15 N	45.23 E
Bacalar, Laguna de (L.), Mex. (lä-go͞o-nä-dĕ-bä-kä-lär')	132a	18.50 N	88.31 W
Bacan, Pulau (I.), Indon.	207	0.30 S	127.00 E
Bacarra, Phil. (bä-kär'rä)	203	18.22 N	120.40 E
Bacău, Rom.	167	46.34 N	27.00 E
Baccarat, Fr. (bȧ-kȧ-rȧ')	169	48.29 N	6.42 E
Bacchus, Ut. (băk'ŭs)	119b	40.40 N	112.06 W
Bachajón, Mex. (bä-chä-hōn')	131	17.08 N	92.18 W
Bachu, China (bä-cho͞o)	198	39.50 N	78.23 E
Back (R.), Can.	96	65.30 N	104.15 W
Bačka Palanka, Yugo. (bäch'kä pälän-kä)	173	45.14 N	19.24 E
Bačka Topola, Yugo. (bäch'kä tō'pō-lä')	173	45.48 N	19.38 E
Back B., India	67e	18.56 N	72.49 E
Back Bay, India (băk)	197b	18.55 N	72.45 E
Back Bay (Neigh.), Ma.	54a	42.21 N	71.05 W
Backstairs Pass., Austl. (băk-stârs')	214	35.50 S	138.15 E
Bac Ninh, Viet. (bäk'nēn')	203	21.10 N	106.02 E
Bacoli, It. (bä-kō-lē')	171c	40.33 N	14.05 E
Bacolod, Phil. (bä-kō'lȯd)	206	10.42 N	123.03 E
Baco, Mt., Phil. (bä'kō)	207a	12.50 N	121.11 E
Bacongo, Con.	71c	4.18 S	15.16 E
Bácsalmás, Hung. (bäch'ôl-mäs)	167	46.07 N	19.18 E
Bacup, Eng. (băk'ŭp)	156	53.42 N	2.12 W
Bad (R.), SD (băd)	114	44.04 N	100.58 W
Badajoz, Sp. (bä-dhä-hōth')	170	38.52 N	6.56 W
Badalona, Sp. (bä-dhä-lō'nä)	171	41.27 N	2.15 E
Badanah, Sau. Ar.	192	30.49 N	40.45 E
Bad Axe, Mi. (băd' ăks)	110	43.50 N	82.55 W
Bad Bramstedt, F.R.G. (bät bräm'shtĕt)	157c	53.55 N	9.53 E
Bad Ems, F.R.G. (bät ĕms)	169	50.20 N	7.45 E
Baden, Aus. (bä'dĕn)	157e	48.00 N	16.14 E
Baden, Switz.	166	47.28 N	8.17 E
Baden-Baden, F.R.G. (bä'dĕn-bä'dĕn)	166	48.46 N	8.11 E
Baden Württemberg (State), F.R.G. (bä'dĕn vür'tĕm-bĕrgh)	166	48.38 N	9.00 E
Bad Freienwalde, G.D.R. (bät frī'ĕn-väl'dĕ)	166	52.47 N	14.00 E
Badger's Mount, Eng.	62	51.20 N	0.09 E
Bad Hersfeld, F.R.G. (bät hĕrsh'fĕlt)	166	50.53 N	9.43 E
Bad Homberg, F.R.G. (bät hōm'bĕrgh)	163	50.14 N	8.35 E
Badin, NC (bă'dĭn)	127	35.23 N	80.08 W
Badīn, Pak.	196	24.47 N	69.51 E
Bad Ischl, Aus. (bät ĭsh''l)	166	47.46 N	13.37 E
Bad Kissingen, F.R.G. (bät kĭs'ĭng-ĕn)	166	50.12 N	10.05 E
Bad Kreuznach, F.R.G. (bät kroits'näk)	166	49.52 N	7.53 E
Badlands (Reg.), ND (băd' lănds)	114	46.43 N	103.22 W
Badlands (Reg.), SD	114	43.43 N	102.36 W
Badlands Natl. Park, SD	114	43.56 N	102.37 W
Badlāpur, India	197b	19.12 N	73.12 E
Bādli, India	67d	28.45 N	77.09 E
Badogo, Mali	228	11.02 N	8.13 W
Bad Oldeslow, F.R.G. (bät ōl'dĕs-lōē)	166	53.48 N	10.21 E
Bad Reichenhall, F.R.G. (bät rī'ĸĕn-häl)	166	47.43 N	12.53 E
Bad River Ind. Res., Wi. (băd)	115	46.41 N	90.36 W
Bad Segeberg, F.R.G. (bät sĕ'gĕ-bo͝orgh)	157c	53.56 N	10.18 E
Bad Tölz, F.R.G. (bät tûltz)	166	47.46 N	11.35 E
Badulla, Sri Lanka	197	6.55 N	81.07 E
Bad Vöslau, Aus.	157e	47.58 N	16.13 E
Badwater Cr., Wy. (băd'wô-tĕr)	117	43.13 N	107.55 W
Baena, Sp. (bä-ā'nä)	170	37.38 N	4.20 W
Baependi, Braz. (bä-å-pĕn'dĭ)	141a	21.57 S	44.51 W
Baerl, F.R.G.	63	51.29 N	6.41 E
Baffin B., Can. (băf'ĭn)	94	72.00 N	65.00 W
Baffin B., Tx.	125	27.11 N	97.35 W
Baffin I., Can.	94	67.20 N	71.00 W
Bafoulabé, Mali (bä-fo͞o-lä-bā')	228	13.48 N	10.50 W
Bāfq, Iran (bäfk)	192	31.48 N	55.23 E
Bafra, Tur. (bäf'rä)	179	41.30 N	35.50 E
Bagabag, Phil. (bä-gä-bäg')	207a	16.38 N	121.16 E
Bāgalkot, India	197	16.14 N	75.40 E
Bagamoyo, Tan. (bä-gä-mō'yō)	231	6.26 S	38.54 E
Bagaryak, Sov. Un. (bä-gȧr-yäk')	182a	56.13 N	61.32 E
Bagbele, Zaire	231	4.21 N	29.17 E
Bagé, Braz. (bä-zhā')	144	31.17 S	54.07 W
Baghdād, Iraq (bȧgh-dȧd') (băg'dăd)	192	33.14 N	44.22 E
Bagheria, It. (bä-gā-rē'ä)	172	38.03 N	13.32 E
Bagley, Mn. (băg'lē)	114	47.31 N	95.24 W
Bagnara, It. (bän-yä'rä)	172	38.17 N	15.52 E
Bagnell Dam, Mo. (băg'nĕl)	123	38.13 N	92.40 W
Bagnères-de-Bigorre, Fr. (bän-yâr'dē-bē-gor')	168	43.40 N	0.70 E
Bagnères-de-Luchon, Fr. (bän-yâr' dē-lu chôɴ')	168	42.46 N	0.36 E
Bagneux, Fr.	64c	48.48 N	2.18 E
Bagnolet, Fr.	64c	48.52 N	2.25 E
Bagnols-sur-Ceze, Fr. (bä-nyȯl')	168	44.09 N	4.37 E
Bagoé R., Mali (bȧ-gō'ȧ)	224	12.22 N	6.34 W
Baguio, Phil. (bä-gē-ō')	207a	16.24 N	120.36 E
Bagzane, Monts (Mtn.), Niger	229	18.40 N	8.40 E
Bahamas, N.A. (bȧ-hā'mȧs)	129	26.15 N	76.00 W
Bahau, Mala.	191b	2.48 N	102.25 E
Bahāwalpur, Pak. (bŭ-hä'wŭl-po͞or)	196	29.29 N	71.41 E
Bahia (State), Braz.	143	11.05 S	43.00 W
Bahía Blanca, Arg. (bä-ē'ä bläŋ'kä)	144	38.45 S	62.07 W
Bahias, Cabo dos (C.), Arg. (kȧ'bô-dôs-bä-ē'äs)	144	44.55 S	65.35 W
Bahia, see Salvador			
Bahi Swp., Tan.	231	6.05 S	35.10 E
Bahía de Caráquez, Ec. (bä-e'ä dā kä-rä'kĕz)	142	0.45 S	80.29 W
Bahía, Islas de la (I.), Hond. (ē's-läs-dĕ-lä-bä-ē'ä)	128	16.15 N	86.30 W
Bahía Negra, Par. (bä-ē'ä nā'grä)	143	20.11 S	58.05 W
Bahoruco, Sierra de (Mts.), Dom. Rep. (sē-ĕ'r-rä-dĕ-bä-ō-ro͞o'kô)	135	18.10 N	71.25 W
Bahrain, Asia (bä-rān')	192	26.15 N	51.17 E
Bahr al Ghazāl (Prov.), Sud. (bär ĕl ghä-zäl')	225	7.56 N	27.15 E
Baḥrīyah (Oasis), Egypt (bȧ-hȧ-rē'yä)	161	28.34 N	29.01 E
Baḥrīyah, Jabal Jalālah al (Plat.), Egypt	191a	29.15 N	32.20 E
Bahtīm, Egypt	71a	30.08 N	31.17 E
Baia de Criş, Rom. (bä'yä dā krēs')	167	46.11 N	22.40 E
Baia Mare, Rom. (bä'yä mä'rā)	167	47.40 N	23.35 E
Baidyabāti, India	196a	22.47 N	88.21 E
Baie-Comeau, Can.	104	49.13 N	68.10 W
Baie de Wasai, Mi. (bā dē wä-sā'ē)	119k	46.27 N	84.15 W
Baie-Saint Paul, Can. (bā'sȧnt-pôl')	103	47.27 N	70.30 W
Baigou, China (bī-gō)	200	39.08 N	116.02 E
Baihe, China (bī-hŭ)	202	32.30 N	110.15 E
Bai Hu (L.), China (bī-ho͞o)	200	31.22 N	117.38 E
Baiju, China (bī-jyo͞o)	200	33.04 N	120.17 E
Baikal. L., see Baykal, Ozero			
Baikal Mts., see Baykal'skiy Khrebet			
Baile Átha Cliath (Dublin), Ire. (bō'lēō'hŏclē'ōh)	162	53.20 N	6.15 W
Bailén, Sp. (bä-ē-lān')	170	38.05 N	3.48 W
Băileşti, Rom. (bȧ-ĭ-lĕsh'tē)	173	44.01 N	23.21 E
Baileys Crossroads, Va.	56d	38.51 N	77.08 W
Bainbridge, Ga. (bān'brĭj)	126	30.52 N	84.35 W
Bainbridge I., Wa.	118a	47.39 N	122.32 W
Bainchipota, India	67a	22.52 N	88.16 E
Baipu, China (bī-po͞o)	200	32.15 N	120.47 E
Baiquan, China (bī-chyuäŋ)	202	47.22 N	126.00 E
Baird, Tx. (bârd)	124	32.22 N	99.28 W
Bairdford, Pa. (bârd'fōrd)	113e	40.37 N	79.53 W
Baird Mts., Ak.	107	67.35 N	160.10 W
Bairnsdale, Austl. (bârnz'dāl)	216	37.50 S	147.39 E
Baïse (R.), Fr. (bä-ēz')	168	43.52 N	0.23 E
Baía dos Tigres, Ang.	230	16.36 S	11.43 E
Baiyang Dian (L.), China (bī-yäŋ-dĭĕn)	200	39.00 N	115.45 E
Baiyunguan, China	67b	39.54 N	116.19 E
Baiyu Shan (Mts.), China (bī-yo͞o shän)	202	37.02 N	108.30 E
Baja, Hung. (bŏ'yŏ)	167	46.11 N	18.55 E
Baja California Norte (State), Mex. (bä-hä)	128	30.15 N	117.25 W
Baja California Sur (State), Mex.	128	26.00 N	113.30 W
Bakal, Sov. Un. (bä'kȧl)	182a	54.57 N	58.50 E
Baker (I.), Oceania	208	1.00 N	176.00 W
Baker (L.), Can.	96	63.51 N	96.10 W
Baker, Mt. (bā'kēr)	117	46.21 N	104.12 W
Baker, Or.	116	44.46 N	117.52 W
Baker Cr., Il.	113a	41.13 N	87.47 W
Baker, Mt., Wa.	116	48.46 N	121.52 W
Bakersfield, Ca. (bā'kērz-fēld)	120	35.23 N	119.00 W
Bakerstown, Pa. (bā'kērz-toun)	113e	40.39 N	79.56 W
Baker Street, Eng.	62	51.30 N	0.21 E
Bakewell, Eng. (bāk'wĕl)	156	53.12 N	1.40 W
Bakhchisaray, Sov. Un. (bȧĸ'chē-sȧ-rī')	175	44.46 N	33.54 E
Bakhmach, Sov. Un. (bȧĸ-mäch')	175	51.09 N	32.47 E
Bakhtarān, Iran	192	34.01 N	47.00 E
Bakhtegan, Daryācheh-ye (L.), Iran	192	29.29 N	54.31 E
Bakhteyevo, Sov. Un. (bȧk-tyĕ'yĕ-vô)	182b	55.35 N	38.32 E
Bakırköy (Neigh.), Tur.	66f	40.59 N	28.52 E
Bako, Eth. (bä'kö)	225	5.47 N	36.39 E
Bakony (Mts.), Hung. (bȧ-kōn'y')	167	46.57 N	17.30 E
Bakoye (R.), Mali (bȧ-kō'ê)	228	12.47 N	9.35 W
Bakr Uzyak, Sov. Un. (bȧkr o͞oz'yȧk)	182a	52.59 N	58.43 E
Baku, Sov. Un. (bȧ-ko͞o')	179	40.28 N	49.45 E
Bakwanga, see Mbuji-Mayi			
Balabac I., Phil. (bä'lä-bäk)	206	8.00 N	116.28 E
Balabac Str., Indon.-Phil.	206	7.23 N	116.30 E
Ba'labakk, Leb.	191a	34.00 N	36.13 E
Balabanovo, Sov. Un. (bȧ-lȧ-bä'nô-vô)	182b	56.10 N	37.44 E
Bala-Cynwyd, Pa.	56b	40.00 N	75.14 W
Balagansk, Sov. Un. (bä-lä-gänsk')	180	53.58 N	103.09 E
Balaguer, Sp. (bä-lä-gĕr')	171	41.48 N	0.50 E
Balakhta, Sov. Un. (bȧ'lȧk-tȧ')	180	55.22 N	91.43 E
Balakleya, Sov. Un. (bȧ'lȧ-klā'yȧ)	175	49.28 N	36.51 E
Balakovo, Sov. Un. (bȧ'lȧ-kô'vŏ)	179	52.00 N	47.40 E
Balancán, Mex. (bä-läŋ-kän')	131	17.47 N	91.32 W
Balanga, Phil. (bä-läŋ'gä)	207a	14.41 N	120.31 E
Balashikha, Sov. Un. (bȧ-lä'shĭ-kȧ)	182b	55.48 N	37.58 E
Balashov, Sov. Un. (bȧ'lȧ-shôf)	179	51.30 N	43.00 E
Balasore, India (bä-lȧ-sōr')	196	21.38 N	86.59 E
Balassagyarmat, Hung. (bô'lôsh-shô-dyôr'môt)	167	48.04 N	19.19 E
Balaton L., Hung. (bô'lô-tôn)	167	46.47 N	17.55 E
Balayan, Phil. (bä-lä-yän')	207a	13.56 N	120.44 E
Balayan B., Phil.	207a	13.46 N	120.46 E
Balboa Heights, Pan. (bäl-bô'ä)	133	8.59 N	79.33 W
Balboa Mt., Pan.	128a	9.05 N	79.44 W
Balcarce, Arg. (bäl-kär'sā)	144	37.49 S	58.17 W
Balchik, Bul.	173	43.24 N	28.13 E
Bald Eagle, Mn. (bôld ē'g'l)	119g	45.06 N	93.01 W
Bald Eagle L., Mn.	119g	45.08 N	93.03 W
Baldock L., Can.	101	56.33 N	97.57 W
Baldwin, NY	55	40.39 N	73.37 W
Baldwin, Pa.	57b	40.23 N	79.58 W
Baldwin Park, Ca. (bôld'wĭn)	119a	34.05 N	117.58 W
Baldwinsville, NY (bôld'wĭns-vĭl)	111	43.10 N	76.20 W
Baldy Mtn., Can.	101	51.28 N	100.44 W
Baldy Pk., Az. (bôl'dē)	121	33.55 N	109.35 W
Baldy Pk., Tx. (bôl'dē pēk)	124	30.38 N	104.11 W
Baleares, Islas (Balearic Is.), Sp. (ē's-läs bä-lĕ-ä'rĕs)	171	39.25 N	1.28 E
Balearic Is., see Baleares, Islas			
Balearic Sea., Eur. (băl-ē-ăr'ĭk)	171	39.40 N	1.05 E
Baleine, Grande Rivière de la (R.), Can.	97	54.45 N	74.20 W
Baler, Phil. (bä-lar')	207a	15.46 N	121.33 E
Baler B., Phil.	207a	15.51 N	121.40 E
Balesin (I.), Phil.	207a	14.28 N	122.10 E
Baley, Sov. Un. (bȧl-yā')	181	51.29 N	116.12 E
Balfate, Hond. (bäl-fä'tē)	132	15.48 N	86.24 W
Balfour, S. Afr. (băl'fo͞or)	223d	26.41 S	28.37 E
Balgowlah, Austl.	70a	33.48 S	151.16 E
Bali (I.), Indon. (bä'lē)	206	8.00 S	115.22 E
Bālihāti, India	67a	22.44 N	88.19 E
Balikesir, Tur. (balĭk'īysĭr)	179	39.40 N	27.50 E
Balikpapan, Indon. (bä'lĕk-pä'pän)	206	1.13 S	116.52 E
Balintang Chan., Phil. (bä-lĭn-täng')	206	19.50 N	121.08 E
Balizhuang, China	67b	39.52 N	116.28 E
Balkan Mts., see Stara Planina			
Balkh, Afg. (bälk)	193	36.48 N	66.50 E
Balkhash, Sov. Un. (bȧl-kăsh')	180	46.58 N	75.00 E
Balkhash, Ozero (L.), Sov. Un.	180	45.58 N	72.15 E
Balki, Sov. Un. (bäl'kĭ)	175	47.22 N	34.56 E
Ballabhpur, India	67a	22.44 N	88.21 E
Ballancourt, Fr. (bä-äɴ-ko͞or')	169b	48.31 N	2.23 E
Ballarat, Austl. (băl'ȧ-răt)	216	37.37 S	144.00 E
Ballard (L.), Austl. (băl'ȧrd)	214	29.15 S	120.45 E
Ballater, Scot. (bäl'ȧ-tēr)	162	57.05 N	3.06 W
Ballé, Mali	228	15.20 N	8.35 W
Ballenato, Punta (C.), Cuba	60b	23.06 N	82.30 W
Balleny Is., Ant. (băl'ĕ nē)	232	67.00 S	164.00 E
Ballina, Austl. (băl-ĭ-nä')	216	28.50 S	153.35 E
Ballina, Ire.	162	54.06 N	9.05 W
Ballinasloe, Ire. (băl'ĭ-nȧ-slō')	162	53.20 N	8.09 W
Ballinger, Tx. (băl'ĭn-jēr)	124	31.45 N	99.58 W
Ballston Spa, NY (bôls'tŭn spä')	111	43.05 N	73.50 W
Ballygunge (Neigh.), India	67a	22.31 N	88.21 E
Balmain, Austl.	70a	33.51 S	151.11 E
Balmazújváros, Hung. (bŏl'mŏz-o͞o'y'vä'rôsh)	167	47.35 N	21.23 E
Balobe, Zaire	231	0.05 N	28.00 E
Balonne (R.), Austl. (băl-ōn')	216	27.00 S	149.10 E
Bālotra, India	196	25.56 N	72.12 E
Balranald, Austl. (băl'-rȧn-ăld)	216	34.42 S	143.30 E
Balş, Rom. (bälsh)	173	44.21 N	24.05 E
Balsam (L.), Can. (bôl'sȧm)	111	44.30 N	78.50 W
Balsas, Braz. (bäl'säs)	143	7.09 S	46.04 W
Balsas (R.), Mex.	128	18.00 N	103.00 W
Balta, Sov. Un. (bäl'tȧ)	175	47.57 N	29.38 E
Baltic Sea, Eur. (bôl'tĭk)	158	55.20 N	16.50 E
Baltimore, Md. (bôl'tĭ-mōr)	112e	39.20 N	76.38 W
Baltimore Highlands, Md.	56c	39.14 N	76.38 W
Baltīm, Egypt (bȧl-tēm')	223b	31.33 N	31.04 E
Baltiysk, Sov. Un. (bäl-tēysk')	165	54.40 N	19.55 E
Baluarte, Río del, Mex. (rē'ō-dĕl-bä-lo͞o'r-tĕ)	130	23.09 N	105.42 W
Baluchistān (Reg.), Pak. (bȧ-lo͞o-chĭ-stän')	193	27.30 N	65.30 E
Balwyn, Austl.	70b	37.49 S	145.05 E
Balzac, Can. (bôl'zăk)	95e	51.10 N	114.01 W
Bama, Nig.	229	11.30 N	13.41 E
Bamako, Mali (bä-mä-kō')	228	12.39 N	8.00 W
Bambang, Phil. (bäm-bäng')	207a	16.24 N	121.08 E
Bambari, Cen. Afr. Rep. (bäm-bȧ-rē)	225	5.44 N	20.40 E
Bamberg, F.R.G. (bäm'bĕrgh)	166	49.53 N	10.52 E
Bamberg, SC (băm'bûrg)	127	33.17 N	81.04 W
Bambuí, Braz. (bä'm-bo͞o-ē)	141a	20.01 S	45.59 W
Bamenda, Cam.	229	5.56 N	10.10 E
Bamingui (R.), Cen. Afr. Rep.	229	7.35 N	19.45 E
Bamingui Bangoran, Parc Nat'l. du (Natl. Park), Cen. Afr. Rep.	229	8.05 N	19.35 E
Bampton, Eng. (băm'tŭn)	156b	51.42 N	1.33 W
Bampūr, Iran (bŭm-po͞or')	192	27.15 N	60.22 E
Bam Yanga, Ngao (Mts.), Cam.	229	8.20 N	14.40 E
Banahao, Mt., Phil. (bä-nä-hä'ō)	207a	14.04 N	121.45 E
Banalia, Zaire	230	1.33 N	25.20 E
Banamba, Mali	228	13.33 N	7.27 W
Bananal, Braz. (bä-nä-näl')	141a	22.42 S	44.17 W
Bananal, Ilha do (I.), Braz. (ē'lä-dô-bä-nä-näl')	143	12.09 S	50.27 W
Banās (R.), India (băn-äs')	196	25.20 N	74.51 E
Banās, Ra's (C.), Egypt	225	23.48 N	36.39 E
Banat (Reg.), Rom.-Yugo. (bä-nät')	173	45.35 N	21.05 E
Banbidian, China	67b	39.54 N	116.32 E

ng-sing; ŋŋ-banŋk; ɴ-nasalized n; nŏd; cŏmmit; ōld; ôbey; ôrder; oi-boil; fo͞od; fo͝ot; ou-out; s-soft; sh-dish; th-thin; pūre; ůnite; ûrn; stŭd; circŭs; ü-as in French tu; '-indeterminate vowel.

PLACE (Pronounciation)	PAGE	Lat. °'	Long. °'
Bancroft, Can. (băn'krŏft)	111	45.05 N	77.55 W
Bancroft, see Chililabombwe			
Bānda, India (bän'dä)	196	25.36 N	80.21 E
Banda Aceh, Indon.	206	5.10 N	95.10 E
Banda Banda, Mt., Austl. (băn'dȧ băn'dȧ)	216	31.09 S	152.15 E
Banda, Kepulauan (Is.), Indon.	207	4.40 S	129.56 E
Banda Laut (Banda Sea), Indon.	207	6.05 S	127.28 E
Bandama Blanc (R.), Ivory Coast (bän-dä'mä)	228	6.15 N	5.00 W
Bandar Abbās, Iran (bän-där' ȧb-bäs')	192	27.04 N	56.22 E
Bandar-e Anzalī, Iran	195	37.28 N	49.27 E
Bandar-e Khomeynī, Iran	192	30.27 N	48.45 E
Bandar-e Lengeh, Iran	192	26.44 N	54.47 E
Bandar-e Torkeman, Iran	192	37.05 N	54.08 E
Bandar Maharani, Mala. (bän-där' mä-hä-rä'nē)	191b	2.02 N	102.34 E
Bandar Seri Begawan, Bru.	211	5.00 N	114.59 E
Bande, Sp.	170	42.02 N	7.58 W
Bandeira, Pico da (Pk.), Braz. (pē'ko͞o dä bän dā'rä)	141a	20.27 S	41.47 W
Bāndel, India	67a	22.56 N	88.22 E
Bandelier Natl. Mon., NM (băn-dĕ-lēr')	121	35.50 N	106.45 W
Banderas, Bahía de (B.), Mex. (bä-ē'ä dĕ bän-dĕ'räs)	130	20.38 N	105.35 W
Bandir C., Indon.	68k	6.11 S	106.49 E
Bandirma, Tur. (bän-dïr'mȧ)	179	40.25 N	27.50 E
Bandon, Or. (băn'dŭn)	116	43.06 N	124.25 W
Bāndra (Neigh), India	197b	19.04 N	72.49 E
Bandundu, Zaire	230	3.18 S	17.20 E
Bandung, Indon.	211	7.00 S	107.22 E
Banes, Cuba (bä'näs)	135	21.00 N	75.45 W
Banff, Can. (bănf)	99	51.10 N	115.34 W
Banff, Scot.	162	57.39 N	2.37 W
Banff Natl. Park, Can.	99	51.38 N	116.22 W
Bánfield, Arg. (bà'n-fyĕ'ld)	144a	34.44 S	58.24 W
Banfora, Upper Volta	228	10.38 N	4.46 W
Bangalore, India (băŋ'gȧ'lôr)	197	13.03 N	77.39 E
Bangassou, Cen. Afr. Rep. (bäɴ-gȧ-so͞o')	225	4.47 N	22.49 E
Bangé, Cam.	229	3.01 N	15.07 E
Bangeta, Mt., Pap. N. Gui.	207	6.20 S	147.00 E
Banggai, Kepulauan (Is.), Indon. (bäng-gī')	207	1.05 N	123.45 E
Banggi, Pulau (I.), Mala.	206	7.12 N	117.10 E
Banghāzī, Libya (bĕn-gä'zē)	225	32.08 N	20.06 E
Bangka (I.), Indon. (bäŋ'kȧ)	206	2.24 S	106.55 E
Bangkalan, Indon. (bäng-kȧ-län')	206	6.07 S	112.50 E
Bang Khun Thian, Thai.	68f	13.42 N	100.28 E
Bangkok, see Krung Thep			
Bangladesh, Asia	193	24.15 N	90.00 E
Bangong Co (L.), China (bäŋ-gōŋ tswo)	196	33.40 N	79.30 E
Bangor, Me. (băn'gẽr)	104	44.47 N	68.47 W
Bangor, Mi.	110	42.20 N	86.05 W
Bangor, Pa.	111	40.55 N	75.10 W
Bangor, Wales (băŋ'ẽr) (băŋ'ŏr)	162	53.13 N	4.05 W
Bangs, Mt., Az. (băngs)	121	36.45 N	113.50 W
Bangu (Neigh.), Braz.	61c	22.52 S	44.27 W
Bangued, Phil. (bän-gād')	207a	17.36 N	120.38 E
Bangui, Cen. Afr. Rep. (bäɴ-gē')	229	4.22 N	18.35 E
Bangweulu, L., Zambia (băng-wē-o͞o'lo͞o)	231	10.55 S	30.10 E
Bangweulu Swp., Zambia	231	11.25 S	30.10 E
Banhā, Egypt	223b	30.24 N	31.11 E
Bani, Dom. Rep. (bä'-nĕ)	135	18.15 N	70.25 W
Bani, Phil. (bä'nē)	207a	16.11 N	119.51 E
Bani (R.), Mali	228	13.07 N	6.15 W
Bánica, Dom. Rep. (bä'-nē-kä)	135	19.00 N	71.35 W
Banī Majdūl, Egypt	71a	30.02 N	31.07 E
Banī Mazār, Egypt	223b	28.29 N	30.48 E
Banī Suwayf, Egypt	223b	29.05 N	31.06 E
Banī Walīd, Libya	194	31.45 N	14.01 E
Banjak, Kepulauan (I.), Indon.	206	2.08 N	97.15 E
Banja Luka, Yugo. (bän-yä-lo͞o'kȧ)	172	44.45 N	17.11 E
Banjarmasin, Indon. (bän-jẽr-mä'sēn)	206	3.18 S	114.32 E
Banjin, China (bän-jyĭn)	200	32.23 N	120.14 E
Banjul (Bathurst), Gam.	228	13.28 N	16.39 W
Bankberg (Mts.), S. Afr. (bȧŋk'bûrg)	227c	32.18 S	25.15 E
Ban Khlong Samrong, Thai.	68f	13.39 N	100.36 E
Banks, Or. (bănks)	118c	45.37 N	123.07 W
Banks, C., Austl.	211b	34.01 S	151.17 E
Banks (Is.), Austl.	215	10.10 S	143.08 E
Banks I., Can.	94	73.00 N	123.00 W
Banks I., Can.	98	53.25 N	130.10 W
Banks Is., Vanuatu	215	13.38 S	168.23 E
Banksmeadow, Austl.	70a	33.58 S	151.13 E
Banks Pen., N.Z.	215a	43.45 S	172.20 E
Banks Str., Austl.	216	40.45 S	148.00 E
Bankstown, Austl.	70a	33.55 S	151.02 E
Ban Lat Phrao, Thai.	68f	13.47 N	100.36 E
Bann (R.), N. Ire. (băn)	162	54.50 N	6.29 W
Banning, Ca. (băn'ĭng)	119a	33.56 N	116.53 W
Bannister (R.), Va. (băn'ĭs-tẽr)	127	36.45 N	79.17 W
Bannockburn, Austl.	211a	38.03 S	144.11 E
Bannu, Pak.	196	33.03 N	70.39 E
Baños, Ec. (bä'-nyôs)	142	1.30 S	78.22 W
Banská Bystrica, Czech. (bän'skä bē'strē-tzä)	167	48.46 N	19.10 E
Bansko, Bul. (bän'skō)	173	41.51 N	23.33 E
Banstala, India	67a	22.32 N	88.25 E
Banstead, Eng. (băn'stĕd)	156b	51.18 N	0.09 W
Banton, Phil. (bän-tōn')	207a	12.54 N	121.55 E
Bantry, Ire. (băn'trĭ)	162	51.39 N	9.30 W
Bantry B., Ire.	162	51.25 N	10.09 W
Banyuwangi, Indon. (bän-jo͞o-wäŋ'gē)	206	8.15 S	114.15 E
Baocheng, China (bou-chŭŋ)	202	33.15 N	106.58 E
Baodi, China (bou-dē)	200	39.44 N	117.19 E
Baoding, China (bou-dĭŋ)	200	38.52 N	115.31 E
Baoji, China (bou-jyē)	202	34.10 N	106.58 E
Baoshan, China (bou-shän)	198	25.14 N	99.03 E
Baoshan, China	201b	31.25 N	121.29 E
Baotou, China (bou-tō)	202	40.28 N	110.10 E
Baoying, China (bou-yĭŋ)	200	33.14 N	119.20 E
Bapsfontein, S. Afr. (băps-fŏn-tān')	227b	26.01 S	28.26 E
Ba 'qūbah, Iraq	195	33.45 N	44.38 E
Ba-queo, Viet.	68m	10.48 N	106.38 E
Baqueroncito, Col. (bä-kē-rō'n-sē-tô)	142a	3.18 N	74.40 W
Bar, Sov. Un. (bär)	175	49.02 N	27.44 E
Bara, India	67a	22.46 N	88.17 E
Baraawe, Som.	223a	1.20 N	44.00 E
Barabinsk, Sov. Un. (bȧ'rȧ-bĭnsk)	180	55.18 N	78.00 E
Baraboo, Wi. (bâr'ȧ-bo͞o)	115	43.29 N	89.44 W
Baracoa, Cuba (bä-rä-kō'ä)	135	20.20 N	74.25 W
Baracoa, Cuba	135a	23.03 N	82.34 W
Baradeo, Arg. (bä-rä-dĕ'ō)	141c	33.50 S	59.30 W
Baradères, Baie des (B.), Hai (bä-rä-dâr')	135	18.35 N	73.35 W
Baragwanath, S. Afr.	71b	26.16 S	27.59 E
Barahona, Dom. Rep. (bä-rä-ô'nä)	135	18.15 N	71.10 W
Barajas de Madrid, Sp. (bä-rä'häs dā mä-drēdh')	171a	40.28 N	3.35 W
Baranagar, India	196a	22.38 N	88.25 E
Baranco, Belize (bä-räŋ'kō)	132	16.01 N	88.55 W
Baranof (I.), Ak. (bä-rä'nôf)	107	56.48 N	136.08 W
Baranovichi, Sov. Un. (bä'rä-nō-vē'chē)	167	53.08 N	25.59 E
Baranpauh, Indon.	191b	0.40 N	103.28 E
Barão de Juperanā, Braz. (bȧ-rou'ɴ-dĕ-zho͞o-pe-rȧ'nȧ)	144b	22.21 S	43.41 W
Barão de Melgaço, Braz. (bä-rouɴ-dĕ-mĕl-gä'sō)	143	16.12 S	55.48 W
Bārāsat, India	67a	22.51 N	88.22 E
Bārāsat, India	196a	22.42 N	88.29 E
Barataria B., La.	125	29.13 N	89.90 W
Baraya, Col. (bä-rȧ'yä)	142a	3.10 N	75.04 W
Barbacena, Braz. (bär-bä-sā'nȧ)	141a	21.15 S	43.46 W
Barbacoas, Col. (bär-bä-kō'äs)	142	1.39 N	78.12 W
Barbacoas, Ven. (bä-bä-kô'ȧs)	143b	9.30 N	66.58 W
Barbados, N.A. (bär-bā'dōz)	129	13.30 N	59.00 W
Barbar, Sud.	225	18.11 N	34.00 E
Barbastro, Sp. (bär-bäs'trō)	171	42.05 N	0.05 E
Barbeau, Mi. (bȧr-bō')	119k	46.17 N	84.16 W
Barberton, Oh. (bär'bẽr-tŭn)	113d	41.01 N	81.37 W
Barberton, S. Afr.	226	25.48 S	31.04 E
Barbezieux, Fr. (bärb'zyû')	168	45.30 N	0.11 W
Barbosa, Col. (bär-bō'-sȧ)	142a	6.26 N	75.19 W
Barboursville, WV (bär'bẽrs-vĭl)	110	38.20 N	82.20 W
Barbourville, Ky. (bär'bẽr-vĭl)	126	36.52 N	83.58 W
Barbuda (I.), Antigua (bär-bo͞o'dȧ)	129	17.45 N	61.15 W
Barcaldine, Austl. (bär'kôl-dīn)	215	23.33 S	145.17 E
Barcarena, Port. (bär-kä-rē'-nä)	171b	38.29 N	9.17 W
Barcarrota, Sp. (bär-kär-rō'tä)	170	38.31 N	6.50 W
Barcellona, It. (bä-chĕl-lō'nä)	172	38.07 N	15.15 E
Barcelona (Neigh.), Sp.	65b	40.22 N	3.34 E
Barcelona, Sp. (bär-thȧ-lō'nä)	171	41.25 N	2.08 E
Barcelona, Ven. (bär-sȧ-lō'nä)	143b	10.09 N	64.41 W
Barcelos, Braz. (bär-sĕ'lôs)	142	1.04 S	63.00 W
Barcelos, Port. (bär-thȧ'lōs)	170e	41.34 N	8.39 W
Barcroft, Lake (Res.), Md.	56d	38.51 N	77.09 W
Bardar-e Pahlavī, Iran	192	37.16 N	49.15 E
Bardawīl, Sabkhat al (B.), Egypt	191a	31.20 N	33.24 E
Bardejov, Czech. (bär'dyĕ-yôf)	167	49.18 N	21.18 E
Bardsey I., Wales (bärd'sē)	162	52.45 N	4.50 W
Bardstown, Ky. (bärds'toun)	110	37.50 N	85.30 W
Bardwell, Ky. (bärd'wĕl)	126	36.51 N	88.57 W
Bare Hills, Md.	56c	39.23 N	76.40 W
Barents Sea, Sov. Un. (bä'rĕnts)	176	72.14 N	37.28 E
Barentu, Eth. (bä-rĕn'to͞o)	225	15.06 N	37.39 E
Barfleur, Pte. de (Pt.), Fr. (bȧr-flûr')	168	49.43 N	1.17 W
Barguzin, Sov. Un. (bär'go͞o-zĭn)	181	53.44 N	109.28 E
Bar Harbor, Me. (bär här'bẽr)	104	44.22 N	68.13 W
Bari, It. (bä'rē)	172	41.08 N	16.53 E
Barinas, Ven. (bä-rē'näs)	142	8.36 N	70.14 W
Baring, C., Can. (bâr'ĭng)	96	70.07 N	119.48 W
Barisan, Pegunungan (Mts.), Indon. (bä-rē-sän')	206	2.38 S	101.45 E
Bariti Bil (L.), India	67a	22.48 N	88.26 E
Barito (Strm.), Indon. (bä-rē'tō)	206	2.10 S	114.38 E
Barka (R.), Eth.	225	16.44 N	37.34 E
Barking (Neigh.), Eng.	62	51.33 N	0.06 E
Barkingside (Neigh.), Eng.	62	51.36 N	0.05 E
Barkley Sd., Can.	98	48.53 N	125.20 W
Barkly East, S. Afr. (bärk'lē ēst)	227c	30.58 S	27.37 E
Barkly Tableland (Plat.), Austl. (bär'klē)	214	18.15 S	137.05 E
Barkol, China (bär-kůl)	198	43.43 N	92.50 E
Barkshire (Co.), Eng.	156b	51.23 N	1.07 W
Bar-le-Duc, Fr. (bär-lē-dük')	168	48.47 N	5.05 E
Barlee (L.), Austl. (bär-lē')	214	29.45 S	119.00 E
Barletta, It. (bär-lĕt'tä)	172	41.19 N	16.20 E
Barmen (Neigh.), F.R.G.	63	51.17 N	7.13 E
Barmstedt, F.R.G. (bärm'shtĕt)	157c	53.47 N	9.46 E
Barnaul, Sov. Un. (bär-nä-o͞ol')	180	53.18 N	83.23 E
Barnes (Neigh.), Eng.	62	51.28 N	0.15 W
Barnesboro, Pa. (bärnz'bẽr-ō)	111	40.45 N	78.50 W
Barnesville, Ga. (bärnz'vĭl)	126	33.03 N	84.10 W
Barnesville, Mn.	114	46.38 N	96.25 W
Barnesville, Oh.	110	39.55 N	81.10 W
Barnet, Vt. (bär'nĕt)	111	44.20 N	72.00 W
Barnetby le Wold, Eng. (bär'nĕt-bĭ)	156	53.34 N	0.26 W
Barnett Hbr., Ba.	134	25.40 N	79.20 W
Barnsdall, Ok. (bärnz'dôl)	123	36.38 N	96.14 W
Barnsley, Eng. (bärnz'lĭ)	156	53.33 N	1.29 W
Barnstaple, Eng. (bärn'stā-p'l)	162	51.06 N	4.05 W
Barnston, Eng.	64a	53.21 N	3.05 W
Barnum Island, NY	55	40.36 N	73.39 W
Barnwell, SC (bärn'wĕl)	127	33.14 N	81.23 W
Baro, Nig. (bä'rō)	229	8.37 N	6.25 E
Baroda, India (bär-rō'dä)	196	22.21 N	73.12 E
Barotse Pln., Zambia	230	15.50 S	22.55 E
Barqah (Cyrenaica) (Prov.), Libya	225	31.09 N	21.45 E
Barquisimeto, Ven. (bär-kē-sē-mā'tō)	142	10.04 N	69.16 W
Barra, Braz. (bär'rä)	143	11.04 S	43.11 W
Barraba, Austl.	216	30.22 S	150.36 E
Barracas (Neigh.), Arg.	60d	34.38 S	58.22 W
Barrackpore, India	67a	22.46 N	88.21 E
Barrackpore Cantonment, India	67a	22.46 N	88.22 E
Barra do Corda, Braz. (bär'rä do͞o cōr-dä)	143	5.33 S	45.13 W
Barra Funda (Neigh.), Braz.	61d	23.31 S	46.39 W
Barra Mansa, Braz. (bär'rä män'sä)	141a	22.35 S	44.09 W
Barrancabermeja, Col. (bär-räŋ'kä-bēr-mā'hä)	142	7.06 N	73.49 W
Barrancas, Chile	61b	33.27 S	70.46 W
Barranco, Peru	60c	12.09 S	77.02 W
Barranquilla, Col. (bär-rän-kēl'yä)	142	10.57 N	75.00 W
Barras, Braz. (bȧ'r-räs)	143	4.13 S	42.14 W
Barre, Vt. (băr'ē)	111	44.15 N	72.30 W
Barre do Piraí, Braz. (bȧr'rē-dô-pē'rä-ē')	141a	22.30 S	43.49 W
Barreiras, Braz. (bär-rā'räs)	143	12.13 S	44.59 W
Barreiro, Port. (bär-rē'ē-ro͞o)	171b	38.39 N	9.05 W
Barren (R.), Ky.	126	37.00 N	86.20 W
Barren, C., Austl. (băr'ĕn)	216	40.20 S	149.00 E
Barren, Nosy (Is.), Mad.	227	18.18 S	43.57 E
Barretos, Braz. (bär-rā'tôs)	143	20.40 S	48.36 W
Barrhead, Can. (băr-hĕd) (băr'ĭd)	99	54.08 N	114.24 W
Barriada Pomar Alto, Sp.	65e	41.29 N	2.14 E
Barrie, Can. (băr'ĭ)	111	44.25 N	79.45 W
Barrington, Can. (bă-rĕng-tŏn)	95a	45.07 N	73.35 W
Barrington, Il.	113a	42.09 N	88.08 W
Barrington, NJ	56b	39.52 N	75.04 W
Barrington, RI	112b	41.44 N	71.16 W
Barrington Tops (Mtn.), Austl.	216	32.00 S	151.25 E
Barrio Obrero Industrial, Peru	60c	12.04 S	77.04 W
Bar River, Can. (bär)	119k	46.27 N	84.02 W
Barron, Wi. (băr'ŭn)	115	45.24 N	91.51 W
Barrow, Ak. (băr'ō)	107	71.20 N	156.00 W
Barrow (I.), Austl.	214	20.50 S	115.00 E
Barrow Creek, Austl.	214	21.23 S	133.55 E
Barrow-in-Furness, Eng.	162	54.10 N	3.15 W
Barrow Pt., Ak.	107	71.20 N	156.00 W
Barrow R., Ire. (bȧ-rȧ)	162	52.35 N	7.05 W
Barstow, Ca. (bär'stō)	120	34.53 N	117.03 W
Barstow, Md.	112e	38.32 N	76.37 W
Barth, G.D.R. (bärt)	166	54.20 N	12.43 E
Bartholomew Bayou, Ar. (bär-thŏl'ō-mū bī-o͞o')	123	33.53 N	91.45 W
Barthurst, Can. (bär-thûrst')	104	47.38 N	65.40 W
Bartica, Guy (bär'tĭ-kȧ)	143	6.23 N	58.32 W
Bartin, Tur. (bär'tĭn)	179	41.35 N	32.12 E
Bartle Frere, Mt., Austl. (bärt''l frēr')	215	17.30 S	145.46 E
Bartlesville, Ok. (bär'tlz-vĭl)	123	36.44 N	95.58 W
Bartlett, Il. (bärt'lĕt)	113a	41.59 N	88.11 W
Bartlett, Tx.	125	30.48 N	97.25 W
Barton, Vt. (bär'tŭn)	111	44.45 N	72.05 W
Barton-upon-Humber, Eng. (bär'tŭn-ŭp'ŏn-hŭm'bẽr)	156	53.41 N	0.26 W
Bartoszyce, Pol. (bär-tô-shĭ'tsȧ)	167	54.15 N	20.50 E
Bartow, Fl. (bär'tō)	127a	27.51 N	81.50 W
Baruta, Ven.	61a	10.26 N	66.53 W
Barú, Volcán (Vol.), Pan.	133	8.48 N	82.37 W
Barvenkovo, Sov. Un. (bär'vĕn-kô'vô)	175	48.55 N	36.59 E
Barwon (R.), Austl. (bär'wŭn)	216	29.45 S	148.25 E
Barwon Heads, Austl.	211a	38.17 S	144.29 E
Barycz R., Pol. (bä'rĭch)	166	51.30 N	16.38 E
Basai Dārāpur (Neigh.), India	67d	28.40 N	77.08 E
Basankusu, Zaire (bä-sän-ko͞o'so͞o)	225	1.14 N	19.45 E
Basbeck, F.R.G. (bäs'bĕk)	157c	53.40 N	9.11 E
Basdahl, F.R.G. (bäs'däl)	157c	53.27 N	9.00 E
Basehor, Ks. (bās'hôr)	119f	39.08 N	94.55 W
Basel, Switz. (bä'z'l)	166	47.32 N	7.35 E
Bashee (R.), S. Afr. (bă-shē')	227c	31.47 S	28.25 E
Bashi Chan, Phil. (băsh'ē)	203	21.20 N	120.22 E
Bashkir (A.S.S.R.), Sov. Un. (bȧsh-kēr')	178	54.12 N	57.15 E
Bashtanka, Sov. Un. (bȧsh-tän'kȧ)	175	47.32 N	32.31 E
Bashtīl, Egypt	71a	30.05 N	31.11 E
Basilan I., Phil.	206	6.37 N	122.07 E
Basildon, Eng.	62	51.35 N	0.25 E
Basilicata (Reg.), It. (bä-zē-lē-kä'tä)	172	40.30 N	15.55 E
Basin, Wy. (bā'sĭn)	117	44.22 N	108.02 W
Basingstoke, Eng. (bā'zĭng-stōk)	156b	51.14 N	1.06 W
Baška, Yugo. (bäsh'ka)	172	44.58 N	14.44 E
Başkale, Tur. (bäsh-kä'lē)	179	38.10 N	44.00 E
Baskatong Res., Can.	103	46.50 N	75.50 W
Baskunchak (L.), Sov. Un.	179	48.20 N	46.40 E
Basoko, Zaire (bȧ-sō'kō)	225	0.52 N	23.50 E
Bassano, Can. (bäs-sän'ō)	99	50.47 N	112.28 W
Bassano del Grappa, It.	172	45.46 N	11.44 E
Bassari, Togo	228	9.15 N	0.47 E
Bassas da India (I.), Afr. (bäs'säs dä ēn'dē-ȧ)	227	21.23 S	39.42 E
Bassein, Bur. (bŭ-sēn')	206	16.46 N	94.47 E
Basse Terre, Guad. (bäs' târ')	133b	16.00 N	61.43 W
Basseterre, Saint Christopher-Nevis	133b	17.20 N	62.42 W
Basse Terre I., Guad.	133b	16.10 N	62.14 W
Bassett, Va. (băs'sĕt)	127	36.45 N	81.58 W
Bass Hill, Austl.	70a	33.54 S	151.00 E
Bass Is., Oh. (băs)	110	41.40 N	82.50 W
Bass Str., Austl.	216	39.40 S	145.40 E
Basswood (L.), Can.-Mn. (băs'wo͝od)	115	48.10 N	91.36 W
Bästad, Swe. (bô'stät)	164	56.26 N	12.46 E
Bastia, Fr. (bäs'tē-ä)	172	42.43 N	9.27 E
Bastogne, Bel. (bäs-tôn'y')	163	50.02 N	5.45 E
Bastrop, La. (bás'trŭp)	125	32.47 N	91.55 W
Bastrop, Tx.	125	30.08 N	97.18 W
Bastrop Bayou, Tx.	125a	29.07 N	95.22 W

PRONOUNCING INDEX

Bāsudebpur – Bella Coola 259

PLACE (Pronounciation)	PAGE	Lat. °′	Long. °′
Bāsudebpur, India	67a	22.49 N	88.25 E
Bata, Equat.Gui. (bä'tä)	230	1.51 N	9.45 E
Batabanó, Cuba (bä-tä-bä-nō')	134	22.45 N	82.20 W
Batabano, Golfo, de (G.), Cuba (gôl-fô-dĕ-bä-tä-bȧ'nō)	134	22.10 N	83.05 W
Batāla, India	196	31.54 N	75.18 E
Bataly, Sov. Un. (bȧ-tä'lĭ)	182a	52.51 N	62.03 E
Batam I., Indon. (bä-täm')	191b	1.03 N	104.00 E
Batang, China (bä-täŋ)	198	30.08 N	99.00 E
Batangan, C., Viet.	203	15.18 N	109.10 E
Batangas, Phil. (bä-tän'gäs)	207a	13.45 N	121.04 E
Batan Is., Phil. (bä-tän')	203	20.58 N	122.20 E
Bátaszék, Hung. (bä'tȧ-sĕk)	167	46.07 N	18.40 E
Batavia, Il. (bȧ-tā'vĭ-ȧ)	113a	41.51 N	88.18 W
Batavia, NY	111	43.00 N	78.15 W
Batavia, Oh.	113f	39.05 N	84.10 W
Bataysk, Sov. Un. (bȧ-tīsk')	175	47.08 N	39.44 E
Bātdâmbâng, Kamp. (bȧt-tȧm-bāng')	206	13.14 N	103.15 E
Batenbrock (Neigh.), F.R.G.	63	51.31 N	6.57 E
Batesburg, SC (bāts'bûrg)	127	33.53 N	81.34 W
Batesville, Ar. (bāts'vĭl)	123	35.46 N	91.39 W
Batesville, In.	110	39.15 N	85.15 W
Batesville, Ms.	126	34.17 N	89.55 W
Batetska, Sov. Un. (bȧ-tĕ'tskȧ)	174	58.36 N	30.21 E
Bath, Can. (bȧth)	104	46.31 N	67.36 W
Bath, Eng.	162	51.24 N	2.20 W
Bath, Me.	104	43.54 N	69.50 W
Bath, NY	111	42.25 N	77.20 W
Bath, Oh.	113d	41.11 N	81.38 W
Bathsheba, Barb.	133b	13.13 N	60.30 W
Bathurst, Austl. (bȧth'ŭrst)	215	33.28 S	149.30 E
Bathurst (I.), Austl.	214	11.19 S	130.13 E
Bathurst, S. Afr. (băt-hûrst)	227c	33.26 S	26.53 E
Bathurst, C., Can. (bȧth'rst)	107	70.33 N	127.55 W
Bathurst Inlet, Can.	96	68.10 N	108.00 W
Bathurst, see Banjul			
Batia, Benin	228	10.54 N	1.29 E
Batian (I.), Indon.	207	1.07 S	127.52 E
Bāţlāq-E Gāvkhūnī (L.), Iran	192	31.40 N	52.48 E
Batley, Eng. (băt'lĭ)	156	53.43 N	1.37 W
Batna, Alg. (bät'nä)	224	35.41 N	6.12 E
Baton Rouge, La. (băt'ŭn ro͞ozh')	125	30.28 N	91.10 W
Batouri, Cam.	229	4.26 N	14.22 E
Battersea (Neigh.), Eng.	62	51.28 N	0.10 W
Batticaloa, Sri Lanka	197	8.40 N	81.10 E
Battle (R.), Can.	99	52.20 N	111.59 W
Battle (R.), Can.	100	53.05 N	109.40 W
Battle Creek, Mi. (băt''l krēk')	110	42.20 N	85.15 W
Battle Ground, Wa. (băt''l ground)	118c	45.47 N	122.32 W
Battle Harbour, Can. (băt''l här'bēr)	97	52.17 N	55.33 W
Battle Mountain, Nv.	116	40.40 N	116.56 W
Battonya, Hung. (bät-tô'nyä)	167	46.17 N	21.00 E
Batu Kepulauan (I.), Indon. (bä'to͞o)	206	0.10 S	99.55 E
Batumi, Sov. Un. (bŭ-to͞o'mē)	179	41.40 N	41.30 E
Batu Pahat., Mala.	191b	1.51 N	102.56 E
Batupanjang, Indon.	191b	1.42 N	101.35 E
Baturité, Braz. (bä-to͞o-rē-tā')	143	4.16 S	38.47 W
Bauang, Phil. (bä'wäng)	207a	16.31 N	120.19 E
Bauchi, Nig. (bȧ-o͞o'chē)	229	10.19 N	9.50 E
Baudouinville, Zaire (bō-dwăN-vēl')	226	7.12 S	29.39 E
Bauernschaft, F.R.G.	63	51.34 N	6.33 E
Bauerstown, Pa.	57b	40.30 N	79.59 W
Baukau (Neigh.), F.R.G.	63	51.33 N	7.12 E
Bauld, C. Can.	105	51.38 N	55.25 W
Baulkham Hills, Austl.	70a	33.46 S	151.00 E
Baumschulenweg (Neigh.), G.D.R.	65a	52.28 N	13.29 E
Bāuria, India	196a	22.29 N	88.08 E
Bauru, Braz. (bou-ro͞o')	143	22.21 S	48.57 W
Bauska, Sov. Un. (bou'skȧ)	165	56.24 N	24.12 E
Bauta, Cuba (bȧ'o͞o-tä)	135a	22.59 N	82.33 W
Bautzen, G.D.R. (bout'sĕn)	166	51.11 N	14.27 E
Bavaria (State), see Bayern			
Baw Baw, Mt., Austl. (bȧ-bȧ)	216	37.50 S	146.17 E
Bawean, Pulau (I.), Indon. (bȧ'vē-än)	206	5.50 S	112.40 E
Bawtry, Eng. (bôtrĭ)	156	53.26 N	1.01 W
Baxley, Ga. (băks'lĭ)	127	31.47 N	82.22 W
Baxter, Austl. (Băks'tēr)	211a	38.12 S	145.10 E
Baxter Springs, Ks. (băks'tēr sprĭngs')	123	37.01 N	94.44 W
Bayaguana, Dom. Rep. (bä-yä-gwä'nä)	135	18.45 N	69.40 W
Bay al Kabīr Wadi (R.), Libya	160	29.52 N	14.28 E
Bayambang, Phil. (bä-yäm-bäng')	207a	15.50 N	120.26 E
Bayamo, Cuba (bä-yä'mō)	134	20.25 N	76.35 W
Bayamón, P.R.	129b	18.27 N	66.13 W
Bayan, China (bä-yän)	202	46.00 N	127.20 E
Bayan-Aul, Sov. Un. (bä'yän-oul')	180	50.43 N	75.37 E
Bayard, Ne. (bā'ērd)	114	41.45 N	103.20 W
Bayard, WV	111	39.15 N	79.20 W
Bayburt, Tur. (bä'ĭ-bo͝ort)	179	40.15 N	40.10 E
Baychabo, Som.	223a	3.19 N	44.20 E
Bay City, Mi. (bā)	110	43.35 N	83.55 W
Bay City, Tx.	125	28.59 N	95.58 W
Baydarag Gol (R.), Mong.	198	46.09 N	98.52 E
Baydaratskaya Guba (B.), Sov. Un.	178	69.20 N	66.10 E
Bay de Verde, Can.	105	48.05 N	52.54 W
Bayern (Bavaria) (State), F.R.G. (bī'ērn) (bȧ-vâ-rĭ-ȧ)	166	49.00 N	11.16 E
Bayeux, Fr. (bȧ-yû')	168	49.19 N	0.41 W
Bayfield, Wi. (bā'fēld)	115	46.48 N	90.51 W
Bayford, Eng.	62	51.46 N	0.06 W
Baykal, Ozero (Baikal, L.), Sov. Un. (bī'käl') (bī'kôl)	181	53.00 N	109.28 E
Baykals'kiy Khrebet (Baikal Mts.), Sov. Un.	181	53.30 N	102.00 E
Baykit, Sov. Un. (bī-kēt')	180	61.43 N	96.39 E
Baykonur, Sov. Un. (bī-kō-no͞or')	180	47.46 N	66.11 E
Baymak, Sov. Un. (bȧy'mäk)	182a	52.35 N	58.21 E
Bay Mills, Mi. (bā mĭlls)	119k	46.27 N	84.36 W
Bay Mills Ind. Res., Mi.	115	46.19 N	85.03 W
Bay Minette, Al. (bā'mĭn-ĕt')	126	30.52 N	87.44 W
Bayombong, Phil. (bä-yôm-bŏng')	207a	16.28 N	121.09 E
Bayonne, Fr. (bȧ-yôn')	168	43.28 N	1.30 W
Bayonne, NJ (bā-yōn')	112a	40.40 N	74.07 W
Bayou Bodcau Res., La. (bī'yo͞o bŏd'kō)	125	32.49 N	93.22 W
Bay Park, NY	55	40.38 N	73.40 W
Bayport, Mn. (bā'pōrt)	119g	45.02 N	92.46 W
Bayramic, Tur.	173	39.48 N	26.35 E
Bayreuth, F.R.G. (bī-roit')	166	49.56 N	11.35 E
Bay Ridge (Neigh.), NY	55	40.37 N	74.02 W
Bay Roberts, Can. (bā rŏb'ērts)	105	47.36 N	53.16 W
Bayrūt, see Beirut			
Bay Saint Louis, Ms. (bā' sȧnt lo͞o'ĭs)	126	30.19 N	89.20 W
Bay Shore, NY (bā' shôr)	112a	40.44 N	73.15 W
Bayside, Ma.	54a	42.18 N	70.53 W
Bayside (Neigh.), NY	55	40.46 N	73.46 W
Bays, L. of, Can. (bās)	111	45.15 N	79.00 W
Bayswater, Austl.	70b	37.51 S	145.16 E
Bayswater North, Austl.	70b	37.49 S	145.17 E
Bayt Lahm (Bethlehem), Jordan (bĕth'lē-hĕm)	191a	31.42 N	35.13 E
Baytown, Tx. (bā'town)	125a	29.44 N	95.01 W
Bayview, Al. (bā'vū)	112h	33.34 N	86.59 W
Bayview (Neigh.), Ca.	58b	37.44 N	122.23 W
Bayview, Wa.	118a	48.29 N	122.28 W
Bay Village, Oh. (bā)	113d	41.29 N	81.56 W
Bayville, NY	55	40.54 N	73.33 W
Baza, Sp. (bä'thä)	170	37.29 N	2.46 W
Bazar-Dyuzi (Mt.), Sov. Un. (bä'zȧr-dyo͞oz'ĕ)	179	41.20 N	47.40 E
Bazaruto, Ilha do (I.), Moz. (bȧ-zȧ-ro͞o'tō)	226	21.42 S	36.10 E
Baza, Sierra de (Mts.), Sp.	170	37.19 N	2.48 W
Baziège, Fr.	168	43.25 N	1.41 E
Beach, ND (bēch)	114	46.55 N	104.00 W
Beachwood, Oh.	56a	41.34 N	81.28 W
Beachy Head, Eng. (bēchē hĕd)	163	50.40 N	0.25 E
Beacon, NY (bē'kŭn)	111	41.30 N	73.55 W
Beacon Hill, Austl.	70a	33.45 S	151.15 E
Beacon Hill (Mtn.), China	68c	22.21 N	114.09 E
Beaconsfield, Can. (bē'kŭnz-fēld)	95a	45.26 N	73.51 W
Beafort Mtn., NJ (bē'fōrt)	112a	41.08 N	74.23 W
Beals Cr., Tx. (bēls)	124	32.10 N	101.14 W
Bean, Eng.	62	51.25 N	0.17 E
Bear (L.), Id.-Ut.	117	41.56 N	111.10 W
Bear Brook (R.), Can.	95c	45.24 N	75.15 W
Bear Cr., Al. (bâr)	126	34.27 N	88.00 W
Bear Cr., Tx.	119c	32.56 N	97.09 W
Bear Creek, Mt. (bâr krēk)	117	45.11 N	109.07 W
Beardstown, Il. (bērds'toun)	123	40.01 N	90.26 W
Bearhead Mtn., Wa. (bâr'hēd)	118a	47.01 N	121.49 W
Bear L., Can.	101	55.08 N	96.00 W
Bear R., Id.	117	42.17 N	111.42 W
Bear R., Ut.	119b	41.28 N	112.10 W
Beas de Segura, Sp. (bā'äs dā sä-go͞o'rä)	170	38.16 N	2.53 W
Beata (I.), Dom. Rep. (bĕ-ä'tä)	135	17.40 N	71.40 W
Beata, Cabo (C.), Dom. Rep. (kȧ'bō-bĕ-ä'tä)	135	17.40 N	71.20 W
Beato (Neigh.), Port.	65d	38.44 N	9.06 W
Beatrice, Ne. (bē'ȧ-trĭs)	123	40.16 N	96.45 W
Beatty, Nv. (bēt'ē)	120	36.58 N	116.48 W
Beattyville, Ky. (bēt'ē-vĭl)	110	37.35 N	83.40 W
Beaucaire, Fr. (bō-kâr')	168	43.49 N	4.37 E
Beaucourt, Fr. (bō-ko͞or')	169	47.30 N	6.54 E
Beaufort, NC (bō'frt)	127	34.43 N	76.40 W
Beaufort, SC	127	32.25 N	80.40 W
Beaufort Sea, Ak.	107	70.30 N	138.40 W
Beaufort West, S. Afr.	226	32.20 S	22.45 E
Beauharnois, Can. (bō-är-nwä')	95a	45.23 N	73.52 W
Beaumont, Ca. (bō'mŏnt)	119a	33.57 N	116.57 W
Beaumont, Can.	95b	46.50 N	71.01 W
Beaumont, Can.	95g	53.22 N	113.18 W
Beaumont, Tx.	125	30.05 N	94.06 W
Beaune, Fr. (bōn)	168	47.02 N	4.49 E
Beauport, Can. (bō-pôr')	95b	46.52 N	71.11 W
Beaupré, Can. (bō-prā')	95b	47.03 N	70.53 W
Beauséjour, Can.	101	50.04 N	96.33 W
Beauvais, Fr. (bō-vĕ')	168	49.25 N	2.05 E
Beaver (I.), Mi.	110	45.40 N	85.30 W
Beaver, Ok. (bē'vēr)	122	36.46 N	100.31 W
Beaver, Pa.	113e	40.42 N	80.18 W
Beaver (R.), Can.	100	54.20 N	111.10 W
Beaver, Ut.	121	38.15 N	112.40 W
Beaver City, Ne.	122	40.08 N	99.52 W
Beaver Cr., Co.	122	39.42 N	103.37 W
Beaver Cr., Ks.	122	39.44 N	101.05 W
Beaver Cr., Mt.	114	46.45 N	104.18 W
Beaver Cr., Wy.	114	43.46 N	104.25 W
Beaver Dam, Wi.	115	43.29 N	88.50 W
Beaverhead Mts., Mt. (bē'vēr-hĕd)	117	44.33 N	112.59 W
Beaverhead R., Mt.	117	45.25 N	112.35 W
Beaver Ind. Res., Mi.	110	45.40 N	85.30 W
Beaverton, Or. (bē'vēr-tŭn)	118c	45.29 N	122.49 W
Bebará', Col. (bĕ-bä-rȧ')	142a	6.07 N	76.39 W
Bebek (Neigh.), Tur.	66f	41.04 N	29.02 E
Bebington, Eng. (bē'bĭng-tŭn)	156	53.20 N	2.59 W
Beccar (Neigh.), Arg.	60d	34.28 S	58.31 W
Bečej, Yugo. (bč'chā)	173	45.36 N	20.03 E
Becerreá, Sp. (bā-thā'rē-ä)	170	42.49 N	7.12 W
Béchar, Alg.	224	31.39 N	2.14 W
Becharof (L.), Ak. (bĕk-ȧ-rôf)	107	57.58 N	156.58 W
Becher B., Can. (bēch'ēr)	118a	48.18 N	123.37 W
Beckenham (Neigh.), Eng.	62	51.24 N	0.02 W
Beckley, WV (bĕk'lĭ)	110	37.40 N	81.15 W
Bédarieux, Fr. (bā-dȧ-ryû')	168	43.36 N	3.11 E
Beddington (Neigh.), Eng.	62	51.22 N	0.08 W
Beddington Cr., Can. (bĕd'ĕng tŭn)	95e	51.14 N	114.13 W
Bedford, Can. (bĕd'fērd)	111	45.10 N	73.00 W
Bedford, Eng.	162	52.10 N	0.25 W
Bedford, Ia.	115	40.40 N	94.41 W
Bedford, In.	110	38.50 N	86.30 W
Bedford, Ma.	105a	42.30 N	71.17 W
Bedford, NY	112a	41.12 N	73.38 W
Bedford, Oh.	113d	41.23 N	81.32 W
Bedford, Pa.	111	40.05 N	78.20 W
Bedford, S. Afr.	227c	32.43 S	26.19 E
Bedford, Va.	127	37.19 N	79.27 W
Bedford Heights, Oh.	56a	41.22 N	81.30 W
Bedford Hills, NY	112a	41.14 N	73.41 W
Bedford Park, Il.	58a	41.46 N	87.49 W
Bedford Park (Neigh.), NY	55	40.52 N	73.53 W
Bedford-Stuyvesant (Neigh.), NY	55	40.41 N	73.55 W
Bedmond, Eng.	62	51.43 N	0.25 W
Bedok, Singapore	67c	1.19 N	103.57 E
Beebe, Ar. (bē'bē)	123	35.04 N	91.54 W
Beecher, Il. (bē'chŭr)	113a	41.20 N	87.38 W
Beechey Hd., Can. (bē'chĭ hĕd)	118a	48.19 N	123.40 W
Beech Grove, In. (bēch grōv)	113g	39.43 N	86.05 W
Beechview (Neigh.), Pa.	57b	40.25 N	80.02 W
Beeck (Neigh.), F.R.G.	63	51.29 N	6.44 E
Beeckerwerth (Neigh.), F.R.G.	63	51.29 N	6.41 E
Beecroft Hd., Austl. (bē'krûft)	216	35.03 S	151.15 E
Beelitz, G.D.R. (bĕ'lētz)	157b	52.14 N	12.59 E
Be'er Sheva', Isr. (bēr-shē'bȧ)	191a	31.15 N	34.48 E
Be'er Sheva' (R.), Isr.	191a	31.23 N	34.30 E
Beestekraal, S. Afr.	223d	25.22 S	27.34 E
Beeston, Eng. (bēs't'n)	156	52.55 N	1.11 W
Beetz R., G.D.R. (bĕtz)	157b	52.28 N	12.37 E
Beeville, Tx. (bē'vĭl)	125	28.24 N	97.44 W
Bega, Austl. (bā'gaă)	216	36.50 S	149.49 E
Beggs, Ok. (bĕgz)	123	35.46 N	96.06 W
Bégles, Fr. (bĕ'gl')	168	44.47 N	0.34 W
Begoro, Ghana	228	6.23 N	0.23 W
Behala, India	196a	22.31 N	88.19 E
Behbehān, Iran	195	30.35 N	50.14 E
Behm Can., Ak.	98	55.41 N	131.35 W
Bei (R.), China (bā)	201a	22.54 N	113.08 E
Bei'an, China (bā-än)	202	48.05 N	126.26 E
Beicai, China (bā-tsī)	201b	31.12 N	121.33 E
Beifei (R.), China (bā-fā)	200	33.14 N	117.03 E
Beihai, China (bā-hī)	203	21.30 N	109.10 E
Beihuangcheng Dao (I.), China (bā-hůäŋ-chŭŋ dou)	200	38.23 N	120.55 E
Beijing (Peking), China (bā-jyĭŋ)	202a	39.55 N	116.23 E
Beijing Shi (Mun.), China (bā-jyĭŋ shr)	200	40.07 N	116.00 E
Beira, Moz. (bā'rȧ)	226	19.45 N	34.58 E
Beira (Reg.), Port. (bĕ'y-rä)	170	40.38 N	8.00 W
Beirut, (Bayrūt), Leb. (bā-ro͞ot')	191a	33.53 N	35.30 E
Beiyuan, China	67b	40.01 N	116.24 E
Beja, Port. (bā'zhä)	170	38.03 N	7.53 W
Béja, Tun.	159	36.52 N	9.20 E
Bejaïa (Bougie), Alg.	224	36.46 N	5.00 E
Bejar, Sp.	170	40.25 N	5.43 W
Bejestān, Iran	192	34.30 N	58.22 E
Bejucal, Cuba (bā-ho͞o-käl')	135a	22.56 N	82.23 W
Bejuco, Pan. (bĕ-ko͞o'kŏ)	133	8.37 N	79.54 W
Békés, Hung. (bā'kāsh)	167	46.45 N	21.08 E
Békéscsaba, Hung. (bā'kāsh-chô'bô)	167	46.39 N	21.06 E
Beketova, Sov. Un. (bĕk'e-to'vȧ)	199	53.23 N	125.21 E
Bela Crkva, Yugo. (bĕ'lä tsĕrk'vä)	173	44.53 N	21.25 E
Bel Air (Neigh.), Ca.	59	34.05 N	118.27 W
Bel Air, Va.	56d	38.52 N	77.10 W
Belalcázar, Sp. (bāl-ȧ-kä'thär)	170	38.35 N	5.12 W
Belas, Port.	65d	38.47 N	9.16 W
Bela Vista (Neigh.), Braz.	61d	23.33 S	46.38 W
Bela Vista de Goia's, Braz.	143	16.57 S	48.47 W
Belawan, Indon. (bā-lä'wȧn)	206	3.43 N	98.43 E
Belaya (R.), Sov. Un. (byĕ'lī-yȧ)	178	52.30 N	56.15 E
Belaya Tserkov', Sov. Un. (byĕ'lī-yȧ tsĕr'kôf)	175	49.48 N	30.09 E
Belcher Is., Can. (bĕl'chēr)	97	56.20 N	80.40 W
Belding, Mi. (bĕl'dĭng)	110	43.05 N	85.25 W
Belebey, Sov. Un. (byĕ'lĕ-bā'ĭ)	178	54.00 N	54.10 E
Belém (Neigh.), Port.	65d	38.42 N	9.12 W
Belém, (Pará), Braz. (bā-lĕN') (pä-rä)	143	1.18 S	48.27 W
Belen, NM (bĕ-lān')	121	34.40 N	106.45 W
Belén, Par. (bā-lān')	144	23.30 S	57.09 W
Belènzinho (Neigh.), Braz.	61d	23.32 S	46.35 W
Bélep, Isles (Is.), N. Cal.	215	19.30 S	160.32 E
Belëv, Sov. Un. (byĕl'yĕf)	174	53.49 N	36.06 E
Belfair, Wa. (bĕl'far)	118a	47.27 N	122.50 W
Belfast, Me. (bĕl'fȧst)	104	44.25 N	69.01 W
Belfast, N. Ire.	162	54.36 N	5.45 W
Belfast, Lough (B.), Ire. (lŏk bĕl'fȧst)	162	54.45 N	6.00 W
Belford Roxo, Braz.	61c	22.46 S	43.24 W
Belfort, Fr. (bā-fôr')	169	47.40 N	7.50 E
Belgaum, India	197	15.57 N	74.32 E
Belgium, Eur. (bĕl'jĭ-ŭm)	154	51.00 N	2.52 E
Belgorod (Oblast), Sov. Un.	175	50.40 N	36.42 E
Belgorod, Sov. Un. (byĕl'gŭ-rut)	175	50.36 N	36.32 E
Belgorod Dnestrovskiy, Sov. Un. (byĕl'gŭ-rŭd nyĕs-trôf'skē)	175	46.09 N	30.19 E
Belgrade, see Beograd			
Belgrano (Neigh.), Arg.	60d	34.34 S	58.28 W
Belgrave, Austl.	70b	37.55 S	145.21 E
Belhaven, NC (bĕl'hā-vĕn)	127	35.33 N	76.37 W
Belington, WV (bĕl'ĭng-tŭn)	111	39.00 N	79.55 W
Beli Timok (R.), Yugo. (bĕ'lē tē'mōk)	173	43.35 N	22.13 E
Belitung (I.), Indon.	206	3.30 S	107.30 E
Belize, N.A.	128	17.00 N	88.40 W
Belize City, Belize (bĕ-lēz')	132a	17.31 N	88.10 W
Belize R., Belize	132a	17.16 N	88.56 W
Bel'kovo, Sov. Un. (byĕl'kô-vô)	182b	56.15 N	38.49 E
Bel'kovskiy (I.), Sov. Un. (byĕl-kôf'skĭ)	181	75.52 N	133.00 E
Bell, Ca.	59	33.58 N	118.11 W
Bell (I.), Can. (bĕl)	105	50.45 N	55.35 W
Bell (R.), Can.	103	49.25 N	77.15 W
Bella Bella, Can.	98	52.10 N	128.07 W
Bella Coola, Can.	98	52.22 N	126.46 W

ng-sing; nŋ-banŋk; N-nasalized n; nŏd; cŏmmit; ōld; ôbey; ôrder; oi-boil; fo͞od; fo͝ot; ou-out; s-soft; sh-dish; th-thin; pūre; ůnite; ûrn; stŭd; circŭs; ü-as in French tu; '-indeterminate vowel.

PLACE (Pronunciation)	PAGE	Lat. °′	Long. °′
Bellaire, Oh. (bĕl-âr′)	110	40.00 N	80.45 W
Bellaire, Tx.	125a	29.43 N	95.28 W
Bellary, India (bĕl-lä′rē)	197	15.15 N	76.56 E
Bella Union, Ur. (bĕ′l-yȧ-ōō-nyô′n)	144	30.18 S	57.26 W
Bella Vista, Arg. (bä′lyȧ vēs′tȧ)	144	27.07 S	65.14 W
Bella Vista, Arg.	144a	34.18 S	58.41 W
Bella Vista, Arg.	144	28.35 S	58.53 W
Bella Vista, Braz.	143	22.16 S	56.14 W
Bellavista, Chile	61b	33.31 S	70.37 W
Bellavista, Peru	60c	12.04 S	77.08 W
Belle-Anse, Hai	135	18.15 N	72.00 W
Belle B., Can. (bĕl)	105	47.35 N	55.15 W
Belle Chasse, La. (bĕl shäs′)	112d	29.52 N	90.00 W
Belle Farm Estates, Md.	56c	39.23 N	76.45 W
Bellefontaine, Oh. (bel-fōn′tån)	110	40.25 N	83.50 W
Bellefontaine Neighbors, Mo.	119e	38.46 N	90.13 W
Belle Fourche (R.), Wy.	114	44.29 N	104.40 W
Belle Fourche, SD (bĕl′ fōōrsh′)	114	44.28 N	103.50 W
Belle Fourche Res., SD	114	44.51 N	103.44 W
Bellegarde, Fr. (bĕl-gärd′)	169	46.06 N	5.50 E
Belle Glade, Fl. (bĕl glād)	127a	26.39 N	80.37 W
Bellehaven, Va.	56d	38.47 N	77.04 W
Belle-Île (I.), Fr. (bĕlēl′)	168	47.15 N	3.30 W
Belle Isle, Str. of, Can.	105	51.35 N	56.30 W
Belle Mead, NJ (bĕl mēd)	112a	40.28 N	74.40 W
Belleoram, Can.	105	47.31 N	55.25 W
Belle Plaine, Ia. (bĕl plān′)	115	41.52 N	92.19 W
Bellerose, NY	55	40.44 N	73.43 W
Belle Vernon, Pa. (bĕl vûr′nŭn)	113e	40.08 N	79.52 W
Belleville, Can. (bĕl′vĭl)	111	44.15 N	77.25 W
Belleville, Il.	119e	38.31 N	89.59 W
Belleville, Ks.	123	39.49 N	97.37 W
Belleville, Mi.	113b	42.12 N	83.29 W
Belleville, NJ	112a	40.47 N	74.09 W
Bellevue, Ia. (bĕl′vū)	115	42.14 N	90.26 W
Bellevue, Ky.	113f	39.06 N	84.29 W
Bellevue, Mi.	110	42.30 N	85.00 W
Bellevue, Oh.	110	41.15 N	82.45 W
Bellevue, Pa.	113e	40.30 N	80.04 W
Bellevue, Wa.	118a	47.37 N	122.12 W
Belley, Fr. (bē-lē′)	169	45.46 N	5.41 E
Bellflower, Ca. (bĕl-flou′ẽr)	119a	33.53 N	118.08 W
Bell Gardens, Ca.	119a	33.59 N	118.11 W
Bell I., Can.	105	50.44 N	55.35 W
Bellingham, Ma. (bĕl′ĭng-hăm)	105a	42.05 N	71.28 W
Bellingham, Wa.	118d	48.46 N	122.29 W
Bellingham B., Wa.	118d	48.44 N	122.34 W
Bellingshausen Sea, Ant. (bĕl′ĭngz houz′n)	232	72.00 S	80.30 W
Bellinzona, Switz. (bĕl-ĭn-tsō′nä)	172	46.10 N	9.09 E
Bellmawr, NJ	56b	39.51 N	75.06 W
Bellmore, NY (bĕl-mōr)	112a	40.40 N	73.31 W
Bello, Col. (bĕ′l-yō)	142a	6.20 N	75.33 W
Bello, Cuba	60b	23.07 N	82.24 W
Bellow Falls, Vt. (bĕl′ōz fôls)	111	43.10 N	72.30 W
Bellpat, Pak.	196	29.08 N	68.00 E
Bell Pen, Can.	97	63.50 N	81.16 W
Bells Corners, Can.	95c	45.20 N	75.49 W
Bells Mtn., Wa. (bĕls)	118c	45.50 N	122.21 W
Belluno, It. (bĕl-lōō′nō)	172	46.08 N	12.14 E
Bell Ville, Arg. (bĕl vēl′)	144	32.33 S	62.36 W
Bellville, S.Afr.	226a	33.54 S	18.38 E
Bellville, Tx. (bĕl′vĭl)	125	29.57 N	96.15 W
Bellwood, Il.	58a	41.53 N	87.52 W
Bélmez, Sp. (bĕl′mĕth)	170	38.17 N	5.17 W
Belmond, Ia. (bĕl′mŏnd)	115	42.49 N	93.37 W
Belmont, Ca.	118b	37.34 N	122.18 W
Belmont, Ma.	54a	42.24 N	71.10 W
Belmonte, Braz. (bĕl-mōn′tå)	143	15.58 S	38.47 W
Belmopan, Belize	128	17.15 N	88.47 W
Belmore, Austl.	70a	33.55 S	151.05 E
Belogorsk, Sov.Un.	181	51.09 N	128.32 E
Belo Horizonte, Braz. (bĕ′lôre-sô′n-tĕ)	141a	19.54 S	43.56 W
Beloit, Ks. (bḗ-loit′)	122	39.26 N	98.06 W
Beloit, Wi.	115	42.31 N	89.04 W
Belomorsk, Sov.Un. (byĕl-ō-môrsk′)	178	64.30 N	34.42 E
Belopol′ye, Sov.Un. (byĕ′lô-pôl′yĕ)	175	51.10 N	34.19 E
Beloretsk, Sov.Un. (byĕ′lô-rĕtsk)	182a	53.58 N	58.25 E
Belorussian (S.S.R.), Sov.Un.	176	53.30 N	25.33 E
Belosarayskaya, Kosa (C.), Sov.Un. (kô-sä′byĕ′lô-sä-räy′skä′yä)	175	46.43 N	37.18 E
Belot, Cuba	60b	23.08 N	82.19 W
Belovo, Sov.Un. (byĕ′lŭ-vû)	180	54.17 N	86.23 E
Belovodsk, Sov.Un. (byĕ-lŭ-vôdsk′)	175	49.12 N	39.36 E
Beloye (L.), Sov.Un.	178	60.10 N	38.05 E
Belozersk, Sov.Un. (byĕ-lŭ-zyôrsk′)	178	60.00 N	38.00 E
Belper, Eng. (bĕl′pẽr)	156	53.01 N	1.28 W
Belt, Mt. (bĕlt)	117	47.11 N	110.58 W
Belt Cr., Mt.	117	47.19 N	110.58 W
Belton, Tx. (bĕl′tŭn)	125	31.04 N	97.27 W
Belton L., Tx.	125	31.15 N	97.35 W
Beltsville, Md. (belts-vĭl)	112e	39.03 N	76.56 W
Bel′tsy, Sov.Un. (bĕl′tsē)	175	47.47 N	27.57 E
Belukha, Gol′tsy (Mtn.), Sov.Un.	180	49.47 N	86.23 E
Belvedere, Ca.	58b	37.52 N	122.28 W
Belvedere (Neigh.), Eng.	62	51.29 N	0.09 E
Belvedere (P. Int.), Aus.	66e	48.11 N	16.23 E
Belvedere, Va.	56d	38.50 N	77.10 W
Belvidere, Il. (bĕl-vē-dēr′)	115	42.14 N	88.52 W
Belvidere, NJ	111	40.50 N	75.05 W
Belyando (R.), Austl. (bĕl-yän′dō)	215	22.09 S	146.48 E
Belyanka, Sov. Un. (byĕl-yȧn-kȧ)	182a	56.04 N	59.16 E
Belynichi, Sov. Un. (byĕl-ĭ-nĭ′chĭ)	174	54.02 N	29.42 E
Belyy (I.), Sov. Un.	180	73.19 N	72.00 E
Belyy, Sov. Un. (byĕ′lē)	174	55.52 N	32.58 E
Belyye Stolby, Sov. Un. (byĕ′lĭ-ye stôl′bĭ)	182b	55.20 N	37.52 E
Belzig, G.D.R. (bĕl′tsēg)	157b	52.08 N	12.35 E
Belzoni, Ms. (bĕl-zō′nē)	126	33.09 N	90.30 W
Bembe, Ang. (bĕɴ′bĕ)	226	7.00 S	14.20 E
Bembézar (R.), Sp. (bĕm-bā-thär′)	170	38.00 N	5.18 W

PLACE (Pronunciation)	PAGE	Lat. °′	Long. °′
Bemidji, Mn. (bḗ-mĭj′ĭ)	115	47.28 N	94.54 W
Bena Dibele, Zaire (bĕn′ȧ dē-bĕ′lĕ)	226	4.00 S	22.49 E
Benalla, Austl. (bĕn-ăl′ȧ)	216	36.30 S	146.00 E
Benares, see Vārānasi			
Benavente, Sp. (bā-nä-vĕn′tā)	170	42.01 N	5.43 W
Ben Avon, Pa.	57b	40.31 N	80.05 W
Benbrook, Tx. (bĕn′brōōk)	119c	32.41 N	97.27 W
Benbrook Res., Tx.	119c	32.35 N	97.30 W
Bend, Or. (bĕnd)	116	44.04 N	121.17 W
Bendeleben, Mt., Ak. (bĕn-dĕl-bĕn)	107	65.18 N	163.45 W
Bender Beyla, Som.	223a	9.40 N	50.45 E
Bendery, Sov. Un. (bĕn-dyĕ′re)	175	46.49 N	29.29 E
Bendigo, Austl. (bĕn′dĭ-gō)	216	36.39 S	144.20 E
Benedict, Md. (bĕnē′dĭct)	112e	38.31 N	76.41 W
Benešov, Czech. (bĕn′ē-shôf)	166	49.48 N	14.40 E
Benevento, It. (bā-nā-vĕn′tō)	172	41.08 N	14.46 E
Benfica (Neigh.), **Braz.**, Braz.	61c	22.53 S	43.15 W
Benfica (Neigh.), **Port.**, Port.	65d	38.45 N	9.12 W
Bengal, B. of, Asia (bĕn-gôl′)	190	17.30 N	87.00 E
Bengamisa, Zaire	230	0.57 N	25.10 E
Bengbu, China (bŭŋ-bōō)	200	32.52 N	117.22 E
Bengkalis, Indon. (bĕng-kä′lĭs)	191b	1.29 N	102.06 E
Bengkulu, Indon.	206	3.46 S	102.18 E
Benguela, Ang. (bĕn-gĕl′ȧ)	230	12.35 S	13.25 E
Beni (R.), Bol. (bā′nē)	142	13.41 S	67.30 W
Béni-Abbas, Alg. (bā′nē ȧ-bĕs′)	224	30.11 N	2.13 W
Benicarló, Sp. (bā-nē-kär-lō′)	171	40.26 N	0.25 E
Benicia, Ca. (bḗ-nĭsh′ĭ-ȧ)	118b	38.03 N	122.09 W
Benin, Afr.	222	8.00 N	2.00 E
Benin (R.), Nig. (bĕn-ēn′)	229	5.55 N	5.15 E
Benin City, Nig.	229	6.19 N	5.41 E
Beni Saf, Alg. (bā′nē säf′)	224	35.23 N	1.20 W
Benito (R.), Equat. Gui.	230	1.35 N	10.45 E
Benkelman, Ne. (bĕn-kĕl-măn)	122	40.05 N	101.35 W
Benkovac, Yugo. (bĕn′kō-vȧts)	172	44.02 N	15.41 E
Ben Macdhui (Mtn.), Leso-S. Afr. (bĕn măk-dōō′ē)	227c	30.38 S	27.54 E
Bennettsville, SC (bĕn′ĕts vĭl)	127	34.35 N	79.41 W
Bennettswood, Austl.	70b	37.51 S	145.07 E
Benninghofen (Neigh.), F.R.G.	63	51.29 N	7.31 E
Bennington, Vt. (bĕn′ĭng-tŭn)	111	42.55 N	73.15 W
Benns Church, Va. (bĕnz′ chûrch′)	112g	36.47 N	76.35 W
Benoni, S. Afr. (bĕ-nō′nī)	227b	26.11 S	28.19 E
Benoni South, S. Afr.	71b	26.13 S	28.18 E
Be,Nosy (I.), Mad.	227	13.14 S	47.28 E
Benoy, Chad	229	8.59 N	16.19 E
Benque Viejo, Belize (bĕn-kĕ bĭĕ′hō)	132a	17.07 N	89.07 W
Benrath (Neigh.), F.R.G.	63	51.10 N	6.52 E
Bensberg, F.R.G.	169c	50.58 N	7.09 E
Bensenville, Il. (bĕn′sĕn-vĭl)	113a	41.57 N	87.56 W
Bensheim, F.R.G. (bĕns-hīm)	166	49.42 N	8.38 E
Benson, Az. (bĕn-sŭn)	121	32.00 N	110.20 W
Benson, Mn.	114	45.18 N	95.36 W
Bensonhurst (Neigh.), NY	55	40.35 N	73.59 E
Bentleigh, Austl.	70b	37.55 S	145.02 E
Bentleyville, Pa. (bent′lē vĭl)	113e	40.07 N	80.01 W
Benton, Ar. (bĕn′tŭn)	123	34.34 N	92.34 W
Benton, Can.	104	45.59 N	67.36 W
Benton, Ca.	120	37.44 N	118.22 W
Benton, Il.	110	38.00 N	88.55 W
Benton Harbor, Mi. (bĕn′tŭn här′bẽr)	110	42.05 N	86.30 W
Bentonville, Ar. (bĕn′tŭn-vĭl)	123	36.22 N	94.11 W
Benue (R.), Nig. (bā′nōō-å)	229	7.55 N	8.55 E
Benut (R.), Mala.	191b	1.43 N	103.20 E
Benwood, WV (bĕn-wŏŏd)	110	39.55 N	80.45 W
Benxi, China (bŭn-shyē)	202	41.25 N	123.50 E
Beograd, (Belgrade), Yugo. (bĕ-ō′gräd) (bĕl′gräd)	173	44.48 N	20.32 E
Beppu, Jap. (bĕ′pōō)	205	33.16 N	131.30 E
Bequia I., N.A. (bĕk-ē′ȧ)	133b	13.00 N	61.08 W
Berakit, Tanjung (C.), Indon.	191b	1.16 N	104.44 E
Berat, Alb. (bĕ-rät′)	173	40.43 N	19.59 E
Berau, Teluk (B.), Indon.	207	2.22 S	131.40 E
Berazategui, Arg. (bĕ-rä-zȧ′tĕ-gē)	144a	34.46 S	58.14 W
Berbera, Som. (bûr′bûr-ȧ)	223a	10.25 N	45.05 E
Berbérati, Cen. Afr. Rep.	229	4.16 N	15.47 E
Berchum, F.R.G.	63	51.23 N	7.32 E
Berck, Fr. (bĕrk)	168	50.26 N	1.36 E
Berd′ansk, Sov. Un.	161	46.45 N	36.47 E
Berdichev, Sov. Un. (bĕ-dē′chĕf)	175	49.53 N	28.32 E
Berdyanskaya, Kosa (C.), Sov. Un. (kô-sä′ bĕ-dyän′skä-yä)	175	46.38 N	36.42 E
Berdyaush, Sov. Un. (bĕr′dyȧûsh)	182a	55.10 N	59.12 E
Berea, Ky. (bḗ-rē′ȧ)	126	37.30 N	84.19 W
Berea, Oh.	113d	41.22 N	81.51 W
Beregovo, Sov. Un. (bĕ′rĕ-gō-vō)	167	48.13 N	22.40 E
Bereku, Tan.	231	4.27 S	35.44 E
Berens (R.), Can. (bĕr′enz)	101	52.15 N	96.30 W
Berens I., Can.	101	52.18 N	97.40 W
Berens River, Can.	101	52.22 N	97.02 W
Beresford, SD (bĕr′ĕs-fẽrd)	114	43.05 N	96.46 W
Berettyóújfalu, Hung. (bĕ′rĕt-tyō-ōō′y′fō-lōō)	167	47.14 N	21.33 E
Berëza, Sov.Un. (bĕ-rā′zȧ)	167	52.29 N	24.59 E
Berezhany, Sov.Un. (bĕr-yĕ′zhȧ-nē)	167	49.25 N	24.58 E
Berezina (R.), Sov.Un. (bĕr-yĕ′zē-nȧ)	174	53.20 N	29.05 E
Berezino, Sov.Un. (bĕr-yä′zē-nô)	174	53.51 N	28.54 E
Berezna, Sov.Un. (bĕr-yôz′nȧ)	175	51.32 N	31.47 E
Bereznegovata, Sov.Un.	175	47.19 N	32.58 E
Berezniki, Sov.Un. (bĕr-yôz′nyḗ-kē)	182a	59.25 N	56.46 E
Berëzovka, Sov.Un. (bĕr-yôz′ôf-kȧ)	175	47.12 N	30.56 E
Berëzovka, Sov.Un.	182a	57.35 N	57.19 E
Berëzovo, Sov.Un. (bĭr-yô′zē-vû)	178	64.10 N	65.10 E
Berëzovskiy, Sov.Un. (bĕr-yô′zôf-skĭ)	182a	56.54 N	60.47 E
Berga, Sp. (bĕr′gä)	171	42.05 N	1.52 E
Bergama, Tur. (bĕr′gä-mä)	179	39.08 N	27.09 E
Bergamo, It. (bĕr′gä-mō)	172	45.43 N	9.41 E
Bergantin, Ven. (bĕr-gän-tē′n)	143b	10.04 N	64.23 W
Bergedorf, F.R.G. (bĕr′gē-dôrf)	157c	53.29 N	10.12 E
Bergen, G.D.R. (bĕr′gĕn)	166	54.26 N	13.26 E
Bergen, Nor.	164	60.24 N	5.20 E

PLACE (Pronunciation)	PAGE	Lat. °′	Long. °′
Bergenfield, NJ	112a	40.55 N	73.59 W
Bergen op Zoom, Neth.	157a	51.29 N	4.16 E
Bergerac, Fr. (bĕr-zhē-rȧk′)	168	44.49 N	0.28 E
Bergfelde, G.D.R.	65a	52.40 N	13.19 E
Berghausen, F.R.G.	63	51.18 N	7.17 E
Bergholtz, NY	57a	43.06 N	78.53 W
Bergisch-Born, F.R.G.	63	51.09 N	7.15 E
Bergisch Gladbach, F.R.G. (bĕrg′ĭsh-glät′bäk)	169c	50.59 N	7.08 E
Bergkamen, F.R.G.	63	51.38 N	7.38 E
Berglern, F.R.G. (bĕrgh′lĕrn)	157d	48.24 N	11.55 E
Bergneustadt, F.R.G.	169c	51.01 N	7.39 E
Bergville, S.Afr. (bĕrg′vĭl)	227c	28.46 S	29.22 E
Berhampur, India	196	19.19 N	84.48 E
Bering Sea, Asia-N.A. (bē′rĭng)	94	58.00 N	175.00 W
Bering Str., Ak.	107	64.50 N	169.50 W
Berislav, Sov.Un. (byĕr′ĭ-slȧf)	175	46.49 N	33.24 E
Berja, Sp. (bĕr′hä)	170	36.50 N	2.56 W
Berkeley, Ca. (bûrk′lĭ)	118b	37.52 N	122.17 W
Berkeley, Il.	58a	41.53 N	87.55 W
Berkeley, Mo.	119e	38.45 N	90.20 W
Berkeley Hills, Pa.	57b	40.32 N	80.00 W
Berkeley Springs, WV (bûrk′lĭ sprĭngz)	111	39.40 N	78.10 W
Berkhamsted, Eng. (bĕk′hăm′stĕd)	156b	51.44 N	0.34 W
Berkley, Mi. (bûrk′lĭ)	113b	42.30 N	83.10 W
Berkovitsa, Bul. (bĕ-kō′vē-tsȧ)	173	43.14 N	23.08 E
Berland (R.), Can.	99	54.00 N	117.10 W
Berlenga (Is.), Port. (bĕr-lĕn′gäzh)	170	39.25 N	9.33 W
Berlin, NH (bûr-lĭn)	111	44.25 N	71.10 W
Berlin, NJ	112f	39.47 N	74.56 W
Berlin, S.Afr. (bĕr-lĭn)	227c	32.53 S	27.36 E
Berlin, Wi. (bûr-lĭn′)	115	43.58 N	88.58 W
Berlin, East, G.D.R. (bĕr-lēn′)	157b	52.31 N	13.28 E
Berlin, West, F.R.G.	157b	52.31 N	13.20 E
Bermejo (R.), Arg. (bĕr-mā′hō)	144	25.05 S	61.00 W
Bermeo, Sp. (bĕr-mā′yō)	170	43.23 N	2.43 W
Bermuda (I.), N.A.	129	32.20 N	65.45 W
Bern, Switz. (bĕrn)	166	46.55 N	7.25 E
Bernal, Arg. (bĕr-näl′)	144a	34.27 S	58.17 W
Bernalillo, NM (bĕr-nä-lē′yō)	121	35.20 N	106.30 W
Bernard (L.), Can. (bĕr-närd′)	111	45.45 N	79.25 W
Bernardsville, NJ (bûr nárds′vĭl)	112a	40.43 N	74.34 W
Bernau, G.D.R. (bĕr′nou)	157b	52.40 N	13.35 E
Bernau bei Berlin, G.D.R.	65a	52.40 N	13.35 E
Bernburg, G.D.R. (bĕrn′bōōrgh)	166	51.48 N	11.43 E
Berndorf, Aus. (bĕrn′dôrf)	166	47.57 N	16.05 E
Berne, In. (bûrn)	110	40.40 N	84.55 W
Berner Alpen (Mts.), Switz.	166	46.29 N	7.30 E
Bernier (I.), Austl. (bĕr-nēr′)	214	24.58 S	113.15 E
Bernina Pizzo (Pk.), Switz.	166	46.23 N	9.58 E
Bero (R.), Ang.	230	15.10 S	12.20 E
Beroun, Czech. (bā′rōn)	166	49.57 N	14.03 E
Berounka R., Czech. (bĕ-rōn′kȧ)	166	49.53 N	13.40 E
Berowra, Austl.	211b	33.36 S	151.10 E
Berre, Étang de (L.), Fr. (ā-tôɴ′ dĕ bâr′)	168a	43.27 N	5.07 E
Berre-l′ Étang, Fr. (bâr′lā-tôɴ′)	168a	43.28 N	5.11 E
Berriozabal, Mex. (bā′rēō-zä-bäl′)	131	16.47 N	93.16 W
Berriyyane, Alg.	160	32.50 N	3.49 E
Berry Creek (R.), Can.	99	51.15 N	111.40 W
Berryessa (R.), Ca. (bĕ′rĭ ĕs′ȧ)	120	38.35 N	122.33 W
Berry Is., Ba.	134	25.40 N	77.50 W
Berryville, Ar. (bĕr′ē-vĭl)	123	36.21 N	93.34 W
Bershad′, Sov.Un. (byĕr′shät)	175	48.22 N	29.31 E
Berthier, Can.	95b	46.56 N	70.44 W
Bertlich, F.R.G.	63	51.37 N	7.04 E
Bertrand (R.), Wa. (bûr′trȧnd)	118d	48.58 N	122.31 W
Berwick, Pa. (bûr′wĭk)	111	41.05 N	76.10 W
Berwick-upon-Tweed, Eng. (bûr′ĭk)	162	55.45 N	2.01 W
Berwyn, Il. (bûr′wĭn)	113a	41.49 N	87.47 W
Berwyn Heights, Md.	56d	38.59 N	76.54 W
Besalampy, Mad. (bĕz-ȧ-lȧm-pē′)	227	16.48 S	40.40 E
Besançon, Fr. (bĕ-säɴ-sôɴ)	169	47.14 N	6.02 E
Besar, Gunong (Mt.), Mala.	191b	2.31 N	103.09 E
Besed′ (R.), Sov.Un. (byĕ′syĕt)	174	52.58 N	31.36 E
Besedy, Sov. Un.	66b	55.37 N	37.47 E
Beshenkovichi, Sov.Un. (byĕ′shĕn-kōvē′chĭ)	174	55.04 N	29.29 E
Beşiktaş (Neigh.), Tur.	66f	41.03 N	29.01 E
Beskid (Mts.), Czech.-Pol.	167	49.23 N	19.00 E
Beskra, Alg.	224	34.52 N	5.39 E
Beskudnikovo (Neigh.), Sov. Un.	66b	55.52 N	37.34 E
Besós (R.), Sp.	65e	41.25 N	2.04 E
Bességes, Fr. (bĕ-sĕzh′)	168	44.20 N	4.07 E
Bessemer, Al. (bĕs′ē-mẽr)	112h	33.24 N	86.58 W
Bessemer, Mi.	115	46.29 N	90.04 W
Bessemer City, NC	127	35.16 N	81.17 W
Bestensee, G.D.R. (bĕs′tĕn-zā)	157b	51.15 N	13.39 E
Betanzos, Sp. (bĕ-tän′thōs)	170	43.18 N	8.14 W
Betatakin Ruin, Az. (bĕt-ȧ-tăk′ĭn)	121	36.40 N	110.29 W
Bethal, S.Afr. (bĕth′ăl)	223d	26.27 S	29.28 E
Bethalto, Il. (bȧ-thăl′tō)	119e	38.54 N	90.03 W
Bethanien, Namibia	226	26.20 S	16.10 E
Bethany, Mo.	123	40.15 N	94.04 W
Bethel, Ak. (bĕth′ĕl)	107	60.50 N	161.50 W
Bethel, Ct.	112a	41.22 N	73.24 W
Bethel, Vt.	111	43.50 N	72.40 W
Bethel Park, Pa.	113e	40.19 N	80.02 W
Bethesda, Md. (bĕ-thĕs′dȧ)	112e	39.00 N	77.10 W
Bethlehem, Pa. (bĕth′lē-hĕm)	111	40.40 N	75.25 W
Bethlehem, S.Afr.	223d	28.14 S	28.18 E
Bethlehem, see Bayt Lahm			
Bethnal Green (Neigh.), Eng.	62	51.32 N	0.03 W
Bethpage, NY	55	40.45 N	73.29 W
Béthune, Fr. (bā-tün′)	168	50.32 N	2.37 E
Betroka, Mad. (bĕ-trŏk′ȧ)	227	23.13 S	46.17 E
Betsham, Eng.	62	51.25 N	0.19 E
Bet She′an, Isr.	191a	32.30 N	35.30 E
Betsiamites, Can.	104	48.57 N	68.36 W
Betsiamites, (R.), Can.	104	49.11 N	69.20 W
Betsiboka (R.), Mad. (bĕt-sĭ-bō′kȧ)	227	16.47 S	46.45 E

PLACE (Pronounciation)	PAGE	Lat. °′	Long. °′
Bettles Field, Ak. (bĕt'tŭls)	107	66.58 N	151.48 W
Betwa (R.), India (bĕt'wȧ)	196	25.00 N	77.37 E
Betz, Fr. (bĕ)	169b	49.09 N	2.58 E
Beveren, Bel.	157a	51.13 N	4.14 E
Beverly, Eng. (bĕv'ēr-lĭ)	156	53.50 N	0.25 W
Beverly, Ma.	105a	42.34 N	70.53 W
Beverly, NJ	112f	40.03 N	74.56 W
Beverly Hills, Austl.	70a	33.57 S	151.05 E
Beverly Hills, Ca.	119a	34.05 N	118.24 W
everly Hills, Mi.	57c	42.32 N	83.15 W
evier, Mo. (bĕ-vēr')	123	39.44 N	92.36 W
ewdley, Eng. (būd'lĭ)	156	52.22 N	2.19 W
exhill, Eng. (bĕks'hĭl)	163	50.49 N	0.25 E
exley, Austl.	70a	33.57 S	151.08 E
Bexley, Eng. (bĕks'ly)	156b	51.26 N	0.09 E
Beyenburg (Neigh.), F.R.G.	63	51.15 N	7.18 E
Beyla, Gui. (bā'lȧ)	228	8.41 N	8.37 W
Beylerbeyi (Neigh.), Tur.	66f	41.03 N	29.03 E
Beylul, Eth.	225	13.15 N	42.21 E
Beyoğlu (Neigh.), Tur.	66f	41.02 N	28.59 E
Beypazari, Tur. (bā-pȧ-zä'rĭ)	179	40.10 N	31.40 E
Beyşehir, Tur. (bā-shĕ'h'r)	179	38.00 N	31.45 E
Beyşehir Gölü (L.), Turk.	179	38.00 N	31.30 E
Beysugskiy, Liman (B.), Sov.Un. (lĭ-män' bĕy-sōōg'skĭ)	175	46.07 N	38.35 E
Bezhetsk, Sov.Un. (byĕ-zhĕtsk')	174	57.46 N	36.40 E
Bezhitsa, Sov.Un. (byĕ-zhĭ'tsȧ)	174	53.19 N	34.18 E
Béziers, Fr. (bā-zyā')	168	43.21 N	3.12 E
Bezons, Fr.	64c	48.56 N	2.13 E
Bhadreswar, India	196a	22.49 N	88.22 E
Bhāgalpur, India (bä'gŭl-pŏŏr)	196	25.15 N	86.59 E
Bhalswa (Neigh.), India	67d	28.44 N	77.10 E
Bhamo, Bur. (bŭ-mō')	198	24.00 N	96.15 E
Bhāngar, India	196a	22.30 N	88.36 E
Bharatpur, India (bērt'pŏŏr)	196	27.21 N	77.33 E
Bhatinda, India (bŭ-tĭn-dȧ)	196	30.19 N	74.56 E
Bhātpāra, India	67a	22.52 N	88.24 E
Bhaunagar, India (bäv-nŭg'ŭr)	196	21.45 N	72.58 E
Bhayandar, India	197a	19.20 N	72.50 E
Bhilai, India	196	21.14 N	81.23 E
Bhīma (R.), India (bē'mȧ)	196	17.15 N	75.55 E
Bhiwandi, India	197a	19.18 N	73.03 E
Bhiwāni, India	196	28.53 N	76.08 E
Bhopāl, India (bō-päl)	196	23.20 N	77.25 E
Bhopura, India	67d	28.42 N	77.20 E
Bhubaneswar, India (bōō-bŭ-nāsh'vŭr)	196	20.21 N	85.53 E
Bhuj, India (bōōj)	196	23.22 N	69.39 E
Bhutan, Asia (bōō-tän')	193	27.15 N	90.30 E
Biafra, Bight of, Afr.	230	4.05 N	7.10 E
Biak (I.), Indon. (bē'äk)	207	1.00 S	136.00 E
Biala Podlaska, Pol. (byä'wä pōd-läs'kä)	167	52.01 N	23.08 E
Bialogard, Pol. (byä-wō'gärd)	166	54.00 N	16.01 E
Bialystok, Pol. (byä-wĭs'tŏk)	167	53.08 N	23.12 E
Biankouma, Ivory Coast	228	7.44 N	7.37 W
Biarritz, Fr. (byä-rēts')	168	43.27 N	1.39 W
Bibā, Egypt (bē'bȧ)	223b	28.54 N	30.59 E
Bibb City, Ga. (bĭb' sĭ'tē)	126	32.31 N	84.56 W
Biberach, F.R.G. (bē'bēräk)	166	48.06 N	9.49 E
Bibiani, Ghana	228	6.28 N	2.20 W
Bic, Can. (bĭk)	104	48.22 N	68.42 W
Bickerstaffe, Eng.	64a	53.32 N	2.50 W
Bickley (Neigh.), Eng.	62	51.24 N	0.03 E
Bicknell, In. (bĭk'nĕl)	110	38.45 N	87.20 W
Bicske, Hung. (bĭsh'kē)	167	47.29 N	18.38 E
Bida, Nig. (bē'dä)	229	9.05 N	6.01 E
Biddeford, Me. (bĭd'ē-fērd)	104	43.29 N	70.29 W
Biddulph, Eng. (bĭd'ŭlf)	156	53.07 N	2.10 W
Bidston, Eng.	64a	53.24 N	3.05 W
Biebrza R., Pol. (byĕb'zhȧ)	167	53.18 N	22.25 E
Biel, Switz. (bēl)	166	47.09 N	7.12 E
Bielefeld, F.R.G. (bē'lē-fĕlt)	166	52.01 N	8.35 E
ella, It. (byĕl'lä)	172	45.34 N	8.05 E
ielsk Podlaski, Pol. (byĕlsk pūd-lä'skĭ)	167	52.47 N	23.14 E
en Hoa, Viet.	206	10.59 N	106.49 E
enville, Lac (L.), Can.	97	55.32 N	72.45 W
esdorf (Neigh.), G.D.R.	65a	52.31 N	13.33 E
esenthal, G.D.R. (bē'sĕn-täl)	157b	52.46 N	13.38 E
èvres, Fr.	64c	48.45 N	2.13 E
ferno (R.), It. (bē-fĕr'nō)	172	41.49 N	14.46 E
foum, Gabon	230	0.22 S	10.23 E
ig (L.), Wa. (bĭg)	118a	48.23 N	122.14 W
ig (R.), Ar.	126	35.55 N	90.10 W
iga, Tur. (bē'ghȧ)	173	40.13 N	27.14 E
ig Bay de Noc, Mi. (bĭg bā dē nŏk')	115	45.48 N	86.41 W
ig Bayou, Ar. (bĭg'bī'yōō)	123	33.04 N	91.28 W
ig Bear City, Ca. (bĭg bâr)	119a	34.16 N	116.51 W
ig Belt Mts., Mt. (bĭg bĕlt)	117	46.53 N	111.43 W
g Bend Dam, SD (bĭg bĕnd)	114	44.11 N	99.33 W
g Bend Natl. Park, Tx.	124	29.15 N	103.15 W
g Black (R.), Ms. (bĭg blăk)	126	32.05 N	90.49 W
g Blue (R.), Ne. (bĭg blōō)	123	40.53 N	97.00 W
g Canyon, Tx. (bĭg kăn'yŭn)	124	30.27 N	102.19 W
g Cr., Oh.	56a	41.27 N	81.41 W
g Cypress Swp., Fl. (bĭg sī'prĕs)	127a	26.02 N	81.20 W
g Delta, Ak. (bĭg dĕl'tȧ)	107	64.08 N	145.48 W
g Fork (R.), Mn. (bĭg fôrk)	115	48.08 N	93.47 W
iggar, Can.	100	52.04 N	108.00 W
iggin Hill (Neigh.), Eng.	62	51.18 N	0.04 E
ig Hole (R.), Mt. (bĭg 'hōl)	117	45.53 N	113.15 W
ig Hole Natl. Battlefield, Mt. (bĭg hōl băt''l-fēld)	117	45.44 N	113.35 W
ig Horn Mts., Wy. (bĭg hôrn)	117	44.47 N	107.40 W
ighorn R., Mt.	117	45.50 N	107.15 W
ig I., Can.	101	49.10 N	94.40 W
ig L., Can.	95g	53.35 N	113.47 W
ig Lake, Wa. (bĭg lăk)	118a	48.24 N	122.14 W
ig Mossy Pt., Can.	101	53.45 N	97.50 W
ig Muddy (R.), Il.	110	37.50 N	89.00 W

PLACE (Pronounciation)	PAGE	Lat. °′	Long. °′
Big Muddy Cr., Mt. (bĭg mud'ĭ)	117	48.53 N	105.02 W
Bignona, Senegal	228	12.49 N	16.14 W
Big Quill L., Can.	100	51.55 N	104.22 W
Big Rapids, Mi. (bĭg răp'ĭdz)	110	43.40 N	85.30 W
Big River, Can.	100	53.50 N	107.01 W
Big Sandy (R.), Az. (bĭg sănd'ē)	121	34.59 N	113.36 W
Big Sandy (R.), Ky.-WV	110	38.15 N	82.35 W
Big Sandy Cr., Co.	122	39.08 N	103.36 W
Big Sandy Cr., Mt.	117	48.20 N	110.08 W
Bigsby I., Can.	101	49.04 N	94.35 W
Big Sioux (R.), SD (bĭg sōō)	114	44.34 N	97.00 W
Big Spring, Tx. (bĭg sprĭng)	124	32.15 N	101.28 W
Big Stone (L.), Mn.-SD (bĭg stōn)	114	45.29 N	96.40 W
Big Stone Gap, Va.	126	36.50 N	82.50 W
Bigtimber, Mt. (bĭg'tĭm-bēr)	117	45.50 N	109.57 W
Big Wood R., Id. (bĭg wŏŏd)	117	43.02 N	114.30 W
Bihać, Yugo. (bē'häch)	172	44.48 N	15.52 E
Bihār (State), India (bē-här')	196	23.48 N	84.57 E
Biharamulo, Tan. (bē-hä-rä-mōō'lō)	231	2.38 S	31.20 E
Bihorului, Munţii (Mts.), Rom.	167	46.37 N	22.37 E
Bijagós, Arquipélago dos (Is.), Guinea-Bissau (är-kē-pā'lä-gō dôs bē-zhä-gôs)	228	11.20 N	17.10 W
Bijāpur, India	197	16.53 N	75.42 E
Bijeljina, Yugo.	173	44.44 N	19.15 E
Bijelo Polje, Yugo. (bē'yĕ-lō pô'lyĕ)	173	43.02 N	19.48 E
Bijiang, China (bē-jyän)	201a	22.57 N	113.15 E
Bijie, China (bē-jyĕ)	203	27.20 N	105.18 E
Bijou Cr., Co. (bē'zhōō)	122	39.41 N	104.13 W
Bikin (R.), Sov.Un.	204	46.37 N	135.55 E
Bikin, Sov.Un. (bē-kēn')	204	46.41 N	134.29 E
Bikoro, Zaire (bē-kō'rō)	230	0.45 S	18.07 E
Bikuar, Parque Nacional do (Natl. Pk.), Ang.	230	15.07 S	14.40 E
Bilāspur, India (bē-läs'pōōr)	196	22.08 N	82.12 E
Bilauktaung (R.), Thai.	206	14.40 N	98.50 E
Bilbao, Sp. (bĭl-bä'ō)	170	43.12 N	2.48 W
Bilbays, Egypt	223b	30.26 N	31.37 E
Bileća, Yugo. (bē'lĕ-chä)	173	42.52 N	18.26 E
Bilecik, Tur. (bē-lĕd-zhĕk')	179	40.10 N	29.58 E
Bilé Karpaty (Mts.), Czech.	167	48.53 N	17.35 E
Bilgoraj, Pol. (bēw-gō'rī)	167	50.31 N	22.43 E
Bilimbay, Sov.Un. (bē'lĭm-bȧy)	182a	56.59 N	59.53 E
Billabong (R.), Austl. (bĭl'ȧ-bŏng)	216	35.15 S	145.20 E
Billerica, Ma. (bĭl'rĭk-ȧ)	105a	42.33 N	71.16 W
Billericay, Eng.	156b	51.38 N	0.25 E
Billings, Mt. (bĭl'ĭngz)	117	45.47 N	108.29 W
Billingsport, NJ	56b	39.51 N	75.14 W
Bill Williams (L.), Az. (bĭl-wĭl'yumz)	121	34.10 N	113.50 W
Bilma, Niger (bēl'mä)	225	18.41 N	13.20 E
Biloxi, Ms. (bĭ-lŏk'sĭ)	126	30.24 N	88.50 W
Bilqās Qism Awwal, Egypt	223b	31.14 N	31.25 E
Bimberi Pk., Austl. (bĭm'bĕrĭ)	216	35.45 S	148.50 E
Binalonan, Phil. (bē-nä-lō'nän)	207a	16.03 N	120.35 E
Binalud (Mtn.) Iran	192	36.32 N	58.34 E
Bingen, F.R.G. (bĭn'gĕn)	166	49.57 N	7.54 E
Bingham, Eng. (bĭng'ăm)	156	52.57 N	0.57 W
Bingham, Me.	104	45.03 N	69.51 W
Bingham Canyon, Ut.	119b	40.33 N	112.09 W
Bingham Farms, Mi.	57c	42.32 N	83.16 W
Binghamton, NY (bĭng'ăm-tŭn)	111	42.05 N	75.55 W
Bingo-Nada (Sea), Jap. (bĭn'gō nä-dä)	205	34.06 N	133.14 E
Binh-dong, Viet.	206m	10.43 N	106.39 E
Binjai, Indon.	206	3.59 N	108.00 E
Binnaway, Austl. (bĭn'ă-wā)	216	31.42 S	149.22 E
Binsheim, F.R.G.	63	51.31 N	6.42 E
Bintan (I.), Indon. (bĭn'tän)	191b	1.09 N	104.43 E
Bintulu, Mala. (bēn'tōō-lōō)	206	3.07 N	113.06 E
Binxian, China (bĭn-shyän)	200	37.27 N	117.58 E
Binxian, China	202	45.40 N	127.20 E
Bio Gorge (Val.), Ghana	228	8.30 N	2.05 W
Bīkaner, India (bĭ-kă'nŭr)	196	28.07 N	73.19 E
Bioko (Fernando Póo)(I.), Equat. Gui.	230	3.35 N	7.45 E
Bīrjand, Iran (bēr'jänd)	192	33.07 N	59.16 E
Bira (R.), Sov.Un.	204	48.55 N	132.25 E
Bira, Sov.Un. (bē'rȧ)	204	49.00 N	133.18 E
Birātnagar, Nep. (bĭ-rät'nŭ-gŭr)	196	26.35 N	87.18 E
Birch, Eng.	64b	53.34 N	2.13 W
Birch B., Wa.	118d	48.55 N	122.52 W
Birch Bay, Wa. (bûrch)	118d	48.55 N	122.45 W
Birch I., Can.	101	52.25 N	99.55 W
Birch Mts., Can.	96	57.36 N	113.10 W
Birch Pt., Wa.	118d	48.57 N	122.50 W
Bird I., S.Afr. (bērd)	227c	33.51 S	26.21 E
Bird Rock (I.), Ba. (bûrd)	135	22.50 N	74.20 W
Birds Hill, Can. (bûrds)	95f	49.58 N	97.00 W
Birdsville, Austl. (bûrdz'vĭl)	216	25.50 S	139.31 E
Birdum, Austl. (bûrd'ŭm)	214	15.45 S	133.25 E
Birecik, Tur. (bē-rĕd-zhĕk')	179	37.10 N	37.50 E
Bir Gara, Chad.	229	13.11 N	15.58 E
Bīrjand, Iran	195	32.53 N	59.13 E
Birkenfeld, Or.	118c	45.59 N	123.20 W
Birkenhead, Eng. (bûr'kĕn-hĕd)	156	53.23 N	3.02 W
Birkenwerder, G.D.R. (bĕr'kĕn-vĕr-dĕr)	157b	52.41 N	13.22 E
Birkholz, G.D.R.	65a	52.38 N	13.34 E
Birling, Eng.	62	51.19 N	0.25 E
Birmingham, Al. (bûr'mĭng-häm)	112h	33.31 N	86.49 W
Birmingham, Eng.	156	52.29 N	1.53 W
Birmingham, Mi.	113b	42.32 N	83.13 W
Birmingham, Mo.	119f	39.10 N	94.22 W
Birmingham Can., Eng.	156	53.07 N	2.40 W
Bi'r Misāhah, Egypt	225	22.16 N	28.04 E
Birnin Kebbi, Nig.	229	12.32 N	4.12 E
Birobidzhan, Sov.Un. (bē'rō-bē-jän')	181	48.42 N	133.28 E
Bîrlad, Rom.	167	46.15 N	27.43 E
Birsk, Sov.Un. (bĭrsk)	178	55.25 N	55.30 E
Birstall, Eng. (bûr'stôl)	156	53.44 N	1.39 W
Biryuchiy (I.), Sov.Un. (bĭr-yōō'chĭ)	175	46.07 N	35.12 E
Biryulëvo, Sov.Un. (bēr-yōōl'yō-vô)	182b	55.35 N	37.39 E
Biryusa (R.), Sov.Un. (bēr-yōō'sä)	180	56.43 N	97.30 E

PLACE (Pronounciation)	PAGE	Lat. °′	Long. °′
Bi'r Za'farānah, Egypt	191a	29.07 N	32.38 E
Biržai, Sov.Un. (bĕr-zhä'ē)	165	56.11 N	24.45 E
Bisbee, Az. (bĭz'bē)	121	31.30 N	109.55 W
Biscay, B. of, Eur. (bĭs'kā')	159	45.19 N	3.51 W
Biscayne B., Fl. (bĭs-kān')	127a	25.22 N	80.15 W
Bischeim, Fr. (bĭsh'hĭm)	169	48.40 N	7.48 E
Biscotasi L., Can.	102	47.20 N	81.55 W
Biser, Sov.Un. (bē'sĕr)	182a	58.24 N	58.54 E
Biševo (Is.), Yugo. (bē'shĕ-vō)	172	42.58 N	15.50 E
Bisho, Ciskei	227	32.50 S	27.20 E
Bishop, Ca. (bĭsh'ŭp)	120	37.22 N	118.25 W
Bishop, Tx.	125	27.35 N	97.46 W
Bishop's Castle, Eng. (bĭsh'ŏps käs'l)	156	52.29 N	2.57 W
Bishopville, SC (bĭsh'ŭp-vĭl)	127	34.11 N	80.13 W
Bismarck, ND (bĭz'märk)	114	46.48 N	100.46 W
Bismarck Arch, Pap. N. Gui.	207	3.15 S	150.45 E
Bismarck Ra., Pap. N. Gui.	207	5.15 S	144.15 E
Bissau, Guinea-Bissau (bē-sa'ōō)	228	11.51 N	15.35 W
Bissett, Can.	101	51.01 N	95.45 W
Bissingheim (Neigh.), F.R.G.	63	51.24 N	6.49 E
Bistineau (L.), La. (bĭs-tĭ-nō')	125	32.19 N	93.45 W
Bistrita, Rom. (bĭs-trĭt-sȧ)	167	47.09 N	24.29 E
Bistrita R., Rom.	167	47.08 N	25.47 E
Bitlis, Tur. (bĭt-lēs')	179	38.30 N	42.00 E
Bitola (Monastir), Yugo. (bē'tô-lä) (mô'nä-stēr)	173	41.02 N	21.22 E
Bitonto, It. (bē-tôn'tō)	172	41.08 N	16.42 E
Bitter Cr., Wy. (bĭt'ēr)	117	41.36 N	108.29 W
Bitterfeld, G.D.R. (bĭt'ēr-fĕlt)	166	51.39 N	12.19 E
Bittermark (Neigh.), F.R.G.	63	51.27 N	7.28 E
Bitterroot R., Mt.	117	46.28 N	114.10 W
Bitterroot Ra., Mt. (bĭt'ēr-ōōt)	116	47.15 N	115.13 W
Bityrug (R.), Sov.Un. (bĭt'yōōg)	175	51.23 N	40.33 E
Biu, Nig.	229	10.35 N	12.13 E
Biwabik, Mn. (bē-wä'bĭk)	115	47.32 N	92.24 W
Biwa-ko (L.), Jap. (bē-wä'kō)	205b	35.03 N	135.51 E
Biya (R.), Sov.Un. (bĭ'yȧ)	180	52.22 N	87.28 E
Biysk, Sov.Un. (bēsk)	180	52.32 N	85.28 E
Bizana, S.Afr. (bĭz-änä)	227c	30.51 S	29.54 E
Bizerte, Tun. (bē-zĕrt')	224	37.23 N	9.52 E
Bjelovar, Yugo. (byĕ-lō'vär)	172	45.54 N	16.53 E
Bjørnafjorden (Fd.), Nor.	164	60.11 N	5.26 E
Björneborg, see Pori			
Bla, Mali	228	12.57 N	5.46 W
Black (L.), Mi. (blăk)	110	45.25 N	84.15 W
Black (L.), NY	111	44.30 N	75.35 W
Black (R.), Ar.	123	35.47 N	91.22 W
Black (R.), Can.	102	49.20 N	81.15 W
Black (R.), NY	111	43.45 N	75.20 W
Black (R.), SC	127	33.55 N	80.10 W
Black (R.), Wi.	115	44.07 N	90.56 W
Blackall, Austl. (blăk'ŭl)	215	24.23 S	145.37 E
Black B., Can. (blăk)	115	48.36 N	88.32 W
Blackburn, Austl.	70b	37.49 S	145.09 E
Blackburn, Eng. (blăk'bûrn)	156	53.45 N	2.28 W
Blackburn Mt., Ak.	107	61.50 N	143.12 W
Black Canyon of the Gunnison Natl. Mon., Co. (blăk kăn'yŭn)	121	38.35 N	107.45 W
Black Creek Pioneer Village (P. Int.), Can.	54c	43.47 N	79.32 W
Black Diamond, Wa. (dī'mŭnd)	118a	47.19 N	122.00 W
Black Down Hills, Eng. (blăk'doun)	162	50.58 N	3.19 W
Blackduck, Mn. (blăk'dŭk)	115	47.41 N	94.33 W
Blackfoot, Id. (blăk'fŏŏt)	117	43.11 N	112.23 W
Blackfoot Ind. Res., Can.	99	50.45 N	113.00 W
Blackfoot Ind. Res., Mt.	117	48.49 N	112.53 W
Blackfoot R., Mt.	117	46.53 N	113.33 W
Blackfoot River Res., Id.	117	42.53 N	111.23 W
Black Hills, SD	114	44.08 N	103.47 W
Black I., Can.	101	51.10 N	96.30 W
Black Lake, Can.	104	46.02 N	71.24 W
Blackley (Neigh.), Eng.	64b	53.31 N	2.13 W
Black Mesa, Az. (blăk mā'sȧ)	121	36.33 N	110.40 W
Blackmore, Eng.	62	51.41 N	0.19 E
Blackmud Cr., Can. (blăk'mŭd)	95g	53.28 N	113.34 W
Blackpool, Eng. (blăk'pōōl)	156	53.49 N	3.02 W
Black R., Viet.	203	20.56 N	104.30 E
Black Ra., NM	121	33.15 N	107.55 W
Black River, Jam. (blăk')	134	18.00 N	77.50 W
Black River Falls, Wi.	115	44.18 N	90.51 W
Black Rock, Austl.	70b	37.59 S	145.01 E
Black Rock Des., Nv. (rŏk)	116	40.55 N	119.00 W
Blacksburg, SC (blăks'bûrg)	127	35.09 N	81.30 W
Black Sea, Eur.-Asia	155	43.01 N	32.16 E
Blackshear, Ga. (blăk'shĭr)	127	31.20 N	82.15 W
Black Springs, Austl.	70b	37.46 S	145.19 E
Blackstone, Va. (blăk'stōn)	127	37.04 N	78.00 W
Black Sturgeon (R.), Can. (stû'jŭn)	115	49.12 N	88.41 W
Blacktown, Austl. (blăk'toun)	211b	33.47 S	150.55 E
Blackville, Can. (blăk'vĭl)	104	46.44 N	65.50 W
Blackville, SC	127	33.21 N	81.19 W
Black Volta (Volta Noire) (R.), Afr. (vōl'tȧ)	228	8.55 N	2.30 W
Black Warrior (R.), Al. (blăk wŏr'ĭ-ēr)	126	32.37 N	87.42 W
Black Warrior (R.), Locust Fk., Al.	126	34.06 N	86.27 W
Black Warrior (R.), Mulberry Fk., Al.	126	34.06 N	86.32 W
Blackwater (R.), Ire. (blăk-wô'tēr)	162	52.05 N	9.02 W
Blackwater (R.), Mo.	123	38.53 N	93.22 W
Blackwater (R.), Va.	127	37.07 N	77.10 W
Blackwell, Ok. (blăk'wĕl)	123	36.47 N	97.19 W
Bladel, Neth.	157a	51.22 N	5.15 E
Bladensburg, Md.	56d	38.56 N	76.55 W
Blagodarnoye, Sov.Un. (blä'gō-där-nō'yē)	179	45.00 N	43.30 E
Blagoevgrad (Gorna Dzhumaya), Bul.	173	42.01 N	23.06 E
Blagoveshchensk, Sov.Un. (blä'gō-vyĕsh'chĕnsk)	181	50.16 N	127.47 E
Blagoveshchensk, Sov.Un.	182a	55.03 N	56.00 E
Blaine, Mn. (blān)	119g	45.11 N	93.14 W
Blaine, Wa.	118d	48.59 N	122.49 W
Blaine, WV	111	39.25 N	79.10 W

262 Blaine Hill – Bonny Lake

PLACE (Pronounciation)	PAGE	Lat. °'	Long. °'
Blaine Hill, Pa.	57b	40.16 N	79.53 W
Blair, Ne. (blâr)	114	41.33 N	96.09 W
Blairmore, Can.	99	49.38 N	114.25 W
Blairsville, Pa. (blârs'vĭl)	111	40.30 N	79.40 W
Blakang Mati (I.), Singapore	67c	1.15 N	103.50 E
Blake (I.), Wa. (blāk)	118a	47.37 N	122.28 W
Blakehurst, Austl.	70a	33.59 S	151.07 E
Blakely, Ga. (blāk'lē)	126	31.22 N	84.55 W
Blanca, Bahia (B.), Arg. (bä-ē'ä-blàn'kä)	144	39.30 S	61.00 W
Blanca Pk., Co. (blăŋ'kà)	122	37.36 N	105.22 W
Blanc, Cap (C.), Mauritania	224	20.39 N	18.08 W
Blanche, (R.), Can.	95c	45.34 N	75.38 W
Blanche, L., Austl. (blănch)	216	29.20 S	139.12 E
Blanchester, Oh. (blăn'chĕs-tẽr)	113f	39.18 N	83.58 W
Blanc, Mt., Fr.-It. (môɴ bläɴ)	169	45.50 N	6.53 E
Blanco (R.), Mex.	130	24.05 N	99.21 W
Blanco (R.), Mex.	131	18.42 N	96.03 W
Blanco, C., Arg. (bläŋ'kô)	144	47.08 S	65.47 W
Blanco, C., Or. (blăn'kō)	116	42.53 N	124.38 W
Blanco, Cabo (C.), C.R. (ká'bô-bläŋ'kō)	132	9.29 N	85.15 W
Blancos, Cayo (I.), Cuba (kä'yō-bläŋ'kōs)	134	23.15 N	80.55 W
Blanding, Ut.	121	37.40 N	109.31 W
Blankenburg, G.D.R. (bläŋ'kĕn-bo͝orgh)	163	51.45 N	11.15 E
Blankenburg (Neigh.), G.D.R.	65a	52.35 N	13.28 E
Blankenfelde, G.D.R. (blän'kĕn-fĕl-dĕ)	157b	52.20 N	13.24 E
Blankenfelde (Neigh.), G.D.R.	65a	52.37 N	13.23 E
Blankenstein, F.R.G.	63	51.24 N	7.14 E
Blanquefort, Fr.	168	44.53 N	0.38 W
Blanquilla, Arrecife (Reef), Mex. (är-rē-sē'fē-blän-kē'l-yä)	131	21.32 N	97.14 W
Blantyre, Malawi (blăn-tīyr)	231	15.47 S	35.00 E
Blasdell, NY (blăz'dĕl)	113c	42.48 N	78.51 W
Blato, Yugo. (blä'tō)	172	42.55 N	16.47 E
Blawnox, Pa.	57b	40.29 N	79.52 W
Blaye-et Sainte Luce, Fr. (blā'ā-săɴt-lüs')	168	45.08 N	0.40 W
Blażowa, Pol. (bwä-zhō'vá)	167	49.51 N	22.05 E
Bleus, Monts (Mts.), Zaire	231	1.10 N	30.10 E
Bliedinghausen (Neigh.), F.R.G.	63	51.09 N	7.12 E
Bliersheim, F.R.G.	63	51.23 N	6.43 E
Blind River, Can. (blīnd)	102	46.10 N	83.09 W
Blissfield, Mi. (blĭs-fēld)	110	41.50 N	83.50 W
Blithe (R.), Eng. (blīth)	156	52.22 N	1.49 W
Blitta, Togo	228	8.19 N	0.59 E
Block (I.), RI (blŏk)	111	41.05 N	71.35 W
Bloedel, Can.	98	50.07 N	125.23 W
Bloemfontein, S.Afr. (blo͞om'fŏn-tān)	223d	29.09 S	26.16 E
Blois, Fr. (blwä)	168	47.36 N	1.21 E
Blombacher Bach (Neigh.), F.R.G.	63	51.15 N	7.14 E
Blood Ind. Res., Can.	99	49.30 N	113.10 W
Bloomer, Wi. (blo͞om'ẽr)	115	45.07 N	91.30 W
Bloomfield, Ia.	115	40.44 N	92.21 W
Bloomfield, In. (blo͞om'fēld)	110	39.00 N	86.55 W
Bloomfield, Mo.	123	36.54 N	89.55 W
Bloomfield, Ne.	114	42.36 N	97.40 W
Bloomfield, NJ	112a	40.48 N	74.12 W
Bloomfield Hills, Mi.	113b	42.35 N	83.15 W
Bloomfield Village, Mi.	57c	42.33 N	83.15 W
Blooming Prairie, Mn. (blo͞om'ĭng prâ'rĭ)	115	43.52 N	93.04 W
Bloomington, Ca. (blo͞om'ĭng-tŭn)	119a	34.04 N	117.24 W
Bloomington, Il.	110	40.30 N	89.00 W
Bloomington, In.	110	39.10 N	86.35 W
Bloomington, Mn.	119g	44.50 N	93.18 W
Bloomsburg, Pa. (blo͞omz'bûrg)	111	41.00 N	76.25 W
Blossburg, Al. (blŏs'bûrg)	112h	33.38 N	86.57 W
Blossburg, Pa.	111	41.45 N	77.00 W
Bloubergstrand, S.Afr.	226a	33.48 S	18.28 E
Blountstown, Fl. (blŭnts'tun)	126	30.24 N	85.02 W
Bludenz, Aus. (bloo-dĕnts')	166	47.09 N	9.50 E
Blue Ash, Oh. (blo͞o ăsh)	113f	39.14 N	84.23 W
Blue Earth, Mn. (blo͞o ûrth)	115	43.38 N	94.05 W
Blue Earth (R.), Mn.	115	43.55 N	94.16 W
Bluefield, WV (blo͞o'fēld)	127	37.15 N	81.11 W
Bluefields, Nic. (blo͞o'fēldz)	133	12.03 N	83.45 W
Blue Island, Il.	113a	41.39 N	87.41 W
Blue Mesa Res., Co.	121	38.25 N	107.00 W
Blue Mosque (P. Int.), Egypt	71a	30.02 N	31.15 E
Blue, Mt., Can.	105	50.28 N	57.11 W
Blue Mts., Austl.	216	33.35 S	149.00 E
Blue Mts., Jam.	134	18.05 N	76.35 W
Blue Mts., Or.	116	45.15 N	118.50 W
Blue Mud B., Austl. (bo͞o mŭd)	214	13.20 S	136.45 E
Blue Nile (Abay) (R.), Eth. (à-bä'ē)	225	9.45 N	37.23 E
Blue Nile (Al-Bahr al-Azraq) (R.), Sud. (bärĕlaz-räk')	225	12.50 N	34.10 E
Blue R., Mo.	119f	38.55 N	94.33 W
Blue Rapids, Ks. (blo͞o răp'ĭdz)	123	39.40 N	96.41 W
Blue Ridge (Mts.), U.S. (blo͞o rĭj)	109	35.30 N	82.50 W
Blue River, Can.	99	52.05 N	119.17 W
Bluff, Ut.	121	37.18 N	109.34 W
Bluff Park, Al.	112h	33.24 N	86.52 W
Bluffton, In. (blŭf-tŭn)	110	40.40 N	85.15 W
Bluffton, Oh.	110	40.50 N	83.55 W
Blumenau, Braz. (blo͞o'mĕn-ou)	144	26.53 S	48.58 W
Blumut, Gunong (Mt.), Mala.	191b	2.03 N	103.34 E
Blyth, Eng. (blĭth)	162	55.03 N	1.34 W
Blythe, Ca.	120	33.37 N	114.37 W
Blytheville, Ar. (blīth'vĭl)	123	35.55 N	89.51 W
Bo, S.L.	228	7.56 N	11.21 W
Boac, Phil.	207a	13.26 N	121.50 E
Boaco, Nic. (bô-ä'kō)	132	12.24 N	85.41 W
Bo'ai, China (bwo-ī)	202	35.10 N	113.08 E
Boa Vista do Rio Branco, Braz. (bō'ä vĕsh'tä do͞o rē'o͞o brän'ko͞o)	143	2.46 N	60.45 W
Boa Vista I., C.V. (bō-ä-vēsh'tà)	224b	16.01 N	23.52 W

PLACE (Pronounciation)	PAGE	Lat. °'	Long. °'
Bobbingworth, Eng.	62	51.44 N	0.13 E
Bobërka, Sov.Un. (bō'bẽr-kà)	167	49.36 N	24.18 E
Bobigny, Fr.	64c	48.54 N	2.27 E
Bobo Dioulasso, Burkina (bō'bô-dyo͞o-làs-sō')	228	11.12 N	4.18 W
Bóbr (R.), Pol. (bŭ'br)	166	51.44 N	15.13 E
Bobr, Sov.Un. (bô'b'r)	174	54.19 N	29.11 E
Bobrinets, Sov.Un. (bô'brē-nyĭts)	175	48.04 N	32.10 E
Bobrov, Sov.Un. (bŭb-rôf')	175	51.07 N	40.01 E
Bobrovitsa, Sov.Un. (bŭb-rō'vē-tsá)	175	50.43 N	31.27 E
Bobruysk, Sov.Un. (bō-bro͞o'ĭsk)	174	53.07 N	29.13 E
Boca (Neigh.), Arg.	60d	34.38 S	58.21 W
Boca del Pozo, Ven. (bô-kä-dĕl-pô'zō)	143b	11.00 N	64.21 W
Boca de Uchire, Ven. (bô-kä-dĕ-o͞o-chē'rĕ)	143b	10.09 N	65.27 W
Bocaina, Serra da (Mtn.), Braz. (sĕ'r-rä-dà-bô-kä'ē-nä)	141a	22.47 S	44.39 W
Bocanegra, Peru	60c	12.01 S	77.07 W
Bocas, Mex. (bō'käs)	130	22.29 N	101.03 W
Bocas del Toro, Pan. (bō'käs dĕl tō'rō)	133	9.24 N	82.15 W
Bochnia, Pol. (bōĸ'nyä)	167	49.58 N	20.28 E
Bocholt, F.R.G. (bō'ĸōlt)	169c	51.50 N	6.37 E
Bochum, F.R.G.-o(bō'ĸo͞om)	169c	51.29 N	7.13 E
Böckel (Neigh.), F.R.G.	63	51.13 N	7.12 E
Bockum, F.R.G.	63	51.20 N	6.44 E
Bockum (Neigh.), F.R.G.	63	51.21 N	6.38 E
Bockum-Hövel, F.R.G. (bō'ĸo͞om-hû'fĕl)	169c	51.41 N	7.45 E
Bodalang, Zaire	230	3.14 N	22.14 E
Bodaybo, Sov.Un. (bō-dī'bō)	181	57.12 N	114.46 E
Bodele (Depression), Chad. (bō-dā-lā')	229	16.45 N	17.05 E
Bodelschwingh (Neigh.), F.R.G.	63	51.33 N	7.22 E
Boden, Swe.	158	65.51 N	21.29 E
Bodensee (L.), F.R.G.-Switz. (bō'dĕn zā)	166	47.48 N	9.22 E
Bodmin, Eng. (bŏd'mĭn)	162	50.29 N	4.45 W
Bodmin Moor, Eng. (bŏd'mĭn mo͞or)	162	50.36 N	4.43 W
Bodø, Nor. (bôd'û)	158	67.13 N	14.19 E
Bodrum, Tur.	179	37.10 N	27.07 E
Boende, Zaire (bô-ĕn'dā)	230	0.13 S	20.52 E
Boerne, Tx. (bō'ẽrn)	124	29.49 N	98.44 W
Boesmans (R.), S.Afr.	227c	33.29 S	26.09 E
Boeuf R., La. (bĕf)	125	32.23 N	91.57 W
Boffa, Gui. (bôf'á)	228	10.10 N	14.02 W
Bōfu, Jap. (bō'fo͞o)	205	34.03 N	131.35 E
Bogalusa, La. (bō-gá-lo͞o'sà)	125	30.48 N	89.52 W
Bogan (R.), Austl. (bŏ'gĕn)	216	32.10 S	147.40 E
Bogense, Den. (bô'gĕn-sĕ)	164	55.34 N	10.09 E
Boggy Pk., Antigua (bŏg'ĭ-pēk)	133b	17.03 N	61.50 W
Bogodukhov, Sov.Un. (bŏ-gō-do͞o'ĸôf)	175	50.10 N	35.31 E
Bogong, Mt., Austl.	216	36.50 S	147.15 E
Bogor, Indon.	206	6.45 S	106.45 E
Bogoroditsk, Sov.Un. (bŏ-gŏ'rô-dĭtsk)	174	53.48 N	38.06 E
Bogorodsk, Sov.Un.	178	56.02 N	43.40 E
Bogorodskoje (Neigh.), Sov. Un.	66b	55.49 N	37.44 E
Bogorodskoye, Sov.Un. (bô-gô-rôd'skô-yĕ)	182a	56.43 N	56.53 E
Bogotá, Col. (bō-gō-tä')	142a	4.38 N	74.06 W
Bogota, NJ	55	40.53 N	74.02 W
Bogotá, Rio (R.), Col. (rē'ō-bō-gō-tä')	142a	4.27 N	74.38 W
Bogotol, Sov.Un. (bŏ'gô-tŏl)	180	56.15 N	89.45 E
Bogoyavlenskoye, Sov.Un. (bŏ'gô-yäf'lĕn-skō'yĕ)	175	48.46 N	33.19 E
Boguchar, Sov.Un. (bō'go͞o-chär)	179	49.40 N	41.00 E
Boguete, Pan. (bô-gĕ'tĕ)	133	8.54 N	82.29 W
Boguslav, Sov.Un. (bō'go͞o-släf)	175	49.34 N	30.51 W
Bohai Haixia (Str.), China (bwo-hī hī-shyä)	202	38.05 N	121.40 E
Bohain-en-Vermandois, Fr. (bô-ăɴ-ŏɴ-vâr-mäɴ-dwä')	168	49.58 N	3.22 E
Bohemia (Prov.), see Cechy			
Bohemian For., F.R.G. (bō-hē'mĭ-ăn)	166	49.35 N	12.27 E
Böhnsdorf (Neigh.), G.D.R.	65a	52.24 N	13.33 E
Bohol (I.), Phil. (bô-hôl')	207	9.28 N	124.35 E
Bohom, Mex. (bŏ-ō'm)	131	16.47 N	92.42 W
Boiestown, Can. (boiz'toun)	104	46.27 N	66.25 W
Bois Blanc (I.), Mi. (boi' blăŋk)	110	45.45 N	84.30 W
Boischâtel, Can. (bwä-shä-tĕl')	95b	46.54 N	71.08 W
Bois-Colombes, Fr.	64c	48.55 N	2.16 E
Bois-des-Filion, Can. (bo͞o-ä'dĕ-fē-yōɴ')	95a	45.40 N	73.46 W
Boise, Id. (boi'zē)	116	43.38 N	116.12 W
Boise (R.), Id.	116	43.43 N	116.30 W
Boise City, Ok.	122	36.42 N	102.30 W
Boissevain, Can. (bois'vān)	101	49.14 N	100.03 W
Boissy-Saint-Léger, Fr.	64c	48.45 N	2.31 E
Bojador, Cabo (C.), W.Sah. (kà'bō-bō-hä-dōr') (bŏj-à-dōr')	224	26.21 N	16.08 W
Bojnūrd, Iran	192	37.29 N	57.13 E
Bokani, Nig.	229	9.26 N	5.13 E
Boké, Gui. (bō-kā')	224	10.58 N	14.15 W
Boknafjorden (Fd.), Nor.	164	59.12 N	5.37 E
Boksburg, S.Afr. (bŏĸs'bûrgh)	227b	26.13 N	28.15 E
Boksburg North, S. Afr.	71b	26.12 S	28.15 E
Boksburg South, S. Afr.	71b	26.14 S	28.15 E
Boksburg West, S. Afr.	71b	26.13 S	28.14 E
Bokungu, Zaire	230	0.41 S	22.19 E
Bol, Chad	229	13.28 N	14.43 E
Bolai I., Cen.Afr.Rep.	229	4.20 N	17.21 E
Bolama, Guinea-Bissau (bô-lä'mä)	224	11.34 S	15.41 W
Bolan (Mt.), Pak. (bô-län')	196	30.13 N	67.09 E
Bolaños, Mex. (bō-län'yōs)	130	21.40 N	103.48 W
Bolaños (R.), Mex.	130	21.26 N	103.54 W
Bolan P., Pak.	196	29.50 N	67.10 E
Bolbec, Fr. (bôl-bĕk')	168	49.37 N	0.26 E
Bole, Ghana (bō'lā)	228	9.02 N	2.29 W
Boleslawiec, Pol. (bō-lĕ-slä'vyĕts)	166	51.15 N	15.35 E

PLACE (Pronounciation)	PAGE	Lat. °'	Long. °'
Bolgatanga, Ghana	228	10.46 N	0.52 W
Bolgrad, Sov.Un. (bŏl-grát)	175	45.41 N	28.38 E
Boli, China (bwo-lē)	202	45.40 N	130.38 E
Bolinao, Phil. (bō-lē-nä'ō)	207a	16.24 N	119.53 E
Bolivar, Mo. (bŏl'ĭ-vár)	123	37.37 N	93.22 W
Bolivar, Tn.	126	35.14 N	88.56 W
Bolivar Pen., Tx. (bŏl'ĭ-vár)	125a	29.25 N	94.40 W
Bolivia, S.A. (bō-lĭv'ĭ-á)	140	17.00 S	64.00 W
Bolívar, Arg. (bô-lē'vär)	141c	36.15 S	61.05 W
Bolívar, Col.	142	1.46 N	76.58 W
Bolívar (La Columna) (Mtn.), Ven. (bô-lē'vär) (lä-kô-lo͞o'm-nä)	142	8.44 N	70.54 W
Bölkenbusch, F.R.G.	63	51.21 N	7.06 E
Bolkhov, Sov. Un. (bŏl-ĸôf')	174	53.27 N	35.59 E
Bollate, It.	65c	45.33 N	9.07 E
Bollensdorf, G.D.R.	65a	52.31 N	13.43 E
Bollin (R.), Eng. (bŏl'ĭn)	156	53.18 N	2.11 W
Bollington, Eng. (bŏl'ĭng-tŭn)	156	53.18 N	2.06 W
Bollington, Eng.	64b	53.22 N	2.25 W
Bollnäs, Swe. (bôl'nĕs)	164	61.22 N	16.20 E
Bollwerk, F.R.G.	63	51.10 N	7.35 E
Bolmen (L.), Swe. (bôl'mĕn)	164	56.58 N	13.25 E
Bolobo, Zaire (bō'lō-bō)	226	2.14 S	16.18 E
Bologna, It. (bō-lōn'yä)	172	44.30 N	11.18 E
Bologoye, Sov. Un. (bŏ-lō-gô'yĕ)	174	57.52 N	34.02 E
Boloncheticul, Mex. (bô-lôn-chĕn-tē-ko͞o'l)	132a	20.03 N	89.47 W
Bolondrón, Cuba (bô-lôn-drōn')	134	22.45 N	81.25 W
Bol'šaja Ochta (Neigh.), Sov. Un.	66a	59.57 N	30.25 E
Bolseno, Lago di (L.), It. (lä'gō-dē-bōl-sä'nō)	172	42.35 N	11.40 E
Bol'shaya Anyuy (R.), Sov. Un.	181	67.58 N	161.15 E
Bol'shaya Chuva (R.), Sov. Un.	181	58.15 N	111.13 E
Bol'shaya Kinel' (R.), Sov. Un.	178	53.20 N	52.40 E
Bol'shaya Lepetikha, Sov. Un. (bôl-shá'yá'lyĕ'phyĕ-tē'ĸä)	175	47.11 N	33.58 E
Bol'shaya Viska, Sov. Un. (vĭs-kä')	175	48.34 N	31.54 E
Bol'shaya Vradiyevka, Sov. Un. (vrá-dyĕf'kä)	175	47.51 N	30.38 E
Bol'she Ust'ikinskoye, Sov. Un. (bôl'she o͞os-tyĭ-kĕn'skô-yĕ)	182a	55.58 N	58.18 E
Bol'shoy Begichev (I.), Sov. Un.	181	74.30 N	114.40 E
Bol'shoye Ivonino, Sov. Un. (ĭ-vô'nĭ-nô)	182a	59.41 N	61.12 E
Bol'shoy Kuyash, Sov. Un. (bôl'-shôy ko͞o'yàsh)	182a	55.52 N	61.07 E
Bolshoy Tokmak, Sov. Un. (bŏl-shôy' tôk-mäk')	175	47.17 N	35.48 E
Bol'šoj Teatr (P. Int.), Sov. Un.	66b	55.46 N	37.37 E
Bolsover, Eng. (bōl'zō-vẽr)	156	53.14 N	1.17 W
Boltaña, Sp. (bōl-tä'nä)	171	42.28 N	0.03 E
Bolton, Can. (bōl'tŭn)	95d	43.53 N	79.44 W
Bolton, Eng.	156	53.35 N	2.26 W
Bolton-upon-Dearne, Eng. (bōl'tŭn-ŭp'ŏn-dûrn)	156	53.31 N	1.19 W
Bolu, Tur. (bō'lo͞o)	179	40.45 N	31.45 E
Bolva (R.), Sov. Un. (bôl'vä)	174	53.30 N	34.30 E
Bolvadin, Tur. (bŏl-vä-dĕn')	179	38.50 N	30.50 E
Bolzano, It. (bôl-tsä'nō)	172	46.31 N	11.22 E
Boma, Zaire (bō'mä)	230	5.51 S	13.03 E
Bombala, Austl. (bŭm-bä'lă)	216	36.55 S	149.07 E
Bombay, India (bŏm-bā')	197b	18.58 N	72.50 E
Bombay Hbr., India	197b	18.55 N	72.52 E
Bomi Hills, Lib.	224	7.00 N	11.00 W
Bom Jardim, Braz. (bôn zhär-dēɴ')	141a	22.10 S	42.25 W
Bom Jesus do Itabapoana, Braz. (bôɴ-zhĕ-so͞o's-dô-ē-tá'bä-pô-á'nä)	141a	21.08 S	41.51 W
Bømlo (I.), Nor. (bûmlô)	164	59.47 N	4.57 E
Bommerholz, F.R.G.	63	51.23 N	7.18 E
Bommern (Neigh.), F.R.G.	63	51.25 N	7.20 E
Bomongo, Zaire	230	1.22 N	18.21 E
Bom Retiro (Neigh.), Braz.	61d	23.32 S	46.38 W
Bom Sucesso, Braz. (bôn-so͞o-sĕ'sō)	141a	21.02 S	44.44 W
Bomu (R.), see Mbomou			
Bon Air, Pa.	56b	39.58 N	75.19 W
Bonaire (I.), Neth. Antilles (bō-nâr')	142	12.10 N	68.15 W
Bonavista, Can. (bŏ-ná-vĭs'tá)	105	48.39 N	53.07 W
Bonavista B., Can.	105	48.45 N	53.20 W
Bon, C., Tun. (bôɴ)	159	37.04 N	11.13 E
Bond, Co. (bŏnd)	122	39.53 N	106.40 W
Bondi, Austl.	70a	33.53 S	151.17 E
Bondo, Zaire (bôn'dô)	230	3.49 N	23.40 E
Bondoc Pen., Phil. (bŏn-dŏk')	207a	13.24 N	122.30 E
Bondoukou, Ivory Coast (bŏn-do͞o'ko͞o)	228	8.02 N	2.48 W
Bonds Cay (I.), Ba. (bŏnds kē)	134	25.30 N	77.45 W
Bondy, Fr.	64c	48.54 N	2.28 E
Bône, see Annaba			
Bonete, Cerro (Mt.), Arg. (bô'nĕtĕh çĕrrô)	144	27.50 S	68.35 W
Bone, Teluk (G.), Indon.	206	4.09 S	121.00 E
Bonfim, Braz. (bôɴ-fē'ɴ)	141a	20.20 S	44.15 W
Bongor, Chad.	229	10.17 N	15.22 E
Bong Son, Viet.	203	14.20 N	109.10 E
Bonham, Tx. (bŏn'ăm)	123	33.35 N	96.09 W
Bonhomme, Pic (Pk.), Hai.	135	19.10 N	72.20 W
Bonifacio, Fr. (bō-nē-fä'chō)	172	41.23 N	9.10 E
Bonifacio, Str. of., Eur.	172	41.14 N	9.02 E
Bonifay, Fl. (bŏn-ĭ-fā')	126	30.46 N	85.40 W
Bonin Is., Asia (bō'nĭn)	208	26.30 N	141.00 E
Bonn, F.R.G. (bŏn)	169c	50.44 N	7.06 E
Bonne B., Can. (bŏn)	105	49.33 N	57.55 W
Bonners Ferry, Id. (bon'erz fĕr'ĭ)	116	48.41 N	116.19 W
Bonner Springs, Ks. (bŏn'ẽr sprĭngz)	119f	39.04 N	94.52 W
Bonne Terre, Mo. (bŏn târ')	123	37.55 N	90.32 W
Bonnet Pk., Can. (bŏn'ĭt)	99	51.26 N	115.53 W
Bonneuil-sur-Marne, Fr.	64c	48.46 N	2.29 E
Bonneville Dam, Or.-Wa. (bŏn'ē-vĭl)	116	45.37 N	121.57 W
Bonnie B., Can. (bŏn'ē)	105	49.38 N	58.15 W
Bonny, Nig. (bŏn'ē)	224	4.29 N	7.13 E
Bonny Lake, Wa. (bŏn'ē lăk)	118a	47.11 N	122.11 W

PRONOUNCING INDEX
Bonnyrigg – Brazil 263

PLACE (Pronounciation)	PAGE	Lat. °′	Long. °′
Bonnyrigg, Austl.	70a	33.54 S	150.54 E
Bonnyville, Can. (bŏn′e-vĭl)	99	54.16 N	110.44 W
Bonorva, It. (bô-nôr′vä)	172	40.26 N	8.46 E
Bonsúcesso (Neigh.), Braz.	61c	22.52 S	43.15 W
Bonthain, Indon. (bôn-tīn′)	206	5.30 S	119.52 E
Bonthe, S.L.	228	7.32 N	12.30 W
Bontoc, Phil. (bŏn-tŏk′)	207a	17.10 N	121.01 E
Booby Rocks (I.), Ba. (bōō′bĭ rŏks)	134	23.55 N	77.00 W
Booker T. Washington Natl. Mon., Va. (bo͝ok′ẽr tē wŏsh′ĭng-tŭn)	127	37.07 N	79.45 W
Boom, Bel.	157a	51.05 N	4.22 E
Boone, Ia. (bōōn)	115	42.04 N	93.51 W
Booneville, Ar. (bōōn′vĭl)	123	35.09 N	93.54 W
Booneville, Ky.	110	37.25 N	83.40 W
Booneville, Ms.	126	34.37 N	88.35 W
Boons, S. Afr.	223d	25.59 S	27.15 E
Boonton, NJ (bōōn′tŭn)	112a	40.54 N	74.24 W
Boonville, In.	110	38.00 N	87.15 W
Boonville, Mo.	123	38.57 N	92.44 W
Boorama, Som.	223a	10.05 N	43.08 E
Boosaaso, Som.	223a	11.19 N	49.10 E
Boothbay Harbor, Me. (bōōth′bā här′bẽr)	104	43.51 N	69.39 W
Boothia, G. of, Can. (bōō′thĭ-å)	97	69.04 N	86.04 W
Boothia Pen., Can.	94	73.30 N	95.00 W
Boothstown, Eng.	64b	53.30 N	2.25 W
Bootle, Eng. (bōōt′l)	156	53.29 N	3.02 W
Booué, Gabon	230	0.06 S	11.56 E
Booysens (Neigh.), S. Afr.	71b	26.14 S	28.01 E
Bor, Sud. (bôr)	225	6.13 N	31.35 E
Bor, Tur. (bôr)	179	37.50 N	34.40 E
Boraha, Nosy (I.), Mad.	227	16.58 S	50.15 E
Borah Pk., Id. (bō′rä)	117	44.12 N	113.47 W
Borås, Swe. (bōō′rōs)	164	57.43 N	12.55 E
Borāzjān, Iran (bō-räz-jän′)	192	29.13 N	51.13 E
Borba, Braz. (bôr′bä)	143	4.23 S	59.31 W
Borbeck (Neigh.), F.R.G.	63	51.29 N	6.57 E
Borborema, Planalto da (Plat.), Braz. (plä-nal′tô-dä-bôr-bō-rē′mä)	143	7.35 S	36.40 W
Bordeaux, Fr. (bôr-dō′)	168	44.50 N	0.37 W
Bordeaux (Neigh.), Can.	54b	45.33 N	73.41 W
Bordeaux, S. Afr.	71b	26.06 S	28.01 E
Bordentown, NJ (bôr′dĕn-toun)	111	40.05 N	74.40 W
Bordj-bou-Arréridj, Alg. (bôrj-bōō-å-rā-rēj′)	159	36.03 N	4.48 E
Bordj Omar Idriss, Alg.	224	28.06 N	6.34 E
Borehamwood, Eng.	62	51.40 N	0.16 W
Borgå, Fin. (bôr′gō)	165	60.26 N	25.41 E
Borgarnes, Ice.	158	64.31 N	21.40 W
Borger, Tx. (bôr′gẽr)	122	35.40 N	101.23 W
Borgholm, Swe. (bôrg-hōlm′)	164	56.52 N	16.40 E
Borgne (L.), La. (bôrn′y′)	125	30.03 N	89.36 W
Borgomanero, It. (bôr′gō-mä-nâ′rō)	172	45.40 N	8.28 E
Borgo Val di Taro, It. (bô′r-zhō-väl-dē-tà′rō)	172	44.29 N	9.44 E
Boring, Or. (bōring)	118c	45.26 N	122.22 W
Borislav, Sov. Un. (bô′rĭs-lôf)	167	49.17 N	23.24 E
Borisoglebsk, Sov. Un. (bŏ-rē sô-glyĕpsk′)	179	51.20 N	42.00 E
Borisov, Sov. Un. (bŏ-rē′sôf)	174	54.16 N	28.33 E
Borisovka, Sov. Un. (bŏ-rē-sôf′kȧ)	175	50.38 N	36.00 E
Borispol′, Sov. Un. (bo-rĭs′pol)	175	50.17 N	30.54 E
Borivli, India	197b	19.15 N	72.48 E
Borja, Sp. (bôr′hä)	170	41.50 N	1.33 W
Borjas Blancas, Sp. (bô′r-кäs-blä′n-käs)	171	41.29 N	0.53 E
Borken, F.R.G. (bôr′kĕn)	169c	51.50 N	6.51 E
Borkou (Reg.), Chad. (bôr-kōō′)	225	18.11 N	18.28 E
Borkum I., F.R.G. (bōr′kōōm)	166	53.31 N	6.50 E
Borlänge, Swe. (bôr-lĕŋ′gĕ)	164	60.30 N	15.24 E
Borle (Neigh.), India	67e	19.02 N	72.55 E
Borneo (I.), Asia (bôr′nē-ō)	206	0.25 N	112.39 E
Bornholm (I.), Den. (bôrn-hôlm)	164	55.16 N	15.15 E
Bornim (Neigh.), G.D.R.	65a	52.26 N	13.00 E
Bornstedt (Neigh.), G.D.R.	65a	52.25 N	13.02 E
Borodayevka, Sov. Un.	175	48.44 N	34.09 E
Boromlya, Sov. Un. (bŏ-rôm′′l-yä)	175	50.36 N	34.58 E
Boromo, Upper Volta	228	11.45 N	2.56 W
Borough Green, Eng.	62	51.17 N	0.19 E
Borough Park (Neigh.), NY	55	40.38 N	74.00 W
Borovan, Bul. (bŏ-rô-vän′)	173	43.24 N	23.47 E
Borovichi, Sov. Un. (bŏ-rō-vē′chē)	174	58.22 N	33.56 E
Borovsk, Sov. Un. (bô′rŏvsk)	174	55.13 N	36.26 E
Borraan, Som.	223a	10.38 N	48.30 E
Borracha, Isla la (I.), Ven. (ē′s-lä-lä-bôr-rä′chä)	143b	10.18 N	64.44 W
Borroloola, Austl. (bŏr-rô-lōō′lȧ)	214	16.15 S	136.19 E
Borshchëv, Sov. Un. (bôrsh-chyôf′)	167	48.47 N	26.04 E
Borth, F.R.G.	63	51.36 N	6.33 E
Bort-les-Orgues, Fr. (bôr-lā-zôrg)	168	45.26 N	2.26 E
Borūjerd, Iran	192	33.45 N	48.53 E
Borzna, Sov. Un. (bôrz′nȧ)	175	51.15 N	32.26 E
Borzya, Sov. Un. (bôrz′yȧ)	181	50.37 N	116.53 E
Bosa, It. (bō′sä)	172	40.18 N	8.34 E
Bosanska Dubica, Yugo. (bō′sän-skä dōō′bĭt-sä)	172	45.10 N	16.49 E
Bosanska Gradiška, Yugo. (bō′sän-skä grä-dĭsh′kä)	172	45.08 N	17.15 E
Bosanski Novi, Yugo. (bō′s sän-skĭ nō′vē)	172	45.00 N	16.22 E
Bosanski Petrovac, Yugo. (bō′sän-skĭ pĕt′rō-väts)	172	44.33 N	16.23 E
Bosanski Šamac, Yugo. (bō′sän-skĭ shä′mȧts)	173	45.03 N	18.30 E
Boscobel, Wi. (bŏs′kô-bĕl)	115	43.08 N	90.44 W
Bose, China (bwo-sŭ)	203	24.00 N	106.38 E
Boshän, China (bwo-shan)	200	36.32 N	117.51 E
Boskol, Sov. Un. (bȧs-kôl′)	182a	53.45 N	61.17 E
Boskoop, Neth.	157a	52.04 N	4.39 E
Boskovice, Czech. (bŏs′kō-vē-tsĕ)	166	49.26 N	16.37 E
Bosna (R.), Yugo.	173	44.19 N	17.54 E
Bosnia (Reg.), Yugo. (bŏs′nĭ-ȧ)	173	44.17 N	16.58 E
Bosobolo, Zaire	230	4.11 N	19.54 E
Bosporous (Str.), see İstanbul Boğazi			
Bossangoa, Cen. Afr. Rep.	229	6.29 N	17.27 E
Bossembélé, Cen. Afr. Rep.	229	5.16 N	17.39 E
Bossier City, La. (bŏsh′ẽr)	125	32.31 N	93.42 W
Bossley Park, Austl.	70a	33.52 S	150.54 E
Bostanci (Neigh.), Tur.	66f	40.57 N	29.05 E
Bosten Hu (L.), China (bwo-stŭn hōō)	198	42.06 N	88.01 E
Boston, Ga. (bôs′tŭn)	126	30.47 N	83.47 W
Boston, Ma.	105a	42.15 N	71.07 W
Boston, Pa.	57b	40.18 N	79.49 W
Boston B., Ma.	54a	42.22 N	70.54 W
Boston Garden (P. Int.), Ma.	54a	42.22 N	71.04 W
Boston Har., Ma.	54a	42.20 N	70.58 W
Boston Heights, Oh.	113d	41.15 N	81.30 W
Boston Mts., Ar.	123	35.46 N	93.32 W
Botafogo (Neigh.), Braz.	61c	22.57 S	43.11 W
Botafogo, Enseada de (B.), Braz.	61c	22.57 S	43.10 W
Botany, Austl.	70a	33.57 S	151.12 E
Botany B., Austl. (bŏt′ȧ-nĭ)	211b	33.58 S	151.11 E
Botany Bay (Neigh.), Eng.	62	51.41 N	0.07 W
Botevgrad, Bul.	173	42.54 N	23.41 E
Bothaville, S. Afr. (bō′tȧ-vĭl)	223d	27.24 S	26.38 E
Bothell, Wa. (bŏth′ĕl)	118a	47.46 N	122.12 W
Bothnia, G. of, Eur. (bŏth′nĭ-ȧ)	158	63.40 N	21.30 E
Botosani, Rom. (bô-tô-shán′ĭ)	167	47.46 N	26.40 E
Botswana, Afr. (bŏtswănȧ)	222	22.10 S	23.13 E
Bottineau, ND (bŏt-ĭ-nō′)	114	48.48 N	100.28 W
Bottrop, F.R.G. (bŏt′trōp)	169c	51.31 N	6.56 E
Botucatú, Braz. (bô-tōō-kä-tōō′)	143	22.50 S	48.23 W
Botwood, Can. (bŏt′wo͝od)	105	49.08 N	55.21 W
Bötzow, G.D.R.	65a	52.39 N	13.08 E
Bouafle, Ivory Coast (bōō-ȧ-flā′)	228	6.59 N	5.45 W
Bouaké, Ivory Coast (bōō-ȧ-kā′)	228	7.41 N	5.00 W
Bouar, Cen. Afr. Rep. (bōō-är)	229	5.57 N	15.36 E
Bou Areg, Sebkha (Marsh), Mor.	170	35.09 N	3.02 W
Boubandjidah, Parc Natl. de (Natl. Pk.), Cam.	229	8.20 N	14.40 E
Boucherville, Can. (bōō-shȧ-vēl′)	95a	45.37 N	73.27 W
Boucherville, Îles de (Is.), Can.	54b	45.37 N	73.28 W
Boucle du Baoulé, Parc Natl. de la (Natl. Pk.), Mali	228	13.50 N	9.15 W
Boudenib, Mor. (bōō-dĕ-nĕb′)	224	32.14 N	3.04 W
Boudette, Mn. (bōō-dĕt)	115	48.42 N	94.34 W
Boudouaou, Alg.	171	36.44 N	3.25 E
Boufarik, Alg. (bōō-fȧ-rēk′)	171	36.35 N	2.55 E
Bougainville Trench, Oceania (bōō-gäN-vēl′)	208	7.00 S	152.00 E
Bougie, see Bejaïa			
Bougouni, Mali (bōō-gōō-nē′)	224	11.27 N	7.30 W
Bouïra, Alg. (boo-ē′rȧ)	160	36.25 N	3.55 E
Bouïra-Sahary, Alg. (bwē-rȧ sȧ′ä-rē)	171	35.16 N	3.23 E
Bouka (R.), Gui.	228	11.05 N	10.40 W
Boukiéro, Con.	71c	4.12 S	15.18 E
Boulder, Austl. (bōl′dẽr)	214	31.00 S	121.40 E
Boulder, Co.	122	40.02 N	105.19 W
Boulder (R.), Mt.	117	46.10 N	112.07 W
Boulder City, Nv.	120	35.57 N	114.50 W
Boulder Cr., Id.	116	42.53 N	116.49 W
Boulder Pk., Id.	117	43.53 N	114.33 W
Boulogne (Neigh.), Arg.	60d	34.31 S	58.34 W
Boulogne-Billancourt, Fr. (bōō-lôn′y′-bē-yäN-kōōr′)	169b	48.50 N	2.14 E
Boulogne-sur-Mer, Fr. (bōō-lôn′y-sür-mâr′)	168	50.44 N	1.37 E
Boumba (R.), Cam.	229	3.20 N	14.40 E
Bouna, Ivory Coast (bōō-nä′)	228	9.16 N	3.00 W
Bouna, Park Natl. de (Natl. Pk.), Ivory Coast	228	9.20 N	3.35 W
Boundary B., Can. (boun′dȧ-rĭ)	118d	49.03 N	122.59 W
Boundary Pk., Nv.	120	37.52 N	118.20 W
Bound Brook, NJ (bound bro͝ok)	112a	40.34 N	74.32 W
Bountiful, Ut. (boun′tĭ-fo͝ol)	119b	40.55 N	111.53 W
Bountiful Pk., Ut. (boun′tĭ-fo͝ol)	119b	40.58 N	111.49 W
Bounty Is., N.Z.	232	47.42 S	179.05 E
Bourem, Mali (bōō-rĕm′)	224	16.43 N	0.15 W
Bourg-en-Bresse, Fr. (bōōr-gĕN-brĕs′)	168	46.12 N	5.13 E
Bourges, Fr. (bōōrzh)	168	47.06 N	2.22 E
Bourget, Can. (bōōr-zhĕ′)	95c	45.26 N	75.09 W
Bourg-la-Reine, Fr.	64c	48.47 N	2.19 E
Bourgoin, Fr. (bōōr-gwăN′)	169	45.46 N	5.17 E
Bourke, Austl. (bŭrk)	216	30.10 S	146.00 E
Bourne, Eng. (bōrn)	156	52.46 N	0.22 W
Bournebridge, Eng.	62	51.38 N	0.11 E
Bourne End, Eng.	62	51.45 N	0.32 W
Bournemouth, Eng. (bôrn′mŭth)	162	50.44 N	1.55 W
Bou Saâda, Alg. (bōō-sä′dä)	160	35.13 N	4.17 E
Bousso, Chad. (bōō-sô′)	225	10.33 N	16.45 E
Boutilimit, Mauritania (bōō-tē-lē-mē′)	224	17.30 N	14.54 W
Bouvert (I.), see Bouvetøya			
Bouvetøya (Bouvert) (I.), Alt. O.	232	54.26 S	3.24 E
Bövinghausen (Neigh.), F.R.G.	63	51.31 N	7.19 E
Bow (R.), Can. (bō)	99	50.35 N	112.15 W
Bowbells, ND (bō′bĕls)	114	48.50 N	102.16 W
Bowdle, SD (bōd′′l)	114	45.28 N	99.42 W
Bowdon, Eng.	64b	53.23 N	2.22 W
Bowen, Austl. (bō′ĕn)	215	20.02 S	148.14 E
Bowie, Md. (bōō′ĭ) (bō′ē)	112e	38.59 N	76.47 W
Bowie, Tx.	122	33.34 N	97.50 W
Bowling Green, Ky. (bōlĭng grēn)	126	37.00 N	86.26 W
Bowling Green, Mo.	123	39.19 N	91.09 W
Bowling Green, Oh.	110	41.25 N	83.40 W
Bowman, ND (bō′mȧn)	114	46.11 N	103.23 W
Bowron (R.), Can. (bō′rŭn)	99	53.20 N	121.10 W
Boxelder Cr., Mt. (bŏks′ĕl-dẽr)	114	45.35 N	104.28 W
Boxelder Cr., Mt.	117	47.17 N	108.37 W
Box Hill, Austl.	70b	37.49 S	145.08 E
Boxian, China (bwo shyĕn)	200	33.52 N	115.47 E
Boxing, China (bwo-shyĭŋ)	200	37.09 N	118.08 E
Boxmoor, Eng.	62	51.45 N	0.29 W
Boxtel, Neth.	157a	51.40 N	5.21 E
Boyabo, Zaire	230	3.43 N	18.46 E
Boyacıköy (Neigh.), Tur.	66f	41.06 N	29.02 E
Boyang, China (bwo-yäŋ)	203	29.00 N	116.42 E
Boyer (R.), Can. (boi′ẽr)	95b	46.26 N	70.56 W
Boyer (R.), Ia.	114	41.45 N	95.36 W
Boyle, Ire. (boil)	162	53.59 N	8.15 W
Boyne (R.), Ire. (boin)	162	53.40 N	6.40 W
Boyne City, Mi.	110	45.15 N	85.05 W
Boyoma Falls, Zaire	230	0.30 N	25.12 E
Bozca Ada (I.), Tur.	173	39.50 N	26.00 E
Bozcaada, Tur. (bōz-cä′dä)	173	39.50 N	26.05 E
Bozeman, Mt. (bōz′mȧn)	117	45.41 N	111.00 W
Bozene, Zaire	230	2.56 N	19.12 E
Bozhen, China (bwo-jŭn)	200	38.05 N	116.35 E
Bozoum, Cen. Afr. Rep.	229	6.19 N	16.23 E
Bra, It. (brä)	172	44.41 N	7.52 E
Brač (I.), Yugo. (bräch)	172	43.18 N	16.36 E
Bracciano, Lago di (L.), It. (lä′gō-dē-brä-chä′nō)	172	42.05 N	12.00 E
Bracebridge, Can. (brās′brĭj)	111	45.05 N	79.20 W
Braceville, Il. (brās′vĭl)	113a	41.13 N	88.16 W
Bräcke, Swe. (brĕk′kĕ)	164	62.44 N	15.28 E
Brackenridge, Pa. (brăk′ĕn-rĭj)	113e	40.37 N	79.44 W
Brackettville, Tx. (brăk′ĕt-vĭl)	124	29.19 N	100.24 W
Braço Maior (R.), Braz.	143	11.00 S	51.00 W
Braço Menor (R.), Braz. (brä′zô-mē-nō′r)	143	11.38 S	50.00 W
Bradano (R.), It. (brä-dä′nō)	172	40.43 N	16.22 E
Braddock, Pa. (brăd′ŭk)	113e	40.24 N	79.52 W
Braddock Hills, Pa.	57b	40.25 N	79.51 W
Bradenburger Tor (P. Int.), G.D.R.	65a	52.31 N	13.23 E
Bradenton, Fl. (brā′dĕn-tŭn)	127a	27.28 N	82.35 W
Bradfield, Eng. (brăd′fēld)	156b	51.25 N	1.08 W
Bradford, Eng. (brăd′fẽrd)	156	53.47 N	1.44 W
Bradford, Oh.	110	40.10 N	84.30 W
Bradford, Pa.	111	42.00 N	78.40 W
Bradley, Il. (brăd′lĭ)	113a	41.09 N	87.52 W
Bradner, Can. (brăd′nẽr)	118d	49.05 N	122.26 W
Bradshaw, Eng.	64b	53.36 N	2.24 W
Brady, Tx. (brā′dĭ)	124	31.09 N	99.21 W
Braga, Port. (brä′gä)	170	41.20 N	8.25 W
Bragado, Arg. (brä-gä′dō)	141c	35.07 S	60.28 W
Bragança, Braz. (brä-gän′sä)	143	1.02 S	46.50 W
Bragança, Port.	170	41.48 N	6.46 W
Bragança Paulista, Braz. (brä-gän′sä-pä′ōō-lē′s-tȧ)	141a	22.58 S	46.31 W
Bragg Creek, Can. (brăg)	95a	50.57 N	114.35 W
Brahmaputra (R.), India (brä′mȧ-pōō′trȧ)	193	26.45 N	92.45 E
Brāhui (Mts.), Pak.	193	28.32 N	66.15 E
Braidwood, Il. (brād′wo͝od)	113a	41.16 N	88.13 W
Brăila, Rom. (brē′ĕlȧ)	175	45.15 N	27.58 E
Brainerd, Mn. (brān′ẽrd)	115	46.20 N	94.09 W
Braintree, Ma. (brān′trē)	105a	42.14 N	71.00 W
Braithwaite, La. (brīth′wīt)	112d	29.52 N	89.57 W
Brakpan, S. Afr. (brăk′păn)	227b	26.15 S	28.22 E
Bralorne, Can. (brā′lôrn)	98	50.47 N	122.49 W
Bramalea, Can.	95d	43.48 N	79.41 W
Bramhall, Eng.	64b	53.22 N	2.10 W
Brampton, Can. (brămp′tŭn)	95d	43.41 N	79.46 W
Branca, Pedra (Mtn.), Braz. (pĕ′drä-brȧ′N-kä)	144b	22.55 S	43.28 W
Branchville, NJ (branch′vĭl)	112a	41.09 S	74.44 W
Branchville, SC	127	33.17 N	80.48 W
Branco (R.), Braz. (bräŋ′kō)	143	2.21 N	60.38 W
Brandberg (Mtn.), Namibia	226	21.15 S	14.15 E
Brandenburg, G.D.R. (brän′dĕn-bo͝orgh)	157b	52.25 N	12.33 E
Brandenburg (Reg.), G.D.R.	166	52.12 N	13.31 E
Brandfort, S. Afr. (brăn′d-fôrt)	223d	28.42 S	26.29 E
Brandon, Can. (brăn′dŭn)	101	49.50 N	99.57 W
Brandon, Vt.	111	43.45 N	73.05 W
Brandon Mtn., Ire. (brăn-dōn)	162	52.15 N	10.12 W
Brandywine, Md. (brăndĭ′wīn)	112e	38.42 N	76.51 W
Branford, Ct. (brăn′fẽrd)	111	41.15 N	72.50 W
Braniewo, Pol. (brä-nyĕ′vô)	167	54.23 N	19.50 E
Brańsk, Pol. (brän′ sk)	167	52.44 N	22.51 E
Brantford, Can. (brănt′fẽrd)	95d	43.09 N	80.17 W
Bras d′Or L., Can. (brä-dôr′)	105	45.52 N	60.50 W
Brasilia Legal (Fordlândia), Braz. (brä-sē′lyä-lĕ-gȧl) (fô′rd-län-dyä)	143	3.45 S	55.46 W
Brasília, Braz. (brä-sē′lvä)	143	15.49 S	47.39 W
Brasópolis, Braz. (brä-sô′pô-lēs)	141a	22.30 S	45.36 W
Braşov (Oraşul-Stalin), Rom.	173	45.39 N	25.35 E
Brass, Nig. (brăs)	224	4.28 N	6.28 E
Bras Saint Michel (R.), Can.	95b	46.47 N	70.51 W
Brasschaat, Bel. (bräs′кät)	157a	51.19 N	4.30 E
Bratcevo (Neigh.), Sov. Un.	66b	55.51 N	37.24 E
Bratenahl, Oh. (bră′tĕn-ôl)	113d	41.34 N	81.36 W
Bratislava, Czech. (brä′tĭs-lä-vä)	157e	48.09 N	17.07 E
Bratsk, Sov. Un. (brätsk)	180	56.10 N	102.04 E
Bratskoye Vdkhr. (Res.), Sov. Un.	180	56.10 N	102.05 E
Bratslav, Sov. Un. (brät′slȧf)	175	48.48 N	28.59 E
Brattleboro, Vt. (brăt′′l-bŭr-ô)	111	42.50 N	72.35 W
Braunau, Aus. (brou′nou)	166	48.15 N	13.05 E
Braunschweig, F.R.G. (broun′shvīgh)	166	52.16 N	10.32 E
Bråviken (R.), Swe.	164	58.40 N	16.40 E
Bravo del Norte, Rio (R.), see Grande, Rio			
Brawley, Ca. (brô′lĭ)	120	32.59 N	115.32 W
Bray, Ire. (brā)	162	53.10 N	6.05 W
Braybrook, Austl.	70b	37.47 S	144.51 E
Braymer, Mo. (brā′mẽr)	123	39.34 N	93.47 W
Brays Bay, Tx. (brās′bĭ′yōō)	125a	29.41 N	95.33 W
Brazeau (R.), Can.	99	52.55 N	116.10 W
Brazeau, Mt., Can. (brä-zō′)	99	52.33 N	117.21 W
Brazil, In. (brȧ-zĭl′)	110	39.30 N	87.00 W
Brazil, S.A.	140	9.00 S	53.00 W

ng-sing; ŋ-baŋk; N-nasalized n; nŏd; cŏmmit; ōld; ôbey; ôrder; oi-boil; fo͞od; fo͝ot; ou-out; s-soft; sh-dish; th-thin; pūre; ûnite; ûrn; stŭd; circŭs; ü-as in French tu; ′-indeterminate vowel.

ăt; fĭnál; rāte; senāte; ärm; ásk; sofá; fâre; ch-choose; dh-as th in other; bē; ĕvent; bĕt; recĕnt; cratĕr; g-gō; gh-guttural g; bĭt; ĭ-short neutral; rīde; ĸ-guttural k as ch in German ich;

PRONOUNCING INDEX

Bucksport – Cabeza 265

PLACE (Pronounciation)	PAGE	Lat. °'	Long. °'
Bucksport, Me. (bŭks'pôrt)	104	44.35 N	68.47 W
Buctouche, Can. (bük-tōōsh')	104	46.28 N	64.43 W
Bucun, China (bōō-tsōōn)	200	36.38 N	117.26 E
Bucureşti (Bucharest), Rom. (bōō-kōō-rĕsh'tĭ) (bōō-kȧ-rĕst')	173	44.23 N	26.10 E
Bucyrus, Oh. (bū-sī'rŭs)	110	40.50 N	82.55 W
Buda (Neigh.), Hung.	66g	47.30 N	19.02 E
Budai-hegység (Mts.), Hung.	66g	47.31 N	19.57 E
Budakeszi, Hung.	66g	47.31 N	18.56 E
Budaörs, Hung.	66g	47.27 N	18.58 E
Budapest, Hung. (bōō'dȧ-pĕsht')	167	47.30 N	19.05 E
Budberg, F.R.G.	63	51.32 N	6.38 E
Büderich, F.R.G.	63	51.37 N	6.34 E
Buderus, F.R.G.	63	51.33 N	7.38 E
Budge Budge, India	196a	22.28 N	88.08 E
Budjala, Zaire	230	2.39 N	19.42 E
Buea, Cam.	229	4.09 N	9.14 E
Buechel, Ky. (bĕ-chōōl')	113h	38.12 N	85.38 W
Bueil, Fr. (bwā')	169b	48.55 N	1.27 E
Buena Park, Ca. (bwā'nȧ pärk)	119a	33.52 N	118.00 W
Buenaventura, Col. (bwä'nä-vĕn-tōō'rȧ)	142	3.46 N	77.09 W
Buenaventura, Bahia de (B.), Col. (bä-ē'ä-dĕ-bwā'nä-vĕn-tōō'rȧ)	142	3.45 N	79.23 W
Buenaventura, Cuba	135a	22.53 N	82.22 W
Buena Vista, Co. (bū'nȧ vĭs'tȧ)	122	38.51 N	106.07 W
Buena Vista, Ga.	126	32.15 N	84.30 W
Buena Vista, Va.	111	37.45 N	79.20 W
Buena Vista, Bahía (B.), Cuba (bä-ē'ä-bwĕ-nä-vē's-tä)	134	22.30 N	79.10 W
Buena Vista Lake Res., Ca. (bū'nȧ vĭs'tȧ)	120	35.14 N	119.17 W
Buendia, Embalse de (Res.), Sp.	170	40.30 N	2.45 W
Buenos Aires, Arg. (bwā'nōs ī'rās)	144	34.20 S	58.30 W
Buenos Aires, Col.	142a	3.01 N	76.34 W
Buenos Aires, C. R.	133	9.10 N	83.21 W
Buenos Aires (L.), Arg.-Chile	144	46.30 S	72.15 W
Buenos Aires (Prov.), Arg.	144	36.15 S	61.45 W
Buer (Neigh.), F.R.G.	63	51.36 N	7.03 E
Buffalo, Mn. (buf'ȧ lō)	115	45.10 N	93.50 W
Buffalo, NY	113c	42.54 N	78.51 W
Buffalo (R.), Ar.	123	35.56 N	92.58 W
Buffalo (R.), S. Afr.	227c	28.35 S	30.27 E
Buffalo (R.), Tn.	126	35.24 N	87.10 W
Buffalo, Tx.	125	31.28 N	96.04 W
Buffalo, Wy.	117	44.19 N	106.42 W
Buffalo Bayou, Tx.	125a	29.46 N	95.32 W
Buffalo Cr., Mn.	115	44.46 N	94.28 W
Buffalo Har., NY	57a	42.51 N	78.52 W
Buffalo Head Hills, Can.	96	57.16 N	116.18 W
Buford, Can. (bū'fûrd)	95g	53.15 N	113.55 W
Buford, Ga. (bū'fĕrd)	126	34.05 N	84.00 W
Bug (R.), Pol. (bōōg)	167	52.29 N	21.20 E
Bug (R.), Sov. Un. (bōōk)	175	48.12 N	30.13 E
Buga, Col. (bōō'gä)	142a	3.54 N	76.17 W
Buggenhout, Bel.	157a	51.01 N	4.10 E
Buggs Island L., NC-Va.	127	36.30 N	78.38 W
Buglandsfjorden (Fd.), Nor.	164	58.53 N	7.55 E
Bugojno, Yugo. (bōō-gō ĭ nō)	172	44.03 N	17.28 E
Bugul'ma, Sov. Un. (bōō-gōōl'mȧ)	178	54.40 N	52.40 E
Buguruslan, Sov. Un. (bōō-gōō-rōōs-lȧn')	178	53.30 N	52.32 E
Buhi, Phil. (bōō'ē)	207a	13.26 N	123.31 E
Buhl, Id. (būl)	116	42.36 N	114.45 W
Buhl, Mn.	115	47.28 N	92.49 W
Buin, Chile (bōō-ēn')	141b	33.44 S	70.44 W
Buinaksk, Sov. Un. (bōō'ē-näksk)	179	42.40 N	47.20 E
Buir Nur (L.), China-Mong. (bōō-ēr nōōr)	202	47.50 N	117.00 E
Bujalance, Sp. (bōō-hä-län'thä)	170	37.54 N	4.22 W
Bujumbura, Burundi	231	3.23 S	29.22 E
Bukama, Zaire (bōō-kä'mä)	226	9.08 S	26.00 E
Bukavu, Zaire	231	2.30 S	28.52 E
Bukhara, Sov. Un. (bōō-kä'rä)	155	39.31 N	64.22 E
Bukitbatu, Indon.	191b	1.25 N	101.58 E
Bukit Panjang, Singapore	67c	1.23 N	103.46 E
Bukit Timah, Singapore	67c	1.20 N	103.47 E
Bukittingg, Indon.	206	0.25 S	100.28 E
Bukoba, Tan.	231	1.20 S	31.49 E
Bukovina (Reg.), Sov. Un. (bōō-kô'vĭ-nȧ)	167	48.06 N	25.20 E
Bula, Indon. (bōō'lä)	207	3.00 S	130.30 E
Bulalacao, Phil. (bōō-lȧ-lä'kä-ô)	207a	12.30 N	121.20 E
Bulawayo, Zimb. (bōō-lȧ-wä'yō)	226	20.12 S	28.43 E
Buldir (I.), Ak. (bŭl dĭr)	107a	52.22 N	175.50 E
Bulgaria, Eur. (bōōl-gā'rĭ-ä)	154	42.12 N	24.13 E
Bulim, Singapore	67c	1.23 N	103.43 E
Bulkley Ra., Can. (bŭlk'lē)	98	54.30 N	127.30 W
Bullaque (R.), Sp. (bōō-lä'kå)	170	39.15 N	4.13 W
Bullas, Sp. (bōōl'yäs)	170	38.07 N	1.48 W
Bulldog Cr., Ut. (bŭl'dŏg')	121	37.45 N	110.55 W
Bull Harbour, Can. (hăr'bēr)	98	50.45 N	127.55 W
Bull Head (Mtn.), Jam.	134	18.10 N	77.15 W
Bulloo (R.), Austl. (bŭ-lōō')	215	25.23 S	143.30 E
Bull Run (R.), Or. (bōōl)	118c	45.26 N	122.11 W
Bull Run Res., Or.	118c	45.29 N	122.11 W
Bull Shoals Res., Ar.-Mo. (bōōl shōlz)	123	36.35 N	92.57 W
Bulmke-Hüllen (Neigh.), F.R.G.	63	51.31 N	7.06 E
Bulphan, Eng. (bōōl'făn)	156b	51.33 N	0.21 E
Bultfontein, S. Afr. (bōōlt'fŏn-tān')	223d	28.18 S	26.10 E
Bulun, Sov. Un. (bōō-lōōn')	181	70.48 N	127.27 E
Bulungu, Zaire (bōō-lōōŋ'gōō)	230	6.04 S	21.54 E
Bulwer, S. Afr. (bōōl-wēr)	227c	29.49 S	29.48 E
Bumba, Zaire (bōōm'bȧ)	230	2.11 N	22.28 E
Bumbles Green, Eng.	62	51.44 N	0.02 E
Bumire I., Tan.	231	1.40 S	32.05 E
Buna, Pap. N. Gui. (bōō'nȧ)	207	8.58 S	148.38 E
Bunbury, Austl. (bŭn'bŭrĭ)	214	33.25 S	115.45 E
Bundaberg, Austl. (bŭn'dȧ-bûrg)	216	24.45 S	152.18 E
Bundoora, Austl.	70b	37.42 S	145.04 E
Bungo-Suidō (Chan.), Jap. (bōōŋ'gō sōō-ē'dō)	205	33.26 N	131.54 E
Bunguran Utara, Kepulauan (Is.), Indon.	206	.322 N	108.00 E
Bunia, Zaire	231	1.34 N	30.15 E
Bunker Hill, Il. (bŭnk'ēr hĭl)	119e	39.03 N	89.57 W
Bunker Hill Monument (P. Int.), Ma.	54a	42.22 N	71.04 W
Bunkie, La. (bŭŋ'kĭ)	125	30.55 N	92.10 W
Bunkyō (Neigh.), Jap.	69a	35.43 N	139.45 E
Bun Plns, Ken.	231	0.55 N	40.35 E
Bununu Dass, Nig.	229	10.00 N	9.31 E
Buona Vista, Singapore	67c	1.16 N	103.47 E
Buor-Khaya, Guba (B.), Sov. Un.	181	71.45 N	131.00 E
Buor Khaya, Mys (C.), Sov. Un.	181	71.47 N	133.22 E
Bura, Ken.	231	1.06 S	39.57 E
Buraydah, Sau. Ar.	192	26.23 N	44.14 E
Burbank, Ca. (bûr'bănk)	119a	34.11 N	118.19 W
Burdekin (R.), Austl. (bûr'dē-kĭn)	215	19.22 S	145.07 E
Burdur, Tur. (bōōr-dōōr')	179	37.50 N	30.15 E
Burdwān, India (bōōd-wän')	196	23.29 N	87.53 E
Bureinskiy, Khrebet (Mts.), Sov. Un.	181	51.15 N	133.30 E
Bures-sur-Yvette, Fr.	64c	48.42 N	2.10 E
Bureya (R.), Sov. Un. (bōō-rä'yä)	181	51.00 N	130.14 E
Bureya, Sov. Un. (bōōrā'ȧ)	181	49.55 N	130.00 E
Burford, Eng. (bûr-fērd)	156b	51.46 N	1.38 W
Burford (L.), NM	121	36.37 N	107.21 W
Burg, F.R.G.	63	51.08 N	7.09 E
Burgas, Bul. (bōōr-gäs')	173	42.29 N	27.30 E
Burgas, Gulf of, Bul.	161	42.30 N	27.40 E
Burgaw, NC (bûr'gô)	127	34.31 N	77.56 W
Burgdorf, Switz. (bōōrg'dôrf)	166	47.04 N	7.37 E
Burgenland (State), Aus.	157e	47.58 N	16.57 E
Burgeo, Can.	105	47.36 N	57.34 W
Burger Township, S. Afr.	71b	26.05 S	27.46 E
Burgess, Va.	111	37.53 N	76.21 W
Burgh Heath, Eng.	62	51.18 N	0.13 W
Burgo, Som.	223a	9.20 N	45.45 E
Burgos, Mex. (bōōr'gōs)	124	24.57 N	98.47 W
Burgos, Phil.	207a	16.03 N	119.52 E
Burgos, Sp. (bōō'r-gôs)	170	42.20 N	3.44 W
Burgsvik, Swe. (bōōrgs'vĭk)	164	57.04 N	18.18 E
Burhānpur, India (bōōr'hān-pōōr)	196	21.26 N	76.08 E
Burholme (Neigh.), Pa.	56b	40.03 N	75.05 W
Burias I., Phil. (bōō'rē-äs)	207a	12.56 N	122.56 E
Burias Pass, Phil. (bōō'rē-äs)	207a	13.04 N	123.11 E
Burica, Punta (Pt.), Pan. (pōō'n-tä-bōō'rē-kä)	133	8.02 N	83.12 W
Burien, Wa. (bū'rĭ-ĕn)	118a	47.28 N	122.20 W
Burin, Can. (bûr'ĭn)	105	47.02 N	55.10 W
Burin Pen., Can.	105	47.00 N	55.40 W
Burkburnett, Tx. (bûrk-bûr'nĕt)	122	34.04 N	98.35 W
Burke, Vt. (bûrk)	111	44.40 N	72.00 W
Burke Chan., Can.	98	52.07 N	127.38 W
Burketown, Austl. (bûrk'toun)	214	17.50 S	139.30 E
Burkina Faso, Afr.	222	11.46 N	3.18 E
Burley, Id. (bûr'lĭ)	117	42.31 N	113.48 W
Burley, Wa.	118a	47.25 N	122.38 W
Burli, Sov. Un.	182a	53.36 N	61.55 E
Burlingame, Ca. (bûr'lĭn-găm)	118b	37.35 N	122.22 W
Burlingame, KS.	123	38.45 N	95.49 W
Burlington, Can. (bûr'lĭng-tŭn)	95d	43.19 N	79.48 W
Burlington, Co.	122	39.17 N	102.26 W
Burlington, Ia.	115	40.48 N	91.05 W
Burlington, Ks.	123	38.10 N	95.46 W
Burlington, Ky.	113f	39.01 N	84.44 W
Burlington, Ma.	105a	42.31 N	71.13 W
Burlington, NC	127	36.05 N	79.26 W
Burlington, NJ	112f	40.04 N	74.52 W
Burlington, Vt.	111	44.30 N	73.15 W
Burlington, Wa.	118a	48.28 N	122.20 W
Burlington, Wi.	113a	42.41 N	88.16 W
Burma, Asia (bûr'mȧ)	190	21.00 N	95.15 E
Burnaby, Can.	98	49.14 N	122.58 W
Burnage, Eng.	64b	53.26 N	2.12 W
Burnet, Tx. (bûrn'ĕt)	124	30.46 N	98.14 W
Burnham, Il.	58a	41.39 N	87.34 W
Burnham on Crouch, Eng. (bûrn'ăm-ŏn-krouch)	156b	51.38 N	0.48 E
Burnhamthorpe, Can.	54c	43.37 N	79.36 W
Burnie, Austl. (bûr'nē)	216	41.15 S	146.05 E
Burning Tree Estates, Md.	56d	39.01 N	77.12 W
Burnley, Eng. (bûrn'lē)	156	53.47 N	2.19 W
Burns, Or. (bûrnz)	116	43.35 N	119.05 W
Burnside, Ky. (bûrn'sīd)	126	36.57 N	84.33 W
Burns Lake, Can. (bûrnz lāk)	98	54.14 N	125.46 W
Burnsville, Can. (bûrnz'vĭl)	104	47.44 N	65.07 W
Burnt R., Or. (bûrnt)	116	44.26 N	117.53 W
Burntwood (R.), Can.	101	55.53 N	97.30 W
Burrard Inlet, Can. (bûr'ȧrd)	118d	49.19 N	123.15 W
Burriana, Sp. (bōōr-rē-ȧ'nä)	171	39.53 N	0.05 W
Burrowhill, Eng.	62	51.21 N	0.36 W
Burr Ridge, Il.	58a	41.46 N	87.55 W
Bursa, Tur. (bōōr'sȧ)	179	40.10 N	28.10 E
Būr Safājah, Egypt	225	26.57 N	33.56 E
Būr Sa'īd (Port Said), Egypt	223c	31.15 N	32.19 E
Burscheid, F.R.G. (bōōr'shīd)	169c	51.05 N	7.07 E
Būr Sūdān, Sud. (sōō-dän')	225	19.30 N	37.10 E
Burt (L.), Mi. (bûrt)	110	45.25 N	84.45 W
Burt, NY (bûrt)	113c	43.19 N	78.45 W
Burton, Eng.	64a	53.16 N	3.01 W
Burton, Wa. (bûr'tŭn)	118a	47.24 N	122.28 W
Burton Res., Ga.	126	34.46 N	83.40 W
Burtonsville, Md. (bûrtŏns-vil)	112e	39.07 N	76.57 W
Burton-upon-Trent, Eng. (bŭr'tŭn-ŭp'-ŏn-trĕnt)	156	52.48 N	1.37 W
Buru (I.), Indon.	207	3.30 S	126.30 E
Burullus (L.), Egypt	223b	31.20 N	30.58 E
Burundi, Afr.	222	3.00 S	29.30 E
Burwell, Ne. (bûr'wĕl)	114	41.46 N	99.08 W
Burwood, Austl.	70b	37.51 S	145.06 E
Bury, Eng. (bĕr'ĭ)	156	53.36 N	2.17 W
Buryat A.S.S.R., Sov. Un.	181	55.15 N	112.00 E
Bury Saint Edmunds, Eng. (bĕr'ĭ-sānt ĕd'mŭndz)	163	52.14 N	0.44 E
Burzaco, Arg. (bōōr-zá'kô)	144a	34.35 S	58.23 W
Busanga Swp., Zambia	231	14.10 S	25.50 E
Busby, Austl.	70a	33.54 S	150.53 E
Buschhausen (Neigh.), F.R.G.	63	51.30 N	6.51 E
Būsh, Egypt (bōōsh)	223b	29.13 N	31.08 E
Būshehr, Iran	192	28.48 N	50.53 E
Bushey, Eng.	62	51.39 N	0.22 W
Bushey Heath, Eng.	62	51.38 N	0.20 W
Bush Hill, Va.	56d	38.48 N	77.07 W
Bushmanland (Reg.), S. Afr. (bōōsh-măn lănd)	226	29.15 S	18.45 E
Bushnell, Il. (bōōsh'nĕl)	123	40.33 N	90.28 W
Bushwick (Neigh.), NY	55	40.42 N	73.55 W
Businga, Zaire (bōō-sĭŋ'gȧ)	230	3.20 N	20.53 E
Busira (R.), Zaire	230	0.05 S	19.20 E
Busk, Sov. Un. (bōō'sk)	167	49.58 N	24.39 E
Busselton, Austl. (bŭs'l-tŭn)	214	33.40 S	115.30 E
Bussum, Neth.	157a	52.16 N	5.10 E
Bustamante, Mex. (bōōs-tȧ-män'tå)	124	26.34 N	100.30 W
Bustleton (Neigh.), Pa.	56b	40.05 N	75.02 W
Busto Arsizio, It. (bōōs'tō är-sēd'zē-ō)	172	45.47 N	8.51 E
Busuanga (I.), Phil. (bōō-swäŋ'gä)	207a	12.20 N	119.43 E
Buta, Zaire (bōō'tȧ)	230	2.48 N	24.44 E
Butantã (Neigh.), Braz.	61d	23.34 S	46.43 W
Butendorf (Neigh.), F.R.G.	63	51.33 N	6.59 E
Butha Buthe, Leso. (bōō-thȧ-bōō'thå)	227c	28.49 S	28.16 E
Butha Qi, China (bōō-thä chē)	204	47.59 N	122.56 E
Butler, Al. (bŭt'lēr)	126	32.05 N	88.10 W
Butler, In.	110	41.25 N	84.50 W
Butler, Md.	112e	39.32 N	76.46 W
Butler, NJ	112a	41.00 N	74.20 W
Butler, Pa.	111	40.50 N	79.55 W
Butovo, Sov. Un. (bōō-tô'vô)	182b	55.33 N	37.36 E
Butsha, Zaire	231	0.57 N	29.13 E
Buttahatchie (R.), Al.-Ms. (bŭt-ȧ-hăch'ē)	126	34.02 N	88.05 W
Butte, Mt. (būt)	117	46.00 N	112.31 W
Butterworth, S. Afr. (bŭ tēr'wûrth)	227c	32.20 S	28.09 E
Büttgen, F.R.G.	63	51.12 N	6.36 E
Butt of Lewis (C.), Scot. (bŭt ŏv lū'ĭs)	162	58.34 N	6.15 W
Butuan, Phil. (bōō-tōō'än)	207	8.40 N	125.33 E
Butung (I.), Indon.	206	5.00 S	122.55 E
Buturlinovka, Sov. Un. (bōō-tōō'lē-nôf'ka)	175	50.47 N	40.35 E
Buuhoodle, Som.	223a	8.15 N	46.20 E
Buulo Berde, Som.	223a	3.53 N	45.30 E
Burr Gaabo, Som.	227	1.14 N	51.47 E
Buxtehude, F.R.G. (bōōks-tĕ-hōō'dĕ)	157c	53.29 N	9.42 E
Buxton, Eng. (bŭks't'n)	156	53.15 N	1.55 W
Buxton, Or.	118c	45.41 N	123.11 W
Buy, Sov. Un. (bwē)	178	58.30 N	41.48 E
Buzău, Rom. (bōō-zĕ'ōō)	173	45.09 N	26.51 E
Buzău (R.), Rom.	175	45.17 N	27.22 E
Buzaymah, Libya	225	25.14 N	22.13 E
Buzi, China (bōō-dz)	200	33.48 N	118.13 E
Buzuluk, Sov. Un. (bōō-zōō-lōōk')	179	52.50 N	52.10 E
Bvkhovo, Sov. Un. (bĭ-κô'vô)	174	53.32 N	30.15 E
Bwendi, Zaire	231	4.01 N	26.41 E
Byala, Bul.	173	43.26 N	25.44 E
Byala Slatina, Bul. (byä'la slä'tēnä)	173	43.26 N	23.56 E
Byblos, see Jubayl			
Byculla (Neigh.), India	67e	18.58 N	72.49 E
Bydgoszcz, Pol. (bĭd'gôshch)	167	53.07 N	18.00 E
Byesville, Oh. (bīz-vĭl)	110	39.55 N	81.35 W
Byfang (Neigh.), F.R.G.	63	51.24 N	7.06 E
Byfleet, Eng.	62	51.20 N	0.29 W
Bygdin (L.), Nor. (bügh-dēn')	164	61.24 N	8.31 E
Byglandsfjord, Nor. (bügh'länds-fyôr)	164	58.40 N	7.49 E
Bykovo, Sov. Un. (bĭ-kô'vô)	182b	55.38 N	38.05 E
Bymea Bay, Austl.	70a	34.03 S	151.06 E
Byrranga, Gory (Mts.), Sov. Un.	180	74.15 N	94.28 E
Bytantay (R.), Sov. Un. (byän'tāy)	181	68.15 N	132.15 E
Bytom, Pol. (bĭ'tŭm)	167	50.21 N	18.55 E
Bytosh', Sov. Un. (bĭ-tôsh')	174	53.48 N	34.06 E
Bytow, Pol. (bĭ'tŭf)	167	54.10 N	17.30 E

C

PLACE (Pronounciation)	PAGE	Lat. °'	Long. °'
Caazapá, Par. (kä-zä-pä')	144	26.14 S	56.18 W
Cabagan, Phil. (kä-bä-gän')	207a	17.27 N	121.50 E
Cabalete (I.), Phil. (kä-bä-lā'tå)	207a	14.19 N	122.00 E
Caballito (Neigh.), Arg.	60d	34.37 S	58.27 W
Caballones, Canal de (Chan.), Cuba (kä-nä'l-dĕ-kä-bäl-yô'nĕs)	134	20.45 N	79.20 W
Caballo Res., NM (kä-bä-lyō')	121	33.00 N	107.20 W
Cabanatuan, Phil. (kä-bä-nä-twän')	207a	15.30 N	120.56 E
Cabano, Can. (kä-bä-nō')	104	47.41 N	68.54 W
Cabarruyan (I.), Phil. (kä-bä-rōō'yän)	207a	16.21 N	120.10 E
Cabedelo, Braz. (kä-bĕ-dā'lōō)	143	6.58 S	34.49 W
Cabeza, Arrecife (Reef), Mex. (är-rĕ-sē'fĕ-kä-bĕ-zä)	131	19.07 N	95.52 W

266 Cabeza del Buey – Cananea

PLACE (Pronunciation)	PAGE	Lat. °′	Long. °′
Cabeza del Buey, Sp. (kä-bā'thä dĕl bwā')	170	38.43 N	5.18 W
Cabimas, Ven. (kä-bē'mäs)	142	10.21 N	71.27 W
Cabinda, Ang. (kä-bĭn'dȧ)	222	5.10 S	10.00 E
Cabinda, Ang.	230	5.33 S	12.12 E
Cabinet Mts., Mt. (kăb'ĭ-nĕt)	116	48.13 N	115.52 W
Cabin John, Md.	56d	38.58 N	77.09 W
Cabo Frio, Braz. (kä'bô-frē'ô)	141a	22.53 S	42.02 W
Cabo Frio, Ilha do, Braz. (ē'lä-dô-kä'bô frē'ô)	141a	23.01 S	42.00 W
Cabonga Res., Can.	103	47.25 N	76.35 W
Cabot Hd., Can. (kăb'ŭt)	110	45.15 N	81.20 W
Cabot Str., Can. (kăb'ŭt)	105	47.35 N	60.00 W
Cabra I., Phil.	207a	13.55 N	119.55 E
Cabra, Sp. (käb'rä)	170	37.28 N	4.29 W
Cabramatta, Austl.	70a	33.54 S	150.56 E
Cabrera (I.), Sp. (kä-brā'rä)	171	39.08 N	2.57 E
Cabrera, Sierra de la (Mts.), Sp.	170	42.15 N	6.45 W
Cabriel (R.), Sp. (kä-brē-ĕl')	170	39.25 N	1.20 W
Cabrillo Natl. Mon., Ca. (kä-brēl'yō)	120a	32.41 N	117.03 W
Cabrobó, Braz. (kä-brō-bô')	143	8.34 S	39.13 W
Cabuçu (R.), Braz. (kä-bōō'-sōō)	144b	22.57 S	43.36 W
Cabugao, Phil. (kä-bōō'gä-ô)	207a	17.48 N	120.28 E
Čačak, Yugo. (chä'chák)	173	43.51 N	20.22 E
Caçapava, Braz. (kä'sä-pá'vä)	141a	23.05 S	45.52 W
Cáceres, Braz. (ká'sĕ-rĕs)	143	16.11 S	57.32 W
Cáceres, Sp. (ká'thå-räs)	170	39.28 N	6.20 W
Cachan, Fr.	64c	48.48 N	2.20 E
Cachapoal (R.), Chile (kä-chä-pô-á'l)	141b	34.23 S	70.19 W
Cacharí, Arg. (kä-chä-rē')	141c	36.23 S	59.29 W
Cache (R.), Ar. (kásh)	123	35.24 N	91.12 W
Cache Cr., Can. (kăsh)	120	38.53 N	122.24 W
Cache Creek, Can.	99	50.48 N	121.19 W
Cache la Poudre (R.), Co. (kásh lá pōōd'r')	122	40.43 N	105.39 W
Cachinal, Chile (kä-chē-näl')	144	24.57 S	69.33 W
Cachi, Nevados de (Pk.), Arg. (nĕ-vá'dôs-dĕ-ká'chē)	144	25.05 S	66.40 W
Cachoeira, Braz. (kä-shô-ā'rä)	143	12.32 S	38.47 W
Cachoeirá do Sul, Braz. (kä-shô-ā'rä-dô-sōō'l)	144	30.02 S	52.49 W
Cachoeiras de Macacu, Braz. (kä-shô-ā'räs-dĕ-mä-ká'kōō)	141a	22.28 S	42.39 W
Cachoeiro de Itapemirim, Braz. (kä-shô-ā'rô-dĕ-ē'tä-pĕmē-rē'ɴ)	141a	20.51 S	41.06 W
Cacilhas, Port.	65d	38.41 N	9.09 W
Caćolo, Ang.	230	10.07 S	19.17 E
Caconda, Ang. (kä-kōn'dä)	230	13.43 S	15.06 E
Cacouna, Can.	104	47.54 N	69.31 W
Cacula, Ang.	230	14.29 S	14.10 E
Cadale, Som.	223a	2.45 N	46.15 E
Caddo (L.), La.-Tx. (kăd'ō)	125	32.37 N	94.15 W
Cadereyta, Mex. (kä-då-rā'tä)	130	20.42 N	99.47 W
Cadereyta Jimenez, Mex. (kä-dä-rā'tä hē-mā'näz)	124	25.36 N	99.59 W
Cadillac, Mi. (kăd'ĭ-lăk)	110	44.15 N	85.25 W
Cadishead, Eng.	64b	53.25 N	2.26 W
Cadi, Sierra de (Mts.), Sp. (sē-ĕ'r-rä-dĕ-kä'dē)	171	42.17 N	1.34 E
Cadiz, Ca. (kā'dĭz)	120	34.33 N	115.30 W
Cadiz, Oh.	110	40.15 N	81.00 W
Cádiz, Sp. (ká'dēz)	170	36.34 N	6.20 W
Cádiz, Golfo de (G.), Sp. (gôl-fô-dĕ-ká'dēz)	170	36.50 N	7.00 W
Caen, Fr. (käɴ)	168	49.13 N	0.22 W
Caernarfon, Wales	162	53.08 N	4.17 W
Caernarfon B., Wales	162	53.09 N	4.56 W
Caeté, Braz. (kä'ĕ-tĕ')	141a	19.53 S	43.41 W
Caetité, Braz. (kä-å-tē-tā')	143	14.02 S	42.14 W
Cagayan, Phil. (kä-gä-yän')	207	8.13 N	124.30 E
Cagayan (R.), Phil.	206	16.45 N	121.55 E
Cagayan Is., Phil.	206	9.40 N	120.30 E
Cagayan Sulu (I.), Phil. (kä-gä-yän sōō'lōō)	206	7.00 N	118.30 E
Cagli, It. (käl'yē)	172	43.35 N	12.40 E
Cagliari, It. (käl'yä-rē)	172	39.16 N	9.08 E
Cagliari, Golfo di (G.), It. (gôl-fô-dē-käl'yä-rē)	172	39.08 N	9.12 E
Cagnes, Fr. (kän'y')	169	43.40 N	7.14 E
Cagua, Ven. (kä'gwä)	143b	10.12 N	67.27 W
Caguas, P.R. (kä'gwäs)	129b	18.12 N	66.01 W
Cahaba (R.), Al. (ká hä-bä)	126	32.50 N	87.15 W
Cahama, Ang. (kä-á'mä)	230	16.17 S	14.19 E
Cahokia, Il. (kȧ-hō'kĭ-ȧ)	119e	38.34 N	90.11 W
Cahora-Bassa (Gorge), Moz.	231	15.40 S	32.50 E
Cahors, Fr. (kȧ-ôr')	168	44.27 N	1.27 E
Cahuacán, Mex. (kä-wä-kä'n)	131a	19.38 N	99.25 W
Cahuita, Punta (Pt.), C.R. (pōō'n-tä-kä-wē'tȧ)	133	9.47 N	82.41 W
Caiapó, Serra do (Mts.), Braz. (sĕ'r-rä-dô-kä-yä-pô')	143	17.52 S	52.37 W
Caibarién, Cuba (kī-bä-rē-ĕn')	134	22.35 N	79.30 W
Caicedonia, Col. (kī-sĕ-dô-nēä)	142a	4.21 N	75.48 W
Caicos Bk., Ba. (kī'kōs)	135	21.35 N	72.00 W
Caicos Is., Turks & Caicos Is.	135	21.45 N	71.50 W
Caicos Passage (Str.), Ba.	135	21.55 N	72.45 W
Caillou B., La. (kȧ-yōō')	125	29.07 N	91.00 W
Caimanera, Cuba (kī-mä-nä'rä)	135	20.00 N	75.10 W
Caiman Pt., Phil. (kī'mán)	207a	15.56 N	119.33 E
Caimito, (R.), Pan. (kä-ē-mē'tô)	128a	8.50 N	79.45 W
Caimito del Guayabal, Cuba (kä-ē-mē'tō-dĕl-gwä-yä-bä'l)	135a	22.57 N	82.36 W
Cairns, Austl. (kârnz)	215	17.02 S	145.49 E
Cairo, C.R. (kī'rō)	133	10.06 N	83.47 W
Cairo, Ga. (kā'rō)	126	30.48 N	84.12 W
Cairo, Il.	123	36.59 N	89.11 W
Cairo, see Al Qāhirah			
Caistor, Eng. (kâs'tēr)	156	53.30 N	0.20 W
Caiundo, Ang.	230	15.46 S	17.28 E
Caiyu, China (tsī-yōō)	202a	39.39 N	116.36 E
Cajamarca, Col. (kä-ĸä-mà'r-kä)	142	4.25 N	75.25 W
Cajamarca, Peru (kä-hä-mär'kä)	142	7.16 S	78.30 W
Čajniče, Yugo. (chī'nĭ-chĕ)	173	43.32 N	19.04 E
Cajon, Ca. (kȧ-hōn')	119a	34.18 N	117.28 W
Caju (Neigh.), Braz.	61c	22.53 S	43.13 W
Çajuru, Braz. (kä-zhōō'rōō)	141a	21.17 S	47.17 W
Čakovec, Yugo. (chá'kō-vĕts)	172	46.23 N	16.27 E
Cala, S. Afr. (cä-lȧ)	227c	31.33 S	27.41 E
Calabar, Nig. (kăl-ȧ-bär')	229	4.57 N	8.19 E
Calabazar, Cuba (kä-lä-bä-zä'r)	135a	23.02 N	82.25 W
Calabozo, Ven. (kä-lä-bō'zō)	142	8.48 N	67.27 W
Calabria (Reg.), It. (kä-lä'brē-ä)	172	39.26 N	16.23 E
Calafat, Rom. (kȧ-lȧ-fát')	173	43.59 N	22.56 E
Calaguas Is., Phil. (kä-läg'wäs)	207a	14.30 N	123.06 E
Calahoo, Can. (kă-lȧ-hōō')	95g	53.42 N	113.58 W
Calahorra, Sp. (kä-lä-ôr'rä)	170	42.18 N	1.58 W
Calais, Fr. (kȧ-lĕ')	168	50.56 N	1.51 E
Calais, Me.	104	45.11 N	67.15 W
Calama, Chile (kä-lä'mä)	144	22.17 S	68.58 W
Calamar, Col. (kä-lä-mär')	142	10.24 N	75.00 W
Calamar, Col.	142	1.55 N	72.33 W
Calamba, Phil. (kä-läm'bä)	207a	14.12 N	121.10 E
Calamian Group (Is.), Phil. (kä-lä-myän')	206	12.14 N	118.38 E
Calañas, Sp. (kä-län'yäs)	170	37.41 N	6.52 W
Calanda, Sp.	171	40.53 N	0.20 W
Calapan, Phil. (kä-lä-pän')	207a	13.25 N	121.11 E
Călăraşi, Rom. (kŭ-lŭ-rásh'ĭ)	161	44.09 N	27.20 E
Calatayud, Sp. (kä-lä-tä-yōōdh')	170	41.23 N	1.37 W
Calauag B., Phil.	207a	14.07 N	122.10 E
Calaveras Res., Ca. (kăl-ȧ-vēr'ăs)	118b	37.29 N	121.47 W
Calavite, C., Phil. (kä-lä-vē'tä)	207a	13.29 N	120.00 E
Calcasieu (R.), La. (kăl'kȧ-shū)	125	30.22 N	93.08 W
Calcasieu L., La.	125	29.58 N	93.08 W
Calcutta, India (kăl-kŭt'ȧ)	196a	22.32 N	88.22 E
Caldas, Col. (kà'l-däs)	142a	6.06 N	75.38 W
Caldas (Dept.), Col.	142a	5.20 N	75.38 W
Caldas da Rainha, Port. (käl'däs dä rīn'yȧ)	170	39.25 N	9.08 W
Calder (R.), Eng. (kôl'dēr)	156	53.39 N	1.30 W
Caldera, Chile (käl-dā'rä)	144	27.02 S	70.53 W
Calder Can., Eng.	156	53.48 N	2.25 W
Caldwell, Id. (kôld'wĕl)	116	43.40 N	116.43 W
Caldwell, Ks.	123	37.04 N	97.36 W
Caldwell, NJ	55	40.51 N	74.17 W
Caldwell, Oh.	110	39.40 N	81.30 W
Caldwell, Tx.	125	30.30 N	96.40 W
Caledon, Can. (kăl'ē-dŏn)	95d	43.52 N	79.59 W
Caledonia, Mn. (kăl-ē-dō'nĭ-ȧ)	115	43.38 N	91.31 W
Calella, Sp. (kä-lĕl'yä)	171	41.37 N	2.39 E
Calera Victor Rosales, Mex. (kä-lā'rä-vē'k-tôr-rō-sá'lĕs)	130	22.57 N	102.42 W
Calexico, Ca. (kȧ-lĕk'sĭ-kō)	120	32.41 N	115.30 W
Calgary, Can. (kăl'gȧ-rĭ)	95e	51.03 N	114.05 W
Calhariz (Neigh.), Port.	65d	38.44 N	9.12 W
Calhoun, Ga. (kăl-hōōn')	126	34.30 N	84.56 W
Cali, Col. (kä'lē)	142a	3.26 N	76.30 W
Calicut, India (kăl'ĭ-kŭt)	197	11.19 N	75.49 E
Caliente, Nv. (käl-yĕn'tā)	121	37.38 N	114.30 W
California, Mo. (kăl-ĭ-fôr'nĭ-ȧ)	123	38.38 N	92.38 W
California, Pa.	113e	40.03 N	79.53 W
California (State), U.S.	108	38.10 N	121.20 W
California, Golfo de (G.), Mex. (gôl-fô-dĕ-kä-lē-fôr-nyä)	128	30.30 N	113.45 W
California, University of (U.C.L.A.) (P. Int.), Ca.	59	34.04 N	118.26 W
Călimani, Munţii (Mts.), Rom.	167	47.05 N	24.47 E
Calimere, Pt., India	197	10.20 N	80.20 E
Calimesa, Ca. (kă-lĭ-mā'sȧ)	119a	34.00 N	117.04 W
Calipatria, Ca. (kăl-ĭ-păt'rĭ-ȧ)	120	33.03 N	115.30 W
Calkini, Mex. (käl-kē-nē')	131	20.21 N	90.06 W
Callabonna, L., Austl. (călă'bŏnȧ)	216	29.35 S	140.28 E
Callao, Peru (käl-yä'ō)	142	12.02 S	77.07 W
Calling (L.), Can. (kôl'ĭng)	99	55.15 N	113.12 W
Calmar, Can. (kăl'mär)	95g	53.16 N	113.49 W
Calmar, Ia.	115	43.12 N	91.54 W
Calnalí, Mex. (käl-nä-lē')	130	20.53 N	98.34 W
Caloocan, Phil.	68g	14.39 N	120.59 E
Caloosahatchee (R.), Fl. (kȧ-loo-sȧ-hăch'ē)	127a	26.45 N	81.41 W
Calotmul, Mex. (kä-lôt-mōōl)	132a	20.58 N	88.11 W
Calpulalpan, Mex. (käl-pōō-lál'pän)	130	19.35 N	98.33 W
Caltagirone, It. (käl-tä-jē-rō'nå)	172	37.14 N	14.32 E
Caltanissetta, It. (käl-tä-nē-sĕt'tä)	172	37.30 N	14.02 E
Caluango, Ang.	230	8.21 S	19.40 E
Calucinga, Ang.	230	11.18 S	16.12 E
Calumet, Mi. (kă-lū-mĕt')	115	47.15 N	88.29 W
Calumet City, Il.	113a	41.37 N	87.33 W
Calumet, L., Il.	113a	41.43 N	87.36 W
Calumet Park, Il.	58a	41.44 N	87.33 W
Calumet Sag Chan., Il.	58a	41.42 N	87.57 W
Calunda, Ang.	230	12.06 S	23.23 E
Caluquembe, Ang.	230	13.47 S	14.44 E
Caluula, Som.	223a	11.53 N	50.40 E
Calvert, Tx. (kăl'vērt)	125	30.59 N	96.41 W
Calvert I., Can.	98	51.35 N	128.00 W
Calvi, Fr. (käl'vē)	172	42.33 N	8.35 E
Calvillo, Mex. (käl-vēl'yō)	130	21.51 N	102.44 W
Calvinia, S. Afr. (kăl-vĭn'ĭ-ȧ)	226	31.20 S	19.50 E
Cam (R.), Eng. (kăm)	162	52.15 N	0.05 E
Camagüey, Cuba (kä-mä-gwā')	134	21.25 N	78.00 W
Camagüey (Prov.), Cuba	134	21.30 N	78.10 W
Camajuani, Cuba (kä-mä-hwä'nē)	134	22.25 N	79.50 W
Camaná, Peru (kä-mä'nä)	142	16.37 S	72.33 W
Camano, Wa. (kä-mä'no)	118a	48.10 N	122.32 W
Camano I., Wa.	118a	48.11 N	122.29 W
Camargo, Mex. (kä-mär gō)	124	26.19 N	98.49 W
Camarón, Cabo (C.), Hond. (ká'bô-kä-mä-rōn')	132	16.06 N	85.05 W
Camas, Wa. (kăm'ȧs)	118c	45.36 N	122.24 W
Camas Cr., Id.	117	44.10 N	112.09 W
Camatagua, Ven. (kä-mä-tá'gwä)	143b	9.49 N	66.55 W
Ca-Mau, Mui (Pt.), Viet.	206	8.36 N	104.43 E
Cambay, India (kăm-bā')	196	22.22 N	72.39 E
Camberwell, Austl.	70b	37.50 S	145.04 E
Cambonda, Serra (Mts.), Ang.	230	12.10 S	14.15 E
Camborne, Eng. (kăm'bôrn)	162	50.15 N	5.28 W
Cambrai, Fr. (käɴ-brĕ')	168	50.10 N	3.15 E
Cambrian Mts., Wales (kăm'brĭ-ăn)	162	52.05 N	4.05 W
Cambridge, Eng. (kām'brĭj)	162	52.12 N	0.11 E
Cambridge, Ma.	105a	42.23 N	71.07 W
Cambridge, Md.	111	38.35 N	76.10 W
Cambridge, Mn.	115	45.35 N	93.14 W
Cambridge, Ne.	122	40.17 N	100.10 W
Cambridge, Oh.	110	40.00 N	81.35 W
Cambridge Bay, Can.	96	69.15 N	105.00 W
Cambridge City, In.	110	39.45 N	85.15 W
Cambridgeshire (Co.), Eng.	156	52.26 N	0.19 W
Cambuci, Braz. (käm-bōō'sē)	141a	21.35 S	41.54 W
Cambuci (Neigh.), Braz.	61d	23.34 S	46.37 W
Cambuí, Braz. (käm-bōō-ē')	141a	22.38 S	46.02 W
Camby, In. (kăm'bē)	113g	39.40 N	86.19 W
Camden, Al. (kăm'dĕn)	126	31.58 N	87.15 W
Camden, Ar.	123	33.36 N	92.49 W
Camden, Austl.	211b	34.03 S	150.42 E
Camden, Me.	104	44.11 N	69.05 W
Camden (Neigh.), Eng.	62	51.33 N	0.10 W
Camden, NJ	112f	39.56 N	75.06 W
Camden, SC	127	34.14 N	80.37 W
Cameia, Parque Nacional da (Natl. Pk.), Ang.	230	11.40 S	21.20 E
Cameron, Mo. (kăm'ēr-ŭn)	123	39.44 N	94.14 W
Cameron, Tx.	125	30.52 N	96.57 W
Cameron, WV	110	39.40 N	80.35 W
Cameron Hills, Can.	96	60.13 N	120.20 W
Cameroon, Afr.	222	5.48 N	11.00 E
Cameroon, (Mtn.), Cam.	229	4.12 N	9.11 E
Cametá, Braz. (kä-mȧ-tä')	143	1.14 S	49.30 W
Camiling, Phil. (kä-mē-lĭng')	207a	15.42 N	120.24 E
Camilla, Ga. (kȧ-mĭl'ȧ)	126	31.13 N	84.12 W
Caminha, Port. (kä-mĭn'yȧ)	170	41.52 N	8.44 W
Camoçim, Braz. (kä-mô-sēɴ')	143	2.56 S	40.55 W
Camooweal, Austl.	214	20.00 S	138.13 E
Campana, Arg. (käm-pä'nä)	141c	34.10 S	58.58 W
Campana (I.), Chile (käm-pän'yä)	144	48.20 S	75.15 W
Campanario, Sp. (kä-pä-nä'rē-ō)	170	38.51 N	5.36 W
Campanella, Punta (C.), It. (pōō'n-tä-käm-pä-nĕ'lä)	171c	40.20 N	14.21 E
Campanha, Braz. (käm-pän-yäɴ')	141a	21.51 S	45.24 W
Campania (Reg.), It. (käm-pän'yä)	172	41.00 N	14.40 E
Campbell, Ca. (kăm'bĕl)	118b	37.17 N	121.57 W
Campbell (Is.), N.Z.	232	52.30 S	169.00 E
Campbell, Mo.	123	36.29 N	90.04 W
Campbellfield, Austl.	70b	37.41 S	144.57 E
Campbellpore, Pak.	196	33.49 N	72.24 E
Campbell River, Can.	98	50.01 N	125.15 W
Campbellsville, Ky. (kăm'bĕlz-vĭl)	126	37.19 N	85.20 W
Campbellton, Can. (kăm'bĕl-tŭn)	104	48.00 N	66.40 W
Campbelltown, Austl. (kăm'bĕl-toun)	211b	34.04 S	150.49 E
Campbelltown, Scot. (kăm'b'l-toun)	162	55.25 N	5.50 W
Camp Dennison, Oh. (dĕ'nĭ-sŏn)	113f	39.12 N	84.17 W
Campeche, Mex. (käm-pā'chå)	131	19.51 N	90.32 W
Campeche (State), Mex.	128	18.55 N	90.20 W
Campeche, Bahia de (B.), Mex. (bä-ē'ä-dĕ-käm-pā'chā)	128	19.30 N	93.40 W
Campechuela, Cuba (käm-på-chwā'lä)	134	20.15 N	77.15 W
Camperdown, S. Afr. (kăm'pēr-doun)	227c	29.14 S	30.33 E
Campina Grande, Braz. (käm-pē'nä grän'dĕ)	143	7.15 S	35.49 W
Campinas, Braz. (käm-pē'näzh)	141a	22.53 S	47.03 W
Camp Ind. Res., Ca. (kămp)	120	32.39 N	116.26 W
Campo, Cam. (käm'pō)	229	2.22 N	9.49 E
Campoalegre, Col. (kä'm-pô-àlĕ'grĕ)	142	2.34 N	75.20 W
Campobasso, It. (käm'pô-bäs'sō)	172	41.35 N	14.39 E
Campo Belo, Braz.	141a	20.52 S	45.15 W
Campo de Criptana, Sp. (käm'pō dā krēp-tä'nä)	170	39.24 N	3.09 W
Campo Florido, Cuba (kä'm-pō flô-rē'dō)	135a	23.07 N	82.07 W
Campo Grande, Braz. (käm-pōō grän'dĕ)	143	20.28 S	54.32 W
Campo Grande, Braz.	144b	22.54 S	43.33 W
Campo Grande (Neigh.), Port.	65d	38.45 N	9.09 W
Campo Maior, Braz. (käm-pōō mä-yôr')	143	4.48 S	42.12 W
Campo Maior, Port.	170	39.03 N	7.06 W
Campo Real, Sp. (käm'pô rå-äl')	171a	40.21 N	3.23 W
Campos, Braz. (kä'm-pôs)	141a	21.46 S	41.19 W
Campos do Jordão, Braz. (kä'm-pôs-dô-zhôr-dou'ɴ)	141a	22.45 S	45.35 W
Campos Gerais, Braz. (kä'm-pôs-zhĕ-rá'es)	141a	21.17 S	45.43 W
Camps Bay, S. Afr. (kămps)	226a	33.57 S	18.22 E
Campsie, Austl.	70a	33.55 S	151.06 E
Camp Springs, Md. (cămp sprĭngz)	112e	38.48 N	76.55 W
Camp Springs, Md.	56d	38.48 N	76.55 W
Camp Wood, Tx. (kămp wŏŏd)	124	29.39 N	100.02 W
Camrose, Can. (kăm-rōz)	100	53.01 N	112.50 W
Camu (R.), Dom. Rep. (kä'mōō)	135	19.05 N	70.15 W
Canada, N.A. (kăn'ȧ-dȧ)	94	50.00 N	100.00 W
Canada B., Can.	105	50.43 N	56.10 W
Cañada de Gómez, Arg. (kä-nyä'dä-dĕ-gō'mĕz)	141c	32.49 S	61.24 W
Canadian, Tx. (kȧ-nā'dĭ-ăn)	122	35.54 N	100.24 W
Canadian R., Ok.	123	34.53 N	97.06 W
Canajoharie, NY (kăn-ȧ-jô-hăr'ē)	111	42.55 N	74.35 W
Çanakkale, Tur. (chä-näk-kä'lĕ)	173	40.10 N	26.26 E
Çanakkale Boğazi (Dardanelles) (Str.), Tur. (chä-näk-kä'lĕ) (där-dȧ-nĕlz')	173	40.05 N	25.50 E
Canandaigua (L.), NY	111	42.45 N	77.20 W
Canandaigua, NY (kăn-ăn-dā'gwȧ)	111	42.55 N	77.20 W
Cananea, Mex. (kä-nä-nĕ'ä)	128	31.00 N	110.20 W

ăt; finăl; rāte; senåte; ärm; ȧsk; sofȧ; fâre; ch-choose; dh-as th in other; bē; ēvent; bĕt; recĕnt; cratēr; g-gō; gh-guttural g; bĭt; ĭ-short neutral; rīde; ĸ-guttural k as ch in German ich;

PRONOUNCING INDEX Canarias – Carron 267

PLACE (Pronounciation)	PAGE	Lat. °'	Long. °'
Canarias, Islas (Is.), Sp. (ē's-läs-kä-nä'ryäs)	224	29.15 N	16.30 W
Canarreos, Arch. de los (Is.), Cuba (är-chē-pyĕ'lä-gô-dĕ-lôs-kä-när-rĕ'ōs)	134	21.35 N	82.20 W
Canarsie (Neigh.), NY	55	40.38 N	73.53 W
Cañas, C.R. (kä'-nyäs)	132	10.26 N	85.06 W
Cañasgordas, Col. (kä'nyäs-gô'r-däs)	142a	6.44 N	76.01 W
Cañas R., C.R.	132	10.20 N	85.21 W
Canastota, NY (kăn-ȧs-tō'tȧ)	111	43.05 N	75.45 W
Canastra, Serra de (Mts.), Braz. (sĕ'r-rä-dĕ-kä-nä's-trä)	143	19.53 S	46.57 W
Canatlán, Mex. (kä-nät-län')	124	24.30 N	104.45 W
Canaveral, C., Fl.	127a	28.30 N	80.23 W
Canavieiras, Braz. (kä-nȧ-vē-ā'räs)	143	15.40 S	38.49 W
Canberra, Austl. (kăn'bĕr-ȧ)	216	35.21 S	149.10 E
Canby, Mn. (kăn'bĭ)	114	44.43 N	96.15 W
Canchyauya, Cerros de (Mts.), Peru (sĕ'r-rôs-dĕ-kän-cho͞o-ȧ'ĭä)	142	7.30 S	74.30 W
Cancuc, Mex. (kän-ko͝ok)	131	16.58 N	92.17 W
Cancún, Mex.	132a	21.25 N	86.50 W
Candelaria, Cuba (kän-dĕ-lä'ryä)	134	22.45 N	82.55 W
Candelaria, Phil. (kän-dȧ-lä'rē-ä)	207a	15.39 N	119.55 E
Candelaria (R.), Mex. (kän-dĕ-lä-ryä)	131	18.25 N	91.21 W
Candeleda, Sp. (kän-dhȧ-lā'dhä)	170	40.09 N	5.18 W
Candia, see **Iráklion**			
Candle, Ak. (kăn'd'l)	107	65.00 N	162.04 W
Cando, ND (kăn'dō)	114	48.27 N	99.13 W
Candon, Phil. (kän-dōn')	207a	17.13 N	120.26 E
Canelones (Dept.), Ur.	141c	34.34 S	56.15 W
Canelones, Ur. (kä-nĕ-lô-nĕs)	141c	34.32 S	56.19 W
Cañete, Peru (kän-yā'tȧ)	142	13.06 S	76.17 W
Caney, Cuba (kä-nā') (kā'nĭ)	135	20.05 N	75.45 W
Caney, Ks. (kā'nĭ)	123	37.00 N	95.57 W
Caney (R.), Tn.	126	36.10 N	85.50 W
Cangamba, Ang.	230	13.40 S	19.54 E
Cangas, Sp. (kän'gäs)	170	42.15 N	8.43 W
Cangas de Narcea, Sp. (kä'n-gäs-dĕ-när-sĕ-ä)	170	43.08 N	6.36 W
Cangzhou, China (tsäŋ-jō)	200	38.21 N	116.53 E
Caniapiscau (L.), Can.	97	54.10 N	71.13 E
Caniapiscau (R.), Can.	97	57.00 N	68.45 W
Canicattì, It. (kä-nē-kät'tē)	172	37.18 N	13.58 E
Canillas (Neigh.), Sp.	65b	40.28 N	3.38 W
Canillejas (Neigh.), Sp.	65b	40.27 N	3.37 W
Cañitas, Mex. (kän-yē'täs)	130	23.38 N	102.44 W
Çankırı, Tur. (chän-kē'rē)	179	40.40 N	33.40 E
Cannell, Can.	95g	53.35 N	113.38 W
Cannelton, In. (kăn'ĕl-tŭn)	110	37.55 N	86.45 W
Cannes, Fr. (kȧn)	169	43.34 N	7.05 E
Canning, Can. (kăn'ĭng)	104	45.09 N	64.25 W
Cannock, Eng. (kăn'ŭk)	156	52.41 N	2.02 W
Cannock Chase (Reg.), Eng. (kăn'ŭk chās)	156	52.43 N	1.54 W
Cannon (R.), Mn. (kăn'ŭn)	115	44.18 N	93.24 W
Cannonball (R.), ND (kăn'ŭn-bäl)	114	46.17 N	101.35 W
Canoe (R.), Can. (kȧ-no͞o)	99	52.20 N	119.00 W
Canoga Park, Ca. (kä-nō'gȧ)	119a	34.07 N	118.36 W
Caño, Isla de (I.), C.R. (ē's-lä-dĕ-kä'nō)	133	8.38 N	84.00 W
Canon City, Co. (kăn'yŭn)	122	38.27 N	105.16 W
Canonsburg, Pa. (kăn'ŭnz-bûrg)	113e	40.16 N	80.11 W
Canoochee (R.), Ga. (kȧ-no͞o'chē)	127	32.25 N	82.11 W
Canora, Can. (kȧ-nōrȧ)	101	51.37 N	102.26 W
Canosa, It. (kä-nō'sä)	172	41.14 N	16.03 E
Canouan (I.), Saint Vincent	133b	12.44 N	61.10 W
Cansaheab, Mex. (kän-sä-ĕ-äb)	132a	21.11 N	89.05 W
Canso, Can. (kăn'sō)	105	45.20 N	61.00 W
Canso, C., Can.	105	45.21 N	60.46 W
Canso, Str. of, Can.	105	45.37 N	61.25 W
Cantabrica, Cordillera (Mts.),Sp. (kôr-dēl-yĕ'rä-kan-tä'brē-kä)	170	43.05 N	6.05 W
Cantagalo, Braz. (kän-tä-gä'lo)	141a	21.59 S	42.22 W
Cantanhede, Port. (kän-täN-yä'dȧ)	170	40.22 N	8.35 W
Canterbury, Eng. (kăn'tĕr-bĕr-ē)	156b	51.17 N	1.06 E
Canterbury, Austl., Austl.	70b	37.49 S	145.05 E
Canterbury Bight, N.Z.	215a	44.15 S	172.08 E
Canterbury Woods, Va.	56d	38.49 N	77.15 W
Cantiles, Cayo (I.), Cuba (ky-ō-kän-tē'lās)	134	21.40 N	82.00 W
Canto do Pontes, Braz.	61c	22.58 S	43.04 W
Canton, Ga.	126	34.13 N	84.29 W
Canton, Il.	123	40.34 N	90.02 W
Canton, Ma.	105a	42.09 N	71.09 W
Canton, Mo.	123	40.08 N	91.33 W
Canton, Ms.	126	32.36 N	90.01 W
Canton, NC	126	35.32 N	82.50 W
Canton, Oh.	110	40.50 N	81.25 W
Canton, Pa.	111	41.50 N	76.45 W
Canton, SD	114	43.17 N	96.37 W
Canton, see **Guangzhou**			
Canton, (I.), see **Kanton** (I.)			
Cantu, It. (kän-to͞o')	172	45.43 N	9.09 E
Cañuelas, Arg. (kä-nyo͞oĕ'-läs)	141c	35.03 S	58.45 W
Canumã (R.), Braz. (kä-no͞o-mä')	143	6.20 S	58.57 W
Canyon, Ca.	58b	37.49 N	122.09 W
Canyon (R.), Wa.	118a	48.09 N	121.48 W
Canyon, Tx. (kăn'yŭn)	122	34.59 N	101.57 W
Canyon De Chelly Natl. Mon., Az.	121	36.14 N	110.00 W
Canyonlands Natl. Park, Ut.	121	38.10 N	110.00 W
Caoxian, China (tsou shyĕn)	200	34.48 N	115.33 E
Capalonga, Phil. (kä-pä-lôŋ'gä)	207a	14.20 N	122.30 E
Capannori, It. (kä-pän'nô-rē)	172	43.50 N	10.30 E
Capão Redondo (Neigh.), Braz.	61d	23.40 S	46.46 W
Caparica, Port.	65d	38.40 N	9.12 W
Capaya (R.), Ven. (kä-pä-ĭä)	143b	10.28 N	66.15 W
Cap-Chat, Can. (kȧp-shä')	97	48.02 N	65.20 W
Cap-de-la-Madeleine, Can. (kȧp dē lȧ mȧ-d'lĕn')	104	46.23 N	72.30 W
Cape (Prov.), S. Afr. (kāp)	226	31.50 S	21.15 E
Cape Breton (I.), Can. (kāp brĕt'ŭn)	105	45.48 N	59.50 W

PLACE (Pronounciation)	PAGE	Lat. °'	Long. °'
Cape Breton Highlands Natl. Park, Can.	105	46.45 N	60.45 W
Cape Charles, Va. (kāp chärlz)	127	37.13 N	76.02 W
Cape Coast, Ghana	228	5.05 N	1.15 W
Cape Fear (R.), NC (kāp fēr)	127	34.43 N	78.41 W
Cape Flats, S. Afr. (kāp flăts)	226a	34.01 S	18.37 E
Cape Girardeau, Mo. (jē-rär-dō')	123	37.17 N	89.32 W
Cape May, NJ (kāp mā)	111	38.55 N	74.50 W
Cape May C.H., NJ	111	39.05 N	75.00 W
Capenhurst, Eng.	64a	53.15 N	2.57 W
Cape Romanzof, Ak. (rō' män zôf)	107	61.50 N	165.45 W
Capesterre, Guad.	133b	16.02 N	61.37 W
Cape Tormentine, Can.	104	46.08 N	63.47 W
Cape Town, S. Afr. (kāp toun)	226a	33.48 S	18.28 E
Cape Verde, Afr.	224b	15.48 N	26.02 W
Cape York Pen., Austl. (kāp yôrk)	215	12.30 S	142.35 E
Cap-Haïtien, Hai. (kȧp ȧ-ē-syăn')	135	19.45 N	72.15 W
Capilla de Señor, Arg. (kä-pēl'yä dā sän-yôr')	141c	34.18 S	59.07 W
Capitachouane, (R.), Can.	103	47.50 N	76.45 W
Capitol Heights, Md.	56d	38.53 N	76.55 W
Capitol Reef Natl. Park, Ut. (kăp'ĭ-tŏl)	121	38.15 N	111.10 W
Capitol View, Md.	56d	39.01 N	77.04 W
Capivari, Braz. (kä-pē-vȧ'rē)	141a	22.59 S	47.29 W
Capivari (R.), Braz.	144b	22.39 S	43.19 W
Capoompeta (Mtn.), Austl. (kȧ-po͞om-pē'tȧ)	216	29.15 S	152.12 E
Capraia (I.), It. (kä-prä'yä)	172	43.02 N	9.51 E
Caprara Pt., It. (kä-prä'rä)	172	41.08 N	8.20 E
Capreol, Can.	102	46.43 N	80.56 W
Caprera (I.), It. (kä-prā'rä)	172	41.12 N	9.28 E
Capri, It.	171c	40.18 N	14.16 E
Capricorn Chan., Austl. (kăp'rĭ-kôrn)	215	22.27 S	151.24 E
Capri, I. di, It. (ē'-sō-lä-dē-kä'prē)	171c	40.19 N	14.10 E
Caprivi Strip (Reg.), Namibia	226	18.00 S	22.00 E
Cap-Rouge, Can. (kȧp ro͞ozh')	95b	46.45 N	71.21 W
Cap-Saint Ignace, Can. (kĭp săN-tē-nyȧs')	95b	47.02 N	70.27 W
Captain Cook Bridge (P. Int.), Austl.	70a	34.00 S	151.08 E
Capua, It. (kä'pwä)	172	41.07 N	14.14 E
Capuáva, Braz.	61d	23.39 S	46.29 W
Capulhuac, Mex. (kä-po͞ol-hwäk')	130	19.33 N	99.43 W
Capulin Mountain Natl. Mon., NM (kȧ-pū'lĭn)	122	36.15 N	103.58 W
Capultitlán, Mex. (kä-po͞ol-tē-tlä'n)	131a	19.15 N	99.40 W
Caputh, G.D.R.	65a	52.21 N	13.00 E
Caquetá (R.), Col. (kä-kä-tä')	142	0.23 S	73.22 W
Caraballeda, Ven.	61a	10.37 N	66.50 W
Carabaña, Sp. (kä-rä-bän'yä)	171a	40.16 N	3.15 W
Carabanchel Alto (Neigh.), Sp.	65b	40.22 N	3.45 W
Carabanchel Bajo (Neigh.), Sp.	65b	40.23 N	3.47 W
Carabelle, Fl. (kăr'ȧ-bĕl)	126	29.50 N	84.40 W
Carabobo (State), Ven. (kä-rä-bô'-bô)	143b	10.07 N	68.06 W
Caracal, Rom. (kȧ-rȧ-kȧl')	173	44.06 N	24.22 E
Caracas, Ven. (kä-rä'käs)	143b	10.30 N	66.58 W
Carácuaro de Morelos, Mex. (kä-rä'kwä-rō-dĕ-mō-rĕ-lôs)	130	18.44 N	101.04 W
Caraguatatuba, Braz. (kä-rä-gwä-tȧ-to͞o'bä)	141a	23.37 S	45.26 W
Carajás, Serra dos (Mts.), Braz. (sĕ'r-rä-dôs-kä-rä-zhá's)	143	5.58 S	51.45 W
Caramanta, Cerro (Mtn.), Col. (sĕ'r-rô-kä-rä-mȧ'n-tä)	142a	5.29 N	76.01 W
Caramarca, Arg. (kä-rä-mȧ'r-kä)	144	28.29 S	65.45 W
Carandaí, Braz. (kä-rän-dȧē')	141a	20.57 S	43.47 W
Carangola, Braz. (kä-rän'gô'lä)	141a	20.46 S	42.02 W
Caransebeş, Rom. (kȧ-rȧn-sā'bĕsh)	173	45.24 N	22.13 E
Carapicuíba, Braz.	61d	23.31 S	46.50 W
Caraquet, Can. (kă-rȧ-kĕt')	104	47.48 N	64.57 W
Carata, Laguna (L.), Nic. (lä-go͞o'nä-kä-rä'tä)	133	13.59 N	83.41 W
Caratasca, Laguna (L.), Hond. (lä-go͞o'nä-kä-rä-täs'kä)	133	15.20 N	83.45 W
Caravaca, Sp. (kä-rä-vä'kä)	170	38.05 N	1.51 W
Caravelas, Braz. (kȧ-rä-vĕl'äzh)	143	17.46 S	39.06 W
Carayaca, Ven. (kȧ-rä-ĭä'kä)	143b	10.32 N	67.07 W
Carazinho, Braz. (kä-rȧ'zē-nyō)	144	28.22 S	52.33 W
Carballino, Sp. (kär-bäl-yē'nō)	170	42.26 N	8.04 W
Carballo, Sp. (kär-bäl'yō)	170	43.13 N	8.40 W
Carbon (R.), Wa. (kär'bŏn)	118a	47.06 N	122.08 W
Carbonado, Wa. (kär-bō-nä'dō)	118a	47.05 N	122.03 W
Carbonara, C., It. (kär-bō-nä'rä)	172	39.08 N	9.33 E
Carbondale, Can. (kär'bŏn-dāl)	95g	53.45 N	113.32 W
Carbondale, Il.	123	37.42 N	89.12 W
Carbondale, Pa.	111	41.35 N	75.30 W
Carbonear, Can. (kär-bō-nēr')	105	47.45 N	53.14 W
Carbon Hill, Al. (kär'bŏn hĭl)	126	33.53 N	87.34 W
Carcagente, Sp. (kär-kä-hĕn'tä)	171	39.09 N	0.29 W
Carcans, Étang de (L.), Fr. (ā-taN-dĕ-kȧr-kăn)	168	45.12 N	1.00 W
Carcassonne, Fr. (kȧr-kȧ-sôn')	168	43.12 N	2.23 E
Carcross, Can. (kär'krôs)	96	60.18 N	134.54 W
Cárdenas, Cuba (kär'dȧ-näs)	134	23.00 N	81.10 W
Cárdenas, Mex. (kȧ'r-dĕ-näs)	131	17.59 N	93.23 W
Cárdenas, Mex.	130	22.01 N	99.38 W
Cardenas, Bahía de (B.), Cuba (bä-ē'ä-dĕ-kär'dȧ-näs)	134	23.10 N	81.10 W
Cardiff, Can. (kär'dĭf)	95g	53.46 N	113.36 W
Cardiff, Wales	162	51.30 N	3.18 W
Cardigan, Wales (kär'dĭ-gȧn)	162	52.05 N	4.40 W
Cardigan B., Wales	162	52.35 N	4.40 W
Cardston, Can. (kärds'tŭn)	99	49.12 N	113.18 W
Carei, Rom. (kä-rĕ')	167	47.42 N	22.28 E
Carentan, Fr. (kä-rôN-täN')	168	49.19 N	1.14 W
Carey (L.), Aust. (kâr'ē)	214	29.20 S	123.35 E
Carey, Oh. (kā'rē)	110	40.55 N	83.25 W
Carhaix-Plouguer, Fr. (kär-ĕ')	168	48.17 N	3.37 W
Caribbean Sea, N.A.-S.A. (kăr-ĭ-bē'ăn)	129	14.30 N	75.30 W
Caribe, Arroyo (R.), Mex. (är-ro'ī-kä-rē'bĕ)	131	18.18 N	90.38 W

PLACE (Pronounciation)	PAGE	Lat. °'	Long. °'
Cariboo Mts., Can. (kă'rĭ-bo͞o)	99	53.00 N	121.00 W
Caribou (I.), Can.	102	47.22 N	85.42 W
Caribou, Me.	104	46.51 N	68.01 W
Caribou L., Mn.	119h	46.54 N	92.16 W
Caribou Mts., Can.	96	59.20 N	115.30 W
Caringbah, Austl.	70a	34.03 S	151.08 E
Carinhanha, Braz. (kä-rĭ-nyăn'yä)	143	14.14 S	43.44 W
Carini, It. (kä-rē'nē)	172	38.09 N	13.10 E
Carinthia (State), see **Kärnten**			
Carleton Place, Can. (kärl'tŭn)	103	45.15 N	76.10 W
Carletonville, S. Afr.	223d	26.20 S	27.23 E
Carlingford, Austl.	70a	33.47 S	151.03 E
Carlinville, Il. (kär'lĭn-vĭl)	123	39.16 N	89.52 W
Carlisle, Eng. (kär-līl')	162	54.54 N	3.03 W
Carlisle, Ky.	110	38.20 N	84.00 W
Carlisle, Pa.	111	40.10 N	77.15 W
Carloforte, It. (kär'lō-fôr-tȧ)	172	39.11 N	8.28 E
Carlos Casares, Arg. (kär-lôs-kä-sȧ'rĕs)	141c	35.38 S	61.17 W
Carlow, Ire. (kär'lō)	162	52.50 N	7.00 W
Carlsbad, NM (kärlz'băd)	124	32.24 N	104.12 W
Carlsbad Caverns Nat'l Park, NM	124	32.08 N	104.30 W
Carlstadt, NJ	55	40.50 N	74.06 W
Carlton, Eng. (kärl'tŭn)	156	52.58 N	1.05 W
Carlton, Mn.	119h	46.40 N	92.26 W
Carlton Center, Mi. (kärl'tŭn sĕn'tĕr)	110	42.45 N	85.20 W
Carlyle, Il. (kärlīl')	123	38.37 N	89.23 W
Carmagnolo, It. (kär-mä-nyô'lä)	172	44.52 N	7.48 E
Carman, Can. (kär'mȧn)	101	49.32 N	98.00 W
Carmarthen, Wales (kär-mär'thĕn)	162	51.50 N	4.20 W
Carmarthen B., Wales (kär-mär'thĕn)	162	51.33 N	4.50 W
Carmaux, Fr. (kär-mō')	168	44.05 N	2.09 E
Carmel, NY (kär'mĕl)	112a	41.25 N	73.42 W
Carmelo, Ur. (kär-mĕ'lo)	141c	33.59 S	58.15 W
Carmen de Areco, Arg. (kär'mĕn' dā ä-rā'kō)	141c	34.21 S	59.50 W
Carmen de Patagones, Arg. (kȧ'r-mĕn-dĕ-pä-tä-gô'nĕs)	144	41.00 S	63.00 W
Carmen, Isla del (I.), Mex. (ē's-lä-dĕl-kȧ'r-mĕn)	131	18.43 N	91.40 W
Carmen, Laguna del (L.), Mex. (lä-go͞o'nä-dĕl-kȧ'r-mĕn)	131	18.15 N	93.26 W
Carmi, Il. (kär'mī)	110	38.05 N	88.10 W
Carmo, Braz. (kȧ'r-mô)	141a	21.57 S	42.06 W
Carmo do Rio Clara, Braz. (kȧ'r-mô-dô-rē'ô-klä'rä)	141a	20.57 S	46.04 W
Carmona, Sp.	170	37.28 N	5.38 W
Carnarvon, Austl. (kär-när'vŭn)	214	24.45 S	113.45 E
Carnarvon, S. Afr.	226	31.00 S	22.15 E
Carnation, Wa. (kär-nā'shŭn)	118a	47.39 N	121.55 W
Carnaxide, Port. (kär-nä-shē'dĕ)	171b	38.44 N	9.15 W
Carndonagh, Ire. (kärn-dō-nä')	162	55.15 N	7.15 W
Carnegie, Ok. (kär-nĕg'ĭ)	122	35.06 N	98.38 W
Carnegie, Pa.	113e	40.24 N	80.06 W
Carnegie Institute (P. Int.), Pa.	57b	40.27 N	79.57 W
Carnetin, Fr.	64c	48.54 N	2.42 E
Carneys Point, NJ (kär'nēs)	111	39.45 N	75.25 W
Carnic Alps (Mts.), Aus.-It.	166	46.43 N	12.38 E
Carnide (Neigh.), Port.	65d	38.46 N	9.11 W
Carnot, Alg. (kär nō')	171	36.15 N	1.40 E
Carnot, Cen. Afr. Rep.	229	5.00 N	15.52 E
Carnsore Pt., Ire. (kärn'sôr)	162	52.10 N	6.16 W
Caro, Mi. (kȧ'rō)	110	43.30 N	83.25 W
Carolina, Braz. (kä-rô-lē'nä)	143	7.26 S	47.16 W
Carolina (L.), Mex. (kä-rō-lē'nä)	132a	18.41 N	89.40 W
Carolina, S. Afr. (kăr-ō-lī'nȧ)	226	26.07 S	30.09 E
Caroline Is., Pac. Is. Trust Ter. (kăr'ō-līn)	208	9.30 N	143.00 E
Caroni (R.), Ven. (kä-rō'nē)	142	5.49 N	62.57 W
Carora, Ven. (kä-rō'rä)	142	10.09 N	70.12 W
Carpathians (Mts.), Eur. (kär-pā'thĭ-ăn)	161	49.23 N	20.14 E
Carpaţii Meridionali (Transylvanian Alps) (Mts.), Rom.	173	45.30 N	23.30 E
Carpentaria, G. of, Austl. (kär-pĕn-târ'ĭȧ)	214	14.45 S	138.50 E
Carpentras, Fr. (kär-päN-träs')	168	44.04 N	5.01 E
Carpi, It.	172	44.48 N	10.54 E
Carrara, It. (kä-rä'rä)	172	44.05 N	10.05 E
Carrauntoohil, Ire. (kă-răn-to͞o'ĭl)	162	52.01 N	9.48 W
Carretas, Punta (Pt.), Peru (po͞o'n-tä-kär-rĕ'tĕ'räs)	142	14.15 S	76.25 W
Carriacou (I.), Grenada (kăr-ē-ȧ-ko͞o')	133b	12.28 N	61.20 W
Carrick-on-Sur, Ire. (kăr'-ĭk)	162	52.20 N	7.35 W
Carrier, Can. (kăr'ĭ-ēr)	95b	46.43 N	71.05 W
Carriere, Ms. (kȧ-rēr')	126	30.37 N	89.37 W
Carrières-sous-Bois, Fr.	64c	48.57 N	2.07 E
Carrières-sous-Poissy, Fr.	64c	48.57 N	2.03 E
Carrières-sur-Seine, Fr.	64c	48.55 N	2.11 E
Carriers Mills, Il. (kăr'ĭ-ērs)	110	37.40 N	88.40 W
Carrington, Eng.	64b	53.26 N	2.24 W
Carrington, ND (kăr'ĭng-tŭn)	114	47.26 N	99.06 W
Carr Inlet, Wa. (kär ĭn'lĕt)	118a	47.20 N	122.42 W
Carrion Crow Hbr., Ba. (kăr'ĭŭn krō)	134	26.35 N	77.55 W
Carrión de los Condes, Sp. (kär-rē-ōn' dā lōs kōn'dās)	170	42.20 N	4.35 W
Carrizo Cr., NM (kär-rē'zō)	122	36.22 N	103.39 W
Carrizo Springs, Tx.	124	28.32 N	99.51 W
Carrizozo, NM (kär-rē-zō'zō)	121	33.40 N	105.55 W
Carroll, Ia. (kăr'ŭl)	115	42.03 N	94.51 W
Carrollton, Ga. (kăr-ŭl-tŭn)	126	33.35 N	84.05 W
Carrollton, Il.	123	39.18 N	90.22 W
Carrollton, Ky.	110	38.45 N	85.15 W
Carrollton, Mi.	110	43.30 N	83.55 W
Carrollton, Mo.	123	39.21 N	93.29 W
Carrollton, Oh.	110	40.35 N	81.10 W
Carrollton, Tx.	119c	32.58 N	96.53 W
Carrols, Wa. (kăr'ŭlz)	118c	46.05 N	122.51 W
Carron (L.), Scot. (kă'rŭn)	162	57.25 N	5.25 W

ŋ-sing; nŋ-banŋk; N-nasalized n; nŏd; cŏmmit; ōld; ôbey; ôrder; oi-boil; fo͞od; fo͝ot; ou-out; s-soft; sh-dish; th-thin; pūre; ûnite; ûrn; stŭd; circŭs; ü-as in French tu; '-indeterminate vowel.

268 Carrot – Céret

PLACE (Pronounciation)	PAGE	Lat. °′	Long. °′
Carrot (R.), Can.	100	53.12 N	103.50 W
Carry-le-Rouet, Fr. (kä-rē′lĕ-rōō-ā′)	168a	43.20 N	5.10 E
Carsamba, Tur. (chär-shäm′bä)	179	41.05 N	36.40 E
Carshalton (Neigh.), Eng.	62	51.22 N	0.10 W
Carson, Ca.	59	33.50 N	118.16 W
Carson (R.), Nv. (kär′sŭn)	120	39.15 N	119.25 W
Carson City, Nv.	120	39.10 N	119.45 W
Carsondale, Md.	56d	38.57 N	76.50 W
Carson Sink, Nv.	120	39.51 N	118.25 W
Cartagena, Col. (kär-tä-hā′nä)	142	10.30 N	75.40 W
Cartagena, Sp. (kär-tä-ĸē′nä)	171	37.46 N	1.00 W
Cartago, Col. (kär-tä′gō)	142a	4.44 N	75.54 W
Cartago, C. R.	133	9.52 N	83.56 W
Cartaxo, Port. (kär-tä′shō)	170	39.10 N	8.48 W
Carteret, NJ (kär′tē-ret)	112a	40.35 N	74.13 W
Cartersville, Ga. (kär′tẽrs-vĭl)	126	34.09 N	84.47 W
Carthage, Il. (kär′thåj)	123	40.27 N	91.09 W
Carthage, Mo.	123	37.10 N	94.18 W
Carthage, NC	127	35.22 N	79.25 W
Carthage, NY	111	44.00 N	75.45 W
Carthage, Tun.	224	37.04 N	10.18 E
Carthage, Tx.	125	32.09 N	94.20 W
Carthcart, S. Afr. (cärth-că′t)	227c	32.18 S	27.11 E
Cartwright, Can. (kärt′rīt)	97	53.36 N	57.00 W
Caruaru, Braz. (kä-rōō-á-rōō′)	143	8.19 S	35.52 W
Carúpano, Ven. (kä-rōō′pä-nō)	142	10.45 N	63.21 W
Caruthersville, Mo. (kȧ-rŭdh′ẽrz-vĭl)	123	36.09 N	89.41 W
Carver, Or. (kärv′ẽr)	118c	45.24 N	122.30 W
Carvoeiro, Cabo (C.), Port. (kȧ′bō-kär-vô-ĕ′y-rō)	170	39.22 N	9.24 W
Cary, Il. (kā′rē)	113a	42.13 N	88.14 W
Casablanca, Chile (kä-sä-bläŋ′kä)	141b	33.19 S	71.24 W
Casablanca, Mor.	224	33.32 N	7.41 W
Casa Branca, Braz. (kȧ′sä-brȧ′ɴ-kä)	141a	21.47 S	47.04 W
Casa Grande, Az. (kä′sä grän′dā)	121	32.50 N	111.45 W
Casa Grande Natl. Mon., Az.	121	33.00 N	111.33 W
Casale Monferrato, It. (kä-sä′lā)	172	45.08 N	8.26 E
Casalmaggiore, It. (kä-säl-mäd-jō′rä)	172	45.00 N	10.24 E
Casa Loma (P. Int.), Can.	54c	43.41 N	79.25 W
Casamance (R.), Senegal (kä-sä-mäɴs′)	228	12.43 N	16.00 W
Cascade Pt., N.Z. (kăs-kād′)	217	43.59 S	168.23 E
Cascade Ra., U.S.	108	42.50 N	122.20 W
Cascade Tun., Wa.	116	47.41 N	120.53 W
Cascais, Port. (käs-kȧ-ēzh)	171b	38.42 N	9.25 W
Case Inlet, Wa. (kās)	118a	47.22 N	122.47 W
Caseros, Arg. (kä-sā′rôs)	144a	34.35 S	58.34 W
Caserta, It. (kä-zĕr′tä)	172	41.04 N	14.21 E
Casey, Il. (kā′sĭ)	110	39.20 N	88.00 W
Cashmere, Wa. (kăsh′mĭr)	116	47.30 N	120.28 W
Casiguran, Phil. (käs-sē-gōō′rän)	207a	16.15 N	122.10 E
Casiguran Sd., Phil.	207a	16.02 N	121.51 E
Casilda, Arg. (kä-sē′l-dä)	141c	33.02 S	61.11 W
Casilda, Cuba	134	21.50 N	80.00 W
Casimiro de Abreu, Braz. (kä′sē-mē′ro-dĕ-á-brĕ′ōō)	141a	22.30 S	42.11 W
Casino, Austl. (kȧ-sē′nō)	216	28.35 S	153.10 E
Casiquiare (R.), Ven. (kä-sē-kyä′rä)	142	2.11 N	66.15 W
Caspe, Sp. (käs′på)	171	41.18 N	0.02 W
Casper, Wy. (kăs′pẽr)	117	42.51 N	106.18 W
Caspian Dep., Sov. Un. (kăs′pĭ-ȧn)	178	47.40 N	52.35 E
Caspian Sea, Asia	176	40.00 N	52.00 E
Cass, WV (kăs)	111	38.25 N	79.55 W
Cass (L.), Mn.	115	47.23 N	94.28 W
Cassai (R.), Ang. (kä-sä′ē)	230	7.30 S	21.45 E
Cass City, Mi. (kăs)	110	43.35 N	83.10 W
Casselman, Can. (kăs′'l-mán)	95c	45.18 N	75.05 W
Casselton, ND (kăs′'l-tŭn)	114	46.53 N	97.14 W
Cássia, Braz. (kȧ′syä)	141a	20.36 S	46.53 W
Cassin, Tx. (kăs′ĭn)	119d	29.16 N	98.29 W
Cassino, It. (käs-sē′nō)	172	41.30 N	13.50 E
Cass Lake, Mn. (kăs)	115	47.23 N	94.37 W
Cassopolis, Mi. (kăs-ŏ′pō-lĭs)	110	41.55 N	86.00 W
Cassville, Mo. (kăs′vĭl)	123	36.41 N	93.52 W
Castanheira de Pêra, Port. (käs-tän-yā′rä-dĕ-pĕ′rä)	170	40.00 N	8.07 W
Castellammare di Stabia, It. (käs-tĕl-läm-mä′rä-dē-stä′byä)	171c	40.26 N	14.29 E
Castellbisbal, Sp.	65e	41.29 N	1.59 E
Castelli, Arg. (kȧs-tĕ′zhē)	141c	36.07 S	57.48 W
Castellón de la Plana, Sp. (käs-tĕl-yō′n-dĕ-lä-plä′nä)	171	39.59 N	0.05 W
Castelnaudary, Fr. (kȧs′tĕl-nō-dȧ-rē′)	168	43.20 N	1.57 E
Castelo, Braz. (käs-tĕ′lô)	141a	21.37 S	41.13 W
Castelo Branco, Port. (käs-tā′lōō bräŋ′kōō)	170	39.48 N	7.37 W
Castelo de Vide, Port. (käs-tā′lōō dĭ vē′dĭ)	170	39.25 N	7.25 W
Castelsarrasin, Fr. (kȧs′tĕl-sȧ-rȧ-zăɴ′)	168	44.03 N	1.05 E
Castelvetrano, It. (käs′tĕl-vē-trä′nō)	172	37.43 N	12.50 E
Castilla, Peru (kȧs-tē′l-yä)	142	5.18 S	80.40 W
Castilla La Nueva (Reg.), Sp. (käs-tē′lyä lä nwä′vä)	170	39.15 N	3.55 W
Castilla La Vieja (Reg.), Sp. (käs-tēl′yä lä vyā′hä)	170	40.48 N	4.24 W
Castillo De San Marcos Natl. Mon., Fl. (kăs-tē′lyā de-sän mär-kōs)	127	29.55 N	81.25 W
Castle (I.), Ba. (kȧs′'l)	135	22.05 N	74.20 W
Castlebar, Ire. (kȧs′'l-bär)	162	53.55 N	9.15 W
Castlecrag, Austl.	70a	33.48 S	151.13 E
Castle Dale, Ut. (kȧs′l dāl)	121	39.15 N	111.00 W
Castle Donington, Eng. (dŏn′ĭng-tŭn)	156	52.50 N	1.21 W
Castleford, Eng. (kȧs′l-fẽrd)	156	53.43 N	1.21 W
Castlegar, Can. (kȧs′'l-gär)	99	49.19 N	117.40 W
Castle Hill, Austl.	70a	33.44 S	151.00 E
Castlemaine, Austl. (kȧs′'l-mān)	216	37.05 S	114.10 E
Castle Pk., Co.	121	39.00 N	106.50 W
Castlerock, Wa. (kȧs′'l-rŏk)	116	46.17 N	122.53 W
Castle Rock Flowage (Res.), Wi.	115	44.03 N	89.48 W
Castle Shannon, Pa. (shăn′ŭn)	113e	40.22 N	80.02 W
Castleton, Eng.	64b	53.35 N	2.11 W
Castleton, In. (kȧs′'l-tŏn)	113g	39.54 N	86.03 W
Castor (R.), Can (kăs′tôr)	95c	45.16 N	75.14 W
Castor (R.), Mo.	123	36.59 N	89.53 W
Castres, Fr. (kȧs′tr′)	168	43.36 N	2.13 E
Castries, Saint Lucia (kȧs-trē′)	133b	14.01 N	61.00 W
Castro, Braz. (käs′trōō)	144	24.56 S	50.00 W
Castro, Chile (käs′tro)	144	42.27 S	73.48 W
Castro Daire, Port. (käs′trōō dīr′ĭ)	170	40.56 N	7.57 W
Castro del Río, Sp. (käs-trô-dĕl rē′ō)	170	37.42 N	4.28 W
Castrop Rauxel, F.R.G. (käs′trōp rou′ksĕl)	169c	51.33 N	7.19 E
Castro Urdiales, Sp. (käs′trō ōōr-dyä′läs)	170	43.23 N	3.11 W
Castro Valley, Ca.	118b	37.42 N	122.05 W
Castro Verde, Port. (käs-trō vĕr′dĕ)	170	37.43 N	8.05 W
Castrovillari, It. (käs′trō-vēl-lyä′rē)	172	39.48 N	16.11 E
Castuera, Sp. (käs-tōō-ā′rä)	170	38.43 N	5.33 W
Casula, Moz.	231	15.25 S	33.40 E
Cat (I.), Ba.	135	25.30 N	75.30 W
Catacamas, Hond. (kä-tä-kȧ′mäs)	132	14.52 N	85.55 W
Cataguases, Braz. (kä-tä-gwȧ′sĕs)	141a	21.23 S	42.42 W
Catahoula (L.), La. (kăt-ȧ-hōō′lȧ)	125	31.35 N	92.20 W
Catalão, Braz. (kä-tä-louɴ′)	143	18.09 S	47.42 W
Catalina (I.), Dom. Rep. (kä-tä-lē′nä)	135	18.20 N	69.00 W
Cataluma (Reg.), Sp. (kä-tä-lōō′mä)	171	41.23 N	0.50 E
Cataluña, Museo de Arte de (P. Int.), Sp.	65e	41.23 N	2.09 E
Catamarca (Prov.), Arg. (kä-tä-mär′kä)	144	27.15 S	67.15 W
Catanaun, Phil. (kä-tä-nä′wän)	207a	13.36 N	122.20 E
Catanduanes I., Phil. (kä-tän-dwä′nĕs)	207	13.55 N	125.00 E
Catanduva, Braz. (kä-tȧn-dōō′vä)	143	21.12 S	48.47 W
Catania, It. (kä-tä′nyä)	172	37.30 N	15.09 E
Catania, Golfo di (G.), It. (gôl-fô-dē-kȧ-tä′nyä)	172	37.24 N	15.28 E
Catanzaro, It. (kä-tän-dzä′rō)	172	38.53 N	16.34 E
Catarroja, Sp. (kä-tär-rō′hä)	171	39.24 N	0.25 W
Catawba (L.), SC	127	35.02 N	81.21 W
Catawba (R.), NC (kȧ-tô′bȧ)	127	35.25 N	80.55 W
Catazajá, Laguna de (L.), Mex. (lä-gōō′nä-dĕ-kä-tä-zä-hȧ′)	131	17.45 N	92.03 W
Catbalogan, Phil. (kät-bä-lō′gän)	207	11.45 N	124.52 E
Catemaco, Mex. (kä-tā-mä′kō)	131	18.26 N	95.06 W
Catemaco, Lago (L.), Mex. (lä′gô-kä-tā-mä′kō)	131	18.23 N	95.04 W
Caterham, Eng. (kā′tẽr-ŭm)	156b	51.16 N	0.04 W
Catete, Ang. (kä-tĕ′tĕ)	230	9.06 S	13.43 E
Catete (Neigh.), Braz.	61c	22.55 S	43.10 W
Catford (Neigh.), Eng.	62	51.27 N	0.01 W
Cathedral Mt., Tx. (kȧ-thē′drăl)	124	30.09 N	103.46 W
Cathedral Pk., S. Afr. (kȧ-thē′drȧl)	227c	28.53 S	29.04 E
Catherine, L., Ar. (kă-thẽr-ĭn)	123	34.26 N	92.47 W
Cathkin Pk., S. Afr. (kăth′kĭn)	227c	29.08 S	29.22 E
Cathlamet, Wa. (kăth-lăm′ĕt)	118c	46.12 N	123.22 W
Catia (Neigh.), Ven.	61a	10.31 N	66.57 W
Catlettsburg, Ky. (kăt′lĕts-bûrg)	110	38.20 N	82.35 W
Catoche, C., Mex. (kä-tō′chĕ)	128	21.30 N	87.15 W
Catonsville, Md. (kā′tŭnz-vĭl)	112e	39.16 N	76.45 W
Catorce, Mex. (kä-tôr′sȧ)	130	23.41 N	100.51 W
Catskill, NY (kăts′kĭl)	111	42.15 N	73.50 W
Catskill Mts., NY	111	42.20 N	74.35 W
Cattaraugus Ind. Res., NY (kăt′tȧ-rȧ-gŭs)	111	42.30 N	79.05 W
Catu, Braz. (kȧ-tōō)	143	12.26 S	38.12 W
Catuala, Ang.	230	16.29 S	19.03 E
Catumbela (R.), Ang. (kă′tŏm-bĕl′ȧ)	230	12.40 S	14.10 E
Cauayan, Phil. (kou-ä′yän)	207a	16.56 N	121.46 E
Cauca (R.), Col. (kou′kä)	142	7.30 N	75.26 W
Caucagua, Ven. (käōō-kȧ′gwä)	143b	10.17 N	66.22 W
Caucasus Mts., Sov. Un. (kô′kȧ-sŭs)	179	43.20 N	42.00 E
Cauchon L., Can. (kô-shŏn′)	101	55.25 N	96.30 W
Caughnawaga, Can.	95a	45.24 N	73.41 W
Caulfield, Austl.	70b	37.53 S	145.03 E
Caulonia, It. (kou-lō′nyä)	172	38.24 N	16.22 E
Cauquenes, Chile (kou-kā′nās)	144	35.54 S	72.14 W
Caura (R.), Ven. (kou′rä)	142	6.48 N	64.40 W
Causapscal, Can.	104	48.22 N	67.14 W
Caution, C., Can. (kô′shŭn)	98	51.10 N	127.47 W
Cauto (R.), Cuba (kou′tō)	135	20.33 N	76.20 W
Cauvery (R.), India	196	11.15 N	78.06 E
Cava, Braz. (kȧ′vä)	144b	22.41 S	43.26 W
Cava de' Tirreni, It. (kȧ′vä-dĕ-tēr-rĕ′nē)	171c	40.27 N	14.43 E
Cávado (R.), Port. (kä-vä′dō)	170	41.43 N	8.08 W
Cavalcante, Braz. (kä-väl-kän′tä)	143	13.45 S	47.33 W
Cavalier, ND (kăv-ȧ-lēr′)	114	48.45 N	97.39 W
Cavally (R.), Ivory Coast-Lib.	228	4.40 N	7.30 W
Cavan, Ire. (kăv′ăn)	162	54.01 N	7.00 W
Cavarzere, It. (kä-vär′dzā-rä)	172	45.08 N	12.06 E
Cavendish, Vt. (kăv′ĕn-dĭsh)	111	43.25 N	72.35 W
Caviana, Ilha (I.), Braz. (kä-vyä′nä)	143	0.45 N	49.33 W
Cavite, Phil. (kä-vē′tä)	207a	14.30 N	120.54 E
Caxambu, Braz. (kä-shá′m-bōō)	141a	22.00 S	44.45 W
Caxias, Braz. (kä′shē-äzh)	143	4.48 S	43.16 W
Caxias, Port.	65d	38.42 N	9.16 W
Caxias do Sul, Braz. (kä′shē-äzh-dô-sōō′l)	144	29.13 S	51.03 W
Caxito, Ang. (kä-shē′tōō)	230	8.33 S	13.36 E
Cayambe, Ec. (kȧ-ïä′m-bĕ)	142	0.03 N	79.09 W
Cayenne, Fr. Gu. (kā-ĕn′)	143	4.56 N	52.18 W
Cayetano Rubio, Mex. (kä-yĕ-tȧ-nô-rōō′byô)	130	20.37 N	100.21 W
Cayey, P. R.	129b	18.05 N	66.12 W
Cayman Brac (I.), Cayman Is. (kī-män′ brȧk)	134	19.45 N	79.50 W
Cayman Is., N. A.	134	19.30 N	80.30 W
Cay Sal Bk., Ba. (kē-săl)	134	23.55 N	80.20 W
Cayuga (L.), NY (kā-yōō′gȧ)	111	42.35 N	76.35 W
Cazalla de la Sierra, Sp. (kä-thäl′yä-dĕ-lä-sē-ĕ′r-rä)	170	37.55 N	5.48
Cazaux, Étang de (L.), Fr. (ā-täɴ′ dĕ kä-zō′)	168	44.32 N	0.59
Cazenovia, NY (kăz-ē-nō′vĭ-ă)	111	42.55 N	75.50
Cazenovia Cr., NY	113c	42.49 N	78.45
Čazma, Yugo. (chäz′mä)	172	45.44 N	16.39
Cazombo, Ang. (kä-zô′m-bŏ)	226	11.54 S	22.52
Cazones (R.), Mex. (kä-zô′nĕs)	131	20.37 N	97.28
Cazones, Ensenada de (B.), Cuba (ĕn-sĕ-nä-dä-dĕ-kä-zō′nås)	134	22.05 N	81.30
Cazones, Golfo de (G.), Cuba (gôl-fô-dĕ-kä-zō′nås)	134	23.55 N	81.15
Cazorla, Sp. (kä-thôr′lå)	170	37.55 N	2.58
Cea (R.), Sp. (thā′ä)	170	42.18 N	5.10
Ceará-Mirim, Braz. (sā-ä-rä′mē-rē′ɴ)	143	6.00 S	35.13
Ceará, see Fortaleza			
Ceará (State), Braz. (sā-å-rä′)	143	5.13 S	39.43
Cebaco, Isla (I.), Pan. (ē′s-lä-så-bä′kō)	133	7.27 N	81.08
Cebolla Cr., Co. (sē-bōl′yä)	121	38.15 N	107.10
Cebreros, Sp. (sĕ-brĕ′rôs)	170	40.28 N	4.28
Cebu, Phil. (sā-bōō′)	207	10.22 N	123.49
Cecchignola (Neigh.), It.	66c	41.49 N	12.29
Čechy (Bohemia) (Prov.), Czech. (bô-hē′mĭ-ȧ)	166	49.51 N	13.55
Cecil, Pa. (sē′sĭl)	113e	40.20 N	80.10
Cecil Park, Austl.	70a	33.52 S	150.51
Cedar (R.), Ia.	115	42.23 N	92.07
Cedar (R.), Wa.	118c	45.56 N	122.32
Cedar, West Fk. (R.), Ia.	115	42.49 N	93.10
Cedar Bayou, Tx.	125a	29.54 N	94.58
Cedar Breaks Natl. Mon., Ut.	121	37.35 N	112.55
Cedarbrook, Pa.	56b	40.05 N	75.10
Cedarburg, Wi. (sē′dẽr bûrg)	115	43.23 N	88.00
Cedar City, Ut.	121	37.40 N	113.10
Cedar Cr., ND	114	46.05 N	102.10
Cedar Falls, Ia.	115	42.31 N	92.29
Cedar Grove, NJ	55	40.51 N	74.14
Cedar Heights, Pa.	56b	40.05 N	75.17
Cedarhurst, NY	55	40.38 N	73.44
Cedar Keys, Fl.	126	29.06 N	83.03
Cedar L., In.	113a	41.23 N	87.25
Cedar Lake, In.	113a	41.22 N	87.27
Cedar Rapids, Ia.	115	42.00 N	91.43
Cedar Springs, Mi.	110	43.15 N	85.40
Cedartown, Ga. (sē′dẽr-toun)	126	34.00 N	85.15
Cedarville, S. Afr. (cēdȧr′vĭl)	227c	30.23 S	29.04
Cedral, Mex. (sā-dräl′)	130	23.47 N	100.42
Cedros, Hond. (sā′drōs)	132	14.36 N	87.07
Cedros (I.), Mex.	128	28.10 N	115.10
Ceduna, Austl. (sē-dōō′nȧ)	214	32.15 S	133.55
Ceel Buur, Som.	223a	4.35 N	46.40
Cefalù, It. (chā-fä-lōō′)	172	38.01 N	14.01
Cega (R.), Sp. (thā′gä)	170	41.25 N	4.27
Cegléd, Hung. (tsā′glād)	167	47.10 N	19.49
Ceglie, It. (chĕ′lyĕ)	173	40.39 N	17.32
Cehegín, Sp. (thā-å-hēn′)	170	38.05 N	1.48
Ceiba del Agua, Cuba (sā′bä-dĕl-ȧ′gwä)	135a	22.53 N	82.38
Cekhira, Tun.	224	34.17 N	10.00
Cela, Ang. (sĕ-lȧ)	230	11.25 S	15.07
Celaya, Mex. (sā-lä′yä)	130	20.33 N	100.49
Celebes (Sulawesi) (I.), Indon.	206	2.15 S	120.30
Celebes Sea, Indon.	206	3.45 N	121.52
Celestún, Mex. (sē-lĕs-tōō′n)	132a	20.57 N	90.18
Celina, Oh. (sēlī′na)	110	40.30 N	84.35
Celje, Yugo. (tsĕl′yĕ)	172	46.13 N	15.17
Celle, F.R.G. (tsĕl′ē)	166	52.37 N	10.05
Cement, Ok. (sē-mĕnt′)	122	34.56 N	98.07
Cenderawasih Teluk (B.), Indon.	207	2.20 S	135.30
Ceniza, Pico (Mtn.), Ven. (pē′kô-sē-nē′zä)	143b	10.24 N	67.26
Center, Tx. (sĕn′tẽr)	125	31.50 N	94.10
Centerhill Res., Tn. (sĕn′tẽr-hĭl)	126	36.02 N	86.00
Center Line, Mi. (sĕn′tẽr līn)	113b	42.29 N	83.01
Centerville, Ia. (sĕn′tẽr-vĭl)	115	40.44 N	92.48
Centerville, Mn.	119g	45.10 N	93.03
Centerville, Pa.	113e	40.02 N	79.58
Centerville, SD	114	43.07 N	96.56
Centerville, Ut.	119b	40.55 N	111.53
Centocelle (Neigh.), It.	66c	41.53 N	12.34
Central African Republic, Afr.	222	7.50 N	21.00
Central America, N. A. (ä-mĕr′ĭ-kȧ)	128	10.45 N	87.15
Central City, Ky. (sĕn′trȧl)	126	37.15 N	87.09
Central City, Ne. (sĕn′trȧl)	114	41.07 N	98.00
Central, Cordillera (Cibao Mts.), Dom. Rep. (kôr-dēl-yā′rȧ sĕn′träl) (sē-bä′ô)	135	19.05 N	71.30
Central, Cordillera (Mts.), Bol. (kôr-dēl-yĕ′rä-sĕn-trä′l)	142	19.18 S	65.29
Central, Cordillera (Mts.), Col.	142a	3.58 N	75.55
Central Cordillera (Mts.), Phil. (kôr-dēl-yĕ′rä-sĕn′träl)	207a	17.05 N	120.55
Central Falls, RI (sĕn′trȧl fôlz)	112b	41.54 N	71.23
Central Highlands, Pa.	57b	40.16 N	79.50
Centralia, Il. (sĕn-trā′lĭ-ȧ)	110	38.35 N	89.05
Centralia, Mo.	123	39.11 N	92.07
Centralia, Wa.	116	46.42 N	122.58
Central Intelligence Agency (P. Int.), Va.	56d	38.57 N	77.09
Central Park (P. Int.), NY	55	40.47 N	73.58
Central Plat, Sov. Un.	178	55.00 N	33.30
Central Valley, NY	112a	41.19 N	74.07
Centre Island, NY	55	40.54 N	73.32
Centreville, Il. (sĕn′tẽr-vĭl)	119e	38.33 N	90.06
Centreville, Md.	111	39.05 N	76.05
Centro Simón Bolívar (P. Int.), Ven.	61a	10.30 N	66.55
Century, Fl. (sĕn′tū-rĭ)	126	30.57 N	87.15
Century City (Neigh.), Ca.	59	34.03 N	118.26
Cephalonia (I.), **see Kefallinéa**			
Céret, Fr. (sā-rĕ′)	168	42.29 N	2.47

ăt; finăl; rāte; senåte; ärm; åsk; sofȧ; fâre; ch-choose; dh-as th in other; bē; ēvent; bĕt; recĕnt; cratẽr; g-gō; gh-guttural g; bĭt; ĭ-short neutral; rīde; ĸ-guttural k as ch in German ich;

PLACE (Pronounciation)	PAGE	Lat. °′	Long. °′
Cereté, Col. (sĕ-rĕ-tĕ′)	142	8.56 N	75.58 W
Cerignola, It. (chā-rē-nyô′lä)	172	41.16 N	15.55 E
Cerknica, Yugo. (tsĕr′knē-tsà)	172	45.48 N	14.21 E
Cern′achovsk, Sov. Un. (chĕr-nyä′kôfsk)	165	55.38 N	21.17 E
Čer′omuski (Neigh.), Sov. Un.	66b	55.41 N	37.35 E
Cerralvo, Mex. (sĕr-räl′vō)	124	26.05 N	99.37 W
Cerralvo (I.), Mex.	128	24.00 N	109.59 W
Cerrito, Col. (sĕr-rē′-tô)	142	3.41 N	76.17 W
Cerritos, Mex. (sĕr-rē′tôs)	130	22.26 N	100.16 W
Cerro de Pasco, Peru (sĕr′rō dā päs′kō)	142	10.45 S	76.14 W
Cerro Gordo, Arroyo de, Mex. (är-rô-yō-dĕ-sĕ′r-rō-gôr-dō)	124	26.12 N	104.06 W
Čertanovo (Neigh.), Sov. Un.	66b	55.38 N	37.37 E
Certegui, Col. (sĕr-tĕ′gē)	142a	5.21 N	76.35 W
Cervantes, Phil. (sĕr-vän′täs)	207a	16.59 N	120.42 E
Cervera del Río Alhama, Sp. (thĕr-vā′rä dĕl rē′ō-äl-ä′mä)	170	42.02 N	1.55 W
Cerveteri, It. (chĕr-vĕ′tĕ-rē)	171d	42.00 N	12.06 E
Cesano Boscone, It.	65c	45.27 N	9.06 E
Cesena, It. (chĕ′sĕ-nä)	172	44.08 N	12.16 E
Cēsis, Sov. Un. (sä′sĭs)	165	57.19 N	25.17 E
Česká Lípa, Czech. (chĕs′kä lē′pa)	166	50.41 N	14.31 E
České Budějovice, Czech. (chĕs′kā bōō′dyĕ-yô-vēt-sĕ)	166	49.00 N	14.30 E
Českomoravaska Vysočina (Mts.), Czech.	166	49.21 N	15.40 E
Český Těšín, Czech.	167	49.43 N	18.22 E
Cesme, Tur. (chĕsh′mĕ)	173	38.20 N	26.20 E
Cessnock, Austl.	216	32.58 S	151.15 E
Cestos (R.), Lib.	228	5.40 N	9.25 W
Cetinje, Yugo. (tsĕt′in-yĕ)	173	42.23 N	18.55 E
Ceuta (Sp.), Aft. (thā-ōō′tä)	224	36.04 N	5.36 W
Cévennes (Reg.), Fr. (sā-vĕn′)	168	44.20 N	3.48 E
Ceyhan (R.), Tur.	161	37.19 N	36.06 E
Ceylon, see Sri Lanka			
Chabot (L.), Ca. (sha′bŏt)	118b	37.44 N	122.06 W
Chacabuco, Arg. (chä-kä-bōō′kō)	141c	34.37 S	60.27 W
Chacaltianguis, Mex. (chä-käl-tē-äŋ′gwĕs)	131	18.18 N	95.50 W
Chacao, Ven.	61a	10.30 N	66.51 W
Chachapoyas, Peru (chä-chä-poi′yäs)	142	6.16 S	77.48 W
Chaco (Prov.), Arg. (chä′kō)	144	26.00 S	60.45 W
Chaco Canyon Natl. Mon., NM (chä′kô)	121	35.38 N	108.06 W
Chad, Afr.	222	17.48 N	19.00 E
Chad, Sov. Un. (chäd)	182a	56.33 N	57.11 E
Chadbourn, NC (chăd′bŭn)	127	34.19 N	78.55 W
Chadderton, Eng.	64b	53.33 N	2.08 W
Chad, L., Afr.	229	13.55 N	13.40 E
Chadron, Ne. (chăd′rŭn)	114	42.50 N	103.10 W
Chadstone, Austl.	70b	37.53 S	145.05 E
Chadwell Saint Mary, Eng.	62	51.29 N	0.22 E
Chafarinas (C.), Mor.	170	35.08 N	2.20 W
Chaffee, Mo. (chăf′ē)	123	37.10 N	89.39 W
Chāgal Hills, Afg.-Pak.	192	29.15 N	63.28 E
Chagodoshcha (R.), Sov. Un. (chä-gō-dôsh-chä)	174	59.08 N	35.13 E
Chagres R., Pan. (chä′grĕs)	133	9.18 N	79.22 W
Chagrin Falls, Oh. (shȧ′grĭn fôls)	113d	41.26 N	81.23 W
Chagrin R., Oh. (shȧ′grĭn)	113d	41.34 N	81.24 W
Chahar (Reg.), China (chä-här)	202	44.25 N	115.00 E
Chahār Borjak, Afg.	195	30.17 N	62.03 E
Chāh Bahār, Iran (chä′h′ bä′hăr)	192	25.18 N	60.45 E
Chakdaha, India	67a	22.20 N	88.20 E
Chake Chake, Tan.	231	5.15 S	39.46 E
Chalatenango, Sal. (chäl-ä-tĕ-näŋ′gō)	132	14.04 N	88.54 W
Chalbi Des., Ken.	231	3.40 N	36.50 E
Chalcatongo, Mex. (chäl-kä-tôŋ′gō)	131	17.04 N	97.41 W
Chalchihuites, Mex. (chäl-chē-wē′tăs)	130	23.28 N	103.57 W
Chalchuapa, Sal. (chäl-chwä′pä)	132	14.01 N	89.39 W
Chalchyn (R.), China-Mong. (chäl-chyn)	181	48.00 N	118.45 E
Chalco, Mex. (chäl-kō)	131a	19.15 N	98.54 W
Chaldon, Eng.	62	51.17 N	0.07 W
Chaleur B., Can. (shȧ-lûr′)	104	47.58 N	65.33 W
Chalfant, Pa.	57b	40.25 N	79.52 W
Chalfont Common, Eng.	62	51.38 N	0.33 W
Chalfont Saint Giles, Eng.	62	51.38 N	0.34 W
Chalfont Saint Peter, Eng.	62	51.37 N	0.33 W
Chalgrove, Eng. (chăl′grôv)	156b	51.38 N	1.05 W
Chaling, China (chä′lĭng)	203	27.00 N	113.31 E
Chalk, Eng.	62	51.26 N	0.25 E
Chalmette, La. (shăl-mĕt′)	112d	29.57 N	89.57 W
Châlons-sur-Marne, Fr. (shȧ-lôN′sür-märn)	168	48.57 N	4.23 E
Chalon-sur-Saône, Fr.	168	46.47 N	4.54 E
Chaltel, Cerro (Mtn.), Arg.-Chile (sĕ′r-rō-chäl′tĕl)	144	48.10 S	73.18 W
Chālūs, Iran	195	36.38 N	51.26 E
Chama (R.), NM (chä′mä)	121	36.19 N	106.31 W
Chamama, Malawi	231	12.55 S	33.43 E
Chaman, Pak. (chŭm-än′)	196	30.58 N	66.21 E
Chama, Sierra de (Mts.), Guat. (sē-ĕ′r-rä-dĕ-chä-mä)	132	15.48 N	90.20 W
Chambal (R.), India (chŭm-bäl′)	196	26.05 N	76.37 E
Chamberlain, SD (chäm′bĕr-lĭn)	114	43.48 N	99.21 W
Chamberlain (L.), Me.	104	46.15 N	69.10 W
Chambersburg, Pa. (chăm′bĕrz-bûrg)	111	40.00 N	77.40 W
Chambéry, Fr. (shäm-bā-rē′)	169	45.35 N	5.54 E
Chambeshi (R.), Zambia	231	10.35 S	31.20 E
Chamblee, Ga. (chăm-blē)	112c	33.55 N	84.18 W
Chambly, Can. (shäN-blē′)	95a	45.27 N	73.17 W
Chambly, Fr.	169b	49.11 N	2.14 E
Chambord, Can.	97	48.22 N	72.01 W
Chambourcy, Fr.	64c	48.54 N	2.03 E
Chamelecón (R.), Hond. (chä-mĕ-lĕ-kō′n)	132	15.09 N	88.42 W
Chame, Punta (Pt.), Pan. (pōō′n-tä-chä′mā)	133	8.41 N	79.27 W
Chamo (L.), Eth.	225	5.58 N	37.00 E
Chamonix-Mont-Blanc, Fr. (shȧ-mô-nē′)	169	45.55 N	6.50 E
Champagne (Reg.), Fr. (shäm-pän′yĕ)	168	48.53 N	4.48 E
Champaign, Il. (shăm-pān′)	110	40.10 N	88.15 W
Champdāni, India	196b	22.48 N	88.21 E
Champerico, Guat. (chäm-pā-rē′kō)	132	14.18 N	91.55 W
Champigny-sur-Marne, Fr.	64c	48.49 N	2.31 E
Champion, Mi. (chăm′pĭ-ŭn)	115	46.30 N	87.59 W
Champlain, L., NY-Vt. (shăm-plān′)	111	44.45 N	73.20 W
Champlan, Fr.	64c	48.43 N	2.16 E
Champlitte-et-le-Prálot, Fr. (shäN-plēt′)	169	47.38 N	5.28 E
Champotón, Mex. (chäm-pō-tōn′)	131	19.21 N	90.43 W
Champotón (R.), Mex.	131	19.19 N	90.15 W
Champs-sur-Marne, Fr.	64c	48.51 N	2.36 E
Chāmrāil, India	67a	22.38 N	88.18 E
Chañaral, Chile (chän-yä-räl′)	144	26.20 S	70.46 W
Chandannagar, India	67a	22.51 N	88.21 E
Chandeleur Is., La. (shăn-dē-lōōr′)	126	29.53 N	88.35 W
Chandeleur Sd., La.	126	29.47 N	89.08 W
Chandīgarh, India	196	30.51 N	77.13 E
Chandler, Can. (chăn′dlẽr)	97	48.21 N	64.41 W
Chandler, Ok.	123	35.42 N	96.52 W
Chandler's Cross, Eng.	62	51.40 N	0.27 W
Chandrapur, India	196	19.58 N	79.21 E
Chang (R.), see Yangtze			
Changane (R.), Moz.	226	22.42 S	32.46 E
Changara, Moz.	231	16.54 S	33.14 E
Changchun, China (chäŋ-chōōn)	202	43.55 N	125.25 E
Changdang Hu (L.), China (chäŋ-däŋ hōō)	200	31.37 N	119.29 E
Changde, China (chäŋ-dŭ)	203	29.00 N	111.38 E
Changdian, China	67b	40.01 N	116.32 E
Changhua, Taiwan (chäng′hwä′)	203	24.02 N	120.32 E
Changi, Singapore	67c	1.23 N	103.59 E
Changjŏn, Kor. (chäng′jŭn′)	204	38.40 N	128.05 E
Changli, China (chäŋ-lē)	200	39.46 N	119.10 E
Changning, China (chäŋ-nĭŋ)	198	24.34 N	99.49 E
Changping, China (chäŋ-pĭŋ)	202	40.12 N	116.10 E
Changqing, China (chäŋ-chyĭŋ)	200	36.33 N	116.42 E
Changsan Cot (I.), Kor.	204	38.06 N	124.50 E
Changsha, China (chäŋ-shä)	203	28.20 N	113.00 E
Changshan Quandao (Is.), China (chäŋ-shän chyōōn-dou)	200	39.08 N	122.26 E
Changshu, China (chäŋ-shōō)	200	31.40 N	120.45 E
Changting, China	203	25.50 N	116.18 E
Changtu, China	204	43.00 N	124.02 E
Changwu, China (chäng′wōō′)	202	35.12 N	107.45 E
Changxindianzhen, China (chäŋ-shyĭn-dĭĕn-jŭn)	202a	39.49 N	116.12 E
Changxing Dǎo (I.), China (chäŋ-shyĭŋ dou)	200	39.38 N	121.10 E
Changyi, China (chäŋ-yē)	200	36.51 N	119.23 E
Changyuan, China (chyäŋ-yuän)	200	35.10 N	114.41 E
Changzhi, China (chäŋ-jr)	202	35.58 N	112.58 E
Changzhou, China (chäŋ-jō)	200	31.47 N	119.56 E
Changzhuyuan, China (chäŋ-jōō-yuän)	200	31.33 N	115.17 E
Chanhassen, Mn. (shăn′hăs-sĕn)	119g	44.52 N	93.32 W
Chanh-hung, Viet.	68m	10.43 N	106.41 E
Channel Is., Eur. (chăn′ĕl)	154	49.15 N	3.30 W
Channel-Port-auz-Basques, Can.	105	47.35 N	59.11 W
Channelview, Tx. (chăn′elvū)	125a	29.46 N	95.07 W
Chantada, Sp. (chän-tä′dä)	170	42.38 N	7.36 W
Chanteloup-les-Vignes, Fr.	64c	48.59 N	2.02 E
Chanthaburi, Thai.	206	12.37 N	102.04 E
Chantilly, Fr. (shäN-tē-yē′)	169b	49.12 N	2.30 E
Chantilly, Va. (shăn′tĭlē)	112e	38.53 N	77.26 W
Chantrey Inlet, Can. (chăn-trē)	96	67.49 N	95.00 W
Chanute, Ks. (shȧ-nōōt′)	123	37.41 N	95.27 W
Chany (L.), Sov. Un. (chä′nē)	180	54.15 N	77.31 E
Chao′an, China (chou-än)	203	23.48 N	116.35 E
Chao Hu (L.), China (chou hōō)	200	31.31 N	117.28 E
Chao Hu (L.), China	203	31.45 N	116.59 E
Chao Phraya, (R.), Thai.	206	16.13 N	99.33 E
Chaor (R.), China (chou-r)	202	47.20 N	121.40 E
Chaoshui, China (chou-shwā)	200	37.43 N	120.56 E
Chaoxian, China (chou shyĕn)	200	31.37 N	117.50 E
Chaoyang, China	202	41.32 N	120.20 E
Chaoyang, China (chou-yäŋ)	203	23.18 N	116.32 E
Chapadão, Serra do (Mtn.), Braz. (sĕ′r-rä-dô-shä-pä-dou′N)	141a	20.31 S	46.20 W
Chapada, Serra da (Mts.), Braz. (sĕ′r-rä-dä-shä-pä′dä)	143	14.57 S	54.34 W
Chapala, Mex. (chä-pä′lä)	130	20.18 N	103.10 W
Chapalagana (R.), Mex. (chä-pä-lä-gä′nä)	130	22.11 N	104.09 W
Chapala, Lago de (L.), Mex. (lä′gô-dĕ-chä-pä′lä)	130	20.14 N	103.02 W
Chaparral, Col. (chä-pär-rä′l)	142a	3.44 N	75.28 W
Chapayevsk, Sov. Un. (chá-pī′ĕfsk)	179	53.00 N	49.30 E
Chapel Hill, NC (chăp′′l hĭl)	127	35.55 N	79.05 W
Chapel Oaks, Md.	56d	38.54 N	76.55 W
Chapeltown, Eng.	64b	53.38 N	2.24 W
Chaplain (L.), Wa. (chăp′lĭn)	118a	47.58 N	121.50 W
Chapleau, Can. (chăp-lō′)	97	47.43 N	83.28 W
Chapman, Mt., Can. (chăp′măn)	99	51.50 N	118.20 W
Chapman's B., S. Afr. (chăp′măns bä)	226a	34.06 S	18.17 E
Chapman Woods, Ca.	59	34.08 N	118.05 W
Chappell, Ne. (chă-pĕl′)	114	41.06 N	102.29 W
Chapultenango, Mex. (chä-pōōl-tē-näŋ′gō)	131	17.19 N	93.08 W
Chapultepec, Castillo de (P. Int.), Mex.	60a	19.25 N	99.11 W
Chá Pungana, Ang.	230	13.44 S	18.39 E
Charcas, Mex. (chär′käs)	130	23.09 N	101.09 W
Charco de Azul, Bahía (B.), Pan. (bä-ē′ä-chä′r-kô-dĕ-ä-zōō′l)	133	8.14 N	82.45 W
Chardzhou, Sov. Un. (chĕr-jô′ōō)	155	38.52 N	63.37 E
Charente (R.), Fr. (shȧ-räNt′)	168	45.48 N	0.28 W
Charenton-le-Pont, Fr.	64c	48.49 N	2.25 E
Chari (R.), Chad (shä-rē′)	229	12.45 N	14.55 E
Charing, Eng. (chă′rĭng)	156b	51.13 N	0.49 E
Chariton, Ia. (châr′ĭ-tŭn)	115	41.02 N	93.16 W
Chariton (R.), Mo.	123	40.24 N	92.38 W
Charlemagne, Can. (shärl-mäny′)	95a	45.43 N	73.29 W
Charleroi, Bel. (shȧr-lē-rwä′)	163	50.25 N	4.35 E
Charleroi, Pa. (shär′lē-roi)	113e	40.08 N	79.54 W
Charles (R.), Ma.	54a	42.22 N	71.03 W
Charlesbourg, Can. (shärl-bōōr′)	95b	46.51 N	71.16 W
Charles, C., Va. (chärlz)	127	37.05 N	75.48 W
Charles City, Ia. (chärlz)	115	43.03 N	92.40 W
Charles de Gaulle, Aéroport (Arpt.), Fr.	64c	49.00 N	2.34 E
Charleston, Il. (chärlz′tŭn)	110	39.30 N	88.10 W
Charleston, Mo.	123	36.53 N	89.20 W
Charleston, Ms.	126	34.00 N	90.02 W
Charleston, SC	127	32.47 N	79.56 W
Charleston, WV	110	38.20 N	81.35 W
Charlestown, In. (chärlz′toun)	113h	38.46 N	85.39 W
Charlestown, Saint Christopher-Nevis	133b	17.10 N	62.32 W
Charleville, Austl. (chär′lē-vĭl)	216	26.16 S	146.28 E
Charleville Mézières, Fr. (shärl-vēl′)	168	49.48 N	4.41 E
Charlevoix, Mi. (shär′lē-voi)	110	45.20 N	85.15 W
Charlevoix, L., Mi.	115	45.17 N	85.43 W
Charlotte, Mi. (shär′lŏt)	110	42.35 N	84.50 W
Charlotte, NC	127	35.15 N	80.50 W
Charlotte Amalie (Saint Thomas), Virgin Is. (U.S.A.) (shär-lŏt′ĕ ä-mä′lĭ-ȧ)	129c	18.21 N	64.54 W
Charlotte Hbr., Fl.	127a	26.49 N	82.00 W
Charlotte L., Can.	98	52.07 N	125.30 W
Charlottenberg, Swe. (shär-lŭt′ĕn-bĕrg)	164	59.53 N	12.17 E
Charlottenburg (Neigh.), F.R.G.	65a	52.31 N	13.16 E
Charlottenburg, Schloss (P. Int.), G.D.R.	65a	52.31 N	13.14 E
Charlottesville, Va. (shär′lŏtz-vĭl)	111	38.00 N	78.25 W
Charlottetown, Can. (shär′lŏt-toun)	105	46.14 N	63.08 W
Charlotte Waters, Austl. (shär′lŏt)	214	26.00 S	134.50 E
Charlton (Neigh.), Eng.	62	51.29 N	0.02 E
Charmes, Fr. (shärm)	169	48.23 N	6.19 E
Charneca (Neigh.), Port.	65d	38.47 N	9.08 W
Charnwood For., Eng. (chärn′wŏŏd)	156	52.42 N	1.15 W
Charny, Can. (shär-nē′)	95b	46.43 N	71.16 W
Chars, Fr. (shär)	169b	49.09 N	1.57 E
Chārsadda, Pak. (chŭr-sä′dä)	193a	34.17 N	71.43 E
Charters Towers, Austl. (chär′tẽrz)	215	20.03 S	146.20 E
Charterwood, Pa.	57b	40.33 N	80.00 W
Chartres, Fr. (shärt′r′)	169b	48.26 N	1.29 E
Chascomús, Arg. (chäs-kō-mōōs′)	141c	35.32 S	58.01 W
Chase City, Va. (chās)	127	36.45 N	78.27 W
Chashniki, Sov. Un. (chäsh′nyē-kē)	174	54.51 N	29.08 E
Chaska, Mn. (chăs′kȧ)	119g	44.48 N	93.36 W
Châteaubriant, Fr. (shȧ-tō-brē-äN′)	168	47.43 N	1.23 W
Châteaudun, Fr. (shȧ-tō-däN′)	168	48.04 N	1.23 E
Châteaufort, Fr.	64c	48.44 N	2.06 E
Château-Gontier, Fr. (chȧ-tō′gôN′tyā′)	168	47.48 N	0.43 W
Châteauguay, Can. (chȧ-tō-gā)	95a	45.22 N	73.45 W
Châteauguay (R.), Can.	95a	45.13 N	73.51 W
Châteauneaut, Fr.	168a	43.23 N	5.11 E
Château-Renault, Fr. (shȧ-tō-rē-nō′)	168	47.36 N	0.57 E
Château-Richer, Can. (shȧ-tō′rē-shā′)	95b	47.00 N	71.01 W
Châteauroux, Fr. (shȧ-tō-rōō′)	168	46.47 N	1.39 E
Château-Thierry, Fr. (shȧ-tō′ty-ĕr-rē′)	168	49.03 N	3.22 E
Châtellerault, Fr. (shȧ-tĕl-rō′)	168	46.48 N	0.31 E
Châtenay-Malabry, Fr.	64c	48.46 N	2.17 E
Chatfield, Mn. (chăt′fēld)	115	43.50 N	92.10 W
Chatham, Can. (chăt′ăm)	102	42.25 N	82.10 W
Chatham, Can.	104	47.02 N	65.28 W
Chatham, Eng. (chăt′ŭm)	156b	51.23 N	0.32 E
Chatham, NJ (chăt′ăm)	112a	40.44 N	74.23 W
Chatham, Oh.	113d	41.06 N	82.01 W
Chatham Is., N. Z.	208	44.00 S	178.00 W
Chatham Sd., Can.	98	54.32 N	130.35 W
Chatham Str., Ak.	107	57.00 N	134.40 W
Châtillon, Fr.	64c	48.48 N	2.17 E
Chatou, Fr.	64c	48.54 N	2.09 E
Chatpur (Neigh.), India	67a	22.36 N	88.23 E
Chatswood, Austl.	70a	33.48 S	151.12 E
Chatsworth, Ca. (chătz′wûrth)	119a	34.16 N	118.36 W
Chatsworth Res., Ca.	119a	34.15 N	118.41 W
Chattahoochee, Fl. (chăt-tȧ-hōō′ chē)	126	30.42 N	84.47 W
Chattahoochee (R.), Al.-Ga.	126	31.17 N	85.10 W
Chattanooga, Tn. (chăt-ȧ-nōō′gȧ)	126	35.01 N	85.15 W
Chattooga (R.), Ga.-SC (chă-tōō′gȧ)	126	34.47 N	83.13 W
Chaudière (R.), Can. (shō-dyĕr′)	103	46.26 N	71.10 W
Chaumont, Fr. (shō-môN′)	168	48.08 N	5.07 E
Chaunskaya Guba (B.), Sov. Un.	181	69.15 N	170.00 E
Chauny, Fr. (shō-nē′)	168	49.40 N	3.09 E
Chau-phu, Kamp.	206	10.49 N	104.57 E
Chausy, Sov. Un. (chou′sĭ)	174	53.57 N	30.58 E
Chautauqua (L.), NY (shȧ-tô′kwȧ)	111	42.10 N	79.25 W
Chavaniga, Sov. Un.	178	66.02 N	37.50 E
Chavenay, Fr.	64c	48.51 N	1.59 E
Chaves, Port. (chä′vĕzh)	170	41.44 N	7.30 W
Chaville, Fr.	64c	48.48 N	2.10 E
Chavinda, Mex. (chä-vē′n-dä)	130	20.01 N	102.27 W
Chazumba, Mex. (chä-zōōm′bä)	131	18.11 N	97.41 W
Cheadle, Eng. (chē′d′l)	156	52.59 N	1.59 W
Cheadle Hulme, Eng.	64b	53.22 N	2.12 W
Cheam (Neigh.), Eng.	62	51.21 N	0.13 W
Cheat R.), WV (chēt)	111	39.35 N	79.40 W
Cheb, Czech. (kĕb)	166	50.05 N	12.23 E

PLACE (Pronounciation)	PAGE	Lat. °′	Long. °′
Chebarkul, Sov. Un. (chĕ-bár-kûl')	182a	54.59 N	60.22 E
Cheboksary, Svo. Un. (chyĕ-bôk-sä'rĕ)	178	56.00 N	47.20 E
Cheboygan, Mi. (shḗ-boi'găn)	110	45.40 N	84.30 W
Chechen' (I.), Sov. Un. (chyĕch'ĕn)	179	44.00 N	48.10 E
Chech, Erg (Dune), Alg.	224	24.45 N	2.07 W
Checotah, Ok. (chḗ-kō'tȧ)	123	35.27 N	95.32 W
Chedabucto B., Can. (chĕd-ȧ-bŭk-tō)	105	45.23 N	61.10 W
Cheduba I., Bur.	206	18.45 N	93.01 E
Cheecham Hills, Can. (chēē'hăm)	100	56.20 N	111.10 W
Cheektowaga, NY (chēk-tō-wä'gȧ)	113c	42.54 N	78.46 W
Cheetham Hill (Neigh.), Eng.	64b	53.31 N	2.15 W
Chefoo, see Yantai			
Chegutu, Zimb	231	18.18 S	30.10 E
Chehalis, Wa. (chḗ-hā'lĭs)	116	46.39 N	122.58 W
Chehalis R., Wa.	116	46.47 N	123.17 W
Cheju, Kor. (chĕ'jōō')	204	33.29 N	126.40 E
Cheju (Quelpart) (I.), Kor.	204	33.20 N	126.25 E
Chekalin, Sov. Un. (chĕ-kä'lĭn)	174	54.05 N	36.13 E
Chelan (L.), Wa.	116	48.09 N	120.20 W
Chelan, Wa. (chḗ-lăn')	116	47.51 N	119.59 W
Chelas (Neigh.), Port.	65d	38.45 N	9.07 W
Chela, Serra da (Mts.), Ang. (sĕr'rȧ dä shā'lȧ)	226	15.30 S	13.30 E
Cheleiros, Port. (shĕ-la'rōzh)	171b	38.54 N	9.19 W
Chéliff (R.), Alg. (shā-lēf)	171	36.17 N	1.22 E
Chelkar (L.), Sov. Un.	179	50.30 N	51.30 E
Chelkar, Sov. Un. (chyĕl'kär)	180	47.52 N	59.41 E
Chelkar Tengiz (L.), Sov. Un. (chyĕl'kär tĕn'yēz)	180	47.42 N	61.45 E
Chelles, Fr.	64c	48.53 N	2.36 E
Chelm, Pol. (ĸĕlm)	167	51.08 N	23.30 E
Chelmno, Pol. (ĸĕlm'nō)	167	53.20 N	18.25 E
Chelmsford, Can.	102	46.35 N	81.12 W
Chelmsford, Eng. (chĕlm's-fērd)	156b	51.44 N	0.28 E
Chelmsford, Ma.	105a	42.36 N	71.21 W
Chelsea, Al. (chĕl'sḗ)	112h	33.20 N	86.38 W
Chelsea, Austl.	211a	38.05 S	145.08 E
Chelsea, Can.	95c	45.30 N	75.46 W
Chelsea, Ma.	105a	42.23 N	71.02 W
Chelsea, Mi.	110	42.20 N	84.00 W
Chelsea, Ok.	123	36.32 N	95.23 W
Cheltenham, Eng. (chĕlt'nŭm)	162	51.57 N	2.06 W
Cheltenham, Md. (chĕltĕn-hăm)	112e	38.45 N	76.50 W
Chelva, Sp. (chĕl'vä)	171	39.43 N	1.00 W
Chelyabinsk, Sov. Un. (chĕl-yä-bḗnsk')	182a	55.10 N	61.25 E
Chelyuskin, Mys (C.), Sov. Un. (chĕl-yōōs'-kĭn)	181	77.45 N	104.45 E
Chemba, Moz.	231	17.08 S	34.52 E
Chembūr (Neigh.), India	67e	19.04 N	72.54 E
Chemillé, Fr. (shē-mē-yā')	168	47.13 N	0.46 W
Chemnitz, see Karl-Marx-Stadt			
Chemung (R.), NY (shḗ-mŭng)	111	42.20 N	77.25 W
Chenāb (R.), Pak. (chḗ-näb)	196	31.33 N	72.28 E
Chenachane, Alg. (shē-ná-shän')	224	26.14 N	4.14 W
Chencun, China (chŭn-tsōōn)	201a	22.58 N	113.14 E
Cheney, Wa. (chē'nā)	116	47.29 N	117.34 W
Chengde, China (chŭŋ-dŭ)	202	40.50 N	117.50 E
Chengdong Hu (L.), China (chŭŋ-dôŋ hōō)	200	32.22 N	116.32 E
Chengdu, China (chŭŋ-dōō)	203	30.30 N	104.10 E
Chenggu, China (chŭŋ-gōō)	202	33.05 N	107.25 E
Chenghai, China (chŭŋ-hī)	203	23.22 N	116.40 E
Chĕn, Gora (Mtn.), Sov. Un.	181	65.13 N	142.12 E
Chengshan Jiao (C.), China (jyou chŭŋ-shän)	202	37.28 N	122.40 E
Chengxi Hu (L.), China (chŭŋ-shyē hōō)	200	32.31 N	116.04 E
Chenies, Eng.	62	51.41 N	0.32 W
Chennevières, Fr.	64c	49.00 N	2.07 E
Chenxian, China (chŭn-shyĕn)	203	25.40 N	113.00 E
Chepén, Peru (chĕ-pĕ'n)	142	7.17 S	79.24 W
Chepo, Pan. (chā'pō)	133	9.12 N	79.06 W
Chepo R., Pan.	133	9.10 N	78.36 W
Cher (R.), Fr. (shâr)	168	47.14 N	1.34 E
Cherán, Mex. (chā-rän')	130	19.41 N	101.54 W
Cherangany Hills, Ken.	231	1.25 N	35.20 E
Cheraw, SC (chē'rô)	127	34.40 N	79.52 W
Cherbourg, Fr. (shär-bōōr')	168	49.39 N	1.43 W
Cherchell, Alg. (shĕr-shĕl')	224	36.38 N	2.09 E
Cherdyn', Sov. Un. (chĕr-dyēn')	178	60.25 N	56.32 E
Cheremkhovo, Sov. Un. (chĕr'yĕm-kô-vō)	180	52.58 N	103.18 E
Cherëmukhovo, Sov. Un. (chĕr-yĕ-mû-kô-vō)	182a	60.20 N	60.00 E
Cherepanovo, Sov. Un. (chĕr'yĕ pä-nô'vō)	180	54.13 N	83.18 E
Cherepovets, Sov. Un. (chĕr-yĕ-pô'vyĕtz)	174	59.08 N	37.59 E
Chereya, Sov. Un. (chĕr-ā'yä)	174	54.38 N	29.16 E
Chergui (I.), Tun.	160	34.50 N	11.40 E
Chergui, Chott ech (L.), Alg. (chĕr gē)	160	34.12 N	0.10 W
Cherikov, Sov. Un. (chĕ'rē-kôf)	174	53.34 N	31.22 E
Cherkassy (Oblast), Sov. Un.	175	48.58 N	30.55 E
Cherkassy, Sov. Un. (chĕr-kä'sĭ)	175	49.26 N	32.03 E
Cherlak, Sov. Un. (chĭr-läk')	180	54.04 N	74.28 E
Chermoz, Sov. Un. (chĕr-môz')	182a	58.47 N	56.08 E
Chern', Sov. Un. (chĕrn)	174	53.28 N	36.49 E
Chërnaya Kalitva (R.), Sov. Un. (chôr'nȧ yȧ kȧ-lēt'vȧ)	175	50.15 N	39.16 E
Chernigov (Oblast), Sov. Un. (chĕr-nē'gôf)	175	51.23 N	31.15 E
Chernigov, Sov. Un. (chĕr-nē'gôf)	175	51.28 N	31.18 E
Chernigovka, Sov. Un.	175	47.08 N	36.20 E
Chernobay, Sov. Un. (chĕr-nō-bī')	175	49.41 N	32.24 E
Chernobyl', Sov. Un. (chĕr-nō-bĭl')	175	51.17 N	30.14 E
Chernogorsk, Sov. Un. (chĕr-nŏ-gôrsk')	180	54.01 N	91.07 E
Chernoistochinsk, Sov. Un. (chĕr-nôy-stô'chĭnsk)	182a	57.44 N	59.55 E
Chĕrnomorskoye, Sov. Un. (chĕr-nô-môr'skô-yĕ)	175	45.29 N	32.43 E
Chernovtsy (Cernăuti), Sov. Un. (chĭr-nôf'tsē) (chĕr-nou'tsḗ)	167	48.18 N	25.56 E
Chernyanka, Sov. Un. (chĕrn-yäŋ'kä)	175	50.56 N	37.48 E
Cherokee, Ia. (chĕr-ô-kē')	114	42.43 N	95.33 W
Cherokee, Ks.	123	37.21 N	94.50 W
Cherokee, Ok.	122	36.44 N	98.22 W
Cherokee (L.), Tn.	126	36.22 N	83.22 W
Cherokee Indian Res., NC	126	35.33 N	83.12 W
Cherokees, L. of the, Ok. (chĕr-ô-kēz')	123	36.32 N	95.14 W
Cherokee Sound Ba.	134	26.15 N	76.55 W
Cherry City, Pa.	57b	40.29 N	79.58 W
Cherryfield, Me. (chĕr'ĭ-fēld)	104	44.37 N	67.56 W
Cherry Grove, Or.	118c	45.27 N	123.15 W
Cherry Hill (Neigh.), Md.	56c	39.15 N	76.38 W
Cherry Hill, NJ	56b	39.55 N	75.01 W
Cherryvale, Ks.	123	37.16 N	95.33 W
Cherryville, NC (chĕr'ĭ-vĭl)	127	35.32 N	81.22 W
Cherskogo, Khrebet (Mts.), Sov. Un.	181	66.15 N	138.30 E
Chertsey, Eng.	62	51.24 N	0.30 W
Cherven', Sov. Un. (chĕr'vyĕn)	174	53.43 N	28.26 E
Chervonoye (L.), Sov. Un. (chĕr-vô'nô-yĕ)	174	52.24 N	28.12 E
Chesaning, Mi. (chĕs'ȧ-nĭng)	110	43.10 N	84.10 W
Chesapeake, Va. (chĕs'â-pēk)	112g	36.48 N	76.16 W
Chesapeake B., Md.	111	38.20 N	76.15 W
Chesapeake Beach, Md.	112e	38.42 N	76.33 W
Chesham, Eng. (chĕsh'ŭm)	156b	51.41 N	0.37 W
Chesham Bois, Eng.	62	51.41 N	0.37 W
Cheshire (Co.), Eng.	156	53.16 N	2.30 W
Cheshire, Mi. (chĕsh'ĭr)	110	42.25 N	86.00 W
Chëshskaya Guba (B.), Sov. Un.	178	67.25 N	46.00 E
Cheshunt, Eng.	62	51.43 N	0.02 W
Chesma, Sov. Un. (chĕs'mȧ)	182a	53.50 N	60.42 E
Chesnokovka, Sov. Un. (chĕs-nŏ-kôf'kȧ)	180	53.28 N	83.41 E
Chessington (Neigh.), Eng.	62	51.21 N	0.18 W
Chester, Eng. (chĕs'tēr)	156	53.12 N	2.53 W
Chester, Il.	123	37.54 N	89.48 W
Chester, Pa.	56b	39.51 N	75.21 W
Chester, Pa.	112f	39.51 N	75.22 W
Chester, SC	127	34.42 N	81.11 W
Chester, Va.	127	37.20 N	77.24 W
Chester, WV	110	40.35 N	80.30 W
Chesterbrook, Va.	56d	38.55 N	77.09 W
Chesterfield, Eng. (chĕs'tēr-fēld)	156	53.14 N	1.26 W
Chesterfield (Inlet), Can.	96	63.59 N	92.09 W
Chesterfield, Iles, N. Cal.	215	19.38 S	160.08 E
Chesterfield Inlet, Can.	96	63.19 N	91.11 W
Chestermere L., Can. (chĕs'tē-mēr)	95e	51.03 N	113.45 W
Chesterton, In. (chĕs'tēr-tŭn)	110	41.35 N	87.05 W
Chestertown, Md. (chĕs'tēr-toun)	111	39.15 N	76.05 W
Chestnut Hill, Ma.	54a	42.20 N	71.10 W
Chestnut Hill, Md.	56c	39.17 N	76.47 W
Chesuncook (L.), Me. (chĕs'ŭn-kŏŏk)	104	46.03 N	69.40 W
Cheswick, Pa.	57b	40.32 N	79.47 W
Chetek, Wi. (chĕ'tĕk)	115	45.18 N	91.41 W
Chetumal, Bahia de (B.), Belize (bä-ē-ä dĕ chĕt-ōō-mäl')	132a	18.07 N	88.05 W
Chevelon Cr., Az. (shĕv'ȧ-lŏn)	121	34.35 N	111.00 W
Chevening, Eng.	62	51.18 N	0.08 E
Cheverly, Md.	56d	38.55 N	76.55 W
Chevilly-Larue, Fr.	64c	48.46 N	2.21 E
Cheviot, Oh. (shĕv'ĭ-ŭt)	113f	39.10 N	84.37 W
Chevreuse, Fr. (shĕ-vrûz')	169b	48.42 N	2.02 E
Chevy Chase, Md. (shĕvĭ chās)	112e	38.58 N	77.06 W
Chevy Chase View, Md.	56d	39.01 N	77.05 W
Chew Bahir (Lake Stefanie), Eth. (stĕf-a-nē)	225	4.46 N	37.31 E
Chewelah, Wa. (chē-wē'lä)	116	48.17 N	117.42 W
Cheyenne (R.), SD	114	44.20 N	102.15 W
Cheyenne, Wy. (shī-ĕn')	114	41.10 N	104.49 W
Cheyenne River Ind. Res., SD	114	45.07 N	100.46 W
Cheyenne Wells, Co.	122	38.46 N	102.21 W
Chhalera Bāngar, India	67d	28.33 N	77.20 E
Chhināmor, India	67a	22.48 N	88.18 E
Chhindwāra, India	196	22.08 N	78.57 E
Chiai, Taiwan (chī'ī')	203	23.28 N	120.28 E
Chiang Mai, Thai.	198	18.38 N	98.44 E
Chiang Rai, Thai.	206	19.53 N	99.48 E
Chiange, Ang.	230	15.45 S	13.48 E
Chiapa de Corzo, Mex. (chḗ-ä'pä dā kôr'zō)	131	16.44 N	93.01 W
Chiapa, Rio de (R.), Mex. (rē'ō-dĕ-chḗ-ä'pä)	132	16.00 N	92.20 W
Chiapas (State), Mex. (chḗ-ä'päs)	128	17.10 N	93.00 W
Chiapas, Cordilla de (Mts.), Mex. (kôr-dēl-yĕ'rä-dĕ-chyȧ'räs)	131	15.55 N	93.15 W
Chiari, It. (kyä'rē)	172	45.31 N	9.57 E
Chiasso, Switz.	166	45.50 N	8.57 E
Chiautla, Mex. (chyä-ōōt'lȧ)	130	18.16 N	98.37 W
Chiavari, It. (kyä-vä'rē)	172	44.18 N	9.21 E
Chiba, Jap. (chē'bȧ)	205a	35.37 N	140.08 E
Chiba (Pref.), Jap.	205a	35.47 N	140.02 E
Chibougamau, Can. (chē-bōō'gä-mou)	103	49.57 N	74.23 W
Chibougamau (L.), Can.	103	49.53 N	74.21 W
Chicago, Il. (shĭ-kô-gō) (chĭ-kä'gō)	113a	41.49 N	87.37 W
Chicago Heights, Il.	113a	41.30 N	87.38 W
Chicago Lawn (Neigh.), Il.	58a	41.47 N	87.41 W
Chicago, North Branch (R.), Il.	58a	41.53 N	87.38 W
Chicago-O'Hare International Arpt., Il.	58a	41.59 N	87.54 W
Chicago Ridge, Il.	58a	41.42 N	87.47 W
Chicago Sanitary and Ship Canal (Can.), Il.	58a	41.42 N	87.58 W
Chicapa (R.), Ang. (chē-kä'pä)	230	7.45 S	20.25 E
Chicbul, Mex. (chēk-bōō'l)	131	18.45 N	90.56 W
Chic-Chocs, Mts., Can.	104	48.38 N	66.37 W
Chichagof (I.), Ak. (chḗ-chä'gôf)	107	57.50 N	137.00 W
Chichâncanab, Lago de (L.), Mex. (lä'gô-dĕ-chē-chän-kä-nä'b)	132a	19.50 N	88.28 W
Chichen Itzá (Ruins), Mex. (chē-chĕ'n-ē-tsä')	132a	20.38 N	88.35 W
Chichester, Eng. (chĭch'ĕs-tēr)	162	50.50 N	0.55 W
Chichimila, Mex. (chē-chē-mḗ'lä)	132a	20.36 N	88.14 W
Chichiriviche, Ven. (chē-chē-rē-vē-chĕ)	143b	10.56 N	68.17 W
Chickamauga, Ga. (chĭk-ȧ-mô'gȧ)	126	34.50 N	85.15 W
Chickamauga, (L.), Tn.	126	35.18 N	85.22 W
Chickasawhay (R.), Ms. (chĭk-ȧ-sô'wā)	126	31.45 N	88.45 W
Chickasha, Ok. (chĭk'ȧ-shā)	122	35.04 N	97.56 W
Chiclana de la Frontera, Sp. (chḗ-klä'nä)	170	36.25 N	6.09 W
Chiclayo, Peru (chḗ-klä'yō)	142	6.46 S	79.50 W
Chico, Ca. (chē'kō)	120	39.43 N	121.51 W
Chico (R.), Arg.	144	44.30 S	66.00 W
Chico (R.), Arg.	144	49.15 S	69.30 W
Chico (R.), Phil.	207a	17.33 N	121.24 E
Chico, Wa.	118a	47.37 N	122.43 W
Chicoa, Moz.	231	15.37 S	32.24 E
Chicoloapan, Mex. (chḗ-kō-lwä'pän)	131a	19.24 N	98.54 W
Chiconautla, Mex. (chḗ-kō-nä-ōō'tlȧ)	131a	19.39 N	99.01 W
Chicontepec, Mex. (chḗ-kōn'tē-pĕk')	130	20.58 N	98.08 W
Chicopee, Ma. (chĭk'ô-pē)	111	42.10 N	72.35 W
Chicoutimi, Can. (shē-kōō'tē-mē')	103	48.26 N	71.04 W
Chicxulub, Mex. (chēk-sōō-lōō'b)	132a	21.10 N	89.30 W
Chidley, C., Can. (chĭd'lĭ)	97	60.32 N	63.56 W
Chief Joseph Dam, Wa.	116	48.00 N	119.39 W
Chiefland, Fl. (chēf'lȧnd)	126	29.30 N	82.50 W
Chiemsee (L.), F.R.G. (ĸēm zā)	166	47.58 N	12.20 E
Chieri, It. (kyâ'rē)	172	45.03 N	7.48 E
Chieti, It. (kyĕ'tē)	172	42.22 N	14.22 E
Chifeng (Ulanhad), China (chr-fŭŋ)	202	42.18 N	118.52 E
Chigirin, Sov. Un. (chḗ-gē'rĕn)	175	49.02 N	32.39 E
Chignall Saint James, Eng.	62	51.46 N	0.25 E
Chignanuapan, Mex. (chē'g-ŋä-nwä-pá'n)	130	19.49 N	98.02 W
Chignecto B., Can. (shĭg-nĕk'tō)	104	45.33 N	64.50 W
Chignik, Ak. (chĭg'nĭk)	107	56.14 N	158.12 W
Chignik B., Ak.	107	56.18 N	157.22 W
Chigu Co (L.), China (chr-gōō tswo)	196	28.55 N	91.47 E
Chigwell, Eng.	62	51.38 N	0.05 E
Chigwell Row, Eng.	62	51.37 N	0.07 E
Chihe, China (chr-hŭ)	200	32.32 N	117.57 E
Chihuahua, Mex. (chḗ-wä'wä)	124	28.37 N	106.06 W
Chihuahua (State), Mex.	128	29.00 N	107.30 W
Chikishlyar, Sov. Un. (chḗ-kēsh-lyär')	179	37.40 N	53.50 E
Chilanga, Zambia	231	15.34 S	28.17 E
Chilapa, Mex. (chḗ-lä'pä)	130	17.34 N	99.14 W
Chilchota, Mex. (chēl-chō'tä)	130	19.40 N	102.04 W
Chilcotin (R.), Can. (chĭl-kō'tĭn)	98	52.20 N	124.15 W
Childer Thornton, Eng.	64a	53.17 N	2.57 W
Childress, Tx. (chĭld'rĕs)	122	34.26 N	100.11 W
Chile, S.A. (chē'lā)	140	35.00 S	72.00 W
Chilecito, Arg. (chē-lȧ-sē'tō)	144	29.06 S	67.25 W
Chilengue, Serra do (Mts.), Ang.	230	13.20 S	15.00 E
Chilibre, Pan. (chē-lḗ'brĕ)	128a	9.09 N	79.37 W
Chililabombwe (Bancroft), Zambia	231	12.18 S	27.43 E
Chilí, Pico de (Pk.), Col. (pē'kô-dĕ chē-lḗ')	142a	4.14 N	75.38 W
Chilka (L.), India	196	19.26 N	85.42 E
Chilko (R.), Can. (chĭl'kō)	98	51.53 N	123.53 W
Chilko L., Can.	98	51.20 N	124.05 W
Chillán, Chile (chēl-yän')	144	36.44 S	72.06 W
Chillicothe, Il. (chĭl-ĭ-kŏth'ḗ)	110	41.55 N	89.30 W
Chillicothe, Mo.	123	39.46 N	93.32 W
Chillicothe, Oh.	110	39.20 N	83.00 W
Chilliwack, Can. (chĭl'ĭ-wăk)	99	49.10 N	121.57 W
Chillum, Md.	56d	38.58 N	76.59 W
Chilly-Mazarin, Fr.	64c	48.42 N	2.19 E
Chiloé, Isla de (I.), Chile (ḗ's-lä-dĕ-chē-lō-ā')	144	43.00 S	75.00 W
Chilpancingo, Mex. (chēl-pän-sēŋ'gō)	130	17.32 N	99.30 W
Chilton, Wi. (chĭl'tŭn)	115	44.00 N	88.12 W
Chilung (Kirin), Taiwan (chĭ'lung)	203	25.02 N	121.48 E
Chilwa, L. Malawi-Moz.	231	15.12 S	36.30 E
Chimacum, Wa. (chĭm'ä-kŭm)	118a	48.01 N	122.47 W
Chimalpa, Mex. (chē-mäl'pä)	131a	19.26 N	99.22 W
Chimaltenango, Guat. (chḗ-mäl-tȧ-näŋ'gō)	132	14.39 N	90.48 W
Chimaltitan, Mex. (chḗmäl-tē-tän')	130	21.36 N	103.50 W
Chimbay, Sov. Un. (chĭm-bī')	155	43.00 N	59.44 E
Chimborazo (Mtn.), Ec. (chḗm-bô-rä'zō)	142	1.35 S	78.45 W
Chimbote, Peru (chēm-bō'tȧ)	142	9.02 S	78.33 W
Chimkent, Sov. Un. (chĭm-kĕnt)	180	42.17 N	69.42 E
Chimki, Sov. Un.	66b	55.54 N	37.26 E
Chimki-Chovrino (Neigh.), Sov. Un.	66b	55.51 N	37.30 E
China, Asia (chī'nȧ)	190	36.45 N	93.00 E
China, Mex. (chē'nä)	124	25.43 N	99.13 W
Chinameca, Sal. (Chē-nä-mā'kä)	132	13.31 N	88.18 W
Chinandega, Nic. (chē-nän-dā'gä)	132	12.38 N	87.08 W
Chinati Pk., Tx. (chĭ-nä'tē)	124	29.56 N	104.29 W
Chinatown (Neigh.), Ca.	58b	37.48 N	122.26 W
Chincha Alta, Peru (chĭn'chä äl'tä)	142	13.24 S	76.04 W
Chinchas, Islas (Is.), Peru (ḗ's-läs-chē'n-chäs)	142	11.27 S	79.05 W
Chinchilla, Austl. (chĭn-chĭl'ȧ)	216	26.44 S	150.36 E
Chinchorro, Banco (Bk.), Mex. (bä'n-kô-chĕn-chô'r-rō)	132a	18.43 N	87.25 W
Chincilla de Monte Aragon, Sp.	170	38.54 N	1.43 W
Chinde, Moz. (shĕn'dĕ)	226	17.39 S	36.34 E
Chin Do (I.), Kor.	204	34.30 N	125.43 E
Chindwin R., Bur. (chĭn-dwĭn)	198	23.30 N	94.34 E
Chingford (Neigh.), Eng.	62	51.38 N	0.01 E
Chingmei, Taiwan	68d	24.59 N	121.32 E
Chingola, Zambia (chĭng-gōlä)	231	12.32 S	27.52 E

PRONOUNCING INDEX
Chinguar – Claresholm 271

PLACE (Pronounciation)	PAGE	Lat. °′	Long. °′
Chinguar, Ang. (chĭng-gär)	226	12.35 S	16.15 E
Chinguetti, Mauritania (chėŋ-gĕt′ė)	224	20.34 N	12.34 W
Chinhoyi, Zimb	231	17.22 S	30.12 E
Chinju, Kor. (chĭn′jo͞o)	204	35.13 N	128.10 E
Chinko (R.), Cen. Afr. Rep. (shĭn′kȯ)	225	6.37 N	24.31 E
Chinmen, see Quemoy			
Chino, Ca. (chē′nō)	119a	34.01 N	117.42 W
Chinon, Fr. (shē-nôɴ′)	168	47.09 N	0.13 E
Chinook, Mt. (shĭn-o͝ok′)	117	48.35 N	109.15 W
Chinook, Wa. (shĭn-o͝ok′)	118c	46.17 N	123.57 W
Chinsali, Zambia	231	10.34 S	32.03 E
Chinteche, Malawi (chĭn-tĕ′chĕ)	226	11.48 S	34.14 E
Chioggia, It. (kyôd′jä)	172	45.12 N	12.17 E
Chipata, Zambia	231	13.39 S	32.40 E
Chipera, Moz. (zhė-pĕ′rä)	226	15.16 S	32.30 E
Chipley, Fl. (chĭp′lĭ)	126	30.45 N	85.33 W
Chipman, Can. (chĭp′mȧn)	104	46.11 N	65.53 W
Chipola (R.), Fl. (chĭ-pō′lȧ)	126	30.40 N	85.14 W
Chippawa, Can. (chĭp′ė-wä)	113c	43.03 N	79.03 W
Chipperfield, Eng.	62	51.42 N	0.29 W
Chippewa (R.), Mn. (chĭp′ė-wä)	114	45.07 N	95.41 W
Chippewa (R.), Wi.	115	45.07 N	91.19 W
Chippewa Falls, Wi.	115	44.55 N	91.26 W
Chippewa Lake, Oh.	113d	41.04 N	81.54 W
Chipping Ongar, Eng.	62	51.43 N	0.15 E
Chipstead, Eng.	62	51.17 N	0.09 E
Chipstead, Eng.	62	51.18 N	0.10 W
Chiputneticook L., Can. (chĭ-po͞ot-nĕt′ĭ-ko͝ok)	104	45.47 N	67.45 W
Chiquimula, Guat. (chē-kė-mo͞o′lä)	132	14.47 N	89.31 W
Chiquimulilla, Guat. (chē-kē-mo͞o-lė′l-yä)	132	14.08 N	90.23 W
Chiquinquira, Col. (chė-kēŋ′kė-rä′)	142	5.33 N	73.49 W
Chiquita, Laguna Mar (L.), Arg. (lä-go͞o′nä-mȧr-chė-kē′tä)	141c	34.25 S	61.10 W
Chirāgh Delhi (Neigh.), India	67d	28.32 N	77.14 E
Chirald, India	197	15.52 N	80.22 E
Chirchik, Sov. Un. (chĭr-chēk′)	180	41.28 N	69.18 E
Chire (R.), Moz.	231	17.15 S	35.25 E
Chiricahua Natl. Mon., Az. (chĭ-rā-cä′hwä)	121	32.02 N	109.18 W
Chirikof (I.), Ak. (chĭ′rĭ-kôf)	107	55.50 N	155.35 W
Chiriqui, Punta (Pt.), Pan. (po͞o′n-tä-chē-rė-kē′)	133	9.13 N	81.39 W
Chiriquí, Golfo de (G.), Pan. (gȯl-fô-dĕ-chē-rė-kē′)	133	7.56 N	82.18 W
Chiriquí Grande, Pan. (chē-rė-kē′ grän′dā)	133	8.57 N	82.08 W
Chiriquí, Laguna de (L.), Pan. (lä-go͞o′nä-dĕ-chē-rė-kē′)	133	9.06 N	82.02 W
Chiri San (Mt.), Kor. (chĭ′rĭ-sän′)	204	35.20 N	127.39 E
Chiromo, Malawi	226	16.34 S	35.13 E
Chirpan, Bul.	173	42.12 N	25.19 E
Chirripó, Cerro (Mtn.), C. R. (chė-rē′pō)	133	9.30 N	83.31 W
Chirripo, Rio (R.), C. R.	133	9.50 N	83.20 W
Chisholm, Mn. (chĭz′ŭm)	115	47.28 N	92.53 W
Chislehurst (Neigh.), Eng.	62	51.25 N	0.04 E
Chistopol′, Sov. Un. (chĭs-tô′pȯl-y′)	178	55.18 N	50.30 E
Chiswellgreen, Eng.	62	51.44 N	0.22 W
Chiswick (Neigh.), Eng.	62	51.29 N	0.16 W
Chita, Sov. Un. (chė-tȧ′)	181	52.09 N	113.39 E
Chitambo, Zambia	231	12.55 S	30.39 E
Chitembo, Ang.	230	13.34 S	16.40 E
Chitina, Ak. (chĭ-tē′nȧ)	107	61.28 N	144.35 W
Chitokoloki, Zambia	230	13.50 S	23.13 E
Chitorgarh, India	196	24.59 N	74.42 E
Chitrāl, Pak. (chē-träl′)	196	35.58 N	71.48 E
Chitré, Pan. (chē′trȧ)	133	7.59 N	80.26 W
Chittagong, Bngl. (chĭt-ȧ-gông′)	196	22.26 N	90.51 E
Chitungwiza, Zimb	226	17.51 S	31.05 E
Chiumbe (R.), Ang. (chė-o͞om′bȧ)	230	9.05 S	21.00 E
Chivasso, It. (kė-väs′sō)	172	45.13 N	7.52 E
Chivhu, Zimb	226	19.59 S	30.58 E
Chivilcoy, Arg. (chē-vėl-koi′)	141c	34.51 S	60.03 W
Chixoy (R.), Guat. (chē-ĸoi′)	132	15.40 N	90.35 W
Chizu, Jap. (chė-zo͞o′)	205	35.16 N	134.15 E
Chloride, Az. (klō′rīd)	121	35.25 N	114.15 W
Chmielnik, Pol. (ĸmyĕl′nėĸ)	167	50.36 N	20.46 E
Choa Chu Kang, Singapore	67c	1.22 N	103.41 E
Choapa (R.), Chile (chȯ-ȧ′pä)	141b	31.56 S	70.48 W
Chobham, Eng.	62	51.21 N	0.36 W
Chocó (Dept.), Col. (chȯ-kô′)	142a	5.33 N	76.28 W
Choctawhatchee (R.), Fl.-Ga.	126	30.37 N	85.56 W
Choctawhatchee, B., Fl. (chôk-tô-hăch′ė)	126	30.15 N	86.32 W
Chodziez, Pol: (ĸōj′yĕsh)	166	52.59 N	16.55 E
Choele Choel, Arg. (chȯ-ĕ′lĕ-chȯĕ′l)	144	39.14 S	66.46 W
Chōfu, Jap. (chō′fo͞o′)	205a	35.39 N	139.33 E
Chōgo, Jap. (chō-gō)	205a	35.25 N	139.28 E
Choisel, Fr.	64c	48.41 N	2.01 E
Choiseul, (I.), Sol. Is. (shwä-zûl′)	215	7.30 S	157.30 E
Choisy-le-Roi, Fr.	64c	48.46 N	2.25 E
Chojnice, Pol. (ĸōĭ-nē-tsĕ)	167	53.41 N	17.34 E
Cholet, Fr. (shȯ-lĕ′)	168	47.06 N	0.54 W
Cho-lon (Neigh.), Viet.	68m	10.46 N	106.40 E
Cholula, Mex. (chō-lo͞o′lä)	130	19.04 N	98.19 W
Choluteca, Hond. (chō-lo͞o-tā′kä)	132	13.18 N	87.12 W
Choluteco (R.), Hond.-Nic.	132	13.34 N	86.59 W
Cho Moi, Viet.	68m	10.51 N	106.38 E
Chomutov, Czech. (kō′mo͞o-tȯf)	166	50.27 N	13.23 E
Chona (R.), Sov. Un. (chō′nä)	181	60.45 N	109.15 E
Chone, Ec. (chô′nĕ)	142	0.48 S	80.06 W
Chŏngjin, Kor. (chŭng-jĭn′)	204	41.48 N	129.46 E
Chŏngju, Kor. (chŭng-jo͞o′)	204	36.35 N	127.30 E
Chongming Dao (I.), China (chȯŋ-mĭŋ dou)	203	31.40 N	122.30 E
Chong Pang, Singapore	67c	1.26 N	103.50 E
Chongqing, China (chȯŋ-chyĭŋ)	203	29.38 N	107.30 E
Chŏnju, Kor. (chŭn-jo͞o′)	204	35.48 N	127.08 E
Chorley, Eng. (chôr′lĭ)	156	53.40 N	2.38 W
Chorleywood, Eng.	62	51.39 N	0.31 W
Chorlton-cum-Hardy (Neigh.), Eng.	64b	53.27 N	2.17 W
Chornaya, Sov. Un.	182b	55.45 N	38.04 E
Chorošovo (Neigh.), Sov. Un.	66b	55.47 N	37.28 E
Chorrera de Managua, Cuba	60b	23.02 N	82.19 E
Chorrillos, Peru (chôr-rē′l-yōs)	142	12.17 S	76.55 W
Chortkov, Sov. Un. (chôrt′kȯf)	167	49.01 N	25.48 E
Chosan, Kor. (chō-sän′)	204	40.44 N	125.48 E
Chosen, Fl. (chō′z′n)	127a	26.41 N	80.41 W
Chōshi, Jap. (chō′shē)	204	35.40 N	140.55 E
Choszczno, Pol. (chȯsh′chnô)	166	53.10 N	15.25 E
Chota Nagpur (Reg.), India	196	23.40 N	82.50 E
Choteau, Mt. (shō′tō)	117	47.51 N	112.10 W
Chowan (R.), NC (chȯ-wän′)	127	36.13 N	76.46 W
Chowilla Res., Austl.	216	34.05 S	141.20 E
Chown, Mt., Can. (choun)	99	53.24 N	119.22 W
Choybalsan, Mong.	202	47.50 N	114.15 E
Christchurch, N.Z. (krīst′chûrch)	215a	43.30 S	172.38 E
Christian (I.), Can. (krĭs′chăn)	110	44.50 N	80.00 W
Christiansburg, Va. (krĭs′chănz-bûrg)	127	37.08 N	80.25 W
Christiansted, Vir. Is. (U.S.A.)	129b	17.45 N	64.44 W
Christmas (I.), **see Kiritimati** (I.)			
Christmas I., Austl.	206	10.35 S	105.40 E
Christopher, Il. (krĭs′tȯ-fēr)	123	37.58 N	89.04 W
Chrudim, Czech. (ĸro͞o′dyēm)	166	49.57 N	15.46 E
Chrzanów, Pol. (ĸzhä′no͝of)	167	50.08 N	19.24 E
Chuansha, China (chůän-shä)	201b	31.12 N	121.41 E
Chubut (Prov.), Arg. (cho͞o-bo͞ot′)	144	44.00 S	69.15 W
Chubut (R.), Arg. (cho͞o-bo͞ot′)	144	43.05 S	69.00 W
Chuckatuck, Va. (chŭck ȧ-tŭck)	112g	36.51 N	76.35 W
Chucunaque (R.), Pan. (cho͞o-ko͞o-nä′kȧ)	133	8.36 N	77.48 W
Chudovo, Sov. Un. (cho͞o′dȯ-vȯ)	174	59.03 N	31.56 E
Chudskoye Oz. (Peipus, L.), Sov. Un. (cho͞ot′skȯ-yĕ)	174	58.43 N	26.45 E
Chuguchak (Reg.), China (cho͞o′go͞o-chäk′)	198	46.09 N	83.58 E
Chuguyev, Sov. Un. (cho͞o′go͝o-yĕf)	175	49.52 N	36.40 E
Chuguyevka, Sov. Un. (cho͞o-go͞o′yĕf-kȧ)	204	43.58 N	133.49 E
Chugwater Cr., Wy. (chŭg′wô-tēr)	114	41.43 N	104.54 W
Chukot Natl. Okrug (Reg.), Sov. Un.	181	68.15 N	170.00 E
Chukotskiy (Chukot) **P-Ov** (Pen.), Sov. Un.	181	66.12 N	175.00 W
Chukotskoye Nagor′ye (Mts.), Sov. Un.	181	66.00 N	166.00 E
Chula Vista, Ca. (cho͞o′lȧ vĭs′tȧ)	120a	32.38 N	117.05 W
Chulkovo, Sov. Un. (cho͞ol-kô vô)	182b	55.33 N	38.04 E
Chulucanas, Peru (cho͞o-lo͞o-kä′näs)	142	5.13 S	80.13 W
Chulum (R.), Sov. Un.	180	57.52 N	84.45 E
Chumikan, Sov. Un. (cho͞o-mē-kän′)	181	54.47 N	135.09 E
Chun′an, China (cho͞on-än)	203	29.38 N	119.00 E
Chunchŏn, Kor. (cho͞on-chŭn′)	204	37.51 N	127.46 E
Chungju, Kor. (chŭng′jo͞o′)	204	37.00 N	128.19 E
Chŭngsanha-ri (Neigh.), Kor.	68b	37.35 N	126.54 E
Chunya (R.), Sov. Un. (cho͞on′yä′)	180	61.45 N	101.28 E
Chunya, Tan.	231	8.32 S	33.25 E
Chūō (Neigh.), Jap.	69a	35.40 N	139.47 E
Chuquicamata, Chile (cho͞o-kė-kä-mä′tä)	144	22.08 S	68.57 W
Chur, Switz. (ko͞or)	166	46.51 N	9.32 E
Churchill, Can. (chûrch′ĭl)	96	58.50 N	94.10 W
Churchill, Pa.	57b	40.27 N	79.51 W
Churchill, Va.	56d	38.54 N	77.10 W
Churchill (R.), Can.	101	57.20 N	96.30 W
Churchill, C., Can.	96	59.07 N	93.50 W
Churchill Falls, Can.	97	53.35 N	64.27 W
Churchill L., Can.	100	56.12 N	108.40 W
Churchill Pk., Can.	96	58.10 N	125.14 W
Church Street, Eng.	62	51.26 N	0.28 E
Church Stretton, Eng. (chûrch strĕt′ŭn)	156	52.32 N	2.49 W
Churchton, Md.	112e	38.49 N	76.33 W
Churu, India	196	28.22 N	75.00 E
Churumuco, Mex. (cho͞o-ro͞o-mo͞o′kō)	130	18.39 N	101.40 W
Chuska Mts., Az.-NM (chŭs-kȧ)	121	36.21 N	109.11 W
Chusovaya R., Sov. Un. (cho͞o-sô-vä′yȧ)	182a	58.08 N	58.35 E
Chusovoy, Sov. Un. (cho͞o-sô-vȯy′)	182a	58.18 N	57.50 E
Chust, Sov. Un. (cho͝ost)	180	41.05 N	71.28 E
Chuvash A. S. S. R., Sov. Un. (cho͞o′vȧsh)	178	55.45 N	46.00 E
Chuviscar (R.), Mex. (cho͞o-vės-kär′)	124	28.34 N	105.36 W
Chuwang, China (cho͞o-wäŋ)	200	36.08 N	114.53 E
Chuxian, China (cho͞o shyĕn)	200	32.19 N	118.19 E
Chuxiong, China (cho͞o-shyȯŋ)	198	25.19 N	101.34 E
Cicero, Il. (sĭs′ēr-ō)	113a	41.50 N	87.46 W
Cide, Pur. (jē′dĕ)	179	41.50 N	33.00 E
Ciechanów, Pol. (tsyĕ-kä′no͝of)	167	52.52 N	20.39 E
Ciego de Avila, Cuba (syā′gō dā ä′vė-lä)	134	21.50 N	78.45 W
Ciego de Avila (Prov.), Cuba	134	22.00 N	78.40 W
Ciempozuelos, Sp. (thyĕm-pȯ-thwā′lōs)	170	40.09 N	3.36 W
Ciénaga, Col. (syā′nä-gä)	142	11.01 N	74.15 W
Cienfuegos, Cuba (syĕn-fwā′gōs)	134	22.10 N	80.30 W
Cienfuegos (Prov.), Cuba	134	22.15 N	80.40 W
Cienfuegos, Bahía (B.), Cuba (bä-ē′ä-syĕn-fwā′gōs)	134	22.00 N	80.35 W
Ciervo, Isla de la (I.), Nic. (ė′s-lä-dĕ-lä-syĕ′r-vô)	133	11.56 N	83.20 W
Cieszyn, Pol. (tsyĕ′shėn)	167	49.47 N	18.45 E
Cieza, Sp. (thyā′thä)	170	38.13 N	1.25 W
Cigüela (R.), Sp.	170	39.53 N	2.54 W
Cihuatlán, Mex. (sē-wä-tlȧ′n)	130	19.13 N	104.36 W
Cihuatlán (R.), Mex.	130	19.11 N	104.30 W
Cijara, Embalse de (Res.), Sp.	170	39.25 N	5.00 W
Cilician Gates P.), Tur.	179	37.30 N	35.30 E
Cimarron (R.), **North Fk.,** Co.	122	37.13 N	102.30 W
Cimarron R., U.S. (sĭm-ȧ-rōn′)	108	36.26 N	98.27 W
Cinca (R.), Sp. (thēŋ′kä)	171	42.09 N	0.08 E
Cincinnati, Oh. (sĭn-sĭ-nȧt′ĭ)	113f	39.08 N	84.30 W
Cinco Balas, Cayos (Is.), Cuba (kä′yōs-thēŋ′kō bä′läs)	134	21.05 N	79.25 W
Cinderella, S. Afr.	71b	26.15 S	28.16 E
Cinisello Balsamo, It.	65c	45.33 N	9.13 E
Cinkota (Neigh.), Hung.	66g	47.31 N	19.14 E
Cintalapa, Mex. (sėn-tä-lä′pä)	131	16.41 N	93.44 W
Cinto, Mt., Fr. (chēn′tō)	172	42.24 N	8.54 E
Circle, Ak. (sûr′k′l)	107	65.49 N	144.22 W
Circleville, Oh. (sûr′k′lvĭl)	110	39.35 N	83.00 W
Cirebon, Indon.	206	6.50 S	108.33 E
Cîmpina, Rom.	173	45.08 N	25.47 E
Cîmpulung, Rom.	173	45.15 N	25.03 E
Cîmpulung Moldovenesc, Rom.	167	47.31 N	25.36 E
Cisco, Tx. (sĭs′kō)	124	32.23 N	98.57 W
Cisliano, It.	65c	45.27 N	8.59 E
Cisneros, Col. (sės-nĕ′rȯs)	142a	6.33 N	75.05 W
Cisterna di Latina, It. (chēs-tĕ′r-nä-dē-lä-tė′nä)	171d	41.36 N	12.53 E
Cistierna, Sp. (thės-tyĕr′nä)	170	42.48 N	5.08 W
Citlaltépetl (Vol.), Mex. (sē-tlȧl-tĕ′pĕtl)	131	19.04 N	97.14 W
Citronelle, Al. (cĭt-rȯ′nēl)	126	31.05 N	88.15 W
Cittadella, It. (chēt-tä-dĕl′lä)	172	45.39 N	11.51 E
Città di Castello, It. (chēt-tä′dē käs-tĕl′lō)	172	43.27 N	12.17 E
City College of New York (P. Int.), NY	55	40.49 N	73.57 W
City Island (Neigh.), NY	55	40.51 N	73.47 W
City of Baltimore, Md.	56d	39.18 N	76.37 W
City of Commerce, Ca.	59	33.59 N	118.08 W
City of Industry, Ca.	59	34.01 N	117.57 W
City of London (Neigh.), Eng.	62	51.31 N	0.05 W
City of Westminster (Neigh.), Eng.	62	51.30 N	0.09 W
Ciudad Altamirano, Mex. (syo͞o-dä′d-äl-tä-mē-rä′nȯ)	130	18.24 N	100.38 W
Ciudad Bolívar, Ven. (syo͞o-dhädh′ bȯ-lē′vär)	142	8.07 N	63.41 W
Ciudad Camargo (Santa Rosalia), Mex. (syo͞o-dhädh′ kä-mär′gō) (sän′tȧ rō-sä′lėȧ)	124	27.42 N	105.10 W
Ciudad Chetumal (Payo Obispo), Mex. (syo͞o-dhädh′ chĕt-o͞o-mäl) (pä′yō ō-bēs′pō)	132a	18.30 N	88.17 W
Ciudad Darío, Nic. (syo͞o-dhädh′dä′rė-ō)	132	12.44 N	86.08 W
Ciudad de la Habana (Prov.), Cuba	134	23.20 N	82.10 W
Ciudad de las Casas, Mex. (syo͞o-dä′d-dĕ-lä-kȧ′säs)	131	16.44 N	92.39 W
Ciudad del Carmen, Mex. (syo͞o-dä′d-dĕl-kȧ′r-mĕn)	131	18.39 N	91.49 W
Ciudad del Maíz, Mex. (syo͞o-dhädh′del mä-ēz′)	130	22.24 N	99.37 W
Ciudad de Naucalpan de Juárez, Mex.	60a	19.28 N	99.14 W
Ciudad Deportive (P. Int.), Mex.	60a	19.24 N	99.06 W
Ciudad de Valles, Mex. (syo͞o-dhädh′dā vä′lyās)	130	21.59 N	99.02 W
Ciudadela, Sp. (thyo͞o-dhä-dhā′lä)	171	40.00 N	3.52 E
Ciudad Fernández, Mex. (syo͞o-dhädh′fĕr-nän′dĕz)	130	21.56 N	100.03 W
Ciudad García Mex. (syo͞o-dhädh′gär-sē′ä)	130	22.39 N	103.02 W
Ciudad General Belgrano, Arg.	60d	34.44 S	58.32 W
Ciudad Guayana Ven.	142	8.30 N	62.45 W
Ciudad Guzmán, Mex. (syo͞o-dhädh′go͞oz-män)	130	19.40 N	103.29 W
Ciudad Hidalgo, Mex. (syo͞o-dä′d-ė-dä′l-gȯ)	130	19.41 N	100.35 W
Ciudad Juárez, Mex. (syo͞o-dhädh hwä′rāz)	125	31.44 N	106.28 W
Ciudad Lineal (Neigh.), Sp.	65b	40.27 N	3.40 W
Ciudad Madero, Mex. (syo͞o-dä′d-mä-dĕ′rȯ)	131	22.16 N	97.52 W
Ciudad Mante, Mex. (syo͞o-dä′d-mȧn′tĕ)	130	22.34 N	98.58 W
Ciudad Manual Doblado, Mex. (syo͞o-dä′d-män-wāl′dō-blä′dō)	130	20.43 N	101.57 W
Ciudad Obregón, Mex. (syo͞o-dhädh-ô-brĕ-gô′n)	128	27.40 N	109.58 W
Ciudad Real, Sp. (thyo͞o-dhädh′rā-äl′)	170	38.59 N	3.55 W
Ciudad Rodrigo, Sp. (thyo͞o-dhädh′rȯ-drē′gō)	170	40.38 N	6.34 W
Ciudad Serdán, Mex. (syo͞o-dä′d-sĕr-dȧ′n)	131	18.58 N	97.26 W
Ciudad Universitaria (Neigh.), Sp.	65b	40.27 N	3.44 W
Ciudad Victoria, Mex. (syo͞o-dhädh′vėk-tō′rė-ä)	130	23.43 N	99.09 W
Civitavecchia, It. (chē′vė-tä-vĕk′kyä)	172	42.06 N	11.49 E
Cixian, China (tsē shyĕn)	200	36.22 N	114.23 E
Clackamas, Or. (klăc-kȧ′măs)	118c	45.25 N	122.34 W
Claire (L.), Can. (klâr)	96	58.33 N	113.16 W
Clair Engle L., Ca.	116	40.51 N	122.41 W
Clairton, Pa. (klărtŭn)	113e	40.17 N	79.53 W
Clamart, Fr.	64c	48.48 N	2.16 E
Clanton, Al. (klăn′tŭn)	126	32.50 N	86.38 W
Clare, Mi. (klâr)	110	43.50 N	84.45 W
Clare I., Ire.	162	53.46 N	10.00 W
Claremont, Ca. (klâr′mŏnt)	119a	34.06 N	117.43 W
Claremont, Eng.	62	51.21 N	0.22 W
Claremont, NH (klâr′mŏnt)	111	43.20 N.	72.20 W
Claremont, WV	110	37.55 N	81.00 W
Claremore, Ok. (klâr′mōr)	123	36.16 N	95.37 W
Claremorris, Ire. (klâr-mŏr′ĭs)	162	53.46 N	9.05 W
Clarence Str., Ak.	98	55.25 N	132.00 W
Clarence Str., Austl. (klăr′ĕns)	214	12.15 S	130.05 E
Clarence Town, Ba.	135	23.05 N	75.00 W
Clarendon, Ar. (klâr′ĕn-dŭn)	123	34.42 N	91.17 W
Clarendon, Tx.	122	34.55 N	100.52 W
Clarens, S. Afr. (clâ-rĕns)	227c	28.34 S	28.26 E
Claresholm, Can. (klâr′ĕs-hōlm)	100	50.02 N	113.35 W

ŋ-sing; nŋ-baŋk; ɴ-nasalized n; nŏd; cŏmmit; ōld; ȯbey; ŏrder; oi-boil; fo͞od; fo͝ot; ou-out; s-soft; sh-dish; th-thin; pūre; ůnite; ûrn; stŭd; circŭs; ü-as in French tu; ′-indeterminate vowel.

272 Clarinda – Colonia

PLACE (Pronounciation)	PAGE	Lat. °′	Long. °′
Clarinda, Ia. (klȧ-rĭn′dȧ)	115	40.42 N	95.00 W
Clarines, Ven. (klä-rē′nĕs)	143b	9.57 N	65.10 W
Clarion, Ia. (klăr′i-ŭn)	115	42.43 N	93.45 W
Clarion, Pa.	111	41.10 N	79.25 W
Clark, NJ	55	40.38 N	74.19 W
Clark, SD (klärk)	114	44.52 N	97.45 W
Clarkdale, Az (klärk-dāl)	121	34.45 N	112.05 W
Clarke City, Can.	104	50.12 N	66.38 W
Clarke Ra, Austl.	215	20.30 S	148.00 E
Clark Fork (R.), Mt.	117	47.50 N	115.35 W
Clark Hill Res., Ga.-SC (klärk-hĭl)	127	33.50 N	82.35 W
Clark, Pt, Can.	110	44.05 N	81.50 W
Clarksburg, WV (klärkz′bûrg)	111	39.15 N	80.20 W
Clarksdale, Ms. (klärks-dāl)	126	34.10 N	90.31 W
Clark's Harbour, Can. (klärks)	104	43.26 N	65.38 W
Clarkson, Can.	54c	43.31 N	79.37 W
Clarkston, Ga. (klärks′tŭn)	112c	33.49 N	84.15 W
Clarkston, Wa.	116	46.24 N	117.01 W
Clarksville, Ar. (klärks-vĭl)	123	35.28 N	93.26 W
Clarksville, Tn.	126	36.30 N	87.23 W
Clarksville, Tx.	123	33.37 N	95.02 W
Clatskanie, Or.	118c	46.04 N	123.11 W
Clatskanie (R.), Or. (klăt-skā′nē)	118c	46.06 N	123.11 W
Clatsop Spit, Or. (klăt-sŏp)	118c	46.13 N	124.04 W
Cláudio, Braz. (klou′-dēō)	141a	20.26 S	44.44 W
Claveria, Phil. (klä-vå-rē′ä)	203	18.38 N	121.08 E
Clawson, Mi. (klô′s′n)	113b	42.32 N	83.09 W
Claxton, Ga. (klăks′tŭn)	127	32.07 N	81.54 W
Clay, Ky. (klā)	126	37.28 N	87.50 W
Clay Center, Ks. (klā sĕn′tēr)	123	39.23 N	97.08 W
Clay City, Ky. (klā sĭ′tĭ)	110	37.50 N	83.55 W
Claycomo, Mo. (kla-kō′mo)	115f	39.12 N	94.30 W
Clay Cross, Eng. (klā krŏs)	156	53.10 N	1.25 W
Claye-Souilly, Fr. (klĕ-sōō-yē′)	169b	48.56 N	2.43 E
Claygate, Eng.	62	51.22 N	0.20 W
Claygate Cross, Eng.	62	51.16 N	0.19 E
Claymont, De. (klā-mŏnt)	112f	39.48 N	75.28 W
Clayton, Al. (klā′tŭn)	126	31.52 N	85.25 W
Clayton, Ca.	118b	37.56 N	121.56 W
Clayton, Eng.	156	53.47 N	1.49 W
Clayton, Mo.	119e	38.39 N	90.20 W
Clayton, NC	127	35.40 N	78.27 W
Clayton, NM	122	36.26 N	103.12 W
Clear (L.), Ca.	120	39.05 N	122.50 W
Clear Boggy Cr., Ok. (klēr bŏg′ĭ krēk)	123	34.21 N	96.22 W
Clear Cr., Az.	121	34.40 N	111.05 W
Clear Cr., Tx.	125a	29.34 N	95.13 W
Clear Cr., Wy.	117	44.35 N	106.20 W
Clearfield, Pa. (klēr-fēld)	111	41.00 N	78.25 W
Clearfield, Ut.	119b	41.07 N	112.01 W
Clear Hills, Can.	96	57.11 N	119.20 W
Clearing (Neigh.), Il.	58a	41.47 N	87.47 W
Clear Lake, Ia.	115	43.09 N	93.23 W
Clear Lake, Wa.	118a	48.27 N	122.14 W
Clear Lake Res., Ca.	116	41.53 N	121.00 W
Clearwater, Fl. (klēr-wô′tēr)	127a	27.43 N	82.45 W
Clearwater (R.), Can.	99	52.00 N	114.50 W
Clearwater (R.), Can.	99	52.00 N	120.10 W
Clearwater (R.), Can.	100	56.10 N	110.40 W
Clearwater (R.), Id.	116	46.27 N	116.33 W
Clearwater (R.) Middle Fork, Id.	116	46.10 N	115.48 W
Clearwater (R.) North Fork, Id.	116	46.34 N	116.08 W
Clearwater (R.) South Fork, Id.	116	45.46 N	115.53 W
Clearwater Mts., Id.	116	45.56 N	115.15 W
Clearwater Res., Mo.	123	37.20 N	91.04 W
Cleburne, Tx. (klē′bŭrn)	125	32.21 N	97.23 W
Cle Elum, Wa. (klē ĕl′ŭm)	116	47.12 N	120.55 W
Clementon, NJ (klē′mĕn-tŭn)	112f	39.49 N	75.00 W
Cleobury Mortimer, Eng. (klēô-bĕr′ĭ môr′tĭ-mēr)	156	52.22 N	2.29 W
Clermont, Austl. (klēr′mŏnt)	215	23.02 S	147.46 E
Clermont, Can.	104	47.45 N	70.20 W
Clermont-Ferrand, Fr. (klĕr-môɴ′fĕr-răɴ′)	168	45.47 N	3.03 E
Cleveland, Ms. (klēv′lănd)	126	33.45 N	90.42 W
Cleveland, Oh.	113d	41.30 N	81.42 W
Cleveland, Ok.	123	36.18 N	96.28 W
Cleveland, Tn.	126	35.09 N	84.52 W
Cleveland, Tx.	125	30.18 N	95.05 W
Cleveland Heights, Oh.	113d	41.30 N	81.35 W
Cleveland Museum of Art (P. Int.), Oh.	56a	41.31 N	81.37 W
Cleveland Park (Neigh.), DC	56d	38.56 N	77.04 W
Cleveland Pen., Ak.	98	55.45 N	132.00 W
Cleves, Oh. (klē′vĕs)	113f	39.10 N	84.45 W
Clew B., Ire. (klōō)	162	53.47 N	9.45 W
Clewiston, Fl. (klē′wis-tŭn)	127a	26.44 N	80.55 W
Clichy, Fr. (klē-shē′)	169b	48.54 N	2.18 E
Clichy-sous-Bois, Fr.	64c	48.55 N	2.33 E
Clifden, Ire. (klĭf′dĕn)	162	53.31 N	10.04 W
Cliffside Park, NJ	55	40.49 N	73.59 W
Clifton, Az. (klĭf′tŭn)	121	33.05 N	109.20 W
Clifton, Ma.	54a	42.29 N	70.53 W
Clifton, NJ	112a	40.52 N	74.09 W
Clifton, SC	127	35.00 N	81.47 W
Clifton, Tx.	125	31.45 N	97.31 W
Clifton Forge, Va.	111	37.50 N	79.50 W
Clifton Heights, Pa.	56b	39.56 N	75.18 W
Clinch (R.), Tn.-Va. (klĭnch)	126	36.30 N	83.19 W
Clingmans Dome (Mtn.), NC (klĭng′măns dōm)	126	35.37 N	83.26 W
Clinton, Can. (klĭn-′tŭn)	99	51.05 N	121.35 W
Clinton, Ia.	115	41.50 N	90.13 W
Clinton, Il.	110	40.10 N	88.55 W
Clinton, In.	110	39.40 N	87.25 W
Clinton, Ky.	126	36.39 N	88.56 W
Clinton, Ma.	105a	42.25 N	71.41 W
Clinton, Md.	112e	38.46 N	76.54 W
Clinton, Mo.	123	38.23 N	93.46 W
Clinton, NC	127	35.58 N	78.20 W
Clinton, Ok.	122	35.31 N	98.56 W
Clinton, SC	127	34.27 N	81.53 W
Clinton, Tn.	126	36.05 N	84.08 W
Clinton, Wa.	118a	47.59 N	122.22 W
Clinton-Colden (L.), Can.	96	63.58 N	106.34 W
Clinton R., Mi.	113b	42.36 N	83.00 W
Clintonville, Wi. (klĭn′tŭn-vĭl)	115	44.37 N	88.46 W
Clio, Mi. (klē′ō)	110	43.10 N	83.45 W
Cloates, Pt., Austl. (klōts)	214	22.47 S	113.45 E
Clocolan, S. Afr.	223d	28.56 S	27.35 E
Clonakilty B., Ire. (klŏn-ȧ-kĭltē)	162	51.30 N	8.50 W
Cloncurry, Austl. (klŏn-kŭr′ē)	214	20.58 S	140.42 E
Clonmel, Ire. (klŏn-mĕl)	162	52.21 N	7.45 W
Clontarf, Austl.	70a	33.48 S	151.16 E
Cloquet, Mn. (klô-kā′)	119h	46.42 N	92.28 W
Closter, NJ (klōs′tēr)	112a	40.58 N	73.57 W
Cloud Pk., Wy. (kloud)	117	44.23 N	107.11 W
Clover, SC (klō′vēr)	127	35.08 N	81.08 W
Clover Bar, Can. (klō′vēr bär)	95g	53.34 N	113.20 W
Cloverdale, Can.	118d	49.06 N	122.44 W
Cloverdale, Ca. (klō′vēr-dāl)	120	38.47 N	123.03 W
Cloverdene, S. Afr.	71b	26.09 S	28.22 E
Cloverport, Ky. (klō′vēr pōrt)	110	37.50 N	86.35 W
Clovis, NM (klō′vĭs)	122	34.24 N	103.11 W
Cluj-Napoca, Rom.	167	46.46 N	23.34 E
Clun (R.), Eng. (klŭn)	156	52.25 N	2.56 W
Cluny, Fr. (klü-nē′)	168	46.27 N	4.40 E
Clutha (R.), N.Z. (klōō′thȧ)	215a	45.52 S	169.30 E
Clwyd (Co.), Wales	156	53.01 N	2.59 W
Clyde, Ks.	123	39.34 N	97.23 W
Clyde, Oh.	110	41.15 N	83.00 W
Clyde (R.), Scot.	162	55.35 N	3.50 W
Clyde, Firth of, Scot. (fûrth ŏv klīd)	162	55.28 N	5.01 W
Côa (R.), Port. (kō′ä)	170	40.28 N	6.55 W
Coacalco, Mex. (kō-ä-käl′kō)	131a	19.37 N	99.06 W
Coachella, Can., Ca. (kō′chĕl-lȧ)	120	33.15 N	115.25 W
Coahuayana, Rio de (R.), Mex. (rē′ō-dĕ-kô-ä-wä-yä′nä)	130	19.00 N	103.33 W
Coahuayutla, Mex. (kō′ä-wī-yōōt′lȧ)	130	18.19 N	101.44 W
Coahuila (State), Mex. (kō-ä-wē′lȧ)	128	27.30 N	103.00 W
Coal City, Il. (kōl sĭ′tĭ)	113a	41.17 N	88.17 W
Coalcomán de Matamoros, Mex. (kō-äl-kō-män′dä mä-tä-mō′rôs)	130	18.46 N	103.10 W
Coalcomán, Rio de (R.), Mex. (rē′ō-dĕ-kō-äl-kō-män′)	130	18.45 N	103.15 W
Coalcomán, Sierra de (Mts.), Mex. (svĕr′rä dā kō-äl-kō-män′)	130	18.30 N	102.45 W
Coaldale, Can. (kōl′dāl)	100	49.43 N	112.37 W
Coaldale, Nv.	120	38.02 N	117.57 W
Coalgate, Ok. (kōl′gāt)	123	34.44 N	96.13 W
Coal Grove, Oh. (kōl grōv)	110	38.20 N	82.40 W
Coal Hill Park (P. Int.), China	67b	39.56 N	116.23 E
Coalinga, Ca. (kō-ȧ-lĭŋ′gȧ)	120	36.09 N	120.23 W
Coalville, Eng. (kōl′vĭl)	156	52.43 N	1.21 W
Coamo, P.R. (kō-ä′mō)	129b	18.05 N	66.21 W
Coari, Braz. (kō-är′ē)	142	4.06 S	63.10 W
Coast Mts., Can. (kōst)	98	54.10 N	128.00 W
Coast Ranges (Mts.), U.S.	108	41.28 N	123.30 W
Coatepec, Mex. (kō-ä-tā-pĕk)	130	19.23 N	98.44 W
Coatepec, Mex.	131d	19.08 N	99.25 W
Coatepec, Mex.	131	19.26 N	96.56 W
Coatepeque, Guat. (kō-ä-tå-pā′kå)	132	14.40 N	91.52 W
Coatepeque, Sal.	132	13.56 N	89.30 W
Coatesville, Pa. (kōts′vĭl)	111	40.00 N	75.50 W
Coatetelco, Mex. (kō-ä-tå-tĕl′kō)	130	18.43 N	99.47 W
Coaticook, Can. (kō′tĭ-kŏŏk)	111	45.10 N	71.55 W
Coatlinchán, Mex. (kô-ä-tlē′n-chä′n)	131a	19.26 N	98.52 W
Coats (I.), Can. (kōts)	97	62.23 N	82.11 W
Coats Land (Reg.), Ant.	232	74.00 S	30.00 W
Coatzacoalcos (Puerto México), Mex. (kô-ät′zä-kô-äl′kōs) (pwĕ′r-tô-mĕ′-kē-kô)	131	18.09 N	94.26 W
Coatzacoalcos (R.), Mex.	131	17.40 N	94.41 W
Coba (Ruins), Mex. (kô′bä)	132a	20.23 N	87.23 W
Cobalt, Can. (kō′bôlt)	97	47.21 N	79.40 W
Cobán, Guat. (kō-bän′)	132	15.28 N	90.19 W
Cobar, Austl.	216	31.28 S	145.50 E
Cobberas, Mt., Austl. (cŏ-bēr-ăs)	216	36.45 S	148.15 E
Cobequid Mts., Can.	104	45.35 N	64.10 W
Cobh, Ire. (kôv)	162	51.52 N	8.09 W
Cobham, Eng.	62	51.23 N	0.24 E
Cobija, Bol. (kō-bē′hä)	142	11.12 S	68.49 W
Cobourg, Can. (kō′bŏŏrgh)	111	43.55 N	78.05 W
Cobre (R.), Jam. (kō′brā)	134	18.05 N	77.00 W
Cóbuè, Moz.	231	12.04 S	34.50 E
Coburg, Austl.	70b	37.45 S	144.58 E
Coburg, F.R.G. (kō′bŏŏrg)	166	50.16 N	10.57 E
Cocentaina, Sp. (kō-thān-tä-ē′nȧ)	171	38.44 N	0.27 W
Cochabamba, Bol. (kō-chä-bäm′bȧ)	142	17.30 S	66.08 W
Cochem, F.R.G. (kō′ĸĕm)	169	50.10 N	7.06 E
Cochin, India (kō-chĭn′)	197	9.58 N	76.19 E
Cochinos, Bahia (B.), Cuba (bä-ē′ä-kô-chē′nōs)	134	22.05 N	81.10 W
Cochinos Bks., Ba.	135	22.20 N	76.15 W
Cochita Res., NM	121	35.45 N	106.10 W
Cochran, Ga. (kŏk′răn)	126	32.23 N	83.23 W
Cochrane, Can. (kŏk′răn)	97	49.01 N	81.06 W
Cochrane, Can.	95e	51.11 N	114.28 W
Cockburn (I.), Can. (kŏk-bûrn)	110	45.55 N	83.25 W
Cockeysville, Md. (kŏk′ĭz-vĭl)	112e	39.30 N	76.40 W
Cockfosters (Neigh.), Eng.	62	51.39 N	0.09 W
Cockrell Hill, Tx. (kŏk′rĕl)	119c	32.44 N	96.53 W
Coco (Segovia) (R.), Hond.-Nic. (kō-kō) (sĕ-gô′vyä)	133	14.55 N	83.45 W
Cocoa, Fl. (kō′kō)	127a	28.21 N	80.44 W
Cocoa Beach, Fl.	127a	28.20 N	80.35 W
Coco, Cayo (I.), Cuba (kä′-yō-kô′kô)	134	22.30 S	78.30 W
Coco, Isla del (I.), C.R. (ē′s-lä-dĕl-kô-kô)	128	5.33 N	87.02 W
Cocoli, Pan. (kŏ-kô′lē)	128a	8.58 N	79.36 W
Coconino, Plat., Az. (kō kō nē′nō)	121	35.45 N	112.28 W
Cocos (Keeling) Is., Oceania (kō′kôs) (kē′lĭng)	7	11.50 S	90.50 E
Coco Solito, Pan. (kô-kô-sŏ-lē′tŏ)	128a	9.21 N	79.53 W
Cocotá (Neigh.), Braz.	61c	22.49 S	43.11 W
Cocula, Mex. (kō-kōō′lä)	130	20.23 N	103.47 W
Cocula (R.), Mex.	130	18.17 N	99.11 W
Codajás, Braz. (kō-dä-häzh′)	142	3.44 N	62.09 W
Codera, Cabo (C.), Ven. (kȧ′bô-kō-dĕ′rä)	143b	10.35 N	66.06 W
Codó, Braz. (kō′dō)	143	4.21 S	43.52 W
Codogno, It. (kô-dō′nyō)	172	45.08 N	9.43 E
Codrington, Antigua (kŏd′rĭng-tŭn)	133	17.39 N	61.49 W
Cody, Wy. (kō′dĭ)	11	44.31 N	109.02 W
Côe d'Or (hill), Fr. (kōr-dŏr′)	168	47.02 N	4.35 E
Coelho da Rocha, Braz.	61c	22.47 S	43.23 W
Coemba, Ang.	230	12.08 S	18.05 E
Coesfeld, F.R.G. (kûs′fĕld)	169c	51.56 N	7.10 E
Coeur d' Alene, Id. (kûr dȧ-lān′)	116	47.43 N	116.35 W
Coeur d' Alene (L.), Id.	116	47.32 N	116.39 W
Coeur d' Alene (R.), Id.	116	47.26 N	116.35 W
Coffeyville, Ks. (kŏf′ĭ-vĭl)	123	37.01 N	95.38 W
Coff's Harbour, Austl.	216	30.20 S	153.10 E
Cofimvaba, S. Afr. (căfĭm′vä-bȧ)	227c	32.01 S	27.37 E
Coghinas (R.), It. (kō′gē-nȧs)	172	40.31 N	9.00 E
Cognac, Fr. (kô-yak′)	168	45.41 N	0.22 W
Cohasset, Ma. (kô-hăs′ĕt)	105a	42.14 N	70.48 W
Cohoes, NY (kô-hōz′)	111	42.50 N	73.40 W
Coig (R.), Arg. (kô′ĕk)	144	51.15 N	71.00 W
Coimbatore, India (kô-ēm-bȧ-tôr′)	197	11.03 N	76.56 E
Coimbra, Port. (kô-ēm′brä)	170	40.14 N	8.23 W
Coina, Port. (kô-ē′nȧ)	171b	38.35 N	9.03 W
Coina (R.), Port. (kô′y-nä)	171b	38.35 N	9.02 W
Coipasa, Salar de (Salt Flat), Chile (sä-lä′r-dĕ-koi-pä′-sä)	142	19.12 S	69.13 W
Coín, Sp. (kô-ēn′)	170	36.40 N	4.45 W
Coixtlahuaca, Mex. (kō-ēks′tlä-wä′kä)	131	17.42 N	97.17 W
Cojedes (State), Ven. (kô-kĕ′dĕs)	143b	9.50 N	68.21 W
Cojimar, Cuba (kō-hē-mär′)	135a	23.10 N	82.19 W
Cojutepeque, Sal. (kô-hōō-tĕ-pā′kå)	132	13.45 N	88.50 W
Cokato, Mn. (kô-kā′tō)	115	45.03 N	94.11 W
Cokeburg, Pa. (kōk bŭgh)	113e	40.06 N	80.03 W
Coker, Nig.	71d	6.29 N	3.20 E
Colāba (Neigh.), India	67e	18.54 N	72.48 E
Colac, Austl. (kŏ′lȧc)	216	38.25 S	143.40 E
Colares, Port. (kô-lä′rĕs)	171b	38.47 N	9.27 W
Colatina, Braz. (kô-lä-tē′nä)	143	19.33 S	40.42 W
Colby, Ks. (kōl′bĭ)	122	39.23 N	101.04 W
Colchagua (Prov.), Chile (kôl-chȧ′gwä)	141b	34.42 S	71.24 W
Colchester, Eng. (kōl′chĕs-tēr)	163	51.52 N	0.50 E
Coldblow (Neigh.), Eng.	62	51.26 N	0.10 E
Cold L., Can. (kōld)	100	54.33 N	110.05 W
Coldwater, Ks. (kōld′wô-tēr)	122	37.14 N	99.21 W
Coldwater, Mi.	110	41.55 N	85.00 W
Coldwater (R.), Ms.	126	34.25 N	90.12 W
Coldwater Cr., Tx.	122	36.10 N	101.45 W
Coleman, Tx. (kōl′mȧn)	124	31.50 N	99.25 W
Colenso, S.Afr. (kŏ-lĕnz′ô)	227c	28.48 S	29.49 E
Coleraine, Mn. (kōl-rān′)	115	47.16 N	93.29 W
Coleraine, N. Ire.	162	55.08 N	6.40 W
Coleshill, Eng. (kōlz′hĭl)	156	52.30 N	1.42 W
Colfax, Ia. (kōl′făks)	115	41.40 N	93.13 W
Colfax, La.	125	31.31 N	92.42 W
Colfax, Wa.	116	46.53 N	117.21 W
Colhué Huapi (L.), Arg. (kôl-wä′ōōȧ′pē)	144	45.30 S	68.45 W
Coligny, S.Afr.	223d	26.20 S	26.18 E
Colima, Mex. (kōlē′mä)	130	19.13 N	103.45 W
Colima (State), Mex.	130	19.10 N	104.00 W
Colima, Nevado de (Mtn.), Mex. (nĕ-vä′dô-dĕ-kô-lē′mä)	130	19.30 N	103.38 W
Coll (I.), Scot. (kōl)	162	56.42 N	6.23 W
College, Ak.	107	64.43 N	147.50 W
College Park, Ga. (kŏl′ĕj)	112c	33.39 N	84.27 W
College Park, Md.	112e	38.59 N	76.58 W
College Point (Neigh.), NY	55	40.47 N	73.51 W
Collegeville, Pa. (kŏl′ĕj-vĭl)	112f	40.11 N	75.27 W
Collie, Austl. (kŏl′ē)	214	33.20 S	116.20 E
Collier B., Austl. (kŏl-yēr)	214	15.30 S	123.30 E
Collier Row (Neigh.), Eng.	62	51.36 N	0.10 E
Collingdale, Pa.	56b	39.55 N	75.17 W
Collingswood, NJ (kŏl′ĭngz-wŏŏd)	112f	39.54 N	75.04 W
Collingwood, Austl.	70b	37.48 S	145.00 E
Collingwood, Can.	110	44.30 N	80.20 W
Collins, Ms. (kŏl′ĭns)	126	31.40 N	89.34 W
Collinsville, Il. (kŏl′ĭnz-vĭl)	119e	38.41 N	89.59 W
Collinsville, Ok.	123	36.21 N	95.50 W
Colmar, Fr. (kôl′mär)	169	48.03 N	7.25 E
Colmenar de Oreja, Sp. (kôl-mā-när′dāōrā′hä)	170	40.06 N	3.25
Colmenar Viejo, Sp. (kôl-mā-när′vyā′hō)	171a	40.40 N	3.46 W
Colnbrook, Eng.	62	51.29 N	0.31 W
Colney Heath, Eng.	62	51.44 N	0.15 W
Colney Street, Eng.	62	51.42 N	0.20 W
Cologne, see Köln			
Cologno Monzese, It.	65c	45.32 N	9.17 E
Colombes, Fr.	64c	48.55 N	2.15 E
Colombia, Col. (kô-lôm′bē-ä)	142a	3.23 N	74.48 W
Colombia, S.A.	140	3.30 N	72.30 W
Colombo, Sri Lanka (kô-lôm′bō)	197	6.58 N	79.52
Colón, Arg. (kō-lōn′)	141c	33.55 S	61.08
Colón, Cuba (kô-lô′n)	134	22.45 N	80.55
Colón, Mex. (kō-lōn′)	130	20.46 N	100.02
Colón, Pan. (kō-lō′n)	128a	9.22 N	79.54
Colonail Park, Md.	56c	39.19 N	76.45
Colon, Arch. de (Galápagos Is.), Ec. (är-chē-pyĕ′l-ägô-dĕ-kō-lōn′) (gä-lä′pȧgōs)	142	0.10 S	87.45
Colonia (Dept.), Ur.	141c	34.08 S	57.50
Colonia, NJ	55	40.35 N	74.18
Colonia, Ur. (kō-lō′nē-ä)	141c	34.27 S	57.50

PRONOUNCING INDEX

Colonial Manor – Cornwall 273

PLACE (Pronounciation)	PAGE	Lat. °′	Long. °′
Colonial Manor, NJ	56b	39.51 N	75.09 W
Colonia Suiza, Ur. (kŏ-lô′nēä-sōōē′zä)	141c	34.17 S	57.15 W
Colōn, Montañas de (Mts.), Hond. (môn-tä′n-yäs-dĕ-kŏ-lô′n)	133	14.58 N	84.39 W
Colonna, Capo (C.), It.	173	39.02 N	17.15 E
Colonsay (I.), Scot. (kŏl-ŏn-sā′)	162	56.08 N	6.08 E
Coloradas, Lomas (Hills), Arg. (lŏ′mäs-kō-lō-rä′däs)	144	43.30 S	68.00 W
Colorado (R.), Tx.	125	30.08 N	97.33 W
Colorado (State), U.S.	108	39.30 N	106.55 W
Colorado City, Tx. (kŏl-ŏ-rä′dō sĭ′tĭ)	124	32.24 N	100.50 W
Colorado Natl. Mon., Co.	121	39.00 N	108.40 W
Colorado Plat, U.S.	108	36.20 N	109.25 W
Colorado R., U.S.	108	36.25 N	112.00 W
Colorado, Rio (R.), Arg.	144	38.30 S	66.00 W
Colorado River Aqueducts, Ca.	120	33.38 N	115.43 W
Colorado River Ind. Res., Az.	121	34.03 N	114.02 W
Colorados, Arch. de los (Is.), Cuba (är-chē-pyĕ-lä-gŏ-dĕ-lŏs-kŏ-lŏ-rä′dōs)	134	22.25 N	84.25 W
Colorado Springs, Co. (kŏl-ŏ-rä′dō)	122	38.49 N	104.48 W
Colosseo (P. Int.), It.	66c	41.54 N	12.29 E
Colotepec (R.), Mex. (kô-lŏ′tĕ-pĕk)	131	15.56 N	96.57 W
Colotlán, Mex. (kŏ-lŏ-tlän′)	130	22.06 N	103.14 W
Colotlán (R.), Mex.	130	22.09 N	103.17 W
Colquechaca, Bol. (kŏl-kā-chä′kä)	142	18.47 S	66.02 W
Colstrip, Mt. (kōl′strip)	117	45.54 N	106.38 W
Colton, Ca. (kōl′tŭn)	119a	34.04 N	117.20 W
Columbia, Il. (kŏ-lŭm′bĭ-ȧ)	119e	38.26 N	90.12 W
Columbia, Ky.	126	37.06 N	85.15 W
Columbia, Md.	112e	39.15 N	76.51 W
Columbia, Mo.	123	38.55 N	92.19 W
Columbia, Ms.	126	31.15 N	89.49 W
Columbia, Pa.	111	40.00 N	76.25 W
Columbia, SC	127	34.00 N	81.00 W
Columbia, TN.	126	35.36 N	87.02 W
Columbia (R.), Can.-U.S.	96	46.20 N	123.00 W
Columbia (R.), Can.	99	51.30 N	119.00 W
Columbia City, In.	110	41.10 N	85.30 W
Columbia City, Or.	118c	45.53 N	112.49 W
Columbia Heights, Mn.	119g	45.03 N	93.15 W
Columbia Icefield, Can.	99	52.08 N	117.26 W
Columbia, Mt., Can.	99	52.09 N	117.25 W
Columbia Mts., Can.	99	51.30 N	118.30 W
Columbiana, Al. (kô-ŭm-bĭ-ă′nȧ)	126	33.10 N	86.35 W
Columbia University (P. Int.), NY	55	40.48 N	73.58 W
Columbretes (I.), Sp. (kŏ-lōōm-brĕ′tĕs)	171	39.54 N	0.54 E
Columbus, Ga. (kŏ-lŭm′bŭs)	126	32.29 N	84.56 W
Columbus, In.	110	39.15 N	85.55 W
Columbus, Ks.	123	37.10 N	94.50 W
Columbus, Ms.	126	33.30 N	88.25 W
Columbus, Mt.	117	45.39 N	109.15 W
Columbus, Ne.	114	41.25 N	97.25 W
Columbus, NM	121	31.50 N	107.40 W
Columbus, Oh.	110	40.00 N	83.00 W
Columbus, Tx.	125	29.44 N	96.34 W
Columbus, Wi.	115	43.20 N	89.01 W
Columbus Bk., Ba. (kŏ-lŭm′büs)	135	22.05 N	75.30 W
Columbus Grove, Oh.	110	40.55 N	84.05 W
Columbus Pt., Ba.	135	24.10 N	75.15 W
Colusa, Ca. (kŏ-lū′sȧ)	120	39.12 N	122.01 W
Colville (R.), Ak.	107	69.00 N	156.25 W
Colville, Wa. (kŏl′vĭl)	116	48.33 N	117.53 W
Colville R, Wa.	116	48.25 N	117.58 W
Colvos Pass., Wa. (kōl′vōs)	118a	47.24 N	122.32 W
Colwood, Can. (kŏl′wōōd)	118a	48.26 N	123.30 W
Colwyn, Pa.	56b	39.55 N	75.15 W
Comacchio, It. (kŏ-mäk′kyō)	172	44.42 N	12.12 E
Comala, Mex. (kō-mä-lä′)	130	19.22 N	103.47 W
Comalapa, Guat. (kō-mä-lä′-pä)	132	14.43 N	90.56 W
Comalcalco, Mex. (kō-mäl-käl′kō)	131	18.16 N	93.13 W
Comanche, Ok. (kŏ-măn′chē)	122	34.20 N	97.58 W
Comanche, Tx.	124	31.54 N	98.37 W
Comanche Cr., Tx.	124	31.02 N	102.47 W
Comas, Peru	60c	11.57 S	77.04 W
Comayagua, Hond. (kō-mä-yä′gwä)	132	14.24 N	87.36 W
Combahee (R.), SC (kŏm-bȧ-hē′)	127	32.42 N	80.40 W
Comer, Ga. (kŭm′ēr)	126	34.02 N	83.07 W
Comete, C., Turks & Caicos (kŏ-mā′tā)	135	21.45 N	71.25 W
Comilla, Bngl. (kŏ-mĭl′ä)	196	23.33 N	91.17 E
Comino, C., It. (kŏ-mē′nō)	172	40.30 N	9.48 E
Comitán, Mex. (kŏ-mē-tän′)	132	16.16 N	92.09 W
Commencement B., Wa. (kŏ-mĕns′mĕnt bā)	118a	47.17 N	122.21 W
Commentry, Fr. (kŏ-mäN-trē′)	168	46.16 N	2.44 E
Commerce, Ga. (kŏm′ērs)	126	34.10 N	83.27 W
Commerce, Ok.	123	36.57 N	94.54 W
Commerce, Tx.	123	33.15 N	95.52 W
Como, Austl.	70a	34.00 S	151.04 E
Como, It. (kō′mō)	172	45.48 N	9.03 E
Comodoro Rivadavia, Arg. (kō′mŏ-dō′rŏ rĕ-vä-dä ′vē-ä)	144	45.47 S	67.31 W
Como-Est, Can.	95a	45.27 N	74.08 W
Como, Lago di (L.), It. (lä′gō-dē-kō′mō)	172	46.00 N	9.30 E
Comonfort, Mex. (kŏ-mōn-fô′rt)	130	20.43 N	100.47 W
Comorin C., India (kŏ′mŏ-rĭn)	197	8.05 N	78.05 E
Comoros, Afr.	222	12.30 S	42.45 E
Comox, Can. (kō′mŏks)	98	49.40 N	124.55 W
Compainalá, Mex. (kŏm-pä-ē-nä-lȧ′)	131	17.05 N	93.11 W
Companario, Cerro (Mtn.), Arg.-Chile (sĕ′r-rŏ-kôm-pä-nä′ryŏ)	141b	35.54 S	70.23 W
Compans, Fr.	64c	49.00 N	2.40 E
Compiègne, Fr. (kôN-pyĕn′y′)	168	49.25 N	2.49 E
Comporta, Port. (kŏm-pŏr′tȧ)	171b	38.24 N	8.48 W
Compostela, Mex. (kōm-pŏ-stā′lä)	130	21.41 N	104.54 W
Compton, Ca. (kŏmpt′tŭn)	119a	33.54 N	118.14 W
Cona (R.), Ga. (kŏ-nȧ)	126	34.40 N	84.51 W
Conakry, Gui. (kŏ-nȧ-krē′)	228	9.31 N	13.43 W
Conanicut (I.), RI (kŏn′ȧ-nĭ-kŭt)	112b	41.34 N	71.20 W
Concarneau, Fr. (kŏN-kär-nō′)	168	47.54 N	3.52 W
Concepción, Bol. (kŏn-sĕp′syōn′)	143	15.47 S	61.08 W
Concepción, Chile	144	36.51 S	72.59 W
Concepción, Pan.	133	8.31 N	82.38 W
Concepción, Par.	144	23.29 S	57.18 W
Concepcion, Phil.	207a	15.19 N	120.40 E
Concepción (R.), Mex.	128	30.25 N	112.20 W
Concepción (Vol.), Nic.	132	11.36 N	85.43 W
Concepción del Mar, Guat. (kŏn-sĕp-syōn′dĕl mär′)	132	14.07 N	91.23 W
Concepción del Oro, Mex. (kŏn-sĕp-syōn′ dĕl ō′rō)	124	24.39 N	101.24 W
Concepción del Uruguary, Arg. (kŏn-sĕp-syô′n-dĕl-ōō-rōō-gwī′)	144	32.31 S	58.10 W
Conceptión (I.), Ba.	135	23.50 N	75.05 W
Conception B., Can. (kŏn-sĕp′shŭn)	105	47.50 N	52.50 W
Conception, Pt., Ca.	120	34.27 N	120.28 W
Conchali, Chile	61b	33.24 S	70.39 W
Concho (R.), Tx. (kŏn′chō)	124	31.34 N	100.00 W
Conchos (R.), Mex. (kōn′chōs)	124	25.03 N	99.00 W
Conchos (R.), Mex.	124	29.08 N	105.02 W
Concord, Austl.	70a	33.52 S	151.06 E
Concord, Ca. (kŏŋ′kŏrd)	118b	37.58 N	122.02 W
Concord, Can., Can.	54c	43.48 N	79.29 W
Concord, Ma.	105a	42.28 N	71.21 W
Concord, NC	127	35.23 N	80.11 W
Concord, NH	111	43.10 N	71.30 W
Concordia, Arg. (kŏn-kôr′dĭ-ȧ)	144	31.18 S	57.59 W
Concordia, Col.	142a	6.04 N	75.54 W
Concordia, Ks.	123	39.32 N	97.39 W
Concordia, Mex. (kŏn-kô′r-dyä)	130	23.17 N	106.06 W
Concord West, Austl.	70a	33.51 S	151.05 E
Concrete, Wa. (kŏn-′krēt)	116	48.33 N	121.44 W
Conde, Fr.	168	48.50 N	0.36 W
Conde, SD (kŏn-dē′)	114	45.10 N	98.06 W
Condega, Nic. (kŏn-dĕ′gä)	132	13.20 N	86.27 W
Condeúba, Braz. (kōn-dā-ōō′bä)	143	14.47 S	41.44 W
Condom, Fr.	168	43.58 N	0.22 E
Condon, Or. (kŏn′dŭn)	116	45.14 N	120.10 W
Conecun (R.), Al. (kŏ-nē′kŭ)	126	31.05 N	86.52 W
Conegliano, It. (kō-nāl-yä′nō)	172	45.59 N	12.17 E
Conejos (R.), Co. (kŏ-nā′hōs)	121	37.07 N	106.19 W
Conemaugh, Pa. (kŏn′ē-mô)	111	40.25 N	78.50 W
Coney I., NY (kō′nĭ)	112a	40.34 N	73.27 W
Coney Island (Neigh.), NY	55	40.34 N	74.00 W
Conflans-Sainte-Honorine, Fr.	64c	48.59 N	2.06 E
Confolens, Fr. (kôN-fä-läN′)	168	46.01 N	0.41 E
Congaree (R.), SC (kŏŋ-gȧ-rē′)	127	33.53 N	80.55 W
Conghua, China (tsŏŋ-hwä)	203	23.30 N	113.40 E
Congleton, Eng. (kŏŋ′g′l-tŭn)	156	53.10 N	2.13 W
Congo, Afr. (kŏn′gō)	222	3.00 S	13.48 E
Congo (Zaire) (R.), Afr.	230	1.10 N	18.25 E
Congo Basin, Zaire	222	2.47 N	20.58 E
Congo, Serra do (Mts.), Ang.	230	6.25 S	18.30 E
Congo, The, see Zaire			
Congress Heights (Neigh.), DC.	56d	38.51 N	77.00 W
Conisbrough, Eng. (kŏn′ĭs-bŭr-ŏ)	156	53.29 N	1.13 W
Coniston, Can.	103	46.29 N	80.51 W
Conklin, Can. (kŏŋk′lĭn)	99	55.38 N	111.05 W
Conley, Ga. (kŏn′lĭ)	112c	33.38 N	84.19 W
Connacht (Reg.), Ire. (cŏn′ăt)	162	53.50 N	8.45 W
Connaughton, Pa.	56b	40.05 N	75.19 W
Conneaut, Oh. (kŏn-ē-ôt′)	110	41.55 N	80.35 W
Connecticut (State), U.S. (kŏ-nĕt′ĭ-kŭt)	109	41.40 N	73.10 W
Connecticut R., U.S.	111	43.55 N	72.15 W
Connellsville, Pa. (kŏn′nĕlz-vĭl)	111	40.00 N	79.40 W
Connemara (Mts.), Ire. (kŏn-nē-mȧ′rȧ)	162	53.30 N	9.54 W
Connersville, In. (kŏn′ērz-vĭl)	110	39.35 N	85.10 W
Conn, Lough (L.), Ire. (lŏk kŏn)	162	53.56 N	9.25 W
Connors Ra., Austl. (kŏn′nŏrs)	215	22.15 S	149.00 E
Conrad, Mt. (kŏn′răd)	117	48.11 N	111.56 W
Conrich, Can. (kŏn′rĭch)	95e	51.06 N	113.51 W
Conroe, Tx. (kŏn′rō)	125	30.18 N	95.23 W
Conselheiro Lafaiete, Braz. (kŏn-sĕ-lā′rô-lȧ-fā′ĕ-tĕ)	141a	20.40 S	43.46 W
Conshohocken, Pa. (kŏn-shŏ-hŏk′ĕn)	112f	40.04 N	75.18 W
Consolação (Neigh.), Braz.	61d	23.33 S	46.39 W
Consolación del Sur, Cuba (kōn-sŏ-lä-syōn′)	134	22.30 N	83.55 W
Consolidated Main Reef Mines (P. Int.), S. Afr.	71b	26.11 S	27.56 E
Con Son (Is.), Viet.	206	8.30 N	106.28 E
Constance, Mt., Wa. (kŏn′stăns)	118a	47.46 N	123.08 W
Constanţa, Rom. (kōn-stȧn′tsȧ)	161	44.12 N	28.36 E
Constantina, Sp. (kŏn-stän-tē′nä)	170	37.52 N	5.39 W
Constantine, Alg. (kôN-stäN′tēn′)	224	36.28 N	6.38 E
Constantine, Mi. (kŏn′stăn-tēn)	110	41.50 N	85.40 W
Constitución, Chile (kōn′stĭ-tōō-syōn′)	144	35.24 S	72.25 W
Constitución (Neigh.), Arg.	60d	34.37 S	58.23 W
Constitution, Ga. (kŏn-stĭ-tū′shŭn)	112c	33.41 N	84.20 W
Contagem, Braz. (kōn-tȧ′zhĕm)	141a	19.54 S	44.05 W
Contepec, Mex. (kōn-tĕ-pĕk′)	130	20.04 N	100.07 W
Contreras, Mex. (kôn-trĕ′räs)	131a	19.18 N	99.14 W
Contwoyto (L.), Can.	96	65.42 N	110.50 W
Converse, Tx. (kōn′vērs)	119d	29.31 N	98.17 W
Conway, Ar. (kŏn′wā)	123	35.06 N	92.27 W
Conway, NH	111	44.00 N	71.10 W
Conway, SC	127	33.49 N	79.01 W
Conway, Wa.	118a	48.20 N	122.20 W
Conyers, Ga. (kŏn′yōrz)	126	33.41 N	84.01 W
Cooch Behār, India (kōōch bē-här′)	196	26.25 N	89.34 E
Coogee, Austl.	70a	33.55 S	151.16 E
Cook, Pt., Austl.	70b	37.55 S	144.48 E
Cook, C., Can. (kōōk)	98	50.08 N	127.55 W
Cookeville, Tn. (kōōk′vĭl)	126	36.07 N	85.30 W
Cooking L., Can.	95g	53.25 N	113.02 W
Cooking Lake, Can. (kōōk′ĭng)	95g	53.10 N	113.08 W
Cook Inlet, Ak.	107	60.50 N	151.38 W
Cook Is., Oceania	209	20.00 S	158.00 W
Cook, Mt., N.Z.	215a	43.27 S	170.13 E
Cooksmill Green, Eng.	62	51.44 N	0.22 E
Cook Str., N.Z.	215a	40.37 S	174.15 E
Cooktown, Austl. (kōōk′toun)	215	15.40 S	145.20 E
Cooleemee, NC (kōō-lē′mē)	127	35.50 N	80.32 W
Coolgardie, Austl. (kōōl-gär′dē)	214	31.00 S	121.25 E
Cooma, Austl. (kōō′mȧ)	216	36.22 S	149.10 E
Coonamble, Austl. (kōō-năm′b′l)	216	31.00 S	148.30 E
Coonoort, India	197	10.22 N	76.15 E
Coon Rapids, Mn. (kōōn)	119g	45.09 N	93.17 W
Cooper, Tx. (kōōp′ēr)	123	33.23 N	95.40 W
Cooper Center, Ak. (kōōp′ēr sĕn′tēr)	107	61.54 N	15.30 W
Coopersale Common, Eng.	62	51.42 N	0.08 E
Coopers Cr., Austl. (kōō′pērz)	216	27.32 N	141.19 E
Cooperstown, ND	114	47.26 N	98.07 W
Cooperstown, NY (kōōp′ērs-toun)	111	42.45 N	74.55 W
Coorong, The (L.), Austl. (kōō′rŏng)	216	36.07 N	319.45 E
Coosa, Al. (kōō′sȧ)	126	32.43 N	86.25 W
Coosa (R.), Al.	126	34.00 N	86.00 W
Coosawattee (R.), Ga. (kōō-sȧ-wôt′ē)	126	34.37 N	84.45 W
Coos B., Or.	116	43.19 N	124.40 W
Coos Bay, Or. (kōōs)	116	43.21 N	124.12 W
Cootamundra, Austl. (kōōtă-mŭnd′ră)	216	34.25 S	148.00 E
Copacabana, Braz. (kô′pä-kȧ-bȧ′nä)	144b	22.57 S	43.11 W
Copalita (R.), Mex. (kŏ-pä-lē′tä)	131	15.55 N	96.06 W
Copán (Ruins), Hond. (kō-pän′)	132	14.50 N	89.10 W
Copano B., Tx. (kō-pän′ō)	125	28.08 N	97.25 W
Copenhagen, see København			
Copiapó, Chile (kō-pyä-pō′)	144	27.16 S	70.28 W
Copley, Oh. (kŏp′lē)	113d	41.06 N	81.38 W
Copparo, It. (kŏp-pä′rō)	172	44.53 N	11.50 E
Coppell, Tx. (kŏp′pēl)	119c	32.57 N	97.00 W
Copper (R.), Ak. (kŏp′ēr)	107	62.38 N	145.00 W
Copper Cliff, Can.	102	46.28 N	81.04 W
Copper Harbor, Mi.	115	47.27 N	87.53 W
Copperhill, Tn. (kŏp′ēr hĭl)	126	35.00 N	84.22 W
Copperinine (R.), Can.	96	66.48 N	114.59 W
Coppermine, Can. (kŏp′ēr-mīn)	96	67.46 N	115.19 W
Copper Mtn., Ak.	98	55.14 N	132.36 W
Copperton, Ut. (kŏp′ēr-tŭn)	119b	40.34 N	112.06 W
Coquilee, Or. (kŏ-kēl′)	116	43.11 N	124.11 W
Coquilhatville, see Mbandaka			
Coquimbo, Chile (kŏ-kēm′bō)	144	29.58 S	71.31 W
Coquimbo (Prov.), Chile	141b	31.50 S	71.05 W
Coquitlam (L.) (kō-kwĭt-lȧm)	118d	49.23 N	122.44 W
Corabia, Rom. (kŏ-rä′bĭ-ȧ)	173	43.45 N	24.29 E
Coracora, Peru (kō′rä-kō′rä)	142	15.12 S	73.42 W
Coral Gables, Fl.	127a	25.43 N	80.14 W
Coral Rapids, Can. (kŏr′ăl)	102	50.18 N	81.49 W
Coral Sea, Oceania (kŏr′ăl)	208	13.30 S	150.00 E
Coralville Res., Ia.	115	41.45 N	91.50 W
Corangamite, L., Austl. (cŏr-ăŋg′ȧ-mît)	216	38.05 S	142.55 E
Coraopolis, Pa. (kō-rä-ŏp′ŏ-lĭs)	113e	40.30 N	80.09 W
Corato, It. (kŏ′rä-tŏ)	172	41.08 N	16.28 E
Corbeil-Essonnes, Fr. (kôr-bā′yĕ-sŏn′)	169b	48.31 N	2.29 E
Corbett, Or. (kôr′bĕt)	118c	45.31 N	122.17 W
Corbie, Fr. (kŏr-bē′)	168	49.55 N	2.27 E
Corbin, Ky. (kôr′bĭn)	126	36.55 N	84.06 W
Corby, Eng. (kôr′bĭ)	156	52.29 N	0.38 W
Corcovado (Mtn.(, Braz. (kôr-kŏ-vä′dōō)	144b	22.57 S	43.13 W
Corcovado, Golfo (G.), Chile (kôr-kŏ-vä′dhō)	144	43.40 S	75.00 W
Cordeiro, Braz. (kôr-dā′rō)	141a	22.03 S	42.22 W
Cordele, Ga. (kôr-dēl′)	126	31.55 N	83.50 W
Cordell, Ok. (kôr-dĕl′)	122	35.19 N	98.58 W
Cordilleran Highlands (Reg.), N.A. (kōr dĭl′lŭr ȧn)	94	55.00 N	125.00 W
Córdoba, Arg. (kôr′dŏ-vä)	144	30.20 S	64.03 W
Córdoba, Mex. (kô′r-dŏ-bä)	131	18.53 N	96.54 W
Córdoba (Prov.), Arg. (kôr′dŏ-vä)	144	32.00 S	64.00 W
Córdoba, Sp. (kŏ′r-dô-bä)	170	37.55 N	4.45 W
Córdoba, Sa. de (Mts.), Arg.	144	31.15 S	64.30 W
Cordova, Ak. (kôr′dŏ-vä)	107	60.34 N	145.38 W
Cordova, Al. (kôr′dŏ-ȧ)	126	33.45 N	86.22 W
Cordova B., Ak.	98	54.55 N	132.35 W
Corfu (I.), see Kérkira			
Corigliano, It. (kō-rē-lyä′nō)	172	39.35 N	16.30 E
Corinth, Ms. (kŏr′ĭnth)	126	34.55 N	88.30 W
Corinth, see Kórinthos			
Corinto, Braz. (kô-rē′n-tō)	143	18.20 S	44.16 W
Corinto, Col.	142a	3.09 N	76.12 W
Corinto, Nic. (kōr-ĭn′to)	132	12.30 N	87.12 W
Corio, Austl.	211a	38.05 S	144.22 E
Corio B., Austl.	211a	38.07 S	144.25 E
Corisco, It.	65c	45.26 N	9.07 E
Corisco, Isal de (I.), Equat. Gui.	230	0.50 N	8.40 E
Cork, Ire. (kôrk)	162	51.54 N	8.25 W
Cork Hbr., Ire.	162	51.44 N	8.15 W
Corleone, It. (kôr-lā-ō′nā)	172	37.48 N	13.18 E
Cormano, It.	65c	45.33 N	9.10 E
Cormeilles-en-Parisis, Fr.	64c	48.59 N	2.12 E
Cormorant L., Can.	101	54.13 N	100.47 W
Cornelia, Ga. (kôr-nē′lyȧ)	126	34.31 N	83.30 W
Cornelis (R.), S. Afr. (kôr-nē′lĭs)	223d	27.48 S	29.15 E
Cornell, Ca. (kôr-nĕl′)	119a	34.06 N	118.46 W
Cornell, Wi.	115	45.10 N	91.10 W
Cornellá, Sp.	65e	41.21 N	2.04 E
Corner Brook, Can. (kôr′nēr)	105	48.57 N	57.57 W
Corner Inlet, Austl.	216	38.55 S	146.45 E
Corning, Ar. (kôr′nĭng)	123	36.26 N	90.35 W
Corning, Ia.	115	40.58 N	94.40 W
Corning, NY	111	42.10 N	77.05 W
Corno, Monte (Mtn.), It. (kôr′nō)	172	42.28 N	13.37 E
Cornwall, Ba.	134	25.55 N	77.15 W
Cornwall, Can. (kôrn′wôl)	111	45.05 N	74.35 W

ng-sing; nŋ-banŋk; N-nasalized n; nŏd; cŏmmit; ōld; ŏbey; ŏrder; oi-boil; fōōd; fŏŏt; ou-out; s-soft; sh-dish; th-thin; pūre; ûnite; ûrn; stŭd; circŭs; ü-as in French tu; ′-indeterminate vowel.

274 Coro – Cruces

PLACE (Pronunciation)	PAGE	Lat. °'	Long. °'
Coro, Ven. (kō'rô)	142	11.22 N	69.43 W
Corocoro, Bol. (kō-rô-kō'rô)	142	17.15 S	68.21 W
Coromandel Coast, India (kŏr-ô-man'dĕl)	197	13.30 N	80.30 E
Coromandel Pen., N.Z.	215a	36.50 S	176.00 E
Corona, Al. (kô-rō'nȧ)	126	33.42 N	87.28 W
Corona, Ca.	119a	33.52 N	117.34 W
Coronada, Bahía de (B.), C.R. (bä-ē'ä-dĕ-kô-rô-nä'dō)	133	8.47 N	84.04 W
Corona del Mar, Ca. (kô-rō'nȧ dĕl mär)	119a	33.36 N	117.53 W
Coronado, Ca. (kŏr-ô-nä'dō)	120a	32.42 N	117.12 W
Coronation G., Can. (kŏr-ô-nā'shŭn)	96	68.07 N	112.50 W
Coronel, Chile (kō-rô-nĕl')	144	37.00 S	73.10 W
Coronel Brandsen, Arg. (kō-rô-nĕl-brä'nd-sĕn)	141c	35.09 S	58.15 W
Coronel Dorrego, Arg. (kŏ-rô-nĕl-dôr-rĕ'gō)	144	38.43 S	61.16 W
Coronel Oviedo, Par. (kō-rô-nĕl-ô-vē'dō)	144	25.28 S	56.22 W
Coronel Pringles, Arg. (kŏ-rô-nĕl-prēn'glĕs)	144	37.54 S	61.22 W
Coronel Suárez, Arg. (kŏ-rô-nĕl-swä'rās)	144	37.27 S	61.49 W
Corowa, Austl. (cŏr-ôwă)	216	36.02 S	146.23 E
Corozal, Belize (cŏr-ŏth-äl')	132a	18.25 N	88.23 W
Corpus Christi, Tx. (kôr'pŭs krĭs'tē)	125	27.48 N	97.24 W
Corpus Christi B., Tx.	125	27.47 N	97.14 W
Corpus Christi L., Tx.	124	28.08 N	98.20 W
Corral, Chile (kō-räl')	144	39.57 S	73.15 W
Corral de Almaguer, Sp. (kô-räl'dā äl-mä-gâr')	170	39.45 N	3.10 W
Corralillo, Cuba (kō-rä-lē-yō)	134	28.00 N	80.40 W
Corregidor I, Phil. (kô-rā-hē-dōr')	207a	14.21 N	120.25 E
Correntina, Braz. (kô-rĕn-tē-nȧ)	143	13.18 S	44.33 W
Corrib, Lough (L.), Ire. (lŏk kŏr'ĭb)	162	53.56 N	9.19 W
Corrientes, Arg. (kō-ryĕn'tās)	144	27.25 S	58.39 W
Corrientes (Prov.)	144	28.45 S	58.00 W
Corrientes, Cabo (C.), Cuba (kä'bô-kôr-rē-ĕn'tĕs)	134	21.50 N	84.25 W
Corrientes, Cabo (C.), Col. (kä'bô-kō-ryĕn'tās)	142	5.34 N	77.35 W
Corrientes, Cabo (C.), Mex.	130	20.25 N	105.41 W
Corringham, Eng.	62	51.31 N	0.28 E
Corroios, Port.	65d	38.38 N	9.09 W
Corry, Pa. (kŏr'ĭ)	111	41.55 N	79.40 W
Corse, C., Fr. (kôrs)	172	42.59 N	9.19 E
Corsica (I.), Fr. (kô'r-sē-kä)	172	42.10 N	8.55 E
Corsicana, Tx. (kôr-sĭ-kăn'ȧ)	125	32.06 N	96.28 W
Cortazar, Mex. (kôr-tä-zär)	130	20.30 N	100.57 W
Corte, Fr. (kôr'tā)	172	42.18 N	9.10 E
Cortegana, Sp. (kôr-tā-gä'nä)	170	37.54 N	6.48 W
Corte Madera, Ca.	58b	37.55 N	122.31 W
Cortes (P. Int.), Sp.	65b	40.25 N	3.41 W
Cortés, Ensenada de (B.), Cuba (ĕn-sĕ-nä-dä-dĕ-kôr-tās')	134	22.05 N	83.45 W
Cortez, Co.	121	37.21 N	108.35 W
Cortland, NY (kôrt'lănd)	111	42.35 N	76.10 W
Cortona, It. (kôr-tō'nä)	172	43.16 N	12.00 E
Corubal (R.), Guinea-Bissau	228	11.43 N	14.40 W
Coruche, Port. (kō-rōō'she)	170	38.58 N	8.34 W
Coruh (R.), Tur. (chō-rōōk')	179	40.30 N	41.10 E
Corum, Tur. (chô-rōōm')	179	40.34 N	34.45 E
Corumbá, Braz. (kô-rōōm-bä')	143	19.01 S	57.28 W
Corunna, Mi. (kô-rŭn'ȧ)	110	43.00 N	84.05 W
Coruripe, Braz. (kō-rōō-rē'pĭ)	143	10.09 S	36.13 W
Corvallis, Or. (kŏr-văl'ĭs)	116	44.34 N	123.17 W
Corve (R.), Eng. (kôr'vē)	156	52.28 N	2.43 W
Corviale (Neigh.), It.	66c	41.52 N	12.25 E
Corydon, Ia.	115	40.45 N	93.20 W
Corydon, In. (kŏr'ĭ-dŭn)	110	38.10 N	86.05 W
Corydon, Ky.	110	37.45 N	87.40 W
Cosamaloápan, Mex. (kô-sä-mä-lwä'pän)	131	18.21 N	95.48 W
Coscomatepec, Mex. (kôs'kōmä-tē-pĕk')	131	19.04 N	97.03 W
Cosenza, It. (kō-zĕnt'sä)	172	39.18 N	16.15 E
Cosfanero, Canal de (Can.), Arg.	60d	34.34 S	58.22 W
Coshocton, Oh. (kô-shŏk'tŭn)	110	40.15 N	81.55 W
Cosigüina (Vol.), Nic.	110	12.59 N	83.35 W
Cosmoledo Group (Is.), Afr. (kŏs-mô-lā'dō)	227	9.42 S	47.45 E
Cosmopolis, Wa. (kŏz-mŏp'ô-lĭs)	116	46.58 N	123.47 W
Cosne-sur-Loire, Fr. (kōn-sür-lwär')	168	47.25 N	2.57 E
Cosoleacaque, Mex. (kō sō lä-ä-kä'kē)	131	18.01 N	94.38 W
Costa de Caparica, Port.	171b	38.40 N	9.12 W
Costa Mesa, Ca. (kŏs'tȧ mā'sȧ)	119a	33.39 N	118.54 W
Costa Rica, N.A. (kŏs'tȧ rē'kȧ)	129	10.30 N	84.30 W
Cosumnes (R.), Ca. (kō-sŭm'nĕz)	120	38.21 N	121.17 W
Cotabambas, Peru (kō-tä-bäm'bäs)	142	13.49 S	72.17 W
Cotabato, Phil. (kō-tä-bä'tō)	207	7.06 N	124.13 E
Cotaxtla, Mex. (kō-täs'tlä)	131	18.49 N	96.22 W
Cotaxtla (R.), Mex.	131	18.54 N	96.21 W
Coteau-du-Lac, Can. (cō-tō'dü-läk)	95a	45.17 N	74.11 W
Coteau-Landing, Can.	95a	45.15 N	74.13 W
Coteaux, Hai.	135	18.15 N	74.05 W
Côte-Saint-Luc, Can.	54b	45.28 N	73.40 W
Côte Visitation (Neigh.), Can.	54b	45.33 N	73.36 W
Cotija de la Paz, Mex. (kô-tē'-ĸä-dĕ-lä-pä'z)	130	19.46 N	102.43 W
Cotonou, Benin (kō-tō-nōō')	229	6.21 N	2.26 E
Cotopaxi (Mtn.), Ec. (kō-tô-păk'sē)	142	0.40 S	78.26 W
Cotorro, Cuba (kô-tôr-rō)	135a	23.03 N	82.17 W
Cotswold Hills, Eng. (kŭtz'wōld)	162	51.35 N	2.16 W
Cottage City, Md.	56d	38.56 N	76.57 W
Cottage Grove, Mn. (kŏt'āj grōv)	119g	44.50 N	92.52 W
Cottage Grove, Or.	116	43.48 N	123.04 W
Cottbus, G.D.R. (kōtt'bōōs)	166	51.47 N	14.20 E
Cottiens Alps (Mts.), Fr.-It.	169	44.46 N	7.02 E
Cottonwood (R.), Mn. (kŏt'ŭn-wŏŏd)	114	44.25 N	95.35 W
Cottonwood Cr., Ca.	116	40.24 N	122.50 W

PLACE (Pronunciation)	PAGE	Lat. °'	Long. °'
Cotuí, Dom. Rep. (kô-tōō'-ē)	135	19.05 N	70.10 W
Cotulla, Tx. (kŏ-tŭl'lȧ)	124	28.26 N	99.14 W
Coubert, Fr. (kōō-bâr')	169b	48.40 N	2.43 E
Coudersport, Pa. (kou'dērz-port)	111	41.45 N	78.00 W
Coudres, Île aux (I.), Can.	104	47.17 N	70.12 W
Coulommiers, Fr. (kōō-lô-myā')	169b	48.49 N	3.05 E
Coulsdon (Neigh.), Eng.	62	51.19 N	0.08 W
Coulto, Serra do (Mts.), Braz. (sĕ'r-rä-dô-kô-ōō'tô)	144b	22.33 S	43.27 W
Council Bluffs, Ia. (koun'sĭl blŭf)	114	41.16 N	95.53 W
Council Grove, Ks. (koun'sĭl grōv)	123	38.39 N	96.30 W
Coupeville, Wa. (kōōp'vĭl)	118a	48.13 N	122.41 W
Courantyne (R.), Guy.-Sur. (kôr'ăntĭn)	143	4.28 N	57.42 W
Courbevoie, Fr.	64c	48.54 N	2.15 E
Courcelle, Fr.	64c	48.42 N	2.06 E
Courtenay, Can. (cōōrt-nā')	98	49.41 N	125.00 W
Courtleigh, Md.	56c	39.22 N	76.46 W
Courtry, Fr.	64c	48.55 N	2.36 E
Coushatta, La. (kou-shăt'ȧ)	125	32.02 N	93.21 W
Coutras, Fr. (kōō-trá')	168	45.02 N	0.07 W
Cova da Piedade, Port.	65d	38.40 N	9.10 W
Covelo, Ang.	230	12.06 S	13.55 E
Cove Neck, NY	55	40.53 N	73.31 W
Coventry, Eng. (kŭv'ĕn-trĭ)	156	52.25 N	1.29 W
Covilhã, Port. (kô-vēl'yăɴ)	170	40.18 N	7.29 W
Covina, Ca. (kô-vē'nȧ)	119a	34.06 N	117.54 W
Covington, Ga. (kŭv'ĭng-tŭn)	126	33.36 N	83.50 W
Covington, In.	110	40.10 N	87.15 W
Covington, Ky.	113f	39.05 N	84.31 W
Covington, La.	125	30.30 N	90.06 W
Covington, Oh.	110	40.10 N	84.20 W
Covington, Ok.	123	36.18 N	97.32 W
Covington, Tn.	126	35.33 N	89.40 W
Covington, Va.	111	37.50 N	80.00 W
Cowal, L., Austl. (kou'ăl)	216	33.30 S	147.10 E
Cowan, (L.), Austl. (kou'ȧn)	214	32.00 S	122.30 E
Cowan Heights, Ca.	59	33.47 N	117.47 W
Cowansville, Can.	104	45.13 N	72.47 W
Cow Cr., Or. (kou)	116	42.45 N	123.35 W
Cowes, Eng. (kouz)	162	50.43 N	1.25 W
Cowichan L., Can.	98	48.54 N	124.20 W
Cowley (Neigh.), Eng.	62	51.32 N	0.29 W
Cowlitz (R.), Wa. (kou'lĭts)	116	46.30 N	122.45 W
Cowra, Austl. (kou'rȧ)	216	33.50 S	148.33 E
Coxim, Braz. (kō-shēɴ')	143	18.32 S	54.43 W
Coxquihui, Mex. (kōz-kē-wē')	131	20.10 N	97.34 W
Cox's Bāzār, Bngl.	190	21.32 N	92.00 E
Coyaima, Col. (kô-yáē'mä)	142a	3.48 N	75.11 W
Coyame, Mex. (kô-yä'mä)	124	29.26 N	105.05 W
Coyanosa Draw, Tx. (kŏ yá-nō'sä)	124	30.55 N	103.07 W
Coyoacán, Mex. (kô-yō-á-kän')	131a	19.21 N	99.10 W
Coyote (R.), Ca. (kī'ōt)	118b	37.37 N	121.57 W
Coyuca de Benítez, Mex. (kō-yōō'kä dā bā-nē'tāz)	130	17.04 N	100.06 W
Coyuca de Catalán, Mex. (kō-yōō'kä dā kä-tä-län')	130	18.19 N	100.41 W
Coyutla, Mex. (kō-yōō'tlä)	131	20.13 N	97.40 W
Cozad, Ne. (kō'zăd)	122	40.53 N	99.59 W
Cozaddale, Oh. (kô-zăd-dāl)	113f	39.16 N	84.09 W
Cozoyoapan Mex. (kō-zō-yô-ä-pá'n)	130	16.45 N	98.17 W
Cozumel, Mex. (kŏ-zōō-mĕ'l)	132a	20.31 N	86.55 W
Cozumel, Isla de (I.), Mex. (ē's-lä-dĕ-kŏ-zōō-mĕ'l)	132a	20.26 N	87.10 W
Crab Cr., Wa. (krăb)	116	46.47 N	119.43 W
Crab Cr., Wa.	116	47.21 N	119.09 W
Cradock, S. Afr. (kră'dŭk)	227c	32.12 S	25.38 E
Crafton, Pa. (krăf'tŭn)	113e	40.26 N	80.04 W
Craig, Co. (krāg)	117	40.32 N	107.31 W
Craighall (Neigh.), S. Afr.	71b	26.07 S	28.02 E
Craighall Park (Neigh.), S. Afr.	71b	26.08 S	28.01 E
Craiova, Rom. (krá-yō'vá)	173	44.18 N	23.50 E
Cranberry (L.), NY (krăn'bĕr-ĭ)	111	44.10 N	74.50 W
Cranbourne, Austl.	211a	38.07 S	145.16 E
Cranbrook, Can. (krăn'brŏŏk)	99	49.31 N	115.46 W
Cranbury, NJ (krăn'bē-rĭ)	112a	40.19 N	74.31 W
Crandon, Wi. (krăn'dŭn)	115	45.35 N	88.55 W
Cranford, NJ	55	40.39 N	74.19 W
Crank, Eng.	64a	53.29 N	2.45 W
Cranston, RI (krăns'tŭn)	112b	41.46 N	71.25 W
Crater L., Or. (krā'tēr)	116	43.00 N	122.08 W
Crater Lake Natl. Park, Or.	116	42.58 N	122.40 W
Craters of the Moon Natl. Mon., Id. (krā'tēr)	117	43.28 N	113.15 W
Crateús, Braz. (krä-tā-ōōzh')	143	5.09 S	40.35 W
Crato, Braz. (krä'tōō)	143	7.19 S	39.13 W
Crawford, Ne. (krô'fērd)	114	42.41 N	103.25 W
Crawford, Wa.	118c	45.49 N	122.24 W
Crawfordsville, In. (krô'fērdz-vĭl)	110	40.00 N	86.55 W
Crazy Mts., Mt. (krā'zĭ)	117	46.11 N	110.25 W
Crazy Woman Cr., Wy.	117	44.08 N	106.40 W
Crecy, S. Afr. (krĕ-sē)	223d	24.38 S	28.52 E
Crécy-en-Brie, Fr. (krā-sē'-ĕɴ-brē')	169b	48.52 N	2.55 E
Crécy-en-Ponthieu, Fr.	168	50.13 N	1.48 E
Credit (R.), Can.	95d	43.41 N	79.55 W
Cree (L.), Can. (krē)	96	57.35 N	107.52 W
Creekmouth (Neigh.), Eng.	62	51.31 N	0.06 E
Creighton, Ne. (krā'tŭn)	114	42.27 N	97.54 W
Creighton, S. Afr. (cre-tŏn)	227c	30.02 S	28.52 E
Creil, Fr. (krĕ'y')	168	49.18 N	2.28 E
Crema, It. (krā'mä)	172	45.21 N	9.53 E
Cremona, It. (krā-mō'nä)	172	45.09 N	10.02 E
Crépy-en-Valois, Fr. (krā-pē'ĕɴ-vä-lwä')	169b	49.14 N	2.53 E
Cres (I.), Yugo.	172	44.50 N	14.31 E
Cres, Yugo. (Tsrĕs)	172	44.58 N	14.21 E
Crescent (L.), Fl. (krĕs'ĕnt)	127	29.33 N	81.30 W
Crescent (L.), Or.	116	43.25 N	121.58 W
Crescent Beach, Can.	118d	49.03 N	122.58 W
Crescent City, Ca. (krĕs'ĕnt)	116	41.46 N	124.13 W
Crescent City, Fl.	127	29.26 N	81.35 W
Crescentville (Neigh.), Pa.	56b	40.02 N	75.05 W

PLACE (Pronunciation)	PAGE	Lat. °'	Long. °'
Cresco, Ia. (krĕs'kō)	115	43.23 N	92.07 W
Cresskill, NJ	55	40.57 N	73.57 W
Crested Butte, Co. (krĕst'ĕd būt)	121	38.50 N	107.00 W
Crest Haven, Md.	56d	39.02 N	76.59 W
Crestline, Ca. (krĕst-līn)	119a	34.15 N	117.17 W
Crestline, Oh.	110	40.50 N	82.40 W
Crestmore, Ca. (krĕst'môr)	119a	34.02 N	117.23 W
Creston, Can. (krĕs'tŭn)	99	49.06 N	116.31 W
Creston, Ia.	115	41.04 N	94.22 W
Creston, Oh.	113d	40.59 N	81.54 W
Crestview, Fl. (krĕst'vū)	126	30.44 N	86.35 W
Crestwood, Il.	58a	41.39 N	87.44 W
Crestwood, Ky. (krĕst'wŏŏd)	113h	38.20 N	85.28 W
Crestwood, Mo.	119e	38.33 N	90.23 W
Crete, Il. (krēt)	113a	41.26 N	87.38 W
Crete (I.), Grc.	172a	35.15 N	24.30 E
Crete, Ne.	123	40.38 N	96.56 W
Créteil, Fr.	64c	48.48 N	2.28 E
Creus, Cabo de (C.), Sp. (kä'-bô-dĕ-krĕ-ōōs)	171	42.16 N	3.18 E
Creuse (R.), Fr. (krûz)	168	46.51 N	0.49 E
Creve Coeur, Mo. (krēv kōōr)	119e	38.40 N	90.27 W
Crevillente, Sp. (krâ-vē-lyĕn'tâ)	171	38.12 N	0.48 W
Crewe, Eng. (krōō)	156	53.06 N	2.27 W
Crewe, Va.	127	37.09 N	78.08 W
Crimea P-Ov (Pen.), **see Krymskiy**			
Crimmitschau, G.D.R. (krĭm'ĭt-shou)	166	50.49 N	12.22 E
Cripple Creek, Co. (krĭp''l)	122	38.44 N	105.12 W
Crisfield, Md. (krĭs-fēld)	111	38.00 N	75.50 W
Cristal, Monts de (Mts.), Gabon	230	0.50 N	10.30 E
Cristina, Braz. (krĕs-tē'-nä)	141a	22.13 S	45.15 W
Cristobal Colón, Pico (Pk.), Col. (pē'kō-krēs-tō'bäl-kō-lōn')	142	11.00 N	74.00 W
Cristo Redentor, Estatua do (P. Int.), Braz.	61c	22.57 S	43.13 W
Crişul Alb (R.), Rom. (krē'shōōl älb)	167	46.20 N	22.15 E
Crna (R.), Yugo. (ts'r'nȧ)	173	41.03 N	21.46 E
Crna Gora (Montenegro)(Reg.), Yugo. (ts'r-nȧ-gō'rȧ) (mōn-tā-nā'grō) (mōn-tē-nē'grō)	173	42.55 N	18.52 E
Črnomelj, Yugo. (ch'r'nō-māl')	172	45.35 N	15.11 E
Croatia (Reg.), **see Hrvatska**			
Crockenhill, Eng.	62	51.23 N	0.10 E
Crockett, Ca. (krŏk'ĕt)	118b	38.03 N	122.14 W
Crockett, Tx.	125	31.19 N	95.28 W
Crofton, Md.	112e	39.01 N	76.43 W
Crofton, Ne.	114	42.44 N	97.32 W
Croissy-Beaubourg, Fr.	64c	48.50 N	2.40 E
Croissy-sur-Seine, Fr.	64c	48.53 N	2.09 E
Croix, Lac la (L.), Can.-Mn. (läk lä krōō-ä')	115	48.19 N	91.53 W
Croker (I.), Austl. (krŏ'kȧ)	214	10.45 S	132.25 E
Cromer, Austl.	70a	33.44 S	151.17 E
Cronenberg (Neigh.), F.R.G.	63	51.12 N	7.08 E
Cronton, Eng.	64a	53.23 N	2.46 W
Cronulla, Austl. (krō-nŭl'ȧ)	211b	34.03 S	151.09 E
Crooked (I.), Ba.	135	22.45 N	74.10 W
Crooked (L.), Can.	105	48.25 N	56.05 W
Crooked (R.), Can.	98	54.30 N	122.55 W
Crooked (R.), Or.	116	44.07 N	120.30 W
Crooked Cr., Il. (krŏŏk'ĕd)	123	40.21 N	90.49 W
Crooked Cr., Or.	116	42.23 N	118.14 W
Crooked Island Passage (Str.), Ba.	135	22.40 N	74.50 W
Crookston, Mn. (krŏŏks'tŭn)	114	47.44 N	96.35 W
Crooksville, Oh. (krŏŏks'vĭl)	110	39.45 N	82.05 W
Crosby, Eng.	64a	53.30 N	3.02 W
Crosby, Mn. (krôz'bĭ)	115	46.29 N	93.58 W
Crosby, ND	114	48.55 N	103.18 W
Crosby (Neigh.), S. Afr.	71b	26.12 S	27.59 E
Crosby, Tx.	125a	29.55 N	95.04 W
Crosne, Fr.	64c	48.43 N	2.28 E
Cross (L.), Can. (krôs)	111	44.55 N	76.55 W
Cross (L.), La.	125	32.33 N	93.58 W
Cross (R.), Nig.	229	5.35 N	8.05 E
Cross City, Fl.	126	29.55 N	83.25 W
Crossett, Ar. (krôs'ĕt)	123	33.08 N	92.00 W
Cross Hbr., Ba.	134	25.55 N	77.105 W
Cross L., Can.	101	54.45 N	97.30 W
Cross Lake, Can.	101	54.37 N	97.47 W
Cross River Res., NY (krôs)	112a	41.14 N	73.34 W
Cross Sd., Ak. (krŏs)	107	58.12 N	137.20 W
Crosswell, Mi. (krŏz'wĕl)	110	43.15 N	82.35 W
Crotch (R.), Can.	103	45.02 N	76.55 W
Crotone, It. (krō-tō'nĕ)	173	39.05 N	17.08 E
Croton Falls Res., NY (krōtŭn)	112a	41.22 N	73.44 W
Croton-on-Hudson, NY (krō'tŭn-ŏn hŭd'sŭn)	112a	41.12 N	73.53 W
Crouse Run (R.), Pa.	57b	40.35 N	79.58 W
Crow (L.), Can.	115	49.13 N	93.29 W
Crow Agency, Mt.	117	45.36 N	107.27 W
Crow Cr., Co.	122	41.08 N	104.25 W
Crow Creek Ind. Res., SD	114	44.17 N	99.17 W
Crow Ind. Res., Mt. (krō)	117	45.26 N	108.12 W
Crowle, Eng. (kroul)	156	53.36 N	0.49 W
Crowley, La. (krou'lē)	125	30.13 N	92.22 W
Crown Mtn., Can. (kroun)	118d	49.24 N	123.05 W
Crown Mtn., Vir.Is.(U.S.A.)	129c	18.22 N	64.58 W
Crown Point, In. (kroun point')	113a	41.25 N	87.22 W
Crown Point, NY	111	44.00 N	73.25 W
Crows Nest, Austl.	70a	33.50 S	151.12 E
Crowsnest P., Can.	99	49.39 N	114.45 W
Crow Wing (R.), Mn. (krō)	115	44.50 N	94.01 W
Crow Wing (R.), Mn.	115	46.42 N	94.48 W
Crow Wing (R.),North Fork, Mn.	115	45.16 N	94.28 W
Crow Wing (R.),South Fork, Mn.	115	44.59 N	94.42 W
Croxley Green, Eng.	62	51.39 N	0.27 W
Croydon, Austl. (kroi'dŭn)	215	18.15 S	142.15 E
Croydon, Austl.	211a	37.48 S	145.17 E
Croydon, Eng.	156b	51.22 N	0.06 W
Croydon, Pa.	112f	40.05 N	74.55 W
Crozet, Îles, Ind. O. (krô-zĕ')	232	46.20 S	51.30 E
Cruces, Cuba (krōō'sås)	134	22.20 N	80.20 W

PLACE (Pronunciation)	PAGE	Lat. °′	Long. °′
Cruces, Arroyo de, Mex. (är-rō'yō-dĕ-krōō'sĕs)	124	26.17 N	104.32 W
Cruillas, Mex. (krōō-ēl'yäs)	124	24.45 N	98.31 W
Crum Lynne, Pa.	56b	39.52 N	75.20 W
Cruz Alta, Braz. (krōōz äl'tä)	144	28.41 S	54.02 W
Cruz, Cabo (C.), Cuba (kä'-bô-krōōz)	134	19.50 N	77.45 W
Cruz, Cayo (I.), Cuba (kä'yō-krōōz)	134	22.15 N	77.50 W
Cruz del Eje, Arg. (krōō's-dĕl-ĕ-kĕ)	144	30.46 S	64.45 W
Cruzeiro, Braz. (krōō-zā'rōō)	141a	22.36 S	44.57 W
Cruzeiro do Sul, Braz. (krōō-zā'rōō dōō sōōl)	142	7.34 S	72.40 W
Crysler, Can.	95c	45.13 N	75.09 W
Crystal Beach, Can.	57a	42.52 N	79.04 W
Crystal City, Tx. (krĭs'tăl sĭ'tĭ)	124	28.40 N	99.90 W
Crystal Falls, Mi. (krĭs'tăl fôls)	115	46.06 N	88.21 W
Crystal Lake, Il. (krĭs'tăl lăk)	113a	42.15 N	88.18 W
Crystal Springs, Ms. (krĭs'tăl sprĭngz)	126	31.58 N	90.20 W
Crystal Sprs., Ca.	118b	37.31 N	122.26 W
Csömör, Hung.	66g	47.33 N	19.14 E
Csongrád, Hung. (chôn'gräd)	167	46.42 N	20.09 E
Csorna, Hung. (chôr'nä)	167	47.39 N	17.11 E
Cúa, Ven. (kōō'ä)	143b	10.10 N	66.54 W
Cuajimalpa, Mex. (kwä-hē-mäl'pä)	131a	19.21 N	99.18 W
Cuale, Sierra del (Mts.), Mex. (sē-ĕ'r-rä-dĕl-kwä'lĕ)	130	20.20 N	104.58 W
Cuamato, Ang. (kwä-mä'tō)	230	17.05 S	15.09 E
Cuamba, Moz.	231	14.49 S	36.33 E
Cuando, Ang. (kwän'dō)	230	16.32 S	22.07 E
Cuando (R.), Ang.	230	16.50 S	22.40 E
Cuangar, Ang.	230	17.36 S	18.39 E
Cuango (Kwango) (R.), Afr. (kwäŋ'gō)	230	6.35 S	16.50 E
Cuanza (R.), Ang. (kwän'zä)	230	9.05 S	13.15 E
Cuarto Saladillo (R.), Arg. (kwär'tō-sä-lä-dē'l-yō)	144	33.00 S	63.25 W
Cuatro Caminos, Cuba (kwä'trô-kä-mē'nôs)	135a	23.01 N	82.13 W
Cuatro Caminos, Cuba	60b	22.54 N	82.23 W
Cuatro Ciénegas, Mex. (kwä'trō syā'nå-gäs)	124	26.59 N	102.03 W
Cuauhtemoc, Mex. (kwä-ōō-tē-mōk')	132	15.43 N	91.57 W
Cuautepec, Mex. (kwä-ōō-tē-pĕk)	130	16.41 N	99.04 W
Cuautepec, Mex.	130	20.01 N	98.19 W
Cuautepec el Alto, Mex.	60a	19.34 N	99.08 W
Cuautitlán, Mex. (kwä-ōō-tēt-län')	131a	19.40 N	99.12 W
Cuautla, Mex. (kwä-ōō'tlä)	130	18.47 N	98.57 W
Cuba, N.A. (kū'bȧ)	129	22.00 N	79.00 W
Cuba, Port. (kōō'bä)	170	38.10 N	7.55 W
Cubagua, Isla (I.), Ven. (ē's-lä-kōō-bä'gwä)	143b	10.48 N	64.10 W
Cubango (Okavango)(R.), Ang.-Namibia (kōō-bäŋ'gō)	230	17.10 S	18.20 E
Cub Hills, Can. (kŭb)	100	54.20 N	104.30 W
Cucamonga, Ca. (kōō-kȧ-mōŋ'gȧ)	119a	34.05 N	117.35 W
Cuchi, Ang.	226	14.40 S	16.50 E
Cuchillo Parado, Mex. (kōō-chē'lyō pä-rä'dō)	124	29.26 N	104.52 W
Cuchumatanes, Sierra de los (Mts.), Guat.	132	15.35 N	91.10 W
Cúcuta, Col. (kōō'kōō-tä)	142	7.56 N	72.30 W
Cudahy, Wi. (kŭd'ȧ-hī)	113a	42.57 N	87.52 W
Cuddalore, India (kŭd ȧ-lōr')	197	11.49 N	79.46 E
Cuddapah, India (kŭd'ȧ-pä)	191	14.31 N	78.52 E
Cudham (Neigh.), Eng.	62	51.19 N	0.05 E
Cue, Austl. (kū)	214	27.30 S	118.10 E
Cuéllar, Sp. (kwā'lyär')	170e	41.24 N	4.15 W
Cuenca, Ec. (kwĕn'kä)	142	2.52 S	78.54 W
Cuenca, Sp.	170	40.05 N	2.07 W
Cuencame, Mex. (kwĕn-kä-mā')	124	24.52 N	103.42 W
Cuenca, Sierra de (Mts.), Sp. (sē-ĕ'r-rä-dĕ-kwĕ'n-kä)	170	40.02 N	1.50 W
Cuerámaro, Mex. (kwä-rä'mä-rō)	130	20.39 N	101.44 W
Cuernavaca, Mex. (kwĕr-nä-vä'kä)	131a	18.55 N	99.15 W
Cuero, Tx. (kwā'rō)	125	29.05 N	97.16 W
Cuetzalá del Progreso, Mex. (kwĕt-zä-lä dĕl prō-grā'sō)	130	18.07 N	99.51 W
Cuetzalan del Progreso, Mex. (kwĕt-zä-län dĕl prō-grā'sō)	131	20.02 N	97.33 W
Cuevas del Almanzora, Sp. (kwĕ'väs-dĕl-äl-män-zō-rä)	170	37.19 N	1.54 W
Cuffley, Eng.	62	51.47 N	0.07 W
Cuglieri, It. (kōō-lyå'rĕ)	172	40.11 N	8.37 E
Cuiabá, Braz. (kōō-yä-bä')	143	15.33 S	56.03 W
Cuicatlán, Mex. (kwē-kä-tlän')	131	17.46 N	96.57 W
Cuigezhuang, China	67b	40.01 N	116.28 E
Cuilapa, Guat. (kōō-ē-lä'pä)	132	14.16 N	90.20 W
Cuilo (R.), Ang.	230	9.15 S	19.30 E
Cuito (R.), Ang. (kōō-ē-'tō)	230	14.15 S	19.00 E
Cuitzeo, Mex. (kwēt'zā-ō)	130	19.57 N	101.11 W
Cuitzeo, Laguna de (L.), Mex. (lä-ōō'nä-dĕ-kwēt'zā-ō)	130	19.58 N	101.05 W
Culcross, Can. (kŭl'rôs)	95f	49.43 N	97.54 W
Cul de Sac (R.), Dom. Rep.-Hai. (kōō'l-dĕ-sä'k)	135	18.35 N	72.05 W
Culebra, (I.), P.R. (kōō-lā'brä)	129b	18.19 N	65.32 W
Culemborg, Neth.	157a	51.57 N	5.14 E
Culgoa (R.), Austl. (kŭl-gō'ȧ)	215	29.21 S	147.00 E
Culiacán, Mex. (kōō-lyä-kä'n)	128	24.45 N	107.30 W
Culion, Phil. (kōō-lē-ōn')	206	11.43 N	119.58 E
Cúllar de Baza, Sp. (kōō'l-yär-dĕ-bä'zä)	170	37.36 N	2.35 W
Cullera, Sp. (kōō-lyā'rä)	171	39.12 N	0.15 W
Cullinan, S. Afr. (kōō'lĭ-nȧn)	227b	25.41 S	28.32 E
Cullman, Ala. (kŭl'mȧn)	126	34.10 N	86.50 W
Culmore, Va.	56d	38.51 N	77.08 W
Culpeper, Va. (kŭl'pĕp-ēr)	111	38.30 N	77.55 W
Culver, In. (kŭl'vēr)	110	41.15 N	86.25 W
Culver City, Ca.	119a	34.00 N	118.23 W
Culverstone Green, Eng.	62	51.20 N	0.21 E
Cumaná, Ven. (kōō-mä-nä')	143b	10.28 N	64.10 W
Cumberland, Can. (kŭm'bēr-lȧnd)	95c	45.31 N	75.25 W
Cumberland, Md.	111	39.40 N	78.40 W
Cumberland, Wa.	118a	47.17 N	121.55 W
Cumberland, Wi.	115	45.31 N	92.01 W
Cumberland (R.), U.S.	126	36.45 N	85.33 W
Cumberland Is., Austl.	215	20.20 S	149.46 E
Cumberland, L., Ky.	126	36.55 N	85.20 W
Cumberland Pen., Can.	97	65.59 N	64.05 W
Cumberland Plat., Tn.	126	35.25 N	85.30 W
Cumberland Sd., Can.	97	65.27 N	65.44 W
Cundinamarca (Dept.), Col. (kōōn-dē-nä-mä'r-kȧ)	142a	4.57 N	74.27 W
Cunduacán, Mex. (kōōn-dōō-ȧ-kän')	131	18.04 N	93.23 W
Cunene (Kunene)(R.), Ang.-Namibia	230	17.05 S	12.35 E
Cuneo, It. (kōō'nå-ō)	172	44.24 N	7.31 E
Cunha, Braz. (kōō'nyȧ)	141a	23.05 S	44.56 W
Cunnamulla, Austl. (kŭn-ȧ-mŭl-ȧ)	216	28.00 S	145.55 E
Cupula, Pico (Mtn.) (pē'kō-kōō'pōō-lä)	128	24.45 N	111.10 W
Cuquío, Mex. (kōō-kē'ō)	130	20.55 N	103.03 W
Curaçao (I.), Neth. Antilles (kōō-rä-sä'ō)	142	12.12 N	68.58 W
Curacautín, Chile (kä-rä-käōō-tē'n)	144	38.25 S	71.53 W
Curacaví, Chile (kōō-rä-kä-vē')	141b	33.23 S	71.09 W
Curaumilla, Punta (Pt.), Chile (kōō-rou-mē'lyä)	141b	33.05 S	71.44 W
Curepto, Chile (kōō-rĕp-tō)	141b	35.06 S	72.02 W
Curicó, Chile (kōō-rē-kō')	141b	34.57 S	71.14 W
Curicó (Prov.), Chile	141b	34.55 S	71.15 W
Curitiba, Braz. (kōō-rē-tē'bȧ)	144	25.20 S	49.15 W
Curly Cut Cays (I.), Ba.	134	23.40 N	77.40 W
Currais Novos, Braz. (kōōr-rä'ēs nō-vōs)	143	6.02 S	36.39 W
Curran, Can. (kü-räN')	95c	45.30 N	74.59 W
Current (I.), Ba. (kŭ-rĕnt)	134	25.20 N	76.50 W
Current (R.), Mo. (kûr'ĕnt)	123	37.18 N	91.21 W
Currie, Mt., S. Afr. (kŭ-rē)	227c	30.28 S	29.23 E
Currituck Sd., NC (kûr'ĭ-tŭk)	127	36.27 N	75.42 W
Curtea-de-Argeş, Rom. (kōōr'tē-ȧ dĕ ȧr'zhĕsh)	173	45.09 N	24.40 E
Curtis (I.), Austl.	215	23.38 S	151.43 E
Curtis, Ne. (kûr'tĭs)	122	40.36 N	100.29 W
Curtis B, Md.	56c	39.13 N	76.35 W
Curtisville, Pa. (kûr'tĭs-vĭl)	113e	40.38 N	79.50 W
Curuá (R.), Braz. (kōō-rōō-ä')	143	6.26 S	54.39 W
Čurug, Yugo. (chōō'rōōg)	173	45.27 N	20.26 E
Curunga, Ang.	230	12.51 S	21.12 E
Curupira, Serra (Mts.), Braz.-Ven. (sĕr'rȧ kōō-rōō-pē'rȧ)	142	1.00 N	65.30 W
Cururupu, Braz. (kōō-rōō-rōō-pōō')	143	1.40 S	44.56 W
Curuzú Cuatiá, Arg. (kōō-rōō-zōō'kwä-tē-ä')	144	29.45 S	57.58 W
Curvelo, Braz. (kōōr-vĕl'ōō)	143	18.47 S	44.14 W
Cusano Milanino, It.	65c	45.33 N	9.11 E
Cushing, Ok. (kŭsh'ĭng)	123	35.58 N	96.46 W
Custer, SD (kŭs'tēr)	114	43.46 N	103.36 W
Custer, Wa.	118d	48.55 N	122.39 W
Custer Battlefield Nat'l Mon., Mt. (kŭs'tēr băt''l-fēld)	117	45.44 N	107.15 W
Cut Bank, Mt. (kŭt bănk)	117	48.38 N	112.19 W
Cuthbert, Ga. (kŭth'bērt)	126	31.47 N	84.48 W
Cuttack, India (kŭ-tăk')	196	20.38 N	85.53 E
Cutzamala (R.), Mex. (kōō-tzä-mä-lä')	130	18.57 N	100.41 W
Cutzamalá de Pinzón, Mex. (kōō-tzä-mä-lä'dĕ-pēn-zō'n)	130	18.28 N	100.36 W
Cuvo (R.), Ang. (kōō'vō)	230	10.55 S	14.00 E
Cuxhaven, F.R.G. (kōōks'hä-fĕn)	166	53.51 N	8.43 E
Cuxton, Eng.	62	51.22 N	0.27 E
Cuyahoga Falls, Oh.	113d	41.08 N	81.29 W
Cuyahoga Heights, Oh.	56a	41.26 N	81.39 W
Cuyahoga R., Oh. (kī-ȧ-hō'gȧ)	113d	41.22 N	81.38 W
Cuyapaire Ind. Res., Ca. (kū-yȧ-pâr)	120	32.46 N	116.20 W
Cuyo Is., Phil. (kōō'yō)	206	10.54 N	120.08 E
Cuyotenango, Guat. (kōō-yō-tĕ-näŋ'gō)	132	14.30 N	91.35 W
Cuyuni (R.), Guy.-Ven. (kōō-yōō'nē)	143	6.40 N	60.44 W
Cuyutlán, Mex. (kōō-yōō-tlän')	130	18.54 N	104.04 W
Cuzco, Peru	142	13.36 S	71.52 W
Cynthiana, Ky. (sĭn-thĭ-ăn'ȧ)	110	38.20 N	84.20 W
Cypress, Ca. (sī'prĕs)	119a	33.50 N	118.03 W
Cypress Hills, Can.	100	49.40 N	110.20 W
Cypress L., Can.	100	49.28 N	109.43 W
Cyprus, Asia (sī'prŭs)	190	35.00 N	31.00 E
Cyrenaica (Prov.), see Barqah			
Cyrildene (Neigh.), S. Afr.	71b	26.11 S	28.06 E
Czechoslovakia, Eur. (chĕk'ō-slō-vä'kĭ-ȧ)	154	49.28 N	16.00 E
Czersk, Pol. (chĕrsk)	167	53.47 N	17.58 E
Częstochowa, Pol. (chăN-stô Kô'vȧ)	167	50.49 N	19.10 E

D

PLACE (Pronunciation)	PAGE	Lat. °′	Long. °′
Da'an, China (dä-än)	202	45.25 N	124.22 E
Dabakala, Ivory Coast (dȧ-bä-kä'lä)	224	8.16 N	4.36 W
Daba Shan (Mts.), China (dä-bä shän)	202	32.25 N	108.20 E
Dabeiba, Col. (dȧ-bā'bä)	142a	7.01 N	76.16 W
Dabie Shan (Mts.), China (dä-bĭē shän)	203	31.40 N	114.50 E
Dabnou, Niger	229	14.09 N	5.22 E
Dabob B., Wa. (dā'bŏb)	118a	47.50 N	122.50 W
Dabola, Gui.	228	10.45 N	11.07 W
Dąbrowa Bialostocka, Pol. (dōN-brō'vȧ)	167	53.37 N	23.18 E
Dacca (Dhaka), Bngl. (dä'kä) (dăk'ȧ)	196	23.45 N	90.29 E
Dachang, China (dä-chäŋ)	201b	31.18 N	121.25 E
Dachangshan Dao (I.), China (dä-chäŋ-shän dou)	200	39.21 N	122.31 E
Dachau, F.R.G. (dä'Kou)	157d	48.16 N	11.26 E
Dacotah, Can. (dȧ-kō'tȧ)	95f	49.52 N	97.38 W
Dadar (Neigh.), India	67e	19.01 N	72.50 E
Dade City, Fl. (dād)	127a	28.22 N	82.09 W
Dadeville, Al. (dād'vĭl)	126	32.48 N	85.44 W
Dādra & Nagar Haveli (Union Ter.), India	196	20.00 N	73.00 E
Dadu (R.), China (dä-dōō)	203	29.20 N	103.03 E
Daet (Mtn.), Phil. (dä'ăt)	207a	14.07 N	122.59 E
Dafoe (R.), Can.	101	55.50 N	95.50 W
Dafter, Mi. (dăf'tēr)	119k	46.21 N	84.26 W
Dagana, Senegal (dä-gä'nä)	228	16.31 N	15.30 W
Dagana (Reg.) Chad	229	12.20 N	15.15 E
Dagang, China (dä-gäŋ)	201a	22.48 N	113.24 E
Dagda, Sov. Un. (dȧg'dȧ)	174	56.04 N	27.30 E
Dagenham, Eng. (dăg'ĕn-ăm)	156b	51.32 N	0.09 E
Dagestan (Reg.), Sov. Un. (dä-gĕs-tän')	179	43.40 N	46.10 E
Daggafontein, S. Afr.	71b	26.18 S	28.28 E
Daggett, Ca. (dăg'ĕt)	120	34.50 N	116.52 W
Dagu, China (dä-gōō)	200	39.00 N	117.42 E
Dagu (R.), China	200	36.29 N	120.06 E
Dagupan, Phil. (dä-gōō'pän)	207a	16.02 N	120.20 E
Daheishan Dao (I.), China (dä-hā-shän dou)	200	37.57 N	120.37 E
Da Hinggan Ling, see Greater Khingan Range			
Dahīrpur (Neigh.), India	67d	28.43 N	77.12 E
Dahl, F.R.G. (däl)	169c	51.18 N	7.33 E
Dahlak Arch. (Is.), Eth.	225	15.45 N	40.30 E
Dahlem (Neigh.), F.R.G.	65a	52.28 N	13.17 E
Dahlerau, F.R.G.	63	51.13 N	7.19 E
Dahlwitz, G.D.R.	65a	52.30 N	13.38 E
Dahomey, see Benin			
Dahra, Libya	194	29.34 N	17.50 E
Daibu, China (dī-bōō)	200	31.22 N	119.29 E
Daigo, Jap. (dī-gō)	205b	34.57 N	135.49 E
Daimiel Manzanares, Sp. (dī-myĕl'män-zä-nä'rĕs)	170	39.05 N	3.36 W
Dairy (R.), East Fk. Or.	118c	45.40 N	123.03 W
Dairy (R.), Or. (dâr'ĭ)	118c	45.33 N	123.04 W
Dai-Sen (Mtn.), Jap. (dī'sĕn')	205	35.22 N	133.35 E
Dai-Tenjo-dake (Mtn.), Jap. (dī-tĕn'jō dä-Kā)	205	36.21 N	137.38 E
Daitō, Jap.	205b	34.42 N	135.38 E
Daiyun Shan (Mtn.), China (dī-yōōn shän)	203	25.40 N	118.08 E
Dajabón, Dom. Rep. (dä-Kä-bô'n)	135	19.35 N	71.40 W
Dajarra, Austl. (dȧ-jăr'ȧ)	214	21.45 S	139.30 E
Dakar, Senegal (dȧ-kär')	228	14.40 N	17.26 W
Dakhla, W. Sah.	224	23.45 N	16.04 W
Dakouraoua, Niger	229	13.58 N	6.15 E
Dakovica, Yugo.	173	42.33 N	20.28 E
Dalälven (R.), Swe.	164	60.26 N	15.50 E
Dalby, Austl. (dôl'bē)	216	27.10 S	151.15 E
Dalcour, La. (dăl-kour)	112d	29.49 N	89.59 W
Dale, Nor. (dä'lĕ)	164	60.35 N	5.55 E
Dale Hollow (L.), Tn. (dāl hŏl'ō)	126	36.33 N	85.03 W
Dalemead, Can. (dä'lĕ-mēd)	95e	50.53 N	113.38 W
Dalen, Nor. (dä'lĕn)	164	59.28 N	8.01 E
Daleside, S. Afr. (dāl'sīd)	223d	26.30 S	28.03 E
Dalesville, Can. (dālz'vĭl)	95a	45.42 N	74.23 W
Daley Waters, Austl. (dā lē)	214	16.15 S	133.30 E
Dalhart, Tx. (dăl härt)	122	36.04 N	102.32 W
Dalhousie, Can. (dăl-hōō'zē)	104	48.04 N	66.23 W
Dali, China (dä-lē)	201a	23.27 N	113.06 E
Dali, China	198	26.00 N	100.08 E
Dali, China	198	35.00 N	109.38 E
Dalian Wan (B.), China (dä-lĭĕn wän)	200	38..55 N	121.50 E
Dalías, Sp. (dä-lē'äs)	170	36.49 N	2.50 W
Dall (I.), Ak. (dăl)	107	54.50 N	133.10 W
Dallas, Or. (dăl'lȧs)	116	44.55 N	123.20 W
Dallas, SD	114	43.13 N	99.34 W
Dallas, Tx.	119c	32.45 N	96.48 W
Dalles Dam, Or.	116	45.36 N	121.08 W
Dallgow, G.D.R.	65a	52.32 N	13.05 E
Dall I., Ak.	98	54.50 N	132.55 W
Dalmacija (Reg.), Yugo. (dăl-mä'tsē-yä)	172	43.25 N	16.37 E
Dalnerechensk, Sov. Un.	181	46.07 N	133.21 E
Daloa, Ivory Coast	228	6.53 N	6.27 W
Dalqū, Sud. (dĕl'gō)	225	20.07 N	30.41 E
Dalroy, Can. (dăl'roi)	95e	51.07 N	113.39 W
Dalrymple, Mt., Austl. (dăl'rĭm-p'l)	215	21.14 S	148.46 E
Dalton, Eng.	64a	53.34 N	2.46 W
Dalton, Ga. (dôl'tŭn)	126	34.46 N	84.58 W
Dalton, S. Afr. (dŏl'tŏn)	227c	29.21 S	30.41 E
Daly (R.), Austl. (dā'lĭ)	214	14.15 S	131.15 E
Daly City, Ca. (dā'lē)	118b	37.42 N	122.27 W
Damān, India	196	20.32 N	72.53 E
Damanhūr, Egypt (dä-män-hōōr')	223b	30.59 N	30.31 E
Damaraland (Reg.), Namibia (dă'nȧ-rȧ-lănd)	226	22.15 S	16.15 E
Damara Rep., Cen. Afr. Rep.	229	4.58 N	18.42 E
Damar, Pulau (I.), Indon.	207	7.15 S	129.15 E
Damas Cays (Is.), Ba. (dä'mäs)	134	23.50 N	79.50 W
Damascus, see Dimashq			
Damba, Ang. (däm'bä)	230	6.41 S	15.08 E
Dame Marie, Cap (C.), Hai. (däm mȧrē')	135	18.35 N	74.50 W
Dāmghān, Iran (dăm-gän')	192	35.50 N	54.15 E

ng-sing; ŋ-baŋk; N-nasalized n; nŏd; cŏmmit; ōld; ôbey; ôrder; oi-boil; fōōd; fŏŏt; ou-out; s-soft; sh-dish; th-thin; pūre; ûnite; ûrn; stŭd; circŭs; ü-as in French tu; '-indeterminate vowel.

276 Dāmghān – Denton

PLACE (Pronounciation)	PAGE	Lat. °′	Long. °′
Dāmghān, Iran	195	39.09 N	54.22 E
Daming, China (dä-mĭŋ)	200	36.15 N	115.09 E
Dammartin-en-Goële, Fr. (däɴ-mär-tăɴ-äɴ-gô-ĕl')	169b	49.03 N	2.40 E
Dampier Arch, Austl. (dän-pyâr')	214	20.15 S	116.25 E
Dampier Land (Penin), Austl.	214	17.30 S	122.25 E
Dampier, Selat (Str.), Indon. (däm'pēr)	207	0.40 S	131.15 E
Dan (R.), NC (dan)	127	36.26 N	79.40 W
Danané, Ivory Coast	228	7.16 N	8.09 W
Da Nang (Tourane), Viet.	203	16.08 N	108.22 E
Danbury, Ct. (dăn'bēr-ĭ)	112a	41.23 N	73.27 W
Danbury, Eng.	156b	51.42 N	0.34 E
Danbury, Tx.	125a	29.14 N	95.22 W
Dandenong, Austl. (dăn'dē-nông)	211a	37.59 S	145.13 E
Dandong, China (dän-dôŋ)	202	40.10 N	124.30 E
Dane (R.), Eng. (dān)	156	53.11 N	2.14 W
Danea, Gui.	228	11.27 N	13.12 W
Danforth, Me.	104	45.38 N	67.53 W
Dongila, Eth.	225	11.17 N	37.00 E
Dan Gora, Nig.	229	11.30 N	8.09 E
Dangtu, China (däŋ-too)	200	31.35 N	118.28 E
Dani, Burkina	228	13.43 N	0.10 W
Dania, Fl. (dā'nĭ-à)	127a	26.01 N	80.10 W
Daniels, Md.	56c	39.26 N	77.03 W
Danilov, Sov. Un. (dä'nē-lôf)	174	58.12 N	40.08 E
Danissa Hills, Ken.	231	3.20 N	40.55 E
Dankov, Sov. Un. (däŋ'kôf)	174	53.17 N	39.09 E
Danlí, Hond. (dän'lē)	132	14.02 N	86.35 W
Dannemora, NY (dăn-ē-mō'rȧ)	111	44.45 N	73.45 W
Dannhauser, S. Afr. (dän'hou-zēr)	227c	28.07 S	30.04 E
Dansville, NY (dănz'vĭl)	111	42.30 N	77.40 W
Danube (Donau,Duna)(R.), Eur.	166	48.35 N	10.38 E
Danube, Mouths of the, Rom. (dăn'ūb)	175	45.13 N	29.37 E
Danvers, Ma. (dăn'vẽrz)	105a	42.34 N	70.57 W
Danville, Ca. (dăn'vĭl)	118b	37.49 N	122.00 W
Danville, Il.	110	40.10 N	87.35 W
Danville, In.	110	39.45 N	86.30 W
Danville, Ky.	110	37.35 N	84.50 W
Danville, Pa.	111	41.00 N	76.35 W
Danville, Va.	127	36.35 N	79.24 W
Danxian, China (dän shyĕn)	203	19.30 N	109.38 E
Danyang, China (dän-yäŋ)	200	32.01 N	119.32 E
Danzig, G. of, Pol. (dàn'tsĭk)	158	54.41 N	19.01 E
Daoxian, China (dou shyĕn)	203	25.35 N	111.27 E
Dapango, Upper Volta	228	10.52 N	0.12 E
Daphnae (Ruins), Egypt	191a	30.43 N	32.12 E
Daqin Dao (I.), China (dä-chyĭn dou)	200	38.18 N	120.50 E
Dar'ā, Syria	191a	32.37 N	36.07 E
Darabani, Rom. (dă-ră-bän'ĭ)	167	48.13 N	26.38 E
Daraj, Libya	224	30.12 N	10.14 E
Darakeh, Iran	68h	35.48 N	51.23 E
Dār as-Salām, Egypt	71a	29.59 N	31.13 E
Darāw, Egypt (dȧ-rä'oo)	223b	24.24 N	32.56 E
Darband, Iran	68h	35.49 N	51.26 E
Darbhanga, India (dŭr-bŭŋ'gä)	196	26.03 N	85.09 E
Darby (I.), Ba.	135	23.50 N	76.20 W
Darby, Pa. (där'bĭ)	112f	39.55 N	75.16 W
Dardanelles (Str.), see Çanakkale Boğazi			
Dar es Salaam, Tan. (där ĕs sȧ-läm')	231	6.48 S	39.17 E
Dārfūr (Prov.), Sud. (där-foor')	225	13.21 N	23.46 E
Dargai, Pak. (dŭr-gä'ē)	193a	34.35 N	72.00 E
D'Arguin, Cap (C.), Mauritania	224	20.28 N	17.46 W
Darien, Col. (dā-rĭ-ĕn')	142a	3.56 N	76.30 W
Darien, Ct. (dâ-rē-ĕn')	112a	41.04 N	73.28 W
Darién, Cordillera de (Mts.), Nic.	132	13.00 N	85.42 W
Darien, Serrania del (Ra.), Pan. (sĕr-ä-nē'ä dĕl dä-rē-ĕn')	133	8.13 N	77.28 W
Darjeeling, India (dŭr-jē'lĭng)	196	27.05 N	88.16 E
Darling(L.), ND (där'lĭng)	114	48.35 N	101.25 W
Darling (R.), Austl.	216	31.50 S	143.20 E
Darling Downs (Reg.), Austl.	216	27.22 S	105.00 E
Darling Ra, Austl.	214	30.30 S	115.45 E
Darlington, Eng. (där'lĭng-tŭn)	162	54.32 N	1.35 W
Darlington, SC	127	34.15 N	79.52 W
Darlington, Wi.	115	42.41 N	90.06 W
Darlowo, Pol. (där-lô'vô)	166	54.26 N	16.23 E
Darmstadt, F.R.G. (därm'shtät)	166	49.53 N	8.40 E
Darnah, Libya	225	32.44 N	22.41 E
Darnley B., Ak. (därn'lē)	107	70.00 N	124.00 W
Daroca, Sp. (dä-rō-kä)	170	41.08 N	1.24 W
Dartford, Eng.	62	51.27 N	0.14 E
Dartmoor, Eng. (därt'moor)	162	50.35 N	4.05 W
Dartmouth, Can. (därt'mŭth)	104	44.40 N	63.34 W
Dartmouth, Eng.	162	50.33 N	3.28 W
Daru I., Pap. N. Gui. (dä'roo)	207	9.04 S	143.21 E
Daruvar, Yugo. (där'roo-vär)	172	45.37 N	17.16 E
Darwen, Eng. (där'wĕn)	156	53.42 N	2.28 W
Darwin, Austl. (där'wĭn)	214	12.25 S	131.00 E
Darwin, Cordillera (Mts.), Chile-Arg. (kôr-dēl-yĕ'rä-där'wĕn)	144	54.40 S	69.30 W
Dash Point, Wa. (dăsh)	118a	47.19 N	122.25 W
Dasht (R.), Pak. (dŭsht)	192	25.30 N	62.30 E
Dasht-e Kavīr Des., Iran (dŭsht-ē-ka-vēr')	192	34.41 N	53.30 E
Dasht-e-Lūt (Des.), Iran (dä'sht-ē-loot)	192	31.47 N	58.38 E
Dasol B., Phil. (dä-sōl')	207a	15.53 N	119.40 E
Datchet, Eng.	62	51.29 N	0.34 W
Datian Ding (Mtn.), China (dä-tĭĕn dĭŋ)	203	22.25 N	111.20 E
Datong, China (dä-tôŋ)	202	40.00 N	113.30 E
Dattapukur, India	196a	22.45 N	88.32 E
Datteln, F.R.G. (dät'tĕln)	169c	51.39 N	7.20 E
Datuan, China (dä-tůän)	201b	30.57 N	121.43 E
Datu, Tandjung (C.), Indon.	206	2.08 N	110.15 E
Daugava (R.), Sov. Un.	165	56.40 N	24.40 E
Daugavpils, Sov. Un. (dä'oo-gäv-pĕls)	174	55.52 N	26.32 E
Dauphin, Can. (dô'fĭn)	101	51.09 N	100.00 W
Dauphin L., Can.	101	51.17 N	99.48 W
Dāvangere, India	197	14.30 N	75.55 E
Davao, Phil. (dä'vä-ô)	207	7.05 N	125.30 E
Davao G., Phil.	207	6.30 N	125.45 E
Davenport, Ia. (dăv'ĕn-pōrt)	115	41.34 N	90.38 W
Davenport, Wa.	116	47.39 N	118.07 W
Daveyton Location, S. Afr.	71b	26.09 S	28.25 E
David, Pan. (dȧ-vēdh')	133	8.27 N	82.27 W
David City, Ne. (dā'vĭd)	114	41.15 N	97.10 W
David-Gorodok, Sov. Un. (dȧ-vēt' gô-rō'dôk)	167	52.02 N	27.14 E
Davis, Ok. (dā'vĭs)	123	34.34 N	97.08 W
Davis, WV	111	39.15 N	79.25 W
Davis L., Or.	116	43.38 N	121.43 W
Davis Mts., Tx.	124	30.45 N	104.17 W
Davisson Lake (Res.), Wa.	116	46.20 N	122.10 W
Davis Str., Can.	94	66.00 N	60.00 W
Davlekanovo, Sov. Un.	178	54.15 N	55.05 E
Davos, Switz. (dä'vōs)	166	46.47 N	9.50 E
Davyhulme, Eng.	64b	53.27 N	2.22 W
Dawa (R.), Eth.	225	4.34 N	41.34 E
Dawāsir, Wādī ad (R.), Sau. Ar.	192	20.48 N	44.07 E
Dawen (R.), China (dä-wŭn)	200	35.58 N	116.53 E
Dawley, Eng. (dô'lĭ)	156	52.38 N	2.28 W
Dawna Ra., Bur. (dô'nȧ)	206	17.02 N	98.01 E
Dawson, Can. (dô'sŭn)	107	64.04 N	139.22 W
Dawson, Ga.	126	31.45 N	84.29 W
Dawson, Mn.	114	44.54 N	96.03 W
Dawson (R.), Austl.	216	24.20 S	149.45 E
Dawson B., Can.	101	52.55 N	100.50 W
Dawson Creek, Can.	99	55.46 N	120.14 W
Dawson Ra., Can.	107	62.15 N	138.10 W
Dawson Springs, Ky.	126	37.10 N	87.40 W
Dawu, China (dä-woo)	200	31.33 N	114.07 E
Dawuji, China	67b	39.51 N	116.30 E
Dax, Fr. (dȧks)	168	43.42 N	1.06 W
Daxian, China (dä-shyĕn)	203	31.12 N	107.30 E
Daxing, China (dä-shyĭŋ)	202a	39.44 N	116.19 E
Dayiqiao, China (dä-yē-chyou)	200	31.43 N	120.40 E
Dayr az Zawr, Syr. (dā-ēr'ez-zôr')	192	35.15 N	40.01 E
Dayrūţ, Egypt	223b	27.33 N	30.48 E
Dayton, Ky. (dā'tŭn)	113f	39.07 N	84.28 W
Dayton, NM	122	32.44 N	104.23 W
Dayton, Oh.	110	39.54 N	84.15 W
Dayton, Tn.	126	35.30 N	85.00 W
Dayton, Tx.	125	30.03 N	94.53 W
Dayton, Wa.	116	46.18 N	117.59 W
Daytona Beach, Fl. (dā-tō'nȧ)	127	29.11 N	81.02 W
Dayu, China (dä-yoo)	203	25.20 N	114.20 E
Da Yunhe (Grand Canal), China (dä yoon-hŭ)	200	34.23 N	117.57 E
Dayville, Ct. (dā'vĭl)	111	41.50 N	71.55 W
De Aar, S. Afr. (dē-är')	226	30.45 S	24.05 E
Dead (L.), Mn. (dĕd)	114	46.28 N	96.00 W
Dead Sea, Isr.-Jordan	191a	31.30 N	35.30 E
Deadwood, SD (dĕd'wood)	114	44.23 N	103.43 W
Deal Island, Md. (dēl-ī'lănd)	111	38.10 N	75.55 W
Dean (R.), Can. (dēn)	98	52.45 N	125.30 W
Dean Chan, Can.	98	52.33 N	127.13 W
Deán Funes, Arg. (dĕ-ä'n-foo-nĕs)	144	30.26 S	64.12 W
Dean Row, Eng.	64b	53.20 N	2.11 W
Dearborn, Mi. (dēr'bŭrn)	113b	42.18 N	83.15 W
Dearborn Heights, Mi.	57c	42.19 N	83.14 W
Dearg, Ben (Mtn.), Scot. (bĕn dŭrg)	162	57.48 N	4.59 W
Dease Str., Can. (dēz)	96	68.50 N	108.20 W
Death Valley, Ca.-Nv.	120	36.55 N	117.12 W
Death Valley Junction, Ca.	120	36.18 N	116.26 W
Death Valley Natl. Mon., Ca.	120	36.34 N	117.00 W
Debal'tsevo, Sov. Un. (dyĕb'ál-tsyĕ'vô)	175	48.23 N	38.29 E
Debao, China (dŭ-bou)	203	23.18 N	106.40 E
Debar (Dibra), Yugo. (dĕ'bär) (dä'brä)	173	41.31 N	20.32 E
Deblin, Pol. (dăɴ'blĭn)	167	51.34 N	21.49 E
Debno, Pol. (dĕb-nô')	166	52.47 N	13.43 E
Debo, Lac (L.), Mali	228	15.15 N	4.40 W
Debrecen, Hung. (dĕ'brĕ-tsĕn)	167	47.32 N	21.40 E
Debre Markos, Eth.	225	10.15 N	37.45 E
Debre Tabor, Eth.	225	11.57 N	38.09 E
Decatur, Al. (dē-kā'tŭr)	126	34.35 N	87.00 W
Decatur, Ga.	112c	33.47 N	84.18 W
Decatur, Il.	123	39.50 N	88.59 W
Decatur, In.	110	40.50 N	84.55 W
Decatur, Mi.	110	42.10 N	86.00 W
Decatur, Tx.	122	33.14 N	97.33 W
Decazeville, Fr. (dē-käz'vēl')	168	44.33 N	2.16 E
Deccan (Plat.), India (dĕk'ăn)	196	19.05 N	76.40 E
Deception L., Can.	100	56.33 N	104.15 W
Deception P., Wa. (dē-sĕp'shŭn)	118a	48.24 N	122.44 W
Děčín, Czech. (dyĕ'chēn)	166	50.47 N	14.14 E
Decorah, Ia. (dē-kō'rȧ)	115	43.18 N	91.48 W
Dedeagats, see Alexandroúpolis			
Dedenevo, Sov. Un. (dyĕ-dyĕ'nyĕ-vô)	182b	56.14 N	37.31 E
Dedham, Ma. (dĕd'ăm)	105a	42.15 N	71.11 W
Dedo do Deus (Mt.), Braz. (dĕ-dô-dô-dĕ'oos)	144b	22.30 S	43.02 W
Dédougou, Burkina (dā-doo-goo')	228	12.38 N	3.28 W
Dee (R.), Scot.	162	57.05 N	2.25 W
Deep (R.), NC (dēp)	127	35.36 N	79.32 W
Deep Fk. (R.), OK.	123	35.35 N	96.42 W
Deep River, Can.	103	46.06 N	77.20 W
Deepwater, Mo. (dep-wô-tēr)	123	38.15 N	93.46 W
Deer (I.), Me.	104	44.07 N	68.38 W
Deerfield, IL. (dēr'fēld)	113a	42.10 N	87.51 W
Deer Island, Or.	118c	45.56 N	122.51 W
Deer L., Can.	101	52.40 N	94.30 W
Deer Lake, Can.	105	49.10 N	57.25 W
Deer Lodge, Mt. (dēr lŏj)	117	46.23 N	112.42 W
Deer Park, Oh.	113f	39.12 N	84.24 W
Deer Park, Wa.	116	47.58 N	117.28 W
Deer River, Mn.	115	47.20 N	93.49 W
Dee Why, Austl.	70a	33.45 S	151.17 E
Dee Why Head, Austl.	70a	33.46 S	151.19 E
Dee Why Lagoon, Austl.	70a	33.45 S	151.18 E
Defiance, Oh. (dē-fī'ăns)	110	41.15 N	84.20 W
DeFuniak Springs, Fl. (dē fū'nĭ-ăk)	126	30.42 N	86.06 W
Deganga, India	196a	22.41 N	88.41 E
Degeh Bur, Eth.	223a	8.10 N	43.25 E
Deggendorf, F.R.G. (dĕ'ghĕn-dôrf)	166	48.50 N	12.59 E
Degollado, Mex. (dā-gô-lyä'dō)	130	20.27 N	102.11 W
DeGrey (R.), Austl. (dē grā')	214	20.20 S	119.25 E
Degtyarsk, Sov. Un. (dĕg-ty'arsk)	182a	56.42 N	60.05 E
Dehiwala-Mount Lavinia, Sri Lanka	197	6.47 N	79.55 E
Dehra Dūn, India (dā'rŭ)	196	30.09 N	78.07 E
Dehua, China (dŭ-hwä)	203	25.30 N	118.15 E
Dej, Rom. (dāzh)	167	47.09 N	23.53 E
De Kalb, Il. (dē kălb')	115	41.54 N	88.46 W
Dekese, Zaire	230	3.27 S	21.24 E
Delacour, Can. (dĕ-lä-koor')	95e	51.09 N	113.45 W
Delagua, Co. (dĕl-ä'gwä)	122	37.19 N	104.42 W
Delair, NJ	56b	39.59 N	75.03 W
De Land, Fl. (dē lănd')	127	29.00 N	81.19 W
Delano, Ca. (dĕl'á-nō)	120	35.47 N	119.15 W
Delano Pk., Ut.	121	38.25 N	112.25 W
Delavan, Wi. (dĕl'á-văn)	115	42.39 N	88.38 W
Delaware, Oh. (dĕl'á-wâr)	110	40.15 N	83.05 W
Delaware (State), U.S.	109	38.40 N	75.30 W
Delaware (R.), Ks.	123	39.45 N	95.47 W
Delaware (R.), U.S.	111	41.50 N	75.20 W
Delaware B., De.-NJ	111	39.05 N	75.10 W
Delaware Res., Oh.	110	40.30 N	83.05 W
Delémont, Switz. (dĕ-lā-môɴ')	166	47.21 N	7.18 E
De Leon, Tx. (dē lē-ŏn')	124	32.06 N	98.33 W
Delfinópolis, Braz. (dĕl-fē'nô'pō'-lēs)	141a	20.20 S	46.50 W
Delft, Neth. (dĕlft)	157a	52.01 N	4.20 E
Delfzijl, Neth.	163	53.20 N	6.50 E
Delgada Pta. (Pt.), Arg. (poo'n-tä-dĕl-gä'dä)	144	43.46 S	63.46 W
Delgado, Cabo (C.), Moz. (kȧ'bô-dĕl-gä'dō)	231	10.40 S	40.35 E
Delhi, Il. (dĕl'hī)	119e	39.03 N	90.16 W
Delhi, India	196	28.54 N	77.13 E
Delhi, La.	125	32.26 N	91.29 W
Delhi (State), India	196	28.30 N	76.50 E
Delhi Cantonment, India	67d	28.36 N	77.08 E
Delitzsch, G.D.R. (dā'lĭch)	166	51.32 N	12.18 E
Delles, Alg. (dĕ'lĕs')	224	36.59 N	3.40 E
Dell Rapids, SD (dĕl)	114	43.50 N	96.43 W
Dellwig (Neigh.), F.R.G.	63	51.29 N	6.56 E
Dellwood, Mn. (dĕl'wood)	119g	45.05 N	92.58 W
Del Mar, Ca. (dĕl mär')	120a	32.57 N	117.16 W
Delmas, S. Afr. (dĕl'mȧs)	223d	26.08 S	28.43 E
Delmenhorst, F.R.G. (dĕl'mĕn-hôrst)	166	53.03 N	8.38 E
Del Norte, Co. (dĕl nôrt')	121	37.40 N	106.25 W
De-Longa (I.), Sov. Un.	181	76.30 N	153.00 E
De Long Mts., Ak. (dē'lŏng)	107	68.38 N	162.30 W
Deloraine, Austl. (dĕ-lŭ-rān)	216	41.30 S	146.40 E
Delphi, In. (dĕl'fī)	110	40.35 N	86.40 W
Delphos, Oh. (dĕl'fŏs)	110	40.50 N	84.20 W
Delran, NJ	56b	40.02 N	74.58 W
Delray Beach, Fl. (dĕl-rā')	127a	26.27 N	80.05 W
Del Rio, Tx. (dĕl rē'ō)	124	29.21 N	100.52 W
Delson, Can. (dĕl'sŭn)	95a	45.24 N	73.32 W
Delta, Co.	121	38.45 N	108.05 W
Delta, Ut.	121	39.20 N	112.35 W
Delta Beach, Can.	95f	50.10 N	98.20 W
Delta Mendota Can, Ca.	120	37.10 N	121.02 W
Delvine, Alb. (dĕl'vē-nȧ)	173	39.58 N	20.10 E
Del Viso, Arg.	60d	34.26 S	58.46 W
Dëma (R.), Sov. Un. (dyĕm'ä)	178	53.40 N	54.30 E
Demarest, NJ	55	40.57 N	73.58 W
Demba, Zaire	230	5.30 S	22.16 E
Dembi Dolo, Eth.	225	8.46 N	34.46 E
Demidov, Sov. Un. (dzyĕ'mē-dô'f)	174	55.16 N	31.32 E
Deming, NM (dĕm'ĭng)	121	32.15 N	107.45 W
Demmeltrath (Neigh.), F.R.G.	63	51.11 N	7.03 E
Demmin, G.D.R. (dĕm'mĕn)	166	53.54 N	13.04 E
Demnat, Mor. (dĕm-nät)	224	31.58 N	7.03 W
Demopolis, Al. (dē-mŏp'ô-lĭs)	126	32.30 N	87.50 W
Demotte, In. (dē'mŏt)	113a	41.12 N	87.13 W
Dempo, Gunung (Vol.), Indon. (dĕm'pô)	206	4.04 S	103.11 E
Dem'yanka (R.), Sov. Un. (dyĕm-yän'kä)	180	59.07 N	72.58 E
Demyansk, Sov. Un. (dyĕm-yänsk')	174	57.39 N	32.26 E
Denain, Fr. (dē-năɴ')	168	50.23 N	3.21 E
Denakil Pln., Eth.	225	12.45 N	41.01 E
Denali Natl. Park, Ak.	107	63.48 N	153.02 W
Denbigh, Wales (dĕn'bĭ)	162	53.15 N	3.25 W
Dendermonde, Bel.	157a	51.02 N	4.04 E
Dendron, Va. (dĕn'drŭn)	127	37.02 N	76.53 W
Denenchōfu (Neigh.), Jap.	69a	35.35 N	139.41 E
Denezhkin Kamen, Gora (Mtn.), Sov. Un. (dzyĕ-ŋĕ'zhkĕn kämĭēŋ)	182a	60.26 N	59.35 E
D'Enfer, Pointe (Pt.), Mart.	133b	14.21 N	60.48 W
Denham, Mt., Jam.	134	18.20 N	77.30 W
Den Helder, Neth. (dĕn hĕl'dēr)	163	52.55 N	5.45 E
Denia, Sp. (dā'nyä)	171	38.48 N	0.06 E
Deniliquin, Austl. (dĕ-nĭl'ĭ-kwĭn)	216	35.20 S	144.52 E
Denison, Ia. (dĕn'ĭ-sŭn)	114	42.01 N	95.22 W
Denison, Tx.	123	33.45 N	97.02 W
Denisovka, Sov. Un. (dĕ-nē'sof-kȧ)	182a	52.26 N	61.45 E
Denizli, Tur. (dĕn-ĭz-lē')	179	37.40 N	29.10 E
Denklingen, F.R.G. (dĕn'klĕn-gĕn)	169c	50.54 N	7.40 E
Denmark, Eur.	154	56.14 N	8.30 E
Denmark, SC (dĕn'märk)	127	33.18 N	81.09 W
Denmark Str., Grnld.	94	66.30 N	27.00 W
Dennilton, S. Afr. (dĕn-ĭl-tŭn)	223d	25.18 S	29.13 E
Dennison, Oh. (dĕn'ĭ-sŭn)	110	40.25 N	81.20 W
Denpasar, Indon.	206	8.35 S	115.10 E
Denshaw, Eng.	64b	53.35 N	2.02 W
Denton, Eng. (dĕn'tŭn)	156	53.27 N	2.07 W
Denton, Md.	111	38.55 N	75.50 W
Denton, Tx.	123	33.12 N	97.06 W

ăt; finăl; rāte; senāte; ärm; ȧsk; sofȧ; fâre; ch-choose; dh-as th in other; bē; ēvent; bĕt; recĕnt; cratẽr; g-gō; gh-guttural g; bĭt; ĭ-short neutral; rīde; ĸ-guttural k as ch in German ich;

PLACE (Pronounciation)	PAGE	Lat. °'	Long. °'
D'Entrecasteaux Is., Pap. N. Gui.			
(dän-tr'-làs-tō')	207	9.45 s	152.00 E
D'Entrecasteaux, Pt., Austl.			
(dän-tr'kás-tō')	214	34.50 s	114.45 E
Denver, Co. (děn'vẽr)	122	39.44 N	104.59 W
Deoli, India	196	25.52 N	75.23 E
De Pere, Wi. (dě pēr')	115	44.25 N	88.04 W
Depew, NY (dē-pū')	113c	42.55 N	78.43 W
Deping, China (dü-pĭŋ)	200	37.28 N	116.57 E
Deptford (Neigh.), Eng.	62	51.28 N	0.02 W
Depue, Il. (dě pū)	110	41.15 N	89.55 W
De Queen, Ar. (dě kwēn')	123	34.02 N	94.21 W
De Quincy, La. (dě kwĭn'sĭ)	125	30.27 N	93.27 W
Dera Ghāzi Khān, Pak.			
(dä'rū gä-zē' кan')	196	30.09 N	70.39 E
Dera Ismāīl Khān, Pak.			
(dä'rū ĭs-mä-ēl' кän')	196	31.55 N	70.51 E
Derbent, Sov. Un. (děr-běnt')	179	42.00 N	48.10 E
Derby, Austl. (där'bě) (dûr'bě)	214	17.20 s	123.40 E
Derby, Ct. (dûr'bě)	111	41.20 N	73.05 W
Derby, Eng. (där'bě)	156	52.55 N	1.29 W
Derby, S. Afr. (där'bǐ)	223d	25.55 s	27.02 E
Derbyshire (Co.), Eng.	156	53.11 N	1.30 W
Derdepoort, S. Afr.	223d	24.39 s	26.21 E
Dere, Lak (R.), Ken.	231	0.45 N	40.15 E
Derendorf (Neigh.), F.R.G.	63	51.15 N	6.48 E
Derg, Lough (L.), Ire. (lŏk děrg)	162	53.00 N	8.09 W
Dermott, Ar. (dûr'mŏt)	123	33.32 N	91.24 W
Derne (Neigh.), F.R.G.	63	51.34 N	7.31 E
Derry, NH (dăr'ĭ)	105a	42.53 N	71.22 W
Derventa, Yugo. (děr'ven-tá)	173	45.58 N	17.58 E
Derwent (R.), Austl.	216	42.21 s	146.30 E
Derwent (R.), Eng.	156	52.54 N	1.24 W
Des Arc, Ar. (dăz ärk')	123	34.59 N	91.31 W
Descalvado, Braz. (děs-käl-vä-dô)	141a	21.55 s	47.37 W
Descartes, Fr.	168	46.58 N	0.42 E
Deschambault L., Can.	100	54.40 N	103.35 W
Deschênes, Can.	95c	45.23 N	75.47 W
Deschenes, L., Can.	95c	54.25 N	75.53 W
Deschutes R., Can.	116	44.25 N	121.21 W
Desdemona, Tx. (děz-dě-mō'ná)	124	32.16 N	98.33 W
Dese, Eth.	225	11.00 N	39.51 E
Deseado, Rio (R.), Arg.			
(rě-ō-dä-sä-ä'dhō)	144	46.50 s	67.45 W
Desirade I., Guad. (dā-zē-räs')	133b	16.21 N	60.51 W
De Smet, SD (dě smět')	114	44.23 N	97.33 W
Des Moines, Ia. (dě moin')	115	41.35 N	93.37 W
Des Moines, NM	122	36.42 N	103.48 W
Des Moines (R.), U.S.	109	43.45 N	94.20 W
Des Moines, Wa.	118a	46.24 N	122.20 W
Desna (R.), Sov. Un. (dyěs-ná')	175	51.05 N	31.03 E
Desolación (I.), Chile (dě-sô-lä-syō'n)	144	53.05 s	74.00 W
De Soto, Mo. (dě sō'tō)	123	38.07 N	90.32 W
Des Peres, Mo. (dě pěr'ěs)	119e	38.36 N	90.26 W
Des Plaines, Il. (děs plänz')	113a	42.02 N	87.54 W
Des Plaines R., Il.	113a	41.39 N	87.56 W
Dessau, G.D.R. (děs'ou)	166	51.50 N	12.15 E
Detmold, G.D.R. (dět'mōld)	166	51.57 N	8.55 E
Detroit, Mi. (dě-troit')	113b	42.22 N	83.10 W
Detroit, Tx.	123	33.41 N	95.16 W
Detroit (R.), Mi.	57c	42.06 N	83.08 W
Detroit Lakes, Mn. (dě-troit'läkz)	114	46.48 N	95.51 W
Detroit Metropolitan-Wayne County			
Arpt., Mi.	57c	42.13 N	83.22 W
Detva, Czech. (dyět'vá)	167	48.32 N	19.21 E
Deuil-la-Barre, Fr.	64c	48.59 N	2.20 E
Deurne, Bel.	157a	51.13 N	4.27 E
Deusen (Neigh.), F.R.G.	63	51.33 N	7.26 E
Deutsch Wagram, Aus.	157e	48.19 N	16.34 E
Deux-Montagnes, Can.	54b	45.33 N	73.53 W
Deux Montagnes, Lac des (L.), Can.	95a	45.28 N	74.00 W
Deva, Rom. (dā'vä)	173	45.52 N	22.52 E
Dévaványa, Hung. (dā'vō-vän-yō)	167	47.01 N	20.58 E
Develi, Tur. (dě'vä-lě)	179	38.20 N	35.10 E
Deventer, Neth. (děv'ěn-tèr)	163	52.14 N	6.07 E
Devils I., see Diable, Ile du			
Devils (L.), ND (děv'ʼlz)	114	47.57 N	99.04 W
Devils Lake, ND	108	48.10 N	98.55 W
Devils Lake Ind. Res., ND	114	48.08 N	99.40 W
Devils Postpile Natl. Mon., Ca.	120	37.42 N	119.12 W
Devils (R.), Tx.	124	29.55 N	101.10 W
Devils Tower Natl. Mon., Wy.	117	44.38 N	105.07 W
Devoll (R.), Alb.	173	40.55 N	20.10 E
Devon, Can.	95g	53.23 N	113.43 W
Devon, S. Afr. (děv'ŭn)	223d	26.23 s	28.47 E
Devonport, Austl. (děv'ŭn-pôrt)	216	41.20 s	146.30 E
Devonport, N.Z.	215a	36.50 s	174.45 E
Devore, Ca. (dě-vôr')	119a	34.13 N	117.24 W
Dewatto, Wa. (dě-wät'ô)	118a	47.27 N	123.04 W
Dewey, Ok. (dū'ĭ)	123	36.48 N	95.55 W
De Witt, Ar. (dě wĭt')	123	34.17 N	91.22 W
De Witt, Ia.	115	41.46 N	90.34 W
Dewsbury, Eng. (dūz'běr-ĭ)	156	53.42 N	1.39 W
Dexter (L.), Fl.	127	29.07 N	81.24 W
Dexter, Me. (děks'tēr)	104	45.01 N	69.19 W
Dexter, Mo.	123	36.46 N	89.56 W
Dezfūl, Iran	192	32.14 N	48.37 E
Dezhnëva, Mys (East Cape), Sov. Un.			
(dyězh'nyĭf)	191	68.00 N	172.00 W
Dezhou, China (dŭ-jō)	200	37.28 N	116.17 E
Dháfni, Grc.	66d	37.48 N	22.01 E
Dhahran, see Az Zahrān			
Dhamtari Cr., India	197b	18.49 N	72.54 E
Dharmavaram, India	197	14.32 N	77.43 E
Dhaulāgiri (Mtn.), Nep.			
(dou-lá-gē'rě)	196	28.42 N	83.31 E
Dhenoúsa (I.), Grc.	173	37.09 N	25.53 E
Dhidhimótikhon, Grc.	173	41.20 N	26.27 E
Dhībān, Jordan	191a	31.30 N	35.46 E
Dhodhekánisos (Dodecanese) (Is.), Grc.	173	38.00 N	26.10 E
Dhule, India	196	20.58 N	74.43 E
Día (I.), Grc. (dě'ä)	172a	35.27 N	25.17 E
Diable, Ile du (Devils I.), Fr. Gu.	143	5.15 N	57.10 W
Diablo Heights, Pan. (dyä'blō)	128a	8.58 N	79.34 W
Diablo, Mt., Ca. (dyä'blŏ)	118b	37.52 N	121.55 W
Diablo Range (Mts.), Ca.	118b	37.47 N	121.50 W
Diaca, Moz.	231	11.30 s	39.59 E
Diaka (R.), Mali	228	14.40 N	5.00 E
Diamantina, Braz.	143	18.14 s	43.32 W
Diamantina (R.), Austl.			
(dĭ'man-tē'nà)	214	25.38 s	139.53 E
Diamantino, Braz. (dě-á-män-tē'no)	143	14.22 s	56.23 W
Diamond Creek, Austl.	70b	37.41 s	145.09 E
Diamond Pk., Or.	116	43.32 N	122.08 W
Diana Bk., Ba. (dĭ'án'á)	135	22.30 N	74.45 W
Dianbai, China (dĭěn-bī)	203	21.30 N	111.20 E
Dian Chi (L.), China (dĭěn chē)	203	24.58 N	103.18 E
Diancun, China	67b	39.55 N	116.14 E
Dibra, see Debar			
Dickinson, ND (dĭk'ĭn-sŭn)	114	46.52 N	102.49 W
Dickinson, Tx. (dĭk'ĭn-sŭn)	125a	29.28 N	95.02 W
Dickinson Bayou, Tx.	125a	29.26 N	95.08 W
Dickson, Tn. (dĭk'sŭn)	126	36.03 N	87.24 W
Dickson City, Pa.	111	41.25 N	75.40 W
Dicle (R.), Tur. (dĭj'lâ)	179	37.50 N	40.40 E
Didcot, Eng. (dĭd'cŏt)	156b	51.35 N	1.15 W
Didiéni, Mali	228	13.53 N	8.06 W
Didsbury (Neigh.), Eng.	64b	53.25 N	2.14 W
Die, Fr. (dě)	169	44.45 N	5.22 E
Diefenbaker (Res.), Can.	96	51.20 N	108.10 W
Diefenbaker L., Can.	100	51.00 N	106.55 W
Diego de Ocampo, Pico (Pk.), Dom. Rep.			
(pě'-kô-dyě'gô-dě-ō-kä'm-pô)	135	19.40 N	70.45 W
Diego Ramírez, Islas (Is.), Chile			
(dě'ä'gô rä-mē'räz)	144	56.15 s	70.15 W
Diéma, Mali	228	14.32 N	9.12 W
Dien Bien Phu, Viet.	198	21.38 N	102.49 E
Diepensee, G.D.R.	65a	52.22 N	13.31 E
Dieppe, Can. (dě-ěp')	104	46.06 N	64.45 W
Dieppe, Fr.	168	49.54 N	1.05 E
Dierks, Ar. (děrks)	123	34.06 N	94.02 W
Diersfordt, F.R.G.	63	51.42 N	6.33 E
Diessem (Neigh.), F.R.G.	63	51.20 N	6.35 E
Diessen, F.R.G. (děs'sěn)	157d	47.57 N	11.06 E
Diest, Bel.	157a	50.59 N	5.05 E
Digby, Can. (dĭg'bĭ)	104	44.37 N	65.46 W
Dighton, Ma. (dĭ-tŭn)	112b	41.49 N	71.05 W
Digmoor, Eng.	64a	53.32 N	2.45 W
Digne, Fr. (děn'y')	169	44.07 N	6.16 E
Digoin, Fr. (dě-gwăn')	168	46.28 N	4.06 E
Digra, India	67a	22.50 N	88.20 E
Digul (R.), Indon.	207	7.00 s	140.27 E
Dijohan Pt., Phil. (dě-kô-än)	207a	16.24 N	122.25 E
Dijon, Fr. (dē-zhôn')	168	47.21 N	5.02 E
Dikson, Sov. Un. (dĭk'sŏn)	180	73.30 N	80.35 E
Dikwa, Nig. (dě'kwä)	225	12.06 N	13.53 E
Dili, Indon. (dĭl'ě)	207	8.35 s	125.35 E
Di Linosa I., It. (dě-lě-nô'sä)	160	36.01 N	12.43 E
Dilizhan, Sov. Un.	179	40.45 N	45.00 E
Dillingham, Ak. (dĭl'ěng-hăm)	107	59.10 N	158.38 W
Dillon, Mt. (dĭl'ŭn)	117	45.12 N	112.40 W
Dillon, SC	127	34.24 N	79.28 W
Dillon Park, Md.	56d	38.52 N	76.56 W
Dillon Res., Oh.	110	40.05 N	82.05 W
Dilolo, Zaire (dě-lō'lô)	226	10.19 s	22.23 E
Dimashq (Damascus), Syria			
(dä-mäs'kŭs)	192	33.31 N	36.18 E
Dimbokro, Ivory Coast	228	6.39 N	4.42 W
Dimbovita (R.), Rom.	173	44.43 N	25.41 E
Dimitrovo, See Pernik			
Dimlang (Mtn.), Nig.	229	8.24 N	11.47 E
Dimona, Isr.	191a	31.03 N	35.01 E
Dinagate (I.), Phil.	207	10.15 N	126.15 E
Dinajpur, Bngl.	196	25.38 N	87.39 E
Dinan, Fr. (dě-näN')	168	48.27 N	2.03 W
Dinant, Bel. (dě-näN')	163	50.17 N	4.50 E
Dinara (Mts.), Yugo. (dě'nä-rä)	172	43.50 N	16.15 E
Dinard, Fr.	168	48.38 N	2.04 W
Dindigul, India	197	10.25 N	78.03 E
Dingalan B., Phil. (dĭn-gä'län)	207a	15.19 N	121.33 E
Dingle, Ire. (dĭng''l)	162	52.10 N	10.13 W
Dingle (Neigh.), Eng.	64a	53.23 N	2.57 W
Dingle B., Ire.	162	52.02 N	10.15 W
Dingo, Austl. (dĭn'gō)	215	23.45 s	149.26 E
Dinguiraye, Gui.	228	11.18 N	10.43 W
Dingwall, Scot. (dĭng'wôl)	162	57.37 N	4.23 W
Dingxian, China (dĭŋ shyěn)	200	38.30 N	115.00 E
Dingxing, China (dĭŋ-shyĭŋ)	200	39.18 N	115.50 E
Dingyuan, China (dĭŋ-yŭän)	200	32.32 N	117.40 E
Dingzi Wan (B.), China	200	36.33 N	121.06 E
Dinosaur Natl. Mon., Co.-Ut.			
(dī'nô-sôr)	117	40.45 N	109.17 W
Dinslaken, F.R.G. (děns'lä-kěn)	169c	51.33 N	6.44 E
Dinslakener Bruch, F.R.G.	63	51.35 N	6.43 E
Dinteloord, Neth.	157a	51.38 N	4.21 E
Dinuba, Ca. (dī-nū'bá)	120	36.33 N	119.29 W
Dinwiddie, S. Afr.	71b	26.16 s	28.10 E
Dios, Cayo de (I.), Cuba			
(kä'yô-dě-dě-ōs')	134	22.05 N	83.05 W
Diourbel, Senegal (dě-ōōr-běl')	228	14.40 N	16.15 W
Diphu Pass, China (dĭ-pōō)	193	28.15 N	96.45 E
Diquis (R.), C.R. (dě-kēs')	133	8.59 N	83.24 W
Dire Dawa, Eth.	223a	9.40 N	41.47 E
Diriamba, Nic. (dē-ryäm'bä)	132	11.52 N	86.15 W
Dirk Hartog (I.), Austl.	214	26.25 s	113.15 E
Dirksland, Neth.	157a	51.45 N	4.04 E
Dirranbandi, Austl. (dĭr-rá-bän'dě)	216	28.24 s	148.29 E
Dirty Devil (R.), Ut. (dûr'tĭ děv''l)	121	38.20 N	110.30 W
Disappointment (L.), Austl.	214	23.20 s	120.20 E
Disappointment, C., Wa.			
(dĭs'á-point'ment)	118c	46.16 N	124.11 W
D'Ischia, I., It. (dē'sh-kyä)	171c	40.26 N	13.55 E
Discovery (Is.), Can. (dĭs-kŭv'ěr-ě)	118a	48.25 N	123.13 W
Discovery, S. Afr. (dĭs-kŭv'ěr-ĭ)	227b	26.10 s	27.53 E
Dishnä, Egypt (děsh'ná)	223b	26.08 N	32.27 E
Disko (I.), Grnld. (dĭs'kō)	94	70.00 N	54.00 W
Dismal Swp., NC-Va. (dĭz'mál)	127	36.35 N	76.34 W
Disna, Sov. Un. (děs'ná)	174	55.34 N	28.15 E
Disneyland (P. Int.), Ca.	59	33.48 N	117.55 W
Dispur, India	196	26.00 N	91.50 E
Disraëli, Can. (dĭs-rä'lĭ)	104	45.53 N	71.23 W
Disteln, F.R.G.	63	51.36 N	7.09 E
District Heights, Md.	56d	38.51 N	76.53 W
District of Columbia, U.S.	109	38.50 N	77.00 W
Distrito Federal (Dist.), Braz.			
(děs-trē'tô-fě-dě-rä'l)	143	15.49 s	47.39 W
Distrito Federal (Dist.), Mex.	131	19.14 N	99.08 W
Disûq, Egypt (dě-sōōk')	223b	31.07 N	30.41 E
Ditton, Eng.	62	51.18 N	0.27 E
Diu, India (dě'ōō)	196	20.48 N	70.58 E
Divilacan B., Phil. (dě-vě-lä'kän)	207a	17.26 N	122.25 E
Divinópolis, Braz. (dě-vē-nô'pô-lěs)	141a	20.10 s	44.53 W
Divo, Ivory Coast	228	5.50 N	5.22 W
Dixie, Can.	54c	43.36 N	79.36 W
Dixon, Il. (dĭks'ŭn)	115	41.50 N	89.30 W
Dixon Entrance, Ak.-Can.	98	54.25 N	132.00 W
Diyarbakir, Tur. (dě-yär-běk'ĭr)	179	38.00 N	40.10 E
Dja (R.), Cam.	229	3.25 N	13.17 E
Djakovo (Neigh.), Sov. Un.	66b	55.39 N	37.40 E
Djambala, Con.	230	2.33 s	14.45 E
Djanet, Alg.	224	24.29 N	9.26 E
Djebob (Mtn.), Ghana	228	8.20 N	0.37 E
Djedi, Oued (R.), Alg.	160	34.18 N	4.39 E
Djelo-Binza, Zaire	71c	4.23 s	15.16 E
Djember, Chad.	229	10.25 N	17.50 E
Djerba, Île de (I.), Tun.	160	33.53 N	11.26 E
Djerid, Chott (L.), Tun. (jěr'ĭd)	224	33.15 N	8.29 E
Djibasso, Burkina	228	13.07 N	4.10 W
Djibo, Burkina	228	14.06 N	1.38 W
Djibouti, Afr.	222	11.35 N	48.08 E
Djibouti, Djibouti (jě-bōō-tě')	223a	11.34 N	43.00 E
Djokoumatombi, Con.	230	0.47 N	15.22 E
Djokupunda, Zaire	230	5.27 s	20.58 E
Djoua (R.), Con.-Gabon	230	1.25 N	13.40 E
Djoué (R.), Con.	71c	4.19 s	15.14 E
Djursholm, Swe. (djōōrs'hôlm)	164	59.26 N	18.01 E
Dmitriyevka, Sov. Un.			
(d'mē-trě-yěf'ká)	175	47.57 N	38.56 E
Dmitriyev-L'govskiy, Sov. Un.			
(d'mē-trī-yěf l'gôf'skĭ)	175	52.07 N	35.05 E
Dmitrov, Sov. Un. (d'mē'trôf)	182b	56.21 N	37.32 E
Dmitrovsk, Sov. Un. (d'mě'trôfsk)	174	52.30 N	35.10 E
Dnepr (Dnieper) (R.), Sov. Un. (ně'pěr)	175	46.47 N	32.57 E
Dneprodzerzhinsk, Sov. Un.			
(d'nyěp'rô-zěr-shĭnsk)	175	48.32 N	34.38 E
Dneprodzerzhinskoye Vdkhr. (Res.), Sov.			
Un.	175	49.00 N	34.10 E
Dnepropetrovsk (Oblast), Sov. Un.	175	48.15 N	34.08 E
Dnepropetrovsk, Sov. Un.			
(d'nyěp'rô-pä-trôfsk)	175	48.23 N	34.10 E
Dnepr Zaliv (B.), Sov. Un.			
(dnyěp'r zá'lĭf)	175	46.33 N	31.45 E
Dnestr (Dniester) (R.), Sov. Un.	175	48.21 N	28.10 E
Dnestrovskiy Líman (B.), Sov. Un.	175	46.13 N	29.50 E
Dnieper (R.), see Dnepr			
Dniester (R.), see Dnestr			
Dno, Sov.Un. (d'nô')	174	57.49 N	29.59 E
Doba, Chad	229	8.39 N	16.51 E
Dobbs Ferry, NY (dŏbz'fě'rě)	112a	41.01 N	73.53 W
Dobbyn, Austl.	214	19.45 s	140.02 E
Dobele, Sov.Un. (dô'bě-lě)	165	56.37 N	23.18 E
Döbeln, G.D.R. (dǔ'běln)	166	51.08 N	13.07 E
Doberai Jazirah (Pen.), Indon.	207	1.25 s	133.15 E
Döbling (Neigh.), Aus.	66e	48.15 N	16.22 E
Dobo, Indon.	207	6.00 s	134.18 E
Doboj, Yugo. (dô'boi)	173	44.42 N	18.04 E
Dobryanka, Sov. Un. (dôb-ryän'ká)	182a	58.27 N	56.26 E
Dobšina, Czech. (dôp'shě-ná)	167	48.48 N	20.25 E
Doce (R.), Braz. (dô'sě)	143	19.01 s	42.14 W
Doce Leguas, Cayos de las (Is.), Cuba			
(kä'yôs-dě-läs-dô-sě-lě'gwäs)	134	20.55 N	79.05 W
Doctor Arroyo, Mex.			
(dôk-tôr' är-rô'yô)	130	23.41 N	100.10 W
Doddinghurst, Eng.	62	51.40 N	0.18 E
Doddington, Eng. (dŏd'dĭng-tŏn)	156b	51.17 N	0.47 E
Dodecanese, Is., see Dhodhekánisos			
Dodge City, Ks. (dŏj)	122	37.44 N	100.01 W
Dodgeville, Wi. (dŏj'vĭl)	115	42.58 N	90.07 W
Dodoma, Tan. (dô'dô-ma)	231	6.11 s	35.45 E
Dog (L.), Can. (dŏg)	115	48.42 N	89.24 W
Dogger Bk., Eur. (dôg'gěr)	158	55.07 N	2.25 E
Dogubayazit, Tur.	179	39.35 N	44.00 E
Dohad, India	196	22.52 N	74.18 E
Doirani (L.), Grc.	173	41.10 N	23.00 E
Dôjô, Jap. (dō-jō)	205b	34.51 N	135.14 E
Dokshitsy, Sov. Un. (dôk-shětsě)	174	54.53 N	27.49 E
Do, Lac (L.), Mali.	228	15.50 N	2.20 W
Dolbeau, Can.	103	48.52 N	72.16 W
Dole, Fr. (dôl)	169	47.07 N	5.28 E
Dolgaya, Kosa (I.), Sov. Un.			
(kô'sá dôl-gä'yä)	175	46.42 N	37.42 E
Dolgeville, NY	111	43.10 N	74.45 W
Dolgiy (I.), Sov. Un.	178	69.20 N	59.20 E
Dolgoprudnyy, Sov. Un.	182b	55.57 N	37.33 E
Dolina, Sov. Un. (dô-lyē'ná)	167	48.57 N	24.01 E
Dolinsk, Sov. Un. (dô-lěnsk')	204	47.29 N	142.31 E
Dollard-des-Ormeaux, Can.	54b	45.29 N	73.49 W
Dollar Hbr., Ba.	134	25.30 N	79.15 W
Dolo, Som.	225	4.01 N	42.14 E
Dolomite, Al. (dŏl'ô-mīt)	111h	33.28 N	86.57 W
Dolomiti, Alpi (Mts.), It.			
(äl-pě'dô'lô'mē-tē)	172	46.16 N	11.43 E
Dolores, Arg. (dô-lô'rěs)	141c	36.20 s	57.42 W
Dolores, Col.	142a	3.33 N	74.54 W

PLACE (Pronunciation)	PAGE	Lat. °'	Long. °'
Dolores, Phil. (dô-lô-rĕs)	207a	17.40 N	120.43 E
Dolores, Tx. (dô-lō'rĕs)	124	27.42 N	99.47 W
Dolores, Ur.	141c	33.32 S	58.15 W
Dolores (R.), Co.-Ut.	121	38.35 N	108.50 W
Dolores Hidalgo, Mex. (dô-lô'rĕs-ē-däl'gō)	130	21.09 N	100.56 W
Dolphin and Union Str., Can. (dŏl'fĭn ūn'yŭn)	96	69.22 N	117.10 W
Dolton, Il.	58a	41.39 N	87.37 W
Domažlice, Czech. (dō'mäzh-lē-tsĕ)	166	49.27 N	12.55 E
Dombasle-sur-Meurthe, Fr. (dôn-bäl')	169	48.38 N	6.18 E
Dombóvár, Hung. (dōm'bō-vär)	167	46.22 N	18.08 E
Domeyko, Cordillera (Mts.), Chile (kôr-dēl-yĕ'rä-dô-mā'kô)	142	20.50 S	69.02 W
Dominguez, Ca.	59	33.50 N	118.31 W
Dominica, N.A. (dŏ-mĭ-nē'kȧ)	129	15.30 N	60.45 W
Dominica Chan., N.A.	133b	15.00 N	61.30 W
Dominican Republic, N.A. (dô-mĭn'ĭ-kăn)	129	19.00 N	70.45 W
Dominion, Can. (dô-mĭn'yŭn)	105	46.13 N	60.01 W
Domiongo, Zaire	230	4.37 S	21.15 E
Domitilla, Catacombe di (P. Int.), It.	66c	41.52 N	12.31 E
Domodedovo, Sov. Un. (dô-mô-dyĕ'do-vô)	182b	55.27 N	37.45 E
Dom Silvério, Braz. (dôn-sēl-vĕ'ryō)	141a	20.09 S	42.57 W
Don (R.), Can.	54c	43.39 N	79.21 W
Don (R.), Eng.	156	53.39 N	0.58 W
Don (R.), Scot.	162	57.19 N	2.39 W
Don (R.), Sov.Un.	176	49.50 N	41.30 E
Don (R.), Eng. (dŏn)	156	53.27 N	1.34 W
Donaldson, Mi. (dŏn'ăl-sŭn)	119k	46.19 N	84.22 W
Donaldsonville, La. (dŏn'ăld-sŭn-vĭl)	123	30.05 N	90.58 W
Donalsonville, Ga.	126	31.02 N	84.50 W
Donau (R.), **See Danube**			
Donaufeld (Neigh.), It.	66c	48.15 N	16.25 E
Donaustadt (Neigh.), Aus.	66e	48.13 N	16.30 E
Donauturm (P. Int.), Aus.	66e	48.14 N	16.25 E
Donawitz, Aus. (dō'nȧ-vĭts)	166	47.23 N	15.05 E
Don Benito, Sp. (dōn'bȧ-nē'tō)	170	38.55 N	6.08 W
Dönberg, F.R.G.	63	51.18 N	7.10 E
Don Bosco (Neigh.), Arg.	60d	34.42 S	58.19 W
Doncaster, Austl. (doŋ'kăs-tēr)	211a	37.47 S	145.08 E
Doncaster, Can.	54c	43.48 N	79.25 W
Doncaster, Eng. (doŋ'kăs-tēr)	156	53.32 N	1.07 W
Doncaster East, Austl.	70b	37.47 S	145.10 E
Dondo, Ang. (dōn'dō)	230	9.38 S	14.25 E
Dondo, Moz.	226	19.33 S	34.47 E
Dondra Hd., Sri Lanka	197	5.52 N	80.52 E
Donegal, Ire. (dŏn-ē-gôl')	162	54.44 N	8.05 W
Donegal Bay, Ire. (dŏn-ē-gôl')	162	54.35 N	8.36 W
Donets (R.), Sov. Un. (dō-nyĕts')	175	48.48 N	38.42 E
Donets Coal Basin (Reg.), Sov. Un. (dō-nyĕts')	175	48.15 N	38.50 E
Donetsk (Stalino), Sov. Un. (dō-nyĕts'k) (stä'lĭ-nō)	175	48.00 N	37.35 E
Donetsk (Oblast), Sov. Un.	175	47.55 N	37.40 E
Dong (R.), China (dôŋ)	199	34.13 N	115.08 E
Dongara, Austl. (dôn-gă'rȧ)	214	29.15 S	115.00 E
Dongba, China	67b	39.58 N	116.32 E
Dongba, China (dôŋ-bä)	200	31.40 N	119.02 E
Dongbahe, China	67b	39.58 N	116.27 E
Dong'e, China (dôŋ-ŭ)	200	36.21 N	116.14 E
Dong'erzen, China (dôŋ-är-dzŭn)	200	36.11 N	116.16 E
Dongfang, China (dôŋ-fäŋ)	203	19.08 N	108.42 E
Donggala, Indon. (dôn-gä'lä)	206	0.45 S	119.32 E
Dongguan, China (dôŋ-gūän)	201a	23.03 N	113.46 E
Dongguang, China (dôŋ-gūäŋ)	200	37.54 N	116.33 E
Donghai, China (dôŋ-hī)	200	34.35 N	119.05 E
Dong Hoi, Viet. (dông-hô-ĕ')	203	17.25 N	106.42 E
Dongming, China (dôŋ-mĭŋ)	200	35.16 N	115.06 E
Dongo, Ang. (dôŋ'gō)	226	14.45 S	15.30 E
Dongon Pt., Phil (dŏng-ôn')	207a	12.43 N	120.35 E
Dongou, Con. (dôŋ-gōō')	230	2.02 N	18.04 E
Dongping, China (dôŋ-pĭŋ)	200	35.50 N	116.24 E
Dongping Hu (L.), China (dôŋ-pĭŋ hōō)	200	36.06 N	116.24 E
Dongsha Dao (I.), **see Pratas**			
Dongshan, China (doŋ-shän)	200	31.05 N	120.24 E
Dongshi, China	67b	39.49 N	116.34 E
Dongtai, China	200	32.51 N	120.20 E
Dongting Hu (L.), China (dôŋ-tĭŋ hōō)	203	29.10 N	112.30 E
Dongxiang, China (dôŋ-shyän)	203	28.18 N	116.38 E
Doniphan, Mo. (dŏn'ĭ-făn)	123	36.37 N	90.50 W
Donji Vakuf, Yugo. (dōn'yĭ väk'ōōf)	172	44.08 N	17.25 E
Don Martin, Presa de (Res.), Mex. (prĕ'sä-dĕ-dôn-mär-tē'n)	124	27.35 N	100.38 W
Donnacona, Can.	104	46.40 N	71.46 W
Donnemarie-en-Montois, Fr. (dôn-mä-rē'ĕN-môN-twä')	169b	48.29 N	3.09 E
Donner und Blitzen (R.), Or. (dŏn'ēr ōōnt'blĭ'tsĕn)	116	42.45 N	118.57 W
Donnybrook, S. Afr. (dŏ-nĭ-brōōk)	227c	29.56 S	29.54 E
Donora, Pa. (dŏ-nō'rȧ)	113e	40.10 N	79.51 W
Don Torcuato, Arg.	60d	34.30 S	58.40 W
Doolow, Som.	223a	4.10 N	42.05 E
Doonerak, Mt., Ak. (dōō'nē-răk)	107	68.00 N	150.34 W
Doorn, Neth.	157a	52.02 N	5.21 E
Door Pen., Wi. (dōr)	115	44.40 N	87.36 W
Dora Baltea (R.), It. (dō'rä bäl'tā-ä)	172	45.40 N	7.34 E
Doraville, Ga. (dō'rȧ-vĭl)	112c	33.54 N	84.17 W
Dorchester, Eng. (dôr'chĕs-tēr)	162	50.45 N	2.34 W
Dorchester Heights National Historic Site (P. Int.), Ma.	54a	42.20 N	71.03 W
Dordogne (R.), Fr. (dôr-dôn'yĕ)	168	44.53 N	0.16 E
Dordrecht, Neth. (dôr'drĕKt)	157a	51.48 N	4.39 E
Dordrecht, S. Afr. (dô'drĕKt)	227c	31.24 S	27.06 E
Doré L., Can.	100	54.31 N	107.06 W
Dorgali, It. (dôr'gä-lē)	172	40.18 N	9.37 E
Dörgön Nuur (L.), Mong	200	47.47 N	94.01 E
Dorion-Vaudreuil, Can. (dôr-yō)	95a	45.23 N	74.01 W
Dorking, Eng. (dôr'kĭng)	156b	51.12 N	0.20 W
D'Orleans, Ile (I.), Can. (yl dôr-lĕ-äN')	95b	46.56 N	71.00 W
Dormont, Pa. (dôr'mŏnt)	113e	40.24 N	80.02 W
Dornap, F.R.G.	63	51.15 N	7.04 E
Dornbirn, Aus. (dôrn'bĕrn)	166	47.24 N	9.45 E
Dornoch, Scot. (dôr'nŏK)	162	57.55 N	4.01 W
Dornoch Firth, Scot. (dôr'nŏK fûrth)	162	57.55 N	3.55 W
Dorogobuzh, Sov. Un. (dôrôgô'-bōō'zh)	174	54.57 N	33.18 E
Dorohoi, Rom. (dō-rô-hoi')	167	47.57 N	26.28 E
Dorpat, see Tartu			
Dorre (I.), Austl. (dôr)	214	25.19 S	113.10 E
Dorseyville, Pa.	57b	40.35 N	79.53 W
Dorstfield (Neigh.), F.R.G.	63	51.31 N	7.25 E
Dorstsen, F.R.G.	169c	51.40 N	6.58 E
Dortmund, F.R.G. (dôrt'mōōnt)	169c	51.31 N	7.28 E
Dortmund-Ems-Kanal (Can.), F.R.G. (dôrt'mōōnd-ĕms'kä-näl')	169c	51.50 N	7.25 E
Dörtyol, Tur. (dûrt'yôl)	179	36.50 N	36.20 E
Dorval, Can. (dôr-vål')	95a	45.26 N	73.44 W
Dos Caminos, Ven. (dôs-kä-mē'nôs)	143b	9.38 N	67.17 W
Dosewallips (R.), Wa. (dō'sē-wäl'lĭps)	118a	47.45 N	123.04 W
Dos Hermanas, Sp. (dōsĕr-mä'näs)	170	37.17 N	5.56 W
Dosso, Niger (dōs-ō')	229	13.03 N	3.12 E
Dothan, Al. (dō'thăn)	126	31.13 N	85.23 W
Douai, Fr. (dōō-å')	168	50.23 N	3.04 E
Douala, Cam. (dōō-ä'lä)	229	4.03 N	9.42 E
Douarnenez, Fr. (dōō-är nē-nĕs')	168	48.06 N	4.18 W
Double Bayou, Tx. (dŭb''l bī'yōō)	125a	29.40 N	94.38 W
Douentza, Mali	228	15.00 N	2.57 W
Douglas, Ak. (dŭg'lăs)	107	58.18 N	134.35 W
Douglas, Ar.	121	31.20 N	109.30 W
Douglas, Ga.	126	31.30 N	82.53 W
Douglas, Isle of Man (dŭg'lȧs)	162	54.10 N	4.24 W
Douglas, Wy. (dŭg'lăs)	117	42.45 N	105.21 W
Douglas (R.), Eng. (dŭg'lȧs)	156	53.38 N	2.48 W
Douglas (R.), Tn. (dŭg'lăs)	126	36.00 N	83.35 W
Douglas Chan, Can.	98	53.30 N	129.12 W
Douglas Lake Ind. Res., Can.	99	50.10 N	120.49 W
Douglasville, Ga. (dŭg'lăs-vĭl)	126	33.45 N	84.47 W
Doumé, Cam. (dōō-mā')	225	4.41 N	13.26 E
Dourada, Serra (Mts.), Braz. (sĕ'r-rä-dōōō-rá'dä)	143	15.11 S	49.57 W
Dourdan, Fr. (dōōr-däN')	169b	48.32 N	2.01 E
Douro (R.), Port. (dō'ōō-rô)	170	41.03 N	8.12 W
Dove (R.), Eng. (dŭv)	156	52.53 N	1.47 W
Dover, De. (dō vēr)	111	39.10 N	75.30 W
Dover, Eng.	163	51.08 N	1.19 E
Dover, NH	111	43.15 N	71.00 W
Dover, NJ	112a	40.53 N	74.33 W
Dover, Oh.	110	40.35 N	81.30 W
Dover, S. Afr.	223d	27.05 S	27.44 E
Dover-Foxcroft, Me. (dō'vēr fôks'krôft)	104	45.10 N	69.15 W
Dover Heights, Austl.	70a	33.53 S	151.17 E
Dover, Str. of, Eur.	163	50.50 N	1.15 W
Doveton, Austl.	70b	38.00 S	145.14 E
Dovlekanovo, Sov. Un. (dŏv'lyĕk-ȧ-nô-vô)	178	54.15 N	55.05 E
Dovre Fjell (Plat.), Nor. (dŏv'rĕ fyĕl')	164	62.03 N	8.36 E
Dow, Il. (dou)	119e	39.01 N	90.20 W
Dowagiac, Mi. (dô-wô'jăk)	110	42.00 N	86.05 W
Dowlatābād, Iran	68h	35.37 N	51.27 E
Downers Grove, Il. (dou'nērz grōv)	113a	41.48 N	88.00 W
Downey, Ca. (dou'nĭ)	119a	33.56 N	118.08 W
Downieville, Ca. (dou'nĭ-nĭl)	120	39.35 N	120.48 W
Downs, Ks. (dounz)	122	39.29 N	98.32 W
Doylestown, Oh. (doilz'toun)	113d	40.58 N	81.43 W
Drâa, C., Mor. (drȧ)	224	28.39 N	12.15 W
Drâa, Oued (R.), Mor.	224	28.00 N	9.31 W
Drabov, Sov. Un. (drä'bôf)	175	49.57 N	32.14 E
Drac (R.), Fr. (dräK)	169	44.50 N	5.47 E
Dracut, Ma. (dră'kŭt)	105a	42.40 N	71.19 W
Draganovo, Bul. (drä-gä-nō'vô)	173	43.13 N	25.45 E
Drăgăşani, Rom. (drä-gȧ-shän'ĭ)	173	44.39 N	24.18 E
Draguignan, Fr. (drä-gēn-yäN')	169	43.35 N	6.28 E
Drakensberg Mts.), Leso-S.Afr. (drä'kĕnz-bĕrgh)	226	29.15 S	29.07 E
Drake Passage, S.A.-Ant. (drāk păs'ĭj)	140	57.00 S	65.00 W
Dráma, Grc. (drä'mä)	173	41.09 N	24.10 E
Drammen, Nor. (dräm'ĕn)	164	59.45 N	10.15 E
Drancy, Fr.	64c	48.56 N	2.27 E
Drau (R.), Aus. (drou)	166	46.44 N	13.45 E
Drava (R.), Yugo. (Drä'vä)	172	46.37 N	15.17 E
Draveil, Fr.	64c	48.41 N	2.25 E
Dravograd, Yugo. (Drä'vô-gräd')	172	46.37 N	15.01 E
Dravosburg, Pa.	57b	40.21 N	79.51 W
Drawsko Pomorskie, Pol. (dräv'skō pō-mōr'skyĕ)	166	53.31 N	15.50 E
Drayton Hbr., Wa. (drā'tŭn)	118d	48.58 N	122.40 W
Drayton Plains, Mi.	113b	42.41 N	83.23 W
Drayton Valley, Can.	99	53.13 N	114.59 W
Drensteinfurt, F.R.G. (drĕn'shtīn-fōōrt)	169c	51.47 N	7.44 E
Dresden, G.D.R. (drās'dĕn)	166	51.05 N	13.45 E
Dreux, Fr. (drû)	169b	48.44 N	1.24 E
Drewitz (Neigh.), G.D.R.	65a	52.22 N	13.08 E
Drexel Hill, Pa.	56b	39.57 N	75.19 W
Driefontein, S. Afr.	223d	25.53 S	29.10 E
Drin (R.), Alb. (drēn)	173	42.13 N	20.13 E
Drina (R.), Yugo. (drē'nä)	173	44.09 N	19.30 E
Drinit, Pelgi (B.), Alb.	173	41.42 N	19.17 E
Dr. Ir. W. J. van Blommestein Meer (Res.), Sur.	143	4.45 N	55.05 W
Drissa (R.), Sov. Un.	174	55.44 N	28.58 E
Drissa, Sov. Un. (drĭs'sä)	174	55.48 N	27.59 E
Driver, Va.	112g	36.50 N	76.30 W
Dröbak, Nor. (drû'bäk)	164	59.40 N	10.35 E
Drobeta-Turnu-Severin, Rom. (sĕ-vĕ-rēn')	173	43.54 N	24.49 E
Drogheda, Ire. (drŏ'hē-dȧ)	162	53.43 N	6.15 W
Drogichin, Sov. Un. (drō-gē'chĭn)	167	52.10 N	25.11 E
Drogobych, Sov. Un. (drō-hô'bĭch)	167	49.21 N	23.31 E
Drôme (R.), Fr. (drōm)	168	44.42 N	4.53 E
Dronfield, Eng. (drŏn'fēld)	156	53.18 N	1.28 W
Droylsden, Eng.	64b	53.29 N	2.10 W
Drumheller, Can. (drŭm-hĕl-ēr)	99	51.28 N	112.42 W
Drummond (I.), Mi. (drŭm'ŭnd)	110	46.00 N	83.50 W
Drummondville, Can. (drŭm'ŭnd-vĭl)	104	45.53 N	72.33 W
Drummoyne, Austl.	70a	33.51 S	151.09 E
Drumright, Ok. (drŭm'rīt)	123	35.59 N	96.37 W
Drunen, Neth.	157a	51.41 N	5.10 E
Drut' (R.), Sov.Un. (drōōt)	174	53.40 N	29.45 E
Druya, Sov.Un. (drōō'yȧ)	174	55.45 N	27.26 E
Družba, Sov. Un.	66b	55.53 N	37.45 E
Drweca R., Pol. (d'r-văn'tsȧ)	167	53.06 N	19.13 E
Dryden, Can. (drī-dĕn)	97	49.47 N	92.50 W
Drysdale, Austl.	211a	38.11 S	144.34 E
Dry Tortugas (I.), Fl. (tôr-tōō'gäz)	127a	24.37 N	82.45 W
Dschang, Cam. (dshäng)	224	5.34 N	10.09 E
Duabo, Lib.	228	5.40 N	8.05 W
Duagh, Can.	95g	53.43 N	113.24 W
Duarte, Ca.	59	34.08 N	117.58 W
Duarte, Pico (Mtn.), Dom. Rep. (dĭŭ'ärtĕh pĕcô)	129	19.00 N	71.00 W
Duas Barras, Braz. (dōō'äs-bà'r-räs)	141a	22.03 S	42.30 W
Dubawnt (L.), Can. (dōō-bônt')	96	63.27 N	103.30 W
Dubawnt (R.), Can.	96	61.30 N	103.49 W
Dubayy, U.A.E.	192	25.18 N	55.26 E
Dubbo, Austl. (dŭb'ō)	216	32.20 S	148.42 E
Dubie, Zaire	231	8.33 S	28.32 E
Dublin, Ca. (dŭb'lĭn)	118b	37.42 N	121.56 W
Dublin, Ga.	126	32.33 N	82.55 W
Dublin, Tx.	124	32.05 N	98.20 W
Dublin, see Baile Átha Cliath			
Dubno, Sov.Un. (dōō'b-nô)	167	50.24 N	25.44 E
Du Bois, Pa. (dōō-bois')	111	41.10 N	78.45 W
Dubossary, Sov. Un. (dōō-bŏ-sä'rĭ)	175	47.16 N	29.11 E
Dubovka, Sov. Un. (dōō-bôf'kȧ)	179	49.00 N	44.50 E
Dubrovka, Sov. Un. (dōō-brôf'kȧ)	182c	59.51 N	30.56 E
Dubrovnik (Ragusa), Yugo. (dōō'brôv-nēk) (rä-gōō'sä)	173	42.40 N	18.10 E
Dubrovno, Sov. Un. (dōō-brôf'nō)	174	54.39 N	30.54 E
Dubuque, Ia. (dōō-būk')	115	42.30 N	90.43 W
Duchesne (R.), Ut.	121	40.20 N	110.50 W
Duchesne, Ut. (dōō-shān')	121	40.12 N	110.23 W
Duchess, Austl. (dŭch'ĕs)	214	21.30 S	139.55 E
Ducie I., Oceania (dü-sē')	209	25.30 S	126.20 W
Duck (R.), Tn.	126	35.55 N	87.40 W
Duckabush (R.), Wa. (dŭk'ȧ-bōōsh)	118a	47.41 N	123.09 W
Duck Lake, Can.	100	52.47 N	106.13 W
Duck Mtn., Can.	101	51.35 N	101.00 W
Ducktown, Tn. (dŭk'toun)	126	35.03 N	84.20 W
Duck Valley Ind. Res., Id.-Nv.	116	42.02 N	115.49 W
Duckwater Pk., Nv. (dŭk-wô-tēr)	120	39.00 N	115.31 W
Duda (R.), Col. (dōō'dä)	142a	3.25 N	74.23 W
Dudinka, Sov. Un. (dōō-dĭn'kȧ)	180	69.15 N	85.42 E
Dudley, Eng. (dŭd'lĭ)	156	52.28 N	2.07 E
Duékoué, Ivory Coast	228	6.45 N	7.21 W
Duero (R.), Sp. (dwĕ'rô)	170	41.30 N	5.10 W
Dugger, In. (dŭg'ēr)	110	39.00 N	87.10 W
Dugi Otok (I.), Yugo. (dōō'gē o'tôk)	172	44.03 N	14.40 E
Dugny, Fr.	64c	48.57 N	2.25 E
Duisburg, F.R.G. (dōō'ĭs-bōōrgh)	169c	51.26 N	6.46 E
Duissern (Neigh.), F.R.G.	63	51.26 N	6.47 E
Dukhān, Qatar	195	25.25 N	50.48 E
Dukhovshchina, Sov. Un. (dōō-Kôfsh-'chēnȧ)	174	55.13 N	32.26 E
Dukinfield, Eng. (dŭk'ĭn-fēld)	156	53.28 N	2.05 W
Dukla P., Pol. (dōō'klä)	167	49.25 N	21.44 E
Dulce, Golfo (G.), C.R. (gōl'fô dōōl'sä)	133	8.25 N	83.13 W
Dulcigno, see Ulcinj			
Dülken, F.G.R. (dül'kĕn)	169c	51.15 N	6.21 E
Dülmen, F.R.G. (dül'mĕn)	169c	51.50 N	7.17 E
Duluth, Mn. (dōō-lōōth')	119h	46.50 N	92.07 W
Dulwich (Neigh.), Eng.	62	51.26 N	0.05 W
Dūmā, Syria	191a	33.34 N	36.17 E
Dumaguete City, Phil. (dōō-mä-gä'tā)	207	9.14 N	123.15 E
Dumai, Indon.	191b	1.39 N	101.30 E
Dumali Pt., Phil. (dōō-mä'lē)	207a	13.07 N	121.42 E
Dumas, Tx.	122	35.52 N	101.58 W
Dumbarton, Scot. (dŭm'bär-tŭn)	162	56.00 N	4.35 W
Dum-Dum, India	196a	22.37 N	88.25 E
Dumfries, Scot. (dŭm-frēs')	162	54.05 N	3.40 W
Dumjor, India	196a	22.37 N	88.14 E
Dumont, NJ (dōō'mŏnt)	112a	40.56 N	74.00 W
Dümpten (Neigh.), F.R.G.	63	51.27 N	6.54 E
Dumyâṭ, Egypt	223b	31.22 N	31.50 E
Dumyâṭ, Maşabb (Chan.), Egypt	223b	31.36 N	31.45 E
Duna (R.), Hung. (dōō'nä)	167	46.07 N	18.45 E
Duna (R.), **see Danube**			
Dunaföldvár, Hung. (dōō'nô-fûld'vär)	167a	46.48 N	18.55 E
Dunajec (R.), Pol. (dōō-nä'yĕts)	167	49.52 N	20.53 E
Dunaújváros, Hung.	167	46.57 N	18.55 E
Dunay, Sov. Un. (dōō'nĭ)	182c	59.59 N	30.57 E
Dunayevtsy, Sov. Un. (dōō-nä'yĕf-tsĭ)	175	48.52 N	26.51 E
Dunbar, WV	110	38.20 N	81.45 W
Duncan, Can. (dŭŋ'kăn)	96.	48.47 N	123.42 W
Duncan, Ok.	122	34.29 N	97.56 W
Duncan (R.), Can.	99	50.30 N	116.45 W
Duncan Dam, Can.	99	50.15 N	116.55 W
Duncan L, Can.	99	50.20 N	117.00 W
Duncansby Hd., Scot. (dŭn'kănz-bĭ)	162a	58.40 N	3.01 W
Duncanville, Tx. (dŭn'kăn-vĭl)	119c	32.39 N	96.55 W
Dundalk, Ire. (dŭn'kôk)	162	54.00 N	6.18 W
Dundalk, Md.	112e	39.16 N	76.31 W

PRONOUNCING INDEX
Dundalk B. – Edgewood 279

PLACE (Pronounciation)	PAGE	Lat. °′	Long. °′
Dundalk B., Ire. (dŭn'dôk)	162	53.55 N	6.15 W
Dundas, Austl.	70a	33.48 S	151.02 E
Dundas, Can. (dŭn-dăs')	95d	43.16 N	79.58 W
Dundas (L.), Austl. (dŭn-dás)	214	32.15 S	122.00 E
Dundas I, Can.	98	54.33 N	130.55 W
Dundas Str., Austl.	214	10.35 S	131.15 E
Dundedin, Fl. (dŭn-ē'dĭn)	127a	28.00 N	82.43 W
Dundee, Il. (dŭn-dē)	113a	42.06 N	88.17 W
Dundee, S. Afr	227c	28.14 S	30.16 E
Dundee, Scot	162	56.30 N	2.55 W
Dundrum B., Ire. (dŭn-drŭm')	162	54.13 N	5.47 W
Dunedin, N.Z.	215a	45.48 S	170.32 E
Dunellen, NJ (dŭn-ĕl'l'n)	112a	40.36 N	74.28 W
Dunfermline, Scot. (dŭn-fĕrm'lĭn)	162	56.05 N	3.30 W
Dungarvan, Ire. (dŭn-gar'văn)	162	52.06 N	7.50 W
Dungeness (R.), Wa.	118a	48.03 N	123.10 W
Dungeness, Wa. (dŭnj-nĕs')	118a	48.09 N	123.07 W
Dungeness Spit, Wa.	118a	48.11 N	123.03 W
Dunham Town, Eng.	64b	53.23 N	2.24 W
Dunheved, Austl.	70a	33.45 S	150.47 E
Dunhua, China (dōōn-hwä)	202	48.18 N	128.10 E
Dunkerque, Fr. (dŭN-kĕrk')	168	51.02 N	2.37 E
Dunkirk, In. (dŭn'kûrk)	110	40.20 N	85.25 W
Dunkirk, NY	111	42.30 N	79.20 W
Dunkwa, Ghana	228	5.22 N	1.12 W
Dun Laoghaire, Ire. (dŭn-lā'rĕ)	162	53.16 N	6.09 W
Dunlap, Ia. (dŭn'lăp)	114	41.53 N	95.33 W
Dunlap, Tn.	126	35.23 N	85.23 W
Dunmore, Pa. (dŭn'mōr)	111	41.25 N	75.30 W
Dunn, NC (dŭn)	127	35.18 N	78.37 W
Dunnellon, Fl. (dŭn-ĕl'ŏn)	127	29.02 N	82.28 W
Dunn Loring, Va.	56d	38.53 N	77.14 W
Dunnville, Can. (dŭn'vĭl)	111	42.55 N	79.40 W
Dunqulah, Sud.	225	19.21 N	30.19 E
Dunsmuir, Ca. (dŭnz'mūr)	116	41.08 N	122.17 W
Dunton Green, Eng.	62	51.18 N	0.11 E
Dunton Wayletts, Eng.	62	51.35 N	0.24 E
Dunvegan, S. Afr.	71b	26.09 S	28.09 E
Dunwoody, Ga. (dŭn-wŏŏd'ĭ)	112c	33.57 N	84.20 W
Duolun, China (dwô-lōōn)	202	42.12 N	116.15 E
Duomo (P. Int.), It.	65c	45.27 N	9.11 E
Du Page R., Il. (dōō pāj)	113a	41.41 N	88.11 W
Du Page R., E. Br., Il.	113a	41.49 N	88.05 W
Du Page R., W. Br., Il.	113a	41.48 N	88.10 W
Dupax, Phil. (dōō'päks)	207a	16.16 N	121.06 E
Dupo, Il. (dū'pō)	119e	38.31 N	90.12 W
Duque de Bragança, Ang. (dōō'kå då brä-gäN'sä)	230	9.06 S	15.57 E
Duque de Caxias, Braz. (dōō'kĕ-dĕ-kå'shyås)	144b	22.46 S	43.18 W
Duquesne, Pa. (dōō-kān')	113e	40.22 N	79.51 W
Du Quoin, Il. (dōō-kwoin')	123	38.01 N	89.14 W
Durance (R.), Fr. (dü-räNs')	169	43.46 N	5.52 E
Durand, Mi. (dů-rănd')	110	42.50 N	84.00 W
Durand, Wi.	115	44.37 N	91.58 W
Durango, Co. (dōō-răŋ'gō)	121	37.15 N	107.55 W
Durango, Mex. (dōō-rä'n-gô)	130	24.02 N	104.42 W
Durango (State), Mex.	128	25.00 N	106.00 W
Durant, Ms. (dů-rănt')	126	33.05 N	89.50 W
Durant, Ok.	123	33.59 N	96.23 W
Duratón (R.), Sp. (dōō-rä-tōn')	170	41.55 N	3.55 W
Durazno (Dept.), Ur.	141c	33.00 S	56.35 W
Durazno, Ur. (dōō-räz'nō)	141c	33.21 S	56.31 W
Durban, S. Afr. (dûr'băn)	227c	29.48 S	31.00 E
Durban Roodepoort Deep Gold Mines (P. Int.), S. Afr.	71b	26.10 S	27.51 E
Durbanville, S. Afr. (dûr-băn'vĭl)	226a	33.50 S	18.39 E
Durbe, Sov. Un. (dōōr'bĕ)	165	56.36 N	21.24 E
Durchholz, F.R.G.	63	51.23 N	7.17 E
Durdevac, Yugo.(dūr'dyĕ-váts')	172	46.03 N	17.03 E
Düren, F.R.G. (dü'rĕn)	169c	50.48 N	6.30 E
Durham, Eng. (dûr'ăm)	162	54.47 N	1.46 W
Durham, NC	127	36.00 N	78.55 W
Durham Downs, Austl.	216	27.30 S	141.55 E
Durrës, Alb. (dŏŏr'ĕs)	173	41.19 N	19.27 E
Duryea, Pa. (dōōr-yā')	111	41.20 N	75.50 W
Dushan, China (dōō-shän)	203	25.50 N	107.42 E
Dushan, China	200	31.38 N	116.16 E
Dushanbe, Sov. Un.	193	38.30 N	68.45 E
Düssel, F.R.G.	63	51.16 N	7.03 E
Düsseldorf, F.R.G. (düs'ĕl-dôrf)	169c	51.14 N	6.47 E
Dussen, Neth.	157a	51.43 N	4.58 E
Dutalan Ula (Mtn.), Mong.	202	49.25 N	112.40 E
Dutch Harbor, Ak. (dŭch här'bĕr)	107a	53.58 N	166.30 W
Duvall, Wa. (dōō'vâl)	118a	47.44 N	121.59 W
Duvergé, Dom. Rep. (dōō-vĕr-hĕ')	135	18.20 N	71.20 W
Duwamish (R.), Wa. (dōō-wăm'ĭsh)	118a	47.24 N	122.18 W
Duyun, China (dōō-yōōn)	203	26.18 N	107.40 E
Dvina, Western, (R.), see **Zapadnaya Dvina**			
Dvinskaya Guba (G.), Sov. Un.	178	65.10 N	38.40 E
Dvŭr Králové, Czech. (dvōōr' krä'lô-vā)	166	50.28 N	15.43 E
Dwārka, India	196	22.18 N	68.59 E
Dwight, Il. (dwĭt)	110	41.00 N	88.20 W
Dworshak Res, Id.	116	46.45 N	115.50 W
Dyat'kovo, Sov. Un. (dyät'kō-vō)	174	53.36 N	34.19 E
Dyer, In. (dī'ēr)	113a	41.30 N	87.31 W
Dyersburg, Tn. (dī'ērz-bûrg)	126	36.02 N	89.23 W
Dyersville, Ia. (dī'ērz-vĭl)	115	42.28 N	91.09 W
Dyes Inlet, Wa. (dīz)	118a	47.37 N	122.45 W
Dyment, Can. (dī'mĕnt)	101	49.37 N	92.19 W
Dzabhan (R.), Mong.	198	48.19 N	94.08 E
Dzamiin Üüd, Mong.	202	44.38 N	111.32 E
Dzaoudzi, Mayotte (dzou'dzĭ)	227	12.44 S	45.15 E
Dzaudzhikau, Sov. Un. (dzou-jĭ-kou')	155	48.00 N	44.52 E
Dzerzhinsk, Sov. Un. (dzhĕr-zhĭnsk')	175	48.24 N	37.58 E
Dzerzhinsk, Sov. Un.	174	53.41 N	27.14 E
Dzerzhinsk, Sov. Un.	178	56.20 N	43.50 E
Dzeržinskij, Sov. Un.	66b	55.38 N	37.50 E
Dzhalal-Abad, Sov. Un. (jă-läl'ă-bät')	180	41.13 N	73.35 E
Dzhambul, Sov. Un. (dzhäm-bōōl')	180	42.51 N	71.29 E
Dzhankoy, Sov. Un. (dzhän'koi)	175	45.43 N	34.22 E
Dzhetygara, Sov. Un. (dzhĕt'-gä'rå)	182a	52.12 N	61.18 E
Dzhizak, Sov. Un. (dzhĕ'zäk)	180	40.13 N	67.58 E
Dzhugdzhur Khrebet (Mts.), Sov. Un. (jōōg-jōōr')	181	56.15 N	137.00 E
Dzialoszyce, Pol. (jyä-wō-shē'tsĕ)	167	50.21 N	20.22 E
Dzibalchén, Mex. (zē-bäl-chĕ'n)	132a	19.25 N	89.39 W
Dzidzantún, Mex. (zēd-zän-tōō'n)	132a	21.18 N	89.00 W
Dzierzoniów, Pol. (dzyĕr-zhôn'yŭf)	166	50.44 N	16.38 E
Dzilam González, Mex. (zē-lä'm-gôn-zä'lĕz)	132a	21.21 N	88.53 W
Dzitás, Mex. (zē-tá's)	132a	20.47 N	88.32 W
Dzitbalché, Mex. (dzēt-bäl-chā')	132a	20.18 N	90.03 W
Dzungaria (Reg.), China (dzōōŋ-gä'rĭ-å)	198	44.39 N	86.13 E
Dzungarian Gate (P.), China	198	45.00 N	88.00 E

E

PLACE (Pronounciation)	PAGE	Lat. °′	Long. °′
Eagle, Ak (ē'g'l)	107	64.42 N	141.20 W
Eagle (R.), Co.	121	39.32 N	106.28 W
Eagle, WV	110	38.10 N	81.20 W
Eaglecliff, Wa (ē'gl-klĭf)	118c	46.10 N	123.13 W
Eagle Cr., In.	113g	39.54 N	86.17 W
Eagle Grove, Ia.	115	42.39 N	93.55 W
Eagle L, Ca.	116	40.45 N	120.52 W
Eagle Lake, Me.	104	47.03 N	68.38 W
Eagle Lake, Tx.	125	29.37 N	96.20 W
Eagle Mountain L, Tx.	119c	32.56 N	97.27 W
Eagle Pass, Tx.	124	28.49 N	100.30 W
Eagle Pk, Ca.	116	41.18 N	120.11 W
Eagle Rock (Neigh.), Ca.	59	34.09 N	118.12 W
Ealing, Eng. (ē'lĭng)	156b	51.29 N	0.19 W
Earle, Ar. (ûrl)	123	35.14 N	90.28 W
Earlington, Ky. (ûr'lĭng-tŭn)	126	37.15 N	87.31 W
Easley, SC (ēz'lĭ)	127	34.48 N	82.37 W
East (R.), NY	55	40.48 N	73.48 W
East Alton, Il. (ôl'tŭn)	119e	38.53 N	90.08 W
East Angus, Can. (ăŋ'gŭs)	103	45.35 N	71.40 W
East Arlington, Ma.	54a	42.25 N	71.08 W
East Aurora, NY (ô-rō'rå)	113c	42.46 N	78.38 W
East B, Tx	125a	29.30 N	94.41 W
East Barnet (Neigh.), Eng.	62	51.38 N	0.09 W
East Bedfont (Neigh.), Eng.	62	51.27 N	0.26 W
East Berlin, G.D.R. (bĕr-lēn')	157b	52.31 N	13.28 E
East Bernstadt, Ky (bûrn'stát)	126	37.09 N	84.08 W
Eastbourne, Eng. (ēst'bôrn)	163	50.48 N	0.16 E
East Braintree, Ma.	54a	42.13 N	70.58 W
East Burwood, Austl.	70b	37.51 S	145.09 E
Eastbury, Eng.	62	51.37 N	0.25 W
East Caicos (I.), Turk & Caicos Is. (kī'kōs)	135	21.40 N	71.35 W
East Cape (C.), N.Z.	217	37.37 S	178.33 E
East Cape, see **Dezhnëva, Mys**			
East Carondelet, Il. (kå-rŏn'dĕ-lĕt)	119e	38.33 N	90.14 W
Eastchester, NY	55	40.57 N	73.49 W
East Chicago, In. (shĭ-kô'gō)	113a	41.39 N	87.29 W
East China Sea, Asia	199	30.28 N	125.52 E
East Cleveland, Oh (klēv'lănd)	113d	41.33 N	81.35 W
Eastcote (Neigh.), Eng.	62	51.35 N	0.24 W
East Cote Blanche B., La. (kōt blăNsh')	125	29.30 N	92.07 W
East Des Moines (R.), Ia. (dē moin')	115	42.57 N	94.17 W
East Detroit, Mi (dē-troit')	113b	42.28 N	82.57 W
Easter (I.), see **Rapa Nui**			
Eastern Ghāts (Mts.), India	197	13.50 N	78.45 E
Eastern Native (Neigh.), S. Afr.	71b	26.13 S	28.05 E
Eastern Turkestan (Reg), China (tōōr-kĕ-stän')(tûr-kĕ-stăn')	198	39.40 N	78.20 E
East Falls (Neigh.), Pa.	56b	40.01 N	75.11 W
East Grand Forks, Mn. (grănd fôrks)	114	47.56 N	97.02 W
East Greenwich, RI (grĭn'ĭj)	112b	41.40 N	71.27 W
Eastham, Eng.	64a	53.19 N	2.58 W
East Ham (Neigh.), Eng.	62	51.32 N	0.03 E
Easthampton, Ma. (ēst-hămp'tŭn)	111	42.15 N	72.45 W
East Hartford, Ct (härt'fērd)	111	41.45 N	72.35 W
East Helena, Mt. (hĕ-hē'nå)	117	46.31 N	111.50 W
East Hills, Austl.	70a	33.58 S	150.59 E
East Hills, NY	55	40.47 N	73.38 W
East Ilsley, Eng. (ĭl'slē)	156b	51.30 N	1.18 W
East Jordan, Mi. (jôr'dăn)	110	45.05 N	85.05 W
East Kansas City, Mo. (kăn'zås)	119f	39.09 N	94.30 W
East Lamma Chan., Asia	68c	22.15 N	114.07 E
Eastland, Tx (ēst'lănd)	124	32.24 N	98.47 W
East Lansdowne, Pa.	56b	39.56 N	75.16 W
East Lansing, Mi (lăn'sĭng)	110	42.45 N	84.30 W
Eastlawn, Mi	113b	42.15 N	83.35 W
East Leavenworth, Mo (lĕv'ĕn-wûrth)	119f	39.18 N	94.50 W
East Liberty (Neigh.), Pa.	57b	40.27 N	79.55 W
East Lindfield, Austl.	70a	33.46 S	151.11 E
East Liverpool, Oh. (lĭv'ēr-pōōl)	110	40.40 N	80.35 W
East London, S. Afr. (lŭn'dŭn)	227c	33.02 S	27.54 E
East Los Angeles, Ca (lōs ăŋ'hå-lās)	119a	34.01 N	118.09 W
Eastmain (R.), Can. (ēst'mān)	97	52.12 N	73.19 W
East Malling, Eng.	62	51.17 N	0.26 E
Eastman, Ga. (ēst'măn)	126	32.10 N	83.11 W
East Meadow, NY	55	40.43 N	73.34 W
East Millstone, NJ (mĭl'stōn)	112a	40.30 N	74.35 W
East Molesey, Eng.	62	51.24 N	0.21 W
East Moline, Il. (mô-lēn')	115	41.31 N	90.28 W
East, Mt., Pan.	128a	9.09 N	79.46 W
East Newark, NJ	55	40.45 N	74.10 W
East New York (Neigh.), NY	55	40.40 N	73.53 W
East Nishnabotna (R.), Ia. (nĭsh-nå-bŏt'nå)	121	40.53 N	95.23 W
East Norwich, NY	55	40.50 N	73.32 W
Easton, Md. (ēs'tŭn)	111	72.45 N	76.05 W
Easton, Pa.	111	40.45 N	75.15 W
Easton L, Ct.	112a	41.18 N	73.17 W
East Orange, NJ (ŏr'ĕnj)	112a	40.46 N	74.12 W
East Palo Alto, Ca	118b	37.27 N	122.07 W
East Peoria, Il. (pē-ō'rĭ-å)	110	40.40 N	89.30 W
East Pittsburgh, Pa (pĭts'bûrg)	113e	40.24 N	79.50 W
East Point, GA	112c	33.41 N	84.27 W
Eastport, Me. (ēst'pōrt)	104	44.53 N	67.01 W
East Providence, RI (prŏv'ĭ-dĕns)	112b	41.49 N	71.22 W
East Retford, Eng. (rĕt'fērd)	156	53.19 N	0.56 W
East Richmond, Ca.	58b	37.57 N	122.19 W
East Rochester, NY (rŏch'ĕs-tēr)	111	43.10 N	77.30 W
East Rockaway, NY	55	40.39 N	73.40 W
East Saint Louis, Il. (sānt lōō'ĭs)(lōō-ĭ)	119e	38.38 N	90.10 W
East Siberian Sea, Sov. Un. (sī-bĭr'y'n)	176	73.00 N	153.28 E
Eastsound, Wa. (ēst-sound)	118d	48.42 N	122.42 W
East Stroudsburg, Pa (stroudz'bûrg)	111	41.00 N	75.10 W
East Syracuse, NY (sĭr'å-kūs)	111	43.05 N	76.00 W
East Tavaputs Plat., Ut. (tă-vă'-pŭts)	121	39.25 N	109.45 W
East Tawas, Mi (tô'wås)	110	44.15 N	83.30 W
East Tilbury, Eng.	62	51.28 N	0.26 E
East Tustin, Ca.	59	33.46 N	117.49 W
East Walker (R.), Nv (wôk'ēr)	120	38.36 N	119.02 W
East Walpole, Ma.	54a	42.10 N	71.13 W
East Watertown, Ma.	54a	42.22 N	71.10 W
East Weymouth, Ma.	54a	42.13 N	70.55 W
Eastwick (Neigh.), Pa.	56b	39.55 N	75.14 W
East Wickham (Neigh.), Eng.	62	51.28 N	0.07 E
Eastwood, Austl.	70a	33.48 S	151.05 E
East York, Can.	95d	43.41 S	79.20 W
Eaton, Co. (ē'tŭn)	113	40.31 N	104.42 W
Eaton, Oh.	110	39.45 N	84.40 W
Eaton Estates, Oh.	113d	41.19 N	82.01 W
Eaton Rapids, Mi. (răp'ĭdz)	110	42.30 N	84.40 W
Eatonton, GA (ē'tŭn-tŭn)	126	33.20 N	83.24 W
Eatontown, NJ (ē'tŭn-toun)	112a	40.18 N	74.04 W
Eaubonne, Fr.	64c	49.00 N	2.17 E
Eau Claire, Wi. (ō klâr')	115	44.47 N	91.32 W
Ebeltoft, Den. (ĕ'bĕl-tŭft)	164	56.11 N	10.39 E
Ebensburg, Pa.	111	40.29 N	78.44 W
Ebersberg, F.R.G. (ĕ'bĕrs-bĕrgh)	157d	48.05 N	11.58 E
Ebina, Jap.	69a	35.26 N	139.25 E
Ebingen, F.R.G. (ā'bĭng-ĕn)	166	48.13 N	9.04 E
Ebinur Hu (L.), China (ä-bē-nōōr hōō)	198	45.09 N	83.15 E
Eboli, It. (ĕb'ô-lē)	172	40.38 N	15.04 E
Ebolowa, Cam.	229	2.54 N	11.09 E
Ebreichsdorf, Aus.	157e	47.58 N	16.24 E
Ebrie, Lagune (Lagoon), Ivory Coast	228	5.20 N	4.50 W
Ebro (R.), Sp. (ā'brō)	171	41.30 N	0.35 W
Ebute-ikorodu, Nig.	71d	6.37 N	3.30 E
Eccles, Eng. (ĕk''lz)	156	53.29 N	2.20 W
Eccles, WV	110	37.45 N	81.10 W
Eccleshall, Eng. (ĕk''lz-hôl)	156	52.51 N	2.15 W
Eccleston, Eng.	64a	53.27 N	2.47 W
Eccleston, Md.	56c	39.24 N	76.44 W
Eceabat (Maidos), Tur.	173	40.10 N	26.21 E
Echague, Phil. (ā-chä'gwä)	207a	16.43 N	121.40 E
Echandi, Cerro (Mt.), Pan. (sĕ'r-rô-ĕ-chä'nd)	133	9.05 N	82.51 W
Ech Cheliff (Orléansville), Alg.	160	36.14 N	1.32 E
Echimamish (R.), Can.	101	54.15 N	97.30 W
Echo Bay, Can. (ĕk'ō)	119k	46.29 N	84.04 W
Echoing (R.), Can. (ĕk'ō-ĭng)	101	55.15 N	91.30 W
Echternach, Lux. (ĕk'tēr-näk)	169	49.48 N	6.25 E
Echuca, Austl. (ē-chōō'kå)	216	36.10 S	144.47 E
Ecija, Sp. (ā'thē-hä)	170	37.20 N	5.07 W
Eckernförde, F.R.G.	166	54.27 N	9.51 E
Eclipse, Va (ē-klĭps')	112g	36.55 N	76.29 W
Ecorse, Mi (ē-kôrs')	113b	42.15 N	83.09 W
Ecuador, S.A. (ĕk'wå-dôr)	140	0.00 N	78.30 W
Ed, Eth.	225	13.57 N	41.37 E
Eda (Neigh.), Jap.	69a	35.34 N	139.34 E
Eddyville, Ky. (ĕd'ĭ-vĭl)	126	37.03 N	88.03 W
Ede, Nig.	229	7.44 N	4.27 E
Edéa, Cam. (ĕ-dā'ä)	229	3.48 N	10.08 E
Eden (R.), Eng. (ē'dĕn)	162	54.40 N	2.35 W
Eden, Tx.	124	31.13 N	99.51 W
Eden, Ut.	119b	41.18 N	111.49 W
Edenbridge, Eng. (ē'dĕn-brĭj)	156b	51.11 N	0.05 E
Edendale, S. Afr.	71b	26.09 S	28.09 E
Edenham, Eng. (ē'd'n-ăm)	156	52.46 N	0.25 W
Eden Prairie, Mn. (prâr'ĭ)	119g	44.51 N	93.29 W
Edenton, NC (ē'dĕn-tŭn)	127	36.02 N	76.37 W
Edenton, Oh	113f	39.14 N	84.02 W
Edenvale, S. Afr. (ēd'ĕn-vāl)	227b	29.06 S	28.10 E
Edenvale Location, S. Afr.	71b	26.08 S	28.11 E
Edenville, S. Afr. (ē'd'n-vĭl)	223d	27.33 S	27.42 E
Eder R., F.R.G. (ā'dēr)	166	51.05 N	8.52 E
Edgefield, SC (ĕj'fēld)	127	33.52 N	81.55 W
Edge Hill (Neigh.), Eng.	64a	53.24 N	2.57 W
Edgeley, ND (ĕj'lĭ)	114	46.24 N	98.43 W
Edgemere, Md.	56c	39.14 N	76.27 W
Edgemont, SD (ĕj'mŏnt)	114	43.19 N	103.50 W
Edgerton, Wi. (ĕj'ēr-tŭn)	115	42.49 N	89.06 W
Edgewater, Al. (ĕj-wô-tēr)	112h	33.31 N	86.52 W
Edgewater, Md.	112e	38.58 N	76.35 W
Edgewater, NJ	55	40.50 N	73.58 W
Edgewood, Can. (ĕj'wŏŏd)	99	49.47 N	118.08 W

ng-sing; ŋ-baŋk; N-nasalized n; nŏd; cŏmmit; ōld; ôbey; ôrder; oi-boil; fōōd; fŏŏt; ou-out; s-soft; sh-dish; th-thin; pūre; ûnite; ûrn; stŭd; circŭs; ü-as in French tu; '-indeterminate vowel.

280 Edgware – Ely

PLACE (Pronounciation)	PAGE	Lat. °′	Long. °′
Edgware (Neigh.), Eng.	62	51.37 N	0.17 W
Edgewater, NY	57a	43.03 N	78.55 W
Edgworth, Eng.	64b	53.39 N	2.24 W
Édhessa, Grc.	173	40.48 N	22.04 E
Edina, Mn. (ē-dī'nȧ)	119g	44.55 N	93.20 W
Edina, Mo.	123	40.10 N	92.11 W
Edinburg, In. (ĕd''n-bûrg)	110	39.20 N	85.55 W
Edinburg, Tx.	124	26.18 N	98.08 W
Edinburgh, Scot. (ĕd''n-bŭr-ō)	162	55.57 N	3.10 W
Edirne (Adrianople), Tur. (ĕ-dĭr'nĕ)(ā-drĭ-ăn-ō'p'l)	173	41.41 N	26.35 E
Edison Park (Neigh.), Il.	58a	42.01 N	87.49 W
Edisto (R.), North Fk, SC	127	33.42 N	81.24 W
Edisto, (R.), SC (ĕd'ĭs-tō)	127	33.10 N	80.50 W
Edisto (R.), South Fk, SC	127	33.43 N	81.35 W
Edisto Island, SC	127	32.32 N	80.20 W
Edmond, Ok. (ĕd'mŭnd)	123	35.39 N	97.29 W
Edmonds, Wa. (ĕd'mŭndz)	118a	47.49 N	122.23 W
Edmonston, Md.	56d	38.57 N	76.56 W
Edmonton, Can.	95g	53.33 N	113.28 W
Edmonton (Neigh.), Eng.	62	51.37 N	0.04 W
Edmundston, Can. (ĕd'mŭn-stŭn)	104	47.22 N	68.20 W
Edna, Tx. (ĕd'nȧ)	125	28.59 N	96.39 W
Edo (R.), Jap.	69a	35.41 N	139.53 E
Edogawa (Neigh.), Jap.	69a	35.42 N	139.52 E
Edremit, Tur. (ĕd-rĕ-mēt')	173	39.35 N	27.00 E
Edremit Körfezi (G.), Tur.	173	39.28 N	26.35 E
Edson, Can. (ĕd'sŭn)	99	53.35 N	116.26 W
Edward (I.), Can. (ĕd'wērd)	102	48.21 N	88.29 W
Edward (L.), Zaire	231	0.25 S	29.40 E
Edwardsville, Il. (ĕd'wērdz-vĭl)	119e	38.49 N	89.58 W
Edwardsville, In	113h	38.17 N	85.53 W
Edwardsville, Ks.	119f	39.04 N	94.49 W
Eel (R.), Ca. (ēl)	116	40.39 N	124.15 W
Eel (R.), In.	110	40.50 N	85.55 W
Efate (I.), Vanuatu (ā-fä'tä)	215	18.02 S	168.29 E
Effigy Mounds Natl. Mon., Ia. (ĕf'ĭ-jŭ mounds)	115	43.04 N	91.15 W
Effingham, Il. (ĕf'ĭng-hăm)	110	39.05 N	88.30 W
Ega (R.), Sp. (ā'gä)	170	42.40 N	2.20 W
Egadi, Isole (Is.), It. (ĕ'sō-lĕ-ĕ'gä-dē)	172	38.01 N	12.00 E
Egea de los Caballeros, Sp. (ā-kā'ā dā lōs kä-bäl-yā'rōs)	170	42.07 N	1.05 W
Egegik, Ak. (ĕg'ĕ-jĭt)	107	58.10 N	157.22 W
Eger, Hung. (ĕ gĕr)	167	47.53 N	20.24 E
Egersund, Nor. (ĕ'ghĕr-sŏŏn')	164	58.29 N	6.01 E
Egg Harbor, NJ (ĕg här'bēr)	111	39.30 N	74.35 W
Egham, Eng. (ĕg'ŭm)	156b	51.24 N	0.33 W
Egiyn (R.), Mong.	198	49.41 N	100.40 E
Egmont, C., N.Z. (ĕg'mŏnt)	217	39.18 S	173.49 E
Egota (Neigh.), Jap.	69a	35.43 N	139.40 E
Egridir Gölü (L.), Tur. (ā-rī-dĭr')	179	38.10 N	30.00 E
Eguilles, Fr (ĕ-gwē')	168a	43.34 N	5.21 E
Egypt, Afr. (ē'jĭpt)	222	26.58 N	27.01 E
Eha-Amufu, Nig.	229	6.40 N	7.46 E
Ehingen (Neigh.), F.R.G.	63	51.22 N	6.42 E
Ehringhausen, F.R.G.	63	51.11 N	7.33 E
Ehringhausen (Neigh.), F.R.G.	63	51.09 N	7.11 E
Eibar, Sp. (ā'ē-bär)	170	43.12 N	2.20 W
Eiche, G.D.R.	65a	52.34 N	13.36 E
Eichlinghofen (Neigh.), F.R.G.	63	51.29 N	7.24 E
Eichstätt, F.R.G. (īk'shtät)	166	48.54 N	11.14 E
Eichwalde, G.D.R. (īĸ'väl-dē)	157b	52.22 N	13.37 E
Eickerend, F.R.G.	63	51.13 N	6.34 E
Eidfjord, Nor. (ĕĭd'fyōr)	164	60.28 N	7.04 E
Eidsvoll, Nor. (īdhs'vôl)	164	60.19 N	11.15 E
Eifel (Plat), F.R.G. (ī'fĕl)	166	50.08 N	6.30 E
Eiffel, Tour (P. Int.), Fr.	64c	48.51 N	2.18 E
Eigen (Neigh.), F.R.G.	63	51.33 N	6.57 E
Eighty Mile Beach, Austl.	214	20.45 S	121.00 E
Eilenburg, G.D.R. (ī'lĕn-bŏŏrgh)	166	51.27 N	12.38 E
Eilliot, S. Afr.	227c	31.19 S	27.52 E
Eilpe (Neigh.), F.R.G.	63	51.21 N	7.29 E
Einbeck, F.R.G. (īn'bĕk)	166	51.49 N	9.52 E
Eindhoven, Neth. (īnd'hō-vĕn)	163	51.29 N	5.20 E
Eirunepé, Braz. (ā-rōō-nĕ-pĕ')	142	6.37 S	69.58 W
Eisenach, G.D.R. (ī'zĕn-äĸ)	166	50.58 N	10.18 E
Eisenhüttenstadt, G.D.R.	166	52.08 N	14.40 E
Eisleben, G.D.R. (īs'lā'bĕn)	166	51.31 N	11.33 E
Ejura, Ghana	228	7.23 N	1.22 W
Ejutla de Crespo, Mex. (ā-hōōt'lä dā krās'pō)	131	16.34 N	96.44 W
Ekanga, Zaire	230	2.23 S	23.14 E
Ekenäs (Tammisaari), Fin. (ĕ'kĕ-nâs)(tȧm'ĭ-sä'rĭ)	165	59.59 N	23.25 E
Ekeren, Bel.	157a	51.17 N	4.27 E
Ekoli, Zaire	230	0.23 S	24.16 E
Eksāra, India	67a	22.38 N	88.17 E
Eksjö, Swe. (ĕk'shû)	164	57.41 N	14.55 E
El Aaiún, W. Sah.	224	26.45 N	13.15 W
El Affroun, Alg. (ĕl ȧf-froun')	171	36.28 N	2.38 E
El Aguacate, Ven.	61a	10.28 N	66.59 W
Elands (R.), S. Afr. (ĕlȧnds)	227c	31.48 S	26.09 E
Elands (R.), S. Afr.	223d	25.11 S	28.52 E
Elandsfontein, S. Afr.	71b	26.10 S	28.12 E
El Arahal, Sp. (ĕl ä-rä-äl')	170	37.17 N	5.32 W
El Arba, Alg.	171	36.35 N	3.10 E
Elat, Isr.	191a	29.34 N	34.57 E
Elâzig, Tur. (ĕl-ä'zĭz)	179	38.40 N	39.00 E
Elba, Al. (ĕl'bȧ)	126	31.25 N	86.01 W
Elba, Isolad' (I.), It. (ē-sō lä-d-ĕl'bȧ)	172d	42.42 N	10.25 E
El Banco, Col. (ĕl băn'cō)	142	8.58 N	74.01 W
Elbansan, Alb. (ĕl-bä-sän')	173	41.08 N	20.05 E
El Barco de Valdeorras, Sp (ĕl bär'kō)	170	42.26 N	6.58 W
Elbe (Labe)(R.), Czech.-G.D.R. (ĕl'bĕ)(lä'bĕ)	166	53.47 N	9.20 E
Elberfeld (Neigh.), F.R.G.	63	51.16 N	7.08 E
Elbert, Mt., Co. (ĕl'bērt)	121	39.05 N	106.25 W
Elberton, Ga. (ĕl'bēr-tŭn)	126	34.05 N	82.53 W
Elbeuf, Fr. (ĕl-bûf')	168	49.16 N	0.59 E
El Beyadh, Alg.	160	33.42 N	1.06 E

PLACE (Pronounciation)	PAGE	Lat. °′	Long. °′
Elbistan, Tur. (ĕl-bē-stän')	179	38.20 N	37.10 E
Elblag, Pol. (ĕl'bläng)	167	54.11 N	19.25 E
El Bonillo, Sp. (ĕl bō-nēl'yō)	170	38.56 N	2.31 W
El Boulaïda, Alg.	224	36.33 N	2.45 E
Elbow (R.), Can. (ĕl'bō)	95e	51.03 N	114.24 W
Elbow Cay (I.), Ba	134	26.25 N	77.55 W
Elbow Lake, Mn.	114	46.00 N	95.59 W
El'brus, Gora (Mt.), Sov. Un. (ĕl'brōōs')	179	43.20 N	42.25 E
El Burgo de Osma, Sp.	170	41.35 N	3.02 W
Elburz Mts., Iran, (ĕl'bōōrz')	179	36.30 N	51.00 E
El Cajon, Ca.	120a	32.48 N	116.58 W
El Cajon, Col (ĕl-kä-kō'n)	142a	4.50 N	76.35 W
El Calvario (Neigh.), Cuba	60b	23.05 N	82.20 W
El Cambur, Ven. (käm-bōōr')	143b	10.24 N	68.06 W
El Campamento (Neigh.), Sp.	65b	40.24 N	3.46 W
El Campo, Tx. (kăm'pō)	125	29.13 N	96.17 W
El Caribe, Ven.	61a	10.37 N	66.49 W
El Carmen, Chile (kȧ'r-mĕn)	141b	34.14 S	71.23 W
El Carmen, Col. (kȧ'r-mĕn)	142	9.54 N	75.12 W
El Casco, Ca. (kȧs'kō)	119a	33.59 N	117.08 W
El Centro, Ca. (sĕn'trō)	120	32.47 N	115.33 W
El Cerrito, Ca. (sĕr-rē'tō)	118b	37.55 N	122.19 W
Elche, Sp. (ĕl'chā)	171	38.15 N	0.42 W
El Cojo, Ven.	61a	10.37 N	66.53 W
El Corozo, Ven.	61a	10.35 N	66.58 W
El Cotorro, Cuba	60b	23.03 N	82.16 W
El Cuyo, Mex.	132a	21.30 N	87.42 W
Elda, Sp. (ĕl'dä)	171	38.28 N	0.44 W
Elder Mills, Can.	54c	43.49 N	79.38 W
El Djazaïr, see Algeirs			
El Djelfa, Alg. (jĕl'fa)	224	34.40 N	3.17 E
El Djouf (Des.), Mauritania (ĕl djōōf)	224	21.45 N	7.05 W
Eldon, Ia. (ĕl-dŭn)	115	40.55 N	92.15 W
Eldon, Mo.	121	38.21 N	92.36 W
Eldora, Ia. (ĕl-dō'rȧ)	115	42.21 N	93.08 W
El Dorado, Ar. (ĕl dō-rä'dō)	123	33.13 N	92.39 W
Eldorado, Il.	110	37.50 N	88.30 W
El Dorado, Ks.	123	37.49 N	96.51 W
Eldorado Springs, Mo. (sprĭngz)	123	37.51 N	94.02 W
Eldoret, Ken. (ĕl-dō-rĕt')	231	0.31 N	35.17 E
El Ebano, Mex. (ā-bä'nō)	130	22.13 N	98.26 W
Electra, Tx. (ē-lĕk'trȧ)	122	34.02 N	98.54 W
Electric Pk., Mt. (ē-lĕk'trĭk)	117	45.03 N	110.52 W
Elektrogorsk, Sov. Un. (ĕl-yĕk'trô-gôrsk)	182b	55.53 N	38.48 E
Elektrostal, Sov. Un. (ĕl-yĕk'trō-stál)	182b	55.47 N	38.27 E
Elektrougli, Sov. Un.	182b	55.43 N	38.13 E
El Encantado, Ven.	61a	10.27 N	66.47 W
Elephanta I. (Ghārāp uri), India	67e	18.57 N	72.55 E
Elephant Butte Res., NM (ĕl'ē-fănt būt)	121	33.25 N	107.10 W
El Escorial, Sp (ĕl-ĕs-kō-ryä'l)	171a	40.38 N	4.08 W
El Espino, Nic. (ĕl-ĕs-pē'nō)	132	13.26 N	86.48 W
Eleuthera (I.), Ba. (ē-lū'thēr-ȧ)	135	25.05 N	76.10 W
Eleuthera Pt., Ba.	135	24.35 N	76.05 W
Eleven Point (R.), Mo. (ē-lĕv'ĕn)	123	36.53 N	91.39 W
El Ferrol, Sp. (fā-rōl')	170	43.30 N	8.12 W
Elgin, Il (ĕl'jĭn)	113a	42.03 N	88.16 W
Elgin, Ne.	114	41.58 N	98.04 W
Elgin, Or.	116	45.34 N	117.58 W
Elgin, Scot.	162	57.40 N	3.30 W
Elgin, Tx.	125	30.21 N	97.22 W
Elgin, Wa.	118a	47.23 N	122.42 W
Elgon, Mt., Ken. (ĕl'gŏn)	231	1.00 N	34.25 E
El Granada, Ca.	58b	37.30 N	122.28 W
El Grara, Alg.	160	32.50 N	4.26 E
El Grullo, Mex. (grōōl-yō)	130	19.46 N	104.10 W
El Guapo, Ven. (gwȧ'pō)	143b	10.07 N	66.00 W
El Guarapo, Ven.	61a	10.36 N	66.58 W
El Hank (Bluffs), Mauritania-Mali	116	23.44 N	6.45 W
El Hatillo, Ven. (ä-tē'l-yō)	143b	10.08 N	65.13 W
Elie, Can. (ē'lē)	95f	49.55 N	97.45 W
Elila (R.), Zaire (ĕ-lē'lȧ)	231	3.00 S	26.50 E
Elisa (I.), Wa. (ē-lĭ'sȧ)	118d	48.43 N	122.37 W
Élisabethville, see Lubumbashi			
Elisenvaara, Sov. Un. (ā-lē'sĕn-vä'rȧ)	165	61.25 N	29.46 E
Elizabeth, La. (ē-lĭz'ȧ-bĕth)	125	30.50 N	92.47 W
Elizabeth, NJ	112a	40.40 N	74.13 W
Elizabeth, Pa.	113e	40.16 N	79.53 W
Elizabeth City, NC	127	36.15 N	76.15 W
Elizabethton, Tn (ē-lĭz-ȧ-bĕth'tŭn)	127	36.19 N	82.12 W
Elizabethtown, Ky. (ē-lĭz'ȧ-bĕth-toun)	110	37.40 N	85.55 W
El Jadida, Mor.	224	33.14 N	8.34 W
Elk, Pol.	167	53.53 N	22.23 E
Elk (R.), Can.	99	50.00 N	115.00 W
Elk (R.), Tn.	126	35.05 N	86.36 W
Elk (R.), WV	110	38.30 N	81.05 W
El Kairouan, Tun. (kĕr-ōō-än)	224	35.46 N	10.04 E
Elk City, Ok. (ĕlk)	122	35.23 N	99.23 W
El Kef, Tun. (xĕf')	159	36.14 N	8.42 E
Elkhart, In. (ĕlk'härt)	110	41.40 N	86.00 W
Elkhart, Ks.	122	37.00 N	101.54 W
Elkhart, Tx	125	31.38 N	95.35 W
Elkhorn (R.), Ne.	114	42.06 N	97.46 W
Elkhorn, Wi (ĕlk'hôrn)	115	42.39 N	88.32 W
Elk I, Can.	101	50.45 N	96.32 W
Elkin, NC (ĕl'kĭn)	127	36.15 N	80.50 W
Elkins, WV (ĕl'kĭnz)	111	38.55 N	79.50 W
Elkins Park, Pa.	56b	40.05 N	75.08 W
Elk Island Natl. Park, Can. (ĕlk ī'lănd)	99	53.37 N	112.45 W
Elko, Nv. (ĕl'kō)	116	40.51 N	115.46 W
Elk Point, SD	114	42.41 N	96.41 W
Elk Rapids, Mi. (răp'ĭdz)	110	44.55 N	85.25 W
Elkridge, Md.	56c	39.13 N	76.42 W
Elk River, Id. (rĭv'ēr)	116	46.47 N	116.11 W
Elk River, Mn.	115	45.17 N	93.33 W
Elkton, Ky. (ĕlk'tŭn)	126	36.47 N	87.08 W
Elkton, Md.	111	39.35 N	75.50 W

PLACE (Pronounciation)	PAGE	Lat. °′	Long. °′
Elkton, SD	114	44.15 N	96.28 W
Elland, Eng. (el'ănd)	156	53.41 N	1.50 W
Ellendale, ND (ĕl'ĕn-dāl)	114	46.01 N	98.33 W
Ellen, Mt., Ut. (ĕl'ĕn)	121	38.05 N	110.50 W
Ellensburg, Wa. (ĕl'ĕnz-bûrg)	116	47.00 N	120.31 W
Ellenville, NY (ĕl'ĕn-vĭl)	111	41.40 N	74.25 W
Ellerslie, Can. (ĕl'ērz-lē)	95g	53.25 N	113.30 W
Ellesmere, Eng. (ĕlz'mēr)	156	52.55 N	2.54 W
Ellesmere I, Can.	94	81.00 N	80.00 W
Ellesmere Park, Eng.	64b	53.29 N	2.20 W
Ellesmere Port, Eng.	156	53.17 N	2.54 W
Ellice Is., see Tuvalu			
Ellicott City, Md. (ĕl'ĭ-kŏt sĭ'tē)	112e	39.16 N	76.48 W
Ellicott Cr., NY	113c	43.00 N	78.46 W
El Limoncito, Ven.	61a	10.29 N	66.47 W
Ellinghorst, (Neigh.), F.R.G.	63	51.34 N	6.57 E
Elliot, Wa. (el'ĭ-ŭt)	118a	47.28 N	122.08 W
Elliotdale, S. Afr. (ĕl-ĭ-ŏt'dāl)	227c	31.58 S	28.42 E
Elliot Lake, Can.	102	46.23 N	82.39 W
Ellis, Ks. (ĕl'ĭs)	122	38.56 N	99.34 W
Ellisville, Ms. (ĕl'ĭs-vĭl)	126	31.37 N	89.10 W
Ellisville, Mo.	119e	38.35 N	90.35 W
Ellsworth, Ks. (ĕlz'wûrth)	122	38.43 N	98.14 W
Ellsworth, Me.	104	44.33 N	68.26 W
Ellsworth Highland, Ant.	232	77.00 S	90.00 W
Ellwangen, F.R.G. (ĕl'väng-gĕn)	166	48.47 N	10.08 E
Elm, F.R.G. (ĕlm)	157c	53.31 N	9.13 E
Elm (R.), SD	114	45.47 N	98.28 W
Elm (R.), WV	110	38.30 N	81.05 W
Elma, Wa. (ĕl'mȧ)	116	47.02 N	123.20 W
El Mahdia, Tun (mä-dē'a)(mä'dē-ȧ)	159	35.30 N	11.09 E
Elm Cr, Tx.	123	33.34 N	97.25 W
Elmendorf, Tx (ĕl'mĕn-dôrf)	119d	29.16 N	98.20 W
El Menia, Alg.	224	30.39 N	2.52 E
Elm Fork, Tx. (ĕlm fôrk)	119c	32.55 N	96.56 W
Elmhurst, Il (ĕlm'hûrst)	113a	41.54 N	87.56 W
Elmhurst (Neigh.), NY	55	40.44 N	73.53 W
El Miliyya, Alg. (mē'ä)	224	36.30 N	6.16 E
Elmira, NY (ĕl-mī'rȧ)	111	42.05 N	76.50 W
Elmira Heights, NY	111	42.10 N	76.50 W
El Misti (Vol.), Peru (mē's-tē)	142	16.04 S	71.20 W
El Modena, Ca. (mō-dē'nō)	119a	33.47 N	117.48 W
El Molinito, Mex.	60a	19.27 N	99.15 W
Elmont, NY	55	40.42 N	73.42 W
El Monte, Ca. (mōn'tā)	119a	34.04 N	118.02 W
El Morro Natl. Mon., NM	121	35.05 N	108.20 W
El Mreyyé (Des.), Mauritania	228	19.15 N	7.50 W
Elmshorn, F.R.G. (ĕlms'hôrn)	157c	53.45 N	9.39 E
Elmwood (Neigh.), Pa.	56b	39.56 N	75.14 W
Elmwood Park, Il.	58a	41.55 N	87.49 W
Elmwood Place, Oh. (ĕlm'wŏŏd plās)	113f	39.11 N	84.30 W
Elokomin (R.), Wa. (ē-lō'kō-mĭn)	118c	46.16 N	123.16 W
El Oro, Mex. (ō-rō)	130	19.49 N	100.04 W
El Palmar, Ven.	61a	10.38 N	66.52 W
El Pao, Ven. (ĕl pȧ'ō)	142	8.08 N	62.37 W
El Paraíso, Hond. (pä-rä-ē'sō)	132	13.55 N	86.35 W
El Pardo, Sp. (pä'r-dō)	171a	40.31 N	3.47 W
El Paso, Tx. (pas'ō)	124	31.47 N	106.27 W
El Pedregal (Neigh.), Ven.	61a	10.30 N	66.51 W
El Pilar, Ven. (pē-lä'r)	143b	9.56 N	64.48 W
El Plantío (Neigh.), Sp.	65b	40.28 N	3.49 W
El Porvenir, Pan. (pôr-vä-nēr')	133	9.34 N	78.55 W
El Puerto de Sta. María, Sp. (pwĕr tō dā sän tä mä-rē'ä)	170	36.36 N	6.18 W
El Qala, Alg.	159	36.52 N	8.23 E
El Qoll, Alg.	224	37.02 N	6.29 E
El Real, Pan. (rā-äl)	133	8.07 N	77.43 W
El Recreo (Neigh.), Ven.	61a	10.30 N	66.53 W
El Reloj, Mex.	60a	19.18 N	99.08 W
El Reno, Ok. (rē'nō)	122	35.31 N	97.57 W
El Rincón de La Florida, Chile	61b	33.33 S	70.34 W
El Roboré, Bol. (rō-bō-rĕ')	143	18.23 S	59.43 W
Elroy, Wi. (ĕl'roi)	115	43.44 N	90.17 W
Elsa, Can.	107	63.55 N	135.25 W
Elsah, Il. (ĕl'zȧ)	119e	38.57 N	90.22 W
El Salto, Mex. (säl'tō)	130	22.48 N	105.22 W
El Salvador, N.A.	128	14.00 N	89.30 W
El Sauce, Nic. (ĕl-sȧ'ōō-sĕ)	132	13.00 N	86.40 W
Elsberry, Mo. (ĕlz'bĕr-ĭ)	123	39.09 N	90.44 W
Elsburg, S. Afr.	71b	26.15 S	28.12 E
Elsdorf, F.R.G. (ĕls'dōrf)	169c	50.56 N	6.35 E
El Segundo, Ca (sĕgŭn'dō)	119a	33.55 N	118.24 W
Elsey, F.R.G.	63	51.22 N	7.34 E
Elsinore, Ca. (ĕl'sĭ-nôr)	119a	33.40 N	117.19 W
Elsinore L., Ca	119a	33.38 N	117.21 W
Elstorf, F.R.G. (ĕls'tōrf)	157c	53.25 N	9.48 E
Elstree, Eng.	62	51.39 N	0.16 W
Eltham, Austl. (ĕl'thăm)	211	37.43 S	145.08 E
Eltham (Neigh.), Eng.	62	51.27 N	0.04 E
El Tigre, Ven. (tē'grĕ)	142	8.49 N	64.15 W
Elton, Eng.	64a	53.16 N	2.49 W
El'ton (L.), Sov. Un.	179	49.10 N	47.00 E
El Toreo (P. Int.), Mex.	60a	19.27 N	99.13 W
El Toro, Ca. (tō'rō)	119a	33.37 N	117.42 W
El Triunfo, Hond. (ĕl-trē-ōō'n-fō)	132	13.06 N	87.00 W
El Triunfo, Sal.	132	13.17 N	88.32 W
Elūru, India	193	16.44 N	80.09 E
El Vado Res, NM	121	36.37 N	106.30 W
El Valle (Neigh.), Ven.	61a	10.27 N	66.55 W
Elvas, Port. (ĕl'väzh)	170	38.53 N	7.11 W
Elverum, Nor. (ĕl'vĕ-rōōm)	164	60.53 N	11.33 E
El Viego, Nic. (ĕl-vyĕ'ĸō)	132	12.10 N	87.10 W
El Viejo (Vol.), Nic.	132	12.44 N	87.03 W
Elvins, Mo. (ĕl'vĭnz)	123	37.49 N	90.31 W
El Wad, Alg.	224	33.23 N	6.49 E
El Wak, Ken. (wäk')	225	3.00 N	41.00 E
Elwood, Il. (ĕ'wŏŏd)	113a	41.24 N	88.07 W
Elwood, In.	110	40.15 N	85.50 W
Ely, Eng. (ē'lĭ)	163	52.25 N	0.17 E
Ely, Mn.	115	47.54 N	91.53 W
Ely, Nv.	120	39.16 N	114.53 W

ăt; finăl; rāte; senāte; ärm; åsk; sofȧ; fâre; ch-choose; dh-as th in other; bē; ēvent; bĕt; recĕnt; cratēr; g-gō; gh-guttural g; bĭt; ĭ-short neutral; rīde; ĸ-guttural k as ch in German ich;

PRONOUNCING INDEX
Elyria – Eure 281

PLACE (Pronounciation)	PAGE	Lat. °'	Long. °'
Elyria, Oh. (ẽ-lĭr'ĭ-ȧ)	113d	41.22 N	82.07 W
El Zamural, Ven.	61a	10.27 N	67.00 W
El Zig-Zag, Ven.	61a	10.33 N	66.58 W
Ema (R.), Sov. Un. (å'mȧ)	165	58.25 N	27.00 E
Emâmshahr, Iran	195	36.25 N	55.01 E
Emån (R.), Swe.	164	57.15 N	15.46 E
Emba (R.), Sov. Un. (yĕm'bȧ)	179	46.50 N	54.10 E
Embalse Guri (L.), Ven.	142	7.30 N	63.00 W
Embarrass (R.), Il. (ĕm-băr'ăs)	110	39.15 N	88.05 W
Embrun, Can. (ĕm'brŭn)	95c	45.16 N	75.17 W
Embrun, Fr. (äɴ-brûɴ')	169	44.35 N	6.32 E
Embu, Braz.	61d	23.39 S	46.51 W
Embu, Ken.	231	0.32 S	37.27 E
Emden, F.R.G. (ĕm'dĕn)	166	53.21 N	7.15 E
Emerald, Austl. (ĕm'ẽr-ăld)	215	28.34 S	148.00 E
Emerson, Can. (ĕm'ẽr-sŭn)	101	49.00 N	97.12 W
Emerson, NJ	55	40.58 N	74.02 W
Emeryville, Ca (ĕm'ẽr-ĭ-vĭl)	118b	37.50 N	122.17 W
Emi Koussi (Mtn.), Chad			
(ā'mē ᴋōō-sē')	229	19.50 N	18.30 E
Emiliano Zapata, Mex.			
(ĕ-mē-lyȧ'nô-zä-pȧ'tȧ)	131	17.45 N	91.46 W
Emilia-Romagna (Reg.), It.			
(ē-mēl'yä rô-mä'n-yä)	172	44.35 N	10.48 E
Eminence, Ky. (ĕm'ĭ-nĕns)	110	38.25 N	85.15 W
Emira I., Pap. N. Gui. (ā-mē-rä')	207	1.40 S	150.28 E
Emmarentia (Neigh.), S. Afr.	71b	26.10 S	28.01 E
Emmen, Neth. (ĕm'ĕn)	163	52.48 N	6.55 E
Emmerich, F.R.G. (ĕm'ẽr-ĭk)	169c	51.51 N	6.16 E
Emmetsburg, Ia. (ĕm'ĕts-bûrg)	115	43.07 N	94.41 W
Emmett, Id. (ĕm'ĕt)	116	43.53 N	116.30 W
Emmons Mt., Ut. (ĕm'ŭnz)	117	40.43 N	110.20 W
Emory Pk., Tx. (ĕ'mō-rē pēk)	124	29.13 N	103.20 W
Empoli, It. (ām'pô-lē)	172	43.43 N	10.55 E
Emporia, Ks. (ĕm-pō'rĭ-ȧ)	123	38.24 N	96.11 W
Emporia, Va.	127	37.40 N	77.34 W
Emporium, Pa. (ĕm-pō'rĭ-ŭm)	111	41.30 N	78.15 W
Ems R., F.R.G. (ĕms)	166	52.52 N	7.16 E
Emst (Neigh.), F.R.G.	63	51.21 N	7.30 E
Ems-Weser (Can.), F.R.G. (vā'zẽr)	166	52.23 N	8.11 E
Emsworth, Pa.	57b	40.30 N	80.04 W
Enånger, Swe. (ĕn-ôŋ'gẽr)	166	61.36 N	16.55 E
Encantada, Cerro de la (Mtn.), Mex.			
(sĕ'r-rô-dĕ-lä-ĕn-kän-tä'dä)	128	31.58 N	115.15 W
Encanto, C., Phil. (ĕn-kän'tō)	207a	15.44 N	121.46 E
Encarnação (Neigh.), Port.	65d	38.47 N	9.06 W
Encarnación, Par. (ĕn-kär-nä-syōn')	144	27.26 S	55.52 W
Encarnación de Diaz, Mex.			
(ĕn-kär-nä-syōn dā dē'áz)	130	21.34 N	102.15 W
Encinal, Tx. (ĕn'sĭ-nôl)	124	28.02 N	99.22 W
Encino (Neigh.), Ca.	59	34.09 N	118.30 W
Encontrados, Ven. (ĕn-kōn-trä'dōs)	142	9.01 N	72.10 W
Encounter B., Austl. (ĕn-koun'tẽr)	216	35.50 S	138.45 E
Endako (R.), Can.	98	54.05 N	125.30 W
Endau (R.), Mala.	191b	2.29 N	103.40 E
Enderbury (I.), Oceania (ĕn'dẽr-bûrĭ)	208	2.00 S	107.50 W
Enderby Land (Reg.), Ant.			
(ĕn'dẽr bĭĭ)	232	72.00 S	52.00 E
Enderlin, ND (ĕn'dẽr-lĭn)	114	46.38 N	97.37 W
Endicott, NY (ĕn'dĭ-kŏt)	111	42.05 N	76.00 W
Endicott Mts., Ak.	107	67.30 N	153.45 W
Enez, Tur.	173	40.42 N	26.05 E
Enfield, Austl.	70a	33.53 S	151.06 E
Enfield, Ct. (ĕn'fēld)	111	41.55 N	72.35 W
Enfield, Eng.	156b	51.38 N	0.06 W
Enfield, NC	127	36.10 N	77.41 W
Engang, Cabo (C.), Dom.Rep.			
(ká'-bô- ĕn-gä-nô)	135	18.40 N	68.30 W
Engcobo, S. Afr. (ĕŋg-cô-bô)	227c	31.41 S	27.59 E
Engel's, Sov. Un. (ĕn'gĕls)	179	51.20 N	45.40 E
Engelskirchen, F.R.G.			
(ĕn'gĕls-kĕr'ĸĕn)	169c	50.59 N	7.25 E
Engenho de Dentro (Neigh.), Braz.	61c	22.54 S	43.18 W
Engenho do Mato, Braz.	61c	22.52 S	43.01 W
Engenho Nôvo (Neigh.), Braz.	61c	22.55 S	43.17 W
Enggano, Pulau (I.), Indon.			
(ĕng-gä'nō)	206	5.22 S	102.18 E
Enghien-les-Bains, Fr.	64c	48.58 N	2.19 E
England, Ar. (ĭŋ'glănd)	123	34.33 N	91.58 W
England (Reg.), U.K. (ĭŋ'glănd)	162	51.35 N	1.40 W
Engleè, Can. (ĕn-gleē)	105	50.44 N	56.06 W
Englefield Green, Eng.	62	51.26 N	0.35 W
Englewood, Co. (ĕn'g'l-wŏŏd)	122	39.39 N	105.00 W
Englewood (Neigh.), Il.	58a	41.47 N	87.39 W
Englewood, NJ	112a	40.54 N	73.59 W
Englewood Cliffs, NJ	55	40.53 N	73.57 W
English, In. (ĭn'glĭsh)	110	38.15 N	86.25 W
English (R.), Can.	97	50.31 N	94.12 W
English Chan, Eng.	159	49.45 N	3.06 W
Enguera, Sp. (ān'gārä)	171	38.58 N	0.42 W
Enid, Ok. (ē'nĭd)	122	36.25 N	97.52 W
Enid Res., Ms.	126	34.13 N	89.47 W
Enkeldoring, S. Afr (ĕŋ'k'l-dôr-ĭng)	223d	25.24 S	28.43 E
Enköping, Swe. (ĕn'kû-pĭng)	164	59.39 N	17.05 E
Ennedi (Plat.), Chad (ĕn-nĕd'ē)	225	16.45 N	22.45 E
Ennepetal, F.R.G.	63	51.18 N	7.22 E
Ennis, Ire. (ĕn'ĭs)	162	52.54 N	9.05 W
Ennis, Tx.	125	32.20 N	96.38 W
Enniscorthy, Ire. (ĕn-ĭs-kôr'thĭ)	162	52.33 N	6.27 W
Enniskillen, N. Ire (ĕn-ĭs-kĭl'ĕn)	162	54.20 N	7.25 W
Enns (R.), Aus. (ĕns)	166	47.37 N	14.35 E
Enoree, SC (ĕ-nō'rē)	127	34.43 N	81.58 W
Enoree (R.), SC	127	34.35 N	81.55 W
Enriquillo, Dom. Rep. (ĕn-rē-kē'l-yô)	135	17.55 N	71.15 W
Enriquillo, Lago (L.), Dom. Rep.			
(lä'gô-ĕn-rē-kē'l-yô)	135	18.35 N	71.35 W
Enschede, Neth. (ĕns'ĸä-dĕ)	163	52.10 N	6.50 E
Enseñada, Arg.	141c	34.50 S	57.55 W
Ensenada, Mex. (ĕn-sĕ-nä'dä)	128	32.00 N	116.30 W
Enshi, China (ŭn-shr)	203x	30.18 N	109.25 E
Enshū-Nada (Sea), Jap.			
(ĕn'shōō nä-dä)	205	34.25 N	137.14 E
Enterprise, Al. (ĕn'tẽr-prīz)	126	31.20 N	85.50 W
Enterprise, Or.	116	45.25 N	117.16 W
Entiat, L, Wa.	116	45.43 N	120.11 W
Entraygues, Fr. (ĕɴ-trĕg')	168	44.39 N	2.33 E
Entre Rios (Prov.), Arg.	144	31.30 S	59.00 W
Enugu, Nig. (ĕ-nōō'gōō)	229	6.27 N	7.27 E
Enumclaw, Wa. (ĕn'ŭm-klô)	118a	47.12 N	121.59 W
Envigado, Col. (ĕn-vē-gá'dô)	142a	6.10 N	75.34 W
Eolie, Isole (Is.), It. (ĕ'sō-lĕ-ĕ-ô'lyĕ)	172	38.43 N	14.43 E
Epe, Nig.	229	6.37 N	3.59 E
Epernay, Fr. (ā-pĕr-nĕ')	168	49.02 N	3.54 E
Epernon, Fr. (ā-pĕr-nôɴ')	169b	48.36 N	1.41 E
Ephraim, Ut. (ē'frâ-ĭm)	121	39.20 N	111.40 W
Ephrata, Wa. (ĕfrā'tȧ)	116	47.18 N	119.35 W
Epi, Vanuatu (ā'pē)	215	16.59 S	168.29 E
Epila, Sp. (ā'pē-lä)	170	41.38 N	1.15 W
Epinal, Fr. (ā-pē-nál')	169	48.11 N	6.27 E
Episkopi, Cyprus	191a	34.38 N	32.55 E
Eppendorf (Neigh.), F.R.G.	63	51.27 N	7.11 E
Eppenhausen (Neigh.), F.R.G.	63	51.21 N	7.31 E
Epping, Austl.	70a	33.46 S	151.05 E
Epping, Eng. (ĕp'ĭng)	156b	51.41 N	0.06 E
Epping Green, Eng.	62	51.44 N	0.05 E
Epping Upland, Eng.	62	51.43 N	0.06 E
Epsom, Eng.	62	51.20 N	0.16 W
Epupa Falls, Ang.	230	17.00 S	13.05 E
Epworth, Eng. (ĕp'wûrth)	156	53.31 N	0.50 W
Equatorial Guinea, Afr.	224	2.00 N	7.15 E
Eramosa (R.), Can. (ĕr-ȧ-mō'sȧ)	95d	43.39 N	80.08 W
Erba, Jabal (Mtn.), Sud. (ĕr-bȧ)	225	20.53 N	36.45 E
Erciyeş Daği (Mtn.), Tur.	161	38.30 N	35.36 E
Erda, Ut. (ẽr'dä)	119b	40.41 N	112.17 W
Erding, F.R.G. (ĕr'dĕng)	157d	48.19 N	11.54 E
Erechim, Braz. (ĕ-rĕ-shē'ɴ)	144	27.43 S	52.11 W
Ereğli, Tur. (ĕ-rā'ĭ-le)	179	37.40 N	34.00 E
Ereğli, Tur.	179	41.15 N	31.25 E
Erenköy (Neigh.), Tur.	66f	40.58 N	29.04 E
Erfurt, G.D.R. (ĕr'fŏŏrt)	166	50.59 N	11.04 E
Ergene (R.), Tur. (ĕr'gĕ-nĕ)	173	41.17 N	26.50 E
Erges (R.), Port.-Sp. (ĕr'-zhĕs)	170	39.45 N	7.01 W
Ergli, Sov. Un.	165	56.54 N	25.38 E
Ergste, F.R.G.	63	51.25 N	7.34 E
Eria (R.), Sp. (ā-rē'ä)	170	42.10 N	6.08 W
Erick, Ok. (âr'ĭk)	122	35.14 N	99.51 W
Erie, Ks. (ē'rĭ)	123	37.35 N	95.17 W
Erie, Pa.	111	42.05 N	80.05 W
Erie, L., U.S.-Can,	109	42.15 N	81.25 W
Erimo Saki (C.), Jap. (ā'rē-mō sä-kē)	204	41.53 N	143.20 E
Erin, Can. (ĕ'rĭn)	95d	43.46 N	80.04 W
Erith (Neigh.), Eng.	62	51.29 N	0.10 E
Eritrea (Reg.), Eth. (ā-rē-trā'á)	225	16.15 N	38.30 E
Erkrath, F.R.G.	63	51.13 N	6.55 E
Erlangen, F.R.G. (ĕr'läng-ĕn)	166	49.36 N	11.03 E
Erlanger, Ky. (ĕr'lăng-ẽr)	113f	39.01 N	84.36 W
Erle (Neigh.), F.R.G.	63	51.33 N	7.05 E
Ermont, Fr.	64c	48.59 N	2.16 E
Ermoúpolis, Grc.	173	37.30 N	24.56 E
Ernākulam, India	197	9.58 N	76.23 E
Erne, Lower Lough (L.), N. Ire.	162	54.30 N	7.40 W
Erne, Upper Lough (L.), N. Ire.			
(lŏk ûrn)	162	54.20 N	7.24 W
Erode, India	197	11.20 N	77.45 E
Eromanga (I.), Vanuatu	215	18.58 S	169.18 E
Eros, La. (ē'rōs)	125	32.23 N	92.22 W
Errego, Moz.	231	16.02 S	37.14 E
Errigal (Mtn.), Ire. (ĕr-ĭ-gôl')	162	55.02 N	8.07 W
Errol Heights, Or.	118c	45.29 N	122.38 W
Erskine Park, Austl.	70a	33.49 S	150.47 E
Erstein, Fr. (ĕr'shtīn)	169	48.27 N	7.40 E
Erwin, NC (ûr'wĭn)	127	35.16 N	78.40 W
Erwin, Tn.	127	36.07 N	82.25 W
Erzgebirge (Ore.Mts.), G.D.R.			
(ĕrts'gĕ-bē'gĕ)	166	50.29 N	12.40 E
Erzincan, Tur. (ĕr-zĭn-jän')	179	39.50 N	39.30 E
Erzurum, Tur. (ĕrz'rōōm')	179	39.55 N	41.10 E
Esambo, Zaire	230	3.40 S	23.24 E
Esashi, Jap. (ĕs'ä-shē)	204	41.50 N	140.10 E
Esbjerg, Den. (ĕs'byĕrgh)	164	55.29 N	8.25 E
Esborn, F.R.G.	63	51.23 N	7.20 E
Escalante (R.), Ut.	121	37.40 N	111.20 W
Escalante, Ut. (ĕs-kȧ-lăn'tē)	121	37.50 N	111.40 W
Escalón, Mex.	124	26.45 N	104.20 W
Escambia (R.), Fl. (ĕs-kăm'bĭ-ȧ)	126	30.38 N	87.20 W
Escanaba, Mi. (ĕs-kȧ-nô'bȧ)	115	45.44 N	87.05 W
Escanaba (R.), Mi.	115	46.10 N	87.22 W
Escarpada Point, Phil.	206	18.40 N	122.45 E
Esch-sur-Alzette, Lux.	169	49.32 N	6.21 E
Eschwege, F.R.G. (ĕsh'vā-gĕ)	166	51.11 N	10.02 E
Eschweiler, F.R.G. (ĕsh'vī-lĕr)	169c	50.49 N	6.15 E
Escocesá, Bahia (B.), Dom. Rep.			
(bä-ē'ä-ĕs-kō-sĕ'sä)	135	19.25 N	69.40 W
Escondido, Ca. (ĕs-kŏn-dē'dō)	120	33.07 N	117.00 W
Escondido R., Nic.	133	12.04 N	84.09 W
Escondido, Rio (R.), Mex.			
(rē'ō-ĕs-kōn-dē'dô)	124	28.30 N	100.45 W
Escuadrón 201, Mex.	60a	19.22 N	99.06 W
Escudo de Veraguas I., Pan.			
(ĕs-kōō'dä dā vā-rä'gwäs)	133	9.07 N	81.25 W
Escuinapa, Mex. (ĕs-kwē-nä'pä)	130	22.49 N	105.44 W
Escuintla, Guat. (ĕs-kwēn'tlä)	132	14.16 N	90.47 W
Escuintla, Mex.	131	15.20 N	92.45 W
Ese, Cayos de (I.), Col.	133	12.24 N	81.07 W
Esfahān, Iran	192	32.38 N	51.30 E
Esgueva (R.), Sp. (ĕs-gĕ'vä)	170	41.48 N	4.10 W
Esher, Eng.	62	51.23 N	0.22 W
Eshowe, S. Afr. (ĕsh'ô-wē)	227c	28.54 S	31.28 E
Esiama, Ghana	228	4.56 N	2.21 W
Eskdale, WV (ĕsk'dāl)	110	38.05 N	81.25 W
Eskifjördur, Ice. (ĕs'kē-fyûr'dōōr)	158	65.04 N	14.01 W
Eskilstuna, Swe. (å'shĕl-stü-na)	164	59.23 N	16.28 E
Eskimo Lakes (L.), Can. (es'kĭ-mō)	96	69.40 N	130.10 W
Eskişehir, Tur. (ĕs-kē-shĕ'h'r)	179	39.40 N	30.20 E
Esko, Mn. (ĕs'kô)	119h	46.27 N	92.22 W
Esla (R.), Sp. (ĕs-lä)	170	41.50 N	5.48 W
Eslöv, Swe. (ĕs'lûv)	164	55.50 N	13.17 E
Esmeraldas, Ec. (ĕs-mȧ-räl'däs)	142	0.58 N	79.45 W
Espada, Punta (Pt.), Dom. Rep.			
(pōō'n-tä-ĕs-pä'dä)	135	18.30 N	68.30 W
Espanola, Can. (ĕs-pȧ-nō'lȧ)	102	46.11 N	81.59 W
Esparta, C.R. (ĕs-pär'tä)	133	9.59 N	84.40 W
Esperance, Austl. (ĕs'pē-răns)	214	33.45 S	122.07 E
Esperanza, Cuba (ĕs-pĕ-rä'n-zä)	134	22.30 N	80.10 W
Espichel, Cabo (C.), Port.			
(kà'bō-ĕs-pē-shĕl')	171b	38.25 N	9.13 W
Espinal, Col. (ĕs-pē-näl')	142a	4.10 N	74.53 W
Espinhaço, Serra do (Mts.), Braz.			
(sĕ'r-rä-dô-ĕs-pē-nä-sô)	143	16.06 S	44.56 W
Espinillo, Punta (Pt.), Ur.			
(pōō'n-tä-ĕs-pē-nē'l-yô)	141c	34.49 S	56.27 W
Espírito Santo, Braz.			
(ĕs-pē'rē-tô-sän'tô)	143	20.27 S	40.18 W
Espírito Santo (State), Braz.	143	19.57 S	40.58 W
Espiritu Santo (I.), Vanuatu			
(ĕs-pē'rē-tōō sän'tō)	215	15.45 S	166.50 E
Espíritu Santo, Bahia del (B.), Mex.			
(bä-ē'ä-dĕl-ĕs-pē'rē-tōō-sän'tô)	132a	19.25 N	87.28 W
Espita, Mex. (ĕs-pē'tä)	132a	20.57 N	88.22 W
Esplugas, Sp.	65e	41.23 N	2.06 E
Espoo, Fin.	165	60.13 N	24.41 E
Esposende, Port. (ĕs-pō-zĕn'dā)	170	41.33 N	8.45 W
Esquel, Arg. (ĕs-kĕ'l)	144	42.47 S	71.22 W
Esquimalt, Can. (ĕs-kwī'mŏlt)	118a	48.26 N	123.24 W
Essaouira, Mor.	224	31.34 N	9.44 W
Essel (Neigh.), F.R.G.	63	51.37 N	7.15 E
Essen, Bel.	157a	51.28 N	4.27 E
Essen, F.R.G. (ĕs'sĕn)	169c	51.26 N	6.59 E
Essenberg, F.R.G.	63	51.26 N	6.42 E
Essendon, Austl.	70b	37.46 S	144.55 E
Essequibo (R.), Guy. (ĕs-ā-kē'bō)	143	4.26 N	58.17 W
Essex, Il.	113a	41.11 N	88.11 W
Essex, Ma.	105a	42.38 N	70.47 W
Essex, Md.	112e	39.19 N	76.29 W
Essex, Vt.	111	44.30 N	73.05 W
Essex Fells, NJ (ĕs'ĕks fĕlz)	112a	40.50 N	74.16 W
Essexville, Mi. (ĕs'ĕks-vĭl)	110	43.35 N	83.50 W
Essington, Pa.	56b	39.52 N	75.18 W
Essling (Neigh.), Aus.	66e	48.13 N	16.32 E
Esslingen, F.R.G. (ĕs'slĕn-gĕn)	166	48.45 N	9.19 E
Estacado, Llano (Plain), U.S.			
(yá-nō ĕs-tácá-dō')	108	33.50 N	103.20 W
Estados, Isla de los, S.A.	144	55.05 S	63.00 W
Estância, Braz. (ĕs-tän'sĭ-ä)	143	11.17 S	37.18 W
Estarreja, Port. (ĕ-tär-rā'zhä)	170	40.44 N	8.39 W
Estats, Pique d' (Pk.), Fr.	171	42.43 N	1.30 E
Estcourt, S. Afr. (ĕst-coort)	227c	29.04 S	29.53 E
Este, It. (ĕs'tā)	172	45.13 N	11.40 E
Estelí, Nic. (ĕs-tā-lē')	132	13.10 N	86.23 W
Estella, Sp. (ĕs-tāl'yä)	170	42.40 N	2.01 W
Estepa, Sp. (ĕs-tā'pä)	170	37.18 N	4.54 W
Estepona, Sp. (ĕs-tā-pō'nä)	170	36.26 N	5.08 W
Esterhazy, Can. (ĕs'tẽr-hā-zē)	101	50.40 N	102.08 W
Esteros, B., Ca. (ĕs-tā'rōs)	120	35.22 N	121.04 W
Estevan, Can. (ĕ-stē'văn)	100	49.07 N	103.05 W
Estevan Group (Is.), Can.	98	53.05 N	129.40 W
Estherville, Ia. (ĕs'tẽr-vĭl)	115	43.24 N	94.49 W
Estill, SC (ĕs'tĭl)	127	32.46 N	81.15 W
Eston, Can.	100	51.10 N	108.45 W
Estonian S.S.R., Sov. Un. (ĕs-tō'nĭ-ăn)	176	59.10 N	25.00 E
Estoril, Port. (ĕs-tô-rēl')	171b	38.45 N	9.24 W
Estrêla (R.), Braz. (ĕs-trĕ'lȧ)	144b	22.39 S	43.16 W
Estrêla, Serra da (Mts.), Port.			
(sĕr'rȧ dä ĕs-trā'lȧ)	170	40.25 N	7.45 W
Estrella, Cerro de la (Mtn.), Mex.	60a	19.21 N	99.05 W
Estremadura (Reg.), Port.			
(ĕs-trā-mä-dōō'rȧ)	170	41.35 N	8.36 W
Estremoz, Port. (ĕs-trā-mōzh')	170	38.50 N	7.35 W
Estrondo, Serra do (Mts.), Braz.			
(sĕr'ȓ dōō ĕs-trôn'dōō)	143	9.52 S	48.56 W
Esumba, Ile (I.), Zaire	230	2.00 N	21.12 E
Esztergom, Hung. (ĕs'tẽr-gōm)	167	47.46 N	18.45 E
Etah, Grnld. (ē'tȧ)	94	78.20 N	72.42 W
Étampes, Fr. (ā-täɴp')	169b	48.26 N	2.09 E
Étaples, Fr. (ā-täp'l')	168	50.32 N	1.38 E
Etchemin (R.), Can. (ĕch'ĕ-mĭn)	95b	46.39 N	71.03 W
Ethiopia, Afr. (ē-thē-ō'pē-ȧ)	222	7.53 N	37.55 E
Eticoga, Guinea-Bissau	228	11.09 N	16.08 W
Etiwanda, Ca. (ĕ-tĭ-wän'dȧ)	119a	34.07 N	117.31 W
Etlatongo, see San Mateo			
Etna, Pa. (ĕt'nȧ)	113e	40.30 N	79.55 W
Etna, Mt. (Vol.), It.	172	37.48 N	15.00 E
Etobicoke, Can.	95d	43.39 N	79.34 W
Etobicoke Cr., Can.	95d	43.44 N	79.48 W
Etolin Str., Ak. (ĕt ō lĭn)	107	60.35 N	165.40 W
Eton, Eng.	62	51.31 N	0.37 W
Etorofu (I.), see Iturop			
Etoshapan (L.), Namibia (ētō'shä)	226	19.07 S	15.30 E
Etowah (R.), Ga.	126	34.23 N	84.19 W
Etowah, Tn. (ĕt'ō-wä)	126	35.18 N	84.31 W
Étréchy, Fr. (ā-trā-shē')	169b	48.29 N	2.12 E
Etten-Leur, Neth.	157a	51.34 N	4.38 E
Etterbeek, Bel. (ĕt'ẽr-bāk)	157a	50.51 N	4.24 E
Etzatlán, Mex. (ĕt-zä-tlän')	130	20.44 N	104.04 W
Eucla, Austl. (ū'klȧ)	214	31.45 S	128.50 E
Euclid, Oh. (ū'klĭd)	113d	41.34 N	81.32 W
Eudora, Ar. (u-dō'rȧ)	123	33.07 N	91.16 W
Eufaula, Al. (ū-fô'lȧ)	126	31.53 N	85.09 W
Eufaula, Ok.	123	35.16 N	95.35 W
Eufaula Res., Ok.	123	35.00 N	94.45 W
Eugene, Or. (ū-jēn')	116	44.02 N	123.06 W
Euless, Tx. (ū'lĕs)	119c	32.50 N	97.05 W
Eunice, La. (ū'nĭs)	125	30.30 N	92.25 W
Eupen, Bel. (oi'pĕn)	163	50.39 N	6.05 E
Euphrates (R.), Asia (ū-frā'tēz)	192	36.00 N	39.30 E
Eure (R.), Fr. (ûr)	168	49.03 N	1.22 E

282 Eureka – Fernandina Beach

PLACE (Pronounciation)	PAGE	Lat. °'	Long. °'
Eureka, Ca. (û-rē'kȧ)	116	40.45 N	124.10 W
Eureka, Ks.	123	37.48 N	96.17 W
Eureka, Mt.	116	48.53 N	115.07 W
Eureka, Nv.	120	39.33 N	115.58 W
Eureka, SD	114	45.46 N	99.38 W
Eureka, Ut.	121	39.55 N	112.10 W
Eureka Springs, Ar.	123	36.24 N	93.43 W
Eurgun (Mtn.), Iran	192	28.47 N	57.00 E
Europe, (ū'rŭp)	154	50.00 N	15.00 E
Eustis, Fl. (ūs'tĭs)	127	28.50 N	81.41 W
Eutaw, Al. (ū-tȧ)	126	32.48 N	87.50 W
Eutsuk L., Can. (o͞ot'sŭk)	98	53.20 N	126.44 W
Evanston, Il. (ĕv'ăn-stŭn)	113a	42.03 N	87.41 W
Evanston, Wy.	117	41.17 N	111.02 W
Evansville, In. (ĕv'ănz-vĭl)	110	38.00 N	87.30 W
Evansville, Wi.	115	42.46 N	89.19 W
Evart, Mi. (ĕv'ērt)	110	43.55 N	85.10 W
Evaton, S. Afr. (ĕv'ȧ-tŏn)	223d	26.32 S	27.53 E
Eveleth, Mn. (ĕv'ē-lĕth)	115	47.27 N	92.35 W
Everard (L.), Austl. (ĕv'ēr-ȧrd)	214	36.20 S	134.10 E
Everard Ra., Austl.	214	27.15 S	132.00 E
Everest, Mt., Nep.-China (ĕv'ēr-ĕst)	196	28.00 N	86.57 E
Everett, Ma. (ĕv'ēr-ĕt)	105a	42.24 N	71.03 W
Everett, Wa. (ĕv'ēr-ĕt)	118a	47.59 N	122.11 W
Everett Mts., Can.	97	62.34 N	68.00 W
Everglades, Fl. (ĕv'ēr-glādz)	127a	25.50 N	81.25 W
Everglades Natl. Park, Fl.	127a	25.39 N	80.57 W
Everglades, The (Swp.), Fl.	134	25.35 N	80.55 W
Evergreen, Al. (ĕv'ēr-grēn)	126	31.25 N	87.56 W
Evergreen Park, Il.	113a	41.44 N	87.42 W
Everman, Tx. (ĕv'ēr-măn)	119c	32.38 N	97.17 W
Everson, Wa. (ĕv'ēr-sŭn)	118d	48.55 N	122.21 W
Everton (Neigh.), Eng.	64a	53.25 N	2.58 W
Eving (Neigh.), F.R.G.	63	51.33 N	7.29 E
Évora, Port. (ĕv'ō-rä)	170	38.35 N	7.54 W
Évreux, Fr. (ā-vrû')	168	49.02 N	1.11 E
Evrótas (R.), Grc. (ĕv-rō'täs)	173	37.15 N	22.17 E
Évvoia (I.), Grc.	173	38.38 N	23.45 E
Ewa Beach, Hi. (ē'wä)	106	21.17 N	158.03 E
Ewaso Ng'iro (R.), Ken.	225	0.59 N	37.47 E
Éden, Braz.	61c	22.48 S	43.24 W
Ewell, Eng.	62	51.21 N	0.15 W
Émerainville, Fr.	64c	48.49 N	2.37 E
Épinay-sous-Sénart, Fr.	64c	48.42 N	2.31 E
Épinay-sur-Seine, Fr.	64c	48.57 N	2.19 E
Ewu, Nig.	71d	6.33 N	3.19 E
Excelsior, Mn. (ĕk-sel'sĭ-ŏr)	119g	44.54 N	93.35 W
Excelsior Springs, Mo.	123	39.20 N	94.13 W
Exe (R.), Eng. (ĕks)	162	50.57 N	3.37 W
Exeter, Ca. (ĕk'sē-tēr)	120	36.18 N	119.09 W
Exeter, Eng.	162	50.45 N	3.33 W
Exeter, NH	111	43.00 N	71.00 W
Exmoor, Eng. (ĕks'mo͝or)	162	51.10 N	3.55 W
Exmouth, Eng. (ĕks'mŭth)	162	50.40 N	3.20 W
Exmouth, G., Austl.	214	21.45 S	114.30 E
Exploits (R.), Can. (ĕks-ploits')	105	48.50 N	56.15 W
Extórrax (R.), Mex. (ĕx-tó'răx)	130	21.04 N	99.39 W
Extrema, Braz. (ĕsh-trĕ'mä)	141a	22.52 S	46.19 W
Extremadura (Reg.), Sp. (ĕks-trā-mä-doo'rä)	170	38.43 N	6.30 W
Exuma Sd, Ba. (ĕk-so͞o'mä)	135	24.20 N	76.20 W
Eyasi, L., Tan. (ā-yä'sē)	231	3.25 S	34.55 E
Eyjafjördur (Fd.), Ice.	158	66.21 N	18.20 W
Eyl, Som.	223a	7.53 N	49.45 E
Eynsford, Eng.	62	51.22 N	0.13 E
Eyrarbakki, Ice.	158	63.51 N	20.52 W
Eyre, Austl. (âr)	214	32.15 S	126.20 E
Eyre (L.), Austl.	216	28.43 S	137.50 E
Eyre Pen, Austl.	214	33.30 S	136.00 E
Eyüp (Neigh.), Tur.	66f	41.03 N	28.55 E
Ezbekīyah (Neigh.), Egypt	71a	30.03 N	31.15 E
Ezeiza, Arg. (ĕ-zā'zä)	144a	34.36 S	58.31 W
Ezine, Tur. (â'zĭ-nâ)	173	39.47 N	26.18 E

F

PLACE (Pronounciation)	PAGE	Lat. °'	Long. °'
Fabens, Tx. (fā'bĕnz)	124	31.30 N	106.07 W
Fåborg, Den. (fô'bôrg)	164	55.06 N	10.19 E
Fabreville (Neigh.), Can.	54b	45.34 N	73.50 W
Fabriano, It. (fä-brē-ä'nō)	172	43.20 N	12.55 E
Facatativá, Col. (fä-kä-tä-tē-vä')	142a	4.49 N	74.09 W
Fada, Chad (fä'dä)	225	17.06 N	21.18 E
Fada Ngourma, Burkina (fä'dä''n go͞or'mä)	228	12.04 N	0.21 E
Faddeya (I.), Sov. Un. (fȧd-yä')	181	76.12 N	145.00 E
Faenza, It. (fä-ĕnd'zä)	172	44.16 N	11.53 E
Faeroe Is., Eur. (fâr'ō)	154	62.00 N	5.45 W
Fafe, Port. (fä'fâ)	170	41.30 N	8.10 W
Fafen (R.), Eth.	223a	8.15 N	42.40 E
Făgăras, Rom. (fȧ-gä'räsh)	173	45.50 N	24.55 E
Fagerness, Nor. (fä'ghĕr-nĕs)	164	61.00 N	9.10 E
Fagnano (L.), Arg.-Chile (fäk-nä'nō)	144	54.35 S	68.20 W
Faguibine, Lac (L.), Mali	228	16.50 N	4.20 W
Fahrland, G.D.R.	65a	52.28 N	13.01 E
Faial I., Acores (fä-yä'l)	224a	38.40 N	29.19 W
Fā'id, Egypt (fä-yēd')	223c	30.19 N	32.18 E
Failsworth, Eng.	64b	53.31 N	2.09 W
Fairbanks, Ak. (fâr'bănks)	107	64.50 N	147.48 W

PLACE (Pronounciation)	PAGE	Lat. °'	Long. °'
Fairbury, Il. (fâr'bĕr-ĭ)	110	40.45 N	88.25 W
Fairbury, Ne.	123	40.09 N	97.11 W
Fairchild Cr., Can. (fâr'chīld)	95d	43.18 N	80.10 W
Fairfax, Mn. (fâr'făks)	115	44.29 N	94.44 W
Fairfax, SC	127	32.29 N	81.13 W
Fairfax, Va.	112e	38.51 N	77.20 W
Fairfield, Al. (fâr'fēld)	112h	33.30 N	86.50 W
Fairfield, Austl.	211b	33.52 S	150.57 E
Fairfield, Ct.	112a	41.08 N	73.22 W
Fairfield, Ia.	115	41.00 N	91.59 W
Fairfield, Il.	110	38.25 N	88.20 W
Fairfield, Me.	104	44.35 N	69.38 W
Fairfield, NJ.	55	40.53 N	74.17 W
Fairhaven, Ma. (fâr-hā'vĕn)	111	41.35 N	70.55 W
Fairhaven, Md.	56d	38.47 N	77.05 W
Fair Haven, Vt.	111	43.35 N	73.15 W
Fair I., Scot. (fâr)	162a	59.34 N	1.41 W
Fair Lawn, NJ	55	40.56 N	74.07 W
Fairlee, Md.	56d	38.52 N	77.16 W
Fairmont, Mn. (fâr'mŏnt)	115	43.39 N	94.26 W
Fairmont, WV	111	39.30 N	80.10 W
Fairmont City, Il.	119e	38.39 N	90.05 W
Fairmount, In.	110	40.25 N	85.45 W
Fairmount, Ks.	119f	39.12 N	95.55 W
Fairmount Heights, Md.	56d	38.54 N	76.55 W
Fair Oaks, Ga. (fâr ōks)	112c	33.56 N	84.33 W
Fairport, NY (fâr'pōrt)	111	43.05 N	77.30 W
Fairport Harbor, Oh.	110	41.45 N	81.15 W
Fairseat, Eng.	62	51.30 N	0.20 E
Fairview, NJ	55	40.49 N	74.00 W
Fairview, Ok. (fâr'vū)	122	36.16 N	98.28 W
Fairview, Or.	118c	45.32 N	112.26 W
Fairview, Ut.	121	39.35 N	111.30 W
Fairview Park, Oh.	113d	41.27 N	81.52 W
Fairweather, Mt., Can. (fâr-wĕdh'ēr)	107	59.12 N	137.22 W
Faisalabad, Pak.	196	31.29 N	73.06 E
Faith, SD (fāth)	114	45.02 N	120.02 W
Faizābād, India	196	26.50 N	82.17 E
Fajardo, P.R.	129b	18.20 N	65.40 W
Fakfak, Indon.	207	2.56 S	132.25 E
Faku, China, (fä-ko͞o)	202	42.28 N	123.20 E
Falalise, C, Viet.	203	19.20 N	106.18 E
Falcón (State), Ven. (fäl-kô'n)	143b	11.00 N	68.28 W
Falconer, NY (fô'k'n-ēr)	111	42.10 N	79.10 W
Falcon Heights, Mn. (fô'k'n)	119g	44.59 N	93.10 W
Falcon Res., Tx. (fôk'n)	124	26.47 N	99.03 W
Falemé (R.), Afr. (fȧ-lȧ-mā')	228	13.40 N	12.00 W
Faleshty, Sov. Un. (fä-lâsh'tĭ)	175	47.33 N	27.46 E
Falfurrias, Tx. (făl'fo͞o-rē'ȧs)	124	27.15 N	98.08 W
Falher, Can. (făl'ēr)	99	55.44 N	117.12 W
Falkenberg, Swe. (fäl'kĕn-bĕrgh)	164	56.54 N	12.25 E
Falkensee, G.D.R. (fäl'kĕn-zā)	157b	52.34 N	13.05 E
Falkenthal, G.D.R. (fäl'kĕn-täl)	157b	52.54 N	13.18 E
Falkirk, Scot. (fôl'kûrk)	162	55.59 N	3.55 W
Falkland Is., S.A. (fôk'lănd)	144	50.45 S	61.00 W
Falköping, Swe. (fäl'chûp-ĭng)	164	58.09 N	13.30 E
Fall City, Wa.	118a	47.34 N	121.53 W
Fall Cr., In. (fôl)	113g	39.52 N	86.04 W
Fallon, Nv. (făl'ŭn)	120	39.30 N	118.48 W
Fall River, Ma.	112b	41.42 N	71.07 W
Falls Church, Va. (fălz chûrch)	112e	38.53 N	77.10 W
Falls City, Ne.	123	40.04 N	95.37 W
Fallston, Md. (făls'ton)	112e	39.32 N	76.26 W
Falmouth, Eng. (făl'mŭth)	162	50.08 N	5.04 W
Falmouth, Jam.	134	18.30 N	77.40 W
Falmouth, Ky.	110	38.40 N	84.20 W
False (B.), see Valsbaai			
False Divi Pt., India	191	15.45 N	80.50 E
Falso, Cabo (C.), Dom.Rep. (kȧ'bō-fäl-sō)	135	17.45 N	71.55 W
Falster (I.), Den. (fäls'tĕr)	164	54.48 N	11.58 E
Fălticeni, Rom. (fŭl-tē-chān'y')	167	47.27 N	26.17 E
Falun, Swe. (fä-lo͞on')	164	60.38 N	15.35 E
Famadas, Sp.	65e	41.21 N	2.05 E
Famagusta, Cyprus (fä-mä-go͞os'tä)	161	35.08 N	33.59 E
Famatina, Sierra de (Mts.), Arg. (sē-ĕ'r-rȧ-dĕ-fä-mä-tē'nä)	144	29.00 S	67.50 W
Fangxian, China (fäŋ-shyĕn)	203	32.05 N	110.45 E
Fanning (I.), see Tabuaeran (I.)			
Fannystelle, Can. (făn'ĭ-stĕl)	95f	49.45 N	97.46 W
Fanø (I.), Den. (fän'û)	164	55.24 N	8.10 E
Fano, It. (fä'nō)	172	43.49 N	13.01 E
Farafangana, Mad. (fä-rä-fäŋ-gä'nä)	227	21.18 S	47.59 E
Farāh, Afg. (fä-rä')	192	32.15 N	62.13 E
Farallón, Punta (Pt.), Mex. (po͞o'n-tä-fä-rä-lōn)	130	19.21 N	105.03 W
Faranah, Gui (fä-rä'nä)	228	10.02 N	10.44 W
Farasān, Jaza'ir (Is.), Eth.	225	16.45 N	41.08 E
Farazād, Iran	68h	35.47 N	51.21 E
Faregh, Wadi al (R.), Libya (wädē ĕl fä-rĕg')	161	30.10 N	19.34 E
Farewell, C., N.Z. (fâr-wĕl')	217	40.37 S	172.40 E
Fargo, ND (fär'gō)	114	46.53 N	96.48 W
Far Hills, NJ (fär hĭlz)	112a	40.41 N	74.38 W
Faribault, Mn. (fă'rĭ-bō)	115	44.19 N	93.16 W
Farilhões (Is.), Port. (fä-rē-lyôɴzh')	170	39.28 N	9.32 W
Faringdon, Eng. (fă'rĭng-dŏn)	156b	51.38 N	1.35 W
Fārīskūr, Egypt (fä-rēs-ko͞or')	223b	31.19 N	31.46 E
Farit, Amba (Mt.), Eth.	225	10.51 N	37.52 E
Farley, Mo (fär'lē)	118f	39.16 N	94.49 W
Farmers Branch, Tx. (fär'mērz brȧnch)	119c	32.56 N	96.53 W
Farmersburg, In. (fär'mērz-bûrg)	110	39.15 N	87.25 W
Farmersville, Tx. (fär'mērz-vĭl)	123	33.11 N	96.22 W
Farmingdale, NJ (färm'ĕng-dāl)	112a	40.11 N	74.10 W
Farmingdale, NY	112a	40.44 N	73.26 W
Farmingham, Ma. (färm-ĭng-hăm)	105a	42.17 N	71.25 W
Farmington, Il. (färm-ĭng-tŭn)	123	40.42 N	90.01 W
Farmington, Me.	104	44.40 N	70.10 W
Farmington, Mi.	113b	42.28 N	83.23 W
Farmington, Mo.	123	37.46 N	90.26 W
Farmington, NM	121	36.40 N	108.10 W

PLACE (Pronounciation)	PAGE	Lat. °'	Long. °'
Farmington, Ut.	119b	40.59 N	111.53 W
Farmington Hills, Mi.	57c	42.28 N	83.23 W
Farmville, NC (färm-vĭl)	127	35.35 N	77.35 W
Farmville, Va.	127	37.15 N	78.23 W
Farnborough, Eng. (färn'bŭr-ô)	156b	51.15 N	0.45 W
Farnborough (Neigh.), Eng.	62	51.21 N	0.04 E
Farne (I.), Eng. (färn)	162	55.40 N	1.32 W
Farnham, Can. (fär'nŭm)	111	45.15 N	72.55 W
Farningham, Eng. (fär'nĭng-ŭm)	156	51.22 N	0.14 E
Farnworth, Eng. (färn'wŭrth)	156	53.34 N	2.24 W
Faro, Braz. (fä'ro͞o)	143	2.05 S	56.32 W
Faro, Port.	170	37.01 N	7.57 W
Farodofay, Mad.	227	24.59 S	46.58 E
Fåron (I.), Swe.	165	57.57 N	19.10 E
Farquhar, C., Austl. (fär'kwȧr)	214	23.50 S	112.55 E
Farrell, Pa. (făr'ĕl)	110	41.10 N	80.30 W
Far Rockaway (Neigh.), NY	55	40.36 N	73.45 W
Farrukhābād, India (fŭ-ro͞ok-hä-bäd')	196	27.29 N	79.35 E
Fársala (Pharsalus), Grc.	173	39.18 N	22.25 E
Farsund, Nor. (fär'so͞on)	164	58.05 N	6.47 E
Fartura, Serra da (Mts.), Braz. (sĕ'r-rä-dȧ-fär-to͞o'rä)	144	26.40 S	53.15 W
Farvel, Kap (C.), Grnld.	94	60.00 N	44.00 W
Farwell, Tx. (fär'wĕl)	122	34.24 N	103.03 W
Fasano, It. (fä-zä'nō)	173	40.50 N	17.22 E
Fastov, Sov. Un. (fäs'tôf)	175	50.04 N	29.57 E
Fatëzh, Sov. Un.	175	52.06 N	35.51 E
Fatima, Port.	170	39.36 N	9.36 E
Fatsa, Tur. (fät'sä)	179	40.50 N	37.30 E
Faucilles, Monts. (Mts.), Fr. (mōɴ' fō-sēl')	169	48.07 N	6.13 E
Fauske, Nor.	158	67.15 N	15.24 E
Faust, Can. (foust)	99	55.19 N	115.38 W
Faustovo, Sov. Un.	182b	55.27 N	38.29 E
Faversham, Eng. (fă'vēr-sh'm)	156b	51.19 N	0.54 E
Favoriten (Neigh.), Aus.	66e	48.11 N	16.23 E
Fawkham Green, Eng.	62	51.22 N	0.17 E
Fawkner, Austl.	70b	37.43 S	144.58 E
Fawsett Farms, Md.	56d	38.59 N	77.14 W
Faxaflói (B.), Ice.	158	64.33 N	22.40 W
Faya, Chad	194	17.55 N	19.07 E
Fayette, Al. (fā-yĕt')	126	33.40 N	87.54 W
Fayette, Ia.	115	42.49 N	91.49 W
Fayette, Mo.	123	39.09 N	92.41 W
Fayette, Ms.	126	31.43 N	91.00 W
Fayetteville, Ar. (fā-yĕt'vĭl)	123	36.03 N	94.08 W
Fayetteville, NC	127	35.02 N	78.54 W
Fayetteville, Tn.	126	35.10 N	86.33 W
Fazao, Forêt Classée du (For.), Togo	228	8.50 N	0.40 E
Fazilka, India	196	30.30 N	74.02 E
Fazzān (Fezzan) (Prov.), Libya	225	26.45 N	13.01 E
Fdérik, Mauritania	224	22.45 N	12.38 W
Fear, C., NC (fēr)	127	33.52 N	77.48 W
Feather (R.), Ca. (fĕth'ēr)	120	38.56 N	121.41 W
Feather, Middle Fk. of (R.), Ca.	120	39.49 N	121.10 W
Feather, North Fk. of (R.), Ca.	120	40.00 N	121.20 W
Featherstone, Eng. (fĕdh'ēr stŭn)	156	53.39 N	1.21 W
Fécamp, Fr. (fā-käɴ')	168	49.45 N	0.20 E
Federal, Distrito (Dist.), Ven. (dēs-trē'tô-fĕ-dĕ-rä'l)	143b	10.34 N	66.55 W
Federal Way, Wa.	118a	47.20 N	122.20 W
Fëdorovka, Sov. Un. (fyô'dô-rôf-kȧ)	182b	56.15 N	37.14 E
Fehmarn I., F.R.G. (fā'märn)	166	54.28 N	11.15 E
Fehrbellin, G.D.R. (fĕr'bĕl-lēn)	157b	52.49 N	12.46 E
Feia, Logoa (L.), Braz. (lô-gôā-fĕ'yä)	141a	21.54 S	41.45 W
Feicheng, China (fā-chŭŋ)	200	36.18 N	116.45 E
Feidong, China (fā-dôŋ)	200	31.53 N	117.28 E
Feira de Santana, Braz. (fĕ'ē-rä dä sänt-än'ä)	143	12.16 S	38.46 W
Feixian, China (fā-shyĕn)	200	35.17 N	117.59 E
Felanitx, Sp. (fā-lä-nēch')	171	39.29 N	3.09 E
Feldkirch, Aus. (fĕlt'kĭrk)	166	47.15 N	9.36 E
Feldkirchen, F.R.G. (fĕld'kēr-ĸĕn)	157d	48.09 N	11.44 E
Felipe Carrillo Puerto, Mex. (fĕ-lē'pĕ-kär-rē'l-yô-pwĕ'r-tô)	132a	19.36 N	88.04 W
Feltre, It. (fĕl'trā)	172	46.02 N	11.56 E
Femunden (L.), Nor.	164	62.17 N	11.40 E
Fengcheng, China (fŭŋ-chŭŋ)	202	40.28 N	124.03 E
Fengcheng, China	201b	30.55 N	121.38 E
Fengdu, China (fŭŋ-do͞o)	203	29.58 N	107.50 E
Fengjie, China (fŭŋ-jyĕ)	203	31.02 N	109.30 E
Fengming Dao (I.), China (fŭŋ-mĭŋ dou)	200	39.19 N	121.15 E
Fengrun, China (fŭŋ-ro͞on)	200	39.51 N	118.06 E
Fengtai, China (fŭŋ-tī)	202a	39.51 N	116.19 E
Fengxian, China (fŭŋ-shyĕn)	201b	30.55 N	121.26 E
Fengxian, China	200	34.41 N	116.36 E
Fengxiang, China (fŭŋ-shyäŋ)	202	34.25 N	107.20 E
Fengyang, China (fŭng'yäng')	200	32.55 N	117.32 E
Fengzhen, China (fŭŋ-jŭn)	202	40.28 N	113.20 E
Fenimore, Pass. Ak. (fĕn-ĭ-mōr)	107a	51.40 N	175.38 W
Fenoarivo Atsinanana, Mad.	227	17.30 S	49.31 E
Fenton, Mi. (fĕn-tŭn)	110	42.50 N	83.40 W
Fenton, Mo.	119e	38.31 N	90.27 W
Fenyang, China	202	37.20 N	111.48 E
Feodosiya (Kefe), Sov. Un. (fĕ-ô-dô'sē'yȧ) (kyĕ'fĕ)	175	45.02 N	35.21 E
Ferbitz, G.D.R.	65a	52.30 N	13.01 E
Ferdows, Iran	192	34.00 N	58.13 E
Ferencváros (Neigh.), Hung.	66g	47.28 N	19.06 E
Ferentino, It. (fā-rĕn-tē'nō)	172	41.42 N	13.18 E
Fergana, Sov. Un.	180	40.16 N	72.07 E
Fergus Falls, Mn. (fûr'gŭs)	114	46.17 N	96.03 W
Ferguson, Mo. (fûr-gŭ-sŭn)	119e	38.45 N	90.18 W
Ferkéssédougou, Ivory Coast	228	9.36 N	5.12 W
Fermo, It. (fĕr'mō)	172	43.10 N	13.43 E
Fermoselle, Sp. (fĕr-mō-säl'yā)	170	41.20 N	6.23 W
Fermoy, Ire. (fûr-moi')	162	52.05 N	8.06 W
Fernandina Beach, Fl. (fûr-năn-dē'nȧ)	127	30.38 N	81.29 W

ăt; finăl; rāte; senāte; ärm; ȧsk; sofȧ; fâre; ch-choose; dh-as th in other; bē; ēvent; bĕt; recĕnt; cratēr; g-gō; gh-guttural g; bĭt; ĭ-short neutral; rīde; ĸ-guttural k as ch in German ich;

PRONOUNCING INDEX

Fernando de Noronha – Fort Benton 283

PLACE (Pronounciation)	PAGE	Lat. °′	Long. °′
Fernando de Noronha (Prov.), Braz. (är-kĕ-pĕ'lä-gô-fĕr-nän-dō-dĕ-nô-rō'n-yä)	143	3.51 S	32.25 W
Fernando Póo (I.), see Bioko			
Fernān-Núñez, Sp. (fĕr-nän'nōōn'yåth)	170	37.42 N	4.43 W
Fernão Veloso, Baia de (B.), Moz.	231	14.20 S	40.55 E
Ferndale, Ca. (fûrn'dāl)	116	40.34 N	124.18 W
Ferndale, Md.	56c	39.11 N	76.38 W
Ferndale, Mi.	57c	42.28 N	83.08 W
Ferndale, Mi.	113b	42.27 N	83.08 W
Ferndale, Wa.	118d	48.51 N	122.36 W
Fernie, Can. (fûr'nĭ)	99	49.30 N	115.03 W
Fern Prairie, Wa. (fûrn prâr'ĭ)	118c	45.38 N	122.25 W
Ferntree Gully, Austl.	211	37.53 S	145.18 E
Ferny Creek, Austl.	70b	37.53 S	145.21 E
Ferrara, It. (fĕr-rä'rä)	172	44.50 N	11.37 E
Ferrat, Cap (C.), Alg. (kăp fĕr-rät)	171	35.49 N	0.29 W
Ferraz de Vasconcelos, Braz.	61d	23.32 S	46.22 W
Ferreira do Alentejo, Port. (fĕr-rĕ'ē-rä dōō ä-lĕn-tā'zhōō)	170	38.03 N	8.06 W
Ferreira do Zezere, Port (fĕr-rĕ'ē-rä dōō zå-zā'rĕ)	170	39.49 N	8.17 W
Ferrelview, Mo. (fĕr'rĕl-vū)	119f	39.18 N	94.40 W
Ferreñafe, Peru (fĕr-rĕn-yà'fĕ)	142	6.38 S	79.48 W
Ferriday, La. (fĕr'ĭ-dā)	125	31.38 N	91.33 W
Ferrières, Fr.	64c	48.49 N	2.42 E
Ferry Village, NY	57a	43.58 N	78.57 W
Fershampenuaz, Sov. Un. (fĕr-shám'pĕn-wäz)	182a	53.32 N	59.50 E
Fertile, Mn. (fur'tĭl)	114	47.33 N	96.18 W
Fès, Mor. (fĕs)	224	34.08 N	5.00 W
Fessenden, ND (fĕs'ĕn-dĕn)	114	47.39 N	99.40 W
Festus, Mo. (fĕst'ŭs)	123	38.12 N	90.22 W
Fetcham, Eng.	62	51.17 N	0.22 W
Fethiye, Turk. (fĕt-hē'yĕ)	179	36.40 N	29.05 E
Feuilles, Rivière aux (R.), Can.	97	58.30 N	70.50 W
Fezzan (Prov.), see Fazzān			
Ffestiniog, Wales	162	52.59 N	3.58 W
Fianarantsoa, Mad. (fyá-nä'rán-tsō'á)	227	21.21 S	47.15 E
Fichtenau, G.D.R.	65a	52.27 N	13.42 E
Ficksburg, S. Afr (fĭks'bûrg)	223d	28.53 S	27.53 E
Fidalgo I., Wa. (fĭ-dăl'gō)	118a	48.28 N	122.39 W
Fiddlers Hamlet, Eng.	62	51.41 N	0.08 E
Fieldbrook, Ca. (fēld'brŏŏk)	118	40.59 N	124.02 W
Fier, Alb. (fyĕr)	173	40.43 N	19.34 E
Fife Ness (C.), Scot. (fīf'nes')	162	56.15 N	2.19 W
Fifth Cataract, Sud.	225	18.27 N	33.38 E
Figeac, Fr. (fē-zhák')	168	44.37 N	2.02 E
Figeholm, Swe. (fē-ghĕ-hōlm)	164	57.24 N	16.33 E
Figueira da Foz, Port. (fē-gwĕy-rä-dá-fô'z)	170	40.10 N	8.50 W
Figuig, Mor.	224	32.20 N	1.30 W
Fiji, Oceania (fē'jē)	208	18.40 S	175.00 E
Filadelfia, C.R. (fĭl-á-dĕl'fĭ-á)	132	10.26 N	85.37 W
Filatovskoye, Sov. Un. (fĭ-lä'tôf-skô-yĕ)	182a	56.49 N	62.20 E
Filbert, WV (fĭl'bērt)	127	37.18 N	81.29 W
Filchner Ice Shelf, Ant. (fĭlk'nēr)	232	80.00 S	35.00 W
Fili (Neigh.), Sov. Un.	66b	55.45 N	37.31 E
Filiatrá, Grc.	173	37.10 N	21.35 E
Filicudi (I.), It. (fē'le-kōō'dē)	172	38.34 N	14.39 E
Filigas (R.), Tur.	161	41.10 N	32.53 E
Filippovskoye, Sov. Un. (fĭ-lĭ-pôf'skô-yĕ)	182b	56.06 N	38.38 E
Filipstad, Swe. (fĭl'ĭps-städh)	164	59.44 N	14.09 E
Fillmore, Ut. (fĭl'mōr)	121	39.00 N	112.20 W
Filsa, Nor.	164	60.35 N	12.03 E
Fimi (R.), Zaire	230	2.43 S	17.50 E
Finaalspan, S. Afr.	71b	26.17 S	28.15 E
Finch, Can. (fĭnch)	95c	45.09 N	75.06 W
Finchley (Neigh.), Eng.	62	51.36 N	0.10 W
Findlay, Oh. (fĭnd'lā)	110	41.05 N	83.40 W
Fingoe, Moz.	231	15.12 S	31.50 E
Finisterre, Cabo de (C.), Sp. (ká'bô-dĕ-fĭn-ĭs-târ')	170	42.52 N	9.48 W
Finke (R.), Austl. (fĭŋ'kē)	214	25.25 S	134.30 E
Finkenkrug, G.D.R.	65a	52.34 N	13.03 E
Finland, Eur. (fĭn'lănd)	154	62.45 N	26.13 E
Finland, G. of, Eur. (fĭn'lănd)	165	59.35 N	23.35 E
Finlandia, Col. (fēn-lä'n-dēä)	142a	4.38 N	75.39 W
Finlay (R.), Can. (fĭn'lā)	96	57.45 N	125.30 W
Finow, G.D.R. (fē'nōv)	157b	52.50 N	13.44 E
Finowfurt, G.D.R. (fē'nō-fōōrt)	157b	52.50 N	13.41 E
Finsterwalde, G.D.R. (fĭn'stĕr-väl-dĕ)	166	51.38 N	13.42 E
Firat (R.), Tur. (fē-rät')	179	39.40 N	38.30 E
Fircrest, Wa. (fûr'krĕst)	118a	47.14 N	122.31 W
Firenze (Florence), It. (fē-rĕnt'sä)	172	43.47 N	11.15 E
Firenzuola, It. (fē-rĕnt-swô'lä)	172	44.08 N	11.21 E
Firgrove, Eng.	64b	53.37 N	2.08 W
Firozpur, India	196	30.58 N	74.39 E
Fischa (R.), Aus.	157e	48.04 N	16.33 E
Fischamend Markt, Aus.	157e	48.07 N	16.37 E
Fischeln (Neigh.), F.R.G.	63	51.18 N	6.35 E
Fish (R.), Namibia (fĭsh)	226	27.30 S	17.45 E
Fish Cay (I.), Ba.	135	22.30 N	74.20 W
Fish Cr., Can. (fĭsh)	95e	50.52 N	114.21 W
Fisher, La. (fĭsh'ēr)	125	31.28 N	93.30 W
Fisher B., Can.	101	51.30 N	97.16 W
Fisher Chan, Can.	98	52.10 N	127.42 W
Fisherman's Wharf (P. Int.), Ca.	58b	37.48 N	122.25 W
Fisher Str., Can.	97	62.43 N	84.28 W
Fisherville, Can.	54c	43.47 N	79.28 W
Fishing L., Can. (fĭsh'ĭng)	101	52.07 N	95.25 W
Fishpool, Eng.	64b	53.35 N	2.17 W
Fitchburg, Ma. (fĭch'bûrg)	105a	42.35 N	71.48 W
Fitri, Lac (L.), Chad	229	12.50 N	17.28 E
Fitzgerald, Ga. (fĭts-jĕr'ăld)	126	31.42 N	83.17 W
Fitz Hugh Sd., Can. (fĭts hū)	98	51.40 N	127.57 W
Fitzroy, Austl.	70b	37.48 S	144.59 E

PLACE (Pronounciation)	PAGE	Lat. °′	Long. °′
Fitzroy (R.), Austl. (fĭts-roi')	214	18.00 S	124.05 E
Fitzroy (R.), Austl.	215	23.45 S	150.02 E
Fitzroy Crossing, Austl.	214	18.08 S	126.00 E
Fitzwilliam (I.), Can. (fĭts-wĭl'yŭm)	110	45.30 N	81.45 W
Fiume, see Rijeka			
Fiumicino, It. (fyōō-mē-chē'nô)	171d	41.47 N	12.19 E
Five Dock, Austl.	70a	33.52 S	151.08 E
Fjällbacka, Swe. (fyĕl'bäk-à)	164	58.37 N	11.17 E
Flagstaff, Az. (flăg-stáf)	121	35.15 N	111.40 W
Flagstaff, S. Afr. (flăg'stäf)	227c	31.06 S	29.31 E
Flagstaff (L.), Me. (flăg-stáf)	111	45.05 N	70.30 W
Flalow, G.D.R. (flä'lōv)	157b	52.44 N	12.58 E
Flåm, Nor. (flôm)	164	60.15 N	7.01 E
Flambeau (R.), Wi. (flăm-bō')	115	45.32 N	91.05 W
Flaming Gorge Res., Wy.	117	41.13 N	109.30 W
Flamingo, Fl. (flá-mĭŋ'gō)	127	25.10 N	80.55 W
Flamingo Cay (I.), Ba. (flá-mĭŋ'gō)	135	22.50 N	75.50 W
Flamingo Pt, Vir. Is. (U.S.A.)	129c	18.19 N	65.00 W
Flanders (Reg.), Fr. (flăn'dērz)	163	50.53 N	2.29 E
Flandreau, SD (flăn'drō)	114	44.02 N	96.35 W
Flatbush (Neigh.), NY	55	40.39 N	73.56 W
Flathead (R.), Can.	99	49.30 N	114.30 W
Flathead L., Mt. (flăt'hĕd)	117	47.57 N	114.20 W
Flathead R., Mt.	117	48.45 N	114.20 W
Flathead R., Middle Fork, Mt.	117	48.30 N	113.47 W
Flathead R., South Fork, Mt.	117	48.05 N	113.45 W
Flat Rock, Mi. (flăt rŏk)	113b	42.06 N	83.17 W
Flattery C., Wa. (flăt'ēr-ĭ)	116	48.22 N	125.45 W
Flat Willow Cr., Mt. (flat wĭl'ō)	117	46.45 N	108.47 W
Flaunden, Eng.	62	51.42 N	0.32 W
Flehe (Neigh.), F.R.G.	63	51.12 N	6.47 E
Flekkefjord, Nor. (flăk'kē-fyôr)	164	58.19 N	6.38 E
Flemingsburg, Ky. (flĕm'ĭngz-bûrg)	110	38.25 N	83.45 W
Flensburg, F.R.G. (flĕns'bōōrgh)	166	54.48 N	9.27 E
Flers, Fr. (flĕr)	168	48.43 N	0.37 W
Fletcher, NC	127	35.26 N	82.30 W
Fley (Neigh.), F.R.G.	63	51.23 N	7.30 E
Flinders (I.), Austl.	216	39.35 S	148.10 E
Flinders (R.), Austl.	215	18.48 S	141.07 E
Flinders (Reg.), Austl. (flĭn'dērz)	214	32.15 S	138.45 E
Flinders Rfs., Austl.	215	17.30 S	149.02 E
Flin Flon, Can. (flĭn flŏn)	110	54.46 N	101.53 W
Flingern (Neigh.), F.R.G.	63	51.14 N	6.49 E
Flint, Mi.	110	43.00 N	83.45 W
Flint (R.), Ga. (flĭnt)	126	31.25 N	84.15 W
Flint, Wales	156	53.15 N	3.07 W
Flora, Il. (flō'rá)	110	38.40 N	88.25 W
Flora, In.	110	40.25 N	86.30 W
Florala, Al. (flŏr-ăl'á)	126	31.01 N	86.19 W
Floral Park, NY (flôr'ál pärk)	112a	40.42 N	73.42 W
Florence, Al. (flŏr'ĕns)	126	34.46 N	87.40 W
Florence, Az.	121	33.00 N	111.25 W
Florence, Ca.	59	33.58 N	118.15 W
Florence, Co.	122	38.23 N	105.08 W
Florence, Ks.	123	38.14 N	96.56 W
Florence, SC	127	34.10 N	79.45 W
Florence, Wa.	118a	48.13 N	122.21 W
Florence, see Firenze			
Florencia, Col. (flō-rĕn'sē-á)	142	1.31 N	75.13 W
Florencio Sanchez, Ur. (flō-rĕn-sēō-sá'n-chĕz)	141c	33.52 S	57.24 W
Florencio Varela, Arg. (flō-rĕn'sē-o vä-rā'lä)	144a	34.34 S	58.16 W
Florentia, S. Afr.	71b	26.16 S	28.08 E
Flores, Braz. (flō'rĕzh)	143	7.57 S	37.48 W
Flores (Dept.), Ur.	141c	33.33 S	57.00 W
Flores, Guat.	132a	16.53 N	89.54 W
Flores (I.), Indon.	206	8.14 S	121.08 E
Flores (Neigh.), Arg.	60d	34.38 S	58.28 W
Flores (R.), Arg.	141c	36.13 S	60.28 W
Flores Laut (Flores Sea), Indon.	206	7.09 N	120.30 E
Floresta (Neigh.), Arg.	60d	34.38 S	58.29 W
Floresville, Tx. (flō'rĕs-vĭl)	124	29.10 N	98.08 W
Floriano, Braz. (flō-rá-ä'nōō)	143	6.17 S	42.58 W
Florianópolis, Braz. (flō-rē-ä-nō'pō-lēs)	144	27.30 S	48.30 W
Florida, Col. (flō-rē'dä)	142a	3.20 N	76.12 W
Florida, Cuba	134	22.10 N	79.50 W
Florida, NY (flŏr'ĭ-dá)	112a	41.20 N	74.21 W
Florida, S. Afr.	227b	26.11 S	27.56 E
Florida, Ur. (flô-rē-dhä)	141c	34.06 S	56.14 W
Florida, (State), U.S. (flŏr'ĭ-dá)	109	30.30 N	84.40 W
Florida (Dept.), Ur. (flô-rē'dhä)	141c	33.48 S	56.15 W
Florida (I.), Sol. Is.	215	8.56 S	159.45 E
Florida B., Fl. (flŏr'ĭ-dá)	127a	24.55 N	80.55 W
Florida Keys (Is.), Fl.	127a	24.33 N	81.20 W
Florida Mts., NM	121	32.10 N	107.35 W
Florida, Strs. of, N.A.	134	24.10 N	81.00 W
Florido, R., Mex. (flô-rē'dō)	124	27.21 N	104.48 W
Floridsdorf, Aus. (flō'rĭds-dôrf)	157e	48.16 N	16.25 E
Florina, Grc. (flō-rē'nä)	173	40.48 N	21.24 E
Florissant, Mo. (flŏr'ĭ-sănt)	119e	38.47 N	90.20 W
Florø, Nor. (flō'ü)	164	61.36 N	5.01 E
Flotantes, Jardines (P. Int.), Mex.	60a	19.16 N	99.06 W
Flourtown, Pa.	56b	40.07 N	75.13 W
Flower Hill, NY	55	40.49 N	73.41 W
Floyd (R.), Ia. (floid)	114	42.38 N	96.15 W
Floydada, Tx. (floi-dā'dá)	122	33.59 N	101.19 W
Floyds Fk. (R.), Ky. (floi-dz)	113h	38.08 N	85.30 W
Flumendosa, R., It. (flōō-mĕn-dō'sä)	172	39.45 N	9.18 E
Flushing, Mi. (flŭsh'ĭng)	110	43.05 N	83.50 W
Flushing (Neigh.), NY	55	40.45 N	73.49 W
Fly (R.), Pap. N. Gui. (flī)	207	8.00 S	141.45 E
Foča, Yugo. (fō'chä)	173	43.29 N	18.48 E
Fochville, S. Afr. (fōk'vĭl)	223d	26.29 S	27.29 E
Focsani, Rom. (fōk-shä'nē)	167	45.41 N	27.17 E
Fogang, China (fwo-gäŋ)	203	23.50 N	113.35 E
Foggia, It. (fôd'jä)	172	41.30 N	15.34 E
Fogo, Can. (fō'gō)	103	49.43 N	54.17 W
Fogo I, Can.	103	49.40 N	54.13 W
Fogo I, C.V.	224b	14.46 N	24.51 W

PLACE (Pronounciation)	PAGE	Lat. °′	Long. °′
Fohnsdorf, Aus. (fōns'dôrf)	166	47.13 N	14.40 E
Föhr I., F.R.G. (fûr)	166	54.47 N	8.30 E
Foix, Fr. (fwä)	168	42.58 N	1.34 E
Fokku, Nig.	229	11.40 N	4.31 E
Folcroft, Pa.	56b	39.54 N	75.17 W
Folgares, Ang.	230	14.54 S	15.08 E
Foligno, It. (fô-lēn'yō)	172	42.58 N	12.41 E
Folkeston, Eng.	163	51.05 N	1.18 E
Folkingham, Eng. (fō'kĭng-ăm)	156	52.53 N	0.24 W
Folkston, Ga.	127	30.50 N	82.01 W
Folsom, NM (fōl'sŭm)	122	36.47 N	103.56 W
Folsom, Pa.	56b	39.54 N	75.19 W
Folsom City, Ca.	120	38.40 N	121.10 W
Fomento, Cuba (fō-mĕ'n-tō)	134	21.35 N	78.20 W
Fómeque, Col. (fô'mĕ-kĕ)	142a	4.29 N	73.52 W
Fonda, Ia. (fŏn'dá)	115	42.33 N	94.51 W
Fond du Lac, Wi. (fŏn dū lăk')	115	43.47 N	88.29 W
Fond du Lac Ind. Res., Mn.	115	46.44 N	93.04 W
Fondi, It. (fōn'dē)	172	41.23 N	13.25 E
Fonsagrada, Sp. (fôn-sä-grä'dhä)	170	43.08 N	7.07 W
Fonseca, Golfo de (G.), Hond. (gôl-fô-dĕ-fôn-sä'kä)	132	13.09 N	87.55 W
Fontainebleau, Fr. (fôɴ-tĕn-blō')	169b	48.24 N	2.42 E
Fontainebleau, S. Afr.	71b	26.07 S	27.59 E
Fontana, Ca. (fŏn-tă'ná)	119a	34.06 N	117.27 W
Fonte Boa, Braz. (fōn'tá bō'á)	142	2.32 S	66.05 W
Fontenay-aux-Roses, Fr.	64c	48.47 N	2.17 E
Fontenay-le-Comte, Fr. (fôɴt-nĕ'lĕ-kôɴt')	168	46.28 N	0.53 W
Fontenay-le-Fleury, Fr.	64c	48.49 N	2.30 E
Fontenay-sous-Bois, Fr.	64c	48.51 N	2.29 E
Fontenay-Trésigny, Fr. (fôɴ-te-hā' tra-sēn-yē')	169b	48.43 N	2.53 E
Fontenelle Res., Wy.	117	42.05 N	110.05 W
Fontera, Punta (Pt.), Mex. (pōō'n-tä-fôn-tĕ'rä)	131	18.36 N	92.43 W
Fontibón, Col. (fōn-tē-bôn')	142a	4.42 N	74.09 W
Fontur (Pt.), Ice.	158	66.21 N	14.02 W
Foothills, S. Afr. (fōōt-hĭls)	227b	25.55 S	27.36 E
Footscray, Austl.	70b	37.48 S	144.54 E
Foraker, Mt., Ak. (fôr'á-kēr)	107	62.40 N	152.40 W
Fora, Ponta de (C.), Braz.	61c	22.57 S	43.07 W
Forbach, Fr. (fôr'bäĸ)	169	49.12 N	6.54 E
Forbes, Austl. (fôrbz)	216	33.24 S	148.05 E
Forbes, Mt., Can.	99	51.52 N	116.56 W
Forbidden City (P. Int.), China	67b	39.55 N	116.23 E
Forchheim, F.R.G. (fôrĸ'hīm)	166	49.43 N	11.05 E
Fordham University (P. Int.), NY	55	40.51 N	73.53 W
Fordlândia, see Brasília Legal			
Fords, NJ	55	40.32 N	74.19 W
Fordsburg (Neigh.), S. Afr.	71b	26.13 S	28.02 E
Fordyce, Ar. (fôr'dīs)	123	33.48 N	92.24 W
Forecariah, Gui. (fōr-ká-rē'ä')	228	9.26 N	13.06 W
Forel, Mt., Grnld.	94	65.50 N	37.41 W
Forest, Ms. (fŏr'ĕst)	126	32.22 N	89.29 W
Forest (R.), ND	114	48.08 N	97.45 W
Forest City, Ia.	115	43.14 N	93.40 W
Forest City, NC	127	35.20 N	81.52 W
Forest City, Pa.	111	41.35 N	75.30 W
Forest Gate (Neigh.), Eng.	62	51.33 N	0.02 E
Forest Grove, Or. (grōv)	118c	45.31 N	123.07 W
Forest Heights, Md.	56d	38.49 N	77.00 W
Forest Hill, Austl.	70b	37.50 S	145.11 E
Forest Hill, Md.	112e	39.35 N	76.26 W
Forest Hill, Tx.	119c	32.40 N	97.16 W
Forest Hill (Neigh.), Can.	54c	43.42 N	79.24 W
Forest Hills, Pa.	57b	40.26 N	79.52 W
Forest Hills (Neigh.), NY	55	40.42 N	73.51 W
Forest Park, Il.	58a	41.53 N	87.50 W
Forest Park (Neigh.), Md.	56c	39.19 N	76.41 W
Forestville, Austl.	70a	33.46 S	151.13 E
Forestville, Can. (fŏr'ĕst-vĭl)	104	48.45 N	69.06 W
Forestville, Md.	112e	38.51 N	76.55 W
Forez, Mts. du, Fr. (môɴ dü fô-rā')	168	44.55 N	3.43 E
Forfar, Scot. (fôr'fár)	162	57.10 N	2.55 W
Forillon, Parc Natl. (Natl. Pk.), Can.	104	48.50 N	64.05 W
Forio (Mtn.), It. (fô'ryō)	171c	40.29 N	13.55 E
Forked Cr., Il. (fôrk'd)	113a	41.16 N	88.01 W
Forked Deer (R.), Tn.	122	35.53 N	89.29 W
Forli, It. (fôr-lē')	172	44.13 N	12.03 E
Formby, Eng. (fôrm'bē)	156	53.34 N	3.04 W
Formby Pt., Eng.	156	53.33 N	3.06 W
Formentera, Isla de (I.), Sp. (ē's-lä-dĕ-fôr-mĕn-tā'rä)	171	38.43 N	1.25 E
Formiga, Braz. (fôr-mē'gä)	141a	20.27 S	45.25 W
Formigas Bk., N.A. (fôr-mē'gäs)	135	18.30 N	75.40 W
Formosa, Arg. (fôr-mō'sä)	144	27.25 S	58.12 W
Formosa, Braz.	143	15.32 S	47.10 W
Formosa (I.), see Taiwan			
Formosa (Prov.), Arg.	144	24.30 S	60.45 W
Formosa B, Ken.	231	2.45 S	40.30 E
Formosa, Serra (Mts.), Braz. (sĕ'r-rä)	143	12.59 S	55.11 W
Formosa Str., see Taiwan Str.			
Fornosovo, Sov. Un. (fôr-nô'sô vô)	182c	59.35 N	30.34 E
Forrest City, Ar. (for'ĕst sĭ'tĭ)	123	35.00 N	90.46 W
Forsayth, Austl. (fôr-sīth')	215	18.33 S	143.42 E
Forshaga, Swe. (fôrs'hä'gä)	164	59.34 N	13.25 E
Forst, G.D.R. (fôrst)	166	51.45 N	14.38 E
Forsyth, Ga. (fôr-sīth')	126	33.02 N	83.56 W
Forsyth, Mt.	117	46.15 N	106.41 W
Fort (Neigh.), India	67e	18.56 N	72.50 E
Fort Albany, Can. (fôrt ôl'bá nĭ)	97	52.20 N	81.30 W
Fort Alexander Ind. Res., Can.	101	50.27 N	96.15 W
Fortaleza (Ceará), Braz. (fôr'tä-lā'zä)	143	3.35 S	38.31 W
Fort Apache Ind. Res., Az. (á-păch'ē)	121	34.02 N	110.27 W
Fort Atkinson, Wi. (ăt'kĭn-sŭn)	115	42.55 N	88.46 W
Fort Beaufort, S. Afr. (bô'fôrt)	227c	32.47 S	26.39 E
Fort Bellefontaine, Mo. (bĕl-fŏn-tān')	119e	38.50 N	90.15 W
Fort Benton, Mt. (bĕn'tŭn)	117	47.51 N	110.40 W

284 Fort Berthold Ind. Res. – Frome

PLACE (Pronounciation)	PAGE	Lat. °′	Long. °′
Fort Berthold Ind. Res., ND (bērth'ôld)	114	47.47 N	103.28 W
Fort Branch, In. (brănch)	110	38.15 N	87.35 W
Fort Chipewyan, Can.	96	58.46 N	111.15 W
Fort Cobb Res., Ok.	122	35.12 N	98.28 W
Fort Collins, Co. (kŏl'ĭns)	122	40.36 N	105.04 W
Fort Crampel, Cen. Afr. Rep. (kràm-pĕl')	229	6.59 N	19.11 E
Fort-de-France, Mart. (dē fräɴs)	133b	14.37 N	61.06 W
Fort Deposit, Al. (dē-pŏz'ĭt)	126	31.58 N	86.35 W
Fort-de-Possel, Cen. Afr. Rep. (dē pô-sĕl')	225	5.03 N	19.11 E
Fort Dodge, Ia. (dŏj)	115	42.31 N	94.10 W
Fort Edward, NY (wẽrd)	111	43.15 N	73.30 W
Fort Erie, Can. (ē'rĭ)	113c	42.55 N	78.56 W
Fortescue (R.), Austl. (fôr'tĕs-kū)	214	21.25 S	116.50 E
Fort Fairfield, Me. (fâr'fēld)	104	46.46 N	67.53 W
Fort Fitzgerald, Can. (fĭts-jĕr'ăld)	96	59.48 N	111.50 W
Fort Frances, Can. (frăn'sĕs)	101	48.36 N	93.24 W
Fort Frederica Natl. Mon., Ga. (frĕd'ē-rĭ-kà)	127	31.13 N	85.25 W
Fort Gaines, Ga. (gānz)	126	31.35 N	85.03 W
Fort George, Can. (jôrj)	97	53.40 N	78.58 W
Fort Gibson, Ok. (gĭb'sŭn)	123	35.50 N	95.13 W
Fort Good Hope, Can. (good hōp)	96	66.19 N	128.52 W
Fort Hall, Ken. (hôl)	225	0.47 S	37.13 E
Fort Hall Ind. Res., Id.	117	43.02 N	112.21 W
Forth, Firth of, Scot. (fûrth ŏv fôrth)	162	56.04 N	3.03 W
Fort Howard, Md.	56c	39.12 N	76.27 W
Fort Huachuca, Az. (wä-chōō'kä)	121	31.30 N	110.25 W
Fortier, Can. (fôr'tyā')	95f	49.56 N	97.55 W
Fort Jameson, Zambia (jäm'sŭn)	226	13.35 S	32.43 E
Fort Jefferson Natl. Mon., Fl. (jĕf'ēr-sŭn)	127a	24.42 N	83.02 W
Fort Johnston, Malawi	226	14.16 S	35.14 E
Fort Kent, Me. (kĕnt)	104	47.14 N	68.37 W
Fort Langley, Can. (lăng'lĭ)	118d	49.10 N	122.35 W
Fort Lauderdale, Fl. (lô'dēr-dāl)	127a	26.07 N	80.09 W
Fort Lee, NJ	112a	40.50 N	73.58 W
Fort Liard, Can.	96	60.16 N	123.34 W
Fort Liberté, Hai. (lē-bĕr-tā')	135	19.40 N	71.50 W
Fort Louden (R.), Tn. (fôrt lou'dĕn)	126	35.52 N	84.10 W
Fort Lupton, Co. (lŭp'tŭn)	122	40.04 N	104.54 W
Fort Matanzas, Fl. (mä-tän'zäs)	127	29.39 N	81.17 W
Fort McDermitt Ind. Res., Or. (măk dēr'mĭt)	116	42.04 N	118.07 W
Fort McHenry National Monument (P. Int.), Md.	56c	39.16 N	76.35 W
Fort Macleod, Can. (mȧ-kloud')	99	49.43 N	113.25 W
Fort McMurray, Can. (mȧk-mŭr'ĭ)	100	56.44 N	111.23 W
Fort McNair (P. Int.), DC	56d	38.52 N	77.04 W
Fort McPherson, Can. (mȧk-fŭr's'n)	96	67.37 N	134.59 W
Fort Madison, Ia. (măd'ĭ-sŭn)	115	40.40 N	91.17 W
Fort Meade, Fl. (mēd)	127a	27.45 N	81.48 W
Fort Mill, SC (mĭl)	127	35.03 N	80.57 W
Fort Mohave Ind. Res., Ca. (mô-hä'vâ)	120	34.59 N	115.02 W
Fort Morgan, Co. (môr'gȧn)	122	40.14 N	103.49 W
Fort Myers, Fl. (mī'ẽrz)	127a	26.36 N	81.45 W
Fort Nelson, Can. (nĕl'sŭn)	96	58.57 N	122.30 W
Fort Nelson (R.), Can. (nĕl'sŭn)	96	58.44 N	122.20 W
Fort Payne, Al. (pān)	126	34.26 N	85.41 W
Fort Peck, Mt. (pĕk)	117	47.58 N	106.30 W
Fort Peck Ind. Res., Mt.	114	48.22 N	105.40 W
Fort Peck Res., Mt.	117	47.52 N	106.59 W
Fort Pierce, Fl. (pērs)	127a	27.25 N	80.20 W
Fort Portal, Ug. (pôr'tâl)	231	0.40 N	30.16 E
Fort Providence, Can. (prŏv'ĭ-dĕns)	96	61.27 N	117.59 W
Fort Pulaski Natl. Mon., Ga. (pu-lăs'kĭ)	127	31.59 N	80.56 W
Fort Qu'Appelle, Can.	100	50.46 N	103.55 W
Fort Randall Dam, U.S.	114	42.48 N	98.35 W
Fort Resolution, Can. (rĕz'ô-lū'shŭn)	96	61.08 N	113.42 W
Fort Riley, Ks. (rī'lĭ)	123	39.05 N	96.46 W
Fort Saint James, Can. (fôrt sānt jāmz)	98	54.26 N	124.15 W
Fort Saint John, Can. (sānt jŏn)	99	56.15 N	120.51 W
Fort Sandeman, Pak. (săn'da-măn)	196	31.28 N	69.29 E
Fort Saskatchewan, Can. (săs-kăt'chōō-ăn)	95g	53.43 N	113.13 W
Fort Scott, Ks. (skŏt)	123	37.50 N	94.43 W
Fort Severn, Can. (sĕv'ērn)	97	56.58 N	87.50 W
Fort Shevchenko, Sov. Un. (shĕv-chĕn'kô)	179	44.30 N	50.18 E
Fort Sibut, Cen. Afr. Rep. (fôr sē-bü')	229	5.44 N	19.05 E
Fort Sill, Ok. (fôrt sĭl)	122	34.41 N	98.25 W
Fort Simpson, Can. (sĭmp'sŭn)	96	61.52 N	121.48 W
Fort Smith, Ar. (smĭth)	123	35.23 N	94.24 W
Fort Smith, Can.	96	60.09 N	112.08 W
Fort Stockton, Tx. (stŏk'tŭn)	124	30.54 N	102.51 W
Fort Sumner, NM (sŭm'nẽr)	122	34.30 N	104.17 W
Fort Sumter Natl. Mon., SC (sŭm'tẽr)	127	32.43 N	79.54 W
Fort Thomas, Ky. (tŏm'ăs)	113f	39.05 N	84.27 W
Fortuna, Ca. (fôr-tū'nȧ)	116	40.36 N	124.10 W
Fortune, Can. (fôr'tŭn)	105	47.04 N	55.51 W
Fortune (I.), Ba.	135	22.35 N	74.20 W
Fortune B, Can.	105	47.25 N	55.25 W
Fort Union Natl. Mon., NM (ūn'yŭn)	122	35.51 N	104.57 W
Fort Valley, Ga. (văl'ĭ)	126	32.33 N	83.53 W
Fort Vermilion, Can. (vẽr-mĭl'yŭn)	96	58.23 N	115.50 W
Fort Victoria, see Mzsvingo.			
Fortville, In. (fôrt-vĭl)	110	40.00 N	85.50 W
Fort Wayne, In. (wān)	110	41.00 N	85.10 W
Fort Wayne Military Museum (P. Int.), Mi.	57c	42.18 N	83.06 W
Fort William (P. Int.), India	67a	22.33 N	88.20 E
Fort William, Scot. (wĭl'yŭm)	162	56.50 N	3.00 W
Fort William, Mt., Austl. (wĭ'ĭ-ăm)	216	24.45 S	151.15 E
Fort Worth, Tx. (wûrth)	119c	32.45 N	97.20 W
Fort Yukon, Ak. (yōō'kŏn)	107	66.30 N	145.00 W
Fort Yuma Ind. Res., Ca. (yōō'mä)	120	32.54 N	114.47 W
Foshan, China	201a	23.02 N	113.07 E
Fossano, It. (fôs-sä'nō)	172	44.34 N	7.42 E
Fossil Cr., Tx. (fŏs-ĭl)	119c	32.53 N	97.19 W
Fossombrone, It. (fôs-sôm-brō'nā)	172	43.41 N	12.48 E
Foss Res, Ok.	122	35.38 N	99.11 W
Fosston, Mn. (fôs'tŭn)	114	47.34 N	95.44 W
Fosterburg, Il. (fôs'tẽr-bûrg)	119e	38.58 N	90.04 W
Foster City, Ca.	58b	37.34 N	122.16 W
Fostoria, Oh. (fŏs-tō'rĭ-ȧ)	110	41.10 N	83.20 W
Fougéres, Fr. (fōō-zhâr')	168	48.23 N	1.14 W
Foula (I.), Scot. (fou'lȧ)	162a	60.08 N	2.04 W
Foulwind, C., N.Z. (foul'wĭnd)	217	41.45 S	171.00 E
Foumban, Cam. (fōōm-bän')	229	5.43 N	10.55 E
Fountain Cr., Co. (foun'tĭn)	122	38.36 N	104.37 W
Fountain Valley, Ca.	119a	33.42 N	117.57 W
Fourche le Fave (R.), Ar. (fōōrsh lä fäv')	123	34.46 N	93.45 W
Fouriesburg, S. Afr. (fōō'rēz-bûrg)	223d	28.38 S	28.13 E
Fourmies, Fr. (fōōr-mē')	168	50.01 N	4.01 E
Four Mts., Is. of the, Ak. (fōr)	107a	52.58 N	170.40 W
Fourqueux, Fr.	64c	48.53 N	2.04 E
Fourth Cataract, Sud.	225	18.52 N	32.07 E
Fouta Djallon (Mts.), Gui. (fōō'tä jä-lôɴ)	224	11.37 N	12.29 W
Foveaux Str., N.Z. (fô-vō')	217	46.30 S	167.43 E
Fowler, Co. (foul'ẽr)	122	38.04 N	104.02 W
Fowler, In.	110	40.35 N	87.20 W
Fowler, Pt., Austl.	214	32.05 S	132.30 E
Fowlerton, Tx. (foul'ẽr-tŭn)	124	28.26 N	98.48 W
Fox (I.), Wa. (fŏks)	118a	47.15 N	122.08 W
Fox (R.), Il.	115	41.35 N	88.43 W
Fox, (R.), Wi.	115	44.18 N	88.23 W
Foxboro, Ma. (fŏks'bŭrô)	105a	42.04 N	71.15 W
Fox Chapel, Pa.	57b	40.30 N	79.55 W
Foxe Basin, Can. (fŏks)	96	67.35 N	79.21 W
Foxe Chan, Can.	97	64.30 N	79.23 W
Foxe Pen, Can.	97	64.57 N	77.26 W
Fox Is., Ak. (fŏks)	107a	53.04 N	167.30 W
Fox L., Il.	113a	42.24 N	88.07 W
Fox Lake, Il. (lăk)	113a	42.24 N	88.11 W
Fox Point, Wi.	113a	43.10 N	87.54 W
Fox Valley, Austl.	70a	33.45 S	151.06 E
Foyle, Lough (B.), Ire. (lŏk foil')	162	55.07 N	7.08 W
Foz do Cunene, Ang.	230	17.16 S	11.50 E
Fraga, Sp. (frä'gä)	171	41.31 N	0.20 E
Fragoso, Cayo (I.), Cuba (kä'yō-frä-gō'sō)	134	22.45 N	79.30 W
Franca, Braz. (frä'n-kä)	143	20.28 S	47.20 W
Francavilla, It. (fräŋ-kä-vēl'lä)	173	40.32 N	17.37 E
France, Eur. (fräns)	154	46.39 N	0.47 E
Frances (L.), Can. (frăn'sĭs)	96	61.27 N	128.28 W
Frances, Cabo (C.), Cuba (kä'bô-frän-sĕ's)	134	21.55 N	84.05 W
Frances, Punta (Pt.), Cuba (pōō'n-tä-frän-sĕ's)	134	21.45 N	83.10 W
Frances Viejo, Cabo (C.), Dom. Rep. (kä'bô-frän'sås vyā'hô)	135	19.40 N	69.35 W
Franceville, Gabon (fräɴs-vēl')	230	1.38 S	13.35 E
Francis Case, L., SD (frăn'sĭs)	114	43.15 N	99.00 W
Francisco Sales, Braz. (frän-sē's-kô-sà'lĕs)	141a	21.42 S	44.26 W
Francistown, Bots. (frăn'sis-toun)	226	21.17 S	27.28 E
Franconville, Fr.	64c	48.59 N	2.14 E
Frank, Pa.	57b	40.16 N	79.48 W
Frankby, Eng.	64a	53.22 N	3.08 W
Frankford (Neigh.), Pa.	56b	40.01 N	75.05 W
Frankfort, Il. (frăŋk'fŭrt)	113a	41.30 N	87.51 W
Frankfort, In.	110	40.15 N	86.30 W
Frankfort, Ks.	123	39.42 N	96.27 W
Frankfort, Ky.	110	38.10 N	84.55 W
Frankfort, Mi.	110	44.40 N	86.15 W
Frankfort, NY	111	43.05 N	75.05 W
Frankfort, S. Afr. (frănk'fŏrt)	227c	32.43 S	27.28 E
Frankfort, S. Afr	223d	27.17 S	28.30 E
Frankfurt (Dist.), G.D.R. (fräŋk'fōōrt)	157b	52.42 N	13.37 E
Frankfurt am Main, F.R.G.	166	50.07 N	8.40 E
Frankfurt an der Oder, G.D.R.	166	52.20 N	14.31 E
Franklin, In. (frănk'lĭn)	110	39.25 N	86.00 W
Franklin, Ky.	126	36.42 N	86.34 W
Franklin, La.	125	29.47 N	91.31 W
Franklin, Ma.	105a	42.05 N	71.24 W
Franklin, Mi.	57c	42.31 N	83.18 W
Franklin, Ne.	122	40.06 N	99.01 W
Franklin, NH	111	43.25 N	71.40 W
Franklin, NJ	112a	41.08 N	74.35 W
Franklin, Oh.	110	39.30 N	84.20 W
Franklin, Pa.	111	41.25 N	79.50 W
Franklin, S. Afr.	227c	30.19 S	29.28 E
Franklin, Tn.	126	35.54 N	86.54 W
Franklin, Va.	127	36.41 N	76.57 W
Franklin (L.), Nv.	120	40.23 N	115.10 W
Franklin, Dist. of, Can.	96	70.46 N	105.22 W
Franklin D. Roosevelt L., Wa.	116	48.12 N	118.43 W
Franklin Mts., Can.	96	65.36 N	125.55 W
Franklin Park, Il.	113a	41.56 N	87.53 W
Franklin Park, Pa.	57b	40.35 N	80.06 W
Franklin Park, Va.	56d	38.55 N	77.09 W
Franklin Roosevelt Park (Neigh.), S. Afr.	71b	26.09 S	27.59 E
Franklin Square, NY	112a	40.43 N	73.40 W
Franklinton, La. (fräŋk'lĭn-tŭn)	125	30.49 N	90.09 W
Frankston, Austl.	211a	38.09 S	145.08 E
Franksville, Wi. (frănkz'vĭl)	113a	42.46 N	87.55 W
Fransta, Swe.	164	62.30 N	16.04 E
Franz Josef Land (Is.), see Zemlya Frantsa Iosifa			
Frascati, It. (fräs-kä'tē)	171d	41.49 N	12.45 E
Fraser (Great Sandy) (I.), Austl. (frā'zẽr)	216	25.12 S	153.00 E
Fraser, Mi. (frā'zẽr)	113b	42.32 N	82.57 W
Fraser (R.), Can.	98	52.20 N	122.35 W
Fraserburgh, Scot. (frā'zẽr-bûrg)	162	57.40 N	2.01 W
Fraser Plateau, Can.	98	51.30 N	122.00 W
Frattamaggiore, It. (frät-tä-mäg-zhyô'rē)	171c	40.41 N	14.16 E
Fray Bentos, Ur. (frī bĕn'tōs)	141c	33.10 S	58.19 W
Frazee, Mn. (frȧ-zē')	114	46.42 N	95.43 W
Fraziers Hog Cay (I.), Ba.	134	25.25 N	77.55 W
Frechen, F.R.G. (frĕ'ĸĕn)	169c	50.54 N	6.49 E
Fredericia, Den. (frĕdh-ĕ-rē'tsē-à)	164	55.35 N	9.45 E
Frederick, Md. (frĕd'ẽr-ĭk)	111	39.25 N	77.25 W
Frederick, Ok.	122	34.23 N	99.01 W
Frederick House (R.), Can.	102	49.05 N	81.20 W
Fredericksburg, Tx. (frĕd'ẽr-ĭkz-bûrg)	124	30.16 N	98.52 W
Fredericksburg, Va.	111	38.20 N	77.30 W
Fredericktown, Mo. (frĕd'ẽr-ĭk-toun)	123	37.32 N	90.16 W
Fredericton, Can. (frĕd'ẽr-ĭk-tŭn)	104	45.48 N	66.39 W
Frederikshavn, Den. (frĕdh'ĕ-rĕks-houn)	164	57.27 N	10.31 E
Frederikssund, Den. (frĕdh'ĕ-rĕks-sōōn)	164	55.51 N	12.04 E
Fredersdorf bei Berlin, G.D.R.	65a	52.31 N	13.44 E
Fredonia, Col. (frē-dō'nyà)	142a	5.55 N	75.40 W
Fredonia, Ks. (frē-dō'nĭ-ȧ)	123	36.31 N	95.50 W
Fredonia, NY	111	42.25 N	79.20 W
Fredrikstad, Nor. (frådh'rĕks-städ)	164	59.14 N	10.58 E
Freeburg, Il. (frē'bûrg)	119e	38.26 N	89.59 W
Freehold, NJ (frē'hōld)	112a	40.15 N	74.16 W
Freeland, Pa. (frē'lănd)	112	41.00 N	75.50 W
Freeland, Wa.	118a	48.01 N	122.32 W
Freels, C., Can. (frēlz)	105	46.37 N	53.45 W
Freelton, Can. (frēl'tŭn)	95d	43.24 N	80.02 W
Freeport, Ba.	134	26.30 N	78.45 W
Freeport, Il. (frē'pōrt)	115	42.19 N	89.30 W
Freeport, NY	112a	40.39 N	73.35 W
Freeport, Tx.	119	28.56 N	95.21 W
Freetown, S.L. (frē'toun)	228	8.30 N	13.15 W
Fregenal de la Sierra, Sp. (frä-hå-näl' dā lä syĕr'rä)	170	38.09 N	6.40 W
Fregene, It. (frĕ-zhĕ'-nĕ)	171d	41.52 N	12.12 E
Freiberg, G.D.R. (frī'bĕrgh)	166	50.54 N	13.18 E
Freiburg, G.D.R.	166	48.00 N	7.50 E
Freienried, F.R.G. (frī'ĕn-rēd)	157d	48.20 N	11.08 E
Freirina, Chile (frå-ĭ-rē'nä)	144	28.35 S	71.26 W
Freisenbruch (Neigh.), F.R.G.	63	51.27 N	7.06 E
Freising, F.R.G. (frī'zĭng)	157d	48.25 N	11.45 E
Fréjus, Fr. (frā-zhüs')	169	43.28 N	6.46 E
Fremantle, Austl. (frē'măn-t'l)	214	32.03 S	116.05 E
Fremont, Ca. (frē-mŏnt')	118b	37.33 N	122.00 W
Fremont, Mi.	110	43.25 N	85.55 W
Fremont, Ne.	114	41.26 N	96.30 W
Fremont, Oh.	110	41.20 N	83.05 W
Fremont (R.), Ut.	121	38.20 N	111.30 W
Fremont Pk., Wy.	117	43.05 N	109.35 W
French Broad (R.), Tn.-NC (frĕnch brôd)	126	35.59 N	83.01 W
French Frigate Shoals (Rocks), Hi.	106b	23.30 N	167.10 W
French Guiana, S.A. (gē-ä'nä)	140	4.20 N	53.00 W
French Lick, In. (frĕnch lĭk)	110	38.35 N	86.35 W
Frenchman (R.), Can.	100	49.25 N	108.30 W
Frenchman Cr., Mt. (frĕnch-măn)	117	48.51 N	107.20 W
Frenchman Cr., Ne.	122	40.24 N	101.50 W
Frenchman Flat, Nv.	120	36.55 N	116.11 W
French Polynesia, Pac. O.	209	15.00 S	140.00 W
French River, Mn.	119h	46.54 N	91.54 W
French's Forest, Austl.	70a	33.45 S	151.14 E
Freshfield, Eng.	64a	53.34 N	3.04 W
Freshfield, Mt., Can. (frĕsh'fēld)	99	51.44 N	116.57 W
Fresh Meadows (Neigh.), NY	55	40.44 N	73.48 W
Fresnillo, Mex. (frås-nēl'yô)	130	23.10 N	102.52 W
Fresno, Ca. (frĕz'nō)	120	36.43 N	119.47 W
Fresno, Col. (frĕs'nô)	142a	5.10 N	75.01 W
Fresno (R.), Ca. (frĕz'nō)	120	37.00 N	120.24 W
Fresno Slough, Ca.	120	36.39 N	120.12 W
Freudenstadt, F.R.G. (froi'den-shtät)	166	48.28 N	8.26 E
Freycinet Pen., Austl. (frā-sē-nĕ')	216	42.13 S	148.56 E
Fria, Gui.	228	10.05 N	13.32 W
Fria (R.), Az. (frē-ä)	121	34.03 N	112.12 W
Fria, C., Namibia (frĭȧ)	226	18.15 S	12.10 E
Frias, Arg. (frē-äs)	144	28.43 S	65.03 W
Fribourg, Switz. (frē-bōōr')	166	46.48 N	7.07 E
Fridley, Mn. (frĭd'lĭ)	119g	45.05 N	93.16 W
Frieburg, F.R.G. (frī'bōōrgh)	166	47.59 N	7.50 E
Friedberg, F.R.G. (frēd'bĕrgh)	157d	48.22 N	11.00 E
Friedenau (Neigh.), F.R.G.	65a	52.28 N	13.20 E
Friedland, G.D.R. (frēt'länt)	166	53.39 N	13.34 E
Friedrichsfeld, F.R.G.	63	51.38 N	6.39 E
Friedrichsfelde (Neigh.), G.D.R.	65a	52.31 N	13.31 E
Friedrichshafen, F.R.G. (frē-drĕks-häf'ĕn)	166	47.39 N	9.28 E
Friedrichshagen (Neigh.), G.D.R.	65a	52.27 N	13.38 E
Friedrichshain (Neigh.), G.D.R.	65a	52.31 N	13.27 E
Friemersheim, F.R.G.	63	51.23 N	6.42 E
Friend, Ne. (frĕnd)	123	40.40 N	97.16 W
Friends Colony (Neigh.), India	67d	28.34 N	77.16 E
Friendship International Arpt., Md.	56c	39.11 N	76.40 W
Friendswood, Tx. (frĕnds'wŏŏd)	125a	29.31 N	95.11 W
Friern Barnet (Neigh.), Eng.	62	51.37 N	0.10 W
Fries, Va. (frēz)	127	36.42 N	80.59 W
Friesack, G.D.R. (frē'säk)	157b	52.44 N	12.35 E
Frillendorf (Neigh.), F.R.G.	63	51.28 N	7.05 E
Frio, Cabo (C.), Braz. (kä'bō-frē'ō)	143	22.58 S	42.08 W
Frio R, Tx.	124	29.00 N	99.15 W
Frisian (Is.), Neth. (frē'zhăn)	163	53.30 N	5.20 E
Friuli-Venezia Giulia (Reg.), It.	172	46.20 N	13.20 E
Frobisher B., Can.	97	62.49 N	66.41 W
Frobisher Bay, Can.	97	63.48 N	68.31 W
Frobisher L., Can. (frŏb'ĭsh'ẽr)	100	56.25 N	108.20 W
Frodsham, Eng. (frŏdz'ăm)	156	53.18 N	2.48 W
Frohavet (Sea), Nor.	158	63.49 N	9.12 E
Frohnau (Neigh.), F.R.G.	65a	52.38 N	13.18 E
Frohnhausen (Neigh.), F.R.G.	63	51.27 N	6.58 E
Frome, L., Austl. (frōōm)	216	30.40 S	140.13 E

ăt; finăl; rāte; senåte; ärm; ȧsk; sofȧ; fâre; ch-choose; dh-as th in other; bē; ēvent; bĕt; recĕnt; cratẽr; g-gō; gh-guttural g; bĭt; ĭ-short neutral; rīde; ĸ-guttural k as ch in German ich;

PRONOUNCING INDEX

Frontenac – Gartenstadt 285

PLACE (Pronounciation)	PAGE	Lat. °'	Long. °'
Frontenac, Ks. (frŏn'tē-năk)	123	37.27 N	94.41 W
Frontera, Mex. (frôn-tā'rä)	131	18.34 N	92.38 W
Front Ra., Wy. (frŭnt)	117	42.17 N	105.53 W
Front Royal, Va. (frŭnt)	111	38.55 N	78.10 W
Frosinone, It. (frō-zē-nō'nā)	172	41.38 N	13.22 E
Frostburg, Md. (frôst'bûrg)	111	39.40 N	78.55 W
Fruita, Co. (fro͞ot-á)	121	39.10 N	108.45 W
Frunze, Sov.Un. (fro͞on'zĕ)	180	42.49 N	74.42 E
Fryanovo, Sov.Un. (f'ryä'nô-vô)	182b	56.08 N	38.28 E
Fryazino, Sov.Un. (f'ryä'zĭ-nô)	182b	55.58 N	38.05 E
Frýdlant, Czech. (frēd'länt)	166	50.56 N	15.05 E
Fryerning, Eng.	62	51.41 N	0.22 E
Fucheng, China (fo͞o-chŭŋ)	200	37.53 N	116.08 E
Fuchu, Jap. (fo͞o'cho͞o)	205a	35.41 N	139.29 E
Fuchun (R.), China (fo͞o-cho͞on)	203	29.50 N	120.00 E
Fuego (Vol.), Guat. (fwā'gō)	132	14.29 N	90.52 W
Fuencarral, Sp. (fuān-kär-räl')	171a	40.29 N	3.42 W
Fuensalida, Sp. (fwān-sä-lē'dä)	170	40.04 N	4.15 W
Fuente, Mex. (fwĕ'n-tĕ')	124	28.39 N	100.34 W
Fuente de Cantos, Sp.			
(fwĕn'tā dā kän'tōs)	170	38.15 N	6.18 W
Fuente el Saz, Sp. (fwĕn'tā ĕl säth')	171a	40.39 N	3.30 W
Fuenteobejuna, Sp.	170	38.15 N	5.30 W
Fuentesaúco, Sp. (fwĕn-tā-sä-o͞o'kō)	170	41.18 N	5.25 W
Fuerte Olimpo, Par.			
(fwĕr'tā ō-lēm-pō)	143	21.10 S	57.49 W
Fuerte, Rio del (R.), Mex.			
(rē'ō-dĕl-fo͞o-ĕ'r-tĕ)	128	26.15 N	108.50 W
Fuerteventura I., Can.Is.			
(fwĕr'tā-vĕn-to͞o'rä)	224	28.24 N	13.21 W
Fuhai, China	198	47.01 N	87.07 E
Fuhlenbrock (Neigh.), F.R.G.	63	51.32 N	6.54 E
Fuji, Jap. (jo͞o'jē)	205	35.11 N	138.44 E
Fuji (R.), Jap.	205	35.20 N	138.23 E
Fujian (Prov.), China (fo͞o-jyĕn)	199	25.40 N	117.30 E
Fujidera, Jap.	205	34.34 N	135.37 E
Fujiidera, Jap.	69b	34.34 N	135.36 E
Fujin, China (fo͞o-jyĭn)	199	47.13 N	132.11 E
Fuji-san (Mtn.), Jap. (fo͞o'jē sän)	205	35.23 N	138.44 E
Fujisawa, Jap. (fo͞o'jē-sä'wa)	205a	35.20 N	139.29 E
Fukagawa (Neigh.), Jap.	69a	35.40 N	139.48 E
Fukiai (Neigh.), Jap.	69b	34.42 N	135.12 E
Fukuchiyama, Jap.			
(fo͞o'ko͞o-chē-yä'ma)	205	35.18 N	135.07 E
Fukue (I.), Jap. (fo͞o-ko͞o'ā)	205	32.40 N	129.02 E
Fukui, Jap. (fo͞o'ko͞o-ē)	205	36.05 N	136.14 E
Fukuoka, Jap. (fo͞o'ko͞o-ō'kä)	205	33.35 N	130.23 E
Fukuoka, Jap.	205a	31.52 N	139.31 E
Fukushima, Jap. (fo͞o'ko͞o-shē'mä)	204	37.45 N	140.29 E
Fukushima (Neigh.), Jap.	69b	34.42 N	135.29 E
Fukuyama, Jap. (fo͞o'ko͞o-yä'mä)	205	34.31 N	133.21 E
Fūlādī, Kūh-e (Mtn.), Afg.	193	34.38 N	67.55 E
Fulda R., F.R.G. (fo͝ol'dä)	166	51.05 N	9.40 E
Fulerum (Neigh.), F.R.G.	63	51.26 N	6.57 E
Fuling, China (fo͞o-lĭŋ)	203	29.40 N	107.30 E
Fullerton, Ca. (fo͝ol'ēr-tŭn)	119a	33.53 N	117.56 W
Fullerton, La.	125	31.00 N	93.00 W
Fullerton, Ne.	114	41.21 N	97.59 W
Fulmer, Eng.	62	51.33 N	0.34 W
Fulton, Ky. (fŭl'tŭn)	126	36.30 N	88.53 W
Fulton, Mo.	123	38.51 N	91.56 W
Fulton, NY	111	43.20 N	76.25 W
Fultondale, Al. (fŭl'tŭn-dāl)	112h	33.37 N	86.48 W
Funabashi, Jap. (fo͞o'nä-bä'shē)	205a	35.43 N	139.59 E
Funasaka, Jap.	69b	34.49 N	135.17 E
Funaya, Jap. (fo͞o-nä'yä)	205b	34.45 N	135.52 E
Funchal, Mad.Is. (fo͞on-shäl')	224	32.41 N	16.15 W
Fundación, Col. (fo͞on-dä-syō'n)	142	10.43 N	74.13 W
Fundão, Port. (fo͞on-douɴ')	170	40.08 N	7.32 W
Fundão, Ilha do (I.), Braz.	61c	22.51 S	43.14 W
Funde, India	67e	18.54 N	72.58 E
Fundy, B. of, Can. (fŭn'dĭ)	102	45.00 N	66.00 W
Fundy Natl.Park, Can.	102	45.38 N	65.00 W
Funing, China, (fo͞o-nĭŋ)	200	33.55 N	119.54 E
Funing, China	200	39.55 N	119.16 E
Funing Wan. (B.), China	203	26.48 N	120.35 E
Funtua, Nig.	229	11.31 N	7.17 E
Furancungo, Moz.	231	14.55 S	33.35 E
Furbero, Mex. (fo͞or-bĕ'rô)	131	20.21 N	97.32 W
Furmanov, Sov.Un. (fûr-mä'nôf)	174	57.14 N	41.11 E
Furnas, Reprêsa de (Res.), Braz.	144b	21.00 S	46.00 W
Furneaux Group (Is.), Austl. (fûr'nō)	215	40.15 S	146.27 E
Fürstenfeld, Aus. (für'stĕn-fĕlt)	166	47.02 N	16.03 E
Fürstenfeldbruck, F.R.G.			
(fur'stĕn-fĕld'bro͝ok)	157d	48.11 N	11.16 E
Fürstenwalde, G.D.R.			
(für'stĕn-väl-dĕ)	166	52.21 N	14.04 E
Fürth, F.R.G. (fürt)	166	49.28 N	11.03 E
Furuichi, Jap. (fo͞o'ro͞o-ē'chē)	205b	34.33 N	135.37 E
Fusa, Jap. (fo͞o'sä)	205a	35.52 N	140.08 E
Fusagasugá, Col.			
(fo͞o-sä-gä-so͞o-gá')	142a	4.22 N	74.22 W
Fuse, Jap.	205b	34.40 N	135.43 E
Fushimi, Jap. (fo͞o'shē-mē)	205b	34.57 N	135.47 E
Fushun, China (fo͞o'sho͞on')	202	41.50 N	124.00 E
Fusong, China (fo͞o-soŋ)	202	42.12 N	127.12 E
Futatsubashi, Jap.	69a	35.29 N	139.30 E
Futtsu, Jap. (fo͞o'tso͞o')	205a	35.19 N	139.49 E
Futtsu Misaki (C.), Jap.			
(fo͞ot'tso͞o' mē-sä'kē)	205a	35.19 N	139.46 E
Fuwah, Egypt (fo͞o'wá)	223b	31.13 N	30.35 E
Fuxian, China (fo͞o shyĕn)	200	39.36 N	121.59 E
Fuxin, China (fo͞o-shyĭn)	202	42.05 N	121.40 E
Fuyang, China (fo͞o-yäŋ)	200	32.53 N	115.48 E
Fuyang, China	203	30.10 N	119.58 E
Fuyang (R.), China (fo͞o-yäŋ)	200	36.59 N	114.48 E
Fuyu, China (fo͞o-yo͞o)	202	45.20 N	125.00 E
Fuzhou, China (fo͞o-jō)	203	26.02 N	119.18 E
Fuzhou (R.), China	200	39.38 N	121.43 E
Fuzhoucheng, China (fo͞o-jō-chŭŋ)	200	39.46 N	121.44 E
Fyfield, Eng.	62	51.45 N	0.16 E
Fyn (I.), Den. (fü''n)	164	55.24 N	10.33 E
Fyne, Loch (L.), Scot. (fīn)	162	56.14 N	5.10 W
Fyresvatn (L.), Nor.	164	59.04 N	7.55 E

G

PLACE (Pronounciation)	PAGE	Lat. °'	Long. °'
Gaalkacyo, Som.	223a	7.00 N	47.30 E
Gabela, Ang.	230	10.48 S	14.20 E
Gabés, Tun. (gä'bĕs)	224	33.51 N	10.04 E
Gabés, Golfe de (G.), Tun.	224	32.22 N	10.59 E
Gabil, Chad	229	11.09 N	18.12 E
Gabin, Pol (gōɴ'bĕn)	167	52.23 N	19.47 E
Gabon, Afr. (gá-bôɴ')	222	0.30 S	10.45 E
Gaborone, Bots.	226	24.28 S	25.59 E
Gabriel R., Tx. (gā'brĭ-ĕl)	125	30.38 N	97.15 W
Gabrovo, Bul. (gäb'rô-vō)	173	42.52 N	25.19 E
Gachetá, Col. (gä-chā'tä)	142a	4.50 N	73.36 W
Gachsārān Iran	195	30.12 N	50.47 E
Gacko, Yugo, (gäts'kô)	173	43.10 N	18.34 E
Gadsden, Al. (gădz'dĕn)	126	34.00 N	86.00 W
Gadyach, Sov.Un. (gäd-yäch')	175	50.22 N	33.59 E
Găeşti, Rom. (gă-yĕsh'tĕ)	173	44.43 N	25.21 E
Gaeta, It. (gä-ā'tä)	172	41.18 N	13.34 E
Gaffney, SC (găf'nĭ)	127	35.04 N	81.47 W
Gafsa, Tun. (găf'sä)	224	34.16 N	8.37 E
Gagarin, Sov.Un.	174	55.32 N	34.58 E
Gagnoa, Ivory Coast	228	6.08 N	5.56 W
Gagny, Fr.	64c	48.53 N	2.32 E
Gagrary (I.), Phil. (gä-grä-rē)	207a	13.23 N	123.58 E
Gahmen (Neigh.), F.R.G.	63	51.36 N	7.32 E
Gaillac-sur-Tarn, Fr.			
(gá-yäk'sür-tärn')	154	43.54 N	1.52 E
Gaillard Cut, Pan. (gä-ēl-yä'rd)	128a	9.03 N	79.42 W
Gainesville, Fl. (gānz'vĭl)	127	29.40 N	82.20 W
Gainesville, Ga.	126	34.16 N	83.48 W
Gainesville, Tx.	123	33.38 N	97.08 W
Gainsborough, Eng. (gānz'bŭr-ô)	156	53.23 N	0.46 W
Gairdner, L., Austl. (gârd'nēr)	216	32.20 S	136.30 E
Gaithersburg, Md. (gā'thērs'bûrg)	112e	39.08 N	77.13 W
Gaixian, China (gī-shyĕn)	200	40.25 N	122.20 E
Galana (R.), Ken.	231	3.00 S	39.30 E
Galapagar, Sp. (gä-lä-pä-gär')	171a	40.36 N	4.00 W
Galápagos Is., see Colon, Arch. de			
Galaria (R.), It.	171d	41.58 N	12.21 E
Galashiels, Scot. (găl-á-shēlz)	162	55.40 N	2.57 W
Galata (Neigh.), Tur.	66f	41.01 N	28.58 E
Galata Köprüsü (P. Int.)	66f	41.00 N	28.57 E
Galati, Rom. (gá-lätz'ĭ)	175	45.25 N	28.05 E
Galatina, It. (gä-lä-tē'nä)	173	40.10 N	18.12 E
Galátsion, Grc.	66d	38.01 N	23.45 E
Galaxídhion, Grc.	173	38.26 N	22.22 E
Galdhopiggen (Mtn.), Nor.	164	61.37 N	8.17 E
Galeana, Mex. (gä-lā-ä'nä)	124	24.50 N	100.04 W
Galena, Il. (gá-lē'ná)	115	42.26 N	90.27 W
Galena, In.	113h	38.21 N	85.55 W
Galená, Ks.	123	37.06 N	94.39 W
Galena Pk., Tx.	125a	29.44 N	95.14 W
Galera, Cerro (Mtn.), Pan.			
(sĕ'r-rô-gä-lĕ'rä)	128a	8.55 N	79.38 W
Galeras (Vol.), Col. (gä-lĕ'räs)	142	0.57 N	77.27 W
Gales (R.), Or. (gālz)	118c	45.33 N	123.11 W
Galesburg, Il. (gālz'bûrg)	123	40.56 N	90.21 W
Galesville, Wi. (gālz'vĭl)	115	44.04 N	91.22 W
Galeton, Pa. (gāl'tŭn)	111	41.45 N	77.40 W
Galich, Sov.Un. (gäl'ĭch)	178	58.20 N	42.38 E
Galicia (Reg.), Pol.-Sov.Un.			
(gá-lĭsh'ĭ-á)	167	49.48 N	21.05 E
Galicia (Reg.), Sp. (gä-lē'thyä)	170	43.35 N	8.03 W
Galilee (L.), Austl. (găl'ĭ-lē)	215	22.23 S	145.09 E
Galilee, Sea of, Isr.	191a	32.53 N	35.45 E
Galina Pt., Jam. (gä-lē'nä)	134	18.25 N	76.50 W
Galion, Oh. (găl'ĭ-ŭn)	110	40.45 N	82.50 W
Galisteo, NM (gä-lĭs-tā'ō)	123	35.20 N	106.00 W
Galite, La. I., Alg. (gä-lēt)	159	37.36 N	8.03 E
Gallarate, It. (gäl-lä-rä'tä)	172	45.37 N	8.48 E
Gallardon, Fr. (gä-lär-dôɴ')	169b	48.31 N	1.40 E
Gallatin, Mo. (găl'á-tĭn)	123	39.55 N	93.58 W
Gallatin, Tn.	126	36.23 N	86.28 W
Gallatin R., Mt.	117	45.12 N	111.10 W
Galle, Sri Lanka (gäl)	197	6.13 N	80.10 E
Gállego (R.), Sp. (gäl-yā'gō)	171	42.27 N	0.37 W
Gallinas, Pta. de (Pt.), Col.			
(gä-lyē'näs)	142	12.10 N	72.10 W
Gallipoli, It. (gäl-lē'pô-lē)	173	40.03 N	17.58 E
Gallipoli Pen., Tur.	173	40.23 N	25.10 E
Gallipolis, Oh. (găl-ĭ-pô-lēs)	110	38.50 N	82.10 W
Gallipoli, see Gelibolu			
Gällivare, Swe. (yĕl-ĭ-vär'ĕ)	158	68.06 N	20.29 E
Gallo (R.), Sp. (gäl'yō)	170	40.43 N	1.42 W
Gallup, NM (găl'ŭp)	123	35.30 N	108.45 W
Galnale Doria R., Eth.	225	5.35 N	40.26 E
Galt, Can.	110	43.22 N	80.19 W
Galty Mts., Ire.	162	52.19 N	8.20 W
Galva, Il. (găl'vá)	123	41.11 N	90.02 W
Galveston, Tx. (găl'vĕs-tŭn)	125a	29.18 N	94.48 W
Galveston B, Tx.	125	29.39 N	94.45 W
Galveston I, Tx.	125a	29.12 N	94.53 W
Galvin, Austl.	70b	37.51 S	144.49 E
Galway, Ire.	162	53.16 N	9.05 W
Galway B., Ire. (gôl'wā)	162	53.10 N	9.47 W
Gamba, China (gäm-bä)	196	28.23 N	89.42 E
Gambaga, Ghana (gäm-bä'gä)	228	10.32 N	0.26 W
Gambela, Eth. (găm-bā'lá)	225	8.15 N	34.33 E
Gambia, Afr. (găm'bē-á)	224	13.38 N	19.38 W
Gambia (R.), (Gambie), Afr.	228	13.20 N	15.55 W
Gambie (R.), (Gambia), Afr.	228	13.20 N	15.55 W
Gamboma, Con. (gäm-bō'mä)	230	1.53 S	15.51 E
Gamleby, Swe. (gäm'lĕ-bü)	164	57.54 N	16.20 E
Gan (R.), China (gän)	203	26.50 N	115.00 E
Gandak (R.), India	196	26.37 N	84.22 E
Gander, Can. (găn'dēr)	105	48.57 N	54.34 W
Gander (R.), Can.	105	49.10 N	54.35 W
Gander L., Can.	105	48.55 N	55.40 W
Gandhinagar, India	196	23.30 N	72.47 E
Gandi, Nig.	229	12.55 N	5.49 E
Gandía, Sp. (gän-dē'ä)	171	38.56 N	0.10 W
Gangdisê Shan (Trans Himalayas)(Mts.),			
China (gäŋ-dē-sŭ shän)			
(trăns-hĭ-mä-lá-yás)	198	30.25 N	83.43 E
Ganges (R.), India (găn'jēz)	196	24.32 N	87.58 E
Ganges, Mouths of, India (găn'jēz)	196	21.18 N	88.40 E
Gangi, It. (gän'jē)	172	37.48 N	14.15 E
Gangtok, India	198	27.15 N	88.30 E
Gannan, China (gän-nän)	202	47.50 N	123.30 E
Gannett Pk., Wy. (găn'ĕt)	117	43.10 N	109.38 W
Gano, Oh. (ğ'nô)	113f	39.18 N	84.24 W
Gänserndorf, Aus.	157e	48.21 N	16.43 E
Gansu (Prov.), China (gän-so͞o)	198	38.50 N	101.10 E
Ganwo, Nig.	229	11.13 N	4.42 E
Ganyu, China (gän-yo͞o)	200	34.52 N	119.07 E
Ganzhou, China (gän-jō)	203	25.50 N	114.30 E
Gao, Mali (gä'ō)	228	16.16 N	0.03 W
Gao'an, China (gou-än)	203	28.30 N	115.02 E
Gaobaita, China	67b	39.53 N	116.30 E
Gaobeidian, China	67b	39.54 N	116.33 E
Gaomi, China, (gou-mē)	200	36.23 N	119.46 E
Gaoqiao, China (gou-chyou)	201b	31.21 N	121.35 E
Gaoshun, China (gou-sho͞on)	200	31.22 N	118.50 E
Gaotang, China (gou-täŋ)	200	36.52 N	116.12 E
Gaoyao, China (gou-you)	203	23.08 N	112.25 E
Gaoyi, China (gou-yē)	200	37.37 N	114.39 E
Gaoyou, China (gou-yō)	200	32.46 N	119.26 E
Gaoyou Hu (L.), China (gou-yō ho͞o)	200	32.59 N	119.04 E
Gap, Fr. (gȧp)	169	44.34 N	6.08 E
Gapan, Phil. (gä-pän)	207a	15.18 N	120.56 E
Garachiné, Pan. (gä-rä-chē'nā)	133	8.02 N	78.22 W
Garachiné, Punta (Pt.), Pan.			
(po͞o'n-tä-gä-rä-chē'nā)	133	8.08 N	78.35 W
Garanhuns, Braz. (gä-rän-yo͞oɴsh')	143	8.49 S	36.28 W
Garbagnate Milanese, It.	65c	45.35 N	9.05 E
Garbatella (Neigh.), It.	66c	41.52 N	12.29 E
Garber, Ok. (gär'bēr)	123	36.28 N	97.35 W
Garches, Fr.	64c	48.51 N	2.11 E
Garching, F.R.G. (gär'ĸĕng)	157d	48.15 N	11.39 E
Garcia, Mex. (gär-sē'ä)	124	25.90 N	100.37 W
Garcia de la Cadena, Mex.			
(dĕ-lä-kä-dĕ-nä)	130	21.14 N	103.26 W
Garda, Lago di (L.), It.			
(lä-gō-dē-gär'dä)	172	45.43 N	10.26 E
Gardanne, Fr. (gȧr-dȧn')	168a	43.28 N	5.29 E
Gardelegen, G.D.R. (gär-dē-lā'ghĕn)	166	52.32 N	11.22 E
Garden (I.), Mi. (gär'd'n)	110	45.50 N	85.50 W
Gardena, Ca. (gär-dē'nā)	119a	33.53 N	118.19 W
Garden City, Ks.	122	37.58 N	100.52 W
Garden City, Mi.	113b	42.20 N	83.21 W
Garden City, NY.	55	40.43 N	73.37 W
Garden City Park, NY	55	40.44 N	73.40 W
Garden Grove, Ca. (gär'd'n grōv)	119a	33.47 N	117.56 W
Garden' Reach., India	196a	22.33 N	88.17 E
Garden River, Can.	119k	46.33 N	84.10 W
Gardēz, Afg.	196	33.43 N	69.09 E
Gardiner, Me. (gärd'nēr)	104	44.12 N	69.46 W
Gardiner, Mt.	117	45.03 N	110.43 W
Gardiner, Wa.	118a	48.03 N	122.55 W
Gardiner Dam, Can.	100	51.17 N	106.51 W
Gardner, Ma.	111	42.35 N	72.00 W
Gardner, Can., Can.	98	53.28 N	128.15 W
Gardner Pinnacles (Rocks), Hi.	106b	25.10 N	167.00 W
Gareloi (I.), Ak. (gär-lo͞o-ä')	107a	51.40 N	178.48 W
Garenfeld, F.R.G.	63	51.24 N	7.31 E
Garfield, NJ (gär'fēld)	112a	40.53 N	74.06 W
Garfield, NJ	55	40.53 N	74.07 W
Garfield, Ut.	119b	40.45 N	112.10 W
Garfield Heights, Oh	113d	41.25 N	81.36 W
Gargaliánoi, Grc. (gȧr-gä-lyä'nē)	173	37.07 N	21.50 E
Garges-lès-Gonesse, Fr.	64c	48.58 N	2.25 E
Gargždai, Sov.Un. (gärgzh'dī)	165	55.43 N	20.09 E
Garibaldi, Mt., Can. (gâr-ĭ-băl'dē)	98	49.51 N	123.01 W
Garin, Arg. (gä-rē'n)	144a	34.10 S	58.44 W
Garissa, Ken.	231	0.28 S	39.38 E
Garland, Md.	56c	39.11 N	76.39 W
Garland, Tx. (gär'lănd)	119c	32.55 N	96.39 W
Garland, Ut.	117	41.45 N	112.10 W
Garm, Sov.Un.	180	39.12 N	70.28 E
Garmisch-Partenkirchen, F.R.G.			
(gär'mēsh pär'tĕn-kēr'ĸĕn)	166	47.38 N	11.10 E
Garnett, Ks. (gär'nĕt)	123	38.16 N	95.15 W
Garonne Riviére (R.), Fr. (gá-rôn)	168	44.43 N	0.25 W
Garoua, Cam. (gär'wä)	229	9.18 N	13.24 E
Garrett, In. (găr'ĕt)	110	41.20 N	85.10 W
Garrison, Md.	56c	39.24 N	76.45 W
Garrison, ND	114	47.38 N	101.24 W
Garrison, NY (găr'ĭ-sŭn)	112a	41.23 N	73.57 W
Garrovillas, Sp. (gä-rô-vēl'yäs)	170	39.42 N	6.30 W
Garry (L.), Can. (găr'ĭ)	96	66.16 N	99.23 W
Garsen, Ken.	231	2.16 S	40.07 E
Garson, Can.	104	46.34 N	80.52 W
Garstedt, F.R.G. (gär'shtĕt)	157c	53.40 N	9.58 E
Garston, Eng.	62	51.41 N	0.23 W
Garston (Neigh.), Eng.	64a	53.21 N	2.53 W
Gartenstadt (Neigh.), F.R.G.	63	51.30 N	7.26 E

ng-sing; ŋ-banŋk; ɴ-nasalized n; nŏd; cŏmmit; ōld; ôbey; ôrder; oi-boil; fo͞od; fo͝ot; ou-out; s-soft; sh-dish; th-thin; pūre; ûnite; ûrn; stŭd; circŭs; ü-as in French tu; '-indeterminate vowel.

286 Gartok – Glacier Pk.

PLACE (Pronounciation)	PAGE	Lat. °′	Long. °′
Gartok, China (gär-tŏk′)	196	31.11 N	80.35 E
Garulia, India	196a	22.48 N	88.23 E
Garwolin, Pol. (gär-vō′lēn)	167	51.54 N	21.40 E
Garwood, NJ	55	40.39 N	74.19 W
Gary, In. (gā′rĭ)	113a	41.35 N	87.21 W
Garza-Little Elm Res., Tx.	125	33.16 N	96.54 W
Garzón, Col. (gär-thōn′)	142	2.13 N	75.44 W
Gasan, Phil. (gä-sän′)	207a	13.19 N	121.52 E
Gasan-Kuli, Sov.Un.	179	37.25 N	53.55 E
Gas City, In. (găs)	110	40.30 N	85.40 W
Gascogne, (Reg.), Fr. (gäs-kôn′yĕ)	168	43.45 N	1.49 W
Gasconade (R.), Mo. (găs-kō-nād′)	123	37.46 N	92.15 W
Gascoyne, (R.), Austl. (găs-koin′)	214	25.15 S	117.00 E
Gashland, Mo. (găsh′-lănd)	119f	39.15 N	94.35 W
Gashua, Nig.	229	12.54 N	11.00 E
Gasny, Fr. (gäs-nē′)	169b	49.05 N	1.36 E
Gaspé, Can.	104	48.50 N	64.29 W
Gaspé, Baie de (B.), Can. (gas′pā)(gȧs-pā′)	104	48.35 N	63.45 W
Gaspé, Cape de (C.), Can.	104	48.45 N	63.34 W
Gaspé, Péninsule de (Pen.), Can.	104	48.23 N	65.42 W
Gasper Hernandez, Dom.Rep. (gäs-pär′ ĕr-nän′dāth)	135	19.40 N	70.15 W
Gassaway, WV (găs′ȧ-wā)	110	38.40 N	80.45 W
Gaston, Or. (găs′tŭn)	118c	45.26 N	123.08 W
Gastonia, NC (găs-tō′nĭ-ȧ)	127	35.15 N	81.14 W
Gastre, Arg. (gäs-trĕ)	144	42.12 S	68.50 W
Gata, Cabo de (C.), Sp. (kȧ′bô-dĕ-gä′tä)	170	36.42 N	2.00 W
Gata, Sierra de (Mts.), Sp. (syĕr′rȧ dā gȧ′tä)	170	40.12 N	6.39 W
Gatchina, Sov.Un. (gä-chē′nȧ)	182c	59.33 N	30.08 E
Gateacre (Neigh.), Eng.	64a	53.23 N	2.51 W
Gátes, Akrotírion (C.), Cyprus	191a	34.30 N	33.15 E
Gateshead, Eng. (gāts′hĕd)	162	54.56 N	1.38 W
Gatesville, Mex. (gāts′vĭl)	125	31.26 N	97.34 W
Gateway of India (P. Int.), India	67e	18.55 N	72.50 E
Gatineau, Can. (gȧ′tē-nō)	95c	45.29 N	75.38 W
Gatineau (R.), Can.	95c	45.45 N	75.50 W
Gatineau, Parc de la (Natl. Pk.), Can.	95c	45.32 N	75.53 W
Gâtine, Hauteurs de (Hills), Fr.	168	46.40 N	0.50 W
Gatley, Eng.	64b	53.23 N	2.14 W
Gato Negro, Ven.	61a	10.33 N	66.57 W
Gattendorf, Aus.	157e	48.01 N	17.00 E
Gatun, Pan. (gä-tōōn′)	128a	9.16 N	79.25 W
Gatun (R.), Pan.	128a	9.21 N	79.10 W
Gatún, L., Pan.	128a	9.13 N	79.24 W
Gatun Locks, Pan.	128a	9.16 N	79.27 W
Gauhāti, India	196	26.09 N	91.51 E
Gauja (R.), Sov.Un. (gå′ōō-yå)	165	57.10 N	24.30 E
Gaula (R.), Nor.	164	62.55 N	10.45 E
Gauttier-Gebergte (Mts.), Indon. (gō-tyā′)	207	2.30 S	138.45 E
Gāvanpāda, India	67e	18.57 N	73.01 E
Gávdhos (I.), Grc. (gäv′dôs)	172a	34.48 N	24.08 E
Gávea (Neigh.), Braz.	61c	22.58 S	43.14 W
Gavins Point Dam, Ne. (gă′-vĭns)	114	42.47 N	97.47 W
Gävle, Swe. (yĕv′lĕ)	164	60.40 N	17.07 E
Gavle-bukten (B.), Swe.	164	60.45 N	17.30 E
Gavrilov Posad, Sov.Un. (gȧ′vrē-lôf′ka po-sȧt)	174	56.34 N	40.09 E
Gavrilov-Yam, Sov.Un. (gȧ′vrē-lôf yäm′)	174	57.17 N	39.49 E
Gawler, Austl. (gô′lēr)	216	34.35 S	138.47 E
Gawler Ra., Austl.	216	32.35 S	136.30 E
Gaya, India (gŭ′yä)(gī′ȧ)	196	24.53 N	85.00 E
Gaya, Nig. (gä′yä)	224	11.58 N	9.05 E
Gaylord, Mi. (gā′lôrd)	110	45.00 N	84.35 W
Gayndah, Austl. (gān′dāh)	216	25.43 S	151.33 E
Gaysin, Sov.Un.	175	48.46 N	29.22 E
Gayton, Eng.	64a	53.19 N	3.06 W
Gaza, see Ghazzah			
Gaziantep, Tur. (gä-zē-än′tĕp)	179	37.10 N	37.30 E
Gbarnga, Lib.	228	7.00 N	9.29 W
Gdańsk (Danzig), Pol. (g′dänsk)(dän′tsĕg)	167	54.20 N	18.40 E
Gdov, Sov.Un. (g′dôf′)	174	58.44 N	27.51 E
Gdynia, Pol. (g′dēn′yȧ)	167	54.29 N	18.30 E
Geary, Ok. (gē′rĭ)	122	35.36 N	98.19 W
Géba (R.), Guinea-Bissau	228	12.25 N	14.35 W
Gebo, Wy. (gĕb′ō)	117	43.49 N	108.13 W
Ged, La. (gĕd)	125	30.07 N	93.36 W
Gediz (R.), Tur.	161	38.44 N	28.45 E
Gedney, (I.), Wa. (gĕd-nē)	118a	48.01 N	122.18 W
Gedser, Den.	166	54.35 N	12.08 E
Gee Cross, Eng.	64b	53.26 N	2.04 W
Geel, Bel.	157a	51.09 N	5.01 E
Geelong, Austl. (jē-lông′)	211a	38.06 S	144.13 E
Geelvink-baai (B.), Indon. (gäl′vĭŋk)	207	2.20 S	135.30 E
Gegu, China (gŭ-gōō)	200	39.00 N	117.30 E
Ge Hu (L.), China (gŭ hōō)	200	31.37 N	119.57 E
Geidam, Nig.	229	12.57 N	11.57 E
Geikie Ra., Austl. (gē′kē)	214	17.35 S	125.32 E
Geislingen, F.R.G. (gis′lĭng-ĕn)	166	48.37 N	9.52 E
Geist Res., In. (gēst)	113g	39.57 N	85.59 W
Geita, Tan.	231	2.52 S	32.10 E
Gejiu, China (gŭ-jĭo)	203	23.32 N	102.50 E
Geldermalsen, Neth.	157a	51.53 N	5.18 E
Geldern, F.R.G. (gĕl′dĕrn)	169c	51.31 N	6.20 E
Gelibolu (Gallipoli), Tur. (gäl-lē′pô-lē)(gĕ-lĭb′ô-lōō)	173	40.25 N	26.40 E
Gellep-Stratum (Neigh.), F.R.G.	63	51.20 N	6.41 E
Gellibrand, Pt., Austl.	70b	37.52 S	144.54 E
Gel′myazov, Sov.Un.	175	49.49 N	31.54 E
Gelsenkirchen, F.R.G. (gĕl-zĕn-kĭrk-ĕn)	169c	51.31 N	7.05 E
Gemas, Mala. (jĕm′ȧs)	191b	2.35 N	102.37 E
Gemena, Zaire	230	3.15 N	19.46 E
Gemlik, Tur. (gĕm′lĭk)	179	40.30 N	29.10 E
Genale (R.), Eth.	223	5.00 N	41.15 E
General Alvear, Arg. (gĕ-nĕ-rȧl′ȧl-vĕ-ȧ′r)	141c	36.04 S	60.02 W
General Arenales, Arg. (ä-rĕ-nä′lĕs)	141c	34.19 S	61.16 W
General Belgrano, Arg. (bĕl-grȧ′nô)	141c	35.45 S	58.32 W
General Cepeda, Mex. (sĕ-pĕ′dä)	124	25.24 N	101.29 W
General Conesa, Arg. (kô-nĕ′sä)	141c	36.30 S	57.19 W
General Guido, Arg. (gē′dô)	141c	36.41 S	57.48 W
General Lavalle, Arg. (lȧ-vȧ′l-yĕ)	141c	36.25 S	56.55 W
General Madariaga, Arg. (män-dȧ-rēä′gä)	144	36.59 S	57.14 W
General Pacheco, Arg.	60d	34.28 S	58.40 W
General Paz, Arg. (pȧ′z)	141c	35.30 S	58.20 W
General Pedro Antonio Santios, Mex. (pĕ′drô-än-tô′nyô-sän-tyōs)	130	21.37 N	98.58 W
General Pico, Arg. (pē′kô)	144	36.46 S	63.44 W
General Roca, Arg. (rô-kä)	144	39.01 S	67.31 W
General San Martín, Arg. (sän-mȧr-tē′n)	144a	34.19 S	58.32 W
General San Martín, Arg.	60d	34.35 S	58.30 W
General Sarmiento (San Miguel), Arg.	60d	34.33 S	58.43 W
General Urquiza (Neigh.)	60d	34.34 S	58.29 W
General Viamonte, Arg. (vēȧ′môn-tĕ)	141c	35.01 S	60.59 W
General Zuazua, Mex. (zwä′zwä)	124	25.54 N	100.07 W
Genesee (R.), NY (jĕn-ē-sē′)	111	42.25 N	78.10 W
Geneseo, Il. (jē-nĕs′eō)	110	41.28 N	90.11 W
Geneva, Al. (jē-nē′vȧ)	126	31.03 N	85.50 W
Geneva, Il.	113a	41.53 N	88.18 W
Geneva, Ne.	123	40.32 N	97.37 W
Geneva, NY	111	42.50 N	77.00 W
Geneva, Oh.	110	41.45 N	80.55 W
Geneva, L., Switz.	166	46.28 N	6.30 E
Geneva, see Génève			
Génève (Geneva), Switz. (zhē-nĕv′)	166	46.14 N	6.04 E
Genichesk, Sov.Un. (gā-nē-chyĕsk′)	175	46.11 N	34.47 E
Genil (R.), Sp. (hā-nēl′)	170	37.15 N	4.05 W
Gennebreck, F.R.G.	63	51.19 N	7.12 E
Gennevilliers, Fr.	64c	48.56 N	2.18 E
Genoa, Ne. (jen′ô-ȧ)	123	41.26 N	97.43 W
Genoa City, Wi.	113a	42.31 N	88.19 W
Genoa, see Genova			
Genova (Genoa), It. (jĕn′ō-vä)	172	44.23 N	9.52 E
Genova, Golfodi (G.), It. (gôl-fô-dē-jĕn′ō-vä)	172	44.10 N	8.45 E
Genovesa (I.), Ec. (ē′s-lä-gĕ-nō-vĕ-sä)	128	0.08 N	90.15 W
Gent, Bel.	163	51.05 N	3.40 E
Genthin, G.D.R. (gĕn-tēn′)	166	52.24 N	12.10 E
Gentilly, Fr.	64c	48.49 N	2.21 E
Genzano di Roma, It., (gzhĕnt-zȧ′-nô-dē-rô′mä)	171d	41.43 N	12.49 E
Geographe B., Austl. (jē-ô-graf′)	214	33.00 S	114.00 E
Geographic Chan., Austl. (jēô′gră-fĭk)	214	24.15 S	112.50 E
Geokchay, Sov. Un. (gĕ-ôk′chī)	179	40.40 N	47.40 E
George (L.), Fl. (jôr-ĭj)	127	29.10 N	81.50 W
George (L.), NY (jôrj)	111	43.40 N	73.30 W
George L., Can.-U.S. (jôrg)	119k	46.26 N	84.09 W
George, L., In.	113a	41.31 N	87.17 W
George, L., Ug.	231	0.02 N	30.25 E
Georges (R.), Austl.	211b	33.57 S	151.00 E
Georges Hall, Austl.	70a	33.55 S	150.59 E
George Town, Ba.	135	23.30 N	75.50 W
Georgetown, Can. (jôrg-toun)	95d	43.39 N	79.56 W
Georgetown, Can. (jôr-ĭj-toun)	105	46.11 N	62.32 W
Georgetown, Cayman Is.	134	19.20 N	81.20 W
Georgetown, Ct.	112	41.15 N	73.25 W
Georgetown, De.	111	38.40 N	75.20 W
Georgetown, Guy. (jôrj′toun)	143	7.45 N	58.04 W
Georgetown, Il.	110	40.00 N	87.40 W
Georgetown, Ky.	110	38.10 N	84.35 W
Georgetown, Ma. (jôrg-toun)	105a	42.43 N	71.00 W
Georgetown, Md.	111	39.25 N	75.55 W
Georgetown (Neigh.), DC	56d	38.54 N	77.03 W
George Town, (Pinang), Mala.	206	5.21 N	100.09 E
Georgetown, S.C. (jôr-ĭj-toun)	127	33.22 N	79.17 W
Georgetown, Tx. (jôrg-toun)	125	30.37 N	97.40 W
Georgetown University (P. Int.), DC	56d	38.54 N	77.04 W
George Washington Birthplace Natl. Mon., Va. (jôrj wŏsh′ĭng-tŭn)	111	38.10 N	77.00 W
George Washington Carver Natl. Mon., Mo. (jôrg wăsh-ĭng-tŭn kär′vēr)	123	36.58 N	94.21 W
George West, Tx.	124	28.20 N	98.07 W
Georgia (State), U.S. (jôr′ji-ă)	109	32.40 N	83.50 W
Georgian (S.S.R.), Sov. Un.	176	42.17 N	43.00 E
Georgiana, Al. (jôr-jē-än′ȧ)	126	31.39 N	86.44 W
Georgian B., Can.	102	45.15 N	80.50 W
Georgian Bay Is. Natl. Pk, Can.	102	45.20 N	81.40 W
Georgia, Str. of, Can.	98	49.20 N	124.00 W
Georgia, Str. of, Wa.	118d	48.56 N	123.06 W
Georgina (R.), Austl. (jôr-jē′nȧ)	214	22.00 S	138.15 E
Georgiyevsk, Sov. Un. (gyôr-gyĕfsk′)	179	44.05 N	43.30 E
Gera, G.D.R. (gā′rä)	166	50.52 N	12.06 E
Geral de Goiás, Serra (Mts.), Braz. (zhā-räl′-dĕ-gô-yȧ′s)	161	14.22 S	45.40 W
Geraldton, Austl. (jĕr′ăld-tŭn)	214	28.40 S	114.35 E
Geraldton, Can.	97	49.43 N	87.00 W
Geral, Serra (Mts.), Braz. (sĕr′rȧ zhā-räl′)	144	28.30 S	51.00 W
Gerdview, S. Afr.	71b	26.10 S	28.11 E
Gérgal, Sp. (gĕr′gäl)	170	37.08 N	2.29 E
Gering, Ne. (gē′rĭng)	114	41.49 N	103.41 W
Gerlachovský Štit (Mtn.), Czech.	167	49.12 N	20.08 E
Gerli (Neigh.), Arg.	60d	34.41 S	58.23 W
German Democratic Republic, Eur.	154	53.30 N	12.30 E
Germantown (Neigh.), Pa.	56b	40.03 N	75.11 W
Germantown, Oh. (jûr′mȧn-toun)	110	39.35 N	84.25 W
Germany, Federal Republic of, Eur. (jûr′mȧ-nĭ)	154	51.45 N	8.30 E
Germiston, S. Afr. (jûr′mĭs-tŭn)	227b	26.19 S	28.11 E
Gerona, Phil. (hā-rō′nä)	207a	15.36 N	120.36 E
Gerona, Sp. (hĕ-rô′nä)	170	41.55 N	2.48 E
Gerrards Cross, Eng. (jĕr′ards krŏs)	156b	51.34 N	0.33 W
Gers (R.), Fr. (zhĕr)	171	43.25 N	0.30 E
Gersthofen, F.R.G. (gĕrst-hō′fĕn)	157d	48.26 N	10.54 E
Getafe, Sp. (hā-tä′fā)	171a	40.19 N	3.44 W
Gettysburg, Pa. (gĕt′ĭs-bûrg)	111	39.50 N	77.15 W
Gettysburg, SD	114	45.01 N	99.59 W
Getzville, NY	57a	43.01 N	78.46 W
Gevelsberg, F.R.G. (gĕ-fĕls′bĕrgh)	169c	51.18 N	7.20 E
Geweke (Neigh.), F.R.G.	63	51.22 N	7.25 E
Ghāghra (R.), India	196	27.19 N	81.22 E
Ghana, Afr. (gän′ä)	222	8.00 N	2.00 W
Ghanzi, Bots. (gän′zē)	226	21.30 S	22.00 E
Ghārāpuri, India	67e	18.54 N	72.56 E
Ghardaïa, Alg. (gär-dä′ē-ä)	224	32.29 N	3.38 E
Gharo, Pak.	196	24.50 N	68.35 E
Ghāt, Libya	224	24.52 N	10.16 E
Ghātkopar (Neigh.), India	67e	19.05 N	72.54 E
Ghazāl, Bahr al- (R.), Sud.	225	9.11 N	29.37 E
Ghazal, Bahr el (R.), Chad. (bär ĕl ghä-zäl′)	229	14.30 N	17.00 E
Ghāzipur (Neigh.), India	67d	28.38 N	77.19 E
Ghaznī, Afg. (gŭz′nē)	196	33.43 N	68.18 E
Ghazzah, Gaza Strip (Gaza)	191a	31.30 N	34.29 E
Gheorgheni, Rom.	167	46.48 N	25.30 E
Gherla, Rom. (gĕr′lä)	167	47.01 N	23.55 E
Ghilizane, Alg.	160	35.43 N	0.43 E
Ghonda (Neigh.), India	67d	28.41 N	77.16 E
Ghondi (Neigh.), India	67d	28.42 N	77.16 E
Ghost Lake, Can.	95e	51.15 N	114.46 W
Ghudāmis, Libya	224	30.07 N	9.26 E
Ghūrīān, Afg.	195	34.21 N	61.30 E
Ghushuri, India	67a	22.37 N	88.22 E
Gia-dinh, Viet.	68m	10.48 N	106.42 E
Giannutri, I. di, It. (jän-nōō′trē)	172	42.15 N	11.06 E
Gibara, Cuba (hē-bä′rä)	135	21.05 N	76.10 W
Gibbsboro, NJ	56b	39.50 N	74.58 W
Gibeon, Namibia (gĭb′ē-ŭn)	226	24.45 S	16.40 E
Gibraleón, Sp. (hē-brä-lā-ōn′)	170	37.24 N	7.00 W
Gibraltar, Eur. (hē-bräl-tä′r)	159	36.08 N	5.22 W
Gibraltar, Bay of, Sp.	170	35.04 N	5.10 W
Gibraltar Pt., Can.	54c	43.36 N	79.23 W
Gibraltar, Str. of, Afr.-Eur.	170	35.55 N	5.45 W
Gibson City, Il. (gĭb′sŭn)	110	40.25 N	88.20 W
Gibson Des, Austl.	214	24.45 S	123.15 E
Gibson Island, Md.	112e	39.05 N	76.26 W
Gibson Res., Ok.	123	36.07 N	95.08 W
Giddings, Tx. (gĭd′ĭngz)	125	30.11 N	96.55 W
Gidea Park (Neigh.), Eng.	62	51.35 N	0.12 E
Gideon, Mo. (gĭd′ē-ŭn)	123	36.27 N	89.56 W
Gien, Fr. (zhē-ăN′)	168	47.43 N	2.37 E
Giessen, F.R.G. (gēs′sĕn)	166	50.35 N	8.40 E
Gif-sur-Yvette, Fr.	64c	48.42 N	2.08 E
Gifu, Jap. (gē′fōō)	205	35.25 N	136.45 E
Gig Harbor, Wa. (gĭg)	118a	47.20 N	122.36 W
Giglio, I. di, It. (jēl′yō)	172	42.23 N	10.55 E
Gijón, Sp. (hē-hōn′)	170	43.33 N	5.37 W
Gila (R.), Az. (hē′lȧ)	121	32.41 N	113.50 W
Gila Bend, Az.	121	32.59 N	112.41 W
Gila Bend Ind. Res., Az.	121	33.02 N	112.48 W
Gila Cliffs Dwellings Natl. Mon., NM	121	33.15 N	108.20 W
Gila River Ind. Res., Az.	121	33.11 N	112.38 W
Gilbert, Mn. (gĭl′bērt)	115	47.27 N	92.29 W
Gilbert (R.), Austl. (gĭl-bĕrt)	215	17.15 S	142.09 E
Gilbert, Mt., Can.	98	50.51 N	124.20 W
Gilbert Islands (I.), Kiribati	208	0.30 S	174.00 E
Gilboa, Mt., S. Afr. (gĭl-bôȧ)	227c	29.13 N	30.17 W
Gilford I., Can. (gĭl′fērd)	98	50.45 N	126.25 W
Gilgit, Pak. (gĭl′gĭt)	196	35.58 N	73.48 E
Gil I., Can. (gĭl)	98	53.13 N	129.15 W
Gillen (I.), Austl. (jĭl′ĕn)	214	26.15 S	125.15 E
Gillett, Ar. (jĭ-lĕt′)	123	34.07 N	91.22 W
Gillette, Wyo.	117	44.17 N	105.30 W
Gillingham, Eng. (gĭl′ĭng ăm)	156b	51.23 N	0.33 E
Gilman, Il. (gĭl′măn)	110	40.45 N	87.55 W
Gilman Hot Springs, Ca.	119a	33.49 N	116.57 W
Gilmer, Tx. (gĭl′mēr)	125	32.43 N	94.57 W
Gilmore, Ga. (gĭl′môr)	112c	33.51 N	84.29 W
Gilo (R.), Eth.	225	7.40 N	34.17 E
Gilroy, Ca. (gĭl-roi′)	120	37.00 N	121.34 W
Giluwe, Mt., Pap. N. Gui.	207	6.04 S	144.00 E
Gimli, Can. (gĭm′lē)	101	50.39 N	97.00 W
Gimone (R.), Fr. (zhē-mōn′)	168	43.26 N	0.36 E
Ginir, Eth.	225	7.13 N	40.44 E
Ginosa, It. (jê-nō′zä)	172	40.35 N	16.48 E
Ginza (Neigh.), Jap.	69a	35.40 N	139.47 E
Ginzo, Sp. (hēn-thō′)	170	42.03 N	7.43 W
Gioia del Colle, It. (jô′yä dĕl kôl′lā)	172	40.48 N	16.55 E
Gi-Paraná (R.), Braz. (zhē-pä-rä-nȧ′)	143	9.33 S	61.35 W
Girard, Ks. (jĭ-rärd′)	123	37.30 N	94.50 W
Girardot, Col. (hē-rär-dōt′)	142a	4.19 N	75.47 W
Giresun, Tur. (ghēr′ĕ-sōōn′)	179	40.55 N	38.20 E
Girgaum (Neigh.), India	67e	18.57 N	72.48 E
Giridih, India (jē-rē-dē)	196	24.12 N	81.18 E
Gironde (Est.), Fr. (zhē-rôNd′)	168	45.31 N	1.00 W
Girvan, Scot. (gûr′văn)	162	55.15 N	5.01 W
Gisborne, N.Z. (gĭz′bŭrn)	217	38.40 S	178,08 E
Gisenyi, Rw.	231	1.43 S	29.15 E
Gisors, Fr. (zhē-zôr′)	168	49.19 N	1.47 E
Gitambo, Zaire	230	4.21 N	24.45 E
Gitega, Burundi	226	3.39 S	30.05 E
Giurgui, Rom. (jōōr′jōō)	173	43.53 N	25.58 E
Givet, Fr. (zhē-vĕ′)	168	50.80 N	4.47 E
Givors, Fr. (zhē-vôr′)	168	45.35 N	4.46 E
Giza Pyramids (P. Int.), Egypt	71a	29.59 N	31.08 E
Gizhiga, Sov. Un. (gē′zhi-gȧ)	181	61.59 N	160.46 E
Gizycko, Pol. (gĭ′zhĭ-ko)	167	54.03 N	21.48 E
Gjirokastër, Alb.	173	40.04 N	20.10 E
Gjøvik, Nor. (gyû′vēk)	164	60.47 N	10.36 E
Glabeek-Zuurbemde, Bel.	157a	50.52 N	4.59 E
Glace Bay, Can. (gläs bā)	105	46.12 N	59.57 W
Glacier Bay Natl. Park, Ak. (glā′shēr)	107	58.40 N	136.50 W
Glacier Natl. Park, Can.	99	51.45 N	117.35 W
Glacier Pk., Wa.	116	48.07 N	121.10 W

ăt; fināl; rāte; senāte; ärm; ȧsk; sofȧ; fâre; ch-choose; dh-as th in other; bē; ēvent; bĕt; recĕnt; cratẽr; g-gō; gh-guttural g; bĭt; ĭ-short neutral; rīde; K-guttural k as ch in German ich;

PLACE (Pronunciation)	PAGE	Lat. °′	Long. °′

Glacier Pt., Can. — 118a — 48.24 N — 123.59 W
Gladbeck, F.R.G. (glăd'bĕk) — 169c — 51.35 N — 6.59 E
Gladdeklipkop, S. Afr. — 223d — 24.17 S — 29.36 E
Gladesville, Austl. — 70a — 33.50 S — 151.08 E
Gladstone, Austl. (glăd'stŏn) — 216 — 23.45 S — 150.00 E
Gladstone, Austl. — 216 — 33.15 S — 138.20 E
Gladstone, Mi. — 115 — 45.50 N — 87.04 W
Gladstone, NJ — 112a — 40.43 N — 74.39 W
Gladstone, Or. — 118c — 45.23 N — 122.36 W
Gladwin, Mi. (glăd'wĭn) — 110 — 44.00 N — 84.25 W
Gladwyne, Pa. — 56b — 40.02 N — 75.17 W
Glåma (R), Nor. — 164 — 61.22 N — 11.02 E
Glamoč, Yugo. (gläm'ŏch) — 172 — 44.03 N — 16.51 E
Glarus, Switz. (glä'rōōs) — 166 — 47.02 N — 9.03 E
Glasgow, Ky. — 126 — 37.00 N — 85.55 W
Glasgow, Mo. — 123 — 39.14 N — 92.48 W
Glasgow, Mt. — 117 — 48.14 N — 106.39 W
Glasgow, Scot. (glas'gō) — 162 — 55.54 N — 4.25 W
Glashütte (Neigh.), F.R.G. — 63 — 51.13 N — 6.52 E
Glassmanor, Md. — 56d — 38.49 N — 76.59 W
Glassport, Pa. — 113e — 40.19 N — 79.53 W
Glassport, Pa. — 57b — 40.19 N — 79.54 W
Glauchau, G.D.R. (glou'кou) — 166 — 50.51 N — 12.28 E
Glazov, Sov. Un. (glä'zôf) — 178 — 58.05 N — 52.52 E
Glehn, F.R.G. — 63 — 51.10 N — 6.35 E
Glen (R.), Eng. (glĕn) — 156 — 52.44 N — 0.18 W
Glénan, Iles de (Is.), Fr. (ĕl-dĕ-glä-näɴ') — 168 — 47.43 N — 4.42 W
Glenarden, Md. — 56d — 38.56 N — 76.52 W
Glen Burnie, Md. (bûr'nē) — 112e — 39.10 N — 76.38 W
Glen Canyon Dam, Az. (glĕn kăn'yŭn) — 121 — 36.57 N — 111.25 W
Glen Carbon, Il. (kär'bŏn) — 119e — 38.45 N — 89.59 W
Glencoe, Il. — 113a — 42.08 N — 87.45 W
Glencoe, Mn. (glĕn'kō) — 115 — 44.44 N — 94.07 W
Glencoe, S. Afr. (glĕn-cô) — 227c — 28.14 S — 30.09 E
Glen Cove, NY (kōv) — 112a — 40.51 N — 73.38 W
Glendale, Az. (glĕn'dāl) — 121 — 33.30 N — 112.15 W
Glendale, Ca. — 119a — 34.09 N — 118.15 W
Glendale, Oh. — 113f — 31.16 N — 84.22 W
Glendive, Mt. (glĕn'dīv) — 117 — 47.08 N — 104.41 W
Glendo, Wy. — 117 — 42.32 N — 104.54 W
Glendora, Ca. (glĕn-dō'rá) — 119a — 34.08 N — 117.52 W
Glendora, NJ — 56b — 39.50 N — 75.04 W
Glen Echo, Md. — 56d — 38.58 N — 77.08 W
Glenelg (R.), Austl. — 216 — 37.20 S — 141.30 E
Glen Ellyn, Il. (glĕn ĕl'-lĕn) — 113a — 41.53 N — 88.04 W
Glenfield, Austl. — 70a — 33.58 S — 150.54 E
Glen Head, NY — 55 — 40.50 N — 73.37 W
Glenhuntly, Austl. — 70b — 37.54 S — 145.03 E
Glen Innes, Austl. (ĭn'ĕs) — 216 — 29.45 S — 152.02 E
Glenmore, Md. — 56c — 39.11 N — 76.36 W
Glenns Ferry, Id. (fĕr'ĭ) — 116 — 42.58 N — 115.21 W
Glen Olden, Pa. (ōl'd'n) — 112f — 39.54 N — 75.17 W
Glenomra, La. (glĕn-mō'rá) — 125 — 30.58 N — 92.36 W
Glen Ridge, NJ — 55 — 40.49 N — 74.13 W
Glen Rock, NJ — 55 — 40.58 N — 74.08 W
Glenrock, Wy. (glĕn'rŏk) — 117 — 42.50 N — 105.53 W
Glenroy, Austl. — 70b — 37.42 S — 144.55 E
Glens Falls, NY (glĕnz fôlz) — 111 — 43.20 N — 73.40 W
Glenshaw, Pa. (glĕn'shô) — 113e — 40.33 N — 79.57 W
Glenside, Pa. — 56b — 40.06 N — 75.09 W
Glen Ullin, ND (glĕn'ŭl'ĭn) — 114 — 46.47 N — 101.49 W
Glen Valley, Can. — 118d — 49.09 N — 122.30 W
Glenview, IL (glĕn'vū) — 113a — 42.04 N — 87.48 W
Glenville, Ga. (glĕn'vĭl) — 127 — 31.55 N — 81.56 W
Glen Waverley, Austl. — 70b — 37.53 S — 145.10 E
Glenwood, Ia. — 114 — 41.03 N — 95.44 W
Glenwood, Mn. — 114 — 45.39 N — 95.23 W
Glenwood Landing, NY — 55 — 40.50 N — 73.39 W
Glenwood Springs, Co. — 121 — 39.35 N — 107.20 W
Glienicke, G.D.R. (glē'nĕ-kĕ) — 157b — 52.38 N — 13.19 E
Glinde, F.R.G. (glĕn'dĕ) — 157c — 53.32 N — 10.13 E
Glittertinden (Mtn.), Nor. — 164 — 61.39 N — 8.12 E
Gliwice, Pol. (gwĭ-wĭt'sĕ) — 167 — 50.18 N — 18.40 E
Globe, Az. (glōb) — 121 — 33.20 N — 110.50 W
Globino, Sov. Un. (glŏb'ē-nô) — 175 — 49.22 N — 33.17 E
Głogów, Pol. (gwō'gŏov) — 166 — 51.40 N — 16.04 E
Glommen (R.), Nor. (glôm'ĕn) — 164 — 60.03 N — 11.15 E
Glonn, F.R.G. (glŏnn) — 157d — 47.59 N — 11.52 E
Glorieuses, Iles (Is.), Afr. — 227 — 11.28 S — 47.50 E
Glossop, Eng. (glŏs'ŭp) — 156 — 53.26 N — 1.57 W
Gloster, Ms. — 126 — 31.10 N — 91.00 W
Gloucester, Eng. (glŏs'tēr) — 162 — 51.54 N — 2.11 W
Gloucester, Ma. — 105a — 42.37 N — 70.40 W
Gloucester City, NJ — 112f — 39.53 N — 75.08 W
Glouster, Oh. (glŏs'tēr) — 110 — 39.35 N — 82.05 W
Glover I., Can. (glŏs'tēr) — 105 — 48.44 N — 57.45 W
Gloversville, NY (glŭv'ērz-vĭl) — 111 — 43.05 N — 74.20 W
Glovertown, Can. (glŭv'ēr-toun) — 105 — 48.41 N — 54.02 W
Glubokoye, Sov. Un. (glōō-bô-kô'yĕ) — 174 — 55.08 N — 27.44 E
Glückstadt, F.R.G. (glük-shtät) — 157c — 53.47 N — 9.25 E
Glukhov, Sov. Un. (glōō'кôf) — 175 — 51.42 N — 33.52 E
Glushkovo, Sov. Un. (glōōsh'kô-vô) — 175 — 51.21 N — 34.43 E
Gmünden, Aus. (g'mōōn'dĕn) — 166 — 47.57 N — 13.47 E
Gniezno, Pol. (g'nyăz'nô) — 167 — 52.32 N — 17.34 E
Gnjilane, Yugo. (g'nyē'lä-nĕ) — 173 — 42.28 N — 21.27 E
Goa (Ter.), India (gō'ä) — 197 — 15.45 N — 74.00 E
Goascorán, Hond. (gō-äs'kō-rän') — 132 — 13.37 N — 87.43 W
Goba, Eth. (gō'bä) — 225 — 7.17 N — 39.58 E
Gobabis, Namibia (gō-bä'bĭs) — 226 — 22.25 S — 18.50 E
Gobi or Shamo (Des.), Mong. (gō'be) — 198 — 43.29 N — 103.15 E
Goble, Or. (gō'b'l) — 118c — 46.01 N — 122.53 W
Goch, F.R.G. (gŏк) — 169c — 51.35 N — 6.10 E
Godāvari, India (gō-dä'vŭ-rĕ) — 196 — 17.42 N — 81.15 E
Goddards Soak (Swp.), Austl. (gŏd'ärdz) — 214 — 31.20 S — 123.30 E
Goderich, Can. (gŏd'rĭch) — 110 — 43.45 N — 81.45 W
Godfrey, Il. (gŏd'frē) — 119e — 38.57 N — 90.12 W
Godhavn, Grnld. (gŏdh'hävn) — 94 — 69.15 N — 53.30 W
Gods (R.), Can. (gŏdz) — 101 — 55.17 N — 93.35 W

Gods Lake, Can. — 101 — 54.40 N — 94.09 W
Godthåb, Grnld. (gŏt'hōōb) — 94 — 64.10 N — 51.32 W
Godwin Austen (Mtn.), See K2
Goéland, Lac au (L.), Can. — 103 — 49.47 N — 76.41 W
Goffs, Ca. (gŏfs) — 120 — 34.57 N — 115.06 W
Goff's Oak, Eng. — 62 — 51.43 N — 0.05 W
Gogebic (L.), Mi. (gô-gē'bĭk) — 115 — 46.24 N — 89.25 W
Gogebic Ra, Mi. — 115 — 46.37 N — 89.48 W
Goggingen, F.R.G. (gŭg'gĕn-gĕn) — 157d — 48.21 N — 10.53 E
Gogland (I.), Sov. Un. — 165 — 60.04 N — 26.55 E
Gogonou, Benin — 229 — 10.50 N — 2.50 E
Gogorrón, Mex. (gō-gô-rōn') — 130 — 21.51 N — 100.54 W
Goiânia, Braz. (gô-vä'nyä) — 143 — 16.41 S — 48.57 W
Goiás, Braz. (gô-yá's) — 143 — 15.57 S — 50.10 W
Goiás (State), Braz. — 143 — 12.35 S — 48.38 W
Goirle, Neth. — 157a — 51.31 N — 5.06 E
Gökçeada (I.), Tur. — 173 — 40.10 N — 25.27 E
Göksu (R.), Tur. (gŭk'sōō') — 179 — 36.40 N — 33.30 E
Gol, Nor. (gŭl) — 164 — 60.58 N — 8.54 E
Golabāri, India — 67a — 22.36 N — 88.20 E
Golax, Va. (gō'läks) — 127 — 36.41 N — 80.56 W
Golcar, Eng. (gŏl'kár) — 156 — 53.38 N — 1.52 W
Golconda, Il. (gŏl-kŏn'dá) — 123 — 37.21 N — 88.32 W
Goldap, Pol. (gŏl'däp) — 167 — 54.17 N — 22.17 E
Golden, Can. — 99 — 51.18 N — 116.58 W
Golden, Co. — 122 — 39.44 N — 105.15 W
Goldendale, Wa. (gŏl'dĕn-dāl) — 116 — 45.49 N — 120.48 W
Golden Gate (Str.), Ca. (gŏl'dĕn gāt) — 118b — 37.48 N — 122.32 W
Golden Hinde, Can. (hīnd) — 98 — 49.40 N — 125.45 W
Golden's Bridge, NY — 112a — 41.17 N — 73.41 W
Golden Valley, Mn. — 119g — 44.58 N — 93.23 W
Golders Green (Neigh.), Eng. — 62 — 51.35 N — 0.12 W
Goldfield, Nv. (gōld'fēld) — 120 — 37.42 N — 117.15 W
Gold Hill (Mtn.), Pan. — 128a — 9.03 N — 79.08 W
Gold Mtn., Wa. (gōld) — 118a — 47.33 N — 122.48 W
Goldsboro, NC (gōldz-bûr'ô) — 127 — 35.23 N — 77.59 W
Goldthwaite, Tx. (gōld'thwät) — 124 — 31.27 N — 98.34 W
Goleniów, Pol. (gô-lĕ-nyŭf') — 166 — 53.33 N — 14.51 E
Golets-Purpula, Gol'tsy (Mtn.), Sov. Un. — 181 — 59.08 N — 115.22 E
Golf, Il. — 58a — 42.03 N — 87.48 W
Golfito, C.R. — 133 — 8.40 N — 83.12 W
Golfo Dulce, see Izabal, L.
Golf Park Terrace, Il. — 58a — 42.03 N — 87.51 W
Goliad, Tx. (gō-lī-ăd') — 125 — 28.40 N — 97.12 W
Golo I., Phil. (gō'lō) — 207a — 13.38 N — 120.17 E
Golo (R.), Fr. — 172 — 42.28 N — 9.18 E
Golovchino, Sov. Un. (gō-lôf'chĕ-nō) — 175 — 50.34 N — 35.52 E
Golyamo Konare, Bul. (gō'lä-mô-kō'nä-rĕ) — 173 — 42.16 N — 24.33 E
Golzow, G.D.R. (gŏl'tsōv) — 157b — 52.17 N — 12.36 E
Gombari, Zaire (gōōm-bä-rĕ) — 231 — 2.45 N — 29.00 E
Gombe, Nig. — 229 — 10.19 N — 11.02 E
Gomel', Sov. Un. (Oblast) — 174 — 52.18 N — 29.00 E
Gomel', Sov. Un. (go'mĕl') — 174 — 52.20 N — 31.03 E
Gomera I., Can. Is. (gô-mā'rä) — 224 — 28.00 N — 18.01 W
Gomez Farias, Mex. (gō'mäz fä-rē'äs) — 124 — 24.59 N — 101.02 W
Gómez Palacio, Mex. (pä-lä'syō) — 124 — 25.35 N — 103.30 W
Gonaïves, Hai. (gō-nä-ēv') — 135 — 19.25 N — 72.45 W
Gonaïves, Golfe des (G.), Hai. (gō-nä-ēv') — 135 — 19.20 N — 73.20 W
Gonâve, Ile De La (I.), Hai. (gō-näv') — 135 — 18.50 N — 73.30 W
Gonda, India — 196 — 27.13 N — 82.00 E
Gondal, India — 196 — 22.02 N — 70.47 E
Gonder, Eth. — 225 — 12.39 N — 37.30 E
Gonesse, Fr. (gō-nĕs') — 169b — 48.59 N — 2.28 E
Gongga Shan (Mtn.), China (gŏŋ-gä shän) — 198 — 29.16 N — 101.46 E
Goniri, Nig. — 229 — 11.30 N — 12.20 E
Gonor, Can. (gō'nŏr) — 95f — 50.04 N — 96.57 W
Gonō (R.), Jap. (gō'nō) — 205 — 35.00 N — 132.25 E
Gonubie, S. Afr. (gôn'ōō-bē) — 227c — 32.56 S — 28.02 E
Gonzales, Mex. (gôn-zä'lēs) — 130 — 22.47 N — 98.26 W
Gonzales, Tx. (gôn-zä'lēz) — 125 — 29.31 N — 97.25 W
González Catán, Arg. (gôn-zä'lēz-kä-tä'n) — 144a — 34.31 S — 58.39 W
Good Hope, C. of, S. Afr. (kăp ov gŏŏd hŏp) — 226a — 34.21 S — 18.29 E
Good Hope Mtn., Can. — 98 — 51.09 N — 124.10 W
Gooding, Id. (gŏŏd'ĭng) — 116 — 42.55 N — 114.43 W
Goodland, Ind. (gŏŏd'lănd) — 110 — 40.50 N — 87.15 W
Goodland, Ks. — 122 — 39.19 N — 101.43 W
Goodwood, S. Afr. (gŏŏd'wŏŏd) — 226a — 33.54 S — 18.33 E
Goole, Eng. (gōōl) — 156 — 53.42 N — 0.52 W
Goose (R.), ND — 114 — 47.40 N — 97.41 W
Goose Bay, Can. — 97 — 53.19 N — 60.33 W
Gooseberry Cr., Wy. (gōōs-bĕr'ĭ) — 117 — 44.04 N — 108.35 W
Goose Cr., Id. (gōōs) — 117 — 42.07 N — 113.53 W
Goose L., Ca. — 116 — 41.56 N — 120.35 W
Gorakhpur, India (gō'rŭk-pōōr) — 196 — 26.45 N — 82.39 E
Gorda Cay, Ba. (gôr'dä) — 134 — 26.05 N — 77.30 W
Gorda, Punta (Pt.), Cuba (pōō'n-tä-gôr-dä) — 134 — 22.25 N — 82.10 W
Gordon, Can. (gôr'dŭn) — 95f — 50.00 N — 97.20 W
Gordon, Ne. — 114 — 42.47 N — 102.14 W
Gordons Corner, Md. — 56d — 39.50 N — 76.57 W
Gore, Eth. (gō'rĕ) — 225 — 8.12 N — 35.34 E
Gore Hill, Austl. — 70a — 33.49 S — 151.11 E
Gorgān, Iran — 192 — 36.44 N — 54.30 E
Gorgona, Isola di, It. (gôr-gō'nä) — 172 — 43.27 N — 9.55 E
Gori, Sov. Un. — 179 — 42.00 N — 44.08 E
Gorinchem, Neth. (gō'rĭn-кĕm) — 157a — 51.50 N — 4.59 E
Goring, Eng. (gō'rĭng) — 156b — 51.30 N — 1.08 W
Gorizia, It. (gō-rē'tsē-ä) — 172 — 45.56 N — 13.40 E
Gor'kiy, Sov. Un. (gôr'kē) — 178 — 56.15 N — 44.05 E
Gor'kovskoye, Sov. Un. — 178 — 56.38 N — 43.40 E
Gor'kovskoye Vdkhr. (Res.), Sov. Un. — 174 — 57.38 N — 41.18 E
Gorlice, Pol. (gôr-lē'tsĕ) — 167 — 49.38 N — 21.11 E
Görlitz, G.D.R. (gûr'lĭts) — 166 — 51.10 N — 15.01 E
Gorlovka, Sov. Un. (gôr'lôf-kà) — 175 — 48.17 N — 38.03 E

Gorman, Tx. (gôr'măn) — 124 — 32.13 N — 98.40 W
Gorna Oryakhovitsa, Bul. (gôr'nä-ôr-yĕk'ô-vē-tsä) — 173 — 43.08 N — 25.40 E
Gornji Milanovac, Yugo (gôr'nyē-mē'lä-nō-väts) — 173 — 44.02 N — 20.29 E
Gorno-Altay Aut. Oblast, Sov. Un. — 180 — 51.00 N — 86.00 E
Gorno-Altaysk, Sov. Un. (gôr'nŭ'ŭl-tīsk') — 180 — 52.28 N — 82.45 E
Gorodënka, Sov. Un. (gô-rô-dĕŋ'kä) — 167 — 48.40 N — 25.30 E
Gorodets (Res.), Sov. Un. — 178 — 57.00 N — 43.55 E
Gorodishche, Sov. Un. (gô-rô'dĭsh-chĕ) — 182a — 57.57 N — 57.03 E
Gorodnya, Sov. Un. (gô-rŏd''nyä) — 175 — 51.54 N — 31.31 E
Gorodok, Sov. Un. (gô-rŏ-dŏk') — 167 — 49.37 N — 23.40 E
Gorodok, Sov. Un. — 174 — 55.27 N — 29.58 E
Gorodok, Sov. Un. — 180 — 50.30 N — 103.58 E
Gorontalo, Indon. (gō-rŏn-tä'lo) — 206 — 0.40 N — 123.04 E
Gorton (Neigh.), Eng. — 64b — 53.27 N — 2.10 W
Goryn' R., Sov. Un. (gō'rĕn') — 167 — 50.55 N — 26.07 E
Gorzow Wielkopolski, Pol. (gô-zhōōv vyĕl-ko-pōl'skĕ) — 166 — 53.44 N — 15.15 E
Gosely, Ind. — 156 — 52.33 N — 2.10 W
Gosen, G.D.R. — 65a — 52.24 N — 13.43 E
Goshen, In. (gō'shĕn) — 110 — 41.35 N — 85.50 W
Goshen, Ky. — 113h — 38.24 N — 85.34 W
Goshen, NY — 112a — 41.24 N — 74.19 W
Goshen, Oh. — 113f — 39.14 N — 84.09 W
Goshute Ind. Res., Ut. (gō-shōōt') — 121 — 39.50 N — 114.00 W
Goslar, F.R.G. (gôs'lär) — 166 — 51.55 N — 10.25 E
Gospa (R.), Ven. (gôs-pä) — 143b — 9.43 N — 64.23 W
Gospić, Yugo. (gôs'pĭch) — 172 — 44.31 N — 15.03 E
Gostivar, Yugo. (gôs'tē-vär) — 173 — 41.46 N — 20.58 E
Gostynin, Pol. (gôs-tē'nĭn) — 167 — 52.24 N — 19.30 E
Göta (R.), Swe. (gŏĕtä) — 164 — 58.11 N — 12.03 E
Göta Kanal (Can.), Swe. (yŭ'tá) — 164 — 58.35 N — 15.24 E
Gotanno (Neigh.), Jap. — 69a — 35.46 N — 139.49 E
Göteborg, Swe. (yŭ'tĕ-bôrgh) — 164 — 57.39 N — 11.56 E
Gotel Mts., Cam.-Nig. — 229 — 7.05 N — 11.20 E
Gotera, Sal. (gō-tä'rä) — 132 — 13.41 N — 88.06 W
Gotha, G.D.R. (gō'tá) — 166 — 50.47 N — 10.43 E
Gothenburg, Ne. (gŏth'ĕn-bûrg) — 122 — 40.57 N — 100.08 W
Gotland (I.), Swe. — 164 — 57.30 N — 17.35 E
Gotō-Rettō (Is.), Jap. (gō'tō rĕt'tō) — 205 — 33.06 N — 128.54 E
Gotska Sandön (I.), Swe. — 165 — 58.24 N — 19.15 E
Götterswickerhamm, F.R.G. — 63 — 51.35 N — 6.40 E
Göttin, G.D.R. — 65a — 52.27 N — 12.54 E
Göttingen, F.R.G. (gŭt'ĭng-ĕn) — 166 — 51.32 N — 9.57 E
Gouda, Neth. (gou'dä) — 157a — 52.00 N — 4.42 E
Gough (I.), Atl. O. (gŏf) — 232 — 40.00 S — 10.00 W
Gouin, Rés, Can. — 95 — 48.35 N — 74.15 W
Goukou, China (gō-kō) — 202 — 48.45 N — 121.42 E
Goulais (R.), Can. — 102 — 46.45 N — 84.10 W
Goulburn, Austl. (gŏl'bûrn) — 216 — 34.47 S — 149.40 E
Goumbati (Mtn.), Senegal — 228 — 13.08 N — 12.06 W
Goumbou, Mali (gōōm-bōō') — 228 — 14.59 N — 7.27 W
Gouna, Cam. — 229 — 8.32 N — 13.34 E
Goundam, Mali (gōōn-däɴ') — 228 — 16.29 N — 3.37 W
Gouré, Niger (gōō-ra') — 224 — 13.53 N — 10.44 E
Gournay-sur-Marne, Fr. — 64c — 48.52 N — 2.34 E
Goussainville, Fr. — 64c — 49.01 N — 2.28 E
Gouverneur, NY (gŭv-ēr-nōōr') — 111 — 44.20 N — 75.25 W
Go-vap, Viet. — 68m — 10.49 N — 106.42 E
Govenlock, Can. (gŭven-lŏk) — 100 — 49.15 N — 109.48 W
Governador Ilhado (I.), Braz. (gō-vĕr-nä-dô-'r-ē-lä'dō) — 144b — 22.48 S — 43.13 W
Governador Portela, Braz. (pōr-tĕ'lá) — 144b — 22.28 S — 43.30 W
Governador Valadares, Braz. (vä-lä-dä'rĕs) — 143 — 18.47 S — 41.45 W
Governor's Harbour, Ba. — 135 — 25.15 N — 76.15 W
Gowanda, NY (gō-wŏn'dá) — 111 — 42.30 N — 78.55 W
Goya, Arg. (gō'yä) — 144 — 29.06 S — 59.12 W
Goyt (R.), Eng. (goit) — 156 — 53.19 N — 2.03 W
Graaff-Reinet, S. Afr. (gräf'rĭ'nĕt) — 226 — 32.10 S — 24.40 E
Gracac, Yugo. (grä'chäts) — 172 — 44.16 N — 15.50 E
Gračanica, Yugo. — 173 — 44.42 N — 18.19 E
Graceville, Fl. (grās'vĭl) — 126 — 30.57 N — 85.30 W
Graceville, Mn. — 114 — 45.33 N — 96.25 W
Gracias, Hond. (grä'sĕ-äs) — 132 — 14.35 N — 88.37 W
Gracias a Dios, Cabo (C.) (kä'bô-grä-syäs-ä-dyô's) — 133 — 15.00 N — 83.13 W
Graciosa I., Açores (grä-syŏ'sä) — 224a — 39.07 N — 27.30 W
Gradačac, Yugo. (grä-dä'chats) — 173 — 44.50 N — 18.28 E
Gradizhsk, Sov. Un. — 175 — 49.12 N — 33.06 E
Grado, Sp. (grä'dō) — 170 — 43.24 N — 6.04 W
Gräfelging, F.R.G. (grä'fĕl-fĕng) — 157d — 48.07 N — 11.27 E
Grafenberg (Neigh.), F.R.G. — 63 — 51.14 N — 6.50 E
Grafing bei München, F.R.G. (grä'fĕng) — 157d — 48.03 N — 11.58 E
Grafton, Austl. (graf'tŭn) — 216 — 29.38 S — 153.05 E
Grafton, Il. — 119e — 38.58 N — 90.26 W
Grafton, Ma. — 105a — 42.13 N — 71.41 W
Grafton, ND — 114 — 48.24 N — 97.25 W
Grafton, Oh. — 113d — 41.16 N — 82.04 W
Grafton, WV — 111 — 39.20 N — 80.00 W
Gragnano, It. (grän-yä'nō) — 171c — 40.27 N — 14.32 E
Graham, NC (grā'ám) — 127 — 36.03 N — 79.23 W
Graham, Tx. — 122 — 33.07 N — 98.34 W
Graham, Wa. — 118a — 47.03 N — 122.18 W
Graham (I.), Can. — 96 — 53.50 N — 132.40 W
Grahamstown, S. Afr. (grä'áms'toun) — 227c — 33.19 S — 26.33 E
Grajaú, Braz. (grä-zhä-ōō') — 143 — 5.59 S — 46.03 W
Grajaú (R.), Braz. — 143 — 4.24 S — 46.04 W
Grajewo, Pol. (grä-yă'vo) — 167 — 53.38 N — 22.28 E
Gramada, Braz. (grä-zhä'dä) — 173 — 43.46 N — 22.41 E
Grama, Serra de (Mtn.), Braz. (sĕ'r-rä-dĕ-grä'mä) — 141a — 23.42 S — 42.28 W
Gramatneusiedl, Aus. — 157e — 48.02 N — 16.29 E
Grammichele, It. (gräm-mē-kĕ'lä) — 172 — 37.15 N — 14.40 E
Grampian Mts., Scot. (grăm'pĭ-án) — 162 — 56.30 N — 4.55 W
Granada, Nic. (grä-nä'dhä) — 132 — 11.55 N — 85.58 W

288 Granada – Grenora

PLACE (Pronounciation)	PAGE	Lat. °′	Long. °′
Granada, Sp. (grä-nä'dä)	170	37.13 N	3.37 W
Gran Bajo (Pln.), Arg. (grán'bä'kō)	144	47.35 S	68.45 W
Granbury, Tx. (grăn'bĕr-ĭ)	125	32.26 N	97.45 W
Granby, Can. (grăn'bĭ)	111	45.30 N	72.40 W
Granby (L.), Co.	122	40.07 N	105.40 W
Granby, Mo.	123	36.54 N	94.15 W
Gran Canal del Desagüe (Can.), Mex.	60a	19.29 N	99.05 W
Gran Canaria I., Can. Is. (grän'kä-nä'rē-ä)	224	27.39 N	15.39 W
Gran Chaco (Reg.), Arg.-Par. (grän'chä'kō)	144	25.30 S	62.15 W
Grand (I.), Mi.	115	46.37 N	86.38 W
Grand (L.), Can.	104	45.17 N	67.42 W
Grand (L.), Can.	104	66.15 N	45.59 W
Grand (R.), Can.	103	43.45 N	80.20 W
Grand (R.), Mi.	110	42.58 N	85.13 W
Grand (R.), Mo.	123	39.50 N	93.52 W
Grand (R.), North Fork, SD	114	45.52 N	102.49 W
Grand (R.), SD	114	45.40 N	101.55 W
Grand (R.), South Fork, SD	114	45.38 N	102.56 W
Grand Bahama (I.), Ba.	134	26.35 N	78.30 W
Grand Bank, Can. (grănd băngk)	105	47.06 N	55.47 W
Grand Bassam, Ivory Coast (grän bá-sän')	228	5.12 N	3.44 W
Grand Bourg, Guad. (grän bōōr')	133b	15.54 N	61.20 W
Grand Caicos (I.), Turks & Caicos Is. (grănd kä-ē'kōs)	135	21.45 N	71.50 W
Grand Canal, Ire.	162	53.21 N	7.15 W
Grand Canal, see Da Yunhe			
Grand Canyon, Az. (grănd kăn yŭn)	121	36.05 N	112.10 W
Grand Canyon (canyon), Az.	121	35.50 N	113.16 W
Grand Canyon Natl. Park, Az.	121	36.15 N	112.20 W
Grand Cayman (I.), Cayman Is. (kā'măn)	134	19.15 N	81.15 W
Grand Coulee Dam, Wa. (kōō'lē)	116	47.58 N	119.28 W
Grande (R.), Chili	141b	35.25 S	70.14 W
Grande, (R.), Mex.	131	17.37 N	96.41 W
Grande (R.), Ur.	141c	33.19 S	57.15 W
Grande, Bahía (B.), Arg. (bä-ē'ä-grán'dē)	144	50.45 S	68.00 W
Grande, Boca (Est.), Ven. (bō'kä-grä'n-dĕ)	143	8.46 N	60.17 W
Grande Cayemite, Ile (I.), Hai.	135	18.45 N	73.45 W
Grande, Ciri (R.), Pan. (sē'rē-grá'n'dĕ)	128a	8.55 N	80.04 W
Grande Comore, Comoros (grä'n-dĕ-kô-mô-rĕ)	227	11.44 S	42.38 E
Grande, Cuchilla (Mts.), Ur. (kōō-chē'l-yä)	144	33.00 S	55.15 W
Grande de Otoro, Hond. (grä'da dā ô-tō'rō)	132	14.42 N	88.21 W
Grande, Ilha (I.), Braz. (grän'dĕ)	141a	23.11 S	44.14 W
Grande Pointe, Can. (grănd point')	95f	49.47 N	97.03 W
Grande Prairie, Can. (prâr'ĭ)	99	55.10 N	118.48 W
Grande R., Nic. (grän'dĕ)	133	13.01 N	84.21 W
Grand Erg Occidental (Dunes), Alg.	224	29.37 N	6.04 E
Grande, Rio (R.), Bol.	142	16.49 S	63.19 W
Grande, Rio (R.), (Bravo del Norte, Rio), Mex.-U.S. (grän'dā)	108	26.50 N	99.10 W
Grande, Rio (R.), Braz.	143	19.48 S	49.54 W
Grande Rivière du Nord, Hai. (rē-vyâr' dü nôr')	135	19.35 N	72.10 W
Grande Ronde R., Or. (rônd')	116	45.32 N	117.52 W
Grande, Salinas (F.), Arg. (sä-lē'näs)	144	29.45 S	65.00 W
Grande, Salto (Falls), Braz. (säl-tô)	143	16.18 S	39.38 W
Gran Desierto (Des.), Mex. (grän-dĕ-syĕ'r-tô)	120	32.14 N	114.28 W
Grande Soufriere Vol., Guad. (sōō-frē-ăr')	133b	16.06 N	61.42 W
Grande Terre I., Guad. (târ')	133b	16.28 N	61.13 W
Grande Vigie, Pointe de la (Pt.), Guad. (gränd vē-gē')	133b	16.32 N	61.25 W
Grand Falls, Can. (fôlz)	105	48.56 N	55.40 W
Grandfather, Mt., NC (grănd-fä-thĕr)	101	36.07 N	81.48 W
Grandfield, Ok. (grănd'fēld)	122	34.13 N	98.39 W
Grand Forks, Can. (fôrks)	99	49.02 N	118.27 W
Grand Forks, ND	114	47.55 N	97.05 W
Grand Haven, Mi (hā'v'n)	110	43.05 N	86.15 W
Grand I, NY	113c	43.03 N	78.58 W
Grand Island, Ne. (ī'lănd)	122	40.56 N	98.20 W
Grand Island, NY	57a	42.49 N	78.58 W
Grand Junction, Co. (jŭngk'shŭn)	121	39.05 N	108.35 W
Grand L., Can. (lāk)	105	49.00 N	57.10 W
Grand L., La.	125	29.57 N	91.25 W
Grand L., Mn.	119h	46.54 N	92.26 W
Grand Ledge, Mi. (lĕj)	110	42.45 N	84.50 W
Grand Lieu, L. de, Fr. (grän'-lyû)	168	46.00 N	1.45 W
Grand Manan (I.), Can. (mā-năn)	104	44.40 N	66.50 W
Grand Mère, Can. (grän mâr')	103	46.36 N	72.43 W
Grand Morin (R.), Fr. (mô-ran')	169b	48.23 N	2.19 E
Grândola, Port. (grän'dô-lá)	170	38.10 N	8.36 W
Grand Portage Ind. Res., Mn. (pōr'tĭj)	115	47.54 N	89.34 W
Grand Portage Natl. Mon., Mi.	115	47.59 N	89.47 W
Grand Prairie, Tx. (prĕ'rē)	119c	32.45 N	97.00 W
Grand Quivira Natl. Mon., NM (kē-vē'rá)	121	34.10 N	106.05 W
Grand Rapids, Can.	101	53.08 N	99.20 W
Grand Rapids, Mi. (răp'ĭdz)	110	43.00 N	85.45 W
Grand Rapids, Mn.	115	47.16 N	93.33 W
Grand Rapids Forebay (Res.), Can.	101	53.10 N	100.00 W
Grand-Riviere, Can.	104	48.26 N	64.30 W
Grand Teton Mt., Wy.	117	43.46 N	110.50 W
Grand Teton Natl. Park, Wy. (tē'tŏn)	117	43.54 N	110.15 W
Grand Traverse B., Mi. (trăv'ĕrs)	110	45.00 N	85.30 W
Grand Turk (I.), Turks & Caicos Is.	125	21.30 N	71.10 W
Grand Turk, Turks & Caicos Is. (tûrk)	135	21.30 N	71.10 W
Grandview, Mo. (grănd'vyōō)	119f	38.53 N	94.32 W
Grand Wash (R.), Az. (wŏsh)	121	36.20 N	113.52 W
Grandyle, NY	57a	43.00 N	78.57 W
Grange Hill, Eng.	62	51.37 N	0.05 E
Granger, Wy. (grān'jĕr)	117	41.37 N	109.58 W
Grangeville, Id. (grānj'vĭl)	116	45.56 N	116.08 W
Granite, Md.	56c	39.21 N	76.51 W
Granite City, Il. (grăn'ĭt sĭt'ĭ)	119e	38.42 N	90.09 W
Granite Falls, Mn. (fôlz)	114	44.46 N	95.34 W
Granite Falls, NC	127	35.49 N	81.25 W
Granite Falls, Wa.	118a	48.05 N	121.59 W
Granite L., Can.	105	48.01 N	57.00 W
Granite Pk., Mt.	117	45.13 N	109.48 W
Graniteville, SC (grăn'ĭt-vĭl)	127	33.35 N	81.50 W
Granito, Braz. (grä-nē'tō)	143	7.39 S	39.34 W
Granma (Prov.), Cuba	134	20.10 N	76.50 W
Gränna, Swe. (grĕn'à)	164	58.02 N	14.38 E
Granollers, Sp. (grä-nôl-yĕrs')	171e	41.36 N	2.19 E
Gran Pajonal (Marsh), Peru (grä'n-pä-kô-näl')	142	11.14 S	71.45 W
Gran Piedra (Mtn.), Cuba (grän-pyĕ'drä)	125	20.00 N	75.40 W
Grantham, Eng. (grăn'tām)	156	52.54 N	0.38 W
Grant Park, Il. (grănt pärk)	113a	41.14 N	87.39 W
Grant Park (P. Int.), Il.	58a	41.52 N	87.37 W
Grants Pass, Or. (grănts pás)	116	42.26 N	123.20 W
Granville, Austl.	70a	33.50 S	151.01 E
Granville, Fr. (grän-vēl')	168	48.52 N	1.35 W
Granville (L.), Can.	101	56.18 N	100.30 W
Granville, NY (grăn'vĭl)	111	43.25 N	73.15 W
Grão Mogol, Braz. (groun' mōō-gôl')	143	16.34 S	42.35 W
Grapevine, Tx. (grāp'vīn)	119c	32.56 N	97.05 W
Gräso (I.), Swe.	164	60.30 N	18.35 E
Grass (R.), NY	111	44.45 N	75.10 W
Grass Cay (I.), Vir. Is.(U.S.A.)	129c	18.22 N	64.50 W
Grasse, Fr. (gräs)	169	43.39 N	6.57 E
Grassendale (Neigh.), Eng.	64a	53.21 N	2.54 W
Grass Mtn., Wa. (grás)	118a	47.13 N	121.48 W
Grates Pt., Can. (grāts)	105	48.09 N	52.57 W
Gravelbourg, Can. (grăv'ĕl-bôrg)	100	49.53 N	106.34 W
Gravesend, Eng. (grāvz'ĕnd')	156b	51.26 N	0.22 E
Gravina, It. (grä-vē'nä)	172	40.48 N	16.27 E
Gravois, Pte., Hai. (grà-vwä')	135	18.00 N	74.20 W
Gray, Fr. (grâ)	169	47.26 N	5.35 E
Grayling, Mi. (grā'lĭng)	110	44.40 N	84.40 W
Grays, Eng.	62	51.29 N	0.20 E
Grayslake, Il. (grāz'lāk)	113a	42.20 N	88.20 W
Grays Pk., Co. (grāz)	122	39.29 N	105.52 W
Grayvoron, Sov. Un. (grá-ē'vô-rôn)	175	50.28 N	35.41 E
Graz, Aus. (gräts)	166	47.05 N	15.26 E
Greasby, Eng.	64a	53.23 N	3.07 W
Great Abaco (I.), Ba. (ä'bä-kō)	134	26.30 N	77.05 W
Great Altcar, Eng.	64a	53.33 N	3.01 W
Great Artesian Basin (Reg.), Austl. (är-tēzh-ăn bā-sĭn)	215	23.16 S	143.37 E
Great Australian Bight, Austl. (ôs-trā'lĭ-ăn bĭt)	214	33.30 S	127.00 E
Great Bahama Bk., Ba (bá-hā'má)	134	25.00 N	78.50 W
Great Barrier (I.), N.Z. (băr'ĭ-ĕr)	217	37.00 S	175.31 E
Great Barrier Rf., Austl. (bá-rĭ-ĕr rēf)	215	16.43 S	146.34 E
Great Basin, U.S. (grāt bā's'n)	108	40.08 N	117.10 W
Great Bear L., Can. (bâr)	96	66.10 N	119.53 W
Great Bend, Ks. (bĕnd)	122	38.41 N	98.46 W
Great Bitter, see Al Buḩayrah al Murrah al Kubrā			
Great Blasket I., Ire. (blăs'kĕt)	162	52.05 N	10.55 W
Great Bookham, Eng.	62	51.16 N	0.22 W
Great Britain, U.K. (brĭt'n)	154	56.53 N	0.02 W
Great Burstead, Eng.	62	51.36 N	0.25 E
Great Corn I., Nic.	133	12.10 N	82.54 W
Great Crosby, Eng.	64a	53.29 N	3.01 W
Great Divide Basin, Wyo. (dĭ-vīd' bā's'n)	117	42.10 N	108.10 W
Great Dividing Ra., Austl. (dĭ-vī-dĭng rānj)	215	35.16 S	146.38 E
Great Duck (I.), Can. (dŭk)	102	45.40 N	83.22 W
Greater Khingan Range (Da Hinggan Ling), China (dä hĭŋ-gän lĭŋ)	202	46.30 N	120.00 E
Greater Leech Ind. Res., Mn. (grāt'ĕr lēch)	115	47.39 N	94.27 W
Greater Manchester (Co.), Eng.	156	53.34 N	2.41 W
Greater Sunda Is., Indon.	206	4.00 S	108.00 E
Great Exuma (I.), Ba. (ĕk-sōō'mä)	135	23.35 N	76.00 W
Great Falls, Mt. (fôlz)	117	47.30 N	111.15 W
Great Falls, SC	127	34.32 N	80.53 W
Great Falls, Va.	56d	39.00 N	77.17 W
Great Guana Cay (I.), Ba. (gwä'nä)	135	24.00 N	76.20 W
Great Harbor Cay (I.), Ba. (kē)	134	25.45 N	77.50 W
Great Inagua (I.), Ba. (ē-nä'gwä)	135	21.00 N	73.15 W
Great Indian Des., India	196	27.35 N	71.37 E
Great Isaac (I.), Ba. (ī'zák)	134	26.05 N	79.05 W
Great Karroo (Mts.), S. Afr. (grāt ká'rōō)	226	32.45 S	22.00 E
Great Kills (Neigh.), NY	55	40.33 N	74.10 W
Great Namaland (Reg.), Namibia	226	25.45 S	16.15 E
Great Neck, NY (nĕk)	112a	40.48 N	73.44 W
Great Nicobar I., Andaman & Nicobar Is. (nĭk-ô-bär')	206	7.00 N	94.18 E
Great Oxney Green, Eng.	62	51.44 N	0.25 E
Great Parndon, Eng.	62	51.45 N	0.05 E
Great Pedro Bluff (Hd.), Jam.	134	17.50 N	78.05 W
Great Plains, The (Reg.), N.A. (plāns)	94	45.00 N	104.00 W
Great Ragged (I.), Ba.	135	22.10 N	75.45 W
Great Ruaha (R.), Tan.	231	7.45 S	34.50 E
Great Saint Bernard Pass, Switz-It. (sānt bĕr-närd')	172	45.53 N	7.15 E
Great Salt L., Ut. (sôlt lāk)	117	41.19 N	112.48 W
Great Salt Lake Des., U.S.	108	41.00 N	113.30 W
Great Salt Plains Res., Ok.	122	36.56 N	98.14 W
Great Sand Dunes Natl. Mon., Co.	122	37.56 N	105.25 W
Great Sand Hills, Can. (sănd)	100	50.35 N	109.05 W
Great Sandy (I.), see Fraser			
Great Sandy Des., Austl. (săn'dē)	214	21.50 S	123.10 E
Great Sandy Des., Or. (săn'dĭ)	116	43.43 N	120.44 W
Great Sitkin (I.), Ak. (sĭt-kĭn)	107a	52.18 N	176.22 W
Great Slave (L.), Can. (slāv)	96	61.37 N	114.58 W
Great Smoky Mts. Natl. Park, NC-Tn. (smōk-ē)	126	35.43 N	83.20 W
Great Stirrup Cay (I.), Ba. (stĭr-ŭp)	134	25.50 N	77.55 W
Great Sutton, Eng.	64a	53.17 N	2.56 W
Great Victoria Des., Austl. (vĭk-tō'rĭ-á)	214	29.45 S	124.30 E
Great Waltham, Eng. (wôl'thŭm)	156	51.47 N	0.27 E
Great Warley, Eng.	62	51.35 N	0.17 E
Great Yarmouth, Eng. (yär-mŭth)	163	52.35 N	1.45 E
Grebbestad, Swe. (grĕb-bĕ-städh)	164	58.42 N	11.15 E
Gréboun, Mont (Mtn.), Niger	229	20.00 N	8.35 E
Greco (Neigh.), It.	65c	45.30 N	9.13 E
Gredos, Sierra de (Mts.) (syĕr'rä dā grā'dōs)	170	40.13 N	5.30 W
Greece, Eur. (grēs)	154	39.00 N	21.30 E
Greeley, Co. (grē'lĭ)	122	40.25 N	104.41 W
Green (R.), Ky (grēn)	126	37.13 N	86.30 W
Green (R.), ND	114	47.05 N	103.05 W
Green (R.), U.S.	108	38.30 N	110.10 W
Green (R.), Ut.	121	38.30 N	110.05 W
Green (R.), Wa.	118a	47.17 N	121.57 W
Green B., U.S.	109	44.55 N	87.40 W
Greenbank, Wa. (grēn'bănk)	118a	48.06 N	122.35 W
Green Bay, Wi.	115	44.30 N	88.04 W
Green Bayou, Tx.	125a	29.53 N	95.13 W
Greenbelt, Md. (grĕn'bĕlt)	112e	38.59 N	76.53 W
Greenbrae, Ca.	58b	37.57 N	122.31 W
Greencastle, In. (grēn-kás''l)	110	39.40 N	86.50 W
Green Cay (I.)	134	24.05 N	77.10 W
Green Cove Springs, Fl. (kōv)	127	29.56 N	81.42 W
Greendale, Wi. (grēn'dāl)	113a	42.56 N	87.59 W
Greenfield, Ia.	115	41.16 N	94.30 W
Greenfield, In. (grēn'fēld)	110	39.45 N	85.40 W
Greenfield, Ma.	111	42.35 N	72.35 W
Greenfield, Mo.	123	37.23 N	93.48 W
Greenfield, Oh.	110	39.15 N	83.25 W
Greenfield, Tn.	126	36.08 N	88.45 W
Greenfield Park, Can.	95a	45.29 N	73.29 W
Greenhills, Oh. (grēn-hĭls)	113f	39.16 N	84.31 W
Greenhithe, Eng.	62	51.27 N	0.17 E
Greenland, N.A. (grēn'lănd)	94	74.00 N	40.00 W
Green Meadows, Md.	56d	38.58 N	76.57 W
Greenmount, Eng.	64b	53.37 N	2.20 W
Green Mountain Res., Co.	121	39.50 N	106.20 W
Green Mtn., Or.	118c	45.52 N	123.24 W
Green Mts., Vt.	111	43.10 N	73.05 W
Greenock, Scot. (grēn'ŭk)	162	55.55 N	4.45 W
Green Pond Mtn., NJ (pŏnd)	112a	41.00 N	74.32 W
Greenport, NY	111	41.06 N	72.22 W
Green R., Blacks Fk, Wy.	117	41.08 N	110.27 W
Green R., Hams Fk., Wy.	117	41.55 N	110.40 W
Green River, Ut. (grēn rĭv'ĕr)	121	39.00 N	110.05 W
Green River, Wy.	117	41.32 N	109.26 W
Greensboro, Al. (grēnz'bŭro)	126	32.42 N	87.36 W
Greensboro, Ga. (grēns-bûr'ô)	126	33.34 N	83.11 W
Greensboro, NC	127	36.04 N	79.45 W
Greensborough, Austl.	70b	37.42 S	145.06 E
Greensburg, In. (grēnz'bûrg)	110	39.20 N	85.30 W
Greensburg, Ks. (grēns-bûrg)	122	37.36 N	99.17 W
Greensburg, Pa.	111	40.20 N	79.30 W
Greenside (Neigh.), S. Afr.	71b	26.09 S	28.01 E
Greenstead, Eng.	62	51.42 N	0.14 E
Green Street, Eng.	62	51.40 N	0.16 W
Green Street Green (Neigh.), Eng.	62	51.21 N	0.04 E
Greenvale, NY	55	40.49 N	73.38 W
Greenville, Al. (grēn'vĭl)	126	31.49 N	86.39 W
Greenville, Il.	123	38.52 N	89.22 W
Greenville, Ky.	126	37.11 N	87.11 W
Greenville, Lib.	228	5.01 N	9.03 W
Greenville, Me.	104	45.26 N	69.35 W
Greenville, Mi.	110	43.10 N	85.25 W
Greenville, Ms.	126	33.25 N	91.00 W
Greenville, NC	127	35.35 N	77.22 W
Greenville, Oh.	110	40.05 N	84.35 W
Greenville, Pa.	110	41.20 N	80.25 W
Greenville, SC	127	34.50 N	82.25 W
Greenville, Tn.	126	36.08 N	82.50 W
Greenville, Tx.	123	33.09 N	96.07 W
Greenwich, Ct.	112a	41.01 N	73.37 W
Greenwich, Eng. (grĭn'ĭj)	156b	51.28 N	0.00
Greenwich (Neigh.), Eng.	62	51.28 N	0.02 E
Greenwich Observatory (P. Int.), Eng.	62	51.28 N	0.00
Greenwich Village (Neigh.), NY	55	40.44 N	74.00 W
Greenwood, Ar. (grēn-wōōd)	123	35.13 N	94.15 W
Greenwood, In.	113g	39.37 N	86.07 W
Greenwood, Ma.	54a	42.29 N	71.04 W
Greenwood, Ms.	126	33.30 N	90.09 W
Greenwood (R.), SC	127	34.17 N	81.55 W
Greenwood, SC	127	34.10 N	82.10 W
Greenwood L., NY	112a	41.13 N	74.20 W
Greer, SC (grēr)	127	34.55 N	81.56 W
Grefrath, F.R.G. (grĕf'rät)	169c	51.20 N	6.21 E
Gregory, SD (grĕg'ō-rĭ)	114	43.12 N	99.27 W
Gregory, L., Austl. (grĕg'ô-rē)	216	29.47 S	139.15 E
Gregory Ra, Austl.	215	19.23 S	143.45 E
Greifenberg, F.R.G. (grī'fĕn-bĕrgh)	157d	48.04 N	11.06 E
Greiffenburg (P. Int.), F.R.G.	63	51.20 N	6.38 E
Greifswald, G.D.R. (grīfs'vält)	166	54.05 N	13.24 E
Greiz, G.D.R. (grīts)	166	50.39 N	12.14 E
Gremyachinsk, Sov. Un. (grâ'myà-chĭnsk)	182a	58.35 N	57.53 E
Grenå, Den. (grĕn'ô)	164	56.25 N	10.51 E
Grenada, Ms. (grē-nä'da)	126	33.45 N	89.47 W
Grenada, N.A.	129	12.02 N	61.15 W
Grenada Res., Ms.	126	33.52 N	89.30 W
Grenadines, The (Is.), Grenada-Saint Vincent (grĕn'á-dēnz)	133b	12.37 N	61.35 W
Grenen (Pt.), Den.	164	57.43 N	10.31 E
Grenoble, Fr. (grē-nō'bl')	169	45.14 N	5.45 E
Grenora, ND (grē-nō'rá)	114	48.38 N	103.55 W

ăt; finăl; rāte; senăte; ärm; àsk; sofá; fâre; ch-choose; dh-as th in other; bē; ēvent; bĕt; recĕnt; cratẽr; g-gō; gh-guttural g; bĭt; ĭ-short neutral; rīde; ĸ-guttural k as ch in German ich;

PRONOUNCING INDEX Grenville – Guntersville L. 289

PLACE (Pronounciation)	PAGE	Lat. °′	Long. °′
Grenville, Can. (grĕn'vĭl)	111	45.40 N	74.35 W
Grenville, Grenada	133b	12.07 N	61.38 W
Gresham, Or. (grĕsh'ăm)	118c	45.30 N	122.25 W
Gretna, La. (grĕt'nȧ)	112d	29.56 N	90.03 W
Grevel (Neigh.), F.R.G.	63	51.34 N	7.33 E
Grevelingen Krammer, R., Neth.	157a	51.42 N	4.03 E
Grevená, Grc. (grĕ'vȧ-nȧ)	173	40.02 N	21.30 E
Grevenbroich, F.R.G. (grĕ'fĕn-broik)	169c	51.05 N	6.36 E
Grey (R.), Can. (grā)	105	47.53 N	57.00 W
Greybull, Wy. (grā'bŏŏl)	117	44.28 N	108.05 W
Greybull R., Wy.	117	44.13 N	108.43 W
Greylingstad, S. Afr. (grā-lĭng'shtȧt)	223d	26.40 S	29.13 E
Greymouth, N.Z. (grā'mouth)	217	42.27 S	171.17 E
Grey, Pt., Can.	118d	49.22 N	123.16 W
Grey Ra., Austl.	216	28.40 S	142.05 E
Greys Hbr., Wa. (grās)	116	46.55 N	124.23 W
Greystanes, Austl.	70a	33.49 S	150.58 E
Greytown, S. Afr. (grā'toun)	227c	29.07 S	30.38 E
Greytown, see **San Juan del Norte**			
Grey Wolf Pk., Wa. (grā wŏŏlf)	118a	48.53 N	123.12 W
Gridley, Ca. (grĭd'lĭ)	120	39.22 N	121.43 W
Griffin, Ga. (grĭf'ĭn)	126	33.15 N	84.16 W
Griffith, Austl. (grĭf-ĭth)	216	34.16 S	146.10 E
Griffith, In.	113a	41.31 N	87.26 W
Grigoriopol', Sov. Un. (grĭ'gor-i-ŏ'pŏl)	175	47.09 N	29.18 E
Grijalva (R.), Mex. (grē-häl'vä)	131	17.25 N	93.23 W
Grim, C., Austl. (grĭm)	216	40.43 S	144.30 E
Grimlinghausen (Neigh.), F.R.G.	63	51.10 N	6.44 E
Grimma, G.D.R. (grĭm'ȧ)	166	51.14 N	12.43 E
Grimsby, Can. (grĭmz'bĭ)	95d	43.11 N	79.33 W
Grimstad, Nor. (grĭm-städh)	164	58.21 N	8.30 E
Grindstone Island, Can.	105	47.25 N	61.51 W
Grinnel, Ia. (grĭ-nĕl')	115	41.44 N	92.44 W
Grinzing (Neigh.), Aus.	66e	48.15 N	16.21 E
Griswold, Ia. (grĭz'wŭld)	115	41.11 N	95.05 W
Griva, Sov. Un. (grē'vȧ)	174	55.51 N	26.31 E
Grímsey (I.), Ice. (grĭms'ȧ)	158	66.30 N	17.50 W
Groais I., Can.	105	50.57 N	55.35 W
Grobina, Sov. Un. (grō'bĭnĭa)	165	56.35 N	21.10 E
Groblersdal, S. Afr.	223d	25.11 S	29.25 E
Grodno, Sov. Un. (grôd'nō)	167	53.40 N	23.49 E
Grodzisk, Pol. (grō'jĕsk)	166	52.14 N	16.22 E
Grodzisk Masowiecki, Pol. (grō'jĕsk mä-zō-vyĕts'ke)	167	52.06 N	20.40 E
Groesbeck, Tx. (grōs'bĕk)	125	31.32 N	96.31 W
Groix, Île de (I.), Fr. (ēl dē grwä')	168	47.39 N	3.28 W
Grójec, Pol. (grōō'yĕts)	167	51.53 N	20.52 E
Gronau, F.R.G. (grō'nou)	166	52.12 N	7.05 E
Groningen, Neth. (grō'nĭng-ĕn)	163	53.13 N	6.30 E
Groote Eylandt (I.), Austl. (grō'tē ī'länt)	214	13.50 S	137.30 E
Grootfontein, Namibia (grōt'fŏn-tān')	226	18.15 S	19.30 E
Groot-Kei, S. Afr. (kē)	227c	32.17 S	27.30 E
Grootkop, (Mtn.), S. Afr.	226a	34.11 S	18.23 E
Groot Marico, S. Afr.	223d	25.36 S	26.23 E
Groot R., S. Afr.	223d	25.13 S	26.20 E
Groot-Vis (R.), S. Afr.	227c	33.04 S	36.08 E
Groot Vloer (L.), S. Afr. (grōt' vlōōr')	227c	33.00 S	20.16 E
Gros Morne (Mtn.), Can. (grō môrn')	105	49.36 N	57.48 W
Gros Morne Natl. Pk., Can.	97	49.45 N	59.15 W
Gros Pate (Mtn.), Can.	105	50.16 N	57.25 W
Grossbeeren, G.D.R.	65a	52.21 N	13.18 E
Grosse I., Mi. (grōs)	113b	42.08 N	83.09 W
Grosse Isle, Can. (īl')	95f	50.04 N	97.27 W
Grossenbaum (Neigh.), F.R.G.	63	51.22 N	6.47 E
Grossenhain, G.D.R. (grōs'ĕn-hīn)	166	51.17 N	13.33 E
Gross-Enzersdorf, Aus.	157e	48.13 N	16.33 E
Grosse Pointe, Mi. (point')	113b	42.23 N	82.54 W
Grosse Pointe Farms, Mi. (färm)	113b	42.25 N	82.53 W
Grosse Pointe Park, Mi. (pärk)	113b	42.23 N	82.55 W
Grosse Pointe Woods, Mi.	57c	42.27 N	82.55 W
Grosseto, It. (grôs-sā'tō)	172	42.46 N	11.09 E
Grossglockner Pk, Aus. (glôk'nĕr)	166	47.06 N	12.45 E
Gross Höbach, F.R.G. (hû'bäk)	157d	48.21 N	11.36 E
Grossjedlersdorf (Neigh.), Aus.	66e	48.17 N	16.25 E
Gross Kreutz, G.D.R. (kroitz)	157b	52.24 N	12.47 E
Gross Schönebeck, G.D.R. (shō'nĕ-bĕk)	157b	52.54 N	13.32 E
Gross Ziethen, G.D.R.	65a	52.24 N	13.27 E
Gros Ventre R., Wy. (grōvĕn't'r)	117	43.38 N	110.34 W
Groton, Ct. (grŏt'ŭn)	111	41.20 N	72.00 W
Groton, Ma.	105a	42.37 N	71.34 W
Groton, SD	114	45.25 N	98.04 W
Grottaglie, It. (grôt-täl'yä)	173	40.32 N	17.26 E
Grouard Mission, Can.	99	55.31 N	116.09 W
Groveland, Ma. (grōv'land)	105a	42.25 N	71.02 W
Groveton, NH (grōv'tŭn)	111	44.35 N	71.30 W
Groveton, Tx.	125	31.04 N	95.07 W
Groznyy, Sov. Un. (grôz'nĭ)	179	43.20 N	45.40 E
Grudziądz, Pol. (grōō'jyŏnts)	167a	53.30 N	18.48 E
Grues, Île aux (I.), Can. (ō grü)	95b	47.05 N	70.32 W
Gruiten, F.R.G.	63	51.14 N	7.01 E
Grumme (Neigh.), F.R.G.	63	51.30 N	7.14 E
Grumpholds-Kirchen, Aus.	157e	48.03 N	16.17 E
Grünau (Neigh.), G.D.R.	65a	52.25 N	13.34 E
Grundy Center, Ia. (grŭn'dĭ sĕn'tēr)	115	42.22 N	92.45 W
Grünewald, F.R.G.	63	51.13 N	7.37 E
Grunewald (Neigh.), F.R.G.	65a	52.30 N	13.17 E
Gruñidora, Mex. (grōō-nyē-dō'rō)	130	24.10 N	101.49 W
Grünwald, F.R.G. (grōōn'väld)	157d	48.04 N	11.34 E
Gryazi, Sov. Un. (gryä'zĭ)	174	52.31 N	39.59 E
Gryazovets, Sov. Un. (gryä'zō-vĕts)	154	58.52 N	40.14 E
Gryfice, Pol. (grĭ'fĭ-tsĕ)	166	53.55 N	15.11 E
Gryfino, Pol. (grĭ'fē-nō)	166	53.16 N	14.30 E
Guabito, Pan. (gwä-bē'tō)	133	9.30 N	82.33 W
Guacanayabo, Golfo de (G.), Cuba (gôl-fô-dĕ-gwä-kä-nä-yä'bō)	134	20.30 N	77.40 W
Guacara, Ven. (gwȧ'kä-rä)	143b	10.16 N	67.48 W
Guacarí, Col. (gwä-kä-rē')	142a	3.45 N	76.20 W
Guaçuí, Braz. (gwä'sōō-ē')	141a	20.47 S	41.40 W
Guadalajara, Mex. (gwä-dhä-lä-hä'rä)	130	20.41 N	103.21 W
Guadalajara, Sp. (gwä-dä-lä-kä'rä)	170	40.37 N	3.10 W
Guadalcanal, Sp. (gwä-dhäl-kä-näl')	170	38.05 N	5.48 W
Guadalcanal (I.), Sol. Is.	215	9.48 S	158.43 E
Guadalcázar, Mex. (gwä-dhäl-kä'zär)	130	22.38 N	100.24 W
Guadalete (R.), Sp. (gwä-dhä-lā'tȧ)	170	38.53 N	5.38 W
Guadalhorce (R.), Sp. (gwä-dhäl-ôr'thā)	170	37.05 N	4.50 W
Guadalimar (R.), Sp. (gwä-dhä-lē-mär')	170	38.29 N	2.53 W
Guadalope (R.), Sp. (gwä-dä-lô-pĕ)	171	40.48 N	0.10 W
Guadalquivir, Río (R.), Sp. (rē'ō-gwä-dhäl-kē-vēr')	170	36.35 N	6.00 W
Guadalupe, Mex.	124	31.23 N	106.06 W
Guadalupe, Basílica de (P. Int.), Mex.	60a	19.29 N	99.07 W
Guadalupe I., Mex.	128	29.00 N	118.45 W
Guadalupe Mts., NM-Tx	124	32.00 N	104.55 W
Guadalupe Pk., Tx.	124	31.55 N	104.55 W
Guadalupe R., Tx. (gwä-dhä-lōō'pȧ)	124	29.54 N	99.03 W
Guadalupe, Sierra de (Mts.), Sp. (syĕr'rä dā gwä-dhä-lōō'pä)	170	39.30 N	5.25 W
Guadarrama (R.), Sp. (gwä-dhär-rä'mä)	171a	40.34 N	3.58 W
Guadarrama, Sierra de (Mts.), Sp. (gwä-dhär-rä'mä)	170	41.00 N	3.40 W
Guadatentin (R.), Sp.	170	37.43 N	1.58 W
Guadeloupe, N.A. (gwä-dē-lōōp)	129	16.40 N	61.10 W
Guadeloupe Pass, N.A.	133b	16.26 N	62.00 W
Guadiana (R.), Port. (gwä-dvä'nä)	170	37.43 N	7.43 W
Guadiana Alto (R.), Sp. (äl'tō)	170	39.02 N	2.52 W
Guadiana, Bahia de (B.), Cuba (bä-ē'ä-dē-gwä-dhē-ä'nä)	134	22.10 N	84.35 W
Guadiana Menor (R.), Sp. (mā'nôr)	170	37.43 N	2.45 W
Guadiaro (R.), Sp. (gwä-dhē-ä'rō)	170	37.38 N	5.25 W
Guadiela (R.), Sp. (gwä-dhē-ā'lä)	170	40.27 N	2.05 W
Guadix, Sp. (gwä-dēsh')	170	37.18 N	3.09 W
Guaianazes (Neigh.), Braz.	61d	23.33 S	46.25 W
Guaira, Braz. (gwä-ē-rä)	143	24.03 S	44.02 W
Guaire (R.), Ven. (gwī'rĕ)	143b	10.25 N	66.43 W
Guajaba, Cayo (I.), Cuba (kä'yō-gwä-hä'bä)	134	21.50 N	77.35 W
Guajará Mirim, Braz. (gwä-zhä-rä'mē-rēɴ')	142	10.58 S	65.12 W
Guajira, Pen. de (Pen.), Col.-Ven. (pĕ-nē'ng-sōō-lä-dĕ-gwä-ĸē'rä)	142	12.35 N	73.00 W
Gualán, Guat. (gwä-län')	132c	15.08 N	89.21 W
Gualeguay, Arg. (gwä-lĕ-gwä'y)	141c	33.10 S	59.20 W
Gualeguay (R.), Arg.	141c	32.49 S	59.05 W
Gualeguaychú, Arg. (gwä-lȧ-gwī-chōō')	141c	33.01 S	58.32 W
Gualeguaychú (R.), Arg.	141c	32.58 S	58.27 W
Gualicho, Salina (F.), Arg. (sä-lē'nä-gwä-lē'chō)	144	40.20 S	65.15 W
Guam, Oceania (gwäm)	208	14.00 N	143.20 E
Guaminí, Arg. (gwä-mē-nē')	144	37.02 S	62.21 W
Guamo, Col. (gwȧ'mō)	142a	4.02 N	74.58 W
Gu'an, China (gōō-än)	202a	39.25 N	116.18 E
Guan (R.), China (gūän)	200	31.56 N	115.19 E
Guanabacoa, Cuba (gwä-nä-bä-kō'ä)	135a	23.08 N	82.19 W
Guanabara, Baia de (B.), Braz.	144b	22.44 S	43.09 W
Guanacaste Cord. (Mts.), C.R. (kôr-dēl-yĕ'rä-gwä-nä-käs'tä)	132	10.54 N	85.27 W
Guanacevi, Mex. (gwä-nä-sē-vē')	128	25.30 N	105.45 W
Guanahacabibes, Pen. de, Cuba (pĕ-nĕn-sōō-lä-dĕ-gwä-nä hä-kä-bē'bås)	134	21.55 N	84.35 W
Guanajay, Cuba (gwäŋä-hī')	134	22.55 N	82.40 W
Guanajuato, Mex. (gwä-nä-hwä'tō)	130	21.01 N	101.16 W
Guanajuato (State), Mex.	128	21.00 N	101.00 W
Guanape (R.), Ven.	143b	9.52 N	65.20 W
Guanape, Ven. (gwä-nä'pĕ)	143b	9.55 N	65.32 W
Guanare, Ven. (gwä-nä'rȧ)	142	8.57 N	69.47 W
Guanduçu (R.), Braz. (gwä'n-dōō'sōō)	144b	22.50 S	43.40 W
Guane, Cuba (gwä'nȧ)	134	22.10 N	84.05 W
Guangchang, China (gūäŋ-chäŋ)	203	25.50 N	116.18 E
Guangde, China (gūäŋ-dŭ)	203	30.40 N	119.20 E
Guangdong (Prov.), China (gūäŋ-dôŋ)	199	23.45 N	113.15 E
Guanglu Dao (I.), China (gūäŋ-lōō dou)	200	39.13 N	122.21 E
Guangping, China (gūäŋ-pĭŋ)	200	36.30 N	114.57 E
Guangrao, China (gūäŋ-rou)	200	37.04 N	118.24 E
Guangshan, China (gūäŋ-shän)	200	32.02 N	114.53 E
Guangxi Zhuangzu (Aut. Reg.), China (gūäŋ-shyē)	198	24.00 N	108.30 E
Guangzhou (Canton), China (gūäŋ-jō)	201a	23.07 N	113.15 E
Guanhu, China (gūän-hōō)	200	34.26 N	117.59 E
Guannan, China (gūän-nän)	200	34.17 N	119.17 E
Guanta, Ven. (gwän'tä)	143b	10.15 N	64.35 W
Guantanamo, Cuba (gwän-tä'nä-mô)	135	20.10 N	75.10 W
Guantánamo (Prov.), Cuba	135	20.10 N	75.05 W
Guantanamo, Bahía de (B.), Cuba (bä-ē'ä-dĕ)	135	19.35 N	75.35 W
Guantao, China (gūän-tou)	200	36.39 N	115.25 E
Guanxian, China (gūän-shyĕn)	200	36.30 N	115.28 E
Guanyao, China (gūän-you)	201a	23.13 N	113.04 E
Guanyintang, China	67b	39.52 N	116.31 E
Guanyun, China (gūän-yōōn)	200	34.28 N	119.16 E
Guapé, Braz. (gwȧ-pĕ)	141a	20.45 S	45.55 W
Guapiles, C.R. (gwä-pē-lĕs)	133	10.05 N	83.54 W
Guapimirim, Braz. (gwä-pē-mē-rē'ɴ)	144b	22.31 S	42.59 W
Guaporé (R.), Bol.-Braz. (gwä-pô-rā')	142	12.11 S	63.47 W
Guaqui, Bol. (guä'kē)	142	16.42 S	68.47 W
Guarabira, Braz. (gwä-rä-bē'rȧ)	143	6.49 S	35.27 W
Guaracarumbo, Ven.	61a	10.34 N	66.59 W
Guaranda, Ec. (gwä-rȧn'dä)	142	1.39 S	78.57 W
Guarapari, Braz. (gwä-rä-pä'rē)	143	20.34 S	40.31 W
Guarapiranga, Represa do (Res.), Braz. (r'ē-prē-sȧ-dô-gwä'rä-pē-rȧ'n-gä)	141a	23.45 S	46.44 W
Guarapuava, Braz. (gwä-rä-pwä'vȧ)	144	25.29 S	51.26 W
Guara, Sierra de (Mts.), Sp. (sē-ĕ'r-rä-dē-gwä'rä)	171	42.24 N	0.15 W
Guaratinguetá, Braz. (guä-rä-tĭɴ-gȧ-tä')	141a	22.49 S	45.10 W
Guarda, Port. (gwär'dä)	170	40.32 N	7.17 W
Guardiato (R.), Sp.	170	38.10 N	5.05 W
Guarena, Sp. (gwä-rā'nyä)	170	38.52 N	6.08 W
Guaribe (R.), Ven. (gwä-rē'bĕ)	143b	9.48 N	65.17 W
Guárico (State), Ven.	143b	9.42 N	67.25 W
Guárico (R.), Ven.	143b	9.50 N	67.07 W
Guarulhos, Braz. (gwȧ-rōō'l-yôs)	141a	32.28 S	46.30 W
Guarus, Braz. (gwä'rōōs)	141a	21.44 S	41.19 W
Guasca, Col. (gwäs'kä)	142a	4.52 N	73.52 W
Guasipati, Ven. (gwä-sē-pä'tē)	143	7.26 N	61.57 W
Guastalla, It. (gwäs-täl'lä)	172	44.53 N	10.39 E
Guasti, Ca. (gwäs'tĭ)	119a	34.04 N	117.35 W
Guatemala, Guat. (guä-tȧ-mä'lä)	132	14.37 N	90.32 W
Guatemala, N.A.	128	15.45 N	91.45 W
Guatire, Ven. (gwä-tē'rē)	143b	10.28 N	66.34 W
Guaxupé, Braz. (gwä-shōō-pĕ')	141a	21.18 S	46.42 W
Guayabal, Cuba (gwä-yä-bä'l)	134	20.40 N	77.40 W
Guayalejo (R.), Mex. (gwä-yä-lĕ'hō)	130	23.24 N	99.09 W
Guayama, P.R. (gwä-yä'mä)	129b	18.00 N	66.08 W
Guayamouc (R.), Hai.	135	19.05 N	72.00 W
Guayaquil, Ec. (gwī-ä-kēl')	142	2.16 S	79.53 W
Guayaquil, Golfo de (G.), Ec. (gôl-fô-dĕ)	142	3.03 S	82.12 W
Guayiare (R.), Col. (gwä-yä'rĕ)	142	3.35 N	69.28 W
Guaymas, Mex. (gwá'y-mäs)	128	27.49 N	110.58 W
Guayubin, Dom. Rep. (gwȧ-yōō-bē'n)	135	19.40 N	71.25 W
Guazacapán, Guat. (gwä-zä-kä-pän')	132	14.04 N	90.26 W
Gubakha, Sov. Un. (gōō-bä'kȧ)	182a	58.53 N	57.35 E
Gubbio, It. (gōōb'byō)	172	43.23 N	12.36 E
Gucheng, China (gōō-chŭŋ)	200	39.09 N	115.43 E
Gudar, Sierra de (Mts.), Sp. (syĕr'rä dā gōō'dhär)	171	40.28 N	0.47 W
Gudena (R.), Den.	164	56.20 N	9.47 E
Gudvangen, Nor. (gōōdh'väŋ-gĕn)	164	60.52 N	6.45 E
Guebwiller, Fr. (gĕb-vē-lâr')	169	47.53 N	7.10 E
Guédi, Mont (Mtn.), Chad	229	12.14 N	18.58 E
Guelma, Alg. (gwĕl'mä)	224	36.32 N	7.17 E
Guelph, Can. (gwĕlf)	95d	43.33 N	80.15 W
Güere (R.), Ven. (gwĕ'rĕ)	143b	9.39 N	65.00 W
Guéret, Fr. (gā-rĕ')	168	46.09 N	1.52 E
Guermantes, Fr.	64c	48.51 N	2.42 E
Guernsey (I.), Eur. (gûrn'zĭ)	168	49.27 N	2.36 W
Guerrero, Mex. (gĕr-rā'rō)	124	26.47 N	99.20 W
Guerrero, Mex.	124	28.20 N	100.24 W
Guerrero (State), Mex.	130	17.45 N	100.15 W
Gueydan, La. (gā'dăn)	125	30.01 N	92.31 W
Guia de Pacobaíba, Braz. (gwē'ä-dĕ-pä'kō-bī'bä)	144b	22.42 S	43.10 W
Guiana Highlands (Mts.), Braz.	140	3.20 N	60.00 W
Guichi, China (gwä-chr)	203	30.35 N	117.28 E
Guichicovi (San Juan), Mex. (gwē-chē-kō'vē)	131	16.58 N	95.10 W
Guidonia, It. (gwē-dō'nyȧ)	171d	42.00 N	12.45 E
Guiglo, Ivory Coast	228	6.33 N	7.29 W
Guignes, Fr. (gēɴ'yĕ)	169b	48.38 N	2.48 E
Güigüe, Ven. (gwē'gwĕ)	143b	10.05 N	67.48 W
Guija, L., Sal. (gē'hä)	132	14.16 N	89.21 W
Guildford, Austl.	70a	33.51 S	150.59 E
Guildford, Eng. (gĭl'fērd)	156b	51.13 N	0.34 W
Guilford, In. (gĭl'fērd)	113f	39.10 N	84.55 W
Guilin, China (gwā-lĭn)	203	25.18 N	110.22 E
Guimarães, Port. (gē-mä-răɴsh')	170	41.27 N	8.22 W
Guinea, Afr. (gĭn'ē)	222	10.48 N	12.28 W
Guinea, G. of, Afr.	222	2.00 N	1.00 E
Guinea-Bissau, Afr. (gĭn'ē)	222	12.00 N	20.00 W
Güines, Cuba (gwē'nās)	134	22.50 N	82.05 W
Guingamp, Fr. (găɴ-gäɴ')	168	48.35 N	3.10 W
Guir (R.), Mor.-Alg.	160	31.55 N	2.48 W
Güira de Melena, Cuba (gwē'rä dā mȧ-lā'nä)	134	22.45 N	82.30 W
Güiria, Ven. (gwē-rē'ä)	142	10.43 N	62.16 W
Guise, Fr. (guēz)	169	49.54 N	3.37 E
Guisisil (Vol.), Nic. (gē-sē-sēl')	132	12.40 N	86.11 W
Guiyang, China (gwā-yäŋ)	203	26.45 N	107.00 E
Guizhou, China (gwā-jō)	201a	22.46 N	113.15 E
Guizhou (Prov.), China	198	27.00 N	106.10 E
Gujānwāla, Pak. (gōōj-rän'va-lȧ)	196	32.08 N	74.14 E
Gujarat (State), India	196	22.54 N	79.00 E
Gulbarga, India (gōōl-bûr'gȧ)	197	17.25 N	76.52 E
Gulbene, Sov. Un. (gōōl-bă'nĕ)	174	57.09 N	26.49 E
Gulfport, Ms. (gŭlf'pōrt)	126	30.24 N	89.05 W
Gulja, see **Yining**			
Gull L., Can.	98	52.35 N	114.00 W
Gull Lake, Can.	100	50.10 N	108.25 W
Gulph Mills, Pa.	56b	40.04 N	75.21 W
Gulu, Ug.	231	2.47 N	32.18 E
Gulyay Pole, Sov. Un.	175	47.39 N	36.12 E
Gumaca, Phil. (gōō-mä-kä')	207a	13.55 N	122.06 E
Gumbeyka R., Sov. Un. (gōōm-bĕy'kȧ)	182a	53.20 N	59.42 E
Gumel, Nig.	229	12.39 N	9.22 E
Gummersbach, F.R.G. (gōōm'ĕrs-bäk)	166	51.02 N	7.34 E
Gummi, Nig.	229	12.09 N	5.09 E
Gumpoldskirchen, Aus.	157	48.04 N	16.15 E
Guna, India	196	24.44 N	77.17 E
Gunisao (R.), Can. (gŭn-ĭ-sā'ō)	101	53.40 N	97.35 W
Gunisao L., Can.	101	53.54 N	97.58 W
Gunnedah, Austl. (gŭ'nē-dȧ)	216	31.00 S	150.10 E
Gunnison, Co. (gŭn'ĭ-sŭn)	121	38.33 N	106.56 W
Gunnison, (R.), Col.	121	38.30 N	106.40 W
Gunnison, Ut.	121	39.10 N	111.50 W
Guntersville, Al. (gŭn'tērz-vĭl)	126	34.20 N	86.19 W
Guntersville L., Al.	126	34.30 N	86.20 W

ng-sing; ŋ-baŋk; ɴ-nasalized n; nŏd; cŏmmit; ōld; ôbey; ôrder; oi-boil; fōōd; fŏŏt; ou-out; s-soft; sh-dish; th-thin; pūre; ůnite; ûrn; stŭd; circŭs; ü-as in French tu; '-indeterminate vowel.

PLACE (Pronounciation)	PAGE	Lat. °′	Long. °′
Guntramsdorf, Aus.	157e	48.04 N	16.19 E
Guntūr, India (go͞on'to͞or)	197	16.22 N	80.29 E
Guo (R.), China (gwô)	200	33.04 N	117.16 E
Guoyang, China (gwô-yäŋ)	200	33.32 N	116.10 E
Gurdon, Ar. (gûr'dŭn)	123	33.56 N	93.10 W
Gurgucia (R.), Braz. (go͞or-go͞o'syä)	143	8.12 S	43.49 W
Gurnee, Il. (gûr'nē)	113a	42.22 N	87.55 W
Gurskøy (I.), Nor. (go͞orskûė)	164	62.18 N	5.20 E
Gurupá, Braz. (go͞o-ro͞o-pä')	143	1.28 S	51.32 W
Gurupi, Serra do (Mts.) (sĕ'r-rä-dô-go͞o-ro͞o-pē')	143	5.32 S	47.02 W
Gurupí (R.), Braz. (go͞o-ro͞o-pē')	143	2.37 S	46.45 W
Guru Sikhar Mt., India	196	29.42 N	72.50 E
Gur'yev, Sov. Un. (go͞or'yĕf)	179	47.10 N	51.50 E
Gur'yevsk, Sov. Un. (go͞or-yĭfsk')	180	54.14 N	86.07 E
Gusau, Nig. (go͞o-zä'o͞o)	229	12.12 N	6.40 E
Gusev, Sov. Un. (go͞o'sĕf)	165	54.35 N	22.15 E
Gushi, China (go͞o-shr)	200	32.11 N	115.39 E
Gushiago, Ghana	228	9.55 N	0.12 W
Gusinje, Yugo. (go͞o-sēn'yĕ)	173	42.34 N	19.54 E
Gus'-Khrustal'nyy, Sov. Un. (go͞os-ĸro͞o-stäl'ny')	174	55.39 N	40.41 E
Gustavo A. Madero, Mex. (go͞os-tä'vô-ä-mä-dĕ'rô)	131a	19.29 N	99.07 W
Güstrow, G.D.R. (güs'trō)	166	53.48 N	12.12 E
Gütersloh, F.R.G. (gü'tĕrs-lo)	166	51.54 N	8.22 E
Guthrie, Ok. (gŭth'rĭ)	123	35.52 N	97.26 W
Guthrie Center, Ia.	115	41.41 N	94.33 W
Gutiérrez Zamora, Mex. (go͞o-tĭ-âr'räz zä-mō'rä)	131	20.27 N	97.17 W
Guttenberg, Ia. (gŭt'ĕn-bûrg)	115	42.48 N	91.09 W
Guttenberg, NJ	55	40.48 N	74.01 W
Guyana, S.A. (gŭy'ănă)	140	7.45 N	59.00 W
Guyancourt, Fr.	64c	48.46 N	2.04 E
Guyang, China (go͞o-yäŋ)	200	34.56 N	114.57 E
Guye, China (go͞o-yŭ)	200	39.46 N	118.23 E
Guymon, Ok. (gī'mŏn)	122	36.41 N	101.29 W
Guysborough, Can. (gīz'bŭr-ô)	105	45.23 N	61.30 W
Guzhen, China (go͞o-jŭn)	200	33.20 N	117.18 E
Gvardeysk, Sov. Un. (gvàr-dĕysk')	165	54.39 N	21.11 E
Gwadabawa, Nig.	229	13.20 N	5.15 E
Gwādar, Pak. (gwä'dŭr)	192	25.15 N	62.29 E
Gwane, Zaire (gwän)	231	4.43 N	25.50 E
Gwda (R.), Pol.	166	53.27 N	16.52 E
Gwembe, Zambia	231	16.30 S	27.35 E
Gweru, Zimb.	226	19.15 S	29.48 E
Gwinn, Mi. (gwĭn)	115	46.15 N	87.30 W
Gyangzê, China (gyäŋdzŭ)	198	29.00 N	89.28 E
Gyaring Co. (L.), China (gyä-rĭŋ)	196	30.37 N	88.33 E
Gydan, Khrebet (Kolymskiy), (Mts.), Sov. Un.	181	61.45 N	155.00 E
Gydanskiy, P-Ov (Pen.), Sov. Un.	180	70.42 N	76.03 E
Gympie, Austl. (gĭm'pē)	216	26.20 S	152.50 E
Gyöngyös, Hung. (dyûn'dvûsh)	167	47.47 N	19.55 E
Györ, Hung. (dyûr)	167	47.40 N	17.37 E
Gyōtoku, Jap. (gyō'tô-ko͞o')	205a	35.42 N	139.56 E
Gypsumville, Can. (jĭp'sŭm'vĭl)	101	51.45 N	98.35 W
Gyula, Hung. (dyo͞o'lä)	167	46.38 N	21.18 E

H

PLACE (Pronounciation)	PAGE	Lat. °′	Long. °′
Haan, F.R.G. (hän)	169c	51.12 N	7.00 E
Haapamäki, Fin. (häp'ä-mĕ-kē)	165	62.16 N	24.20 E
Haapsalu, Sov. Un. (häp'sä-lo͞o)	165	58.56 N	23.33 E
Haar, F.R.G. (här)	157d	48.06 N	11.44 E
Haar (Neigh.), F.R.G.	63	51.26 N	7.13 E
Ha 'Arava (Wādī al Jayb), Isr.	191a	30.33 N	35.10 E
Haarlem, Neth. (här'lĕm)	157a	52.22 N	4.37 E
Habana (Prov.), Cuba (hä-vä'nä)	134	22.45 N	82.25 W
Haberfield, Austl.	70a	33.53 S	151.08 E
Habikino, Jap.	205b	34.32 N	135.37 E
Hābra, India	196a	22.49 N	88.38 E
Hachinohe, Jap. (hä'chē-nō'hå)	204	40.29 N	141.40 E
Hachiōji, Jap. (hä'chē-ō'jē)	205	35.39 N	139.18 E
Hacienda Heights, Ca.	59	33.58 N	117.58 W
Hackensack, NJ (hăk'ĕn-săk)	112a	40.54 N	74.03 W
Hacketts, Eng.	62	51.45 N	0.05 W
Hackney (Neigh.), Eng.	62	51.33 N	0.03 W
Haddonfield, NJ (hăd'ŭn-fēld)	112f	39.53 N	75.02 W
Haddon Heights, NJ (hăd'ŭn hīts)	112f	39.53 N	75.03 W
Hadd, Ra's al (C.), Om.	192	22.29 N	59.46 E
Hadejia, Nig. (hä-dā'jä)	229	12.30 N	9.59 E
Hadejia (R.), Nig.	229	12.15 N	9.40 E
Hadera, Isr. (ĸă-dĕ'rà)	191a	32.26 N	34.55 E
Hadersdorf (Neigh.), Aus.	66e	48.13 N	16.14 E
Haderslev, Den. (hä'dhĕrs-lĕv)	164	55.17 N	9.28 E
Hadfield, Austl.	70b	37.42 S	144.56 E
Hadibu, P.D.R. of Yem.	223a	12.40 N	53.50 E
Hadlock, Wa. (hăd'lŏk)	118a	48.02 N	122.46 W
Ḩaḑramawt (Reg.), P.D.R. of Yem.	192	15.22 N	48.40 E
Hadur Shuayb, Jabal (Mtn.), Yemen	192	15.45 N	43.45 E
Haeju, Kor. (hä'ĕ-jŭ)	204	38.03 N	125.42 E
Haemgon-ni (Neigh.), Kor.	68b	37.35 N	126.49 E
Hafnarfjördur, Ice.	158	64.02 N	21.32 W
Haft Gel, Iran	195	31.27 N	49.27 E
Hafun, Ras. (C.), Som. (hä-fo͞on')	223a	10.15 N	51.35 E
Hageland, Mt. (hăge'lând)	117	48.53 N	108.43 W
Hagen, F.R.G. (hä'gĕn)	169c	51.21 N	7.29 E

PLACE (Pronounciation)	PAGE	Lat. °′	Long. °′
Hagerstown, In. (hā'gĕrz-toun)	110	39.55 N	85.10 W
Hagerstown, Md.	111	39.40 N	77.45 W
Hagi, Jap. (hä'gĭ)	205	34.25 N	131.25 E
Hague, C. de la, Fr. (dĕ lä ȧg')	168	49.44 N	1.55 W
Haguenau, Fr. (ȧg'nō')	169	48.47 N	7.48 E
Hague, The, see 's Gravenhagen			
Hahnenberg, F.R.G.	63	51.12 N	7.24 E
Hai'an, China (hī-än)	200	32.35 N	120.25 E
Haibara, Jap. (hä'ē-bä'rä)	205	34.29 N	135.57 E
Haicheng, China (hī-chŭŋ)	202	40.58 N	122.45 E
Haidārpur (Neigh.), India	67d	28.43 N	77.09 E
Haidian, China (hī-dĭĕn)	202a	39.59 N	116.17 E
Haifa (Hefa), Isr. (hä'ē-fȧ)	191a	32.48 N	35.00 E
Haifeng, China (hä'ē-fĕng')	203	23.00 N	115.20 E
Haifuzhen, China (hī-fo͞o-jŭn)	200	31.57 N	121.48 E
Haijima, Jap.	69a	35.42 N	139.21 E
Haikou, China (hī-kō)	203	20.00 N	110.20 E
Ḩā'il, Sau. Ar. (hāl)	190	27.30 N	41.47 E
Hailaerh, China	202	49.10 N	118.40 E
Hailey, Id. (hā'lĭ)	117	43.31 N	114.19 W
Haileybury, Can.	103	47.27 N	79.38 W
Haileyville, Ok. (hā'lĭ-vĭl)	123	34.51 N	95.34 W
Hailin, China (hä'ē-lĕn')	204	44.31 N	129.11 E
Hailing Dao (I.), China (hī-lĭŋ dou)	203	21.30 N	112.15 E
Hailong, China (hī-loŋ)	202	42.32 N	125.52 E
Hailun, China (hä'ē-lo͞on')	202	47.18 N	126.50 E
Hainan Dao (I.), China (hī-nän dou)	203	19.00 N	111.10 E
Hainault (Neigh.), Eng.	62	51.36 N	0.06 E
Hainburg an der Donau, Aus.	157e	48.09 N	16.57 E
Haines, Ak. (hānz)	107	59.10 N	135.38 W
Haines City, Fl.	127a	28.05 N	81.38 W
Haiphong, Viet. (hī'fông')(hä'ēp-hŏng)	203	20.52 N	106.40 E
Haiti, N.A. (hā'tĭ)	129	19.00 N	72.15 W
Haizhou Wan (B.), China	202	35.49 N	120.35 E
Hajdúböszormény, Hung. (hôl'do͞o-bû'sûr-mān')	167	47.41 N	21.30 E
Hajdúhadház, Hung. (hô'ĭ-do͞o-hôd'häz)	167	47.32 N	21.32 E
Hajdúnánás, Hung. (hô'ĭ-do͞o-nä'näsh)	167	47.52 N	21.27 E
Hajduszoboszló, Hung. (hô'ĭ-do͞o-sô'bôs-lō)	167	47.24 N	21.25 E
Hakodate, Jap. (hä-kō-dä't å)	204	41.46 N	140.42 E
Haku-San (Mtn.), Jap. (hä'ko͞o-sän')	205	36.11 N	136.45 E
Halachó, Mex. (ä-lä-chŏ')	131	20.28 N	90.06 W
Halā'ib, Egypt (hä-lä'ĕb)	225	22.10 N	36.40 E
Ḩalbā, Leb.	191a	34.33 N	36.03 E
Halbe, G.D.R. (häl'bĕ)	157b	52.07 N	13.43 E
Halberstadt, G.D.R. (häl'bĕr-shtät)	166	51.54 N	11.07 E
Halcon, Mt., Phil. (häl-kōn')	207a	13.19 N	120.55 E
Halden (Neigh.), F.R.G.	63	51.23 N	7.31 E
Halden, Nor. (häl'dĕn)	164	59.10 N	11.21 E
Haldensleben, G.D.R.	166	52.18 N	11.23 E
Hale, Eng. (hāl)	156	53.22 N	2.20 W
Haleakala Crater, Hi. (hä'lā-ä'kä-lä)	106a	20.44 N	156.15 W
Haleakala Natl. Park, Hi.	106a	20.46 N	156.00 W
Halebarns, Eng.	64b	53.22 N	2.19 W
Haledon, NJ	55	40.56 N	74.11 W
Hales Corners, Wi. (hālz kôr'nĕrz)	113a	42.56 N	88.03 W
Halesowen, Eng. (hālz'ô-wĕn)	156	52.26 N	2.03 W
Halethorpe, Md. (hāl-thôrp)	112e	39.15 N	76.40 W
Halewood, Eng.	64a	53.22 N	2.49 W
Haleyville, Al. (hā'lĭ-vĭl)	126	34.11 N	87.36 W
Half Moon Bay, Ca. (hăf'mo͞on)	118b	37.28 N	122.26 W
Halfway House, S. Afr. (häf-wā hous)	227b	26.00 S	28.08 E
Halfweg, Neth.	157a	52.23 N	4.45 E
Haliç (B.), Tur.	66f	41.02 N	28.58 E
Halifax, Can. (hăl'ĭ-făks)	104	44.39 N	63.36 W
Halifax, Eng.	156	53.44 N	1.52 W
Halifax B., Austl. (hăl'ĭ-făx)	215	18.56 S	147.07 E
Halifax Hbr., Can.	104	44.35 N	63.31 W
Halkett, C., Ak.	107	70.50 N	151.15 W
Hallam, Austl.	70b	38.01 S	145.06 E
Hallam Park, Can.	99	52.11 N	118.46 E
Halla San (Mt.), Kor. (häl'lȧ-sän)	204	33.20 N	126.37 E
Halle, Bel. (häl'lĕ)	157a	50.45 N	4.13 E
Halle, G.D.R.	166	51.30 N	11.59 E
Hallettsville, Tx. (hăl'ĕts-vĭl)	125	29.26 N	96.55 W
Hallock, Mn. (hăl'ŭk)	114	48.46 N	96.57 W
Hall Pen, Can. (hôl)	97	63.14 N	65.40 W
Halls Bayou, Tx.	125a	29.55 N	95.23 W
Hallsberg, Swe. (häls'bĕrgh)	164	59.04 N	15.04 E
Halls Creek, Austl. (hôlz)	214	18.15 S	127.45 E
Halmahera (I.), Indon. (häl-mä-hä'rä)	207	0.45 N	128.45 E
Halmahera, Laut (Halmahera Sea), Indon.	207	1.00 S	129.00 E
Halmstad, Swe. (hälm'städ)	164	56.40 N	12.46 E
Halsafjorden, Nor. (häl'sĕ fyôrd)	164	63.03 N	8.23 E
Halstead, Eng.	62	51.20 N	0.08 E
Halstead, Ks. (hôl'stĕd)	123	38.02 N	97.36 W
Haltern, F.R.G. (häl'tĕrn)	169c	51.45 N	7.10 E
Haltom City, Tx. (hôl'tŏm)	119c	32.48 N	97.13 W
Halvarenbeek, Neth.	157a	51.29 N	5.10 E
Halver, F.R.G.	63	51.11 N	7.30 E
Ham (Neigh.), Eng.	62	51.26 N	0.19 W
Hamadān, Iran (hŭ-mŭ-dän')	192	34.45 N	48.07 E
Ḩamāh, Syr. (hä'mä)	161	35.08 N	36.53 E
Hamamatsu, Jap. (hä'mä-mät'so͞o)	205	34.41 N	137.43 E
Hamar, Nor. (hä'mär)	164	60.49 N	11.05 E
Hamasaka, Jap. (hä'mȧ-sä'kȧ)	201	35.57 N	134.27 E
Hamberg, S. Afr.	71b	26.11 S	27.53 E
Hamborn, F.R.G. (häm'bōrn)	169c	51.30 N	6.43 E
Hamburg, Ar. (hăm'bûrg)	123	33.15 N	91.49 W
Hamburg, F.R.G. (häm'bo͞orgh)	157c	53.34 N	10.02 E
Hamburg, Ia.	114	40.39 N	95.40 W
Hamburg, NJ	112a	41.09 N	74.35 W
Hamburg, NY	113c	42.44 N	78.51 W
Hamburg, S. Afr. (hăm'bûrg)	227c	33.18 S	27.28 E
Hamburg (State), F.R.G.	157c	53.35 N	10.00 E
Hamden, Ct. (hăm'dĕn)	111	41.20 N	72.55 W

PLACE (Pronounciation)	PAGE	Lat. °′	Long. °′
Hämeenlinna, Fin. (hĕ'mān-lĭn-nȧ)	165	61.00 N	24.29 E
Hameln, F.R.G. (hä'mĕln)	166	52.06 N	9.23 E
Hamelwörden, F.R.G. (hä'mĕl-vûr-dĕn)	157c	53.47 N	9.19 E
Hamersley ., Austl. (hăm'ĕrz-lē)	214	22.15 S	117.50 E
Hamhŭng, Kor. (häm'ho͞ong')	204	39.57 N	127.35 E
Hami (Kumul), China (hä-mē)(kô-mo͞ol')	198	42.58 N	93.14 E
Hamilton, Al.	126	34.09 N	88.01 W
Hamilton, Austl. (hăm'ĭl-tŭn)	216	37.50 S	142.10 E
Hamilton, Can.	95d	43.15 N	79.52 W
Hamilton, Ma.	105a	42.37 N	70.52 W
Hamilton, Mo.	123	39.43 N	93.59 W
Hamilton, Mt.	117	46.15 N	114.09 W
Hamilton, N.Z.	217	37.45 S	175.28 E
Hamilton, Oh.	113f	39.22 N	84.33 W
Hamilton, Tx.	124	31.42 N	98.07 W
Hamilton Hbr., Can.	95d	43.17 N	79.50 W
Hamilton Inlet, Can.	97	54.20 N	56.57 W
Hamilton, L., Ar.	123	34.25 N	93.32 W
Hamina, Fin. (hȧ'mē-nȧ)	165	60.34 N	27.15 E
Hamlet, NC (hăm'lĕt)	127	35.52 N	79.46 W
Hamlin, Tx. (hăm'lĭn)	122	32.54 N	100.08 W
Hamm, F.R.G. (häm)	169c	51.40 N	7.48 E
Hamm (Neigh.), F.R.G.	63	51.12 N	6.44 E
Hammanskraal, S. Afr. (hä-mȧns-kräl')	223d	25.24 S	28.17 E
Hamme, Bel.	157a	51.06 N	4.07 E
Hamme-Oste Kanal (Can.), F.R.G. (hä'mĕ-ōs'tĕ kä-näl)	157c	53.20 N	8.59 E
Hammerfest, Nor. (hä'mĕr-fĕst)	158	70.38 N	23.59 E
Hammersmith (Neigh.), Eng.	62	51.30 N	0.14 W
Hammond, In. (hăm'ŭnd)	113a	41.37 N	87.31 W
Hammond, La.	125	30.30 N	90.28 W
Hammond, Or.	118c	46.12 N	123.57 W
Hammondville, Austl.	70a	33.57 S	150.57 E
Hammonton, NJ (hăm'ŭn-tŭn)	111	39.40 N	74.45 W
Hampden, Me. (hăm'dĕn)	104	44.44 N	68.51 W
Hampshire Downs, Eng. (hămp'shĭr dounz)	162	51.01 N	1.05 W
Hampstead, Md.	112e	39.36 N	76.54 W
Hampstead (Neigh.), Eng.	62	51.33 N	0.11 W
Hampstead Heath (P. Int.), Eng.	62	51.34 N	0.10 W
Hampstead Norris, Eng. (hămp-stĕd nŏ'rĭs)	156b	51.27 N	1.14 W
Hampton, Austl.	70b	37.56 S	145.00 E
Hampton, Can. (hămp'tŭn)	104	45.32 N	65.51 W
Hampton, Ia.	115	42.43 N	93.15 W
Hampton (Neigh.), Eng.	62	51.25 N	0.22 W
Hampton, Va.	112g	37.02 N	76.21 W
Hampton National Historic Site (P. Int.), Md.	56c	39.25 N	76.35 W
Hampton Roads (Inlet), Va.	112g	36.56 N	76.23 W
Ḩamrā, Al- Ḩammadah al- (Plat.), Libya	224	29.39 N	10.53 E
Hamtramck, Mi. (hăm-trăm'ĭk)	113b	42.24 N	83.03 W
Hāmūn-i Māshkel (L.), Pak. (hä-mo͞on'ē mäsh-kĕl')	192	28.28 N	64.13 E
Han (R.), China (hän)	203	25.00 N	116.35 E
Han (R.), China	203	31.40 N	112.04 E
Han (R.), Kor.	204	37.10 N	127.40 E
Hana, Hi. (hä'nä)	106a	20.43 N	155.59 W
Hanábana (R.), Cuba (hä-nä-bä'nä)	134	22.30 N	80.55 W
Hanalei B., Hi. (hä-nä-lä'ē)	106a	22.15 N	159.40 W
Hanang (Mtn.), Tan.	231	4.26 S	35.24 E
Hanau, F.R.G. (hä'nou)	166	50.08 N	8.56 E
Hancock, Mi. (hăn'kŏk)	115	47.08 N	88.37 W
Handan, China (hän-dän)	200	36.37 N	114.30 E
Handforth, Eng.	64b	53.21 N	2.13 W
Haney, Can. (hā-nē)	99	49.13 N	122.36 W
Hanford, Ca. (hăn'fērd)	120	36.20 N	119.38 W
Han-gang (R.), Kor.	68b	37.36 N	126.47 E
Hangayn Nuruu (Khangai Mts.), Mong.	198	48.03 N	99.45 E
Hangchou, China (hăng'chō')	203	30.17 N	120.12 E
Hang Hau Town, China	68c	22.19 N	114.16 E
Hango, Fin. (häŋ'gû)	165	59.49 N	22.56 E
Hangzhou Wan (B.), China (häŋ-jō wän)	203	30.20 N	121.25 E
Hankamer, Tx. (hăn'kȧ-mĕr)	125a	29.52 N	94.42 W
Hankinson, ND (hăŋ'kĭn-sŭn)	114	46.04 N	96.54 W
Hankou, China (hän-kō)	203	30.42 N	114.22 E
Hanna, Can. (hăn'ȧ)	99	51.38 N	111.54 W
Hanna, Wy.	117	41.51 N	106.34 W
Hannah, ND	114	48.58 N	98.42 W
Hannibal, Mo. (hăn'ĭ bȧl)	123	39.42 N	91.22 W
Hann, Mt., Austl. (hän)	214	16.05 S	126.07 E
Hannover, F.R.G. (hän-ō'vĕr)	166	52.22 N	9.45 E
Hanö-bukten (B.), Swe.	164	55.54 N	14.55 E
Hanoi, Viet. (hä-noi')	203	21.04 N	105.50 E
Hanover, Can. (hăn'ô-vĕr)	110	44.10 N	81.05 W
Hanover (I.), Chile	144	51.00 S	74.45 W
Hanover, Ma.	105a	42.07 N	70.49 W
Hanover, Md.	56c	39.11 N	76.42 W
Hanover, NH	111	43.45 N	72.15 W
Hanover, Pa.	111	39.50 N	77.00 W
Hanshan, China (hän'shän')	200	31.43 N	118.06 E
Hans Lollick (I.), Vir. Is. (U.S.A.) (häns'lôl'ĭk)	129c	18.24 N	64.55 W
Hanson, Ma. (hăn'sŭn)	105a	42.04 N	70.53 W
Hansville, Wa. (hăns'-vĭl)	118a	47.55 N	122.33 W
Hantengri Feng (Mtn.), China (hän-tŭŋ-rē fŭŋ)	198	42.10 N	80.20 E
Hantsport, Can. (hănts'pōrt)	104	45.04 N	64.11 W
Hanworth (Neigh.), Eng.	62	51.26 N	0.23 W
Hanyang, China (han'yäng')	203	30.30 N	114.10 E
Hanzhong, China (hän-jôŋ)	202	33.02 N	107.00 E
Haocheng, China (hou-chŭŋ)	200	33.19 N	117.33 E
Haparanda, Swe. (hä-pa-rän'dä)	158	65.54 N	23.57 E
Hapeville, Ga. (hăp'vĭl)	112c	33.39 N	84.25 W
Hapsford, Eng.	64a	53.16 N	2.48 W
Haql, Sau. Ar.	191a	29.15 N	34.57 E
Haramachida, Jap.	69a	35.33 N	139.27 E

ăt; finăl; rāte; senåte; ärm; åsk; sofȧ; fâre; ch-choose; dh-as th in other; bē; ėvent; bĕt; recĕnt; cratẽr; g-gō; gh-guttural g; bĭt; ĭ-short neutral; rīde; ĸ-guttural k as ch in German ich;

PLACE (Pronounciation)	PAGE	Lat. °′	Long. °′
Harar (Prov.), Eth.	225	8.15 N	41.00 E
Harare (Salisbury), Zimb.	231	17.50 S	31.03 E
Harbin, China	202	45.40 N	126.30 E
Harbor Beach, Mi. (här'bẽr bēch)	110	43.50 N	82.40 W
Harbor City (Neigh.), Ca.	59	33.48 N	118.17 W
Harbord, Austl.	70a	33.45 S	151.26 E
Harbor Isle, NY	55	40.36 N	73.40 W
Harbor Springs, Mi.	110	45.25 N	85.05 W
Harbour Breton, Can. (brĕt'ŭn) (brē-tôN')	105	47.29 N	55.48 W
Harbour Grace, Can. (grās)	105	47.32 N	53.13 W
Harburg, F.R.G. (här-bŏŏrgh)	157c	53.28 N	9.58 E
Hardangerfjorden (Fd.), Nor. (här-däng'ẽr fyôrd)	164	59.58 N	6.30 E
Hardin, Mt. (här'dĭn)	117	45.44 N	107.36 W
Harding (L.), Al.-Ga.	126	32.43 N	85.00 W
Harding, S. Afr. (här'dĭng)	227c	30.34 S	29.54 E
Hardwār, India (hŭr'dwär)	196	29.56 N	78.06 E
Hardy (R.), Mex. (här'dĭ)	120	32.04 N	115.10 W
Hare B., Can. (hâr)	103	51.18 N	55.50 W
Harefield (Neigh.), Eng.	62	51.36 N	0.29 W
Harerge, Eth.	225	9.43 N	42.10 E
Hargeysa, Som. (här-gā'ē-sȧ)	223a	9.20 N	43.57 E
Harghita, Munţii (Mts.), Rom.	167	46.25 N	25.40 E
Harima-Nada (Sea), Jap. (hä'rē-mä nä-dä)	205	34.34 N	134.37 E
Haringey (Neigh.), Eng.	62	51.35 N	0.07 W
Haringvliet (R.), Neth.	157a	51.49 N	4.03 E
Harker Village, NJ	56b	39.51 N	75.09 W
Har, Laga (R.), Ken.	231	2.15 N	39.30 E
Harlan, Ia. (här'lăn)	124	41.40 N	95.10 W
Harlan, Ky.	126	36.50 N	83.19 W
Harlan Co. Res., Ne.	122	40.03 N	99.51 W
Harlem, Mt. (hàr'lĕm)	117	48.33 N	108.50 W
Harlem (Neigh.), NY	55	40.49 N	73.56 W
Harlesden (Neigh.), Eng.	62	51.32 N	0.15 W
Harlingen, Neth. (här'lĭng-ĕn)	163	53.10 N	5.24 E
Harlingen, Tx.	125	26.12 N	97.42 W
Harlington (Neigh.), Eng.	62	51.29 N	0.26 W
Harlow, Eng. (här'lō)	156b	51.46 N	0.08 E
Harlowton, Mt. (hár'lô-tun)	117	46.26 N	109.50 W
Harmar Heights, Pa.	57b	40.33 N	79.49 W
Harmarville, Pa.	57b	40.32 N	79.51 W
Harmony, In. (här'mô-nĭ)	110	39.35 N	87.00 W
Harney Basin, Or. (här'nĭ)	116	43.26 N	120.19 W
Harney L., Or.	116	43.11 N	119.23 W
Harney Pk., SD	114	43.52 N	103.32 W
Härnosand, Swe. (hĕr-nû-sänd)	164	62.37 N	17.54 E
Haro, Sp. (ä'rō)	170	42.35 N	2.49 W
Harola, India	67d	28.36 N	77.19 E
Harold Hill (Neigh.), Eng.	62	51.36 N	0.13 E
Harold Wood (Neigh.), Eng.	62	51.36 N	0.14 E
Haro Str., Can.-U.S. (hă'rō)	118a	48.27 N	123.11 W
Harpen (Neigh.), F.R.G.	63	51.29 N	7.16 E
Harpenden, Eng. (här'pĕn-d'n)	156b	51.48 N	0.22 W
Harper, Ks. (här'pẽr)	122	37.17 N	98.02 W
Harper, Lib.	228	4.25 N	7.43 W
Harper, Wa.	118a	47.31 N	122.32 W
Harpers Ferry, WV (här'pẽrz)	111	39.20 N	77.45 W
Harper Woods, Mi.	57c	42.24 N	82.55 W
Harpurhey (Neigh.), Eng.	64b	53.31 N	2.13 W
Harricana (R.), Can.	103	50.10 N	78.50 W
Harriman, Tn. (hă'ĭ-măn)	126	35.55 N	84.34 W
Harrington, De. (hăr'ĭng-tŭn)	111	38.55 N	75.35 W
Harri Rud (R.), Afg.	192	34.29 N	61.16 E
Harris (I.), Scot. (hăr'ĭs)	162	57.55 N	6.40 W
Harris (L.), Fl.	127a	28.43 N	81.40 W
Harrisburg, Il. (hăr'ĭs-bûrg)	110	37.45 N	88.35 W
Harrisburg, Pa.	111	40.15 N	76.50 W
Harrismith, S. Afr. (hă-rĭs'mĭth)	223d	28.17 S	29.08 E
Harrison, Ar. (hăr'ĭ-sŭn)	123	36.13 N	93.06 W
Harrison, NJ	55	40.45 N	74.10 W
Harrison, NY	55	40.58 N	73.43 W
Harrison, Oh.	113f	39.16 N	84.45 W
Harrisonburg, Va. (hăr'ĭ-sŭn-bûrg)	111	38.30 N	78.50 W
Harrison L., Can.	99	49.31 N	121.59 W
Harrisonville, Md.	56c	39.23 N	77.50 W
Harrisonville, Mo. (hăr-ĭ-sŭn-vĭl)	123	38.39 N	94.21 W
Harris Park, Austl.	70a	33.49 S	151.01 E
Harrisville, Ut. (hăr'ĭs-vĭl)	119b	41.17 N	112.00 W
Harrisville, WV	110	39.10 N	81.05 W
Harrodsburg, Ky. (hăr'ŭdz-bûrg)	110	37.45 N	84.50 W
Harrods Cr., Ky. (hăr'ŭdz)	113h	38.24 N	85.33 W
Harrow, Eng. (hăr'ō)	156b	51.34 N	0.21 W
Harrow on the Hill (Neigh.), Eng.	62	51.34 N	0.20 W
Harsefeld, F.R.G. (här'zĕ-fĕld')	157c	53.27 N	9.30 E
Harstad, Nor. (här'städh)	158	68.49 N	16.10 E
Hart, Mi. (härt)	110	43.40 N	86.25 W
Hartbeesfontein, S. Afr.	223d	26.46 S	26.25 E
Hartbeespoortdam (L.), S. Afr.	227b	25.47 S	27.43 E
Hartford, Al. (härt'fẽrd)	126	31.05 N	85.42 W
Hartford, Ar.	123	35.01 N	94.21 W
Hartford, Ct.	111	41.45 N	72.40 W
Hartford, Il.	119e	38.50 N	90.06 W
Hartford, Ky.	126	37.25 N	86.50 W
Hartford, Mi.	110	42.15 N	86.15 W
Hartford, Wi.	115	43.19 N	88.25 W
Hartford City, In.	110	40.35 N	85.25 W
Hartington, Eng. (härt'ĭng-tŭn)	156	53.08 N	1.48 W
Hartington, Ne.	114	42.37 N	97.18 W
Hartland Pt., Eng.	162	51.03 N	4.40 W
Hartlepool, Eng. (här't'l-pōōl)	162	54.40 N	1.12 W
Hartley, Eng.	62	51.23 N	0.19 E
Hartley, Ia. (härt'lĭ)	114	43.12 N	95.29 W
Hartley Bay, Can.	98	53.25 N	129.15 W
Hart Mtn., Can. (härt)	101	52.25 N	101.30 W
Hartsbeespoort, S. Afr.	227b	25.44 S	27.51 E
Hartselle, Al. (härt'sĕl)	126	34.24 N	86.55 W
Hartshorne, Ok. (härts'hôrn)	123	34.49 N	95.34 W
Hartsville, SC (härts'vĭl)	127	34.20 N	80.04 W
Hartwell, Ga. (härt'wĕl)	126	34.21 N	82.56 W
Hartwell Res., Ga.	126	34.30 N	83.00 W
Hārua, India	196a	22.36 N	88.40 E
Har Us Nuur (L.), Mong	198	48.00 N	92.32 E
Harvard, Il. (här'vȧrd)	115	42.25 N	88.39 W
Harvard, Ma.	105a	42.30 N	71.35 W
Harvard, Ne.	122	40.36 N	98.08 W
Harvard, Mt., Co.	121	38.55 N	106.20 W
Harvel, Eng.	62	51.21 N	0.22 E
Harvey, Can.	104	45.44 N	64.46 W
Harvey, Il.	113a	41.37 N	87.39 W
Harvey, La.	112d	29.54 N	90.05 W
Harvey, ND	114	47.46 N	99.55 W
Harwich, Eng. (här'wĭch)	163	51.53 N	1.13 E
Harwick, Pa.	57b	40.34 N	79.48 W
Harwood, Eng.	64b	53.35 N	2.23 W
Harwood, Md.	56c	38.52 N	76.37 W
Harwood Heights, Il.	58a	41.59 N	87.48 W
Harwood Park, Md.	56c	39.12 N	76.44 W
Haryana (State), India	196	29.00 N	75.45 E
Harz Mts., G.D.R. (härts)	166	51.42 N	10.50 E
Hasanābād, Iran	68h	35.44 N	51.19 E
Hasā, Wādī al (R.), Jordan	191a	30.55 N	35.50 E
Hasbrouck Heights, NJ	55	40.52 N	74.04 W
Hashimoto, Jap. (hä'shē-mō'tō)	205	34.19 N	135.37 E
Haskayne, Eng.	64a	53.34 N	2.58 W
Haskell, Ok. (hăs'kĕl)	123	35.49 N	95.41 W
Haskell, Tx.	122	33.09 N	99.43 W
Hasköy (Neigh.), Tur.	66f	41.02 N	28.58 E
Haslingden, Eng. (hăz'lĭng dĕn)	156	53.43 N	2.19 W
Hasselbeck-Schwarzbach, F.R.G.	63	51.16 N	6.53 E
Hasseleholm, Swe. (häs'lĕ-hōlm)	164	56.10 N	13.44 E
Hassels (Neigh.), F.R.G.	63	51.10 N	6.53 E
Hasselt, Bel. (häs'ĕlt)	157a	50.56 N	5.23 E
Hassi Messaoud, Alg.	224	31.17 N	6.13 E
Hasslinghausen, F.R.G.	63	51.20 N	7.17 E
Hästen (Neigh.), F.R.G.	63	51.09 N	7.06 E
Hasten (Neigh.), F.R.G.	63	51.12 N	7.09 E
Hastings, Eng. (hās'tĭngz)	163	50.52 N	0.28 E
Hastings, Mi.	110	42.40 N	85.20 W
Hastings, Mn.	119g	44.44 N	92.51 W
Hastings, Ne.	122	40.34 N	98.42 W
Hastings, N.Z.	217	39.33 S	176.53 E
Hastings-on-Hudson, NY (ŏn-hŭd'sŭn)	112a	40.59 N	75.53 W
Hastingwood, Eng.	62	51.45 N	0.09 E
Hatchie (R.), Tn. (hăch'ē)	126	35.28 N	89.14 W
Hateg, Rom. (kät-sāg')	173	45.35 N	22.57 E
Hatfield Broad Oak, Eng. (hăt-fēld brôd ōk)	156	51.50 N	0.14 E
Hatogaya, Jap. (hä'tō-gä-yä)	205a	35.50 N	139.45 E
Hatsukaichi, Jap. (hät'sōō-kȧ'ē-chē)	205	34.22 N	132.19 E
Hatteras, C., NC (hăt'ẽr-ȧs)	127	35.15 N	75.24 W
Hattiesburg, Ms. (hăt'ĭz-bûrg)	126	31.20 N	89.18 W
Hattingen, F.R.G. (hä'tĕn-gĕn)	169c	51.24 N	7.11 E
Hatton (Neigh.), Eng.	62	51.28 N	0.25 W
Hattori, Jap.	69b	34.46 N	135.27 E
Hatvan, Hung. (hôt'vôn)	167	47.39 N	19.44 E
Hatzfeld (Neigh.), F.R.G.	63	51.17 N	7.11 E
Haugesund, Nor. (hou'gĕ-soon')	164	59.26 N	5.20 E
Haughton Green, Eng.	64b	53.27 N	2.06 W
Haukivesi (L.), Fin. (hou'kē-vĕ'sē)	165	62.02 N	29.02 E
Haultain (R.), Can.	100	56.15 N	106.35 W
Hauptsrus, S. Afr.	223d	26.35 S	26.16 E
Hauraki, G., N.Z. (hä-ōō-rä'kē)	217	36.30 S	175.00 E
Haut Atlas (Mts.), Mor.	160	32.10 N	5.49 W
Hauterive, Can.	104	49.11 N	68.16 W
Haut, Isle au, Me. (hō)	104	44.03 N	68.13 W
Hauula, Hi.	106a	21.37 N	157.45 W
Hauz Rāni (Neigh.), India	67d	28.32 N	77.13 E
Havana, Cuba	60b	23.08 N	82.22 W
Havana, Il. (hȧ-vă'nȧ)	123	40.17 N	90.02 W
Havana, see La Habana			
Havasu L., Az. (hăv'ȧ-sōō)	121	34.26 N	114.09 W
Havel-Kanal (Can.), G.D.R.	65a	52.36 N	13.12 E
Havel R., G.D.R. (hä'fĕl)	166	53.09 N	13.10 E
Haverford, Pa.	56b	40.01 N	75.18 W
Haverhill, Ma. (hā'vẽr-hĭl)	105a	42.46 N	71.05 W
Haverhill, NH	111	44.00 N	72.05 W
Havering (Neigh.), Eng.	62	51.34 N	0.14 E
Havering-atte-Bower (Neigh.), Eng.	62	51.37 N	0.11 E
Havering's Grove, Eng.	62	51.38 N	0.23 E
Haverstraw, NY (hā'vẽr-strô)	112a	41.11 N	73.58 W
Havertown, Pa.	56b	39.59 N	75.18 W
Havlíckuv Brod, Czech.	166	49.38 N	15.34 E
Havre, Mt. (hăv'ẽr)	117	48.34 N	109.42 W
Havre-Bouche Boucher, Can. (hăv'rȧ-bōō-shā')	105	45.42 N	61.30 W
Havre de Grace, Md. (hăv'ẽr dē grās')	111	39.35 N	76.05 W
Havre-Saint Pierre, Can.	105	50.15 N	63.36 W
Haw (R.), NC (hô)	127	36.17 N	79.46 W
Hawaii (State), U.S.	108c	20.00 N	157.40 W
Hawaii (I.), Hi (häw wī'ē)	106b	19.50 N	157.15 W
Hawaiian Gardens, Ca.	59	33.50 N	118.04 W
Hawaiian Is., U.S. (hä-wī'ăn)	108c	22.00 N	158.00 W
Hawaii Volcanoes Natl. Pk., Hi.	106a	19.30 N	155.25 W
Hawarden, Ia. (hā'wȧr-dĕn)	114	43.00 N	96.28 W
Hawf, Jabal (Hills), Egypt	71a	29.55 N	31.21 E
Hawi, Hi. (hä'wē)	106a	20.16 N	155.48 W
Hawick, Scot. (hô'ĭk)	162	55.25 N	2.55 W
Hawke B., N.Z. (hôk)	217	39.17 S	177.20 E
Hawker, Austl. (hô'kẽr)	216	31.58 S	138.12 E
Hawkesbury, Can. (hôks'bẽr-ĭ)	111	45.35 N	74.35 W
Hawkinsville, Ga. (hô'kĭnz-vĭl)	126	32.15 N	83.30 W
Hawks Nest Pt., Ba.	135	24.05 N	75.30 W
Hawley, Eng.	62	51.25 N	0.14 E
Hawley, Mn. (hô'lĭ)	114	46.52 N	96.18 W
Haworth, Eng. (hā'wûrth)	156	53.50 N	1.57 W
Haworth, NJ	55	40.58 N	73.59 W
Hawtah, Sau. Ar.	192	15.58 N	48.26 E
Hawthorn, Austl.	70b	37.49 S	145.02 E
Hawthorne, Ca. (hô'thôrn)	119a	33.55 N	118.22 W
Hawthorne, NJ	55	40.57 N	74.09 W
Hawthorne, Nv.	120	38.33 N	118.39 W
Haxtun, Co. (hăks'tŭn)	122	40.39 N	102.38 W
Hay (R.), Austl. (hā)	214	23.00 S	136.45 E
Hay (R.), Can.	96	60.21 N	117.14 W
Hayama, Jap. (hä-yä'mä)	205a	35.16 N	139.35 E
Hayashi, Jap. (hä-yä'shē)	205a	35.13 N	139.38 E
Hayden, Az. (hā'dĕn)	121	33.00 N	110.50 W
Hayes (Neigh.), Eng.	62	51.23 N	0.01 E
Hayes (R.), Can.	111	55.25 N	93.55 W
Hayes, Mt., Ak. (hāz)	107	63.32 N	146.40 W
Haynesville, La. (hānz'vĭl)	125	32.55 N	93.08 W
Hayrabolu, Tur.	173	41.14 N	27.05 E
Hay River, Can.	106	60.50 N	115.53 W
Hays, Ks. (hāz)	122	38.51 N	99.20 W
Haysī, Wādī al (R.), Egypt	191	29.24 N	34.32 E
Haystack Mtn., Wa. (hā-stăk')	118a	48.26 N	122.07 W
Hayward, Ca. (hā'wẽrd)	118b	37.40 N	122.06 W
Hayward, Wi.	115	46.01 N	91.31 W
Hazard, Ky. (hăz'ȧrd)	126	37.13 N	83.10 W
Hazel Grove, Eng.	64b	53.23 N	2.08 W
Hazelhurst, Ga. (hā'z'l-hûrst)	127	31.50 N	82.36 W
Hazelhurst, Ms.	126	31.52 N	90.23 W
Hazel Park, Mi.	113b	42.28 N	83.06 W
Hazelton, Can. (hā'z'l-tŭn)	98	55.15 N	127.40 W
Hazelton Mts., Can.	98	55.00 N	128.00 W
Hazleton, Pa.	111	41.00 N	76.00 W
Headland, Al. (hĕd'lănd)	126	31.22 N	85.20 W
Headley, Eng.	62	51.17 N	0.16 W
Heald Green, Eng.	64b	53.22 N	2.14 W
Healdsburg, Ca. (hēldz'bûrg)	120	38.37 N	122.52 W
Healdton, Ok. (hēld'tŭn)	123	34.13 N	97.28 W
Heanor, Eng. (hēn'ŏr)	156	53.01 N	1.22 W
Heard I., Ind. O. (hûrd)	232	53.10 S	74.35 E
Hearne, Tx. (hûrn)	125	30.53 N	96.35 W
Hearst, Can. (hûrst)	97	49.36 N	83.40 W
Heart (R.), ND (härt)	114	46.46 N	102.34 W
Heart Lake Ind. Res., Can.	99	55.02 N	111.30 W
Heart's Content, Can. (härts kŏn'tĕnt)	105	47.52 N	53.22 W
Heathmont, Austl.	70b	37.49 S	145.15 E
Heath Pte., Can. (hēth)	105	49.06 N	61.45 W
Heaton Moor, Eng.	64b	53.25 N	2.11 W
Heavener, Ok. (hēv'nẽr)	123	34.52 N	94.36 W
Heaverham, Eng.	62	51.18 N	0.15 E
Heaviley, Eng.	64b	53.24 N	2.09 W
Hebbronville, Tx. (hē'brŭn-vĭl)	124	27.18 N	98.40 W
Hebbville, Md.	56c	39.20 N	77.46 W
Hebei (Prov.), China (hŭ-bā)	199	39.15 N	115.40 E
Heber, Ut. (hē'bẽr)	121	40.30 N	111.25 W
Heber Springs, Ar.	123	35.28 N	91.59 W
Hebgen Res., Mt. (hĕb'gĕn)	117	44.47 N	111.38 W
Hebrides, Sea of, Scot.	162	57.00 N	7.00 W
Hebron, Can. (hĕb'rŭn)	97	58.11 N	62.56 W
Hebron, In.	113a	41.19 N	87.13 W
Hebron, Ky.	113f	39.04 N	84.43 W
Hebron, ND	114	46.54 N	102.04 W
Hebron, Ne.	123	40.11 N	97.36 W
Hebron, see Al Khalīl			
Heby, Swe. (hĭ'bü)	164	59.56 N	16.48 E
Hecate Str., Can. (hĕk'ȧ-tē)	98	53.00 N	131.00 W
Hecelchakán, Mex. (ā-sĕl-chä-kän')	131	20.10 N	90.09 W
Hechi, China (hŭ-chr)	203	24.50 N	108.18 E
Hechuan, China (hŭ-chyuän)	203	30.00 N	106.20 E
Hecla I., Can.	101	51.08 N	96.45 W
Hedemora, Swe. (hĭ-dĕ-mō'rä)	164	60.16 N	15.55 E
Hedon, Eng. (hĕ-dŭn)	156	53.44 N	0.12 W
Heemstede, Neth.	157a	52.20 N	4.36 E
Heerdt (Neigh.), F.R.G.	63	51.13 N	6.43 E
Heerlen, Neth.	163	50.55 N	5.58 E
Hefa, see Haifa			
Hefei, China (hŭ-fā)	200	31.51 N	117.15 E
Heflin, Al. (hĕf'lĭn)	126	33.40 N	85.33 W
Heide, F.R.G. (hī'dē)	166	54.13 N	9.06 E
Heide (Neigh.), F.R.G.	63	51.31 N	6.52 E
Heidelberg, Austl. (hī'dĕl-bûrg)	211	37.45 S	145.04 E
Heidelberg, F.R.G. (hīdĕl-bĕrgh)	166	49.24 N	8.43 E
Heidelberg, Pa.	57b	40.23 N	80.05 W
Heidenheim, F.R.G. (hī'dĕn-hīm)	166	48.41 N	10.09 E
Heil, F.R.G.	63	51.38 N	7.35 E
Heilbron, S. Afr. (hĭl'brōn)	223d	27.17 S	27.58 E
Heilbronn, F.R.G. (hīl'brōn)	166	49.09 N	9.16 E
Heiligenhaus, F.R.G. (hī'lē-gĕn-houz)	169c	51.19 N	6.58 E
Heiligensee (Neigh.), F.R.G.	65a	52.36 N	13.13 E
Heiligenstadt, G.D.R. (hī'lē-gĕn-shtät)	166	51.21 N	10.10 E
Heilong (R.), China-Sov. Un. (hā-loŋ)	202	49.38 N	127.25 E
Heilongjiang, China (hā-lôŋ-jyäŋ)	199	46.36 N	128.07 E
Heinersdorf, G.D.R.	65a	52.23 N	13.20 E
Heinersdorf (Neigh.), G.D.R.	65a	52.34 N	13.27 E
Heinola, Fin. (hā-nō'lá)	165	61.13 N	26.03 E
Heinsberg, F.R.G. (hīnz'bĕrgh)	169c	51.04 N	6.07 E
Heisingen (Neigh.), F.R.G.	63	51.25 N	7.04 E
Heist-op-den-Berg, Bel.	157a	51.05 N	4.14 E
Hejaz, see Al Hijāz			
Hejian, China (hŭ-jyĕn)	200	38.28 N	116.05 E
Hel, Pol. (hāl)	167	54.37 N	18.53 E
Helagsfjället (Mtn.), Swe.	164	62.54 N	12.24 E
Helan Shan (Mts.), China (hŭ-län shän)	198	38.02 N	105.20 E
Helena, Ar. (hē-lē'nȧ)	123	34.33 N	90.35 W
Helena, Mt. (hĕ-lē'nȧ)	117	46.35 N	112.01 W
Helensburgh, Austl. (hĕl'ĕnz-bŭr-ō)	211b	34.11 S	150.59 E
Helensburgh, Scot.	162	56.01 N	4.53 W
Helgoland I., F.R.G. (hĕl'gō-länd)	166	54.13 N	7.30 E
Heliopolis (P. Int.), Egypt	71a	30.08 N	31.17 E
Heliopolis, see Misr al-Jadīdah (Neigh.), Egypt	71a	30.06 N	31.20 E
Helka (Vol.), Ice. (hĕl'kȧ)	158	63.53 N	19.37 W
Hellier, Ky. (hĕl'yẽr)	127	37.16 N	82.27 W
Hellín, Sp. (ĕl-yén')	170	38.30 N	1.40 W
Helmand (R.), Afg. (hĕl'mŭnd)	192	31.00 N	63.48 E

ng-sing; ŋ-baŋk; N-nasalized n; nŏd; cŏmmit; ōld; ôbey; ôrder; oi-boil; fōōd; fŏŏt; ou-out; s-soft; sh-dish; th-thin; pūre; ůnite; ûrn; stŭd; circŭs; ü-as in French tu; '-indeterminate vowel.

PLACE (Pronounciation)	PAGE	Lat. °'	Long. °'
Helmond, Neth. (hĕl'mōnt) (ĕl'môɴ')	163	51.35 N	5.04 E
Helmstedt, F.R.G. (hĕlm'shtĕt)	166	52.14 N	11.03 E
Helotes, Tx. (hē'lōts)	119d	29.35 N	98.41 W
Helper, Ut. (hĕlp'ēr)	121	39.40 N	110.55 W
Helsby, Eng.	64a	53.16 N	2.46 W
Helsingborg, Swe. (hĕl'sĭng-bôrgh)	164	56.04 N	12.40 E
Helsingfors, see Helsinki			
Helsingør, Den. (hĕl-sĭng-ŭr')	164	56.03 N	12.33 E
Helsinki (Helsingfors), Fin. (hĕl'sēn-kē) (hĕl'sĭng-fôrs')	165	60.10 N	24.53 E
Hemel Hempstead, Eng. (hĕm'ĕl hĕmp'stĕd)	156b	51.43 N	0.29 W
Hemer, F.R.G.	169c	51.32 N	7.46 E
Hemet, Ca. (hĕm'ĕt)	119a	33.45 N	116.57 W
Hemingford, Ne. (hĕm'ĭng-fērd)	114	42.21 N	103.30 W
Hemphill, Tx. (hĕmp'hĭl)	125	31.20 N	93.48 W
Hempstead, NY (hĕmp'stĕd)	112a	40.42 N	73.37 W
Hempstead, Tx.	125	30.07 N	96.05 W
Hemse, Swe. (hĕm'sē)	164	57.15 N	18.25 E
Hemsön (I.), Swe.	164	62.43 N	18.22 E
Henan (Prov.), China (hŭ-nän)	199	33.58 N	112.33 E
Henares (R.), Sp. (å-nä'rås)	170	40.50 N	2.55 W
Henderson, Ky. (hĕn'dēr-sŭn)	110	37.50 N	87.30 W
Henderson, NC	127	36.18 N	78.24 W
Henderson, Nv.	120	36.09 N	115.04 W
Henderson, Tn.	126	35.25 N	88.40 W
Henderson, Tx.	125	32.09 N	94.48 W
Hendersonville, NC (hĕn'dēr-sŭn-vĭl)	127	35.17 N	82.28 W
Hendon, Eng. (hĕn'dŭn)	156b	51.34 N	0.13 W
Hendrina, S. Afr. (hĕn-drē'nȧ)	223d	26.10 S	29.44 E
Hengch'un, Taiwan (hĕng'chŭn')	203	22.00 N	120.42 E
Hengelo, Neth. (hĕngē-lō)	163	52.20 N	6.45 E
Hengshan, China (hĕng'shän')	203	27.20 N	112.40 E
Hengshui, China (hĕng'shōō-ē')	200	37.43 N	115.42 E
Hengxian, China (hŭŋ shyĕn)	203	22.40 N	104.20 E
Hengyang, China	203	26.58 N	112.30 E
Henley on Thames, Eng. (hĕn'lē ŏn tĕmz)	156b	51.31 N	0.54 W
Henlopen, C., De. (hĕn-lō'pĕn)	111	38.45 N	75.05 W
Hennebont, Fr. (ĕn-bôɴ')	168	47.47 N	3.16 W
Hennenman, S. Afr.	223d	27.59 S	27.03 E
Hennessey, Ok. (hĕn'ĕ-sĭ)	122	36.04 N	97.53 W
Hennigsdorf, G.D.R. (hĕ'nĕngz-dōrf))	157b	52.39 N	13.12 E
Hennops (R.), S. Afr. (hĕn'ŏps)	227b	25.51 S	27.57 E
Hennopsrivier, S. Afr.	227b	25.50 S	27.59 E
Henrietta, Ok. (hĕn-rĭ-ĕt'ȧ)	123	35.25 N	95.58 W
Henrietta, Tx. (hen-rĭ-ĕ'tȧ)	122	33.47 N	98.11 W
Henrietta Maria, C., Can. (hĕn-rĭ-ĕt'ȧ)	97	55.10 N	82.20 W
Henry Mts., Ut. (hĕn'rĭ)	121	38.55 N	110.45 W
Henteyn Nuruu (Mts.), Sov. Un.	202	49.40 N	111.00 E
Hentiyn Nuruu (Mts.), Mong.	198	49.25 N	107.51 E
Henzada, Bur.	206	17.38 N	95.28 E
Heppner, Or. (hĕp'nēr)	116	45.21 N	119.33 W
Hepu, China (hŭ-pōō)	203	21.28 N	109.10 E
Herāt, Afg. (hĕ-rät')	192	34.28 N	62.13 E
Herbede, F.R.G.	63	51.25 N	7.16 E
Hercegovina (Reg.), Yugo. (hĕr-tsĕ-gô'vē-nȧ)	173	43.23 N	17.52 E
Hercules, Can.	95g	53.27 N	113.20 W
Herdecke, F.R.G. (hĕr'dĕ-kĕ)	169c	51.24 N	7.26 E
Heredia, C.R. (ā-rā'dhē-ä)	133	10.04 N	84.06 W
Hereford, Eng. (hĕrĕ'fērd)	162	52.05 N	2.44 W
Hereford, Md.	112e	39.35 N	76.42 W
Hereford, Tx. (hĕr'ĕ-fērd)	122	34.47 N	102.25 W
Hereford and Worcester (Co.), Eng.	156	52.24 N	2.15 W
Herencia, Sp. (å-rān'thē-ä)	170	39.23 N	3.22 W
Herentals, Bel.	157a	51.10 N	4.51 E
Herford, F.R.G. (hĕr'fôrt)	166	52.06 N	8.42 E
Herington, Ks. (hĕr'ĭng-tŭn)	123	38.41 N	96.57 W
Herisau, Switz. (hā'rē-zou)	166	47.23 N	9.18 E
Herk-de-Stad, Bel.	157a	50.56 N	5.13 E
Herkimer, NY (hûr'kĭ-mēr)	111	43.05 N	75.00 W
Hermann, Mo. (hûr'mȧn)	123	38.41 N	91.27 W
Hermannskogel (Mtn.), Aus.	66e	48.16 N	16.18 E
Hermansville, Mi. (hûr'mȧns-vĭl)	110	45.40 N	87.35 W
Hermantown, Mn. (hēr'mȧn-toun)	119h	46.46 N	92.12 W
Hermanusdorings, S. Afr.	223d	24.08 S	27.46 E
Herminie, Pa. (hûr-mĭ'nē)	113e	40.16 N	79.45 W
Hermitage B., Can. (hûr'mĭ-tĕj)	105	47.35 N	56.05 W
Hermit Is., Pap. N. Gui. (hûr'mĭt)	207	1.48 S	144.55 E
Hermosa Beach, Ca. (hēr-mō'sȧ)	119a	33.51 N	118.24 W
Hermosillo, Mex. (ĕr-mô-sē'l-yō)	128	29.00 N	110.57 W
Hermsdorf (Neigh.), F.R.G.	65a	52.37 N	13.18 E
Hernals (Neigh.), Aus.	66e	48.13 N	16.20 E
Herndon, Va. (hērn'don)	112e	38.58 N	77.22 W
Herne, F.R.G. (hĕr'nĕ)	169c	51.32 N	7.13 E
Herning, Den. (hĕr'nĭng)	164	56.08 N	8.55 E
Hernwood Heights, Md.	56c	39.22 N	77.50 W
Héroes Chapultepec, Cuba	60a	19.28 N	99.04 W
Héroes de Churubusco, Cuba	60a	19.22 N	99.06 W
Heron (L.), Mn. (hĕr'ŭn)	114	43.42 N	95.23 W
Herongate, Eng.	62	51.36 N	0.21 E
Heron Lake, Mn.	114	43.48 N	95.20 W
Heronsgate, Eng.	62	51.38 N	0.31 W
Herrero, Punta (pt.), Mex. (pōō'n-tä-ĕr-rĕ'rô)	132	19.18 N	87.24 W
Herrin, Il. (hĕr'ĭn)	110	37.50 N	89.00 W
Herschel, S. Afr. (hēr'-shĕl)	227c	30.37 S	27.12 E
Herscher, Il. (hēr'shēr)	113a	41.03 N	88.06 W
Hersham, Eng.	62	51.22 N	0.23 W
Herstal, Bel. (hĕr'stäl)	163	50.42 N	5.32 E
Herten, F.R.G.	63	51.35 N	7.07 E
Hertford, NC (hûrt'fērd)	127	36.10 N	76.30 W
Hertfordshire (Co.), Eng.	156	51.46 N	0.05 W
Hertzberg, G.D.R. (hĕrtz'bĕrgh)	157b	52.54 N	12.58 E
Hervás, Sp.	170	40.16 N	5.51 W
Herzliyya, Isr.	191a	32.10 N	34.49 E
Hessen, (State), F.R.G. (hĕs'ĕn)	166	50.42 N	9.00 E

PLACE (Pronounciation)	PAGE	Lat. °'	Long. °'
Heswall, Eng.	64a	53.20 N	3.06 W
Hetch Hetchy Aqueduct, Ca. (hĕtch hĕt'chĭ ȧk'wē-dŭkt)	120	37.27 N	120.54 W
Hettinger, ND (hĕt'ĭn-jēr)	114	45.58 N	102.36 W
Hetzendorf (Neigh.), Aus.	66e	48.10 N	16.18 E
Heuningspruit, S. Afr.	223d	27.28 S	27.26 E
Heven (Neigh.), F.R.G.	63	51.26 N	7.17 E
Hewlett, NY	55	40.38 N	73.42 W
Hewlett Harbor, NY	55	40.38 N	73.41 W
Hexian, China (hŭ shyĕn)	203	24.20 N	111.28 E
Hexian, China	200	31.44 N	118.20 E
Hextable, Eng.	62	51.25 N	0.11 E
Heyang, China (hŭ-yäŋ)	202	35.18 N	110.18 E
Heystekrand, S. Afr.	223d	25.16 S	27.14 E
Heyuan, China (hŭ-yůän)	203	23.48 N	114.45 E
Heywood, Eng. (hā'wŏŏd)	156	53.36 N	2.12 W
Heze, China (hŭ-dzŭ)	200	35.13 N	115.28 E
Hialeah, Fl. (hī-ȧ-lē'ăh)	127a	25.49 N	80.18 W
Hiawatha, Ks. (hī-ȧ-wô'thȧ)	123	39.50 N	95.33 W
Hiawatha, Ut.	121	39.25 N	111.05 W
Hibbing, Mn. (hĭb'ĭng)	115	47.26 N	92.58 W
Hickman, Ky. (hĭk'mȧn)	126	34.33 N	89.10 W
Hickory, NC (hĭk'ô-rĭ)	127	35.43 N	81.21 W
Hickory Hills, Il.	58a	41.43 N	87.49 W
Hicksville, NY (hĭks'vĭl)	112a	40.47 N	73.25 W
Hicksville, OH	110	41.15 N	84.45 W
Hico, Tx. (hī'kō)	124	32.00 N	98.02 W
Hidalgo, Mex. (ē-dhäl'gō)	120	24.14 N	99.25 W
Hidalgo, Mex.	124	27.49 N	99.53 W
Hidalgo (State), Mex.	128	20.45 N	99.30 W
Hidalgo del Parral, Mex. (ē-dä'l-gō-dĕl-pär-rä'l)	124	26.55 N	105.40 W
Hidalgo Yalalag, Mex. (ē-dhäl'gō-yä-lä-läg)	131	17.12 N	96.11 W
Hiddinghausen, F.R.G.	63	51.22 N	7.17 E
Hiedelberg, S. Afr.	223d	26.32 S	28.22 E
Hierro I., Can.Is. (yĕ'r-rô)	224	27.37 N	18.29 W
Hiesfeld, F.R.G.	63	51.33 N	6.46 E
Hietzing (Neigh.), Aus.	66e	48.11 N	16.18 E
Higashi (Neigh.), Jap.	69b	34.41 N	135.31 E
Higashimurayama, Jap.	205a	35.46 N	139.28 E
Higashinada (Neigh.), Jap.	69b	34.43 N	135.16 E
Higashinakano, Jap.	69a	35.38 N	139.25 E
Higashinari (Neigh.), Jap.	69b	34.40 N	135.33 E
Higashiōizumi (Neigh.), Jap.	69a	35.45 N	139.36 E
Higashiōsaka, Jap.	205b	34.40 N	135.44 E
Higashisumiyoshi (Neigh.), Jap.	69b	34.37 N	135.32 E
Higashiyama (Neigh.), Jap.	68e	34.52 N	135.48 E
Higashiyodogawa (Neigh.) Jap.	69b	34.44 N	135.29 E
Higgins (L.), Mi. (hĭg'ĭnz)	110	44.20 N	84.45 W
Higginsville, Mo. (hĭg'ĭnz-vĭl)	123	39.05 N	93.44 W
High (I.), Mi.	110	45.45 N	85.45 W
Higham Upshire, Eng.	62	51.26 N	0.28 E
High Beach, Eng.	62	51.39 N	0.02 E
High Bluff, Can.	95f	50.01 N	98.08 W
Highborne Cay, Ba. (hībôrn kē)	134	24.45 N	76.50 W
Highcliff, Pa.	57b	40.32 N	80.03 W
Higher Broughton (Neigh.), Eng.	64b	53.30 N	2.15 W
Highgrove, Ca. (hī'grōv)	119a	34.01 N	117.20 W
High Island, Tx.	125a	29.34 N	94.24 W
Highland, Ca. (hī'lȧnd)	119a	34.08 N	117.13 W
Highland, Il.	123	38.44 N	89.41 W
Highland, In.	113a	41.33 N	87.28 W
Highland, Mi.	113b	42.38 N	83.37 W
Highland, Pa.	57b	40.33 N	80.04 W
Highland Park, Il.	113a	42.11 N	87.47 W
Highland Park, Md.	56d	38.54 N	76.54 W
Highland Park, Mi.	113b	42.24 N	83.06 W
Highland Park, NJ	112a	40.30 N	74.25 W
Highland Park, Tx.	119c	32.49 N	96.48 W
Highlands, NJ (hī-lăndz)	112a	40.24 N	73.59 W
Highlands, Tx.	125a	29.49 N	95.01 W
Highlands North (Neigh.), S. Afr.	71b	26.09 S	28.05 E
High Laver, Eng.	62	51.45 N	0.13 E
Highmore, SD (hī'mōr)	114	44.30 N	99.26 W
High Ongar, Eng. (on'gēr)	156b	51.43 N	0.15 E
High Pk., Phil.	207a	51.38 N	120.05 E
High Point, NC	127	35.55 N	80.00 W
High Prairie, Can.	99	55.26 N	116.29 W
High Ridge, Mo.	115e	38.27 N	90.32 W
High River, Can.	99	50.35 N	113.52 W
Highrock (R.), NC (hī'-rŏk)	127	35.40 N	80.15 W
High Springs, Fl.	127	29.48 N	82.38 W
High Tatra Mts., Czech.-Pol.	167	49.15 N	19.40 E
Hightown, Eng.	64a	53.32 N	3.04 W
Hightstown, NJ (hīts-toun)	112a	40.16 N	74.32 W
High Wycombe, Eng. (wĭ-kŭm)	156b	51.36 N	0.45 W
Higuero, Pta (Pt.), P.R.	129b	18.21 N	67.11 W
Higuerote, Ven. (ē-gĕ-rô'tĕ)	143b	10.29 N	66.06 W
Higüey, Dom. Rep. (ē-gwĕ'y)	135	18.40 N	68.45 W
Hiiumaa (D'Ago), Sov. Un. (hē'ōōm-ô)	165	58.47 N	22.05 E
Hikone, Jap. (hē'kō-nĕ)	205	35.15 N	136.15 E
Hildburghausen, G.D.R. (hĭld'bōōrg hou-zĕn)	166	50.26 N	10.45 E
Hilden, F.R.G. (hēl'dĕn)	169c	51.10 N	6.56 E
Hildesheim, F.R.G. (hĭl'dĕs-hīm)	166	52.08 N	9.56 E
Hillaby, Mt., Barb. (hĭl'ȧ-bĭ)	133b	13.15 N	59.35 W
Hillbrow (Neigh.), S. Afr.	71b	26.11 S	28.03 E
Hill City, Ks. (hĭl)	122	39.22 N	99.54 W
Hill City, Mn.	115	46.58 N	93.38 W
Hill Crest, Pa.	56b	40.05 N	75.11 W
Hillcrest Heights, Md.	56d	38.52 N	76.57 W
Hillegersberg, Neth.	157a	51.57 N	4.29 E
Hillen (Neigh.), F.R.G.	63	51.37 N	7.13 E
Hillerød, Den. (hē'lĕ-rûdh)	164	55.56 N	12.17 E
Hillingdon (Neigh.), Eng.	62	51.32 N	0.27 W
Hillsboro, IL. (hĭlz'bŭr-ō)	123	39.09 N	89.28 W
Hillsboro, Ks.	123	38.22 N	97.11 W
Hillsboro, ND	114	47.23 N	97.05 W
Hillsboro, NH	111	43.05 N	71.55 W
Hillsboro, Oh.	110	39.10 N	83.40 W

PLACE (Pronounciation)	PAGE	Lat. °'	Long. °'
Hillsboro, Or.	118c	45.31 N	122.59 W
Hillsboro, Tx.	125	32.01 N	97.06 W
Hillsboro, Wi.	115	43.39 N	90.20 W
Hillsburgh, Can. (hĭlz'bûrg)	95d	43.48 N	80.09 W
Hills Creek Res., Or.	116	43.41 N	122.26 W
Hillsdale, Mi. (hĭls-dāl)	120	41.55 N	84.35 W
Hillside, Md.	56d	38.52 N	76.55 W
Hillside (Neigh.), NY	55	40.42 N	73.47 W
Hillwood, Va.	56d	38.52 N	77.10 W
Hilo, Hi. (hē'lō)	106a	19.44 N	155.01 W
Hiltrop (Neigh.), F.R.G.	63	51.30 N	7.15 E
Hilversum, Neth. (hĭl'vēr-sŭm)	157a	52.13 N	5.10 E
Himachal Pradesh (State), India	196	36.03 N	77.41 E
Himalaya Mts., Asia (hĭ-mä'lȧ-yȧ)	193	29.30 N	85.02 E
Himeji, Jap. (hē'mȧ-jē)	205	34.50 N	134.42 E
Himmelgeist (Neigh.), F.R.G.	63	51.10 N	6.49 E
Himmelpforten, F.R.G. (hē'mĕl-pfôr-tĕn)	157c	53.37 N	9.19 E
Hims, Syr.	195	34.44 N	36.43 E
Hinche, Hai. (hēn'chȧ) (ăɴsh)	135	19.10 N	72.05 W
Hinchinbrook (I.), Austl. (hĭn-chĭn-brŏŏk)	215	18.23 S	146.57 W
Hinckley, Eng. (hĭnk'lĭ)	156	52.32 N	1.21 W
Hindley, Eng. (hĭnd'lĭ)	156	53.32 N	2.35 W
Hindu Kush (Mts.), Asia (hĭn'dōō kōōsh')	193	35.15 N	68.44 E
Hindupur, India (hĭn'dōō-pōōr)	197	13.52 N	77.34 E
Hingham, Ma. (hĭng'ăm)	105a	42.14 N	70.53 W
Hinkley, Oh. (hĭnk'-lĭ)	113d	41.14 N	81.45 W
Hino, Jap.	69a	35.41 N	139.24 E
Hinojosa del Duque, Sp. (ē-nô-kō'sä)	170	38.30 N	5.09 W
Hinsdale, Il. (hĭnz'dāl)	113a	41.48 N	87.56 W
Hinsel (Neigh.), F.R.G.	63	51.26 N	7.05 E
Hinton, Can. (hĭn'tŭn)	99	53.25 N	117.34 W
Hinton, WV (hĭn'tŭn)	110	37.40 N	80.55 W
Hirado (I.), Jap. (hē'rä-dō)	205	33.19 N	129.18 E
Hirakata, Jap. (hē'rä-kä'tä)	205b	34.49 N	135.40 E
Hiratsuka, Jap. (hē-rät-sōō'kȧ)	205	35.20 N	139.19 E
Hirosaki, Jap. (hē'rô-sä'kē)	204	40.31 N	140.38 E
Hirose, Jap. (hē'rô-sä)	205	35.20 N	133.11 E
Hiroshima, Jap. (hē-rô-shē'mȧ)	205	34.22 N	132.25 E
Hirota, Jap.	69b	34.45 N	135.21 E
Hirschstetten (Neigh.), Aus.	66e	48.14 N	16.29 E
Hirson, Fr. (ēr-sôɴ')	168	49.54 N	4.00 E
Hisar, India	199	29.15 N	75.47 E
Hispaniola (I.), N.A. (hĭ'spăn-ĭ-ō-lȧ)	129	17.30 N	73.15 W
Hitachi, Jap. (hē-tä'chē)	204	36.42 N	140.47 E
Hitchcock, Tx. (hĭch'kŏk)	125a	29.21 N	95.01 W
Hitdorf, F.R.G. (hēt'dōrf)	169c	51.04 N	6.56 E
Hither Green (Neigh.), Eng.	62	51.27 N	0.01 W
Hitoyoshi, Jap. (hē'tô-yō'shē)	205	32.13 N	130.45 E
Hitra (I.), Nor. (hĭträ)	158	63.34 N	7.37 E
Hittefeld, F.R.G. (hē'tĕ-fĕld)	157c	53.23 N	9.59 E
Hiwasa, Jap. (hē'wȧ-sä)	205	33.44 N	134.31 E
Hiwassee (R.), Tn. (hī-wôs'sē)	126	35.10 N	84.35 W
Hjälmaren (L.), Swe.	164	59.07 N	16.05 E
Hjo, Swe. (yō)	164	58.19 N	14.11 E
Hjørring, Den. (jûr'ĭng)	164	57.27 N	9.59 E
Hlohovec, Czech. (hlō'ho-vĕts)	167	48.24 N	17.49 E
Hobart, Austl. (hō'bȧrt)	216	43.00 S	147.30 E
Hobart, In.	113a	41.31 N	87.15 W
Hobart, Ok.	122	35.02 N	99.06 W
Hobart, Wa.	118a	47.25 N	121.58 W
Hobbs, NM (hŏbs)	122	32.41 N	104.04 W
Hoboken, Bel. (hō'bō-kĕn)	157a	51.11 N	4.20 E
Hoboken, NJ	112a	40.43 N	74.03 W
Hobro, Den. (hô-brô')	164	56.38 N	9.47 E
Hobson, Va. (hŏb'sŭn)	112g	36.54 N	76.31 W
Hobson's B., Austl. (hŏb'sŭnz)	211a	37.54 S	144.45 E
Hobsons B., Austl.	70b	37.51 S	144.56 E
Hobyo, Som.	223a	5.24 N	48.28 E
Hochdahl, F.R.G.	63	51.13 N	6.56 E
Hochheide, F.R.G.	63	51.27 N	6.41 E
Ho Chi Minh City (Saigon), Viet.	206	10.46 N	106.34 E
Hochlar (Neigh.), F.R.G.	63	51.36 N	7.10 E
Höchsten, F.R.G.	63	51.27 N	7.29 E
Hockinson, Wa. (hŏk'ĭn-sŭn)	118c	45.44 N	122.29 W
Hoctún, Mex. (ôk-tōō'n)	132a	20.52 N	89.10 W
Hodgenville, Ky. (hŏj'ĕn-vĭl)	110	37.35 N	85.45 W
Hodges Hill (Mtn.), Can. (hŏj'ĕz)	103	49.04 N	55.53 W
Hodgkins, Il.	58a	41.46 N	87.51 W
Hódmezövásárhely, Hung. (hōd'mĕ-zû-vô'shôr-hĕl-y')	167	46.24 N	20.21 E
Hodna, Chott el (L.), Alg.	159	35.20 N	3.27 E
Hodonin, Czech. (hĕ'dô-nén)	167	48.50 N	17.06 E
Hoegaarden, Bel.	157a	50.46 N	4.55 E
Hoek van Holland, Neth.	157a	51.59 N	4.05 E
Hoeryŏng, Kor. (hwĕr'yŭng)	204	42.28 N	129.39 E
Hof, F.R.G. (hōf)	166	50.19 N	11.55 E
Hofburg (P. Int.), Aus.	66e	48.12 N	16.22 E
Hofsjökull (Gl.), Ice. (hôfs'yü'kōōl)	158	64.55 N	18.40 W
Hog (I.), Mi.	110	45.50 N	85.20 W
Hogansville, Ga. (hō'gȧnz-vĭl)	126	33.10 N	84.54 W
Hogar y Redención, Mex.	60a	19.22 N	99.13 W
Hog Cay (I.), Ba.	135	23.35 N	75.30 W
Hogsty Rf., Ba.	135	21.45 N	73.50 W
Hohenbrunn, F.R.G. (hō'hĕn-brōōn)	157d	48.03 N	11.42 E
Hohenlimburg, F.R.G. (hō'hĕn lĕm'bōōrg)	169c	51.20 N	7.35 E
Hohen Neuendorf, G.D.R. (hō'hĕn noi'ĕn-dōrf)	157b	52.40 N	13.22 E
Hohenschönhausen (Neigh.), G.D.R.	65a	52.33 N	13.30 E
Hohensyburg (P. Int.), F.R.G.	63	51.25 N	7.29 E
Hohe Tauern (Mts.), Aus. (hō'ĕ tou'ĕrn)	166	47.11 N	12.12 E
Hohhot, China (hŭ-hōō-tŭ)	202	41.05 N	111.50 E
Hohoe, Ghana	228	7.09 N	0.28 E
Hohokus, NJ (hō-hō-kŭs)	112a	41.01 N	74.08 W
Höhscheid (Neigh.), F.R.G.	63	51.09 N	7.04 E
Hoisington, Ks. (hoi'zĭng-tŭn)	122	38.30 N	98.46 W
Hoisten, F.R.G.	63	51.08 N	6.42 E

ăt; finăl; rāte; senåte; ärm; åsk; sofȧ; fâre; ch-choose; dh-as th in other; bē; ēvent; bĕt; recĕnt; cratēr; g-gō; gh-guttural g; bĭt; ĭ-short neutral; rīde; ĸ-guttural k as ch in German ich;

ng-sing; nn-bannk; N-nasalized n;   nŏd; cŏmmit; ōld; ô̇bey; ôṙder; oi-boil; fōōd; foŏt; ou-out;   s-soft; sh-dish;   th-thin;   pūre; ûnite; ûrn; stŭd; circŭs; ü-as in French tu;   '-indeterminate vowel.

ăt; finăl; rāte; senâte; ärm; àsk; sofà; fâre;   ch-choose;   dh-as th in other;   bē; ĕvent; bĕt; recĕnt; cratēr;   g-gō; gh-guttural g;   bĭt; ĭ-short neutral; rīde;   ĸ-guttural k as ch in German ich;

PLACE (Pronounciation)	PAGE	Lat. °′	Long. °′
Ilan, Taiwan (ē'län')	203	24.50 N	121.42 E
Ilawa, Pol. (ē-lä'vá)	167	53.35 N	19.36 E
Ilchester, Md.	56c	39.15 N	76.46 W
Ile-á-la-Crosse, Can.	100	55.34 N	108.00 W
Ilebo (Port-Franqui), Zaire	230	4.19 S	20.35 E
Ile-Cadieux, Can.	54b	45.25 N	74.01 W
Ilek (R.), Sov. Un.	179	51.20 N	53.10 E
Ilek, Sov. Un. (ē'lyĕk)	179	51.30 N	53.10 E
Ile-Perrot, Can. (yl-pĕ-rōt')	95a	45.21 N	73.54 W
Ilesha, Nig.	229	7.38 N	4.45 E
Ilford, Eng. (ĭl'fĕrd)	156b	51.33 N	0.06 E
Ilfracombe, Eng. (ĭl-frá-kōōm')	162	51.13 N	4.08 W
Ilhabela, Braz. (ē'lä-bĕ'lä)	141a	23.47 S	45.21 W
Ilha Grande, Baia de (B.), Braz. (ēl'yá grän'dĕ)	141a	23.17 S	44.25 W
Ilhavo, Port. (ēl'yá-vò)	170	40.36 N	8.41 E
Ilhéus, Braz. (ē-lā'ōōs)	143	14.52 S	39.00 W
Iliamna, Ak. (ē-lē-ăm'ná)	107	59.45 N	155.05 W
Iliamna (L.), Ak.	107	59.25 N	155.30 W
Iliamna (Vol.), Ak.	107	60.18 N	153.25 W
Ilim (R.), Sov. Un. (ē-lyĕm')	180	57.28 N	103.00 E
Ilimsk, Sov. Un. (ē-lyĕmsk')	180	56.47 N	103.43 E
Ilin I., Phil. (ē-lyĕn')	207a	12.16 N	120.57 E
Il'intsiy, Sov.Un.	175	49.07 N	29.13 E
Ilion, NY (ĭl'ĭ-ŭn)	111	43.00 N	75.05 W
Ilioúpolis, Grc.	66d	37.56 N	23.45 E
Ili R., Sov. Un. (ē'lē)	198	43.46 N	77.41 E
Ilkeston, Eng. (ĭl'kĕs-tŭn)	156	52.58 N	1.19 W
Illampu, Nevado (Pk.), Bol. (nĕ-vá'dô-ēl-yäm-pōō')	142	15.50 S	68.15 W
Illapel, Chile (ē-zhä-pĕ'l)	141b	31.37 S	71.10 W
Iller R., F.R.G. (ĭl'er)	166	47.52 N	10.06 E
Illimani, Nevado (Pk.), Bol. (nĕ-vá'dô-ēl-yĕ-mä'nĕ)	142	16.50 S	67.38 W
Illinois (R.), Il.	123	40.52 N	89.31 W
Illinois (State), U. S. (ĭl-ĭ-noi')	109	40.25 N	90.40 W
Illizi, Alg.	224	26.35 N	8.24 E
Illovo, S. Afr.	71b	26.08 S	28.03 E
Il'men', Ozero (L.), Sov. Un. (ô'zĕ-rô el''men'') (ĭl'mĕn)	174	58.18 N	32.00 E
Ilo, Peru	142	17.46 S	71.13 W
Ilobasco, Sal. (ē-lô-bäs'kô)	132	13.57 N	88.46 W
Iloilo, Phil. (ē-lô-ē'lô)	206	10.49 N	112.33 E
Ilopango, L., Sal. (ē-lô-päṅ'gō)	132	13.48 N	88.50 W
Ilorin, Nig. (ē-lô-rēn')	229	8.30 N	4.32 E
Ilūkste, Sov. Un.	174	55.59 N	26.20 E
Ilverich, F.R.G.	63	51.17 N	6.42 E
Ilwaco, Wa. (ĭl-wä'kô)	118c	46.19 N	124.02 W
Ilych (R.), Sov. Un. (ē'l'ĭch)	178	62.30 N	57.30 E
Imabari, Jap. (ē'mä-bä'rē)	205	34.05 N	132.58 E
Imai, Jap. (ē-mī')	205b	34.31 N	135.47 E
Iman (R.), Sov. Un. (ē-män')	204	45.40 N	134.31 E
Imandra (L.), Sov. Un. (ē-män'drá)	178	67.40 N	32.30 E
Imbābah, Egypt (ēm-bä'bá)	223b	30.06 N	31.09 E
Imbarié, Braz. (ēm-bä-ryĕ')	144b	22.38 S	43.13 W
Imeni Morozova, Sov. Un. (ĭm-yĕ'nyĭ mô rô'zô vá)	182c	59.58 N	31.02 E
Imeni Moskvy, Kanal (Moscow Can.), Sov. Un. (ká-näl'ĭm-yä'nĭ môs-kvĭ)	174	56.33 N	37.15 E
Imeni Tsyurupy, Sov. Un.	182b	55.30 N	38.39 E
Imeni Vorovskogo, Sov. Un.	182b	55.43 N	38.21 E
Imlay City, Mi. (ĭm'lā)	110	43.00 N	83.15 W
Immenstadt, F.R.G. (ĭm'ĕn-shtät)	166	47.34 N	10.12 E
Immerpan, S. Afr. (ĭmēr-pän)	223d	24.29 S	29.14 E
Imola, It. (ē'mô-lä)	172	44.19 N	11.43 E
Imotski, Yugo. (ē-môts'kē)	172	43.25 N	17.15 E
Impamperi, Braz.	143	17.44 S	48.03 W
Impendle, S. Afr. (ĭm-pĕnd'lá)	227c	29.38 S	29.54 E
Imperia, It. (ēm-pā'rē-á)	172	43.52 N	8.00 E
Imperial, Pa. (ĭm-pē'rĭ-ál)	113e	40.27 N	80.15 W
Imperial Beach, Ca.	120a	32.34 N	117.08 W
Imperial Res., Az.	121	32.57 N	114.19 W
Imperial Valley, Ca.	120	33.00 N	115.22 W
Impfondo, Con. (ĭmp-fôn'dô)	230	1.37 N	18.04 E
Imphal, India (ĭmp'hŭl)	193	24.42 N	94.00 E
Ina (R.), Jap. (ē-nä')	205b	34.56 N	135.21 E
Inagi, Jap.	69a	35.38 N	139.30 E
Inaja Ind. Res., Ca. (ē-nä'hä)	120	32.56 N	116.37 W
Inari (L.), Fin.	158	69.02 N	26.22 E
Inatsuke (Neigh.), Jap.	69a	35.46 N	139.43 E
Inca, Sp. (ēṅ'kä)	171	39.43 N	2.53 E
Ince, Eng.	64a	53.17 N	2.49 W
Ince Blundell, Eng.	64a	53.31 N	3.02 W
Ince Burun (C.), Tur. (ĭn'jä)	179	42.00 N	35.00 E
Inch'ŏn, Kor. (ĭn'chŭn)	204	37.26 N	126.46 E
Incudine, Mt. (Mtn.), Fr. (ĕn-kōō-dē'nä) (äN-kü-dĕn')	172	41.53 N	9.17 E
Indalsälven (R.), Swe.	164	62.50 N	16.50 E
Indé, Mex. (ēn'dä)	124	25.53 N	105.15 W
Independence, Ks. (ĭn-dĕ-pĕn'dĕns)	123	37.14 N	95.42 W
Independence, Mo.	119f	39.06 N	94.26 W
Independence, Oh.	113d	41.23 N	81.39 W
Independence, Or.	116	44.49 N	123.13 W
Independence Mts., Nv.	116	41.15 N	116.02 W
Independence National Historical Park NJ (P. Int.), Md.	56b	39.57 N	75.09 W
Inder (L.), Sov. Un.	179	48.20 N	52.10 E
In der Bredde, F.R.G.	63	51.20 N	7.23 E
India, Asia (ĭn'dĭ-á)	190	23.00 N	77.30 E
India Gate (P. Int.), India	67d	28.37 N	77.18 E
Indian (L.), Mi. (ĭn'dĭ-án)	115	46.04 N	86.34 W
Indian (L.), NY	111	44.05 N	75.45 W
Indiana, Pa. (ĭn-dĭ-än'á)	111	40.40 N	79.10 W
Indiana (State), U. S.	109	39.50 N	86.45 W
Indianapolis, In. (ĭn-dĭ-án-ăp'ô-lĭs)	113g	39.45 N	86.08 W
Indian Arm (R.), Can. (ĭn'dĭ-án ärm)	118d	49.21 N	122.55 W
Indian Head, Can.	100	50.29 N	103.44 W
Indian Head Park, Il.	58a	41.47 N	87.54 W
Indian L., Can.	102	47.00 N	82.00 W
Indianola, Ia. (ĭn-dĭ-án-ō'lá)	115	41.22 N	93.33 W
Indianola, Ms.	126	33.29 N	90.35 W
Indianola, Pa.	57b	40.34 N	79.51 W
Indianópolis (Neigh.), Braz.	61d	23.36 S	46.38 W
Indian O.	190	0	70.00 E
Indian Springs, Va.	56d	38.49 N	77.10 W
Indigirka (R.), Sov. Un. (ĕn-dē-gēr'ká)	181	67.45 N	145.45 E
Indio (R.), Pan. (ē'n-dyô)	128a	9.13 N	78.28 W
Indochina (Reg.), Asia (ĭn-dô-chī'ná)	206	17.22 N	105.18 E
Indonesia, Asia (ĭn'dô-nē-zhá)	206	4.38 S	118.45 E
Indonesian Culture, Museum of (P. Int.), Indon.	68k	6.09 S	106.49 E
Indore, India (ĭn-dōr')	196	22.48 N	76.51 E
Indragiri (R.), Indon. (ĭn-drá-jē'rē)	206	0.27 S	102.05 E
Indrāvati (R.), India (ĭn-drŭ-vä'tē)	132	19.15 N	80.54 E
Indre (R.), Fr. (äN'dr')	168	47.13 N	0.29 E
Indus, Can. (ĭn'dŭs)	95e	50.55 N	113.45 W
Indus (R.), Pak.	196	26.43 N	67.41 E
Industria (Neigh.), S. Afr.	71b	26.12 S	27.59 E
Indwe, S. Afr. (ĭnd'wä)	227c	31.30 S	27.21 E
Inebolu, Tur. (ē-nâ-bô'lōō)	179	41.50 N	33.40 E
Inego, Tur. (ē'nä-gū)	179	40.05 N	29.20 E
Infanta, Phil. (ēn-fän'tä)	207a	14.44 N	121.39 E
Infanta, Phil.	207a	15.50 N	119.53 E
Inferror, Laguna (L.), Mex. (lä-gōō'nä-ĕn-fĕr-rôr)	131	16.18 N	94.40 W
Infiernillo, Presa de (Res.), Mex.	131	18.50 N	101.50 W
Infiesto, Sp. (ēn-fyĕ's-tô)	170	43.21 N	5.24 W
I-n-Gall, Niger	229	16.47 N	6.56 E
Ingatestone, Eng.	62	51.41 N	0.22 E
Ingeniero Budge (Neigh.), Arg.	60d	34.43 S	58.28 W
Ingersoll, Can. (ĭn'gĕr-sôl)	110	43.05 N	81.00 W
Ingham, Austl. (ĭng'ăm)	215	18.45 S	146.14 E
Ingleburn, Austl.	70a	34.00 S	150.52 E
Ingles, Cayos (Is.), Cuba (kä-yôs-ē'n-glē's)	134	21.55 N	82.35 W
Ingleside (Neigh.), Ca.	58b	37.43 N	122.28 W
Inglewood, Ca. (ĭn'g'l-wōōd)	119a	33.57 N	118.22 W
Inglewood, Can.	95d	43.48 N	79.56 W
Ingoda (R.), Sov. Un. (ēn-gô'dä)	181	51.29 N	112.32 E
Ingolstadt, F.R.G. (ĭṅ'gôl-shtät)	166	48.46 N	11.27 E
Ingomar, Pa.	57b	40.35 N	80.05 W
Ingram, Pa.	57b	40.26 N	80.04 W
Ingrave, Eng.	62	51.36 N	0.21 E
Ingul (R.), Sov. Un. (ēn-gōōl')	175	47.22 N	32.52 E
Ingulets (R.), Sov. Un. (ēn-gōōl'yĕts')	175	47.12 N	33.12 E
Ingur (R.), Sov. Un.	179	42.30 N	42.00 E
Inhambane, Moz. (ēn-äm-bä'-nĕ)	226	23.47 S	35.28 E
Inhambupe, Braz. (ēn-yäm-bōō'pä)	143	11.47 S	38.13 W
Inharrime, Moz. (ēn-yär-rē'mä)	226	24.17 S	35.07 E
Inhomirim, Braz. (ē-nô-mē-rē'N)	144b	22.34 S	43.11 W
Iniridía (R.), Col. (ē-nē-rē'dä)	142	2.25 N	70.38 W
Injune, Austl. (ĭn'jōōn)	216	25.52 S	148.30 E
Inkeroinen, Fin. (ĭn'kĕr-oi-nĕn)	165	60.42 N	26.50 E
Inkster, Mi. (ĭngk'stĕr)	113b	42.18 N	83.19 W
Innamincka, Austl. (ĭnn-á'mĭn-ká)	216	27.50 S	140.48 E
Inner Brass (I.), Vir. Is. (U.S.A.) (bräs)	129c	18.23 N	64.58 W
Inner Hebrides (Is.), Scot.	162	57.20 N	6.20 W
Inner Mongolia, (Aut. Reg.), see Nei Monggol			
Innisfail, Can.	99	52.02 N	113.57 W
Inn R., F.R.G.-Aus. (ĭn)	166	48.19 N	13.16 E
Innsbruck, Aus. (ĭns'brōōk)	166	47.15 N	11.25 E
Ino, Jap. (ē'nô)	205	33.34 N	133.23 E
Inongo, Zaire (ē-nôṅ'gô)	230	1.57 S	18.16 E
Inowroctaw, Pol. (ē-nô-vrôts'läf)	167	52.48 N	18.16 E
In Salah, Alg.	224	27.13 N	2.22 E
Inscription House Ruin, Az. (ĭn'skrĭp-shŭn hous rōō'ĭn)	121	36.45 N	110.47 W
Inter-American Hy., Mex. (ĭn'tĕr á-mĕr'ĭ-kán)	130	22.30 N	99.08 W
International Falls, Mn. (ĭn'tĕr-nâsh'ŭn-ál fôlz)	115	48.34 N	93.26 W
Inuvik, Can.	96	68.40 N	134.10 W
Inuyama, Jap. (ē'nōō-yä'mä)	205	35.24 N	137.01 E
Invercargil, N. Z. (ĭn-vĕr-kár'gĭl)	217	46.25 S	68.27 E
Inverell, Austl. (ĭn-vĕr-el')	216	29.50 S	151.32 E
Invergrove Hts., Mn. (ĭn'vĕr-grōv)	119g	44.51 N	93.01 W
Inverness, Can. (ĭn-vĕr-nĕs')	105	46.14 N	61.18 W
Inverness, Fl.	127	28.48 N	82.22 W
Inverness, Scot.	162	57.30 N	4.07 W
Investigator Str., Austl. (ĭn-vĕst'ĭ'gä-tôr)	216	35.33 S	137.00 E
Inwood, NY	55	40.37 N	73.45 W
Inyangani, Mt., Zimb. (ēn-yän-gä'nĕ)	226	18.06 S	32.37 E
Inyokern, Ca.	120	35.39 N	117.51 W
Inyo Mts., Ca. (ĭn'yō)	120	36.55 N	118.04 W
Inzer R., Sov. Un. (ĭn'zĕr)	182a	54.24 N	57.17 E
Inzersdorf (Neigh.), Aus.	66e	48.09 N	16.21 E
Inzia (R.), Zaire	230	5.55 S	17.50 E
Iō (I.), Jap. (ē'wō)	205	30.46 N	130.15 E
Ioánnina (Yannina), Grc. (yô-ä'nĕ-nä) (yä'nē-nä)	173	39.39 N	20.52 E
Ioco, Can.	118d	49.18 N	122.53 W
Iola, Ks. (ī-ō'lá)	123	37.55 N	95.23 W
Iôna, Parque Nacional do (Natl. Pk.), Ang.	230	16.35 S	12.00 E
Ionia, Mi.	110	43.00 N	85.10 W
Ionian Is., Grc. (ī-ō'nĭ-án)	173	39.10 N	20.05 E
Ionian Sea, Eur.	161	38.59 N	18.48 E
Ios (I.), Grc. (ī'ôs)	173	36.48 N	25.25 E
Iowa (State), U.S. (ī'ô-wá)	109	42.05 N	94.20 W
Iowa (R.), Ia.	115	41.55 N	92.20 W
Iowa City, Ia.	115	41.39 N	91.31 W
Iowa Falls, Ia.	115	42.32 N	93.16 W
Iowa Park, Tx.	122	33.57 N	98.39 W
Ipala, Tan.	231	4.30 S	32.53 E
Ipanema (Neigh.), Braz.	61c	22.59 S	43.12 W
Ipeiros (Reg.), Grc.	173	39.35 N	20.45 E
Ipel' (R.), Czech.-Hung. (ē'pĕl)	167	48.08 N	19.00 E
Ipiales, Col. (ē-pĕ-ä'läs)	142	0.48 N	77.45 W
Ipoh, Mala.	206	4.45 N	101.05 E
Ipswich, Austl. (ĭps'wĭch)	216	27.40 S	152.50 E
Ipswich, Eng.	163	52.05 N	1.05 E
Ipswich, Ma.	105a	42.41 N	70.50 W
Ipswich, SD	114	45.26 N	99.01 W
Ipu, Braz. (ē-pōō)	143	4.11 S	40.45 W
Iput' (R.), Sov. Un. (ē-pōōt')	174	52.53 N	31.57 E
Iquique, Chile (ē-kē'kē)	142	20.16 S	70.07 W
Iquitos, Peru (ē-kē'tōs)	142	3.39 S	73.18 W
Iráklion (Candia), Grc.	172a	35.20 N	25.10 E
Iran, Asia (ē-rän')	190	31.15 N	53.30 E
Iran Mts., Mala.	206	2.30 N	114.30 E
Iran, Plat. of, Iran	192	32.28 N	58.00 E
Irapuato, Mex. (ē-rä-pwä'tò)	130	20.41 N	101.24 W
Iraq, Asia (ē-räk')	190	32.00 N	42.30 E
Irazu Vol, C.R. (ē-rä-zōō')	133	9.58 N	83.54 W
Irbid, Jordan (ĕr-bēd')	191a	32.33 N	35.51 E
Irbil, Iraq	179	36.10 N	44.00 E
Irbit, Sov. Un. (ĕr-bĕt')	178	57.40 N	63.10 E
Irby, Eng.	64b	53.21 N	3.07 W
Irébou, Zaire (ē-rä'bōō)	226	0.40 S	17.48 E
Ireland, Eur. (ī-r-länd)	154	53.33 N	8.00 W
Iremel', Gora (Mt.), Sov. Un. (gä-rä'ĭ-rĕ'mĕl)	182a	54.32 N	58.52 E
Irene, S. Afr. (ī-rē-nē)	227b	25.53 S	28.13 E
Irgiz, Sov. Un. (ĭr-gēz')	180	48.30 N	61.17 E
Irgiz (R.), Sov. Un.	180	49.30 N	60.32 E
Iriklinskoye Vdkhr (Res.), Sov. Un.	178	52.20 N	58.50 E
Iringa, Tan. (ē-rĭṅ'gä)	231	7.46 S	35.42 E
Iriomote Jima (I.), Jap. (ērē'-ō-mō-tä)	203	24.20 N	123.30 E
Iriona, Hond. (ē-rē-ō'nä)	132	15.53 N	85.12 W
Irīgui (Reg.), Mali-Mauritania	228	16.45 N	5.35 W
Irish Sea, Eur. (ī'rĭsh)	162	53.55 N	5.25 W
Irkutsk, Sov. Un. (ĭr-kōōtsk')	180	52.16 N	104.00 E
Irlam, Eng. (ĭr'lăm)	156	53.26 N	2.26 W
Irois, Cap des (C.), Hai.	135	18.25 N	74.50 W
Iron Cove (B.), Austl.	70a	33.52 S	151.10 E
Irondale, Al. (ī'ĕrn-dāl)	112h	33.32 N	86.43 W
Iron Gate (Gorge), Yugo.-Rom.	173	44.43 N	22.32 E
Iron Knob, Austl. (ī-án nôb)	216	32.47 S	137.10 E
Iron Mountain, Mi. (ī'ĕrn)	115	45.49 N	88.04 W
Iron River, Mi.	115	46.09 N	88.39 W
Ironton, Oh. (ī'ĕrn-tŭn)	110	38.30 N	82.45 W
Ironwood, Mi. (ī'ĕrn-wōōd)	115	46.28 N	90.10 W
Iroquois (R.), Il.-In. (ĭr'ô-kwoi)	110	40.55 N	87.20 W
Iroquois Falls, Can.	97	48.41 N	80.39 W
Irō-Saki (C.), Jap. (ē'rō sä'kē)	205	34.35 N	138.54 E
Irpen' (R.), Sov. Un. (ĭr-pĕn')	175	50.13 N	29.55 E
Irrawaddy (R.), Bur. (ĭr-á-wäd'ē)	193	23.27 N	96.25 E
Irtysh (R.), Sov. Un. (ĭr-tĭsh')	180	58.32 N	68.31 E
Irumu, Zaire (ē-rōō'mōō)	225	1.30 N	29.52 E
Irun, Sp. (ē-rōōn')	170	43.20 N	1.47 W
Irvine, Ca. (ûr'vīn)	119a	33.40 N	117.45 W
Irvine, Ky.	110	37.40 N	84.00 W
Irvine, Scot.	162	55.39 N	4.40 W
Irving, Tx. (ûr'vĕng)	119c	32.49 N	96.57 W
Irving Park (Neigh.), Il.	58a	41.57 N	87.43 W
Irvington (Neigh.), NY	56c	39.17 N	76.41 W
Irvington, NJ (ûr'vĕng-tŭn)	112a	40.43 N	74.15 W
Irwin, Pa. (ûr'wĭn)	113e	40.19 N	79.42 W
Is, Sov. Un. (ēs)	182a	58.48 N	59.44 E
Isa, Nig.	229	13.14 N	6.24 E
Isaacs, Mt., Pan. (ē-sä-á'ks)	128a	9.22 N	79.01 W
Isabela (I.), Ec. (ē-sä-bä'lä)	142	0.47 S	91.35 W
Isabela (I.), Mex. (ē-sä-bĕ'-lä)	130	21.56 N	105.53 W
Isabela, Cabo (C.), Dom. Rep. (kä'bô-ē-sä-bĕ'lä)	135	20.00 N	71.00 W
Isabella, Cord. (Mts.), Nic. (kôr-dēl-yĕ'rä-ē-sä-bĕlä)	132	13.20 N	85.37 W
Isabella Ind. Res., Mi. (ĭs-á-bĕl'-lä)	110	43.35 N	84.55 W
Isaccea, Rom. (ē-säk'chä)	175	45.16 N	28.26 E
Isafjördur, Ice. (ēs'á-fy̆r-dōōr)	158	66.09 N	22.39 W
Isando, S. Afr.	71b	26.09 S	28.12 E
Isangi, Zaire (ē-säṅ'gĕ)	230	0.46 N	24.15 E
Isarco (R.), It. (ē-sär'kô)	172	46.37 N	11.25 E
Isarog, Mt., Phil. (ē-sä-rô-g)	207a	13.40 N	123.23 E
Isar R., F.R.G. (ē'zär)	166	48.27 N	12.02 E
Ischia, It. (ēs'kyä)	171c	40.29 N	13.58 E
Ise (Uji-Yamada), Jap. (ĭs'hĕ) (ū'gē-yä'mä'dä)	205	34.30 N	136.43 E
Iselin, NJ	55	40.34 N	74.19 W
Iseo, Lago d' (L.), It. (lä-gô'dĕ-ē-zĕ'ô)	172	45.50 N	9.55 E
Isére (R.), Fr. (ē-zâr')	169	45.24 N	6.04 E
Iserlohn, F.R.G. (ē'zĕr-lôn)	169c	51.22 N	7.42 E
Isernia, It. (ē-zĕr'nē-á)	172	41.35 N	14.14 E
Ise-Wan (B), Jap. (ē'sĕ wän)	205	34.49 N	136.44 E
Iseyin, Nig.	229	7.58 N	3.36 E
Ishikari Wan (B.), Jap. (ē'shĕ-kä-rē wän)	204	43.30 N	141.05 E
Ishim, Sov. Un. (ĭsh-ēm')	180	56.07 N	69.13 E
Ishim (R.), Sov. Un.	180	53.17 N	67.45 E
Ishimbay, Sov. Un. (ē-shēm-bī')	182a	53.28 N	56.02 E
Ishinomaki, Jap. (ĭsh-nō-mä'kē)	204	38.22 N	141.22 E
Ishinomaki Wan (B.), Jap. (ē-shĕ-nō-mä'kĕ wän)	204	38.10 N	141.40 E
Ishly, Sov. Un. (ĭsh'lĭ)	182a	54.13 N	55.55 E
Ishlya, Sov. Un. (ĭsh'lyá)	182a	53.54 N	57.48 E
Ishmant, Egypt	223b	29.17 N	31.15 E
Ishpeming, Mi. (ĭsh'pĕ-mĭng)	115	46.28 N	87.42 W
Isidro Casanova, Arg.	60d	34.42 S	58.35 W
Isipingo, S. Afr. (ĭs-ĭ-pĭṅg-gô)	227c	29.59 S	30.58 E
Isiro (Paulis), Zaire	231	2.47 N	27.37 E
Iskenderun, Tur. (ĭs-kĕn'dĕr-ōōn)	179	36.45 N	36.15 E
Iskenderun Körfezi (G.), Turk.	161	36.22 N	35.25 E
Iskilip, Tur. (ĭs'kĭ-lĕp')	179	40.40 N	34.30 E
İskür (R.), Bul. (ĭs'k'r)	173	43.05 N	23.37 E
Isla-Cristina, Sp. (ē'lä-krē-stē'nä)	170	37.13 N	7.20 W
Islamābād, India	193	33.55 N	73.05 E
Isla Mujeres, Mex. (ē's-lä-mōō-kĕ'rĕs)	132a	21.25 N	86.53 W
Island L., Can.	101	53.47 N	94.25 W
Island Park, NY	55	40.36 N	73.40 W
Islands, B. of, Can. (ī'lăndz)	105	49.10 N	58.15 W

PLACE (Pronounciation)	PAGE	Lat. °'	Long. °'
Islay (I.), Scot. (ī'lā)	162	55.55 N	6.35 W
Isle (R.), Fr. (ēl)	168	45.02 N	0.29 E
Isle of Axholme (Reg.), Eng. (ăks'-hōm)	156	53.33 N	0.48 W
Isle of Man, Eur. (măn)	162	54.26 N	4.21 W
Isle Royale Nat'l Park, U. S. (īl'roi-ăl')	115	47.57 N	88.37 W
Isleta, NM (ēs-lā'tȧ) (ī-lē'tȧ)	121	34.55 N	106.45 W
Isle Verte, Can. (ēl vĕrt')	104	48.01 N	69.20 W
Isleworth (Neigh.), Eng.	62	51.28 N	0.20 W
Islington (Neigh.), Can.	54c	43.39 N	79.32 W
Islington (Neigh.), Eng.	62	51.34 N	0.06 W
Ismailia (Al Isma 'īlīyah), Egypt (ēs-mā-ēl'ēȧ)	223c	30.35 N	32.17 E
Ismā'īlīyah (Neigh.), Egypt	71a	30.03 N	31.14 E
Ismā'īlīyah Can., Egypt	223c	30.25 N	31.45 E
Ismaning, F.R.G. (ēz'mä-nēng)	157d	48.14 N	11.41 E
Isnā, Egypt (ēs'nȧ)	223b	25.17 N	32.33 E
Isparta, Tur. (ē-spär'tȧ)	179	37.50 N	30.40 E
Israel, Asia	192	32.40 N	34.00 E
Issaquah, Wa. (ĭz'să-kwăh)	118a	47.32 N	122.02 W
Isselburg, F.R.G. (ē'sĕl-bōōrg)	169c	51.50 N	6.28 E
Issoire, Fr. (ē-swȧr')	168	45.32 N	3.13 E
Issoudun, Fr. (ē-sōō-dăN')	168	46.56 N	2.00 E
Issum, F.R.G. (ē'sōōm)	169c	51.32 N	6.24 E
Issyk-Kul, Ozero (L.), Sov. Un.	180	42.13 N	76.12 E
Issy-les-Moulineaux, Fr.	64c	48.49 N	2.17 E
Istādeh-ye Moqor, Ab-e (L.), Afg.	196	32.35 N	68.00 E
Istanbul, Tur. (ē-stän-bōōl')	179	41.02 N	29.00 E
Istanbul Boğazi (Bosporous) (Str.), Tur.	179	41.10 N	29.10 E
Istead Rise, Eng.	62	51.24 N	0.22 E
Istiaía, Grc. (ĭs-tyī'yä)	173	38.58 N	23.11 E
Istmina, Col. (ēst-mē'nä)	142a	5.10 N	76.40 W
Istokpoga (L.), Fl. (īs-tōk-pō'gȧ)	127a	27.20 N	81.33 W
Istra (Pen.), Yugo. (ē-strä)	172	45.18 N	13.48 E
Istranca Dağlari (Mts.), Bul.-Turk. (ī-strän'jȧ)	173	41.50 N	27.25 E
Istres, Fr. (ēs'tr')	168a	43.30 N	5.00 E
Itá, Par. (ē-tȧ')	144	25.39 S	57.14 W
Itabaiana, Braz. (ē-tä-bä-yȧ-nä)	143	10.42 S	37.17 W
Itabapoana, Braz. (ē-tä'-bä-pôȧ'nä)	141a	21.19 S	40.58 W
Itabapoana (R.), Braz.	141a	21.11 S	41.18 W
Itabirito, Braz. (ē-tä-bē-rē'tō)	141a	20.15 S	43.46 W
Itaboraí, Braz. (ē-tä-bō-rȧē')	141a	22.46 S	42.50 W
Itabuna, Braz. (ē-tä-bōō'nȧ)	143	14.47 S	39.17 W
Itacoara, Braz. (ē-tä-kō'ä-rä)	141a	21.41 S	42.04 W
Itacoatiara, Braz. (ē-tȧ-kwȧ-tyä'rȧ)	143	3.03 S	58.18 W
Itaguaí, Braz. (ē-tä-gwä-ē')	141a	22.52 S	43.46 W
Itagüí, Col. (ē-tä'gwē)	142a	6.11 N	75.36 W
Itagui (R.), Braz.	144b	22.53 S	43.43 W
Itaipava, Braz. (ē-tī-pȧ'-vä)	144b	22.23 S	43.09 W
Itaipu, Braz. (ē-tī'pōō)	144b	22.58 S	43.02 W
Itaipu, Ponta de (C.), Braz.	61c	22.59 S	43.03 W
Itaituba, Braz. (ē-tä'ī-tōō'bȧ)	143	4.12 S	56.00 W
Itajái, Braz. (ē-tä-zhī')	144	26.52 S	48.39 W
Itajubá, Braz. (ē-tä-zhōō-bȧ')	141a	22.26 S	45.27 W
Italy, Eur. (ĭt'ȧ-lē)	154	43.58 N	11.14 E
Italy, Tx.	125	32.11 N	96.51 W
Itambi, Braz. (ē-tä'm-bē)	144b	22.44 S	42.57 W
Itami, Jap. (ē'tä'mē')	205b	34.47 N	135.25 E
Itapecerica, Braz. (ē-tä-pĕ-sĕ-rē'kȧ)	141a	21.29 S	45.08 W
Itapecurú (R.), Braz. (ē-tä-pĕ-kōō-rōō')	143	4.05 S	43.49 W
Itapēcuru-Mirim, Braz. (ē-tä-pĕ'kōō-rōō-mē-rēN')	143	3.17 S	44.15 W
Itaperuna, Braz. (ē-tȧ-pâ-rōō'nä)	141a	21.12 S	41.53 W
Itapetininga, Braz. (ē-tä-pĕ-tē-nē'N-gä)	141a	23.37 S	48.03 W
Itapira, Braz. (ē-tȧ-pē'rȧ)	143	20.42 S	51.19 W
Itapira, Braz.	141a	21.27 S	46.47 W
Itaquaquecetuba, Braz.	61d	23.29 S	46.21 W
Itarsi, India	196	22.43 N	77.45 E
Itasca (L.), Mn.	115	47.13 N	95.14 W
Itasca, Tx. (ī-tăs'kȧ)	125	32.09 N	97.08 W
Itatiaia, Pico da (Pk.), Braz. (pē'-kō-dȧ-ē-tä-tyȧ'ēä)	141a	22.18 S	44.41 W
Itatiba, Braz. (ē-tä-tē'bä)	141a	23.01 S	46.48 W
Itaúna, Braz. (ē-tä-ōō'nä)	141a	20.05 S	44.35 W
Itaverá, Braz. (ē-tä-vĕ-rȧ')	141a	22.44 S	44.07 W
Ithaca, Mi. (ĭth'ȧ-kȧ)	110	43.20 N	84.35 W
Ithaca, NY	111	42.25 N	76.30 W
Itháka (I.), Grc. (ē'thä-kē)	173	38.27 N	20.48 E
Itigi, Tan.	231	5.42 S	34.29 E
Itimbiri (R.), Zaire	230	2.40 N	23.30 E
Itire, Nig.	71d	6.31 N	3.21 E
Itoko, Zaire (ē-tō'kō)	226	1.13 S	22.07 E
Itsā, Egypt (ēt'sȧ)	223b	29.13 N	30.47 E
Itu, Braz. (ē-tōō')	141a	23.16 S	47.16 W
Ituango, Col. (ē-twäŋ'gō)	142a	7.07 N	75.44 W
Ituiutaba, Braz. (ē-tōō-ēōō-tä'bä)	143	18.56 S	49.17 W
Itumirim, Braz. (ē-tōō-mē-rē'N)	141a	21.20 S	44.51 W
Itundujia Santa Cruz, Mex. (ē-tōōn-dōō-hē'ȧ sä'n-tä krōō'z)	131	16.50 N	97.43 W
Iturbide, Mex. (ē'tōōr-bē'dhȧ)	132a	19.38 N	89.31 W
Iturup (Etorofu) (I.), Sov. Un. (ē-tōō-rōōp')	181	45.35 N	147.15 E
Ituzaingo, Arg. (ē-tōō-zä-ē'n-gō)	144a	34.24 S	58.40 W
Itzehoe, F.R.G. (ē'tzĕ-hō)	157c	53.55 N	9.31 E
Iuka, Ms. (ī-ū'kȧ)	126	34.47 N	88.10 W
Iúna, Braz. (ē-ōō'-nä)	141a	20.22 S	41.32 W
Iupeba, Braz.	61d	23.41 S	46.22 W
Iva (R.),	180	53.45 N	99.30 E
Ivanhoe, Austl. (ĭv'ăn-hō)	216	32.53 S	144.10 E
Ivanhoe, Austl.	70b	37.46 S	145.03 E
Ivano-Frankovsk, Sov. Un. (ē-vä'nō frän-kôvsk')	167	48.53 N	24.46 E
Ivanovo (Oblast), Sov. Un.	174	56.55 N	40.30 E
Ivanovo, Sov. Un. (ē-vä'nô-vō)	174	57.02 N	41.54 E
Ivanpol', Sov. Un. (ē-vän'pôl)	175	49.51 N	28.11 E
Ivanteyevka, Sov. Un. (ē-vȧn-tyē'yĕf-kȧ)	182b	55.58 N	37.56 E
Ivdel', Sov. Un. (ĭv'dyĕl)	182a	60.42 N	60.27 E
Iver, Eng.	62	51.31 N	0.30 W
Iver Heath, Eng.	62	51.32 N	0.31 W
Iviza (I.), see **Ibiza**			
Ivohibé, Mad. (ē-vô-hē-bā')	227	22.28 S	46.59 E
Ivory Coast, Afr.	222	7.43 N	6.30 W
Ivrea, It. (ē-vrĕ'ä)	172	45.25 N	7.54 E
Ivry-sur-Seine, Fr.	64c	48.49 N	2.23 E
Ivujivik, Can.	97	62.17 N	77.52 W
Iwaki (Taira), Jap.	204	37.03 N	140.57 E
Iwate Yama (Mt.), Jap. (ē-wä-tē-yä'mä)	204	39.50 N	140.56 E
Iwatsuki, Jap.	205a	35.48 N	139.43 E
Iwaya, Jap. (ē'wȧ-yȧ)	205b	34.35 N	135.01 E
Iwo, Nig.	229	7.38 N	4.11 E
Ixcateopán, Mex. (ēs-kä-tä-ō-pän')	130	18.29 N	99.49 W
Ixelles, Bel.	157a	50.49 N	4.23 E
Ixhautlán, Mex. (ēs-wȧt-län')	130	20.41 N	98.01 W
Ixhuatán (San Francisco), Mex. (ēs-hwä-tän')	131	16.19 N	94.30 W
Ixmiquilpan, Mex. (ēs-mē-kēl'pän)	130	20.30 N	99.12 W
Ixopo, S. Afr.	227c	30.10 S	30.04 E
Ixtacalco, Mex. (ēs-tȧ-käl'kō)	131a	19.23 N	99.07 W
Ixtaltepec (Asunción), Mex. (ēs-täl-tē-pĕk')	131	16.33 N	95.04 W
Ixtapalapa, Mex. (ēs'tä-pä-lä'pä)	131a	19.21 N	99.06 W
Ixtapaluca, Mex. (ēs'tä-pä-lōō'kä)	131a	19.18 N	98.53 W
Ixtepec, Mex. (ēks-tē'pĕk)	131	16.37 N	95.09 W
Ixtlahuaca, Mex. (ēs-tlä-wä'kä)	131a	19.34 N	99.46 W
Ixtlán de Juárez, Mex. (ēs-tlän' dā hwä'räz)	131	17.20 N	96.29 W
Ixtlán del Río, Mex. (ēs-tlän'dĕl rē'ō)	130	21.05 N	104.22 W
Iyo-Nada (Sea), Jap. (ē'yō nä-dä)	205	33.33 N	132.07 E
Izabal, Guat. (ē'zä-bäl')	132	15.23 N	89.10 W
Izabal, L. (Golfo Dulce), Guat. (gôl'fō dōōl'sā)	132	15.30 N	89.04 W
Izalco, Sal. (ē-zäl'kō)	132	13.50 N	89.40 W
Izamal, Mex. (ē-zä-mä'l)	132a	20.55 N	89.00 W
Izhevsk, see **Ustinov**			
Izhma (R), Sov. Un.	178	64.00 N	53.00 E
Izhma, Sov. Un. (ĭzh'mȧ)	178	65.00 N	54.05 E
Izhora R., Sov. Un. (ēz'hô-rȧ)	182c	59.36 N	30.20 E
Izmail, Sov. Un. (ēz-mȧ-ēl)	175	45.00 N	28.49 E
İzmir, Tur. (ĭz-mēr')	179	38.25 N	27.05 E
İzmir Körfezi (G.), Tur.	173	38.43 N	26.37 E
İzmit, Tur. (ĭz-mēt')	179	40.45 N	29.45 E
Iznajar, Embalse de (Res.), Sp.	170	37.15 N	4.30 W
Iztaccíhuatl (Mtn.), Mex.	131a	19.10 N	98.38 W
Izu (I.), Jap. (ē'zōō)	205	34.32 N	139.25 E
Izuhara, Jap. (ē'zōō-hä'rä)	205	34.11 N	129.18 E
Izumi-Ōtsu, Jap. (ē'zōō-mōō ō'tsōō)	205b	34.30 N	135.24 E
Izumo, Jap. (ē'zōō-mō)	205	35.22 N	132.45 E

J

PLACE (Pronounciation)	PAGE	Lat. °'	Long. °'
Jaachimsthal, G.D.R. (yä'Kēm-stäl)	157b	52.58 N	13.45 E
Jabal, Bahr al (R.), Sud.	225	7.02 N	30.45 E
Jabalpur, India	196	23.18 N	79.59 E
Jabavu, S. Afr.	71b	26.15 S	27.53 E
Jablonec nad Nisou, Czech. (yäb'lô-nyĕts)	166	50.43 N	15.12 E
Jablunkov P., Czech. (yäb'lōōn-kôf)	167	49.31 N	18.35 E
Jaboatão, Braz. (zhä-bô-ȧ-touN)	143	8.14 S	35.08 W
Jaca, Sp. (hä'kä)	171	42.35 N	0.30 W
Jacala, Mex. (hä-kȧ'lä)	130	21.01 N	99.11 W
Jacaltenango, Guat. (hä-kȧl-tĕ-näŋ'gō)	132	15.39 N	91.41 W
Jacareí, Braz. (zhä-kȧ-rĕ-ē')	141a	23.19 S	45.57 W
Jacarepaguá, Braz. (zhä-kȧ-rä'pä-gwä')	144b	22.55 S	43.22 W
Jacarézinho, Braz. (zhä-kä-rĕ'zē-nyō)	143	23.13 S	49.58 W
Jachymov, Czech. (yä'chĭ-môf)	166	50.22 N	12.51 E
Jacinto City, Tx. (hä-sĕn'tō) (jȧ-sĭn'tō)	125a	29.45 N	95.14 W
Jacksboro, Tx. (jăks'bŭr-ō)	122	33.13 N	98.11 W
Jackson, Al. (jăk'sŭn)	126	31.31 N	87.52 W
Jackson, Ca.	120	38.22 N	120.47 W
Jackson, Ga.	126	33.19 N	83.55 W
Jackson, Ky.	126	37.32 N	83.17 W
Jackson, La.	125	30.50 N	91.13 W
Jackson, Mi.	110	42.15 N	84.25 W
Jackson, Mn.	115	43.37 N	95.00 W
Jackson, Ms.	126	32.17 N	90.10 W
Jackson, Mo.	123	37.23 N	89.40 W
Jackson, Oh.	110	39.00 N	82.40 W
Jackson, Tn.	126	35.37 N	88.49 W
Jackson Heights (Neigh.), NY	55	40.45 N	73.53 W
Jackson L., Wy.	117	43.57 N	110.28 W
Jackson, Port., Austl.	211b	33.50 S	151.18 E
Jacksonville, Al. (jăk'sŭn-vĭl)	126	33.52 N	85.45 W
Jacksonville, Fl.	127	30.20 N	81.40 W
Jacksonville, Il.	123	39.43 N	90.12 W
Jacksonville, Tx.	125	31.58 N	95.18 W
Jacksonville Beach, Fl.	127	31.18 N	81.25 W
Jacmel, Hai. (zhȧk-mĕl')	125	18.15 N	72.30 W
Jacobābād, Pak.	196	28.22 N	68.30 E
Jacobina, Braz. (zhä-kô-bē'nȧ)	143	11.13 S	40.30 W
Jaco, L., Mex. (hä'kō)	124	27.51 N	103.50 W
Jacomino, Cuba	60b	23.06 N	82.20 W
Jacques-Cartier (R.), Can.	95b	47.04 N	71.28 W
Jacques Cartier, Détroit de (Str.), Can.	105	50.07 S	63.58 W
Jacques Cartier, Mt., Can.	104	48.59 N	66.00 W
Jacquet River, Can. (zhȧ-kĕ') (jăk'ĕt)	104	47.55 N	66.00 W
Jacuí, Braz. (zhä-kōō-ē')	141a	21.03 S	46.43 W
Jacutinga, Braz. (zhä-kōō-tēn'gä)	141a	21.17 S	46.36 W
Jade B., F.R.G. (yä'dē)	166	53.28 N	8.17 E
Jade Buddha, Temple of the (Yufosi) (P. Int.), China	68a	31.14 N	121.26 E
Jadotville, see **Likasi**			
Jaén, Peru (Kä-ĕ'n)	142	5.38 S	78.49 W
Jaen, Sp.	170	37.45 N	3.48 W
Jaffa, C., Austl. (jăf'ȧ)	216	36.58 S	139.29 E
Jaffna, Sri Lanka (jäf'nȧ)	197	9.44 N	80.09 E
Jagüey Grande, Cuba (hä'gwā grän'dā)	134	22.35 N	81.05 W
Jahore Str., Mala.	191b	1.22 N	103.37 E
Jahrom, Iran	192	28.30 N	53.28 E
Jaibo (R.), Cuba (hä-ē'bō)	125	20.10 N	75.20 W
Jaipur, India	196	27.00 N	75.50 E
Jaisaimer, India	196	27.00 N	70.54 E
Jajce, Yugo. (yī'tsĕ)	172	44.20 N	17.19 E
Jajpur, India	196	20.49 N	86.37 E
Jakarta, Indon. (yȧ-kär'tä)	206	6.17 S	106.45 E
Jakobstad, Fin. (yȧ'kôb-stȧdh)	158	63.33 N	22.31 E
Jalacingo, Mex. (hä-lä-sĭŋ'gō)	131	97.16 N	19.47 W
Jalālābād, Afg. (jŭ-lä-lȧ-bäd)	193a	34.25 N	70.27 E
Jalālah al Baḩrīyah, Jabal, (Mts.), Egypt	223b	29.20 N	32.00 E
Jalapa, Guat. (hä-lä'pȧ)	132	14.38 N	89.58 W
Jalapa de Diaz (San Felipe), Mex. (dā dē-äz') (sän fā-lē'pā)	131	18.06 N	96.33 W
Jalapa del Marqués, Mex. (dĕl mär-kās')	131	16.30 N	95.29 W
Jalapa Enríquez, Mex. (ĕn-rē'kāz)	131	19.32 N	96.53 W
Jaleswar, Nep.	196	26.50 N	85.55 E
Jalgaon, India	196	21.08 N	75.33 E
Jalisco, Mex. (hä-lēs'kō)	130	21.27 N	104.54 W
Jalisco (State), Mex.	128	20.07 N	104.45 W
Jalón (R.), Sp. (hä-lōn')	170	41.22 N	1.46 W
Jalostotitlán, Mex. (hä-lōs-tē-tlȧn')	130	21.09 N	102.30 W
Jalpa, Mex. (häl'pä)	131	18.12 N	93.06 W
Jalpa, Mex. (häl'pä)	130	21.40 N	103.04 W
Jalpan, Mex. (häl'pän)	130	21.13 N	99.31 W
Jaltepec, Mex. (häl-tȧ-pĕk')	131	17.20 N	95.15 W
Jaltipan, Mex. (häl-tȧ-pän')	131	17.59 N	94.42 W
Jaltocan, Mex. (häl-tō-kän')	130	21.08 N	98.32 W
Jālū, Wāḩat (Oasis), Libya	225	28.58 N	21.45 E
Jamaare (R.), Nig.	229	11.50 N	10.10 E
Jamaica, N. A.	129	17.45 N	78.00 W
Jamaica B., NY	55	40.36 N	73.51 W
Jamaica Cay (I.), Ba.	135	22.45 N	75.55 W
Jamālīyah (Neigh.), Egypt	71a	30.03 N	31.16 E
Jamālpur, Bngl.	196	24.56 N	89.58 E
Jamay, Mex. (hä-mī')	130	20.16 N	103.43 W
Jambi, Indon. (mäm'bē)	206	1.45 S	103.28 E
James (R.), Mo.	123	36.51 N	93.22 W
James (R.), NC	127	36.07 N	81.48 W
James (R.), U.S.	108	46.25 N	98.55 W
James (R.), Va.	111	37.35 N	77.50 W
James B., Can. (jāmz)	97	53.53 N	80.40 W
Jamesburg, NJ (jāmz'bûrg)	112a	40.21 N	74.26 W
Jameson Raid Memorial (P. Int.), S. Afr.	71b	26.11 S	27.49 E
James Pt., Ba.	135	25.20 N	76.30 W
James Ra., Austl.	214	24.15 S	133.30 E
James Ross (I.), Ant.	140	64.20 S	58.20 W
Jamestown, ND	114	46.54 N	98.42 W
Jamestown, NY (jāmz'toun)	111	42.05 N	79.15 W
Jamestown, RI	112b	41.30 N	71.21 W
Jamestown, S. Afr.	227c	31.07 S	26.49 E
Jamestown Res., ND	114	47.16 N	98.40 W
Jamiltepec, Mex. (hä-mēl-tȧ-pĕk)	131	16.16 N	97.54 W
Jammerbagten (B.), Den.	164	57.20 N	9.28 E
Jammu, India	196	32.50 N	74.52 E
Jammu and Kashmīr (Disputed Reg.), India-Pak. (kȧsh-mēr')	196	39.10 N	75.05 E
Jāmnagar, India (jäm-nŭ'gŭr)	196	22.33 N	70.03 E
Jamshedpur, India (jăm'shăd-pōōr)	196	22.52 N	86.11 E
Jamundí, Col. (hä-mōō'n-dē')	142a	3.15 N	76.32 W
Jándula (R.), Sp. (hän'dōō-lȧ)	170	38.28 N	3.52 W
Janesville, Wi. (jānz'vĭl)	115	42.41 N	89.03 W
Janin, Jordon	191a	32.27 N	35.19 E
Jan Mayen (I.), Nor. (yän mī'ĕn)	158	70.59 N	8.05 W
Jánoshalma, Hung. (yä'nôsh-hôl-mô)	167	46.17 N	19.18 E
Janów Lubelski, Pol. (yä'nōōf lŭ-bĕl'skĭ)	167	50.40 N	22.25 E
Januária, Braz. (zhä-nwä'rē-ä)	143	15.31 S	44.17 W
Japan, Asia (jȧ-păn')	191	36.30 N	133.30 E
Japan, Sea of, Asia (jȧ-păn')	204	40.08 N	132.55 E
Japeri, Braz. (zhȧ-pĕ'rē)	144b	22.38 S	43.40 W
Japurá (R.), Braz. (zhä-pōō-rä')	142	1.30 S	67.54 W
Jarabacoa, Dom. Rep. (Kä-rä-bä-kō'ä)	125	19.05 N	70.40 W
Jaral del Progreso, Mex. (hä-räl dĕl prō-grä'sō)	130	20.21 N	101.05 W
Jarama (R.), Sp. (hä-rä'mä)	170	40.33 N	3.30 W
Jarash, Jordan	191a	32.17 N	35.53 E
Jardim Paulista (Neigh.), Braz.	61d	23.35 S	46.40 W
Jardines, Banco (Bk.), Cuba (bä'n-kō-här-dē'nȧs)	134	21.45 N	81.40 W
Jardines del Pedregal de San Angel, Mex.	60a	19.18 N	99.13 W
Jari (R.), Braz. (zhä-rē)	143	0.28 N	53.00 W
Jarocin, Pol. (yä-rō'tsyēn)	167	51.58 N	17.31 E
Jaroslaw, Pol. (yȧ-rôs-wȧf)	167	50.01 N	22.41 E
Jargalant, Mong.	202	46.28 N	115.10 E
Jarud Qi, China (jya-lōō-tŭ shyē)	202	44.35 N	120.40 E
Jasenevo (Neigh.), Sov. Un.	66b	55.36 N	37.33 E
Jasin, Mala.	191b	2.19 N	102.26 E

PRONOUNCING INDEX Jašiūnai – Jugo-Zapad 297

PLACE (Pronounciation)	PAGE	Lat. °'	Long. °'
Jašiūnai, Sov. Un. (dzȧ-sho͞o-nȧ'ē)	165	54.27 N	25.25 E
Jāsk, Iran (jäsk)	192	25.46 N	57.48 E
Jaslo, Pol. (yäs'wō)	167	49.44 N	21.28 E
Jason B., Mala.	191 b	1.53 N	104.14 E
Jasonville, In. (jā'sŭn-vĭl)	110	39.10 N	87.15 W
Jasper, Al. (jăs'pēr)	126	33.50 N	87.17 W
Jasper, Can.	99	52.53 N	118.05 W
Jasper, Fl.	126	30.30 N	82.56 W
Jasper, In.	110	38.20 N	86.55 W
Jasper, Mn.	114	43.51 N	96.22 W
Jasper, Tx.	125	30.55 N	93.59 W
Jasper Natl. Park, Can.	99	53.09 N	117.45 W
Jászapáti, Hung. (yäs'ô-pä-tē)	167	47.29 N	20.10 E
Jászberény, Hung.	167	47.30 N	19.56 E
Jatate (R.), Mex. (hä-tä-tä')	131	16.30 N	91.29 W
Jatibonico, Cuba (hä-tē-bô-nē'kô)	134	22.00 N	79.15 W
Játiva, Sp. (hä'tē-vä)	171	38.58 N	0.31 W
Jaú, Braz. (zhȧ-o͞o')	144	22.16 S	48.31 W
Jauja, Peru (ká-o͞o'ĸ)	142	11.43 S	75.32 W
Jaumave, Mex. (hou-mä'vå)	130	23.23 N	99.24 W
Jaunjelgava, Sov. Un. (youn'yĕl'gȧ-vȧ)	165	56.37 N	25.06 E
Javari (R.), Col.-Peru (ĸȧ-vä-rē)	142	4.25 S	72.07 W
Java Trench, Indon.	206	9.45 S	107.30 E
Jávea, Sp. (hȧ-vā'ä)	171	38.45 N	0.07 E
Jawa (I.), Indon.	206	8.35 S	111.11 E
Jawa, Laut (Java Sea), Indon.	206	5.10 S	110.30 E
Jawor, Pol. (yä'vôr)	166	51.04 N	16.12 E
Jaworzno, Pol. (yä-vôzh'nô)	167	50.11 N	19.18 E
Jaya, Puncak (Pk.), Indon.	207	4.00 S	131.15 E
Jayapura (Sukarnapura), Indon.	207	2.30 S	140.45 W
Jayb, Wādī al (R.), see Ha 'Arava			
Jazīrat Muhammad, Egypt	71 a	30.07 N	31.12 E
Jazzīn, Leb.	191 a	33.34 N	35.37 E
Jeanerette, La. (jĕn-ĕr-et') (zhän-rĕt')	125	29.54 N	91.41 W
Jebba, Nig. (jĕb'ȧ)	224	9.07 N	4.46 E
Jeddore L., Can.	105	48.07 N	55.35 W
Jedlesee (Neigh.), Aus.	66 e	48.16 N	16.23 E
Jędrzejów, Pol. (yăɴ-dzhā'yo͝of)	167	50.38 N	20.18 E
Jefferson, Ga. (jĕf'ēr-sŭn)	126	34.05 N	83.35 W
Jefferson, Ia.	115	42.10 N	94.22 W
Jefferson, La.	112 d	29.57 N	90.04 W
Jefferson, Pa.	57 b	39.56 N	80.04 W
Jefferson, Tx.	125	32.47 N	94.21 W
Jefferson, Wi.	115	42.59 N	88.45 W
Jefferson City, Mo.	123	38.34 N	92.10 W
Jefferson, Mt., Or.	116	44.41 N	121.50 W
Jefferson Park (Neigh.), Il.	58 a	41.59 N	87.46 W
Jefferson R., Mt.	117	45.37 N	112.22 W
Jeffersontown, Ky. (jĕf'ēr-sŭn-toun)	113 h	38.11 N	85.34 W
Jeffersonville, In. (jĕf'ēr-sŭn-vĭl)	113 h	38.17 N	85.44 W
Jega, Nig.	229	12.15 N	4.23 E
Jehol (Reg.), China (jē-hōl)	199	42.31 N	118.12 E
Jeib, Wadi el (R.), Jordan-Isr.	161	30.30 N	35.20 E
Jēkabpils, Sov. Un. (yĕk'ăb-pĭls)	165	56.29 N	25.50 E
Jelenia Góra, Pol. (yĕ-lĕn'yȧ go͞o'rȧ)	166	50.53 N	15.43 E
Jelgava, Sov. Un. (yĕl'gȧ-vȧ)	165	56.39 N	23.40 E
Jellico, Tn. (jĕl'ĭ-kō)	126	36.34 N	84.06 W
Jena, G.D.R. (yā'nä)	166	50.55 N	11.37 E
Jenkins, Ky. (jĕŋ'kĭnz)	127	37.09 N	82.38 W
Jenkintown, Pa. (jĕŋ'kĭn-toun)	112 f	40.06 N	75.08 W
Jennings, La. (jĕn'ĭngz)	125	30.14 N	92.40 W
Jennings, Mi.	110	44.20 N	85.20 W
Jennings, Mo.	119 e	38.43 N	90.16 W
Jequié, Braz. (zhĕ-kyĕ')	143	13.53 S	40.06 W
Jequitinhonha (R.), Braz. (zhĕ-kē-tēŋ-ō'n-yä)	143	16.47 S	41.19 W
Jérémie, Hai. (zhā-rā-mē')	135	18.40 N	74.10 W
Jeremoabo, Braz. (zhĕ-rä-mō-ȧ'bō)	143	10.03 S	38.13 W
Jerez de la Frontera, Sp. (ĸē-rāth' dā lä frôn-tä'rä)	170	36.42 N	6.09 W
Jerez de Los Caballeros, Sp. (ĸē-rath'dā lōs kä-väl-yä'rôs)	170	38.20 N	6.45 W
Jerez, Punta (Pt.), Mex. (po͞o'n-tä-ĸē-räz')	131	23.04 N	97.44 W
Jericho, Austl. (jĕr'ĭ-kō)	215	28.38 S	146.24 E
Jericho, NY	55	40.48 N	73.32 W
Jericho, S. Afr. (jĕr-ĭkō)	223 d	25.16 N	27.47 E
Jericho, see Arīḥā			
Jerome, Az. (jē-rōm')	121	34.45 N	112.10 W
Jerome, Id.	117	42.44 N	114.31 W
Jersey (I.), Eur. (jûr'zĭ)	168	49.13 N	2.07 W
Jersey City, NJ	112 a	40.43 N	74.05 W
Jersey Shore, Pa.	111	41.10 N	77.15 W
Jerseyville, Il. (jēr'zē-vĭl)	123	39.07 N	90.18 W
Jerusalem, Isr.-Jordan (jē-ro͞o'sȧ-lĕm)	191 a	31.46 N	35.14 E
Jesup, Ga. (jĕs'ŭp)	127	31.36 N	81.53 W
Jesús Carranza, Mex. (hē-so͞o's-kär-rä'n-zä)	131	17.26 N	95.01 W
Jesús del Monte (Neigh.)	60 b	23.06 N	82.22 W
Jésus, Ile (I.), Can.	54 b	45.35 N	73.45 W
Jesús María, Peru	60 c	12.04 S	77.04 W
Jewel, Or. (jū'ĕl)	118 c	45.56 N	123.30 W
Jewel Cave Natl. Mon., SD	114	43.44 N	103.52 W
Jhālawār, India	196	24.29 N	79.09 E
Jhang Maghiāna, Pak.	196	31.21 N	72.19 E
Jhānsi, India (jän'sē)	196	25.29 N	78.32 E
Jhārsuguda, India	196	22.51 N	86.13 E
Jhelum (R.), Pak. (jā'lŭm)	196	31.40 N	71.51 E
Jhenkāri, India	67 a	22.46 N	88.18 E
Jhil Kuranga (Neigh.), India	67 d	28.40 N	77.17 E
Jiache, China (jyä-chŭ)	200	38.03 N	116.18 E
Jiading, China (jyä-dĭŋ)	201 a	31.23 N	121.15 E
Jialing (R.), China (jyä-lĭŋ)	203	30.30 N	106.20 E
Ji'an, China (jyē-än)	203	27.15 N	115.10 E
Ji'an, China	202	41.00 N	126.04 E
Jianchangying, China (jyĕn-chäŋ-yĭŋ)	200	40.09 N	119.47 E
Jiangcun, China (jyän-tso͞on)	201 a	23.16 N	113.14 E
Jiangling, China (jyäŋ-lĭŋ)	203	30.30 N	112.10 E
Jiangshanzhen, China (jyäŋ-shän-jŭn)	200	36.39 N	120.31 E
Jiangsu (Prov.), China (jyäŋ-so͞o)	199	33.45 N	120.30 E
Jiangwan, China (jyäŋ-wän)	201 b	31.18 N	121.29 E
Jiangxi (Prov.), China (jyäŋ-shyē)	199	28.15 N	116.00 E
Jiangyin, China (jyäŋ-yĭn)	200	31.54 N	120.15 E
Jianli, China (jyĕn-lē)	203	29.50 N	112.52 E
Jianning, China (jyĕn-nĭŋ)	203	26.50 N	116.55 E
Jian'ou, China (jyĕn-ō)	203	27.10 N	118.18 E
Jianshi, China (jyĕn-shr)	203	30.40 N	109.45 E
Jiaohe, China (jyou-hŭ)	202	43.40 N	127.20 E
Jiaoxian, China (jyou shyĕn)	200	36.18 N	120.01 E
Jiaozuo, China (jyou-dzwô)	200	35.15 N	113.18 E
Jiashan, China (jyä-shän)	200	32.41 N	118.00 E
Jiaxing, China (jyä-shyĭŋ)	203	30.45 N	120.50 E
Jiayu, China (jyä-yo͞o)	203	33.00 N	114.00 E
Jiazhou Wan (B.), China (jyä-jō wän)	200	36.10 N	119.55 E
Jicarilla Ind. Res., NM (ĸē-kȧ-rēl'yȧ)	121	36.45 N	107.00 W
Jicaron, Isla (I.), Pan. (ĸē-kä-rōn')	133	7.14 N	81.41 W
Jiddah, Sau. Ar.	192	21.30 N	39.15 E
Jieshou, China	200	33.17 N	115.20 E
Jieyang, China (jyĕ-yäŋ)	203	23.38 N	116.20 E
Jiggalong, Austl. (jĭg'ȧ-lông)	214	23.20 S	120.45 E
Jiguani, Cuba (ĸē-gwä-nē')	135	20.20 N	76.30 W
Jigüey, Bahía (B.), Cuba (bä-ē'ä-ĸē'gwā)	134	22.15 N	78.10 W
Jihlava, Czech. (yē'hlȧ-vȧ)	166	49.23 N	15.33 E
Jijel, Alg.	159	36.49 N	5.47 E
Jijia (R.), Rom.	167	47.35 N	27.02 E
Jijiashi, China (jyē-jyä-shr)	200	32.10 N	120.17 E
Jijiga, Eth.	223 a	9.15 N	42.48 E
Jijona, Sp. (ĸē-hō'nä)	171	38.31 N	0.29 W
Jilf al-Kabīr, Hadabat al (Plat.), Egypt	225	24.09 N	25.29 E
Jilin, China (jyē-lĭn)	202	43.58 N	126.40 E
Jilin (Prov.), China	199	44.20 N	124.50 E
Jiloca (R.), Sp. (ĸē-lō'kä)	170	41.13 N	1.30 W
Jilotepeque, Guat. (ĸē-lô-tĕ-pĕ'kĕ)	132	14.39 N	89.36 W
Jima, Eth.	225	7.41 N	36.52 E
Jimbolia, Rom. (zhĭm-bô'lyä)	173	45.45 N	20.44 E
Jiménez, Mex. (ĸē-mā'nāz)	130	24.12 N	98.29 W
Jimenez, Mex.	124	27.09 N	104.55 W
Jiménez, Mex.	124	29.03 N	100.42 W
Jiménez del Téul, Mex. (tē-o͞o'l)	130	21.28 N	103.51 W
Jimo, China (jyē-mwo)	200	36.22 N	120.28 E
Jim Thorpe, Pa. (jĭm' thôrp')	111	40.50 N	75.45 W
Jinan, China (jyē-nän)	200	36.40 N	117.01 E
Jincheng, China (jyĭn-chŭŋ)	202	35.30 N	112.50 E
Jindřichov Hradec, Czech. (yēn'd'r-zhĭ-ko͞of hrä'dĕts)	166	49.09 N	15.02 E
Jing (R.), China (jyĭŋ)	202	34.40 N	108.20 E
Jing'anji, China (jyĭŋ-än-jē)	200	34.30 N	116.55 E
Jingdezhen, China (jyĭn-dŭ-jŭn)	203	29.18 N	117.18 E
Jingjiang, China (jyĭŋ-jyäŋ)	200	32.02 N	120.15 E
Jingning, China (jyĭŋ-nĭŋ)	202	35.28 N	105.50 E
Jingpo Hu (L.), China (jyĭŋ-pwo ho͞o)	202	44.10 N	129.00 E
Jingxian, China (jyĭŋ shyĕn)	203	26.32 N	109.45 E
Jingxian, China	200	37.43 N	116.17 E
Jingxing, China (jyĭŋ-shyĭŋ)	202	47.00 N	123.00 E
Jingzhi, China (jyĭŋ-jr)	200	36.19 N	119.23 E
Jinhua, China (jyĭn-hwä)	203	29.10 N	119.42 E
Jining, China (jyē-nĭŋ)	200	35.26 N	116.34 E
Jining, China	202	41.00 N	113.10 E
Jinja, Ug. (jĭn'jä)	231	0.26 N	33.12 E
Jinotega, Nic. (ĸē-nô-tā'gä)	132	13.07 N	86.00 W
Jinotepe, Nic. (ĸē-nô-tā'pā)	132	11.52 N	86.12 W
Jinqiao, China (jyĭn-chyou)	200	31.46 N	116.46 E
Jinshan, China (jyĭn-shän)	201 b	30.53 N	121.09 E
Jinta, China (jyĭn-tä)	198	40.11 N	98.45 E
Jintan, China (jyĭn-tän)	200	31.47 N	119.34 E
Jin Xian, China (jyĭn shyĕn)	200	39.04 N	121.40 E
Jinxiang, China (jyĭn-shyäŋ)	200	35.03 N	116.20 E
Jinyun, China (jyĭn-yo͞on)	203	28.40 N	120.08 E
Jinzhai, China (jyĭn-jī)	200	31.41 N	115.51 E
Jinzhou, China (jyĭn-jō)	202	41.00 N	121.00 E
Jinzhou Wan (B.), China (jyĭn-jō wän)	200	39.07 N	121.17 E
Jinzū-Gawa (Strm.), Jap. (jĕn'zo͞o gä'wä)	205	36.26 N	137.18 E
Jipijapa, Ec. (ĸē-pē-hä'pä)	142	1.36 S	80.52 W
Jiquilisco, Sal. (ĸē-kē-lē's-kô)	132	13.18 N	88.32 W
Jiquilpan de Juarez, Mex. (ĸē-kēl'pän dā hwä'rāz)	130	20.00 N	102.43 W
Jiquipilco, Mex. (hē-kē-pē'l-kô)	131 a	19.32 N	99.37 W
Jirjā, Egypt (jēr'gȧ)	223 b	26.20 N	31.51 E
Jitotol, Mex. (ĸē-tô-tōl')	131	17.03 N	92.54 W
Jiu (R.), Rom.	173	44.45 N	23.17 E
Jiugang, China	67 b	39.49 N	116.27 E
Jiujiang, China (jyô-jyän)	201 a	22.50 N	113.02 E
Jiujiang, China	203	29.43 N	116.00 E
Jiuquan, China (jyô-chyän)	198	39.46 N	98.26 E
Jiurongcheng, China (jyô-rôŋ-chŭŋ)	200	37.23 N	122.31 E
Jiushouzhang, China (jyô-shō-jäŋ)	200	35.59 N	115.52 E
Jiuwuqing, China (jyô-wo͞o-chyĭŋ)	202 a	32.39 N	116.51 E
Jiuyongnian, China (jyô-yôŋ-nĭĕn)	200	36.41 N	114.46 E
Jixian, China (jyē shyĕn)	200	35.25 N	114.03 E
Jixian, China	200	37.37 N	115.33 E
Jixian, China	200	40.03 N	117.25 E
Jiyum (R.), China (jyē-yo͞om)	200	39.35 N	117.34 E
Jīzān, Sau. Ar.	195	16.54 N	42.29 E
João Pessoa (Paraíba), Braz. (shô-ouɴ'pĕ-sōō') (pä-rä-ē'bȧ)	143	7.09 S	34.45 W
João Ribeiro, Braz. (zhô-uɴ-rē-bā'rō)	141 a	20.42 S	44.03 W
Jobabo (R.), Cuba (hō-bä'bä)	134	20.50 N	77.15 W
Jock (R.), Can. (jŏk)	95 c	45.08 N	75.51 W
Jocotepec, Mex. (jô-kō-tā-pĕk')	130	20.17 N	103.26 W
Jodar, Sp. (hō'där)	170	37.54 N	3.20 W
Jodhpur, India (hōd'po͞or)	196	26.23 N	73.00 E
Joensuu, Fin. (yô-ĕn'so͞o)	165	62.35 N	29.46 E
Joffre, Mt., Can. (jŏ'f'r)	99	50.32 N	115.13 W
Jōga-Shima(I.), Jap. (jō'gä shē'mä)	205 a	35.07 N	139.37 E
Jõgeva, Sov. Un. (yû'gĕ-vȧ)	174	58.45 N	26.23 E
Joggins, Can. (jŏ'gĭnz)	102	45.42 N	64.27 W
Johannesburg, S. Afr. (yô-hän'ĕs-bo͞orgh)	227 b	26.08 S	27.54 E
Johannisthal (Neigh.), G.D.R.	65 a	52.26 N	13.30 E
John Carroll University (P. Int.), Oh.	56 a	41.29 N	81.32 W
John Day Dam, Or.	116	45.40 N	120.15 W
John Day R., Or. (jŏn'dā)	116	44.46 N	120.15 W
John Day R., Middle Fork, Or.	116	44.53 N	119.04 W
John Day R., North Fork, Or.	116	45.03 N	118.50 W
John F. Kennedy International Arpt., NY	55	40.38 N	73.47 W
John Martin Res., Co. (jŏn mär'tĭn)	122	37.57 N	103.04 W
Johns Hopkins University (P. Int.), Md.	56 c	39.20 N	76.37 W
Johnson (R.), Or. (jŏn'sŭn)	118 c	45.27 N	122.20 W
Johnsonburg, Pa. (jŏn'sŭn-bûrg)	111	41.30 N	78.40 W
Johnson City, Il. (jŏn'sŭn)	110	37.50 N	88.55 W
Johnson City, NY	111	42.10 N	76.00 W
Johnson City, Tn.	127	36.17 N	82.23 W
Johnston (I.), Oceania (jŏn'stŭn)	208	17.00 N	168.00 W
Johnstone Saint, Can.	98	50.25 N	126.00 W
Johnston Falls, Afr.	231	10.35 S	28.50 E
Johnstown, NY (jonz'toun)	111	43.00 N	74.20 W
Johnstown, Pa.	111	40.20 N	78.50 W
Johor (R.), Mala. (jŭ-hōr')	191 b	1.39 N	103.52 E
Johor Bahru, Mala. (bȧ-hŭ-ro͞o')	191 b	1.28 N	103.46 E
Johor, Selat (Str.), Asia	67 c	1.28 N	103.48 E
Jõhvi, Sov. Un. (yû'vĭ)	174	59.21 N	27.21 E
Joigny, Fr. (zhwȧn-yē')	168	47.58 N	3.26 E
Joinville, Braz. (zhwăɴ-vēl')	144	26.18 S	48.47 W
Joinville, Fr.	168	48.28 N	5.05 E
Joinville (I.), Ant.	140	63.00 S	53.30 W
Joinville-le-Pont, Fr.	64 c	48.49 N	2.28 E
Jojutla, Mex. (hō-ho͞o'tlä)	130	18.39 N	99.11 W
Jola, Mex. (ĸô'lä)	130	21.08 N	104.26 W
Joliet, Il. (jō-lĭ-ĕt')	113 a	41.37 N	88.05 W
Joliette, Can. (zhô-lyĕt')	103	46.01 N	73.30 W
Jolo Phil. (hō-lō)	206	5.59 N	121.05 E
Jolo I., Phil.	206	5.55 N	121.15 E
Jomalig (I.), Phil. (hô-mä'lĕg)	207 a	14.44 N	122.34 E
Jomulco, Mex. (hô-mo͞ol'kō)	130	21.08 N	104.24 W
Jonacatepec, Mex. (hō-nä-kä-tā-pĕk')	130	18.39 N	98.46 W
Jonava, Sov. Un. (yō-nä'vȧ)	165	55.05 N	24.15 E
Jones, Phil. (jōnz)	207 a	13.56 N	122.05 E
Jones, Phil.	207 a	16.35 N	121.39 E
Jonesboro, Ar. (jōnz'bûro)	123	35.49 N	90.42 W
Jonesboro, La.	125	32.14 N	92.43 W
Jonesville, La. (jōnz'vĭl)	125	31.35 N	91.50 W
Jonesville, Mi.	110	42.00 N	84.45 W
Jong (R.), S.L.	228	8.10 N	12.10 W
Joniškis, Sov. Un. (yô'nĭsh-kĭs)	165	56.14 N	23.36 E
Jönköping, Swe. (yûn'chû-pĭng)	164	57.47 N	14.10 E
Jonquiere, Can. (zhôɴ-kyâr')	103	48.25 N	71.15 W
Jonuta, Mex. (hô-no͞o'tä)	131	18.07 N	92.09 W
Jonzac, Fr. (zhôɴ-zȧk')	168	45.27 N	0.27 W
Joplin, Mo. (jŏp'lĭn)	123	37.05 N	94.31 W
Jordan, Asia (jôr'dăn)	190	30.15 N	38.00 E
Jordan (R.), Jordan	191 a	31.58 N	35.36 E
Jordan R., Ut.	119 b	40.42 N	111.56 W
Jorhāt, India (jōr-hät')	193	26.43 N	94.16 E
Jorullo, Vol. de, Mex. (vôl-kä'n-dĕ-hô-ro͞ol'yō)	130	18.54 N	101.38 W
José C. Paz, Arg.	60 d	34.32 S	58.44 W
Joseph Bonaparte, G., Austl. (jō'sĕf bō'nȧ-pärt)	214	13.30 S	128.40 E
Josephburg, Can.	95 g	53.45 N	113.06 W
Joseph L., Can. (jō'sĕf lăk)	95 g	53.18 N	113.06 W
Joshua Tree Natl. Mon., Can. (jō'shū-ȧ trē)	120	34.02 N	115.53 W
Jos Plat., Nig. (jôs)	229	9.53 N	9.05 E
Jostedalsbreen (Gl.), Nor. (yôstĕ-däls-brĕĕn)	164	61.40 N	6.55 E
Jotunheimen (Mts.), Nor.	164	61.44 N	8.11 E
Joulter's Cays (Is.), Ba. (jōl'tērz)	134	25.20 N	78.10 W
Jouy-en-Josas, Fr.	64 c	48.46 N	2.10 E
Jouy-le-Chatel, Fr. (zhwē-lĕ-shä-tĕl')	169 b	48.40 N	3.07 E
Jovellanos, Cuba (hō-vĕl-yä'nōs)	134	22.50 N	81.10 W
Jōyō, Jap.	205 b	34.51 N	135.48 E
J. Percy Priest Res., Tn.	126	36.00 N	86.45 W
Juan Aldama, Mex. (ko͞oȧ'n-äl-dä'mä)	130	24.16 N	103.21 W
Juan Anchorena (Neigh.), Arg.	60 d	34.29 S	58.30 W
Juan de Fuca, Str. of, Wa.-Can. (hwän' dā fo͞o'kä)	116	48.25 N	124.37 W
Juan de Nova, Ile (I.), Afr.	227	17.18 S	43.07 E
Juan Diaz, (R.), Pan. (ĸo͞oȧ'n-dē'äz)	128 a	9.05 N	79.30 W
Juan Fernández, Islas de (Is.), Chile (ē's-läs-dĕ-hwän' fĕr-nän'dāth)	140	33.30 S	79.00 W
Juan González Romero, Mex.	60 a	19.30 N	99.04 W
Juan L. Lacaze, Ur. (ho͞oȧ'n-ĕ'lĕ-lä-kä'zĕ)	141 c	34.25 S	57.28 W
Juan Luis, Cayos de (Is.), Cuba (ka-yōs-dĕ-hwän lo͞o-ēs')	134	22.15 N	82.00 W
Juárez, Arg. (ho͞oä'rĕz)	144	37.42 S	59.46 W
Juàzeiro, Braz. (zho͞oȧ'zā'rô)	143	9.27 S	40.28 W
Juazeiro do Norte, Braz. (zho͞oȧ'zā'rô-dô-nôr-tĕ)	143	7.16 S	38.57 W
Jūbā, Sud.	225	4.58 N	31.37 E
Jubayl (Byblos), Leb. (jo͞o-bĭl')	191 a	34.07 N	35.38 E
Jubba (R.), Som.	223 a	1.30 N	42.25 E
Júcar (R.), Sp. (ho͞o'kär)	170	39.10 N	1.22 W
Júcaro, Cuba (ho͞o'kȧ-rô)	134	21.40 N	78.50 W
Juchipila, Mex. (ho͞o-chē-pē'lä)	130	21.26 N	103.09 W
Juchitán, Mex. (ho͞o-chē-tän')	128	16.15 N	95.00 W
Juchitán de Zaragoza, Mex. (ho͞o-chē-tän' dā thä-rä-gō'thä)	131	16.27 N	95.03 W
Juchitlán, Mex. (ho͞o-chē-tlän)	130	20.05 N	104.07 W
Jucuapa, Sal. (ĸo͞o-kwä'pä)	132	13.30 N	88.24 W
Judenburg, Aus. (jo͞o'dĕn-bûrg)	166	47.10 N	14.40 E
Judith R., Mt. (jo͞o'dĭth)	117	47.20 N	109.36 W
Jugo-Zapad (Neigh.), Sov. Un.	66 b	55.40 N	37.32 E

PLACE (Pronunciation)	PAGE	Lat. °′	Long. °′
Juhua Dao (I.), China (jyōō-hwä dou)	200	40.30 N	120.47 E
Juigalpa, Nic. (hwē-gäl'pä)	132	12.02 N	85.24 W
Juilly, Fr.	64c	49.01 N	2.42 E
Juist (I.), F.R.G. (yōō'ēst)	163	53.41 N	6.50 E
Juiz de Fora, Braz. (zhōō-ēzh' dā fō'rä)	141a	21.47 S	43.20 W
Jujuy, Arg. (hōō-hwē')	144	24.14 S	65.15 W
Jujuy (Prov.), Arg. (hōō-hwē')	144	23.00 S	65.45 W
Jukskei (R.), S. Afr.	227b	25.58 S	27.58 E
Julesburg, Co. (jōōlz'bûrg)	122	40.59 N	102.16 W
Juliaca, Peru (hōō-lē-ä'kä)	142	15.26 S	70.12 W
Julian Alps (Mts.), Yugo.	172	46.05 N	14.05 E
Julianehåb, Grnld.	94	60.07 N	46.20 W
Jülich, F.R.G. (yü'lēk)	169c	50.55 N	6.22 E
Jullundur, India	196	31.29 N	75.39 E
Julpaiguri, India	196	26.35 N	88.48 E
Jumento Cays (Is.), Ba. (hōō-mĕn'tō)	135	23.05 N	75.40 W
Jumilla, Sp. (hōō-mēl'yä)	170	38.28 N	1.20 W
Jump (R.), Wi. (jŭmp)	115	45.18 N	90.53 W
Jumpingpound Cr., Can. (jŭmp-ĭng-pound)	95e	51.01 N	114.34 W
Jumrah, Indon.	191b	1.48 N	101.04 E
Jumundá (R.), Braz. (zhōō-mōō'n-dä')	143	1.33 S	57.42 W
Junagādh, India (jōō-nä'gŭd)	196	21.33 N	70.25 E
Junayfah, Egypt	223c	30.11 N	32.26 E
Junaynah, Ra's al (Mt.), Egypt	191a	29.02 N	33.58 E
Junction, Tx. (jŭngk'shŭn)	124	30.29 N	99.48 W
Junction City, Ks.	123	39.01 N	96.49 W
Jundiaí, Braz. (zhōō'n-dyä-ē')	141a	23.12 S	46.52 W
Juneau, Ak. (jōō'nō)	107	58.25 N	134.30 W
Jungfrau (Pk.), Switz. (yōōng'frou)	166	46.30 N	7.59 E
Juniata (Neigh.), Pa.	56b	40.01 N	75.07 W
Junín, Arg. (hōō-nē'n)	141c	34.35 S	60.56 W
Junín, Col.	142a	4.47 N	73.39 W
Juniyah, Leb. (jōō-nē'ĕ)	191a	33.59 N	35.38 E
Jupiter (R.), Can.	105	49.40 N	63.20 W
Jupiter, Mt., Wa.	118a	47.42 N	123.04 W
Jur (R.), Sud. (jōōr)	225	6.38 N	27.52 E
Jura (I.), Scot. (jōō'rá)	162	56.09 N	6.45 W
Jura (Mts.), Switz. (zhü-rá')	169	46.55 N	6.49 E
Jura, Sd. of, Scot. (jōō'rá)	162	55.45 N	5.55 W
Jurbarkas, Sov. Un. (yōōr-bär'käs)	165	55.06 N	22.50 E
Jūrmala, Sov. Un.	165	56.57 N	23.37 E
Jurong, China (jyōō-rôŋ)	200	31.58 N	119.12 E
Jurong, Singapore	67c	1.21 N	103.42 E
Juruá (R.), Braz. (zhōō-rōō-ä')	142	5.27 S	67.39 W
Juruena (R.), Braz. (zhōō-rōōĕ'nä)	143	12.22 S	58.34 W
Justice, Il.	58a	41.45 N	87.50 W
Jutaí (R.), Braz. (zhōō-táy)	142	4.26 S	68.16 W
Jutiapa, Guat. (hōō-tē-ä'pä)	132	14.16 N	89.55 W
Juticalpa, Hond. (hōō-tē-käl'pä)	132	14.35 N	86.17 W
Juventino Rosas, Mex. (κōō-vĕn-tē'nô-rô-säs)	130	20.38 N	101.02 W
Juventud, Isla de la (I.), Cuba	134	21.40 N	82.45 W
Juvisy-sur-Orge, Fr.	64c	48.41 N	2.23 E
Juxian, China (jyōō shyĕn)	200	35.35 N	118.50 E
Juxtahuaca, Mex. (hōōs-tlá-hwä'kä)	130	17.20 N	98.02 W
Juye, China (jyōō-yū)	200	35.25 N	116.05 E
Južna Morava (R.), Yugo. (ū'zhnä mô'rä-vä)	173	42.30 N	22.00 E
Jwālahari (Neigh.), India	67d	28.40 N	77.06 E
Jylland (Reg.), Den.	164	56.04 N	9.00 E
Jyväskylä, Fin. (yû'vĕs-kû-lĕ)	165	62.14 N	25.46 E

K

PLACE (Pronunciation)	PAGE	Lat. °′	Long. °′
Kaabong, Ug.	231	3.31 N	34.08 E
Kaalfontein, S. Afr. (kärl-fōn-tān)	227b	26.02 S	28.16 E
Kaappunt (C.), S. Afr.	226a	34.21 S	18.30 E
Kaarst, F.R.G.	63	51.14 N	6.37 E
Kabaena, Pulau (I.), Indon. (kä-bá-ä'ná)	206	5.35 S	121.07 E
Kabala, S. L. (ká-bá'lá)	224	9.43 N	11.39 W
Kabale, Ug.	231	1.15 S	29.59 E
Kabalega Falls, Ug.	231	2.15 N	31.41 E
Kabalo, Zaire (kä-bä'lō)	231	6.03 S	26.55 E
Kabambare, Zaire (kä-bäm-bä'rå)	226	4.47 S	27.45 E
Kabba, Nig.	229	7.50 N	6.03 E
Kabe, Jap. (kä'bā)	205	34.32 N	132.30 E
Kabel (Neigh.), F.R.G.	63	51.24 N	7.29 E
Kabinakagami (R.), Can.	102	49.00 N	84.15 W
Kabinda, Zaire (kä-bēn'dä)	230	6.08 S	24.29 E
Kabompo (R.), Zambia (ká-bôm'pō)	230	14.00 S	23.40 E
Kabongo, Zaire (ká-bông'ō)	226	7.58 S	25.10 E
Kabot, Gui.	228	10.48 N	14.57 W
Kaboudia, Ra's (C.), Tun.	160	35.17 N	11.28 E
Kābul, Afg. (kä'bōōl)	196	34.39 N	69.14 E
Kabul (R.), Asia (kä'bōōl)	193	34.44 N	69.43 E
Kabunda, Zaire	231	12.25 S	29.22 E
Kabwe (Broken Hill), Zambia	231	14.27 S	28.27 E
Kachuga, Sov. Un. (kå-chōō-gå)	181	54.09 N	105.43 E
Kadei (R.), Cam.-Cen. Afr. Rep.	229	4.00 N	15.10 E
Kadıköy (Neigh.), Tur.	66f	40.59 N	29.01 E
Kadiyevka, Sov. Un. (ká-dĭ-yĕf'ká)	175	48.34 N	38.37 E
Kadnikov, Sov. Un. (käd'nē-kôf)	178	59.30 N	40.10 E
Kadoma, Jap.	205b	34.43 N	135.36 E
Kadoma, Zimb.	231	18.21 S	29.55 E
Kaduna, Nig. (kä-dōō'nä)	229	10.33 N	7.27 E
Kaduna (R.), Nig.	229	9.30 N	6.00 E
Kaédi, Mauritania (kä-ā-dē')	228	16.09 N	13.30 W
Kaena Pt., Hi. (kä'å-nä)	106a	21.33 N	158.19 W
Kaesŏng (Kaijo), Kor. (kä'ĕ-sŭng) (kī'jō)	204	38.00 N	126.35 E
Kafanchan, Nig.	229	9.36 N	8.17 E
Kafia Kingi, Sud. (kä'fē-á kĭŋ'gē)	225	9.17 N	24.28 E
Kafue (R.), Zambia	231	15.45 S	26.30 E
Kafue, Zambia (kä'fōō)	226	15.45 S	28.17 E
Kafue Flats (Pln.), Zambia	231	16.15 S	26.30 E
Kafue Natl. Pk., Zambia	231	15.00 S	25.35 E
Kafwira, Zaire	231	12.10 S	27.33 E
Kagal'nik (R.), Sov. Un. (kä-gäl''nēk)	175	46.58 N	39.25 E
Kagera (R.), Tan. (kä-gā'rá)	231	1.10 S	31.10 E
Kagoshima, Jap. (kä'gô-shē'má)	205	31.35 N	130.31 E
Kagoshima-Wan (B.), Jap. (kä'gô-shē'mä wän)	205	31.24 N	130.39 E
Kagran (Neigh.), Sov. Un.	66a	48.15 N	16.27 E
Kagul, Sov. Un. (ka-gōōl')	175	45.49 N	28.17 E
Kahayan (R.), Indon.	206	1.45 S	113.40 E
Kahemba, Zaire	230	7.17 S	19.00 E
Kahia, Zaire	231	6.21 S	28.24 E
Kahoka, Mo. (ká-hō'ká)	123	40.26 N	91.42 W
Kahoolawe (I), Hi. (kä-hōō-lä'wē)	106a	20.28 N	156.48 W
Kahoué, Mont (Mtn.), Ivory Coast	228	7.06 N	7.15 W
Kahshahpiwi (R.), Can.	115	48.24 N	90.56 W
Kahuku Pt., Hi. (kä-hōō'kōō)	106a	21.50 N	157.50 W
Kahului, Hi.	106a	20.53 N	156.28 W
Kaiang, Mala.	191b	3.00 N	101.47 E
Kaiashk (R.), Can.	102	49.40 N	89.30 W
Kaibab Ind. Res., Az. (kä'ē-băb)	121	36.55 N	112.45 W
Kaibab Plat, Az.	121	36.30 N	112.10 W
Kaidori, Jap.	69a	35.37 N	139.27 E
Kaidu (R.), China (kī-dōō)	198	42.35 N	84.04 E
Kaieteur Fall, Guy. (kī-ē-tōōr')	143	4.48 N	59.24 W
Kaifeng, China (kī-fŭŋ)	200	34.48 N	114.22 E
Kaijo, see **Kaesong**			
Kai Kecil (I.), Indon.	207	5.45 S	132.40 E
Kai, Kepulauan (Is.), Indon.	207	5.35 S	132.45 E
Kaikyō, Sōya (Str.), Sov. Un. (sō'yá ká-ē'kī-ô)	177	45.45 N	141.20 E
Kailua, Hi. (kä'ē-lōō'ä)	106a	21.18 N	157.43 W
Kailua Kona, Hi.	106a	19.49 N	155.59 W
Kaimana, Indon.	207	3.32 S	133.47 E
Kaimanawa Mts., N.Z.	217	39.10 S	176.00 E
Kainan, Jap. (kä'ē-nän')	205	34.09 N	135.14 E
Kainji L., Nig.	229	10.25 N	4.50 E
Kaisarianí, Grc.	66d	37.58 N	23.47 E
Kaisermühlen (Neigh.), Aus.	66e	48.14 N	16.26 E
Kaiserslautern, F.R.G. (kī-zĕrs-lou'tĕrn)	166	49.26 N	7.46 E
Kaiserwerth (Neigh.), F.R.G.	63	51.18 N	6.44 E
Kaitaia, N. Z. (kä-ē-tä'ē-á)	217	35.30 S	173.28 E
Kaiwi Chan.,Hi. (kaē-wē)	106a	21.10 N	157.38 W
Kaiyuan, China (kū-yuän)	203	23.42 N	103.20 E
Kaiyuan, China	202	42.30 N	124.00 E
Kaiyuh Mts., Ak. (kī-yōō')	107	64.25 N	157.38 W
Kajaani, Fin. (kä'yá-nē)	158	64.15 N	27.16 E
Kajang, Gunong (Mt.), Mala.	191b	2.47 N	104.05 E
Kajiki, Jap. (kä'jē-kē)	205	31.44 N	130.41 E
Kakhovka, Sov. Un. (kä-κôf'ká)	175	46.46 N	33.32 E
Kakhovskoye (L.), Sov. Un. (ká-κôf'skô-yē)	175	47.21 N	33.33 E
Kākināda, India	193	16.58 N	82.18 E
Kaktovik, Ak. (kăk-tō'vĭk)	107	70.08 N	143.51 W
Kakwa (R.), Can. (kăk'wá)	99	54.00 N	118.55 W
Kalach, Sov. Un. (ká-lách')	179	50.15 N	40.55 E
Kaladan (R.), Bur.	198	21.07 N	93.04 E
Kalahari Des., Bots. (kä-lä-hä'rē)	226	23.00 S	22.03 E
Kalama (R.), Wa.	118c	46.03 N	122.47 W
Kalama, Wa. (ká-lăm'á)	118c	46.01 N	122.50 W
Kalámai, Grc. (kä-lä-mī')	173	37.04 N	22.08 E
Kalamákion, Grc.	66d	37.55 N	23.43 E
Kalamazoo, Mi. (kăl-á-má-zōō')	110	42.20 N	85.40 W
Kalamazoo (R.), Mi.	110	42.35 N	86.00 W
Kalanchak, Sov. Un. (kä-län-chäk')	175	46.17 N	33.14 E
Kalapana, Hi. (kä-lä-pá'nä)	106a	19.25 N	155.00 W
Kalar (Mtn.), Iran	192	31.43 N	51.41 E
Kalāt, Pak. (kŭ-lät')	196	29.05 N	66.36 E
Kalatoa, Pulau (I.), Indon.	206	7.22 S	122.30 E
Kalemie (Albertville), Zaire	231	5.56 S	29.12 E
Kalgan, see **Zhangjiakou**			
Kalgoorlie, Austl. (kăl-gōōr'lē)	214	30.45 S	121.35 E
Kaliakra, Nos (Pt.), Rom.	161	43.25 N	28.42 E
Kalima, Zaire	231	2.34 S	26.37 E
Kalina (Neigh.), Zaire	71c	4.18 S	15.16 E
Kalinin (Oblast), Sov. Un.	174	56.50 N	33.08 E
Kalinin (Tver), Sov. Un. (kä-lē'nĕn) (tvĕr)	174	56.52 N	35.57 E
Kaliningrad (Königsberg), Sov. Un. (kä-lē-nēn'grät) (kû'nĕks-bĕrgh)	165	54.42 N	20.32 E
Kaliningrad, Sov. Un. (kä-lē-nēn'grät)	182b	55.55 N	37.49 E
Kalinkovichi, Sov. Un. (kä-lēn-ko-vē'chē)	175	52.07 N	29.19 E
Kalispel Ind. Res., Wa. (kăl-ĭ-spĕl')	116	48.25 N	117.30 W
Kalispell, Mt. (kăl'ĭ-spĕl)	117	48.12 N	114.18 W
Kalisz, Pol. (kä'lēsh)	167	51.45 N	18.05 E
Kaliua, Tan.	231	5.04 S	31.48 E
Kalixälven (R.), Swe.	158	67.12 N	22.00 E
Kālkāji (Neigh.), India	67d	28.33 N	77.16 E
Kalksburg (Neigh.), Aus.	66e	48.08 N	16.15 E
Kalkum, F.R.G.	63	51.18 N	6.46 E
Kallithéa, Grc.	66d	37.57 N	23.42 E
Kalmar, Swe. (käl'mär)	164	56.40 N	16.19 E
Kalmarsund (Sd.), Swe. (käl'mär)	164	56.30 N	16.17 E
Kal'mius (R.), Sov. Un. (käl''myōōs)	175	47.15 N	37.38 E
Kalmthout, Bel.	157a	51.23 N	4.28 E
Kalmyk A. S. S. R., Sov. Un. (kál'mĭk)	179	46.56 N	46.00 E
Kalocsa, Hung. (kä'lô-chä)	167	46.32 N	19.00 E
Kalohi Chan., Hi. (kä-lō'hĭ)	106a	20.55 N	157.15 W
Kaloko, Zaire	231	6.47 S	25.48 E
Kalomo, Zambia (kä-lō'mō)	231	17.02 S	26.30 E
Kalsubai Mt., India	196	24.43 N	73.47 E
Kaltenkirchen, F.R.G. (käl'tĕn-kēr-κĕn)	157c	53.50 N	9.57 E
Kālu (R.), India	197b	19.18 N	73.14 E
Kaluga (Oblast), Sov. Un.	174	54.10 N	34.30 E
Kaluga, Sov. Un. (ká-lōō'gä)	174	54.29 N	36.12 E
Kalundborg, Den. (ká-lōōn''bôr')	164	55.42 N	11.07 E
Kalush, Sov. Un. (kä'lōōsh)	167	49.02 N	24.24 E
Kalvarija, Sov. Un. (käl-vä-rē'yá)	165	54.24 N	23.17 E
Kalwa, India	197b	19.12 N	72.59 E
Kal'ya, Sov. Un. (käl'yá)	182a	60.17 N	59.58 E
Kalyān, India	197b	19.16 N	73.07 E
Kalyazin, Sov. Un. (käl-yá'zēn)	174	57.13 N	37.55 E
Kalyma (R.), Sov. Un.	181	66.32 N	152.46 E
Kama (L.), Sov. Un.	178	55.28 N	51.00 E
Kama (R.), Sov. Un. (kä'mä)	178	56.10 N	53.50 E
Kamaishi, Jap. (kä'mä-ē'shē)	204	39.16 N	142.03 E
Kamakura, Jap. (kä'mä-kōō'rä)	205a	35.19 N	139.33 E
Kamarān (I.), P. D. R. of Yem.	192	15.19 N	41.47 E
Kāmārhāti, India	196a	22.41 N	88.23 E
Kamata (Neigh.), Jap.	69a	35.33 N	139.43 E
Kambove, Zaire (käm-bō'vē)	226	10.58 S	26.43 E
Kamchatka (R.), Sov. Un.	181	54.15 N	158.38 E
Kamchatka, P-Ov (Pen.), Sov. Un.	181	55.19 N	157.45 E
Kāmdebpur, India	67a	22.54 N	88.20 E
Kameari (Neigh.), Jap.	69a	35.46 N	139.51 E
Kameido (Neigh.), Jap.	69a	35.42 N	139.50 E
Kamen, F.R.G. (kä'mĕn)	169c	51.35 N	7.40 E
Kamenets-Podol'skiy, Sov. Un. (ká-mă'nĕts pô-dôl'skĭ)	175	48.41 N	26.34 E
Kamenjak, Rt (C.), Yugo. (κä'mĕ-nyäk)	172	44.45 N	13.57 E
Kamenka, Sov. Un. (kä-mĕŋ'ká)	175	48.02 N	28.43 E
Kamenka, Sov. Un.	167	50.06 N	24.20 E
Kamen'-na-Obi, Sov. Un. (kä-mĭny'nŭ ô'bē)	180	53.43 N	81.28 E
Kamensk-Shakhtinskiy, Sov. Un. (kä'mĕnsk shäk'tĭn-skĭ)	175	48.17 N	40.16 E
Kamensk-Ural'skiy, Sov. Un. (kä'mĕnsk ōō-räl'skĭ)	182a	56.27 N	61.55 E
Kamenz, G.D.R. (kä'mĕnts)	166	51.16 N	14.05 E
Kameoka, Jap. (kä'mā-ōkä)	205b	35.01 N	135.35 E
Kāmet (Mt.), India	196	35.50 N	79.42 E
Kamiakatsuka (Neigh.), Jap.	69a	35.46 N	139.39 E
Kamiasao, Jap.	69a	35.35 N	139.30 E
Kamień Pomorski, Pol.	166	53.57 N	14.48 E
Kamiishihara, Jap.	69a	35.39 N	139.32 E
Kamikitazawa (Neigh.), Jap.	69a	35.40 N	139.38 E
Kamikoma, Jap. (kä'mē-kō'mä)	205b	34.45 N	135.50 E
Kamina, Zaire	230	8.44 S	25.00 E
Kaministikwia (R.), Can. (ká-mĭ-nĭ-stĭk'wĭ-á)	115	48.40 N	89.41 W
Kamioyamada, Jap.	69a	35.35 N	139.24 E
Kamitsuruma, Jap.	69a	35.31 N	139.25 E
Kamituga, Zaire	231	3.04 S	28.11 E
Kamloops, Can. (kăm'lōōps)	99	50.40 N	120.20 W
Kamoshida (Neigh.), Jap.	69a	35.34 N	139.30 E
Kampala, Ug. (käm-pä'lä)	231	0.19 N	32.25 E
Kampar (R.), Indon. (käm'pär)	206	0.30 N	101.30 E
Kampene, Zaire	230	3.36 S	26.40 E
Kampenhout, Bel.	157a	50.56 N	4.33 E
Kamp-Lintfort, F.R.G. (kämp-lĕnt'fōrt)	169c	51.30 N	6.34 E
Kampong Kranji, Singapore	67c	1.26 N	103.46 E
Kampong Loyang, Singapore	67c	1.22 N	103.58 E
Kâmpóng Saôm, Kamp.	206	10.40 N	103.50 E
Kampong Tanjong Keling, Singapore	67c	1.18 N	103.42 E
Kâmpóng Thum, Kamp. (kŏm'pŏng-tŏm)	206	12.41 N	104.29 E
Kâmpôt, Kamp. (käm'pōt)	206	10.41 N	104.07 E
Kamp R., Aus. (kämp)	166	48.30 N	15.45 E
Kampuchea, Asia	206	12.15 N	104.00 E
Kamsack, Can. (kăm'săk)	101	51.34 N	101.54 W
Kamskoye (Res.), Sov. Un.	178	59.08 N	56.30 E
Kamskoye Vdkhr. (Res.), Sov. Un.	182a	59.03 N	56.48 E
Kamudilo, Zaire	231	7.42 S	27.18 E
Kamuela, Hi.	106a	20.01 N	155.40 W
Kamuk, Cerro (Mt.), C. R. (sĕ'r-rô-kä-mōō'k)	133	9.18 N	83.02 W
Kamu Misaki (C.), Jap. (kä'mōō mē-sä'kē)	204	43.25 N	139.35 E
Kamyshevatskaya, Sov. Un. (ká-mwēsh'ĕ-vät'skä-yá)	175	46.24 N	37.58 E
Kamyshin, Sov. Un. (kä-mwēsh'ĭn)	179	50.08 N	45.20 E
Kamyshlov, Sov. Un. (kä-mēsh'lôf)	178	56.50 N	62.32 E
Kan (R.), Sov. Un. (kän)	180	56.30 N	94.17 E
Kanab, Ut. (kăn'ăb)	121	37.00 N	112.30 W
Kanabeki, Sov. Un. (ká-nä'byĕ-kĭ)	182a	57.48 N	57.16 E
Kanab Plat., Az.	121	36.31 N	112.55 W
Kanaga (I.), Ak. (kă-nă'gă)	107a	52.02 N	177.38 W
Kanagawa (Pref.), Jap. (kä'nä-gä'wä)	205a	35.29 N	139.32 E
Kanai, Jap.	69a	35.35 N	139.28 E
Kanā'is, Ra's al (C.), Egypt	161	31.14 N	28.08 E
Kanamachi, Jap. (kä-nä-mä'chē)	205a	35.46 N	139.52 E
Kanamori, Jap.	69a	35.32 N	139.28 E
Kananga (Luluabourg), Zaire (lōō'lōō-a-bōōrg')	230	6.14 S	22.17 E
Kananikol'skoye, Sov. Un. (kä-ná-nĭ-kôl'skô-yē)	182a	52.48 N	57.29 E
Kanasín, Mex. (kä-nä-sē'n)	132a	20.54 N	89.31 W
Kanatak, Ak. (kă-nă'tŏk)	107	57.35 N	155.48 W
Kanawha (R.), U. S. (ká-nô'wá)	109	37.55 N	81.50 W
Kanaya, Jap. (kä-nä'yá)	205a	35.10 N	139.49 E
Kanazawa, Jap. (kä'ná-zä'wá)	205	36.34 N	136.38 E
Kānchenjunga (Mtn.), India-Nep. (kĭn-chĭn-jōōŋ'gá)	196	27.30 N	88.18 E
Kānchipuram, India	197	12.55 N	79.43 E
Kanda Kanda, Zaire (kän'dá kän'dá)	230	6.56 S	23.36 E

PRONOUNCING INDEX

Kandalaksha – Kellogg 299

PLACE (Pronounciation)	PAGE	Lat. °′	Long. °′
Kandalaksha, Sov. Un. (kȧn-dȧ-lȧk'shȧ)	178	67.10 N	33.05 E
Kandalakshskiy Zaliv (B.), Sov. Un.	178	66.20 N	35.00 E
Kandava, Sov. Un. (kän'dȧ-vȧ)	165	57.03 N	22.45 E
Kandi, Benin (käN-dē')	229	11.08 N	2.56 E
Kandiāro, Pak.	196	27.09 N	68.12 E
Kandla, India (kŭnd'lŭ)	196	23.00 N	70.20 E
Kandy, Sri Lanka (kän'dė)	197	7.18 N	80.42 E
Kane, Pa. (kān)	111	41.40 N	78.50 W
Kaneohe, Hi. (kä-nā-ō'hā)	106a	21.25 N	157.47 W
Kaneohe B., Hi.	106a	21.32 N	157.40 W
Kanëv, Sov. Un. (kä-nyôf')	175	49.46 N	31.27 E
Kanevskaya, Sov. Un. (kȧ-nyĕf'skȧ)	175	46.07 N	38.58 E
Kanevskoye Vdkhr. (Res.), Sov. Un.	179	50.10 N	30.40 E
Kangaroo (I.), Austl. (kăŋ-gȧ-rōō')	216	36.05 S	137.05 E
Kangaroo Ground, Austl.	70b	37.41 S	145.13 E
Kangāvar, Iran (kŭŋ'gā-vär)	192	34.37 N	46.45 E
Kangding, China (käŋ-dĭŋ)	198	30.15 N	101.58 E
Kangean, Kepulauan (I.), Indon. (käŋ'gė-än)	206	6.50 S	116.22 E
Kanggye, Kor. (käng'gyĕ)	204	40.55 N	126.40 E
Kanghwa (I.), Kor. (käng'hwä)	204	37.38 N	126.00 E
Kangnŭng, Kor. (käng'nōō ng)	204	37.42 N	128.50 E
Kango, Gabon (käN-gō)	230	0.09 N	10.08 E
Kangowa, Zaire	230	9.55 S	22.48 E
Kaningo, Ken.	231	0.49 S	38.32 E
Kanin Nos, Mys (G.), Sov. Un.	178	68.40 N	44.00 E
Kanin, P-Ov. (Pen.), Sov. Un. (kȧ-nēn')	178	68.00 N	45.00 E
Kanjiža, Yugo. (kä'nyė-zhä)	173	46.05 N	20.02 E
Kankakee, Il. (kăŋ-kȧ-kē')	113a	41.07 N	87.53 W
Kankakee (R.), Il.	110	41.15 N	88.15 W
Kankan, Gui (kāN-käN) (kän-kän')	228	10.23 N	9.18 W
Kannapolis, NC (kăn-ăp'ȯ-lĭs)	127	35.30 N	80.38 W
Kannoura, Jap. (kä'nō-ōō'rä)	205	33.34 N	134.18 E
Kano, Nig. (kä'nō)	229	12.00 N	8.30 E
Kanonkop (Mtn.), S. Afr.	226a	33.49 S	18.37 E
Kanopolis Res., Ks. (kăn-ŏp'ȯ-lĭs)	122	38.44 N	98.01 W
Kānpur, India (kän'pûr)	196	26.00 N	82.45 E
Kansas (State), U. S. (kăn'zȧs)	108	38.30 N	99.40 W
Kansas (R.), Ks.	123	39.08 N	95.52 W
Kansas City, Ks.	119f	39.06 N	94.39 W
Kansas City, Mo.	119f	39.05 N	94.35 W
Kansk, Sov. Un.	180	56.14 N	95.43 E
Kansōng, Kor.	204	38.09 N	128.29 E
Kantang, Thai. (kän'täng')	206	7.26 N	99.28 E
Kantchari, Burkina	228	12.29 N	1.31 E
Kanton (I.), Oceania	208	3.50 S	174.00 E
Kantunilkin, Mex. (kän-tōō-nēl-kē'n)	132a	21.07 N	87.30 W
Kanzaki (R.), Jap.	69b	34.42 N	135.25 E
Kanzhakovskiy Kamen Gora, (Mt.), Sov. Un. (kȧn-zhă'kôvs-kēė kămĭen)	182a	59.38 N	59.12 E
Kaohsiung, Taiwan (kä-ȯ-syōōng')	203	22.35 N	120.25 E
Kaolack, Senegal	228	14.09 N	16.04 W
Kaouar (Oasis), Niger	225	19.16 N	13.09 E
Kaoyu Hu (L.), China (kä'ō-yōō'hōō)	203	32.42 N	118.40 E
Kapaa, Hi.	106a	22.06 N	159.20 W
Kapal, Sov. Un. (kȧ-päl')	180	45.13 N	79.08 E
Kapanga, Zaire	230	8.21 S	22.35 E
Kapchagay, Sov. Un.	191	43.55 N	77.45 E
Kapellen, F.R.G.	63	51.25 N	6.35 E
Kapfenberg, Aus. (kȧp'fĕn-bērgh)	166	47.27 N	15.16 E
Kapiri Mposhi, Zambia	231	13.58 S	28.41 E
Kapoeta, Sud.	225	4.45 N	33.35 E
Kaposvár, Hung. (kô'pȯsh-vär)	167	46.21 N	17.45 E
Kapotn'a (Neigh.), Sov. Un.	66b	55.38 N	37.48 E
Kapsan, Kor. (käp'sän')	204	40.59 N	128.22 E
Kapuskasing, Can.	97	49.28 N	82.22 W
Kapuskasing (R.), Can.	102	48.55 N	82.55 W
Kapustin Yar, Sov. Un. (kä'pōōs-tėn yär')	179	48.30 N	45.40 E
Kaputar, Mt., Austl. (kă-pû-tăr)	216	30.11 S	150.11 E
Kapuvár, Hung. (kô'pōō-vär)	166	47.35 N	17.02 E
Kara (R.), Sov. Un.	178	68.30 N	65.20 E
Kara, Sov. Un. (kärȧ)	180	68.42 N	65.30 E
Karabalā', Iraq (kŭr'bȧ-lä)	192	32.31 N	43.58 E
Karabanovo, Sov. Un. (kä'rȧ-bȧ-nō-vȯ)	182b	56.19 N	38.43 E
Karabash, Sov. Un. (kó-rȧ-bäsh')	182a	55.27 N	60.14 E
Kara-Bogaz-Gol, Zaliv (B.), Sov. Un. (kȧ-rä' bŭ-gäs')	179	41.30 N	53.40 E
Karachev, Sov. Un. (kȧ-rȧ-chôf')	174	53.08 N	34.54 E
Karāchi, Pak.	196	24.59 N	68.56 E
Karacumy (Des.), Sov. Un.	155	39.08 N	59.53 E
Karaganda, Sov. Un. (kȧ-rȧ-gän'dä)	180	49.42 N	73.18 E
Karaidel, Sov. Un. (kä'rī-dĕl)	182a	55.52 N	56.54 E
Kara-Khobda (R.), Sov. Un. (kä-rȧ Kôb'dȧ)	179	50.40 N	55.00 E
Karakoram Pass, India-Pak.	193	35.35 N	77.45 E
Karakoram Ra., India-Pak. (kä'rä kō'rōōm)	198	35.24 N	76.38 E
Karakorum (Ruins), Mong.	198	47.25 N	102.22 E
Karakumy (Des.), Sov. Un. (kara-kum)	176	40.00 N	57.00 E
Karaman, Tur. (kä-rä-män')	179	37.10 N	33.00 E
Karamay, China (kär-äm-ā)	198	45.37 N	84.53 E
Karamea Bight, N.Z. (kȧ-rȧ-mē'ȧ bīt)	217	41.20 S	171.30 E
Kara Sea, see Karskoye More			
Karashahr (Yanqi), China (kä-rä-shä-är) (yän-chyē)	198	42.14 N	86.28 E
Karatsu, Jap. (kä'rȧ-tsōō)	205	33.28 N	129.59 E
Karaul, Sov. Un. (kä-rä-ōōl')	180	70.13 N	83.46 E
Karave, India	67e	19.01 N	73.01 E
Karawanken Mts., Aus.	166	46.32 N	14.07 E
Karcag, Hung. (kär'tsäg)	167	47.18 N	20.58 E
Kardhítsa, Grc.	173	39.23 N	21.57 E
Kärdla, Sov. Un. (kĕrd'lȧ)	165	58.59 N	22.44 E
Karelian (A. S. S. R.), Sov. Un.	176	62.30 N	32.35 E
Karema, Tan.	231	6.49 S	30.26 E
Kargat, Sov. Un. (kär-gät')	180	55.17 N	80.07 E
Karghalik, see Yecheng			
Kargopol', Sov. Un. (kär-gō-pōl'')	178	61.30 N	38.50 E
Kariaí, Grc.	173	40.14 N	24.15 E
Kariba, L., Afr.	231	17.15 S	27.55 E
Karibib, Namibia (kȧr'ȧ-bĭb)	226	21.55 S	15.50 E
Kārikāl, India (kä-rė-käl')	197	10.58 N	79.49 E
Karimata, Pulau-Pulau (Is.), Indon. (kä-rė-mä'tȧ)	206	1.08 S	108.10 E
Karimata, Selat (Karimata Strait), Indon.	206	1.00 S	107.10 E
Karimun Besar (I.), Indon.	191b	1.10 N	103.28 E
Karimunjawa, Kepulauan (Is.), Indon. (kä'rė-mōōn-yä'vä)	206	5.36 S	110.15 E
Karin, Som. (kȧr'ĭn)	223a	10.43 N	45.50 E
Karkaralinsk, Sov. Un. (kär-kär-ä-lēnsk')	180	49.18 N	75.28 E
Karkar Dūmān (Neigh.), India	67d	28.39 N	77.18 E
Karkar I., Pap. N. Gui. (kär'kär)	207	4.50 S	146.45 E
Karkheh (R.), Iran	192	32.45 N	47.50 E
Karkinitskiy Zailv (B.), Sov. Un. (kär-kė-net'skĭ-ė zä'lĭf)	175	45.50 N	32.45 E
Karl-Marx-Stadt (Chemnitz), G.D.R.	166	50.48 N	12.53 E
Karlobag, Yugo. (kär-lō-bäg')	172	44.30 N	15.03 E
Karlovac, Yugo. (kär'lȯ-vȧts)	172	45.29 N	15.16 E
Karlovka, Sov. Un. (kȧr'lôv-kȧ)	175	49.26 N	35.08 E
Karlovo, Bul. (kär'lȯ-vō)	173	42.39 N	24.48 E
Karlovy Vary, Czech. (kär'lȯ-vė vä'rė)	166	50.13 N	12.53 E
Karlshamn, Swe. (kärls'häm)	164	56.11 N	14.50 E
Karlskrona, Swe. (kärls'krȯ-nä)	164	56.10 N	15.33 E
Karlsruhe, F.R.G. (kärls'rōō-ĕ)	166	49.00 N	8.23 E
Karlstad, Swe. (kärl'städ)	164	59.25 N	13.28 E
Karluk, Ak. (kär'lŭk)	107	57.30 N	154.22 W
Karmøy (I.), Nor. (kärm-ûe)	164	59.14 N	5.00 E
Karnap, F.R.G.	63	51.09 N	6.56 E
Karnataka (State), India	197	14.55 N	75.00 E
Karnobat, Bul. (kär-nȯ'bät)	173	42.39 N	26.59 E
Kärnten (Carinthia) (State), Aus. (kĕrn'tĕn)	166	46.55 N	13.42 E
Karolinenhof (Neigh.), G.D.R.	65a	52.23 N	13.38 E
Karonga, Malawi (kȧ-rōŋ'gȧ)	226	9.52 S	33.57 E
Kárpathos (I.), Grc.	161	35.34 N	27.26 E
Karpinsk, Sov. Un. (kär'pĭnsk)	182a	59.46 N	60.00 E
Kars, Tur. (kärs)	179	40.35 N	43.00 E
Karsakpay, Sov. Un. (kär-säk-pī')	180	47.47 N	67.07 E
Kārsava, Sov. Un. (kär'sä-vä)	174	56.46 N	27.39 E
Karshi, Sov. Un. (kär'shē)	193	38.30 N	66.08 E
Karskiye Vorota, Proliv (Str.), Sov. Un.	180	70.30 N	58.07 E
Karskoye More (Kara Sea), Sov. Un.	180	74.00 N	68.00 E
Kartaly, Sov. Un. (kȧr'tá lė)	182a	53.05 N	60.40 E
Karunagapalli, India	197	9.09 N	76.34 E
Karvina, Czech.	167	49.50 N	18.30 E
Kasaan, Ak.	98	55.32 N	132.24 E
Kasai (Neigh.), Jap.	69a	35.39 N	139.53 E
Kasai (R.), Zaire	230	3.45 S	19.10 E
Kasama, Zambia (kȧ-să'mȧ)	231	10.13 S	31.12 E
Kasanga, Tan. (kȧ-säŋ'gȧ)	231	8.28 S	31.09 E
Kasaoka, Jap. (kä'sȧ-ō'kȧ)	205	34.33 N	133.29 E
Kasba-Tadla, Mor. (käs'bȧ-täd'lȧ)	224	32.37 N	5.57 W
Kasempa, Zambia (kȧ-sĕm'pȧ)	231	13.27 S	25.50 E
Kasenga, Zaire (kȧ-seŋ'gȧ)	231	10.22 S	28.38 E
Kasese, Ug.	231	0.10 N	30.05 E
Kasese, Zaire	231	1.38 S	27.07 E
Kāshān, Iran (kā-shān')	192	33.52 N	51.15 E
Kashgar, see Kashi			
Kashi (Kashgar), China (kä-shr) (käsh-gär)	198	39.29 N	76.00 E
Kashihara, Jap. (kä'shė-hä'rä)	205b	34.31 N	135.48 E
Kashiji Pln. Zambia	230	13.25 S	22.30 E
Kashin, Sov. Un. (kä-shēn')	174	57.20 N	37.38 E
Kashira, Sov. Un. (kä-shē'rȧ)	174	54.49 N	38.11 E
Kashiwa, Jap. (kä'shė-wä)	205a	35.51 N	139.58 E
Kashiwara, Jap.	205b	34.35 N	135.38 E
Kashiwazaki, Jap. (kä'shē-wä-zä'kė)	178	37.06 N	138.17 E
Kāshmar, Iran	195	35.12 N	58.27 E
Kashmir (Disputed Reg.), see Jammu and Kashmir			
Kashmor, Pak.	196	28.33 N	69.34 E
Kashtak, Sov. Un. (käsh'tȧk)	182a	55.18 N	61.25 E
Kasimov, Sov. Un. (kȧ-sē'môf)	174	54.56 N	41.23 E
Kaskanak, Ak. (kăs-kă'năk)	107	60.00 N	158.00 W
Kaskaskia (R.), Il. (kăs-kăs'kĭ-ȧ)	110	39.10 N	88.50 W
Kaskattama (R.), Can. (kăs-kă-tä'mȧ)	101	56.28 N	90.55 W
Kaskinen, see Kaskö			
Kaskö (Kaskinen), Fin. (käs'kû) (käs'kē-nĕn)	165	62.24 N	21.18 E
Kasli, Sov. Un. (käs'lĭ)	182a	55.54 N	60.46 E
Kasongo, Zaire (kä-sȯŋ'gō)	226	4.31 S	26.42 E
Kásos (I.), Grc.	161	35.20 N	26.55 E
Kassalā, Sud. (kä-sä'lä)	225	15.26 N	36.28 E
Kassándras, Kólpos (G.), Grc.	173	40.10 N	23.35 E
Kassel, F.R.G. (käs'ĕl)	166	51.19 N	9.30 E
Kassinga. Ang.	226	15.05 S	16.15 E
Kasslerfeld (Neigh.), F.R.G.	63	51.26 N	6.45 E
Kasson, Mn. (kăs'ŭn)	115	44.01 N	92.45 W
Kastamonu, Tur. (kä-stȧ-mō'nōō)	179	41.20 N	33.50 E
Kastoría, Grc. (kȧs-tō'rĭ-ȧ)	173	40.28 N	21.17 E
Kasūr, Pak.	196	31.10 N	74.29 E
Kataba, Zambia	230	16.05 S	25.10 E
Katahdin, Mt., Me. (kȧ-tä'dĭn)	104	45.56 N	68.57 W
Katanga (Reg.), Zaire (kȧ-täŋ'gȧ)	226	8.30 S	25.00 E
Katanning, Austl. (kȧ-tăn'ĭng)	214	33.45 S	117.45 E
Katano, Jap.	69b	34.48 N	135.42 E
Katav-Ivonovski, Sov. Un. (kä'tăf ĭ-vä'nȯfsk)	182a	54.46 N	58.13 E
Katayama (Neigh.), Jap.	69a	35.46 N	139.34 E
Kateninskiy, Sov. Un. (kȧtyĕ'nĭs-kĭ)	182a	53.12 N	61.05 E
Kateríni, Grc.	173	40.18 N	22.36 E
Katernberg (Neigh.), F.R.G.	63	51.29 N	7.04 E
Katete, Zambia	231	14.05 S	32.07 E
Katherine, Austl. (kăth'ēr-ĭn)	214	14.15 S	132.20 E
Kāthiāwār (Pen.), India (kä'tyȧ-wär')	196	22.10 N	70.20 E
Kathmandu, Nep. (kāt-mān-dōō')	196	27.49 N	85.21 E
Kathryn, Can. (kăth'rĭn)	95e	51.13 N	113.42 W
Kathryn, Ca.	119a	33.42 N	117.45 W
Katihār, India	196	25.39 N	87.39 E
Katiola, Ivory Coast	228	8.08 N	5.06 W
Katmai Natl. Park, Ak. (kăt'mī)	107	58.38 N	155.00 W
Katompi, Zaire	231	6.11 S	26.20 E
Katopa, Zaire	230	2.45 S	25.06 E
Katowice, Pol.	167	50.15 N	19.00 E
Katrineholm, Swe. (kȧ-trē'nĕ-hōlm)	164	59.01 N	16.10 E
Kātrīnā, Jabal (Mtn.), Egypt	225	28.43 N	34.00 E
Katsbakhskiy, Sov. Un. (kȧts-băk'skĭ)	182a	52.57 N	59.37 E
Katsina, Nig. (kät'sė-nȧ)	229	13.00 N	7.32 E
Katsura (R.), Jap. (kä'tsōō-rä)	205b	34.55 N	135.43 E
Katsushika (Neigh.), Jap.	69a	35.43 N	139.51 E
Katta-Kurgan, Sov. Un. (kȧ-tȧ-kōōr-gän')	180	39.45 N	66.42 E
Kattegat (Str.), Eur. (kăt'ĕ-gät)	164	56.57 N	11.25 E
Katternberg (Neigh.), F.R.G.	63	51.09 N	7.02 E
Katumba, Zaire	231	7.45 S	25.18 E
Katun' (R.), Sov. Un. (kȧ-tōōn')	180	51.30 N	86.18 E
Katwijkaan Zee, Neth.	157a	52.12 N	4.23 E
Kauai (I.), Hi.	106a	22.09 N	159.15 W
Kauai Chan., Hi. (kä-ōō-ä'ė)	106a	21.35 N	158.52 W
Kaufbeuren, F.R.G. (kouf'boi-rĕn)	166	47.52 N	10.38 E
Kaufman, Tx. (kôf'măn)	125	32.36 N	96.18 W
Kaukauna, Wi. (kô-kô'nȧ)	115	44.17 N	88.15 W
Kaulakahi Chan., Hi. (kä'ōō-lȧ-kä'hė)	106a	22.00 N	159.55 W
Kaulsdorf-Süd (Neigh.), G.D.R.	65a	52.29 N	13.34 E
Kaunakakai, Hi. (kä'ōō-nȧ-kä'kī)	106a	21.06 N	156.59 W
Kaunas (Kovno), Sov. Un. (kou'nȧs) (kȯv'nȯ)	165	54.42 N	23.54 E
Kaura Namoda, Nig.	229	12.35 N	6.35 E
Kavajë, Alb. (kȧ-vä'yŭ)	173	41.11 N	19.36 E
Kavála, Grc. (kä-vä'lä)	173	40.55 N	24.24 E
Kavieng, Pap. N. Gui. (kä-vė-ĕng')	207	2.44 S	151.02 E
Kawagoe, Jap. (kä-wă-gō'ȧ)	205a	35.55 N	139.29 E
Kawaguchi, Jap. (kä-wä-gōō-chē)	205a	35.48 N	139.44 E
Kawaikini (Mtn.), Hi. (kä-wä'ė-kĭ-nĭ)	106a	22.05 N	159.33 W
Kawanishi, Jap. (kä-wä'nė-shē)	205b	34.49 N	135.26 E
Kawasaki, Jap. (kä-wä-sä'kė)	205a	35.32 N	139.43 E
Kawashima (Neigh.), Jap.	69a	35.28 N	139.35 E
Kawm Umbū, Egypt	223b	24.30 N	32.59 E
Kaxgar (R.), China	198	39.26 N	74.30 E
Kaya, Burkina (kä'yä)	228	13.05 N	1.05 W
Kayan (R.), Indon.	206	1.45 N	115.38 E
Kaycee, Wy. (kā-sē')	117	43.43 N	106.38 W
Kayes, Mali (kāz)	228	14.27 N	11.26 W
Kayseri, Tur. (kī'sĕ-rē)	179	38.45 N	35.20 E
Kaysville, Ut. (kāz'vĭl)	119b	41.02 N	111.56 W
Kazach'ye, Sov. Un.	181	70.46 N	135.47 E
Kazakh S.S.R., Sov. Un. (kȧ-zäk')	176	48.45 N	59.00 E
Kazan', Sov. Un. (kȧ-zän')	178	55.50 N	49.18 E
Kazanka, Sov. Un. (kȧ-zän'kȧ)	175	47.49 N	32.50 E
Kazanlŭk, Bul. (kȧ'zȧn-lėk)	173	42.47 N	25.23 E
Kazatin, Sov. Un.	175	49.43 N	28.50 E
Kazbek, Gora (Mt.), Sov. Un. (kȧz-bĕk')	179	42.45 N	44.30 E
Kāzerūn, Iran	192	29.37 N	51.44 E
Kazincbarcika, Hung. (kô'zĭnts-bôr-tsĭ-ko)	167	48.15 N	20.39 E
Kazungula, Zambia	231	17.45 S	25.20 E
Kazusa Kameyama, Jap. (kä-zōō-sä kä-mȧ'yä-mä)	205a	35.14 N	140.06 E
Kazym (R.), Sov. Un. (kä-zēm')	180	63.30 N	67.41 E
Kéa (I.), Grc.	173	37.36 N	24.13 E
Kealaikahiki Chan., Hi. (kā-ä'lä-ė-kä-hē'kē)	106a	20.38 N	157.00 W
Keansburg, NJ (kēnz'bûrg)	112a	40.26 N	74.08 W
Kearney, Ne. (kär'nĭ)	122	40.42 N	99.05 W
Kearny, NJ	112a	40.46 N	74.09 W
Kearsley, Eng.	64b	53.32 N	2.23 W
Keasey, Or. (kēz'ĭ)	118c	45.51 N	123.20 W
Keban Gölü (L.), Tur.	179	38.20 N	39.50 E
Kebayoram (Neigh.), Indon.	68k	6.12 S	106.46 E
Kebnekaise Mt., Swe. (kĕp'nĕ-kȧ-ēs'ĕ)	158	67.53 N	18.10 E
Kecskemét, Hung. (kĕch'kĕ-māt)	167	46.52 N	19.42 E
Kedah State, Mala. (kā'dä)	206	6.00 N	100.31 E
Kédainiai, Sov. Un. (kē-dī'nĭ-ī)	165	55.16 N	23.58 E
Kedgwick, Can. (kĕdj'wĭk)	104	47.39 N	67.21 W
Keenbrook, Ca. (kēn'brōōk)	119a	34.16 N	117.29 W
Keene, NH (kēn)	111	42.55 N	72.15 W
Keetmanshoop, Namibia (kāt'mȧns-hōp)	226	26.30 S	18.05 E
Keet Seel Ruin, Az. (kēt sēl)	121	36.46 N	110.32 W
Keewatin, Mn. (kē-wä'tĭn)	115	47.24 N	93.03 W
Keewatin, Dist. of, Can.	96	61.26 N	97.54 W
Kefallinía (Cephalonia) (I.), Grc.	173	38.08 N	20.58 E
Kefe, see Feodosiya			
Keffi, Nig. (kĕf'ė)	229	8.51 N	7.52 E
Ke-Ga, Mui (Pt.), Viet.	206	12.58 N	109.50 E
Kei (R.), S. Afr. (kā)	227c	32.57 S	26.50 E
Keila, Sov. Un. (kā'lȧ)	165	59.19 N	24.25 E
Keilor, Austl.	70b	37.43 S	144.50 E
Kei Mouth, S. Afr.	227c	32.40 S	28.23 E
Keiskammahoek, S. Afr. (kās'kämä-hōōk')	227c	32.42 S	27.11 E
Kéita, Bahr (R.), Chad.	229	9.30 N	19.17 E
Keitele (L.), Fin. (kā'tĕ-lĕ)	165	62.50 N	25.40 E
Kekaha, Hi.	106a	21.57 N	159.42 W
Kelafo, Eth.	223a	5.40 N	44.00 E
Kelang, Mala.	191b	3.20 N	101.27 E
Kelang (R.), Mala.	191b	3.00 N	101.40 E
Kelenföld (Neigh.), Hung.	66g	47.28 N	19.03 E
Kelkit (R.), Tur.	161	40.38 N	37.03 E
Keller, Tx. (kĕl'ēr)	119c	32.56 N	97.15 W
Kellinghusen, F.R.G. (kĕ'lēng-hōō-zĕn)	157c	53.57 N	9.43 E
Kellogg, Id. (kĕl'ŏg)	116	47.32 N	116.07 W

ng-sing; nŋ-banŋk; N-nasalized n; nŏd; cŏmmit; ōld; ȯbey; ôrder; oi-boil; fōōd; fŏŏt; ou-out; s-soft; sh-dish; th-thin; pūre; u̇nite; ûrn; stŭd; circŭs; ü-as in French tu; '-indeterminate vowel.

300 Kellyville – King of Prussia

PLACE (Pronounciation)	PAGE	Lat. °′	Long. °′
Kellyville, Austl.	70a	33.43 S	150.57 E
Kelme', Sov. Un. (kĕl-må)	165	55.36 N	22.53 E
Kélo, Chad	229	9.19 N	15.48 E
Kelowna, Can.	99	49.53 N	119.29 W
Kelsey Bay, Can. (kĕl'sē)	98	50.24 N	125.57 W
Kelso, Wa.	118c	46.09 N	122.54 W
Keluang, Mala.	191b	2.01 N	103.19 E
Kelvedon Hatch, Eng.	62	51.40 N	0.16 E
Kem', Sov. Un. (kĕm)	178	65.00 N	34.48 E
Kemah, Tx. (kē'må)	125a	29.32 N	95.01 W
Kemerovo, Sov. Un.	180	55.31 N	86.05 E
Kemi, Fin. (kā'mē)	158	65.48 N	24.38 E
Kemi (R.), Fin.	158	67.02 N	27.50 E
Kemigawa, Jap. (kĕ'mē-gä'wä)	205a	35.38 N	140.07 E
Kemijarvi, Fin. (kā'mē-yĕr-vē)	158	66.48 N	27.21 E
Kemi-joki (L.), Fin.	158	66.37 N	28.13 E
Kemmerer, Wy. (kĕm'ēr-ēr)	117	41.48 N	110.36 W
Kemminghausen (Neigh.), F.R.G.	63	51.34 N	7.29 E
Kemp (L.), Tx. (kĕmp)	122	33.55 N	99.22 W
Kempen, F.R.G. (kĕm'pĕn)	169c	51.22 N	6.25 E
Kempsey, Austl. (kĕmp'sē)	216	30.59 S	152.50 E
Kempt (L.), Can. (kĕmpt)	104	47.28 N	74.00 W
Kempten, F.R.G. (kĕmp'tĕn)	166	47.44 N	10.17 E
Kempton Park, S. Afr. (kĕmp'tŏn pärk)	227b	26.07 S	28.29 E
Kemsing, Eng.	62	51.18 N	0.14 E
Ken (R.), India	196	25.00 N	79.55 E
Kenai, Ak. (kĕ-nī')	107	60.38 N	151.18 W
Kenai Mts., Ak.	107	60.00 N	150.00 W
Kenai Pen, Ak.	107	64.40 N	150.18 W
Kenberma, Ma.	54a	42.17 N	70.52 W
Kendal, Eng. (kĕn'dăl)	162	54.20 N	1.48 W
Kendal, S. Afr.	223d	26.03 S	28.58 E
Kendallville, In. (kĕn'dăl-vĭl)	110	41.25 N	85.20 W
Kenedy, Tx. (kĕn'ĕ-dĭ)	119	28.49 N	97.50 W
Kenema, S.L.	228	7.52 N	11.12 W
Kenilworth, Il.	58a	42.05 N	87.43 W
Kenilworth, NJ	55	40.41 N	74.18 W
Kenitra (Port Lyautey), Mor. (kĕ-nē'trå)	160	34.21 N	6.34 W
Kenley (Neigh.), Eng.	62	51.19 N	0.06 W
Kenmare, ND (kĕn-mâr')	114	48.41 N	102.05 W
Kenmore, NY (kĕn'mōr)	113c	42.58 N	78.53 W
Kennebec (R.), Me. (kĕn-ē-bĕk')	104	44.23 N	69.48 W
Kennebunk, Me. (kĕn-ē-buŋk')	104	43.24 N	70.33 W
Kennedale, Tx. (kĕn'-ē-dāl)	119c	32.38 N	97.13 W
Kennedy, C., see Canaveral			
Kennedy, Mt., Can.	107	60.25 N	138.50 W
Kenner, La. (kĕn'ēr)	125	29.58 N	90.15 W
Kennett, Mo. (kĕn'ĕt)	123	36.14 N	90.01 W
Kennewick, Wa. (kĕn'ē-wĭk)	116	46.12 N	119.06 W
Kenney Dam, Can.	98	53.37 N	124.58 W
Kennydale, Wa. (kĕn-nē'dāl)	118a	47.31 N	122.12 W
Kénogami, Can. (kĕn-ŏ'gä-mē)	103	48.26 N	71.14 W
Kenogamissi L., Can.	102	48.15 N	81.31 W
Keno Hill, Can.	107	63.58 N	135.18 W
Kenora, Can. (kē-nō'rå)	101	49.47 N	94.29 W
Kenosha, Wi. (kē-nō'shå)	113a	42.34 N	87.50 W
Kenova, WV (kē-nō'vå)	110	38.20 N	82.35 W
Kensico Res., NY (kĕn'sĭ-kō)	112a	41.08 N	73.45 W
Kensington, Austl.	70a	33.55 S	151.14 E
Kensington, Ca.	58b	37.54 N	122.16 W
Kensington, Md.	56d	39.02 N	77.03 W
Kensington (Neigh.), NY.	55	40.39 N	73.58 W
Kensington (Neigh.), Pa.	56b	39.58 N	75.08 W
Kensington (Neigh.), S. Afr.	71b	26.12 S	28.06 E
Kensington and Chelsea (Neigh.), Eng.	62	51.29 N	0.11 W
Kent, Oh. (kĕnt)	110	41.05 N	81.20 W
Kent, Wa.	118a	47.23 N	122.14 W
Kentani, S. Afr. (kĕnt-änĭ')	227c	32.31 S	28.19 E
Kentland, In. (kĕnt'lănd)	110	40.50 N	87.25 W
Kentland, Md.	56d	38.55 N	76.53 W
Kenton, Oh. (kĕn'tŭn)	110	40.40 N	83.35 W
Kent Pen, Can.	96	68.28 N	108.10 W
Kentucky (State), U. S. (kĕn-tŭk'ĭ)	109	37.30 N	87.35 W
Kentucky (L.), U. S.	109	36.20 N	88.50 W
Kentucky (R.), U. S.	109	38.15 N	85.01 W
Kentwood, La. (kĕnt'wŏŏd)	125	30.56 N	90.31 W
Kenya, Afr. (kĕn'yå)	222	1.00 N	36.53 E
Kenya, Mt., see Kirinyaga			
Kenyon, Mn. (kĕn'yŭn)	115	44.15 N	92.58 W
Keokuk, Ia. (kē'ō-kŭk)	123	40.24 N	91.34 W
Keoma, Can. (kē-ō'må)	95e	51.13 N	113.39 W
Keon Park, Austl.	70b	37.42 S	145.01 E
Kepenkeck L., Can.	105	48.13 N	54.45 W
Kepno, Pol. (kaŋ'pnō)	167	51.17 N	17.59 E
Kerala (State), India	197	16.38 N	76.00 E
Kerang, Austl. (kē-răng')	216	35.32 S	143.58 E
Keratsinion, Grc.	66d	37.58 N	23.37 E
Kerch', Sov. Un. (kĕrch)	175	45.20 N	36.26 E
Kerchenskiy Proliv (Str.) (Kerch Str.), Sov. Un. (kĕr-chĕn'skĭ prō'lĭf)	175	45.08 N	36.35 E
Kerempe Burun (C.), Tur.	179	42.00 N	33.20 E
Keren, Eth.	225	15.46 N	38.28 E
Kerguélen, Îles, Ind. O. (kĕr'gā-lĕn)	232	49.50 S	69.30 E
Kericho, Ken.	231	0.22 S	35.17 E
Kerinci, Gunung (Mtn.), Indon.	206	1.45 S	101.18 E
Keriya (R.), China (kē'rē-yä)	198	37.13 N	81.59 E
Keriya, see Yütian			
Kerkebet, Eth.	195	16.18 N	37.24 E
Kerkenna, Îles (I.), Tun. (kĕr'kĕn-nä)	225	34.49 N	11.37 E
Kerki, Sov. Un. (kĕr'kē)	193	37.52 N	65.15 E
Kérkira, Grc.	173	39.36 N	19.56 E
Kérkira (I.), Grc.	173	39.33 N	19.36 E
Kermadec Is., N. Z. (kĕr-måd'ĕk)	208	30.30 S	177.00 E
Kermadec Tonga Trench, Oceania (kĕr-måd'ĕk tŏŋ'gå)	208	23.00 S	172.30 W
Kermān, Iran (kĕr-män')	192	30.23 N	57.08 E
Kermānshāh, see Bakhtarān			
Kern (R.), Ca.	120	35.31 N	118.37 W
Kern Can., Ca. (kûrn)	120	36.57 N	119.37 W
Kern, South Fork of (R.), Ca.	120	35.40 N	118.15 W
Kérouané, Gui.	228	9.16 N	9.01 W
Kerpen, F.R.G. (kĕr'pĕn)	169c	50.52 N	6.42 E
Kerrobert, Can.	100	51.53 N	109.13 W
Kerrville, Tx. (kûr'vĭl)	124	30.02 N	99.07 W
Kerulen (R.), Mong. (kĕr'ōō-lĕn)	199	47.52 N	113.22 E
Kesagami L., Can.	103	50.23 N	80.15 W
Kesan, Tur. (kĕ'shån)	173	40.50 N	26.37 E
Keshan, China (kŭ-shän)	202	48.00 N	126.30 E
Kesour, Monts des (Mts.), Alg.	160	32.51 N	0.30 W
Kestell, S. Afr. (kĕs'tĕl)	223d	28.19 S	28.43 E
Keszthely, Hung. (kĕst'hĕl-lĭ)	167	46.46 N	17.12 E
Ket' (R.), Sov. Un. (kyĕt)	180	58.30 N	84.15 E
Keta, Ghana	224	6.00 N	1.00 E
Ketamputih, Indon.	191b	1.25 N	102.19 E
Ketapang, Indon. (kĕ-tå-päng')	206	2.00 S	109.57 E
Ketchikan, Ak. (kĕch-ĭ-kăn')	98	55.21 N	131.35 W
Ketrzyn, Pol. (kaŋ't'r-zĭn)	167	54.04 N	21.24 E
Kettering, Eng. (kĕt'ēr-ĭng)	156	52.23 N	0.43 W
Kettering, Oh.	110	39.40 N	84.15 W
Kettle (R.), Can.	99	49.40 N	119.00 W
Kettle (R.), Mn. (kĕt''l)	115	46.20 N	92.57 W
Kettwig, F.R.G. (kĕt'vēg)	169c	51.22 N	6.56 E
Kety, Pol. (kaŋ tĭ)	167	49.54 N	19.16 E
Ketzin, G.D.R. (kē'tzēn)	157b	52.29 N	12.51 E
Keuka (L.), NY (kē-ū'kå)	111	42.30 N	77.10 W
Kevelaer, F.R.G. (kĕ'fĕ-lăr)	169c	51.35 N	6.15 E
Kew, Austl.	70b	37.49 S	145.02 E
Kew, S. Afr.	71b	26.08 S	28.06 E
Kewanee, Il. (kē-wä'nē)	115	41.15 N	89.55 W
Kewaunee, Wi. (kē-wô'nē)	115	44.27 N	87.33 W
Keweenaw B., Mi. (kē'wē-nô)	115	46.59 N	88.15 W
Keweenaw Pen., Mi.	115	47.28 N	88.12 W
Kew Gardens (P. Int.), Eng.	62	51.28 N	0.18 W
Keya Paha (R.), S.D. (kē-yå pä'hä)	114	43.11 N	100.10 W
Key Largo (I.), Fl.	127a	25.11 N	80.15 W
Keyport, NJ (kē'pōrt)	112a	40.26 N	74.12 W
Keyport, Wa.	118a	47.42 N	122.38 W
Keyser, WV (kī'sēr)	111	39.25 N	79.00 W
Key West, Fl. (kē wĕst')	127a	24.31 N	81.47 W
Kežmarok, Czech. (kĕzh'må-rôk)	167	49.10 N	20.27 E
Khabarovo, Sov. Un. (kŭ-bár-ôvŏ)	180	69.31 N	60.41 E
Khabarovsk, Sov. Un. (Kä-bä'rôfsk)	181	48.35 N	135.12 E
Khaïdhárion, Grc.	66d	37.33 N	22.53 E
Khajuri (Neigh.), India	67d	28.43 N	77.16 E
Khakass Aut. Oblast, Sov. Un.	180	52.32 N	89.33 E
Khalándrion, Grc.	66d	38.01 N	23.48 E
Khālāpur, India	197b	18.48 N	73.17 E
Khalkidhiki (Pen.), Grc.	173	40.30 N	23.18 E
Khalkís, Grc. (Käl'kĭs)	173	38.28 N	23.38 E
Khal'mer-Yu, Sov. Un. (kŭl-myĕr'-yōō')	180	67.52 N	64.25 E
Khalturin, Sov. Un. (Käl'tōō-rēn)	178	58.28 N	49.00 E
Khambhāt, G. of, India	196	21.20 N	72.27 E
Khammam, India	197	17.09 N	80.13 E
Khānābād, Afg.	196	36.43 N	69.11 E
Khānaqīn, Iraq	195	34.21 N	45.22 E
Khandwa, India	196	21.53 N	76.22 E
Khangai Mts., see Hangayn Nuruu			
Khanh-Hung, Viet.	206	9.45 N	105.50 E
Khaniá, Grc. (kä-nē'á)	172a	35.29 N	24.04 E
Khaníon, Kólpos (G.), Grc.	172a	35.35 N	23.55 E
Khanka (L.), Sov. Un. (Kän'kå)	199	45.09 N	133.28 E
Khānpur, Pak.	196	28.42 N	70.42 E
Khanty-Mansiysk, Sov. Un. (Kŭn-te'mŭn-sēsk')	180	61.02 N	69.01 E
Khān Yūnus, Gaza Strip	191a	31.21 N	34.19 E
Kharagpur, India (kŭ-rŭg'pŏŏr)	196	22.26 N	87.21 E
Khardah, India	67a	22.44 N	88.22 E
Khar'kov (Oblast), Sov. Un.	175	49.33 N	35.55 E
Khar'kov, Sov. Un. (Kär'kôf)	175	50.00 N	36.10 E
Kharlovka, Sov. Un.	178	68.47 N	37.20 E
Kharmanli, Bul. (Kår-män'lē)	173	41.54 N	25.55 E
Khartoum (Al Kharṭūm), Sud.	225	15.34 N	32.36 E
Khāsh, Iran	192	28.08 N	61.08 E
Khāsh (R.), Afg.	192	32.30 N	64.27 E
Khasi Hills, India	196	25.38 N	91.55 E
Khaskovo, Bul. (Kås'kô-vô)	173	41.56 N	25.32 E
Khatanga, Sov. Un. (Kå-tän'gå)	181	71.48 N	101.47 E
Khatangskiy Zaliv (B.), Sov. Un. (kä-täŋ'g-skē)	181	73.45 N	108.30 E
Khayāla (Neigh.), India	67d	28.40 N	77.06 E
Khemis Miliana, Alg.	159	36.19 N	1.56 E
Kherson (Oblast), Sov. Un.	175	46.32 N	32.55 E
Kherson, Sov. Un. (Kĕr-sôn')	175	46.38 N	32.34 E
Khetan (R.), India	196	10.57 N	78.23 E
Khichripur (Neigh.), India	67d	28.37 N	77.19 E
Khiitola, Sov. Un. (khē'tō-lå)	165	61.14 N	29.40 E
Khimki, Sov. Un. (Kēm'kĭ)	182b	55.54 N	37.27 E
Khiva, Sov. Un. (kē'vå)	155	41.15 N	60.30 E
Khíos, Grc. (kē'ôs)	173	38.23 N	26.09 E
Khíos (I.), Grc.	173	38.20 N	25.45 E
Khmel'nik, Sov. Un.	175	49.34 N	27.58 E
Khmel'nitskiy, Sov. Un. (kmĭē'lnē'ts-kēē)	179	49.29 N	26.54 E
Khmel'nitskiy (Oblast), Sov. Un. (Kmĕl-nēt'skĭ ôb'låst')	175	49.27 N	26.30 E
Kholargós, Grc.	66d	38.00 N	23.48 E
Kholm, Sov. Un. (Kôlm)	174	57.09 N	31.07 E
Kholmsk, Sov. Un. (Kŭlmsk)	181	47.09 N	142.33 E
Khomeynīshahr, Iran	195	32.41 N	51.31 E
Khopër (R.), Sov. Un. (Kô'pēr)	179	52.00 N	43.00 E
Khor (R.), Sov. Un.	204	47.23 N	135.20 E
Khor, Sov. Un. (Kôr')	204	47.50 N	134.52 E
Khóra Sfakíon, Grc.	172a	35.12 N	24.10 E
Khorel, India	67a	22.42 N	88.19 E
Khorog, Sov. Un. (Kôr'ôg)	180	37.30 N	71.47 E
Khorog, Sov. Un.	196	37.10 N	71.43 E
Khorol, Sov. Un. (Kô'rôl)	175	49.48 N	33.17 E
Khorol (R.), Sov. Un.	175	49.50 N	33.21 E
Khorramābād, Iran	195	33.30 N	48.20 E
Khorramshahr, Iran (kō-ram'shär)	192	30.36 N	48.15 E
Khotin, Sov. Un. (Kô'tĕn)	175	48.29 N	26.32 E
Khot'kovo, Sov. Un.	182b	56.15 N	38.00 E
Khoybār, Sau. Ar.	192	25.45 N	39.28 E
Khoyniki, Sov. Un.	175	51.54 N	30.00 E
Khulna, Bngl.	196	22.50 N	89.38 E
Khūryān Mūryān (Is.), Om.	192	17.27 N	56.02 E
Khust, Sov. Un. (Kŏŏst)	167	48.10 N	23.18 E
Khvalynsk, Sov. Un. (Kvå-lĭnsk')	179	52.30 N	48.00 E
Khvoy, Iran	192	38.32 N	45.01 E
Khyber Pass, Pak. (kī'bēr)	193a	34.28 N	71.18 E
Kialwe, Zaire	231	9.22 S	27.08 E
Kiambi, Zaire (kyäm'bē)	231	7.20 S	28.01 E
Kiamichi (R.), Ok. (kyå-mē'chē)	123	34.31 N	95.34 W
Kianta (L.), Fin. (kyån'tå)	178	65.00 N	28.15 E
Kibenga, Zaire	230	7.55 S	17.35 E
Kibiti, Tan.	231	7.44 S	38.57 E
Kibombo, Zaire	231	3.54 S	25.55 E
Kibondo, Tan.	231	3.35 S	30.42 E
Kibouendé, Con.	71c	4.19 S	15.11 E
Kičevo, Yugo. (kē'chĕ-vô)	173	41.30 N	20.59 E
Kichijōji, Jap.	69a	35.42 N	139.35 E
Kickapoo (R.), Wi. (kĭk'å-pōō)	115	43.20 N	90.55 W
Kicking Horse P., Can.	99	51.25 N	116.10 W
Kidal, Mali (kē-dål')	224	18.33 N	1.00 E
Kidderminster, Eng. (kĭd'ēr-mĭn-stēr)	156	52.23 N	2.14 W
Kidderpore (Neigh.), India	67a	22.31 N	88.19 E
Kidd's Beach, S. Afr. (kĭdz)	227c	33.09 S	27.43 E
Kidsgrove, Eng. (kĭdz'grōv)	156	53.05 N	2.30 W
Kiel, F.R.G. (kēl)	166	54.19 N	10.08 E
Kiel, Wi.	115	43.52 N	88.04 W
Kiel B., F.R.G.	166	54.33 N	10.19 E
Kiel Can., see Nord-Ostsee Kan.			
Kielce, Pol. (kyĕl'tsĕ)	167	50.50 N	20.41 E
Kieldrecht, Bel. (kēl'drĕKt)	157a	51.17 N	4.09 E
Kierspe, F.R.G.	63	51.08 N	7.35 E
Kiev (Oblast), Sov. Un. (kē'yĕf) (ôb'låst')	175	50.05 N	30.40 E
Kiev, see Kiyev			
Kievskoye Vdkhr. (Res.), Sov. Un.	179	51.00 N	30.20 E
Kiffa, Mauritania (kēf'å)	228	16.37 N	11.24 W
Kigali, Rw. (kē-gä'lē)	226	1.59 S	30.05 E
Kigoma, Tan. (kē-gō'mä)	231	4.57 S	29.38 E
Kii-Suido (Chan.), Jap. (kē sōō-ē'dō)	205	33.53 N	134.55 E
Kikaiga (I.), Jap.	204	28.25 N	130.10 E
Kikinda, Yugo. (Kē'kĕn-dä)	173	45.49 N	20.30 E
Kikládhes (Is.), Grc.	173	37.30 N	24.45 E
Kikwit, Zaire (kē'kwĕt)	230	5.02 S	18.49 E
Kil, Swe. (kēl)	164	59.30 N	13.15 E
Kilauea, Hi. (kē-lä-ōō-ā'ä)	106a	22.12 N	159.25 W
Kilauea Crater, Hi.	106a	19.28 N	155.18 W
Kilbuck Mts., Ak. (kĭl-bŭk)	107	60.05 N	160.00 W
Kilchu, Kor. (kĭl'chōō)	204	40.59 N	129.23 E
Kildare, Ire. (kĭl-dār')	161	53.09 N	7.05 W
Kilembe, Zaire	230	5.42 S	19.55 E
Kilgore, Tx.	125	32.23 N	94.53 W
Kilifi, Ken.	231	3.38 S	39.51 E
Kilimanjaro (Mtn.), Tan. (kyl-ē-măn-jä'rō)	227	3.09 S	37.19 E
Kilimatinde, Tan. (kĭl-ē-mä-tĭn'då)	226	5.48 S	34.58 E
Kilindoni, Tan.	231	7.55 S	39.39 E
Kilingi-Nõmme, Sov. Un. (kē'lĭn-gē-nôm'mĕ)	165	58.08 N	25.03 E
Kilis, Tur. (kē'lēs)	179	36.50 N	37.20 E
Kiliya, Sov. Un. (kē'lyå)	175	45.28 N	29.17 E
Kilkenny, Ire. (kĭl-kĕn-ĭ)	162	52.40 N	7.30 W
Kilkis, Grc. (kĭl'kĭs)	173	40.59 N	22.51 E
Killala, Ire. (kĭ-lä'lå)	162	54.11 N	9.10 W
Killara, Austl.	70a	33.46 S	151.09 E
Killarney, Ire.	162	52.03 N	9.05 W
Killarney Heights, Austl.	70a	33.46 S	151.13 E
Killdeer, ND (kĭl'dēr)	114	47.22 N	102.45 W
Kilmarnock, Scot. (kĭl-mär'nŭk)	162	55.38 N	4.25 W
Kilokri (Neigh.), India	67d	28.35 N	77.16 E
Kilrush, Ire. (kĭl'rŭsh)	162	52.40 N	9.16 W
Kilwa Kisiwani, Tan.	231	8.58 S	39.30 E
Kilwa Kivinje, Tan.	227	8.43 S	39.18 E
Kim (R.), Cam.	229	5.40 N	11.17 E
Kimamba, Tan.	231	6.47 S	37.08 E
Kimba, Austl. (kĭm'bå)	216	33.08 S	136.25 E
Kimball, Ne. (kĭm-băl)	114	41.14 N	103.41 W
Kimball, SD	114	43.44 N	98.58 W
Kimberley, Can. (kĭm'bēr-lĭ)	99	49.41 N	115.59 W
Kimberley, S. Afr.	226	28.40 S	24.50 E
Kimi, Cam.	229	6.05 N	11.30 E
Kimry, Sov. Un. (kĭm'rē)	174	56.53 N	37.24 E
Kimvula, Zaire	230	5.44 S	15.58 E
Kinabalu, Gunong (Mtn.), Mala.	206	5.45 N	115.26 E
Kincardine, Can. (kĭn-kär'dĭn)	110	44.10 N	81.15 W
Kinda, Zaire	230	9.18 S	25.04 E
Kindanba, Con.	230	3.44 S	14.31 E
Kinder, La. (kĭn'dēr)	125	30.30 N	92.50 W
Kindersley, Can. (kĭn'dērz-lē)	100	51.27 N	109.10 W
Kindia, Gui. (kĭn'dē-å)	228	10.04 N	12.51 W
Kindu, Zaire	231	2.57 S	25.56 E
Kinel'-Cherkassy, Sov. Un.	178	53.32 N	51.32 E
Kineshma, Sov. Un. (kē-nĕsh'må)	174	57.27 N	41.02 E
King (I.), Austl. (kĭng)	216	39.35 S	143.40 E
Kingaroy, Austl. (kĭŋ'gå-roi)	216	26.37 S	151.50 E
King City, Ca. (kĭng sĭ'tĭ)	120	36.12 N	121.08 W
King City, Can.	95d	43.56 N	79.32 W
Kingcome Inlet, Can. (kĭng'kŭm)	98	50.50 N	126.10 W
Kingfisher, Ok. (kĭng'fĭsh-ēr)	122	35.51 N	97.55 W
King George, Mt., Can.	99	50.35 N	115.24 W
King George Sd., Austl. (jôrj)	214	35.17 S	118.30 E
King George's Res., Eng.	62	51.39 N	0.01 W
Kingisepp, Sov. Un. (kĭŋ-gē-sep')	174	59.22 N	28.38 E
King Leopold Ranges, Austl. (lē'ō-pōld)	214	16.25 S	125.00 E
Kingman, Az. (kĭng'măn)	121	35.10 N	114.05 W
Kingman, Ks. (kĭng'măn)	122	37.38 N	98.07 W
King of Prussia, Pa.	56b	40.05 N	75.23 W

PRONOUNCING INDEX

Kings – Kolomenskoje 301

PLACE (Pronounciation)	PAGE	Lat. °′	Long. °′
Kings (R.), Ca.	120	36.28 N	119.43 W
Kingsbury (Neigh.), Eng.	62	51.35 N	0.17 W
Kings Canyon Natl. Park, Ca. (kăn'yŭn)	120	36.52 N	118.53 W
Kingsclere, Eng. (kĭngs-clēr)	156b	51.18 N	1.15 W
Kingscote, Austl. (kĭngz'kŭt)	216	35.45 S	137.32 E
King Sd., Austl.	214	16.50 S	123.35 E
Kingsdown, Eng.	62	51.21 N	0.17 E
Kingsford, Austl.	70a	33.56 S	151.14 E
Kingsgrove, Austl.	70a	33.57 S	151.06 E
Kings Langley, Eng.	62	51.43 N	0.28 W
King's Lynn, Eng. (kĭngz lĭn')	163	52.45 N	0.20 E
Kings Mt., NC	127	35.13 N	81.30 W
Kings Norton, Eng. (nôr'tŭn)	156	52.25 N	1.54 W
Kings Park, NY (kĭngz pärk)	112a	40.53 N	73.16 W
Kings Park, Va.	56d	38.48 N	77.15 W
Kings Pk., Ut.	117	40.46 N	110.20 W
Kings Point, NY	55	40.49 N	73.45 W
Kingsport, Tn. (kĭngz'pōrt)	127	36.33 N	82.36 W
Kingston, Austl. (kĭngz'tŭn)	216	37.52 S	139.52 E
Kingston, Can.	111	44.15 N	76.30 W
Kingston, Jam.	134	18.00 N	76.45 W
Kingston, NY	111	42.00 N	74.00 W
Kingston, Pa.	111	41.15 N	75.50 W
Kingston, Wa.	118a	47.04 N	122.29 W
Kingston upon Hull, Eng.	156	53.45 N	0.25 W
Kingston upon Thames (Neigh.), Eng.	62	51.25 N	0.19 W
Kingstown, Saint Vincent (kĭngz'toun)	133b	13.10 N	61.14 W
Kingstree, SC (kĭngz'trē)	127	33.30 N	79.50 W
Kingsville, Tx. (kĭngz'vĭl)	124	27.32 N	97.52 W
King William I., Can. (kĭng wĭl'yăm)	96	69.25 N	97.00 W
King William's Town, S. Afr. (kĭng-wĭl'-yŭmz-toun)	217c	32.53 S	27.24 E
Kinira (R.), S. Afr.	227c	30.37 S	28.52 E
Kinloch, Mo. (kĭn-lŏk)	119e	38.44 N	90.19 W
Kinnaird, Can. (kĭn-ärd')	99	49.17 N	117.39 W
Kinnairds Hd., Scot. (kĭn-ârds'hĕd)	162	57.42 N	3.55 W
Kinomoto, Jap. (kē'nō-mōtō)	205	33.53 N	136.07 E
Kinosaki, Jap. (kē'nō-sä'kē)	205	35.38 N	134.47 E
Kinshasa (Léopoldville), Zaire	230	4.18 S	15.18 E
Kinshasa-Est (Neigh.), Zaire	71c	4.18 S	15.18 E
Kinshasa-Quest (Neigh.), Zaire	71c	4.20 S	15.15 E
Kinsley, Ks. (kĭnz'lĭ)	122	37.55 N	99.24 W
Kinston, NC (kĭnz'tŭn)	127	35.15 N	77.35 W
Kintamo, Rapides de, Afr.	71c	4.19 S	15.15 E
Kintampo, Ghana (kĕn-täm'pō)	228	8.03 N	1.43 W
Kintsana, Con.	71c	4.19 S	15.10 E
Kintyre (Pen), Scot.	162	55.50 N	5.40 W
Kioroshi, see Ōmori			
Kirthar Ra., Pak. (kĭr-tŭr)	196	27.00 N	67.10 E
Kiowa, Ks. (kī'ô-wȧ)	122	37.01 N	98.30 W
Kiowa, Ok.	123	34.42 N	95.53 W
Kiyose, Jap.	205a	35.47 N	139.32 E
Kiparissiakós Kólpos (G.), Grc.	173	37.28 N	21.15 E
Kiparissía, Grc.	173	37.17 N	21.43 E
Kipawa Lac (L.), Can.	103	46.55 N	79.00 W
Kipembawe, Tan. (kē-pĕm-bä'wȧ)	231	7.39 S	33.24 E
Kipengere Ra., Tan.	231	9.10 S	34.00 E
Kipili, Tan.	231	7.26 S	30.36 E
Kipusha, Zaire	231	11.46 S	27.14 E
Kipushi, Zaire	231	11.46 S	27.14 E
Kirby, Tx. (kŭr'bĭ)	119d	29.29 N	98.23 W
Kirbyville, Tx. (kŭr'bĭ-vĭl)	125	30.39 N	93.54 W
Kirchderne (Neigh.), F.R.G.	63	51.33 N	7.30 E
Kirchende, F.R.G.	63	51.25 N	7.26 E
Kirchhellen, F.R.G.	63	51.36 N	6.55 E
Kirchhellen Heide (For.), F.R.G.	63	51.36 N	6.53 E
Kirchhörde (Neigh.), F.R.G.	63	51.27 N	7.27 E
Kirchlinde (Neigh.), F.R.G.	63	51.32 N	7.22 E
Kirdāsah, Egypt	71a	30.02 N	31.07 E
Kirenga (R.), Sov. Un. (kĕ-rĕŋ'gȧ)	181	56.30 N	103.18 E
Kirensk, Sov. Un. (kē-rĕnsk')	181	57.47 N	108.22 E
Kirghiz S. S. R., Sov. Un. (kĭr-gēz')	176	41.45 N	74.38 E
Kirghiz Steppe (Plain), Sov. Un.	176	49.28 N	57.07 E
Kirgizskiy Khrebet (Kirgiz) (Mts.), Sov. Un.	193	37.58 N	72.23 E
Kiri, Zaire	230	1.27 S	19.00 E
Kiribati, Oceania	208	1.30 S	173.00 E
Kirin, see Chilung			
Kirinyaga (Kenya) (Mtn.), Ken.	231	0.10 S	37.20 E
Kiritimati (I.), Oceania	209	2.20 N	157.40 W
Kirkby, Eng.	64a	53.29 N	2.54 W
Kirkby-in-Ashfield, Eng. (kûrk'bē-ĭn-ăsh'fēld)	156	53.06 N	1.16 W
Kirkcaldy, Scot. (kĕr-kô'dĭ)	162	56.06 N	3.15 W
Kirkdale (Neigh.), Eng.	64a	53.26 N	2.59 W
Kirkenes, Nor.	158	69.40 N	30.03 E
Kirkham, Eng. (kûrk'ăm)	156	53.47 N	2.53 W
Kirkland, Can.	54b	45.27 N	73.52 W
Kirkland, Wa. (kûrk'lănd)	118a	47.41 N	122.12 W
Kirklareli, Tur. (kêrk'lär-ĕ'lĕ)	173	41.44 N	27.15 E
Kirksville, Mo. (kûrks'vĭl)	123	40.12 N	92.35 W
Kirkūk, Iraq (kĭr-kōōk')	192	35.28 N	44.22 E
Kirkwall, Scot. (kûrk'wôl)	162a	58.58 N	2.59 W
Kirkwood, Md.	56d	38.57 N	76.58 W
Kirkwood, Mo. (kûrk'wŏŏd)	119e	38.35 N	90.24 W
Kirkwood, S. Afr.	227c	33.26 S	25.24 E
Kirn, F.R.G. (kērn)	166	49.47 N	7.23 E
Kirov, Sov. Un.	174	54.04 N	34.19 E
Kirov, Sov. Un.	178	58.35 N	49.35 E
Kirovabad, Sov. Un. (kē-rŭ-vŭ-bät')	179	40.40 N	46.20 E
Kirovgrad, Sov. Un. (kē'rŭ-vŭ-grad)	182a	57.26 N	60.03 E
Kirovograd, Sov. Un. (kē-rŭ-vŭ-grät')	175	48.33 N	32.17 E
Kirovograd (Oblast), Sov. Un.	175	48.23 N	31.10 E
Kirovsk, Sov. Un. (kē-rôfsk')	182c	59.52 N	30.59 E
Kirovsk, Sov. Un.	178	67.40 N	33.58 E
Kirsanov, Sov. Un. (kêr-sȧ'nôf)	179	52.40 N	42.40 E
Kirsehir, Tur. (kêr-shĕ'hēr)	179	39.10 N	34.00 E
Kirtachi Seybou, Niger	229	12.48 N	2.29 E
Kirton, Eng. (kûr'tŭn)	156	53.29 N	0.35 W
Kiruna, Swe. (kē-rōō'nä)	158	67.49 N	20.08 E
Kirundu, Zaire	231	0.44 S	25.32 E
Kirwan Heights, Pa.	57b	40.22 N	80.06 W
Kirwin Res., Ks. (kûr'wĭn)	122	39.34 N	99.04 W
Kiryū, Jap. (kē'rĭ-ōō)	205	36.26 N	139.18 E
Kirzhach, Sov. Un. (kêr-zhȧk')	174	56.08 N	38.53 E
Kisaki, Tan. (kē-sȧ'kē)	227	7.37 S	37.43 E
Kisangani (Stanleyville), Zaire	230	0.30 S	25.12 E
Kisarazu, Jap. (kē'sȧ-rȧ'zōō)	205a	35.23 N	139.55 E
Kiselëvsk, Sov. Un. (kē-sĭ-lyôfsk')	180	54.05 N	86.19 E
Kishar Bāla, Iran	68h	35.49 N	51.13 E
Kishinëv, Sov. Un. (ke-shē-nyôf')	175	47.02 N	28.52 E
Kishiwada, Jap. (kē'shē-wä'dä)	205	34.25 N	135.18 E
Kishkino, Sov. Un. (kēsh'kĭ-nô)	182b	55.15 N	38.04 E
Kısıklı (Neigh.), Tur.	66f	41.01 N	29.03 E
Kisiwani, Tan.	231	4.08 S	37.57 E
Kiska (I.), Ak. (kĭs'kä)	107a	52.08 N	177.10 E
Kiskatinaw (R.), Can.	99	55.10 N	120.20 W
Kiskittogisu L., Can.	101	54.05 N	99.00 W
Kiskitto L., Can. (kĭs-kĭ'tō)	101	54.16 N	98.34 W
Kiskunfélegyháza, Hung. (kĭsh'kōōn-fā'lĕd-y'hä'zô)	167	46.42 N	19.52 E
Kiskunhalas, Hung. (kĭsh'kōōn-hô'lôsh)	167	46.24 N	19.26 E
Kiskunmajsa, Hung. (kĭsh'kōōn-mī'shô)	167	46.29 N	19.42 E
Kismaayo, Som.	227	0.18 S	42.30 E
Kiso, Jap.	69a	35.34 N	139.26 E
Kiso-Gawa (Strm.), Jap. (kē'sō-gä'wä)	205	35.29 N	137.12 E
Kiso-Sammyaku (Mts.), Jap. (kē'sō säm'myȧ-kōō)	205	35.47 N	137.39 E
Kissamos, Grc.	172a	35.13 N	24.11 E
Kissidougou, Gui. (kē'sē-dōō'gōō)	228	9.11 N	10.06 W
Kissimmee, Fl. (kĭ-sĭm'ē)	127a	28.17 N	81.25 W
Kissimmee (L.), Fl.	127a	27.58 N	81.17 W
Kissimmee (R.), Fl.	127a	27.45 N	81.07 W
Kistarcsa, Hung.	66g	47.33 N	19.16 E
Kistrand, Nor. (kē'stränd)	158	70.29 N	25.01 E
Kisujszallás, Hung. (kĭsh'ōō'y'sä'läsh)	167	47.12 N	20.47 E
Kisumu, Ken. (kē'sōō-mōō)	231	0.06 S	34.45 E
Kita, Mali (kē'tȧ)	228	13.03 N	9.29 W
Kita (Neigh.), Jap.	69a	35.45 N	139.44 E
Kitakami Gawa (R.), Jap. (kē'tȧ-kä'mē gä-wä)	204	39.20 N	141.10 E
Kitakyūshū, Jap. (kē'tȧ-kyōō'shōō')	205	34.15 N	130.23 E
Kitale, Ken.	231	1.01 N	35.00 E
Kitamachi (Neigh.), Jap.	69a	35.46 N	139.39 E
Kitamba (Neigh.), Zaire	71c	4.19 S	15.14 E
Kitatawara, Jap.	69b	34.44 N	135.42 E
Kit Carson, Co.	122	38.46 N	102.48 W
Kitchener, Can. (kĭch'ĕ-nēr)	110	43.25 N	80.35 W
Kitenda, Zaire	230	6.53 S	17.21 E
Kitgum, Ug. (kĭt'gōōm)	225	3.29 N	33.04 E
Kitimat, Can. (kĭ'tĭ-māt)	98	54.03 N	128.33 W
Kitimat (R.), Can.	98	53.50 N	129.00 W
Kitimat Ra., Can.	98	53.30 N	128.50 W
Kitlope (R.), Can. (kĭt'lōp)	98	53.00 N	128.00 W
Kitsuki, Jap. (kēt'sōō-kē)	205	33.24 N	131.35 E
Kittanning, Pa. (kĭ-tăn'ĭng)	111	40.50 N	79.30 W
Kittatinny Mts., NJ (kĭ-tȧ-tĭ'nē)	112a	41.16 N	74.44 W
Kittery, Me. (kĭt'ēr-ĭ)	104	43.07 N	70.45 W
Kittsee, Aus.	157e	48.05 N	17.05 E
Kitty Hawk, NC (kĭt'tē hôk)	127	36.04 N	75.42 W
Kitunda, Tan.	231	6.48 S	33.13 E
Kitwe, Zambia	231	12.49 S	28.13 E
Kitzingen, F.R.G. (kĭt'zĭng-ĕn)	166	49.44 N	10.08 E
Kiunga, Ken.	231	1.45 S	41.29 E
Kivu, Lac (L.), Zaire	231	1.45 S	28.55 E
Kími, Grc.	173	38.38 N	24.05 E
Kímolos (I.), Grc. (kē'mô-lôs)	173	36.52 N	24.20 E
Kíthira (I.), Grc.	161	36.15 N	22.56 E
Kíthnos (I.), Grc.	173	37.24 N	24.10 E
Kiyev (Kiev), Sov. Un. (kē'yĕf)	179	50.27 N	30.30 E
Kizel, Sov. Un. (kē'zĕl)	182a	59.05 N	57.42 E
Kizil Irmak (R.), Tur. (kĭz'ĭl ĭr-măk')	179	40.15 N	34.00 E
Kizil'skoye, Sov. Un. (kĭz'ĭl-skô-yĕ)	182a	52.43 N	58.53 E
Kizlyar, Sov. Un. (kĭz-lyär')	179	44.00 N	46.50 E
Kizu, Jap. (kē'zōō)	205b	34.43 N	135.49 E
Kizuki, Jap.	69a	35.34 N	139.40 E
Kizuri, Jap.	69b	34.39 N	135.34 E
Kizyl Arvat, Sov. Un. (kē'zĭl-ŭr-vät')	155	38.55 N	56.33 E
Klaas Smits (R.), S. Afr.	227c	31.45 S	26.33 E
Klaaswaal, Neth.	157a	51.46 N	4.25 E
Kladno, Czech. (kläd'nō)	166	50.10 N	14.05 E
Klagenfurt, Aust. (klä'gĕn-fōōrt)	166	46.38 N	14.19 E
Klaipéda (Memel), Sov. Un. (klī'pȧ-dȧ) (mā'mĕl)	165	55.43 N	21.10 E
Klamath Falls, Or.	116	42.13 N	121.49 W
Klamath Mts., Ca.	116	42.00 N	123.25 W
Klamath R., Ca.	116	41.40 N	122.25 W
Klarälven (R.), Swe.	164	60.40 N	13.00 E
Klaskanine (R.), Or. (klăs'kȧ-nīn)	118c	46.02 N	123.43 W
Klatovy, Czech. (klȧ'tô-vē)	166	49.23 N	13.18 E
Klawock, Ak. (klā'wăk)	107	55.32 N	133.10 W
Kledering (Neigh.), Aus.	66e	48.08 N	16.26 E
Kleef, F.R.G.	63	51.11 N	6.56 E
Kleinbeeren, G.D.R.	65a	52.22 N	13.20 E
Kleinebroich, F.R.G.	63	51.12 N	6.35 E
Klein Elandsvlei, S. Afr.	71b	26.09 S	27.39 E
Kleinmachnow, G.D.R. (klīn-mäĸ'nō)	157b	52.22 N	13.12 E
Klein Ziethen, G.D.R.	65a	52.23 N	13.27 E
Klerksdorp, S. Afr. (klērks'dôrp)	223d	26.52 S	26.40 E
Klerksraal, S. Afr. (klērks'kräl)	223d	26.15 S	27.10 E
Kletnya, Sov. Un. (klyĕt'nyȧ)	174	52.19 N	33.14 E
Kletsk, Sov. Un. (klĕtsk)	174	53.04 N	26.43 E
Kleve, F.R.G. (klĕ'fĕ)	169c	51.47 N	6.09 E
Kley (Neigh.), F.R.G.	63	51.30 N	7.22 E
Klickitat R., Wa.	116	46.01 N	121.07 W
Klimovichi, Sov. Un. (klē-mô-vē'chē)	174	53.37 N	31.21 E
Klimovsk, Sov. Un. (klĭ'môfsk)	182b	55.21 N	37.32 E
Klin, Sov. Un. (klēn)	174	56.18 N	36.43 E
Klintehamn, Swe. (klēn'tē-häm)	164	57.24 N	18.14 E
Klintsy, Sov. Un. (klĭn'tsĭ)	174	52.46 N	32.14 E
Klip (R.), S. Afr. (klĭp)	223d	27.18 N	29.25 E
Klipgat, S. Afr.	223d	25.26 S	27.57 E
Klippan, Swe. (klyp'pȧn)	164	56.08 N	13.09 E
Klippoortje, S. Afr.	71b	26.17 S	28.14 E
Kliptown, S. Afr.	71b	26.17 S	27.53 E
Ključ, Yugo. (klyōōch)	172	44.32 N	16.48 E
Klodzko, Pol. (klôd'skô)	166	50.26 N	16.38 E
Klondike Reg., Ak.-Can. (klŏn'dīk)	107	64.12 N	142.38 W
Klosterfelde, G.D.R. (klōs'tĕr-fĕl-dē)	157b	52.47 N	13.29 E
Klosterneuburg, Aus. (klōs-tĕr-noi'bōōrgh)	157e	48.19 N	16.20 E
Kluane (L.), Can.	96	61.15 N	138.40 W
Kluane Natl. Pk., Can.	96	60.25 N	137.53 W
Kluczbork, Pol. (klōōch'bŏrk)	167	50.59 N	18.15 E
Klyaz'ma (R.), Sov. Un. (klyäz'mȧ)	174	55.49 N	39.19 E
Klyuchevskaya (Vol.), Sov. Un. (klyōō-chĕfskä'yä)	181	56.13 N	160.00 E
Klyuchi, Sov. Un. (klyōō'chĭ)	182a	57.03 N	57.20 E
Knezha, Bul. (knyä'zhȧ)	173	43.27 N	24.03 E
Knife (R.), ND (nīf)	114	47.06 N	102.33 W
Knight Inlet, Can. (nīt)	98	50.41 N	125.40 W
Knightstown, In. (nīts'toun)	110	39.45 N	85.30 W
Knin, Yugo. (knēn)	172	44.02 N	16.14 E
Knittelfeld, Aus.	166	47.13 N	14.50 E
Knob Pk., Phil. (nŏb)	207a	12.30 N	121.20 E
Knockholt, Eng.	62	51.18 N	0.06 E
Knockholt Pound, Eng.	62	51.19 N	0.08 E
Knoppiesfontein, S. Afr.	71b	26.05 S	28.25 E
Knottingley, Eng. (nŏt'ĭng-lĭ)	156	53.42 N	1.14 W
Knott's Berry Farm (P. Int.), Ca.	59	33.50 N	118.00 W
Knotty Ash (Neigh.), Eng.	64a	53.25 N	2.54 W
Knowsley, Eng.	64a	53.27 N	2.51 W
Knowsley Hall (P. Int.), Eng.	64a	53.26 N	2.50 W
Knox, Austl.	70b	37.53 S	145.18 E
Knox, In. (nŏks)	110	41.15 N	86.40 W
Knox, C., Can.	98	54.12 N	133.20 W
Knoxville, Ia. (nŏks'vĭl)	115	41.19 N	93.05 W
Knoxville, Tn.	126	35.58 N	83.55 W
Knutsford, Eng. (nŭts'fērd)	156	53.18 N	2.22 W
Knyszyn, Pol. (knĭ'shĭn)	167	53.16 N	22.59 E
Kobayashi, Jap. (kō'bȧ-yä'shē)	205	31.58 N	130.59 E
Kōbe, Jap. (kō'bĕ)	205b	34.30 N	135.10 E
Kobelyaki, Sov. Un. (kō-bĕl-yä'kē)	175	49.11 N	34.12 E
København (Copenhagen), Den. (kû-b'n-houn')	164	55.43 N	12.27 E
Koblenz, F.R.G. (kō'blĕntz)	166	50.18 N	7.36 E
Kobozha (R.), Sov. Un. (kô-bō'zhȧ)	174	58.55 N	35.18 E
Kobrin, Sov. Un. (kō'brĕn')	167	52.13 N	24.23 E
Kobrinskoye, Sov. Un. (kô-brĭn'skô-yĕ)	182c	59.25 N	30.07 E
Kobuk (R.), Ak. (kō'bŭk)	107	66.58 N	158.48 W
Kobuleti, Sov. Un. (kô-bōō-lyā'tē)	179	41.50 N	41.40 E
Kočani, Yugo. (kô'chä-nĕ)	173	41.54 N	22.25 E
Kočevje, Yugo. (kô'chāv-ye)	172	45.38 N	14.51 E
Kocher R., F.R.G. (kôĸ'ĕr)	166	49.00 N	9.52 E
Kōchi, Jap. (kō'chē)	205	33.35 N	133.32 E
Kodaira, Jap.	205a	35.43 N	139.29 E
Kodiak, Ak. (kō'dyăk)	107	57.50 N	152.30 W
Kodiak (I.), Ak.	107	57.24 N	153.32 W
Kodok, Sud. (ko'dŏk)	225	9.57 N	32.08 E
Koforidua, Ghana (kō fô-rĭ-dōō'ȧ)	228	6.03 N	0.17 W
Kōfu, Jap. (kō'fōō')	205	35.41 N	138.34 E
Koga, Jap. (kō'gȧ)	205	36.13 N	139.40 E
Kogan (R.), Gui.	228	11.30 N	14.05 W
Kogane, Jap. (kō'gä-nȧ)	205a	35.50 N	139.56 E
Koganei, Jap. (kō'gä-nā)	205a	35.42 N	139.31 E
Kogarah, Austl.	70a	33.58 S	151.08 E
Køge, Den. (kû'gĕ)	164	55.27 N	12.09 E
Køge Bugt (B.), Den.	164	55.30 N	12.25 E
Kogil'nik (R.), Sov. Un. (kô-gĕl-nēk')	175	46.08 N	29.10 E
Kogoni, Mali	228	14.44 N	6.02 W
Koh-i Baba Mt., Afg.	196	39.39 N	67.09 E
Kohīma, India (kô-ē'mȧ)	193	25.45 N	94.41 E
Koito (R.), Jap. (kô'ē-tō)	205a	35.19 N	139.58 E
Kōje (I.), Kor. (kû'jĕ)	204	34.53 N	129.00 E
Kokand, Sov. Un. (kô-känt')	180	40.27 N	71.07 E
Kokchetav, Sov. Un. (kôk'chĕ-tȧf)	180	53.15 N	69.13 E
Kokemäenjoki (R.), Fin.	165	61.23 N	22.03 E
Kokhma, Sov. Un. (kôĸ'mȧ)	174	56.57 N	41.08 E
Kokkola, Fin. (kôk'kô-lȧ)	158	63.47 N	22.58 E
Kokomo, In. (kō'kô-mō)	110	40.30 N	86.20 W
Koko Nor (Qinghai Hu) (L.), China (kō'kô nor) (chyĭŋ-hī hōō)	198	37.26 N	98.30 E
Kokopo, Pap. N. Gui. (kô-kô'pō)	207	4.25 S	152.27 E
Koksoak (R.), Can. (kôk'sô-ăk)	97	57.42 N	69.50 W
Kokstad, S. Afr. (kôk'shtät)	227c	30.33 S	29.27 E
Kokubu, Jap. (kō'kōō-bōō)	205	31.42 N	130.46 E
Kokubunji, Jap.	69a	35.42 N	139.29 E
Kokuou, Jap. (kô'kōō-ô'ōō)	205b	34.34 N	135.39 E
Kola Pen., see Kol'skiy P-Ov.			
Kolār, (Kolār Gold Fields), India (kôl-är')	197	13.39 N	78.33 E
Kolárovo, Czech. (kôl-árôvō)	167	47.54 N	17.59 E
Kolbio, Ken.	231	1.10 S	41.15 E
Kol'chugino, Sov. Un. (kôl-chōō'gē-nô)	174	56.19 N	39.29 E
Kolda, Sen.	228	12.53 N	14.57 W
Kolding, Den. (kŭl'dĭng)	164	55.29 N	9.24 E
Kole, Zaire (kō'lȧ)	226	3.19 S	22.46 E
Kolguyev (I.), Sov. Un. (kôl-gōō'yĕf)	178	69.00 N	49.00 E
Kolin, Czech. (kō'lēn)	166	50.01 N	15.11 E
Kolkasrags (Pt.), Sov. Un. (kôl-käs'rägz)	165	57.46 N	22.39 E
Köln (Cologne), F.R.G.	169c	50.56 N	6.57 E
Kolno, Pol. (kôw'nô)	167	53.23 N	21.56 E
Kolo, Pol. (kō'wô)	167	52.11 N	18.37 E
Kolobrzeg, Pol. (kô-lôb'zhĕk)	166	54.10 N	15.35 E
Kolomenskoje (Neigh.), Sov. Un.	66b	55.40 N	37.41 E

ŋ-sing; nŋ-banŋk; ɴ-nasalized n; nŏd; cŏmmit; ōld; ôbey; ôrder; oi-boil; fōōd; fŏŏt; ou-out; s-soft; sh-dish; th-thin; pūre; ûnite; ûrn; stŭd; circŭs; ü-as in French tu; '-indeterminate vowel.

PLACE (Pronounciation)	PAGE	Lat. °′	Long. °′
Kolomna, Sov. Un. (kȧl-ôm'nȧ)	182b	55.06 N	38.47 E
Kolomyya, Sov. Un. (kō'lô-mē'yȧ)	167	48.32 N	25.04 E
Kolonie Stolp, G.D.R.	65a	52.28 N	13.46 E
Kolp' (R.), Sov. Un. (kôlp)	174	59.29 N	35.32 E
Kolpashevo, Sov. Un. (kŭl pȧ shô'vȧ)	180	58.16 N	82.43 E
Kolpino, Sov. Un. (kôl'pē-nô)	182c	59.45 N	30.37 E
Kolpny, Sov. Un. (kôlp'nyē)	174	52.14 N	36.54 E
Kol'skiy P-Ov. (Kola Pen.), Sov. Un.	178	67.15 N	37.40 E
Kolva (R.), Sov. Un.	178	61.00 N	57.00 E
Kolwezi, Zaire (kōl-wĕ'zē)	231	10.43 S	25.28 E
Kolyberovo, Sov. Un. (kô-lĭ-byâ'rô-vô)	182b	55.16 N	38.45 E
Kolyma (R.), Sov. Un.	181	66.30 N	151.45 E
Kolymskiy (Mts.), see **Gydan**, Khrebet			
Kolyvan', Sov. Un. (kôl-ē-vän')	180	55.28 N	82.59 E
Kom (R.), Cam.-Gabon	230	2.15 N	12.05 E
Komadougou Yobé (R.), Niger-Nig.	229	13.20 N	12.45 E
Komadugu Gana (R.), Nig.	229	12.15 N	11.10 E
Komae, Jap.	205a	35.37 N	139.35 E
Komagome (Neigh.), Jap.	69a	35.44 N	139.45 E
Komandorskie Ostrova (Is.), Sov. Un.	93	55.40 N	167.13 E
Komárno, Czech. (kô'mär-nô)	167	47.46 N	18.08 E
Komarno, Sov. Un.	167	49.38 N	23.43 E
Komárom, Hung. (kô'mä-rôm)	167	47.45 N	18.06 E
Komatipoort, S. Afr. (kō-mä'tē-pōrt)	226	25.21 S	32.00 E
Komatsu, Jap. (kō-mät'sōō)	205	36.23 N	136.26 E
Komatsushima, Jap. (kō-mät'sōō-shē'mä)	205	34.04 N	134.32 E
Komeshia, Zaire	231	8.01 S	27.07 E
Komga, S. Afr. (kōm'gȧ)	227c	32.36 S	27.54 E
Komi (A.S.S.R.), Sov. Un. (kômē)	176	61.31 N	53.15 E
Kommetjie, S. Afr.	226a	34.09 S	18.19 E
Kommunizma, Pik (Pk.), Sov. Un.	198	39.46 N	71.23 E
Komoe (R.), Ivory Coast	228	5.40 N	3.40 W
Komotiní, Grc.	173	41.07 N	25.22 E
Komrat, Sov. Un. (kôm-rät')	175	46.17 N	28.38 E
Komsomolets, Sov. Un. (kôm-sô-mô'lĕts)	182a	53.45 N	63.04 E
Komsomolets Zaliv (B.), Sov. Un.	179	45.40 N	52.00 E
Komsomol'sk-na-Amure, Sov. Un. (kŭm-sŭ-môlsk'nŭ-ŭ-mōōr'yĭ)	181	50.46 N	137.14 E
Komsomol'skoye, Sov. Un. (kôm-sô-môl'skô-yĕ)	175	48.42 N	28.44 E
Kona, Mali	228	14.57 N	3.53 W
Konda (R.), Sov. Un. (kôn'dȧ)	178	60.50 N	64.00 E
Kondas R., Sov. Un. (kôn'dȧs)	182a	59.30 N	56.28 E
Kondli (Neigh.), India	67d	28.37 N	77.19 E
Kondoa, Tan. (kôn-dō'ȧ)	226	4.52 S	36.00 E
Kondolole, Zaire	231	1.20 N	25.58 E
Kong, Ivory Coast (kông)	224	9.05 N	4.41 W
Kongbo, Cen. Afr. Rep.	230	4.44 N	21.23 E
Kongolo, Zaire (kôŋ'gō'lō)	231	5.23 S	27.00 E
Kongsberg, Nor. (kŭngs'bĕrg)	164	59.40 N	9.36 E
Kongsvinger, Nor. (kŭngs'vĭŋ-gẽr)	164	60.12 N	12.00 E
Koni, Zaire (kō'nē)	226	10.32 S	27.27 E
Königsberg, see **Kaliningrad**			
Königsbrunn, F.R.G. (kû'nĕgs-brōōn)	157d	48.16 N	10.53 E
Königshardt (Neigh.), F.R.G.	63	51.33 N	6.51 E
Königs Wusterhausen, G.D.R. (kû'nĕgs vōōs'tĕr-hou-zĕn)	157b	52.18 N	13.38 E
Konin, Pol. (kô'nyĕn)	167	52.11 N	18.17 E
Kónitsa, Grc. (kô'nyē'tsȧ)	173	40.03 N	20.46 E
Konjic, Yugo. (kôn'yĕts)	173	43.38 N	17.59 E
Konju, Kor.	205	36.21 N	127.05 E
Konkouré (R.), Gui.	228	10.30 N	13.25 W
Konnagar, India	196a	22.41 N	88.22 E
Konohana (Neigh.), Jap.	69b	34.41 N	135.16 E
Kōnoike, Jap.	69b	34.42 N	135.37 E
Konotop, Sov. Un. (kô-nô-tôp')	175	51.13 N	33.14 E
Konpienga (R.), Burkina	228	11.15 N	0.35 E
Konqi (R.), China (kôn-chyē)	198	41.09 N	87.46 E
Końskie, Pol. (koin''skyĕ)	167	51.12 N	20.26 E
Konstantinovka, Sov. Un. (kôn-stȧn-tē'nôf-kȧ)	175	48.33 N	37.42 E
Konstanz, F.R.G. (kôn'shtänts)	166	47.39 N	9.10 E
Kontagora, Nig. (kōn-tȧ-gō'rä)	229	10.24 N	5.28 E
Konya, Tur. (kōn'yȧ)	179	36.55 N	32.25 E
Kootenay (R.), Can.	99	49.45 N	117.05 W
Kootenay L., Can.	99	49.35 N	116.50 W
Kootenay Natl. Park, Can. (kōō'tē-nā)	96	51.06 N	117.02 W
Kooyong, Austl.	70b	37.50 S	145.02 E
Kōō-zan (Mtn.), Jap. (kōō'zän)	205b	34.53 N	135.32 E
Kopervik, Nor. (kô'pĕr-vēk)	164	59.18 N	5.20 E
Kopeysk, Sov. Un. (kô-pāsk')	182a	55.07 N	61.36 E
Köping, Swe. (chû'pĭng)	164	59.32 N	15.58 E
Kopparberg, Swe. (kōp'pȧr-bĕrgh)	164	59.53 N	15.00 E
Koppeh Dāgh (Mts.), Iran	192	37.28 N	58.29 E
Koppies, S. Afr.	223d	27.15 S	27.35 E
Koprivnica, Yugo. (kô'prēv-nē'tsȧ)	172	46.10 N	16.48 E
Kopychintsy, Sov. Un. (kô-pē-chēn'tsĕ)	167	49.06 N	25.55 E
Korçë, Alb. (kôr'chĕ)	173	40.37 N	20.48 E
Korčula (I.), Yugo. (kôr'chōō-lȧ)	172	42.50 N	17.05 E
Korea B., China-Kor.	204	39.18 N	123.50 E
Korean Arch., Kor.	204	34.05 N	125.35 E
Korea, North, Asia	191	40.00 N	127.00 E
Korea, South, Asia	191	36.30 N	128.00 E
Korea Str., Kor.-Jap.	204	33.30 N	128.30 E
Korets, Sov. Un. (kô-rĕts')	167	50.35 N	27.13 E
Korhogo, Ivory Coast (kôr-hō'gō)	228	9.27 N	5.38 W
Kōri, Jap.	69b	34.47 N	135.39 E
Koridhallós, Grc.	66d	37.59 N	23.39 E
Korinthiakós Kólpos (G.), Grc.	173	38.15 N	22.33 E
Kórinthos (Corinth), Grc. (kô-rēn'thôs) (kŏr'ĭnth)	173	37.56 N	22.54 E
Kōriyama, Jap. (kō'rē-yȧ'mä)	204	37.18 N	140.25 E
Korkino, Sov. Un. (kôr'kē-nŭ)	182a	54.53 N	61.25 E
Korla, China (kōr-lä)	198	41.37 N	86.03 E
Körmend, Hung. (kûr'mĕnt)	166	47.02 N	16.36 E
Kornat (I.), Yugo. (kôr-nät')	172	43.46 N	15.10 E
Korneuburg, Aus. (kôr'noi-bŏŏrgh)	157e	48.22 N	16.21 E
Koro, Mali	228	14.04 N	3.05 W
Korocha, Sov. Un. (kô-rō'chȧ)	175	50.50 N	37.13 E
Korop, Sov. Un. (kō'rôp)	175	51.33 N	33.54 E
Korosten', Sov. Un. (kô'rôs-tĕn)	175	50.51 N	28.39 E
Korostyshev, Sov. Un. (kô-rôs'tē-shôf)	175	50.19 N	29.05 E
Koro Toro, Chad	229	16.05 N	18.30 E
Korotoyak, Sov. Un. (kô'rô-tô-yȧk')	175	51.00 N	39.06 E
Korsakov, Sov. Un. (kôr'sȧ-kôf')	181	46.42 N	143.16 E
Korsnäs, Fin. (kôrs'nĕs)	165	62.51 N	21.17 E
Korsør, Den. (kôrs'ûr')	159	55.19 N	11.08 E
Kortrijk, Bel.	163	50.49 N	3.10 E
Koryakskiy Khrebet (Mts.), Sov. Un.	181	62.00 N	168.45 E
Koryukovka, Sov. Un. (kôr-yōō-kôf'kȧ)	175	51.44 N	32.24 E
Kościan, Pol. (kŭsh'tsyȧn)	166	52.05 N	16.38 E
Kościerzyna, Pol. (kŭsh-tsyĕ-zhĕ'nȧ)	167	54.08 N	17.59 E
Kosciusko, Ms. (kŏs-ĭ-ŭs'kō)	126	33.04 N	89.35 W
Kosciusko, Mt., Austl.	216	36.26 S	148.20 E
Kosel'sk, Sov. Un. (kō-zĕlsk')	174	54.01 N	35.49 E
Kosha, Sud.	225	20.49 N	30.27 E
Koshigaya, Jap. (kō'shē-gä'yä)	205a	35.53 N	139.48 E
Koshiki-Rettō (Is.), Jap. (kō-shē'kē rȧt'tō)	205	31.51 N	129.40 E
Kosi (R.), India (kô'sē)	196	26.00 N	86.20 E
Košice, Czech. (kō'shē-tsĕ')	167	48.43 N	21.17 E
Kosino, Sov. Un.	66b	55.43 N	37.52 E
Kosmos, S. Afr. (kŏz'mŏs)	227b	25.45 S	27.51 E
Kosmosa, Monument (P. Int.), Sov. Un.	66b	55.49 N	37.38 E
Kosobrodskiy, Sov. Un. (kä-sô'brôd-skĭ)	182a	54.14 N	60.53 E
Koso Lake, see **Hövsgöl Nuur**			
Kosovska Mitrovica, Yugo. (kô'sôv-skä' mē'trô-vē-tsä')	173	42.51 N	20.50 E
Kostajnica, Yugo. (kôs'tä-ē-nē'tsȧ)	172	45.14 N	16.32 E
Koster, S. Afr.	223d	25.52 S	26.52 E
Kostino, Sov. Un. (kôs'tĭ-nô)	182b	55.54 N	37.51 E
Kostroma, Sov. Un. (kôs-trô-mȧ')	174	57.46 N	40.55 E
Kostroma (Oblast), Sov. Un.	174	57.50 N	41.10 E
Kostrzyn, Pol. (kôst'chĕn)	166	52.35 N	14.38 E
Kos'va R., Sov. Un. (kôs'vȧ)	182a	58.44 N	57.08 E
Koszalin, Pol. (kô-shä'lĭn)	166	54.12 N	16.10 E
Köszeg, Hung. (kû'sĕg)	166	47.21 N	16.32 E
Kota, India	196	25.17 N	75.49 E
Kota Baharu, Mala. (kō'tä bä'rōō)	206	6.15 N	102.23 E
Kotabaru, Indon.	206	3.22 S	116.15 E
Kota Kinabalu, Mala.	206	5.55 N	116.05 E
Kota Kota, Malawi (kō-tȧ kō-tȧ)	226	12.52 S	34.16 E
Kota Tinggi, Mala.	191b	1.43 N	103.54 E
Kotel, Bul. (kō-tĕl')	173	42.54 N	26.28 E
Kotel'nich, Sov. Un. (kô-tyĕl'nēch)	178	58.15 N	48.20 E
Kotel'nyy (I.), Sov. Un. (kō-tyĕl'nē)	181	74.51 N	134.09 E
Kothapur, India	197	16.48 N	74.15 E
Kotka, Fin. (kŏt'kȧ)	165	60.28 N	26.56 E
Kotlas, Sov. Un. (kôt'lȧs)	178	61.10 N	46.50 E
Kotlin, Ostrov (I.), Sov. Un. (ôs-trôf' kôt'lĭn)	182c	60.02 N	29.49 E
Kōtō (Neigh.), Jap.	69a	35.41 N	139.48 E
Kotor, Yugo. (kō'tôr)	173	42.26 N	18.48 E
Kotorosl' (R.), Sov. Un. (kô-tô'rôsl)	174	57.18 N	39.08 E
Kotor Varoš, Yugo. (kō'tôr vä'rôsh)	172	44.37 N	17.23 E
Kotovsk, Sov. Un. (kô-tôfsk')	175	47.49 N	29.31 E
Kotte, Sri Lanka	197	6.50 N	80.05 E
Kotto (R.), Cen. Afr. Rep.	225	5.17 N	22.04 E
Kotuy (R.), Sov. Un. (kô-tōō')	181	71.00 N	103.15 E
Kotzebue, Ak. (kŏt'sē-bōō)	107	66.48 N	162.42 W
Kotzebue Sd., Ak.	107	67.00 N	164.28 W
Koualé, Mali	228	11.24 N	7.01 W
Kouchibouguac Natl. Pk., Can.	104	46.53 N	65.35 W
Koudougou, Burkina (kōō-dōō'gōō)	228	12.15 N	2.22 W
Kouilou (R.), Con.	230	4.00 S	12.05 E
Koula-Moutou, Gabon	230	1.08 S	12.29 E
Koulikoro, Mali (kōō-lē-kō'rō)	228	12.53 N	7.33 W
Koulouguidi, Mali	228	13.27 N	17.33 E
Koumra, Chad	229	8.55 N	17.33 E
Koundara, Gui.	228	12.29 N	13.18 W
Koundé, Cen. Afr. Rep. (kōōn-dā')	225	6.08 N	14.32 E
Kounradskiy, Sov. Un. (kŭ-ōōn-rät'skē)	180	47.25 N	75.10 E
Kouroussa, Gui. (kōō-rōō'sä)	228	10.39 N	9.53 W
Koutiala, Mali (kōō-tē-ä'lä)	224	12.29 N	5.29 W
Kouvola, Fin. (kō'ōō-vô-lä)	165	60.51 N	26.40 E
Kouzhen, China (kō-jŭn)	200	36.19 N	117.37 E
Kovda (L.), Sov. Un. (kôv'dȧ)	178	66.45 N	32.00 E
Kovel' Sov. Un. (kō'vĕl)	167	51.13 N	24.45 E
Kovno, see **Kaunas**			
Kovrov, Sov. Un. (kôv-rôf')	174	56.23 N	41.21 E
Kowie, see **Port Alfred**			
Kowloon, Hong Kong (kō'lōōn')	203	22.28 N	114.20 E
Kowloon City, Hong Kong	68c	22.19 N	114.11 E
Kowloon (Jiulong), Hong Kong	68c	22.18 N	114.10 E
Koyuk, Ak. (kô-yōōk')	107	65.00 N	161.18 W
Koyukuk (R.), Ak. (kô-yōō'kōōk)	107	66.25 N	153.50 W
Kozáni, Grc.	173	40.16 N	21.51 E
Kozelets, Sov. Un. (kôzĕ-lyĕts)	175	50.53 N	31.07 E
Kozienice, Pol. (kō-zyĕ-nē'tsĕ)	167	51.34 N	21.35 E
Koźle, Pol. (kôzh'lĕ)	167	50.19 N	18.10 E
Kozloduy, Bul. (kŭz'lô-dwē)	173	43.45 N	23.42 E
Kōzu (I.), Jap. (kō'zōō)	205	34.16 N	139.03 E
Kozukue (Neigh.), Jap.	69a	35.30 N	139.36 E
Kraai (R.), S. Afr. (krä'ē)	227c	30.50 S	27.03 E
Krabbendijke, Neth.	157a	51.26 N	4.05 E
Krâchéh, Kamp.	206	12.28 N	106.06 E
Kragerö, Nor. (krä'gĕr-û)	164	58.53 N	9.21 E
Kragujevac, Yugo. (krä'gōō'yĕ-vȧts)	173	44.01 N	20.55 E
Krahenhöhe (Neigh.), F.R.G.	63	51.10 N	7.06 E
Kra, Isth. of, Thai.	206	9.30 S	99.45 E
Kraków, Pol. (krä'kōōf)	167	50.05 N	20.00 E
Kraljevo, Yugo. (kräl'ye-vô)	159	43.39 N	20.48 E
Kramatorsk, Sov. Un. (krȧ-mä'tôrsk)	175	48.43 N	37.32 E
Kramfors, Swe. (kräm'fôrs)	164	62.54 N	17.49 E
Krampnitz, G.D.R.	65a	52.28 N	13.04 E
Kranj, Yugo. (krän')	172	46.16 N	14.23 E
Kranskop, S. Afr. (kränz'kŏp)	227c	28.57 S	30.54 E
Kransnaya Gorka, Sov. Un. (kräs'nȧ-yȧ gôr'kȧ)	182a	55.13 N	56.43 E
Krāslava, Sov. Un. (kräs'lä-vä)	174	55.53 N	27.12 E
Kraslice, Czech. (kräs'lē-tsĕ)	166	50.19 N	12.30 E
Krasnaya Sloboda, Sov. Un.	179	48.25 N	44.35 E
Kraśnik, Pol. (kräsh'nĭk)	167	50.53 N	22.15 E
Krasnoarmeysk, Sov. Un. (kräs'nô-ȧr-maśk')	182b	56.06 N	38.09 E
Krasnoarmeyskoye, Sov. Un.	175	48.19 N	37.04 E
Krasnodar, Sov. Un. (kräs'nô-dȧr)	175	45.03 N	38.55 E
Krasnodarskiy (Oblast) Province, Sov. Un. (krȧs-nô-där'skĭ ôb'lȧst)	175	47.28 N	38.13 E
Krasnogorsk, Sov. Un.	182b	55.49 N	37.20 E
Krasnogorskiy, Sov. Un. (kräs-nô-gôr'skĭ)	182a	54.36 N	61.25 E
Krasnograd, Sov. Un. (kräs'nô-grät)	175	49.23 N	35.26 E
Krasnogvardeyskiy, Sov. Un. (krȧ'sno-gvȧr-dzyĕ ĕs-kēē)	182a	57.17 N	62.05 E
Krasnokamsk, Sov. Un. (kräs-nô-kȧmsk')	178	58.00 N	55.45 E
Krasnokutsk, Sov. Un. (krȧs-nô-kōōtsk')	175	50.03 N	35.05 E
Krasnosel'ye, Sov. Un. (kräs'nô-sĕl'yĕ)	175	48.44 N	32.24 E
Krasnoslobodsk, Sov. Un. (kräs'nô-slôbôtsk')	178	54.20 N	43.50 E
Krasnotur'insk, Sov. Un. (krŭs-nŭ-tōō-rensk')	182a	59.47 N	60.15 E
Krasnoufimsk, Sov. Un. (krŭs-nŭ-ōō-fēmsk')	182a	56.38 N	57.46 E
Krasnoural'sk, Sov. Un. (kräs'nô-ōō-rälsk')	182a	58.21 N	60.05 E
Krasnousol'skiy, Sov. Un. (kräs-nô-ōō-sôl'skĭ)	182a	53.53 N	56.30 E
Krasnovishersk, Sov. Un. (kräs-nô-vēshersk')	178	60.22 N	57.20 E
Krasnovodsk, Sov. Un. (kräs-nô-vôtsk')	179	40.00 N	52.50 E
Krasnoyarsk, Sov. Un. (kräs-nô-yȧrsk')	180	56.13 N	93.12 E
Krasnoye Selo, Sov. Un. (kräs'nŭ-yŭ sâ'lô)	182c	59.44 N	30.06 E
Krasnyj Stroitel' (Neigh.), Sov. Un.	66b	55.35 N	37.37 E
Krasny Kholm, Sov. Un. (kräs'nē ĸôlm)	174	58.03 N	37.11 E
Krasnystaw, Pol. (kräs-nē-stäf')	167	50.59 N	23.11 E
Krasnyy Bor, Sov. Un. (kräs'nē bôr)	182c	59.41 N	30.40 E
Krasnyy Klyuch, Sov. Un. (kräs'nē'klyûch')	182a	55.24 N	56.43 E
Krasnyy Kut, Sov. Un. (krȧs-nē kōōt')	179	50.50 N	47.00 E
Kratovo, Sov. Un. (krä'tô-vô)	182b	55.35 N	38.10 E
Kratovo, Yugo. (krä'tô-vô)	173	42.04 N	22.12 E
Kray (Neigh.), F.R.G.	63	51.28 N	7.05 E
Krefeld, F.R.G. (krā'fĕlt)	169c	51.20 N	6.34 E
Kremenchug, Sov. Un. (krĕm'ĕn-chōōgh')	175	49.04 N	33.26 E
Kremenchugskoye (Res.), Sov. Un. (krĕm-ĕn-chōōgh'skô-ye)	175	49.20 N	32.45 E
Kremenets, Sov. Un. (krĕ-mĕn-yĕts')	167	50.06 N	25.43 E
Kreml' (P. Int.), Sov. Un.	66b	55.45 N	37.37 E
Kremmen, G.D.R. (krĕ'mĕn)	157b	52.45 N	13.02 E
Krempe, F.R.G. (krĕm'pĕ)	157c	53.50 N	9.29 E
Krems, Aus. (krĕms)	166	48.25 N	15.36 E
Krestsy, Sov. Un.	165	58.18 N	32.26 E
Kresttsy, Sov. Un. (krâst'sē)	174	58.16 N	32.25 E
Kretinga, Sov. Un. (krĕ-tĭŋ'gȧ)	165	55.55 N	21.17 E
Kreuzberg, F.R.G.	63	51.09 N	7.27 E
Kreuzberg (Neigh.), F.R.G.	65a	52.30 N	13.23 E
Kribi, Cam. (krē'bē)	229	2.57 N	9.55 E
Krichëv, Sov. Un. (krē'chôf)	174	53.44 N	31.39 E
Krilon, Mys (Pt.), Sov. Un. (mĭs krĭl'ôn)	204	45.58 N	142.00 E
Krimpen aan de IJssel, Neth.	157a	51.55 N	4.34 E
Krishna (R.), India	193	16.23 N	75.00 E
Krishnanagar, India	196	23.29 N	88.33 E
Krishnapur, India	67a	22.36 N	88.26 E
Kristiansand, Nor. (krĭs-tyȧn-sän'')	164	58.09 N	7.59 E
Kristianstad, Swe. (krĭs-tyȧn-städ')	164	56.02 N	14.09 E
Kristiansund, Nor. (krĭs-tyȧn-sōōn'')	164	63.07 N	7.49 E
Kristinehamn, Swe. (krēs-tē'nē-häm')	164	59.20 N	14.05 E
Kristinestad, Fin. (krĭs-tē'nĕ-städh)	165	62.16 N	21.28 E
Kriva-Palanka, Yugo. (krē-vȧ-pȧ-läŋ'kȧ)	173	42.12 N	22.21 E
Krivoye Ozero, Sov. Un.	175	47.57 N	30.21 E
Krivoy Rog, Sov. Un. (krē-voi' rôgh')	175	47.54 N	33.22 E
Križevci, Yugo. (krē'zhĕv-tsĭ)	172	46.02 N	16.30 E
Krk (I.), Yugo. (k'rk)	172	45.06 N	14.33 E
Krnov, Czech. (k'r'nôf)	167	50.05 N	17.41 E
Krokodil (R.), S. Afr. (krŏ'kō-dī)	223d	24.25 S	27.08 E
Krolevets, Sov. Un. (krô-lĕ'vyĕts)	175	51.33 N	33.21 E
Kroměříž, Czech. (krô'myĕr-zhēzh)	167	49.18 N	17.23 E
Kromy, Sov. Un. (krô'mē)	174	52.44 N	35.41 E
Kronshtadt, Sov. Un. (krōn'shtät)	182c	59.59 N	29.47 E
Kroonstad, S. Afr. (krōn'shtät)	223d	27.40 S	27.15 E
Kropotkin, Sov. Un. (krȧ-pôt'kĭn)	179	45.25 N	40.30 E
Krosno, Pol. (krôs'nō)	167	49.41 N	21.46 E
Krotoszyn, Pol. (krô-tô'shĭn)	167	51.41 N	17.25 E
Krško, Yugo. (k'rsh'kō)	172	45.58 N	15.30 E
Kruger Natl. Park, S. Afr. (krōō'gẽr) (krü'gẽr)	226	23.22 S	30.18 E
Krugersdorp, S. Afr. (krōō'gẽrz-dôrp)	227b	26.06 S	27.46 E
Krugersdorp West, S. Afr.	71b	26.06 S	27.45 E
Krujë, Alb. (krōō'yȧ)	173	41.32 N	19.49 E
Krummenerl, F.R.G.	63	51.05 N	7.45 E

PRONOUNCING INDEX Krummensee – Lafayette 303

PLACE (Pronounciation)	PAGE	Lat. °′	Long. °′
Krummensee, G.D.R.	65a	52.36 N	13.42 E
Krung Thep (Bangkok), Thai.	206	13.50 N	100.29 E
Kruševac, Yugo. (kro͞o'shĕ-vȧts)	173	43.34 N	21.21 E
Kruševo, Yugo.	173	41.20 N	21.15 E
Krylatskoje (Neigh.), Sov. Un.	66b	55.45 N	37.26 E
Krylbo, Swe. (krŭl'bô)	164	60.07 N	16.14 E
Krymskaya, Sov. Un. (krĭm'skȧ-yȧ)	175	44.58 N	38.01 E
Krymskaya (Oblast), Sov. Un.	175	45.08 N	34.05 E
Krymskiy P-Ov (Crimea) (Pen.), Sov. Un. (krĕm-skĭ pô-lo͞o-ôs'trôf)	175	45.18 N	33.30 E
Krynki, Pol. (krĭn'kė)	167	53.15 N	23.47 E
Kryukov, Sov. Un. (k'r'yo͞o-kôf')	175	49.02 N	33.26 E
Ksar Chellala, Alg.	171	35.12 N	2.20 E
Ksar-el-Kebir, Mor.	160	35.01 N	5.48 W
Ksar-es-Souk, Mor.	160	31.58 N	4.25 W
K2 (Godwin Austen), Pak. (gŏd wĭn ôs'tĕn)	198	36.06 N	76.38 E
Kuai (R.), China (ko͞o-ī)	200	33.30 N	116.56 E
Kuala Klawang, Mala.	191b	2.57 N	102.04 E
Kuala Lumpur, Mala. (kwä'lä lo͞om-po͞or')	191b	3.08 N	101.42 E
Kuandian, China (ku̇än-dĭĕn)	202	40.40 N	124.50 E
Kuba, Sov. Un. (ko͞o'bȧ)	179	41.05 N	48.30 E
Kuban' (R.), Sov. Un. (ko͞o-bȧn'')	175	45.10 N	37.55 E
Kuban (R.), Sov. Un.	179	45.20 N	40.05 E
Kuban R., Sov. Un.	161	45.14 N	38.20 E
Kubenskoye (L.), Sov. Un.	178	59.40 N	39.40 E
Kuching, Mala. (ko͞o'chĭng)	206	1.30 N	110.26 E
Kuchinoerabo (I.), Jap. (ko͞o'chê nō ĕr'ä-bō)	205	30.31 N	129.53 E
Küçükbakkal, Tur.	66f	40.58 N	29.06 E
Kudamatsu, Jap. (ko͞o'dȧ-mä'tso͞o)	205	34.00 N	131.51 E
Kudap, Indon.	191b	1.14 N	102.30 E
Kudat, Mala. (ko͞o-dät')	206	6.56 N	116.48 E
Kudbrooke (Neigh.), Eng.	62	51.28 N	0.03 E
Kudirkos Naumietis, Sov. Un. (ko͞odĭr-kôs nå'o͞o-mĕ'tĭs)	165	54.51 N	23.00 E
Kudymkar, Sov. Un. (ko͞o-dĭm-kär')	180	58.43 N	54.52 E
Kufstein, Aus. (ko͞of'shtīn)	166	47.34 N	12.11 E
Kuhstedt, F.R.G. (ko͞o'shtĕ)	157c	53.23 N	8.58 E
Kuibyshev, see Kuybyshev			
Kuilsrivier, S. Afr.	226a	33.56 S	18.41 E
Kuito, Ang.	230	12.22 S	16.56 E
Kuji, Jap.	205	33.57 N	131.18 E
Kujū-san (Mt.), Jap. (ko͞o'jo͞o-sän')	205	33.07 N	131.14 E
Kukës, Alb. (ko͞o'kĕs)	173	42.03 N	20.25 E
Kula, Bul. (ko͞o'lȧ)	173	43.52 N	23.13 E
Kula, Tur.	179	38.32 N	28.30 E
Kula Kangri Mt., China	196	33.11 N	90.36 E
Kular, Khrebet (Mts.), Sov. Un. (ko͞o-lär')	181	69.00 N	131.45 E
Kuldīga, Sov. Un. (ko͞ol'dê-gȧ)	165	56.59 N	21.59 E
Kulebaki, Sov. Un. (ko͞o-lĕ-bäk'ĭ)	178	55.22 N	42.30 E
Küllenhahn (Neigh.), F.R.G.	63	51.14 N	7.08 E
Kulmbach, F.R.G. (klo͞olm'bäκ)	166	50.07 N	11.28 E
Kulunda, Sov. Un. (ko͞o-lo͞on'dȧ)	180	52.38 N	74.00 E
Kulundinskoye (L.), Sov. Un.	180	52.45 N	77.18 E
Kum (R.), Kor. (ko͞om)	204	36.50 N	127.30 E
Kuma (R.), Sov. Un. (ko͞o'mä)	179	44.50 N	45.10 E
Kumamoto, Jap. (ko͞o'mä-mō'tô)	205	32.49 N	130.40 E
Kumano-Nada (Sea), Jap. (ko͞o-mä'nō nä-dä)	205	34.03 N	136.36 E
Kumanovo, Yugo. (ko͞o-mä'nô-vô)	173	42.10 N	21.41 E
Kumasi, Ghana (ko͞o-mä'sė)	228	6.41 N	1.35 W
Kumba, Cam. (ko͞om'bȧ)	229	4.38 N	9.25 E
Kumbakonam, India (ko͞om'bŭ-kō'nŭm)	197	10.59 N	79.25 E
Kumkale, Tur.	173	39.59 N	26.10 E
Kumo, Nig.	229	10.03 N	11.13 E
Kumta, India	197	14.19 N	75.28 E
Kumul, see Hami			
Kunashak, Sov. Un. (kû-nä'shȧk)	182a	55.43 N	61.35 E
Kunashir (Kunashiri) (I.), Sov. Un. (ko͞o-nŭ-shēr')	199	44.40 N	145.45 E
Kunashiri (I.), see Kunashir			
Kunda, Sov. Un. (ko͞on'dȧ)	174	59.30 N	26.28 E
Kundelungu, Plateau des (Plat.), Zaire	222	9.00 S	25.30 E
Kundravy, Sov. Un. (ko͞on'drȧ-vĭ)	182a	54.50 N	60.14 E
Kundur (I.), Indon.	191b	0.49 N	103.20 E
Kunene (Cunene) (R.), Ang.-Namibia	230	17.05 S	12.35 E
Kungälv, Swe. (kŭng'ĕlf)	164	57.53 N	12.01 E
Kungrad, Sov. Un. (ko͞on-grät')	155	42.59 N	59.00 E
Kungsbacka, Swe. (kŭngs'bä-kȧ)	164	57.31 N	12.04 E
Kungur, Sov. Un. (ko͞on-go͞or')	182a	57.27 N	56.53 E
Kunitachi, Jap.	69a	35.41 N	139.26 E
Kunlun Shan (Mts.), China (ko͞on-lo͞on shän)	198	35.26 N	83.09 E
Kunming, China (ko͞on-mĭŋ)	203	25.10 N	102.50 E
Kunsan, Kor. (ko͞on'sän')	203	35.54 N	126.46 E
Kunshan, China (ko͞onshän)	201b	31.23 N	120.57 E
Kuntsëvo, Sov. Un. (ko͞on-tsyô'vô)	182b	55.43 N	37.27 E
Kun'ya (R.), Sov. Un. (ko͞on'yȧ)	174	56.45 N	30.53 E
Kun'ya, Sov. Un.	182a	58.42 N	56.47 E
Kuopio, Fin. (ko͞o-ô'pê-ŏ)	158	62.48 N	28.30 E
Kupa (R.), Yugo.	172	45.32 N	14.50 E
Kupang, Indon.	207	10.14 S	123.37 E
Kupavna, Sov. Un.	182b	55.49 N	38.11 E
Kupferdreh (Neigh.), F.R.G.	63	51.23 N	7.05 E
Kupino, Sov. Un. (ko͞o-pī'nô)	180	54.00 N	77.47 E
Kupiškis, Sov. Un. (ko͞o-pĭsh'kĭs)	141	55.50 N	24.55 E
Kupyansk, Sov. Un. (ko͞op-yänsk')	175	49.44 N	37.38 E
Kuqa, China (ko͞o-chyä)	198	41.34 N	82.44 E
Kura (R.), Sov. Un. (ko͞o'rȧ)	179	41.10 N	45.40 E
Kurashiki, Jap. (ko͞o'rä-shē'kė)	205	34.37 N	133.44 E
Kuraymah, Sud.	225	18.34 N	31.49 E
Kurayoshi, Jap. (ko͞o'rȧ-yō'shė)	205	35.25 N	133.49 E
Kurdistan (Reg.), Tur.-Iran (kûrd'ĭ-stăn)	179	37.40 N	43.30 E
Kurdufān (Prov.), Sud. (kôr-dô-fän')	225	14.08 N	28.39 E
Kŭrdzhali, Bul.	173	41.39 N	25.21 E
Kure, Jap. (ko͞o'rĕ)	205	34.17 N	132.35 E
Kuressaare, Sov. Un. (ko͞o'rĕ-sä'rĕ)	165	58.15 N	22.26 E
Kurgan, Sov. Un. (ko͞or-găn')	180	55.28 N	65.14 E
Kurgan Tyube, Sov. Un. (ko͞or-găn' tyo͞o'bĕ)	180	38.00 N	68.49 E
Kurihama, Jap. (ko͞o-rē-hä'mä)	205a	35.14 N	139.42 E
Kuril Is., Sov. Un. (ko͞o'rĭl)	181	46.20 N	149.30 E
Ku-ring-gai, Austl.	70a	33.45 S	151.08 E
Kurisches Haff (Bay), Sov. Un.	165	55.10 N	21.08 E
Kurl (Neigh.), F.R.G.	63	51.35 N	7.35 E
Kurla (Neigh.), India	197b	19.03 N	72.53 E
Kurmuk, Sud. (ko͞or'mo͝ok)	225	10.40 N	34.13 E
Kurnell, Austl.	70a	34.01 S	151.13 E
Kurnool, India (ko͞or-no͞ol')	197	16.00 N	78.04 E
Kuro (I.), Jap. (ko͞o'rô)	205	30.49 N	129.56 E
Kurrajong, Austl.	211b	33.33 S	150.40 E
Kuršenai, Sov. Un. (ko͞or'shȧ-nī)	155	56.01 N	22.56 E
Kursk (Oblast), Sov. Un. (ko͞orsk)	165	51.30 N	35.13 E
Kursk, Sov. Un. (ko͞orsk)	165	51.44 N	36.08 E
Kuršumlija, Yugo. (ko͞or'sho͞om'lĭ-yȧ)	163	43.08 N	21.18 E
Kūrtī, Sud.	225	18.08 N	31.39 E
Kuruçeşme (Neigh.), Tur.	66f	41.03 N	29.02 E
Kuruman, S. Afr. (ko͞o-ro͞o-män')	226	27.25 S	23.30 E
Kurume, Jap.	69a	35.45 N	139.32 E
Kurume, Jap. (ko͞o'ro͞o-mĕ)	205	33.10 N	130.30 E
Kururi, Jap. (ko͞o'ro͞o-rê)	205a	35.17 N	140.05 E
Kusa, Sov. Un. (ko͞o'sȧ)	182a	55.19 N	59.27 E
Kushchëvskaya, Sov. Un.	175	46.34 N	39.40 E
Kushikino, Jap. (ko͞o'shĭ-kē'nō)	205	31.44 N	130.19 E
Kushimoto, Jap. (ko͞o'shĭ-mō'tō)	205	33.29 N	135.47 E
Kushiro, Jap. (ko͞o'shē-rō)	204	43.00 N	144.22 E
Kush-Murun (L.), Sov. Un. (ko͞osh-mo͞o-ro͞on')	180	52.30 N	64.15 E
Kushum (R.), Sov. Un. (ko͞o-sho͞om')	179	50.30 N	50.40 E
Kushva, Sov. Un. (ko͞osh'vȧ)	182a	58.18 N	59.51 E
Kuskokwim (R.), Ak.	107	61.32 N	160.36 W
Kuskokwim B., Ak. (kŭs'kô-kwĭm)	107	59.25 N	163.14 W
Kuskokwim Mts., Ak.	107	62.08 N	158.00 W
Kuskovak, Ak. (kŭs-kō'văk)	107	60.10 N	162.50 W
Kuskovo (Neigh.), Sov. Un.	66b	55.44 N	37.49 E
Kustanay, Sov. Un. (ko͞os-tȧ-nī')	180	53.10 N	63.39 E
Kūstī, Sud.	225	13.09 N	32.39 E
Kütahya, Tur. (kû-tä'hyȧ)	179	39.20 N	29.50 E
Kutaisi, Sov. Un. (ko͞o-tŭ-ē'sē)	179	42.15 N	42.40 E
Kutaradja, Indon.	206	5.30 N	95.20 E
Kutch, Gulf of, India	196	22.45 N	68.33 E
Kutch, Rann of (Swp.), India	196	23.59 N	69.13 E
Kutenholz, F.R.G. (ko͞o'tĕn-hōlts)	157c	53.29 N	9.20 E
Kutim, Sov. Un. (ko͞o'tĭm)	182a	60.22 N	58.51 E
Kutina, Yugo. (ko͞o'tĕ-nȧ)	172	45.29 N	16.48 E
Kutno (L.), Sov. Un.	178	65.15 N	31.30 E
Kutno, Pol. (ko͞ot'nō)	167	52.14 N	19.22 E
Kutulik, Sov. Un. (ko͞o to͞o'lyĭk)	179	53.12 N	102.51 E
Kuty, Sov. Un. (ko͞o'tė)	167	48.16 N	25.12 E
Kuusamo, Fin. (ko͞o'sȧ-mô)	158	65.59 N	29.10 E
Kuvshinovo, Sov. Un. (ko͞ov-shē'nō-vō)	174	57.01 N	34.09 E
Kuwait, Asia	190	29.00 N	48.45 E
Kuwait, see Al Kuwayt			
Kuwana, Jap. (ko͞o'wȧ-nȧ)	205	35.02 N	136.40 E
Kuybyshev, (Kuibyshev), Sov. Un. (ko͞o'ē-bĭ-shĭf)	178	53.10 N	50.05 E
Kuybyshevskoye (Res.), Sov. Un.	178	53.40 N	49.00 E
Kuz'minki (Neigh.), Sov. Un.	66b	55.42 N	37.48 E
Kuzneckovo, Sov. Un.	182b	55.29 N	38.22 E
Kuznetsk, Sov. Un. (ko͞oz-nyĕtsk')	179	53.00 N	46.30 E
Kuznetsk Basin, Sov. Un.	180	57.15 N	86.15 E
Kuznetsovka, Sov. Un. (ko͞oz-nyĕt'sôf-kȧ)	182a	54.41 N	56.40 E
Kuznetsovo, Sov. Un. (ko͞oz-nyĕt-sô'vô)	174	56.39 N	36.55 E
Kuznetsy, Sov. Un.	182b	55.50 N	38.39 E
Kvarner Zaliv (B.), Yugo. (kvär'nĕr)	172	44.41 N	14.05 E
Kvichak, Ak. (vĭc'-hȧk)	107	59.00 N	156.48 W
Kwa (R.), Zaire	230	3.00 S	16.45 E
Kwahu Plat., Ghana	228	7.00 N	1.35 W
Kwando (R.), Zambia	230	16.50 S	22.40 E
Kwango (Cuango) (R.), Afr. (kwäng'ō')	230	6.35 S	16.50 E
Kwangwazi, Tan.	231	7.47 S	38.15 E
Kwa-Thema, S. Afr.	71b	26.18 S	28.23 E
Kwekwe, Zimb.	226	18.49 S	29.45 E
Kwenge (R.), Zaire (kwĕŋ'gē)	230	6.45 S	18.23 E
Kwidzyń, Pol. (kvē'dzĭn)	167	53.45 N	18.56 E
Kwilu (R.), Zaire (kwē'lo͞o)	230	3.22 S	17.22 E
Kyakhta, Sov. Un. (kyäκ'ta)	181	51.00 N	107.30 E
Kyaukpyu, Bur. (chouk'pyoo')	198	19.19 N	93.33 E
Kyayisu (R.), India	196	38.05 N	74.36 E
Kybartai, Sov. Un. (kē'bär-tī')	165	54.40 N	22.46 E
Ky Lam, Viet.	203	15.48 N	108.30 E
Kyn, Sov. Un. (kĭn')	182a	57.52 N	58.42 E
Kynuna, Austl. (kī-no͞o'nȧ)	215	21.30 S	142.12 E
Kyoga, L., Ug.	231	1.30 N	32.45 E
Kyōga-Saki (C.), Jap. (kyō'gä sa'kė)	205	35.46 N	135.14 E
Kyŏngju, Kor. (kyŭng'yo͞o)	204	35.48 N	129.12 E
Kyōto, Jap. (ky 'tō')	205b	35.00 N	135.46 E
Kyōto (Pref.), Jap.	205b	34.56 N	135.42 E
Kyren, Sov. Un. (kĭ-rĕn')	180	51.46 N	102.13 E
Kyrönjoki (R.), Fin.	165	63.03 N	22.20 E
Kyrya, Sov. Un. (kĕr'yȧ)	182a	59.18 N	59.03 E
Kyshtym, Sov. Un. (kĭsh-tĭm')	182a	55.43 N	60.33 E
Kytlym, Sov. Un. (kĭt'lĭm)	182a	59.30 N	59.15 E
Kyūhōji (Neigh.), Jap.	69b	34.38 N	135.35 E
Kyūshū (I.), Jap. (kyo͞o'sho͞o')	205	32.27 N	131.03 E
Kyustendil, Bul. (kyo͞os-tĕn-dĭl')	173	42.16 N	22.39 E
Kyzyl, Sov. Un. (kĭ zĭl)	180	51.37 N	93.38 E
Kyzyl Kum, Peski (Des.), Sov. Un. (kĭ zĭl ko͞om)	155	42.47 N	64.45 E
Kzyl-Orda, Sov. Un. (kzĕl-ôr'dȧ)	180	44.58 N	65.45 E

L

PLACE (Pronounciation)	PAGE	Lat. °′	Long. °′
Laa, Aus.	166	48.42 N	16.23 E
Laab im Walde, Aus.	66e	48.09 N	16.11 E
Laaken (Neigh.), F.R.G.	63	51.15 N	7.15 E
La Almunia de Doña Godina, Sp. (lä'äl-mo͞on'yä dā dō nyä gô-dē'nä)	170	41.29 N	1.22 W
Laas Caanood, Som.	223a	8.24 N	47.20 E
La Asunción, Ven. (lä ä-so͞on-syōn')	142	11.02 N	63.57 W
La Baie, Can.	103	48.21 N	70.53 W
La Banda, Arg. (lä bän'dä)	144	27.48 S	64.12 W
La Bandera, Chile	61b	33.34 S	70.39 W
La Barca, Mex. (lä bär'kȧ)	130	20.17 N	102.33 W
Labé, Gui. (lȧ-bā')	228	11.19 N	12.17 W
Labe (R.), see Elbe			
Laberge (L.), Can. (lȧ-bĕrzh')	96	61.08 N	136.42 W
Laberinto de las Doce Leguas (Is.), Cuba (lä-bå-rēn tô dä läs dō'så lā'gwäs)	134	20.40 N	78.35 W
Labinsk, Sov. Un.	179	44.30 N	40.40 E
Labis, Mala. (läb'ĭs)	191b	2.23 N	103.01 E
La Bisbal, Sp. (lä bēs-bäl')	171	41.55 N	3.00 E
Labo, Phil. (lä'bô)	207a	14.11 N	122.49 E
La Boissière, Fr.	64c	48.46 N	1.59 E
Labo, Mt., Phil.	207a	14.00 N	122.47 E
Labouheyre, Fr. (lȧ-bo͞o-âr')	168	44.14 N	0.58 W
Laboulaye, Arg. (lä-bô'o͞o-lä-yĕ)	144	34.01 S	63.10 W
Labrador (Reg.), Can. (lăb'rȧ-dôr)	97	53.05 N	63.30 W
Labrador Sea, Can.	105	50.38 N	55.00 W
Lábrea, Braz. (lä-brā'ä)	142	7.28 S	64.39 W
Labuan, Pulau (I.), Mala. (lä-bo͞o-än')	206	5.28 N	115.11 E
Labuha, Indon.	207	0.43 S	127.35 E
L'Acadie, Can. (lȧ-kȧ-dē')	95a	45.18 N	73.22 W
L'Acadie (R.), Can.	95a	45.24 N	73.21 W
La Calera, Chile (lä-kä-lĕ-rä)	141b	32.47 S	71.11 W
La Calera, Col.	142a	4.43 N	73.58 W
Lac Allard, Can.	105	50.38 N	63.28 W
La Canada, Ca. (lä kän-yä'dä)	119a	34.13 N	118.12 W
La Candelaria, Mex.	60a	19.20 N	99.09 W
Lacantum (R.), Mex. (lä-kän-to͞o'm)	131	16.13 N	90.52 W
La Carolina, Sp. (lä kä-rô-lē'nä)	170	38.16 N	3.48 W
La Catedral, Cerro (Mtn.), Mex. (sĕ'r-rô-lä-kä-tĕ-drȧ'l)	131a	19.32 N	99.31 W
Lac-Beauport, Can. (läk-bō-pōr')	95b	46.58 N	71.17 W
Laccadive Sea, Asia	196	9.10 N	75.17 E
Laccodive Is., see Lakshadweep			
Lac Court Oreille Ind. Res., Wi. (lăk kôrt-ô-rĕl) (lăk ko͞or tô-rā'y')	115	46.04 N	91.18 W
Lac du Flambeau Ind. Res., Wi.	115	46.12 N	89.50 W
La Ceiba, Hond. (lä sēbä)	132	15.45 N	86.52 W
La Ceja, Col. (lä-sĕ-κä)	142a	6.02 N	75.25 W
Lac-Frontière, Can.	97	46.42 N	70.00 W
Lacha (L.), Sov. Un. (lá'chä)	178	61.15 N	39.05 E
La Chaux de Fonds, Switz. (lȧ shō dē-fôɴ')	166	47.07 N	6.47 E
Lach Dera (R.), Som. (läk dā'rä)	223a	0.45 N	41.26 E
L'Achigan (R.), Can. (lä-shē-gäɴ)	95a	45.49 N	73.48 W
Lachine, Can. (lȧ-shēn')	95a	45.26 N	73.40 W
Lachlan (R.), Austl. (läk'lăn)	216	33.54 S	145.15 E
La Chorrera, Pan. (làchôr-rā'rä)	128a	8.54 N	79.47 W
Lachta (Neigh.), Sov. Un.	66a	60.00 N	30.09 E
Lachute, Can. (lȧ-sho͞ot')	95a	45.39 N	74.20 W
La Ciotat, Fr. (lȧ syô-tȧ')	169	43.13 N	5.35 E
La Cisterna, Chile	61b	33.33 S	70.41 W
Lackawanna, NY (lak-ȧ-wŏn'ȧ)	113c	42.49 N	78.50 W
Lac la Biche, Can.	99	54.46 N	112.58 W
La Columna (Mtn.), see Bolivar			
Lacombe, Can.	99	52.28 N	113.44 W
La Concordia, Mex. (lä-kôn-kô'r-dyä)	131	16.07 N	92.40 W
Laconia, NH (lȧ-kō'nĭ-ȧ)	111	43.30 N	71.30 W
La Conner, Wa. (lȧ kŏn'ĕr)	118a	48.23 N	122.30 W
La Coruña, Sp. (lä kô-ro͞on'yä)	170	43.20 N	8.20 W
La Courneuve, Fr.	64c	48.56 N	2.23 E
Lacreek (L.), SD (lă'krēk)	114	43.04 N	101.46 W
La Cresenta, Ca. (lȧ krĕs'ĕnt-ȧ)	119a	34.14 N	118.13 W
La Cross, Ks. (lȧ-krôs')	122	38.30 N	99.20 W
La Crosse, Wi.	115	43.48 N	91.14 W
La Cruz, Col. (lȧ kro͞oz')	142	1.37 N	77.00 W
La Cruz, C. R. (lä-kro͞o'z)	132	11.05 N	85.37 W
Lac Simard, (L.), Can.	103	47.38 N	78.40 W
Lacs, Riviere des (R.), ND (rē-vyĕr' de läk)	114	48.30 N	101.45 W
La Cuesta, C. R. (lä-kwĕ's-tä)	133	8.32 N	82.51 W
La Culebra, Sierra de (Mts.), Sp. (sē-ĕ'r-rä-dĕ-lä-ko͞o-lĕ-brä)	170	41.52 N	6.21 W
La Cygne, Ks. (lȧ-sēn'y') (lȧ-sēn')	123	38.20 N	94.45 W
Ladd, Il. (lăd)	110	41.25 N	89.25 W
Ladíspoli, It. (lä-dē's-pô-lē)	171d	41.57 N	12.05 E
Lādīz, Iran	195	28.56 N	61.19 E
Ladner, Can. (lăd'nĕr)	118d	49.05 N	123.05 W
Lādnun, India (läd'no͞on)	196	27.45 N	74.20 E
Ladoga, Lake, see Ladozhskoye Ozero			
La Dolorita, Ven.	61a	10.29 N	66.47 W
La Dorado, Col. (lä dô-rä'dä)	142a	5.28 N	74.42 W
Ladozhskoye Ozero (Ladoga, L.), Sov. Un. (lȧ-dôsh'skô-yĕ ô'zĕ-rô)	165	60.59 N	31.30 E
La Durantaye, Can. (lä dü-răɴ-tā')	95b	46.51 N	70.51 W
Lady Frere, S. Afr. (lā-dē frâ'r')	227c	31.48 S	27.16 E
Lady Grey, S. Afr.	227c	30.44 S	27.17 E
Ladysmith, Can. (lā'dĭ-smĭth)	98	48.58 N	123.49 W
Ladysmith, S. Afr.	227c	28.38 S	29.48 E
Ladysmith, Wi.	115	45.27 N	91.07 W
Lae, Pap. N. Gui. (lä'ā)	207	6.15 S	146.57 E
Laerdalsøyri, Nor.	164	61.08 N	7.26 E
Laesø (I.), Den. (lâs'û)	164	57.17 N	10.57 E
La Esperanza, Hond. (lä ĕs-pȧ-rän'zä)	132	14.20 N	88.21 W
La Estrada, Sp. (lä ĕs-trä'dä)	170	42.42 N	8.29 W
Lafa, China (lä'fä)	204	43.49 N	127.19 E
Lafayette, Al.	126	32.52 N	85.25 W

ŋ-sing; ŋ-baŋk; ɴ-nasalized n; nŏd; cŏmmit; ōld; ôbey; ôrder; oi-boil; fo͞od; fo͝ot; ou-out; s-soft; sh-dish; th-thin; pūre; ůnite; ûrn; stŭd; circŭs; ü-as in French tu; '-indeterminate vowel.

PLACE (Pronounciation)	PAGE	Lat. °′	Long. °′
Lafayette, Ca.	118b	37.53 N	122.07 W
Lafayette, Ga. (lă-fā-yĕt′)	126	34.41 N	85.19 W
Lafayette, In.	110	40.25 N	86.55 W
Lafayette, La.	125	30.15 N	92.02 W
La Fayette, RI	112b	41.34 N	71.29 W
Lafayette Hill, Pa.	56b	40.05 N	75.15 W
Laferrere, Arg.	60d	34.45 S	58.35 W
La Ferté-Alais, Fr. (lä-fĕr-tā′ä-lā′)	169b	48.29 N	2.19 E
La Ferté-sous-Jouarre, Fr. (lá fĕr-tā′sōō-zhōō-är′)	169b	48.56 N	3.07 E
Lafia, Nig.	229	8.30 N	8.30 E
Lafiagi, Nig.	229	8.52 N	5.25 E
Laflèche, Can.	54b	45.30 N	73.28 W
La Flèche, Fr. (lá flâsh′)	168	47.43 N	0.03 W
La Floresta, Sp.	65e	41.27 N	2.04 E
La Florida, Chile	61b	33.27 S	70.33 W
La Follete, Tn. (lä-fŏl′ĕt)	126	36.23 N	84.07 W
Lafourche, Bay., La. (bä-yōō′lá-fōōrsh′)	125	29.25 N	90.15 W
La Frette-sur-Seine, Fr.	64c	48.58 N	2.11 E
La Gaiba, Braz. (lä-gī′bä)	143	17.54 S	57.32 W
Lagan, N. Ire. (lā′găn)	162	54.30 N	6.00 W
Lågan (R.), Nor. (lô′ghĕn)	164	59.15 N	9.47 E
Lagan (R.), Swe.	164	56.34 N	13.25 E
La Garenne-Colombes, Fr.	64c	48.55 N	2.15 E
Lagarto, R., Pan. (lä-gä′r-tô)	128a	9.08 N	80.05 W
Lagartos L., Mex. (lä-gä′r-tôs)	132a	21.32 N	88.15 W
Laghouat, Alg. (lä-gwät′)	224	33.45 N	2.49 E
Lagny, Fr. (län-yē′)	169b	48.53 N	2.41 E
Lagoa da Prata, Braz. (lä-gô′ä-dä-prä′tä)	141a	20.04 S	45.33 W
Lagoa Dourada, Braz. (lä-gô′ä-dōō-rä′dä)	141a	20.55 S	44.03 W
Lagogne, Fr. (laN-gōn′y′)	168	44.43 N	3.50 E
Lagonay, Phil.	207a	13.44 N	123.31 E
Lagonoy G., Phil. (lä-gô-noi′)	207a	13.34 N	123.46 E
Lagos, Nig. (lä′gōs)	229	6.27 N	3.24 E
Lagos, Port. (lä′gōzh)	170	37.08 N	8.43 W
Lagos de Moreno, Mex. (lä′gōs dā mō-rā′nō)	130	21.21 N	101.55 W
La Grand′ Combe, Fr. (lá grän kaNb′)	168	44.12 N	4.03 E
La Grande, Or. (lá grănd′)	116	45.20 N	118.06 W
La Grande (R.), Can.	97	53.55 N	77.30 W
La Grange, Austl. (lä grānj)	214	18.40 S	122.00 E
La Grange, Ga. (lá-grānj′)	126	33.01 N	85.00 W
La Grange, Il.	113a	41.49 N	87.53 W
Lagrange, In.	110	41.40 N	85.25 W
La Grange, Ky.	110	38.20 N	85.25 W
La Grange, Mo.	123	40.04 N	91.30 W
Lagrange, Oh.	113d	41.14 N	82.07 W
Lagrange, Tx.	125	29.55 N	96.50 W
La Grange Highlands, Il.	58a	41.48 N	87.53 W
La Grange Park, Il.	58a	41.50 N	87.52 W
La Granja, Chile	61b	33.32 S	70.39 W
La Grita, Ven. (lä grē′tä)	142	8.02 N	71.59 W
La Guaira, Ven. (lä gwä′ē-rä)	143b	10.36 N	66.54 W
La Guardia, Sp. (lä gwär′dē-ä)	170	41.55 N	8.48 W
La Guardia Arpt., NY	55	40.46 N	73.53 W
Laguna, Braz. (lä-gōō′nä)	144	28.19 S	48.42 W
Laguna, Cayos (Is.), Cuba (kä′yōs-lä-gōō′nä)	134	22.15 N	82.45 W
Laguna de Bay (L.), Phil. (lä-gōō′nä dā bä′ē)	207a	14.24 N	121.13 E
Laguna Ind. Res., NM	121	35.00 N	107.30 W
Lagunillas, Bol. (lä-gōō-nēl′yäs)	142	19.42 S	63.38 W
Lagunillas, Mex. (lä-gōō-nē′l-yäs)	130	21.34 N	99.41 W
La Habana (Havana), Cuba (lä-ä-bä′nä)	135a	23.08 N	82.23 W
La Habra, Ca. (lá hăb′rá)	119a	34.56 N	117.57 W
La Habra Heights, Ca.	59	33.57 N	117.57 W
Lahaina, Hi. (lä-hä′ē-nä)	106a	20.52 N	156.39 W
La Häy-les-Roses, Fr.	64c	48.47 N	2.21 E
Lāhījān, Iran	195	37.12 N	50.01 E
Laholm, Swe. (lä′hôlm)	164	56.30 N	13.00 E
La Honda, Ca. (lä hôn′dä)	118b	37.20 N	122.16 W
Lahore, Pak. (lä-hōr′)	196	32.00 N	74.18 E
Lahr, F.R.G. (lär)	166	48.19 N	7.52 E
Lahti, Fin. (lä′tē)	165	60.59 N	27.39 E
Lai, Chad.	229	9.29 N	16.18 E
Lai′an, China (lī-än)	200	32.27 N	118.25 E
Laibin, China (lī-bĭn)	203	23.42 N	109.20 E
Lai, C., Viet.	203	17.08 N	107.30 E
L′Aigle, Fr. (lĕ′gl′)	168	48.45 N	0.37 E
Lainate, It.	65c	45.34 N	9.02 E
Lainz (Neigh.), Aus.	66e	48.11 N	16.17 E
Laisamis, Ken.	231	1.36 N	37.48 E
Laiyang, China (läī′yäng)	200	36.59 N	120.42 E
Laizhou Wan (B.), China (lī-jō wän)	200	37.22 N	119.19 E
Laja, Río de la (R.), Mex. (rē′ō-dĕ-lä-lá′Kä)	130	20.17 N	100.57 W
Lajas, Cuba (lä′häs)	134	22.25 N	80.20 W
Lajeado, Braz. (lä-zhĕä′dô)	144	29.24 S	51.46 W
Lajeado Velho (Neigh.), Braz.	61d	23.32 S	46.23 W
Laje, Ponta da (C.), Port.	65d	38.40 N	9.19 W
Lajes, Braz. (lá′zhĕs)	144	27.47 S	50.17 W
Lajinha, Braz. (lä-zhē′nyä)	141a	20.08 S	41.36 W
La Jolla, Ca. (lá hoi′yá)	120a	32.51 N	117.16 W
La Jolla Ind. Res., Ca.	120	33.19 N	116.21 W
La Junta, Co. (lá hōōn′tá)	122	37.59 N	103.35 W
Lake Arrowhead, Ca.	59	33.52 N	118.05 W
Lake Arthur, La. (är′thŭr)	125	30.06 N	92.40 W
Lake Barcroft, Va.	56d	38.51 N	77.09 W
Lake Barkley (Res.), Tn.	126	36.45 N	88.00 W
Lake Benton, Mn. (bĕn′tŭn)	114	44.15 N	96.17 W
Lake Bluff, Il. (blŭf)	113a	42.17 N	87.50 W
Lake Brown, Austl. (broun)	214	31.03 S	118.30 E
Lake Charles, La. (chärlz′)	125	30.15 N	93.14 W
Lake City, Fl.	127	30.09 N	82.40 W
Lake City, Ia.	115	42.14 N	94.43 W
Lake City, Mn.	115	44.28 N	92.19 W
Lake City, SC	127	33.57 N	79.45 W
Lake Cowichan, Can. (kou′ĭ-chán)	98	48.50 N	124.03 W
Lake Crystal, Mn. (krĭs′tál)	115	44.05 N	94.12 W
Lake Dist., Eng. (lāk)	162	54.25 N	3.20 W
Lake Elmo, Mn. (ĕlmō)	119g	45.00 N	92.53 W
Lake Forest, Il. (fŏr′ĕst)	113a	42.16 N	87.50 W
Lake Fork (R.), Ut.	121	40.30 N	110.25 W
Lake Geneva, Wi. (jĕ-nē′vá)	115	42.36 N	88.28 W
Lake Harbour, Can. (här′bĕr)	97	62.43 N	69.40 W
Lake Havasu City, Az.	120	34.27 N	114.22 W
Lake June, Tx. (jōōn)	119c	32.43 N	96.45 W
Lakeland, Fl. (lāk′lănd)	127a	28.02 N	81.58 W
Lakeland, Ga.	126	31.02 N	83.02 W
Lakeland, Mn.	119g	44.57 N	92.47 W
Lake Linden, Mi. (lĭn′dĕn)	115	47.11 N	88.26 W
Lake Louise, Can. (lōō-ēz′)	99	51.26 N	116.11 W
Lakemba, Austl.	70a	33.55 S	151.05 E
Lake Mills, Ia. (mĭlz′)	115	43.25 N	93.32 W
Lakemore, Oh. (lāk-mōr)	113d	41.01 N	81.24 W
Lake Odessa, Mi.	110	42.50 N	85.15 W
Lake Oswego, Or. (ŏs-wē′go)	118c	45.25 N	122.40 W
Lake Placid, NY	111	44.17 N	73.59 W
Lake Point, Ut.	119b	40.41 N	112.16 W
Lakeport, Ca. (lāk′pōrt)	120	39.03 N	122.54 W
Lake Preston, SD (prēs′tŭn)	114	44.21 N	97.23 W
Lake Providence, La. (prŏv′ĭ-dĕns)	125	32.48 N	91.12 W
Lake Red Rock (Res.), Ia.	115	41.30 N	93.15 W
Lake Sharpe (Res.), SD	114	44.30 N	100.00 W
Lakeside, Ca. (lāk′sīd)	120a	32.52 N	116.55 W
Lakeside, S. Afr.	71b	26.06 S	28.09 E
Lake Station, In.	113a	41.34 N	87.15 W
Lake Stevens, Wa.	118a	48.01 N	122.04 W
Lake Success, NY (sŭk-sĕs′)	112a	40.46 N	73.43 W
Lakeview, Ca. (lāk-vū′)	119a	33.50 N	117.07 W
Lakeview (Neigh.), Il.	58a	41.57 N	87.39 W
Lakeview, Or.	116	42.11 N	120.21 W
Lake Village, Ar.	123	33.20 N	91.17 W
Lake Wales, Fl. (wālz′)	127a	27.54 N	81.35 W
Lakewood, Ca. (lāk′wŏŏd)	119a	33.50 N	118.09 W
Lakewood, Co.	122	39.44 N	105.06 W
Lakewood, Oh.	113d	41.29 N	81.48 W
Lakewood, Pa.	111	40.05 N	74.10 W
Lakewood, Wa.	118a	48.09 N	122.13 W
Lakewood Center, Wa.	118a	47.10 N	122.31 W
Lake Worth, Fl. (wûrth′)	127a	26.37 N	80.04 W
Lake Worth Village, Tx.	119c	32.49 N	97.26 W
Lake Zürich, Il. (tsü′rĭk)	113a	42.11 N	88.05 W
Lakhdenpokh′ya, Sov. Un. (l′äk-dĭe′npōKyá)	165	61.33 N	30.10 E
Lakhtinskiy, Sov. Un. (lák-tĭn′skĭ)	182c	59.59 N	30.10 E
Lakota, ND (lá-kō′tá)	114	48.04 N	98.21 W
Lakshadweep (State), India	197	10.10 N	72.50 E
Lakshadweep Is. (Laccadive Is.), India	197	11.00 N	73.02 E
Laleham, Eng.	62	51.25 N	0.30 W
La Libertad, Guat. (lä lē-bĕr-tädh′)	132	15.31 N	91.44 W
La Libertad, Guat.	132a	16.46 N	90.12 W
La Libertad, Sal.	132	13.29 N	89.20 W
La Ligua, Chile (lä lē′gwä)	141b	32.21 S	71.13 W
La Lisa, Cuba	60b	23.04 N	82.26 W
Lalitpur, Nep.	196	27.23 N	85.24 E
Lalín, Sp. (lä-lē′n)	170	42.40 N	8.05 W
La Línea, Sp. (lä lē′nā-ä)	170	36.11 N	5.22 W
La Louviere, Bel. (lá lōō-vyâr′)	163	50.30 N	4.10 E
La Luz, Mex. (lä lōōz′)	130	21.04 N	101.19 W
Lama-Kara, Togo	228	9.33 N	1.12 E
La Malbaie, Can. (lá mäl-bâ′)	103	47.39 N	70.10 W
La Mancha (Mts.), Sp. (lä män′chä)	170	38.55 N	4.20 W
Lamar, Co. (lá-mär′)	122	38.04 N	102.44 W
Lamar, Mo.	123	37.28 N	94.15 W
La Marmora, Pta. (Mtn.), It. (lä-mä′r-mô-rä)	174	40.00 N	9.28 E
La Marque, Tx. (lâ-märk)	125a	29.23 N	94.58 W
Lamas, Peru (lä′más)	142	6.24 S	76.41 W
Lamballe, Fr. (läN-bäl′)	168	48.29 N	2.36 W
Lambaréné, Gabon (läN-bá-rā-nā′)	230	0.42 S	10.13 E
Lambari, Braz. (läm-bá′rē)	141a	21.58 S	45.22 W
Lambayeque, Peru (läm-bä-yā′kå)	142	6.41 S	79.58 W
Lambert, Ms. (lăm′bērt)	126	34.10 N	90.16 W
Lambertville, NJ (lăm′bērt-vĭl)	111	40.20 N	75.00 W
Lambeth (Neigh.), Eng.	62	51.30 N	0.07 W
Lambourne End, Eng.	62	51.38 N	0.08 E
Lambrate (Neigh.), It.	65c	45.29 N	9.15 E
Lambro (R.), It.	65c	45.26 N	9.16 E
Lambton, S. Afr.	71b	26.15 S	28.10 E
Lame Deer, Mt. (lām dēr′)	117	45.36 N	106.40 W
Lamego, Port. (lä-mā′gō)	170	41.07 N	7.47 W
La Mesa, Ca. (lä mā′sä)	120a	32.46 N	117.01 W
La Mesa, Col.	142a	4.38 N	74.27 W
Lamesa, Tx.	122	32.44 N	101.54 W
La Mirada, Ca.	59	33.54 N	118.01 W
Lamía, Grc. (lá-mē′á)	173	38.54 N	22.25 E
Lamon B., Phil. (lä-mōn′)	207a	14.35 N	121.52 E
La Mora, Chile (lä-mō′rä)	141b	32.28 S	70.56 W
La Mott, Pa.	56b	40.04 N	75.08 W
La Moure, ND (lá mōōr′)	114	46.23 N	98.17 W
Lampa (R.), Chile (lá′m-pä)	141b	33.15 S	70.55 W
Lampasas, Tx. (lăm-păs′ás)	124	31.06 N	98.10 W
Lampasas R., Tx.	124	31.18 N	98.08 W
Lampazos, Mex. (läm-pä′zōs)	124	27.03 N	100.30 W
Lampedusa (I.), It. (läm-på-dōō′sä)	159	35.29 N	12.58 E
Lamstedt, F.R.G. (läm′shtĕt)	157c	53.38 N	9.06 E
Lamu, Ken. (lä′mōō)	231	2.16 S	40.54 E
Lamu I., Ken.	231	2.25 S	40.50 E
La Mure, Fr. (lá mür′)	169	44.55 N	5.50 E
Lan′ (R.), Sov. Un. (lán′)	174	52.38 N	27.05 E
Lanai (I.), Hi. (lä-nä′ē)	106a	20.48 N	157.06 W
Lanai City, Hi.	106a	20.50 N	156.56 W
Lanak La (P.), China	196	34.40 N	79.50 E
La Nao, Cabo de (C.), Sp. (ká′bô-dĕ-lä-nä′ō)	171	38.43 N	0.14 E
Lanark, Scot. (lăn′árk)	162	55.40 N	3.50 W
Lancashire (Co.), Scot. (lăŋ′ká-shĭr)	156	53.49 N	2.42 W
Lancaster, Can. (lăŋ′kás-tēr)	104	45.15 N	66.06 W
Lancaster, Eng.	162	54.04 N	2.55 W
Lancaster, Ky.	110	37.35 N	84.30 W
Lancaster, Ma.	105a	42.28 N	71.40 W
Lancaster, NH	111	44.25 N	71.30 W
Lancaster, NY	113c	42.54 N	78.42 W
Lancaster, Oh.	110	39.40 N	82.35 W
Lancaster, Pa.	111	40.05 N	76.20 W
Lancaster, Tx.	119c	32.36 N	96.45 W
Lancaster, Wi.	115	42.51 N	90.44 W
Lândana, Ang. (län-dä′nä)	226	5.15 S	12.07 E
Landau, F.R.G. (län′dou)	166	49.13 N	8.07 E
Lander, Wy. (lăn′dēr)	117	42.49 N	108.24 W
Landerneau, Fr. (läN-dĕr-nō′)	168	48.28 N	4.14 W
Landes (Plain), Fr. (läNd)	168	44.22 N	0.52 W
Landover, Md.	56d	38.56 N	76.54 W
Landsberg, F.R.G. (länds′bĕrgh)	157d	48.03 N	10.53 E
Lands End Pt., Eng.	162	50.03 N	5.45 W
Landshut, F.R.G. (länts′hōōt)	166	48.32 N	12.09 E
Landskrona, Swe. (láns-krōō′ná)	164	55.51 N	12.47 E
Lane Cove, Austl.	70a	33.49 S	151.10 E
Lanett, Al. (lá-nĕt′)	126	32.52 N	85.13 W
Langadhás, Grc.	173	40.44 N	24.10 E
Langat (R.), Mala.	191b	2.46 N	101.33 E
Langdon, Can. (lăng′dŭn)	95e	50.58 N	113.40 W
Langdon, Mn.	119g	44.49 N	92.56 W
Langdon Hills, Eng.	62	51.34 N	0.25 E
L′Ange-Gardien, Can. (läNzh gár-dyăN′)	95b	46.55 N	71.06 W
Langeland (I.), Den.	164	54.52 N	10.46 E
Langenberg, F.R.G.	63	51.21 N	7.09 E
Langenbochum, F.R.G.	63	51.37 N	7.07 E
Langendreer (Neigh.), F.R.G.	63	51.28 N	7.19 E
Langenhorst, F.R.G.	63	51.22 N	7.02 E
Langenthal, Switz.	169	47.11 N	7.50 E
Langenzersdorf, Aus.	157e	48.30 N	16.22 E
Langesund, Nor. (läng′ĕ-sŏŏn′)	164	58.59 N	9.38 E
Langfjorden (Fd.), Nor.	164	62.40 N	7.45 E
Langhorne, Pa. (lăng′hôrn)	112f	40.10 N	74.55 W
Langhorne Acres, Md.	56d	38.51 N	77.16 W
Langia Mts., Ug.	231	3.35 N	33.35 E
Langjökoll (Glacier), Ice. (läng-yû′kōōl)	158	64.40 N	20.31 W
Langla Co. (L.), China (läŋ-lä tswo)	196	30.42 N	80.40 E
Langlade (I.), Saint Pierre & Miquelon	103	46.50 N	56.20 W
Langley, Can. (lăng′lĭ)	118d	49.06 N	122.39 W
Langley, Md.	56d	38.57 N	77.10 W
Langley, SC	127	33.32 N	81.52 W
Langley, Wa.	118a	48.02 N	122.25 W
Langley Ind. Res., Can.	118d	49.12 N	122.31 W
Langley Park, Md.	56d	38.59 N	76.59 W
Langnau, Switz. (läng′nou)	166	46.56 N	7.46 E
Langon, Fr. (läN-gôN′)	168	44.34 N	0.16 W
Langres, Fr. (läN′gr′)	168	47.53 N	5.20 E
Langres, Plateau de (Plat.), Fr. (plä-tō′dĕ-läN′grĕ)	168	47.39 N	5.00 E
Langsa, Indon. (läng′sá)	206	4.33 N	97.52 E
Lang Son, Viet. (läng′sŏn′)	206	21.52 N	106.42 E
Langst-Kierst, F.R.G.	63	51.18 N	6.43 E
L′Anguille (R.), Ar. (läN-gē′y′)	123	35.23 N	90.52 W
Langxi, China (läŋ-shyē)	200	31.10 N	119.09 E
Langzhong, China (läŋ-jôŋ)	203	31.40 N	106.05 E
Lanham, Md. (lăn′ăm)	112e	38.58 N	76.54 W
Lanigan, Can. (lăn′ĭ-gán)	100	51.52 N	105.02 W
Lank-Latum, F.R.G.	63	51.18 N	6.41 E
Lankoviri, Nig.	229	9.00 N	11.25 E
Lankwitz (Neigh.), F.R.G.	65a	52.26 N	13.21 E
Lansdale, Pa. (lănz′dāl)	111	40.20 N	75.15 W
Lansdowne, Austl.	70a	33.54 S	150.59 E
Lansdowne, Md.	56c	39.15 N	76.40 W
Lansdowne, Pa.	112f	39.57 N	75.17 W
L′Anse, Mi. (láns)	115	46.43 N	88.28 W
L′Anse and Vieux Desert Ind. Res., Mi.	115	46.41 N	88.12 W
Lansford, Pa. (lănz′fērd)	120	40.50 N	75.50 W
Lansing, Ia.	115	43.22 N	91.16 W
Lansing, Il.	113a	41.34 N	87.33 W
Lansing, Ks.	119f	39.15 N	94.53 W
Lansing, Mi.	110	42.45 N	84.35 W
Lansing (Neigh.), Can.	54c	43.45 N	79.25 W
Lantianchang, China	67b	39.58 N	116.17 E
Lanús, Arg. (lä-nōōs′)	144a	34.27 S	58.24 W
Lanusei, It. (lä-nōō-sĕ′y)	172	39.51 N	9.34 E
Lanúvio, It. (lä-nōō′vyô)	171d	41.41 N	12.42 E
Lanzarote I., Can. Is. (län-zá-rō′tä)	224	29.04 N	13.03 W
Lanzhou, China (län-jō)	202	35.55 N	103.55 E
Laoag, Phil. (lä-wäg′)	206	18.13 N	120.38 E
Lao Ho (R.), China (lä′ō hō′)	199	43.37 N	120.05 E
Laohumiao, China	67b	39.58 N	116.20 E
Laon, Fr. (läN)	168	49.36 N	3.35 E
La Oroya, Peru (lä-ô-rō′yä)	142	11.30 S	76.00 W
Laos, Asia (lä-ōs) (lá-ōs′)	206	20.15 N	102.00 E
Laoshan Wan (B.), China (lou-shän wän)	200	36.21 N	120.48 E
Lapa (Neigh.), Braz.	61c	22.55 S	43.11 W
La Palma, Pan. (lä-päl′mä)	133	8.25 N	78.07 W
La Palma, Sp.	170	37.24 N	6.36 W
La Palma I., Can. Is.	224	28.42 N	19.03 W
La Pampa (Prov.), Arg.	144	37.25 S	67.00 W
Lapa Rio Negro, Braz. (lä-pä-rē′ō-nĕ′grô)	144	26.12 S	49.56 W
La Paternal (Neigh.), Arg.	60d	34.36 S	58.28 W
La Paz, Arg. (lä päz′)	144	30.48 S	59.47 W
La Paz, Bol.	143	16.31 S	68.03 W
La Paz, Hond.	132	14.15 N	87.40 W
La Paz, Mex. (lä-pá′z)	130	23.39 N	100.44 W
La Paz, Mex.	128	24.00 N	110.15 W
Lapeer, Mi. (lá-pēr′)	110	43.05 N	83.15 W
La-Penne-sur-Huveaune, Fr. (la-pĕn′sür-ü-vōn′)	168a	43.18 N	5.33 E
La Perouse, Austl.	70a	33.59 S	151.14 E
La Piedad Cabadas, Mex. (lä pyå-dhädh′ kä-bä′dhäs)	130	20.20 N	102.04 W

ăt; finăl; rāte; senāte; ärm; àsk; sofá; fâre; ch-choose; dh-as th in other; bē; ēvent; bĕt; recĕnt; cratēr; g-gō; gh-guttural g; bĭt; ĭ-short neutral; rīde; K-guttural k as ch in German ich;

PRONOUNCING INDEX

Lapland – Le Moule 305

PLACE (Pronounciation)	PAGE	Lat. °'	Long. °'
Lapland (Reg.), Eur. (lăp'lănd)	158	68.20 N	22.00 E
La Plata, Arg. (lä plä'tä)	141c	34.54 S	57.57 W
La Plata, Mo. (lȧ plā'tȧ)	123	40.03 N	92.28 W
La Plata Pk., Co.	121	39.00 N	106.25 W
La Playa, Cuba	60b	23.06 N	82.27 W
La Pocatière, Can. (lȧ pō-kȧ-tyâr')	104	47.24 N	70.01 W
La Poile B., Can. (lȧ pwäl')	105	47.38 N	58.20 W
La Porte, In. (lȧ pōrt')	110	41.35 N	86.45 W
Laporte, Oh.	113d	41.19 N	82.05 W
La Porte, Tx.	125a	29.40 N	95.01 W
La Porte City, Ia.	115	42.20 N	92.10 W
Lappeenranta, Fin. (lä'pēn-rän'tä)	165	61.04 N	28.08 E
La Prairie, Can. (lȧ-prâ-rē')	95a	45.24 N	73.30 W
Lâpseki, Tur. (läp'sȧ-kē)	173	40.20 N	26.41 E
Laptev Sea, Sov. Un. (läp'tyĭf)	176	75.39 N	120.00 E
La Puebla, Sp. (lä pwā'blä)	171	39.46 N	3.02 E
La Puebla de Montalbán, Sp. (lä pwā'blä dā mōnt-äl-bän')	170	39.54 N	4.21 W
La Puente, Ca. (pwĕn'tē)	119a	34.01 N	117.57 W
La Punta, Peru	60c	12.05 S	77.10 W
Lapusul (R.), Rom. (lä'pōō-shōōl)	167	47.29 N	23.46 E
La Queue-en-Brie, Fr.	64c	48.47 N	2.35 E
La Quiaca, Arg. (lä kē-ä'kä)	144	22.15 S	65.44 W
L'Aquila, It. (lä'kē-lä)	172	42.22 N	13.24 E
Lār, Iran (lär)	192	27.31 N	54.12 E
Lara, Austl.	211a	38.02 S	144.24 E
Larache, Mor. (lä-räsh')	224	35.15 N	6.09 W
Laramie (R.), Co.	122	40.56 N	105.55 W
Laramie, Wy. (lăr'ȧ-mĭ)	108	41.20 N	105.40 W
Laranjeiras (Neigh.), Braz.	61c	22.56 S	43.11 W
Larchmont, NY (lärch'mŏnt)	112a	40.56 N	73.46 W
Larch Mtn., Or. (lärch)	118c	45.32 N	122.06 W
Laredo, Sp. (lȧ-rā'dhō)	170	43.24 N	3.24 W
Laredo, Tx.	124	27.31 N	99.29 W
La Reina, Chile	61b	33.27 S	70.33 W
La Réole, Fr. (lȧ rā-ōl')	168	44.37 N	0.03 W
Largeau, Chad (lär-zhō')	229	17.55 N	19.07 E
Largo, Cayo, Cuba (kä'yō-lär'gō)	134	21.40 N	81.30 W
Larimore, ND (lăr'ĭ-môr)	114	47.53 N	97.38 W
Larino, It. (lä-rē'nō)	172	41.48 N	14.54 E
La Rioja, Arg. (lä rē-ōhä)	144	29.18 S	67.42 W
La Rioja (Prov.), Arg. (lä-rē-ō'kä)	144	28.45 S	68.00 W
Lárisa, Grc. (lä'rē-sȧ)	173	39.38 N	22.25 E
Lārkāma, Pak.	196	27.40 N	68.12 E
Larkspur, Ca.	58b	37.56 N	122.32 W
Lárnakos, Kólpos (B.), Cyprus	191a	36.50 N	33.45 E
Lárnax, Cyprus	191a	34.55 N	33.37 E
Larned, Ks. (lär'nĕd)	122	38.09 N	99.07 W
La Robla, Sp. (lä rōb'lä)	170	42.48 N	5.36 W
La Rochelle, Fr. (lȧ rō-shĕl')	168	46.10 N	1.09 W
La Roche-sur-Yon, Fr. (lȧ rôsh'sûr-yôn')	168	46.39 N	1.27 W
La Roda, Sp. (lä rō'dä)	170	39.13 N	2.08 W
La Romona, Dom. Rep. (lä-rä-mô'nä)	135	18.25 N	69.00 W
Larrey Pt., Austl. (lăr'ē)	214	19.15 S	118.15 E
Laruns, Fr. (lȧ-răns')	168	42.58 N	0.28 W
Larvik, Nor. (lär'vēk)	164	59.06 N	10.03 E
La Sabana, Ven. (lä-sä-bȧ'nä)	143b	10.38 N	66.24 W
La Sabina, Cuba (lä-sä-bē'nä)	135a	22.51 N	82.16 W
La Sagra (Mtn.), Sp. (lä sä'grä)	170	37.56 N	2.35 E
La Sal, Ut. (lȧ sȧl')	121	38.10 N	109.20 W
La Salle, Can. (lȧ säl')	113b	42.14 N	83.06 W
La Salle, Can.	95a	45.26 N	73.39 W
La Salle, Can.	95f	49.41 N	97.16 W
La Salle, Il.	110	41.20 N	89.05 W
Las Animas, Co. (lȧs ä'nĭ-mȧs)	122	38.03 N	103.16 W
La Sarre, Can.	103	48.43 N	79.12 W
Lascahobas, Hai. (läs-kä-ō'bȧs)	135	19.00 N	71.55 W
Las Cruces, Mex. (läs-krōō'sĕs)	131	16.37 N	93.54 W
Las Cruces, NM	121	32.20 N	106.50 W
La Selle, Massif De (Mts.), Hai. (lä'sĕl')	135	18.25 N	72.05 W
La Serena, Chile (lä-sĕ-rĕ'nä)	144	29.55 S	71.24 W
La Seyne, Fr. (lä-sân')	169	43.07 N	5.52 E
Las Flores, Arg. (läs flō'rĕs)	141c	36.01 S	59.07 W
Las Flores, Ven.	61a	10.34 N	66.56 W
Lashio, Bur. (lăsh'ē-ō)	198	22.58 N	98.03 E
Lashkarak, Iran	68h	35.49 N	51.36 E
Las Juntas, C. R. (läs-kōō'n-täs)	132	10.15 N	85.00 W
Las Maismas (Reg.), Sp. (läs-mī's-mäs)	170	37.05 N	6.25 W
Las Minas, Ven.	61a	10.27 N	66.52 W
La Solana, Sp. (lä-sō-lä-nä)	170a	38.56 N	3.13 W
Las Palmas, Pan.	133	8.08 N	81.30 W
Las Palmas de Gran Canaria, Can. Is. (läs päl'mäs)	224	28.07 N	15.28 W
La Spezia, It. (lä-spĕ'zyä)	172	44.07 N	9.48 E
Las Piedras, Ur. (läs-pyĕ'drȧs)	141c	34.42 S	56.08 W
Las Pilas (Vol.), Nic. (läs-pē'läs)	132	12.32 N	86.43 W
Las Rejas, Chile	61b	33.28 S	70.44 W
Las Rosas, Mex. (läs rō thäs)	131	16.24 N	92.23 W
Las Rozas de Madrid, Sp. (läs rō'thas dā mä-dhrēd')	171a	40.29 N	3.53 W
Lassee, Aus.	157e	48.14 N	16.50 E
Lassen Pk., Ca. (lăs'ĕn)	116	40.30 N	121.32 W
Lassen Volcanic Natl. Park, Ca.	116	40.43 N	121.35 W
L'Assomption, Can. (lȧs-sôm-syôn)	95a	45.50 N	73.25 W
Lass Qoray, Som.	223a	11.13 N	48.19 E
Las Tablas, Pan. (läs tä'bläs)	133	7.48 N	80.16 W
Last Mountain (L.), Can. (lȧst moun'tĭn)	100	51.05 N	105.10 W
Lastoursville, Gabon (lȧs-tōōr-vēl')	226	1.00 S	12.49 E
Las Tres Virgenes, Vol., Mex. (vē'r-hĕ-nĕs)	128	26.00 N	111.45 W
Las Tunas (Prov.), Cuba	134	21.05 N	77.00 W
Las Vacas, Mex. (läs-vȧ'käs)	131	16.24 N	95.48 W
Las Vegas, Chile (läs-vĕ'gäs)	141b	30.50 S	70.59 W
Las Vegas, Nv. (läs vā'gȧs)	120	36.12 N	115.10 W
Las Vegas, NM	122	35.36 N	105.13 W
Las Vegas, Ven. (läs-vĕ'gäs)	143b	10.26 N	64.08 W
Las Vigas, Mex.	130	19.38 N	97.03 W
Las Vizcachas, Meseta de (Plat.), Arg. (mĕ-sĕ'tä-dĕ-läs-vēz-kä'chȧs)	144	49.35 S	71.00 W
Latacunga, Ec. (lä-tä-kōōŋ'gä)	142	1.02 S	78.33 W
Latakia, see Al Lādhiqīah			
La Teste-de-Buch, Fr. (lä-tĕst-dĕ-büsh)	168	44.38 N	1.11 W
Lathrop, Mo. (lā'thrŭp)	123	39.32 N	94.21 W
Latimer, Eng.	62	51.41 N	0.33 W
Latium (Reg.), see Lazio			
Latoritsa R., Sov. Un. (lȧ-tô'rĭ-tsȧ)	167	48.27 N	22.30 E
Latourell, Or. (lȧ-tou'rĕl)	118c	45.32 N	122.13 W
La Tremblade, Fr. (lä-trĕn-bläd')	168	45.45 N	1.12 W
Latrobe, Pa. (lȧ-trōb')	111	40.25 N	79.15 W
Lattingtown, NY	55	40.54 N	73.36 W
La Tuque, Can. (lȧ'tük')	97	47.27 N	72.49 W
Lātūr, India (lä-tōōr')	197	18.20 N	76.35 E
Latvian (S. S. R.), Sov. Un.	176	57.28 N	24.29 E
Launceston, Austl. (lôn'sĕs-tŭn)	216	41.35 S	147.22 E
Launceston, Eng. (lôrn'stŏn)	162	50.38 N	4.26 W
La Unión, Chile (lä-ōō-nyō'n)	144	40.15 S	73.04 W
La Unión, Mex. (lä ōōn-nyōn')	130	17.59 N	101.48 W
La Unión, Sal.	132	13.18 N	87.51 W
La Unión, Sp.	171	37.38 N	0.50 W
Laupendahl, F.R.G.	63	51.21 N	6.56 E
Laura, Austl. (lôrȧ)	215	15.40 S	144.45 E
Laura, Sov. Un. (lou'rȧ)	174	57.36 N	27.29 E
Laurel, De. (lô'rĕl)	111	38.30 N	75.40 W
Laurel, Md.	112e	39.06 N	76.51 W
Laurel, Ms.	126	31.42 N	89.07 W
Laurel, Mt.	117	45.41 N	108.45 W
Laurel, Wa.	118d	48.52 N	122.29 W
Laurel Gardens, Pa.	57b	40.31 N	80.01 W
Laurel Hollow, NY	55	40.52 N	73.28 W
Laurelwood, Or. (lô'rĕl-wŏŏd)	118c	45.25 N	123.05 W
Laurens, SC (lô'rĕnz)	127	34.29 N	82.03 W
Laurentian Highlands (Reg.), Can. (lô'rĕn-tĭ-ăn)	94	49.00 N	74.50 W
Laurentides, Can. (lô'rĕn-tīdz)	95a	45.51 N	73.46 W
Lauria, It. (lou'rē-ä)	172	40.03 N	15.02 E
Laurinburg, NC (lô'rĭn-bûrg)	127	34.45 N	79.27 W
Laurium, Mi. (lô'rĭ-ŭm)	115	47.13 N	88.28 W
Lausanne, Switz. (lō-zȧn')	166	46.32 N	6.35 E
Lautaro, Chile (lou-tä'rō)	144	38.40 S	72.24 W
Laut Kecil, Kepulauan (Is.), Indon.	206	4.44 S	115.43 E
Laut, Pulau (I.), Indon.	206	3.39 S	116.07 E
Lauzon, Can. (lō-zōn')	95b	46.50 N	71.10 W
Lava Beds Natl. Mon., Ca. (lä'vȧ bĕds)	116	41.38 N	121.44 W
Lavaca R., Tx. (lȧ-văk'ȧ)	125	29.05 N	96.50 W
Lava Hot Springs, Id.	117	42.37 N	111.58 W
Laval, Can.	95a	45.31 N	73.44 W
Laval, Fr. (lä-väl')	168	48.05 N	0.47 W
Laval-des-Rapides (Neigh.), Can.	54b	45.33 N	73.42 W
Laval-Ouest (Neigh.), Can.	54b	45.33 N	73.52 W
La Vecilla de Curueno, Sp.	170	42.53 N	5.18 W
La Vega, Dom. Rep. (lä-vĕ'gä)	135	19.15 N	70.35 W
La Vega (Neigh.), Ven.	61a	10.28 N	66.57 W
Lavella (I.), Sol. Is.	215	7.50 S	155.45 E
Lavello, It. (lä-vĕl'lō)	172	41.05 N	15.50 E
La Verne, Ca. (lȧ vûrn')	119a	34.06 N	117.46 W
Laverton, Austl. (lā'vẽr-tŭn)	214	28.45 S	122.30 E
La Victoria, Peru	60c	12.04 S	77.02 W
La Victoria, Ven. (lä vēk-tō'rē-ä)	143b	10.14 N	67.20 W
Lavonia, Ga. (lȧ-vō'nĭ-ȧ)	126	34.26 N	83.05 W
Lavon Res., Tx.	125	33.06 N	96.20 W
Lavras, Braz. (lä'vräzh)	141a	21.15 S	44.59 W
Lávrion, Grc. (läv'rĭ-ôn)	173	37.44 N	24.05 E
Lawndale, Ca. (lôn'dāl)	119a	33.54 N	118.22 W
Lawndale (Neigh.), Il.	58a	41.51 N	87.43 W
Lawndale (Neigh.), Pa.	56b	40.03 N	75.05 W
Lawnside, NJ	56b	39.52 N	75.03 W
Lawra, Ghana	228	10.39 N	2.52 W
Lawrence, In. (lô'rĕns)	113g	39.59 N	86.01 W
Lawrence, Ks.	123	38.57 N	95.13 W
Lawrence, Ma.	105a	42.42 N	71.09 W
Lawrence, Pa.	113e	40.18 N	80.07 W
Lawrenceburg, In. (lô'rĕns-bûrg)	113f	39.06 N	84.47 W
Lawrenceburg, Ky.	110	38.00 N	85.00 W
Lawrenceburg, Tn.	126	35.13 N	87.20 W
Lawrenceville, Ga. (lô-rĕns-vĭl)	126	33.56 N	83.57 W
Lawrenceville, Il.	110	38.45 N	87.45 W
Lawrenceville, NJ	112a	40.17 N	74.44 W
Lawrenceville (Neigh.), Pa.	57b	40.28 N	79.57 W
Lawrenceville, Va.	127	36.43 N	77.52 W
Lawsonia, Md. (lô-sō'nĭ-ȧ)	111	38.00 N	75.50 W
Lawton, Ok. (lô'tŭn)	122	34.36 N	98.25 W
Lawz, Jabal al (Mtn.), Sau. Ar.	192	28.46 N	35.37 E
Layang Layang, Mala. (lä-yäng' lä-yäng')	191b	1.49 N	103.28 E
Laysan (I.), Hi.	107b	26.00 N	171.00 W
Layton, Ut. (lā'tŭn)	119b	41.04 N	111.58 W
Lazdijai, Sov. Un. (läzh'dē-yī')	165	54.12 N	23.35 E
Lazio (Latium) (Reg.), It. (lä'zyô) (lȧ't-zēōōm)	172	42.05 N	12.25 E
Lead, SD (lēd)	114	44.22 N	103.47 W
Leader, Can.	100	50.55 N	109.32 W
Leadville, Co. (lĕd'vĭl)	122	39.14 N	106.18 W
Leaf (R.), Ms. (lēf)	126	31.43 N	89.20 W
League City, Tx. (lēg)	125a	29.31 N	95.05 W
Leamington, Can. (lĕm'ĭng-tŭn)	110	42.05 N	82.35 W
Leamington, Eng. (lĕ'mĭng-tŭn)	162	52.17 N	1.25 W
Leatherhead, Eng. (lĕdh'ẽr-hĕd')	156b	51.17 N	0.20 W
Leavenworth, Ks. (lĕv'ĕn-wûrth)	119f	39.19 N	94.54 W
Leavenworth, Wa.	116	47.35 N	120.39 W
Leawood, Ks. (lē'wŏŏd)	119f	38.58 N	94.37 W
Leba, Pol. (lā'bä)	167	54.45 N	17.34 E
Lebam R., Mala.	191b	1.35 N	104.09 E
Lebango, Con.	230	0.22 N	14.49 E
Lebanon, Asia	192	34.00 N	34.00 E
Lebanon, Il. (lĕb'ȧ-nŭn)	119e	38.36 N	89.49 W
Lebanon, In.	110	40.00 N	86.30 W
Lebanon, Ky.	126	37.32 N	85.15 W
Lebanon, Mo.	123	37.40 N	92.43 W
Lebanon, NH	111	43.40 N	72.15 W
Lebanon, Oh.	110	39.25 N	84.10 W
Lebanon, Or.	116	44.31 N	122.53 W
Lebanon, Pa.	111	40.20 N	76.20 W
Lebanon, Tn.	126	36.10 N	86.16 W
Lebanon Mts., Leb.	161	33.30 N	35.32 E
Lebedin, Sov. Un. (lyĕ'bĕ-dĕn)	175	48.56 N	31.35 E
Lebedin, Sov. Un.	175	50.34 N	34.27 E
Lebedyan', Sov. Un. (lyĕ'bĕ-dyän')	174	53.03 N	39.08 E
Le Blanc, Fr. (lĕ-blän')	168	46.38 N	0.59 E
Le Blanc-Mesnil, Fr.	64c	48.56 N	2.28 E
Leblon (Neigh.), Braz.	61c	22.59 S	43.13 W
Le Borgne, Hai. (lē bōrn'y')	135	19.50 N	72.30 W
Lebork, Pol. (lăn-bōōrk')	167	54.33 N	17.46 E
Le Bourget, Fr.	64c	48.56 N	2.26 E
Lebrija, Sp. (lå-brē'hä)	170	36.55 N	6.06 W
Lebú, Chile (lĕ-bōō')	144	37.35 S	73.37 W
Lecce, It. (lĕt'chā)	173	40.22 N	18.11 E
Lecco, It. (lĕk'kō)	172	45.52 N	9.28 E
Le Châtelet-en-Brie, Fr. (lĕ-shä-tĕ-lā'ĕn-brē')	169b	48.29 N	2.50 E
Leche, Laguna de (L.), Cuba (lä-gōō'nä-dĕ-lĕ'chĕ)	134	22.10 N	78.30 W
Leche, Laguna de la (L.), Mex.	124	27.16 N	102.45 W
Lech R., F.R.G. (lĕk)	166	47.41 N	10.52 E
Lecompte, La.	125	31.06 N	92.25 W
Le Creusot, Fr. (lĕkrû-zō')	168	46.48 N	4.23 E
Ledesma, Sp. (lå-dĕs'mä)	170	41.05 N	5.59 W
Ledsham, Eng.	64a	53.16 N	2.58 W
Leduc, Can. (lĕ-dōōk')	99	53.16 N	113.33 W
Leech (L.), Mn. (lēch)	115	47.06 N	94.16 W
Leeds, Al. (lēdz)	112h	33.33 N	86.33 W
Leeds, Eng.	156	53.48 N	1.33 W
Leeds, ND	114	48.18 N	99.24 W
Leeds and Liverpool Can., Eng. (lĭv'ẽr-pōōl)	156	53.36 N	2.38 W
Leegebruch, G.D.R. (lĕh'gĕn-brōōk)	157b	52.43 N	13.12 E
Leek, Eng. (lēk)	156	53.06 N	2.01 W
Lee Manor, Va.	56d	38.52 N	77.15 W
Leer, F.R.G. (lār)	166	53.14 N	7.27 E
Lees, Eng.	64b	53.32 N	2.04 W
Leesburg, Fl. (lēz'bûrg)	127	28.49 N	81.53 W
Leesburg, Va.	111	39.10 N	77.30 W
Lees Ferry, Az.	121	36.55 N	111.45 W
Lees Summit, Mo.	119f	38.55 N	94.23 W
Lee Stocking (I.), Ba.	135	23.45 N	76.05 W
Leesville, La. (lēz'vĭl)	125	31.09 N	93.17 W
Leetonia, Oh. (lē-tō'nĭ-ȧ)	110	40.50 N	80.45 W
Leeuwarden, Neth. (lā'wär-dĕn)	163	52.12 N	5.50 E
Leeuwin, C., Austl. (lōō'wĭn)	214	34.15 S	114.30 E
Leeward Is., N. A. (lē'wẽrd)	125	12.25 N	62.15 W
Le Francois, Mart.	133b	14.37 N	60.55 W
Lefroy (L.), Austl. (lē-froi')	214	31.30 S	122.00 E
Leganés, Sp. (lå-gä'nås)	171a	40.20 N	3.46 W
Legazpi, Phil. (lå-gäs'pē)	207a	13.09 N	123.44 E
Legge Pk., Austl. (lĕg)	216	41.33 S	148.10 E
Leghorn, see Livorno			
Legnano, It. (lå-nyä'nō)	172	45.35 N	8.53 E
Legnica, Pol. (lĕk-nĭt'sȧ)	166	51.13 N	16.10 E
Leh, India (lā)	196	34.10 N	77.40 E
Le Havre, Fr. (lē ȧv'r')	168	49.31 N	0.07 E
Lehi, Ut. (lē'hī)	121	40.25 N	111.55 W
Lehman Caves Natl. Mon., Nv. (lē'măn)	121	38.54 N	114.08 W
Lehnin, G.D.R. (lĕh'nēn)	157b	52.19 N	12.45 E
Leião, Port.	65d	38.44 N	9.18 W
Leicester, Eng. (lĕs'tẽr)	156	52.37 N	1.08 W
Leicestershire, (Co.), Eng.	156	52.40 N	1.12 W
Leichhardt, Austl.	70a	33.53 S	151.07 E
Leichhardt, (R.), Austl. (līk'härt)	214	18.30 S	139.45 E
Leiden, Neth. (lī'dĕn)	157a	52.09 N	4.29 E
Leigh Creek, Austl. (lē krēk)	216	30.33 S	138.30 E
Leikanger, Nor. (lī'kän'gẽr)	164	61.11 N	6.51 E
Leimuiden, Neth.	157a	52.13 N	4.40 E
Leine R., F.R.G. (lī'nĕ)	166	51.58 N	9.56 E
Leinster, Ire. (lĕn-stẽr)	162	52.45 N	7.19 W
Leipsic, Oh. (līp'sĭk)	110	41.05 N	84.00 W
Leipzig, G.D.R. (līp'tsĭk)	166	51.20 N	12.24 E
Leiria, Port. (lā-rē'ä)	170	39.45 N	8.50 W
Leitchfield, Ky. (lĕch'fēld)	126	37.28 N	86.20 W
Leitha (R.), Aus.	157e	48.04 N	16.57 E
Leithe (Neigh.), F.R.G.	63	51.29 N	7.06 E
Leitrim, Can.	95c	45.20 N	75.36 W
Leizhou Bandao (Pen.), China (lā-jō bän-dou)	203	20.42 N	109.10 E
Lékéti, Monts de la (Mts.), Con.	230	2.34 S	14.17 E
Le Kremlin-Bicêtre, Fr.	64c	48.49 N	2.21 E
Leksand, Swe. (lĕk'sänd)	164	60.45 N	14.56 E
Leland, Wa. (lē'lănd)	118a	47.54 N	122.53 W
Leliu, China (lŭ-lĭō)	201a	22.52 N	113.09 E
Le Locle, Switz. (lē lô'kl')	166	47.03 N	6.43 E
Le Maire, Estrecho de (Str.), Arg. (ĕs-trĕ'chō-dĕ-lĕ-mī'rĕ)	144	55.15 S	65.30 W
Le Mans, Fr. (lē män')	168	48.01 N	0.12 E
Le Marin, Mart.	133b	14.28 N	60.55 W
Le Mars, Ia. (lē märz')	114	42.46 N	96.09 W
Lemay, Mo.	119e	38.32 N	90.17 W
Lemdiyya, Alg.	224	36.18 N	2.40 E
Leme, Morro do (Hill), Braz.	61c	22.58 S	43.10 W
Lemery, Phil. (lā-mā-rē')	207a	13.51 S	120.55 E
Le Mesnil-Amelot, Fr.	64c	49.01 N	2.36 E
Le Mesnil-le-Roi, Fr.	64c	48.56 N	2.08 E
Lemesós, Cyprus	191a	34.39 N	33.02 E
Lemhi R., Id.	117	44.40 N	113.27 W
Lemhi Ra. (Mts.), Id. (lĕm'hī)	117	44.35 N	113.33 W
Lemmon, SD (lĕm'ŭn)	114	45.55 N	102.10 W
Le Môle, Hai. (lē mōl')	135	19.50 N	73.20 W
Lemon Grove, Ca. (lĕm'ŭn-grōv)	120a	32.44 N	117.02 W
Lemon Heights, Ca.	59	33.46 N	117.48 W
Lemont, Il. (lē'mŏnt)	113a	41.40 N	87.59 W
Le Moule, Guad. (lē mōōl')	133b	16.19 N	61.22 W

ng-sing; nŋ-baŋk; N-nasalized n; nŏd; cŏmmit; ōld; ôbey; ôrder; oi-boil; fōōd; fŏŏt; ou-out; s-soft; sh-dish; th-thin; pūre; ůnite; ûrn; stŭd; circŭs; ü-as in French tu; '-indeterminate vowel.

PLACE (Pronunciation)	PAGE	Lat. °'	Long. °'
LeMoyne, Can.	54b	45.31 N	73.29 W
Lempa R., Sal. (lĕm'pä)	132	13.20 N	88.46 W
Lemvig, Den. (lĕm'vĕgh)	164	56.33 N	8.16 E
Lena, Swe. (lĭ'nä)	164	60.01 N	17.40 E
Lençóes Paulista, Braz. (lĕɴ-sôɴs' pou-lēs'tá)	144	22.30 S	48.45 W
Lençóis, Braz. (lĕn-sóis)	143	12.38 S	41.28 W
Lenexa, Ks. (lē'nĕx-ă)	119f	38.58 N	99.44 W
Lenger, Sov. Un. (lyĭn'gyĕr)	155	41.38 N	70.00 E
Lengyandong, China (lŭŋ-yän-dôŋ)	201a	23.12 N	113.21 E
Lenik (R.), Mala.	191b	1.59 N	102.51 E
Leninabad, Sov. Un. (lĕ-nyē-ná bät')	180	40.15 N	69.49 E
Lenina, Gora (Hill), Sov. Un.	66b	55.42 N	37.31 E
Leninakan, Sov. Un. (lĕ-nyē-ná-kän')	179	40.40 N	43.50 E
Leningrad (Oblast), Sov. Un.	174	59.15 N	30.30 E
Leningrad, Sov. Un. (lyĕ-nĕn-grät')	182c	59.57 N	30.20 E
Leningradskaya, Sov. Un. (lyĕ-nĭn-gräd'ská-yá)	175	46.19 N	39.23 E
Lenino, Sov. Un. (lyĕ'nĭ-nô)	182b	55.37 N	47.41 E
Leninogorsk, Sov. Un. (lyĕ-nĭn ŭ gôrsk')	180	50.29 N	83.25 E
Leninsk, Sov. Un. (lyĕ-nēnsk')	179	48.40 N	45.10 E
Leninsk-Kuznetski, Sov. Un. (lyĕ-nēnsk'kōōz-nyĕt'skĭ)	180	54.28 N	86.48 E
Lenkoran', Sov. Un. (lĕn-kô-rän')	179	38.52 N	48.58 E
Lennox, Ca.	59	33.56 N	118.21 W
Lennox, SD (lĕn'ŭks)	114	43.22 N	96.53 W
Lenoir, NC (lē-nōr')	127	35.54 N	81.35 W
Lenoir City, Tn.	126	35.47 N	84.16 W
Lenox, Ia.	115	40.51 N	94.29 W
Lenz, S. Afr.	71b	26.19 S	27.49 E
Léo, Upper Volta	228	11.06 N	2.06 W
Leoben, Aus. (lå-ō'bĕn)	166	47.22 N	15.09 E
Léogane, Hai. (lā-ô-gan')	135	18.30 N	72.35 W
Leola, SD (lē-ō'lá)	114	45.43 N	99.55 W
Leominster, Ma. (lĕm'ĭn-stēr)	105a	42.32 N	71.45 W
Leon, Ia. (lē'ŏn)	115	40.43 N	93.44 W
León, Mex. (lå-ōn')	130	21.08 N	101.41 W
León, Nic. (lĕ-ô'n)	132	12.28 N	86.53 W
Leon (Reg.), Sp. (lĕ-ô'n)	170	41.18 N	5.50 W
León, Sp. (lĕ-ô'n)	170	42.38 N	5.33 W
Leonforte, It. (lā-ôn-fôr'tā)	172	37.40 N	14.27 E
Leonia, NJ	55	40.52 N	73.59 W
Leon R., Tx. (lē'ŏn)	124	31.54 N	98.20 W
Leopoldau (Neigh.), Aus.	66e	48.16 N	16.27 E
Leopold II, L., see Mai-Ndombe			
Leopoldina, Braz. (lā-ô-pôl-dē'nä)	141a	21.32 S	42.38 W
Léopold, Mont (Hill), Zaire	71c	4.19 S	15.15 E
Leopoldsburg, Bel.	157a	51.07 N	5.18 E
Leopoldsdorf im Marchfelde, Aus. (lā'ô-pôlts-dôrf')	157e	48.14 N	16.42 E
Leopoldstadt (Neigh.), Aus.	66e	48.13 N	16.23 E
Léopoldville, see Kinshasa			
Leovo, Sov. Un. (lå-ō'vô)	175	46.30 N	28.16 E
Lepe, Sp. (lā'pā)	170	37.15 N	7.12 W
Le Pecq, Fr.	64c	48.54 N	2.07 E
Lepel', Sov. Un. (lyĕ-pĕl')	174	54.52 N	28.41 E
Le Perreux-sur-Marne, Fr.	64c	48.51 N	2.30 E
Leping, China (lŭ-pĭŋ)	203	29.02 N	117.12 E
L'Épiphanie, Can. (lā-pē-fä-nē')	95a	45.51 N	73.29 W
Le Plessis-Belleville, Fr. (lĕ-plĕ-sē'bĕl-vēl')	169b	49.05 N	2.46 E
Le Plessis-Bouchard, Fr.	64c	49.00 N	2.14 E
Le Plessis-Trévise, Fr.	64c	48.49 N	2.34 E
Lepontine Alpi (Mts.), Switz. (lĕ-pŏn'tĭn)	166	46.28 N	8.38 E
Le Port-Marly, Fr.	64c	48.53 N	2.06 E
Lepreau, Can. (lĕ-prō')	104	45.10 N	66.28 W
Le Pré-Saint-Gervais, Fr.	64c	48.53 N	2.25 E
Lepsinsh, Sov. Un.	180	45.32 N	80.47 E
Le Puy, Fr. (lĕ pwē')	168	45.02 N	3.54 E
Le Raincy, Fr.	64c	48.54 N	2.31 E
Lercara Friddi, It. (lĕr-kä'rä)	172	36.47 N	13.36 E
Lerdo, Mex. (lĕr'dō)	124	25.31 N	103.30 W
Léré, Chad (lā-rā')	225	9.42 N	14.14 E
Léré, Mali	228	15.43 N	4.55 W
Leribe, Leso.	227c	28.53 S	28.02 E
Lérida, Sp. (lā'rē-dhä)	171	41.38 N	0.37 E
Lerma, Mex. (lĕr'mä)	131	19.49 N	90.34 W
Lerma, Mex.	131a	19.17 N	99.30 W
Lerma (R.), Mex.	130	20.14 N	101.50 W
Lerma, Sp. (lĕ'r-mä)	170	42.03 N	3.45 W
Le Roy, NY (lĕ roi')	111	43.00 N	78.00 W
Lerwick, Scot. (lĕr'ĭk) (lûr'wĭk)	162a	60.08 N	1.27 W
Léry, Can. (lā-rī')	95a	45.21 N	73.49 W
Lery, L., La. (lĕ'rē)	112d	29.48 N	89.45 W
Les Andelys, Fr. (lā-zäɴ-dĕ-lē')	169b	49.15 N	1.25 E
Les Cayes, Hai.	135	18.15 N	73.45 W
Les Cèdres, Can. (lā-sĕdr'')	95a	45.18 N	74.03 W
Les Clayes-sous-Bois, Fr.	64c	48.49 N	1.59 E
Les Grésillons, Fr.	64c	48.56 N	2.01 E
Lesh (Alessio), Alb. (lĕshĕ) (ä-lĕ'sē-ō)	173	41.47 N	19.40 E
Leshan, China (lŭ-shän)	203	29.40 N	103.40 E
Lésigny, Fr.	64c	48.45 N	2.37 E
Lésina, Lago di (L.), It. (lä'gō dē lā'zē-nä)	172	41.48 N	15.12 E
Leskovac, Yugo. (lĕs'kô-váts)	173	43.00 N	21.58 E
Leslie, Ar. (lĕz'lĭ)	123	35.49 N	92.32 W
Leslie, S. Afr.	223d	26.23 S	28.57 E
Les Lilas, Fr.	64c	48.53 N	2.25 E
Les Loges-en-Josas, Fr.	64c	48.46 N	2.09 E
Lesnoj (Neigh.), Sov. Un.	66a	60.00 N	30.19 E
Lesnoy, Sov. Un. (lĕs'noi)	178	66.45 N	34.45 E
Lesogorsk, Sov. Un. (lyĕs'ô-gôrsk)	204	49.28 N	141.59 E
Lesotho, Afr. (lĕsō'thō)	226	29.45 S	28.07 E
Lesozavodsk, Sov. Un. (lyĕ-sô-zá-vôdsk')	204	45.21 N	133.19 E
Les Pavillons-sous-Bois, Fr.	64c	48.55 N	2.30 E
Les Sables-d'Olonne, Fr. (lā sá'bl'dô-lŭn')	168	46.30 N	1.47 W
Les Saintes Is., Guad. (lā-săɴt')	133b	15.50 N	61.40 W
Lesser Khingan Range (Xiao Hinggan Ling), China (shyou hĭŋyän lĭŋ)	199	69.50 N	129.26 E
Lesser Slave (R.), Can.	99	55.15 N	114.30 W
Lesser Slave L., Can. (lĕs'ēr slāv)	99	55.25 N	115.30 W
Lesser Sunda Is., Indon.	206	9.00 S	120.00 E
L'Estaque, Fr. (lĕs-täl)	168a	43.22 N	5.20 E
Lester, Pa.	56b	39.52 N	75.17 W
Les Thilliers-en-Vexin, Fr. (lā-tē-yā'ĕɴ-vĕ-săɴ')	169b	49.19 N	1.36 E
Le Sueur, Mn. (lĕ sōōr')	115	44.27 N	93.53 W
Lésvos (I.), Grc.	173	39.15 N	25.40 E
Leszno, Pol. (lĕsh'nô)	166	51.51 N	16.35 E
Letchmore Heath, Eng.	62	51.40 N	0.20 W
Le Teil, Fr. (lĕ tā'y')	168	44.34 N	4.39 E
Le Temple, Fr.	64c	49.00 N	1.58 E
Lethbridge, Austl.	70a	33.44 S	150.48 E
Lethbridge, Can. (lĕth'brĭj)	99	49.42 N	112.50 W
Le Thillay, Fr.	64c	49.00 N	2.28 E
Letichev, Sov. Un. (lyĕ-tē-chĕf')	175	49.22 N	27.29 E
Leticia, Col. (lĕ-tē'syá)	142	4.04 S	69.57 W
Leting, China (lŭ-tĭŋ)	200	39.26 N	118.53 E
Letmathe, F.R.G. (lĕt'mät-hĕ)	169c	51.22 N	7.37 E
Le Tréport, Fr. (lē-trā'pôr')	168	50.03 N	1.21 E
Leuven (Louvain), Bel.	157a	50.53 N	4.42 E
Levack, Can.	102	46.38 N	81.23 W
Levádhia, Grc.	173	38.25 N	22.51 E
Le Val-d'Albian, Fr.	64c	48.45 N	2.11 E
Levallois-Perret, Fr. (lĕ-vål-wä'pĕ-rĕ')	169b	48.53 N	2.17 E
Levanger, Nor. (lĕ-väng'ĕr)	158	63.42 N	11.01 E
Levanna (Mtn.), Fr.-It. (lå-vä'nä)	172	45.25 N	7.14 E
Levenshulme (Neigh.), Eng.	64b	53.27 N	2.10 W
Leveque, C., Austl. (lē-vĕk')	214	16.26 S	123.08 E
Leverkusen, F.R.G. (lĕ'fĕr-kōō-zĕn)	169c	51.01 N	6.59 E
Le Vésinet, Fr.	64c	48.54 N	2.08 E
Levice, Czech. (lā'vĕt-sĕ)	167	48.13 N	18.37 E
Levico, It. (lā'vē-kō)	172	46.02 N	11.20 E
Le Vigan, Fr. (lĕ vē-gäɴ')	168	43.59 N	3.36 E
Lévis, Can. (lā-vē') (lē'vĭs)	95b	46.49 N	71.11 W
Levittown, NY	55	40.41 N	73.31 W
Levittown, Pa. (lĕ'vĭt-toun)	112f	40.08 N	74.50 W
Levkás, Grc. (lyĕfkäs')	173	38.49 N	20.43 E
Levkás (I.), Grc.	173	38.42 N	20.22 E
Levoča, Czech. (lā'vô-chá)	167	49.03 N	20.38 E
Levy (L.), Fl. (lē'vĭ)	127	29.31 N	82.23 W
Lewes, De. (lōō'ĭs)	111	38.45 N	75.10 W
Lewes, Eng.	162	50.51 N	0.01 E
Lewinsville, Va.	56d	38.54 N	77.12 W
Lewinsville Heights, Va.	56d	38.53 N	77.12 W
Lewis (R.) East Fk., Wa.	118c	45.52 N	122.40 W
Lewisburg, Tn. (lū'ĭs-bûrg)	126	35.27 N	86.47 W
Lewisburg, WV	110	37.50 N	80.20 W
Lewisdale, Md.	56d	38.58 N	76.58 W
Lewisham (Neigh.), Eng.	62	51.27 N	0.01 E
Lewisham, S. Afr.	71b	26.07 S	27.49 E
Lewis Hills, Can.	105	48.48 N	58.30 W
Lewis, I. of, Scot. (lōō'ĭs)	162	58.05 N	6.07 W
Lewisporte, Can. (lū'ĭs-pōrt)	105	49.15 N	55.04 W
Lewis R., Wa.	116	46.05 N	122.09 W
Lewis Ra., Mt. (lū'ĭs)	117	48.05 N	113.06 W
Lewiston, Id. (lū'ĭs-tŭn)	116	46.24 N	116.59 W
Lewiston, Me.	104	44.05 N	70.14 W
Lewiston, NY	113c	43.11 N	79.02 W
Lewiston, Ut.	117	41.58 N	111.51 W
Lewistown, Il. (lū'ĭs-toun)	123	40.23 N	90.06 W
Lewistown, Mt.	117	47.05 N	109.25 W
Lewistown, Pa.	111	40.35 N	77.30 W
L'Étang-la-Ville, Fr.	64c	48.52 N	2.05 E
Lexington, Ky. (lĕk'sĭng-tŭn)	110	38.05 N	84.30 W
Lexington, Ma.	105a	42.27 N	71.14 W
Lexington, Ms.	126	33.08 N	90.02 W
Lexington, Mo.	123	39.11 N	93.52 W
Lexington, Nb.	122	40.46 N	99.44 W
Lexington, NC	127	35.47 N	80.15 W
Lexington, Tn.	126	35.37 N	88.24 W
Lexington, Va.	111	37.45 N	79.20 W
Leybourne, Eng.	62	51.18 N	0.25 E
Leyte (I.), Phil. (lā'tā)	207	10.35 N	125.35 E
Lezajsk, Pol. (lĕ-zhä-ĭsk)	167	50.14 N	22.25 E
Lezha (R.), Sov. Un. (lĕ-zhä')	174	58.59 N	40.27 E
L'gov, Sov. Un. (lgôf)	175	51.42 N	35.15 E
Lhasa, China (läs'ä)	196	29.41 N	91.12 E
L'Hautil, Fr.	64c	49.00 N	2.01 E
Liangxiangzhen, China (lĭäŋ-shyäŋ-jŭn)	202a	39.43 N	116.08 E
Lianjiang, China (lĭĕn-jyäŋ)	203	21.38 N	110.15 E
Lianozovo, Sov. Un. (lĭ-a-nô'zô-vô)	182b	55.54 N	37.36 E
Lianshui, China (lĭĕn-shwā)	200	33.46 N	119.15 E
Lianyungang, China (lĭĕn-yōōn-gäŋ)	200	34.35 N	119.09 E
Liaocheng, China (lĭou-chŭŋ)	200	36.27 N	115.56 E
Liaodong Bandao (Pen.), China (lĭou-dôŋ bän-dou)	200	39.45 N	122.22 E
Liaodong Wan (B.), China (lĭou-dôŋ wäŋ)	202	40.25 N	121.15 E
Liaoning (Prov.), China	199	41.31 N	122.11 E
Liaoyang, China (lyä'ō-yäng')	202	41.18 N	123.10 E
Liaoyuan, China (lĭou-yüän)	202	43.00 N	124.59 E
Liard (R.), Can. (lē-är')	119	59.43 N	126.42 W
Libano, Col. (lē'bá-nô)	142a	4.55 N	75.05 W
Libby, Mt. (lĭb'ē)	116	48.27 N	115.35 W
Libenge, Zaire (lē-bĕŋ'gā)	225	3.39 N	18.40 E
Liberal, Ks. (lĭb'ēr-ăl)	122	37.01 N	100.56 W
Liberdade (Neigh.), Braz.	61d	23.35 S	46.37 W
Liberec, Czech. (lē'bĕr-ĕts)	166	50.45 N	15.06 E
Liberia, Afr. (lī-bē'rĭ-ă)	222	6.30 N	9.55 W
Liberia, C. R.	132	10.38 N	85.28 W
Libertad, Arg.	60d	34.42 S	58.38 W
Libertad de Orituco, Ven. (lē-bĕr-tä'd-dĕ-ô-rē-tōō'kô)	143b	9.32 N	66.24 W
Liberty, In. (lĭb'ēr-tĭ)	110	39.35 N	84.55 W
Liberty, Mo.	119f	39.15 N	94.25 W
Liberty, Pa.	57b	40.20 N	79.51 W
Liberty, SC	127	34.47 N	82.41 W
Liberty, Tx.	125	30.03 N	94.46 W
Liberty, Ut.	119b	41.20 N	111.52 W
Liberty B., Wa.	118a	47.43 N	122.41 W
Liberty L., Md.	112e	39.25 N	76.56 W
Liberty Manor, Md.	56c	39.21 N	76.47 W
Libertyville, Il. (lĭb'ēr-tĭ-vĭl)	113a	42.17 N	87.57 W
Libode, S. Afr. (lĭ-bō'dĕ)	227c	31.33 S	29.03 E
Libón, R., Hai.	135	19.30 N	71.45 W
Libourne, Fr. (lē-bōōrn')	168	44.55 N	0.12 W
Library, Pa.	57b	40.18 N	80.02 W
Libres, Mex. (lē'brās)	131	19.26 N	97.41 W
Libreville, Gabon (lē-br'vēl')	230	0.23 N	9.27 E
Liburn, Ga. (lĭb'ûrn)	112c	33.53 N	84.09 W
Libya, Afr. (lĭb'ē-ä)	222	27.38 N	15.00 E
Libyan Des. (Aş Şahrā' al Lībīyah), Libya (lĭb'ē-ăn)	225	28.23 N	23.34 E
Libyan Plat., Egypt	161	30.58 N	26.20 E
Licancábur, Cerro (Mtn.), Chile (sĕ'r-rô-lē-kán-ká'bōōr)	144	22.45 S	67.45 W
Licanten, Chile (lē-kän-tĕ'n)	141b	34.58 S	72.00 W
Lichfield, Eng. (lĭch'fēld)	156	52.41 N	1.49 W
Lichinga, Moz.	231	13.18 S	35.14 E
Lichtenberg (Neigh.), G.D.R.	65a	51.31 N	13.29 E
Lichtenburg, S. Afr. (lĭk'tĕn-bĕrgh)	223d	26.09 S	26.10 E
Lichtendorf, F.R.G.	63	51.28 N	7.37 E
Lichtenplatz (Neigh.), F.R.G.	63	51.15 N	7.12 E
Lichtenrade (Neigh.), F.R.G.	65a	52.23 N	13.25 E
Lichterfelde (Neigh.), F.R.G.	65a	52.26 N	13.19 E
Lick Cr., In. (lĭk)	113g	39.43 N	86.06 W
Licking (R.), Ky. (lĭk'ĭng)	110	38.30 N	84.10 W
Lida, Sov. Un. (lē'dá)	167	53.53 N	25.19 E
Lidcombe, Austl.	70a	33.52 S	151.03 E
Lidgerwood, ND (lĭj'ēr-wood)	114	46.04 N	97.10 W
Lidköping, Swe. (lēt'chû-pĭng)	164	58.31 N	13.06 E
Lido Beach, NY	55	40.35 N	73.38 W
Lido di Roma, It. (lē'dô-dē-rô'mä)	171d	41.19 N	12.17 E
Lidzbark, Pol. (lĭts'bärk)	167	54.07 N	20.36 E
Liebenbergsvlei (R.), S. Afr.	223d	27.35 S	28.25 E
Liebenwalde, G.D.R. (lē'bĕn-väl-dĕ)	157b	52.52 N	13.24 E
Liechou Pan-Tao (Pen.), China	203	20.40 N	109.25 E
Liechtenstein, Eur. (lēk'tĕn-shtīn)	159	47.10 N	10.00 E
Liège, Bel. (lē-āzh')	163	50.40 N	5.30 E
Lienyün, China (lĭan'yün)	199	33.10 N	120.01 E
Lienz, Aus. (lē-ĕnts')	166	46.49 N	12.45 E
Liepāja, Sov. Un. (le'pä-yä')	165	56.31 N	20.59 E
Lier, Bel.	157a	51.08 N	4.34 E
Lierenfeld (Neigh.), F.R.G.	63	51.13 N	6.51 E
Liesing, Aus. (lē'sĭng)	157e	48.09 N	16.17 E
Liestal, Switz. (lēs'täl)	166	47.28 N	7.44 E
Lievre, Rivière du (R.), Can.	111	45.00 N	75.25 W
Lifanga, Zaire	230	0.19 N	21.57 E
Lifou, (I.), N. Cal.	215	21.15 S	167.32 E
Ligao, Phil. (lē-gä'ô)	207a	13.14 N	123.33 E
Lightning Ridge, Austl.	216	29.23 S	147.50 E
Ligonha (R.), Moz. (lē-gō'nyá)	227	16.14 S	39.00 E
Ligonier, In. (lĭg-ô-nēr)	110	41.30 N	85.35 W
Ligovo, Sov. Un. (lē'gô-vô)	182c	59.51 N	30.13 E
Liguria (Reg.), It. (lē-gōō-rē-ä)	172	44.24 N	8.27 E
Ligurian Sea, Eur. (lĭ-gū'rĭ-ăn)	172	43.42 N	8.32 E
Lihou Rfs., Austl. (lē-hōō')	215	17.23 S	152.43 E
Lihuang, China (lē'hōōäng)	200	31.32 N	115.46 E
Lihue, Hi. (lē-hōō'ā)	106a	21.59 N	159.23 W
Lihula, Sov. Un. (lē'hōō-lá)	165	58.41 N	23.50 E
Liji, China (lē-jyē)	200	33.47 N	117.47 E
Lijiang, China (lē-jyäŋ)	200	27.00 N	100.08 E
Lijin, China (lē-jyĭn)	200	37.30 N	118.15 E
Likasi (Jadotville), Zaire	231	10.59 S	26.44 E
Likhoslavl', Sov. Un. (lyē-kôsläv''l)	174	57.07 N	35.27 E
Likhovka, Sov. Un. (lyē-ĸôf'ká)	175	48.52 N	33.57 E
Likouala (R.), Con.	230	0.10 S	16.30 E
Lille, Fr. (lēl)	168	50.38 N	3.01 E
Lille Baelt (str.), Den.	164	55.09 N	9.53 E
Lillehammer, Nor. (lēl'ē-häm'mĕr)	164	61.07 N	10.25 E
Lillesand, Nor. (lēl'ĕ-sän')	164	58.16 N	8.19 E
Lilleström, Nor. (lēl'ĕ-strûm)	164	59.56 N	11.04 E
Lilliwaup, Wa. (lĭl'ĭ-wŏp)	118a	47.28 N	123.07 W
Lillooet, Can. (lĭ'lōō-ĕt)	99	50.30 N	121.55 W
Lillooet (R.), Can.	99	49.50 N	122.10 W
Lilongwe, Malawi (lē-lô-än)	231	13.59 S	33.44 E
Liluāh, India	67a	22.35 N	88.23 E
Lilydale, Austl.	70b	37.45 S	145.21 E
Lilyfield, Austl.	70a	33.52 S	151.10 E
Lima, Oh. (lī'má)	110	40.40 N	84.05 W
Lima, Peru (lē'mä)	142	12.06 S	76.55 W
Lima, Swe.	164	60.54 N	13.24 E
Lima (R.), Port.	170	41.45 N	8.22 W
Lima Duarte, Braz. (dwä'r-tĕ)	141a	21.52 S	43.47 W
Limão (Neigh.), Braz.	61d	23.30 S	46.40 W
Lima Res., Mt.	117	44.45 N	112.15 W
Limay (R.), Arg. (lē-mä'ē)	144	39.50 S	69.15 W
Limbazi, Sov. Un. (lēm'bä-zĭ)	165	57.32 N	24.44 E
Limbdi, India	196	22.37 N	71.52 E
Limbé, Hai.	135	19.45 N	72.30 W
Limburg an der Lahn, F.R.G. (lem-bōōrg')	166	50.22 N	8.03 E
Limefield, Eng.	64b	53.37 N	2.18 W
Limeira, Braz. (lē-mā'rä)	141a	22.34 S	47.24 W
Limestone Bay, Can. (lĭm'stōn)	101	53.50 N	98.50 W
Limfjorden (Fd.), Den.	164	56.55 N	8.56 E
Limmen Bght., Austl. (lĭm'ĕn)	214	14.45 S	136.00 E
Limni, Grc. (lĕm'nē)	173	38.47 N	23.22 E
Limnos (I.), Grc.	173	39.58 N	24.48 E
Limoges, Can. (lē-môzh')	95c	45.20 N	75.15 W
Limon, Co. (lĭ'mŏn)	122	39.15 N	103.41 W
Limón, C. R. (lē-mōn')	133	10.01 N	83.02 W
Limón, Hond. (lē-mô'n)	132	15.53 N	85.34 W
Limón B., Pan.	128a	9.21 N	79.58 W
Limon (R.), Dom. Rep.	135	18.20 N	71.40 W
Limours, Fr. (lē-mōōr')	169b	48.39 N	2.05 E
Limousin, Plateaux du (Plat.), Fr. (plä-tō' dü lē-mōō-zăɴ')	168	45.44 N	1.09 E

ăt; finăl; rāte; senåte; ärm; åsk; sofá; fâre; ch-choose; dh-as th in other; bē; ēvent; bĕt; recĕnt; cratēr; g-gō; gh-guttural g; bĭt; ĭ-short neutral; rīde; ĸ-guttural k as ch in German ich;

PLACE (Pronounciation)	PAGE	Lat. °'	Long. °'
moux, Fr. (lē-mōō')	168	43.03 N	2.14 E
mpopo R., Afr. (lĭm-pō'pō)	226	23.15 S	27.46 E
nares, Chile (lē-nä'rās)	141b	35.51 S	71.35 W
nares, Mex.	124	24.53 N	99.34 W
nares (Prov.), Chile	141b	35.53 S	71.30 W
nares, Sp. (lē-nä'rĕs)	170	38.07 N	3.38 W
naro, C., It. (lē-nä'rä)	172	42.02 N	11.53 E
nce, Peru	60c	12.05 S	77.03 W
nchuan, China (lĭn-chůän)	203	27.58 N	116.18 E
ncoln, Arg. (lĭŋ'kŭn)	141c	34.51 S	61.29 W
ncoln, Can.	95d	43.10 N	79.29 W
ncoln, Ca.	120	38.51 N	121.19 W
ncoln, Eng.	156	53.14 N	0.33 W
ncoln, Il.	123	40.09 N	89.21 W
ncoln, Ks.	122	39.02 N	98.08 W
ncoln, Me.	104	45.23 N	68.31 W
ncoln, Ma.	105a	42.25 N	71.19 W
ncoln, Ne.	123	40.49 N	96.43 W
ncoln, Pa.	57b	40.18 N	79.51 W
ncoln Center (P. Int.), NY	55	40.46 N	73.59 W
ncoln Heath (Reg.), Eng.	156	53.23 N	0.39 W
ncolnia Heights, Va.	56d	38.50 N	77.09 W
ncoln, Mt., Co.	122	39.20 N	106.19 W
ncoln Park, Mi.	113b	42.14 N	83.11 W
ncoln Park, NJ	112a	40.56 N	74.18 W
ncoln Park (P. Int.), Il.	58a	41.56 N	87.38 W
ncoln Place (Neigh.), Pa.	57b	40.22 N	79.55 W
ncolnshire (Co.), Eng.	156	53.12 N	0.29 W
ncolnshire Wolds (Hills), Eng. (woldz')	162	53.25 N	0.23 W
ncolnton, NC (lĭŋ'kŭn-tŭn)	127	35.27 N	81.15 W
ncolnwood, Il.	58a	42.00 N	87.46 W
nda-a-Velha, Port.	65d	38.43 N	9.14 W
ndale, Ga. (lĭn'dāl)	126	34.10 N	85.10 W
ndau, F.R.G. (lĭn'dou)	166	47.33 N	9.40 E
nden, Al. (lĭn'dĕn)	126	32.16 N	87.47 W
nden, Ma.	54a	42.26 N	71.02 W
nden, Mo.	119f	39.13 N	94.35 W
nden, NJ	112a	40.39 N	74.14 W
nden (Neigh.), S. Afr.	71b	26.08 S	28.00 E
ndenberg, G.D.R.	65a	52.36 N	13.31 E
nden-dahlhausen (Neigh.), F.R.G.	63	51.26 N	7.09 E
ndenhorst (Neigh.), F.R.G.	63	51.33 N	7.27 E
ndenhurst, NY (lĭn'dĕn-hûrst)	112a	40.41 N	73.23 W
ndenwold, NJ (lĭn'dĕn-wōld)	112f	39.50 N	75.00 W
nderhausen, F.R.G.	63	51.18 N	7.17 E
ndesberg, Swe. (lĭn'dĕs-bĕrgh)	164	59.37 N	15.14 E
ndesnes (C.), Nor. (lĭn'ĕs-nĕs)	163	58.00 N	7.05 E
ndfield, Austl.	70a	33.47 S	151.10 E
ndho, China	202	40.45 N	107.30 E
ndi, Tan. (lĭn'dē)	231	10.00 S	39.43 E
ndian, China (lĭn-dĭĕn)	202	42.08 N	124.59 E
ndi R., Zaire	225	1.00 N	27.13 E
ndley, S. Afr. (lĭnd'lē)	223d	27.52 S	27.55 E
ndow, G.D.R. (lĕn'dōv)	157b	52.58 N	12.59 E
ndsay, Can. (lĭn'zē)	111	44.20 N	78.45 W
ndsay, Ok.	122	34.50 N	97.38 W
ndsborg, Ks. (lĭnz'bôrg)	122	38.34 N	97.42 W
neville, Al. (lĭn'vĭl)	126	33.18 N	85.45 W
nfen, China	202	36.00 N	111.38 E
nga, Kepulauan (Is.), Indon.	206	0.35 S	105.05 E
ngao, China (lĭn-gou)	203	19.58 N	109.40 E
ngayen, Phil. (lĭŋ'gä-yän')	207a	16.01 N	120.13 E
ngayen G., Phil.	207a	16.18 N	120.11 E
ngbi, China (lĭŋ-bē)	200	33.33 N	117.33 E
ngdianzhen, China	200	31.52 N	121.28 E
ngen, F.R.G. (lĭŋ'gĕn)	166	52.32 N	7.20 E
ngling, China (lĭŋ-lĭŋ)	203	26.10 N	111.40 E
ngshou, China (lĭŋ-shō)	200	38.21 N	114.41 E
nguère, Senegal (lĭŋ-gěr')	228	15.24 N	15.07 W
ngwu, China	202	38.05 N	106.18 E
ngyuan, China (lĭŋ-yůän)	202	41.12 N	119.20 E
nhai, China	203	28.52 N	121.08 E
nhe, China (lĭn-hŭ)	202	40.49 N	107.45 E
nhó, Port.	65d	38.46 N	9.23 W
nhuaiguan, China (lĭn-hwī-gůän)	200	32.55 N	117.38 E
nhuanj, China (lĭ-hwī-jyĕ)	200	33.42 N	116.33 E
njiangi, China (lĭn-jyäŋ)	202	41.45 N	127.00 E
nköping, Swe. (lĭn'chû-pĭng)	164	58.25 N	15.35 E
nksfield (Neigh.), S. Afr.	71b	26.10 S	28.06 E
nmeyer, S. Afr.	71b	26.16 S	28.04 E
nn (Neigh.), F.R.G.	63	51.20 N	6.38 E
nnhe, Loch (L.), Scot. (lĭn'ē)	162	56.35 N	4.30 W
nqing, China (lĭn-chyĭŋ)	200	36.49 N	115.42 E
nqux, China (lĭn-chyōō)	200	36.31 N	118.33 E
ns, Braz. (lē'ɴs)	143	21.42 S	49.41 W
nthicum Heights, Md. (lĭn'thĭ-kŭm)	112e	39.12 N	76.39 W
nton, In. (lĭn'tŭn)	110	39.05 N	87.15 W
nton, ND	114	46.16 N	100.15 W
ntorf, F.R.G.	63	51.20 N	6.49 E
nwu, China (lĭn'wōō')	203	25.20 N	112.30 E
nxi, China (lĭn-shyē)	202	43.30 N	118.02 E
nyi, China (lĭn-yē)	200	35.04 N	118.21 E
nying, China (lĭn'yĭng')	200	33.48 N	113.56 E
nz, Aus. (lĭnts)	166	48.18 N	14.18 E
nzhang, China (lĭn-jäŋ)	200	36.19 N	114.40 E
vâni, Sov. Un. (lē'vá-nē)	174	56.24 N	26.12 E
pa, Phil. (lē-pä')	207a	13.55 N	121.10 E
pari, It. (lē'pä-rē)	172	38.29 N	15.00 E
pari (I.), It.	172	38.32 N	15.04 E
petsk, Sov. Un. (lyē'pĕtsk)	174	52.26 N	39.34 E
petsk, (Oblast), Sov. Un.	174	52.18 N	38.30 E
ping, China (lē-pĭŋ)	203	26.18 N	109.00 E
pno, Pol. (lēp'nō)	167	52.50 N	19.12 E
ppe (R.), F.R.G. (lĭp'ē)	163	51.36 N	6.45 E
ppolthausen (Neigh.), F.R.G.	63	51.37 N	7.29 E
ppstadt, F.R.G. (lĭp'shtät)	166	51.39 N	8.20 E
pscomb, Al. (lĭp'skŭm)	112h	33.26 N	86.56 W
ptsy, Sov. Un. (lyĕp'tsē)	175	50.11 N	36.25 E
pu, China (lē-pōō)	203	24.38 N	110.35 E
ra, Ug.	231	2.15 N	32.54 E
Liri (R.), It. (lē'rē)	172	41.49 N	13.30 E
Liria, Sp. (lē'ryä)	171	39.35 N	0.34 W
Lisala, Zaire (lē-sä'lä)	230	2.09 N	21.31 E
Lisboa (Lisbon), Port. (lēzh-bō'ä) (lĭz'bŭn)	171b	38.42 N	9.05 W
Lisbon, ND	114	46.21 N	97.43 W
Lisbon, Oh.	110	40.45 N	80.50 W
Lisbon, see Lisboa			
Lisbon Falls, Me.	104	43.59 N	70.03 W
Lisburn, N. Ire. (lĭs'bŭrn)	162	54.35 N	6.05 W
Lisburne, C., Ak.	107	68.20 N	165.40 W
Lishi, China (lē-shr)	202	37.32 N	111.12 E
Lishu, China	202	43.12 N	124.18 E
Lishui, China (lĭ'shwĭ')	200	31.41 N	119.01 E
Lishui, China	203	28.28 N	120.00 E
Lisianski I., Hi.	107b	25.30 N	174.00 W
Lisieux, Fr. (lē-zyû')	168	49.10 N	0.13 E
Lisiy Nos, Sov. Un. (lĭ'sĭy-nôs)	182c	60.01 N	30.00 E
Liski, Sov. Un. (lyēs'kē)	175	50.56 N	39.28 E
Lisle, Il. (lĭl)	113a	41.48 N	88.04 W
L'Isle-Adam, Fr. (lēl-ädäɴ')	169b	49.05 N	2.13 E
Lismore, Austl. (lĭz'môr)	216	28.48 S	153.18 E
Lister, Mt., Ant. (lĭs'tēr)	232	78.05 S	163.00 E
Litani (R.), Lib.	191a	33.28 N	35.42 E
Litchfield, Il. (lĭch'fēld)	123	39.10 N	89.38 W
Litchfield, Mn.	115	45.08 N	94.34 W
Litchfield, Oh.	113d	41.10 N	82.01 W
Litherland, Eng.	64a	53.28 N	2.59 W
Lithgow, Austl. (lĭth'gō)	216	33.23 S	149.31 E
Lithinon Akra (C.), Grc.	172a	34.59 N	24.35 E
Lithonia, Ga. (lĭ-thō'nĭ-à)	112c	33.43 N	84.07 W
Lithuanian S. S. R., Sov. Un. (lĭth-ů-ā-'nĭ-à)	178	55.42 N	23.30 E
Litin, Sov. Un. (lē-tēn)	175	49.16 N	28.11 E
Litókhoron, Grc. (lē'tô-ĸō'rôn)	173	40.05 N	22.29 E
Litoko, Zaire,	230	1.13 S	24.47 E
Litoměřice, Czech. (lē'tô-myĕr'zhĭ-tsĕ)	166	50.33 N	14.10 E
Litomyšl, Czech. (lē'tô-mēsh'l)	166	49.52 N	16.14 E
Litoo, Tan.	231	9.45 S	38.24 E
Little (R.), Austl.	211a	37.54 S	144.27 E
Little (R.), Tn.-Mo.	126	36.28 N	89.39 W
Little R., Tx.	125	30.48 N	96.50 W
Little Abaco (I.), Ba. (ä'bä-kō)	134	26.55 N	77.45 W
Little Abitibi (R.), Can.	102	50.15 N	81.30 W
Little America, Ant.	232	78.30 S	161.30 W
Little Andama I., Andaman & Nicobar Is. (ăn-dá-măn')	206	10.39 N	93.08 E
Little Bahama Bk., Ba. (bá-hā'má)	134	26.55 N	78.40 W
Little Belt Mts., Mt. (bĕlt)	117	47.00 N	110.50 W
Little Berkhamsted, Eng.	62	51.45 N	0.08 W
Little Bighorn R., Mt. (bĭg-hôrn)	115	45.08 N	107.30 W
Little Bitterroot R., Mt. (bĭt'ēr-ōōt)	116	47.45 N	114.45 W
Little Bitter, see Al Buhayrah al Murrah aş Şughrá			
Little Blue R., Mo. (blōō)	119f	38.52 N	94.25 W
Little Blue (R.), Ne.	122	40.15 N	98.01 W
Littleborough, Eng. (lĭt''l-bŭr-ô)	156	53.39 N	2.06 W
Little Burstead, Eng.	62	51.36 N	0.24 E
Little Calumet R., Il. (kăl-ů-mĕt')	113a	41.38 N	87.38 W
Little Cayman (I.), Cayman Is. (kā'màn)	134	19.40 N	80.05 W
Little Chalfont, Eng.	62	51.40 N	0.34 W
Little Colorado (R.), Az. (kŏl-ô-rä'dō)	121	36.05 N	111.35 W
Little Compton, RI (kŏmp'tŏn)	112b	41.31 N	71.07 W
Little Corn I., Nic.	133	12.19 N	82.50 W
Little End, Eng.	62	51.41 N	0.14 E
Little Exuma (I.), Ba. (ĕk-sōō'mä)	135	23.25 N	75.40 W
Little Falls, Mn. (fôlz)	115	45.58 N	94.23 W
Little Falls, NJ	55	40.53 N	74.14 W
Little Falls, NY	111	43.05 N	74.55 W
Little Ferry, NJ	55	40.51 N	74.03 W
Littlefield, Tx. (lĭt''l-fēld)	122	33.55 N	102.17 W
Little Fork (R.), Mn. (fôrk)	115	48.24 N	93.30 W
Little Hans Lollick (I.), Vir. Is (U.S.A.) (häns lŏl'lĭk)	129c	18.25 N	64.54 W
Little Hulton, Eng.	64b	53.32 N	2.25 W
Little Humboldt R., Nv. (hŭm'bōlt)	116	41.10 N	117.40 W
Little Inagua (I.), Ba. (ē-nä'gwä)	135	21.30 N	73.00 W
Little Isaac (I.), Ba. (ī'zák)	134	25.55 N	79.00 W
Little Kanawha (R.), WV (ká-nô'wá)	110	39.05 N	81.30 W
Little Karroo (Mts.), S. Afr. (kä-rōō)	226	33.50 S	21.02 E
Little Lever, Eng.	64b	53.34 N	2.22 W
Little Mecatina (R.), Can. (mē cá tĭ nä')	97	52.40 N	62.21 W
Little Miami R., Oh. (mī-ăm'ĭ)	113f	39.19 N	84.15 W
Little Minch (Chan.), Scot.	162	57.35 N	6.45 W
Little Missouri (R.), Ar. (mĭ-sōō'rĭ)	123	34.15 N	93.54 W
Little Missouri (R.), SD	114	45.46 N	103.48 W
Little Nahant, Ma.	54a	42.25 N	70.56 W
Little Neck (Neigh.), NY	55	40.46 N	73.44 W
Little Pee Dee (R.), SC (pē-dē')	127	34.35 N	79.21 W
Little Powder R., Wy. (pou'dēr)	115	44.51 N	105.20 W
Little Red (R.), Ar. (rĕd)	123	35.25 N	91.55 W
Little Red R., Ok.	123	33.53 N	94.38 W
Little Rock, Ar. (rŏk)	123	34.42 N	92.16 W
Little Sachigo L., Can. (să'chĭ-gō)	101	54.09 N	92.11 W
Little San Salvador (I.), Ba. (săn săl'vá-dôr)	135	24.35 N	75.55 W
Little Satilla (R.), Ga. (sá-tĭl'á)	114	31.43 N	82.47 W
Little Sioux (R.), Ia. (sōō)	114	42.22 N	95.47 W
Little Smoky (R.), Can. (smōk'ĭ)	99	55.10 N	116.55 W
Little Snake R., Co. (snāk)	117	40.40 N	108.21 W
Little Stanney, Eng.	64b	53.15 N	2.53 W
Little Sutton, Eng.	64a	53.17 N	2.57 W
Little Tallapoosa (R.), Al. (tăl-á-pōō'sá)	126	32.25 N	85.28 W
Little Tennessee (R.), Tn. (tĕn-ĕ-sē')	126	35.36 N	84.05 W
Little Thurrock, Eng.	62	51.28 N	0.21 E
Littleton, Co. (lĭt''l-tŭn)	122	39.34 N	105.01 W
Littleton, Eng.	62	51.24 N	0.28 W
Littleton, Ma.	105a	42.32 N	71.29 W
Littleton, NH	103	44.15 N	71.45 W
Little Wabash (R.), Il. (wô'băsh)	110	38.50 N	88.30 W
Little Warley, Eng.	62	51.35 N	0.19 E
Little Wood R., Id. (wŏŏd)	117	43.00 N	114.08 W
Liuhe, China	202	42.10 N	125.38 E
Liuli, Tan.	231	11.05 S	34.38 E
Liulicun, China	67b	39.56 N	116.28 E
Liup'an Shan (Mts.), China	202	36.20 N	105.30 E
Liuwa Pln., Zambia	230	14.30 S	22.40 E
Liuyang, China (lyōō'yäng')	203	28.10 N	113.35 E
Liuyuan, China (lĭō-yůän)	200	36.09 N	114.37 E
Liuzhou, China (lĭō-jō)	203	24.25 N	109.30 E
Lively, Can.	102	46.26 N	81.09 W
Livengood, Ak. (lĭv'ĕn-gŏŏd)	107	65.30 N	148.35 W
Live Oak, Fl. (lĭv'ōk)	126	30.15 N	83.00 W
Livermore, Ca. (lĭv'ēr-mōr)	118b	37.41 N	121.46 W
Livermore, Ky.	110	37.30 N	87.05 W
Liverpool, Austl. (lĭv'ēr-pōōl)	211b	33.55 S	150.56 E
Liverpool, Can.	104	44.02 N	64.41 W
Liverpool, Eng.	156	53.25 N	2.52 W
Liverpool, Tx.	125a	29.18 N	95.17 W
Liverpool B., Can.	107	69.45 N	130.00 W
Liverpool Ra., Austl.	215	31.47 S	31.00 E
Livindo R., Gabon	225	1.09 N	13.30 E
Livingston, Al. (lĭv'ĭng-stŭn)	126	32.35 N	88.09 W
Livingston, Guat.	132	15.50 N	88.45 W
Livingston, Il.	119e	38.58 N	89.51 W
Livingston, Mt.	117	45.40 N	110.35 W
Livingston, NJ	112a	40.47 N	74.20 W
Livingston, Tn.	126	36.23 N	85.20 W
Livingstone, Zambia (lĭv-ĭng-stŏn)	231	17.50 S	25.53 E
Livingstone, Chutes de (Livingstone Falls), Con.-Zaire	230	4.50 S	14.30 E
Livingstone Mts., Tan.	231	9.30 S	34.10 E
Livingstonia, Malawi (lĭv-ĭng-stō'nĭ-á)	231	10.36 S	34.07 E
Livno, Yugo. (lēv'nô)	172	43.50 N	17.03 E
Livny, Sov. Un. (lēv'nē)	174	52.28 N	37.36 E
Livonia, Mi. (lĭ-vō-nĭ-á)	113b	42.25 N	83.23 W
Livorno (Leghorn), It. (lē-vôr'nō) (lĕg'hôrn)	172	43.32 N	11.18 E
Livramento, Braz. (lē-vrá-mē'n-tô)	144	30.46 S	55.21 W
Livry-Gargan, Fr.	64c	48.56 N	2.33 E
Límoges, Fr.	168	45.50 N	1.15 E
Lixian, China (lē shyĕn)	203	29.42 N	111.40 E
Lixian, China	200	38.30 N	115.38 E
Liyang, China (lē'yäng')	200	31.30 N	119.29 E
Lizard Pt., Eng. (lĭz'árd)	162	49.55 N	5.09 W
Lizy-sur-Ourcq, Fr. (lēk-sē'sür-ōōrk')	169b	49.01 N	3.02 E
Ljmuiden, Neth.	157a	52.27 N	4.35 E
Ljubljana, Yugo. (lyōō'blyä'na)	172	46.04 N	14.29 E
Ljubuški, Yugo. (lyōō'bōōsh-kē)	172	43.11 N	17.29 E
Ljungan (R.), Swe.	164	62.50 N	13.45 E
Ljungby, Swe. (lyōōng'bü)	164	56.49 N	13.56 E
Ljusdal, Swe. (lyōōs'dāl)	164	61.50 N	16.11 E
Ljusnan (R.), Swe.	164	61.55 N	15.33 E
Llandudno, Wales (lăn-dŭd'nō)	162	53.20 N	3.46 W
Llanelli, Wales (lá-nĕl'ĭ)	162	51.44 N	4.09 W
Llanes, Sp. (lyä'nās)	170	43.25 N	4.41 W
Llano, Tx. (lä'nō) (lyä'nō)	124	30.45 N	98.41 W
Llano R., Tx.	124	30.38 N	99.04 W
Llanos (Reg.), Col.-Ven. (lyá'nōs)	142	4.00 N	71.15 W
Llera, Mex. (lyā'rä)	130	23.16 N	99.03 W
Llerena, Sp. (lyā-rā'nä)	170	38.14 N	6.02 W
Llobregat (R.), Sp. (lyô-brē-gät')	171	41.55 N	1.55 E
Lloyd L., Can. (loid)	95e	50.52 N	114.13 W
Lloydminster, Can.	102	53.17 N	110.00 W
Lluchmayor, Sp. (lyōōch-mä-yôr')	171	39.28 N	2.53 E
Llullaillaco (Vol.), Arg. (lyōō-lyī-lyä'kō)	144	24.50 S	68.30 W
Loange (R.), Zaire (lô-äŋ'gä)	230	6.10 S	19.40 E
Lo Aranguiz, Chile	61b	33.23 S	70.40 W
Lobatsi, Bots. (lō-bä'tsē)	226	25.13 S	25.35 E
Lobau (Pln.), Aus.	66e	48.10 N	16.32 E
Lobería, Arg. (lô-bĕ'rē'ä)	144	38.13 S	58.48 W
Lobito, Ang. (lô-bē'tō)	230	12.30 S	13.34 E
Lobnya, Sov. Un. (lôb'nyá)	182b	56.01 N	37.29 E
Lobo, Phil.	207a	13.39 N	121.14 E
Lobos, Arg. (lō'bôs)	141c	35.10 S	59.08 W
Lobos, Cayo (I.), Ba. (lō'bôs)	134	22.25 N	77.40 W
Lobos de Tierra (I.), Peru (lô'bō-dĕ-tyĕ'r-rä)	142	6.29 S	80.55 W
Lobos, Isla de (I.), Mex. (ē's-lä-dĕ-lô'bōs)	131	21.24 N	97.11 W
Lobva, Sov. Un. (lôb'vá)	182a	59.12 N	60.28 E
Lobva R., Sov. Un.	182a	59.14 N	60.17 E
Locarno, Switz. (lô-kär'nō)	166	46.10 N	8.43 E
Lochearn, Md.	56c	39.21 N	76.43 W
Loches, Fr. (lôsh)	168	47.08 N	0.56 E
Lochloosa (L.), Fl. (lŏk-lō'sá)	127	29.33 N	82.07 W
Loch Raven Res., Md.	112e	39.28 N	76.38 W
Lockeport, Can.	104	43.42 N	65.07 W
Lockhart, SC (lŏk'hârt)	127	34.47 N	81.30 W
Lockhart, Tx.	125	29.54 N	97.40 W
Lock Haven, Pa. (lŏk'hā-vĕn)	111	41.05 N	77.30 W
Lockland, Oh. (lŏk'lănd)	113f	39.14 N	84.27 W
Lockport, Can. (lŏk'pōrt)	95f	50.05 N	96.56 W
Lockport, Il.	113a	41.35 N	88.04 W
Lockport, NY	113c	43.11 N	78.43 W
Lockwillow, S. Afr.	71b	26.17 S	27.50 E
Loc-ninh, Viet. (lōk'nĭng')	206	12.00 N	106.30 E
Locust Grove, NY	55	40.48 N	73.30 W
Locust Valley, NY	55	40.53 N	73.36 W
Lod, Isr. (lōd)	191a	31.57 N	34.55 E
Lodève, Fr. (lô-dĕv')	168	43.43 N	3.18 E
Lodeynoye Pole, Sov. Un. (lô-dĕy-nô'yĕ)	165	60.43 N	33.24 E
Lodge Cr., Can. (lŏj)	100	49.20 N	110.20 W
Lodge Cr., Mt.	117	48.51 N	109.30 W
Lodgepole Cr., Wy. (lŏj'pōl)	114	41.22 N	104.48 W
Lodhran, Pak.	196	29.40 N	71.39 E
Lodi, Ca. (lō'dī)	120	38.07 N	121.17 W

ŋ-sing; ŋ-baŋk; ɴ-nasalized n; nŏd; cŏmmit; ōld; ôbey; ôrder; oi-boil; fōōd; fŏŏt; ou-out; s-soft; sh-dish; th-thin; pūre; ûnite; ûrn; stŭd; circŭs; ü-as in French tu; '-indeterminate vowel.

PLACE (Pronounciation)	PAGE	Lat. °′	Long. °′
Lodi, It. (lô'dē)	172	45.18 N	9.30 E
Lodi, NJ	55	40.53 N	74.05 W
Lodi, Oh. (lō'dī)	113d	41.02 N	82.01 W
Lodosa, Sp. (lô-dô'sä)	170	42.27 N	2.04 W
Lodwar, Ken.	231	3.07 N	35.36 E
Łódź, Pol. (wōōdzh)	167	51.46 N	19.13 E
Loeches, Sp. (lô-āch'ĕs)	171a	40.22 N	3.25 W
Loffa (R.), Lib.	228	7.10 N	10.35 W
Lofoten (Is.), Nor. (lô'fō-tĕn)	158	68.26 N	13.42 E
Logan, Oh. (lō'găn)	110	39.35 N	82.25 W
Logan, Ut.	117	41.46 N	111.51 W
Logan, WV	110	37.50 N	82.00 W
Logan, Mt., Can.	96	60.54 N	140.33 W
Logansport, In. (lō'gănz-pōrt)	110	40.45 N	86.25 W
Logan Square (Neigh.), Il.	58a	41.56 N	87.42 W
Lognes, Fr.	64c	48.50 N	2.38 E
Logone (R.), Afr. (lō-gō'nä) (lô-gōn')	229	11.15 N	15.10 E
Logroño, Sp. (lô-grō'nyō)	170	42.28 N	2.25 W
Logrosán, Sp. (lô-grô-sän')	170	39.22 N	5.29 W
Løgstør, Den. (lügh-stûr')	164	56.56 N	9.15 E
Lohausen (Neigh.), F.R.G.	63	51.16 N	6.44 E
Lohberg, F.R.G.	63	51.35 N	6.46 E
Lo Hermida, Chile	61b	33.29 S	70.33 W
Lohheide, F.R.G.	63	51.30 N	6.40 E
Löhme, G.D.R.	65a	52.37 N	13.40 E
Lohmühle, F.R.G.	63	51.31 N	6.40 E
Löhnen, F.R.G.	63	51.36 N	6.39 E
Loir (R.), Fr. (lwår)	168	47.40 N	0.07 E
Loire (R.), Fr.	168	47.19 N	1.11 W
Loja, Ec. (lō'hä)	142	3.49 S	79.13 W
Loja, Sp. (lô'-kä)	170	37.10 N	4.11 W
Loka, Zaire	230	0.20 N	17.57 E
Lokala Drift, Bots. (lô'kä-lȧ drĭft)	223d	24.00 S	26.38 E
Lokandu, Zaire	231	2.31 S	25.47 E
Lokhvitsa, Sov. Un. (lôk-vĭt'sȧ)	175	50.21 N	33.16 E
Lokichar, Ken.	231	2.23 N	35.39 E
Lokitaung, Ken.	231	4.16 N	35.45 E
Lokofa-Bokolongo, Zaire	230	0.12 N	19.22 E
Lokoja, Nig. (lô-kō'yä)	229	7.47 N	6.45 E
Lokolama, Zaire	230	2.34 S	19.53 E
Lokosso, Burkina	228	10.19 N	3.40 W
Loliondo, Tan.	231	2.03 S	35.37 E
Lolland, Den. (lôl'än')	164	54.41 N	11.00 E
Lolo, Mt.	117	46.45 N	114.05 W
Lol R., Sud. (lōl)	225	9.06 N	28.09 E
Lom, Bul. (lōm)	173	43.48 N	23.15 E
Loma Linda, Ca. (lō'mȧ lĭn'dȧ)	119a	34.04 N	117.16 W
Loma Mansa (Mtn.), S.L.	228	9.13 N	11.07 W
Lomami (R.), Zaire	230	0.50 S	24.40 E
Lomas Chapultepec (Neigh.), Mex.	60a	19.26 N	99.13 W
Lomas de Zamora, Arg. (lō'mäs dā zä-mō'rä)	144a	34.31 S	58.24 W
Lombard, Il. (lŏm-bärd)	113a	41.53 N	88.01 W
Lombardia (Reg.), It. (lôm-bär-dē'ä)	172	45.20 N	9.30 E
Lombardy, S. Afr.	71b	26.07 S	28.08 E
Lomblen, Pulau (I.), Indon. (lŏm-blĕn')	207	8.08 S	123.45 E
Lombok (I.), Indon. (lŏm-bŏk')	206	9.15 S	116.15 E
Lomé, Togo. (lō-mā') (lô'mā)	228	6.08 N	1.13 E
Lomela, Zaire (lô-mā'lȧ)	226	2.19 S	23.33 E
Lomela (R.), Zaire	230	0.35 S	21.20 E
Lometa, Tx. (lō-mē'tȧ)	124	31.10 N	98.25 W
Lomie, Cam. (lô-mē-ā')	229	3.10 N	13.37 E
Lomita, Ca. (lō-mē'tȧ)	119a	33.48 N	118.20 W
Lommel, Bel.	157a	51.14 N	5.21 E
Lommond, Loch (L.), Scot. (lôk lō'mŭnd)	162	56.15 N	4.40 W
Lomonosov, Sov. Un. (lô-mô'nô-sof)	182c	59.54 N	29.47 E
Lompoc, Ca. (lŏm-pōk')	120	34.39 N	120.30 W
Lomza, Pol. (lôm'zhȧ)	167	53.11 N	22.04 E
Lonaconing, Md. (lō-nȧ-kō'nĭng)	111	39.35 N	78.55 W
London, Can. (lŭn'dŭn)	110	43.00 N	81.20 W
London, Eng.	156b	51.30 N	0.07 W
London, Ky.	126	37.07 N	84.06 W
London, Oh.	110	39.50 N	83.30 W
London Colney, Eng.	62	51.43 N	0.18 W
Londonderry, Can. (lŭn'dŭn-dĕr-ĭ)	104	45.29 N	63.36 W
Londonderry, N. Ire.	162	55.00 N	7.19 W
Londonderry, C., Austl.	214	13.30 S	127.00 E
London Zoo (P. Int.), Eng.	62	51.32 N	0.09 W
Londrina, Braz. (lôn-drē'nä)	143	21.53 S	51.17 W
Lonely (I.), Can. (lōn'lĭ)	110	45.35 N	81.30 W
Lone Pine, Ca.	120	36.36 N	118.03 W
Lone Star, Nic.	133	13.58 N	84.25 W
Long (I.), Ba.	135	23.25 N	75.10 W
Long (I.), Can.	104	44.21 S	66.25 W
Long (L.), ND	114	46.47 N	100.14 W
Long (L.), Wa.	118a	47.29 N	122.36 W
Longa, Ang.	230	14.42 S	18.32 E
Longa (R.), Ang. (lôŋ'gȧ)	230	10.20 S	13.50 E
Long B., SC	127	33.30 N	78.54 W
Long Beach, Ca. (lông bēch)	119a	33.46 N	118.12 W
Long Beach, NY	112a	40.35 N	73.38 W
Long Branch, NJ (lông brȧnch)	112a	40.18 N	73.59 W
Long Ditton, Eng.	62	51.23 N	0.20 W
Longdon, ND (lông'-dŭn)	114	48.45 N	98.23 W
Long Eaton, Eng. (ē'tŭn)	156	52.54 N	1.16 W
Longfield, Eng.	62	51.24 N	0.18 E
Longford, Ire. (lŏng'fẽrd)	162	53.43 N	7.40 W
Longgu, China (lôŋ-gōō)	200	34.52 N	116.48 E
Longhorn, Tx. (lông-hôrn)	119d	29.33 N	98.23 W
Longhua, China	68a	31.09 N	121.26 E
Long I., Ak.	98	54.54 N	132.45 W
Long I., NY (lông)	111	40.50 N	72.50 W
Long I., Pap. N. Gui.	207	5.10 S	147.30 E
Longido, Tan.	231	2.44 S	36.41 E
Long Island City (Neigh.), NY	55	40.45 N	73.56 W
Long Island Sd., Ct.-NY (lông ī'lănd)	111	41.05 N	72.45 W
Longjumeau, Fr. (lôn-zhü-mō')	169b	48.42 N	2.17 E
Longkou, China (lôŋ-kō)	200	37.39 N	120.21 E
Long L., Can.	102	49.10 N	86.45 W
Longlac, Can. (lông'lȧk)	102	49.41 N	86.28 W

PLACE (Pronounciation)	PAGE	Lat. °′	Long. °′
Longlake, SD (lông-lāk)	114	45.52 N	99.06 W
Longmont, Co. (lông'mŏnt)	122	40.11 N	105.07 W
Longnor, Eng. (lông'nôr)	156	53.11 N	1.52 W
Long Pine, Ne. (lông pīn)	114	42.31 N	99.42 W
Long Point, Austl.	70a	34.01 S	150.54 E
Long Point B., Can.	111	42.40 N	80.10 W
Long Prairie, Mn. (lông prâr'ĭ)	115	45.58 N	94.49 W
Long Pt., Can.	101	53.02 N	98.40 W
Long Pt., Can.	105	48.48 N	58.46 W
Long Pt., Can.	111	42.35 N	80.05 W
Long Range Mts., Can.	105	48.00 N	58.30 W
Longreach, Austl. (lông'rēch)	215	23.32 S	144.17 E
Long Reach (R.), Can.	104	45.26 N	66.05 W
Long Reef Point, Austl.	70a	33.45 S	151.19 E
Long Rf., Austl.	211b	33.45 S	151.22 E
Longridge, Eng. (lông'rĭj)	156	53.51 N	2.37 W
Longs Pk., Co. (lôngz)	122	40.17 N	105.37 W
Longtansi, China (lôŋ-tä-sz)	200	32.12 N	115.53 E
Longton, Eng. (lông'tŭn)	156	52.59 N	2.08 W
Longueuil, Can. (lôn-gû'y')	95a	45.32 N	73.30 W
Longueville, Austl.	70a	33.50 S	151.10 E
Longview, Tx.	125	32.29 N	94.44 W
Longview, Wa. (lông-vū)	118c	46.06 N	123.02 W
Longville, La. (lông'vĭl)	125	30.36 N	93.14 W
Longwy, Fr. (lôn-wē')	169	49.32 N	6.14 E
Longxi, China (lôŋ-shyē)	202	35.00 N	104.40 E
Long-xuyen, Viet. (loung' sōō'yĕn)	206	10.31 N	105.28 E
Longzhen, China (lôŋ-jŭn)	181	48.47 N	126.43 E
Longzhou, China (lôŋ-jō)	203	22.20 N	107.02 E
Lonoke, Ar. (lō'nōk)	123	34.48 N	91.52 W
Lons-le-Saunier, Fr. (lôn-lē-sō-nyā')	169	46.40 N	5.33 E
Lontue, (R.), Chile (lôn-tōō'ē')	141b	35.20 S	70.45 W
Looc, Phil. (lô-ōk')	207a	12.16 N	121.59 E
Loogootee, In.	110	38.40 N	86.55 W
Lookout, C., NC (lŏŏk'out)	127	34.34 N	76.38 W
Lookout Pt. Res., Or.	116	43.51 N	122.38 W
Loolmalasin (Mtn.), Tan.	231	3.03 S	35.46 E
Looma, Can. (ōō'mȧ)	95g	53.22 N	113.15 W
Loop (Neigh.), Il.	58a	41.53 N	87.38 W
Loop Head, Ire. (lōōp)	162	52.32 N	9.59 W
Loosahatchie (R.), Tn. (lōz-ȧ-hă'chē)	126	35.20 N	89.45 W
Loosdrechtsche Plassen (L.), Neth.	157a	52.11 N	5.09 E
Lopatka, Mys (C.), Sov. Un. (lô-pät'kȧ)	177	51.00 N	156.52 E
Lopez B., Phil. (lō'pāz)	207a	14.04 N	122.00 E
Lopez, Cap (C.), Gabon	230	0.37 N	8.43 E
Lopez I, Wa.	118a	48.25 N	122.53 W
Lopori (R.), Zaire (lō-pō'rē)	230	1.35 N	20.43 E
Lo Prado Arriba, Chile	61b	33.26 S	70.45 W
Lora, Sp. (lō'rä)	170	37.40 N	5.31 W
Lorain, Oh. (lô-rān')	113d	41.28 N	82.10 W
Loralai, Pak. (lō-rŭ-lī')	196	30.31 N	68.35 E
Lorca, Sp. (lôr'kä)	170	37.39 N	1.40 W
Lord Howe (I.), Austl. (lôrd hou)	215	31.44 S	157.56 W
Lordsburg, NM (lôrdz'bûrg)	121	32.20 N	108.45 W
Lorena, Braz. (lô-rā'nȧ)	141a	22.45 S	45.07 W
Loreto, Braz. (lô-rā'tō)	143	7.09 S	45.10 W
Loretteville, Can. (lô-rĕt-vēl')	95b	46.51 N	71.21 W
Lorica, Col. (lô-rē'kä)	142	9.14 N	75.54 W
Lorient, Fr. (lô-rē'än')	168	47.45 N	3.22 W
Lorn, Firth of, Scot. (fûrth ŏv lôrn')	162	56.10 N	6.09 W
Lörrach, F.R.G. (lûr'äk)	166	47.36 N	7.38 E
Los Alamitos, Ca. (lōs ȧl-ȧ-mē'tôs)	119a	33.48 N	118.04 W
Los Alamos, NM (ȧl-ȧ-môs')	121	35.53 N	106.20 W
Los Altos, Ca. (ȧl-tôs')	118b	37.23 N	122.06 W
Los Andes, Chile (ȧn'dĕs)	141b	32.44 S	70.36 W
Los Angeles, Ca. (ăŋ'gĕl-ĕs) (ă'jĕl-ĕs) (äŋ'hȧ-lâs)	119a	34.00 N	118.15 W
Los Angeles, Chile (äŋ'hȧ-lās)	144	37.27 S	72.15 W
Los Angeles Aqueduct, Ca.	120	35.12 N	118.02 W
Los Angeles Arpt., Ca.	59	33.56 N	118.24 W
Los Angeles R., Ca.	119a	33.50 N	118.13 W
Los Bronces, Chile (lôs brō'n-sĕs)	141b	33.09 S	70.18 W
Loscha R., Id. (lŏs'chȧ)	116	46.20 N	115.11 W
Los Chonos, Archipielago de, Chile (är-chē-pyĕ'lä-gô dĕ lŏs chô'nôs)	144	44.35 N	76.15 W
Los Cuatro Álamos, Chile	61b	33.32 S	70.44 W
Los Dos Caminos, Ven.	61a	10.31 N	66.50 W
Los Estados, Isla de (I.), Arg. (ē's-lä dĕ lôs ĕs-dôs)	144	54.45 S	64.25 W
Los Gatos, Ca. (gä'tôs)	120	37.13 N	121.59 W
Los Herreras, Mex. (ĕr-rä-räs)	124	25.55 N	99.23 W
Los Ilanos, Dom. Rep. (lôs ē-lä'nōs)	135	18.35 N	69.30 W
Los Indios, Cayos de (Is.), Cuba (kä'vōs dĕ lôs ē'n-dvō's)	134	21.50 N	83.10 W
Lošinj (I.), Yugo.	172	44.35 N	14.34 E
Losino Petrovskiy, Sov. Un.	182b	55.52 N	38.12 E
Los Nietos, Ca. (nyā'tôs)	119a	33.57 N	118.05 W
Los Palacios, Cuba	134	22.35 N	83.15 W
Los Pinos (R.), Co.-NM (pē'nōs)	121	36.58 N	107.35 W
Los Reyes Mex.(rā'yĕs)	130	19.35 N	102.29 W
Los Reyes, Mex.	131a	19.21 N	98.58 W
Los Santos, Pan. (săn'tôs)	133	7.57 N	80.24 W
Los Santos de Maimona Sp. (săn'tōs)	170	38.38 N	6.30 W
Los Teques, Ven. (tĕ'kĕs)	143b	10.22 N	67.04 W
Lost R., Id. (lôst)	117	43.56 N	113.38 W
Lost R, Or.	116	42.07 N	121.30 W
Lost River Mts., Id. (rĭ'vẽr)	117	44.23 N	113.48 W
Los Vilos, Chile (vē'lôs)	141b	31.56 S	71.29 W
Lot (R.), Fr. (lôt)	168	44.32 N	1.08 E
Lota, Chile (lō'tä)	144	37.11 S	73.14 W
Lothian, Md. (lōth'ĭăn)	112e	38.50 N	76.38 W
Lotikipi Pln, Ken.	231	4.25 N	34.55 E
Lötschberg Tunnel, Switz.	166	46.26 N	7.54 E
Louangphrabang, Laos (lōō-ang'prä-băng')	206	19.47 N	102.15 E
Loudon, Tn. (lou'dŭn)	126	35.43 N	84.20 W
Loudonville, Oh. (lou'dŭn-vĭl)	110	40.40 N	82.15 W
Loudun, Fr. (lōō-dŭn')	168	47.03 N	0.00
Louga, Senegal (lōō'gä)	228	15.37 N	16.13 W
Loughborough, Eng. (lŭf'bŭr-ô)	156	56.46 N	1.12 W

PLACE (Pronounciation)	PAGE	Lat. °′	Long.
Loughton, Eng.	62	51.39 N	0.03
Louisa, Ky. (lōō'ēz-ȧ)	110	38.05 N	82.40
Louisade Arch., Pap. N. Gui. (lōō-ĭs-äd är-kĭ-pĕl-ĭ-gō)	215	10.44 S	153.58
Louisberg, NC (lōō'ĭs-bûrg)	127	36.05 N	79.19
Louisburg, Can. (lōō'ĭs-bourg)	105	45.55 N	59.58
Louiseville, Can.	104	46.17 N	72.58
Louisiana, Mo. (lōō-ē-zē-ăn'ȧ)	123	39.24 N	91.03
Louisiana (State), U. S.	109	30.50 N	92.50
Louis Trichardt, S. Afr. (lōō'ĭs trĭch'art)	226	22.52 S	29.53
Louisville, Co. (lōō'ĭs-vĭl) (lōō'ē-vĭl)	122	39.58 N	105.08
Louisville, Ga.	127	33.00 N	82.25
Louisville, Ky.	113h	38.15 N	85.45
Louisville, Ms.	126	33.07 N	89.02
Louis XIV, Pte., Can.	97	54.35 N	79.51
Loulé, Port. (lō-lā')	170	37.08 N	8.03
Louny, Czech. (lō'nē)	166	50.20 N	13.47
Loup (R.), Ne. (lōōp)	114	41.17 N	97.58
Loup City, Ne.	114	41.15 N	98.59
Lourdes, Fr. (lōōrd)	170	43.06 N	0.03
Lourenço Marques, see Maputo			
Loures, Port. (lō'rĕzh)	171b	38.49 N	9.10
Lousa, Port. (lō'zȧ)	170	40.05 N	8.12
Louth, Eng. (louth)	162	53.27 N	0.02
Louvain, see Leuven			
Louveciennes, Fr.	64c	48.52 N	2.07
Louviers, Fr. (lōō-vyā')	168	49.13 N	1.11
Louvre (P. Int.), Fr.	64c	48.52 N	2.20
Louvres, Fr. (lōōv'r')	169b	49.03 N	2.30
Lovat', Sov. Un. (lô-vȧt'y')	174	57.23 N	31.18
Lovech, Bul. (lō'vĕts)	173	43.10 N	24.40
Lovedale, Pa.	57b	40.17 N	79.52
Loveland, Co. (lŭv'lănd)	122	40.24 N	105.04
Loveland, Oh.	113	39.16 N	84.15
Lovell, Wy. (lŭv'ĕl)	117	44.50 N	108.23
Lovelock, Nv. (lŭv'lŏk)	120	40.10 N	118.37
Loves Green, Eng.	62	51.43 N	0.24
Lovick, Al. (lŭ'vĭk)	112h	33.34 N	86.38
Loviisa, Fin. (lô'vē-sȧ)	165	60.28 N	26.10
Low, C., Can. (lō)	97	62.58 N	86.50
Lowa, Zaire (lō'wȧ)	226	1.30 S	27.18
Lowell, In.	113a	41.17 N	87.26
Lowell, Ma.	105a	42.38 N	71.18
Lowell, Mi.	110	42.55 N	85.20
Löwenberg, G.D.R. (lû'vĕn-bĕrgh)	157b	52.53 N	13.09
Lower Arrow (L.), Can. (ăr'ō)	99	49.40 N	118.80
Lower Austria (State), see Niederösterreich			
Lower Broughton (Neigh.), Eng.	64b	53.29 N	2.15
Lower Brule Ind. Res., SD (brü'lā)	114	44.15 N	100.21
Lower Higham, Eng.	62	51.26 N	0.28
Lower Hutt, N.Z. (hŭt)	217	41.55 S	174.55
Lower Klamath L., Ca. (klăm'ăth)	116	41.55 N	121.50
Lower L., Ca.-Nv.	116	41.21 N	119.53
Lower Marlboro, Md. (lō'ẽr mărl'bōrō)	112e	38.40 N	76.42
Lower Monumental Res., Wa.	116	46.45 N	118.50
Lower Nazeing, Eng.	62	51.44 N	0.01
Lower New York Bay (B.), NY	55	40.33 N	74.02
Lower Otay Res., Ca. (ō'tā)	120a	32.37 N	116.46
Lower Place, Eng.	64b	53.36 N	2.09
Lower Red. (L.), Mn. (rĕd)	115	47.58 N	94.31
Lower Saxony (State), see Niedersachsen			
Lowestoft, Eng. (lō'stŏft)	163	52.31 N	1.45
Lowicz, Pol. (lô'vĭch)	167	52.06 N	19.57
Lowville, NY (lou'vĭl)	111	43.45 N	75.30
Loxicha (Santa Catarina), Mex. (lô-zē'chä) (sän-tä kä-tä-rē'nä)	131	16.03 N	96.46
Loxton, Austl. (lŏks'tŭn)	216	34.25 S	140.38
Loyauté, Iles, N. Cal.	215	21.17 S	168.16
Loznica, Yugo. (lōz'nē-tsȧ)	173	44.31 N	19.16
Lozorno, Czech.	157e	48.21 N	17.03
Lozova, Sov. Un. (lô-zô'vȧ)	175	48.54 N	36.17
Lozovatka, Sov. Un. (lô-zô-vät'kä)	175	48.03 N	33.19
Lozovaya, Sov. Un. (lô-zo-vä'yä)	175	48.27 N	38.37
Lozoya, Canal de, Sp. (kä-nä'l dĕ lô-thō'yä)	171a	40.36 N	3.41
Luachimo, Ang.	230	7.20 S	20.47
Lualaba (R.), Zaire (lōō-ȧ-lä'bȧ)	231	1.00 S	25.45
Luama (R.), Zaire (lōō'ä-mȧ)	231	4.17 S	27.45
Lu'an, China (lōō-än)	200	31.45 N	116.29
Luan (R.), China	202	41.25 N	117.15
Luanda, Ang. (lōō-än'dȧ)	230	8.48 S	13.14
Luanguinga (R.), Ang. (lōō-ä-gĭŋ'gȧ)	226	14.00 S	20.45
Luangwa (R.), Zambia (lōō-äŋ'gwȧ)	231	11.25 S	32.55
Luanshya, Zambia	231	13.08 S	28.24
Luanxian, China (luän shyĕn)	200	39.47 N	118.40
Luao, Ang.	230	10.42 S	22.12
Luarca, Sp. (lwä'kä)	170	43.33 N	6.30
Lubaczów, Pol. (lōō-bä'chōōf)	177	50.08 N	23.10
Lubán, Pol. (lōō'bän')	166	51.08 N	15.17
Lubānas Ezers (L.), Sov. Un. (lōō-bä'nás ā'zĕrs)	165	56.48 N	26.30
Lubang, Phil. (lōō-bäng')	207a	13.49 N	120.07
Lubang (Is.), Phil.	207a	13.47 N	119.56
Lubango, Ang.	230	14.55 S	13.30
Lubao, Phil. (lōō-bä'ō)	207a	14.55 N	120.36
Lubartow, Pol. (lōō-bär'tōōf)	167	51.27 N	22.37
Lubawa, Pol. (lōō-bä'vȧ)	167	53.31 N	19.47
Lübben, G.D.R. (lüb'ĕn)	166	51.56 N	13.53
Lubbock, Tx. (lŭb'ŭk)	122	33.35 N	101.50
Lubec, Me. (lū'bĕk)	104	44.49 N	67.01
Lübeck, F.R.G. (lü'bĕk)	166	53.53 N	10.42
Lübecker Bucht (B.), G.D.R. (lü'bĕ-kĕr bōōkt)	166	54.10 N	11.20
Lubilash (R.), Zaire (lōō-bē-lásh'-)	230	7.35 S	23.55
Lubin, Pol. (lyōō'bĭn)	166	51.24 N	16.14
Lublin, Pol. (lyōō'blĕn')	167	51.14 N	22.33
L'ublino (Neigh.), Sov. Un.	66b	55.41 N	37.44
Lubny, Sov. Un. (lōōb'nē)	175	50.01 N	33.02

ăt; finȧl; rāte; senȧte; ärm; ȧsk; sofȧ; fâre; ch-choose; dh-as th in other; bē; ēvent; bĕt; recĕnt; cratẽr; g-gō; gh-guttural g; bĭt; ĭ-short neutral; rīde; K-guttural k as ch in German ich;

PRONOUNCING INDEX
Lubuagan – Madera 309

PLACE (Pronounciation)	PAGE	Lat. °′	Long. °′
Lubuagan, Phil. (lōō-bwä-gä'n)	207a	17.24 N	121.11 E
Lubudi, Zaire	231	9.57 S	25.58 E
Lubudi (R.), Zaire (lōō-bōō'dē)	231	9.20 S	25.20 E
Lubumbashi (Élisabethville), Zaire	231	11.40 S	27.28 E
Lucano, Ang.	231	11.16 S	21.38 E
Lucca, It. (lōōk'kä)	172	43.51 N	10.29 E
Lucea, Jam.	134	18.25 N	78.10 W
Luce B., Scot. (lūs)	162	54.45 N	4.45 W
Lucena, Phil. (lōō-sä'nä)	207a	13.55 N	121.36 E
Lucena, Sp. (lōō-thā'nä)	170	37.25 N	4.28 W
Lucena del Cid, Sp. (lōō'thā'nä dā thēdh')	171	40.08 N	0.18 W
Lučenec, Czech. (lōō'chå-nyĕts)	167	48.19 N	19.41 E
Lucera, It. (lōō-châ'rä)	172	41.31 N	15.22 E
Luchi, China	203	28.18 N	110.10 E
Luchou, Taiwan	68d	25.05 N	121.28 E
Lucin, Ut. (lů-sēn')	117	41.23 N	113.59 W
Lucipara, Kepulauan (I.), Indon. (lōō-sē-pä'rȧ)	207	5.45 S	128.15 E
Luckenwalde, G.D.R. (lōōk-ĕn-väl'dĕ)	157b	52.05 N	13.10 E
Lucknow, India (lŭk'nou)	196	26.54 N	80.58 E
Luçon, Fr. (lü-sôN')	168	46.27 N	1.12 W
Lucrecia, Cabo (C.), Cuba (kä'bô-lōō-krā'sē-ä)	135	21.05 N	75.30 W
Lüda, China (lů-dä)	200	38.54 N	121.35 E
Luda Kamchiya (R.), Bul.	173	42.46 N	27.13 E
Luddesdown, Eng.	62	51.22 N	0.24 E
Lüdenscheid, F.R.G. (lü'dĕn-shīt)	169c	51.13 N	7.38 E
Lüderitz, Namibia (lü'dēr-ĭts) (lü'dē-rīts)	226	26.35 S	15.15 E
Lüderitz Bucht (B.), Namibia	226	26.35 S	14.30 E
Ludhiāna, India	196	31.00 N	75.52 E
Lüdinghausen, F.R.G. (lü'dēng-hou-zĕn)	169c	51.46 N	7.27 E
Ludington, Mi. (lŭd'ĭng-tŭn)	110	44.00 N	86.25 W
Ludlow, Eng. (lŭd'lō)	156	52.22 N	2.43 W
Ludlow, Ky.	113f	39.05 N	84.33 W
Ludvika, Swe. (loodh-vē'kȧ)	164	60.10 N	15.09 E
Ludwigsburg, F.R.G. (lōōt'vēks-bōōrgh)	166	48.53 N	9.14 E
Ludwigsfelde, G.D.R. (lōōd'vēgs-fĕl-dĕ)	157b	52.18 N	13.16 E
Ludwigshafen, F.R.G. (lōōt'vēks-hä'fĕn)	166	49.29 N	8.26 E
Ludwigslust, G.D.R. (lōōt'vēks-lōōst)	166	53.18 N	11.31 E
Ludza, Sov. Un. (lōōd'zȧ)	174	56.33 N	27.45 E
Luebo, Zaire (lōō-ā'bô)	226	5.15 S	21.22 E
Luena, Ang.	230	11.45 S	19.55 E
Luena, Zaire	231	9.27 S	25.47 E
Lufira (R.), Zaire (lōō-fē'rȧ)	226	9.32 S	27.15 E
Lufkin, Tx. (lŭf'kĭn)	125	31.21 N	94.43 W
Luga, Sov. Un. (lōō'gȧ)	174	58.43 N	29.52 E
Luga (R.), Sov. Un.	174	59.00 N	29.25 E
Lugano, Switz. (lōō-gä'nō)	166	46.01 N	8.52 E
Lugarno, Austl.	70a	33.59 S	151.03 E
Lugenda (R.), Moz. (lōō-zhĕn'dä)	231	12.05 S	38.15
Lugnaquilla Mtn., Ire. (lōōk-nȧ-kwĭ-lȧ)	162	52.56 N	6.30 W
Lugo, It. (lōō'gô)	172	44.28 N	11.57 E
Lugo, Sp. (lōō'gō)	170	43.01 N	7.32 W
Lugoj, Rom.	173	45.51 N	21.56 E
Lugouqiao, China	67b	39.51 N	116.13 E
Luhe, China (lōō-hŭ)	200	32.22 N	118.50 E
Luhe, see Winsen			
Luiana, Ang.	230	17.23 S	23.03 E
Luilaka (R.), Zaire (lōō-ē-lä'kȧ)	226	2.18 S	21.15 E
Luimneach, Ire. (lĭm'nȧk)	162	52.39 N	8.35 W
Luis Moya, Mex. (lōōē's-mô-yä)	130	22.26 N	102.14 W
Luján, Arg. (lōō'hän')	141c	34.36 S	59.07 W
Luján (R.), Arg.	141c	34.33 S	58.59 W
Lujchow Pen., China	199	20.40 N	100.30 E
Lujia, China (lōō-jyä)	200	31.17 N	120.54 W
Lukanga Swp., Zambia (lōō-kăŋ'gȧ)	231	14.30 S	27.25 E
Lukenie (R.), Zaire (lōō-kā'ynȧ)	230	3.10 S	19.05 E
Lukolela, Zaire	226	1.03 S	17.01 E
Lukovit, Bul. (lōō'kō-vēt')	173	43.13 N	24.07 E
Łuków, Pol. (wōō'kōōf)	167	51.57 N	22.25 E
Lukuga (R.), Zaire (lōō-kōō'gȧ)	231	5.50 S	27.35 E
Lule (R.), Swe.	178	66.20 N	20.25 E
Luleå, Swe. (lōō-lĕ-ô)	158	65.39 N	21.52 E
Lüleburgaz, Tur. (lü'lĕ-bōōr-gäs')	173	41.25 N	27.23 E
Luling, Tx. (lū'lĭng)	125	29.41 N	97.38 W
Lulong, China (lōō-lôŋ)	200	39.54 N	118.53 E
Lulonga (R.), Zaire	230	1.00 N	18.37 E
Lulu (I.), Can. (lū'lōō)	118d	49.09 N	123.05 W
Lulua (R.), Zaire (lōō'lōō-ȧ)	230	15.40 N	22.07 E
Luluabourg, see Kananga			
Lulu I, Ak.	96	55.28 N	133.30 W
Lulu I, Can.	98	49.09 N	123.05 W
Lumajangdong Co. (L.), China (lōō-ma-jäŋ-dôŋtswo)	196	34.00 N	81.47 E
Lumber (R.), NC (lŭm'bēr)	127	35.12 N	79.35 W
Lumberton, Ms. (lŭm'bēr-tŭn)	126	31.00 N	89.25 W
Lumberton, NC	127	34.47 N	79.00 W
Luminárias, Braz. (lōō-mē-nȧ'ryäs)	141a	21.32 S	44.53 W
Lummi (I.), Wa.	118d	48.42 N	122.43 W
Lummi B., Wa. (lŭm'ĭ)	118d	48.47 N	122.44 W
Lummi Island, Wa.	118d	48.44 N	122.42 W
Lumwana, Zambia	230	11.50 S	25.10 E
Lün, Mong.	198	47.58 N	104.52 E
Luna, Phil. (lōō'nȧ)	207a	16.51 N	120.22 E
Lund, Swe. (lŭnd)	164	55.42 N	13.10 E
Lunda (Reg.), Ang. (lōōn'dȧ)	222	8.53 S	20.00 E
Lundi (R.), Zimb. (lōōn'dē)	226	21.09 S	30.10 E
Lundy (I.), Eng. (lŭn'dē)	162	51.12 N	4.50 W
Lüneberger Heide (Reg.), F.R.G. (lü'nĕ-bōōr-gĕr hī'dĕ)	166	53.08 N	10.00 E
Lüneburg, F.R.G. (lü'nē-bōōrgh)	166	53.16 N	10.25 E
Lunel, Fr. (lü-nĕl')	168	43.41 N	4.07 E
Lünen, F.R.G. (lü'nĕn)	169c	51.36 N	7.30 E
Lunenburg, Can. (lōō'nĕn-bûrg)	104	44.23 N	64.19 W
Lunenburg, Ma.	105a	42.36 N	71.44 W
Lunéville, Fr. (lü-nā-vel')	169	48.37 N	6.29 E
Lunga (R.), Zambia (lōōŋ'gȧ)	226	12.58 S	26.18 E
Lungué-Bungo (R), Ang.	230	13.00 S	21.27 E
Lūni (R), India	196	25.20 N	72.00 E
Luninets (R), Sov. Un. (lōō-nēn'yets)	174	52.14 N	26.54 E
Lunsar, S.L.	228	8.41 N	12.32 W
Lunt, Eng.	64a	53.31 N	2.59 W
Luodian, China (lwô-dĭĕn)	201a	31.25 N	121.20 E
Luoding, China (lwô-dĭŋ)	203	23.42 N	111.35 E
Luohe, China (lwô-hŭ)	200	33.35 N	114.02 E
Luoyang, China (lwô-yäŋ)	202	34.45 N	112.32 E
Luozhen, China (lwô-jŭn)	200	37.45 N	118.29 E
Luque, Par. (loo'kä)	144	25.18 S	57.17 W
Lūrah (R), Afg.	196	32.10 N	67.20 E
Luray, Va. (lū-rā')	111	38.40 N	78.25 W
Lurgan, N. Ire. (lûr'găn)	162	54.27 N	6.28 W
Lurigancho, Peru	60c	12.02 S	77.01 W
Lúrio, Moz. (lōō'rē-ô)	227	13.17 S	40.29 E
Lúrio (R), Moz.	231	14.00 S	38.45 E
Lurnea, Austl.	70a	33.56 S	150.54 E
Lusaka, Zaire	231	7.10 S	29.27 E
Lusaka, Zambia (lōō-sä'kȧ)	231	15.25 S	28.17 E
Lusambo, Zaire (lōō-säm'bō)	230	4.58 S	23.27 E
Lusanga, Zaire	226	5.13 S	18.43 E
Lusangi, Zaire	231	4.37 S	27.08 E
Lushai Hills, Bur.	196	28.28 N	92.50 E
Lushan, China	202	33.45 N	113.00 E
Lushiko (R), Zaire	230	6.35 S	19.45 E
Lushoto, Tan. (lōō-shō'tō)	227	4.47 S	38.17 E
Lüshun, China (lü-shŭn)	200	38.49 N	121.15 E
Lusikisiki, S. Afr. (lōō-sē-kē-sē'kē)	227c	31.22 S	29.37 E
Lusk, Wy. (lŭsk)	114	42.46 N	104.27 W
Lutcher, La. (lŭch'ēr)	125	30.03 N	90.43 W
Lütgendortmund (Neigh.), F.R.G.	63	51.30 N	7.21 E
Luton, Eng. (lū'tŭn)	162	51.55 N	0.28 W
Lutsk, Sov. Un. (lōōtsk)	167	50.45 N	25.20 E
Lüttringhausen (Neigh.), F.R.G.	63	51.13 N	7.14 E
Luuq, Som.	223a	3.38 N	42.35 E
Luverne, Al. (lū-vûn')	126	31.42 N	86.15 W
Luverne, Mn.	114	43.40 N	96.13 W
Luvua (R), Zaire (lōō'vōō-ȧ)	231	7.00 S	27.45 E
Luwingu, Zambia	231	10.15 S	29.55 E
Luxapalila Cr., Al. (lŭk-sȧ-pôl'ĭ-lȧ)	126	33.36 N	88.08 W
Luxembourg, Eur.	154	49.30 N	6.22 E
Luxembourg, Lux. (lŭk-sĕm-bûrg) (lük sän-bōōr') (look-sĕm-bōōrgh)	169	49.38 N	6.30 E
Luxeuil-les-Baines, Fr.	169	47.49 N	6.19 E
Luxomni, Ga. (lŭx'ŏm-nī)	112c	33.54 N	84.07 W
Luxor, see Al Uqşur			
Lu Xun Museum (P. Int.), China	68a	31.16 N	121.28 E
Luya Shan (Mtn.), China	202	38.50 N	111.40 E
Luyi, China (lōō-yē)	200	33.52 N	115.32 E
Luyuan, China	67b	39.54 N	116.27 E
Luz, Braz.	61c	22.48 S	43.05 W
Luz (Neigh.), Port.	65d	38.46 N	9.10 W
Luza (R.), Sov. Un. (lōō'zä)	178	60.30 N	47.10 E
Luzern, Switz. (lōō-tsĕrn)	166	47.03 N	8.18 E
Luzhou, China (lōō-jō)	203	28.58 N	105.25 E
Luziânia, Braz. (lōō-zyȧ'nēȧ)	143	16.17 S	47.44 W
Lužniki (Neigh.), Sov. Un.	66b	55.43 N	37.33 E
Luzon (I.), Phil. (lōō-zŏn')	206	17.10 N	119.45 E
Luzon Str., Phil.	203	20.40 N	121.00 E
L'vov, Sov. Un. (l'vōōf)	167	49.51 N	24.01 E
Lyakhovskiye (Is.), Sov. Un. (lya'kô'v-skyĕ)	181	73.45 N	145.15 E
Lyalta, Can.	95e	51.07 N	113.36 W
Lyalya R., Sov. Un. (lyȧ'lyȧ)	182a	58.58 N	60.17 E
Lyaskovets, Bul.	173	43.07 N	25.41 E
Lydenburg, S. Afr. (lī'dĕn-bûrg)	226	25.06 S	30.21 E
Lydiate, Eng.	64a	53.32 N	2.57 W
Lye Green, Eng.	62	51.43 N	0.35 W
Lyell, Mt., Ca. (lī'ĕl)	120	37.44 N	119.22 W
Lykens, Pa. (lī'kĕnz)	111	40.35 N	76.45 W
Lyna R., Pol. (lĭn'ȧ)	167	53.56 N	20.30 E
Lynbrook, NY	55	40.39 N	73.41 W
Lynch, Ky. (lĭnch)	126	36.56 N	82.55 W
Lynchburg, Va. (lĭnch'bûrg)	127	37.23 N	79.08 W
Lynch Cove, Wa. (lĭnch)	118a	47.26 N	122.54 W
Lynden, Can. (lĭn'dĕn)	95d	43.14 N	80.08 W
Lynden, Wa.	118d	48.56 N	122.27 W
Lyndhurst, Austl.	211a	38.03 S	145.14 E
Lyndhurst, NJ	55	40.49 N	74.07 W
Lyndhurst, Oh.	56a	41.31 N	81.30 W
Lyndon, Ky. (lĭn'dŭn)	113h	38.15 N	85.36 W
Lyndonville, Vt. (lĭn'dŭn-vĭl)	111	44.35 N	72.00 W
Lyne, Eng.	62	51.23 N	0.33 W
Lynn, Ma. (lĭn)	105a	42.28 N	70.57 W
Lynnewood Gardens, Pa.	56b	40.04 N	75.09 W
Lynnfield, Ma.	54a	42.32 N	71.03 W
Lynn Lake, Can. (lāk)	101	56.51 N	100.30 W
Lynwood, Ca. (lĭn'wōōd)	119a	33.56 N	118.13 W
Lyon, Fr. (lē-ôN')	168	45.44 N	4.52 E
Lyons, Ga. (lī'ŭnz)	127	32.08 N	82.19 W
Lyons, Il.	58a	41.49 N	87.50 W
Lyons, Ks.	122	38.20 N	98.11 W
Lyons, Ne.	114	41.57 N	96.28 W
Lyons, NJ	112a	40.41 N	74.33 W
Lyons, NY	111	43.05 N	77.00 W
Lysefjorden (Fd.), Nor.	164	58.59 N	6.35 E
Lysekil, Swe. (lü'sĕ-kĕl)	164	58.17 N	11.22 E
Lysterfield, Austl.	70b	37.56 S	145.18 E
Lys'va, Sov. Un. (lĭs'vȧ)	182a	58.07 N	57.47 E
Lytham, Eng. (lĭth'ăm)	156	53.44 N	2.58 W
Lytkarino, Sov. Un.	182b	55.25 N	37.55 E
Lyttelton, S. Afr. (lĭt'l'tŏn)	227b	25.51 S	28.13 E
Lyuban', Sov. Un. (lyōō'bȧn)	182c	59.21 N	31.15 E
Lyubar, Sov. Un. (lyōō'bär)	175	49.56 N	27.44 E
Lyubertsy, Sov. Un. (lyōō'bĕr-tsĕ)	182b	55.40 N	37.55 E
Lyubim, Sov. Un. (lyōō-bēm')	174	58.24 N	40.39 E
Lyublino, Sov. Un. (lyōōb'lĭ-nô)	182b	55.41 N	37.45 E
Lyudinovo, Sov. Un. (lū-dē'novō)	174	53.52 N	34.28 E

M

PLACE (Pronounciation)	PAGE	Lat. °′	Long. °′
Ma'ān, Jordan (mä-än')	191a	30.12 N	35.45 E
Maartensdijk, Neth.	157a	52.09 N	5.10 E
Maas (R.), Neth.	169c	51.32 N	6.07 E
Maastricht, Neth. (mäs'trĭKt)	163	50.51 N	5.35 E
Mabaia, Ang.	230	7.13 S	14.03 E
Mabana, Wa. (mä-bä-nä)	118a	48.06 N	122.25 W
Mabank, Tx. (mă'bănk)	125	32.21 N	96.05 W
Mabeskraal, S. Afr.	223d	25.12 S	26.47 E
Mableton, Ga. (mā'b'l-tŭn)	112c	33.49 N	84.34 W
Mabrouk, Mali	224	19.27 N	1.16 W
Mabula, S. Afr. (mă'bōō-la)	223d	24.49 S	27.59 E
Macaé, Braz. (mä-kä-ā')	141a	22.22 S	41.47 W
Macaira (R.), Ven. (mä-kī'rä)	143b	9.37 N	66.16 W
Macalelon, Phil. (mä-kä-lā-lōn')	207a	13.46 N	122.09 E
Macao, Asia	199	22.00 N	113.00 E
Macapá, Braz. (mä-kä-pä')	143	0.08 N	50.02 W
Macau, Braz. (mä-kä'ōō)	143	5.12 S	36.34 W
Macaya, Pico de (Pk.), Hai.	135	18.25 N	74.00 W
Macclesfield, Eng. (măk''lz-fēld)	156	53.15 N	2.07 W
Macclesfield Can., Eng. (măk''lz-fēld)	156	53.14 N	2.07 W
Macdona, Tx. (măk-dō'nȧ)	119d	29.20 N	98.42 W
Macdonald (I.), Austl. (măk-dŏn'ăld)	214	23.40 S	127.40 E
Macdonnell Ra., Austl. (măk-dŏn'ĕl)	214	23.40 S	131.30 E
MacDowell L., Can. (măk-dou ĕl)	101	52.15 N	92.45 W
Macdui, Ben (Mtn.), Scot. (bĕn măk-dōō'ē)	162	57.06 N	3.45 W
Macedonia, Oh. (măs-ē-dō'nĭ-ȧ)	113d	41.19 N	81.30 E
Macedonia (Reg.), Eur. (măs-ē-dō'nĭ-ȧ)	173	41.05 N	22.15 E
Maceió, Braz. (mä-sȧ-yō')	143	9.33 S	35.35 W
Macerata, It. (mä-chå-rä'tä)	172	43.18 N	13.28 E
Macfarlane, L., Austl. (măc'fär-lān)	216	32.10 S	137.00 E
Machache (Mtn.), Leso.	223c	29.22 S	27.53 E
Machado, Braz. (mä-shȧ-dō)	141a	21.42 S	45.55 W
Machakos, Ken.	231	1.31 S	37.16 E
Machala, Ec. (mä-chȧ'lä)	142	3.18 S	78.54 W
Machens, Mo. (măk'ĕns)	119e	38.54 N	90.20 W
Machias, Me. (mȧ-chī'ȧs)	104	44.22 N	67.29 W
Machida, Jap. (mä-chē'dä)	205a	35.32 N	139.28 E
Machilīpatnam, India	197	16.22 N	81.10 E
Machu Picchu, Peru (mȧ'chōō-pē'k-chōō)	142	13.07 S	72.34 W
Măcin, Rom. (mȧ-chēn')	175	45.15 N	28.09 E
Macina (Depression), Mali	228	14.50 N	4.40 W
Mackay, Austl. (mȧ-kī')	215	21.15 S	149.08 E
Mackay, Id. (măk-kā')	117	43.55 N	113.38 W
Mackay (l), Austl. (mȧ-kī')	214	22.30 S	127.45 E
MacKay (L.), Can. (măk-kā')	96	64.10 N	112.35 W
Mackay (R.), Can.	100	56.50 N	112.30 W
Mackenzie (R.), Can.	96	63.38 N	124.23 W
Mackenzie B., Ak.	107	69.20 N	137.10 W
Mackenzie, Dist. of, Can.	96	63.48 N	125.25 W
Mackenzie Mts., Can. (mȧ-kĕn'zĭ)	96	63.41 N	129.27 W
Mackinac, Str. of, Mi. (măk'ĭ-nô) (măk'ĭ-năk)	110	45.50 N	84.40 W
Mackinaw (R.), Il.	110	40.35 N	89.25 W
Mackinaw City, Mi. (măk'ĭ-nô)	110	45.45 N	84.45 W
Mackinnon Road, Ken.	231	3.44 S	39.03 E
Macleantown, S. Afr. (măk-lăn'toun)	227c	32.48 S	27.48 E
Maclear, S. Afr. (mȧ-klēr')	227c	31.06 S	28.23 E
Macleod, Austl.	70b	37.43 S	145.04 E
Macomb, Il. (mȧ-kōōm')	123	40.27 N	90.40 W
Mâcon, Fr. (mä-KôN)	168	46.19 N	4.51 E
Macon, Ga. (mā'kŏn)	126	32.49 N	83.39 W
Macon, Ms.	126	32.07 N	88.31 W
Macon, Mo.	123	39.42 N	92.29 W
Macquarie (R.), Austl.	216	31.43 S	148.04 E
Macquarie Fields, Austl.	70a	33.59 S	150.53 E
Macquarie Is., Austl. (mȧ-kwŏr'ĕ)	232	54.36 S	158.45 E
Macquarie University (P. Int.), Austl.	70a	33.46 S	151.06 E
Macritchie Res., Singapore	67c	1.21 N	103.50 E
Macuelizo, Hond. (mä-kwĕ-lē'zô)	132	15.22 N	88.32 W
Macuto, Ven.	61a	10.37 N	66.53 W
Ma'dabā, Jordan	191a	31.43 N	34.47 E
Madagascar, Afr. (măd-ȧ-găs'kȧr)	222	18.05 S	43.12 E
Madame (I.), Can. (mȧ-dȧm')	105	45.33 N	61.02 W
Madanapalle, India	197	13.06 N	78.09 E
Madang, Pap. N. Gui. (mä-däng')	207	5.15 S	145.45 E
Madaoua, Niger (mȧ-dou'ȧ)	224	14.04 N	6.03 E
Madawaska (R.), Can. (măd-ȧ-wôs'kȧ)	111	45.20 N	77.25 W
Madeira (R.), Braz.	142	6.48 S	62.43 W
Madeira, Arquipelado da (Is.), Port. (är-kē-pĕ'lä-gō-dä-mä-dĕý-rä)	224	33.26 N	16.44 W
Madeira, Ilha da (I.), Mad. Is. (mä-dā'rä)	224	32.41 N	16.15 W
Madelia, Mn. (mȧ-dē'lĭ-ȧ)	115	44.03 N	94.23 W
Madeline (I.), Wi. (măd'ĕ-lĭn)	115	46.47 N	91.30 W
Madera, Ca. (mȧ-dā'rȧ)	120	36.57 N	120.04 W
Madera (Vol.), Nic.	132	11.27 N	85.30 W

ng-sing; nŋ-banŋk; N-nasalized n; nŏd; cŏmmit; ōld; ôbey; ôrder; oi-boil; fōōd; fŏŏt; ou-out; s-soft; sh-dish; th-thin; pūre; ůnite; ûrn; stŭd; circŭs; ü-as in French tu; '-indeterminate vowel.

310 Madgaon – Mamburao

PLACE (Pronounciation)	PAGE	Lat. °′	Long. °′
Madgaon, India	197	15.09 N	73.58 E
Madhya Pradesh (State), India (mŭd'vŭ prŭ-dāsh')	196	22.04 N	77.48 E
Madill, Ok. (mȧ-dĭl')	123	34.04 N	96.45 W
Madīnat ash Sha'b, P.D.R. of Yem.	192	12.45 N	44.00 E
Madingo, Con.	230	4.07 S	11.22 E
Madingou, Con.	230	4.09 S	13.34 E
Madison, Fl. (măd'ĭ-sŭn)	126	30.28 N	83.25 W
Madison, Ga.	126	33.34 N	83.29 W
Madison, Il.	119e	38.40 N	90.09 W
Madison, In.	110	38.45 N	85.25 W
Madison, Ks.	123	38.08 N	96.07 W
Madison, Me.	104	44.47 N	69.52 W
Madison, Mn.	114	44.59 N	96.13 W
Madison, NC	127	36.22 N	79.59 W
Madison, Ne.	114	41.49 N	97.27 W
Madison, NJ	112a	40.46 N	74.25 W
Madison, SD	114	44.01 N	97.08 W
Madison, Wi.	115	43.05 N	89.23 W
Madison Heights, Mi.	57c	42.30 N	83.06 W
Madison R, Mt.	117	45.15 N	111.30 W
Madison Res, Mt.	117	45.25 N	111.28 W
Madisonville, Ky. (măd'ĭ-sŭn-vĭl)	110	37.20 N	87.30 W
Madisonville, La.	119	30.22 N	90.10 W
Madisonville, Tx.	119	30.57 N	95.55 W
Madjori, Burkina	228	11.26 N	1.15 E
Mado Gashi, Ken.	231	0.44 N	39.10 E
Madona, Sov. Un. (mȧ'dô'nȧ)	174	56.50 N	26.14 E
Mad R., Ca. (măd)	116	40.38 N	123.37 W
Madrakah, Ra's al (C.), Om.	192	18.53 N	57.48 E
Madras, India (mȧ-drȧs') (mŭ-drŭs')	197	13.08 N	80.15 E
Madre de Dios, Arch., Chile (mä'drå dā dē-ōs')	144	50.40 S	76.30 W
Madre de Dios, Rio (R.), Bol. (rē'ō-mä'drå dā dē-ōs')	142	12.07 S	68.02 W
Madre del Sur, Sierra (Mts.), Mex. (sē-ĕ'r-rä-mä'drå dĕlsōōr')	130	17.35 N	100.35 W
Madre, Laguna L., Mex. (lä-gōō'nä mä'drå)	119	25.08 N	97.41 W
Madre, Sierra (Mts.), Mex. (sē-ĕ'r-rä-mȧ'drĕ)	130	15.55 N	92.40 W
Madre, Sierra (Mts.), Phil.	207a	16.40 N	122.10 E
Madrid, Ia. (măd'rĭd)	115	41.51 N	93.48 W
Madrid, Sp. (mä-drē'd)	171a	40.26 N	3.42 W
Madridejos, Sp. (mä-dhrē-dhā'hōs)	170	39.29 N	3.32 W
Madrillon, Va.	56d	38.55 N	77.14 W
Madura (I.), Indon. (mȧ-dōō'rä)	206	6.45 S	113.30 E
Madurai, India (mä-dōō'rä)	197	9.57 N	78.04 E
Madureira (Neigh.), Braz.	61c	22.53 S	43.21 W
Madureira, Serra do, (Mtn.), Braz. (sĕ'r-rä-dô-mä-dōō-rā'rȧ)	144b	22.49 S	43.30 W
Maebashi, Jap. (mä-ē-bä'shē)	205	36.26 N	139.04 E
Maeno (Neigh.), Jap.	69a	35.46 N	139.42 E
Maestra, Sierra (Mts.), Cuba (sē-ĕ'r-rȧ-mä-ās'trä)	134	20.05 N	77.05 W
Maewo (I.), Vanuatu	215	15.17 S	168.16 E
Mafeking, S. Afr. (mäf'ē-kĭng)	226	25.46 S	24.45 E
Mafia (I.), Tan. (mä-fē'ä)	231	7.47 S	40.00 E
Mafra, Braz. (mä'frä)	144	26.21 S	49.59 W
Mafra, Port. (mäf'rȧ)	171b	38.56 N	9.20 W
Magadan, Sov. Un. (mȧ-gȧ-dän')	181	59.39 N	150.43 E
Magadan Oblast, Sov. Un.	181	63.00 N	170.30 E
Magadi, Ken.	231	1.54 S	36.17 E
Magadi (L.), Ken. (mȧ-gä'dē)	231	1.50 S	36.00 E
Magalhães Bastos (Neigh.), Braz.	61c	22.53 S	43.23 W
Magalies (R), S. Afr. (mä-gä'lyĕs)	227b	25.51 S	27.42 E
Magaliesberg (Mts.), S. Afr.	227b	25.45 S	27.43 E
Magaliesburg, S. Afr.	223d	26.01 S	27.32 E
Magallanes, Phil. (mä-gäl-yä'näs)	207a	12.48 N	123.52 E
Magallanes, Estrecho de (Str.), Arg.-Chile (ĕs-trĕ'chô-dĕ-mä-gäl-yä'nĕs)	144	52.30 S	68.45 W
Magangué, Col. (mä-gän'gā)	142	9.08 N	74.56 W
Magat (R.), Phil. (mä-gät')	207a	16.45 N	121.16 E
Magdalena, Arg. (mäg-dä-lā'nä)	141c	35.05 S	57.32 W
Magdalena, Bol.	142	13.17 S	63.57 W
Magdalena (I.), Chile	144	44.45 S	73.15 W
Magdalena, Mex.	108	30.34 N	110.50 W
Magdalena, NM	121	34.10 N	107.45 W
Magdalena, Bahia (B.), Mex. (bä-ē'ä-mäg-dä-lā'nä)	128	24.30 N	114.00 W
Magdalena Contreras, Mex.	60a	19.18 N	99.17 W
Magdalena del Mar, Peru	60c	12.06 S	77.05 W
Magdalena, Rio (R.), Col.	142	7.45 N	74.04 W
Magdalen Is., Can. (măg'dȧ-lĕn)	105	47.27 N	61.25 W
Magdalen Laver, Eng.	62	51.45 N	0.11 E
Magdeburg, G.D.R. (mäg'dĕ-bŏŏrgh)	166	52.07 N	11.39 E
Magé, Braz. (mä-zhā')	144b	22.39 S	43.02 W
Magenta, It. (mȧ-jĕn'tȧ)	172	45.26 N	8.53 E
Mageroya (I.), Nor.	158	71.10 N	24.11 E
Maggiore, Lago (L.), It.	172	46.03 N	8.25 E
Maghāghah, Egypt	223b	28.38 N	30.50 W
Maghniyya, Alg.	160	34.52 N	1.40 W
Maghull, Eng.	64a	53.32 N	2.57 W
Maginu, Jap.	69a	35.35 N	139.36 E
Magiscatzin, Mex. (mä-kēs-kät-zēn')	130	22.48 N	98.42 W
Maglaj, Yugo. (mȧ'glä-ē)	173	44.34 N	18.12 E
Magliana (Neigh.), It.	66c	41.50 N	12.25 E
Maglić, Yugo. (mäg'lēch)	173	43.36 N	20.36 E
Maglie, It. (mäl'yā)	173	40.06 N	18.20 E
Magna, Ut. (măg'nȧ)	119b	40.43 N	112.06 W
Magnitogorsk, Sov. Un. (mȧg-nyē'tô-gôrsk)	182a	53.26 N	59.05 E
Magnolia, Ar. (măg-nō'lĭ-ȧ)	123	33.16 N	93.13 W
Magnolia, Ms.	126	31.08 N	90.27 W
Magnolia, NJ	56b	39.51 N	75.02 W
Magny-en-Vexin, Fr. (mä-nyē'ĕN-vĕ-sȧN')	169b	49.09 N	1.45 E
Magny-les-Hameaux, Fr.	64c	48.44 N	2.04 E
Magog, Can. (mȧ-gŏg')	111	45.15 N	72.10 W
Magome (Neigh.), Jap.	69a	35.35 N	139.43 E
Magpie (R.), Can.	102	50.40 N	64.30 W
Magpie (R.), Can.	115	48.13 N	84.50 W
Magpie Lac (L.), Can.	104	50.55 N	64.39 W
Magrath, Can.	99	49.25 N	112.52 W
Maguanying, China	67b	39.52 N	116.17 E
Magude, Moz. (mä-gōō'dȧ)	226	24.58 S	32.39 E
Magwe, Bur. (mŭg-wā')	198	20.19 N	94.57 E
Mahābād, Iran	179	36.55 N	45.50 E
Mahahi Port, Zaire (mä-hä'gē)	225	2.14 N	31.12 E
Mahajanga, Mad.	227	15.12 S	46.26 E
Mahakam (Strm.), Indon.	206	0.30 S	116.15 E
Mahali Mts., Tan.	231	6.20 S	30.00 E
Mahaly, Mad. (mȧ-hȧl-ē')	227	24.09 S	46.20 E
Mahameru, Gunung (Mtn.), Indon.	206	8.00 S	112.50 E
Mahānadi (R.), India (mŭ-hä-nŭd'ē)	196	20.50 N	84.27 E
Mahanoro, Mad. (mȧ-hȧ-nō'rō)	227	19.57 S	48.47 E
Mahanoy City, Pa. (mä-hȧ-noi')	111	40.50 N	76.10 W
Mahārāshtra (State), India	196	19.06 N	75.00 E
Maḥaṭṭat al-Hilmīyah (Neigh.), Egypt	71a	30.07 N	31.19 E
Maḥaṭṭat al Qaṭrānah, Jordan	191a	31.15 N	36.04 E
Maḥaṭṭat 'Aqabat al Hijāzīyah, Jordan	191a	29.45 N	35.55 E
Maḥaṭṭat ar Ramlah, Jordan	191	29.31 N	35.57 E
Maḥaṭṭat Jurf ad Darāwīsh, Jordan	191a	30.41 N	35.51 E
Mahavavy (R.), Mad. (mä-hä-vä'vē)	227	17.42 S	46.06 E
Mahaweli (R.), India	196	7.47 N	80.43 E
Mahd adh-Dhahab, Sau. Ar.	195	23.30 N	40.52 E
Mahe, India (mä-ā')	197	11.42 N	75.39 E
Mahenge, Tan. (mä-hĕŋ'gȧ)	231	7.38 S	36.16 E
Mahi (R.), India	196	23.16 N	73.20 E
Māhīm (Neigh.), India	67e	19.03 N	72.49 E
Māhīm Bay, India	197b	19.03 N	72.45 E
Mahlabatini, S. Afr. (mä'lȧ-bȧ-tē'nē)	227c	28.15 S	31.29 E
Mahlow, G.D.R. (mä'lōv)	157b	52.23 N	13.24 E
Mahlsdorf (Neigh.), G.D.R.	65a	52.31 N	13.37 E
Mahlsdorf-Süd (Neigh.), G.D.R.	65a	52.29 N	13.36 E
Mahnomen, Mn. (mô-nō'mĕn)	114	47.18 N	95.58 W
Mahón, Sp. (mä-ōn')	171	39.52 N	4.15 E
Mahone B., Can.	104	44.30 N	64.15 W
Mahone Bay, Can. (mȧ-hōn')	104	44.27 N	64.23 W
Mahopac, L., NY (mā-hō'păk)	112a	41.24 N	73.45 W
Mahrauli (Neigh.), India	67d	28.31 N	77.11 E
Māhul (Neigh.), India	67e	19.01 N	72.53 E
Mahwah, NJ (mȧ-wä')	112a	41.05 N	74.09 W
Maidenhead, Eng. (mād'ĕn-hĕd)	156b	51.30 N	0.44 W
Maidstone, Austl.	70b	37.47 S	144.52 E
Maidstone, Eng.	156b	51.17 N	0.32 E
Maiduguri, Nig. (mä'ē-dȧ-gōō'rē)	229	11.51 N	13.10 E
Maigualida Sierra (Mts.), Ven. (sē-ĕ'r-rȧ-mī-gwä'lē-dĕ)	142	6.30 N	65.50 W
Maijdi, Bngl.	196	22.59 N	91.08 E
Maikop, see Maykop			
Main (R.), F.R.G. (mīn)	166	49.49 N	9.20 E
Main Barrier Ra., Austl. (băr'ĭ'ēr)	216	31.25 S	141.40 E
Mai-Ndombe, Lac (Leopold II, L.), Zaire	226	2.16 S	19.00 E
Maine (State), U. S. (mān)	109	45.25 N	69.50 W
Mainland (I.), Scot. (mān-lănd)	162a	60.19 N	2.40 W
Maintenon, Fr. (mäN-tĕ-nôN')	169b	48.35 N	1.35 E
Maintirano, Mad. (mä'ēn-tē-rä'nō)	227	18.05 S	44.08 E
Mainz, F.R.G. (mīnts)	166	49.59 N	8.16 E
Maio I., C. V. (mä'yo)	224b	15.15 N	22.50 W
Maipo (R.), Chile (mī'pô)	141b	33.45 S	71.08 W
Maipo (Vol.), Arg.	144	34.08 S	69.51 W
Maipú, Arg. (mī'pōō')	141c	36.51 S	57.54 W
Maipú, Chile	61b	33.31 S	70.46 W
Maiquetía, Ven. (mī-kĕ-tē'ä)	143b	10.37 N	66.56 W
Maisí, Punta (Pt.), Cuba (pōōn'n-tä-mī-sē')	135	20.10 N	74.00 W
Maison-Rouge, Fr. (mā-zôN-rōōzh')	169b	48.34 N	3.09 E
Maisons-Alfort, Fr.	64c	48.48 N	2.26 E
Maisons-Laffitte, Fr.	64c	48.57 N	2.09 E
Maitani, Jap.	69b	34.49 N	135.22 E
Maitland, Austl. (māt'lănd)	216	32.45 S	151.40 E
Maizuru, Jap. (mä-ĭ'zōō-rōō)	205	32.26 N	135.15 E
Majene, Indon.	206	3.34 S	119.00 E
Maji, Eth.	225	6.14 N	35.34 E
Majorca (I.), see Mallorca			
Makah Ind. Res., Wa. (mȧ kī')	116	48.17 N	124.52 W
Makala, Zaire	71c	4.25 S	15.15 E
Makanya, Tan. (mä-kän'yä)	227	4.15 S	37.49 E
Makanza, Zaire	225	1.42 N	19.08 E
Makarska, Yugo. (mȧ'kär-skȧ)	172	43.17 N	17.05 E
Makar'yev, Sov. Un.	178	57.50 N	43.48 E
Makasar, see Ujung Pandang			
Makasar, Selat (Makassar Strait), Indon.	206	2.00 S	118.07 E
Makati, Phil.	68g	14.34 N	121.01 E
Makaw, Zaire	230	3.29 S	18.19 E
Make (I.), Jap. (mä'kȧ)	205	30.43 N	130.49 E
Makeni, S. L.	228	8.53 N	12.03 W
Makeyevka, Sov. Un. (mŭk-yä'ūf-kŭ)	175	48.03 N	38.00 E
Makgadikgadi Pans (L.), Bots.	223	20.38 S	21.31 E
Makhachkala, Sov. Un. (mäK'äch-kä'lä)	179	43.00 N	47.40 E
Makhaleng (R.), Leso.	227c	29.53 S	27.33 E
Makindu, Ken.	231	2.17 S	37.49 E
M'akino, Sov. Un.	66b	55.48 N	37.22 E
Makkah (Mecca), Sau. Ar. (mĕk'ȧ)	192	21.27 N	39.45 E
Makkovik, Can.	97	55.01 N	59.10 W
Makó, Hung. (mô'kō)	167	46.13 N	20.30 E
Makokou, Gabon (mȧ-kô-kōō')	230	0.34 N	12.52 E
Maków Mazowiecki, Pol. (mä'kōov mä-zō-vyĕts'kē)	167	52.51 N	21.07 E
Makuhari, Jap. (mä-kōō-hä'rē)	205a	35.39 N	140.04 E
Makurazaki, Jap. (mä'kōō-rä-zä'kē)	205	31.16 N	130.18 E
Makurdi, Nig.	229	7.45 N	8.32 E
Makushin, Ak. (mȧ-kōō'shĭn)	107	53.57 N	166.28 W
Makushino, Sov. Un. (mȧ-kōō-shē'nô)	180	55.03 N	67.43 E
Malabar Coast, India (măl'ȧ-bär)	197	11.19 N	75.33 E
Malabar Pt., India	67e	18.57 N	72.47 E
Malabo, Equat. Gui.	230	3.45 N	8.47 E
Malabon, Phil.	207a	14.39 N	120.57 E
Malacca, Str. of, Asia (mȧ-lăk'ȧ)	206	4.15 N	99.44 E
Malad, Id. (mȧ-läd')	117	42.11 N	112.15 W
Málaga, Col. (mä'lä-gȧ)	142	6.41 N	72.46 W
Málaga, Sp.	170	36.45 N	4.25 W
Malagón, Sp. (mä-lä-gōn')	170	39.12 N	3.52 W
Malaita (I.), Sol. Is. (mȧ-lä'ē-tȧ)	215	8.38 S	161.15 E
Malakāl, Sud. (mȧ-lȧ-käl')	225	9.46 N	31.54 E
Malakhovka, Sov. Un. (mȧ-läk'ôf-kȧ)	182b	55.38 N	38.01 E
Malakoff, Fr.	64c	48.49 N	2.19 E
Malakpur (Neigh.), India	67d	28.42 N	77.12 E
Malang, Indon.	206	8.06 S	112.50 E
Malange, Ang. (mä-läŋ-gȧ)	230	9.32 S	16.20 E
Malanville, Benin	224	12.04 N	3.09 E
Malapedia (R.), Can.	104	48.11 N	67.08 W
Mala Punta (Pt.), Pan. (pōō'n-tä-mä'lä)	133	7.32 N	79.44 W
Mälaren (L.), Swe.	164	59.38 N	16.55 E
Malartic, Can.	97	48.07 N	78.11 W
Malaspina Str. Can. (măl-ȧ-spē'nȧ)	98	49.44 N	124.20 W
Malatya, Tur. (mȧ-lä'tyȧ)	179	38.30 N	38.15 E
Malawi, Afr.	222	11.15 S	33.45 E
Malawi, L., see Nyasa, L.			
Malaya (Reg.), Mala. (mȧ-lā'yä)	206	3.35 N	101.30 E
Malaya Vishera, Sov. Un. (vē-shä'rä)	174	58.51 N	32.13 E
Malay Pen., Asia (mȧ-lā') (mā'lā)	206	7.46 N	101.06 E
Malaysia, Asia (mȧ-lā'zhȧ)	206	4.10 N	101.22 E
Mal B., Ire. (măl)	162	52.51 N	9.45 W
Malbon, Austl. (măl'bŭn)	214	21.15 S	140.30 E
Malbork, Pol. (mäl'bôrk)	167	54.02 N	19.04 E
Malcabran (R.), Port. (mäl-kä-brän')	171b	38.47 N	8.46 W
Malden (I.), Oceania	209	4.20 S	154.30 W
Malden, Ma. (môl'dĕn)	105a	42.26 N	71.04 W
Malden, Mo.	123	36.32 N	89.56 W
Maldives, Asia	190	4.30 N	71.30 E
Maldon, Eng. (môrl'dŏn)	156b	51.44 N	0.39 E
Maldonado, Ur. (mäl-dô-nȧ'dô)	144	34.54 S	54.57 W
Maldonado, Punta (Pt.), Mex. (pōō'n-tä)	130	16.18 N	98.34 W
Maléa, Ákra (C.), Grc.	173	37.31 N	23.13 E
Mālegaon, India	196	20.35 N	74.30 E
Male Karpaty (Mts.), Czech.	167	48.31 N	17.15 E
Malekula (I.), Vanuatu (mä-lā-kōō'lä)	215	16.44 S	167.45 E
Malema, Moz.	231	14.57 S	37.20 E
Malhão da Estrêla (Mtn.), Sp. (mäl-you'N-dȧ-ĕs-trē'lä)	170	40.20 N	7.38 W
Malheur L., Or. (mȧ-lōōr')	116	43.16 N	118.37 W
Malheur R., Or. (mȧ-lōōr')	116	43.45 N	117.41 W
Mali, Afr.	222	15.45 N	0.15 W
Malibu, Ca. (mă'lĭ-bōō)	119a	34.03 N	118.38 W
Malimba, Monts (Mts.), Zaire	231	7.45 S	29.15 E
Malin, Sov. Un. (mȧ-lēn')	175	50.44 N	29.15 E
Malinalco, Mex. (mä-lē-näl'kō)	130	18.54 N	99.31 W
Malinaltepec, Mex. (mä-lē-näl-tȧ-pĕk')	130	17.01 N	98.41 W
Malindi, Ken. (mä-lēn'dē)	227	3.14 S	40.04 E
Malin Hd., N. Ire.	162	55.23 N	7.24 W
Malino, Sov. Un. (mä'lĭ-nô)	182b	55.07 N	38.12 E
Malinovka, Sov. Un. (mȧ-lē-nôf'kȧ)	175	49.50 N	36.43 E
Malkara, Tur. (mäl'Kȧ-rȧ)	173	40.51 N	26.52 E
Malko Tŭrnovo, Bul. (mäl'kō-t'r'nô-vȧ)	173	41.59 N	27.28 E
Mallaig, Scot.	162	56.59 N	5.55 W
Mallawī, Egypt (mȧ-lä'wē)	223b	27.43 S	30.49 E
Mallet Creek, Oh. (măl'ĕt)	113d	41.10 N	81.55 W
Mallorca (Majorca) (I.), Sp. (mäl-yô'r-kä)	171	39.18 N	2.22 E
Mallorquinas, Sp.	65e	41.28 N	2.16 E
Mallow, Ire. (măl'ō)	162	52.07 N	9.04 W
Malmédy, Bel. (mȧl-mā-dē')	163	50.25 N	6.01 E
Malmesbury, S. Afr. (mämz'bēr-ĭ)	226	33.30 S	18.35 E
Malmköping, Swe. (mälm'chû'pĭng)	164	59.09 N	16.39 E
Malmö, Swe. (mälm'û)	164	55.36 N	12.58 E
Malmyzh, Sov. Un. (mȧl-mēzh')	181	49.58 N	137.07 E
Malmyzh, Sov. Un.	178	56.30 N	50.48 E
Malnoue, Fr.	64c	48.50 N	2.36 E
Maloarkhangelsk, Sov. Un. (mä'lô-ȧr-Käŋ'gĕlsk)	174	52.26 N	36.29 E
Malolos, Phil. (mä-lô'lôs)	207a	14.51 N	120.49 E
Malomal'sk, Sov. Un. (mȧ-lô-mälsk'')	182a	58.47 N	59.55 E
Malone, NY (mȧ-lōn')	111	44.50 N	74.20 W
Malonga, Zaire	230	10.24 S	23.10 E
Maloti Mts., Leso	227c	29.00 S	28.29 E
Maloyaroslavets, Sov. Un. (mä'lô-yä-rô-slä-vyĕts)	174	55.01 N	36.25 E
Malozemel'skaya Tundra (Plains), Sov. Un.	178	67.30 N	50.00 E
Malpas, Eng. (măl'pȧz)	144	53.01 N	2.46 W
Malpelo, Isla de (I.), Col. (mäl-pā'lō)	142	3.55 N	81.30 W
Malpeque B., Can. (môl-pĕk')	104	46.30 N	63.47 W
Malta, Eur.	154	35.52 N	13.30 E
Malta, Mt. (môl'tȧ)	117	48.20 N	107.50 W
Maltahöhe, Namibia (mäl'tä-hō'ē)	226	24.45 S	16.45 E
Maltrata, Mex. (mäl-trä'tä)	131	18.48 N	97.16 W
Maluku (Moluccas) (Is.), Indon.	207	2.22 S	128.25 E
Maluku, Laut (Molucca) (Sea), Indon.	207	0.15 N	125.41 E
Malūt, Sud.	225	10.30 N	32.17 E
Mālvan, India	197	16.08 N	73.32 E
Malvern, Ar. (măl'vērn)	123	34.21 N	92.47 W
Malvern (Neigh.), S. Afr.	71b	26.12 S	28.06 E
Malverne, NY	55	40.40 N	73.40 W
Malvern East, S. Afr.	71b	26.12 S	28.08 E
Malyy Anyuy (R.), Sov. Un.	181	67.52 N	164.30 E
Malyy Lyakhovskiye (I.), Sov. Un.	181	74.15 N	142.30 E
Malyy Tamir (I.), Sov. Un.	181	78.10 N	107.30 E
Mamantel, Mex. (mä-män-tĕl')	131	18.36 N	91.06 W
Mamaroneck, NY (măm'ȧ-rō-nĕk)	112a	40.57 N	73.44 W
Mamau, Gui.	224	10.26 N	12.07 W
Mambasa, Zaire,	231	1.21 N	29.03 E
Mamberamo (R.), Indon. (mäm-bȧ-rä'mō)	207	2.30 S	138.00 E
Mamburao, Phil. (mäm-bōō'rä-ō)	207a	13.14 N	120.35 E

PLACE (Pronounciation)	PAGE	Lat. °′	Long. °′
Mamera, Ven.	61a	10.27 N	66.59 W
Mamfe, Cam. (mäm′fĕ)	224	5.46 N	9.17 E
Mamihara, Jap. (mä′mē-hä-rä)	205	32.41 N	131.12 E
Mammoth Cave, Ky. (măm′ŏth)	126	37.10 N	86.04 W
Mammoth Cave Natl. Park, Ky.	126	37.20 N	86.21 W
Mammoth Hot Springs, Wy. (măm′ŭth hôt sprĭngz)	117	44.55 N	110.50 W
Mamnoli, India	197b	19.17 N	73.15 E
Mamoré (R.), Bol. (mä-mô-rā′)	142	13.19 S	65.27 W
Mampong, Ghana	228	7.04 N	1.24 W
Mamry, Jezioro (L.), Pol. (mäm′rĭ)	167	54.10 N	21.28 E
Man, Ivory Coast	228	7.24 N	7.33 W
Manacor, Sp. (mä-nä-kôr′)	171	39.35 N	3.15 E
Manado, Indon.	207	1.29 N	124.50 E
Managua, Cuba (mä-nä′gwä)	135a	22.58 N	82.17 W
Managua, Nic.	132	12.10 N	86.16 W
Managua, Lago de (L.), Nic. (lä′gô-dĕ)	132	12.28 N	86.10 W
Manakara, Mad. (mä-nä-kä′rŭ)	227	22.17 S	48.06 E
Mananara (R.), Mad. (mä-nä-nä′rŭ)	227	23.15 S	48.15 E
Mananjary, Mad. (mä-nän-zhä′rē)	227	20.16 S	48.13 E
Manáos, see Manaus			
Manas, China (mä-nä-sz)	198	44.30 N	86.00 E
Manas (R.), China	198	45.00 N	85.45 E
Manas Hu (L.), China (mä-nä-sü hōō)	198	45.49 N	86.08 E
Manassas, Va. (mȧ-năs′ȧs)	111	38.45 N	77.30 W
Manaus (Manáos), Braz. (mä-nä′ōōzh)	143	3.01 S	60.00 W
Manayunk (Neigh.), Pa.	56b	40.01 N	75.13 W
Mancelona, Mi. (măn-sē-lō′nȧ)	110	44.50 N	85.05 W
Mancha Real, Sp. (män′chä rā-äl′)	170	37.48 N	3.37 W
Manchazh, Sov. Un. (män′chȧsh)	182a	56.30 N	58.10 E
Manchester, Ct. (măn′chĕs-tẽr)	111	41.45 N	72.30 W
Manchester, Eng.	156	53.28 N	2.14 W
Manchester, Ga.	126	32.50 N	84.37 W
Manchester, Ia.	115	42.30 N	91.30 W
Manchester, Ma.	105a	42.35 N	70.47 W
Manchester, Mo.	119e	38.36 N	90.31 W
Manchester, NH	111	43.00 N	71.30 W
Manchester, Oh.	110	38.40 N	83.35 W
Manchester Docks (P. Int.), Eng.	64b	53.28 N	2.17 W
Manchester Ship Canal, Eng.	156	53.20 N	2.40 W
Manchuria (Reg.), China (măn-chōō′rē-ȧ)	199	48.00 N	124.58 E
Mand (R.), Iran	192	28.20 N	52.30 E
Mandal, Nor. (män′däl)	164	58.03 N	7.28 E
Mandalay, Bur. (măn′dȧ-lā)	198	22.00 N	96.08 E
Mandalselva (R.), Nor.	164	58.25 N	7.30 E
Mandaluyong, Phil.	68g	14.35 N	121.02 E
Mandan, ND (măn′dăn)	114	46.49 N	100.54 W
Mandāoli (Neigh.), India	67d	28.38 N	77.18 E
Mandara Mts., Cam.-Nig. (män-dä′rä)	229	10.15 N	13.23 E
Mandau Siak (R.), Indon.	191b	1.03 N	101.25 E
Mandimba, Moz.	231	14.21 S	35.39 E
Mandinga, Pan. (män-dĭŋ′gä)	133	9.32 N	79.04 W
Mandla, India	196	22.43 N	80.23 E
Mándra, Grc. (män′drä)	173	38.06 N	23.32 E
Mandres-les-Roses, Fr.	64c	48.42 N	2.33 E
Mandritsara, Mad. (mȧn-drēt-sä′rȧ)	227	15.49 S	48.47 E
Manduria, It. (män-dōō′rē-ä)	173	40.23 N	17.41 E
Mandve, India	197b	18.47 N	72.52 E
Māndvi, India (mŭnd′vē)	197b	19.29 N	72.53 E
Māndvi, India (mŭnd′vē)	196	22.54 N	69.23 E
Mandvi (Neigh.), India	67e	18.57 N	72.50 E
Mandya, India	197	12.40 N	77.00 E
Manfalūṭ, Egypt (män-fȧ-loot′)	223b	27.18 N	30.59 E
Manfredonia, It. (män-frå-dô′nyä)	172	41.39 N	15.55 E
Manfredónia, Golfo di (G.), It. (gôl-fô-dē)	172	41.34 N	16.05 E
Manga (Reg.), Niger	229	14.00 N	11.50 E
Mangabeiras, Chap. das (Plains), Braz. (shä-pä′däs-däs-mäŋ-gä-bĕ′ē-räzh)	143	8.05 S	47.32 W
Mangalore, India (mŭŋ-gŭ-lōr′)	197	12.53 N	74.52 E
Manganji, Jap.	69a	35.40 N	139.26 E
Mangaratiba, Braz. (män-gä-rä-tē′bȧ)	141a	22.56 S	44.03 W
Mangatarem, Phil. (män′gȧ-tä′rĕm)	207a	15.48 N	120.18 E
Mange, Zaire	230	0.54 N	20.30 E
Mangkalihat, Tandjoeng (C.), Indon. (mäng′kȧ-lē-hät′)	206	1.25 N	119.55 E
Mangles, Islas de, Cuba (ē′s-läs-dĕ-mäŋ′gläs) (măŋ′g′lz)	134	22.05 N	83.50 W
Mangoky (R.), Mad. (män-gō′kē)	227	22.02 S	44.11 E
Mangole, Pulau (I.), Indon.	207	1.35 S	126.22 E
Mangualde, Port. (män-gwäl′dĕ)	170	40.38 N	7.44 W
Mangueira, L. da (L.), Braz. (män-gā′ē-rȧ)	144	33.15 S	52.45 W
Mangum, Ok. (măŋ′gŭm)	122	34.52 N	99.31 W
Mangyshlak, P-Ov. (Pen.), Sov. Un.	179	44.30 N	50.40 E
Mangzhangdian, China (mäŋ-jäŋ-dĭĕn)	200	32.07 N	114.44 E
Manhasset, NY	55	40.48 N	73.42 W
Manhattan, Il.	113a	41.25 N	87.29 W
Manhattan, Ks. (măn-hăt′ăn)	123	39.11 N	96.34 W
Manhattan Beach, Ca.	119a	33.53 N	118.24 W
Manhuaçu, Braz. (män-ōōȧ′sōō)	141a	20.17 S	42.01 W
Manhumirim, Braz. (män-ōō-mē-rē′N)	141a	22.02 S	41.57 W
Mania (R.), Mad. (män′yä)	227	19.52 S	46.02 E
Manicoré, Braz. (mä-nē-kō-rā′)	143	5.53 S	61.13 W
Manicouagane (R.), Can.	97	50.00 N	68.35 W
Manicouagane, Lac (L.), Can.	97	51.30 N	68.19 W
Manicuare, Ven. (mä-nē-kwä′rē)	143b	10.35 N	64.10 W
Manihiki Is., Oceania (mä′nē-hē′kē)	209	9.40 S	158.00 W
Manikuagen, Rivière (R.), Can.	102	49.30 N	68.30 W
Manila, Phil.	207a	14.37 N	121.00 E
Manila B., Phil. (mȧ-nĭl′ȧ)	207a	14.38 N	120.46 E
Manipur (State), India	198	25.00 N	94.00 E
Manique de Baixo, Port.	65d	38.44 N	9.22 W
Manisa, Tur. (mä′nē-sȧ)	179	38.40 N	27.30 E
Manistee, Mi. (măn-ĭs-tē′)	110	44.15 N	86.20 W
Manistee (R.), Mi	110	44.25 N	85.45 W
Manistique, Mi. (măn-ĭs-tēk′)	115	45.58 N	86.16 W
Manistique (L.), Mi	115	46.14 N	85.30 W
Manistique (R.), Mi	115	46.05 N	86.09 W
Manitoba (Prov.), Can. (măn-ĭ-tō′bȧ)	96	55.12 N	97.29 W
Manitoba (L.), Can.	101	51.00 N	98.45 W
Manito L., Can. (măn′ĭ-tō)	100	52.45 N	109.45 W
Manitou (I.), Mi. (măn′ĭ-tōō)	115	47.21 N	87.33 W
Manitou (L.), Can.	115	49.21 N	93.01 W
Manitou Is., Mi.	110	45.05 N	86.00 W
Manitoulin I., Can. (măn-ĭ-tōō′lĭn)	110	45.45 N	81.30 W
Manitou Springs, Co.	122	38.51 N	104.58 W
Manitowoc, Wi. (măn-ĭ-tô-wŏk′)	115	44.05 N	87.42 W
Manitqueira, Serra da (Mts.), Braz. (sĕr′rä dä män-tē-kä′ē-rȧ)	141a	22.40 S	45.12 W
Maniwaki, Can.	103	46.23 N	76.00 W
Manizales, Col. (mä-nē-zä′läs)	142a	5.05 N	75.31 W
Manjacaze, Moz. (man′yä-kä′zĕ)	226	24.37 S	33.49 E
Mānjra (R.), India	196	18.18 N	77.00 E
Mankato, Ks. (măn-kā′tō)	122	39.45 N	98.12 W
Mankato, Mn.	115	44.10 N	93.59 W
Mankim, Cam.	229	5.01 N	12.00 E
Manlléu, Sp. (män-lyā′ōō)	171	42.00 N	2.16 E
Manly, Austl.	70a	33.48 S	151.17 E
Mannar, Sri Lanka (mȧ-när′)	197	9.48 N	80.03 E
Mannar, G. of, India	197	8.47 N	78.33 E
Mannersdorf am Leithagebirge, Aus.	157e	47.58 N	16.36 E
Mannheim, F.R.G. (män′hīm)	166	49.30 N	8.31 E
Manning, Ia. (măn′ĭng)	115	41.53 N	95.04 W
Manning, SC	127	33.41 N	80.12 W
Mannington, WV (măn′ĭng-tŭn)	110	39.30 N	80.55 W
Mannswörth (Neigh.), Aus.	66e	48.09 N	16.31 E
Mannu (R.), It. (mä′n-nōō)	172	39.32 N	9.03 E
Mano (R.), Lib.	228	7.00 N	11.25 W
Man of War B., Ba.	125	21.05 N	74.05 W
Man of War Chan., Ba.	125	22.45 N	76.10 W
Manokwari, Indon. (mȧ-nōk-wä′rē)	207	0.56 S	134.10 E
Manono, Zaire	231	7.18 S	27.25 E
Manor, Can. (măn′ẽr)	101	49.36 N	102.05 W
Manor, Wa.	118c	45.45 N	122.36 W
Manorhaven, NY	55	40.50 N	73.42 W
Manori (Neigh.) India	197b	19.13 N	72.43 E
Manosque, Fr. (mȧ-nôsh′)	169	43.51 N	5.48 E
Manotick, Can.	95c	45.13 N	75.41 W
Manresa, Sp. (män-rā′sä)	171	41.44 N	1.52 E
Mansa, Zambia	231	11.12 S	28.53 E
Mansabá, Guinea-Bissau	228	12.18 N	15.15 W
Mansel (I.), Can. (măn′sĕl)	97	61.56 N	81.10 W
Manseriche, Pongo de (Water Gap), Peru (pŏ′n-gô-dĕ-män-sĕ-rē′chĕ)	142	4.15 S	77.45 W
Mansfield, Eng. (mănz′fēld)	156	53.08 N	1.12 W
Mansfield, La.	125	32.02 N	93.43 W
Mansfield, Oh.	110	40.45 N	82.30 W
Mansfield, Wa.	116	47.48 N	119.39 W
Mansfield, Mt., Vt.	111	44.30 N	72.45 W
Mansfield Woodhouse, Eng. (wŏŏd-hous)	156	53.08 N	1.12 W
Manso (R.), Braz.	143	13.30 S	51.45 W
Manta, Ec. (män′tä)	142	1.03 S	80.16 W
Manteno, Il. (măn-tē-nō)	113a	41.15 N	87.50 W
Manteo, NC	127	35.55 N	75.40 W
Mantes-la-Jolie, Fr. (mäNt-ĕ-lä-zhŏ-lē′)	169b	48.59 N	1.42 E
Manti, Ut. (măn′tī)	121	39.15 N	111.40 W
Mantilla (Neigh.), Cuba	60b	23.04 N	82.20 W
Mantova (Mantua), It. (män′tô-vä) (măn′tū-ȧ)	172	45.09 N	10.47 E
Mantua, Cuba (män-tōō′ȧ)	134	22.20 N	84.15 W
Mantua, Md.	56d	38.51 N	77.15 W
Mantua, Ut. (măn′tū-ȧ)	119b	41.30 N	111.57 W
Mantua, see Mantova			
Manuan (L.), Can. (mä-nōō′ăn)	104	50.36 N	70.50 W
Manuan (R.), Can.	104	50.15 N	70.30 W
Manui, Pulau (Is.), Indon. (mä-nōō′ē)	207	3.35 S	123.38 E
Manus, (I.), Pap. N. Gui. (mä′nōōs)	207	2.22 S	146.22 E
Manvel, Tx. (măn′vel)	125a	29.28 N	95.22 W
Manville, NJ (măn′vĭl)	112a	40.33 N	74.36 W
Manville, RI	112b	41.57 N	71.27 W
Manyal Shīhah, Egypt	71a	29.57 N	31.14 E
Manych (R.), Sov. Un. (mä-nĭch′)	179	47.00 N	41.10 E
Manych Dep., Sov. Un.	155	46.32 N	42.44 E
Manych-Gudilo (Lake), Sov. Un.	179	46.40 N	42.50 E
Manzala L., Egypt	223b	31.14 N	32.04 E
Manzanares, Col. (män-sä-nä′rĕs)	142a	5.15 N	75.09 W
Manzanares (R.), Sp. (mänz-nä′rĕs)	171a	40.36 N	3.48 W
Manzanares, Canal del, Sp. (kä-nä′l-dĕl-män-thä-nä′rĕs)	171a	40.20 N	3.38 W
Manzanillo, Cuba (män′zä-nēl′yō)	134	20.20 N	77.05 W
Manzanillo, Mex.	130	19.02 N	104.21 W
Manzanillo, Bahía de (B.), Hai.	135	19.55 N	71.50 W
Manzanillo, Bahía de (B.), Mex. (bä-ē′ä-dĕ-män-zä-nē′l-yō)	130	19.00 N	104.38 W
Manzanillo, Punta (Pt.), Pan.	133	9.40 N	79.33 W
Manzhouli, China (män-jō-lē)	202	49.25 N	117.15 E
Manzovka, Sov. Un. (mȧn-zhô′f-kȧ)	204	44.16 N	132.13 E
Mao, Chad (mä′ō)	229	14.07 N	15.19 E
Mao, Dom. Rep.	135	19.35 N	71.10 W
Maoke, Pegunungan (Mtn.), Indon.	207	4.00 S	138.00 E
Maoming, China	203	21.55 N	110.40 E
Maoniu Shan (Mtn.), China (mou-nĭō shän)	202	32.45 N	104.09 E
Mapastepec, Mex. (ma-päs-tā-pĕk′)	131	15.24 N	92.52 W
Mapia, Kepulauan (I.), Indon. (mä′pē-ä)	207	0.57 N	134.22 E
Mapimi, Mex. (mä-pē-mē′)	124	25.50 N	103.50 W
Mapimi, Bolsón de (Des.), Mex. (bôl-sŏ′n-dĕ-mä-pē′mē)	124	27.27 N	103.20 W
Maple Creek, Can. (mā′p′l) (crēk)	100	49.55 N	109.27 W
Maple Cross, Eng.	62	51.37 N	0.30 W
Maple Grove, Can. (grōv)	95a	45.19 N	73.51 W
Maple Heights, Oh.	113d	41.25 N	81.34 W
Maple Leaf Gardens (P. Int.), Can.	54c	43.40 N	79.23 W
Maple Shade, NJ (shād)	112f	39.57 N	75.01 W
Maple Valley, Wa. (văl′ē)	118a	47.24 N	122.02 W
Maplewood, Mn. (wŏŏd)	119g	45.00 N	93.03 W
Maplewood, Mo.	119e	38.37 N	90.20 W
Maplewood, NJ	55	40.44 N	74.17 W
Mapocho (R.), Chile	61b	33.25 S	70.47 W
Mapumulo, S. Afr. (mä-pä-mōō′lō)	227c	29.12 S	31.05 E
Maputo (Lourenço Marques), Moz.	226	26.50 S	32.30 E
Maqueda Chan., Phil. (mä-kā′dä)	207a	13.40 N	123.52 E
Maquela do Zombo, Ang. (mȧ-kā′lȧ dōō zôm′bōō)	226	6.08 S	15.15 E
Maquoketa, Ia. (mȧ-kō-kē-tȧ)	115	42.04 N	90.42 W
Maquoketa (R.), Ia.	115	42.08 N	90.40 W
Maracaibo, Ven. (mä-rä-kī′bō)	142	10.38 N	71.45 W
Maracaibo, Lago de (L.), Ven. (lä′gô-dĕ-mä-rä-kī′bō)	142	9.55 N	72.13 W
Maracay, Ven. (mä-rä-käy′)	143b	10.15 N	67.35 W
Marādah, Libya	225	29.10 N	19.07 E
Maradi, Niger (mȧ-rȧ-dē′)	229	13.29 N	7.06 E
Marāgheh, Iran	179	37.20 N	46.10 E
Maraisburg, S. Afr.	227b	26.12 S	27.57 E
Marais des Cygnes (R.), Ks.	123	38.30 N	95.30 W
Marajó, Ilha de (I.), Braz. (mȧ-rä-zhō′)	143	0.30 N	50.00 W
Maralal, Ken.	231	1.06 N	36.42 E
Marali, Cen. Afr. Rep.	229	6.01 N	18.24 E
Marand, Iran	195	38.26 N	45.46 E
Maranguape, Braz. (mä-rȧŋ-gwä′pĕ)	143	3.48 S	38.38 W
Maranhão (State), Braz. (mä-rän-youN)	143	5.15 S	45.52 W
Maranhão see São Luis			
Maranoa (R.), Austl. (mä-rä-nō′ä)	216	27.01 S	148.03 E
Marano di Napoli, It. (mä-rä′nō-dē-nä′pô-lē)	171c	40.39 N	14.12 E
Marañón, Rio (R.), Peru (rē′ō-mä-rä-nyōn′)	142	4.26 S	75.08 W
Maraoli (Neigh.), India	67e	19.03 N	72.54 E
Marapanim, Braz. (mä-rä-pä-nē′N)	143	0.45 S	47.42 W
Maras, Tur. (mä-räsh′)	179	37.40 N	36.50 E
Marathon, Can.	102	48.50 N	86.10 W
Marathon, Fl. (măr′ȧ-thŏn)	127a	24.41 N	81.06 W
Marathon, Oh.	113f	39.09 N	83.59 W
Maravatio, Mex. (mä-rȧ-vä′tē-ō)	130	19.54 N	100.25 W
Marawi, Sud.	225	18.07 N	31.57 E
Marayong, Austl.	70a	33.45 S	150.54 E
Marble Bar, Austl. (märb″l bär)	214	21.15 S	119.15 E
Marble Can., Az. (mär′b′l)	121	36.21 N	111.48 W
Marble Hall, S. Afr. (hȧll)	223d	24.59 S	29.19 E
Marblehead, Ma. (mär′b′l-hĕd)	105a	42.30 N	70.51 W
Marburg an der Lahn, F.R.G.	166	50.49 N	8.46 E
Marcala, Hond. (mär-kä-lä)	132	14.08 N	88.01 W
Marca, Ponta da (Pt.), Ang.	230	16.31 S	11.42 E
Marceline, Mo. (mär-sē-lēn′)	123	39.42 N	92.56 W
Marche (Reg.), It. (mär′kā)	174	43.35 N	12.33 E
Marchegg, Aus.	157e	48.18 N	16.55 E
Marchena (I.), Ec. (ē′s-lä-mär-chē′nä)	142	0.29 N	90.31 W
Marchena, Sp. (mär-chä′nä)	170	37.20 N	5.25 W
Marchfeld (Reg.), Aus.	157e	48.14 N	16.37 E
Marco Polo Bridge (P. Int.), China	67b	39.52 N	116.12 E
Marcos Paz, Arg. (mär-kōs′ päz)	141c	34.49 S	58.51 W
Marcus (I.), Asia (mär′kŭs)	208	24.00 N	155.00 E
Marcus Hook, Pa. (mär′kŭs hŏŏk)	112f	39.49 N	75.25 W
Marcy, Mt., NY (mär′sē)	111	44.10 N	73.55 W
Mar de Espanha, Braz. (mär-dĕ-ĕs-pȧ′nyȧ)	141a	21.53 S	43.00 W
Mar del Plata, Arg. (mär dĕl- plä′ta)	144	37.59 S	57.35 W
Mardin, Tur. (mär-dēn′)	179	37.25 N	40.40 E
Mare (I.), N. Cal. (mȧ-rā′)	215	21.53 S	168.30 E
Maree, Loch (L.), Scot. (mä-rē′)	162	57.40 N	5.44 W
Mareil-Marly, Fr.	64c	48.53 N	2.05 E
Marengo, Ia. (mȧ-rĕŋ′gō)	115	41.47 N	92.04 W
Marennes, Fr. (mȧ-rĕn′)	168	45.49 N	1.08 W
Marfa, Tx. (mär′fȧ)	124	30.19 N	104.01 W
Marganets, Sov. Un.	175	47.41 N	34.33 E
Margarethenhöhe (Neigh.), F.R.G.	63	51.26 N	6.58 E
Margaretting, Eng.	62	51.41 N	0.25 E
Margarita, Pan. (mär-gōō-rē′tä)	128a	9.20 N	79.55 W
Margarita, Isla de (I.), Ven. (mä-gȧ-rē′tȧ)	143b	11.00 N	64.15 W
Margate, Eng. (mär′gāt)	162	51.21 N	1.17 E
Margate, S. Afr. (mä-gāt′)	227c	30.52 S	30.21 E
Margherita Pk., Afr.	231	0.22 N	29.51 E
Marguerite (R.), Can.	104	50.39 N	66.42 W
Mari (A. S. S. R.), Sov. Un. (mä′rē)	178	56.20 N	48.00 E
Maria, Can. (mȧ-rē′ȧ)	104	48.10 N	66.04 W
María Cleofas (I.), Mex. (mä-rē′ä klā′ō-fäs)	130	21.17 N	106.14 W
Mariager, Den. (mä-rē-ägh′ẽr)	164	56.38 N	10.00 E
María Magdalena (I.), Mex. (mä rē′ä mäg-dä-lā′nä)	130	21.25 N	106.23 W
Mariana, Braz. (mä-ryä′nä)	141a	20.23 S	43.24 W
Mariana Is., Oceania (mä-rē-ä′nȧ)	208	17.20 N	145.00 E
Marianao, Cuba (mä-rē-ä-nä′ō)	135a	23.05 N	82.26 W
Mariana Trench, Oceania	208	12.00 N	144.00 E
Marianna, Ar. (mä-rĭ-ăn′ȧ)	123	34.45 N	90.45 W
Marianna, Fl.	126	30.46 N	85.14 W
Marianna, Pa.	113e	40.01 N	80.05 W
Mariano Acosta, Arg. (mä-rēä′nō-ȧ-kōs′tä)	144a	34.28 S	58.48 W
Mariano Acosta, Arg.	60d	34.40 S	58.50 W
Mariano J. Haedo, Arg.	60d	34.39 S	58.36 W
Mariánské Lázne, Czech. (mär′yan-skĕ′läz′nyĕ)	156	49.58 N	12.42 E
Maria Paula, Braz.	61c	22.54 S	43.02 W
Marias, Islas (Is.), Mex. (mä-rē′äs)	128	21.30 N	106.40 W
Marias R., Mt. (mȧ-rī′ȧz)	117	48.15 N	110.50 W
Mariato, Punta (Pt.), Pan.	133	7.17 N	81.09 W
Maribo, Den. (mä′rē-bō)	164	54.46 N	11.29 E
Maribor, Yugo. (mä′re-bôr)	172	46.33 N	15.37 E

PLACE (Pronounciation)	PAGE	Lat. °′	Long. °′
Maribyrnong, Austl.	70b	37.46 S	144.54 E
Maricá, Braz. (mä-rē-kä′)	141a	22.55 S	42.49 W
Maricaban (I.), Phil. (mä-rē-kä-bän′)	207a	13.40 N	120.44 E
Marico R., S. Afr. (mä′rĭ-cô)	223d	24.53 S	26.22 E
Marie Byrd Land, Ant. (mȧ rē′bûrd′)	232	78.00 S	130.00 W
Mariefred, Swe. (mä-rē′ĕ-frĭd)	164	59.17 N	17.09 E
Marie Galante I., Guad. (mȧ-rē′ gȧ-läɴt′)	133b	15.58 N	61.05 W
Mariehamn, Fin. (mȧ-rē′ĕ-hām′′n)	164	60.07 N	19.57 E
Mariehamn, see Maarianhamina			
Mariendorf (Neigh.), F.R.G.	65a	52.26 N	13.23 E
Marienfelde (Neigh.), F.R.G.	65a	52.25 N	13.22 E
Mariestad, Swe. (mä-rē′ĕ-städ′)	164	58.43 N	13.45 E
Marietta, Ga. (mā-rĭ′-ĕt′ȧ)	112c	33.57 N	84.33 W
Marietta, Oh.	110	39.25 N	81.30 W
Marietta, Ok.	123	33.53 N	97.07 W
Marietta, Wa.	118d	48.48 N	122.35 W
Mariinsk, Sov. Un. (mȧ-re′ĭnsk)	180	56.15 N	87.28 E
Marijampole, Sov. Un. (mä-rē-yäm-pô′lĕ)	165	54.33 N	23.26 E
Marikana, S. Afr. (mă′-rĭ-kä-nă)	223d	25.40 S	27.28 E
Marikina, Phil.	68g	14.37 N	121.06 E
Marília, Braz. (mä-rē′lyȧ)	143	22.02 S	49.48 W
Marimba, Ang.	230	8.28 S	17.08 E
Marina del Rey, Ca.	59	33.59 N	118.28 W
Marina del Rey (B.), Ca.	59	33.58 N	118.27 W
Marin City, Ca.	58b	37.52 N	122.21 W
Marinduque I., Phil. (mä-rēn-dōō′kā)	207a	13.14 N	121.45 E
Marine, Il. (mȧ-rēn′)	119e	38.48 N	89.47 W
Marine City, Mi.	110	42.45 N	82.30 W
Marine L., Mn.	119g	45.13 N	92.55 W
Marineland of the Pacific (P. Int.), Ca.	59	33.44 N	118.24 W
Marine on Saint Croix, Mn. (äɴ sĕɴ krōō-ä)	119g	45.11 N	92.47 W
Marinette, Wi. (măr-ĭ-nĕt′)	115	45.04 N	87.40 W
Maringa (R.), Zaire (mă-riŋ′gä)	230	1.15 N	20.05 E
Marinha Grande, Port. (mä-rēn′yȧ grän′dĕ)	170	39.49 N	8.53 W
Marion, Al. (măr′ĭ-ŭn)	126	32.36 N	87.19 W
Marion, Ia.	115	42.01 N	91.39 W
Marion, Il.	110	37.40 N	88.55 W
Marion, In.	110	40.35 N	85.45 W
Marion, Ks.	123	38.21 N	97.02 W
Marion, Ky.	126	37.19 N	88.05 W
Marion, NC	127	35.40 N	82.00 W
Marion, ND	114	46.37 N	98.20 W
Marion, Oh.	110	40.35 N	83.10 W
Marion, SC	127	34.08 N	79.23 W
Marion, Va.	127	36.48 N	81.33 W
Marion (R.), SC	127	33.25 N	80.35 W
Marion Rf., Austl.	215	18.57 S	151.31 E
Mariposa, Chile (mä-rē-pô′sä)	141b	35.33 S	71.21 W
Mariposa Cr., Ca.	120	37.14 N	120.30 W
Mariquita, Col. (mä-rē-kē′tä)	142a	5.13 N	74.52 W
Mariscal Estigarribia, Par. (mä-rēs-käl′ĕs-tē-gär-rē′byä)	143	22.03 S	60.28 W
Marisco, Ponta do (Pt.), Braz. (pô′n-tä-dô-mä-rē′s-kö)	144b	23.01 S	43.17 W
Maritime Alps (Mts.), Fr.-It. (mȧ′rĭ-tīm ălps)	169	44.20 N	7.02 E
Mariveles, Phil.	207a	14.27 N	120.29 E
Marj Uyan, Leb.	191a	33.21 N	35.36 E
Marka, Som.	223a	1.45 N	44.47 E
Marka Kul′ (L.), Sov. Un.	198	49.15 N	85.48 E
Markaryd, Swe. (mär′kä-rüd)	164	56.30 N	13.34 E
Marked Tree, Ar. (märkt trē)	123	35.31 N	90.26 W
Marken, I., Neth.	157a	52.26 N	5.08 E
Market Bosworth, Eng. (bŏz′wûrth)	156	52.37 N	1.23 W
Market Deeping, Eng. (dēp′ĭng)	156	52.40 N	0.19 W
Market Drayton, Eng. (drā′tŭn)	156	52.54 N	2.29 W
Market Harborough, Eng. (här′bŭr-ô)	156	52.28 N	0.55 W
Market Rasen, Eng. (rā′zĕn)	156	53.23 N	0.21 W
Markham, Can. (märk′ȧm)	95d	43.53 N	79.15 W
Markham, Mt., Ant.	232	82.59 S	159.30 E
Markovka, Sov. Un. (mȧr-kôf′kȧ)	175	49.32 N	39.34 E
Markovo, Sov. Un. (mär′kô-vô)	181	64.46 N	170.48 E
Markrāna, India	196	27.08 N	74.43 E
Marks, Sov. Un.	179	51.40 N	46.40 E
Marksville, La. (märks′vĭl)	125	31.09 N	92.05 W
Markt Indersdorf, F.R.G. (märkt ēn′dĕrs-dōrf)	157d	48.22 N	11.23 E
Marktredwitz, F.R.G. (märk-rĕd′vēts)	166	50.02 N	12.05 E
Markt Schwaben, F.R.G. (märkt shvä′bĕn)	157d	48.12 N	11.52 E
Marl, F.R.G. (märl)	169c	51.40 N	7.05 E
Marlboro, NJ	112a	40.18 N	74.15 W
Marlborough, Ma.	105a	42.21 N	71.33 W
Marlette, Mi. (mär-lĕt′)	110	43.25 N	83.05 W
Marlin, Tx. (mär′lĭn)	125	31.18 N	96.52 W
Marlinton, WV (mär′lĭn-tŭn)	111	38.15 N	80.10 W
Marlow, Eng. (mär′lō)	156b	51.33 N	0.46 W
Marlow, Ok.	122	34.38 N	97.56 W
Marls, The (Shoals), Ba. (märls)	134	26.30 N	77.15 W
Marly-le-Roi, Fr.	64c	48.52 N	2.05 E
Marmande, Fr. (mȧr-mäɴd′)	168	44.30 N	0.10 E
Marmara (I.), Tur. (mär′mȧ-rȧ)	173	40.38 N	27.35 E
Marmara Denizi (Sea), Tur.	179	40.40 N	28.00 E
Marmarth, ND (mär′mȧrth)	114	46.19 N	103.57 W
Mar Muerto (L.), Mex. (mär-mōōĕ′r-tô)	131	16.13 N	94.22 W
Marne, F.R.G. (mär′nĕ)	157c	53.57 N	9.01 E
Marne (R.), Fr. (märn)	168	49.08 N	3.39 E
Maroa, Ven. (mä-rō′ä)	142	2.43 N	67.37 W
Maroantsetra, Mad. (mȧ-rō-äŋ-tsā′trȧ)	227	15.18 S	49.48 E
Maro Jarapeto (Mtn.), Col. (mä-rô-hä-rä-pĕ′tô)	142a	6.29 N	76.39 W
Marolles-en-Brie, Fr.	64c	48.44 N	2.33 E
Maromokotro (Mtn.), Mad.	227	14.00 S	49.11 E
Marondera, Zimb.	231	18.10 S	31.36 E

PLACE (Pronounciation)	PAGE	Lat. °′	Long. °′
Maroni (R.), Fr. Gu.-Sur. (mȧ-rō′nē)	143	3.02 N	53.54 W
Maro Rf., Hi.	106b	25.15 N	170.00 W
Maroua, Cam. (mär′wä)	229	10.36 N	14.20 E
Maroubra, Austl.	70a	33.57 S	151.16 E
Marple, Eng. (mär′p′l)	157	53.24 N	2.04 W
Marquard, S. Afr.	223d	28.41 S	27.26 E
Marquesas Is., Fr. Polynesia (mär-kĕ′säs)	209	8.50 S	141.00 W
Marquesas Keys (Is.), Fl. (mȧr-kē′zȧs)	127a	24.37 N	82.15 W
Marquês de Valença, Braz. (mȧr-kĕ′s-dĕ-vä-lĕ′n-sȧ)	141a	22.16 S	43.42 W
Marquette, Can. (mȧr-kĕt′)	95f	50.04 N	97.43 W
Marquette, Mi.	115	46.32 N	87.25 W
Marquez, Tx. (mär-kāz′)	125	31.14 N	96.15 W
Marra, Jabal (Mt.), Sud. (jĕb′ĕl mär′ä)	225	13.00 N	23.47 E
Marrakech, Mor. (mȧr-rä′kĕsh)	224	31.38 N	8.00 W
Marree, Austl. (măr′rē)	216	29.38 S	137.55 E
Marrero, La.	112d	29.55 N	90.06 W
Marrickville, Austl.	70a	33.55 S	151.09 E
Marrupa, Moz.	231	13.08 S	37.30 E
Mars, Pa. (märz)	113e	40.42 N	80.01 W
Marsā al Burayqah, Libya	194	30.25 N	19.34 E
Marsabit, Ken.	231	2.20 N	37.59 E
Marsala, It. (mär-sä′lä)	172	37.48 N	12.28 E
Marsā Maṭrūḥ, Egypt	225	31.19 N	27.14 E
Marscheid (Neigh.), F.R.G.	63	51.14 N	7.14 E
Marsden, Eng. (märz′dĕn)	156	53.36 N	1.55 W
Marseille, Fr. (mȧr-sâ′y′)	168a	43.18 N	5.25 E
Marseilles, Il. (mär-sĕlz′)	110	41.20 N	88.40 W
Mar, Serra do (Mts.), Braz. (sĕr′rȧ dōō mär′)	144	26.30 S	49.15 W
Marsfield, Austl.	70a	33.47 S	151.07 E
Marshall, Il. (mär′shăl)	110	39.20 N	87.40 W
Marshall, Mi.	110	42.20 N	84.55 W
Marshall, Mn.	114	44.28 N	95.49 W
Marshall, Mo.	123	39.07 N	93.12 W
Marshall, Tx.	125	32.33 N	94.22 W
Marshall Is., Pac. Is. Trust Ter.	208	10.00 N	165.00 E
Marshalltown, Ia. (mär′shȧl-toun)	115	42.02 N	92.55 W
Marshallville, Ga. (mär′shȧl-vĭl)	126	32.29 N	83.55 W
Marshfield, Ma. (märsh′fēld)	105a	42.06 N	70.43 W
Marshfield, Mo.	123	37.20 N	92.53 W
Marshfield, Wi.	115	44.40 N	90.10 W
Marsh Harbour, Ba.	134	26.30 N	77.00 W
Mars Hill, In. (märz′hĭl′)	113g	39.43 N	86.15 W
Mars Hill, Me.	104	46.34 N	67.54 W
Marstrand, Swe. (mär′stränd)	164	57.54 N	11.33 E
Marsyaty, Sov. Un. (märs′yȧ-tĭ)	182a	60.03 N	60.28 E
Mart, Tx. (märt)	125	31.32 N	96.49 W
Martaban, G. of, Bur. (mär-tŭ-bän′)	206	16.34 N	96.58 E
Martapura, Indon.	206	3.19 S	114.45 E
Marten (Neigh.), F.R.G.	63	51.31 N	7.23 E
Marthas Vineyard (I.), Ma. (mär′thȧz vĭn′yȧrd)	107	41.25 N	70.35 W
Martí, Cuba (mär-tē′)	134	23.00 N	80.55 W
Martigny, Switz. (mȧr-tē-nyē′)	166	46.06 N	7.00 E
Martigues, Fr.	168a	43.24 N	5.05 E
Martin (R.), Al.	126	32.40 N	86.05 W
Martin, Tn. (mär′tĭn)	126	36.20 N	88.45 W
Martina Franca, It. (mär-tē′nä fräŋ′kä)	173	40.43 N	17.21 E
Martinez, Ca. (mär-tē′nĕz)	118b	38.01 N	122.08 W
Martinez, Tx.	119d	29.25 N	98.20 W
Martinique, N. A. (mȧr-tē-nēk′)	129	14.50 N	60.40 W
Martin Pt., Ak.	107	70.10 N	142.00 W
Martinsburg, WV (mär′tĭnz-bûrg)	111	39.30 N	78.00 W
Martins Ferry, Oh. (mär′tĭnz)	110	40.05 N	80.45 W
Martinsville, In. (mär′tĭnz-vĭl)	110	39.25 N	86.25 W
Martinsville, Va.	127	36.40 N	79.53 W
Martínez (Neigh.), Arg.	60d	34.29 S	58.30 W
Martos, Sp. (mär′tōs)	170	37.43 N	3.58 W
Martre, Lac la (L.), Can. (läk la märtr)	96	63.24 N	119.58 W
Marugame, Jap. (mä′rōō-gä′mā)	205	34.19 N	133.48 E
Marungu (Mts.), Tan.	231	7.50 S	29.50 E
Marve (Neigh.), India	197b	19.12 N	72.43 E
Marvila (Neigh.), Port.	65d	38.44 N	9.06 W
Marvín, Sp. (mär-vē′n)	170	42.24 N	8.40 W
Marwitz, G.D.R.	65a	52.41 N	13.09 E
Mary, Sov. Un. (mä′rē)	176	37.45 N	61.47 E
Mar′yanskaya, Sov. Un. (mȧr-yän′skȧ-yȧ)	175	45.04 N	38.39 E
Maryborough, Austl. (mā′rĭ-bŭr-ô)	216	25.35 S	152.40 E
Maryborough, Austl.	216	37.00 S	143.50 E
Maryland (State), U. S. (mĕr′ĭ-lănd)	109	39.10 N	76.25 W
Maryland Park, Md.	56d	38.53 N	76.54 W
Mary′s R., Nv. (mā′rĭz)	116	41.25 N	115.10 W
Marystown, Can. (mâr′ĭz-toun)	105	47.11 N	55.10 W
Marysville, Ca.	120	39.09 N	121.37 W
Marysville, Can.	104	45.59 N	66.35 W
Marysville, Oh.	110	40.15 N	83.25 W
Marysville, Wa.	118a	48.03 N	122.11 W
Maryūṭ (L.), Egypt	223b	31.09 N	30.10 E
Maryville, Il. (mā′rĭ-vĭl)	119e	38.44 N	89.57 W
Maryville, Mo.	123	40.21 N	94.51 W
Maryville, Tn.	126	35.44 N	83.59 W
Marzahn (Neigh.), G.D.R.	65a	52.33 N	13.33 E
Mārzuq, Libya	225	26.00 N	14.09 E
Marzūq, Idehan (Dunes), Libya	225	24.30 N	13.00 E
Masai Steppe (Plat.), Tan.	231	4.30 S	36.40 E
Masaka, Ug.	231	0.20 S	31.44 E
Masalasef, Chad	229	11.43 N	17.08 E
Masalembo-Besar (I.), Indon.	206	5.40 S	114.28 E
Masan, Kor. (mä-sän′)	204	35.10 N	128.31 E
Masangwe, Tan.	231	5.28 S	30.05 E
Masasi, Tan. (mä-sä′sē)	231	10.43 S	38.48 E
Masatepe, Nic. (mä-sä-tĕ′pĕ)	132	11.57 N	86.10 W
Masaya, Nic. (mä-sä′yä)	132	11.58 N	86.05 W
Masbate, Phil. (mäs-bä′tā)	207a	12.21 N	123.38 E
Masbate (I), Phil.	207a	12.19 N	123.03 E

PLACE (Pronounciation)	PAGE	Lat. °′	Long. °′
Mascarene Is., Mauritius	232	20.20 S	56.40 E
Mascot, Austl.	70a	33.56 S	151.12 E
Mascot, Tn. (măs′kŏt)	126	36.04 N	83.45 W
Mascota, Mex. (mäs-kō′tä)	130	20.33 N	104.45 W
Mascota (R.), Mex.	130	20.33 N	104.52 W
Mascouche, Can. (mȧs-kōōsh′)	95a	45.45 N	73.36 W
Mascouche (R.), Can.	95a	45.44 N	73.45 W
Mascoutah, Il. (măs-kū′tā)	119e	38.29 N	89.48 W
Maseru, Leso. (măz′ēr-ōō)	226	29.09 S	27.11 E
Mashhad, Iran.	192	36.17 N	59.30 E
Mashra′ar-Ragg, Sud.	225	8.28 N	29.15 E
Masi-Manimba, Zaire	230	4.46 S	17.55 E
Masindi, Ug. (mä-sēn′dē)	225	1.44 N	31.43 E
Masjed Soleymān, Iran	192	31.45 N	49.17 E
Mask, Lough (B.), Ire. (lŏk mȧsk)	162	53.35 N	9.23 W
Maslovo, Sov. Un. (mäs′lô-vô)	182a	60.08 N	60.28 E
Mason, Mi. (mā′sŭn)	110	42.35 N	84.25 W
Mason, Oh.	113f	39.22 N	84.18 W
Mason, Tx.	124	30.46 N	99.14 W
Mason City, Ia.	115	43.08 N	93.14 W
Masonville, Va.	56d	38.51 N	77.12 W
Maspeth (Neigh.), NY	55	40.43 N	73.55 W
Masquaro (L.), Can.	105	50.34 N	60.40 W
Massa, It. (mäs′sä)	172	44.02 N	10.08 E
Massachusetts (State), U. S. (măs-ȧ-chōō′sĕts)	109	42.20 N	72.30 W
Massachusetts B., Ma.	104	42.26 N	70.20 W
Massachusetts Institute of Technology (P. Int.), Ma.	54a	42.21 N	71.06 W
Massafra, It. (mäs-sä′frä)	172	40.35 N	17.05 E
Massa Marittima, It.	172	43.03 N	10.55 E
Massapequa, NY	112a	40.41 N	73.28 W
Massaua, see Mitsiwa			
Massena, NY (mă-sē′nȧ)	111	44.55 N	74.55 W
Masset, Can. (măs′ĕt)	96	54.02 N	132.09 W
Masset Inlet, Can.	98	53.42 N	132.20 E
Massif Central (Plat.), Fr. (mȧ-sēf′ säɴ-trȧl′)	168	45.12 N	3.02 E
Massillon, Oh. (măs′ĭ-lŏn)	110	40.50 N	81.35 W
Massinga, Moz. (mä-sĭn′gä)	226	23.18 S	35.18 E
Massive, Mt., Co. (mȧs′ĭv)	121	39.05 N	106.30 W
Masson, Can. (măs-sŭn)	95c	45.33 N	75.25 W
Massy, Fr.	64c	48.44 N	2.17 E
Masuda, Jap. (mä-sōō′dȧ)	205	34.42 N	131.53 E
Masuria (Reg.), Pol.	167	53.40 N	21.10 E
Matadi, Zaire (mȧ-tä′dē)	230	5.49 S	13.27 E
Matagalpa, Nic. (mä-tä-gäl′pä)	132	12.52 N	85.57 W
Matagami (L.), Can. (mâ-tä-gä′mē)	97	50.10 N	78.28 W
Matagorda B., Tx. (măt-ȧ-gôr′dȧ)	125	28.32 N	96.13 W
Matagorda I., Tx.	125	28.13 N	96.27 W
Matam, Senegal (mä-täm′)	228	15.40 N	13.15 W
Matamoros, Mex. (mä-tä-mō′rōs)	124	25.32 N	103.13 W
Matamoros, Mex.	125	25.52 N	97.30 W
Matandu (R.), Tan.	231	8.55 S	38.35 E
Matane, Can. (mȧ-tȧn′)	104	48.51 N	67.32 W
Matanzas, Cuba (mä-tän′zäs)	134	23.05 N	81.35 W
Matanzas (Prov.), Cuba	134	22.45 N	81.20 W
Matanzas, Bahía (B.), Cuba (bä-ē′ä)	134	23.10 N	81.30 W
Matapalo, Cabo (C.), C. R. (kȧ′bô-mä-tä-pä′lō)	133	8.22 N	83.25 W
Matapédia, Can. (mă-tȧ-pā′dē-ȧ)	104	47.58 N	66.56 W
Matapédia, (L.), Can.	104	48.33 N	67.32 W
Matapédia, (R.), Can.	104	48.10 N	67.10 W
Mataquito (R.), Chile (mä-tä-kē′tô)	141b	35.08 S	71.35 W
Matara, Sri Lanka (mä-tä′rä)	197	5.59 N	80.35 E
Mataram, Indon.	206	8.45 S	116.15 E
Mataró, Sp. (mä-tä-rō′)	171	41.33 N	2.27 E
Matatiele, S. Afr. (mä-tä-tyā′lā)	227c	30.21 S	28.49 E
Matawan, NJ	112a	40.24 N	74.13 W
Matawin (R.), Can. (măt ȧ-wĭn)	104	46.46 N	73.25 W
Matehuala, Mex. (mä-tȧ-wä′lä)	130	23.38 N	100.39 W
Matera, It. (mä-tȧ′rä)	172	40.42 N	16.37 E
Mateur, Tun. (mȧ-tûr′)	159	37.09 N	9.43 E
Mātherān, India	197b	18.58 N	73.16 E
Matheson, Can.	103	48.35 N	80.33 W
Mathews, L., Ca. (măth ūz)	119a	33.50 N	117.24 W
Mathura, India (mu-tōō′rŭ)	196	27.39 N	77.39 E
Matias Barbosa, Braz. (mä-tē′äs-bȧr-bô-sä)	139a	21.53 S	43.19 W
Matillas, Laguna (L.), Mex. (lä-gōō′nä-mä-tē′l-yäs)	131	18.02 N	92.36 W
Matina, C. R. (mä-tē′nä)	133	10.06 N	83.20 W
Matiši, Sov. Un. (mä′tē-sē)	165	57.43 N	25.09 E
Matlalcueyetl, Cerra, Mex. (sĕ′r-rä-mä-tläl-kwĕ′yĕtl)	130	19.13 N	98.02 W
Matlock, Eng. (măt′lŏk)	156	53.08 N	1.33 W
Matochkin Shar, Sov. Un. (mä′tŏch-kĭn)	180	73.57 N	56.16 E
Mato Grosso, Braz. (mät′ōō grōs′ōō)	143	15.04 S	59.58 W
Mato Grosso (State), Braz.	143	14.38 S	55.36 W
Mato Grosso, Chapada de (Plain), Braz. (shä-pä′dä-dĕ)	143	13.39 S	55.42 W
Mato Grosso do Sul (State), Braz.	143	20.00 S	56.00 W
Matosinhos, Port.	170	41.10 N	8.48 W
Matrah, Om. (mȧ-trä′)	192	23.36 N	58.27 E
Matsubara, Jap.	205b	34.34 N	135.34 E
Matsudo, Jap. (mät′sōō-dô)	205a	35.48 N	139.55 E
Matsue, Jap. (mät′sōō-ĕ)	205	35.29 N	133.04 E
Matsumoto, Jap. (mät′sōō-mō′tô)	205	36.15 N	137.59 E
Matsuyama, Jap. (mät′sōō-yä′mä)	205	33.48 N	132.45 E
Matsuzaka, Jap. (mät′sōō-zä′kä)	205	34.35 N	136.34 E
Mattamuskeet (R.), NC (măt-tȧ-mŭs′kēt)	127	35.34 N	76.03 W
Mattaponi (R.), Va. (măt′ȧ-ponī′)	111	37.45 N	77.00 W
Mattawa, Can. (măt′ȧ-wȧ)	103	46.15 N	78.49 W
Matternhorn (Mtn.), Switz. (mät′ēr-hôrn)	166	45.57 N	7.36 E
Matteson, Il. (mătt′ē-sŭn)	113a	41.30 N	87.42 W
Matthew Town, Ba. (măth′ū toun)	135	21.00 N	73.40 W
Mattoon, Il. (mă-tōōn′)	110	39.30 N	88.20 W
Maturín, Ven. (mä-tōō-rēn′)	142	9.48 N	63.16 W
Mátyásföld (Neigh.), Hung.	66g	47.31 N	19.13 E

PRONOUNCING INDEX
Mátyas-Templom – Melville Pen 313

PLACE (Pronounciation)	PAGE	Lat. °'	Long. °'
Mátyas-Templom (P. Int.), Hung.	66g	47.30 N	19.02 E
Maúa, Moz	221	13.51 S	37.10 E
Mauá, Braz.	61d	23.40 S	46.27 W
Mauban, Phil. (mä'o͞o-bän')	207a	14.11 N	121.44 E
Maubeuge, Fr. (mô-bûzh')	168	50.18 N	3.57 E
Maud, Oh. (môd)	113f	39.21 N	84.23 W
Mauer, Aus. (mou'ẽr)	157e	48.09 N	16.16 E
Mauer (Neigh.), Aus.	66e	48.09 N	16.16 E
Maués, Braz. (mȧ-wĕ's)	143	3.34 S	57.30 W
Mau Escarpment (Cliff), Ken.	231	0.45 S	35.50 E
Maui (I.), Hi. (mä'o͞o-ē)	106a	20.52 N	156.02 W
Maule (R.), Chile (mȧ'o͞o-lĕ)	141b	35.45 S	70.50 W
Maumee, Oh. (mô-mē')	110	41.30 N	83.40 W
Maumee (R.), In.-Oh.	110	41.10 N	84.50 W
Maumee B., Oh.	110	41.50 N	83.20 W
Maun, Bots. (mä-o͞on')	226	19.52 S	23.40 E
Mauna Kea (Vol.), Hi. (mä'o͞o-näkā'ä)	106a	19.52 N	155.30 W
Mauna Loa (Vol.), Hi. (mä'o͞o-nälō'ä)	106a	19.28 N	155.38 W
Maung Nakhon Sawan, Thai.	206	16.00 N	99.52 E
Maurecourt, Fr.	64c	49.00 N	2.04 E
Maurepas L., La. (mō-rē-pä')	125	30.18 N	90.40 W
Mauricie, Parc Natl. de la (Natl. Pk.), Can.	104	46.46 N	73.00 W
Mauritania, Afr. (mô-rē̇-tā'nĭ-ȧ)	222	19.38 N	13.30 W
Mauritius, Afr. (mô-rĭsh'ĭ-ŭs)	232	20.18 S	57.36 E
Maury, Wa. (mô'rĭ)	118a	47.22 N	122.23 W
Mauston, Wi. (môs'tŭn)	115	43.46 N	90.05 W
Maverick, (R.), Az. (mā-vûr'ĭk)	121	33.40 N	109.30 W
Mavinga, Ang.	230	15.50 S	20.21 E
Maxcanú, Mex. (mäs-kä-no͞o')	131	20.35 N	89.59 W
Maxville, Can. (măks'vĭl)	95c	45.17 N	74.52 W
Maxville, Mo.	119e	38.26 N	90.24 W
Maya (R.), Sov. Un. (mä'yä)	181	58.00 N	135.45 E
Mayaguana (I.), Ba.	135	22.25 N	73.00 W
Mayaguana Passage (Str.), Ba.	135	22.20 N	73.25 W
Mayagüez, P. R. (mä-yä-gwāz')	129b	18.12 N	67.10 W
Mayarí, Cuba (mä-yä-rē')	125	20.45 N	75.40 W
Mayari (R.), Cuba	125	20.25 N	75.35 W
Mayas, Montañas (Mts.), Belize (mŏntăŋ'ăs mā'ăs)	132a	16.43 N	89.00 W
Mayd (I.), Som.	223a	11.24 N	46.38 E
Mayen, F.R.G. (mī'ĕn)	166	50.19 N	7.14 E
Mayenne (R.), Fr. (mȧ-yĕn)	168	48.14 N	0.45 W
Mayfair (Neigh.), Pa.	56b	40.02 N	75.03 W
Mayfair (Neigh.), S. Afr.	71b	26.12 S	28.01 E
Mayfair West (Neigh.), S. Afr.	71b	26.12 S	28.00 E
Mayfield, Ky. (mā'fēld)	126	36.44 N	88.19 W
Mayfield Cr., Ky.	127	36.54 N	88.47 W
Mayfield Heights, Oh.	113d	41.31 N	81.26 W
Mayfield Res., Wa.	116	46.31 N	122.34 W
Maykop (Maikop), Sov. Un. (mī-kôp')	179	44.35 N	40.10 E
Maykor, Sov. Un. (mī-kôr')	182a	59.01 N	55.52 E
Maymyo, Bur. (mī'myō)	198	22.14 N	96.32 E
Maynard, Ma. (mā'nȧrd)	105a	42.25 N	71.27 W
Mayne, Can. (mān)	118d	48.51 N	123.18 W
Mayne (I), Can.	118d	48.52 N	123.14 W
Mayo, Can. (mā-yō')	96	63.40 N	135.51 W
Mayo, Fl.	126	30.02 N	83.08 W
Mayo, Md.	112e	38.54 N	76.31 W
Mayodan, NC (mā-yō'dăn)	127	36.25 N	79.59 W
Mayon (Vol.), Phil. (mä-yōn')	207a	13.21 N	123.43 E
Mayotte (I.), France (mȧ-yȯt')	227	13.07 S	45.32 W
May Pen, Jam	134	18.00 N	77.25 W
Mayraira Pt., Phil.	203	18.40 N	120.45 E
Mayran, Laguna de (L.), Mex. (lä-o͞o'nä-dĕ-mī-rän')	124	25.40 N	102.35 W
Maysville, Ky. (māz'vĭl)	110	38.35 N	83.45 W
Mayumba, Gabon	230	3.25 S	10.39 E
Mayville, NY (mā'vĭl)	111	42.15 N	79.30 W
Mayville, ND	114	47.30 N	97.20 W
Mayville, Wi.	115	43.30 N	88.45 W
Maywood, Ca. (mā'wo͝od)	119a	33.59 N	118.11 W
Maywood, Il.	113a	41.53 N	87.51 W
Maywood, NJ.	55	40.56 N	74.04 W
Mazabuka, Zambia (mä-zä-bo͞o'kä)	231	15.51 S	27.46 E
Mazagão, Braz. (mä-zȧ-gou'ɴ)	143	0.05 S	51.27 W
Mazapil, Mex. (mä-zä-pēl')	124	24.40 N	101.30 W
Mazara del Vallo, It. (mät-sä'rä dĕl väl'lō)	172	37.40 N	12.37 E
Mazār-i-Sharīf, Afg. (mȧ-zär'-ē-shȧ-rēf')	196	36.48 N	67.12 E
Mazarrón, Sp. (mä-zär-rô'n)	170	36.37 N	1.29 W
Mazaruni (R.), Guy. (mä-zä-ro͞o'nē̇)	143	5.58 N	59.37 W
Mazatenango, Guat. (mä-zä-tā-näŋ'gō)	132	14.30 N	91.30 W
Mazatla, Mex.	131a	10.30 N	99.24 W
Mazatlán, Mex.	130	23.14 N	106.27 W
Mazatlán (San Juan), Mex. (mä-zä-tlän') (saṅ hwän')	131	17.05 N	95.26 W
Mažeikiai, Sov. Un. (mȧ-zhā'kē̇-ī)	165	56.19 N	22.24 E
Mazhafah, Jabal (Mts.), Sau. Ar.	191a	28.56 N	35.05 E
Mazilovo (Neigh.), Sov. Un.	66b	55.44 N	37.26 E
Mazoe (R.), Moz.	231	16.40 S	32.50 E
Mazorra, Cuba	60b	23.01 N	82.24 W
Mazzarino, It. (mät-sä-rē'nō)	172	37.16 N	14.15 E
Mbabane, Swaz. (m'bä-bä'nĕ)	226	26.18 S	31.14 E
Mbaiki, Cen. Afr. Rep. (m'bȧ-ē'kē̇)	229	3.53 N	18.00 E
Mbakana, Montagne de (Mts.), Cam.	229	7.55 N	14.40 E
Mbakaou, Barrage de, Cam.	229	6.10 N	12.55 E
Mbala (Abercorn), Zambia	231	8.50 S	31.22 E
Mbale, Ug.	231	1.05 N	34.10 E
Mbamba Bay, Tan.	231	11.17 S	34.46 E
Mbandaka (Coquilhatville), Zaire	230	0.04 N	18.16 E
Mbanza Congo, Ang.	230	6.30 N	14.10 E
Mbanza-Ngungu, Zaire	230	5.20 S	10.55 E
Mbarara, Ug.	231	0.37 S	30.39 E
Mbasay, Chad	229	7.39 N	15.40 E
Mbeya, Tan.	231	8.54 S	33.27 E
Mbigou, Gabon (m-bē-go͞o')	226	2.07 S	11.30 E
Mbinda, Con.	230	2.00 S	12.55 E
Mbogo, Tan.	231	7.26 S	33.26 E
Mbomou (Bomu) (R.), Cen. Afr. Rep.-Zaire (m'bō'mo͞o)	230	4.50 S	23.35 E
Mbout, Mauritania (m'bo͞o')	224	16.03 N	12.31 W
Mbuji-Mayi (Bakwanga), Zaire	230	6.09 S	23.28 E
McAdam, Can. (măk-ăd'ăm)	104	45.36 N	67.20 W
McAfee, NJ (măk-ȧ'fē)	112a	41.10 N	74.32 W
McAlester, Ok. (măk ăl'ĕs-tēr)	123	34.55 N	95.45 W
McAllen, Tx. (măk-ăl'ĕn)	124	26.12 N	98.14 W
McBride, Can. (măk-brīd')	99	53.18 N	120.10 W
McCalla, Al. (măk-kăl'lā)	112h	33.20 N	87.00 W
McCamey, Tx. (mă-kā'mĭ)	124	31.08 N	102.13 W
McCaysville, Ga. (mă-kāz'vĭl)	126	34.57 N	84.21 W
McColl, SC (mȧ-kól')	127	34.40 N	79.34 W
McComb, Ms. (mȧ-kōm')	126	31.14 N	90.27 W
McConaughy, L., Ne. (măk kō'nō ĭ')	114	41.24 N	101.40 W
McCook, Il.	58a	41.48 N	87.50 W
McCook, Ne. (mȧ-ko͝ok')	122	40.13 N	100.37 W
McCormick, SC (mȧ-kôr'mĭk)	127	33.56 N	82.20 W
McCormick Place (P. Int.), Il.	58a	41.51 N	87.37 W
McDonald, Pa. (măk-dŏn'ăid)	113e	40.22 N	80.13 W
McDonald I, Austl.	232	53.00 S	72.45 E
McDonald L., Can. (măk-dŏn-ăld)	95e	51.12 N	113.53 W
McGehee, Ar. (mȧ-gē')	123	33.39 N	91.22 W
McGill, Nv. (mȧ-gĭl')	120	39.25 N	114.47 W
McGill University (P. Int.), Can.	54b	45.30 N	73.35 W
McGowan, Wa. (măk-gou'ăn)	118c	46.15 N	123.55 W
McGrath, Ak. (măk'grȧth)	107	62.58 N	155.20 W
McGregor, Can. (măk-grĕg'ēr)	113b	42.08 N	82.58 W
McGregor, Ia.	115	42.58 N	91.12 W
McGregor, Tx	125	31.26 N	97.23 W
McGregor L., Can. (măk-grĕg'ēr)	95c	45.38 N	75.44 W
McGregor (R.), Can.	99	54.10 N	121.00 W
McHenry, Il. (măk-hĕn'rĭ)	113a	42.21 N	88.16 W
Mchinji, Malawi	231	13.42 S	32.50 E
McIntosh, SD (măk'ĭn-tŏsh)	114	45.54 N	101.22 W
McKay (R), Or.	118	45.43 N	123.00 W
McKeesport, Pa. (mȧ-kez'pōrt)	113e	40.21 N	79.51 W
McKees Rocks, Pa. (mȧ-kēz' rŏks)	113e	40.29 N	80.05 W
McKenzie, Tn. (mȧ-kĕn'zĭ)	126	36.07 N	88.30 W
McKenzie R., Or.	116	44.07 N	122.20 W
McKinley, Mt., Ak. (mȧ-kĭn'lĭ)	107	63.00 N	151.02 W
McKinney, Tx. (mȧ-kĭn'ĭ)	123	33.12 N	96.35 W
McKnight Village, Pa.	57b	40.31 N	80.00 W
McLaughlin, SD (mȧk-lŏf'lĭn)	114	45.48 N	100.45 W
McLean, Va. (mă̇c'lān)	112e	38.56 N	77.11 W
McLeansboro, Il. (mȧ-klānz'bŭr-ȯ)	110	38.10 N	88.35 W
McLennan, Can. (măk-lĭn'nȧn)	96	55.42 N	116.54 W
McLeod (R), Can.	99	53.45 N	115.15 W
McLeod Lake, Can.	98	54.59 N	123.02 W
McLoughlin, Mt., Or. (mȧk-lŏk'lĭn)	116	42.27 N	122.20 W
McMillan L., Tx. (măk-mĭl'ȧn)	124	32.40 N	104.09 W
McMillin, Wa. (mȧk-mĭl'ĭn)	118a	47.08 N	122.14 W
McMinnville, Or. (măk-mĭn'vĭl)	116	45.13 N	123.13 W
McMinnville, Tn.	126	35.41 N	85.47 W
McMurray, Pa.	57b	40.17 N	80.05 W
McMurray, Wa. (mȧk-mŭr'ĭ)	118a	48.19 N	122.15 W
McNary, Az. (mȧk-nâr'ē̇)	121	34.10 N	109.55 W
McNary, La.	125	30.58 N	92.32 W
McNary Dam, Or.-Wa.	116	45.57 N	119.15 W
McPherson, Ks. (mȧk-fŭr's'n)	123	38.21 N	97.41 W
McRae, Ga. (mȧk-rā')	126	32.02 N	82.55 W
McRoberts, Ky. (mȧk-rŏb'ērts)	126	37.12 N	82.40 W
Mead, Ks. (mēd)	122	37.17 N	100.21 W
Mead, L., Az.-Nv.	121	36.20 N	114.14 W
Meade Pk., Id.	117	42.19 N	111.16 W
Meadow Lake, Can. (mĕd'ō lāk)	100	54.08 N	108.26 W
Meadowlands, S. Afr.	71b	26.13 S	27.54 E
Meadows, Can. (mĕd'ōz)	95f	50.02 N	97.35 W
Meadville, Pa. (mēd'vĭl)	111	41.40 N	80.10 W
Meaford, Can. (mĕ'fērd)	110	44.35 N	80.40 W
Mealy Mts., Can. (mē'lē)	97	53.32 N	57.58 W
Meandarra, Austl. (mē-ȧn-dä'rȧ)	216	27.47 S	149.40 E
Meaux, Fr. (mō)	169b	48.58 N	2.53 E
Mecapalapa, Mex. (mă-kä-pä-lä'pä)	131	20.32 N	97.52 W
Mecatina (I.), Can. (mā-kȧ-tē'nȧ)	105	50.50 N	58.33 W
Mecatina (R.), Can. (mā-kȧ-tē'nȧ)	105	50.50 N	59.45 W
Mecca, see Makkah			
Mechanic Falls, Me. (mē̇-kăn'ĭk)	104	44.05 N	70.23 W
Mechanicsburg, Pa. (mē̇-kăn'ĭks-bŭrg)	111	40.15 N	77.00 W
Mechanicsville, Md. (mē̇-kăn'ĭks-vĭl)	112e	38.27 N	76.45 W
Mechanicville, NY (mē̇kăn'ĭk-vĭl)	111	42.55 N	73.45 W
Mechelen, Bel.	157a	51.01 N	4.28 E
Méchérial, Mor.	160	33.30 N	0.13 W
Mecicine Bow Ra., Co.-Wy. (mĕd'ĭ-sĭn bō)	122	40.55 N	106.02 W
Meckinghoven, F.R.G.	63	51.37 N	7.19 E
Mecklenburg (Reg.), G.D.R. (mĕk'lĕn-bo͝orgh)	166	53.34 N	12.18 E
Medan, Indon. (mā̇-dän')	206	3.35 N	98.35 E
Medanosa, Punta (Pt.), Arg. (po͞o'n-tä-mĕ-dä-nô'sä)	144	47.50 S	65.53 W
Medden (R.), Eng. (mĕd'ĕn)	156	53.14 N	1.05 W
Medellín, Col. (mā̇-dhĕl-yēn')	142a	6.15 N	75.34 W
Medellin, Mex. (mĕ-dĕl-yē'n)	131	19.03 N	96.08 W
Medenine, Tun. (mā-dē-nēn')	160e	33.22 N	10.33 E
Medfeld, Ma. (mĕd'fēld)	105a	42.11 N	71.19 W
Medford, Ma. (mĕd'fērd)	105a	42.25 N	71.07 W
Medford, NJ	112f	39.54 N	74.50 W
Medford, Ok.	122	36.47 N	97.44 W
Medford, Or.	116	42.19 N	122.52 W
Medford, Wi.	115	45.09 N	90.22 W
Medford Hillside, Ma.	54a	42.24 N	71.07 W
Media, Pa. (mē'dĭ-ȧ)	112f	39.55 N	75.24 W
Medias, Rom. (mĕd-yäsh')	167	46.09 N	24.21 E
Medical Lake, Wa. (mĕd'ĭ-kăl)	116	47.34 N	117.40 W
Medicine Bow R., Wy.	117	41.58 N	106.30 W
Medicine Hat, Can. (mĕd'ĭ-sĭn hăt)	100	50.03 N	110.40 W
Medicine L., Mt. (mĕd'ĭ-sĭn)	117	48.24 N	104.15 W
Medicine Lodge, Ks.	122	37.17 N	98.37 W
Medina, NY (mē̇-dī'nȧ)	111	43.15 N	78.20 W
Medina, Oh.	113d	41.08 N	81.52 W
Medina del Campo, Sp. (mā̇-dē'nä dĕl käm'pō)	170	41.18 N	4.54 W
Medina de Ríoseco, Sp. (mā̇-dē'nä dā rē̇-ô-sā'kȯ)	170	41.53 N	5.05 W
Médina Gonassé, Sen.	228	13.08 N	13.45 W
Medina L., Tx.	124	29.36 N	98.47 W
Medina R., Tx.	124	29.45 N	99.13 W
Medina, see Al Madīnah			
Medina Sidonia, Sp. (sē̇-dō'nyä)	170	36.28 N	5.58 W
Medio (R.), Arg. (mĕ'dyȯ)	141c	33.40 S	60.30 W
Mediterranean Sea, Afr.-Asia-Eur. (mĕd-ĭ-tēr-ā'nē̇-ăn)	160	36.22 N	13.25 E
Medjerda (R.), Tun. (mĕ-jĕr'dȧ)	159	36.43 N	9.54 E
Mednogorsk, Sov. Un.	180	51.27 N	57.22 E
Medvedista (R.), Sov. Un. (mĕd-vyĕ'dē̇ tsȧ)	179	50.10 N	43.40 E
Medvedkovo (Neigh.), Sov. Un.	66b	55.53 N	37.38 E
Medvezhegorsk, Sov. Un. (mĕd-vyĕzh'yĕ-gôrsk')	178	63.00 N	34.20 E
Medvezh'y (Is.), Sov. Un.	181	71.00 N	161.25 E
Medway, Ma. (mĕd'wā)	105a	42.08 N	71.23 W
Medyn', Sov. Un. (mĕ-dēn')	174	54.58 N	35.53 E
Medzhibozh, Sov. Un. (mĕd-zhē̇-bōzh')	175	49.23 N	27.29 E
Meekatharra, Austl. (mē-kȧ-thăr'ȧ)	214	26.30 S	118.38 E
Meeker, Co. (mēk'ēr)	121	40.00 N	107.55 W
Meelpaeg L., Can. (mēl'pȧ-ĕg)	105	48.22 N	56.52 W
Meerane, G.D.R. (mā-rä'nē)	166	50.51 N	12.27 E
Meerbusch, F.R.G.	169c	51.15 N	6.41 E
Meerut, India (mē'ro͞ot)	196	28.59 N	77.43 E
Megalópolis, Grc. (mĕg-ȧ lŏ'pȯ-lĭs)	173	37.22 N	22.08 E
Meganom, M.(C.), Sov. Un. (mĕ-gȧ-nôm')	175	44.48 N	35.17 E
Mégara, Grc. (mĕg'ȧ-rȧ)	173	37.59 N	23.21 E
Megget, SC (mĕg'ĕt)	127	32.44 N	80.15 W
Meghelaya (State), India	198	25.30 N	91.30 E
Megler, Wa. (mĕg'lēr)	118c	46.15 N	123.52 W
Meglino (L.), Sov. Un. (mā̇-glē'nȯ)	174	58.32 N	35.27 E
Meguro (Neigh.), Jap.	69a	35.38 N	139.42 E
Meherrin (R.), Va. (mē̇-hĕr'ĭn)	127	36.40 N	77.49 W
Mehlville, Mo.	119e	38.30 N	90.19 W
Mehpālpur (Neigh.), India	67d	28.33 N	77.08 E
Mehrābād, Iran	68h	35.40 N	51.20 E
Mehram Nagar (Neigh.), India	67d	28.34 N	77.07 E
Mehrow, G.D.R.	65a	52.34 N	13.37 E
Mehrum, F.R.G.	63	51.35 N	6.37 E
Mehsāna, India	196	23.42 N	72.23 E
Mehun-sur-Yévre, Fr. (mē-ŭɴ-sür-yĕvr')	168	47.11 N	2.14 E
Meide, F.R.G.	63	51.11 N	6.55 E
Meiderich (Neigh.), F.R.G.	63	51.28 N	6.46 E
Meidling (Neigh.), Aus.	66e	48.11 N	16.20 E
Meiersberg, F.R.G.	63	51.17 N	6.57 E
Meiji Shrine (P. Int.), Jap.	69a	35.41 N	139.42 E
Meiling Pass, China (mā'lĭng')	203	25.22 N	115.00 E
Meinerzhagen, F.R.G. (mī'nĕrts-hä-gĕn)	169c	51.06 N	7.39 E
Meiningen, G.D.R. (mī'nĭng-ĕn)	166	50.35 N	10.25 E
Meiringen, Switz.	166	46.45 N	8.11 E
Meissen, G.D.R.	166	51.11 N	13.28 E
Meizhu, China (mā-jo͞o)	200	31.17 N	119.12 E
Mejillones, Chile (mā̇-ᴋē̇-lyō'nā̇s)	144	23.07 S	70.31 W
Mekambo, Gabon	230	1.01 N	13.56 E
Mekele, Eth.	225	13.31 N	39.19 E
Meknés, Mor. (mĕk'nĕs) (mĕk-nĕs')	224	33.56 N	5.44 W
Mekong (Lancang) (R.), China (län-tsäŋ)	198	24.45 N	100.31 E
Mekong R., Thai.-Laos	206	17.53 N	103.57 E
Mékrou (R.), Afr.	229	11.35 N	2.25 E
Melaka (Malacca), Mala.	191b	2.11 N	102.15 E
Melaka (State), Mala.	191b	2.19 N	102.09 E
Melbourne, Austl. (mĕl'bŭrn)	211a	37.52 S	145.08 E
Melbourne, Eng.	156	52.49 N	1.26 W
Melbourne, Fl.	127a	28.05 N	80.37 W
Melbourne, Ky.	113f	39.02 N	84.22 W
Melcher, Ia. (mĕl'chēr)	115	41.13 N	93.11 W
Melekess, Sov. Sov. Un. (mĕl-yĕk ĕs)	178	54.20 N	49.30 E
Melenki, Sov. Un. (mĕ-lyĕŋ'kē̇)	174	55.25 N	41.34 E
Melfort, Can. (mĕl'fôrt)	100	52.52 N	104.36 W
Melghir Chott (L.), Alg.	224	33.52 N	5.22 E
Melik, Wadi el (R.), Sud.	225	16.48 N	29.30 E
Melilla (Sp.), Afr. (mā-lēl'yä)	224	35.24 N	3.30 W
Melipilla, Chile (mā̇-lē̇-pē'lyä)	141b	33.40 S	71.12 W
Melita, Can.	101	49.11 N	101.09 W
Melitopol', Sov. Un. (mā-lē̇-tô'pȯl-y')	175	46.49 N	35.19 E
Melívoia, Grc.	173	39.42 N	22.47 E
Melkrivier, S. Afr.	223d	24.01 S	28.23 E
Mellen, Wi. (mĕl'ĕn)	115	46.20 N	90.40 W
Mellerud, Swe. (mål'ĕ-ro͞odh)	164	58.43 N	12.25 E
Melling, Eng.	64a	53.30 N	2.56 W
Melmoth, S. Afr.	227c	28.38 S	31.26 E
Melo, Ur. (mā'lō)	144	32.18 S	54.07 W
Melocheville, Can. (mĕ-lôsh-vēl')	95a	45.24 N	73.56 W
Melozha R., Sov. Un. (myĕ'lô-zhȧ)	182b	56.06 N	38.34 E
Melrose, Ma. (mĕl'rōz)	105a	42.29 N	71.06 W
Melrose, Mn.	115	45.39 N	94.49 W
Melrose Highlands, Ma.	54a	42.28 N	71.04 W
Melrose Park, Il.	113a	41.54 N	87.52 W
Melsetter, Zimb. (mĕl-sĕt'ēr)	226	19.44 S	32.51 E
Meltham, Eng. (mĕl'thăm)	156	53.35 N	1.51 W
Melton, Austl. (mĕl'tŭn)	211a	37.41 S	144.35 E
Melton Mowbray, Eng. (mō'brâ)	156	52.45 N	0.52 W
Melúli (R.), Moz.	231	16.10 S	39.30 E
Melun, Fr. (mē-lŭɴ')	169b	48.32 N	2.40 E
Melunga, Ang.	230	17.16 S	16.24 E
Melville, Can. (mĕl'vĭl)	100	50.55 N	102.48 W
Melville, La.	119	30.39 N	91.45 W
Melville (I.), Austl.	214	11.30 S	131.12 E
Melville (R.), Can.	97	53.46 N	59.31 W
Melville, C., Austl.	215	14.15 S	145.50 E
Melville Hills, Can.	96	69.18 N	124.57 W
Melville Pen, Can.	97	67.44 N	84.09 W

ng-sing; nŋ-banŋk; ɴ-nasalized n; nŏd; cŏmmit; ōld; ȯbey; ŏrder; oi-boil; fo͞od; fo͝ot; ou-out; s-soft; sh-dish; th-thin; pūre; ůnite; ûrn; stŭd; circŭs; ü-as in French tu; '-indeterminate vowel.

314 Melvindale – Miguel Pereira

PLACE (Pronounciation)	PAGE	Lat. °'	Long. °'
Melvindale, Mi. (mĕl'vĭn-dāl)	113b	42.17 N	83.11 W
Mélykút, Hung. (mā'l'ko͞ot)	167	46.14 N	19.21 E
Memba, Moz. (mĕm'bȧ)	227	14.12 N	40.35 E
Memel, S. Afr. (mĕ'mĕl)	223d	27.42 S	29.35 E
Memel, see Klaipėda			
Memmingen, F.R.G. (mĕm'ĭng-ĕn)	166	47.59 N	10.10 E
Memo (R.), Ven. (mĕ'mō)	143b	9.32 N	66.30 W
Memphis, Mo. (mĕm'fĭs)	123	40.27 N	92.11 W
Memphis, Tn. (mĕm'fĭs)	126	35.07 N	90.03 W
Memphis, Tx.	122	34.42 N	100.33 W
Memphis (Ruins), Egypt	223b	29.50 N	31.12 E
Memphremagog (L.), Can. (mĕm'frē-mā'gŏg)	111	45.05 N	72.10 W
Mena, Ar. (mē'nȧ)	123	34.35 N	94.09 W
Mena, Sov. Un. (mē-nä')	175	51.31 N	32.14 E
Menangle, Austl.	211b	34.08 S	150.48 E
Menard, Tx. (mē-närd')	124	30.56 N	99.48 W
Menasha, Wi. (mē-năsh'ȧ)	115	44.12 N	88.29 W
Mende, Fr. (mäNd)	168	44.31 N	3.30 E
Menden, F.R.G. (mĕn'dĕn)	169c	51.26 N	7.47 E
Menden (Neigh.), F.R.G.	63	51.24 N	6.54 E
Menderes (R).), Tur. (mĕn'dĕr-ĕs)	179	37.50 N	28.20 E
Mendes, Braz. (mĕ'n-dĕs)	144b	22.32 S	43.44 W
Mendocino, C., Ca. (mĕn'dō-sē'nō)	116	40.25 N	124.22 W
Mendota, Il. (mĕn-dō'tȧ)	115	41.34 N	89.06 W
Mendota (L.), Wi.	115	43.09 N	89.41 W
Mendoza, Arg. (mĕn-dō'sä)	144	32.48 S	68.45 W
Mendoza (Prov.), Arg.	144	35.10 S	69.00 W
Mengcheng, China (mŭŋ-chŭŋ)	200	33.15 N	116.34 E
Mengede (Neigh.), F.R.G.	63	51.34 N	7.23 E
Menglinghausen (Neigh.), F.R.G.	63	51.28 N	7.25 E
Meng Shan (Mts.), China (mŭŋ shän)	200	35.47 N	117.23 E
Mengzi, China	198	23.22 N	103.20 E
Menindee, Austl. (mē-nĭn-dē)	216	32.23 S	142.30 E
Menlo Park, Ca. (mĕn'lō pärk)	118b	37.27 N	122.11 W
Menlo Park Terrace, NJ	55	40.32 N	74.20 W
Menno, SD (mĕn'ō)	114	43.14 N	97.34 W
Menominee, Mi. (mē-nŏm'ĭ-nē)	115	45.08 N	87.40 W
Menominee (R.), Mi.-Wi.	115	45.37 N	87.54 W
Menominee Falls, Wi. (fôls)	113a	43.11 N	88.06 W
Menominee Ra, Mi.	115	46.07 N	88.53 W
Menomonee R., Wi.	113a	43.09 N	88.06 W
Menomonie, Wi.	115	44.53 N	91.55 W
Menongue, Ang.	230	14.36 S	17.48 E
Menorca (I.) (Minorca), Sp. (mĕ-nō'r-kä)	171	40.05 N	3.58 E
Mentana, It. (mĕn-tä'nä)	171d	42.02 N	12.40 E
Mentawai, Kepulauan (Is.), Indon. (mĕn-tä-vī')	206	1.08 S	98.10 E
Menton, Fr. (mäN-tôN')	169	43.46 N	7.37 E
Mentone, Austl.	70b	37.59 S	145.05 E
Mentone, Ca. (mĕn'tōne)	119a	34.05 N	117.08 W
Mentz (R.), S. Afr. (mĕnts)	227c	33.13 S	25.15 E
Menzel Bourguiba, Tun.	159	37.12 N	9.51 E
Menzelinsk, Sov. Un. (mĕn'zyĕ-lĕnsk')	178	55.40 N	53.15 E
Menzies, Austl. (mĕn'zēz)	214	29.45 S	122.15 E
Meogui, Mex. (mȧ-ō'gē)	124	28.17 N	105.28 W
Meopham, Eng.	62	51.22 N	0.22 E
Meopham Station, Eng.	62	51.23 N	0.21 E
Meppel, Neth. (mĕp'ĕl)	163	52.41 N	6.08 E
Meppen, F.R.G. (mĕp'ĕn)	166	52.40 N	7.18 E
Merabéllou, Kólpos (G.), Grc.	172a	35.16 N	25.55 E
Meramec (R.), Mo. (mĕr'ȧ-mĕk)	123	38.06 N	91.06 W
Merano, It. (mȧ-rä'nō)	172	46.39 N	11.10 E
Merasheen (I), Can. (mē'rȧ-shēn)	105	47.30 N	54.15 W
Merauke, Indon. (mȧ-rou'kȧ)	207	8.32 S	140.17 E
Meraux, La. (mē-ro')	108d	29.56 N	89.56 W
Mercader y Millás, Sp.	65e	41.21 N	2.05 E
Mercato San Severino, It. (mĕr-kä'tō sän sĕ-vĕ-rē'nō)	171c	40.34 N	14.38 E
Merced, Ca. (mĕr-sĕd')	120	37.17 N	120.30 W
Merced (R), Ca.	120	37.25 N	120.31 W
Mercedario, Cerro (Mtn.), Chile (mĕr-sȧ-dhä'rē-ō)	141b	31.58 S	70.07 W
Mercedes, Arg. (mĕr-sā'dhās)	144	29.04 S	58.01 W
Mercedes, Arg.	141c	34.41 S	59.26 W
Mercedes, Tx.	124	26.09 N	97.55 W
Mercedes, Ur.	141c	33.17 S	58.04 W
Mercedita, Chile (mĕr-sĕ-dē'tä)	141b	33.51 S	71.10 W
Mercer Island, Wa. (mûr'sēr)	118a	47.35 N	122.15 W
Mercês, Braz. (mĕ-sĕ's)	141a	21.13 S	43.20 W
Mercês, Port.	65d	38.47 N	9.19 W
Merchong (R.), Mala.	191b	3.08 N	103.13 E
Merchtem, Bel.	157a	50.57 N	4.13 E
Mercier, Can.	95a	45.19 N	73.45 W
Mercier-Lacombe, Alg. (mĕr-syā' lȧ-kôNb)	171	35.18 N	0.11 W
Mercy, C., Can.	97	64.48 N	63.22 W
Merdeka Palace (P. Int.), Indon.	68k	6.10 S	106.49 E
Mere, Eng.	64b	53.20 N	2.25 W
Meredale, S. Afr.	71b	26.17 S	27.59 E
Meredith, NH (mĕr'ē-dĭth)	111	43.35 N	71.35 W
Merefa, Sov. Un. (mȧ-rĕf'ȧ)	175	49.49 N	36.04 E
Merendón, Serrania de (Mts.), Hond. (sĕr-rä-nē'ä-dä mȧ-rĕn-dōn')	132	15.01 N	89.05 W
Mereworth, Eng. (mĕ-rē wûrth)	156b	51.15 N	0.23 E
Mergui, Bur. (mĕr-gē')	206	12.29 N	98.39 E
Mergui Arch, Asia	206	12.04 N	97.02 E
Meric (R.), Grc.-Tur.	164	40.43 N	26.19 E
Mérida, Mex.	132a	20.58 N	89.37 W
Mérida, Ven.	142	8.30 N	71.15 W
Mérida, Cordillera de (Mts.), Ven. (mĕ'rē-dhä)	142	8.30 N	70.45 W
Meriden, Ct. (mĕr'ĭ-dĕn)	111	41.30 N	72.50 W
Meridian, Ms. (mē-rĭd-ĭ-ăn)	126	32.21 N	88.41 W
Meridian, Tx.	125	31.56 N	97.37 W
Mérignac, Fr.	168	44.50 N	0.40 W
Merikarvia, Fin. (mā'rē-kȧr'vē-ä)	165	61.51 N	21.30 E
Mering, F.R.G. (mĕ'rēng)	157d	48.16 N	11.00 E
Merion Station, Pa.	56b	40.00 N	75.15 W
Meriwether Lewis Natl. Mon., Tn. (mĕr'ĭ-wĕth-ēr lo͞o'ĭs)	126	35.25 N	87.25 W
Merkel, Tx. (mûr'kĕl)	124	32.26 N	100.02 W
Merkiné, Sov. Un. (mĕr'kĭ-nē)	165	54.09 N	24.10 E
Merksem, Bel.	157a	51.15 N	4.27 E
Merkys R., Sov. Un. (măr'kĭs)	167	54.23 N	25.00 E
Merlo, Arg. (mĕr-lô)	144a	34.35 S	58.44 W
Merlynston, Austl.	70b	37.43 S	144.58 E
Merri (Cr.), Austl.	70b	37.48 S	145.01 E
Merriam, Ks. (mĕr-rĭ-yȧm)	119f	39.01 N	94.42 W
Merriam, Mn.	119g	44.44 N	93.36 W
Merrick, NY (mĕr'ĭk)	112a	40.40 N	73.33 W
Merrifield, Va. (mĕr'ĭ-fēld)	112e	38.50 N	77.12 W
Merrill, Wi. (mĕr'ĭl)	115	45.11 N	89.42 W
Merrimac, Ma. (mĕr'ĭ-măk)	105a	45.20 N	71.00 W
Merrimack, NH	105a	42.51 N	71.25 W
Merrimack (R.), Ma.-NH (mĕr'ĭ-măk)	111	43.10 N	71.30 W
Merrimack R., Ma.	105a	42.49 N	70.44 W
Merrionette Park, Il.	58a	41.41 N	87.42 W
Merritt, Can. (mĕr'ĭt)	99	50.07 N	120.47 W
Merrylands, Austl.	70a	33.50 S	150.59 E
Merryville, La. (mĕr'ĭ-vĭl)	125	30.46 N	93.34 W
Mersa Fatma, Eth.	225	14.54 N	40.14 E
Merscheid (Neigh.), F.R.G.	63	51.10 N	7.01 E
Merseburg, G.D.R. (mĕr'zĕ-bo͞orgh)	166	51.21 N	11.59 E
Mersey (R.), Eng. (mûr'zē)	156	52.52 N	2.04 W
Merseyside (Co.), Eng.	156	53.29 N	2.59 W
Mersin, Tur. (mĕr-sēn')	179	37.00 N	34.40 E
Mersing, Mala.	191b	2.25 N	103.51 E
Merta Road, India (mār'tŭ rōd)	196	26.50 N	73.54 E
Merthyr Tydfil, Wales (mûr'thēr tĭd'vĭl)	162	51.46 N	3.30 W
Mértola Almodóvar, Port. (mĕr-tô-lȧ-äl-mō-dō'vär)	170	37.39 N	8.04 W
Merton (Neigh.), Eng.	62	51.25 N	0.12 W
Méru, Fr. (mā-rü')	169b	49.14 N	2.08 E
Meru, Ken. (mä'ro͞o)	225	0.01 N	37.45 E
Merume Mts., Guy. (mĕr-ū'mē)	143	5.45 N	60.15 W
Meru, Mt., Tan.	231	3.15 S	36.43 E
Merwerde, Kanal (Can.), Neth.	157a	52.15 N	5.01 E
Merwin (L.), Wa. (mĕr'wĭn)	118c	45.58 N	122.27 W
Merzifon, Tur. (mĕr'ze-fōn)	179	40.50 N	35.30 E
Merzig, F.R.G. (mĕr'tsēg)	169	49.27 N	6.54 E
Mesa, Az. (mā'sȧ)	121	33.25 N	111.50 W
Mesabi Ra., Mn. (mā-sŏb'bē)	115	47.17 N	93.04 W
Mesagne, It. (mā-sän'yâ)	173	40.34 N	17.51 E
Mesa Verde Natl. Park, Co. (vĕr'dē)	121	37.22 N	108.27 W
Mescalero Ind. Res., NM (mĕs-kä-lā'rō)	121	33.10 N	105.45 W
Meščerskij, Sov. Un.	66b	55.40 N	37.25 E
Meshchovsk, Sov. Un. (myĕsh'chĕfsk)	174	54.17 N	35.19 E
Mesilla, NM (mȧ-sē'yä)	121	32.15 N	106.45 W
Meskine, Chad	229	11.25 N	15.21 E
Mesolóngion, Grc. (mĕ-sô-lôŋ'gē-ôn)	173	38.23 N	21.28 E
Mesquita, Braz.	61c	22.48 S	43.26 W
Messina, It. (mĕ-sē'nȧ)	172	38.11 N	15.34 E
Messina, S. Afr.	226	22.17 S	30.13 E
Messina, Stretto di (Str.), It. (stĕ't-tô dē)	172	38.10 N	15.34 E
Messíni, Grc.	173	37.05 N	22.00 E
Messiniakós Kólpos (G.), Grc.	173	36.59 N	22.00 E
Messy, Fr.	64c	48.58 N	2.42 E
Mesta (R.), Bul. (mĕ-stä')	173	41.42 N	23.40 E
Mestre, It. (mĕs'trā)	172	45.29 N	12.15 E
Meta (Dept.), Col. (mĕ'tä)	142a	3.28 N	74.07 W
Meta (R.), Col.	142	4.33 N	72.09 W
Métabetchouane (R.), Can. (mĕ-tȧ-bĕt-cho͞o-än')	104	47.45 N	72.00 W
Metairie, La.	125	30.00 N	90.11 W
Metán, Arg. (mĕ-tȧ'n)	144	25.32 S	64.51 W
Metangula, Moz.	226	12.42 S	34.48 E
Metapán, Sal. (mȧ-täpän')	132	14.21 N	89.26 W
Metcalfe, Can. (mĕt-käf)	95c	45.14 N	75.27 W
Metchosin, Can.	118a	48.22 N	123.33 W
Metepec, Mex. (mȧ-tĕ-pĕk')	130	18.56 N	98.31 W
Metepec, Mex.	131a	19.15 N	99.36 W
Methow R., Wa. (mĕt'hou) (mĕt hou')	116	48.26 N	120.15 W
Methuen, Ma. (mē-thū'ĕn)	105a	42.44 N	71.11 W
Metković, Yugo. (mĕt'kô-vĭch)	173	43.02 N	17.40 E
Metlakatla, Ak. (mĕt-lȧ-kăt'lȧ)	107	55.08 N	131.35 W
Metropolis, Il. (mē-trŏp'ô-lĭs)	123	37.09 N	88.46 W
Metropolitan Museum of Art (P. Int.), NY	55	40.47 N	73.58 W
Metter, Ga. (mĕt'ēr)	127	32.21 N	82.05 W
Mettmann, F.R.G. (mĕt'män)	169c	51.15 N	6.58 E
Metuchen, NJ (mē-tŭ'chĕn)	112a	40.32 N	74.21 W
Metz, Fr. (mĕtz)	169	49.08 N	6.10 E
Metztitlán, Mex. (mĕtz-tĕt-län)	130	20.36 N	98.45 W
Meuban, Cam.	229	2.27 N	12.41 E
Meudon, Fr.	64c	48.48 N	2.14 E
Meuse (R.), Eur. (mûz) (müz)	168	50.32 N	5.22 E
Mexborough, Eng. (mĕks'bŭr-ô)	156	53.30 N	1.17 W
Mexia, Tx. (mȧ-hē'ä)	125	31.32 N	96.29 W
Mexian, China	203	24.20 N	116.10 E
Mexicalcingo, Mex. (mĕ-kē-käl-sĕn'gō)	131a	19.13 N	99.34 W
Mexicali, Mex. (māk-sē-kä'lē)	120	32.28 N	115.29 W
Mexican Hat, Ut. (mĕk'sĭ-kăn hăt)	121	37.10 N	109.55 W
Mexico, Me. (mĕk'sĭ-kō)	104	44.34 N	70.33 W
Mexico, Mo.	123	39.09 N	91.51 W
Mexico, N. A.	94	23.45 N	104.00 W
Mexico (State), Mex. (māk'sē-kō)	128	19.50 N	99.50 W
Mexico City, Mex. (mĕk'sĭ-kō)	131a	19.28 N	99.09 W
Mexico, G. of, N. A.	128	25.15 N	93.45 W
Mexticacán, Mex. (mĕs'tē-kä-kän')	130	21.12 N	102.43 W
Meyers Chuck, Ak.	98	55.44 N	132.15 W
Meyersdale, Pa. (mī'ērz-dāl)	111	39.55 N	79.00 W
Meyerton, S. Afr. (mī'ēr-tŭn)	223d	26.35 S	28.01 E
Meymaneh, Afg.	192	35.53 N	64.38 E
Mezen', Sov. Un.	178	65.50 N	44.05 E
Mezen' (R), Sov. Un.	178	65.20 N	44.45 E
Mézenc, Mt., Fr. (mōN-mä-zĕN')	168	44.55 N	4.12 E
Mezha (R.), Sov. Un. (myā'zhȧ)	174	55.53 N	31.44 E
Mézieres-sur-Seine, Fr. (mā-zyâr'sür-sân')	169b	48.58 N	1.49 E
Mezőkövesd, Hung. (mĕ'zû-kû'vĕsht)	167	47.49 N	20.36 E
Mezőtur, Hung. (mĕ'zû-to͞or)	167	47.00 N	20.36 E
Mezquital, Mex. (māz-kē-täl')	130	23.30 N	104.20 W
Mezquital (R.), Mex.	130	23.07 N	104.52 W
Mezquitic, Mex. (māz-kē-tēk')	130	22.25 N	103.43 W
Mezquitic (R.), Mex.	130	22.25 N	103.45 W
Mfangano I., Ken.	231	0.28 S	33.35 E
Mga, Sov. Un. (m'gȧ)	182c	59.45 N	31.04 E
Mgeni (R.), S. Afr.	227c	29.38 S	30.53 E
Mglin, Sov. Un. (m'glĕn')	174	53.03 N	32.52 E
Mia, Oued (R.), Alg.	160	29.26 N	3.15 E
Miacatlán, Mex. (mē'ä-kä-tlän')	130	18.42 N	99.17 W
Mia-dong (Neigh.), Kor.	68b	37.37 N	127.01 E
Miahuatlán, Mex. (mē'ä-wä-tlän')	131	16.20 N	96.38 W
Miajadas, Sp. (mē-ä-hä'däs)	170	39.10 N	5.53 W
Miami, Az.	121	33.20 N	110.55 W
Miami, Fl.	127a	25.45 N	80.11 W
Miami, Ok.	123	36.51 N	94.51 W
Miami, Tx.	122	35.41 N	100.39 W
Miami (R.), Oh.	110	39.20 N	84.45 W
Miami Beach, Fl.	127a	25.47 N	80.07 W
Miami Drainage Can., Fl.	134	26.25 N	80.50 W
Miamisburg, Oh. (mī-ăm'iz-bûrg)	110	39.40 N	84.20 W
Miamitown, Oh. (mī-ăm'ĭ-toun)	113f	39.13 N	84.43 W
Mīāneh, Iran	192	37.15 N	47.13 E
Miangos, Pulau, (I.), Phil. (myä'n-gäs)	207	5.30 N	127.00 E
Miaodao Qundao (Is.), China (mĭou-dou chyo͞on-dou)	200	38.06 N	120.35 E
Miaoli, Taiwan (mē-ou'lĭ)	203	24.30 N	120.48 E
Miaozhen, China (mĭou-jŭn)	200	31.44 N	121.28 E
Miass, Sov. Un. (mī-äs')	182a	55.00 N	60.03 E
Miastko, Pol. (my»äst'kô)	166	54.01 N	17.00 E
Michajlovskoje, Sov. Un.	66b	55.35 N	37.35 E
Michalovce, Czech. (mē'Kä-lôf'tsĕ)	167	48.44 N	21.56 E
Michel Pk., Kan.	98	53.35 N	125.25 W
Michelson, Mt. Ak. (mĭch'ĕl-sŭn)	107	69.11 N	144.12 W
Michendorf, F.R.G. (mē'Kĕn-dōrf)	157b	52.19 N	13.02 E
Miches, Dom. Rep. (mē'chĕs)	135	19.00 N	69.05 W
Michigan (State), U. S. (mĭsh-'ĭ-găn)	109	45.55 N	87.00 W
Michigan, L., U. S.	109	43.20 N	87.10 W
Michigan City, In.	110	41.40 N	86.55 W
Michikamau (L.), Can.	97	54.11 N	63.21 W
Michillinda, Ca.	59	34.07 N	118.05 W
Michipicoten (I.), Can. (mĕ-shĭ-pĭ-kō'tĕn)	115	47.49 N	85.50 W
Michipicoten (R.), Can.	115	47.56 N	84.42 W
Michipicoten Harbour, Can.	115	47.58 N	84.58 W
Michoacán (State), Mex.	130	19.15 N	101.30 W
Michurinsk, Sov. Un. (mĭ-cho͞o-rĭnsk')	174	52.53 N	40.32 E
Mico, Punta (Pt.), Nic. (po͞o'n-tä-mē'kô)	133	11.38 N	83.24 W
Midas, Nv. (mī'dȧs)	116	41.15 N	116.50 W
Middelfart, Den. (mēd'l-fȧrt)	164	55.30 N	9.45 E
Middle (R.), Can.	98	55.00 N	125.50 W
Middle Andaman I., Andaman & Nicobar Is. (ăn-dȧ-măn')	206	12.44 N	93.21 E
Middle Bayou, Tx.	125a	29.38 N	95.06 W
Middle Bight (B.), Ba. (bīt)	134	24.20 N	77.35 W
Middleburg, S. Afr. (mĭd'ĕl-bûrg)	226	31.30 S	25.00 E
Middleburg, S. Afr.	223d	25.47 S	29.30 E
Middleburgh Heights, Oh.	56a	41.22 N	81.48 W
Middlebury, Vt. (mĭd''l-bĕr-ĭ)	111	44.00 N	73.10 W
Middle Concho, Tx. (kōn'chō)	124	31.21 N	100.50 W
Middle Loup (R.), Ne. (lo͞op)	114	41.49 N	100.20 W
Middleport, Oh. (mĭd''l-pōrt)	110	39.00 N	82.05 W
Middle River., Md.	112e	39.20 N	76.27 W
Middlesboro, Ky. (mĭd''lz-bŭr-ō)	126	36.36 N	83.42 W
Middlesbrough, Eng. (mĭd''lz-brŭ)	162	54.35 N	1.18 W
Middlesex, NJ (mĭd''l-sĕks)	112a	40.34 N	74.30 W
Middleton, Can. (mĭd''l-tŭn)	104	44.57 N	65.04 W
Middleton, Eng.	156	53.04 N	2.12 W
Middleton (I.), Ak.	107	59.35 N	146.35 W
Middletown, Ct.	111	41.35 N	72.40 W
Middletown, De.	111	39.30 N	75.40 W
Middletown, Ma.	105a	42.35 N	71.01 W
Middletown, NY	112a	41.26 N	74.25 W
Middletown, Oh.	110	39.30 N	84.25 W
Middlewich, Eng. (mĭd''l-wĭch)	156	53.11 N	2.27 W
Middlewit, S. Afr. (mĭd'l'wĭt)	223d	24.50 S	27.00 E
Midfield, Al.	112h	33.28 N	86.54 W
Midi, Canal du, Fr. (kä-näl-dü-mē-dē')	171	43.22 N	1.35 E
Midicine Lodge (R.), Ks.	122	37.20 N	98.57 W
Mid Illovo, S. Afr. (mĭd ĭl'ô-vō)	227c	29.59 S	30.32 E
Midland, Can. (mĭd'lănd)	111	44.45 N	79.50 W
Midland, Mi.	110	43.40 N	84.20 W
Midland, Tx.	124	32.05 N	102.05 W
Midland Beach (Neigh.), NY	55	40.34 N	74.05 W
Midlothian, Il.	58a	41.38 N	87.42 W
Midvale, Ut. (mĭd'vāl)	119b	40.37 N	111.54 W
Midway, Al. (mĭd'wā)	126	32.03 N	85.30 W
Midway, S. Afr.	71b	26.18 S	27.51 E
Midway City, Ca.	59	33.45 N	118.00 W
Midway Is., Pac. O.	208	28.00 N	179.00 W
Midwest, Wy. (mĭd-wĕst')	117	43.25 N	106.15 W
Midye, Tur. (mēd'yĕ)	179	41.35 N	28.10 E
Midzyrzecz, Pol. (myăn-dzû'zhĕch)	166	52.26 N	15.35 E
Mielec, Pol. (myĕ'lĕts)	167	50.17 N	21.27 E
Mier, Mex. (myâr)	124	26.26 N	99.08 W
Mieres, Sp. (myā'rās)	170	43.14 N	5.45 W
Mier y Noriega, Mex. (myâr'ē nô-rē-ā'gä)	130	22.28 N	100.08 W
Miguel Auza, Mex. (mē-gĕ'l-ä-o͞o'zä)	130	24.17 N	103.27 W
Miguel Pereira, Braz. (pĕ-rā'rä)	144b	22.27 S	43.28 W

ăt; finăl; rāte; senâte; ärm; ȧsk; sofȧ; fâre; ch-choose; dh-as th in other; bē; ēvent; bĕt; recĕnt; cratēr; g-gō; gh-guttural g; bĭt; ĭ-short neutral; rīde; K-guttural k as ch in German ich;

PRONOUNCING INDEX
Mijares (R.) – Mjösa 315

PLACE (Pronounciation)	PAGE	Lat. °'	Long. °'
Mijares (R.), Sp. (mē-hä'räs)	171	40.05 N	0.42 W
Mikage, Jap. (mē'kä-gā)	205b	34.42 N	135.15 E
Mikawa-Wan (B.), Jap. (mē'kä-wä wän)	205	34.43 N	137.09 E
Mikhaylov, Sov. Un. (mē-ĸäy'lôf)	174	54.14 N	39.03 E
Mikhaylovka, Sov. Un. (mē-kä'ē-laf-kȧ)	175	47.16 N	35.12 E
Mikhaylovka, Sov. Un.	182a	55.35 N	55.57 E
Mikhaylovka, Sov. Un.	182c	59.20 N	30.21 E
Mikhaylovka, Sov. Un.	179	50.05 N	43.10 E
Mikhnëvo, Sov. Un. (mĭk-nyô'vô)	182b	55.08 N	37.57 E
Miki, Jap. (mē'kē)	205b	34.47 N	134.59 E
Mikindani, Tan. (mē-kēn-dä'nē)	231	10.17 S	40.07 E
Mikkeli, Fin. (mĕk'ĕ-lĭ)	165	61.42 N	27.14 E
Míkonos (I.), Grc.	173	37.26 N	25.30 E
Mikulov, Czech. (mĭ'kōō-lôf)	166	48.47 N	16.39 E
Mikumi, Tan.	231	7.24 S	36.59 E
Mikuni, Jap. (mē'kōō-nē)	205	36.09 N	136.14 E
Mikuni-Sammyaku (Mts.), Jap. (säm'myä-kōō)	205	36.51 N	138.38 E
Mikura (I.), Jap. (mē'kōō-rȧ)	205	33.53 N	139.26 E
Milaca, Mn. (mē-lăk'ȧ)	115	45.45 N	93.41 W
Milan, Mi. (mĭ'lăn)	110	42.05 N	83.40 W
Milan, Mo.	123	40.13 N	93.07 W
Milan, Tn.	126	35.54 N	88.47 W
Milan, see Milano			
Milano (Milan), It. (mē-lä'nō)	172	45.29 N	9.12 E
Milâs, Tur. (mē'läs)	179	37.10 N	27.25 E
Milazzo, It. (mē-lät'sô)	172	38.13 N	15.17 E
Milbank, SD (mĭl'băŋĸ)	114	45.13 N	96.38 W
Mildura, Austl. (mĭl-dū'rȧ)	216	34.10 S	142.18 E
Miles City, Mt. (mīlz)	117	46.24 N	105.50 W
Milford, Ct. (mĭl'fērd)	111	41.15 N	73.05 W
Milford, De.	111	38.55 N	75.25 W
Milford, Md.	56c	39.21 N	76.44 W
Milford, Ma.	105a	42.09 N	71.31 W
Milford, Mi.	113b	42.35 N	83.36 W
Milford, NH	111	42.50 N	71.40 W
Milford, Oh.	113f	39.11 N	84.18 W
Milford, Ut.	121	38.20 N	113.05 W
Miling, Austl. (mĭl''ng)	214	30.30 S	116.25 E
Milipitas, Ca. (mĭl-ĭ-pĭ'tăs)	118b	37.26 N	121.54 W
Milk R., Can.-U.S.	117	48.25 N	108.45 W
Milk River, Can. (mĭlk)	99	49.09 N	112.05 W
Millau, Fr. (mē-yō')	168	44.06 N	3.04 E
Millbourne, Pa.	56b	39.58 N	75.15 W
Millbrae, Ca. (mĭl'brā)	118b	37.36 N	122.23 W
Millburn, NJ	55	40.44 N	74.20 W
Millbury, Ma. (mĭl'bēr-ĭ)	105a	42.12 N	71.46 W
Mill Cr., Can. (mĭl)	95g	53.13 N	113.25 W
Mill Cr., Ca.	120	40.07 N	121.55 W
Milledgeville, Ga. (mĭl'ĕj-vĭl)	126	33.05 N	83.15 W
Mille Iles, R. des, Can. (rē-vyâr' dā mĭl'ĭl')	95a	45.41 N	73.40 W
Mille Lac Ind. Res., Mn. (mĭl lăk')	115	46.14 N	94.13 W
Mille Lacs (L.), Mn.	115	46.25 N	93.22 W
Mille Lacs, Lac des (L.), Can. (läk dē mēl läks)	115	48.52 N	90.53 W
Millen, Ga. (mĭl'ĕn)	127	32.47 N	81.55 W
Miller, SD (mĭl'ēr)	114	44.31 N	99.00 W
Millerovo, Sov. Un. (mĭl'ē-rô-vô)	175	48.58 N	40.27 E
Millersburg, Ky. (mĭl'ērz-bûrg)	103	38.15 N	84.10 W
Millersburg, Oh.	103	40.35 N	81.55 W
Millersburg, Pa.	111	40.35 N	76.55 W
Millers Ferry Lake (Res.), Al.	126	32.10 N	87.15 W
Millerton, Can. (mĭl'ēr-tŭn)	104	46.56 N	65.40 W
Millertown, Can. (mĭl'ēr-toun)	105	48.49 N	56.32 W
Mill Green, Eng.	62	51.41 N	0.22 E
Mill Hill (Neigh.), Eng.	62	51.37 N	0.13 W
Millicent, Austl. (mĭl-ĭ-sĕnt)	216	37.30 S	140.20 E
Millinocket, Me. (mĭl-ĭ-nŏk'ĕt)	104	45.40 N	68.44 W
Millis, Ma. (mĭl-ĭs)	105a	42.10 N	71.22 W
Mill Neck, NY	55	40.52 N	73.34 W
Millstadt, Il. (mĭl'stăt)	119e	38.27 N	90.06 W
Millstone (R.), NJ (mĭl'stōn)	112a	40.27 N	74.38 W
Millstream, Austl. (mĭl'strēm)	214	21.45 S	117.10 E
Milltown, Can. (mĭl'toun)	104	45.13 N	67.19 W
Millvale, Pa.	57b	40.29 N	79.58 W
Mill Valley, Cal. (mĭl)	118b	37.54 N	122.32 W
Millwood Res., Ar.	123	33.00 N	94.00 W
Milly-la-Forêt, Fr. (mē-yē'-la-fō-rĕ')	169b	48.24 N	2.28 E
Milmont Park, Pa.	56b	39.53 N	75.20 W
Milnerton, S. Afr. (mĭl'nēr-tŭn)	226a	33.52 S	18.30 E
Milnor, ND (mĭl'nēr)	114	46.17 N	97.29 W
Milnrow, Eng.	64b	53.37 N	2.06 W
Milo, Me.	104	44.16 N	69.01 W
Milo (I.), see Mílos			
Milon-la-Chapelle, Fr.	64c	48.44 N	2.03 E
Milos, (Milo) (I.), Grc. (mē'lŏs)	173	36.45 N	24.35 E
Milpa Alta, Mex. (mē'l-pä-ä'l-tä)	131a	19.11 N	99.01 W
Milspe, F.R.G.	63	51.18 N	7.21 E
Milton, Can.	95d	43.31 N	79.53 W
Milton, Fl. (mĭl'tŭn)	126	30.37 N	87.02 W
Milton, Ma.	105a	42.15 N	71.05 W
Milton, Pa.	111	41.00 N	76.50 W
Milton, Ut.	119b	41.04 N	111.44 W
Milton, Wa.	118a	47.15 N	122.20 W
Milton, Wi.	115	42.45 N	89.00 W
Milton-Freewater, Or.	116	45.57 N	118.25 W
Milvale, Pa. (mĭl'vāl)	113e	40.29 N	79.58 W
Milville, NJ (mĭl'vĭl)	111	39.25 N	75.00 W
Milwaukee, Or. (mĭl-wô'kē)	118c	45.27 N	122.38 W
Milwaukee, Wi.	113a	43.03 N	87.55 W
Milwaukee R., Wi.	113a	43.10 N	87.56 W
Mimiapan, Mex. (mē-myä-pȧn')	131a	19.26 N	99.28 W
Mimoso do Sul, Braz. (mē-mô'sō-dō-sōō'l)	141a	21.03 S	41.21 W
Min (R.), China (mēn)	203	26.03 N	118.30 E
Min (R.), China	203	29.30 N	104.00 E
Mina (R.), Alg. (mē'nȧ)	171	35.24 N	0.51 E
Minago (R.), Can. (mĭ-nä'gō)	101	54.25 N	98.45 W
Minakuchi, Jap. (mē'nȧ-kōō'chē)	205	34.59 N	136.06 E
Minami (Neigh.), Jap.	68e	34.58 N	135.45 E
Minamisenju (Neigh.), Jap.	69a	35.44 N	139.48 E
Minas, Cuba (mē'näs)	134	21.03 N	77.35 W
Minas, Indon.	191b	0.52 N	101.29 E
Minas, Ur. (mē'näs)	144	34.18 S	55.12 W
Minas Basin, Can. (mĭ'nȧs)	104	45.20 N	64.00 W
Minas Chan., Can.	104	45.15 N	64.45 W
Minas de Oro, Hond. (mē'näs-dĕ-dĕ-ō-rô)	132	14.52 N	87.19 W
Minas de Riotinto, Sp. (mē'näs dā rē-ō-tēn'tō)	170	37.43 N	6.35 W
Minas Gerais (State), Braz. (mē'näzh-zhĕ-rȧ'ēs)	143	17.45 S	43.50 W
Minas Nova, Braz. (mē'näzh nō'väzh)	143	17.20 S	42.19 W
Minas, Sierra de las (Mts.), Guat. (syĕr'rȧ dā läs mē'näs)	132	15.08 N	90.25 W
Minatare (L.), Ne. (mĭn'ȧ-târ)	114	41.56 N	103.07 W
Minatitlan, Mex. (mē-nä-tē-tlän')	131	17.59 N	94.33 W
Minatitlan, Mex.	130	19.21 N	104.02 W
Minato, Jap. (mē'nȧ-tô)	205a	35.13 N	139.52 E
Minato (Neigh.), Jap.	69a	35.39 N	139.45 E
Minato (Neigh.), Jap.	69b	34.39 N	135.26 E
Minch, The (Chan.), Scot.	162	58.04 N	6.04 W
Mindanao (I.), Phil. (mĭn-dä-nou')	207	7.30 N	125.10 E
Mindanao Sea, Phil.	207	8.55 N	124.00 E
Minden, F.R.G. (mĭn'dĕn)	166	52.17 N	8.58 E
Minden, La.	125	32.36 N	93.19 W
Minden, Ne.	122	40.30 N	98.54 W
Mindoro (I.), Phil. (mĭn-dō'rō)	207a	13.04 N	121.06 E
Mindoro Str., Phil.	207a	12.28 N	120.33 E
Mindyak, Sov. Un. (mēn'dyȧk)	182a	54.01 N	58.48 E
Mineola, NY (mĭn-ē-ō'lȧ)	112a	40.43 N	73.38 W
Mineola, Tx.	125	32.39 N	95.31 W
Mineral del Chico, Mex. (mē-nä-räl'dĕl chē'kô)	130	20.13 N	98.46 W
Mineral del Monte, Mex. (mē-nä-räl dĕl mōn'tā)	130	20.18 N	98.39 W
Mineral'nyye Vody, Sov. Un.	179	44.10 N	43.15 E
Mineral Point, Wi. (mĭn'ēr-ăl)	115	42.50 N	90.10 W
Minerál Wells, Tx. (mĭn'ēr-ăl wĕlz)	124	32.48 N	98.06 W
Minerva, Oh. (mĭ-nur'vȧ)	110	40.45 N	81.10 W
Minervino, It. (mē-nĕr-vē'nô)	172	41.07 N	16.05 E
Mineyama, Jap. (mē-nĕ-yä'mä)	205	35.38 N	135.05 E
Mingan, Can.	104	50.18 N	64.02 W
Mingechaur (R.), Sov. Un.	179	41.00 N	47.20 E
Mingenew, Austl. (mĭn'gĕ-nū)	214	29.15 S	115.45 E
Mingo Junction, Oh. (mĭŋ'gō)	110	40.15 N	80.40 W
Minho (Reg.), Port. (mēn yōō)	170	41.32 N	8.13 W
Minho (R.), Jam.	134	17.55 N	77.20 W
Minho, Rio (R.), Port. (rē'ō mē'n-yô)	170	41.28 N	9.05 W
Ministik L., Can. (mĭ-nĭs'tĭk)	95g	53.23 N	113.05 W
Minna, Nig. (mĭn'ȧ)	229	9.37 N	6.33 E
Minneapolis, Ks. (mĭn-ē-ăp'ō-lĭs)	123	39.07 N	97.41 W
Minneapolis, Mn.	119g	44.58 N	93.15 W
Minnedosa, Can. (mĭn-ē-dō'sȧ)	101	50.14 N	99.51 W
Minneota, Mn. (mĭn-ē-ō'tȧ)	114	44.34 N	95.59 W
Minnesota (State), U. S. (mĭn-ē-sō'tȧ)	109	46.10 N	90.20 W
Minnesota (R), Mn.	114	45.04 N	96.03 W
Minnetonka (L.), Mn. (mĭn-ē-tôŋ'kȧ)	115	44.52 N	93.34 W
Minnie Maud Cr., Ut. (mĭn'ĭmôd')	121	39.50 N	110.30 W
Minnitaki L., Can. (mĭ'nĭ-tä'kē)	101	49.58 N	92.00 W
Minō, Jap. (mē'nō)	205b	34.49 N	135.28 E
Mino (R.), Jap.	205b	34.56 N	135.06 E
Miño (R.), Sp. (mē'nyō)	170	42.28 N	7.48 W
Minonk, Il. (mĭ'nŏnk)	110	40.55 N	89.00 W
Minooka, Il. (mĭ-nōō'kȧ)	113a	41.27 N	88.15 W
Minorca (I.), see Menorca			
Minot, ND (mĭ'nŏt)	114	48.13 N	101.16 W
Minsk, Sov. Un. (mēnsk)	174	53.54 N	27.35 E
Minsk (Oblast), Sov. Un.	174	53.50 N	27.43 E
Mińsk Mazowiecki, Pol. (mēn'sk mä-zō-vyĕt'skĭ)	167	52.10 N	21.35 E
Minsterley, Eng. (mĭnstēr-lē)	156	52.38 N	2.55 W
Mintard, F.R.G.	63	51.22 N	6.54 E
Minto, Austl.	70a	34.01 S	150.51 E
Minto, Can.	104	46.05 N	66.05 W
Minto (L.), Can.	97	57.18 N	75.50 W
Minturno, It. (mēn-tōōr'nō)	172	41.17 N	13.44 E
Minūf, Egypt (mē-nōōf')	223b	30.26 N	30.55 E
Minusinsk, Sov. Un. (mē-nōō-sĕnsk')	180	53.47 N	91.45 E
Min'yar, Sov. Un. (mēn'yär)	182	55.06 N	57.33 E
Miquelon (I.), Saint Pierre & Miquelon, (mĭk-ē-lôn')	105	47.00 N	56.40 W
Miquelon L., Can. (mĭ'kē-lôn)	95g	53.16 N	112.55 W
Miquihuana, Mex. (mē-kē-wä'nä)	130	23.36 N	99.45 W
Miquon, Pa.	56b	40.04 N	75.16 W
Mir, Sov. Un. (mēr)	167	53.27 N	26.25 E
Mira (R.), Port. (mē'rä)	170	37.29 N	8.15 W
Miracema, Braz. (mē-rä-sĕ'mä)	141a	21.24 S	42.10 W
Mirador, Braz. (mē-rȧ-dōr')	143	6.19 S	44.12 W
Miraflores, Col. (mē-rä-flō'räs)	142	5.10 N	73.13 W
Miraflores, Peru	60c	12.08 S	77.03 W
Miraflores, Peru	142	16.19 S	71.20 W
Miraflores Locks, Pan.	128a	9.00 N	79.35 W
Miragoâne, Hai. (mē-rȧ-gwän')	135	18.25 N	73.05 W
Miraí, Braz. (mē-rȧ-ē')	141a	21.13 S	42.36 W
Mira Loma, Ca. (mĭ'rȧ lō'mȧ)	119a	34.01 N	117.32 W
Miramar, Ca. (mĭr'ȧ-mär)	120a	32.53 N	117.08 W
Miramar (Neigh.), Cuba	60b	23.07 N	82.25 W
Miramas, Fr.	168a	43.35 N	5.00 E
Miramichi B., Can. (mĭr'ȧ-mē'shē)	104	47.08 N	65.08 W
Miranda, Austl.	70a	34.02 S	151.06 E
Miranda, Col. (mē-rä'n-dä)	142a	3.14 N	76.11 W
Miranda, Ven.	143b	10.09 N	68.24 W
Miranda (State), Ven.	143b	10.17 N	66.41 W
Miranda de Ebro, Port. (mē-rän'dä dōō-dwĕ'rô)	170	41.30 N	6.17 W
Miranda de Ebro, Sp. (mē-rä'n-dä-dĕ-ĕ'brô)	170	42.42 N	2.59 W
Mirandela, Port. (mē-rän-dā'lȧ)	170	41.28 N	7.10 W
Mirando City, Tx. (mĭr-ăn'dō)	124	27.25 N	99.03 W
Mira Por Vos Islets (Is.), Ba. (mē'rä pôr vōs)	135	22.05 N	74.30 W
Mira Por Vos Pass (Str.), Ba.	135	22.10 N	74.35 W
Mirbāt, Om.	192	16.58 N	54.42 E
Mirebalais, Hai. (mēr-bȧ-lĕ')	135	18.50 N	72.05 W
Mirecourt, Fr. (mēr-kōōr')	169	48.20 N	6.08 E
Mirfield, Eng. (mûr'fēld)	156	53.41 N	1.42 W
Mirgorod, Sov. Un.	175	49.56 N	33.36 E
Miri, Mala. (mē'rē)	206	4.13 N	113.56 E
Mirim, L., Braz.-Ur. (mē-rēɴ')	144	33.00 S	53.15 W
Mírina, Grc.	173	39.52 N	25.01 E
Miropol'ye, Sov. Un. (mē-rô-pôl'yĕ)	175	51.02 N	35.13 E
Mīrpur Khās, Pak. (mēr'pōōr ĸäs)	196	25.36 N	69.10 E
Mirzāpur, India (mēr'zä-pōōr)	196	25.12 N	82.38 E
Mirzāpur, India	67a	22.50 N	88.24 E
Misailovo, Sov. Un.	66b	55.34 N	37.49 E
Misantla, Mex. (mē-sän'tlä)	131	19.55 N	96.49 W
Miscou (I.), Can. (mĭs'kō)	104	47.58 N	64.35 W
Miscou Pt., Can.	104	48.04 N	64.32 W
Miseno, C., It. (mē-zĕ'nō)	171c	40.33 N	14.12 E
Misery, Mt., Saint Kitts-Nevis (mĭz'rē-ĭ)	133b	17.28 N	62.47 W
Mishan, China (mĭ'shäɴ)	204	45.32 N	132.19 E
Mishawaka, In. (mĭsh-ȧ-wôk'ȧ)	110	41.45 N	86.15 W
Mishima, Jap. (mē'shē-mä)	205	35.09 N	138.56 E
Misiones (Prov.), Arg. (mē-syō'nās)	144	27.00 S	54.30 W
Miskito, Cayos (Is.), Nic.	133	14.34 N	82.30 W
Miskolc, Hung. (mĭsh'kōlts)	167	48.07 N	20.50 E
Misr al-Qadīmah (Old Cairo) (Neigh.), Egypt	71a	30.00 N	31.14 E
Misool (I.), Pulau, Indon. (mē-sōōl')	207	2.00 S	130.05 E
Misquah Hills, Mn. (mĭs-kwä' hĭlz)	115	47.50 N	90.30 W
Mişr al Jadīdah (Ruins), Egypt	223b	30.06 N	31.35 E
Misr al-Jadīdah (Heliopolis) (Neigh.), Egypt	71a	30.06 N	31.20 E
Misrātah, Libya	225	32.23 N	14.58 E
Missinaibi L., Can.	102	48.23 N	83.40 W
Missinaibi (R.), Can. (mĭs'ĭn-ä'ē-bē)	97	50.27 N	83.01 W
Mission, Ks. (mĭsh'ŭn)	119f	39.02 N	94.39 W
Mission, Tx.	124	26.14 N	98.19 W
Mission City, Can. (sĭ'tĭ)	118d	49.08 N	112.18 W
Mississagi (R.), Can.	102	46.35 N	83.30 W
Mississauga, Can.	95d	43.34 N	79.37 W
Mississinewa (R.), In. (mĭs-ĭ-sĭn'ē-wä)	110	40.30 N	85.45 W
Mississippi (State), U.S. (mĭs-ĭ-sĭp'ē)	109	32.30 N	89.45 W
Mississippi (L.), Can.	111	45.05 N	76.15 W
Mississippi (R.), U. S.	109	31.50 N	91.30 W
Mississippi Sd., Ms.	126	34.16 N	89.10 W
Missoula, Mt. (mĭ-zōō'lȧ)	117	46.25 N	114.00 W
Missouri (State), U. S. (mĭ-sōō'rē)	109	38.00 N	93.40 W
Missouri (R.), U. S.	109	40.40 N	96.00 W
Missouri City, Tx.	125a	29.37 N	95.32 W
Missouri Coteau, (Plat.), U. S.	108	47.30 N	101.00 W
Missouri Valley, Ia.	114	41.35 N	95.53 W
Mist, Or. (mĭst)	118c	46.00 N	123.15 W
Mistassibi (R.), Can. (mĭs-tȧ-sĭ'bē)	104	49.44 N	69.58 W
Mistassini, Can. (mĭs-tȧ-sĭ'nē)	104	48.56 N	71.55 W
Mistassini (L.), Can. (mĭs-tȧ-sĭ'nē)	97	50.48 N	73.30 W
Mistassini (R.), Can.	104	50.02 N	72.38 W
Mistelbach, Aust. (mĭs'tĕl-bäk)	166	48.34 N	16.33 E
Misteriosa, L., Mex. (mēs-tĕ-ryô'sä)	132a	18.05 N	90.15 W
Mistretta, It. (mē-strĕt'tä)	172	37.54 N	14.22 E
Mitaka, Jap. (mē'tä-kä)	205a	35.42 N	139.34 E
Mita, Punta de (Pt.), Mex. (pōō'n-tä-dĕ-mē'tä)	130	20.44 N	105.34 W
Mitcham, Austl.	70b	37.49 S	145.12 E
Mitcham (Neigh.), Eng.	62	51.24 N	0.10 W
Mitchell, Il. (mĭch'ĕl)	119e	38.46 N	90.05 W
Mitchell, In.	110	38.45 N	86.25 W
Mitchell, Ne.	114	41.56 N	103.49 W
Mitchell, SD	114	43.42 N	98.01 W
Mitchell (R.), Austl.	215	15.30 S	142.15 E
Mitchell, Mt., NC	127	35.47 N	82.15 W
Mit Ghamr, Egypt	223b	30.43 N	31.20 E
Mitilíni, Grc.	173	39.09 N	26.35 E
Mitla P., Egypt	191a	30.03 N	32.40 E
Mito, Jap. (mē'tō)	205	36.20 N	140.23 E
Mitry-Mory, Fr.	64c	48.59 N	2.37 E
Mitsiwa (Massaua), Eth.	225	15.40 N	39.19 E
Mitsu, Jap. (mēt'sōō)	205	34.21 N	132.49 E
Mitte (Neigh.), G.D.R.	65a	52.31 N	13.24 E
Mittelland (Can.), G.D.R. (mĭt'ĕl-lănd)	166	52.18 N	10.42 E
Mittenwalde, G.D.R. (mē'tĕn-väl-dĕ)	157b	52.16 N	13.33 E
Mittweida, G.D.R. (mĭt-vī'dä)	166	50.59 N	12.58 E
Mitumba, Monts (Mts.), Zaire	231	10.50 S	27.00 E
Mityayevo, Sov. Un. (mĭt-yä'yĕ-vô)	182a	60.17 N	61.02 E
Miura, Jap.	205a	35.08 N	139.37 E
Mius (R.), Sov. Un. (mē-ōōs')	175	47.30 N	38.48 W
Miwa, Jap. (mē'wä)	205b	34.32 N	135.51 E
Mixcoac (Neigh.), Mex.	60a	19.23 N	99.12 W
Mixico, Guat. (mēs'kō)	132	14.37 N	90.37 W
Mixquiahuala, Mex. (mēs-kē-wä'lä)	130	20.12 N	99.13 W
Mixteco (R.), Mex. (mēs-tä'kō)	130	17.45 N	98.10 W
Miyake (I.), Jap. (mē'yä-kā)	205	34.06 N	139.21 E
Miyake, Jap. (mē'yä-kā)	205b	34.35 N	135.34 E
Miyakojima (Neigh.), Jap.	69b	34.43 N	135.33 E
Miyakonojō, Jap. (mē'yȧ-kô'nô-jô)	205	31.42 N	131.03 E
Miyazaki, Jap. (mē'yä-zä'kē)	205	31.55 N	131.27 E
Miyoshi, Jap. (mē-yō'shē')	205	34.48 N	132.49 E
Mizdah, Libya (mēz'dä)	160	31.29 N	13.09 E
Mizil, Rom. (mē'zēl)	173	45.01 N	26.30 E
Mizonokuchi, see Takatsu			
Mizonuma, Jap.	69a	35.48 N	139.36 E
Mizoram (Union Ter.), India	196	23.25 N	92.45 E
Mizue (Neigh.), Jap.	69a	35.41 N	139.54 E
Mizuho, Jap.	69a	35.46 N	139.21 E
Mjölby, Swe. (myûl'bü)	164	58.20 N	15.09 E
Mjörn (L.), Swe.	164	57.55 N	12.22 E
Mjösa, Nor. (myûsä)	164	60.41 N	11.25 E

ng-sing; ŋg-baŋk; ɴ-nasalized n; nŏd; cŏmmit; ōld; ôbey; ôrder; oi-boil; fōōd; fŏŏt; ou-out; s-soft; sh-dish; th-thin; pūre; ûnite; ûrn; stŭd; circŭs; ü-as in French tu; '-indeterminate vowel.

316 Mkalama – Monticello

PLACE (Pronounciation)	PAGE	Lat. °′	Long. °′
Mkalama, Tan.	226	4.07 S	34.38 E
Mkomazi (R.), S. Afr.	227c	30.10 S	30.30 E
Mkushi, Zambia	231	13.40 S	29.20 E
Mkwaja, Tan.	231	5.47 S	38.51 E
Mladá Boleslav, Czech. (mlä'dä bô'lĕ-släf)	166	50.26 N	14.52 E
Mlala Hills, Tan.	231	6.47 S	31.45 E
Mlanje Mts., Malawi	231	15.55 S	35.30 E
Mlawa, Pol. (mwä'vá)	167	53.07 N	20.25 E
Mlazi (R.), S. Afr.	227c	29.52 S	30.42 E
Mljet (I.), Yugo. (mlyĕt)	173	42.40 N	17.45 E
Mmabatho, Boph.	222	25.42 S	25.43 E
Mnevniki (Neigh.), Sov. Un.	66b	55.45 N	37.28 E
Mo (R.), Togo	228	9.05 N	0.55 E
Moa (R.), S. L.	228	7.40 N	11.15 W
Moab, Ut. (mō'ăb)	121	38.35 N	109.35 W
Moanda, Gabon	226	1.37 S	13.09 E
Moapa River Ind. Res., Nv. (mō-ăp'á)	120	36.44 N	115.01 W
Moa, Pulau, (I.), Indon.	207	8.30 S	128.30 E
Moar L., Can. (môr)	101	52.00 N	95.09 W
Moba, Nig.	71d	6.27 N	3.28 E
Mobaye, Cen. Afr. Rep. (mô-bä'y')	230	4.19 N	21.11 E
Mobayi-Mbongo, Zaire	225	4.14 N	21.11 E
Moberly, Mo. (mō'bēr-lĭ)	123	39.24 N	92.25 W
Moberly (R.), Can.	99	55.40 N	121.15 W
Mobile, Al. (mô-bēl')	126	30.42 N	88.03 W
Mobile B., Al.	126	30.26 N	87.56 W
Mobile (R.), Al.	126	31.15 N	88.00 W
Mobridge, SD (mō'brĭj)	114	45.32 N	100.26 W
Moca, Dom. Rep. (mô'kä)	135	19.25 N	70.35 W
Moçambique, Moz. (mō-säɴ-bē'kĕ)	231	15.03 S	40.42 E
Moçâmedes, Ang. (mō-zá-mĕ-dĕs)	230	15.10 S	12.09 E
Moçâmedes (Reg.), Ang.	226	16.00 S	12.15 E
Mocha, Yemen (mō'kȧ)	192	13.11 N	43.20 E
Mochitlán, Mex. (mō-chē-tlän')	130	17.10 N	99.19 W
Mochudi, Bots. (mō-chōō'dē)	226	24.13 S	26.07 E
Mocímboa da Praia, Moz. (mô-sē'ēm-bô-à prä'ēȧ)	231	11.20 S	40.21 E
Moclips, Wa.	116	47.14 N	124.13 W
Mococa, Braz. (mô-kô'kȧ)	141a	21.29 S	46.58 W
Môco, Serra (Mts.), Arg.	230	12.25 S	15.10 E
Moctezuma, Mex. (mōk'tā-zōō'mä)	130	22.44 N	101.06 W
Mocuba, Moz.	231	16.50 S	36.59 E
Modderbee, S. Afr.	71b	26.10 S	28.24 E
Modderfontein, S. Afr.	227b	26.06 S	28.10 E
Modena, It. (mô'dĕ-nä)	172	44.38 N	10.54 E
Modesto, Ca. (mô-dĕs'tō)	120	37.39 N	121.00 W
Modica, It. (mô'dē-kä)	159	36.50 N	14.43 E
Modjeska, Ca.	59	33.43 N	117.37 W
Mödling, Aust. (mûd'lĭng)	157e	48.06 N	16.17 E
Moelv, Nor.	164	60.55 N	10.40 E
Moengo, Sur.	143	5.43 N	54.19 W
Moenkopi, Az.	121	36.07 N	111.13 W
Moers, F.R.G. (mûrs)	169c	51.27 N	6.38 E
Moffat Tun., Co. (môf'ăt)	122	39.52 N	106.20 W
Mofolo, S. Afr.	71b	26.14 S	27.53 E
Mogadore, Oh. (mŏg-á-dōr')	113d	41.04 N	81.23 E
Mogaung, Bur. (mô-gä'ōōng)	198	25.30 N	96.52 E
Mogi das Cruzes, Braz. (mô-gē-däs-krōō'sĕs)	141a	23.33 S	46.10 W
Mogi-Guaçu (R.), Braz. (mô-gē-gwá'sōō)	141a	22.06 S	47.12 W
Mogilëv, Sov. Un. (mô-gē-lyôf')	174	53.53 N	30.22 E
Mogilëv (Oblast), Sov. Un. (mô-gē-lyôf')	174	53.28 N	30.15 E
Mogilëv-Podol'skiy, Sov. Un. (mô-gē-lyôf) (pô-dôl'skĭ)	175	48.27 N	27.51 E
Mogilno, Pol. (mô-gēl'nô)	167	52.38 N	17.58 W
Mogi-Mirim, Braz. (mô-gē-mē-rē'ɴ)	141a	22.26 S	46.57 W
Mogincual, Moz.	231	15.35 S	40.25 E
Mogok, Bur. (mô-gōk')	198	23.14 N	96.38 E
Mogollon, NM (mō-gô-yōn')	121	33.25 N	108.45 W
Mogollon, Plat., Az. (mō-gô-yōn')	121	34.26 N	111.17 W
Mogol R., S. Afr. (mô-gŏl)	223d	24.12 S	27.55 E
Moguer, Sp. (mô-gĕr')	170	37.15 N	6.50 W
Mohács, Hung. (mô'häch)	167	45.59 N	18.38 E
Mohale's Hoek, Leso.	227c	30.09 S	27.28 E
Mohall, ND (mō'hôl)	114	48.46 N	101.29 W
Mohammadia, Alg.	171	35.35 N	0.05 E
Mohave (L.), Nv. (mô-hä'vä)	120	35.23 N	114.40 W
Mohawk (R.), NY (mō'hôk)	111	43.15 N	75.20 W
Mohe, China (mwo-hŭ)	199	53.33 N	122.30 E
Moheli (I.), Comoros (mô-ā-lē') (mô-hä'lē)	227	12.23 S	43.38 E
Mohenjo-Dero (Ruins), Pak.	196	27.20 N	68.10 E
Mohili (Neigh.), India	67e	19.06 N	72.53 E
Mõisaküla, Sov. Un. (mĕē'sá-kü'lă)	165	58.07 N	25.12 E
Moisie (R.), Can. (mwá-zē')	105	50.35 N	66.25 W
Moissac, Fr. (mwä-sák')	168	44.07 N	1.05 E
Moita, Port. (mô-ē'tá)	171b	38.39 N	9.00 W
Mojave, Ca.	120	35.06 N	118.09 W
Mojave (R.), Ca. (mô-hä'vä)	120	34.46 N	117.24 W
Mojave Desert, Ca.	120	35.05 N	117.30 W
Mokelumne (R.), Ca. (mô-kē-lŭm'nē)	120	38.30 N	120.17 W
Mokhotlong, Leso.	227c	29.18 S	29.06 E
Mokp'o, Kor. (môk'pō')	204	34.50 N	126.30 E
Moksha (R.), Sov. Un. (môk-shä')	178	54.40 N	43.20 E
Mol, Bel.	157a	51.21 N	5.09 E
Molat (I.), Yugo. (mô'lät)	172	44.15 N	14.40 E
Moldavia (Reg.), Rom.	167	47.20 N	27.12 E
Moldavian S. S. R., Sov. Un.	176	48.00 N	28.00 E
Molde, Nor. (môl'dē)	164	62.44 N	7.15 E
Moldova R., Rom.	167	47.17 N	26.27 E
Moldoveanu (Mtn.), Rom.	173	45.33 N	24.38 E
Molepolole, Bots. (mō-lā-pô-lō'lā)	226	24.15 S	25.33 W
Molfetta, It. (môl-fĕt'tä)	172	41.11 N	16.38 E
Molina, Chile (mŏ-lē'nä)	141b	35.07 S	71.17 W
Molina de Aragón, Sp. (mô-lē'nä dē ä-rä-gō'n)	170	41.40 N	1.54 W
Molina de Segura, Sp. (mô-lē'nä dē sĕ-gōō'rä)	170	38.03 N	1.07 W

PLACE (Pronounciation)	PAGE	Lat. °′	Long. °′
Moline, Il. (mô-lēn')	115	41.31 N	90.34 W
Molino de Rosas, Mex.	60a	19.22 N	99.13 W
Moliro, Zaire	231	8.13 S	30.34 E
Moliterno, It. (môl-ē-tĕr'nô)	172	40.13 N	15.54 W
Molins de Rey, Sp.	65e	41.25 N	2.01 E
Möllen, F.R.G.	63	51.35 N	6.42 E
Mollendo, Peru (mô-lyĕn'dō)	142	17.02 S	71.59 W
Moller, Port, Ak. (pōrt mōl'ēr)	107	56.18 N	161.30 W
Mölndal, Swe. (mûln'däl)	164	57.39 N	12.01 E
Molochnaya (R.), Sov. Un. (mô-lôch'ná-yá) (rē-kä')	175	47.05 N	35.22 E
Molochnoye, Ozero (L.), Sov. Un. (ô'zē-rô mô-lôch'nô-yē)	175	46.35 N	35.32 E
Molodechno, Sov. Un. (mô-lô-dĕch'nô)	174	54.18 N	26.57 E
Molodechno (Oblast), Sov. Un.	174	54.27 N	27.38 E
Molody Tud, Sov. Un. (mô-lô-dô'ē tōō'd)	182b	55.17 N	37.31 E
Mologa (R.), Sov. Un. (mô-lô'gá)	174	58.05 N	35.43 E
Molokai (I.), Hi. (mō-lô kä'ē)	106a	21.15 N	157.05 E
Molokcha R., Sov. Un. (mô'lôk-chä)	182b	56.15 N	38.29 E
Molopo (R.), S. Afr. (mō-lō-pô)	226	27.45 S	20.45 E
Molson L., Can. (mōl'sŭn)	101	54.12 N	96.45 W
Molteno, S. Afr. (môl-tā'nô)	227c	31.24 S	26.23 E
Moma, Moz.	231	16.44 S	39.14 E
Mombasa, Ken. (mōm-bä'sä)	231	4.03 N	39.40 E
Mombetsu, Jap. (môm'bĕt-sōō')	204	44.21 N	142.48 E
Momboyo (R.), Zaire	230	0.20 S	19.20 E
Momence, Il. (mô-mĕns')	113a	41.09 N	87.40 W
Momostenango, Guat. (mô-môs-tā-näŋ'gô)	132	15.02 N	91.25 W
Momotombo, Nic.	132	12.25 N	86.43 W
Mompog Pass, Phil. (mŏm-pŏg')	207a	13.35 N	122.09 E
Mompos, Col. (mōm-pōs')	142	8.05 N	74.30 W
Møn (I.), Den. (mûn)	164	54.54 N	12.30 E
Monaca, Pa. (mŏ-ná'kŏ)	113e	40.41 N	80.17 W
Monaco, Eur. (mŏn'á-kō)	159	43.43 N	7.47 E
Monaghan, Ire. (mŏ'á-găn)	162	54.16 N	7.20 W
Mona Pass, N.A. (mō'nä)	129	18.00 N	68.10 W
Monarch Mtn., Can. (mŏn'ērk)	98	51.41 N	125.53 W
Monashee Mts., Can. (mŏ-nä'shē)	99	50.30 N	118.30 W
Monastir, Tun. (môn-ás-tēr')	159	35.49 N	10.56 E
Monastir, see Bitola			
Monastyrishche, Sov. Un. (mô-nás-tē-rēsh'chā)	175	48.57 N	29.53 E
Monastyrshchina, Sov. Un. (mô-nás-tērsh'chĭ-ná)	174	54.19 N	31.49 E
Moncada, Sp.	65e	41.29 N	2.11 E
Monçao, Braz. (mon-souɴ')	143	3.39 S	45.23 W
Moncayo (Mtn.), Sp. (môn-kä'yō)	170	41.44 N	1.48 W
Monchegorsk, Sov. Un. (mōn'chĕ-gôrsk)	178	69.00 N	33.35 E
Mönchengladbach, F.R.G. (mûn'ĸĕn gläd'bäĸ)	169c	51.12 N	6.28 E
Monchique, Serra de (Mts.), Port. (sĕr'rä dä môn-chē'kē)	170	37.22 N	8.37 W
Monclova, Mex. (môn-klō'vä)	124	26.53 N	101.25 W
Moncton, Can. (mŭŋk'tŭn)	104	46.06 N	64.47 W
Mondego, Cabo (C.), Port. (ká'bō môn-dā'gōō)	170	40.12 N	8.55 W
Mondêgo (R.), Port. (mōn-dĕ'gō)	170	40.10 N	8.36 W
Mondeor, S. Afr.	71b	26.17 S	28.00 E
Mondombe, Zaire (môn-dôm'bā)	226	0.45 S	23.06 E
Mondoñedo, Sp. (môn-dô-nyā'dō)	170	43.35 N	7.18 W
Mondoví, It. (môn-dô'vē)	172	44.23 N	7.53 E
Mondovi, Wi. (mŏn-dō'vĭ)	115	44.35 N	91.42 W
Monee, Il. (mŏ-nī)	113a	41.25 N	87.45 W
Monessen, Pa. (mŏ'nĕs'sen)	113e	40.09 N	79.53 W
Monett, Mo. (mô-nĕt')	123	36.55 N	93.55 W
Monforte de Lemos, Sp. (môn-fôr'tä dē lĕ'môs)	170	42.30 N	7.30 W
Monga, Chad	229	4.12 N	22.49 E
Mongala R., Zaire (mŏn-gál'á)	225	3.20 N	21.30 E
Mongalla, Sud.	225	5.11 N	31.46 E
Mongat, Sp.	65e	41.28 N	2.17 E
Monghyr, India (mŏn-gēr')	196	25.23 N	86.34 E
Mongo, Chad	194	12.11 N	18.42 E
Mongo (R.), S.L.	228	9.50 N	11.50 W
Mongolia, Asia (mŏŋ-gō'lĭ-á)	190	46.00 N	100.00 E
Mongos, Chaîne des (Mts.), Cen. Afr. Rep.	225	8.04 N	21.59 E
Mongoumba, Cen. Afr. Rep. (mŏŋ-gōōm'bá)	230	3.38 N	18.36 E
Mongu, Zambia (mŏŋ-gōō')	230	15.15 S	23.09 E
Monken Hadley (Neigh.), Eng.	62	51.40 N	0.11 W
Monkey Bay, Malawi	231	14.05 S	34.55 E
Monkey River, Belize (mŭŋ'kĭ)	132a	16.22 N	88.33 W
Monkland, Can. (mŭngk-lănd)	95c	45.12 N	74.52 W
Monkoto, Zaire (môn-kō'tô)	230	1.38 S	20.39 E
Monmouth, Il. (mŏn'mŭth)(mŏn'mouth)	123	40.54 N	90.38 W
Monmouth Junction, NJ (mŏn'mouth jŭngk'shŭn)	112a	40.23 N	74.33 W
Monmouth Mtn., Can. (mŏn'mŭth)	98	51.00 N	123.47 W
Mono (L.), Can. (mŏ'nō)	120	38.04 N	119.00 W
Mono (R.), Togo	228	7.20 N	1.25 E
Monon, In. (mō'nŏn)	110	40.55 N	86.55 W
Monongah, WV (mô-nŏŋ'gá)	111	39.25 N	80.10 W
Monongahela, Pa. (mô-nŏn-gá-hē'lá)	113e	40.11 N	79.55 W
Monongahela (R.), Pa.	57b	40.27 N	80.00 W
Monongahela (R.), WV	111	39.30 N	80.10 W
Monopoli, It. (mô-nô'pô-lē)	173	40.55 N	17.17 E
Monóvar, Sp. (mô-nō'vär)	171	38.26 N	0.50 W
Monreale, It. (mōn-rā-ä'lā)	172	38.04 N	13.15 E
Monroe, Ga. (mŭn-rō')	126	33.47 N	83.43 W
Monroe, La.	125	32.30 N	92.06 W
Monroe, Mi.	110	41.55 N	83.25 W
Monroe, NC	127	34.58 N	80.34 W
Monroe, NY	112a	41.19 N	74.11 W
Monroe, Ut.	121	38.35 N	112.10 W
Monroe, Wa.	118a	47.52 N	121.58 W

PLACE (Pronounciation)	PAGE	Lat. °′	Long. °′
Monroe, Wi.	115	42.35 N	89.40 W
Monroe (L.), Fl.	127	28.50 N	81.15 W
Monroe City, Mo.	123	39.38 N	91.41 W
Monroeville, Al. (mŭn-rō'vĭl)	126	31.33 N	87.19 W
Monrovia, Ca. (mŏn-rō'vĭ-á)	119a	34.09 N	118.00 W
Monrovia, Lib.	228	6.18 N	10.47 W
Mons, Bel. (môɴ')	163	50.29 N	3.55 E
Monson, Me. (mŏn'sŭn)	104	45.17 N	69.28 W
Mönsterås, Swe. (mŭn'stĕr-ôs)	164	57.04 N	16.24 E
Montagh Ata (Mt.), China	198	38.26 N	75.23 E
Montagne Tremblante Prov. Pk., Can.	109	46.30 N	75.51 W
Montague, Can. (mŏn'tá-gū)	105	46.10 N	62.39 W
Montague, Mi.	110	43.30 N	86.25 W
Montague (I.), Ak.	107	60.10 N	147.00 W
Montalbán, Ven. (mônt-äl-bän)	143b	10.14 N	68.19 W
Montalbancito, Ven.	61a	10.28 N	66.59 W
Montalcone, It. (môn-täl-kô'nĕ)	172	45.49 N	13.30 E
Montalegre, Port. (mōn-tä-lā'grĕ)	170	41.49 N	7.48 W
Montana (State), U.S. (mŏn-tăn'á)	108	47.10 N	111.50 W
Montánchez, Sp. (môn-tän'chāth)	170	39.18 N	6.09 W
Montara, Ca.	58b	37.33 N	122.31 W
Montargis, Fr. (môɴ-tár-zhē')	168	47.59 N	2.42 E
Montataire, Fr. (môɴ-tá-târ)	169b	49.15 N	2.26 E
Montauban, Fr. (môɴ-tô-bäɴ')	168	44.01 N	1.22 E
Montauk, NY	111	41.03 N	71.57 W
Montauk Pt., NY (mŏn-tôk')	111	41.05 N	71.55 W
Montbanch, Sp. (mônt-bän'ch)	171	41.20 N	1.08 E
Montbard, Fr. (môɴ-bár')	168	47.40 N	4.19 E
Montbéliard, Fr. (môɴ-bā-lyár')	169	47.32 N	6.45 E
Mont Belvieu, Tx. (mŏnt bĕl'vū)	125a	29.51 N	94.53 W
Montbrison, Fr. (môɴ-brē-zoɴ')	168	45.38 N	4.06 E
Montceau, Fr. (môɴ-sō')	168	46.39 N	4.22 E
Montclair, Ca.	59	34.06 N	117.41 W
Montclair, NJ (mŏnt-klâr')	112a	40.49 N	74.13 W
Mont-de-Marsan, Fr. (môɴ-dē-már-säɴ')	168	43.54 N	0.32 W
Montdidier, Fr. (môɴ-dē-dyā')	168	49.42 N	2.33 E
Monte, Arg. (mŏ'n-tĕ)	141c	35.25 S	58.49 W
Monteagudo, Bol. (mōn'tā-ä-gōō'dhō)	142	19.49 S	63.48 W
Montebello, Ca. (mŏn-tē-bĕl'ō)	119a	34.01 N	118.06 W
Montebello, Can.	95c	45.40 N	74.56 W
Monte Bello (Is.), Austl.	214	20.30 S	114.10 E
Monte Caseros, Arg. (mŏ'n-tĕ-kä-sĕ'rôs)	144	30.16 S	57.39 W
Monte Chingolo (Neigh.), Arg.	60d	34.45 S	58.20 W
Mont Ecillos, Cord. de (Mts.), Hond. (kôr-dĕl-yĕ'rä dĕ mô'nt ĕ-sē'l-yōs)	132	14.19 N	87.52 W
Monte Cristi, Dom. Rep. (mŏ'n-tĕ-krē's-tē)	135	19.50 N	71.40 W
Montecristo, I. di, It. (mōn'tā-krēs'tō)	172	42.20 N	10.19 E
Monte Escobedo, Mex. (mōn'tā ĕs-kô-bā'dhō)	130	22.18 N	103.34 W
Monteforte Irpino, It. (môn-tē-fô'r-tē ē'r-pē'nō)	171c	40.39 N	14.42 E
Montefrío, Sp. (mōn-tā-frē'ō)	170	37.20 N	4.02 W
Montego Bay, Jam. (mŏn-tē'gō)	134	18.30 N	77.55 W
Monte Grande, Arg. (mŏ'n-tĕ grän'dĕ)	144a	34.34 S	58.28 W
Montelavar, Port. (mōn-tĕ-lá-vär')	171b	38.51 N	9.20 W
Montélimar, Fr. (môɴ-tā-lē-mär')	168	44.33 N	4.47 E
Montellano, Sp. (mōn-tā-lyä'nō)	170	37.00 N	5.34 W
Montello, Wi. (mŏn-tĕl'ō)	115	43.47 N	89.20 W
Montemorelos, Mex. (mōn'tā-mō-rā'lōs)	124	25.14 N	99.50 W
Montemor-o-Novo, Port. (mōɴ-tĕ-môr'ōō-nô'vōō)	170	38.39 N	8.11 W
Montenegro (Reg.), **see Crna Gora**			
Montepuez, Moz.	231	13.07 S	39.00 E
Montepulciano, It. (môn'tā-pōōl-chä'nō)	172	43.05 N	11.48 E
Montereau-faut-Yonne, Fr. (môɴ-t'rō'fō-yōn')	168	48.24 N	2.57 E
Monterey, Ca. (mŏn-tē-rā')	120	36.36 N	121.53 W
Monterey, Tn.	126	36.06 N	85.15 W
Monterey B., Ca.	120	36.48 N	122.01 W
Monterey Park, Ca.	119a	34.04 N	118.08 W
Montería, Col. (mōn-tā-rā'ä)	142	8.47 N	75.57 W
Monteros, Arg. (môn-tĕ'rôs)	144	27.14 S	65.29 W
Monterotondo, It. (môn-tē-rô-tô'n-dō)	171d	42.03 N	12.39 E
Monterrey, Mex. (mōn-tĕr-rā')	124	25.43 N	100.19 W
Montesano, Wa. (mŏn-tē-sä'nō)	116	46.59 N	123.35 W
Monte Sant' Angelo, It. (mô'n-tĕ săn ä'n-gzhĕ-lô)	172	41.43 N	15.59 E
Montes Claros, Braz. (môn-tĕs-klä'rôs)	143	16.44 S	43.41 W
Montespaccato (Neigh.), It.	66c	41.54 N	12.23 E
Montevallo, Al. (mŏn-tē-văl'ō)	126	33.05 N	86.49 W
Montevarchi, It. (mōn-tā-vär'kē)	172	43.30 N	11.45 E
Monteverde Nuovo (Neigh.), It.	66c	41.51 N	12.27 E
Montevideo, Ur. (mōn'tā-vē-dhā'ō)	141c	34.50 S	56.10 W
Monte Vista, Co. (mŏn'tē vĭs'tá)	121	37.35 N	106.10 W
Montezuma, Ga. (mŏn-tē-zōō'má)	126	32.17 N	84.00 W
Montezuma Castle Natl. Mon., Az.	121	34.38 N	111.50 W
Montfermeil, Fr.	64c	48.54 N	2.34 E
Montflorit, Sp.	65e	41.29 N	2.08 E
Montfoort, Neth.	157a	52.02 N	4.56 E
Montfor-l'Amaury, Fr. (môɴ-fôr'lä-mō-rē')	169b	48.47 N	1.49 E
Montfort, Fr. (mŏn-fôr)	168	48.09 N	1.58 W
Montgeron, Fr.	64c	48.42 N	2.27 E
Montgomery, Al. (mŏnt-gŭm'ēr-ĭ)	126	32.23 N	86.17 W
Montgomery, WV	110	38.10 N	81.25 W
Montgomery City, Mo.	123	38.58 N	91.29 W
Montgomery Knolls, Md.	56c	39.14 N	76.48 W
Monticello, Ar. (mŏn-tĭ-sĕl'ō)	123	33.38 N	91.47 W
Monticello, Fl.	126	30.32 N	83.53 W
Monticello, Ga.	126	33.00 N	83.11 W
Monticello, Ia.	115	42.14 N	91.13 W
Monticello, Il.	110	40.05 N	88.35 W

ăt; finăl; rāte; senāte; ärm; ȧsk; sofȧ; fâre; ch-choose; dh-as th in other; bē; ēvent; bĕt; recĕnt; cratēr; g-gō; gh-guttural g; bĭt; ĭ-short neutral; rīde; ĸ-guttural k as ch in German ich;

PRONOUNCING INDEX

Monticello – Mount Moriac 317

PLACE (Pronounciation)	PAGE	Lat. °′	Long. °′
Monticello, In.	110	40.40 N	86.50 W
Monticello, Ky.	126	36.47 N	84.50 W
Monticello, Me.	104	46.19 N	67.53 W
Monticello, Mn.	115	45.18 N	93.48 W
Monticello, NY	111	41.35 N	74.40 W
Monticello, Ut.	121	37.55 N	109.25 W
Montigny-le-Bretonneux, Fr.	64c	48.46 N	2.02 E
Montigny-lés-Cormeilles, Fr.	64c	48.59 N	2.12 E
Montijo, Port. (mȯn-tė′zhō)	171b	38.42 N	8.58 W
Montijo, Sp. (mȯn-tē′hō)	170	38.55 N	6.35 W
Montijo, Bahia (B.), Pan. (bä-ē′ä mȯn-tē′hō)	133	7.36 N	81.11 W
Mont-Joli, Can. (môN zhȯ-lē′)	104	48.35 N	68.11 W
Montjuich, Castillo de (P. Int.), Sp.	65e	41.22 N	2.10 E
Montluçon, Fr. (môN-lü-sôN′)	168	46.20 N	2.35 E
Montmagny, Can. (môN-màn-yē′)	95b	46.59 N	70.33 W
Montmagny, Fr.	64c	48.58 N	2.21 E
Montmartre (Neigh.), Fr.	64c	48.53 N	2.21 E
Montmorency, Austl.	70b	37.43 S	145.07 E
Montmorency, Fr. (môN′mȯ-räN-sē′)	169b	48.59 N	2.19 E
Montmorency (R.), Can. (mŏnt-mȯ-rĕn′sĭ)	95b	47.30 N	71.10 W
Montmorillon, Fr. (môN′mȯ-rė-yôN′)	168	46.26 N	0.50 E
Montone (R.), It. (mȯn-tȯ′nĕ)	172	44.03 N	11.45 E
Montoro, Sp. (mȯn-tō′rȯ)	170	38.01 N	4.22 W
Montpelier, Id.	117	42.19 N	111.19 W
Montpelier, In. (mŏnt-pēl′yẽr)	110	40.35 N	85.20 W
Montpelier, Oh.	110	41.35 N	84.35 W
Montpelier, Vt.	111	44.20 N	72.35 W
Montpellier, Fr. (môN-pĕ-lyā′)	168	43.38 N	3.53 E
Montréal, Can. (mŏn-trė-ôl′)	95a	45.30 N	73.35 W
Montreal (R.), Can.	103	47.50 N	80.30 W
Montreal (R.), Can.	102	47.15 N	84.20 W
Montreal L., Can.	100	54.20 N	105.40 W
Montréal-Nord, Can.	95a	45.36 N	73.38 W
Montréal-Quest, Can.	54b	45.27 N	73.39 W
Montreuil, Fr.	64c	48.52 N	2.27 E
Montreux, Switz. (môn-trû′)	166	46.26 N	6.52 E
Montrose, Austl.	70b	37.49 S	145.21 E
Montrose, Ca. (mŏnt-rōz)	119a	34.13 N	118.13 W
Montrose, Co. (mŏn-trōz′)	121	38.30 N	107.55 W
Montrose, Oh.	113d	41.08 N	81.38 W
Montrose, Pa. (mŏnt-rōz′)	111	41.50 N	75.50 W
Montrose, Scot.	162	56.45 N	2.25 W
Montrose Hill, Pa.	57b	40.30 N	79.51 W
Montrouge, Fr.	64c	48.49 N	2.19 E
Mont-Royal, Can.	95a	47.31 N	73.39 W
Mont Saint Martin, Fr. (mŏN săN mär-tăN′)	169	49.34 N	6.13 E
Montserrat, N.A. (mŏnt-sĕ-răt′)	129	16.48 N	63.15 W
Monts, Pointe des (Pt.), Can. (pwăNt′ dā môN′)	104	49.19 N	67.22 W
Montvale, NJ (mŏnt-vāl′)	112a	41.02 N	74.01 W
Monywa, Bur. (mŏn′yōō-wȧ)	206	22.02 N	95.16 E
Monza, It. (mōn′tsä)	172	45.34 N	9.17 E
Monzón, Sp. (mōn-thōn′)	171	41.54 N	1.09 E
Moóca (Neigh.), Braz.	61d	23.33 S	46.35 W
Moody, Tx. (mōō′dĭ)	125	31.18 N	97.20 W
Mooi (R.), S. Afr. (mōō′ĭ)	223d	26.34 S	27.03 E
Mooi (R.), S. Afr.	227c	29.00 S	30.15 E
Mooirivier, S. Afr.	227c	29.14 S	29.59 E
Moolap, Austl.	211a	38.11 S	144.26 E
Moonachie, NJ	55	40.50 N	74.03 W
Moonta, Austl. (mōōn′tȧ)	216	34.05 S	137.42 E
Moora, Austl. (mōōr′ȧ)	214	30.35 S	116.12 E
Moorabbin, Austl.	70b	37.56 S	145.02 E
Moorcroft, Wy. (mōr′krôft)	117	44.17 N	104.59 W
Moore (L.), Austl. (mōr)	214	29.50 S	128.12 E
Moorebank, Austl.	70a	33.56 S	150.56 E
Moorenweis, F.R.G. (mō′rĕn-vīz)	157d	48.10 N	11.05 E
Moore Res., Vt.-NH	111	44.20 N	72.10 W
Moorestown, NJ (morz′toun)	112f	39.58 N	74.56 W
Mooresville, In. (mōrz′vĭl)	113g	39.37 N	86.22 W
Mooresville, NC	127	35.34 N	80.48 W
Moorhead, Mn. (mōr′hĕd)	114	46.52 N	96.44 W
Moorhead, Ms.	126	33.25 N	90.30 W
Moorland (Plain), **see Landes**			
Mooroolbark, Austl.	70b	37.47 S	145.19 E
Moorside, Eng.	64b	53.34 N	2.04 W
Moose (L.), Can. (mōōs)	96	54.14 N	99.28 W
Moose (R.), Can.	97	51.01 N	80.42 W
Moose Creek, Can.	95c	45.16 N	74,58 W
Moosehead, Me. (mōōs′hĕd)	104	45.37 N	69.15 W
Moose I., Can.	101	51.50 N	97.09 W
Moose Jaw, Can. (mōōs jô)	100	50.23 N	105.32 W
Moose Jaw (Cr.), Can.	100	50.34 N	105.17 W
Moose Lake, Can.	101	53.40 N	100.28 W
Moose Mtn., Can.	101	49.45 N	102.37 W
Moose Mtn. Cr., Can.	100	49.12 N	102.10 W
Moosilauke (Mtn.), NH (mōō-sĭ-lȧ′kē)	111	44.00 N	71.50 W
Moosinning, F.R.G. (mō′zē-nēng)	157d	48.17 N	11.51 E
Moosomin, Can. (mōō′sȯ-mĭn)	101	50.07 N	101.40 W
Moosonee, Can. (mōō′sȯ-nė)	97	51.20 N	80.44 W
Mopti, Mali (mŏp′tė)	228	14.30 N	4.12 W
Moquegua, Peru (mȯ-kā′gwä)	142	17.15 S	70.54 W
Mór, Hung. (mōr)	167	47.51 N	18.14 E
Mora, India	197b	18.54 N	72.56 E
Mora, Mn. (mō′rȧ)	115	45.52 N	93.18 W
Mora, NM	122	35.58 N	105.17 W
Mora, Sp. (mȯ-rä)	170	39.42 N	3.45 W
Mora, Swe. (mō′rä)	164	61.00 N	14.29 E
Morādābād, India (mȯ-rä-dä-bäd′)	196	28.57 N	78.48 E
Morales, Guat. (mȯ-rä′lĕs)	132	15.29 N	88.46 W
Moramanga, Mad. (mō-rä-mäŋ′gä)	227	18.48 S	48.09 E
Morangis, Fr.	64c	48.42 N	2.20 E
Morant Pt., Jam. (mȯ-rănt′)	135	17.55 N	76.10 W
Morata de Tajuña, Sp. (mȯ-rä′tä dā tä-hōō′nyä)	171a	40.14 N	3.27 W
Moratuwa, Sri Lanka	197	6.35 N	79.59 E
Morava (Moravia) (Prov.), Czech. (mȯ′rä-vä)(mȯ-rā′vĭ-ȧ)	167	49.21 N	16.57 E
Morava R., Czech.	166	49.53 N	16.53 E
Moravia, see Morava			
Morawhanna, Guy. (mȯ-rȧ-hwä′nȧ)	143	8.12 N	59.33 W
Moray Firth, Scot. (mŭr′ȧ)	162	57.41 N	3.55 W
Mörbylånga, Swe. (mûr′bü-lȯŋ′gȧ)	164	56.32 N	16.23 E
Morden, Can. (môr′dĕn)	101	49.11 N	98.05 W
Mordialloc, Austl. (mȯr-dĭ-ăl′ŏk)	211a	38.00 S	145.05 E
Mordvin, (A.S.S.R.), Sov. Un.	178	54.18 N	43.50 E
Moreau (R.), SD (mȯ-rō′)	114	45.13 N	102.22 W
More, Ben (Mtn.), Scot. (bĕn môr)	162	58.09 N	5.01 W
Moree, Austl. (mō′rē)	216	29.20 S	149.50 E
Morehead, Ky.	110	38.10 N	83.25 W
Morehead City, NC (mōr′hĕd)	127	34.43 N	76.43 W
Morehouse, Mo. (mōr′hous)	123	36.49 N	89.41 W
Morelia, Mex. (mȯ-rā′lyä)	130	19.43 N	101.12 W
Morella, Sp. (mȯ-rāl′yä)	171	40.38 N	0.07 W
Morelos, Mex. (mȯ-rā′lōs)	130	22.46 N	102.36 W
Morelos, Mex.	131a	19.41 N	99.29 W
Morelos, Mex.	124	28.24 N	100.51 W
Morelos (Neigh.), Mex.	60a	19.27 N	99.07 W
Morelos, R., Mex.	124	25.27 N	99.35 W
Morena, Sierra (Mt.), Ca. (syĕr′rä mȯ-rā′nä)	118b	37.24 N	122.19 W
Morena, Sierra (Mts.), Sp. (syĕr′rä mȯ-rā′nä)	170	38.15 N	5.45 W
Morenci, Az. (mȯ-rĕn′sĭ)	121	33.05 N	109.25 W
Morenci, Mi.	110	41.50 N	84.50 W
Moreno, Arg. (mȯ-rĕ′nō)	144a	34.39 S	58.47 W
Moreno, Ca.	119a	33.55 N	117.09 W
Mores (I.), Ba. (mōrz)	134	26.20 N	77.35 W
Moresby (I.), Can. (mōrz′bĭ)	118b	48.43 N	123.15 W
Moresby I., Can.	96	52.50 N	131.55 W
Moreton, Eng.	64a	53.24 N	3.07 W
Moreton B., Austl. (môr′tŭn)	216	27.12 S	153.10 E
Moreton (I.), Austl. (môr′tŭn)	216	26.53 S	152.42 E
Morewood, Can. (mōr′wŏŏd)	95c	45.11 N	75.17 W
Morgan, Mt. (môr′găn)	117	48.55 N	107.56 W
Morgan, Ut.	117	41.04 N	111.42 W
Morgan City, La.	125	29.41 N	91.11 W
Morganfield, Ky. (môr′găn-fēld)	110	37.40 N	87.55 W
Morgan's Bay, S. Afr.	227c	32.42 S	28.19 E
Morganton, NC (môr′găn-tŭn)	127	35.44 N	81.42 W
Morgantown, WV (môr′găn-toun)	111	39.40 N	79.55 W
Morga Ra, Afg.	193a	34.02 N	70.38 E
Morgenzon, S. Afr. (môr′gănt-sŏn)	223d	26.44 S	29.39 E
Moriac, Austl.	211a	38.15 S	14.12 E
Morice L., Can.	98	54.00 N	127.37 W
Moriguchi, Jap. (mō′rė-gōō′chė)	205b	34.44 N	135.34 E
Morinville, Can. (mō′rĭn-vĭl)	95g	53.48 N	113.39 W
Morioka, Jap. (mō′rė-ō′kȧ)	204	39.40 N	141.21 E
Morivione (Neigh.), It.	65c	45.26 N	9.12 E
Morkoka (R.), Sov. Un. (mȯr-kô′kȧ)	181	65.35 N	111.00 E
Morlaix, Fr. (mŏr-lĕ′)	168	48.36 N	3.48 W
Morley, Can. (mŏr′lė)	95e	51.10 N	114.51 W
Morley Green, Eng.	64b	53.20 N	2.16 W
Mormant, Fr.	169	48.35 N	2.54 E
Morne Diablotin, Mt. Dominica (mȯrn dė-ȧ-blȯ-tăN′)	133b	15.31 N	61.24 W
Morne Gimie, Mt., Saint Lucia (mȯrn′ zhė-mē′)	133b	13.53 N	61.03 W
Morningside, Md.	56d	38.50 N	76.53 W
Mornington, Austl.	211a	38.13 S	145.02 E
Morobe, Pap. N. Gui.	207	8.03 S	147.45 E
Morocco, Afr. (mȯ-rŏk′ō)	222	32.00 N	7.00 W
Morogoro, Tan. (mō-rȯ-gō′rō)	231	6.49 S	37.40 E
Moroleón, Mex. (mȯ-rō-lā-ōn′)	130	20.07 N	101.15 W
Morombe, Mad. (mōō-rōōm′bā)	227	21.39 S	43.34 E
Morón, Arg. (mo-rŏ′n)	144a	34.24 S	58.37 W
Morón, Cuba (mȯ-rōn′)	134	22.05 N	78.35 W
Morón, Ven. (mȯ-rŏ′n)	143b	10.29 N	68.11 W
Morondava, Mad. (mȯ-rōn-dȧ′vȧ)	227	20.17 S	44.18 E
Morón de la Frontera, Sp. (mȯ-rōn′dā läf rȯn-tā′rä)	170	37.08 N	5.20 W
Morongo Ind. Res., Ca. (mō-rôŋ′gō)	120	33.54 N	116.47 W
Moroni, Comoros	226	11.41 S	43.16 E
Moroni, Ut. (mȯ-rō′nĭ)	121	39.30 N	111.40 W
Morotai (I.), Indon. (mō-rȯ-tä′ė)	207	2.12 N	128.30 E
Moroto, Ug.	231	2.32 N	34.39 E
Morozovsk, Sov. Un.	179	48.20 N	41.50 E
Morrill, Ne. (mŏr′ĭl)	114	41.59 N	103.54 W
Morrilton, Ar. (mŏr′ĭl-tŭn)	123	35.09 N	92.42 W
Morrinhos, Braz. (mȯ-rēn′yōzh)	143	17.45 S	48.56 W
Morris, Can. (mŏr′ĭs)	101	49.21 N	97.22 W
Morris, Il.	110	41.20 N	88.25 W
Morris, Mn.	114	45.35 N	95.53 W
Morris (R.), Can.	101	49.30 N	97.30 W
Morrison, Il. (mŏr′ĭ-sŭn)	115	41.48 N	89.58 W
Morris Plains, NJ (mŏr′ĭs pláns)	112a	40.49 N	74.29 W
Morris Res., Ca.	119a	34.11 N	117.49 W
Morristown, NJ (mŏr′rĭs-toun)	112a	40.48 N	74.29 W
Morristown, Tn.	126	36.10 N	83.18 W
Morrisville, Pa. (mŏr′ĭs-vĭl)	112f	40.12 N	74.46 W
Morro, Castillo del (P. Int.), Cuba	60b	23.09 N	82.21 W
Morro do Chapéu, Braz. (mȯr-ŏŏ dōō-shä-pĕ′ōō)	143	11.34 S	41.03 W
Morrow, Oh. (mŏr′ō)	113f	39.21 N	84.07 W
Mors (I.), Den.	164	56.46 N	8.38 E
Mörsenbroich (Neigh.), F.R.G.	63	51.15 N	6.48 E
Morshansk, Sov. Un. (môr-shȧnsk′)	179	53.25 N	41.35 E
Mortara, It. (mȯr-tä′rä)	172	45.13 N	8.47 E
Morteros, Arg. (mȯr-tĕ′tôs)	144	30.47 S	62.00 W
Mortes, Rio das (R.), Braz. (rē′o-däs-mô′r-tĕs)	141a	21.04 S	44.29 W
Mortlake, Austl.	70a	33.51 S	151.07 E
Mortlake (Neigh.), Eng.	62	51.28 N	0.16 W
Morton, Pa.	56b	39.55 N	75.20 W
Morton Grove, Il.	58a	42.02 N	87.47 W
Morton Ind. Res., Mn. (mŏr′tŭn)	115	44.35 N	94.48 W
Mortsel, Bel. (mȯr-sĕl′)	157a	51.10 N	4.28 E
Morvan (Mts.), Fr. (mōr-väN′)	168	47.11 N	4.10 E
Morzhovets (I.), Sov. Un. (mȯr′zhô-vyĕts′)	178	66.40 N	42.30 E
Mosal′sk, Sov. Un. (mō-zȧlsk′)	174	54.27 N	34.57 E
Moscavide, Port.	65d	38.47 N	9.06 W
Moscow, Id. (mŏs′kō)	116	46.44 N	116.57 W
Moscow, see Moskva			
Moscow Can., see Imeni Moskvy, Kanal			
Mosel R., F.R.G. (mō′sĕl) (mȯ-zĕl)	166	49.49 N	7.00 E
Moses Lake, Wa.	116	47.08 N	119.15 W
Moses L., Wa. (mō′zĕz)	116	47.09 N	119.30 W
Moses R., S. Afr.	223d	25.17 S	29.04 E
Moshchnyy (Is.), Sov. Un. (môsh′chnĭ)	165	59.56 N	28.07 E
Moshi, Tan. (mō′shė)	231	3.21 S	37.20 E
Mosiøen, Nor.	158	65.50 N	13.10 E
Moskháton, Grc.	66d	37.57 N	23.41 E
Moskva (Moscow), Sov. Un. (mŏs-kvä′)	182b	55.45 N	37.37 E
Moskva (Oblast), Sov. Un.	174	55.38 N	36.48 E
Moskva (R.), Sov. Un.	174	55.50 N	37.05 E
Mosman, Austl.	70a	33.49 S	151.14 E
Mosonmagyaróvár, Hung.	167	47.51 N	17.16 E
Mosquitos, Costa de, Nic. (kȯs-tä-dĕ-mŏs-kē′tō)	133	12.05 N	83.49 W
Mosquitos, Gulfo de los (G.), Pan. (gōō′l-fô-dĕ-lȯs-mŏs-kē′tōs)	133	9.17 N	80.59 W
Moss, Nor. (môs)	164	59.29 N	10.39 E
Moss Bank, Eng.	64a	53.29 N	2.44 W
Moss Beach, Ca. (môs bēch)	118b	37.32 N	122.31 W
Moss Crest (Mtn.), Va.	56d	38.55 N	77.15 W
Mosselbaai, S. Afr. (mô′sul bā)	226	34.06 S	22.23 E
Mossendjo, Con.	230	2.57 S	12.44 E
Mossley, Eng. (môs′lĭ)	156	53.31 N	2.02 W
Mossley Hill (Neigh.), Eng.	64a	53.23 N	2.55 W
Mossoró, Braz. (mō-sȯ-rōō′)	143	5.13 S	37.14 W
Moss Point, Ms. (môs)	126	30.25 N	88.32 W
Most, Czech. (mȯst)	166	50.32 N	13.37 E
Mostaganem, Alg. (mŏs′tä-gȧ-nĕm′)	224	36.04 N	0.11 E
Mostar, Yugo. (môs′tär)	173	43.20 N	17.51 E
Móstoles, Sp. (mȯs-tō′lās)	171a	40.19 N	3.52 W
Mostoos Hills, Can. (mŏs′tōōs)	100	54.50 N	108.45 W
Mosvatnet, Nor.	164	59.55 N	7.50 E
Motagua R., Guat. (mȯ-tä′gwä)	132	15.29 N	88.39 W
Motala, Swe. (mȯ-tô′lä)	164	58.34 N	15.00 E
Motherwell, Scot. (mŭdh′ẽr-wĕl)	162	55.45 N	4.05 W
Motril, Sp. (mȯ-trēl′)	170	36.44 N	3.32 W
Mottingham (Neigh.), Eng.	62	51.26 N	0.03 E
Motul, Mex. (mō-tōō′l)	132a	21.07 N	89.14 W
Mouaskar, Alg.	224	35.25 N	0.08 E
Mouchoir Bk., Ba. (mōō-shwȧr′)	135	21.35 N	70.40 W
Mouchoir Passage (Str.), Ba.	135	21.05 N	71.05 W
Moudjéria, Mauritania	228	17.53 N	12.20 W
Moudon, Switz.	169	46.40 N	6.47 E
Mouila, Gabon,	230	1.52 S	11.01 E
Mouille Pt., S. Afr.	226a	33.54 S	18.19 E
Moulins, Fr. (mōō-lăN′)	168	46.34 N	3.19 E
Moulmein, Bur. (mōl-mān′)	206	16.30 N	97.39 E
Moulouya, Oued (R.), Mor. (mōō-lōō′yȧ)	160	34.07 N	3.27 W
Moultrie, Ga. (mōl′trĭ)	126	31.10 N	83.48 W
Moultrie (Dam), SC	127	33.12 N	80.00 W
Mound City, Mo.	123	40.08 N	95.13 W
Mound City (Mound), Il.	123	37.06 N	89.13 W
Mound City Group Natl. Mon., Oh.	110	39.25 N	83.00 W
Moundon, Chad	229	8.34 N	16.05 E
Moundsville, WV (moundz′vĭl)	110	39.50 N	80.50 W
Mountain Brook, Al. (moun′tĭn brŏŏk)	112h	33.30 N	86.45 W
Mountain Creek L., Tx.	119c	32.43 N	97.03 W
Mountain Grove, Mo. (grōv)	123	37.07 N	92.16 W
Mountain Home, Id. (hōm)	116	43.08 N	115.43 W
Mountain Park, Can. (pärk)	99	52.55 N	117.14 W
Mountain View, Ca. (moun′tĭn vū)	118b	37.25 N	122.07 W
Mountain View, Mo.	123	36.59 N	91.46 W
Mount Airy, NC (âr′ĭ)	127	36.28 N	80.37 W
Mount Athos (Reg.), see **Áyion Óros**			
Mount Ayliff, S. Afr. (ā′lĭf)	227c	30.48 S	29.24 E
Mount Ayr, Ia. (âr)	115	40.43 N	94.06 W
Mount Baldy, Ca.	59	34.14 N	117.40 W
Mount, C., Lib.	228	6.47 N	11.20 W
Mount Carmel, Il. (kär′mĕl)	110	38.25 N	87.45 W
Mount Carmel, Pa.	111	40.50 N	76.25 W
Mount Carooll, Il.	115	42.05 N	89.55 W
Mount Clemens, Mi. (klĕm′ĕnz)	113b	42.36 N	82.52 W
Mount Dennis (Neigh.), Can.	54c	43.42 N	79.30 W
Mount Desert (I.), Me. (dė-zûrt′)	104	44.15 N	68.08 W
Mount Dora, Fl. (dō′rȧ)	127a	28.45 N	81.38 W
Mount Druitt, Austl.	70a	33.46 S	150.49 E
Mount Duneed, Austl.	211a	38.15 S	144.20 E
Mount Eliza, Austl.	211a	38.11 S	145.05 E
Mount Ephraim, NJ	56b	39.53 N	75.06 W
Mountevideo, Mn. (mōn′tȧ-vė-dhā′ō)	114	44.56 N	95.42 W
Mount Fletcher, S. Afr. (flĕ′chẽr)	227c	30.42 S	28.32 E
Mount Forest, Can. (fŏr′ĕst)	110	44.00 N	80.45 W
Mount Frere, S. Afr. (frâr′)	227c	30.54 S	29.02 E
Mount Gambier, Austl. (găm′bēr)	216	37.30 S	140.53 E
Mount Gilead, Oh. (gĭl′ė̆ăd)	110	40.30 N	82.50 W
Mount Greenwood (Neigh.), Il.	58a	41.42 N	87.43 W
Mount Healthy, Oh. (hĕlth′ė)	113f	39.14 N	84.32 W
Mount Hebron, Md.	56c	39.18 N	76.50 W
Mount Holly, NJ (hŏl′ĭ)	112f	39.59 N	74.47 W
Mount Hope, Can.	95d	43.09 N	79.55 W
Mount Hope, NJ (hōp)	112a	40.55 N	74.32 W
Mount Hope, WV	110	37.55 N	81.10 W
Mount Isa, Austl. (ī′zȧ)	214	21.00 S	139.45 E
Mount Kisco, NY (kĭs′ko)	112a	41.12 N	73.44 W
Mountlake Terrace, Wa. (mount lāk tĕr′ĭs)	118a	47.48 N	122.19 W
Mount Lebanon, Pa. (lĕb′ȧ-nŭn)	113e	40.22 N	80.03 W
Mount Magnet, Austl. (măg-nĕt)	214	28.00 S	118.00 E
Mount Martha, Austl.	211a	38.17 S	145.01 E
Mount Morgan, Austl. (môr-găn)	215	23.42 S	150.45 E
Mount Moriac, Austl.	211a	38.13 S	144.12 E

ng-sing; nŋ-baŋk; N-nasalized n; nŏd; cŏmmit; ōld; ȯbey; ôrder; oi-boil; fōōd; fŏŏt; ou-out; s-soft; sh-dish; th-thin; pūre; ůnite; ûrn; stŭd; circŭs; ü-as in French tu; ′-indeterminate vowel.

PLACE (Pronunciation)	PAGE	Lat. °′	Long. °′
Mount Morris, Mi. (mĭr′ĭs)	110	43.10 N	83.45 W
Mount Morris, NY	111	42.45 N	77.50 W
Mountnessing, Eng.	62	51.39 N	0.21 E
Mount Olive, NC (ŏl′ĭv)	127	35.11 N	78.05 W
Mount Oliver, Pa.	57b	40.28 N	79.59 W
Mount Peale, Ut.	121	38.26 N	109.16 W
Mount Pleasant, Ia. (plĕz′ănt)	115	40.59 N	91.34 W
Mount Pleasant, Mi.	110	43.35 N	84.45 W
Mount Pleasant, SC	127	32.46 N	79.51 W
Mount Pleasant, Tn.	126	35.31 N	87.12 W
Mount Pleasant, Tx.	123	33.10 N	94.56 W
Mount Pleasant, Ut.	121	39.35 N	111.20 W
Mount Pritchard, Austl.	70a	33.54 S	150.54 E
Mount Prospect, Il. (prŏs′pĕkt)	113a	42.03 N	87.56 W
Mount Rainier, Md.	56d	38.56 N	76.58 W
Mount Rainier Natl. Park, Wa. (rȧ-nēr′)	116	46.47 N	121.17 W
Mount Revelstoke Natl. Park, Can. (rĕv′ĕl-stōk)	96	51.22 N	120.15 W
Mount Savage, Md. (săv′āj)	111	39.45 N	78.55 W
Mount Shasta, Ca. (shăs′tȧ)	116	41.18 N	122.17 W
Mount Sterling, Il. (stûr′lĭng)	123	39.59 N	90.44 W
Mount Sterling, Ky.	110	38.05 N	84.00 W
Mount Stewart, Can. (stū′ȧrt)	115	46.22 N	62.52 W
Mount Union, Pa. (ūn′yŭn)	111	40.25 N	77.50 W
Mount Vernon, Il. (vûr′nŭn)	110	38.20 N	88.50 W
Mount Vernon, In.	110	37.55 N	87.50 W
Mount Vernon, Mo.	123	37.09 N	93.48 W
Mount Vernon, NY	112a	40.55 N	73.51 W
Mount Vernon, Oh.	110	40.25 N	82.30 W
Mount Vernon, Pa.	57b	40.17 N	79.48 W
Mount Vernon, Va.	112e	38.43 N	77.06 W
Mount Vernon, Wa.	118a	48.25 N	122.20 W
Mount Washington (Neigh.), Md.	56c	39.22 N	76.40 W
Mount Washington Summit, Md.	56c	39.23 N	76.40 W
Mount Waverley, Austl.	70b	37.53 S	145.08 E
Moura, Braz. (mō′rȧ)	143	1.33 S	61.38 W
Moura, Port.	170	38.08 N	7.28 W
Mourenx, Fr. (mōō-răn)	168	43.24 N	0.40 W
Mourne, Mts., N. Ire. (môrn)	162	54.10 N	6.09 W
Moussoro, Chad	229	13.39 N	16.29 E
Moûtiers, Fr. (mōō-tyâr′)	169	45.31 N	6.34 E
Mowbullan, Mt., Austl. (mō′bōō-lȧn)	216	26.50 S	151.34 E
Moyahua, Mex. (mô-yä′wä)	130	21.16 N	103.10 W
Moyale, Ken. (mô-yä′lä)	225	3.28 N	39.04 E
Moyamba, S.L. (mô-yäm′bä)	228	8.10 N	12.26 W
Moyen Atlas (Mts.), Mor.	160	32.49 N	5.28 W
Moyeuvre-Grande, Fr.	169	49.15 N	6.26 E
Moyie R., Id. (moi′yē)	116	38.50 N	116.10 W
Moylan, Pa.	56b	39.54 N	75.23 W
Moyobamba, Peru (mō-yō-bäm′bä)	142	6.12 S	76.56 W
Moyuta, Guat. (mô-ē-ōō′tä)	132	14.01 N	90.05 W
Moyyero (R.), Sov. Un.	181	67.15 N	104.10 E
Mozambique, Afr. (mō-zăm-bēk′)	222	20.15 S	33.53 E
Mozambique Chan., Afr. (mō-zăm-bek′)	227	24.00 S	38.00 E
Mozdok, Sov. Un. (môz-dôk′)	179	43.45 N	44.35 E
Mozhaysk, Sov. Un. (mô-zhäysk′)	174	55.31 N	36.02 E
Mozhayskiy, Sov. Un. (mô-zhäy′skĭ)	182c	59.42 N	30.08 E
Mozyr′, Sov. Un. (mô-zür′)	175	52.03 N	29.14 E
Mpanda, Tan.	231	6.22 S	31.02 E
Mpika, Zambia	231	11.54 S	31.26 E
Mpimbe, Malawi	231	15.18 S	35.04 E
Mporokoso, Zambia ('m-pō-rō-kō′sō)	231	9.23 S	30.05 E
Mpwapwa, Tan. ('m-pwä′pwä)	231	6.21 S	36.29 E
Mqanduli, S. Afr. ('m-kän′dōō-lē)	227c	31.50 S	28.42 E
Mragowo, Pol. (mräŋ′gô-vô)	167	53.52 N	21.18 E
M′Sila, Alg. (m′sē′lȧ)	224	35.47 N	4.34 E
Msta (R.), Sov. Un. (m′stä′)	174	58.33 N	32.08 E
Mstislavl′, Sov. Un. (m′stē-slävl′)	174	54.01 N	31.42 E
Mtakataka, Malawi	231	14.12 S	34.32 E
Mtamvuna (R.), S. Afr.	227c	30.43 S	29.53 E
Mtata (R.), S. Afr.	227c	31.48 S	29.03 E
Mt. Nimba Natl. Pk., Gui.-Ivory Coast	228	7.35 N	8.10 W
Mtsensk, Sov. Un. (m′tsĕnsk)	174	53.17 N	36.33 E
Mtwara, Tan.	231	10.16 S	40.11 E
Muang Khon Kaen, Thai.	206	16.37 N	102.41 E
Muang Lamphum, Thai.	206	18.40 N	98.59 E
Muar (R.), Mala.	191b	2.18 N	102.43 E
Mubende, Ug.	231	0.35 N	31.23 E
Mubi, Nig.	229	10.18 N	13.20 E
Mucacata, Moz.	231	13.20 S	39.59 E
Much, F.R.G. (mōōĸ)	169c	50.54 N	7.24 E
Muchinga Mts., Zambia	231	12.40 S	30.50 E
Much Wenlock, Eng. (mŭch wĕn′lŏk)	156	52.35 N	2.33 W
Muckalee Cr., Ga. (mŭk′ȧ lē)	126	31.55 N	84.10 W
Mucking, Eng.	62	51.30 N	0.26 E
Muckleshoot Ind. Res., Wa. (mŭck′′l-shōōt)	118a	47.21 N	122.04 W
Mucubela, Moz.	231	16.55 S	37.52 E
Mucugê, Braz. (mōō-kōō-zhĕ′)	143	13.02 S	41.19 W
Mud (L.), Mi. (mŭd)	115	46.12 N	84.32 W
Mud (L.), Nv.	120	40.28 N	119.11 W
Mudan (R.), China (mōō-dän)	202	45.30 N	129.40 E
Mudanjiang, China (mōō-dän-jyäŋ)	202	44.28 N	129.38 E
Muddy (R.), Nv. (mŭd′ĭ)	120	36.56 N	114.42 W
Muddy Boggy Cr., Ok. (mud′ĭ bôg′ĭ)	123	34.42 N	96.11 W
Muddy Cr., Ut. (mŭd′ĭ)	121	38.45 N	111.10 W
Mudgee, Austl. (mŭ-jē)	216	32.47 S	149.10 E
Mudjatik (R.), Can.	100	56.23 N	107.40 W
Mufulira, Zambia	231	12.33 S	28.14 E
Muğla, Tur. (mōōg′lä)	179	37.10 N	28.20 E
Mühileiten, Aus.	66e	48.10 N	16.34 E
Mühldorf, F.R.G. (mül-dôrf)	166	48.15 N	12.33 E
Mühlenbeck, G.D.R.	65a	52.40 N	13.22 E
Mühlhausen, G.D.R. (mül′hou-zĕn)	166	51.13 N	10.25 E
Muhu (I.), Sov. Un. (mōō′hōō)	165	58.41 N	22.55 E
Mui Ron, C., Viet.	203	18.05 N	106.45 E
Muir Woods Natl. Mon., Ca. (mūr)	120	37.54 N	123.22 W
Muizenberg, S. Afr. (mwĭz-ĕn-bûrg′)	226a	34.07 S	18.28 E
Mujāhidpur (Neigh.), India	67d	28.34 N	77.13 E
Mukachëvo, Sov. Un. (mōō-kȧ-chyô′vô)	167	48.25 N	22.43 E
Mukhtuya, Sov. Un. (mōōk-tōō′yȧ)	181	61.00 N	113.00 E
Mukilteo, Wa. (mū-kĭl-tā′ō)	118a	47.57 N	122.18 W
Muko, Jap. (mōō′kô)	205b	34.57 N	135.43 E
Muko (R.), Jap. (mōō′kô)	205b	34.52 N	135.17 E
Mukutawa (R.), Can.	101	53.10 N	97.28 W
Mukwonago, Wi. (mū-kwō-nȧ′gō)	113a	42.52 N	88.19 W
Mula, Al. (mŭl′gȧ)	112h	33.33 N	86.59 W
Mula, Sp. (mōō′lä)	170	38.05 N	1.12 W
Mulde R., G.D.R. (mōōl′dē)	166	50.30 N	12.30 E
Muleros, Mex. (mōō-lā′rōs)	130	23.44 N	104.00 W
Muleshoe, Tx.	122	34.13 N	102.43 W
Mulgrave, Can. (mŭl′grāv)	105	45.37 N	61.23 W
Mulgrave (I.), Austl.	215	10.08 S	142.14 E
Mulhacén, (Mtn.), Sp.	170	37.04 N	3.18 W
Mülheim, F.R.G. (mül′hīm)	169c	51.25 N	6.53 E
Mülheim an der Ruhr, F.R.G.	63	51.24 N	6.54 E
Mulhouse, Fr. (mü-lōōz′)	169	47.46 N	7.20 E
Muling, China (mōō-lĭŋ)	202	44.32 N	130.18 E
Muling (R.), China	202	44.40 N	130.30 E
Mullan, Id. (mŭl′ăn)	116	47.26 N	115.50 W
Müller, Pegunungan (Mts.), Indon. (mŭl′ĕr)	206	0.22 N	113.05 E
Mullingar, Ire. (mŭl-ĭn-gär)	162	53.31 N	7.26 W
Mullins, SC (mŭl′ĭnz)	127	34.11 N	79.13 W
Mullins River, Belize	132a	17.08 N	88.18 W
Mull, I. of, Scot. (mŭl)	162	56.40 N	6.19 W
Multān, Pak. (mōō-tän′)	196	30.17 N	71.13 E
Multnomah Chan., Or. (mŭl nō mȧ)	118c	45.41 N	122.53 W
Mulumbe, Monts (Mts.), Zaire	231	8.47 S	27.20 E
Mulvane, Ks. (mŭl-vān′)	123	37.30 N	97.13 W
Mumbwa, Zambia (mōōm′bwä)	231	14.59 S	27.04 E
Mumias, Ken.	231	0.20 N	34.29 E
Muna, Mex. (mōō′nȧ)	132a	20.28 N	89.42 W
Münchehofe, G.D.R.	65a	52.30 N	13.40 E
München (Munich), F.R.G. (mün′kĕn)	157d	48.08 N	11.35 E
Muncie, In. (mŭn′sĭ)	110	40.10 N	85.30 W
Mundelein, Il. (mŭn-dē-lĭn′)	113a	42.16 N	88.00 W
Mündelheim (Neigh.), F.R.G.	63	51.21 N	6.41 E
Mundonueva, Pico de (Pk.), Col. (pē′kō-dĕ-mōō′n-dō-nwĕ′vä)	142a	4.18 N	74.12 W
Muneco, Cerro (Mtn.), Mex. (sĕ′r-rô-mōō-nĕ′kō)	131a	19.13 N	99.20 W
Mungana, Austl. (mŭn-găn′ȧ)	215	17.15 S	144.18 E
Mungbere, Zaire	231	2.38 N	28.30 E
Munger, Mn. (mŭn′gēr)	119h	46.48 N	92.20 W
Mungindi, Austl. (mŭn-gĭn′dē)	216	32.00 S	148.45 E
Munhall, Pa. (mŭn′hôl)	113e	40.24 N	79.53 W
Munhango, Ang. (mōōn-häŋ′gȧ)	226	12.15 S	18.55 E
Munich, see **München**			
Munirka (Neigh.), India	67d	28.34 N	77.10 E
Munising, Mi. (mū′nĭ-sĭng)	115	46.24 N	86.41 W
Munku Sardyk (Mtn.), Sov. Un.-Mong. (mōōn′kōō sär-dĭk′)	180	51.45 N	100.30 E
Muñoz, Phil. (mōōn-nyōth′)	207a	15.44 N	120.53 E
Munro (Neigh.), Arg.	60d	34.32 S	58.31 W
Münster, F.R.G. (mün′stĕr)	169c	51.57 N	7.38 E
Munster, In. (mŭn′stĕr)	113a	41.34 N	87.31 W
Munster, Ire. (mŭn-stēr)	162	52.30 N	9.24 W
Muntok, Indon. (mōōn-tŏk′)	206	2.05 S	105.11 E
Munzi Freire, Braz. (mōō-nē′z-frā′rĕ)	141a	20.29 S	41.25 W
Muong Sing, Laos (mōō′ông-sĭng′)	206	21.06 N	101.17 E
Muping, China (mōō-pĭŋ)	200	37.23 N	121.36 E
Muqdisho, Som.	223a	2.08 N	45.22 E
Muqui, Braz. (mōō-kōōē)	141a	20.56 S	41.20 W
Muradiye, Tur. (mōō-rä′dē-yĕ)	179	39.00 N	43.40 E
Murat, Fr. (mü-rä′)	168	45.05 N	2.56 E
Murat (R.), Tur. (mōō-rät′)	179	38.50 N	40.40 E
Murayama, Jap.	69a	35.45 N	139.23 E
Murchison (R.), Austl. (mûr′chĭ-sŭn)	214	26.45 S	116.15 E
Murcia, Sp. (mōōr′thyä)	170	38.00 N	1.10 W
Murcia (Reg.), Sp.	170	38.35 N	1.51 W
Murdo, SD (mûr′dô)	114	43.53 N	100.42 W
Mureș R., Rom. (mōō′rĕsh)	167	46.02 N	21.50 E
Muret, Fr. (mü-rĕ′)	168	43.28 N	1.17 E
Murfreesboro, Tn. (mûr′frēz-bŭr-ô)	126	35.50 N	86.19 W
Murgab (R.), Sov. Un. (mōōr-gäb′)	143	37.07 N	62.32 E
Muriaé, Braz. (mōō-ryä-ĕ′)	141a	21.10 S	42.21 W
Muriaé (R.), Braz.	141a	21.20 S	41.40 W
Murino, Sov. Un. (mōō′rĭ-nô)	182c	60.03 N	30.28 E
Müritz (L.), G.D.R. (mür′its)	166	53.20 N	12.33 E
Murku Sardyk (Pk.), Sov. Un.-Mong.	198	51.56 N	100.21 E
Murmansk, Sov. Un. (mōōr-mänsk′)	178	69.00 N	33.20 E
Murom, Sov. Un. (mōō′rôm)	178	55.30 N	42.00 W
Muroran, Jap. (mōō′rô-rän)	204	42.21 N	141.05 E
Muros, Sp. (mōō′rōs)	170	42.48 N	9.00 W
Muroto-Zaki (Pt.), Jap. (mōō′rô-tō zä′kē)	205	33.14 N	134.12 E
Murphy, Mo. (mŭr′fĭ)	119e	38.29 N	90.29 W
Murphy, NC	126	35.05 N	84.00 W
Murphysboro, Il. (mŭr′fĭz-bŭr-ô)	123	37.46 N	89.21 W
Mur R., Aus. (mōōr)	166	47.10 N	14.08 E
Murray, Ky. (mŭr′ĭ)	126	36.39 N	88.17 W
Murray, Ut.	119b	40.40 N	111.53 W
Murray (R.), Can.	99	55.00 N	121.00 W
Murray (R.), SC (mŭr′ĭ)	127	34.07 N	81.18 W
Murray Bridge, Austl.	216	35.10 S	139.35 E
Murray Harbour, Can.	104	46.00 N	62.31 W
Murray R., Austl.	216	34.20 S	142.21 W
Murray Reg., Austl. (mŭ′rē)	215	33.20 S	142.30 E
Murrumbidgee (R.), Austl. (mŭr-ŭm-bĭd′jē)	216	34.30 S	145.20 E
Murrupula, Moz.	231	15.27 S	38.47 E
Murshidābād, India (mōōr′shē-dä-bäd′)	196	24.08 N	87.11 E
Murska Sobota, Yugo. (mōōr′skä sô′bô-tä)	172	46.40 N	16.14 E
Murtal, Port.	65d	38.42 N	9.22 W
Muruasigar (Mtn.), Ken.	231	3.08 N	35.02 E
Murwāra, India	196	23.54 N	80.23 E
Murwillumbah, Austl. (mŭr-wĭl′lŭm-bŭ)	216	28.15 S	153.30 E
Mürz R., Aus. (mürts)	166	47.30 N	15.21 E
Murzzuschlag, Aus. (mürts′tsōō-shlägh)	166	47.37 N	15.41 E
Mus, Tur. (mōōsh)	179	38.55 N	41.30 E
Musala (Mtn.), Bul.	173	42.05 N	23.24 E
Musan, Kor. (mōō′sän)	204	41.11 N	129.10 E
Musashino, Jap. (mōō-sä′shē-nō)	205a	35.43 N	139.35 E
Muscat, Om. (mŭs-kăt′)	192	23.23 N	58.30 E
Muscatine, Ia. (mŭs-kȧ-tēn)	115	41.26 N	91.00 W
Muscat & Oman, see **Oman**			
Muscle Shoals, Al. (mŭs′′l shōlz)	126	34.44 N	87.38 W
Musgrave Ra., Austl. (mŭs′grāv)	214	26.15 S	131.15 E
Mushie, Zaire (mŭsh′ē)	226	3.04 S	16.50 E
Mushin, Nig.	229	6.32 N	3.22 E
Musi (Strm.), Indon. (mōō′sē)	206	2.40 S	103.42 E
Musinga, Alto (Ht.), Col. (ä′l-tô-mōō-sē′n-gä)	142a	6.40 N	76.13 W
Muskego L., Wi. (mŭs-kē′gō)	113a	42.53 N	88.10 W
Muskegon, Mi. (mŭs-kē′gŭn)	110	43.15 N	86.20 W
Muskegon (R.), Mi.	110	43.20 N	85.55 W
Muskegon Heights, Mi.	110	43.10 N	86.20 W
Muskingum (R.), Oh. (mŭs-kĭŋ′gŭm)	110	39.45 N	81.55 W
Muskogee, Ok. (mŭs-kō′gē)	123	35.44 N	95.21 W
Muskoka (L.), Can. (mŭs-kō′kȧ)	111	45.00 N	79.30 W
Musoma, Tan.	231	1.30 S	33.48 E
Mussau I., Pap. N. Gui. (mōō-sä′ōō)	207	1.30 S	149.32 E
Musselshell R., Mt. (mŭs′′l-shĕl)	117	46.25 N	108.20 W
Mussende, Ang.	230	10.32 S	16.05 E
Mussuma, Ang.	230	14.14 S	21.59 E
Mustafakemalpasa, Tur.	179	40.05 N	28.30 E
Mustang Bayou, Tx.	125a	29.22 N	95.12 W
Mustang Cr., Tx. (mŭs′tăng)	122	36.22 N	102.46 W
Mustang I., Tx.	125	27.43 N	97.00 W
Mustique I., Saint Vincent (müs-tēk′)	133b	12.53 N	61.03 W
Musturud, Egypt	71a	30.08 N	31.17 E
Mustvee, Sov. Un. (mōōst′vĕ-ĕ)	165	38.50 N	26.54 E
Musu Dan (C.), Kor. (mōō′sōō dän)	199	40.51 N	130.00 E
Musu Dan (Pt.), Kor. (mōō′sōō dän)	204	40.48 N	129.50 E
Muswellbrook, Austl. (mŭs′wŭnl-brōōk)	216	32.15 S	150.50 E
Mutare, Zimb.	226	18.49 S	32.39 E
Mutombo Mukulu, Zaire (mōō-tôm′bō mōō-kōō′lōō)	226	8.12 S	23.56 E
Mutsu Wan (B.), Jap. (mōōt′sōō wän)	204	41.20 N	140.55 E
Mutton Bay, Can. (mŭt′′n)	105	50.48 N	59.02 W
Mutum, Braz. (mōō-tōō′m)	141a	19.48 S	41.24 W
Muyun-Kum, Peski (Des.), Sov. Un. (mōō-yōōn′kōōm′)	180	44.30 N	70.00 E
Muzaffargarh, Pak.	196	30.09 N	71.15 E
Muzaffarpur, India	196	26.13 N	85.20 E
Muzon, C., Ak.	98	54.41 N	132.44 W
Múzquiz, Mex. (mōōz′kēz)	124	27.53 N	101.31 W
Muztagata (Mtn.), China	198	38.20 N	75.28 E
Mvomero, Tan.	231	6.20 S	37.25 E
Mvoti (R.), S. Afr.	227c	29.18 S	30.52 E
Mwanza, Tan. (mwän′zä)	231	2.31 S	32.54 E
Mwaya, Tan. (mwä′yä)	226	9.19 S	33.51 E
Mwenga, Zaire	231	3.02 S	28.26 E
Mweru (L.), Zaire-Zambia	231	8.50 S	28.50 E
Mwingi, Ken.	231	0.56 S	38.04 E
Myingyan, Bur. (myĭng-yŭn′)	198	21.37 N	95.26 E
Myitkyina, Bur. (myĭ′chē-nȧ)	198	25.33 N	97.25 E
Myjava, Czech. (mûē′yȧ-vä)	167	48.45 N	17.33 E
Mymensingh, Bngl.	196	24.48 N	90.28 E
Mynämäki, Fin.	165	60.41 N	21.58 E
Myohyang San (Mtn.), Kor. (myō′hyang)	204	40.00 N	126.12 E
Mýrdalsjökull (Gl.), Ice. (mür′däls-yû′kōōl)	158	63.34 N	18.04 W
Myrtle Beach, SC (mûr′t′l)	127	33.42 N	78.53 W
Myrtle Point, Or.	116	43.04 N	124.08 W
Mysen, Nor.	164	59.32 N	11.16 E
Myshikino, Sov. Un. (mēsh′kē-nô)	174	57.48 N	38.21 E
Mysore, India (mī-sōr′)	197	12.31 N	76.42 E
Mysovka, Sov. Un. (mē′ sôf-kȧ)	165	55.11 N	21.17 E
Mystic, Ia. (mĭs′tĭk)	115	40.47 N	92.54 W
Mytishchi, Sov. Un. (mē-tēsh′chi)	182b	55.55 N	37.46 E
Mziha, Tan.	231	5.54 S	37.47 E
Mzimba, Malawi ('m-zĭm′bä)	231	11.52 S	33.34 E
Mzimkulu (R.), S. Afr.	227c	30.12 S	29.57 E
Mzimvubu (R.), S. Afr.	227c	31.22 S	29.20 E
Mzsvingo, Zimb.	226	20.07 S	30.47 E
Mzuzu, Malawi	231	11.30 S	34.10 E

N

PLACE (Pronunciation)	PAGE	Lat. °′	Long. °′
Naab R., F.R.G. (näp)	166	49.38 N	12.15 E
Naaldwijk, Neth.	157a	52.00 N	4.11 E
Naalehu, Hi.	106a	19.00 N	155.35 W
Naantali, Fin. (nän′tȧ-lē)	165	60.29 N	22.03 E
Nabberu (L.), Austl. (năb′ēr-ōō)	214	26.05 S	120.35 E
Nabeul, Tun. (nā-bûl′)	224	36.34 N	10.45 E
Nabiswera, Ug.	231	1.28 N	32.16 E

ăt; finăl; rāte; senāte; ärm; åsk; sofȧ; fâre; ch-choose; dh-as th in other; bē; ēvent; bĕt; recĕnt; cratēr; g-gō; gh-guttural g; bĭt; ĭ-short neutral; rīde; ĸ-guttural k as ch in German ich;

PRONOUNCING INDEX
Naboomspruit – Navidad Bk. 319

PLACE (Pronounciation)	PAGE	Lat. °′	Long. °′
Naboomspruit, S. Afr.	223d	24.32 s	28.43 E
Nābulus, Jordan	191a	32.13 N	35.16 E
Nacala, Moz. (nă-kȧ'lȧ)	231	14.34 s	40.41 E
Nacaome, Hond. (nä-kä-ō'mȧ)	132	13.32 N	87.28 W
Naceur, Bou Mt., Mor.	160	33.50 N	3.55 W
Na Cham, Viet. (nä chäm')	203	22.02 N	106.30 E
Naches R., Wa. (năch'ĕz)	116	46.51 N	121.03 W
Náchod, Czech. (näk'ôt)	166	50.25 N	16.08 E
Nächstebreck (Neigh.), F.R.G.	63	51.18 N	7.14 E
Nacimiento (R.), Ca. (nȧ-sĭ-myĕn'tô)	120	35.50 N	121.00 W
Nacogdoches, Tx. (năk'ô-dō'chĕz)	125	31.36 N	94.40 W
Nadadores, Mex. (nä-dä-dō'rās)	124	27.04 N	101.36 W
Nadiād, India	196	22.45 N	72.51 E
Nadir, Vir. Is. (U.S.A.)	129c	18.19 N	64.53 W
Nădlac, Rom.	173	46.09 N	20.52 E
Nad Nisou, see Jablonec			
Nad Váhom, see Nové Mesto			
Nadvornaya, Sov. Un. (näd-vo͞or'nȧ-yȧ)	167	48.37 N	24.35 E
Nadym (R.), Sov. Un. (nȧ'dĭm)	180	64.30 N	72.48 E
Naestved, Den. (nĕst'vĭdh)	164	55.14 N	11.46 E
Nafada, Nig.	229	11.08 N	11.20 E
Nafishah, Egypt	223c	30.34 N	32.15 E
Nafūd ad Daḩy (Des.), Sau. Ar.	193	22.15 N	44.15 E
Naga, Phil. (nä'gä)	207a	13.37 N	123.12 E
Naga (I.), Jap.	205	32.09 N	130.16 E
Nagahama, Jap. (nä'gä-hä'mä)	205	33.32 N	132.29 E
Nagahama, Jap.	205	35.23 N	136.16 E
Nagaland (State), India	198	25.47 N	94.15 E
Nagano, Jap. (nä'gä-nô)	205	36.42 N	138.12 E
Nagao, Jap.	69b	34.50 N	135.43 E
Nagaoka, Jap. (nä'gȧ-ō'kȧ)	205	37.22 N	138.49 E
Nagaoka, Jap.	205b	34.54 N	135.42 E
Nāgappattinam, India	197	10.48 N	79.51 E
Nagarote, Nic. (nä-gä-rô'tĕ)	132	12.17 N	86.35 W
Nagasaki, Jap. (nä'gȧ-sä'kē)	205	32.48 N	129.53 E
Nagata (Neigh.), Jap.	69b	34.40 N	135.09 E
Nagatino (Neigh.), Sov. Un.	66b	55.41 N	37.41 E
Nagatsuta (Neigh.), Jap.	69a	35.32 N	139.30 E
Nāgaur, India	196	27.19 N	73.41 E
Nagaybakskiy, Sov. Un. (nȧ-gȧy-bäk'skĭ)	182a	53.33 N	59.33 E
Nagcarlan, Phil. (näg-kär-län')	207a	14.07 N	121.24 E
Nag, Co (L.), China	196	31.38 N	91.18 E
Nāgercoil, India	197	8.15 N	77.29 E
Nagorno Karabakh (Reg.), Sov. Un. (nu-gôr'nŭ-kŭ-rŭ-bäk')	179	40.10 N	46.50 E
Nagoya, Jap. (nä'gō'yȧ)	205	35.09 N	136.53 E
Nāgpur, India (näg'po͞or)	196	21.12 N	79.09 E
Nagua, Dom. Rep. (nȧ'gwä)	135	19.20 N	69.40 W
Nagykanizsa, Hung. (nôd'y'kô'nē-shô)	166	46.27 N	17.00 E
Nagykōrōs, Hung. (nôd'y'kŭ-rŭsh)	167	47.02 N	19.46 E
Nagytarcsa, Hung.	66g	47.32 N	19.17 E
Naha, Jap. (nä'hä)	199	26.02 N	127.43 E
Nahanni Natl. Pk., Can.	96	62.10 N	125.15 W
Nahant, Ma. (nȧ-hănt)	105a	42.26 N	70.55 W
Nahant B., Ma.	54a	42.27 N	70.55 W
Nahariyya, Isr.	191a	33.01 N	35.06 E
Nahaut, Ma.	54a	42.25 N	70.55 W
Nahmer, F.R.G.	63	51.20 N	7.35 E
Nahr al Khābur (R.), Syr.	179	35.50 N	41.00 E
Nahuel Huapi (L.), Arg. (nä'wĕl wä'pē)	144	41.00 s	71.30 W
Nahuizalco, Sal. (nä-wē-zäl'kō)	132	13.50 N	89.43 W
Nāhyā, Egypt	71a	30.03 N	31.07 E
Naic, Phil. (nä-ēk)	207a	14.20 N	120.46 E
Naica, Mex. (nä-ē'kä)	124	27.53 N	105.30 W
Naiguatá, Ven. (nī-gwä-tȧ')	143b	10.37 N	66.44 W
Naiguata, Pico (Mtn.), Ven. (pē'kô)	143b	10.32 N	66.44 W
Naihāti, India	196a	22.54 N	88.25 E
Nain, Can. (nīn)	97	56.29 N	61.52 W
Nā'īn, Iran	195	32.52 N	53.05 E
Nairn, Scot. (nârn)	162	57.35 N	3.54 W
Nairobi, Ken. (nī-rō'bē)	231	1.17 s	36.49 E
Naivasha, Ken. (nī-vä'shȧ)	227	0.47 s	36.29 E
Najd (Des.), Sau. Ar.	192	25.18 N	42.38 E
Naj 'Ḩammādī, Egypt (näg'hä-mä'dē)	223b	26.02 N	32.12 E
Najin, Kor. (nä'jĭn)	204	42.04 N	130.35 E
Najran (Des.), Sau. Ar. (nŭj-rän')	192	17.29 N	45.30 E
Naju, Kor. (nä'jo͞o')	204	35.02 N	126.42 E
Najusa (R.), Cuba (nä-ho͞o'sä)	134	21.55 N	77.55 W
Naka (R.), Jap.	69a	35.39 N	139.51 E
Nakadorishima (I.), Jap. (nä'kä'dô'rē-shē'mä)	202	33.00 N	128.20 E
Nakagyō (Neigh.), Jap.	68e	35.01 N	135.45 E
Nakajima, Jap.	69a	35.26 N	139.56 E
Nakanobu (Neigh.), Jap.	69a	35.36 N	139.43 E
Nakatsu, Jap. (nä'käts-o͞o)	205	33.34 N	131.10 E
Nakhichevan, Sov. Un. (nȧ-kē-chĕ-vȧn')	179	39.10 N	45.30 E
Nakhodka, Sov. Un. (nŭ-kôt'kŭ)	181	43.03 N	133.08 E
Nakhon Ratchasima, Thai.	206	14.56 N	102.14 E
Nakhon Sawan, Thai.	206	15.42 N	100.06 E
Nakhon Si Thammarat, Thai.	206	8.27 N	99.58 E
Nakskov, Den. (näk'skou)	164	54.51 N	11.06 E
Nakto nad Notecia, Pol. (näk'wō näd nō-tĕ'chōn)	167	53.10 N	17.35 E
Naktong (R.), Kor. (näk'tŭng)	204	36.10 N	128.30 E
Nal'chik, Sov. Un. (nȧl-chēk')	179	43.30 N	43.35 E
Nalón (R.), Sp. (nä-lōn')	170	43.15 N	5.38 W
Nālūt, Libya (nä-lo͞ot')	224	31.51 N	10.49 E
Namakan (L.), Mn. (nă'mȧ-kȧn)	115	48.20 N	92.43 W
Namak, Daryacheh-ye (L.), Iran	192	34.58 N	51.33 E
Namakzār-e Shāhdād (L.), Iran (nŭ-mŭk-zär')	192	31.00 N	58.30 E
Namamugi (Neigh.), Jap.	69a	35.29 N	139.41 E
Namangan, Sov. Un. (nȧ-mȧn-gän')	180	41.08 N	71.59 E
Namao, Can.	95g	53.43 N	113.30 W
Namatanai, Pa. N. Gui. (nä'mä-tȧ-nä'ē)	207	3.43 s	152.26 E
Nambe Pueblo Ind. Res., NM (näm'bā pwĕb'lô)	121	35.52 N	105.39 W
Nambour, Austl. (năm'bo͝or)	216	26.48 s	153.00 E
Nam Co (L.), China (näm tswo)	196	30.30 N	91.10 E
Nam-Dinh, Viet. (näm dēnk')	206	20.30 N	106.10 E
Nametil, Moz.	231	15.43 s	39.21 E
Namhae (I.), Kor. (näm'hī')	204	34.23 N	128.05 E
Namib (Des.), Namibia (nä-mēb')	226	18.45 s	12.45 E
Namibia, Afr.	222	19.30 s	16.13 E
Namoi (R.), Austl. (năm'oi)	216	30.10 s	148.43 E
Namous, Oued en (R.), Alg. (nȧ-mo͞os')	160	31.48 N	00.19 W
Nampa, Id. (năm'pȧ)	116	43.35 N	116.35 W
Namp'o, Kor.	202	38.47 N	125.28 E
Nampuecha, Moz.	231	13.59 s	40.18 E
Nampula, Moz.	231	15.07 s	39.15 E
Namsos, Nor. (näm'sôs)	158	64.28 N	11.14 E
Namu, Can.	98	51.03 N	127.50 W
Namuli, Serra (Mts.), Moz.	231	15.05 s	37.05 E
Namur, Bel. (nȧ-mür')	163	50.29 N	4.55 E
Namutoni, Namibia (nȧ-mo͞o-tō'nē)	226	18.45 s	17.00 E
Nan (R.), Thai	206	18.11 N	100.29 E
Nanacamilpa, Mex. (nä-nä-kä-mē'l-pä)	131a	19.30 N	98.33 W
Nanaimo, Can. (nȧ-nī'mō)	98	49.10 N	123.56 W
Nanam, Kor. (nä'nän')	204	41.38 N	129.37 E
Nanao, Jap. (nä'nä-ō)	205	37.03 N	136.59 E
Nan'ao Dao, China (nän-ou dou)	203	23.30 N	117.30 E
Nancefield, S. Afr.	71b	26.17 s	27.53 E
Nanchang, China (nən-chəŋ)	203	28.38 N	115.48 E
Nanchangshan Dao (I.), China (nän-chäŋ-shän dou)	200	37.56 N	120.42 E
Nancheng, China (nän-chäŋ)	203	26.50 N	116.40 E
Nanchong, China (nän-chôŋ)	203	30.45 N	106.05 E
Nancy, Fr. (näN-sē')	169	48.42 N	6.11 E
Nancy Cr., Ga. (năn'cē)	112c	33.51 N	84.25 W
Nanda Devi (Mt.), India (nän'dä dā'vē)	196	30.30 N	80.25 E
Nānded, India	196	19.13 N	77.21 E
Nandurbār, India	196	21.29 N	74.13 E
Nandyāl, India	197	15.54 N	78.09 E
Nanga Parbat, Pak.	196	35.20 N	74.35 E
Nangi, India	196a	22.30 N	88.14 E
Nangis, Fr. (näN-zhē')	169b	48.33 N	3.01 E
Nangong, China (nän-gôŋ)	200	37.22 N	115.22 E
Nangweshi, Zambia	230	16.26 s	23.17 E
Nanhuangcheng Dao (I.), China (nän-hūäŋ-chŭŋ dou)	200	38.22 N	120.54 E
Nanhui, China	201b	31.03 N	121.45 E
Nani Dinh, Viet.	203	20.25 N	106.08 E
Nani Hu (L.), China (näN'yi' ho͞o)	200	31.12 N	119.05 E
Naniwa (Neigh.), Jap.	69b	34.39 N	135.30 E
Nanjing, China (nän-jyĭŋ)	200	32.04 N	118.46 E
Nanjuma (R.), China (nän-jyo͞o-mä)	200	39.37 N	115.45 E
Nanle, China (nän-lŭ)	200	36.03 N	115.13 E
Nan Ling (Mts.), China	203	25.15 N	111.40 E
Nanliu (R.), China (nän-lĭô)	203	22.00 N	109.18 E
Nannine, Austl. (nă-nēn')	214	25.50 s	118.30 E
Nanning, China (nän'nĭng')	203	22.56 N	108.10 E
Nānole (Neigh.), India	67e	19.01 N	72.55 E
Nanpan (R.), China (nän-pän)	203	24.50 N	105.30 E
Nanping, China (nän-pĭŋ)	203	26.40 N	118.05 E
Nansei-shotō (Ryukyu Islands), Jap.	199	27.30 N	127.00 E
Nansemond, Va. (năn'sē-mŭnd)	112g	36.46 N	76.32 W
Nansemond R., Va.	112g	36.50 N	76.34 W
Nantai Zan (Mtn.), Jap. (nän-täē zän)	205	36.47 N	139.28 E
Nanterre, Fr.	64c	48.53 N	2.12 E
Nantes, Fr. (näNt')	168	47.13 N	1.37 W
Nanteuil-le-Haudouin, Fr. (näN-tû-lĕ-ō-dwȧN')	169b	49.08 N	2.49 E
Nanticoke, Pa. (năn'tĭ-kōk)	111	41.10 N	76.00 W
Nantong, China (nän-tôŋ)	200	32.02 N	120.51 E
Nantong, China	200	32.08 N	121.06 E
Nantouillet, Fr.	64c	49.00 N	2.42 E
Nantucket (I.), Ma. (năn-tŭk'ĕt)	111	41.15 N	70.05 W
Nantwich, Eng. (nănt'wĭch)	156	53.04 N	2.31 W
Nanxiang, China (nän-shyäŋ)	201b	31.17 N	121.17 E
Nanxiong, China (nän-shôŋ)	203	25.10 N	114.20 E
Nanyang, China	202	33.00 N	112.42 E
Nanyang, Hu (L.), China (nän-yäŋ ho͞o)	200	35.14 N	116.24 E
Nanyuan, China (nän-yūän)	202a	39.48 N	116.24 E
Naoābād, India	67a	22.28 N	88.27 E
Naolinco, Mex. (nä-o-lēŋ'kō)	131	19.39 N	96.50 W
Naopukuria, India	67a	22.55 N	88.16 E
Náousa, Grc. (nä'o͞o-sȧ)	173	40.38 N	22.05 E
Naozhou Dao (I.), China (nou-jō dou)	203	20.58 N	110.58 E
Napa, Ca. (năp'ȧ)	120	38.20 N	122.17 W
Napanee, Can. (năp'ȧ-nē)	111	44.15 N	77.00 W
Naperville, Il. (nā'pēr-vĭl)	113a	41.46 N	88.09 W
Napier, N.Z. (nā'pĭ-ēr)	217	39.30 s	177.00 E
Napierville, Can. (nā'pĭ-ē-vĭl)	95a	45.11 N	73.24 W
Naples, Fl. (nă'p'lz)	127a	26.07 N	81.46 W
Naples, see Napoli			
Napo (R.), Peru (nä'pō)	142	1.49 s	74.20 W
Napoleon, Oh. (nȧ-pō'lē-ŭn)	110	41.20 N	84.10 W
Napoleonville, La. (nȧ-pō'lē-ŭn-vĭl)	125	29.56 N	91.03 W
Napoli (Naples), It. (nä'pô-lē)	171c	40.37 N	14.12 E
Napoli, Golfo de (G.), It. (gôl-fô-dē)	171c	40.29 N	14.08 E
Nappanee, In. (năp'ȧ-nē)	110	41.30 N	86.00 W
Nara, Jap. (nä'rä)	205b	34.41 N	135.50 E
Nara, Mali	224	15.09 N	7.27 W
Nara (Pref.), Jap.	205b	34.36 N	135.49 E
Nara (R.), Sov. Un.	174	55.05 N	37.16 E
Naracoorte, Austl. (nȧ-rȧ-ko͞on'tē)	216	36.50 s	140.50 E
Narashino, Jap.	205a	35.41 N	140.01 E
Naraspur, India	197	16.32 N	81.43 E
Nārāyanpāra, India	67a	22.54 N	88.19 E
Narbėrth, Pa. (när'bûrth)	112f	40.01 N	75.17 W
Narbonne, Fr. (nȧr-bôn')	168	43.12 N	3.00 E
Nardò, It. (när-dô')	173	40.11 N	18.02 E
Nare, Col. (nä'rĕ)	142a	6.12 N	74.37 W
Narew R., Pol. (när'ĕf)	167	52.43 N	21.19 E
Narmada (R.), India	196	22.17 N	74.45 E
Naroch' (L.), Sov. Un. (nä'rôch)	174	54.51 N	27.00 E
Narodnaya, Gora (Mtn.), Sov. Un. (nȧ-rôd'nȧ-yȧ)	178	65.10 N	60.10 E
Naro-Fominsk, Sov. Un. (nä'rô-mēnsk')	174	55.23 N	36.43 E
Narrabeen, Austl. (năr-ȧ-bĭn)	211b	33.44 s	151.18 E
Narragansett, RI (năr-ă-găn'sĕt)	112b	41.26 N	71.27 W
Narragansett B., RI	111	41.20 N	71.15 W
Narrandera, Austl. (nȧ-rȧn-dē'rȧ)	216	34.40 s	146.40 E
Narraweena, Austl.	70a	33.45 s	151.16 E
Narre Warren North, Austl.	70b	37.59 s	145.19 E
Narrogin, Austl. (năr'ô-gĭn)	214	33.00 s	117.15 E
Naruo, Jap.	69b	34.43 N	135.23 E
Narva, Sov. Un. (nȧr'vȧ)	174	59.24 N	28.12 E
Narvacan, Phil. (när-vä-kän')	207a	17.27 N	120.29 E
Narva Jõesuu, Sov. Un. (nȧr'vȧ o͞o-ô-ă'so͞o-o͞o)	174	59.26 N	28.02 E
Narvik, Nor. (när'vēk)	158	68.21 N	17.18 E
Narvskiy Zaliv (B.), Sov. Un. (nȧr'vskĭ zä'lĭf)	165	59.35 N	27.25 E
Nar'yan-Mar, Sov. Un. (när'yȧn mär')	178	67.42 N	53.30 E
Naryilco, Austl. (năr-ĭl'kô)	216	28.40 s	141.50 E
Narym, Sov. Un. (nä-rēm')	180	58.47 N	82.05 E
Naryn (R.), Sov. Un. (nŭ-rĭn')	193	41.46 N	73.00 E
Naseby, Eng. (nāz'bĭ)	156	52.23 N	0.59 W
Nashua, Mo. (năsh'ŭ-ȧ)	119f	39.18 N	94.34 W
Nashua, NH	105a	42.47 N	71.23 W
Nashville, Ar. (năsh'vĭl)	123	33.56 N	93.50 W
Nashville, Ga.	126	31.12 N	83.15 W
Nashville, Il.	123	38.21 N	89.42 W
Nashville, Mi.	110	42.35 N	85.50 W
Nashville, Tn.	126	36.10 N	86.48 W
Nashwauk, Mn. (năsh'wôk)	115	47.21 N	93.12 W
Našice, Yugo. (nä'shē-tsĕ)	173	45.29 N	18.06 E
Nasielsk, Pol. (nä'syĕlsk)	167	52.35 N	20.50 E
Näsijärvi (L.), Fin. (nĕ'sē-yĕr'vē)	178	61.42 N	24.05 E
Nāsik, India (nä'sĭk)	196	20.02 N	73.49 E
Nāşir, Sud. (nä-zēr')	225	8.30 N	33.06 E
Nasirabād, India	196	26.13 N	74.48 E
Nāşir, Buḩayrat, see Nasser, L.			
Naskaupi (R.), Can. (näs'kô-pĭ)	97	53.59 N	61.10 W
'Nasondoye, Zaire	230	10.22 s	25.06 E
Nass (R.), Can. (năs)	98	55.00 N	129.30 W
Nassau, Ba. (năs'ô)	134	25.05 N	77.20 W
Nassenheide, G.D.R. (nä'sĕn-hī-dĕ)	157b	52.49 N	13.13 E
Nasser, L., (Nāşir, Buḩayrat), Egypt	223b	23.50 N	32.50 E
Nässjö, Swe. (nĕs'shû)	164	57.39 N	14.39 E
Nasugbu, Phil. (nȧ-so͞og-bo͞o')	207a	14.05 N	120.37 E
Nasworthy L., Tx. (năz'wûr-thē)	124	31.17 N	100.30 W
Natá, Pan. (nä-tȧ')	133	8.20 N	80.30 W
Natagaima, Col. (nä-tä-gī'mä)	142a	3.38 N	75.07 W
Nātāgarh, India	67a	22.42 N	88.25 E
Natal, Braz. (nä-täl')	143	6.00 s	35.13 W
Natal (Prov.), S. Afr. (nȧ-täl')	226	28.50 s	30.07 E
Natalspruit, S. Afr.	71b	26.19 s	28.09 E
Natashquan, Can. (nä-täsh'kwän)	105	50.11 N	61.49 W
Natashquan (R.), Can.	105	50.35 N	61.35 W
Natchez, Ms. (năch'ĕz)	126	1.35 N	91.20 W
Natchitoches, La. (năk'ĭ-tŏsh)(nȧch-ĭ-tōsh')	125	31.46 N	93.06 W
Natick, Ma. (nā'tĭk)	105a	42.17 N	71.21 W
National Area (Reg.), Sov. Un.	181	66.30 N	170.30 E
National Bison Ra. (Mts.), Mt. (năsh'ŭn-ăl bī's'n)	117	47.18 N	113.58 W
National City, Ca.	120a	32.38 N	117.01 W
National Park, Pa.	56b	39.51 N	75.12 W
Natitingou, Benin	228	10.19 N	1.22 E
Natividade, Braz. (nä-tē-vē-dä'dĕ)	143	11.43 s	47.34 W
Natrona Hts., Pa. (nā'trŏ nā)	113e	40.38 N	79.43 W
Natron, L., Tan. (nā'trŏn)	231	2.17 s	36.10 E
Naţrūn, Wādī an, Egypt	223b	30.33 N	30.12 E
Natuna Besar (I.), Indon.	206	4.00 N	106.50 E
Natural Bridges Natl. Mon., Ut. (năt'ū-răl brĭj'ĕs)	121	37.20 N	110.20 W
Naturaliste, C., Austl. (năt-ū-rȧ-lĭst')	214	33.30 s	115.10 E
Naucalpan, Mex. (nä'o͞o-käl-pȧ'n)	131a	19.28 N	99.14 W
Nauchampatepetl (Mtn.), Mex. (näo͞o-chäm-pä-tĕ'pĕtl)	131	19.32 N	97.09 W
Nauen, G.D.R. (nou'ĕn)	157b	52.36 N	12.53 E
Naugatuck, Ct. (nô'gȧ-tŭk)	111	41.25 N	73.05 W
Naujan, Phil. (nä-o͞o-hän')	207a	13.19 N	121.17 E
Naumburg, G.D.R. (noum'bo͝orgh)	166	51.10 N	11.50 E
Naupada (Neigh.), India	67e	19.04 N	72.50 E
Nauru, Oceania	208	0.30 s	167.00 E
Nautla, Mex. (nä-o͞ot'lä)	131	20.14 N	96.44 W
Nava, Mex. (nä'vä)	124	28.25 N	100.44 W
Nava del Rey, Sp. (nä-vä dĕl rā'ē)	170	41.22 N	5.04 W
Navahermosa, Sp. (nä-vä-ĕr-mō'sä)	170	39.39 N	4.28 W
Navajas, Cuba (nä-vä-häs')	134	22.40 N	81.20 W
Navajo Ind. Res., Az.-NM (năv'ȧ-hō)	121	36.31 N	109.24 W
Navajo Natl. Mon., Az.	121	36.43 N	110.39 W
Navajo Res., NM	121	36.57 N	107.26 W
Navalcarnero, Sp. (nä-väl'kär-nā'rō)	171a	40.17 N	4.05 W
Navalmoral de la Mata, Sp. (nä-väl'mōräl' dā lä mä'tä)	170	39.53 N	5.32 W
Navan, Can. (nă'vȧn)	95c	45.25 N	75.26 W
Navarino, (I.), Chile (nȧ-vä-rē'nô)	144	55.30 s	68.15 W
Navarra (Reg.), Sp. (nä-vär'rä)	170	42.40 N	1.35 W
Navarro, Arg. (nä-vȧ'r-rō)	141c	35.00 s	59.16 W
Navasota, Tx. (năv-aȧ-sō'tȧ)	125	30.24 N	96.05 W
Navasota R., Tx.	125	31.03 N	96.11 W
Navassa (I.), N.A. (nȧ-vȧs'ȧ)	135	18.25 N	75.15 W
Navestock, Eng.	62	51.39 N	0.13 E
Navestock Side, Eng.	62	51.39 N	0.16 E
Navia (R.), Sp. (nä-vē'ä)	170	43.10 N	6.45 W
Navidad, Chile (nä-vē-dä'd)	141b	34.57 s	71.51 W
Navidad Bk., Ba. (nä-vē-dädh')	135	20.05 N	69.00 W

ng-sing; nŋ-banŋk; N-nasalized n; nŏd; cŏmmit; ōld; ôbey; ôrder; oi-boil; fo͞od; fo͝ot; ou-out; s-soft; sh-dish; th-thin; pūre; ûnite; ûrn; stŭd; circŭs; ü-as in French tu; -indeterminate vowel.

320 Navidade do Carangola – New Hebrides

PLACE (Pronounciation)	PAGE	Lat. °′	Long. °′
Navidade do Carangola, Braz. (nä-vē-dä'dô-kä-rän-gô'la)	141a	21.04 S	41.58 W
Navojoa, Mex. (nä-vô-kô'ä)	128	27.00 N	109.40 W
Navotas, Phil.	68g	14.40 N	120.57 E
Návplion, Grc.	173	37.33 N	22.46 E
Nawābshāh, Pak. (nȧ-wäb'shä)	196	26.20 N	68.30 E
Náxos (I.), Grc. (näk'sôs)	173	37.15 N	25.20 E
Nayābās, India	67d	28.45 N	77.19 E
Nayarit (State), Mex. (nä-yä-rēt')	128	22.00 N	105.15 W
Nayarit, Sierra de (Mts.), Mex. (sē-ĕ'r-rä-dĕ)	130	23.20 N	105.07 W
Naye, Senegal	228	14.25 N	12.12 W
Naylor, Md. (nā'lōr)	112e	38.43 N	76.46 W
Nazaré, Braz. (nä-zä-rĕ')	143	13.04 S	38.49 W
Nazaré da Mata, Braz. (dä-mä-tä)	143	7.46 S	35.13 W
Nazaré, Port. (nä-zä-rā')	170	39.38 N	9.04 W
Nazas, Mex. (nä'zäs)	124	25.14 N	104.08 W
Nazas, R., Mex.	124	25.08 N	104.20 W
Nazerat, Isr.	191a	32.43 N	35.19 E
Nazilli, Tur. (nȧ-zĭ-lē')	179	37.40 N	28.10 E
Naziya R., Sov. Un. (nȧ-zē'yȧ)	182c	59.48 N	31.18 E
Nazko (R.), Can.	98	52.35 N	123.10 W
Nazlat as-Sammān, Egypt	71a	29.59 N	31.08 E
Nazlat Khalīfah, Egypt	71a	30.01 N	31.10 E
Ndalatando, Ang.	230	9.18 S	14.54 E
Ndali, Benin	229	9.51 N	2.43 E
Ndélé, Cen. Afr. Rep. (n'dā-lā')	225	8.21 N	20.43 E
Ndikiniméki, Cam.	229	4.46 N	10.50 E
N'Djamena, Chad	229	12.07 N	15.03 E
Ndjili (Neigh.), Zaire	71c	4.20 S	15.22 E
Ndjolé, Gabon (n'dzhô-lā')	226	0.15 S	10.45 E
Ndola, Zambia (n'dō'lä)	231	12.58 S	28.38 E
Ndoto Mts., Ken.	231	1.55 N	37.05 E
Ndrhamcha, Sebkha de (L.), Mauritania	228	18.50 N	15.15 W
Nduye, Zaire	231	1.50 N	29.01 E
Neagh Lough (L.), N. Ire. (lŏk nā)	162	54.40 N	6.47 W
Néa Ionía, Grc.	66d	38.02 N	23.45 E
Néa Liósia, Grc.	66d	38.02 N	23.42 E
Néa Páfos, Cyprus	191a	34.46 N	32.27 E
Neapean (R.), Austl.	211b	33.40 S	150.39 E
Neápolis, Grc. (nā-ŏp' ô-lĭs)	173	36.35 N	23.08 E
Neápolis, Grc.	172a	35.17 N	25.37 E
Near Is., Ak. (nēr)	107a	52.20 N	172.40 E
Near North Side (Neigh.), Il.	58a	41.54 N	87.38 W
Néa Smírni, Grc.	66d	37.57 N	23.43 E
Neath, Wales (nēth)	162	51.41 N	3.50 W
Nebine Cr., Austl. (nĕ-bēne')	216	27.50 S	147.00 E
Nebit-Dag, Sov. Un. (nyĕ-bēt'däg')	179	39.30 N	54.20 E
Nebraska (State), U.S. (nē-brăs'kȧ)	108	41.45 N	101.30 W
Nebraska City, Ne.	123	40.40 N	95.50 W
Nechako (R.), Can.	98	52.45 N	124.55 W
Nechako Plat., Can. (nĭ-chă'kō)	98	54.00 N	124.30 W
Nechako Ra., Can.	98	53.20 N	124.30 W
Nechako Res., Can.	98	53.25 N	125.10 W
Neches R., Tx. (nĕch'ĕz)	125	31.03 N	94.40 W
Neckar R., F.R.G. (nĕk'är)	166	49.16 N	9.06 E
Necker I., Hi.	106b	24.00 N	164.00 W
Necochea, Arg. (nā-kô-chā'ä)	144	38.30 S	58.45 W
Nedlitz (Neigh.), G.D.R.	65a	52.26 N	13.03 E
Nedrigaylov, Sov. Un. (nĕ-drĭ-gī'lôf)	175	50.49 N	33.52 E
Needham, Ma. (nēd'ăm)	105a	42.17 N	71.14 W
Needham Heights, Ma.	54a	41.28 N	71.14 W
Needles, Ca. (nē'd'lz)	120	34.51 N	114.39 W
Neenah, Wi. (nē'nȧ)	115	44.10 N	88.30 W
Neepawa, Can.	101	50.13 N	99.29 W
Nee Res., Co. (nee)	122	38.26 N	102.56 W
Nee Soon, Singapore	67c	1.24 N	103.49 E
Negareyama, Jap. (nå'gä-rå-yä'mä)	205a	35.52 N	139.54 E
Negaunee, Mi. (nē-gô'nē)	115	46.30 N	87.37 W
Negeri Sembilan (State), Mala. (nā'grē-sĕm-bē-län')	191b	2.46 N	101.54 E
Negev (Des.), Isr. (nĕ'gĕv)	191a	30.34 N	34.43 E
Negombo, Sri Lanka	197	7.39 N	79.49 E
Negotin, Yugo. (nĕ'gô-tēn)	173	44.13 N	22.33 E
Negro (R.), Arg.	144	39.50 S	65.00 W
Negro (R.), Ur.	141c	33.17 S	58.18 W
Negro, Cerro (Mt.), Pan. (sĕ'r»rô-nā'grô)	133	8.44 N	80.37 W
Negro R., Nic.	132	13.01 N	87.10 W
Negro, Rio (R.), Braz. (rē'ō nā'grōō)	142	0.18 S	63.21 W
Negros (I.), Phil. (nā'grōs)	206	9.50 N	121.45 E
Neguá, Col. (nĕ-gwä')	142a	5.51 N	76.36 W
Nehalem R., Or. (nē-hăl'ĕm)	116	45.52 N	123.37 W
Nehaus an der Oste, F.R.G. (noi'houz)(ōz'tē)	157c	53.48 N	9.02 E
Nehbandān, Iran	195	31.32 N	60.02 E
Nehe, China (nŭ-hŭ)	202	48.23 N	124.58 E
Neheim-Hüsten, F.R.G. (nĕ'hīm)	169c	51.28 N	7.58 E
Neiba, Dom. Rep. (nå-ē'bä)	135	18.30 N	71.20 W
Neiba, Bahai de (B.), Dom. Rep. (bä-ä'ē-dĕ)	135	18.10 N	71.00 W
Neiba, Sierra de (Mts.), Dom. Rep. (sē-ĕr'rä-dĕ)	135	18.40 N	71.40 W
Neihart, Mt. (nī'härt)	117	46.54 N	110.39 W
Neijiang, China (nā-jyäŋ)	203	29.38 N	105.01 E
Neillsville, Wi. (nēlz'vĭl)	115	44.35 N	90.37 W
Nei Monggol (Inner Monglia)(Aut. Reg.), China (nā-mŭŋ-gol)	198	40.15 N	105.00 E
Neiqiu, China (nā-chyō)	200	37.17 N	114.32 E
Neira, Col. (nā'rä)	142a	5.10 N	75.32 W
Neisse (R.), Pol. (nēs)	166	51.30 N	15.00 E
Neiva, Col. (nå-ē'vä)(nā'vä)	142a	2.55 N	75.16 W
Nexiang, China (nā-shyäŋ)	202	33.00 N	111.38 E
Nekemte, Eth.	225	9.09 N	36.29 E
Nekoosa, Wi. (nē-kōō'sȧ)	115	44.19 N	89.54 W
Neksø, Den. (nĕk'sû)	164	55.05 N	15.05 E
Neligh, Ne. (nē'lĭg)	114	42.06 N	98.02 W
Nel'kan, Sov. Un. (nĕl-kän')	181	57.45 N	136.36 E
Nellore, India (nĕl-lōr')	197	14.28 N	79.59 E
Nel'ma, Sov. Un. (nĕl-mä')	204	47.34 N	139.05 E
Nelson, Can. (nĕl'sŭn)	99	49.29 N	117.17 W

PLACE (Pronounciation)	PAGE	Lat. °′	Long. °′
Nelson, Eng.	156	53.50 N	2.13 W
Nelson, N.Z.	217	41.15 S	173.22 E
Nelson (I.), Ak.	107	60.38 N	164.42 W
Nelson (R.), Can.	101	56.50 N	93.40 W
Nelson, C., Austl.	216	38.29 S	141.20 E
Nelson Cr., Nv.	120	40.22 N	114.43 W
Nelsonville, Oh. (nĕl'sŭn-vĭl)	110	39.30 N	82.15 W
Néma, Mauritania (nā'mä)	228	16.37 N	7.15 W
Nemadji R., Wi. (nē-măd'jē)	119h	46.33 N	92.16 W
Neman, Sov. Un. (ŋĕ'-mȧn)	165	55.02 N	22.01 E
Neman R., Sov. Un.	167	53.28 N	24.45 E
Nematābād, Iran	68h	35.38 N	51.12 E
Nembe, Nig.	229	4.35 N	6.26 E
Nemčinovka, Sov. Un.	66b	55.43 N	37.23 E
Nemeiban L., Can. (nĕ-mē'bȧn)	100	55.20 N	105.20 W
Nemirov, Sov. Un. (nyå-mē'rôf)	175	48.56 N	28.51 E
Nemours, Fr.	168	48.16 N	2.41 E
Nemuro, Jap. (nā'mōō-rō)	204	43.13 N	145.10 E
Nemuro Str., Jap.	204	43.07 N	145.10 E
Nen (R.), China (nŭn)	199	47.07 N	123.28 E
Nen (R.), Eng. (nĕn)	156	52.32 N	0.19 W
Nenagh, Ire. (nē'nȧ)	162	52.50 N	8.05 W
Nenana, Ak. (nå-nä'nȧ)	107	64.28 N	149.18 W
Nenikyul', Sov. Un. (nĕ-nyē'kyûl)	182c	59.26 N	30.40 E
Nenjiang, China (nŭn-jyäŋ)	202	49.02 N	125.15 E
Neodesha, Ks. (nē-ô-dĕ-shô')	123	37.24 N	95.41 W
Néon Psikhikón, Grc.	66d	38.00 N	23.47 E
Neosho, Mo.	123	36.51 N	94.22 W
Neosho (R.), Ks. (nē-ō'shō)	123	38.07 N	95.40 W
Nepal, Asia (nĕ-pôl')	190	28.45 N	83.00 E
Nephi, Ut. (nē'fī)	121	39.40 N	111.50 W
Nepisiguit (R.), Can. (nĭ-pĭ'sĭ-kwĭt)	104	47.25 N	66.28 W
Nepomuceno, Braz. (nĕ-pô-mōō-sĕ'no)	141a	21.15 S	45.13 W
Nera (R.), It. (nā'rä)	172	42.45 N	12.54 E
Nérac, Fr. (nā-rȧk')	168	44.08 N	0.19 E
Nerchinsk, Sov. Un. (nyĕr' chĕnsk)	181	51.47 N	116.17 E
Nerchinskiy Khrebet (Mts.), Sov. Un.	181	50.30 N	118.30 E
Nerchinskiy Zavod, Sov. Un. (nyĕr'chĕn-skĭzȧ-vôt')	181	51.35 N	119.46 E
Nerekhta, Sov. Un. (nyĕ-rĕĸ'tȧ)	174	57.29 N	40.34 E
Neretva (R.), Yugo. (nĕ'rĕt-vȧ)	173	43.08 N	17.50 E
Nerja, Sp. (nĕr'hä)	170	36.45 N	3.53 W
Nerl' (R.), Sov. Un. (nyĕrl)	174	56.59 N	37.57 E
Nerskaya R., Sov. Un. (nyĕr'skȧ-yȧ)	182b	55.31 N	38.46 E
Nerussa (R.), Sov. Un. (nyå-rōō'sȧ)	174	52.24 N	34.20 E
Ness, Eng.	64a	53.17 N	3.03 W
Ness City, Ks. (nĕs)	122	38.27 N	99.55 W
Ness, Loch (L.), Scot. (lŏĸ nĕs)	162	37.23 N	4.20 W
Nesterov, Sov. Un. (nyĕs-tā'rôf)	165	54.39 N	22.38 E
Nesterov, Sov. Un. (ŋĕs'-tzhyé-rôf)	167	50.03 N	23.58 E
Neston, Eng.	64a	53.18 N	3.04 W
Néstos (R.), Grc. (nās'tōs)	173	41.25 N	24.12 E
Nesvizh, Sov. Un. (nyĕs'vēsh)	174	53.13 N	26.44 E
Netanya, Isr.	191a	32.19 N	34.52 E
Netcong, NJ (nĕt'cŏnj)	112a	40.54 N	74.42 W
Netherlands, Eur. (nĕdh'ēr-lăndz)	154	53.01 N	3.57 E
Netherlands Guiana, see Suriname			
Netherton, Eng.	64a	53.30 N	2.58 W
Nette (Neigh.), F.R.G.	63	51.33 N	7.25 E
Nettilling (L.), Can.	97	66.30 N	70.40 W
Nett Lake Ind. Res., Mn. (nĕt lăk)	115	48.23 N	93.19 W
Nettuno, It. (nĕt-tōō'nô)	171d	41.28 N	12.40 E
Neubeckum, F.R.G. (noi'bĕ-kōōm)	169c	51.48 N	8.01 E
Neubrandenburg, G.D.R. (noi-brän'dĕn-bŏŏrgh)	166	53.33 N	13.16 E
Neuburg, F.R.G. (noi'bŏŏrgh)	166	48.43 N	11.12 E
Neuchâtel, Switz. (nû-shȧ-tĕl')	166	47.00 N	6.52 E
Neuchatel, Lac de (L.), Switz.	166	46.48 N	6.53 E
Neudorf (Neigh.), F.R.G.	63	51.25 N	6.47 E
Neuenhagen, G.D.R. (noi'ĕn-hä-gĕn)	157b	52.31 N	13.41 E
Neuenhagen bei Berlin, G.D.R.	65a	52.32 N	13.41 E
Neuenhof (Neigh.), F.R.G.	63	51.10 N	7.13 E
Neuenkamp (Neigh.), F.R.G.	63	51.26 N	6.44 E
Neuenrade, F.R.G. (noi'ĕn-rä-dĕ)	169c	51.17 N	7.47 E
Neu-Erlaa (Neigh.), Aus.	66e	48.08 N	16.19 E
Neu Fahrland, G.D.R.	65a	52.26 N	13.03 E
Neufchâtel-en-Bray, Fr. (nû-shä-tĕl'ĕɴ-brā')	168	49.43 N	1.25 E
Neuilly-sur-Marne, Fr.	64c	48.51 N	2.32 E
Neuilly-sur-Seine, Fr.	64c	48.53 N	2.16 E
Neukirchen-Vluyn, F.R.G.	63	51.27 N	6.33 E
Neulengbach, Aus.	157e	48.13 N	15.55 E
Neumarkt, F.R.G. (noi'märkt)	166	49.17 N	11.30 E
Neumünster, F.R.G. (noi'münstĕr)	166	54.04 N	10.00 E
Neunkirchen, Aust. (noin'kĭrĸ-ĕn)	166	47.43 N	16.05 E
Neunkirchen, F.R.G.	169	49.21 N	7.20 E
Neuquén, Arg. (nĕ-ōō-kān')	144	38.52 S	68.12 W
Neuquen (Prov.), Arg.	144	39.40 S	70.45 W
Neuquén (R.), Arg.	144	38.45 S	69.00 W
Neuruppin, G.D.R. (noi'rōō-pēn)	157b	52.55 N	12.48 E
Neuse (R.), NC (nūz)	127	36.12 N	78.50 W
Neusiedler See (L.), Aus. (noi-zēd'lēr)	166	47.54 N	16.31 E
Neuss, F.R.G. (nois)	169c	51.12 N	6.41 E
Neusserweyhe (Neigh.), F.R.G.	63	51.13 N	6.39 E
Neustadt, F.R.G. (noi'shtät)	166	49.21 N	8.08 E
Neustadt bei Coburg, F.R.G. (bī kō'bŏŏrgh)	166	50.20 N	11.09 E
Neustadt in Holstein, F.R.G.	166	54.06 N	10.50 E
Neustift am Walde (Neigh.), Aus.	66e	48.15 N	16.18 E
Neustrelitz, G.D.R. (noi-strā'lĭts)	166	53.21 N	13.05 E
Neutral Hills, Can. (nū'trȧl)	100	52.10 N	110.50 W
Neu Ulm, F.R.G. (noi ōō lm')	166	48.23 N	10.01 E
Neuva Pompeya (Neigh.), Arg.	60d	34.39 S	58.25 W
Neuville, Can. (nū'vĭl)	95b	46.39 N	71.35 W
Neuville-sur-Oise, Fr.	64c	49.01 N	2.04 E
Neuwaldegg (Neigh.), Aus.	66e	48.14 N	16.17 E
Neuwied, F.R.G. (noi'vēdt)	166	50.26 N	7.28 E
Neva (R.), Sov. Un. (nyĕ-vä')	182c	59.49 N	30.54 E
Nevada, Ia. (nē-vä'dȧ)	115	42.01 N	93.27 W
Nevada, Mo.	123	37.49 N	94.21 W

PLACE (Pronounciation)	PAGE	Lat. °′	Long. °′
Nevada (State), U.S. (nĕ vä'dȧ)	108	39.30 N	117.00 W
Nevada City, Ca.	120	39.16 N	120.01 W
Nevada, Sierra (Mts.), Sp. (syĕr'rä nā-vä'dhä)	170	37.01 N	3.28 W
Nevada, Sierra (Mts.), U.S. (sē-ĕ'r-rä nĕ-vä'dȧ)	108	39.20 N	120.05 W
Nevado, Cerro el (Mtn.), Col. (sĕ'r-rô-ĕl-nĕ-vä'dô)	142a	4.02 N	74.08 W
Nevado de Colima (Mtn.), Mex. (nä-vä'dhô dā kô-lē'mä)	130	19.34 N	103.39 W
Neva Stantsiya, Sov. Un. (nyĕ-vä' stän'tsĭ-yȧ)	162c	59.53 N	30.30 E
Nevel', Sov. Un. (nyĕ'vĕl)	174	56.03 N	29.57 E
Neveri (R.), Ven. (nĕ-vĕ-rē)	143b	10.13 N	64.18 W
Nevers, Fr. (nē-vȧr')	168	46.59 N	3.10 E
Neves, Braz.	61c	22.51 S	43.06 W
Neve, Serra da (Mts.), Ang.	230	13.40 S	13.20 E
Nevesinje, Yugo. (nĕ-vĕ'sĕn-yĕ)	173	43.15 N	18.08 E
Neviges, F.R.G.	63	51.19 N	7.05 E
Neville I., Pa.	57b	40.31 N	80.08 W
Nevis, Ben (Mtn.), Scot. (bĕn)	162	56.47 N	5.00 W
Nevis I., Saint Kitts-Nevis (nē'vĭs)	133b	17.05 N	62.38 W
Nevis Pk., Saint Kitts-Nevis	133b	17.11 N	62.33 W
Nevşehir, Tur. (nĕv-shĕ'hĕr)	179	38.40 N	34.35 E
Nev'yansk, Sov. Un. (nĕv-yänsk')	182a	57.29 N	60.14 E
New (R.), Va. (nū)	127	37.20 N	80.35 W
Newabāgam, India	67a	22.48 N	88.24 E
New Addington (Neigh.), Eng.	62	51.21 N	0.01 W
Newala, Tan.	231	10.56 S	39.18 E
New Albany, In. (nû ôl'bȧ-nĭ)	113h	38.17 N	85.49 W
New Albany, Ms.	126	34.28 N	39.00 W
New Amsterdam, Guy. (ăm'stēr-dăm)	143	6.14 N	57.30 W
Newark, Ca. (nū'ērk)	118b	37.32 N	122.02 W
Newark, De. (nōō'ärk)	111	39.40 N	75.45 W
Newark, Eng. (nū'ērk)	156	53.04 N	0.49 W
Newark, NJ (nōō'ûrk)	112a	40.44 N	74.10 W
Newark, NY (nū'ērk)	111	43.05 N	77.10 W
Newark, Oh.	110	40.05 N	82.25 W
Newaygo, Mi. (nū'wā-go)	110	43.25 N	85.50 W
New Bedford, Ma. (bĕd'fērd)	111	41.35 N	70.55 W
Newberg, Or. (nū'bûrg)	116	45.17 N	122.58 W
New Bern, NC (bûrn)	127	35.05 N	77.05 W
Newbern, Tn.	126	36.05 N	89.12 W
Newberry, Mi. (nū'bĕr-ĭ)	115	46.22 N	85.31 W
Newberry, SC	127	34.15 N	81.40 W
New Boston, Mi. (bôs'tŭn)	113b	42.10 N	83.24 W
New Boston, Oh.	110	38.45 N	82.55 W
New Braunfels, Tx. (nū broun'fĕls)	124	29.43 N	98.07 W
New Brighton, Eng.	64a	53.26 N	3.03 W
New Brighton, Mn. (brī'tŭn)	119g	45.04 N	93.12 W
New Brighton, Pa.	113e	40.34 N	80.18 W
New Brighton (Neigh.), NY	55	40.38 N	74.06 W
New Britain, Ct. (brĭt''n)	111	41.40 N	72.45 W
New Britain (I.), Pap. N. Gui.	207	6.45 S	149.38 E
New Brunswick, NJ (brŭnz'wĭk)	112a	40.29 N	74.27 W
New Brunswick (Prov.), Can.	97	47.14 N	66.30 W
Newburg, In.	110	38.00 N	87.25 W
Newburg, Mo.	123	37.54 N	91.53 W
Newburgh, NY	111	41.30 N	74.00 W
Newburgh Heights, Oh.	113d	41.27 N	81.40 W
Newbury, Eng. (nū'bĕr-ĭ)	162	51.24 N	1.26 W
Newbury, Ma.	105a	42.48 N	70.52 W
Newburyport, Ma. (nū'bēr-ĭ-pōrt)	105a	42.48 N	70.53 W
New Caledonia, Oceania	215	21.28 S	164.40 E
New Canaan, Ct. (kā-nȧn)	112a	41.06 N	73.30 W
New Carlisle, Can. (kär-lĭl')	104	48.01 N	65.20 W
New Carrollton, Md.	56d	35.58 N	76.53 W
Newcastle, Austl. (nū-kȧs''l)	216	33.00 S	151.55 E
Newcastle, Can.	104	47.00 N	65.34 W
New Castle, De.	111	39.40 N	75.35 W
Newcastle, Eng. (nû-käs''l)	156	53.01 N	2.14 W
New Castle, In.	110	39.55 N	82.25 W
New Castle, Oh.	110	40.20 N	82.10 W
New Castle, Pa.	110	41.00 N	80.25 W
Newcastle, Tx.	122	33.13 N	98.44 W
Newcastle, Wy.	114	43.51 N	104.11 W
Newcastle upon Tyne, Eng.	162	55.00 N	1.45 W
Newcastle Waters, Austl. (wô'tērz)	214	17.10 S	133.25 E
Newclare (Neigh.), S. Afr.	71b	26.11 S	27.58 E
Newcomerstown, Oh. (nū'kŭm-ērz-toun)	110	40.15 N	81.40 W
New Croton Res., NY (krŏ'tôn)	112a	41.15 N	73.47 W
New Delhi, India (dĕl'hī)	196	28.43 N	77.18 E
Newell, SD (nū'ĕl)	114	44.43 N	103.26 W
New Eltham (Neigh.), Eng.	62	51.26 N	0.04 E
New England Ra., Austl. (nû ĭŋ'glȧnd)	215	29.32 S	152.30 E
Newenham, C., Ak. (nū-ĕn-hăm)	107	58.40 N	162.32 W
Newfane, NY (nū-fān)	113c	43.17 N	78.44 W
New Ferry, Eng.	64a	53.22 N	2.59 W
Newfoundland (Prov.), Can. (nū-fŭn'lănd')(nū'fŭnd-lănd) (nū'found-lănd')	97a	48.15 N	56.53 W
Newgate, Can. (nū'gāt)	99	49.01 N	115.10 W
Newgate Street, Eng.	62	51.44 N	0.07 W
New Georgia (I.), Sol. Is. (jôr'jĭ-ȧ)	215	8.08 S	158.00 E
New Glasgow, Can. (glȧs'gō)	115	45.35 N	62.36 W
New Guinea (I.), Asia (gĭne)	207	5.45 S	140.00 E
Newhalem, Wa. (nū hā'lŭm)	116	48.44 N	121.11 W
Newham (Neigh.), Eng.	62	51.32 N	0.03 E
New Hampshire (State), U. S. (hămp'shĭr)	109	43.55 N	71.40 W
New Hampton, Ia. (hămp'tŭn)	115	43.03 N	92.20 W
New Hanover, S. Afr. (hăn'ôvēr)	227c	29.23 S	30.32 E
New Hanover (I.), Pap. N. Gui.	207	2.37 S	150.15 E
New Harmony, In. (nū här'mô-nĭ)	110	38.10 N	87.55 W
New Haven, Ct. (hā'vĕn)	111	41.20 N	72.55 W
Newhaven, Eng.	163	50.45 N	0.10 E
New Haven, In. (nū hăv''n)	110	41.05 N	85.00 W
New Hebrides (Is.), Vanuatu	215	16.00 S	167.00 E

ăt; finȧl; rāte; senȧte; ärm; ȧsk; sofȧ; fâre; ch-choose; dh-as th in other; bē; ēvent; bĕt; recĕnt; cratēr; g-gō; gh-guttural g; bĭt; ĭ-short neutral; rīde; ĸ-guttural k as ch in German ich;

PRONOUNCING INDEX

New Hey – Nobeoka 321

PLACE (Pronounciation)	PAGE	Lat. °′	Long. °′
New Hey, Eng.	64b	50.36 N	2.06 W
New Holland, Eng. (hŏl'ănd)	156	53.42 N	0.21 W
New Holland, NC	127	35.27 N	76.14 W
New Hope Mtn., Al. (hōp)	112h	33.23 N	86.45 W
New Hudson, Mi. (hŭd'sŭn)	113b	42.30 N	83.36 W
New Hyde Park, NY	55	40.44 N	73.41 W
New Hythe, Eng.	62	51.19 N	0.27 E
New Iberia, La. (ī-bē'rĭ-ȧ)	125	30.00 N	91.50 W
Newington, Can. (nū'ĕng-tŏn)	95c	45.07 N	75.00 W
New Ireland (I.), Pap. N. Gui. (ĭr'lănd)	207	3.15 S	152.30 E
New Jersey (State), U. S. (jûr'zĭ)	109	40.30 N	74.50 W
New Kensington, Pa. (kĕn'zĭng-tŭn)	113e	40.34 N	79.35 W
Newkirk, Ok. (nū'kûrk)	123	36.52 N	97.03 W
New Kowloon (Xinjiulong), China	68c	22.20 N	114.10 E
New Lagos (Neigh.), Nig.	71d	6.30 N	3.22 E
New Lenox, Il. (lĕn'ŭk)	113a	41.31 N	87.58 W
New Lexington, Oh. (lĕk'sĭng-tŭn)	110	39.40 N	82.10 W
New Lisbon, Wi. (lĭz'bŭn)	115	43.52 N	90.11 W
New Liskeard, Can.	103	47.30 N	79.40 W
New London, Ct. (lŭn'dŭn)	111	41.20 N	72.05 W
New London, Wi.	115	44.24 N	88.45 W
New Madrid, Mo. (măd'rĭd)	123	36.34 N	89.31 W
Newman (L.), Fl.	127	29.41 N	82.13 W
Newman's Grove, Ne. (nū'măn grōv)	114	41.46 N	97.44 W
Newmarket, Can. (nū'mär-kĕt)	111	44.00 N	79.30 W
Newmarket, S. Afr.	71b	26.17 S	28.08 E
New Martinsville, WV (mär'tĭnz-vĭl)	110	39.35 N	80.50 W
New Meadows, Id.	116	44.58 N	116.20 W
New Mexico (State), U. S. (mĕk'sĭ-kō)	108	34.30 N	107.10 W
New Milford, NJ	55	40.56 N	74.01 W
New Mills, Eng. (mĭlz)	156	53.22 N	2.00 W
New Munster, Wi. (mŭn'stēr)	113a	42.35 N	88.13 W
Newnan, Ga. (nū'năn)	126	33.22 N	84.47 W
New Norfolk, Austl. (nôr'fŏk)	216	42.50 S	147.17 E
New Orleans, La. (ôr'lē-ănz)	112d	30.00 N	90.05 W
New Philadelphia, Oh. (fĭl-ȧ-dĕl'fĭ-ȧ)	110	40.30 N	81.30 W
New Plymouth, N. Z. (plĭm'ŭth)	217	39.04 S	174.13 E
Newport, Ar. (nū'pōrt)	123	35.35 N	91.16 W
Newport, Austl.	70b	37.51 S	144.53 E
Newport, Austl.	211b	33.39 S	151.19 E
Newport, Eng. (nū-pôrt)	162	50.41 N	1.25 W
Newport, Eng.	156	52.46 N	2.22 W
Newport, Ky.	113f	39.05 N	84.30 W
Newport, Me.	104	44.49 N	69.20 W
Newport, Mn.	119g	44.52 N	92.59 W
Newport, NH	111	43.20 N	72.10 W
Newport, Or.	116	44.39 N	124.02 W
Newport, RI	112b	41.29 N	71.16 W
Newport, Tn.	126	35.55 N	83.12 W
Newport, Vt.	111	44.55 N	72.15 W
Newport, Wales	162	51.36 N	3.05 W
Newport, Wa.	116	48.12 N	117.01 W
Newport Beach, Ca. (bēch)	119a	33.36 N	117.55 W
Newport News, Va.	112g	36.59 N	76.24 W
New Prague, Mn. (nū prāg)	115	44.33 N	93.35 W
New Providence (I.), Ba. (prŏv'ĭ-dĕns)	134	25.00 N	77.25 W
New Redruth, S. Afr.	71b	26.16 S	28.07 E
New Richmond, Oh. (rĭch'mŭnd)	110	38.55 N	84.15 W
New Richmond, Wi.	115	45.07 N	92.34 W
New Roads, La. (rōds)	125	30.42 N	91.26 W
New Rochelle, NY (rū-shĕl')	112a	40.55 N	73.47 W
New Rockford, ND (rŏk'fōrd)	114	47.40 N	99.08 W
New Ross, Ire. (rôs)	166	52.25 N	6.55 W
New Sarepta, Can.	95g	53.17 N	113.09 W
New Siberian Is., see Novosibirskiye O-va			
New Smyrna Beach, Fl. (smûr'nȧ)	127	29.00 N	80.57 W
New South Wales (State), Austl. (wālz)	215	32.45 S	146.14 E
Newton, Can. (nū'tŭn)	95f	49.56 N	98.04 W
Newton, Eng.	156	53.27 N	2.37 W
Newton, Ia.	115	41.42 N	93.04 W
Newton, Il.	110	39.00 N	88.10 W
Newton, Ks.	123	38.03 N	97.22 W
Newton, Ma.	105a	42.21 N	71.13 W
Newton, Ms.	126	32.18 N	89.10 W
Newton, NJ	112a	41.03 N	74.45 W
Newton, NC	127	35.40 N	81.19 W
Newton, Tx.	125	30.47 N	93.45 W
Newton (Neigh.), Austl.	70a	33.54 S	151.11 E
Newton Brook (Neigh.), Can.	54c	43.48 N	79.24 W
Newton Highlands, Ma.	54a	41.19 N	71.13 W
Newton Lower Falls, Ma.	54a	42.19 N	71.23 W
Newtonsville, Oh. (nū'tŭnz-vĭl)	113f	39.11 N	84.04 W
Newton Upper Falls, Ma.	54a	42.19 N	71.13 W
Newtonville, Ma.	54a	42.21 N	71.13 W
Newtown, ND (nū'toun)	114	47.57 N	102.25 W
Newtown, Oh.	113f	39.08 N	84.22 W
Newtown, Pa.	112f	40.13 N	74.56 W
Newtownards, Ire. (nu-t'n-ardz')	162	54.35 N	5.39 W
New Ulm, Mn. (ŭlm)	115	44.18 N	94.27 W
New Utrecht (Neigh.), NY	55	40.36 N	73.59 W
New Waterford, Can. (wô'tēr-fērd)	105	46.15 N	60.05 W
New Westminster, Can. (wĕst'mĭn-stēr)	118d	49.12 N	122.55 W
New York, NY (yôrk)	112a	40.40 N	73.58 W
New York (State), U. S.	109	42.45 N	78.05 W
New Zealand, Oceania (zē'lănd)	215a	42.00 S	175.00 E
Nexapa (R.), Mex. (nĕks-ä'pä)	130	18.32 N	98.29 W
Neya-gawa, Jap. (nā'yȧ gä'wä)	205b	34.47 N	135.38 E
Neyshābūr, Iran	192	36.06 N	58.45 E
Neyva R., Sov. Un. (nĕy'vȧ)	182a	57.39 N	60.37 E
Nezhin, Sov. Un. (nyĕzh'ĕn)	175	50.03 N	31.52 E
Nez Perce, Id. (nĕz' pûrs')	116	46.16 N	116.15 W
Ngami (R.), Bots. (n'gä'mē)	226	20.56 S	22.31 E
Ngamouéri, Con.	71c	4.14 S	15.14 E
Ngangerabeli Pln., Ken.	231	1.20 S	40.10 E

PLACE (Pronounciation)	PAGE	Lat. °′	Long. °′
Ngangla Ringco (L.), China (ŋäŋ-lä rĭŋ-tswo)	196	31.42 N	82.53 E
Ngaoundéré, Cam. (n'gōn-dȧ-rā')	229	7.19 N	13.35 E
Ngarimbi, Tan.	231	8.28 S	38.36 E
Ngoko (R.), Afr.	230	1.55 N	15.53 E
Ngol-Kedju Hill, Cam.	229	6.20 N	9.45 E
Ngombe, Zaire	71c	4.24 S	15.11 E
Ngong, Ken. ('n-gông)	227	1.27 S	36.39 E
Ngounié (R.), Gabon	230	1.15 S	10.43 E
Ngoywa, Tan.	231	5.56 S	32.48 E
Ngqeleni, S. Afr. ('ng-kĕ-lā'nē)	227c	31.41 S	29.04 E
Nguigmi, Niger ('n-gēg'mē)	229	14.15 N	13.07 E
Ngunza, Ang.	230	11.13 S	13.50 E
Ngurore, Nig.	229	9.18 N	12.14 E
Nguru, Nig. ('n-gōō'rōō)	224	12.53 N	10.26 E
Nguru Mts., Tan.	231	6.10 S	37.35 E
Nha-trang, Viet. (nyä-träng')	206	12.08 N	108.56 E
Niafounke, Mali	224	16.03 N	4.17 W
Niagara, Wi. (nī-ăg'ȧ-rȧ)	115	45.45 N	88.05 W
Niagara Falls, Can.	113c	43.05 N	79.05 W
Niagara Falls, NY	113c	43.06 N	79.02 W
Niagara-on-the-Lake, Can.	95d	43.16 N	79.05 W
Niagara R., U. S.-Can.	113c	43.12 N	79.03 W
Niakaramandougou, Ivory Coast	228	8.40 N	5.17 W
Niamey, Niger (nē-ä-mā')	229	13.31 N	2.07 E
Niamtougou, Togo	228	9.46 N	1.06 E
Niangara, Zaire (nē-äŋ-gá'rá)	231	3.42 N	27.52 E
Niangua (R.), Mo. (nī-ăŋ'gwá)	123	37.30 N	93.05 W
Nias, Pulau (I.), Indon. (nē'äs')	206	0.58 N	97.43 E
Nibe, Den. (nē'bĕ)	164	56.57 N	9.36 E
Nicaragua, N. A. (nĭk-ȧ-rä'gwȧ)	128	12.45 N	86.15 W
Nicaragua, Lago de (L.), Nic. (lä'gô dĕ)	132	11.45 N	85.28 W
Nicastro, It. (nē-käs'trō)	172	38.39 N	16.15 E
Nicchehabin, Punta (Pt.), Mex. (pōō'n-tä-nĕk-chĕ-ä-bē'n)	132a	19.50 N	87.20 W
Nice, Fr. (nēs)	169	43.42 N	7.21 E
Nicheng, China (nē-chŭŋ)	201b	30.54 N	121.48 E
Nichicun (L.), Can. (nĭch'ĭ-kŭn)	97	53.07 N	72.10 W
Nicholas Chan., Ba. (nĭk'ô-lȧs)	134	23.30 N	80.20 W
Nicholasville, Ky. (nĭk'ô-lȧs-vĭl)	110	37.55 N	84.35 W
Nicobar Is., Andaman & Nicobar Is. (nĭk-ô-bär')	206	8.28 N	94.04 E
Nicolai Mtn., Or. (nē-cō lī')	118c	46.05 N	123.27 W
Nicolás Romero, Mex. (nē-kô-lá's rô-mĕ'rô)	131a	19.38 N	99.20 W
Nicolet, L., Mi. (nĭ'kŏ-lĕt)	119k	46.22 N	84.14 W
Nicolls Town, Ba.	134	25.10 N	78.00 W
Nicols, Mn. (nĭk'ĕls)	119g	44.50 N	93.12 W
Nicomeki (R.), Can.	118d	49.04 N	122.47 W
Nicosia, Cyprus (nē-kô-sē'á)	161	35.10 N	33.22 E
Nicoya, C. R. (nē-kō'yä)	132	10.08 N	85.27 W
Nicoya, Golfo de (G.), C. R. (gôl-fô-dĕ)	132	10.03 N	85.04 W
Nicoya, Pen. de, C. R.	132	10.05 N	86.00 W
Nidaros, see Trondheim			
Nidzica, Pol. (nē-jēt'sá)	167	53.21 N	20.30 E
Niederaden (Neigh.), F.R.G.	63	51.36 N	7.34 E
Niederbonsfeld, F.R.G.	63	51.23 N	7.08 E
Niederdonk, F.R.G.	63	51.14 N	6.41 E
Niederelfringhausen, F.R.G.	63	51.21 N	7.10 E
Niedere Tauern (Mts.), Aus.	166	47.15 N	13.41 E
Niederkrüchten, F.R.G. (nē'dēr-krük-tĕn)	169c	51.12 N	6.14 E
Nieder-Neuendorf, G.D.R.	65a	52.37 N	13.12 E
Niederösterreich (Lower Austria) (State), Aus.	157e	48.24 N	16.20 E
Niedersachsen (Lower Saxony) (State), F.R.G. (nē'dēr-zäĸ-sĕn)	166	52.52 N	8.27 E
Niederschöneweide (Neigh.), G.D.R.	65a	52.27 N	13.31 E
Niederschönhausen (Neigh.), G.D.R.	65a	52.35 N	13.23 E
Niélé, Ivory Coast	228	10.12 N	5.38 W
Niellim, Chad	229	9.42 N	17.49 E
Niemeyer (Neigh.), Braz.	61c	23.00 S	43.15 W
Nienburg, F.R.G. (nē'ĕn-bōōrgh)	166	52.40 N	9.15 E
Niénokoué, Mont (Mtn.), Ivory Coast	228	5.26 N	7.10 W
Nierst, F.R.G.	63	51.19 N	6.43 E
Nietverdiend, S. Afr.	223d	25.02 S	26.10 E
Nieuw Nickerie, Sur. (nē-nē'kē-rē')	143	5.51 N	57.00 W
Nieves, Mex. (nyā'vās)	130	24.00 N	102.57 W
Niğde, Tur. (nĭg'dĕ)	179	37.55 N	34.40 E
Nigel, S. Afr. (nī'jĕl)	223d	26.26 S	28.27 E
Niger, Afr. (nī'jēr)	222	18.02 N	8.30 E
Niger (R.), Afr.	229	5.33 N	6.33 E
Niger Delta, Nig.	229	4.45 N	5.20 E
Nigeria, Afr. (nī-jē'rĭ-ȧ)	222	8.57 N	6.30 E
Nihoa (I.), Hi.	106b	23.15 N	161.30 W
Nihonbashi (Neigh.), Jap.	69a	35.41 N	139.47 E
Nii (I.), Jap. (nē)	205	34.26 N	139.23 E
Niigata, Jap. (nē'ē-gä'tȧ)	204	37.47 N	139.04 E
Niihau (I.), Hi. (nē'ē-ha'ōō)	106a	21.50 N	160.05 W
Niimi, Jap. (nē'mē)	205	34.59 N	133.28 E
Niiza, Jap.	205a	35.48 N	139.34 E
Nijmegen, Neth. (nī'mā-gĕn)	163	51.50 N	5.52 E
Nikaidō, Jap. (nē'ki-dô)	205b	34.36 N	135.48 E
Nikitinka, Sov. Un. (nē-kĭ'tĭn-kȧ)	174	55.33 N	33.19 E
Nikkō, Jap. (nĕk'kō)	205	36.44 N	139.35 E
Nikolayev, Sov. Un. (nē-kô-lä'yĕf)	175	46.58 N	32.02 E
Nikolayev (Oblast), Sov. Un. (ôb'lȧst)	175	47.27 N	31.25 E
Nikolayevka, Sov. Un. (nē-kô-lä'yĕf-kȧ)	182c	59.29 N	29.48 E
Nikolayevka, Sov. Un.	204	48.37 N	134.09 E
Nikolayevskiy, Sov. Un.	179	50.00 N	45.30 E
Nikolayevsk-na-Amure, Sov. Un.	181	53.18 N	140.49 E
Nikolo-Chovanskoje, Sov. Un.	66b	55.36 N	37.27 E
Nikol'sk, Sov. Un. (nē-kôlsk')	178	59.30 N	45.40 E
Nikol'skoye, Sov. Un. (nē-kôl'skô-yĕ)	182c	59.27 N	30.00 E
Nikopol, Bul. (nē'kô-pôl')	173	43.41 N	24.52 E
Nikopol', Sov. Un.	175	47.36 N	34.24 E
Nikšić, Yugo. (nēk'shēch)	173	42.45 N	18.57 E
Nilahue (R.), Chile (nē-lá'wĕ)	141b	36.36 S	71.50 W
Nile (R.), Afr. (nīl)	225	19.15 N	32.30 E

PLACE (Pronounciation)	PAGE	Lat. °′	Long. °′
Niles, Il.	58a	42.01 N	87.49 W
Niles, Mi. (nīlz)	110	41.50 N	86.15 W
Niles, Oh.	110	41.15 N	80.45 W
Nileshwar, India	197	12.08 N	74.14 E
Nilgani, India	67a	22.46 N	88.26 E
Nilgiri Hills, India	197	17.05 N	76.22 E
Nilópolis, Braz. (nē-lô'pō-lēs)	144b	22.48 S	43.25 W
Nimba, Mont (Mtn.), Ivory Coast (nĭm'bȧ)	224	7.40 N	8.33 W
Nimba Mts., Gui.-Ivory Coast	228	7.30 N	8.35 W
Nimrod Res., Ar. (nĭm'rŏd)	123	34.58 N	93.46 W
Nimule, Sud. (nē-mōō'lā)	225	3.38 N	32.12 E
Ninda, Ang.	230	14.47 S	21.24 E
Nine Ashes, Eng.	62	51.42 N	0.18 E
Ninety Mile Bch., Austl.	216	38.20 S	147.30 E
Nineveh (Ruins), Iraq (nĭn'ĕ-vȧ)	179	36.30 N	43.10 E
Ning'an, China (nĭŋ-än)	202	44.20 N	129.20 E
Ningbo, China (nĭŋ-bwo)	203	29.56 N	121.30 E
Ningde, China (nĭŋ-dŭ)	203	26.38 N	119.33 E
Ninghai, China (nĭng'hī')	203	29.20 N	121.20 E
Ninghe, China (nĭŋ-hŭ)	200	39.20 N	167.50 E
Ningjin, China (nĭŋ-jyĭn)	200	37.39 N	116.47 E
Ningjin, China	200	37.37 N	114.55 E
Ningming, China	203	22.22 N	107.06 E
Ningwu, China (nĭng'wōō')	202	39.00 N	112.12 E
Ningxia Huizu (Aut. Reg.), China (nĭŋ-shyä)	198	37.10 N	106.00 E
Ningyang, China (nĭng'yäng')	200	35.46 N	116.48 E
Ninh Binh, Viet. (nĕn bĕnk')	203	20.22 N	106.00 E
Ninigo Group (Is.), Pap. N. Gui.	207	1.15 S	143.30 E
Ninnescah (R.), Ks. (nĭn'ĕs-kä)	122	37.37 N	98.31 W
Nioaque, Braz. (nēō-à'-kĕ)	143	21.14 S	55.41 W
Niobrara (R.), Ne. (nī-ô-brâr'ȧ)	114	42.46 N	98.46 W
Niokolo Koba, Parc Natl. du (Natl. Pk.), Senegal	228	13.05 N	13.00 W
Nīl, Nahr an-, see Nile (R.)			
Nīmach, India	196	24.32 N	74.51 E
Nioro du Sahel, Mali (nē-ō'rō)	228	15.15 N	9.35 W
Nipawin, Can.	100	53.22 N	104.00 W
Nipe, Bahía de (B.), Cuba (bä-ē'ä-dĕ-nē'pā)	135	20.50 N	75.30 W
Nipe, Sierra de (Mts.), Cuba (sē-ĕ'r-rȧ-dĕ)	135	20.20 N	75.50 W
Nipigon, Can. (nĭp'ĭ-gŏn)	110	48.58 N	88.17 W
Nipigon B., Can.	115	48.56 N	88.00 W
Nipigon (L.), Can.	102	49.37 N	89.55 W
Nipisiguit (R.), Can. (nĭ-pĭ'sĭ-kwĭt)	104	47.26 N	66.15 W
Nipissing (L.), Can. (nĭp'ĭ-sĭng)	103	45.59 N	80.19 W
Niquero, Cuba (nē-kā'rō)	134	20.00 N	77.35 W
Nirmali, India	196	26.30 N	86.43 E
Nîmes, Fr. (nēm)	168	43.49 N	4.22 E
Niš, Yugo. (nēsh)	173	43.18 N	21.55 E
Nisa, Port. (nē'sȧ)	170	39.32 N	7.41 W
Nišava (R.), Yugo. (nē'shá-vá)	173	43.17 N	22.17 E
Nishi, Jap.	69b	34.41 N	135.30 E
Nishinari (Neigh.), Jap.	69b	34.38 N	135.28 E
Nishino (I.), Jap. (nēsh'ē-nō)	205	36.06 N	132.49 E
Nishinomiya, Jap. (nēsh'ē-nô-mē'yȧ)	205b	34.44 N	135.21 E
Nishinoomote, Jap. (nēsh'ē-nô-mō'tô)	205	30.44 N	130.59 E
Nishio, Jap. (nēsh'ē-ô)	205	34.50 N	137.01 E
Nishionmiya, Jap.	69b	34.43 N	135.20 E
Nishiyodogawa (Neigh.), Jap.	69b	34.42 N	135.27 E
Niska L., Can. (nĭs'kȧ)	100	55.35 N	108.38 W
Nisko, Pol. (nēs'kô)	167	50.30 N	22.07 E
Nisku, Can. (nĭs-kū')	95g	53.21 N	113.33 W
Nisqually R., Wa. (nĭs-kwôl'ĭ)	116	46.51 N	122.33 W
Nissan (R.), Swe.	164	57.06 N	13.22 E
Nisser (L.), Nor. (nĭs'ĕr)	164	59.14 N	8.35 E
Nissum Fd., Den.	164	56.24 N	7.35 E
Niterói, Braz. (nē-tĕ-rô'ĭ)	144b	22.53 S	43.07 W
Nith (R.), Scot. (nĭth)	162	55.13 N	3.55 W
Nitra, Czech. (nē'trȧ)	167	48.18 N	18.04 E
Nitra R., Czech.	167	48.13 N	18.14 E
Nitro, WV (nī'trô)	110	38.25 N	81.50 W
Niue, Oceania (nĭ'ōō)	209	19.50 S	167.00 W
Nivelles, Bel. (nē'vĕl')	163	50.33 N	4.17 E
Níkaia, Grc.	66d	37.58 N	23.39 E
Nízke Tatry (Mts.), Czech.	167	48.57 N	19.18 E
Nixon, Tx. (nĭk'sŭn)	125	29.16 N	97.48 W
Nizāmābād, India	196	18.48 N	78.07 E
Nizhne-Angarsk, Sov. Un. (nyēzh'nyĭ-ŭngärsk')	181	55.49 N	108.46 E
Nizhne-Chirskaya, Sov. Un. (nyĭ-ŭn-gärsk')	179	48.20 N	42.50 E
Nizhne-Kolymsk, Sov. Un. (kô-lēmsk')	181	68.32 N	160.56 E
Nizhneudinsk, Sov. Un. (nēzh'nyĭ-ōōdēnsk')	180	54.58 N	99.15 E
Nizhniye Sergi, Sov. Un. (nyēzh' nyē sĕr'gē)	182a	56.41 N	59.19 E
Nizhniye Serogozy, Sov. Un. (nyēzh'nyĭ sĕ-rô-gô'zĭ)	175	46.51 N	34.25 E
Nizhniy Tagil, Sov. Un. (tŭgēl')	182a	57.54 N	59.59 E
Nizhnyaya (Lower) Tunguska (R.), Sov. Un. (tōōn-gōōs'kȧ)	180	64.13 N	91.30 E
Nizhnyaya Kur'ya, Sov. Un. (nyē'zhnyȧ-yȧ koor'yȧ)	182a	58.01 N	56.00 E
Nizhnyaya Salda, Sov. Un. (nyē'zhnya'ya säl'da')	182a	58.05 N	60.43 E
Nizhnyaya Taymyra (R.), Sov. Un.	180	72.30 N	95.18 E
Nizhnyaya Tura, Sov. Un. (tōō'rȧ)	182a	58.38 N	59.50 E
Nizhnyaya Us'va, Sov. Un. (ōō'vȧ)	182a	59.05 N	58.53 E
Njombe, Tan.	231	9.20 S	34.46 E
Njurunda, Swe. (nyōō-rōōn'dȧ)	164	62.15 N	17.24 E
Nkala Mission, Zambia	231	15.55 S	26.00 E
Nkandla, S. Afr. ('n-kănd'lä)	227c	28.40 S	31.06 E
Nkawkaw, Ghana	228	6.33 N	0.47 W
Noākhāli, Bngl.	196	22.52 N	91.08 E
Noatak, Ak. (nō-ȧ'tȧk)	107	67.22 N	163.28 W
Noatak (R.), Ak.	107	67.58 N	162.15 W
Nobeoka, Jap. (nō-bȧ-ō'kȧ)	205	32.36 N	131.41 E

ng-sing; ŋ-baŋk; ɴ-nasalized n; nŏd; cŏmmit; ōld; ôbey; ôrder; oi-boil; fōōd; fŏŏt; ou-out; s-soft; sh-dish; th-thin; pūre; ûnite; ûrn; stŭd; circŭs; ü-as in French tu; '-indeterminate vowel.

322 Noblesville – Noshiro

PLACE (Pronounciation)	PAGE	Lat. °′	Long. °′
Noblesville, In. (nō'bl'z-vĭl)	110	40.00 N	86.00 W
Nobleton, Can. (nō'bl'tŭn)	95d	43.54 N	79.39 W
Noborito, Jap.	69a	35.37 N	139.34 E
Nocera Inferiore, It. (ēn-fē-ryô'rĕ)	171c	40.30 N	14.38 E
Nochistlán, Mex. (nô-chēs-tlän')	130	21.23 N	102.52 W
Nochixtlón (Asunción), Mex. (ä-sōōn-syōn')	131	17.28 N	97.12 W
Nogales, Az. (nô-gä'lĕs)	121	31.20 N	110.55 W
Nogales, Mex. (nô-gä'lĕs)	131	18.49 N	97.09 W
Nogales, Mex.	128	31.15 N	111.00 W
Nogal Val., Som. (nô'gäl)	223a	8.30 N	47.50 E
Nogaysk, Sov. Un. (nô-gīsk')	175	46.43 N	36.21 E
Nogent-le-Roi, Fr. (nō-zhōN-lē-rwä')	169b	48.39 N	1.32 E
Nogent-le-Rotrou, Fr. (rō-trōō')	168	48.22 N	0.47 E
Nogent-sur-Marne, Fr.	64c	48.50 N	2.29 E
Noginsk, Sov. Un. (nô-gēnsk')	182b	55.52 N	38.28 E
Noguera Pallares (R.), Sp.	171	42.18 N	1.03 E
Noirmoutier, Île de (I.), Fr. (nwȧr-mōō-tyā')	168	47.03 N	3.08 W
Noisy-le-Grand, Fr.	64c	48.51 N	2.33 E
Noisy-le-Roi, Fr.	64c	48.51 N	2.04 E
Noisy-le-Sec, Fr.	64c	48.53 N	2.28 E
Nojimä-Zaki (Pt.), Jap. (nō'jē-mä zä-kē)	205	35.54 N	139.48 E
Nokomis, Il. (nô-kō'mĭs)	110	39.15 N	89.10 W
Nola, It. (nô'lä)	171c	40.41 N	14.32 E
Nolinsk, Sov. Un. (nô-lênsk')	178	57.32 N	49.50 E
Noma Misaki (C.), Jap. (nō'mä mē'sä-kē)	205	31.25 N	130.09 E
Nombre de Dios, Mex. (nôm-brĕ-dĕ-dyô's)	130	23.50 N	104.14 W
Nombre de Dios, Pan. (nô'm-brĕ)	133	9.34 N	79.28 W
Nome, Ak. (nōm)	107	64.30 N	165.20 W
Nonacho (L.), Can.	96	61.48 N	111.20 W
Nonantum, Ma.	54a	42.20 N	71.12 W
Nong'an, China (nôŋ-än)	202	44.25 N	125.10 E
Nongoma, S. Afr. (nôn-gō'mȧ)	226	27.48 S	31.45 E
Nooksack, Wa. (nōōk'săk)	118d	48.55 N	122.19 W
Nooksack (R.), Wa.	118d	48.54 N	122.31 W
Noordwijk aan Zee, Neth.	157a	52.14 N	4.25 E
Noordzee, Kanal, (Can.), Neth.	157a	52.27 N	4.42 E
Nootka (I.), Can. (nōōt'kȧ)	96	49.32 N	126.42 W
Nootka Sd., Can.	98	49.33 N	126.38 W
Nóqui, Ang. (nô-kē')	230	5.51 S	13.25 E
Nor (R.), China (nou')	204	46.55 N	132.45 E
Nora, In. (nō'rä)	113g	39.54 N	86.08 W
Nora, Swe.	164	59.32 N	14.56 E
Noranda, Can.	103	48.15 N	79.01 W
Norbeck, Md. (nōr'bĕk)	112e	39.06 N	77.05 W
Norborne, Mo. (nôr'bôrn)	123	39.17 N	93.39 W
Norco, Ca. (nôr'kô)	119a	33.57 N	117.33 W
Norcross, Ga. (nôr'krôs)	112c	33.56 N	84.13 W
Nordegg, Can. (nûr'dĕg)	99	52.28 N	116.04 W
Norden, Eng.	64b	53.38 N	2.13 W
Norden, F.R.G. (nôr'dĕn)	166	53.35 N	7.14 E
Norderney I., F.R.G. (nōr'dĕr-nĕy)	166	53.45 N	6.58 E
Nord Fd., Nor. (nō'fyôr)	164	61.50 N	5.35 E
Nordhausen, G.D.R. (nôrt'hau-zĕn)	166	51.30 N	10.48 E
Nordhorn, F.R.G. (nôrt'hôrn)	166	52.26 N	7.05 E
Nordland, Wa. (nôrd'lȧnd)	118a	48.03 N	122.41 W
Nördlingen, F.R.G. (nûrt'lĭng-ĕn)	166	48.51 N	10.30 E
Nord-Ostsee Kan. (Kiel) Can., F.R.G. (nōrd-ōzt-zā) (kēl)	166	54.03 N	9.23 E
Nordrhein-Westfalen (North Rhine-Westphalia) (State), F.R.G. (nōrd'hīn-vĕst-fä-lĕn)	166	50.50 N	6.53 E
Nord, Riviere du, Can. (rēv-yĕr' dü nōr)	95a	45.45 N	74.02 W
Nordvik, Sov. Un. (nôrd'vēk)	181	73.57 N	111.15 E
Nore R., Ire. (nōr)	162	52.34 N	7.15 W
Norf, F.R.G.	63	51.09 N	6.43 E
Norfield, Ms. (nôr'fēld)	126	31.24 N	90.25 W
Norfolk, Ma. (nôr'fŏk)	105a	42.07 N	71.19 W
Norfolk, Ne.	114	42.10 N	97.25 W
Norfolk, Oceania	208	27.10 S	166.50 E
Norfolk, Va.	112g	36.55 N	76.15 W
Norfork, L., Ar.	123	36.25 N	92.09 W
Noria, Mex. (nō'rē-ȧ)	130	23.04 N	106.20 W
Noril'sk, Sov. Un. (nô rēlsk')	180	69.00 N	87.11 E
Normal, Il. (nôr'mȧl)	110	40.35 N	89.00 W
Norman, Ok. (nôr'mȧn)	123	35.13 N	97.25 W
Norman (R.), Austl.	215	18.27 S	141.29 E
Normandie (Reg.), Fr. (nōr-mäN-dē')	168	49.02 N	0.17 E
Normandie, Collines de (Hills), Fr. (kō-lēn'dĕ-nōr-män-dē')	168	48.46 N	0.50 W
Normandy Heights, Md.	56c	39.17 N	76.48 W
Normanhurst, Austl.	70a	33.43 S	151.06 E
Norman, L., NC	127	35.30 N	80.53 W
Normanton, Austl. (nôr'mȧn-tŭn)	215	17.45 S	141.10 E
Normanton, Eng.	156	53.40 N	1.21 W
Norman Wells, Can.	96	65.26 N	127.00 W
Nornalup, Austl. (nôr-năl'ŭp)	214	35.00 S	117.00 E
Norra Dellen (L.), Swe.	164	61.57 N	16.25 E
Nørresundby, Den. (nû-rĕ-sōōn'bü)	164	57.04 N	9.55 E
Norridge, Il.	58a	41.57 N	87.49 W
Norris, Tn. (nŏr'ĭs)	126	36.09 N	84.05 W
Norris (R.), Tn.	126	36.17 N	84.10 W
Norristown, Pa. (nŏr'ĭs-town)	112f	40.07 N	75.21 W
Norrköping, Swe. (nôr'chûp'ĭng)	164	58.37 N	16.10 E
Norrtälje, Swe. (nôr-tĕl'yĕ)	164	59.47 N	18.39 E
Norseman, Austl. (nôrs'mȧn)	214	32.15 S	122.00 E
Norte, Punta (Pt.), Arg. (pōō'n-tä-nōr'tĕ)	141c	36.17 S	56.46 W
Norte, Serra do (Mts.), Braz. (sĕ'r-rä-dô-nôr'te)	143	12.04 S	59.08 W
North Abington, Ma.	54a	42.08 N	70.57 W
North Adams, Ma. (ăd'ămz)	111	42.40 N	73.05 W
Northam, Austl. (nôr-dhăm)	214	31.50 S	116.45 E
Northam, S. Afr. (nôr'thăm)	223d	24.52 S	27.16 E
North America (ȧ-mĕr'ĭ-kȧ)	94		
North American Basin, Atl. O. (ȧ-mĕr'ĭ-kȧn)	129	23.45 N	62.45 W
Northampton, Austl. (nôr-thămp'tŭn)	214	28.22 S	114.45 E
Northampton, Eng. (nôrth-ămp'tŭn)	162	52.14 N	0.56 W
Northampton, Ma.	111	42.20 N	72.45 W
Northampton, Pa.	111	40.45 N	75.30 W
Northamptonshire (Co.), Eng.	156	52.25 N	0.47 W
North Andaman I., Andaman & Nicobar Is. (ăn-dȧ-măn')	206	13.15 N	93.30 E
North Andover, Ma. (ăn'dô-vēr)	105a	42.42 N	71.07 W
North Arlington, NJ	55	40.47 N	74.08 W
North Arm, Can. (ärm)	118d	49.13 N	123.01 W
North Atlanta, Ga. (ăt-lăn'tȧ)	112c	33.52 N	84.20 W
North Attleboro, Ma. (ăt''l-bŭr-ô)	112b	41.59 N	71.18 W
North Auburn, Austl.	70a	33.50 S	151.02 E
North Baltimore, Oh. (bôl'tĭ-môr)	110	41.10 N	83.40 W
North Balwyn, Austl.	70b	37.48 S	145.05 E
North Barnaby, Md.	56d	38.49 N	76.57 W
North Barrackpore, India	67a	22.46 N	88.22 E
North Basque, Tx. (băsk)	124	31.56 N	98.01 W
North Battleford, Can. (băt''l-fērd)	100	52.47 N	108.17 W
North Bay, Can.	103	46.13 N	79.26 W
North Beach (Neigh.), Ca.	58b	37.48 N	122.25 W
North Bellmore, NY	55	40.41 N	73.32 W
North Bend, Or. (bĕnd)	116	43.23 N	124.13 W
North Bergen, NJ	55	40.48 N	74.01 W
North Berwick, Me. (bûr'wĭk)	104	43.18 N	70.46 W
North Bight, Ba. (bīt)	134	24.30 N	77.40 W
North Bimini (I.), Ba. (bĭ'mĭ-nē)	134	25.45 N	79.20 W
North Borneo (Reg.), see Sabah			
Northborough, Ma. (nôrth'bûr-ô)	105a	42.19 N	71.39 W
North Box Hill, Austl.	70b	37.48 S	145.07 E
North Braddock, Pa.	57b	40.24 N	79.52 W
Northbridge, Austl.	70a	33.49 S	151.13 E
Northbridge, Ma. (nôrth'brĭj)	105a	42.09 N	71.39 W
North C., Can.	105c	47.02 N	60.25 W
North C., N.Z.	217	34.31 S	173.02 E
North Caicos (I.), Turks & Caicos (kī'kōs)	135	21.55 N	72.00 W
North Caldwell, NJ	55	40.52 N	74.16 W
North Carolina (State), U. S. (kăr-ô-lī'nȧ)	109	35.40 N	81.30 W
North Cascades Natl. Pk., Wa.	99	48.50 N	120.50 W
North Cat Cay (I.), Ba.	134	25.35 N	79.20 W
North Chan, N. Ire.-Scot.	162	55.15 N	7.56 W
North Chan (B.), Can. (chăn)	110	46.10 N	83.20 W
North Charleston, SC (chärlz'tŭn)	127	32.49 N	79.57 W
North Chicago, Il. (shĭ-kô'gō)	113a	42.19 N	87.51 W
Northcliff (Neigh.), S. Afr.	71b	26.09 S	27.58 E
North College Hill, Oh. (kŏl'ĕj hĭl)	113f	39.13 N	84.33 W
North Concho, Tx. (kŏn'chō)	124	31.40 N	100.48 W
North Cooking Lake, Can. (kōōk'ĭng lāk)	95g	53.28 N	112.57 W
Northcote, Austl.	70b	37.46 S	145.00 E
North Dakota (State), U. S. (dȧ-kō'tȧ)	108	47.20 N	101.55 W
North Downs, Eng. (dounz)	162	51.11 N	0.01 W
North Downs (Plat.), Eng.	62	51.10 N	0.10 E
North Dum-Dum, India	196a	22.38 N	88.23 E
Northeast C., Ak. (nôrth-ēst)	107	63.15 N	169.04 W
Northeast Providence Chan., Ba. (prŏv'ĭ-dĕns)	134	25.45 N	77.00 W
Northeast Pt., Ba.	135	21.25 N	73.00 W
Northeast Pt., Ba.	135	22.45 N	73.50 W
Northeim, F.R.G. (nôrt'hīm)	166	51.42 N	9.59 E
North Elbow Cays (Is.), Ba.	134	23.55 N	80.30 W
North Englewood, Md.	56d	38.55 N	76.55 W
Northern Cheyenne Ind. Res., Mt.	117	45.32 N	106.43 W
Northern Dvina (R.), see Severnaya Dvina			
Northern Ireland, U. K. (īr'lănd)	162	54.48 N	7.00 W
Northern Land (Is.), see Severnaya Zemlya			
Northern Territory, Austl.	214	18.15 S	133.00 E
North Essendon, Austl.	70b	37.45 S	144.54 E
Northfield, Il.	58a	42.06 N	87.46 W
Northfield, Mn. (nôrth'fēld)	115	44.28 N	93.11 W
North Fitzroy, Austl.	70b	37.47 S	144.59 E
Northfleet, Eng.	62	51.27 N	0.21 E
North Flinders, Ra., Austl. (flĭn'dērz)	216	31.55 S	138.45 E
North Foreland, Eng. (dōr'lȧnd)	163	51.20 N	1.30 E
North Franklin Mt., Tx. (frăŋ'klĭn)	124	31.55 N	106.30 W
North Frisian Is., Den.	164	55.16 N	8.15 E
North Gamboa, Pan. (gäm-bô'ä)	128a	9.07 N	79.40 W
North Germiston, S. Afr.	71b	26.14 S	28.09 E
North Gower, Can. (gŏw'ēr)	95c	45.08 N	75.43 W
North Haledon, NJ	55	40.58 N	74.11 W
North Hanover, Ma.	54a	42.09 N	70.52 W
North Hills, NY	55	40.47 N	73.41 W
North Hollywood, Ca. (hŏl'ē-wōōd)	119a	34.10 N	118.23 W
North I., Ca.	120a	32.39 N	117.14 W
North I., N. Z.	217	37.20 S	173.30 E
North Judson, In. (jŭd'sŭn)	110	41.15 N	86.50 W
North Kamloops, Can. (kăm'lōōps)	99	50.41 N	120.22 W
North Kansas City, Mo. (kăn'zȧs)	119f	39.08 N	94.34 W
North Kingstown, RI	112b	41.34 N	71.26 W
Northlake, Il.	58a	41.55 N	87.54 W
North Little Rock, Ar. (lĭt''l rŏk)	123	34.46 N	92.13 W
North Loup (R.), Ne. (lōōp)	114	42.05 N	100.10 W
North Manchester, In. (măn'chĕs-tēr)	110	41.00 N	85.45 W
North Manly, Austl.	70a	33.46 S	151.16 E
Northmead, Austl.	70a	33.47 S	151.00 E
Northmead, S. Afr.	71b	26.10 S	28.20 E
North Merrick, NY	55	40.41 N	73.34 W
Northmoor, Mo. (nôth'mōōr)	119f	39.10 N	94.37 W
North Moose L., Can.	101	54.09 N	100.20 W
North Mount Lofty Ranges, Austl.	216	33.50 S	138.30 E
North Ockendon (Neigh.), Eng.	62	51.32 N	0.18 E
North Ogden, Ut. (ŏg'dĕn)	119b	41.18 N	111.58 W
North Ogden Pk., Ut.	119b	41.23 N	111.59 W
North Olmsted, Oh. (ōlm-stĕd)	113d	41.25 N	81.55 W
North Parramatta, Austl.	70a	33.48 S	151.00 E
North Pease (R.), Tx. (pēz)	122	34.19 N	100.58 W
North Pender (I.), Can. (pĕn'dēr)	118d	48.48 N	123.16 W
North Philadelphia (Neigh.), Pa.	56b	39.58 N	75.09 W
North Plains, Or. (plānz)	118c	45.36 N	123.00 W
North Platte, Ne. (plăt)	114	41.08 N	100.45 W
North Platte, (R.), U. S.	108	41.20 N	102.40 W
North Point, Hong Kong	68c	22.17 N	114.12 E
Northport, Al. (nôrth'pōrt)	126	33.12 N	87.35 W
Northport, NY	112a	40.53 N	73.20 W
Northport, Wa.	116	48.53 N	117.47 W
North Pt., Barb.	133b	13.22 N	59.36 W
North Pt., Mi.	110	45.00 N	83.20 W
North Quincy, Ma.	54a	42.17 N	71.01 W
North Randolph, Ma.	54a	42.12 N	71.04 W
North Reading, Ma. (rĕd'ĭng)	105a	42.34 N	71.04 W
North Rhine-Westphalia (State), see Nordrhein-Westfalen			
North Richland Hills, Tx.	119c	32.50 N	97.13 W
North Richmond, Ca.	58b	37.57 N	122.22 W
Northridge, Ca. (nôrth'ridj)	119a	34.14 N	118.32 W
North Ridgeville, Oh. (rĭj-vĭl)	113d	41.23 N	82.01 W
North Riverside, Il.	58a	41.51 N	87.49 W
North Royalton, Oh. (roi'ăl-tŭn)	113d	41.19 N	81.44 W
North Ryde, Austl.	70a	33.48 S	151.07 E
North Saint Paul, Mn. (sånt pôl')	115g	45.01 N	92.59 W
North Saskatchewan (R.), Can. (săn-kăch'ē-wän)	100	52.40 N	106.45 W
North Sea, Eur.	158	56.09 N	3.16 E
North Side (Neigh.), Pa.	57b	40.28 N	80.01 W
North Skunk (R.), Ia. (skŭnk)	115	41.39 N	92.46 W
North Springfield, Va.	56d	38.48 N	77.13 W
North Stradbroke I., Austl. (străd'brōk)	215	27.45 S	154.18 E
North Sydney, Austl.	70a	33.50 S	151.13 E
North Sydney, Can. (sĭd'nē)	105	46.13 N	60.15 W
North Taranaki Bight, N. Z. (tä-rȧ-nä'kĭ bīt)	217	38.40 S	174.00 E
North Tarrytown, NY (tăr'ĭ-toun)	112a	41.05 N	73.52 W
North Thompson (R.), Can.	99	50.50 N	120.10 W
North Tonawanda, NY (tŏn-ȧ-wŏn'dȧ)	113c	43.02 N	78.53 W
North Truchas Pks. (Mts.), NM (trōō'chäs)	205	37.18 N	137.03 E
North Twillingate (I.), Can. (twĭl'ĭn-gāt)	121	35.58 N	105.37 W
North Uist (I.), Scot. (ū'ĭst)	162	57.37 N	7.22 W
Northumberland, NH	111	44.30 N	71.30 W
Northumberland, Is., Austl.	215	21.42 S	151.30 E
Northumberland Str., Can. (nôr thŭm'bēr-lȧnd)	104	46.25 N	64.20 W
North Umpqua R., Or. (ŭmp'kwȧ)	116	43.20 N	122.50 W
North Valley Stream, NY	55	40.41 N	73.41 W
North Vancouver, Can. (văn-kōō'vēr)	118d	49.19 N	123.04 W
North Vernon, In. (vûr'nŭn)	110	39.05 N	85.45 W
North Versailles, Pa.	57b	40.22 N	79.48 W
Northville, Mi. (nôrth-vĭl)	113b	42.26 N	83.28 W
North Wales, Pa. (wālz)	112f	40.12 N	75.16 W
North Weald Bassett, Eng.	62	51.43 N	0.10 E
North West C., Austl. (nôrth'wĕst)	214	21.50 S	112.25 E
Northwest Cape Fear, (R.), NC (cāp fēr)	127	34.34 N	79.46 W
Northwestern University (P. Int.), Il.	58a	42.04 N	87.40 W
North West Gander (R.), Can. (găn'dēr)	105	48.40 N	55.15 W
Northwest Har., Md.	56c	39.16 N	76.35 W
Northwest Highlands, Scot.	162	56.50 N	5.20 W
Northwest Providence Chan., Ba. (prŏv'ĭ-dĕns)	134	26.15 N	78.45 W
Northwest Territories, Can. (tĕr'ĭ-tō'rĭs)	96	64.42 N	119.09 W
North Weymouth, Ma.	54a	42.15 N	70.57 W
Northwich, Eng. (nôrth'wĭch)	163	53.15 N	2.31 W
North Wilkesboro, NC (wĭlks'bûrô)	127	36.08 N	81.10 W
North Wilmington, Ma.	54a	42.34 N	71.10 W
Northwood, Ia. (nôrth'wōōd)	115	43.26 N	93.13 W
Northwood, ND	114	47.44 N	97.36 W
Northwood (Neigh.), Eng.	62	51.37 N	0.25 W
North Wood Cr., Wy.	117	44.02 N	107.37 W
North Yamhill (R.), Or. (yăm' hĭl)	118c	45.22 N	123.21 W
North York, Can.	95d	43.47 N	79.25 W
North York Moors, Eng. (yôrk mōōrz')	162	54.20 N	0.40 W
North Yorkshire (Co.), Eng.	156	53.50 N	1.10 W
Norton, Ks. (nôr'tŭn)	122	39.40 N	99.54 W
Norton, Ma.	112b	41.58 N	71.08 W
Norton, Va.	127	36.54 N	82.36 W
Norton B., Ak.	107	64.22 N	162.18 W
Norton Heath, Eng.	62	51.43 N	0.19 E
Norton Res., Ma.	112b	42.01 N	71.07 W
Norton Sd., Ak.	107	63.48 N	164.50 W
Norval, Can. (nôr'vål)	95d	43.39 N	79.52 W
Norwalk, Ca. (nôr'wôk)	119a	33.54 N	118.05 W
Norwalk, Ct.	112a	41.06 N	73.25 W
Norwalk, Oh.	110	41.15 N	82.35 W
Norway, Eur. (nôr'wā)	154	63.48 N	11.17 E
Norway, Me.	104	44.11 N	70.35 W
Norway, Mi.	115	45.47 N	87.55 W
Norway House, Can.	101	53.59 N	97.50 W
Norwegian Sea, Eur. (nôr-wē'jăn)	158	66.54 N	1.43 E
Norwell, Ma. (nôr'wĕl)	105a	42.10 N	70.47 W
Norwich, Ct. (nôr'wĭch)	111	41.20 N	72.00 W
Norwich, Eng.	163	52.40 N	1.15 E
Norwich, NY	111	42.35 N	75.30 W
Norwood, Ma. (nôr'wōōd)	105a	42.11 N	71.13 W
Norwood, NC	127	35.15 N	80.08 W
Norwood, Oh.	113f	39.10 N	84.27 W
Norwood, Pa.	56b	39.53 N	75.18 W
Norwood Park (Neigh.), Il.	58a	41.59 N	87.48 W
Nose (Neigh.), Jap.	69b	34.49 N	135.09 E
Nose Cr., Can. (nōz)	95e	51.09 N	114.02 W
Noshiro, Jap. (nō'shē-rō)	204	40.09 N	140.02 E

ăt; finăl; rāte; senåte; ärm; ȧsk; sofȧ; fâre; ch-choose; dh-as th in other; bē; ēvent; bĕt; recĕnt; cratēr; g-gō; gh-guttural g; bĭt; ĭ-short neutral; rīde; K-guttural k as ch in German ich;

PRONOUNCING INDEX
Nosovka – Oberwengern 323

PLACE (Pronounciation)	PAGE	Lat. °′	Long. °′
Nosovka, Sov. Un. (nô'sôf-kà)	175	50.54 N	31.35 E
Nossa Senhora do Ó (Neigh.), Braz.	61d	23.30 S	46.41 W
Nossob (R.), Namibia (nŏ'sŏb)	226	24.15 S	19.10 E
Noteć R., Pol. (nô'tĕcn)	166	52.50 N	16.19 E
Noto, It. (nô'tô)	159	36.49 N	15.08 E
Notodden, Nor. (nōt'ôd'n)	164	59.35 N	9.15 E
Noto-Hantō (Pen.), Jap. (nô'tō hän'tō)	205	37.18 N	137.03 E
Notre-Dame (P. Int.), Fr.	64c	48.51 N	2.21 E
Notre Dame B., Can. (nō't'r dàm')	105	49.45 N	55.15 W
Notre-Dame-des-Victoires (Neigh.), Can.	54b	45.35 N	73.34 W
Notre-Dame-du-Lac, Can.	104	47.37 N	68.51 W
Notre Dame, Monts (Mts.), Can.	104	46.35 N	70.35 W
Nottawasaga B., Can. (nŏt'á-wá-sä'gá)	110	44.45 N	80.35 W
Nottaway (R.), Can. (nôt'á-wā)	97	50.58 N	78.02 W
Nottingham, Eng. (nŏt'ĭng-ăm)	156	52.58 N	1.09 W
Nottingham, Pa.	56b	40.07 N	74.58 W
Nottingham I., Can.	97	62.58 N	78.53 W
Nottingham Park, Il.	58a	41.46 N	87.48 W
Nottinghamshire (Co.), Eng.	156	53.03 N	1.05 W
Notting Hill, Austl.	70b	37.54 S	145.08 E
Nottoway, (R.), Va. (nôt'á-wā)	127	36.53 N	77.47 W
Notukeu Cr., Can.	100	49.55 N	106.30 W
Nouadhibou, Mauritania	224	21.02 N	17.09 W
Nouakchott, Mauritania	228	18.06 N	15.57 W
Nouamrhar, Mauritania	228	19.22 N	16.31 W
Noumea, N. Cal. (nōō-mā'ä)	215	22.18 S	166.48 E
Nouvelle, Can. (nōō-vĕl')	104	48.09 N	66.22 W
Nouvelle-France, Cap de (C.), Can.	97	62.03 N	74.00 W
Nouzonville, Fr. (nōō-zôN-vēl')	168	49.51 N	4.43 E
Nova Cachoeirinha (Neigh.), Braz.	61d	23.28 S	46.40 W
Nova Cruz, Braz. (nō'vá-krōō'z)	143	6.22 S	35.20 W
Nova Friburgo, Braz. (frē-bōōr'gōō)	141a	22.18 S	42.31 W
Nova Gaia, Ang.	230	10.09 S	17.31 E
Nova Iguaçu, Braz. (nō'vä-ē-gwä-sōō')	144b	22.45 S	43.27 W
Nova Lima, Braz. (lē'mä)	141a	19.59 S	43.51 W
Nova Lisboa, see Huambo			
Nova Mambone, Moz. (nō'vá-màm-bō'nĕ)	226	21.04 S	35.13 E
Novara, It. (nô-vä'rä)	172	45.24 N	8.38 E
Nova Resende, Braz.	141a	21.12 S	46.25 W
Nova Scotia (Prov.), Can. (skō'shà)	97	44.28 N	65.00 W
Novate Milanese, It.	65c	45.32 N	9.08 E
Nova Varoš, Yugo. (nô'vä vä'rôsh)	173	43.24 N	19.53 E
Novaya Ladoga, Sov. Un. (nô'vá-ya lá-dô-gá)	165	60.06 N	32.16 E
Novaya Lyalya, Sov. Un. (lyá'lyá)	182a	59.03 N	60.36 E
Novaya Odessa, Sov. Un. (ô-dĕs'ä)	175	47.18 N	31.48 E
Novaya Praga, Sov. Un. (prä'gá)	175	48.34 N	32.54 E
Novaya Sibir (I.), Sov. Un. (sē-bēr')	181	75.42 N	150.00 E
Novaya Vodolaga, Sov. Un. (vô-dôl'á-gá)	175	49.43 N	35.51 E
Novaya Zemlya (I.), Sov. Un. (zĕm-lyá')	180	72.00 N	54.46 E
Nova Zagora, Bul. (zä'gô-rá)	173	42.30 N	26.01 E
Novelda, Sp. (nō-vĕl'dá)	171	38.22 N	0.46 W
Nové Mesto nad Váhom, Czech. (nô'vĕ myĕs'tô)	167	48.44 N	17.47 E
Nové Zámky, Czech. (zám'kĕ)	167	47.58 N	18.10 E
Novgorod, Sov. Un. (nôv'gô-rôt)	174	58.32 N	31.16 E
Novgorod (Oblast), Sov. Un.	174	58.27 N	31.55 E
Novgorod-Severskiy, Sov. Un.	175	52.01 N	33.14 E
Novi, Mi. (nō'vĭ)	113b	42.29 N	83.28 W
Novigrad, Yugo. (nō'vĭ gràd)	172	44.09 N	15.34 E
Novi Ligure, It. (nô'vē)	172	44.43 N	8.48 E
Novinger, Mo. (nŏv'ĭn-jēr)	123	40.14 N	92.43 W
Novi Pazar, Bul. (pá-zär')	173	43.22 N	27.26 E
Novi Pazar, Yugo. (pá-zär')	173	43.08 N	20.30 E
Novi Sad, Yugo. (säd')	173	45.15 N	19.53 E
Novoarchangel'skoje, Sov. Un.	66b	55.55 N	37.33 E
Novoasbest, Sov. Un. (nô-vô-äs-bĕst')	182a	57.43 N	60.14 E
Novoaydar, Sov. Un. (nô'vô-ī-där')	175	48.57 N	39.01 E
Novocherkassk, Sov. Un. (nô'vô-chĕr-kásk')	175	47.25 N	40.04 E
Novochovrino (Neigh.), Sov. Un.	66b	55.52 N	37.30 E
Novogirejevo (Neigh.), Sov. Un.	66b	55.45 N	37.49 E
Novogrudok, Sov. Un. (nô-vô-grōō'dôk)	167	53.35 N	25.51 E
Novo-Kazalinsk, Sov. Un. (nô-vŭ-kŭ-zá-lyēnsk')	176	45.47 N	62.00 E
Novokuznetsk (Stalinsk), Sov. Un. (nō'vô-kōō'z-nyĕ'tsk) (stá'lēnsk)	180	53.43 N	86.59 E
Novoladozhskiy Kanal (Can.), Sov. Un. (nô-vô-lä'dôzh-skĭ ká-näl')	182c	59.54 N	31.19 E
Novo Mesto, Yugo. (nôvô mās'tô)	172	45.48 N	15.13 E
Novomirgorod, Sov. Un. (nô'vô-mēr'gô-rôt)	175	48.46 N	31.44 E
Novomoskovsk, Sov. Un. (nô'vô-môs-kôfsk')	174	54.06 N	38.08 E
Novomoskovsk, Sov. Un.	175	48.37 N	35.12 E
Novonikol'skiy, Sov. Un. (nô'vô-nyĭ-kôl'skĭ)	182a	52.28 N	57.12 E
Novorossiysk, Sov. Un. (nô'vô-rô-sēsk')	175	44.43 N	37.48 E
Novorzhev, Sov. Un. (nô'vô-rzhĕv')	174	57.01 N	29.17 E
Novo-Selo, Bul. (nô'vô-sĕ'lô)	173	44.09 N	22.46 E
Novosibirsk, Sov. Un. (nô'vô-sē-bērsk')	180	55.09 N	82.58 E
Novosibirskiye O-va (New Siberian Is.), Sov. Un. (no'vŭ-sĭ-bĭr'skē-ē)	181	76.45 N	140.30 E
Novosil', Sov. Un. (nô'vô-sĭl)	174	52.58 N	37.03 E
Novosokol'niki, Sov. Un. (nô'vô-sô-kôl'nē-kē)	174	56.18 N	30.07 E
Novotatishchevskiy, Sov. Un. (nô'vô-tá-tyĭsh'chĕv-skĭ)	182a	53.22 N	60.24 E
Novoukrainka, Sov. Un.	175	48.18 N	31.33 E
Novouzensk, Sov. Un. (nô-vô-ōō-zĕnsk')	179	50.40 N	48.08 E
Novozybkov, Sov. Un. (nô'vô-zēp'kôf)	174	52.31 N	31.54 E
Nový Jičín, Czech. (nô'vē yē'chēn)	167	49.36 N	18.02 E
Novyy Bug, Sov. Un. (bōōk)	175	47.43 N	32.33 E
Novyy Oskol, Sov. Un. (ôs-kôl')	175	50.46 N	37.53 E
Novyy Port, Sov. Un. (nô'vē)	180	67.19 N	72.28 E
Nowa Sól, Pol. (nô'vá sül')	166	51.49 N	15.41 E
Nowata, Ok. (nô-wä'tá)	123	36.42 N	95.38 W
Nowra, Austl. (nou'rá)	216	34.55 S	150.45 E
Nowy Dwór Mazowiecki, Pol. (nō'vĭ dvōōr mä-zo-vyĕts'ke)	167	52.26 N	20.46 E
Nowy Sacz, Pol. (nô'vē sôNch')	167	49.36 N	20.42 E
Nowy Targ, Pol. (tärk')	167	49.29 N	20.02 E
Noxon Res., Mt.	116	47.50 N	115.40 W
Noxubee (R.), Ms. (nŏks'ū-bē)	126	33.20 N	88.55 W
Noya, Sp. (no'yä)	170	42.46 N	8.50 W
Noyes I., Ak. (noiz)	98	55.30 N	133.40 W
Nozaki, Jap. (nō'zä-kē)	205b	34.43 N	135.39 E
Nozuta, Jap.	69a	35.35 N	139.27 E
No. 1, Canal, Arg.	141c	36.43 S	58.14 W
No. 9, Canal, Arg.	141c	36.22 S	58.19 W
No. 12, Canal, Arg.	141c	36.47 S	57.20 W
Nqamakwe, S. Afr. ('n-gä-mä'kwå)	227c	32.13 S	27.57 E
Nqutu, S. Afr. ('n-kōō'tōō)	227c	28.17 S	30.41 E
Nsawam, Ghana	228	5.50 N	0.20 W
Nsouélé, Con.	71c	4.12 S	15.11 E
Nsukka, Nig.	229	6.52 N	7.24 E
Ntshoni (Mtn.), S. Afr.	227c	29.34 S	30.03 E
Ntwetwe Pan (Salt Flat), Bots.	226	20.00 S	24.18 E
Nu (Salween) (R.), China (nōō)	198	30.08 N	96.38 E
Nubah, Jibāl an-(Mts.), Sud.	225	12.22 N	30.39 E
Nubian Des., Sud. (nōō'bĭ-ăn)	225	21.13 N	33.09 E
Nudo Coropuna (Mt.), Peru (nōō'dô kō-rō-pōō'nä)	142	15.53 S	72.04 W
Nudo de Pasco (Mt.), Peru (dĕ päs'kô)	142	10.34 S	76.12 W
Nueces R., Tx. (nû-ā'sås)	124	28.20 N	98.08 W
Nueltin (L.), Can. (nwĕl'tin)	96	60.14 N	101.00 W
Nueva Armenia, Hond. (nwä'vä är-mä'nē-á)	132	15.47 N	86.32 W
Nueva Atzacoalco, Mex.	60a	19.29 N	99.05 W
Nueva Chicago (Neigh.), Arg.	60d	34.40 S	58.30 W
Nueva Coronela, Cuba	60b	23.04 N	82.28 W
Nueva Esparta (State), Ven. (nwĕ'vä ĕs-pä'r-tä)	143b	10.50 N	64.35 W
Nueva Gerona, Cuba (kĕ-rô'nä)	134	21.55 N	82.45 W
Nueva Palmira, Ur. (päl-mē'rä)	141c	33.53 S	58.23 W
Nueva Rosita, Mex. (nōōĕ'vä rô-sĕ'tä)	108	27.55 N	101.10 W
Nueva San Salvador (Santa Tecla), Sal. (sän' säl-vá-dōr) (sän'tä tĕ'klä)	132	13.41 N	89.16 W
Nueve de Julio, Arg. (nwā'vå dā hōō'lyô)	141c	35.26 S	60.51 W
Nuevitas, Cuba (nwä-vē'tás)	134	21.35 N	77.15 W
Nuevitas, Bahía de, Cuba (bä-ē'ä dĕ nwä-vē'täs)	134	21.30 N	77.05 W
Nuevo, Ca. (nwā'vō)	119a	33.48 N	117.09 W
Nuevo Laredo, Mex. (lä-rā'dhō)	124	27.29 N	99.30 W
Nuevo Leon (State), Mex. (lå-ōn')	128	26.00 N	100.00 W
Nuevo San Juan, Pan. (nwĕ'vô sän kōō-ä'n)	128a	9.14 N	79.43 W
Nugumanovo, Sov. Un. (nû-gû-mä'nô-vô)	182a	55.28 N	61.50 E
Nulato, Ak. (nōō-lä'tō)	107	64.40 N	158.18 W
Nullagine, Austl. (nŭ-lă'jēn)	214	22.00 S	120.07 E
Nullarbor Plain (Reg.), Austl. (nŭ-lär'bôr)	214	31.45 S	126.30 E
Numabin B., Can. (nōō-mä'bĭn)	100	56.30 N	103.08 W
Numansdorp, Neth.	157a	51.43 N	4.25 E
Numazu, Jap. (nōō'mä-zōō)	205	35.06 N	138.55 E
Numfoor, Pulau (I.), Indon.	207	1.20 S	134.48 E
Nun (R.), Nig.	229	5.05 N	6.10 E
Nunawading, Austl.	70b	37.49 S	145.10 E
Nuneaton, Eng. (nŭn'ē-tŭn)	156	52.31 N	1.28 W
Nunivak (I.), Ak. (nōō'nĭ-văk)	107	60.25 N	167.42 W
Nunkiní, Mex. (nōōn-kē-nē')	132a	20.19 N	90.14 W
Ñuñoa, Chile	61b	33.28 S	70.36 W
Nunyama, Sov. Un. (nûn-yä'má)	107	65.49 N	170.32 W
Nuoro, It. (nwô'rō)	172	40.29 N	9.20 E
Nura (R.), Sov. Un. (nōō'rä)	180	49.48 N	73.54 E
Nurata, Sov. Un. (nōōr'ät'á)	180	40.33 N	65.28 E
Nürnberg, F.R.G. (nürn'bĕrgh)	166	49.28 N	11.07 E
Nurse Cay (I.), Ba.	135	22.30 N	75.50 W
Nusabyin, Tur. (nōō'sĭ-bēn)	179	37.05 N	41.10 E
Nushagak (R.), Ak. (nū-shă-găk')	107	59.28 N	157.40 W
Nushan Hu (L.), China (nü'shän hōō)	200	32.50 N	117.59 E
Nushki, Pak. (nŭsh'kē)	193	29.30 N	66.02 E
Nussdorf (Neigh.), Aus.	66e	48.15 N	16.22 E
Nuthe R., G.D.R. (nōō'tĕ)	157b	52.15 N	13.11 E
Nutley, NJ (nŭt'lē)	112a	40.49 N	74.09 W
Nutter Fort, WV (nŭt'ēr fôrt)	111	39.15 N	80.15 W
Nutwood, Il. (nŭt'wŏŏd)	119e	39.05 N	90.34 W
Nuwaybi 'al Muzayyinah, Egypt	191a	28.59 N	34.40 E
Nuweland, S. Afr.	226a	33.58 S	18.28 E
Nyack, NY (nī'ăk)	112a	41.05 N	73.55 W
Nyaiqêntanglha Shan (Mts.), China (nyä-ĭn-chyŭn-täŋ-lä shän)	198	29.55 N	88.08 E
Nyakanazi, Tan.	231	3.00 S	31.15 E
Nyala, Sud.	225	12.00 N	24.52 E
Nyanga (R.), Gabon	230	2.45 S	10.30 E
Nyanza, Rw.	231	2.21 S	29.45 E
Nyasa, L. (Malawi, L.), Afr. (nyä'sä)	231	10.45 S	34.30 E
Nyazepetrovsk, Sov. Un. (nyä'zĕ-pĕ-trôvsk')	182a	56.04 N	59.38 E
Nyborg, Den. (nü'bôr'')	164	55.20 N	10.45 E
Nybro, Swe. (nü'brō)	164	56.44 N	15.56 E
Nyeri, Ken.	231	0.25 S	36.57 E
Nyika Plat, Malawi	231	10.30 S	35.50 E
Nyíregyháza, Hung. (nyē'rĕd-y'hä'zä)	167	47.58 N	21.45 E
Nykøbing, Den. (nü'kû-bĭng)	164	56.46 N	8.47 E
Nykøbing, Den.	164	54.45 N	11.54 E
Nykøbing Sjaelland, Den.	164	55.55 N	11.37 E
Nyköping, Swe. (nü'chû-pĭng)	164	58.46 N	16.58 E
Nylstroom, S. Afr. (nĭl'strōm)	223d	24.42 S	28.25 E
Nymagee, Austl. (nī-mà-gē')	216	32.17 S	146.18 E
Nymburk, Czech. (nĕm'bŏŏrk)	166	50.12 N	15.03 E
Nynäshamn, Swe. (nü-nĕs-hàm'n)	164	58.53 N	17.55 E
Nyngan, Austl. (nĭŋ'gán)	216	31.31 S	147.25 E
Nyong (R.), Cam. (nyông)	229	3.40 N	10.25 E
Nyou, Burkina	228	12.46 N	1.56 W
Nyrány, Czech. (nĕr-zhä'nĕ)	166	49.43 N	13.13 E
Nysa, Pol. (nē'sá)	167	50.29 N	17.20 E
Nystad, see Uusikaupunki			
Nytva, Sov. Un.	178	58.00 N	55.10 E
Nyungwe, Malawi	231	10.16 S	34.07 E
Nyunzu, Zaire	231	5.57 S	28.01 E
Nyuya (R.), Sov. Un. (nyōō'yá)	181	60.30 N	111.45 E
Nzega, Tan.	231	4.13 S	33.11 E
Nzérékoré, Gui.	228	7.45 N	8.49 W
Nzeto, Ang.	230	7.14 S	12.52 E
Nzi (R.), Ivory Coast	228	7.00 N	4.27 W

O

PLACE (Pronounciation)	PAGE	Lat. °′	Long. °′
Oahe Dam, SD (ō-á-hē)	114	44.28 N	100.34 W
Oahe Res., SD	114	45.20 N	100.00 W
Oahu (I.), Hi. (ō-ä'hōō) (ō-ä'hü)	106a	21.38 N	157.48 W
Oak Bay, Can.	98	48.27 N	123.18 W
Oak Bluff, Can. (ōk blŭf)	95f	49.47 N	97.21 W
Oak Creek, Co. (ōk krēk')	117	40.20 N	106.50 W
Oakdale, Ca. (ōk'dāl)	120	37.45 N	120.52 W
Oakdale, Ky.	110	38.15 N	85.50 W
Oakdale, La.	125	30.49 N	92.40 W
Oakdale, Pa.	113e	40.24 N	80.11 W
Oakengates, Eng. (ōk'ĕn-gāts)	156	52.41 N	2.27 W
Oakes, ND (ōks)	114	46.10 N	98.50 W
Oakfield, Me. (ōk'fēld)	104	46.08 N	68.10 W
Oakford, Pa. (ōk'fōrd)	112f	40.08 N	74.58 W
Oak Forest, Il.	58a	41.36 N	87.45 W
Oak Grove, Or. (grōv)	118c	45.25 N	122.38 W
Oakham, Eng. (ōk'ăm)	156	52.40 N	0.38 W
Oakharbor, Oh. (ōk'här'bēr)	110	41.30 N	83.05 W
Oak Harbor, Wa.	118a	48.18 N	122.39 W
Oakland, Ca. (ōk'lănd)	118b	37.48 N	122.16 W
Oakland, Md.	56d	38.52 N	76.55 W
Oakland, Ne.	114	41.50 N	96.28 W
Oakland (Neigh.), Pa.	57b	40.26 N	79.58 W
Oakland City, In.	110	38.20 N	87.20 W
Oakland Gardens (Neigh.), NY	55	40.45 N	73.45 W
Oaklawn, Il. (ōk'lôn)	113a	41.43 N	87.45 W
Oakleigh, Austl. (ōk'lå)	211a	37.54 S	145.05 E
Oakleigh South, Austl.	70b	37.56 S	145.05 E
Oakley, Id. (ōk'lĭ)	117	42.15 N	135.53 W
Oakley, Ks.	122	39.08 N	100.49 W
Oakman, Al. (ōk'măn)	126	33.42 N	87.20 W
Oakmont, Pa. (ōk'mōnt)	113e	40.31 N	79.50 W
Oak Mtn., Al.	112h	33.22 N	86.42 W
Oak Park, Il. (pärk)	113a	41.53 N	87.48 W
Oak Park, Mi.	57c	42.28 N	83.11 W
Oak Point, Wa.	118c	46.11 N	123.11 W
Oak Ridge, Tn. (rĭj)	126	36.01 N	84.15 W
Oak View, Md.	56d	39.01 N	76.59 W
Oakview, NJ	56b	39.51 N	75.09 W
Oakville, Can. (ōk'vĭl)	95d	43.27 N	79.40 W
Oakville, Can.	95f	49.56 N	97.58 W
Oakville, Mo.	119e	38.27 N	90.18 W
Oakville Cr., Can.	95d	43.34 N	79.54 W
Oakwood, Oh.	56a	41.06 N	84.23 W
Oakwood, Tx. (ōk'wŏŏd)	125	31.36 N	95.48 W
Oatley, Austl.	70a	33.59 S	151.05 E
Oatman, Az. (ōt'măn)	121	34.00 N	114.25 W
Oaxaca (State), Mex. (wä-hä'kä)	128	16.45 N	97.00 W
Oaxaca de Juárez, Mex. (kōōá'rĕz)	131	17.03 N	96.42 W
Oaxaca, Sierra de (Mts.), Mex. (sē-ĕ'r-rä dĕ)	131	16.15 N	97.25 W
Ob' (R.), Sov. Un.	180	62.15 N	67.00 E
Oba, Can. (ō'bá)	102	48.58 N	84.09 W
Obama, Jap. (ō'bá-mä)	205	35.29 N	135.44 E
Oban, Scot. (ō'băn)	162	56.25 N	5.35 W
Oban Hills, Nig.	229	5.35 N	8.30 E
O'Bannon, Ky. (ō-băn'nŏn)	113h	38.17 N	85.30 W
Obatogamau (L.), Can. (ō-bá-tō'găm-ô)	103	49.38 N	74.10 W
Oberbauer, F.R.G.	63	51.17 N	7.26 E
Oberbonsfeld, F.R.G.	63	51.22 N	7.08 E
Oberelfringhausen, F.R.G.	63	51.20 N	7.11 E
Oberhaan, F.R.G.	63	51.13 N	7.02 E
Oberhausen, F.R.G. (ō'bĕr-hou'zĕn)	169c	51.27 N	6.51 E
Ober-Kassel (Neigh.), F.R.G.	63	51.14 N	6.46 E
Ober-kirchbach, Aus.	66e	48.17 N	16.12 E
Oberlaa (Neigh.), Aus.	66e	48.08 N	16.24 E
Oberlin, Ks. (o'bēr-lĭn)	122	39.49 N	100.30 W
Oberlin, Oh.	110	41.15 N	82.15 W
Oberösterreich (Prov.), Aus.	166	48.05 N	13.15 E
Oberroth, F.R.G. (ō'bĕr-rōt)	157d	48.19 N	11.20 E
Ober Sankt Veit (Neigh.), Aus.	66e	48.11 N	16.16 E
Oberschöneweide (Neigh.), G.D.R.	65a	52.28 N	13.31 E
Oberwengern, F.R.G.	63	51.23 N	7.22 E

PLACE (Pronounciation)	PAGE	Lat. °′	Long. °′
Obgruiten, F.R.G.	63	51.13 N	7.01 E
Óbidos, Braz. (ỏ'bĕ-dōōzh)	143	1.57 s	55.32 w
Obihiro, Jap. (ỏ'bē-hē'rō)	204	42.55 N	142.50 E
Obi, Kepulauan (Is.), Indon. (ỏ'bĕ)	207	1.25 s	128.15 E
Obion (R.), Tn.	126	36.10 N	89.25 w
Obion (R.), North Fk., Tn. (ỏ-bī'ŏn)	126	35.49 N	89.06 w
Obi, Pulau (I.), Indon.	207	1.30 s	127.45 E
Obitochnaya, Kosa (C.), Sov. Un. (kô-sä' ỏ-bē-tôch'nà-yá)	175	46.32 N	36.07 E
Obitsu (R.), Jap. (ỏ'bĕt'sōō)	205a	35.19 N	140.03 E
Obock, Djibouti (ỏ-bòk')	223a	11.55 N	43.15 E
Obol' (R.), Sov. Un.	174	55.24 N	29.24 E
Oboyan, Sov. Un. (ỏ-bỏ-yän')	175	51.14 N	36.16 E
Obskaya Guba (B.), Sov. Un.	180	67.13 N	73.45 E
Obu (Neigh.), Jap.	69b	34.44 N	135.09 E
Obuasi, Ghana	228	6.14 N	1.39 w
Obukhov, Sov. Un. (ỏ'bōō-κôf)	175	50.07 N	30.36 E
Obukhovo, Sov. Un.	182b	55.50 N	38.17 E
Očakovo (Neigh.), Sov. Un.	66b	55.41 N	37.27 E
Ocala, Fl. (ỏ-kä'lá)	127	29.11 N	82.09 w
Ocampo, Mex. (ỏ-käm'pō)	130	22.49 N	99.23 w
Ocaña, Col. (ỏ-kän'yä)	142	8.15 N	73.37 w
Ocaña, Sp. (ỏ-kä'n-yä)	170	39.58 N	3.31 w
Occidental, Cordillera (Mts.), Col. (kôr-dĕl-yĕ'rä ôk-sĕ-dĕn-täl')	142a	5.05 N	76.04 w
Occidental, Cordillera (Mts.), Peru	142	10.12 s	76.58 w
Occidental, Grand Erg (Dunes), Alg.	224	29.30 N	00.45 w
Occidental, Sierra Madre (Mts.), Mex. (sĕ-ĕ'r-rä-mä'drĕ-ôk-sĕ-dĕn-tä'l)	128	29.30 N	107.30 w
Ocean Beach, Ca. (ỏ'shän bēch)	120a	32.44 N	117.14 w
Ocean Bight (B.), Ba.	125	21.15 N	73.15 w
Ocean City, Md.	111	38.20 N	75.10 w
Ocean City, NJ	111	39.15 N	74.35 w
Ocean Falls, Can. (Fôls)	98	52.21 N	127.40 w
Ocean Grove, Austl.	211a	38.16 s	144.32 E
Ocean Grove, NJ (grōv)	111	40.10 N	74.00 w
Oceanside, Ca. (ỏ'shän-sīd)	120	33.11 N	117.22 w
Oceanside, NY	112a	40.38 N	73.39 w
Ocean Springs, Ms. (sprĭngs)	126	30.25 N	88.49 w
Ocenele Mari, Rom.	173	45.05 N	24.17 E
Ochakov, Sov. Un. (ỏ-chä'kôf)	175	46.38 N	31.33 E
Ochiai (Neigh.), Jap.	69a	35.43 N	139.42 E
Ochlockonee R., Fl.-Ga. (ỏk-lỏ-kỏ'nē)	126	30.10 N	84.38 w
Ocilla, Ga. (ỏ-sĭl'á)	126	31.36 N	83.15 w
Ockelbo, Swe. (ôk'ĕl-bỏ)	164	60.54 N	16.35 E
Ockham, Eng.	62	51.18 N	0.27 w
Ocmulgee (R.), Ga.	127	32.25 N	83.30 w
Ocmulgee Natl. Mon., Ga. (ỏk-mŭl'gē)	126	32.45 N	83.28 w
Ocna-Sibiului, Rom. (ôck'nä-sĕ-byōō-lōō-ĕ')	173	45.52 N	24.04 E
Ocoa, Bahai de (B.), Dom. Rep. (bä-ä'ĕ-ỏ-kỏ'ä)	135	18.20 N	70.40 w
Ococingo, Mex. (ỏ-kỏ-sĕ'n-gỏ)	131	17.03 N	92.18 w
Ocom, L., Mex. (ỏ-kỏ'm)	132a	19.26 N	88.18 w
Oconee, (R.), Ga. (ỏ-kỏ'nē)	126	32.45 N	83.00 w
Oconomowoc, Wi. (ỏ-kôn'ỏ-mỏ-wôk')	115	43.06 N	88.24 w
Oconto, Wi. (ỏ-kôn'tỏ)	115	44.54 N	87.55 w
Oconto (R.), Wi.	115	45.08 N	88.24 w
Oconto Falls, Wi.	115	44.53 N	88.11 w
Ocós, Guat. (ỏ-kỏs')	132	14.31 N	92.12 w
Ocotal, Nic. (ỏ-kỏ-täl')	132	13.36 N	86.31 w
Ocotepeque, Hond. (ỏ-kỏ-tå-pä'kå)	132	14.25 N	89.13 w
Ocotlán, Mex. (ỏ-kỏ-tlän')	130	20.19 N	102.44 w
Ocotlán de Morelos, Mex. (dä mỏ-rä'lōs)	131	16.46 N	96.41 w
Ocozocoautla, Mex. (ỏ-kỏ'zỏ-kwä-ōō'tlä)	131	16.44 N	93.22 w
Ocumare del Tuy, Ven. (ỏ-kōō-mä'ra del twĕ')	143b	10.07 N	66.47 w
Oda, Ghana	228	5.55 N	0.59 w
Odawara, Jap. (ỏ'dà-wä'rä)	205	35.15 N	139.10 E
Odda, Nor. (ôdh-ä)	164	60.04 N	6.30 E
Odebolt, Ia. (ỏ'dĕ-bôlt)	114	42.20 N	95.14 w
Odemira, Port. (ỏ-då-mē'rà)	170	37.35 N	8.40 w
Odemis, Tur. (ỏ-dĕ'mĕsh)	179	38.12 N	28.00 E
Odendaalsrus, S. Afr. (ỏ'dĕn-däls-rūs')	223d	27.52 s	26.41 E
Odense, Den. (ỏ'dhĕn-sĕ)	164	55.24 N	10.20 E
Odenton, Md. (ỏ'dĕn-tŭn)	112e	39.05 N	76.43 w
Odenwald (For.), F.R.G. (ỏ'dĕn-väld)	166	49.39 N	8.55 E
Oderhaff (L.), G.D.R.	166	53.47 N	14.02 E
Oder R., G.D.R. (ỏ'dĕr)	166	52.40 N	14.19 E
Odessa, Sov. Un. (ỏ-dĕs'á)	175	46.28 N	30.44 E
Odessa, Tx.	124	31.52 N	102.21 w
Odessa, Wa.	116	47.20 N	118.42 w
Odessa (Oblast), Sov. Un.	175	46.05 N	29.48 E
Odiel (R.), Sp. (ỏ-dĕ-ĕl')	170	37.47 N	6.42 w
Odienné, Ivory Coast	228	9.30 N	7.34 w
Odiham, Eng. (ỏd'ē-ám)	156b	51.14 N	0.56 w
Odintsovo, Sov. Un. (ỏ-dĕn'tsỏ-vỏ)	182b	55.40 N	37.16 E
Odiongan, Phil. (ỏ-dĕ-ỏn'gän)	207a	12.24 N	121.59 E
Odivelas, Port. (ỏ-dĕ-vä'lyäs)	171b	38.47 N	9.11 w
Odobesti, Rom. (ỏ-dỏ-bĕsh't')	167	45.46 N	27.08 E
O'Donnell, Tx. (ỏ-dön'ĕl)	122	32.59 N	101.51 w
Odorhei, Rom. (ỏ-dỏr-hä')	167	46.18 N	25.17 E
Odra R., Pol. (ỏ'drä)	167	50.28 N	17.55 E
Oeiras, Braz. (wå-ĕ-räzh')	143	7.05 s	42.01 w
Oeirás, Port. (ỏ-ĕ'y-rá's)	171b	38.42 N	9.18 w
Oella, Md.	56c	39.16 N	76.47 w
Oelwein, Ia. (ỏl'wīn)	115	42.40 N	91.56 w
Oespel (Neigh.), F.R.G.	63	51.30 N	7.23 E
Oestrich, F.R.G.	63	51.22 N	7.38 E
Oestrich (Neigh.), F.R.G.	63	51.34 N	7.22 E
Oestrum, F.R.G.	63	51.25 N	6.40 E
O'Fallon, Il. (ỏ-fäl'ŭn)	119e	38.36 N	89.55 w
O'Fallon Cr., Mt.	117	46.25 N	104.47 w
Ofanto (R.), It. (ỏ-fän'tỏ)	172	41.08 N	15.33 E
Offa, Nig.	229	8.09 N	4.44 E
Offenbach, F.R.G. (ôf'ĕn-bäk)	166	50.06 N	8.50 E
Offenburg, F.R.G. (ôf'ĕn-bōōrgh)	166	48.28 N	7.57 E
Ofin, Nig.	71d	6.33 N	3.30 E
Ofuna, Jap. (ỏ'fōō-nä)	205a	35.21 N	139.32 E
Ogaden Plat., Eth.	223a	6.45 N	44.53 E
Ogaki, Jap.	205	35.21 N	136.36 E
Ogallala, Ne. (ỏ-gä-lä'lä)	114	41.08 N	101.44 w
Ogawa, Jap.	69a	35.44 N	139.28 E
Ogbomosho, Nig. (ôg-bỏ-mỏ'shỏ)	229	8.08 N	4.15 E
Ogden, Ia. (ôg'dĕn)	115	42.10 N	94.20 w
Ogden, Ut.	119b	41.14 N	111.58 w
Ogden Pk., Ut.	119b	41.11 N	111.51 w
Ogden R., Ut.	119b	41.16 N	111.54 w
Ogdensburg, NJ (ôg'dĕnz-bûrg)	112a	41.05 N	74.36 w
Ogdensburg, NY	111	44.40 N	75.30 w
Ogeechee, (R.), Ga. (ỏ-gē'chĕ)	127	32.35 N	81.50 w
Ogies, S. Afr.	223d	26.03 s	29.04 E
Ogilvie Mts., Can. (ỏ'g'l-vĭ)	96	64.45 N	138.10 w
Oglesby, Il. (ỏ'g'lz-bĭ)	110	41.20 N	89.00 w
Oglio (R.), It. (ỏl'yỏ)	172	45.15 N	10.19 E
Ogo, Jap. (ỏ'gỏ)	205b	34.49 N	135.06 E
Ogooué (R.), Gabon	230	0.50 s	9.20 E
Ogou (R.), Togo	228	8.05 N	1.30 E
Ogoyo, Nig.	71d	6.26 N	3.29 E
Ogudnévo, Sov. Un. (ôg-ōōd-nyỏ'vỏ)	182b	56.04 N	38.17 E
Ogudu, Nig.	71d	6.34 N	3.24 E
Ogulin, Yugo. (ỏ-gōō-lēn')	172	45.17 N	15.11 E
Ogwashi-Uku, Nig.	229	6.10 N	6.31 E
O'Higgins (Prov.), Chile (ô-kĕ'gēns)	141b	34.17 s	70.52 w
Ohio, (State), U. S. (ỏ'hī'ỏ)	109	40.30 N	83.15 w
Ohio R., U. S.	110	37.25 N	88.05 w
Ohoopee (R.), Ga. (ỏ-hōō'pe-mc)	127	32.32 N	82.38 w
Ohře (R.), Czech. (ôr'zhĕ)	166	50.08 N	12.45 E
Ohrid, Yugo. (ỏ'κrĕd)	173	41.08 N	20.46 E
Ohrid, L., Alb.-Yugo.	173	40.58 N	20.35 E
Ôi, Jap. (oi')	205a	35.51 N	139.31 E
Oi-Gawa (Strm.), Jap. (ỏ'ĕ-gä'wä)	205	35.09 N	138.05 E
Oil City, Pa. (oil sĭ'tĭ)	111	41.25 N	79.40 w
Oirschot, Neth.	157a	51.30 N	5.20 E
Oise (R.), Fr. (wäz)	168	49.30 N	2.56 E
Oisterwijk, Neth.	157a	51.34 N	5.13 E
Oita, Jap. (ỏ'ē-tä)	205	33.14 N	131.38 E
Oji, Jap. (ỏ'jĕ)	205b	34.36 N	135.43 E
Ojinaga, Mex. (ỏ-κĕ-nä'gä)	124	29.34 N	104.26 w
Ojo Caliente, Mex. (ỏκô käl-yĕn'tå)	130	21.50 N	100.43 w
Ojocaliente, Mex. (ỏ-κô-kä-lyĕ'n-tĕ)	130	22.39 N	102.15 w
Ojo del Toro, Pico (Pk.), Cuba (pĕ'kỏ-ỏ-κỏ-dĕl-tỏ'rỏ)	134	19.55 N	77.25 w
Oka, Can. (ỏ-kä')	95a	45.28 N	74.05 w
Oka (R.), Sov. Un. (ỏ-kä')	178	55.10 N	42.10 E
Oka (R.), Sov. Un. (ỏ-kä')	179	52.10 N	35.20 E
Oka (R.), Sov. Un. (ỏ-kä')	180	53.28 N	101.09 E
Okahandja, Namibia	226	21.50 s	16.45 E
Okanagan L., Can.	99	50.00 N	119.28 w
Okanagan (R.), Can. (ỏ'kà-näg'án)	99	49.06 N	119.43 w
Okano (R.), Gabon (ỏ'kä'nỏ)	224	0.15 N	11.08 E
Okanogan, Wa.	116	48.20 N	119.34 w
Okanogan R., Wa.	116	48.36 N	119.33 w
Okatibbee (R.), Ms. (ỏ'kä-tĭb'ĕ)	126	32.37 N	88.54 w
Okatoma Cr., Ms. (ỏ-kä-tỏ'mä)	126	31.43 N	89.34 w
Okavango (Cubango) (R.), Ang. Namibia	226	17.10 s	18.20 E
Okavango Swp., Bots.	226	19.30 s	23.02 E
Okaya, Jap. (ỏ'kà-yä)	205	36.04 N	138.01 E
Okayama, Jap. (ỏ'kä-yä'mä)	205	34.39 N	133.54 E
Okazaki, Jap. (ỏ'kä-zä'kĕ)	205	34.58 N	137.09 E
Okeechobee, Fl. (ỏ-kĕ-chỏ'bē)	127	27.15 N	80.50 w
Okeechobee, L., Fl.	127a	27.00 N	80.49 w
O'Keefe Centre (P. Int.), Can.	54c	43.37 N	79.22 w
Okeene, Ok. (ỏ-kēn')	122	36.06 N	98.19 w
Okefenokee Swp., Ga. (ỏ'kĕ-fĕ-nỏ'kĕ)	127	30.54 N	82.20 w
Okemah, Ok. (ỏ-kĕ'mä)	123	35.26 N	96.18 w
Okene, Nig.	229	7.33 N	6.15 E
Oke Ogbe, Nig.	71d	6.24 N	3.23 E
Okha, Sov. Un. (ù-κä')	181	53.44 N	143.12 E
Okhotino, Sov. Un. (ỏ-κô'tĭ-nỏ)	182b	56.14 N	38.24 E
Okhotsk, Sov. Un. (ỏ-κôtsk')	181	59.28 N	143.32 E
Okhotsk, Sea of, Asia (ỏ-kôtsk')	191	56.45 N	146.00 E
Oki Guntō (Arch.), Jap. (ỏ'kĕ gōōn'tỏ)	205	36.17 N	133.05 E
Okinawa (I.), Jap. (ỏ'kĕ-nä'wä)	204	26.30 N	128.00 E
Okinawa Guntō (Is.), Jap. (gōōn'tỏ')	204	26.50 N	127.25 E
Okino (I.), Jap. (ỏ'kĕ)	205	36.22 N	133.27 E
Ôkino Erabu (I.), Jap. (ỏ-kĕ'nỏ-å-rä'bōō)	204	27.18 N	129.00 E
Oklahoma (State), U. S. (ỏ-klá-hỏ'mä)	108	36.00 N	98.20 w
Oklahoma City, Ok.	123	35.27 N	97.32 w
Oklawaha (R.), Fl. (ỏk-lá-wô'hỏ)	127	29.13 N	82.00 w
Okmulgee, Ok. (ỏk-mŭl'gē)	123	35.37 N	95.58 w
Okolona, Ky. (ỏ-kỏ-lỏ'ná)	113h	38.08 N	85.41 w
Okolona, Ms.	126	33.59 N	88.43 w
Okushiri (I.), Jap. (ỏ'koo-shē'rĕ)	204	42.12 N	139.30 E
Okuta, Nig.	229	9.14 N	3.15 E
Olalla, Wa. (ỏ-lä'lä)	118a	47.26 N	122.33 w
Olanchito, Hond. (ỏ'län-chē'tỏ)	132	15.28 N	86.35 w
Öland (I.), Swe. (ù-länd')	164	57.03 N	17.15 E
Olathe, Ks. (ỏ-lä'thĕ)	119f	38.53 N	94.49 w
Olavarría, Arg. (ỏ-lä-vär-rē'ä)	144	36.49 s	60.15 w
Oława, Pol (ỏ-lä'vä)	167	50.57 N	17.18 E
Olazoago, Arg. (ỏ-läz-kôä'gỏ)	141c	35.14 s	60.37 w
Olbia, It. (ỏ'l-byä)	172	40.55 N	9.28 E
Olching, F.R.G. (ỏl'κēng)	157d	48.13 N	11.21 E
Old Bahama Chan., N. A. (bá-hä'mä)	134	22.45 N	78.30 w
Old Bight, Ba.	135	24.15 N	75.20 w
Old Bridge, NJ (brĭj)	112a	40.24 N	74.22 w
Old Brookville, NY	55	40.49 N	73.35 w
Old Crow, Can. (crỏ)	96	67.51 N	139.58 w
Oldenburg, F.R.G. (ỏl'dĕn-bōōrgh)	166	53.09 N	8.13 E
Old Forge, Pa. (fôrj)	111	41.20 N	75.50 w
Oldham, Eng. (ỏld'ám)	156	53.32 N	2.07 w
Oldham Pond (L.), Ma.	54a	42.03 N	70.51 w
Old Harbor, Ak. (här'bĕr)	107	57.18 N	153.20 w
Old Head of Kinsale, Ire. (ỏld hĕd ŏv kĭn-sāl)	162	51.35 N	8.35 w
Old Malden (Neigh.), Eng.	62	51.23 N	0.15 w
Old North Church (P. Int.), Ma.	54a	42.22 N	71.03 w
Old R., Tx.	125a	29.54 N	94.52 w
Olds, Can. (ỏldz)	99	51.47 N	114.06 w
Old Tate, Bots.	226	21.18 s	27.43 E
Old Town, Me. (toun)	104	44.55 N	68.42 w
Old Westbury, NY	55	40.47 N	73.37 w
Old Windsor, Eng.	62	51.28 N	0.35 w
Old Wives L., Can. (wīvz)	100	50.56 N	106.00 w
Olean, NY (ỏ-lē-ăn')	111	42.05 N	78.25 w
Olecko, Pol. (ỏ-lĕt'skỏ)	167	54.02 N	22.29 E
Olekma (R.), Sov. Un. (ỏ-lyĕk-má')	181	56.51 N	120.33 E
Olëkminsk, Sov. Un. (ỏ-lyĕk-mĕnsk')	181	60.39 N	120.40 E
Olenëk (R.), Sov. Un. (ỏ-lyĕ-nyôk')	181	70.18 N	121.15 E
Oléron Ile, d' (I.), Fr. (ĕl' dỏ lä-rôn')	168	45.52 N	1.58 w
Oleśnica, Pol. (ỏ-lĕsh-nĭ'tsä)	167	51.13 N	17.24 E
Olfen, F.R.G. (ỏl'fĕn)	169c	51.43 N	7.22 E
Ol'ga, Sov. Un. (ỏl'gá)	181	43.48 N	135.44 E
Ol'gi, Zaliv (B.), Sov. Un. (zä'lĭf ỏl'gī)	204	43.43 N	135.25 E
Ol'gopol, Sov. Un. (ỏl-gỏ-pỏl'y')	175	48.11 N	29.28 E
Olhão, Port. (ỏl-youn')	170	37.02 N	7.54 w
Olievenhoutpoort, S. Afr.	227b	25.58 s	27.55 E
Olifants (R.), S. Afr. (ỏl'ĭ-fánts)	226	23.58 s	31.00 E
Ólimbos, Grc.	173	40.03 N	22.22 E
Ólimbos (Mtn.), Cyprus	191a	34.56 N	32.52 E
Olinalá, Mex. (ỏ-lĕ-nä-lä')	130	17.47 N	98.51 w
Olinda, Austl.	70b	37.51 s	145.22 E
Olinda, Braz. (ỏ-lĕ'n-dä)	143	8.00 s	34.58 w
Olinda, Braz.	61c	22.49 s	43.25 w
Oliva, Sp. (ỏ-lĕ'vä)	171	38.54 N	0.07 w
Oliva de la Frontera, Sp. (ỏ-lĕ'vä dä)	170	38.33 N	6.55 w
Olivais (Neigh.), Port.	65d	34.46 N	9.06 w
Olive Hill, Ky. (ỏl'ĭv)	110	38.15 N	83.10 w
Oliveira, Braz. (ỏ-lē-vä'rä)	141a	20.42 s	44.49 w
Olive Mount (Neigh.), Eng.	64a	53.24 N	2.55 w
Olivenza, Sp. (ỏ-lĕ-vĕn'thä)	170	38.42 N	7.06 w
Oliver, Can. (ỏ'lĭ-vĕr)	99	49.11 N	119.33 w
Oliver, Can.	95g	53.38 N	113.21 w
Oliver, Wi. (ỏ'lĭvĕr)	119h	46.39 N	92.12 w
Oliver L., Can.	95g	53.19 N	113.00 w
Olivia, Mn. (ỏ-lĭv'ē-á)	106	44.46 N	95.00 w
Olivos, Arg. (ỏ-lē'vỏs)	144a	34.15 s	58.29 w
Ollagüe, Chile (ỏ-lyä'gå)	142	21.17 s	68.17 w
Ollerton, Eng. (ỏl'ĕr-tŭn)	156	53.12 N	1.02 w
Olmos Park, Tx. (ỏl'mŭs pärk')	119d	29.27 N	98.32 w
Olmsted, Oh.	56a	41.24 N	81.44 w
Olmsted Falls, Oh.	56a	41.22 N	81.55 w
Olney, Il. (ỏl'nĭ)	110	38.45 N	88.05 w
Olney, Or. (ỏl'nĕ)	118c	46.06 N	123.45 w
Olney, Tx.	122	33.24 N	98.43 w
Olney (Neigh.), Pa.	56b	40.02 N	75.08 w
Olomane (R.), Can. (ỏ'lỏ má'nĕ)	105	51.05 N	60.50 w
Olomouc, Czech. (ỏ'lỏ-mōts)	167	49.37 N	17.15 E
Olonets, Sov. Un. (ỏ-lỏ'nĕts)	165	60.58 N	32.54 E
Olongapo, Phil.	207a	14.49 s	120.17 E
Oloron, Gave d' (Strm.), Fr. (gäv-dỏ-lỏ-rôn')	168	43.21 N	0.44 w
Oloron-Sainte-Marie, Fr. (ỏ-lỏ-rôn't'sänt má-rē')	168	43.11 N	1.37 w
Olot, Sp. (ỏ-lỏt')	171	42.09 N	2.30 E
Olpe, F.R.G. (ỏl'pĕ)	169c	51.02 N	7.51 E
Ol'shanka, Sov. Un. (ỏl'shäņ-kä)	175	48.14 N	30.52 E
Ol'shany, Sov. Un. (ỏl'shän-ĕ)	175	50.02 N	35.54 E
Olsnitz, G.D.R. (ôlz'nĕtz)	166	50.25 N	12.11 E
Olsztyn, Pol. (ỏl'shtĕn)	167	53.47 N	20.28 E
Olten, Switz. (ỏl'tĕn)	166	47.20 N	7.53 E
Oltenita, Rom. (ỏl-tä'nĭ-tsä)	173	44.05 N	26.39 E
Oltul (R.), Rom.	161	44.09 N	24.40 E
Olvera, Sp. (ỏl-vĕ'rä)	170	36.55 N	7.16 w
Olympia, Wa. (ỏ-lĭm'pĭ-á)	116	47.02 N	122.52 w
Olympic Mts., Wa.	116	47.54 N	123.58 w
Olympic Natl. Park, Wa. (ỏ-lĭm'pĭk)	116	47.54 N	123.00 w
Olympeion (P. Int.), Grc.	66d	37.58 N	23.44 E
Olympus Mt., Wa. (ỏ-lĭm'pŭs)	116	47.43 N	123.30 w
Olyphant, Pa. (ỏl'ĭ-fánt)	111	41.30 N	75.40 w
Olyutorskiy, Mys (C.), Sov. Un. (ŭl-yōō'tôr-skĕ)	181	59.49 N	167.16 E
Omae-Zaki (Pt.), Jap. (ỏ'mä-å zä'kĕ)	205	34.37 N	138.15 E
Omagh, N. Ire. (ỏ'mä)	162	54.35 N	7.25 w
Omaha, Ne. (ỏ'mä-hä)	114	41.18 N	95.57 w
Omaha Ind. Res., Ne.	114	42.09 N	96.08 w
Oman, Asia	190	20.00 N	57.45 E
Oman, G. of, Asia	192	24.24 N	58.58 E
Omaruru, Namibia (ỏ-mä-rōō'rōō)	226	21.25 s	16.50 E
Omboué, Gabon	230	1.34 s	9.15 E
Ombrone (R.), It. (ỏm-brỏ'nä)	172	42.48 N	11.18 E
Omealca, Mex. (ỏmä-äl'kä)	131	18.44 N	96.45 w
Ometepec, Mex. (ỏ-mä-tå-pĕk')	130	16.41 N	98.27 w
Om Hajer, Eth.	225	14.06 N	36.46 E
Omineca (R.), Can. (ỏ-mĭ-nĕk'á)	98	55.10 N	125.45 w
Omineca Mts., Can.	98	56.00 N	125.00 w
Ômiya, Jap. (ỏ'mē-yä)	205a	35.54 s	139.38 E
Omoa, Hond. (ỏ-mỏ'rä)	132	15.43 N	88.03 w
Omoko, Nig.	229	5.20 N	6.39 E
Omolon (R.), Sov. Un. (ỏ'mỏ)	181	67.43 N	159.15 E
Omo R., Eth.	225	5.54 N	36.09 E
Ômori (Kiroshi), Jap. (ỏ'mỏ-rē)(kĕ'ỏ-rỏ'shē)	205a	35.50 N	140.09 E
Omotepe, Isla de (I.), Nic. (ĕ's-lä-dĕ-ỏ-mỏ-tĕ'pĕ)	132	11.32 N	85.30 w
Omro, Wi. (ỏm'rỏ)	115	44.01 N	89.46 w
Omsk, Sov. Un. (ỏmsk)	180	55.12 N	73.19 E
Ômuta, Jap. (ỏ'mōō-tä)	205	32.56 N	129.57 E
Ômuta, Jap.	203	33.01 N	130.28 E
Omutninsk, Sov. Un. (ỏ'mōō-tnĕnsk)	178	58.38 N	52.10 E
Onawa, Ia. (ỏn-á-wá)	114	42.02 N	96.05 w

ăt; finăl; rāte; senăte; ärm; ásk; sofá; fâre; ch-choose; dh-as th in other; bē; ěvent; bět; recěnt; cratēr; g-gō; gh-guttural g; bĭt; ĭ-short neutral; rīde; κ-guttural k as ch in German ich;

PLACE (Pronounciation)	PAGE	Lat. °′	Long. °′
Onaway, Mi.	110	45.25 N	84.10 W
Once (Neigh.), Arg.	60d	34.36 S	58.24 W
Oncócua, Ang.	230	16.34 S	13.28 E
Onda, Sp. (ōn'dä)	171	39.58 N	0.13 W
Ondava (R.), Czech. (ōn'dȧ-vȧ)	167	48.51 N	21.40 E
Ondo, Nig.	229	7.04 N	4.47 E
Ondörhaan, Mong.	202	47.20 N	110.40 E
Onega, Sov. Un. (ō̍-nyĕ'gȧ)	178	63.50 N	38.08 E
Onega, L., see Onezhskoye Ozero			
Onega (R.), Sov. Un.	178	63.20 N	39.20 E
Oneida, NY (ō̍-nī'dȧ)	111	43.05 N	75.40 W
Oneida, (L.), NY	111	43.10 N	76.00 W
O'Neill, Ne. (ō-nēl')	114	42.28 N	98.38 W
Onekotan (I.), Sov. Un. (ŭ-nyĕ-kŭ-tän')	181	49.45 N	153.45 E
Oneonta, NY (ō-nē̍-ŏn'tȧ)	111	42.25 N	75.05 W
Onezhskaja Guba (B.), Sov. Un.	178	64.30 N	36.00 E
Onezhskiy, P-Ov. (Pen.), Sov. Un.	178	64.30 N	37.40 E
Onezhskoye Ozero (Onega, L.), Sov. Un. (ō̍-năsh'skō̍-yĕ ô'zĕ-rō̍)	178	62.02 N	34.35 E
Ongiin Hiid, Mong.	198	46.00 N	102.46 E
Ongole, India	197	15.36 N	80.03 E
Onilahy (R.), Mad.	227	23.41 S	45.00 E
Onitsha, Nig. (ō̍-nĭt'shȧ)	229	6.09 N	6.47 W
Onomichi, Jap. (ō'nō̍-mē'chē̍)	205	34.27 N	133.12 E
Onon (R.), Sov. Un. (ô'nō̍n)	181	50.33 N	114.18 E
Onon (R.), Sov. Un. (ô'nō̍n)	181	48.30 N	110.38 E
Onoto, Ven. (ô-nŏ'tō̍)	143b	9.38 N	65.03 W
Onslow, Austl. (ŏnz'lō)	214	21.53 S	115.00 E
Onslow B, NC (ō̍nz'lō)	127	34.22 N	77.35 W
Ontake San (Mtn.), Jap. (ō̍n'tä-kā̍ sän)	205	35.55 N	137.29 E
Ontario, Ca. (ŏn-tā'rĭ-ō)	119a	34.04 N	117.39 E
Ontario, Or.	116	44.02 N	116.57 W
Ontario (Prov.), Can.	97	50.47 N	88.50 W
Ontario, L., U. S.-Can.	109	43.35 N	79.05 W
Ontario Science Centre (P. Int.), Can.	54c	43.43 N	79.21 W
Onteniente, Sp. (ōn-tā̍-nyĕn'tā)	171	38.48 N	0.35 W
Ontonagon, Mi. (ŏn-tō̍-năg'ŏn)	115	46.50 N	89.20 W
Ōnuki, Jap. (ō'no͞o-kē̍)	205a	35.17 N	139.51 E
Oodnadatta, Austl. (o͞od'nȧ-dȧ'tȧ)	214	27.38 S	135.40 E
Ooldea Station, Austl. (o͞ol-dā'ä)	214	30.35 S	132.08 E
Oologah Res., Ok.	123	36.43 N	95.32 W
Ooltgensplaat, Neth.	157a	51.41 N	4.19 E
Ōmori (Neigh.), Jap.	69a	35.34 N	139.44 E
Ōsaka-wan (B.), Jap.	69b	34.30 N	135.18 E
Oostanaula (R.), Ga. (o͞o-stȧ-nô'lȧ)	126	34.25 N	85.10 W
Oostende, Bel. (ōst-ĕn'dē)	163	51.14 N	2.55 E
Oosterhout, Neth.	157a	51.38 N	4.52 E
Ooster Schelde (R.), Neth.	163	51.40 N	3.40 E
Ootsa L., Can.	98	53.49 N	126.18 W
Ōyodo (Neigh.), Jap.	69b	34.43 N	135.30 E
Opalaca, Sierra de (Mts.), Hond. (sē-sĕ'r-rä-dĕ-ō̍-pä-lä'kä)	132	14.30 N	88.29 W
Opasquia, Can. (ō-păs'kwē̍-ȧ)	101	53.16 N	93.53 W
Opatow, Pol. (ō̍-pä'to͝of)	167	50.47 N	21.25 E
Opava, Czech. (ō'pä-vä)	167	49.56 N	17.52 E
Opelika, Al. (ŏp-ē̍-lī'kȧ)	126	32.39 N	85.23 W
Opelousas, La. (ŏp-ē-lo͞o'sȧs)	125	30.33 N	92.04 W
Opeongo (L.), Can. (ŏp-ē̍-ôŋ'gō)	111	45.40 N	78.20 W
Opheim, Mt. (ō̍-fīm')	117	48.51 N	106.19 W
Ophir, Ak. (ō'fēr)	107	63.10 N	156.28 W
Ophir, Mt., Mala.	191b	2.22 N	102.37 E
Ophirton (Neigh.), S. Afr.	71b	26.14 S	28.01 E
Opico, Sal. (ō̍-pē'kō)	132	13.50 N	89.23 W
Opinaca (R.), Can. (ŏp-ĭ-nä'kȧ)	97	52.28 N	77.40 W
Opladen, F.R.G. (ōp'lä-dĕn)	169c	51.04 N	7.00 E
Opobo, Nig.	229	4.34 N	7.27 E
Opochka, Sov. Un. (ō-pôch'kȧ)	174	56.43 N	28.39 E
Opoczno, Pol. (ō̍-pôch'nō̍)	167	51.22 N	20.18 E
Opole, Pol. (ō̍-pôl'ä)	167	50.42 N	17.55 E
Opole Lubelskie, Pol. (ō-pō'lă lo͞o-bĕl'skyĕ)	167	51.09 N	21.58 E
Oposhnya, Sov. Un. (ō̍-pôsh'nyȧ)	175	49.57 N	34.34 E
Opp, Al. (ŏp)	126	31.18 N	86.15 W
Oppdal, Nor. (ôp'däl)	164	62.37 N	9.41 E
Opportunity, Wa. (ŏp-ŏr tū'nĭ tĭ)	116	47.37 N	117.20 W
Oppum (Neigh.), F.R.G.	63	51.19 N	6.37 E
Oquirrh Mts., Ut. (ō'kwēr)	119b	40.38 N	112.11 W
Oradea, Rom. (ō̍-räd'yä)	167	47.02 N	21.55 E
Oradell, NJ	55	40.57 N	74.02 W
Oran (Wahran), Alg. (ō-rän)(ō̍-räN')	160	35.46 N	0.45 W
Orán, Arg. (ō̍-rȧ'n)	144	23.13 S	64.17 W
Oran, Mo. (ôr'ȧn)	123	37.05 N	89.39 W
Orange, Austl. (ŏr'ĕnj)	216	33.15 S	149.08 E
Orange, Ca.	119a	33.48 N	117.51 W
Orange, Ct.	111	41.15 N	73.00 W
Orange, Fr. (ô-raNzh')	168	44.08 N	4.48 E
Orange, NJ	112a	40.46 N	74.14 W
Orange, Tx.	122	30.07 N	93.44 W
Orange (L.), Fl.	127	29.30 N	82.12 W
Orange (R.), Namibia-S. Afr.	226	29.15 S	17.30 E
Orangeburg, SC (ŏr'ĕnj-bûrg)	127	33.30 N	80.50 W
Orange, Cabo (C.), Braz. (kȧ-bô-rȧ'n-zhĕ)	143	4.25 N	51.30 W
Orange Cay (I.), Ba. (ŏr-ĕnj kē)	134	24.55 N	79.05 W
Orange City, Ia.	114	43.01 N	96.06 W
Orange Free State (Prov.), S. Afr.	226	28.15 S	26.00 E
Orange Grove (Neigh.), S. Afr.	71b	26.10 S	28.05 E
Orangeville, Can. (ŏr'ĕnj-vĭl)	95d	43.55 N	80.06 W
Orangeville, S. Afr.	223d	27.05 S	28.13 E
Orange Walk, Belize (wôl''k)	132a	18.09 N	88.32 W
Orani, Phil. (ō-rä'nē̍)	207a	14.47 N	120.32 E
Oranienburg, G.D.R. (ō-rä'nē̍-ĕn-bo͝orgh)	157b	52.45 N	13.14 E
Oranjemund, Namibia	226	28.33 S	16.20 E
Oran, Sebkhan d' (L.), Alg.	171	35.28 N	0.28 W
Orăştie, Rom. (ō̍-rûsh'tyā̍)	173	45.50 N	23.14 E
Oraşul-Stalin, see Braşov			
Orbetello, It. (ôr-bȧ-tĕl'lō)	172	42.27 N	11.15 E
Orbigo (R.), Sp. (ôr-bē'gō)	170	42.30 N	5.55 W
Orbost, Austl. (ôr'bŭst)	216	37.43 S	148.20 E
Orcas (I.), Wa. (ôr'kȧs)	118d	48.43 N	122.52 W
Orchard Farm, Mo. (ôr'chērd färm)	119e	38.53 N	90.27 W
Orchard Park, NY	113c	42.46 N	78.46 W
Orchards, Wa. (ôr'chēdz)	118c	45.40 N	122.33 W
Orchilla I., Ven. (ôr-kĭl-ȧ)	142	11.47 N	66.34 W
Ord, Ne. (ôrd)	114	41.35 N	98.57 W
Ord (R.), Austl.	214	17.30 S	128.40 E
Orda, Sov. Un. (ôr'dȧ)	182a	56.50 N	57.12 E
Ordenes, Sp. (ōr'dā̍-nās)	170	43.46 N	8.24 W
Ordos Des., China	202	39.12 N	108.10 E
Ord Pk., Az.	121	33.55 N	109.40 W
Ordu, Tur. (ō̍r'do͞o)	179	41.00 N	37.50 E
Ordway, Co. (ôrd'wā)	122	38.11 N	103.46 W
Ordzhonikidze, Sov. Un. (ora ghō NĬ kĭd ze)	179	43.05 N	44.35 E
Örebro, Swe. (û'rē-brō)	164	59.16 N	15.11 E
Oredezh R., Sov. Un. (ô'rĕ-dĕzh)	182c	59.23 N	30.21 E
Oregon, Il.	115	42.01 N	89.21 W
Oregon (State), U.S.	108	43.40 N	121.50 W
Oregon Caves Natl. Mon., Or. (cāvz)	116	42.05 N	123.13 W
Oregon City, Or.	118c	45.21 N	122.36 W
Öregrund, Swe. (û-rĕ-gro͝ond)	164	60.20 N	18.26 E
Orekhov, Sov. Un. (ôr-yĕ'Kôf)	175	47.34 N	35.51 E
Orekhovo, Bul.	173	43.43 N	23.59 E
Orekhovo-Zuyevo, Sov. Un. (ō̍r-yĕ'Kō̍-vō̍ zo͞o'yĕ-vō̍)	174	55.46 N	39.00 E
Orël, Sov. Un. (ôr-yôl')	174	52.54 N	36.03 E
Orël (Oblast), Sov. Un.	174	52.35 N	36.08 E
Orel' (R.), Sov. Un.	175	49.08 N	34.55 E
Oreland, Pa.	56b	40.07 N	75.11 W
Orem, Ut. (ŏ'rĕm)	121	40.15 N	111.50 W
Ore Mts., see Erzgebirge			
Orenburg, Sov. Un. (ô'rĕn-bo͞org)	179	51.50 N	55.05 E
Orense, Sp. (ō̍-rĕn'sā)	170	42.20 N	7.52 W
Orfanoú, Kólpos (G.), Grc.	173	40.40 N	23.55 E
Organos, Sierra de los (Mts.), Cuba (sē-ĕ'r-rȧ-dĕ-lō̍s-ŏ'r-gä-nō̍s)	134	22.20 N	84.10 W
Organ Pipe Cactus Natl. Mon., Az. (ôr'găn pīp kăk'tŭs)	121	32.14 N	113.05 W
Orgãos, Serra das (Mtn.), Braz. (sĕ'r-rä-däs-ôr-gouN's)	141a	22.30 S	43.01 W
Orgeyev, Sov. Un. (ôr-gyĕ'yĕf)	175	47.27 N	28.49 E
Orhon (R.), Mong.	198	48.33 N	103.07 E
Oriental, Cordillera (Mts.), Bol. (kō̍r-dēl-yĕ'rä ō-rē̍-ĕn-täl')	142	14.00 S	68.33 W
Oriental, Cordillera (Mts.), Col. (kō̍r-dēl-yĕ'rä)	142a	3.30 N	74.27 W
Oriental, Cordillera (Mts.), Dom. Rep. (kō̍r-dēl-yĕ'rä-ō̍-ryĕ'n-täl)	135	18.55 N	69.40 W
Oriental, Sierra Madre, (Mts.), Mex. (sē-ĕ'r-rä-mä'drĕ-ô-ryĕ'n-täl')	128	25.30 N	100.45 W
Orihuela, Sp. (ō'rē̍-wā'lä)	171	38.04 N	0.55 W
Orillia, Can. (ō̍-rĭl'ĭ-ȧ)	111	44.35 N	79.25 W
Orin, Wy.	117	42.40 N	105.10 W
Orinda, Ca.	118b	37.53 N	122.11 W
Orinoco, Rio (R.), Ven. (rē̍'ō-ō̍-rĭ-nō'kō̍)	142	8.32 N	63.13 W
Orion, Phil. (ō-rē̍-ōn')	207a	14.37 N	120.34 E
Orissa (State), India (ŏ-rĭs'ȧ)	196	25.09 N	83.50 E
Oristano, It. (ō̍-rē̍s-tä'nō)	172	39.53 N	8.38 E
Oristano, Golfo di (G.), It. (gō̍l-fō̍-dē-ō̍-rē̍s-tä'nō)	172	39.53 N	8.12 E
Orituco (R.), Ven. (ō̍-rē-to͞o'kō)	143b	9.37 N	66.25 W
Oriuco, (R.), Ven. (ō̍-rē̍o͞o'kō)	143b	9.36 N	66.25 W
Orivesi (L.), Fin.	165	62.15 N	29.55 E
Orizaba, Mex. (ō̍-rē̍-zä'bä)	131	18.52 N	97.05 E
Orkanger, Nor.	164	63.19 N	9.54 W
Orkla (R.), Nor. (ôr'klȧ)	164	62.55 N	9.50 E
Orkney, S. Afr. (ôrk'nĭ)	223d	26.58 S	26.39 E
Orkney (Is.), Scot.	162a	59.01 N	2.08 W
Orlando, Fl. (ôr-lăn'dō)	127a	28.32 N	81.22 W
Orlando, S. Afr. (ôr-lăn-dō̍)	227b	26.15 S	27.56 E
Orlando West Extension, S. Afr.	71b	26.15 S	27.54 E
Orland Park, Il. (ôr-lăn')	113a	41.38 N	87.52 W
Orleans, Can. (ō̍r-lā̍-äN')	95c	45.28 N	75.31 W
Orléans, Fr. (ō̍r-lā-äN')	168	47.55 N	1.56 E
Orleans, In. (ō̍r-lēnz')	110	38.40 N	86.25 W
Orléans, Île d' (I.), Can.	95b	46.56 N	70.57 W
Orléansville, see Ech Cheliff			
Orly, Fr.	64c	48.45 N	2.24 E
Ormond, Austl.	70b	37.54 S	145.03 E
Ormond Beach, Fl. (ôr'mŏnd)	127	29.15 N	81.05 W
Ormskirk, Eng. (ôrms'kērk)	156	53.34 N	2.53 W
Ormstown, Can. (ôrms'toun)	95a	45.07 N	74.00 W
Orneta, Pol. (ôr-nyĕ'tä)	167	54.07 N	20.10 E
Ornö (I.), Swe.	164	59.02 N	18.35 E
Örnsköldsvik, Swe. (ûrn'skôlts-vēk)	158	63.10 N	18.32 E
Orobie, Alpi (Mts.), It. (äl'pē-ô-rŏ'byĕ)	172	46.05 N	9.47 E
Orocué, Col. (ō̍-rō̍-kwā')	142	4.48 N	71.26 W
Oron, Nig.	229	4.48 N	8.14 E
Oro, Rio del (R.), Mex. (rē'ō dĕl ō'rō)	130	18.04 N	100.59 W
Oro, Rio del (R.), Mex.	114	26.04 N	105.40 W
Orosei, Golfo di (G.), It. (gō̍l-fō̍-dē-ō-rō̍-sā'ē)	172	40.12 N	9.45 E
Orosháza, Hung. (ō̍-rō̍sh-hä'sô)	167	46.33 N	20.31 E
Orosi Vol., C. R. (ō-rō'sē)	132	11.00 N	85.30 W
Oroville, Ca. (ōr'ō̍-vĭl)	120	39.29 N	121.34 W
Oroville, Wa.	116	48.55 N	119.25 W
Orpington (Neigh.), Eng.	62	51.23 N	0.06 E
Orrville, Oh. (ôr'vĭl)	110	40.45 N	81.50 W
Orsa, Swe. (ōr'sä)	164	61.08 N	14.35 E
Orsay, Fr.	64c	48.48 N	2.11 E
Orsett, Eng.	62	51.31 N	0.22 E
Orsha, Sov. Un. (ôr'shȧ)	174	54.29 N	30.28 E
Orsk, Sov. Un. (ôrsk)	179	51.15 N	58.50 E
Orsova, Rom. (ō̍r'shô-vä)	173	44.43 N	22.26 E
Orsoy, F.R.G.	63	51.31 N	6.41 E
Ortega, Col. (ôr-tĕ'gä)	142a	3.56 N	75.12 W
Ortegal, Cabo (C.), Sp. (kȧ'bō̍-ôr-tā̍-gäl')	170	43.46 N	8.15 W
Orth, Aus.	157e	48.09 N	16.42 E
Orthez, Fr. (ō̍r-tĕz')	171	43.29 N	0.43 W
Ortigueira, Sp. (ôr-tē̍-gā'ē̍-rä)	170	43.40 N	7.50 W
Orting, Wa. (ôrt'ĭng)	118a	47.06 N	122.12 W
Ortona, It. (ō̍r-tō'nä)	172	42.22 N	14.22 E
Ortonville, Mn. (ō̍r-tŭn-vĭl)	114	45.18 N	96.26 W
Oruba, Nig.	71d	6.35 N	3.25 E
Orūmīyeh, Iran	192	37.30 N	45.15 E
Orūmīyeh, Daryacheh-ye (L.), Iran	192	38.01 N	45.17 E
Oruro, Bol. (ō̍-ro͞o'rō)	142	17.57 S	66.59 W
Orvieto, It. (ō̍r-vyā̍'tō)	172	42.43 N	12.08 E
Oryu-dong (Neigh.), Kor.	68b	37.29 N	126.51 E
Osa, Sov. Un. (ô'sȧ)	178	57.18 N	55.25 E
Osage, Ia. (ō'sāj)	115	43.16 N	92.49 W
Osage, NJ	56b	39.51 N	75.01 W
Osage (R.), Mo.	123	38.10 N	93.12 W
Osage City, Ks. (ō'sāj sĭ'tĭ)	123	38.28 N	95.53 W
Ōsaka, Jap. (ō'sä-kä)	205b	34.40 N	135.27 E
Ōsaka (Pref.), Jap.	205b	34.45 N	135.36 E
Osaka Castle (P. Int.), Jap.	69b	34.41 N	135.32 E
Ōsaka-Wan (B.), Jap. (wän)	205	34.34 N	135.16 E
Osakis, Mn. (ō̍-sā'kĭs)	115	45.51 N	95.09 W
Osakis (L.), Mn.	115	45.55 N	94.55 W
Osa, Pen. de, C. R. (ō'sä)	133	8.30 N	83.25 W
Osasco, Braz.	61d	23.32 S	46.46 W
Osawatomie, Ks. (ŏs-ȧ-wăt'ō̍-mē̍)	123	38.29 N	94.57 W
Osborne, Ks. (ŏz'bŭrn)	122	39.25 N	98.42 W
Osceola, Ar. (ŏs-ē̍-ō'lȧ)	123	35.42 N	89.58 W
Osceola, Ia.	115	41.04 N	93.45 W
Osceola, Mo.	123	38.02 N	93.41 W
Osceola, Ne.	114	41.11 N	97.34 W
Osceola, Tn.	123	35.42 N	89.58 W
Oscoda, Mi. (ŏs-kō'dȧ)	110	44.25 N	83.20 W
Osëtr (R.), Sov. Un. (ō̍'sĕt'r)	174	54.27 N	38.15 E
Osgood, In. (ŏz'go͝od)	110	39.10 N	85.20 W
Osgoode, Can.	95c	45.09 N	75.37 W
Osh, Sov. Un. (ôsh)	180	40.28 N	72.47 E
Oshawa, Can. (ŏsh'ȧ-wȧ)	111	43.50 N	78.50 W
Ōshima (I.), Jap. (ō'shē'mä)	205	34.47 N	139.35 E
Oshkosh, Ne. (ŏsh'kŏsh)	114	41.24 N	102.22 W
Oshkosh, Wi.	115	44.01 N	88.35 W
Oshmyany, Sov. Un. (ō̍sh-myä'nĭ)	165	54.27 N	25.55 E
Oshodi, Nig.	71d	6.34 N	3.21 E
Oshogbo, Nig.	229	7.47 N	4.34 E
Osijek, Yugo. (ō̍s'ĭ-yĕk)	173	45.33 N	18.48 E
Osinniki, Sov. Un. (ŭ-sē'nyĭ-kē)	180	53.29 N	85.19 E
Oskaloosa, Ia. (ŏs-kȧ-lo͞o'sȧ)	115	41.16 N	92.40 W
Oskarshamm, Swe. (ôs'kärs-häm'n)	164	57.16 N	16.24 E
Oskarström, Swe. (ôs'kärs-strûm)	164	56.48 N	12.55 E
Oskol (R.), Sov. Un. (ôs-kôl')	175	51.00 N	37.41 E
Oslo, Nor. (ō̍s'lō)	164	59.56 N	10.41 E
Oslofjorden (Fd.), Nor.	164	59.03 N	10.35 E
Osmaniye, Tur.	179	37.10 N	36.30 E
Osnabrück, F.R.G. (ôs-nä-brük')	166	52.16 N	8.05 E
Osorno, Chile (ō̍-sō'r-nō)	144	40.42 S	73.13 W
Osorun, Nig.	71d	6.33 N	3.29 E
Osøyra, Nor.	164	60.24 N	5.22 E
Osprey Reef (I.), Austl. (ŏs'prā̍)	215	14.00 S	146.45 E
Ossa, Mt., Austl. (ŏsȧ)	216	41.45 S	146.05 E
Ossenberg, F.R.G.	63	51.34 N	6.35 E
Osseo, Mn. (ŏs'sĕ-ō)	119g	45.07 N	93.24 W
Ossining, NY (ŏs'ĭ-nĭng)	112a	41.09 N	73.51 W
Ossipee, NH (ŏs'ĭ-pē̍)	104	43.42 N	71.08 W
Ossjøen (L.), Nor. (ō̍s-syûĕn)	164	61.20 N	12.00 E
Ossum-Bösinghoven, F.R.G.	63	51.18 N	6.39 E
Ostankino (Neigh.), Sov. Un.	66b	55.49 N	37.37 E
Ostashkov, Sov. Un. (ō̍s-täsh'kôf)	174	57.07 N	33.04 E
Ost-Berlin, G.D.R.	65a	52.30 N	13.25 E
Oster, Sov. Un. (ōs'tĕr)	175	50.55 N	30.52 E
Osterdalälven (R.), Swe.	164	61.40 N	13.00 E
Oster Fd., Nor. (ûs'tēr fyō̍r')	175	60.40 N	5.25 E
Osterfeld (Neigh.), F.R.G.	63	51.30 N	6.53 E
Östersund, Swe. (ûs'tēr-so͞ond)	164	63.09 N	14.49 E
Östhammar, Swe. (ûst'häm'är)	164	60.16 N	18.21 E
Ostrava, Czech.	167	49.51 N	18.18 E
Ostróda, Pol. (ôs'tro͝ot-ȧ)	167	53.41 N	19.58 E
Ostróg, Sov. Un. (ŏs-trôk')	175	50.21 N	26.40 E
Ostrogozhsk, Sov. Un. (ôs-tr-gôzhk')	175	50.53 N	39.03 E
Ostrołęka, Pol. (ō̍s-trō̍-woN'kȧ)	167	53.04 N	21.35 E
Ostropol', Sov. Un. (ō̍s-trō̍-pō̍l')	175	49.48 N	27.32 E
Ostrov, Sov. Un. (ō̍s-trôf')	174	57.21 N	28.22 E
Ostrov, Sov. Un.	66b	55.35 N	37.51 E
Ostrowiec Świetokrzyski, Pol. (ōs-trō'vyĕts shvyĕN-tō-kzhĭ'ske)	167	50.55 N	21.24 E
Ostrów Lubelski, Pol. (ôs'tro͝of lo͞o'bĕl-skĭ)	167	51.32 N	22.49 E
Ostrów Mazowiecka, Pol. (mä-zō̍-vyĕt'skä)	167	52.47 N	21.54 E
Ostrów Wielkopolski, Pol. (ōs'tro͝of vyĕl-kō-pōl'skē)	167	51.38 N	17.49 E
Ostrzeszów, Pol. (ō̍s-tzhā'sho͝of)	167	51.26 N	17.56 E
Ostuni, It. (ō̍s-to͞o'nē)	173	40.44 N	17.35 E
Osum (R.), Alb. (ō'so͞om)	173	40.37 N	20.00 E
Ōsumi-Guntō (Arch.), Jap. (ō'so͞o-mē̍ go͞on'tō)	205	30.34 N	130.30 E
Ōsumi Kaikyō (Van Diemen)(Str.), Jap. (käē̍'kyō̍)(văn dē'mĕn)	205	31.02 N	130.10 E
Osuna, Sp. (ō̍-so͞o'nä)	170	37.18 N	5.05 W
Osveya, Sov. Un. (ôs'vĕ-yȧ)	174	56.00 N	28.08 E
Oswaldtwistle, Eng. (ŏz-wȧld-twĭs''l)	156	53.44 N	2.23 W
Oswegatchie (R.), NY (ŏs-wē̍-găch'ĭ)	111	44.15 N	75.20 W
Oswego, Ks. (ŏs-wē'gō)	123	37.10 N	95.08 W
Oswego, NY	111	43.25 N	76.30 W
Oświęcim, Pol. (ō̍sh-vyăN'tsyĭm)	167	50.02 N	19.17 E
Otapää, Sov. Un. (ô'tĕ-pâ)	174	58.03 N	26.31 E
Otaru, Jap. (ō̍'tȧ-ro͞o)	204	43.07 N	141.00 E
Otavalo, Ec. (ōtä-vä'lō)	142	0.14 N	78.16 W
Otavi, Namibia (ō̍-tä'vē̍)	226	19.35 S	17.20 E
Otay, Ca. (ō'tā)	120a	32.36 N	117.04 W
Otford, Eng.	62	51.19 N	0.12 E
Othonoí (I.), Grc.	173	39.51 N	19.26 E

ng-sing; nŋ-baŋk; N-nasalized n; nŏd; cŏmmit; ōld; ôbey; ôrder; oi-boil; fo͞od; fo͝ot; ou-out; s-soft; sh-dish; th-thin; pūre; ů̍nite; ûrn; stŭd; circŭs; ü-as in French tu; '-indeterminate vowel.

326 Óthris – Palmer

PLACE (Pronunciation)	PAGE	Lat. °'	Long. °'
Óthris, Óros (Mts.), Grc.	173	39.00 N	22.15 E
Oti (R.), Ghana	228	9.00 N	0.10 E
Otish, Mts., Can. (ō-tĭsh')	97	52.15 N	70.20 W
Otjiwarongo, Namibia (ŏt-jē-wȧ-rôn'gō)	226	20.20 S	16.25 E
Otočac, Yugo. (ō'tô-chȧts)	172	44.53 N	15.15 E
Otra (R.), Nor.	164	59.13 N	7.20 E
Otradnoye, Sov. Un. (ô-trȧ'd-nôyě)	182	59.46 N	30.50 E
Otranto, It. (ô'trän-tô) (ô-trän'tō)	173	40.07 N	18.30 E
Otranto, Strait of, It.-Alb.	173	40.30 N	18.45 E
Otra R., Sov. Un. (ôt'rȧ)	182b	55.22 N	38.20 E
Otsego, Mi. (ŏt-sē'gō)	110	42.25 N	85.45 W
Otsu, Jap. (ō'tsōō)	205b	35.00 N	135.54 E
Otta (L.), Nor. (ôt'tȧ)	164	61.53 N	8.40 E
Ottakring (Neigh.), Aus.	66e	48.12 N	16.19 E
Ottavia (Neigh.), It.	66c	41.58 N	12.24 E
Ottawa, Can. (ŏt'ȧ-wȧ)	95c	45.25 N	75.43 W
Ottawa, Il.	110	41.20 N	88.50 W
Ottawa, Ks.	123	38.37 N	95.16 W
Ottawa, Oh.	110	41.00 N	84.00 W
Ottawa (R.), Can.	97	46.05 N	77.20 W
Ottawa Is., Can.	97	59.50 N	81.00 W
Otter Cr., Ut. (ŏt'ēr)	121	38.20 N	111.55 W
Otter Cr., Vt.	111	44.05 N	73.15 W
Otter Pt., Can.	118a	48.21 N	123.50 W
Ottershaw, Eng.	62	51.22 N	0.32 W
Otter Tail (L.), Mn.	114	46.21 N	95.52 W
Otterville, Il. (ŏt'ēr-vĭl)	119e	39.03 N	90.24 W
Ottery, S. Afr. (ŏt'ēr-ĭ)	226a	34.02 S	18.31 E
Ottumwa, Ia. (ô-tŭm'wȧ)	115	41.00 N	92.26 W
Otukpa, Nig.	229	7.09 N	7.41 E
Otumba, Mex. (ô-tŭm'bä)	131a	19.41 N	98.46 W
Otway, C., Austl. (ŏt'wā)	216	38.55 S	153.40 E
Otway, Seno (B.), Chile (sě'nō-ô't-wä'y)	144	53.00 S	73.00 W
Otwock, Pol. (ôt'vôtsk)	167	52.05 N	21.18 E
Ouachita, (R.), U. S.	109	33.25 N	92.30 W
Ouachita Mts., Ok. (wŏsh'ĭ-tô)	123	34.29 N	95.01 W
Ouaddaï (Reg.), Chad (wä-dī')	225	13.04 N	20.00 E
Ouagadougou, Burkina (wä'gȧ-dōō'gōō)	228	12.22 N	1.31 W
Ouahigouya, Burkina (wä-ē-gōō'yä)	228	13.35 N	2.25 W
Oualâta, Mauritania (wä-lä'tä)	224	17.11 N	6.50 W
Ouallene, Alg. (wäl-lân')	224	24.43 N	1.15 E
Ouanaminthe, Hai.	135	19.35 N	71.45 W
Ouanda Djallé, Cen. Afr. Rep. (wän'dȧ jä' lā')	225	8.56 N	22.46 E
Ouarane (Dunes), Mauritania	224	20.44 N	10.27 W
Ouarkoye, Burkina	228	12.05 N	3.40 W
Ouassel (R.), Alg.	171	35.30 N	1.55 E
Oubangui (Ubangi) (R.), Afr. (ōō-bäŋ'gē)	230	4.30 N	20.35 E
Oude Rijn (R.), Neth.	157a	52.09 N	4.33 E
Oudewater, Neth.	157a	52.01 N	4.52 E
Oud-Gastel, Neth.	157a	51.35 N	4.27 E
Oudtshoorn, S. Afr. (outs'hōrn)	226	33.33 S	23.36 E
Oued Rhiou, Alg.	171	35.55 N	0.57 E
Oued Tlelat, Alg.	171	35.33 N	0.28 W
Ouellé, Ivory-Coast	228	7.18 N	4.01 W
Ouenzé (Neigh.), Con.	71c	4.14 S	15.17 E
Ouessant, I. d', Fr. (ēl-dwě-säN')	168	48.28 N	5.00 W
Ouesso, Con.	230	1.37 N	16.04 E
Ouest, Pt., Hai.	135	19.00 N	73.25 W
Ouezzane, Mor. (wě-zan')	224	34.48 N	5.40 W
Ouham (R.), Cen. Afr. Rep.-Chad	229	8.30 N	17.50 E
Ouidah, Benin (wē-dä')	224	6.25 N	2.05 E
Oujda, Mor.	224	34.41 N	1.45 W
Oulins, Fr. (ōō-lăN')	169b	48.52 N	1.27 E
Oullins, Fr. (ōō-lăN')	168	45.44 N	4.46 E
Oulu, Fin. (ō'lōō)	158	64.58 N	25.43 E
Oulujärvi, (L.), Fin.	158	64.20 N	25.48 E
Oum Chalouba, Chad (ōōm shä-lōō'bä)	225	15.48 N	20.30 E
Oum Hadjer, Chad.	229	13.18 N	19.41 E
Ounas (R.), Fin. (ō'nȧs)	158	67.46 N	24.40 E
Oundle, Eng. (ôn'd'l)	156	52.28 N	0.28 W
Ounianga Kébir, Chad (ōō-nē-äŋ'gȧ kē-bēr')	225	19.04 N	20.22 E
Ouray, Co. (ōō-rā')	123	38.00 N	107.40 W
Ourinhos, Braz. (ôōō-rē'nyôs)	143	23.04 S	49.45 W
Ourique, Port. (ō-rē'kě)	170	37.39 N	8.10 W
Ouro Fino, Braz. (ōŭ-rô-fē'nō)	141a	22.18 S	46.21 W
Ouro Prêto, Braz. (ō'rōō prā'tōō)	141a	20.24 S	43.30 W
Outardes, Rivière aux. (R.), Can.	105	50.53 N	68.50 W
Outer (I.), Wi. (out'ēr)	115	47.03 N	90.20 W
Outer Brass (I.), Vir. Is.(U. S. A.) (bräs)	129c	18.24 N	64.58 W
Outer Hebrides (Is.), Scot.	162	57.20 N	7.50 W
Outjo, Namibia (ōt'yō)	226	20.05 S	17.10 E
Outlook, Can.	100	51.31 N	107.05 W
Outremont, Can. (ōō-trē-môN')	95a	45.31 N	73.36 W
Ouyen, Austl. (ōō-ĕn)	216	35.05 S	142.10 E
Ovalle, Chile (ō-väl'yā)	144	30.43 S	71.16 W
Ovando, Bahía de (B.), Cuba (bä-ē'ä-dě-ô-vä'n-dō)	135	20.10 N	74.05 W
Ovar, Port. (ô-vär')	170	40.52 N	8.38 W
Overbrook (Neigh.), Pa.	56b	39.58 N	75.16 W
Overbrook (Neigh.), Pa.	57b	40.24 N	79.59 W
Overijse, Bel.	157a	50.46 N	4.32 E
Overland, Mo. (ō-vēr-lănd)	119e	38.42 N	90.22 W
Overland Park, Ks.	119f	38.59 N	94.40 W
Overlea, Md. (ō'vēr-lā)(ō'vēr-lē)	112e	39.21 N	76.31 W
Övertornea, Swe.	158	66.19 N	23.31 E
Ovidiopol', Sov. Un. (ô-vē-dē-ô'pôl')	175	46.15 N	03.28 E
Oviedo, Dom. Rep. (ô-vyě'dō)	135	17.50 N	71.25 W
Oviedo, Sp. (ō-vē-ā'dhō)	170	43.22 N	5.50 W
Ovruch, Sov. Un. (ôv'rōōch)	175	51.19 N	28.51 E
Owada, Jap. (ō'wä-dȧ)	205a	35.49 N	139.33 E
Owambo (Reg.), Namibia	226	18.10 S	15.00 E
Owando, Con.	230	0.29 S	15.55 E
Owasco (L.), NY (ō-wăsk'kō)	111	42.50 N	76.30 W
Owase, Jap. (ō'wä-shě)	205	34.03 N	136.12 E
Óbuda (Neigh.), Hung.	66g	47.33 N	19.02 E
Owego, NY (ō-wē'gō)	111	42.05 N	76.15 W
Owen, Wi. (ō'ĕn)	115	44.56 N	90.35 W
Owens (L.), Ca. (ō'ĕnz)	120	36.27 N	117.45 W
Owens (R.), Ca.	120	37.13 N	118.20 W
Owensboro, Ky. (ō'ĕnz-bŭr-ô)	110	37.45 N	87.05 W
Owen Sound, Can. (ō'ĕn)	110	44.30 N	80.55 W
Owen Stanley Ra., Pap. N. Gui (stăn'lē)	207	9.00 S	147.30 E
Owensville, In. (ō'ĕnz-vĭl)	110	38.15 N	87.40 W
Owensville, Mo.	123	38.20 N	91.29 W
Owensville, Oh.	113f	39.08 N	84.07 W
Owenton, Ky. (ō'ĕn-tŭn)	110	38.35 N	84.55 W
Owerri, Nig. (ô-wĕr'ē)	224	5.26 N	7.04 E
Owings Mill, Md. (ōwĭngz mĭl)	112e	39.25 N	76.50 W
Owl Cr., Wy. (oul)	117	43.45 N	108.46 W
Owo, Nig.	229	7.15 N	5.37 E
Oworonsoki, Nig.	71d	6.33 N	3.24 E
Owosso, Mi. (ô-wŏs'ō)	110	43.00 N	84.15 W
Owyhee Mts., Id. (ô-wī'hē)	116	43.15 N	116.48 W
Owyhee R., Or.	116	43.04 N	117.45 W
Owyhee Res., Or.	116	43.27 N	117.30 W
Owyhee R., South Fork, Id.	116	42.07 N	116.43 W
Oxbow, Can.	101	49.12 N	102.11 W
Oxchuc, Mex. (ôs-chōōk')	131	16.47 N	92.24 W
Oxford, Al. (ŏks'fērd)	126	33.38 N	80.46 W
Oxford, Can. (ŏks'fērd)	103	45.44 N	63.52 W
Oxford, Eng.	156b	51.43 N	1.16 W
Oxford, Ma.	105a	42.07 N	71.52 W
Oxford, Mi.	110	42.50 N	83.15 W
Oxford, Ms.	126	34.22 N	89.30 W
Oxford, NC	127	36.17 N	78.35 W
Oxford, Oh.	110	39.30 N	84.45 W
Oxford Falls, Austl.	70a	33.44 S	151.15 E
Oxford L., Can.	101	54.51 N	95.37 W
Oxfordshire (CO.), Eng.	156b	51.36 N	1.30 W
Oxkutzcab, Mex. (ôx-kōō'tz-käb)	132a	20.18 N	89.22 W
Oxmoor, Al. (ŏks'mōōr)	112h	33.25 N	86.52 W
Oxnard, Ca. (ŏks'närd)	120	34.08 N	119.12 W
Oxon Hill, Md. (ōks'ōn hĭl)	112e	38.48 N	77.00 W
Oxshott, Eng.	62	51.20 N	0.21 W
Oxtotepec, Mex. (ôx-tô-tě'pěk)	131a	19.10 N	99.04 W
Oyama, Jap.	69a	35.36 N	139.22 E
Oyapock (R.), Braz.-Fr. Gu. (ō-yȧ-pŏk')	143	2.45 N	52.15 W
Oyem, Gabon (ô-yěm)(ô-yăN')	230	1.37 N	11.35 E
Øyeren (L.), Nor. (ûĭěrěn)	164	59.50 N	11.25 E
Oymyakon, Sov. Un. (oi-myŭ-kôn')	181	63.14 N	142.58 E
Oyo, Nig. (ō'yō)	229	7.51 N	3.56 E
Oyonnax, Fr. (ô-yô-nȧks')	169	46.16 N	5.40 E
Oyster Bay, NY	112a	40.52 N	73.32 W
Oyster Bay Cove, NY	55	40.52 N	73.31 W
Oyster Bayou, Tx.	125a	29.41 N	94.33 W
Oyster Cr., Tx. (ois'tēr)	125a	29.13 N	95.29 W
Ozama (R.), Dom. Rep. (ô-zä'mä)	135	18.45 N	69.55 W
Ozamiz, Phil. (ô-zä'mēz)	207	8.06 N	123.43 E
Ozark, Al. (ō'zärk)	126	31.28 N	85.28 W
Ozark, Ar.	123	35.29 N	93.49 W
Ozark Plat, Mo.	123	36.37 N	93.56 W
Ozarks, L. of the, Mo. (ō'zärksz)	123	38.06 N	93.26 W
Ozëry, Sov. Un. (ô-zyô'rě)	174	54.53 N	38.31 E
Ozgol, Iran	68h	35.47 N	51.30 E
Ozieri, It.	172	40.38 N	8.53 E
Ozoir-la-Ferrière, Fr.	64c	48.46 N	2.40 E
Ozone Park (Neigh.), NY	55	40.40 N	73.51 W
Ozorkow, Pol. (ô-zôr'kōōf)	167	51.58 N	19.20 E
Ozuluama, Mex. (ô'zōō-lōō-ä'mä)	131	21.34 N	97.52 W
Ozumba, Mex. (ô-zōō'm-bä)	131a	19.02 N	98.48 W

P

PLACE (Pronunciation)	PAGE	Lat. °'	Long. °'
Paarl, S. Afr. (pärl)	226	33.45 S	18.55 E
Paarlshoop (Neigh.), S. Afr.	71b	26.13 S	27.59 E
Pauilo, Hi. (pä-ä-ōō'ē-lō)	106a	20.03 N	155.25 W
Pabianice, Pol. (pä-byȧ-nē'tsě)	167	51.40 N	19.29 E
Pacaás Novos, Massiço de (Mts.), Braz. (mä-sē'sô-dě-pä-kä's-nô'vôs)	142	11.03 S	64.02 W
Pacaraima, Serra (Mts.), Braz.-Ven. (sěr'rȧ pä-kä-rä-ē'mȧ)	142	3.45 N	62.30 W
Pacasmayo, Peru (pä-käs-mä'yō)	142	7.24 S	79.30 W
Pachuca, Mex. (pä-chōō'kä)	131	20.07 N	98.43 W
Pacific, Wa. (pȧ-sĭf'ĭk)	118a	47.16 N	122.15 W
Pacifica, Ca. (pȧ-sĭf'ĭ-kä)	118b	37.38 N	122.29 W
Pacific Beach, Ca.	120a	32.47 N	117.22 W
Pacific Grove, Ca.	120	36.37 N	121.54 W
Pacific O.,	208	0	170.00 W
Pacific Palisades (Neigh.), Ca.	59	34.03 N	118.32 W
Pacific Ra., Can.	98	51.00 N	125.30 W
Pacific Rim Natl. Pk., Can.	98	49.00 N	126.00 W
Paço de Arcos, Port.	65d	38.42 N	9.17 W
Pacolet (R.), SC (pă'cō-lĕt)	127	34.55 N	81.49 W
Pacy-sur-Eure, Fr. (pä-sē-sür-ûr')	169b	49.01 N	1.24 E
Padang, Indon. (pä-däng')	206	1.01 S	100.28 E
Padang Endau, Mala.	191b	2.39 N	103.38 E
Padang, Palau (I.), Indon.	191b	1.12 N	102.21 E
Paddington (Neigh.), Eng.	62	51.31 N	0.10 W
Paden City, WV (pā'děn)	110	39.30 N	80.55 W
Paderborn, F.R.G. (pä-děr-bôrn')	166	51.43 N	8.46 E
Paderno Dugnano, It.	65c	45.34 N	9.10 E
Padibe, Ug.	231	3.28 N	32.50 E
Padiham, Eng. (păd'ĭ-hăm)	156	53.48 N	2.19 W
Padilla, Mex. (pä-dēl'yä)	130	24.00 N	98.45 W
Padilla B., Wa. (pä-děl'lȧ)	118a	48.31 N	122.34 W
Padova (Padua), It. (pä'dô-vä)(păd'ū-ȧ)	172	45.24 N	11.53 E
Padre I., Tx. (pä'drā)	125	27.09 N	97.15 W
Padre Miguel (Neigh.), Braz.	61c	22.53 S	43.26 W
Padstow, Austl.	70a	33.57 S	151.02 E
Padua, see Padova			
Paducah, Ky. (pȧ-dū'kȧ)	126	37.05 N	88.36 W
Paducah, Tx.	122	34.01 N	100.18 W
Paektu San (Mt.), China-Kor. (pâk'tōō-sän')	204	42.00 N	128.03 E
Pag (I.), Yugo (päg)	172	44.30 N	14.48 E
Pagai Selatan, Pulau (I.), Indon.	206	2.48 S	100.22 E
Pagai Utara, Pulau (I.), Indon.	206	2.45 S	100.02 E
Pagasitikós Kólpos (G.), Grc.	173	39.15 N	23.00 E
Page, Az.	123	36.57 N	111.27 W
Pagosa Springs, Co. (pȧ-gō'sȧ)	123	37.15 N	107.05 W
Pagote, India	67e	18.54 N	72.59 E
Pahala, Hi. (pä-hä'lä)	106a	19.11 N	155.28 W
Pahang (State), Mala.	191b	3.02 N	102.57 E
Pahang R., Mala.	206	3.39 N	102.41 E
Pahokee, Fl. (pȧ-hō'kē)	127a	26.45 N	80.40 W
Paide, Sov. Un. (pī'dě)	165	58.54 N	25.30 E
Päijänne (L.), Fin. (pě'ē-yěn-ně)	165e	61.38 N	25.05 E
Pailolo Chan., Hi. (pä-ē-lō'lō)	106a	21.05 N	156.41 W
Paine, Chile (pī'nĕ)	141b	33.49 S	70.44 W
Painesville, Oh. (pānz'vĭl)	110	41.40 N	81.15 W
Painted Des., Az. (pānt'ĕd)	123	36.15 N	111.35 W
Painted Rock Res., Az.	123	33.00 N	113.05 W
Paintsville, Ky. (pānts'vĭl)	110	37.50 N	82.50 W
Paisley, Austl.	70b	37.51 S	144.51 E
Paisley, Scot. (pāz'lĭ)	162	55.50 N	4.30 W
Paita, Peru (pä-ē'tä)	142	5.11 S	81.12 W
Pai T'ou Shan (Mts.), Korea	202	40.30 N	127.20 E
Paiute Ind. Res., Ut.	123	38.17 N	113.50 W
Pajápan, Mex. (pä-hä'pän)	131	18.16 N	94.41 W
Pakanbaru, Indon.	206	0.43 N	101.15 E
Pakhra R., Sov. Un. (päK'rȧ)	182b	55.29 N	37.51 E
Pakistan, Asia	190	28.00 N	67.30 E
Pakistan East, see Bangladesh			
Pakokku, Bur. (pȧ-kŏk'kōō)	206	21.29 N	95.00 E
Paks, Hung. (pôksh)	167	46.38 N	18.53 E
Pala, Chad	229	9.22 N	14.54 E
Palacios, Tx. (pä-lä'syōs)	125	28.42 N	96.12 W
Palagruža (Is.), Yugo (pä'lä-grōō'zhä)	172	42.20 N	16.23 E
Palaión Fáliron, Grc.	66d	37.55 N	23.41 E
Palaiseau, Fr. (pȧ-lě-zō')	169b	48.44 N	2.16 E
Palana, Sov. Un.	181	59.07 N	159.58 E
Palanan B., Phil. (pä-lä'nän)	207a	17.14 N	122.35 E
Palanan Pt., Phil.	207a	17.12 N	122.40 E
Palanpur, India (pä'lŭn-pōōr)	196	24.08 N	73.29 E
Palapye, Bots (pȧ-läp'yě)	226	22.34 S	27.28 E
Palatine, Il. (păl'ȧ-tīn)	113a	42.07 N	88.03 W
Palatka, Fl. (pȧ-lăt'kȧ)	127	29.39 N	81.40 W
Palauig, Phil. (pȧ-lou'ĕg)	207a	15.27 N	119.54 E
Palau Is., Pac. Is. Trust. Ter. (pä-lä'ōō)	207	7.15 N	134.30 E
Palawan (I.), Phil. (pä-lä'wȧn)	206	9.50 N	117.38 E
Pālayankottai, India	197	8.50 N	77.50 E
Paldiski, Sov. Un. (päl'dĭ-skĭ)	165	59.22 N	24.04 E
Palembang, Indon. (pä-lěm-bäng')	206	2.57 S	104.40 E
Palencia, Guat. (pä-lěn'sē-ȧ)	132	14.40 N	90.22 W
Palencia, Sp. (pä-lě'n-syä)	170	42.02 N	4.32 W
Palengue, Mex. (pä-lěŋ'kä)	131	17.34 N	91.58 W
Palenque, Punta (Pt.), Dom. Rep. (pōō'n-tä)	135	18.10 N	70.10 W
Palermo, Col. (pä-lěr'mô)	142a	2.53 N	75.26 W
Palermo, It.	172	38.08 N	13.24 E
Palermo (Neigh.), Arg.	60d	34.35 S	58.25 W
Palestine, Tx.	125	31.46 N	95.38 W
Palestine (Reg.), Asia (păl'ěs-tīn)	191a	31.33 N	35.00 E
Paletwa, Bur. (pŭ-lět'wä)	198	21.19 N	92.52 E
Palghāt, India	197	10.49 N	76.40 E
Pāli, India	196	25.53 N	73.18 E
Palimé, Togo	228	6.54 N	0.38 E
Palín, Guat. (pä-lēn')	132	14.42 N	90.42 W
Palisade, Nv. (păl-ĭ-sād')	116	40.39 N	116.11 W
Palisades Park, NJ	55	40.51 N	74.00 W
Palizada, Mex. (pä-lē-zä'dä)	131	18.17 N	92.04 W
Palk Str., India (pôk)	196	10.00 N	79.23 E
Pallejá, Sp.	65e	41.25 N	2.00 E
Palma, Braz. (päl'mä)	141a	21.23 S	42.18 W
Palma, Sp.	171	39.35 N	2.38 E
Palma, Ba, de (B.), Sp. (bä-ē'ä-dě)	171	39.24 N	2.37 E
Palma del Rio, Sp. (děl rē'ō)	170	37.43 N	5.19 W
Palmar de Cariaco, Ven.	61a	10.34 N	66.55 W
Palmares, Braz. (päl-mȧ'rěs)	143	8.46 S	35.28 W
Palmas, Braz. (päl'mäs)	144	26.20 S	51.56 W
Palmas, C., Lib.	228	4.22 N	7.44 W
Palma Soriano, Cuba (sô-ré-ä'nō)	135	20.15 N	76.00 W
Palm Beach, Fl. (päm bēch')	127a	26.43 N	80.03 W
Palmeira dos Índios, Braz. (pä-mā'rä-dôs-ē'n-dyôs)	143	9.26 S	36.33 W
Palmeirinhas, Ponta das (Pt.), Arg.	230	9.05 S	13.00 E
Palmela, Port. (päl-mā'lä)	171b	38.34 N	8.54 W
Palmer, Ak. (päm'ēr)	107	61.38 N	149.15 W

PRONOUNCING INDEX Palmer – Passau 327

PLACE (Pronounciation)	PAGE	Lat. °′	Long. °′
Palmer, Wa.	118a	47.19 N	121.53 W
Palmer Park, Md.	56d	38.55 N	76.52 W
Palmerston North, N. Z. (päm′ẽr-stŭn)	217	40.20 S	175.35 W
Palmerville, Austl. (päm′ẽr-vĭl)	215	16.08 S	144.15 E
Palmetto, Fl. (pȧl-mĕt′ō)	127a	27.32 N	82.34 W
Palmetto Pt., Ba.	135	21.15 N	73.25 W
Palmi, It. (päl′mē)	172	38.21 N	15.54 E
Palmira, Col. (päl-mē′rä)	142a	3.33 N	76.17 W
Palmira, Cuba	134	22.15 N	80.25 W
Palmyra, Mo. (păl-mī′rȧ)	123	39.45 N	91.32 W
Palmyra, NJ	112f	40.01 N	75.00 W
Palmyra (I.), Oceania	209	6.00 N	162.20 W
Palmyra (Ruins), Syr.	192	34.25 N	38.28 E
Palmyras Pt., India	196	20.42 N	87.45 E
Palmyre, Syr.	155	30.35 N	37.58 E
Palo Alto, Ca. (pä′lō äl′tō)	118b	37.27 N	122.09 W
Paloduro Cr., Tx. (pä-lô-do͞o′rô)	122	36.16 N	101.12 W
Paloh, Mala.	191b	2.11 N	103.12 E
Paloma, L., Mex. (pä-lō′mä)	124	26.53 N	104.02 W
Palomar Park, Ca.	58b	37.29 N	122.16 W
Palomo, Cerro el (Mtn.), Chile (sĕ′r-rô-ĕl-pä-lō′mô)	141b	34.36 S	70.20 W
Palos, Cabo de (C.), Sp. (kȧ′bô-dĕ-pä′lôs)	171	39.38 N	0.43 W
Palos Heights, Il.	58a	41.40 N	87.48 W
Palos Hills, Il.	58a	41.41 N	87.49 W
Palos Park, Il.	58a	41.40 N	87.50 W
Palos Verdes Estates, Ca. (pă′lŭs vûr′dĭs)	119a	33.48 N	118.24 W
Palouse, Wa. (pȧ-lo͞oz′)	116	46.54 N	117.04 W
Palouse Hills, Wa.	116	46.48 N	117.47 W
Palouse R., Wa.	116	47.02 N	117.35 W
Palu, Tur. (pä-loo′)	179	38.55 N	40.10 E
Paluan, Phil. (pä-lo͞o′än)	207a	13.25 N	120.29 E
Pamamushir (I.), Sov. Un.	181	50.42 N	153.45 E
Pamiers, Fr. (pȧ-myā′)	168	43.07 N	1.34 E
Pamirs (Plat), Sov. Un.	193	38.14 N	72.27 E
Pamlico R., NC (păm′lĭ-kō)	127	35.25 N	76.59 W
Pamlico Sd., NC	127	35.10 N	76.10 W
Pampa, Tx. (păm′pȧ)	122	35.32 N	100.56 W
Pampa de Castillo (Plat), Arg. (pä′m-pä-dĕ-käs-tē′l-yô)	144	45.30 S	67.30 W
Pampana (R.), S. L.	228	8.35 N	11.55 W
Pampanga (R.), Phil. (päm-päŋ′gä)	207a	15.20 N	120.48 E
Pampas (Reg.), Arg. (päm′päs)	144	37.00 S	64.30 W
Pampilhosa do Botão, Port. (päm-pē-lyō′sȧ-dô-bō-to′uɴ)	170	40.21 N	8.32 W
Pamplona, Col. (päm-plō′nä)	142	7.19 N	72.41 W
Pamplona, Sp. (päm-plō′nä)	170	42.49 N	1.39 W
Pamunkey (R.), Va. (pȧ-mŭŋ′kĭ)	111	37.40 N	77.20 W
Pana, Il. (pā′nȧ)	110	39.25 N	89.05 W
Panabá, Mex. (pä-nä-bȧ′)	132a	21.18 N	88.15 W
Panagyurishte, Bul. (pȧ-nȧ-gyo͞o′rĕsh-tĕ)	173	42.30 N	24.11 E
Panaji (Panjim) India,	197	15.33 N	73.52 E
Panamá, N.A. (păn-ȧ-mä′)	129	8.35 N	81.08 W
Panamá, B. de, Pan.	133	8.50 N	79.08 W
Panama City, Fl. (păn-ȧ mä′ sĭ′tĭ)	126	30.08 N	85.39 W
Panamá, G. de, Pan.	129	7.45 N	79.20 W
Panamá, Istmo de, Pan.	129	9.00 N	81.00 W
Panamint Ra., Ca. (păn-ȧ-mĭnt′)	120	36.40 N	117.30 W
Panaria (Is.), It. (pä-nä′rē-a)	172	38.37 N	15.05 E
Panaro (R.), It. (pä-nä′rô)	172	44.47 N	11.06 E
Panay (I.), Phil. (pä-nī′)	206	11.15 N	121.38 E
Pančevo, Yugo, (pȧn′chĕ-vô)	173	44.52 N	20.42 E
Pānchghara, India	67a	22.44 N	88.16 E
Panch′iao, Taiwan	68d	25.01 N	121.27 E
Panchor, Mala.	191b	2.10 N	103.43 E
Pānchur, India	196a	22.31 N	88.17 E
Panda, Zaire (pän′dä′)	226	10.59 S	27.24 E
Pandar-e Pahlavī, Iran	179	37.30 N	49.30 E
Pan de Guajaibon (Mtn.), Cuba (pän dā gwä-jȧ-bōn′)	134	22.50 N	83.20 W
Pandu, Zaire	230	5.00 N	19.15 E
Panevėžys, Sov. Un. (pä′nyĕ-vāzh′ēs)	165	55.44 N	24.21 E
Panfilov, Sov. Un. (pŭn-fē′lôf)	180	44.12 N	79.58 E
Panga, Zaire (päŋ′gä)	231	1.51 N	26.25 E
Pangani, Tan. (pän-gä′nē)	227	5.28 S	38.58 E
Pangani (R.), Tan.	231	4.40 S	37.45 E
Pangkalpinang, Indon. (päng-käl′pē-näng′)	206	2.11 S	106.04 E
Pangnirtung, Can.	97	66.08 N	65.26 W
Panguitch, Ut. (pän′gwĭch)	123	37.50 N	112.30 W
Panimávida, Chile (pä-nē-mȧ′vē-dä)	141b	36.44 S	71.26 W
Pānināti, India	196a	22.42 N	88.23 E
Panje, India	67e	18.54 N	72.57 E
Panjim, see Panaji			
Pankow (Neigh.), G.D.R.	65a	52.34 N	13.24 E
Panshi, China (pän-shē)	202	42.50 N	126.48 E
Pan Si Pan (Mtn.), Viet.	203	22.25 N	103.50 E
Pantar, Pulau (I.), Indon. (pän′tär)	207	8.40 N	123.45 E
Pantelleria (I.), It. (pän-tĕl-lā-rē′ä)	159	36.43 N	11.59 E
Pantepec, Mex. (pän-tā-pĕk′)	131	17.11 N	93.04 W
Pantheon (P. Int.), It.	66c	41.55 N	12.29 E
Pantitlán, Mex.	60a	19.25 N	99.05 W
Pantjoran (Neigh.), Indon.	68k	6.14 S	106.50 E
Panuco, Mex. (pä′no͞o-kô)	130	22.04 N	98.11 W
Pánuco, Mex. (pä′no͞o-kô)	130	29.47 N	105.55 W
Panuco (R.), Mex.	130	21.59 N	98.20 W
Pánuco de Coronado, Mex. (pä′no͞o-kô dā kō-rō-nä′dhō)	124	24.33 N	104.20 W
Panvel, India	197b	18.59 N	73.06 E
Panyu, China (pä-yo͞o)	201a	22.56 N	113.22 E
Panzós, Guat. (pä-zós′)	132	15.26 N	89.40 W
Pao, (R.), Ven. (pá′ō)	143b	9.52 N	67.57 W
Paola, Ks. (pā-ō′lȧ)	123	38.34 N	94.51 W
Paoli, In. (pā-ō′lī)	110	38.35 N	86.30 W
Paoli, Pa.	112f	40.03 N	75.29 W
Paonia, Co. (pā-ō′nyȧ)	121	38.50 N	107.40 W
Paoting, China	202	42.04 N	125.00 E

PLACE (Pronounciation)	PAGE	Lat. °′	Long. °′
Pápa, Hung. (pä′pô)	167	47.18 N	17.27 E
Papagayo (R.), Mex. (pä-pä-gä′yō)	130	16.52 N	99.41 W
Papagayo, Golfo del (G.), C. R. (gôl-fô-dĕl-pä-pä-gȧ′yō)	132	10.44 N	85.56 W
Papagayo, Laguna (L.), Mex. (lä-o͞o-nä)	130	16.44 N	99.44 W
Papago Ind. Res., Az. (pä′pä′gō)	121	32.33 N	112.12 W
Papantla de Olarte, Mex. (pä-pän′tlä dā-ô-lä′r-tĕ)	128	20.30 N	97.15 W
Papatoapan (R.), Mex. (pä-pä-tô-ā-pȧ′n)	131	18.00 N	96.22 W
Papelón, Ven.	61a	10.27 N	66.47 W
Papenburg, F.R.G. (päp′ĕn-bo͝orgh)	166	53.05 N	7.23 E
Papinas, Arg. (pä-pē′näs)	141c	35.30 S	57.19 W
Papineauville, Can. (pä-pē-nō′vĕl)	95c	45.38 N	75.01 W
Papua, Gulf of, Pap. N. Gui. (păp-o͞o-ȧ)	207	8.20 S	144.45 E
Papua New Guinea, Oceania (păp-o͞o-ȧ)(gĭne)	207	7.00 S	142.15 E
Papudo, Chile (pä-po͞o′dô)	141b	32.30 S	71.25 W
Paquequer Pequeno, Braz. (pä-kĕ-kĕ′r-pĕ-kĕ′nô)	144b	22.19 S	43.02 W
Pará (State), Braz. (pä-rä′)	143	4.45 S	53.30 W
Pará (R.), Braz. (pä-rä′)	141a	20.21 S	44.38 W
Para (R.), Sov. Un.	174	53.45 N	40.58 E
Paracale, Phil. (pä-rä-kä′lå)	207a	14.17 N	122.47 E
Paracambi, Braz. (pä-rä-kȧ′m-bē)	144b	22.36 S	43.43 W
Paracatu, Braz. (pä-rä-kä-to͞o′)	143	17.17 S	46.43 W
Paraćin, Yugo. (pȧ′rä-chēn)	173	43.51 N	21.26 E
Para de Minas, Braz. (pä-rä-dĕ-mē′näs)	141a	19.52 S	44.37 W
Paradise (I.), Ba.	134	25.05 N	77.20 W
Paradise Valley, Ny. (păr′ȧ-dīs)	116	41.28 N	117.32 W
Parados, Cerro de los (Mtn.), Col. (sĕ′r-rô-dĕ-lôs-pä-rä′dōs)	142a	5.44 N	75.13 W
Paragould, Ar. (păr′ȧ-go͞old)	123	36.03 N	90.29 W
Paraguaçu (R.), Braz. (pä-rä-gwä-zo͞o′)	143	12.25 S	39.46 W
Paraguaná, Pen. de (Pen.), Ven. (pĕ-nē′ng-so͞o-lä-dĕ-pä-rä-gwä-nȧ′)	142	12.00 N	69.55 W
Paraguay, S. A. (păr′ȧ-gwā)	140	24.00 S	57.00 W
Paraguay, Rio (R.), S.A. (rē′ō-pä-rä-gwä′y)	143	21.12 S	57.31 W
Paraíba (State), Braz. (pä-rä-ē′bä)	143	7.11 S	37.05 W
Paraíba (R.), Braz.	141a	23.02 S	45.43 W
Paraíba do Sul, Braz. (dô-so͞o′l)	141a	22.10 S	43.18 W
Paraíba, see João Pessoa			
Paraibuna, Braz. (pä-räē-bo͞o′nä)	141a	23.23 S	45.38 W
Paraíso, C. R.	133	9.50 N	83.53 W
Paraíso, Mex.	131	18.24 N	93.11 W
Paraiso, Pan. (pä-rä-ē′sô)	128a	9.02 N	79.38 W
Paraisópolis, Braz. (pä-räē-sô′pō-lēs)	141a	22.35 S	45.45 W
Paraitinga, Braz. (pä-rä-ē-tē′n-gä)	141a	23.15 S	45.24 W
Parakou, Benim (pȧ-rȧ-ko͞o′)	229	9.21 N	2.37 E
Paramaribo, Sur. (pȧ-rȧ-mȧ′rē-bō)	143	5.50 N	55.15 W
Paramatta, Austl. (păr-ȧ-măt′ȧ)	211b	33.49 S	150.59 E
Paramillo (Mtn.), Col. (pä-rä-mē′l-yō)	142a	7.06 N	75.55 W
Paramount, Ca.	59	33.53 N	118.09 W
Paramus, NJ	112a	40.56 N	74.04 W
Paramushir (I.), Sov. Un.	181	50.45 N	154.00 E
Paran (R.), Isr.	191a	30.05 N	34.50 E
Paraná, Arg. (pä-rä-nä′)	144	31.44 S	60.29 W
Paraná (State), Braz.	144	24.25 S	52.00 W
Paraná (R.), Braz.	143	13.05 S	47.11 W
Paranaguá, Braz. (pä-rä′nä-gwȧ′)	143	25.39 S	48.42 W
Paranaíba, Braz. (pä-rä-nȧ-ē′bȧ)	143	19.43 S	51.13 W
Paranaíba (R.), Braz.	143	18.58 S	50.44 W
Parana Ibicuy (R.), Arg. (ē-bē-ko͞o′ē)	141c	33.27 S	59.26 W
Paranam, Sur.	143	5.39 N	55.13 W
Paranápanema (R.), Braz. (pä-rä′nȧ′pä-nē-mä)	144	22.28 S	52.15 W
Parañaque, Phil.	68g	14.30 N	120.59 E
Paraná, Rio (R.), Arg.	144	32.15 S	60.55 W
Paraopeda (R.), Braz. (pä-rä-o-pĕ′dä)	141a	20.09 S	44.14 W
Parapara, Ven. (pä-rä-pä-rä)	143b	9.44 N	67.17 W
Pará, Rio do (R.), Braz. (rē′ō-dô-pä-rä′)	143	1.09 S	48.48 W
Pará, see Belém			
Parati, Braz. (pä-rätē)	141a	23.14 S	44.43 W
Paray-le-Monial, Fr. (pȧ-rē′lē-mô-nyäl′)	168	46.27 N	4.14 E
Pārbati (R.), India	196	24.50 N	76.44 E
Parcel Is., China	206	16.40 N	113.00 E
Parchim, G.D.R. (par′kĭm)	166	53.25 N	11.52 E
Parczew, Pol. (pär′chĕf)	167	51.38 N	22.53 E
Pardo (R.), Braz. (pär′dō)	143	15.25 S	39.40 W
Pardo (R.), Braz.	141a	21.32 S	46.40 W
Pardubice, Czech. (pär′do͞o-bĭt-sĕ)	166	50.02 N	15.47 E
Parecis, Serra dos (Mts.), Braz. (sĕr′rȧ dōs pä-rā-sēzh′)	143	13.45 S	59.28 W
Paredes de Nava, Sp (pä-rā′dās dā nä′vä)	170	42.10 N	4.41 W
Paredón, Mex.	124	25.56 N	100.58 W
Parent, Can.	103	47.59 N	74.30 W
Parent, Lac (L.), Can.	103	48.40 N	77.00 W
Pare Pare, Indon.	206	4.01 S	119.38 E
Pargolovo, Sov. Un. (pȧr-gô′lô vô)	182c	60.04 N	30.18 E
Pari (Neigh.), Braz.	61d	23.32 S	46.37 W
Paria (R.), Az.-Ut.	121	37.07 N	111.51 W
Paria, Golfo de (G.), Ven. (gôl-fô-dĕ-br-pä-rē-ä)	142	10.33 N	62.14 W
Paricutín, Vol., Mex. (pä-rē-ko͞o-tē′n)	130	19.27 N	102.14 W
Parida, Rio de la (R.), Mex. (rē′ō-dĕ-lä-pä-rē′dä)	124	26.23 N	104.40 W
Parima, Serra (Mts.), Braz.-Ven. (sĕr′rȧ pä-rē′mȧ)	142	3.45 N	64.00 W
Pariñas, Punta (Pt.), Peru (po͞o′n-tä-pä-rē′n-yäs)	142	4.30 S	81.23 W
Parintins, Braz. (pä-rĭn-tĭɴzh′)	143	2.34 S	56.30 W
Paris, Ar. (păr′ĭs)	119	35.17 N	93.43 W
Paris, Can.	110	43.15 N	80.23 W

PLACE (Pronounciation)	PAGE	Lat. °′	Long. °′
Paris, Fr. (pȧ-rē′)	169b	48.51 N	2.20 E
Paris, Il.	110	39.35 N	87.40 W
Paris, Ky.	110	38.15 N	84.15 W
Paris, Mo.	123	39.27 N	91.59 W
Paris, Tn.	126	36.16 N	88.20 W
Paris, Tx.	123	33.39 N	95.33 W
Paris-le-Bourget, Aéroport de (Arpt.), Fr.	64c	49.00 N	2.25 E
Paris-Orly, Aéroport de (Arpt.), Fr.	64c	48.45 N	2.25 E
Parita, Golfo de (G.), Pan. (gôl-fô-dĕ-pä-rē′tä)	133	8.06 N	80.10 W
Park City, Ut.	117	40.39 N	111.33 W
Parkdene, S. Afr.	71b	26.14 S	28.16 E
Parker, SD (pär′kẽr)	114	43.24 N	97.10 W
Parker Dam, Az.-Ca.	123	34.20 N	114.00 W
Parkersburg, WV (pär′kẽrz-bûrg)	110	39.15 N	81.35 W
Parkes, Austl. (pärks)	216	33.10 S	148.10 E
Park Falls, Wi. (pärk)	115	45.55 N	90.29 W
Park Forest, Il.	113a	41.29 N	87.41 W
Parkgate, Eng.	64a	53.18 N	3.05 W
Parkhill Gardens, S. Afr.	71b	26.14 S	28.11 E
Parkland, Wa. (pärk′lȧnd)	118a	47.09 N	122.26 W
Parklawn, Va.	56d	38.50 N	77.09 W
Parklea, Austl.	70a	33.44 S	150.57 E
Park Orchards, Austl.	70b	37.46 S	145.13 E
Park Ra., Co.	117	40.54 N	106.40 W
Park Rapids, Mn.	115	46.53 N	95.05 W
Park Ridge, Il.	113a	42.00 N	87.50 W
Park Ridge Manor, Il.	58a	42.02 N	87.50 W
Park River, ND	114	48.22 N	97.43 W
Parkrose, Or. (pärk′rōz)	118c	45.33 N	122.33 W
Park Rynie, S. Afr.	227c	30.22 S	30.43 E
Parkston, SD (pärks′tŭn)	114	43.22 N	97.59 W
Park Town (Neigh.), S. Afr.	71b	26.11 S	28.03 E
Parktown North (Neigh.), S. Afr.	71b	26.09 S	28.02 E
Park View, NM (vū)	121	36.45 N	106.30 W
Parkview, Pa.	57b	40.30 N	79.56 W
Parkville, Md.	112e	39.22 N	76.32 W
Parkville, Mo.	119f	39.12 N	94.41 W
Parkwood, Md.	56d	39.01 N	77.05 W
Parla, Sp. (pär′lä)	171a	40.14 N	3.46 W
Parliament, Houses of (P. Int.), Eng.	62	51.30 N	0.07 W
Parma, It. (pär′mä)	172	44.48 N	10.20 E
Parma, Oh.	113d	41.23 N	81.44 W
Parma Heights, Oh.	113d	41.23 N	81.36 W
Parnaguá, Braz. (pär-nä-gwȧ′)	143	9.52 S	44.27 W
Parnaíba, Braz. (pär-nä-ē′bä)	143	3.00 S	41.42 W
Parnaíba (R.), Braz.	143	3.57 S	42.30 W
Parnassós (Mtn.), Grc.	173	38.36 N	22.35 E
Parndorf, Aus.	157e	48.00 N	16.52 E
Pärnu, Sov. Un. (pĕr′no͞o)	165	58.24 N	24.29 E
Pärnu (R.), Sov. Un.	165	58.40 N	25.05 E
Pärnu Laht (B.), Sov. Un. (läĸt)	165	58.15 N	24.17 E
Paro, Bhu. (pä′rô)	196	27.30 N	89.30 E
Paroo (R.), Austl. (pä′ro͞o)	216	29.40 S	144.24 E
Paropamisus (Mts.), Afg.	192	34.45 N	63.58 E
Páros, Grc. (pä′rôs) (pā′rŏs)	173	37.05 N	25.14 E
Páros (I.), Grc.	173	37.11 N	25.00 E
Parow, S. Afr. (pȧ′rô)	226a	33.54 S	18.36 E
Parowan, Ut. (păr′ô-wăn)	121	37.50 N	112.50 W
Parral, Chile (pär-rä′l)	144	36.07 S	71.47 W
Parral, R., Mex.	124	27.25 N	105.08 W
Parramatta, Austl.	70a	33.49 S	151.00 E
Parramatta (R.), Aust. (păr-ȧ-măt′ȧ)	211b	33.42 S	150.58 E
Parras, Mex. (pär-räs′)	124	25.28 N	102.08 W
Parrita, C. R. (pär-rē′tä)	133	9.32 N	84.17 W
Parrsboro, Can. (pärz′bŭr-ô)	104	45.24 N	64.20 W
Parry (I.), Can. (păr′ĭ)	110	45.15 N	80.00 W
Parry Is., Can.	94	75.30 N	110.00 W
Parry, Mt., Can.	98	52.53 N	128.45 W
Parry Sound, Can.	111	45.20 N	80.00 W
Parsnip (R.), Can. (pärs′nĭp)	98	54.45 N	122.20 W
Parsons, Ks. (pär′s′nz)	123	37.20 N	95.16 W
Parsons, WV	111	39.05 N	79.40 W
Parthenay, Fr. (pȧr-t′nĕ′)	168	46.39 N	0.16 W
Partington, Eng.	64b	53.25 N	2.26 W
Partinico, It. (pär-tē′nē-kô)	172	38.02 N	13.11 E
Partizansk, Sov. Un.	204	43.15 N	133.19 E
Parys, S. Afr. (pȧ-rĭs′)	223d	26.53 S	27.28 E
Pasadena, Ca. (păs-ȧ-dē′nȧ)	119a	34.09 N	118.09 W
Pasadena, Md.	112e	39.06 N	76.35 W
Pasadena, Tx.	125a	29.43 N	95.13 W
Pasay, Phil.	68g	14.33 N	121.00 E
Pascagoula, Ms. (păs-kȧ-go͞o′lȧ)	126	30.22 N	88.33 W
Pascagoula (R.), Ms.	126	30.52 N	88.48 W
Paşcani, Rom. (päsh-kän′)	167	47.46 N	26.42 E
Pasco, Wa. (păs′kō)	116	46.13 N	119.04 W
Pascoe Vale, Austl.	70b	37.44 S	144.56 E
Pasewalk, G.D.R. (pä′zē-välk)	166	53.31 N	14.01 E
Pashiya, Sov. Un. (pä′shĭ-yȧ)	182a	58.27 N	58.17 E
Pashkovo, Sov. Un. (pȧsh-kô′vô)	204	48.52 N	131.09 E
Pashkovskaya, Sov. Un. (pȧsh-kôf′skȧ-yȧ)	175	45.29 N	39.04 E
Pasig, Phil.	207a	14.34 N	121.05 E
Pasión, Rio de la (R.), Guat. (rē′ō-dĕ-lä-pä-syōn′)	132a	16.31 N	90.11 W
Pasir Gudang, Mala.	67c	1.27 N	103.53 E
Pasir Panjang, Singapore	67c	1.17 N	103.47 E
Pasir Puteh, Mala.	67c	1.26 N	103.56 E
Paso de los Libres, Arg. (pä-sô-dĕ-lôs-lē′brĕs)	144	29.33 S	57.05 W
Paso de los Toros, Ur. (tō′rôs)	141c	32.43 S	56.33 W
Paso del Rey, Arg.	60d	34.39 S	58.45 W
Paso Robles, Ca. (pă′sō rō′blĕs)	120	35.38 N	120.44 W
Pasquia Hills, Can. (păs′kwē-ȧ)	102	53.13 N	102.37 W
Passaic, NJ (pă-sā′ĭk)	112a	40.52 N	74.08 W
Passaic R., NJ	112a	40.42 N	74.26 W
Passamaquoddy B., Can. (păs′ȧ-mȧ-kwŏd′ĭ)	104	45.06 N	66.59 W
Passa Tempo, Braz. (pä′s-sä-tĕ′m-pô)	141a	21.40 S	44.29 W
Passau, F.R.G. (päs′ou)	166	48.34 N	13.27 E

328 Pass Christian – Perris

PLACE (Pronounciation)	PAGE	Lat. °′	Long. °′
Pass Christian, Ms. (pȧs krĭs'tyĕn)	126	30.20 N	89.15 W
Passero, C., It. (päs-sĕ'rô)	159	36.34 N	15.13 E
Passo Fundo, Braz. (pä'sō fo͞on'do͞o)	144	28.16 S	52.13 W
Passos, Braz. (pä's-sōs)	141a	20.45 S	46.37 W
Pastaza (R.), Peru (päs-tä'zä)	142	3.05 S	76.18 W
Pasto, Col. (päs'tô)	142	1.15 N	77.19 W
Pastora, Mex. (päs-tô-rä)	130	22.08 N	100.04 W
Pasuruan, Indon.	206	7.45 S	112.50 E
Pasvalys, Sov. Un. (päs-vä-lēs')	165	56.04 N	24.23 E
Patagonia (Reg.), Arg. (păt-ȧ-gō'nĭ-ȧ)	144	46.45 S	69.30 W
Pātālganga (R.), India	197b	18.52 N	73.08 E
Patapsco R., Md. (pȧ-tăps'kō)	112e	39.12 N	76.30 W
Paternò, It. (pä-tĕr-nô')	172	37.25 N	14.58 E
Paterson, NJ (păt'ēr-sŭn)	112a	40.55 N	74.10 W
Pathfinder Res., Wy. (păth'fīn-dēr)	117	42.22 N	107.10 W
Patiāla, India (pŭt-ē-ä'lŭ)	196	30.25 N	76.28 E
Pati do Alferes, Braz. (pä-tē-dô-ȧl-fĕ'rĕs)	144a	22.25 S	43.25 W
Patna, India (pŭt'nŭ)	196	25.33 N	85.18 E
Patnanongan, Phil. (pät-nä-nôŋ'gän)	207a	14.50 N	122.25 E
Patoka (R.), Ind. (pȧ-tō'kȧ)	110	38.25 N	87.25 W
Patom Plat., Sov. Un.	181	59.30 N	115.00 E
Patos, Braz. (pä'tōzh)	143	7.03 S	37.14 W
Patos, Wa. (pä'tōs)	118d	48.47 N	122.57 W
Patos de Minas, Braz. (dĕ-mē'näzh)	143	18.39 S	46.31 W
Patos, Lago dos (L.), Braz. (lä'gō-ȧ dozh pä'tōzh)	144	31.15 S	51.30 W
Pátrai (Patras), Grc. (pä-trī') (pä-träs')	173	38.15 N	21.48 E
Patraïkós Kólpos (G.), Grc.	173	38.16 N	21.19 E
Patras, see Pátrai			
Patrocínio, Braz. (pä-trō-sē'nē-o͞o)	143	18.48 S	46.47 W
Pattani, Thai. (pät'ȧ-nē)	206	6.56 N	101.13 E
Patten, Me. (păt''n)	104	45.59 N	68.27 W
Patterson, La. (păt'ēr-sŭn)	125	29.41 N	91.20 W
Patton, Pa.	111	40.40 N	78.45 W
Patuca, Punta (Pt.), Hond. (po͞o'n-tä-pä-to͞o'kä)	133	15.23 N	84.05 W
Patuca R., Hond.	133	15.22 N	84.31 W
Patuxent (R.), Md. (pȧ-tŭk'sĕnt)	111	39.10 N	77.10 W
Pátzcuaro, Mex. (päts'kwä-rô)	130	19.30 N	101.36 W
Pátzcuaro, Lago de (L.), Mex. (lä'gô-dĕ)	130	19.36 N	101.38 W
Patzicía, Guat. (pät-zē'syä)	132	14.36 N	90.57 W
Patzún, Guat. (pät-zo͞on')	132	14.40 N	91.00 W
Pau, Fr. (pō)	168	43.18 N	0.23 W
Pau, Gave de (Strm.), Fr. (gäv-dē)	168	43.33 N	0.51 W
Paulding, Oh. (pôl'dĭng)	110	41.05 N	84.35 W
Paulinenaue, G.D.R. (pou'lē-nĕ-nou-ĕ)	157b	52.40 N	12.43 E
Paulis, see Isiro			
Paulistana, Braz. (pȧ'o͞o-lēs-tá-nä)	143	8.13 S	41.06 W
Paulo Afonso, Salto (falls), Braz. (säl-tô-pou'lo͞o äf-fôɴ'so͞o)	143	9.33 S	38.32 W
Paul Roux, S. Afr. (pôrl ro͞o)	223d	28.18 S	27.57 E
Paulsboro, NJ (pôlz'bē-rô)	112f	39.50 N	75.16 W
Pauls Valley, Ok. (pôlz văl'ē)	123	34.43 N	97.13 W
Pavarandocito, Col. (pä-vä-rän-dô-sē'tô)	142a	7.18 N	76.32 W
Pavda, Sov. Un. (päv'da)	182a	59.16 N	59.32 E
Pavia, It. (pä-vē'ä)	172	45.12 N	9.11 E
Pavlodar, Sov. Un. (pȧv-lô-dȧr')	180	52.17 N	77.23 E
Pavlo'f B., Ak. (păv-lōf)	107	55.20 N	161.20 W
Pavlograd, Sov. Un. (pȧv-lô-grȧt')	175	48.32 N	35.52 E
Pavlovsk, Sov. Un. (pȧv-lôfsk')	175	50.28 N	40.05 E
Pavlovsk, Sov. Un.	182c	59.41 N	30.27 E
Pavlovskiy Posad, Sov. Un. (pȧv-lôf'skĭ pô-sȧt')	182b	55.47 N	38.39 E
Pavuna, Braz. (pä-vo͞o'nȧ)	144b	22.48 S	43.21 W
Päwesin, G.D.R. (pȧ'vĕ-zēn)	157b	52.31 N	12.44 E
Pawhuska, Ok. (pô-hŭs'kȧ)	123	36.41 N	96.20 W
Pawnee, Ok. (pô-nē')	123	36.20 N	96.47 W
Pawnee (R.), Ks.	122	38.18 N	99.42 W
Pawnee City, Ne.	123	40.08 N	96.09 W
Paw Paw, Mi. (pô'pô)	110	42.15 N	85.55 W
Paw Paw (R.), Mi.	115	42.14 N	86.21 W
Pawtucket, RI (pô-tŭk'ĕt)	112b	41.53 N	71.23 W
Paxoí (I.), Grc.	173	39.14 N	20.15 E
Paxton, Il. (păks'tŭn)	110	40.35 N	88.00 W
Paya Lebar, Singapore	67c	1.22 N	103.53 E
Payette, Id. (pȧ-ĕt')	116	44.05 N	116.55 W
Payette R., Id.	116	43.57 N	116.26 W
Payette R., North Fork, Id.	116	44.35 N	116.10 W
Payette R., South Fork, Id.	116	44.07 N	115.43 W
Pay-Khoy, Khrebet (Mts.), Sov. Un.	178	68.08 N	63.04 E
Payne (L.), Can. (pān)	97	59.22 N	73.16 W
Paynesville, Mn. (pānz'vĭl)	115	45.23 N	94.43 W
Paynesville, S. Afr.	71b	26.14 S	28.28 E
Payo Obispo, see Cuidad Chetumal			
Paysandú, Ur. (pī-sän-do͞o')	144	32.16 S	57.55 W
Payson, Ut. (pā's'n)	121	40.05 N	111.45 W
Pazardzhik, Bul. (pä-zȧr-dzhek')	173	42.10 N	24.22 E
Pazin, Yugo. (pä'zēn)	172	45.14 N	13.57 E
Peabody, Ks. (pē'bŏd-ĭ)	123	38.09 N	97.09 W
Peabody, Ma.	105a	42.32 N	70.56 W
Peabody Institute (P. Int.), Md.	56c	39.18 N	76.37 W
Peace (R.), Can.	99	55.40 N	118.30 W
Peace Cr., Fl. (pēs)	127a	27.16 N	81.53 W
Peace Dale, RI (dāl)	112b	41.27 N	71.30 W
Peace River, Can. (rĭv'ēr)	99	56.14 N	117.17 W
Peacock Hills, Can. (pē-kŏk' hĭlz)	96	66.08 N	109.55 W
Peak Hill, Austl.	214	25.38 S	118.50 E
Peakhurst, Austl.	70a	33.58 S	151.04 E
Peak, The (Mt.), Eng. (pēk)	156	53.23 N	1.52 W
Pearl (R.), La.-Ms. (pûrl)	126	31.06 N	89.44 W
Pearland, Tx. (pûrl'ănd)	125a	29.34 N	95.17 W
Pearl Harbor, Hi.	106a	21.20 N	157.53 W
Pearsall, Tx. (pēr'sôl)	124	28.53 N	99.06 W
Pearse I., Can. (pērs)	98	54.51 N	130.21 W
Pearston, S. Afr. (pē'ērstŏn)	227c	32.36 S	25.09 E
Peary Land (Reg.), Grnld. (pēr'ĭ)	93	82.00 N	40.00 W
Pease (R.), Tx. (pēz)	122	34.07 N	99.53 W
Peason, La. (pēz''n)	125	31.25 N	93.19 W
Pebane, Moz. (pĕ-bȧ'nē)	231	17.10 S	38.08 E
Peć, Yugo. (pĕch)	173	42.39 N	20.18 E
Pecan Bay, Tx. (pē̇-kăn')	124	32.04 N	99.15 W
Peçanha, Braz. (pā-kän'yȧ)	143	18.37 S	42.26 W
Pecatonica (R.), Il. (pĕk-ȧ-tŏn-ĭ-kȧ)	115	42.21 N	89.28 W
Pechenga, Sov. Un. (pyĕ'chĕŋ-gȧ)	178	69.30 N	31.10 E
Pechincha (Neigh.), Braz.	61c	22.56 S	43.21 W
Pechora (R.), Sov. Un.	178	66.00 N	52.30 E
Pechora Basin, Sov. Un. (pyĕ-chô'rȧ)	180	67.55 N	58.37 E
Pechorskaya Guba (B.), Sov. Un.	178	68.40 N	55.00 E
Pecos, NM (pā'kôs)	121	35.29 N	105.41 W
Pecos, Tx.	124	31.26 N	103.30 W
Pecos (R.), U.S.	108	31.10 N	103.10 W
Pécs, Hung. (pāch)	167	46.04 N	18.15 E
Peddie, S. Afr.	227c	33.13 S	27.09 E
Pededze (R.), Sov. Un. (pă'dĕd-zĕ)	174	57.18 N	27.13 E
Pedley, Ca. (pĕd'lē)	119a	33.59 N	117.29 W
Pedra Azul, Braz. (pā'drä-zo͞o'l)	143	16.03 S	41.13 W
Pedreiras, Braz. (pĕ-drā'räs)	143	4.30 S	44.31 W
Pedro Antonio Santos (Sta. Cruz Chico), Mex. (pā'drō än-tō'nē-ō sän'tōs) (sän'tä kro͞oz' chē'kô)	132a	18.55 N	88.13 W
Pedro Betancourt, Cuba (bā-täŋ-kōrt')	134	22.40 N	81.15 W
Pedro de Valdivia, Chile (pĕ'drô-dĕ-väl-dē'vē-ä)	144	22.32 S	69.55 W
Pedro do Rio, Braz. (dô-rē'rō)	144b	22.20 S	43.09 W
Pedro II, Braz. (pä'dro͞o sȧ-go͞on'do͞o)	143	4.20 S	41.27 W
Pedro Juan Caballero, Par. (ho͞oȧ'n-kä-bäl-yĕ'rō)	143	22.40 S	55.42 W
Pedro Miguel, Pan. (mē̇-gäl')	128a	9.01 N	79.36 W
Pedro Miguel Locks, Pan. (mē̇-gäl')	128a	9.01 N	79.36 W
Pedro, Pt., Sri Lanka (pē'drô)	197	9.50 N	80.14 E
Peebinga, Austl. (pē-bĭng'ȧ)	216	34.43 S	140.55 E
Peebles, Scot. (pē'b'lz)	162	55.40 N	3.15 W
Pee Dee (R.), NC-SC (pē-dē')	127	34.01 N	79.26 W
Peekskill, NY (pēks'kĭl)	112a	41.17 N	73.55 W
Pegasus B., N.Z. (pĕg'ȧ-sŭs)	217	43.18 S	173.25 E
Pegnitz R., F.R.G. (pĕgh-nēts)	166	49.38 N	11.40 E
Pego, Sp. (pā'gō)	171	38.50 N	0.09 W
Pegu, Bur. (pĕ-go͞o')	206	17.17 N	96.29 E
Peguis Ind. Res., Can.	101	51.20 N	97.35 W
Pegu Yoma (Mt.), Bur. (pĕ-go͞o'yō'mä)	198	19.16 N	95.59 E
Pehčevo, Yugo. (pĕĸ'chĕ-vô)	173	41.42 N	22.57 E
Pehladpur (Neigh.), India	67d	28.35 N	77.06 E
Peigan Ind. Res., Can.	99	49.35 N	113.40 W
Peipus, L., see Chudskoye Ozero			
Peit'ou, Taiwan	68d	25.08 N	121.29 E
Pekin, Il. (pē'kĭn)	110	40.35 N	89.30 W
Peking, see Beijing			
Pelagie, Isole I., It.	160	35.46 N	12.32 E
Pélagos (I.), Grc.	173	39.17 N	24.05 E
Pelahatchee, Ms. (pĕl-ȧ-hăch'ē)	126	32.17 N	89.48 W
Pelat, Mt., Fr. (pē-lȧ')	169	44.16 N	6.43 E
Peleduy, Sov. Un. (pyĕl-yĭ-do͞o'ē)	181	59.50 N	112.47 E
Pelee I., Can. (pē'lē)	110	41.45 N	82.30 W
Pelee, Mt. (Vol.), Mart. (pē-lā')	133b	14.49 N	61.10 W
Pelee, Pt., Can.	110	41.55 N	82.30 W
Pelequén, Chile (pĕ-lĕ-kĕ'n)	141b	34.26 S	71.52 W
Pelew (Is.), see Palau			
Pelham, Ga. (pĕl'hăm)	126	31.07 N	84.10 W
Pelham, NH	105a	42.43 N	71.22 W
Pelham, NY	55	40.55 N	73.49 W
Pelham Manor, NY	55	40.54 N	73.48 W
Pelican (L.), Mn.	115	46.36 N	94.00 W
Pelican B., Can.	101	52.45 N	100.20 W
Pelican Hbr., Ba. (pĕl'ĭ-kăn)	134	26.20 N	76.45 W
Pelican Rapids, Mn. (pĕl'ĭ-kăn)	114	46.34 N	96.05 W
Pella, Ia. (pĕl'ȧ)	115	41.25 N	92.50 W
Pell-Worm I., F.R.G. (pĕl'vôrm)	166	54.33 N	8.25 E
Pelly (L.), Can.	96	66.08 N	102.57 W
Pelly (R.), Can.	96	62.20 N	133.00 W
Pelly B., Can. (pĕl'ĭ)	96	68.57 N	91.05 W
Pelly Crossing, Can.	107	62.50 N	136.50 W
Pelly Mts., Can.	96	61.50 N	133.05 W
Peloncillo Mts., Az. (pĕl-ôn-sĭl'lō)	121	32.40 N	109.20 W
Peloponnisos (Reg.), Grc.	173	37.28 N	22.14 E
Pelotas, Braz. (pā-lō'tăzh)	144	31.45 S	52.18 W
Pelton, Can. (pĕl'tŭn)	113b	42.15 N	82.57 W
Pelym (R.), Sov. Un.	178	60.20 N	63.05 E
Pelzer, SC (pĕl'zēr)	127	34.38 N	82.30 W
Pemanggil (I.), Mala.	191b	2.37 N	104.41 E
Pematangsiantar, Indon.	206	2.58 N	99.03 E
Pemba, Moz. (pĕm'bȧ)	231	12.58 S	40.30 E
Pemba, Zambia	226	15.29 S	27.22 E
Pemba (I.), Tan	231	5.20 S	39.57 E
Pemba Chan., Afr.	231	5.10 S	39.30 E
Pembina, ND (pĕm'bĭ-nȧ)	114	48.58 N	97.15 W
Pembina (R.), Can.	101	49.08 N	98.20 W
Pembina (R.), Can.	99	53.05 N	114.30 W
Pembroke, Can. (pĕm' brŏk)	111	45.50 N	77.00 W
Pembroke, Ma. (pĕm'brŏk)	105a	42.05 N	70.49 W
Pembroke, Wales	162	51.40 N	5.00 W
Pen, India	197b	18.44 N	73.06 E
Penafiel, Port. (pā-nȧ-fyĕl')	170	41.12 N	8.19 W
Peñafiel, Sp. (pā-nyȧ-fyĕl')	170	41.38 N	4.08 W
Peña Grande (Neigh.), Sp.	65b	40.29 N	3.44 W
Peñalara (Mtn.), Sp. (pā-nyä-lä'rä)	170	40.52 N	3.57 W
Pena Nevada, Cerro, Mex.	130	23.47 N	99.52 W
Peñaranda de Bracamonte, Sp. (pā-nyä-rän'dä dā brä-kä-mōn'tā)	170	40.54 N	5.11 W
Peñarroya-Peublonuevo, Sp. (pĕn-yär-rô'yä-pwĕ'blô-nwĕ'vô)	170	38.18 N	5.18 W
Peñas, Cabo de (C.), Sp. (kȧ'bô-dĕ-pā'nyäs)	170	43.42 N	6.12 W
Penasco R., Tx. (pā-nás'kō)	124	32.50 N	104.45 W
Penas, Golfo de, Chile (gôl-fô-dĕ-pĕ'n-äs)	144	47.15 S	77.30 W
Pendembu, S. L. (pĕn-dĕm'bo͞o)	228	8.06 N	10.42 W
Pender, Ne. (pĕn'dēr)	114	42.08 N	96.43 W
Penderisco (R.), Col. (pĕn-dĕ-rē's-kô)	142a	6.30 N	76.21 W
Pendjari, Parc Natl. de la (Natl. Pk.), Benin	228	11.25 N	1.30 E
Pendlebury, Eng.	64b	53.31 N	2.20 W
Pendleton, Or. (pĕn'd'l-tŭn)	116	45.41 N	118.47 W
Pend Oreille L., Id. (pŏn-dô-rā') (pĕn-dô-rĕl')	116	48.09 N	116.38 W
Pend Oreille R., Wa.	116	48.44 N	117.20 W
Penedo, Braz. (pā-nā'do͞o)	143	10.17 S	36.28 W
Penetanguishene, Can. (pĕn'ē̇-tăŋ-gĭ-shēn')	111	44.45 N	79.55 W
Pengcheng, China (pŭŋ-chŭŋ)	200	36.24 N	114.11 E
Penglai, China (pŭŋ-lī)	200	37.49 N	120.45 E
Penha (Neigh.), Braz.	61c	22.49 S	43.17 W
Penha de França (Neigh.), Braz.	61d	23.32 S	46.32 W
Peniche, Port. (pĕ-nē'chȧ)	170	39.22 N	9.24 W
Peninsula, Oh. (pĕn-ĭn'sū-lȧ)	113d	41.14 N	81.32 W
Penistone, Eng. (pĕn'ĭ-stŭn)	156	53.31 N	1.38 W
Penjamillo, Mex. (pĕn-hä-mēl'yō)	130	20.06 N	101.56 W
Penjamo, Mex. (pān'hä-mō)	130	20.27 N	101.43 W
Penk (R.), Eng. (pĕnk)	156	52.41 N	2.10 W
Penkridge, Eng. (pĕnk'rĭj)	156	52.43 N	2.07 W
Pennant Hills, Austl.	70a	33.44 S	151.04 E
Penne, It. (pĕn'nā)	172	42.28 N	13.57 E
Penner (R.), India (pĕn'ēr)	196	14.43 N	79.09 E
Penn Hills, Pa.	57b	40.28 N	79.53 W
Pennines (Mts.), Eng. (pĕn-īn')	162	54.30 N	2.10 W
Pennines, Alpes (Mts.), Switz.	166	46.02 N	7.07 E
Pennsauken, NJ	56b	39.58 N	75.04 W
Pennsboro, WV (pĕnz'bŭr-ô)	110	39.10 N	81.00 W
Penns Grove, NJ (pĕnz grōv)	112f	39.44 N	75.28 W
Pennsylvania (State), U. S. (pĕn-sĭl-vā'nĭ-ȧ)	109	41.00 N	78.10 W
Penn Valley, Pa.	56b	40.01 N	75.16 W
Penn Wynne, Pa.	56b	39.59 N	75.16 W
Penn Yan, NY (pĕn yăn')	111	42.40 N	77.00 W
Pennycutaway (R.), Can.	101	56.10 N	93.25 W
Peno (L.), Sov. Un. (pā'nô)	174	56.55 N	32.28 E
Penobscot (R.), Me.	104	45.00 N	68.36 W
Penobscot B., Me. (pē-nŏb'skŏt)	104	44.20 N	69.00 W
Penong, Austl. (pē̇-nông')	214	32.00 S	133.00 E
Penonomé, Pan. (pā-nō-nō-mā')	133	8.32 N	80.21 W
Penrith, Austl.	211b	33.45 S	150.42 E
Pensacola, Fl. (pĕn-sȧ-kō'lȧ)	126	30.25 N	87.13 W
Pensacola Dam, Ok.	123	36.27 N	95.02 W
Pensby, Eng.	64a	53.21 N	3.06 W
Pensilvania, Col. (pĕn-sēl-vȧ'nyä)	142a	5.31 N	75.05 W
Pentagon (P. Int.), Va.	56d	38.52 N	77.03 W
Pentecost (I.), Vanuatu (pĕn'tē̇-kŏst)	215	16.05 S	168.28 E
Penticton, Can.	99	49.30 N	119.35 W
Pentland Firth, Scot. (pĕnt'lănd)	162a	58.44 N	3.25 W
Penza, Sov. Un. (pĕn'zȧ)	179	53.10 N	45.00 E
Penzance, Eng. (pĕn-zăns')	162	50.07 N	5.40 W
Penzberg, F.R.G. (pĕnts'bĕrgh)	166	47.43 N	11.21 E
Penzhina (R.), Sov. Un. (pyĭn-zē-nŭ)	181	62.15 N	166.30 E
Penzhino, Sov. Un.	181	63.42 N	168.00 E
Penzhinskay'a Guba (B.), Sov. Un.	181	60.30 N	161.30 E
Penzing (Neigh.), Aus.	66e	48.12 N	16.18 E
Peoria, Il. (pē-ō'rĭ-ȧ)	110	40.45 N	89.35 W
Peotillos, Mex. (pā-ō-tel'yōs)	130	22.30 N	100.39 W
Peotone, Il. (pē'ō-tōn)	113a	41.20 N	87.47 W
Pepacton Res., NY (pĕp-ȧc'tŭn)	111	42.05 N	74.40 W
Pepe, Cabo (C.), Cuba (kä'bô-pĕ'pĕ)	134	21.30 N	83.10 W
Pepperell, Ma. (pĕp'ēr-ĕl)	105a	42.40 N	71.36 W
Peqin, Alb. (pĕ-kēn')	173	41.03 N	19.48 E
Pequannock, NJ	55	40.57 N	74.18 W
Perales (R.), Sp. (pā-rä'lās)	171	40.24 N	4.07 W
Perales de Tajuña, Sp. (dā tä-ho͞o'nyä)	171a	40.14 N	3.22 W
Percé, Can. (pĕr'sā')	104	48.31 N	64.13 W
Perche, Collines du (Hills), Fr.	168	48.25 N	0.40 E
Perchtoldsdorf, Aus. (pĕrk'tôlts-dôrf)	157e	48.07 N	16.17 E
Perdekop, S. Afr.	223d	27.11 S	29.38 E
Perdido (R.), Al.-Fl. (pĕr-dī'dō)	126	30.45 N	87.38 W
Perdido, Mt., Sp. (pĕr-dē'dō)	171	42.40 N	0.00 W
Perdões, Braz. (pĕr-dô'ĕs)	141a	21.05 S	45.05 W
Pereira, Col. (pā-rā'rä)	142a	4.49 N	75.42 W
Perekop, Sov. Un. (pĕr-ā-kôp')	175	46.08 N	33.39 E
Pere Marquette, Mi.	110	43.55 N	86.10 W
Pereshchepino, Sov. Un. (pā'rāsh-chē'pē-nô)	175	49.02 N	35.19 E
Pereslavl'-Zalesskiy, Sov. Un. (pā-rā-slav''l zä-lyĕs'kĭ)	174	56.43 N	38.52 E
Pereyaslav, Sov. Un. (pĕ-rā-yäs'läv)	175	50.05 N	31.25 E
Pergamino, Arg. (pĕr-gä-mē'nō)	141c	33.53 S	60.36 W
Perham, Mn. (pĕr'hăm)	114	46.37 N	95.35 W
Peribonca (R.), Can. (pĕr-ĭ-bŏŋ'kȧ)	103	49.10 N	71.20 W
Périgueux, Fr. (pā-rē-gû')	168	45.12 N	0.43 E
Perija, Sierra de (Mts.), Col. (sē-ĕ'r-rä-dĕ-pĕ-rē'ĸä)	142	9.25 N	73.30 W
Peristérion, Grc.	66d	38.01 N	23.42 E
Perivale (Neigh.), Eng.	62	51.32 N	0.19 W
Perkam, Tandjung (C.), Indon.	207	1.20 S	138.45 E
Perkins, Can. (pĕr'kĕns)	95c	45.37 N	75.37 W
Perlas, Arch. de Las, Pan. (är-chē-pyĕ'lä-gô-dĕ-läs-pĕr'läs)	133	8.29 N	79.15 W
Perlas, Laguna las (L.), Nic. (lä-go͞o'nä-dĕ-läs)	133	12.34 N	83.19 W
Perleberg, G.D.R. (pĕr'lĕ-bĕrg)	166	53.06 N	11.51 E
Perm', Sov. Un. (pĕrm)	182a	58.00 N	56.15 E
Pernambuco (State), Braz. (pĕr-näm-bo͞o'kō)	143	8.08 S	38.54 W
Pernambuco, see Recife			
Pernik, Bul. (pĕr-nēk')	173	42.36 N	23.04 E
Péronne, Fr. (pā-rôn')	168	49.57 N	2.49 E
Perote, Mex. (pĕ-rō'tĕ)	131	19.33 N	97.13 W
Perouse Str., Jap.-Sov. Un.	204	45.45 N	141.38 E
Perovo, Sov. Un. (pā'rô-vô)	182b	55.43 N	37.47 E
Perpignan, Fr. (pĕr-pē-nyäɴ')	168	42.42 N	2.48 E
Perris, Ca. (pĕr'ĭs)	119a	33.46 N	117.14 W

ăt; finăl; rāte; senāte; ärm; ȧsk; sofȧ; fâre; ch-choose; dh-as th in other; bē; ē̇vent; bĕt; recĕnt; cratēr; g-gō; gh-guttural g; bĭt; ĭ-short neutral; rīde; ĸ-guttural k as ch in German ich;

PRONOUNCING INDEX

Perros – Pinheiros 329

PLACE (Pronounciation)	PAGE	Lat. °′	Long. °′
Perros, Bahia (B.), Cuba (bä-ē'ä-pā'rōs)	134	22.25 N	78.35 W
Perrot Île (I.), Can. (pěr'ŭt)	95a	45.23 N	73.57 W
Perry, Fl. (pěr'ĭ)	126	30.06 N	83.35 W
Perry, Ga.	126	32.27 N	83.44 W
Perry, Ia.	115	41.49 N	94.40 W
Perry, NY	111	42.45 N	78.00 W
Perry, Ok.	123	36.17 N	97.18 W
Perry, Ut.	119b	41.27 N	112.02 W
Perry Hall, Md.	112e	39.24 N	76.29 W
Perrymont, Pa.	57b	40.33 N	80.02 W
Perryopolis, Pa. (pě-rē-ŏ'pō-lĭs)	113e	40.05 N	79.45 W
Perrysburg, Oh. (pěr ĭz-bûrg)	110	41.35 N	83.35 W
Perryton, Tx. (pěr'ĭ-tŭn)	122	36.23 N	100.48 W
Perryville, Ak. (pěr-ĭ-vĭl)	107	55.58 N	159.28 W
Perryville, Mo.	123	37.41 N	89.52 W
Persan, Fr. (pěr-säN')	169b	49.09 N	2.15 E
Persepolis (Ruins), Iran (pēr-sěp'o-lĭs)	155	30.15 N	53.08 E
Persian G., Asia (pûr'zhǎn)	192	27.38 N	50.30 E
Persia, see Iran			
Perth, Austl. (pûrth)	214	31.50 S	116.10 E
Perth, Can.	111	44.40 N	76.15 W
Perth, Scot.	162	56.24 N	3.25 W
Perth Amboy, NJ (äm'boi)	112a	40.31 N	74.16 W
Pertuis, Fr. (pěr-tüē')	169	43.43 N	5.29 E
Peru, Il. (pē-rōō')	110	41.20 N	89.10 W
Peru, In.	110	40.45 N	86.00 W
Peru, S. A.	140	10.00 S	75.00 W
Perugia, It. (pā-rōō'jä)	172	43.08 N	12.24 E
Peruque, Mo. (pě rō'kē)	119e	38.52 N	90.36 W
Pervomaysk, Sov. Un. (pěr-vô-mīsk')	175	48.04 N	30.52 E
Pervoural'sk, Sov. Un. (pěr-vô-ōō-rálsk')	182a	56.54 N	59.58 E
Pervyy Kuril'skiy Proliv (Str.), Sov. Un.	181	51.43 N	154.32 E
Perwenitz, G.D.R.	65a	52.40 N	13.01 E
Pesaro, It. (pā'zä-rō)	172	43.54 N	12.55 E
Pescado (R.), Ven. (pěs-kä'dō)	143b	9.33 N	65.32 W
Pescara, It. (pās-kä'rä)	172	42.26 N	14.15 E
Pescara (R.), It.	172	42.18 N	13.22 E
Peschanyy, Mys (C.), Sov. Un.	179	43.10 N	51.20 E
Pescia, It. (pā'shä)	172	43.53 N	11.42 E
Peshāwar, Pak. (pě-shä'wŭr)	193a	34.01 N	71.34 E
Peshtera, Bul.	173	42.03 N	24.19 E
Peshtigo (R.), Wi.	115	45.15 N	88.14 W
Peshtigo, Wi. (pěsh'tē-gō)	115	45.03 N	87.46 W
Pesing, Indon.	68k	6.10 S	106.45 E
Peski, Sov. Un. (pyâs'kĭ)	182b	55.13 N	38.48 E
Pêso da Régua, Port. (pā-sōō-dä-rā'gwä)	170	41.09 N	7.47 W
Pespire, Hond. (pås-pē'rå)	132	13.35 N	87.20 W
Pesqueria, R., Mex. (pås-kå-rē'ä)	124	25.55 N	100.25 W
Pessac, Fr.	168	44.48 N	0.38 W
Pesterzsébet (Neigh.), Hung.	66g	47.26 N	19.07 E
Pestlorinc (Neigh.), Hung.	66g	47.26 N	19.12 E
Pestújhely (Neigh.), Hung.	66g	47.32 N	19.07 E
Petacalco, Bahía de (B.), Mex. (bä-ē'ä-dě-pě-tä-kàl'kô)	130	17.55 N	102.00 W
Petah Tiqwa, Isr.	191a	32.05 N	34.53 E
Petaluma, Ca. (pět-ȧ-lōō'mȧ)	120	38.15 N	122.38 W
Petare, Ven. (pě-tä'rē)	143b	10.28 N	66.48 W
Petatlán, Mex. (pā-tä-tlän')	130	17.31 N	101.17 W
Petawawa, Can.	103	45.54 N	77.17 W
Petén, Laguna de (L.), Guat. (lä-gōō'nä-dě-pā-tān')	132a	17.05 N	89.54 W
Petenwell Res., Wi.	115	44.10 N	89.55 W
Peterborough, Austl.	216	32.53 S	138.58 E
Peterborough, Can. (pē'tēr-bŭr-ō)	111	44.20 N	78.20 W
Peterborough, Eng.	156	52.35 N	0.14 W
Peterhead, Scot. (pē-tēr-hěd')	162	57.36 N	3.47 W
Peter Pond L., Can. (pŏnd)	100	55.55 N	108.44 W
Peter Pt., Can.	111	43.50 N	77.00 W
Petersburg, Ak. (pē'tērz-bûrg)	107	56.52 N	133.10 W
Petersburg, Il.	123	40.01 N	89.51 W
Petersburg, In.	110	38.30 N	87.15 W
Petersburg, Ky.	113f	39.04 N	84.52 W
Petersburg, Va.	127	37.12 N	77.30 W
Peters Creek (R.), Pa.	57b	40.18 N	79.52 W
Petershagen, G.D.R. (pě'tērs-hä-gěn)	157b	52.32 N	13.46 E
Petersham, Austl.	70a	33.54 S	151.09 E
Petershausen, F.R.G. (pě'tērs-hou-zěn)	157d	48.25 N	11.29 E
Pétionville, Hai.	135	18.30 N	72.20 W
Petit, S. Afr.	71b	26.06 S	28.22 E
Petitcodiac, Can. (pē-tē-kô-dyåk')	104	45.56 N	65.10 W
Petite Terre I., Guad. (pē-tēt'târ')	133b	16.12 N	61.00 W
Petit Goâve, Hai. (pē-tē' gô-áv')	135	18.25 N	72.50 W
Petit Jean Cr., Ar. (pē-tē'zhäN')	123	35.05 N	93.55 W
Petit Loango, Gabon	230	2.16 S	9.35 E
Petlalcingo, Mex. (pě-tläl-sěŋ'gô)	131	18.05 N	97.53 W
Peto, Mex. (pě'tô)	132a	20.07 N	88.49 W
Petorca, Chile (pā-tōr'kå)	141	32.14 S	70.55 W
Petoskey, Mi. (pē-tŏs-kĭ)	110	45.25 N	84.55 W
Petra, Jordan	191a	30.21 N	35.25 E
Petra Velikogo, Zaliv (B.), Sov. Un. (zä'lĭf pět-rä' vě-lĭ'kô-vô)	204	42.40 N	131.50 E
Petrich, Bul. (pā'trĭch)	173	41.24 N	23.13 E
Petrified Forest Natl. Park, Az. (pět'rĭ-fīd fôr'ěst)	121	34.58 N	109.35 W
Petrikov, Sov. Un. (pyě'trē-kô-v)	175	52.09 N	28.30 E
Petrikovka, Sov. Un. (pyě'trē-kôf-kä)	175	48.43 N	34.29 E
Petrinja, Yugo. (pā'trěn-yå)	172	45.25 N	16.17 E
Petrodvorets, Sov. Un. (pyě-trô-dvô-ryěts')	182c	59.53 N	29.55 E
Petrokrepost', Sov. Un. (pyě'trô-krě-pôst)	182c	59.56 N	31.03 E
Petrolia, Can. (pē-trō'lĭ-ȧ)	110	42.50 N	82.10 W
Petrolina, Braz. (pě-trō-lē'nȧ)	143	9.18 S	40.28 W
Petronell, Aus.	157e	48.07 N	16.52 E
Petropavlovka, Sov. Un. (pyě'trô-päv'lôf-kȧ)	175	48.24 N	36.23 E
Petropavlovka, Sov. Un.	182a	54.10 N	59.50 E
Petropavlovsk, Sov. Un. (pyě-trô-päv'lôfsk)	180	54.44 N	69.07 E
Petropavlovsk-Kamchatskiy, Sov. Un. (käm-chät'skĭ)	181	53.13 N	158.56 E
Petrópolis, Braz. (på-trô-pô-lēzh')	144b	22.31 S	43.10 W
Petroşani, Rom.	173	45.24 N	23.24 E
Petrovsk, Sov. Un. (pyě-trôfsk')	179	52.20 N	45.15 E
Petrovskaya, Sov. Un. (pyě-trôf'skå-yå)	175	45.25 N	37.50 E
Petrovsko-Razumovskoje (Neigh.), Sov. Un.	66b	55.50 N	37.34 E
Petrovskoye, Sov. Un.	179	45.20 N	43.00 E
Petrovsk-Zabaykal'skiy, Sov. Un. (pyě-trôfskzä-bĭ-käl'skĭ)	181	51.13 N	109.08 E
Petrozavodsk, Sov. Un. (pyā'trô-zå-vôtsk')	165	61.46 N	34.25 E
Petrus Steyn, S. Afr. (pā'trōōs stän')	223d	27.40 S	28.09 E
Petseri, Sov. Un. (pět'sě-rē)	174	57.48 N	27.33 E
Pewaukee, Wi. (pĭ-wô'kē)	113a	43.05 N	88.15 W
Pewaukee L., Wi.	113a	43.03 N	88.18 W
Pewee Valley, Ky. (pe wē)	113h	38.19 N	85.29 W
Peza (R.), Sov. Un. (pyå'zå)	178	65.35 N	46.50 E
Pézenas, Fr. (pā-zē-nä')	168	43.26 N	3.24 E
Pforzheim, F.R.G. (pfôrts'hīm)	166	48.52 N	8.43 E
Phalodi, India	196	27.13 N	72.22 E
Phan-thiet, Viet. (p'hän')	206	11.30 N	108.43 E
Pharsalus, see Fársala			
Phelps Corner, Md.	56d	38.48 N	76.58 W
Phenix City, Al. (fē'nĭks)	126	32.29 N	85.00 W
Philadelphia, Ms. (fĭl-ȧ-děl'phĭ-ȧ)	126	32.45 N	89.07 W
Philadelphia, Pa.	112f	40.00 N	75.13 W
Philip, SD (fĭl'ĭp)	114	44.03 N	101.35 W
Philippeville, see Skikda			
Philippines, Asia (fĭl'ĭ-pēnz)	191	14.25 N	125.00 E
Philippine Sea, Asia (fĭl'ĭ-pēn)	208	16.00 N	133.00 E
Philippine Trench, Phil.	207	10.30 N	127.15 E
Philippopolis, see Plovdiv			
Philipsburg, Pa. (fĭl'lĭps-bērg)	111	40.55 N	78.10 W
Philipsburg, Wy.	117	46.19 N	113.19 W
Phillip (I.), Austl. (fĭl'ĭp)	216	38.32 S	145.10 E
Phillip Chan., Indon.	191b	1.04 N	103.40 E
Phillipi, WV (fĭ-lĭp'ĭ)	111	39.10 N	80.00 W
Phillips, Wi. (fĭl'ĭps)	115	45.41 N	90.24 W
Phillipsburg, Ks. (fĭl'lĭps-bērg)	122	39.44 N	99.19 W
Phillipsburg, NJ	111	40.45 N	75.10 W
Phinga, India	67a	22.41 N	88.25 E
Phitsanulok, Thai.	206	16.51 N	100.15 E
Phnum Pénh, Kamp. (nŏm'pěn')	206	11.39 N	104.53 E
Phoenix, Az. (fē'nĭks)	121	33.30 N	112.00 W
Phoenix, Md.	112e	39.31 N	76.40 W
Phoenix Is., Oceania	208	4.00 S	174.00 W
Phoenixville, Pa. (fē'nĭks-vĭl)	112f	40.08 N	75.31 W
Phra Nakhon Si Ayutthaya, Thai.	206	14.16 N	100.37 E
Phu Bia (Pk.), Laos	206	19.36 N	103.00 E
Phuket, Thai.	206	7.57 N	98.19 E
Phu-Quoc, Dao (I.), Kamp.	206	10.13 N	104.00 E
Phu-tho-hoa, Viet.	68m	10.46 N	106.39 E
Pi (R.), China (bē)	200	32.06 N	116.31 E
Piacenza, It. (pyä-chěnt'sä)	172	45.02 N	9.42 E
Pianosa (I.), It. (pyä-nō'sä)	172	42.13 N	15.45 E
Piatra-Neamţ, Rom. (pyä'trȧ-nå'åmts')	167	46.54 N	26.24 E
Piauí (State), Braz. (pyou'ē)	143	7.40 S	42.25 W
Piauí, Serra do (Mts.), Braz. (sěr'rȧ dōō pyou'ē)	143	10.45 S	44.36 W
Piave (R.), It. (pyä'vā)	172	45.45 N	12.15 E
Piazza Armerina, It. (pyät'sä är-må-rē'nä)	172	37.23 N	14.26 E
Pibor R., Sud. (pē'bôr)	225	7.21 N	32.54 E
Pic (R.), Can. (pěk)	115	48.48 N	86.28 W
Picara Pt. (U. S. A.), Vir. Is. (pē-kä'rä)	129c	18.23 N	64.57 W
Picayune, Ms. (pĭk'ȧ yōōn)	126	30.32 N	89.41 W
Picher, Ok. (pĭch'ēr)	123	36.58 N	94.49 W
Pichilemu, Chile (pē-chē-lě'mōō)	141b	34.22 S	72.01 W
Pichucalco, Mex. (pē-chōō-käl'kô)	131	17.34 N	93.06 W
Pichucalco (R.), Mex.	131	17.40 N	93.02 W
Pickerel (L.), Can. (pĭk'ēr-ěl)	115	48.35 N	91.10 W
Pickwick (R.), Tn. (pĭk'wĭck)	126	35.04 N	88.05 W
Pico, Ca. (pē'kô)	119a	34.01 N	118.05 W
Pico de Aneto (Mtn.), Sp. (pē'kō-dě-ä-ně'tô)	171	42.35 N	0.38 E
Pico I., Açores (pē'kōō)	224a	38.16 N	28.49 W
Pico Riveria, Ca.	119a	34.01 N	118.05 W
Picos, Braz. (pē'kōzh)	143	7.13 S	41.23 W
Picton, Austl. (pĭk'tŭn)	211b	34.11 S	150.37 E
Picton, Can.	103	44.00 N	77.15 W
Pictou, Can. (pĭk-tōō')	104	45.41 N	62.43 W
Pidálion, Akrotírion (C.), Cyprus	191a	34.50 N	34.05 E
Pidurutalagala Mt., Sri Lanka (pē'dōō-rōō-tä'lá-gä'lä)	197	7.00 N	80.46 E
Pie (I.), Can. (pī)	115	48.10 N	89.07 W
Piedade, Braz. (pyā-dä'dě)	141a	23.42 S	47.25 W
Piedade do Baruel, Braz.	61d	23.37 S	46.18 W
Piedmont, Al. (pēd'mŏnt)	126	33.54 N	85.36 W
Piedmont, Ca.	118b	37.50 N	122.14 W
Piedmont, Mo.	123	37.09 N	90.42 W
Piedmont, SC	127	34.40 N	82.27 W
Piedmont, WV	111	39.30 N	79.05 W
Piedrabuena, Sp. (pyā-drä-bwā'nä)	170	39.01 N	4.10 W
Piedras Negras, Mex. (pyā'dräs nā'gräs)	124	28.41 N	100.33 W
Piedras, Punta (Pt.), Arg. (pōō'n-tä-pyě'dräs)	141c	35.25 S	57.10 W
Pieksämäki, Fin. (pyěk'sě-mě-kē)	165	62.18 N	27.14 E
Piemonte (Reg.), It. (pyě-mô'n-tě)	172	44.30 N	7.42 E
Pienaars R., S. Afr.	223d	25.13 S	28.05 E
Pienaarsrivier, S. Afr.	223d	25.12 S	28.18 E
Pierce, Ne. (pērs)	114	42.11 N	97.33 W
Pierce, WV	111	39.15 N	79.30 W
Piermont, NY (pēr'mŏnt)	112a	41.03 N	73.55 W
Pierre, SD (pēr)	114	44.22 N	100.20 W
Pierrefitte-sur-Seine, Fr.	64c	48.58 N	2.22 E
Pierrefonds, Can.	95a	45.29 N	73.52 W
Pieštany, Czech. (pyěsh'tyȧ-nûĭ)	167	48.36 N	17.48 E
Pietermaritzburg, S. Afr. (pē-tēr-mȧ-rĭts-bûrg)	227c	29.36 S	30.23 E
Pietersburg, S. Afr. (pē'tērz-bûrg)	223d	23.56 S	29.30 E
Pietersfield, S. Afr.	71b	26.14 S	28.26 E
Piet Retief, S. Afr. (pēt rĕ-tēf')	226	27.00 S	30.58 E
Pietrosul Pk., Rom.	167	47.35 N	24.49 E
Pieve di Cadore, It. (pyā'vå dē kä-dō'rå)	172	46.26 N	12.22 E
Pigeon (R.), Can.-Mn. (pĭj'ŭn)	115	48.05 N	90.13 W
Pigeon L., Can.	99	53.00 N	114.00 W
Pigeon Lake, Can.	95f	49.57 N	97.36 W
Piggott, Ar. (pĭg-ŭt)	123	36.22 N	90.10 W
Pijijiapan, Mex. (pēκē-kē-ä'pän)	131	15.40 N	93.12 W
Pijnacker, Neth.	157a	52.01 N	4.25 E
Pikes Pk., Co. (pīks)	122	38.49 N	105.03 W
Pikesville, Md.	56c	39.23 N	76.44 W
Pikeville, Ky. (pīk'vĭl)	127	37.28 N	82.31 W
Pikou, China (pē-kō)	200	39.25 N	122.19 E
Pikwitonei, Can. (pĭk'wĭ-tōn)	101	55.35 N	97.09 W
Pila, Pol. (pē'lå)	166	53.09 N	16.44 E
Pilansberg, S. Afr. (pē'ǎns'bûrg)	223d	25.08 S	26.55 E
Pilar, Arg. (pē'lär)	141c	34.27 S	58.55 W
Pilar, Par.	144	27.00 S	58.15 W
Pilar de Goiás, Braz. (dě-gô'yà's)	143	14.47 S	49.33 W
Pilchuck (R.), Wa.	118a	48.03 N	121.58 W
Pilchuck Cr., Wa. (pĭl'chŭck)	118a	48.19 N	122.11 W
Pilchuck Mtn., Wa.	118a	48.03 N	121.48 W
Pilcomayo (R.), Par. (pēl-cō-mī'ō)	144	24.45 S	69.15 W
Pilgrim Gardens, NJ	56b	39.57 N	75.19 W
Pilgrims Hatch, Eng.	62	51.38 N	0.17 E
Pili, Phil. (pē'lē)	207a	13.34 N	123.17 E
Pilica R., Pol. (pē-lēt'sä)	167	51.00 N	19.48 E
Pillar Pt., Can. (pĭl'ǎr)	118a	48.14 N	124.06 W
Pillar Rocks, Wa.	118c	46.16 N	123.35 W
Pilón (R.), Mex. (pē-lōn')	130	24.13 N	99.03 W
Pilot Point, Tx. (pī'lŭt)	123	33.24 N	97.00 W
Pilsen, see Plzeň			
Piltene, Sov. Un. (pĭl'tě-ně)	165	57.17 N	21.40 E
Pimal, Cerra (Mtn.), Mex. (sě'r-rä-pē-mäl')	130	22.58 N	104.19 W
Pimba, Austl. (pĭm'bȧ)	214	31.15 S	146.50 E
Pimville (Neigh.), S. Afr. (pĭm'vĭl)	227b	26.17 S	27.54 E
Pinacate, Cerro (Mtn.), Mex. (sě'r-rô-pē-nä-kä'tě)	128	31.45 N	113.30 W
Pinamalayan, Phil. (pē-nä-mä-lä'yän)	207a	13.04 N	121.31 E
Pinang, see George Town			
Pinarbasi, Tur. (pē'när-bä'shĭ)	179	38.50 N	36.10 E
Pinar del Río, Cuba (pē-när' děl rē'ō)	134	22.25 N	83.35 W
Pinar del Río (Prov.), Cuba	134	22.45 N	83.25 W
Pinatubo (Mtn.), Phil. (pē-nä-tōō'bô)	207a	15.09 N	120.19 E
Pincher Creek, Can. (pĭn'chēr krēk)	99	49.29 N	113.57 W
Pinckneyville, Il. (pĭnk'nĭ-vĭl)	123	38.06 N	89.22 W
Pińczów, Pol. (pēn''chōōf)	167	50.32 N	20.33 E
Pindamonhangaba, Braz. (pē'n-dä-mōnyá'n-gä-bä)	141a	22.56 S	45.26 W
Pinder Pt., Ba.	134	26.35 N	78.35 W
Píndhos Óros (Mts.), Grc.	173	39.48 N	21.19 E
Pindiga, Nig.	229	9.59 N	10.54 E
Pine (R.), Can. (pīn)	98	55.30 N	122.20 W
Pine (R.), Wi.	115	45.50 N	88.37 W
Pine Bluff, Ar. (pīn blŭf)	123	34.13 N	92.01 W
Pine Brook, NJ	55	40.52 N	74.20 W
Pine City, Mn. (pīn)	115	45.50 N	93.01 W
Pine Cr., Nv.	120	40.15 N	116.17 W
Pine Creek, Austl.	214	13.45 S	132.00 E
Pinecrest, Va.	56d	38.50 N	77.09 W
Pine Falls, Can.	101	50.35 N	96.15 W
Pine Forest Ra., Nv.	116	41.35 N	118.45 W
Pinega, Sov. Un. (pē-nyě'gȧ)	178	64.40 N	43.30 E
Pinega (R.), Sov. Un.	178	64.10 N	42.30 E
Pine Grove, Can.	54c	43.48 N	79.35 W
Pine Hill, NJ (pīn hĭl)	112f	39.47 N	74.59 W
Pinehurst, Ma.	54a	42.32 N	71.14 W
Pine Is., Fl.	127a	24.48 N	81.32 W
Pine Island Sd., Fl.	127a	26.32 N	82.30 W
Pine Lake Estates, Ga. (lāk ěs-tāts')	112c	33.47 N	84.13 W
Pinelands, S. Afr. (pīn'lǎnds)	226a	33.57 S	18.30 E
Pine Lawn, Mo. (lôn)	119e	38.42 N	90.17 W
Pine Pass, Can.	98	55.22 N	122.40 W
Pine Ridge, Va.	56d	38.52 N	77.14 W
Pine Ridge Ind. Res., SD (rĭj)	114	43.33 N	102.13 W
Pinerolo, It. (pē-nå-rô'lō)	172	44.47 N	7.18 E
Pines, Lake o' the, Tx.	125	32.50 N	94.40 W
Pinetown, S. Afr. (pīn'toun)	227c	29.47 S	30.52 E
Pine View Res., Ut. (vū)	119b	41.17 N	111.54 W
Pineville, Ky. (pīn'vĭl)	126	36.48 N	83.43 W
Pineville, La.	125	31.20 N	92.25 W
Ping (R.), Thai.	206	17.54 N	98.29 E
Pingding, China (pĭŋ-dĭŋ)	202	37.50 N	113.30 E
Pingdu, China (pĭŋ-dōō)	200	36.46 N	119.57 E
Pingfang, China	67b	39.56 N	116.33 E
Pinggir, Indon.	191b	1.05 N	101.12 E
Pinghe, China (pĭŋ-hŭ)	203	24.30 N	117.02 E
Pingle, China (pĭŋ-lŭ)	203	24.30 N	110.22 E
Pingliang, China (pĭng'lyäng')	202	35.12 N	106.50 E
Pingquan, China (pĭŋ-chyůän)	202	40.58 N	118.40 E
Pingtan, China (pĭŋ-tän)	203	25.30 N	119.45 E
Pingtan Dao (I.), China (pĭŋ-tän dou)	203	25.40 N	119.45 E
P'ingtung, Taiwan	203	22.40 N	120.35 E
Pingwu, China (pĭŋ-wōō)	202	32.20 N	104.40 E
Pingxiang, China (pĭŋ-shyäŋ)	203	27.40 N	113.50 E
Pingyi, China (pĭŋ-yē)	200	35.30 N	117.38 E
Pingyuan, China (pĭŋ-yůän)	200	37.11 N	116.26 E
Pingzhou, China (pĭŋ-jō)	201a	23.01 N	113.11 E
Pinhal, Braz. (pē-nyá'l)	141a	22.11 S	46.43 W
Pinhal Novo, Port. (nô vōō)	171b	38.38 N	8.54 W
Pinheiros (R.), Braz.	61d	23.32 S	46.44 W

PLACE (Pronounciation)	PAGE	Lat. °′	Long. °′
Pinhel, Port. (pēn-yĕl′)	170	40.45 N	7.03 W
Piniós (R.), Grc.	173	40.33 N	21.40 E
Pini, Pulau (I.), Indon.	206	0.07 S	98.38 E
Pinnacles Natl. Mon., Ca. (pĭn′ȧ-k′lz)	120	36.30 N	121.00 W
Pinneberg, F.R.G. (pĭn′ĕ-bĕrg)	157c	53.40 N	9.48 E
Pinner (Neigh.), Eng.	62	51.36 N	0.23 W
Pinole, Ca. (pĭ-nō′lē̇)	118b	38.01 N	122.17 W
Pinos-Puente, Sp. (pwān′tā̇)	170	37.15 N	3.43 W
Pinotepa Nacional, Mex. (pē-nō̇-tā′pä nä-syō̇-näl′)	130	16.21 N	98.04 W
Pins, Ile des, N. Cal.	215	22.44 S	167.44 E
Pinsk, Sov. Un. (pē̇n′sk)	167	52.07 N	26.05 E
Pinta (I.), Ec.	142	0.41 N	90.47 W
Pintendre, Can. (pĕɴ-täɴdr′)	95b	46.45 N	71.07 W
Pinto, Sp. (pēn′tō)	171a	40.14 N	3.42 W
Pinto Butte, Can. (pĭn′tō)	100	49.22 N	107.25 W
Pioche, Nv. (pī-ō′chē̇)	121	37.56 N	114.28 W
Piombino, It. (pyō̇m-bē′nō)	172	42.56 N	10.33 E
Pioneer Mts., Mt. (pī′ō̇-nēr′)	117	45.23 N	112.51 W
Piotrków Trybunalski, Pol. (pyōtr′ko͞ov trĭ-bo͞o-nal′skē)	167	51.23 N	19.44 E
Piper, Al. (pī′pēr)	126	33.04 N	87.00 W
Piper, Ks.	119f	39.09 N	94.51 W
Pipéri (I.), Grc. (pē′per-ē̇)	173	39.19 N	24.20 E
Pipe Spring Natl. Mon., Az. (pīp sprĭng)	121	36.50 N	112.45 W
Pipestone, Mn. (pīp′stōn)	114	44.00 N	96.19 W
Pipestone Natl. Mon., Mn.	114	44.03 N	96.24 W
Pipmaucan, Rés., Can. (pĭp-mä-kän′)	104	49.45 N	70.00 W
Piqua, Oh. (pĭk′wȧ)	110	40.10 N	84.15 W
Piracaia, Braz. (pē-rä-kȧ′yä)	141a	23.04 S	46.20 W
Piracicaba, Braz. (pē̇-rä-sē̇-kä′bä)	141a	22.43 S	47.39 W
Piraeus (Piraiévs), Grc.	66d	37.57 N	23.38 E
Piraí, Braz. (pē-rä-ē′)	141a	22.38 S	43.54 W
Piraíba (R.), Braz. (pä-rä-ē′bȧ)	141a	21.38 S	41.29 W
Piramida, Gol′tsy (Mtn.), Sov. Un.	180	54.00 N	96.00 E
Pirámide de Cuicuilco (P. Int.), Mex.	60a	19.18 N	99.11 W
Piran, Yugo. (pē-rā̇′n)	172	45.31 N	13.34 E
Piranga, Braz. (pē-rä′n-gä)	141a	20.41 S	43.17 W
Pirapetinga, Braz. (pē-rä-pĕ-tē′n-gä)	141a	21.40 S	42.20 W
Pirapora, Braz. (pē̇-rȧ-pō′rȧ)	143	17.39 S	44.54 W
Pirassununga, Braz. (pē-rä-so͞o-no͞o′n-gä)	141a	22.00 S	47.24 W
Pirenópolis, Braz. (pē-rĕ-nô′pō-lē̇s)	143	15.56 S	48.49 W
Pírgos, Grc.	173	37.51 N	21.28 E
Piritu, Laguna de (L.), Ven. (lä-go͞o′nä-dĕ-pē-rē′to͞o)	143b	10.00 N	64.57 W
Pirmasens, F.R.G. (pĭr-mä-zĕns′)	166	49.12 N	7.34 E
Pirna, G.D.R. (pĭr′nä)	166	50.57 N	13.56 E
Pirot, Yugo. (pē′rōt)	173	43.09 N	22.35 E
Pirtleville, Az. (pûr′t′l-vĭl)	121	31.25 N	109.35 W
Piru, Indon. (pē̇-ro͞o′)	207	3.15 S	128.25 E
Piryatin, Sov. Un. (pēr-yä-tēn′)	175	50.13 N	32.31 E
Pisa, It. (pē′sä)	172	43.52 N	10.24 E
Pisagua, Chile (pē̇-sä′gwä)	142	18.43 S	70.12 W
Piscataway, Md. (pĭs-kă-tă-wā)	112e	38.42 N	76.59 W
Piscataway, NJ	112a	40.35 N	74.27 W
Pisco, Peru (pēs′kō)	142	13.43 S	76.07 W
Pisco, Bahia de (B.), Peru (bä-ē′ä-dĕ)	142	13.43 S	77.48 W
Piseco (L.), NY (pĭ-sā′kō̇)	111	43.25 N	74.35 W
Pisek, Czech. (pē′sĕk)	166	49.18 N	14.08 E
Pisticci, It. (pē̇s-tē′chē̇)	172	40.24 N	16.34 E
Pistoia, It. (pē̇s-tô′yä)	172	43.57 N	11.54 E
Pisuerga (R.), Sp. (pē̇-swĕr′gä)	170	41.48 N	4.28 W
Pitalito, Col. (pē-tä-lē′tō)	142	1.45 N	75.09 W
Pitampura Kālan (Neigh.), India	67d	28.42 N	77.08 E
Pitcairn, Oceania	209	25.04 S	130.05 W
Pitcairn, Pa. (pĭt′kârn)	113e	40.29 N	79.47 W
Pitch′ (R.), Sov. Un. (p′tē̇ch)	174	53.17 N	28.16 E
Piteå, Swe. (pē′tĕ-ô′)	158	65.21 N	21.10 E
Pitealven (R.), Swe.	158	66.08 N	18.51 E
Pitesti, Rom. (pē̇-tĕsht′′)	173	44.51 N	24.51 E
Pithara, Austl. (pĭt′ără)	214	30.27 S	116.45 E
Pithiviers, Fr. (pē̇-tē-vyā′)	168	48.12 N	2.14 E
Pitman, NJ (pĭt′mȧn)	112f	39.44 N	75.08 W
Pitons du Carbet, Mt., Mart.	133b	14.40 N	61.05 W
Pit R., Ca. (pĭt)	116	40.58 N	121.42 W
Pitseng, Leso.	227c	29.03 S	28.13 E
Pitt (R.), Can.	118d	49.19 N	122.39 W
Pitt I., Can.	98	53.35 N	129.45 W
Pittsburg, Ca. (pĭts′bûrg)	118b	38.01 N	121.52 W
Pittsburg, Ks.	123	37.25 N	94.43 W
Pittsburg, Tx.	123	32.00 N	94.57 W
Pittsburgh, Pa.	113e	40.26 N	80.01 W
Pittsfield, IL. (pĭts′fēld)	123	39.37 N	90.47 W
Pittsfield, Me.	104	44.45 N	69.44 W
Pittsfield, Ma.	111	42.25 N	73.15 W
Pittston, Pa. (pĭts′tŭn)	111	41.20 N	75.50 W
Piũi, Braz. (pē-o͞o′ē)	141a	20.27 S	45.57 W
Piura, Peru (pē̇-o͞o′rä)	142	5.13 S	80.46 W
Piya, Sov. Un. (pē′yȧ)	182a	58.34 N	61.12 E
Placentia, Ca. (plă-sĕn′shĭ-ȧ)	119a	33.52 N	117.50 W
Placentia, Can.	105	47.15 N	53.58 W
Placentia B., Can.	105	47.14 N	54.30 W
Placerville, Ca. (plăs′ēr-vĭl)	120	38.43 N	120.47 W
Placetas, Cuba (plä-thā′täs)	134	22.10 N	79.40 W
Placid (L.), NY (plăs′ĭd)	111	44.20 N	74.00 W
Plain City, Ut. (plān)	119b	41.18 N	112.06 W
Plainfield, Il. (plān′fēld)	113a	41.37 N	88.12 W
Plainfield, In.	113g	39.42 N	86.23 W
Plainfield, NJ	112a	40.38 N	74.25 W
Plainview, Ar. (plān′vū)	123	34.59 N	93.15 W
Plainview, Mn.	115	44.09 N	93.12 W
Plainview, Ne.	114	42.20 N	97.47 W
Plainview, NY	112a	40.47 N	73.28 W
Plainview, Tx.	122	34.11 N	101.42 W
Plainwell, Mi. (plan′wĕl)	110	42.25 N	85.40 W
Plaisance, Can. (plĕ-zäɴs′)	95c	45.37 N	75.07 W
Plana or Flat Cays (Is.), Ba. (plä′nä)	135	22.35 N	73.35 W
Plandome Manor, NY	55	40.49 N	73.42 W
Planegg, F.R.G. (plä′nĕg)	157b	48.06 N	11.27 E
Plano, Tx. (plā′nō)	123	33.01 N	96.42 W
Plantagenet, Can. (pläɴ-täzh-nĕ′)	95c	45.33 N	75.00 W
Plant City, Fl. (plȧnt sĭ′tĭ)	127a	28.00 N	82.07 W
Plaquemine, La. (pläk′mēn′)	125	30.17 N	91.14 W
Plasencia, Sp. (plä-sĕn′thē̇-ä)	170	40.02 N	6.07 W
Plast, Sov. Un. (plȧst)	182a	54.22 N	60.48 E
Plaster Rock, Can. (plȧs′tēr rŏk)	104	46.54 N	67.24 W
Plastun, Sov. Un. (plȧs-to͞on′)	204	44.41 N	136.08 E
Platani (R.), It. (plä-tä′nē)	172	37.26 N	13.28 E
Plata, R. de la (R.), Arg.-Urg. (dālä plä′tä)	144	34.35 S	58.15 W
Plateforme, Pte., Hai.	135	19.35 N	73.50 W
Platinum, Ak. (plăt′ĭ-nŭm)	107	59.00 N	161.27 W
Plato, Col. (plä′tō)	142	9.49 N	74.48 W
Platón Sánchéz, Mex. (plä-tōn′ sän′chĕz)	130	21.14 N	98.20 W
Platt, Eng.	62	51.17 N	0.20 E
Platte, SD (plăt)	114	43.22 N	98.51 W
Platte (R.), Mo.	123	40.09 N	94.40 W
Platte (R.), U. S.	108	40.50 N	100.40 W
Platteville, Wi. (plăt′vĭl)	115	42.44 N	90.31 W
Plattsburg, Mo. (plăts′bûrg)	123	39.33 N	94.26 W
Plattsburg, NY	111	44.40 N	73.30 W
Plattsmouth, Ne. (plăts′mŭth)	114	41.00 N	95.53 W
Plauen, G.D.R. (plou′ĕn)	166	50.30 N	12.08 E
Playa de Guanabo, Cuba (plä-yä-dĕ-gwä-nä′bō̇)	135a	23.10 N	82.07 W
Playa del Rey (Neigh.), Ca.	59	33.58 N	118.26 W
Playa de Santa Fe, Cuba (sä′n-tä-fĕ′)	135a	23.05 N	82.31 W
Playas (L.), NM (plä′yȧs)	121	31.50 N	108.30 W
Playa Vicente, Mex. (vē-sĕn′tā̇)	131	17.49 N	95.49 W
Playa Vicente (R.), Mex.	131	17.36 N	96.13 W
Playgreen L., Can. (plā′grēn)	101	54.00 N	98.10 W
Plaza de Toros Monumental (P. Int.), Sp.	65e	41.24 N	2.11 E
Pleasant (L.), NY (plĕz′ănt)	111	43.25 N	74.25 W
Pleasant Grove, Al.	112h	33.29 N	86.57 W
Pleasant Hill, Ca.	118b	37.57 N	122.04 W
Pleasant Hill, Mo.	123	38.46 N	94.18 W
Pleasant Hills, Pa.	57b	40.20 N	79.58 W
Pleasanton, Ca. (plĕz′ăn-tŭn)	118b	37.40 N	121.53 W
Pleasanton, Ks.	123	38.10 N	94.41 W
Pleasanton, Tx.	124	28.58 N	98.30 W
Pleasant Plain, Oh. (plĕz′ănt)	113f	39.17 N	84.06 W
Pleasant Ridge, Mi.	113b	42.28 N	83.09 W
Pleasant View, Ut. (plĕz′ănt vū)	119b	41.20 N	112.02 W
Pleasantville, Md.	56c	39.11 N	76.38 W
Pleasantville, NY (plĕz′ănt-vĭl)	112a	41.08 N	73.47 W
Pleasure Ridge Park, Ky. (plĕzh′ēr rĭj)	113h	38.09 N	85.49 W
Plenty, Bay of, N. Z. (plĕn′tē̇)	217	37.30 S	177.10 E
Plentywood, Mt. (plĕn′tē̇-wo͝od)	117	48.47 N	104.38 W
Ples, Sov. Un. (plyĕs)	174	57.26 N	41.29 E
Pleshcheyevo (L.), Sov. Un. (plĕsh-chă′yĕ-vō̇)	174	56.50 N	38.22 E
Plessisville, Can. (plĕ-sē′vēl′)	104	46.12 N	71.47 W
Pleszew, Pol. (plĕ′zhĕf)	167	51.54 N	17.48 E
Plettenberg, F.R.G. (plĕ′tĕn-bĕrgh)	169c	51.13 N	7.53 E
Pleven, Bul. (plĕ′vĕn)	173	43.24 N	24.26 E
Pljevlja, Yugo. (plĕv′lyä)	173	43.20 N	19.21 E
Plock, Pol. (pwôtsk)	167	52.32 N	19.44 E
Ploërmel, Fr. (plō̇-ĕr-mêl′)	168	47.56 N	2.25 W
Ploieşti, Rom. (plō̇-yĕsht′′)	173	44.56 N	26.01 E
Plomárion, Grc. (plō̇-mä′rĭ-ŏn)	173	38.51 N	26.24 E
Plomb du Cantal (Mt.), Fr. (plôɴ′dükäɴ-täl′)	168	45.30 N	2.49 E
Plonge, Lac la (L.), Can. (plōɴzh)	100	55.08 N	107.25 W
Plovdiv (Philippopolis), Bul. (plôv′dĭf) (fĭl-ĭp-ŏp′ō̇-lĭs)	173	42.09 N	24.43 E
Pluma Hidalgo, Mex. (plo͞o′mä ē-däl′gō)	131	15.54 N	96.23 W
Plumpton, Austl.	70a	33.45 S	150.50 E
Plunge, Sov. Un. (plo͞on′gā)	165	55.56 N	21.45 E
Plymouth, Eng. (plĭm′ŭth)	162	50.25 N	4.14 W
Plymouth, In.	110	41.20 N	86.20 W
Plymouth, Ma.	111	42.00 N	70.45 W
Plymouth, Mi.	113b	42.23 N	83.27 W
Plymouth, Montserrat	133b	16.43 N	62.12 W
Plymouth, NH	111	43.50 N	71.40 W
Plymouth, NC	127	35.50 N	76.44 W
Plymouth, Pa.	111	41.15 N	75.55 W
Plymouth, Wi.	115	43.45 N	87.59 W
Plyussa (R.), Sov. Un. (plyo͞o′sȧ)	174	58.33 N	28.30 E
Plzeň (Pilsen), Czech.	166	49.46 N	13.25 E
Pô, Burkina	228	11.10 N	1.09 W
Po (R.), It.	172	44.57 N	12.38 E
Poá, Braz.	61d	23.32 S	46.20 W
Pobé, Benin (pō̇-bā′)	229	6.58 N	2.41 E
Pocahontas, Ar. (pō-kȧ-hŏn′tȧs)	123	36.15 N	91.01 W
Pocahontas, Ia.	115	42.43 N	94.41 W
Pocatello, Id. (pō-kȧ-tĕl′ō)	117	42.54 N	112.30 W
Pochëp, Sov. Un. (pō̇-chĕp′)	174	52.56 N	32.27 E
Pochinok, Sov. Un. (pō̇-chē′nôk)	174	54.14 N	32.27 E
Pochinski, Sov. Un.	178	54.40 N	44.50 E
Pochotitán, Mex. (pô-chō̇-tē-tȧ′n)	130	21.37 N	104.33 W
Pochutla (San Pedro), Mex. (pō-cho͞o′tlä) (sän pā′drō)	131	15.46 N	96.28 W
Pocomoke City, Md. (pō-kō-mōk′)	111	38.05 N	75.35 W
Pocono Mts., Pa. (pō-cō′nō)	111	41.10 N	75.05 W
Poços de Caldas, Braz. (pō-sôs-dĕ-käl′dȧs)	141a	21.48 S	46.34 W
Poder, Senegal (pō̇-dôr′)	224	16.35 N	15.04 W
Podkamennaya (Stony) (R.) Tunguska, Sov. Un.	180	61.43 N	93.45 E
Podol′sk, Sov. Un. (pō̇-dôl′′sk)	182b	55.26 N	37.33 E
Podvolochisk, Sov. Un.	175	49.32 N	26.16 E
Poggibonsi, It. (pō̇d-jē̇-bôn′sē̇)	172	43.27 N	11.12 E
Pogodino, Sov. Un. (pō̇-gô′dē̇-nō̇)	174	54.17 N	31.00 E
P′ohang, Kor.	204	35.57 N	129.23 E
Point Cook, Austl.	70b	37.56 S	144.45 E
Pointe-à-Pitre, Guad. (pwăɴt′ ȧ pē-tr′)	133b	16.15 N	61.32 W
Pointe-aux-Trembles, Can. (po͞o-äɴt′ ō-träɴbl)	95a	45.39 N	73.30 W
Pointe Claire, Can. (po͞o-äɴt′ klĕr)	95a	45.27 N	73.48 W
Pointe-des-Cascades, Can. (kăs-kādz′)	95a	45.19 N	73.58 W
Pointe Fortune, Can. (fôr′tūn)	95a	45.34 N	74.23 W
Pointe-Gatineau, Can. (po͞o-äɴt′gä-tē-nō′)	95c	45.28 N	75.42 W
Pointe Noire, Con.	230	4.48 S	11.51 E
Point Hope, Ak. (hōp)	107	68.18 N	166.38 W
Point Pleasant, Md.	56c	39.11 N	76.35 W
Point Pleasant, WV (plĕz′ănt)	110	38.50 N	82.10 W
Point Roberts, Wa. (rŏb′ērts)	118d	48.59 N	123.04 W
Poissy, Fr. (pwȧ-sē′)	169b	48.55 N	2.02 E
Poitiers, Fr. (pwȧ-tyā′)	168	46.35 N	0.18 E
Pokaran, India (pō′kŭr-ŭn)	196	27.00 N	72.05 E
Pokrov, Sov. Un. (pō̇-krôf)	174	55.56 N	39.09 E
Pokrovsko-Strešnevo (Neigh.), Sov. Un.	66b	55.49 N	37.29 E
Pokrovskoye, Sov. Un. (pō̇-krôf′skō̇-yĕ)	175	47.27 N	38.54 E
Pola (R.), Sov. Un. (pō′lä)	174	54.44 N	31.53 E
Pola de Laviana, Sp. (dĕ-lä-vyä′nä)	170	43.15 N	5.29 W
Pola de Siero, Sp.	170	43.24 N	5.39 W
Poland, Eur. (pō′lănd)	154	52.37 N	17.01 E
Polangui, Phil. (pô-läŋ′gē)	207a	13.18 N	123.29 E
Polazna, Sov. Un. (pô′lȧz-nȧ)	182a	58.18 N	56.25 E
Polessk, Sov. Un. (pô′lĕsk)	165	54.50 N	21.14 E
Poles′ye (Pripyat Marshes), Sov. Un.	179	52.10 N	27.30 E
Polevskoy, Sov. Un. (pô-lĕ′vs-kô′ē̇)	182a	56.28 N	60.14 E
Polgár, Hung. (pō̇l′gär)	167	47.54 N	21.10 E
Policastro, Golfo di (G.), It.	172	41.00 N	13.23 E
Poligny, Fr. (pō-lē-nyē′)	169	46.48 N	5.42 E
Polikhnitos, Grc.	173	39.05 N	26.11 E
Polillo, Phil. (pō̇-lēl′yō)	207a	14.42 N	121.56 W
Polillo Is., Phil.	207a	15.05 N	122.15 E
Polillo Str., Phil.	207a	15.02 N	121.40 E
Polist′ (R.), Sov. Un. (pô′lĭst)	174	57.42 N	31.02 E
Polistena, It. (pō-lē̇s-tā′nä)	172	40.25 N	16.05 E
Poliyiros, Grc.	173	40.23 N	23.27 E
Polkan, Gol′tsy (Mtn.), Sov. Un.	180	60.18 N	92.08 E
Pollensa, Sp. (pōl-yĕn′sä)	171	39.50 N	3.00 E
Polochic R., Guat. (pō-lō̇-chēk′)	132	15.19 N	89.45 W
Polonnoye, Sov. Un. (pō̇′lô-nō̇-yĕ)	175	50.07 N	27.31 E
Polotsk, Sov. Un. (pô′lō̇tsk)	174	55.30 N	28.48 E
Polpaico, Chile (pō̇l-pȧ′y-kō̇)	141b	33.10 S	70.53 W
Polson, Mt. (pōl′sŭn)	117	47.40 N	114.10 W
Polsum, F.R.G.	63	51.37 N	7.03 E
Poltava, Sov. Un. (pō̇l-tä′vä)	175	49.35 N	34.33 E
Poltava (Oblast), Sov. Un.	175	49.53 N	32.58 E
Pōltsamaa, Sov. Un. (pŏlt′sȧ-mä)	174	58.39 N	26.00 E
Pōltsamaa (R.), Sov. Un.	174	58.35 N	25.55 E
Polunochnoye, Sov. Un. (pô-lo͞o-nō̇′ch-nô′yĕ)	182a	60.52 N	60.27 E
Poluy (R.), Sov. Un. (pôl′wē̇)	180	65.45 N	68.15 E
Polyakovka, Sov. Un. (pŭl-yä′kō̇v-kȧ)	182a	54.38 N	59.42 E
Polyarnyy, Sov. Un. (pŭl-yär′nē)	178	69.10 N	33.30 E
Pomba (R.), Braz. (pô′m-bȧ)	141a	21.28 S	42.28 W
Pomerania (Reg.), Pol. (pŏm-ē̇-rā′nĭ-ȧ)	166	53.50 N	15.20 E
Pomeranian B., G.D.R. (pō′mĕ-rä-ny-än)	164	54.10 N	14.20 E
Pomeroy, S. Afr. (pŏm′ēr-roi)	227c	28.36 S	30.26 E
Pomeroy, Wa. (pŏm′ēr-oi)	116	46.28 N	117.35 W
Pomezia, It. (pō̇-mĕ′t-zyä)	171d	41.41 N	12.31 E
Pomigliano d′ Arco, It. (pō̇-mē-lyȧ′nō̇-d-ä′r-kō̇)	171c	40.39 N	14.23 E
Pomme de Terre, Mn. (pō̇m dē tĕr′)	114	45.22 N	95.52 W
Pomona, Ca. (pō̇-mō′nȧ)	119a	34.04 N	117.45 W
Pomona Estates, S. Afr.	71b	26.06 S	28.15 E
Pomorie, Bul.	173	42.24 N	27.41 E
Pompano Beach, Fl. (pŏm′pă-nō̇)	127a	26.12 N	80.07 W
Pompeii Ruins, It.	171c	40.31 N	14.29 E
Pomponne, Fr.	64c	48.53 N	2.41 E
Pompton Lakes, NJ (pŏmp′tŏn)	112a	41.01 N	74.16 W
Pompton Plains, NJ	55	40.58 N	74.18 W
Pomuch, Mex. (pô-mo͞o′ch)	132a	20.12 N	90.10 W
Ponca, Ne. (pŏn′kȧ)	114	42.34 N	96.43 W
Ponca City, Ok.	123	36.42 N	97.07 W
Ponce, P. R. (pōn′sā)	129b	18.01 N	66.43 W
Ponders End (Neigh.), Eng.	62	51.39 N	0.03 W
Pondicherry, India (pôn-dĭ-shĕr′ē′) (pŏn-dĭ-shĕr′ē̇)	197	11.58 N	79.48 E
Pondicherry (State), India	197	11.50 N	74.50 E
Ponferrada, Sp. (pōn-fĕr-rä′dhä)	170	42.33 N	6.38 W
Ponoka, Can. (pŏ-nō′kȧ)	99	52.42 N	113.35 W
Ponoy, Sov. Un.	178	66.58 N	41.00 E
Ponoy (R.), Sov. Un.	178	65.50 N	38.40 E
Ponta Delgada, Açores (pō̇n′tȧ dĕl-gä′dȧ)	224a	37.40 N	25.45 W
Ponta Grossa, Braz. (grō′sȧ)	144	25.09 S	50.05 W
Pont-à-Mousson, Fr. (pôɴ′tȧ-mo͞osôɴ′)	169	48.55 N	6.02 E
Ponta Porã, Braz.	143	22.30 S	55.31 W
Pontarlier, Fr. (pôɴ′tȧr-lyā′)	169	46.53 N	6.22 E
Pont-Audemer, Fr. (pôɴ′tōd′mâr′)	168	49.23 N	0.28 E
Pontault-Combault, Fr.	64c	48.47 N	2.36 E
Pontcarré, Fr. (pôɴ-kȧ-rā′)	169b	48.48 N	2.42 E
Pontchartrain L., La. (pôɴ-shȧr-trăn′)	125	30.10 N	90.10 W
Pontedera, It. (pōn-tā̇-dā′rä)	172	43.37 N	10.37 E
Ponte de Sor, Port. (pōŋ′tĕ dā̇ sōr′)	170	39.14 N	8.03 W
Pontefract, Eng. (pŏn′tē̇-frăkt)	156	53.41 N	1.18 W
Ponte Nova, Braz. (pô′n-tĕ-nô′vȧ)	141a	20.26 S	42.52 W
Pontevedra, Arg.	60d	34.46 S	58.43 W
Pontevedra, Sp. (pō̇n-tĕ-vĕ-drä)	170	42.28 N	8.38 W
Ponthierville, see Ubundi			
Pontiac, Il. (pŏn′tĭ-ăk)	110	40.55 N	88.35 W
Pontiac, Mi.	113b	42.37 N	83.17 W

ăt; finăl; rāte; senā̇te; ärm; ȧsk; sofȧ; fâre; ch-choose; dh-as th in other; bē; ē̇vent; bĕt; recĕnt; cratēr; g-gō; gh-guttural g; bĭt; ĭ-short neutral; rīde; ᴋ-guttural k as ch in German ich;

PRONOUNCING INDEX Pontianak – Pressbaum 331

PLACE (Pronounciation)	PAGE	Lat. °′	Long. °′
ontianak, Indon. (pôn-tê-ä'näk)	206	0.04 S	109.20 E
ontian Kechil, Mala.	191b	1.29 N	103.24 E
ontic Mts., Turk.	179	41.20 N	34.30 E
ontinha (Neigh.), Port.	65d	38.46 N	9.11 W
ontivy, Fr. (pôN-tê-vē')	168	48.05 N	2.57 W
ont-l'Abbé, Fr. (pôN-lȧ-bā')	168	47.53 N	4.12 W
ontoise, Fr. (pôN-twȧz')	169b	49.03 N	2.05 E
ontonnyy, Sov. Un. (pôn'tôn-nyĭ)	182c	59.47 N	30.39 E
ontotoc, Ms. (pŏn-tô-tŏk')	126	34.11 N	88.59 W
ontremoli, It. (pôn-trĕm'ô-lē)	172	44.21 N	9.50 E
onziane, Isole (I.), It. (ē'sō-lĕ)	172	40.55 N	12.58 E
oole, Eng. (pōōl)	162	50.43 N	2.00 W
oolesville, Md. (poolĕs-vĭl)	112e	39.08 N	77.26 W
ooley I., Can. (pōō'lē)	98	52.44 N	128.16 W
oopó, Lago de (L.), Bol. (lä'gô-dĕ-pō-ô-pō')	142	18.16 S	67.57 W
opayán, Col. (pō-pä-yän')	142	2.21 N	76.43 W
oplar, Mt. (pŏp'lẽr)	117	48.08 N	105.10 W
oplar (Neigh.), Eng.	62	51.31 N	0.01 W
oplar Bluff, Mo. (blŭf)	123	36.43 N	90.22 W
oplar Heights, Va.	56d	38.53 N	77.12 W
oplar Plains, Ky. (plāns)	110	38.20 N	83.40 W
oplar Point, Can.	95f	50.04 N	97.57 W
oplar R., Mt.	117	48.34 N	105.20 W
oplar R., West Fork, Mt.	117	48.59 N	106.06 W
oplarville, Ms. (pŏp'lẽr-vĭl)	126	30.50 N	89.33 W
opocatépetl Volcán (Vol.), Mex. (pô-pô-kä-tā'pĕ't'l)	131a	19.01 N	98.38 W
opokabaka, Zaire (pō'pô-kȧ-bä'kȧ)	230	5.42 S	16.35 E
opovka, Sov. Un. (pô'pôf-kȧ)	175	50.03 N	33.41 E
opovka, Sov. Un.	175	51.13 N	33.08 E
opovo, Bul. (pô'pô-vō)	173	43.23 N	26.17 E
orbandar, India (pōr-bŭn'dŭr)	196	21.44 N	69.40 E
orce (R.), Col. (pôr-sĕ)	142a	7.11 N	74.55 W
orcher I., Can. (pôr'kẽr)	98	53.57 N	130.30 W
orcuna, Sp. (pôr-kōō'nä)	170	37.54 N	4.10 W
orcupine (R.), Ak.	107	67.00 N	143.25 W
orcupine (R.), Can.	96	67.38 N	140.07 W
orcupine Cr., Mt. (pôr'kū-pīn)	117	46.38 N	107.04 W
orcupine Cr., Mt.	117	48.27 N	106.24 W
orcupine Hills, Can.	101	52.30 N	101.45 W
ordenone, It. (pōr-dā-nō'nā)	172	45.58 N	12.38 E
oreč, Yugo. (pô'rĕch)	172	45.13 N	13.37 E
ori, Fin. (pô'rē)	165	61.29 N	21.45 E
oriúncula, Braz. (po-rēōō'n-kōō-lä)	141a	20.58 S	42.02 W
orkhov, Sov. Un. (pôr'κôf)	174	57.46 N	29.33 E
orlamar, Ven. (pôr-lä-mär')	142	11.00 N	63.55 W
ornic, Fr. (pôr-nēk')	168	47.08 N	2.07 W
oronaysk, Sov. Un. (pô'rô-nīsk)	181	49.21 N	143.23 E
orrentruy, Switz. (pô-räN-trüē')	166	47.25 N	7.02 E
orsgrunn, Nor. (pôrs'grōōn')	164	59.09 N	9.36 E
ortachuelo, Bol. (pôrt-ä-chwā'lô)	142	17.20 S	63.12 W
ortage, Pa. (pôr'tāj)	111	40.25 N	78.35 W
ortage, Wi.	115	43.33 N	89.29 W
ortage Des Sioux, Mo. (dē sōō)	119e	38.56 N	90.21 W
ortage-la-Prairie, Can. (lä-prā'rĭ)	95f	49.57 N	98.25 W
ort Alberni, Can. (pōr äl-bĕr-nē')	98	49.14 N	124.48 W
ortalegre, Port. (pôr-tä-lā'grĕ)	170	39.18 N	7.26 W
ortales, NM (pôr-tä'lĕs)	122	34.10 N	103.11 W
ort Alfred (Kowie), S. Afr. (kou'ĭ)	227c	33.36 S	26.55 E
ort Alice, Can. (ăl'ĭs)	98	50.23 N	127.27 W
ort Allegany, Pa. (ăl-ê-gā'nĭ)	111	41.50 N	78.10 W
ort Angeles, Wa. (ăn'jê-lĕs)	116	48.07 N	123.26 W
ort Antonio, Jam.	135	18.10 N	76.25 W
ortarlington, Austl.	211a	38.07 S	144.39 E
ort Arthur, Tx.	125	29.52 N	93.59 W
ort Augusta, Austl. (ô-gŭs'tă)	216	32.28 S	137.50 E
ort au Port B., Can. (pŏr'tō pōr')	105	48.41 N	58.45 W
ort-au-Prince, Hai. (prăNs')	135	18.35 N	72.20 W
ort Austin, Ml. (ôs'tĭn)	110	44.00 N	83.00 W
ort aux Basques, Can.	105	47.36 N	59.09 W
ort Blair, Andaman & Nicobar Is. (blâr)	206	12.07 N	92.45 E
ort Bolivar, Tx. (bŏl'ĭ-vȧr)	125a	29.22 N	94.46 W
ort Borden, Can. (bôr'dĕn)	104	46.15 N	63.42 W
ort-Bouët, Ivory Coast	224	5.24 N	3.56 W
ort-Cartier, Can.	104	50.01 N	66.53 W
ort Chester, NY (chĕs'tẽr)	112a	40.59 N	73.40 W
ort Chicago, Ca. (shĭ-kô'gō)	118b	38.03 N	122.01 W
ort Clinton, Oh. (klĭn'tŭn)	110	41.30 N	83.00 W
ort Colborne, Can.	103	42.53 N	79.13 W
ort Coquitlam, Can. (kô-kwĭt'lȧm)	118d	49.16 N	122.46 W
ort Credit, Can. (krĕd'ĭt)	95d	43.33 N	79.35 W
ort-de-Bouc, Fr. (pôr-dē-bōōk')	168a	43.24 N	5.00 E
ort de Paix, Hai. (pē)	135	19.55 N	72.50 W
ort Dickson, Mala. (dĭk'sŭn)	191b	2.33 N	101.49 E
ort Discovery (B.), Wa. (dĭs-kŭv'ẽr-ĭ)	118a	48.05 N	122.55 W
ort Edward, S. Afr. (ĕd'wẽrd)	227c	31.04 S	30.14 E
ort Elgin, Can. (ĕl'jĭn)	104	46.03 N	64.05 W
ort Elizabeth, S. Afr. (ê-lĭz'ȧ-bĕth)	227c	33.57 S	25.37 E
orterdale, Ga. (pōr'tẽr-dāl)	126	33.34 N	83.53 W
orterville, Ca. (pōr'tẽr-vĭl)	120	36.03 N	119.05 W
ortezuelo de Tupungato (Vol.), Arg.-Chile (pōr-tē-zwĕ-lō-dĕ-tōō-pōō'n-gä-tô)	144	33.30 S	69.52 W
ort Francqui, see Ilebo			
ort Gamble, Wa. (găm'bŭl)	118a	47.52 N	122.36 W
ort Gamble Ind. Res., Wa.	118a	47.54 N	122.33 W
ort-Gentil, Gabon (zhäN-tē')	230	0.43 S	8.47 E
ort Gibson, Ms.	126	31.56 N	90.57 W
ort Harcourt, Nig. (här'kŭrt)	229	4.43 N	7.05 E
ort Hardy, Can. (här'dĭ)	98	50.43 N	127.29 W
ort Hawkesbury, Can.	105	45.37 N	61.21 W
ort Hedland, Austl. (hĕd'lănd)	214	20.30 S	118.30 E
orthill, Id.	116	49.00 N	116.30 W
ort Hood, Can. (hŏŏd)	105	46.01 N	61.32 W
ort Hope, Can. (hōp)	111	43.55 N	78.10 W
ort Huron, Mi. (hū'rŏn)	110	43.00 N	82.30 W
ortici, It. (pôr'tê-chē)	171c	40.34 N	14.20 E
ortillo, Chile (pôr-tē'l-yô)	141b	32.51 S	70.09 W
ortimão, Port. (pôr-tē-mo'uN)	170	37.09 N	8.34 W

PLACE (Pronounciation)	PAGE	Lat. °′	Long. °′
Port Jervis, NY (jûr'vĭs)	112a	41.22 N	74.41 W
Portland, Austl. (pōrt'lănd)	216	38.20 S	142.40 E
Portland, In.	110	40.25 N	85.00 W
Portland, Me.	104	43.40 N	70.16 W
Portland, Mi.	110	42.50 N	85.00 W
Portland, Or.	118c	45.31 N	122.41 W
Portland, Tx.	125	27.53 N	97.20 W
Portland Bight (B.), Jam.	134	17.45 N	77.05 W
Portland Can., Ak.	98	55.10 N	130.08 W
Portland Inlet, Can.	98	54.50 N	130.15 W
Portland Pt., Jam	134	17.40 N	77.20 W
Port Lavaca, Tx. (lȧ-vä'kȧ)	125	28.36 N	96.38 W
Port Lincoln, Austl. (lĭŋ-kŭn)	216	34.39 S	135.50 E
Port Ludlow, Wa. (lŭd'lō)	118a	47.26 N	122.41 W
Port Lyautey, see Kenitra			
Port Macquarie, Austl. (mȧ-kwŏ'rĭ)	216	31.25 S	152.45 E
Port Madison Ind. Res., Wa. (măd'ĭ-sŭn)	118a	47.46 N	122.38 W
Port Maria, Jam. (mȧ-rī'ȧ)	134	18.20 N	76.55 W
Port Melbourne, Austl.	70b	37.51 S	144.56 E
Port-Menier, Can. (mē-nyā')	104	49.49 N	64.20 W
Port Moody, Can. (mōōd'ĭ)	118d	49.17 N	122.51 W
Port Moresby, Pap. N. Gui. (mōrz'bē)	207	9.34 S	147.20 E
Port Neches, Tx. (nĕch'ĕz)	125	29.59 N	93.57 W
Port Nelson, Can. (nĕl'sŭn)	101	57.03 N	92.36 W
Portneuf-Sur-Mer, Can. (pôr-nûf'sür mĕr)	104	48.36 N	69.06 W
Port Nolloth, S. Afr. (nŏl'ŏth)	226	29.10 S	17.00 E
Porto, Port. (pōr'tōō)	170	41.10 N	8.38 W
Porto Acre, Braz. (ä'krĕ)	142	9.38 S	67.34 W
Porto Alegre, Braz. (ä-lā'grĕ)	144	29.58 S	51.11 W
Porto Alexandre, Ang. (ȧ-lē-zhän'drĕ)	230	15.49 S	11.53 E
Porto Amboim, Ang.	230	11.01 S	13.45 E
Portobelo, Pan. (pôr'tô-bā'lô)	133	9.32 N	79.40 W
Pôrto de Pedras, Braz. (pā'dräzh)	143	9.09 S	35.20 W
Pôrto Feliz, Braz. (fē-lē's)	141a	23.12 S	47.30 W
Portoferraio, It. (pōr'tô-fĕr-rä'yō)	172	42.47 N	10.20 E
Port of Spain, Trin. (spān)	143	10.44 N	61.24 W
Portogruaro, It. (pōr'tô-grōō-ä'rō)	172	45.48 N	12.49 E
Portola, Ca. (pôr'tō-lȧ)	120	39.47 N	120.29 W
Porto Mendes, Braz. (mĕ'n-dĕs)	143	24.41 S	54.13 W
Porto Murtinho, Braz. (mōōr-tēn'yōō)	143	21.43 S	57.43 W
Pôrto Nacional, Braz. (nȧ-syô-näl')	143	10.43 S	48.14 W
Porto Novo, Benin (pōr'tô-nō'vō)	229	6.29 N	2.37 E
Port Orchard, Wa. (ôr'chẽrd)	118a	47.32 N	122.38 W
Port Orchard (B.), Wa.	118a	47.40 N	122.39 W
Porto Salvo, Port.	65d	38.43 N	9.18 W
Porto Santo, Ilha de (I.), Mad. Is. (säN'tōō)	224	32.41 N	16.15 W
Porto Seguro, Braz. (sā-gōō'rōō)	143	16.26 S	38.59 W
Porto Torres, It. (tôr'rĕs)	172	40.49 N	8.25 E
Porto-Vecchio, Fr. (vĕk'ē-ô)	172	41.36 N	9.17 E
Porto Velho, Braz. (väl'yōō)	142	8.45 S	63.43 W
Portoviejo, Ec. (pôr-tô-vyā'hō)	142	1.11 S	80.28 W
Port Phillip B., Austl. (fĭl'ĭp)	216	37.57 S	144.50 E
Port Pirie, Austl. (pĭ'rē)	216	33.10 S	138.00 E
Port Radium, Can. (rā'dē-ŭm)	96	66.06 N	118.03 W
Port Reading, NJ	55	40.34 N	74.16 W
Port Royal (B.), Jam. (roi'ăl)	134	17.50 N	76.45 W
Port Said, see Bûr Sa'îd			
Port Saint Johns, S. Afr. (sânt jŏnz)	227c	31.37 S	29.32 E
Port Shepstone, S. Afr. (shĕps'tŭn)	227c	30.45 S	30.23 E
Portsmouth, Dominica	133b	15.33 N	61.28 W
Portsmouth, Eng. (pôrts'mŭth)	162	50.45 N	1.03 W
Portsmouth, NH	111	43.05 N	70.50 W
Portsmouth, Oh.	110	38.45 N	83.00 W
Portsmouth, Va.	112g	36.50 N	76.19 W
Port Sulphur, La. (sŭl'fẽr)	126	29.28 N	89.41 W
Port Sunlight, Eng.	64a	53.21 N	2.59 W
Port Susan (B.), Wa. (sū-zȧn')	118a	48.11 N	122.25 W
Port Tampa, Fl. (tăm'pȧ)	127a	27.50 N	82.30 W
Port Townsend, Wa. (tounz'ĕnd)	118a	48.07 N	122.46 W
Port Townsend (B.), Wa.	118a	48.05 N	122.47 W
Portugal, Eur. (pōr'tu-găl)	154	38.15 N	8.08 W
Portugalete, Sp. (pōr-tōō-gä-lā'tā)	170	43.18 N	3.05 W
Portuguese East Africa, see Mozambique			
Portuguese India, see Gôa, Daman & Diu			
Portuguese West Africa, see Angola			
Port Vendres, Fr. (pôr väN'dr')	168	42.32 N	3.07 E
Port Vue, Pa.	57b	40.20 N	79.52 W
Port Wakefield, Austl. (wāk'fēld)	216	34.12 S	138.10 E
Port Washington, NY (wôsh'ĭng-tŭn)	112a	40.49 N	73.42 W
Port Washington, Wi.	115	43.24 N	87.52 W
Posadas, Arg. (pō-sä'dhäs)	144	27.32 S	55.56 W
Posadas, Sp. (pô-sä-däs)	170	37.48 N	5.09 W
Poshekhon 'ye Volodarsk, Sov. Un. (pô-shyĕ'κôn-yĕ vôl'ô-dȧrsk)	174	58.31 N	39.07 E
Poso, Danau (L.), Indon. (pō'sō)	206	2.00 S	119.40 E
Pospelokova, Sov. Un. (pôs-pyĕl'kô-vȧ)	182a	59.25 N	60.50 E
Possession Sd., Wa. (pŏ-zĕsh-ŭn)	118a	47.59 N	122.17 W
Possum Kingdom Res., Tx. (pŏs'ŭm kĭng'dŭm)	124	32.58 N	98.12 W
Post, Tx. (pōst)	122	33.12 N	101.21 W
Postojna, Yugo. (pōs-tōynȧ)	172	45.45 N	14.13 E
Pos'yet, Sov. Un. (pos-yĕt')	204	42.27 N	130.47 E
Potawatomi Ind. Res., Ks. (pŏt-ȧ-wä'tō mē)	123	39.30 N	96.11 W
Potchefstroom, S. Afr. (pŏch'ĕf-strōm)	223d	26.42 S	27.06 E
Poteau, Ok. (pô-tō')	123	35.03 N	94.37 W
Poteet, Tx. (pô-tēt)	124	29.05 N	98.35 W
Potenza, It. (pô-tĕnt'sä)	172	40.39 N	15.49 E
Potenza (R.), It.	172	43.09 N	13.00 E
Potgietersrus, S. Afr. (pŏt-κē'tẽrs-rûs)	223d	24.09 S	29.04 E
Potholes Res., Wa.	116	47.00 N	119.20 W

PLACE (Pronounciation)	PAGE	Lat. °′	Long. °′
Poti, Sov. Un. (pô'tē)	179	42.10 N	41.40 E
Potiskum, Nig.	229	11.43 N	11.05 E
Potomac, Md. (pô-tō'măk)	112e	39.01 N	77.13 W
Potomac (R.), Va. (pô-tō'măk)	111	38.15 N	76.55 W
Poto Poto (Neigh.), Con.	71c	4.15 S	15.18 E
Potosí, Bol. (pō-tô-sē')	142	19.42 S	65.42 W
Potosi, Mo. (pō-tō'sĭ)	123	37.56 N	90.46 W
Potosí, R., Mex. (pō-tô-sē')	124	25.04 N	99.36 W
Potrerillos, Hond. (pō-trȧ-rēl'yôs)	132	15.13 N	87.58 W
Potsdam, G.D.R. (pôts'däm)	157b	52.24 N	13.04 E
Potsdam, NY (pŏts'dăm)	111	44.40 N	75.00 W
Potsdam (Dist.), G.D.R. (pôts'däm)	157b	52.31 N	12.45 E
Pottenstein, Aus.	157e	47.58 N	16.06 E
Potters Bar, Eng. (pŏt'ẽz bär)	156b	51.41 N	0.12 W
Potter Street, Eng.	62	51.46 N	0.08 E
Pottstown, Pa. (pŏts'toun)	111	40.15 N	75.40 W
Pottsville, Pa. (pŏts'vĭl)	111	40.40 N	76.15 W
Poughkeepsie, NY (pŏ-kĭp'sē)	111	41.45 N	73.55 W
Poulsbo, Wa. (pōlz'bōō)	118a	47.44 N	122.38 W
Poulton-le-Fylde, Eng. (pōl'tŭn-lē-fīld')	156	53.52 N	2.59 W
Pouso Alegre, Braz. (pō'zōō ä-lā'grĕ)	141a	22.13 S	45.56 W
Póvoa de Varzim, Port. (pō-vō'ȧ dā vär'zēN)	170	41.23 N	8.44 W
Powder R., Mt.-Wy. (pou'dẽr)	117	45.18 N	105.37 W
Powder R., Or.	116	44.55 N	117.35 W
Powder River, Wy.	117	43.06 N	106.55 W
Powder R., South Fk., Wy.	117	43.13 N	106.54 W
Powell, Wy. (pou'ĕl)	117	44.44 N	108.44 W
Powell L., Can.	98	50.10 N	124.13 W
Powell, L., Ut.	121	37.26 N	110.25 W
Powell Pt., Ba.	125	24.50 N	76.20 W
Powell Res., Ky.-Tn.	126	36.30 N	83.35 W
Powell River, Can.	98	49.52 N	124.33 W
Poyang Hu (L.), China (pwo-yän-hōō)	203	29.20 N	116.28 E
Poygan (R.), Wi. (poi'găn)	115	44.10 N	89.05 W
Poyle, Eng.	62	51.28 N	0.31 W
Poynton, Eng.	64b	53.21 N	2.07 W
Požarevac, Yugo. (pô'zhä'rĕ-vȧts)	173	44.38 N	21.12 E
Poznań, Pol. (pôz'nän')	166	52.24 N	16.55 E
Pozoblanco, Sp. (pô-thō-bläŋ'kō)	170	38.23 N	4.50 W
Pozo Rica, Mex. (pô-zô-rē'kä)	131	20.32 N	97.25 W
Pozos, Mex. (pô'zōs)	130	22.05 N	100.50 W
Pozuelo de Alarcón, Sp. (pô-thwā'lō dā ä-lär-kōn')	171a	40.27 N	3.49 W
Pozzuoli, It. (pôt-swô'lē)	171c	40.34 N	14.08 E
Pra (R.), Ghana (prȧ)	228	5.45 N	1.35 W
Pra (R.), Sov. Un.	174	55.00 N	40.13 E
Prachin Buri, Thai. (prä'chĕn)	206	13.59 N	101.15 E
Pradera, Col. (prä-dĕ'rä)	142a	3.24 N	76.13 W
Prades, Fr. (prȧd)	168	42.37 N	2.23 E
Prado, Col. (prä'dô)	142a	3.44 N	74.55 W
Prado Churubusco, Mex.	60a	19.21 N	99.07 W
Prado, Museo del (P. Int.), Sp.	65b	40.25 N	3.41 W
Prado Res., Ca. (prä'dō)	119a	33.45 N	117.40 W
Prados, Braz. (prȧ'dôs)	141a	21.05 S	44.04 W
Prague, see Praha			
Praha (Prague), Czech. (prä'hȧ) (präg)	166	50.05 N	14.26 E
Prahran, Austl.	70b	37.51 S	144.59 E
Praia, C. V. (prä'yȧ)	224b	15.00 N	23.30 W
Praia da Cruz Quebrada, Port.	65d	38.42 N	9.14 W
Praia Funda, Ponta da (Pt.), Braz. (pôn'tä-dȧ-prä'yȧ-fōō'n-dä)	144b	23.04 S	43.34 W
Prairie du Chien, Wi. (prā'rĭ dōō shēn')	115	43.02 N	91.10 W
Prairie Grove, Can. (prā'rĭ grōv)	95f	49.48 N	96.57 W
Prairie Island Ind. Res., Mn.	115	44.42 N	92.32 W
Prairies, R. des, Can. (rē-vyâr' dā prȧ-rē')	95a	45.40 N	73.34 W
Pratas (Dongsha Dao) (I.), China (dôŋ-shä dou)	203	20.40 N	116.30 E
Prat del Llobregat, Sp.	65e	41.20 N	2.06 E
Prato, It. (prä'tō)	172	43.53 N	11.03 E
Pratt, Ks. (prăt)	122	37.37 N	98.43 W
Pratt's Bottom (Neigh.), Eng.	62	51.20 N	0.07 E
Prattville, Al. (prăt'vĭl)	126	32.28 N	86.27 W
Pravdinsk, Sov. Un.	165	54.26 N	20.11 E
Pravdinskiy, Sov. Un. (prȧv-dĕn'skĭ)	182b	56.03 N	37.52 E
Pravia, Sp. (prä'vē-ä)	170	43.30 N	6.08 W
Pregolya (R.), Sov. Un. (prĕ-gô'lȧ)	165	54.37 N	20.50 E
Premont, Tx. (prē-mŏnt')	124	27.20 N	98.07 W
Prenton, Eng.	64a	53.22 N	3.03 W
Prenzlau, G.D.R. (prĕnts'lou)	166	53.19 N	13.52 E
Prenzlauer Berg (Neigh.), G.D.R.	65a	52.32 N	13.26 E
Přerov, Czech. (przhĕ'rôf)	167	49.28 N	17.28 E
Presa Aleman (L.), Mex. (prä'sä-lĕ-mà'n)	131	18.20 N	96.35 W
Presa de Infiernillo (Res.), Mex.	131	18.50 N	101.50 W
Prescot, Eng. (prĕs'kŭt)	156	53.25 N	2.48 W
Prescott, Az. (prĕs'kŏt)	121	34.30 N	112.30 W
Prescott, Ar.	123	33.47 N	93.23 W
Prescott, Can. (prĕs'kŭt)	111	44.45 N	75.35 W
Prescott, Wi. (prĕs'kŏt)	119g	44.45 N	92.48 W
Presho, SD (prĕsh'ô)	114	43.56 N	100.04 W
Presidencia Roque Sáenz Peña, Arg. (prĕ-sē-dĕ'n-sēä-rō'kĕ-sä'ĕnz-pĕ'n-yȧ)	144	26.52 S	60.15 W
Presidente Epitácio, Braz. (prā-sē-dĕn'tĕ ȧ-pē-tä'syōō)	143	21.56 S	52.01 W
Presidente Roosevelt, (Estacgao) (P. Int.), Braz.	61d	23.33 S	46.36 W
Presidio, Tx. (prĕ-sĭ'dĭ-ô)	124	29.33 N	104.23 W
Presidio of San Francisco (P. Int.), Ca.	58b	37.48 N	122.28 W
Presidio, Rio del (R.), Mex. (rē'ō-dĕl-prĕ-sē'dyō)	130	23.54 N	105.44 W
Prešov, Czech. (prĕ'shôf)	167	49.00 N	21.18 E
Prespa, L., Alb.-Yugo. (prĕs'pä)	173	40.49 N	20.50 E
Prespuntal (R.), Ven. (prĕs-pōōn-täl')	143b	9.55 N	64.32 W
Presque Isle, Me. (prĕsk'ēl')	104	46.41 N	68.03 W
Pressbaum, Aus.	157e	48.12 N	16.06 E

332 Prestea – Puulavesi

PLACE (Pronounciation)	PAGE	Lat. °'	Long. °'
Prestea, Ghana	228	5.27 N	2.08 W
Preston, Austl.	70b	37.45 S	145.01 E
Preston, Eng. (prĕs'tŭn)	144	53.46 N	2.42 W
Preston, Id. (pres'tŭn)	117	42.05 N	111.54 W
Preston, Mn. (prĕs'tŭn)	115	43.42 N	92.06 W
Preston, Wa.	118a	47.31 N	121.56 W
Prestonburg, Ky. (prĕs'tŭn-bûrg)	110	37.35 N	82.50 W
Prestwich, Eng. (prĕst'wĭch)	144	53.32 N	2.17 W
Pretoria, S. Afr. (prē-tō'rĭ-ȧ)	227b	25.43 S	28.16 E
Pretoria North, S. Afr. (prĕ-tô'rĭ-ȧ nōōrd)	227b	25.41 S	28.11 E
Préveza, Grc. (prĕ'vå-zä)	173	38.58 N	20.44 E
Pribilof (Is.), Ak. (prĭ'bĭ-lof)	107	57.00 N	169.20 W
Priboj, Yugo. (prē'boi)	173	43.33 N	19.33 E
Price (R.), Ut.	121	39.21 N	110.35 W
Price, Ut. (prīs)	121	39.35 N	110.50 W
Priddis, Can. (prĭd'dĭs)	95e	50.53 N	114.20 W
Priddis Cr., Can.	95e	50.56 N	114.32 W
Priego, Sp. (prē-ā'gō)	170	37.27 N	4.13 W
Prienai, Sov. Un. (prē-ĕn'ī)	165	54.38 N	23.56 E
Prieska, S. Afr. (prē-ĕs'kȧ)	226	29.40 S	22.50 E
Priest L., Id. (prēst)	116	48.30 N	116.43 W
Priest Rapids Dam, Wa.	116	46.39 N	119.55 W
Priest Rapids Res., Wa.	116	46.42 N	119.58 W
Priiskovaya, Sov. Un. (prĭ-ēs'kô-va-yȧ)	182a	60.50 N	58.55 E
Prijedor, Yugo. (prē'yĕ-dôr)	172	44.58 N	16.43 E
Prijepolje, Yugo. (prē'yĕ-pô'lyĕ)	173	43.22 N	19.41 E
Prilep, Yugo. (prē'lĕp)	173	41.20 N	21.35 E
Priluki, Sov. Un. (prē-lōō'kē)	175	50.36 N	32.21 E
Primorsk, Sov. Un. (prē-môrsk')	165	60.24 N	28.35 E
Primorsko-Akhtarskaya, Sov. Un. (prē-môr'skô äк-tär'skĭ-ĕ)	175	46.03 N	38.09 E
Primos, Pa.	56b	39.55 N	75.18 W
Primrose, S. Afr.	227b	26.11 S	28.11 E
Primrose L., Can.	100	54.55 N	109.45 W
Prince Albert, Can. (prĭns ăl'bērt)	100	53.12 N	105.46 W
Prince Albert Natl. Park, Can.	96	54.10 N	105.25 W
Prince Albert Sd., Can.	97	70.23 N	116.57 W
Prince Charles I., Can. (chärlz)	97	67.41 N	74.10 W
Prince Edward I. (Prov.), Can.	97	46.45 N	63.10 W
Prince Edward Is., S. Afr.	232	46.36 S	37.57 E
Prince Edward Natl. Park, Can. (ĕd'wērd)	104	46.33 N	63.35 W
Prince Edward Pen., Can.	111	44.00 N	77.15 W
Prince Frederick, Md. (prĭnce frĕdĕrĭk)	112e	38.33 N	76.35 W
Prince George, Can. (jôrj)	98	53.51 N	122.57 W
Prince of Wales (I.), Ak.	98	55.47 N	132.50 W
Prince of Wales (I.), Austl.	215	10.47 S	142.15 E
Prince of Wales, C., Ak. (wālz)	107	65.48 N	169.08 W
Prince Rupert, Can. (roo'pērt)	98	54.19 N	130.19 W
Princes Risborough, Eng. (prĭns'ĕz rĭz'brŭ)	156b	51.41 N	0.51 W
Princess Charlotte B., Austl. (shär'lŏt)	215	13.45 S	144.15 E
Princess Martha Coast, Ant. (mär'thȧ)	232	72.00 S	5.00 W
Princess Royal Chan., Can. (roi'ăl)	98	53.10 N	128.37 W
Princess Royal I., Can.	98	52.57 N	128.49 W
Princeton, Can. (prĭns'tŭn)	99	49.27 N	120.31 W
Princeton, IL.	110	41.20 N	89.25 W
Princeton, In.	110	38.20 N	87.35 W
Princeton, Ky.	126	37.07 N	87.52 W
Princeton, Mi.	115	46.16 N	87.33 W
Princeton, Mn.	115	45.34 N	93.36 W
Princeton, Mo.	123	40.23 N	93.34 W
Princeton, NJ	112a	40.21 N	74.40 W
Princeton, WV	127	37.21 N	81.05 W
Princeton, Wi.	115	43.50 N	89.09 W
Prince William Sd., Ak. (wĭl'yăm)	107	60.40 N	147.10 W
Principe Chan., Can. (prĭn'sĭ-pē)	98	53.28 N	129.45 W
Prineville, Or. (prīn'vĭl)	116	44.17 N	120.48 W
Prineville Res., Or.	116	44.07 N	120.45 W
Prinzapolca, Nic. (prēn-zä-pōl'kä)	133	13.18 N	83.35 W
Prinzapolca R., Nic.	133	13.23 N	84.23 W
Prior Lake, Mn. (prī'ēr)	119g	44.43 N	93.26 W
Priozërsk, Sov. Un. (prĭ-ô'zĕrsk)	165	61.03 N	30.08 E
Pripyat (Pripet) (R.), Sov. Un. (prē'pyät)	179	51.50 N	29.45 E
Pripyat Marshes, see Poles'ye			
Priština, Yugo. (prēsh'tĭ-nä)	173	42.39 N	21.12 E
Pritchard, Al. (prĭt'chârd)	126	30.44 N	87.04 W
Pritzwalk, G.D.R. (prēts'välk)	166	53.09 N	12.12 E
Privas, Fr. (prē-väs')	168	44.44 N	4.37 E
Privol'noye, Sov. Un. (prē'vôl-nô-yĕ)	175	47.30 N	32.21 E
Principe (I.), Afr. (prēn'sē-pĕ)	230	1.37 N	7.25 E
Prizren, Yugo. (prē'zrĕn)	173	42.11 N	20.45 E
Procida, It. (prō'chē-dä)	171c	40.31 N	14.02 E
Procida, I. di, It.	171c	40.32 N	13.57 E
Proctor, Mn. (prŏk'tēr)	119h	46.45 N	92.14 W
Proctor, Vt.	111	43.40 N	73.00 W
Proebstel, Wa. (prōb'stĕl)	118c	45.40 N	122.29 W
Proenca-a-Nova, Port. (prô-ān'sȧ-ä-nō'vȧ)	170	39.44 N	7.55 W
Progreso, Hond. (prô-grĕ'sô)	132	15.28 N	87.49 W
Progreso, Mex. (prô-grä'sō)	131	21.14 N	89.39 W
Progreso, Mex.	124	27.29 N	101.05 W
Prokop'yevsk, Sov. Un.	180	53.52 N	86.38 E
Prokuplje, Yugo. (prô'kōōp'l-yĕ)	173	43.16 N	21.40 E
Prome (Pye), Bur.	206	18.46 N	95.15 E
Pronya (R.), Sov. Un. (prô'nyä)	174	54.08 N	30.58 E
Pronya (R.), Sov. Un.	174	54.08 N	39.30 E
Propriá, Braz. (prō-prē-ä')	143	10.17 S	36.47 W
Prospect, Austl.	70a	33.48 S	150.56 E
Prospect, Ky. (prŏs'pĕkt)	113h	38.21 N	85.36 W
Prospect Heights, Il.	58a	42.06 N	87.56 W
Prospect Park, NJ	55	40.56 N	74.10 W
Prospect Park, Pa. (prŏs'pĕkt pärk)	112f	39.53 N	75.18 W
Prosser, Wa. (prŏs'ēr)	116	46.10 N	119.46 W
Prostějov, Czech. (prôs'tyĕ-yôf)	167	49.28 N	17.08 E
Protea, S. Afr.	71b	26.17 S	27.51 E
Protection (I.), Wa. (prô-tĕk'shŭn)	118a	48.07 N	122.56 W
Protoka (R.), Sov. Un. (prôt'ô-kȧ)	174	55.00 N	36.42 E
Provadiya, Bul. (prō-väd'ē-yȧ)	173	43.13 N	27.28 E
Providence, Ky. (prŏv'ĭ-dĕns)	110	37.25 N	87.45 W
Providence, RI	112b	41.50 N	71.23 W
Providence, Ut.	117	41.42 N	111.50 W
Providencia, Chile	61b	33.26 S	70.37 W
Providencia, Isla de (I.), Col.	133	13.21 N	80.55 W
Providenciales (I.), Turks & Caicos Is. (prō-vē-dĕn-sē-ä'lås) (prŏ-vĭ-dĕn'shȧlz)	125	21.50 N	72.15 W
Provideniya, Sov. Un. (prô-vĭ-dä'nĭ-yȧ)	107	64.30 N	172.54 W
Provincetown, Ma.	111	42.03 N	70.11 W
Provo, Ut. (prō'vō)	121	40.15 N	111.40 W
Prozor, Yugo. (prô'zôr)	172	43.48 N	17.59 E
Prudence I., RI (prōō'dĕns)	112b	41.38 N	71.20 W
Prudhoe B., Ak.	107	70.40 N	147.25 W
Prudnik, Pol. (prōōd'nĭk)	167	50.19 N	17.34 E
Prussia (Reg.), G.D.R. (prŭsh'ȧ)	166	50.43 N	8.35 E
Pruszków, Pol. (prōōsh'kōōf)	167	52.09 N	20.50 E
Prut (R.), Sov. Un. (prōōt)	175	48.05 N	27.07 E
Pryor, Ok. (prī'ēr)	123	36.16 N	95.19 W
Prypeć (R.), Sov. Un.	179	51.50 N	25.35 E
Przasnysz, Pol.	167	51.05 N	19.53 E
Przemyśl, Pol. (pzhĕ'mĭsh'l)	167	49.47 N	22.45 E
Przheval'sk, Sov. Un. (p'r-zhĭ-välsk')	180	42.25 N	78.18 E
Psará (I.), Grc. (psä'rȧ)	173	38.39 N	25.26 E
Psël (R.), Sov. Un. (psĕl)	175	49.45 N	33.42 E
Pskov, Sov. Un. (pskôf)	174	57.48 N	28.19 E
Pskov (Oblast), Sov. Un.	174	57.33 N	29.05 E
Pskovskoye Ozero (L.), Sov. Un. (p'skôv'skô'yĕ ôzĕ-rô)	174	58.05 N	28.15 E
Ptuj, Yugo. (ptōō'ē)	172	46.24 N	15.54 E
Pucheng, China (pōō'chĕng')	203	28.02 N	118.25 E
Pucheng, China (pōō-chŭŋ)	200	35.43 N	115.22 E
Puck, Pol. (pōōtsk)	167	54.43 N	18.23 E
Puddington, Eng.	64a	53.15 N	3.00 W
Pudog, China	198	33.29 N	79.26 E
Pudozh, Sov. Un. (pōō'dôzh)	178	61.50 N	36.50 E
Puebla, Mex. (pwā'blä)	130	19.02 N	98.11 W
Puebla (State), Mex.	130	19.00 N	97.45 W
Puebla de Don Fadrique, Sp. (pwĕ'blä dā dōn fä-drē'kā)	170	37.55 N	2.55 W
Pueblo, Co. (pwā'blō)	122	38.15 N	104.36 W
Pueblo Libre, Peru	60c	12.08 S	77.05 W
Pueblo Nuevo, Mex. (nwā'vô)	130	23.23 N	105.21 W
Pueblo Nuevo (Neigh.), Sp.	65b	40.26 N	3.39 W
Pueblo Viejo, Mex. (vyā'hô)	131	17.23 N	93.46 W
Puente Alto, Chile (pwĕ'n-tĕ ȧl'tô)	141b	33.36 S	70.34 W
Puenteareas, Sp. (pwĕn-tā-ä-rā'äs)	170	42.09 N	8.23 W
Puentedeume, Sp. (pwĕn-tå-dhå-ōō'må)	170	43.28 N	8.09 W
Puente-Genil, Sp. (pwĕn'tå-hå-nēl')	170	37.25 N	4.18 W
Puerco (R.), NM (pwĕr'kō)	121	35.15 N	107.05 W
Puerto Aisén, Chile (pwĕ'r-tō ä'y-sĕ'n)	144	45.28 S	72.44 W
Puerto Angel, Mex. (pwĕ'r-tô äŋ'hål)	131	15.42 N	96.32 W
Puerto Armuelles, Pan. (pwe'r-tô är-mōō-ā'lyās)	133	8.18 N	82.52 W
Puerto Barrios, Guat. (pwĕ'r-tô bär'rē-ôs)	132	15.43 N	88.36 W
Puerto Bermúdez, Peru (pwĕ'r-tō bĕr-mōō'dāz)	142	10.17 S	74.57 W
Puerto Berrío, Col. (pwĕ'r-tô bĕr-rē'ō)	142a	6.29 N	74.27 W
Puerto Cabello, Ven. (pwĕ'r-tô kä-bĕl'yō)	143b	10.28 N	68.01 W
Puerto Cabezas, Nic. (pwĕ'r-tô kä-bā'zäs)	133	14.01 N	83.26 W
Puerto Casado, Par. (pwĕ'r-tô kä-sä'dō)	144	22.16 S	57.57 W
Puerto Castilla, Hond. (pwĕ'r-tô käs-tēl'yō)	132	16.01 N	86.01 W
Puerto Chicama, Peru (pwĕ'r-tō chē-kä'mä)	142	7.46 S	79.18 W
Puerto Columbia, Col. (pwĕ'r-tô kô-lôm'bē-ȧ)	142	11.08 N	75.09 W
Puerto Cortés, C. R. (pwĕ'r-tô kôr-tās')	133	9.00 N	83.37 W
Puerto Cortés, Hond. (pwĕ'r-tô kôr-tās')	132	15.48 N	87.57 W
Puerto Cumarebo, Ven. (pwĕ'r-tô kōō-mä-rĕ'bô)	142	11.25 N	69.17 W
Puerto de Luna, NM (pwĕr'tô dȧ lōō'nä)	122	34.49 N	104.36 W
Puerto de Nutrias, Ven. (pwĕ'r-tô dĕ nōō-trē-äs')	142	8.02 N	69.19 W
Puerto Deseado, Arg. (pwĕ'r-tô dā-så-ä'dhō)	144	47.38 S	66.00 W
Puerto de Somport (P.), Fr.-Sp.	171	42.51 N	0.25 W
Puerto Eten, Peru (pwĕ'r-tô ĕ-tĕ'n)	142	6.59 S	79.51 W
Puerto Jimenez, C. R. (pwĕ'r-tô кē-mĕ'nĕz)	133	8.35 N	83.23 W
Puerto La Cruz, Ven. (pwĕ'r-tô lä krōō'z)	143b	10.14 N	64.38 W
Puertollano, Sp. (pwĕ-tôl-yä'nō)	170	38.41 N	4.05 W
Puerto Madryn, Arg. (pwĕ'r-tô mä-drĕ'n)	144	42.45 S	65.01 W
Puerto Maldonado, Peru (pwĕ'r-tō mäl-dō-nä'dô)	142	12.43 S	69.01 W
Puerto Mexico, see Coatzacoalcos			
Puerto Miniso, Mex. (pwĕ'r-tô mē-nē'sô)	130	16.06 N	98.02 W
Puerto Montt, Chile (pwĕ'r-tō mô'nt)	144	41.29 S	73.00 W
Puerto Natales, Chile (pwĕ'r-tô nä-tä'lĕs)	144	51.48 S	72.01 W
Puerto Niño, Col. (pwĕ'r-tô nē'n-yô)	142a	5.57 N	74.36 W
Puerto Padre, Cuba (pwĕ'r-tō pä'drā)	134	21.10 N	76.40 W
Puerto Peñasco, Mex. (pwĕ'r-tô pĕn-yä's-kô)	128	31.39 N	113.15 W
Puerto Pinasco, Par. (pwĕ'r-tō pē-nä's-kô)	144	22.31 S	57.50 W
Puerto Píritu, Ven. (pwĕ'r-tô pē'rē-tōō)	143b	10.05 N	65.04 W
Puerto Plata, Dom. Rep. (pwĕ'r-tô plä'tä)	135	19.50 N	70.40 W
Puerto Princesa, Phil. (pwĕr-tô prēn-sā'sä)	206	9.45 N	118.41 E
Puerto Rico, N. A. (pwĕr'tô rē'kō)	129	18.16 N	66.50 W
Puerto Rico Trench, N. A.	129	19.45 N	66.30 W
Puerto Salgar, Col. (pwĕ'r-tō säl-gär')	142a	5.30 N	74.39 W
Puerto Santa Cruz, Arg. (pwĕ'r-tō sän'tä krōōz')	144	50.04 S	68.32 W
Puerto Suárez, Bol. (pwĕ'r-tô swä'rāz)	143	18.55 S	57.39 W
Puerto Tejada, Col. (pwĕ'r-tô tĕ-кä'dä)	142a	3.13 N	76.23 W
Puerto Vallarta, Mex. (pwĕ'r-tō väl-yär'tä)	130	20.36 N	105.13 W
Puerto Varas, Chile (pwĕ'r-tō vä'räs)	144	41.16 S	73.03 W
Puerto Wilches, Col. (pwĕ'r-tō vēl'c-hĕs)	142	7.19 N	73.54 W
Pugachëv, Sov. Un. (pōō'gȧ-chyôf)	179	52.00 N	48.40 E
Puget, Wa. (pū'jĕt)	118c	46.10 N	123.23 W
Puget Sd., Wa.	116	47.49 N	122.26 W
Puglia (Apulia) (Reg.), It. (pōō'lyä) (ä-pōō'lyä)	172	41.13 N	16.10 E
Pukaskwa Natl. Pk., Can.	102	48.22 N	85.55 W
Pukeashun Mtn., Can.	99	51.12 N	119.14 W
Pukin (R.), Mala.	191b	2.53 N	102.54 E
Pula, Yugo. (pōō'lä)	172	44.52 N	13.55 E
Pulacayo, Bol. (pōō-lä-kä'yō)	142	20.12 N	66.33 W
Pulaski, Tn. (pû-lăs'kĭ)	126	35.11 N	87.03 W
Pulaski, Va.	127	37.00 N	81.45 W
Pulawy, Pol. (pōō-wä'vē)	167	51.24 N	21.59 E
Pulizat (R.), India	196	13.58 N	79.52 E
Pullman, Wa. (pōōl'măn)	116	46.44 N	117.10 W
Pullman (Neigh.), Il.	58a	41.43 N	87.36 W
Pulog (Mtn.), Phil. (pōō'lôg)	207a	16.38 N	120.53 E
Pultusk, Pol. (pōōl'tōōsk)	158	52.40 N	21.09 E
Puma Yumco (L.), China (pōō-mä yōōm-tswo)	196	28.30 N	90.10 E
Pumphrey, Md.	56c	39.13 N	76.38 W
Pumpkin Cr., Mt. (pŭmp'kĭn)	117	45.47 N	105.35 W
Punakha, Bhu. (pōō-nŭk'ŭ)	196	27.45 N	89.59 E
Punata, Bol. (pōō-nä'tä)	142	17.43 S	65.43 W
Punchbowl, Austl.	70a	33.56 S	151.03 E
Pune, India	196	18.38 N	73.53 E
Punggol, Singapore	67c	1.25 N	103.55 E
Punjab (State), India (pŭn'jäb')	196	31.00 N	75.30 E
Puno, Peru (pōō'nô)	142	15.58 S	7.02 W
Punta Arenas, Chile (pōō'n-tä-rĕ'näs)	144	53.09 S	70.48 W
Punta Brava, Cuba	60b	23.01 N	82.30 W
Punta de Piedras, Ven. (pōō'n-tä dĕ pyĕ'dräs)	143b	10.54 N	64.06 W
Punta Gorda, Belize (pōōn'tä gôr'dä)	132	16.07 N	88.50 W
Punta Gorda, Fl. (pŭn'tȧ gôr'dȧ)	127a	26.55 N	82.02 W
Punta Gorda, Rio (R.), Nic. (pōō'n-tä gô'r-dä)	133	11.34 N	84.13 W
Punta Indio, Can., Arg. (pōō'n-tä- ē'n-dyô)	141c	34.56 S	57.20 W
Puntarenas, C. R. (pōōnt-ä-rā'näs)	133	9.59 N	84.49 W
Punto Fijo, Ven. (pōō'n-tô fē'кô)	142	11.48 N	70.14 W
Punxsutawney, Pa. (pŭnk-sŭ-tô'nē)	111	40.55 N	79.00 W
Puquio, Peru (pōō'kyô)	142	14.43 S	74.02 W
Pur (R.), Sov. Un.	180	65.30 N	77.30 E
Purcell, Ok. (pûr-sĕl')	123	35.01 N	97.22 W
Purcell Mts., Can. (pûr-sĕl')	99	50.00 N	116.30 W
Purdy, Wa. (pûr'dē)	118a	47.23 N	122.37 W
Purépero, Mex. (pōō-rā'pā-rō)	130	19.56 N	102.02 W
Purfleet, Eng.	62	51.29 N	0.15 E
Purgatoire (R.), Colo. (pûr-gȧ-twär')	122	37.25 N	103.53
Puri, India (pōō'rē)	196	19.52 N	85.51
Purial, Sierra de (Mts.), Cuba (sē-ĕ'r-rȧ-dĕ-pōō-rē-äl')	135	20.15 N	74.40
Purificacion, Col. (pōō-rē-fē-kä-syōn')	142a	3.52 N	74.54
Purificación, Mex. (pōō-rē-fē-kä-syô'n)	130	19.44 N	104.38
Purificación (R.), Mex.	130	19.30 N	104.54
Purkersdorf, Aus.	157e	48.13 N	16.11
Purley (Neigh.), Eng.	62	51.20 N	0.07
Puruandiro, Mex. (pōō-rōō-än'dē-rō)	130	20.04 N	101.33
Purús (R.), Braz. (pōō-rōō's)	142	6.45 S	64.34
Pusan, Kor.	204	35.08 N	129.05
Pushkin, Sov. Un. (pōōsh'kĭn)	182c	59.43 N	30.25
Pushkino, Sov. Un. (pōōsh'kē-nô)	182b	56.01 N	37.51
Pustoshka, Sov. Un. (pûs-tôsh'kȧ)	174	56.20 N	29.33
Pustunich, Mex. (pōōs-tōō'nēch)	131	19.10 N	90.29
Putaendo, Chile (pōō-tä-ĕn-dô)	141b	32.37 S	70.42
Puteaux, Fr. (pü-tō')	169b	48.52 N	2.12
Putfontein, S. Afr. (pōōt'fŏn-tān)	227b	26.08 S	28.24
Puth Kalān (Neigh.), India	67d	28.43 N	77.05
Putian, China (pōō-tĭĕn)	203	25.40 N	119.02
Putilkovo, Sov. Un.	66b	55.52 N	37.23
Putivl', Sov. Un. (pōō-tēv'l')	175	51.22 N	33.24
Putla de Guerrero, Mex. (pōō'tlä-dĕ-gĕr-rĕ'rō)	131	17.03 N	97.55
Putnam, Ct. (pŭt'năm)	111	41.55 N	71.55
Putney (Neigh.), Eng.	62	51.28 N	0.13
Putorana, Gory (Mts.), Sov. Un.	180	68.45 N	93.15
Pütt, F.R.G.	63	51.11 N	6.59
Puttalam, Sri Lanka	197	8.02 N	79.44
Putumayo (R.), Col.-Peru (pōō-tōō-mä'yō)	142	1.02 S	73.50
Putung, Tandjung (C.), Indon.	206	3.35 S	111.50
Puulavesi (L.), Fin.	165	61.49 N	27.10

PRONOUNCING INDEX

Puyallup – Rajang 333

PLACE (Pronounciation)	PAGE	Lat. °'	Long. °'
Puyallup, Wa. (pū-ăl'ŭp)	118a	47.12 N	122.18 W
Puyang, China (pōō-yäŋ)	200	35.42 N	114.58 E
Pweto, Zaire (pwā'tō)	226	8.29 S	28.58 E
Pyasina (R.), Sov. Un. (pyä-sē'nȧ)	180	72.45 N	87.37 E
Pyatigorsk, Sov. Un. (pyȧ-tē-gôrsk')	179	44.00 N	43.00 E
Pye, see Prome			
Pyhäjärvi (L.), Fin.	165	60.57 N	21.50 E
Pyinmana, Bur. (pyēn-mä'nŭ)	198	19.47 N	96.15 E
Pymatuning Res., Pa. (pī-mȧ-tûn'ĭng)	110	41.40 N	80.30 W
Pymble, Austl.	70a	33.45 S	151.09 E
Pyŏnggang, Kor. (pyŭng'gäng')	204	38.21 N	127.18 E
P'yŏngyang, Kor.	204	39.03 N	125.48 E
Pyramid (L.), Nv. (pī'rȧ-mĭd)	120	40.02 N	119.50 W
Pyramid Lake Ind. Res., Nv.	120	40.17 N	119.52 W
Pyramids, Egypt	223b	29.53 N	31.10 E
Pyrenees (Mts.), Fr.-Sp. (pĭr-e-nēz')	171	43.00 N	0.05 E
Pyrford, Eng.	62	51.19 N	0.30 W
Pyrzyce, Pol. (pĕzhĭ'tsĕ)	166	53.09 N	14.53 E

Q

PLACE (Pronounciation)	PAGE	Lat. °'	Long. °'
Qal'at Bishah, Sau. Ar.	192	20.01 N	42.30 E
Qallābāt, Sud.	225	12.55 N	36.12 E
Qana el Suweis (Suez Can.), Egypt	223c	30.53 N	32.21 E
Qandahār, Afg.	193	31.43 N	65.58 E
Qandala, Som.	195	11.28 N	49.52 E
Qārah (Oasis), Egypt	161	29.28 N	26.29 E
Qareh Sū (R.), Iran	179	38.50 N	47.10 E
Qarqan, see Qiemo			
Qarqan (R.), China	198	38.55 N	87.15 E
Qārūn, Birket (L.) Egypt	223b	29.34 N	30.34 E
Qasr al-Burayqah, Libya	225	30.25 N	19.20 E
Qasr al-Farāfirah, Egypt	225	27.04 N	28.13 E
Qaşr Banī Walīd, Libya	225	31.45 N	14.04 E
Qaşr-e Fīrūzeh, Iran	68h	35.40 N	51.32 E
Qasrel-Boukhari, Alg.	160	35.50 N	2.48 E
Qatar, Asia (kä'tȧr)	190	25.00 N	52.45 E
Qaţţārah, Munkhafaḍ (Dep.), Egypt	225	30.07 N	27.30 E
Qāyen, Iran	192	33.45 N	59.08 E
Qazvīn, Iran	195	36.16 N	50.00 E
Qeshm, Iran	192	26.51 N	56.10 E
Qeshm (I.), Iran	192	26.52 N	56.15 E
Qezel Owzan, Iran	192	37.00 N	48.23 E
Qezel Owzan, (R.), Iran	179	37.00 N	47.35 E
Qezi'ot, Egypt-Isr.	191a	30.53 N	34.28 E
Qianwei, China (chyĕn-wā)	200	40.11 N	120.05 E
Qi'anzhen, China (chyē-än-jŭn)	200	32.16 N	120.59 E
Qibao, China (chyē-bou)	201b	31.06 N	121.16 E
Qiblīyah, Jabal al Jalālat al (Plat.), Egypt	191a	28.49 N	32.21 E
Qiemo (Qargan), China (chyär-chyän)	198	38.02 N	85.16 E
Qieshikou, China	67b	39.59 N	116.24 E
Qifţ, Egypt (kĕft)	223b	25.58 N	32.52 E
Qijiang, China (chyē-jyäŋ)	203	29.05 N	106.40 E
Qikou, China (chyē-kō)	200	38.37 N	117.33 E
Qilian Shan (Mts.), China (chyē-lĭĕn shän)	198	38.43 N	98.00 E
Qiliping, China (chyē-lē-pĭŋ)	200	31.28 N	114.41 E
Qinā, Egypt (kä'nȧ)	223b	26.10 N	32.48 E
Qinā, Wādī, Egypt	223b	26.38 N	32.53 E
Qindao (Tsingtao), China (chyĭn-dou)	200	36.05 N	120.10 E
Qing'an, China (chyĭŋ-än)	202	46.50 N	127.30 E
Qingcheng, China (chyĭŋ-chŭŋ)	200	37.12 N	117.43 E
Qingfeng, China (chyĭŋ-fŭŋ)	200	35.52 N	115.05 E
Qinghai (Prov.), China (chyĭŋ-hī)	198	36.14 N	95.30 E
Qinghai Hu (L.), see Koko Nor			
Qinghe, China (chyĭŋ-hŭ)	202a	40.08 N	116.16 E
Qinghuayuan, China	67b	40.00 N	116.19 E
Qingjiang, China (chyĭŋ-jyäŋ)	203	28.00 N	115.30 E
Qingjiang, China	200	33.34 N	118.58 E
Qingliu, China (chyĭŋ-lĭō)	203	26.15 N	116.50 E
Qingningsi, China (chyĭŋ-nĭŋ-sz)	201b	31.16 N	121.33 E
Qingping, China (chyĭŋ-pĭŋ)	200	36.46 N	116.03 E
Qingpu, China (chyĭŋ-pōō)	201b	31.08 N	121.06 E
Qingxian, China (chyĭŋ shyĕn)	200	38.37 N	116.48 E
Qingyang, China (chyĭŋ-yäŋ)	202	36.02 N	107.42 E
Qingyuan, China (chyĭŋ-yōän)	203	23.43 N	113.10 E
Qingyuan, China	202	42.05 N	125.00 E
Qingyun, China (chyĭŋ-yōōn)	200	37.52 N	117.26 E
Qingyundian, China (chĭŋ-yōōn-dĭĕn)	202a	39.41 N	116.31 E
Qinhuangdao, China (chyĭn-huäŋ-dou)	200	39.57 N	119.34 E
Qin Ling (Mts.), China (chyĭn lĭŋ)	191	33.25 N	108.58 E
Qin Ling (Mts.), China	202	33.35 N	108.25 E
Qinyang, China (chyĭn-yäŋ)	200	35.00 N	112.55 E
Qinzhou, China (chyĭn-jō)	203	22.00 N	108.35 E
Qionghai, China (chyôŋ-hī)	203	19.10 N	110.28 E
Qiqian, China (chyē-chyĕn)	199	52.23 N	121.04 E
Qiqihar, China	202	47.18 N	124.00 E
Qiryat Gat, Isr.	191a	31.38 N	34.36 E
Qiryat Shemona, Isr.	191a	33.12 N	35.34 E
Qitai, China (chyē-tī)	198	44.07 N	89.04 E
Qiuxian, China (chyô shyĕn)	200	36.43 N	115.13 E
Qixian, China (chyē-shyĕn),	200	34.33 N	114.47 E
Qixian, China	200	35.36 N	114.13 E
Qiyang, China (chyē-yäŋ)	203	26.40 N	112.00 E
Qolleh-ye, Damāvand (Mtn.), Iran	179	36.05 N	52.05 E
Qom, Iran	192	34.28 N	50.53 E
Quabbin Res., Ma. (kwā'bĭn)	111	42.20 N	72.10 W
Quachita, L., Ar. (kwä shĭ'tô)	123	34.47 N	93.37 W
Quadra, Boca de, Str., Ak. (bōk'ȧ dĕ kwŏd'rȧ)	98	55.08 N	130.50 W
Quadra I., Can.	98	50.08 N	125.16 W
Quadraro (Neigh.), It.	66c	41.51 N	12.33 E
Quahran, see Oran			
Quakers Hill, Austl.	70a	33.43 S	150.53 E
Quakertown, Pa. (kwā'kēr-toun)	111	40.30 N	75.20 W
Quamdo, China (chyäm-dwō)	198	31.06 N	96.30 E
Quanah, Tx. (kwä'nȧ)	122	34.19 N	99.43 W
Quang Ngai, Viet. (kwäng n'gä'ē)	203	15.05 N	108.58 E
Quang Ngai (Mtn.), Viet.	203	15.10 N	108.20 E
Quanjiao, China (chyuän-jyou)	200	32.06 N	118.17 E
Quanzhou, China (chyuän-jō)	203	24.58 N	118.40 E
Quanzhou, China	203	25.58 N	111.02 E
Qu'Appelle (R.), Can.	100	50.35 N	103.25 W
Qu'Appelle Dam, Can.	100	51.00 N	106.25 W
Quartu Sant' Elena It. (kwär-tōō' sänt a'lâ-nä)	172	39.16 N	9.12 E
Quartzsite, Az.	121	33.40 N	114.13 W
Quatsino Sd, Can. (kwŏt-sē'nō)	98	50.25 N	128.10 W
Qūchān, Iran	195	37.06 N	58.30 E
Qudi, China	200	37.06 N	117.15 E
Québec, Can. (kwē-bĕk') (kâ-bĕk')	95b	46.49 N	71.13 W
Quebec (Prov.), Can.	97	51.07 N	70.25 W
Quedlinburg, G.D.R. (kvĕd'lēn-bōōrgh)	166	51.45 N	11.10 E
Qued-Zem, Mor. (wĕd-zĕm')	224	33.05 N	5.49 W
Queen Bess, Mt., Can.	98	51.16 N	124.34 W
Queen Charlotte Is., Can. (kwēn shär'lŏt)	98	53.30 N	132.25 W
Queen Charlotte Ra., Can.	98	53.00 N	132.00 W
Queen Charlotte Sd., Can.	98	51.30 N	129.30 W
Queen Charlotte Str., Can. (strāt)	98	50.40 N	127.25 W
Queen Elizabeth Is., Can. (ê-lĭz'ȧ-bĕth)	94	78.20 N	110.00 W
Queen Maud G., Can. (mäd)	96	68.27 N	102.55 W
Queen Maud Land, Ant.	232	75.00 S	10.00 E
Queen Maud Mts., Ant.	232	85.00 S	179.00 W
Queens Chan., Austl. (kwēnz)	214	14.25 S	129.10 E
Queenscliff, Austl.	211a	38.16 S	144.39 E
Queensland (state), Austl. (kwēnz'lănd)	215	22.45 S	141.01 E
Queenstown, Austl. (kwēnz'toun)	216	42.00 S	145.40 E
Queenstown, S. Afr.	227c	31.54 S	26.53 E
Queimados, Braz. (kā-mȧ'dôs)	144b	22.42 S	43.34 W
Quela, Ang.	230	9.16 S	17.02 E
Quelimane, Moz. (kā-lê-mä'nĕ)	216	17.48 S	37.05 E
Quelpart (I.), see Cheju			
Queluz, Port.	65d	38.45 N	9.15 W
Quemado de Güines, Cuba (kā-mä'dhä-dĕ-gwē'nĕs)	134	22.45 N	80.20 W
Quemoy (Chinmen), Taiwan	203	24.30 N	118.20 E
Quemoy (I.), Taiwan	203	24.35 N	118.45 E
Quepos, C.R. (kā'pôs)	133	9.26 N	84.10 W
Quepos, Punta (Pt.), C.R. (pōō'n-tä)	133	9.23 N	84.20 W
Querenburg (Neigh.), F.R.G.	63	51.27 N	7.16 E
Querétaro, Mex. (kâ-rā'tä-rō)	130	20.37 N	100.25 W
Querétaro (State), Mex.	130	21.00 N	100.00 W
Quesada, Sp. (kâ-sä'dhä)	170	37.51 N	3.04 W
Quesnel, Can. (kā-nĕl')	98	52.59 N	122.30 W
Quesnel L., Can.	99	52.32 N	121.05 W
Quesnel (R.), Can.	98	52.15 N	122.00 W
Quetame, Col. (kĕ-tä'mĕ)	142a	4.20 N	73.50 W
Quetta, Pak. (kwĕt'ä)	196	30.19 N	67.01 E
Quezaltenango, Guat. (kâ-zäl'tâ-näŋ'gō)	132	14.50 N	91.30 W
Quezaltepeque, Guat. (kâ-zäl'tâ-pā'kâ)	132	14.39 N	89.26 W
Quezaltepeque, Sal. (kĕ-zäl'tĕ-pĕ-kĕ)	132	13.50 N	89.17 W
Quezon City, Phil. (kā-zōn)	207a	14.40 N	121.02 E
Qufu, China (chyōō-fōō)	200	35.37 N	116.54 E
Quibdo, Col. (kēb'dō)	142a	5.42 N	76.41 W
Quiberon, Fr. (kē-bē-rôN')	168	47.29 N	3.08 W
Quiçama, Parque Nacional de (Natl. Pk.), Ang.	230	10.00 S	13.25 E
Quiché, Guat. (kē-shā')	132	15.05 N	91.08 W
Quicksborn, F.R.G. (kvēks'bōrn)	157c	53.44 N	9.54 E
Quilcene, Wa. (kwĭl-sēn')	118a	47.50 N	122.53 W
Quilimari, Chile (kē-lē-mä'rē)	141b	32.06 S	71.28 W
Quillan, Fr. (kē-yäN')	168	43.53 N	2.13 E
Quillota, Chile (kēl-yō'tä)	141b	32.52 S	71.14 W
Quilmes, Arg. (kēl'mās)	144b	34.43 S	58.16 W
Quilon, India (kwē-lōn')	197	8.58 N	76.16 E
Quilpie, Austl. (kwĭl'pē)	216	26.34 S	149.20 E
Quilpué, Chile (kēl-pōō ĕ')	141b	33.03 S	71.22 W
Quimbaya, Col. (kēm-bä'yä)	142a	4.38 N	75.46 W
Quimbele, Ang.	230	6.28 S	16.13 E
Quimbonge, Ang.	230	8.36 S	18.30 E
Quimper, Fr. (kăN-pĕr')	168	47.59 N	4.04 W
Quinalt R., Wa.	116	47.23 N	124.10 W
Quinault Ind. Res., Wa.	116	47.27 N	124.34 W
Quincy, Fl. (kwĭn'sē)	126	30.35 N	84.35 W
Quincy, Il.	123	39.55 N	91.23 W
Quincy, Ma.	105a	42.15 N	71.00 W
Quincy, Mi.	110	42.00 N	84.50 W
Quincy, Or.	118c	46.08 N	123.10 W
Quincy B., Ma.	54a	42.17 N	70.58 W
Qui-nhon, Viet. (kwĭnyôn)	206	13.51 N	109.03 E
Quinn R., Nv. (kwĭn)	116	41.42 N	117.45 W
Quintanar de la Orden, Sp. (kēn-tä-när')	170	39.36 N	3.02 W
Quintana Roo (State), Mex. (rô'ô)	132a	19.30 N	88.30 W
Quinta Normal, Chile	61b	33.27 S	70.42 W
Quintero, Chile (kēn-tĕ'rô)	141b	32.48 S	71.30 W
Quinto Romano (Neigh.), It.	65c	45.29 N	9.05 E
Quionga, Moz.	231	10.37 S	40.30 E
Quiroga, Mex. (kē-rō'gä)	130	19.39 N	101.30 W
Quiroga, Sp. (kē-rô'gä)	170	42.28 N	7.18 W
Quitaúna, Braz.	61d	23.31 S	46.47 W
Quitman, Ga. (kwĭt'măn)	126	30.46 N	83.35 W
Quitman, Ms.	126	33.02 N	88.43 W
Quito, Ec. (kē'tō)	142	0.17 S	78.32 W
Quixadá, Braz. (kē-shä-dä')	143	4.58 S	38.58 W
Qulūşanā, Egypt (kōō-lōōs'nä)	223b	28.22 N	30.44 E
Qumbu, S. Afr. (kōōm'bōō)	227c	31.10 S	28.48 E
Quorn, Austl. (kwôrn)	216	32.20 S	138.00 E
Qurayyah, Wādī (R.), Egypt	191a	30.08 N	34.27 E
Qūş, Egypt (kōōs)	223b	25.53 N	32.48 E
Qutang, China (chyōō-täŋ)	200	32.33 N	120.07 E
Quthing, Leso.	227c	30.35 S	27.42 E
Quvea (I.), N. Cal.	215	20.43 S	166.48 E
Quxian, China (chyōō-shyĕn)	203	28.58 N	118.58 E
Quxian, China	203	30.40 N	106.48 E
Quzhou, China (chyoô-jō)	200	36.47 N	114.58 E
Quzvīn, Iran	192	36.10 N	49.59 E

R

PLACE (Pronounciation)	PAGE	Lat. °'	Long. °'
Raab R., Aus. (räp)	166	46.55 N	15.55 E
Raadt (Neigh.), F.R.G.	63	51.24 N	6.56 E
Raahe, Fin. (rä'ĕ)	158	64.39 N	24.22 E
Raasdorf, Aus.	66e	48.15 N	16.34 E
Rab (I.), Yugo. (räb)	172	44.45 N	14.40 E
Raba, Indon.	206	8.32 S	118.49 E
Raba R., Hung.	167	47.28 N	17.12 E
Rabat, Mor. (rȧ-bät')	224	33.59 N	6.47 W
Rabaul, Pap. N. Gui. (rä'boul)	207	4.15 S	152.19 E
Rābigh, Sau. Ar.	195	22.48 N	39.01 E
Raby, Eng.	64a	53.19 N	3.02 W
Raccoon (R.), Ia. (ră-kōōn')	115	42.07 N	94.45 W
Raccoon Cay (I.), Ba.	135	22.25 N	75.50 W
Race, C., Can. (rās)	105	46.40 N	53.10 W
Raceview, S. Afr.	71b	26.17 S	28.08 E
Rachado, C., Mala.	191b	2.26 N	101.29 E
Racibórz, Pol. (rä-chē'bōōzh)	167	50.06 N	18.14 E
Racine, Wi. (rȧ-sēn')	113a	42.43 N	87.49 W
Raco, Mi. (rȧ cō)	119k	46.22 N	84.43 W
Rădăuţi, Rom.'(rû-dû-ōōts'')	167	47.53 N	25.55 E
Radcliffe, Eng. (răd'klĭf)	156	53.34 N	2.20 W
Radevormwald, F.R.G. (rä'dĕ-fōrm-väld)	169c	51.12 N	7.22 E
Radford, Va. (răd'fērd)	127	37.06 N	81.33 W
Rādhanpur, India	196	23.57 N	71.38 E
Radium, S. Afr. (rā'dĭ-ŭm)	223d	25.06 S	28.18 E
Radlett, Eng.	62	51.42 N	0.20 W
Radnor, Pa.	56b	40.02 N	75.21 W
Radom, Pol. (rä'dôm)	167	51.24 N	21.11 E
Radomir, Bul. (rä'dō-mēr)	173	42.33 N	22.58 E
Radomsko, Pol. (rä-dôm'skô)	167	51.04 N	19.27 E
Radomyshl, Sov. Un. (rä-dô-mēsh''l)	175	50.30 N	29.13 E
Radoviš, Yugo. (rä-dô-vēsh)	173	41.39 N	22.28 E
Radul', Sov. Un. (rä-dōōl)	175	51.52 N	30.46 E
Radviliškis, Sov. Un. (răd'vē-lēsh'kēs)	165	55.49 N	23.31 E
Radwah, Jabal (Mtn.), Sau. Ar.	192	24.44 N	38.14 E
Radzyń Podlaski, Pol. (räd'zēn-y' pŭd-lä'skĭ)	167	51.49 N	22.40 E
Raeford, NC (rā'fērd)	127	34.57 N	79.15 W
Raesfeld, F.R.G. (răz'fĕld)	169c	51.46 N	6.50 E
Raeside, Austl. (rā'sīd)	214	29.20 S	122.30 E
Rae Str., Can. (rā)	96	68.40 N	95.03 W
Rafaela, Arg. (rä-fä-ĕ'lä)	144	31.15 S	61.21 W
Rafael Castillo, Arg.	60d	34.42 S	58.37 W
Rafah, Egypt (rä'fä)	191a	31.14 N	34.12 E
Rafaï, Cen. Afr. Rep. (rä-fī')	225	4.59 N	23.58 E
Rafḥā, Sau. Ar.	192	29.43 N	43.13 E
Rafsanjān, Iran	192	30.45 N	56.30 E
Raft R., Id. (răft)	117	42.20 N	113.17 W
Ragay, Phil. (rä-gī')	207a	13.49 N	122.45 E
Ragay G., Phil.	207a	13.44 N	122.38 E
Ragga, Egypt	179	36.00 N	39.00 E
Ragunda, Swe. (rä-gōōn'dä)	164	63.07 N	16.24 E
Ragusa, It. (rä-gōō'sä)	159	36.58 N	14.41 E
Ragusa, see Dubrovnik			
Rahm (Neigh.), F.R.G.	63	51.21 N	6.47 E
Rahnsdorf (Neigh.), G.D.R.	65a	52.26 N	13.42 E
Rahway, NJ (rô'wā)	112a	40.37 N	74.16 W
Rāichūr, India (rä'ē-chōōr')	197	16.23 N	77.18 E
Raigarh, India (rī'gŭr)	196	21.57 N	83.32 E
Rainbow Bridge Natl. Mon., Ut. (rān'bō)	121	37.05 N	111.00 W
Rainbow City, Pan.	128a	9.20 N	79.23 W
Rainford, Eng.	64a	53.30 N	2.48 W
Rainhill, Eng.	64a	53.26 N	2.46 W
Rainhill Stoops, Eng.	64a	53.24 N	2.45 W
Rainier, Or.	118c	46.05 N	122.56 W
Rainier, Mt., Wa. (rā-nēr')	116	46.52 N	121.46 W
Rainy (L.), Can.-Mn. (rān'ē)	101	48.43 N	94.29 W
Rainy (R.), Can.-Mn.	101	48.50 N	94.41 W
Rainy River, Can.	101	48.43 N	94.29 W
Raipur, India (rä'jŭ-bōō-rē')	196	21.25 N	81.37 E
Raisin (R.), Mi. (rā'zĭn)	110	42.00 N	83.35 W
Raitan, NJ (rā-tăn)	112a	40.34 N	74.40 W
Rājahmundry, India (räj-ŭ-mŭn'drē)	197	17.03 N	81.51 E
Rajang (Strm.), Mala.	206	2.10 N	113.30 E

ng-sing; nŋ-baŋk; N-nasalized n; nŏd; cŏmmit; ōld; ôbey; ôrder; oi-boil; fōōd; fŏŏt; ou-out; s-soft; sh-dish; th-thin; pūre; ûnite; ûrn; stŭd; circŭs; ü-as in French tu; '-indeterminate vowel.

334 Rājapālaiyam – Reni

PLACE (Pronounciation)	PAGE	Lat. °′	Long. °′
Rājapālaiyam, India	196	9.30 N	77.33 E
Rājasthān (State), India (rä'jŭs-tän)	196	31.20 N	72.00 E
Rājkot, India (räj'kôt)	196	22.20 N	70.48 E
Rājpur, India	196a	22.24 N	88.25 E
Rājpur (Neigh.), India	67d	28.41 N	77.12 E
Rājshāhi, Bngl.	196	24.26 S	88.39 E
Rakhov, Sov. Un. (rä'ĸôf)	167	48.02 N	24.13 E
Rakh'ya, Sov. Un. (räk'yȧ)	182c	60.06 N	30.50 E
Rakitnoye, Sov. Un. (rȧ-kēt'nô-yĕ)	175	50.51 N	35.53 E
Rákoscsaba (Neigh.), Hung.	66g	47.29 N	19.17 E
Rákoshegy (Neigh.), Hung.	66g	47.28 N	19.14 E
Rákoskeresztúr (Neigh.), Hung.	66g	47.29 N	19.15 E
Rákosliget (Neigh.), Hung.	66g	47.30 N	19.16 E
Rákospalota (Neigh.), Hung.	66g	47.34 N	19.08 E
Rákosszentmihály (Neigh.), Hung.	66g	47.32 N	19.11 E
Rakovnik, Czech. (rä'kôk-nyēk)	166	50.07 N	13.45 E
Rakvere, Sov. Un. (rȧk'vĕ-rĕ)	174	59.22 N	26.14 E
Raleigh, NC	127	35.45 N	78.39 W
Raleigh, B., NC	127	34.50 N	76.15 W
Ram (R.), Can.	99	52.10 N	115.05 W
Rama, Nic. (rä'mä)	133	12.11 N	84.14 W
Ramallo, Arg. (rä-mä'l-yô)	141c	33.28 S	60.02 W
Ramanāthapuram, India	197	9.13 N	78.52 E
Rambouillet, Fr. (räɴ-bōō-yĕ')	169b	48.39 N	1.49 E
Rame Hd, S. Afr.	227c	31.48 S	29.22 E
Ramenka (Neigh.), Sov. Un.	66b	55.41 N	37.30 E
Ramenskoye, Sov. Un. (rá'mĕn-skô-yĕ)	182b	55.34 N	38.15 E
Ramlat as Sab'atayn (Reg.), Sau. Ar.	192	16.08 N	45.15 E
Ramm, Jabal (Mts.), Jordan	191a	29.37 N	35.32 E
Ramos, Mex. (rä'mōs)	130	22.46 N	101.52 W
Ramos (R.), Nig.	229	5.10 N	5.40 E
Ramos Arizpe, Mex. (ä-rēz'pȧ)	124	25.33 N	100.57 W
Rampart, Ak. (răm'pȧrt)	107	65.28 N	150.18 W
Rampo Mts., NJ-NY (răm'pō)	112a	41.06 N	74.12 W
Rāmpur, India (räm'pōōr)	196	28.53 N	79.03 E
Ramree I., Bur. (räm'rē')	206	19.01 N	93.23 E
Ramsayville, Can. (răm'zē vĭl)	95c	45.23 N	75.34 W
Ramsbottom, Eng. (rămz'bŏt-ŭm)	156	53.39 N	2.20 W
Ramsden Heath, Eng.	62	51.38 N	0.28 E
Ramsey, Isle of Man (răm'zē)	162	54.20 N	4.25 W
Ramsey, NJ	112a	41.03 N	74.09 W
Ramsey L., Can.	102	47.15 N	82.16 W
Ramsgate, Austl.	70a	33.59 S	151.08 E
Ramsgate, Eng. (rămz''gāt)	163	51.19 N	1.20 E
Ramsjö, Swe. (räm'shû)	164	62.11 N	15.44 E
Ramu (R.), Pap. N. Gui. (rä'mōō)	207	5.35 S	145.16 E
Rancagua, Chile (rän-kä'gwä)	141b	34.10 S	70.43 W
Rance (R.), Fr. (räɴs)	168	48.17 N	2.30 W
Rānchī, India (rän'chē)	196	23.24 N	85.18 E
Ranchleigh, Md.	56c	39.22 N	76.40 W
Rancho Boyeros, Cuba (rä'n-chô-bô-yĕ'rôs)	135a	23.00 N	82.23 W
Rancho Palos Verdes, Ca.	59	33.45 N	118.24 W
Randallstown, Md. (răn'dȧlz-toun)	112e	39.22 N	76.48 W
Randburg, S. Afr.	71b	26.06 S	27.59 E
Randers, Den. (rän'ĕrs)	164	56.28 N	10.03 E
Randfontein, S. Afr. (rănt'fŏn-tān)	227b	26.10 S	27.42 E
Randleman, NC (răn'd'l-măn)	127	35.49 N	79.50 W
Randolph, Ma. (răn'dŏlf)	105a	42.10 N	71.03 W
Randolph, Ne.	114	42.22 N	97.22 W
Randolph, Vt.	111	43.55 N	72.40 W
Random I., Can. (răn'dŭm)	105	48.12 N	53.25 W
Randsfjorden (Fd.), Nor.	164	60.35 N	10.10 E
Randwick, Austl.	70a	33.55 S	151.15 E
Ranérou, Senegal	228	15.18 N	13.58 W
Rangeley, Me. (ränj'lē)	104	44.56 N	70.38 W
Rangeley (L.), Me.	104	45.00 N	70.25 W
Ranger, Tx. (rān'jēr)	124	32.26 N	98.41 W
Rangia, India	196	26.32 N	91.39 E
Rangoon, Bur. (răŋ-gōōn')	206	16.46 N	96.09 E
Rangpur, Bngl. (rŭng'pōōr)	196	25.48 N	89.19 E
Rangsang (I.), Indon. (räng'säng')	191b	0.53 N	103.05 E
Rangsdorf, G.D.R. (rängs'dōrf)	157b	52.17 N	13.25 E
Ranholas, Port.	65d	38.47 N	9.22 W
Rānīganj, India (rä-nē-gŭnj')	196	23.40 N	87.08 E
Rankin, Pa.	57b	40.25 N	79.53 W
Rankin Inlet, Can. (răŋ'kĕn)	96	62.45 N	94.27 W
Ranova (R.), Sov. Un. (rä'nô-vȧ)	174	53.55 N	40.03 E
Ransomville, NY (răn'sum-vĭl)	113c	43.15 N	78.54 W
Rantau, Mala.	191b	2.35 N	101.58 E
Rantelkomboa, Bulu (Mtn.), Indon.	206	3.22 S	119.50 E
Rantoul, Il. (răn-tōōl')	110	40.25 N	88.05 W
Raoyang, China (rou-yäŋ)	200	38.16 N	115.45 E
Rapallo, It. (rä-päl'lô)	172	44.21 N	9.14 E
Rapa Nui (Easter) (I.), Chile (rä'pä nōō'ē) (ēs'tēr)	209	26.50 S	109.00 W
Rapel (R.), Chile (rä-pål')	141b	34.05 S	71.30 W
Rapid (R.), Mn. (răp'ĭd)	115	48.21 N	94.50 W
Rapid City, SD	114	44.06 N	103.14 W
Rapla, Sov. Un. (räp'lȧ)	165	59.02 N	24.46 E
Rappahannock (R.), Va. (răp'ȧ-hăn'ŭk)	111	38.20 N	75.25 W
Raquette (L.), NY (răk'ĕt)	111	43.50 N	74.35 W
Rara Mazowiecka, Pol. (rä'rä mä-zō-vyĕts'kä)	167	51.46 N	20.17 E
Raritan R., NJ (răr'ĭ-tăn)	112a	40.32 N	74.27 W
Rarotonga, Cook Is. (rä'rô-tŏŋ'gȧ)	209	20.40 S	163.00 W
Ra's an Naqb, Jordan	191a	30.00 N	35.29 E
Ras Dashen Terara (Mtn.), Eth. (räs dä-shän')	225	12.49 N	38.14 E
Raseiniai, Sov. Un. (rä-syā'nyĭ)	165	55.23 N	23.04 E
Ra's Fartak (C.), P. D. R. of Yem.	192	15.43 N	52.17 E
Rashayya, Leb.	191a	33.30 N	35.50 E
Rashīd (Rosetta), Egypt (rȧ-shēd') (rô-zĕt'ȧ)	223b	31.22 N	30.25 E
Rashīd, Masabb (R. Mth.), Egypt	223b	31.30 N	29.58 E
Rashkina, Sov. Un. (rȧsh'kĭ-nȧ)	182a	59.57 N	61.30 E
Rashkov, Sov. Un. (räsh'kôf)	175	47.55 N	28.51 E
Rasht, Iran	192	37.13 N	49.45 E
Raška, Yugo. (räsh'kȧ)	173	43.16 N	20.40 E
Ras Kuh Mt., Pak.	196	34.03 N	65.10 E
Rasskazovo, Sov. Un. (räs-kä'sô-vô)	179	52.40 N	41.40 E
Rastatt, F.R.G. (rä-shtät)	166	48.51 N	8.12 E
Rastes, Sov. Un. (rȧs'tĕs)	182a	59.24 N	58.49 E
Rastunovo, Sov. Un. (rȧs-tōō'nô-vô)	182b	55.15 N	37.50 E
Ras Uarc (C.), Mor.	170	35.28 N	2.58 W
Ratangarh, India (rŭ-tŭn'gŭr)	196	28.10 N	74.30 E
Ratcliff, Tx. (răt'klĭf)	125	31.22 N	95.09 W
Rath (Neigh.), F.R.G.	63	51.17 N	6.49 E
Rathenow, G.D.R. (rä'tĕ-nō)	166	52.36 N	12.20 E
Rathlin I., Ire. (răth-lĭn)	162	55.18 N	6.13 W
Rathmecke, F.R.G.	63	51.15 N	7.38 E
Ratingen, F.R.G. (rä'tēn-gĕn)	169	51.18 N	6.51 E
Rat Is., Ak. (răt)	107a	51.35 N	176.48 E
Ratlām, India	196	23.19 N	75.05 E
Ratnāgiri, India	197	17.04 N	73.24 E
Raton, NM (rȧ-tōn')	122	36.52 N	104.26 W
Rattlesnake Cr., Or. (răt''l snāk)	116	42.38 N	117.39 W
Rättvik, Swe. (rĕt'vēk)	164	60.54 N	15.07 E
Rauch, Arg. (rȧ'ōōch)	141c	36.47 S	59.05 W
Raufoss, Nor. (rou'fôs)	164	60.44 N	10.30 E
Raúl Soares, Braz. (rä-ōō'l-sôä'rĕs)	141a	20.05 S	42.28 W
Rauma, Fin. (rä'ōō-mȧ)	165	61.07 N	21.31 E
Rauna, Sov. Un. (råŭ'nȧ)	165	57.21 N	25.31 E
Raurkela, India	196	22.15 N	84.53 E
Rautalampi, Fin. (rä'ōō-tĕ-lăm'pô)	165	62.39 N	26.25 E
Rava-Russkaya, Sov. Un. (rä'vȧ rōōs'kä-yȧ)	167	50.14 N	23.40 E
Ravenna, It. (rä-vĕn'nä)	172	44.27 N	12.13 E
Ravenna, Ne. (rȧ-vĕn'ȧ)	114	41.20 N	98.50 W
Ravenna, Oh.	110	41.10 N	81.20 W
Ravensburg, F.R.G. (rä'vĕns-bōōrgh)	166	47.48 N	9.35 E
Ravensdale, Wa. (rā'vĕnz-dāl)	118a	47.22 N	121.58 W
Ravensthorpe, Austl. (rā'vĕns-thôrp)	214	33.30 S	120.20 E
Ravenswood, S. Afr.	71b	26.11 S	28.15 E
Ravenswood, WV (rā'vĕnz-wōōd)	110	38.55 N	81.50 W
Ravensworth, Va.	56d	38.48 N	77.13 W
Ravenwood, Va.	56d	38.52 N	77.09 W
Rāwalpindi, Pak. (rä-wŭl-pēn'dē)	196	33.40 N	73.10 E
Rawāndūz, Iraq	192	36.37 N	44.30 E
Rawicz, Pol. (rä'vēch)	166	51.36 N	16.51 E
Rawlina, Austl. (rôr-lēnȧ)	214	31.13 S	125.45 E
Rawlins, Wy. (rô'lĭnz)	117	41.46 N	107.15 W
Rawson, Arg. (rô'sŭn)	144	43.16 S	65.09 W
Rawson, Arg.	141c	34.36 S	60.03 W
Rawtenstall, Eng. (rô'tĕn-stôl)	156	53.42 N	2.17 W
Raya, Bukit (Mtn.), Indon.	206	0.45 S	112.11 E
Ray, C., Can. (rā)	105	47.40 N	59.18 W
Raychikinsk, Sov. Un. (rī'chĭ-kēnsk)	181	49.52 N	129.17 E
Rayleigh, Eng. (rā'lē)	156b	51.35 N	0.36 E
Raymond, Can. (rā'mŭnd)	99	49.27 N	112.39 W
Raymond, Wa.	116	46.41 N	123.42 W
Raymondville, Tx. (rā'mŭnd-vĭl)	122	26.30 N	97.46 W
Ray Mts., Ak.	107a	65.40 N	151.45 W
Rayne, La. (rān)	125	30.12 N	92.15 W
Rayón, Mex. (rä-yōn')	130	21.49 N	99.39 W
Rayton, S. Afr. (rā'tŭn)	227b	25.45 S	28.33 E
Raytown, Mo. (rā'toun)	119f	39.01 N	94.48 W
Rayville, La. (rā-vĭl)	125	32.28 N	91.46 W
Razdel'naya, Sov. Un. (räz-dĕl'nä-yȧ)	175	46.47 N	30.08 E
Razdol'noye, Sov. Un. (räz-dôl'nô-yĕ)	204	43.38 N	131.58 E
Razgrad, Bul.	173	43.32 N	26.32 E
Razlog, Bul. (räz'lôk)	173	41.54 N	23.32 E
Razorback Mtn., Can. (rā'zēr-băk)	98	51.35 N	124.42 W
Raz, Pte. du (Pt.), Fr. (pwäɴt dü rä)	168	48.02 N	4.43 W
Rea (R.), Eng. (rē)	156	52.25 N	2.31 W
Reaburn, Can. (rā'bûrn)	95f	50.06 N	97.53 W
Reading, Eng. (rĕd'ĭng)	156b	51.25 N	0.58 W
Reading, Ma.	105a	42.32 N	71.07 W
Reading, Mi.	110	41.45 N	84.45 W
Reading, Oh.	113f	39.14 N	84.26 W
Reading, Pa.	111	40.20 N	75.55 W
Readville (Neigh.), Ma.	54a	42.14 N	71.08 W
Realengo, Braz. (rē-ä-län-gô)	144b	23.50 S	43.25 W
Real Felipe, Castillo (P. Int.), Peru	60c	12.04 S	77.09 W
Rebel Hill, Pa.	56b	40.04 N	75.20 W
Rebiana (Oasis), Libya	225	24.10 N	22.03 E
Rebun (I.), Jap. (rē'bōōn)	204	45.25 N	140.54 E
Recanati, It. (rā-kä-nä'tē)	172	43.25 N	13.35 E
Recherche, Arch. of the, Austl. (rē-shârsh')	214	34.17 S	122.30 E
Rechitsa, Sov. Un. (ryĕ'chēt-sȧ)	174	52.22 N	30.24 E
Recife (Pernambuco), Braz. (rȧ-sē'fĕ) (pĕr-näm-bōō'kô)	143	8.09 S	34.59 W
Recife, Kapp (C.), S. Afr. (rȧ-sē'fĕ)	227c	34.03 S	25.43 E
Recklinghausen, F.R.G.	63	51.36 N	7.13 E
Recklinghausen-Süd (Neigh.), F.R.G.	63	51.34 N	7.13 E
Reconquista, Arg. (rä-kōn-kēs'tä)	144	29.01 S	59.41 W
Reconquista (R.), Arg.	60d	34.27 S	58.36 W
Rector, Ar. (rĕk'tēr)	123	36.16 N	90.21 W
Red (Basin), see **Szechwan**			
Red (R.), Can.-U. S. (rĕd)	101	49.11 N	97.18 W
Red (R.), **North Fk.**, Tx.	122	35.20 N	100.08 W
Red (R.), Tn.	126	36.35 N	86.55 W
Red (R.), U.S.	109	31.40 N	92.55 W
Red (R.), Viet.	206	22.25 N	103.50 E
Redan, Ga. (rē-dăn') (rĕd'ăn)	112c	33.44 N	84.09 W
Red Bank, NJ (băngk)	112a	40.21 N	74.06 W
Red Bank National Park, NJ.	56b	39.52 N	75.10 W
Red Bluff, Ca. (blŭf)	118	40.10 N	122.14 W
Red Bluff Res., Tx.	124	32.03 N	103.52 W
Redbridge (Neigh.), Eng.	62	51.34 N	0.05 E
Redby, Mn. (rĕd'bē)	115	47.52 N	94.55 W
Red Cedar (R.), Wi. (sē'dēr)	115	45.03 N	91.48 W
Redcliff, Can. (rĕd'clĭf)	100	50.05 N	110.47 W
Redcliffe, Austl. (rĕd'clĭf)	207	27.20 S	153.12 E
Red Cliff Ind. Res., Wi.	115	46.48 N	91.22 W
Red Cloud, Ne. (kloud)	122	40.06 N	98.32 W
Red Deer, Can. (dēr)	99	52.16 N	113.48 W
Red Deer (R.), Can.	99	52.05 N	113.00 W
Red Deer (R.), Can.	100	52.55 N	102.10 W
Red Deer L., Can.	101	52.58 N	101.28 W
Reddick, Il. (rĕd'dĭk)	113a	41.06 N	88.16 W
Redding, Ca. (rĕd'ĭng)	116	40.36 N	122.25 W
Reddish, Eng.	64b	53.26 N	2.09 W
Redenção da Serra, Braz. (rĕ-dĕn-souɴ-dä-sĕ'r-rä)	141a	23.17 S	45.31 W
Redfield, SD (rĕd'fēld)	114	44.53 N	98.30 W
Red Fish Bar, Tx.	125a	29.29 N	94.53 W
Redford (Neigh.), Mi.	57c	42.25 N	83.16 W
Redford Township, Mi.	57c	42.25 N	83.16 W
Red Hill, Ca.	59	33.45 N	117.48 W
Red Indian L., Can. (ĭn'dĭ-ăn)	105	48.40 N	56.50 W
Redklinghausen, F.R.G. (rĕk'lĭng-hou-zĕn)	169c	51.36 N	7.13 E
Red Lake, Can. (lāk)	101	51.02 N	93.49 W
Red Lake (R.), Mn.	114	48.02 N	96.04 W
Red Lake Falls, Mn. (lāk fôls)	114	47.52 N	96.17 W
Red Lake Ind. Res., Mn.	114	48.09 N	95.55 W
Redlands, Ca. (rĕd'lăndz)	119a	34.04 N	117.11 W
Red Lion, Pa. (lī'ŭn)	111	39.55 N	76.30 W
Red Lodge, Mt.	117	45.13 N	107.16 W
Redmond, Wa. (rĕd'mŭnd)	118a	47.40 N	122.07 W
Rednitz R., F.R.G. (rĕd'nētz)	166	49.10 N	11.00 E
Red Oak, Ia. (ōk)	114	41.00 N	95.12 W
Redon, Fr. (rē-dôɴ')	168	47.42 N	2.03 W
Redonda I., Antigua (rĕ-dŏn'dȧ)	133b	16.55 N	62.28 W
Redonda, Isla, Braz. (ē's-lä-rĕ-dô'n-dä)	144b	23.05 S	43.11 W
Redondela, Sp. (rä-dhôn-dā'lä)	170	42.16 N	8.34 W
Redondo, Port. (rȧ-dôn'dōō)	170	38.40 N	7.32 W
Redondo, Wa. (rē-dŏn'dō)	118a	47.21 N	122.19 W
Redondo Beach, Ca.	119a	33.50 N	118.23 W
Red Pass, Can. (pȧs)	99	52.59 N	118.59 W
Red Rock Cr., Mt.	117	44.54 N	112.44 W
Red R., Prairie Dog Town Fk., Tx. (prā'rĭ)	122	34.54 N	101.31 W
Red R., Salt Fk., Tx.	122	35.04 N	100.31 W
Red Sea, Afr.-Asia	225	23.15 N	37.00 E
Redstone, Can. (rĕd'stōn)	98	52.08 N	123.42 W
Red Sucker L., Can. (sŭk'ēr)	101	54.09 N	93.40 W
Redwater Cr., Mt.	117	47.37 N	105.25 W
Red Willow Cr., Ne.	122	40.34 N	100.48 W
Red Wing, Mn.	115	44.34 N	92.35 W
Redwood City, Ca. (rĕd' wōōd)	118b	37.29 N	122.13 W
Redwood Falls, Mn.	115	44.32 N	95.06 W
Reed City, Mi. (rēd)	110	43.50 N	85.35 W
Reed L., Can.	101	54.37 N	100.30 W
Reedley, Ca. (rēd'lē)	120	36.37 N	119.27 W
Reedsburg, Wi. (rēdz'bûrg)	115	43.32 N	90.01 W
Reedsport, Or. (rēdz'pôrt)	116	43.42 N	124.08 W
Reelfoot (R.), Tn. (rēl'fōōt)	126	36.18 N	89.20 W
Ree, Lough (B.), Ire. (lŏĸ'rē')	162	53.30 N	7.45 W
Rees, F.R.G. (rĕz)	169c	51.46 N	6.25 E
Reeves, Mt., Austl. (rēv's)	216	33.50 S	149.56 E
Reform, Al. (rē-fôrm')	126	33.23 N	88.00 W
Refugio, Tx. (rȧ-fōō'hyō) (rē-fū'jō)	125	28.18 N	97.15 W
Rega (R.), Pol. (rĕ-gä)	166	53.48 N	15.30 E
Regen R., F.R.G. (rā'ghĕn)	166	49.09 N	12.21 E
Regensburg, F.R.G. (rā'ghĕns-bōōrgh)	166	49.02 N	12.06 E
Regents Park, Austl.	70a	33.53 S	151.02 E
Regent's Park (P. Int.), Eng.	62	51.32 N	0.09 W
Reggane, Alg.	224	27.08 N	0.06 E
Reggio, La. (rĕg'jĭ-ō)	112d	29.50 N	89.46 W
Reggio di Calabria, It. (rĕ'jô dē kä-lä'brē-ä)	172	38.07 N	15.42 E
Reggio nell' Emilia, It.	172	44.43 N	10.34 E
Reghin, Rom. (rȧ-gēn')	167	46.47 N	24.44 E
Regina, Can. (rē-jī'nȧ)	100	50.25 N	104.39 W
Regla, Cuba (răg'lä)	135a	23.08 N	82.20 W
Regnitz (R.), F.R.G. (rĕg'nētz)	166	49.50 N	10.55 E
Rego Park (Neigh.), NY	55	40.44 N	73.52 W
Reguengos de Monsaraz, Port. (rȧ-gĕŋ'gōzh dā mōn-sä-räzh')	170	38.26 N	7.30 W
Reh, F.R.G.	63	51.22 N	7.33 E
Rehoboth, Namibia	226	23.10 S	17.15 E
Rehovot, Isr.	191a	31.53 N	34.49 E
Reichenbach, G.D.R. (rī'ĸĕn-bäĸ)	166	50.36 N	12.18 E
Reidsville, NC (rēdz'vĭl)	127	36.20 N	79.37 W
Reigate, Eng. (rī'gāt)	156b	51.12 N	0.12 W
Ré, Ile de (I.), Fr. (ēl dē rā')	168	46.10 N	1.53 W
Reims, Fr. (răɴs)	168	49.16 N	4.00 E
Reina Adelaida, Arch., Chile (är-chē'pyĕ'lȧ-gô-rā'nä-ä-dĕ-lī'dä)	144	52.00 S	74.15 W
Reinbeck, Ia. (rīn'bĕk)	115	42.22 N	92.34 W
Reindeer (L.), Can. (rān'dēr)	96	57.36 N	101.23 W
Reindeer (R.), Can.	100	55.45 N	103.30 W
Reindeer I., Can.	101	52.25 N	98.00 W
Reindeer L., Can.	101	57.15 N	102.40 W
Reinosa, Sp. (rȧ-ē-nō'sä)	170	43.01 N	4.08 W
Reisholz (Neigh.), F.R.G.	63	51.11 N	6.52 E
Reistertown, Md. (rēs'tēr-toun)	112e	39.28 N	76.50 W
Reitz, S. Afr.	223d	27.48 S	28.25 E
Rema, Jabal (Mtn.), Yemen	192	14.13 N	44.38 E
Rembau, Mala.	191b	2.36 N	102.06 E
Remedios, Col. (rĕ-mĕ'dyôs)	142a	7.03 N	74.42 W
Remedios, Cuba (rä-mā'dhē-ōs)	134	22.30 N	79.35 W
Remedios, Pan. (rĕ-mĕ'dyōs)	133	8.14 N	81.46 W
Remedios de Escalada (Neigh.), Arg.	60d	34.43 S	58.23 W
Remiremont, Fr. (rē-mēr-môɴ')	169	48.01 N	6.35 E
Rempang I., Indon.	191b	0.51 N	104.04 E
Remscheid, F.R.G. (rĕm'shīt)	169c	51.10 N	7.11 E
Rena, Nor.	164	61.08 N	11.17 E
Renca, Chile	61b	33.24 S	70.44 W
Renca, Cerro (Mtn.), Chile	61b	33.23 S	70.43 W
Rendova (I.), Sol. Is. (rĕn'dô-vȧ)	215	8.38 S	156.26 E
Rendsburg, F.R.G. (rĕnts'bōōrgh)	166	54.19 N	9.39 E
Renfrew, Can. (rĕn'frōō)	111	45.30 N	76.30 W
Rengam, Mala. (rĕn'gäm')	191b	1.53 N	103.24 E
Rengo, Chile (rĕn'gō)	141b	34.22 S	70.50 W
Reni, Sov. Un. (ran')	175	45.26 N	28.18 E

ăt; finăl; rāte; senâte; ärm; åsk; sofȧ; fâre; ch-choose; dh-as th in other; bē; ēvent; bĕt; recĕnt; cratēr; g-gō; gh-guttural g; bĭt; ĭ-short neutral; rīde; ĸ-guttural k as ch in German ich;

RONOUNCING INDEX		Renmark – Río Gallegos 335

.ACE (Pronounciation)	PAGE	Lat. °′	Long. °′
enmark, Austl. (rĕn′märk)	216	34.10 S	140.50 E
ennel (I.), Sol. Is. (rĕn-nĕl′)	215	11.50 S	160.38 E
ennes, Fr. (rĕn)	168	48.07 N	1.02 W
ennselaer, NY (rĕn′sĕ-lâr)	111	42.40 N	73.45 W
eno, Nv. (rē′nō)	120	39.32 N	119.49 W
eno (R.), It. (rā′nô)	172	44.10 N	10.55 E
enovo, Pa. (rē-nō′vō)	111	41.20 N	77.50 W
enqiu, China (rŭn-chyô)	200	38.44 N	116.05 E
ensselaer, In. (rĕn′sĕ-lâr)	110	41.00 N	87.10 W
entchler, Il. (rĕnt′chlēr)	119e	38.30 N	89.52 W
enton, Wa. (rĕn′tŭn)	118a	47.29 N	122.13 W
enville, Mn. (rĕn′vĭl)	115	44.44 N	95.13 W
epentigny, Can.	95a	45.47 N	73.26 W
epublic, Al. (rē-pŭb′lĭk)	112h	33.37 N	86.54 W
epublic, Wa.	116	48.38 N	118.44 W
epublican (R.), Ks.	123	39.40 N	97.40 W
epublican (R.), South Fk., Co. (rē-pŭb′lĭ-kăn)	122	39.35 N	102.28 W
epulse B., Austl. (rē-pŭls′)	215	20.56 S	149.22 E
equena, Sp. (rå-kā′nä)	170	39.29 N	1.03 W
eseda (Neigh.), Ca.	59	34.12 N	118.31 W
esende, Braz. (rĕ-sĕ′n-dĕ)	141a	22.30 S	44.26 W
esende Costa, Braz. (kôs-tä)	141a	20.55 S	44.12 W
eservoir, Austl.	70b	37.43 S	145.00 E
eshetilovka, Sov. Un. (ryĕ′ shĕ-tē-lôf-kå)	175	49.34 N	34.04 E
esistencia, Arg. (rā-sēs-tĕn′syä)	144	27.24 S	58.54 W
esita, Rom. (rå′shē-tå)	173	45.18 N	21.56 E
esolute, Can. (rĕz-ō-lūt′)	94	74.41 N	95.00 W
esolution (I.), Can. (rĕz-ō-lū′shŭn)	97	61.30 N	63.58 W
esolution I., N.Z. (rĕz-ŏl-ûshûn)	217	45.43 S	166.20 E
esse (Neigh.), F.R.G.	63	51.34 N	7.07 E
estigouche (R.), Can. (rĕs-tē-gōōsh′)	104	47.35 N	67.35 W
estrepo, Col. (rĕs-trĕ′pô)	142a	3.49 N	76.31 W
estrepo, Col.	142a	4.16 N	73.32 W
etalhuleu, Guat. (rā-täl-ōō-lān′)	132	14.31 N	91.41 W
ethel, Fr. (r-tl′)	168	49.34 N	4.20 E
éthimnon, Grc.	172a	35.21 N	24.30 E
etie, Bel.	157a	51.16 N	5.08 E
etiro, Parque del (P. Int.), Sp.	65b	40.25 N	3.41 W
etsil, Wa. (rĕt′sĭl)	118a	47.33 N	122.37 W
eunion, Afr. (rā-ü-nyôn′)	232	21.06 S	55.36 E
eus, Sp. (rā′ōōs)	171	41.08 N	1.05 E
eusrath, F.R.G.	63	51.06 N	6.57 E
eutlingen, F.R.G. (roit′lĭng-ĕn)	166	48.29 N	9.14 E
eutov, Sov. Un. (rĕ-ōō′ôf)	182b	55.45 N	37.52 E
eval, see Tallinn			
evda, Sov. Un. (ryâv′då)	182a	56.48 N	59.57 E
evelstoke, Can. (rĕv′ĕl-stōk)	99	51.59 N	118.12 W
eventazon, R., C.R. (rå-vĕn-tä-zōn′)	133	10.10 N	83.30 W
evere, Ma. (rē-vēr′)	105a	42.24 N	71.01 W
evesby, Austl.	70a	33.57 S	151.01 E
evillagigedo Chan, Ak. (rĕ-vĭl′å-gĭ-gē′dō)	98	55.10 N	131.13 W
evillagigedo I., Ak.	98	55.35 N	131.23 W
evillagigedo, Islas (I.), Mex. (ē′s-läs-rĕ-vĕl-yä-hĕ′gĕ-dô)	128	18.45 N	111.00 W
evin, Fr. (rē-văN)	168	49.56 N	4.34 E
ewa, India (rā′wä)	196	24.41 N	81.11 E
ewāri, India	196	28.19 N	76.39 E
exburg, Id. (rĕks′bûrg)	117	43.50 N	111.48 W
ey, Iran	68h	35.35 N	51.25 E
eyes, Bol. (rā′yĕs)	142	14.19 S	67.16 W
eyes, Pt., Ca.	120	38.00 N	123.00 W
ey, Isla del (I.), Pan. (ē′s-lä-dĕl-rā′ē)	133	8.20 N	78.40 W
eykjanes (C.), Ice. (rā′kyå-nĕs)	154	63.37 N	24.33 W
eykjavik, Ice. (rā′kyå-vĕk)	158	64.09 N	21.39 W
ey, L., Mex. (rā)	124	27.00 N	103.33 W
eynosa, Mex. (rā-ē-nō′sä)	124	26.05 N	98.21 W
ezekne, Sov. Un. (rå′zĕk-nĕ)	174	56.31 N	27.19 E
ezh, Sov. Un. (rĕzh′)	182a	57.22 N	61.23 E
ezina, Sov. Un. (ryĕzh′ĕ-nĭ)	175	47.44 N	28.56 E
haetien Alps (Mts.), It.	172	46.22 N	10.33 E
heinberg, F.R.G. (rīn′bĕrgh)	169c	51.33 N	6.37 E
heine, F.R.G. (rī′nĕ)	166	52.16 N	7.26 E
heinen, F.R.G.	63	51.27 N	7.38 E
heinhausen, F.R.G.	63	51.24 N	6.44 E
hein-Herne-Kanal (Can.), F.R.G.	63	51.27 N	6.47 E
heinkamp, F.R.G.	63	51.30 N	6.37 E
heinland-Pfalz (Rhineland-Palatinate) (State), F.R.G.	166	50.05 N	6.40 E
hein R., F.R.G. (rīn)	166	50.34 N	7.21 E
heydt, F.R.G. (rĕ′yt)	169c	51.10 N	6.28 E
hine (R.), Eur.	154	50.34 N	7.21 E
hinelander, Wi. (rīn′lăn-dēr)	115	45.39 N	89.25 W
hin Kanal (Can.), G.D.R. (rĕn kä-näl′)	157b	52.47 N	12.40 E
hin R., G.D.R. (rĕn)	157b	52.52 N	12.49 E
hiou (R.), Alg.	171	35.45 N	1.18 E
ho, It.	65c	45.32 N	9.02 E
hode Island (State), U.S. (rōd ī′lănd)	109	41.35 N	71.40 W
hode I., RI	112b	41.31 N	71.14 W
hodes, Austl.	70a	33.50 S	151.05 E
hodes, Eng.	64b	53.33 N	2.14 W
hodes, S. Afr. (rôdz)	227c	30.48 S	27.56 E
hodon, Fr.	64c	48.43 N	2.04 E
hodope Mts., Bul. (rô′dô-pĕ)	173	42.00 N	24.08 E
hondda, Wales (rŏn′dhå)	162	51.40 N	3.40 W
hône (R.), Fr. (rōn)	168	45.14 N	4.53 E
hoon, Neth.	157a	51.52 N	4.24 E
hum (I.), Scot. (rŭm)	162	57.00 N	6.20 W
iachão, Braz. (rē-ä-chouN′)	143	7.15 S	46.30 W
ialto, Ca. (rē-ăl′tō)	119a	34.06 N	117.23 W
iau (Prov.), Indon.	191b	0.56 N	101.25 E
iau, Kepulauan (I.), Indon.	206	0.30 N	104.55 E
iau, Selat (Str.), Indon.	191b	0.40 N	104.27 E
iaza (R.), Sp. (rē-ä′thä)	170	41.25 N	3.25 W
ibadavia, Sp. (rē-bä-dhä′vē-ä)	170	42.18 N	8.06 W
ibadeo, Sp. (rē-bä-dhā′ō)	170	37.32 N	7.05 W
Ribadesella, Sp. (rē′bä-dā-sāl′yä)	170	43.30 N	5.02 W
Ribauè, Moz.	231	14.57 S	38.17 E
Ribe, Den. (rē′bĕ)	164	55.20 N	8.45 E
Ribeirão Prêto, Braz. (rē-bä-rouN-prē′tô)	141a	21.11 S	47.47 W
Ribera, NM (rē-bē′rä)	122	35.23 N	105.27 W
Riberalta, Bol. (rē-bå-räl′tä)	142	11.06 S	66.02 W
Rib Lake, Wi. (rĭb lāk)	115	45.20 N	90.11 W
Rice, Ca. (rīs)	120	34.05 N	114.50 W
Rice (L.), Can.	111	44.05 N	78.10 W
Rice L., Mn.	119g	45.10 N	93.09 W
Rice Lake, Wi.	115	45.30 N	91.44 W
Richards I., Can. (rĭch′ērds)	107	69.45 N	135.30 W
Richards Landing, Can. (lănd′ĭng)	119k	46.18 N	84.02 W
Richardson, Tx. (rĭch′ērd-sŭn)	119c	32.56 N	96.44 W
Richardson, Wa.	118a	48.27 N	122.54 W
Richardson Mts., Can.	96	66.58 N	136.19 W
Richardson Mts., N.Z.	217	44.50 S	168.30 E
Richardson Park, De. (pärk)	111	39.45 N	75.35 W
Richelieu (R.), Can. (rēsh′lyû′)	111	45.05 N	73.25 W
Richfield, Mn.	119g	44.53 N	93.17 W
Richfield, Oh.	113d	41.14 N	81.38 W
Richfield, Ut.	121	38.45 N	112.05 W
Richford, Vt. (rĭch′fērd)	111	45.00 N	72.35 W
Rich Hill, Mo. (rĭch hĭl)	123	38.05 N	94.21 W
Richibucto, Can. (rĭ-chĭ-bŭk′tō)	104	46.41 N	64.52 W
Richland, Ga. (rĭch′lănd)	126	32.05 N	84.40 W
Richland, Wa.	116	46.17 N	119.19 W
Richland Center, Wi. (sĕn′tēr)	115	43.20 N	90.25 W
Richmond, Austl. (rĭch′mŭnd)	215	20.47 S	143.14 E
Richmond, Austl.	70b	37.49 S	145.00 E
Richmond, Austl.	211b	33.36 S	150.45 E
Richmond, Ca.	118b	37.56 N	122.21 W
Richmond, Can.	95c	45.12 N	75.49 W
Richmond, Can.	104	45.40 N	72.07 W
Richmond, Il.	113a	42.29 N	88.18 W
Richmond, In.	110	39.50 N	85.00 W
Richmond, Ky.	110	37.45 N	84.20 W
Richmond, Mo.	123	39.16 N	93.58 W
Richmond, S. Afr.	227c	29.52 S	30.17 E
Richmond, Tx.	125	29.35 N	95.45 W
Richmond, Ut.	117	41.55 N	111.50 W
Richmond, Va.	111	37.35 N	77.30 W
Richmond (Neigh.), Eng.	62	51.28 N	0.18 W
Richmond (Neigh.), NJ	56b	39.59 N	75.06 W
Richmond Beach, Wa.	118a	47.47 N	122.23 W
Richmond Heights, Mo.	119e	38.38 N	90.20 W
Richmond Heights, Oh.	56a	41.33 N	81.29 W
Richmond Highlands, Wa.	118a	47.46 N	122.22 W
Richmond Hill, Can. (hĭl)	95d	43.53 N	79.26 W
Richmond Hill (Neigh.), NY	55	40.42 N	73.49 W
Richmondtown Restoration (P. Int.), NY	55	40.34 N	74.09 W
Richmond Valley (Neigh.), NY	55	40.31 N	74.13 W
Richton, Ms. (rĭch′tŭn)	126	31.20 N	89.54 W
Richwood, WV (rĭch′wŏŏd)	110	38.10 N	80.30 W
Ricketts Pt., Austl.	70b	38.00 S	145.02 E
Rickmansworth, Eng.	62	51.39 N	0.29 W
Ridderkerk, Neth.	157a	51.52 N	4.35 E
Rideau (R.), Can.	95c	45.17 N	75.41 W
Rideau L., Can. (rē-dō′)	111	44.40 N	76.20 W
Ridge, Eng.	62	51.41 N	0.15 W
Ridgefield, Ct. (rĭj′fēld)	112a	41.16 N	73.30 W
Ridgefield, NJ	55	40.50 N	74.00 W
Ridgefield, Wa.	118c	45.49 N	122.40 W
Ridgefield Park, NJ	55	40.51 N	74.01 W
Ridgeway, Can. (rĭj′wā)	113c	42.53 N	79.02 W
Ridgewood, NJ (rĭdj′wŏŏd)	112a	40.59 N	74.08 W
Ridgewood (Neigh.), NY	55	40.42 N	73.53 W
Ridgway, Pa.	111	41.25 N	78.40 W
Riding Mountain Natl. Park, Can. (rīd′ĭng)	96	50.59 N	99.19 W
Riding Mtn., Can. (rīd′ĭng)	101	50.37 N	99.37 W
Riding Rocks (Is.), Ba.	134	25.20 N	79.10 W
Ridley Park, Pa.	56b	39.53 N	75.19 W
Riebeek-Oos, S. Afr.	227c	33.14 S	26.09 E
Ried, Aus. (rēd)	166	48.13 N	13.30 E
Riemke (Neigh.), F.R.G.	63	51.30 N	7.13 E
Riesa, G.D.R. (rē′zå)	166	51.17 N	13.17 E
Rieti, It. (rē-â′tē)	172	42.25 N	12.51 E
Rietvlei, S. Afr.	71b	26.18 S	28.03 E
Rievleidam (L.), S. Afr.	227b	25.52 S	28.18 E
Rifle, Co. (rī′f′l)	121	39.35 N	107.50 W
Riga, G. of, Sov. Un.	165	57.56 N	23.05 E
Rigaud, Can. (rē-gō′)	95a	45.29 N	74.18 W
Rigby, Id. (rĭg′bē)	117	43.40 N	111.55 W
Rigeley, WV (rĭj′lē)	111	39.40 N	78.45 W
Rigolet, Can. (rĭg-ō-lā′)	97	54.10 N	58.40 W
Riihimäki, Fin.	165	60.44 N	24.44 E
Rijeka (Fiume), Yugo. (rĭ-yĕ′kä)	172	45.22 N	14.24 E
Rijkevorsel, Bel.	157a	51.21 N	4.46 E
Rijswijk, Neth.	157a	52.03 N	4.19 E
Rika R., Sov. Un. (rē′kå)	167	48.21 N	23.37 E
Rima (R.), Nig.	229	13.30 N	5.50 E
Rimavska Sobota, Czech. (rē′måf-skå sô′bô-tå)	167	48.25 N	20.01 E
Rimbo, Swe. (rēm′bōō)	164	59.45 N	18.22 E
Rimini, It. (rē′mē-nē)	172	44.03 N	12.33 E
Rimouski, Can. (rē-mōōs′kē)	104	48.27 N	68.32 W
Rinc n de Romos, Mex. (rēn-kōn dā rō-mōs′)	130	22.13 N	102.21 W
Rincón, Cuba	60b	22.57 N	82.25 W
Ringkøbing, Den. (rĭng′kûb-ĭng)	164	56.06 N	8.14 E
Ringkøbing Fd., Den.	164	55.55 N	8.04 E
Ringsted, Den. (rĭng′stĕdh)	164	55.27 N	11.49 E
Ringvassøya (I.), Nor. (rĭng′väs-ûê)	158	69.58 N	16.43 E
Ringwood, Austl.	211a	37.49 S	145.14 E
Ringwood North, Austl.	70b	37.48 S	145.14 E
Rinjani, Gunung (Mtn.), Indon.	206	8.39 S	116.22 E
Rio Abajo, Pan. (rē′ō-ä-bä′kō)	128a	9.01 N	78.30 W
Rio Balsas, Mex. (rē′ō-bäl-säs)	130	17.59 N	99.45 W
Riobamba, Ec. (rē′ō-bäm-bä)	142	1.45 S	78.37 W
Rio Bonito, Braz. (rē′ōō bō-nē′tōō)	141a	22.44 S	42.38 W
Rio Branco, Braz. (rē′ōō bräŋ′kōō)	142	9.57 S	67.50 W
Rio Branco (Ter.), Braz.	143	2.35 N	61.25 W
Rio Casca, Braz. (rē′ō-kå′s-kä)	141a	20.15 S	42.39 W
Rio Chico, Ven. (rē′ō chē′kō)	143b	10.20 N	65.58 W
Rio Claro, Braz. (rē′ōō klä′rōō)	141a	21.25 S	47.33 W
Rio Comprido (Neigh.), Braz.	61c	22.55 S	43.12 W
Rio das Flores, Braz. (rē′ō-däs-flō-rĕs)	141a	22.10 S	43.35 W
Rio de Janeiro, Braz. (rē′ōō dā zhä-nā′ê-rōō)	144b	22.50 S	43.20 W
Rio de Janeiro (State), Braz.	143	22.27 S	42.43 W
Rio de Mouro, Port.	65d	38.46 N	9.20 W
Rio Frío, Mex. (rē′ō-frē′ô)	131a	19.21 N	98.40 W
Rīga, Sov. Un. (rē′gå)	165	56.55 N	24.05 E
Rīgān, Iran	192	28.45 N	58.55 E
Rīgestān (Reg.), Afr.	192	30.53 N	64.42 E
Rio Grande, Braz. (rē′ōō grän′dĕ)	144	31.04 S	52.14 W
Rio Grande, Mex. (rē′ō grän′dä)	130	23.51 N	102.59 W
Rio Grande (R.), Co. (rē′ōō grän′dĕ)	121	37.44 N	106.51 W
Riogrande, Tx. (rē′ō grån-dä)	124	26.23 N	98.48 W
Rio Grande do Norte (State), Braz. (rē′ōō grän′dĕ dōō nôr′tĕ)	143	5.26 S	37.20 W
Rio Grande do Sul (State), Braz. (rē′ōō grän′dĕ-dô-sōō′l)	144	29.00 S	54.00 W
Riom, Fr. (rē-ôN′)	168	45.54 N	3.08 E
Rio Muni (Prov.), Equat. Gui. (rē′ō mōō′nē)	222	1.47 N	8.33 E
Rio Negro, Embalse del (Res.), Ur. (ĕm-bä′l-sĕ-dĕl-rē′ō-nĕ′grō)	144	32.45 S	55.50 W
Rionero, It. (rē-ō-nâ′rô)	172	40.55 N	15.42 E
Rio Novo, Braz. (rē′ō-nô′vô)	141a	21.30 S	43.08 W
Rio Pardo de Minas, Braz. (rē′ō pär′dō-dĕ-mē′näs)	143	15.43 S	42.24 W
Rio Pombo, Braz. (rē′ō pôm′bä)	141a	21.17 S	43.09 W
Rio Sorocaba, Represado (Res.), Braz. (rĕ-prĕ-sä-dô-rē′ō-sô-rô-kä′bä)	141a	23.37 S	47.19 W
Rio Verde, Braz. (vĕr′dĕ)	143	17.47 S	50.49 W
Ripley, Eng. (rĭp′lē)	156	53.03 N	1.24 W
Ripley, Eng.	62	51.18 N	0.29 W
Ripley, Ms.	126	34.44 N	88.55 W
Ripley, Tn.	126	35.44 N	89.34 W
Ripoll, Sp. (rē-pōl′)	171	42.10 N	2.10 E
Ripon, Wi. (rĭp′ŏn)	115	43.49 N	88.50 W
Ripon (I.), Austl.	214	20.05 S	118.10 E
Ripon Falls, Ug.	225	0.38 N	33.02 E
Rîmnicu-Sărat, Rom.	173	45.24 N	27.06 E
Rîmnicu-Vîlcea, Rom.	173	45.07 N	24.22 E
Risaralda (Dept.), Col.	142a	6.45 S	76.00 W
Risdon, Austl. (rĭz′dŭn)	215	42.37 S	147.32 E
Rishiri (I.), Jap. (rē-shē′rē)	204	45.10 N	141.08 E
Rishon le Ziyyon, Isr.	191a	31.57 N	34.48 E
Rishra, India	196a	22.42 N	88.22 E
Rising Sun, In. (rīz′ĭng sŭn)	110	38.55 N	84.55 W
Risle (R.), Fr.	168	49.12 N	0.43 E
Risor, Nor. (rēs′ûr)	164	58.44 N	9.10 E
Ritacuva, Alto (Mtn.), Col. (ä′l-tô-rē-tä-kōō′vä)	142	6.22 N	72.13 W
Ritchie, Va.	56d	38.52 N	76.52 W
Rithāla (Neigh.), India	67d	28.43 N	77.06 E
Rittman, Oh. (rĭt′năn)	113d	40.58 N	81.47 W
Ritzville, Wa. (rĭts′vĭl)	116	47.08 N	118.23 W
Riva, Dom. Rep. (rē′vä)	135	19.10 N	69.55 W
Riva, It. (rē′vä)	172	45.54 N	10.49 E
Riva, Md. (rĭ′vä)	112e	38.57 N	76.36 W
Rivas, Nic. (rē′väs)	132	11.25 N	85.51 W
Rive-de-Gier, Fr. (rēv-dĕ-zhē-ā′)	168	45.32 N	4.37 E
Rivera, Ur. (rē-vā′rä)	144	30.52 S	55.32 W
River Cess, Lib. (rĭv′ēr sĕs)	224	5.46 N	9.52 W
Riverdale, Il. (rĭv′ēr dāl)	113a	41.38 N	87.36 W
Riverdale, Md.	56d	38.58 N	76.55 W
Riverdale, Ut.	119b	41.11 N	112.00 W
Riverdale (Neigh.), NY	55	40.54 N	73.54 W
River Edge, NJ	55	40.56 N	74.02 W
River Falls, Al.	126	31.20 N	86.25 W
River Falls, Wi.	115	44.48 N	92.38 W
River Forest, Il.	58a	41.53 N	87.49 W
River Grove, Il.	58a	41.56 N	87.50 W
Riverhead, Eng.	62	51.17 N	0.10 E
Riverhead, NY (rĭv′ēr hĕd)	111	40.55 N	72.40 W
Riverina (Reg.), Austl. (rĭv-ēr-ē′nä)	216	34.55 S	144.30 E
River Jordan, Can. (jôr′dăn)	118a	48.25 N	124.03 W
River Oaks, Tx. (ōkz)	119c	32.47 N	97.24 W
River Rouge, Mi. (rōōzh)	113b	42.16 N	83.09 W
Rivers, Can.	101	50.01 N	100.15 W
Riverside, Ca. (rĭv′ēr-sīd)	119a	33.59 N	117.21 W
Riverside, Il.	58a	41.50 N	87.49 W
Riverside, NJ	112f	40.02 N	74.58 W
Rivers Inlet, Can.	98	51.45 N	127.15 W
Riverstone, Austl.	211b	33.41 S	150.52 E
Riverton, Va.	111	39.00 N	78.15 W
Riverton, Wy.	117	43.02 N	108.24 W
Rivesaltes, Fr. (rēv′zält′)	168	42.48 N	2.48 E
Riviera Beach, Fl. (rĭv-ĭ-ēr′å bēch)	127a	26.46 N	80.04 W
Riviera Beach, Md.	112e	39.10 N	76.32 W
Rivie′re Beaudette, Can. (bō-dĕt′)	95a	45.14 N	74.20 W
Rivière-du-Loup, Can. (rē-vyâr′ dü lōō′)	104	47.50 N	69.32 W
Rivière Que Barre, Can. (rēv-yĕr′ kē-bär)	95g	53.47 N	113.51 W
Rivière-Trois-Pistoles, Can. (trwä′pēs-tôl′)	104	48.07 N	69.10 W
Rímac, Peru	60c	12.02 S	77.03 W
Rímac (R.), Peru	60c	12.02 S	77.09 W
Río Branco, Ur. (rīō brănçō)	144	32.33 S	53.29 W
Río Cuarto, Arg. (rē′ō kwär′tō)	144	33.05 S	64.15 W
Río de Jesús, Pan. (rē′ō-dĕ-kĕ-sōō′s)	133	7.54 N	80.59 W
Río Dercero, Arg. (rē′ō dĕr-sĕ′rô)	144	32.12 S	63.59 W
Río Gallegos, Arg. (rē′ō gä-lā′gōs)	144	51.43 S	69.15 W

336 Río Grande – Rossel

PLACE (Pronounciation)	PAGE	Lat. °′	Long. °′
Río Grande, Ven.	61a	10.35 N	66.57 W
Ríohacha, Col. (rē'ō-ä'chä)	142	11.30 N	72.54 W
Río Hato, Pan. (rē'ō-ä'tô)	133	8.19 N	80.11 W
Ríonegro, Col. (rē'ō-nĕ'grō)	142a	6.09 N	75.22 W
Río Negro (Dept.), Ur. (rē'ō-nĕ'grō)	141c	32.48 S	57.45 W
Río Negro (Prov.), Arg. (rē'ō nā'grō)	144	40.15 S	68.15 W
Ríosucio, Col. (rē'ō-sōō'syô)	142a	5.25 N	75.41 W
Ríoverde, Mex. (rē'ō-vĕr'dā)	130	21.54 N	99.59 W
Riyadh (Ar Riyāḑ), Sau. Ar.	192	24.31 N	46.47 E
Rize, Tur. (rē'zĕ)	179	41.00 N	40.30 E
Rizhao, China (rĕ-jou)	200	35.27 N	119.28 E
Rizzuto, C., It. (rēt-sōō'tô)	173	38.53 N	17.05 E
Rjukan, Nor. (ryōō'kän)	164	59.53 N	8.30 E
Roanne, Fr. (rō-än')	168	46.02 N	4.04 E
Roanoke, Al. (rō'à-nōk)	126	33.08 N	85.21 W
Roanoke, Va.	127	37.16 N	79.55 W
Roanoke (R.), NC-Va.	127	36.17 N	77.22 W
Roanoke (Staunton) (R.), Va.	127	37.05 N	79.20 W
Roanoke Rapids, NC	127	36.25 N	77.40 W
Roanoke Rapids, L., NC	127	36.28 N	77.37 W
Roan Plat., Co. (rōn)	121	39.25 N	108.50 W
Roatan, Hond. (rō-ä-tän')	132	16.18 N	86.33 W
Roatan I., Hond.	132	16.19 N	86.46 W
Robbeneiland (I.), S. Afr.	226a	33.48 S	18.22 E
Robbins, Il. (rŏb'ĭnz)	113a	41.39 N	87.42 W
Robbinsdale, Mn. (rŏb'ĭnz-dāl)	119g	45.03 N	93.22 W
Robe, Wa. (rōb)	118a	48.06 N	121.50 W
Robertsham (Neigh.), S. Afr.	71b	26.15 S	28.00 E
Roberts, Mt., Austl. (rŏb'ẽrts)	215	32.05 S	152.30 E
Robertson, Lac (L.), Can.	105	51.00 N	59.10 W
Robertsport, Lib. (rŏb'ẽrts-pōrt)	228	6.45 N	11.22 W
Roberts, Pt., Wa. (rŏb'ẽrts)	118d	48.58 N	123.05 W
Roberval, Can. (rŏb'ẽr-văl) (rô-bĕr-vȧl')	97	48.32 N	72.15 W
Robinson, Il. (rŏb'ĭn-sŭn)	110	39.00 N	87.45 W
Robinson, S. Afr.	71b	26.09 S	27.43 E
Robinson's, Can.	105	48.16 N	58.50 W
Robinvale, Austl. (rŏb-ĭn'văl)	216	34.45 S	142.45 E
Roblin, Can.	101	51.15 N	101.25 W
Robson, Mt., Can. (rŏb'sŭn)	99	53.07 N	119.09 W
Robstown, Tx. (rŏbz'toun)	125	27.46 N	97.41 W
Roca, Cabo da (C.), Port. (kä'bō-dä-rô'kä)	171b	38.47 N	9.30 W
Rocas, Atol das (Atoll), Braz. (ä-tôl-däs-rō'käs)	143	3.50 S	33.46 W
Rocedos São Pedro E São Paulo, (I.), Braz. (rō-zĕ'dôs-souN-pĕ'drô-ĕ-souN-pä'ōō-lô)	140	1.50 N	30.00 W
Rocha, Ur. (rō'chäs)	144	34.26 S	54.14 W
Rocha Miranda (Neigh.), Braz.	61c	22.52 S	43.22 W
Rocha Sobrinho, Braz.	61c	22.47 S	43.25 W
Rochdale, Eng. (rŏch'dāl)	156	53.37 N	2.09 W
Roche à Bateau, Hai. (rôsh à bȧ-tō')	135	18.10 N	74.00 W
Rochefort, Fr. (rôsh-fōr')	168	45.55 N	0.57 W
Rochelle, Il. (rô-shĕl')	115	41.53 N	89.06 W
Rochelle Park, NJ	55	40.55 N	74.04 W
Rochester, In. (rŏch'ĕs-tẽr)	110	41.05 N	86.20 W
Rochester, Mi.	113b	42.41 N	83.09 W
Rochester, Mn.	115	44.01 N	92.30 W
Rochester, NH	111	43.20 N	71.00 W
Rochester, NY	111	43.15 N	77.35 W
Rochester, Pa.	113e	40.42 N	80.16 W
Rock (R.), Ia.	114	43.17 N	96.13 W
Rock (R.), Il.	115	41.40 N	89.52 W
Rock (R.), Or.	118c	45.34 N	122.52 W
Rock (R.), Or.	118c	45.52 N	123.14 W
Rockaway, NJ (rŏck'ȧ-wā)	112a	40.54 N	74.30 W
Rockaway Park (Neigh.), NY	55	40.35 N	73.50 W
Rockaway Point (Neigh.), NY	55	40.33 N	73.55 W
Rockbank, Austl.	211a	37.44 S	144.40 E
Rockcliffe Park, Can. (rok'klĭf pärk)	95c	45.27 N	75.40 W
Rock Cr., Can. (rŏk)	100	49.01 N	107.00 W
Rock Cr., Il.	113a	41.16 N	87.54 W
Rock Cr., Mt.	117	46.25 N	113.40 W
Rock Cr., Or.	116	45.30 N	120.06 W
Rock Cr., Wa.	116	47.09 N	117.50 W
Rock Creek Park (P. Int.), DC.	56d	38.58 N	77.03 W
Rockdale, Austl., Egypt	71a	33.57 S	151.08 E
Rockdale, Md.	112e	39.22 N	76.49 W
Rockdale, Tx. (rŏk'dāl)	125	30.39 N	97.00 W
Rockefeller Center (P. Int.), NY	55	40.45 N	74.00 W
Rock Falls, Il. (rŏk fôlz)	115	41.45 N	89.42 W
Rock Ferry, Eng.	64a	53.22 N	3.00 W
Rockford, Il. (rŏk'fẽrd)	115	42.16 N	89.07 W
Rockhampton, Austl. (rŏk-hămp'tŭn)	215	23.26 S	150.29 E
Rockhill, SC (rŏk'hĭl)	127	34.55 N	81.01 W
Rockingham, NC (rŏk'ĭng-hăm)	127	34.54 N	79.45 W
Rockingham For., Eng. (rok'ĭng-hăm)	156	52.29 N	0.43 W
Rock Island, Il.	115	41.31 N	90.37 W
Rock Island Dam, Wa. (ī lănd)	116	47.17 N	120.33 W
Rockland, Can. (rŏk'lănd)	95c	45.33 N	75.17 W
Rockland, Me.	104	44.06 N	69.09 W
Rockland, Ma.	105a	42.07 N	70.55 W
Rockland Res., Austl.	216	36.55 S	142.20 E
Rockledge, Pa.	56b	40.03 N	75.05 W
Rockmart, Ga. (rŏk'märt)	126	33.58 N	85.00 W
Rockmont, Wi. (rŏk'mŏnt)	119h	46.34 N	91.54 W
Rockport, In. (rŏk'pōrt)	110	38.20 N	87.00 W
Rockport, Ma.	105a	42.39 N	70.37 W
Rockport, Mo.	123	40.25 N	95.30 W
Rockport, Tx.	125	28.03 N	97.03 W
Rock Rapids, Ia. (răp'ĭdz)	114	43.26 N	96.10 W
Rock Sd., Ba.	135	24.50 N	76.05 W
Rocksprings, Tx. (rŏk sprĭngs)	124	30.02 N	100.12 W
Rock Springs, Wy.	117	41.35 N	109.13 W
Rockstone, Guy. (rŏk'stôn)	143	5.55 N	57.27 W
Rock Valley, Ia. (văl'ĭ)	114	43.13 N	96.17 W
Rockville, In. (rŏk'vĭl)	110	39.45 N	87.15 W
Rockville, Md.	112e	39.05 N	77.11 W
Rockville Centre, NY (sĕn'tẽr)	112a	40.39 N	73.39 W
Rockwall, Tx. (rŏk'wôl)	123	32.55 N	96.23 W
Rockwell City, Ia. (rŏk'wĕl)	115	42.22 N	94.37 W
Rockwood, Can. (rŏk-wŏŏd)	95d	43.37 N	80.08 W
Rockwood, Me.	104	45.39 N	69.45 W
Rockwood, Tn.	126	35.51 N	84.41 W
Rocky (R.), Oh.	56a	41.30 N	81.49 W
Rocky Boys Ind. Res., Mt.	117	48.08 N	109.34 W
Rocky Ford, Co.	122	38.02 N	103.43 W
Rocky Hbr., Hong Kong	68c	22.20 N	114.19 E
Rocky Hill, NJ (hĭl)	112a	40.24 N	74.38 W
Rocky Island L., Can.	102	46.56 N	83.04 W
Rocky Mount, NC	127	35.55 N	77.47 W
Rocky Mountain House, Can.	99	52.22 N	114.55 W
Rocky Mountain Natl. Park, Co.	122	40.29 N	106.06 W
Rocky Mts., N.A.	94	50.00 N	114.00 W
Rocky R., East Br., Oh.	113d	41.13 N	81.43 W
Rocky River, Oh.	56a	41.30 N	81.40 W
Rocky River, Oh.	113d	41.29 N	81.51 W
Rocky R., West Br., Oh.	113d	41.17 N	81.54 W
Rocquencourt, Fr.	64c	48.50 N	2.07 E
Rodas, Cuba (rō'dhäs)	135	22.20 N	80.35 W
Roden (R.), Eng. (rō'dĕn)	156	52.49 N	2.38 W
Rodeo, Ca. (rō'dēō)	118b	38.02 N	122.16 W
Rodeo, Mex. (rô-dā'ō)	124	25.12 N	104.34 W
Roderick I., Can. (rŏd'ĕ-rĭk)	98	52.40 N	128.22 W
Rodez, Fr. (rô-dĕz')	168	44.22 N	2.34 E
Ródhos, Grc.	161	36.24 N	28.15 E
Ródhos (I.), Grc.	161	36.00 N	28.29 E
Rodniki, Sov. Un. (rôd'nē-kē)	174	57.08 N	41.48 E
Rodonit, Kep I (C.), Alb.	173	41.38 N	19.01 E
Rodosto, see Tekirdağ			
Roebling, NJ (rōb'lĭng)	112f	40.07 N	74.48 W
Roebourne, Austl. (rō'bŭrn)	214	20.50 S	117.15 E
Roebuck, B. Austl. (rō'bŭck)	214	18.15 S	121.10 E
Roedtan, S. Afr.	223d	24.37 S	29.08 E
Roehampton (Neigh.), Eng.	62	51.27 N	0.14 W
Roeselare, Bel.	163	50.55 N	3.05 E
Roesiger (L.), Wa. (rōz'ĭ-gẽr)	118a	47.59 N	121.56 W
Roes Welcome Sd., Can. (rōz)	97	64.10 N	87.23 W
Rogachëv, Sov. Un. (rôg'á-chyôf)	174	53.07 N	30.04 E
Rogans Hill, Austl.	70a	33.44 S	151.01 E
Rogatica, Yugo. (rô-gä'tē-tsä)	173	43.46 N	19.00 E
Rogatin, Sov. Un. (rō-gä'tĭn)	167	49.22 N	24.37 E
Rogers, Ar. (rŏj-ẽrz)	123	36.19 N	94.07 W
Rogers City, Mi.	110	45.30 N	83.50 W
Rogers Park (Neigh.), Il.	58a	42.01 N	87.40 W
Rogersville, Tn.	126	36.21 N	83.00 W
Rognac, Fr. (rôn-yäk')	168a	43.29 N	5.15 E
Rogoaguado (L.), Bol. (rō'gō-ä-gwä-dō)	142	12.42 S	66.46 W
Rogovskaya, Sov. Un. (rô-gôf'skȧ-yȧ)	175	45.43 N	38.42 E
Rogózno, Pol. (rô'gôzh-nô)	166	52.44 N	16.53 E
Rogue R., Or. (rōg)	116	42.32 N	124.13 W
Rohdenhaus, F.R.G.	63	51.18 N	7.01 E
Röhlinghausen (Neigh.), F.R.G.	63	51.36 N	7.14 E
Rohrbeck, G.D.R.	65a	52.32 N	13.02 E
Roissy, Fr.	64c	48.47 N	2.39 E
Roissy-en-France, Fr.	64c	49.00 N	2.31 E
Rojas, Arg. (rō'häs)	141c	34.11 S	60.42 W
Rojo, Cabo (C.), Mex. (rō'hō)	131	21.35 N	97.16 W
Rojo, Cabo (C.), P. R. (rō'hō)	129b	17.55 N	67.14 W
Rokel (R.), S. L.	228	9.00 N	11.55 W
Rokkō-Zan (Mtn.), Jap. (rôk'kō zän)	205b	34.46 N	135.16 E
Roksana, S. Afr.	71b	26.07 S	28.04 E
Rokugō (Neigh.), Jap.	69a	35.33 N	139.43 E
Rokycany, Czech. (rō'kĭ'tsä-nĭ)	166	49.44 N	13.37 E
Roldanillo, Col. (rôl-dä-nē'l-yō)	142a	4.24 N	76.09 W
Rolla, Mo.	123	37.56 N	91.45 W
Rolla, ND	114	48.52 N	99.32 W
Rolleville, Ba.	135	23.40 N	76.00 W
Rolling Acres, Md.	56c	39.17 N	76.52 W
Röllinghausen (Neigh.), F.R.G.	63	51.31 N	7.08 E
Rolling Hills, Ca.	59	33.46 N	118.21 W
Roma, Austl. (rō'mȧ)	216	26.30 S	148.48 E
Roma, Leso.	227c	29.28 S	27.43 E
Roma (Rome), It. (rō'mä) (rōm)	171d	41.52 N	12.37 E
Romaine (R.), Can. (rô-mĕn')	105	51.22 N	63.23 W
Romainville, Fr.	64c	48.53 N	2.26 E
Roman, Rom. (rō'män)	167	46.56 N	26.57 E
Romania, Eur. (rō-mä'nē-ȧ)	154	46.18 N	22.53 E
Romano, C., Fl. (rō-mä'nō)	127a	25.48 N	82.00 W
Romano, Cayo (I.), Cuba (kä'yō-rô-mä'nō)	134	22.15 N	78.00 W
Romanovo, Sov. Un. (rô-mä'nô-vô)	182a	59.09 N	61.24 E
Romans, Fr. (rô-mäN')	168	45.04 N	4.49 E
Romblon, Phil. (rōm-blōn')	207a	12.34 N	122.16 E
Romblon I., Phil.	207a	12.33 N	122.17 E
Rome, Ga. (rōm)	126	34.14 N	85.10 W
Rome, NY	111	43.15 N	75.25 W
Romeo, Mi. (rō'mē-ō)	110	42.50 N	83.00 W
Rome, see Roma			
Romford, Eng. (rŭm'fẽrd)	156b	51.35 N	0.11 E
Romiley, Eng.	64b	53.25 N	2.05 W
Romilly-sur-Seine, Fr. (rô-mē-yē'sür-sān')	168	48.32 N	3.41 E
Romita, Mex. (rō-mē'tä)	130	20.53 N	101.32 W
Romny, Sov. Un. (rôm'nĭ)	175	50.46 N	33.31 E
Rømø (I.), Den. (rûm'ö)	164	55.08 N	8.17 E
Romoland, Ca. (rō'mō'lănd)	119a	33.44 N	117.11 W
Romorantin-Lanthenay, Fr. (rô-mô-räN-tăN')	168	47.24 N	1.46 E
Rompin, Mala.	191b	2.42 N	102.30 E
Rompin (R.), Mala.	191b	2.54 N	103.10 E
Romsdalsfjorden (Fd.), Nor.	164	62.40 N	7.05 W
Romulus, Mi. (rom'ū lŭs)	113b	42.14 N	83.24 W
Ronaldsay, North (I.), Scot.	162	59.21 N	2.23 W
Ronaldsay, South (I.), Scot. (rŏn'ăld-s'ā)	162	59.48 N	2.55 W
Ronan, Mt. (rō'năn)	117	47.28 N	114.03 W
Roncador, Serra do (Mts.), Braz. (sĕr'rá dŏŏ rôn-kä-dōr')	143	12.44 S	52.19 W
Roncesvalles, Sp. (rôn-sĕs-vä'l-yĕs)	170	43.00 N	1.17
Ronceverte, WV (rŏn'sē-vûrt)	110	37.45 N	80.30
Ronda, Sp. (rōn'dä)	170	37.45 N	5.10
Ronda, Sierra de (Mts.), Sp.	170	36.35 N	5.03
Rondebult, S. Afr.	71b	26.18 S	28.14
Rondônia (Ter.), Braz.	142	10.15 S	63.07
Ronge, Lac la (L.), Can. (rŏnzh)	100	55.10 N	105.00
Rongjiang, China (rôŋ-jyäŋ)	203	25.52 N	108.45
Rongxian, China	203	22.50 N	110.32
Rønne, Den. (rûn'ĕ)	164	55.08 N	14.46
Ronneby, Swe. (rōn'ĕ-bü)	164	56.13 N	15.17
Ronne Ice Shelf, Ant.	232	77.30 S	38.00
Ronsdorf (Neigh.), F.R.G.	63	51.14 N	7.12
Ront Ra. (Mts.), Co. (rŏnt)	122	40.59 N	105.29
Roodepoort, S. Afr. (rō'dĕ-pōrt)	227b	26.10 S	27.52
Roodhouse, Il. (rōōd'hous)	123	39.29 N	90.21
Rooiberg, S. Afr.	223d	24.46 S	27.42
Roosendaal, Neth. (rō'zĕn-däl)	157a	51.32 N	4.27
Roosevelt, NY	55	40.41 N	73.36
Roosevelt, Ut. (rōz''vĕlt)	121	40.20 N	110.00
Roosevelt (R.), Az.	121	33.45 N	111.00
Roosevelt (R.), Braz. (rô'sĕ-vĕlt)	143	9.22 S	60.28
Roosevelt I., Ant.	232	79.30 S	168.00
Root R., Wi.	113a	42.49 N	87.54
Rooty Hill, Austl.	70a	33.46 S	150.50
Roper (R.), Austl. (rōp'ẽr)	214	14.50 S	134.00
Ropsha, Sov. Un. (rôp'shȧ)	182c	59.44 N	29.53
Roque Pérez, Arg. (rô'kĕ-pĕ'rĕz)	141c	35.23 S	59.22
Roques, Islas los (Is.), Ven.	142	21.25 N	67.40
Roraima (Ter.), Braz. (rô'rīy-mă)	142	2.00 N	62.15
Roraima, Mtn., Ven.-Guy. (rô-rä-ē'mä)	143	5.12 N	60.52
Røros, Nor. (rûr'ôs)	164	62.36 N	11.25
Ros' (R.), Sov. Un. (rôs)	175	49.40 N	30.22
Rosales, Mex. (rō-zä'lās)	124	28.15 N	100.43
Rosales, Phil. (rô-sä'lĕs)	207a	15.54 N	120.38
Rosa, Monte (Mt.), It. (mōn'tā rō'zä)	166	45.56 N	7.51
Rosamorada, Mex. (rō'zä-mō-rä'dhä)	130	22.06 N	105.16
Rosanna, Austl.	70b	37.45 S	145.04
Rosaria, Laguna (L.), Mex. (lä-gōō'nä-rô-sȧ'ryä)	131	17.50 N	93.51
Rosario, Arg. (rô-zä'rē-ō)	141c	32.58 S	60.42
Rosario, Braz. (rô-zä'rē-ōō)	143	2.49 S	44.15
Rosario, Mex.	124	26.31 N	105.40
Rosario, Mex.	130	22.58 N	105.54
Rosario, Phil.	207a	13.49 N	121.13
Rosario, Ur.	141c	34.19 S	57.24
Rosario, Cayo (I.), Cuba (kä'yō-rô-sä'ryō)	134	21.40 N	81.55
Rosário do Sul, Braz. (rô-zä'rē-ōō-dô-sōō'l)	144	30.17 S	54.5
Rosário Oeste, Braz. (ō'ĕst'ĕ)	143	14.47 S	56.2
Rosario Str., Wa.	118a	48.27 N	122.45
Rosas, Golfo de (G.), Sp. (gôl-fô-dĕ-rō'zäs)	171	42.10 N	3.2
Rosbach, F.R.G. (rōz'bäĸ)	169c	50.47 N	7.38
Roscoe, Tx. (rôs'kō)	124	32.26 N	100.38
Roseau, Dominica	133b	15.17 N	61.2
Roseau, Mn. (rô-zō')	114	48.52 N	95.4
Roseau (R.), Mn.	114	48.52 N	96.1
Rosebank (Neigh.), S. Afr.	71b	26.09 S	28.0
Roseberg, Or. (rōz'bûrg)	116	43.13 N	123.3
Rosebery (Neigh.), Austl.	70a	33.55 S	151.1
Rosebud (R.), Can. (rōz'bŭd)	99	51.20 N	112.2
Rosebud Cr., Mt.	117	45.48 N	106.3
Rosebud Ind. Res., SD	114	43.13 N	100.4
Rosedale, Ms.	126	33.49 N	90.5
Rosedale, Wa.	118a	47.20 N	122.3
Rosedale (Neigh.), Can.	54c	43.41 N	79.2
Rosedale (Neigh.), NY	55	40.39 N	73.4
Roseires Res., Sud.	224	11.15 N	34.4
Roseland (Neigh.), Il.	58a	41.42 N	87.3
Roselle, Il. (rō-zĕl')	113a	41.59 N	88.0
Roselle, NJ	55	40.40 N	74.1
Rosemead, Ca.	59	34.04 N	118.0
Rosemere, Can. (rōz'mēr)	95a	45.38 N	73.4
Rosemont, Il.	58a	41.59 N	87.5
Rosemont, Pa.	56b	40.01 N	75.1
Rosemount, Mn. (rōz'mount)	119g	44.44 N	93.0
Rosendal, S. Afr. (rô-sĕn'täl)	223d	28.32 S	27.5
Roseneath, S. Afr.	71b	26.17 S	28.1
Rosenheim, F.R.G. (rō'zĕn-hīm)	166	47.52 N	12.0
Rosenthal (Neigh.), G.D.R.	65a	52.36 N	13.2
Rosetown, Can. (rōz'toun)	100	51.33 N	108.0
Rose Tree, Pa.	56b	39.56 N	75.2
Rosetta, see Rashīd,			
Rosettenville (Neigh.), S. Afr.	227b	26.15 S	28.0
Roseville, Austl.	70a	33.47 S	151.1
Roseville, Ca. (rōz'vĭl)	120	38.44 N	121.1
Roseville, Mi.	113b	42.30 N	82.5
Roseville, Mn.	119g	45.01 N	93.1
Rosiclare, Il. (rōz'y-klâr)	110	37.30 N	88.1
Rosignol, Guy. (rôs-ĭg-nćl)	143	6.16 N	57.3
Roșiori-de-Vede, Rom. (rô-shôr'ē dĕ vĕ-dĕ)	173	44.06 N	25.0
Roskilde, Den. (rôs'kēl-dĕ)	164	55.39 N	12.0
Roslavl', Sov. Un. (rôs'läv'l)	174	53.56 N	32.5
Roslyn, NY	55	40.48 N	73.3
Roslyn, Wa. (rŏz'lĭn)	116	47.14 N	121.0
Roslyn Estates, NY	55	40.47 N	73.4
Roslyn Heights, NY	55	40.47 N	73.3
Rosny-sous-Bois, Fr.	64c	48.53 N	2.2
Rosovka, Sov. Un.	175	47.14 N	36.3
Rösrath, F.R.G. (rûz'rät)	169c	50.53 N	7.1
Ross, Oh. (rôs)	113f	39.19 N	84.3
Rossano, It. (rô-sä'nō)	172	39.34 N	16.3
Rossan Pt., Ire.	162	54.45 N	8.3
Ross Cr., Can.	95g	53.50 N	113.0
Ross Dam, Wa.	116	48.40 N	121.0
Rosseau (L.), Can. (rôs-sō')	103	45.15 N	79.3
Rossel (I.), Pap. N. Gui. (rô-sĕl')	215	11.31 S	154.0

ăt; finăl; rāte; senāte; ärm; ȧsk; sofȧ; fâre; ch-choose; dh-as th in other; bē; ēvent; bĕt; recĕnt; cratẽr; g-gō; gh-guttural g; bĭt; ĭ-short neutral; rīde; ĸ-guttural k as ch in German ich;

ONOUNCING INDEX

Rosser – Safford 337

CE (Pronounciation)	PAGE	Lat. °′	Long. °′
sser, Can. (rôs'sēr)	95f	49.59 N	97.27 W
ss I., Can.	101	54.14 N	97.45 W
ssignol, L., Can.	104	44.10 N	65.10 W
ssland, Can. (rôs'lȧnd)	99	49.05 N	118.48 W
ssmore, Austl.	70a	33.57 S	150.46 E
sso, Mauritania	228	16.30 N	15.49 W
ssosh', Sov. Un. (rôs'sŭsh)	175	50.12 N	39.32 E
ssouw, S. Afr.	227c	31.12 S	27.18 E
ss Sea, Ant.	232	76.00 S	178.00 W
ss Shelf Ice, Ant.	232	81.30 S	175.00 W
ssvatnet (L.), Nor.	158	65.36 N	13.08 E
ssville, Ga. (rôs'vĭl)	126	34.57 N	85.22 W
ssville, Md.	56c	39.20 N	76.29 W
sthern, Can.	100	52.41 N	106.25 W
stherne, Eng.	64b	53.21 N	2.23 W
stock, G.D.R. (rôs'tŭk)	166	54.04 N	12.06 E
stov, Sov. Un.	174	57.13 N	39.23 E
stov (Oblast), Sov. Un.	175	47.38 N	39.15 E
stov-na-Donu, Sov. Un. rôstôv-nȧ-dô-nōō)	179	47.16 N	39.47 E
swell, Ga. (rôz'wĕl)	126	34.02 N	84.21 W
swell, NM	122	33.23 N	104.32 W
syln, Pa.	56b	40.07 N	75.08 W
an, Tx. (rô-tăn')	122	32.51 N	100.27 W
henburg, F.R.G.	166	49.20 N	10.10 E
herham, Eng. (rŏdh'ēr-ăm)	156	53.26 N	1.21 W
hesay, Can. (rôth'så)	104	45.23 N	66.00 W
hesay, Scot.	162	55.50 N	3.14 W
h-neusiedl (Neigh.), Aus.	66e	48.08 N	16.23 E
hwell, Eng.	156	53.44 N	1.30 W
i, Pulau (I.), Indon. (rō'tē)	206	10.30 S	122.52 E
o, Austl. (rō'tô)	216	33.07 S	145.30 E
orua, N.Z.	217	38.07 S	176.17 E
terdam, Neth. (rôt'ĕr-däm')	157a	51.55 N	4.27 E
tweil, F.R.G. (rōt'vīl)	166	48.10 N	8.36 E
ubaix, Fr. (rōō-bĕ')	168	50.42 N	3.10 E
uen, Fr. (rōō-äɴ')	168	49.25 N	1.05 E
uge (R.), Can. (rōōzh)	95d	43.53 N	79.21 W
uge (R.), Can.	103	46.40 N	74.50 W
uge, R., Mi.	113b	42.30 N	83.15 W
ugh River Res., Ky.	110	37.45 N	86.10 W
und Lake, Il.	113a	42.21 N	88.05 W
und Pd., Can.	105	48.15 N	55.57 W
und Rock, Tx.	125	30.31 N	97.41 W
und Top (Mtn.), Or. (tŏp)	118c	45.41 N	123.22 W
undup, Mt. (round'ŭp)	117	46.25 N	108.35 W
usay (I.), Scot. (rōō'zå)	162a	59.10 N	3.04 W
uyn, Can. (rōōn)	97	48.22 N	79.03 W
vaniemi, Fin. (rô'vȧ-nyĕ'mĭ)	158	66.29 N	25.45 E
vato, It. (rô-vä'tō)	172	45.33 N	10.00 E
ven'ki, Sov. Un. (rô-vĕn'ki')	175	48.06 N	39.44 E
ven'ki, Sov. Un.	175	49.54 N	38.54 E
vereto, It. (rō-vå-rā'tô)	172	45.53 N	11.05 E
vigo, It. (rô-vē'gô)	172	45.05 N	11.48 E
vinj, Yugo. (rô'ēn')	172	45.05 N	13.40 E
vira, Col. (rô-vē'rä)	142a	4.14 N	75.13 W
vno, Sov. Un. (rôv'nô)	167	50.37 N	26.17 E
vno (Oblast), Sov. Un.	175	50.55 N	27.00 E
vnoye, Sov. Un. (rôv'nô-yĕ)	175	48.11 N	31.46 E
vuma (Ruvuma) (R.), Moz.-Tan.	231	10.50 S	39.50 E
wland Heights, Ca.	59	33.59 N	117.54 W
wley, Ma. (rou'lē)	105a	42.43 N	70.53 W
wville, Austl.	70b	37.56 S	145.14 E
xana, Il. (rŏks'ăn-nȧ)	119e	38.51 N	90.05 W
xas, Phil. (rô-xäs)	206	11.30 N	122.47 E
xboro, Can.	54b	45.31 N	73.48 W
xboro, NC (rŏks' bŭr-ô)	127	36.22 N	78.58 W
xborough (Neigh.), Pa.	56b	40.02 N	75.13 W
xbury (Neigh.), NY	55	40.34 N	73.54 W
xo, Cap (C.), Senegal	228	12.20 N	16.43 W
y, NM (roi)	122	35.54 N	104.09 W
y, Ut.	119b	41.10 N	112.02 W
yal (I.), Ba.	134	25.30 N	76.50 W
yal Albert Hall (P. Int.), Eng.	62	51.30 N	0.11 W
yal Can., Ire. (roi-ȧl)	162	53.28 N	6.45 W
yal Natal Natl. Pk., S. Afr. (roi'ăl)	227c	28.35 S	28.54 E
yal Naval College (P. Int.), Eng.	62	51.29 N	0.01 W
yal Oak, Can. (roi'ȧl ōk)	118a	48.30 N	123.24 W
yal Oak, Mi.	113b	42.29 N	83.09 W
yal Oak Township, Mi.	57c	42.27 N	83.10 W
yal Ontario Museum (P. Int.), Can.	54c	43.40 N	79.24 W
yalton, Mi. (roi'ăl-tŭn)	110	42.00 N	86.25 W
yan, Fr. (rwä-yäɴ')	168	45.40 N	1.02 W
ye, Fr. (rwä)	168	49.43 N	2.40 E
yersford, Pa. (rô' yērz-fērd)	112f	40.11 N	75.32 W
yston, Ga. (roiz'tŭn)	126	34.15 N	83.06 W
yton, Eng. (roi'tŭn)	156	53.34 N	2.07 W
zay-en-Brie, Fr. (rô-zā-ĕɴ-brē')	169b	48.41 N	2.57 E
zelle, Austl.	70a	33.52 S	151.10 E
zhaya R., Sov. Un. (rô'zhȧ-yȧ)	182b	55.20 N	37.37 E
žňava, Czech. (rôzh'nyȧ-vȧ)	167	48.39 N	20.32 E
shchevo, Sov. Un. ('r-tĭsh'chĕ-vô)	179	52.15 N	43.40 E
(R.), China (rōō)	200	33.07 N	114.18 E
acana Falls, Ang.-Namibia	226	17.15 S	14.45 E
aha Natl. Pk., Tan.	231	7.15 S	34.50 E
apehu (Vol.), N.Z. (rōō-ȧ-pā'hōō)	217	39.15 S	175.37 E
beho Mts., Tan.	231	6.45 S	36.15 E
bidoux, Ca.	119a	33.59 N	117.24 W
bondo I., Tan.	231	2.10 S	31.55 E
btsovsk, Sov. Un.	180	51.31 N	81.17 E
by, Ak. (rōō'bē)	107	64.38 N	155.22 W
by (L.), Nv.	120	40.11 N	115.20 W
by Mts., Nv.	120	40.11 N	115.36 W
by R., Mt.	117	45.06 N	112.10 W
dersdorf, G.D.R.	65a	52.29 N	13.47 E
dge Ramos, Braz.	61d	23.41 S	46.34 W
dinghausen (Neigh.), F.D.R.	63	51.27 N	7.25 E
dkøbing, Den. (rōōdh'kûb-ĭng)	164	54.56 N	10.44 E
dnitz, G.D.R. (rüd'nētz)	157b	52.44 N	13.38 E
dolf, L., Ken.-Eth. (rōō'dŏlf)	231	3.30 N	36.05 E
dolstadt, G.D.R. (rōō'dôl-shtät)	163	50.46 N	13.30 E
dow (Neigh.), F.R.G.	65a	52.25 N	13.30 E

PLACE (Pronounciation)	PAGE	Lat. °′	Long. °′
Rueil-Malmaison, Fr.	64c	48.53 N	2.11 E
Rufā'ah, Sud. (rōō-fä'ä)	225	14.52 N	33.30 E
Ruffec, Fr. (rü-fĕk')	168	46.03 N	0.11 E
Rufiji (R.), Tan. (rōō-fē'jē)	231	8.00 S	39.20 E
Rufisque, Senegal (rü-fēsk')	228	14.43 N	17.17 W
Rufunsa, Zambia	231	15.05 S	29.40 E
Rufus Woods, Wa.	116	48.02 N	119.33 W
Rugao, China (rōō-gou)	200	32.24 N	120.33 E
Rugby, Eng. (rŭg'bē)	156	52.22 N	1.15 W
Rugby, ND	114	48.22 N	100.00 W
Rugeley, Eng. (rōōj'lē)	156	52.46 N	1.56 W
Rügen (Pen.), G.D.R. (rü'ghĕn)	166	54.28 N	13.47 E
Rüggeberg, F.R.G.	63	51.16 N	7.22 E
Ruhlsdorf, G.D.R.	65a	52.23 N	13.16 E
Ruhnu-Saar (I.), Sov. Un. (rōōnōō-så'år)	165	57.46 N	23.15 E
Ruhrort (Neigh.), F.R.G.	63	51.26 N	6.45 E
Ruhr R., F.R.G. (rōōr)	166	51.18 N	8.17 E
Rui'an, China (rwā-än)	203	27.48 N	120.40 E
Ruislip (Neigh.), Eng.	62	51.34 N	0.25 W
Ruiz, Mex. (rōōē'z)	130	21.55 N	105.09 W
Ruiz, Nevado del (Pk.), Col. (nĕ-vȧ'dô-dĕl-rōōē'z)	142a	4.52 N	75.20 W
Rūjiena, Sov. Un. (rōō'yĭ-ă-nȧ)	165	57.54 N	25.19 E
Ruki (R.), Zaire	230	0.05 S	18.55 E
Rukwa, L., Tan. (rōōk-wä')	231	8.00 S	32.25 E
Rum (R.), Mn. (rŭm)	115	45.52 N	93.45 W
Ruma, Yugo. (rōō'mȧ)	173	45.00 N	19.53 E
Rum'ancevo, Sov. Un.	66b	55.38 N	37.26 E
Rumbek, Sud. (rŭm'bĕk)	225	6.52 N	29.43 E
Rum Cay (I.), Ba.	135	23.40 N	74.50 W
Rumelihisari (Neigh.), Tur.	66f	41.05 N	29.03 E
Rumeln-Kaldenhausen, F.R.G.	63	51.24 N	6.40 E
Rumford, Me. (rŭm'fērd)	104	44.32 N	70.35 W
Rummah, Wādī ar (R.), Sau. Ar.	192	26.17 N	41.45 E
Rummānah, Egypt	191a	31.01 N	32.39 E
Rummelsburg (Neigh.)	65a	52.30 N	13.29 E
Rummenohl, F.R.G.	63	51.17 N	7.32 E
Runan, China (rōō-nän)	200	32.59 N	114.22 E
Runcorn, Eng. (rŭŋ'kôrn)	156	53.20 N	2.44 W
Runnemede, NJ	56b	39.51 N	75.04 W
Runnymede (P. Int.), Eng.	62	51.26 N	0.34 W
Ruo (R.), China (rwô)	198	41.15 N	100.46 E
Rupat, Palau (I.), Indon. (rōō'pät)	191b	1.55 N	101.35 E
Rupat, Selat (Str.), Indon.	191b	1.55 N	101.17 E
Rupert, Id. (rōō'pērt)	117	42.36 N	113.41 W
Rupert, Rivière de (R.), Can.	97	51.35 N	76.30 W
Rural Ridge, Pa.	57b	40.35 N	79.50 W
Ruse (Russe), Bul. (rōō'sĕ) (rōō'sĕ)	173	43.50 N	25.59 E
Rushan, China (rōō-shän)	200	36.54 N	121.31 E
Rush City, Mn.	115	45.40 N	92.59 W
Rusholme (Neigh.), Eng.	64b	53.27 N	2.12 W
Rushville, Il. (rŭsh'vĭl)	123	40.08 N	90.34 W
Rushville, In.	110	39.35 N	85.30 W
Rushville, Ne.	114	42.43 N	102.27 W
Rusizi (R.), Zaire,	231	3.00 S	29.05 E
Rusk, Tx. (rŭsk)	125	31.49 N	95.09 W
Ruskin, Can. (rŭs'kĭn)	118d	49.10 N	122.25 W
Russ (R.), Aus.	157e	48.12 N	16.55 E
Russas, Braz. (rōō's-säs)	143	4.48 S	37.50 W
Russel L., Can.	101	56.15 N	101.30 W
Russell, Ca.	118b	37.39 N	122.08 W
Russell, Can. (rŭs'ĕl)	101	50.47 N	101.15 W
Russell, Can.	95c	45.15 N	75.22 W
Russell, Ks.	122	38.51 N	98.51 W
Russell, Ky.	110	38.30 N	82.45 W
Russell Gardens, NY	55	40.47 N	73.43 W
Russell Is., Sol. Is.	215	9.16 S	158.30 E
Russellville, Al. (rŭs'ĕl-vĭl)	126	34.29 N	87.44 W
Russellville, Ar.	123	35.16 N	93.08 W
Russelville, Ky.	126	36.48 N	86.51 W
Russe, see Ruse			
Russian (R.), Ca. (rŭsh'ăn)	120	38.59 N	123.10 W
Russian S. F. S. R., Sov. Un.	176	61.00 N	60.00 E
Rustenburg, S. Afr. (rŭs'tĕn-bûrg)	223d	25.40 S	26.15 E
Ruston, La. (rŭs'tŭn)	125	32.32 N	92.39 W
Ruston, Wa.	118a	47.18 N	122.30 W
Rusville, S. Afr.	71b	26.10 S	28.18 E
Rutchenkovo, Sov. Un. (rōō-chĕn'kô-vô)	175	47.54 N	37.36 E
Rute, Sp. (rōō'tā)	170	37.20 N	4.34 W
Ruth, Nv. (rōōth)	120	39.17 N	115.00 W
Ruthenia (Reg.), Sov. Un.	167	48.25 N	23.00 E
Rutherford, NJ	55	40.49 N	74.07 W
Rutherfordton, NC (rŭdh'ēr-fērd-tŭn)	127	35.23 N	81.58 W
Rutland, Vt.	111	43.35 N	72.55 W
Rutledge, Md. (rût'lĕdj)	112e	39.34 N	76.33 W
Rutledge, Pa.	56b	39.54 N	75.20 W
Rutog, China (rōō-tô-gŭ)	196	33.42 N	79.56 E
Rutshuru, Zaire (rōōt-shōō'rōō)	231	1.11 S	29.27 E
Rüttenscheid (Neigh.), F.R.G.	63	51.26 N	7.00 E
Ruvo, It. (rōō'vô)	172	41.07 N	16.32 E
Ruvuma (Rovuma) (R.), Moz.-Tan.	231	10.50 S	39.50 E
Ruza, Sov. Un. (rōō'zȧ)	174	55.42 N	36.12 E
Ruzhany, Sov. Un. (rōō-zhän'ĭ)	167	52.49 N	24.54 E
Rwanda, Afr.	222	2.10 S	29.37 E
Ryabovo, Sov. Un. (ryä'bô-vô)	182c	59.24 N	31.08 E
Ryarsh, Eng.	62	51.19 N	0.24 E
Ryazan', Sov. Un. (ryä-zän'')	174	54.37 N	39.43 E
Ryazan' (Oblast), Sov. Un.	174	54.10 N	39.37 E
Ryazhsk, Sov. Un. (ryäzh'sk')	174	53.43 N	40.04 E
Rybachiy, P-Ov. (Pen.), Sov. Un.	178	69.50 N	33.20 E
Rybatskoye, see Andropov	182c	59.50 N	30.31 E
Rybinsk, see Andropov			
Rybinskoye Vdkhr. (Res.), Sov. Un.	174	58.23 N	38.15 E
Rybnik, Pol. (rĭb'nēk)	167	50.06 N	18.37 E
Rybnitsa, Sov. Un. (rĭb'nēt-sȧ)	175	47.45 N	29.02 E
Rydal, Pa.	56b	40.06 N	75.06 W
Rydalmere, Austl.	70a	33.49 S	151.02 E
Ryde, Austl.	70a	33.49 S	151.06 E
Ryde, Eng. (rīd)	162	50.43 N	1.16 W

PLACE (Pronounciation)	PAGE	Lat. °′	Long. °′
Rye, NY (rī)	112a	40.58 N	73.42 W
Ryl'sk, Sov. Un. (rēl''sk)	175	51.33 N	34.42 E
Rynfield, S. Afr.	71b	26.09 S	28.20 E
Ryōtsu, Jap. (ryōt'sōō)	204	38.02 N	138.23 E
Rypin, Pol. (rĭ'pēn)	167	53.04 N	19.25 E
Ryukyu, see Nansei-shotō			
Rzeszów, Pol. (zhå-shōōf)	167	50.02 N	22.00 E
Rzhev, Sov. Un. ('r-zhĕf)	174	56.16 N	34.17 E
Rzhishchëv, Sov. Un. ('r-zhĭsh'chĕf)	175	49.58 N	31.05 E

S

PLACE (Pronounciation)	PAGE	Lat. °′	Long. °′
Saale R., G.D.R. (sä-lĕ)	166	51.14 N	11.52 E
Saalfeld, G.D.R. (säl'fĕlt)	166	50.38 N	11.20 E
Saarbrücken, F.R.G. (zähr'brü-kĕn)	166	49.15 N	7.01 E
Saaremaa (Ezel) (I.), Sov. Un. (sä'rĕ-mä)	165	58.28 N	21.30 E
Saarland (State), F.R.G.	166	49.25 N	6.50 E
Saarn (Neigh.), F.R.G.	63	51.24 N	6.53 E
Saarnberg (Neigh.), F.R.G.	63	51.25 N	6.53 E
Şaavedra, Arg. (sä-ä-vā'drä)	144	37.45 S	62.23 W
Šabac, Yugo. (shä'bȧts)	173	44.45 N	19.49 E
Sabadell, Sp. (sä-bä-dhål')	171	41.32 N	2.07 E
Sabah (Reg.), Mala.	206	5.10 N	116.25 E
Saba I., Neth. Antilles (sä'bä)	133b	17.39 N	63.20 W
Sabana, Arch. de, Cuba (är-chē-pyĕ'lä-gô dĕ sä-bä'nä)	134	23.05 N	80.00 W
Sabana de la Mar, Dom. Rep. (sä-bä'nä dā lä mär')	135	19.05 N	69.30 W
Sabana de Uchire, Ven. (sä-bȧ'nä dĕ ōō-chē'rĕ)	143b	10.02 N	65.32 W
Sabanagrande, Hond. (sä-bä'nä-grä'n-dĕ)	132	13.47 N	87.16 W
Sabanalarga, Col. (sä-bȧ'nä-lär'gä)	142	10.38 N	75.02 W
Sabana, R., Pan. (sä-bä'nä)	133	8.40 N	78.02 W
Sabanas Páramo (Mtn.), Col. (sä-bȧ'näs pȧ'rä-mô)	142a	6.28 N	76.08 W
Sabancuy, Mex. (sä-bäŋ-kwē')	131	18.58 N	91.09 W
Sabang, Indon. (sä'bäng)	206	5.52 N	95.26 E
Sabaudia, It. (sȧ-bou'dē-ä)	174	41.19 N	13.00 E
Sabetha, Ks. (sȧ-bĕth'ȧ)	123	39.54 N	95.49 W
Sabhā, Libya	194	27.03 S	14.26 E
Sabi (R.), Zimb. (sä'bē)	226	20.18 S	32.07 E
Sabile, Sov. Un. (sȧ'bē-lĕ)	165	57.03 N	22.34 E
Sabinal, Tx. (sȧ-bī'nȧl)	124	29.19 N	99.27 W
Sabinal, Cayo (I.), Cuba (kä'yō sä-bē-näl')	134	21.40 N	77.20 W
Sabinas, Mex.	128	28.05 N	102.30 W
Sabinas, R., Mex. (sä-bē'näs)	124	26.37 N	99.52 W
Sabinas, Rio (R.), Mex. (rē'ō sä-bē'näs)	124	27.25 N	100.33 W
Sabinas Hidalgo, Mex. (ē-däl'gô)	124	26.30 N	100.10 W
Sabine, Tx. (sȧ-bēn')	125	29.44 N	93.54 W
Sabine (R.), U.S.	109	31.35 N	94.00 W
Sabine L., La.-Tx.	125	29.53 N	93.41 W
Sabine, Mt., Ant.	232	72.05 S	169.10 E
Sablayan, Phil. (säb-lä-yän')	207a	12.49 N	120.47 E
Sable, C., Can. (sā'b'l)	104	43.25 N	65.24 W
Sable, C., Fl.	127a	25.12 N	81.10 W
Sables, Rivière aux (R.), Can.	103	49.00 N	70.20 W
Sablé-sur-Sarthe, Fr. (säb-lā-sür-särt')	168	47.50 N	0.17 W
Sablya, Gora (Mtn.), Sov. Un.	178	64.50 N	59.00 E
Sàbor (R.), Port. (sä-bōr')	170	41.18 N	6.54 W
Saburovo (Neigh.), Sov. Un.	66b	55.38 N	37.42 E
Sabzevār, Iran	195	36.13 N	57.42 E
Sac (R.), Mo. (sôk)	123	38.11 N	93.45 W
Sacandaga Res., NY (să-kăn-dâ'gȧ)	111	43.10 N	74.15 W
Sacavém, Port. (sä-kä-vĕɴ')	171b	38.47 N	9.06 W
Sacavém (R.), Port.	165b	38.52 N	9.06 W
Sac City, Ia. (sŏk)	115	42.25 N	95.00 W
Sachigo L., Can. (săch'ĭ-gō)	101	53.49 N	92.08 W
Sachsen (Reg.), G.D.R. (zäĸ'sĕn)	166	50.45 N	12.17 E
Sacketts Harbor, NY (săk'ĕts)	111	43.55 N	76.05 W
Sackville, Can. (săk'vĭl)	104	45.54 N	64.22 W
Saco, Me. (sô'kô)	104	43.30 N	70.28 W
Saco (R.), Braz. (sä'kô)	144b	22.20 S	43.26 W
Saco (R.), Me.	104	43.53 N	70.46 W
Sacra Famalia do Tinguá, Braz. (sä-krä fä-mä'lyä dô tēn-gwȧ')	144b	22.29 S	43.36 W
Sacramento, Ca. (săk-rȧ-mĕn'tō)	120	38.35 N	121.30 W
Sacramento, Mex.	124	25.45 N	103.22 W
Sacramento, Mex.	124	27.05 N	101.45 W
Sacramento (R.), Ca.	120	40.20 N	122.07 W
Sacré-Cœur (P. Int.), Fr.	64c	48.53 N	2.21 E
Sacrow (Neigh.), G.D.R.	65a	52.26 N	13.06 E
Şa'dah, Yemen	192	16.50 N	43.45 E
Saddle Brook, NJ	55	40.54 N	74.06 W
Saddle Lake Ind. Res., Can.	99	54.00 N	111.40 W
Saddle Mtn., Or. (săd''l)	118c	45.58 N	123.40 W
Saddle Rock, NY	55	40.48 N	73.45 W
Sadiya, India (sŭ-dē'yä)	193	27.53 N	95.35 E
Sado (I.), Jap. (sä'dō)	204	38.05 N	138.26 E
Sado (R.), Port. (sä'dōō)	170	38.15 N	8.20 W
Saeby, Den. (sĕ'bü)	164	57.21 N	10.29 E
Saeki, Jap. (sä'å-kē)	205	32.56 N	131.51 E
Safdar Jang's Tomb (P. Int.), India	67d	28.36 N	77.13 E
Safford, Az. (săf'fērd)	121	32.50 N	109.45 W

PLACE (Pronounciation)	PAGE	Lat. °′	Long. °′
Safi (Asfi), Mor. (sä'fė) (äs'fė)	224	32.24 N	9.09 W
Safid Rud (R.), Iran	179	36.50 N	49.40 E
Saga, Jap. (sä'gä)	205	33.15 N	130.18 E
Sagamihara, Jap.	69a	35.32 N	139.23 E
Sagami-Nada (Sea), Jap. (sä'gä'mė nä-dä)	205	35.06 N	139.24 E
Sagamore Hills, Oh. (săg'ȧ-môr hĭlz)	113d	41.19 N	81.34 W
Saganaga (L.), Can.-Mn. (să-gȧ-nă'gȧ)	115	48.13 N	91.17 W
Sāgar, India	196	23.55 N	78.45 E
Sagauche Cr., Co.	111	38.05 N	106.40 W
Saginaw, Mi. (săg'ĭ-nô)	110	43.25 N	84.00 W
Saginaw, Mn.	119h	46.51 N	92.26 W
Saginaw, Tx.	119c	32.52 N	97.22 W
Saginaw B., Mi.	110	43.50 N	83.40 W
Sagiz (R.), Sov. Un. (sä'gēz)	179	48.30 N	56.10 E
Saguache, Co. (sȧ-wăch') (sȧ-gwä'chė)	111	38.05 N	106.10 W
Sagua de Tánamo, Cuba (sä-gwä dĕ tá'nä-mō)	135	20.40 N	75.15 W
Sagua la Grande, Cuba (sä-gwä lä grä'n-dĕ)	134	22.45 N	80.05 W
Saguaro Natl. Mon., Az. (säg-wä'rō)	121	32.12 N	110.40 W
Saguenay (R.), Can. (săg-ē-nā')	102	48.20 N	70.15 W
Sagunto, Sp. (sä-gōōn'tō)	171	39.40 N	0.17 W
Sahara Des., Afr. (sȧ-hä'rȧ)	222	23.44 N	1.40 W
Saharan Atlas (Mts.), Mor.-Alg.	160	32.51 N	1.02 W
Sahāranpur, India (sŭ-hä'rŭn-pōōr')	196	29.58 N	77.41 E
Sahara Village, Ut. (sȧ-hä'rȧ)	119b	41.06 N	111.58 W
Sāhiwāl, Pak.	196	30.43 N	73.04 E
Sahuayo de Dias, Mex.	130	20.03 N	102.43 W
Saigon, see Ho Chi Minh City			
Saijō, Jap. (sä'ė-jȯ)	205	33.55 N	133.13 E
Saimaa, Fin. (sä'ĭ-mä)	165	61.24 N	28.45 E
Sain Alto, Mex. (sä-ēn' äl'tō)	130	23.35 N	103.13 W
Saint Adolphe, Can. (sånt a'dŏlf) (săN' tȧ-dȯlf')	95f	49.40 N	97.07 W
Saint Afrique, Fr. (săN' tȧ-frēk')	168	43.58 N	2.52 E
Saint Albans, Austl. (sånt ôl'bănz)	211a	37.44 S	144.47 E
Saint Albans, Eng.	156b	51.44 N	0.20 W
Saint Albans, Vt.	111	44.50 N	73.05 W
Saint Albans, WV	110	38.20 N	81.50 W
Saint Albans (Neigh.), NY	55	40.42 N	73.46 W
Saint Albans Cathedral (P. Int.), Eng.	62	51.45 N	0.20 W
Saint Albert, Can. (sånt ăl'bērt)	95g	53.38 N	113.38 W
Saint Amand-MontRond, Fr. (săN't ȧ-mäN' môN-rôN')	168	46.44 N	2.28 E
Saint André, Cap (C.), Mad.	227	16.15 S	44.31 E
Saint André-Est., Can.	95a	45.33 N	74.19 W
Saint Andrew, B., Fl.	126	30.20 N	85.45 W
Saint Andrews, Can.	104	45.05 N	67.03 W
Saint Andrews, Scot.	162	56.20 N	2.40 W
Saint Andrew's Chan., Can. (ăn'drōōz)	105	46.06 N	60.28 W
Saint Anicet, Can. (sĕNt ä-nē-sĕ')	95a	45.07 N	74.23 W
Saint Ann, Mo. (sånt ăn')	119e	38.44 N	90.23 W
Saint Anne, Il.	113a	41.01 N	87.44 W
Saint Anne of the Congo (P. Int.), Con.	71c	4.16 S	15.17 E
Saint Anns B., Can. (ănz)	105	46.20 N	60.30 W
Saint Ann's Bay, Jam.	134	18.25 N	77.15 W
Saint Anselme, Can. (săN' täN-sĕlm')	95b	46.37 N	70.58 W
Saint Anthony, Can. (säN ăn'thȯ-nė)	105	51.24 N	55.35 W
Saint Anthony, Id. (sånt ăn'thȯ-nė)	117	43.59 N	111.42 W
Saint Antoine-de-Tilly, Can.	95b	46.00 N	71.31 W
Saint Apollinaire, Can. (săN' tȧ-pȯl-ė-nâr')	95b	46.36 N	71.30 W
Saint Arnoult-en-Yvelines, Fr. (sȧN-tär-nōō'ĕN-nēv-lēn')	169b	48.33 N	1.55 E
Saint Augustin-de-Québec, Can. (sĕn tō-güs-tēn')	95b	46.45 N	71.27 W
Saint Augustin-Deux-Montagnes, Can.	95a	45.38 N	73.59 W
Saint Augustine, Fl. (sånt ô'gŭs-tēn)	127	29.53 N	81.21 W
Saint Barthelemy I., Guad.	133b	17.55 N	62.32 W
Saint Bees Hd., Eng. (sånt bēz' hĕd)	162	54.30 N	3.40 W
Saint Benoit, Can. (sĕN bĕ-nōō-ä')	95a	45.34 N	74.05 W
Saint Bernard, La. (bēr-närd')	112d	29.52 N	89.52 W
Saint Bernard, Oh.	113f	39.10 N	84.30 W
Saint-Brice-sous-Forêt, Fr.	64c	49.00 N	2.21 E
Saint Bride Mt., Can. (sånt brīd)	99	51.30 N	115.57 W
Saint Brieuc, Fr. (săN' brēs')	168	48.32 N	2.47 W
Saint Bruno, Can. (brū'nō)	95a	45.31 N	73.40 W
Saint Canut, Can. (săN' kȧ-nū')	95a	45.43 N	74.04 W
Saint Casimir, Can. (kȧ-zė-mēr')	104	46.45 N	72.34 W
Saint Catharines, Can. (kăth'å-rĭnz)	95d	43.10 N	79.14 W
Saint Catherine, Mt., Grenada	133b	12.10 N	62.42 W
Saint Chamas, Fr. (sȧN-shä-mä')	168a	43.32 N	5.03 E
Saint Chamond, Fr. (săN' shȧ-môN')	168	45.30 N	4.17 E
Saint Charles, Can. (săN' shärlz')	95b	46.47 N	70.57 W
Saint Charles, Il. (sånt chärlz')	113a	41.55 N	88.19 W
Saint Charles, Mi.	110	43.20 N	84.10 W
Saint Charles, Mn.	115	43.56 N	92.05 W
Saint Charles, Mo.	119e	38.47 N	90.29 W
Saint Charles, Lac (L.), Can.	95b	46.56 N	71.21 W
Saint Christopher-Nevis, N.A.	129	17.24 N	63.30 W
Saint Christopher-Nevis (I.), Saint Christopher-Nevis	129	17.24 N	63.30 W
Saint Clair, Mi. (sånt klâr)	110	42.55 N	82.30 W
Saint Clair (L.), Can.-Mi.	110	42.25 N	82.30 W
Saint Clair (R.), Can.-Mi.	110	42.45 N	82.25 W
Saint Clair Shores, Mi.	113b	42.30 N	82.54 W
Saint Claude, Fr. (săN' klōd')	169	46.24 N	5.53 E
Saint Clet, Can. (săNt' klā')	95a	45.22 N	74.21 W
Saint Cloud, Fl. (sånt kloud')	127a	28.13 N	81.17 W
Saint-Cloud, Fr.	64c	48.51 N	2.13 E
Saint Cloud, Mn.	115	45.33 N	94.08 W
Saint Constant, Can. (kŏn'stănt)	95a	45.23 N	73.34 W
Saint Croix (I.), Vir. Is. (U.S.A.) (sånt kroi')	129b	17.40 N	64.43 W
Saint Croix (R.), Can.-Me. (kroi')	104	45.28 N	67.32 W
Saint Croix I., S. Afr. (săN krwă)	227c	33.48 S	25.45 E
Saint Croix Ind. Res., Wi.	115	45.40 N	92.21 W
Saint Croix R., Mn.-Wi. (sånt kroi')	115	45.00 N	92.44 W
Saint-Cyr-l'Ecole, Fr.	64c	48.48 N	2.04 E
Saint Damien-de-Buckland, Can. (sånt dā'mė-ĕn)	95b	46.37 N	70.39 W
Saint David, Can. (dā'vĭd)	95b	46.47 N	71.11 W
Saint Davids, Pa.	56b	40.02 N	75.22 W
Saint David's Hd., Wales	162	51.54 N	5.25 W
Saint-Denis, Fr. (săN'dē-nē')	169b	48.26 N	2.22 E
Saint Dié, Fr. (dė-ā')	169	48.18 N	6.55 E
Saint Dizier, Fr. (dė-zyā')	168	48.49 N	4.55 E
Saint Dominique, Can. (sĕN dō-mē-nēk')	95a	45.19 N	74.09 W
Sainte Anne, Can. (săNt'ȧn') (sånt ăn')	104	46.55 N	71.46 W
Sainte Anne, Guad.	133b	16.15 N	61.23 W
Sainte-Anne (R.), Can.	95b	47.07 N	70.50 W
Sainte Anne-de-Beaupré, Can. (dē bō-prā')	95b	47.02 N	70.56 W
Sainte Anne-des-Plaines, Can. (dā plĕN)	95a	45.46 N	73.49 W
Sainte Barbe, Can. (sånt bärb')	95a	45.14 N	74.12 W
Sainte Claire, Can.	95b	46.36 N	70.52 W
Sainte-Dorothée (Neigh.), Can.	54b	45.32 N	73.49 W
Saint Edouard-de-Napierville, Can. (sĕN-tĕ-dōō-är')	95a	45.14 N	73.31 W
Sainte Euphémie, Can. (sĕNt û-fĕ-mē')	95b	46.47 N	70.27 W
Sainte Famille, Can. (săN't fȧ-mē'y')	95b	46.58 N	70.58 W
Sainte Felicite, Can.	104	48.54 N	67.20 W
Sainte Foy, Can. (săNt fwä)	95b	46.47 N	71.18 W
Sainte-Geneviève, Can.	54b	45.29 N	73.52 W
Sainte Genevieve, Mo. (sånt jĕn'ĕ-vēv)	123	37.58 N	90.02 W
Sainte-Hélène, Île (I.), Can.	54b	45.31 N	73.32 W
Sainte Justine-de-Newton, Can. (sånt jŭs-tēn')	95a	45.22 N	74.22 W
Saint Elias, Mt., Can. (sånt ė-lī'ăs)	107	60.25 N	141.00 W
Sainte-Marie-aux-Mines, Fr. (sȧN'tĕ-mä-rē'ō-mēn')	169	48.14 N	7.08 E
Sainte Marie-Beauce, Can. (săNt'mȧ-rē')	104	46.27 N	71.03 W
Sainte Marie, Cap (C.), Mad.	227	25.31 S	45.00 E
Sainte Martine, Can.	95a	45.14 N	73.37 W
Sainte Pétronille, Can. (sĕNt pĕt-rō-nēl')	95b	46.51 N	71.08 W
Sainte Rose, Guad.	133b	16.19 N	61.45 W
Sainte-Rose (Neigh.), Can.	54b	45.36 N	73.47 W
Saintes, Fr.	168	45.44 N	0.41 W
Sainte Scholastique, Can. (skȯ-lȧs-tēk')	95a	45.39 N	74.05 W
Saint Étienne, Fr.	168	45.26 N	4.22 E
Saint Etienne-de-Lauzon, Can. (săN' tā-tyĕn')	95b	46.39 N	71.19 W
Saint Eustache, Can. (săN' tû-stȧsh')	95a	45.34 N	73.54 W
Saint Eustache, Can.	95f	49.58 N	97.47 W
Saint Eustatius I., Neth. Antilles (sånt u-stā'shŭs)	133b	17.32 N	62.45 W
Saint Félicíen, Can. (săN fā-lė-syăN')	105	48.39 N	72.28 W
Saint Féréol, Can. (fa-rā-ȯl')	95b	47.07 N	70.52 W
Saint Florent-sur-Cher, Fr. (săN' flȯ-räN'sür-shâr')	168	46.58 N	2.15 E
Saint Flour, Fr. (săN flōōr')	168	45.02 N	3.09 E
Saint Francis L., Can. (săN frăn'sĭs)	111	45.00 N	74.20 W
Saint Francis (R.), Ar.	123	35.56 N	90.27 W
Saint François, Can. (săN'fräN-swä')	95b	47.01 N	70.49 W
Saint François de Boundji, Con.	223	1.03 S	15.22 E
Saint Francois Xavier, Can.	95f	49.55 N	97.32 W
Saint Gaudens, Fr. (gō-dăNs')	168	43.07 N	0.43 E
Saint George, Austl. (sånt jôrj')	216	28.02 S	148.40 E
Saint George, Can. (săN jôrj')	104	45.08 N	66.49 W
Saint George, Can. (săN'zhôrzh')	95d	43.14 N	80.15 W
Saint George, SC (sånt jôrj')	127	33.11 N	80.35 W
Saint George, Ut.	121	37.05 N	113.40 W
Saint George, C., Can.	105	48.28 N	59.15 W
Saint George, C., Fl.	126	29.30 N	85.20 W
Saint George (I.), Ak.	107	56.30 N	169.40 W
Saint George (Neigh.), NY	55	40.39 N	74.05 W
Saint George's, Can. (jôrj'ēs)	105	48.26 N	58.29 W
Saint Georges, Fr. Gu.	143	3.48 N	51.47 W
Saint Georges, Grenada	133b	12.02 N	61.57 W
Saint Georges B., Can.	105	45.49 N	61.45 W
Saint George's B., Can.	105	48.20 N	59.00 W
Saint George's Chan., Eng.-Ire. (jôr-jĕz)	162	51.45 N	6.30 W
Saint Germain-en-Laye, Fr. (săN' zhĕr-măN-äN-lā')	169b	48.53 N	2.05 E
Saint Gervais, Can. (zhĕr-vĕ')	95b	46.43 N	70.53 W
Saint Girons, Fr. (zhē-rôN')	168	42.58 N	1.08 E
Saint-Gratien, Fr.	64c	48.58 N	2.17 E
Saint Gregory, Mt., Can. (sånt grĕg'ēr-ė)	105	49.19 N	58.13 W
Saint Helena, Atl. O.	222	16.01 S	5.16 W
Saint Helenabaai (B.), Afr.	226	32.25 S	17.15 E
Saint Helens, Eng. (sånt hĕl'ĕnz)	156	53.27 N	2.44 W
Saint Helens, Or. (hĕl'ĕnz)	118c	45.52 N	122.49 W
Saint Helens, Mt., Wa.	116	46.13 N	122.10 W
Saint Helier, Jersey (hyĕl'yĕr)	168	49.12 N	2.06 W
Saint Henri, Can. (săN' hĕn'rė)	95b	46.41 N	71.04 W
Saint Hubert, Can.	95a	45.29 N	73.24 W
Saint Hyacinthe, Can. (săN' tė-ä-săNt') (sånt hī'ȧ-sĭnth)	111	45.35 N	72.55 W
Saint-Ignace, Can.	104	46.42 N	70.30 W
Saint Ignace, Mi. (sånt ĭg'nȧs)	115	45.51 N	84.39 W
Saint Ignace (I.), Can. (săN' ĭg'nȧs)	115	48.47 N	88.14 W
Saint Irenee, Can. (săN' tē-rȧ-nā')	104	47.34 N	70.15 W
Saint Isidore-de-Laprairie, Can. (saN' tē-zė-dōr') (sånt ĭz'ĭ-dôr)	95a	45.18 N	73.41 W
Saint Isidore-de-Prescott, Can. (săN' ĭz'ĭ-dôr-prĕs-kŏt)	95c	45.23 N	74.54 W
Saint Isidore-Dorchester, Can. (dŏr-chĕs'tēr)	95b	46.35 N	71.0
Saint Ives, Austl.	70a	33.44 S	151.1
Saint Jacob, Il. (jā-kŏb)	119e	38.43 N	89.4
Saint James, Mn. (sånt jāmz')	115	43.58 N	94.3
Saint James, Mo.	113	37.59 N	91.3
Saint James, C., Can.	98	51.58 N	131.0
Saint Janvier, Can. (săN' zhän-vyā')	95a	45.43 N	73.5
Saint Jean, Can. (săN' zhäN')	111	45.20 N	73.1
Saint Jean, Can.	95b	46.55 N	70.5
Saint Jean-Chrysostome, Can. (krĭ-zōs-tōm')	95b	46.43 N	71.1
Saint Jean-d'Angely, Fr. (däN-zhå-lē')	168	45.56 N	0.3
Saint Jean-de-Luz, Fr. (dē lüz')	168	43.23 N	1.4
Saint Jean, Lac (L.), Can.	103	48.35 N	72.0
Saint Jérôme, Can. (sånt jĕ-rōm') (săN zhā-rōm')	95a	45.47 N	74.0
Saint Joachim-de-Montmorency, Can. (sånt jō'ȧ-kĭm)	95b	47.04 N	70.5
Saint John, Can. (sånt jŏn)	104	45.16 N	66.0
Saint John, In.	113a	41.27 N	87.2
Saint John, Ks.	122	37.59 N	98.4
Saint John, ND	114	48.57 N	99.4
Saint John B., Can.	105	50.54 N	57.0
Saint John, C., Can.	105	50.00 N	55.3
Saint John I., Can.	105	50.49 N	57.1
Saint John (I.), Vir. Is. (U.S.A.)	129b	18.16 N	64.4
Saint John (R.), Can.	104	46.39 N	67.4
Saint John (R.), N.A.	97	45.15 N	67.4
Saint Johns, Antigua	133b	17.07 N	61.5
Saint Johns, Az. (jŏnz)	121	34.30 N	109.2
Saint John's, Can. (jŏns)	105	47.34 N	52.4
Saint Johns, Mi.	110	43.05 N	84.3
Saint Johns (R.), Fl.	127	29.54 N	81.3
Saint Johnsburg, NY	57a	43.05 N	78.5
Saint Johnsbury, Vt. (jŏnz'bĕr-ė)	111	44.25 N	72.0
Saint John's University (P. Int.), NY	55	40.43 N	73.4
Saint Joseph, Can. (jō'zhûf)	104	46.17 N	70.5
Saint Joseph, Dominica	133b	15.25 N	61.2
Saint Joseph, Mi.	110	42.05 N	86.3
Saint Joseph, Mo. (sånt jȯ-sĕf)	123	39.44 N	94.4
Saint Joseph (I.), Can.	110	46.15 N	83.5
Saint Joseph (L.), Can. (jō'zhûf)	97	51.31 N	90.4
Saint Joseph (R.), Mi. (sånt jȯ'sĕf)	110	41.45 N	85.5
Saint Joseph, B., Fl. (jō'zhûf)	126	29.48 N	85.2
Saint Joseph-de-Beauce, Can. (sĕN zhō-zĕf'dĕ bōs)	103	46.18 N	70.5
Saint Joseph-du-Lac, Can. (sĕN zhō-zĕf' dü läk)	95a	45.32 N	74.0
Saint Joseph I., Tx. (sånt jȯ-sĕf)	125	27.58 N	96.5
Saint Junien, Fr. (săN'zhü-nyăN')	168	45.53 N	0.5
Saint Kilda, Austl.	70b	37.52 S	144.5
Saint Kilda (I.), Scot. (kĭl'dȧ)	162	57.10 N	8.3
Saint Kitts (I.), Saint Kitts-Nevis (sānt kĭtts)	129	17.24 N	63.3
Saint Lambert, Can. (săN' läN-bĕr') (sånt lăm'bērt)	95a	45.29 N	73.2
Saint Lambert-de-Lévis, Can.	95b	46.35 N	71.1
Saint Laurent, Can. (săN'lō-rän)	95a	45.31 N	73.4
Saint Laurent, Fr. Gu.	143	5.27 N	53.5
Saint Laurent-d'Orleans, Can.	95b	46.52 N	71.0
Saint Lawrence, Can. (sānt lô'rĕns)	105	46.55 N	55.2
Saint Lawrence (I.), Ak. (sånt lô'rĕns)	107	63.10 N	172.1
Saint Lawrence, Gulf of, Can.	105	48.00 N	62.0
Saint Lawrence R. (Fleuve Saint-Laurent), Can.-U.S.	97	48.24 N	69.3
Saint Lazare, Can. (săN'lȧ-zȧr')	95b	46.39 N	70.4
Saint Lazare-de-Vaudreuil, Can.	95a	45.24 N	74.0
Saint Léger-en-Yvelines, Fr. (sȧN-lā-zhĕ'ĕN-nēv-lēn')	169b	48.43 N	1.4
Saint Leonard, Can. (sånt lĕn'ȧrd)	104	47.10 N	67.5
Saint Léonard, Can.	95a	45.36 N	73.3
Saint Leonard, Md.	112e	38.29 N	76.3
Saint-Lô, Fr. (săN'lō')	168	49.08 N	1.0
Saint Louis, Mi. (sånt lōō'ĭs)	110	43.25 N	84.3
Saint Louis, Mo. (sånt lōō'ĭs) (lōō'ė)	119e	38.39 N	90.1
Saint-Louis, Senegal	228	16.02 N	16.3
Saint Louis (R.), Mn. (sånt lōō'ĭs)	115	46.57 N	92.5
Saint Louis-de-Gonzague, Can. (săN' lōō ē')	95a	45.13 N	74.0
Saint Louis, Lac (L.), Can. (săN' lōō-ē')	95a	45.24 N	73.5
Saint Louis Park, Mn.	119g	44.56 N	93.2
Saint Lucia, N. A.	129	13.54 N	60.4
Saint Lucia Chan., N. A. (lū'shĭ-ȧ)	133b	14.15 N	61.0
Saint Lucie Can., Fl. (lū'sė)	127a	26.57 N	80.2
Saint Magnus B., Scot. (măg'nŭs)	162a	60.25 N	2.0
Saint Malo, Fr. (săN' mȧ-lȯ')	168	48.40 N	2.0
Saint Malo, Golfe de (G.), Fr. (gôlf-dĕ-sȧN-mä-lō')	168	48.50 N	2.4
Saint-Mandé, Fr.	64c	48.50 N	2.2
Saint Marc, Hai. (săN' mȧrk')	135	19.10 N	72.4
Saint-Marc, Canal de (Chan.), Hai.	135	19.05 N	73.1
Saint Marcellin, Fr. (mär-sĕ-lăN')	169	45.08 N	5.1
Saint Margarets, Md.	112e	39.02 N	76.3
Saint Maries, Id. (sånt mā'rēs)	116	47.18 N	116.3
Saint Martin I., Guad.-Neth-Antilles (mär'tĭn)	133b	18.06 N	62.5
Saint Martins, Can. (mär'tĭnz)	104	45.21 N	65.3
Saint Martinville, La. (mär'tĭn-vĭl)	125	30.08 N	91.5
Saint Mary, C., Gam.	228	13.28 N	16.4
Saint Mary (R.), Can. (mā'rė)	99	49.25 N	113.0
Saint Mary (Res.), Can.	99	49.30 N	113.0
Saint Mary Cray (Neigh.), Eng.	62	51.23 N	0.0
Saint Marylebone (Neigh.), Eng.	62	51.31 N	0.1
Saint Marys, Austl. (mā'rėz)	216	41.40 S	148.1
Saint Marys, Austl.	70a	33.47 S	150.4
Saint Marys, Can.	110	43.15 N	81.1
Saint Marys, Ga.	127	30.43 N	81.3
Saint Mary's, Ks.	123	39.12 N	96.0

ăt; finăl; rāte; senåte; ärm; ȧsk; sofȧ; fâre; ch-choose; dh-as th in other; bē; ėvent; bĕt; recĕnt; cratēr; g-gō; gh-guttural g; bĭt; ĭ-short neutral; rīde; K-guttural k as ch in German ich;

PRONOUNCING INDEX

Saint Mary's – San Angelo 339

PLACE (Pronounciation)	PAGE	Lat. °'	Long. °'
Saint Mary's, Oh.	110	40.30 N	84.25 W
Saint Marys, Pa.	111	41.25 N	78.30 W
Saint Marys, WV	110	39.20 N	81.15 W
Saint Mary's B., Can.	104	44.20 N	66.10 W
Saint Mary's B., Can.	105	46.50 N	53.47 W
Saint Marys Is., Can.	105	50.19 N	59.17 W
Saint Marys R., Can.-U.S.	119k	46.27 N	84.33 W
Saint Marys (R.), Ga.-Fl.	127	30.37 N	82.05 W
Saint Mathew, SC (măth'ū)	127	33.40 N	80.46 W
Saint Matthew (I.), Ak.	107	60.25 N	172.10 W
Saint Matthews, Ky. (măth'ūz)	113h	38.15 N	85.39 W
Saint Maur-des-Fossés, Fr.	169b	48.48 N	2.29 E
Saint-Maurice, Fr.	64c	48.49 N	2.25 E
Saint Maurice (R.), Can. (săN' mô-rēs') (sânt mô'rĭs)	104	47.20 N	72.55 W
Saint-Mesmes, Fr.	64c	48.59 N	2.42 E
Saint Michael, Ak. (sânt mī'kĕl)	107	63.22 N	162.20 W
Saint Michel, Can. (săN'mē-shĕl')	95b	46.52 N	70.54 W
Saint-Michel, Can.	54b	45.35 N	73.35 W
Saint Michel-de-l'Atalaye, Hai.	135	19.25 N	72.20 W
Saint Michel-de-Napierville, Can.	95a	45.14 N	73.34 W
Saint Mihiel, Fr. (săN' mē-yĕl')	169	48.53 N	5.30 E
Saint Moritz, Switz. (sânt mō'rĭts) (zăŋkt mō'rĭts)	166	46.31 N	9.50 E
Saint Nazaire, Fr. (săN'nà-zâr')	168	47.18 N	2.13 W
Saint Nérée, Can. (nā-rā')	95b	46.43 N	70.43 W
Saint Nicolas, Can. (ne-kô-lä')	95b	46.42 N	71.32 W
Saint Nicolas, Cap (C.), Hai.	135	19.45 N	73.35 W
Saint-Nom-la-Bretèche, Fr.	64c	48.51 N	2.01 E
Saint Omer, Fr. (săN'tô-mâr')	168	50.44 N	2.16 E
Saint-Ouen, Fr.	64c	48.54 N	2.20 E
Saint Pancras (Neigh.), Eng.	62	51.32 N	0.07 W
Saint Pascal, Can. (sĕN pă-skål')	104	47.32 N	69.48 W
Saint Paul, Can. (sânt pôl')	99	53.59 N	111.17 W
Saint Paul, Mn.	119g	44.57 N	93.05 W
Saint Paul, Ne.	114	41.13 N	98.28 W
Saint Paul (I.), Ak.	107	57.10 N	170.20 W
Saint Paul (R.), Lib.	228	7.10 N	10.00 W
Saint Paul I, Can.	105	47.15 N	60.10 W
Saint Paul, Île (I.), Ind. O.	232	38.43 S	77.31 E
Saint Paul Park, Mn. (pärk)	119g	44.51 N	93.00 W
Saint Pauls, NC (pôls)	127	34.47 N	78.57 W
Saint Paul's Cathedral (P. Int.), Eng.	62	51.31 N	0.06 W
Saint Paul's Cray (Neigh.), Eng.	62	51.24 N	0.07 E
Saint Peter, Mn. (pē tēr)	115	44.20 N	93.56 W
Saint Peter Port, Guernsey	168	49.27 N	2.35 W
Saint Petersburg, Fl. (pē'tērz-bûrg)	127a	27.47 N	82.38 W
Saint Philémon, Can. (sĕN fēl-mōN')	95b	46.41 N	70.28 W
Saint Philippe-d'Argenteuil, Can. (săn'fe-lēp')	95a	45.20 N	73.28 W
Saint Philippe-de-Lapairie, Can.	95a	45.38 N	74.25 W
Saint-Pierre, Can.	54b	45.27 N	73.39 W
Saint Pierre, Mart. (săn'pyâr')	133b	14.45 N	61.12 W
Saint Pierre (I.), Saint Pierre & Miquelon	105	46.47 N	56.11 W
Saint Pierre-d'Orléans, Can.	95b	46.53 N	71.04 W
Saint Pierre, Lac (L.), Can.	104	46.07 N	72.45 W
Saint Pierre & Miquelon, N. A.	105	46.53 N	56.40 W
Saint Pierre-Montmagny, Can.	95b	46.55 N	70.37 W
Saint Placide, Can. (plăs'ĭd)	95a	45.32 N	74.11 W
Saint Pol-de-Léon, Fr. (săN-pô'dĕ-lā-ôN')	168	48.41 N	4.00 W
Saint Pölten, Aus. (zăŋkt-pûl'tĕn)	166	48.12 N	15.38 E
Saint-Prix, Fr.	64c	49.01 N	2.16 E
Saint Quentin, Fr. (săN'käN-tăN')	168	49.52 N	3.16 E
Saint Raphaël, Can. (rä-fà-él')	95b	46.48 N	70.46 W
Saint Raymond, Can. (săN' rā-mōN') (sânt rā'mŭnd)	104	46.50 N	71.51 W
Saint Rédempteur, Can. (săN rā-däNp-tûr')	95b	46.42 N	71.18 W
Saint Rémi, Can. (sĕN rē-mē')	95a	45.15 N	73.36 W
Saint-Rémy-lès-Chevreuse, Fr.	64c	48.42 N	2.04 E
Saint Romuald-d'Etchemin, Can. (sĕN rŏ'mōō-äl)	95b	46.45 N	71.14 W
Saint Siméon, Can.	104	47.51 N	69.55 W
Saint Stanislas-de-Kostka, Can. (sĕN stä-nēs-läz' de kōst'kä)	95a	45.11 N	74.08 W
Saint Stephen, Can. (stē'vĕn)	104	45.12 N	66.17 W
Saint Sulpice, Can.	95a	45.50 N	73.21 W
Saint Thérèse-de-Blainville, Can. (tĕ-rĕz' dĕ blĕN-vēl')	95a	45.38 N	73.51 W
Saint-Thibault-des-Vignes, Fr.	64c	48.52 N	2.41 E
Saint Thomas, Can. (tŏm'ăs)	110	42.45 N	81.15 W
Saint Thomas (I.), Vir. Is. (U.S.A.)	129c	18.22 N	64.57 W
Saint Thomas Hbr., Vir. Is. (U.S.A.) (tŏm'ăs)	129c	18.19 N	64.56 W
Saint Thomas, see Charlotte Amalie			
Saint Timothée, Can. (tē-mô-tā')	95a	45.17 N	74.03 W
Saint Tropez, Fr. (trô-pĕ')	169	43.15 N	6.42 E
Saint Valentin, Can. (väl-ĕn-tīn)	95a	45.07 N	73.19 W
Saint Valéry-sur-Somme, Fr. (vá-lā-rē')	168	50.10 N	1.39 E
Saint Vallier, Can. (väl-yā')	95b	46.54 N	70.49 W
Saint Veit, Aus. (zăŋkt vīt')	166	46.46 N	14.20 E
Saint Victor, Can. (vĭk'tēr)	104	46.09 N	70.56 W
Saint Vincent and the Grenadines, N. A.	129	13.20 N	60.50 W
Saint-Vincent-de-Paul (Neigh.) Can.	54b	45.37 N	73.39 W
Saint Vincent, G., Austl. (vĭn'sĕnt)	216	34.55 S	138.00 E
Saint Vincent Pass, N. A.	133b	13.35 N	61.10 W
Saint Walburg, Can.	100	53.39 N	109.12 W
Saint Yrieix-la-Perche, Fr. (ē-rē-ĕ)	168	45.30 N	1.08 E
Saitama (Pref.), Jap. (sī'tä-mä)	205a	35.52 N	139.40 E
Saitbaba, Sov. Un. (sá-ĕt'bá-bá)	182a	54.06 N	56.42 E
Saïda, Alg. (sä'ē-dà)	224	34.51 N	00.07 E
Sajama, Nevada (Pk.), Bol. (nĕ-vá'dä-sä-há'mä)	142	18.13 S	68.53 W
Sakai, Jap. (sä'kä-ē)	205b	34.34 N	135.28 E
Sakaiminato, Jap.	205	35.33 N	133.15 E
Sakākah, Sau. Ar.	192	29.58 N	40.03 E
Sakakawea, Lake, ND	114	47.49 N	101.58 W
Sakania, Zaire (sá-kä'nĭ-á)	231	12.45 S	28.34 E
Sakarya (R.), Tur. (sá-kär'yá)	179	40.10 N	31.00 E
Sakata, Jap. (sä'kä-tä)	204	38.56 N	139.57 E
Sakchu, Kor. (säk'chōō)	204	40.29 N	125.09 E
Sakhalin (I.), Sov. Un. (sá-ká-lēn')	181	51.52 N	144.15 E
Šakiai, Sov. Un. (shä'kĭ-ī)	165	54.59 N	23.05 E
Sakishima-Gunto (Is.), Jap. (sä'kē-shē'ma gōōn'tō')	203	24.25 N	125.00 E
Sakmara (R.), Sov. Un.	179	52.00 N	56.10 E
Sakomet R., RI (sä-kō'mĕt)	112b	41.32 N	71.11 W
Sakurai, Jap.	205b	34.31 N	135.51 E
Sakwaso L., Can. (sá-kwá'sō)	101	53.01 N	91.55 W
Sal (R.), Sov. Un. (sál)	179	47.20 N	42.10 E
Sala, Swe. (sô'lä)	164	59.56 N	16.34 E
Sala Consilina, It. (sä'lä kôn-sē-lē'nä)	172	40.24 N	15.38 E
Salada, Laguna (L.), Mex. (lä-gōō'nä-sä-lä'dä)	120	32.34 N	115.45 W
Saladillo, Arg. (sä-lä-dēl'yô)	141c	35.38 S	59.48 W
Salado, Hong. (sä-lä'dhō)	132	15.44 N	87.03 W
Salado (R.), Arg. (sä-lä'dô)	144	26.05 S	63.35 W
Salado (R.), Arg.	141c	35.53 S	58.12 W
Salado (R.), Mex. (sä-lä'dô)	131	18.30 N	97.29 W
Salado Cr., Tx.	119d	29.23 N	98.25 W
Salado de los Nadadores Rio (R.), Mex. (dĕ-lôs-nä-dä-dō'rĕs)	124	27.26 N	101.35 W
Salado, Rio (R.), Mex. (rē'ō)	124	26.55 N	99.36 W
Salal, Chad	229	14.51 N	17.13 E
Salamá, Guat. (sä-lä'mä)	132	15.06 N	90.19 W
Salamá, Hond. (sä-lä-mä')	132	14.43 N	86.30 W
Salamanca, Chile (sä-lä-mä'n-kä)	141b	31.48 S	70.57 W
Salamanca, Mex.	130	20.36 N	101.10 W
Salamanca, NY (săl-á-măŋ'ká)	111	42.10 N	78.45 W
Salamanca, Sp. (sä-lä-mä'n-ká)	170	40.54 N	5.42 W
Salamat, Bahr (R.), Chad. (bär sä-lä-mät')	225	10.06 N	19.16 E
Salamina, Col. (sä-lä-mē'-nä)	142a	5.25 N	75.29 W
Salamis, Grc. (săl'á-mĭs)	173	37.58 N	23.30 E
Salat-la-Canada, Fr.	168	44.52 N	1.13 E
Salaverry, Peru (sä-lä-vä'rē)	142	8.16 S	78.54 W
Salawati (I.), Indon. (sä-lä-wä'tē)	207	1.22 N	130.15 E
Salawe, Tan.	231	3.19 S	32.52 E
Sala-y-Gómez I. Chile	209	26.50 S	105.50 W
Sal, Cay (I.), Ba. (kē săl)	134	23.45 N	80.25 W
Salcedo, Dom. Rep. (säl-sä'dō)	135	19.25 N	70.30 W
Saldaña (R.), Col. (säl-dá'n-yä)	142a	3.42 N	75.16 W
Saldanha, S. Afr.	226	32.55 S	18.05 E
Saldus, Sov. Un. (sál'dŏŏs)	165	56.39 N	22.30 E
Sale, Austl. (sāl)	216	38.10 S	147.07 E
Sale, Eng.	156	53.24 N	2.20 W
Salé, Mor. (sá-lā')	224	34.09 N	6.42 W
Sale (R.), Can. (sál'rē-vyâr')	95f	49.44 N	97.11 W
Salekhard, Sov. Un. (sŭ-lyĭ-kärt)	178	66.35 N	66.50 E
Salem, Il. (sā'lĕm)	110	38.40 N	89.00 W
Salem, India	197	11.39 N	78.11 E
Salem, In.	110	38.35 N	86.00 W
Salem, Ma.	105a	42.31 N	70.54 W
Salem, Mo.	123	37.36 N	91.33 W
Salem, NH	105a	42.46 N	71.16 W
Salem, NJ	111	39.35 N	75.30 W
Salem, Oh.	110	40.55 N	80.50 W
Salem, Or.	116	44.55 N	123.03 W
Salem, S. Afr.	227c	33.29 S	26.30 E
Salem, SD	114	43.43 N	97.23 W
Salem, Va.	127	37.16 N	80.05 W
Salem, WV	110	39.15 N	80.35 W
Salemi, It. (sä-lå'mē)	172	37.49 N	12.48 E
Salerno, It. (sä-lĕr'nô)	171c	40.27 N	14.46 E
Salerno, Golfo di (G.), It. (gôl-fô-dē)	172	40.30 N	14.40 E
Salford, Eng. (săl'fērd)	156	53.26 N	2.19 W
Salgir (R.), Sov. Un. (sál'gēr)	175	45.25 N	34.22 E
Salgótarján, Hung. (shôl'gô-tôr-yän)	167	48.06 N	19.50 E
Sal. I., C. V. Is. (säal)	224b	16.45 N	22.39 W
Salida, Co. (sá-lī'dá)	122	38.31 N	106.01 W
Salies-de-Béan, Fr.	168	43.27 N	0.58 W
Salima, Malawi	231	13.47 S	34.26 E
Salina (I.), It. (sä-lē'nä)	172	38.35 N	14.48 E
Salina, Ks. (sá-lī'ná)	123	38.50 N	97.37 W
Salina, Ut.	121	39.00 N	111.55 W
Salina Cruz, Mex. (sä-lē'nä krōōz')	131	16.10 N	95.12 W
Salina Pt., Ba.	135	22.10 N	74.20 W
Salinas, Ca. (sá-lē'nás)	120	36.41 N	121.40 W
Salinas, Mex.	130	22.38 N	101.42 W
Salinas, P. R.	129b	17.58 N	66.16 W
Salinas (R.), Ca.	120	36.33 N	121.29 W
Salinas (R.), Mex. (sä-lē'näs)	131	16.15 N	90.31 W
Salinas, Bahia de (B.), Nic.-C. R. (bä-ē'ä-dĕ-sá-lē'nás)	132	11.05 N	85.55 W
Salinas, Cape, Sp. (sä-lēnäs)	171	39.14 N	1.02 E
Salinas Victoria, Mex. (sä-lē'näs vēk-tō'rē-ä)	124	25.59 N	100.19 W
Saline (R.), Ak. (sá-lēn')	123	34.06 N	92.30 W
Saline (R.), Ks.	122	39.05 N	99.43 W
Salins-les-Bains, Fr. (sá-lăN'-lā-băN')	169	46.55 N	5.54 E
Salisbury, Can.	104	46.03 N	65.05 W
Salisbury, Eng. (sôlz'bē-rē)	162	50.35 N	1.51 W
Salisbury, Md.	111	38.20 N	75.40 W
Salisbury, Mo.	123	39.24 N	92.47 W
Salisbury, NC	127	35.40 N	80.29 W
Salisbury, see Harare			
Salisbury (I.), Can.	97	63.36 N	76.20 W
Salisbury Plain, Eng.	162	51.15 N	1.52 W
Salkehatchie (R.), SC (sô-kē-hăch'ē)	127	33.09 N	81.10 W
Salkhia, India	67a	22.35 N	88.21 E
Sallisaw, Ok. (săl'ĭ-sô)	123	35.27 N	94.48 W
Salmon, Id. (săm'ŭn)	117	45.11 N	113.54 W
Salmon (R.), Can.	104	46.19 N	65.36 W
Salmon (R.), Can.	98	54.00 N	123.50 W
Salmon (R.), Id.	116	45.30 N	115.45 W
Salmon (R.), Middle Fork, Id.	116	44.54 N	114.50 W
Salmon (R.), NY	111	44.35 N	74.15 W
Salmon (R.), South Fork, Id.	116	44.51 N	115.47 W
Salmon (R.), Wa.	118c	45.44 N	122.36 W
Salmon Arm, Can.	99	50.42 N	119.16 W
Salmon Falls (R.), Id.	116	42.22 N	114.53 W
Salmon Gums, Austl. (gŭmz)	214	33.00 S	122.00 E
Salmon River Mts., Id.	116	44.15 N	115.44 W
Salon-de-Provence, Fr. (sá-lôN-dē-prô-văNs')	169	43.48 N	5.09 E
Salonta, Rom. (sä-lôn'tä)	167	46.46 N	21.38 E
Salop (Co.), Eng.	156	52.36 N	2.45 W
Saloum (R.), Senegal	228	14.10 N	15.45 W
Salsette I., India	197b	19.12 N	72.52 E
Sal'sk, Sov. Un. (sälsk)	179	46.30 N	41.20 E
Salt, (R.), Az. (sôlt)	121	33.28 N	111.35 W
Salt (R.), Mo.	123	39.54 N	92.11 W
Salta, Arg. (säl'tä)	144	24.50 S	65.16 W
Salta (Prov.), Arg.	144	25.15 S	65.00 W
Saltair, Ut. (sôlt'âr)	119b	40.46 N	112.09 W
Salt Cay (I.), Turks & Caicos Is.	135	21.20 N	71.15 W
Salt Cr., Il. (sôlt)	113a	42.01 N	88.01 W
Saltillo, Mex. (säl-tēl'yo-mc)	124	25.24 N	100.59 W
Salt Lake City, Ut. (sôlt lāk sĭ'tĭ)	119b	40.45 N	111.52 W
Salto, Arg. (säl'tō)	141c	34.17 S	60.15 W
Salto, Ur.	144	31.18 S	57.45 W
Salto (R.), Mex.	130	22.16 N	99.18 W
Salto Grande, Braz. (grän'dā)	143	22.57 S	49.58 W
Salton Sea, Ca. (sôlt'ŭn)	120	33.28 N	115.43 W
Salto, Serra do (Mtn.), Braz. (sĕ'r-rä-dô)	141a	20.26 S	43.28 W
Saltpond, Ghana	224	5.16 N	1.07 W
Salt River Ind. Res., Az. (sôlt rĭv'ēr)	121	33.40 N	112.01 W
Saltsjöbaden, Swe. (sält'shû-bäd'ĕn)	164	59.15 N	18.20 E
Saltspring I, Can. (sâlt'sprĭng)	98	48.47 N	123.30 W
Saltville, Va. (sôlt'vĭl)	127	36.50 N	81.45 W
Saltykovka, Sov. Un. (sál-tĕ'kôf-ká)	182b	55.45 N	37.56 E
Saluda, SC (sá-lōō'dá)	127	34.02 N	81.46 W
Saluda (R.), SC	127	34.07 N	81.48 W
Salud, Mt., Pan. (sä-lōō'th)	128a	9.14 N	79.42 W
Saluzzo, It. (sä-lōōt'sō)	172	44.39 N	7.31 E
Salvador (Bahia), Braz. (säl-vä-dōr') (bä-ē'á)	143	12.59 S	38.27 W
Salvador L., La.	125	29.45 N	90.20 W
Salvador Pt., Ba.	134	24.30 N	77.45 W
Salvatierra, Mex. (säl-vä-tyĕr'rä)	130	20.13 N	100.52 W
Salwā Baḩrī, Egypt	223b	24.43 N	32.58 E
Salween R., Bur. (săl-wēn')	198	26.46 N	98.19 E
Sal'yany, Sov. Un.	179	39.40 N	49.10 E
Salzburg, Aus. (sälts'bŏŏrgh)	166	47.48 N	13.04 E
Salzburg (State), Aus.	166	47.30 N	13.18 E
Salzwedel, G.D.R. (sälts-vā'dĕl)	166	52.51 N	11.10 E
Samāika (Neigh.), India	67d	28.32 N	77.05 E
Samālūt, Egypt (sä-mä-lōōt')	223b	28.17 N	30.43 E
Samaná, Dom. Rep. (sä-mä-nä')	135	19.15 N	69.25 W
Samana Cabo (C.), Dom. Rep. (ká'bô)	135	19.20 N	69.00 W
Samana or Atwood Cay (I.), Ba.	135	23.05 N	73.45 W
Samar (I.), Phil. (sä'mär)	207	11.30 N	126.07 E
Samara (R.), Sov. Un. (sá-mä'rá)	175	48.47 N	35.30 E
Samara (R.), Sov. Un.	179	52.50 N	50.35 E
Samarai, Pap. N. Gui. (sä-mä-rä'ē)	207	10.45 S	150.49 E
Samarkand, Sov. Un. (sá-már-känt')	180	39.42 N	67.00 E
Sāmarrā', Iraq	195	34.12 N	43.52 E
Samba, Zaire	231	4.38 S	26.22 E
Sambalpur, India (sŭm'bŭl-pŏŏr)	196	21.30 N	84.05 E
Sāmbhar (R.), India	196	27.00 N	74.58 E
Sambor, Sov. Un. (säm'bôr)	167	49.31 N	23.12 E
Samborombón (R.), Arg.	141c	35.20 S	57.52 W
Samborombón, Bahia (B.), Arg. (bä-ē'ä-säm-bô-rôm-bô'n)	141c	35.57 S	57.05 W
Sambre (R.), Bel. (säN'br')	163	50.20 N	4.15 E
Sambungo, Ang.	230	8.39 S	20.43 E
Sammamish (R.), Wa.	118a	47.43 N	122.08 W
Sammamish, L., Wa. (sá-măm'ĭsh)	118a	47.35 N	122.02 W
Samoa (I.), Oceania	208	15.00 S	170.00 W
Samokov, Bul. (sä'mô-kôf)	173	42.20 N	23.33 E
Samora Correia, Port. (sä-mō'rä-kôr-rĕ'yä)	171b	38.55 N	8.52 W
Samorovo, Sov. Un. (sá-má-rô'vô)	180	60.47 N	69.13 E
Sámos (I.), Grc. (sä'mŏs)	173	37.53 N	26.35 E
Samothráki (I.), Grc.	173	40.23 N	25.10 E
Sampaloc Pt., Phil. (säm-pä'lôk)	207a	14.43 N	119.56 E
Sam Rayburn Res, Tx.	125	31.10 N	94.15 W
Samsø (I.), Den. (säm'sû)	164	55.49 N	10.47 E
Samson, Al. (săm'sŭn)	126	31.06 N	86.02 W
Samsu, Kor. (säm'sōō')	204	41.12 N	128.00 E
Samsun, Tur. (säm'sōōn')	179	41.20 N	36.05 E
Samtredia, Sov. Un. (sám'trĕ-dē)	179	42.18 N	42.25 E
Samuel (I.), Can. (săm'ū-ĕl)	118d	48.50 N	123.10 W
Samur (R.), Sov. Un. (sä-mōōr')	179	41.40 N	47.20 E
San, Mali (sän)	228	13.18 N	4.54 W
Şan'ā', Yemen (sän'ä)	192	15.17 N	44.05 E
Sanaga (R.), Cam. (sä-nä'gä)	229	4.10 N	10.40 E
San Ambrosio, Isla (I.), Chile (ē's-lä-dĕ-sän äm-brō'zē-ō)	140	26.40 S	80.00 W
Sanana, Pulau (I.), Indon.	207	2.15 S	126.38 E
Sanandaj, Iran	192	36.44 N	46.43 E
San Andreas, Ca. (săn ăn'drē-ăs)	120	38.10 N	120.42 W
San Andreas (L.), Ca.	118b	37.36 N	122.26 W
San Andrés, Col. (sän-än-drĕ's)	142a	6.57 N	75.41 W
San Andrés, Mex. (sän än-drās')	131a	19.15 N	99.10 W
San Andrés (L.), see Petén, Laguna de			
San Andrés de Giles, Arg. (sän-än-drĕ's-dĕ-gē'lĕs)	141c	34.26 S	59.28 W
San Andres I., Col.	133	12.32 N	81.34 W
San Andres, Laguna de (L.), Mex.	131	22.40 N	97.50 W
San Andres Mts., NM	121	33.45 N	106.40 W
San Andres, Mts., U. S. (săn ăn'drē-ăs)	108	33.00 N	106.40 W
San Andrés Totoltepec, Mex.	60a	19.15 N	99.10 W
San Andrés Tuxtla, Mex. (sän-än-drā's-tōōs'tlä)	131	18.27 N	95.12 W
San Angelo, Tx. (săn ăn'jĕ-lō)	124	31.28 N	100.22 W

340 San Antioco – San Juan Martinez

PLACE (Pronounciation)	PAGE	Lat. °′	Long. °′
San Antioco, I. di, It. (ē'sō-lä-dē-sän-än-tyō'kô)	172	39.00 N	8.25 E
San Antonio, Chile (sän-àn-tô'nyō)	141b	33.34 S	71.36 W
San Antonio, Col.	142a	2.57 N	75.06 W
San Antonio, Col.	142a	3.55 N	75.28 W
San Antonio, Phil.	207a	14.57 N	120.05 E
San Antonio, Tx. (săn ăn-tō'nē-ō)	119d	29.25 N	98.30 W
San Antonio (R.), Ca.	120	36.00 N	121.13 W
San Antonio Abad, Sp. (sän än-tō'nyô ä-bädh')	171	38.59 N	1.17 E
San Antonio B., Tx.	125	28.20 N	97.08 W
San Antonio, Cabo (C.), Cuba (kà'bô-sän-än-tô'nyô)	134	21.55 N	84.55 W
San Antonio de Areco, Arg. (dā ä-rā'kô)	141c	34.16 S	59.30 W
San Antonio de Galipán, Ven.	61a	10.33 N	66.53 W
San Antonio de las Vegas, Cuba (sän än-tō'nyô-dĕ-läs-vĕ'gäs)	135a	22.51 N	82.16 W
San Antonio de los Baños, Cuba (dā lōs bän'yōs)	135a	22.54 N	82.30 W
San Antonio de los Cobres, Arg. (dā lōs kō'brās)	144	24.15 S	66.29 W
San Antônio de Pádua, Braz. (dĕ-pà'dwä)	141a	21.32 S	42.09 W
San Antonio de Tamanaco, Ven. (sän-àn-tô-nyō-dĕ-tà-mä-nà'kô)	143b	9.42 N	66.03 W
San Antonio Heights, Ca.	59	34.10 N	117.40 W
San Antonio Oeste, Arg. (sän-nä-tō'nyô ô-ĕs'tā)	144	40.49 S	64.56 W
San Antonio Pk., Ca. (săn ăn-tō'nĭ-ō)	119a	34.17 N	117.39 W
San Antonio R., Tx.	124	29.00 N	97.58 W
Sanarate, Guat. (sä-nä-rä'tĕ)	132	14.47 N	90.12 W
San Augustine, Tx. (săn ô'gŭs-tēn)	125	31.33 N	94.08 W
San Bartolo, Mex. (sän bär-tō'lô)	131a	19.36 N	99.43 W
San Bartolo, Mex.	124	24.43 N	103.12 W
San Bartolomé de la Cuadra, Sp.	65e	41.26 N	2.02 E
San Bartolomeo, It. (bär-tô-lô-mā'ô)	172	41.25 N	15.04 E
San Baudilio de Llobregat, Sp.	65e	41.21 N	2.03 E
San Benedetto del Tronto, It. (bā'nā-dĕt'tô dĕl trōn'tô)	172	42.58 N	13.54 E
San Benito, Tx. (săn bĕ-nē'tô)	125	26.07 N	97.37 W
San Benito (R.), Ca.	120	36.40 N	121.20 W
San Bernardino, Ca. (bûr-när-dē'nô)	119a	34.07 N	117.19 W
San Bernardino Mts., Ca.	120	34.05 N	116.23 W
San Bernardo, Chile (sän bĕr-när'dô)	141b	33.35 S	70.42 W
San Blas, Mex. (sän bläs')	130	21.33 N	105.19 W
San Blas, C., Fl.	126	29.38 N	85.38 W
San Blas, Cord. de (Mts.), Pan. (kôr-dēl-yĕ'rä-dĕ)	133	9.17 N	78.20 W
San Blas,Golfo de (G.), Pan.	133	9.33 N	78.42 W
San Blas, Punta (Pt.), Pan.	133	9.35 N	78.55 W
San Bruno, Ca. (săn brū-nō)	118b	37.38 N	122.25 W
San Buenaventura, Mex. (bwā'nà-vĕn-tōō'rà)	124	27.07 N	101.30 W
San Carlos, Ca. (săn kär'lōs)	118b	37.30 N	122.15 W
San Carlos, Chile (sän-kà'r-lōs')	144	36.23 S	71.58 W
San Carlos, Col.	142a	6.11 N	74.58 W
San Carlos, Equat. Gui.	230	3.27 N	8.33 E
San Carlos, Mex. (sän kär'lōs)	131	17.49 N	92.33 W
San Carlos, Mex.	124	24.36 N	98.52 W
San Carlos, Nic. (sän-kä'r-lôs)	133	11.08 N	84.48 W
San Carlos, Phil.	207a	15.56 N	120.20 E
San Carlos, Ven.	142	9.36 N	68.35 W
San Carlos de Bariloche, Arg. (sän-kà'r lōs-dĕ-bä-rē' lô'chĕ)	144	41.15 S	71.26 W
San Carlos Ind. Res, Az. (săn kär'lōs)	121	33.27 N	110.15 W
San Carlos R., C. R.	133	10.36 N	84.18 W
San Carlos Res, Az.	121	33.05 N	110.29 W
San Casimiro, Ven. (kä-sē-mē'rō)	143b	10.01 N	67.02 W
San Cataldo, It. (kä-täl'dō)	172	37.30 N	13.59 E
Sánchez, Dom. Rep. (sän'chĕz)	135	19.15 N	69.40 W
Sanchez, Río de los (R.), Mex. (rē'ō-dĕ-lôs)	130	20.31 N	102.29 W
Sánchez Román (Tlaltenango), Mex. (rô-mà'n) (tlä'l-tĕ-nän-gō)	130	21.48 N	103.20 W
Sanchung, Taiwan	68d	25.04 N	121.29 E
San Clemente, Sp. (sän klå-mĕn'tå)	170	39.25 N	2.24 W
San Clemente (I.), Ca.	120	33.02 N	118.36 W
San Clemente de Llobregat, Sp.	65e	41.20 N	2.00 E
San Cristobal, Dom. Rep. (krēs-tō'bäl)	135	18.25 N	70.05 W
San Cristóbal, Guat.	132	15.22 N	90.26 W
San Cristóbal, Ven.	142	7.43 N	72.15 W
San Cristobal (I.), Ec.	142	1.05 S	89.15 W
San Cristobal (I.), Sol. Is.	215	10.47 S	162.17 E
Sancti Spíritus, Cuba (säŋk'tē spē'rē-tōōs)	134	21.55 N	79.25 W
Sancti Spiritus (Prov.), Cuba	134	22.05 N	79.20 W
San Cugat del Vallés, Sp.	65e	41.28 N	2.05 E
Sancy, Puy de (Pk.), Fr. (pwē-dĕ-säN-sē')	168	45.30 N	2.53 E
Sand (I.), Or. (sănd)	118c	46.16 N	124.01 W
Sand (I.), Wi.	115	46.03 N	91.09 W
Sand (R.), S. Afr.	223d	28.09 S	26.46 E
Sand (R.), S. Afr.	227c	28.30 S	29.30 E
Sanda, Jap. (sän'dä)	205b	34.53 N	135.14 E
Sandakan, Mala. (sàn-dä'kàn)	206	5.51 N	118.03 E
Sanday (I.), Scot. (sănd'ā)	162a	59.17 N	2.25 W
Sandbach, Scot. (sănd'băch)	156	53.08 N	2.22 W
Sandefjord, Nor. (sän'dĕ-fyôr')	164	59.09 N	10.14 E
San de Fuca, Wa. (de-fōō-cä)	118a	48.14 N	122.44 W
Sanders, Az.	121	35.13 N	109.20 W
Sanderson, Tx. (săn'dĕr-sŭn)	124	30.09 N	102.24 W
Sanderstead (Neigh.), Eng.	62	51.20 N	0.05 W
Sandersville, Ga. (săn'dĕrz-vĭl)	126	32.57 N	82.50 W
Sandhammar, C., Swe. (sänt'häm-màr)	164	55.24 N	14.37 E
Sand Hills (Reg.), Ne. (sănd)	114	41.57 N	101.29 W
Sand Hook, NJ (sănd hŏŏk)	112a	40.29 N	74.05 W
Sandhurst, Eng. (sănd'hûrst)	156b	51.20 N	0.48 W
San Diego, Ca. (săn dē-ā'gô)	120a	32.43 N	117.10 W
San Diego, Tx.	122	27.47 N	98.13 W
San Diego (R.), Ca.	120	32.53 N	116.57 W
San Diego de la Unión, Mex. (sän dē-ā-gô dā lä ōō-nyōn')	130	21.27 N	100.52 W
Sandies Cr., Tx. (sănd'ēz)	125	29.13 N	97.34 W
San Dimas, Ca. (săn dē-màs)	119a	34.07 N	117.49 W
San Dimas, Mex. (dē-mäs')	122	24.08 N	105.57 W
Sandnes, Nor. (sänd'nĕs)	164	58.52 N	5.44 E
Sandoa, Zaire (sän-dō'à)	226	9.39 S	23.00 E
Sandomierz, Pol. (sàn-dô'myĕzh)	167	50.39 N	21.45 E
San Doná di Piave, It. (sän dô nà' dē pyä'vē)	172	45.38 N	12.34 E
Sandoway, Bur. (sän-dô-wī')	198	18.24 N	94.28 E
Sandpoint, Id. (sănd point)	116	48.17 N	116.34 W
Sandringham, Austl. (săn'drĭng-ăm)	211a	37.57 S	145.01 E
Sandringham (Neigh.), S. Afr.	71b	26.09 S	28.07 E
Sandrio, It. (sä'n-dryô)	172	46.11 N	9.53 E
Sands Point, NY	55	40.51 N	73.43 W
Sand Springs, Ok. (sănd sprĭnz)	123	36.08 N	96.06 W
Sandstone, Austl. (sănd'stōn)	214	28.00 S	119.25 E
Sandstone, Mn.	113	46.08 N	92.53 W
Sanduo, China (sän-dwō)	200	32.49 N	119.39 E
Sandusky, Al. (săn-dŭs'kē)	112h	33.32 N	86.50 W
Sandusky, Mi.	110	43.25 N	82.50 W
Sandusky, Oh.	110	41.25 N	82.45 W
Sandusky (R.), Oh.	110	41.10 N	83.20 W
Sandwich, Il. (sănd'wĭch)	110	42.35 N	88.53 W
Sandy, Or. (sănd'ē)	118c	45.24 N	122.16 W
Sandy, Ut.	119b	40.36 N	111.53 W
Sandy C., Austl.	216	24.25 S	153.10 E
Sandy Cr., Wy.	117	42.08 N	109.35 W
Sandy (R.), Or.	118c	45.28 N	122.17 W
Sandy Hook, Ct. (hŏŏk)	112a	41.25 N	73.17 W
Sandy L., Can.	95g	53.46 N	113.58 W
Sandy L., Can.	101	53.00 N	93.07 W
Sandy L., Can.	105	49.16 N	57.00 W
Sandy Point, Tx.	125a	29.22 N	95.27 W
Sandy Pt., Wa.	118d	48.48 N	122.42 W
Sandy Springs, Ga. (springz)	112c	33.55 N	84.23 W
San Enrique, Arg. (sän-ĕn-rē'kĕ)	141c	35.47 S	60.22 W
San Estanislao, Par. (ĕs-tä-nēs-lä'ō)	144	24.38 S	56.20 W
San Esteban, Hond. (ĕs-tĕ'bän)	132	15.13 N	85.53 W
San Fabian, Phil. (fä-byä'n)	207a	16.14 N	120.28 E
San Felipe, Chile (fĕ-lē'pā)	141b	32.45 S	70.43 W
San Felipe, Mex. (fĕ-lē'pĕ)	130	21.29 N	101.13 W
San Felipe, Mex.	130	22.21 N	105.26 W
San Felipe, Ven. (fĕ-lē'pĕ)	142	10.13 N	68.45 W
San Felipe, Cayos de (Is.), Cuba (kä'yōs-dĕ-sän-fĕ-lē'pĕ)	134	22.00 N	83.30 W
San Felipe, Cr., Ca. (săn fĕ-lēp'ā)	120	33.10 N	116.03 W
San Felipe Terremotos, Mex.	60a	19.22 N	99.04 W
San Feliu de Guixols, Sp. (sän fā-lē'ōō dā gē-hôls)	171	41.45 N	3.01 E
San Feliu de Llobregat, Sp.	65e	41.23 N	2.03 E
San Félix, Isla (I.), Chile (ē's-lä-dĕ-sän fā-lēks')	140	26.20 S	80.10 W
San Fernanda, Sp. (fĕr-nä'n-dä)	170	36.28 N	6.13 W
San Fernando, Arg. (fĕr-nà'n-dô)	144a	34.11 S	58.34 W
San Fernando, Ca. (fĕr-nän'dō)	119a	34.17 N	118.27 W
San Fernando, Chile	141b	36.36 S	70.58 W
San Fernando, Mex. (fĕr-nän'dô)	124	24.52 N	98.10 W
San Fernando, Phil. (sän fĕr-nä'n-dô)	207a	16.38 N	120.19 E
San Fernando de Apure, Ven. (sän-fĕr-nä'n-dō-dĕ-ä-pōō'rå)	142	7.46 N	67.29 W
San Fernando de Atabapo, Ven. (dĕ-ä-tä-bä'pô)	142	3.58 N	67.41 W
San Fernando de Henares, Sp. (dĕ-ā-nä'rås)	171a	40.23 N	3.31 W
San Fernando R., Mex. (sän fĕr-nän'dô)	124	25.07 N	98.25 W
Sånfjället (Mtn.), Swe.	164	62.19 N	13.30 E
Sanford, Can. (săn'fērd)	95f	49.41 N	97.27 W
Sanford, Fl. (săn'fôrd)	127a	28.46 N	81.18 W
Sanford, Me. (săn'fērd)	104	43.26 N	70.47 W
Sanford, NC	127	35.26 N	79.10 W
San Francisco, Arg. (sän frän'sĭs'kô)	144	31.23 S	62.09 W
San Francisco, Ca.	118b	37.45 N	122.26 W
San Francisco, Sal.	132	13.48 N	88.11 W
San Francisco (R.), NM	121	33.35 N	108.55 W
San Francisco B., Ca. (săn frăn'sĭs'kô)	118b	37.45 N	122.21 W
San Francisco Culhuacán, Mex.	60a	19.20 N	99.06 W
San Francisco del Oro, Mex. (dĕl ō'rō)	128	27.00 N	106.37 W
San Francisco del Rincón, Mex. (dĕl rēn-kōn')	130	21.01 N	101.51 W
San Francisco de Macaira, Ven. (dĕ-mä-kī'rä)	143b	9.58 N	66.17 W
San Francisco de Macoris, Dom. Rep. (dā-mä-kō'rēs)	135	19.20 N	70.15 W
San Francisco de Paula, Cuba (dā pou'là)	135a	23.04 N	82.18 W
San Francisco el Grande, Iglesia de (P. Int.), Sp.	65b	40.25 N	3.43 W
San Francisco, see Ixhuatán			
San Gabriel, Ca. (săn gä-brē-ēl') (gā'brē-ĕl)	119a	34.06 N	118.06 W
San Gabriel Chilac, Mex. (sän-gä-brē-ĕl-chē-läk')	130	18.19 N	97.22 W
San Gabriel Mts, Ca.	119a	34.17 N	118.03 W
San Gabriel R., Ca.	119a	33.47 N	118.06 W
San Gabriel Res., Ca.	119a	34.14 N	117.48 W
Sangamon (R.), Il. (săn'gà-mŭn)	123	40.08 N	90.08 W
Sangenjaya (Neigh.), Jap.	69a	35.38 N	139.40 E
Sanger, Ca. (săng'ēr)	120	36.42 N	119.33 W
Sangerhausen, G.D.R. (säng'ĕr-hou-zĕn)	166	51.28 N	11.17 E
Sangha (R.), Afr.	229	2.40 N	16.10 E
Sangihe Pulau (I.), Indon. (säŋ'gē-ā)	207	3.30 N	125.30 E
San Gil, Col. (sän-Kē'l)	142	6.32 N	73.13 W
San Giovanni in Fiore, It. (sän jô-vän'nē ēn fyō'rå)	172	39.15 N	16.40 E
San Giuseppe Vesuviano, It. (sän-zhĕōō-sĕ'p-pĕ-vĕ-sōō-vyà'nô)	171c	40.36 N	14.31 E
Sangju, Kor. (säng'jōō')	204	36.20 N	128.07 E
Sāngli, India	197	16.56 N	74.38 E
Sangmélima, Cam.	229	2.56 N	11.59 E
San Gorgonio Mt., Ca. (săn gôr-gō'nĭ-ō)	119a	34.06 N	116.50 W
Sangre De Cristo Ra., U. S. (săng'ēr-de-krēs-tō)	108	37.45 N	105.50 W
San Gregoria, Ca. (săn grĕ-gôr'ā)	118b	37.20 N	122.23 W
San Gregorio Atlapulco, Mex.	60a	19.15 N	99.03 W
Sangro (R.), It. (säŋ'grô)	172	41.38 N	13.56 E
Sangüesa, Sp. (sän-gwĕ'sä)	170	42.36 N	1.15 W
Sanhe, China (sän-hŭ)	200	39.59 N	117.06 E
Sanibel I., Fl. (săn'ĭ-bĕl)	127a	26.26 N	82.15 W
San Ignacio, Belize	132a	17.11 N	89.04 W
San Ildefonso, C. Phil. (sän-ēl-dĕ-fōn-sô)	207a	16.03 N	122.10 E
San Ildefonso o la Granja, Sp. (ō lä grän'khä)	170	40.54 N	4.02 W
San Ildefonso, see Villa Alta			
San Isidro, Arg. (ē-sē'drô)	144a	34.13 S	58.31 W
San Isidro, C.R.	133	9.24 N	83.43 W
San Isidro, Peru	60c	12.07 S	77.03 W
San Jacinto, Ca. (săn jà-sĭn'tô)	119a	33.47 N	116.57 W
San Jacinto, Phil. (sän hä-sēn'tô)	207a	12.33 N	123.43 E
San Jacinto (R.), West Fork, Tx.	125	30.35 N	95.37 W
San Jacinto R., Ca. (săn jà-sĭn'tô)	119a	33.44 N	117.14 W
San Jacinto R., Tx.	125	30.25 N	95.05 W
San Javier, Chile (sän-há-vē'ĕr)	141b	35.35 S	71.43 W
San Jerónimo, Mex.	131a	19.31 N	98.46 W
San Jerónimo de Juárez, Mex. (hå-rō'nē-mô då hwä'råz)	130	17.08 N	100.30 W
San Jerónimo Lídice, Mex.	60a	19.20 N	99.13 W
San Joaquin, Ven.	143b	10.16 N	67.47 W
San Joaquin (R.), Ca. (săn hwä-kēn')	120	37.10 N	120.51 W
San Joaquin Valley, Ca.	120	36.45 N	120.30 W
San Jorge, Golfo (G.), Arg. (gôl-fô-sän-Kô'r-Kĕ)	144	46.15 S	66.45 W
San José, Bol. (sän-hô-sā')	143	17.54 S	60.42 W
San Jose, Ca. (săn hô-zā')	118b	37.20 N	121.54 W
San Jose, C. R. (sän hô-sā')	133	9.57 N	84.05 W
San José, Guat.	132	13.56 N	90.49 W
San Jose, Phil.	207a	12.22 N	121.04 E
San Jose, Phil.	207a	15.49 N	120.57 E
San José, Ur. (hô-sĕ')	141c	34.20 S	56.43 W
San Jose (I.), Mex. (Kô-sĕ')	128	25.00 N	110.35 W
San Jose (R.), NM (săn hô-zā')	121	35.15 N	108.10 W
San José de Feliciano, Arg. (då ĕs-kē'nà)	144	30.26 S	58.44 W
San José de Galipán, Ven.	61a	10.35 N	66.54 W
San José de Gauribe, Ven. (sän-hô-sĕ'dĕ-gàōō-rē'bĕ)	143b	9.51 N	65.49 W
San Jose de las Lajas, Cuba (sän-Kô-sĕ'dĕ-läs-lä'käs)	135a	22.58 N	82.10 W
San José (Dept.), Ur.	141c	34.17 S	56.23 W
San Jose, Isla de (I.), Pan. (ē's-lä-dĕ-sän hō-sä')	133	8.17 N	79.20 W
San José Iturbide, Mex. (ē-tōōr-bē'dĕ)	130	21.00 N	100.24 W
San José (R.), Ur. (sän-hô-sĕ')	141c	34.05 S	56.47 W
San Juan, Arg. (hwän')	144	31.36 S	68.29 W
San Juan, Col. (hōōà'n)	142a	3.23 N	73.48 W
San Juan, Dom. Rep. (sän hwän')	135	18.50 N	71.15 W
San Juan, Phil.	207a	16.41 N	120.20 E
San Juan, P. R. (sän hwän')	129b	18.30 N	66.10 W
San Juan (Prov.), Arg.	144	31.00 S	69.30 W
San Juan (R.), Mex. (sän-hōō-än')	131	18.10 N	95.23 W
San Juan (R.), Ut.	121	37.10 N	110.30 W
San Juan Bautista, Par. (sän hwän' bou-tēs'tä)	144	26.48 S	57.09 W
San Juan, Cabezas de (C.), P. R.	129b	18.29 N	65.30 W
San Juan, Cabo (C.), Equat. Gui.	230	1.08 N	9.23 E
San Juan Capistrano, Mex. (sän-hōō-än' kä-pēs-trä'nô)	130	22.41 N	104.07 W
San Juan Cr., Ca. (săn hwän')	120	35.24 N	120.12 W
San Juan de Aragón, Mex.	60a	19.28 N	99.05 W
San Juan de Aragón, Bosque (P. Int.), Mex.	60a	19.28 N	99.04 W
San Juan de Aragón, Zoologico de (P. Int.), Mex.	60a	19.28 N	99.05 W
San Juan de Dios, Ven.	61a	10.35 N	66.57 W
San Juan de Guadalupe, Mex. (sän hwan då gwä-dhä-lōō'på)	124	24.37 N	102.43 W
San Juan del Monte, Phil.	68g	14.36 N	121.02 E
San Juan del Norte (Greytown), Nic. (dĕl nôr-tå) (grā'toun)	133	10.55 N	83.44 W
San Juan del Norte Bahia de (B.), Nic. (bä-ē'ä-dĕ-sän hwän dĕl nôr'tå)	133	11.12 N	83.40 W
San Juan de los Lagos, Mex. (sän-hōō-än'då lōs lä'gôs)	130	21.15 N	102.18 W
San Juan de los Lagos (R.), Mex. (då lōs lä'gôs)	130	21.13 N	102.12 W
San Juan de los Morros, Ven. (dĕ-lōs-mô'r-rôs)	143b	9.54 N	67.22 W
San Juan del Rio, Mex. (dĕl rē'ô)	130	20.21 N	99.59 W
San Juan del Rio, Mex. (sän hwän del rē'ô)	124	24.47 N	104.29 W
San Juan del Sur, Nic. (dĕl sōōr)	132	11.15 N	85.53 W
San Juan de Sabinas, Mex. (dĕ-sä-bē'näs)	124	27.56 N	101.23 W
San Juan Despí, Sp.	65e	41.22 N	2.04 E
San Juan Evangelista, Mex. (sän-hōō-ä'n-ā-väŋ-kå-lēs'ta')	131	17.57 N	95.08 W
San Juan I., Wa.	118a	48.28 N	123.08 W
San Juan Is., Can. (sän hwän)	118d	48.49 N	123.14 W
San Juan Ixtenco, Mex. (ēx-tĕ'n-kô)	131	19.14 N	97.52 W
San Juan Martinez, Cuba (sän kōō'ä'n-mär-tē'nĕz)	134	22.15 N	83.50 W

ăt; finăl; rāte; senåte; ärm; àsk; sofà; fâre; ch-choose; dh-as th in other; bē; ēvent; bĕt; recĕnt; cratēr; g-gō; gh-guttural g; bĭt; ĭ-short neutral; rīde; K-guttural k as ch in German ich;

RONOUNCING INDEX

San Juan Mts. – Santarém 341

ACE (Pronounciation)	PAGE	Lat. °′	Long. °′
an Juan Mts., Co. (san hwán′)	121	37.50 N	107.30 W
an Juan, Pico (Pk.), Cuba (pē′kô-sän-koōȧ′n)	134	21.55 N	80.00 W
an Juan R., Nic.	133	10.58 N	84.18 W
an Juan, Rio (R.), Mex. (rē′ō-sän-hwän)	124	25.35 N	99.15 W
an Juan, see Guichicovi			
an Juan, see Mazatlán			
an Julián, Arg. (sän hōō-lyȧ′n)	144	49.17 S	68.02 W
an Justo, Arg. (hōōs′tô)	144a	34.25 S	58.33 W
an Justo Desvern, Sp.	65e	41.23 N	2.05 E
ankanbiriwa (Mtn.), S. L.	228	8.56 N	10.48 W
ankarani R., Gui.-Mali (sän′kä-rä′nē)	228	11.10 N	8.35 W
ankt Gallen, Switz.	166	47.25 N	9.22 E
ankuru (R.), Zaire (sän-kōō′rōō)	230	4.00 S	22.35 E
an Lazaro, C., Mex. (sän-lȧ′zä-rō)	128	24.58 N	113.30 W
an Leandro, Ca. (săn lē-ăn′drô)	118b	37.43 N	122.10 W
an Lorenzo, Arg. (sän lô-rĕn′zô)	141c	32.46 S	60.44 W
an Lorenzo, Ca. (săn lô-rĕn′zô)	118b	37.41 N	122.08 W
an Lorenzo, Hond. (sän lô-rĕn′zô)	132	13.24 N	87.24 W
an Lorenzo de El Escorial, Sp. (sän lôrĕn′tho dĕl ĕs-kō-rē-äl′)	171a	40.36 N	4.09 W
an Lorenzo Tezonco, Mex.	60a	19.18 N	99.04 W
anlúcar de Barrameda, Sp. (sän-lōō′kär)	170	36.46 N	6.21 W
an Lucas, Bol. (lōō′kȧs)	142	20.12 S	65.06 W
an Lucas, C., Mex.	128	22.45 N	109.45 W
an Lucas, see Ojitlán			
an Luis, Arg. (lōō-ēs′)	144	33.16 S	66.15 W
an Luis, Col. (lōōē′s)	142a	6.03 N	74.57 W
an Luis, Cuba	135	20.15 N	75.50 W
an Luis, Guat.	132	14.38 N	89.42 W
an Luis (Neigh.), Cuba	60b	23.05 N	82.20 W
an Luis (Prov.), Arg.	144	32.45 S	66.00 W
an Luis (State), Mex.	128	22.45 N	101.45 W
an Luis de la Paz, Mex. (dā lä päz′)	130	21.17 N	100.32 W
an Luis del Cordero, Mex. (dĕl kôr-dā′rô)	124	25.25 N	104.20 W
an Luis Obispo, Ca. (ô-bĭs′pō)	120	35.18 N	120.40 W
an Luis Obispo, B., Ca.	120	35.07 N	121.05 W
an Luis Potosi, Mex. (pō-tô-sē′)	130	22.08 N	100.58 W
an Luis Potosí (State), Mex.	128	22.45 N	101.45 W
an Luis Rey (R.), Ca. (rā′ē)	120	33.22 N	117.06 W
an Luis Tlaxialtemalco, Mex.	60a	19.15 N	99.03 W
an Manuel, Az. (sän măn′ū-ĕl)	121	32.30 N	110.45 W
an Marcial, NM (săn mȧr-shäl′)	121	33.40 N	107.00 W
an Marco, It. (sän mär′kô)	172	41.53 N	15.50 E
an Marcos, Guat. (mär′kôs)	132	14.57 N	91.49 W
an Marcos, Mex.	130	16.46 N	99.23 W
an Marcos, Tx. (săn mär′kôs)	124	29.53 N	97.56 W
an Marcos de Colón, Hond. (sän-mȧ′r-kōs-dĕ-kô-lô′n)	132	13.17 N	86.50 W
an Marcos R., Tx.	124	30.08 N	98.15 W
an Marcos, Universidad de (P. Int.), Peru	60c	12.03 S	77.05 W
an Maria (Vol.), Guat. (sän-mä-rē′ä)	132	14.45 N	91.33 W
an Maria di Léuca, C., It. (dē-lĕ′ōō-kä)	173	39.47 N	18.20 E
an Marino, Ca. (săn mĕr-ē′nô)	119a	34.07 N	118.06 W
an Marino, Eur.	159	43.40 N	13.00 E
an Marino, San Marino (sän mä-rē′nô)	172	44.55 N	12.26 E
an Martin Chalchicuautla, Mex. (sän mär-tē′n chäl-chē-kwä-ōō′tlä)	130	21.22 N	98.39 W
an Martin de la Vega, Sp. (sän mär ten′ dā lä vā′gä)	171a	40.12 N	3.34 W
an Martín, Col. (sän mär-tē′n)	142a	3.42 N	73.44 W
an Martín, Mex. (mär-tē′n)	131	18.36 N	95.11 W
an Martín (L.), Arg.-Chile	144	48.15 S	72.30 W
an Martín Hidalgo, Mex. (sän mär-tē′n-ē-däl′gô)	130	20.27 N	103.55 W
an Mateo, Ca. (săn mä-tā′ô)	118b	37.34 N	122.20 W
an Mateo (Etlatongo), Mex. (sän-mä-tĕ′ô) (ĕ-tlä-tô′n-gō)	131	16.59 N	97.04 W
an Mateo, Sp. (sän mä-tā′ō)	171	40.26 N	0.09 E
an Mateo, Ven. (sän mȧ-tĕ′ô)	143b	9.45 N	64.34 W
an Matías, Golfo (G.), Arg. (sän mä-tē′äs)	144	41.30 S	63.45 W
anmen Wan (B.), China	203	29.00 N	122.15 E
an Miguel, Arg. (sän mē-gĕ′l)	144a	34.17 S	58.43 W
an Miguel, Chile	61b	33.30 S	70.40 W
an Miguel, Mex. (sän mē-gäl′)	131	18.18 N	97.09 W
an Miguel, Pan.	133	8.26 N	78.55 W
an Miguel, Peru	60c	12.06 S	77.06 W
an Miguel, Phil. (sän mē-gĕ′l)	207a	15.09 N	120.56 E
an Miguel, Sal. (sän mē-gäl′)	132	13.28 N	88.11 W
an Miguel, Ven. (sän mē-gĕ′l)	143b	9.56 N	64.58 W
an Miguel (I.), Ca.	120	34.03 N	120.23 W
n Miguel (R.), Bol. (sän-mē-gĕl′)	142	13.34 S	63.58 W
n Miguel (R.), Co. (săn mē-gĕl′)	121	38.15 N	108.40 W
n Miguel (R.), Mex. (sän mē-gäl′)	131	15.27 N	92.00 W
n Miguel (Vol.), Sal.	132	13.27 N	88.17 W
n Miguel B., Phil.	207a	13.55 N	123.12 E
n Miguel, Bahia (B.), Pan. (bä-ē′ä-sän mē-gäl′)	133	8.17 N	78.26 W
n Miguel de Allende, Mex. (dā ä-lyĕn′dā)	130	20.54 N	100.44 W
n Miguel del Padrón, Cuba	60b	23.05 N	82.19 W
n Miguel el Alto, Mex. (ĕl äl′tô)	130	21.03 N	102.26 W
n Miguel, see Sola de Vega			
n Miguel, see Talea de Castro			
nnār, Sud.	225	13.34 N	33.32 E
n Narcisco, Phil. (sän när-sē′sô)	207a	15.01 N	120.05 E
n Narcisco, Phil.	207a	13.34 N	122.33 E
n Nicolás, Arg. (sän nē-kô-lȧ′s)	141c	33.20 S	60.14 W
n Nicolas, Phil. (nē-kô-läs′)	207a	16.05 N	120.45 E
n Nicolas (I.), Ca. (săn nĭ′kô-lȧ)	120	33.14 N	119.10 W
n Nicolás (R.), Mex.	130	19.40 N	105.08 W
nniquellie, Ivory Coast	228	7.22 N	8.43 W
nnois, Fr.	64c	48.58 N	2.15 E

PLACE (Pronounciation)	PAGE	Lat. °′	Long. °′
Sannūr, Wādī, Egypt	223b	28.48 N	31.12 E
Sanok, Pol. (sä′nôk)	167	49.31 N	22.13 E
San Pablo, Ca. (săn păb′lô)	118b	37.58 N	122.21 W
San Pablo, Phil. (sän-pä-blô)	207a	14.05 N	121.20 E
San Pablo, Ven. (sän-pȧ′blô)	143b	9.46 N	65.04 W
San Pablo B., Ca. (săn păb′lô)	118b	38.04 N	122.25 W
San Pablo R., Pan. (sän päb′lô)	133	8.12 N	81.12 W
San Pablo Res, Ca.	118b	37.55 N	122.12 W
San Pascual, Phil. (päs-kwäl′)	207a	13.08 N	122.59 E
San Pedro, Arg. (sän pā′drô)	144	24.15 S	64.15 W
San Pedro, Arg.	141c	33.41 S	59.42 W
San Pedro, Ca. (săn pē′drô)	119a	33.44 N	118.17 W
San Pedro, Chile (sän pĕ′drô)	141b	33.54 S	71.27 W
San Pedro, Mex. (sän pā′drô)	131	18.38 N	92.25 W
San Pedro, Par. (sän-pĕ′drô)	144	24.13 S	57.00 W
San Pedro, Sal. (sän pā′drô)	132	13.49 N	88.58 W
San Pedro (R.), Az.	121	32.48 N	110.37 W
San Pedro (R.), Cuba (sän-pĕ′drô)	134	21.05 N	78.15 W
San Pedro (R.), Mex. (sän pā′drô)	130	22.08 N	104.59 W
San Pedro B., Ca. (săn pē′drô)	119a	33.42 N	118.12 W
San Pedro de las Colonias, Mex. (dĕ-läs-kô-lô′nyäs)	124	25.47 N	102.58 W
San Pedro de Macorís, Dom. Rep. (sän-pĕ′drō-dā mä-kô-rēs′)	135	18.30 N	69.30 W
San Pedro Lagunillas, Mex. (sän pā′drô lä-gōō-nēl′yäs)	130	21.12 N	104.47 W
San Pedro R., Guat. (sän pā′drô)	132a	17.11 N	90.23 W
San Pedro R., Mex.	124	27.56 N	105.50 W
San Pedro, Rio de (R.), Mex. (rē′ō-dĕ-sän-pĕ′drô)	131	18.23 N	92.13 W
San Pedro, Río de (R.), Mex.	130	21.51 N	102.24 W
San Pedro, see Amusgos			
San Pedro, see Pochutla			
San Pedro Sula, Hond. (sän pā′drô sōō′lä)	132	15.29 N	88.01 W
San Pedro Xalostoc, Mex.	60a	19.32 N	99.05 W
San Pedro y San Pablo, see Teposcolula			
San Pedro Zacatenco, Mex.	60a	19.31 N	99.08 W
San Pietro, I. di, It. (ē′sō-lä-dē-sän pyā′trô)	172	39.09 N	8.15 E
San Pietro in Vaticano (P. Int.), It.	66c	41.54 N	12.28 E
San Quentin, Ca. (sän kwĕn-tēn′)	118b	37.57 N	122.29 W
San Quintin, Phil. (sän kĕn-tēn′)	207a	15.59 N	120.47 E
San R, Pol.	167	50.33 N	22.12 E
San Rafael, Arg. (sän rä-fä-āl′)	144	34.30 S	68.13 W
San Rafael, Ca. (săn rȧ-fĕl)	118b	37.58 N	122.31 W
San Rafael, Col. (sän-rä-fȧ-ĕ′l)	142a	6.18 N	75.02 W
San Rafael (R.), Ut. (săn rȧ-fĕl′)	121	39.05 N	110.50 W
San Rafael, Cabo (C.), Dom. Rep. (kȧ′bô)	135	19.00 N	68.50 W
San Ramon, Ca. (sän rä-mōn′)	118b	37.47 N	122.59 W
San Ramōn, C. R.	133	10.07 N	84.30 W
San Remo, It. (sän rā′mô)	172	43.48 N	7.46 E
San Roman, C., Ven. (sän-rô-mä′n)	129	12.00 N	69.45 W
San Roque, Col. (sän-rô′kĕ)	142a	6.29 N	75.00 W
San Roque, Sp.	170	36.13 N	5.23 W
San Saba, Tx. (săn sä′bȧ)	124	31.12 N	98.43 W
San Saba R., Tx.	124	30.58 N	99.12 W
San Salvador, Sal. (sän säl-vä-dōr′)	132	13.45 N	89.11 W
San Salvador (I.), Ec.	142	0.14 S	90.50 W
San Salvador (R.), Ur. (sän-säl-vä-dô′r)	141c	33.42 S	58.04 W
San Salvador (Watling) (I.), Ba. (săn săl′vȧ-dôr)	135	24.05 N	74.30 W
Sansanné-Mango, Togo (sän-sȧ-nā′ mäɴ′gô)	228	10.21 N	0.28 E
San Sebastian, Can. Is. (sän sā-bäs-tyän′)	224	28.09 N	17.11 W
San Sebastián, Sp.	170	43.19 N	1.59 W
San Sebastián, Ven. (sän-sĕ-bäs-tyȧ′n)	143b	9.58 N	67.11 W
San Sebastiàn de los Reyes, Sp. (sän sā-bäs-tyän′dā lōs rā′yĕs)	171a	40.33 N	3.38 W
San Severo, It. (sän sĕ-vâ′rō)	172	41.43 N	15.24 E
Sanshui, China (sän-shwā)	199	23.14 N	112.51 E
San Simon (R.), Az. (sȧn sī-mōn′)	121	32.45 N	109.30 W
San Siro (Neigh.), It.	65c	45.29 S	9.07 E
Sanssouci, Schloss (P. Int.), Sp.	65a	52.24 N	13.02 E
Santa Ana, Ca. (săn′tȧ ăn′ȧ)	119a	33.45 N	117.52 W
Santa Ana, Mex. (sän′tä ä′nä)	130	19.18 N	98.10 W
Santa Ana, Sal.	132	14.02 N	89.35 W
Santa Ana Mts., Ca.	119a	33.44 N	117.36 W
Santa Ana R., Ca.	119a	33.41 N	117.57 W
Santa Anna, Tx.	124	31.44 N	99.18 W
Santa Anna, Cochilha de (Mts.), Braz. (kô-chē′lä dĕ sän-tä-nä)	144	30.30 S	56.30 W
Santa Antāo (I.), C. V. Is. (sä-tä-ȧ′n-zhĕ-lô)	224b	17.20 N	26.05 W
Santa Bárbara, Braz. (sän-tä-bȧ′r-bä-rä)	141a	19.57 S	43.25 W
Santa Barbara, Ca. (săn′tȧ bär′bȧ-rȧ)	120	34.26 N	119.43 W
Santa Barbara, Hond. (sän′tȧ bär′bȧ-rȧ)	132	14.52 N	88.20 W
Santa Barbara, Mex.	124	26.48 N	105.50 W
Santa Barbara (I.), Ca.	120	33.30 N	118.44 W
Santa Barbara (Is.), Ca.	120	33.45 N	119.46 W
Santa Barbara Chan., Ca.	120	34.15 N	120.00 W
Santa Branca, Braz. (sän-tä-brä′ɴ-kä)	139a	23.25 S	45.52 W
Santa Catalina (I.), Ca.	120	33.29 N	118.37 W
Santa Catalina, Cerro de (Mt.), Pan. (sĕ′r-rô-dĕ-sän-tä-kä-tä-lē′nä)	133	8.39 N	81.36 W
Santa Catalina, G. of, Ca. (săn′tȧ kă-tȧ-lē′nȧ)	120	33.00 N	117.58 W
Santa Catarina, Mex. (sän′tȧ kä-tä-rē′nä)	124	25.41 N	100.27 W
Santa Catarina (R.), Mex.	130	16.31 N	98.39 W
Santa Catarina (State), Braz. (sän-tä-kä-tä-rē′nȧ)	144	27.15 S	50.30 W

PLACE (Pronounciation)	PAGE	Lat. °′	Long. °′
Santa Catarina, see Loxicha			
Santa Catarina, see Yosonotú			
Santa Clara, Ca. (săn′tȧ klârȧ)	116b	37.21 N	121.56 W
Santa Clara, Cuba (sän′t klä′rá)	134	22.25 N	80.00 W
Santa Clara, Mex.	124	24.29 N	103.22 W
Santa Clara, Ur.	144	32.46 S	54.51 W
Santa Clara (R.), Ca. (săn′tȧ klă′rȧ)	120	34.22 N	118.53 W
Santa Clara, (Vol.), Nic.	132	12.44 N	87.00 W
Santa Clara, Bahía de (B.), Cuba (bä-ē′ä-dĕ-sän-tä-klä-rä)	134	23.05 N	80.50 W
Santa Clara, Sierra, (Mts.), Mex. (sē-ĕ′r-rä-sän′tȧ klä′rȧ)	128	27.30 N	113.50 W
Santa Coloma de Cervelló, Sp.	65e	41.22 N	2.01 E
Santa Coloma de Gramanet, Sp.	65e	41.27 N	2.13 E
Santa Cruz, Bol. (sän′tȧ krōōz′)	142	17.45 S	63.03 W
Santa Cruz, Braz. (sän-tä-krōō′s)	144	29.43 S	52.15 W
Santa Cruz, Braz.	144b	22.55 S	43.41 W
Santa Cruz, Ca.	120	36.59 N	122.02 W
Santa Cruz, Chile	141b	34.38 S	71.21 W
Santa Cruz, C. R.	132	10.16 N	85.37 W
Santa Cruz, Mex.	124	25.50 N	105.25 W
Santa Cruz, Phil.	203a	13.28 N	122.02 E
Santa Cruz, Phil.	203a	14.17 N	121.25 E
Santa Cruz, Phil.	203a	15.46 N	119.53 E
Santa Cruz (Prov.), Arg.	144	48.00 S	70.00 W
Santa Cruz (I.), Ec. (sän-tä-krōō′z)	142	0.38 S	90.20 W
Santa Cruz (R.), Arg. (sän′tȧ krōōz′)	144	50.05 S	66.30 W
Santa Cruz (R.), Az. (săn′tȧ krōōz′)	121	32.30 N	111.30 W
Santa Cruz Barillas, Guat. (sän-tä-krōō′z-bä-rē′l-yäs)	132	15.47 N	91.22 W
Santa Cruz Chico, see Pedro Antonio Santos			
Santa Cruz del Sur, Cuba (sän-tä-krōō′s-dĕl-sōō′r)	134	20.45 N	78.00 W
Santa Cruz de Tenerife, Can. Is. (sän′tä krōōz dā tā-nā-rē′fā)	224	28.07 N	15.27 W
Santa Cruz Is., Sol. Is.	215	10.58 S	166.47 E
Santa Cruz Meyehualco, Mex.	60a	19.20 N	99.03 W
Santa Cruz Mts., Ca. (săn′tȧ krōōz′)	118b	37.30 N	122.19 W
Santa Domingo, Cay (I.), Ba.	135	21.50 N	75.45 W
Santa Eduviges, Chile	61b	33.33 S	70.39 W
Santa Elena del Gomero, Chile	61b	33.29 S	70.46 W
Santa Eugenia de Ribeira, Sp. (sän-tä-ĕōō-hĕ′nyä-dĕ-rē-bĕ′y-rä)	170	42.34 N	8.55 W
Santa Eulalia del Rio, Sp. (sän′ta ā-ōō-lä′lē-ä dĕl rē′ô)	171	38.58 N	1.29 E
Santa Fe, Arg. (sän′tä fā′)	144	31.33 S	60.45 W
Santa Fe, Cuba (sän-tä-fĕ′)	134	21.45 N	82.40 W
Santa Fé, Cuba	60b	23.05 N	82.31 W
Santa Fe, Mex.	60a	19.23 N	99.14 W
Santa Fe, NM (săn′tȧ fā′)	121	35.10 N	106.00 W
Santa Fe, Sp. (sän′tä-fā′)	170	37.12 N	3.43 W
Santa Fe (Prov.), Arg. (sän′tä fā′)	144	32.00 S	61.15 W
Santa Filomena, Braz. (sän-tä-fē-lô-mĕ′nä)	143	9.09 S	44.45 W
Santa Genoveva, (Mtn.), Mex. (sän-tä-hĕ-nō-vĕ′vä)	128	23.30 N	110.00 W
Santai, China (san-tī)	203	31.02 N	105.02 E
Santa Inés, Ven. (sän′tä ē-nĕ′s)	143b	9.54 N	64.21 W
Santa Inés (I.), Chile (sän′tä ē-nās′)	144	53.45 S	74.15 W
Santa Isabel (I.), Sol. Is.	215	7.57 S	159.28 E
Santa Lucia, Cuba (sän′tȧ lōō-sē′ȧ)	134	21.50 N	77.30 W
Santa Lucia, Ur. (sän-tä-lōō-sē′ä)	141c	34.27 S	56.23 W
Santa Lucia, Ven.	143b	10.18 N	66.40 W
Santa Lucia B., Cuba (sän′tȧ lōō-sē′ȧ)	134	22.55 N	84.20 W
Santa Lucia (R.), Ur. (sän-tä-lōō-sē′ä)	141c	34.19 S	56.13 W
Santa Magarita (I.), Mex. (sän′tȧ mär-gȧ-rē′tȧ)	128	24.15 N	112.00 W
Santa Maria, Braz. (sän′tȧ mä-rē′ȧ)	144	29.40 S	54.00 W
Santa Maria, Ca. (săn-tȧ mȧ-rē′ȧ)	120	34.57 N	120.28 W
Santa Maria, It. (sän-tä mä-rē′ä)	172	41.05 N	14.15 E
Santa Maria, Phil. (sän-tä-mä-rē′ä)	207a	14.48 N	120.57 E
Santa Maria (R.), Mex. (sän′tȧ mä-rē′ȧ)	130	21.33 N	100.17 W
Santa Maria, C, Ba.	135	23.45 N	75.30 W
Santa Maria, Cabo de (C.), Port. (kȧ′bō-dĕ-sän-tä-mä-rē′ä)	170	36.58 N	7.54 W
Santa Maria, Cayo (I.), Cuba (kä′yō-săn′tȧ mȧ-rē′ȧ)	134	22.40 N	79.00 W
Santa Maria de los Angeles, Mex. (dĕ-lôs-ȧ′n-hĕ-lĕs)	130	22.10 N	103.34 W
Santa Maria de Ocotán, Mex. (sän′tä-mä-rē′ä-dĕ-ô-kô-tȧ′n)	130	22.56 N	104.30 W
Santa Maria I., Açores (sän-tä-mä-rē′ä)	224a	37.09 N	26.02 W
Santa Maria Madalena, Braz. (sän-tä-mȧ-rē′ä-mȧ-dȧ-lĕ-nä)	141a	22.00 S	42.00 W
Santa Maria, see Huazolotitlán			
Santa María del Oro, Mex. (sän′tä-mä-rē′ä-dĕl-ô-rô)	130	21.21 N	104.35 W
Santa María del Rio, Mex. (sän′tȧ mä-rē′ȧ dĕl rē′ō)	130	21.46 N	100.43 W
Santa María del Rosario, Cuba	60b	23.04 N	82.15 W
Santa María Tulpetlac, Mex.	60a	19.34 N	99.03 W
Santa Marta, Col. (sän′tȧ mär′tȧ)	142	11.15 N	74.13 W
Santa Marta, Peru	60c	12.02 S	76.56 W
Santa Marta, Cabo de (C.), Ang.	230	13.52 S	12.25 E
Santa Martha Acatitla, Mex.	60a	19.22 N	99.01 W
Santa Monica, Ca. (săn′tȧ mŏn′ĭ-kȧ)	119a	34.01 N	118.29 W
Santa Mónica (Neigh.), Ven.	61a	10.29 N	66.53 W
Santa Monica B., Ca.	59	33.54 N	118.25 W
Santa Monica Mts., Ca.	119a	34.08 N	118.38 W
Santana (R.), Braz. (sän-tä′nä)	144b	22.33 S	43.37 W
Santander, Col. (sän-tän-dĕr′)	142a	3.00 N	76.25 W
Santander, Sp. (sän-tän-dâr′)	170	43.27 N	3.50 W
Sant′ Antimo, It.	171c	40.40 N	14.11 E
Santañy, Sp. (sän-tän′yē)	171	39.21 N	3.08 E
Santa Paula, Ca. (săn′tȧ pô′lȧ)	120	34.24 N	119.05 W
Santarém, Braz. (sän-tä-rĕɴ′)	143	2.28 S	54.37 W
Santarém, Port.	170	39.18 N	8.48 W

PLACE (Pronounciation)	PAGE	Lat. °′	Long. °′
Santaren Chan., Ba. (săn-tȧ-rĕn′)	134	24.15 N	79.30 W
Santa Rita, NM (săn′tȧ rē′tȧ)	121	32.45 N	108.05 W
Santa Rita do Passo Quatro, Braz. (sän-tä-rē̍′tȧ-dō̍-kwȧ′trô)	141a	21.43 S	47.27 W
Santa Rita do Sapucai, Braz. (sä-po͞o-kȧ′ē)	141a	22.15 S	45.41 W
Santa Rosa, Arg. (sän-tä-rō̍-sä)	144	36.45 S	64.10 W
Santa Rosa, Ca. (săn′tȧ rō′zȧ)	120	38.27 N	122.42 W
Santa Rosa, Col. (sän-tä-rō̍-sä)	142a	6.38 N	75.26 W
Santa Rosa, Ec.	142	3.29 S	78.55 W
Santa Rosa, Guat. (sän′tȧ rō′sȧ)	132	14.21 N	90.16 W
Santa Rosa, Hond.	132	14.45 N	88.51 W
Santa Rosa, NM (săn′tȧ rō′sȧ)	122	34.55 N	104.41 W
Santa Rosa, Ven. (sän-tä-rō̍-sä)	143b	9.37 N	64.10 W
Santa Rosa de Cabal, Col. (sän-tä-rō̍-sä-dĕ-kä-bä′l)	142a	4.53 N	75.38 W
Santa Rosa de Huechuraba, Chile	61b	33.21 S	70.41 W
Santa Rosa de Locobe, Chile	61b	33.26 S	70.33 W
Santa Rosa de Viterbo, Braz. (sän-tä-rô-sȧ-dĕ-vē-tĕr′-bō̍)	141a	21.30 S	47.21 W
Santa Rosa Ind. Res., Ca. (săn′tȧ rō′zȧ′)	120	33.28 N	116.50 W
Santa Rosalia, see Ciudad Camargo			
Santa Rosalía, Mex. (sän′tȧ rō̍-zä′lē̍-ȧ)	128	27.13 N	112.15 W
Santa Rosa Mts., Nv. (săn′tȧ rō′zȧ)	116	41.33 N	117.50 W
Santa Susana, Ca. (săn′tȧ so͞o-ză′nȧ)	119a	34.16 N	118.42 W
Santa Tecla, see Nueva San Salvador			
Santa Teresa, Arg. (sän-tä-tĕ-rĕ′sä)	141c	33.27 S	60.47 W
Santa Teresa, Ven.	143b	10.14 N	66.40 W
Santa Teresa de lo Ovalle, Chile	61b	33.23 S	70.47 W
Santa Úrsula Coapa, Mex.	60a	19.17 N	99.11 W
Santa Vitória do Palmar, Braz. (sän-tä-vē-tŏ′ryä-dō̍-pəl-mȧr)	144	33.30 S	53.16 W
Santa Ynez (R.), Ca. (săn′tȧ ē-nĕz′)	120	34.40 N	120.20 W
Santa Ysabel Ind. Res., Ca. (săn-tȧ ĭ-zȧ-bĕl′)	120	33.05 N	116.46 W
Santee, Ca. (săn tē′)	120a	32.50 N	116.58 W
Santee (R.), SC	127	33.27 N	80.02 W
Santeny, Fr.	64c	48.43 N	2.34 E
Sant′ Eufemia, Golfo di (G.), It. (gō̍l-fō̍-dē-sän-tĕ′o͞o-fĕ′myä)	172	38.53 N	15.53 E
Santiago, Braz. (sän-tyȧ′gô)	144	29.05 S	54.46 W
Santiago, Chile (sän-tē̍-ä′gō̍)	141b	33.26 S	70.40 W
Santiago, Pan.	133	8.07 N	80.58 W
Santiago, Phli. (sän-tyä′gō̍)	207a	16.42 N	121.33 E
Santiago (Prov.), Chile (sän-tyȧ′gō)	141b	33.28 S	70.55 W
Santiago (I.), Phil.	207a	16.29 N	120.03 E
Santiago Acahualtepec, Mex.	60a	19.21 N	99.01 W
Santiago de Compostela, Sp.	170	42.52 N	8.32 W
Santiago de Cuba, Cuba (sän-tyȧ′gō̍-dā ko͞o′bȧ)	135	20.00 N	75.50 W
Santiago de Cuba (Prov.), Cuba	135	20.20 N	76.05 W
Santiago de las Vegas, Cuba (sän-tyȧ′gō̍-dĕ-läs-vĕ′gäs)	135a	22.58 N	82.23 W
Santiago del Estero, Arg. (sän-tē-ȧ′gō-dĕl ĕs-tā′rō̍)	144	27.50 S	64.14 W
Santiago del Estero (Prov.), Arg. (sän-tē-ȧ′gō-dĕl ĕs-tā-rō̍)	144	27.15 S	63.30 W
Santiago de los Cabelleros, Dom. Rep. (sän-tyȧ′gō̍-dā̍ lōs kȧ-bä-yā′rō̍s)	135	19.30 N	70.45 W
Santiago Mts., Tx. (sän-tē̍-ä′gō̍)	124	30.00 N	103.30 W
Santiago Res., Ca.	119a	33.47 N	117.42 W
Santiago, Rio Grande de (R.), Mex. (rē̍′o-grä′n-dĕ-dĕ-sän-tyȧ′gô)	130	21.15 N	104.05 W
Santiago Rodriguez, Dom. Rep. (sän-tyȧ′gō̍-rô-drē̍′gĕz)	135	19.30 N	71.25 W
Santiago, see Zacatepec			
Santiago Tepalcatlalpan, Mex.	60a	19.15 N	99.08 W
Santiago Tuxtla, Mex. (sän-tyȧ′gô-to͞o′x-tlä)	131	18.28 N	95.18 W
Santiaguillo, Laguna de (L.), Mex. (lä-oô′nä-dĕ-sän-tē̍-a-gēl′yō̍)	124	24.51 N	104.43 W
Santiam R., Or. (săn′tyăm)	116	44.42 N	122.26 W
Santissimo (Neigh.), Braz.	61c	22.53 S	43.31 W
Santisteban del Puerto, Sp. (sän′tē̍ stā̍-bän′dĕl pwĕr′tō̍)	170	38.15 N	3.12 W
Santo Amaro, Braz. (sän′to͞o ä-mä′ro͞o)	143	12.32 S	38.33 W
Santo Amaro (Neigh.), Braz.	61d	23.39 S	46.42 W
Santo Amaro de Campos, Braz. (sän-tô-ä-mä′rō̍-dĕ-kȧm′pôs)	141a	22.01 S	41.05 W
Santo André, Braz. (sän-tô-än-drĕ′)	141a	23.40 S	46.31 W
Santo Angelo, Braz. (sän-tô-ȧ′n-zhĕ-lō̍)	144	28.16 S	53.59 W
Santo Antônio do Monte, Braz. (sän-tô-än-tô′nyō̍-dō̍-môn′tĕ)	141a	20.06 S	45.18 W
Santo Domingo, Cuba (sän′tō̍-dōmĭŋ′gō̍)	134	22.35 N	80.20 W
Santo Domingo, Dom. Rep. (sän′tō̍ dō̍-mĭn′gō̍)	135	18.30 N	69.55 W
Santo Domingo, Nic. (sän-tō̍-dō̍-mē̍′n-gō)	132	12.15 N	84.56 W
Santo Domingo de la Caizada, Sp. (dā lä käl-thä′dä)	170	42.27 N	2.55 W
Santo Domingo, see Zanatepec			
Santoña, Sp. (sän-tō′nyä)	170	43.25 N	3.27 W
Sant′ Onofrio (Neigh.), It.	66c	41.56 N	12.25 E
Santos, Braz. (sän′tozh)	141a	23.58 S	46.20 W
Santos Dumont, Braz. (sän′tō̍s-do͞o-mô′nt)	141a	21.28 S	43.33 W
Santo Tomé, Arg. (sän-tō̍-tō̍-mĕ′)	144	28.32 S	56.04 W
Sanuki, Jap. (sä′no͞o-kē̍)	205a	35.16 N	139.53 E
San Urbano, Arg. (sän-o͞or-bä′nō̍)	141c	33.39 S	61.28 W
San Valentin, M. (Mtn.), Chile (sän-vä-lĕn-tē′n)	144	46.41 S	73.30 W
San Vicente, Arg. (sän-vē-sĕn′tĕ)	141c	35.00 S	58.26 W
San Vicente, Chile	141b	34.25 S	71.06 W
San Vicente, Sal. (sän vē̍-sĕn′tā̍)	132	13.41 N	88.43 W
San Vicente de Alcántara, Sp. (sän vē̍-thĕn′tā̍ dā̍ äl-kän′tä-rä)	170	39.24 N	7.08 W
San Vicente dels Horts, Sp.	65e	41.24 N	2.01 E
San Vito al Tagliamento, It. (san vē′tô)	172	45.53 N	12.52 E
San Xavier Ind. Res., Az. (x-ā′vĭēr)	121	32.07 N	111.12 W
San Ysidro, Ca. (sän ysĭ-drō′)	120a	32.33 N	117.02 W
Sanyuanli, China (sän-yṻän-lē)	202a	23.11 N	113.16 E
São Bernado do Campo, Braz. (souɴ-bĕr-nȧr′dō̍-dō̍-kȧ′m-pô)	141a	23.44 S	46.33 W
São Borja, Braz. (souɴ-bôr-zhä)	144	28.44 S	55.59 W
São Caetano do Sul, Braz.	61d	23.26 S	46.34 W
São Carlos, Braz. (souɴ kär′lōzh)	141a	22.02 S	47.54 W
São Cristovão, Braz. (souɴ-krē̍s-tō-vouɴ)	143	11.04 S	37.11 W
São Cristóvão (Neigh.), Braz.	61c	22.54 S	43.14 W
São Fidélis, Braz. (souɴ-fē-dĕ′lēs)	141a	21.41 S	41.45 W
São Francisco, Braz. (souɴ fräɴ-sēsh′ko͞o)	143	15.59 S	44.42 W
São Francisco do Sul, Braz. (souɴ fräɴ-sēsh′ko͞o-dō̍-so͞o′l)	144	26.15 S	48.42 W
São Francisco, Rio (R.), Braz. (rē′ō-sän-frän-sē̍′s-kō)	143	8.56 S	40.20 W
São Gabriel, Braz. (souɴ′gä-brē̍-ĕl′)	144	30.28 S	54.11 W
São Geraldo, Braz. (souɴ-zhĕ-rä′l-dō̍)	141a	21.01 S	42.49 W
São Gonçalo, Braz. (souɴ′gōŋ-sä′lo͞o)	144b	22.55 S	43.04 W
São Gonçalo do Sapucaí, Braz. (souɴ-gôn-sä′lō-dō̍-sä-po͞o-kī′)	141a	21.55 S	45.34 W
São Hill, Tan.	231	8.20 S	35.12 E
Sao Joao, Guinea-Bissau,	228	11.32 N	15.26 W
São João da Barra, Braz. (souɴ-zhō̍uɴ-dä-bȧ′rä)	144b	21.40 S	41.03 W
São João da Boa Vista, Braz. (souɴ-zhō̍uɴ-dä-bôä-vē̍′s-tä)	141a	21.58 S	46.45 W
São João del Rei, Braz. (souɴ zhō̍-ouɴ′dĕl-rā)	141a	21.08 S	44.14 W
São João de Meriti, Braz. (souɴ-zhō̍uɴ-dĕ-mĕ-rē-tē̍)	144b	22.47 S	43.22 W
São João do Arguaia, Braz. (souɴ zhō̍-ouɴ′dō̍-ä-rä-gwä′yä)	141	5.29 S	48.44 W
São João dos Lampas, Port. (souɴ′ zhō̍-ouɴ′ dōzh län-päzh′)	171b	38.52 N	9.24 W
São João Nepomuceno, Braz. (souɴ-zhō̍uɴ-nĕ-pō̍-mo͞o-sĕ-nō)	141a	21.33 S	43.00 W
São Jorge I., Açores (souɴ zhôr′zhĕ)	224a	38.28 N	27.34 W
São José do Rio Pardo, Braz. (souɴ-zhô-sĕ′dō̍-rē′ō-pȧ′r-dō)	141a	21.36 S	46.50 W
São José do Rio Prêto, Braz. (souɴ zhō̍-zĕ′dō̍-re′ō-prĕ-tō)	143	20.57 S	49.12 W
São José dos Campos, Braz. (souɴ zhō̍-zā′dōzh käɴ pōzh′)	141a	23.12 S	45.53 W
São Julião da Barra, Port.	65d	38.40 N	9.21 W
São Leopoldo, Braz. (souɴ-lĕ-ō̍-pôl′dō̍)	144	29.46 S	51.09 W
São Luis (Maranhão), Braz. (souɴ-lo͞oē̍′s-mä-rän-youɴ′)	143	2.31 S	43.14 W
São Luis do Paraitinga, Braz. (souɴ-lo͞oē̍′s-dō̍-pä-rä-ē-tē′n-gä)	141a	23.15 S	44.18 W
São Manuel (R.) Braz.	143	8.28 S	57.07 E
São Mateus, Braz. (souɴ mä-tā′o͞ozh)	143	18.44 S	39.45 W
São Mateus, Braz.	61c	22.49 S	43.23 W
São Miguel Arcanjo, Braz. (souɴ-mē-gĕ′l-ȧr-kän-zhō)	141a	23.54 S	47.59 W
São Miguel I., Açores	224a	37.59 N	26.38 W
São Miguel Paulista (Neigh.), Braz.	61d	23.30 S	46.26 W
Saona (I.), Dom. Rep. (sä-ō̍′nä)	135	18.10 N	68.55 W
Saône (R.), Ra. (sōn)	168	46.27 N	4.58 E
São Nicolau, Ang.	230	14.15 S	12.21 E
São Nicolau, C. V. (souɴ′ nē̍-kō̍-louɴ′)	224b	16.19 N	25.19 W
São Paulo, Braz. (souɴ′ pou′lo͞o)	141a	23.34 S	46.38 W
São Paulo (State), Braz. (souɴ pou′lo͞o)	143	21.45 S	50.47 W
São Paulo de Olivença, Braz. (souɴ′pou′lo͞odā̍ ō-lē̍-vĕn′sȧ)	142	3.32 S	68.46 W
São Pedro, Braz. (souɴ-pĕ′drō̍)	141a	22.34 S	47.54 W
São Pedro de Aldeia, Braz. (souɴ-pĕ′drō̍-dĕ-äl-dĕ′yä)	141a	22.50 S	42.04 W
São Raimundo Nonato, Braz. (souɴ′ rī-mo͞o′n-do nō̍-nä′to͞o)	143	9.09 S	42.32 W
São Roque, Braz. (souɴ′ rō′kĕ)	141a	23.32 S	47.08 W
São Roque, Cabo de (C.), Braz. (kä′bo-dĕ-souɴ′ rō′kĕ)	143	5.06 S	35.11 W
São Sebastião, Braz. (souɴ sā̍-bäs-tē̍-ouɴ′)	141a	23.48 S	45.25 W
São Sebastião do Paraíso, Braz. (souɴ-sĕ-bäs-tē-ouɴ-dō̍-pä-rä-ē′sō)	141a	20.54 S	46.58 W
São Sebastião, Ilha de (I.), Braz. (ēl′yȧ dā̍ souɴ′ sā̍-bäs-tē̍-ouɴ′)	141a	23.52 S	45.22 W
São Simão, Braz. (souɴ-sē-mouɴ)	141a	21.30 S	47.33 W
São Tiago I., C. V. (souɴ tē̍-ä′go͞o)	224b	15.09 N	24.45 W
São Tomé, São Tomé & Príncipe (souɴ tō̍-mā′)	230	0.20 N	6.44 E
São Tomé (I.), São Tomé & Príncipe	230	0.20 N	7.00 E
São Tomé, Cabo de (C.), Braz. (kä′bō-dĕ-souɴ-tō̍-mĕ′)	141a	22.00 S	40.00 W
Sao Tome & Principe, Afr. (prēn′sē̍-pĕ)	222	1.00 N	6.00 E
Saoura, Oued (R.), Alg.	160	29.39 N	1.42 W
São Vicente, Braz. (souɴ ve-se′n-tĕ)	141a	23.57 S	46.25 W
Sao Vincente I., C. V. (souɴ vē̍-sĕn′tā̍)	224b	16.51 N	24.35 W
São Vinente, Cabo de (C.), Port. (kȧ′bō-dĕ-sän-vē̍-sĕ′n-tĕ)	170	37.03 N	9.31 W
Sapele, Nig. (sä-pā′lā)	229	5.54 N	5.41 E
Sapitwa (Mtn.), Malawi	231	15.58 S	35.38 E
Sapozhok, Sov. Un. (sä-pō̍-zhôk′)	174	53.58 N	40.44 E
Sapporo, Jap. (säp-pô′rō̍)	204	43.02 N	141.29 E
Sapronovo, Sov. Un. (sȧp-rô′nô-vô)	182b	55.13 N	38.25 E
Sapucaia, Braz. (sä-po͞o-kä′yȧ)	141a	22.01 S	42.54 W
Sapucaí (R.), Braz. (sä-po͞o-kȧ-ē′)	141a	21.07 S	45.53 W
Sapucaí Mirim (R.), Braz. (sä-po͞o-kȧ-ē′mē-rē̍ɴ)	141a	21.06 S	47.0
Sapulpa, Ok. (sȧ-pŭl′pȧ)	123	36.01 N	96.0
Sāqiyat Makkī, Egypt	71a	30.00 N	31.1
Saqqez, Iran	195	36.14 N	46.1
Saquarema, Braz. (sä-kwä-rĕ-mä)	141a	22.56 S	42.3
Sara, Wa. (sä′rä)	118c	45.45 N	122.4
Sara, Bahr (R.), Chad-Cen. Afr. Rep. (bär)	225	8.19 N	17.4
Sarajas de Madrid (Neigh.), Sp.	65b	40.28 N	3.3
Sarajevo, Yugo. (sä-rȧ-yĕv′ō̍) (sȧ-rä′ya-vō̍)	173	43.15 N	18.2
Sarakhs, Iran	195	36.32 N	61.1
Sarana, Sov. Un. (sá-rä′ná)	182a	56.31 N	57.4
Saranac L., NY (săr′ȧ-năk)	111	44.15 N	74.2
Saranac Lake, NY	111	44.20 N	74.0
Sarandi, Arg. (sä-rän′dē̍)	144a	34.36 S	58.2
Sarandi Grande, Ur. (sä-rän′dē-grän′dĕ)	141c	33.42 S	56.2
Sārangpur, India	196	23.39 N	76.3
Saranley, Som.	223a	2.28 N	42.1
Saransk, Sov. Un. (sȧ-ränsk′)	178	54.10 N	45.1
Sarany, Sov. Un. (sȧ-rȧ′nĭ)	182a	58.33 N	58.4
Sara Pk., Nig.	229	9.37 N	9.2
Sarapul, Sov. Un. (sä-räpo͞ol′)	178	56.28 N	53.5
Sarasota, Fl. (săr-ȧ-sōtȧ)	127a	27.27 N	82.3
Saratoga, Tx. (săr-ȧ-tō′gȧ)	125	30.17 N	94.3
Saratoga, Wa.	118a	48.04 N	122.2
Saratoga Pass, Wa.	118a	48.09 N	122.3
Saratoga Springs, NY (sprĭngz)	111	43.05 N	74.5
Saratov, Sov. Un. (sȧ rä′tôf)	179	51.30 N	45.3
Saravane, Laos	203	15.48 N	106.4
Sarawak (Reg.), Mala. (sȧ-rä′wäk)	206	2.30 N	112.4
Sárbogárd, Hung. (shär′bō̍-gärd)	167	46.53 N	18.3
Sarcee Ind. Res., Can. (sär′sē̍)	95e	50.58 N	114.2
Sarcelles, Fr.	64c	49.00 N	2.2
Sardalas, Libya	224	25.59 N	10.3
Sardinia (I.), It. (sär-dĭn′ĭȧ)	172	40.08 N	9.0
Sardis, Ms. (sär′dĭs)	126	34.26 N	89.5
Sargent, Ne. (sär′jĕnt)	114	41.40 N	99.3
Sarh (Fort-Archambault), Chad. (är-chaɴ-bō̍′)	229	9.09 N	18.2
Sarikamis, Tur.	179	40.30 N	42.4
Sariñena, Sp. (sä-rĕn-yĕ′nä)	171	41.46 N	0.1
Sariwŏn, Korea (sä′rē̍-wŭn′)	202	38.40 N	125.4
Sark (I.), Guernsey (särk)	168	49.28 N	2.2
Şarkoy, Tur. (shär′kû-ē̍)	173	40.39 N	27.0
Šarmiento, Monte (Mt.), Chile (mō̍′n-tĕ-sär-myĕn′tō)	144	54.28 S	70.4
Sarnia, Can. (sär′nē̍-ȧ)	110	43.00 N	82.2
Sarno, It. (sä′r-nô)	171c	40.35 N	14.3
Sarny, Sov. Un. (sär′nē̍)	167	51.17 N	26.3
Saronikós Kólpos (G.), Grc.	173	37.51 N	23.3
Saros Körfezi (G.), Tur. (sä′rō̍s)	173	40.30 N	26.2
Şárospatak, Hung. (shä′rō̍sh-pô′tôk)	167	48.19 N	21.3
Šar Planina (Mts.), Yugo. (shär plä′nē̍-na)	173	42.07 N	21.5
Sarpsborg, Nor. (särps′bôrg)	164	59.17 N	11.0
Sarratt, Eng.	62	51.41 N	0.2
Sarrebourg, Fr. (sär-bo͞or′)	169	48.44 N	7.0
Sarreguemines, Fr. (sär-gē-mēn′)	169	49.06 N	7.0
Sarria, Sp. (sär′ē̍-ä)	170	42.14 N	7.1
Sarstun R., Guat. (särs-to͞o′n)	132	15.50 N	89.2
Sartène, Fr. (sär-tĕn′)	172	41.36 N	8.5
Sarthe (R.), Fr. (särt)	168	47.44 N	0.3
Sartrouville, Fr.	64c	48.57 N	2.1
Sárvár, Hung. (shär′vär)	166	47.14 N	16.5
Saryche, Mys (C.), Sov. Un. (mĭs sȧ-rēch′)	179	44.25 N	33.0
Sary-Ishikotrau, Peski (Des.), Sov. Un. (sä′rē̍ ē′ shē̍k-ō′trou)	180	46.12 N	75.3
Sarysu (R.), Sov. Un. (sä′rē̍-so͞o)	180	47.47 N	69.1
Sasarām, India (sŭs-ŭ-räm′)	196	25.00 N	84.0
Sasayama, Jap. (sä′sä-yä′mä)	205	35.05 N	135.1
Sasebo, Jap. (sä′sā̍-bō̍)	205	33.12 N	129.4
Sashalom (Neigh.), Hung.	66g	47.31 N	19.1
Sašice, Czech.	166	49.14 N	13.3
Saskatchewan (Prov.), Can.	96	54.46 N	107.4
Saskatchewan (R.), Can. (săs-kăch′ē̍-wän)	100	53.45 N	103.2
Saskatoon, Can. (săs-kȧ-to͞on′)	100	52.07 N	106.3
Sasolburg, S, Afr.	223d	26.52 S	27.4
Sasovo, Sov. Un. (sȧs′ō̍-vō̍)	178	54.20 N	42.0
Saspamco, Tx. (săs-păm′cō)	119d	29.13 N	98.1
Sassafras, Austl.	70b	37.52 S	145.2
Sassandra, Ivory Coast	228	4.58 N	6.0
Sassandra (R.), Ivory Coast (sȧs-sän′drȧ)	228	5.35 N	6.2
Sassari, It. (säs′sä-rē̍)	172	40.44 N	8.3
Sassnitz, G.D.R. (säs′nē̍ts)	166	54.31 N	13.3
Satadougou, Mali (sä-tȧ-do͞o-goȯ′)	228	12.21 N	10.0
Säter, Swe. (sĕ′tēr)	164	60.21 N	15.5
Sātghara, India	67a	22.44 N	88.2
Satilla (R.), Ga. (sȧ-tĭl′ȧ)	127	31.15 N	82.1
Satka, Sov. Un. (sät′kȧ)	182a	55.03 N	59.0
Sátoraljaujhely, Hung. (shä′tō̍-rô-lyô-o͞o′yĕl′)	167	48.24 N	21.4
Satu-Mare, Rom. (sȧ′to͞o-mȧ′rĕ)	167	47.50 N	22.5
Saturna, Can. (să-tûr′nȧ)	118d	48.48 N	123.1
Saturna (I.), Can.	118d	48.47 N	123.0
Sauda, Nor.	164	59.40 N	6.2
Saudárkrókur, Ice.	158	65.41 N	19.3
Saudi Arabia, Asia (sȧ-o͞o′dĭ ȧ-rä′bĭ-ȧ)	190	22.40 N	46.0
Sauerlach, F.R.G. (zou′ĕr-läᴋ)	157d	47.58 N	11.3
Saugatuck, Mi. (sô′gȧ-tŭk)	110	42.40 N	86.1
Saugeer (R.), Can. (sô′gēr)	110	44.20 N	81.2
Saugerties, NY (sô′gēr-tēz)	111	42.05 N	73.5
Saugus, Ma. (sô′gŭs)	105a	42.28 N	71.0
Sauk (R.), Mn. (sôk)	115	45.30 N	94.4
Sauk Centre, Mn.	115	45.43 N	94.5
Sauk City, Wi.	115	43.16 N	89.4

ăt; finăl; rāte; senāte; ärm; ȧsk; sofȧ; fâre; ch-choose; dh-as th in other; bē; ē̍vent; bĕt; recĕnt; cratēr; g-gō; gh-guttural g; bĭt; ĭ-short neutral; rīde; ᴋ-guttural k as ch in German ich;

PRONOUNCING INDEX

Sauk Rapids – Semiahmoo Spit 343

PLACE (Pronounciation)	PAGE	Lat. °′	Long. °′
Sauk Rapids, Mn. (răp'ĭd)	115	45.35 N	94.08 W
Sault Sainte Marie, Can.	102	46.31 N	84.20 W
Sault Sainte Marie, Mi. (sōō sānt mȧ-rē')	119k	46.29 N	84.21 W
Saumatre, Etang (L.), Hai.	135	18.40 N	72.10 W
Saunders L., Can. (sän'dẽrs)	95g	53.18 N	113.25 W
Saurimo, Ang.	230	9.39 S	20.24 E
Sausalito, Ca. (sô-sȧ-lē'tô)	118b	37.51 N	122.29 W
Sausset-les-Pins, Fr. (sō-sĕ'lā-păN')	168a	43.20 N	5.08 E
Saútar, Ang.	230	11.06 S	18.27 E
Sauvie I., Or. (sô'vē)	118c	45.43 N	123.49 W
Sava (R.), Yugo. (sä'vä)	173	44.50 N	17.00 E
Savage, Md. (să'vĕj)	112e	39.07 N	76.49 W
Savage, Mn.	119g	44.47 N	93.20 W
Savalan (Mtn.), Iran	179	38.20 N	48.00 E
Savalen (L.), Nor.	164	62.19 N	10.15 E
Savalou, Benin	229	7.56 N	1.58 E
Savanna, Il. (sȧ-văn'ȧ)	115	42.05 N	90.09 W
Savannah, Ga. (sȧ-văn'ȧ)	127	32.04 N	81.07 W
Savannah, Mo.	115	39.58 N	94.49 W
Savannah, Tn.	126	35.13 N	88.14 W
Savannah (R.), Ga.-SC	127	33.11 N	81.51 W
Savannakhét, Indo China	206	16.33 N	104.45 E
Savanna la Mar, Jam. (sȧ-văn'ȧ lȧ mär')	134	18.10 N	78.10 W
Sávara R., Czech.	166	49.36 N	15.24 E
Savé, Benin (sȧ-vā')	224	8.09 N	2.03 E
Save (R.), Fr.	168	43.32 N	0.50 E
Save, Rio (R.), Moz. (rē'ō-sä'vē)	226	21.28 S	34.14 E
Sāveh, Iran	195	35.01 N	50.20 E
Saverne, Fr. (sȧ-vĕrn')	169	48.40 N	7.22 E
Savigliano, It. (sä-vēl-yä'nô)	172	44.38 N	7.42 E
Savigny-sur-Orge, Fr.	169b	48.41 N	2.22 E
Savona, It. (sä-nō'nä)	172	44.19 N	8.28 E
Savonlinna, Fin. (sȧ'vôn-lēn'nȧ)	165	61.53 N	28.49 E
Savran', Sov. Un. (säv-rän')	175	48.07 N	30.09 E
Sawahlunto, Indon.	206	0.37 S	100.50 E
Sawākin, Sud.	225	19.02 N	37.19 E
Sawda, Jabal as (Mts.), Libya	225	28.14 N	13.46 E
Sawhāj, Egypt	223b	26.34 N	31.40 E
Sawknah, Libya	225	29.04 N	15.53 E
Sawu, Laut (Savu Sea), Indon.	206	9.15 S	122.15 E
Sawu, Pulau (I.), Indon.	206	10.15 S	122.00 E
Sawyer, (L.), Wa. (sô'yẽr)	118a	47.20 N	122.02 W
Say, Niger (sä'ē)	224	13.09 N	2.16 E
Sayan Khrebet (Mts.), Sov. Un. (sŭ-yän')	180	51.30 N	90.00 E
Saydā (Sidon), Leb. (sä'ē-dä) (sī'dŏn)	191a	33.34 N	35.23 E
Sayhūt, P. D. R. of Yem.	192	15.23 N	51.28 E
Sayre, Ok. (sā'ēr)	122	35.19 N	99.40 W
Sayre, Pa.	111	41.55 N	76.30 W
Sayreton, Al. (sā'ēr-tŭn)	112h	33.34 N	86.51 W
Sayreville, NJ (sâr'vĭl)	112a	40.28 N	74.21 W
Sayr Usa, Mong.	198	44.15 N	107.00 E
Sayula, Mex. (sä-yōō'lä)	131	17.51 N	94.56 W
Sayula, Mex.	130	19.50 N	101.33 W
Sayula, Luguna de (L.), Mex. (lä-gōō'nä-dē)	130	20.00 N	103.33 W
Say'un, P.D.R. of Yem.	192	16.00 N	48.59 E
Sayville, NY (sā'vĭl)	111	40.45 N	73.10 W
Saywūn, P.D.R. of Yem.	195	15.56 N	48.47 E
Sazanit (I.), Alb.	173	40.30 N	19.17 E
Sazhino, Sov. Un. (sáz-hē'nô)	182a	56.20 N	58.15 E
Scäffle, Swe.	164	59.10 N	12.55 E
Scala, Teatro alla (P. Int.), It.	65c	45.28 N	9.11 E
Scandinavian Pen., Eur.	190	62.00 N	14.00 E
Scanlon, Mn. (skăn'lŏn)	119h	46.27 N	92.26 W
Scappoose, Or. (skă-pōōs')	118c	45.46 N	122.53 W
Scappoose (R.), Or.	118c	45.47 N	122.57 W
Scarborough, Can. (skär'bẽr-ô)	95d	43.45 N	79.12 W
Scarborough, Eng. (skär'bŭr-ô)	162	54.16 N	0.19 W
Scarsdale, NY (skärz'dāl)	112a	41.01 N	73.47 W
Scarth Hill, Eng.	64a	53.33 N	2.52 W
Scatari I, Can. (skăt'ȧ-rē)	103	46.00 N	59.44 W
Sceaux, Fr.	64c	48.47 N	2.17 E
Schaerbeek, Bel. (skär'bāk)	157a	50.33 N	4.23 E
Schaffhausen, Switz. (shäf'hou-zĕn)	166	47.42 N	8.38 E
Schalksmühle, F.R.G.	63	51.14 N	7.31 E
Schapenrust, S. Afr.	71b	26.16 S	28.22 E
Scharl, F.R.G.	63	51.06 N	7.40 E
Scharnhorst (Neigh.), F.R.G.	63	51.32 N	7.32 E
Schefferville, Can.	97	54.52 N	67.01 W
Scheiblingstein, Aus.	66e	48.16 N	16.13 E
Schelde, R., Bel.	163	51.04 N	3.55 E
Schenectady, NY (skĕ-nĕk'tȧ-dē)	111	42.50 N	73.55 W
Scheveningen, Neth.	157a	52.06 N	4.15 E
Schiedam, Neth.	157a	51.55 N	4.23 E
Schildow, G.D.R.	65a	52.38 N	13.23 E
Schiller Park, Il.	58a	41.58 N	87.52 W
Schiltigheim, Fr. (shēl'tegh-hīm)	169	48.48 N	7.47 E
Schio, It. (skē'ô)	172	45.43 N	11.23 E
Schleswig, F.R.G. (shlĕs'vĭgh)	166	54.32 N	9.32 E
Schleswig-Holstein (State), F.R.G. (shlĕs'vĭgh-hōl'shtīn)	166	54.40 N	9.10 E
Schmalkalden, G.D.R. (shmäl'käl-dĕn)	166	50.41 N	10.25 E
Schneider, In. (schnīd'ēr)	113a	41.12 N	87.26 W
Schofield, Wi. (skō'fēld)	115	44.52 N	89.37 W
Schöller, F.R.G.	63	51.14 N	7.01 E
Scholven (Neigh.), F.R.G.	63	51.36 N	7.01 E
Schönbrunn, Schloss (P. Int.), Aus.	66e	48.11 N	16.19 E
Schönebeck, G.D.R. (shû'nĕ-bergh)	166	52.01 N	11.44 E
Schönebeck (Neigh.), F.R.G.	63	51.28 N	6.56 E
Schöneberg (Neigh.), F.R.G.	65a	52.29 N	13.21 E
Schönefeld, G.D.R.	65a	52.23 N	13.30 E
Schöneiche, G.D.R.	65a	52.28 N	13.41 E
Schönerlinde, G.D.R.	65a	52.39 N	13.27 E
Schonnebeck (Neigh.), F.R.G.	63	51.29 N	7.04 E
Schönow, G.D.R.	65a	52.40 N	13.32 E
Schönwalde, G.D.R.	65a	52.37 N	13.07 E
Schoonhoven, Neth.	157a	51.56 N	4.51 E
Schramberg, F.R.G. (shräm'bĕrgh)	166	48.14 N	8.24 E
Schreiber, Can.	102	48.50 N	87.10 W
Schroon (L.), NY (skrōōn)	111	43.50 N	73.50 W
Schultzendorf, G.D.R. (shōōl'tzĕn-dōrf)	157b	52.21 N	13.55 E
Schumacher, Can.	102	48.30 N	81.30 W
Schüren (Neigh.), F.R.G.	63	51.30 N	7.32 E
Schuyler, Ne. (slī'lẽr)	114	41.28 N	97.05 W
Schuylkill (R.), Pa. (skōōl'kĭl)	112	40.10 N	75.31 W
Schuylkill-Haven, Pa. (skōōl'kĭl hā-vĕn)	111	40.35 N	76.10 W
Schwabach, F.R.G. (shvä'bäk)	166	49.19 N	11.02 E
Schwäbische Alb (Mts.), F.R.G. (shvă'bē-shĕ ălb)	166	48.11 N	9.09 E
Schwäbisch Gmünd, F.R.G. (shvă'bēsh gmünd)	166	48.47 N	9.49 E
Schwäbisch Hall, F.R.G. (häl)	166	49.08 N	9.44 E
Schwafheim, F.R.G.	63	51.25 N	6.39 E
Schwandorf, F.R.G. (shvän'dôrf)	166	49.19 N	12.08 E
Schwanebeck, G.D.R.	65a	52.37 N	13.32 E
Schwanenwerder (Neigh.), F.R.G.	65a	52.27 N	13.10 E
Schwaner, Pegunungan Mts., Indon. (sKvän'ẽr)	206	1.05 S	112.30 E
Schwarzenberg, F.R.G.	63	51.24 N	6.42 E
Schwarzwald (For.), F.R.G. (shvärts'väld)	166	47.54 N	7.57 E
Schwaz, Aus.	166	47.20 N	11.45 E
Schwechat, Aus. (shvĕk'ät)	157e	48.09 N	16.29 E
Schwedt, G.D.R. (shvĕt)	166	53.04 N	14.17 E
Schweflinghausen, F.R.G.	63	51.16 N	7.25 E
Schweinfurt, F.R.G. (shvīn'fōōrt)	166	50.03 N	10.14 E
Schwelm, F.R.G. (shvĕlm)	169c	51.17 N	7.18 E
Schwenke, F.R.G.	63	51.11 N	7.26 E
Schwerin, G.D.R. (shvĕ-rēn')	166	53.36 N	11.25 E
Schwerin (Neigh.), F.R.G.	63	51.33 N	7.20 E
Schweriner See (L.), G.D.R. (shvĕ'rē-nĕr zā)	166	53.40 N	11.06 E
Schwerte, F.R.G. (shvĕr'tĕ)	169c	51.26 N	7.34 E
Schwielowsee (L.), G.D.R. (shvē'lōv zā)	157b	52.20 N	12.52 E
Schwyz, Switz. (schēts)	166	47.01 N	8.38 E
Sciacca, It. (shē-äk'kä)	172	37.30 N	13.09 E
Science and Industry, Museum of (P. Int.), Il.	58a	41.47 N	87.35 W
Scilly, Isles of (Is.), Eng. (sĭl'ē)	162	49.56 N	6.50 W
Scioto (R.), Oh. (sī-ō'tō)	110	39.10 N	82.55 W
Scituate, Ma. (sĭt'ū-āt)	105a	42.12 N	70.45 W
Scobey, Mt. (skō'bē)	117	48.48 N	105.29 W
Scoggin, Or. (skō'gĭn)	118c	45.28 N	123.14 W
Scoresby, Austl.	70b	37.54 S	145.14 E
Scotch (R.), Can. (skŏch)	95c	45.21 N	74.56 W
Scotia, Ca. (skō'shȧ)	116	40.29 N	124.06 W
Scotland, SD	114	43.08 N	97.43 W
Scotland, U. K. (skŏt'lȧnd)	162	57.05 N	5.10 W
Scotland Neck, NC (nĕk)	127	36.06 N	77.25 W
Scotstown, Can. (skŏts'toun)	111	45.35 N	71.15 W
Scott Air Force Base, Il.	119e	38.33 N	89.52 W
Scottburgh, S. Afr. (skŏt'bŭr-ô)	227c	30.18 S	30.42 E
Scott, C., Can. (skŏt)	96	50.47 N	128.26 W
Scott City, Ks.	122	38.28 N	100.54 W
Scottdale, Ga. (skŏt'dāl)	112c	33.47 N	84.16 W
Scott Is., Ant.	232	67.00 S	178.00 E
Scott, Mt., Or.	118c	45.27 N	122.33 W
Scott, Mt., Or.	116	42.55 N	122.00 W
Scott Ra., Ant.	232	68.00 S	55.00 E
Scottsbluff, Ne. (skŏts'blŭf)	114	41.52 N	103.40 W
Scotts Bluff Natl. Mon., Ne.	114	41.45 N	103.47 W
Scottsboro, Al. (skŏts'bŭro)	101	34.40 N	86.03 W
Scottsburg, In. (skŏts'bûrg)	110	38.40 N	85.50 W
Scottsdale, Austl. (skŏts'dāl)	216	41.12 S	147.37 E
Scottsville, Ky. (skŏts'vĭl)	101	36.45 N	86.10 W
Scott Township, Pa.	57b	40.24 N	80.06 W
Scottville, Mi.	110	44.00 N	86.20 W
Scranton, Pa. (skrăn'tŭn)	111	41.45 N	75.45 W
Scugog (L.), Can. (skū'gôg)	111	44.05 N	78.55 W
Scunthorpe, Eng. (skŭn'thôrp)	156	53.36 N	0.38 W
Scutari, L., Alb. (skōō'tä-rē)	173	42.14 N	19.33 E
Scutari, see Shkodër			
Seabeck, Wa. (sē'bĕck)	128a	47.38 N	122.50 W
Sea Bright, NJ (sē brīt)	112a	40.22 N	73.58 W
Seabrook, Md.	56d	38.58 N	76.51 W
Seabrook, Tx. (sē'brŏŏk)	125	29.34 N	95.01 W
Sea Cliff, NY	55	40.51 N	73.38 W
Seacombe, Eng.	64a	53.25 N	3.01 W
Seaford, De. (sē'fērd)	111	38.35 N	75.40 W
Seaford, NY	55	40.40 N	73.30 W
Seaforth, Austl.	70a	33.48 S	151.15 E
Seaforth, Eng.	64a	53.28 N	3.01 W
Seagraves, Tx. (sē'grāvs)	122	32.51 N	102.38 W
Sea, Is., Ga.-SC (sē)	127	31.21 N	81.05 W
Seal, Eng.	62	51.17 N	0.14 E
Seal (R.), Can.	96	59.08 N	96.37 W
Seal Beach, Ca.	119a	33.44 N	118.06 W
Seal Cays (Is.), Ba.	135	22.40 N	75.55 W
Seal Cays (Is.), Turks & Caicos Is.	135	21.10 N	71.45 W
Seal I., S. Afr. (sēl)	226a	34.07 S	18.36 E
Seal Rocks (Rocks), Ca.	58b	37.47 N	122.31 W
Sealy, Tx. (sē'lē)	125	29.46 N	96.10 W
Searcy, Ar. (sûr'sē)	123	35.13 N	91.43 W
Searles (L.), Ca. (sûrl's)	120	35.44 N	117.22 W
Searsport, Me. (sērz'pōrt)	104	44.28 N	68.55 W
Seaside, Or. (sē'sīd)	116	45.59 N	123.55 W
Seat Pleasant, Md.	56d	38.53 N	76.52 W
Seattle, Wa. (sē-ăt''l)	118a	47.36 N	122.20 W
Sebaco, Nic. (sē-bä'kô)	132	12.50 N	86.03 W
Sebago, Me. (sē-bā'gō)	104	43.52 N	70.20 W
Sebastion Vizcaino, Bahia (B.), Mex. (bä-ē'ä-sē-bäs-tyô'n-vēs-kä-ē'nō)	128	28.45 N	115.15 W
Sebastopol, Ca. (sē-bȧs'tô-pôl)	120	38.27 N	122.50 W
Sebderat, Eth.	225	15.30 N	36.45 E
Sébé (R.), Gabon	230	0.45 S	13.30 E
Sebeş, Rom.	173	45.58 N	23.34 E
Sebewaing, Mi. (se'bē-wăng)	110	43.45 N	83.25 W
Sebezh, Sov. Un. (syĕ'bĕzh)	174	56.16 N	28.29 E
Sebinkarahisar, Tur.	179	40.15 N	38.10 E
Sebnitz, G.D.R. (zĕb'nēts)	166	51.01 N	14.16 E
Sebou, Oued (R.), Mor.	160	34.23 N	5.18 W
Sebree, Ky. (sē-brē')	110	37.35 N	87.30 W
Sebring, Fl. (sē'brĭng)	127a	27.30 N	81.26 W
Sebring, Oh.	110	40.55 N	81.05 W
Secane, Pa.	56b	39.55 N	75.18 W
Secaucus, NJ	55	40.47 N	74.04 W
Secchia (R.), It. (sĕ'kyä)	172	44.25 N	10.25 E
Seco (R.), Mex. (sĕ'kô)	131	18.11 N	93.18 W
Sedalia, Mo.	123	38.42 N	93.12 W
Sedan, Fr. (sē-däN)	168	49.49 N	4.55 E
Sedan, Ks. (sē-dăn')	123	37.07 N	96.08 W
Sedom, Isr.	191a	31.04 N	35.24 E
Sedro Woolley, Wa. (sē'drô-wōōl'ē)	118a	48.30 N	122.14 W
Šeduva, Sov. Un. (shĕ'dōō-vȧ)	165	55.46 N	23.45 E
Seeberg, G.D.R.	65a	52.33 N	13.41 E
Seeburg, G.D.R.	65a	52.31 N	13.07 E
Seefeld, G.D.R.	65a	52.37 N	13.40 E
Seekoevlei (L.), S. Afr. (zā'kōōf-lī)	226a	34.04 S	18.33 E
Seer Green, Eng.	62	51.37 N	0.36 W
Seestall, F.R.G. (zā'shtäl)	157d	47.58 N	10.52 E
Sefrou, Mor. (sē-frōō')	160	33.49 N	4.46 W
Sefton, Eng.	64a	53.30 N	2.58 W
Seg (L.), Sov. Un. (syĕgh)	178	64.00 N	33.30 E
Segamat, Mala. (sā'gȧ-mȧt)	191b	2.30 N	102.49 E
Segang, China (sŭ-gäŋ)	200	31.59 N	114.13 E
Segbana, Benin	229	10.56 N	3.42 E
Segorbe, Sp. (sĕ-gôr-bĕ)	171	39.50 N	0.30 W
Ségou, Mali (sā-gōō')	228	13.27 N	6.16 W
Segovia, Col. (sĕ-gô'vēä)	142a	7.08 N	74.42 W
Segovia, Sp. (sā-gō'vē-ä)	170	40.58 N	4.05 W
Segovia (R.), see Coco			
Segre (R.), Sp. (sā'grä)	171	41.54 N	1.10 E
Seguam (I.), Ak. (sē'gwäm)	107a	52.16 N	172.10 W
Seguam Pass., Ak.	107a	52.20 N	173.00 W
Séguédine, Niger	229	20.12 N	12.59 E
Séguéla, Ivory Coast (sā-gā-lä')	228	7.57 N	6.40 W
Seguin, Tx. (sĕ-gēn')	124	29.35 N	97.58 W
Segula (I.), Ak. (sē-gū'lȧ)	107a	52.08 N	178.35 E
Segura (R.), Sp.	170	38.24 N	2.12 W
Segura (R.), Sp. (sā-gōō'rä)	171	38.07 N	0.33 W
Segura, Sierra de (Mts.), Sp. (sē-ĕ'r-rä-dē)	170	38.05 N	2.45 W
Sehwān, Pak.	196	26.33 N	67.51 E
Seibeeshiden, Jap.	69a	35.34 N	139.22 E
Seibo, Dom. Rep. (sĕ'y-bō)	135	18.45 N	69.05 W
Seiling, Ok.	122	36.09 N	98.56 W
Seinäjoki, Fin. (sâ'ē-nĕ-yô'kē)	165	62.47 N	22.50 E
Seine (R.), Can. (sān)	102	49.04 N	91.00 W
Seine (R.), Can. (sān)	95f	49.48 N	96.30 W
Seine (R.), Fr.	168	49.21 N	1.17 E
Seine, Baie de la (B.), Fr. (bī dē lä sān)	168	49.37 N	0.53 W
Seio do Venus (Mtn.), Braz. (sē-yô-dô-vē'nōōs)	144b	22.28 S	43.12 W
Seixal, Port. (sā-ē-shäl')	171b	38.38 N	9.06 W
Sekenke, Tan.	231	4.16 S	34.10 E
Sekondi-Takoradi, Ghana (sē-kôn'dē tä-kô-rä'dē)	228	4.59 N	1.43 W
Sekota, Eth.	225	12.47 N	38.59 E
Selangor (State), Mala. (sā-län'gōr)	191b	2.53 N	101.29 E
Selanovtsi, Bul. (sāl'ȧ-nôv-tsĭ)	173	43.42 N	24.05 E
Selaru I., Indon.	207	8.30 S	130.30 E
Selatan, Tandjung (C.), Indon. (sā-lä'tän)	206	4.09 S	114.40 E
Selawik, Ak. (sē-lȧ-wĭk)	107	66.30 N	160.09 W
Selayar, Pulau (I.), Indon.	206	6.15 S	121.15 E
Selbecke (Neigh.), F.R.G.	63	51.20 N	7.28 E
Selbusjøen (L.), Nor. (sĕl'bōō)	164	63.18 N	11.55 E
Selby, Eng. (sĕl'bē)	156	53.47 N	1.03 W
Selby (Neigh.), S. Afr.	71b	26.13 S	28.02 E
Seldovia, Ak. (sĕl-dō'vē-ȧ)	107	59.26 N	151.42 W
Selection Park, S. Afr.	71b	26.18 S	28.27 E
Selemdzha (R.), Sov. Un. (sâ-lĕmt-zhä')	181	52.28 N	131.50 E
Selenga (R.), Sov. Un. (sĕ lĕŋ gä')	181	51.00 N	106.40 E
Selenge, Mong.	198	49.04 N	102.23 E
Selennyakh (R.), Sov. Un. (sĕl-yĭn-yäk)	181	67.42 N	141.45 E
Sélestat, Fr. (sē-lē-stä')	169	48.16 N	7.27 E
Selibaby, Mauritania (sȧ-lē-bȧ-bē')	224	15.21 N	12.11 W
Seliger (L.), Sov. Un. (sĕl'lē-gĕr)	174	57.14 N	33.18 E
Selizharovo, Sov. Un. (sâ'lē-zhä'rô-vô)	174	56.51 N	33.28 E
Selkirk, Can. (sĕl'kûrk)	101	50.09 N	96.52 W
Selkirk Mts., Can.	96	51.00 N	117.40 W
Selleck, Wa. (sĕl'ĕck)	118a	47.22 N	121.52 W
Sellersburg, In. (sĕl'ĕrs-bûrg)	113h	38.25 N	85.45 W
Sellya Khskaya, Guba (B.), Sov. Un. (sĕl-yäk'sKȧ-yȧ)	181	72.30 N	136.00 E
Selma, Al. (sĕl'mȧ)	126	32.25 N	87.00 W
Selma, Ca.	120	36.34 N	119.37 W
Selma, NC	127	35.33 N	78.16 W
Selma, Tx.	119d	29.33 N	98.19 W
Selmer, Tn.	126	35.11 N	88.36 W
Selsingen, F.R.G. (zĕl'zĕn-gĕn)	157c	53.22 N	9.13 E
Seltar, Singapore	67c	1.25 N	103.53 E
Selway R., Id. (sĕl'wȧ)	116	46.07 N	115.12 W
Selwyn (L.), Can. (sĕl'wĭn)	96	59.41 N	104.30 W
Seman (R.), Alb.	173	40.48 N	19.53 E
Semarang, Indon. (sĕ-mä'räng)	206	7.03 S	110.27 E
Semarinda, Indon.	206	0.30 S	117.10 E
Sembawang, Singapore	67c	1.27 N	103.50 E
Semendria, see Smederevo			
Semënovka, Sov. Un. (sĕ-myôn'ôf-kȧ)	175	52.10 N	32.34 E
Semeru, Gunung (Mtn.), Indon.	206	8.06 S	112.55 E
Semiahmoo Ind. Res., Can.	118d	49.01 N	122.43 W
Semiahmoo Spit, Wa. (sĕm'ĭ-ȧ-mōō)	118d	48.59 N	122.52 W

ng-sing; ŋ-baŋk; N-nasalized n; nŏd; cŏmmit; ōld; ôbey; ôrder; oi-boil; fōōd; fŏŏt; ou-out; s-soft; sh-dish; th-thin; pūre; ůnite; ûrn; stŭd; circŭs; ü-as in French tu; '-indeterminate vowel.

344 Semichi Is. – Shenze

PLACE (Pronounciation)	PAGE	Lat. °'	Long. °'
Semichi Is., Ak. (sē-mē'chī)	107a	52.40 N	174.50 W
Seminoe Res., Wy. (sĕm'ĭ nō)	117	42.08 N	107.10 W
Seminole, Ok. (sĕm'ĭ-nōl)	123	35.13 N	96.41 W
Seminole, Tx.	124	32.43 N	102.39 W
Seminole Ind. Res., Fl.	127a	26.19 N	81.11 W
Seminole Ind. Res., Fl.	127a	27.05 N	81.25 W
Seminole, L., Fl.-Ga.	126	30.57 N	84.46 W
Semipalatinsk, Sov. Un. (sĕ'mē-pá-lá-tyēnsk')	180	50.28 N	80.29 E
Semisopochnoi (I.), Ak. (sĕ-mē-sá-pōsh' noi)	107a	51.45 N	179.25 W
Semiyarskoye, Sov. Un. (sĕ'mē-yär'skô-yĕ)	180	51.03 N	78.28 E
Semliki R., Ug.-Zaire (sĕm'lē-kē)	225	0.45 N	29.36 E
Semlin, see **Zemun**			
Semmering P., Aus. (sĕm'ĕr-ĭng)	166	47.39 N	15.50 E
Semnān, Iran	179	35.30 N	53.30 E
Senador Pompeu, Braz. (sĕ-nä-dōr-pôm-pĕ'ōō)	143	5.34 S	39.18 W
Senatobia, Ms. (sĕ-ná-tō'bē-á)	126	34.36 N	89.56 W
Send, Eng.	62	51.17 N	0.31 W
Sendai, Jap. (sĕn-dī')	204	38.18 N	141.02 E
Seneca, Ks. (sĕn'ē-ká)	123	39.49 N	96.03 W
Seneca, Md.	112e	39.04 N	77.20 W
Seneca, SC	126	34.40 N	82.58 W
Seneca (L.), NY	111	42.30 N	76.55 W
Seneca Falls, NY	111	42.55 N	76.55 W
Senegal, Afr. (sĕn-ĕ-gôl')	222	14.53 N	14.58 W
Sénégal (R.), Afr.	228	16.00 N	14.00 W
Senekal, S. Afr. (sĕn'ē-kál)	223d	28.20 S	27.37 E
Senftenberg, G.D.R. (zĕnf'tĕn-bĕrgh)	166	51.32 N	14.00 E
Sengunyane (R.), Leso	227c	29.35 S	28.08 E
Senhor do Bonfim, Braz. (sĕn-yôr dô bôn-fē'n)	143	5.21 S	40.09 W
Senigallia, It. (så-nē-gäl'lyä)	172	43.42 N	13.16 E
Senj, Yugo. (sĕn')	172	44.58 N	14.55 E
Senja (I.), Nor. (sĕnyä)	158	69.28 N	16.10 E
Senlis, Fr. (sän-lēs')	169b	49.13 N	2.35 E
Sennar Dam, Sud.	225	13.38 N	33.38 E
Senneterre, Can.	97	48.20 N	77.22 W
Senno, Sov. Un. (syĕ'nô)	174	54.48 N	29.43 E
Senriyama, Jap.	69b	34.47 N	135.30 E
Sens, Fr. (säns)	168	48.05 N	3.18 E
Sensuntepeque, Sal. (sĕn-sōōn-tå-pā'kå)	132	13.53 N	88.34 W
Senta, Yugo. (sĕn'tä)	173	45.54 N	20.05 E
Sentosa (I.), Singapore	67c	1.15 N	103.50 E
Senzaki, Jap. (sĕn'zä-kē)	205	34.22 N	131.09 E
Seoul, see **Sŏul**			
Sepang, Mala.	191b	2.43 N	101.45 E
Sepetiba, Baia de (B.), Braz. (bäē'ä dĕ så-på-tē'bá)	144b	23.01 S	43.42 W
Sepik (R.), Pap. N. Gui. (sĕp-ēk')	207	4.07 S	142.40 E
Septentrional, Cordillera (Mts.), Dom. Rep. (kôr-dēl-yĕ'rä sĕp-tĕn-tryô-nä'l)	135	19.50 N	71.15 W
Septeuil, Fr. (sĕ-tû')	169b	48.53 N	1.40 E
Sept-Îles, Can. (sĕ-tēl')	104	50.12 N	66.23 W
Sequatchie (R.), Tn. (sē-kwăch'ē)	126	35.33 N	85.14 W
Sequim, Wa. (sē'kwĭm)	118a	48.05 N	123.07 W
Sequim B., Wa.	118a	48.04 N	122.58 W
Sequoia Natl. Park, Ca. (sē-kwoi'á)	120	36.34 N	118.37 W
Seragoon Hbr., Singapore	67c	1.23 N	103.57 E
Seraing, Bel. (sē-răn')	163	50.38 N	5.28 E
Seram (I.), Indon.	207	2.45 S	129.30 E
Serāmpore, India	196a	22.44 N	88.21 E
Serang, Indon. (så-räng')	206	6.13 S	106.10 E
Seranggung, Indon.	191b	0.49 N	104.11 E
Serangoon, Singapore	67c	1.22 N	103.54 E
Serbia (Reg.), see **Srbija**			
Serdobsk, Sov. Un. (sĕr-dôpsk')	179	52.30 N	44.20 E
Serebr'anyj Bor (Neigh.), Sov. Un.	66b	55.48 N	37.30 E
Sered', Czech.	167	48.17 N	17.43 E
Seredina-Buda, Sov. Un. (sĕ-rå-dē'ná-bōō'dá)	175	52.11 N	34.03 E
Seremban, Mala. (sĕr-ĕm-bän')	191b	2.44 N	101.57 E
Serengeti Natl. Pk., Tan.	231	2.20 S	34.50 E
Serengeti Pln., Tan.	231	2.40 S	34.55 E
Serenje, Zambia (sĕ-rĕn'yĕ)	226	13.12 S	30.49 E
Seres, see **Sérrai**			
Seret, Czech.	167	48.17 N	17.43 E
Seret R., Sov. Un. (sĕr'ĕt)	167	49.45 N	25.30 E
Sergeya Kirova (I.), Sov. Un. (sĕr-gyē'yá kē'rô-vå)	180	77.30 N	86.10 E
Sergipe (State), Braz. (sĕr-zhē'pĕ)	143	10.27 S	37.04 W
Sergiyevsk, Sov. Un.	178	53.58 N	51.00 E
Sérifos, Grc.	173	37.10 N	24.32 E
Sérifos (I.), Grc.	173	37.42 N	24.17 E
Serodino, Arg. (sĕ-rô-dē'nō)	141c	32.36 S	60.56 W
Seropédica, Braz. (sĕ-rô-pĕ'dē-kä)	144b	22.44 S	43.43 W
Serov, Sov. Un. (syĕ-rôf')	182a	59.36 N	60.30 E
Serowe, Bots. (sĕ-rō'wĕ)	226	22.18 S	26.39 E
Serpa, Port. (sĕr-pä)	170	37.56 N	7.38 W
Serpukhov, Sov. Un. (syĕr'pōō-kôf)	174	54.53 N	37.27 E
Sérrai (Seres), Grc. (sĕr'rĕ) (sĕr'ĕs)	173	41.06 N	23.36 E
Serranias Del Burro, Mex. (sĕr-rä-nē'äs dĕl bōō'r-rô)	124	29.39 N	102.07 W
Serrinha, Braz. (sĕr-rēn'yá)	143	11.43 S	38.49 W
Serta, Port. (sĕr'tá)	170	39.48 N	8.01 W
Sertânia, Braz. (sĕr-tá'nyä)	143	8.28 S	37.13 W
Sertãozinho, Braz. (sĕr-toun-zē'n-yô)	141a	21.10 S	47.58 W
Serting (R.), Mala.	191b	3.01 N	102.32 E
Seruí, Braz. (sĕ-rōō-ē')	144b	22.40 S	43.08 W
Servon, Fr.	64c	48.43 N	2.35 E
Sese Is., Ug.	231	0.30 S	32.30 E
Sesia (R.), It. (sâz'yä)	172	45.33 N	8.25 E
Sesimbra, Port. (sĕ-sē'm-brä)	171b	38.27 N	9.06 W
Sesmyl (R.), S. Afr.	227b	25.51 S	28.06 E
Sesto San Giovanni, It.	65c	45.32 N	9.14 E
Sestri Levante, It. (sĕs'trē lå-vän'tå)	172	44.15 N	9.24 E

PLACE (Pronounciation)	PAGE	Lat. °'	Long. °'
Sestroretsk, Sov. Un. (sĕs-trô-rĕtsk)	182c	60.06 N	29.58 E
Sestroretskiy Razliv, Ozero (L.), Sov. Un. (ô'zĕ-rô sĕs-trô' rĕts-kĭ-räz'lĭf)	182c	60.05 N	30.07 E
Seta, Jap. (sĕ'tä)	205b	34.58 N	135.56 W
Setagaya (Neigh.), Jap.	69a	35.39 N	139.40 E
Séte, Fr. (sĕt)	168	43.24 N	3.42 E
Sete Lagoas, Braz. (sĕ-tĕ lä-gô'äs)	143	19.23 S	43.58 W
Sete Pontes, Braz.	61c	22.51 S	43.05 W
Seto, Jap. (sĕ'tō)	205	35.11 N	137.07 E
Seto-Naikai (Sea), Jap. (sĕ'tô nī'kī)	205	33.50 N	132.25 E
Seton Hall University (P. Int.), NY	55	40.45 N	74.15 W
Settat, Mor. (sĕt-ät') (sĕ-tá')	224	33.02 N	7.30 W
Sette-Cama, Gabon. (sĕ-tĕ-kä-mä')	226	2.29 S	9.40 E
Settecamini (Neigh.), It.	66c	41.56 N	12.37 E
Settimo Milanese, It.	65c	45.29 N	9.03 E
Settlement Pt., Ba. (sĕt'l-mĕnt)	134	26.40 N	79.00 W
Settlers, S. Afr. (sĕt'lērs)	223d	24.57 S	28.33 E
Settsu, Jap.	205b	34.46 N	135.33 E
Setúbal, Port. (så-tōō'bäl)	171b	30.32 N	8.54 W
Setúbal, B. de, Port. (bä-ē'ä)	170	38.27 N	9.08 W
Seul, Lac (L.), Can. (låk sûl)	101	50.20 N	92.30 W
Sevan (L.), Sov. Un. (syĭ-vän')	179	40.10 N	45.20 E
Sevastopol' (Akhiar), Sov. Un. (syĕ-vás-tô'pôl'') (äk'yár)	175	44.34 N	33.34 E
Seven Hills, Austl.	70a	33.46 S	150.57 E
Seven Hills, Oh.	56a	41.22 N	81.41 W
Seven Is., see Shichitō			
Seven Kings (Neigh.), Eng.	62	51.34 N	0.05 E
Sevenoaks, Eng. (sĕ-vĕn-ôks')	156b	51.16 N	0.12 E
Severka R., Sov. Un. (sâ'vĕr-ká)	182b	55.11 N	38.41 E
Severn (R.), Can. (sĕv'ērn)	97	55.21 N	88.42 W
Severna Park, Md. (sĕv'ērn-á)	112e	39.04 N	76.33 W
Severnaya Dvina (Northern Dvina) (R.), Sov. Un.	178	63.00 N	42.40 E
Severnaya Zemlya (Northern Land) (Is.), Sov. Un. (sĕ-vyĭr-nī'u zĭ-m'lyä')	177	79.33 N	101.15 E
Severoural'sk, Sov. Un. (sĕ-vyĭ-rŭ-ōō-rälsk')	182a	60.08 N	59.53 E
Sevier (L.), Ut. (sē-vēr')	121	38.55 N	113.10 W
Sevier R., Ut.	121	39.25 N	112.20 W
Sevier R., East Fork, Ut.	121	37.45 N	112.10 W
Sevilla, Col. (sĕ-vē'l-yä)	142a	4.16 N	75.56 W
Sevilla, Sp. (så-vēl'yä)	170	37.29 N	5.58 W
Seville, Oh. (sĕ'vĭl)	113d	41.01 N	81.45 W
Sevlievo, Bul. (sĕv'lyĕ-vô)	173	41.02 N	25.05 E
Sevran, Fr.	64c	48.56 N	2.32 E
Sèvres, Fr.	64c	48.49 N	2.12 E
Sevsk, Sov. Un. (syĕfsk)	174	52.08 N	34.28 E
Seward, Ak. (sū'ărd)	107	60.18 N	149.28 W
Seward, Ne.	123	40.55 N	97.06 W
Seward Pen., Ak.	107	65.40 N	164.00 W
Sewell, Chile (sĕ'ōō-ĕl)	144	34.01 S	70.18 W
Sewickley, Pa. (sē-wĭk'lē)	113e	40.33 N	80.11 W
Seybaplaya, Mex. (sā-ē-bä-plä'yä)	131	19.38 N	90.40 W
Seychelles, Afr. (sā-shĕl')	224	5.20 S	55.10 E
Seydisfjördur, Ice. (sā'dēs-fyûr-dōōr)	158	65.21 N	14.08 W
Seyé, Mex. (sĕ-yĕ')	132a	20.51 N	89.22 W
Seyhan (R.), Tur.	161	37.28 N	35.40 E
Seylac, Som.	223a	11.19 N	43.20 E
Seym (R.), Sov. Un. (sĕym)	175	51.23 N	33.22 E
Seymour, In. (sē'mōr)	103	38.55 N	85.55 W
Seymour, Ia.	115	40.41 N	93.03 W
Seymour, S. Afr. (sē'môr)	227c	32.33 S	26.48 E
Seymour, Tx.	122	33.35 N	99.16 W
Sezela, S. Afr.	227c	30.33 S	30.37 W
Sezze, It. (sĕt'så)	172	41.32 N	13.30 E
Sfaz, Tun. (sfäks)	224	34.51 N	10.45 E
Sfîntu-Gheorghe, Rom.	173	45.53 N	25.49 E
's-Gravenhage (The Hague), Neth. ('s krä'vĕn-hä'kĕ) (hāg)	157a	52.05 N	4.16 E
Sha (R.), China (shä)	199	33.33 N	114.30 E
Shaanxi (Prov.), China (shän-shyē)	198	35.30 N	109.10 E
Shabeelle (R.), Som.	223a	1.38 N	43.50 E
Shablykino, Sov. Un. (sháb-lē'kĭ-nô)	182b	56.22 N	38.37 E
Shache (Yarkand), China (shä-chū)	198	38.15 N	77.15 E
Shackleton Shelf Ice, Ant. (shăk''l-tŭn)	232	65.00 S	100.00 E
Shades Cr., Al. (shādz)	112h	33.20 N	86.55 W
Shades Mtn., Al.	112h	33.22 N	86.51 W
Shagamu, Nig.	229	6.51 N	3.39 E
Shāhdara (Neigh.), India	67d	28.40 N	77.18 E
Shāhjahānpur, India (shä-jŭ-hän'pōōr)	196	27.58 N	79.58 E
Shah Mosque (P. Int.), Iran	68h	35.40 N	51.25 E
Shahrezā, Iran (shä-rā'zä)	192	31.47 N	51.47 E
Shajing, China (shä-jyĭŋ)	201a	22.44 N	113.48 E
Shakarpur Khās (Neigh.), India	67d	28.38 N	77.17 E
Shaker Hts., Oh. (shā'kēr)	113d	41.28 N	81.34 W
Shakhty, Sov. Un. (shäk'tē)	175	47.41 N	40.11 E
Shaki, Nig.	229	8.39 N	3.25 E
Shakopee, Mn. (shăk'ô-pe)	119g	44.48 N	93.31 W
Shakūrpur (Neigh.), India	67d	28.41 N	77.09 E
Shala L., Eth. (shä'lå)	225	7.34 N	39.00 E
Shambe, Sud. (shäm'bå)	225	7.08 N	30.46 E
Shām, Jabal ash (Mtn.), Om.	192	23.01 N	57.45 E
Shammar, Jabal (Mts.), Sau. Ar. (jĕb'ĕl shŭm'ár)	192	27.13 N	40.16 E
Shamokin, Pa. (shá-mō'kĭn)	111	40.45 N	76.30 W
Shamrock, Tx. (shăm'rŏk)	122	35.14 N	100.12 W
Shamva, Zimb (shäm'vá)	226	17.18 S	31.35 E
Shandī, Sud.	225	16.44 N	33.29 E
Shandon, Oh. (shăn-dŭn)	113f	39.20 N	84.13 W
Shandong (Prov.), China (shän-dôŋ)	199	36.08 N	117.09 E
Shandong Bandao (Pen.), China (shän-dôŋ bän-dou)	202	37.00 N	120.10 E
Shangcai, China (shäŋ-tsī)	200	33.16 N	114.16 E
Shangcheng, China (shäŋ-chŭŋ)	200	31.47 N	115.22 E
Shangdu, China (shäŋ-dōō)	202	41.38 N	113.22 E
Shanghai, China (shäng'hī')	201b	31.14 N	121.27 E
Shanghai-Shi (Mun.), China (shäŋ-hī shr)	199	31.30 N	121.45 E

PLACE (Pronounciation)	PAGE	Lat. °'	Long. °'
Shanghe, China (shäŋ-hŭ)	200	37.18 N	117.10 E
Shanglin, China (shäŋ-lĭn)	200	38.20 N	116.05 E
Shangqiu, China (shäŋ-chyô)	200	34.24 N	115.39 E
Shangrao, China (shäŋ-rou)	203	28.25 N	117.58 E
Shangzhi, China (shäŋ-jr)	202	45.18 N	127.52 E
Shanhaiguan, China	200	40.01 N	119.45 E
Shannon, Al. (shăn'ŭn)	112h	33.23 N	86.52 W
Shannon (R.), Ire. (shăn'ŏn)	162	52.30 N	9.58 W
Shanshan, China (shän'shän')	198	42.51 N	89.53 E
Shantar (I.), Sov. Un. (shän'tär)	181	55.13 N	138.42 E
Shantou (Swatow), China (shän-tō)	203	23.20 N	116.40 E
Shanxi (Prov.), China (shän-shyē)	199	37.30 N	112.00 E
Shan Xian, China (shän shyĕn)	200	34.47 N	116.04 E
Shaobo, China (shou-bwo)	200	32.33 N	119.30 E
Shaobo Hu (L.), China (shou-bwo hōō)	200	32.07 N	119.13 E
Shaoguan, China (shou-gŭän)	203	24.58 N	113.42 E
Shaoxing, China (shou-shyĭŋ)	203	30.00 N	120.40 E
Shapki, Sov. Un. (shäp'kĭ)	182c	59.36 N	31.11 E
Shaqrā', P.D.R. of Yem.	195	13.21 N	45.42 E
Shark B., Austl. (shärk)	214	25.30 S	113.00 E
Sharon, Ma. (shăr'ŏn)	105a	42.07 N	71.11 W
Sharon, Pa.	110	41.15 N	80.30 W
Sharon Hill, Pa.	56b	39.55 N	75.16 W
Sharon Springs, Ks.	122	38.51 N	101.45 W
Sharonville, Oh. (shăr'ŏn vĭl)	113f	39.16 N	84.24 W
Sharpsburg, Pa. (shärps'bûrg)	113e	40.30 N	79.54 W
Sharps Hill, Pa.	57b	40.30 N	79.56 W
Sharr, Jabal (Mtn.), Sau. Ar.	192	28.00 N	36.07 E
Shashi, China (shä-shē)	203	30.20 N	112.18 E
Shasta L., Ca. (shăs'tá)	116	40.51 N	122.32 W
Shasta, Mt., Ca.	116	41.35 N	122.12 W
Shatsk, Sov. Un. (shátsk)	178	54.00 N	41.40 E
Shattuck, Ok. (shăt'ŭk)	122	36.16 N	99.53 W
Shaunavon, Can.	100	49.40 N	108.25 W
Shaw, Eng.	64b	53.35 N	2.06 W
Shaw, Ms. (shô)	126	33.36 N	90.44 W
Shawano, Wi. (shá-wô'nō)	115	44.41 N	88.13 W
Shawinigan, Can.	97	46.32 N	72.46 W
Shawnee, Ks. (shô-nē')	119f	39.01 N	94.43 W
Shawnee, Ok.	123	35.20 N	96.54 W
Shawneetown, Il. (shô'nē-toun)	110	37.40 N	88.05 W
Shayang, China	203	31.00 N	112.38 E
Shchara (R.), Sov. Un. (sh-chä'rå)	167	53.17 N	25.12 E
Shchëlkovo, Sov. Un. (shchĕl'kô-vô)	182b	55.55 N	38.00 E
Shchëtovo, Sov. Un. (shchĕ'tô-vô)	175	48.11 N	39.13 E
Shchigry, Sov. Un. (shchē'grē)	175	51.52 N	36.54 E
Shchors, Sov. Un. (shchôrs)	175	51.38 N	31.58 E
Shchuch'ye Ozero, Sov. Un. (shchōōch'yĕ ô'zĕ-rō)	182a	56.31 N	56.35 E
Sheakhala, India	196a	22.47 N	88.10 E
Shebele R., Eth. (shā'bå-lē)	223a	6.07 N	43.10 E
Sheboygan, Wi. (shē-boi'găn)	115	43.45 N	87.44 W
Sheboygan Falls, Wi.	115	43.43 N	87.51 W
Shechem (Ruins), Jordan	191a	32.15 N	35.22 E
Shedandoah, Pa.	111	40.50 N	76.15 W
Shediac, Can. (shĕ'dē-ăk)	104	46.13 N	64.32 W
Shedin Pk., Can. (shĕd'ĭn)	98	55.55 N	127.32 W
Sheepshead Bay (Neigh.), NY	55	40.35 N	73.56 W
Sheerness, Eng. (shēr'nĕs)	156b	51.26 N	0.46 E
Sheffield, Al. (shĕf'fēld)	126	35.42 N	87.42 W
Sheffield, Can.	95d	43.20 N	80.13 W
Sheffield, Eng.	156	53.23 N	1.28 W
Sheffield, Oh.	113d	41.26 N	82.05 W
Sheffield Lake, Oh.	113d	41.30 N	82.03 W
Sheksna (R.), Sov. Un. (shĕks'ná)	178	59.50 N	38.40 E
Shelagskiy, Mys (C.), Sov. Un. (shĭ-läg'skē)	181	70.08 N	170.52 E
Shelbina, Ar. (shĕl-bī'ná)	123	39.41 N	92.03 W
Shelburn, In. (shĕl'bŭrn)	110	39.10 N	87.30 W
Shelburne, Can.	104	43.46 N	65.19 W
Shelburne, Can.	111	44.04 N	80.12 W
Shelby, In. (shĕl'bē)	113a	41.12 N	87.21 W
Shelby, Mi.	110	43.35 N	86.20 W
Shelby, Ms.	126	33.56 N	90.44 W
Shelby, Mt.	117	48.35 N	111.55 W
Shelby, NC	127	35.16 N	81.35 W
Shelby, Oh.	110	40.50 N	82.40 W
Shelbyville, Il. (shĕl'bē-vĭl)	110	39.20 N	88.45 W
Shelbyville, In.	110	39.30 N	85.45 W
Shelbyville, Ky.	110	38.10 N	85.15 W
Shelbyville, Tn.	126	35.30 N	86.28 W
Shelbyville Res., Il.	192	39.30 N	88.45 W
Sheldon, Ia. (shĕl'dŭn)	114	43.10 N	95.50 W
Sheldon, Tx.	125a	29.52 N	95.07 W
Shelekhova, Zaliv (B.), Sov. Un.	181	60.00 N	156.00 E
Shelikof Str., Ak. (shĕ'lē-kôf)	107	57.56 N	154.20 W
Shellbrook, Can.	100	53.15 N	106.22 W
Shelley, Id. (shĕl'lē)	117	43.24 N	112.06 W
Shellow Bowells, Eng.	62	51.45 N	0.20 E
Shellrock (R.), Ia. (shĕl'rŏk)	115	43.25 N	93.19 W
Shelon' (R.), Sov. Un. (shå'lôn)	174	57.50 N	29.40 E
Shelter, Port (B.), China	68c	22.21 N	114.17 E
Shelton, Ct. (shĕl'tŭn)	111	41.15 N	73.05 W
Shelton, Ne.	122	40.46 N	98.41 W
Shelton, Wa.	116	47.14 N	123.05 W
Shemakha, Sov. Un. (shĕ-má-kä')	182a	56.16 N	59.19 E
Shemakha, Sov. Un.	179	40.35 N	48.40 E
Shenandoah, Ia. (shĕn-ăn-dō'á)	123	40.46 N	95.23 W
Shenandoah, Va.	111	38.30 N	78.30 W
Shenandoah (R.), Va.	111	38.55 N	78.05 W
Shenandoah Natl. Park., Va.	111	38.35 N	78.25 W
Shendam, Nig.	229	8.53 N	9.32 E
Shenfield, Eng.	62	51.38 N	0.19 E
Shengfang, China (shengfäng)	200	39.05 N	116.40 E
Shenkursk, Sov. Un. (shĕn-kōōrsk')	182	62.10 N	43.08 E
Shenmu, China	202	38.55 N	110.35 E
Shenqiu, China	200	33.11 N	115.06 E
Shenxian, China (shŭn shyän)	200	38.02 N	115.33 E
Shenxian, China (shŭn shyĕn)	200	36.14 N	115.38 E
Shenyang, China (shŭn-yäŋ)	202	41.45 N	123.22 E
Shenze, China (shŭn-dzŭ)	200	38.12 N	115.12 E

ăt; finăl; rāte; senåte; ärm; àsk; sofá; fâre; ch-choose; dh-as th in other; bē; ėvent; bĕt; recĕnt; cratēr; g-gō; gh-guttural g; bĭt; ĭ-short neutral; rīde; K-guttural k as ch in German ich;

PRONOUNCING INDEX

Sheopur – Simpson Des. 345

PLACE (Pronunciation)	PAGE	Lat. °′	Long. °′
Sheopur, India	196	25.37 N	78.10 E
Shepard, Can. (shĕ'pärd)	95e	50.57 N	113.55 W
Shepetovka, Sov. Un. (shĕ-pĕ-tôf'kȧ)	175	50.10 N	27.01 E
Shepparton, Austl. (shĕp'ăr-tŭn)	216	36.15 S	145.25 E
Shepperton, Eng.	62	51.24 N	0.27 W
Sherborn, Ma. (shûr'bŭrn)	105a	42.15 N	71.22 W
Sherbro I., S. L.	228	7.30 N	12.55 W
Sherbrooke, Can.	111	45.24 N	71.54 W
Sherburn, Eng. (shûr'bŭrn)	156	53.47 N	1.15 W
Shereshevo, Sov. Un. (shĕ-rĕ-shĕ-vô)	167	52.31 N	24.08 E
Sheridan, Ar. (shĕr'ĭ-dăn)	123	34.19 N	92.21 W
Sheridan, Or.	116	45.06 N	123.22 W
Sheridan, Wy.	117	44.48 N	106.56 W
Sherman, Tx. (shĕr'măn)	123	33.39 N	96.37 W
Sherman Oaks (Neigh.), Ca.	59	34.09 N	118.26 W
Sherna R., Sov. Un. (shĕr'nȧ)	182b	56.08 N	38.45 E
Sherridon, Can.	101	55.10 N	101.10 W
's Hertogenbosch, Neth. (sĕr-tō'ghĕn-bôs)	157a	51.41 N	5.19 E
Sherwood, Or.	118c	45.21 N	122.50 W
Sherwood For., Eng.	156	53.11 N	1.07 W
Sherwood Park, Can.	99	53.31 N	113.19 W
Shetland (Is.), Scot. (shĕt'lănd)	162a	60.35 N	2.10 W
Sheva, India	67e	18.56 N	72.57 E
Shevchenko, Sov. Un.	192	44.00 N	51.10 E
Shewa Gimira, Eth.	225	7.13 N	35.49 E
Shexian, China (shŭ shyĕn)	200	36.34 N	113.42 E
Sheyang (R.), China (she-yäŋ)	200	33.42 N	119.40 E
Sheyenne (R.), ND (shī-ĕn')	114	46.42 N	97.52 W
Shi (R.), China (shr)	200	31.58 N	115.50 E
Shi (R.), China	200	32.09 N	114.11 E
Shiawassee (R.), Mi. (shī-á-wôs'ē)	110	43.15 N	84.05 W
Shibām, P. D. R. of Yem. (shē'bäm)	192	16.02 N	48.40 E
Shibīn al Kawn, Egypt (shē-bēn'ĕl kōm')	223b	30.31 N	31.01 E
Shibīn al Qanāţir, Egypt (kȧ-nä'tĕr)	223b	30.18 N	31.21 E
Shibuya (Neigh.), Jap.	69a	35.40 N	139.42 E
Shichitō (Seven Is.), Jap. (shē'chē-tō)	205	34.18 N	139.28 E
Shicun, China (shr-tso͞on)	200	33.47 N	117.18 E
Shields R., Mt. (shēldz)	117	45.54 N	110.40 W
Shifnal, Eng. (shĭf'năl)	156	52.40 N	2.22 W
Shihlin, Taiwan	68d	25.05 N	121.31 E
Shijian, China (shr-jyĕn)	200	31.27 N	117.51 E
Shijiazhuang, China (shr-jyä-jůäŋ)	200	38.04 N	114.31 E
Shijiu Hu (L.), China (shr-jyō ho͞o)	200	31.29 N	119.07 E
Shijōnawate, Jap.	69b	34.45 N	135.39 E
Shikārpur, Pak.	196	27.51 N	68.52 E
Shiki, Jap. (shē'kē)	205a	35.50 N	139.35 E
Shikoku (I.), Jap. (shē'kō'ko͞o)	205	33.43 N	133.33 E
Shilibao, China	67b	39.55 N	116.29 E
Shilka (R.), Sov. Un. (shĭl'kȧ)	181	53.00 N	118.45 E
Shilla (Mt.), India	196	37.18 N	78.17 E
Shillong, India (shēl-lông')	196	25.39 N	91.58 E
Shiloh, Il. (shī'lō)	119e	38.34 N	89.54 W
Shilong, China (shr-lôŋ)	203	23.05 N	113.58 E
Shilou, China	201a	22.58 N	113.29 E
Shimabara, Jap. (shē'mä-bä'rä)	205	32.46 N	130.22 E
Shimada, Jap. (shē'mä-dä)	205	34.49 N	138.13 E
Shimber Berris (Mtn.), Som	223a	10.40 N	47.23 E
Shimizu, Jap. (shē'mē-zo͞o)	205	35.00 N	138.29 E
Shimminato, Jap. (shēm'mē'nä-tô)	205	36.47 N	137.05 E
Shimoda, Jap. (shē'mô-dȧ)	205	34.41 N	138.58 E
Shimoga, India	197	13.59 N	75.38 E
Shimohōya, Jap.	69a	35.45 N	139.34 E
Shimoigusa (Neigh.), Jap.	69a	35.43 N	139.37 E
Shimomizo, Jap.	69a	35.31 N	139.23 E
Shimoni, Ken.	231	4.39 S	39.23 E
Shimonoseki, Jap. (shē'mô-nō-sĕ'kē) (shē-mô-nô'sē-kĭ)	205	33.58 N	130.55 E
Shimo-Saga, Jap. (shē'mô sä'gä)	205b	35.01 N	135.41 E
Shimoshakujii (Neigh.), Jap.	69a	35.45 N	139.37 E
Shimotsuruma, Jap.	69a	35.29 N	139.28 E
Shimoyugi, Jap.	69a	35.38 N	139.23 E
Shinagawa-Wan (B.), Jap. (shē'nä-gä'wä wän)	205a	35.37 N	139.49 E
Shinano-Gawa (Strm.), Jap. (shē-nä'nō gä'wä)	205	36.43 N	138.22 E
Shinbārī, Egypt	71a	30.07 N	31.09 E
Shindand, Afg.	195	33.18 N	62.08 E
Shingū, Jap. (shĭn'go͞o)	205	33.43 N	135.59 E
Shinji (L.), Jap. (shĭn'jē)	205	35.23 N	133.05 E
Shinjuku (Neigh.), Jap.	69a	35.41 N	139.42 E
Shinkolobwe, Zaire	231	11.02 S	26.35 E
Shin, Loch (L.), Scot. (lŏĸ shĭn)	162	58.08 N	4.02 W
Shinyanga, Tan. (shĭn-yäŋ'gä)	225	3.40 S	33.26 E
Shiono Misaki (C.), Jap. (shē-ô'nō mē'sä-kē)	204	33.20 N	136.10 E
Shīrāz, Iran (shē-räz')	192	29.32 N	52.27 E
Shipai, China (shr-pī)	201a	23.07 N	113.23 E
Ship Channel Cay (I.), Ba. (shĭp chă-nĕl kē)	134	24.50 N	76.50 W
Shipley, Eng. (shĭp'lē)	156	53.50 N	1.47 W
Shippegan, Can. (shĭ'pē-găn)	104	47.45 N	64.42 W
Shippegan I., Can.	104	47.50 N	64.38 W
Shippenburg, Pa. (shĭp'ĕn bûrg)	111	40.00 N	77.30 W
Shipshaw (R.), Can. (shĭp'shô)	104	48.50 N	71.03 W
Shiqma (R.), Isr.	191a	31.31 N	34.40 E
Shirane-san (Mtn.), Jap. (shē'rä'nå-sän')	205	35.44 N	138.14 E
Shira Saki (C.), Jap. (shē'rä sä'kē)	204	41.25 N	142.10 E
Shirati, Tan. (shē-rä'tē)	226	1.15 S	34.02 E
Shīrāz, Iran	195	29.36 N	52.32 E
Shire (R.), Malawi (shē'rā)	231	16.20 S	35.05 E
Shirley, Ma. (shûr'lē)	105a	42.33 N	71.39 W
Shirokoye, Sov. Un. (shē'rô-kô-yĕ)	175	47.40 N	33.18 E
Shishaldin Vol., Ak. (shī-shăl'dĭn)	107a	54.48 N	164.00 W
Shively, Ky. (shīv'lē)	113h	38.11 N	85.47 W
Shivpuri, India	196	25.31 N	77.46 E
Shivta, Horvot (Ruins), Isr.	191a	30.54 N	34.36 E
Shivwits (Shebit) Ind. Res., Ut. (shĭv'wĭts) (shĕ'bĭt)	121	37.10 N	113.50 W
Shivwits Plat, Az.	121	36.13 N	113.42 W
Shiwan, China (shr-wän)	201a	23.01 N	113.04 E
Shiwan Dashan (Mts.), China (shr-wän dä-shän)	203	22.10 N	107.30 E
Shizuki, Jap. (shĭ'zo͞o-kē)	205	34.29 N	134.51 E
Shizuoka, Jap. (shē'zo͞o'ōkȧ)	205	34.58 N	138.24 E
Shklov, Sov. Un. (shklôf)	174	54.11 N	30.23 E
Shkodër (Scutari), Alb. (shkô'dûr) (sko͞o'tȧrē)	173	42.04 N	19.30 E
Shkotovo, Sov. Un. (shkô'tô-vô)	204	43.15 N	132.21 E
Shoal Cr., Il. (shōl)	123	38.37 N	89.25 W
Shoal L., Can.	101	49.32 N	95.00 W
Shoals, In. (shōlz)	110	38.40 N	86.45 W
Shōdai, Jap.	69b	34.51 N	135.42 E
Shōdo (I.), Jap. (shō'dō)	205	34.27 N	134.27 E
Shogunle, Nig.	71d	6.35 N	3.21 E
Sholāpur, India (shō'lä-po͞or)	197	17.42 N	75.51 E
Shomolu, Nig.	71d	6.32 N	3.23 E
Shoreham, Eng.	62	51.20 N	0.11 E
Shorewood, Wi. (shōr'wo͝od)	113a	43.05 N	87.54 W
Shoshone, Id. (shô-shōn'tē)	117	42.56 N	114.24 W
Shoshone L., Wy.	117	44.17 N	110.50 W
Shoshone R., Wy.	117	44.20 N	109.28 W
Shoshoni, Wy.	117	43.14 N	108.05 W
Shostka, Sov. Un. (shôst'kȧ)	175	51.51 N	33.31 E
Shougouang, China (shō-gůäŋ)	200	36.53 N	118.45 E
Shouxian, China (shō shyĕn)	200	32.36 N	116.45 E
Shpola, Sov. Un. (shpô'lȧ)	175	49.01 N	31.36 E
Shreveport, La. (shrēv'pôrt)	125	32.30 N	93.46 W
Shrewsbury, Eng. (shro͞oz'bēr-ĭ)	156	52.43 N	2.44 W
Shrewsbury, Ma.	105a	42.18 N	71.43 W
Shroud Cay (I.) (shroud), Ba.	134	24.20 N	76.40 W
Shu (R.), China (sho͞o)	200	34.47 N	118.27 E
Shuangcheng, China (shůäŋ-chŭŋ)	202	45.18 N	126.18 E
Shuanghe, China (shůäŋ-hŭ)	200	31.33 N	116.48 E
Shuangliao, China	199	43.37 N	123.30 E
Shuangyang, China	202	43.28 N	125.45 E
Shubrā al-Khaymah, Egypt	71a	30.06 N	31.15 E
Shuhedun, China (sho͞o-hŭ-do͞on)	200	31.33 N	117.01 E
Shuiye, China (shwā-yŭ)	200	36.08 N	114.07 E
Shule (R.), China (sho͞o-lŭ)	198	40.53 N	94.55 E
Shullsburg, Wi. (shŭlz'bûrg)	115	42.35 N	90.16 W
Shumagin (Is.), Ak. (sho͞o'mȧ-gĕn)	107	55.22 N	159.20 W
Shumen, Bul.	173	43.15 N	26.54 E
Shunde, China (sho͞on-dŭ)	201a	22.50 N	113.15 E
Shungnak, Ak. (shŭng'nȧk)	107	66.55 N	157.20 W
Shunut, 'Gora (Mt.), Sov. Un. (gȧ-rä sho͞o'no͞ot)	182a	56.33 N	59.45 E
Shunyi, China (sho͞on-yē)	202a	40.09 N	116.38 E
Shuqrah, P. D. R. of Yem.	192	13.32 N	46.02 E
Shūrāb (R.), Iran (sho͞o räb)	192	31.08 N	55.30 E
Shuri, Jap. (sho͞o'rē)	204	26.10 N	127.48 E
Shur R., Iran (sho͞or)	179	35.40 N	50.10 E
Shurugwi, Zimb	226	19.34 S	30.03 E
Shūshtar, Iran (sho͞osh'tûr)	192	31.50 N	48.46 E
Shuswap L., Can. (sho͞os'wŏp)	99	50.57 N	119.15 W
Shuya, Sov. Un. (sho͞o'yȧ)	174	56.52 N	41.23 E
Shuyang, China (sho͞o yäng)	200	34.09 N	118.47 E
Shweba, Bur.	203	22.23 N	96.13 E
Shyaulyay, see Šiauliai			
Siak Ketjil (R.), Indon.	191b	1.01 N	101.45 E
Siaksriinderapura, Indon. (sē-äks'rĭ ĕn'drȧ-po͞o'rä)	191b	0.48 N	102.05 E
Siālkot, Pak. (sē-äl'kōt)	196	32.39 N	74.30 E
Śiátista, Grc. (syä'tĭs-ta)	173	40.15 N	21.32 E
Šiauliai (Shyaulyay), Sov. Un. (shē-ou'lē-ī)	165	55.57 N	23.19 E
Siau, Pulau (I.), Indon.	207	2.40 N	126.00 E
Šibay, Sov. Un. (sē'báy)	182a	52.41 N	58.40 E
Šibenik, Yugo. (shē-bā'nēk)	172	43.44 N	15.55 E
Siberia (Reg.), Asia	190	57.00 N	97.00 E
Siberut, Pulau (I.), Indon. (sē'bā-ro͞ot)	206	1.22 S	99.45 E
Sibī, Pak.	196	29.41 N	67.52 E
Sibiti, Con. (sē-bē-tē')	230	3.41 S	13.21 E
Sibiu, Rom. (sē-bĭ-o͞o')	173	45.47 N	24.09 E
Sibley, Ia. (sĭb'lē)	114	43.24 N	95.33 W
Sibolga, Indon. (sē-bō'gā)	206	1.45 N	98.45 E
Sibpur, India	67a	22.34 N	88.19 E
Sibsāgar, India (sēb-sŭ'gŭr)	193	26.47 N	94.45 E
Sibutu I., Phil.	206	4.40 N	119.30 E
Sibuyan (I.), Phil. (sē-bo͞o-yän')	207a	12.19 N	122.25 E
Sibuyan Sea, Phil.	206	12.43 N	122.38 E
Sichuan (Prov.), China (sz-chůän)	198	31.20 N	103.00 E
Sicily (I.), It. (sĭs'ĭ-lē)	159	37.38 N	13.30 E
Sickingmühle, F.R.G.	63	51.42 N	7.07 E
Sico R., Hond. (sē-kô)	132	15.32 N	85.42 W
Sicuani, Peru (sē-kwä'nē)	142	14.12 S	71.12 W
Sidamo (Prov.), Eth. (sē-dä'mô)	223	5.08 N	37.45 E
Sidao, China	67b	39.51 N	116.26 E
Sidcup (Neigh.), Eng.	62	51.25 N	0.06 E
Siderno Marina, It. (sē-dĕr'nô mä-rē'nä)	172	38.18 N	16.19 E
Sidhirókastron, Grc.	173	41.13 N	23.27 E
Sidi Aïssa, Alg.	171	35.53 N	3.44 E
Sīdī Barrānī, Egypt	194	31.36 N	25.55 E
Sidi bel Abbès, Alg. (sē'dē-bĕl à-bĕs')	224	35.15 N	0.43 W
Sidi Ifni, Mor. (ēf'nē)	224	29.22 N	10.15 W
Sidley, Mt., Ant. (sĭd'lē)	232	77.25 S	129.00 W
Sidney, Can.	98	48.39 N	123.24 W
Sidney, Mt. (sĭd'nē)	117	47.43 N	104.07 W
Sidney, Ne.	114	41.10 N	103.00 W
Sidney, Oh.	110	40.20 N	84.10 W
Sidney Lanier, L., Ga. (lăn'yēr)	126	34.27 N	83.56 W
Sido, Mali	228	11.40 N	7.36 W
Sidon, see Saydā			
Sidr, Wādī (R.), Egypt	191a	29.43 N	32.58 E
Siedlce, Pol. (syĕd''l-tsĕ)	167	52.09 N	22.20 E
Siegburg, F.R.G. (zĕg'bo͞orgh)	169c	50.48 N	7.13 E
Siegen, F.R.G. (zē'ghĕn)	169c	50.52 N	8.01 E
Sieghartskirchen, Aus.	157e	48.16 N	16.00 E
Siemensstadt (Neigh.), F.R.G.	65a	52.32 N	13.17 E
Siemiatycze, Pol. (syĕm'yä'tē-chĕ)	167	52.26 N	22.52 E
Siemionówka, Pol. (sĕĕ-mēō'nôf-kä)	167	52.53 N	23.50 E
Siem Reap, Kamp. (syĕm'rā'ap)	206	13.32 N	103.54 E
Siena, It. (sē-ĕn'ä)	172	43.19 N	11.21 E
Sieradz, Pol. (syĕ'rädz)	167	51.35 N	18.45 E
Sierpc, Pol. (syĕrpts)	167	52.51 N	19.42 E
Sierra Blanca, Tx. (sē-ĕ'rȧ blaŋ-kä)	124	31.10 N	105.20 W
Sierra Blanca Pk., NM (blăn'kȧ)	121	33.25 N	105.50 W
Sierra Leone, Afr. (sē-ĕr'rä lā-ō'nā)	222	8.48 N	12.30 W
Sierra Madre, Ca. (mä'drē)	119a	34.10 N	118.03 W
Sierra Mojada, Mex. (sē-ĕ'r-rä-mô-Ká'dä)	124	27.22 N	103.42 W
Sigean, Fr. (sē-zhŏɴ')	168	43.02 N	2.56 E
Sigeurney, Ia. (sē-gûr-nĭ)	115	41.16 N	92.10 W
Sighetu Marmatiei, Rom.	167	47.57 N	23.55 E
Sighisoara, Rom. (sē-gē-shwä'rȧ)	167	46.11 N	24.48 E
Siglufjördur, Ice.	158	66.06 N	18.45 W
Signakhi, Sov. Un.	179	41.45 N	45.50 E
Signal Hill, Ca. (sĭg'năl hĭl)	119a	33.48 N	118.11 W
Sigsig, Ec. (sēg-sēg')	142	3.04 S	78.44 W
Sigtuna, Swe. (sēgh-to͞o'nȧ)	164	59.40 N	17.39 E
Siguanea, Ensenada de la (B.), Cuba (ĕn-sĕ-nä-dä-dĕ-lä-sē-gwä-nā'ä)	134	21.45 N	83.15 W
Siguatepeque, Hond. (sē-gwä'tĕ-pĕ-kĕ)	132	14.33 N	87.51 W
Sigüenza, Sp. (sē-gwĕ'n-zä)	170	41.03 N	2.38 W
Siguiri, Gui. (sē-gē-rē')	228	11.25 N	9.10 W
Sihong, China (sz-hôŋ)	200	33.25 N	118.13 E
Siirt, Tur. (sĭ-ērt')	179	38.00 N	42.00 E
Sikalongo, Zambia	231	16.46 S	27.07 E
Sikasso, Mali (sē-käs'sō)	228	11.19 N	5.40 W
Sikeston, Mo. (sīks'tŭn)	123	36.50 N	89.35 W
Sikhote Alin', Khrebet (Mts.), Sov. Un. (se-Kô'ta a-lēn')	181	45.00 N	135.45 E
Sikinos (I.), Grc. (sĭ'kĭ-nōs)	173	36.45 N	24.55 E
Sikkim (State), India	196	27.42 N	88.25 E
Siklós, Hung. (sĭ'klōsh)	167	45.51 N	18.18 E
Sil (R.), Sp. (sē'l)	170	42.20 N	7.13 W
Silāmpur (Neigh.), India	67d	28.40 N	77.16 E
Silang, Phil. (sē-läng')	207a	14.14 N	120.58 E
Silao, Mex. (sē-lä'ō)	130	20.56 N	101.25 W
Silchar, India (sĭl-chär')	196	24.52 N	92.50 E
Silent Valley, S. Afr. (sī'lĕnt vă'lē)	223d	24.32 S	26.40 E
Siler City, NC (sī'lēr)	127	35.45 N	79.29 W
Silesia (Reg.), Pol. (sĭ-lē'shȧ)	167	50.58 N	16.53 E
Silifke, Tur.	179	36.20 N	34.00 E
Siling Co (L.), China	196	32.05 N	89.10 E
Silistra, Bul. (sē-lēs'trȧ)	161	44.01 N	27.13 E
Siljan (R.), Swe. (sēl'yän)	164	60.48 N	14.28 E
Silkeborg, Den. (sĭl'kĕ-bôr')	164	56.10 N	9.33 E
Sillery, Can. (sēl'-re')	95b	46.46 N	71.15 W
Siloam Springs, Ar. (sī-lōm)	123	36.10 N	94.32 W
Siloana Plns., Zambia	230	16.55 S	23.10 E
Silocayoápan, Mex. (sē-lō-kä-yō-á'pän)	130	17.29 N	98.09 W
Silsbee, Tx. (sĭlz' bē)	125	30.19 N	94.09 W
Šilschede, F.R.G.	63	51.21 N	7.19 E
Šilutė, Sov. Un. (shĭ-lo͞o'tā)	165	55.23 N	21.26 E
Silva Jardim, Braz. (sē'l-vä-zhär-dēɴ)	141a	22.40 N	42.24 W
Silvana, Wa. (sĭ-văn'ȧ)	118a	48.12 N	122.16 W
Silvânia, Braz. (sēl-vá'nyä)	143	16.43 S	48.33 W
Silvassa, India	196	20.10 N	73.00 E
Silver (L.), Mo.	123	39.38 N	93.12 W
Silverado, Ca. (sĭl-vēr-ä'dō)	118a	33.45 N	117.40 W
Silver Bank Passage (Str.), Ba.	135	20.40 N	70.20 W
Silver Bay, Mn.	115	47.24 N	91.07 W
Silver Bk., Ba.	135	20.40 N	69.40 W
Silver City, NM (sĭl'vēr sĭ'tĭ)	121	32.45 N	108.20 W
Silver City, Pan.	133	9.20 N	79.54 W
Silver Cr., Az.	121	34.30 N	110.05 W
Silver Cr., In.	113h	38.20 N	85.45 W
Silver Creek, NY (crēk)	111	42.35 N	79.10 W
Silver Cr., Muddy Fk., In.	113h	38.26 N	85.52 W
Silverdale, Wa. (sĭl'vēr-dāl)	118a	47.39 N	122.42 W
Silver Hill, Md.	56d	38.51 N	76.57 W
Silver L., Wi.	113a	42.35 N	88.08 W
Silver Lake, Ma.	54a	42.00 N	70.48 W
Silver Lake, Wi. (lāk)	113a	42.33 N	88.10 W
Silver Spring, Md. (sprĭng)	112e	39.00 N	77.00 W
Silver Star Mtn., Wa.	118c	45.45 N	122.15 W
Silverthrone Mtn., Can. (sĭl'vēr-thrōn)	98	51.31 N	126.06 W
Silverton, Co. (sĭl'vēr-tŭn)	121	37.50 N	107.40 W
Silverton, Oh.	113f	39.12 N	84.24 W
Silverton, Or.	116	45.02 N	122.46 W
Silverton, S. Afr.	227b	25.45 S	28.13 E
Silves, Port. (sēl'vĕzh)	170	37.15 N	8.24 W
Silvies R., Or. (sĭl'vēz)	116	43.44 N	119.15 W
Sim, Sov. Un. (sĭm)	182a	55.00 N	57.42 E
Simao, China (sz-mou)	198	22.56 N	101.07 E
Simba, Zaire	230	0.36 N	22.55 E
Simcoe, Can. (sĭm'kō)	111	42.50 N	80.20 W
Simcoe (L.), Can.	111	44.30 N	79.20 W
Simeulue, Pulau (I.), Indon.	206	2.27 N	95.30 E
Simferopol' (Akmechet), Sov. Un. (sēm-fĕ-rô'pôl') (ák-mĕch'ĕt)	175	44.58 N	34.04 E
Simi (I.), Grc.	161	36.27 N	27.41 E
Similk Beach, Wa. (sē'mĭlk)	118a	48.27 N	122.35 W
Simla, India (sĭm'lȧ)	196	31.09 N	77.15 E
Simla (Neigh.), India	67a	22.35 N	88.22 E
Simleul-Silvaniei, Rom. (shēm-lä'o͞ol-sēl-vä'nyĕ-ē)	167	47.14 N	22.46 E
Simms Pt., Ba.	134	25.00 N	77.40 W
Simojovel, Mex. (sē-mō-hō-vĕl')	131	17.12 N	92.43 W
Simonésia, Braz. (sē-mō-nĕ'syä)	141a	20.04 S	41.53 W
Simonette (R.), Can. (sī-mŏn-ĕt')	99	54.15 N	118.00 W
Simonstad, S. Afr.	226a	34.11 S	18.25 E
Simood Sound, Can.	98	50.45 N	126.25 W
Simplon P., Switz. (sĭm'plŏn) (săɴ-plôɴ')	166	46.13 N	7.53 E
Simpson (I.), Can.	115	48.43 N	87.44 W
Simpson Des., Austl. (sĭmp-sŭn)	214	24.40 S	136.40 E

346 Sim R. – Solheim

PLACE (Pronounciation)	PAGE	Lat. °'	Long. °'
Sim R., Sov. Un.	182a	55.00 N	57.42 E
Simrishamn, Swe. (sēm'rēs-häm'n)	164	55.35 N	14.19 E
Sims Bayou, Tx. (sĭmz bī-yōō')	125a	29.37 N	95.23 W
Simushir (I.), Sov. Un. (se-mōō'shēr)	199	47.15 N	150.47 E
Sinaia, Rom. (sĭ-nä'yȧ)	173	45.20 N	25.30 E
Sinai Pen., Egypt (sī'nī)	225	29.24 N	33.29 E
Sinaloa (State), Mex. (sē-nä-lô-ä)	128	25.15 N	107.45 W
Sinan, China (sz-nän)	203	27.50 N	108.30 E
Sinanju, Kor. (sĭ'nän-jōō')	204	39.39 N	125.41 E
Sinap, Tur.	179	42.00 N	35.05 E
Sincé, Col. (sēn'sā)	142	9.15 N	75.14 W
Sincelejo, Col. (sēn-sā-lā'hō)	142	9.12 N	75.30 W
Sinclair Inlet, Wa. (sĭn-klâr')	118a	47.31 N	122.41 W
Sinclair Mills, Can.	98	54.02 N	121.41 W
Sindi, Sov. Un. (sēn'dē)	165	58.20 N	24.40 E
Sinel'nikovo, Sov. Un. (sē'nye-brl-nē'kô'vô)	175	49.19 N	35.33 E
Sines, Port. (sē'nāzh)	170	37.57 N	8.50 W
Singapore, Singapore (sĭn'gȧ-pōr')	191b	1.18 N	103.52 E
Singapore, Asia	191b	1.22 N	103.45 E
Singapore Str., Indon.	191b	1.14 N	104.20 E
Singlewell or Ifield, Eng.	62	51.25 N	0.23 E
Singu, Bur. (sĭn'gŭ)	198	22.37 N	96.04 E
Siniye Lipyagi, Sov. Un. (sēn'ē lēp'yä-gē)	175	51.24 N	38.29 E
Sinj, Yugo. (sēn')	172	43.42 N	16.39 E
Sinjah, Sud.	225	13.09 N	33.52 E
Sinkāt, Sud.	195	18.50 N	36.50 E
Sinking (Aut. Reg.), see **Xinjiang**			
Sin'kovo, Sov. Un. (sĭn-kô'vô)	182b	56.23 N	37.19 E
Sinnamary, Fr. Gu.	143	5.15 N	57.52 W
Sinni (R.), It. (sēn'nē)	172	40.05 N	16.15 E
Sinnūris, Egypt	223b	29.25 N	30.52 E
Sino, Pedra de (Mtn.), Braz. (pě'drä-dô-sē'nô)	144b	22.27 S	43.02 W
Sino-Soviet Friendship, Palace of (P. Int.), China	68a	31.14 N	121.25 E
Sint Niklaas, Bel.	157a	51.10 N	4.07 E
Sinton, Tx. (sĭn'tŭn)	125	28.03 N	97.30 W
Sintra, Port. (sēn'trȧ)	171b	38.48 N	9.23 W
Sint Truiden, Bel.	125a	50.49 N	5.14 E
Sinŭiju, Kor. (sĭ'nōōĭ-jōō)	204	40.04 N	124.33 E
Sinyavino, Sov. Un. (sĭn-yä'vĭ-nô)	182c	59.50 N	31.07 E
Sinyaya (R.), Sov. Un. (sēn'yȧ-yȧ)	174	56.40 N	28.20 E
Sinyukha (R.), Sov. Un. (sē'nyōō-ĸȧ)	175	48.34 N	30.49 E
Sīdī Barrānī, Egypt	225	31.41 N	26.09 E
Sion, Switz. (sē'ôɴ')	166	46.15 N	7.17 E
Sioux City, Ia. (sōō sĭ'tĭ)	114	42.30 N	96.25 W
Sioux Falls, SD (fôlz)	114	43.33 N	96.43 W
Sioux Lookout, Can.	101	50.06 N	91.55 W
Sipí, Col. (sē-pē')	142a	4.39 N	76.38 W
Siping, China (sz-pĭŋ)	202	43.05 N	124.24 E
Sipiwesk, Can.	96	55.27 N	97.24 W
Sipsey (R.), Al. (sĭp'sē)	126	33.26 N	87.42 W
Sipura, Pulau (I.), Indon.	206	2.15 S	99.33 E
Siqueros, Mex. (sē-kā'rōs)	130	23.19 N	106.14 W
Siquia, R., Nic. (sē-kē'ä)	133	12.23 N	84.36 W
Siracusa, It. (sē-rä-koo'sä)	159	37.02 N	15.19 E
Sirājganj, Bngl. (sĭ-räj'gŭnj)	196	24.23 N	89.43 E
Sirama, Sal. (Sē-rä-mä)	132	13.23 N	87.55 W
Sir Douglas, Mt., Can. (sûr dŭg'lăs)	99	50.44 N	115.20 W
Sir Edward Pellew Group (Is.), Austl. (pēl'ū)	214	15.15 S	137.15 E
Siret, Rom.	167	47.58 N	26.01 E
Siret (R.), Rom.	167	46.10 N	27.18 E
Sirhān, Wadi (R.), Sau. Ar.	192	31.02 N	37.16 E
Sirsa, India	196	29.39 N	75.02 E
Sir Sandford, Mt., Can. (sûr sănd'fērd)	99	51.40 N	117.52 W
Sirvintos, Sov. Un. (shēr'vĭn-tôs)	165	55.02 N	24.59 E
Sir Wilfrid Laurier, Mt., Can. (sûr wĭl'frĭd lôr'yēr)	99	52.47 N	119.45 W
Sisak, Yugo. (sē'sȧk)	172	45.29 N	16.20 E
Sisal, Mex. (sē-säl')	131	21.09 N	90.03 W
Sishui, China (sz-shwā)	200	35.40 N	117.17 E
Sisquoc (R.), Ca. (sĭs'kwŏk)	120	34.47 N	120.13 W
Sisseton, SD (sĭs'tŭn)	114	45.39 N	97.04 W
Sistān, Daryacheh-ye (L.), Iran-Afg.	192	31.45 N	61.15 E
Sisteron, Fr. (sēst'rôɴ')	169	44.10 N	5.55 E
Sisterville, WV (sĭs'tēr-vĭl)	110	39.30 N	81.00 W
Sitía, Grc. (sē'tĭ-ȧ)	172a	35.09 N	26.10 E
Sitka, Ak. (sĭt'kȧ)	107	57.08 N	135.18 W
Sittingbourne, Eng. (sĭt-ĭng-bôrn)	156b	51.20 N	0.44 E
Sittwe, Bur.	206	20.09 N	92.54 E
Sivas, Tur. (sē'väs)	179	39.50 N	36.50 E
Sivash (L.), Sov. Un. (sē'vȧsh)	175	45.55 N	34.42 E
Siverek, Tur. (sē'vě-rěk)	179	37.50 N	39.20 E
Siverskaya, Sov. Un. (sē'vēr-skȧ-yȧ)	165	59.17 N	30.03 E
Siwah (Oasis), Egypt (sē'wä)	225	29.33 N	25.11 E
Sídheros, Ákra (C.), Grc.	172a	35.19 N	26.20 E
Sífnos (I.), Grc.	173	36.58 N	24.30 E
Síros (I.), Grc.	173	37.23 N	24.55 E
Sīwah, Egypt	194	29.12 N	25.31 E
Sixaola R., C. R. (sē-ĸä-ō'lä) (sēk-sä-ō'lä)	133	9.31 N	83.07 W
Sixian, China (sz shyěn)	200	33.29 N	116.57 E
Sixth Cataract, Sud.	225	16.26 N	32.44 E
Siyang, China (sz-yäŋ)	200	33.43 N	118.42 E
Sjaelland (I.), Den. (shĕl'lán')	164	55.34 N	11.35 E
Sjenica, Yugo. (syě'nē-tsä)	173	43.15 N	20.02 E
Skadovsk, Sov. Un. (skä'dôfsk)	175	46.08 N	32.54 E
Skagen, Den. (skä'ghěn)	164	57.43 N	10.32 E
Skagerrak (Str.), Eur. (skä-ghě-räk')	164	57.43 N	8.28 E
Skagit B., Wa. (skăg'ĭt)	118a	48.20 N	122.32 W
Skagit R., Wa.	116	48.29 N	121.52 W
Skagway, Ak. (skăg-wā)	107	59.30 N	135.28 W
Skälderviken (B.), Swe.	164	56.20 N	12.25 E
Skalistyy, Golets (Mtn.), Sov. Un.	181	57.28 N	119.48 E
Skamania, Wa. (skȧ-mā'nĭ-ȧ)	118c	45.37 N	112.03 W
Skamokawa, Wa.	118c	46.16 N	123.27 W
Skanderborg, Den. (skän-ěr-bôr')	164	56.04 N	9.55 E
Skaneateles, NY (skăn-ē-ăt'lēs)	111	42.55 N	76.25 W
Skaneateles (L.), NY	111	42.50 N	76.20 W
Skänninge, Swe. (shěn'ĭng-ě)	164	58.24 N	15.02 E
Skanör-Falsterbo, Swe. (skän'ûr)	164	55.24 N	12.49 E
Skara, Swe. (skä'rȧ)	164	58.25 N	13.24 E
Skeena (R.), Can. (skē'nă)	98	54.10 N	129.40 W
Skeena Mts., Can.	98	56.00 N	128.00 W
Skeerpoort, S. Afr.	227b	25.49 S	27.45 E
Skeerpoort (R.), S. Afr.	227b	25.58 S	27.41 E
Skeldon, Guy. (skěl'dŭn)	143	5.49 N	57.15 W
Skelleftea, Swe. (shěl'ěf-tě-a')	158	64.47 N	20.48 E
Skellefteälven (R.), Swe.	158	62.25 N	19.28 E
Skelmersdale, Eng.	64a	53.33 N	2.48 W
Skhodnya, Sov. Un. (skôd'nyȧ)	182b	55.57 N	37.21 E
Skhodnya R., Sov. Un.	182b	55.55 N	37.16 E
Skíathos (I.), Grc. (skē'á-thôs)	173	39.15 N	23.25 E
Skibbereen, Ire. (skĭb'ēr-ēn)	162	51.32 N	9.25 W
Skidegate Inlet, Can. (skĭ'-dē-găt')	98	53.15 N	132.00 W
Skidmore, Tx. (skĭd'môr)	125	28.16 N	97.40 W
Skien, Nor. (skē'ěn)	164	59.13 N	9.35 E
Skierniewice, Pol. (skyěr-nyě-vēt'sě)	167	51.58 N	20.13 E
Skihist Mtn., Can.	98	50.11 N	121.54 W
Skikda (Philippeville), Alg.	160	36.58 N	6.51 E
Skilpadfontein, S. Afr.	223d	25.02 S	28.50 E
Skíros, Grc.	173	38.53 N	24.32 E
Skiros (I.), Grc.	173	38.50 N	24.43 E
Skive, Den. (skē'vě)	164	56.34 N	8.56 E
Skjálfandafljót (R.), Ice. (skyäl'fänd-ô)	158	65.24 N	16.40 W
Skjerstad, Nor. (skyěr-städ)	158	67.12 N	15.37 E
Škofja Loka, Yugo. (shkôf'yȧ lō'kȧ)	172	46.10 N	14.20 E
Skokie, Il. (skō'kē)	113a	42.02 N	87.45 W
Skokomish Ind. Res., Wa. (Skō-kō'mĭsh)	118a	47.22 N	123.07 W
Skole, Sov. Un. (skô'lē)	167	49.03 N	23.32 E
Skópelos (I.), Grc. (skô'pā-lôs)	173	39.04 N	23.31 E
Skopin, Sov. Un. (skô'pēn)	174	53.49 N	39.35 E
Skopje, Yugo. (skôp'yě)	173	42.02 N	21.26 E
Skövde, Swe. (shûv'dě)	164	58.25 N	13.48 E
Skovorodino, Sov. Un. (skô'vô-rô'dĭ-nô)	181	53.53 N	123.56 E
Skowhegan, Me. (skou-hē'găn)	104	44.45 N	69.27 W
Skradin, Yugo. (skrä'dēn)	172	43.49 N	17.58 E
Skreia, Nor. (skrā'ȧ)	164	60.40 N	10.55 E
Skudeneshavn, Nor. (skōō'dě-nes-houn')	164	59.10 N	5.19 E
Skuilte, S. Afr.	71b	26.07 S	28.19 E
Skull Valley Ind. Res., Ut. (skŭl)	121	40.25 N	112.50 W
Skuna, (R.), Ms. (skû'nȧ)	126	33.57 N	89.36 W
Skunk (R.), Ia. (skŭnk)	115	41.12 N	92.14 W
Skuodas, Sov. Un. (skwô'dȧs)	165	56.16 N	21.32 E
Skurup, Swe. (skû'rōōp)	164	55.29 N	13.27 E
Skvira, Sov. Un. (skvē'rȧ)	175	49.43 N	29.41 E
Skwierzyna, Pol. (skvē-ěr'zhĭ-nȧ)	166	52.35 N	15.30 E
Skye, I. of, Scot. (skī)	162	57.25 N	6.17 W
Skykomish (R.), Wa. (skī'kō-mĭsh)	118a	47.50 N	121.55 W
Skyring, Seno (B.), Chile (sě'nô-s-krē'ng)	144	52.35 S	72.30 W
Slade Green (Neigh.), Eng.	62	51.28 N	0.12 E
Slagese, Den.	164	55.25 N	11.19 E
Slamet, Gunung (Mtn.), Indon. (slä'mět)	206	7.15 S	109.15 E
Slănic, Rom. (slŭ'nēk)	173	45.13 N	25.56 E
Slate (I.), Can. (slāt)	115	48.38 N	87.14 W
Slater, Mo. (slāt'ēr)	123	39.13 N	93.03 W
Slatina, Rom. (slä'tē-nä)	173	44.26 N	24.21 E
Slaton, Tx. (slā'tŭn)	122	33.26 N	101.38 W
Slattocks, Eng.	64b	53.35 N	2.10 W
Slave (R.), Can. (slāv)	96	59.40 N	111.21 W
Slavgorod, Sov. Un. (sláf'gô-rôt)	180	52.58 N	78.43 E
Slavonija (Reg.), Yugo. (slä-vô'nē-yä)	173	45.29 N	17.31 E
Slavonska Požega, Yugo. (slä-vôn'skä pô'zhě-gä)	172	45.18 N	17.42 E
Slavonski Brod, Yugo. (skä-vôn'skē brôd)	173	45.10 N	18.01 E
Slavuta, Sov. Un. (slȧ-vōō'tȧ)	175	50.18 N	27.01 E
Slavyansk, Sov. Un. (slȧv'yänsk')	175	48.52 N	37.34 E
Slavyanskaya, Sov. Un. (slȧv-yȧn'skȧ-yȧ)	175	45.14 N	38.09 E
Slayton, Mn. (slā'tŭn)	114	44.00 N	95.44 W
Sleaford, Eng. (slē'fērd)	156	53.00 N	0.25 W
Sleepy Eye, Mn. (slēp'ĭ ī)	115	44.17 N	94.44 W
Sleepy Hollow, Ca.	59	33.57 N	117.47 W
Slidell, La. (slī-děl')	125	30.17 N	89.47 W
Sliedrecht, Neth.	157a	51.49 N	4.46 E
Sligo, Ire. (slī'gō)	162	54.17 N	8.19 W
Slite, Swe. (slē'tě)	164	57.41 N	18.47 E
Sliven, Bul. (slē'vĕn)	173	42.41 N	26.20 E
Sloan, NY	57a	42.54 N	78.47 W
Sloatsburg, NY (slōts'bŭrg)	112a	41.09 N	74.11 W
Slobodka, Sov. Un. (slô'bôd-kȧ)	165	54.34 N	26.12 E
Slobodskoy, Sov. Un. (slô'bôt-skoi)	178	58.48 N	50.02 E
Sloka, Sov. Un. (slô'kȧ)	165	56.57 N	23.37 E
Slonim, Sov. Un. (swô'nēm)	167	53.05 N	25.19 E
Slough, Eng. (slou)	156b	51.29 N	0.36 E
Slovakia (Prov.), see **Slovensko**			
Slovenija (Reg.), Yugo. (slô-vě'nē-yä)	172	45.58 N	14.43 E
Slovensko (Slovakia) (Prov.), Czech. (slô-věn'skô) (slô-vȧk'ĭ-ă)	167	48.40 N	19.00 E
Sluch' (R.), Sov. Un.	167	50.56 N	26.48 E
Slunj, Yugo. (slōōn')	172	45.08 N	15.46 E
Slupsk, Pol. (swōōpsk)	167	54.28 N	17.02 E
Slutsk, Sov. Un. (slōōtsk)	174	53.02 N	27.34 E
Slyne Head, Ire. (slīn)	162	53.25 N	10.05 W
Smackover, Ar. (smăk'ô-vēr)	123	33.22 N	92.42 W
Smederevo (Semendria), Yugo. (smě'de-rě-vô) (sě-měn'drĭ-ă)	173	44.39 N	20.54 E
Smederevska Palanka, Yugo. (smě-dě-rěv'skä pä-län'kä)	173	44.21 N	21.00 E
Smedjebacken, Swe. (smĭ'tyě-bä-kěn)	164	60.09 N	15.19 E
Smela, Sov. Un. (smyā'lȧ)	175	49.14 N	31.52 E
Smeloye, Sov. Un. (smyā'lô-ě)	175	50.55 N	33.36 E
Smethport, Pa. (smĕth'pōrt)	111	41.50 N	78.25 W
Smethwick (Warley), Eng.	156	52.31 N	2.04 W
Smiltene, Sov. Un. (smēl'tě-ně)	174	57.26 N	25.57 E
Smith, Can. (smĭth)	99	55.10 N	114.02 W
Smith (I.), Wa.	118a	48.20 N	122.53 W
Smith Center, Ks. (sěn'tēr)	122	39.45 N	98.46 W
Smithers, Can. (smĭth'ērs)	98	54.47 N	127.10 W
Smithfield, Austl.	70a	33.51 S	150.57 E
Smithfield, NC (smĭth'fēld)	127	35.30 N	78.21 W
Smithfield, Ut.	117	41.50 N	111.49 W
Smithland, Ky. (smĭth'lănd)	110	37.10 N	88.25 W
Smith Mountain Lake (Res.), Va.	127	37.00 N	79.45 W
Smith Point, Tx.	125a	29.32 N	94.45 W
Smith R., Mt.	117	47.00 N	111.20 W
Smiths Falls, Can. (smĭths)	103	44.55 N	76.05 W
Smithton, Austl. (smĭth'tŭn)	216	40.55 S	145.12 E
Smithton, Il.	119e	38.24 N	89.59 W
Smithville, Tx. (smĭth'vĭl)	125	30.00 N	97.08 W
Smitswinkelvlakte, S. Afr.	226a	34.16 S	18.25 E
Smoke Creek Des., Nv. (smōk crēk)	120	40.28 N	119.40 W
Smoky (R.), Can. (smōk'ĭ)	99	55.30 N	117.30 W
Smoky Hill (R.), Ks. (smōk'ĭ hĭl)	123	38.40 N	97.32 W
Smøla (I.), Nor. (smûlä)	164	63.16 N	7.40 E
Smolensk, Sov. Un. (smô-lyěnsk')	174	54.46 N	32.03 E
Smolensk (Oblast), Sov. Un.	174	55.00 N	32.18 E
Smyadovo, Bul.	173	43.04 N	27.00 E
Smyrna, De. (smûr'nȧ)	111	39.20 N	75.35 W
Smyrna, Ga.	112c	33.53 N	84.31 W
Snag, Can. (snăg)	107	62.18 N	140.30 W
Snake (R.), Mn. (snāk)	115	45.58 N	93.20 W
Snake (R.), Wa.	116	46.35 N	117.20 W
Snake Ra., Nv.	121	39.20 N	114.15 W
Snake R., Henrys Fork, Id.	117	43.52 N	111.55 W
Snake River Pln., Id.	117	43.08 N	114.46 W
Snap Pt., Ba.	134	23.45 N	77.30 W
Sneffels Pk., Co. (sněf'ělz)	121	38.00 N	107.50 W
Snelgrove, Can. (sněl'grōv)	95d	43.44 N	79.50 W
Sniardwy, Jezioro (L.), Pol. (snyärt'vĭ)	167	53.46 N	21.59 E
Snodland, Eng.	62	51.20 N	0.27 E
Snöhetta (Mtn.), Nor. (snû-hěttä)	164	62.18 N	9.12 E
Snohomish, Wa.	118a	47.53 N	122.04 W
Snohomish (R.), Wa. (snô-hō'mĭsh)	118a	47.55 N	122.05 W
Snoqualmie, Wa. (snō qwäl'mē)	118a	47.32 N	121.50 W
Snoqualmie R., Wa.	116	47.32 N	121.53 W
Snov (R.), Sov. Un. (snôf)	175	51.38 N	31.38 E
Snowden, Pa.	57b	40.16 N	79.58 W
Snowdon (Mtn.), Wales	162	53.05 N	4.04 W
Snow Hill, Md. (hĭl)	111	38.15 N	75.20 W
Snow Lake, Can.	101	54.50 N	100.10 W
Snowy Mts., Austl. (snō'ē)	215	36.17 S	148.30 E
Snyder, Ok. (snī'dēr)	122	34.40 N	98.57 W
Snyder, Tx.	124	32.48 N	100.53 W
Soar (R.), Eng. (sōr)	156	52.44 N	1.09 W
Sobat R., Sud. (sō'bȧt)	225	9.04 N	32.02 E
Sobinka, Sov. Un. (sô-bĭŋ'kȧ)	174	55.59 N	40.02 E
Sobo Zan (Mt.), Jap. (sô'bô zän)	205	32.47 N	131.27 E
Sobral, Braz. (sô-brä'l)	143	3.39 S	40.16 W
Sochaczew, Pol. (sô-ĸä'chěf)	167	52.14 N	20.18 E
Sochi, Sov. Un. (sôch'ĭ)	179	43.35 N	39.50 E
Society Is., Fr. Polynesia (sô-sī'ě-tē)	209	15.00 S	157.30 W
Socoltenango, Mex. (sô-kôl-tě-näŋ'gō)	131	16.17 N	92.20 W
Socorro, Braz. (sô-kô'r-rō)	141a	22.35 S	46.32 W
Socorro, Col. (sô-kôr'rō)	142	6.23 N	73.19 W
Socorro, NM	121	34.05 N	106.55 W
Socotra I., P. D. R. of Yem. (sô-kō'trȧ)	223a	13.00 N	52.30 E
Socúellamos, Sp. (sô-kōō-äl'yä-môs)	170	39.18 N	2.48 W
Soda (L.), Ca. (sō'dȧ)	120	35.12 N	116.25 W
Soda Pk., Wa.	118c	45.53 N	122.04 W
Soda Springs, Id. (sprĭngz)	117	42.39 N	111.37 W
Söderhamn, Swe. (sû-děr-häm''n)	164	61.20 N	17.00 E
Söderköping, Swe.	164	58.30 N	16.14 E
Södertälje, Swe. (sû-děr-těl'yě)	164	59.12 N	17.35 E
Sodingen (Neigh.), F.R.G.	63	51.32 N	7.15 E
Sodo, Eth.	225	7.03 N	37.46 E
Sodpur, India	67a	22.42 N	88.23 E
Södra Dellen (L.), Swe.	164	61.45 N	16.30 E
Soest, F.R.G. (zōst)	166	51.35 N	8.05 E
Soeurs, Île des (I.), Can.	54b	45.28 N	73.33 W
Sofia, see **Sofiya**			
Sofiya (Sofia), Bul. (sô'fē-yȧ) (sô'fē-ȧ)	173	42.43 N	23.20 E
Sofiyevka, Sov. Un. (sô-fē'yěf-kȧ)	175	48.03 N	33.53 E
Soga, Jap. (sô'gä)	205a	35.35 N	140.08 E
Sogamoso, Col. (sô-gä-mô'sō)	142	5.42 N	72.51 W
Sognafjorden (Fd.), Nor.	164	61.09 N	5.30 E
Sogozha (R.), Sov. Un. (sô'gô-zhȧ)	174	58.35 N	39.08 E
Soissons, Fr. (swä-sôɴ')	168	49.23 N	3.17 E
Soisy-sous-Montmorency, Fr.	64c	48.59 N	2.18 E
Sōka, Jap. (sō'kä)	205a	35.50 N	139.49 E
Sokal', Sov. Un. (sô'käl')	167	50.28 N	24.20 E
Soke, Tur. (sû'kě)	179	37.40 N	27.10 E
Sokodé, Togo (sô-kô-dā')	228	8.59 N	1.08 E
Sokolka, Pol. (sô-kōōl'kȧ)	167	53.23 N	23.30 E
Sokol'niki (Neigh.), Sov. Un.	66b	55.48 N	37.41 E
Sokolo, Mali (sô-kô-lō')	224	14.51 N	6.09 W
Sokone, Senegal	228	13.53 N	16.22 W
Sokoto, Nig. (sō'kô-tō)	229	13.04 N	5.16 E
Sokotów Podlaski, Pol. (sô-kô-wōōf' pŭd-lä'skĭ)	167	52.24 N	22.15 E
Sola de Vega (San Miguel), Mex. (sō'lä dā vā'gä) (sän mē-gāl')	131	16.31 N	96.58 W
Solander, C., Austl.	211b	34.03 S	151.16 E
Solano, Phil. (sō-lä'nō)	207a	16.31 N	121.11 E
Sölderholz (Neigh.), F.R.G.	63	51.29 N	7.35 E
Soledad, Col. (sō-lě-dä'd)	142	10.47 N	75.00 W
Soledad Díez Gutierrez, Mex. (sô-lā-dhädh'dē'äz gōō-tyā'rēz)	130	22.19 N	100.54 W
Soleduck R., Wa. (sōl'dŭk)	116	47.59 N	124.28 W
Solentiname, Islas de (Is.), Nic. (ē's-läs-dě-sō-lěn-tě-nä'mȧ)	132	11.15 N	85.16 W
Solheim, S. Afr.	71b	26.11 S	28.10 E

RONOUNCING INDEX

Solihull – Speldorf 347

ACE (Pronounciation)	PAGE	Lat. °′	Long. °′
lihull, Eng. (sō'lĭ-hŭl)	156	52.25 N	1.46 W
likamsk, Sov. Un. (sô-lē-kȧmsk')	182a	59.38 N	56.48 E
l'-Iletsk, Sov. Un.	179	51.10 N	55.05 E
limões, Rio (R.), Braz. (rē'ō-sô-lē-mô'ĕs)	142	2.45 S	67.44 W
lingen, F.R.G. (zô'lĭng-ĕn)	169c	51.10 N	7.05 E
lleftea, Swe. (sôl-lĕf'tē-ô)	164	63.06 N	17.17 E
ller, Sp. (sō'lyĕr)	171	39.45 N	2.40 E
lncevo, Sov. Un.	66b	55.39 N	37.24 E
logne (Reg.), Fr. (sō-lōn'yĕ)	168	47.36 N	1.53 E
lola, Guat. (sô-lō'lä)	132	14.45 N	91.12 W
lomon Is., Oceania (sŏ'lō-mŭn)	208	7.00 S	160.00 E
lomon R., Ks.	122	39.24 N	98.19 W
lomon R. North Fk., Ks.	122	39.34 N	99.52 W
lomon R., South Fk., Ks.	122	39.19 N	99.52 W
lon, China (swo-lo͞on)	202	47.32 N	121.18 E
lon, Oh. (sō'lŭn)	113d	41.23 N	81.26 W
lothurn, Switz. (zō'lō-tho͞orn)	166	47.13 N	7.30 E
lovetskiye (I.), Sov. Un.	178	65.10 N	35.40 E
lta (I.), Yugo. (shôl'tä)	172	43.20 N	16.15 E
ltau, F.R.G. (sōl'tou)	166	53.00 N	9.50 E
l'tsy, Sov. Un. (sôl'tsĕ)	174	58.04 N	30.13 E
lvay, NY (sŏl'vā)	111	43.05 N	76.10 W
lvesborg, Swe. (sûl'vĕs-bôrg)	164	56.04 N	14.35 E
l'vychegodsk, Sov. Un. (sôl'vē-chĕ-gôtsk')	178	61.18 N	46.58 E
lway Firth, Eng.-Scot. (sŏl'wā fûrth')	162	54.42 N	3.55 W
lwezi, Zambia	231	12.11 S	26.25 E
malia, Afr. (sō-mä'lē-ȧ)	222	3.28 N	44.47 E
manga, Tan.	231	8.24 S	39.17 E
mbor, Yugo. (sôm'bôr)	173	45.45 N	19.10 E
mbrerete, Mex. (sōm-brā-rā'tā)	130	23.38 N	103.37 W
mbrero, Cayo (C.), Ven. (kä-yô-sôm-brĕ'rô)	143b	10.52 N	68.12 W
merdale, NJ	56b	39.51 N	75.01 W
merset, Ky. (sŭm'ēr-sĕt)	126	37.05 N	84.35 W
merset, Md.	56d	38.58 N	77.05 W
merset, Ma.	112b	41.46 N	71.05 W
merset, Pa.	111	40.00 N	79.05 W
merset, Tx.	119d	29.13 N	98.39 W
merset East, S. Afr.	227c	32.44 S	25.36 E
mersworth, NH (sŭm'ērz-wûrth)	104	43.16 N	70.53 W
merton, Az. (sŭm'ēr-tŭn)	120	32.36 N	114.43 W
merton (Neigh.), Pa.	56b	40.06 N	75.01 W
merville, Ma. (sŭm'ēr-vĭl)	105a	42.23 N	71.06 W
merville, NJ	112a	40.34 N	74.37 W
merville, Tn.	126	35.14 N	89.21 W
merville, Tx.	125	30.21 N	96.31 W
mesul R., Rom. (sô-mă'sho͞ol)	167	47.43 N	23.09 E
mma Vesuviana, It. (sôm'mä vā-zo͞o-vē-ä'nä)	171c	40.38 N	14.27 E
mme (R.), Fr. (sŏm)	168	50.02 N	2.04 E
mmerberg, F.R.G.	63	51.27 N	7.32 E
mmerfeld, G.D.R. (zō'mĕr-fĕld)	157b	52.48 N	13.02 E
mmerville, Austl.	211a	38.14 S	145.10 E
moto, Nic. (sô-mō'tō)	132	13.28 N	86.37 W
muncurá, Meseta de (Plat.), Arg. (mĕ-sĕ'tä-dĕ-sô-mo͞o'n-ko͞o-rá')	144	41.15 S	68.00 W
n (R.), India (sōn)	196	24.40 N	82.35 E
ná, Pan. (sō'nä)	133	8.00 N	81.19 W
nari, India	67e	18.52 N	72.59 E
nchŏn, Kor. (sŭn'shŭn)	204	39.49 N	124.56 E
ndags, S. Afr.	227c	33.17 S	25.14 E
nderborg, Den. (sûn''ĕr-bôrgh)	164	54.55 N	9.47 E
ndershausen, G.D.R. (zôn'dĕrz-hou'zĕn)	166	51.17 N	10.45 E
ng Ca (R.), Viet.	203	19.15 N	105.00 E
ngea, Tan. (sôn-gā'ȧ)	231	10.41 S	35.39 E
nghua (R.), see Sungari			
ngjiang, China (sôŋ-jyäŋ)	201b	31.01 N	121.14 E
ngjin, Kor. (sŭng'jĭn')	204	40.38 N	129.10 E
ngkhla, Thai. (sông'klä')	206	7.09 N	100.34 E
ngwe, Zaire	231	12.25 S	29.40 E
nneberg, G.D.R. (sôn'ē-bĕrgh)	166	50.20 N	11.14 E
nora, Ca. (sō-nō'rȧ)	120	37.58 N	120.22 W
nora, Tx.	124	30.33 N	100.38 W
nora (State), Mex.	128	29.45 N	111.15 W
nora (R.), Mex.	128	28.45 N	111.35 W
nora Pk., Ca.	120	38.22 N	119.39 W
nseca, Sp. (sôn-sä'kä)	170	39.41 N	3.56 W
nsón, Col. (sôn-sôn')	142a	5.42 N	75.28 W
nsonate, Sal. (sōn-sō-nä'tā)	132	13.46 N	89.43 W
nsorol Is., Pac. Is. Trust Ter. (sŏn-sō-rōl')	207	5.03 N	132.33 E
oke Basin, Can. (so͞ok)	118a	48.21 N	123.47 W
o Locks, Can.-U. S. (so͞o lŏks)	119	46.30 N	84.30 W
petrán, Col. (sô-pĕ-trä'n)	142a	6.30 N	75.44 W
pot, Pol. (sô'pôt)	164	54.26 N	18.25 E
pron, Hung. (shŏp'rŏn)	166	47.41 N	16.36 E
ra, It. (sô'rä)	172	41.43 N	13.37 E
rbas, Sp. (sôr'bäs)	170	37.05 N	2.07 W
rbonne (P. Int.), Fr.	64c	48.51 N	2.21 E
rdo (R.), Mex. (sô'r-dô)	131	16.39 N	97.33 W
rel, Can. (sô-rĕl')	103	46.01 N	73.07 W
rell, C., Austl.	216	42.10 S	144.50 E
resina, It. (sō-rā-zē'nä)	172	45.17 N	9.51 E
ria, Sp. (sō'rē-ä)	170	41.46 N	2.28 W
riano (Dept.), Ur. (sō-rēä'nô)	141c	33.25 S	58.00 W
rocaba, Braz. (sô-rô-kä'bȧ)	141a	23.29 S	47.27 W
roki, Sov. Un. (sŏ-rō'kē)	175	48.09 N	28.17 E
rong, Indon. (sō-rông')	207	1.00 S	131.20 E
rot' (R.), Sov. Un. (sō-rō'tzh)	174	57.08 N	29.23 E
roti, Ug. (sō-rō'tē)	231	1.43 N	33.37 E
røya (I.), Nor.	158	70.37 N	20.58 E
rraia (R.), Port. (sôr-rī'ȧ)	170	38.55 N	8.42 W
rrento, It. (sôr-rĕn'tō)	171c	40.23 N	14.23 E
rsogon, Phil. (sôr-sōgōn')	207	12.51 N	124.02 E
rtavala, Sov. Un. (sôr'tä-vä-lä)	165	61.43 N	30.40 E
san, Korea (sŭ'sän)	202	36.40 N	126.25 E
senki, Sov. Un.	66b	55.34 N	37.26 E
sna (R.), Sov. Un. (sôs'nȧ)	175	50.33 N	38.15 E
Sosnitsa, Sov. Un. (sôs-nē'tsȧ)	175	51.30 N	32.29 E
Sosnogorsk, Sov. Un.	180	63.13 N	54.09 E
Sosnowiec, Pol. (sôs-nô'vyĕts)	167	50.17 N	19.10 E
Sosunova, Mys (Pt.), Sov. Un. (mĭs sô'so͞o-nôf'ȧ)	204	46.28 N	138.06 E
Sos'va (R.), Sov. Un. (sôs'vȧ)	178	63.10 N	63.30 E
Sos'va R., Sov. Un. (sôs'vȧ)	182a	59.55 N	60.40 E
Sota (R.), Benin	229	11.10 N	3.20 E
Sota la Marina, Mex. (sô-tä-lä-mä-rē'nä)	130	22.45 N	98.11 W
Soteapan, Mex. (sō-tā-ä'pän)	131	18.14 N	94.51 W
Soto la Marina, Rio (R.), Mex. (rē'ō-so'tō lä mä-rē'nä)	130	23.55 N	98.30 W
Sotuta, Mex. (sô-to͞o'tä)	132a	20.35 N	89.00 W
Souanké, Con.	230	2.05 N	14.03 E
Soublette, Ven. (sō-o͞o-blĕ'tĕ)	143b	9.55 N	66.06 W
Souflion, Grc.	173	41.12 N	26.17 E
Soufriere, Saint Lucia (so͞o-frē-âr')	133b	13.50 N	61.03 W
Soufrière (Vol.), Montserrat	133b	16.43 N	62.10 W
Soufríere, Mt., Saint Vincent	133b	13.19 N	61.12 W
Sŏul (Seoul), Kor.	204	37.35 N	127.03 E
Soulanges, Can.	54b	45.20 N	74.15 W
Sounding Cr., Can. (soun'dĭng)	100	51.35 N	111.00 W
Souq Ahras, Alg.	159	36.23 N	8.00 E
Sources, Mt. aux, Leso.-S. Afr. (môN'tō so͞ors')	223c	28.47 S	29.04 E
Soure, Port. (sōr-ĕ)	170	40.04 N	8.37 W
Souris, Can. (so͞o'rē')	105	46.20 N	62.17 W
Souris, Can.	101	49.38 N	100.15 W
Souris (R.), Can.	101	49.10 N	102.00 W
Sourlake, Tx. (sour'lāk)	125	30.09 N	94.24 W
Sousse, Tun. (so͞os)	224	36.00 N	10.39 E
South (R.), NC	127	34.49 N	78.33 W
South Africa, Afr.	222	28.00 S	24.50 E
Southall (Neigh.), Eng.	62	51.31 N	0.23 W
South Amboy, NJ (south'ăm'boi)	112a	40.28 N	74.17 W
South America	138		
Southampton, Eng. (south-ămp'tŭn)	162	50.54 N	1.30 W
Southampton, NY	111	40.53 N	72.24 W
Southampton I., Can.	97	64.38 N	84.00 W
South Andaman I., Andaman & Nicobar Is. (ăn-dȧ-măn')	206	11.57 N	93.24 E
South Australia (State), Austl. (ôs-trā'lĭ-ȧ)	214	29.45 S	132.00 E
South B., Ba.	135	20.55 N	73.35 W
South Bend, In. (bĕnd)	110	41.40 N	86.20 W
South Bend, Wa. (bĕnd)	116	46.39 N	123.48 W
South Bight (B.), Ba.	134	24.20 N	77.35 W
South Bimini (I.), Ba. (bē'mē-nē)	134	25.40 N	79.20 W
Southborough, Ma. (south'bŭr-ô)	105a	42.18 N	71.33 W
South Boston, Va. (bôs'tŭn)	127	36.41 N	78.55 W
South Boston (Neigh.), Ma.	54a	42.20 N	71.03 W
Southbridge, Ma. (south'brĭj)	111	42.05 N	72.00 W
South Brooklyn (Neigh.), NY	55	40.41 N	73.59 W
South Caicos (I.), Turks & Caicos (kī'kōs)	135	21.30 N	71.35 W
South Carolina (State), U. S. (kăr-ô-lī'nȧ)	109	34.15 N	81.10 W
South Cave, Eng. (cāv)	156	53.45 N	0.35 W
South Charleston, WV (chärlz'tŭn)	110	38.20 N	81.40 W
South Chicago (Neigh.), Il.	58a	41.44 N	87.33 W
South China Sea, Asia (chī'nȧ)	206	15.23 N	114.12 E
South Cr., Austl.	211b	33.43 S	167.00 E
Southcrest, S. Afr.	71b	26.15 S	28.07 E
South Dakota (State), U. S. (dȧ-kō'tȧ)	108	44.20 N	101.55 W
South Darenth, Eng.	62	51.24 N	0.15 E
South Downs, Eng. (dounz)	162	50.55 N	1.13 W
South Dum-Dum, India	196a	22.36 N	88.25 E
Southeast Asia Treaty Organization Headquarters (P. Int.), Thai	68f	13.45 N	100.31 E
Southeast, C., Austl.	215	43.47 S	146.03 E
Southend-on-Sea, Eng. (south-ĕnd')	156b	51.33 N	0.41 E
Southern Alps (Mts.), N. Z. (sŭ-thûrn ălps)	217	43.35 S	170.00 E
Southern California, University of (P. Int.), Ca.	59	34.02 N	118.17 W
Southern Cross, Austl.	214	31.13 S	119.30 E
Southern Indian (L.), Can. (sŭth'ērn ĭn'dĭ-ăn)	99	56.46 N	98.57 W
Southern Pines, NC (sŭth'ērn pīnz)	127	35.10 N	79.23 W
Southern Ute Ind. Res., Co. (ūt)	121	37.05 N	108.23 W
Southern Yemen, see Yemen, People's Democratic Republic of			
South Euclid, Oh. (ū'klĭd)	113d	41.30 N	81.34 W
Southfield, Mi.	57c	42.29 N	83.17 W
Southfleet, Eng.	62	51.25 N	0.19 E
South Fox (I.), Mi. (fŏks)	110	45.25 N	85.55 W
South Gate, Ca. (gāt)	119a	33.57 N	118.13 W
Southgate (Neigh.), Eng.	62	51.38 N	0.08 W
South Georgia (I.), Falk Is. (jôr'jȧ)	140	54.00 S	37.00 W
South Germiston, S. Afr.	71b	26.15 S	28.10 E
South Green, Eng.	62	51.37 N	0.26 E
South Haven, Mi. (hāv''n)	110	42.25 N	86.15 W
South Head (C.), Austl.	70a	33.50 S	151.17 E
South Hempstead, NY	55	40.41 N	73.37 W
South Hill, Va.	127	36.44 N	78.08 W
South Hills (Neigh.), S. Afr.	71b	26.15 S	28.05 E
South I., N. Z.	217	42.40 S	169.00 E
South Indian Lake, Can.	101	56.50 N	99.00 W
Southington, Ct. (sŭdh'ĭng-tŭn)	111	41.35 N	72.55 W
South Loup (R.), Ne. (lo͞op)	114	41.21 N	100.08 W
South Lynnfield, Ma.	54a	42.31 N	71.00 W
South Media, Pa.	56b	39.54 N	75.23 W
South Melbourne, Austl.	70b	37.50 S	144.57 E
South Merrimack, NH (mĕr'ĭ-măk)	105a	42.47 N	71.36 W
South Milwaukee, Wi. (mĭl-wô'kē)	113a	42.55 N	87.52 W
South Mimms, Eng.	62	51.42 N	0.14 W
South Moose L., Can.	101	53.51 N	100.20 W
South Nation (R.), Can. (nā'shŭn)	95c	45.12 N	75.07 W
South Negril Pt., Jam. (nā-grēl')	134	18.15 N	78.25 W
South Ockendon, Eng.	62	51.32 N	0.18 E
South Ogden, Ut. (ŏg'dĕn)	119b	41.12 N	111.58 W
South Orange, NJ	55	40.45 N	74.15 W
South Orkney Is., B. A. T.	232	57.00 S	45.00 W
South Oxhey, Eng.	62	51.38 N	0.23 W
South Paris, Me. (păr'ĭs)	104	44.13 N	70.32 W
South Park, Ky. (pärk)	113h	38.06 N	85.43 W
South Pasadena, Ca. (păs-ȧ-dē'nȧ)	119a	34.06 N	118.08 W
South Pease (R.), Tx. (pēz)	121	33.54 N	100.45 W
South Pender (I.), Can. (pĕn'dēr)	118d	48.45 N	123.09 W
South Philadelphia (Neigh.), Pa.	56b	39.56 N	75.10 W
South Pittsburgh, Tn. (pĭs'bûrg)	126	35.00 N	85.42 W
South Platte (R.), U. S. (plăt)	108	40.40 N	102.40 W
South Porcupine, Can.	102	48.28 N	81.13 W
Southport, Austl. (south'pōrt)	216	27.57 S	153.27 E
Southport, Eng. (south'pôrt)	156	53.38 N	3.00 W
Southport, In.	113g	39.40 N	86.07 W
Southport, NC	127	35.55 N	78.02 W
South Portland, Me. (pōrt-lănd)	104	43.37 N	70.15 W
South Prairie, Wa. (prā'rĭ)	118a	47.08 N	122.06 W
South Pt., Barb.	133b	13.00 N	59.43 W
South Pt., Mi.	110	44.50 N	83.20 W
South R., Ga.	112c	33.40 N	84.15 W
South Range, Wi. (rānj)	119h	46.37 N	91.59 W
South River, NJ (rĭv'ēr)	112a	40.27 N	74.23 W
South Saint Paul, Mn.	119g	44.54 N	93.02 W
South Salt Lake, Ut. (sôlt lāk)	119b	40.44 N	111.53 W
South Sandwich Is., Falk. Is. (sănd'wĭch)	140	58.00 S	27.00 W
South Sandwich Trench, S. A.-Ant.	140	55.00 S	27.00 W
South San Francisco, Ca. (săn frăn-sĭs'kô)	118d	37.39 N	122.24 W
South San Francisco, Ca.	58b	37.39 N	122.24 W
South San Jose Hills, Ca.	59	34.01 N	117.55 W
South Saskatchewan (R.), Can. (sás-kach'ē-wän)	100	53.15 N	105.05 W
South Shetland Is., B. A. T.	232	62.00 S	70.00 W
South Shields, Eng. (shēldz)	162	55.00 N	1.22 W
South Shore (Neigh.), Il.	58a	41.46 N	87.35 W
South Side (Neigh.), Pa.	57b	40.26 N	79.58 W
South Sioux City, Ne. (so͞o sĭt'ē)	114	42.48 N	96.26 W
South Taranaki Bight, N. Z. (tä-rä-nä'kē)	217	39.35 S	173.50 E
South Thompson (R.), Can. (tŏmp'sŭn)	99	50.41 N	120.21 W
Southton, Tx. (south'tŭn)	119d	29.18 N	98.26 W
South Uist (I.), Scot. (û'ĭst)	162	57.15 N	7.24 W
South Umpqua R., Or. (ŭmp'kwȧ)	116	43.00 N	122.54 W
South Walpole, Ma.	54a	42.06 N	71.16 W
South Waltham, Ma.	54a	42.22 N	71.15 W
Southwark (Neigh.), Eng.	62	51.30 N	0.06 W
South Weald, Eng.	62	51.37 N	0.16 E
Southwell, Eng. (south'wĕl)	156	53.04 N	0.56 W
South West Africa, see Namibia			
South Westbury, NY	55	40.45 N	73.35 W
Southwest Miramichi (R.), Can. (mĭr ȧ-mē'shē)	104	46.35 N	66.17 W
Southwest Pt., Ba.	134	25.50 N	77.10 W
Southwest Pt., Ba.	135	23.55 N	74.30 W
South Weymouth, Ma.	54a	42.10 N	70.57 W
South Whittier, Ca.	59	33.56 N	118.03 W
South Yorkshire (Co.), Eng.	156	53.29 N	1.35 W
Sovetsk (Tilsit), Sov. Un. (sô-vyĕtsk')	165	55.04 N	21.54 E
Sovetskaya Gavan', Sov. Un. (sŭ-vyĕt'skĭ-u gä'vŭn')	181	48.59 N	140.14 E
Soviet Union, Eur.-Asia (sō-vĭ-ĕt')	190	60.30 N	64.00 E
Sow (R.), Eng. (sou)	156	52.45 N	2.12 W
Soweto (Neigh.), S. Afr.	71b	26.14 S	27.54 E
Sōya Misaki (C.), Jap. (sō'yȧ mē'sä-kē)	204	45.35 N	141.25 E
Soyo, Ang	230	6.10 S	12.25 E
Sozh (R.), Sov. Un. (sôzh)	174	52.17 N	31.00 E
Sozopol, Bul. (sôz'ô-pôl')	173	42.18 N	27.50 E
Spa, Bel. (spä)	163	50.30 N	5.50 E
Spain, Eur. (spān)	154	40.15 N	4.30 W
Spalding, Ne. (spôl'dĭng)	114	41.43 N	98.23 W
Spanaway, Wa. (spăn'ȧ-wā)	118a	47.06 N	122.26 W
Spandau (Neigh.), F.R.G.	65a	52.32 N	13.12 E
Spangler, Pa. (spăng'lēr)	111	40.40 N	78.50 W
Spanish Fork, Ut. (spăn'ĭsh fôrk)	121	40.10 N	111.40 W
Spanish Town, Jam.	134	18.00 N	76.55 W
Sparks, Nv. (spärks)	120	39.34 N	119.45 W
Sparrows Point, Md. (spăr'ōz)	112e	39.13 N	76.29 W
Sparta, Ga. (spär'tȧ)	126	33.16 N	82.59 W
Sparta, Il.	123	38.07 N	89.42 W
Sparta, Mi.	110	43.10 N	85.45 W
Sparta, Tn.	126	35.54 N	85.26 W
Sparta, Wi.	115	43.56 N	90.50 W
Sparta Mts., NJ	112a	41.00 N	74.38 W
Spartanburg, SC (spär'tăn-bûrg)	127	34.57 N	82.13 W
Sparta, see Spárti			
Spartel (C.), Mor. (spär-tĕl')	170	35.48 N	5.50 W
Spárti, Grc. (Sparta)	173	37.07 N	22.28 E
Spartivento, C., It. (spär-tē-vĕn'tô)	172	37.55 N	16.09 E
Spartivento, C., It.	172	38.54 N	8.52 E
Spas-Demensk, Sov. Un. (spȧs dyĕ-mĕnsk')	174	54.24 N	34.02 E
Spas-Klepiki, Sov. Un. (spȧs klĕp'ē-kē)	174	55.09 N	40.11 E
Spassk-Ryazanskiy, Sov. Un. (ryä-zän'skĭ)	174	54.24 N	40.21 E
Spassk-Dal'niy, Sov. Un. (spŭsk'dál'nyē)	181	44.30 N	133.00 E
Spátha, Ákra (C.), Grc.	172a	35.42 N	24.45 E
Spaulding, Al. (spôl'dĭng)	112h	33.27 N	86.50 W
Spear, C., Can. (spēr)	105	47.32 N	52.32 W
Spearfish, SD (spēr'fĭsh)	114	44.28 N	103.52 W
Speed, In. (spēd)	113h	38.25 N	85.45 W
Speedway, In. (spēd'wā)	113g	39.47 N	86.14 W
Speichersee (L.), F.R.G.	157d	48.12 N	11.47 E
Speke (Neigh.), Eng.	64b	53.21 N	2.51 W
Speldorf (Neigh.), F.R.G.	63	51.25 N	6.52 E

-sing; ŋ-baŋk; N-nasalized n; nŏd; cŏmmit; ōld; ôbey; ôrder; oi-boil; fo͞od; fo͝ot; ou-out; s-soft; sh-dish; th-thin; pūre; ûnite; ûrn; stŭd; circŭs; ü-as in French tu; '-indeterminate vowel.

348 Spellen – Stornoway

PLACE (Pronounciation)	PAGE	Lat. °′	Long. °′
Spellen, F.R.G.	63	51.37 N	6.37 E
Spencer, In. (spĕn'sẽr)	110	39.15 N	86.45 W
Spencer, Ia.	115	43.09 N	95.08 W
Spencer, NC	127	35.43 N	80.25 W
Spencer, WV	110	38.55 N	81.20 W
Spencer G., Austl. (spĕn'sẽr)	216	34.20 S	136.55 E
Sperenberg, G.D.R. (shpĕ'rĕn-bĕrgh)	157b	52.09 N	13.22 E
Sperkhiós (R.), Grc.	173	38.54 N	22.02 E
Spey (L.), Scot. (spā)	162	57.25 N	3.29 W
Speyer, F.R.G. (shpī'ẽr)	166	49.18 N	8.26 E
Sphinx (Pyramid), Egypt (sfĭnks)	223b	29.57 N	31.08 E
Spijkenisse, Neth.	157a	51.51 N	4.18 E
Spinazzola, It. (spē-nät'zô-lä)	172	40.58 N	16.05 E
Spirit Lake, Id. (spĭr'ĭt)	116	47.58 N	116.51 W
Spirit Lake, Ia. (lāk)	115	43.25 N	95.08 W
Spišská Nová Ves, Czech. (spēsh'skä nō'vä vĕs)	167	48.56 N	20.35 E
Spitsbergen (Is.), **see Svalbard**			
Spittal, Aus. (shpē-täl')	166	46.48 N	13.28 E
Split, Yugo. (splēt)	172	43.30 N	16.28 E
Split L., Can.	101	56.08 N	96.15 W
Spokane, Wa. (spōkăn')	116	47.39 N	117.25 W
Spokane R., Wa.	116	47.47 N	118.00 W
Spoleto, It. (spô-lā'tō)	172	42.44 N	12.44 E
Spoon (R.), Il. (spo͞on)	123	40.36 N	90.22 W
Spooner, Wi. (spo͞on'ẽr)	115	45.50 N	91.53 W
Sporádhes (Is.), Grc.	173	38.55 N	24.05 E
Sportswood, Austl.	70b	37.50 S	144.53 E
Spotswood, NJ (spŏtz'wo͝od)	112a	40.23 N	74.22 W
Sprague R., Or. (sprāg)	116	42.30 N	121.42 W
Spratly (I.), China (sprăt'lē)	206	8.38 N	11.54 E
Spray, NC (sprā)	127	36.30 N	79.44 W
Spree R., G.D.R. (shprā)	166	51.53 N	14.08 E
Spremberg, G.D.R. (shprĕm'bĕrgh)	166	51.35 N	14.23 E
Spring (R.), Ar.	123	36.25 N	91.35 W
Springbok, S. Afr. (sprĭng'bŏk)	226	29.35 S	17.55 E
Spring, Cr., Nv. (sprĭng)	120	40.18 N	117.45 W
Spring Cr., Tx.	125	30.03 N	95.43 W
Spring Cr., Tx.	124	31.08 N	100.50 W
Springdale, Ar. (sprĭng'dāl)	123	36.10 N	94.07 W
Springdale, Can.	105	49.30 N	56.05 W
Springdale, Pa.	113e	40.33 N	79.46 W
Springer, NM (sprĭng'ẽr)	122	36.21 N	104.37 W
Springerville, Az.	121	34.08 N	109.17 W
Springfield, Co. (sprĭng'fēld)	122	37.24 N	102.04 W
Springfield, Il.	123	39.46 N	89.37 W
Springfield, Ky.	110	37.35 N	85.10 W
Springfield, Ma.	111	42.05 N	72.35 W
Springfield, Mn.	115	44.14 N	94.59 W
Springfield, Mo.	123	37.13 N	93.17 W
Springfield, NJ	55	40.43 N	74.19 W
Springfield, Oh.	110	39.55 N	83.50 W
Springfield, Or.	116	44.01 N	123.02 W
Springfield, Pa.	56b	39.55 N	75.24 W
Springfield, Tn.	126	36.30 N	86.53 W
Springfield, Vt.	111	43.20 N	72.35 W
Springfield, Va.	56d	38.45 N	77.13 W
Springfontein, S. Afr. (sprĭng'fôn-tīn)	226	30.16 S	25.45 E
Springhill, Can. (sprĭng-hĭl')	105	45.39 N	64.03 W
Spring Mill, Pa.	56b	40.04 N	75.17 W
Spring Mts., Nv.	120	36.18 N	115.49 W
Springs, S. Afr. (sprĭngs)	227b	26.16 S	28.27 E
Springstein, Can. (sprĭng'stīn)	95f	49.49 N	97.29 W
Springton Res., Pa. (sprĭng-tŭn)	112f	39.57 N	75.26 W
Springvale, Austl.	211a	37.57 N	145.09 E
Springvale South, Austl.	70b	37.58 S	145.09 E
Spring Valley, Ca.	120a	32.46 N	117.01 W
Springvalley, Il. (sprĭng-văl'ĭ)	110	41.20 N	89.15 W
Spring Valley, Mn.	115	43.41 N	92.26 W
Spring Valley, NY	112a	41.07 N	74.03 W
Springville, Ut. (sprĭng-vĭl)	121	40.10 N	111.40 W
Springwood, Austl.	211b	33.42 S	150.34 E
Sprockhövel, F.R.G.	63	51.22 N	7.15 E
Spruce Grove, Can. (spro͞os grōv)	95g	53.32 N	113.55 W
Spur, Tx. (spûr)	122	33.29 N	100.51 W
Squam (L.), NH (skwôm)	111	43.45 N	71.30 W
Squamish, Can. (skwō'mĭsh)	98	49.42 N	123.09 W
Squamish (R.), Can.	98	50.10 N	124.30 W
Squillace, Gulfo di (G.), It. (go͞o'l-fô-dē skwēl-lä'chā)	172	38.44 N	16.47 E
Squirrel Hill (Neigh.), Pa.	57b	40.26 N	79.55 W
Squirrel's Heath (Neigh.)	62	51.35 N	0.13 E
Srbija (Serbia) (Reg.), Yugo. (sr bē-yä) (sẽr'bē-ä)	173	44.05 N	20.35 E
Srbobran, Yugo. (s'r'bō-brän')	173	45.32 N	19.50 E
Sredne-Kolymsk, Sov. Un. (s'rĕd'nyĕ kô-lēmsk')	181	67.49 N	154.55 E
Sredne Rogatka, Sov. Un. (s'red'ná-ya) (rô gär'tkå)	182c	59.49 N	30.20 E
Sredniy Ik (R.), Sov. Un. (srĕd'nĭ ĭk)	182a	55.46 N	58.50 E
Sredniy Ural (Mts.), Sov. Un. (o͞o'răl)	182a	57.47 N	59.00 E
Šrem, Pol. (shrĕm)	167	52.06 N	17.01 E
Sremska Karlovci, Yugo. (srĕm'skē kär'lov-tsē)	173	45.10 N	19.57 E
Sremska Mitrovica, Yugo. (srĕm'skä mē'trō-vē-tsä')	173	44.59 N	19.39 E
Sretensk, Sov. Un. (s'rĕ'tĕnsk)	181	52.13 N	117.39 E
Sri Lanka (Ceylon), Asia	190	8.45 N	82.30 E
Srīnagar, India (srē-nŭg'ŭr)	196	34.11 N	74.49 E
Sroda, Pol. (shrô'dá)	167	52.14 N	17.17 E
Staaken (Neigh.), G.D.R.	65a	52.32 N	13.08 E
Stabroek, Bel.	157a	51.20 N	4.21 E
Stade, F.R.G. (shtä'dĕ)	157c	53.36 N	9.28 E
Städjan (Mtn.), Swe. (stĕd'yän)	164	61.53 N	12.50 E
Stadlau (Neigh.), Aus.	66e	48.14 N	16.28 E
Stafford, Eng. (stăf'fẽrd)	156	52.48 N	2.06 W
Stafford, Ks.	122	37.58 N	98.37 W
Staffordshire (Co.), Eng.	156	52.45 N	2.00 W
Stahnsdorf, G.D.R. (shtäns'dôrf)	157b	52.22 N	13.10 E
Staines, Eng.	62	51.26 N	0.13 W
Stains, Fr.	64c	48.57 N	2.23 E
Stalinabad, see Dushanbe			
Stalingrad, see Volgograd			
Stalino, see Donetsk			
Stalin, see Varna			
Stalinsk, see Novokuznetsk			
Stalybridge, Eng. (stā'lē-brĭj)	156	53.29 N	2.03 W
Stambaugh, Mi. (stăm'bô)	115	46.03 N	88.38 W
Stamford, Ct. (stăm'fẽrd)	112a	41.03 N	73.32 W
Stamford, Eng.	156	52.39 N	0.28 W
Stamford, Tx.	122	32.57 N	99.48 W
Stammersdorf, Aus. (shtäm'ẽrs-dôrf)	157e	48.19 N	16.25 E
Stamps, Ar. (stămps)	123	33.22 N	93.31 W
Stanberry, Mo. (stan'bĕr-ē)	123	40.12 N	94.34 W
Standerton, S. Afr. (stăn'dẽr-tŭn)	223d	26.57 S	29.17 E
Standing Rock Ind. Res., ND (stănd'ĭng rŏk)	114	47.07 N	101.05 W
Standish, Eng. (stăn'dĭsh)	156	53.36 N	2.39 W
Stanford, Ky. (stăn'fẽrd)	126	37.29 N	84.40 W
Stanford le Hope, Eng.	62	51.31 N	0.26 E
Stanford Rivers, Eng.	62	51.41 N	0.13 E
Stanger, S. Afr. (stăŋ-ger)	227c	29.22 S	31.18 E
Staniard Creek, Ba.	134	24.50 N	77.55 W
Stanislaus (R.), Ca. (stăn'ĭs-lô)	120	38.10 N	120.16 W
Stanley, Can. (stăn'lē)	104	46.17 N	66.44 W
Stanley, Falk. Is.	144	51.46 S	57.59 W
Stanley, Hong Kong	68c	22.13 N	114.12 E
Stanley, ND	114	48.20 N	102.25 W
Stanley, Wi.	115	44.56 N	90.56 W
Stanley Mound (Hill), Hong Kong	68c	22.14 N	114.12 E
Stanley Pool (L.), Zaire	229	4.07 S	15.40 E
Stanley Res., India (stăn'lē)	196	12.07 N	77.27 E
Stanleyville, see Kisangani			
Stanlow, Eng.	64a	53.17 N	2.52 W
Stanmore (Neigh.), Eng.	62	51.37 N	0.19 W
Stann Creek, Belize (stăn krēk)	132a	17.01 N	88.14 W
Stanovoy Khrebet (Mts.), Sov. Un. (stŭn-à-voi')	181	56.12 N	127.12 E
Stansted, Eng.	62	51.20 N	0.18 E
Stanton, Ca. (stăn'tŭn)	119a	33.48 N	118.00 W
Stanton, Ne.	114	41.57 N	97.15 W
Stanton, Tx.	124	32.08 N	101.46 W
Stanwell, Eng.	62	51.27 N	0.29 W
Stanwell Moor, Eng.	62	51.28 N	0.30 W
Stanwood, Wa. (stăn'wo͝od)	118a	48.14 N	122.23 W
Stapleford Abbots, Eng.	62	51.38 N	0.10 E
Stapleford Tawney, Eng.	62	51.40 N	0.11 E
Staples, Mn. (stā'p'lz)	115	46.21 N	94.48 W
Stapleton, Al.	126	30.45 N	87.48 W
Stara Planina (Balkan Mts.), Bul.	154	42.50 N	24.45 E
Staraya Kupavna, Sov. Un. (stä'rá-yá kû-päf'ná)	182b	55.48 N	38.10 E
Staraya Russa, Sov. Un. (stä'rá-yá ro͞o'sá)	174	57.58 N	31.21 E
Stara Zagora, Bul. (zä'gô-rá)	173	42.26 N	25.37 E
Starbuck, Can. (stär'bŭk)	95f	49.46 N	97.36 W
Stargard Szczeciński, Pol. (shtär'gärt shchĕ-chyn'skē)	166	53.19 N	15.03 E
Staritsa, Sov. Un. (stä'rē-tså)	174	56.29 N	34.58 E
Starke, Fl. (stärk)	127	29.55 N	82.07 W
Starkville, Co. (stärk'vĭl)	122	37.06 N	104.34 W
Starkville, Ms.	126	33.27 N	88.47 W
Starnberg, F.R.G. (shtärn-bĕrgh)	157d	47.59 N	11.20 E
Starnberger See (L.), F.R.G.	166	47.58 N	11.30 E
Starobel'sk, Sov. Un. (stä-rô-byĕlsk')	175	49.19 N	38.57 E
Starodub, Sov. Un. (stä-rô-dro͞op')	174	52.25 N	32.49 E
Starogrød Gdański, Pol. (stä'rō-grad gdĕn'skē)	167	53.58 N	18.33 E
Staro-Konstantinov, Sov. Un. (stä'rô kôn-stán-tē'nôf)	175	49.45 N	27.12 E
Staro-Minskaya, Sov. Un. (stä'rô mĭn'ská-yá)	175	46.19 N	38.51 E
Staro-Shcherbinovskaya, Sov. Un.	175	46.38 N	38.38 E
Staro-Subkhangulovo, Sov. Un. (stäro-so͞ob-kan-go͞o'lōvō)	182a	53.08 N	57.24 E
Staroutkinsk, Sov. Un. (stá-rô-o͞ot'kĭnsk)	182a	57.14 N	59.21 E
Staroverovka, Sov. Un.	175	49.31 N	35.48 E
Start Pt., Eng. (stärt)	162	50.14 N	3.34 W
Stary Sacz, Pol. (stä-rē sôṇch')	167	49.32 N	20.36 E
Staryy Oskol, Sov. Un. (stä'rē ôs-kôl')	175	51.18 N	37.51 E
Stassfurt, G.D.R. (shtäs'fo͞ort)	166	51.52 N	11.35 E
Staszów, Pol. (stä'sho͞of)	167	50.32 N	21.13 E
State College, Pa. (stāt kŏl'ĕj)	111	40.50 N	77.55 W
State Line, Mn. (līn)	119h	46.36 N	92.18 W
Staten I., NY (stăt'ĕn)	112a	40.35 N	74.10 W
Statesboro, Ga. (stāts'bŭr-ô)	127	32.26 N	81.47 W
Statesville, NC (stās'vĭl)	127	34.45 N	80.54 W
Statue of Liberty National Monument (P. Int.), NY	55	40.41 N	74.03 W
Staunton, Il. (stôn'tŭn)	119e	39.01 N	89.47 W
Staunton, Va.	111	38.10 N	79.05 W
Stavanger, Nor. (stä'väng'ẽr)	158	58.59 N	5.44 E
Stave (R.), Can. (stāv)	118d	49.12 N	122.24 W
Staveley, Eng. (stāv'lē)	156	53.17 N	1.21 W
Stavenisse, Neth.	157a	51.35 N	3.59 E
Stavropol', Sov. Un.	179	45.05 N	41.50 E
Stawno, Pol. (swav'nō)	166	54.21 N	16.38 E
Steamboat Springs, Co. (stēm'bōt')	122	40.30 N	106.48 W
Steblëv, Sov. Un. (styĕp'lyôf)	175	49.23 N	31.03 E
Steel (R.), Can. (stēl)	115	49.08 N	86.55 W
Steelton, Pa. (stēl'tŭn)	111	40.15 N	76.45 W
Steenbergen, Neth.	157a	51.35 N	4.18 E
Steens Mts., Or. (stēnz)	116	42.15 N	118.52 W
Steep Pt., Austl. (stēp)	214	26.15 N	112.05 E
Stefaniee, L., see Chew Bahir			
Steger, Il. (stē'gẽr)	113a	41.28 N	87.38 W
Steglitz (Neigh.), F.R.G.	65a	52.28 N	13.19 E
Steiermark (Styria) (State), Aus. (shtī'ẽr-märk)	166	47.22 N	14.40 E
Steinbach, Can.	96	49.32 N	96.4
Steinkjer, Nor. (stĕĭn-kyĕr)	158	64.00 N	11.1
Steinstücken (Neigh.), G.D.R.	65a	52.23 N	13.0
Stella, Wa. (stĕl'á)	118c	46.11 N	123.1
Stellarton, Can. (stĕl'ár-tŭn)	104	45.34 N	62.4
Stendal, G.D.R (shtĕn'däl)	166	52.37 N	11.5
Stepanakert, Sov. Un. (styĕ'pän-á-kĕrt)	179	39.50 N	46.4
Stephens, Port, Austl. (stē'fĕns)	216	32.43 N	152.5
Stephenville, Can. (stē'vĕn-vĭl)	105	48.33 N	58.3
Stepney (Neigh.), Eng.	62	51.31 N	0.0
Stepnyak, Sov. Un. (styĭp-nyäk')	180	52.37 N	70.4
Sterkrade, F.R.G. (shtĕr'krädĕ)	169c	51.31 N	6.5
Sterkrade (Neigh.), F.R.G.	63	51.31 N	6.5
Sterkstroom, S. Afr.	227c	31.33 S	26.3
Sterling, Co. (stûr'lĭng)	122	40.38 N	103.1
Sterling, Il.	115	41.48 N	89.4
Sterling, Ks.	122	38.11 N	98.1
Sterling, Ma.	105a	42.26 N	71.4
Sterling, Tx.	124	31.53 N	100.5
Sterling Park, Ca.	58b	37.41 N	122.2
Sterlitamak, Sov. Un. (styĕr'lē-ta-mák')	182a	53.38 N	55.5
Šternberk, Czech. (shtĕrn'bĕrk)	167	49.44 N	17.1
Stettin, see Szczecin			
Stettler, Can.	99	52.19 N	112.4
Steubenville, Oh. (stū'bĕn-vĭl)	110	40.20 N	80.4
Stevens (L.), Wa. (stē'vĕnz)	118a	47.59 N	122.0
Stevens Point, Wi.	115	44.30 N	89.3
Stevensville, Mt. (stē'vĕnz-vĭl)	117	46.31 N	114.0
Stewart (R.), Can. (stū'ẽrt)	96	63.27 N	138.4
Stewart I., N. Z.	217	46.56 S	167.4
Stewart Manor, NY	55	40.43 N	73.4
Stewiacke, Can. (stū'wē-ăk)	104	45.08 N	63.2
Steynsrus, S. Afr. (stīns'ro͞os)	223d	27.58 S	27.3
Steyr, Aus. (shtīr)	166	48.03 N	14.2
Stickney, Il.	58a	41.49 N	87.4
Stiepel (Neigh.), F.R.G.	63	51.25 N	7.1
Stif, Alg.	224	36.18 N	5.2
Stikine (R.), Can. (stĭ-kēn')	96	58.17 N	130.1
Stikine Ranges, Can.	96	59.05 N	130.0
Stillaguamish (R.), South Fk. Wa. (stĭl-á-gwä'mĭsh)	118a	48.05 N	121.5
Stillaguamish (R.), Wa.	118a	48.11 N	122.1
Stillwater, Mn. (stĭl'wô-tẽr)	119g	45.04 N	92.4
Stillwater, Mt.	117	45.23 N	109.4
Stillwater, Ok.	123	36.06 N	97.0
Stillwater R., Mt.	116	48.47 N	114.4
Stillwater Ra., Nv.	120	39.43 N	118.1
Stintonville, S. Afr.	71b	26.14 S	28.1
Štip, Yugo. (shtĭp)	173	41.43 N	22.0
Stirling, Scot. (stûr'lĭng)	162	56.05 N	3.5
Stittsville, Can. (stĭts'vĭl)	95c	45.15 N	75.5
Stjördalshalsen, Nor. (styûr-däls-hälsĕn)	164	63.26 N	11.0
Stockbridge Munsee Ind. Res., Wi. (stŏk'brĭdj mŭn-sē)	115	44.49 N	89.0
Stockerau, Aus. (shtô'kĕ-rou)	157e	48.24 N	16.1
Stockholm, Me. (stŏk'hōlm)	104	47.05 N	68.0
Stockholm, Swe. (stôk'hôlm)	164	59.23 N	18.0
Stockport, Eng. (stŏk'pôrt)	156	53.24 N	2.0
Stockton, Ca. (stŏk'tŭn)	120	37.56 N	121.1
Stockton, Eng.	162	54.35 N	1.2
Stockton, Ks.	122	39.26 N	99.1
Stockton (I.), Wi.	115	46.56 N	90.2
Stockton Plat., Tx.	124	30.34 N	102.3
Stockton Res., Mo.	123	37.40 N	93.4
Stockum (Neigh.), F.R.G.	63	51.28 N	7.2
Stöde, Swe. (stû'dĕ)	164	62.26 N	16.3
Stoke D'Abernon, Eng.	62	51.19 N	0.2
Stoke Newington (Neigh.), Eng.	62	51.34 N	0.0
Stoke-on-Trent, Eng. (stōk-ŏn-trĕnt)	156	53.01 N	2.1
Stoke Poges, Eng.	62	51.33 N	0.3
Stokhod (R.), Sov. Un. (stō-kōd)	167	51.24 N	25.2
Stolac, Yugo. (stô'láts)	173	43.03 N	17.5
Stolbovy (Is.), Sov. Un. (stôl-bô-voi')	181	73.43 N	133.0
Stolin, Sov. Un. (stô'lēn)	167	51.54 N	26.5
Stolpe, G.D.R.	65a	52.40 N	13.1
Stömstad, Swe.	164	58.58 N	11.0
Stondon Massey, Eng.	62	51.41 N	0.1
Stone, Eng.	62	51.27 N	0.1
Stone, Eng.	156	52.54 N	2.0
Stoneham, Can. (stōn'ám)	95b	46.59 N	71.2
Stoneham, Ma.	105a	42.30 N	71.0
Stonehaven, Scot. (stōn'hā-v'n)	162	56.57 N	2.0
Stone Mountain, Ga. (stōn)	112c	33.49 N	84.1
Stone Park, Il.	58a	41.45 N	87.5
Stonewall, Can. (stōn'wôl)	95f	50.09 N	97.2
Stonewall, Ms.	126	32.08 N	88.4
Stoney Creek, Can. (stō'nē)	95d	43.13 N	79.4
Stonington, Ct. (stōn'ĭng-tŭn)	111	41.20 N	71.5
Stony Cr., Ca. (stō'nē)	120	39.28 N	122.3
Stony Indian Res., Can.	95e	51.10 N	114.4
Stony Mountain, Can.	95f	50.05 N	97.1
Stony Plain, Can. (stō'nē plān)	95g	53.02 N	114.0
Stony Plain Ind. Res., Can.	95g	53.29 N	113.4
Stony Point, NY	112a	41.13 N	73.5
Stony Run, Md.	56c	39.11 N	76.4
Storå (R.), Den.	164	56.22 N	8.3
Stora Lule (R.), Swe. (sto͞o'rä lo͞o'lĕ)	178	67.00 N	19.3
Stora Sotra (I.), Nor.	164	60.24 N	4.3
Stord (I.), Nor. (stôrd)	164	59.54 N	5.1
Store Baelt (Str.), Den.	164	55.25 N	10.5
Storeton, Eng.	64a	53.21 N	3.0
Storfjorden (Fd.), Nor.	164	62.17 N	6.1
Stormberg (Mts.), S. Afr. (stôrm'bûrg)	227c	31.28 S	26.3
Storm Lake, Ia.	115	42.39 N	95.1
Stormy Pt., Vir. Is. (U.S.A.) (stôr'mē)	129c	18.22 N	65.0
Stornoway, Scot. (stôr'nô-wā)	162	58.13 N	6.2

ăt; finăl; rāte; senāte; ärm; ȧsk; sofȧ; fâre; ch-choose; dh-as th in other; bē; ēvent; bĕt; recĕnt; cratẽr; g-gō; gh-guttural g; bĭt; ĭ-short neutral; rīde; K-guttural k as ch in German ich;

PRONOUNCING INDEX

Storozhinets – Sutton-at-Hone 349

PLACE (Pronounciation)	PAGE	Lat. °′	Long. °′
Storozhinets, Sov. Un. (stô-rô'zhēn-yĕts)	167	48.10 N	25.44 E
Störsjo, Swe. (stôr'shû)	164	62.49 N	13.08 E
Storsjoen (L.), Nor. (stôr-syûěn)	164	61.32 N	11.30 E
Storsjon (L.), Swe.	164	63.06 N	14.00 E
Storvik, Swe. (stôr'vēk)	164	60.37 N	16.31 E
Stoughton, Ma. (stō'tŭn)	105a	42.07 N	71.06 W
Stoughton, Wi.	115	42.54 N	89.15 W
Stour (R.), Eng. (stour)	163	52.09 N	0.29 E
Stourbridge, Eng. (stour'brĭj)	156	52.27 N	2.08 W
Stow, Ma. (stō)	105a	42.56 N	71.31 W
Stow, Oh.	113d	41.09 N	81.26 W
Stowe Township, Pa.	57b	40.29 N	80.04 W
Straatsdrif, S. Afr.	223d	25.19 S	26.22 E
Strabane, N. Ire. (stră-băn')	162	54.59 N	7.27 W
Straelen, F.R.G. (shtră'lĕn)	169c	51.26 N	6.16 E
Strahan, Austl. (strā'ăn)	215	42.08 S	145.28 E
Strakonice, Czech. (strä'kô-nyē-tsĕ)	166	49.18 N	13.52 E
Straldzha, Bul. (sträl'dzhȧ)	173	42.37 N	26.44 E
Stralsund, G.D.R. (shräl'so͞ont)	166	54.18 N	13.04 E
Strangford, Lough (B.), Ire. (lŏk străng'fērd)	162	54.30 N	5.34 W
Strängnäs, Swe. (strĕng'nĕs)	164	59.23 N	16.59 E
Stranraer, Scot. (străn-rär')	162	54.55 N	5.05 W
Strasbourg, Fr. (strȧs-bo͞or')	169	48.36 N	7.49 E
Stratford, Can. (străt'fērd)	110	43.20 N	81.05 W
Stratford, Ct.	111	41.10 N	73.05 W
Stratford, Wi.	115	44.16 N	90.02 W
Stratford-upon-Avon, Eng.	162	52.13 N	1.41 W
Strathcona Prov. Pk., Can.	98	49.40 N	125.50 W
Strathfield, Austl.	70a	33.52 S	151.06 E
Strathmoor (Neigh.), Mi.	57c	42.23 N	83.11 W
Straubing, F.R.G. (strou'bĭng)	166	48.52 N	12.36 E
Strauch, F.R.G.	63	51.09 N	6.56 E
Strausberg, G.D.R. (strous'bĕrgh)	166	52.35 N	13.50 E
Strawberry (R.), Ut.	121	40.05 N	110.55 W
Strawberry Mts., Or. (strô'bĕr'ĭ)	116	44.19 N	119.20 W
Strawberry Point, Ca.	58b	37.54 N	122.31 W
Strawn, Tx. (strôn)	124	32.38 N	98.28 W
Streatham (Neigh.), Eng.	62	51.26 N	0.08 W
Streator, Il. (strē'tēr)	110	41.05 N	88.50 W
Streeter, ND	114	46.40 N	99.22 W
Streetsville, Can. (strētz'vĭl)	95d	43.34 N	79.43 W
Strehaia, Rom. (strĕ-kä'yȧ)	173	44.37 N	23.13 E
Strel'na, Sov. Un. (strĕl'nȧ)	182c	59.52 N	30.01 E
Stretford, Eng. (strĕt'fērd)	156	53.25 N	2.19 W
Strickland (R.), Pap. N. Gui. (strĭk'lănd)	207	6.15 S	142.00 E
Strijen, Neth.	157a	51.44 N	4.23 E
Stromboli (Vol.), It. (strôm'bô-lē)	172	38.46 N	15.16 E
Stromyn, Sov. Un. (strô'mĭn)	182b	56.02 N	38.29 E
Strong (R.), Ms. (strông)	126	32.03 N	89.42 W
Strongsville, Oh. (strôngz'vĭl)	113d	41.19 N	81.50 W
Stronsay (I.), Scot. (strŏn'sā)	162a	59.09 N	2.35 W
Stroudsburg, Pa. (stroudz'bûrg)	111	41.00 N	75.15 W
Strubenvale, S. Afr.	71b	26.16 S	28.28 E
Struer, Den.	164	56.29 N	8.34 E
Strugi Krasnyye, Sov. Un. (stro͞o'gĭ krä's-ny'yĕ)	174	58.14 N	29.10 E
Struisbelt, S. Afr.	71b	26.19 S	28.29 E
Struma (R.), Bul. (stro͞o'mȧ)	173	41.55 N	23.05 E
Strumica, Yugo. (stro͞o'mĭ-tsȧ)	173	41.26 N	22.38 E
Strümp, F.R.G.	63	51.17 N	6.40 E
Strunino, Sov. Un.	182b	56.23 N	38.34 E
Struthers, Oh. (strŭdh'ērz)	110	41.00 N	80.35 W
Struvenhütten, F.R.G. (shtro͞o'vĕn-hü-tĕn)	157c	53.52 N	10.04 E
Strydpoortberge (Mts.), S. Afr.	223d	24.08 N	29.18 E
Stryy, Sov. Un. (strē')	167	49.16 N	23.51 E
Strzelce Opolskie, Pol. (stzhĕl'tsĕ o-pŏl'skyĕ)	167	50.31 N	18.20 E
Strzelin, Pol. (stzhĕ-lĭn)	167	50.48 N	17.06 E
Strzelno, Pol. (stzhål'nô)	167	52.37 N	18.10 E
Stuart, Fl. (stū'ērt)	127a	27.10 N	80.14 W
Stuart, Ia.	115	41.31 N	94.20 W
Stuart (I.), Ak.	107	63.25 N	162.45 W
Stuart (I.), Wa.	118d	48.42 N	123.10 W
Stuart L., Can.	98	54.32 N	124.35 W
Stuart Ra., Austl.	214	29.00 S	134.30 E
Stung Treng, Kamp. (sto͝ong'trĕng')	206	13.36 N	106.00 E
Stupava, Czech.	157e	48.17 N	17.02 E
Stupsk, Pol. (swo͝opsk)	167	54.28 N	17.02 E
Sturgeon (R.), Can.	95g	53.41 N	113.46 W
Sturgeon (R.), Mi.	115	46.43 N	88.43 W
Sturgeon B., Can.	101	52.00 N	98.00 W
Sturgeon Bay, Wi.	115	44.50 N	87.22 W
Sturgeon Falls, Can.	97	46.19 N	79.49 W
Sturgis, Ky.	110	37.35 N	88.00 W
Sturgis, Mi.	110	41.45 N	85.25 W
Sturgis, SD	114	44.25 N	103.31 W
Sturt Cr., Austl.	214	19.40 S	127.40 E
Sturtevant, Wi. (stŭr'tē-vănt)	113a	42.42 N	87.54 W
Stutterheim, S. Afr. (stŭrt'ēr-hĭm)	227c	32.34 S	27.27 E
Stuttgart, Ar. (stŭt'gärt)	123	34.30 N	91.33 W
Stuttgart, F.R.G. (shto͞ot'gärt)	166	48.48 N	9.15 E
Styal, Eng.	64b	53.21 N	2.15 W
Stykkisholmur, Ice.	158	65.00 N	21.48 W
Styria, see Steiermark			
Styr' R., Sov. Un. (stēr)	167	51.44 N	26.07 E
Styrum (Neigh.), F.R.G.	63	51.27 N	6.51 E
Suao, Taiwan (so͞o'ou)	203	24.35 N	121.45 E
Subarnarakha (R.), India	196	22.38 N	86.26 E
Subata, Sov. Un. (so͞o'bȧ-tȧ)	165	56.02 N	25.54 E
Subic, Phil. (so͞o'bĭk)	207a	14.52 N	120.15 E
Subic B., Phil.	207a	14.41 N	120.11 E
Subotica, Yugo. (so͞o'bô'tē-tsȧ)	173	46.06 N	19.41 E
Subugo (Mtn.), Ken.	231	1.40 S	35.49 E
Succasunna, NJ (sŭk'kȧ-sŭn'nȧ)	112a	40.52 N	74.37 W
Suceava, Rom. (so͞o-chȧ-ä'vȧ)	167	47.39 N	26.17 E
Suceava R., Rom.	167	47.45 N	26.10 E
Sucha, Pol. (so͞o'kȧ)	167	49.44 N	19.40 E
Suchiapa, Mex. (so͞o-chē-ä'pä)	131	16.38 N	93.08 W
Suchiapa (R.), Mex.	131	16.27 N	93.26 W
Suchitoto, Sal. (so͞o-chē-tō'tō)	132	13.58 N	89.03 W
Sucia Is., Wa. (soū'sē-ȧ)	118d	48.46 N	122.54 W
Sucio (R.), Col. (so͞o'syō)	142a	6.55 N	76.15 W
Suck, Ire. (sŭk)	162	53.34 N	8.16 W
Sucre, Bol. (so͞o'krā)	142	19.06 S	65.16 W
Sucre (State), Ven. (so͞o'krĕ)	143b	10.18 N	65.12 W
Sucy-en-Brie, Fr.	64c	48.46 N	2.32 E
Suda, Sov. Un. (so͞o'dȧ)	182a	56.58 N	56.45 E
Suda (R.), Sov. Un. (so͞o'dȧ)	174	59.24 N	36.40 E
Sudair, Sau. Ar. (sŭ-dä'ēr)	192	25.48 N	46.28 E
Sudalsvatnet (L.), Nor.	164	59.35 N	6.59 E
Sudan, Afr.	222	14.00 N	28.00 E
Sudan (Reg.), Afr. (so͞o-dän')	229	15.00 N	7.00 E
Sudberg (Neigh.), F.R.G.	63	51.11 N	7.08 E
Sudbury, Can. (sŭd'bēr-ē)	97	46.28 N	81.00 W
Sudbury, Ma.	105a	42.23 N	71.25 W
Sud, Canal du (Chan.), Hai.	135	18.40 N	73.15 W
Suderwich (Neigh.), F.R.G.	63	51.37 N	7.15 E
Sudetes (Mts.), Czech.	166	50.41 N	15.37 E
Sudogda, Sov. Un. (so͞o'dôk-dȧ)	174	55.57 N	40.29 E
Sudost' (R.), Sov. Un. (so͞o-dôst')	174	52.43 N	33.13 E
Sud, Rivière du, Can. (rē-vyâr' dü süd')	95b	46.56 N	70.35 W
Sudzha, Sov. Un. (so͝od'zhȧ)	175	51.14 N	35.11 E
Sueca, Sp. (swā'kä)	171	39.12 N	0.18 W
Suemez I., Ak.	98	55.17 N	133.21 W
Suez Can., see Qana el Suweis			
Suez, G. of, Egypt (so͞o-ĕz')	223c	29.53 N	32.33 E
Suez, see As Suways			
Suffern, NY (sŭf'fērn)	112a	41.07 N	74.09 W
Suffolk, Va. (sŭf'ŭk)	112g	36.43 N	76.35 W
Sugandha, India	67a	22.54 N	88.20 E
Sugar (Cr.), In.	110	39.55 N	87.10 W
Sugar City, Co.	122	38.12 N	103.42 W
Sugar Cr., Il. (sho͝og'ēr)	123	40.14 N	89.28 W
Sugar Creek, Mo.	119f	39.07 N	94.27 W
Sugar I., Mi.	119k	46.31 N	84.12 W
Sugarloaf Pt., Austl. (so͝ogēr'lôf)	216	32.19 S	153.04 E
Suggi L., Can.	101	54.22 N	102.47 W
Suginami (Neigh.), Jap.	69a	35.42 N	139.38 E
Sūhānak, Iran	68h	35.48 N	51.32 E
Suhaymī, Wādī as (R.), Egypt	191a	29.48 N	33.12 E
Sühbaatar, Mong	181	50.18 N	106.31 E
Suhl, G.D.R. (zo͞ol)	166	50.37 N	10.41 E
Suichuan (Mtn.), China	203	26.25 N	114.10 E
Suide, China (swā-dŭ)	202	37.32 N	110.12 E
Suifenhe, China (swā-fŭn-hŭ)	181	44.47 N	131.13 E
Suihua, China,	202	46.38 N	126.50 E
Suining, China (so͞o'ē-nĭng')	200	33.54 N	117.57 E
Suipacha, Arg. (swē-pä'chȧ)	141c	34.45 S	59.43 W
Suiping, China (swā-pĭŋ)	200	33.09 N	113.58 E
Suir R., Ire. (sūr)	162	52.20 N	7.32 W
Suisun B., Ca. (so͞o-ē-so͞on')	118b	38.07 N	122.02 W
Suita, Jap. (so͞o'ē-tä)	205b	34.45 N	135.32 E
Suitland, Md. (so͞ot'lănd)	112e	38.51 N	76.57 W
Suixian, China (swā shyĕn)	203	31.42 N	113.20 E
Suiyüan (Reg.), China (swā-yüĕn)	198	41.31 N	107.04 E
Suizhong, China (swā-jôŋ)	200	40.22 N	120.20 E
Sukabumi, Indon.	206	6.52 S	106.56 E
Sukadana, Indon.	206	1.15 S	110.30 E
Sukagawa, Jap. (so͞o'kä-gä'wä)	205	37.08 N	140.07 E
Sukarnapura, see Jayapura			
Sukhinichi, Sov. Un. (so͞o'kē'nē-chē)	174	54.07 N	35.18 E
Sukhona (R.), Sov. Un. (so͞o-kô'nȧ)	178	59.30 N	42.20 E
Sukhoy Log, Sov. Un. (so͞o'kôy lôg)	182a	56.55 N	62.03 E
Sukhumi, Sov. Un. (so͞o-ko͞om')	179	43.00 N	41.00 E
Sukkur, Pak. (sŭk'ŭr)	196	27.49 N	68.50 E
Sukkwan I., Ak.	98	55.05 N	132.45 W
Suksun, Sov. Un. (so͝ok'so͞on)	182a	57.08 N	57.22 E
Sukumo, Jap. (so͞o'ko͞o-mô)	205	32.58 N	132.45 E
Sukunka (R.), Can.	99	55.00 N	121.50 W
Sula (R.), Sov. Un. (so͞o-lȧ')	175	50.36 N	33.13 E
Sulaco R., Hond. (so͞o-lä'kō)	132	14.55 N	87.31 W
Sulaimān Ra., Pak. (so͞o-lä-ē-män')	196	29.47 N	69.10 E
Sulak (R.), Sov. Un. (so͞o-lȧk')	179	43.30 N	47.00 E
Sula, Kepulauan (I.), Indon.	207	2.20 S	125.20 E
Sulawesi (I.), see Celebes			
Suleya, Sov. Un. (so͞o-lē'ya)	182a	55.12 N	58.52 E
Sulfeld, F.R.G. (zo͞o'fĕld)	157c	53.48 N	10.13 E
Sūlgan, Iran	68h	35.49 N	51.15 E
Sulina, Rom. (so͞o-lē'nȧ)	175	45.08 N	29.38 E
Sulitelma (Mtn.), Nor.-Swe. (so͞o-lē-tyĕl'mȧ)	158	67.03 N	16.35 E
Sullana, Peru (so͞o-lyä'nä)	142	4.57 N	80.47 W
Sulligent, Al. (sŭl'ĭ-jĕnt)	126	33.52 N	88.06 W
Sullivan, Il. (sŭl'ĭ-văn)	110	41.35 N	88.35 W
Sullivan, In.	110	39.05 N	87.20 W
Sullivan, Mo.	123	38.13 N	91.09 W
Sulmona, It. (so͞ol-mō'nä)	172	42.02 N	13.58 E
Sulphur, Ok. (sŭl'fŭr)	123	34.31 N	96.58 W
Sulphur (R.), Tx.	123	33.26 N	95.06 W
Sulphur Springs, Tx. (sprĭngz)	123	33.09 N	95.36 W
Sultan, Wa. (sŭl'tăn)	118a	47.52 N	121.49 W
Sultan (R.), Wa.	118a	47.55 N	121.49 W
Sultepec, Mex. (so͞ol-tȧ-pĕk')	130	18.50 N	99.51 W
Sulu Arch., Phil. (so͞o'lo͞o)	206	5.52 N	122.00 E
Suluntah, Libya	161	32.39 N	21.49 E
Sulūq, Libya.	194	31.39 N	20.15 E
Sulu Sea, Phil.	206	8.25 N	119.00 E
Suma, Jap. (so͞o'mä)	205b	34.39 N	135.08 E
Suma (Neigh.), Jap.	69b	34.39 N	135.08 E
Sumas, Wa. (sū'mȧs)	118d	49.00 N	122.16 W
Sumatera (I.), see Sumatra			
Sumatra (Sumatera) (I.), Indon. (so͞o-mä'trȧ)	206	2.06 N	99.40 E
Sumba (I.), Indon. (sŭm'bȧ)	206	9.52 S	119.00 E
Sumba, Ile (I.), Zaire	230	1.44 N	19.32 E
Sumbawa (I.), Indon. (so͞om-bä'wä)	206	9.00 S	118.18 E
Sumbawa-Besar, Indon.	206	8.32 S	117.20 E
Sumbawanga, Tan.	231	7.58 S	31.37 E
Sümeg, Hung. (shü'mĕg)	167	46.59 N	17.19 E
Sumida (R.), Jap. (so͞o'mē-dä)	205	36.01 N	139.24 E
Sumidouro, Braz. (so͞o-mē-dō'ro͞o)	141a	22.04 S	42.41 W
Sumiyoshi, Jap. (so͞o'mē-yō'shē)	205b	34.43 N	135.16 E
Sumiyoshi (Neigh.), Jap.	69b	34.36 N	135.31 E
Summer L., Or. (sŭm'ēr)	116	42.50 N	120.35 W
Summerland, Can. (sŭ'mēr-lănd)	99	49.39 N	117.33 W
Summerseat, Eng.	64b	53.38 N	2.19 W
Summerside, Can. (sŭm'ēr-sīd)	104	46.25 N	63.47 W
Summerton, SC (sŭm'ēr-tŭn)	127	33.37 N	80.22 W
Summerville, SC (sŭm'ēr-vĭl)	127	33.00 N	80.10 W
Summit, Il. (sŭm'mĭt)	113a	41.47 N	87.48 W
Summit, NJ	112a	40.43 N	74.21 W
Summit Lake Ind. Res., Nv.	116	41.35 N	119.30 W
Summit Park, Md.	56c	39.23 N	76.41 W
Summit Pk., Co.	121	37.20 N	106.40 W
Sumner, Wa. (sŭm'nēr)	118a	47.12 N	122.14 W
Šumperk, Czech. (sho͞om'pĕrk)	166	49.57 N	17.02 E
Sumrall, Ms. (sŭm'rôl)	126	31.25 N	89.34 W
Sumter, SC (sŭm'tēr)	127	33.55 N	80.21 W
Sumy, Sov. Un. (so͞o'mĭ)	175	50.54 N	34.47 E
Sumy (Oblast), Sov. Un.	175	51.02 N	34.05 E
Sunburst, Mt.	117	48.53 N	111.55 W
Sunbury, Eng.	62	51.25 N	0.26 W
Sunbury, Pa. (sŭn'bēr-ē)	111	40.50 N	76.45 W
Sundance, Wy. (sŭn'dăns)	117	44.24 N	104.27 W
Sundarbans (Swp.), Bngl.-India (so͝on'dēr-bŭns)	196	21.50 N	89.00 E
Sunda Selat (Str.), Indon.	206	5.45 S	106.15 E
Sunday Str., Austl. (sŭn'dā)	214	15.50 S	122.45 E
Sundbyberg, Swe. (so͞on'bü-bĕrgh)	164	59.24 N	17.56 E
Sunderland, Eng. (sŭn'dēr-lănd)	162	54.55 N	1.25 W
Sunderland, Md.	112e	38.41 N	76.36 W
Sundridge, Eng.	62	51.17 N	0.18 E
Sundsvall, Swe. (so͞onds'väl)	164	62.24 N	19.19 E
Sunflower, (R.), Ms. (sŭn-flou'ēr)	126	32.57 N	90.40 W
Sungari (Songhua) (R.), China (so͞oŋ-hwä)	199	46.09 N	127.53 E
Sungari Res., China	202	42.55 N	127.50 E
Sungurlu, Tur. (so͞on'go͞or-lo͞o')	179	40.08 N	34.20 E
Sun Kosi (R.), Nep.	196	27.13 N	85.52 E
Sunland, Ca. (sŭn-lănd)	119a	34.16 N	118.18 W
Sunne, Swe. (so͞on'ĕ)	164	59.51 N	13.07 E
Sunninghill, Eng. (sŭnĭng'hĭl)	156b	51.23 N	0.40 W
Sunnymead, Ca. (sŭn'ĭ-mēd)	119a	33.56 N	117.15 W
Sunnyside, Ut.	121	39.35 N	110.20 W
Sunnyside, Wa.	116	46.19 N	120.00 W
Sunnyvale, Ca. (sŭn-nē-văl)	118b	37.23 N	122.02 W
Sunol, Ca. (so͞o'nŭl)	118b	37.36 N	122.53 W
Sun R., Mt. (sŭn)	117	47.34 N	111.53 W
Sunset, Ut. (sŭn-sĕt)	119b	41.08 N	112.02 W
Sunset Beach, Ca.	59	33.43 N	118.04 W
Sunset Crater Natl. Mon., Az. (krā'tēr)	121	35.20 N	111.30 W
Sunshine, Austl.	211a	37.47 S	144.50 E
Suntar, Sov. Un. (so͞on-tär')	181	62.14 N	117.49 E
Sunyani, Ghana	228	7.20 N	2.20 W
Suoyarvi, Sov. Un. (so͞o'ô-yĕr'vē)	165	62.12 N	32.29 E
Superior, Az. (su-pē'rĭ-ēr)	121	33.15 N	111.10 W
Superior, Ne.	122	40.04 N	98.05 W
Superior, Wi.	119h	46.44 N	92.06 W
Superior, Wy.	117	41.45 N	108.57 W
Superior, L., Can.-U.S.	97	47.38 N	89.20 W
Superior, Laguna (L.), Mex. (lä-go͞o'nȧ so͞o-pä-rē-ōr')	131	16.20 N	94.55 W
Superior Village, Wi.	119h	46.38 N	92.07 W
Sup'ung Res., Kor.-China (so͞o'po͞ong)	204	40.35 N	126.00 E
Suqian, China (so͞o-chyĕn)	200	33.57 N	118.17 E
Suquamish, Wa. (so͞o-gwä'mĭsh)	118a	47.44 N	122.34 W
Şūr (Tyre), Leb. (so͞or) (tīr)	191a	33.16 N	35.13 E
Şūr, Om.	192	22.23 N	59.28 E
Sura (Neigh.), India	67a	22.33 N	88.25 E
Surabaya, Indon.	206	7.23 S	112.45 E
Surakarta, Indon.	206	7.35 S	110.45 E
Šurany, Czech. (sho͞o'rȧ-nû')	167	48.05 N	18.11 E
Surat, Austl. (sŭ-răt)	216	27.18 S	149.00 E
Surat, India (so͞o'rŭt)	196	21.08 N	73.22 E
Surat Thani, Thai.	206	8.59 N	99.14 E
Surazh, Sov. Un. (so͞o-rȧzh')	174	53.02 N	32.27 E
Surazh, Sov. Un.	174	55.24 N	30.46 E
Surbiton (Neigh.), Eng.	62	51.24 N	0.18 W
Surco, Peru	60c	12.09 S	77.01 W
Suresnes, Fr.	64c	48.52 N	2.14 E
Surgères, Fr. (sür-zhâr')	168	46.06 N	0.51 W
Surgut, Sov. Un. (so͞or-go͞ot')	180	61.18 N	73.38 E
Suriname, S.A. (so͞o-rē-näm')	140	4.00 N	56.00 W
Surquillo, Peru	60c	12.07 S	77.02 W
Sürmaq, Iran	195	31.03 N	52.48 E
Surt, Libya	225	31.14 N	16.37 E
Surt, Khalīj (G.), Afr.	161	31.30 N	18.28 E
Suruga-Wan (B.), Jap. (so͞o'ro͞o-gä wän)	205	34.52 N	138.36 E
Suru-Lere (Neigh.), Nig.	71d	6.31 N	3.22 E
Susa, It. (so͞o'sä)	172	45.01 N	7.09 E
Susa, Jap.	205	34.40 N	131.39 E
Sušak (I.), Yugo.	172	42.45 N	16.30 E
Susaki, Jap. (so͞o'sä-kē)	205	33.23 N	133.16 E
Susak, Otok (I.), Yugo. (so͞o'shȧk)	172	44.31 N	14.15 E
Susitna, Ak. (so͞o-sĭt'nȧ)	107	61.28 N	150.28 W
Susitna (R.), Ak.	107	62.00 N	150.28 W
Susong, China (so͞o-sôŋ)	203	30.18 N	116.08 E
Susquehanna, Pa. (sŭs'kwē-hăn'ȧ)	111	41.55 N	73.55 W
Susquehanna (R.), Pa.	111	39.50 N	76.20 W
Sussex, Can. (sŭs'ĕks)	104	45.43 N	65.31 W
Sussex, NJ	112a	41.12 N	74.36 W
Sussex, Wi.	113a	43.08 N	88.12 W
Sutherland, Austl. (sŭdh'ēr-lănd)	211b	34.02 S	151.04 E
Sutherland, S. Afr. (sŭ'thēr-lănd)	226	32.25 S	20.40 E
Sutlej (R.), Pak.-India (sŭt'lĕj)	196	30.15 N	72.25 E
Sutton, Eng. (sut''n)	156b	51.21 N	0.12 W
Sutton, Ma.	105a	42.09 N	71.46 W
Sutton-at-Hone, Eng.	62	51.25 N	0.14 E

ng-sing; ŋ-baŋk; N-nasalized n; nŏd; cŏmmit; ōld; ôbey; ôrder; oi-boil; fo͞od; fo͝ot; ou-out; s-soft; sh-dish; th-thin; pūre; ûnite; ûrn; stŭd; circŭs; ü-as in French tu; '-indeterminate vowel.

350 Sutton Coldfield – Talata Mafara

PLACE (Pronounciation)	PAGE	Lat. °′	Long. °′
Sutton Coldfield, Eng. (kōld'fēld)	156	52.34 N	1.49 W
Sutton-in-Ashfield, Eng. (ĭn-ăsh'fēld)	156	53.07 N	1.15 W
Suurbekom, S. Afr.	71b	26.19 S	27.44 E
Suurberge (Mts.), S. Afr.	227c	33.15 S	25.32 E
Suwa, Jap. (sōō'wä)	205	36.03 N	138.08 E
Suwanee L., Can.	101	56.08 N	100.10 W
Suwannee (R.), Fl.-Ga. (sōō-wô'nē)	126	29.42 N	83.00 W
Suwatki, Pol. (sōō-vou'kē)	167	54.05 N	22.58 E
Suways al Ḩulwah, Tur'at as (Can.), Egypt	223c	30.15 N	32.20 E
Suxian, China (sōō shyĕn)	200	33.37 N	117.51 E
Suzdal', Sov. Un. (sōōz'dál)	174	56.26 N	40.29 E
Suzhou, China (sōō-jō)	200	31.19 N	120.37 E
Suzuki-shinden, Jap.	69a	35.43 N	139.31 E
Suzu Misaki (C.), Jap. (sōō'zōō mē'sä-kē)	204	37.30 N	137.35 E
Svalbard (Spitsbergen) (Is.), Eur. (sväl'bärt) (spĭts'bûr-gĕn)	176	77.00 N	20.00 E
Svaneke, Den. (svä'nĕ-kĕ)	164	55.08 N	15.07 E
Svatovo, Sov. Un. (svä'tô-vô)	175	49.23 N	38.10 E
Svedala, Swe. (svĕ'dä-lä)	164	55.29 N	13.11 E
Sveg, Swe.	164	62.03 N	14.22 E
Svelvik, Nor. (svĕl'vĕk)	164	59.37 N	10.18 E
Svenčionys, Sov. Un.	165	55.09 N	26.09 E
Svendborg, Den. (svĕn-bôrgh)	164	55.05 N	10.35 E
Svensen, Or. (svĕn'sĕn)	118c	46.10 N	123.39 W
Sverdlovsk, Sov. Un. (svĕrd-lôfsk')	182a	56.51 N	60.36 E
Svetlaya, Sov. Un. (svyĕt'lá-yá)	204	46.09 N	137.53 E
Svilajnac, Yugo. (svē'lá-ē-náts)	173	44.12 N	21.14 E
Svilengrad, Bul. (svĕl'ĕn-grát)	173	41.44 N	26.11 E
Svir' (R.), Sov. Un.	178	60.55 N	33.40 E
Svir Kanal (Can.), Sov. Un. (ká-näl')	165	60.10 N	32.40 E
Svishtov, Bul. (svĕsh'tôf)	173	43.36 N	25.21 E
Svisloch' (R.), Sov. Un. (svēs'lôk)	174	53.38 N	28.10 E
Svitavy, Czech.	166	49.46 N	16.28 E
Svitsa (R.), Sov. Un. (svĭ-tsá)	167	49.09 N	24.10 E
Svobodnyy, Sov. Un. (svô-bôd'nĭ)	181	51.28 N	128.28 E
Svolvaer, Nor. (svôl'vĕr)	158	68.15 N	14.29 E
Svyatoy Nos, Mys (C.), Sov. Un. (svyŭ'toi nôs)	181	72.18 N	139.28 E
Swadlincote, Eng. (swŏd'lĭn-kôt)	156	52.46 N	1.33 W
Swain Rfs., Austl. (swān)	215	22.12 S	152.08 E
Swainsboro, Ga. (swānz'bŭr-ô)	127	32.37 N	82.21 W
Swakopmund, Namibia (svä'kôp-mōōnt) (swa'kôp-mōōnd)	226	22.40 S	14.30 E
Swallowfield, Eng. (swŏl'ō-fēld)	156b	51.21 N	0.58 W
Swampscott, Ma. (swômp'skŏt)	105a	42.28 N	70.55 W
Swan (R.), Austl.	214	31.30 S	126.30 E
Swan (R.), Can.	101	51.58 N	101.45 W
Swan Acres, Pa.	57b	40.33 N	80.02 W
Swan Hill, Austl.	216	35.20 S	143.30 E
Swan Hills, Can. (hĭlz)	99	54.52 N	115.45 W
Swan, I., Austl. (swŏn)	211a	38.15 S	144.41 E
Swan L., Can.	101	52.30 N	100.45 W
Swanland (Reg.), Austl. (swŏn'lănd)	214	31.45 S	119.15 E
Swanley, Eng.	62	51.24 N	0.12 E
Swan R., Mt.	117	47.50 N	113.40 W
Swan Ra., Mt.	117	47.50 N	113.40 W
Swan River, Can. (swŏn rĭv'ẽr)	101	52.06 N	101.16 W
Swanscombe, Eng.	62	51.26 N	0.18 E
Swansea, Il. (swŏn'sē)	119e	38.32 N	89.59 W
Swansea, Ma.	112b	41.45 N	71.09 W
Swansea, Wales	162	51.37 N	3.59 W
Swansea (Neigh.), Can.	54c	43.38 N	79.28 W
Swanson Res., Ne. (swŏn'sŭn)	122	40.13 N	101.30 W
Swartberg (Mtn.), S. Afr.	227c	30.08 S	29.34 E
Swarthmore, Pa.	56b	39.54 N	75.21 W
Swartkop (Mtn.), S. Afr.	226a	34.13 S	18.27 E
Swartruggens, S. Afr.	223d	25.59 S	26.40 E
Swartspruit, S. Afr.	227b	25.44 S	28.01 E
Swatow, see Shantou			
Swaziland, Afr. (Swä'zē-lănd)	226	26.45 S	31.30 E
Sweden, Eur. (swē'dĕn)	154	60.10 N	14.10 E
Swedesboro, NJ (swēdz'bē-rô)	112f	39.45 N	75.22 W
Sweetwater, Tn. (swēt'wô-tẽr)	126	35.36 N	84.29 W
Sweetwater, Tx.	124	32.28 N	100.25 W
Sweetwater (L.), ND	114	48.15 N	98.35 W
Sweetwater R., Wy.	117	42.19 N	108.35 W
Sweetwater Res., Ca.	120a	32.42 N	116.54 W
Świebodziec, Pol. (shvyĕN-bo'jĕts)	166	52.16 N	15.36 E
Świdnica, Pol. (shvĭd-nē'tsá)	166	50.50 N	16.30 E
Świdwin, Pol. (shvĭd'vĭn)	166	53.46 N	15.48 E
Świebodzin, Pol. (shvyăN-bôd'jēn)	166	50.51 N	16.17 E
Świecie, Pol. (shvyăN'tsyĕ)	167	53.23 N	18.26 E
Świętokrzyskie Góry (Mts.), Pol. (shvyĕN-tō-kzhĭ'skyĕ gōō'rĭ)	167	50.57 N	21.02 E
Swift (R.), Eng.	156	52.26 N	1.08 W
Swift (R.), Me. (swĭft)	104	44.42 N	70.40 E
Swift Current, Can. (swĭft kûr'ĕnt)	100	50.17 N	107.50 W
Swift Res., Wa.	116	46.03 N	122.10 W
Swindle I., Can.	98	52.32 N	128.35 W
Swindon, Eng. (swĭn'dŭn)	162	51.35 N	1.55 W
Swinomish Ind. Res., Wa. (swĭ-nō'mĭsh)	118a	48.25 N	122.27 W
Świnoujście, Pol. (shvĭ-nĭ-ō-wĕsh'chyĕ)	166	53.56 N	14.14 E
Swinton, Eng. (swĭn'tŭn)	156	53.30 N	1.19 W
Swinton, Eng.	64b	53.31 N	2.20 W
Swissvale, Pa. (swĭs'vāl)	113e	40.25 N	79.53 W
Switzerland, Eur. (swĭt'zẽr-lănd)	154	46.30 N	7.43 E
Syas' (R.), Sov. Un. (syäs)	174	59.28 N	33.24 E
Sycamore, Il. (sĭk'ȧ-mōr)	115	42.00 N	88.42 W
Sychëvka, Sov. Un. (sē-chôf'ká)	174	55.52 N	34.18 E
Sydenham, Austl.	70b	37.42 S	144.46 E
Sydenham (Neigh.), Eng	62	51.26 N	0.03 W
Sydenham (Neigh.), S. Afr.	71b	26.09 S	28.06 E
Sydney, Austl. (sĭd'nē)	211b	33.55 S	151.17 E
Sydney, Can.	103	46.09 N	60.11 W
Sydney Mines, Can.	103	46.14 N	60.14 W
Syktyvkar, Sov. Un. (sük-tüf'kär)	178	61.35 N	50.40 E
Sylacauga, Al. (sĭl-ȧ-kô'gȧ)	126	33.10 N	86.15 W

PLACE (Pronounciation)	PAGE	Lat. °′	Long. °′
Sylarna (Mtn.), Swe.	164	63.00 N	12.10 E
Sylt I., F.R.G. (sĭlt)	166	54.55 N	8.30 E
Sylvania, Austl.	70a	34.01 S	151.07 E
Sylvania, Ga. (sĭl-vā'nĭ-ȧ)	127	32.44 N	81.40 W
Sylvania Heights, Austl.	70a	34.02 S	151.06 E
Sylvester, Ga. (sĭl-vĕs'tẽr)	126	31.32 N	83.50 W
Syndal, Austl.	70b	37.53 S	145.09 E
Syosset, NY	55	40.50 N	73.30 W
Syracuse, Ks. (sĭr'ȧ-kūs)	122	37.59 N	101.44 W
Syracuse, NY	111	43.05 N	76.10 W
Syracuse, Ut.	119b	41.06 N	112.04 W
Syr-Dar'ya (R.), Sov. Un.	176	44.15 N	65.45 E
Syria, Asia (sĭr'ĭ-ȧ)	190	35.00 N	37.15 E
Syrian Des. (Bādiyat ash Shām), Asia (sĭr'ĭ-ăn)	192	32.03 N	39.30 E
Sysert', Sov. Un. (sĕ'sĕrt)	182a	56.30 N	60.48 E
Syso'la (R.), Sov. Un.	178	60.50 N	50.40 E
Syukunosho, Jap.	69b	34.50 N	135.32 E
Syzran', Sov. Un. (sĕz-rän')	179	53.10 N	48.10 E
Szamotuty, Pol. (shá-mô-tōō'wē)	166	52.36 N	16.34 E
Szarvas, Hung. (sôr'vôsh)	167	46.51 N	20.36 E
Szczebrzeszyn, Pol. (shchĕ-bzhä'shĕn)	167	50.41 N	22.58 E
Szczecin (Stettin), Pol. (shchĕ'tsĭn) (shtĕ-tēn')	166	53.25 N	14.35 E
Szczecinek, Pol. (shchĕ'tsĭ-nĕk)	166	53.41 N	16.42 E
Szczuczyn, Pol. (shchōō'chēn)	167	53.32 N	22.17 E
Szczytno, Pol. (shchĭt'nô)	167	53.33 N	21.00 E
Szechwan Basin (Red), China	198	30.45 N	104.40 E
Szeged, Hung. (sĕ'gĕd)	167	46.15 N	20.12 E
Székesfehérvár, Hung. (sā'kĕsh-fĕ'hār-vär)	167	47.12 N	18.26 E
Szekszárd, Hung. (sĕk'särd)	167	46.19 N	18.42 E
Szentendre, Hung. (sĕnt'ĕn-drĕ)	167	47.40 N	19.07 E
Szentes, Hung. (sĕn'tĕsh)	167	46.38 N	20.18 E
Szigetvar, Hung. (sĕ'gĕt-vär)	167	46.05 N	17.50 E
Szolnok, Hung. (sôl'nôk)	167	47.11 N	20.12 E
Szombathely, Hung. (sôm'bôt-hĕl')	166	47.13 N	16.35 E
Szprotawa, Pol. (shprō-tä'vä)	166	51.34 N	15.29 E
Szydlowiec, Pol. (shid-wô'vyets)	167	51.13 N	20.53 E

T

PLACE (Pronounciation)	PAGE	Lat. °′	Long. °′
Taal (L.), Phil. (tä-äl')	207a	13.58 N	121.06 E
Tabaco, Phil. (tä-bä'kō)	207a	13.27 N	123.40 E
Tabankulu, S. Afr. (tă-băn-kōō'la)	227c	30.56 S	29.19 E
Tabasara, Serrania de (Ra.), Pan. (sĕr-rä-nē'ä dā tä-bä-sä'rä)	133	8.29 N	81.22 W
Tabasco, Mex. (tä-bäs'kō)	130	21.47 N	103.04 W
Tabasco (State), Mex.	131	18.10 N	83.00 W
Taber, Can.	99	49.47 N	112.08 W
Tablas (I.), Phil. (tä'bläs)	207a	12.26 N	112.15 E
Tablas Str., Phil.	207a	12.17 N	121.41 E
Table B., S. Afr. (tā'b'l)	226a	33.41 S	18.27 E
Table Mt., S. Afr.	226a	33.58 S	18.26 E
Table Rock Lake, Mo.	123	36.37 N	93.29 W
Tabligbo, Togo	228	6.35 N	1.30 E
Taboão da Serra, Braz.	61d	23.38 S	46.46 W
Taboga (I.), Pan. (tä-bō'gä)	128a	8.48 N	79.35 W
Taboguilla (I.), Pan. (tä-bō-gē'l-yä)	128a	8.48 N	79.31 W
Taboleiro (Plat.), Braz. (tä-bō-lā'rō)	143	9.34 S	39.22 W
Tábor, Czech. (tä'bôr)	166	49.25 N	14.40 E
Tabora, Tan. (tä-bō'rä)	231	5.01 S	32.48 E
Tabou, Ivory Coast (tȧ-bōō')	228	4.25 N	7.21 W
Tabrīz, Iran (tȧ-brēz')	192	38.00 N	46.13 E
Tabuaeran (I.), Oceania	209	3.52 N	159.20 W
Tacámbaro (R.), Mex. (tä-käm'bä-rō)	130	18.55 N	101.25 W
Tacambaro de Codallos, Mex. (dā kō-däl'yōs)	130	19.12 N	101.28 W
Tacaná (Vol.), Mex.-Guat. (tä-kä-nä')	132	15.09 N	92.07 W
Tacarigua, Laguna de la (L.), Ven. (lä-gōō'nä-dĕ-lä-tä-kä-rē'gwä)	143b	10.18 N	65.43 W
Tacheng, China (tä-chŭŋ)	198	46.50 N	83.24 E
Tachie (R.), Can.	98	54.30 N	125.00 W
Tachikawa, Jap.	69a	35.42 N	139.25 E
Tacloban, Phil. (tä-klō'bän)	207	11.06 N	124.58 E
Tacna, Peru (täk'nä)	142	18.34 S	70.16 W
Tacoma, Wa. (tȧ-kō'mȧ)	118a	47.14 N	122.27 W
Taconic Ra., NY (tȧ-kŏn'ĭk)	111	41.55 N	73.40 W
Tacony (Neigh.), Pa.	56b	40.02 N	75.03 W
Tacotalpa, Mex. (tä-kō-täl'pä)	131	17.37 N	92.51 W
Tacotalpa (R.), Mex.	131	17.24 N	92.38 W
Tacuarembó, Ur. (tä-kwä-rĕm'bō)	144	31.44 S	55.56 W
Tacuba (Neigh.), Mex.	60a	19.28 N	99.12 W
Tacubaya (Neigh.), Mex.	60a	19.25 N	99.12 W
Tademaït, Plat. du, Alg. (tä-dē-mä'ēt)	224	28.00 N	2.15 E
Tadio, Lagune (Lagoon), Ivory Coast	228	5.20 N	5.25 W
Tadjoura, Djibouti (tȧd-zhōō'rȧ)	223a	11.48 N	42.54 E
Tadley, Eng. (tăd'lē)	156b	51.19 N	1.08 W
Tadó, Col. (tä-dō')	142a	5.15 N	76.30 W
Tadotsu, Jap. (tä'dô-tsōō)	205	34.14 N	133.43 E
Tadoussac, Can. (tȧ-dōō-sȧk')	103	48.09 N	69.43 W
Tadworth, Eng.	62	51.17 N	0.14 W
Taebaek Sanmaek (Mts.), Kor. (tī-bĭk' sän-mīk')	204	37.20 N	128.50 E
Taedong R., Kor. (tī-dŏng)	204	38.38 N	124.32 E
Taegu, Kor. (tī'gōō')	204	35.49 N	128.41 E

PLACE (Pronounciation)	PAGE	Lat. °′	Long. °′
Taejŏn, Kor.	204	36.20 N	127.26 E
Tafalla, Sp. (tä-fäl'yä)	170	42.30 N	1.42 W
Tafna (R.), Alg. (täf'nä)	171	35.28 N	1.00 W
Taft, Ca. (tȧft)	120	35.09 N	119.27 W
Tagama (Reg.), Niger	229	15050 N	6.30 E
Taganrog, Sov. Un. (tȧ-gȧn-rôk')	175	47.13 N	38.44 E
Taganrogskiy Zaliv (B.), Sov. Un. (tȧ-gȧn-rôk'skĭ zä'lĭf)	175	46.55 N	38.17 E
Tagula (I.), Pap. N. Gui. (tä'gōō-lȧ)	215	11.45 S	153.46 E
Tagus (R.), Port.	170	39.23 N	8.01 W
Tagus (Tajo) (R.), Sp. (tā'gŭs)	170	39.40 N	5.07 W
Tahan, Gunong (Pk.), Mala.	206	4.33 N	101.52 E
Tahat (Mtn.) Alg. (tä-hät')	224	23.22 N	5.21 E
Tahiti (I.), Fr. Polynesia (tä-hē'tē) (tä'ē-tē')	209	17.30 S	149.30 W
Tahkuna Nina, Sov. Un. (tȧh-kōō'nȧ nē'nȧ)	165	59.08 N	22.03 E
Tahlequah, Ok. (tă-lĕ-kwä')	123	35.54 N	94.58 W
Tahoe (L.), Ca.-Nv. (tä'hō)	120	39.09 N	120.18 W
Tahoua, Niger (tä'ōō-ä)	229	14.54 N	5.16 E
Ṭahṭā, Egypt (tä'tä)	223b	26.48 N	31.29 E
Tahtsa (L.), Can. (tŏt'-sȧ-pĕk)	98	53.33 N	127.47 W
Tahuya, Wa. (tȧ-hū-yä')	118a	47.23 N	123.03 W
Tahuya (R.), Wa.	118a	47.28 N	122.55 W
Tai'an, China (tī-än)	200	36.13 N	117.08 E
Taibai Shan (Mtn.), China (tī-bī shän)	202	33.42 N	107.25 E
Taibus Qi, China (tī-bōō-sz chyē)	202	41.52 N	115.25 E
Taicang, China (tī-tsäŋ)	201b	31.26 N	121.06 E
T'aichung, Taiwan (tī'chōōng)	203	24.10 N	120.42 E
Tai'erzhuang, China (tī-är-jŭäŋ)	200	34.34 N	117.44 E
Taigu, China (tī-gōō)	202	37.25 N	112.35 E
Taihang Shan (Mts.), China (tī-häŋ shän)	202	35.45 N	112.00 E
Taihe, China (tī-hŭ)	200	33.10 N	115.38 E
Tai Hu (L.), China (tī hōō)	200	31.13 N	120.00 E
Tailagoin (Reg.), Mong. (tī'lȧ-gän' kä'rä)	198	43.39 N	105.54 E
Tailai, China (tī-lī)	202	46.20 N	123.10 E
Tailem Bend, Austl. (tā-lĕm)	216	35.15 S	139.30 E
Taimyr, P-Ov (Pen.), see Taymyr			
T'ainan, Taiwan (tī'nan')	203	23.08 N	120.18 E
Tainaron, Akra (C.), Grc.	161	36.20 N	21.20 E
Taining, China (tī'nĭng')	203	26.58 N	117.15 E
T'aipei, Taiwan (tī'pā')	203	25.02 N	121.38 E
Taipei Institute of Technology (P. Int.), Taiwan	68d	25.02 N	121.32 E
Taiping, Mala.	206	4.56 N	100.39 E
Taiping, Ling (Mtn.), China (lĭŋ tī-pĭŋ)	202	47.03 N	120.30 E
Tai Po Tsai, China	68c	22.21 N	114.15 E
Taira, see Iwaki			
Taisha, Jap. (tī'shä)	205	35.23 N	132.40 E
Taishan, China (tī-shän)	203	22.15 N	112.50 E
Tai Shan (Mtn.), China (tī shän)	200	36.16 N	117.05 E
Taishet, see Tayshet			
Taitao, Peninsula de, Chile (pĕ-nē'ng-sōō-lä-dĕ-tä-ē-tä'ō)	144	46.20 S	77.15 W
Taitō (Neigh.), Jap.	69a	35.43 N	139.47 E
T'aitung, Taiwan (tī'tōōng')	203	22.45 N	121.02 E
Taiwan (Formosa), Asia (tī-wän) (fôr-mō'sȧ)	191	23.30 N	122.20 E
Taiwan Normal University (P. Int.), Taiwan	68d	25.02 N	121.31 E
Taiwan Str., Asia	203	24.30 N	120.00 E
Tai Wan Tau, China	68c	22.18 N	114.17 E
Tai Wan Tsun, China	68c	22.19 N	114.12 E
Taínaron, Ákra (C.), Grc.	173	37.45 N	22.00 E
Taixian, China (tī shyĕn)	200	32.31 N	119.54 E
Taixing, China (tī-shyĭŋ)	200	32.12 N	119.58 E
Taiyanggong, China	67b	39.58 N	116.25 E
Taiyuan, China (tī-yŭän)	202	37.32 N	112.38 E
Taizhou, China (tī-jō)	200	32.23 N	119.41 E
Ta'izz, Yemen	195	13.38 N	44.04 E
Tajano de Morais, Braz. (tĕ-zhä'nô-dĕ-mô-rä'ēs)	141a	22.05 S	42.04 W
Tajik (S.S.R.), Sov. Un.	176	39.22 N	69.30 E
Tajninka, Sov. Un.	66b	55.54 N	37.45 E
Tajo (R.), see Tagus			
Tajrīsh, Iran	68h	35.48 N	51.25 E
Tajumulco (Vol.), Guat. (tä-hōō-mōōl'kō)	132	15.03 N	91.53 W
Tajuña (R.), Sp. (tä-kōō'n-yä)	170	40.23 N	2.36 W
Tājūrā', Libya	160	32.56 N	13.24 E
Tak, Thai.	206	16.57 N	99.12 E
Taka (I.), Jap. (tä'kä)	205	30.47 N	130.23 E
Takada, Jap. (tä'kȧ-dä)	205	37.08 N	138.30 E
Takahashi, Jap. (tä'kä'hä-shĭ)'	205	34.47 N	133.35 E
Takaishi, Jap.	205b	34.32 N	135.27 E
Takamatsu, Jap. (tä'kä'mä-tsōō')	205	34.20 N	134.02 E
Takamori, Jap. (tä'kä'mô-rē')	205	32.50 N	131.08 E
Takaoka, Jap. (ta'kä'ô-kä')	205	36.45 N	136.59 E
Takapuna, N.A.	217	36.48 S	174.47 E
Takarazuka, Jap. (tä'kä-rä-zōō'kä)	205b	34.48 N	135.22 E
Takasaki, Jap. (tä'kät'sōō-kē')	205	36.20 N	139.00 E
Takatsu (Mizonokuchi), Jap. (tä-kät'sōō) (mē'zō-nō-kōō'chē)	205a	35.36 N	139.37 E
Takatsuki, Jap. (tä'kät'sōō-kē')	205b	34.51 N	135.38 E
Takaungu, Ken. (tä'kä'ōōŋ-gōō')	197	3.41 S	39.48 E
Takayama, Jap. (tä'kä'yä'mä)	205	36.11 N	137.16 E
Takefu, Jap. (tä'kĕ-fōō)	205	35.57 N	136.09 E
Takenotsuka (Neigh.), Jap.	69a	35.48 N	139.48 E
Takla L., Can.	98	55.25 N	125.53 W
Takla Makan (Des.), China (mä-kän')	198	39.22 N	82.34 E
Takoma Park, Md. (tă'kōmă pärk)	112e	38.59 N	77.00 W
Takum, Nig.	229	7.17 N	9.59 E
Tala, Mex. (tä'lä)	130	20.39 N	103.42 W
Talagante, Chile (tä-lä-gá'n-tĕ)	141b	33.39 S	70.54 W
Talanga, Hond. (tä-lä'n-gä)	132	14.21 N	87.09 W
Talara, Peru (tä-lä'rä)	142	4.32 S	81.17 W
Talasea, Pap. N. Gui. (tä-lä-sä'ä)	207	5.20 S	150.00 E
Talata Mafara, Nig.	229	12.35 N	6.04 E

ACE (Pronunciation)	PAGE	Lat. °'	Long. °'
aud, Kepulauan (Is.), Indon. (tä-lout')	207	4.17 N	127.30 E
avera de la Reina, Sp. (tä-lä-vä'rä dä lä rå-ē'nä)	170	39.58 N	4.51 W
awdī, Sud.	225	10.41 N	30.21 E
ca, Chile (täl'kä)	141b	35.25 S	71.39 W
ca (Prov.), Chile	141b	35.23 S	71.15 W
cahuano, Chile (täl-kä-wä'nō)	144	36.41 S	73.05 W
ca, Punta (Pt.), Chile (pōō'n-tä-täl'kä)	139b	33.25 S	71.42 W
dom, Sov. Un. (täl-dôm)	174	56.44 N	37.33 E
dy-Kurgan, Sov. Un. (täl'dĭ-koor-gän')	180	45.03 N	77.18 E
ea de Castro (San Miguel), Mex. (tä'lå-ä dä käs'trō)	131	17.22 N	96.14 W
ibu, Pulau (I.), Indon.	207	1.30 S	125.00 E
im (I.), Phil. (tä-lēm')	207a	14.21 N	121.14 E
isay, Phil. (tä-lē'sī)	207a	14.08 N	122.56 E
keetna, Ak. (tål-kēt'nȧ)	107	62.18 N	150.02 W
kheh Rūd (R.), Iran	179	38.00 N	46.50 E
ladega, Al. (tăl-ȧ-dē'gȧ)	126	33.25 N	86.06 W
lahassee, Fl. (tăl-ȧ-hăs'ē)	126	30.25 N	84.17 W
lahatchie (R.), Ms. (tal-ȧ hăch'ē)	126	34.21 N	90.03 W
lapoosa, Ga. (tăl-ȧ-pōō'sȧ)	126	33.44 N	85.15 W
lapoosa (R.), Al.	126	32.22 N	86.08 W
lassee, Al. (tăl'ȧ-sē)	126	32.30 N	85.54 W
linn (Reval), Sov. Un. (tål'lĕn) (rä'väl)	165	59.26 N	24.44 E
lmadge, Oh. (tăl'mĭj)	113d	41.06 N	81.26 W
lulah, La. (tȧ-lōō'lȧ)	125	32.25 N	91.13 W
ly Ho, Austl.	70b	37.52 S	145.09 E
manca, Cord. de (Mts.), C. R. (kôr-dēl-yĕ'rä-dĕ-täl-mä'n-kä)	133	9.37 N	83.55 W
'noye, Sov. Un. (tål'nô-yĕ)	175	48.52 N	30.43 E
o (Mt.), Eth.	225	10.45 N	37.55 E
oje Budrukh, India	197b	19.05 N	73.05 E
pa de Allende, Mex. (täl'pä dä äl-yĕn'då)	130	20.25 N	104.48 W
si, Sov. Un. (tal'sĭ)	165	57.16 N	22.35 E
tal, Chile (täl-täl')	144	25.26 S	70.32 W
y, Sov. Un. (täl'ĭ)	175	49.51 N	40.07 E
ma, Ia. (tā'mä)	115	41.57 N	92.36 W
ma (R.), Jap.	69a	35.32 N	139.47 E
ma (R.), Jap.	205a	35.38 N	139.35 E
magawa (Neigh.), Jap.	69a	35.37 N	139.39 E
ma-kyūryō (Hills), Jap.	69a	35.35 N	139.30 E
male, Ghana (tä-mä'lå)	228	9.25 N	0.50 W
man', Sov. Un. (tå-män'')	175	45.13 N	36.46 E
maná, Cerro (Mtn.), Col. (sĕ'r-rô-tä-mä-ná')	142a	5.06 N	76.10 W
manaco (R.), Ven. (tä-mä-nä'kō)	143b	9.32 N	66.00 W
maqua, Pa. (tȧ-mô'kwȧ)	111	40.45 N	75.50 W
mar (R.), Eng. (tā'mär)	162	50.35 N	4.15 W
marite de Litera, Sp. (tä-mä-rē'tä)	171	41.52 N	0.24 E
maulipas (State), Mex. (tä-mä-ōō-lē'päs')	130	23.45 N	98.30 W
mazula de Gordiano, Mex. (tä-mä-zoo'lä dä gôr-dē-ä'nô)	130	19.44 N	103.09 W
mazulapan del Progreso, Mex. (tä-mä-zōō-lä'päm-dĕl-prô-grĕ-sō)	131	17.41 N	97.34 W
mazunchale, Mex. (tä-mä-zōōn-chä'lå)	130	21.16 N	98.46 W
mbacounda, Senegal (täm-bä-kōōn'dä)	228	13.47 N	13.40 W
mbador, Serra do (Mts.), Braz. (sĕ'r-rä-dô-täm'bä-dōr)	143	10.33 S	41.16 W
mbelan, Kepulauan (Is.), Indon. (täm-bå-län')	206	0.38 N	107.38 E
mbo, Austl. (tăm'bō)	216	24.50 S	146.15 E
mbov, Sov. Un. (tåm-bôf')	179	52.45 N	41.10 E
mbov (Oblast), Sov. Un.	174	52.50 N	40.42 E
mbre (R.), Sp. (täm'brā)	170	42.59 N	8.33 W
mbura, Sud. (täm-bōō'rä)	225	5.34 N	27.30 E
me (R.), Eng. (tām)	156	52.41 N	1.42 W
mega (R.), Port. (tå-mā'gå)	170	41.30 N	7.45 W
menghest, Alg.	224	22.34 N	5.34 E
menghest, Oued (R.), Alg.	224	22.15 N	2.51 E
mesí (R.), Mex. (tä-mĕ-sē')	130	22.36 N	98.32 W
mgak, Monts (Mtn.), Niger (tam-gäk')	229	18.40 N	8.40 E
mgue, Massif du (Mtn.), Gui.	228	12.15 N	12.35 W
miahua, Mex. (tä-myä-wä)	131	21.17 N	97.26 W
miahua, Laguna (L.), Mex. (lä-gōō'nä-tä-myä-wä)	131	21.38 N	97.33 W
miami, Can., Fl. (tä-mī-ăm'ĭ)	127a	25.52 N	80.08 W
mil Nadu (State), India	197	11.30 N	78.00 E
mmisaari, see Ekenäs			
mpa, Fl. (tăm'pȧ)	127a	27.57 N	82.25 W
mpa B., Fl.	127a	27.35 N	82.38 W
mpere, Fin. (tåm'pĕ-rĕ)	158	61.21 N	23.39 E
mpico, Mex. (täm-pē'kō)	131	22.14 N	97.51 W
mpico Alto, Mex. (täm-pē'kō äl'tō)	131	22.07 N	97.48 W
mpin, Mala.	191b	2.28 N	102.15 E
muín, Mex. (tä-mōō-ē'n)	130	22.04 N	98.47 W
mworth, Austl. (tăm'wûrth)	216	31.01 S	151.00 E
mworth, Eng.	156	52.58 N	1.41 W
na (I.), Vanuatu	215	19.32 S	169.27 E
na (R.), Ken. (tä'nä)	231	2.00 S	40.15 E
na (R.), Nor.-Fin.	158	69.20 N	24.54 E
nabe, Jap. (tä-nä'bā)	205	33.45 N	135.21 E
nabe, Jap.	205b	34.49 N	135.46 E
nacross, Ak. (tă'nȧ-crŏs)	107	63.20 N	143.30 W
naga (I.), Ak. (tä-nä'gä)	107a	51.28 N	178.10 W
nahbala, Pulau (I.), Indon. (tä-nä-bä'lä)	206	0.30 S	98.22 E
nahmasa, Pulau (I.), Indon. (tä-nä-mä'sä)	206	0.03 S	97.30 E
nakpur, India (tŭn'ăk-pōōr)	196	29.10 N	80.07 E
na L., Eth.	225	12.09 N	36.41 E
nami, Austl. (tȧ-nä'mē)	214	19.45 S	129.50 E
nana, Ak. (tă'nȧ-nô)	107	65.18 N	152.20 W

PLACE (Pronounciation)	PAGE	Lat. °'	Long. °'
Tanana (R.), Ak.	107	64.26 N	148.40 W
Tanaro (R.), It. (tä-nä'rô)	172	44.45 N	8.02 E
Tanashi, Jap.	205a	35.44 N	139.34 E
Tan-binh, Viet.	68m	10.48 N	106.40 E
Tanbu, China (tän-bōō)	201a	23.20 N	113.06 E
Tancheng, China (tän-chŭŋ)	200	34.37 N	118.22 E
Tanchŏn, Kor. (tän'chŭn)	204	40.29 N	128.50 E
Tancítaro, Mex. (tän-sē'tä-rō)	130	19.16 N	102.24 W
Tancítaro, Cerro de, Mex. (sĕ'r-rô-dĕ)	130	19.24 N	102.19 W
Tancoco, Mex. (tän-kō'kō)	131	21.16 N	99.45 W
Tandil, Arg. (tän-dēl')	132	36.16 S	59.01 W
Tandil, Sierra del (Mts.), Arg.	132	38.40 S	59.40 W
Tanega (I.), Jap. (tä'nå-gä')	205	30.36 N	131.11 E
Tanezrouft (Reg.), Alg. (tä'nĕz-rōōft)	224	24.17 N	0.30 W
Tang (R.), China (täŋ)	200	33.38 N	117.29 E
Tang (R.), China	200	39.13 N	114.45 E
Tanga, Tan. (tăŋ'gȧ)	231	5.04 S	39.06 E
Tangancícuaro, Mex. (täŋ-gän-sē'kwa»um rô)	130	19.52 N	102.13 W
Tanganyika, L., Afr.	231	5.15 S	29.40 E
Tanger (Tangier), Mor. (tăn-jēr')	224	35.52 N	5.55 W
Tangermünde, G.D.R. (täŋ'ĕr-mün'de)	166	52.33 N	11.58 E
Tanggu, China (täŋ-gōō)	200	39.04 N	117.41 E
Tanggula Shan (Mts.), China (täŋ-gōō-lä shän)	198	33.15 N	89.07 E
Tangho, China	202	32.40 N	112.50 E
Tangier, see Tanger			
Tangipahoa R., La. (tăn'jē-pȧ-hō'ȧ)	125	30.48 N	90.28 W
Tangra Yumco (L.), China (täŋ-rä yōōm-tswo)	196	30.50 N	85.40 E
T'angshan, China	200	39.38 N	118.11 E
Tangxian, China (täŋ shyĕn)	200	38.09 N	115.00 E
Tangzha, China (täŋ-jä)	200	32.06 N	120.48 E
Tanimbar, Kepulauan (Is.), Indon.	207	8.00 S	132.00 E
Tanjong (C.), Mala.	191b	1.53 N	102.29 E
Tanjong Piai (I.), Mala.	191b	1.16 N	103.11 E
Tanjong Ramunia (C.), Mala.	191b	1.27 N	104.44 E
Tanjungbalai, Indon. (tän'jông-bä'lä)	191b	1.00 N	103.26 E
Tanjungkarand, Indon.	206	5.16 S	105.06 E
Tanjungpandan, Indon.	206	2.47 S	107.51 E
Tanjungpinang, Indon. (tän'jŏng-pē'näng)	191b	0.55 N	104.29 E
Tanjungpriok (Neigh.), Indon.	68k	6.06 S	106.53 E
Tannu-Ola (Mts.), Sov. Un.	177	51.00 N	94.00 E
Tannūrah, Ra's al (C.), Sau. Ar.	192	26.45 N	49.59 E
Tano (R.), Ghana	228	5.40 N	2.30 W
Tan-qui-dong, Viet.	68m	10.44 N	106.43 E
Tanquijo, Arrecife (Reef), Mex. (är-rĕ-sē'fĕ-tän-kē'kô)	131	21.07 N	97.16 W
Tanshui Ho (R.), Taiwan	68d	25.08 N	121.27 E
Tan Son Nhut, Viet.	68m	10.49 N	106.40 E
Ṭanṭā, Egypt (tän'tä)	223b	30.50 N	31.00 E
Tan-thoi-nhut, Viet.	68m	10.50 N	106.36 E
Tan-thuan-dong, Viet.	68m	10.45 N	106.44 E
Tantoyuca, Mex. (tän-tō-yōō'kä)	130	21.22 N	98.13 W
Tanyang, Kor.	204	36.53 N	128.20 E
Tanzania, Afr.	222	6.48 S	33.58 E
Tao (R.), China (tou)	202	35.30 N	103.40 E
Tao'an, China (tou-än)	202	45.15 N	122.45 E
Tao'er (R.), China (tou-är)	202	45.40 N	122.00 E
Taormina, It. (tä-ôr-mē'nä)	172	37.53 N	15.18 E
Taos, NM (tä'ôs)	121	36.25 N	105.35 W
Taoudenni, Mali (tä'ōō-dĕ-nē')	224	22.57 N	3.37 W
Taoussa, Mali	228	16.55 N	0.35 W
Taoyuan, China (tou-yüän)	203	29.00 N	111.15 E
Tapa, Sov. Un. (tá'pȧ)	165	59.16 N	25.56 E
Tapachula, Mex.	132	14.55 N	92.20 W
Tapajós (R.), Braz. (tä-pä-zhô's)	143	3.27 S	55.33 W
Tapalque, Arg. (tä-päl-kĕ')	141c	36.22 S	60.05 W
Tapanatepec, Mex. (tä-pä-nä-tĕ-pĕk)	131	16.22 N	94.19 W
Tāpi (R.), India	196	21.33 N	74.30 E
Tapiales, Arg.	60d	34.44 S	58.30 W
Tappi Saki (C.), Jap. (täp'pē sä'kē)	204	41.05 N	139.40 E
Tapps (L.), Wa. (tăpz)	118a	47.20 N	122.12 W
Tapsiā (Neigh.), India	67a	22.32 N	88.22 E
Taqātu' Hayyā, Sud.	225	18.10 N	36.17 E
Taquara (Neigh.), Braz.	61c	22.55 S	43.21 W
Taquara, Serra de (Mts.), Braz. (sĕ'r-rä-dĕ-tä-kwä'rä)	143	15.28 S	54.33 W
Taquari (R.), Braz. (tä-kwä'rĭ)	143	18.35 S	56.50 W
Tar (R.), NC (tär)	127	35.58 N	78.06 W
Tara, Sov. Un. (tä'rȧ)	180	56.58 N	74.13 E
Tara (I.), Phil. (tä'rä)	207a	12.18 N	120.28 E
Tara (R.), Sov. Un. (tä'rȧ)	180	56.32 N	76.13 E
Ṭarābulus (Tripoli), Leb. (tȧ-rä'bōō-lōōs)	191a	34.25 N	35.50 E
Tarābulus (Tripoli), Libya	225	32.50 N	13.13 E
Tarābulus (Tripolitania) (Prov.), Libya	225	31.00 N	12.26 E
Tarakan, Indon.	206	3.17 N	118.04 E
Tarancón, Sp. (tä-rän-kōn')	170	40.01 N	3.00 W
Taranto, It. (tä'rän-tô)	172	40.30 N	17.15 E
Taranto, Golfo di (G.), It. (gôl-fô-dē tä'rän-tô)	172	40.03 N	17.10 E
Tarapoto, Peru (tä-rä-pô'tō)	142	6.29 S	76.26 W
Tarare, Fr. (tȧ-rär')	168	45.55 N	4.23 E
Tarascon, Fr. (tȧ-räs-kôN')	168	42.53 N	1.35 E
Tarascon, Fr. (tä-räs-kôN)	168	43.47 N	4.41 E
Tarashcha, Sov. Un. (tä'rȧsh-chȧ)	175	49.34 N	30.52 E
Tarasht, Iran	68h	35.42 N	51.21 E
Tarata, Bol. (tä-rä'tä)	142	17.43 S	66.00 W
Taravo (R.), Fr.	172	41.54 N	8.58 E
Tarazit, Massif de (Mts.), Niger	229	20.05 N	7.35 E
Tarazona, Sp. (tä-rä-thō'nä)	170	41.54 N	1.45 W
Tarazona de la Mancha, Sp. (tä-rä-zō'nä-dĕ-lä-mä'n-chä)	170	39.13 N	1.50 W
Tarbat Ness (Hd.), Scot. (tår'bȧt)	162	57.51 N	3.50 W
Tarbes, Fr. (tårb)	168	43.04 N	0.05 E
Tarbock Green, Eng.	64a	53.23 N	2.49 W
Tarboro, NC (tär'bŭr-ô)	127	35.53 N	77.34 W
Tarbū, Libya	225	26.07 N	15.49 E

PLACE (Pronounciation)	PAGE	Lat. °'	Long. °'
Taredo (Neigh.), India	67e	19.58 N	72.49 E
Taree, Austl. (tȧ-rē')	216	31.52 S	152.21 E
Tarentum, Pa. (tȧ-rĕn'tŭm)	113e	40.36 N	79.44 W
Tarfa, Wādī at, Egypt	223b	28.14 N	31.00 E
Tarfaya, Mor.	224	27.58 N	12.55 W
Tarhūnah, Libya	194	32.26 N	13.38 E
Tarija, Bol. (tär-rē'hä)	142	21.42 S	64.52 W
Tarīm, P. D. R. of Yem. (tȧ-rīm')	192	16.13 N	49.08 E
Tarim (R.), China (tȧ-rĭm')	198	40.45 N	85.39 E
Tarim Basin, China (tȧ-rĭm')	198	39.52 N	82.34 E
Tarkastad, S. Afr.	227c	32.01 S	26.18 E
Tarkhankut, Mys (C.), Sov. Un. (mĭs tär-Kän'koot)	175	45.18 N	32.08 E
Tarkio, Mo. (tär'kĭ-ō)	123	40.27 N	95.22 W
Tarks (R.), S. Afr. (tä'kȧ)	227c	32.15 S	26.00 E
Tarkwa, Ghana (tärk'wä)	228	5.19 N	1.59 W
Tarlac, Phil. (tär'läk)	207	15.29 N	120.36 E
Tarlton, S. Afr. (tärl'tŭn)	227b	26.05 S	27.38 E
Tarma, Peru (tär'mä)	142	11.26 S	75.40 W
Tarn (R.), Fr. (tärn)	168	44.03 N	2.41 E
Târnava Mica R., Rom. (tĕr-nä'vȧ mē'kō)	169	46.17 N	24.20 E
Tarnów, Pol. (tär'nōōf)	169	50.02 N	21.00 E
Taro (R.), It. (tä'rō)	172	44.41 N	10.03 E
Taroudant, Mor. (tȧ-rōō-dänt')	224	30.39 N	8.52 W
Tarpon Springs, Fl. (tär'pŏn)	127a	28.07 N	82.44 W
Tarporley, Eng. (tär'pēr-lē)	156	53.09 N	2.40 W
Tarpum B., Ba. (tär'pŭm)	135	25.05 N	76.20 W
Tarquinia (Corneto), It. (tär-kwē'nē-ä) (kôr-nä'tô)	172	42.16 N	11.46 E
Tarragona, Sp. (tär-rä-gō'nä)	171	41.05 N	1.15 E
Tarrant, Al. (tăr'ănt)	112h	33.35 N	86.46 W
Tarrasa, Sp. (tär-rä'sä)	171	41.34 N	2.01 E
Tárrega, Sp. (tä rå-gä)	171	41.40 N	1.09 E
Tarrejón de Ardoz, Sp. (tär-rĕ-Kô'n-dĕ-är-dôz)	171a	40.28 N	3.29 W
Tarrytown, NY (tăr'ĭ-toun)	112a	41.04 N	73.52 W
Tarsus, Tur. (tår'sōōs) (tär'sŭs)	179	37.00 N	34.50 E
Tartagal, Arg. (tär-tä-gá'l)	144	23.31 S	63.47 W
Tartu (Dorpat), Sov. Un. (tär'tōō) (dôr'pät)	174	58.23 N	26.44 E
Ṭarṭūs, Egypt	161	34.54 N	35.59 E
Tarumi, Jap. (tä'rōō-mē)	205b	34.38 N	135.04 E
Tarusa, Sov. Un. (tä-rōōs'ȧ)	174	54.43 N	37.11 E
Tarzana, Ca. (tär-ză'ȧ)	119a	34.10 N	118.32 W
Tashauz, Sov. Un. (tŭ-shŭ-ōōs')	155	41.50 N	59.45 E
Tashkent, Sov. Un. (tåsh'kĕnt)	180	41.23 N	69.04 E
Tasman B., N. Z. (tăz'măn)	217	40.50 S	173.20 E
Tasmania (State), Austl. (tăz-mā'nĭ-ȧ)	216	38.20 S	146.30 E
Tasmania (I.), Austl.	215	41.28 S	142.30 E
Tasman Pen, Austl.	216	43.00 S	148.30 E
Tasman Sea, Oceania	208	29.30 S	155.00 E
Tasquillo, Mex. (täs-kē'lyō)	130	20.34 N	99.21 W
Tassili-n-Ajjer (Plat.), Alg. (tȧs'ē-lē ä'jĕr)	224	25.40 N	6.57 E
Tatar (A. S. S. R.), Sov. Un. (tȧ-tär')	178	55.30 N	51.00 E
Tatarsk, Sov. Un. (tȧ-tärsk')	180	55.15 N	75.00 E
Tatar Str., Sov. Un.	181	51.00 N	141.45 E
Tate Gallery (P. Int.), Eng.	62	51.29 N	0.08 W
Tater Hill (Mtn.), Or. (tāt'ēr hĭl)	118c	45.47 N	123.02 W
Tateyama, Jap. (tä'tē-yä'mä)	205	35.04 N	139.52 E
Tathong Chan., Asia	68c	22.15 N	114.15 E
Tatlow, Mt., Can.	98	51.23 N	123.52 W
Tatsfield, Eng.	62	51.18 N	0.02 E
Tatuí, Braz. (tä-tōō-ē')	141a	23.21 S	47.49 W
Tau, Nor.	164	59.05 N	5.59 E
Taubaté, Braz. (tou-bȧ-tā')	141a	23.03 S	45.32 W
Tauern Tun, Aus.	166	47.12 N	13.17 E
Taung, S. Afr. (tä'ōōng)	226	27.25 S	24.47 E
Taunton, Ma. (tän'tŭn)	112b	41.54 N	71.03 W
Taunton R., RI	112b	41.50 N	71.02 W
Taupo, L., N. Z. (tä'ōō-pō)	217	38.42 S	175.55 E
Taurage, Sov. Un. (tou'rȧ-gā)	165	55.15 N	22.18 E
Taurus Mts., see Toros Dağlari			
Tauste, Sp. (tä-ōōs'tå)	170	41.55 N	1.15 W
Tavda, Sov. Un. (tåv-dá')	180	58.00 N	64.44 E
Tavda (R.), Sov. Un.	178	59.20 N	63.28 E
Taverny, Fr. (tȧ-vĕr-nē')	169b	49.02 N	2.13 E
Taviche, Mex. (tä-vē'chĕ)	131	16.43 N	96.35 W
Tavira, Port. (tä-vē'rȧ)	170	37.09 N	7.42 W
Tavistock, NJ	56b	39.53 N	75.02 W
Tavoy, Bur.	206	14.04 N	98.19 E
Tavşanli, Tur. (tav'shän-lĭ)	179	39.30 N	29.30 E
Tawakoni (L.), Tx.	125	32.51 N	95.59 W
Tawaramoto, Jap. (tä'wä-rä-mô-tô)	205b	34.33 N	135.48 E
Tawas City, Mi.	110	44.15 N	83.30 W
Tawas Pt., Mi. (tô'wȧs)	110	44.15 N	83.25 W
Tawitawi Group (Is.), Phil. (tä'wē-tä'wē)	206	4.52 N	120.35 E
Tawkar, Sud.	225	18.28 N	37.46 E
Taxco de Alarcón, Mex. (täs'kō dĕ ä-lär-kô'n)	130	18.34 N	99.37 W
Tay (R.), Scot.	162	56.35 N	3.37 W
Tayabas B., Phil. (tä-yä'bäs)	207a	13.44 N	121.40 E
Tayga, Sov. Un. (tī'gä)	180	56.12 N	85.47 E
Taygonos, Mys (Taigonos) (C.), Sov. Un.	181	60.37 N	160.17 E
Tay, Loch (L.), Scot.	162	56.25 N	5.07 W
Taylor, Mi.	57c	42.13 N	83.16 W
Taylor, Tx.	125	30.35 N	97.25 W
Taylor, Mt., NM	121	35.20 N	107.40 W
Taylorville, Il. (tā'lēr-vĭl)	110	39.30 N	89.20 W
Taymā, Sua. Ar.	192	27.45 N	38.55 E
Taymyr (Taimyr) (L.), Sov. Un. (tī-mĭr')	181	74.13 N	100.45 E
Taymyr, P-Ov (Taimyr) (Pen.), Sov. Un.	180	75.15 N	95.00 E
Táyros, Grc.	66d	37.58 N	23.42 E
Tayshet (Taishet), Sov. Un. (tī-shĕt')	180	56.09 N	97.49 E
Taytay, Phil (tī-tī)	180	10.37 N	119.10 E
Taytay, Phil.	68g	14.34 N	121.08 E
Tayung, Phil. (tä-yōōng')	207a	16.01 N	120.45 E

PLACE (Pronounciation)	PAGE	Lat. °'	Long. °'
Taz (R.), Sov. Un. (táz)	180	67.15 N	80.45 E
Taza, Mor. (tä'zä)	224	34.08 N	4.00 W
Tazovskoye, Sov. Un.	180	66.58 N	78.28 E
Tbessa, Alg.	224	35.27 N	8.13 E
Tbilisi, Sov. Un. ('tbĭl-yĕ'sĕ)	179	41.40 N	44.45 E
Tchibanga, Gabon (chĕ-bäŋ'gä)	230	2.51 S	11.02 E
Tchien, Lib.	228	6.04 N	8.08 W
Tchigai, Plat. du (Plat.), Chad-Niger	229	21.20 N	14.50 E
Tczew, Pol. (t'chĕf')	167	54.06 N	18.48 E
Teabo, Mex. (tĕ-ä'bô)	132a	20.25 N	89.14 W
Teague, Tx.	125	31.39 N	96.16 W
Teaneck, NJ	55	40.53 N	74.01 W
Teapa, Mex. (tĕ-ä'pä)	131	17.35 N	92.56 W
Tebing Tinggi (I.), Indon. (teb'ĭng-tĭng'gä)	191b	0.54 N	102.39 E
Tebukbetung, Indon.	206	5.30 S	105.04 E
Tecalitlán, Mex. (tā-kä-lē'-tlän')	130	19.28 N	103.17 W
Techiman, Ghana	228	7.35 N	1.56 W
Tecoanapa, Mex. (tā-kwä-nä-pä')	130	16.33 N	98.46 W
Tecoh, Mex. (tĕ-kŏ)	132a	20.46 N	89.27 W
Tecolotlán, Mex. (tā-kô-lô-tlän')	130	20.13 N	103.57 W
Tecolutla, Mex. (tā-kô-lōō'tlä)	131	20.33 N	97.00 W
Tecolutla (R.), Mex.	131	20.16 N	97.14 W
Tecomán, Mex. (tā-kô-män')	130	18.53 N	103.53 W
Tecómitl, Mex. (tĕ-kŏ'mĕtl)	131a	19.13 N	98.59 W
Tecozautla, Mex. (tā'kô-zä-ōō'tlä)	130	20.33 N	99.38 W
Tecpan de Galeana, Mex. (tĕk-pän' dä gä-lä-ä'nä)	130	17.13 N	100.41 W
Tecpatán, Mex. (tĕk-pä-tä'n)	131	17.08 N	93.18 W
Tecuala, Mex. (tĕ-kwä-lä)	130	22.24 N	105.29 W
Tecuci, Rom. (ta-kōōch')	167	45.51 N	27.30 E
Tecumseh, Can. (tĕ-kŭm'sĕ)	113b	42.19 N	82.53 W
Tecumseh, Mi.	110	42.00 N	84.00 W
Tecumseh, Ne.	124	40.21 N	96.09 W
Tecumseh, Ok.	123	35.18 N	96.55 W
Teddington (Neigh.), Eng.	62	51.25 N	0.20 W
Tees (R.), Eng. (tēz)	162	54.40 N	2.10 W
Tefé, Braz. (tĕf-ā')	142	3.27 S	64.43 W
Teganuna (L.), Jap. (tĕ'gä-nōō'nä)	205a	35.50 N	140.02 E
Tegel (Neigh.), F.R.G.	65a	52.35 N	13.17 E
Tegeler See (L.), G.D.R.	65a	52.35 N	13.15 E
Tegucigalpa, Hond. (tå-gōō-sē-gäl'pä)	132	14.08 N	87.15 W
Tehachapi Mts., Ca.	120	34.50 N	118.55 W
Tehar (Neigh.), India	67d	28.38 N	77.07 E
Tehentlo L., Can.	98	55.11 N	125.00 W
Tehrān, Iran (tĕ-hrän')	192	35.45 N	51.30 E
Tehuacan, Mex. (tā-wä-kän')	131	18.27 N	97.23 W
Tehuantepec (Sto. Domingo), Mex. (tå-wän-tå-pĕk') (sän-tô dô-mē'n-gô)	131	16.20 N	95.14 W
Tehuantepec, Mex.	131	16.30 N	95.23 W
Tehuantepec, Golfo de (G.), Mex. (gôl-fô dĕ)	128	15.45 N	95.00 W
Tehuantepec, Istmo de (Isth.), Mex. (ē'st-mô dĕ)	131	17.55 N	94.35 W
Tehuehuetla Arroyo (R.), Mex. (tĕ-wĕ-wĕ'tlä är-rô-yô)	130	17.54 N	100.26 W
Tehuitzingo, Mex. (tā-wē-tzĭŋ'gô)	130	18.21 N	98.16 W
Tejeda, Sierra de (Mts.), Sp. (sē-ĕ'r-rä dĕ tĕ-kĕ'dä)	170	36.55 N	5.57 W
Tejúpan (Santiago), Mex. (tĕ-κōō-pá'n) (sän-tyä'gô)	131	17.39 N	97.34 W
Tejúpan, Punta (Pt.), Mex. (pōō'n-tä)	130	18.19 N	103.30 W
Tejupilco de Hidalgo, Mex. (tā-hōō-pēl'kô dä ē-dhäl'gô)	130	18.52 N	100.07 W
Tekamah, Ne. (tĕ-kä'má)	114	41.46 N	96.13 W
Tekax de Alvaro Obregon, Mex. (tĕ-kä'x dĕ ä'l-vä-rô-brĕ-gô'n)	132a	20.12 N	89.11 W
Tekeze (R.), Eth.	225	13.38 N	38.00 E
Tekirdağ (Rodosto), Tur. (tĕ-kĕr'dägh')	173	41.00 N	27.28 E
Tekit, Mex. (tĕ-kē't)	132a	20.35 N	89.18 W
Tekoa, Wa. (tĕ-kō'ä)	116	47.15 N	117.03 W
Tekstil'ščiki (Neigh.), Sov. Un.	66b	55.42 N	37.44 E
Tela, Hond. (tā'lä)	132	15.45 N	87.25 W
Tela, India	67d	28.44 N	77.20 E
Tela, Bahia de (B.), Hond. (bä-ē'ä dĕ)	132	15.53 N	87.29 W
Telapa Burok, Gunong (Mt.), Mala.	191b	2.51 N	102.04 E
Telavi, Sov. Un.	179	42.00 N	45.20 E
Tel Aviv-Yafo, Isr. (tĕl-ä-vēv'já'já'fá)	191a	32.03 N	34.46 E
Telegraph Creek, Can. (tĕl'ē-gráf)	96	57.59 N	131.22 W
Teleneshty, Sov. Un.	175	47.31 N	28.22 E
Telescope Pk., Ca. (tĕl'ē skōp)	120	36.12 N	117.05 W
Telesung, Indon.	191b	1.07 N	102.53 E
Telica (Vol.), Nic. (tā-lē'kä)	132	12.38 N	86.52 W
Telimélé, Gui.	228	10.54 N	13.02 W
Tell City, In. (tĕl)	110	38.00 N	86.45 W
Teller, Ak. (tĕl'ẽr)	107	65.17 N	166.28 W
Tello, Col. (tĕl'y-ô)	142a	3.05 N	75.08 W
Telluride, Co. (tĕl'ū-rīd)	121	37.55 N	107.50 W
Telok Datok, Mala.	191b	2.51 N	101.33 E
Teloloapan, Mex. (tā'lô-lô-ä'pän)	130	18.19 N	99.54 W
Tel'pos-Iz, Gora (Mtn.), Sov. Un. (tyĕl'pôs-ēz')	178	63.50 N	59.20 E
Telšiai, Sov. Un. (tĕl'sha'ĕ)	165	55.59 N	22.17 E
Teltow, G.D.R. (tĕl'tō)	157b	52.24 N	13.12 E
Teltower Hochfläche (Plat.), G.D.R.	65a	52.22 N	13.20 E
Teluklecak, Indon.	191b	1.53 N	101.45 E
Tema, Ghana	228	5.38 N	0.01 E
Temascalcingo, Mex. (tā'mäs-käl-sĭŋ'gô)	130	19.55 N	100.00 W
Temascaltepec, Mex. (tā'mäs-käl-tå pĕk)	130	19.00 N	100.03 W
Temax, Mex. (tĕ'mäx)	132a	21.10 N	88.51 W
Temir, Sov. Un. (tyĕ'mĕr)	179	49.10 N	57.15 E
Temir-Tau, Sov. Un.	180	50.08 N	73.13 E
Témiscaming, Can. (tĕ-mĭs'ká-mĭng)	103	46.40 N	78.50 W
Temiscouata (L.), Can.	104	47.40 N	68.50 W
Temoaya, Mex. (tĕ-mô-a-um-yä)	131a	19.28 N	99.36 W

PLACE (Pronounciation)	PAGE	Lat. °'	Long. °'
Tempelhof (Neigh.), F.R.G.	65a	52.28 N	13.23 E
Temperley, Arg. (tĕ'm-pĕr-lä)	144a	34.32 S	58.24 W
Tempio Pausania, It. (tĕm'pē-ō pou-sä'nĕ-ä)	172	40.55 N	9.05 E
Temple, Tx. (tĕm'p'l)	125	31.06 N	97.20 W
Temple City, Ca.	119a	34.07 N	118.02 W
Temple Hills, Md.	56d	38.49 N	76.57 W
Temple of Heaven (P. Int.), China	67b	39.53 N	116.25 E
Templestowe, Austl.	70b	37.45 S	145.07 E
Templeton, Can. (tĕm'p'l-tŭn)	95c	45.29 N	75.37 W
Temple University (P. Int.), Pa.	56b	39.59 N	75.09 W
Templin, G.D.R. (tĕm-plēn')	166	53.08 N	13.30 E
Tempoal (R.), Mex. (tĕm-pô-ä'l)	130	21.38 N	98.23 W
Temryuk, Sov. Un. (tyĕm-ryōōk')	175	45.17 N	37.21 E
Temuco, Chile (tå-mōō'kō)	144	38.46 S	72.38 W
Temyasovo, Sov. Un. (tĕm-yä'sô-vô)	182a	53.00 N	58.06 E
Tenabó, Mex. (tĕ-nä-bô')	132a	20.05 N	90.11 W
Tenafly, NJ	55	40.56 N	73.58 W
Tenāli, India	197	16.10 N	80.32 E
Tenamaxtlán, Mex. (tä'nä-mäs-tlän')	130	20.13 N	104.06 W
Tenancingo, Mex. (tā-nän-sēŋ'gô)	130	18.54 N	99.36 W
Tenango, Mex. (tå-näŋ'gô)	131a	19.09 N	98.51 W
Tenasserim, Bur. (tĕn-äs'ĕr-ĭm)	206	12.09 N	99.01 E
Tenderovskaya Kosa (C.), Sov. Un. (tĕn-dĕ-fôf'ská-yä kô-sä')	175	46.12 N	31.17 E
Tenéré (Des.), Niger	229	19.23 N	10.15 E
Tenerife I., Can. Is. (tå-nå-rē'få) (tĕn-ĕr-īf')	224	28.41 N	17.02 W
Ténès, Alg. (tä-nĕs')	159	36.28 N	1.22 E
Tengiz (L.), Sov. Un. (tyĭn-gēz')	180	50.45 N	68.39 E
Tengxian, China (tŭŋ shyĕn)	200	35.07 N	117.08 E
Tenjin, Jap. (tĕn'jĕn)	205b	34.54 N	135.04 E
Tenke, Zaire (tĕŋ'kå)	231	11.26 S	26.45 E
Tenkiller Ferry Res., Ok. (tĕn-kĭl'ĕr)	123	35.42 N	94.47 W
Tenkodogo, Burkina (tĕn-kô-dô'gô)	228	11.47 N	0.22 W
Tenmile (R.), Wa. (tĕn mīl)	118d	48.52 N	122.32 W
Tennant Creek, Austl. (tĕn'ănt)	214	19.45 S	134.00 E
Tennessee (State), U. S. (tĕn-ĕ-sē')	109	35.50 N	88.00 W
Tennessee (L.), U. S.	109	35.35 N	88.20 W
Tennessee (R.), U. S.	126	35.10 N	88.20 W
Tennille, Ga. (tĕn'ĭl)	126	32.55 N	86.50 W
Tennōji (Neigh.), Jap.	69b	34.39 N	135.31 E
Teno (R.), Chile (tĕ'nô)	141b	34.55 S	71.00 W
Tenora, Austl. (tĕn-ôrá)	216	34.23 S	147.33 E
Tenosique, Mex. (tā-nô-sē'kå)	131	17.27 N	91.25 W
Tenri, Jap.	205b	34.36 N	135.50 E
Tenryū-Gawa (Strm.), Jap. (tĕn'ryōō'gä'wä)	205	35.16 N	137.54 E
Tensas R., La. (tĕn'sô)	125	31.54 N	91.30 W
Tensaw, Al. (tĕn'sô)	126	30.45 N	87.52 W
Tenterfield, Austl. (tĕn'tĕr-fēld)	216	29.00 S	152.06 E
Ten Thousand, Is., Fl. (tĕn thou'zănd)	127a	25.45 N	81.35 W
Teocaltiche, Mex. (tā'ô-käl-tē'chå)	130	21.27 N	102.38 W
Teocelo, Mex. (tā-ô-sā'lô)	131	19.22 N	96.57 W
Teocuitlatlán de Corona, Mex. (tā'ô-kwē'tä-tlän' dä kô-rō'nä)	130	20.06 N	103.22 W
Teófilo Otoni, Braz. (tĕ-ô'fē-lô-tô'nĕ)	143	17.49 S	41.18 W
Teoloyucan, Mex. (tā-ô-lô-yōō'kän)	130	19.43 N	99.12 W
Teopisca, Mex. (tā-ô-pēs'kä)	131	16.30 N	92.33 W
Teotihuacán,, Mex. (tĕ-ô-tē-wä-kà'n)	131a	19.40 N	98.52 W
Teotitlán del Camino, Mex. (tā-ô-tē-tlän' dĕl kä-mē'nô)	131	18.07 N	97.04 W
Tepalcatepec, Mex. (tā'pál-kä-tĕ'pĕk)	130	19.11 N	102.51 W
Tepalcatepec (R.), Mex.	130	18.54 N	102.25 W
Tepalcates, Mex.	60a	19.23 N	99.04 W
Tepalcingo, Mex. (tā-päl-sēŋ'gô)	130	18.34 N	98.49 W
Tepatitlan de Morelos, Mex. (tā-pä-tē-tlän' dä mô-rā'los)	130	20.15 N	102.47 W
Tepeaca, Mex. (tā-pä-ä'kä)	131	18.57 N	97.54 W
Tepecoacuiloc de Trujano, Mex. (tā'på-kô-ä-kwēl'kô dä trōō-hä'nô)	130	19.15 N	99.29 W
Tepeji del Rio, Mex. (tā-på-κē' dĕl rē'ô)	131	19.55 N	99.22 W
Tepelmeme, Mex. (tā'pĕl-mā'må)	131	17.51 N	97.23 W
Tepepan, Mex.	60a	19.16 N	99.08 W
Tepetlaoxtoc, Mex. (tā'på-tlä'ôs-tôk')	131a	19.34 N	98.49 W
Tepezala, Mex. (tā-på-zä-lä')	130	22.12 N	102.12 W
Tepic, Mex. (tā-pēk')	130	21.32 N	104.53 W
Teplaya Gora, Sov. Un. (tyôp'lä-yä gô-rá)	182a	58.32 N	59.08 W
Teplice Sanov, Czech. (tĕp'li-tsĕ shá'nôf)	166	50.39 N	13.50 E
Teposcolula (San Pedro y San Pablo), Mex. (tā-pôs-kô-lōō'lä) (sän pā'drô ē sän pä'blô)	131	17.33 N	97.29 W
Tequendama, Salto de (Falls), Col. (sä'l-tô dĕ tĕ-kĕn-dä'mä)	142a	4.34 N	74.18 W
Tequila, Mex. (tå-kē'lä)	130	20.53 N	103.48 W
Tequisistlán (R.), Mex. (tā-kē-sēs-tlä'n)	131	16.20 N	95.40 W
Tequisquiapan, Mex. (tā-kēs-kē-ä'pän)	130	20.33 N	99.57 W
Ter (R.), Sp. (tĕr)	171	42.04 N	2.52 E
Téra, Niger	228	14.01 N	0.45 E
Tera (R.), Sp. (tä'rä)	170	42.05 N	6.24 W
Teramo, It. (tä'rä-mô)	172	42.40 N	13.41 E
Terborg, Neth. (tĕr-bôrg)	169c	51.55 N	6.23 E
Tercan, Tur. (tĕr'jän)	179	39.40 N	40.12 E
Terceira I., Acores (tĕr-sä'rä)	224a	38.49 N	26.36 W
Terebovlya, Sov. Un. (tĕ-rä'bôv-lyä)	167	49.18 N	25.43 E
Terek (R.), Sov. Un. (tĕ-rĕk')	179	43.30 N	45.10 E
Terenkul', Sov. Un. (tĕ-rĕn'kōōl)	182a	55.38 N	62.18 E
Teresina, Braz. (tĕr-ā-sē'nä)	143	5.04 S	42.42 W
Teresópolis, Braz. (tĕr-ā-sô'pō-lĕzh)	144b	22.25 S	42.59 W
Teribërka, Sov. Un. (tĕr-ē-byôr'ká)	178	69.00 N	35.15 E
Terme, Tur. (tĕr'mĕ)	179	41.05 N	42.00 E
Termez, Sov. Un. (tyĕr'mĕz)	193	37.19 N	67.20 E
Terminal I., Ca.	59	33.45 N	118.15 W

PLACE (Pronounciation)	PAGE	Lat. °'	Long. °'
Termini, It. (tĕr'mĕ-nĕ)	172	37.58 N	13.39 E
Términos, Laguna de (L.), Mex. (lä-gōō'nä dĕ ĕ'r-mē-nôs)	131	18.37 N	91.32 W
Termoli, It. (tĕr'mô-lĕ)	172	42.00 N	15.01 E
Tern (R.), Eng. (tûrn)	156	52.49 N	2.31 W
Ternate, Indon. (tĕr-nä'tä)	207	0.52 N	127.25 E
Terni, It. (tĕr'nē)	172	42.38 N	12.41 E
Ternopol', Sov. Un. (tĕr-nô-pôl')	167	49.32 N	25.36 E
Terpeniya, Mys (C.), Sov. Un.	181	48.44 N	144.42 E
Terpeniya, Zaliv (B.), Sov. Un. (zä'lĭf tĕr-pä'nĭ-yä)	204	49.10 N	143.05 E
Terrace, Can. (tĕr'ĭs)	98	54.31 N	128.35 W
Terracina, It. (tĕr-rä-chē'nä)	172	41.18 N	13.14 E
Terra Nova Natl. Park, Can.	105	48.37 N	54.15 W
Terrebonne, Can. (tĕr-bŏn')	95a	45.42 N	73.38 W
Terrebonne B., La.	125	28.55 N	90.30 W
Terre Haute, In. (tĕr-ĕ' hōt')	110	39.25 N	87.25 W
Terrell, Tx. (tĕr'ĕl)	125	32.44 N	96.15 W
Terrell, Wa.	118d	48.53 N	122.44 W
Terrell Hills, Tx. (tĕr'ĕl hĭlz)	119d	29.28 N	98.27 W
Terschelling (I.), Neth. (tĕr-skĕl'ĭng)	163	53.25 N	5.12 E
Teruel, Sp. (tā-rōō-ĕl')	170	40.20 N	1.05 W
Tešanj, Yugo. (tĕ'shän')	173	44.36 N	17.59 E
Teschendorf, G.D.R. (tĕ'shĕn-dôrf)	157b	52.51 N	13.10 E
Tesecheacan, Mex. (tĕ-sĕ-chĕ-ä-ká'n)	131	18.10 N	95.41 W
Teshekpuk (L.), Ak. (tĕ-shĕk'pŭk)	107	70.18 N	152.36 W
Teshio Dake (Mt.), Jap. (tĕsh'ē-ô-dä'kä)	204	44.00 N	142.50 E
Teshio Gawa (R.), Jap. (tĕsh'ē-ô gä'wä)	204	44.53 N	144.55 E
Tesiin Gol (R.), Mong.	198	50.14 N	94.30 E
Teslin, Can. (tĕs-lĭn)	107	60.10 N	132.30 W
Teslin (L.), Can.	96	60.12 N	132.08 W
Teslin (R.), Can.	96	61.18 N	134.14 W
Tessalon, Can.	102	46.20 N	83.35 W
Tessaoua, Niger (tĕs-sä'ōō-ä)	224	13.53 N	7.53 E
Tessenderlo, Bel.	157a	51.04 N	5.08 E
Test (R.), Eng. (tĕst)	162	51.10 N	2.20 W
Testa del Gargano (Pt.), It. (tās'tä dĕl gär-gä'nô)	172	41.48 N	16.13 E
Tetachuck L., Can.	98	53.20 N	125.50 W
Tete, Moz. (tä'tĕ)	231	16.13 S	33.35 E
Tête Jaune Cache, Can. (tĕt'zhôn-käsh)	99	52.57 N	119.26 W
Tetepiskaw, Lac (L.), Can.	102	51.02 N	69.23 W
Teterboro, NJ	55	40.52 N	74.03 W
Teterev (R.), Sov. Un. (tyĕ'tyĕ-rĕf)	175	50.35 N	29.18 E
Teterow, G.D.R. (tä'tĕ-rō)	166	53.46 N	12.33 E
Teteven, Bul. (tĕt'ĕ-ven)	174	42.57 N	24.15 E
Teton R., Mt. (tĕ'tôn)	117	47.54 N	111.37 W
Tetouan, Mor.	224	35.42 N	5.34 W
Tetovo, Yugo. (tä'tô-vô)	173	42.01 N	21.00 E
Tetyukhe-Pristan, Sov. Un. (tĕt-yōō'κĕ prī-stän')	204	44.21 N	135.44 E
Tetyushi, Sov. Un. (tyĭt-yōō'shĭ)	178	54.58 N	48.40 E
Teupitz, G.D.R. (toĭ'pĕtz)	157b	42.08 N	13.37 E
Tevere (Tiber) (R.), It.	66c	44.19 N	12.25 E
Tévere (Tiber) (R.), It. (tā'vå-rä)	172	42.30 N	12.14 E
Teverya, Isr. (tĭ'bĕr)	191a	32.48 N	35.32 E
Tewksbury, Ma. (tūks'bĕr-ĭ)	105a	42.37 N	71.14 W
Texada I., Can.	98	49.40 N	124.24 W
Texarkana, Ar. (tĕk-sär-kän'á)	123	33.26 N	94.02 W
Texarkana, Tx.	123	33.26 N	94.04 W
Texas (State), U. S.	108	31.00 N	101.00 W
Texas City, Tx.	125	29.23 N	94.54 W
Texcaltitlán, Mex. (tās-käl'tĕ-tlän')	130	18.54 N	99.51 W
Texcoco, Mex. (tås-kō'kô)	131a	19.31 N	98.53 W
Texel (I.), Neth. (tĕk'sĕl)	163	53.10 N	4.45 E
Texistepec, Mex. (tĕk-sēs-tä-pĕk')	131	17.51 N	94.46 W
Texiutlán, Mex. (tå-zĕ-ōō-tlän')	131	19.48 N	97.21 W
Texmelucan, Mex. (tās-mä-lōō'kän)	131a	19.17 N	98.26 W
Texoma, L., Ok. (tĕk'ô-mä)	123	34.03 N	96.28 W
Texontepec, Mex. (tå-zōn-tå-pĕk')	130	19.52 N	98.48 W
Texontepec de Aldama, Mex. (dä äl-dä'mä)	130	20.19 N	99.19 W
Teyateyaneng, Leso.	227c	29.11 S	27.43 E
Teykovo, Sov. Un. (tĕy-kô-vô)	174	56.52 N	40.34 E
Tezpur, India	196	26.42 N	92.52 E
Tha-anne (R.), Can.	96	60.50 N	96.56 W
Thabana Ntlenyana (Mtn.), Leso.	227c	29.28 S	29.17 E
Thabazimbi, S. Afr.	223d	24.36 S	27.22 E
Thailand, Asia	190	16.30 N	101.00 E
Thailand, G. of, Asia	206	11.37 N	100.46 E
Thākurpukur, India	67a	22.28 N	88.19 E
Thale Luang (L.), Thai.	206	7.51 N	99.39 E
Thame, Eng. (tām)	156b	51.43 N	0.59 W
Thames (R.), Can. (tĕmz)	110	42.40 N	81.45 W
Thames (R.), Eng.	163	51.26 N	0.54 W
Thames Ditton, Eng.	62	51.23 N	0.21 W
Thāmit, Wadi (R.), Libya	161	30.39 N	16.23 E
Thāna, India (thä'nŭ)	197b	19.13 N	72.58 E
Thāna (R.), India	197b	19.13 N	72.58 E
Thanh-Hoa, Viet. (tän'hô'á)	203	19.46 N	105.42 E
Thanjāvūr, India	197	10.51 N	79.11 E
Thann, Fr. (tän)	169	47.49 N	7.05 E
Thaon-les-Vosges, Fr. (tä-ôN-lä-vôzh')	169	48.16 N	6.24 E
Thargomindah, Austl. (thär'gô-mĭn'dá)	216	27.58 S	143.57 E
Thásos (I.), Grc. (thä'sôs)	173	40.41 N	24.53 E
Thatch Cay (I.), Vir. Is. (U. S. A.) (thăch)	129c	18.22 N	64.53 W
Thatto Heath, Eng.	64a	53.26 N	2.45 W
Thaya R., Aus.-Czech. (tä'yä)	166	48.48 N	15.40 E
Thayer, Mo. (thä'ĕr)	123	36.30 N	91.34 W
The Basin, Austl.	70b	37.51 S	145.19 E
Thebes (Ruins), Egypt (thēbz)	223b	25.47 N	32.39 E
Thebes, see Thivai			
The Brothers (Mtn.), Wa. (brŭth'ĕrs)	118a	47.39 N	123.08 W

ăt; finăl; rāte; senăte; ärm; ásk; sofá; fâre;   ch-choose;   dh-as th in other;   bē; ĕvent; bĕt; recĕnt; cratēr;   g-gō; gh-guttural g;   bīt; ĭ-short neutral; rīde;   κ-guttural k as ch in German ich;

PRONOUNCING INDEX

The Capital – Tlaxiaco Sta. Maria Asunción 353

PLACE (Pronounciation)	PAGE	Lat. °′	Long. °′
The Capital (P. Int.), DC	56d	38.53 N	77.00 W
The Coteau (Hills), Can.	100	51.10 N	107.30 W
The Dalles, Or. (dălz)	116	45.36 N	121.10 W
The Father (Mtn.), Pap. N. Gui.	207	5.05 S	151.30 E
The Hague, see 's Gravenhage			
Thelum, Pak.	196	32.59 N	73.43 E
The Narrows (Str.), NY	55	40.37 N	74.03 W
The Oaks, Austl.	211b	34.04 S	150.36 E
Theodore, Austl. (thēō'dôr)	216	24.51 S	150.09 E
Theodore Roosevelt Dam, Az. (thē-ô-dōr rōō-sȧ-vělt)	121	33.46 N	111.25 W
Theodore Roosevelt Natl. Park, ND	114	47.20 N	103.42 W
Theológos, Grc.	173	40.37 N	24.41 E
The Oval (P. Int.), Eng.	62	51.29 N	0.07 W
The Pas, Can. (pä)	101	53.50 N	101.15 W
The Rajah (Mtn.), Can.	99	53.15 N	118.31 W
Thermopolis, Wy. (thēr-mŏp'ô-lĭs)	117	43.38 N	108.11 W
The Round Mtn., Austl.	216	30.17 S	152.19 E
The Sound (Str.), Austl.	70a	33.49 S	151.17 E
Thessalía (Reg.), Grc.	173	39.50 N	22.09 E
Thessalon, Can.	97	46.11 N	83.37 W
Thessaloníki, Grc. (thěs-sá-lô-nē'kē)	173	40.38 N	22.59 E
Thetford Mines, Can. (thět'fērd mīns)	104	46.05 N	71.20 W
The Twins (Mtn.), Leso.-S. Afr. (twĭnz)	227c	30.09 S	28.29 E
Theunissen, S. Afr.	223d	28.25 S	26.44 E
Theydon Bois, Eng.	62	51.40 N	0.06 E
Thiais, Fr.	64c	48.46 N	2.23 E
Thibaudeau, Can. (tĭ'bō-dō')	101	57.05 N	94.08 W
Thibodaux, La. (tē-bô-dō')	125	29.48 N	90.48 W
Thief (L.), Mn. (thēf)	114	48.32 N	95.46 W
Thief (R.), Mn.	114	48.18 N	96.07 E
Thief Rivers Falls, Mn. (thēf rĭv'ēr fôlz)	114	48.07 N	96.11 W
Thier, F.R.G.	63	51.05 N	7.22 E
Thiers, Fr. (tyâr)	168	45.51 N	3.32 E
Thiès, Senegal (tē-ĕs')	228	14.48 N	16.56 W
Thika, Ken.	231	1.03 S	37.05 E
Thimbu, Bhu.	196	27.33 N	89.42 E
Thingvallavatn (L.), Ice.	158	64.12 N	20.22 W
Thionville, Fr. (tyôN-vēl')	169	49.23 N	6.31 E
Third Cataract, Sud.	225	19.53 N	30.11 E
Thisted, Den. (tēs'tědh)	164	56.57 N	8.38 E
Thistilfjördur (Fd.), Ice.	158	66.29 N	14.59 W
Thistle (I.), Austl. (thĭs''l)	216	34.55 S	136.11 E
Thistletown (Neigh.), Can.	54c	43.44 N	79.33 W
Thívai (Thebes), Grc.	173	38.20 N	23.18 E
Thjórsá (R.), Ice. (tyûr'sá)	158	64.23 N	19.18 W
Thohoyandou, Venda	222	23.00 S	30.29 E
Tholen, Neth.	157a	51.32 N	4.11 E
Thomas, Ok. (tŏm'ăs)	122	35.44 N	98.43 W
Thomas, WV	111	39.15 N	79.30 W
Thomaston, Ga. (tŏm'ăs-tŭn)	126	32.51 N	84.17 W
Thomaston, NY	55	40.47 N	73.43 W
Thomastown, Austl.	70b	37.41 S	145.01 E
Thomasville, Al. (tŏm'ăs-vĭl)	126	31.55 N	87.43 W
Thomasville, NC	127	35.52 N	80.05 W
Thomlinson, Mt., Can.	98	55.33 N	127.29 W
Thompson, Can.	101	55.48 N	97.59 W
Thompson (R.), Can.	99	50.15 N	121.20 W
Thompson (R.), Mo.	123	40.32 N	93.49 W
Thompson Falls, Mt.	116	47.35 N	115.20 W
Thomson, Ga. (tŏm'sŭn)	127	33.28 N	82.29 W
Thomson (R.) Austl. (tŏm-sŏn)	215	29.30 S	143.07 E
Thomson's Falls, Ken.	231	0.02 N	36.22 E
Thon Buri (Neigh.), Thai.	68f	13.43 N	100.29 E
Thong, Eng.	62	51.24 N	0.24 E
Thong Hoe, Singapore	67c	1.25 N	103.42 E
Thong-tay-hoi, Viet.	68m	10.50 N	106.39 E
Thonon-les-Bains, Fr. (tô-nôN'lå-băN')	169	46.22 N	6.27 E
Thorigny-sur-Marne, Fr.	64c	48.53 N	2.42 E
Thórisvatn (L.), Ice.	158	64.02 N	19.09 W
Thornbury, Austl.	70b	37.45 S	145.00 E
Thorne, Eng. (thôrn)	156	53.37 N	0.58 W
Thornhill, S. Afr.	71b	26.07 S	28.09 E
Thornleigh, Austl.	70a	33.44 S	151.05 E
Thornton, Eng.	64a	53.30 N	3.00 W
Thornton Hough, Eng.	64a	53.19 N	3.03 W
Thornton-le-Moors, Eng.	64a	53.16 N	2.50 W
Thorntown, In. (thôrn'tŭn)	110	40.05 N	86.35 W
Thornwood Common, Eng.	62	51.43 N	0.08 E
Thorold, Can. (thō'rōld)	95d	43.13 N	79.12 W
Thouars, Fr. (tōō-är')	168	47.00 N,	0.17 W
Thousand Is., NY-Can. (thou'zănd)	111	44.15 N	76.10 W
Thrace (Reg.), Grc.-Tur. (thrās)	173	41.20 N	26.07 E
Thrapston, Eng. (thrăp'stŭn)	156	52.23 N	0.32 W
Three Forks, Mt. (thrē fôrks)	117	45.56 N	111.35 W
Three Oaks, Mi. (thrē ōks)	110	41.50 N	86.40 W
Three Points, C., Ghana	228	4.45 N	2.06 W
Three Rivers, Mi.	110	42.00 N	83.40 W
Thule, Grnld.	75	76.34 N	68.47 W
Thun, Switz. (tōōn)	166	46.46 N	7.34 E
Thunder B., Can. (thŭn'dēr)	115	48.29 N	88.52 W
Thunder Bay, Can.	102	48.28 N	89.12 W
Thunder Hills, Can.	100	54.30 N	106.00 W
Thunersee (L.), Switz.	166	46.40 N	7.30 E
Thurber, Tx. (thûr'bēr)	124	32.30 N	98.23 W
Thüringen (Thuringia) (former state or region), G.D.R. (tü'rĭng-ĕn)	166	51.07 N	10.45 E
Thurles, Ire. (thûrlz)	162	52.44 N	7.45 W
Thurrock, Eng. (thŭ'rŏk)	156b	51.28 N	0.19 E
Thursday (I.), Austl. (thûrz-dā)	215	10.17 S	142.23 E
Thurso, Can. (thŭn'sô)	95c	45.36 N	75.15 W
Thurso, Scot.	162	58.35 N	3.40 W
Thurston Pen. Ant. (thûrs'tŭn)	232	71.20 S	98.00 W
Thysville, Zaire (tēs-vēl')	226	5.08 S	14.58 E
Tiandong, China (tĭĕn-dôŋ)	203	23.32 N	107.10 E
Tianjin, China	200	39.08 N	117.14 E
Tianjin Shi (Mun.), China (tĭĕn-jyĭn shr)	200	39.30 N	117.13 E

PLACE (Pronounciation)	PAGE	Lat. °′	Long. °′
Tianmen, China (tĭĕn-mŭn)	203	30.40 N	113.10 E
Tianshui, China (tĭĕn-shwā)	202	34.25 N	105.40 E
Tibagi, Braz. (tē'bá-zhē)	144	24.40 S	50.35 W
Tibasti, Sarir (Des.), Chad	225	24.00 N	16.30 E
Tibati, Cam.	229	6.27 N	12.38 E
Tiber (R.), see Tevere			
Tibesti Massif (Mts.), Chad	225	20.40 N	17.48 E
Tibet (Aut. Reg.), see Xizang			
Tibet, Plat. of, China (tĭ-bět')	198	32.22 N	83.30 E
Ţibleşului, Munţii (Mts.), Rom	167	47.41 N	24.05 E
Tibnīn, Leb.	191a	33.12 N	35.23 E
Tiburon, Ca. (tē-bōō-rōn')	118b	37.53 N	122.27 W
Tiburon, Ca.	58b	36.04 N	119.19 W
Tiburon, Hai.	135	18.35 N	74.25 W
Tiburón (I.), Mex.	128	28.45 N	113.10 W
Tiburon, Cabo (C.), Pan. (ká'bô)	133	8.42 N	77.19 W
Tiburon I., Ca.	118b	37.52 N	122.26 W
Ticaco Pass, Phil. (tē-kä-kô)	207a	12.38 N	123.50 E
Ticao I., Phil. (tē-kä'ō)	207a	12.40 N	123.30 E
Tickhill, Eng. (tĭk'ĭl)	156	53.26 N	1.06 W
Ticonderoga, NY (tī-kŏn-dēr-ō'gȧ)	111	43.50 N	73.30 W
Ticul, Mex. (tē-kōō'l)	132a	20.22 N	89.32 W
Tidaholm, Swe. (tē'dá-hōlm)	164	58.11 N	13.53 E
Tideswell, Eng. (tīdz'wĕl)	156	53.17 N	1.47 W
Tidikelt (Reg.), Alg. (tē-dē-kĕlt')	224	25.53 N	2.11 E
Tidjikdja, Mauritania (tē-jĭk'jä)	228	18.33 N	11.25 W
Tiefenbroich, F.R.G.	63	51.18 N	6.49 E
Tieling, China (tĭĕ-liŋ)	202	42.18 N	123.50 E
Tielmes, Sp. (tyâl-màs')	171a	40.15 N	3.20 W
Tienen, Bel. (Brussels In.)	157	50.49 N	4.58 E
Tienshan Hu (L.), China (dĭăn'shän'hōō)	200	31.08 N	120.30 E
Tien Shan (Mts.), Sov. Un.-China	198	42.00 N	78.46 E
Tiergarten (Neigh.), F.R.G.	65a	52.31 N	13.21 E
Tiergarten (P. Int.), F.R.G.	65a	52.30 N	13.21 E
Tierp, Swe. (tyěrp)	164	60.21 N	17.28 E
Tierpoort, S. Afr.	227b	25.53 N	28.26 E
Tierra Blanca, Mex. (tyě'r-rä-blä'n-kä)	131	18.28 N	96.19 W
Tierra del Fuego (Reg.), Chile-Arg. (tyěr'rä děl fwā'gō)	144	53.50 S	68.45 W
Tiétar (R.), Sp. (tē-ā'tär)	170	39.56 N	5.44 W
Tietê, Braz. (tyā-tā')	141a	23.08 S	47.42 W
Tieté, (R.), Braz.	143	20.46 S	50.46 W
Tietê (R.), Braz.	61d	23.29 S	46.51 W
Tiffin, Oh. (tĭf'ĭn)	110	41.10 N	83.15 W
Tifton, Ga. (tĭf'tŭn)	126	31.25 N	83.34 W
Tigard, Or. (tī'gärd)	118c	45.25 N	122.46 W
Tignish, Can. (tĭg'nĭsh)	104	46.57 N	64.02 W
Tigoda (R.), Sov. Un. (tē'gô-dá)	182c	59.29 N	31.15 E
Tigre, Arg. (tē'grĕ)	144	34.09 S	58.35 W
Tigre (R.), Peru	142	2.20 S	75.41 W
Tigres, Península dos (Pen.), Ang. (pĕ-nē'ŋ-sōō-lä-dôs-tē'grĕs)	226	16.30 S	11.45 E
Tigris (R.), Asia	192	34.45 N	44.10 E
Tihert, Alg.	224	35.28 N	1.15 E
Tihuatlán, Mex. (tē-wä-tlän')	131	20.43 N	97.34 W
Tijuana, Mex. (tē-hwä'nä)	120a	32.32 N	117.02 W
Tijuca, Pico da (Mtn.), Braz. (pē'kō-dä-tē-zhōō'kà)	144b	22.56 S	43.17 W
Tikal (Ruins), Guat. (tē-käl')	132a	17.16 N	89.49 W
Tikhoretsk, Sov. Un. (tē-kôr-yĕtsk')	179	45.55 N	40.05 E
Tikhvin, Sov. Un. (tēk-vēn')	174	59.36 N	33.38 E
Tikrīt, Iraq	192	34.36 N	43.31 E
Tiksi, Sov. Un. (tĕk-sē')	181	71.42 N	128.32 E
Tilburg, Neth. (tĭl'bûrg)	157a	51.33 N	5.05 E
Tilbury, Eng.	62	51.28 N	0.23 E
Tilemsi, Vallée du (Val.), Mali	228	17.50 N	0.25 E
Tilichiki, Sov. Un. (tyĭ-le-chĭ-kē)	181	60.49 N	166.14 E
Tiligul (R.), Sov. Un. (tē'lĭ-gûl)	175	47.25 N	30.27 E
Tilimsen, Alg.	224	34.53 N	1.21 W
Tillabéry, Niger (tē-yà-bā-rē')	224	14.14 N	1.30 E
Tillamook, Or. (tĭl'à-mŏŏk)	116	45.27 N	123.50 W
Tillamook B., Or.	116	45.32 N	124.26 W
Tillberga, Swe. (tĕl-bĕr'ghá)	164	59.40 N	16.34 E
Tillsonburg, Can. (tĭl'sŭn-bûrg)	103	42.50 N	80.50 W
Tilsit, see Sovetsk			
Tim, Sov. Un. (tēm)	175	51.39 N	37.07 E
Timaru, N.Z. (tĭm'á-rōō)	217	44.26 S	171.17 E
Timashevskaya, Sov. Un. (tēmä-shĕfs-kä'yä)	175	45.47 N	38.57 E
Timbalier B., La. (tĭm'bá-lēr)	125	28.55 N	90.14 W
Timber, Or. (tĭm'bēr)	118c	45.43 N	123.17 W
Timberview, Md.	56c	39.13 N	76.45 W
Timbo, Gui. (tĭm'bō)	224	10.41 N	11.51 W
Timbuktu, see Tombouctou			
Times Square (P. Int.), NY	55	40.45 N	74.00 W
Timétrine Monts (Mts.), Mali.	228	19.50 N	0.30 W
Timimoun, Alg. (tē-mē-mōōn')	224	29.14 N	0.22 E
Timiris, Cap (C.), Mauritania	228	19.23 N	16.32 W
Timis (R.), Rom.	173	45.28 N	21.06 E
Timiskaming Station, Can. (tē-mĭs'kȧ-mĭng)	97	46.41 N	79.01 W
Timişoara, Rom.	173	45.44 N	21.21 E
Timmins, Can. (tĭm'ĭnz)	97	48.25 N	81.22 W
Timmonsville, SC (tĭm'ŭnz-vĭl)	127	34.09 N	79.55 W
Timor (I.), Indon. (tē-mōr')	207	10.08 S	125.00 E
Timor Sea, Asia	208	12.40 S	125.00 E
Timpanogos Cave Natl. Mon., Ut. (tĭ-măn'ō-gŏz)	121	40.25 N	111.45 W
Timperley, Eng.	64b	53.24 N	2.19 W
Timpson, Tx. (tĭmp'sŭn)	125	31.55 N	94.24 W
Timpton (R.), Sov. Un. (tēmp'tôn)	181	57.15 N	126.35 E
Timsāh (L.), Egypt (tĭm'sä)	223c	30.34 N	32.22 E
Tina (R.), S. Afr. (tē'nȧ)	227c	30.50 S	28.44 E
Tinaguillo, Ven. (tē-nä-gē'l-yō)	143b	9.55 N	68.18 W
Tina, Monte (Mtn.), Dom. Rep. (mô'n-tē-tē'nä)	135	18.50 N	70.40 W
Tindouf, Alg. (tēn-dōōf')	224	27.43 N	7.44 W
Tinggi, Palau (I.), Mala.	191b	2.16 N	104.16 E
Tinghert, Plat. du, Alg.	224	27.30 N	7.30 E
Tingi Mts., S. L.	228	9.00 N	10.50 W

PLACE (Pronounciation)	PAGE	Lat. °′	Long. °′
Ting Kau, Hong Kong	68c	22.23 N	114.04 E
Tinglin, China	201b	30.53 N	121.18 E
Tingo María, Peru (tē'ngô-mä-rē'ä)	142	9.15 S	76.04 W
Tingréla, Ivory Coast	228	10.29 N	6.24 W
Tingsryd, Swe. (tĭngs'rüd)	164	56.32 N	14.58 E
Tingtzu Wan (B.), China (dĭng'tze wän)	200	36.33 N	121.06 E
Tinguindio Paracho, Mex. (tēn'kē'n-dyō-pärä-chô)	130	19.38 N	102.02 W
Tinguiririca (R.), Chile (tē'n-gē-rē-rē'kä)	141b	36.48 S	70.45 W
Tinley Park, Il. (tĭn'lē)	113a	41.34 N	87.47 W
Tinnoset, Nor. (tĕn'nôs'sĕt)	164	59.44 N	9.00 E
Tinnsjø, Nor. (tĭnnsyû)	164	59.55 N	8.49 E
Tinogasta, Arg. (tē-nô-gäs'tä)	144	28.07 S	67.30 W
Tinsukia, India (tin-sōō'kĭ-à)	193	27.18 N	95.29 W
Tintic, Ut. (tĭn'tĭk)	121	39.55 N	112.15 W
Tioga (Neigh.), Pa.	56b	40.00 N	75.10 W
Tīh, Jabal at (Mts.), Egypt	191a	29.23 N	34.05 E
Tioman (I.), Mala.	191b	2.25 N	104.30 E
Tīnah, Khalīj at (G.), Egypt	191a	31.06 N	32.42 E
Tio, Pic de (Pk.), Gui.	228	8.55 N	8.55 W
Tipitapa, Nic. (tē-pē-tä'pä)	132	12.14 N	86.05 W
Tipitapa R., Nic.	132	12.13 N	85.57 W
Tippah Cr., (R.), Ms. (tĭp'pȧ)	126	34.43 N	88.15 W
Tippecanoe (R.), In. (tĭp-ē-kȧ-nōō')	110	40.55 N	86.45 W
Tipperary, Ire. (tĭ-pē-râ'rē)	162	52.28 N	8.13 W
Tippo Bay, Ms. (tĭp'ō bīōō')	123	33.35 N	90.06 W
Tipton, In.	110	40.15 N	86.00 W
Tipton, Ia.	115	41.46 N	91.10 W
Tirane, Alb. (tē-rä'nä)	173	41.48 N	19.50 E
Tirano, It. (tē-rä'nō)	172	46.12 N	10.09 E
Tiraspol', Sov. Un. (tē-räs'pôl')	175	46.52 N	29.38 E
Tire, Tur. (tē'rĕ)	179	38.05 N	27.48 E
Tiree (I.), Scot. (tī-rē')	162	56.34 N	6.30 W
Tires, Port.	65d	38.43 N	9.21 W
Tirich Mir (Mt.), Pak.	196	36.50 N	71.48 E
Tirlyanskiy, Sov. Un. (tĭr-lyän'skĭ)	182a	54.13 N	58.37 E
Tirol (State), Aus. (tē-rōl')	166	47.13 N	11.10 E
Tîrgovişte, Rom.	173	44.54 N	25.29 E
Tîrgu-Jiu, Rom.	173	45.02 N	23.17 E
Tîrgu-Mureş, Rom.	167	46.33 N	24.35 E
Tîrgu Neamt, Rom.	167	47.14 N	26.23 E
Tîrgu-Ocna, Rom.	167	46.18 N	26.38 E
Tîrgu-Secuiesc, Rom.	167	46.04 N	26.06 E
Tirso (R.), It. (tēr'sô)	172	40.15 N	9.03 E
Tiruchchirāppalli, India (tĭr'ōō-chĭ-rä'pà-lĭ)	197	10.49 N	78.48 E
Tirunelveli, India	197	8.53 N	77.43 E
Tiruppur, India	197	11.11 N	77.08 E
Tisa (R.), Hung.-Yugo. (tē'sä)	173	45.50 N	20.13 E
Tisdale, Can. (tĭz'dāl)	100	52.51 N	104.04 W
Tista (R.), India	196	26.03 N	88.52 E
Titāgarh, India	196a	22.44 N	88.23 E
Titicaca, Lago (L.), Bol.-Peru (lä'gō-tē-tē-kä'kä)	142	16.12 S	70.33 W
Titiribi, Col. (tē-tē-rē-bē')	142a	6.05 N	75.47 W
Titograd, Yugo.	173	42.25 N	20.42 E
Tito, Lagh (R.), Ken.	231	2.25 N	39.05 E
Titovo Užice, Yugo. (tē'tô-vô ōō'zhē-tsĕ)	173	43.51 N	19.53 E
Titov Veles, Yugo. (tē'tôv vĕ'lĕs)	173	41.42 N	21.50 E
Titterstone Clee Hill, Eng. (klē)	156	52.24 N	2.37 W
Titule, Zaire	230	3.17 N	25.32 E
Titusville, Fl. (tĭ'tŭs-vĭl)	127a	28.37 N	80.44 W
Titusville, Pa.	111	40.40 N	79.40 W
Titz, F.R.G. (tētz)	169c	51.00 N	6.26 E
Tiu Keng Wan, China	68c	22.18 N	114.15 E
Tiverton, RI (tĭv'ēr-tun)	112b	41.38 N	71.11 W
Tivoli, It. (tē'vô-lē)	171d	41.38 N	12.48 E
Tínos (I.), Grc.	173	37.45 N	25.12 E
Tîrnăveni, Rom.	167	46.19 N	24.18 E
Tírnavos, Grc.	173	39.50 N	22.14 E
Tixkokob, Mex. (tēx-kō-kō'b)	132a	21.01 N	89.23 W
Tixtla de Guerrero, Mex. (tē'x-tlä-dē-gĕr-rē'rô)	130	17.36 N	99.24 W
Tizapán, Mex.	60a	19.20 N	99.13 W
Tizard Bk. and Rf., China (tĭz'ărd)	206	10.51 N	113.20 E
Tizimín, Mex. (tē-zē-mē'n)	132a	21.08 N	88.10 W
Tizi-Ouzou, Alg. (tē'zē-ōō-zōō')	224	36.44 N	4.04 E
Tiznados (R.), Ven. (tēz-nä'dōs)	143b	9.53 N	67.49 W
Tiznit, Mor. (tēz-nēt)	224	29.52 N	9.39 W
Tlacolula de Matamoros, Mex. (tlä-kô-lōō'lä dā mätä-mō'rōs)	131	16.56 N	96.29 W
Tlacotálpan, Mex. (tlä-kô-täl'pän)	131	18.39 N	95.40 W
Tlacotepec, Mex. (tlä-kô-tä-pĕ'k)	130	17.46 N	99.57 W
Tlacotepec, Mex.	130	19.11 N	99.41 W
Tlacotepec, Mex.	131	18.41 N	97.40 W
Tláhuac, Mex. (tlä-wäk')	131a	19.16 N	99.00 W
Tlajomulco de Zúñiga, Mex. (tlä-hô-mōō'l-ko-dĕ-zōō'n-yē-gä)	130	20.30 N	103.27 W
Tlalchapa, Mex. (tläl-chä'pä)	130	18.26 N	100.29 W
Tlalixcoyan, Mex. (tlä-lēs'kô-yän')	131	18.53 N	96.04 W
Tlalmanalco, Mex. (tläl-mä-nä'l-kô)	131a	19.12 N	98.48 W
Tlalnepantla, Mex. (täl-nĕ-pá'n-tyä)	131a	19.32 N	99.13 W
Tlalnepantla, Mex. (tläl-nå-pán'tlä)	131a	18.59 N	99.01 W
Tlalpan, Mex. (tläl-pä'n)	131a	19.17 N	99.10 W
Tlalpujahua, Mex. (tläl-pōō-кä'wä)	130	19.15 N	100.10 W
Tlaltenango, see Sánchez Román			
Tlaltenco, Mex.	60a	19.17 N	99.01 W
Tlapa, Mex. (tlä'pä)	130	17.30 N	98.09 W
Tlapacoyan, Mex. (tlä-pä-kô-yä'n)	131	19.57 N	97.11 W
Tlapaneco (R.), Mex. (tlä-pänĕ'kô)	130	17.59 N	98.44 W
Tlapehuala, Mex. (tlä-pâ-wä'lä)	130	18.17 N	100.30 W
Tlaquepaque, Mex. (tlä-kĕ-pä'kĕ)	130	20.39 N	103.17 W
Tlatlaya, Mex. (tlä-tlä'yä)	130	18.36 N	100.14 W
Tlaxcala, Mex. (tläs-kä'lä)	130	19.16 N	98.14 W
Tlaxcala (State), Mex.	130	19.30 N	98.15 W
Tlaxco, Mex. (tläs'kō)	130	19.37 N	98.06 W
Tlaxiaco Sta. María Asunción, Mex. (tläk-sē-ä'kō sän'tä mä-rē'ä ä-sōōn-syōn')	131	17.16 N	95.41 W

ng-sing; ŋ-baŋk; N-nasalized n; nŏd; cŏmmit; ōld; ôbey; ôrder; oi-boil; fōōd; fŏŏt; ou-out; s-soft; sh-dish; th-thin; pūre; ûnite; ûrn; stŭd; circŭs; ü-as in French tu; '-indeterminate vowel.

354 Tlayacapan – Trakiszki

PLACE (Pronounciation)	PAGE	Lat. °'	Long. °'
Tlayacapan, Mex. (tlä-yä-kä-pä'n)	131a	18.57 N	99.00 W
Tlevak Str., Ak.	98	53.03 N	132.58 W
Tlumach, Sov. Un. (t'lû-mäch')	167	48.47 N	25.00 E
Toa (R.), Cuba (tō'ä)	135	20.25 N	74.35 W
Toamasina, Mad.	227	18.14 S	49.25 E
Toana Ra. (Mts.), Nv. (tō-ȧ-nō')	117	40.45 N	114.11 W
Toar, Cuchillas de (Mtn.), Cuba (kōō-chē'l-lyäs-dĕ-tô-ä'r)	135	18.20 N	74.50 W
Tobago (I.), N. A. (tô-bā'gō)	129	11.15 N	60.30 W
Toba Inlet, Can.	98	50.20 N	124.50 W
Tobarra, Sp. (tô-bär'rä)	170	38.37 N	1.42 W
Tobol (R.), Sov. Un. (tô-bôl')	180	56.02 N	65.30 E
Tobol'sk, Sov. Un. (tô-bôlsk')	180	58.09 N	68.28 E
Tocaima, Col. (tô-kä'y-mä)	142a	4.28 N	74.38 W
Tocantinópolis, Braz. (tô-kän-tē-nō'pō-lês)	143	6.27 S	47.18 W
Tocantins (R.), Braz. (tō-kän-tēns')	143	3.28 S	49.22 W
Toccoa, Ga. (tŏk'ō-ȧ)	126	34.35 N	83.20 W
Toccoa (R.), Ga.	126	34.53 N	84.24 W
Tochigi, Jap. (tō'chē-gĭ)	205	36.25 N	139.45 E
Tocoa, Hond. (tô-kô'ä)	132	15.37 N	86.01 W
Tocopilla, Chile (tō-kô-pēl'yä)	144	22.03 S	70.08 W
Tocuyo de la Costa, Ven. (tô-kōō'yô-dĕ-lä-kôs'tä)	143b	11.03 N	68.24 W
Toda, Jap.	205d	35.48 N	139.42 E
Todmorden, Eng. (tŏd'môr-dĕn)	156	53.43 N	2.05 W
Tóecé, Burkina	228	11.50 N	1.16 W
Tofino, Can. (tō-fē'nō)	98	49.09 N	125.54 W
Töfsingdalens (Natl. Park), Swe.	164	62.09 N	13.05 E
Tōgane, Jap. (tō'gä-nä)	205	35.29 N	140.16 E
Togian, Kepulauan (Is.), Indon.	206	0.20 S	122.00 E
Togo, Afr. (tō'gō)	222	8.00 N	0.52 E
Toguzak R., Sov. Un. (tô'gōō-zák)	182a	53.40 N	61.42 E
Tohopekaliga (L.), Fl. (tō'hō-pē'kȧ-lī'gȧ)	127a	28.16 N	81.09 W
Toijala, Fin. (toi'yȧ-lȧ)	165	61.11 N	21.46 E
Toi-Misaki (C.), Jap. (toi mē'sä-kê)	205	31.20 N	131.20 E
Toiyabe Ra., Nv. (toi'yă-bē)	120	38.59 N	117.22 W
Tokachi Gawa (R.), Jap. (tō-kä'chē gä'wä)	204	43.10 N	142.30 E
Tokaj, Hung. (tô'kô-ê)	167	48.06 N	21.24 E
Tokara Guntō (Is.), Jap. (tō-kä'rä gōōn'tō')	204	29.45 N	129.15 E
Tokara Kaikyo (Str.), Jap. (tō'kä'rä kī'kyō)	204	30.20 N	129.50 E
Tokat, Tur. (tô-кät')	179	40.20 N	36.30 E
Tokelau Is., Oceania (tō-kē-lä'ōō)	208	8.00 S	176.00 W
Tokmak, Sov. Un. (tôk'mák)	180	42.44 N	75.41 E
Tokorozawa, Jap. (tô'kô-rô-zä'wä)	205a	35.47 N	139.29 E
Toksu Palace (P. Int.), Kor.	68b	37.35 N	126.58 E
Tokuno (I.), Jap. (tô-kōō'nō)	204	27.42 N	129.25 E
Tokushima, Jap. (tō'kōō'shē-mä)	205	34.06 N	134.31 E
Tokuyama, Jap. (tō'kōō'yä-mä)	205	34.04 N	131.49 E
Tōkyō, Jap. (tō'kē-ō)	205a	35.41 N	139.44 E
Tōkyō (Pref.), Jap.	205a	35.42 N	139.40 E
Tōkyō-Wan (B.), Jap. (tō'kyō wän)	205a	35.56 N	139.56 E
Tolbukhin, Bul.	173	43.33 N	27.52 E
Tolcayuca, Mex. (tôl-kä-yōō'kä)	130	19.55 N	98.54 W
Toledo, Ia. (tô-lē'dō)	115	41.59 N	92.35 W
Toledo, Oh.	110	41.40 N	83.35 W
Toledo, Or.	116	44.37 N	123.58 W
Toledo, Sp. (tô-lĕ'dô)	170	39.53 N	4.02 W
Toledo Bend Res., La.-Tx.	109	31.30 N	93.30 W
Toledo, Montes de (Mts.), Sp. (mô'n-tĕs-dĕ-tô-lĕ'dô)	170	39.33 N	4.40 W
Toliara, Mad.	227	20.16 S	43.44 E
Tolima (Dept.), Col. (tô-lē'mä)	142a	4.07 N	75.20 W
Tolimán, Mex. (tô-lê-män')	130	20.54 N	99.54 W
Tolima, Nevado del (Pk.), Col. (nĕ-vä-dô-dĕl-tô-lē'mä)	142a	4.40 N	75.20 W
Tollesbury, Eng. (tōl'z-bĕrĭ)	156b	51.46 N	0.49 E
Tollygunge (Neigh.), India	67a	22.30 N	88.21 E
Tolmezzo, It. (tôl-mĕt'zô)	172	46.25 N	13.03 E
Tolmin, Yugo. (tôl'mên)	172	46.12 N	13.45 E
Tolna, Hung. (tôl'nô)	167	46.25 N	18.47 E
Tolosa, Sp. (tô-lō'sä)	170	43.10 N	2.05 W
Tolo, Teluk (B.), Indon. (tō'lō)	206	2.00 S	122.06 E
Tolt (R.), Wa. (tōlt)	118a	47.13 N	121.49 W
Toluca, Il. (tô-lōō'kȧ)	110	41.00 N	89.10 W
Toluca, Mex. (tô-lōō'kä)	131a	19.17 N	99.40 W
Toluca, Nevado de (Mtn.), Mex. (nĕ-vä-dô-dĕ-tô-lōō'kä)	131a	19.09 N	99.42 W
Tolworth (Neigh.), Eng.	62	51.23 N	0.17 W
Tolyatti, Sov. Un.	178	53.30 N	49.10 E
Tom' (R.), Sov. Un.	180	55.33 N	85.00 E
Tomah, Wi. (tō'mȧ)	115	43.58 N	90.31 W
Tomahawk, Wi. (tŏm'ȧ-hôk)	115	45.27 N	89.44 W
Tomakovka, Sov. Un. (tō-mä'kôf-kȧ)	175	47.49 N	34.43 E
Tomar, Port. (tō-mär')	170	39.36 N	8.26 W
Tomashevka, Sov. Un. (tô-mȧ'shĕf-kȧ)	167	51.34 N	23.37 E
Tomaszow Lubelski, Pol. (tô-mä'shōōf lōō-bĕl'skĭ)	167	50.20 N	23.27 E
Tomaszów Mazowiecki, Pol. (tô-mä'shōōf mä-zō'vyĕt-skĭ)	167	51.33 N	20.00 E
Tomatlán, Mex. (tô-mä-tlä'n)	130	19.54 N	105.14 W
Tomatlán (R.), Mex.	130	19.56 N	105.14 W
Tombadonkéa, Gui.	228	11.00 N	14.23 W
Tombador, Serra do (Mts.), Braz. (sĕr'rȧ dōō tōm-bä-dôr')	143	11.31 S	57.33 W
Tombigbee (R.), Al. (tŏm-bĭg'bē)	126	31.45 N	88.02 W
Tombos, Braz. (tô'm-bōs)	141a	20.53 S	42.00 W
Tombouctou (Timbuktu), Mali (tôm-bōōk-tōō')	228	16.46 N	3.01 W
Tombs of the Caliphs (P Int.), Egypt	71a	30.03 N	31.17 E
Tombstone, Az. (tōōm'stōn)	121	31.40 N	110.00 W
Tomelilla, Swe. (tô'mĕ-lēl-lä)	164	55.34 N	13.55 E
Tomelloso, Sp. (tō-mâl-lyō'sō)	170	39.09 N	3.02 W
Tomini, Teluk (B.), Indon. (tô-mē'nê)	206	0.10 N	121.00 E
Tommot, Sov. Un. (tŏm-mŏt')	181	59.13 N	126.22 E
Tomsk, Sov. Un. (tŏmsk)	180	56.29 N	84.57 E
Tonalá, Mex. (tō-nä-lä')	131	16.05 N	93.45 W
Tonala, Mex.	130	20.38 N	103.14 W
Tonalá (R.), Mex.	131	18.05 N	94.08 W
Tonawanda, NY (tôn-ȧ-wŏn'dȧ)	113c	43.01 N	78.53 W
Tonawanda Cr., NY	113c	43.05 N	78.43 W
Tonawanda, Town of, NY	57a	42.59 N	78.52 W
Tonbei, China (tôŋ-bā)	202	48.00 N	126.48 E
Tonbridge, Eng. (tŭn-brĭj)	156b	51.11 N	0.17 E
Tonda, Jap. (tôn'dä)	205b	34.51 N	135.38 E
Tondabayashi, Jap. (tôn-dä-bä'yä-shê)	205b	34.29 N	135.36 E
Tondano, Indon. (tôn-dä'nō)	207	1.15 N	124.50 E
Tønder, Den. (tûn'nēr)	164	54.47 N	8.49 E
Tondlá, Mex.	131	16.04 N	93.57 W
Tone (R.), Jap. (tō'nē)	205a	35.55 N	139.57 E
Tone-Gawa (Strm.), Jap. (tō'nē gä'wa)	205	36.12 N	139.19 E
Tonekābon, Iran	179	36.40 N	51.00 E
Tonga, Oceania (tŏŋ'gȧ)	208	18.50 S	175.20 W
Tong'an, China (tôŋ-än)	203	24.48 N	118.02 E
Tongguan, China (tôŋ-gūän)	202	34.48 N	110.25 E
Tonghe, China (tôŋ-hŭ)	202	45.58 N	128.40 E
Tonghua, China (tôŋ-hwä)	202	41.43 N	125.50 E
Tongjiang, China (tôŋ-jyäŋ)	199	47.38 N	132.54 E
Tongliao, China (tôŋ-lĭou)	202	43.30 N	122.15 E
Tongo, Cam.	229	5.11 N	14.00 E
Tongoy, Chile (tōn-goi')	144	30.16 S	71.29 W
Tongren, China (tôŋ-rŭn)	203	27.45 N	109.12 E
Tongshan, China (tôŋ-shän)	200	34.27 N	116.27 E
Tongtian (R.), China (tôŋ-tĭĕn)	198	34.11 N	96.08 E
Tongue of Arabat (Spit), **see Arabatskaya Strelka**			
Tongue of the Ocean (Chan.), Ba. (tŭng ŏv thē ōshŭn)	134	24.05 N	77.20 W
Tongue R., Mt. (tŭng)	117	45.08 N	106.40 W
Tongxian, China (tôŋ shyĕn)	202a	39.55 N	116.40 E
Tonj R., Sud. (tônj)	225	6.18 N	28.33 E
Tonk, India (Tŏŋk)	196	26.13 N	75.45 E
Tonkawa, Ok. (tŏŋ kȧ-wô)	123	36.42 N	97.19 W
Tonkin, Gulf of, Viet. (tôn-kăn')	203	20.30 N	108.10 E
Tonle Sap (L.), Kamp. (tôn'lā săp')	206	13.03 N	102.49 E
Tonneins, Fr. (tô-năn')	168	44.24 N	0.18 E
Tönning, F.R.G. (tû'nēng)	166	54.20 N	8.55 E
Tonopah, Nv. (tō-nô-pä')	120	38.04 N	117.15 W
Tönsberg, Nor. (tûns'bĕrgh)	164	59.19 N	10.25 E
Tonsholt, F.R.G.	63	51.38 N	6.58 E
Tonto (R.), Mex. (tōn'tō)	131	18.15 N	96.13 W
Tonto Cr., Az.	121	34.05 N	111.15 W
Tonto Natl. Mon., Az. (tôn'tô)	121	33.33 N	111.08 W
Tooele, Ut. (tōō-ĕl ē)	119b	40.33 N	112.17 W
Toohsien, China	203	25.30 N	111.32 W
Toongabbie, Austl.	70a	33.47 S	150.57 E
Toot Hill, Eng.	62	51.42 N	0.12 E
Toowoomba, Austl. (tōō wōōm'bȧ)	216	23.72 S	152.10 E
Topanga, Ca. (tō'păn-gȧ)	119a	34.05 N	118.36 W
Topeka, Ks. (tô-pē'kȧ)	123	39.02 N	95.41 W
Topilejo, Mex. (tô-pē-lĕ'hô)	131a	19.12 N	99.09 W
Topkapi (Neigh.), Tur.	66f	41.02 N	28.54 E
Topkapi Müzesi (P. Int.), Tur.	66f	41.00 N	28.59 E
T'oplyj Stan (Neigh.), Sov. Un.	66b	55.37 N	37.30 E
Topock, Az.	121	34.40 N	114.20 W
Top of Hebers, Eng.	64b	53.34 N	2.12 W
Topol'čany, Czech. (tô-pôl'chä-nü)	167	48.38 N	18.10 E
Topolobampo, Mex. (tō-pō-lô-bä'm-pô)	128	25.45 N	109.00 W
Topolovgrad, Bul.	173	42.05 N	26.19 E
Toppenish, Wa. (tôp'ĕn-ĭsh)	116	46.22 N	120.00 W
Toppings, Eng.	64b	53.37 N	2.25 W
Tora, Île (I.), Mauritania	228	19.50 N	16.45 W
Torbat-e Heydarīyeh, Iran	195	35.16 N	59.13 E
Torbat-e Jām, Iran	195	35.14 N	60.36 E
Torbay, Can. (tôr-bā')	105	47.40 N	52.43 W
Torbay, see Torquay			
Torbreck, Mt., Austl. (tōr-brĕk)	216	37.05 S	146.55 E
Torch (L.), Mi. (tôrch)	110	45.00 N	85.30 W
Torcy, Fr.	64c	48.51 N	2.39 E
Tor di Quinto (Neigh.), It.	66c	41.56 N	12.28 E
Töreboda, Swe. (tû'rĕ-bō'dä)	164	58.44 N	14.04 E
Torhout, Bel.	163	51.01 N	3.04 E
Toribío, Col. (tô-rē-bē'ō)	142a	2.58 N	76.14 W
Toride, Jap. (tō'rē-dā)	205a	35.54 N	104.04 E
Torino (Turin), It. (tô-rē'no) (tū'rĭn)	172	45.05 N	7.44 E
Tormes (R.), Sp. (tōr'mās)	170	41.12 N	6.15 W
Torneälven (R.), Swe.	158	67.29 N	22.05 E
Torneträsk (L.), Swe. (tôr'nĕ trĕsk)	152	68.10 N	20.36 E
Torngat Mts., Can.	97	59.18 N	64.35 W
Tornio, Fin. (tôr'nĭ-ô)	158	65.55 N	24.09 E
Toro, Lac (L.), Can.	104	46.53 N	73.46 W
Toronto, Can. (tô-rŏn'tō)	95d	43.40 N	79.23 W
Toronto, Oh.	110	40.30 N	80.35 W
Toronto, L., Mex. (lä'gô-tô-rô'n-tō)	124	27.35 N	105.37 W
Toropets, Sov. Un. (tō'rô-pyĕts)	174	56.31 N	31.37 E
Toros Dağlari (Taurus Mts.), Tur. (tô'rŭs)	179	37.00 N	32.40 E
Torote (R.), Sp. (tô-rō'tä)	171a	40.36 N	3.24 W
Tor Pignatara (Neigh.), It.	66c	41.52 N	12.32 E
Torquay (Torbay), Eng. (tôr-kē')	162	50.30 N	3.26 W
Torra, Cerro (Mtn.), Col. (sĕ'r-rô-tō'r-rä)	142a	4.41 N	76.22 W
Torrance, Ca. (tŏr'rănc)	119a	33.50 N	118.20 W
Torre Annunziata, It. (tôr'rä ä-nōōn-tsē-ä'tä)	171c	40.31 N	14.27 E
Torreblanca, Sp.	171	40.18 N	0.12 E
Torre del Greco, It. (tôr'rå dĕl grā'kô)	171c	40.32 N	14.23 E
Torrejoncillo, Sp. (tôr'rā-hōn-thē'lyō)	170	39.54 N	6.26 W
Torrelavega, Sp. (tôr-rā'lä-vä'gä)	170	43.22 N	4.02 W
Torrellas de Llobregat, Sp.	65e	41.21 N	1.59 E
Torre Maggiore, It. (tôr'rā mäd-jō'rā)	172	40.41 N	15.18 E
Torrens, L., Austl. (tŏr-ĕns)	216	30.07 S	137.40 E
Torrente, Sp. (tôr-rĕn'tā)	171	39.25 N	0.28 W
Torreon, Mex. (tôr-rå-ōn')	124	25.32 N	103.26 W
Torres Is., Vanuatu (tôr'rĕs) (tŏr'ĕz)	215	13.18 N	165.59 E
Torres Martinez Ind. Res., Ca. (tôr'ĕz mär-tē'nĕz)	120	33.33 N	116.21 W
Torres Novas, Port. (tôr'rĕzh nō'väzh)	170	39.28 N	8.37 W
Torres Str., Austl. (tôr'rĕs)	207	10.30 S	141.30 E
Torres Vedras, Port. (tôr'rĕsh vă'drăzh)	170	39.08 N	9.18 W
Torrevieja, Sp. (tôr-rā-vyā'hä)	171	37.58 N	0.40 W
Torrijos, Phil. (tôr-rē'hōs)	207a	13.19 N	122.06 E
Torrington, Ct. (tŏr'ĭng-tŭn)	111	41.50 N	73.10 W
Torrington, Wy.	114	42.04 N	104.11 W
Torro, Sp. (tŏ'r-rō)	170	41.27 N	5.23 W
Tor Sapienza (Neigh.), It.	66c	41.54 N	12.35 E
Torsby, Swe. (tôrs'bü)	164	60.07 N	12.56 E
Torshälla, Swe. (tôrs'hĕl-ä)	164	59.26 N	16.21 E
Tórshavn, Faer. (tôrs-houn')	158	62.00 N	6.55 W
Tortola (I.), Vir. Is. (Br.) (tôr-tō'lä)	129b	18.34 N	64.40 W
Tortona, It. (tôr-tō'nä)	172	44.52 N	8.52 W
Tortosa, Sp. (tôr-tō'sä)	171	40.59 N	0.33 E
Tortosa, Cabo de (C.), Sp. (kä'bô-dĕ-tôr-tō-sä)	171	40.42 N	0.55 E
Tortue, Canal de la (Chan.), Hai. (tôr-tü')	135	20.05 N	73.20 W
Tortue, Ile de la (I.), Hai.	135	20.10 N	73.00 W
Tortue, Rivière de la (R.), Can. (lä tôr-tü')	95a	45.12 N	73.32 W
Tortuga, Isla la (I.), Ven. (ê's-lä-lä-tôr-tōō'gä)	143b	10.55 N	65.18 W
Tortuguitas, Arg.	60d	34.28 S	58.45 W
Toruń, Pol. (tō'rōōn')	167	53.01 N	18.37 E
Tõrva, Sov. Un. (t'r'vȧ)	174	58.02 N	25.56 E
Torzhok, Sov. Un. (tôr'zhôk)	174	57.03 N	34.53 E
Tosa-Wan (B.), Jap. (tō'sä wän)	205	33.14 N	133.39 E
Toscana (Reg.), It. (tôs-kä'nä)	172	43.23 N	11.08 E
Toshima (Neigh.), Jap.	69a	35.44 N	139.43 E
Tosna R., Sov. Un.	182c	59.38 N	30.52 E
Tosno, Sov. Un. (tôs'nô)	182c	59.32 N	30.52 E
Tostado, Arg. (tôs-tä'dô)	144	29.10 S	61.43 W
Tosya, Tur. (tôz'yȧ)	179	41.00 N	34.00 E
Totana, Sp. (tô-tä-nä)	170	37.45 N	1.28 W
Tot'ma, Sov. Un. (tôt'mȧ)	178	60.00 N	42.20 E
Totness, Sur.	143	5.51 N	56.17 W
Totonicapán, Guat. (tô-tō-nē-kä'pän)	132	14.55 N	91.20 W
Totoras, Arg. (tô-tô'räs)	141c	32.33 S	61.13 W
Totowa, NJ	55	40.54 N	74.13 W
Totsuka, Jap. (tôt'sōō-kä)	205	35.24 N	139.32 E
Tottenham, Eng. (tŏt'ĕn-ȧm)	156b	51.35 N	0.06 W
Tottenville (Neigh.), NY	55	40.31 N	74.15 W
Totteridge (Neigh.), Eng.	62	51.38 N	0.12 W
Tottington, Eng.	64b	53.37 N	2.20 W
Tottori, Jap. (tô'tô-rē)	205	35.30 N	134.15 E
Touba, Ivory Coast	228	8.17 N	7.41 W
Touba, Senegal	228	14.51 N	15.53 W
Toubkal Jebel (Mtn.), Mor.	224	31.15 N	7.46 W
Tougan, Burkina	228	13.04 N	3.04 W
Touggourt, Alg. (tōō-gōōrt') (tōō-gōōr')	224	33.09 N	6.07 E
Touil, Oued (R.), Alg. (tōō-ĕl')	160	34.42 N	21.6 E
Toul, Fr. (tōōl)	169	48.39 N	5.51 E
Toulnustouc (R.), Can.	104	50.23 N	67.55 W
Toulon, Fr. (tōō-lôn')	169	43.09 N	5.54 E
Toulouse, Fr. (tōō-lōōz')	168	43.37 N	1.27 E
Toungoo, Bur. (tŏ-ōōŋ-gōō')	206	19.00 N	96.29 E
Tourane, see Da Nang			
Tourcoing, Fr. (tōōr-kwan')	168	50.44 N	3.06 E
Tournan-en-Brie, Fr. (tōōr-nän-ĕn-brē')	169b	48.45 N	2.47 E
Tours, Fr. (tōōr)	168	47.23 N	0.39 E
Touside, Pic (Pk.), Chad (tōō-sē-dā')	225	21.10 N	16.30 E
Toussus-le-Noble, Fr.	64c	48.45 N	2.07 E
Tovdalselva (R.), Nor. (tôv-däls-ĕlvä)	164	58.23 N	8.16 E
Towaco, NJ	55	40.56 N	74.21 W
Towanda, Pa. (tô-wän'dȧ)	111	41.45 N	76.30 W
Tower Hamlets (Neigh.), Eng.	62	51.32 N	0.03 W
Tower of London (P. Int.), Eng.	62	51.30 N	0.05 W
Towers of Silence (P. Int.), India	67e	18.58 N	72.48 E
Town Bluff L., Tx.	125	30.52 N	94.30 W
Towner, ND (tou'nēr)	114	48.21 N	100.24 W
Town Reach (Str.), Asia	67c	1.28 N	103.44 E
Townsend, Ma. (toun'zĕnd)	105a	42.41 N	71.42 W
Townsend, Mt.	117	46.19 N	111.35 W
Townsend, Mt., Wa.	118a	47.52 N	123.03 W
Townsville, Austl. (tounz'vĭl)	143	19.18 S	146.50 E
Towson, Md. (tou'sŭn)	112e	39.24 N	76.36 W
Towuti, Danau (L.), Indon. (tô-wōō'tē)	206	3.00 S	121.45 E
Toxkan (R.), China	198	40.34 N	77.15 E
Toyah, Tx. (tô'yȧ)	124	31.19 N	103.46 W
Toyama, Jap. (tō'yä-mä)	205	36.42 N	137.14 E
Toyama-Wan (B.), Jap.	205	36.58 N	137.16 E
Toyoda, Jap.	69a	35.39 N	139.23 E
Toyohashi, Jap. (tō'yô-hä'shê)	205	34.44 N	137.21 E
Toyonaka, Jap. (tō'yô-nä'kȧ)	205b	34.47 N	135.28 E
Tozeur, Tun. (tô-zûr')	160	33.59 N	8.11 E
Traar (Neigh.), F.R.G.	63	51.23 N	6.36 E
Trabzon, Tur. (tráb'zôn)	179	41.00 N	39.45 E
Tracy, Ca. (trā'sē)	120	37.45 N	121.27 W
Tracy, Can.	104	46.00 N	73.13 W
Tracy, Mn.	114	44.13 N	95.37 W
Tracy City, Tn.	126	35.15 N	85.44 W
Trafalgar, Cabo (C.), Sp. (kä'bô-trä-fäl-gä'r)	170	36.10 N	6.02 W
Trafaria, Port.	65d	38.40 N	9.14 W
Trafford Park, Eng.	64b	53.28 N	2.20 W
Trafonomby (Mtn.), Mad.	227	24.32 S	46.35 E
Trail, Can. (trāl)	99	49.06 N	117.42 W
Traisen (R.), Aus.	157e	48.15 N	15.55 E
Traiskirchen, Aus.	157e	48.01 N	16.18 E
Trakai, Sov. Un. (trȧ-kāy)	165	54.38 N	24.59 E
Trakiszki, Pol. (trȧ-kē'-sh-kê)	167	54.16 N	23.07 E

PRONOUNCING INDEX

Tralee – Tunja 355

PLACE (Pronounciation)	PAGE	Lat. °′	Long. °′
Tralee, Ire. (trȧ-lē′)	162	52.16 N	9.20 W
Tranas, Swe. (trän′ôs)	164	58.03 N	14.56 E
Trancoso, Port. (träŋ-kō′so͞o)	170	40.46 N	7.23 W
Trangan, Pulau (I.), Indon. (träŋ′gän)	207	6.52 S	133.30 E
Trani, It. (trä′nē)	172	41.15 N	16.25 E
Tranmere, Eng.	64a	53.23 N	3.01 W
Transcaucasia (Reg.), Sov. Un.	155	41.17 N	44.30 E
Trans Himalayas (Mts.), **see Gangdisê Shan**			
Transvaal (Prov.), S. Afr. (trăns-väl′)	226	24.21 S	28.18 E
Transylvania (Reg.), Rom. (trăn-sĭl-vā′nĭ-ȧ)	167	46.30 N	22.35 E
Transylvanian Alps (Mts.), **see Carpaţii Meridionali**			
Trapani, It. (trä′pä-nė)	172	38.02 N	12.34 E
Trappes, Fr. (tráp)	169b	48.47 N	2.01 E
Traralgon, Austl. (tră′răl-gŏn)	216	38.15 S	146.33 E
Trarza (Reg.), Mauritania	228	17.35 N	15.15 W
Trasimeno, Lago (L.), Ir. (lä′gō trä-sė-mā′nō)	172	43.00 N	12.12 E
Trás-os-Montes (Mts.), Port. (träzh′ōzh mȯn′tāzh)	170	41.33 N	7.13 W
Traun R., Aus. (troun)	166	48.10 N	14.15 E
Traunstein, F.R.G. (troun′stīn)	166	47.52 N	12.38 E
Traverse City, Mi.	110	44.45 N	85.40 W
Traverse, L., Mn.-SD (trăv′ērs)	114	45.46 N	96.53 W
Travnik, Yugo. (träv′nēk)	172	44.13 N	17.43 E
Treasure I., Ca. (trĕzh′ēr)	118b	37.49 N	122.22 W
Trebbin, G.D.R. (trĕ′bēn)	157b	52.13 N	13.13 E
Třebič, Czech. (t′rzhĕ′bēch)	166	49.13 N	15.53 E
Trebinje, Yugo. (trȧ′bēn-yĕ)	173	42.43 N	18.21 E
Trebisov, Czech. (trĕ′bė-shôf)	167	48.36 N	21.32 E
Třeboň, Czech. (t′rzhĕ′bȯn′)	166	49.00 N	14.48 E
Tregrosse Is., Austl. (trė-grōs′)	215	18.08 S	150.53 E
Treinta y Tres, Ur. (trȧ-ēn′tā ē trās′)	144	33.14 S	54.17 W
Trélazé, Fr. (trā-lá-zā′)	168	47.27 N	0.32 W
Trelew, Arg. (trē′lū)	144	43.15 S	65.25 W
Trelleborg, Swe.	164	55.24 N	13.07 E
Tremblay-lès-Gonnesse, Fr.	64c	48.59 N	2.34 E
Tremiti, Isole (Is.), It. (ė′sō-lĕ trā-mē′tē)	172	42.07 N	16.33 E
Tremont (Neigh.), NY	55	40.51 N	73.55 W
Trenčín, Czech. (trĕn′chēn)	167	48.52 N	18.02 E
Trenque Lauquén, Arg. (trĕn′kĕ-lä′o͞o-kĕ′n)	144	35.50 S	62.44 W
Trent (R.), Can. (trĕnt)	103	44.15 N	77.55 W
Trent and Mersey Can., Eng. (trĕnt) (mûr zē)	156	53.11 N	2.24 W
Trentino-Alto Adige (Reg.), It.	172	46.16 N	10.47 E
Trento, It. (trĕn′tô)	172	46.04 N	11.07 E
Trenton, Can. (trĕn′tŭn)	97	44.05 N	77.35 W
Trenton, Can.	105	45.37 N	62.38 W
Trenton, Mi.	113b	42.08 N	83.12 W
Trenton, Mo.	123	40.05 N	93.36 W
Trenton, NJ	112a	40.13 N	74.46 W
Trenton, Tn.	126	35.57 N	88.55 W
Trepassey, Can. (trė-păs′ė)	105	46.44 N	53.22 W
Trepassey B., Can.	105	46.40 N	53.20 W
Treptow (Neigh.), G.D.R.	65a	52.29 N	13.29 E
Tres Arroyos, Arg. (trās′är-rō′yōs)	144	38.18 S	60.16 W
Três Coracoes, Braz. (trĕ′s kō-rä-zô′ĕs)	141a	21.41 S	45.14 W
Tres Cumbres, Mex. (trĕ′s ko͞o′m-brĕs)	131a	19.03 N	99.14 W
Três Lagoas, Braz. (trĕ′s lä-gô′ás)	143	20.48 S	51.42 W
Três Marias, Represa (Res.), Braz. (rĕ-prā′sä trĕs′ mä-rē′äs)	143	18.15 S	45.30 W
Tres Morros, Alto de (Mtn.), Col. (á′l-tō dĕ trĕ′s mô′r-rôs)	142a	7.08 N	76.10 W
Três Pontas, Braz. (trĕ′pô′n-täs)	141a	21.22 S	45.30 W
Três Pontas, Cabo das (C.), Ang.	230	10.23 S	13.32 E
Três Rios, Braz. (trĕ′s rė′ōs)	141a	22.07 S	43.13 W
Très-Saint Rédempteur, Can. (săɴ rā-dăɴp-tûr′)	95a	45.26 N	74.23 W
Tressancourt, Fr.	64c	48.55 N	2.00 E
Treuenbrietzen, G.D.R. (troi′ĕn-brē-tzĕn)	157b	52.06 N	12.52 E
Treviglio, It. (trā-vē′lyô)	172	45.30 N	9.34 E
Treviso, It. (trĕ-vė′sō)	172	45.39 N	12.15 E
Triangle, The (Reg.), Asia	198	26.00 N	98.00 E
Trichardt, S. Afr. (trĭ-ĸärt′)	223	26.32 N	29.16 E
Triel-sur-Seine, Fr.	64c	48.59 N	2.00 E
Trieste, It. (trė-ĕs′tā)	172	45.39 N	13.48 E
Trigueros, Sp. (trė-gā′rōs)	170	37.23 N	6.50 W
Trikala, Grc.	173	39.33 N	21.49 E
Trikora, Puncak (Pk.), Indon.	207	4.15 S	138.45 E
Trim Cr., Il. (trĭm)	113a	41.19 N	87.39 W
Trincomalee, Sri Lanka (trĭŋ-kȯ-mȧ-lē′)	197	8.39 N	81.12 E
Tring, Eng. (trĭng)	156b	51.46 N	0.40 W
Trinidad, Bol. (trē-nė-dhädh′)	142	14.48 S	64.43 W
Trinidad, Col. (trĭn′ĭdăd)	122	37.11 N	104.31 W
Trinidad, Cuba (trē-nė-dhädh′)	134	21.50 N	80.00 W
Trinidad, Ur.	141c	33.29 S	56.55 W
Trinidad (I.), Trin. (trĭn′ĭ-dăd)	143	10.00 N	61.00 W
Trinidad and Tobago, N. A. (trĭn′ĭ-dăd) (tȯ-bā′gō)	129	11.00 N	61.00 W
Trinidade, Ilha da (I.), Braz. (ė′lä dă trė-nē-dä-dĕ)	140	21.00 S	32.00 W
Trinidad R., Pan.	128a	8.55 N	80.01 W
Trinidad, Sierra de (Mts.), Cuba (sē-ĕ′r-rá dĕ trė-nė-dä′d)	134	21.50 N	79.55 W
Trinitaria, Mex. (trē-nē-tä′ryä)	131	16.09 N	92.04 W
Trinité, Mart.	133b	14.47 N	61.00 W
Trinity, Can. (trĭn′ĭ-tė)	105	48.59 N	53.55 W
Trinity, Tx.	125	30.52 N	95.27 W
Trinity (Is.), Ak.	107	56.25 N	153.15 W
Trinity (R.), **East Fk.,** Tx.	122	33.24 N	96.42 W
Trinity (R.), **West Fk.,** Tx.	123	33.22 N	98.26 W
Trinity B., Can.	105	48.00 N	53.40 W
Trinity R., Ca.	116	40.50 N	123.20 W
Trinity R., Tx.	125	30.50 N	95.09 W
Trino, It. (trē′nô)	172	45.11 N	8.16 E
Trion, Ga. (trī′ŏn)	126	34.32 N	85.18 W
Trípolis, Grc. (trĭ′pȯ-lĭs)	173	37.32 N	22.32 E
Tripoli, see Ţarābulus			
Tripolitania (Prov.), **see Tarābulus**			
Tripp, SD (trĭp)	114	43.13 N	97.58 W
Tripura (State), India	196	24.00 N	92.00 E
Tristan da Cunha Is., Alt. O. (trės-tän′dä ko͞on′yȧ)	232	35.30 S	12.15 W
Triste, Golfo (G.), Ven. (gȯl-fô trē′s-tĕ)	143b	10.40 N	68.05 W
Triticus Res., NY (trī tĭ-cŭs)	112a	41.20 N	73.36 W
Trivandrum, India (trė-vŭn′drŭm)	197	8.34 N	76.58 E
Trnava, Czech. (t′r′nȧ-vȧ)	167	48.22 N	17.34 E
Trobriand Is., Pap. N. Gui. (trō-brė-ănd′)	207	8.25 S	151.45 E
Trogir, Yugo. (trȯ′gēr)	172	43.32 N	16.17 E
Troice-Lykovo (Neigh.), Sov. Un.	66b	55.47 N	37.24 E
Trois-Rivières, Can. (trwä′rė-vyâ′)	97	46.21 N	72.35 W
Troitsk, Sov. Un. (trô′ėtsk)	182a	54.06 N	61.34 E
Troitsko-Pechorsk, Sov. Un. (trô′ĭtsk-ȯ-pyĕ-chôrsk′)	180	62.18 N	56.07 E
Troitskoye, Sov. Un.	175	47.39 N	30.16 E
Trollhättan, Swe. (trôl′hĕt-ĕn)	164	58.17 N	12.17 E
Trollheim (Mts.), Nor. (trȯll-hĕĭm)	164	62.48 N	9.05 E
Trombay (Neigh.), India	67e	19.02 N	72.57 E
Tromsö, Nor. (trôm′sû)	158	69.38 N	19.12 E
Trona, Ca. (trō′nȧ)	120	35.49 N	117.20 W
Tronador, Cerro (Mtn.), Arg. (sĕ′r-rȯ trō-nä′dȯr)	144	41.17 S	71.56 W
Troncoso, Mex. (trȯn-kȯ′sō)	130	22.43 N	102.22 W
Trondheim, Nor. (trôn′hȧm)	164	63.25 N	11.35 E
Tropar′ovo (Neigh.), Sov. Un.	66b	55.39 N	37.29 E
Trosa, Swe. (trȯ′sä)	164	58.54 N	17.25 E
Trottiscliffe, Eng.	62	51.19 N	0.21 E
Trout (L.), Can.	97	51.16 N	92.46 W
Trout (L.), Can.	96	61.10 N	121.30 W
Trout Cr., Or.	116	42.18 N	118.31 W
Troutdale, Or. (trout′dāl)	118c	45.32 N	122.23 W
Trout L., Can.	101	51.13 N	93.20 W
Trout Lake, Mi.	115	46.20 N	85.02 W
Trouville, Fr. (tro͞o-vēl′)	168	49.23 N	0.05 E
Troy, Al. (troi)	126	31.47 N	85.46 W
Troy, Il.	119e	38.44 N	89.53 W
Troy, Ks.	123	39.46 N	95.07 W
Troy, Mo.	123	38.56 N	99.57 W
Troy, Mt.	116	48.28 N	115.56 W
Troy, NY	111	42.45 N	73.45 W
Troy, NC	127	35.21 N	79.58 W
Troy, Oh.	110	40.00 N	84.10 W
Troyes Fr. (trwä)	168	48.18 N	4.03 E
Troy Ruins, Tur.	173	39.59 N	26.14 E
Troyville (Neigh.), S. Afr.	71b	26.12 S	28.04 E
Trstenik, Yugo. (t′r′stĕ-nėk)	173	43.36 N	20.00 E
Trst, see Trieste			
Trubchëvsk, Sov. Un. (tro͝op′chĕfsk)	174	52.36 N	32.46 E
Trucial States, see United Arab Emirates			
Truckee, Ca. (trŭk′ė)	120	39.20 N	120.12 W
Truckee (R.), Ca.-Nv.	120	39.25 N	120.07 W
Truganina, Austl.	211a	37.49 N	144.44 E
Trujillo, Col. (tro͞o-ĸė′l-yō)	142a	4.10 N	76.20 W
Trujillo, Hond. (tro͞o-ĸēl′yō)	132	15.55 N	85.58 W
Trujillo, Peru	142	8.08 S	79.00 W
Trujillo, Sp. (tro͞o-ĸė′l-yȯ)	170	39.27 N	5.50 W
Trujillo, Ven.	142	9.15 N	70.28 W
Trujillo (R.), Mex.	130	23.12 N	103.10 W
Trujin, L., Dom. Rep. (tro͞o-ĸēn′)	135	17.45 N	71.25 W
Trumann, Ar. (tro͞o′măn)	123	35.41 N	90.31 W
Trŭn, Bul. (trŭn)	173	42.49 N	22.39 E
Truro, Can. (tro͞o′rō)	104	45.22 N	63.16 W
Truro, Eng.	162	50.17 N	5.05 W
Trussville, Al. (trŭs′vĭl)	112h	33.37 N	86.37 W
Trust Territory of the Pacific Islands, Pac. O.	208	10.00 N	155.00 E
Truth or Consequences, NM (tro͞oth ŏr kŏn′sė-kwĕn-sĭs)	121	33.10 N	107.20 W
Trutnov, Czech. (tro͝ot′nȯf)	166	50.36 N	15.36 E
Trzcianka, Pol. (tchyän′kȧ)	166	53.02 N	16.27 E
Trzebiatow, Pol. (tchĕ-byä′to͞o-v)	166	54.03 N	15.16 E
Tsaidam Basin, China (tsī-däm)	198	37.19 N	94.08 E
Tsala Apopka (R.), Fl. (tsä′lȧ ă-pŏp′kȧ)	127	28.57 N	82.11 W
Tsast Bogd (Mt.), Mong.	198	46.44 N	92.34 E
Tsavo Natl. Pk., Ken.	231	2.35 S	38.45 E
Tsawwassen Ind. Res., Can.	118d	49.03 N	123.11 W
Tselinograd, Sov. Un. (tsĕ′lē-nȯ-gră′d)	180	51.10 N	71.43 E
Tsentral′nyy-Kospashskiy, Sov. Un. (tsĕn-träl′nyĭ-kôs-pȧsh′skĭ)	182a	59.03 N	57.48 E
Tshela, Zaire (tshā′lȧ)	230	4.59 S	12.56 E
Tshikapa, Zaire (tshė-kä′pä)	230	6.25 S	20.48 E
Tshofa, Zaire	230	5.14 S	25.15 E
Tshuapa (R.), Zaire	230	10.15 S	21.25 E
Tsiafajovona (Mtn.), Mad.	227	19.17 S	47.27 E
Tsimlyanskiy (Res.), Sov. Un. (tsym-lyă′ns-kēė)	179	47.50 N	43.40 E
Tsing I., China	68c	22.21 N	114.05 E
Tsin Shui Wan (B.), Hong Kong	68c	22.13 N	114.10 E
Tsiribihina (R.), Mad. (tsē′rė-bē-hė-nä′)	227	19.45 S	43.30 E
Tsitsa (R.), S. Afr. (tsė′tsȧ)	227c	31.28 S	28.53 E
Tsolo, S. Afr. (tsō′lō)	227c	31.19 S	28.47 E
Tsomo, S. Afr.	227c	32.03 S	27.49 E
Tsomo (R.), S. Afr.	227c	31.53 S	27.48 E
Tsu, Jap. (tso͞o)	205	34.42 N	136.31 E
Tsuchiura, Jap. (tso͞o′chė-o͞o-rä)	205	36.04 N	140.09 E
Tsuda, Jap. (tso͞o′dä)	205b	34.48 N	135.43 E
Tsugaru Kaikyō (Str.), Jap. (tso͞o′gä-ro͞o kī′kyō)	204	41.25 N	140.20 E
Tsukumono (Neigh.), Jap.	69b	34.50 N	135.11 E
Tsumeb, Namibia (tso͞o′mĕb)	226	19.10 S	17.45 E
Tsunashima, Jap. (tso͞o′nä-shė′mä)	205a	35.32 N	139.37 E
Tsunashima (Neigh.), Jap.	69a	35.32 N	139.38 E
Tsuruga, Jap. (tso͞o′ro͞o-gä)	205	35.39 N	136.04 E
Tsurugi San (Mtn.), Jap. (tso͞o′ro͞o-gė sän)	205	33.52 N	134.07 E
Tsurumi (R.), Jap.	69a	35.29 N	139.41 E
Tsuruoka, Jap. (tso͞o′ro͞o-ō′kä)	204	38.43 N	139.51 E
Tsurusaki, Jap. (tso͞o′ro͞o-sä′kė)	205	33.15 N	131.42 E
Tsu Shima (I.), Jap. (tso͞o shė′mä)	205	34.28 N	129.30 E
Tsushima Kaikyō (Str.), Asia (tso͞o′shė-mä kī′kyō)	205	33.52 N	129.30 E
Tsuwano, Jap. (tso͞o′wȧ-nȯ′)	205	34.28 N	131.47 E
Tsu Wan (Quanwan), China	68c	22.22 N	114.07 E
Tsuyama, Jap. (tso͞o′yä-mä′)	205	35.05 N	134.00 E
Tua (R.), Port. (to͞o′ä)	170	41.23 N	7.18 W
Tualatin (R.), Or. (to͞o′ȧ-lā-tĭn)	118c	45.25 N	122.54 W
Tuamoto, Iles, Fr. Polynesia (to͞o-ä-mō′to͞o)	209	19.00 S	141.20 W
Tuapse, Sov. Un. (to͞o′ȧp-sĕ)	179	44.00 N	39.10 E
Tuareg (Reg.), Alg.	224	21.26 N	2.51 E
Tubarão, Braz. (to͞o-bä-rouɴ′)	144	28.23 N	48.56 W
Tübingen, F.R.G. (tü′bĭng-ĕn)	166	48.33 N	9.05 E
Tubinskiy, Sov. Un. (tû bĭn′skĭ)	182a	52.53 N	58.15 E
Tubruq, Libya	225	32.03 N	24.04 E
Tucacas, Ven. (to͞o-kä′käs)	143b	10.48 N	68.20 W
Tuckahoe, NY	55	40.57 N	73.50 W
Tucker, Ga. (tŭk′ēr)	112c	33.51 N	84.13 W
Tucson, Az. (to͞o-sŏn′)	121	32.15 N	111.00 W
Tucumán, Arg. (to͞o-ko͞o-män′)	144	26.52 S	65.08 W
Tucumán (Prov.), Arg.	144	26.30 S	65.30 W
Tucumcari, NM (to͞o′kŭm-kâr-ė)	122	35.11 N	103.43 W
Tucupita, Ven. (to͞o-ko͞o-pė′tä)	142	9.00 N	62.09 W
Tucuruí, Braz. (to͞o-ko͞o-to͞o-ē′)	143	3.34 S	49.44 W
Tudela, Sp. (to͞o-dhā′lä)	170	42.03 N	1.37 W
Tugaloo (R.), Ga.-SC (tŭg′ȧ-lo͞o)	126	34.35 N	83.05 W
Tugela (R.), S. Afr. (to͞o-gel′ȧ)	227c	28.50 S	30.52 E
Tugela Ferry, S. Afr.	227c	28.44 S	30.27 E
Tug Fork (R.), WV (tŭg)	110	37.50 N	82.30 W
Tuguegarao, Phil. (to͞o-gā-gȧ-rä′ō)	207a	17.37 N	121.44 E
Tuhai (R.), China (to͞o-hī)	200	37.05 N	116.56 E
Tuinplaas, S. Afr.	223d	24.54 S	28.46 E
Tujunga, Ca. (to͞o-jŭŋ′gȧ)	119a	34.15 N	118.16 W
Tukan, Sov. Un. (to͞o′kȧn)	182a	53.52 N	57.25 E
Tukangbesi, Kepulauan (Is.), Indon.	207	6.00 S	124.15 E
Tūkrah, Libya	225	32.34 N	20.47 E
Tuktoyaktuk, Can. (to͞ok-tō-yăk′to͞ok)	96	69.32 N	132.37 W
Tukums, Sov. Un. (to͞o′ko͞oms)	165	56.57 N	23.09 E
Tukuyu, Tan. (to͞o-ko͞o′yȧ)	226	9.13 S	33.43 E
Tukwila, Wa. (tŭk′wĭ-lȧ)	118a	47.28 N	122.16 W
Tula, Mex. (to͞o′lä)	130	20.04 N	99.22 W
Tula, Sov. Un. (to͞o′lȧ)	174	54.12 N	37.37 E
Tula (Oblast), Sov. Un.	174	53.45 N	37.19 E
Tula (R.), Mex. (to͞o′lä)	130	20.40 N	99.27 W
Tulagai (I.), Sol. Is. (to͞o-lä′gē)	215	9.15 S	160.17 E
Tulalip, Wa. (tū-lă′lĭp)	118a	48.04 N	122.18 W
Tulalip Ind. Res., Wa.	118a	48.06 N	122.16 W
Tulancingo, Mex. (to͞o-län-sĭŋ′gō)	130	20.04 N	98.24 W
Tulangbawang (R.), Indon.	206	4.17 S	105.00 E
Tulare, Ca. (to͞o-lä′rȧ) (tul-âr′)	120	36.12 N	119.22 W
Tulare Basin, Ca.	120	35.57 N	120.18 W
Tularosa, NM (to͞o-lȧ-rō′zȧ)	121	33.05 N	106.05 W
Tulcán, Ec. (to͞ol-kän′)	142	0.44 N	77.52 W
Tulcea, Rom. (to͞ol′chȧ)	175	45.10 N	28.47 E
Tul′chin, Sov. Un. (to͞ol′chĕn)	175	48.42 N	28.53 E
Tulcingo, Mex. (to͞ol-sĭŋ′gō)	130	18.03 N	98.27 W
Tule (R.), Ca. (to͞ol′lȧ)	120	36.08 N	118.50 W
Tule River Ind. Res., Ca. (to͞o′lȧ)	120	36.05 N	118.35 W
Tuli, Zimb. (to͞o′lė)	226	20.58 S	29.12 E
Tulia, Tx. (to͞o′lĭ-ȧ)	122	34.32 N	101.46 W
Tulijá (R.), Mex. (to͞o-lē-ĸȧ′)	131	17.28 N	92.11 W
Tulik Vol., Ak. (to͞o′lĭk)	107a	53.28 N	168.10 W
Tūlkarm, Jordan (to͞ol kärm)	191a	32.19 N	35.02 E
Tullahoma, Tn. (tŭl-ȧ-hō′mȧ)	126	35.21 N	86.12 W
Tullamarine, Austl.	70b	37.41 S	144.52 E
Tullamore, Ire. (tŭl-ȧ-mōr′)	162	53.15 N	7.29 W
Tulle, Fr. (tül)	168	45.15 N	1.45 E
Tulln, Aus. (to͞oln)	157e	48.21 N	16.04 E
Tullner Feld (Reg.), Aus.	157e	48.20 N	15.59 E
Tulpetlac, Mex. (to͞ol-pȧ-tlȧk′)	131a	19.33 N	99.04 W
Tulsa, Ok. (tŭl′sȧ)	123	36.08 N	95.58 W
Tuluá, Col. (to͞o-lo͞o-ȧ′)	142a	4.06 N	76.12 W
Tulum, Mex. (to͞o-lo͞o′m)	132a	20.17 N	87.26 W
Tulun, Sov. Un. (to͞o-lo͞on′)	180	54.29 N	100.43 E
Tumaco, Col. (to͞o-mä′kô)	142	1.41 N	78.44 W
Tuma R., Nic. (to͞o′mä)	132	13.07 N	85.32 W
Tumba, Lac (L.), Zaire (to͞om′bä)	230	0.50 S	17.45 E
Tumbes, Peru (to͞o′m-bĕs)	142	3.39 S	80.27 W
Tumbiscatío, Mex. (to͞om-bė-skȧ-tē′ō)	130	18.32 N	102.23 W
Tumbo (I.), Can.	118d	48.49 N	123.04 W
Tumen, China (to͞o-mŭn)	202	43.00 N	129.50 E
Tumen (R.), China	204	42.08 N	128.40 E
Tumeremo, Ven. (to͞o-mȧ-rā′mō)	143	7.15 N	61.28 W
Tumkūr, India	197	13.22 N	77.05 E
Tumuacacori Natl. Mon., Az. (to͞o-mä-kä′kȧ-rē)	121	31.36 N	110.20 W
Tumuc-Humac Mts., S. A. (to͞o-mo͞ok′o͞o-mäk′)	143	2.15 N	54.50 W
Tunas de Zaza, Cuba (to͞o′näs dā zä′zä)	134	21.40 N	79.35 W
Tunbridge Wells, Eng. (tŭn′brĭj welz′)	162	51.05 N	0.09 E
Tundra (Reg.), Sov. Un.	180	70.45 N	84.00 E
Tunduru, Tan.	231	11.07 S	37.21 E
Tungabhadra Res., India	196	15.26 N	75.57 E
Tungpa, China (to͞ong-bä)	200	35.56 N	116.19 E
Tuni, India	197	17.29 N	82.38 E
Tunica, Ms. (tū′nĭ-kȧ)	126	34.41 N	90.23 W
Tunis, Tun. (tū′nĭs)	224	36.59 N	10.06 E
Tunis, Golfe de (G.), Tun.	159	37.06 N	10.43 E
Tunisia, Afr. (tu-nĭzh′ė-ȧ)	222	35.00 N	10.11 E
Tunja, Col. (to͞o′n-hȧ)	142	5.32 N	73.19 W

ng-sing; nŋ-banŋk; ɴ-nasalized n; nŏd; cŏmmit; ōld; ȯbey; ŏrder; oi-boil; fo͞od; fo͝ot; ou-out; s-soft; sh-dish; th-thin; pūre; ůnite; ûrn; stŭd; circŭs; ü-as in French tu; ′-indeterminate vowel.

356 Tunkhannock – Union de Tula

PLACE (Pronounciation)	PAGE	Lat. °′	Long. °′
Tunkhannock, Pa. (tŭnk-hăn'ŭk)	111	41.35 N	75.55 W
Tunnel (R.), Wa. (tŭn'ĕl)	118a	47.48 N	123.04 W
Tuoji Dao (I.), China (twô-jyē dou)	200	38.11 N	120.45 E
Tuolumne (R.), Ca. (twô-lŭm'nē)	120	37.35 N	120.37 W
Tuostakh (R.), Sov. Un.	181	67.09 N	137.30 E
Tupã, Braz. (tōō-pá)	143	21.47 S	50.33 W
Tupelo, Ms. (tū'pĕ-lō)	126	34.14 N	88.43 W
Tupinambaranas, Ilha (I.), Braz. (ē'lä-tōō-pē-näɴ-bä-rä'näs)	143	3.04 S	58.09 W
Tupiza, Bol. (tōō-pē'zä)	142	21.26 S	65.43 W
Tupper Lake, NY (tŭp'ēr)	111	44.15 N	74.25 W
Tuquerres, Col. (tōō-kĕ'r-rĕs)	142	1.12 N	77.44 W
Tura, Sov. Un. (tŏŏr'á)	180	64.08 N	99.58 E
Turbio (R.), Mex. (tōōr-byō)	130	20.28 N	101.40 W
Turbo, Col. (tōō'bō)	142	8.02 N	76.43 W
Turda, Rom. (tŏŏr'dä)	167	46.35 N	23.47 E
Turfan Depression, China	198	42.16 N	90.00 E
Turffontein (Neigh.), S. Afr.	71b	26.15 S	28.02 E
Turgay, Sov. Un. (tōōr'gī)	180	49.42 N	63.39 E
Turgayka (R.), Sov. Un. (tōōr-gī'kă)	155	49.44 N	66.15 E
Tŭrgovishte, Bul.	173	43.14 N	26.36 E
Turgutlu, Tur.	179	38.30 N	27.20 E
Türi, Sov. Un. (tü'rĭ)	165	58.49 N	25.29 E
Turia (R.), Sp. (tōō'ryä)	170	40.12 N	1.18 W
Turicato, Mex. (tōō-rē-kä'tō)	130	19.03 N	101.24 W
Turiguano (I.), Cuba (tōō-rē-gwä'nō)	134	22.20 N	78.35 W
Turin, see Torino			
Turka, Sov. Un. (tōōr'kå)	167	49.10 N	23.02 E
Turkestan, Sov. Un. (tûr-kĕ-stăn') (tōōr-kĕ-stan')	180	42.40 N	65.00 E
Turkestan (Reg.), Sov. Un.	176	43.27 N	62.14 E
Turkey, Eur.-Asia	190	38.45 N	32.00 E
Turkey (R.), Ia. (tûrk'ē)	115	43.20 N	92.16 W
Turkmen (S. S. R.), Sov. Un. (tōōrk-mĕn')	176	40.46 N	56.01 E
Turks (Is.), Turks & Caicos Is. (tûrks)	129	21.40 N	71.45 W
Turks I. Pass, Turks & Caicos Is.	135	21.15 N	71.25 W
Turku (Åbo), **Fin.** (tōōr'kōō) (ô'bō)	165	60.28 N	22.12 E
Turlock, Ca. (tûr'lŏk)	120	37.30 N	120.51 W
Turneffe (I.), Belize	132a	17.25 N	87.43 W
Turner, Ks. (tûr'nēr)	119f	39.05 N	94.42 W
Turner Sd., Ba.	134	24.20 N	78.05 W
Turners Pen, S.L.	228	7.20 N	12.40 W
Turnhout, Bel. (tŭrn-hout')	157a	51.19 N	4.58 E
Turnov, Czech. (tōōr'nôf)	166	50.36 N	15.12 E
Turnu-Măgurel, Rom.	173a	43.54 N	24.49 E
Turpan, China (tōō-är-pän)	198	43.06 N	88.41 E
Turquino, Pico de (Pk.), Cuba (pē'kō dā tōōr-kē'nō)	134	20.00 N	76.50 W
Turranmurra, Austl.	70a	33.44 S	151.08 E
Turrialba, C. R. (tōōr-ryä'l-bä)	133	9.54 N	83.41 W
Turtkul', Sov. Un. (tōōrt-kōōl')	155	41.28 N	61.02 E
Turtle (R.), Can.	101	49.20 N	92.30 W
Turtle B., Tx.	125a	29.48 N	94.38 W
Turtle Cr., SD	114	44.40 N	98.53 W
Turtle Creek, Pa.	57b	40.25 N	79.49 W
Turtle Mountain Ind. Res., ND	114	48.45 N	99.57 W
Turtle Mts., ND	114	48.57 N	100.11 W
Turukhansk, Sov. Un. (tōō-rōō-ĸänsk')	180	66.03 N	88.39 E
Turya R., Sov. Un. (tōōr'yá)	167	51.18 N	24.55 E
Tuscaloosa, Al. (tŭs-kå-lōō'så)	126	33.10 N	87.35 W
Tuscarora, Nv. (tŭs-kå-rō'rå)	116	41.18 N	116.15 W
Tuscarora Ind. Res., NY	113c	43.10 N	78.51 W
Tuscola, Il. (tŭs-kō-lå)	110	39.50 N	88.20 W
Tuscumbia, Al. (tŭs-kŭm'bĭ-å)	126	34.41 N	87.42 W
Tushino, Sov. Un. (tōō'shĭ-nô)	182b	55.51 N	37.24 E
Tuskegee, Al. (tŭs-kē'gē)	126	32.25 N	85.40 W
Tustin, Ca. (tŭs'tĭn)	119a	33.44 N	117.49 W
Tutayev, Sov. Un. (tōō-tå-yĕf')	174	57.53 N	39.34 E
Tutbury, Eng. (tŭt'bēr-ē)	156	52.52 N	1.51 W
Tuticorin, India (tōō-tē-kô-rĭn')	197	8.51 N	78.09 E
Tutitlan, Mex. (tōō-tē-tlä'n)	131a	19.38 N	99.10 W
Tutóia, Braz. (tōō-tō'yá)	143	2.42 S	42.21 W
Tutrakan, Bul.	173	44.02 N	26.36 E
Tuttle Creek Res., Ks.	123	39.30 N	96.38 W
Tuttlingen, F.R.G. (tŏŏt'lĭng-ĕn)	166	47.58 N	8.50 E
Tutwiler, Ms. (tŭt'wĭ-lēr)	126	34.01 N	90.25 W
Tuva Aut. Oblast, Sov. Un.	180	51.15 N	90.45 E
Tuvalu, Oceania	208	5.20 S	174.00 E
Tuwayq, Jabal (Mts.), Sau. Ar.	192	20.45 N	46.30 E
Tuxedo, Md.	56d	38.55 N	76.55 W
Tuxedo Park, NY (tŭk-sē'dō pärk)	112a	41.11 N	74.11 W
Tuxford, Eng. (tŭks'fērd)	156	53.14 N	0.54 W
Tuxpan, Mex. (tōōs'pän)	130	19.34 N	103.22 W
Túxpan, Mex.	131	20.57 N	97.26 W
Túxpan (R.), Mex. (tōōs'pän)	131	20.55 N	97.52 W
Túxpan, Arrecife (Rf.), Mex. (är-rē-sē'fē-tōō'x-pä'n)	131	21.01 N	97.12 W
Tuxtepec, Mex. (tōōs-tå-pĕk')	131	18.06 N	96.09 W
Tuxtla Gutiérrez, Mex. (tōōs'tlä gōō-tyår'rĕs)	131	16.44 N	93.08 W
Tuy, Sp.	158	42.07 N	8.49 W
Tuy (R.), Ven. (tōō'ē)	143b	10.15 N	66.03 W
Tuyra R., Pan. (tōō-ē'rá)	133	7.55 N	77.37 W
Tuz Gölü (L.), Tur.	179	39.00 N	33.30 E
Tuzigoot Natl. Mon., Az.	121	34.40 N	111.52 W
Tuzla, Yugo. (tōōz'lå)	173	44.33 N	18.46 E
Tvedestrand, Nor. (tvĭ'dhĕ-stränd)	164	58.39 N	8.54 E
Tveitsund, Nor. (tvåt'sōōnd)	164	59.03 N	8.29 E
Tver, see Kalinin			
Tvertsa (L.), Sov. Un. (tvĕr'tså)	154	56.58 N	35.22 E
Tweed (R.), Scot. (twēd)	162	55.32 N	2.35 W
Tweeling, S. Afr. (twē'lĭng)	223d	27.34 S	28.31 E
Twelvemile Cr., NY (twĕlv'mīl)	113c	43.13 N	78.58 W
Twenty Mile Cr., Can. (twĕn'tĭ mīl)	95d	43.09 N	79.49 W
Twickenham, Eng. (twĭk''n-ăm)	156b	51.26 N	0.20 W
Twillingate, Can. (twĭl'ĭn-gāt)	105	49.39 N	54.46 W
Twin Bridges, Mt. (twĭn brĭ-jĕz)	117	45.34 N	112.17 W
Twin Falls, Id. (fôls)	117	42.33 N	114.29 W
Twinsburg, Oh. (twĭnz'bûrg)	113d	41.19 N	81.26 W
Twitchell Res., Ca.	120	34.50 N	120.10 W
Two Butte Cr., Co. (tōō būt)	122	37.39 N	102.45 W
Two Harbors, Mn.	115	47.00 N	91.42 W
Two Prairie Bay, Ar. (prâ'rĭ bī ōō')	123	34.48 N	92.07 W
Two Rivers, Wi. (rĭv'ērz)	115	44.09 N	87.36 W
Tyabb, Austl.	211a	38.16 S	145.11 E
Tyachev, Sov. Un. (tyä'chĕf)	167	48.01 N	23.42 E
Tyasmin (R.), Sov. Un. (tyås-mĭn')	175	49.14 N	32.23 E
Tylden, S. Afr. (tĭl-dĕn)	227c	32.08 S	27.06 E
Tyldesley, Eng. (tĭldz'lē)	156	53.32 N	2.28 W
Tyler, Mn. (tī'lēr)	114	44.18 N	96.08 W
Tyler, Tx.	125	32.21 N	95.19 W
Tyler Park, Va.	56d	38.52 N	77.12 W
Tylertown, Ms. (tī'lēr-toun)	126	31.08 N	90.06 W
Tyndall, SD (tĭn'dål)	114	42.58 N	97.52 W
Tyndinskiy, Sov. Un.	181	55.22 N	124.45 E
Tyne (R.), Eng. (tīn)	162	54.59 N	1.56 W
Tynemouth, Eng. (tīn'mŭth)	162	55.04 N	1.39 W
Tynest, Nor. (tün'sĕt)	164	62.17 N	10.45 E
Tyngsboro, Ma. (tĭnj-bûr'ô)	105a	42.40 N	71.27 W
Tyre, see Şūr			
Tyrifjorden (Fd.), Nor.	164	60.03 N	10.25 E
Tyrone, NM (tī'rōn)	121	32.40 N	108.20 W
Tyrone, Pa.	111	40.40 N	78.15 W
Tyrrell, L., Austl. (tir'ĕll)	216	35.12 S	143.00 E
Tyrrhenian Sea, It. (tĭr-rē'nĭ-ăn)	159	40.10 N	12.15 E
Tysons Corner, Va.	56d	38.55 N	77.14 W
Tyub-Karagan, Mys (C.), Sov. Un.	179	44.30 N	50.10 E
Tyukalinsk, Sov. Un. (tyōō-kå-lĭnsk')	180	56.03 N	71.43 E
Tyukyan (R.), Sov. Un. (tyōōk'yán)	181	65.42 N	116.09 E
Tyuleniy (I.), Sov. Un.	179	44.30 N	48.00 E
Tyumen', Sov. Un. (tyōō-mĕn')	180	57.02 N	65.28 E
Tyura-Tam, Sov. Un.	180	46.00 N	63.15 E
Tzucacab, Mex. (tzōō-kä-kä'b)	132a	20.06 N	89.03 W

U

PLACE (Pronounciation)	PAGE	Lat. °′	Long. °′
Uarc, Ras (C.), Mor.	160	35.31 N	2.45 W
Uaupés, Braz. (wä-ōō'pās)	142	0.02 S	67.03 W
Ubá, Braz. (ōō-bå')	141a	21.08 S	42.55 W
Ubangi (Oubangui) (R.), Afr. (ōō-bäŋ'gē)	230	4.30 N	20.35 E
Ubatuba, Braz. (ōō-bå-tōō'bá)	141a	23.25 S	45.06 W
Ubeda, Sp. (ōō'bå-dä)	170	38.01 N	3.23 W
Uberaba, Braz. (ōō-bå-rä'bá)	143	19.47 S	47.47 W
Uberlândia, Braz. (ōō-bĕr-lá'n-dyä)	143	18.54 S	48.11 W
Ubombo, S. Afr. (ōō-bôm'bô)	226	27.33 S	32.13 E
Ubon Ratchathani, Thai. (ōō'bŭn rä'chätá-nē)	206	15.15 N	104.52 E
Ubort' (R.), Sov. Un. (ōō-bôrt')	175	51.18 N	27.43 E
Ubrique, Sp. (ōō-brē'kå)	170	36.43 N	5.36 W
Ubundi (Ponthierville), Zaire	231	00.21 S	25.29 E
Ucayali (R.), Peru (ōō'kä-yä'lē)	142	8.58 S	74.13 W
Uccle, Bel. (ū'kl')	157a	50.48 N	4.17 E
Uchaly, Sov. Un. (û-chä'lĭ)	182a	54.22 N	59.28 E
Uch-Aral, Sov. Un. (ŏŏch'å-ral')	180	46.14 N	80.58 E
Uchiko, Jap. (ōō'chē-kō)	205	33.30 N	132.39 E
Uchinoura, Jap. (ōō'chē-nô-ōō'rá)	205	31.16 N	131.03 E
Uchinskoye Vdkhr. (Res.), Sov. Un. (ōōch-ĕn'skô-yĕ vô-dô-ĸrá-nĭ'li-shchĕ)	182b	56.08 N	37.44 E
Uchiura-Wan (B.), Jap. (ōō'chē-ōō'rä wän)	204	42.20 N	140.44 E
Uchur (R.), Sov. Un. (ōō-chŏŏr')	181	58.27 N	131.34 E
Ückendorf (Neigh.), F.R.G.	63	51.30 N	7.07 E
Uda (R.), Sov. Un. (ōō'dá)	181	52.28 N	110.51 E
Uda (R.), Sov. Un.	181	53.54 N	131.29 E
Udaipur, India (ōō-dŭ'ē-pōōr)	196	24.41 N	73.41 E
Uday (R.), Sov. Un. (ōō-dī')	175	50.45 N	32.13 E
Uddevalla, Swe. (ŏŏd'dĕ-väl-á)	164	58.21 N	11.55 E
Udine, It. (ōō'dē-nå)	172	46.05 N	13.14 E
Udmurt (A. S. S. R.), Sov. Un.	180	57.00 N	53.00 E
Udon Thani, Thai.	206	17.31 N	102.51 E
Udskaya Guba (B.), Sov. Un.	143	55.00 N	136.30 E
Ueda, Jap. (wä'dä)	205	36.26 N	138.16 E
Uedesheim (Neigh.), F.R.G.	63	51.10 N	6.48 E
Uekermünde, G.D.R. (ü'kĕr-mün-dĕ)	166	53.43 N	14.01 E
Uele R., Zaire (wä'lå)	230	3.55 N	23.30 E
Uerdingen (Neigh.), F.R.G.	63	51.21 N	6.39 E
Ufa, Sov. Un. (ōō'fa)	182a	54.45 N	55.57 E
Ufa (R.), Sov. Un.	178	56.00 N	57.05 E
Ugab (R.), Namibia (ōō'gäb)	226	21.10 S	14.00 E
Ugalla (R.), Tan. (ōō-gä'lä)	231	6.15 S	32.30 E
Uganda, Afr. (ōō-gän'dä) (û-găn'då)	222	2.00 N	32.28 E
Ugashik L., Ak. (ōō'gá-shĕk)	107	57.36 N	157.10 W
Ugie, S. Afr. (ōō'jē)	227c	31.13 S	28.14 E
Uglegorsk, Sov. Un. (ōō-gl-gôrsk)	181	49.00 N	142.31 E
Ugleural'sk, Sov. Un. (ōōg-lĕ-ōō-rálsk')	182a	58.58 N	57.35 E
Uglich, Sov. Un. (ōōg-lĕch')	174	57.33 N	38.19 E
Uglitskiy, Sov. Un. (ōōg-lĭt'skĭ)	182a	53.50 N	60.18 E
Uglovka, Sov. Un. (ōōg-lôf'ká)	174	58.14 N	33.24 E
Ugra (R.), Sov. Un. (ōōg'rá)	174	54.43 N	34.20 E
Ugŭrchin, Bul.	173	43.06 N	24.23 E
Uhrichsville, Oh. (ū'rĭks-vĭl)	110	40.25 N	81.20 W
Uiju, Kor. (ōō'ējōō)	204	40.09 N	124.33 E
Uil (R.), Sov. Un. (ōō-ēl')	179	49.30 N	55.10 E
Uinkaret Plat., Az. (ū-ĭn'kâr-ĕt)	121	36.43 N	113.15 W
Uinskoye, Sov. Un. (ōō-ĭn'skô-yĕ)	182a	56.53 N	56.25 E
Uinta (R.), Ut. (ū-ĭn'tá)	121	40.25 N	109.55 W
Uintah, Ut. (ū-ĭn'tå)	119b	41.09 N	111.56 W
Uintah and Ouray Ind. Res., Ut.	121	39.55 N	109.20 W
Uitenhage, S. Afr.	227c	33.46 S	25.26 E
Uithoorn, Neth.	157a	52.13 N	4.49 E
Uíge, Ang.	230	7.37 S	15.03 E
Uji, Jap. (ōō'jē)	205b	34.53 N	135.49 E
Ujiji, Tan. (ōō-jē'jē)	231	4.55 S	29.41 E
Ujjain, India (ōō-jŭēn)	196	23.18 N	75.37 E
Ujung Pandang (Makasar), Indon.	206	5.08 S	119.28 E
Ukerewe I., Tan.	231	2.00 S	32.40 E
Ukhta, Sov. Un. (ōōk'tá)	178	65.22 N	31.30 E
Ukhta, Sov. Un.	180	63.08 N	53.42 E
Ukiah, Ca. (ū-kī'å)	120	35.09 N	122.12 W
Ukita (Neigh.), Jap.	69a	35.40 N	139.52 E
Ukmerge, Sov. Un. (ōōk'mĕr-ghå)	165	55.16 N	24.45 E
Ukrainian (S. S. R.), Sov. Un.	176	49.15 N	30.15 E
Uku (I.), Jap. (ōōk'ōō)	205	33.18 N	129.02 E
Ulan Batar, (Ulaanbaatar) Mong.	198	47.56 N	107.00 E
Ulanhad, see Chifeng			
Ulan-Ude, Sov. Un. (ōō'län ōō'då)	181	51.59 N	107.41 E
Ulchin, Kor. (ōōl'chĕn')	204	36.57 N	129.26 E
Ulcinj (Dulcigno), Yugo. (ōōl'tsĕn')	173	41.56 N	19.15 E
Ulhās (R.), India	197b	19.13 N	73.03 E
Ulhāsnagar, India	197b	19.10 N	73.07 E
Uliastay, Mong.	198	47.49 N	97.00 E
Ulindi (R.), Zaire (ōō-lĭn'dē)	230	1.55 S	26.17 E
Ulla, Sov. Un. (ōōl'á)	174	55.14 N	29.15 E
Ulla (R.), Sov. Un.	174	54.58 N	29.03 E
Ulla (R.), Sp. (ōō'lä)	170	42.45 N	8.33 W
Üllendahl (Neigh.), F.R.G.	63	51.19 N	7.18 E
Ullŭng (I.), Kor. (ōōl'lōōng')	204	37.29 N	130.50 E
Ulm, F.R.G. (ōōlm)	166	48.24 N	9.59 E
Ulmer, Mt., Ant. (ŭl'mûr')	232	77.30 S	86.00 W
Ulricehamn, Swe. (ōōl-rē'sĕ-häm)	164	57.49 N	13.23 E
Ulsan, Kor. (ōōl'sän')	204	35.35 N	129.22 E
Ulster (Reg.), Ire.-N. Ire. (ŭl'stēr)	162	54.41 N	7.10 W
Ulua R., Hond. (ōō-lōō'á)	132	15.49 N	87.45 W
Ulubāria, India	196a	22.27 N	88.09 E
Uluguru Mts., Tan.	231	7.15 S	37.30 E
Ulukişla, Tur. (ōō-lōō-kēsh'lá)	179	36.40 N	34.30 E
Ulunga, Sov. Un. (ōō-lōōn'gá)	204	46.16 N	136.29 E
Ulungur (R.), China (ōō-lōōn-gûr)	198	46.31 N	149.00 E
Ulu-Telyak, Sov. Un. (ōō lōō'tĕlyăk)	182a	54.54 N	57.01 E
Ulverstone, Austl. (ŭl'vēr-stŭn)	216	41.20 S	146.22 E
Ul'yanovka, Sov. Un. (ōō-lyä'nôf-kå)	182c	59.38 N	30.47 E
Ul'yanovsk, Sov. Un. (ōō-lyä'nôfsk)	178	54.20 N	48.05 E
Ulysses, Ks. (ū-lĭs'ēz)	122	37.34 N	101.25 W
Ulzangom, Mong.	198	50.23 N	92.14 E
Ülzen, F.R.G. (ült'sĕn)	166	52.58 N	10.34 E
Umán, Mex. (ōō-män')	131	20.52 N	89.44 W
Uman', Sov. Un. (ōō-mán')	175	48.44 N	30.13 E
Umatilla Ind. Res., Or. (ū-má-tĭl'á)	116	45.38 N	118.35 W
Umberpāda, India	197b	19.28 N	73.04 E
Umbria (Reg.), It. (ŭm'brĭ-á)	172	42.53 N	12.22 E
Umeå, Swe. (ōō'mĕ-ô)	158	63.48 N	20.29 E
Umeälven (R.), Swe.	158	64.57 N	18.51 E
Umhlatuzi (R.), S. Afr. (ōōm'hlá-tōō'zĭ)	227c	28.47 S	31.17 E
Umiat, Ak. (ōō'mĭ-ăt)	107	69.20 N	152.28 W
Umkomaas, S. Afr. (ōōm-kō'mäs)	227c	30.12 S	30.48 E
Umm Durmān, see Omdurman			
Umnak (I.), Ak. (ōōm'nák)	107a	53.10 N	169.08 W
Umnak Pass, Ak.	107a	53.10 N	168.04 W
Umniati (R.), Zimb.	226	17.08 S	29.11 E
Umpqua R., Or. (ŭmp'kwá)	116	43.42 N	123.50 W
Umtata, Trans. (ōōm-tä'tä)	227c	31.36 S	28.47 E
Umtentweni, S. Afr.	227c	30.41 S	30.29 E
Umzimkulu, S. Afr. (ōōm-zĕm-kōō'lōō)	227c	30.12 S	29.53 E
Umzinto, S. Afr. (ōōm-zĭn'tô)	227c	30.19 S	30.41 E
Una (R.), Yugo. (ōō'ná)	172	44.38 N	16.10 E
Unalakleet, Ak. (ū-ná-lák'lēt)	107	63.50 N	160.42 W
Unalaska, Ak. (ū-ná-lás'ká)	107a	53.30 N	166.20 W
Unare (R.), Ven.	143b	9.45 N	65.12 W
Unare, Laguna de (L.), Ven. (lä-gōō'nä-de-ōō-ná'rĕ)	143b	10.07 N	65.23 W
Unayzah, Sau Ar.	192	25.50 N	44.02 E
Uncas, Can. (ŭŋ'kás)	95g	53.30 N	113.02 W
Uncia, Bol. (ōōn'sē-ä)	142	18.28 S	66.32 W
Uncompahgre (R.), Co.	121	38.20 N	107.45 W
Uncompahgre Pk., Co. (ŭn-kŭm-pä'grē)	121	38.00 N	107.30 W
Uncompahgre Plat., Co.	121	38.40 N	108.40 W
Underberg, S. Afr. (ŭn'dēr-bûrg)	227c	29.51 S	29.32 E
Undo, Eth.	225	6.37 N	38.29 E
Unecha, Sov. Un. (ōō-nĕ'chá)	174	32.51 N	32.44 E
Ungava B., Can. (ŭŋ-gä'vá)	97	59.46 N	67.18 W
Ungava, Péninsule d' (Pen.), Can.	97	59.55 N	74.00 W
União da Vitória, Braz. (ōō-nē-ouɴ' dä vē-tô'ryä)	144	26.17 S	51.13 W
Unidad Sante Fe, Mex.	60a	19.23 N	99.15 W
Unije (I.), Yugo. (ōō'nē-yĕ)	172	44.39 N	14.10 E
Unimak (I.), Ak. (ōō-nē-mák')	107a	54.30 N	163.35 W
Unimak Pass, Ak.	107a	54.22 N	165.22 W
Union, Ms. (ūn'yŭn)	126	32.35 N	89.07 W
Union, Mo.	123	38.28 N	90.59 W
Union, NC	127	34.42 N	81.40 W
Union, NJ	55	40.42 N	74.16 W
Union, Or.	116	45.13 N	117.52 W
Union City, Ca.	118b	37.36 N	122.01 W
Union City, Ind.	110	40.10 N	85.00 W
Union City, Mi.	110	42.00 N	85.10 W
Union City, NJ	55	40.46 N	74.02 W
Union City, Pa.	111	41.50 N	79.50 W
Union City, Tn.	126	36.25 N	89.04 W
Uniondale, NY	55	40.43 N	73.36 W
Union de Reyes, Cuba (ōō-nyô'n-dĕ-rĕ-yĕ's)	134	22.45 N	81.30 W
Union de San Antonio, Mex. (sän än-tō'nyō)	130	21.07 N	101.56 W
Union de Tula, Mex. (tōō'lä)	130	19.57 N	104.14 W

ăt; finăl; rāte; senāte; ärm; åsk; sofá; fâre; ch-choose; dh-as th in other; bē; ēvent; bĕt; recĕnt; cratēr; g-gō; gh-guttural g; bĭt; ĭ-short neutral; rīde; ĸ-guttural k as ch in German ich;

PRONOUNCING INDEX

Union Grove – Valsbaai 357

PLACE (Pronounciation)	PAGE	Lat. °′	Long. °′
Union Grove, Wi. (ūn-yŭn grōv)	113a	42.41 N	88.03 W
Unión Hidalgo, Mex. (ē-dä'lgô)	131	16.29 N	94.51 W
Union Point, Ga.	126	33.37 N	83.08 W
Union Springs Al. (sprĭngz)	126	32.08 N	85.43 W
Uniontown, Al. (ūn'yŭn-toun)	126	32.26 N	87.30 W
Uniontown, Oh.	113d	40.58 N	81.25 W
Uniontown, Pa.	111	39.55 N	79.45 W
Unionville, Mo. (ūn'yŭn-vĭl)	123	40.28 N	92.58 W
Unisan, Phil. (ōō-nē'sän)	207a	13.50 N	121.59 E
Unitas, Mts., U. S. (ū-nĭ'tăs)	108	40.35 N	111.00 W
United Arab Emirates, Asia	190	24.00 N	54.00 E
United Arab Republic, see Egypt			
United Kingdom, Eur.	158	56.30 N	1.40 W
United Nations Headquarters (P. Int.), NY	55	40.45 N	73.58 W
United Pueblo Ind. Res., NM (u-nīt'ĕd pōō-ĕb'lō) (pwā'blō)	121	35.30 N	107.00 W
United States, N. A.	94	38.00 N	110.00 W
Unity, Can.	100	52.27 N	109.10 W
Universal, In. (ū-nĭ-vûr'săl)	110	39.35 N	87.30 W
University City, Mo. (ū'nĭ-vûr'sĭ-tĭ)	119e	38.40 N	90.19 W
University Heights, Oh.	56a	41.30 N	81.32 W
University Park, Md.	56d	38.58 N	76.57 W
University Park, Tx.	119c	32.51 N	96.48 W
Unna, F.R.G. (ōō'nä)	169c	51.32 N	7.41 E
Unst (I.), Scot. (ōōnst)	162a	60.50 N	1.24 W
Unterhaching, F.R.G. (ōōn'tĕr-hä-kĕng)	157d	48.03 N	11.38 E
Untermauerbach, Aus.	66e	48.14 N	16.12 E
Unye, Tur. (ün'yĕ)	179	41.00 N	37.10 E
Unzha (R.), Sov. Un. (ōōn'zhá)	178	57.45 N	44.10 E
Upa (R.), Sov. Un. (ōō'pá)	174	53.54 N	36.48 E
Upanda, Sierra do (Mts.), Ang. (sē-ĕ'r-rä-dô-ōō-pä'n-dä)	222	13.15 S	14.15 E
Upata, Ven. (ōō-pä'tä)	142	7.58 N	62.27 W
Upemba, Parc Natl. de l' (Natl. Pk.), Zaire	231	9.10 S	26.15 E
Up Holland, Eng.	64a	53.33 N	2.44 W
Upington, S. Afr. (ŭp'ĭng-tŭn)	226	28.25 S	21.15 E
Upland, Ca. (ŭp'lănd)	119a	34.06 N	117.38 W
Upland, Pa.	56b	39.51 N	75.23 W
Upolu Pt., Hi. (ōō-pô'lōō)	106a	20.15 N	155.48 W
Upper Arrow L., Can. (ăr'ō)	99	50.30 N	117.55 W
Upper Brookville, NY	55	40.51 N	73.34 W
Upper Darby, Pa. (där'bĭ)	112f	39.58 N	75.16 W
Upper de Lacs (R.), ND (dē läk)	114	48.58 N	101.55 W
Upper Ferntree Gully, Austl.	70b	37.54 S	145.19 E
Upper Kapuas Mts., Mala.	206	1.45 N	112.06 E
Upper L., Nv. (ŭp'ēr)	116	41.42 N	119.59 W
Upper Marlboro, Md. (ūpēr mărl'bōrô)	112e	38.49 N	76.46 W
Upper Mill, Wa. (mĭl)	118a	47.11 N	121.55 W
Upper New York B., NY	55	40.41 N	74.03 W
Upper Red L., Mn. (rĕd)	115	48.14 N	94.53 W
Upper Saint Clair, Pa.	57b	40.21 N	80.05 W
Upper Sandusky, Oh. (săn-dŭs'kē)	110	40.50 N	83.20 W
Upper San Leandro Res., Ca. (ŭp'ĕr săn lē-ăn'drô)	118b	37.47 N	122.04 W
Upper Tooting (Neigh.), Eng.	62	51.26 N	0.10 W
Upper Volta, see Burkina Faso			
Uppingham, Eng. (ŭp'ĭng-ăm)	156	52.35 N	0.43 W
Uppsala, Swe. (ōōp'sá-lä)	164	59.53 N	17.39 E
Upton, Eng.	62	51.30 N	0.35 W
Uptown, Ma. (ŭp'toun)	105a	42.10 N	71.36 W
Uptown (Neigh.), Il.	58a	41.58 N	87.40 W
Upwey, Austl.	70b	37.54 S	145.20 E
Uraga, Jap. (ōō'rá-gá')	205a	35.15 N	139.43 E
Uraga-Kaikyō (Str.), Jap. (ōō'rä-gä kī'kyō)	205a	35.11 N	139.44 W
Ural (R.), Sov. Un. (ōō-räl'') (ū-rôl)	179	49.50 N	51.30 E
Urals (Mts.), Sov. Un.	176	56.28 N	58.13 E
Ural'sk, Sov. Un. (ōō-rálsk')	179	51.15 N	51.10 E
Uran, India (ōō-rän')	197b	18.53 N	72.46 E
Uranium City, Can.	96	59.34 N	108.59 W
Urawa, Jap. (ōō'rä-wä')	205a	35.52 N	139.39 E
Urayasu, Jap. (ōō'rä-yä'sōō)	205a	35.40 N	139.54 W
Urazovo, Sov. Un. (ōō-rá'zô-vô)	175	50.08 N	38.03 E
Urbana, Il. (ûr-băn'á)	110	40.10 N	88.15 W
Urbana, Oh.	110	40.05 N	83.50 W
Urbino, It. (ōōr-bē'nô)	172	43.43 N	12.37 E
Urda, Sov. Un. (ōōr'dá)	179	48.50 N	47.30 E
Urdaneta, Phil. (ōōr-dä-nä'tä)	207a	15.59 N	120.34 E
Urdinarrain, Arg. (ōōr-dē-när-rāē'n)	141c	32.43 S	58.53 W
Urdzhar, Sov. Un. (ōōrd-zhär')	180	47.28 N	82.00 E
Urfa, Tur. (ōōr'fá)	179	37.20 N	38.45 E
Urgench, Sov. Un. (ōōr-gĕnch')	155	41.32 N	60.33 E
Uritsk, Sov. Un. (ōō'rĭtsk)	182c	59.50 N	30.11 E
Urla, Tur. (ōōr'lá)	173	38.20 N	26.44 E
Urman, Sov. Un. (ōōr'mán)	182a	54.53 N	56.52 E
Urmi (R.), Sov. Un. (ōōr'mē)	204	48.50 N	134.00 E
Urmston, Eng.	64b	53.27 N	2.21 W
Uromi, Nig.	229	6.44 N	6.18 E
Urrao, Col. (ōōr-rá'ô)	142a	6.19 N	76.11 W
Urshel'skiy, Sov. Un. (ōōr-shĕl'skēē)	174	55.50 N	40.11 E
Ursus, Pol.	167	52.12 N	20.53 E
Urubamba (R.), Peru (ōō-rōō-bäm'bä)	142	11.48 S	72.34 W
Uruguaiana, Braz. (ōō-rōō-gwī-ä'ná)	144	29.45 S	57.00 W
Uruguay, S. A. (ōō-rōō-gwī') (ū'rōō-gwā)	140	32.45 S	56.00 W
Uruguay, Rio (R.), Braz. (rē'ō-ōō-rōō-gwī)	144	27.05 S	55.15 W
Ürümqi, China (ū-rŭm-chyē)	198	43.49 N	87.43 E
Urup (I.), Sov. Un. (ōō'rōōp')	181	46.08 N	149.00 E
Uryupinsk, Sov. Un. (ōōr'yōō-pēn-sk')	179	50.50 N	42.00 E
Urziceni, Rom. (ōō-zē-chĕn'')	173	44.45 N	26.42 E
Usa, Jap.	204	33.31 N	131.22 E
Usa (R.), Sov. Un. (ōō'sá)	178	66.00 N	58.20 E
Uşak, Tur. (ōō'shák)	179	39.50 N	29.15 E
Usakos, Namibia (ōō-sä'kōs)	226	22.00 S	15.40 E
Usambara Mts., Tan.	231	4.40 S	38.25 E
Usangu Flats (Pln.), Tan.	231	8.10 S	34.00 E
Ushaki, Sov. Un. (ōō'shá-kĭ)	182c	59.28 N	31.00 E
Ushakovskoye, Sov. Un. (ōō-shá-kôv'skô-yĕ)	182a	56.18 N	62.23 E
Ushashi, Tan.	231	2.00 S	33.57 E
Ushiku, Jap. (ōō'shē-kōō)	205a	35.24 N	140.09 E
Ushimado, Jap. (ōō'shē-mä'dō)	205	34.37 N	134.09 E
Ushuaia, Arg. (ōō-shōō-ī'ä)	144	54.46 S	68.24 W
Üsküdar, Tur.	179	40.55 N	29.00 E
Usman', Sov. Un. (ōōs-mán')	174	52.03 N	39.40 E
Usol'ye, Sov. Un. (ōō-sô'lyĕ)	182a	59.24 N	56.40 E
Usol'ye-Sibirskoye, Sov. Un. (ōō-sô'lyĕsĭ bēr'skô-yĕ)	180	52.44 N	103.46 E
Uspallata P., Arg.-Chile (ōōs-pä-lyä'tä)	144	32.47 S	70.08 W
Uspanapa (R.), Mex. (ōōs-pä-nä'pä)	131	17.43 N	94.14 W
Ussel, Fr. (üs'ĕl)	168	45.33 N	2.17 E
Ussuri (R.), China (ōō-sōō'rē)	199	46.30 N	133.56 E
Ussuriysk, Sov. Un.	181	43.48 N	132.09 E
Ust'-Bol'sheretsk, Sov. Un.	181	52.41 N	157.00 E
Ustica, I. di, It. (ē'sō-lä-dē-ōōs'tē-kä)	172	38.43 N	12.11 E
Ustinov, Sov. Un.	178	56.50 N	53.15 E
Ustinovka, Sov. Un. (ōōs-tē'nôf-kä)	175	47.59 N	32.31 E
Usti, Czech. (ōōs'tē)	166	50.39 N	14.02 E
Ust'-Izhora, Sov. Un. (ōōst-ēz'hô-rá)	182c	59.49 N	30.35 E
Ustka, Pol. (ōōst'ká)	166	54.34 N	16.52 E
Ust'-Kamchatsk, Sov. Un.	181	56.13 N	162.18 E
Ust'-Kamenogorsk, Sov. Un.	180	49.58 N	80.43 E
Ust'-Katav, Sov. Un. (ōōst ká'táf)	182a	54.55 N	58.12 E
Ust'-Kishert', Sov. Un. (ōōst kē'shĕrt)	182a	57.21 N	57.13 E
Ust'-Kulom, Sov. Un. (kōō'lŭm)	178	61.38 N	54.00 E
Ust'-Maya, Sov. Un. (má'yá)	181	60.33 N	134.43 E
Ust' Olenëk, Sov. Un.	181	72.52 N	120.15 E
Ust-Ordynskiy, Sov. Un. (ōōst-ôr-dyēnsk'ĭ)	181	52.47 N	104.39 E
Ust' Penzhino, Sov. Un.	181	63.00 N	165.10 E
Ust' Port, Sov. Un. (ōōst'pôrt')	180	69.20 N	83.41 E
Ust'-Tsil'ma, Sov. Un. (tsĭl'má)	178	65.25 N	52.10 E
Ust'-Tyrma, Sov. Un. (tur'má)	181	50.27 N	131.17 E
Ust'Uls, Sov. Un. (ōōls)	182a	60.35 N	58.32 E
Ust'-Urt, Plato (Plat.), Sov. Un. (ōōrt)	176	44.03 N	54.58 E
Ustyuzhna, Sov. Un. (yōōzh'ná)	174	58.49 N	36.19 E
Usu, China (ů-sōō)	198	44.28 N	84.07 E
Usuki, Jap. (ōō'sōō-kē')	205	33.06 N	131.47 E
Usulutan, Sal. (ōō-sōō-lä-tän')	132	13.22 N	88.25 W
Usumacinta (R.), Mex. (ōō'sōō-mä-sēn'tō)	131	18.24 N	92.30 W
Us'va, Sov. Un. (ōōs'vá)	182a	58.41 N	57.38 E
Utah (State), U. S. (ū'tô)	108	39.25 N	112.40 W
Utah (L.), Ut.	121	40.10 N	111.55 W
Utan, India	197b	19.27 N	72.43 E
Ute Mtn. Ind. Res., NM	121	36.57 N	108.34 W
Utena, Sov. Un. (ōō'tā-nä)	165	55.32 N	25.40 E
Utete, Tan. (ōō-tā'tā)	227	8.05 S	38.47 E
Utfort, F.R.G.	63	51.28 N	6.38 E
Utica, In. (ū'tĭ-ká)	113h	38.20 N	85.39 W
Utica, NY	111	43.05 N	75.10 W
Utiel, Sp. (ōō-tyål')	170	39.34 N	1.13 W
Utika, Mi. (ū'tĭ-ká)	113b	42.37 N	83.02 W
Utik L., Can.	101	55.16 N	96.00 W
Utikuma L., Can.	100	55.50 N	115.25 W
Utila I., Hond. (ōō-tē'lä)	132	16.07 N	87.05 W
Utinga, Braz.	61d	23.38 S	46.32 W
Uto, Jap. (ōō'tō')	205	32.43 N	130.39 E
Utrecht, Neth. (ü'trĕkt) (ū'trĕkt)	157a	52.05 N	5.06 E
Utrera, Sp. (ōō-trā'rä)	170	37.12 N	5.48 W
Utsunomiya, Jap. (ōōt'sōō-nō-mē-yá')	205	36.35 N	139.52 E
Uttaradit, Thai.	206	17.47 N	100.10 E
Uttarpara-Kotrung, India	196a	22.40 N	88.21 E
Uttar Pradesh (State), India (ōōt-tär-prä-dĕsh)	196	27.00 N	80.00 E
Uttoxeter, Eng. (ŭt-tôk'sē-tēr)	156	52.54 N	1.52 W
Utuado, P. R. (ōō-tōō-ä'dhō)	129b	18.16 N	66.40 W
Uusikaupunki (Nystad), Fin. (ōō'sĭ-kou'pōōn-kĭ) (nü'städh)	165	60.48 N	21.24 E
Uvalde, Tx. (ū-väl'dē)	124	29.14 N	99.47 W
Uvel'skiy, Sov. Un. (ōō-vyĕl'skĭ)	182a	54.27 N	60.22 E
Uvinza, Tan.	231	5.06 S	30.22 E
Uvira, Zaire (ōō-vē'rä)	226	3.28 S	29.03 E
Uvod' (R.), Sov. Un. (ōō-vôd')	174	56.52 N	41.03 E
Uvongo Beach, S. Afr.	227c	30.49 S	30.23 E
Uvs Nuur (L.), Mong.	198	50.29 N	93.32 E
Uwajima, Jap. (ōō-wä'jē-mä)	205	33.12 N	132.35 E
Uxbridge, Ma. (ŭks'brĭj)	105a	42.05 N	71.38 W
Uxbridge (Neigh.), Eng.	62	51.33 N	0.29 W
Uxmal (Ruins), Mex. (ōō'x-mä'l)	132a	20.22 N	89.44 W
Uyama, Jap.	69b	34.50 N	135.41 E
Uy R., Sov. Un. (ōōy)	182a	54.05 N	62.11 E
Uyskoye, Sov. Un. (ûy'skô-yĕ)	182a	54.22 N	60.01 E
Uyuni, Bol. (ōō-yōō'nē)	142	20.28 S	66.45 W
Uyuni, Salar de (Salt Flat), Bol. (sä-lär-dē)	142	20.58 S	67.09 W
Uzbek S. S. R., Sov. Un. (ōōz-bĕk')	176	42.42 N	60.00 E
Uzen, Bol'shoy (R.), Sov. Un.	179	49.50 N	49.35 E
Uzh (R.), Sov. Un. (ōōzh)	175	51.07 N	29.05 E
Uzhgorod, Sov. Un. (ōōzh'gô-rôt)	167	48.38 N	22.18 E
Uzunköpru, Tur. (ōō'zōōn'kû-prü)	173	41.17 N	26.42 E
V			
Vaal (R.), S. Afr. (väl)	226	28.15 S	24.30 E
Vaaldam (L.), S. Afr.	223d	26.58 S	28.37 E
Vaalplaas, S. Afr.	223d	25.39 S	28.56 E
Vaalwater, S. Afr.	223d	24.17 S	28.08 E
Vaasa, Fin. (vä'sá)	165	63.06 N	21.39 E
Vác, Hung. (väts)	167	47.46 N	19.10 E
Vache, Île À (I.), Hai. (väsh)	135	18.05 N	73.40 W
Vadsø, Nor. (vädh'sû)	158	70.08 N	29.52 E
Vadstena, Swe. (väd'stĭ'ná)	164	58.27 N	14.53 E
Vaduz, Liech. (vä'dōōts)	166	47.10 N	9.32 E
Vaga (R.), Sov. Un. (va'gá)	178	61.55 N	42.30 E
Vah R., Czech. (väk)	167	48.07 N	17.52 E
Vaigai (R.), India	196	10.20 N	78.13 E
Vaires-sur-Marne, Fr.	64c	48.52 N	2.39 E
Vakh (R.), Sov. Un. (vák)	180	61.30 N	81.33 E
Valachia (Reg.), Rom.	173	44.45 N	24.17 E
Valcanuta (Neigh.), It.	66c	41.53 N	12.25 E
Valcartier-Village, Can. (väl-kärt-yĕ'vē-lāzh')	95b	46.56 N	71.28 W
Valdai Hills, Sov. Un. (vál-dī' gô'rĭ)	174	57.50 N	32.35 E
Valday (Valdai), Sov. Un. (vál-dī')	174	57.58 N	33.13 E
Valdecañas, Embalse de (Res.), Sp.	170	39.15 N	5.30 W
Valdemārpils, Sov. Un.	165	57.22 N	22.34 E
Valdemorillo, Sp. (väl-dā-mô-rēl'yō)	171a	40.30 N	4.04 W
Valdepeñas, Sp. (väl-dā-pān'yäs)	170	38.46 N	3.22 W
Valderaduey (R.), Sp. (väl-dĕ-rä-dwĕ'y)	170	41.39 N	5.35 W
Valdés, Pen., Arg. (väl-dĕ's)	144	42.15 S	63.15 W
Valdez, Ak. (văl'dēz)	107	61.10 N	146.18 W
Valdilecha, Sp. (väl-dē-lā'chä)	171a	40.17 N	3.19 W
Valdivia, Chile (väl-dē'vä)	144	39.47 S	73.13 W
Valdivia, Col. (väl-dē'vēä)	142a	7.10 N	75.26 W
Val-d' Or., Can.	103	48.03 N	77.50 W
Valdosta, Ga. (väl-dŏs'tá)	126	30.50 N	83.18 W
Valdoviño, Sp. (väl-dô-vē'nō)	170	43.36 N	8.05 W
Vale, Or. (vāl)	116	43.59 N	117.14 W
Valença, Braz. (vä-lĕn'sá)	143	13.43 S	38.58 W
Valença, Port.	170	42.03 N	8.36 W
Valence, Fr. (vä-lĕnns)	168	44.56 N	4.54 E
Valencia, Sp. (vä-lĕn'thē-ä)	171	39.26 N	0.23 W
Valencia, Ven. (vä-lĕn'syä)	143b	10.11 N	68.00 W
Valencia (Reg.), Sp. (vä-lĕn'thē-ä)	171	39.08 N	0.43 W
Valencia de Alcántara, Sp.	170	39.34 N	7.13 W
Valencia I., Ire. (vá-lĕn'shá)	162	51.55 N	10.26 W
Valencia, Lago de (L.), Ven.	143b	10.11 N	67.45 W
Valenciennes, Fr. (vá-län-syĕn')	168	50.24 N	3.36 E
Valentine, Ne. (vá län-tē-nyē')	114	42.52 N	100.34 W
Valentín Alsina (Neigh.), Arg.	60d	34.40 S	58.25 W
Valera, Ven. (vä-lĕ'rä)	142	9.12 N	70.45 W
Valerianovsk, Sov. Un. (vá-lĕ-rĭ-ä'nôvsk)	182a	58.47 N	59.34 E
Valérien, Mont (Hill), Fr.	64c	48.53 N	2.13 E
Valga, Sov. Un. (väl'gá)	174	57.47 N	26.03 E
Valhalla, S. Afr. (vál-hăl-á)	227b	25.49 S	28.09 E
Valier, Mt. (vă-lēr')	117	48.17 N	112.14 W
Valjevo, Yugo. (väl'yá-vô)	173	44.17 N	19.57 E
Valki, Sov. Un. (väl'kē)	175	49.49 N	35.40 E
Valladolid, Mex. (väl-yä-dhô-lēdh')	132a	20.39 N	88.13 W
Valladolid, Sp. (väl-yä-dhô-lēdh')	170	41.41 N	4.41 W
Vall de Uxó, Sp. (väl-dĕ-ōōx-ô')	171	39.50 N	0.15 W
Valldoreix, Sp.	65e	41.28 N	2.04 E
Valle, Arroyo del, Ca. (ä-rō'yō dĕl väl'yå)	120	37.36 N	121.43 W
Vallecas, Sp. (väl-yā'käs)	171a	40.23 N	3.37 W
Vallecas (Neigh.), Sp.	65b	40.23 N	3.37 W
Valle de Allende, Mex. (väl'yā dā äl-yĕn'då)	124	26.55 N	105.25 W
Valle de Bravo, Mex. (brä'vô)	130	19.12 N	100.07 W
Valle de Guanape, Ven. (vä'l-yĕ-dĕ-gwä-nä'pĕ)	143b	9.54 N	65.41 W
Valle de la Pascua, Ven. (lä-pä's-kōōä)	142	9.12 N	65.08 W
Valle del Cauca, Col. (vä'l-yĕ del kou'kä)	142a	4.03 N	76.13 W
Valle de Santiago, Mex. (sän-tē-ä'gô)	130	20.23 N	101.11 W
Valledupar, Col. (dōō-pär')	142	10.13 N	73.39 W
Valle Grande, Bol. (grän'dā)	142	18.27 S	64.03 W
Vallejo, Ca. (vä-yā'hō) (vă-lā'hō)	118b	38.06 N	122.15 W
Vallejo, Sierra de (Mts.), Mex. (sē-ĕ'r-rä-dĕ-väl-yĕ'kô)	130	21.00 N	105.10 W
Vallenar, Chile (väl-yā-när')	144	28.39 S	70.52 W
Valletta, Malta (väl-lĕt'ä)	160	35.50 N	14.29 E
Valle Vista, Ca. (väl'yā vĭs'tá)	119a	33.45 N	116.53 W
Valley City, ND	114	46.55 N	97.59 W
Valley City, Oh. (văl'ĭ)	113d	41.14 N	81.56 W
Valleydale, Ca.	59	34.06 N	117.56 W
Valley Falls, Ks.	123	39.25 N	95.26 W
Valleyfield, Can. (văl'ē-fēld)	95a	45.16 N	74.09 W
Valley Mede, Md.	56c	39.17 N	76.50 W
Valley Park, Mo. (văl'ē pärk)	119e	38.33 N	90.30 W
Valley Stream, NY (văl'ĭ strēm)	112a	40.39 N	73.42 W
Valli di Comácchio (L.), It. (vä'lē-dē-kô-má'chyô)	172	44.38 N	12.15 E
Vallière, Hai. (väl-yâr')	135	19.30 N	71.55 W
Vallimanca (R.), Arg. (väl-yē-mä'n-kä)	141c	36.21 S	60.55 W
Valls, Sp. (väls)	171	41.15 N	1.15 E
Valmiera, Sov. Un. (vál'myĕ-rá)	165	57.34 N	25.54 E
Valognes, Fr. (vá-lôn'y')	168	49.32 N	1.30 W
Valona, see Vlorë			
Valparaíso, Chile (väl'pä-rä-ē'sô)	141b	33.02 S	71.32 W
Valparaiso, In. (văl-pá-rā'zō)	110	41.25 N	87.05 W
Valparaiso, Mex.	130	22.49 N	103.33 W
Valpariso (Prov.), Chile	141b	32.58 S	71.23 W
Valréas, Fr. (vál-rā-ä')	168	45.25 N	4.56 E
Vals (R.), S. Afr.	223d	27.32 S	26.51 E
Valsbaai (False Bay), S. Afr.	226a	34.14 S	18.35 E

ng-sing; ŋ-baŋk; ɴ-nasalized n; nŏd; cŏmmit; ōld; ôbey; ôrder; oi-boil; fōōd; fŏŏt; ou-out; s-soft; sh-dish; th-thin; pūre; ûnite; ûrn; stŭd; circŭs; ü-as in French tu; '-indeterminate vowel.

358 Vals – Victoria

PLACE (Pronounciation)	PAGE	Lat. °′	Long. °′
Vals, Tandjung (C.), Indon.	207	8.30 S	137.15 E
Valuyevo, Sov. Un. (vȧ-lo͞o′yě-vô)	182b	55.34 N	37.21 E
Valuyki, Sov. Un. (vȧ-lo͞o-ē′ke̍)	175	50.14 N	38.04 E
Valverde del Camino, Sp. (väl-věr-dě-děl-kä-me̍′nō)	170	37.34 N	6.44 W
Vambanād (R.), India	196	10.00 N	76.03 E
Vammala, Fin.	165	61.19 N	22.51 E
Van, Tur. (vȧn)	179	38.04 N	43.10 E
Van Buren, Ar. (văn bū′rĕn)	123	35.26 N	94.20 W
Van Buren, Me.	104	47.09 N	67.58 W
Vanceburg, Ky. (văns′bûrg)	110	38.35 N	83.20 W
Vancouver, Can. (văn-ko͞o′vẽr)	118d	49.16 N	123.06 W
Vancouver, Wa.	118c	45.37 N	122.40 W
Vancouver I., Can.	98	49.50 N	125.05 W
Vancouver Island Ra., Can.	98	49.25 N	125.25 W
Vandalia, Il. (văn-dā′lĭ-ȧ)	110	39.00 N	89.00 W
Vandalia, Mo.	123	39.19 N	91.30 W
Vanderbijlpark, S. Afr.	223d	26.43 S	27.50 E
Vanderhoof, Can.	98	54.01 N	124.01 W
Van Diemen (Str.), see Ōsumi Kaikyō			
Van Diemen, C., Austl. (văndē′mĕn)	214	11.05 S	130.15 E
Van Diemen G., Austl.	214	11.50 S	131.30 E
Vandreuil, Can. (vô-drû′y′)	95a	45.24 N	74.02 W
Vanegas, Mex. (vä-nĕ′gäs)	130	23.54 N	100.54 W
Vänern (L.), Swe.	164	58.52 N	13.17 E
Vänersborg, Swe. (vĕ′nẽrs-bôr′)	164	58.24 N	12.15 E
Vanga, Ken. (väŋ′gä)	227	4.38 S	39.10 E
Vangani, India	197b	19.07 N	73.15 E
Van Gölü (L.), Tur.	179	38.45 N	43.00 E
Van Horn, Tx.	124	31.03 N	104.50 W
Vanier, Can.	95c	45.27 N	75.39 W
Vaniköy (Neigh.), Tur.	66f	41.04 N	29.04 E
Van Lear, Ky. (văn lēr′)	110	37.45 N	82.50 W
Vannes, Fr. (vȧn)	168	47.42 N	2.46 W
Van Nuys, Ca. (văn nīz′)	119a	34.11 N	118.27 W
Van Rees, Pegunungan (Mtn.), Indon.	207	2.30 S	138.45 E
Vantaan (R.), Fin.	165	60.25 N	24.43 E
Vanuatu, Oceania	215	16.02 S	169.15 E
Vanves, Fr.	64c	48.50 N	2.18 E
Van Wert, Oh. (văn wûrt′)	110	40.50 N	84.35 W
Vanzago, It.	65c	45.32 N	9.00 E
Vara, Swe. (vä′rä)	164	58.17 N	12.55 E
Varaklāni, Sov. Un.	172	56.38 N	26.46 E
Varallo, It. (vä-räl′lô)	172	45.44 N	8.14 E
Vārānasi (Benares), India	196	25.25 N	83.00 E
Varanerfjorden (Fd.), Nor.	158	70.05 N	30.20 E
Varano, Lago di (L.), It. (lä′gō-dē-vä-rä′nō̍)	172	41.52 N	15.55 E
Varaždin, Yugo. (vä′räzh′de̍n)	172	46.17 N	16.20 E
Varazze, It. (vä-rät′sā)	172	44.23 N	8.34 E
Varberg, Swe. (vär′bĕrg)	164	57.06 N	12.16 E
Vardar (R.), Yugo. (vär′där)	173	41.40 N	21.50 E
Vardø, Nor. (värd′û)	158	70.23 N	30.15 E
Varėna, Sov. Un. (vä-rä′nȧ)	165	54.16 N	24.35 E
Varennes, Can. (vȧ-rĕn′)	95a	45.41 N	73.27 W
Varĕs, Yugo. (vä′rĕsh)	173	44.10 N	18.20 E
Varese, It. (vä-rā′sā̍)	172	45.45 N	8.49 E
Vargem Grande (Neigh.), Braz.	61c	22.59 S	43.29 W
Varginha, Braz. (vär-zhe̍′n-yä)	141a	21.33 S	45.25 W
Varkaus, Fin. (vär′kous)	165	62.19 N	27.51 E
Varlamovo, Sov. Un. (vár-lȧ′mô-vô)	182a	54.37 N	60.41 E
Varna (Stalin), Bul. (vär′nȧ) (stä′lĭn)	173	43.14 N	27.58 E
Varna, Sov. Un.	182a	53.22 N	60.59 E
Värnamo, Swe. (vĕr′nȧ-mō̍)	164	57.11 N	13.45 E
Varnsdorf, Czech. (värns′dôrf)	166	50.54 N	14.36 E
Varnville, SC (värn′vĭl)	127	32.49 N	81.05 W
Várpalota (P. Int.), Hung.	66g	47.30 N	19.02 E
Vars, Can. (värz)	95c	45.21 N	75.21 W
Varvaropolye, Sov. Un. (vȧr′vȧr′ō̍-pô-lyě)	175	48.38 N	38.37 E
Vasa, India	197b	19.20 N	72.47 E
Vascongadas (Reg.), Sp. (väs-kō̍n-gä′däs)	170	42.35 N	2.46 W
Vashka (R.), Sov. Un.	178	63.20 N	47.50 E
Vashon, Wa. (văsh′ŭn)	118a	47.27 N	122.28 W
Vashon Heights, Wa. (hītz)	118a	47.30 N	122.28 W
Vashon I., Wa.	118a	47.27 N	122.27 W
Vasiljevskij, Ostrov (I.), Sov. Un.	66a	59.56 N	30.15 E
Vasil′kov, Sov. Un. (vȧ-se̍l′-kôf′)	175	50.10 N	30.22 E
Vaslui, Rom. (vȧs-lo͞o′e̍)	167	46.39 N	27.49 E
Vassar, Mi. (văs′ẽr)	110	43.25 N	83.35 W
Vassouras, Braz. (väs-sō′räzh)	144b	22.25 S	43.40 W
Västerås, Swe. (vĕs′tĕr-ō̍s)	164	59.39 N	16.30 E
Västerdalälven (R.), Swe.	164	61.06 N	13.10 E
Västervik, Swe. (vĕs′tĕr-vēk)	164	57.45 N	16.35 E
Vasto, It. (väs′tô)	172	42.06 N	12.42 E
Vasyugan (R.), Sov. Un. (vȧs-yo͞o-gȧn′)	180	58.52 N	77.30 E
Vatican City (Città del Vaticano), Eur. (văt′ĭ-kăn sĭt′e̍) (chē-tȧ′del vä-te̍-kä′nô)	171d	41.54 N	12.22 E
Vaticano, C., It. (vä-te̍-kä′nô)	172	38.38 N	15.52 E
Vatnajökull (Gl.), Ice. (vät′nȧ-yû-ko͝ol)	158	64.34 N	16.41 W
Vatomandry, Mad. (vä-to͞o-män′drē)	227	18.53 S	48.13 E
Vatra Dornei, Rom. (vät′rȧ dôr′nā̍′)	167	47.22 N	25.20 E
Vättern (L.), Swe.	164	58.15 N	14.24 E
Vattholma, Swe.	164	60.01 N	17.40 E
Vaucluse, Austl.	70a	33.51 S	151.17 E
Vaugh, Wa. (vôn)	118a	47.21 N	122.47 W
Vaughan, Can.	95d	43.47 N	79.36 W
Vaughn, NM	122	34.37 N	105.13 W
Vauhallan, Fr.	64c	48.44 N	2.12 E
Vaujours, Fr.	64c	48.56 N	2.35 E
Vaupés (R.), Col. (vȧ′o͞o-pĕ′s)	142	1.18 N	71.14 W
Vaxholm, Swe. (väks′hō̍lm)	164	59.26 N	18.19 E
Växjo, Swe. (vĕks′shû)	164	56.53 N	14.46 E
Vaygach (I.), Sov. Un. (vī-gȧch′)	178	70.00 N	59.00 E
Veadeiros, Chapadas dos (Mts.), Braz. (shä-pä′däs-dō̍s-vě-ȧ-dā′rōs)	143	15.20 S	48.43 W
Vedea (R.), Rom. (vā̍′dyȧ)	173	44.25 N	24.45 E
Vedia, Arg. (vĕ′dyä)	141c	34.29 S	61.30 W
Veedersburg, In. (vē′dẽrz-bûrg)	110	40.05 N	87.15 W
Vega (I.), Nor.	158	65.38 N	10.51 E
Vega de Alatorre, Mex. (vā′gä dā ä-lä-tōr′rā̍)	131	20.02 N	96.39 W
Vega Real (Mts.), Dom. Rep. (vĕ′gä-rĕ-ä′l)	135	19.30 N	71.05 W
Vegreville, Can.	100	53.30 N	112.03 W
Vehār L., India	197b	19.11 N	72.52 E
Veinticinco de Mayo, Arg. (vā̍-ēn′te̍-sēn′kō dā mä′yō)	141c	35.26 S	60.09 W
Vejer de la Frontera, Sp.	170	36.15 N	5.58 W
Vejle, Den. (vī′lĕ)	164	55.41 N	9.29 E
Velbert, F.R.G. (fĕl′bĕrt)	169c	51.20 N	7.03 E
Velebit (Mts.), Yugo. (vā′lĕ-be̍t)	172	44.25 N	15.23 E
Velen, F.R.G. (fĕ′lĕn)	169c	51.54 N	7.00 E
Vélez-Málaga, Sp. (vā′lāth-mä′lä-gä)	170	36.48 N	4.05 W
Vélez-Rubio, Sp. (ro͞o′be̍-ō̍)	170	37.38 N	2.05 W
Velika Kapela (Mts.), Yugo. (vĕ′le̍-kä kä-pĕ′lä)	172	45.03 N	15.20 E
Velika Morava (R.), Yugo. (mō̍′rä-vä)	173	44.20 N	21.10 E
Velikaya (R.), Sov. Un. (vā̍-lē′kȧ-yȧ)	174	57.25 N	28.07 E
Velikiy Bychkov, Sov. Un. (vĕ-lē′kē bo͝och-kôf′)	167	47.59 N	24.01 E
Velikiye Luki, Sov. Un. (vyē-lē′-kye̍ lo͞o′ke)	174	56.19 N	30.32 E
Velikiy Ustyug, Sov. Un. (vā̍-lē′kĭ o͞os-tyo͝og′)	178	60.45 N	46.38 E
Veliko Tŭrnovo, Bul.	173	43.06 N	25.38 E
Velikoye, Sov. Un. (vā̍-lē′kō̍-yĕ)	174	57.21 N	39.45 E
Velikoye (L.), Sov. Un.	174	57.00 N	36.53 E
Veli Lošinj, Yugo (lô′she̍n′)	172	44.30 N	14.29 E
Velizh, Sov. Un. (vā̍′le̍zh)	174	55.37 N	31.11 E
Velke Meziřičí, Czech. (vĕl′kā mĕzh′′r-zhyĭ-chĭ)	166	49.21 N	16.01 E
Vella (I.), Sol. Is. (vāl′yä)	215	8.00 S	156.42 E
Velletri, It. (vĕl-lā′trē)	171d	41.42 N	12.48 E
Vellore, India (vĕl-lōr′)	197	12.57 N	79.09 E
Vels, Sov. Un. (vĕls)	182a	60.35 N	58.47 E
Vel′sk, Sov. Un. (vĕlsk)	178	61.00 N	42.18 E
Velten, G.D.R. (fel′tĕn)	157b	52.41 N	13.11 E
Velya R., Sov. Un. (vĕl′yȧ)	182b	56.23 N	37.54 E
Venadillo, Col. (vĕ-nä-de̍′l-yō)	142a	4.43 N	74.55 W
Venado, Mex. (vā̍-mä′dō)	130	22.54 N	101.07 W
Venado Tuerto, Arg. (vĕ-nä′dô-to͞oĕ′r-tô)	144	33.28 S	61.47 W
Vendôome, Fr. (väɴ-dōm′)	168	47.46 N	1.05 E
Veneto (Reg.), It. (vĕ-nĕ′tō̍)	172	45.58 N	11.24 E
Venëv, Sov. Un. (vĕn-ĕf′)	174	54.19 N	38.14 E
Venezia (Venice), It. (vā̍-nāt′se̍-ä)	172	45.25 N	12.18 E
Venezuela, S.A. (vĕn-e̍-zwē′lȧ)	140	8.00 N	65.00 W
Venezuela, Golfo de (G.), Ven. (gôl-fô-dĕ)	142	11.34 N	71.02 W
Veniaminof, Mt., Ak.	107	56.12 N	159.20 W
Venice, Ca. (vĕn′ĭs)	119a	33.59 N	118.28 W
Venice, Il.	119e	38.40 N	90.10 W
Venice, see Venezia			
Venice (Neigh.), Ca.	59	34.00 N	118.29 W
Venice, Gulf of (G.), It.	172	45.23 N	13.00 E
Venlo, Neth.	169c	51.22 N	6.11 E
Vennhausen (Neigh.), F.R.G.	63	51.13 N	6.51 E
Venta (R.), Sov. Un. (vĕn′tȧ)	165	57.05 N	21.45 E
Ventana, Sierra de la (Mts.), Arg. (sē-ĕ-rȧ-dĕ-lä-vĕn-tȧ′nä)	144	38.00 S	63.00 W
Ventersburg, S. Afr. (vĕn-tẽrs′bûrg)	223d	28.06 S	27.10 E
Ventersdorp, S. Afr. (vĕn-tẽrs′dôrp)	223d	26.20 S	26.48 E
Venterspos Location, S. Afr.	71b	26.18 S	27.42 E
Ventimiglia, It. (vĕn-te̍-mēl′yä)	172	43.46 N	7.37 E
Ventnor, NJ (vĕnt′nẽr)	111	39.20 N	74.25 W
Ventspils, Sov. Un. (vĕnt′spe̍ls)	165	57.24 N	21.41 E
Ventuari (R.), Ven. (vĕn-to͞oȧ′rē)	142	4.47 N	65.56 W
Ventura, Ca. (vĕn-to͞o′rȧ)	120	34.18 N	119.18 W
Venukovsky, Sov. Un. (vĕ-no͞o′kôv-skĭ)	182b	55.10 N	37.26 E
Venustiano Carranza, Mex. (vĕ-no͞os-tyä′nō-kär-rä′n-zä)	130	19.44 N	103.48 W
Venustiano Carranzo, Mex. (kär-rä′n-zō̍)	131	16.21 N	92.36 W
Vera, Arg. (vĕ-rä)	144	29.22 S	60.09 W
Vera, Sp. (vā′rä)	170	37.18 N	1.53 W
Veracruz, Mex.	131	19.13 N	96.07 W
Vera Cruz, (State), Mex. (vā-rä-kro͞oz′)	128	20.30 N	97.15 W
Verāval, India (vĕr′vŭ-väl)	196	20.59 N	70.49 E
Verberg (Neigh.), F.R.G.	63	51.22 N	6.36 E
Vercelli, It. (vĕr-chĕl′le̍)	172	45.18 N	8.27 E
Verchères, Can. (vĕr-shâr′)	95a	45.46 N	73.21 W
Verde (I.), Phil. (vĕr′dā̍)	207a	13.34 N	121.11 E
Verde (R.), Az. (vûrd)	121	34.04 N	111.40 W
Verde (R.), Mex.	130	21.48 N	99.50 W
Verde (R.), Mex.	131	16.05 N	97.44 W
Verde (R.), Mex.	130	20.50 N	103.00 W
Verde, Cap (C.), Ba.	135	22.50 N	75.00 W
Verde, Cay (I.), Ba.	135	22.00 N	75.05 W
Verde Island Pass., Phil. (vĕr′dē)	207a	13.36 N	120.39 E
Verdemont, Ca. (vûr′de̍-mŏnt)	119a	34.12 N	117.22 W
Verden, F.R.G. (fĕr′dĕn)	166	52.55 N	9.15 E
Verdigris (R.), Ok. (vûr′de̍-grēs)	123	36.50 N	95.29 W
Verdun, Can. (vĕr′dŭɴ′)	95a	45.27 N	73.34 W
Verdun, Fr. (vâr-dûɴ′)	168	49.09 N	5.21 E
Verdun, Fr.	171	43.48 N	1.10 E
Vereeniging, S. Afr. (vĕ-rā′nĭ-gĭng)	223d	26.40 S	27.56 E
Verena, S. Afr. (vĕr-e̍n ȧ)	223d	25.30 S	29.02 E
Vereya, Sov. Un. (vĕ-rā̍′yȧ)	174	55.21 N	36.08 E
Verga, NJ	56b	39.52 N	75.10 W
Vergara, Sp. (vĕr-gä′rä)	170	43.08 N	2.23 W
Verín, Sp. (vā̍-rēn′)	170	41.56 N	7.26 W
Verkhne-Kamchatsk, Sov. Un. (vyĕrk′nyĕ kȧm-chatsk′)	181	54.42 N	158.41 E
Verkhne Neyvinskiy, Sov. Un. (nā-vĭn′skĭ)	182a	57.17 N	60.10 E
Verkhne Ural′sk, Sov. Un. (o͞o-ralsk′)	182a	53.53 N	50.15 E
Verkhneye, Sov. Un. (vyĕrĸ′nĕ-yĕ)	175	48.53 N	38.29 E
Verkhniy Avzyan, Sov. Un. (vyĕrk′nyĕ ȧv-zyȧn′)	182a	53.32 N	57.30 E
Verkhniye Kigi, Sov. Un. (vyĕrk′nĭ-yĕ kĭ′gĭ)	182a	55.23 N	58.37 E
Verkhniy Ufaley, Sov. Un. (o͞o-fȧ′lā)	182a	56.04 N	60.15 E
Verkhnyaya Pyshma, Sov. Un. (vyĕrk′nyä-yä po͞osh′mȧ)	182a	56.57 N	60.37 E
Verkhnyaya Salda, Sov. Un. (säl′dȧ)	182a	58.03 N	60.33 E
Verkhnyaya Tunguska (Angara), (R.), Sov. Un. (to͞on-go͞os′kȧ)	180	58.13 N	97.00 E
Verkhnyaya Tura, Sov. Un. (to͞o′rȧ)	182a	58.22 N	59.51 E
Verkhnyaya Yayva, Sov. Un. (yäy′vȧ)	182a	59.28 N	59.38 E
Verkhotur′ye, Sov. Un. (vyĕr-kô-to͞or′yĕ)	182a	58.52 N	60.47 E
Verkhoyansk, Sov. Un. (vyĕr-ĸō̍-yänsk′)	181	67.43 N	133.33 E
Verkhoyanskiy Khrebet (Mts.), Sov. Un. (vyĕr-ĸō̍-yänskĭ)	181	67.45 N	128.00 E
Vermilion, Can. (vẽr-mĭl′yŭn)	99	53.22 N	110.51 W
Vermilion (L.), Mn.	115	47.49 N	92.35 W
Vermilion (R.), Can.	104	47.30 N	73.15 W
Vermilion (R.), Can.	99	53.30 N	111.00 W
Vermilion (R.), Il.	110	41.05 N	89.00 W
Vermilion (R.), Mn.	115	48.09 N	92.31 W
Vermilion Hills, Can.	100	50.43 N	106.50 W
Vermilion Ra, Mn.	115	47.55 N	91.59 W
Vermillion, SD	114	42.46 N	96.56 W
Vermillion (R.), SD	114	43.54 N	97.14 W
Vermillion B., La.	125	29.47 N	92.00 W
Vermont, Austl.	70b	37.50 S	145.12 E
Vermont (State), U.S. (vẽr-mŏnt′)	109	43.50 N	72.50 W
Vernal, Ut. (vûr′nȧl)	117	40.29 N	109.40 W
Verneuk Pan (L.), S. Afr. (vĕr-nŭk′)	226	30.10 S	21.46 E
Vernon, Ca. (vŭr′nŭn)	119a	34.01 N	118.12 W
Vernon, Can. (vĕr-nôɴ′)	99	50.18 N	119.15 W
Vernon, Can.	95c	45.10 N	75.27 W
Vernon, In. (vûr′nŭn)	110	39.00 N	85.40 W
Vernon, NJ	112a	39.00 N	85.40 W
Vernon, Tx.	122	34.09 N	99.16 W
Vernonia, Or. (vûr-nō′nyȧ)	118c	45.52 N	123.12 W
Vero Beach, Fl. (vē′rō̍)	127a	27.36 N	80.25 W
Véroia, Grc.	173	40.30 N	22.13 E
Verona, It. (vā-rō′nä)	172	45.28 N	11.02 E
Verona, NJ	55	40.50 N	74.12 W
Verona, Pa.	57b	40.30 N	79.50 W
Verrières-le-Buisson, Fr.	64c	48.45 N	2.16 E
Versailles, Fr. (vĕr-sī′y′)	169b	48.48 N	2.07 E
Versailles, Ky. (vẽr-sālz′)	110	38.05 N	84.45 W
Versailles, Mo.	123	38.27 N	92.52 W
Versailles, Pa.	57b	40.21 N	79.51 W
Versailles (Neigh.), Arg.	60d	34.38 S	58.31 W
Versailles, Château de (P. Int.), Fr.	64c	48.48 N	2.07 E
Vert, Cap (C.), Senegal	228	14.43 N	17.30 W
Verulam, S. Afr. (vĕ-ro͞o-lăm)	227c	29.39 S	31.08 E
Verulamium (P. Int.), Eng.	62	51.45 N	0.22 W
Verviers, Bel. (vĕr-vyā′)	163	50.35 N	5.57 E
Vesëloye, Sov. Un. (vĕ-syô′lō̍-yĕ)	175	46.59 N	34.56 E
Vesijärvi (L.), Fin.	165	61.09 N	25.10 E
Vesn′aki (Neigh.), Sov. Un.	66b	55.44 N	37.49 E
Vesoul, Fr. (vē-so͞ol′)	169	47.38 N	6.11 E
Vestavia Hills, Al.	112h	33.26 N	86.46 W
Vesterålen (Is.), Nor. (vĕs′tẽr ō̍′lĕn)	158	68.54 N	14.03 E
Vestfjord, Nor.	158	67.33 N	12.59 E
Vestmannaeyjar, Ice. (vĕst′män-ä-ā′yär)	158	63.12 N	20.17 W
Vesuvio, (Mtn.), It. (vĕ-so͞o′vyä)	171c	40.35 N	14.26 E
Ves′yegonsk, Sov. Un. (vĕ-syĕ-gônsk′)	174	58.42 N	37.09 E
Veszprem, Hung. (vĕs′prām)	167	47.05 N	17.53 E
Vészto, Hung. (vĕs′tû)	167	46.55 N	21.18 E
Vetka, Sov. Un. (vyĕt′kȧ)	174	52.36 N	31.05 E
Vetlanda, Swe. (vĕt-län′dä)	164	57.26 N	15.05 E
Vetluga, Sov. Un. (vyĕt-lo͞o′gȧ)	178	57.50 N	45.42 E
Vetluga (R.), Sov. Un.	178	56.50 N	45.50 E
Vetovo, Bul. (vā′tō̍-vō̍)	173	43.42 N	26.18 E
Vet R., S. Afr. (vĕt)	223d	28.25 S	26.37 E
Vetren, Bul. (vĕt′rĕn′)	173	42.16 N	24.04 E
Vevay, In. (vē′vā)	110	38.45 N	85.05 W
Veynes, Fr. (vān′′)	169	44.31 N	5.47 E
Vézère (R.), Fr. (vā-zer′)	168	45.01 N	1.00 E
Viacha, Bol. (vēȧ′chȧ)	142	16.43 S	68.16 W
Viadana, It. (ve̍-ä-dä′nä)	172	44.55 N	10.30 E
Vian, Ok. (vī′ăn)	123	35.30 N	95.00 W
Viana, Braz. (vē-ä′nä)	143	3.09 S	44.44 W
Viana del Bollo, Sp. (ve̍-ä′nä dĕl bō̍l′yō̍)	170	42.10 N	7.07 W
Viana do Alentejo, Port. (ve̍-ä′nȧ do͞o ä-lĕɴ-tā′ho͞o)	170	38.20 N	8.02 W
Viana do Castelo, Port. (do͞o käs-tā′lo͞o)	170e	41.41 N	8.45 W
Viangchan, Laos	206	18.07 N	102.33 E
Viar (R.), Sp. (ve̍-ä′rä)	170	38.15 N	6.08 W
Viareggio, It. (ve̍-ä-rĕd′jô)	172	43.52 N	10.14 E
Viborg, Den. (vē′bôr)	164	56.27 N	9.22 E
Vibo Valentia, It. (ve̍′bō̍-vä-lĕ′n-tyä)	172	38.47 N	16.06 E
Vicálvaro, Sp.	171a	40.25 N	3.37 W
Vicente Lòpez, Arg. (vē-sĕ′n-tĕ-lŏ′pĕz)	144a	34.15 S	58.20 W
Vicenza, It. (ve̍-chĕnt′sä)	172	45.33 N	11.33 E
Vich, Sp. (vēch)	171	41.55 N	2.14 E
Vichuga, Sov. Un. (vē-cho͞o′gȧ)	174	57.13 N	41.58 E
Vichy, Fr. (ve̍-shē′)	168	46.06 N	3.28 E
Vickersund, Nor.	164	60.00 N	9.59 E
Vicksburg, Mi. (vĭks′bûrg)	110	42.10 N	85.30 W
Vicksburg, Ms.	126	32.20 N	90.50 W
Viçosa, Braz. (vē-sô′sä)	141a	23.46 S	42.51 W
Victoria, Arg. (vēk-tô′re̍ä)	141c	32.36 S	60.09 W
Victoria, Cam. (vĭk-tō′rĭ-ȧ)	229	4.01 N	9.12 E
Victoria, Can. (vĭk-tō′rĭ-ȧ)	98	48.26 N	123.23 W
Victoria, Chile (vēk-tô-re̍ä)	144	38.15 S	72.16 W
Victoria, Col. (vēk-tô′re̍ä)	142a	5.19 N	74.54 W

ăt; finăl; rāte; senāte; ärm; ȧsk; sofȧ; fâre; ch-choose; dh-as th in other; bē; e̍vent; bĕt; recĕnt; cratẽr; g-gō; gh-guttural g; bĭt; ĭ-short neutral; rīde; ĸ-guttural k as ch in German ich;

RONOUNCING INDEX

Victoria – Vladimir 359

ACE (Pronounciation)	PAGE	Lat. °'	Long. °'
ictoria, Phil. (vê̆k-tô-ryä)	207a	15.34 N	120.41 E
ictoria, Tx. (vĭk-tō'rĭ-ȧ)	125	28.48 N	97.00 W
ictoria, Va.	127	36.57 N	78.13 W
ictoria (Neigh.), Arg.	60d	34.28 S	58.31 W
ictoria (State), Austl.	215	36.46 S	143.15 E
ictoria I., Nig.	71d	6.26 N	3.26 E
ictoria (L.), Afr.	231	0.50 S	32.50 E
ictoria (R.), Austl.	214	17.25 S	130.50 E
ictoria de las Tunas, Cuba (vê̆k-tō'rê-ä dā läs to͞o'näs)	134	20.55 N	77.05 W
ctoria Falls, Zambia	231	17.56 S	25.50 E
ctoria Falls, Zimb.	231	17.55 S	25.51 E
ictoria I., Can.	96	70.13 N	107.45 W
ictoria L., Can.	105	48.20 N	57.40 W
ictoria Land, Ant.	232	75.00 S	160.00 E
ictoria Lawn Tennis Association Courts (P. Int.), Austl.	70b	37.51 S	145.02 E
ictoria, Mt., Bur.	198	21.26 N	93.59 E
ictoria, Mt., Pap. N. Gui.	207	9.35 S	147.45 E
ictoria Nile (R.), Ug.	231	2.20 N	31.35 E
ictoria Peak (Mtn.), Hong Kong	68c	22.17 N	114.08 E
ictoria Pk., Belize (vê̆k-tōrĭ'ȧ)	132a	16.47 N	88.40 W
ictoria Pk., Can.	98	50.03 N	126.06 W
ictoria River Downs, Austl. (vĭc-tôr'ĭȧ)	214	16.30 S	131.10 E
ictoria Station (P. Int.), Eng.	64b	53.29 N	2.15 W
ictoria Str., Can. (vĭk-tō'rĭ-ȧ)	96	69.10 N	100.58 W
ictoriaville, Can. (vĭk-tō'rĭ-ȧ-vĭl)	103	46.04 N	71.59 W
ictoria West, S. Afr. (wĕst)	226	31.25 S	23.10 E
idalia, Ga. (vĭ-dā'lĭ-ȧ)	127	32.10 N	82.26 W
idalia, La.	125	31.33 N	91.28 W
idin, Bul. (vĭ'dên)	173	44.00 N	22.53 E
idnoye, Sov. Un.	182b	55.33 N	37.41 E
idzy, Sov. Un. (vê'dzĭ)	174	55.23 N	26.46 E
iedma, Arg. (vyād'mä)	144	40.55 S	63.03 W
iedma (L.), Arg.	144	49.40 S	72.35 W
iejo R., Nic. (vyā'hō)	132	12.45 N	86.19 W
ienna, Ga. (vê-ĕn'ȧ)	126	32.03 N	83.50 W
ienna, Il.	123	37.24 N	88.50 W
ienna, Va.	112e	38.54 N	77.16 W
ienna, see Wien			
ienne, Fr. (vyĕn')	168	45.31 N	4.54 E
ienne (R.), Fr.	168	47.06 N	0.20 E
ieques, P.R. (vyā'kâs)	129b	18.09 N	65.27 W
ieques (I.), P.R. (vyā'kâs)	129b	18.05 N	65.28 W
ierfontien, S. Afr. (vēr'fôn-tān)	223d	27.06 S	26.45 E
ieringhausen (Neigh.), F.R.G.	63	51.11 N	7.10 E
iersen, F.R.G. (fēr'zĕn)	169c	51.15 N	6.24 E
ierwaldstätter See (L.), Switz.	166	46.54 N	8.36 E
ierzon, Fr. (vyâr-zôɴ')	168	47.14 N	2.04 E
iesca, Mex. (vê-ās'kä)	124	25.21 N	102.47 W
iesca, Laguna de (L.), Mex. (lä-o͞o'nä-dĕ)	124	25.30 N	102.40 W
ieste, It. (vyĕs'tâ)	172	41.52 N	161.0 E
ietnam, Asia (vyĕt'näm')	206	18.00 N	107.00 E
iew Park, Ca.	59	34.00 N	118.21 W
igan, Phil. (vēgän)	207a	17.36 N	120.22 E
igevano, It. (vê-jâ-vä'nô)	172	45.18 N	8.52 E
igentino (Neigh.), It.	65c	45.25 N	9.11 E
igny, Fr. (vên-y'ē')	169b	49.05 N	1.54 E
igo, Sp. (vē'gō)	170	42.18 N	8.42 W
ihti, Fin. (vē'tĭ)	165	60.27 N	24.18 E
iipuri, see Vyborg			
ijayawāda, India	197	16.31 N	80.37 E
ijosë, (R.), Alb.	173	40.15 N	20.30 E
iksøyri, Nor.	164	61.06 N	6.35 E
ila, Vanuatu	215	18.00 S	168.30 E
ila Augusta, Braz.	61d	23.28 S	46.32 W
ila Boacaya (Neigh.), Braz.	61d	23.29 S	46.44 W
ila Caldas Xavier, Moz.	231	15.59 S	34.12 E
ila de Manica, Moz. (vē'lä dā mä-nē'kȧ)	226	18.48 S	32.49 E
ila de Rei, Port. (vē'lȧ dā rā'ĭ)	170	39.42 N	8.03 W
ila do Conde, Port. (vē'lȧ do͞o kôn'dĕ)	170	41.21 N	8.44 W
ilafranca de Xira, Port. (fräŋ'kȧ dā shē'rȧ)	170	38.58 N	8.59 W
ila Guilherme (Neigh.), Braz.	61d	23.30 S	46.36 W
ilaine (R.), Fr. (vē-lȧn')	168	47.34 N	0.20 W
ila Isabel (Neigh.), Braz.	61c	22.55 S	43.15 W
ila Jaguára (Neigh.), Braz.	61d	23.31 S	46.45 W
ila Madalena (Neigh.) Braz.	61d	23.33 S	46.42 W
ila Mariana (Neigh.), Braz.	61d	23.35 S	46.38 W
ilanculos, Moz. (vê-län-ko͞o'lôs)	226	22.03 S	35.13 E
ilāni, Sov. Un. (vē'lȧ-nĭ)	174	56.31 N	27.00 E
ila Nova de Foz Côa, Port. (nō'vȧ dā fôz-kō'ȧ)	170	41.08 N	7.11 W
ila Nova de Gaia, Port. (vē'lȧ nō'vȧ dā gä'yä)	170	41.08 N	8.40 W
ila Nova de Milfontes, Port. (nō'vȧ dā mêl-fôn'tāzh)	170	37.44 N	8.48 W
ila Progresso, Braz.	61c	22.55 S	43.03 W
ila Prudente (Neigh.), Braz.	61d	23.35 S	46.33 W
ila Real, Port. (rā-äl')	170	41.18 N	7.48 W
ila Real de Santo Antonio, Port. (vê'lä-rĕ-ä'l-dĕ-sän-tô-än-tô'nyô)	170	37.14 N	7.25 W
ila Viçosa, Port. (vê-sō'zȧ)	170	38.47 N	7.24 W
ileyka, Sov. Un. (vê-lā'ê-kȧ)	174	54.19 N	26.58 E
ilhelmina, Swe.	158	64.37 N	16.30 E
iljandi, Sov. Un. (vēl'yän-dê)	165	58.24 N	25.34 E
iljoenskroon, S. Afr.	223d	27.13 S	26.58 E
ilkaviškis, Sov. Un. (vêl-kȧ-vēsh'kês)	165	54.40 N	23.08 E
ilkija, Sov. Un. (vêl-kē'ēȧ)	165	55.04 N	23.30 E
il'kitskogo (I.), Sov. Un. (vyl-kēts-kōgō)	180	73.25 N	76.00 E
ilkovo, Sov. Un. (vĭl-kô-vô)	179	45.24 N	29.36 E
illa Acuña, Mex. (vêl'yä-ko͞o'n-yä)	124	29.20 N	100.56 W
illa Adelina (Neigh.), Arg.	60d	34.31 S	58.32 W
illa Ahumada, Mex. (ä-o͞o-mä'dä)	124	30.43 N	106.30 W
illa Alta (San Ildefonso), Mex. (äl'tä)(sän ēl-dâ-fōn'sō)	131	17.20 N	96.08 W

PLACE (Pronounciation)	PAGE	Lat. °'	Long. °'
Villa Angela, Arg. (vê'l-yä ȧ'n-ᴋĕ-lä)	144	27.31 S	60.42 W
Villa Ballester, Arg. (vê'l-yä-bȧl-yĕs-tĕr)	144a	34.18 S	58.33 W
Villa Bella, Bol. (bĕ'l-yä)	142	10.25 S	65.22 W
Villablino, Sp. (vêl-yä-blē'nô)	170	42.58 N	6.18 W
Villa Borghese (P. Int.), It.	66c	41.55 N	12.29 E
Villa Bosch (Neigh.), Arg.	60d	34.36 S	58.34 W
Villacañas, Sp. (vêl-yä-kän'yäs)	170	39.39 N	3.20 W
Villacarrillo, Sp. (vêl-yä-kä-rēl'yô)	170	38.09 N	3.07 W
Villach, Aus. (fê'läᴋ)	166	46.38 N	13.50 E
Villacidro, It. (vē-lä-chē'drô)	172	39.28 N	8.41 E
Villa Ciudadela (Neigh.), Arg.	60d	34.38 S	58.34 W
Villa Clara (Prov.), Cuba	134	22.40 N	80.10 W
Villa Constitución, Arg. (kōn-stê-to͞o-syōn')	141c	33.15 S	60.19 W
Villa Coronado, Mex. (kō-rō-nä'dhô)	124	26.45 N	105.10 W
Villa Cuauhtémoc, Mex. (vêl'yä-ko͞o-äo͞o-tĕ'môk)	131	22.11 N	97.50 W
Villa de Allende, Mex. (vēl'yä'dā äl-yĕn'dâ)	124	25.18 N	100.01 W
Villa de Alvarez, Mex. (vêl'yä-dĕ-ä'l-vä-rĕz)	130	19.17 N	103.44 W
Villa de Cura, Ven. (dĕ-ko͞o'rä)	143b	10.03 N	67.29 W
Villa de Guadalupe, Mex. (dĕ-gwä-dhä-lo͞o'pâ)	130	23.22 N	100.44 W
Villa de Mayo, Arg.	60d	34.31 S	58.41 W
Villa Devoto (Neigh.), Arg.	60d	34.36 S	58.31 W
Villa Diamante (Neigh.), Arg.	60d	34.41 S	58.26 W
Villa Dolores, Arg. (vēl'yä dô-lō'rās)	144	31.50 S	65.05 W
Villa Domínico (Neigh.), Arg.	60d	34.41 S	58.20 W
Villa Escalante, Mex. (vêl'yä-ĕs-kä-lȧn'tĕ)	130	19.24 N	101.36 W
Villa Flores, Mex. (vêl'yä-flō'rās)	131	16.13 N	93.17 W
Villafranca, It. (vēl-lä-fräŋ'kä)	172	45.22 N	10.53 E
Villafranca del Bierzo, Sp. (vēl'yä-fräŋ'kä dĕl byĕr'thō)	170	42.37 N	6.49 W
Villafranca de los Barros, Sp. (vēl-yä-fräŋ'kä dā lōs bär'rōs)	170	38.34 N	6.22 W
Villafranca del Panadés, Sp. (vēl-yäfrän'kä dĕl pä-nä-dās')	171	41.20 N	1.40 E
Villafranche-de-Rouergue, Fr. (dē-ro͞o-ĕrg')	168	44.21 N	2.02 E
Villa García, Mex. (gär-sē'ä)	130	22.07 N	101.55 W
Villagarcia, Sp. (vēl'yä-gär-thē'ä)	170	42.38 N	8.43 W
Villagram, Mex. (vēl-yä-gräm')	124	24.28 N	99.30 W
Villa Grove, Il. (vĭl'ȧ grōv')	110	39.55 N	88.15 W
Villaguay, Arg. (vê'l-yä-gwī)	144	31.47 S	58.53 W
Villa Hayes, Par. (vēl'yä äyâs)(hāz)	144	25.07 S	57.31 W
Villahermosa, Mex. (vēl'yä-ĕr-mō'sä)	131	17.59 N	92.56 W
Villa Hidalgo, Mex. (vēl'yäē-däl'gō)	130	21.39 N	102.41 W
Villa José L. Suárez (Neigh.)	60d	34.32 S	58.34 W
Villajoyosa, Sp. (vēl'yä-hô-yō'sä)	171	38.30 N	0.14 W
Villalba, Sp.	170	43.18 N	7.43 W
Villaldama, Mex. (vēl-yäl-dä'mä)	124	26.30 N	100.26 W
Villa Lopez, Mex. (vēl'yä lō'pĕz)	124	27.00 N	105.02 W
Villalpando, Sp. (vēl-yäl-pän'dō)	170	41.54 N	5.24 W
Villa Lugano (Neigh.), Arg.	60d	34.41 S	58.28 W
Villa Lynch (Neigh.), Arg.	60d	34.36 S	58.32 W
Villa Madero, Arg.	60d	34.41 S	58.30 W
Villa María, Arg. (vê'l-yä-mä-rē'ä)	144	32.17 S	63.08 W
Villamatín, Sp. (vēl-yä-mä-tê'n)	170	36.50 N	5.38 W
Villa Mercedes, Arg. (mĕr-sā'dâs)	144	33.38 S	65.16 W
Villa Montes, Bol. (vê'l-yä-mô'n-tĕs)	142	21.13 S	63.26 W
Villa Morelos, Mex. (mô-rĕ'lomcs)	130	20.01 N	101.24 W
Villa Nova, Md.	56c	39.21 N	76.44 W
Villanova, Pa.	56b	40.02 N	75.21 W
Villanueva, Col. (vê'l-yä-no͞oĕ'vä)	142	10.44 N	73.08 W
Villanueva, Hond. (vēl'yä-nwā'vä)	132	15.19 N	88.02 W
Villanueva, Mex. (vêl'yä-no͞oĕ'vä)	130	22.25 N	102.53 W
Villanueva de Córdoba, Sp. (vêl-yä-nwĕ'vä-dā kôr'dô-bä)	170	38.18 N	4.38 W
Villanueva de la Serena, Sp. (lä sā-rā'nä)	170	38.59 N	5.56 W
Villanueva y Geltrú, Sp. (ēᴋĕl-tro͞o')	171	41.13 N	1.44 E
Villa Obregón, Mex. (vē'l-yä-ô-brĕ-gô'n)	131a	19.21 N	99.11 W
Villa Ocampo, Mex. (ô-käm'pō)	124	26.26 N	105.30 W
Villa Pedro Montoya, Mex. (vêl'yä-pĕ'drô-môn-tô'yȧ)	130	21.38 N	99.51 W
Villard-Bonnot, Fr. (vēl-yär'bôn-nô')	169	45.15 N	5.53 E
Villa Real (Neigh.), Arg.	60d	34.37 S	58.31 W
Villarreal, Sp. (vêl-yär-rĕ-äl)	171	39.55 N	0.07 W
Villarrica, Par. (vēl-yä-rē'kä)	144	25.55 S	56.23 W
Villarrobledo, Sp. (vēl-yär-rô-blā'dhō)	170	39.15 N	2.37 W
Villa Sáenz Peña (Neigh.), Arg.	60d	34.46 S	58.31 W
Villa San Andrés (Neigh.), Arg.	60d	34.33 S	58.32 W
Villa Santos Lugares (Neigh.), Arg.	60d	34.36 S	58.32 W
Villa Turdera (Neigh.), Arg.	60d	34.48 S	58.25 W
Villa Union, Mex. (vêl'yä-o͞o-nyōn')	130	23.10 N	106.14 W
Villaverde (Neigh.), Sp.	65b	40.21 N	3.42 W
Villavicencio, Col. (vê'l-yä-vē-sĕ'n-syō)	142a	4.09 N	73.38 W
Villaviciosa de Odón, Sp. (vēl'yä-vê-thê-ō'sä dā ō-dōn')	171a	40.22 N	73.38 W
Villavieja, Col. (vê'l-yä-vē-ĕ'ᴋȧ)	142a	3.13 N	75.13 W
Villazón, Bol. (vê'l-yä-zô'n)	144	22.02 S	65.42 W
Villecresnes, Fr.	64c	48.43 N	2.32 E
Ville-d'Avray, Fr.	64c	48.50 N	2.11 E
Villefranche, Fr.	168	45.59 N	4.43 E
Villejuif, Fr. (vēl'zhüst')	169b	48.48 N	2.22 E
Ville-Maríe, Can.	103	47.18 N	79.22 W
Villemomble, Fr.	64c	48.53 N	2.31 E
Villena, Sp. (vē-lyā'nȧ)	171	38.37 N	0.52 W
Villenbon-sur-Yvette, Fr.	64c	48.42 N	2.15 E
Villeneuve, Can. (vēl'nûv')	95g	53.40 N	113.49 W
Villeneuve-la-Garenne, Fr.	64c	48.56 N	2.20 E
Villeneuve-le-Roi, Fr.	64c	48.44 N	2.25 E
Villeneuve-Saint Georges, Fr. (săɴ-zhôrzh')	169b	48.43 N	2.27 E
Villeneuve-sur-Lot, Fr. (sür-lō')	168	44.25 N	0.41 E

PLACE (Pronounciation)	PAGE	Lat. °'	Long. °'
Villeparisis, Fr.	64c	48.56 N	2.37 E
Ville Platte, La. (vēl plȧt')	125	30.41 N	92.17 W
Villers Cotterêts, Fr. (vē-ār'kô-trā')	168a	49.15 N	3.05 E
Villers-sur-Marne, Fr.	64c	48.50 N	2.33 E
Villerupt, Fr. (vēl'rüp')	169	49.28 N	6.16 E
Ville-Saint Georges, Can. (vĭl-sĕɴ-zhôrzh')	103	46.07 N	70.40 W
Villeta, Col. (vē'l-yĕ'tȧ)	142a	5.02 N	74.29 W
Villeurbanne, Fr. (vēl-ûr-bän')	168	45.43 N	4.55 E
Villevaudé, Fr.	64c	48.55 N	2.39 E
Villiers, S. Afr. (vĭl'ĭ-ērs)	223d	27.03 S	28.38 E
Villiers-le-Bâcle, Fr.	64c	48.44 N	2.08 E
Villiers-le-Bel, Fr.	64c	49.00 N	2.23 E
Villingen-Schwenningen, F.R.G.	166	48.04 N	8.33 E
Villisca, Ia. (vĭ'lĭs'kȧ)	115	40.56 N	94.56 W
Villupuram, India	197	11.59 N	79.33 E
Vilnius (Wilno), Sov. Un. (vĭl'nê-o͞os)	165	54.40 N	25.26 E
Vilppula, Fin. (vĭl'pŭ-lȧ)	165	62.01 N	24.24 E
Vilvoorde, Bel.	157a	50.56 N	4.25 E
Vilyuy (R.), Sov. Un. (vēl'yĭ)	181	65.22 N	108.45 E
Vilyuysk, Sov. Un. (vê-lyo͞o'ĭsk')	181	63.41 N	121.47 E
Vimmerby, Swe. (vĭm'ēr-bü)	164	57.41 N	15.51 E
Vimperk, Czech. (vĭm-pĕrk')	166	49.04 N	13.41 E
Viña del Mar, Chile (vē'nyä dĕl mär')	141b	33.00 S	71.33 W
Vinalhaven, Me. (vī-năl-hā'vĕn)	104	44.03 N	68.49 W
Vinaroz, Sp. (vē-nä'rōth)	171	40.29 N	0.27 E
Vincennes, Fr. (văɴ-sĕn')	169b	48.51 N	2.27 E
Vincennes, In. (vĭn-zĕnz')	110	38.40 N	87.30 W
Vincennes, Château de (P. Int.), Fr.	64c	48.51 N	2.26 E
Vincent, Al. (vĭn'sĕnt)	126	33.21 N	86.25 W
Vindelälven (R.), Swe.	158	65.02 N	18.30 E
Vindeln, Swe. (vĭn'dĕln)	158	64.10 N	19.52 E
Vindhya Ra., India (vĭnd'yä)	196	22.30 N	75.50 E
Vineland, NJ (vīn'lănd)	111	39.30 N	75.00 W
Vinh, Viet. (vên'y')	203	18.38 N	105.42 E
Vinhais, Port. (vên-yä'ēzh)	170	41.51 N	7.00 W
Vinings, Ga. (vī'nĭngz)	112c	33.52 N	84.28 W
Vinita, Ok. (vĭ-nē'tȧ)	123	36.38 N	95.09 W
Vinkovci, Yugo. (vēn'kôv-tsê)	173	45.17 N	18.47 E
Vinnitsa, Sov. Un. (vê'nêt-sȧ)	175	49.13 N	28.31 E
Vinnitsa (Oblast), Sov. Un.	175	48.45 N	28.01 E
Vinogradovo, Sov. Un. (vĭ-nô-grä'do-vô)	182b	55.25 N	38.33 E
Vinson Massif (Mtn.), Ant.	232	77.40 S	87.00 W
Vinton, Ia. (vĭn'tŭn)	115	42.08 N	92.01 W
Vinton, La.	125	30.12 N	93.35 W
Violet, La. (vī'ô-lĕt)	112d	29.54 N	89.54 W
Virac, Phil. (vê-räk')	203	13.38 N	124.20 E
Virbalis, Sov. Un. (vêr'bȧ-lês)	165	54.38 N	22.55 E
Virden, Can. (vûr'dĕn)	96	49.51 N	101.55 W
Virden, Il.	123	39.28 N	89.46 W
Virgin (R.), U.S.	121	36.51 N	113.50 W
Virginia, Mn. (vēr-jĭn'yȧ)	115	47.32 N	92.36 W
Virginia, S. Afr.	223d	28.07 S	26.54 E
Virginia (State), U.S.	109	37.00 N	80.45 W
Virginia Beach, Va.	112g	36.50 N	75.58 W
Virginia City, Nv.	120	39.18 N	119.40 W
Virginia Hills, Va.	56d	38.47 N	77.06 W
Virginia Water, Eng.	62	51.24 N	0.34 W
Virgin Is., N.A. (vûr'jĭn)	129	18.15 N	64.00 W
Viroflay, Fr.	64c	48.48 N	2.10 E
Viroqua, Wi. (vĭ-rō'kwȧ)	115	43.33 N	90.54 W
Virovitica, Yugo. (vê-rô-vē'tê-tsȧ)	172	45.50 N	17.24 E
Virpazar, Yugo. (vêr'pä-zär')	173	42.16 N	19.06 E
Virrat, Fin. (vĭr'ät)	165	62.15 N	23.45 E
Virserum, Swe. (vĭr'sĕ-ro͞om)	164	57.22 N	15.35 E
Vis, Yugo. (vês)	172	43.03 N	16.11 E
Vis (I.), Yugo.	172	43.00 N	16.10 E
Visalia, Ca. (vĭ-sā'lĭ-ȧ)	120	36.20 N	119.18 W
Visby, Swe. (vĭs'bü)	164	57.39 N	18.19 E
Viscount Mellville Sound, Can.	94	74.80 N	110.00 W
Visêgrad, Yugo. (vē'shĕ-gräd)	173	43.45 N	19.19 E
Vishākhapatnam, India	197	17.48 N	83.21 E
Vishera R., Sov. Un. (vĭ'shĕ-rȧ)	182a	60.40 N	58.46 E
Vishnyakovo, Sov. Un.	182b	55.44 N	38.10 E
Vishoek, S. Afr.	226a	34.13 S	18.26 E
Visim, Sov. Un. (vē'sĭm)	182a	57.38 N	59.32 E
Viskan (R.), Swe.	164	57.20 N	12.25 E
Viški, Sov. Un. (vēs'kĭ)	174	56.02 N	26.47 E
Vislinskij Zaliv (B.), Pol.	167	54.22 N	19.39 E
Visoko, Yugo. (vē'sô-kô)	173	43.59 N	18.10 E
Vistula (R.), see Wisla			
Vitacura, Chile	61b	33.24 S	70.36 W
Vitarte, Peru	60c	12.02 S	76.54 W
Vitebsk, Sov. Un. (vē'tyĕpsk)	174	55.12 N	30.16 E
Vitebsk (Oblast), Sov. Un.	174	55.05 N	29.18 E
Viterbo, It. (vê-tĕr'bō)	172	42.24 N	12.08 E
Vitim, Sov. Un. (vē'têm)	181	59.22 N	112.43 E
Vitim (R.), Sov. Un. (vē'têm)	181	56.12 N	115.30 E
Vitino, Sov. Un. (vē'tĭ-nô)	182c	59.40 N	29.51 E
Vitória, Braz. (vê-tō'rê-ä)	143	20.09 S	40.17 W
Vitoria, Sp. (vē-tô-ryä)	170	42.43 N	2.43 W
Vitória de Conquista, Braz. (vê-tō'rê-ä-dä-kōn-kwē's-tä)	143	14.51 S	40.44 W
Vitré, Fr. (vê-trā')	168	48.09 N	1.15 W
Vitry-le-François, Fr. (vê-trē'lĕ-fräɴ-swȧ')	168	48.44 N	4.34 E
Vitry-sur-Seine, Fr.	64c	48.48 N	2.24 E
Vittoria, It. (vê-tô'rê-ô)	159	37.01 N	14.31 E
Vittorio, It. (vê-tô'rê-ô)	172	45.59 N	12.17 E
Vivero, Sp. (vê-vā'rō)	170	43.39 N	7.37 W
Vivian, La. (vĭv'ĭ-ȧn)	125	32.51 N	93.59 W
Vírgen del San Cristó bal (P. Int.), Chile	61b	33.26 S	70.39 W
Víron, Grc.	66d	37.57 N	23.45 E
Vize, Tur. (vē'zĕ)	173	41.34 N	27.46 E
Vizianagaram, India	197	18.10 N	83.29 E
Vlaardingen, Neth. (vlär'dĭng-ĕn)	157a	51.54 N	4.20 E
Vladimir, Sov. Un. (vlȧ-dyē'mēr)	174	56.08 N	40.24 E
Vladimir (Oblast), Sov. Un. (vlä-dyē'mēr)	174	56.08 N	39.53 E

360 Vladimiro-Aleksandrovskoye – Wandoan

PLACE (Pronounciation)	PAGE	Lat. °′	Long. °′
Vladimiro-Aleksandrovskoye, Sov. Un. (vlȧ-dyē'mē-rô ȧ-lĕk-săn'drôf-skô-yĕ)	204	42.50 N	133.00 E
Vladimir-Volynskiy, Sov. Un. (vlȧ-dyē'mēr vô-lēn'skĭ)	167	50.50 N	24.20 E
Vladivostok, Sov. Un. (vlȧ-dē-vôs-tŏk')	181	43.06 N	131.47 E
Vladykino (Neigh.), Sov. Un.	66b	55.52 N	37.36 E
Vlasenica, Yugo. (vlä'sĕ-nēt'sȧ)	173	44.11 N	18.58 E
Vlasotince, Yugo. (vlä'sô-tēn-tsĕ)	173	42.58 N	22.08 E
Vlieland (I.), Neth. (vlē'länt)	163	53.19 N	4.55 E
Vlissingen, Neth. (vlĭs'sĭng-ĕn)	163	51.30 N	3.34 E
Vlorë (Valona), Alb. (vlō'rŭ)	173	40.28 N	19.31 E
Vltava (R.), Czech.	166	49.24 N	14.18 E
Vodl (L.), Sov. Un. (vôd''l)	178	62.20 N	37.20 E
Voël (R.), S. Afr.	226	32.52 S	25.12 E
Voerde, F.R.G.	63	51.35 N	6.41 E
Voesch, F.R.G.	63	51.24 N	6.26 E
Vogelheim (Neigh.), F.R.G.	63	51.29 N	6.59 E
Voghera, It. (vô-gā'rä)	172	44.58 N	9.02 E
Vohwinkel (Neigh.), F.R.G.	63	51.14 N	7.09 E
Voight (R.), Wa.	118a	47.03 N	122.08 W
Voinjama, Lib.	228	8.25 N	9.45 W
Voiron, Fr. (vwȧ-rôN')	171	45.23 N	5.48 E
Voisin, Lac (L.), Can. (vwŏ'-zĭn)	100	54.13 N	107.15 W
Voisins-le-Bretonneux, Fr.	64c	48.45 N	2.03 E
Volcán Misti (Vol.), Peru	142	16.04 S	71.20 W
Volchansk, Sov. Un. (vôl-chänsk')	175	50.18 N	36.56 E
Volchonka-Zil (Neigh.), Sov. Un.	66b	55.40 N	37.37 E
Volch'ya (R.), Sov. Un. (vôl-chyä')	175	49.42 N	34.39 E
Volga (R.), Sov. Un. (vôl'gä)	179	47.30 N	46.20 E
Volga, Mouths of the, Sov. Un.	179	46.00 N	49.10 E
Volgograd (Stalingrad), Sov. Un. (vŏl-gō-grä't)(stá'lên-grat)	179	48.40 N	42.20 E
Volgogradskoye (Res.), Sov. Un. (vôl-gô-grad'skô-yĕ)	179	51.10 N	45.10 E
Volkhov, Sov. Un. (vôl'kôf)	174	59.54 N	32.21 E
Volkhov (R.), Sov. Un.	174	58.45 N	31.40 E
Volkovysk, Sov. Un. (vôl-kô-vēsk')	167	53.11 N	24.29 E
Vollme, F.R.G.	63	51.10 N	7.36 E
Volmarstein, F.R.G.	63	51.22 N	7.23 E
Volmerswerth (Neigh.), F.R.G.	63	51.11 N	6.46 E
Volodarskiy, Sov. Un. (vô-lô-där'skĭ)	182c	59.49 N	30.06 E
Vologda, Sov. Un. (vô'lôg-dȧ)	174	59.12 N	39.52 E
Vologda (Oblast), Sov. Un.	174	59.00 N	37.26 E
Volokolamsk, Sov. Un. (vô-lô-kôlȧmsk)	174	56.02 N	35.58 E
Volokonovka, Sov. Un. (vô-lô-kô'nôf-kȧ)	175	50.28 N	37.52 E
Vólos, Grc. (vô'lôs)	173	39.23 N	22.56 E
Volozhin, Sov. Un. (vô'lô-shēn)	174	54.04 N	26.38 E
Vol'sk, Sov. Un. (vôl'sk)	179	52.10 N	47.00 E
Volta (R.), Ghana	228	6.05 N	0.30 E
Volta Blanche (R.), Burkina	228	11.30 N	0.40 W
Volta, La., Ghana (vōl'tȧ)	228	7.10 N	0.30 W
Volta Noire (Black Volta) (R.), Afr.	228	10.30 N	2.55 W
Volta Redonda, Braz. (vōl'tä-rā-dôn'dä)	141a	22.32 S	44.05 W
Volterra, It. (vôl-tĕr'rä)	172	43.22 N	10.51 E
Voltri, It. (vōl'trē)	172	44.25 N	8.45 E
Volturno (R.), It. (vōl-tōōr'nō)	172	41.12 N	14.20 E
Vólvi, Límni (L.), Grc.	173	40.41 N	23.23 E
Volzhskoye (L.), Sov. Un. (vôl'sh-skô-yĕ)	174	56.43 N	36.18 E
Von Ormy, Tx. (vŏn ôr'mē)	119d	29.18 N	98.36 W
Võõpsu, Sov. Un. (vōōp'sōō)	174	58.06 N	27.30 E
Voorberg, Neth.	157a	52.04 N	4.21 E
Voortrekkerhoogte, S. Afr.	227b	25.48 S	28.10 E
Vop' (R.), Sov. Un. (vôp)	174	55.20 N	32.40 E
Vopnafjördur, Ice.	158	65.43 N	14.58 W
Vorarlberg (Prov.), Aus.	166	47.20 N	9.55 E
Vordingborg, Den. (vôr'dĭng-bôr)	164	55.10 N	11.55 E
Vorhalle (Neigh.), F.R.G.	63	51.23 N	7.28 E
Voríai (Is.), Grc.	173	39.12 N	24.03 E
Vorkuta, Sov. Un. (vôr-kōō'tȧ)	178	67.28 N	63.40 E
Vormholz, F.R.G.	63	51.24 N	7.18 E
Vormsi (I.), Sov. Un. (vôrm'sĭ)	165	59.06 N	23.05 E
Vórois Evvoïkós Kólpos (G.), Grc	173	38.48 N	23.02 E
Vorona (R.), Sov. Un. (vô-rô'na)	179	51.50 N	42.00 E
Voronezh, Sov. Un. (vô-rô'nyĕzh)	175	51.39 N	39.11 E
Voronezh (Oblast), Sov. Un.	175	51.10 N	39.13 E
Voronezh (R.), Sov. Un.	174	52.17 N	39.32 E
Voronovo, Sov. Un. (vô'rô-nô-vô)	167	54.07 N	25.16 E
Vorontsovka, Sov. Un. (vô-rônt'sôv-kȧ)	182a	59.40 N	60.14 E
Voron'ya (R.), Sov. Un. (vô-rônyȧ)	178	68.20 N	35.20 E
Voroshilovgrad, Sov. Un.	179	48.34 N	39.18 E
Voroshilovgrad (Oblast), Sov. Un.	175	49.08 N	38.37 E
Võrts-Järv (L.), Sov. Un. (vôrts yärv)	174	58.15 N	26.12 E
Võru, Sov. Un. (vô'rû)	174	57.50 N	26.58 E
Vorya R., Sov. Un. (vôr'yȧ)	182b	55.55 N	38.15 E
Vosges (Mts.), Fr. (vōzh)	169	48.09 N	6.57 E
Voskresensk, Sov. Un. (vôs-krē-sĕnsk')	182b	55.20 N	38.42 E
Voss, Nor. (vôs)	164	60.40 N	6.24 E
Vostryakovo, Sov. Un.	182b	55.23 N	37.49 E
Votkinsk, Sov. Un. (vôt-kēnsk')	178	57.00 N	54.00 E
Votkinskoye Vdkhr (Res.), Sov. Un.	178	57.30 N	55.00 E
Vouga (R.), Port. (vō'gȧ)	170	40.43 N	7.51 W
Vouziers, Fr. (vōō-zyā')	168	49.25 N	4.40 E
Voxnan (R.), Swe.	164	61.30 N	15.24 E
Voyageurs Natl. Park, Mn.	115	48.30 N	92.40 W
Vozhe (L.), Sov. Un. (vôzh'yĕ)	178	60.40 N	39.00 E
Voznesensk, Sov. Un. (vôz-nyĕ-sĕnsk')	175	47.34 N	31.22 E
Vrangelya (Wrangel) (I.), Sov. Un.	176	71.25 N	178.30 E
Vranje, Yugo. (vrän'yĕ)	173	42.33 N	21.55 E
Vratsa, Bul. (vrät'tsȧ)	173	43.12 N	23.31 E
Vrbas, Yugo. (v'r'bäs)	173	45.34 N	19.43 E
Vrbas (R.), Yugo.	172	44.25 N	17.17 E
Vrchlabi, Czech. (v'r'chlä-bē)	168	50.32 N	15.51 E
Vrede, S. Afr. (vrĭ'dĕ)(vrēd)	223d	27.25 S	29.11 E
Vredefort, S. Afr. (vrĭ'dĕ-fôrt)(vrēd'fōrt)	223d	27.00 S	27.21 E
Vreeswijk, Neth.	157a	52.00 N	5.06 E
Vršac, Yugo. (v'r'shȧts)	173	45.08 N	21.18 E
Vrutky, Czech. (vrōōt'kē)	167	49.09 N	18.55 E
Vryburg, S. Afr. (vrī'bûrg)	226	26.55 S	29.45 E
Vryheid, S. Afr. (vrī'hīt)	226	27.43 S	30.58 E
Vsetín, Czech. (fsĕt'yēn)	167	49.21 N	18.01 E
Vsevolozhskiy, Sov. Un. (vsyĕ'vôlô'zh-skēē)	182c	60.01 N	30.41 E
Vuelta Abajo (Mts.), Cuba (vwĕl'tä ä-bä'hō)	134	22.20 N	83.45 W
Vught, Neth.	157a	51.38 N	5.18 E
Vukovar, Yugo. (vōō'kô-vär)	173	45.20 N	19.00 E
Vulcan, Mi. (vŭl'kăn)	110	45.45 N	87.50 W
Vulcano (I.), It. (vōōl-kä'nô)	172	38.23 N	15.00 E
Vŭlchedrŭma, Bul.	173	43.43 N	23.29 E
Vyartsilya, Sov. Un. (vyȧr-tsē'lyȧ)	165	62.10 N	30.40 E
Vyatka (R.), Sov. Un. (vyát'kȧ)	178	58.25 N	51.25 E
Vyazemskiy, Sov. Un. (vyȧ-zĕm'skĭ)	204	47.29 N	134.39 E
Vyaz'ma, Sov. Un. (vyȧz'mȧ)	174	55.12 N	34.17 E
Vyazniki, Sov. Un. (vyȧz'nē-kē)	178	56.10 N	42.10 E
Vyborg (Viipuri), Sov. Un. (vwē'bôrk)	165	60.43 N	28.46 E
Vychegda (R.), Sov. Un. (vē'chĕg-dȧ)	178	61.40 N	48.00 E
Vym (R.), Sov. Un. (vwēm)	178	63.15 N	51.20 E
Vyritsa, Sov. Un. (vē'rĭ-tsȧ)	182c	59.24 N	30.20 E
Vyshnevolotskoye (L.), Sov. Un. (vŭy'sh-ŋē'vôlôt's-kô'yĕ)	174	57.30 N	34.27 E
Vyshniy Volochëk, Sov. Un. (vĕsh'nyĭ vôl-ô-chĕk')	174	57.34 N	34.35 E
Vyskov, Czech. (vĕsh'kôf)	166	49.17 N	16.58 E
Vysoké Mýto, Czech. (vû'sô-kā mû'tô)	166	49.58 N	16.07 E
Vysokovsk, Sov. Un. (vĭ-sô'kôfsk)	174	56.16 N	36.32 E
Vytegra, Sov. Un. (vû'tĕg-rȧ)	178	61.00 N	36.20 E
Vyur, Sov. Un.	178	57.55 N	27.00 E

W

PLACE (Pronounciation)	PAGE	Lat. °′	Long. °′
Wa, Ghana	228	10.04 N	2.29 W
Waal (R.), Neth. (väl)	163	51.46 N	5.00 E
Waalwijk, Neth.	157a	51.41 N	5.05 E
Wabamuno, Can. (wŏ'bă-mŭn)	99	53.33 N	114.28 W
Wabasca, Can. (wŏ-bás'kȧ)	99	56.00 N	113.53 W
Wabash, In. (wô'băsh)	110	40.45 N	85.50 W
Wabash (R.), Il.-In.	110	38.00 N	88.00 W
Wabasha, Mn. (wä'bȧ-shô)	115	44.24 N	92.04 W
Wabowden, Can. (wȧ-bō'd'n)	101	54.55 N	98.38 W
Wabrzeźno, Pol. (vôŋ-bzĕzh'nô)	167	53.17 N	18.59 E
Wabu Hu (L.), China (wä-bōō hōō)	200	32.25 N	116.35 E
W. A. C. Bennett Dam, Can.	99	56.01 N	122.10 W
Waccamaw (R.), SC (wăk'ȧ-mô)	127	33.47 N	78.55 W
Waccasassa B., Fl. (wă-kȧ-să'sȧ)	126	29.02 N	83.10 W
Wachow, G.D.R. (vä'κōv)	157b	53.32 N	12.46 E
Waco, Tx. (wā'kō)	125	31.35 N	97.06 W
Waconda Lake (Res.), Ks.	122	39.45 N	98.15 W
Wadayama, Jap. (wä'dä'yä-mä)	205	35.19 N	134.49 E
Waddenzee (Sea), Neth.	163	53.00 N	4.50 E
Waddington, Mt., Can. (wŏd'dĭng-tŭn)	98	51.23 N	125.15 W
Wadena, Can.	100	51.57 N	103.50 W
Wadena, Mn. (wŏ-dē'nȧ)	115	46.26 N	95.09 W
Wadesboro, NC (wādz'bŭr-ô)	127	34.57 N	80.05 W
Wadeville, S. Afr.	71b	26.16 S	28.11 E
Wadi Gestro (R.), Eth.	225	6.25 N	41.21 E
Wādī Mūsā, Jordan	191a	30.19 N	35.29 E
Wadley, Ga. (wŭd'lē)	127	32.54 N	82.25 W
Wad Madani, Sud. (wäd mē-dä'nē)	225	14.27 N	33.31 E
Wadowice, Pol. (vȧ-dō'vēt-sĕ)	167	49.53 N	19.31 E
Wadsworth, Oh. (wŏdz'wûrth)	113d	41.01 N	81.44 W
Wager B., Can. (wā'jēr)	97	65.48 N	88.19 W
Wagga Wagga, Austl. (wôg'ȧ wôg'ȧ)	216	35.10 S	147.30 E
Wagoner, Ok. (wăg'ŭn-ēr)	123	35.58 N	95.22 W
Wagon Mound, NM (wăg'ŭn mound)	122	35.59 N	104.45 W
Wągrowiec, Pol. (vôŋ-grō'vyĕts)	167	52.47 N	17.14 E
Waha, Libya	194	28.16 N	19.54 E
Wahiawa, Hi.	106a	21.30 N	158.03 W
Wahoo, Ne (wä-hōō')	114	41.14 N	96.39 W
Wahpeton, ND (wô'pē-tŭn)	114	46.17 N	96.38 W
Währing (Neigh.), Aus.	66e	48.14 N	16.21 E
Wahroonga, Austl.	70a	33.43 S	150.07 E
Waialua, Hi. (wä'ē-ä-lōō'ä)	106a	21.33 N	158.08 W
Waianae, Hi. (wä'ē-ȧ-nä'ä)	106a	21.25 N	158.11 W
Waidhofen, Aus. (vīd'hôf-ĕn)	166	47.58 N	14.46 E
Waidmannslust (Neigh.), F.R.G.	65a	52.36 N	13.20 E
Waigeo, Pulau (I.), Indon. (wä-ē-gä'ô)	181	0.07 N	131.00 E
Waikato (R.), N.Z. (wä'ē-kä'to)	217	38.10 S	175.35 E
Waikerie, Austl. (wā'kēr-ē)	216	34.15 S	140.00 E
Wailuku, Hi. (wä'ē-lōō'kōō)	106a	20.55 N	156.30 W
Waimanalo, Hi. (wä-ē-mä'nä-lo)	106a	21.19 N	157.53 W
Waimea, Hi. (wä-ē-mä'ä)	106a	21.56 N	159.38 W
Wainganga (R.), India (wä-ēn-gŭŋ'gä)	196	20.24 N	79.41 E
Waingapu, Indon.	206	9.32 S	120.00 E
Wainwright, Ak. (wān-rīt)	107	74.40 N	159.00 W
Wainwright, Can.	99	52.49 N	110.52 W
Waipahu, Hi. (wä'ē-pä'hōō)	106a	21.20 N	158.02 W
Waiska R., Mi. (wȧ-ĭz-kȧ)	119k	46.20 N	84.38 W
Waitara, Austl.	70a	33.43 S	150.06 E
Waitsburg, Wa. (wāts'bûrg)	116	46.17 N	118.08 W
Wajima, Jap. (wä'jē-mȧ)	205	37.23 N	136.56 E
Wajir, Ken.	231	1.45 N	40.04 E
Wakamatsu, Jap. (wä-kä'mät-sōō)	205	33.54 N	130.44 E
Wakami (R.), Can.	102	47.43 N	82.22 W
Wakasa-Wan (B.), Jap. (wä'kä-sä wän)	205	35.43 N	135.39 E
Wakatipu (L.), N.Z. (wä-kä-tē'pōō)	217	45.04 S	168.30 E
Wakayama, Jap. (wä-kä'yä-mä)	205	34.14 N	135.11 E
Wake (I.), Oceania (wāk)	208	19.25 N	167.00 E
Wa Keeney, Ks. (wô-kē'nē)	122	39.01 N	99.53 W
Wakefield, Can. (wāk-fēld)	95c	45.39 N	75.55 W
Wakefield, Eng.	156	53.41 N	1.25 W
Wakefield, Ma.	105a	42.31 N	71.05 W
Wakefield, Mi.	115	46.28 N	89.55 W
Wakefield, Ne.	114	42.15 N	96.52 W
Wakefield, RI	112b	41.26 N	71.30 W
Wake Forest, NC (wāk fŏr'ĕst)	127	35.58 N	78.31 W
Waki, Jap. (wä'kē)	205	34.05 N	134.10 E
Wakkanai, Jap. (wä'kä-nä'ē)	204	45.19 N	141.43 E
Wakkerstroom, S. Afr. (vák'ēr-strôm)(wăk'ēr-strōōm)	226	27.19 S	30.04 E
Wakonassin (R.), Can.	102	46.35 N	82.10 W
Walbrzych, Pol. (väl'bzhûk)	166	50.46 N	16.16 E
Waldbauer (Neigh.), F.R.G.	63	51.18 N	7.28 E
Waldoboro, Me. (wôl'dô-bŭr-ô)	104	44.06 N	69.22 W
Waldo L., Or. (wôl'dō)	116	43.46 N	122.10 W
Waldorf, Md. (wăl'dôrf)	112e	38.37 N	76.57 W
Waldron, Mo.	119f	39.14 N	94.47 W
Waldron (I.), Wa.	118d	48.42 N	123.02 W
Wales, Ak. (wālz)	107	65.35 N	168.14 W
Wales, U.K.	162	52.12 N	3.40 W
Walewale, Ghana	228	10.21 N	0.48 W
Walcz, Pol. (välch)	166	53.61 N	16.30 E
Walgett, Austl. (wôl'gĕt)	216	30.00 S	148.10 E
Walgreen Coast, Ant. (wôl'grēn)	232	73.00 N	110.00 W
Walhalla, SC (wŭl-hăl'ȧ)	126	34.45 N	83.04 W
Walikale, Zaire	231	1.25 S	28.03 E
Walkden, Eng.	64b	53.32 N	2.24 W
Walker, Mn. (wôk'ēr)	115	47.06 N	94.37 W
Walker L, Can.	101	54.42 N	96.57 W
Walker L., Nv.	120	38.46 N	118.30 W
Walker (R.), Nv.	120	39.07 N	119.10 W
Walker, Mt., Wa.	118a	47.47 N	122.54 W
Walker River Ind. Res., Nv.	120	39.06 N	118.20 W
Walkerville, Mt. (wôk'ēr-vĭl)	117	46.20 N	112.32 W
Wallace, Id. (wŏl'ăs)	116	47.27 N	115.55 W
Wallaceburg, Can.	102	42.39 N	82.25 W
Wallach, F.R.G.	63	51.35 N	6.34 E
Wallacia, Austl.	211b	33.52 S	150.40 E
Wallapa B., Wa. (wŏl ȧ pă)	116	46.39 N	124.30 W
Wallaroo, Austl. (wŏl-ȧ-rōō)	216	33.52 S	137.45 E
Wallasey, Eng. (wŏl'ȧ-sē)	156	53.25 N	3.03 W
Walla Walla, Wa. (wŏl'ȧ wŏl'ȧ)	116	46.03 N	118.20 W
Walled Lake, Mi. (wôl'd lāk)	113b	42.32 N	83.29 W
Wallel, Tulu (Mt.), Eth.	225	9.00 N	34.52 E
Wallgrove, Austl.	70a	33.47 S	150.51 E
Wallingford, Eng. (wŏl'ĭng-fērd)	156b	51.34 N	1.08 W
Wallingford, Pa.	56b	39.54 N	75.22 W
Wallingford, Vt.	111	43.30 N	72.55 W
Wallington, NJ	55	40.51 N	74.07 W
Wallington (Neigh.), Eng.	62	51.21 N	0.09 W
Wallis and Funtuna Is., Oceania	208	13.00 S	176.10 E
Wallisville, Tx. (wŏl'ĭs-vĭl)	125a	29.50 N	94.44 W
Wallowa, Or. (wôl'ô-wȧ)	116	45.34 N	117.32 W
Wallowa Mts., Or.	116	45.10 N	117.22 W
Wallowa R., Or.	116	45.28 N	117.28 W
Wallula, Wa.	116	46.08 N	118.55 W
Walmersley, Eng.	64b	53.37 N	2.18 W
Walnut, Ca. (wôl'nŭt)	119a	34.00 N	117.51 W
Walnut (R.), Ks.	123	37.28 N	97.06 W
Walnut Canyon Natl. Mon, Az.	121	35.10 N	111.30 W
Walnut Cr., Tx.	119c	32.37 N	97.03 W
Walnut Creek, Ca.	118b	37.54 N	122.04 W
Walnut Park, Ca.	59	33.58 N	118.13 W
Walnut Ridge, Ar. (rĭj)	123	36.04 N	90.56 W
Walpole, Ma. (wôl'pōl)	105a	42.09 N	71.15 W
Walpole, NH	111	43.05 N	72.25 W
Walsall, Eng. (wôl-sôl)	156	52.35 N	1.58 W
Walsenburg, Co. (wôl'sĕn-bûrg)	122	37.38 N	104.46 W
Walsum, F.R.G.	63	51.32 N	6.41 E
Walter F. George Res., Al.-Ga.	126	32.00 N	85.00 W
Walter Reed Army Medical Center (P. Int.), DC	56d	38.58 N	77.02 W
Walters, Ok. (wôl'tērz)	122	34.21 N	98.19 W
Waltersdorf, G.D.R.	65a	52.22 N	13.35 E
Waltham, Ma. (wôl'thȧm)	105a	42.22 N	71.14 W
Waltham Forest (Neigh.), Eng.	62	51.35 N	0.01 W
Walthamstow, Eng. (wôl'tȧm-stō)	156b	51.34 N	0.01 W
Walton, Eng.	62	51.24 N	0.25 W
Walton, NY	111	42.10 N	75.05 W
Walton-le-Dale, Eng. (lē-dāl')	156	53.44 N	2.40 W
Walton on the Hill, Eng.	62	51.17 N	0.15 W
Waltrop, F.R.G.	63	51.37 N	7.23 E
Walt Whitman Homes, NJ	56b	39.52 N	75.11 W
Walvis Bay, S. Afr. (wôl'vĭs)	226	22.50 S	14.30 E
Walworth, Wi. (wôl'wûrth)	115	42.33 N	88.39 W
Walze, F.R.G.	63	51.16 N	7.31 E
Wamba (R.), Zaire	230	5.30 N	17.05 E
Wambel (Neigh.), F.R.G.	63	51.32 N	7.32 E
Wamego, Ks. (wŏ-mē'gō)	123	39.13 N	96.17 W
Wami (R.), Tan. (wä'mē)	227	6.31 S	37.17 E
Wanapitei L., Can.	103	46.45 N	80.45 W
Wanaque, NJ (wŏn'ȧ-kū)	112a	41.03 N	74.16 W
Wanaque Res., NJ	112a	41.06 N	74.20 W
Wanda Shan (Mts.), China (wän-dä shän)	199	45.54 N	131.45 E
Wandhofen, F.R.G.	63	51.26 N	7.33 E
Wandoan, Austl.	216	26.09 S	149.51 E

PRONOUNCING INDEX
Wandsbek – Welper 361

PLACE (Pronounciation)	PAGE	Lat. °′	Long. °′
Wandsbek, F.R.G. (vänds'bĕk)	157c	53.34 N	10.07 E
Wandsworth, Eng. (wôndz'wûrth)	156	51.26 N	0.12 W
Wanganui, N.Z. (wôŋ'gȧ-nōō'ē)	217	39.53 S	175.01 E
Wangaratta, Austl. (wŏŋ'gȧ-răt'ȧ)	216	36.23 S	146.18 E
Wangeroog, I., F.R.G. (vän'gĕ-rōg)	166	53.49 N	7.57 E
Wangqing, China (wäŋ-chyĭŋ)	204	43.14 N	129.33 E
Wangqingtuo, China (wäŋ-chyĭŋ-twô)	200	39.14 N	116.56 E
Wangsi, China (wäŋ-sē)	200	37.59 N	116.57 E
Wangsim-ni (Neigh.), Kor.	68b	37.36 N	127.03 E
Wanheimerort (Neigh.), F.R.G.	63	51.24 N	6.46 E
Wanne-Eickel, F.R.G.	63	51.32 N	7.09 E
Wannsee (Neigh.), F.R.G.	65a	52.25 N	13.09 E
Wansdorf, G.D.R.	65a	52.38 N	13.05 E
Wanstead (Neigh.), Eng.	62	51.34 N	0.02 E
Wantage, Eng. (wŏn'tȧj)	156b	51.33 N	1.26 W
Wantagh, NY	112a	40.41 N	73.30 W
Wantirna, Austl.	70b	37.51 S	145.14 E
Wantirna South, Austl.	70b	37.52 S	145.14 E
Wanxian, China (wän shyĕn)	200	38.51 N	115.10 E
Wanxian, China (wän-shyĕn)	203	30.48 N	108.22 E
Wanzai, China (wän-dzī)	203	28.05 N	114.25 E
Wanzhi, China (wän-jr)	200	31.11 N	118.31 E
Waodoan, Austl. (wŏd'ŏn)	216	26.12 S	149.52 E
Wapakoneta, Oh. (wä'pȧ-kō-nĕt'ȧ)	110	40.35 N	84.10 W
Wapawekka Hills, Can. (wŏ'pă-wē'kă-hĭlz)	100	54.45 N	104.20 W
Wapawekka L., Can.	100	54.55 N	104.40 W
Wapello, Ia. (wŏ-pĕl'ō)	115	41.10 N	91.11 W
Wapesi L., Can. (wŏ-pē'zē)	101	50.34 N	92.21 W
Wappapello Res., Mo. (wă'pȧ-pĕl-lō)	123	37.07 N	90.10 W
Wappingers Falls, NY (wŏp'ĭn-jērz)	111	41.35 N	73.55 W
Wapsipinicon (R.), Ia. (wŏp'sĭ-pĭn'ĭ-kŏn)	115	42.16 N	91.35 W
Warabi, Jap. (wä'rä-bē)	205a	35.50 N	139.41 E
Warangal, India (wŭ'răŋ-gȧl)	196	18.03 N	79.45 E
Warburton, The (R.), Austl. (wŏr'bûr-tŭn)	214	27.30 S	138.45 E
Ward, Iran	68h	35.48 N	51.10 E
Wardān, Wādī (R.), Egypt	191a	29.22 N	33.00 E
Ward Cove, Ak.	98	55.24 N	131.43 W
Warden, S. Afr. (wôr'dĕn)	223d	27.52 S	28.59 E
Wardha, India (wŭr'dä)	196	20.46 N	78.42 E
Wardle, Eng.	64b	53.39 N	2.08 W
War Eagle, WV (wôr ē'g'l)	110	37.30 N	81.50 W
Waren, F.R.G. (vä'rĕn)	166	53.32 N	12.43 E
Warendorf, F.R.G. (vä'rĕn-dōrf)	169c	51.57 N	7.59 E
Wargla, Alg.	224	32.00 N	5.18 E
Warialda, Austl.	216	29.32 S	150.34 E
Warley, see Smethwick			
Warlingham, Eng.	62	51.19 N	0.04 W
Warmbad, Namibia (värm'bäd) (wôrm'băd)	226	28.25 S	18.45 E
Warmbad, S. Afr.	223d	24.52 S	28.18 E
Warm Beach, Wa. (wôrm)	118a	48.10 N	122.22 W
War Memorial Stadium (P. Int.), NY	57a	42.54 N	78.52 W
Warm Springs Ind. Res., Or. (wôrm sprĭnz)	116	44.55 N	121.30 W
Warm Springs Res., Or.	116	43.42 N	118.40 W
Warnemünde, G.D.R. (vär'nĕ-mün-dĕ)	164	54.11 N	12.04 E
Warner Ra. (Mts.), Ca.-Or.	116	41.30 N	120.17 W
Warnow R., G.D.R. (vär'nō)	166	53.51 N	11.55 E
Warracknabeal, Austl.	216	36.20 S	142.28 E
Warragamba Res., Austl.	216	33.40 S	150.00 E
Warrandyte, Austl.	70b	37.45 S	145.13 E
Warrandyte South, Austl.	70b	37.46 S	145.14 E
Warrāq al-'Arab, Egypt	71a	30.06 N	31.12 E
Warrāq al-Hadar, Egypt	71a	30.06 N	31.13 E
Warrāq al-Hadar wa Ambūtbah wa Mīt an-Naṣārā, Egypt	71a	30.06 N	31.13 E
Warrawee, Austl.	70a	33.44 S	151.07 E
Warrego (R.), Austl. (wôr'ē-gō)	215	27.13 S	145.58 E
Warren, Ar. (wŏr'ĕn)	123	33.37 N	92.03 W
Warren, Can.	95f	50.08 N	97.32 W
Warren, In.	110	40.40 N	85.25 W
Warren, Mi.	113b	42.33 N	83.03 W
Warren, Mn.	114	48.11 N	96.44 W
Warren, Oh.	110	41.15 N	80.50 W
Warren, Or.	118c	45.49 N	122.51 W
Warren, Pa.	111	41.50 N	79.10 W
Warren, RI	112b	41.44 N	71.14 W
Warrendale, Pa. (wŏr'ĕn-dāl)	113e	40.39 N	80.04 W
Warrensburg, Mo. (wŏr'ĕnz-bûrg)	123	38.45 N	93.42 W
Warrensville Heights, Oh.	56a	41.26 N	81.29 W
Warrenton, Ga. (wŏr'ĕn-tŭn)	127	33.26 N	82.37 W
Warrenton, Or.	118c	46.10 N	123.56 W
Warrenton, Va.	111	38.45 N	77.50 W
Warri, Nig. (wär'ē)	224	5.33 N	5.43 E
Warrington, Eng.	156	53.22 N	2.30 W
Warrington, Fl. (wŏ'ĭng-tŭn)	126	30.21 N	87.15 W
Warrnambool, Austl. (wôr'năm-bōōl)	216	36.20 S	142.28 E
Warroad, Mn. (wôr'rōd)	115	48.55 N	95.20 W
Warrumbungle Ra., Austl. (wôr'ŭm-bŭŋ-g'l)	215	31.18 S	150.00 E
Warsaw, Il. (wŏr'sô)	123	40.21 N	91.26 W
Warsaw, In.	110	41.15 N	85.50 W
Warsaw, NY	111	42.45 N	78.10 W
Warsaw, NC	127	35.00 N	78.07 W
Warsaw, see Warszawa			
Warsop, Eng. (wôr'sŭp)	156	53.13 N	1.05 W
Warszawa (Warsaw), Pol. (vȧr-shä'vȧ)	167	52.15 N	21.05 E
Warta R., Pol. (vär'tȧ)	166	52.35 N	15.07 E
Wartburg, S. Afr.	227c	29.26 S	30.39 E
Wartenberg (Neigh.), G.D.R.	65a	52.34 N	13.31 E
Warwick, Austl. (wŏr'ĭk)	216	28.05 S	152.10 E
Warwick, Can.	104	45.58 N	71.57 W
Warwick, Eng.	162	52.19 N	1.46 W
Warwick, NY	112a	41.15 N	74.22 W
Warwick, RI	112b	41.42 N	71.27 W
Warwickshire (Co.), Eng.	156	52.30 N	1.35 W
Wasatch Mts., Ut. (wô'săch)	119b	40.45 N	111.46 W
Wasatch Plat., Ut.	121	38.55 N	111.40 W
Wasatch Ra., U.S.	108	39.10 N	111.30 W
Wasbank, S. Afr.	227c	28.27 S	30.09 E
Wasco, Or. (wäs'kō)	116	45.36 N	120.42 W
Waseca, Mn. (wô-sē'kȧ)	115	44.04 N	93.31 W
Waseda University (P. Int.), Jap.	69a	35.42 N	139.43 E
Washburn, Me. (wŏsh'bŭrn)	104	46.46 N	68.10 W
Washburn, Wi.	115	46.41 N	90.55 W
Washburn, Mt., Wy.	117	44.55 N	110.10 W
Washington, DC (wŏsh'ĭng-tŭn)	112e	38.50 N	77.00 W
Washington, Ga.	126	33.43 N	82.46 W
Washington, In.	110	38.40 N	87.10 W
Washington, Ia.	115	41.17 N	91.42 W
Washington, Ks.	123	39.48 N	97.04 W
Washington, Mo.	123	38.33 N	91.00 W
Washington, NC	127	35.32 N	77.01 W
Washington, Pa.	113e	40.10 N	80.14 W
Washington (State), U.S.	108	47.30 N	121.10 W
Washington (I.), Wi.	115	45.18 N	86.42 W
Washington Court House, Oh.	110	39.30 N	83.25 W
Washington, L., Wa.	118a	47.34 N	122.12 W
Washington Monument (P. Int.), DC	56d	38.53 N	77.03 W
Washington, Mt., NH	111	44.15 N	71.15 W
Washington National Arpt., Va.	56d	38.51 N	77.02 W
Washington Park, Il.	119e	38.38 N	90.06 W
Washita (R.), Ok. (wŏsh'ĭ-tô)	122	35.33 N	99.16 W
Washougal, Wa. (wŏ-shōō'gȧl)	118c	45.35 N	122.21 W
Washougal (R.), Wa.	118c	45.38 N	122.17 W
Wash, The (Est.), Eng. (wŏsh)	163	53.00 N	0.20 E
Wasilkow, Pol. (vȧ-sēl'kōōf)	167	53.12 N	23.13 E
Waskaiowaka L., Can. (wŏ'skă-yō'wŏ-kă)	101	56.30 N	96.20 W
Wassenberg, F.R.G. (vä'sĕn-bĕrgh)	169c	51.06 N	6.07 E
Wass L., Can. (wŏs)	101	53.40 N	95.25 W
Wassmannsdorf, G.D.R.	65a	52.22 N	13.28 E
Wassuk Ra., Nv. (wȧs'sŭk)	120	38.58 N	119.00 W
Waswanipi, Lac (L.), Can.	103	49.35 N	76.15 W
Water (I.), Vir. Is. (U.S.A.) (wô'tēr)	129c	18.20 N	64.57 W
Waterberge (Mts.), S. Afr. (wôrtēr'bûrg)	223d	24.25 S	27.53 E
Waterboro, SC (wô'tēr-bûr-ō)	127	32.50 N	80.40 W
Waterbury, Ct. (wô'tēr-bĕr-ē)	111	41.30 N	73.00 W
Water Cay (I.), Ba.	135	22.55 N	75.50 W
Waterdown, Can. (wô'tēr-doun)	95d	43.20 N	79.54 W
Wateree (R.), SC (wô'tēr-ē)	127	34.40 N	80.48 W
Waterford, Ire. (wô'tēr-fērd)	162	52.20 N	7.03 W
Waterford, Wi.	113a	42.46 N	88.13 W
Waterloo, Bel.	157a	50.44 N	4.24 E
Waterloo, Can. (wô-tēr-lōō')	103	43.30 N	80.40 W
Waterloo, Can.	103	45.25 N	72.30 W
Waterloo, Eng.	64a	53.28 N	3.02 W
Waterloo, Il.	123	38.19 N	90.08 W
Waterloo, Ia.	113	42.30 N	92.22 W
Waterloo, Md.	112e	39.11 N	76.50 W
Waterloo, NY	111	42.55 N	76.50 W
Waterton-Glacier Intl. Peace Park, Mt.-Can. (wô'ter-tŭn-glā'shûr)	96	48.55 N	114.10 W
Waterton Lakes Nat. Pk., Can.	99	49.05 N	113.50 W
Watertown, Ma. (wô'tēr-toun)	105a	42.22 N	71.11 W
Watertown, NY	111	44.00 N	75.55 W
Watertown, SD	114	44.53 N	97.07 W
Watertown, Wi.	113	43.13 N	88.40 W
Water Valley, Ms. (väl'ē)	126	34.08 N	89.38 W
Waterville, Me.	104	44.34 N	69.37 W
Waterville, Mn.	113	44.10 N	93.35 W
Waterville, Wa.	116	47.38 N	120.04 W
Watervliet, NY (wô'tēr-vlēt')	111	42.45 N	73.54 W
Watford, Eng. (wŏt'fōrd)	156b	51.38 N	0.24 W
Wathaman L., Can.	100	56.55 N	103.43 W
Watling (I.), see San Salvador			
Watlington, Eng. (wŏt'lĭng-tŭn)	156b	51.37 N	1.01 W
Watonga, Ok. (wŏ-tôŋ'gȧ)	122	35.50 N	98.26 W
Watsa, Zaire (wät'sä)	231	3.03 N	29.32 E
Watseka, Il. (wŏt-sē'kȧ)	110	40.45 N	87.45 W
Watson, In. (wŏt'sŭn)	113h	38.21 N	85.42 W
Watsonia, Austl.	70b	37.43 S	145.05 E
Watson Lake, Can.	96	60.18 N	128.50 W
Watsons Bay, Austl.	70a	33.51 S	151.17 E
Watsonville, Ca. (wŏt'sŭn-vĭl)	120	36.55 N	121.46 W
Wattenscheid, F.R.G. (vä'tĕn-shīd)	169c	51.30 N	7.07 E
Watts, Ca. (wŏts)	119a	33.56 N	118.15 W
Watts Bar (R.), Tn. (bär)	126	35.45 N	84.49 W
Wattville, S. Afr.	71b	26.13 S	28.18 E
Waubay, SD (wô'bā)	114	45.19 N	97.18 W
Wauchula, Fl. (wô-chōō'lȧ)	127a	27.32 N	81.48 W
Wauconda, Il. (wô-kŏn'dȧ)	113a	42.15 N	88.08 W
Waukegan, Il. (wô-kē'gȧn)	113a	42.22 N	87.51 W
Waukesha, Wi. (wô'kē-shô)	113a	43.01 N	88.13 W
Waukon, Ia. (wô kŏn)	115	43.15 N	91.30 W
Waupaca, Wi. (wô-păk'ȧ)	115	44.22 N	89.06 W
Waupun, Wi. (wô-pŭn')	115	43.37 N	88.45 W
Waurika, Ok. (wô-rē'kȧ)	122	34.09 N	97.59 W
Wausau, Wi. (wô'sô)	115	44.58 N	89.40 W
Wausaukee, Wi. (wô-sô'kē)	115	45.22 N	87.58 W
Wauseon, Oh. (wô'sē-ŏn)	110	41.30 N	84.10 W
Wautoma, Wi. (wô-tō'mȧ)	115	44.04 N	89.11 W
Wauwatosa, Wi. (wô-wȧ-t'ō'sȧ)	113a	43.03 N	88.00 W
Waveland, Ma.	54a	42.17 N	70.53 W
Waveney (R.), Eng. (wāv'nē)	163	52.27 N	1.17 E
Waverley, Austl.	70a	33.54 S	151.16 E
Waverly, Ia. (wā'vēr-lē)	115	42.43 N	92.29 W
Waverly, Ma.	54a	42.23 N	71.11 W
Waverly, S. Afr.	227c	31.54 S	26.29 E
Waverly, Tn.	126	36.04 N	87.46 W
Wāw, Sud.	225	7.41 N	28.00 E
Wawa, Can.	102	47.59 N	84.47 W
Wāw al-Kabir, Libya	225	25.23 N	16.52 E
Wawanesa, Can. (wŏ'wŏ-nē'sȧ)	101	49.36 N	99.41 W
Wawasee (L.), In. (wô-wô-sē')	110	41.25 N	85.45 W
Waxahachie, Tx. (wăk-sȧ-hăch'ē)	125	32.23 N	96.50 W
Waycross, Ga. (wā'krôs)	127	31.11 N	82.24 W
Wayland, Ky. (wā'lănd)	126	37.25 N	82.47 W
Wayland, Ma.	105a	42.23 N	71.22 W
Wayne, Mi.	113b	42.17 N	83.23 W
Wayne, Ne.	114	42.13 N	97.03 W
Wayne, NJ	112a	40.56 N	74.16 W
Wayne, Pa.	112f	40.03 N	75.22 W
Waynesboro, Ga. (wānz'bŭr-ô)	127	33.05 N	82.02 W
Waynesboro, Pa.	111	39.45 N	77.35 W
Waynesboro, Va.	111	38.05 N	78.50 W
Waynesburg, Pa. (wānz'bûrg)	111	39.55 N	80.10 W
Waynesville, NC (wānz'vĭl)	126	35.28 N	82.58 W
Waynoka, Ok. (wā-nō'kȧ)	122	36.34 N	98.52 W
Wayzata, Mn. (wā-zä-tȧ)	119g	44.58 N	93.31 W
Wazīrbad, Pak.	196	32.39 N	74.11 E
Wazirābād (Neigh.), India	67d	28.43 N	77.14 E
Wāzirpur (Neigh.), India	67d	28.41 N	77.10 E
Weagamow L., Can. (wē'ăg-ă-mou)	101	52.53 N	91.22 W
Wealdstone (Neigh.), Eng.	62	51.36 N	0.20 W
Weald, The (Reg.), Eng. (wēld)	162	50.58 N	0.15 W
Weatherford, Ok. (wĕ-dhēr-fērd)	122	85.32 N	98.41 W
Weatherford, Tx.	125	32.45 N	97.46 W
Weaver (R.), Eng. (wē'vēr)	156	53.09 N	2.31 W
Weaverville, Ca. (wē'vēr-vĭl)	116	40.44 N	122.55 W
Webb City, Mo.	123	37.10 N	94.26 W
Weber R., Ut.	119b	41.13 N	112.07 W
Webster, Ma.	105a	42.04 N	71.52 W
Webster, SD	114	45.19 N	97.30 W
Webster City, Ia.	115	42.28 N	93.49 W
Webster Groves, Mo. (grōvz)	119e	38.36 N	90.22 W
Webster Springs, WV (sprĭngz)	111	38.30 N	80.20 W
Wedau (Neigh.), F.R.G.	63	51.24 N	6.48 E
Weddell Sea, Ant. (wĕd'ĕl)	232	73.00 S	45.00 W
Wedding (Neigh.), F.R.G.	65a	52.33 N	13.22 E
Weddinghofen, F.R.G.	63	51.36 N	7.37 E
Wedel, F.R.G. (vā'dĕl)	157c	53.35 N	9.42 E
Wedge Mtn., Can. (wĕj)	98	50.10 N	122.50 W
Wedgeport, Can. (wĕj'pōrt)	104	43.44 N	65.59 W
Wednesfield, Eng. (wĕd''nz-fēld)	156	52.36 N	2.04 W
Weed, Ca. (wēd)	116	41.35 N	122.21 W
Weehawken, NJ	55	40.46 N	74.01 W
Weenen, S. Afr. (vā'nĕn)	227c	28.52 S	30.05 E
Weert, Neth.	163	51.16 N	5.39 E
Weesow, G.D.R.	65a	52.39 N	13.43 E
Weesp, Neth.	157a	52.18 N	5.01 E
Wegendorf, G.D.R.	65a	52.36 N	13.45 E
Wegorzewo, Pol. (vôŋ-gô'zhĕ-vô)	167	54.14 N	21.46 E
Wegrow, Pol. (vôŋ'grōōf)	167	52.23 N	22.02 E
Wehofen (Neigh.), F.R.G.	63	51.32 N	6.46 E
Wehringhausen (Neigh.), F.R.G.	63	51.21 N	7.27 E
Wei (R.), China (wā)	200	35.47 N	114.27 E
Wei (R.), China (wā)	202	34.00 N	108.10 E
Weichang, China (wā-chäŋ)	202	41.50 N	118.00 E
Weidling, Aus.	66e	48.17 N	16.19 E
Weidlingau (Neigh.), Aus.	66e	48.13 N	16.13 E
Weidlingbach, Aus.	66e	48.16 N	16.15 E
Weifang, China	200	36.43 N	119.08 E
Weihai, China (wa'hăī')	200	37.30 N	122.05 E
Weilheim, F.R.G. (vīl'hīm')	166	47.50 N	11.06 E
Weimar, G.D.R. (vī'mär)	166	50.59 N	11.20 E
Weinan, China	202	34.32 N	109.40 E
Weipa, Austl.	215	12.25 S	141.54 E
Weir River, Can. (wēr-rĭv-ēr)	101	56.49 N	94.04 W
Weirton, WV	110	40.25 N	80.35 W
Weiser, Id. (wē'zēr)	116	44.15 N	116.58 W
Weiser R., Id.	116	44.26 N	116.40 W
Weishi, China (wā-shr)	200	34.23 N	114.12 E
Weissenburg, F.R.G. (vī'sĕn-bōōrgh)	166	49.04 N	11.20 E
Weissenfels, G.D.R. (vī'sĕn-fĕlz)	166	51.13 N	11.58 E
Weitmar (Neigh.), F.R.G.	63	51.27 N	7.12 E
Weixi, China (wā-shyē)	199	27.27 N	99.30 E
Weixian, China (wā shyĕn)	200	36.59 N	115.17 E
Wejherowo, Pol. (vā-hĕ-rô'vô)	167	54.36 N	18.15 E
Welch, WV (wĕlch)	127	37.24 N	81.28 W
Welcome Monument (P. Int.), Indon.	68k	6.11 S	106.49 E
Weldon, NC (wĕl'dŭn)	127	36.24 N	77.36 W
Weldon (R.), Mo.	123	40.22 N	93.39 W
Weleetka, Ok. (wē-lĕt'kȧ)	123	35.19 N	96.08 W
Welford, Austl. (wĕl'fērd)	216	25.08 S	144.43 E
Welhamgreen, Eng.	62	51.44 N	0.13 W
Welheim (Neigh.), F.R.G.	63	51.32 N	6.59 E
Welhemina, Kanal (Can.), Neth.	157a	51.37 N	4.55 E
Welkom, S. Afr. (wĕl'kŏm)	223d	27.57 S	26.45 E
Welland, Can. (wĕl'ănd)	113c	42.59 N	79.13 W
Wellesley, Ma. (wĕlz'lē)	105a	42.18 N	71.17 W
Wellesley Hills, Ma.	54a	42.19 N	71.17 W
Wellesley Is., Austl.	214	16.15 S	139.25 E
Well Hill, Eng.	62	51.21 N	0.09 E
Wellinghofen (Neigh.), F.R.G.	63	51.28 N	7.29 E
Wellington, Austl. (wĕl'lĭng-tŭn)	216	32.40 S	148.50 E
Wellington, Eng.	156	52.42 N	2.30 W
Wellington, Ks.	123	37.16 N	97.24 W
Wellington, N.Z.	215a	41.15 S	174.45 E
Wellington, Oh.	110	41.10 N	82.10 W
Wellington, Tx.	122	34.51 N	100.12 W
Wellington (I.), Chile (ōōĕ'lĕng-tŏn)	144	49.30 S	76.30 W
Wells, Austl. (wĕlz)	214	26.35 S	123.40 E
Wells, Can.	99	53.06 N	121.34 W
Wells, Mi.	110	45.50 N	87.00 W
Wells, Mn.	115	43.44 N	93.43 W
Wells, Nv.	116	41.07 N	115.04 W
Wellsboro, Pa. (wĕlz'bŭ-rô)	111	41.45 N	77.15 W
Wellsburg, WV (wĕlz'bûrg)	110	40.10 N	80.40 W
Wells Res., Wa.	116	48.05 N	119.45 W
Wellston, Oh. (wĕlz'tŭn)	110	39.05 N	82.30 W
Wellsville, Mo. (wĕlz'vĭl)	123	39.04 N	91.33 W
Wellsville, NY	111	42.10 N	78.00 W
Wellsville, Oh.	110	40.35 N	80.40 W
Wellsville, Ut.	117	41.38 N	111.57 W
Welper, F.R.G.	63	51.25 N	7.12 E

362 Wels – White Sands Natl. Mon.

PLACE (Pronounciation)	PAGE	Lat. °′	Long. °′
Wels, Aus. (věls)	166	48.10 N	14.01 E
Welshpool, Wales (wělsh'pōōl)	162	52.44 N	3.10 W
Welverdiend, S. Afr. (věl-vēr-děnd')	223d	26.23 S	27.16 E
Welwyn Garden City, Eng. (wělĭn)	156b	51.46 N	0.17 W
Wem, Eng. (wěm)	156	52.51 N	2.44 W
Wembere (R.), Tan.	231	4.35 S	33.55 E
Wembley (Neigh.), Eng.	62	51.33 N	0.18 W
Wen (R.), China (wŭn)	200	36.24 N	119.00 E
Wenan Wa (Swp.), China (wěn'än' wä)	200	38.56 N	116.29 E
Wenatchee, Wa. (wě-năch'ē)	116	47.24 N	120.18 W
Wenatchee Mts., Wa.	116	47.28 N	121.10 W
Wenchang, China (wŭn-chäŋ)	203	19.32 N	110.42 E
Wenchi, Ghana	228	7.42 N	2.07 W
Wendelville, NY	57a	43.04 N	78.47 W
Wendeng, China (wŭn-dŭŋ)	200	37.14 N	122.03 E
Wendo, Eth.	225	6.37 N	38.29 E
Wendorer, Ut.	117	40.47 N	114.01 W
Wendover, Can. (wěn-dōv'ēr)	95c	45.34 N	75.07 W
Wendover, Eng.	156b	51.44 N	0.45 W
Wengern, F.R.G.	63	51.24 N	7.21 E
Wenham, Ma. (wěn'ăm)	105a	42.36 N	70.53 W
Wennington (Neigh.), Eng.	62	51.30 N	0.13 E
Wenonah, NJ (wěn'ō-nä)	112f	39.48 N	75.08 W
Wenquan, China (wŭn-chyůän)	202	47.10 N	120.00 E
Wenshan, China	203	23.20 N	104.15 E
Wenshang, China (wěn'shäng)	200	35.43 N	116.31 E
Wensu, China (wěn-sōō)	198	41.45 N	80.30 E
Wentworth, Austl. (wěnt'wûrth)	216	24.03 S	141.53 E
Wentworthville South, Austl.	70a	33.49 S	150.58 E
Wenzhou, China (wŭn-jō)	203	28.00 N	120.40 E
Wepener, S. Afr. (wē'pěn-ēr) (vā'pěn-ěr)	226	29.43 S	27.04 E
Werden (Neigh.), F.R.G.	63	51.23 N	7.00 E
Werder, G.D.R. (věr'děr)	157b	52.23 N	12.56 E
Were Ilu, Eth.	225	10.39 N	39.21 E
Werl, F.R.G. (věrl)	169c	51.33 N	7.55 E
Wermelskirchen, F.R.G.	63	51.08 N	7.13 E
Werne (Neigh.), F.R.G.	63	51.29 N	7.18 E
Werneuchen, G.D.R. (věr'hoi-ĸěn)	157b	52.38 N	13.44 E
Wernsdorf, G.D.R.	65a	52.22 N	13.43 E
Werra R., F.R.G. (věr'ä)	166	51.16 N	9.54 E
Werribee, Austl.	211a	37.54 S	144.40 E
Werribee (R.), Austl.	211a	37.40 S	144.37 E
Wersten (Neigh.), F.R.G.	63	51.11 N	6.49 E
Wertach R., F.R.G. (věr'täk)	166	48.12 N	10.40 E
Weseke, F.R.G. (vě'zē-kě)	169c	51.54 N	6.51 E
Wesel, F.R.G. (vā'zěl)	169c	51.39 N	6.37 E
Weser R., F.R.G. (vā'zěr)	166	53.08 N	8.35 E
Weslaco, Tx. (wěs-lā'kō)	124	26.10 N	97.59 W
Weslemkoon (L.), Can.	103	45.02 N	77.25 W
Wesleyville, Can. (wěs'lē-vĭl)	105	49.09 N	53.34 W
Wessel (Is.), Austl. (wěs'ěl)	214	11.45 S	136.25 E
Wesselsbron, S. Afr. (wěs'ěl-brŏn)	223d	27.51 S	26.22 E
Wessington Springs, SD (wěs'ĭng-tŭn)	114	44.06 N	98.35 W
West Abington, Ma.	54a	42.08 N	70.59 W
West Allis, Wi. (wěst-ăl'ĭs)	113a	43.01 N	88.01 W
West Alton, Mo. (ôl'tŭn)	119e	38.52 N	90.13 W
West Athens, Ca.	59	33.55 N	118.18 W
West B., Tx.	125a	29.11 N	95.03 W
West Bend, Wi. (wěst běnd)	115	43.25 N	88.13 W
West Bengal (State), India (běn-gôl')	196	23.30 N	87.30 E
West Berlin, F.R.G. (běr-lēn')	157b	52.31 N	13.20 E
West Blocton, Al. (blŏk'tŭn)	126	33.05 N	87.05 W
Westborough, Ma. (wěst'bŭr-ô)	105a	42.17 N	71.37 W
West Boylston, Ma. (boil'stŭn)	105a	42.22 N	71.46 W
West Branch, Mi. (wěst branch)	110	44.15 N	84.10 W
West Bridgford, Eng. (brĭj'fērd)	156	52.55 N	1.08 W
West Bromwich, Eng. (wěst brŭm'ĭj)	156	52.32 N	1.59 W
Westbrook, Me. (wěst'brŏŏk)	104	43.41 N	70.23 W
Westbury, NY	55	40.45 N	73.35 W
Westby, Wi. (wěst'bē)	115	43.40 N	90.52 W
West Caicos (I.), Turks & Caicos (käē'kō) (kī'kōs)	135	21.40 N	72.30 W
West Caldwell, NJ	55	40.51 N	74.17 W
West Cape Howe (C.), Austl.	214	35.15 S	117.30 E
West Carson, Ca.	59	33.50 N	118.18 W
Westchester, Il.	58a	41.51 N	87.53 W
West Chester, Oh. (chěs'tēr)	113f	39.20 N	84.24 W
West Chester, Pa.	112f	39.57 N	75.36 W
Westchester (Neigh.), Ca.	59	33.55 N	118.25 W
Westchester (Neigh.), NY.	55	40.51 N	73.52 W
West Chicago, Il. (chĭ-kä'gō)	113a	41.53 N	88.12 W
West Collingswood, NJ	56b	39.54 N	75.06 W
West Collingswood Heights, NJ.	56b	39.59 N	75.07 W
West Columbia, SC (cŏl'ŭm-bē-ȧ)	127	33.58 N	81.05 W
West Columbia, Tx.	125	29.08 N	95.39 W
West Conshohocken, NJ	56b	40.04 N	75.19 W
West Cote Blanche B., La. (kōt blănch)	125	29.30 N	92.17 W
West Covina, Ca. (wěst kō-vē'nȧ)	119a	34.04 N	117.55 W
Westdale, Il.	58a	41.56 N	87.55 W
West Derby (Neigh.), Eng.	64a	53.26 N	2.54 W
West Des Moines, Ia. (dē moin')	115	41.35 N	93.42 W
West Des Moines (R.), Ia.	115	42.52 N	94.32 W
West Drayton (Neigh.), Eng.	62	51.30 N	0.29 W
West Elizabeth, Pa.	57b	40.17 N	79.54 W
West End., Ba.	134	26.40 N	78.55 W
West End, Eng.	62	51.44 N	0.04 W
West End (Neigh.), Eng.	62	51.32 N	0.24 W
West End (Neigh.), Pa.	57b	40.27 N	80.02 W
Westende, F.R.G.	63	51.25 N	7.24 E
Westenfeld (Neigh.), F.R.G.	63	51.28 N	7.09 E
Westerbauer (Neigh.), F.R.G.	63	51.20 N	7.23 E
Westerham, Eng. (wě'stēr'ŭm)	156b	51.15 N	0.05 E
Westerholt, F.R.G.	63	51.36 N	7.05 E
Westerhörn, F.R.G. (věs'tēr-hōrn)	157c	53.52 N	9.41 E
Westerlo, Bel.	157a	51.05 N	4.57 E
Westerly, RI (wěs'tēr-lē)	111	41.25 N	71.50 W
Western Australia (State), Austl. (ôs-trā'lĭ-ȧ)	214	24.15 S	121.30 E
Western Ghāts (Mts.), India	197	17.35 N	74.00 E
Western Port, Md. (wěs'tērn pōrt)	111	39.30 N	79.00 W
Western Sahara, Afr. (sȧ-hä'rȧ)	222	23.05 N	15.33 W
Western Samoa, Oceania	208	14.30 S	172.00 W
Western Siberian Lowland, Sov. Un.	176	63.37 N	72.45 E
Western Springs, Il.	58a	41.47 N	87.53 W
Westerville, Oh. (wěs'tēr-vĭl)	110	40.10 N	83.00 W
Westerwald (For.), F.R.G. (věs'tēr-väld)	166	50.35 N	7.45 E
Westfalenhalle (P. Int.), F.R.G.	63	51.30 N	7.27 E
Westfield, Ma. (wěst'fēld)	111	42.05 N	72.45 W
Westfield, NJ	112a	40.39 N	74.21 W
Westfield, NY (wěst'fēld)	112	42.20 N	79.40 W
Westford, Ma. (wěst'fērd)	105a	42.35 N	71.26 W
West Frankfort, Il. (frăŋk'fŭrt)	112	37.55 N	88.55 W
West Ham, Eng.	156b	51.30 N	0.00 W
West Hanover, Ma.	54a	42.07 N	70.53 W
West Hartford, Ct. (härt'fērd)	111	41.45 N	72.45 W
Westhead, Eng.	64a	53.34 N	2.15 W
West Heidelberg, Austl.	70b	37.45 S	145.02 E
West Helena, Ar. (hěl'ěn-ȧ)	123	34.32 N	90.39 W
West Hempstead, NY	55	40.42 N	73.39 W
Westhofen, F.R.G.	63	51.25 N	7.31 E
West Hollywood, Ca.	59	34.05 N	118.24 W
West Homestead, Pa.	57b	40.24 N	79.55 W
West Horndon, Eng.	62	51.34 N	0.21 E
West Hoxton, Austl.	70a	33.55 S	150.51 E
West Hyde, Eng.	62	51.37 N	0.30 W
Westick, F.R.G.	63	51.35 N	7.38 E
West Indies (Reg.), N. A. (ĭn'dēz)	129	19.00 N	78.30 W
West Jordon, Ut. (jôr'dăn)	119b	40.37 N	111.56 W
West Kirby, Eng. (kûr'bē)	156	53.22 N	3.11 W
West Lafayette, In. (lä-fâ-yět')	110	40.25 N	86.55 W
Westlake, Oh.	113d	41.27 N	81.55 W
Westland, Mi.	57c	42.19 N	83.23 W
West Lawn, Va.	56d	38.52 N	77.11 W
Westleigh, S. Afr. (wěst-lē)	223d	27.39 S	27.18 E
West Liberty, Ia. (wěst lĭb'ēr-tĭ)	115	41.34 N	91.15 W
West Liberty (Neigh.), Pa.	57b	40.24 N	80.01 W
West Linn, Or. (lĭn)	118c	45.22 N	122.37 W
Westlock, Can. (wěst'lŏk)	99	54.09 N	113.52 W
West Los Angeles (Neigh.), Ca.	59	34.03 N	118.28 W
West Malling, Eng.	62	51.18 N	0.25 E
West Manayunk, Pa.	56b	40.01 N	75.14 W
West Medford, Ma.	54a	42.25 N	71.08 W
West Memphis, Ar.	123	35.08 N	90.11 W
West Midlands (Co.), Eng.	156	52.26 N	1.50 W
West Mifflin, Pa.	57b	40.22 N	79.52 W
Westminster, Ca. (wěst'min-stēr)	119a	33.45 N	117.59 W
Westminster, Md.	111	39.40 N	76.55 W
Westminster, SC	126	34.38 N	83.10 W
Westminster Abbey (P. Int.), Eng.	62	51.30 N	0.07 W
Westmont, Ca.	59	33.56 N	118.18 W
Westmount, Can. (wěst'mount)	95a	45.29 N	73.36 W
West, Mt., Pan.	128a	9.10 N	79.52 W
West Newbury, Ma. (nū'běr-ē)	105a	42.47 N	70.57 W
West Newton, Ma.	54a	42.21 N	71.14 W
West Newton, Pa. (nū'tŭn)	113e	40.12 N	79.45 W
West New York, NJ (nů yŏrk)	112a	40.47 N	74.01 W
West Nishnabotna (R.), Ia. (nĭsh-nȧ-bŏt'nȧ)	123	40.56 N	95.37 W
West Norwood (Neigh.), Eng.	62	51.26 N	0.06 W
Weston, Ma. (wěs'tŭn)	105a	42.22 N	71.18 W
Weston, WV	110	39.00 N	80.30 W
Westonaria, S. Afr.	223d	26.19 S	27.38 E
Weston-super-Mare, Eng. (wěs'tŭn sū'pēr-mā'rē)	162	51.23 N	3.00 W
West Orange, NJ (wěst ŏr'ěnj)	112a	40.46 N	74.14 W
West Palm Beach, Fl. (päm bēch)	127a	26.44 N	80.04 W
West Peabody, Ma.	54a	42.30 N	70.57 W
West Pensacola, Fl. (pěn-sȧ-kō'lȧ)	126	30.24 N	87.18 W
West Pittsburg, Ca. (pĭts'bûrg)	118b	38.02 N	121.56 W
Westplains, Mo. (wěst-plānz')	123	36.42 N	91.51 W
West Point Ga.	126	32.52 N	85.10 W
West Point, Ms.	126	33.36 N	88.39 W
Westpoint, Ne.	114	41.50 N	96.00 W
West Point, NY	112a	41.23 N	73.58 W
West Point, Ut.	119b	41.07 N	112.05 W
West Point, Va.	111	37.25 N	76.50 W
Westport, Ct. (wěst'pōrt)	112a	41.07 N	73.22 W
Westport, Ire.	162	53.44 N	9.36 W
Westport, Or. (wěst'pôrt)	118c	46.08 N	123.22 W
West Puente Valley, Ca.	59	34.04 N	117.59 W
West Pymble, Austl.	70a	33.46 S	151.08 E
Westray (I.), Scot. (wěs'trā)	162a	59.19 N	3.05 W
West Road (R.), Can. (rōd)	98	53.00 N	124.00 W
West Ryde, Austl.	70a	33.48 S	151.05 E
West Saint Paul, Mn. (sånt pôl')	119g	44.55 N	93.05 W
West Sand Spit (I.), Ba.	135	21.25 N	72.10 W
West Schelde (R.), Neth.	163	51.25 N	3.30 E
West Seneca, NY	57a	42.50 N	78.45 W
West Slope, Or.	118c	45.30 N	122.46 W
West Somerville, Ma.	54a	42.24 N	71.07 W
West Tavaputs Plat., Ut. (wěst tăv'ȧ-pōōts)	121	39.45 N	110.35 W
West Terre Haute, In. (těr-ē hōt')	110	39.30 N	87.30 W
West Thurrock, Eng.	62	51.29 N	0.16 E
West Tilbury, Eng.	62	51.29 N	0.24 E
West Turffontein (Neigh.), S. Afr.	71b	26.16 S	28.02 E
West Union, Ia. (ūn'yŭn)	115	42.58 N	91.48 W
West University Place, Tx.	125a	29.43 N	95.26 W
Westview, Oh. (wěst'vů)	113d	41.21 N	81.54 W
West View, Pa.	113e	40.31 N	80.02 W
Westville, Can. (wěst'vĭl)	105	45.34 N	62.43 W
Westville, Il.	110	40.00 N	87.40 W
Westville, NJ.	56b	39.52 N	75.08 W
Westville Grove, NJ	56b	39.51 N	75.07 W
West Virginia (State), U.S. (wěst vēr-jĭn'ĭ-ȧ)	109	39.00 N	80.50 W
West Walker (R.), Ca. (wôk'ēr)	120	38.25 N	119.25 W
West Warwick, RI (wŏr'ĭk)	112b	41.42 N	71.31
Westwego, La. (wěst-wē'gō)	112d	29.55 N	90.09
West Whittier, Ca.	59	33.59 N	118.04
West Wickham (Neigh.), Eng.	62	51.22 N	0.01
Westwood, Ca. (wěst'wŏŏd)	120	40.18 N	121.00
Westwood, Ks.	119f	39.03 N	94.37
Westwood, Ma.	105a	42.13 N	71.14
Westwood, NJ	112a	40.59 N	74.02
Westwood (Neigh.), Ca.	59	34.04 N	118.27
West Wyalong, Austl. (wī'alông)	216	34.00 S	147.20
West Yorkshire (Co.), Eng.	156	53.37 N	1.48
Wetar, Pulau (I.), Indon. (wět'ár)	207	7.34 S	126.00
Wetaskiwin, Can. (wě-tăs'kē-wŏn)	99	52.58 N	113.22
Wetherill Park, Austl.	70a	33.51 S	150.54
Wethmar, F.R.G.	63	51.37 N	7.33
Wetmore, Tx. (wět'mōr)	119d	29.34 N	98.25
Wetter, F.R.G.	169c	51.23 N	7.23
Wetumpka, Al. (wē-tŭmp'kȧ)	126	32.33 N	86.12
Wetzlar, F.R.G. (vets'lär)	169	50.35 N	8.30
Wewak, Pap. N. Gui. (wā-wäk')	207	3.19 S	143.30
Wewoka, Ok. (wē-wō'kȧ)	123	35.09 N	96.30
Wexford, Ire. (wěks'fērd)	162	52.20 N	6.30
Weybridge, Eng. (wā'brĭj)	156b	51.20 N	0.26
Weyburn, Can. (wā'bûrn)	100	49.41 N	103.52
Weyer (Neigh.), F.R.G.	63	51.10 N	7.01
Weymouth, Eng. (wā'mŭth)	162	50.37 N	2.34
Weymouth, Ma.	105a	42.44 N	70.57
Weymouth, Oh.	113d	41.11 N	81.48
Whalan, Austl.	70a	33.45 S	150.49
Whale Cay (I.), Ba.	134	24.50 N	77.45
Whale Cay Chans, Ba.	134	26.45 N	77.10
Wharton, NJ (hwôr'tŭn)	112a	40.54 N	74.35
Wharton, Tx.	125	29.19 N	96.06
What Cheer, Ia. (hwŏt chēr)	115	41.23 N	92.24
Whatcom, L., Wa. (hwät'kŭm)	118c	48.44 N	123.34
Whatshan L., Can. (wŏt'shăn)	99	50.00 N	118.03
Wheatland, Wy. (hwēt'lănd)	117	42.04 N	104.52
Wheaton, Il. (hwē'tŭn)	113a	41.52 N	88.06
Wheaton, Md.	112e	39.05 N	77.05
Wheaton, Mn.	114	45.48 N	96.29
Wheeler Pk., Nv.	121	38.58 N	114.15
Wheeling, Il. (hwēl'ĭng)	113a	42.08 N	87.54
Wheeling, WV	110	40.05 N	80.45
Wheelwright, Arg. (ōōē'l-rē'gt)	141c	33.46 S	61.14
Whelpleyhill, Eng.	62	51.44 N	0.33
Whidbey I., Wa. (hwĭd'bē)	118a	48.13 N	122.50
Whippany, NJ (hwĭp'á-nē)	112a	40.49 N	74.25
Whistler, Al. (hwĭs'lēr)	126	30.46 N	88.07
Whiston, Eng.	64a	53.25 N	2.50
Whitaker, Pa.	57b	40.24 N	79.53
Whitby, Can. (hwĭt'bē)	103	43.50 N	79.00
Whitby, Eng.	64a	53.17 N	2.54
Whitchurch, Eng. (hwĭt'chûrch)	156	52.58 N	2.49
White (L.), Can.	102	48.47 N	85.50
White (L.), Can.	103	45.15 N	76.35
White (R.), Ar.	123	34.32 N	91.11
White (R.), Can.	102	48.34 N	85.46
White (R.), Co.	121	40.10 N	108.55
White (R.), In.	110	39.15 N	86.45
White (R.), SD	114	43.41 N	99.48
White (R.), South Fork, SD	114	43.13 N	101.04
White (R.), Tx.	122	36.25 N	102.20
White (R.), Vt.	111	43.45 N	72.35
White B., Can.	105	50.00 N	56.30
White Bear Ind. Res., Can.	101	49.15 N	102.15
White Bear L., Mn.	119g	45.04 N	92.58
White Bear Lake, Mn.	119g	45.05 N	93.01
White Castle, La.	125	30.10 N	91.09
White Center, Wa.	118a	47.31 N	122.21
White Cloud, Mi.	110	43.35 N	85.45
Whitecourt, Can. (wĭt'côrt)	99	54.09 N	115.41
White Earth (R.), ND	114	48.30 N	102.44
White Earth Ind. Res., Mn.	114	47.18 N	95.42
Whiteface (R.), Mn. (whĭt'fās)	115	47.12 N	92.13
Whitefield, Eng.	64b	53.33 N	2.18
Whitefield, NH (hwĭt'fēld)	111	44.20 N	71.35
Whitefish (B.), Mi.	115	46.36 N	84.50
Whitefish (R.), Mi.	115	46.12 N	86.56
Whitefish B., Can.	101	49.26 N	94.14
Whitefish Bay, Wi.	113a	43.07 N	77.54
Whitefish, Mt. (hwĭt'fĭsh)	117	48.24 N	114.25
White Hall, Il.	123	39.26 N	90.23
Whitehall, Mi. (hwĭt'hôl)	110	43.20 N	86.20
Whitehall, NY	111	43.30 N	73.25
Whitehall, Pa.	57b	40.22 N	79.59
Whitehaven, Eng. (hwĭt'hā-věn)	162	54.35 N	3.30
Whitehead, Ma.	54a	42.17 N	70.52
Whitehorn, Pt., Wa. (hwĭt'hôrn)	118d	48.54 N	122.48
Whitehorse, Can. (whĭt'hôrs)	96	60.39 N	135.01
White House (P. Int.), DC	56d	38.54 N	77.02
White L., La.	125	29.40 N	92.35
Whiteley Village, Eng.	62	51.21 N	0.26
Whiteman, Ma.	54a	42.05 N	70.56
Whitemarsh, Pa.	56b	40.07 N	75.13
Whitemouth (L.), Can.	114	49.14 N	95.40
White, Mt., Ca.	120	37.38 N	118.13
White Mts., Me.	104	44.22 N	71.15
White Mts., NH	111	42.20 N	71.05
White Nile (Abyad, Al-Bahr al-) (R.), Sud.	225	14.00 N	32.35
White Oak, Pa.	57b	40.21 N	79.48
White Otter (L.), Can.	115	49.15 N	91.48
White P., Ak.-Can.	96	59.35 N	135.03
White Plains NY	112a	41.02 N	73.47
White R., Wa.	116	47.07 N	121.48
White R., East Fork, In.	110	38.45 N	86.20
White River, Can.	102	48.38 N	85.23
White River Plat., Co.	121	39.45 N	107.50
White Rock, Can.	118d	49.01 N	122.49
Whiterock Res., Tx. (hwĭt'rŏk)	119c	32.51 N	96.40
Whitesail L., Can. (whīt'sāl)	98	53.30 N	127.00
White Sands Natl. Mon., NM	121	32.50 N	106.20

PLACE (Pronounciation)	PAGE	Lat. °'	Long. °'
White Sea, Sov. Un.	178	66.00 N	40.00 E
White Settlement, Tx.	119c	32.45 N	97.28 W
Whitestone (Neigh.), NY	55	40.47 N	73.49 W
White Sulphur Springs, Mt.	117	46.32 N	110.49 W
White Umfolzi (R.), S. Afr. (ŭm-fô-lō'zē)	227c	28.12 S	30.55 E
Whiteville, NC (hwīt'vĭl)	127	34.18 N	78.45 W
White Volta (R.), Ghana	228	9.40 N	1.10 W
Whitewater (L.), Can.	114	49.14 N	100.39 W
Whitewater, Wi. (whīt-wŏt'ēr)	115	42.49 N	88.40 W
Whitewater B., Fl.	127a	25.16 N	80.21 W
Whitewater Cr., Mt.	117	48.50 N	107.50 W
Whitewater L., Can.	101	49.15 N	100.20 W
Whitewater R., In.	113f	39.19 N	84.55 W
Whitewell, Tn. (hwĭt'wĕl)	126	35.11 N	85.31 W
Whitewright, Tx. (hwīt'rīt)	123	33.33 N	96.25 W
Whitham (R.), Eng. (wĭth'ŭm)	162	53.08 N	0.15 W
Whiting, In. (hwīt'ĭng)	113a	41.41 N	87.30 W
Whitinsville, Ma. (hwĭt'ĕns-vĭl)	105a	42.06 N	71.40 W
Whitman, Ma. (hwĭt'măn)	105a	42.05 N	70.57 W
Whitmire, SC (hwĭt'mīr)	127	34.30 N	81.40 W
Whitney L., Tx. (hwĭt'nē)	125	32.02 N	97.36 W
Whitney, Mt., Ca.	120	36.34 N	118.18 W
Whitstable, Eng. (wĭt'stăb'l)	156b	51.22 N	1.03 E
Whitsunday (I.), Austl. (hwĭt's'n-dā)	215	20.16 S	149.00 E
Whittier, Ca. (hwĭt'ĭ-ēr)	119a	33.58 N	118.02 W
Whittier South, Ca.	59	33.57 N	118.01 W
Whittlesea, S. Afr. (wĭt'l'sē)	227c	32.11 S	26.51 E
Whitworth, Eng. (hwĭt'wŭrth)	156	53.40 N	2.10 W
Whyalla, Austl. (hwī-ăl'ȧ)	216	33.00 S	137.32 E
Whymper, Mt., Can. (wĭm'pēr)	98	48.57 N	124.10 W
Wiarton, Can. (wī'ăr-tŭn)	102	44.45 N	80.45 W
Wichita, Ks. (wĭch'ĭ-tô)	123	37.42 N	97.21 W
Wichita (R.), Tx.	122	33.50 N	99.38 W
Wichita Falls, Tx. (fôls)	122	33.54 N	98.29 W
Wichita Mts., Ok.	162	34.48 N	98.43 W
Wichlinghofen (Neigh.), F.R.G.	63	51.27 N	7.30 E
Wick, Scot. (wĭk)	162	58.25 N	3.05 W
Wickatunk, NJ (wĭk'ȧ-tŭnk)	112a	40.21 N	74.15 W
Wickede (Neigh.), F.R.G.	63	51.32 N	7.37 E
Wickenburg, Az.	121	33.58 N	112.44 W
Wickliffe, Oh. (wĭk'klĭf)	113d	41.37 N	81.29 W
Wicklow, Ire.	162	52.59 N	6.06 W
Wicklow Mts., Ire. (wĭk'lō)	162	52.49 N	6.20 W
Wickup Mtn., Or. (wĭk'ŭp)	118c	46.06 N	123.35 W
Wiconisco, Pa. (wĭ-kŏn'ĭs-kō)	111	43.35 N	76.45 W
Widen, WV (wī'dĕn)	110	38.25 N	80.55 W
Widnes, Eng. (wĭd'nĕs)	156	53.21 N	2.44 W
Wieden, F.R.G. (vē'dĕn)	166	49.41 N	12.09 E
Wiegan, Eng. (wĭg'ăn)	156	53.33 N	2.37 W
Wieliczka, Pol. (vyĕ-lēch'kȧ)	167	49.58 N	20.06 E
Wieluń, Pol. (vyĕ'lo͞on')	167	51.13 N	18.33 E
Wiemelhausen (Neigh.), F.R.G.	63	51.28 N	7.13 E
Wien (Vienna), Aus. (vēn) (vē-ĕn'ä)	157e	48.13 N	16.22 E
Wien (State), Aus.	157e	48.11 N	16.23 E
Wiener Berg (Hill), Aus.	66e	48.10 N	16.22 E
Wiener Neustadt, Aus. (vē'nēr noi'shtät)	166	47.48 N	16.15 E
Wiener Wald (For.), Aus.	157e	48.09 N	16.05 E
Wienerwald (Mts.), Aus.	66e	48.16 N	16.12 E
Wieprz, R., Pol (vyĕpzh)	167	51.25 N	22.45 E
Wiergate, Tx. (wēr'gāt)	125	31.00 N	93.42 W
Wiesbaden, F.R.G. (vēs'bä-dĕn)	166	50.05 N	8.15 E
Wiggins, Ms. (wĭg'ĭnz)	126	30.51 N	89.05 W
Wight, Isle of (I.), Eng. (wīt)	162	50.44 N	1.17 W
Wilber, Ne. (wĭl'bēr)	123	40.29 N	96.57 W
Wilburton, Ok. (wĭl'bēr-tŭn)	123	34.54 N	95.18 W
Wilcannia, Austl. (wĭl-căn-ĭȧ)	216	31.30 S	143.30 E
Wildau, G.D.R. (vēl'dou)	157b	52.20 N	13.39 E
Wildberg, G.D.R. (vēl'bĕrgh)	157b	52.52 N	12.39 E
Wildcat Hill, Can. (wīld'kăt)	100	53.17 N	102.30 W
Wildercroft, Md.	56d	38.58 N	76.53 W
Wildhay (R.), Can. (wīld'hā)	99	53.15 N	117.20 W
Wildomar, Ca. (wĭl'dô-mär)	119a	33.35 N	117.17 W
Wild Rice (R.), Mn.	114	47.10 N	96.40 W
Wild Rice (R.), ND	114	46.10 N	97.12 W
Wild Rice L., Mn.	119h	46.54 N	92.10 W
Wildspitze (Mtn.), Aus.	166	46.55 N	10.50 E
Wildwood, NJ	111	39.00 N	74.50 W
Wildwood Manor, Md.	56d	39.01 N	77.07 W
Wiley, Co. (wī'lē)	122	38.08 N	102.41 W
Wilge R., S. Afr. (wĭl'jē)	223d	25.38 S	29.09 E
Wilge R., S. Afr.	223d	27.27 S	28.46 E
Wilhelmina Gebergte (Mts.), Sur.	143	4.30 N	57.00 W
Wilhelm, Mt., Pap. N. Gui.	215	5.58 S	144.58 E
Wilhelmshaven, F.R.G. (vĕl-hĕlms-hä'fĕn)	166	53.30 N	8.10 E
Wilhelmstadt (Neigh.), F.R.G.	65a	52.31 N	13.11 E
Wilkes-Barre, Pa. (wĭlks'băr-ē)	111	41.15 N	75.50 W
Wilkes Land, Ant.	232	71.00 S	126.00 E
Wilkeson, Wa. (wĭl-kē'sŭn)	118a	47.06 N	122.03 W
Wilkie, Can. (wĭlk'ē)	100	52.25 N	108.43 W
Wilkinsburg, Pa. (wĭl'kĭnz-bûrg)	113e	40.26 N	79.53 W
Wilkins Township, Pa.	57b	40.25 N	79.50 W
Willamette R., Or.	116	44.15 N	123.13 W
Willapa B., Wa.	116	46.37 N	124.00 W
Willard, Oh. (wĭl'ȧrd)	110	41.00 N	82.50 W
Willard, Ut.	119b	41.24 N	112.02 W
Willaston, Eng.	64a	53.18 N	3.00 W
Willcox, Az. (wĭl'kŏks)	121	32.15 N	109.50 W
Willemstad, Neth. Antilles	142	12.12 N	68.58 W
Willesden, Eng. (wĭlz'dĕn)	156b	51.31 N	0.17 W
William Creek, Austl. (wĭl'yăm)	214	28.45 S	136.20 E
Williams, Az. (wĭl'yămz)	121	35.15 N	112.15 W
Williams (I.), Ba.	134	25.30 N	78.30 W
Williamsburg, Ky. (wĭl'yămz-bûrg)	126	36.42 N	84.09 W
Williamsburg, Oh.	113f	39.04 N	84.02 W
Williamsburg, Va.	127	37.15 N	76.41 W
Williamsburg (Neigh.), NY	55	40.42 N	73.57 W
Williams Lake, Can.	99	52.08 N	122.09 W
Williamson, WV (wĭl'yăm-sŭn)	110	37.40 N	82.15 W
Williamsport, Md.	111	39.35 N	77.45 W
Williamsport, Pa.	111	41.15 N	77.05 W
Williamston, NC (wĭl'yămz-tŭn)	127	35.50 N	77.04 W
Williamston, SC	127	34.36 N	82.30 W
Williamstown, Austl.	70b	37.52 S	144.54 E
Williamstown, WV (wĭl'yămz-toun)	110	39.20 N	81.30 W
Williamsville, NY (wĭl'yăm-vĭl)	113c	42.58 N	78.46 W
Willich, F.R.G.	63	51.16 N	6.33 E
Willimantic, Ct. (wĭl-ĭ-măn'tĭk)	111	41.40 N	72.10 W
Willingale, Eng.	62	51.44 N	0.19 E
Willis, Tx. (wĭl'ĭs)	125	30.24 N	95.29 W
Willis Is., Austl.	215	16.15 S	150.30 E
Williston, ND (wĭl'ĭs-tŭn)	114	48.08 N	103.38 W
Williston, L., Can.	98	55.40 N	123.40 W
Williston Park, NY	55	40.45 N	73.39 W
Willmar, Mn. (wĭl'mär)	99	45.07 N	95.05 W
Willmersdorf, G.D.R.	65a	52.40 N	13.41 E
Willoughby, Austl.	70a	33.48 S	151.12 E
Willoughby, Oh. (wĭl'ō-bē)	113d	41.39 N	81.25 W
Willow, Ak.	107	61.50 N	150.00 W
Willow Brook, Ca.	59	33.55 N	118.14 W
Willow Cr., Mt. (wĭl'ō)	117	48.45 N	111.34 W
Willow Cr., Or.	116	44.21 N	117.34 W
Willow Grove, Pa.	112f	40.07 N	75.07 W
Willowick, Oh. (wĭl'ō-wĭk)	113d	41.39 N	81.28 W
Willowmore, S. Afr. (wĭl'ō-môr)	226	33.15 S	23.37 E
Willow Run, Mi. (wĭl'ō rŭn)	113b	42.16 N	83.34 W
Willow Run, Va.	56d	38.49 N	77.10 W
Willows, Ca. (wĭl'ōz)	120	39.32 N	122.11 W
Willow Springs, Il.	58a	41.44 N	87.52 W
Willow Springs, Mo. (sprĭngz)	123	36.59 N	91.56 W
Willowvale, S. Afr. (wĭ-lō'vāl)	227c	32.17 S	28.32 E
Wills Point, Tx. (wĭlz point)	125	32.42 N	96.02 W
Wilmer, Tx. (wĭl'mēr)	119c	32.35 N	96.40 W
Wilmette, Il. (wĭl-mĕt')	113a	42.04 N	87.42 W
Wilmington, Austl.	216	32.39 S	138.07 E
Wilmington, Ca. (wĭl'mĭng-tŭn)	119a	33.46 N	118.16 W
Wilmington, De.	112f	39.45 N	75.33 W
Wilmington, Eng.	62	51.26 N	0.12 E
Wilmington, Il.	113a	41.19 N	88.09 W
Wilmington, Ma.	105a	42.34 N	71.10 W
Wilmington, NC	127	34.12 N	77.56 W
Wilmington, Oh.	110	39.20 N	83.50 W
Wilmore, Ky. (wĭl'mōr)	110	37.50 N	84.35 W
Wilmslow, Eng. (wĭlmz'lō)	156	53.19 N	2.14 W
Wilno, see Vilnius			
Wilpoort, S. Afr.	223d	26.57 S	26.17 E
Wilson, Ar. (wĭl'sŭn)	123	35.35 N	90.02 W
Wilson, NC	127	35.42 N	77.55 W
Wilson, Ok.	123	34.09 N	97.27 W
Wilson (R.), Al.	126	34.53 N	87.28 W
Wilson, L., Al.	126	34.45 N	86.58 W
Wilson, Mt., Ca.	119a	34.15 N	118.06 W
Wilson Pk., Ut.	117	40.46 N	110.27 W
Wilson, Pt., Austl.	211a	38.05 S	144.31 E
Wilson's Prom., Austl. (wĭl'sŭnz)	216	39.05 S	146.50 E
Wilsonville, Il. (wĭl'sŭn-vĭl)	119e	39.04 N	89.52 W
Wilstedt, F.R.G. (vēl'shtĕt)	157c	53.45 N	10.04 E
Wilster, F.R.G. (vēl'stēr)	157c	53.55 N	9.23 E
Wilton, Ct. (wĭl'tŭn)	112a	41.11 N	73.25 W
Wilton, ND	114	47.09 N	100.47 W
Wilton Woods, Va.	56d	38.47 N	77.06 W
Wiluna, Austl. (wĭ-lo͞o'nȧ)	214	26.35 S	120.25 E
Wimbledon (Neigh.), Eng.	62	51.25 N	0.12 W
Wimbledon Common (P. Int.), Eng.	62	51.26 N	0.14 W
Winamac, In. (wĭn'ȧ măk)	110	41.05 N	86.40 W
Winburg, S. Afr. (wĭm-bûrg)	223d	28.31 S	27.02 E
Winchester, Ca. (wĭn'chĕs-tēr)	119a	33.41 N	117.06 W
Winchester, Eng.	162	51.04 N	1.20 W
Winchester, Id.	116	46.14 N	116.39 W
Winchester, In.	110	40.10 N	84.50 W
Winchester, Ky.	110	38.00 N	84.15 W
Winchester, Ma.	105a	42.28 N	71.09 W
Winchester, NH	111	42.45 N	72.25 W
Winchester, Tn.	121	35.11 N	86.06 W
Winchester, Va.	111	39.10 N	78.10 W
Windber, Pa. (wĭnd'bēr)	111	40.15 N	78.45 W
Wind Cave Natl. Park, SD	114	43.36 N	103.53 W
Winder, Ga. (wīn'dēr)	121	33.58 N	83.43 W
Windermere, Eng. (wĭn'dēr-mēr)	162	54.25 N	2.59 W
Windfall, Can. (wĭnd'fôl)	99	54.11 N	116.15 W
Windham, Ct. (wĭnd'ăm)	111	41.45 N	72.05 W
Windham, NH	105a	42.49 N	71.21 W
Windhoek, Namibia (vĭnt'ho͝ok)	226	22.05 S	17.10 E
Wind L., Wi.	113a	42.49 N	88.06 W
Wind Mtn., NM	124	32.02 N	105.30 W
Windom, Mn. (wĭn'dŭm)	115	43.50 N	95.04 W
Windora, Austl. (wĭn-dō'rȧ)	216	25.15 S	142.50 E
Wind R., Wy.	117	43.17 N	109.02 W
Wind River Ind. Res., Wy.	117	43.07 N	109.08 W
Wind River Ra., Wy.	117	43.19 N	109.47 W
Windsor, Austl. (wĭn'zēr)	211b	33.37 S	150.49 E
Windsor, Can.	113b	42.19 N	83.00 W
Windsor, Can.	104	44.59 N	64.08 W
Windsor, Can.	105	48.57 N	55.40 W
Windsor, Co.	122	40.27 N	104.51 W
Windsor, Eng.	156b	51.27 N	0.37 W
Windsor, Mo.	123	38.32 N	93.31 W
Windsor, NC	127	35.58 N	76.57 W
Windsor, Vt.	104	43.30 N	72.25 W
Windsor Arpt., (P. Int.), Can.	57c	42.17 N	82.58 W
Windsor Hills, Ca.	59	33.59 N	118.21 W
Windsor, University of (P. Int.), Can.	57c	42.18 N	83.04 W
Windward Is., N. A. (wind'wērd)	129	12.45 N	61.40 W
Windward Pass, N. A.	135	19.30 N	74.20 W
Winefred L., Can.	100	55.30 N	110.35 W
Winfield, Ks.	123	37.14 N	97.00 W
Wing Lake Shores, Mi.	57c	42.33 N	83.17 W
Winifred, Mt. (wĭn ĭ frĕd)	117	47.35 N	109.20 W
Winisk (R.), Can.	97	54.30 N	86.30 W
Wink, Tx. (wĭŋk)	124	31.48 N	103.06 W
Winkler, Can. (wĭnk'lēr)	101	49.11 N	97.56 W
Winneba, Ghana (wĭn'ē-bȧ)	228	5.25 N	0.36 W
Winnebago, Mn. (wĭn'ē-bā'gō)	115	43.45 N	94.08 W
Winnebago Ind. Res., Ne.	114	42.15 N	96.06 W
Winnebago, L., Wi.	115	44.09 N	88.10 W
Winnemucca, Nv. (wĭn-ē-mŭk'ȧ)	116	40.59 N	117.43 W
Winnemucca (L.), Nv.	120	40.06 N	119.07 W
Winner, SD (wĭn'ēr)	114	43.22 N	99.50 W
Winnetka, Il. (wĭ-nĕtkȧ)	113a	42.07 N	87.44 W
Winnett, Mt. (wĭn'ĕt)	117	47.01 N	108.20 W
Winnfield, La. (wĭn'fēld)	125	31.56 N	92.39 W
Winnibigoshish (L.), Mn. (wĭn'ĭ-bĭ-gō'shĭsh)	115	47.30 N	93.45 W
Winnipeg, Can. (wĭn'ĭ-pĕg)	95f	49.53 N	97.09 W
Winnipeg (R.), Can.	96	52.20 N	95.54 W
Winnipeg Beach, Can.	101	50.31 N	96.58 W
Winnipeg, L., Can.	101	52.00 N	97.00 W
Winnipegosis, Can. (wĭn'ĭ-pē-gō'sĭs)	101	51.39 N	99.56 W
Winnipegosis (L.), Can.	101	52.30 N	100.00 W
Winnipesaukee (L.), NH (wĭn'ē-pē-sô'kē)	111	43.40 N	71.20 W
Winnsboro, La. (wĭnz'bŭr'ō)	125	32.09 N	91.42 W
Winnsboro, SC	127	34.29 N	81.05 W
Winnsboro, Tx.	123	32.56 N	95.15 W
Winona, Can. (wĭ-nō'nȧ)	95d	43.13 N	79.39 W
Winona, Mn.	115	44.03 N	91.40 W
Winona, Ms.	126	33.29 N	89.43 W
Winooski, Vt. (wĭ-no͞os'kē)	111	44.30 N	73.10 W
Winsen (Luhe), F.R.G. (vēn'zĕn) (lo͞o'hē)	157c	53.22 N	10.13 E
Winsford, Eng. (wĭnz'fērd)	156	53.11 N	2.30 W
Winslow, Az. (wĭnz'lō)	121	35.00 N	110.45 W
Winslow, Wa.	118a	47.38 N	122.31 W
Winsted, Ct. (wĭn'stĕd)	111	41.55 N	73.05 W
Winster, Eng. (wĭn'stēr)	156	53.08 N	1.38 W
Winston-Salem, NC (wĭn stŭn-sā'lĕm)	127	36.05 N	80.15 W
Winterberg, F.R.G.	63	51.17 N	7.18 E
Winterberge (Mts.), S. Afr.	227c	32.18 S	26.25 E
Winter Garden, Fl. (wĭn'tēr gär'd'n)	127a	28.32 N	81.35 W
Winter Harbour, Can.	98	50.31 N	128.02 W
Winter Haven, Fl. (hā'vĕn)	127a	28.01 N	81.38 W
Wintering L., Can. (wĭn'tēr-ĭng)	101	55.24 N	97.42 W
Winter Park, Fl. (pärk)	127a	28.35 N	81.21 W
Winters, Tx. (wĭn'tērz)	124	31.59 N	99.58 W
Winterset, Ia. (wĭn'tēr-sĕt)	115	41.19 N	94.03 W
Winterswijk, Neth.	169c	51.58 N	6.44 E
Winterthur, Switz. (vĭn'tēr-to͞or)	166	47.30 N	8.32 E
Winterton, S. Afr.	227c	28.51 S	29.33 E
Winthrop, Me. (wĭn'thrŭp)	104	44.19 N	70.00 W
Winthrop, Ma.	105a	42.23 N	70.59 W
Winthrop, Mn.	115	44.31 N	94.20 W
Winton, Austl. (wĭn-tŭn)	215	22.17 S	143.08 E
Winz, F.R.G.	63	51.23 N	7.09 E
Wipperfürth, F.R.G. (vē'pĕr-fürt)	169c	51.07 N	7.23 E
Wirksworth, Eng. (wûrks'wûrth)	156	53.05 N	1.35 W
Wisconsin (State), U. S. (wĭs-kŏn'sĭn)	109	44.30 N	91.00 W
Wisconsin (R.), Wi.	115	43.14 N	90.34 W
Wisconsin Dells, Wi.	115	43.38 N	89.46 W
Wisconsin Rapids, Wi.	115	44.24 N	89.50 W
Wishek, ND (wĭsh'ĕk)	114	46.15 N	99.34 W
Wisła (Vistula) R., Pol. (vēs'wȧ) (vĭs'tū-lȧ)	167	52.48 N	19.02 E
Wisłoka R., Pol. (vēs-wô'kȧ)	167	49.55 N	21.26 E
Wismar, G.D.R. (vĭs'mär)	166	53.53 N	11.28 E
Wismar, Guy. (wĭs'mȧr)	143	5.58 N	58.15 W
Wisner, Ne. (wĭz'nēr)	114	42.00 N	96.55 W
Wissembourg, Fr. (vē-säN-bo͞or')	169	49.03 N	7.58 E
Wissinoming, (Neigh.), Pa.	56b	40.01 N	75.04 W
Wissous, Fr.	64c	48.44 N	2.20 E
Wister, L., Ok. (vĭs'tēr)	123	35.02 N	94.52 W
Witbank, S. Afr. (wĭt-băŋk)	223d	25.53 S	29.14 E
Witberg (Mtn.), S. Afr.	227c	30.32 S	27.18 E
Witfield, S. Afr.	71b	26.11 S	28.12 E
Witham, Eng. (wĭdh'ăm)	156b	51.48 N	0.37 E
Witham (R.), Eng.	156	53.11 N	0.20 W
Withamsville, Oh. (wĭdh'ămz-vĭl)	113f	39.04 N	84.16 W
Withington (Neigh.), Eng.	64b	53.26 N	2.14 W
Withlacoochee (R.), Fl. (wĭth-lȧ-ko͞o'chē)	127a	28.58 N	82.30 W
Withlacoochee (R.), Ga.	126	31.15 N	83.30 W
Withrow, Mn. (wĭdh'rō)	119g	45.08 N	92.54 W
Witney, Eng. (wĭt'nē)	156b	51.45 N	1.30 W
Witpoortje, S. Afr.	71b	26.08 S	27.50 E
Witt, Il. (vĭt)	110	39.10 N	89.15 W
Witten, F.R.G. (vē'tĕn)	169c	51.26 N	7.19 E
Wittenau (Neigh.), F.R.G.	65a	52.35 N	13.20 E
Wittenberg, G.D.R. (vē'tĕn-bĕrgh)	166	51.53 N	12.40 E
Wittenberge, G.D.R. (vĭt-ĕn-bĕr'gē)	166	52.59 N	11.45 E
Wittlaer, F.R.G.	63	51.19 N	6.44 E
Wittlich, F.R.G. (vĭt'lĭk)	166	49.58 N	6.54 E
Witu, Ken. (wē'to͞o)	227	2.18 S	40.28 E
Witu Is., Pap. N. Gui.	207	4.45 S	149.50 E
Witwatersberg (Mts.), S. Afr. (wĭt-wôr-tērz-bûrg)	227b	25.58 S	27.53 E
Witwatersrand (Ridge), S. Afr. (wĭt-wôr'tērs-rănd)	223d	25.55 S	26.27 E
Witwatersrand, Gold Mine, (P. Int.), S. Afr.	71b	26.12 S	28.15 E
Witwatersrand, University of (P. Int.), S. Afr.	71b	26.12 S	28.02 E
Wkra R., Pol. (f'krȧ)	167	52.40 N	20.35 E
Włocławek, Pol. (vwô-tswä'vĕk)	167	52.38 N	19.08 E
Włodawa, Pol. (vwô-dä'vä)	167	51.33 N	23.33 E
Włoszczowa, Pol. (vwôsh-chô'vä)	167	50.51 N	19.58 E
Woburn, Ma. (wo͞o'bŭrn) (wō'bŭrn)	105a	42.29 N	71.10 W
Woburn, (Neigh.), Can.	54c	43.46 N	79.13 W
Woerden, Neth.	157a	52.05 N	4.52 E
Woking, Eng.	156b	51.18 N	0.33 W
Wokingham, Eng. (wō'kĭng-hăm)	156b	51.23 N	0.50 W
Wolcott, Ks. (wōl'kŏt)	119f	39.12 N	94.47 W
Woldingham, Eng.	62	51.17 N	0.02 W
Wolf (I.), Can. (wo͝olf)	111	44.10 N	76.25 W

ng-sing; ŋ-baŋk; N-nasalized n; nŏd; cŏmmit; ōld; ôbey; ôrder; oi-boil; fo͞od; fo͝ot; ou-out; s-soft; sh-dish; th-thin; pūre; ůnite; ûrn; stŭd; circŭs; ü-as in French tu; '-indeterminate vowel.

364 Wolf – Yakima

PLACE (Pronunciation)	PAGE	Lat. °′	Long. °′
Wolf (R.), Ms.	126	30.45 N	89.36 W
Wolf (R.), Wi.	115	45.14 N	88.45 W
Wolfenbüttel, F.R.G. (vôl'fĕn-büt-ĕl)	166	52.10 N	10.32 E
Wolf L., Il.	113a	41.39 N	87.33 W
Wolf Point, Mt. (wo͝olf point)	117	48.07 N	105.40 W
Wolfratshausen, F.R.G. (vōlf'räts-hou-zĕn)	157d	47.55 N	11.25 E
Wolfsburg, F.R.G. (vōlfs'bo͞orgh)	166	52.30 N	10.37 E
Wolfville, Can. (wo͝olf'vĭl)	104	45.05 N	64.22 W
Wolgast, G.D.R. (vôl'gäst)	166	54.04 N	13.46 E
Wolhuterskop, S. Afr.	227b	25.41 S	27.40 E
Wolkersdorf, Aus.	157e	48.24 N	16.31 E
Wollaston, Ma.	54a	42.16 N	71.01 W
Wollaston (L.), Can. (wo͝ol'ȧs-tŭn)	96	58.15 N	103.20 W
Wollaston Pen., Can.	96	70.00 N	115.00 W
Wollongong, Austl. (wo͝ol'ŭn-gông)	216	34.26 S	151.05 E
Wolomin, Pol. (vô-wō'mēn)	167	52.19 N	21.17 E
Wolseley, Can.	100	50.25 N	103.15 W
Wolstanton, Eng. (wo͝ol-stăn'tŭn)	156	53.02 N	2.13 W
Woltersdorf, G.D.R. (vōl'tĕs-dôrf)	157b	52.07 N	13.13 E
Woltersdorf, G.D.R.	65a	52.26 N	13.45 E
Wolverhampton, Eng. (wo͝ol'vēr-hămp-tŭn)	156	52.35 N	2.07 W
Wolverine, Mi.	57c	42.33 N	83.29 W
Wolwehoek, S. Afr.	223d	26.55 S	27.50 E
Wonga Park, Austl.	70b	37.44 S	145.16 E
Wŏnsan, Kor. (wŭn'sän')	204	39.08 N	127.24 E
Wonthaggi, Austl. (wônt-hăg'ē)	216	38.45 S	145.42 E
Wood, SD (wo͝od)	114	43.26 N	100.25 W
Woodbine, Ia. (wo͝od'bīn)	114	41.44 N	95.42 W
Woodbridge, NJ (wo͝od'brĭj')	112a	40.33 N	74.18 W
Woodbrook, Md.	56c	39.23 N	76.37 W
Wood Buffalo Natl. Park, Can.	96	59.50 N	118.53 W
Woodburn, Il. (wo͝od'bûrn)	119e	39.03 N	90.01 W
Woodburn, Or.	116	45.10 N	122.51 W
Woodbury, NJ (wo͝od'bĕr-ē)	112f	39.50 N	75.14 W
Woodbury, NY	55	40.49 N	73.28 W
Woodbury Terrace, NJ	56b	39.51 N	75.08 W
Woodcrest, Ca. (wo͝od'krĕst)	119a	33.53 N	117.18 W
Woodford, Eng.	64b	53.21 N	2.10 W
Woodford Bridge (Neigh.), Eng.	62	51.36 N	0.04 E
Wood Green (Neigh.), Eng.	62	51.36 N	0.07 W
Woodhaven (Neigh.), NY	55	40.41 N	73.51 W
Woodinville, Wa. (wo͝od'ĭn-vĭl)	118a	47.46 N	122.09 W
Woodland, Ca. (wo͝od'lănd)	120	38.41 N	121.47 W
Woodland, Wa.	118c	45.54 N	122.45 W
Woodland Hills, Ca.	119a	34.10 N	118.36 W
Woodlands, Singapore	67c	1.27 N	103.46 E
Woodlark I., Pap. N. Gui. (wo͝od'lärk)	207	9.07 S	152.00 E
Woodlawn, Md.	56c	39.19 N	76.43 W
Woodlawn, Md.	56d	38.57 N	76.53 W
Woodlawn (Neigh.), Il.	58a	41.47 N	87.36 W
Woodlawn Beach, NY (wo͝od'lôn bēch)	113c	42.48 N	78.51 W
Woodlawn Heights, Md.	56c	39.11 N	76.39 W
Woodlyn, Pa.	56b	39.52 N	75.21 W
Woodlynne, NJ	56b	39.55 N	75.05 W
Woodmansterne, Eng.	62	51.19 N	0.10 W
Woodmere, NY	55	40.38 N	73.43 W
Woodmoor, Md.	56c	39.20 N	76.44 W
Wood Mountain, Can.	100	49.14 N	106.20 W
Wood Ridge, NJ	55	40.51 N	74.05 W
Wood River, Il.	119e	38.52 N	90.06 W
Woodroffe, Mt., Austl. (wo͝od'rŭf)	214	26.05 S	132.00 E
Woodruff, SC (wo͝od'rŭf)	127	34.43 N	82.03 W
Woods (L.), Austl. (wo͝odz)	214	18.00 S	133.18 E
Woodsburgh, NY	55	40.37 N	73.42 W
Woods Cross, Ut. (krôs)	119b	40.53 N	111.54 W
Woodsfield, Oh. (wo͝odz-fēld)	110	39.45 N	81.10 W
Woodside (Neigh.), NY	55	40.45 N	73.55 W
Woods, L. of the, Can.-Mn.	109	49.25 N	93.25 W
Woodson, Or. (wo͝odsŭn)	118c	46.07 N	123.20 W
Woodstock, Can. (wo͝od'stŏk)	104	43.10 N	80.50 W
Woodstock, Can.	104	46.09 N	67.34 W
Woodstock, Eng.	156b	51.48 N	1.22 W
Woodstock, Il.	115	42.20 N	88.29 W
Woodstock, Va.	111	38.55 N	78.25 W
Woodsville, NH (wo͝odz'vĭl)	111	44.10 N	72.00 W
Woodville, Ms. (wo͝od'vĭl)	126	31.06 N	91.11 W
Woodville, Tx.	125	30.48 N	94.25 W
Woodward, Ok. (wo͝od'wôrd)	122	36.25 N	99.24 W
Woollahra, Austl.	70a	33.53 S	151.15 E
Woolton (Neigh.), Eng.	64a	53.23 N	2.52 W
Woolwich, Eng. (wo͝ol'ĭj)	156b	51.28 N	0.05 E
Woomera, Austl. (wo͞om'ēra)	216	31.15 S	136.43 E
Woonsocket, RI (wo͞on-sŏk'ĕt)	112b	42.00 N	71.30 W
Woonsocket, SD	114	44.03 N	98.17 W
Wooster, Oh. (wo͞os'tēr)	110	40.50 N	81.55 W
Worcester, Eng. (wo͞o'stēr)	162	52.09 N	2.14 W
Worcester, Ma. (wo͞os'tēr)	105a	42.16 N	71.49 W
Worcester, S. Afr. (wo͞os'tēr)	226	33.35 S	19.31 E
Worden, Il. (wôr'dĕn)	119e	38.56 N	89.50 W
Workington, Eng. (wûr'kĭng-tŭn)	162	54.40 N	3.30 W
Worksop, Eng. (wûrk'sŏp) (wûr'sŭp)	156	53.18 N	1.07 W
Worland, Wy. (wûr'lănd)	117	44.02 N	107.56 W
Wormley, Eng.	62	51.44 N	0.01 W
Worms, F.R.G. (vōrms)	166	49.37 N	8.22 E
Worona Res., Austl.	211b	34.12 S	150.55 E
Woronora, Austl.	70a	34.01 S	151.03 E
Worsley, Eng.	64b	53.30 N	2.23 W
Worth, Il. (wûrth)	113a	41.42 N	87.47 W
Wortham, Tx. (wûr'dhăm)	125	31.46 N	96.22 W
Worthing, Eng. (wûr'dhĭng)	162	50.48 N	0.29 W
Worthington, In. (wûr'dhĭng-tŭn)	110	39.05 N	87.00 W
Worthington, Md.	56c	39.14 N	76.47 W
Worthington, Mn.	114	43.38 N	95.36 W
Worth L., Tx.	119c	32.48 N	97.32 W
Wowoni, Pulau (I.), Indon. (wō-wō'nē)	207	4.05 S	123.45 E
W, Parcs Nationaux du (Natl. Pk.), Dahomey-Niger	229	12.20 N	2.40 E
Wragby, Eng. (răg'bē)	156	53.17 N	0.19 W
Wrangell, Ak. (răn'gĕl)	107	56.28 N	132.25 W
Wrangell, Mt., Ak.	107	61.58 N	143.50 W
Wrangell Mts., Ak.-Can.	107	62.28 N	142.40 W
Wrath, C., Scot. (răth)	162	58.34 N	5.01 W
Wray, Co. (rā)	122	40.06 N	102.14 W
Wraysbury, Eng.	62	51.27 N	0.33 W
Wreak (R.), Eng. (rēk)	141	52.45 N	0.59 W
Wreck Rfs., Austl. (rĕk)	215	22.00 S	155.52 E
Wrekin, The (Mt.), Eng. (rĕk'ĭn)	156	54.20 N	2.33 W
Wrens, Ga. (rĕnz)	127	33.15 N	82.25 W
Wrentham, Ma.	105a	42.04 N	71.20 W
Wrexham, Wales (rĕk'săm)	156	53.03 N	3.00 W
Wrights Corners, NY (rītz kôr'nērz)	113c	43.14 N	78.42 W
Wrightsville, Ga. (rīts'vĭl)	127	32.44 N	82.44 W
Writtle, Eng.	62	51.44 N	0.26 E
Wroclaw (Breslau), Pol. (vrô'tsläv) (brĕs'lou)	167	51.07 N	17.10 E
Wrotham, Eng. (ro͞ot'ŭm)	156b	51.18 N	0.19 E
Wrotham Heath, Eng.	62	51.18 N	0.21 E
Wrzesnia, Pol. (vzhăsh'nyȧ)	167	52.19 N	17.33 E
Wuchang, China	202	44.59 N	127.00 E
Wuchang, China (wo͞o-chäŋ)	203	30.32 N	114.25 E
Wucheng, China (wo͞o-chŭŋ)	200	37.14 N	116.03 E
Wuhan, China	203	30.30 N	114.15 E
Wuhu, China (wo͞o'ho͞o)	200	31.22 N	118.22 E
Wuji, China (wo͞o-jyī)	200	38.12 N	114.57 E
Wujiang, China (wo͞o-jyäŋ)	200	31.10 N	120.38 E
Wulajie, China (wo͞o-lä-jyĕ)	204	44.08 N	126.25 E
Wuleidao Wan (C.), China (wo͞o-lā-dou wän)	200	36.55 N	122.00 E
Wülfrath, F.R.G.	63	51.17 N	7.02 E
Wu Liang Shan (Mts.), China	206	23.07 N	100.45 E
Wulidian, China (wo͞o-lē-dĭĕn)	200	32.09 N	114.17 E
Wünsdorf, G.D.R. (vüns'dorf)	157b	52.10 N	13.29 E
Wupatki Nat'l Mon., Az.	121	35.35 N	111.45 W
Wuping, China (wo͞o-pĭŋ)	203	25.05 N	116.01 E
Wupper (R.), F.R.G.	63	51.05 N	7.00 E
Wuppertal, F.R.G. (vo͝op'ĕr-täl)	169c	51.16 N	7.14 E
Wuqiao, China (wo͞o-chyou)	200	37.37 N	116.29 E
Wu R., China (wo͞o')	203	27.30 N	108.00 E
Würm (R.), F.R.G. (Würm)	157d	48.07 N	11.20 E
Würselen, F.R.G. (vür'zĕ-lĕn)	169d	50.49 N	6.09 E
Würzburg, F.R.G. (vürts'bo͝orgh)	166	49.48 N	9.57 E
Wurzen, G.D.R. (vo͝ort'sĕn)	166	51.22 N	12.45 E
Wushi, China (wo͞o-shr)	198	41.13 N	79.08 E
Wusong, China (wo͞o-sôŋ)	201b	31.23 N	121.29 E
Wusong (R.), China	68a	31.15 N	121.29 E
Wustermark, G.D.R. (vo͞os'tĕr-märk)	157b	52.33 N	12.57 E
Wustrau, G.D.R. (vo͞ost'rou)	157b	52.15 N	12.51 E
Wuustwezel, Bel.	157a	51.23 N	4.36 E
Wuwie, China (wo͞o'wā')	200	31.19 N	117.53 E
Wuxi, China (wo͞o-shyē)	200	31.36 N	120.17 E
Wuxing, China (wo͞o-shyĭŋ)	203	30.38 N	120.10 E
Wuyi Shan (Mts.), China (wo͞o-yē shän)	203	26.38 N	116.35 E
Wuyou, China (wo͞o-yō)	200	33.18 N	120.15 E
Wuzhi Shan (Mtn.), China (wo͞o-jr shän)	203	18.48 N	109.30 E
Wuzhou, China (wo͞o-jō)	203	23.32 N	111.25 E
Wyandotte, Mi. (wī'ăn-dŏt)	113b	42.12 N	83.10 W
Wye, Eng. (wī)	156b	51.12 N	0.57 E
Wye (R.), Eng.	156	53.14 N	1.46 W
Wymore, Ne. (wī'mōr)	123	40.09 N	96.41 W
Wynberg, S. Afr. (wīn'bĕrg)	226a	34.00 S	18.28 E
Wyncote, Pa.	56b	40.05 N	75.09 W
Wyndham, Austl. (wĭnd'ăm)	214	15.30 S	128.15 E
Wyndmoor, Pa.	56b	40.05 N	75.12 W
Wynne, Ar. (wĭn)	123	35.12 N	90.46 W
Wynnewood, Ok. (wĭn'wo͝od)	123	34.39 N	97.10 W
Wynnewood, Pa.	56b	40.01 N	75.17 W
Wynona, Ok. (wī-nō'nȧ)	123	36.33 N	96.19 W
Wynyard, Can. (wĭn'yērd)	100	51.47 N	104.10 W
Wyoming, Oh. (wī-ō'mĭng)	113f	39.14 N	84.28 W
Wyoming (State), U. S.	108	42.50 N	108.30 W
Wyoming Ra., Wy.	117	42.43 N	110.35 W
Wyre For., Eng. (wīr)	156	52.24 N	2.24 W
Wysokie Mazowieckie, Pol. (vē-sô'kyĕ mä-zô-vyĕts'kyĕ)	166	52.55 N	22.42 E
Wyszkow, Pol. (vēsh'ko͞of)	166	52.35 N	21.29 E
Wythenshawe (Neigh.), Eng.	64b	53.24 N	2.17 W
Wytheville, Va. (wĭth'vĭl)	127	36.55 N	81.06 W

X

PLACE (Pronunciation)	PAGE	Lat. °′	Long. °′
Xabregas (Neigh.), Port.	65d	38.44 N	9.07 W
Xagua, Banco (Bk.), Cuba (bä'n-kō-sä'gwä)	134	21.35 N	80.50 W
Xai Xai, Moz.	226	25.00 S	33.45 E
Xangongo, Ang.	226	16.50 S	15.05 E
Xanten, F.R.G. (ksän'tĕn)	169c	51.40 N	6.28 E
Xánthi, Grc.	173	41.08 N	24.53 E
Xau, L., Bots.	226	21.15 S	24.38 E
Xcalak, Mex. (sä-lä'k)	132a	18.15 N	87.50 W
Xenia, Oh. (zē'nĭ-ȧ)	110	39.40 N	83.55 W
Xi (R.), China (shyē)	203	23.15 N	112.10 E
Xiajin, China (shyä-jyĭn)	200	36.58 N	115.59 E
Xiamen (Amoy), China	203	24.30 N	118.10 E
Xiamen (I.), China (shyä-mŭn)	203	24.28 N	118.20 E
Xi'an, China (shyē-än)	202	34.20 N	109.00 E
Xiang (R.), China (shyäŋ)	203	26.18 N	112.25 E
Xiangcheng, China (shyäŋ-chŭŋ)	200	33.52 N	113.31 E
Xianghe, China (shyäŋ-hŭ)	202a	39.46 N	116.59 E
Xiangtan, China (shyäŋ-tän)	203	27.55 N	112.45 E
Xianyang, China (shyĕn-yäŋ)	202	34.20 N	108.40 E
Xiao Hinggan Ling (Ra.), see Lesser Khingan			
Xiaohongmen, China	67b	39.49 N	116.26 E
Xiaoxingkai Hu (L.), China (shyou-shyĭŋ-kī ho͞o)	204	42.25 N	132.45 E
Xiaoxintian, China	67b	39.58 N	116.22 E
Xiapu, China (shyä-po͞o)	203	27.00 N	120.00 E
Xiayi, China (shyä-yē)	200	34.15 N	116.07 E
Xicotencatl, Mex. (sē-kô-tĕn-kät'l)	130	32.00 N	98.58 W
Xifeng, China (shyē-fŭŋ)	202	42.40 N	124.40 E
Xigazê, China (shyē-gä-dzŭ)	196	29.22 N	88.57 E
Xiheying, China (shyē-hŭ-yĭŋ)	200	39.58 N	114.50 E
Xiliao (R.), China (shyē-lĭou)	202	41.40 N	122.40 E
Xilitla, Mex. (sē-lē'tlä)	130	21.24 N	98.59 W
Xinchang, China (shyĭn-chäŋ)	201b	31.02 N	121.38 E
Xing'an, China (shyĭŋ-än)	203	25.44 N	110.32 E
Xingcheng, China (shyĭŋ-chŭŋ)	200	40.38 N	120.41 E
Xinghua, China (shyĭŋ-hwä)	200	32.58 N	119.48 E
Xingjiawan, China (shyĭŋ-jyä-wän)	200	37.16 N	114.54 E
Xingtai, China (shyĭŋ-tī)	200	37.04 N	114.33 E
Xingu (R.), Braz. (zhĕŋ-go͞o')	143	6.20 S	52.34 W
Xinhai, China (shyĭn-hī)	200	36.59 N	117.33 E
Xinhua, China (shyĭn-hwä)	203	27.45 N	111.20 E
Xinhuai (R.), China (shyĭn-hwī)	200	33.48 N	119.39 E
Xinhui, China (shyn-hwā)	203	22.40 N	113.08 E
Xining, China (shyē-nĭŋ)	198	36.52 N	101.36 E
Xinjiang Uygur (Sinkiang) (Aut. Reg.), China (shyĭn-jyäŋ)	198	40.15 N	82.15 E
Xinjin, China (shyĭn-jyĭn)	200	39.23 N	121.57 E
Xinmin, China (shyĭn-mĭn)	202	42.00 N	122.42 E
Xintai, China (shyĭn-tī)	200	35.55 N	117.44 E
Xintang, China (shyĭn-täŋ)	201a	23.08 N	113.36 E
Xinxian, China (shyĭn shyĕn)	200	31.47 N	114.50 E
Xinxian, China	202	38.20 N	112.45 E
Xinxiang, China (shyĭn-shyäŋ)	200	35.17 N	113.49 E
Xinyang, China (shyĭn-yäŋ)	200	32.08 N	114.04 E
Xinye, China (shyĭn-yŭ)	202	32.40 N	112.20 E
Xinzao, China (shyĭn-dzou)	201a	23.01 N	113.25 E
Xinzheng, China (shyĭn-jŭŋ)	200	34.24 N	113.43 E
Xinzhuang, China	67b	39.56 N	116.31 E
Xiongyuecheng, China (shyôŋ-yûĕ-chŭŋ)	200	40.10 N	122.08 E
Xiping, China (shyē-pĭŋ)	200	33.21 N	114.01 E
Xishui, China (shyē-shwā)	203	30.30 N	115.10 E
Xixian, China (shyē shyĕn)	200	32.20 N	114.42 E
Xiyang, China (shyē-yäŋ)	200	37.37 N	113.42 E
Xiying, China (shyē-yĭŋ)	200	31.26 N	119.57 E
Xiyou, China (shyē-yō)	200	37.21 N	119.59 E
Xizang (Tibet) (Aut. Reg.), China (shyē-dzäŋ)	198	31.15 N	87.30 E
Xizhong Dao (I.), China (shyē-jôŋ dou)	200	39.27 N	121.06 E
Xochihuehuetlan, Mex. (sô-chē-wĕ-wĕ-tlä'n)	130	17.53 N	98.29 E
Xochimilco, Mex. (sō-chē-mēl'kô)	131a	19.05 N	99.06 W
Xochimilco, Lago de (L.), Mex.	60a	19.16 N	99.06 W
Xuancheng, China (shyůän-chŭŋ)	203	30.52 N	118.48 E
Xuanhua, China (shyůän-hwä)	202	40.35 N	115.05 E
Xuanhuadian, China (shyůän-hwä-dĭĕn)	200	31.42 N	114.29 E
Xuchang, China (shyo͞o-chäŋ)	200	34.02 N	113.49 E
Xuddur, Som.	223a	3.55 N	43.45 E
Xun (R.), China (shyo͞on)	203	23.28 N	110.30 E
Xuyi, China (shyo͞o-yē)	200	31.02 N	113.49 E
Xuzhou, China	200	34.17 N	117.10 E

Y

PLACE (Pronunciation)	PAGE	Lat. °′	Long. °′
Ya'an, China (yä-än)	203	30.00 N	103.20 E
Yablonitskiy Pereval (P.), Sov. Un. (yȧb-lô'nĭt-skĭ pĕ-rĕ-väl')	167	48.20 N	24.25 E
Yablonovyy Khrebet (Mts.), Sov. Un. (yȧ-blô-nô-vē')	181	51.15 N	111.30 E
Yacheng, China (yä-chŭŋ)	203	18.20 N	109.10 E
Yachiyo, Jap.	205a	35.43 N	140.07 E
Yacolt, Wa. (yă'kôlt)	118c	45.52 N	122.24 W
Yacolt (Mt.), Wa.	118c	45.52 N	122.27 W
Yacona (R.), Ms. (yá'cō nă)	126	34.13 N	89.30 W
Yacuiba, Arg. (yȧ-ko͞o-ē'bȧ)	144	22.02 S	63.44 W
Yadkin (R.), NC (yăd'kĭn)	127	36.12 N	80.40 W
Yafran, Libya,	225	31.57 N	12.04 E
Yagotin, Sov. Un. (yä'gô-tēn)	175	50.18 N	31.46 E
Yaguajay, Cuba (yä-guä-hä'ē)	134	22.20 N	79.20 W
Yahagi-Gawa (Strm.), Jap. (yä'hä-gē gä'wä)	205	35.16 N	137.22 E
Yaho, Jap.	69a	35.41 N	139.27 E
Yahongqiao, China (yä-hôŋ-chyou)	200	39.45 N	117.52 E
Yahualica, Mex. (yä-wä-lē'kä)	130	21.08 N	102.53 W
Yajalon, Mex. (yä-hä-lōn')	131	17.16 N	92.20 W
Yakhroma, Sov. Un. (yäl'rô-ma)	182b	56.17 N	37.30 E
Yakhroma R., Sov. Un.	182b	56.15 N	37.38 E
Yakima, Wa. (yăk'ĭmȧ)	116	46.35 N	120.30 W

ăt; finăl; rāte; senāte; ärm; ȧsk; sofȧ; fâre; ch-choose; dh-as th in other; bē; ēvent; bĕt; recĕnt; cratēr; g-gō; gh-guttural g; bĭt; ĭ-short neutral; rīde; K-guttural k as ch in German ich;

RONOUNCING INDEX

Yakima R. – Yuncheng 365

LACE (Pronounciation)	PAGE	Lat. °′	Long. °′
akima R., Wa. (tăk′ĭ-mȧ)	116	46.48 N	120.22 W
akoma, Zaire	230	4.05 N	22.27 E
akō (Neigh.), Jap.	69a	35.32 N	139.41 E
aku (I.), Jap. (yä′ko͞o)	205	30.15 N	130.41 E
akut A.S.S.R., Sov. Un.	181	65.21 N	117.13 E
akutat, Ak. (yăk′o͞o-tăt)	107	59.32 N	139.35 W
akutsk, Sov. Un. (yȧ-ko͞otsk′)	181	62.13 N	129.49 E
ale, Mi.	110	43.05 N	82.45 W
ale, Ok.	123	36.07 N	96.42 W
ale Res., Wa.	116	46.00 N	122.20 W
alinga, Cen. Afr. Rep. (yȧ-lĭŋ′gȧ)	225	6.56 N	23.22 E
alobusha (R.), Ms. (yȧ-lô-bo͞osh′ȧ)	126	33.48 N	90.02 W
along (R.), China (yä-lôŋ)	198	32.29 N	98.41 E
alta, Sov. Un. (yäl′tȧ)	179	44.29 N	34.12 E
alu (Amnok) (R.), China-Kor.	204	41.20 N	126.35 E
alu (R.), China (yä-lo͞o)	204	48.20 N	122.35 E
alutorovsk, Sov. Un. (yä-lo͞o-tô′rôfsk)	180	56.42 N	66.32 E
amada, Jap. (yä′mȧ-dȧ)	205	33.37 N	133.39 E
amagata, Jap. (yä-mȧ′gä-tȧ)	204	38.12 N	140.24 E
amaguchi, Jap. (yä-mȧ′go͞o-chē)	205	34.10 N	131.30 E
amaguchi, Jap.	69b	34.50 N	135.15 E
amal, P-ov (Pen.), Sov. Un. (yä-mäl′)	180	71.15 N	70.00 E
amantau, Gora (Mt.), Sov. Un. (gȧ-rä′ yä′man-tȧw)	182a	54.16 N	58.08 E
amasá, Dom. Rep. (yä-mä′sä)	135	18.50 N	70.00 W
amasaki, Jap. (yä′mȧ′sä-kē)	205	35.01 N	134.33 E
amasaki, Jap.	205b	34.53 N	135.41 E
amashina, Jap. (yä′mä-shē′nä)	205b	34.59 N	135.50 E
amashita, Jap. (yä′mä-shē′tä)	205b	34.53 N	135.25 E
amato, Jap.	69a	35.44 N	139.26 E
amato, Jap.	69a	35.47 N	139.37 E
amato, Jap.	205a	35.28 N	139.28 E
amato (R.), Jap.	69b	34.36 N	135.26 E
amato-Kōriyama, Jap.	205b	34.39 N	135.48 E
amato-takada, Jap. (yä′mä-tô tä′kä-dä)	205b	34.31 N	135.45 E
ambi, Mesa de, Col. (mĕ′sä-dĕ-yȧ′m-bē)	142	1.55 N	71.45 W
ambol, Bul. (yȧm′bôl)	173	42.28 N	26.31 E
amdena (I.), Indon.	207	7.23 S	130.30 E
amenkou, China	67b	39.53 N	116.12 E
amethin, Bur. (yŭ-mē′thēn)	198	20.14 N	96.27 E
amhill, Or. (yăm′hĭl)	118c	45.20 N	123.11 W
amkino, Sov. Un. (yäm′kĭ-nô)	182b	55.56 N	38.25 E
amma Yamma, L., Austl. (yäm′ȧ yäm′ȧ)	216	26.15 S	141.30 E
amoussoukro, Ivory Coast	228	6.49 N	5.17 W
amsk, Sov. Un. (yämsk)	181	59.41 N	154.09 E
amuna (R.), India	196	26.50 N	80.10 E
amzho Yumco (L.), China (yäm-jwo yo͞om-tswo)	203	29.11 N	91.26 E
ana (R.), Sov. Un. (yä′nȧ)	181	69.42 N	135.45 E
anac, Austl. (yăn′ȧk)	216	36.10 S	141.30 E
anagawa, Jap. (yä-nä′gä-wä)	205	33.11 N	130.24 E
anam, India (yŭnŭm′)	196	16.48 N	82.15 E
an′an, China (yän-än)	198	36.46 N	109.15 E
an′an, China	202	36.35 N	109.32 E
anbu′, Sau. Ar.	192	23.57 N	38.02 E
ancheng, China (yän-chŭŋ)	200	33.23 N	120.11 E
ancheng, China	200	33.38 N	113.59 E
andongi, Zaire	230	2.51 N	22.16 E
angcheng Hu (L.), China (yäŋ-chŭŋ ho͞o)	200	31.30 N	120.31 E
angchun, China (yäŋ-cho͞on)	203	22.08 N	111.48 E
ang′erzhuang, China (yäŋ-är-jūäŋ)	200	38.18 N	117.31 E
anggezhuang, China (yäŋ-gŭ-jūäŋ)	202a	40.10 N	116.48 E
anggu, China (yäŋ-go͞o)	200	36.06 N	115.46 E
anghe, China (yäŋ-hŭ)	200	33.48 N	118.23 E
angjiang, China (yäŋ-jyäŋ)	203	21.52 N	111.58 E
angjiaogou, China (yäŋ-jyou-gō)	200	36.17 N	118.53 E
angquan, China (yäŋ-chyūän)	200	37.52 N	113.36 E
angtze (Chang) (R.), China (yăng′tse) (chäŋ)	199	30.30 N	117.25 E
angxin, China (yäŋ-shyĭn)	200	37.39 N	117.34 E
angyang, Kor. (yäng′yäng′)	204	38.02 N	128.38 E
angzhou, China (yäŋ-jō)	199	32.24 N	119.24 E
anji, China (yän-jyē)	202	42.55 N	129.35 E
anjiahe, China (yän-jyä-hŭ)	200	31.55 N	114.47 E
anjin, China (yän-jyĭn)	200	35.09 N	114.13 E
ankton, SD (yănk′tŭn)	114	42.51 N	97.24 W
anling, China (yän-lĭŋ)	200	34.07 N	114.12 E
annina, see Ioánnina			
anqi, see Karashahr			
anshan, China (yän-shän)	200	38.05 N	117.15 E
anshou, China (yän-shō)	202	45.25 N	128.43 E
antai, China (yän-tī)	200	37.32 N	121.22 E
anychi, Sov. Un. (yä′nĭ-chĭ)	182a	57.42 N	56.24 E
anzhou, China (yäŋ-jō)	200	35.35 N	116.50 E
anzhuang, China (yän-jūäŋ)	200	36.08 N	117.47 E
ao, Chad (yä′ō)	215	13.00 N	17.38 E
ao, Jap.	205b	34.37 N	135.76 E
aoundé, Cam. (yȧ-o͞on-dā′)	229	3.52 N	11.31 E
ap (I.), Pac. Is. Trust Ter. (yăp)	208	11.00 N	138.00 E
apen, Pulau (I.), Indon.	207	1.30 S	136.15 E
aque del Norte (R.), Dom. Rep. (yä′kā dĕl nôr′tā)	135	19.40 N	71.25 W
aque del Sur (R.), Dom. Rep. (yä-kĕ-dĕl-so͞o′r)	135	18.35 N	71.05 W
aqui (R.), Mex. (yä′kē)	128	28.15 N	109.40 W
aracuy (State), Ven. (yä-rä-ko͞o′ē)	143b	10.10 N	68.31 W
araka, Austl. (yȧ-răk′ȧ)	216	24.50 S	144.08 E
aransk, Sov. Un. (yä-ränsk′)	178	57.18 N	48.05 E
arda (Well), Chad (yär′dȧ)	225	18.29 N	19.13 E
are (R.), Eng.	163	52.40 N	1.32 E
arkand (R.), India (yär-känt′)	196	36.11 N	76.10 E
arkand, see Shache			
arlung Zangbo (R.), see Brahmaputra			
armouth, Can. (yär′mŭth)	104	43.50 N	66.07 W
aroslavka, Sov. Un. (yȧ-rô-släv′kȧ)	182a	55.52 N	57.59 E
aroslavl′, Sov. Un. (yȧ-rô-släv′′l)	174	57.57 N	39.54 E
Yaroslavl′ (Oblast), Sov. Un.	174	58.05 N	38.05 E
Yarra (R.), Austl.	70b	37.51 S	144.54 E
Yarra Can., Austl.	70b	37.49 S	144.55 E
Yarra-to (L.), Sov. Un. (yȧ′rô-tô′)	178	68.30 N	71.30 E
Yarraville, Austl.	70b	37.49 S	144.53 E
Yartsevo, Sov. Un. (yär′tsyē-vô)	174	55.04 N	32.38 E
Yartsevo, Sov. Un.	180	60.13 N	89.52 E
Yarumal, Col. (yä-ro͞o-mäl′)	142a	6.57 N	75.24 W
Yasel′da R., Sov. Un. (yä-syŭl′dȧ)	167	53.13 N	25.53 E
Yasinya, Sov. Un.	167	48.17 N	24.21 E
Yateras, Cuba (yä-tā′räs)	135	20.00 N	75.00 W
Yates Center, Ks. (yāts)	123	37.53 N	95.44 W
Yathkyed (L.), Can. (yȧth-kī-ĕd′)	96	62.41 N	98.00 W
Yatsuga-take (Mtn.), Jap. (yät′so͞o-gä dä′kā)	205	36.01 N	138.21 W
Yatsushiro, Jap. (yät′so͞o′shē-rô)	205	32.30 N	130.35 E
Yatta Plat., Ken.	231	1.55 S	38.10 E
Yautepec, Mex. (yä-o͞o-tā-pĕk′)	130	18.53 N	99.04 W
Yavorov, Sov. Un.	167	49.56 N	23.24 E
Yawata, Jap. (yä′wä-tä)	205b	34.52 N	135.43 E
Yawatahama, Jap. (yä′wä′tä′hä-mä)	205	33.24 N	132.25 E
Yaxian, China (yä shyĕn)	203	18.10 N	109.32 E
Yayama, Zaire	230	1.16 S	23.07 E
Yayao, China (yä-you)	201a	23.10 N	113.40 E
Yazd, Iran	192	31.59 N	54.03 E
Yazoo (R.), Ms. (yă′zo͞o)	126	32.32 N	90.40 W
Yazoo City, Ms.	126	32.50 N	90.18 W
Ye, Bur. (yā)	206	15.13 N	97.52 E
Yeading (Neigh.), Eng.	62	51.32 N	0.24 W
Yeadon, Pa. (yē′dŭn)	112f	39.56 N	75.16 W
Yecheng, see Karghalik			
Yecla, Sp. (yā′klä)	170	38.35 N	1.09 W
Yedikule (Neigh.), Tur.	66f	40.59 N	28.55 E
Yefremov, Sov. Un. (yĕ-fră′môf)	174	53.08 N	38.04 E
Yegor′yevsk, Sov. Un. (yĕ-gôr′yĕfsk)	174	55.23 N	38.59 E
Yeji, China (yŭ-jyē)	200	31.52 N	115.57 E
Yelabuga, Sov. Un. (yĕ-lä′bo͞o-gȧ)	178	55.50 N	52.18 E
Yelan, Sov. Un.	179	50.50 N	44.00 E
Yelets, Sov. Un. (yĕ-lyĕts′)	174	52.35 N	38.28 E
Yelizavetpol′skiy, Sov. Un. (yĕ′lĭ-za-vĕt-pôl-skĭ)	182a	52.51 N	60.38 E
Yelizavety, Mys (C.), Sov. Un. (yĕ-lyē-sȧ-vyĕ′tĭ)	181	54.28 N	142.59 E
Yell (I.), Scot. (yĕl)	162a	60.35 N	1.27 W
Yellow (R.), Fl. (yĕl′ō)	126	30.33 N	86.53 W
Yellowhead Pass, Can. (yĕl′ō-hĕd)	99	52.52 N	118.35 W
Yellowknife, Can. (yĕl′ō-nīf)	96	62.29 N	114.38 W
Yellow R., see Huang			
Yellow Sea, Asia	202	35.20 N	122.15 E
Yellowstone L., Wy.	117	44.27 N	110.03 W
Yellowstone Natl. Park, Wy. (yĕl′ō-stōn)	117	44.45 N	110.35 W
Yellowstone R., Mt.	117	46.28 N	105.39 W
Yellowstone R., Clark Fk., Wy.	117	44.55 N	109.05 W
Yellowtail Res., Mt.-Wy.	117	45.00 N	108.10 W
Yel′nya, Sov. Un. (yĕl′nyȧ)	174	54.34 N	33.12 E
Yemanzhelinsk, Sov. Un. (yĕ-mȧn-zhâ′lĭnsk)	182a	54.47 N	61.24 E
Yemen, Asia (yĕm′ĕn)	190	15.45 N	44.30 E
Yemen, People′s Democratic Republic of., Asia	190	14.45 N	46.45 E
Yemetsk, Sov. Un.	178	63.28 N	41.28 E
Yenakiyevo, Sov. Un. (yĕ-nä′kĭ-yĕ-vô)	175	48.14 N	38.12 E
Yenangyaung, Bur. (yā′nän-d oung)	193	20.27 N	94.59 E
Yencheng, China (yŭ-chŭn)	198	37.30 N	79.26 E
Yendi, Ghana (yĕn′dē)	228	9.26 N	0.01 W
Yengisar, China (yŭn-gē-sär)	198	39.01 N	75.29 E
Yenice (R.), Tur.	179	41.10 N	33.00 E
Yenikapi (Neigh.), Tur.	66f	41.00 N	28.57 E
Yeniköy (Neigh.), Tur.	66f	41.07 N	29.04 E
Yenisey (R.), Sov. Un. (yĕ-nē-sĕ′ē)	180	67.48 N	87.15 E
Yeniseysk, Sov. Un. (yĕ-nĭĕsā′ĭsk)	180	58.27 N	90.28 E
Yeo (I.), Austl. (yō)	214	28.15 S	124.00 E
Yerevan, Sov. Un. (yĕ-rĕ-vän′)	179	40.10 N	44.30 E
Yerington, Nv. (yē′rĭng-tŭn)	162	38.59 N	119.10 W
Yermak (I.), Sov. Un.	178	66.30 N	71.30 E
Yeste, Sp. (yĕs′tā)	170	38.23 N	2.19 W
Yeu, Île d′ (I.), Fr. (ēl dyû)	168	46.43 N	2.45 W
Yevpatoriya, Sov. Un. (yĕf-pä′tô-rĭ-yȧ)	175	45.13 N	33.22 E
Yevrey Aut. Oblast., Sov. Un.	181	48.45 N	132.00 E
Yexian, China (yŭ-shyĕn)	200	37.09 N	119.57 E
Yeya (R.), Sov. Un. (yă′yȧ)	175	46.25 N	39.17 E
Yeysk, Sov. Un. (yĕysk)	175	46.41 N	38.13 E
Yg (R.), see Yug			
Yiannitsá, Grc.	173	40.47 N	22.26 E
Yiaros (I.), Grc.	173	37.52 N	24.42 E
Yibin, China (yē-bĭn)	203	28.50 N	104.40 E
Yichang, China (yē-chäŋ)	203	30.38 N	111.22 E
Yidu, China (yē-do͞o)	200	36.42 N	118.30 E
Yiewsley (Neigh.), Eng.	62	51.31 N	0.28 W
Yi He (R.), China (yē hŭ)	200	34.38 N	118.07 E
Yilan, China (yē-län)	202	46.10 N	129.40 E
Yimianpo, China (yē-mĭĕn-pwo)	204	44.59 N	127.56 E
Yinchuan, China (yĭn-chūän)	202	38.22 N	106.22 E
Yingkou, China (yĭŋ-kō)	202	40.35 N	122.10 E
Yining (Gulja), China (yē-nĭŋ)	198	43.58 N	80.40 E
Yin Shan (Mtn.), China (yĭng′shän′)	202	40.50 N	110.30 E
Yio Chu Kang, Singapore	67c	1.23 N	103.51 E
Yishan, China (yē-shän)	203	24.32 N	108.42 E
Yishui, China (yē-shwā)	200	35.49 N	118.40 E
Yitong, China (yē-tôŋ)	204	43.15 N	125.10 E
Yíthion, Grc.	173	36.50 N	22.37 E
Yixian, China (yē shyĕn)	202	41.30 N	121.15 E
Yiyang, China (yē-yäŋ)	203	28.52 N	112.12 E
Ymir, Can. (wī′mēr)	99	49.17 N	117.13 W
Yoakum, Tx. (yō′kŭm)	125	29.18 N	97.09 W
Yockanookany, (R.), Ms. (yŏk′ȧ-no͞o-kă-nī)	126	32.47 N	89.38 W
Yodo-Gawa (Str.), Jap. (yō′dō′gä-wä)	205b	34.46 N	135.35 E
Yog Pt., Phil. (yōg)	203	14.00 N	124.30 E
Yogyakarta, Indon. (yŏg-yȧ-kär′tȧ)	206	7.50 S	110.20 E
Yoho Natl. Park, Can. (yō′hō)	99	51.26 N	116.30 W
Yojoa, Lago de (L.), Hond. (lä′gô dĕ yô-hō′ä)	132	14.49 N	87.53 W
Yokkaichi, Jap. (yô′kä′ē-chē)	205	34.58 N	136.35 E
Yokohama, Jap. (yō′kô-hä′mą)	205a	35.37 N	139.40 E
Yokosuka, Jap. (yô-kō′so͞o-kä)	205a	35.17 N	139.40 E
Yokota, Jap. (yō-kō′tä)	205a	35.23 N	140.02 E
Yola, Nig. (yō′lä)	224	9.13 N	12.27 E
Yolaina, Cord. de (Mts.), Nic. (kôr-dēl-yĕ′rä dĕ yō-lä-ē′nä)	133	11.34 N	84.34 W
Yolombó, Col. (yô-lôm-bŏ′)	142a	6.37 N	74.59 W
Yomon, Gui.	228	7.34 N	9.16 W
Yonago, Jap. (yō′nä-gō)	205	35.27 N	133.19 E
Yŏnch′on (Neigh.), Kor.	68b	37.38 N	127.04 E
Yonezawa, Jap. (yō′nĕ′zȧ-wä)	204	37.50 N	140.07 E
Yong′an, China (yôŋ-än)	203	26.00 N	117.22 E
Yongding (R.), China (yôŋ-dĭŋ)	202	40.25 N	115.00 E
Yŏngdŏk, Kor. (yŭng′dŭk′)	204	36.28 N	129.25 E
Yongdŭngp′o (Neigh.), Kor.	68b	37.32 N	126.54 E
Yŏnghŭng, Kor. (yŭng′ho͞ong′)	204	39.31 N	127.11 E
Yonghŭng Man (B.), Kor.	204	39.10 N	128.00 E
Yongnian, China (yôŋ-nĭĕn)	200	36.47 N	114.32 E
Yongqing, China (yôŋ-chyĭŋ)	202a	39.18 N	116.27 E
Yongshun, China (yôŋ-sho͞on)	203	29.05 N	109.58 E
Yonkers, NY (yŏŋ′kērz)	112a	40.57 N	73.54 W
Yonne (R.), Fr. (yôn)	168	48.18 N	3.15 E
Yono, Jap. (yō′nō)	205a	35.53 N	139.36 E
Yorba Linda, Ca. (yôr′bă lĭn′dȧ)	119a	33.55 N	117.51 W
York, Al. (yôrk)	126	32.33 N	88.16 W
York, Austl.	214	32.00 S	117.00 E
York, Can.	95d	43.41 N	79.29 W
York, Eng.	162	53.58 N	1.10 W
York, Ne.	123	40.52 N	97.36 W
York, Pa.	111	40.00 N	76.40 W
York, SC	127	34.59 N	81.14 W
York, C., Austl.	215	10.45 S	142.35 E
Yorketown, Austl.	216	35.00 S	137.28 E
York Factory, Can.	101	57.05 N	92.18 W
Yorkfield, Il.	58a	41.52 N	87.56 W
York, Kap (C.), Grnld.	94	75.30 N	73.00 W
York Pen, Austl.	216	34.24 S	137.20 E
Yorkshire Wolds (Hills), Eng. (yôrk′shĭr)	162	54.00 N	0.35 W
Yorkton, Can. (yôrk′tŭn)	100	51.13 N	102.28 W
Yorktown, Tx. (yôrk′toun)	125	28.57 N	97.30 W
Yorktown, Va.	127	37.12 N	76.31 W
Yorkville (Neigh.), Can.	54c	43.40 N	79.24 W
Yoro, Hond. (yō′rô)	132	15.09 N	87.05 W
Yoron (I.), Jap.	208	26.48 N	128.40 E
Yosemite Natl. Park, Ca. (yô-sĕm′ĭ-tē)	120	38.03 N	119.36 W
Yoshida, Jap. (yō′shē-dȧ)	205	34.39 N	132.41 E
Yoshikawa, Jap. (yō-shē′kä′wä′)	205a	35.53 N	139.51 E
Yoshino (R.), Jap. (yō′shē-nō)	205	34.04 N	133.57 E
Yoshkar-Ola, Sov. Un. (yôsh-kär′ô-lä′)	178	56.35 N	48.05 E
Yosonotú (Santa Catarina), Mex. (yô-sō-nô-to͞o′) (sän′tä kä-tä-rē′nä)	131	16.51 N	97.37 W
Yos Sudarsa, Pulau (I.), Indon.	207	7.20 S	138.30 E
Yŏsu, Kor. (yŭ′so͞o′)	204	34.42 N	127.42 W
You (R.), China (yō)	203	23.55 N	106.50 E
Youghal, Ire. (yo͞o′ôl) (yôl)	162	51.58 N	7.57 E
Youghal B., Ire.	162	51.52 N	7.46 W
Young, Austl. (yŭng)	216	34.15 S	148.18 E
Young, Ur. (yô-o͞o′ng)	141c	32.42 S	57.38 W
Youngs (L.), Wa. (yŭngz)	118a	47.25 N	122.08 W
Youngstown, NY	113c	43.15 N	79.02 W
Youngstown, Oh.	110	41.05 N	80.40 W
Yozgat, Tur. (yôz′gȧd)	179	39.50 N	34.50 E
Ypsilanti, Mi. (ĭp-sĭ-lăn′tĭ)	113b	42.15 N	83.37 W
Yreka, Ca. (wī-rē′kȧ)	116	41.43 N	122.36 W
Ysleta, Tx. (ēz-lĕ′tȧ)	124	31.42 N	106.18 W
Yssingeaux, Fr. (ē-săɴ-zhō)	168	45.09 N	4.08 E
Ystad, Swe. (ü′städ)	164	55.29 N	13.28 E
Yu′alliq, Jabal (Mts.), Egypt	191a	30.12 N	33.42 E
Yuan (R.), China (yūän)	203	28.50 N	110.50 E
Yuan′an, China (yūän-än)	203	31.08 N	111.28 E
Yuan Huan (P. Int.), Taiwan	68d	25.03 N	121.31 E
Yuanling, China (yūän-lĭŋ)	203	28.30 N	110.18 E
Yuanshi, China (yūän-shr)	200	37.45 N	114.32 E
Yuasa, Jap.	205	34.02 N	135.10 E
Yuba City, Ca. (yo͞o′bȧ)	120	39.08 N	121.38 W
Yuby, C., Mor. (yo͞o′bē)	224	28.01 N	13.21 W
Yucaipa, Ca. (yŭ-kȧ-ē′pȧ)	119a	34.02 N	117.02 W
Yucatán (State), Mex. (yo͞o-kä-tän′)	128	20.45 N	89.00 W
Yucatán Chan, Mex.	128	22.30 N	87.00 W
Yucheng, China (yo͞o-chŭŋ)	200	34.31 N	115.54 E
Yucheng, China	200	36.55 N	116.39 E
Yuci, China (yo͞o-tsz)	202	37.32 N	112.40 E
Yudoma (R.), Sov. Un. (yo͞o-dō′mȧ)	181	59.13 N	137.00 E
Yueqing, China (yūĕ-chyĭn)	203	28.02 N	120.40 E
Yueyang, China (yūĕ-yäŋ)	203	92.25 N	113.05 E
Yuezhuang, China (yūĕ-jūäŋ)	200	36.13 N	118.17 E
Yug (R.), Sov. Un. (yo͞og)	178	59.50 N	45.55 E
Yugoslavia, Eur. (yo͞o-gô-slä-vĭ-ȧ)	154	44.48 N	17.29 E
Yukhnov, Sov. Un. (yo͞ok′nof)	174	54.44 N	35.15 E
Yukon (Ter.), Can. (yo͞o′kŏn)	96	63.16 N	135.30 W
Yukon R., Ak.-Can.	107	62.10 N	143.00 W
Yukutat B., Ak. (yo͞o-kū tăt′)	107	59.34 N	140.50 W
Yuldybayevo, Sov. Un. (yo͞old′bä′yĕ-vô)	182a	52.20 N	57.52 E
Yulin, China (yo͞o-lĭn)	203	22.38 N	110.10 E
Yulin, China	202	38.18 N	109.45 E
Yuma, Az. (yo͞o′mä)	121	32.40 N	114.40 W
Yuma, Co.	122	40.08 N	102.50 W
Yuma (R.), Dom. Rep.	135	19.05 N	70.05 W
Yuma, Bahia de (B.), Dom. Rep. (bä-ē′ä-dĕ-yo͞o′mä)	135	18.20 N	68.05 W
Yumbi, Zaire	231	1.14 S	26.14 E
Yumen, China (yo͞o-mŭn)	198	40.14 N	96.56 E
Yuncheng, China (yo͞on-chŭŋ)	202	35.00 N	110.40 E

g-sing; nŋ-baŋk; ɴ-nasalized n; nŏd; cŏmmit; ōld; ôbey; ôrder; oi-boil; fo͞od; fo͝ot; ou-out; s-soft; sh-dish; th-thin; pūre; ūnite; ûrn; stŭd; circŭs; ü-as in French tu; ′-indeterminate vowel.

ăt; finăl; râte; senåte; ärm; àsk; sofà; fâre;   ch-choose;   dh-as th in other;   bē; ĕvent; bĕt; recĕnt; cratēr;   g-gō; gh-guttural g;   bĭt; ĭ-short neutral; rīde;   ĸ-guttural k as ch in German ich;

PLACE (Pronounciation)	PAGE	Lat. °′	Long. °′
Zubtsov, Sov. Un. (zo͞op-tsôf′)	174	56.13 N	34.34 E
Zuera, Sp. (thwä′rä)	171	41.40 N	0.48 W
Zuger See (L.), Switz. (tso͞og)	166	47.10 N	8.40 E
Zugló (Neigh.), Hung.	66g	47.31 N	19.08 E
Zugspitze Pk., Aus.-F.R.G.	166	47.25 N	11.00 E
Zuidelijk Flevoland (Reg.), Neth.	157a	52.22 N	5.20 E
Zuishavane, Zimb.	226	20.15 S	30.28 E
Zújar (R.), Sp. (zo͞o′ẋär)	170	38.55 N	5.05 W
Zújar, Embalse del (Res.), Sp.	170	38.50 N	5.20 W
Zulueta, Cuba (zo͞o-lo͞o-ě′tä)	134	22.20 N	79.35 W
Zululand (Reg.), S. Afr. (zo͞o′lo͞o-lånd)	226	27.45 S	31.29 E
Zumbo, Moz. (zo͞om′bo͞o)	231	15.36 S	30.25 E
Zumbro (R.), Mn. (zŭm′brŏ)	115	44.18 N	92.14 W

PLACE (Pronounciation)	PAGE	Lat. °′	Long. °′
Zumbrota, Mn. (zŭm-brŏ′tȧ)	115	44.16 N	92.39 W
Zumpango, Mex. (so͞om-päṇ-gŏ)	130	19.48 N	99.06 W
Zundert, Neth.	157a	51.28 N	4.39 E
Zungeru, Nig. (zo͞oṇ-gä′ro͞o)	229	9.48 N	6.09 E
Zunhua, China (dzo͞on-hwä)	200	40.12 N	117.55 E
Zuni (R.), Az.-NM	121	34.40 N	109.30 W
Zuni Ind. Res., NM (zo͞o′ně)	121	35.10 N	108.40 W
Zuni Mts., NM	121	35.10 N	108.10 W
Zunyi, China	198	27.58 N	106.40 E
Zürich, Switz. (tsü′rĭk)	166	47.22 N	8.32 E
Zürichsee (L.), Switz.	166	47.18 N	8.47 E
Zushi, Jap. (zo͞o′shě)	205a	35.17 N	139.35 E
Zuurbekom, S. Afr.	71b	26.19 S	27.49 E
Zuwārah, Libya	225	32.58 N	12.07 E

PLACE (Pronounciation)	PAGE	Lat. °′	Long. °′
Zuwayzā, Jordan	191a	31.42 N	35.58 E
Zvenigorod, Sov. Un. (zvä-ně′gô-rŏt)	174	55.46 N	36.54 E
Zvenigorodka, Sov. Un. (zvä-ně′gô-rŏt′kä)	175	49.07 N	30.59 E
Zvolen, Czech. (zvô′lěn)	167	48.35 N	19.10 E
Zvornik, Yugo. (zvôr′někˉ)	173	44.24 N	19.08 E
Zweckel (Neigh.), F.R.G.	63	51.36 N	6.59 E
Zweibrücken, F.R.G. (tsvī-brük′ěn)	166	49.16 N	7.20 E
Zwickau, G.D.R. (tsvĭk′ou)	166	50.43 N	12.30 E
Zwolle, Neth. (zvŏl′ě)	163	52.33 N	6.05 E
Zyradow, Pol. (zhě-rär′do͞of)	167	52.04 N	20.28 E
Zyryanka, Sov. Un. (zě-ryän′kȧ)	181	65.45 N	151.15 E
Zyryanovsk, Sov. Un. (zě-ryä′nôfsk)	180	49.43 N	83.52 E

ng-sing; nn-bannk; N-nasalized n;   nŏd; cŏmmit; ōld; ôbey; ôrder; oi-boil; fo͞od; fo͝ot; ou-out;   s-soft; sh-dish;   th-thin;   pūre; ûnite; ûrn; stŭd; circŭs; ü-as in French tu;   ′-indeterminate vowel.